D1480607

The Official NFL Encyclopedia

The Official NFL Encyclopedia

Beau Riffenburgh

NAL BOOKS
NEW AMERICAN LIBRARY
TIMES MIRROR
NEW YORK AND SCARBOROUGH, ONTARIO

NAL BOOKS TRADEMARK REG. U.S. PAT. OFF. AND FOREIGN COUNTRIES
REGISTERED TRADEMARK—MARCA REGISTRADA
HECHO EN CRAWFORDSVILLE, INDIANA, Y WILLARD, OHIO, U.S.A.

SIGNET, SIGNET CLASSIC, MENTOR, PLUME, MERIDIAN, and NAL BOOKS are published *in the United States* by New American Library, 1633 Broadway, New York, New York 10019; *in Canada* by The New American Library of Canada Limited, 81 Mack Avenue, Scarborough, Ontario M1L 1M8

Riffenburgh, Beau
The Official NFL Encyclopedia
1. National Football League. 2. Football—United States.
I. Title
Library of Congress Catalog Card Number: 86-42634
ISBN 0-453-00524-1
First printing, August 1986
1 2 3 4 5 6 7 8 9
PRINTED IN THE UNITED STATES OF AMERICA

A National Football League Book

Major Contributors
Bill Barron
David Boss
Jim Campbell
Chuck Garrity, Sr.
Joe Horrigan
John Wiebusch

Designers
David Johnston
Glen Iwasaki

Production Coordinator
Jere Wright

CONTENTS

INTRODUCTION

The Official NFL Encyclopedia represents a major effort to produce the most comprehensive and entertaining history of pro football ever published. Admittedly, it has an advantage that other similar books don't have—the source, subject, and creator are the same. This is the NFL's book about itself. It has been written, however, with objectivity, with the desire to record the truth even when not popular or previously accepted, and with an attempt to appeal to both the football novice and the serious aficionado.

Although *The Official NFL Encyclopedia* should be understandable even to fans with a minimal knowledge of the history of pro football, it does presuppose a certain knowledge of the basic precepts of the game.

From a historical standpoint, researchers, most notably those associated with the Pro Football Researchers Association, constantly are uncovering new material about the early days of pro football and the infancy of the NFL. What is generally accepted to be historical fact at one time might be proven wrong at a later date. For example, the Chicago Bears under coach George Halas and with the assistance of Clark Shaugnessy did not "invent" the T-formation with man-in-motion in 1940. The Bears' success with it that year merely popularized it. As early as 1930, the Bears, under coach Ralph Jones, were using the T-formation. Many colleges had played it since the turn of the century.

Much confusion has occurred because throughout the history of the NFL there have been periodic changes in the ways positions, team records, and a number of statistical categories have been kept.

To avoid this confusion, positions from the pre-modern era generally have been changed to their T-formation equivalents throughout this book. Thus, blocking backs are listed as quarterbacks, and tailbacks and wingbacks as halfbacks. T-formation players are recorded as what they were known as at the time, although there were several positions that changed names in the 1960s. Prior to 1960, the backfield included a left halfback, a right halfback, and a fullback, while the line included left and right ends. From 1960-66, those positions were known as halfback, flanker, fullback, split end, and tight end. In 1967-68, two running backs joined the flanker, split end, and tight end. Since 1969, the positions have been two running backs, two wide receivers, and a tight end. In starting lineups, the player who would be considered the fullback under the old designation systems is listed first among running backs.

In 1964, the defensive positions left safety and right safety were replaced by free safety and strong safety, except on certain teams that kept the old designations, such as the Minnesota Vikings under Harry (Bud) Grant. The emergence of the 3-4 defense in the 1970s brought about the position designations of nose tackle and inside linebacker.

In the contemporary method of figuring pro football percentages, ties count as a half game won and a half game lost; that has been the rule since 1972. The all-time totals for teams and coaches in this history are figured that way, while year-by-year percentages before 1972 don't include ties at all, as was the rule during that period.

The all-time and year-to-year player records in this book include marks set since NFL statistics were kept and all AFL records from 1960-69. AAFC marks are not included in player records. However, the records of AAFC coaches are included in the Coaches section. Individual statistics for scoring, rushing, passing, and receiving first were kept officially in the NFL in 1932, with punting (1939), interceptions (1940), and punt and kickoff returns (1941) started later. These categories always have used the same criteria for individual championships, except for passing, which has changed numerous times. Since 1973, passers have been rated based on performance standards established for completion percentage, interception percentage, touchdown percentage, and yards per attempt. Passers are allocated points according to how their marks compare with those standards; then the points are converted to a scale.

To be considered for an individual passing, punt return, or kickoff return title, an individual had to have recorded a minimum number of passes or returns for that year, minimums that have changed many times. Similarly the year-to-year leaders in yards per carry or reception had to have a minimum number of carries or receptions to qualify.

ACKNOWLEDGMENTS

A project the size of *The Official NFL Encyclopedia* could not have been completed without the contributions of many people.

The most important editorial assistance came from the six individuals who are listed as major contributors on the legal page. Four—Bill Barron, David Boss, Chuck Garrity, Sr., and John Wiebusch—are members of the staff of the Creative Services Division of National Football League Properties, Inc. Each made important contributions during the initial planning stages of the book. In addition, Wiebusch and Garrity served as primary editors, Boss was in charge of photo selection, and Barron compiled the Rules of the NFL section. Barron also oversaw the schedule and budget for the project, with assistance from Nancy James.

Jim Campbell, now of the Little League Baseball Museum but formerly of NFL Properties and the Pro Football Hall of Fame, compiled the All-Time Roster section and did much of the original research for the NFL Draft section and the Extinct Leagues section. Joe Horrigan of the Hall of Fame contributed enormous amounts of information about the early years of the NFL, which was incorporated into the Seven Decades of the NFL and the Teams of the NFL sections. The author constantly used the seemingly endless knowledge of both Campbell and Horrigan, who also served as fact checkers. Jack Hand, former director of information for the NFC, also read the book for errors.

A number of independent researchers made significant contributions as well. The works of David Neft and Richard Cohen, perhaps the preeminent NFL historians, served as a basis for much of the fact checking of copy. Bob Carroll and Bob Braunwart compiled much of the information on the origins of the APFA and the 1920 season, including the results of that season, which are recognized by the NFL for the first time in this book. John Hogrogian put together the listing of the early all-pros. Denny Lynch compiled the AAFC drafts of 1947-49, an enormously important piece of material previously thought lost to the ages. Larry Eldridge updated the AFC team histories and gave consultation on the existing histories.

Additional research or editorial assistance was given by Chuck Garrity, Jr., Jeff Fellenzer, and Jim Natal of NFL Properties; Pete Abitante, Joel Bussert, and Art McNally of the National Football League; and Seymour Siwoff and Steve Hirdt of Elias Sports Bureau. Don Smith of the Pro Football Hall of Fame, Tom Bennett, and Rick Smith contributed to earlier editions.

Jane Morrissey, Gretchen Meyer, and Alicia Eastlake assisted with the inputting of the rosters and other information. Morrissey also coordinated the dissemination of this information for checking, and Meyer compiled and verified the photo credits.

The Official NFL Encyclopedia was designed by David Johnston and Glen Iwasaki.

Jere Wright managed the entire production process, working with a staff that included Joan Borgman, Laurel Burden, Barbara Hager, Violet Lee, Charlene Narita, Joanne Parsh-Fuller, Sandra Todd, Debra Uttal-Leifer, Hillary Weiss, and James Whitaker.

Typesetting was done by Marilyn Arai, Rick Wadholm, and Marlene Reicheg of NFL Properties, and by CAPCO of Los Angeles. The proofreader was Sheryl Strauss. Darkroom services were handled by Jim Chaffin, Miguel Elliott, and Mark Sherengo. Stan James, Stanley Wing, and Charles Prince were in charge of reproduction of copy and mailing services. Phil Barber, Sharon Kuthe, and Paul Tsuchiya of the NFL Properties library looked the other way when the author borrowed reference material for overly long periods of time.

Dick Falk and Tina Thompson maintained quality control responsibilities and handled the production coordination with the printer. Scott Kabak served as the liaison between NFL Properties and the publisher.

The book was printed at R.R. Donnelley's Crawfordsville, Indiana, and Willard, Ohio, plants.

To all of these people, and to the author's wife Mary—who for nine months put up with 544 pages instead of one husband—sincere thanks.

—Beau Riffenburgh

Roots of Pro Football

GROWTH OF COLLEGE FOOTBALL

American football comes from English soccer and rugby. Soccer is called football on other continents; it is the most popular game in the world. Rugby also is played practically everywhere, the by-product of British imperialism. American football is the cousin of these games and they all involve, in one way or another, the kicking of some object up and down a field. The kicking games of primitive tribes, *harpaston* in the Greek city-state of Sparta, *calcio* in ancient Rome, and the varieties of soccer that have been played for perhaps 2,000 years, can be considered ancestors of football. The ball used in those games might have been leather filled with sawdust, the bladder of some slaughtered animal, or the skull of an adversary slain in battle.

Soccer football was played in the American colonies, according to John Allen Krout in *Annals of American Sport*. "Here and there in the records of colonial days," he wrote, "one catches glimpses of boys and young men, occasionally young women, playing a game known as football. It might more accurately have been called handball, for throwing and passing the inflated bladder or sawdust-filled leather seems to have been more important than kicking it. In the latter part of the eighteenth century this haphazard game assumed a place with fisticuffs, wrestling matches, and drinking bouts, enjoyed by undergraduates as a means of relief from the severe mental discipline of college life."

Two important steps in the evolution of football occurred in the mother country of England. First, rugby was invented. At the Rugby School, a student named William Webb Ellis picked up the ball and ran with it during a soccer game in 1823. The rules forbade advancing the ball any way except kicking it, and the other players in the game were outraged at Ellis for breaking the rules. His innovation, however, became the basis for a new game, one that would influence American football greatly because the runner could carry the ball and not just kick it.

The second thing that happened in England was the formation of the London Football Association in 1862. It was organized by the proponents of the kicking game. They drew up rules forbidding the carrying of the ball. From then on their game was called association football or soccer. But that was not their largest contribution to American football. More importantly, they wrote rules that independent-minded Americans would overhaul and rewrite. And by having a rules convention the British established a rite of the sport, a tradition as much a part of it as bringing the uniforms out of storage for the first practice each year and blowing up the footballs.

There was high school soccer football before there was college soccer football. Boston secondary schools were playing games against each other on the Common as early as 1860, according to Allison Danzig in *The History of American Football*. Gerritt Smith Miller, a student at the Dixwell School from Peterboro, New York, organized the Oneida Football Club of Boston, "the first definite and formal football organization in the United States," in 1862.

College football began November 6, 1869. Rutgers and Princeton both had soccer football teams and they were close to each other, so they played a game. It vaguely resembled what we know as football today. Each team had 25 players, the ball was advanced by kicking it or butting it with the head, and there were goal posts that were 25 yards apart. These were modified London Football Association rules. The first team to make six goals won, and Rutgers triumphed six goals to four.

Yale and Columbia also had soccer football teams. Princeton and Yale formed football associations for games between classes. Harvard, however, played a different game, one more like rugby, called the "Boston Game." Canada then made the next and one of the most important contributions of all to the evolution of football. McGill University in Montreal played rugby; the sport probably had been brought to Canada by the British army. McGill played three games against Harvard in 1874, two at Cambridge and one at Montreal. As a result of these games Harvard took up rugby completely instead of soccer. The rugby principles of running with the ball and tackling had a foot in the door of American football.

It seemed as if everyone had different rules, and the sport was in a state of confusion. Then came the Massasoit convention of 1876 at which the first rules for American football were written. That same year the imposing figure of the man who would become the father of the game as we know it today, Walter Camp of Yale, appeared on the stage.

In a football game today, the ball does not pass back and forth at random but instead is held by each team. Each has to make a given number of yards, 10, in those four downs or lose the ball. Each has 11 players on the field. The principal handler of the ball is the "quarterback." The center snaps the ball to him. Walter Camp was responsible for all these innovations. Parke Davis wrote, "What Washington was to his country, Camp was to American football—the friend, the founder, and the father."

A Yale athlete and coach, Camp was so heroic and romantic a figure, so chivalrous, so simon-pure of motive and deed, that he was said to have been the model for the fictional character "Frank Merriwell of Yale" on which a whole generation of American boys was weaned.

Camp was so respected as a football authority that, while he wore the hat of magazine writer, he alone was archbishop at the annual coronation in *Collier's Weekly* of the knights of the gridiron, the All-Americas.

He ruled over the first college football juggernaut, Yale, before 1910. And he created the Daily Dozen exercise program for a feeble and flabby American public. He was aristocratic, a *bon vivant* and raconteur who was a celebrity and living legend everywhere he went.

When Walter Camp entered Yale in 1876, he was the product of one of the correct New Haven families and of the exclusive Hopkins Grammar School. He learned the variety of football then being played at Yale from Gene Baker, the captain of the team. Baker was Yale's delegate to the convention at the Massasoit House, a hotel in Springfield, Massachusetts. Playing rules were adopted there and an intercollegiate association was formed; it was the forerunner of the National Collegiate Athletic Association. The rules it adopted resembled those of rugby and it was called rugby football.

Camp played halfback in rugby football. He was a brilliant runner and kicker, a dashing figure with a flowing mustache and long hair held in place by a headband; in actuality he looked very much like many young men a century later. With Camp making dropkicks or picking up the ball and darting through the entire opposing team, Yale won 25, lost 1, and tied 6 in six years of intercollegiate play. At last, in a move aimed directly at him, the annual rules convention limited eligibility to five years. By then, Camp was in the Yale Medical School, and captain of the football team for the third time. He left medical school just one year short of his degree. He gave as his reason the fact that he could not stand the sight of blood, but it really may have been because he could no longer captain the Yale team and also compete, as he had, in baseball, track (he is credited by some with having been the first to run the hurdles and not jump each of them), tennis, and gymnastics.

The most remarkable fact of Camp's student days, however, is that he represented his university at the annual rules convention as a sophomore, in 1877. At that point, the game was one in which the ball was put down on the field with both teams clustering around it and all of them kicking at the ball and trying to drive it free. Someone finally would succeed in picking it up and starting off on a run. Then he probably would meet opposition and kick the ball away or make a lateral or backward pass. But he also may have been knocked to the turf before doing any of these things.

In 1880, Camp had an idea to give one side undisputed possession of the ball until that side, of its own volition, gave the ball up. This was passed by the rules convention, and Camp had invented scrimmage. In the same year, he convinced his colleagues that a team should number 11, not 15, players. Further, the person receiving the ball from a "snapback," later called a center, should be called the "quarterback." Snaps were first made with the foot. Later, players were allowed to guide the ball with a hand. Finally they came to center entirely with the hands.

Having created the position of quarterback, Camp, as Yale captain, then became the first to have his quarterback call signals. For example, the quarterback would say, "Play up sharp, Charlie!" if a kick was about to be made.

But Camp's conviction that the chivalrous Ivy Leaguers gladly would give up the ball when they could not gain ground during scrimmage was ill-founded. The "block game" resulted; one team kept the ball the whole first half and the other the whole second half. This led Camp to suggest—and the convention to pass—a rule requiring a team to make five yards in three downs; it was increased later to 10 yards in four downs.

After leaving medical school Camp took a position with his uncle's business, the New Haven Clock Company. He also kept his affiliation with Yale; indeed, he soon dominated its athletic department. And he continued to be a member of one committee of football rulesmakers or another until he died.

Camp never was a paid coach nor did he ever assume the title. Instead, a series of coaches drew their authority from him. And he held the purse strings of the fund made from Yale Field gate receipts.

Tad Jones, who had been a Camp player and was later Yale's coach, explained that, "Camp coached through the coaches. He seldom took an active part on the field. He had no more authoritative position than treasurer of the Yale Field Association, but his advice had authority because it was good advice. The practice then was to have the former year's captain return as head coach, and Camp, by serving every year as adviser, gave unity and continuity to these shifting assistants."

In 1888 Camp proposed—and the convention passed—a rule permitting tackling as low as the knees. Its effect on football was stupefying. Runners who were tackled that way went down to stay. The savage mass play era dawned. Offenses contracted and bunched themselves around the runner. The dangerous "wedge" appeared. Lorin Deland of Harvard created the even more dangerous flying wedge. Camp and Yale fostered the shoving wedge. Play became brutal, fights proliferated, and there were deaths on the gridiron.

A public outcry arose. The mass play era split intercollegiate football and led to the White House conference of 1905 and the subsequent formation of the NCAA.

President Theodore Roosevelt called representatives of Yale, Harvard, and Princeton to the White House and told them to clean up football. "Brutality and foul play should receive the same summary punishment given to a man who cheats at cards," he said.

The President could provide moral leadership but the real reform of football occurred in the nuts-and-bolts work of the rules committees. There were two meetings in December, 1905, and as a result an old and new committee combined themselves and the Intercollegiate Athletic Association was formed. The name later was changed to National Collegiate Athletic Association.

Camp headed the old committee, Captain Palmer Pierce of West Point the new, and they sat down together for the first time in January, 1906. They legalized the forward pass. More reforms were made in succeeding years. But the game of football had been defined by Camp and his associates, and it was this game that the National Football League adopted in 1920 and did not change for more than a decade.

THE ROOTS OF PRO FOOTBALL

Sports took root in America after the Civil War. People fled the factories and went outdoors to ride bicycles and play golf and other sports. One of the most important aspects of this movement was the advent of the athletic club. The first was the New York Athletic Club in 1868. Virtually every other city acquired one after that. These clubs sponsored teams in a great variety of sports. They gave tremendous impetus to competition in all of them. And they probably started pro football.

The photographs are still with us today, legions of them in seemingly endless supply, with players reclining somber-faced in their uniforms in front of pastoral studio backdrops, a melon-shaped football at their feet with lettering such as "Johnstown A.C. 1891" on it. It is astonishing how many team pictures remain. Clearly, club football teams were everywhere. Were they all, every club and every player, amateurs? Probably not.

One of their number, William (Pudge) Heffelfinger of the Allegheny Athletic Association of Pittsburgh, received what history records as the first payment to play football in 1892. But he was the most famous player of his day; others more obscure than Heffelfinger may have received payments earlier than he did. And it is known that some athletic clubs bent the rules and awarded their players in ways that carried the clubs to the brink of professionalism—and perhaps beyond.

Baseball had gone professional with the formation of the American Association in 1871 and the new Amateur Athletic Union was determined to stop this "evil" from spreading to other sports, and rid them all of the "tramp athlete," the opportunist who moved about and sold his services to college or athletic club. He was the bane of the athletic world and the AAU gained much support. It grew into an organization with great power. Each year it held a sports carnival in New York City where athletes could compete for national championships in their respective sports.

But the AAU inadvertently helped bring about the rise of pro football. In 1889, six athletic clubs in the East decided to copy the parent AAU and form their own union, or league. They were the Baltimore Athletic Club, the Boston Athletic Association, the New York Athletic Club, the New York Crescents Athletic Club, the New York Manhattans, and the Orange (New Jersey) Athletic Club. They played for the "amateur title of America" each year for more than a decade. There was now a league of amateur teams. The next step was to begin talking about going professional.

The AAU moved against what it believed to be professionalism on two fronts in 1890. The San Francisco Olympic Athletic Club was accused by a rival of obtaining jobs for its players in order to get them to jump to the Olympic Club. The AAU decreed, however, that while San Francisco's action was not to be commended, it was not actually professionalism, only a "semi" form of it; the Olympic Club got off with a reprimand, and the term "semipro" was born.

In New Jersey, the Orange Athletic Club awarded trophies or watches to its best players at the end of each season. Accusations were made against Orange but apparently this was the practice of several clubs in the New York City area. According to Dr. Harry March, the recipient of the gift then could be seen "threading his way to some well-known pawnbroker where the watch was placed in hock, the usual sum received thereby being a sawbuck—twenty smackers. Then the player, still strictly amateur, somehow ran across the man who managed those amateur games and sold him the pawn ticket for another twenty dollars. By some special sense of divination, second sightedness or mental telepathy, the promoter found himself urged towards the same pawn shop and under an irresistible impulse, retrieved the pawned watch, paying a small interest and twenty dollars. Then, after the next game, the player received as his trophy the same gold watch, which then went through the same identical loaning experience."

The AAU ruled that clubs could no longer award trophies; they had to limit their gifts to banners costing 25 cents apiece. But the big athletic clubs continued to find ways to get around the rules. One way was to hand out travel expenses equal to double the amount of the fare. There obviously were professional players on athletic clubs in other cities before Heffelfinger was paid $500 by a club in Pittsburgh and started the recorded history of pro football.

THE PENNSYLVANIA PERIOD

Pennsylvania is an historic state. It was one of the 13 original colonies. The Articles of Confederation, Declaration of Independence, and Constitution were signed there. General George Washington and his troops encamped there at Valley Forge in 1777. Later, the Civil War reached its turning point when a Confederate army led by General Robert E. Lee advanced as far north as Gettysburg—and met defeat.

Much westward expansion moved across Pennsylvania's breadth. In the west, the Allegheny and Monongahela rivers meet in Pittsburgh and form the mighty Ohio River. This great waterway was the gateway to the West for American settlers.

Similarly, the game of football moved toward becoming a professional game westward from colleges such as Yale, Princeton, Rutgers, and Harvard, across Pennsylvania to Pittsburgh where, through the phenomenon of the athletic club, the first known pro football was played. Pro football then moved directly westward into Ohio, into towns such as Akron, Canton, and Massillon. And they and others formed what became the NFL.

Pittsburgh's first athletic clubs were the Allegheny Athletic Association and the Pittsburgh Athletic Club. Such clubs emerged after the Civil War, according to researcher Thomas Jable, as an antidote to Victorianism. Through competitive athletics at their clubs, American men could "countermand the Victorian principles of delicacy and refinement." Football, aggressive and sometimes violent, served this need especially well; it "represented a significant triumph of robust manliness over tender and fragile femininity." Membership in an athletic club also meant prestige and an opportunity to identify vicariously with the big names in college football.

Anyone who has ever arrived at a city park all set for a good, hard-fought touch football game, only to see that the opposition has brought along a few surprise players all of whom are better and more experienced than anyone else there, is familiar with the term "ringer." And ringers hired by the Allegheny Athletic Association of Pittsburgh in 1892 were the first pro football players.

In Jable's words, "As competition increased in intensity and winning became important, the athletic club turned to the established athlete from the outside. . . . In hiring the gifted player or professional, the athletic club shattered the amateur ideal upon which it was founded, that is, participation for the sheer love of the game. Victory meant fame, glory, and increased income for the athletic club. Big money was made by individual members who wagered heavily on their club's eleven. From this atmosphere at the athletic club, professionalism crept into football as the Allegheny Athletic Association and the Pittsburgh Athletic Club vied for notoriety, prestige, and profits."

The Allegheny Athletic Association was organized by two Pittsburgh businessmen, John Moorehead and O. D. Thompson, who were graduates of Yale and who had played football there. The club was called "AAA," the "AAA's," "Three A's," and, as it edged nearer professionalism, sometimes "Four A's" with a tongue-in-cheek extra "A" for "amateur." It had the first club football team in Pittsburgh in about 1890.

The Pittsburgh Athletic Club's gym was the largest and best in western Pennsylvania; for that reason the team was sometimes called the "Gyms." The Pittsburgh Athletic Club was older than the AAA. It formed a football team in 1891 because it felt the AAA team was getting more than its share of publicity in the Pittsburgh newspapers.

Professor William Kirschner was the physical director of the PAC and became its star football player. Researcher Nelson Ross writes that Kirschner "had little football experience, but he possessed tremendous strength and size and learned quickly." And he was probably a semi-professional.

"Professor Kirschner received a regular salary for teaching his gym classes," Ross writes. "It was noted, however, that during the football season his 'teaching' salary went up considerably. It was denied that this had any connection with his playing on the PAC football team, but rivals noted that while his salary doubled, his classes were only half their normal size during the football season. Pittsburgh papers were at times critical of Kirschner's status but no one accused him outright."

PAC challenged AAA to a game. AAA ignored the challenge. The feud grew hotter when AAA lured away four of PAC's best players. At last a game was scheduled for Columbus Day, October 12, 1892, at the PAC field in Pittsburgh's East Liberty section. More than 3,000 spectators flocked to the grounds, Jable wrote, "in drags, tallyhos, dog carts, street cars, and railroad cars. They filled the seating accommodations at PAC Park to more than capacity. Hundreds more packed the surrounding buildings from the first floor to the roof, viewing the game at no expense. More spectators would have been in attendance had not the lengthy Columbus Day parade prevented a number of street cars and other public conveyances from reaching East Liberty. The fashionable crowd was evenly split between the two teams, though each faction was easily distinguishable by the colors it wore. PAC rooters wore red and white ribbons, while the AAA followers donned blue and white colors."

The game ended in a 6-6 tie. George Proctor, a physician, scored the only goal for PAC and Norman McClintock of Yale, playing for AAA, scored its goal. The same players also kicked their teams' goals; a touchdown counted four points and a successful placekick counted two. The teams divided $1,200 in gate receipts, and as a result of the great interest in the game each club processed about 100 new members during the weeks that followed.

The news that PAC had played a ringer, however, stirred new hostilities. A.C. Read, captain of the Penn State team and a shotputter, had played for PAC under the name of "Stayer." The PAC captain had misled AAA, saying "Stayer" was an old friend he had met on the street and invited to play in the game. AAA was incensed, and, as AAA plotted how to get even, a famous Yale All-America who was then in faraway Chicago loomed in the future of Pittsburgh football.

William Walter (Pudge) Heffelfinger played guard for Yale in 1888-1891. Walter Camp was his mentor and Amos Alonzo Stagg his teammate. Heffelfinger made the first All-America team ever selected, in 1889. He also made the team for two more years and has been one of the guards on virtually every all-time All-America team selected. In 1892, his Yale days behind him, he was working in a nondescript railroad office job in Omaha, Nebraska, when he grew bored and joined a Chicago amateur club called the Chicago AA on an Eastern tour in which it would play teams in Cleveland, Rochester, Princeton, Philadelphia, Cambridge, and Brooklyn. The Chicago AA was a controversial member of the AAU. Its playing manager, Billy Crawford, was paying ample expenses to players and enraging the AAU with talk of a "professional football league" in cities such as Chicago, Detroit, Cleveland, Pittsburgh, and New York; he was a man 28 years ahead of his time.

The Chicago AA's tour was not scheduled to stop in Pittsburgh, but it was the talk of the athletic clubs there, and when the tour reached Cleveland two members of the Pittsburgh Athletic Club were in the stands. "Both cheered wildly," wrote Ross, "when the magnificent Heffelfinger hit the Cleveland fullback so hard that he fumbled the ball, with William grabbing it and streaking with incredible speed for a man so large, over the Cleveland goal line."

The big rematch in Pittsburgh between the PAC and AAA was a few weeks away. The people of Pittsburgh were shocked to read in the *Press* that PAC was rumored to be offering $250 each to Heffelfinger and another Chicago AA player, Knowlton (Snake) Ames, to play against AAA. The rumors persisted as the game drew nearer.

Many years have gone by since that fateful game, and as time has passed football teams have learned to squash rumors that they are close to signing a player to a contract. Negotiations always can go sour at the last minute and the team is left with nothing except an unsigned contract and a credibility gap. This postulate of present-day football was not there for the Pittsburgh Athletic Club to follow in 1892. And when the archrivals of club football lined up against each other at Recreation Park on Pittsburgh's North Side November 13, Heffelfinger was there all right, but not with PAC. He was with the AAA. So were his former Chicago AA teammates Ed Malley, a shot-putter from Detroit, and Ben (Sport) Donnelly, former Princeton star; Ames had decided to forgo the game rather than risk his amateur status.

It was a cold day and there was snow on the ground. A crowd of about 3,000 watched as the Pittsburgh Athletic Club angrily protested the presence of AAA ringers. All bets were off, PAC declared. It offered to play a scrub game. While the crowd grew restive, the substitutes of each team began to play while the regulars argued. O.D. Thompson, the manager of AAA, pointed out that PAC planned to play A.C. Read, "Stayer" in the first game, this time under his real name, and PAC also had Clarence Lomax of Cornell and Simon Martin of the Steelton, Pennsylvania, Athletic Club in its lineup. The arguments continued until the two teams at last agreed to play an "exhibition" game with all bets canceled. They settled on two 30-minute halves. AAA won 4-0. Heffelfinger picked up a fumble by one of his teammates, ran around end, and went 25 yards for a touchdown. Malley missed the kick for goal. The bickering had delayed the game, and darkness ended it 18 minutes into the second half.

Heffelfinger demonstrated a vicious method for breaking PAC's wedge. When PAC wedged down the field, he ran and jumped at it with full speed, bringing his knees against the mass. The wedge didn't last long.

The PAC captain, Charley Aull, left the game with a badly injured back. His brother, Burt, retired after receiving "a fierce blow to the head." Sport Donnelly received "a terrific smash in the eye."

After the game Heffelfinger was paid $500 for playing and $25 for expenses, Malley and Donnelly $25 for travel. Heffelfinger was thus the first professional football player on record. Gross receipts totaled $1,683. After Heffelfinger's fee, a visitors' guarantee of $428, and miscellaneous expenses, the AAA made a profit of $621.

A furor over professionalism raged for weeks in Pittsburgh's newspapers. O.D. Thompson, AAA manager, a skillful lawyer, and the man primarily responsible for making Heffelfinger a professional, left town. He went to New York to defend AAA track stars named E.V. Pant and J.B. McKennan against AAU charges that *they* were professionals.

A guard and assistant manager on the football team named Billy Kountz was left to fend off the questions the press was asking about pros on the AAA. Thompson returned too late for a rubber match to be played against PAC. Heffelfinger and Malley left Pittsburgh but Sport Donnelly stayed and one week after the PAC game played for AAA against Washington and Jefferson College; he was paid $250 and thus became the second known pro football player in history. The next year three players named Rafferty, Van Cleve, and Wright (their first names are not known) became the third, fourth, and fifth when they received contracts to play for AAA for $50 a game—the first pro football contracts in history. The athletic clubs threw caution and their AAU affiliation to the wind and ended forever the pretense that they were amateur. Allegheny Athletic Association was barred permanently from the AAU in 1895. Many of its members resigned. The others, who openly admitted their professionalism, imported Heffelfinger, Donnelly, other members of the touring Chicago AA, and other well-known football players such as Tom (Doggie) Trenchard and Langdon (Biffy) Lea of Princeton. They played back-to-back games in 1896 against PAC and the new Pittsburgh Duquesnes and won both games, 18-0 and 12-0. Heffelfinger and the other imports apparently were paid a staggering $100 a game. The players who had been together in 1892 enjoyed their reunion and held marathon beer-drinking sessions talking over old times. AAA finished the season playing a barnstorming tour against amateur teams in western Pennsylvania, West Virginia, and Ohio. But the payroll for the back-to-back games in November had bankrupted the club. By 1897, "for all practical purposes, it ceased to exist as a functioning year-round club," Ross wrote. "Professionalism and its opponents had dealt it a death blow." There was one more uneventful season before the club broke up when its most patriotic members left to fight in the Spanish-American War. When the war veterans returned there were high-priced bidding contests as they sold their services to the Duquesnes or PAC. What was left of AAA sponsored an amateur team made up of Western Pennsylvania Theological Seminary students, a team that must have been quite different in character from the rollicking Alleghenies of earlier years.

America's first known pro football team had come and gone. It was, however, just the beginning for the sport. Open football professionalism spread to the clubs of the small towns in the surrounding coal region, pro football appeared in other states, and a "World Series" was played indoors at Madison Square Garden in both 1902 and 1903, giving rise to the same event in the game of professional baseball.

William Chase Temple was an industrialist who donated the "Temple Cup," a portentous silver trophy, to the winner of a playoff between the first-place and second-place finishers in the National League of Professional Baseball Clubs between 1894 and 1897 (there was no American League in baseball until 1901). Temple also gave a cup to the winner of the football "Challenge Cup" competition among Pittsburgh's three athletic club football teams. The newest of them was the Duquesne Country and Athletic Club, or Pittsburgh Duquesnes. This team ran up a huge payroll in signing players returning from the Spanish-American War. In 1899, it found itself in the unique position of having every player on the team salaried. It looked to Temple for help. He bought the football team from the athletic club and thus became pro football's first owner.

William E. Corey and A. C. Dinkey were next. They were Pittsburgh steel barons and friends of Temple. They formed teams to play his Duquesnes. But while he had a big-city team, theirs were located in the grimy steel mill towns of Braddock and Homestead east of the city. Interest in club football ran high there among the miners and mill laborers who dug the ore and worked the blast furnaces. Corey's team was the Braddock Carnegies, the original club team having been named earlier for steel magnate Andrew Carnegie; Dinkey's was the Homestead Library and Athletic Club, or Athletics, or, later, Homestead Steelers.

Corey was a generous, kindly man whose team was made up mostly of steelworkers; it had only a few token college products. The steelworkers got a football bonus in addition to their regular salaries and were excused from work in the mills during football season.

Dinkey, in contrast, went after the big college All-Americas. He also raided Temple's Duquesnes for players. With such high-priced talent, Dinkey won the "world's championship," which actually meant the championship of the athletic clubs in and around Pittsburgh, in 1900 and 1901.

Friendships among wealthy men often are tested by sports competition. Temple was outraged by Dinkey's actions. Temple and owner Barney Dreyfuss of the baseball Pittsburgh Pirates—a name gained through pirating the players of other teams—formed a new football club called the Pittsburgh Professionals, or Pros. For the first time a team openly admitted it was professional. It immediately began raiding back the players Dinkey had stolen. And to stir interest and support, Temple and Dreyfuss decided to use their contacts in baseball and get an intrastate rivalry going with Philadelphia.

There is still one team in American sports whose name goes all the way back to the era of athletic clubs and their preeminence. It is the Oakland Athletics. This baseball team, which a famous manager named Connie Mack led for a half-century, played in Philadelphia until 1954, in Kansas City until 1968, and is now in Oakland.

In 1902, Mack's team was American League champion. He and Ben Shibe, the owner, then decided to field a football team, too. So did the rival Philadelphia Nationals or Phillies of the National League. During the 1902 season, the Athletics, Phillies, and the Pittsburgh team that was known that year either as the Pros or the Stars played games against each other. Mack's team was 11-2-1 in all games for the season, according to researcher Milt Roberts; 2-1 against the Phillies and 1-1-1 against Pittsburgh.

Pitcher Rube Waddell played on Mack's football team some of the time. In one of the three games against Pittsburgh, pitcher Christy Mathewson played fullback for Pittsburgh. Because of the presence of these famous baseball personages, the one-year foray of Mack into football is given perhaps more importance than it deserves in some histories. Nevertheless, he could rightfully claim the pro football championship of 1902.

The first World Series was played in football, not baseball. Pro football was growing in popularity not only in Pennsylvania in 1902, but in other states as well. The New York Knickerbockers, a football team about which little else is known, was impressed with the interest shown in the Philadelphia-Pittsburgh games and conceived the idea of a World Series. It was actually to be a four-team tournament, and a promoter named Tom O'Rourke arranged for it to be held in Madison Square Garden, the original Garden at Madison Avenue and Twenty-Sixth Street in New York City.

There was one World Series in 1902 and another in 1903. The first was played between the Knickerbockers, the Philadelphia Athletics, the Watertown (New York) Red and Blacks, and the Syracuse Athletic Club. Syracuse won. Glenn (Pop) Warner, later a famous coach of the Carlisle Indian School, Stanford, and other college teams, played center for Syracuse in the first World Series.

The second was in 1903 and included Philadelphia, Watertown, the Orange (New Jersey) Athletic Club, and the Franklin (Pennsylvania) Athletic Club, which had lured away many of the best players from Pittsburgh with high salaries. Franklin defeated every other team and won the tournament.

Football's World Series did not become a lasting event but baseball adopted the idea, and, in its first series, Boston of the American League defeated Dreyfuss's Pittsburgh team of the National League in 1903, five games to three. There was no series in 1904, but it was resumed in 1905 and there has been one ever since.

There was professional football in other Pennsylvania cities, too. Pro teams included the Olympic Athletic Club of McKeesport, the Jeanette Athletic Association, the Pitcairn Quakers, the Conshohocken Pros, the Coaldale Big Green, and the Pottsville All-Service. There also were noted individuals. Lawson Fiscus, a celebrated Princeton player, apparently got $20 a game in 1894 to play for the Greensburg Athletic Association. John Brallier, a quarterback at Indiana College (Pennsylvania) in 1895, accepted $10 and "cakes"—expenses—to play for the Latrobe Athletic Club.

Brallier later became a dentist in Latrobe. He corresponded with Dr. Henry March, the New York Giants' doctor and a dabbler in pro football. Brallier wrote that he had been the first professional football player in history in 1895 with Latrobe. March published Brallier's claim in his 1934 book, the rambling, often misinformed *Pro Football's Ups and Downs*. Brallier became a figure of history. The game in which he had played for the first time for Latrobe was called the first pro game in history. The myth grew; the Pro Football Hall of Fame almost was located in Latrobe instead of the city of the founding of the NFL, Canton, Ohio.

In 1971, however, Nelson Ross's research, which originally had been given to Dan Rooney of the Steelers and later filed away at the Hall of Fame, was "rediscovered." Together with the actual expense sheet of the Allegheny Athletic Association showing it paid Heffelfinger $500 in 1892, it proved that Heffelfinger, not Brallier, was the first known pro. Subsequent research by Thomas Jable corroborated Ross's findings and added new details in the account of Heffelfinger and the AAA.

Pro football declined in Pittsburgh after 1903. The Alleghenies had faded from view. The Duquesne Country and Athletic Club had been absorbed by the Pros or Stars and they in turn by the Franklin team that won the second World Series. The mill teams at Braddock and Homestead disappeared when their owners, Corey and Dinkey, lost interest; Corey, one of the first three club owners in pro football, became president of United States Steel in August, 1903.

THE OHIO PERIOD

Athletic clubs and their ringers ushered in pro football. It "came out of the closet" in Pennsylvania when teams there openly declared themselves pros. And it grew into a league in Ohio. This was one of the most important steps in American sports history.

The game grew up in prosperous, growing cities; the population of rubber capital Akron was 69,067 in 1910 and Canton's was 50,217. And these cities were in the eye of the press and public. McKinley and Harding both ran their presidential campaigns from their front porches, McKinley in Canton and Harding in Marion, and they kept their homes in those Ohio cities while they were president.

In this setting, pro football arrived. Predictably, it had its roots in athletic club teams. According to Ross, there were club teams in Dayton in 1889, Cleveland in 1890, Cincinnati in 1891, Akron in 1894, and Canton and Youngstown in 1895. Other club teams appeared in Alliance, Byesville, Columbus, Lorain, Marion, Newark, Sandusky, Salem, Shelby, and Toledo. There was a state champion proclaimed every year after 1896.

The Shelby team, known as the Blues, was one of the first Ohio teams to turn pro. As early as 1902, the squad was composed entirely of ex-college players who were purely professional. Included was the first known black pro football player, Charles Follis.

"But in 1903 a new team appeared on the horizon named the Massillon Tigers," Ross wrote. "That town had never had an independent football team before, but organized one for the '03 season, defeated amateur Canton in the first of many blood battles between them, and then promptly challenged defending and unscored-on state champion East Akron AA to a game for the amateur title of Ohio."

Massillon imported professionals from the Pittsburgh Athletic Club and won the game 12-0. Within one year, the state had at least eight pro teams, and in 1904 there was an abortive attempt to form a league and end cutthroat bidding for players. It became the second known discussion of a pro league, the first having been by Billy Crawford of the Chicago AA in 1892. Ohio's attempts to form a league in 1904 never amounted to anything, either, and the all-out scrambling for players continued.

Eddie Stewart, the city editor of the *Massillon Independent,* and Charles (Cy) Rigler were prominent managers of the football team in Massillon. It got the name "Tigers" when Stewart bought a supply of jerseys with striped sleeves, in the style of Princeton University, at a cut rate from a sporting goods store. Massillon was state champion in 1904, 1905, and 1906. It suffered a stinging defeat at the hands of Canton in 1911, dropped out of football for a while, and returned in 1916.

A.A. (Buzz) Wesbacker, who was a high school coach in Greensburg, Pennsylvania, in 1917, also played for the Massillon Tigers. "The pro games were always on Sunday," he recalled, "and each team would get together Sunday morning with the coach, who would map out the plays and signals. We would practice for an hour, and that was it. If the coach liked the way you played in the actual game, you were signed up for the following week.

"I got fifty dollars a game and expenses. The crowds were mostly rubber, steel, and factory workers. The games were played on baseball fields with stands on one side and a rope stretched on the other; that was standing room only, where most of the betting took place. The bets were placed on the ground, just inside the rope, anchored with a rock, never to be touched until the game ended. At times some young punk would try his luck at getting the loot, only to be warned with a big juicy spit of tobacco near his feet. It certainly was effective."

Akron was such a hotbed of football that in the days of amateur teams it had not one but two of them. When East Akron lost to Massillon in 1903, Akron pretended to disdain the hiring of pros for a while. By the end of 1904, however, it was one of the cities pushing the hardest in the ill-fated attempt to organize a pro league.

The Akron Indians, state champions in 1909, were a team of players from southeast Akron who had played football together since they were boys. They lost the championship in 1910, however, to the Shelby Blues, who were led by George (Peggy) Parrott, a former star player for Case Western Reserve in Cleveland. By 1913, however, Parrott had switched his allegiance to Akron; he led that team to a victory over Shelby. Parrott became a celebrated player-manager who was a lively promoter of the game and recruiter of talent. He wanted to beat the rival Canton Bulldogs at any cost. In 1914, he imported the entire left side of Notre Dame's 1913 line, including end Knute Rockne, and Akron beat Canton 21-0 and was named the state champion.

Pro football players came from varied backgrounds. The players for the Columbus Panhandles were, in their regular jobs, mechanics for the Panhandle Division of the Pennsylvania Railroad. "They had free transportation and so they were an inexpensive team to play," Harry March wrote. "The boys worked in the shop until four o'clock Saturday afternoon, got their suppers at home, grabbed the rattlers [trains] to any point within twelve hours' ride of Columbus, played the Sunday game, took another train to Columbus, and punched the time clock at seven Monday morning."

The Panhandles first gained notoriety as amateurs in 1902, when Luke Westwater instructed the players in the "fine points" of football, and developed them into one of the premier teams in Ohio. In 1903, they went 6-3, losing only to Ohio State, Ohio Medical University, and the Shelby Blues.

Joe Carr took over the Panhandles in 1904 when he was assistant sports editor of the *Ohio State Journal* in Columbus. Under Carr, the Panhandles, turned pro. Carr's sports involvement grew and he became the manager of the minor league baseball team in Columbus and a professional basketball team. He later became president of the National Football League from 1921 until his death in 1939.

Katherine and Theodore Nesser, German immigrants who lived in Columbus, had six sons and each of them—Al, Frank, Fred, John, Phil, and Ted—played professionally with the Panhandles.

The Dover Canals got their name because Dover was a port on the Ohio and Erie Canals. The Elyria Athletics represented Elyria, named for the Ely family that founded the town. Elyria came out of nowhere and shocked Canton to win the Ohio championship in 1912.

No other Ohio team, however, made as much history or contributed as much to professional football before 1920 as the Canton Bulldogs. They turned pro in 1905. Outsiders were imported with the express purpose of beating the archrival Massillon Tigers, seven miles to the west, and taking the Stark County and Ohio professional championships. The ringers didn't help, however; Massillon went undefeated, beat Canton 14-4, and won the state championship again. More Canton-Massillon battles, and an eventful 1906 football season, loomed ahead.

In 1906, Peggy Parrott joined Massillon. Canton's playing coach, Bill Laub, was injured and did not return. He was replaced by Blondy Wallace, who would become a figure of notoriety almost unparalleled among all pro football coaches. Wallace, according to March, "knew where to get the right men, how to condition them, and how to build up an attack and defense, but he never won their confidence in his integrity and honesty."

Wallace raided Massillon's team and landed four of its players—Clark Schrontz, Jack Lang, Jack Hayden, and Herman Kerchoffe. It was the year that the rules committee of Walter Camp and his associates legalized the forward pass, and Wallace took the Canton Bulldogs to Penn State to learn the new maneuver from the coach there.

Canton and Massillon played a two-game series in 1906. The games were eagerly awaited in the neighboring cities and even far outside their realm of Stark County and Ohio. Grantland Rice, the most eminent of sportswriters, wrote grandly before the first game: "There have been a few football games before. Yale has faced Princeton, Harvard has tackled Penn, and Michigan and Chicago have met in one or two steamy affairs. But these were not the Real Product when measured by the football standard set by the warring factions of Stark County, Ohio, now posing in the football limelight."

The two titans of pro football squared off for the first time at the Tigers' field on the grounds of the Ohio state asylum in Massillon. A big crowd watched. Some stood atop a trolley car stopped on the tracks nearby, others along the top of the rickety wooden fence that surrounded the field. Massillon won 10-5. The second game was at Canton two weeks later and the Tigers won again 13-6.

Controversy swelled around both games. "Canton players had been drawing very little money from Wallace," March wrote, "letting him keep their funds for fear a big poker game or other luxuries would lead them to extravagance. They had asked him to bet the money on the first game with Massillon.

"When the game resulted in a Massillon victory he told the fellows he had bet it on the second game."

Wallace's troubles had just begun. The *Massillon Independent* accused him of having tried to throw the second game by influencing the Massillon players and, failing that, persuaded a Canton player to throw it. "When accused by his teammates," March wrote, "this player said he had simply obeyed orders as he was accustomed to do. At any rate he left town hurriedly, on the first train, in his playing togs—his belongings following later—maybe."

A Canton fan who lost heavily on the second game confronted the Bulldogs' players at the Courtland Hotel bar in Canton. Angry words were exchanged. Punches were thrown, and soon a brawl was in progress. The crowd surged through a plate glass window and out into Court Street, where police arrived and broke it up with their night sticks.

Blondy Wallace sued the *Massillon Independent* for libel. The suit was thrown out of court.

Shamed, Canton quit pro football. Its "big team" (there were neighborhood teams that sprang up periodically) did not return for five years, until 1911. In 1912, a 21 year-old clerk at the Canton gas company named Jack Cusack became the secretary-treasurer of the team.

Cusack accepted the job as a favor to Roscoe Oberlin, who owned the team. H. H. Halter was manager and resented the intrusion of a man as young as Cusack. Halter was having trouble negotiating a contract for games with Peggy Parrott and the Akron Indians; Parrott felt Akron was a bigger drawing card than Canton and therefore did not have to divide the gate receipts evenly with the Bulldogs. Cusack entered the negotiations and, after five hours of dealing with Parrott, came away with the half-and-half arrangement. Halter was ousted as manager.

The team took the name "Professionals," to make fans forget the tainted past of the Bulldogs. It moved out to lease a new field, League Park. Cusack was made a full partner with Oberlin. They added 1,500 seats to the park in 1913 and sold season tickets for the first time in 1914. Cusack quit his job at the gas company to work full-time for the team. There were hard times as Cusack struggled to make a profit. He found a financial angel in J. J. Frey of the Home Brewing Company, who opened a $10,000 line of credit for the team at the Canton Bank. But Cusack's troubles continued. Center Harry Turner died of injuries he received in a game in 1914; Canton played out the season amid protests and before small crowds.

Jim Thorpe came to Canton in November, 1915. Cusack signed him for $250 a game just before the first game of the season against Massillon. Thorpe was the world's most celebrated athlete. A Sac and Fox Indian from Oklahoma, he had been an All-America halfback for the Carlisle Indian Industrial School in Carlisle, Pennsylvania, coached by Glenn (Pop) Warner. In 1912, he won the decathlon and pentathlon for the United States in the fifth modern Olympiad at Stockholm, Sweden. "Sir, you are the greatest athlete in the world," King Gustav V of Sweden told Thorpe as he presented him his medals. But heartbreaking sadness followed for Thorpe; his Olympic medals were taken from him when it was learned that he had played semipro baseball in Rocky Mount, North Carolina, for $25 a game in 1911 during the summer months while a student at Carlisle; unlike countless other college athletes who did the same thing, he had not played the pro sport under an assumed name. (Thorpe's medals since have been restored posthumously.) When Jack Cusack signed him for Canton, Thorpe was the veteran of one season of pro football with Pine Village, Indiana, in 1913, was a reserve outfielder with the New York Giants during the summer, and was employed in the fall as backfield coach for the University of Indiana.

His one season with Pine Village had been insignificant; he now found in the Canton Bulldogs the right supporting cast to become a sensational professional player. Cusack also signed other notables from college football that year such as Hube Wagner of Pittsburgh, Bill Gardner of Carlisle, Earle (Greasy) Neale, the coach at West Virginia Wesleyan, and his line coach, John Kellison. Neale and Kellison played as pros under aliases.

Cusack's friends warned him he had made a terrible mistake in signing Thorpe for so much money. The Bulldogs, however, played before 6,000 fans at Massillon, losing 16-0. Thorpe is supposed to have slipped on the wet field on the way to two touchdowns. There were 8,000 fans for the second game at League Park in Canton. So many fans clamored to get into the park for the second meeting of the two teams that the Bulldogs sold standing-room-only tickets in the end zones and the two teams agreed on the ground rule that any player crossing the goal line into the crowd must be in possession of the ball when he emerged from it.

Thorpe dropkicked two field goals and Canton led 6-0. Three quarters went by and the Bulldogs were on the verge of a great victory. Massillon's passing attack began working, however, and an end named Briggs caught a pass on the 15-yard line and raced across the end zone, disappearing into the surging crowd. Gideon (Charley) Smith, the first black player on the Canton team, followed Briggs in mad pursuit into the crowd. There, out of sight, a Canton trolley-car conductor kicked the ball out of Briggs's hands and into the arms of Smith, who emerged from the sea of humanity onto the playing field, the ball in his hands. It was a touchback and Canton's victory was preserved.

Massillon fans streamed onto the field in protest. The officials called the game. Massillon demanded that the officials settle the matter by making a statement about the referee's decision awarding the touchback. The officials agreed but only if it could be placed in a sealed envelope and opened by the manager of the Massillon team at 30 minutes after midnight at the Courtland Hotel that night.

A tense crowd divided equally among Canton and Massillon supporters was on hand at 12:30 A.M. as the envelope with the statement was opened. It was read aloud and Canton's victory was upheld. Years later, the conductor whose kicking game equaled Thorpe's that day confessed to his crime while riding a streetcar through Canton with Jack Cusack.

The next season, 1916, was the best of all for Canton and Thorpe. "The 1916 Bulldogs," Cusack wrote in the 1960s, "were one of the greatest teams ever assembled, one I would match against any team in professional football today if they played under the rules and with the same ball in vogue at that time."

Thorpe missed the first two games because he was playing baseball for the Giants; Canton defeated Altoona (Pennsylvania) 23-0 and Pitcairn (Pennsylvania) 7-0. In Thorpe's first game with the team, the Bulldogs swamped a team called the Buffalo All-Stars 77-0. The New York All-Stars fell 67-0. Canton then won a tough game against the Columbus Panhandles by the score of 12-0; Cusack says in his memoirs that Thorpe made an 85-yard punt that day.

Canton defeated Peggy Parrott and the Cleveland Indians twice, 27-0 and 14-7. Thorpe made a 71-yard punt return in the first game and won the second on a touchdown run around end. Youngstown fell to Canton 13-0. The first game of the year against Massillon ended in a 0-0 tie when Thorpe left the game after the first quarter with a foot injury. For the second, Cusack signed Carlisle star Pete Calac, and Calac and Thorpe led Canton to a 24-0 shutout of the Tigers. The season ended with Canton the professional champion of the world, undefeated in 10 games; its defense had allowed only seven points, while its offense had scored 264.

Early pro football in Pittsburgh had suffered when some of its players left the game to fight in the Spanish-American War in 1897. In 1917, 20 years later, Cusack and other pro managers in Ohio lost some of their best players to World War I. The Bulldogs still fielded another strong team, however, and played two stirring games against Massillon. Charlie Brickley, former Harvard All-America and a dropkicker of renown, now led Massillon. He imported "an entire Army Ambulance Corps team from Allentown, Pennsylvania" to play against Canton, but the Bulldogs won the first game of the year between the two teams 14-3. In the second game, Thorpe and Stan Cofall, a former Notre Dame star now with Massillon, waged a dropkicking duel that Thorpe lost; Cofall's two field goals won the game for Massillon 6-0. Thorpe was later named the first president and Cofall the vice president of the American Professional Football Association, forerunner of the NFL.

Cusack's strange and ill-timed departure from the Bulldogs followed. Apparently because of the war and the difficulties football managers were having in signing players, Cusack left the Bulldogs and went to Oklahoma to become an oilfield wildcatter. He caught malaria in Arkansas in 1921.

He eventually returned to Canton to recover from his illness and soon thereafter went to Cleveland, where he became Jim Thorpe's personal business manager; Thorpe played for the Cleveland Indians at the time.

It remained for an automobile dealer named Ralph Hay to take over Cusack's Canton Bulldogs interests. In 1920, it was Hay who was the owner of record when it was his Hupmobile agency showroom in Canton that was the site of the organizational meeting of the league that would become the NFL.

Seven Decades of the NFL

1920 Professional football had existed in the United States for at least 28 years, since Pudge Heffelfinger played for the Allegheny Athletic Association in Pittsburgh for $500 in 1892. The sport still was loosely organized, although the best teams—particularly those in the informal "Ohio League"—generally played each other once or twice a season, allowing for the selection of a champion. The top teams in this unofficial league were so strong that each year the best of them was able to call itself, deservedly, the "U.S. Professional Champion."

But there was a need for a better-regulated league to deal with three major problems that threatened to destroy professional football.

The most urgent problem was that of rising salaries. Because most stadiums used by the pros seated only a few thousand people, and infrequently were filled at that, the increasing salaries of the day—$50 to $75 per game for most players and often $100 or more for stars—threatened to bankrupt many clubs.

Some sort of salary cap was needed. That was an unlikely proposition, however, due to the second problem—players continually jumping from one team to another, following the highest bidder. Team managers were willing to pay to have the best possible teams, and the players wanted to make the most they could. In that scenario, salaries just went higher and higher.

Pro football's third problem was its use of college players who still were enrolled in school. These players would play in college games on Saturdays and, under assumed names, in pro games on Sundays. The use of college players generated a negative image for the professional sport, which was seen by the public as enticing honorable young men with illicit inducements.

A league in which all the member teams would follow the same rules of operation seemed the answer. There had been talk of forming such a league as early as 1892, when the era of athletic clubs and their semiprofessional teams was at its peak. A serious attempt at organization failed in Ohio in 1904.

A second attempt to form a league was initiated in 1920. On August 20, representatives from four teams met in the offices of Ralph Hay, the business manager of the reigning professional champions, the Canton Bulldogs. At the meeting, Hay and Jim Thorpe represented Canton, Frank Neid and Art Ranney the Akron Pros, Carl Storck the Dayton Triangles, and Jimmy O'Donnell and Stanley Cofall the Cleveland Indians.

This first organizational meeting resulted in the founding of the American Professional Football Conference, the stated purposes of which, according to the *Canton Evening Repository,* were: "to raise the standard of professional football in every way possible, to eliminate bidding for players between rival clubs, and to secure cooperation in the formation of schedules, at least for the bigger teams." The members of the new league agreed to refrain from signing any player still attending college or offering inducements to any players attached to one of the member clubs. It also was decided that if two clubs were dealing with the same player, terms would be agreed upon between the clubs. However, the most important thing the representatives did, according to the *Cleveland Plain Dealer,* was to place a "maximum on financial terms for players."

Joining the four clubs at the meeting as charter members of the APFC were teams from Buffalo, Rochester (New York), and Hammond (Indiana). Each team was unable to be represented at the meeting, but officially applied by letter instead. However, there since has been much confusion about just which teams actually did apply. The Rochester entry certainly came from Leo Lyons, the manager of the city's most successful team, the Jeffersons. The Hammond entry most likely was sent by A.A. Young, the owner of the Hammond Pros, although that is debatable because the 1920 Hammond team was a different club from the Hammond Pros of 1919, who became the Chicago Tigers in 1920. The Buffalo entry remains a mystery. Although the Buffalo All-Americans of Frank McNeil officially were admitted to the league in 1921, they weren't even in existence in 1919, and they played the early part of the 1920 season without openly acknowledging the operation of any pro organization. However, they did play Canton in November, and historians traditionally have included them as an original member.

The members of the APFC had hoped that F.J. Griffiths, the vice president and general manager of the Central Steel Company, would back the Massillon Tigers and enter the team in the new league. However, Griffiths declined, thereby withdrawing Massillon from the sport for the season. Because Canton-Massillon games had generated the greatest fan interest in pro football, Hay, who was appointed temporary secretary, kept prospective dates on the schedule open for the Tigers, who would be replaced by the Hammond team should Massillon indeed not play.

A second meeting was scheduled for September 17, and Hay invited a large number of teams to attend, many of which, including Buffalo's entry, did not show up. Ten teams did: Akron; Canton; Cleveland; Dayton; Hammond; Rochester; the Decatur (Illinois) Staleys, with George Halas and Morgan O'Brien representing A.E. Staley's interests; the Muncie (Indiana) Flyers, represented by Earl Ball; the Racine Cardinals, represented by painting and decorating contractor Chris O'Brien, who had run the team since 1899; and the Rock Island (Illinois) Independents, represented by manager Walter Flannigan. There was some confusion about the Cardinals, who were named for Racine Avenue in south Chicago rather than for Racine, Wisconsin, as was assumed when a record was made of the teams that were present.

Again, Massillon didn't send a representative to the meeting. However, Vernon (Mac) McGinnis, an Akron promoter, attempted to obtain a franchise named the Massillon Tigers. McGinnis intended for his club to be a traveling team, playing its entire schedule on the road. However, the plan for a "Massillon" team backed by outside financing and really having nothing to do with Massillon was not viewed favorably by the member clubs, who didn't allow McGinnis's representative into the meeting. Instead, Hay spoke for Massillon and said that the city would not operate a team in 1920.

Hay operated a Hupmobile automobile dealership, and the meeting was held in his showroom. There were not enough chairs in the room and some of the representatives of the clubs had to sit on the running boards and fenders of the automobiles.

Early in the meeting, the APFC changed its four-week-old name to the American Professional Football Association, or APFA. Hoping to capitalize on his fame, the members elected Jim Thorpe of Canton as league president. Stanley Cofall of Cleveland was elected vice president and Art Ranney of Akron secretary-treasurer, while A.A. Young of Hammond was appointed the chairman of the rules committee.

A membership fee of $100 per team was charged to give an appearance of respectability, but no team ever paid it. Each team also agreed to print the words "Member of American Professional Football Association" on its stationery. Each club also agreed to mail a list of all players used in the 1920 season to Ranney, so each would have first choice in 1921 of the same players it used in 1920.

A Mr. Marshall of the Brunswick-Dalke Collender Company, Tire Division, presented a silver loving cup to be given to the team awarded the championship by the APFA. Any team winning the cup three times was to become its permanent owner. However, the issue of a champion was to prove tricky due to the difficulty of determining standings. The association had not reached the stage at which an equal schedule could be drawn up by every club. Scheduling was left up to the clubs themselves, and there was a wide variation both in the overall number of games played and in the number played against association teams. The second organizational meeting ended with the understanding that the president would call another meeting in January.

Near the start of the 1920 season, three more teams traditionally listed as charter members of the APFA entered the picture. On October 2, Hay announced that he had received a letter from the Detroit Heralds, who were joining the Association. The Columbus Panhandles, who had been invited to the second meeting but hadn't attended, and the Chicago Tigers also apparently joined, although the exact dates of their entries never have been determined.

It long has been a source of debate just which teams to include when discussing the APFA in 1920. Amazingly, mention of the organization virtually disappeared from the sports pages, even in game stories, until it met again in 1921. Moreover, the APFA didn't keep standings, choosing to determine its champion by the same method the Ohio League had used, not by won-loss record, but by a consensus of which was the strongest team. The 10 teams at the second organizational meeting certainly were members, although it later was inaccurately claimed Muncie hadn't fielded a team. The three teams that joined near the beginning of the season also were members. Buffalo, while not attending the early meetings, played several late-season games it claimed were leading to a championship, so by that time the team apparently considered itself a member. But many of the other teams that played the members or tried to schedule games with Canton or Akron were certainly not interested in the league, but only in playing teams that would attract big crowds. Therefore, the most accurate accounting of clubs in the 1920 APFA would seem to be the traditional 14 teams.

On September 26, the first game featuring an APFA team was played at Rock Island's Douglas Park. A crowd of 800 watched the Independents defeat the St. Paul Ideals 48-0 in the rain.

A week later, October 3, the first games matching two APFA teams were held. After a scoreless first half at Triangle Park in Dayton, what can be considered the first touchdown in a game between two NFL opponents was scored. Early in the third period, Lou Partlow of Dayton ran seven yards for the score. George Kinderdine kicked the extra point. The Triangles went on to defeat the Columbus Panhandles 14-0.

That same day, Rock Island scored three touchdowns through blocked punts in the first quarter and whipped the Muncie Flyers 45-0. The Muncie team played so poorly that Halas, the Decatur player-coach-manager, immediately canceled a game that had been scheduled against the Flyers for the next week. At the same time, the team's financial backers pulled out, and the Flyers folded.

By early in the season, the Racine Cardinals generally had come to be known as the Chicago Cardinals. On November 7, Paddy Driscoll ran 40 yards for a touchdown to lead the Cardinals to a 6-3 victory over the Chicago Tigers. Legend has it that Cardinals owner Chris O'Brien had bet the APFA franchise rights to Chicago on the game, with the loser being forced to fold. Indeed, at the end of the season, the Tigers did just that. But the story still is questionable. In 1920, the APFA didn't have the kind of franchise rights that existed later. In addition, the newspapers of the day make it clear that the game was for the pro championship of Chicago, a title with more prestige than rights to anything in the little-known APFA.

The Cardinals' victory certainly helped push the Tigers into oblivion. Before the game, most of the city's newspaper coverage had gone to the Tigers. After the Cardinals won, they surpassed the Tigers in both media attention and attendance. The dwindling attendance and an expensive roster forced the Tigers to fold because they lost too much money.

By the beginning of December, most of the teams in the association had abandoned hope for a championship, and some of them, including the Tigers and Detroit Heralds, had finished their seasons, disbanded, and had their franchises canceled by the association. Four teams—Akron (the only undefeated team), Buffalo, Canton, and Decatur—still had championship aspirations, however. Frank McNeil of Buffalo came up with a plan to give his team the championship, playing Canton in New York City and Akron in Buffalo on back-to-back days, December 4 and 5. The plan started well, when the All-Americans defeated the Bulldogs 7-3. The next day, however, in a storm that alternated between dumping rain and snow, Buffalo and Akron struggled to a scoreless tie. The game not only eliminated Buffalo from the championship picture, it also marked the first APFA player deal. Either directly before or immediately after the game, Akron sold tackle Bob (Nasty) Nash to Buffalo for $300 and five percent of the gate receipts.

Also on December 5, the Staleys staked their claim with a 10-0 victory over the Cardinals, the only team that had beaten them during the regular season. The 1920 season reached its climax in a game on December 12 between Akron and Decatur. Despite hiring Paddy Driscoll from the Cardinals for the game, however, the Staleys could achieve no more than a scoreless tie against a team they had to beat to win the championship.

Akron not only finished the season undefeated, the team made history by having Fritz Pollard as its co-coach, along with Elgie Tobin. Although it hardly was noted at the time, Pollard was the first black coach in the NFL. Only in later years was much made of the fact, and an effort made to ascertain the role Pollard played in the handling of the team.

While most of the teams in the APFA realized their most important goal—to survive through 1920—the season wasn't totally successful. Salaries had continued to rise, players still had jumped from team to team, and some teams had continued to use college players.

1920 STANDINGS	W	L	T	Pct.
Akron Pros	8	0	3	1.000
Decatur Staleys	10	1	2	.909
Buffalo All-Americans	9	1	1	.900
Chicago Cardinals	6	2	2	.750
Rock Island Independents	6	2	2	.750
Dayton Triangles	5	2	2	.714
Rochester Jeffersons	6	3	2	.667
Canton Bulldogs	7	4	2	.636
Detroit Heralds	2	3	3	.400
Cleveland Tigers	2	4	2	.333
Chicago Tigers	2	5	1	.286
Hammond Pros	2	5	0	.286
Columbus Panhandles	2	6	2	.250
Muncie Flyers	0	1	0	.000

1921 The league meeting that had been scheduled for January wasn't held until April 30, at the Portage Hotel in Akron. Missing were the APFA's top two officers, President Jim Thorpe and vice president Stanley Cofall. Thorpe, the APFA's nominal head, never had been involved in any major policy decisions and apparently had lost interest in any off-field involvement with the league. Cofall, the former Cleveland player-coach, wasn't even associated with the APFA anymore, having been cut by manager Jimmy O'Donnell in late October after the Tigers didn't score a point in their first three games.

The teams represented at the meeting were Akron, Buffalo, Canton, the Chicago Cardinals, Columbus, Dayton, Decatur, Hammond, Rochester, and the Philadelphia Quakers. Letters requesting entrance into the association were received from the Breckenridge Company Team of Louisville, Kentucky, and from the Cincinnati Celts.

The first order of business at the meeting was to award the championship trophy for the 1920 season to the Akron Pros. The next was to plan for the 1921 season.

Realizing that they needed more experienced leadership than Thorpe could supply, the team owners and managers installed Joe Carr as president. Carr, a Columbus sportswriter, was the manager of the Panhandles, a minor league baseball executive, and a pioneer in professional basketball; he would supply the firm control that the new league needed in its formative years. Morgan O'Brien, A.E. Staley's top assistant, was named vice president, and Carl Storck of Dayton became the secretary-treasurer.

The naming of new officers was just part of the APFA's general reorganization that was approved at the Akron meeting. Under the reorganization, the team representatives reaffirmed the league's goals while better defining its parameters. They passed a number of rules, including one that prevented players from playing for two clubs in the same week. They also charged Carr, O'Brien, and Storck to draft a league constitution and by-laws.

Under Carr's sure but stern hand, the association developed into more than the loose, haphazard collection of teams it had been in 1920. Carr freely borrowed from major league baseball in designing the APFA constitution and by-laws. He gave teams territorial rights within the league. He restricted player movements and developed membership criteria for the franchises themselves. He established a permanent league office in Columbus. He issued standings so that the league would have one champion. And he increased the national popularity of the sport by scheduling more interstate games.

The league's membership increased to 22 teams. Twelve of the original 14 teams returned for a second season, including Muncie, which had played only one game in 1920. The first two new teams to enter the association were the Louisville Brecks and the Cincinnati Celts, who appear to have been admitted at the April meeting. On June 18, a new team from Detroit, the Panthers, was granted a franchise, as was Toledo, which was supposed to be operated by Jim Thorpe. A Toledo team never was fielded, however, and the franchise is assumed to have been canceled at the beginning of the season.

Another four franchises—the Green Bay Packers, the Evansville (Indiana) Crimson Giants, the Minneapolis Marines, and the Tonawanda (New York) Kardex (who were called the Lumberjacks in the newspapers)—entered the association on August 27.

That same day, Frank McNeil of the Buffalo All-Americans was granted a franchise. Although McNeil had not attended any league meetings in 1920, the action undoubtedly was more than a formality. During the 1920 season, many Buffalo players spent their Saturdays playing for the Philadelphia Quakers, a non-APFA team that couldn't play on Sunday because of Pennsylvania blue laws. At the April meeting, the Philadelphia franchise indicated its intent to get into the association. Aware of the new league rule that no player could play for two teams the same week, McNeil convinced Philadelphia to withdraw its application; if the Quakers weren't league members, the Buffalo-Philadelphia players wouldn't have to adhere to the rule preventing double use.

Two other franchises located in cities that later would become hotbeds of pro football also were granted before the start of the 1921 season—one in Washington and one in New York. The exact dates of their entries into the association are unknown.

Chicago kept two association teams despite losing the Tigers. The A.E. Staley Manufacturing Company, which sponsored the Decatur Staleys, was forced to drop its football program due to a decline in business. A.E. Staley, the company's owner, suggested to player-coach George Halas that he move the team to Chicago. Staley also paid Halas $5,000 to keep the name Staleys for one season. Halas moved the new Chicago Staleys into Cubs Park, where the Chicago Tigers had played the year before. In order to cut his risks, Halas made halfback Ed (Dutch) Sternaman his partner. The two of them brought many of the former Decatur players with them, including two future Pro Football Hall of Famers, Guy Chamberlin and George Trafton. The new team immediately became one of the best in the league.

The season started off as a three-team race among Akron, Buffalo, and the Staleys, but the Pros faded late in the year, leaving the All-Americans and the Staleys to play for the title. On Thanksgiving Day, Buffalo defeated the Staleys 7-6 to take the league lead. But on December 4, in a rematch in Chicago, Sternaman kicked a 20-yard field goal to provide the margin of victory as the Staleys won 10-7. Buffalo claimed that the second game was merely a postseason exhibition, noted that one of the Staleys' victories had been against a non-association team, and argued it had won the championship. But Carr ruled in favor of the Staleys, giving Halas his first championship.

While the All-Americans and the Staleys were contending for the championship, many teams were having problems. Canton was hurt at the gate by the loss of Jim Thorpe, who became player-coach at Cleveland and took teammates Joe Guyon and Pete Calac with him. Then Thorpe was injured early in the season and played very little after that; Cleveland lost the rest of its games and was devastated at the box office.

A number of franchises didn't play full APFA seasons, and their records were stricken from the league standings for a time. The league had determined to establish its champion based on percentage, and if a minimum number of games (six) to be played to qualify for the championship wasn't met, that team wasn't listed in the order of finish for the championship. Those teams and their records since have been added back into the standings.

Four teams—Evansville, Louisville, Hammond, and Minneapolis—played full schedules, but not enough of the games were within the league to qualify for the championship. Each returned for the 1922 season.

One team—the Muncie Flyers—actually dropped out of the association after only two games. Four others—Cincinnati, Tonawanda, the New York Giants, and the Washington Senators—played only partial seasons but didn't drop their franchises immediately, as Muncie had done. These four, plus Muncie, Detroit, and Cleveland, each had its franchise canceled by the league for failure to post necessary league fees for the 1922 season.

1921 STANDINGS	W	L	T	Pct.
Chicago Staleys	9	1	1	.900
Buffalo All-Americans	9	1	2	.900
Akron Pros	8	3	1	.727
Canton Bulldogs	5	2	3	.714
Rock Island Independents	4	2	1	.667
Evansville Crimson Giants	3	2	0	.600
Green Bay Packers	3	2	1	.600
Dayton Triangles	4	4	1	.500
Chicago Cardinals	3	3	2	.500
Rochester Jeffersons	2	3	0	.400
Cleveland Indians	3	5	0	.375

	W	L	T	Pct.
Washington Senators	1	2	0	.333
Cincinnati Celts	1	3	0	.250
Hammond Pros	1	3	1	.250
Minneapolis Marines	1	3	1	.250
Detroit Heralds	1	5	1	.167
Columbus Panhandles	1	8	0	.111
Tonawanda Kardex	0	1	0	.000
Muncie Flyers	0	2	0	.000
Louisville Brecks	0	2	0	.000
New York Giants	0	2	0	.000

1922 There were more shifts of APFA franchises at the January 28 league meeting, including the changing of owners for one already established. The team actually was the same as that which had operated as the Chicago Staleys in 1921, but the franchise was granted anew to George Halas and Ed Sternaman, after being held previously by A.E. Staley. Philadelphia and New Haven (Connecticut) also were granted franchises, although neither ever fielded teams.

After admitting the use of players who had college eligibility remaining during the 1921 season, John Clair and the Green Bay management submitted a formal apology and withdrew from the league. A $1,000 bond was required from all clubs thereafter to guard against such violations.

Five months later, at the June 24 meeting, the Packers were back. Player-coach Curly Lambeau promised to obey league rules and then used $50 of his own money to buy back the franchise. Milwaukee, Youngstown, Racine (Wisconsin), and LaRue (Ohio) also were granted franchises, although Youngstown never fielded a team.

The LaRue franchise never actually played in LaRue. The all-Indian team featured Jim Thorpe, Joe Guyon, and Pete Calac, and was known as the Oorang Indians. The franchise was granted to Walter Lingo, who owned the Oorang Kennels (Oorang is a strain of Airedale). The kennel was in LaRue, but the games were played in Marion, the home of Warren Harding, then the President of the United States.

At the June meeting, two name changes were made. The APFA officially became the National Football League, and, to create a relationship with the successful baseball Chicago Cubs in the public mind, Halas renamed the Chicago Staleys the Chicago Bears.

On August 20, Bill Harley, who seven months earlier had lost his bid to operate the Chicago franchise that was granted to Halas and Sternaman, was granted a franchise for Toledo, which brought to 18 the number of teams actually playing in the 1922 season.

As in 1921, there was a wide variation in the quality and number of opponents NFL teams faced. The Evansville Crimson Giants played only two league games, and the franchise was canceled at the end of the season. The most games (11 or 12) were played by the three best teams—Canton and the two Chicago clubs.

Canton emerged as the league's first true powerhouse. The Bulldogs had virtually a new team, led by player-coach Guy Chamberlin (who had left the Staleys after playing with them two years), and future Hall of Fame tackles Link Lyman and Wilbur (Pete) Henry. After an early tie with Dayton, Canton beat the previously undefeated Bears 7-6 when a heavy rush forced Joey Sternaman, the co-owner's younger brother, to miss an extra point. A tie with Toledo set up important back-to-back games between the Bulldogs and the undefeated Cardinals. The Bulldogs won 7-0 and 20-3, and went on to win the championship with a 10-0-2 record. The Cardinals later defeated the Bears twice, and both Chicago teams ended up with three losses.

Despite some success, the sport still was hard on its owners. The Bears made just $1,476.92, while Ralph Hay lost money despite his team's championship. The Packers were plagued by bad weather and low attendance, and Lambeau went broke. But Green Bay businessmen, realizing the value of the team to a small community, arranged for a $2,500 loan to the club. A public non-profit corporation then was set up to operate the Packers, with Lambeau remaining as manager and coach. At $5 for a share of the team and a season ticket, the people of Green Bay contributed enough to insure future solvency for their team.

1922 STANDINGS	W	L	T	Pct.
Canton Bulldogs	10	0	2	1.000
Chicago Bears	9	3	0	.750
Chicago Cardinals	8	3	0	.727
Toledo Maroons	5	2	2	.714
Rock Island Independents	4	2	1	.667
Racine Legion	6	4	1	.600
Dayton Triangles	4	3	1	.571
Green Bay Packers	4	3	3	.571
Buffalo All-Americans	5	4	1	.556
Akron Pros	3	5	2	.375
Milwaukee Badgers	2	4	3	.333
Oorang Indians	2	6	0	.250
Minneapolis Marines	1	3	0	.250
Louisville Brecks	1	3	0	.250
Evansville Crimson Giants	0	3	0	.000
Rochester Jeffersons	0	4	1	.000
Hammond Pros	0	5	1	.000
Columbus Panhandles	0	7	0	.000

1923 Three new franchises were granted—to Cleveland, Duluth, and St. Louis—bringing the total number of teams to 20. The Columbus franchise changed its team name from Panhandles to Tigers. For the first time, all of the franchises considered to be part of the league fielded teams, although the league still did not regulate the schedules. Canton, Milwaukee, and the Chicago teams again led the way with 12 league games, while Rochester played only 2.

Canton went undefeated again, and the Bears were runners-up again. The Bulldogs earned their championship the hard way—three times defeating contenders on the road. Canton overcame the Bears 6-0 with two fourth-quarter field goals by Wilbur (Pete) Henry. Two weeks later, the Bulldogs traveled to Comiskey Park. The Cardinals had a 5-0 record, including a 60-0 victory over Rochester. But Lou Smythe, who would become the only player in NFL history to lead the league in both rushing and passing touchdowns, supplied the late fireworks for the Bulldogs in a 7-3 victory. After a 3-3 tie with Buffalo gave Canton the only blemish on its record, a 46-10 victory over previously undefeated Cleveland left the Bulldogs the only unbeaten team in the NFL, a record it would maintain in an 11-0-1 season.

At the other end of the spectrum were two teams that didn't win a game—the Rochester Jeffersons and the Louisville Brecks—and 1-10 Oorang. In a 26-0 loss to the Bears, the Indians (who scored only a safety in their first eight games) were on the verge of a touchdown when Jim Thorpe fumbled a bad snap, which George Halas picked up on the 2-yard line and carried 98 yards for a touchdown. "I could feel Thorpe breathing down my neck all the way," Halas said. The return was an NFL record that lasted until 1972.

1923 STANDINGS	W	L	T	Pct.
Canton Bulldogs	11	0	1	1.000
Chicago Bears	9	2	1	.818
Green Bay Packers	7	2	1	.778
Milwaukee Badgers	7	2	3	.778
Cleveland Indians	3	1	3	.750
Chicago Cardinals	8	4	0	.667
Duluth Kelleys	4	3	0	.571
Columbus Tigers	5	4	1	.556
Buffalo All-Americans	4	4	3	.500
Racine Legion	4	4	2	.500
Toledo Maroons	2	3	2	.400
Rock Island Independents	2	3	3	.400
Minneapolis Marines	2	5	2	.286
St. Louis All-Stars	1	4	2	.200
Hammond Pros	1	5	1	.167
Dayton Triangles	1	6	1	.143
Akron Indians	1	6	0	.143
Oorang Indians	1	10	0	.091
Rochester Jeffersons	0	2	0	.000
Louisville Brecks	0	3	0	.000

1924 In January, the league admitted a new franchise, representing Kansas City, Missouri. The team played its first season as the Blues, but changed its name to Cowboys before the 1925 season.

At the July meeting, Frankford, a section of Philadelphia, was granted a franchise. Meanwhile, St. Louis's franchise was canceled; the Buffalo franchise tranferred owners and received a new team name (Bisons); the Oorang Indians were given permission to suspend operations for a year (after which time a new team never was reformed); and the league ordered the Toledo franchise to transfer or suspend operations for a year.

The Toledo team did not operate again. There are no exact dates of transfer and many details are unclear, but it appears likely that the franchise was transferred to Kenosha, Wisconsin, where many of Toledo's players showed up with a new team, as did Toledo's team name, "Maroons."

Another team, the Louisville Brecks, also suspended operations before the season and missed both the 1924 and 1925 seasons, although the franchise continued to be a league member and to be represented at meetings.

A seemingly insignificant action at the July meeting, but one that later would have definite repercussions, was the owners' vote that the season's schedule begin September 27 and close November 30, and that the championship standings be decided on a percentage basis of all games between league teams played between and including those dates.

On August 3, Sam Deutsch, a Cleveland sports promoter who owned the Cleveland Indians, purchased the Canton Bulldogs for $2,500. Despite consecutive championships for the Bulldogs, high salaries and increasing traveling expenses had combined with a small stadium to make the franchise a financial disaster. Deutsch kept Canton inactive in 1924, and invited the team's 10 best players to join his Cleveland team. Seven did, including Guy Chamberlin and Link Lyman, although three of the biggest names—Wilbur (Pete) Henry, Harry Robb, and Larry Conover—joined the independent Pottsville (Pennsylvania) Maroons.

The season opened with 20 franchises, although only 18 fielded teams. The championship race came down to three teams—the newly renamed Cleveland Bulldogs, the Chicago Bears, and the Frankford Yellow Jackets.

Starting with a 16-14 victory over the Bears on October 5, Cleveland went undefeated in its first six games, finishing with a 7-1-1 record (both the loss and tie came in games against Frankford). The Yellow Jackets lost two games early in the year, but their schedule kept them in contention. Because of a Philadelphia law preventing spectator sports on Sunday, they played home games on Saturday and away games on Sunday. This double scheduling allowed them to run up an 11-2-1 record, with almost twice as many games as some teams. The Bears began with a scoreless tie with Rock Island and a loss to Cleveland, then didn't lose again, winning their November 30 season finale for a 6-1-4 record.

Two other teams had been in contention early in the season. Rock Island, featuring a seemingly rejuvenated Jim Thorpe, shut out its first four opponents before losing 23-7 in Kansas City. In that game, the Independents had to play without star tackle Duke Slater, because Kansas City wouldn't allow a black player in the game. Rock Island was defeated by Duluth late in the season to finish 6-2-2. The Kelleys were hurt by a short schedule. They lost only once, 13-0 in Green Bay, but their 5-1 record didn't include enough victories to challenge Cleveland.

After seemingly winning the championship, Cleveland scheduled another game against the runner-up Bears. When the Bears won 23-0, they claimed the title. Player-coach George Halas insisted both teams had agreed that the game was to be played for the championship. But the Bulldogs weren't willing to give up their claim to the title, and the issue wasn't resolved until the league meeting in January, 1925. There, President Joe Carr declared Cleveland the champion, ruling that the clubs didn't have the right to schedule games without league permission. Thus, any games played after November 30 were simply exhibition games. To insure against such problems in the future, the 1925 season was extended to December 20.

1924 STANDINGS	W	L	T	Pct.
Cleveland Bulldogs	7	1	1	.875
Chicago Bears	6	1	4	.857
Frankford Yellow Jackets	11	2	1	.846
Duluth Kelleys	5	1	0	.833
Rock Island Independents	6	2	2	.750
Green Bay Packers	7	4	0	.636
Racine Legion	4	3	3	.571
Chicago Cardinals	5	4	1	.556
Buffalo Bisons	6	5	0	.545
Columbus Tigers	4	4	0	.500
Hammond Pros	2	2	1	.500
Milwaukee Badgers	5	8	0	.385
Akron Indians	2	6	0	.333
Dayton Triangles	2	6	0	.333
Kansas City Blues	2	7	0	.222
Kenosha Maroons	0	5	1	.000
Minneapolis Marines	0	6	0	.000
Rochester Jeffersons	0	7	0	.000

1925 The most momentous season in the NFL's brief history was preceded by a continuation of the league's growth. Two teams—Kenosha and Racine—failed to field teams and forfeited their franchises. Minneapolis apparently suspended league operations for the year. However, on August 1, five new teams were admitted to the NFL—the Detroit Panthers, featuring Jimmy Conzelman as owner, coach, and tailback; the Providence Steam Roller; a new Canton Bulldogs team, which Sam Deutsch had sold back to the Canton Professional Football Company after one year; a New York team that, like the one in 1921, was named the Giants; and the Pottsville (Pennsylvania) Maroons, who had been perhaps the most successful independent pro team in 1923-24.

Late in the season, the NFL scored its greatest coup in gaining national public acceptance. Red Grange, the "Galloping Ghost" of Illinois and the most celebrated player in the history of college football, signed a pro contract. Grange and his fast-talking manager, C.C. (Cash and Carry) Pyle, held secret negotiations with George Halas; shortly after his last college game in mid-November, Grange signed a contract with the Bears. In return for a large share of the gate receipts, Grange agreed to join the Chicago team for the remainder of its schedule and for a postseason barnstorming tour.

Much of the public still viewed pro football as a tasteless, unnatural business. Grange helped change that. On Thanksgiving Day, he played in his first game, against the league-leading Chicago Cardinals. More than 36,000 people—the largest crowd in pro football history—turned out to see Grange, but the punting of Paddy Driscoll kept the Bears pinned in their own territory all day, and the game ended a scoreless tie.

At the beginning of December, the Bears left on an exhausting tour that saw them play eight games in 12 days. Five of the games were against NFL opponents and three weren't, but all were financial windfalls. The Bears traveled to St. Louis, Philadelphia, New York City, Washington, Boston, Pittsburgh, and Detroit, before playing a final game in Chicago. In New York, the Giants were on the verge of financial collapse in their first year in the NFL. But an unbelievable crowd of 73,000 turned out at the Polo Grounds to see Grange, saving Tim Mara's team. After a week off, the Bears left for another tour, playing nine games in the South and the West, including a game in Los Angeles on January 16, where 75,000 fans watched the Bears defeat the Los Angeles Tigers in the Coliseum.

In much of the country, the race for the league championship was lost amid the publicity given to the Grange tour. But that race took on one of the strangest twists in the history of the NFL, and it ended with a roaring dispute because of a disagreement over which games counted in the standings.

After the problems encountered with late season games in 1924, the NFL had extended the 1925 season to December 20. However, league games were only scheduled until December 6. The rationale was that by that time all league teams would have played the minimum number of games (eight) needed to qualify for the championship. Those teams doing poorly could end their seasons. But those teams who had a shot at the championship or who could make money for another couple of weeks still could schedule each other until December 20.

On December 6, a week and a half after Red Grange's debut, the top two teams in the league, the 9-1-1 Cardinals and 9-2-0 Pottsville, met for a game the Chicago newspapers proclaimed was for the league championship. The Maroons stopped Driscoll and won 21-7, putting themselves in first place and winning the championship, as far as they were concerned.

Just because the scheduled games were over, however, didn't mean the season had ended. Chris O'Brien, the owner of the Cardinals, had another big pay day in mind, namely a season-ending game with the Bears and Grange. To enhance his chances of scheduling such a game, he also scheduled two more games first—against Milwaukee on December 10 and Hammond on December 12. He hoped that victories in those two games would put his team back in first place, and they did. Playing two teams that had been disbanded and then pulled back together on a moment's notice, the Cardinals won 59-0 and 13-0. Despite the victories, O'Brien's maneuvering was unsuccessful. Grange suffered an arm injury in a game at Pittsburgh and was ordered to the sideline until after December 20.

Meanwhile, Pottsville manager J.G. Striegel scheduled a game with Providence for December 13. He also scheduled another game he figured would be a money-maker, signing to play a team of former Notre Dame players, including the Four Horsemen, at Shibe Park in Philadelphia.

As soon as President Joe Carr heard about the Notre Dame game, he warned Striegel that it couldn't be played. Frankford lodged a formal complaint with the Commissioner—not only was the game being played in an area within Frankford's territorial rights, it was being played the same day as a Yellow Jackets home game.

On December 12, the Maroons defeated the All-Stars 9-7. That same day, Carr fined the club $500, suspended it from all rights and privileges (including the right to compete for the championship), and returned its franchise to the league. He also canceled Pottsville's scheduled game with Providence.

Several days later, when it was revealed that four Chicago high school players had competed for Milwaukee in the hastily arranged Cardinals-Badgers game, Carr punished those offenders, too. Ambrose McGurk, the Milwaukee owner, was given 90 days to sell the club; Art Folz, a Cardinals player who had procured the high schoolers, was banned from the NFL for life; and, although O'Brien hadn't known about the arrangement, the Cardinals were fined $1,000.

At the same time, Striegel asked Carr to reconsider his actions against the Maroons. Carr agreed to let the owners decide at the next league meeting. On February 6, Carr presented the facts to the owners, including the most important statement: "Three different notices forbidding the Pottsville club to play were given, and management elected to play regardless." The owners voted to uphold Carr's actions, and Pottsville remained out of the league.

When the owners awarded the 1925 championship, however, a problem developed. Even without the Milwaukee game, the Cardinals had the best record in the NFL. But when it was moved that the Cardinals be awarded the championship, Chris O'Brien let it be known he would not accept it. The vote was tabled, and the NFL never went through the formality of awarding the 1925 championship to any team.

As the team with the best record in 1925, the Cardinals since have been regarded as that season's champions, despite O'Brien's rejection. Pottsville may have had the best team in the league, but it made the mistake of flaunting league rules in favor of some fast money.

1925 STANDINGS	W	L	T	Pct.
Chicago Cardinals	11	2	1	.846
Pottsville Maroons	10	2	0	.833
Detroit Panthers	8	2	2	.800
New York Giants	8	4	0	.667
Akron Indians	4	2	2	.667
Frankford Yellow Jackets	13	7	0	.650
Chicago Bears	9	5	3	.643
Rock Island Independents	5	3	3	.625
Green Bay Packers	8	5	0	.615
Providence Steam Roller	6	5	1	.545
Canton Bulldogs	4	4	0	.500
Cleveland Bulldogs	5	8	1	.385
Kansas City Cowboys	2	5	1	.286
Hammond Pros	1	4	0	.200
Buffalo Bisons	1	6	2	.143
Duluth Kelleys	0	3	0	.000
Rochester Jeffersons	0	6	1	.000
Milwaukee Badgers	0	6	0	.000
Dayton Triangles	0	7	1	.000
Columbus Tigers	0	9	0	.000

1926 Red Grange's manager, C.C. Pyle, told the Chicago Bears that Grange wouldn't play for them in 1926 unless he was paid a five-figure salary and was given one-third ownership of the team. George Halas and Ed Sternaman refused.

At the league's February meeting in Detroit, Pyle announced that he and Grange had secured a lease to Yankee Stadium. He requested a New York franchise to showcase Grange. Tim Mara, who held exclusive territorial rights to New York, objected. Because Joe Carr had made a firm decision on the issue of territorial rights regarding Pottsville's game in Philadelphia, the league had a precedent, to which it adhered. Pyle was turned down. Pyle then announced that he would form a rival league for the 1926 season.

By mid-summer, the NFL was in serious conflict with the new American Football League. In addition to Pyle's New York Yankees, new franchises in Boston and Newark joined four teams that competed directly with new or established NFL franchises in Brooklyn, Chicago, Los Angeles, and Philadelphia.

At the July league meeting, the NFL had one public relations bonus. Co-existence with college football was assured when George Halas pushed through a rule prohibiting any team from having in its lineup a player whose college class had not graduated. The rest of the news was not as positive, and the new league caused distinct changes in the setup of the NFL. Four teams—Cleveland, Minneapolis, Rochester, and Rock Island—suspended operations for a year with league permission. Rock Island then jumped directly to the AFL, while a number of Cleveland's top players formed the AFL's ninth and final team.

The NFL gained six new franchises, however. Brooklyn, Hartford, and Los Angeles entered the league for the first time; Racine was readmitted to league membership; Louisville fielded its first team in three years; and, in an effort to avoid having them

1920s, 1930s: A Photographic Portfolio

Fritz Pollard was Akron's co-coach (with Elgie Tobin) in 1920, when the Pros won the APFA title.

George Halas, the player-coach-owner of the Chicago Bears, won 325 games in 40 years as coach.

The Pittsburgh Lyceums were an independent football team in the 1920s for which Art Rooney (far right, front row) and his brother Dan (third from right, front row) played. Art Rooney also was signed by baseball's Boston Red Sox and was selected to the 1920 United States Olympic boxing team.

Red Grange (with ball) played his first pro game for the Chicago Bears on Thanksgiving Day, November 22, 1925, against the Chicago Cardinals. The game at Wrigley Field was watched by 38,000 and ended a scoreless tie. Grange was held to 40 yards rushing by a defense that included John (Paddy) Driscoll.

In 1925, Jim Thorpe (right) joined the New York Giants for their first season in the NFL. The team's first coach was Bob Folwell (left).

The first NFL Championship Game was held in 1932 at Chicago Stadium, which featured an 80-yard field. The Bears defeated Portsmouth 9-0.

In 1943, Beattie Feathers became the first pro player to rush for 1,000 yards in a season (1,004).

On November 29, 1934, the Chicago Bears beat the Detroit Lions 19-16 to clinch the Western Division. The Bears included Bronko Nagurski, Bill Hewitt, and helmetless George Musso and Roy (Link) Lyman.

In 1936, George Preston Marshall, the owner of the Boston Redskins, transferred the NFL Championship Game to New York's Polo Grounds, because he was angered by lack of attendance in Boston. The site of the game proved to be of little consequence, as the Green Bay Packers defeated the Redskins 21-6.

The first pro franchise of a nationwide league to regularly schedule and play games in California was the Los Angeles Bulldogs (dark uniforms) of the 1936-37 American Football League.

Little (5-7, 150) Davey O'Brien set an NFL record for passing yards (1,324) as a rookie in 1939.

Cecil Isbell (shown passing) led Green Bay to the 1938 NFL Championship Game against the New York Giants. The Packers outgained the Giants 379-212, but two blocked punts set up nine New York points and helped the Giants win 23-17. Arnie Herber (38) threw a touchdown pass for the Packers.

join the AFL, the Pottsville Maroons were conditionally re-admitted to the league. The moves left the NFL with 22 active teams.

Despite its seemingly good health, as expressed by continued growth, the NFL was in a state of confusion and concern in 1926. The Milwaukee and Duluth franchises each had new ownership, and Duluth had a new nickname—the Eskimos—as did the Buffalo Rangers and the Louisville Colonels. Neither Louisville nor the Los Angeles Buccaneers actually had anything to do with its official city. Both were traveling teams based in Chicago, as were the Los Angeles Wildcats of the AFL.

The AFL teams helped put the financial squeeze on the NFL before the season even rolled around. Chris O'Brien experienced serious problems in Chicago, with the AFL's Bulls joining the Bears as competition. In order to help O'Brien, the league rescinded his $1,000 fine. But that wasn't enough. The Bulls leased Comiskey Park, forcing the Cardinals back to Normal Field, their home of earlier years, and then went after Paddy Driscoll. O'Brien couldn't afford to pay Driscoll what the Bulls could, so he traded him to the Bears. Without Driscoll, the Cardinals fell into mediocrity, while the Bears became even stronger.

When the season was actually played, it turned out to be one of the most exciting in NFL history. At the end of November, the Bears were 11-0-2, Frankford (led by former Canton coach Guy Chamberlin) was 12-1-1, and Pottsville was 10-1-1. Two late games decided the championship. On December 4, the Bears broke a scoreless tie with less than five minutes to play, but the Yellow Jackets blocked Driscoll's extra point, then drove to a touchdown and extra point to gain a 7-6 victory. The next weekend, while Frankford defeated Providence, the Bears beat Pottsville, which had recorded 10 shutouts in 12 games, 9-7.

The Yellow Jackets won the NFL championship with a 14-1-1 mark, but they could not equal the number of games or the media attention of Ole Haugsrud's Duluth team. The Eskimos played at home on September 19, when the weather permitted it, but then went on a tour that didn't end until February 5, after they had played 29 league and exhibition games on the road. Before the season, Haugsrud signed Ernie Nevers, the All-America fullback on Pop Warner's Rose Bowl entry from Stanford. One of the most glamorous players in the country, the big, blond, handsome Nevers was the NFL's answer as a gate attraction to Grange. Because Haugsrud paid Nevers a high fee, plus a percentage of the gate, he had little money left to pay the rest of his team. Thus, for most of the season he carried no more than 15 players. Nevers played all but 29 minutes of the season, and sportswriter Grantland Rice dubbed him and his teammates "the Iron Men of the North."

Despite the exciting championship race and the financial success of the Eskimos, by the end of the season the NFL was awash in red ink. Jim Thorpe had returned to Canton at age 36, but the Bulldogs went broke, disbanded at the end of the season, and saw their franchise canceled. The Racine franchise also folded. Tackle Steve Owen left a faltering Kansas City team for the New York Giants club, which, going up against Grange and the Yankees, had lost $40,000. Even the champion Yellow Jackets were in trouble, having been outdrawn by the AFL champion Philadelphia Quakers. Perhaps the only thing that saved the NFL was that the AFL, itself plagued by financial problems, folded one team at a time and drifted into obscurity.

1926 STANDINGS	**W**	**L**	**T**	**Pct.**
Frankford Yellow Jackets	14	1	1	.933
Chicago Bears	12	1	3	.923
Pottsville Maroons	10	2	1	.833
Kansas City Cowboys	8	3	0	.727
Green Bay Packers	7	3	3	.700
Los Angeles Buccaneers	6	3	1	.667
New York Giants	8	4	1	.667
Duluth Eskimos	6	5	3	.545
Buffalo Rangers	4	4	2	.500
Chicago Cardinals	5	6	1	.455
Providence Steam Roller	5	7	1	.417
Detroit Panthers	4	6	2	.400
Hartford Blues	3	7	0	.300
Brooklyn Lions	3	8	0	.273
Milwaukee Badgers	2	7	0	.222
Akron Indians	1	4	3	.200
Dayton Triangles	1	4	1	.200
Racine Tornadoes	1	4	0	.200
Columbus Tigers	1	6	0	.143
Canton Bulldogs	1	9	3	.100
Hammond Pros	0	4	0	.000
Louisville Colonels	0	4	0	.000

1927 The February 5 league meeting offered little to help the financially troubled NFL, although one franchise, Rock Island, was officially forfeited to the league, and another, Pottsville, had its conditional probation lifted and was restored as a member in good standing.

Two months later, however, President Joe Carr took the first step to save the faltering league by making sweeping moves that changed the look of professional football forever. On April 23, Carr called a special meeting in Cleveland to consider proposals for the reorganization of the NFL. At this meeting, it was decided that to secure the NFL's future the league should eliminate the financially weaker teams and consolidate the quality players onto a limited number of more successful teams.

It was further decided that in order to reduce the number of league teams and franchises, selected franchise holders would be given the option of retiring from the league or suspending operations. While inactive, a franchise could be sold, providing the prospective buyer was approved by the league, and the players could be sold, providing that a franchise disbanded its team. If a franchise elected to retire from the league, it would be given its pro-rated share of the league treasury. The sale or reactivation of a suspended franchise had to be completed by July 7, 1928, or the franchise would be considered canceled. The league promised that it would not admit any new franchises until all those suspended had been sold or canceled.

On July 16, with league permission, 12 of the NFL's 23 franchises suspended operations for a year. Gone from the playing fields were teams from Akron, Brooklyn, Columbus, Detroit, Hammond, Hartford, Kansas City, Los Angeles, Louisville, Milwaukee, Minneapolis, and Rochester. Shortly thereafter, Kansas City officially disbanded its team, sold some of its players' contracts, and retired from the league.

The new-look NFL had 12 teams in 1927. Joining the 10 returning from 1926 were the Cleveland Bulldogs, back after having suspended operations for a year, and the New York Yankees of Pyle and Grange. On September 4, the suspended Brooklyn franchise was transferred to Tim Mara in lieu of payments owed him. Mara allowed Pyle to enter the NFL and operate under the authority of the Brooklyn franchise, the rights to which Mara still held. The Yankees appeased Mara's territorial rights to New York by agreeing to play 13 of their 16 games on the road.

For the first time, the center of gravity of the NFL had left the Midwest, where the league had started. Now there were six eastern teams and six midwestern teams, one of each (the Yankees and Duluth) primarily a road team.

The road teams, which promised to bring in huge sums of money to the league, were big disappointments. Grange suffered a knee injury in the fourth game of the season, and, although he missed only three weeks, he never was the same runner again. The Yankees became a mediocre team with little draw. Duluth was even worse as both a draw and on the field. The team had Ernie Nevers, but little else, and it slumped to eleventh place in the standings.

The championship race came down to three teams in late November. The Giants had been tied and defeated early in the season by Cleveland and its rookie sensation at tailback, Benny Friedman. But then the New York club won six games in a row to take a slim lead (8-1-1) over the Bears (7-1-1) and Packers (6-1-1). On November 20, the Bears defeated the Packers 14-6, setting up a game for the title the next weekend with the Giants. Before the two teams played, however, the Cardinals (now coached by Guy Chamberlin) upset the Bears 3-0 on Thanksgiving Day. Then the Giants finished any Chicago hopes with a 13-7 victory in a game that Pro Football Hall of Fame tackle Steve Owen called, "the toughest, roughest football game I ever played." The champion Giants completed the season having posted 10 shutouts in 13 games.

1927 STANDINGS	**W**	**L**	**T**	**Pct.**
New York Giants	11	1	1	.917
Green Bay Packers	7	2	1	.778
Chicago Bears	9	3	2	.750
Cleveland Bulldogs	8	4	1	.667
Providence Steam Roller	8	5	1	.615
New York Yankees	7	8	1	.467
Frankford Yellow Jackets	6	9	3	.400
Pottsville Maroons	5	8	0	.385
Chicago Cardinals	3	7	1	.300
Dayton Triangles	1	6	1	.143
Duluth Eskimos	1	8	0	.111
Buffalo Bisons	0	5	0	.000

1928 The NFL contracted even further, dropping to 10 teams on the field. On July 7, those franchises that had suspended operations the year before but hadn't been sold or re-admitted were canceled—Akron, Columbus, Hammond, Hartford, Louisville, Milwaukee, Minneapolis, and Rochester. The next month, Los Angeles withdrew from the league. The Detroit franchise shifted ownership and agreed to field a team for 1928.

Three franchises that had fielded teams in 1927 disappeared. Ernie Nevers pitched for the St. Louis Browns in the offseason and then decided to coach for Glenn (Pop) Warner at Stanford. Without Nevers, and thus without any prospects, Duluth suspended operations for the year. Cleveland also suspended operations, and Buffalo simply didn't field a team. Like Nevers, Red Grange didn't return to the sport, spending the season nursing his injured knee and starring in a Hollywood movie.

The top three teams from the year before—the Giants, Bears, and Packers—were eliminated from the championship race in the opening weeks of the season. The Providence Steam Roller, coached by Jimmy Conzelman; the Detroit Wolverines, which had picked up many of the Cleveland players, including Benny Friedman; and the Frankford Yellow Jackets remained in contention through much of the season. Detroit was in first place until it suffered back-to-back losses to Frankford and Providence in early November.

The season came down to a Saturday-Sunday pair of games between Frankford and Providence. Despite being in a large city, the Yellow Jackets still kept the small-town flavor of some early NFL teams. "It is worth the time of anyone to wander out to Frankford on a Saturday afternoon in the autumn," Bill Roper wrote in *Football Today and Tomorrow.* "A steady stream of men and women flow toward the football field. On the arms of girls are the colors of the Yellow Jackets, in their hands, pennants. They cheer for the players because they know them, because it is their team. They have a clannishness that is refreshing, that would put most colleges to shame, and very few of them ever saw a college."

The home field advantage didn't provide much

help for the Yellow Jackets in a 6-6 tie. The next day, after an overnight train ride to Providence, the two teams played again. The Steam Roller played home games at the Cycledrome, a 10,000-seat oval that had been built for bicycle races. The stadium was so small that players tackled near the sidelines often went into the crowd. One end zone had to be shortened to five yards because of the track. The visiting team had no locker room facilities, and had to change and shower at the hotel, while the 18-man Steam Roller team used the Cycledrome dressing room that had been built to accommodate two to four bicycle racers. Again the game was close, but the Steam Roller, whose only loss had come in the second week to Frankford, won 6-0 on a 46-yard touchdown pass from George (Wildcat) Wilson to Curly Oden. Providence was undefeated in its last three games, and won the title with an 8-1-2 record.

1928 STANDINGS	W	L	T	Pct.
Providence Steam Roller	8	1	2	.889
Frankford Yellow Jackets	11	3	2	.786
Detroit Wolverines	7	2	1	.778
Green Bay Packers	6	4	3	.600
Chicago Bears	7	5	1	.583
New York Giants	4	7	2	.364
New York Yankees	4	8	1	.333
Pottsville Maroons	2	8	0	.200
Chicago Cardinals	1	5	0	.167
Dayton Triangles	0	7	0	.000

1929 At the July league meeting, an era ended when Chris O'Brien, the founder and owner of the Cardinals, sold the club to Dr. David Jones. The same month, a number of other league franchises were shuffled around. The Pottsville franchise, having serious financial problems due to its small stadium, was transferred to Boston, where the team was named the Bulldogs. The Duluth franchise, which had missed the 1928 season, was transferred to Orange, New Jersey, where the team became the Tornadoes. The New York Yankees' franchise, unable to turn a profit without Grange, was abandoned by C.C. Pyle and reverted back to Tim Mara. As he did while allowing the Yankees to play under the authority of the Brooklyn franchise, Mara transferred the franchise to Staten Island, bringing into the league a former independent team named the Stapletons. Mara also purchased the Detroit Wolverines. Mara wanted the services of Benny Friedman, but he was forced to buy the entire franchise in order to obtain the star quarterback.

Two earlier franchises—Buffalo and Minneapolis—fielded teams after not playing in 1928. It is not known whether Minneapolis's previous franchise was reinstated or if a new one was awarded. Cleveland's franchise, which also hadn't had a team in 1928, was canceled.

At the same league meeting in July, the NFL made another change. After eight years of playing with three officials—the referee, umpire, and head linesman—the league added a fourth, the field judge.

Green Bay and New York dominated play in the NFL. The Packers added three players—each of whom eventually would be selected to the Pro Football Hall of Fame—who helped them establish the best defense in the league. The first was tackle Cal Hubbard, who had enjoyed Green Bay when he had played there with the Giants, and had asked to be traded to the Wisconsin franchise. The second Green Bay acquisition was guard Mike Michalske, a former college star who had signed with the New York Yankees of the AFL and now was a free agent. The third was a colorful, enigmatic, and unconventional rule and curfew breaker who also happened to be one of the most talented backs in the league, Johnny Blood (McNally). He signed as a free agent, after his Pottsville team was transferred. The Giants, meanwhile, developed the best offense in the league behind the passing of Friedman.

Green Bay and New York both stormed through the first nine weeks of the season undefeated. In that span, the Packers recorded five shutouts and twice more gave up only a safety. The Giants opened with a scoreless tie in Orange, then won eight in a row. The showdown between the two came on November 24 at the Polo Grounds. Johnny Blood scored one touchdown and set up another with a fumble recovery as the Packers won 20-6. The Packers still couldn't afford to lose any of their remaining games, and they didn't. Despite a scoreless tie with Frankford the week after the game in New York, they finished the season undefeated (12-0-1). The Giants also won their remaining games, for a 13-1-1 record.

The individual highlight of the season occurred in a game between two also-rans, the Cardinals and the Bears. The Bears featured Red Grange, who had been prompted back into the league by losses in the stock market. The Cardinals were led by Ernie Nevers, who had returned from baseball when Dewey Scanlon, the former Duluth coach, had been hired to lead the Chicago team back to prominence. On Thanksgiving Day, the Cardinals, who had jelled into a power late in the season, thrashed the Bears 40-6 as Nevers scored all 40 points, on six rushing touchdowns and four extra points. Nevers's 40 points set a record that remains the oldest mark in the *NFL Record and Fact Book.*

1929 STANDINGS	W	L	T	Pct.
Green Bay Packers	12	0	1	1.000
New York Giants	13	1	1	.923
Frankford Yellow Jackets	9	4	5	.692
Chicago Cardinals	6	6	1	.500
Boston Bulldogs	4	4	0	.500
Orange Tornadoes	3	4	4	.429
Staten Island Stapletons	3	4	3	.429
Providence Steam Roller	4	6	2	.400
Chicago Bears	4	9	2	.333
Buffalo Bisons	1	7	1	.125
Minneapolis Red Jackets	1	9	0	.100
Dayton Triangles	0	6	0	.000

1930 In July, one of the NFL's newest franchises (Boston) and one of its oldest (Buffalo) became memories, when they were forfeited to the league. A number of other team transactions happened that month. The Orange team moved to Newark, where it was known as the Newark Tornadoes. John Dwyer, a Brooklyn businessman, purchased the Dayton franchise, moved it, and renamed the team the Brooklyn Dodgers. And the Portsmouth (Ohio) Spartans entered the league.

Although 11 teams played the season, only two ever were in contention for the championship. The first two months of the season Green Bay and New York combined for only one loss, a 14-7 Packers victory over the Giants in Green Bay. Both teams lost on November 16, setting up their rematch at the Polo Grounds the next week. Before a crowd of 45,000 and featuring former Army All-America halfback Chris Cagle for the first time, the Giants defeated the Packers 13-6 to take over the league lead with an 11-2 record compared to Green Bay's 8-2. Four days later, New York gave the lead back to Green Bay, dropping a 7-6 contest at Staten Island. Given a second chance, the Packers maintained their lead the rest of the season and won the championship with a 10-3-1 record despite a late-season loss to the Bears.

The Bears had started the season slowly after George Halas had retired as head coach and had hired Ralph Jones from Lake Forest College as his replacement. But once the team got used to Jones's new refinements of the T-formation—moving the ends out wide and putting a halfback in motion—and his new strategies—using more end runs and passing frequently—they were unstoppable. Rookie fullback Bronko Nagurski and a line that included eventual Pro Football Hall of Famers Link Lyman and George Trafton led the way as the Bears closed their season with five consecutive victories.

Perhaps the most important game of the year for the NFL included only one league team. On December 14, in a game in which all proceeds were to go to the New York Unemployment Fund to help those suffering because of the Great Depression, the Giants played an all-star team of Notre Dame graduates coached by Knute Rockne. Rockne, Notre Dame fans, and most of the public in general held the pro game in low esteem and expected the Notre Dame team to win easily. But before 55,000 fans, Benny Friedman led the Giants to an easy 22-0 victory. The game helped give the league credibility with the press and the public as a quality product.

1930 STANDINGS	W	L	T	Pct.
Green Bay Packers	10	3	1	.769
New York Giants	13	4	0	.765
Chicago Bears	9	4	1	.692
Brooklyn Dodgers	7	4	1	.636
Providence Steam Roller	6	4	1	.600
Staten Island Stapletons	5	5	2	.500
Chicago Cardinals	5	6	2	.455
Portsmouth Spartans	5	6	3	.455
Frankford Yellow Jackets	4	13	1	.235
Minneapolis Red Jackets	1	7	1	.125
Newark Tornadoes	1	10	1	.091

1931 The Depression continued to hurt the NFL, as two more teams left the field. The Minneapolis franchise suspended operations for a year, but wasn't able to come back in 1932 and was canceled. The Newark franchise was forfeited to the league, which, for the first time in history, ordered it to be disposed of to the highest bidder; no bidder appeared before the season.

A new franchise began play in Cleveland, bringing the number of teams starting the season to 10. The Cleveland franchise actually was a league-sponsored traveling team managed by Jerry Corcoran, the former manager of the Columbus Tigers. The NFL's intention was to make it a permanent league member located in Cleveland if there was an approved backer and demonstrated fan support for the team. Neither developed, and the franchise was discontinued at the end of a 2-8 season.

The season was another success story for the Packers. With the Bears hurt by injuries and the Giants by the retirement of Benny Friedman (who returned, but too late to help get them back into contention), the only challenger to Green Bay was Portsmouth. Coach George (Potsy) Clark used rookie backs Earl (Dutch) Clark and Glenn Presnell to lead the Spartans to eight consecutive victories to open the season, but they still couldn't shake the undefeated Packers. Then back-to-back losses the first week of November dropped Portsmouth behind Green Bay, and a Portsmouth loss to the Cardinals clinched the third title in a row for the Packers, who finished with a 12-2 record despite a loss to the Bears in the season finale.

The Frankford Yellow Jackets didn't even make it to the end of the season. They were plagued with problems both on the field and at the gate. On November 10, the franchise folded.

1931 STANDINGS	W	L	T	Pct.
Green Bay Packers	12	2	0	.857
Portsmouth Spartans	11	3	0	.786
Chicago Bears	8	5	0	.667
Chicago Cardinals	5	4	0	.556
New York Giants	7	6	1	.538
Providence Steam Roller	4	4	3	.500
Staten Island Stapletons	4	6	1	.400
Cleveland Indians	2	8	0	.200
Brooklyn Dodgers	2	12	0	.143
Frankford Yellow Jackets	1	6	1	.143

1932 In the depths of the Depression, the NFL's membership fell to eight teams, the smallest in its history. Providence, which only four years before had won the championship, suspended operations for a year with league permission. But the Steam Roller never played again in the NFL, and the franchise was forfeited to the league in 1933. In July, a four-man Boston syndicate composed of George Preston Marshall, Vincent Bendix, Jay O'Brien, and M. Dorland Doyle, was granted a franchise. There are indications that the new Boston franchise—known as the Braves—was the same one that had been located in Newark in 1930. It wasn't a good time to start a team. By the end of the season, the Braves had lost $46,000, and Marshall was left as the sole owner of the team.

There were some bright spots for Boston, however. Two future Pro Football Hall of Fame players joined the team as rookies, halfback Cliff Battles and tackle Glen (Turk) Edwards. Battles led the NFL in rushing with 576 yards in the first year that the league office kept official statistics. The other league leaders, in the categories that were kept that first year, were Ray Flaherty of the Giants, with 21 receptions; Earl (Dutch) Clark of Portsmouth, with 55 points; and Arnie Herber of Green Bay, the passing leader with 639 yards and nine touchdowns.

The shortcomings of the standings in pro football in 1932 cost the Packers a fourth consecutive NFL championship and led to a playoff game that changed the sport profoundly.

Green Bay added rookie fullback Clarke Hinkle to its array of stars and ran up a 10-1-1 record with two games left to play. However, the Packers were shut out in their last two games by the two teams chasing them, 19-0 by Portsmouth and 9-0 by the Bears. Green Bay's 10-3-1 record included almost double the victories of the Spartans and Bears (six each), but the championship was determined on a percentage basis, not including ties. Green Bay finished with a .769 percentage.

The Bears and Spartans, meanwhile, each recorded .857 percentages. The Bears, who had started the season with three scoreless ties and a 2-0 loss to the Packers, were 6-1-6, while the Spartans, who also had lost a 15-10 decision to Green Bay, were 6-1-4. Under today's rules, in which a tie counts as half a win and half a loss, the Packers would have won the title, but they were shunted off to third place behind Portsmouth and the Bears.

After the season finale, the league office arranged for a championship game one week later in Chicago, between the Bears and the Spartans. The Bears' victory over Green Bay was played in the snow at Wrigley Field, and the playoff game was scheduled for the same site.

The weather grew continually worse that week, however. The bitter cold and heavy snow prompted George Halas to move the game indoors to Chicago Stadium—a hockey arena. The conditions were new to football. There was a layer of dirt on the arena floor, left over from a circus that had just left. There was room only for an 80-yard field, so each team was penalized 20 yards as soon as it crossed midfield. Goal posts were moved to the goal lines from the end lines, and inbounds lines were created because the walls came up to the field.

A crowd of 11,198 saw the game. Portsmouth played without Dutch Clark, who already had left the team for a job as basketball coach at his alma mater, Colorado College. Nonetheless, the Spartans stayed even with the Bears for three quarters. Then in the fourth quarter, the Bears scored on a touchdown pass from Bronko Nagurski to Red Grange. The Spartans contested the call, but the touchdown stood. Chicago added a safety and won the first NFL Championship Game 9-0.

1932 STANDINGS	W	L	T	Pct.
Chicago Bears	6	1	6	.857
Portsmouth Spartans	6	1	4	.857
Green Bay Packers	10	3	1	.769
Boston Braves	4	4	2	.500
New York Giants	4	6	2	.400
Brooklyn Dodgers	3	9	0	.250
Chicago Cardinals	2	6	2	.250
Staten Island Stapletons	2	7	3	.222

NFL championship: Chicago Bears 9, Portsmouth 0

LEADING RUSHERS	Att.	Yards	Avg.	TD
Cliff Battles, Boston	148	576	3.9	3
Bob Campiglio, Staten Island	104	504	4.8	2
Bronko Nagurski, Chi. Bears	109	486	4.5	4
Dutch Clark, Portsmouth	112	461	4.1	3
Ken Strong, Staten Island	96	375	3.9	2

LEADING PASSER	Att.	Comp.	Yards	TD	Int.
Arnie Herber, Green Bay	101	37	639	9	9

LEADING RECEIVER	No.	Yards	Avg.	TD
Luke Johnsos, Chi. Bears	24	321	13.4	2

LEADING SCORER	TD	FG	PAT	TP
Dutch Clark, Portsmouth	6	3	10	55

1933 The NFL, which long had followed the rules of college football, made a number of significant changes from the college game for the first time and began to independently develop rules serving its needs and the style of play it preferred.

As a result of successful use of inbounds lines (or hashmarks) in the 1932 Championship Game, the league owners passed a rule that the ball would be moved in 10 yards to an inbounds line whenever it was in play within five yards of the sidelines. The goal posts were moved from the end lines to the goal lines to promote field-goal attempts, increase scoring, and reduce the number of tie games. Passing from anywhere behind the line of scrimmage (instead of from at least five yards behind the line) was permitted. These rules changes had their desired effect—there was a dramatic increase in passing, scoring, and wide-open, exciting play in the NFL in 1933.

There was one other major change that spurred interest in the league both at the box office and with the media. At the July meeting, George Preston Marshall and George Halas pushed through a proposal that divided the NFL into two divisions. Not only did the new structure allow more teams to be in contention later in the season, it set up a yearly championship game that rivaled the interest in Major League Baseball's World Series.

At the same meeting, the NFL grew to 10 teams. Philadelphia, Pittsburgh, and Cincinnati each were granted a franchise. Meanwhile, Staten Island suspended operations for one year, and then suspended operations again in 1934. The franchise was canceled in 1935.

The new Philadelphia franchise was awarded to Bert Bell and Lud Wray, who named their team the Eagles, adopting the symbol of the National Recovery Administration of the "New Deal" of President Franklin D. Roosevelt. Before the league owners approved Philadelphia's bid for a franchise, they made a stipulation that Bell and Wray pay 25 percent of the outstanding liens against the former Frankford Yellow Jackets club, which had been forfeited to the league with large debts.

The new Pittsburgh team was the first in the NFL for the city that had hosted the first-known pro football game in 1892. The new franchise was granted to Art Rooney, who founded the team with the winnings from a successful day at a race track. Rooney named the team the Pirates, after Pittsburgh's baseball team. Cincinnati's new team was named the Reds, also after the baseball team.

Before the season started, Halas bought out his partner, Ed (Dutch) Sternaman, to become sole owner of the Bears. Marshall, meanwhile, changed the name of his team from the Braves to the Redskins.

The new divisional format set up two run-away title races. In the east, the Giants won with the best offense in the league, paced by rookie Harry Newman, who led the NFL with 11 touchdown passes, and Ken Strong, who led the league in scoring, after joining the Giants from the defunct Stapletons. Neither Brooklyn, which had the league's top receiver in halfback John (Shipwreck) Kelley (the last halfback to lead the league in receiving for 41 years, until 1974), nor Boston, which featured the top two rushers in the NFL, Jim Musick and Cliff Battles, had the overall talent to challenge the Giants.

In the west, the Bears had Halas on the sidelines again, and that was enough to leave behind Portsmouth, which was forced to play without Dutch Clark when he decided to remain at his job as the coach at Colorado College. On December 17, before 26,000 fans, the Bears hosted the Giants at Wrigley Field in the first NFL Championship Game that had been planned before the season. The Bears won 23-21 on a touchdown in the fourth quarter, when Bronko Nagurski threw a pass to end Bill Hewitt, who lateraled the ball to end Bill Karr, who scored.

1933 STANDINGS						
Eastern Division	**W**	**L**	**T**	**Pct.**	**Pts.**	**OP**
New York Giants	11	3	0	.786	244	101
Brooklyn Dodgers	5	4	1	.556	93	54
Boston Redskins	5	5	2	.500	103	97
Philadelphia Eagles	3	5	1	.375	77	158
Pittsburgh Pirates	3	6	2	.333	67	208
Western Division	**W**	**L**	**T**	**Pct.**	**Pts.**	**OP**
Chicago Bears	10	2	1	.833	133	82
Portsmouth Spartans	6	5	0	.545	128	87
Green Bay Packers	5	7	1	.423	170	107
Cincinnati Reds	3	6	1	.333	38	110
Chicago Cardinals	1	9	1	.100	52	101

NFL championship: Chicago Bears 23, New York Giants 21

LEADING RUSHERS	Att.	Yards	Avg.	TD
Jim Musick, Boston	173	809	4.7	5
Cliff Battles, Boston	146	737	5.0	3
Bronko Nagurski, Chi. Bears	128	533	4.2	1
Glenn Presnell, Portsmouth	118	522	4.4	6
Swede Hanson, Philadelphia	133	494	3.7	3

LEADING PASSERS	Att.	Comp.	Yards	TD	Int.
Harry Newman, NY Giants	136	53	973	9	17
Glenn Presnell, Portsmouth	125	47	774	4	12
Arnie Herber, Green Bay	126	50	656	4	12
Benny Friedman, Brooklyn	80	42	597	5	7
Keith Molesworth, Chi. Bears	50	19	421	5	4

LEADING RECEIVERS	No.	Yards	Avg.	TD
John (Shipwreck) Kelly, Brooklyn	22	246	11.2	3
Bill Hewitt, Chi. Bears	16	274	17.1	2
Roger Grove, Green Bay	15	217	14.5	0
Ray Tesser, Pittsburgh	14	274	19.6	0
Lavern Dilweg, Green Bay	14	225	16.1	0

LEADING SCORERS	TD	FG	PAT	TP
Ken Strong, NY Giants	6	5	13	64
Glenn Presnell, Portsmouth	6	6	10	64

SUPERLATIVES		
Rushing average	6.2	Kink Richards, NY Giants
Receiving average	29.5	Paul Moss, Pittsburgh
Completion percentage	52.5	Benny Friedman, Brooklyn
Touchdowns	7	Kink Richards, NY Giants Shipwreck Kelly, Brooklyn Buckets Goldenberg, Green Bay

1934 In June, G.A. (Dick) Richards bought the Portsmouth Spartans, moved them to Detroit to play in the University of Detroit Stadium, and renamed them the Lions.

Two months later, professional football gained new prestige when the champion Chicago Bears were matched against the best college football players in the first Chicago College All-Star Game. The *Chicago Tribune* sponsored the game, and the college all-stars were selected in a poll of 105 newspapers throughout the country. Noble Kizer of Purdue accepted the job coaching the All-Stars despite the fact that some of his colleagues urged him not to coach a game against professionals. The game, at Soldier Field, was a scoreless tie and there were only nine first downs, but a crowd of 79,432 attended.

When the regular season started, the Bears and the Lions were the class of the west, and of the league. The Bears featured a high-powered offense, led by rookie Beattie Feathers, who became the first NFL back ever to gain 1,000 yards in a season, finishing with 1,004 on only 101 carries. In the same backfield, Bronko Nagurski finished fourth in the league with 586 yards, and Gene Ronzani tenth with 485. The Bears won their first 11 games. The Lions, with

Dutch Clark returning to finish third in the league in rushing and fourth in passing, also had the league's best defense. They shut out their first seven opponents and kept pace with the Bears by winning their first 10 games, before a 3-0 upset by Green Bay.

Back-to-back games between the Bears and the Lions closed the season. In the first, won by Chicago 19-16, they met in the first Thanksgiving Day game in Detroit, starting a pro football tradition that still continues. It also was the first NFL game broadcast nationally; Graham McNamee was the announcer for CBS radio. The Bears also won the second game, 10-7, to finish 13-0.

At the other end of the spectrum in the Western Division was Cincinnati. The Reds lost eight games in a row to open the season, scoring a total of only 10 points. When the franchise defaulted on payments to its players, it was suspended by the league. The St. Louis Gunners, an independent team that had gone 14-2 in 1933, joined the league, which still had three games left, by purchasing the Cincinnati franchise. In their first game, the Gunners fielded the same team that had played as an independent a week earlier, and defeated Pittsburgh 6-0. Five Reds players joined the Gunners for their last two games and must have carried ill fortune with them—reminiscent of the Reds, the Gunners lost both times.

In the NFL Championship Game, the Bears met the Giants, who had won the weak Eastern Division with an 8-5 record, including a 1-4 mark against teams from the west and an 0-2 record against the Bears. The Giants were given no chance on an extremely cold day with an icy field at the Polo Grounds, and trailed 10-3 at halftime. But some of the Giants' players put on basketball shoes at halftime for better footing, and they went on to defeat the Bears 30-13. The game was dubbed the "Sneakers Game."

1934 STANDINGS

Eastern Division	W	L	T	Pct.	Pts.	OP
New York Giants	8	5	0	.615	147	107
Boston Redskins	6	6	0	.500	107	94
Brooklyn Dodgers	4	7	0	.364	61	153
Philadelphia Eagles	4	7	0	.364	127	85
Pittsburgh Pirates	2	10	0	.167	51	206
Western Division	**W**	**L**	**T**	**Pct.**	**Pts.**	**OP**
Chicago Bears	13	0	0	1.000	286	86
Detroit Lions	10	3	0	.769	238	59
Green Bay Packers	7	6	0	.538	156	112
Chicago Cardinals	5	6	0	.455	80	84
St. Louis Gunners	1	2	0	.333	27	61
Cincinnati Reds	0	8	0	.000	10	243

NFL championship: New York Giants 30, Chicago Bears 13

LEADING RUSHERS	Att.	Yards	Avg.	TD
Beattie Feathers, Chi. Bears	101	1,004	9.9	8
Swede Hanson, Philadelphia	147	805	5.5	7
Dutch Clark, Detroit	122	763	6.3	8
Bronko Nagurski, Chi. Bears	123	586	4.8	7
Warren Heller, Pittsburgh	132	528	4.0	1

LEADING PASSERS	Att.	Comp.	Yards	TD	Int.
Arnie Herber, Green Bay	115	42	799	8	12
Warren Heller, Pittsburgh	112	31	511	2	15
Dutch Clark, Detroit	49	23	383	0	3
Harry Newman, NY Giants	91	35	366	1	5
Ed Matesic, Philadelphia	60	20	272	3	5
Harp Vaughan, Pittsburgh	39	14	272	2	5

LEADING RECEIVERS	No.	Yards	Avg.	TD
Joe Carter, Philadelphia	16	238	14.9	4
Red Badgro, NY Giants	16	206	12.9	1
Ben Smith, Pittsburgh	12	190	15.8	0
Charley Malone, Boston	11	121	11.0	2
Joe Skladany, Pittsburgh	10	222	22.2	2
Milt Gantenbein, Green Bay	10	165	16.5	0
Jack Grossman, Brooklyn	10	158	15.8	1
Bill Hewitt, Chi. Bears	10	151	15.1	5
Clarke Hinkle, Green Bay	10	110	11.0	1

LEADING SCORER	TD	FG	PAT	TP
Jack Manders, Chi. Bears	3	10	31	79

SUPERLATIVES		
Rushing average	9.9	Beattie Feathers, Chi. Bears
Receiving average	28.6	Harry Ebding, Detroit
Completion percentage	46.9	Dutch Clark, Detroit
Touchdowns	9	Beattie Feathers, Chi. Bears

1935 Alarmed by the domination of the Giants and the Bears, Bert Bell of Philadelphia proposed in May that NFL teams institute a draft of college players, held in an inverse order of the teams' finish of the previous season. The proposal was accepted, and the first draft was scheduled for a time prior to the 1936 season.

In June, the St. Louis franchise was offered a conditional acceptance as a permanent NFL club, but the owners refused the conditions, and the franchise was rejected by the league. St. Louis wouldn't have another NFL team until the Chicago Cardinals moved there in 1960.

End Don Hutson of the University of Alabama joined the Green Bay Packers and made a feared passing combination with tailback Arnie Herber.

The inbounds lines or hashmarks, established at 10 yards from each sideline in 1933, were moved nearer the center of the field, 15 yards from each sideline. The player limit was increased from 20 to 24.

Detroit ousted the Chicago Bears as Western Division champions and, led by Dutch Clark and Leroy (Ace) Gutowsky, defeated the New York Giants 26-7 in the NFL Championship Game on a raw, snowy day at the University of Detroit Stadium before a sparse crowd of 15,000 fans. Raymond (Buddy) Parker, a rookie back for the Lions, scored his team's final touchdown. The victory gave Detroit the football and baseball championships of 1935; the baseball Tigers had won their first World Series earlier.

1935 STANDINGS

Eastern Division	W	L	T	Pct.	Pts.	OP
New York Giants	9	3	0	.750	180	96
Brooklyn	5	6	1	.455	90	141
Pittsburgh	4	8	0	.333	100	209
Boston	2	8	1	.200	65	123
Philadelphia	2	9	0	.182	60	179
Western Division	**W**	**L**	**T**	**Pct.**	**Pts.**	**OP**
Detroit	7	3	2	.700	191	111
Green Bay	8	4	0	.667	181	96
Chicago Bears	6	4	2	.600	192	106
Chicago Cardinals	6	4	2	.600	99	97

NFL championship: Detroit 26, New York Giants 7
One game between Boston and Philadelphia was canceled.

LEADING RUSHERS	Att.	Yards	Avg.	TD
Doug Russell, Chi. Cardinals	140	499	3.6	0
Ernie Caddel, Detroit	87	450	5.2	6
Kink Richards, NY Giants	149	449	3.0	4
Bill Shepherd, Boston-Detroit	143	425	3.0	4
Dutch Clark, Detroit	120	412	3.4	4

LEADING PASSERS	Att.	Comp.	Yards	TD	Int.
Ed Danowski, NY Giants	113	57	795	11	9
Arnie Herber, Green Bay	106	40	729	8	6
Johnny Gildea, Pittsburgh	95	28	529	2	20
Bernie Masterson, Chi. Bears	44	18	456	7	4
Bob Monnett, Green Bay	65	31	454	2	6

LEADING RECEIVERS	No.	Yards	Avg.	TD
Tod Goodwin, NY Giants	26	432	16.6	4
J. Blood (McNally), Green Bay	25	404	16.2	3
Bill Smith, Chi. Cardinals	24	318	13.3	2
Charley Malone, Boston	22	433	19.7	2
Luke Johnsos, Chi. Bears	19	298	15.7	4

LEADING SCORER	TD	FG	PAT	TP
Dutch Clark, Detroit	6	1	16	55

SUPERLATIVES		
Rushing average	5.2	Ernie Caddel, Detroit
Receiving average	23.6	Joe Carter, Philadelphia
Completion percentage	50.4	Ed Danowski, NY Giants
Touchdowns	7	Don Hutson, Green Bay

1936 There were no franchise transactions for the first time since the formation of the NFL. It also was the first year in which all member teams played the same number of games. The player limit was increased to 25.

The Philadelphia Eagles of Bert Bell finished last with a 2-9 record, so the man who had proposed the draft now made the first choice in the first draft. Philadelphia chose Jay Berwanger, All-America halfback of the University of Chicago. The Eagles, however, traded the negotiation rights to him to the Chicago Bears in exchange for tackle Art Buss. Berwanger never agreed to terms with the Bears and never played pro football. The Bears, however, made exceptional choices when they took two future Hall of Famers, tackle Joe Stydahar of West Virginia and guard Dan Fortmann of Colgate.

A rival league was formed and it became the second organization to call itself the American Football League. The Boston Shamrocks were its champion and the other teams were the Brooklyn Tigers, Cleveland Rams, New York Yankees, Pittsburgh Americans, and Rochester Tigers.

Green Bay had Arnie Herber and Clarke Hinkle in its backfield and Don Hutson at end. Hutson scored eight touchdowns and the Packers easily won the Western Division,with their only loss coming to the second-place Bears. The Boston Redskins emerged as a strong team and captured the weak Eastern Division championship.

There were only 5,000 fans at Fenway Park in Boston when the Redskins defeated Pittsburgh in the team's last home game of the season. Despite the team's chances of winning a championship, the fans had stayed away in protest because Marshall had raised ticket prices on the day of a previous game without advance notice. With the newspapers and fans berating him, Marshall moved the championship game with Green Bay to the Polo Grounds in New York. A crowd of 29,545 attended as Herber and Hutson led Green Bay to a 21-6 victory over the Redskins.

1936 STANDINGS

Eastern Division	W	L	T	Pct.	Pts.	OP
Boston	7	5	0	.583	149	110
Pittsburgh	6	6	0	.500	98	187
New York Giants	5	6	1	.455	115	163
Brooklyn	3	8	1	.273	92	161
Philadelphia	1	11	0	.083	51	206
Western Division	**W**	**L**	**T**	**Pct.**	**Pts.**	**OP**
Green Bay	10	1	1	.909	248	118
Chicago Bears	9	3	0	.750	222	94
Detroit	8	4	0	.667	235	102
Chicago Cardinals	3	8	1	.273	74	143

NFL championship: Green Bay 21, Boston 6

LEADING RUSHERS	Att.	Yards	Avg.	TD
Tuffy Leemans, NY Giants	206	830	4.0	2
Ace Gutowsky, Detroit	191	827	4.3	6
Dutch Clark, Detroit	123	628	5.1	7
Cliff Battles, Boston	176	614	3.5	5
G. Grosvenor, Chi. Bears-Card.	170	612	3.6	4

LEADING PASSERS	Att.	Comp.	Yards	TD	Int.
Arnie Herber, Green Bay	173	77	1,239	11	13
Ed Matesic, Pittsburgh	138	64	850	5	16
Phil Sarboe, Chi. Card.-Brooklyn	114	47	680	3	13
Pug Vaughan, Chi. Cardinals	79	30	546	3	10
Ed Danowski, NY Giants	104	47	515	6	10

LEADING RECEIVERS	No.	Yards	Avg.	TD
Don Hutson, Green Bay	34	536	15.8	8
Bill Smith, Chi. Cardinals	20	414	20.7	1
Ernie Caddel, Detroit	19	150	7.9	1
Wayne Millner, Boston	18	211	11.7	0
Eggs Manske, Philadelphia	17	325	19.1	0

LEADING SCORER	TD	FG	PAT	TP
Dutch Clark, Detroit	7	4	19	73

SUPERLATIVES		
Rushing average	6.4	Ernie Caddel, Detroit
Receiving average	23.9	Bill Hewitt, Chi. Bears
Completion percentage	53.5	Dutch Clark, Detroit
Touchdowns	9	Don Hutson, Green Bay

1937 In February, George Preston Marshall moved the Redskins from Boston to his hometown of Washington, D.C. Griffith Stadium was leased for the Redskins' games. Washington signed All-America tailback Sammy Baugh of TCU to a contract for $8,000.

The nation's capital embraced the exciting Redskins. A Friday night game against the New York Giants was moved up to Thursday night so it would not conflict with one of President Franklin D. Roosevelt's "fireside chats" on the radio.

There had been a Cleveland Rams team in the 1936 season of the second American Football League. A new team called the Cleveland Rams, which had no relationship to the former team other than it had the same name, was formed by Homer Marshman and joined the NFL. The league once more had 10 teams.

Dutch Clark became the coach of the Detroit Lions and Johnny Blood (McNally) the coach of the Pittsburgh Pirates.

Philadelphia made the first draft choice again, selecting back Sam Francis of Nebraska but trading the rights to him to the Chicago Bears.

The Los Angeles Bulldogs had an 8-0 record in the American Football League, which then folded. The other 1937 teams were the Boston Shamrocks, Cincinnati Bengals, New York Yankees, Pittsburgh Americans, and Rochester Tigers.

Baugh was the NFL's leading passer and the Redskins won six of their last seven games en route to the Eastern Division championship. The title wasn't clinched until the last day of the season, when the Redskins, accompanied by 8,000 fans, traveled to New York to play the second-place Giants. The Redskins won easily 49-14. In the Western Division, the Bears also had a close race with the Packers, who gave the Chicago team its only loss of the season. But Green Bay dropped its last two games of the year to give the Bears the title. In the championship game, the Bears met the Redskins on a frigid day at Wrigley Field in Chicago. Despite the bitter cold, Baugh had a sensational passing game in which he completed 18 of 33 for an unprecedented 335 yards. The Redskins were the NFL champions, 28-21.

At the end of the season Bronko Nagurski retired from football.

1937 STANDINGS

Eastern Division	**W**	**L**	**T**	**Pct.**	**Pts.**	**OP**
Washington	8	3	0	.727	195	120
New York Giants	6	3	2	.667	128	109
Pittsburgh	4	7	0	.364	122	145
Brooklyn	3	7	1	.300	82	174
Philadelphia	2	8	1	.200	86	177
Western Division	**W**	**L**	**T**	**Pct.**	**Pts.**	**OP**
Chicago Bears	9	1	1	.900	201	100
Green Bay	7	4	0	.636	220	122
Detroit	7	4	0	.636	180	105
Chicago Cardinals	5	5	1	.500	135	165
Cleveland	1	10	0	.091	75	207

NFL championship: Washington 28, Chicago Bears 21

LEADING RUSHERS	**Att.**	**Yards**	**Avg.**	**TD**
Cliff Battles, Washington	216	874	4.0	5
Clarke Hinkle, Green Bay	129	552	4.3	5
John Karcis, Pittsburgh	128	511	4.0	3
Dutch Clark, Detroit	96	468	4.9	5
George Grosvenor, Chi. Cardinals	137	461	3.4	2

LEADING PASSERS	**Att.**	**Comp.**	**Yards**	**TD**	**Int.**
Sammy Baugh, Washington	171	81	1,127	8	14
Ed Danowski, NY Giants	134	66	814	8	5
Pat Coffee, Chi. Cardinals	119	52	804	5	11
Arnie Herber, Green Bay	104	47	676	7	10
Bernie Masterson, Chi. Bears	72	26	615	8	7

LEADING RECEIVERS	**No.**	**Yards**	**Avg.**	**TD**
Don Hutson, Green Bay	41	552	13.5	7
Gaynell Tinsley, Chi. Cardinals	36	675	18.8	5
Charley Malone, Washington	28	419	15.0	4
Jeff Barrett, Brooklyn	20	461	23.1	3
Bill Hewitt, Philadelphia	16	197	12.3	5

LEADING SCORER	**TD**	**FG**	**PAT**	**TP**
Jack Manders, Chi. Bears	5	8	15	69

SUPERLATIVES		
Rushing average	5.6	Ernie Caddel, Detroit
Receiving average	23.1	Jeff Barrett, Brooklyn
Completion percentage	50.7	Bob Monnett, Green Bay
Touchdowns	7	Cliff Battles, Washington Clark Hinkle, Green Bay Don Hutson, Green Bay

1938 Sammy Baugh had gotten rough treatment at times during his rookie season, and, as a result, the rules were changed. A new rule called for a 15-yard penalty for roughing the passer after the ball had left his hand. The player limit increased to 30.

Hugh (Shorty) Ray, a Chicago school teacher, coach, and supervisor of football officials, became a technical advisor to the NFL on rules, at the suggestion of George Halas.

Corbett Davis, back from Indiana, was the first choice in the NFL draft. He was the selection of the Cleveland Rams, who had finished 1-10. Sid Luckman was a rookie with the Bears, Ward Cuff with the Giants, Frank (Bruiser) Kinard with Brooklyn, and Alex Wojciechowicz with Detroit. Pittsburgh shocked the other teams when owner Art Rooney gave a $15,800 contract to All-America Byron (Whizzer) White of Colorado to play for the Pirates. White had a storied career in college, scoring 34 points in his last game. He became the NFL's leading rusher with 567 yards as a rookie, but the Pirates won only two games and finished last in the Eastern Division.

The New York Giants won in the East, defeating the Redskins 36-0 on the last day of the season. Despite a late-season loss to Detroit, Green Bay won the Western Division when the Lions lost their season finale to Philadelphia. The Giants defeated Green Bay 23-17 in the NFL Championship Game before a record crowd of 48,120 at the Polo Grounds.

George Preston Marshall of the Redskins had met in Los Angeles during the summer with two notable sports figures to discuss a pet idea of his. He wanted an annual all-star game between the league champions and a team of all-stars. He sold the idea to sports editor Bill Henry of the *Los Angeles Times* and promoter Tom Gallery. The first Pro Bowl was played at Wrigley Field in Los Angeles on January 15, 1938. The Giants defeated the Pro All-Stars 13-10 before a crowd of 20,000.

1938 STANDINGS

Eastern Division	**W**	**L**	**T**	**Pct.**	**Pts.**	**OP**
New York Giants	8	2	1	.800	194	79
Washington	6	3	2	.667	148	154
Brooklyn	4	4	3	.500	131	161
Philadelphia	5	6	0	.455	154	164
Pittsburgh	2	9	0	.182	79	169
Western Division	**W**	**L**	**T**	**Pct.**	**Pts.**	**OP**
Green Bay	8	3	0	.727	223	118
Detroit	7	4	0	.636	119	108
Chicago Bears	6	5	0	.545	194	148
Cleveland	4	7	0	.364	131	215
Chicago Cardinals	2	9	0	.182	111	168

NFL championship: New York Giants 23, Green Bay 17

LEADING RUSHERS	**Att.**	**Yards**	**Avg.**	**TD**
Byron (Whizzer) White, Pittsburgh	152	567	3.7	4
Tuffy Leemans, NY Giants	121	463	3.8	4
Bill Shepherd, Detroit	100	455	4.6	3
Cecil Isbell, Green Bay	85	445	5.2	2
Ace Gutowsky, Detroit	131	444	3.4	2

LEADING PASSERS	**Att.**	**Comp.**	**Yards**	**TD**	**Int.**
Ed Danowski, NY Giants	129	70	848	7	8
Sammy Baugh, Washington	128	63	853	6	11
Ace Parker, Brooklyn	148	63	865	5	7
Jack Robbins, Chi. Cardinals	97	52	577	2	9
Bernie Masterson, Chi. Bears	112	46	848	7	9

LEADING RECEIVERS	**No.**	**Yards**	**Avg.**	**TD**
Gaynell Tinsley, Chi. Cardinals	41	516	12.6	1
Don Hutson, Green Bay	32	548	17.1	9
Joe Carter, Philadelphia	27	386	14.3	7
Charley Malone, Washington	24	257	10.7	1
Jim Benton, Cleveland	21	418	19.9	5

LEADING SCORER	**TD**	**FG**	**PAT**	**TP**
Clarke Hinkle, Green Bay	7	3	7	58

SUPERLATIVES		
Rushing average	5.2	Cecil Isbell, Green Bay
Receiving average	19.9	Jim Benton, Cleveland
Completion percentage	54.4	Bob Monnett, Green Bay
Touchdowns	9	Don Hutson, Green Bay

1939 Joe F. Carr, president of the National Football League since 1921, died May 20. Secretary-treasurer Carl Storck was named to succeed Carr as acting president.

An NFL game was televised for the first time when the National Broadcasting Company took a camera to Ebbets Field in Brooklyn October 22 and beamed the game between the Dodgers and the Philadelphia Eagles back to the approximately 1,000 sets then in New York.

Sid Luckman replaced Bernie Masterson as the starting quarterback for the Chicago Bears. They played the T-formation with man-in-motion while other clubs played long-snap formations such as the A-formation and Double and Single Wing. Clark Shaughnessy of the University of Chicago was assisting George Halas and his Bears' coaching staff in developing new plays. Luckman became the smart leader and good ball-handler Halas needed to run the system, which was becoming more and more complex. Bill Osmanski, the Bears' rookie fullback from Holy Cross, led the league in rushing with 699 yards.

New York and Washington were strong again and George Preston Marshall of the Redskins led both a parade of some 12,000 fans from Washington and the Redskins' Band up Broadway on the way to the Polo Grounds at 151st Street for the final game of the regular season. Sportswriter Bill Corum wrote later that, "At the head of a 150-piece brass band and 12,000 fans, George Preston Marshall slipped unobtrusively into New York today."

New York won the game, however, 9-7 and Marshall was angry afterwards, yelling foul over a call by referee Bill Halloran that a Redskins' field goal attempt by Bo Russell was no good with only 45 seconds left.

The Giants were Eastern champions. They went to Wisconsin to meet the Western Division champion Green Bay Packers. There was limited seating in City Stadium in Green Bay, so the game was moved to the Wisconsin State Fair Park in Milwaukee and the ticket price increased to $4.40. A crowd of 32,279 watched as coach Earl (Curly) Lambeau gained revenge for the previous year's defeat with a 27-0 triumph for the NFL championship.

League attendance set a record—1,071,200.

1939 STANDINGS

Eastern Division	**W**	**L**	**T**	**Pct.**	**Pts.**	**OP**
New York Giants	9	1	1	.900	168	85
Washington	8	2	1	.800	242	94
Brooklyn	4	6	1	.400	108	219
Philadelphia	1	9	1	.100	105	200
Pittsburgh	1	9	1	.100	114	216
Western Division	**W**	**L**	**T**	**Pct.**	**Pts.**	**OP**
Green Bay	9	2	0	.818	233	153
Chicago Bears	8	3	0	.727	298	157
Detroit	6	5	0	.545	145	150
Cleveland	5	5	1	.500	195	164
Chicago Cardinals	1	10	0	.091	84	254

NFL championship: Green Bay 27, New York Giants 0

LEADING RUSHERS	**Att.**	**Yards**	**Avg.**	**TD**
Bill Osmanski, Chi. Bears	121	699	5.8	7
Andy Farkas, Washington	139	547	3.9	5
Joe Maniaci, Chi. Bears	77	544	7.1	4
Pug Manders, Brooklyn	114	482	4.2	2
Parker Hall, Cleveland	120	458	3.8	2

LEADING PASSERS	**Att.**	**Comp.**	**Yards**	**TD**	**Int.**
Parker Hall, Cleveland	208	106	1,227	9	13
Davey O'Brien, Philadelphia	201	99	1,324	6	17
Ace Parker, Brooklyn	157	72	977	4	13
Arnie Herber, Green Bay	139	57	1,107	8	9
Frank Filchock, Washington	89	55	1,094	11	7

LEADING RECEIVERS	**No.**	**Yards**	**Avg.**	**TD**
Don Hutson, Green Bay	34	846	24.9	6
Perry Schwartz, Brooklyn	33	550	16.7	3
Vic Spadaccini, Cleveland	32	292	9.1	1
Red Ramsey, Philadelphia	31	359	11.6	1
Jim Benton, Cleveland	27	388	14.4	7

LEADING SCORER	**TD**	**FG**	**PAT**	**TP**
Andy Farkas, Washington	11	0	2	68

LEADING PUNTER	**No.**	**Avg.**	**Long**
Parker Hall, Cleveland	58	40.8	80

SUPERLATIVES		
Rushing average	7.1	Joe Maniaci, Chi. Bears
Receiving average	27.3	Andy Farkas, Washington
Completion percentage	61.8	Frank Filchock, Washington
Touchdowns	11	Andy Farkas, Washington

1940 After being tipped off about an unheralded college center, owner George Richards of Detroit ordered coach Gus Henderson to select Clyde (Bulldog) Turner of Hardin-Simmons on the first round of the draft. Richards then paid Turner to tell the other NFL teams that he wasn't interested in pro football. At the draft, however, Henderson, who had coached at USC, selected Trojans quarterback Doyle Nave, and George Halas then took Turner. Richards fired Henderson, who then told President Carl Storck about the payment to Turner. When the league fined Richards $5,000, he sold the team to Fred Mandel.

Mandel hired former Lions coach George (Potsy) Clark as his coach, one of only several significant coaching changes. Dr. John Bain (Jock) Sutherland, the former coach of national championship teams at the University of Pittsburgh, moved into pro football as coach of the Brooklyn Dodgers. Jimmy Conzelman took over as coach of the Chicago Cardinals.

For the third time, a rival league appeared to challenge the NFL. Just as the earlier rival leagues had done, this one took the name "American Football League." The Columbus Bullies won its championship with an 8-1-1 record; the other teams were the Boston Bears, Buffalo Indians, Cincinnati Bengals, Milwaukee Chiefs, and New York Yankees.

Byron (Whizzer) White had been in England for studies as a Rhodes scholar. He returned to pro football, this time with Detroit, and again led the league in rushing, gaining 514 yards. Quarterback Davey O'Brien of Philadelphia threw 60 passes in one game. End Don Looney of the Eagles caught 58 passes for the season.

The Chicago Bears won the Western Division, the Washington Redskins the Eastern Division. Chicago lost only three games, one of them to the Redskins by the score of 7-3; there was a disputed play late in the game in which the Bears demanded a pass interference call and were denied. George Preston Marshall of the Redskins later commented to the press, "The Bears are front runners, quitters. They're not a second-half team, just a bunch of cry-babies." The comment gave the Bears something to think about when the two teams met again three weeks later in the NFL Championship Game in Washington.

Clark Shaughnessy, who had become coach at Stanford and won 10 straight games using the T-formation with man-in-motion, rejoined the Bears for their preparations. He studied film of the 7-3 game and saw that the Redskins had a predictable defense. They stayed in a five-three and always shifted their linebackers toward the man-in-motion. He and the Bears' coaches saw that it was an easy defense to exploit. Counter plays were put in the game plan to send Bears' runners away from the movement of the linebackers. The Bears would control the ball, it was decided, and keep it away from Washington's great passer, Sammy Baugh. Shaughnessy also wrote new terminology for Bears' play-calling that made the team's blocking more efficient.

Fullback Bill Osmanski ran 68 yards for a touchdown on the second play of the game. It was not a counter play. Rather, it was to the same side as the man-in-motion, George McAfee, and Osmanski started off left guard but then cut outside. End George Wilson made a great block clearing the last Redskins' defender out of the way downfield.

Chicago's offense continued to work efficiently and mow down the Redskins. Baugh and other Washington tailbacks threw three passes that the Bears returned for touchdowns. When it was over, the Bears had won the NFL championship by the astounding score of 73-0, the most one-sided pro game ever and the most celebrated victory in football history.

The championship game was the first ever carried on network radio. Red Barber broadcast it to 120 stations of the Mutual Broadcasting System, which paid $2,500 for the rights to the game.

1940 STANDINGS

Eastern Division	**W**	**L**	**T**	**Pct.**	**Pts.**	**OP**
Washington	9	2	0	.818	245	142
Brooklyn	8	3	0	.727	186	120
New York Giants	6	4	1	.600	131	133
Pittsburgh	2	7	2	.222	60	178
Philadelphia	1	10	0	.091	111	211
Western Division	**W**	**L**	**T**	**Pct.**	**Pts.**	**OP**
Chicago Bears	8	3	0	.727	238	152
Green Bay	6	4	1	.600	238	155
Detroit	5	5	1	.500	138	153
Cleveland	4	6	1	.400	171	191
Chicago Cardinals	2	7	2	.273	139	222

NFL championship: Chicago Bears 73, Washington 0

LEADING RUSHERS	**Att.**	**Yards**	**Avg.**	**TD**
Byron (Whizzer) White, Detroit	146	514	3.5	5
Johnny Drake, Cleveland	134	480	3.6	9
Tuffy Leemans, NY Giants	132	474	3.6	1
Banks McFadden, Brooklyn	65	411	6.3	1
Dick Todd, Washington	76	408	5.4	4

LEADING PASSERS	**Att.**	**Comp.**	**Yards**	**TD**	**Int.**
Sammy Baugh, Washington	177	111	1,367	12	10
Davey O'Brien, Philadelphia	277	124	1,290	5	17
Cecil Isbell, Green Bay	150	68	1,037	9	12
Sid Luckman, Chi. Bears	105	48	941	4	9
Ace Parker, Brooklyn	111	49	817	10	7

LEADING RECEIVERS	**No.**	**Yards**	**Avg.**	**TD**
Don Looney, Philadelphia	58	707	12.2	4
Don Hutson, Green Bay	45	664	14.8	7
Jimmy Johnston, Washington	29	350	12.1	3
Jim Benton, Cleveland	22	351	16.0	3
Vic Spadaccini, Cleveland	22	276	12.5	2

LEADING SCORER	**TD**	**FG**	**PAT**	**TP**
Don Hutson, Green Bay	7	0	15	57

LEADING INTERCEPTORS	**No.**	**Yards**	**Avg.**	**TD**
Ace Parker, Brooklyn	6	146	24.3	1
Kent Ryan, Detroit	6	65	10.8	0
Don Hutson, Green Bay	6	24	4.0	0

LEADING PUNTER	**No.**	**Avg.**	**Long**
Sammy Baugh, Washington	35	51.4	85

SUPERLATIVES

Rushing average	6.3	Banks McFadden, Brooklyn
Receiving average	26.3	Paul McDonough, Cleveland
Completion percentage	62.7	Sammy Baugh, Washington
Touchdowns	9	Johnny Drake, Cleveland Dick Todd, Washington

1941 On March 1, Elmer Layden, head coach and athletic director at Notre Dame, and one of that university's famous "Four Horsemen" backfield of the 1920s, was named the first commissioner of the NFL. The title of president was discarded. Layden moved the NFL office to Chicago. Carl Storck, acting president of the league since the death of Joe Carr in 1939, resigned.

After the 1940 season, Art Rooney was so discouraged that he sold the Pirates to Alexis Thompson. Rooney then bought a half interest in the Philadelphia Eagles from his friend Bert Bell. But in April, Thompson mentioned his preference for the Philadelphia franchise, and Rooney, eager to return to Pittsburgh, talked Bell into swapping the Eagles for the Pirates. The Pittsburgh franchise entered the 1941 season with two owners and a new name, the Steelers.

Another franchise changed hands when Homer Marshman sold the Cleveland Rams to Dan Reeves and Fred Levy, Jr.

The league by-laws were revised to provide for playoffs in case there were ties in division races, and sudden-death overtime in case a playoff game was tied after four quarters.

An official *Record Manual* was published by the NFL for the first time. It replaced the pro football guides that had been published by the Spalding sporting goods company in the 1930s.

Earle (Greasy) Neale became the head coach and Tommy Thompson the quarterback of the Eagles, and they became the second team to change from a long-snap formation to the T-formation.

Co-owner Bert Bell began the season as coach of the Steelers but stepped down after losing two games and was succeeded by Aldo (Buff) Donelli. Donelli had been coach of Duquesne University and did not resign from that job; he continued to coach Duquesne in the afternoons and the Steelers in the mornings. The situation came to a head when Duquesne was scheduled to play a game at St. Mary's (California) on a Saturday and the Steelers were scheduled to play the Eagles in Philadelphia on Sunday. Donelli chose to attend the college game instead of the professional game and was dismissed from his duties with the Steelers. Walt Kiesling coached the team for the rest of the season.

The New York Giants had already clinched the Eastern Division championship and were playing the final game of the season against Brooklyn, December 7. News of the Japanese attack on Pearl Harbor was announced on the public address system and servicemen were instructed to report to their bases. Although the Dodgers went on to win that game, and had beaten the Giants earlier in the year, a loss to Pittsburgh (the Steelers' only victory of the year) cost them the title.

The Chicago Bears and Green Bay finished in a tie for the Western Division championship, setting up the first divisional playoff game in league history. The Bears, who earlier had split games with the Packers, defeated Green Bay 33-14 the Sunday following the attack on Pearl Harbor. The Bears then crushed the Giants 37-9 in the NFL Championship Game.

After a season in which the Columbus Bullies won their second consecutive title, the third American Football League folded.

1941 STANDINGS

Eastern Division	**W**	**L**	**T**	**Pct.**	**Pts.**	**OP**
New York Giants	8	3	0	.727	238	114
Brooklyn	7	4	0	.636	158	127
Washington	6	5	0	.545	176	174
Philadelphia	2	8	1	.200	119	218
Pittsburgh	1	9	1	.100	103	276
Western Division	**W**	**L**	**T**	**Pct.**	**Pts.**	**OP**
Chicago Bears	10	1	0	.909	396	147
Green Bay	10	1	0	.909	258	120
Detroit	4	6	1	.400	121	195
Chicago Cardinals	3	7	1	.300	127	197
Cleveland	2	9	0	.182	116	244

Western Division playoff: Chicago Bears 33, Green Bay 14
NFL championship: Chicago Bears 37, New York Giants 9

LEADING RUSHERS	**Att.**	**Yards**	**Avg.**	**Long**	**TD**
Pug Manders, Brooklyn	111	486	4.4	46	6
George McAfee, Chi. Bears	65	474	7.3	70	6
Marshall Goldberg, Chi. Cardinals	117	427	3.6	25	3
Norm Standlee, Chi. Bears	81	414	5.1	46	5
Clarke Hinkle, Green Bay	129	393	3.0	20	5

LEADING PASSERS	**Att.**	**Comp.**	**Yards**	**TD**	**Int.**
Cecil Isbell, Green Bay	206	117	1,479	15	11
Sammy Baugh, Washington	193	106	1,236	10	19
Sid Luckman, Chi. Bears	119	68	1,181	9	6
Tommy Thompson, Philadelphia	162	86	974	8	14
Ace Parker, Brooklyn	102	51	642	2	8

LEADING RECEIVERS	**No.**	**Yards**	**Avg.**	**Long**	**TD**
Don Hutson, Green Bay	58	738	12.7	45	10
Dick Humbert, Philadelphia	29	332	11.4	33	3
Bill Dewell, Chi. Cardinals	28	262	9.4	30	1
Perry Schwartz, Brooklyn	25	362	14.5	36	2
Lou Brock, Green Bay	22	307	14.0	36	2

LEADING SCORER	**TD**	**FG**	**PAT**	**TP**
Don Hutson, Green Bay	12	1	20	95

LEADING INTERCEPTORS	**No.**	**Yards**	**Avg.**	**Long**	**TD**
M. Goldberg, Chi. Cardinals	7	54	7.7	16	0
Art Jones, Pittsburgh	7	35	5.0	12	0

LEADING PUNTER	**No.**	**Avg.**	**Long**
Sammy Baugh, Washington	30	48.7	75

LEADING PUNT RETURNER	**No.**	**Yards**	**Avg.**	**Long**	**TD**
Whizzer White, Detroit	19	262	13.8	64	0

LEADING KICKOFF RETURNER	**No.**	**Yards**	**Avg.**	**Long**	**TD**
M. Goldberg, Chi. Cardinals	12	290	24.2	41	0

SUPERLATIVES

Rushing average	7.3	George McAfee, Chi. Bears
Receiving average	28.5	Ken Kavanaugh, Chi. Bears
Completion percentage	57.1	Sid Luckman, Chi. Bears
Touchdowns	12	Don Hutson, Green Bay George McAfee, Chi. Bears

LONGEST

Run	70	George McAfee, Chi. Bears
Pass	80	Ray Mallouf to John Hall, Chi. Cardinals
Interception	91	Hal Van Every, Green Bay
Punt	75	Sammy Baugh, Washington
Punt return	90	Andy Uram, Green Bay
Field goal	43	Clarke Hinkle, Green Bay

1942 World War II ravaged the rosters and staffs of NFL teams. Numerous players, coaches, and team owners departed to serve in the Armed Forces. Teams became filled with men who had failed the draft physical examination or older players who were beyond military age.

Don Hutson of the Green Bay Packers had a spectacular year, catching 74 passes for 1,211 yards and 17 touchdowns and scoring 138 points. Bill Dudley, star tailback in Pittsburgh's Single Wing, gained 696 yards rushing.

Washington was still strong with Ray Flaherty as coach and Sammy Baugh as the team's tailback. The Redskins dropped the second game of the year to the Giants, then won nine in a row to finish 10-1. The Chicago Bears still had Sid Luckman as quarterback, but owner and coach George Halas left the team in midseason to join the Armed Forces. Assistants Heartley (Hunk) Anderson and Luke Johnsos became co-coaches of the Bears. The change didn't faze the club a bit, as the Bears swept to 11 consecutive victories, including two thrashings of second-place Green Bay.

The Redskins gained a small measure of revenge for the 73-0 defeat in 1940 when they defeated the Bears 14-6 for the NFL championship.

1942 STANDINGS

Eastern Division	W	L	T	Pct.	Pts.	OP
Washington	10	1	0	.909	227	102
Pittsburgh	7	4	0	.636	167	119
New York Giants	5	5	1	.500	155	139
Brooklyn	3	8	0	.273	100	168
Philadelphia	2	9	0	.182	134	239
Western Division	**W**	**L**	**T**	**Pct.**	**Pts.**	**OP**
Chicago Bears	11	0	0	1.000	376	84
Green Bay	8	2	1	.800	300	215
Cleveland	5	6	0	.455	150	207
Chicago Cardinals	3	8	0	.273	98	209
Detroit	0	11	0	.000	38	263

NFL championship: Washington 14, Chicago Bears 6

LEADING RUSHERS	Att.	Yards	Avg.	Long	TD
Bill Dudley, Pittsburgh	162	696	4.3	66	5
Merlyn Condit, Brooklyn	129	647	5.0	63	3
Gary Famiglietti, Chi. Bears	118	503	4.3	21	8
Andy Farkas, Washington	125	468	3.7	22	4
Dick Riffle, Pittsburgh	115	467	4.1	44	4
LEADING PASSERS	**Att.**	**Comp.**	**Yards**	**TD**	**Int.**
Cecil Isbell, Green Bay	268	146	2,021	24	14
Sammy Baugh, Washington	225	132	1,524	16	11
Sid Luckman, Chi. Bears	105	57	1,023	10	13
Tommy Thompson, Philadelphia	203	95	1,410	8	16
Wilson Schwenk, Chi. Cardinals	295	126	1,350	6	27
LEADING RECEIVERS	**No.**	**Yards**	**Avg.**	**Long**	**TD**
Don Hutson, Green Bay	74	1,211	16.4	73	17
Frank (Pop) Ivy, Chi.Cardinals	27	259	9.6	18	0
Dante Magnani, Cleveland	24	276	11.5	67	4
Jim Benton, Cleveland	23	345	15.0	45	1
Dick Todd, Washington	23	328	14.3	53	4
LEADING SCORER	**TD**	**FG**	**PAT**		**TP**
Don Hutson, Green Bay	17	1	33		138
LEADING INTERCEPTOR	**No.**	**Yards**	**Avg.**	**Long**	**TD**
Bulldog Turner, Chi. Bears	8	96	12.0	42	1
LEADING PUNTER	**No.**		**Avg.**		**Long**
Sammy Baugh, Washington	37		48.2		74
LEADING PUNT RETURNER	**No.**	**Yards**	**Avg.**	**Long**	**TD**
Merlyn Condit, Brooklyn	21	210	10.0	23	0
LEADING KICKOFF RETURNER	**No.**	**Yards**	**Avg.**	**Long**	**TD**
M. Goldberg, Chi. Cardinals	15	393	26.2	95	1

SUPERLATIVES

Rushing average	6.4	Frank Maznicki, Chi. Bears
Receiving average	30.1	Ray McLean, Chi. Bears
Completion percentage	58.7	Sammy Baugh, Washington
Touchdowns	17	Don Hutson, Green Bay

LONGEST

Run	80	Lloyd Cardwell, Detroit
Pass	73	Cecil Isbell to Don Hutson, Green Bay
Interception	66	Neal Adams, NY Giants
Punt	74	Sammy Baugh, Washington Dean McAdams, Brooklyn
Punt return	89	Ray McLean, Chi. Bears
Kickoff return	98	Andy Uram, Green Bay
Field goal	46	Chet Adams, Cleveland

1943 The first major franchise moves since 1938 occurred. In April, with co-owners Dan Reeves and Fred Levy in the Armed Forces, the Rams were granted permission to suspend operations for a year. Ten days later, Levy transferred his stock in the Rams to Reeves. In June, the Philadelphia and Pittsburgh franchises merged. Although neither franchise gave up any of its players' rights while the merger was in effect, Pittsburgh could vote in owners' meetings only on topics that directly affected the Steelers or the league constitution. During the season, the franchise officially was known as Phil-Pitt, although newspapers dubbed the team the "Steagles." Also at the June meeting, Ted Collins was granted a franchise for Boston, which was to become active in the season of 1944, or as soon thereafter as the league deemed advisable.

Playing talent was scarce. Some players worked at defense plants during the day and practiced with their teams at night. Fathers now were being drafted for the war, and the NFL, concerned about the effect that would have on its roster, increased the player limit from 25 to 28.

One of the most profound rules changes in NFL history was made when the league voted to permit free substitution. "Platoonery" was one of the most disputed subjects in the game's history and was widely opposed by those who believed the "iron man" who played both ways was more consistent with the rugged nature of the game. Abbreviated NFL rosters during World War II prevented its effects from taking place immediately, but free substitution made possible the development of separate platoons for offense and defense and the appearance of specialists at all positions in pro football.

Bronko Nagurski rejoined the Chicago Bears. He was 34 years old and had not played pro football since his retirement from the game in 1937. He played tackle and fullback and while at fullback gained 84 yards on 16 carries. Bill Hewitt, 34, was another retired player who returned to the game. He played for Phil-Pitt, which divided its home games between Philadelphia and Pittsburgh. Earle (Greasy) Neale and Walt Kiesling were co-coaches of the team.

Although Sid Luckman set a league record with seven touchdown passes against the Giants on November 14, he didn't lead the league in passing. That honor went to Sammy Baugh, who also led the NFL in interceptions and punting.

Washington tied for the Eastern title with the Giants and a playoff was necessary for the second consecutive year. Baugh led the Redskins to an easy 28-0 victory.

The Redskins and Bears played for the championship for the third time in four years. The Redskins had administered the Bears' only loss of the year, but Luckman threw five touchdown passes as Chicago won the championship game 41-21. Luckman's touchdown passes set a championship game record. The winning share in the championship game exceeded $1,000 for the first time. Each Bears player earned $1,146, each Redskins player $765.

1943 STANDINGS

Eastern Division	W	L	T	Pct.	Pts.	OP
Washington	6	3	1	.667	229	137
New York Giants	6	3	1	.667	197	170
Phil-Pitt	5	4	1	.556	225	230
Brooklyn	2	8	0	.200	65	234
Western Division	**W**	**L**	**T**	**Pct.**	**Pts.**	**OP**
Chicago Bears	8	1	1	.889	303	157
Green Bay	7	2	1	.778	264	172
Detroit	3	6	1	.333	178	218
Chicago Cardinals	0	10	0	.000	95	238

Eastern Division playoff: Washington 28, New York Giants 0
NFL championship: Chicago Bears 41, Washington 21

LEADING RUSHERS	Att.	Yards	Avg.	Long	TD
Bill Paschal, NY Giants	147	572	3.9	54	10
Clarke Hinkle, Phil-Pitt	116	571	4.9	56	4
Harry Clark, Chi. Bears	120	556	4.6	20	3
Ward Cuff, NY Giants	80	523	6.5	65	3
Tony Canadeo, Green Bay	94	489	5.2	35	3
LEADING PASSERS	**Att.**	**Comp.**	**Yards**	**TD**	**Int.**
Sammy Baugh, Washington	239	133	1,754	23	19
Sid Luckman, Chi. Bears	202	110	2,194	28	12
Irv Comp, Green Bay	92	46	662	7	4
Ron Cahill, Chi. Cardinals	109	50	608	3	21
Dean McAdams, Brooklyn	75	37	315	0	7
LEADING RECEIVERS	**No.**	**Yards**	**Avg.**	**Long**	**TD**
Don Hutson, Green Bay	47	776	16.5	79	11
Joe Aguirre, Washington	37	420	11.4	44	7
Wilbur Moore, Washington	30	537	17.9	72	7
Ed Rucinski, Chi. Cardinals	26	398	15.3	47	3
Harry Jacunski, Green Bay	24	528	22.0	86	3
LEADING SCORER	**TD**	**FG**	**PAT**		**TP**
Don Hutson, Green Bay	12	3	36		117
LEADING INTERCEPTOR	**No.**	**Yards**	**Avg.**	**Long**	**TD**
Sammy Baugh, Washington	11	112	10.2	23	0
LEADING PUNTER	**No.**		**Avg.**		**Long**
Sammy Baugh, Washington	50		45.9		81
LEADING PUNT RETURNER	**No.**	**Yards**	**Avg.**	**Long**	**TD**
Andy Farkas, Washington	15	168	11.2	33	0
LEADING KICKOFF RETURNER	**No.**	**Yards**	**Avg.**	**Long**	**TD**
Ken Heineman, Brooklyn	16	444	27.8	69	0

SUPERLATIVES

Rushing average	6.5	Ward Cuff, NY Giants
Receiving average	24.6	Tony Bova, Phil-Pitt
Completion percentage	57.7	Sammy Baugh, Washington
Touchdowns	12	Don Hutson, Green Bay Bill Paschal, NY Giants

LONGEST

Run	79	Dante Magnani, Chi. Bears
Pass	86	Lou Brock to Harry Jacunski, Green Bay
Interception	91	Clarke Hinkle, Phil-Pitt
Punt	81	Sammy Baugh, Washington
Punt return	77	Frank Sinkwich, Detroit
Kickoff return	98	Ned Mathews, Detroit
Field goal	45	Ward Cuff, NY Giants

1944 The league's shortage of teams and players remained an acute problem. The Philadelphia-Pittsburgh merger was dissolved at the end of the 1943 season, and the Eagles began to operate on their own once more. In April, however, the Steelers merged with the Chicago Cardinals, forming a team called Card-Pitt that had a 0-10 season.

The Cleveland Rams resumed operations. The Brooklyn Dodgers changed their name to Brooklyn Tigers. Ted Collins's Boston franchise fielded a team. Collins had wanted a club that would occupy Yankee Stadium in New York. Failing that, he named his team the Boston Yanks.

The manpower shortage was so acute that only 12 of the 330 players selected in the NFL draft actually played for their teams in 1944. Center Mel Hein and kicker Ken Strong were brought back to pro football by the Giants. The Giants also signed tailback Arnie Herber, who had retired in 1940. Sammy Baugh of Washington spent part of the season operating his ranch in Rotan, Texas, and alternated in the Redskins' backfield with Frank Filchock. Clark Shaughnessy, coach of the University of Maryland, was an advisor to coach Dudley DeGroot of the Redskins as they adopted the T-formation. The coaches around the league benefited from a rule legalizing coaching from the bench.

In the East, the Eagles raced through their first seven games unbeaten and administered the only loss of the year to the Giants. But a one-sided loss to the Bears left them half a game behind New York, which kept winning to win the title by half a game. In the West, the Packers raced to six consecutive victories, and then coasted home. Although they had been beaten by the Giants 24-0 in the next-to-last game of the season, the Packers beat them 14-7 in New York to win the NFL Championship Game.

1944 STANDINGS

Eastern Division	W	L	T	Pct.	Pts.	OP
New York Giants	8	1	1	.889	206	75
Philadelphia	7	1	2	.875	267	131
Washington	6	3	1	.667	169	180
Boston Yanks	2	8	0	.200	82	233
Brooklyn	0	10	0	.000	69	166
Western Division	**W**	**L**	**T**	**Pct.**	**Pts.**	**OP**
Green Bay	8	2	0	.800	238	141
Chicago Bears	6	3	1	.667	258	172
Detroit	6	3	1	.667	216	151
Cleveland	4	6	0	.400	188	224
Card-Pitt	0	10	0	.000	108	328

NFL championship: Green Bay 14, New York Giants 7

LEADING RUSHERS	Att.	Yards	Avg.	Long	TD
Bill Paschal, NY Giants	196	737	3.8	68t	9
John Grigas, Card-Pitt	185	610	3.3	29	3
Frank Sinkwich, Detroit	150	563	3.8	72t	6
Henry Margarita, Chi. Bears	88	463	5.3	47t	4
Steve Van Buren, Philadelphia	80	444	5.6	70t	5
LEADING PASSERS	**Att.**	**Comp.**	**Yards**	**TD**	**Int.**
Frank Filchock, Washington	147	84	1,139	13	9
Sammy Baugh, Washington	146	82	849	4	8
Sid Luckman, Chi. Bears	143	71	1,018	11	11
Irv Comp, Green Bay	177	80	1,159	12	21
Al Reisz, Cleveland	113	49	777	8	10
LEADING RECEIVERS	**No.**	**Yards**	**Avg.**	**Long**	**TD**
Don Hutson, Green Bay	58	866	14.9	55t	9
Jim Benton, Cleveland	39	505	12.9	36	6
Joe Aguirre, Washington	34	410	12.1	58t	4
Wilbur Moore, Washington	33	424	12.8	59t	5
Les Dye, Washington	24	281	11.7	61t	2
George Wilson, Chi. Bears	24	265	11.0	24t	4
Bob Masterson, Brooklyn	24	258	10.8	30	1

LEADING SCORER	TD	FG	PAT	TP
Don Hutson, Green Bay	9	0	31	85

LEADING INTERCEPTOR	No.	Yards	Avg.	Long	TD
Howard Livingston, NY Giants	9	172	19.1	40	1

LEADING PUNTER	No.	Avg.	Long
Frank Sinkwich, Detroit	45	41.0	73

LEADING PUNT RETURNER	No.	Yards	Avg.	Long	TD
Steve Van Buren, Philadelphia	15	230	15.3	55t	1

LEADING KICKOFF RETURNER	No.	Yards	Avg.	Long	TD
Bob Thurbon, Card-Pitt	12	291	24.3	55	0

SUPERLATIVES		
Rushing average	6.1	Al Grygo, Chi. Bears
Receiving average	37.3	Mel Bleeker, Philadelphia
Completion percentage	57.1	Frank Filchock, Washington
Touchdowns	9	Don Hutson, Green Bay Bill Paschal, NY Giants

LONGEST		
Run	80	Bob Davis, Boston
Pass	86t	Sid Luckman to Ray McLean, Chi. Bears
Interception	83t	Don Perkins, Green Bay
Punt	76	Sammy Baugh, Washington Cecil Johnson, Brooklyn
Punt return	60	Frank Seno, Washington
Kickoff return	97t	Steve Van Buren, Philadelphia
Field goal	49	Roy Zimmerman, Philadelphia

1945 German armies surrendered between May 4 and May 8. The Japanese surrendered aboard the U.S.S. Missouri in the Tokyo harbor September 2. The war had taken a heavy toll among all Americans and among National Football League players: 638 had served in the war, 69 had been decorated, and 19 had died.

The NFL restored the pre-war player limit of 33. The hashmarks or inbounds lines were moved from 15 yards to 20 yards in from each sideline.

The Steelers and the Cardinals played the season as independent teams again, but the league had its third merger in as many years. Brooklyn and Boston merged into a team that played part of its games in each city, but was known simply as The Yanks.

Don Hutson of Green Bay led the NFL in receiving for the fifth consecutive year and scored a record 29 points in one quarter—four touchdowns and five extra points, in the second quarter of a 57-21 Green Bay victory over Detroit.

Bob Waterfield was a sensational rookie quarterback for Cleveland. His favorite receiver, Jim Benton, caught 10 passes for 303 yards in one game against Detroit, a record that would last until 1985. The Rams won the Western Division championship and Waterfield was awarded the Joe F. Carr trophy given to the most valuable player in the league.

The Chicago Bears fell to 3-7 and finished fourth in the West. Owner and coach George Halas rejoined them late in the season after his service with the U.S. Navy in the Pacific.

Steve Van Buren won the rushing title for the first time and Philadelphia gave Cleveland its only loss, but the Eagles were runners-up to the Redskins in the Eastern Division. Sammy Baugh, now accustomed to Washington's new T-formation, set a record with an incredible 70.3 percent completion rate.

Washington met Cleveland in the title game at Municipal Stadium in Cleveland on a frigid day when the temperature was six degrees. Baugh threw a pass from his own end zone in the first quarter. The pass hit the goal post and it was ruled a safety and two points for Cleveland. The Rams went on to win 15-14.

In December, Dan Topping, the owner of the Brooklyn franchise, announced he was leaving the NFL to join the new All-America Football Conference. Shortly thereafter, Brooklyn's franchise was declared forfeit, and all of the players on its active and reserve lists were assigned to The Yanks, who once again became known as the Boston Yanks.

1945 STANDINGS

Eastern Division	W	L	T	Pct.	Pts.	OP
Washington	8	2	0	.800	209	121
Philadelphia	7	3	0	.700	272	133
New York Giants	3	6	1	.333	179	198
Boston	3	6	1	.333	123	211
Pittsburgh	2	8	0	.200	79	220
Western Division	**W**	**L**	**T**	**Pct.**	**Pts.**	**OP**
Cleveland	9	1	0	.900	244	136
Detroit	7	3	0	.700	195	194
Green Bay	6	4	0	.600	258	173
Chicago Bears	3	7	0	.300	192	235
Chicago Cardinals	1	9	0	.100	98	228

NFL championship: Cleveland 15, Washington 14

LEADING RUSHERS	Att.	Yards	Avg.	Long	TD
Steve Van Buren, Philadelphia	143	832	5.8	69t	15
Frank Akins, Washington	147	797	5.4	45	6
Henry Margarita, Chi. Bears	112	497	4.4	38	3
Fred Gehrke, Cleveland Rams	74	467	6.3	72t	7
Fred Gillette, Cleveland Rams	63	390	6.2	52	1

LEADING PASSERS	Att.	Comp.	Yards	TD	Int.
*Sammy Baugh, Washington	182	128	1,669	11	4
*Sid Luckman, Chi. Bears	217	117	1,725	14	10
Bob Waterfield, Cleveland Rams	171	88	1,609	14	16
Leroy Zimmerman, Philadelphia	132	67	991	9	8
Paul Christman, Chi. Cardinals	219	89	1,147	5	12

*Tied for passing title.

LEADING RECEIVERS	No.	Yards	Avg.	Long	TD
Don Hutson, Green Bay	47	834	17.7	75t	9
Jim Benton, Cleveland Rams	45	1,067	23.7	84t	8
Steve Bagarus, Washington	35	623	17.8	70t	5
George Wilson, Chi. Bears	28	259	9.3	18	3
John Greene, Detroit	26	550	21.2	63t	4
Bill Dewell, Chi. Cardinals	26	370	14.2	70	1

LEADING SCORER	TD	FG	PAT	TP
Steve Van Buren, Philadelphia	18	0	2	110

LEADING INTERCEPTOR	No.	Yards	Avg.	Long	TD
Roy Zimmerman, Philadelphia	7	90	12.9	23	0

LEADING PUNTER	No.	Avg.	Long
Roy Dale McKay, Green Bay	44	41.2	73

LEADING PUNT RETURNER	No.	Yards	Avg.	Long	TD
Dave Ryan, Detroit	15	220	14.7	56	0

LEADING KICKOFF RETURNER	No.	Yards	Avg.	Long	TD
Steve Van Buren, Philadelphia	13	373	28.7	98t	1

SUPERLATIVES		
Rushing average	6.3	Fred Gehrke, Cleveland
Receiving average	26.9	Frank Liebel, NY Giants
Completion percentage	70.3	Sammy Baugh, Washington
Touchdowns	18	Steve Van Buren, Philadelphia

LONGEST		
Run	77t	Bill Paschal, NY Giants
Pass	84t	Bob Waterfield to Jim Benton, Cleveland
Interception	74	Sammy Baugh, Washington
Punt	73	Roy Dale McKay, Green Bay
Punt return	81t	Chuck DeShane, Detroit
Kickoff return	98t	Steve Van Buren, Philadelphia
Field goal	49	Ted Fritsch, Green Bay

1946 In January, the NFL took on a truly national appearance for the first time. Dan Reeves had considered moving his team to Los Angeles for several years, and, on January 12, the league gave him permission to do so. The new Los Angeles Rams became the first NFL team to actually play its home games on the West Coast.

The NFL had waited for years for the return of peace and prosperity. It arrived at last, but when it did it had to be shared with the rival All-America Football Conference. Founded by sports editor Arch Ward of the *Chicago Tribune*, it began play in Brooklyn, Buffalo, Chicago, Cleveland, Los Angeles, Miami, New York, and San Francisco.

There was direct competition between NFL and AAFC teams in three cities. The New York Giants were in competition with the Brooklyn Dodgers and New York Yankees of the AAFC. The Chicago Bears and Cardinals had competition from the Chicago Rockets of the AAFC. And the Los Angeles Rams were in competition with the Los Angeles Dons of the AAFC.

The contract of NFL Commissioner Elmer Layden was not renewed, and Bert Bell, co-owner of the Pittsburgh Steelers, was named to replace him. Bell received a three-year contract and accepted the job of leading the league against its new rival. He moved the NFL headquarters from Chicago to Bala Cynwyd, a suburb of Philadelphia.

The rule that cost the Washington Redskins a safety in the 1945 championship game was changed so that a forward pass hitting the goal posts was now an incomplete pass. Free substitution was being debated hotly, especially in college football, and the NFL restricted its rule, limiting substitutions to three men at a time.

The Los Angeles Rams averaged 38,700 fans in Memorial Coliseum. They added backs Tom Harmon and Kenny Washington to their lineup but failed to repeat as champions. The Chicago Bears won the Western Division, recapturing the glory they had known before World War II. They had a backfield of Sid Luckman at quarterback, Hugh Gallerneau and Dante Magnani at halfbacks, and Bill Osmanski at fullback.

Frank Filchock, acquired from Washington, led the New York Giants to the Eastern championship. Philadelphia finished second for the third consecutive year. The Chicago Cardinals, coached by Jimmy Conzelman, were growing stronger and had Paul Christman, Marshall Goldberg, and Pat Harder in their backfield.

Jock Sutherland returned from military service and became coach of the Pittsburgh Steelers. Tailback Bill Dudley of the Steelers had a great season, leading the league in rushing, interceptions, and punt returns and winning the most valuable player award. But Dudley and Sutherland feuded and the Steelers remained unsuccessful.

There were reports of a betting scandal on the eve of the championship game in New York between the Giants and the Bears. The Giants' Filchock and Merle Hapes were questioned about an attempt by a New York man to fix the game. Hapes was suspended for failing to report the contact, but Filchock was permitted to play the game. He played well but Chicago won 24-14. Luckman ran 19 yards on a keeper play for the decisive touchdown. A title game record crowd of 58,346 watched.

The league was in competition with a rival organization and a number of its players had jumped to the other league. The NFL nevertheless set an attendance record of 1,732,135, an average of 31,494 a game.

1946 STANDINGS

Eastern Division	W	L	T	Pct.	Pts.	OP
New York Giants	7	3	1	.700	236	162
Philadelphia	6	5	0	.545	231	220
Washington	5	5	1	.500	171	191
Pittsburgh	5	5	1	.500	136	117
Boston	2	8	1	.200	189	273
Western Division	**W**	**L**	**T**	**Pct.**	**Pts.**	**OP**
Chicago Bears	8	2	1	.800	289	193
Los Angeles Rams	6	4	1	.600	277	257
Green Bay	6	5	0	.545	148	158
Chicago Cardinals	6	5	0	.545	260	198
Detroit	1	10	0	.091	142	310

NFL championship: Chicago Bears 24, New York Giants 14

LEADING RUSHERS	Att.	Yards	Avg.	Long	TD
Bill Dudley, Pittsburgh	146	604	4.1	41	3
Pat Harder, Chi. Cardinals	106	545	5.1	55	4
Steve Van Buren, Philadelphia	116	529	4.6	58	5
Hugh Gallarneau, Chi. Bears	112	476	4.3	52t	7
Tony Canadeo, Green Bay	122	476	3.9	27	0

LEADING PASSERS	Att.	Comp.	Yards	TD	Int.
Bob Waterfield, LA Rams	251	127	1,747	18	17
Sid Luckman, Chi. Bears	229	110	1,826	17	16
Paul Governali, Boston	192	83	1,293	13	10
Paul Christman, Chi. Cardinals	229	100	1,656	13	18
Sammy Baugh, Washington	161	87	1,163	8	17

LEADING RECEIVERS	No.	Yards	Avg.	Long	TD
Jim Benton, LA Rams	63	981	15.5	57	6
Harold Crisler, Boston	32	385	12.0	62	5
Steve Bagarus, Washington	31	438	14.1	51t	3
Jack Ferrante, Philadelphia	28	451	16.1	48	4
Bill Dewell, Chi. Cardinals	27	643	23.8	82t	7
Mal Kutner, Chi. Cardinals	27	634	23.5	63	5

LEADING SCORER	TD	FG	PAT	TP
Ted Fritsch, Green Bay	10	9	13	100

LEADING INTERCEPTOR	No.	Yards	Avg.	Long	TD
Bill Dudley, Pittsburgh	10	242	24.2	80t	1

LEADING PUNTER	No.	Avg.	Long
Roy Dale McKay, Green Bay	64	42.7	64

LEADING PUNT RETURNER	No.	Yards	Avg.	Long	TD
Bill Dudley, Pittsburgh	27	385	14.3	52	0

LEADING KICKOFF RETURNER	No.	Yards	Avg.	Long	TD
Abe Karnofsky, Boston	21	599	28.5	97t	1

SUPERLATIVES		
Rushing average	6.8	Elmer Angsman, Chi. Cardinals
Receiving average	23.8	Bill Dewell, Chi. Cardinals

1940s, 1950s: A Photographic Portfolio

Byron (Whizzer) White (with ball) led the NFL in rushing in 1940 with Detroit. Two years earlier, he had led the league as a rookie with Pittsburgh.

On the second play of the 1940 NFL Championship Game, Bill Osmanski (with ball) of the Bears ran 68 yards for a touchdown. The next two times Chicago had the ball, Sid Luckman and Joe Maniaci scored, and the Bears went on to score the most lopsided victory in NFL history, 73-0 over Washington.

Tom Harmon made his pro football debut with the New York Americans of the AFL in 1941.

In 1947, Paul Christman's passing and play-calling led the Chicago Cardinals to the NFL championship. He was joined in the backfield by Pat Harder (34), Charley Trippi, and Elmer Angsman.

Conditions rarely have been as extreme as in the 1948 NFL Championship Game. Steve Van Buren accounted for the game's only score on a five-yard run, as the Philadelphia Eagles beat the Chicago Cardinals 7-0.

In 1947, Spec Sanders of the New York Yankees (AAFC) rushed for 1,432 yards and passed for 1,442.

Buddy Young was short (5-5), but he was one of the biggest offensive threats in pro football.

Deacon Dan Towler (with ball), who led the NFL with 894 yards in 1952 and ran for the most touchdowns in 1952 and 1954, joined Paul (Tank) Younger and Dick Hoerner in the Rams' ''Bull Elephant'' backfield.

Otto Graham, who had announced he would retire after the game, scored three touchdowns and passed for three more to lead Cleveland to a 56-10 victory over Detroit in the 1954 NFL Championship Game. Graham returned the next year to lead the Browns to their tenth championship-game appearance in his 10 years.

Despite playing for weak teams, Fred Cone (with ball) of the Green Bay Packers was one of the best fullbacks in pro football in the 1950s. Teammate Al Carmichael (42) also was an outstanding player.

Versatile Lynn Chandnois of Pittsburgh remains the number-two kickoff returner in NFL history.

Touchdown Tommy Wilson was signed by the Rams as a free agent in 1956 despite not playing college football. Against the Packers his rookie season, he set an NFL record by rushing for 223 yards.

In 1956, Rick Casares led the NFL in rushing with 1,126 yards, second-highest total ever at the time.

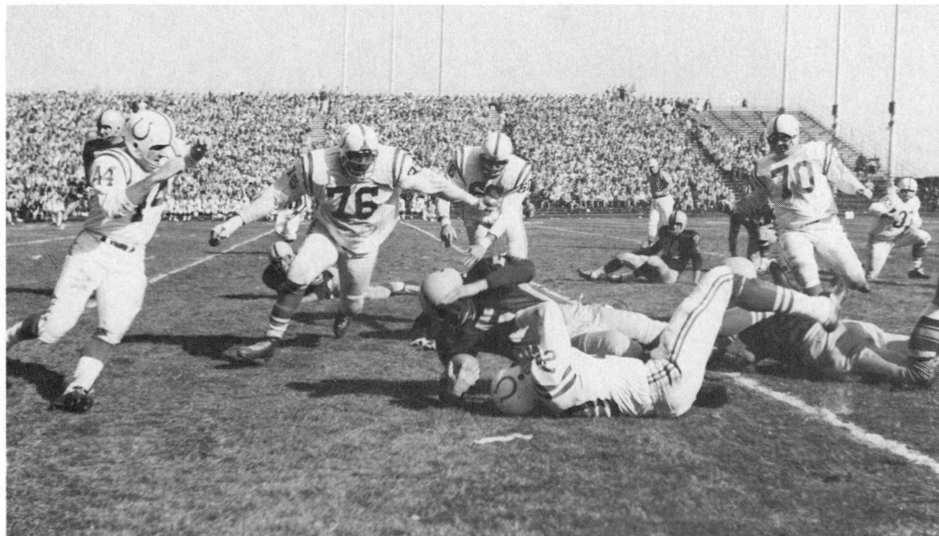

The Baltimore defense of the late 1950s was one of the best ever. It included Eugene (Big Daddy) Lipscomb (76), Art Donovan (70), Bert Rechichar (44), Don Shinnick (66), and Milt Davis (20).

Tobin Rote (18) led Detroit's miracle 31-27 comeback over San Francisco in a 1957 playoff game.

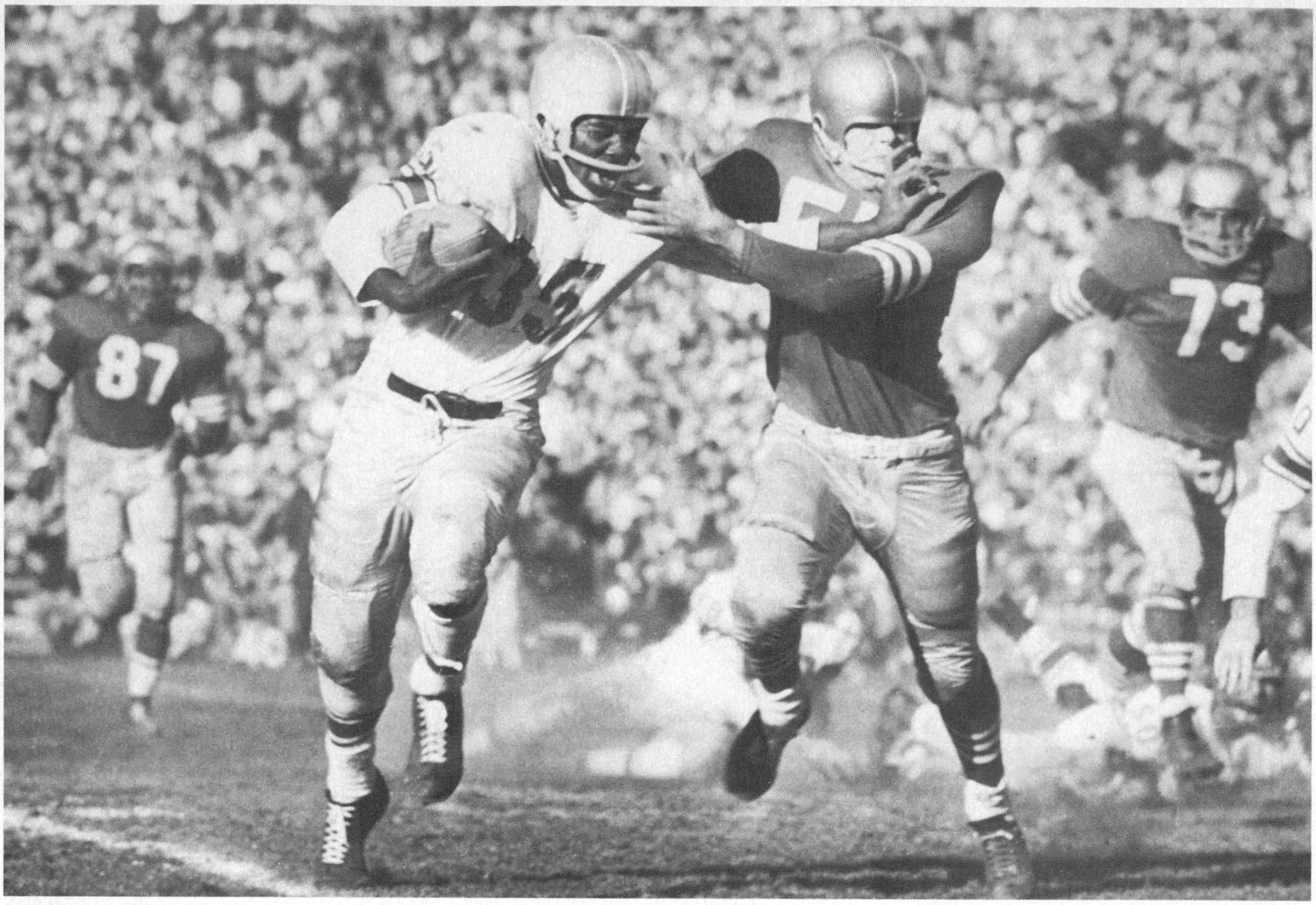

John Henry Johnson (with ball) is perhaps the best back not enshrined in the Pro Football Hall of Fame. He was a star with San Francisco, Detroit, and Pittsburgh, rushing for more than 1,000 yards two times with the Steelers and helping the Lions to the NFL championship in 1957. He finished his career with Houston.

Eddie LeBaron (14) became famous partially because of his height (5-8). However, he was an outstanding quarterback for both Washington and the Dallas Cowboys. He led the NFL in passing in 1958.

Charlie Conerly helped lead the Giants to four NFL Championship Games in six years.

J.D. Smith of thc 49crs followed the blocks of Ted Connolly to the second-most rushing yards (1,036) in the NFL in 1959. Smith started his career on defense.

Del Shofner was one of the best receivers in the NFL with the Los Angeles Rams and the New York Giants. He had four 1,000-yard receiving seasons.

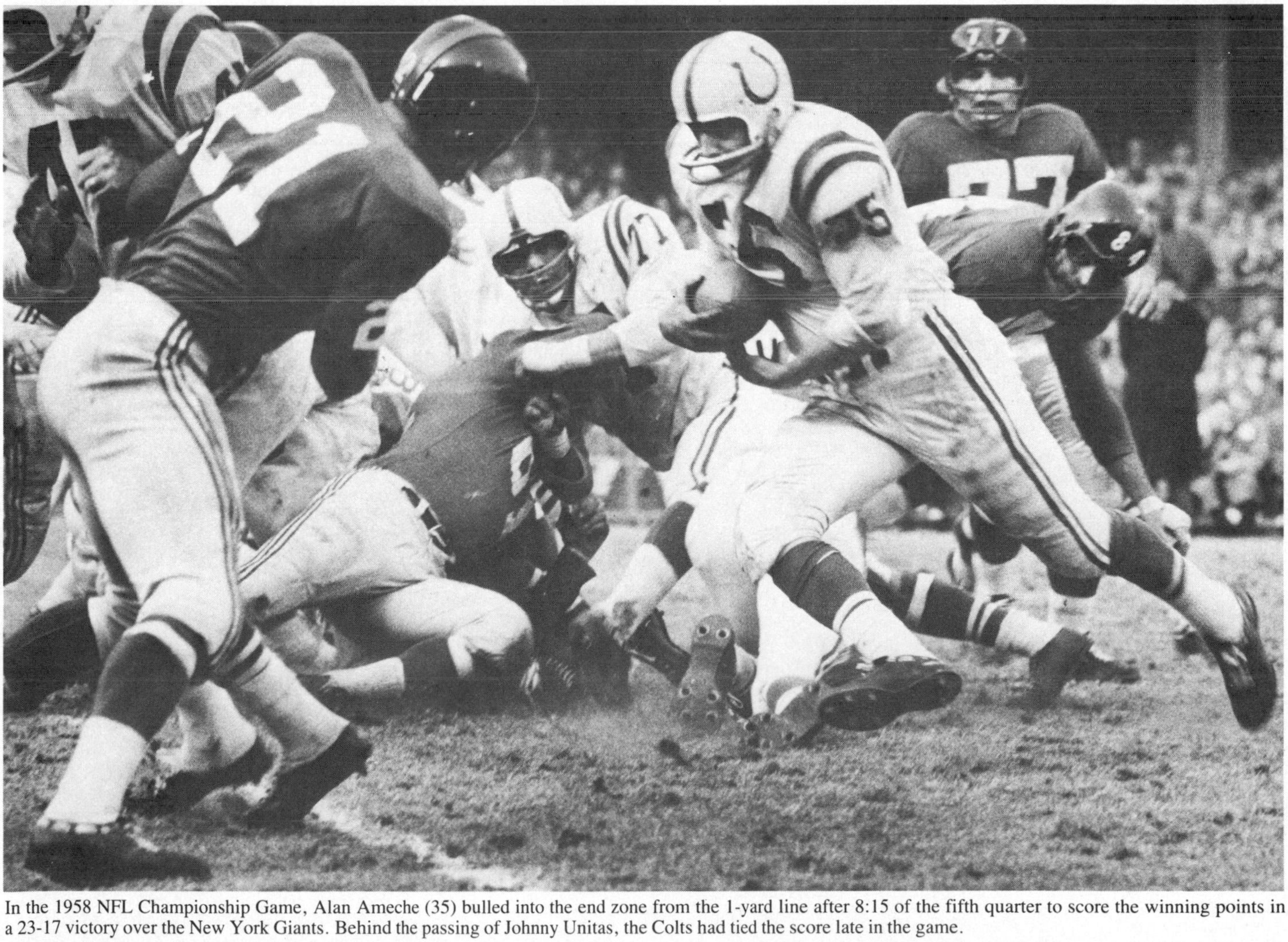

In the 1958 NFL Championship Game, Alan Ameche (35) bulled into the end zone from the 1-yard line after 8:15 of the fifth quarter to score the winning points in a 23-17 victory over the New York Giants. Behind the passing of Johnny Unitas, the Colts had tied the score late in the game.

Completion percentage	55.3	Tommy Thompson, Philadelphia
Touchdowns	10	Ted Fritsch, Green Bay

LONGEST

Run	84t	Tom Harmon, LA Rams
Pass	88t	Dave Ryan to John Greene, Detroit
Interception	85t	Tom Harmon, LA Rams
Punt	81	Bill deCorrevont, Detroit
Punt return	70	Jack Wilson, LA Rams
Kickoff return	105t	Frank Seno, Chi. Cardinals
Field goal	46	Ted Fritsch, Green Bay

1947 Charles W. Bidwill, owner of the Chicago Cardinals, won a bidding war with the New York Yankees of the All-America Football Conference and signed star halfback Charley Trippi of Georgia. It gave the NFL a decisive victory over the AAFC.

A bonus draft choice was made for the first time. One team a year would get a special bonus choice before the first round began in exchange for its thirtieth-round pick. The Chicago Bears won rights to the first bonus and chose back Bob Fenimore of Oklahoma State, but he lasted only one season with them.

Sudden death was adopted for championship games. A fifth official, the back judge, was added. The player limit was increased to 35 for the first three games and 34 for the rest of the season.

Jock Sutherland traded tailback Bill Dudley to Detroit and installed Johnny Clement as the Steelers' tailback.

Charles Bidwill, Sr., died. Bidwill's wife and sons retained ownership of the team that became the strongest in the league. The Cardinals had what was called a "dream backfield" made up of Trippi, Elmer Angsman, Paul Christman, and Pat Harder. They defeated the Bears 30-21 in a climactic game that gave the Cardinals the division championship. Harder scored 102 points to lead the league.

The Cardinals had won a title at last after years as an also-ran. The same thing happened in the Eastern Division, where the Eagles of coach Earle (Greasy) Neale won the championship. Left halfback Steve Van Buren gained 1,008 yards rushing, becoming the first 1,000-yard rusher in the NFL since 1934. Van Buren went off the right side time after time on power plays from the T-formation. The Eagles finished with the same record as Pittsburgh, which still played the Single-Wing formation. They met in a playoff and Philadelphia won 21-0.

The Western champions, the Cardinals, changed from their usual passing attack to a running game and made 282 yards on the ground in the championship game against the Eagles. The running of Chicago's Trippi and Angsman offset the passing of Philadelphia's Tommy Thompson, and the Cardinals won the NFL championship 28-21.

1947 STANDINGS

Eastern Division	**W**	**L**	**T**	**Pct.**	**Pts.**	**OP**
Philadelphia	8	4	0	.667	308	242
Pittsburgh	8	4	0	.667	240	259
Boston	4	7	1	.364	168	256
Washington	4	8	0	.333	295	367
New York Giants	2	8	2	.200	190	309
Western Division	**W**	**L**	**T**	**Pct.**	**Pts.**	**OP**
Chicago Cardinals	9	3	0	.750	306	231
Chicago Bears	8	4	0	.667	363	241
Green Bay	6	5	1	.545	274	210
Los Angeles Rams	6	6	0	.500	259	214
Detroit	3	9	0	.250	231	305

Eastern Division playoff: Philadelphia 21, Pittsburgh 0
NFL championship: Chicago Cardinals 28, Philadelphia 21

LEADING RUSHERS	**Att.**	**Yards**	**Avg.**	**Long**	**TD**
Steve Van Buren, Philadelphia	217	1,008	4.6	45	14
Johnny Clement, Pittsburgh	129	670	5.2	43	4
Tony Canadeo, Green Bay	103	464	4.5	35	2
Kenny Washington, LA Rams	60	444	7.4	92t	5
Walt Schlinkman, Green Bay	115	439	3.8	20	2
LEADING PASSERS	**Att.**	**Comp.**	**Yards**	**TD**	**Int.**
Sammy Baugh, Washington	354	210	2,938	25	15
Tommy Thompson, Philadelphia	201	106	1,680	16	15
Sid Luckman, Chi. Bears	323	176	2,712	24	31
Jack Jacobs, Green Bay	242	108	1,615	16	17
Paul Christman, Chi. Cardinals	301	138	2,191	17	22
LEADING RECEIVERS	**No.**	**Yards**	**Avg.**	**Long**	**TD**
Jim Keane, Chi. Bears	64	910	14.2	50	10
Bob Nussbaumer, Washington	47	597	12.7	55t	4
Mal Kutner, Chi. Cardinals	43	944	22.0	70t	7
Nolan Luhn, Green Bay	42	696	16.6	44	7
Bill Dewell, Chi. Cardinals	42	576	13.7	46t	4
LEADING SCORER	**TD**	**FG**	**PAT**	**TP**	
Pat Harder, Chi. Cardinals	7	7	39	102	
LEADING INTERCEPTORS	**No.**	**Yards**	**Avg.**	**Long**	**TD**
Frank Reagan, NY Giants	10	203	20.3	71	0
Frank Seno, Boston	10	100	10.0	38	0
LEADING PUNTER	**No.**	**Avg.**	**Long**		
Jack Jacobs, Green Bay	57	43.5	74		
LEADING PUNT RETURNER	**No.**	**Yards**	**Avg.**	**Long**	**TD**
Walt Slater, Pittsburgh	28	435	15.5	33	0
LEADING KICKOFF RETURNER	**No.**	**Yards**	**Avg.**	**Long**	**TD**
Eddie Saenz, Washington	29	797	27.5	94t	2

SUPERLATIVES

Rushing average	7.4	Kenny Washington, LA Rams
Receiving average	32.6	Don Currivan, Boston
Completion percentage	59.3	Sammy Baugh, Washington
Touchdowns	14	Steve Van Buren, Philadelphia

LONGEST

Run	92t	Kenny Washington, LA Rams
Pass	88t	Frank Reagan to George Franck, NY Giants
Interception	96t	Bulldog Turner, Chi. Bears
Punt	86	Bob Waterfield, LA Rams
Punt return	88t	Tom Harmon, LA Rams
Kickoff return	95t	Steve Van Buren, Philadelphia
Field goal	50	Ted Fritsch, Green Bay

1948 The National Football League and All-America Football Conference were at war for players. Their clubs were strained to their financial limits as they vied to sign stars. Washington had the bonus choice in the NFL and used it to draft tailback Harry Gilmer of Alabama, who was supposed to be the eventual successor to Sammy Baugh. George Preston Marshall of the Redskins now had both Baugh and Gilmer, so he sold the rights to Charlie Conerly of Mississippi to the New York Giants. The Giants finally signed Conerly after a fight with the Brooklyn Dodgers of the AAFC and Dodgers' owner Branch Rickey.

Baugh was nearing the end of his NFL career, and so was another quarterbacking great, Sid Luckman of the Chicago Bears. Owner George Halas of the Bears signed both Bobby Layne of Texas and Johnny Lujack of Notre Dame.

Prominent rookies included tackle George Connor with the Chicago Bears, safety Emlen Tunnell with the New York Giants, and end Tom Fears with the Los Angeles Rams. Fears caught 51 passes to lead the league.

Fred Mandel sold the Detroit Lions to a syndicate headed by D. Lyle Fife.

Halfback Fred Gehrke of the Los Angeles Rams, who had studied art in college at Utah, painted horns on the leather helments of the Rams, the first helmet emblems in pro football.

Each division champion repeated. Tommy Thompson threw 25 touchdown passes and Steve Van Buren gained 945 yards as the Philadelphia Eagles had a 9-2-1 record in the East. Pat Harder scored 110 points and the Chicago Cardinals ran up an 11-1 record, clinching the division in the season finale with a 24-21 victory over the Bears, who had been tied for first.

A blizzard blanketed the field at Shibe Park in Philadelphia before the Eagles and Cardinals met in the championship game. The yard lines were obliterated, making officiating extremely difficult. The teams struggled for three quarters without any points until tackle Frank (Bucko) Kilroy of the Eagles recovered a Cardinals' fumble at the Chicago 17-yard line. Van Buren later scored from the 5 and the Eagles won 7-0.

1948 STANDINGS

Eastern Division	**W**	**L**	**T**	**Pct.**	**Pts.**	**OP**
Philadelphia	9	2	1	.818	376	156
Washington	7	5	0	.583	291	287
New York Giants	4	8	0	.333	297	388
Pittsburgh	4	8	0	.333	200	243
Boston	3	9	0	.250	174	372
Western Division	**W**	**L**	**T**	**Pct.**	**Pts.**	**OP**
Chicago Cardinals	11	1	0	.917	395	226
Chicago Bears	10	2	0	.833	375	151
Los Angeles Rams	6	5	1	.545	327	269
Green Bay	3	9	0	.250	154	290
Detroit	2	10	0	.167	200	407

NFL championship: Philadelphia 7, Chicago Cardinals 0

LEADING RUSHERS	**Att.**	**Yards**	**Avg.**	**Long**	**TD**
Steve Van Buren, Philadelphia	201	945	4.7	29	10
Charley Trippi, Chi. Cardinals	128	690	5.4	50t	6
Elmer Angsman, Chi. Cardinals	131	638	4.9	72t	8
Warren Wilson, Detroit	157	612	3.9	38	2
Tony Canadeo, Green Bay	123	589	4.8	49	4
LEADING PASSERS	**Att.**	**Comp.**	**Yards**	**TD**	**Int.**
Tommy Thompson, Philadelphia	246	141	1,965	25	11
Jim Hardy, LA Rams	211	112	1,390	14	7
Charlie Conerly, NY Giants	299	162	2.175	22	13
Sammy Baugh, Washington	315	185	2,599	22	23
Ray Mallouf, Chi. Cardinals	143	73	1,160	13	6
LEADING RECEIVERS	**No.**	**Yards**	**Avg.**	**Long**	**TD**
Tom Fears, LA Rams	51	698	13.7	80t	4
Pete Pihos, Philadelphia	46	766	16.7	48	11
Mal Kutner, Chi. Cardinals	41	943	23.0	71t	14
Val Jansante, Pittsburgh	39	623	16.0	66t	3
Bill Swiacki, NY Giants	39	550	14.1	65t	10
LEADING SCORER	**TD**	**FG**	**PAT**	**TP**	
Pat Harder, Chi. Cardinals	6	7	53	110	
LEADING INTERCEPTOR	**No.**	**Yards**	**Avg.**	**Long**	**TD**
Dan Sandifer, Washington	13	258	19.8	54	2
LEADING PUNTER	**No.**	**Avg.**	**Long**		
Joe Muha, Philadelphia	57	47.3	82		
LEADING PUNT RETURNER	**No.**	**Yards**	**Avg.**	**Long**	**TD**
George McAfee, Chi. Bears	30	417	13.9	60t	1
LEADING KICKOFF RETURNER	**No.**	**Yards**	**Avg.**	**Long**	**TD**
Joe Scott, NY Giants	20	569	28.5	99t	1

SUPERLATIVES

Rushing average	5.4	Charley Trippi, Chi. Cardinals
Receiving average	23.0	Mal Kutner, Chi. Cardinals
Completion percentage	58.7	Sammy Baugh, Washington
Touchdowns	15	Mal Kutner, Chi. Cardinals

LONGEST

Run	74t	Noah Mullins, Chi. Bears
Pass	86t	Sammy Baugh to Dan Sandifer, Washington
Interception	89t	Joe Golding, Boston
Punt	88	Bob Waterfield, LA Rams
Punt return	70t	Jerome Davis, Chi. Cardinals
Kickoff return	99t	Joseph Scott, NY Giants
Field goal	47	Bob Waterfield, LA Rams

1949 The attrition of the NFL-AAFC war was felt by every team. The champion Philadelphia Eagles, at the peak of their greatness, lost money and were sold by Alexis Thompson to a syndicate headed by James P. Clark. The Green Bay Packers were in financial straits, having been hit the hardest of any NFL team in the bidding war with the AAFC to sign players.

In January, Ted Collins asked that his Boston franchise be canceled and that he be granted a new franchise in New York. The league approved his request, and the New York Bulldogs were born. Although the reason for this unusual maneuver is not clear, it is believed to have been done so the financially troubled Collins could write off the Boston franchise as a tax loss while still remaining in the league. The new team played in the Polo Grounds, but, despite the presence of Bobby Layne, who had been obtained from the Bears, still stayed in the red.

The league had two 1,000-yard rushers for the first time. Steve Van Buren gained 1,146 for Philadelphia and Tony Canadeo 1,052 for Green Bay.

In addition to Van Buren, Philadelphia also had Bosh Pritchard at halfback, quarterback Tommy Thompson passing to ends Pete Pihos and Jack Ferrante, and rookie center Chuck Bednarik. The Eagles raced to an 11-1 record, winning the East by four-and-a-half games.

Los Angeles, coached by Clark Shaughnessy, won the Western Division due to two wins over the second-place Bears. Elroy (Crazylegs) Hirsch joined the Rams from the AAFC Chicago Rockets and he and ends Tom Fears and Bob Shaw became a great passing combination with quarterbacks Bob Waterfield and Norm Van Brocklin, a rookie from Oregon. Fears set a record by catching 77 passes.

Another rookie of note was the Bears' third quarterback, George Blanda.

Peace came to pro football December 9. Bert Bell announced a merger agreement in which three teams of the AAFC—the Cleveland Browns, San Francisco 49ers, and Baltimore Colts—would join the NFL in 1950. The players from the other teams would be divided up in an allocation draft.

The Los Angeles Memorial Coliseum was the site for the championship game between the Rams and the Eagles. Heavy rain drenched the field and there were only 22,945 fans in attendance as Van Buren gained 196 yards on 31 carries, leading the Eagles to a 14-0 victory and their second straight NFL championship, both by shutouts.

At the end of the season, Earl (Curly) Lambeau, Green Bay's head coach since 1921, left the Packers.

1949 STANDINGS

Eastern Division	**W**	**L**	**T**	**Pct.**	**Pts.**	**OP**
Philadelphia	11	1	0	.917	364	134
Pittsburgh	6	5	1	.545	224	214
New York Giants	6	6	0	.500	287	298
Washington	4	7	1	.364	268	339
New York Bulldogs	1	10	1	.091	153	368
Western Division	**W**	**L**	**T**	**Pct.**	**Pts.**	**OP**
Los Angeles Rams	8	2	2	.800	360	239
Chicago Bears	9	3	0	.750	332	218
Chicago Cardinals	6	5	1	.545	360	301
Detroit	4	8	0	.333	237	259
Green Bay	2	10	0	.167	114	329

NFL championship: Philadelphia 14, Los Angeles Rams 0

LEADING RUSHERS	**Att.**	**Yards**	**Avg.**	**Long**	**TD**
Steve Van Buren, Philadelphia	263	1,146	4.4	41	11
Tony Canadeo, Green Bay	208	1,052	5.1	54	4
Elmer Angsman, Chi. Cardinals	125	674	5.4	82t	6
Gene Roberts, NY Giants	152	634	4.2	63t	9
Jerry Nuzum, Pittsburgh	139	611	4.4	64t	5
LEADING PASSERS	**Att.**	**Comp.**	**Yards**	**TD**	**Int.**
Sammy Baugh, Washington	255	145	1,903	18	14
Johnny Lujack, Chi. Bears	312	162	2,658	23	22
Tommy Thompson, Philadelphia	214	116	1,727	16	11
Bob Waterfield, LA Rams	296	154	2,168	17	24
Charlie Conerly, NY Giants	305	152	2,138	17	20
LEADING RECEIVERS	**No.**	**Yards**	**Avg.**	**Long**	**TD**
Tom Fears, LA Rams	77	1,013	13.2	51t	9
Bob Mann, Detroit	66	1,014	15.4	64t	4
Bill Chipley, NY Bulldogs	57	631	11.1	69	2
Jim Keane, Chi. Bears	47	696	14.8	39	6
Bill Swiacki, NY Giants	47	652	13.9	42	4
LEADING SCORERS	**TD**	**FG**	**PAT**		**TP**
Pat Harder, Chi. Cardinals	8	3	45		102
Gene Roberts, NY Giants	17	0	0		102
LEADING INTERCEPTOR	**No.**	**Yards**	**Avg.**	**Long**	**TD**
Bob Nussbaumer, Chi. Cardinals	12	157	13.1	68	0
LEADING PUNTER	**No.**		**Avg.**		**Long**
Mike Boyda, NY Bulldogs	56		44.2		61
LEADING PUNT RETURNER	**No.**	**Yards**	**Avg.**	**Long**	**TD**
Vitamin T Smith, LA Rams	27	427	15.8	85	1
LEADING KICKOFF RETURNER	**No.**	**Yards**	**Avg.**	**Long**	**TD**
Don Doll, Detroit	21	536	25.5	56	0

SUPERLATIVES

Rushing average	6.0	Bosh Pritchard, Philadelphia
Receiving average	22.6	Ken Kavanaugh, Chi. Bears
Completion percentage	56.9	Sammy Baugh, Washington
Touchdowns	17	Gene Roberts, NY Giants

LONGEST

Run	97t	Bob Gage, Pittsburgh
Pass	85t	Charlie Conerly to Gene Roberts, NY Giants
Interception	102t	Bob Smith, Detroit
Punt	82	Joe Geri, Pittsburgh
Punt return	85	Vitamin T Smith, LA Rams
Kickoff return	95t	Jack Salscheider, NY Giants
Field goal	48	John Patton, Philadelphia

1950 The complicated terms were worked out for the assimilation of three new teams into the league. The new name adopted for the league was the National-American Football League. The old NFL Eastern Division became the American Conference, and the Western Division the National Conference. The Cleveland Browns entered the American and the San Francisco 49ers and the Baltimore Colts the National. The Chicago Cardinals moved to the American Conference, switching with the team that had been the New York Bulldogs. On March 3, the name of the league returned to the National Football League.

Ted Collins still owned a New York franchise, but it had a new name, the New York Yanks; a new stadium, Yankee Stadium; and a new head coach, Red Strader. Almost the entire team was new, too. The Bulldogs' players had been eligible to be taken with college seniors in the draft; the team had divided the players from the AAFC Yankees with the Giants; and a number of new players came in a special allocation draft that allowed the 13 teams to draft the remaining AAFC players, with Baltimore being granted special consideration with 15 choices compared to 10 for the other teams. All-in-all, the Yanks returned only three players from the Bulldogs' team.

For the first time in history, an NFL team, the Los Angeles Rams, contracted to have all its games televised. The arrangement covered both home and away games and the sponsor agreed to make up the difference in home game income if it was lower than it had been the season before. Attendance fell and the cost to the sponsor was $307,000. The Washington Redskins followed the Rams in arranging to televise their games; other teams made deals to put selected games on television.

Unlimited free substitution was restored in the NFL and the way opened for the era of two platoons and specialization in pro football.

An exceptional number of talented players entered the league. Defensive tackle Arnie Weinmeister and defensive backs Tom Landry, Otto Schnellbacher, and Harmon Rowe joined the New York Giants from the defunct AAFC Yankees. Cleveland's array of stars such as quarterback Otto Graham, backs Marion Motley and Dub Jones, ends Dante Lavelli and Mac Speedie, and linemen Lou Groza and Bill Willis moved into the NFL, and so did San Francisco stars such as quarterback Frankie Albert and fullback Joe Perry, and quarterback Y.A. Tittle of Baltimore.

The NFL draft yielded tackle Art Donovan for Baltimore; end Leon Hart and back Doak Walker for Detroit (Walker had actually been drafted as a future in 1949 but did not join Detroit until 1950); quarterback Tobin Rote for Green Bay; tackle Ernie Stautner for Pittsburgh; tackle Leo Nomellini and end Gordy Soltau for San Francisco; and halfback Charlie (Choo-Choo) Justice and quarterback Eddie LeBaron for Washington.

Commissioner Bert Bell set up a first-weekend test of strength between the NFL and AAFC when he scheduled champion Philadelphia against four-time AAFC champion Cleveland on Saturday night before the regular opening day of the season. Cleveland won 35-10 before 71,237 fans. The Browns, coached by Paul Brown, went on to compile a 10-2 regular-season record. The Giants beat them 6-0 and 17-13, throwing an Umbrella defense over the Browns' passing attack of Graham to Lavelli, Speedie, and Jones.

Motley of the Browns won the league rushing championship with 810 yards. Tom Fears of the Rams had a great season, catching 84 passes. Rookie Walker of the Lions—who also placekicked—scored 128 points in the 12-game season.

For the first time ever, there were deadlocks in each conference, and playoffs were necessary in each. Cleveland gained revenge against the Giants, winning the American Conference playoff 8-3 on two field goals by Groza and a safety. Los Angeles defeated the Chicago Bears 24-14 in the National Conference playoff.

The Browns edged the Rams 30-28 on a 16-yard field goal by Groza with 28 seconds to play at Cleveland Municipal Stadium in one of the most exciting title games ever played.

The Pro Bowl game, dormant since 1942, was revived under a new format in which the all-stars of each conference would be matched against each other. The game would be played in Los Angeles at the Memorial Coliseum each year after the championship game, and would be sponsored by the *Los Angeles Times*. Otto Graham, quarterback of the champion Cleveland Browns, completed 19 of 27 passes for 252 yards and a touchdown, and ran for two touchdowns, to lead the American Conference to a 28-27 victory over the National Conference in the first Pro Bowl game with this new format. It was one of the most exciting of all-star games, with Graham's quarterback rivals, teammates Bob Waterfield and Norm Van Brocklin of Los Angeles, combining for 21 completions in 44 pass attempts for 294 yards and three touchdowns.

1950 STANDINGS

American Conference	**W**	**L**	**T**	**Pct.**	**Pts.**	**OP**
Cleveland	10	2	0	.833	310	144
New York Giants	10	2	0	.833	268	150
Philadelphia	6	6	0	.500	254	141
Pittsburgh	6	6	0	.500	180	195
Chicago Cardinals	5	7	0	.417	233	287
Washington	3	9	0	.250	232	326
National Conference	**W**	**L**	**T**	**Pct.**	**Pts.**	**OP**
Los Angeles Rams	9	3	0	.750	466	309
Chicago Bears	9	3	0	.750	279	207
New York Yanks	7	5	0	.583	366	367
Detroit	6	6	0	.500	321	285
Green Bay	3	9	0	.250	244	406
San Francisco	3	9	0	.250	213	297
Baltimore	1	11	0	.083	213	462

American Conference playoff: Cleveland 8, New York Giants 3
National Conference playoff: Los Angeles Rams 24, Chicago Bears 14
NFL championship: Cleveland 30, Los Angeles Rams 28

LEADING RUSHERS	**Att.**	**Yards**	**Avg.**	**Long**	**TD**
Marion Motley, Cleveland	140	810	5.8	69t	3
Frank Ziegler, Philadelphia	172	733	4.3	52	1
Joe Geri, Pittsburgh	188	705	3.8	47	2
Eddie Price, NY Giants	126	703	5.6	74	4
Joe Perry, San Francisco	124	647	5.2	78t	5
LEADING PASSERS	**Att.**	**Comp.**	**Yards**	**TD**	**Int.**
Norm Van Brocklin, LA Rams	233	127	2,061	18	14
Otto Graham, Cleveland	253	137	1,943	14	20
Joe Geri, Pittsburgh	113	41	866	6	15
George Ratterman, NY Yanks	294	140	2,251	22	24
Charlie Conerly, NY Giants	132	56	1,000	8	7
LEADING RECEIVERS	**No.**	**Yards**	**Avg.**	**Long**	**TD**
Tom Fears, LA Rams	84	1,116	13.3	53t	7
Dan Edwards, NY Yanks	52	775	14.9	82t	6
Cloyce Box, Detroit	50	1,009	20.2	82t	11
Paul Salata, Baltimore	50	618	12.4	57t	4
Bob Shaw, Chi. Cardinals	48	971	20.2	65t	12
LEADING SCORER	**TD**	**FG**	**PAT**		**TP**
Doak Walker, Detroit	11	8	38		128
LEADING INTERCEPTOR	**No.**	**Yards**	**Avg.**	**Long**	**TD**
Spec Sanders, NY Yanks	13	199	15.3	29	0
LEADING PUNTER	**No.**		**Avg.**		**Long**
Curly Morrison, Chi. Bears	57		43.3		65
LEADING PUNT RETURNER	**No.**	**Yards**	**Avg.**	**Long**	**TD**
Herb Rich, Baltimore	12	276	23.0	86t	1
LEADING KICKOFF RETURNER	**No.**	**Yards**	**Avg.**	**Long**	**TD**
Vitamin T Smith, LA Rams	22	742	33.7	97t	3

SUPERLATIVES

Rushing average	6.3	Johnny Lujack, Chi. Bears
Receiving average	21.4	Hugh Taylor, Washington
Completion percentage	57.3	Bob Waterfield, LA Rams
Touchdowns	12	Bob Shaw, Chi. Cardinals

LONGEST

Run	96t	Bob Hoernschemeyer, Detroit
Pass	96t	Tobin Rote to Billy Grimes, Green Bay
Interception	94t	Roy Steiner, Green Bay
Punt	76	Jim Hardy, Chi. Cardinals
Punt return	96t	Bill Dudley, Washington
Kickoff return	103t	Russ Craft, Philadelphia
Field goal	52	Ted Fritsch, Green Bay

1951 The Baltimore Colts' franchise that had come into the NFL from the All-America Football Conference died after one season. Abraham Watner, its owner, turned the franchise and player contracts back to the NFL for $50,000. Baltimore's former pro players were made available for drafting at the same time as college players January 18. Four former Colts were among the 13 players selected in the first round—quarterback Y. A. Tittle by San Francisco, back Billy Stone by the Chicago Bears, back Jim Spavital by the New York Giants, and back Chet Mutryn by Philadelphia.

Tailback Kyle Rote of SMU was the bonus choice in the draft. He was selected by the Giants.

The Rams had their greatest season. They had a great passing attack with quarterbacks Bob Waterfield and Norm Van Brocklin, who shared the position, and ends Tom Fears and Bob Boyd and flanker Elroy (Crazylegs) Hirsch as pass targets. The runners—big, fast Dan Towler, Dick Hoerner, and Paul (Tank) Younger—were nicknamed the "Bull Elephant" backfield. The "pony backs" were in reserve. They were Glenn Davis, Volney (Skeet) Quinlan, and Verda (Vitamin T) Smith.

Van Brocklin had an NFL record 554 yards passing in a game against the New York Yanks. Waterfield, however, ended the season as the NFL's leading passer. Waterfield also was the Rams' placekicker and Van Brocklin the punter. Hirsch caught 66 passes for a record 1,495 yards and 17 touchdowns.

The Rams' attendance went up as they reversed their television policy and aired only road games.

The Rams had to fight to win their conference championship. The Detroit Lions had Raymond (Buddy) Parker as coach and players such as quarterback Bobby Layne, fullback Pat Harder, and halfbacks Bob Hoernschemeyer and Doak Walker. Detroit beat Los Angeles 24-22 in a key game one week before the end of the season and took over first place. The Lions then lost their final game to San Francisco while the Rams defeated Green Bay and captured the National Conference title.

The Cleveland Browns were the strongest team in the American Conference. Dub Jones, the Browns' versatile halfback, scored six touchdowns in one game against the Chicago Bears, tying an NFL record set by Ernie Nevers in 1929. Cleveland lost its opening game to San Francisco and then roared back, winning 11 straight.

The championship game was televised coast-to-coast for the first time. It was on the DuMont network, which paid $75,000 for the rights to it. The Rams defeated the Browns 24-17 before 57,522 at Los Angeles Memorial Coliseum. Van Brocklin and Fears combined for a 73-yard touchdown pass in the final quarter to win the game. The winning and losing shares set records, $2,108 for each member of the Rams and $1,483 for each member of the Browns.

1951 STANDINGS

American Conference	**W**	**L**	**T**	**Pct.**	**Pts.**	**OP**
Cleveland	11	1	0	.917	331	152
New York Giants	9	2	1	.818	254	161
Washington	5	7	0	.417	183	296
Pittsburgh	4	7	1	.364	183	235
Philadelphia	4	8	0	.333	234	264
Chicago Cardinals	3	9	0	.250	210	287
National Conference	**W**	**L**	**T**	**Pct.**	**Pts.**	**OP**
Los Angeles Rams	8	4	0	.667	392	261
Detroit	7	4	1	.636	336	259
San Francisco	7	4	1	.636	255	205
Chicago Bears	7	5	0	.583	286	282
Green Bay	3	9	0	.250	254	375
New York Yanks	1	9	2	.100	241	382

NFL championship: Los Angeles Rams 24, Cleveland 17

LEADING RUSHERS	**Att.**	**Yards**	**Avg.**	**Long**	**TD**
Eddie Price, NY Giants	271	971	3.6	80t	7
Rob Goode, Washington	208	951	4.6	33	9
Dan Towler, LA Rams	126	854	6.8	79t	6
Bob Hoernschemeyer, Detroit	132	678	5.1	85t	2
Joe Perry, San Francisco	136	677	5.0	58t	3

LEADING PASSERS	**Att.**	**Comp.**	**Yards**	**TD**	**Int.**
Bob Waterfield, LA Rams	176	88	1,566	13	10
Norm Van Brocklin, LA Rams	194	100	1,725	13	11
Otto Graham, Cleveland	265	147	2,205	17	16
Steve Romanik, Chi. Bears	101	43	791	3	9
Bob Celeri, NY Yanks	238	102	1,797	12	15

LEADING RECEIVERS	**No.**	**Yards**	**Avg.**	**Long**	**TD**
Elroy Hirsch, LA Rams	66	1,495	22.7	91t	17
Gordy Soltau, San Francisco	59	826	14.0	48t	7
Fran Polsfoot, Chi. Cardinals	57	796	14.0	80t	4
Bob Mann, Green Bay	50	696	13.9	52	8
Dante Lavelli, Cleveland	43	586	13.6	47	6

LEADING SCORER	**TD**	**FG**	**PAT**	**TP**
Elroy Hirsch, LA Rams	17	0	0	102

LEADING INTERCEPTOR	**No.**	**Yards**	**Avg.**	**Long**	**TD**
Otto Schnellbacher, NY Giants	11	194	17.6	46t	2

LEADING PUNTER	**No.**	**Avg.**	**Long**
Horace Gillom, Cleveland	73	45.5	66

LEADING PUNT RETURNER	**No.**	**Yards**	**Avg.**	**Long**	**TD**
Buddy Young, NY Yanks	12	231	19.3	79t	1

LEADING KICKOFF RETURNER	**No.**	**Yards**	**Avg.**	**Long**	**TD**
Lynn Chandnois, Pittsburgh	12	390	32.5	55	0

SUPERLATIVES		
Rushing average	6.9	Tobin Rote, Green Bay
Receiving average	22.7	Elroy Hirsch, LA Rams
Completion percentage	56.6	Bobby Thomason, Green Bay
Touchdowns	17	Elroy Hirsch, LA Rams

LONGEST		
Run	85t	Bob Hoernschemeyer, Detroit
Pass	91t	Bob Waterfield to Elroy Hirsch, LA Rams
Interception	88t	Bob Summerhays, Green Bay
Punt	75	Verl Lillywhite, San Francisco
Punt return	89t	Jack Christiansen, Detroit
Kickoff return	100t	Emlen Tunnell, NY Giants
Field goal	47	Bob Waterfield, LA Rams

1952 After eight years of futility and money losses, Ted Collins sold the New York Yanks' franchise back to the league on January 19. Five days later, a new franchise was awarded to a group from Dallas after it purchased the assets of the Yanks from the league. Long a hotbed of high school and college football, Texas seemed to be a certain success for the NFL. But the venture ended in disaster. The new Dallas Texans went through their first four home games averaging fewer than 15,000 per game. The owners bailed out immediately, turning the club back to the league in midseason. For the last five games of the year, the commissioner's office operated the Texans as a road team, using Hershey, Pennsylvania, as a home base. The Texans had one moment, however. On Thanksgiving Day, they upset the Bears 27-23 before a crowd of only 3,000 in Akron, Ohio. At the end of the season, the club disbanded and the franchise was canceled. It was the last time an NFL team failed.

One of the best groups of rookie players in history entered the NFL. It included the bonus draft choice, quarterback Bill Wade of Los Angeles; halfback Frank Gifford of the Giants, linebacker Bill George of the Bears, defensive end Gino Marchetti of Dallas, back Ollie Matson of the Cardinals, back Hugh McElhenny of San Francisco, and back Ed Modzelewski of Pittsburgh. Marchetti and Matson were from the same college, San Francisco.

Joe Bach replaced John Michelosen as coach at Pittsburgh and the Steelers abandoned the Single-Wing for the T-formation, the last professional team to do so.

Bob Waterfield of the Rams led one of the most spectacular comebacks in the history of the league when he rallied the Rams from a 28-6 deficit with 12 minutes to play to beat Green Bay 30-28.

Detroit lost two of its first three games but then stormed back to finish in a tie with Los Angeles for the National Conference championship. They met in a playoff, and Pat Harder scored 19 points to lead Detroit, which had already beaten the Rams twice, to a 31-21 victory.

Cleveland lost four games but still won the American Conference title when the Giants lost three of their last five games. The first NFL Championship Game between two growing rivals, the Lions and Browns, followed. Detroit won 17-7 and claimed its first NFL championship in 17 years. Raymond (Buddy) Parker, coach of the Lions, had been their blocking back when they won the championship the last time in 1935.

Two of the greatest NFL players in history, Sammy Baugh of the Washington Redskins and Steve Van Buren of the Philadelphia Eagles, retired.

1952 STANDINGS

American Conference	**W**	**L**	**T**	**Pct.**	**Pts.**	**OP**
Cleveland	8	4	0	.667	310	213
New York Giants	7	5	0	.583	234	231
Philadelphia	7	5	0	.583	252	271
Pittsburgh	5	7	0	.417	300	273
Chicago Cardinals	4	8	0	.333	172	221
Washington	4	8	0	.333	240	287
National Conference	**W**	**L**	**T**	**Pct.**	**Pts.**	**OP**
Detroit	9	3	0	.750	344	192
Los Angeles Rams	9	3	0	.750	349	234
San Francisco	7	5	0	.583	285	221
Green Bay	6	6	0	.500	295	312
Chicago Bears	5	7	0	.417	245	326
Dallas Texans	1	11	0	.083	182	427

National Conference playoff: Detroit 31, Los Angeles Rams 21
NFL championship: Detroit 17, Cleveland 7

LEADING RUSHERS	**Att.**	**Yards**	**Avg.**	**Long**	**TD**
Dan Towler, LA Rams	156	894	5.7	44t	10
Eddie Price, NY Giants	183	748	4.1	75t	5
Joe Perry, San Francisco	158	725	4.6	78t	8
Hugh McElhenny, San Francisco	98	684	7.0	89t	6
Bob Hoernschemeyer, Detroit	106	457	4.3	41	4

LEADING PASSERS	**Att.**	**Comp.**	**Yards**	**TD**	**Int.**
Norm Van Brocklin, LA Rams	205	113	1,736	14	17
Tobin Rote, Green Bay	157	82	1,268	13	8
Babe Parilli, Green Bay	177	77	1,416	13	17
Otto Graham, Cleveland	364	181	2,816	20	24
Frankie Albert, San Francisco	129	71	964	8	10

LEADING RECEIVERS	**No.**	**Yards**	**Avg.**	**Long**	**TD**
Mac Speedie, Cleveland	62	911	14.7	50	5
Bud Grant, Philadelphia	56	997	17.8	84t	7
Elbie Nickel, Pittsburgh	55	884	16.1	54t	9
Gordy Soltau, San Francisco	55	774	14.1	49t	7
Don Stonesifer, Chi. Cardinals	54	617	11.4	26	0

LEADING SCORER	**TD**	**FG**	**PAT**	**TP**
Gordy Soltau, San Francisco	7	6	34	94

LEADING INTERCEPTOR	**No.**	**Yards**	**Avg.**	**Long**	**TD**
Night Train Lane, LA Rams	14	298	21.3	80t	2

LEADING PUNTER	**No.**	**Avg.**	**Long**
Horace Gillom, Cleveland	61	45.7	73

LEADING PUNT RETURNER	**No.**	**Yards**	**Avg.**	**Long**	**TD**
Jack Christiansen, Detroit	15	322	21.5	79t	2

LEADING KICKOFF RETURNER	**No.**	**Yards**	**Avg.**	**Long**	**TD**
Lynn Chandnois, Pittsburgh	17	599	35.2	93t	2

SUPERLATIVES		
Rushing average	7.0	Hugh McElhenny, San Francisco
Receiving average	23.4	Hugh Taylor, Washington
Completion percentage	55.1	Norm Van Brocklin, LA Rams
Touchdowns	15	Cloyce Box, Detroit

LONGEST		
Run	89t	Hugh McElhenny, San Francisco
Pass	90t	Babe Parilli to Billy Howton, Green Bay
Interception	97t	Herb Rich, LA Rams
Punt	73	Horace Gillom, Cleveland
Punt return	94t	Hugh McElhenny, San Francisco
Kickoff return	100t	Ollie Matson, Chi. Cardinals
Field goal	52	Lou Groza, Cleveland

1953 Baltimore had been trying to get a new NFL team since the Colts had been sold back to the league in January, 1951. In December, 1952, Commissioner Bert Bell had said if Baltimore could sell 15,000 season tickets, the city could have a new franchise. It took only 31 days to reach the quota.

On January 23, a group headed by Carroll Rosenbloom was granted a franchise and was awarded the holdings of the former Dallas Texans organization.

Before the season, the Colts put together the largest trade in NFL history, acquiring 10 players from the Browns in exchange for five new Colts. When the season started, only 13 players from the Texans had caught on with the Colts, but the new team nevertheless won its first game, 13-9 over the Bears when Bert Rechichar ran back an interception for a touchdown and kicked a record 56-yard field goal.

Before the season, the names of the American and National Conferences were changed to Eastern Conference and Western Conference. Mickey McBride, founder of the Cleveland Browns, sold the team to a group headed by Dave R. Jones.

In March, Jim Thorpe, pro football's first great player and the first president of the American Professional Football Association, died.

The league had another fine collection of rookies. Roosevelt Brown, Jack Stroud, and Ray Wietecha joined the Giants; Joe Schmidt joined Detroit, Jim Ringo Green Bay, Doug Atkins the Bears, Bob St. Clair San Francisco, and Gene (Big Daddy) Lipscomb, who had not played college football, was in his first year with the Rams.

Lou Groza of Cleveland kicked a record 23 field goals. Joe Perry of San Francisco gained 1,018 yards rushing and won a bonus of $5,090, $5 for every yard he gained. Harry (Bud) Grant, an end for Philadelphia, left the Eagles to sign a contract with the Canadian Football League, and his successor, Pete Pihos, led the NFL with 63 pass receptions.

Detroit won the Western Conference on the strength of two close victories over second-place San Francisco. Cleveland appeared on its way to a perfect season but lost the last game of the year, to Philadelphia, and finished 11-1. The Browns still won the Eastern Division easily. In the championship game, quarterback Bobby Layne of the Lions brought them from behind in the closing minutes and threw the winning touchdown pass to end Jim Doran for a 17-16 victory.

In November, the NFL won an important court victory when Commissioner Bert Bell's policy of blacking out television of home games was upheld by Judge Allan K. Grim of the United States District Court for the Eastern District of Philadelphia.

Steve Owen of the Giants suffered through a long season and one of his losses was a 62-14 drubbing at the hands of the Browns. He departed the Giants after 23 years as their head coach. Bob Waterfield of the Rams and Clyde (Bulldog) Turner of the Bears retired.

1953 STANDINGS

Eastern Conference	W	L	T	Pct.	Pts.	OP
Cleveland	11	1	0	.917	348	162
Philadelphia	7	4	1	.636	352	215
Washington	6	5	1	.545	208	215
Pittsburgh	6	6	0	.500	211	263
New York Giants	3	9	0	.250	179	277
Chicago Cardinals	1	10	1	.091	190	337
Western Conference	**W**	**L**	**T**	**Pct.**	**Pts.**	**OP**
Detroit	10	2	0	.833	271	205
San Francisco	9	3	0	.750	372	237
Los Angeles Rams	8	3	1	.727	366	236
Chicago Bears	3	8	1	.273	218	262
Baltimore	3	9	0	.250	182	350
Green Bay	2	9	1	.182	200	338

NFL championship: Detroit 17, Cleveland 16

LEADING RUSHERS	Att.	Yards	Avg.	Long	TD
Joe Perry, San Francisco	192	1,018	5.3	51t	10
Dan Towler, LA Rams	152	879	5.8	73t	7
Skeet Quinlan, LA Rams	97	705	7.3	74t	4
Charlie Justice, Washington	115	616	5.4	43	2
Fran Rogel, Pittsburgh	137	527	3.8	58	2
LEADING PASSERS	**Att.**	**Comp.**	**Yards**	**TD**	**Int.**
Otto Graham, Cleveland	258	167	2,722	11	9
Norm Van Brocklin, LA Rams	286	156	2,393	19	14
Y.A. Tittle, San Francisco	259	149	2.121	20	16
Bobby Thomason, Philadelphia	304	162	2,462	21	20
Bobby Layne, Detroit	273	125	2,088	16	21
LEADING RECEIVERS	**No.**	**Yards**	**Avg.**	**Long**	**TD**
Pete Pihos, Philadelphia	63	1,049	16.7	59	10
Elbie Nickel, Pittsburgh	62	743	12.0	40	4
Elroy Hirsch, LA Rams	61	941	15.4	70	4
Don Stonesifer, Chi. Cardinals	56	684	12.2	46	2
Jim Dooley, Chi. Bears	53	841	15.9	72	4

LEADING SCORER	TD	FG	PAT	TP
Gordy Soltau, San Francisco	6	10	48	114

LEADING INTERCEPTOR	No.	Yards	Avg.	Long	TD
Jack Christiansen, Detroit	12	238	19.8	92t	1

LEADING PUNTER	No.	Avg.	Long
Pat Brady, Pittsburgh	80	46.9	64

LEADING PUNT RETURNER	No.	Yards	Avg.	Long	TD
Charley Trippi, Chi. Cardinals	21	239	11.4	38	0
LEADING KICKOFF RETURNER	**No.**	**Yards**	**Avg.**	**Long**	**TD**
Joe Arenas, San Francisco	16	551	34.4	82	0

SUPERLATIVES		
Rushing average	7.3	Skeet Quinlan, LA Rams
Receiving average	22.8	Bob Boyd, LA Rams
Completion percentage	64.7	Otto Graham, Cleveland
Touchdowns	13	Joe Perry, San Francisco

LONGEST		
Run	74t	Skeet Quinlan, LA Rams
Pass	97t	Bobby Layne to Cloyce Box, Detroit
Interception	92t	Jack Christiansen, Detroit
Punt	69	Clarence Avinger, NY Giants
Punt return	78t	Woodley Lewis, LA Rams
Kickoff return	104t	Buddy Young, Baltimore
Field goal	56	Bert Rechichar, Baltimore

1954 Commissioner Bert Bell was given a new 12-year contract by the NFL, and two of its teams made significant coaching moves. The Giants named Jim Lee Howell head coach. He hired Vince Lombardi as offensive coach and had Tom Landry as player-coach of his defensive team. The Colts hired Weeb Ewbank, an assistant to Paul Brown at Cleveland, as head coach.

Brown was concerned that his quarterback, Otto Graham, was near retirement and drafted Bobby Garrett of Stanford as the NFL bonus choice. Garrett's availability became uncertain because of military commitments, however, and Brown traded him to Green Bay for Babe Parilli. Parilli himself was in the army but was due to return to pro football in two years.

Canadian Football League teams were raiding NFL teams and signed quarterback Eddie LeBaron and defensive end Gene Brito of Washington, and defensive tackle Arnie Weinmeister of the Giants.

Quarterback Adrian Burk of Philadelphia threw seven touchdown passes in one game against Washington, tying the record set by Sid Luckman in 1943. Joe Perry of the San Francisco 49ers became the first back in league history to gain 1,000 yards rushing in consecutive seasons. He led the league with 1,049.

Cleveland and Detroit headed for their third straight meeting in the championship game. The Browns again started slowly, losing two of their first three games before winning eight in a row. A game with the Lions, postponed because of a conflict with the Cleveland Indians' baseball World Series against the New York Giants, was rescheduled for December 19, a week after the other clubs finished their seasons. Detroit won 14-10 in a blizzard.

Raymond (Buddy) Parker of Detroit was gaining a reputation as one who held a jinx over his coaching rival, Brown of Cleveland. Parker had his alter ego, Bobby Layne, at quarterback. Huge tackle Les Bingaman anchored Detroit's five-man line on defense. Safety Jack Christiansen led a superb secondary nicknamed "Chris's Crew." It was an exceptional team but it was not the equal of the Browns in the 1954 title game. Graham, playing what he said was his last game, made it one of his greatest ever when he threw three touchdown passes and scored three times himself as the Browns routed the Lions 56-10.

1954 STANDINGS

Eastern Conference	W	L	T	Pct.	Pts.	OP
Cleveland	9	3	0	.750	336	162
Philadelphia	7	4	1	.625	284	230
New York Giants	7	5	0	.583	293	184
Pittsburgh	5	7	0	.417	219	263
Washington	3	9	0	.250	207	432
Chicago Cardinals	2	10	0	.167	183	347
Western Conference	**W**	**L**	**T**	**Pct.**	**Pts.**	**OP**
Detroit	9	2	1	.818	337	189
Chicago Bears	8	4	0	.667	301	279
San Francisco	7	4	1	.636	313	251
Los Angeles Rams	6	5	1	.545	314	285
Green Bay	4	8	0	.333	234	251
Baltimore	3	9	0	.250	131	279

NFL championship: Cleveland 56, Detroit 10

LEADING RUSHERS	Att.	Yards	Avg.	Long	TD
Joe Perry, San Francisco	173	1,049	6.1	58	8
John Henry Johnson, San Fran.	129	681	5.3	38t	9
Tank Younger, LA Rams	91	610	6.7	75t	8
Dan Towler, LA Rams	149	599	4.0	24	11
Maurice Bassett, Cleveland	144	588	4.1	22	6
LEADING PASSERS	**Att.**	**Comp.**	**Yards**	**TD**	**Int.**
Norm Van Brocklin, LA Rams	260	139	2,637	13	21
Otto Graham, Cleveland	240	142	2,092	11	17
Zeke Bratkowski, Chi. Bears	130	67	1,087	8	17
Tom Dublinski, Detroit	138	77	1,073	8	7
Bob Clatterbuck, NY Giants	101	50	781	6	7
LEADING RECEIVERS	**No.**	**Yards**	**Avg.**	**Long**	**TD**
Pete Pihos, Philadelphia	60	872	14.5	34	10
Billy Wilson, San Francisco	60	830	13.8	43	5
Bob Boyd, LA Rams	53	1,212	22.9	80t	6
Billy Howton, Green Bay	52	768	14.8	59	2
Dante Lavelli, Cleveland	47	802	17.1	64	7

LEADING SCORER	TD	FG	PAT	TP
Bobby Walston, Philadelphia	11	4	36	114

LEADING INTERCEPTOR	No.	Yards	Avg.	Long	TD
Night Train Lane, Chi. Cards.	10	181	18.1	64	0

LEADING PUNTER	No.	Avg.	Long
Pat Brady, Pittsburgh	66	43.2	72

LEADING PUNT RETURNER	No.	Yards	Avg.	Long	TD
Veryl Switzer, Green Bay	24	306	12.8	93t	1
LEADING KICKOFF RETURNER	**No.**	**Yards**	**Avg.**	**Long**	**TD**
Billy Reynolds, Cleveland	14	413	29.5	51	0

SUPERLATIVES		
Rushing average	8.0	Hugh McElhenny, San Francisco
Receiving average	25.0	Harlon Hill, Chi. Bears
Completion percentage	59.2	Otto Graham, Cleveland
Touchdowns	12	Harlon Hill, Chi. Bears

LONGEST		
Run	88t	Billy Wells, Washington
Pass	84t	Adrian Burk to Jerry Williams, Philadelphia
Interception	81t	Russ Craft, Pittsburgh
Punt	80	Horace Gillom, Cleveland
Punt return	93t	Veryl Switzer, Green Bay
Kickoff return	100t	Bill Bowman, Detroit
Field goal	50	Pat Summerall, Chi. Cardinals

1955 The Washington expatriates, Eddie LeBaron and Gene Brito, returned from the Canadian Football League and rejoined the Redskins. Paul Brown talked Otto Graham out of retirement. Quarterback Johnny Unitas was drafted by the Pittsburgh Steelers but was cut; Walt Kiesling, the Steelers' coach, chose quarterbacks Jim Finks and Ted Marchibroda over Unitas. The Baltimore Colts made an 80-cent telephone call to the rejected quarterback and signed him as a free agent.

George Halas announced he was coaching his last season for the Chicago Bears. And Sid Gillman, a little-known college coach at Cincinnati, took over as head coach of the Los Angeles Rams.

The league's sudden-death overtime rule was used for the first time in a preseason game at Portland, Oregon. The promoter of the game there between the Rams and Giants convinced them to play under the rule of sudden death, and also an oddball system of numbering the field yard lines from 1 to 100. To the dismay of both coaches, Gillman and Jim Lee Howell, the game was tied 17-17 after four quarters and an overtime period was necessary. The Rams scored three minutes later on a two-yard run by Paul (Tank) Younger and won 23-17.

Graham started slowly for Cleveland but hit his stride and led the league in passing. Cleveland won its sixth straight NFL division championship and tenth title in a row counting its four years in the All-America Football Conference.

Detroit did not do as well. It went into a tailspin after middle guard Les Bingaman retired and Bobby Layne strained his shoulder while lassoing a calf in the offseason in Texas. The Lions struggled to a 3-9 record and finished last in the Western Conference.

Rookie coach Gillman of Los Angeles lost twice to the Chicago Bears but still won the West in his first season. The Bears' attempts to win a title for Halas in his last season failed when the crosstown Cardinals crushed them 53-14.

The Los Angeles Memorial Coliseum, where the Rams and Browns had played their classic 1951 championship, was the scene once more for the title game. Graham of Cleveland, as he had the year before against Detroit, was once more playing what he said was his last game of professional football. He dominated the Rams, running for two touchdowns and passing for two others to swamp Los Angeles 38-14 before a championship game record crowd of 85,693.

The National Broadcasting Company replaced the DuMont network as the network carrying the title game, for which it paid a rights fee of $100,000.

An organization that later would gain prominence, the NFL Players Association, was founded.

1955 STANDINGS

Eastern Conference	W	L	T	Pct.	Pts.	OP
Cleveland	9	2	1	.818	349	218
Washington	8	4	0	.667	246	222
New York Giants	6	5	1	.545	267	223
Chicago Cardinals	4	7	1	.364	224	252
Philadelphia	4	7	1	.364	248	231
Pittsburgh	4	8	0	.333	195	285

Western Conference	W	L	T	Pct.	Pts.	OP
Los Angeles Rams	8	3	1	.727	260	231
Chicago Bears	8	4	0	.667	294	251
Green Bay	6	6	0	.500	258	276
Baltimore	5	6	1	.455	214	239
San Francisco	4	8	0	.333	216	298
Detroit	3	9	0	.250	230	275

NFL championship: Cleveland 38, Los Angeles Rams 14

LEADING RUSHERS	Att.	Yards	Avg.	Long	TD
Alan Ameche, Baltimore	213	961	4.5	79t	9
Howie Ferguson, Green Bay	192	859	4.5	57	4
Curley Morrison, Cleveland	156	824	5.3	56	3
Ron Waller, LA Rams	151	716	4.7	55t	7
Joe Perry, San Francisco	156	701	4.5	42	2

LEADING PASSERS	Att.	Comp.	Yards	TD	Int.
Otto Graham, Cleveland	185	98	1,721	15	8
Ed Brown, Chi. Bears	164	85	1,307	9	10
Bobby Thomason, Philadelphia	171	88	1,337	10	7
Y.A. Tittle, San Francisco	287	147	2,185	17	28
Eddie LeBaron, Washington	178	79	1,270	9	15

LEADING RECEIVERS	No.	Yards	Avg.	Long	TD
Pete Pihos, Philadelphia	62	864	13.9	40t	7
Billy Wilson, San Francisco	53	831	15.7	72t	7
Billy Howton, Green Bay	44	697	15.8	60	5
Dave Middleton, Detroit	44	663	15.1	77t	3
Tom Fears, LA Rams	44	569	12.9	31	2
Lew Carpenter, Detroit	44	312	7.1	34t	2

LEADING SCORER	TD	FG	PAT	TP
Doak Walker, Detroit	7	9	27	96

LEADING INTERCEPTOR	No.	Yards	Avg.	Long	TD
Will Sherman, LA Rams	11	101	9.2	36	0

LEADING PUNTER	No.	Avg.	Long
Norm Van Brocklin, LA Rams	60	44.6	61

LEADING PUNT RETURNER	No.	Yards	Avg.	Long	TD
Ollie Matson, Chi. Cardinals	13	245	18.8	78	2

LEADING KICKOFF RETURNER	No.	Yards	Avg.	Long	TD
Al Carmichael, Green Bay	14	418	29.9	100t	1

SUPERLATIVES		
Rushing average	5.4	Rick Casares, Chi. Bears
Receiving average	20.8	Ray Renfro, Cleveland
Completion percentage	53.0	Otto Graham, Cleveland
Touchdowns	9	Alan Ameche, Baltimore Harlon Hill, Chi. Bears

LONGEST		
Run	81t	Rick Casares, Chi. Bears
Pass	98t	Ogden Compton to Night Train Lane, Chi. Cardinals
Interception	92t	Leo Sanford, Chi. Cardinals
Punt	75	Adrian Burk, Philadelphia
Punt return	78t	Ollie Matson, Chi. Cardinals
Kickoff return	100t	Al Carmichael, Green Bay
Field goal	52	Bert Rechichar, Baltimore

1956 The rules were changed so that it became illegal to grab an opponent's facemask. Using radio receivers to communicate with players on the field, a practice initiated by Paul Brown, was banned. A brown ball with white stripes, not a white ball with black stripes, was ordered for use in night games.

The championship teams of 1955, the Cleveland Browns and Los Angeles Rams, went from greatness to mediocrity. Otto Graham made good his retirement from pro football and the Browns tried unsuccessfully to replace him with Tommy O'Connell, Babe Parilli, and George Ratterman, finishing with their first losing season and failing to win a divisional championship for the first time in club history.

Los Angeles plunged to last place in the Western Conference. Sid Gillman vacillated between Norm Van Brocklin and Bill Wade at quarterback and had trouble replacing defensive linemen Andy Robustelli, who had been traded to the Giants, and Gene (Big Daddy) Lipscomb, who had been waived.

The season belonged, instead, to the Giants and Bears. The Giants moved from the Polo Grounds to Yankee Stadium. Trades brought them Robustelli and kicker Don Chandler. Linebacker Sam Huff and defensive end Jim Katcavage were Giants' rookies. Frank Gifford, Kyle Rote, Mel Triplett, and Alex Webster were in the Giants' backfield to run the ball and catch passes. And Jim Lee Howell had a novel system in which he would start Don Heinrich at quarterback to probe the defense and determine how it was playing, and then send in Charlie Conerly to play the rest of the game.

Paddy Driscoll, a former teammate and a longtime friend and coaching associate of George Halas, replaced him as coach of the Bears. They were humiliated 42-10 early in the season by the revived Detroit Lions, but came back to win the conference championship by beating Detroit 38-21 in the final week of the season. The second game was marred by controversy when defensive end Ed Meadows hit Bobby Layne and put him out of action. Ed Brown established himself as Chicago's quarterback and led the league in passing. Fullback Rick Casares gained 1,126 yards rushing.

Other teams had new looks. Johnny Unitas took over as quarterback of the Baltimore Colts after George Shaw suffered a broken leg, and Lenny Moore joined the team as a rookie. In San Francisco, former quarterback Frankie Albert became head coach.

The Giants and Bears met for the championship at Yankee Stadium. Clark Shaughnessy, the Bears' offensive coach, changed to an entirely different game plan the day of the game and it backfired. New York got a quick touchdown when Gene Filipski returned the opening kickoff 58 yards and Triplett scored on a 17-yard run moments later. The Giants went on to rout the Bears 47-7.

1956 STANDINGS

Eastern Conference	W	L	T	Pct.	Pts.	OP
New York Giants	8	3	1	.727	264	197
Chicago Cardinals	7	5	0	.583	240	182
Washington	6	6	0	.500	183	225
Cleveland	5	7	0	.417	167	177
Pittsburgh	5	7	0	.417	217	250
Philadelphia	3	8	1	.273	143	215
Western Conference	**W**	**L**	**T**	**Pct.**	**Pts.**	**OP**
Chicago Bears	9	2	1	.818	363	246
Detroit	9	3	0	.750	300	188
San Francisco	5	6	1	.455	233	284
Baltimore	5	7	0	.417	270	322
Green Bay	4	8	0	.333	264	342
Los Angeles Rams	4	8	0	.333	291	307

NFL championship: New York Giants 47, Chicago Bears 7

LEADING RUSHERS	Att.	Yards	Avg.	Long	TD
Rick Casares, Chi. Bears	234	1,126	4.8	68t	12
Ollie Matson, Chi. Cardinals	192	924	4.8	79t	5
Hugh McElhenny, San Francisco	185	916	5.0	86t	8
Alan Ameche, Baltimore	178	858	4.8	43	8
Frank Gifford, NY Giants	159	819	5.2	69	5

LEADING PASSERS	Att.	Comp.	Yards	TD	Int.
Ed Brown, Chi. Bears	168	96	1,667	11	12
Bill Wade, LA Rams	178	91	1,461	10	13
Bobby Layne, Detroit	244	129	1,909	9	17
Norm Van Brocklin, LA Rams	124	68	966	7	12
Lamar McHan, Chi. Cardinals	152	72	1,159	10	8

LEADING RECEIVERS	No.	Yards	Avg.	Long	TD
Billy Wilson, San Francisco	60	889	14.8	77t	5
Billy Howton, Green Bay	55	1,188	21.6	66t	12
Frank Gifford, NY Giants	51	603	11.8	48	4
Harlon Hill, Chi. Bears	47	1,128	24.0	79t	11
Jim Mutscheller, Baltimore	44	715	16.3	53t	6

LEADING SCORER	TD	FG	PAT	TP
Bobby Layne, Detroit	5	12	33	99

LEADING INTERCEPTOR	No.	Yards	Avg.	Long	TD
Lindon Crow, Chi. Cardinals	11	170	15.5	42	0

LEADING PUNTER	No.	Avg.	Long
Norm Van Brocklin, LA Rams	48	43.1	72

LEADING PUNT RETURNER	No.	Yards	Avg.	Long	TD
Ken Konz, Cleveland	13	187	14.4	65t	1

LEADING KICKOFF RETURNER	No.	Yards	Avg.	Long	TD
Tommy Wilson, LA Rams	15	477	31.8	103t	1

SUPERLATIVES		
Rushing average	7.5	Lenny Moore, Baltimore
Receiving average	24.0	Harlon Hill, Chi. Bears
Completion percentage	57.1	Ed Brown, Chi. Bears
Touchdowns	14	Rick Casares, Chi. Bears

LONGEST		
Run	86t	Hugh McElhenny, San Francisco
Pass	79t	Bill McColl to Harlon Hill, Chi. Bears
Interception	95t	Will Sherman, LA Rams
Punt	72	Norm Van Brocklin, LA Rams
Punt return	95t	Frank Bernardi, Chi. Cardinals
Kickoff return	106t	Al Carmichael, Green Bay
Field goal	49	Sam Baker, Washington

1957 Raymond (Buddy) Parker, coach of the Detroit Lions, shocked the team, the city, and all pro football when he resigned while at the podium addressing a "Meet the Lions" banquet at a Detroit hotel before the season. He moved to Pittsburgh as head coach and was replaced in Detroit by his former assistant, George Wilson. In Los Angeles, Pete Rozelle was named general manager of the Rams.

The Baltimore Colts, Pittsburgh Steelers, and Cleveland Browns each had had 5-7 records in 1956. They had coin flips to determine order of selection in the draft, and Cleveland came in last, and first. The Colts selected guard Jim Parker of Ohio State, who went on to a Hall of Fame career. The Steelers then selected the player the Browns really wanted, Len Dawson of Purdue. Dawson became a substitute with the Steelers, who traded with San Francisco to get Earl Morrall as their starting quarterback. The Browns, meanwhile, were left with a player who would go on to be a legendary running back, Jim Brown of Syracuse.

Other notable first-year players included halfback Jon Arnett of Los Angeles, quarterback John Brodie of San Francisco, bonus draft choice halfback Paul Hornung and end Ron Kramer of Green Bay, quarterback Sonny Jurgensen and flanker Tommy McDonald of Philadelphia, and guard-tackle Jim Parker of Baltimore.

Cleveland ascended to the championship of the Eastern Conference again with Tommy O'Connell playing quarterback and the rookie Brown leading the league with 942 yards rushing and setting an NFL record with 237 yards in one game against the Los Angeles Rams.

The coaching change in Detroit did not affect the Lions adversely. They battled with San Francisco for the Western Conference title. Detroit coach Wilson used Bobby Layne and Tobin Rote in a two-quarterback system. Fullback John Henry Johnson was the major offensive weapon for the Lions. Layne suffered a broken ankle late in the season and Rote had the quarterback job to himself.

San Francisco went through one of the most momentous seasons any NFL team ever had. The 49ers had Hugh McElhenny and Joe Perry in the backfield with quarterback Y. A. Tittle, who had a sensational new passing target in end R. C. Owens. Owens stood 6 feet 5 inches. Tittle threw "alley-oop" passes high in the air and Owens, a college basketball player, leaped above smaller defensive backs to make the catches.

Tony Morabito, founder and co-owner of the 49ers, suffered a heart attack and died during their game at Kezar Stadium against the Chicago Bears, October 28. The 49ers were a big gate attraction everywhere they played and an NFL-record crowd of 102,368 watched them play the Rams at Los Angeles Memorial Coliseum, November 10.

Detroit and San Francisco tied for the Western Conference lead and the Lions won an amazing playoff victory, coming from behind for a 31-27 victory after trailing 27-7 in the third quarter.

Detroit met Cleveland for the NFL title and, with quarterback Tobin Rote throwing four touchdown passes and running for another, smashed the Browns 59-14. It was the worst defeat Cleveland ever suffered and avenged the Lions' one-sided loss to the Browns in the 1954 title game.

1957 STANDINGS

Eastern Conference	W	L	T	Pct.	Pts.	OP
Cleveland	9	2	1	.818	269	172
New York Giants	7	5	0	.583	254	211
Pittsburgh	6	6	0	.500	161	178
Washington	5	6	1	.455	251	230
Philadelphia	4	8	0	.333	173	230
Chicago Cardinals	3	9	0	.250	200	299
Western Conference	**W**	**L**	**T**	**Pct.**	**Pts.**	**OP**
Detroit	8	4	0	.667	251	231
San Francisco	8	4	0	.667	260	264
Baltimore	7	5	0	.583	303	235
Los Angeles Rams	6	6	0	.500	307	278
Chicago Bears	5	7	0	.417	203	211
Green Bay	3	9	0	.250	218	311

Western Conference playoff: Detroit 31, San Francisco 27
NFL championship: Detroit 59, Cleveland 14

LEADING RUSHERS	Att.	Yards	Avg.	Long	TD
Jim Brown, Cleveland	202	942	4.7	69t	9
Rick Casares, Chi. Bears	204	700	3.4	25t	6
Don Bosseler, Washington	167	673	4.0	28	7
John Henry Johnson, Detroit	129	621	4.8	62	5
Tommy Wilson, LA Rams	127	616	4.9	46	3
LEADING PASSERS	**Att.**	**Comp.**	**Yards**	**TD**	**Int.**
Tommy O'Connell, Cleveland	110	63	1,229	9	8
Eddie LeBaron, Washington	167	99	1,508	11	10
Johnny Unitas, Baltimore	301	172	2,550	24	17
Norm Van Brocklin, LA Rams	265	132	2,105	20	21
Lamar McHan, Chi. Cardinals	200	87	1,568	10	15
LEADING RECEIVERS	**No.**	**Yards**	**Avg.**	**Long**	**TD**
Billy Wilson, San Francisco	52	757	14.6	40	6
Raymond Berry, Baltimore	47	800	17.0	67t	6
Jack McClairen, Pittsburgh	46	630	13.7	48t	2
Frank Gifford, NY Giants	41	588	14.3	63	4
Lenny Moore, Baltimore	40	687	17.2	82t	7
LEADING SCORERS	**TD**	**FG**	**PAT**	**TP**	
Sam Baker, Washington	1	14	29	77	
Lou Groza, Cleveland	0	15	32	77	
LEADING INTERCEPTORS	**No.**	**Yards**	**Avg.**	**Long**	**TD**
Milt Davis, Baltimore	10	219	21.9	75t	2
Jack Christiansen, Detroit	10	137	13.7	52	1
Jack Butler, Pittsburgh	10	85	8.5	20	0
LEADING PUNTER	**No.**	**Avg.**	**Long**		
Don Chandler, NY Giants	60	44.6	61		
LEADING PUNT RETURNER	**No.**	**Yards**	**Avg.**	**Long**	**TD**
Bert Zagers, Washington	14	217	15.5	76t	2
LEADING KICKOFF RETURNER	**No.**	**Yards**	**Avg.**	**Long**	**TD**
Jon Arnett, LA Rams	18	504	28.0	98t	1

SUPERLATIVES

Rushing average	5.0	Lenny Moore, Baltimore
Receiving average	29.0	Ray Renfro, Cleveland
Completion percentage	63.1	Y.A. Tittle, San Francisco
Touchdowns	11	Lenny Moore, Baltimore

LONGEST

Run	76	Hon Waller, LA Rams
Pass	83t	Lamar McHan to Gern Nagler, Chi. Cardinals
Interception	99t	Jerry Norton, Philadelphia
Punt	86	Larry Barnes, San Francisco
Punt return	76t	Bert Zagers, Washington
Kickoff return	98t	Jon Arnett, LA Rams
Field goal	50	Ben Agajanian, NY Giants

1958 The league's four new coaches took their teams in different directions. George Halas reinstated himself with the Bears and the team finished only a game out of first place. Frank (Pop) Ivy of the Cardinals and Buck Shaw of Philadelphia each guided his team to a share of the poorest record in the Eastern Division, a position the Cardinals would maintain. Shaw, on the other hand, began to turn the Eagles' fortunes around by obtaining Norm Van Brocklin from the Rams. In Green Bay, Ray McLean led the Packers to the poorest record in the NFL, and was replaced by Vince Lombardi at the end of the year.

Raymond (Buddy) Parker, coach of the Pittsburgh Steelers, traded quarterback Earl Morrall to Detroit in exchange for Bobby Layne, the quarterback of the Lions' great teams when Parker was their coach.

Quarterback King Hill was selected by the Cardinals as the last bonus draft choice. The practice was then abolished.

Another quarterback in the news was Johnny Unitas of the Colts. A collapsed lung and three broken ribs kept him out of two games but when he returned he threw a 58-yard touchdown pass to halfback Lenny Moore on the first play against Green Bay. Baltimore beat the Bears 17-0 in an important game in November; it was the first time the Bears had been shut out since 1946. Despite two losses to end the season, the Colts finished in first place, a game ahead of the Bears.

The Giants won the Eastern Conference after a bitter fight with Cleveland. Jim Brown of the Browns broke Steve Van Buren's NFL rushing record with 1,527 yards and led the league in scoring with 18 touchdowns and 108 points. He also had a good running mate when rookie Bobby Mitchell joined him in the Browns' backfield.

The Giants got into a playoff against Cleveland by beating the Browns 13-10 in the last week of the season. Pat Summerall of New York kicked a 49-yard field goal in the snow for the victory. In the playoff game, the Giants held Jim Brown to eight yards and the entire Browns' offense to 86, and won 10-0.

Baltimore and New York met for the championship at Yankee Stadium. The Giants rallied from a 14-3 halftime deficit for a 17-14 lead only to have Unitas complete pass after pass to end Raymond Berry, setting up a tying 20-yard field goal by Steve Myhra with 7 seconds to play. The game entered sudden death, the first time in history a title game had gone into overtime. New York had the ball first but had to punt. The Colts then went all the way, with Unitas driving them 80 yards in 13 plays. A second-down pass from Unitas to end Jim Mutscheller set up a one-yard touchdown plunge by fullback Alan Ameche, winning it for Baltimore 23-17.

A dramatic sudden-death championship game on national television captured the imagination of millions. Tex Maule's story on the game for *Sports Illustrated* in its January 5, 1959 issue was headlined, "The Best Football Game Ever Played."

NBC's live telecast of the game, with Chuck Thompson of Baltimore and Chris Schenkel of New York calling the plays, reached an estimated 10,820,000 homes in America. It was not shown in the largest market, however; New York City was blacked out. New Yorkers also could not read about it because the city was in the midst of a newspaper strike.

1958 STANDINGS

Eastern Conference	W	L	T	Pct.	Pts.	OP
New York Giants	9	3	0	.750	246	183
Cleveland	9	3	0	.750	302	217
Pittsburgh	7	4	1	.636	261	230
Washington	4	7	1	.304	214	268
Chicago Cardinals	2	9	1	.182	261	356
Philadelphia	2	9	1	.182	235	306
Western Conference	**W**	**L**	**T**	**Pct.**	**Pts.**	**OP**
Baltimore	9	3	0	.750	381	203
Chicago Bears	8	4	0	.667	298	230
Los Angeles Rams	8	4	0	.667	344	278
San Francisco	6	6	0	.500	257	324
Detroit	4	7	1	.364	261	276
Green Bay	1	10	1	.091	193	382

Eastern Conference playoff: New York Giants 10, Cleveland 0
NFL championship: Baltimore 23, New York Giants 17, overtime

LEADING RUSHERS	Att.	Yards	Avg.	Long	TD
Jim Brown, Cleveland	257	1,527	5.9	65t	17
Alan Ameche, Baltimore	171	791	4.6	28	8
Joe Perry, San Francisco	125	758	6.1	73t	4
Tom Tracy, Pittsburgh	169	714	4.2	64	5
Jon Arnett, LA Rams	133	683	5.1	57	6
LEADING PASSERS	**Att.**	**Comp.**	**Yards**	**TD**	**Int.**
Eddie LeBaron, Washington	145	79	1,365	11	10
Milt Plum, Cleveland	189	102	1,619	11	11
Bobby Layne, Pittsburgh	294	145	2,510	14	12
Bill Wade, LA Rams	341	181	2,875	18	22
Johnny Unitas, Baltimore	263	136	2,007	19	7
LEADING RECEIVERS	**No.**	**Yards**	**Avg.**	**Long**	**TD**
Raymond Berry, Baltimore	56	794	14.2	54	9
Pete Retzlaff, Philadelphia	56	766	13.7	49	2
Del Shofner, LA Rams	51	1,097	21.5	92t	8
Lenny Moore, Baltimore	50	938	18.5	77t	7
Clyde Conner, San Francisco	49	512	10.4	26	5
LEADING SCORER	**TD**	**FG**	**PAT**	**TP**	
Jim Brown, Cleveland	18	0	0	108	
LEADING INTERCEPTOR	**No.**	**Yards**	**Avg.**	**Long**	**TD**
Jim Patton, NY Giants	11	183	16.6	42	0
LEADING PUNTER	**No.**	**Avg.**	**Long**		
Sam Baker, Washington	48	45.4	64		
LEADING PUNT RETURNER	**No.**	**Yards**	**Avg.**	**Long**	**TD**
Jon Arnett, LA Rams	18	223	12.4	58	0
LEADING KICKOFF RETURNER	**No.**	**Yards**	**Avg.**	**Long**	**TD**
Ollie Matson, Chi. Cardinals	14	497	35.5	101t	2

SUPERLATIVES

Rushing average	7.3	Lenny Moore, Baltimore
Receiving average	27.6	Jimmy Orr, Pittsburgh
Completion percentage	59.9	John Brodie, San Francisco
Touchdowns	18	Jim Brown, Cleveland

LONGEST

Run	83t	John David Crow, Chi. Cardinals
Pass	93t	Bill Wade to Red Phillips, LA Rams
Interception	70t	Will Sherman, LA Rams
Punt	67	Don Chandler, NY Giants
Punt return	71t	Yale Lary, Detroit
Kickoff return	103t	Lenny Lyles, Baltimore
Field goal	49	Pat Summerall, NY Giants

1959 On February 17, Tim Mara, the founder of the New York Giants, died at the age of 71.

General manager Pete Rozelle of the Rams traded eight players and a draft choice—the rights to nine players—to the Chicago Cardinals in exchange for running back Ollie Matson.

Lamar Hunt, a Dallas, Texas, businessman who had been unsuccessful in attempts to buy the Cardinals, announced his intentions to form a second professional football league. He found interested parties for franchises and the first meeting of the league was held at the Conrad Hilton Hotel in Chicago, August 14. The representatives and their cities were: Hunt, Dallas; Bob Howsam, Denver; K. S. (Bud) Adams, Houston; Barron Hilton, Los Angeles; Max Winter and William Boyer, Minneapolis; and Harry Wismer, New York City. They made plans to begin league play in 1960. Eight days later at another meeting in Dallas, they announced that the league would be called the "American Football League."

Buffalo became the seventh AFL team, October 28, and Boston the eighth, November 22. Buffalo was represented by Ralph C. Wilson and Boston by William H. Sullivan.

In November, the AFL held an initial draft and named former World War II flying ace and South Dakota governor Joe Foss as its commissioner.

NFL Commissioner Bert Bell died of a heart attack while attending a Philadelphia Eagles game at Franklin Field, October 11. Austin Gunsel, the league treasurer, was named interim commissioner.

In the West, Baltimore and the Chicago Bears each had slow starts, the Colts 3-3 and the Bears 1-4. But neither lost again, and the Colts edged the Bears for the title. Johnny Unitas led the league with 2,899 yards and 32 touchdown passes, while Raymond Berry led with 66 catches and 14 touchdown receptions. Green Bay was the West's most improved team despite the loss of Randy Duncan, the league's number-one draft choice, who signed with the Canadian Football League. Vince Lombardi established Bart Starr as his quarterback, Paul Hornung as his left halfback, and Jim Taylor as his fullback. Hornung led the league in scoring.

Quarterback Charlie Conerly led the league in passing and led the Giants to another Eastern Conference championship. They beat the Browns 10-6 and 48-7. Cleveland's Jim Brown had another season over 1,000 yards with 1,329.

Baltimore again defeated the Giants in the NFL title game. New York led 9-7 going into the last quarter, but Unitas and Lenny Moore were the principal figures as the Colts put together a 24-point fourth period and Baltimore won 31-16, claiming its second straight championship.

1959 STANDINGS

Eastern Conference	W	L	T	Pct.	Pts.	OP
New York Giants	10	2	0	.833	284	170
Cleveland	7	5	0	.583	270	214
Philadelphia	7	5	0	.583	268	278
Pittsburgh	6	5	1	.545	257	216
Washington	3	9	0	.250	185	350
Chicago Cardinals	2	10	0	.167	234	324
Western Conference	**W**	**L**	**T**	**Pct.**	**Pts.**	**OP**
Baltimore	9	3	0	.750	374	251
Chicago Bears	8	4	0	.667	252	196
Green Bay	7	5	0	.583	248	246
San Francisco	7	5	0	.583	255	237
Detroit	3	8	1	.273	203	275
Los Angeles Rams	2	10	0	.167	242	315

NFL championship: Baltimore 31, New York Giants 16

LEADING RUSHERS	Att.	Yards	Avg.	Long	TD
Jim Brown, Cleveland	290	1,329	4.6	70t	14
J.D. Smith, San Francisco	207	1,036	5.0	73t	10
Ollie Matson, LA Rams	161	863	5.4	50	6
Tom Tracy, Pittsburgh	199	794	4.0	51	3
Bobby Mitchell, Cleveland	131	743	5.7	90t	5
LEADING PASSERS	**Att.**	**Comp.**	**Yards**	**TD**	**Int.**
Charlie Conerly, NY Giants	194	113	1,706	14	4
Earl Morrall, Detroit	137	65	1,102	5	6
Johnny Unitas, Baltimore	367	193	2,899	32	14

	Att.	Comp.	Yards	TD	Int.
Norm Van Brocklin, Philadelphia	340	191	2,617	16	14
Bill Wade, LA Rams	261	153	2,001	12	17

LEADING RECEIVERS	**No.**	**Yards**	**Avg.**	**Long**	**TD**
Raymond Berry, Baltimore	66	959	14.5	55t	14
Del Shofner, LA Rams	47	936	19.9	72t	7
Lenny Moore, Baltimore	47	846	18.0	71	6
Tommy McDonald, Philadelphia	47	846	18.0	71	10
Jim Mutscheller, Baltimore	44	699	15.9	40t	8
Billy Wilson, San Francisco	44	540	12.3	57t	4

LEADING SCORER	**TD**	**FG**	**PAT**	**TP**
Paul Hornung, Green Bay	7	7	31	94

LEADING INTERCEPTORS	**No.**	**Yards**	**Avg.**	**Long**	**TD**
Dean Derby, Pittsburgh	7	127	18.1	24	0
Milt Davis, Baltimore	7	119	17.0	57t	1
Don Shinnick, Baltimore	7	70	10.0	23	0

LEADING PUNTER	**No.**	**Avg.**	**Long**
Yale Lary, Detroit	45	47.1	67

LEADING PUNT RETURNER	**No.**	**Yards**	**Avg.**	**Long**	**TD**
Johnny Morris, Chi. Bears	14	171	12.2	78t	1

LEADING KICKOFF RETURNER	**No.**	**Yards**	**Avg.**	**Long**	**TD**
Abe Woodson, San Francisco	13	382	29.4	105t	1

SUPERLATIVES

Rushing average	6.6	Johnny Olszewski, Washington
Receiving average	23.2	Max McGee, Green Bay
Completion percentage	58.6	Milt Plum, Cleveland
Touchdowns	14	Raymond Berry, Baltimore Jim Brown, Cleveland

LONGEST

Run	90t	Bobby Mitchell, Cleveland
Pass	88t	Ed Brown to Harlon Hill, Chi. Bears
Interception	70t	Harland Svare, NY Giants
Punt	71	Tommy Davis, San Francisco Rick Casares, Chi. Bears
Punt return	84t	Ken Hall, Chi. Cardinals
Kickoff return	105t	Abe Woodson, San Francisco
Field goal	50	Jim Martin, Detroit

1960 At the league meeting, the owners were hopelessly deadlocked in an attempt to elect a new commissioner to succeed Bert Bell. The older owners wanted acting commissioner Austin Gunsel, while a number of the younger owners supported Marshall Leahy, an attorney from San Francisco. On January 26, Wellington Mara nominated Pete Rozelle of the Rams as a compromise choice. On the twenty-third ballot, but the first in which he was mentioned, Rozelle was elected commissioner. The same day, Lamar Hunt was elected the first president of the AFL.

The next day, Minneapolis withdrew from the AFL, and the day after that, the same ownership was granted a franchise to start play in the NFL in 1961. At the same time, another franchise was granted to Dallas to start play in 1960. Owned by Clint Murchison, Dallas hired Tex Schramm as general manager and Tom Landry, the defensive coach of the Giants, as head coach. On January 30, the Minneapolis franchise of the AFL was replaced by one located in Oakland. The new franchise was owned by an eight-man syndicate headed by Y.C. (Chet) Soda.

More changes occurred before the two leagues' seasons started. In March, the Chicago Cardinals moved to St. Louis. The AFL, meanwhile, established a number of rules and practices different than those of the NFL. There would be a two-point option on points-after-touchdown for successfully running or passing the ball across the goal line, players' names would be on their jerseys, and the teams would play 14-game, not 12-game, schedules. Also a non-tampering pact was agreed on between the leagues.

In July, the AFL signed a five-year contract with ABC to televise games. In the same month, a Los Angeles court ruled that the Rams' contract with Heisman Trophy-winning halfback Billy Cannon was invalid, freeing Cannon to sign with the Houston Oilers and setting a precedent for other cases that eventually gave the AFL rights to John Robinson and Charley Flowers. Quarterback Don Meredith of SMU, who had been sought both by the Dallas Cowboys and Dallas Texans, settled on the Cowboys.

The Boston Patriots defeated the Buffalo Bills 28-7 at Buffalo in the first AFL preseason game before 16,000, July 30, and the Denver Broncos defeated Boston 13-10 at Boston in the first AFL regular season game before 21,597, September 9.

The Houston Oilers, coached by Lou Rymkus and quarterbacked by NFL castoff George Blanda, compiled a 10-4 record and won the Eastern Division. The Los Angeles Chargers, coached by the former boss of the NFL Rams, Sid Gillman, also had a 10-4 record and won the Western championship. Blanda threw three touchdown passes as Houston defeated Los Angeles 24-16 in the first AFL Championship Game.

Vince Lombardi won his first division championship as coach of the Packers, who won a title for the first time since 1944. Halfback Paul Hornung had a sensational season, scoring 176 points on 15 touchdowns, 15 field goals, and 41 extra points in a 12-game regular season.

The Eagles, coached by Lawrence (Buck) Shaw and led by quarterback Norm Van Brocklin and linebacker Chuck Bednarik, won the Eastern Conference with the best record in football, 10-2.

Three NFL runners had over 1,000 yards. They were Jim Brown of Cleveland, Jim Taylor of Green Bay, and John David Crow of St. Louis.

The new Dallas Cowboys finished with an 0-11-1 record, tying the Giants 31-31.

The San Francisco 49ers adopted a Shotgun offense for their last five games and won four of them.

Chuck Bednarik went both ways, playing 60 minutes of offense and defense, during five games for Philadelphia. He accomplished the same feat in the NFL Championship Game against Green Bay. It was one of the most hard-fought title games ever, and Philadelphia won 17-13. Time ran out after Bednarik tackled the Packers' Taylor at the Eagles' 9-yard line. Shaw, the coach, and Van Brocklin, the quarterback, announced their retirements.

The Lions won the first Bert Bell Benefit Bowl, known as the Playoff Bowl (a game between second-place finishers), defeating the Browns 17-16.

The NFL attendance for the 1960 season was 3,128,296 for 78 games and the AFL's was 926,156 for 56 games.

1960 AFL STANDINGS

Eastern Division	**W**	**L**	**T**	**Pct.**	**Pts.**	**OP**
Houston	10	4	0	.714	379	285
New York Titans	7	7	0	.500	382	399
Buffalo	5	8	1	.358	296	303
Boston	5	9	0	.357	286	349
Western Division	**W**	**L**	**T**	**Pct.**	**Pts.**	**OP**
Los Angeles Chargers	10	4	0	.714	373	336
Dallas Texans	8	6	0	.571	362	253
Oakland	6	8	0	.429	319	388
Denver	4	9	1	.308	309	393

AFL championship: Houston 24, Los Angeles Chargers 16

LEADING RUSHERS	**Att.**	**Yards**	**Avg.**	**Long**	**TD**
Abner Haynes, Dallas Texans	156	875	5.6	57	9
Paul Lowe, LA Chargers	136	855	6.3	69	9
Billy Cannon, Houston	152	644	4.2	60	1
Dave Smith, Houston	154	643	4.2	65	5
Tony Teresa, Oakland	139	608	4.4	83	6

LEADING PASSERS	**Att.**	**Comp.**	**Yards**	**TD**	**Int.**
Jack Kemp, LA Chargers	406	211	3,018	20	25
Al Dorow, NY Titans	396	201	2,748	26	26
Frank Tripucka, Denver	478	248	3,038	24	34
Butch Songin, Boston	392	187	2,476	22	15
Cotton Davidson, Dallas Texans	379	179	2,474	15	16

LEADING RECEIVERS	**No.**	**Yards**	**Avg.**	**Long**	**TD**
Lionel Taylor, Denver	92	1,235	13.4	80	12
Bill Groman, Houston	72	1,473	20.5	92	12
Don Maynard, NY Titans	72	1,265	17.6	65	6
Art Powell, NY Titans	69	1,167	16.9	76	14
Abner Haynes, Dallas Texans	55	576	10.5	34	3

LEADING SCORER	**TD**	**FG**	**PAT**	**TP**
Gene Mingo, Denver	6	18	33	123

LEADING INTERCEPTOR	**No.**	**Yards**	**Avg.**	**TD**
Goose Gonsoulin, Denver	11	98	8.9	0

LEADING PUNTER	**No.**	**Avg.**	**Long**
Paul Maguire, LA Chargers	43	40.5	61

LEADING PUNT RETURNER	**No.**	**Yards**	**Avg.**	**Long**	**TD**
Abner Haynes, Dallas Texans	14	215	15.4	46	0

LEADING KICKOFF RETURNER	**No.**	**Yards**	**Avg.**	**Long**	**TD**
Ken Hall, Houston	19	594	31.3	104	1

SUPERLATIVES

Rushing average	6.3	Paul Lowe, LA Chargers
Receiving average	20.5	Bill Groman, Houston
Completion percentage	54.0	Tom Flores, Oakland
Touchdowns	14	Art Powell, NY Titans

LONGEST

Run	87t	Jack Larscheid, Oakland
Pass	92t	Jacky Lee to Bill Groman, Houston
Interception	80t	David Webster, Dallas Texans
Punt	72	Wayne Crow, Oakland
Punt return	76t	Gene Mingo, Denver
Kickoff return	104t	Ken Hall, Houston
Field goal	53	George Blanda, Houston

1960 NFL STANDINGS

Eastern Conference	**W**	**L**	**T**	**Pct.**	**Pts.**	**OP**
Philadelphia	10	2	0	.833	321	246
Cleveland	8	3	1	.727	362	217
New York Giants	6	4	2	.600	271	261
St. Louis	6	5	1	.545	288	230
Pittsburgh	5	6	1	.455	240	275
Washington	1	9	2	.100	178	309
Western Conference	**W**	**L**	**T**	**Pct.**	**Pts.**	**OP**
Green Bay	8	4	0	.667	332	209
Detroit	7	5	0	.583	239	212
San Francisco	7	5	0	.583	208	205
Baltimore	6	6	0	.500	288	234
Chicago Bears	5	6	1	.455	194	299
Los Angeles Rams	4	7	1	.364	265	297
Dallas Cowboys	0	11	1	.000	177	369

NFL championship: Philadelphia 17, Green Bay 13

LEADING RUSHERS	**Att.**	**Yards**	**Avg.**	**Long**	**TD**
Jim Brown, Cleveland	215	1,257	5.8	71t	9
Jim Taylor, Green Bay	230	1,101	4.8	32	11
John David Crow, St. Louis	183	1,071	5.9	57	6
Nick Pietrosante, Detroit	161	872	5.4	57	8
J.D. Smith, San Francisco	174	780	4.5	41	5

LEADING PASSERS	**Att.**	**Comp.**	**Yards**	**TD**	**Int.**
Milt Plum, Cleveland	250	151	2,297	21	5
Norm Van Brocklin, Philadelphia	284	153	2,471	24	17
Johnny Unitas, Baltimore	378	190	3,099	25	24
Bill Wade, LA Rams	182	106	1,294	12	11
Bobby Layne, Pittsburgh	209	103	1,814	13	17

LEADING RECEIVERS	**No.**	**Yards**	**Avg.**	**Long**	**TD**
Raymond Berry, Baltimore	74	1,298	17.5	70t	10
Sonny Randle, St. Louis	62	893	14.4	57t	15
Red Phillips, LA Rams	52	883	17.0	61t	8
Jim Gibbons, Detroit	51	604	11.8	65t	2
Pete Retzlaff, Philadelphia	46	826	18.0	57t	5

LEADING SCORER	**TD**	**FG**	**PAT**	**TP**
Paul Hornung, Green Bay	15	15	41	176

LEADING INTERCEPTORS	**No.**	**Yards**	**Avg.**	**Long**	**TD**
Dave Baker, San Francisco	10	96	9.6	28	0
Jerry Norton, St. Louis	10	96	9.6	26	0

LEADING PUNTER	**No.**	**Avg.**	**Long**
Jerry Norton, St. Louis	39	45.6	62

LEADING PUNT RETURNER	**No.**	**Yards**	**Avg.**	**Long**	**TD**
Abe Woodson, San Francisco	13	174	13.4	48	0

LEADING KICKOFF RETURNER	**No.**	**Yards**	**Avg.**	**Long**	**TD**
Tom Moore, Green Bay	12	397	33.1	84	0

SUPERLATIVES

Rushing average	5.9	John David Crow, St. Louis
Receiving average	24.3	Buddy Dial, Pittsburgh
Completion percentage	60.4	Milt Plum, Cleveland
Touchdowns	15	Paul Hornung, Green Bay Sonny Randle, St. Louis

LONGEST

Run	87t	John Henry Johnson, Pittsburgh
Pass	91t	Bart Starr to Boyd Dowler, Green Bay Ed Brown to Willard Dewveall, Chi. Bears
Interception	92t	Bernie Parrish, Cleveland
Punt	75	Bob Green, Pittsburgh
Punt return	48	Abe Woodson, San Francisco
Kickoff return	97t	Lenny Lyles, Baltimore
Field goal	52	Jim Martin, Detroit

1961 Commissioner Pete Rozelle signed a two-year contract awarding NBC radio and television rights to the NFL Championship Game for $615,000 annually. Congress then passed a bill legalizing single network television contracts by professional sports leagues.

On April 27, Canton, Ohio, where the NFL was formed in 1920, was selected as the site for the construction of the Pro Football Hall of Fame.

Norm Van Brocklin, quarterback of the champion Philadelphia Eagles, was named head coach of the new Minnesota Vikings. His former understudy, Sonny Jurgensen, took over at quarterback for the Eagles. Y. A. Tittle, one of four quarterbacks on the roster of the San Francisco 49ers, was traded to the Giants because rookie Billy Kilmer and veterans

John Brodie and Bobby Waters were better suited for the needs of the 49ers' new Shotgun offense. The Tittle trade was just one of several made by New York. It also acquired defensive back Erich Barnes from the Bears and ends Del Shofner from the Rams and Joe Walton from the Redskins.

The first American Football League franchise shift occurred when the Los Angeles Chargers were moved and became the San Diego Chargers. Ed McGah, Wayne Valley, and Robert Osborne bought out their partners in the ownership of the Oakland Raiders; McGah was named Raiders' president. Bob and Lee Howsam sold the Denver Broncos to a group headed by Calvin Kunz.

In the NFL, Art Modell bought controlling interest in the Cleveland Browns and the Redskins moved to the new District of Columbia Stadium.

Three original AFL coaches departed during the season. Wally Lemm replaced Lou Rymkus at Houston, Mike Holovak replaced Lou Saban at Boston, and Marty Feldman replaced Eddie Erdelatz at Oakland.

End Willard Dewveall of the Chicago Bears played out his option and joined Houston of the AFL, the first player to voluntarily move from one league to the other.

The Chargers, playing in a new city, won the Western Division title by six games. The Oilers repeated as Eastern champions, due to a victory over and a tie with second-place Boston. San Diego had two giant rookie linemen in Earl Faison and Ernie Ladd and won its first 11 games in a row. Houston's George Blanda completed seven touchdown passes in one game and a pro record 36 for the season. He also broke Johnny Unitas's record with 3,330 yards while his receivers, Charley Hennigan and Bill Groman, set records with 1,746 yards and 17 touchdown receptions, respectively. Lionel Taylor of the Denver Broncos caught a pro football record 100 passes.

Late in the season, AFL Commissioner Joe Foss had the first major challenge to his authority. To get a jump on the NFL in signing college seniors, the owners had a secret draft in November, with each team selecting six players. Foss already had set the official date for the draft in December, and when he found out about the secret draft, he declared it invalid. Several of the owners who had had outstanding drafts objected strenuously, the most vocal being Harry Wismer of the Titans. Wismer's first selection was Heisman Trophy winner Ernie Davis, who was then selected by Buffalo in the official draft (and later signed with Cleveland of the NFL). Wismer demanded that Foss be fired, but the Commissioner weathered the storm and actually was given a new five-year contract at the end of the season. Surprisingly, in the spring of 1962, Foss served as the best man at Wismer's wedding.

In late December, Houston defeated San Diego 10-3 for its second straight AFL title.

The Green Bay Packers of Vince Lombardi ruled the NFL. Halfback Paul Hornung led the league in scoring for the third year in a row despite the fact that it was the time of the Berlin crisis and he was on active duty in the army reserve, stationed at Fort Riley, Kansas; he had to travel back and forth each weekend to the Packers' games. He scored 33 points in one game against Baltimore.

San Francisco's Shotgun offense was the talk of the league. Coach Red Hickey alternated John Brodie, Billy Kilmer, and Bobby Waters at quarterback in the unusual formation in which they took the snap from center seven to nine yards back and then ran, passed, or handed off. The 49ers ran up a 4-1 record until the Chicago Bears stopped them 31-0, playing middle linebacker Bill George at middle guard, where he befuddled the 49ers' center and put pressure on their passers. San Francisco went back to an ordinary pro formation, and became an ordinary team, after that.

Detroit won six games on the road but only two at home. The new Minnesota Vikings had a respectable 3-11 record and their rookie quarterback, Fran Tarkenton, starred as they won their first regular-season game 37-13 over the Chicago Bears. Tarkenton passed for four touchdowns and ran for a fifth.

Tittle, the new leader of the New York Giants, had 17 touchdown passes as they won the Eastern Conference. Sonny Jurgensen of Philadelphia set a pro record by passing for 3,723 yards (almost 400 more than Blanda in the AFL), but the Eagles lost both their games against New York and missed the title by half a game. Jim Brown of Cleveland led the NFL in rushing for the fifth straight time and tied his own single-game mark with 237 yards against Philadelphia.

Hornung set a championship record when he scored 19 points to lead the Green Bay Packers to their first NFL championship since 1944 and first under Lombardi 37-0 over the Giants in the title game, December 31.

1961 AFL STANDINGS

Eastern Division	W	L	T	Pct.	Pts.	OP
Houston	10	3	1	.769	513	242
Boston	9	4	1	.692	413	313
New York Titans	7	7	0	.500	301	390
Buffalo	6	8	0	.429	294	342
Western Division	**W**	**L**	**T**	**Pct.**	**Pts.**	**OP**
San Diego	12	2	0	.857	396	219
Dallas Texans	6	8	0	.429	334	343
Denver	3	11	0	.214	251	432
Oakland	2	12	0	.143	237	458

AFL championship: Houston 10, San Diego 3

LEADING RUSHERS	Att.	Yards	Avg.	Long	TD
Billy Cannon, Houston	200	948	4.7	61	6
Bill Mathis, NY Titans	202	846	4.2	30	7
Abner Haynes, Dallas Texans	179	841	4.7	59	9
Paul Lowe, San Diego	175	767	4.4	87	9
Charlie Tolar, Houston	157	577	3.7	28	4
LEADING PASSERS	**Att.**	**Comp.**	**Yards**	**TD**	**Int.**
George Blanda, Houston	362	187	3,330	36	22
Tom Flores, Oakland	366	190	2,176	15	19
Jack Kemp, San Diego	364	165	2,686	15	22
Al Dorow, NY Titans	438	197	2,651	19	30
Babe Parilli, Boston	198	104	1,314	13	9
LEADING RECEIVERS	**No.**	**Yards**	**Avg.**	**Long**	**TD**
Lionel Taylor, Denver	100	1,176	11.8	52	4
Charley Hennigan, Houston	82	1,746	21.3	80	12
Art Powell, NY Titans	71	881	12.4	48	5
Dave Kocourek, San Diego	55	1,055	19.2	76	4
Chris Burford, Dallas	51	850	16.7	54	5
LEADING SCORER	**TD**	**FG**	**PAT**		**TP**
Gino Cappelletti, Boston	8	17	48		147
LEADING INTERCEPTOR	**No.**	**Yards**	**Avg.**	**Long**	**TD**
Billy Atkins, Buffalo	10	158	15.8	29	0
LEADING PUNTER	**No.**		**Avg.**		**Long**
Billy Atkins, Buffalo	85		44.5		70
LEADING PUNT RETURNER	**No.**	**Yards**	**Avg.**	**Long**	**TD**
Dick Christy, NY Titans	18	383	21.3	70	2
LEADING KICKOFF RETURNER	**No.**	**Yards**	**Avg.**	**Long**	**TD**
Dave Grayson, Dallas Texans	16	453	28.3	73	0

SUPERLATIVES

Rushing average	8.6	Jack Spikes, Dallas Texans
Receiving average	23.5	Bill Groman, Houston
Completion percentage	52.5	Babe Parilli, Boston
Touchdowns	18	Bill Groman, Houston

LONGEST

Run	87t	Paul Lowe, San Diego
Pass	91t	Jack Kemp to Keith Lincoln, San Diego
Interception	99t	Dave Grayson, Dallas Texans
Punt	82	Paul Maguire, San Diego
Punt return	70t	Dick Christy, NY Titans
Kickoff return	93t	Fred Brown, Buffalo
Field goal	55	George Blanda, Houston

1961 NFL STANDINGS

Eastern Conference	W	L	T	Pct.	Pts.	OP
New York Giants	10	3	1	.769	368	220
Philadelphia	10	4	0	.714	361	297
Cleveland	8	5	1	.615	319	270
St. Louis	7	7	0	.500	279	267
Pittsburgh	6	8	0	.429	295	287
Dallas Cowboys	4	9	1	.308	236	380
Washington	1	12	1	.077	174	392
Western Conference	**W**	**L**	**T**	**Pct.**	**Pts.**	**OP**
Green Bay	11	3	0	.786	391	223
Detroit	8	5	1	.615	270	258
Baltimore	8	6	0	.571	302	307
Chicago Bears	8	6	0	.571	326	302
San Francisco	7	6	1	.538	346	272
Los Angeles Rams	4	10	0	.286	263	333
Minnesota	3	11	0	.214	285	407

NFL championship: Green Bay 37, New York Giants 0

LEADING RUSHERS	Att.	Yards	Avg.	Long	TD
Jim Brown, Cleveland	305	1,408	4.6	38	8
Jim Taylor, Green Bay	243	1,307	5.4	53	15
Alex Webster, NY Giants	196	928	4.7	59	2
Nick Pietrosante, Detroit	201	841	4.2	42	5
J.D. Smith, San Francisco	167	823	4.9	33	8
LEADING PASSERS	**Att.**	**Comp.**	**Yards**	**TD**	**Int.**
Milt Plum, Cleveland	302	177	2,416	18	10
Sonny Jurgensen, Philadelphia	416	235	3,723	32	24
Bart Starr, Green Bay	295	172	2,418	16	16
John Brodie, San Francisco	283	155	2,588	14	12
Bill Wade, Chi. Bears	250	139	2,258	22	13
LEADING RECEIVERS	**No.**	**Yards**	**Avg.**	**Long**	**TD**
Red Phillips, LA Rams	78	1,092	14.0	69t	5
Raymond Berry, Baltimore	75	873	11.6	44	0
Del Shofner, NY Giants	68	1,125	16.5	46t	11
Tommy McDonald, Philadelphia	64	1,144	17.9	66	13
Mike Ditka, Chi. Bears	56	1,076	19.2	76t	12
Billy Howton, Dallas	56	785	14.0	53	4
LEADING SCORER	**TD**	**FG**	**PAT**		**TP**
Paul Hornung, Green Bay	10	15	41		146
LEADING INTERCEPTOR	**No.**	**Yards**	**Avg.**	**Long**	**TD**
Dick Lynch, NY Giants	9	60	6.7	36	0
LEADING PUNTER	**No.**		**Avg.**		**Long**
Yale Lary, Detroit	52		48.4		71
LEADING PUNT RETURNER	**No.**	**Yards**	**Avg.**	**Long**	**TD**
Willie Wood, Green Bay	14	225	16.1	72t	2
LEADING KICKOFF RETURNER	**No.**	**Yards**	**Avg.**	**Long**	**TD**
Dick Bass, LA Rams	23	698	30.3	64	0

SUPERLATIVES

Rushing average	7.0	Lenny Moore, Baltimore
Receiving average	22.4	Frank Clarke, Dallas
Completion percentage	58.6	Milt Plum, Cleveland
Touchdowns	16	Jim Taylor, Green Bay

LONGEST

Run	73t	Dick Bass, LA Rams
Pass	98t	Bill Wade to John Farrington, Chi. Bears
Interception	102t	Erich Barnes, NY Giants
Punt	78	Jerry Norton, St. Louis
Punt return	90t	Dick Bass, LA Rams
Kickoff return	105t	Timmy Brown, Philadelphia
		Jon Arnett, LA Rams
Field goal	52	Steve Myhra, Baltimore
		John Aveni, Washington

1962 Pete Rozelle was given a new five-year contract.

Dan Reeves bought out his partners and took complete control of the Los Angeles Rams. In the AFL, Ed McGah and Wayne Valley acquired controlling interest in the Raiders from partner Robert Osborne. There was an unusual coaching change when Wally Lemm left the Houston Oilers of the AFL after winning a championship and moved to the St. Louis Cardinals. Frank (Pop) Ivy, coach of the Cardinals, moved to the Oilers. Sid Gillman of the San Diego Chargers tried to slip quarterback Jack Kemp, who had a broken hand, through waivers to the reserve list. For the $100 fee, Kemp was picked up by the Buffalo Bills. A strong contingent of NFL rookies included quarterback Roman Gabriel and defensive tackle Merlin Olsen of Los Angeles and end Gary Collins of Cleveland. Two old pros, quarterback Bobby Layne of Pittsburgh and linebacker Chuck Bednarik of Philadelphia, retired.

There was intense competition between the two leagues for college players. The NFL signed most of the big-name players and also won a court victory after a two-and-a-half-year battle when a U.S. District judge ruled against the AFL's charges of monopoly and conspiracy in expansion, television, and signings.

Len Dawson requested and was granted his release from the Browns. He signed with the Dallas Texans and was reunited with Hank Stram, who had been the backfield coach when Dawson was at Purdue.

The NFL entered into a single network agreement with CBS for telecasting of all regular-season games for $4,650,000 annually.

The rules were changed in both leagues, making it illegal to grab another player's facemask. The AFL voted to make the scoreboard clock the official timer of the game.

Ivy, the new Oilers' coach, became the third to guide them to a division championship and had an 11-3 record. The Dallas Texans won the West as the Chargers fell to 4-10.

Cookie Gilchrist, who had been playing in the Canadian Football League, came into the AFL as a rookie with Buffalo and led the league in rushing with 1,096 yards.

The Texans defeated the Oilers 20-17 for the AFL championship in the longest pro game ever played up to that point. It went into a second quarter of sudden-death overtime, 77 minutes and 54 seconds, before Tommy Brooker of Dallas kicked a 25-yard field goal to win it.

Green Bay withstood a challenge from Detroit to once again win the NFL's Western Conference, with a 13-1 record. The Packers prevailed even though the Lions upset them 26-14 on Thanksgiving Day, sacking quarterback Bart Starr for 110 yards in losses. Starr led the NFL in passing and fullback Jim Taylor had his greatest season, gaining 1,474 yards to oust Jim Brown of Cleveland as the league rushing leader. Taylor also led the league with an NFL-record 19 touchdowns.

Quarterback Y.A. Tittle of the New York Giants passed for seven touchdowns and 505 yards against Washington, October 28.

Sam Huff, the Giants' middle linebacker, waged a fierce personal duel with the Packers' Taylor as the two teams played for the NFL championship. It was bitterly cold and the wind was blowing 40 miles an hour at Yankee Stadium in New York. Taylor gained 85 yards and Jerry Kramer kicked three field goals as the Packers won their second consecutive NFL title 16-7.

1962 AFL STANDINGS

Eastern Division	**W**	**L**	**T**	**Pct.**	**Pts.**	**OP**
Houston	11	3	0	.786	387	270
Boston	9	4	1	.692	346	295
Buffalo	7	6	1	.538	309	272
New York Titans	5	9	0	.357	278	423
Western Division	**W**	**L**	**T**	**Pct.**	**Pts.**	**OP**
Dallas Texans	11	3	0	.786	389	233
Denver	7	7	0	.500	353	334
San Diego	4	10	0	.286	314	392
Oakland	1	13	0	.071	213	370

AFL championship: Dallas Texans 20, Houston 17, overtime

LEADING RUSHERS	**Att.**	**Yards**	**Avg.**	**Long**	**TD**
Cookie Gilchrist, Buffalo	214	1,096	5.1	44	13
Abner Haynes, Dallas Texans	221	1,049	4.7	71	13
Charley Tolar, Houston	244	1,012	4.1	25	7
Clem Daniels, Oakland	161	766	4.8	72	7
Curtis McClinton, Dallas Texans	111	604	5.4	69	2
LEADING PASSERS	**Att.**	**Comp.**	**Yards**	**TD**	**Int.**
Len Dawson, Dallas Texans	310	189	2,759	29	17
Babe Parilli, Boston	253	140	1,988	18	8
Frank Tripucka, Denver	440	240	2,917	17	25
George Blanda, Houston	418	197	2,810	27	42
Johnny Green, NY Titans	258	128	1,741	10	18
LEADING RECEIVERS	**No.**	**Yards**	**Avg.**	**Long**	**TD**
Lionel Taylor, Denver	77	908	11.8	45	4
Art Powell, NY Titans	64	1,130	17.7	80	8
Dick Christy, NY Titans	62	538	8.7	41	3
Bo Dickinson, Denver	60	554	9.2	33	4
Don Maynard, NY Titans	56	1,041	18.6	86	8
LEADING SCORER	**TD**	**FG**	**PAT**		**TP**
Gene Mingo, Denver	4	27	32		137
LEADING INTERCEPTOR	**No.**	**Yards**	**Avg.**	**Long**	**TD**
Lee Riley, NY Titans	11	122	11.1	30	0
LEADING PUNTER	**No.**		**Avg.**		**Long**
Jim Fraser, Denver	55		43.6		75
LEADING PUNT RETURNER	**No.**	**Yards**	**Avg.**	**Long**	**TD**
Dick Christy, NY Titans	15	250	16.7	73	2
LEADING KICKOFF RETURNER	**No.**	**Yards**	**Avg.**	**Long**	**TD**
Bobby Jancik, Houston	24	726	30.3	61	0

SUPERLATIVES

Rushing average	5.8	Larry Garron, Boston
Receiving average	21.7	Jim Colclough, Boston
Completion percentage	60.9	Len Dawson, Dallas Texans
Touchdowns	19	Abner Haynes, Dallas Texans

LONGEST

Run	86t	Keith Lincoln, San Diego
Pass	98t	Jacky Lee to Willard Dewveall, Houston
Interception	91t	Fred Williamson, Oakland
Punt	75	Jim Fraser, Denver
Punt return	73t	Dick Christy, NY Titans
Kickoff return	103t	Keith Lincoln, San Diego
Field goal	54	George Blanda, Houston

1962 NFL STANDINGS

Eastern Conference	**W**	**L**	**T**	**Pct.**	**Pts.**	**OP**
New York Giants	12	2	0	.857	398	283
Pittsburgh	9	5	0	.643	312	363
Cleveland	7	6	1	.538	291	257
Washington	5	7	2	.417	305	376
Dallas Cowboys	5	8	1	.385	398	402
St. Louis	4	9	1	.308	287	361
Philadelphia	3	10	1	.231	282	356
Western Conference	**W**	**L**	**T**	**Pct.**	**Pts.**	**OP**
Green Bay	13	1	0	.929	415	148
Detroit	11	3	0	.786	315	177
Chicago Bears	9	5	0	.643	321	287
Baltimore	7	7	0	.500	293	288
San Francisco	6	8	0	.429	282	331
Minnesota	2	11	1	.154	254	410
Los Angeles Rams	1	12	1	.077	220	334

NFL championship: Green Bay 16, New York Giants 7

LEADING RUSHERS	**Att.**	**Yards**	**Avg.**	**Long**	**TD**
Jim Taylor, Green Bay	272	1,474	5.4	51	19
John Henry Johnson, Pittsburgh	251	1,141	4.5	40	7
Dick Bass, LA Rams	196	1,033	5.3	57	6
Jim Brown, Cleveland	230	996	4.3	31	13
Don Perkins, Dallas	222	945	4.3	35	7
LEADING PASSERS	**Att.**	**Comp.**	**Yards**	**TD**	**Int.**
Bart Starr, Green Bay	285	178	2,438	12	9
Y.A. Tittle, NY Giants	375	200	3,224	33	20
Eddie LeBaron, Dallas	166	95	1,436	16	9
Frank Ryan, Cleveland	194	112	1,541	10	7
Sonny Jurgensen, Philadelphia	366	196	3,261	22	26
LEADING RECEIVERS	**No.**	**Yards**	**Avg.**	**Long**	**TD**
Bobby Mitchell, Washington	72	1,384	19.2	81t	11
Sonny Randle, St. Louis	63	1,158	18.4	86t	7
Bobby Joe Conrad, St. Louis	62	954	15.4	72t	4
Red Phillips, LA Rams	60	875	14.6	65t	5
Tommy McDonald, Philadelphia	58	1,146	19.8	60t	10
Mike Ditka, Chi. Bears	58	904	15.6	69t	5
Johnny Morris, Chi. Bears	58	889	15.3	73t	5
LEADING SCORER	**TD**	**FG**	**PAT**		**TP**
Jim Taylor, Green Bay	19	0	0		114
LEADING INTERCEPTOR	**No.**	**Yards**	**Avg.**	**Long**	**TD**
Willie Wood, Green Bay	9	132	14.7	37	0
LEADING PUNTER	**No.**		**Avg.**		**Long**
Tommy Davis, San Francisco	48		45.6		82
LEADING PUNT RETURNER	**No.**	**Yards**	**Avg.**	**Long**	**TD**
Pat Studstill, Detroit	29	457	15.8	44	0
LEADING KICKOFF RETURNER	**No.**	**Yards**	**Avg.**	**Long**	**TD**
Abe Woodson, San Francisco	37	1,157	31.3	79	0

SUPERLATIVES

Rushing average	5.6	Amos Marsh, Dallas
Receiving average	22.2	Frank Clarke, Dallas
Completion percentage	62.5	Bart Starr, Green Bay
Touchdowns	19	Jim Taylor, Green Bay

LONGEST

Run	77t	Willie Galimore, Chi. Bears
Pass	89t	Fran Tarkenton to Charley Ferguson, Minnesota
Interception	101t	Richie Petitbon, Chi. Bears
Punt	82	Tommy Davis, San Francisco
Punt return	85t	Abe Woodson, San Francisco
Kickoff return	103t	Herb Adderley, Green Bay
Field goal	53	Sam Baker, Dallas

1963 In April, Commissioner Pete Rozelle indefinitely suspended Paul Hornung of Green Bay and Alex Karras of Detroit for placing bets on their own teams and also fined five other Detroit players $2,000 each for betting on games in which they did not participate. The Detroit Lions Football Company was fined $2,000 on each of two counts for failure to report information promptly and for lack of proper sideline supervision.

On May 10, Gene (Big Daddy) Lipscomb, one of the greatest defensive tackles of all time, was found dead of an overdose of heroin.

The competition between the NFL Cowboys and AFL Texans for Dallas football fans ended with the Texans moving to Kansas City and becoming the Chiefs. The struggling New York franchise of the AFL, the Titans, was taken over by the league from owner Harry Wismer and then passed to the control of a group headed by David (Sonny) Werblin, who changed their name to the Jets. The Patriots moved their games from Boston University Field to larger Fenway Park. The Jets and Oakland Raiders, losers of 19 straight games at one point, were allowed to select players from other franchises in hopes of giving the league more competitive balance.

Paul Brown, coach of the Browns since their inception, was fired and replaced by Blanton Collier. Don Shula became coach of the Colts and Weeb Ewbank coach of the Jets. Linebackers Lee Roy Jordan of Dallas and Dave Robinson of Green Bay were notable rookies in the NFL and defensive tackle Buck Buchanan and guard Ed Budde started their careers with Kansas City.

The Pro Football Hall of Fame was dedicated at Canton, Ohio. Seventeen charter members were inducted.

NFL Properties was founded to serve as the licensing arm of the NFL. It was granted exclusive rights to the league and club trademarks for commercial application. The company later came to represent the NFL in licensing, marketing, and publishing.

San Diego won the AFL Western Division title again, but only after a struggle with Oakland. The Raiders, coached by former Chargers assistant Al Davis, won their last eight games and finished second with a 10-4 record. Clem Daniels of Oakland led the league with 1,099 yards rushing and Paul Lowe of San Diego was second with 1,010. Cookie Gilchrist of Buffalo set a professional record with 243 yards rushing in a game against the New York Jets.

The Boston Patriots and Buffalo Bills finished in a tie for the Eastern Division title, and the Patriots won a playoff 26-8 on a snow-covered field at Buffalo.

San Diego crushed Boston 51-10 in the championship game behind 206 yards rushing and 329 combined net yards by halfback Keith Lincoln.

The Chicago Bears, coached by George Halas, denied Green Bay another NFL championship. The Bears had a solid defense led by linebackers Joe Fortunato, Bill George, and Larry Morris and won the Western Conference. Green Bay stayed close behind despite losing quarterback Bart Starr with a broken hand. The difference was the Bears' two victories over the Packers, Green Bay's only losses of the year. Los Angeles had a massive defensive line called the Fearsome Foursome, made up of ends David (Deacon) Jones and Lamar Lundy and tackles Roosevelt Grier and Merlin Olsen.

Y. A. Tittle of the New York Giants had another brilliant season, throwing a record 36 touchdown passes, and the Giants won their third straight Eastern Conference championship. Jim Brown thrived under Blanton Collier and had his most productive season with 1,863 yards and games of 232 against Dallas and 223 against Philadelphia on the way to his sixth rushing title in seven years.

The domination of the Western Conference in the title game continued. The Chicago Bears stopped the Giants 14-10, intercepting five passes by Tittle, who twisted a knee in the second quarter but nevertheless played the second half in a losing effort.

1963 AFL STANDINGS

Eastern Division	**W**	**L**	**T**	**Pct.**	**Pts.**	**OP**
Boston	7	6	1	.538	317	257
Buffalo	7	6	1	.538	304	291
Houston	6	8	0	.429	302	372
New York Jets	5	8	1	.385	249	399
Western Division	**W**	**L**	**T**	**Pct.**	**Pts.**	**OP**
San Diego	11	3	0	.786	399	256
Oakland	10	4	0	.714	363	288
Kansas City	5	7	2	.417	347	263
Denver	2	11	1	.154	301	473

Eastern Division playoff: Boston 26, Buffalo 8
AFL championship: San Diego 51, Boston 10

LEADING RUSHERS	**Att.**	**Yards**	**Avg.**	**Long**	**TD**
Clem Daniels, Oakland	215	1,099	5.1	74	3
Paul Lowe, San Diego	177	1,010	5.7	66	8
Cookie Gilchrist, Buffalo	232	979	4.2	32	12
Keith Lincoln, San Diego	128	826	6.5	76	5
Larry Garron, Boston	179	750	4.2	47	2
LEADING PASSERS	**Att.**	**Comp.**	**Yards**	**TD**	**Int.**
Tobin Rote, San Diego	286	170	2,510	20	17
Tom Flores, Oakland	247	113	2,101	20	13
Jack Kemp, Buffalo	384	194	2,914	13	20

Len Dawson, Kansas City	352	190	2,389	26	19
George Blanda, Houston	423	224	3,003	24	25

LEADING RECEIVERS	**No.**	**Yards**	**Avg.**	**Long**	**TD**
Lionel Taylor, Denver	78	1,101	14.1	72	10
Art Powell, Oakland	73	1,304	17.8	85	16
Bake Turner, NY Jets	71	1,007	14.2	53	6
Bill Miller, Buffalo	69	860	12.5	36	3
Chris Burford, Kansas City	68	824	12.1	69	9

LEADING SCORER	**TD**	**FG**	**PAT**	**TP**
Gino Cappelletti, Boston	2	22	35	113

LEADING INTERCEPTOR	**No.**	**Yards**	**Avg.**	**Long**	**TD**
Fred Glick, Houston	12	180	15.0	45	1

LEADING PUNTER	**No.**	**Avg.**	**Long**
Jim Fraser, Denver	81	44.4	66

LEADING PUNT RETURNER	**No.**	**Yards**	**Avg.**	**Long**	**TD**
Hoot Gibson, Oakland	26	307	11.8	85	2

LEADING KICKOFF RETURNER	**No.**	**Yards**	**Avg.**	**Long**	**TD**
Bobby Jancik, Houston	45	1,317	29.3	53	0

SUPERLATIVES		
Rushing average	6.4	Keith Lincoln, San Diego
Receiving average	22.8	Clem Daniels, Oakland
Completion percentage	59.4	Tobin Rote, San Diego
Touchdowns	16	Art Powell, Oakland

LONGEST		
Run	76	Keith Lincoln, San Diego
Pass	93t	Tom Flores to Dobie Craig, Oakland
Interception	98t	Bob Suci, Boston
Punt	72	Jerrel Wilson, Kansas City
Punt return	93t	Bill Baird, NY Jets
Kickoff return	99t	Dave Grayson, Kansas City
Field goal	52	Gene Mingo, Denver

1963 NFL STANDINGS

Eastern Conference	**W**	**L**	**T**	**Pct.**	**Pts.**	**OP**
New York Giants	11	3	0	.786	448	280
Cleveland	10	4	0	.714	343	262
St. Louis	9	5	0	.643	341	283
Pittsburgh	7	4	3	.636	321	295
Dallas	4	10	0	.286	305	378
Washington	3	11	0	.214	279	398
Philadelphia	2	10	2	.167	242	381
Western Conference	**W**	**L**	**T**	**Pct.**	**Pts.**	**OP**
Chicago Bears	11	1	2	.917	301	144
Green Bay	11	2	1	.846	369	206
Baltimore	8	6	0	.571	316	285
Detroit	5	8	1	.385	326	265
Minnesota	5	8	1	.385	309	390
Los Angeles Rams	5	9	0	.357	210	350
San Francisco	2	12	0	.143	198	391

NFL championship: Chicago Bears 14, New York Giants 10

LEADING RUSHERS	**Att.**	**Yards**	**Avg.**	**Long**	**TD**
Jim Brown, Cleveland	291	1,863	6.4	80t	12
Jim Taylor, Green Bay	248	1,018	4.1	40t	9
Timmy Brown, Philadelphia	192	841	4.4	34	6
John Henry Johnson, Pittsburgh	186	773	4.2	48	4
Tommy Mason, Minnesota	166	763	4.6	70t	7

LEADING PASSERS	**Att.**	**Comp.**	**Yards**	**TD**	**Int.**
Y.A. Tittle, NY Giants	367	221	3,145	36	14
Johnny Unitas, Baltimore	410	237	3,481	20	12
Earl Morrall, Detroit	328	174	2,621	24	14
Frank Ryan, Cleveland	256	135	2,026	25	13
Charley Johnson, St. Louis	423	222	3,280	28	21

LEADING RECEIVERS	**No.**	**Yards**	**Avg.**	**Long**	**TD**
Bobby Joe Conrad, St. Louis	73	967	13.2	48	10
Bobby Mitchell, Washington	69	1,436	20.8	99t	7
Terry Barr, Detroit	66	1,086	16.5	75t	13
Del Shofner, NY Giants	64	1,181	18.5	70t	9
Buddy Dial, Pittsburgh	60	1,295	21.6	83t	9

LEADING SCORER	**TD**	**FG**	**PAT**	**TP**
Don Chandler, NY Giants	0	18	52	106

LEADING INTERCEPTORS	**No.**	**Yards**	**Avg.**	**Long**	**TD**
Dick Lynch, NY Giants	9	251	27.9	82t	3
Roosevelt Taylor, Chi. Bears	9	172	19.1	46	1

LEADING PUNTER	**No.**	**Avg.**	**Long**
Yale Lary, Detroit	35	48.9	73

LEADING PUNT RETURNER	**No.**	**Yards**	**Avg.**	**Long**	**TD**
Dick James, Washington	16	214	13.4	39	0

LEADING KICKOFF RETURNER	**No.**	**Yards**	**Avg.**	**Long**	**TD**
Abe Woodson, San Francisco	29	935	32.2	103t	3

SUPERLATIVES		
Rushing average	6.4	Jim Brown, Cleveland
Receiving average	21.6	Buddy Dial, Pittsburgh
Completion percentage	60.2	Y.A. Tittle, NY Giants
Touchdowns	15	Jim Brown, Cleveland

LONGEST		
Run	80t	Jim Brown, Cleveland
Pass	99t	George Izo to Bobby Mitchell, Washington
Interception	87t	Leroy Caffey, Philadelphia
Punt	73	Yale Lary, Detroit Gary Collins, Cleveland
Punt return	90t	Tommy Watkins, Detroit
Kickoff return	103t	Abe Woodson, San Francisco
Field goal	53	Don Chandler, NY Giants Sam Baker, Dallas

1964 There was a reshuffling of NFL owners in January. William Clay Ford, the president of the Lions, purchased the team. A group headed by Jerry Wolman purchased the Eagles. And Carroll Rosenbloom, the majority owner of the Colts since 1953, acquired complete ownership of the franchise.

The NFL signed a new contract with CBS television for a total of $14.1 million for the rights to regular-season games for the next two years. Each NFL club would receive more than $1 million a year. In addition, CBS acquired the rights to the 1964 and 1965 NFL Championship Games for $1.8 million each.

The AFL signed a new five-year, $36-million television contract with NBC. The deal assured each team approximately $900,000 a year from television rights.

Wolman of the Eagles hired Joe Kuharich as head coach. Kuharich shook up the Eagles, trading quarterback Sonny Jurgensen to Washington for quarterback Norm Snead and also dealing with Green Bay for center Jim Ringo and Detroit for halfback Ollie Matson.

The New York Giants traded linebacker Sam Huff to Washington and defensive tackle Ed Modzelewski to Cleveland. In addition to Jurgensen and Huff, the Redskins also acquired rookie halfback Charley Taylor.

Soccer player Pete Gogolak of Cornell University became the first soccer-style kicker in pro football, signing a contract with the Buffalo Bills of the AFL. Gogolak had 19 field goals but was overshadowed by Gino Cappelletti of Boston, who had 25, along with 38 extra points and seven touchdowns as a pass receiver to lead the league in scoring with 155 points. New York managed no better than third in the Eastern Division but set a club attendance record of 298,972 in its new stadium, despite having to play some home games on Saturday nights to avoid conflict with the baseball Mets. Three times during the season, the Jets set club single-game attendance records. Buffalo won the Eastern title by beating Boston 24-14 on the last day of the season at snow-covered Fenway Park in a near-blizzard. The Bills finished 12-2 to Boston's 10-3-1.

The AFL's reputation for wide-open football grew as San Diego's Lance Alworth became perhaps the best wide receiver in the game, and as Houston quarterback George Blanda attempted 505 passes for the season, including 68 in one game against Buffalo that the Oilers lost 24-10. Charley Hennigan caught 101 of Blanda's passes, breaking the single-season record set by Lionel Taylor of Denver in 1961.

San Diego won the West behind the pass catching of Alworth, the passing of young John Hadl, and the running of Keith Lincoln. Kansas City embarrassed the Chargers late in the season, however, beating them 49-6.

In the championship game, Cookie Gilchrist of Buffalo gained 144 yards rushing on a foggy day at War Memorial Stadium in Buffalo and the Bills defeated the Chargers 20-7.

Blanton Collier continued to build Cleveland into a powerful team. Fullback Jim Brown led the league in rushing for the seventh time in eight years and boosted his career touchdown total to 105. Frank Ryan was the Browns' quarterback and he had Gary Collins at flanker and first-round draft choice Paul Warfield at split end. Warfield caught 52 passes and the Browns held off a challenge from St. Louis to win the Eastern Conference. The Cardinals offset a victory over and a tie with the Browns with a loss to and a tie with the Giants, who fell to the worst record in the NFL.

A similar fate befell the Chicago Bears, defending Western champions. Halfback Willie Galimore and end John Farrington were killed in an auto crash near the Bears' training camp at Rensselaer, Indiana. Deprived of a running game and shaken by the accident, the Bears dropped to sixth place despite a passing attack that ranked second in the NFL, featuring Johnny Morris, who caught an NFL record 93 passes, and Mike Ditka, who set a record for tight ends with 75 receptions.

Paul Hornung of Green Bay, suspended the previous season, rejoined the Packers. Quarterback Bart Starr led the league's passers and fullback Jim Taylor had his fifth consecutive season gaining more than 1,000 yards. Minnesota became a contending team in only its fourth season, tying the Packers for second place in the West behind 22 touchdown passes by Fran Tarkenton. Alex Karras, who, like Hornung, had been suspended, rejoined Detroit.

The Baltimore Colts were the Western champions and had the best record in the NFL, 12-2. Quarterback Johnny Unitas guided the Colts' attack that included halfback Lenny Moore, who scored an NFL record 20 touchdowns.

Baltimore was favored in the title game against the surprising Browns. Cleveland, however, pulled off one of the biggest upsets in the game's history. Ryan threw three touchdown passes to Collins, and Cleveland won 27-0 before 79,544 at Cleveland Stadium. The winning and losing shares were records, $8,052 for each member of the Browns and $5,571 for each member of the Colts.

Y.A. Tittle and Andy Robustelli, two of the greatest players in Giants' history, retired.

1964 AFL STANDINGS

Eastern Division	**W**	**L**	**T**	**Pct.**	**Pts.**	**OP**
Buffalo	12	2	0	.857	400	242
Boston	10	3	1	.769	365	297
New York Jets	5	8	1	.385	278	315
Houston	4	10	0	.286	310	355
Western Division	**W**	**L**	**T**	**Pct.**	**Pts.**	**OP**
San Diego	8	5	1	.615	341	300
Kansas City	7	7	0	.500	366	306
Oakland	5	7	2	.417	303	350
Denver	2	11	1	.154	240	438

AFL championship: Buffalo 20, San Diego 7

LEADING RUSHERS	**Att.**	**Yards**	**Avg.**	**Long**	**TD**
Cookie Gilchrist, Buffalo	230	981	4.3	67	6
Matt Snell, NY Jets	215	948	4.4	42	5
Clem Daniels, Oakland	173	824	4.8	42	2
Sid Blanks, Houston	145	756	5.2	91	6
Abner Haynes, Kansas City	139	697	5.0	80	4

LEADING PASSERS	**Att.**	**Comp.**	**Yards**	**TD**	**Int.**
Len Dawson, Kansas City	354	199	2,879	30	18
Babe Parilli, Boston	473	228	3,465	31	27
George Blanda, Houston	505	262	3,287	17	27
John Hadl, San Diego	274	147	2,157	18	15
Cotton Davidson, Oakland	320	155	2,497	21	19

LEADING RECEIVERS	**No.**	**Yards**	**Avg.**	**Long**	**TD**
Charley Hennigan, Houston	101	1,546	15.3	53	8
Art Powell, Oakland	76	1,361	17.9	77	11
Lionel Taylor, Denver	76	873	11.5	57	7
Frank Jackson, Kansas City	62	943	15.2	72	9
Lance Alworth, San Diego	61	1,235	20.2	82	13

LEADING SCORER	**TD**	**FG**	**PAT**	**TP**
Gino Cappelletti, Boston	7	25	37#	155

#includes one two-point conversion

LEADING INTERCEPTOR	**No.**	**Yards**	**Avg.**	**Long**	**TD**
Dainard Paulson, NY Jets	12	157	13.1	42	1

LEADING PUNTER	**No.**	**Avg.**	**Long**
Jim Fraser, Denver	73	44.2	67

LEADING PUNT RETURNER	**No.**	**Yards**	**Avg.**	**Long**	**TD**
Bobby Jancik, Houston	12	220	18.3	82	1

LEADING KICKOFF RETURNER	**No.**	**Yards**	**Avg.**	**Long**	**TD**
Bo Roberson, Oakland	36	975	27.1	59	0

SUPERLATIVES		
Rushing average	5.5	Mack Lee Hill, Kansas City
Receiving average	27.1	Elbert Dubenion, Buffalo
Completion percentage	56.2	Len Dawson, Kansas City
Touchdowns	15	Lance Alworth, San Diego

LONGEST		
Run	91t	Sid Blanks, Houston
Pass	94t	Jack Kemp to Glenn Bass, Buffalo
Interception	98t	Pete Jaquess, Houston
Punt	79	Jim Norton, Houston
Punt return	82t	Bobby Jancik, Houston
Kickoff return	93t	Ode Burrell, Houston
Field goal	51	Gino Cappelletti, Boston Gene Mingo, Denver

1960s: A Photographic Portfolio

Paul Lowe of the Los Angeles Chargers was the number-two rusher in the AFL in 1960, with 855 yards. The Houston defender is linebacker Dennit Morris.

The first regular-season game the Cardinals played after moving to St. Louis in 1960 was against the Los Angeles Rams. Flanker Bobby Joe Conrad (returning a punt) and halfback John David Crow, former college teammates at Texas A&M, helped lead the Cardinals to a 43-21 victory in the game and a 6-5-1 season.

The new Dallas Cowboys, winless in their first 10 games, tied New York 31-31, on December 4, 1960, as Eddie LeBaron threw three touchdown passes.

One of the stars of the expansion Minnesota Vikings in 1961 was rookie halfback Tommy Mason, who had been the first selection in the 1961 NFL draft.

Lionel Taylor (87) caught 92 passes for Denver in 1960. He led the AFL in receiving five times.

Tommy McDonald was a key to the Eagles' championship in 1960; he scored 13 touchdowns.

Abner Haynes was the AFL's most valuable player as a rookie in 1960 with 875 yards rushing.

The New York Giants' defense helped carry the team to the NFL Championship Game six times between 1956 and 1963. The best-known defender was linebacker Sam Huff, but the heart of the defense was the front four, which included (from left) Andy Robustelli, Dick Modzelewski, Jim Katcavage, and Rosey Grier.

Charley Hennigan set records with 1,746 yards receiving in 1961 and with 101 receptions in 1964.

Billy Cannon (with ball) was one of the offensive stars for Houston in the 1962 AFL Championship Game, and E.J. Holub shone for the Dallas Texans' defense. The Texans won 20-17 in a game that lasted 77:54.

Charley Johnson, one of the best passers of the 1960s, led the NFL with 3,045 yards in 1964.

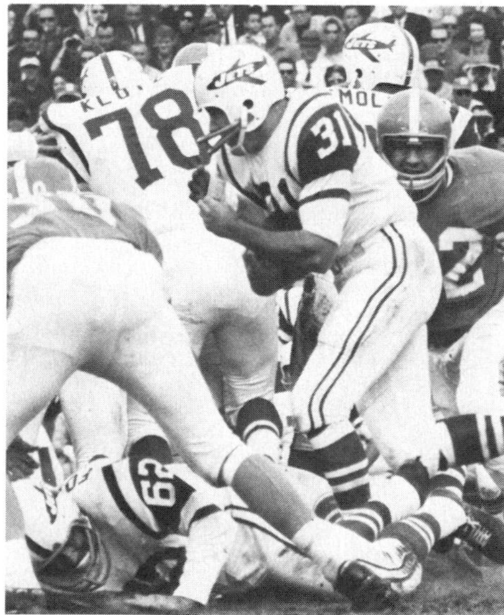

In 1963, Bill Mathis (31) was an outstanding runner for the renamed and re-helmeted New York Jets.

Billy Shaw (66) leading for Cookie Gilchrist was one of the most feared sights in the early AFL.

Timmy Brown (22) of the Philadelphia Eagles was one of the most versatile halfbacks of the 1960s. In Brown's best season—1965—he led the NFL with a 5.4-yard rushing average and made 50 pass receptions.

Flanker Johnny Morris of the Chicago Bears set an NFL record with 93 receptions in 1964.

San Diego had two of the AFL's best defensive linemen. Ernie Ladd (77) and Earl Faison (86) helped the Chargers to five championship games.

There were many reasons for Jim Brown's success in Cleveland. Two of the more important ones were guards Gene Hickerson (66) and John Wooten (60).

The Atlanta Falcons weren't overly successful (3-11) in their initial season (1966). They did, however, unveil the NFL's top draft selection—Tommy Nobis of Texas—who became an almost-immediate all-pro and was one of the best linebackers ever to play the game. Nobis is shown stopping Ken Willard of the 49ers.

Bob Griese had a trying season as a rookie in 1967, but he later led the Dolphins to three Super Bowls.

Fullback Jim Nance of Boston set the AFL rushing record with 1,458 yards in 1966.

Late in his career, John Mackey of the Colts already was considered the best tight end ever.

Bob Hayes brought a new dimension to the Dallas offense and became one of the most-feared receivers of all-time. The ''world's fastest human,'' Hayes led the league in average per reception as a rookie. He led the NFL (or NFC) in touchdown catches in 1965, 1966, and 1971, and in punt returns in 1968.

Daryle Lamonica, the AFL's most valuable player in 1967 and 1969, led the league in passing both those years and led Oakland to Super Bowl II.

John Gilliam (with ball) returned the opening kickoff 94 yards for a touchdown against the Rams in the Saints' first regular-season game, September 17, 1967.

In the 1967 NFL Championship Game, nicknamed the Ice Bowl, Don Meredith (rolling out behind tackle Ralph Neely) had the Cowboys ahead until Bart Starr's touchdown won it 21-17 for Green Bay.

Leroy Kelly of Cleveland succeeded Jim Brown and became one of the best runners ever in the NFL.

If injuries hadn't ended Greg Cook's career with Cincinnati prematurely, he might be remembered as one of the best passers ever.

Matt Snell's powerful running and Joe Namath's (12) passing led the New York Jets to the greatest upset of all-time, 16-7 over Baltimore in Super Bowl III.

1964 NFL STANDINGS

Eastern Conference	W	L	T	Pct.	Pts.	OP
Cleveland	10	3	1	.769	415	293
St. Louis	9	3	2	.750	357	331
Philadelphia	6	8	0	.429	312	313
Washington	6	8	0	.429	307	305
Dallas	5	8	1	.385	250	289
Pittsburgh	5	9	0	.357	253	315
New York Giants	2	10	2	.167	241	399
Western Conference	**W**	**L**	**T**	**Pct.**	**Pts.**	**OP**
Baltimore	12	2	0	.857	428	225
Green Bay	8	5	1	.615	342	245
Minnesota	8	5	1	.615	355	296
Detroit	7	5	2	.583	280	260
Los Angeles Rams	5	7	2	.417	283	339
Chicago Bears	5	9	0	.357	260	379
San Francisco	4	10	0	.286	236	330

NFL championship: Cleveland 27, Baltimore 0

LEADING RUSHERS	Att.	Yards	Avg.	Long	TD
Jim Brown, Cleveland	280	1,446	5.2	71	7
Jim Taylor, Green Bay	235	1,169	5.0	84t	12
John Henry Johnson, Pittsburgh	235	1,048	4.5	45t	7
Bill Brown, Minnesota	226	866	3.8	48	7
Don Perkins, Dallas	174	768	4.4	59	6

LEADING PASSERS	Att.	Comp.	Yards	TD	Int.
Bart Starr, Green Bay	272	163	2,144	15	4
Fran Tarkenton, Minnesota	306	171	2,506	22	11
Sonny Jurgensen, Washington	385	207	2,934	24	13
Johnny Unitas, Baltimore	305	158	2,824	19	6
Milt Plum, Detroit	287	154	2,241	18	15

LEADING RECEIVERS	No.	Yards	Avg.	Long	TD
Johnny Morris, Chi. Bears	93	1,200	12.9	63t	10
Mike Ditka, Chi. Bears	75	897	12.0	34	5
Frank Clarke, Dallas	65	973	15.0	49	5
Bobby Joe Conrad, St. Louis	61	780	12.8	53	6
Bobby Mitchell, Washington	60	904	15.1	60	10

LEADING SCORER	TD	FG	PAT	TP
Lenny Moore, Baltimore	20	0	0	120

LEADING INTERCEPTOR	No.	Yards	Avg.	Long	TD
Paul Krause, Washington	12	140	11.7	35t	1

LEADING PUNTER	No.	Avg.	Long
Bobby Walden, Minnesota	72	46.4	73

LEADING PUNT RETURNER	No.	Yards	Avg.	Long	TD
Tommy Watkins, Detroit	16	238	14.9	68t	2

LEADING KICKOFF RETURNER	No.	Yards	Avg.	Long	TD
Clarence Childs, NY Giants	34	987	29.0	100t	1

SUPERLATIVES		
Rushing average	5.2	Jim Brown, Cleveland
Receiving average	19.9	Gary Ballman, Philadelphia
Completion percentage	61.9	Rudy Bukich, Chi. Bears
Touchdowns	20	Lenny Moore, Baltimore

LONGEST		
Run	84t	Jim Taylor, Green Bay
Pass	95t	Bill Munson to Bucky Pope, LA Rams
Interception	97t	Bobby Smith, LA Rams
Punt	75	Billy Lothridge, Dallas
Punt return	90	Brady Keys, Pittsburgh
Kickoff return	100t	Clarence Childs, NY Giants
Field goal	53	Tommy Davis, San Francisco

1965 In January, Sonny Werblin signed quarterback Joe Namath of Alabama to a record contract reported to be $400,000 a year. The Jets also signed Heisman Trophy-winner John Huarte of Notre Dame. Namath was the most talked-about member of an exceptional class of rookies that also included halfback Gale Sayers and linebacker Dick Butkus of the Bears, end Bob Hayes of the Cowboys, end Fred Biletnikoff of the Raiders, and fullback Ken Willard of the 49ers.

Raymond (Buddy) Parker quit as coach of the Steelers and George Wilson as coach of the Lions. They were succeeded by Mike Nixon and Harry Gilmer, respectively.

CBS signed a new television contract with the NFL calling for $18.8 million a year, plus $2 million for the championship game. The network also received permission to telecast three night games in prime time and also to modify the blackout so that one game could be seen in a city when the club was home.

Over the summer, each league decided to expand. The NFL added Atlanta and the AFL added Miami, both for 1966.

NFL rules were changed increasing the number of officials for each game from five to six; the sixth official was called the line judge. Officials' penalty flags were changed in color from white to bright gold.

The Houston Oilers, who had been playing their home games at Jeppesen Stadium, a 38,000-seat high school facility, announced they would not play in the new Astrodome because of "an unrealistic lease agreement" and signed a five-year lease for the use of 70,000-seat Rice Stadium.

Buffalo and San Diego repeated as champions of their divisions in the AFL, the Bills by five games over the Jets, and the Chargers with a season-closing victory over second-place Oakland. Namath took over as the Jets' starter and threw 18 touchdown passes; wide receiver Don Maynard caught 14 touchdown passes for the Jets, the same number Lance Alworth had for the Chargers. Alworth had 1,602 yards receiving, the second-most ever, and a 23.2-yard average.

Buffalo won the title game for the second year in a row, shutting out San Diego 23-0.

Jim Brown's ninth season for Cleveland was another great one but the Browns got a challenge from the Dallas Cowboys in the Eastern Conference for the first time. Dallas reached .500 with a 7-7 record. Quarterback Don Meredith threw 22 touchdown passes and brilliant rookie split end Bob Hayes caught 46 for 1,003 yards and 12 touchdowns.

Chicago finished third in the Western Conference but halfback Gale Sayers was almost unstoppable. He scored six touchdowns in one game against San Francisco and had a record 22 for the year.

Norm Van Brocklin quit as coach of the Vikings in midseason, then changed his mind and returned a few days later.

Green Bay and Baltimore were the Western Conference's best teams but wound up deadlocked. The Packers missed a chance to clinch the title when they were tied by the 49ers on the last day of the season. The Colts went through a difficult season, losing quarterback Johnny Unitas with a knee injury and his replacement, Gary Cuozzo, with a shoulder separation. Halfback Tom Matte, who had played quarterback in college at Ohio State, took over the position for Baltimore and, reading his plays off a wristband, led the Colts to a victory over Los Angeles. That set up a playoff against the Packers at Green Bay. Matte again was the makeshift quarterback for the Colts, and the Packers' starter, Bart Starr, was injured early in the game and replaced by Zeke Bratkowski. The Colts argued unsuccessfully that a field goal by Don Chandler that tied the game 10-10 in the fourth quarter was wide of the goal posts. The teams played 13 minutes and 39 seconds of sudden-death overtime before another field goal by Chandler won the game 13-10 for Green Bay.

Wintry Green Bay was the site of the title game between the Packers and Browns. A morning storm made roads nearly impassable, delayed the arrival of the Browns, and sent a work crew using shovels and snow plows into action. Playing on the muddy turf, the Packers used their ball-control game, with Paul Hornung gaining 105 yards and Jim Taylor 96, while Jim Brown was held to 50 in a 23-12 Green Bay victory, its third NFL championship under coach Vince Lombardi.

Except for the Pro Bowl it was the last game for Cleveland's Brown. He left behind a career total of 12,312 yards rushing, seven 1,000-yard seasons, 58 100-yard games, four 200-yard games, a career average of 5.2 yards per rush, and 126 touchdowns.

Brown ended his career appropriately in the Pro Bowl, scoring three touchdowns and winning the outstanding back award in the East's 36-7 victory.

After the season, the AFL All-Star game ran into trouble in New Orleans when some players charged they were racially discriminated against. The game was shifted to Houston.

Two men who played important roles in NFL history died. They were Earl (Curly) Lambeau, founder and former coach of the Green Bay Packers, and Jack Mara, co-owner of the New York Giants.

1965 AFL STANDINGS

Eastern Division	W	L	T	Pct.	Pts.	OP
Buffalo	10	3	1	.769	313	226
New York Jets	5	8	1	.385	285	303
Boston	4	8	2	.333	244	302
Houston	4	10	0	.286	298	429
Western Division	**W**	**L**	**T**	**Pct.**	**Pts.**	**OP**
San Diego	9	2	3	.818	340	227
Oakland	8	5	1	.615	298	239
Kansas City	7	5	2	.583	322	285
Denver	4	10	0	.286	303	392

AFL championship: Buffalo 23, San Diego 0

LEADING RUSHERS	Att.	Yards	Avg.	Long	TD
Paul Lowe, San Diego	222	1,121	5.0	59	7
Cookie Gilchrist, Denver	252	954	3.8	44	6
Clem Daniels, Oakland	219	884	4.0	57	5
Matt Snell, NY Jets	169	763	4.5	44	4
Curtis McClinton, Kansas City	175	661	3.8	48	6

LEADING PASSERS	Att.	Comp.	Yards	TD	Int.
John Hadl, San Diego	348	174	2,798	20	21
Len Dawson, Kansas City	305	163	2,262	21	14
Joe Namath, NY Jets	340	164	2,220	18	15
Jack Kemp, Buffalo	391	179	2,368	10	18
George Blanda, Houston	442	186	2,542	20	30

LEADING RECEIVERS	No.	Yards	Avg.	Long	TD
Lionel Taylor, Denver	85	1,131	13.3	63	6
Lance Alworth, San Diego	69	1,602	23.2	85	14
Don Maynard, NY Jets	68	1,218	17.9	56	14
Ode Burrell, Houston	55	650	11.8	52	4
Art Powell, Oakland	52	800	15.4	66	12

LEADING SCORER	TD	FG	PAT	TP
Gino Cappelletti, Boston	9	17	27	132

LEADING INTERCEPTOR	No.	Yards	Avg.	Long	TD
W.K. Hicks, Houston	9	156	17.3	31	0

LEADING PUNTER	No.	Avg.	Long
Jerrel Wilson, Kansas City	69	45.4	64

LEADING PUNT RETURNER	No.	Yards	Avg.	Long	TD
Speedy Duncan, San Diego	30	464	15.5	66	2

LEADING KICKOFF RETURNER	No.	Yards	Avg.	Long	TD
Abner Haynes, Denver	34	901	26.5	60	0

SUPERLATIVES		
Rushing average	5.0	Paul Lowe, San Diego
Receiving average	23.2	Lance Alworth, San Diego
Completion percentage	53.4	Len Dawson, Kansas City
Touchdowns	14	Lance Alworth, San Diego Don Maynard, NY Jets

LONGEST		
Run	80t	Wray Carlton, Buffalo
Pass	95t	George Blanda to Dick Compton, Houston
Interception	79t	Dave Grayson, Oakland
Punt	79	Jim Norton, Houston
Punt return	82t	Bobby Jancik, Houston
Kickoff return	102t	Charley Warner, Buffalo
Field goal	53	Gino Cappelletti, Boston

1965 NFL STANDINGS

Eastern Conference	W	L	T	Pct.	Pts.	OP
Cleveland	11	3	0	.786	363	325
Dallas	7	7	0	.500	325	280
New York Giants	7	7	0	.500	270	338
Washington	6	8	0	.429	257	301
Philadelphia	5	9	0	.357	363	359
St. Louis	5	9	0	.357	296	309
Pittsburgh	2	12	0	.143	202	397
Western Conference	**W**	**L**	**T**	**Pct.**	**Pts.**	**OP**
Green Bay	10	3	1	.769	316	224
Baltimore	10	3	1	.769	389	284
Chicago Bears	9	5	0	.643	409	275
San Francisco	7	6	1	.538	421	402
Minnesota	7	7	0	.500	383	403
Detroit	6	7	1	.462	257	295
Los Angeles Rams	4	10	0	.286	269	328

Western Conference playoff: Green Bay 13, Baltimore 10, overtime

NFL championship: Green Bay 23, Cleveland 12

LEADING RUSHERS	Att.	Yards	Avg.	Long	TD
Jim Brown, Cleveland	289	1,544	5.3	67	17
Gale Sayers, Chi. Bears	166	867	5.2	61t	14
Timmy Brown, Philadelphia	158	861	5.4	54t	6
Ken Willard, San Francisco	189	778	4.1	32	5
Jim Taylor, Green Bay	207	734	3.5	35	4

LEADING PASSERS	Att.	Comp.	Yards	TD	Int.
Rudy Bukich, Chi. Bears	312	176	2,641	20	9
Johnny Unitas, Baltimore	282	164	2,530	23	12
John Brodie, San Francisco	391	242	3,112	30	16
Bart Starr, Green Bay	251	140	2,055	16	9
Earl Morrall, NY Giants	302	155	2,446	22	12

LEADING RECEIVERS	No.	Yards	Avg.	Long	TD
Dave Parks, San Francisco	80	1,344	16.8	53t	12
Tommy McDonald, LA Rams	67	1,036	15.5	51	9
Pete Retzlaff, Philadelphia	66	1,190	18.0	78	10
Bobby Mitchell, Washington	60	867	14.5	80t	6
Bernie Casey, San Francisco	59	765	13.0	59t	8

LEADING SCORER	TD	FG	PAT	TP
Gale Sayers, Chi. Bears	22	0	0	132

LEADING INTERCEPTOR	No.	Yards	Avg.	Long	TD
Bobby Boyd, Baltimore	9	78	8.7	24	1

LEADING PUNTER	No.	Avg.	Long
Gary Collins, Cleveland	65	46.7	71

LEADING PUNT RETURNER	No.	Yards	Avg.	Long	TD
Leroy Kelly, Cleveland	17	265	15.6	67t	2

LEADING KICKOFF RETURNER	No.	Yards	Avg.	Long	TD
Tommy Watkins, Detroit	17	584	34.4	94	0

SUPERLATIVES

Rushing average	5.4	Timmy Brown, Philadelphia
Receiving average	21.8	Bob Hayes, Dallas
Completion percentage	61.9	John Brodie, San Francisco
Touchdowns	22	Gale Sayers, Chi. Bears

LONGEST

Run	67	Jim Brown, Cleveland
Pass	89t	Earl Morrall to Homer Jones, NY Giants
Interception	96t	Larry Wilson, St. Louis
Punt	90	Don Chandler, Green Bay
Punt return	85t	Gale Sayers, Chi. Bears
Kickoff return	101t	Lance Rentzel, Minnesota
Field goal	53	Fred Cox, Minnesota
		Tommy Davis, San Francisco

1966 What was perhaps the most eventful year for pro football since 1920 started off with a bang. On January 2, Lou Saban, the coach of AFL champion Buffalo, resigned to become head coach at Maryland. Saban was replaced by Joe Collier. Before the season, six other pro coaches were hired: George Allen with the Rams (succeeding Harland Svare), Johnny Rauch in Oakland (Al Davis), Charley Winner in St. Louis (Wally Lemm), Lemm in Houston (Hugh Taylor), Otto Graham in Washington (Bill McPeak), and Bill Austin in Pittsburgh (Mike Nixon).

The AFL and NFL spent a combined total of $7 million to sign 1966 draft choices. Three NFL rookies—Donny Anderson and Jim Grabowski of Green Bay and Tommy Nobis of Atlanta—each signed contracts more lucrative than that Joe Namath had signed in 1965 with the Jets.

The NFL signed 75 percent of its 232 draftees, the AFL 46 percent of its 181. Of 111 common draft choices, 79 signed with the NFL, 28 with the AFL, and 4 went unsigned.

The heat of the war was turned up in April, after the Giants signed kicker Pete Gogolak, who had become a free agent after playing with the Bills. On April 7, Joe Foss resigned as AFL Commissioner. The next day, Foss was replaced by Al Davis, the coach and general manager of the Raiders. An all-out effort was begun to raid NFL teams, taking star players and particularly quarterbacks. John Brodie of San Francisco, Roman Gabriel of Los Angeles, and tight end Mike Ditka of Chicago were the first NFL players to sign with the AFL. With the cost of signing college players already skyrocketing, the specter of having to bid for the services of established pros brought visions of bankruptcy to NFL owners.

Meanwhile, Lamar Hunt of Kansas City and Tex Schramm of Dallas held a series of secret meetings discussing the possibility of a merger. On June 8, NFL Commissioner Pete Rozelle announced a merger of the AFL and NFL. Under the agreement, the two leagues would combine to form an expanded league with 24 teams, expanding to 26 teams by 1968 and to 28 by 1970 or shortly thereafter. All existing franchises would be retained, and no franchise would be transferred. While maintaining separate schedules through 1969, the two leagues agreed to play a yearly championship game beginning in January, 1967, and to hold a combined draft, also beginning in 1967. Preseason games would be held between teams of each league starting in 1967, and official regular-season play would start in 1970, when the two leagues officially would merge to form one league with two conferences. Rozelle was named Commissioner of the expanded league setup.

Before the 1966 season, several other changes occurred. In July, Al Davis resigned as AFL commissioner and returned to Oakland, with Milt Woodard becoming the AFL president. The next month Barron Hilton sold the San Diego Chargers for $10 million to a group headed by Eugene Klein and Samuel Schulman.

When the leagues lined up for regular-season play, there were two new teams, the first two ever in the Deep South. The Atlanta Falcons, owned by Rankin Smith, were in the NFL, and the Miami Dolphins, owned by Minneapolis attorney Joe Robbie and entertainer Danny Thomas, were in the AFL. The Falcons were placed in the Eastern Conference for purposes of standings, but played a round-robin schedule in which they met every other NFL team. The Dolphins also were in the Eastern Division. Another team, the Raiders, had a new stadium, as Oakland-Alameda County Coliseum opened for football.

In October, Congress approved the merger, passing special legislation exempting the agreement between the AFL and NFL from antitrust action. The next month, New Orleans was selected as the sixteenth NFL franchise city, and the franchise subsequently was awarded to a group of 19 businessmen headed by John Mecom, Jr. With the entry of New Orleans, the NFL owners voted to realign into four four-team divisions for the 1967 through 1969 seasons.

On the field, Kansas City dominated the AFL. With Len Dawson leading the league in passing, rookie Mike Garrett in rushing average, and the defense in interceptions, the Chiefs won the West by three games. In the East, Buffalo, featuring rookie of the year halfback Bobby Burnett, edged Boston by half a game when the Patriots lost the season finale to the Jets. Boston's fullback, Jim Nance, set an AFL record with 1,458 yards rushing. Miami got off to a fast start when Joe Auer returned the opening kickoff of the Dolphins' first game for a touchdown. Despite going though five quarterbacks, the Dolphins won three games.

In the AFL Championship Game, the Chiefs overwhelmed the two-time defending champion Bills 31-7 to qualify for the first AFL-NFL World Championship Game.

In the NFL, Green Bay used the league's top defense, top passer (Bart Starr), and leading active rusher (Jim Taylor) to build the best record in football (12-2) and win the Western Conference title. Dallas came of age in the East, edging Cleveland for the title and becoming the first expansion team ever to win a division or conference championship. The Cowboys offset the Browns' Leroy Kelly with a sound pair of backs, Dan Reeves and Don Perkins, and a passing game that featured Don Meredith and Bob Hayes.

The experience of the Packers proved too much in the NFL Championship Game. Tom Brown intercepted Meredith's pass in the Green Bay end zone during the waning moments of the game to preserve a 34-27 Green Bay victory.

The Los Angeles Memorial Coliseum was the site for the first AFL-NFL World Championship Game (the name Super Bowl was not yet official for the event). Both CBS and NBC broadcast the game, which was not a sellout (63,035 attended). Green Bay held a 14-10 lead at halftime and broke the game open in the second half to win 35-10. The player of the game was Bart Starr, who threw two touchdown passes to end Max McGee.

1966 AFL STANDINGS

Eastern Division	W	L	T	Pct.	Pts.	OP
Buffalo	9	4	1	.692	358	255
Boston	8	4	2	.667	315	283
New York Jets	6	6	2	.500	322	312
Houston	3	11	0	.214	335	396
Miami	3	11	0	.214	213	362
Western Division	**W**	**L**	**T**	**Pct.**	**Pts.**	**OP**
Kansas City	11	2	1	.846	448	276
Oakland	8	5	1	.615	315	288
San Diego	7	6	1	.538	335	284
Denver	4	10	0	.286	196	381

AFL championship: Kansas City 31, Buffalo 7

LEADING RUSHERS	Att.	Yards	Avg.	Long	TD
Jim Nance, Boston	299	1,458	4.9	65	11
Mike Garrett, Kansas City	147	801	5.4	77	6
Clem Daniels, Oakland	204	801	3.9	64	7
Bobby Burnett, Buffalo	187	766	4.1	32	4
Wray Carlton, Buffalo	156	696	4.5	23	6

LEADING PASSERS	Att.	Comp.	Yards	TD	Int.
Len Dawson, Kansas City	284	159	2,527	26	10
John Hadl, San Diego	375	200	2,846	23	14
Tom Flores, Oakland	306	151	2,638	24	14
Joe Namath, NY Jets	471	232	3,379	19	27
Babe Parilli, Boston	382	181	2,721	20	20

LEADING RECEIVERS	No.	Yards	Avg.	Long	TD
Lance Alworth, San Diego	73	1,383	18.9	78	13
George Sauer, NY Jets	63	1,079	17.1	77	5
Otis Taylor, Kansas City	58	1,297	22.4	89	8
Chris Burford, Kansas City	58	758	13.1	38	8
Willie Frazier, Houston	57	1,129	19.8	79	12

LEADING SCORER	TD	FG	PAT	TP
Gino Cappelletti, Boston	6	16	35	119

LEADING INTERCEPTORS	No.	Yards	Avg.	Long	TD
Johnny Robinson, Kansas City	10	136	13.6	29	1
Bobby Hunt, Kansas City	10	113	11.3	33	0

LEADING PUNTER	No.	Avg.	Long
Bob Scarpitto, Denver	76	45.8	70

LEADING PUNT RETURNER	No.	Yards	Avg.	Long	TD
Speedy Duncan, San Diego	18	238	13.2	81	1

LEADING KICKOFF RETURNER	No.	Yards	Avg.	Long	TD
Goldie Sellers, Denver	19	541	28.5	100	2

SUPERLATIVES

Rushing average	5.4	Mike Garrett, Kansas City
Receiving average	22.4	Otis Taylor, Kansas City
Completion percentage	56.0	Len Dawson, Kansas City
Touchdowns	13	Lance Alworth, San Diego

LONGEST

Run	77t	Mike Garrett, Kansas City
Pass	89t	Len Dawson to Otis Taylor, Kansas City
Interception	87	Ron Hall, Boston
Punt	70	Bob Scarpitto, Denver
Punt return	81t	Speedy Duncan, San Diego
Kickoff return	100t	Goldie Sellers, Denver
		Nemiah Wilson, Denver
Field goal	51	George Blanda, Houston

1966 NFL STANDINGS

Eastern Conference	W	L	T	Pct.	Pts.	OP
Dallas	10	3	1	.769	445	239
Cleveland	9	5	0	.643	403	259
Philadelphia	9	5	0	.643	326	340
St. Louis	8	5	1	.615	264	265
Washington	7	7	0	.500	351	355
Pittsburgh	5	8	1	.385	316	347
Atlanta	3	11	0	.214	204	437
New York Giants	1	12	1	.077	263	501
Western Conference	**W**	**L**	**T**	**Pct.**	**Pts.**	**OP**
Green Bay	12	2	0	.857	335	163
Baltimore	9	5	0	.643	314	226
Los Angeles Rams	8	6	0	.571	289	212
San Francisco	6	6	2	.500	320	325
Chicago Bears	5	7	2	.417	234	272
Detroit	4	9	1	.308	206	317
Minnesota	4	9	1	.308	292	304

NFL championship: Green Bay 34, Dallas 27
Super Bowl I: Green Bay (NFL) 35, Kansas City (AFL) 10

LEADING RUSHERS	Att.	Yards	Avg.	Long	TD
Gale Sayers, Chi. Bears	229	1,231	5.4	58t	8
Leroy Kelly, Cleveland	209	1,141	5.5	70t	15
Dick Bass, LA Rams	248	1,090	4.4	50	8
Bill Brown, Minnesota	251	829	3.3	33t	6
Ken Willard, San Francisco	191	763	4.0	49	5

LEADING PASSERS	Att.	Comp.	Yards	TD	Int.
Bart Starr, Green Bay	251	156	2,257	14	3
Sonny Jurgensen, Washington	436	254	3,209	28	19
Frank Ryan, Cleveland	382	200	2,974	29	14
Don Meredith, Dallas	344	177	2,805	24	12
Johnny Unitas, Baltimore	348	195	2,748	22	24

LEADING RECEIVERS	No.	Yards	Avg.	Long	TD
Charley Taylor, Washington	72	1,119	15.5	86t	12
Pat Studstill, Detroit	67	1,266	18.9	99t	5
Dave Parks, San Francisco	66	974	14.8	65t	5
Bob Hayes, Dallas	64	1,232	19.3	95t	13
Tom Moore, LA Rams	60	433	7.2	30t	3

LEADING SCORER	TD	FG	PAT	TP
Bruce Gossett, LA Rams	0	28	29	113

LEADING INTERCEPTOR	No.	Yards	Avg.	Long	TD
Larry Wilson, St. Louis	10	180	18.0	91t	2

LEADING PUNTER	No.	Avg.	Long
David Lee, Baltimore	49	45.6	64

LEADING PUNT RETURNER	No.	Yards	Avg.	Long	TD
Johnny Roland, St. Louis	20	221	11.1	86t	1

LEADING KICKOFF RETURNER	No.	Yards	Avg.	Long	TD
Gale Sayers, Chi. Bears	23	718	31.2	93t	2

SUPERLATIVES

Rushing average	5.5	Leroy Kelly, Cleveland
Receiving average	21.8	Homer Jones, NY Giants

Completion percentage	62.2	Bart Starr, Green Bay
Touchdowns	16	Leroy Kelly, Cleveland
		Dan Reeves, Dallas
LONGEST		
Run	70t	Leroy Kelly, Cleveland
Pass	99t	Karl Sweetan to Pat Studstill, Detroit
Interception	101t	Henry Carr, NY Giants
Punt	70	Bobby Walden, Minnesota
Punt return	86t	Johnny Roland, St. Louis
Kickoff return	94t	Roy Shivers, St. Louis
	94	Dick Gordon, Chi. Bears
Field goal	51	Sam Baker, Philadelphia

1967 The NFL had four divisions for the first time. Its 16 teams were divided into the Century and Capitol divisions of the Eastern Conference and the Central and Coastal divisions of the Western Conference. New Orleans began play in the Capitol Division with Tom Fears as its head coach. Cincinnati was awarded a franchise as the tenth AFL team, to begin competition in 1968. Paul Brown, former head coach of the Browns, was head coach, general manager, and part owner of the new club.

The first combined AFL-NFL draft was held March 14. The Baltimore Colts traded with New Orleans for the first pick and chose defensive end Bubba Smith of Michigan State. Running backs Floyd Little of Denver and Mel Farr of Detroit, linebacker George Webster of Houston, cornerback Lem Barney of Detroit, quarterback Bob Griese of Miami, and guard Gene Upshaw of Oakland were other notable rookies.

Coach Norm Van Brocklin and quarterback Fran Tarkenton of Minnesota had a falling out. Van Brocklin quit as coach and was replaced by Bud Grant. Tarkenton was traded to the Giants.

The San Diego Chargers moved into the new San Diego Stadium.

An NFL team lost to an AFL team for the first time when Denver beat Detroit 13-7 in a preseason game August 5.

Quarterback Daryle Lamonica led the Oakland Raiders to a 13-1 record and the AFL West title. Lamonica, who had been a reserve at Buffalo, led the AFL in passing with 3,228 yards and 30 touchdowns. George Blanda, 39 years old, signed as a free agent after being released by Houston and became the Raiders' kicker and Lamonica's backup at quarterback. Houston, with a bruising ground game led by Hoyle Granger, took the Eastern title despite a great year by quarterback Joe Namath for the New York Jets. Namath had 4,007 yards and 26 touchdowns passing. Oakland whipped Houston 40-7 in the championship game.

Green Bay won the NFL Central Division with the league's best defense and with rookie Travis Williams setting a record by running back four kickoffs for touchdowns. In the Coastal Division, the Rams and Colts tied for the league's best record at 11-1-2. The two teams tied early in the season, but, in the last game of the year, the Rams destroyed the previously unbeaten Colts 34-10 to win the title. The Packers beat the Rams 28-7 for the Western Conference title.

Dallas won the Capitol and Cleveland the Century Division, each by comfortable margins. Sonny Jurgensen of Washington completed 288 passes for 3,747 yards (both NFL records), Jim Bakken of St. Louis kicked seven field goals in one game against Pittsburgh, and Leroy Kelly of the Browns led the league in rushing. In the Eastern Conference title game, the Cowboys won a one-sided 52-14 victory over Cleveland.

Lambeau Field in Green Bay was the site for the title game. The temperature was 13 degrees below zero and the wind chill 40 below. Trailing 17-14 with 13 seconds to play, the Packers scored when quarterback Bart Starr went over on a one-yard sneak behind a tremendous block by guard Jerry Kramer on Dallas defensive tackle Jethro Pugh. Later, Lombardi said he had passed up an almost sure field goal in favor of the sneak for the touchdown because, "I couldn't see going for a tie and making all those people in the stands suffer through sudden death in this weather."

The temperature was 65 degrees, 78 higher than it had been two weeks earlier in Green Bay, when the Packers beat Oakland 33-14 at the Orange Bowl in Miami in the second AFL-NFL World Championship Game. Don Chandler kicked four field goals for the Packers and Starr directed an offense that ran up 325 yards.

It was Lombardi's second consecutive world championship, coming on the heels of his third straight NFL championship. He stunned the football world by announcing his retirement as Packers' head coach.

George Halas, 73, also retired for the fourth and last time as head coach of the Bears.

End Raymond Berry and guard Jim Parker of the Colts, kicker Lou Groza of the Browns (for the second time), fullback Jim Taylor of the Saints, and center Jim Ringo of the Eagles were notable players who retired from football.

1967 AFL STANDINGS

Eastern Division	**W**	**L**	**T**	**Pct.**	**Pts.**	**OP**
Houston	9	4	1	.692	258	199
New York Jets	8	5	1	.615	371	329
Buffalo	4	10	0	.286	237	285
Miami	4	10	0	.286	219	407
Boston	3	10	1	.231	280	389
Western Division	**W**	**L**	**T**	**Pct.**	**Pts.**	**OP**
Oakland	13	1	0	.929	468	233
Kansas City	9	5	0	.643	408	254
San Diego	8	5	1	.615	360	352
Denver	3	11	0	.214	256	409

AFL championship: Oakland 40, Houston 7

LEADING RUSHERS	**Att.**	**Yards**	**Avg.**	**Long**	**TD**
Jim Nance, Boston	269	1,216	4.5	53	7
Hoyle Granger, Houston	236	1,194	5.1	67	6
Mike Garrett, Kansas City	236	1,087	4.6	58	9
Dickie Post, San Diego	161	663	4.1	67t	7
Brad Hubbert, San Diego	116	643	5.5	80t	2
LEADING PASSERS	**Att.**	**Comp.**	**Yards**	**TD**	**Int.**
Daryle Lamonica, Oakland	425	220	3,228	30	20
Len Dawson, Kansas City	357	206	2,651	24	17
Joe Namath, NY Jets	491	258	4,007	26	28
John Hadl, San Diego	427	217	3,365	24	22
Bob Griese, Miami	331	166	2,005	15	18
LEADING RECEIVERS	**No.**	**Yards**	**Avg.**	**Long**	**TD**
George Sauer, NY Jets	75	1,189	15.9	61t	6
Don Maynard, NY Jets	71	1,434	20.2	75t	10
Jack Clancy, Miami	67	868	13.0	44t	2
Otis Taylor, Kansas City	59	958	16.2	71t	11
Hewritt Dixon, Oakland	59	563	9.5	48	2
LEADING SCORER	**TD**	**FG**	**PAT**		**TP**
George Blanda, Oakland	0	20	56		116
LEADING INTERCEPTORS	**No.**	**Yards**	**Avg.**	**Long**	**TD**
Miller Farr, Houston	10	264	26.4	67	3
Tom Janik, Buffalo	10	222	22.2	46	2
Dick Westmoreland, Miami	10	127	12.7	29	1
LEADING PUNTER	**No.**		**Avg.**		**Long**
Bob Scarpitto, Denver	105		44.9		73
LEADING PUNT RETURNER	**No.**	**Yards**	**Avg.**	**Long**	**TD**
Floyd Little, Denver	16	270	16.9	72t	1
LEADING KICKOFF RETURNER	**No.**	**Yards**	**Avg.**	**Long**	**TD**
Zeke Moore, Houston	14	405	28.9	92t	1

SUPERLATIVES		
Rushing average	5.5	Brad Hubbert, San Diego
Receiving average	20.2	Don Maynard, NY Jets
Completion percentage	57.7	Len Dawson, Kansas City
Touchdowns	13	Emerson Boozer, NY Jets
LONGEST		
Run	80t	Brad Hubbert, San Diego
Pass	79t	Babe Parilli to Art Graham, Boston
Interception	100t	Speedy Duncan, San Diego
Punt	73	Bob Scarpitto, Denver
Punt return	78	Rodger Bird, Oakland
Kickoff return	106t	Noland Smith, Kansas City
Field goal	54	Jan Stenerud, Kansas City

1967 NFL STANDINGS

EASTERN CONFERENCE

Capitol Division	**W**	**L**	**T**	**Pct.**	**Pts.**	**OP**
Dallas	9	5	0	.643	342	268
Philadelphia	6	7	1	.462	351	409
Washington	5	6	3	.455	347	353
New Orleans	3	11	0	.214	233	379
Century Division	**W**	**L**	**T**	**Pct.**	**Pts.**	**OP**
Cleveland	9	5	0	.643	334	297
New York Giants	7	7	0	.500	369	379
St. Louis	6	7	1	.462	333	356
Pittsburgh	4	9	1	.308	281	320
WESTERN CONFERENCE						
Coastal Division	**W**	**L**	**T**	**Pct.**	**Pts.**	**OP**
Los Angeles Rams	11	1	2	.917	398	196
Baltimore	11	1	2	.917	394	198
San Francisco	7	7	0	.500	273	337
Atlanta	1	12	1	.077	175	422
Central Division	**W**	**L**	**T**	**Pct.**	**Pts.**	**OP**
Green Bay	9	4	1	.692	332	209
Chicago Bears	7	6	1	.538	239	218
Detroit	5	7	2	.417	260	259
Minnesota	3	8	3	.273	233	294

Conference championships: Dallas 52, Cleveland 14; Green Bay 28, Los Angeles Rams 7

NFL championship: Green Bay 21, Dallas 17

Super Bowl II: Green Bay (NFL) 33, Oakland (AFL) 14

LEADING RUSHERS	**Att.**	**Yards**	**Avg.**	**Long**	**TD**
Leroy Kelly, Cleveland	235	1,205	5.1	42t	11
Dave Osborn, Minnesota	215	972	4.5	73	2
Gale Sayers, Chi. Bears	186	880	4.7	70	7
Johnny Roland, St. Louis	234	876	3.7	70	10
Mel Farr, Detroit	206	860	4.2	57	3
LEADING PASSERS	**Att.**	**Comp.**	**Yards**	**TD**	**Int.**
Sonny Jurgensen, Washington	508	288	3,747	31	16
Johnny Unitas, Baltimore	436	255	3,428	20	16
Fran Tarkenton, NY Giants	377	204	3,088	29	19
Roman Gabriel, LA Rams	371	196	2,779	25	13
Norm Snead, Philadelphia	434	240	3,399	29	24
LEADING RECEIVERS	**No.**	**Yards**	**Avg.**	**Long**	**TD**
Charley Taylor, Washington	70	990	14.1	86t	9
Jerry Smith, Washington	67	849	12.7	43	12
Willie Richardson, Baltimore	63	860	13.7	31t	8
Bobby Mitchell, Washington	60	866	14.4	65t	6
Ben Hawkins, Philadelphia	59	1,265	21.4	87t	10
LEADING SCORER	**TD**	**FG**	**PAT**		**TP**
Jim Bakken, St. Louis	0	27	36		117
LEADING INTERCEPTORS	**No.**	**Yards**	**Avg.**	**Long**	**TD**
Lem Barney, Detroit	10	232	23.2	71t	3
Dave Whitsell, New Orleans	10	178	17.8	41t	2
LEADING PUNTER	**No.**		**Avg.**		**Long**
Billy Lothridge, Atlanta	87		43.7		62
LEADING PUNT RETURNER	**No.**	**Yards**	**Avg.**	**Long**	**TD**
Ben Davis, Cleveland	18	229	12.7	52t	1
LEADING KICKOFF RETURNER	**No.**	**Yards**	**Avg.**	**Long**	**TD**
Travis Williams, Atlanta	18	739	41.1	104t	4

SUPERLATIVES		
Rushing average	5.1	Leroy Kelly, Cleveland
Receiving average	24.7	Homer Jones, NY Giants
Completion percentage	58.5	Johnny Unitas, Baltimore
Touchdowns	14	Homer Jones, NY Giants
LONGEST		
Run	73	Bill Asbury, Pittsburgh
		Dave Osborn, Minnesota
Pass	96	Billy Kilmer to Walter Roberts, New Orleans
Interception	94t	Rick Volk, Baltimore
Punt	78	Pat Studstill, Detroit
Punt return	81	Bob Grim, Minnesota
Kickoff return	104t	Travis Williams, Green Bay
Field goal	53	Lou Michaels, Baltimore

1968 Sonny Werblin sold his interest in the New York Jets to four partners, and one of them, Don Lillis, became the acting head of the corporation. Lillis died two months later and Phil Iselin was named Jets' president.

The Houston Oilers left Rice Stadium and began playing their games in the Astrodome.

The AFL reached an agreement with its players association for a pension increase but a prolonged dispute between NFL owners and the newly recognized NFL Players' Association turned into a strike in July. It was settled a few days before training camps opened.

The New York Jets easily won the AFL East behind a strong passing attack featuring league most valuable player Joe Namath throwing to George Sauer and Don Maynard. New York also had strong running with Matt Snell and Emerson Boozer.

The Jets played a tense game with the Raiders at Oakland on November 17. New York led 32-29 with two minutes to play when NBC television switched from the game to begin the movie, *Heidi*. The network's switchboard lit up with angry protests while the Raiders came back with two late touchdowns to win what was dubbed the "Heidi Game" 43-32. NBC tried to make amends by repeatedly running the final minutes on their news shows and by promising never to leave a game early again.

Oakland and Kansas City tied for first place in the Western Division with 12-2 records. The Raiders had the best offense in the league, while the Chiefs had the toughest defense. They had split their regular-season games. The Raiders recorded an overwhelming playoff victory 41-6 as Daryle Lamonica bombed the Chiefs with five touchdown passes.

The Jets met the Raiders for the AFL championship. Namath outpassed Lamonica, throwing for three touchdowns, and the Jets won 27-23.

Earl Morrall, acquired from the Giants, took over as quarterback of Baltimore when Johnny Unitas went out with an elbow injury. Morrall had a sensational 26-touchdown season and the Colts, coached by Don Shula, lost only to Cleveland 30-20 while compiling a 13-1 record, one of the best in NFL history. Baltimore won the Coastal Division easily, despite the Rams' 10-3-1 record being the second-best in the NFL. Minnesota had an excellent front four that was nicknamed the Purple People Eaters. It consisted of ends Carl Eller and Jim Marshall and tackles Alan Page and Gary Larsen. Led by their strong defense and the running and receiving of fullback Bill Brown, the Vikings won the Central Division, their first title of any kind. The Colts won a playoff from the Vikings 24-14 for the Western Conference championship.

There was an important quarterback switch in the Eastern Conference, too. Bill Nelsen replaced Frank Ryan as quarterback of the Cleveland Browns and led them to the Century Division title. The Browns won by a half game despite losing both games to second-place St. Louis. In the Capitol Division, the Cowboys overcame a midseason slump to post the second-best record in the NFL (12-2). The league's second-toughest defense to score against was complemented by quarterback Don Meredith, who finished second in the NFL in passing. In the Eastern Conference championship game, the Browns used several Dallas turnovers and the running of Leroy Kelly to beat the Cowboys 31-20.

The Browns met their match in the NFL title game, however. Baltimore swamped them 34-0 with an offensive barrage that included three touchdowns by Tom Matte.

Super Bowl was now the official name for what had been called the AFL-NFL World Championship Game, and the Colts, 15-1 in regular and postseason games, were solid favorites as they faced the AFL champion Jets at Miami. Three days before the game, however, Namath of the Jets was attending a sports dinner when he said, "We are going to win on Sunday, I guarantee you."

Namath made his boast reality when he completed 17 of 28 passes, sent Matt Snell rushing for 121 yards, and the Jets won 16-7 to become the first AFL team to win a Super Bowl.

1968 AFL STANDINGS

Eastern Division	**W**	**L**	**T**	**Pct.**	**Pts.**	**OP**
New York Jets	11	3	0	.786	419	280
Houston	7	7	0	.500	303	248
Miami	5	8	1	.385	276	355
Boston	4	10	0	.286	229	406
Buffalo	1	12	1	.077	199	367
Western Division	**W**	**L**	**T**	**Pct.**	**Pts.**	**OP**
Oakland	12	2	0	.857	453	233
Kansas City	12	2	0	.857	371	170
San Diego	9	5	0	.643	382	310
Denver	5	9	0	.357	255	404
Cincinnati	3	11	0	.214	215	329

Western Division playoff: Oakland 41, Kansas City 6
AFL championship: New York Jets 27, Oakland 23

LEADING RUSHERS	**Att.**	**Yards**	**Avg.**	**Long**	**TD**
Paul Robinson, Cincinnati	238	1,023	4.3	87t	8
Robert Holmes, Kansas City	174	866	5.0	76t	7
Hewritt Dixon, Oakland	206	865	4.2	28	2
Hoyle Granger, Houston	202	848	4.2	47t	7
Dickie Post, San Diego	151	758	5.0	62t	3

LEADING PASSERS	**Att.**	**Comp.**	**Yards**	**TD**	**Int.**
Len Dawson, Kansas City	224	131	2,019	17	9
Daryle Lamonica, Oakland	416	206	3,245	25	15
Joe Namath, NY Jets	380	187	3,147	15	17
Bob Griese, Miami	355	186	2,473	21	16
John Hadl, San Diego	440	208	3,473	27	32

LEADING RECEIVERS	**No.**	**Yards**	**Avg.**	**Long**	**TD**
Lance Alworth, San Diego	68	1,312	19.3	80t	10
George Sauer, NY Jets	66	1,141	17.3	43	3
Fred Biletnikoff, Oakland	61	1,037	17.0	82	6
Karl Noonan, Miami	58	760	13.1	50t	11
Don Maynard, NY Jets	57	1,297	22.8	87t	10

LEADING SCORER	**TD**	**FG**	**PAT**	**TP**
Jim Turner, NY Jets	0	34	43	145

LEADING INTERCEPTOR	**No.**	**Yards**	**Avg.**	**Long**	**TD**
Dave Grayson, Oakland	10	195	19.5	54	1

LEADING PUNTER	**No.**	**Avg.**	**Long**
Jerrel Wilson, Kansas City	63	45.1	70

LEADING PUNT RETURNER	**No.**	**Yards**	**Avg.**	**Long**	**TD**
Noland Smith, Kansas City	18	270	15.0	80t	1

LEADING KICKOFF RETURNER	**No.**	**Yards**	**Avg.**	**Long**	**TD**
George Atkinson, Oakland	32	802	25.1	60	0

SUPERLATIVES		
Rushing average	5.0	Dickie Post, San Diego
Receiving average	22.8	Don Maynard, NY Jets
Completion percentage	58.5	Len Dawson, Kansas City
Touchdowns	12	Warren Wells, Oakland

LONGEST		
Run	87t	Paul Robinson, Cincinnati
Pass	94t	George Blanda to Warren Wells, Oakland
Interception	100t	Tom Janik, Buffalo
Punt	87	Bob Scarpitto, Denver
Punt return	95t	Speedy Duncan, San Diego
Kickoff return	100t	Max Anderson, Buffalo
Field goal	52	Jan Stenerud, Kansas City

1968 NFL STANDINGS
EASTERN CONFERENCE

Capitol Division	**W**	**L**	**T**	**Pct.**	**Pts.**	**OP**
Dallas	12	2	0	.857	431	186
New York Giants	7	7	0	.500	294	325
Washington	5	9	0	.357	249	358
Philadelphia	2	12	0	.143	202	351
Century Division	**W**	**L**	**T**	**Pct.**	**Pts.**	**OP**
Cleveland	10	4	0	.714	394	273
St. Louis	9	4	1	.692	325	289
New Orleans	4	9	1	.308	246	327
Pittsburgh	2	11	1	.154	244	397

WESTERN CONFERENCE

Coastal Division	**W**	**L**	**T**	**Pct.**	**Pts.**	**OP**
Baltimore	13	1	0	.929	402	144
Los Angeles Rams	10	3	1	.769	312	200
San Francisco	7	6	1	.538	303	310
Atlanta	2	12	0	.143	170	389
Central Division	**W**	**L**	**T**	**Pct.**	**Pts.**	**OP**
Minnesota	8	6	0	.571	282	242
Chicago Bears	7	7	0	.500	250	333
Green Bay	6	7	1	.462	281	227
Detroit	4	8	2	.333	207	241

Conference championships: Cleveland 31, Dallas 20;
Baltimore 24, Minnesota 14
NFL championship: Baltimore 34, Cleveland 0
Super Bowl III: New York Jets (AFL) 16, Baltimore (NFL) 7

LEADING RUSHERS	**Att.**	**Yards**	**Avg.**	**Long**	**TD**
Leroy Kelly, Cleveland	248	1,239	5.0	65	16
Ken Willard, San Francisco	227	967	4.3	69t	7
Tom Woodeshick, Philadelphia	217	947	4.4	54t	3
Dick Hoak, Pittsburgh	175	858	4.9	77t	3
Gale Sayers, Chi. Bears	138	856	6.2	63	2

LEADING PASSERS	**Att.**	**Comp.**	**Yards**	**TD**	**Int.**
Earl Morrall, Baltimore	317	182	2,909	26	17
Don Meredith, Dallas	309	171	2,500	21	12
John Brodie, San Francisco	404	234	3,020	22	21
Bart Starr, Green Bay	171	109	1,617	15	8
Fran Tarkenton, NY Giants	337	182	2,555	21	12

LEADING RECEIVERS	**No.**	**Yards**	**Avg.**	**Long**	**TD**
Clifton McNeil, San Francisco	71	994	14.0	65t	7
Roy Jefferson, Pittsburgh	58	1,074	18.5	62	11
Lance Rentzel, Dallas	54	1,009	18.7	65t	6
Dan Abramowicz, New Orleans	54	890	16.5	47t	7
Bob Hayes, Dallas	53	909	17.2	54t	10

LEADING SCORER	**TD**	**FG**	**PAT**	**TP**
Leroy Kelly, Cleveland	20	0	0	120

LEADING INTERCEPTOR	**No.**	**Yards**	**Avg.**	**Long**	**TD**
Willie Williams, NY Giants	10	103	10.3	24	0

LEADING PUNTER	**No.**	**Avg.**	**Long**
Billy Lothridge, Atlanta	75	44.3	70

LEADING PUNT RETURNER	**No.**	**Yards**	**Avg.**	**Long**	**TD**
Bob Hayes, Dallas	15	312	20.8	90t	2

LEADING KICKOFF RETURNER	**No.**	**Yards**	**Avg.**	**Long**	**TD**
Preston Pearson, Baltimore	15	527	35.1	102t	2

SUPERLATIVES		
Rushing average	6.2	Gale Sayers, Chi. Bears
Receiving average	23.5	Homer Jones, NY Giants
Completion percentage	63.7	Bart Starr, Green Bay
Touchdowns	20	Leroy Kelly, Cleveland

LONGEST		
Run	77t	Dick Hoak, Pittsburgh
Pass	99t	Sonny Jurgensen to Gerry Allen, Washington
Interception	96t	Roosevelt Taylor, Chi. Bears
Punt	84	Ron Widby, Dallas
Punt return	98t	Charlie West, Minnesota
Kickoff return	102t	Preston Pearson, Baltimore
Field goal	50	Mike Clark, Dallas Don Cockroft, Cleveland

1969 There were a number of coaching moves before the season. George Allen, fired as coach of the Rams by owner Dan Reeves, was rehired after his players protested the firing. Vince Lombardi left the general managership of the Packers and became part-owner, executive vice president, and head coach of the Redskins. John Madden became head coach of the Raiders succeeding John Rauch, who went to the Bills, and Chuck Noll became head coach of the Steelers.

O. J. Simpson of USC, winner of the Heisman Trophy, was the first choice in the draft, by Buffalo.

In May, the Eagles obtained a new owner when Jerry Wolman sold the team to Leonard Tose, a trucking magnate, for $16.1 million.

Commissioner Pete Rozelle announced a new television contract with the ABC network for 13 regular-season Monday night games in prime time during 1970, 1971, and 1972.

It was necessary to thrash out the format under which the 26 teams would compete once they were all in one league starting in 1970. The owners alternately argued, dozed, agreed, ate, and eventually compromised in a marathon 35-hour, 45-minute realignment meeting in May. As a result of the meeting, Baltimore, Cleveland, and Pittsburgh joined the 10 AFL teams in a new 13-team American Football Conference, and the remaining 13 teams from the 16-club NFL became the National Football Conference. There would also be a "wild card" or best second-place team in each conference going into the playoffs each year. All this was to become effective the next year.

For 1969 only, the AFL played under a format in which the second-place team in each division would play the champion of the other division in the first round of the playoffs.

In the AFL East, the Jets and Oilers qualified for the playoffs. The Jets went 10-4 with much the same team that had won the Super Bowl the year before. The Oilers finished second with a 6-6-2 record. In the West, Paul Brown's Bengals beat both the Raiders and the Chiefs once, but the two teams still finished with the best records in the AFL. Oakland won two close games over Kansas City in the last month of the season to clinch the title with a 12-1-1 record, best in pro football. The Raiders won on the arm of Daryle Lamonica, who passed for 3,302 yards and 34 touchdowns. The Chiefs won behind a stifling defense and a host of "mini-backs," including Mike Garrett, Warren McVea, and Robert Holmes. Sid Gillman, the coach of the Chargers since 1960, was forced to step down after nine games because of ulcers; he was succeeded by assistant Charlie Waller. Lance Alworth of the Chargers finished a string in which he caught at least one pass in 96 consecutive games.

The two first-round playoff games couldn't have been more different. In New York, Len Dawson hit Gloster Richardson with a 19-yard pass for the only touchdown of the day, as the Chiefs upset the Jets 13-6. The next day, Lamonica threw six touchdown passes as the Raiders thrashed the Oilers 56-7.

Kansas City won the AFL title game, stopping Oakland 17-7. Lamonica was injured and 42-year-old George Blanda took over in a losing effort. The Chiefs and their coach, Hank Stram, advanced to the Super Bowl and a chance to avenge their loss in the first world championship game four seasons before.

Behind the play of league most valuable player

Roman Gabriel, the Rams won their first 11 games and ousted the Colts as Coastal Division champions. Minnesota's withering defense and gutsy quarterback Joe Kapp helped the Vikings to the NFC's best record (12-2). The Cowboys and Browns each won their division again, with the new-look Cowboys featuring a backfield of quarterback Craig Morton and running backs Calvin Hill and Walt Garrison. In the Capitol Division, Washington placed second with a 7-5-2 record, as Lombardi and rookie running back Larry Brown added to Sonny Jurgensen's always potent passing attack.

George Preston Marshall, the founder of the team, died at the age of 72.

Quarterback Bill Nelsen led Cleveland to a rousing victory over Dallas, 38-14, for the Eastern Conference title. Kapp led the Vikings from a 17-7 deficit to a 23-20 victory over Los Angeles to claim the Western Conference championship.

In the NFL title game, Kapp threw a touchdown pass and scored once as Minnesota defeated Cleveland 27-7.

Minnesota met Kansas City in Super Bowl IV at New Orleans. The Vikings were favored but Garrett and Otis Taylor scored touchdowns and Jan Stenerud kicked three field goals, giving the Chiefs a 23-7 victory. Losers in the first Super Bowl, Kansas City won the last game played between the champions of the two leagues before their reorganization.

1969 AFL STANDINGS

Eastern Division	**W**	**L**	**T**	**Pct.**	**Pts.**	**OP**
New York Jets	10	4	0	.714	353	269
Houston	6	6	2	.500	278	279
Boston	4	10	0	.286	266	316
Buffalo	4	10	0	.286	230	359
Miami	3	10	1	.231	233	332
Western Division	**W**	**L**	**T**	**Pct.**	**Pts.**	**OP**
Oakland	12	1	1	.923	377	242
Kansas City	11	3	0	.786	359	177
San Diego	8	6	0	.571	288	276
Denver	5	8	1	.385	297	344
Cincinnati	4	9	1	.308	280	367

Divisional playoffs: Kansas City 13, New York Jets 6; Oakland 56, Houston 7

AFL championship: Kansas City 17, Oakland 7

LEADING RUSHERS	**Att.**	**Yards**	**Avg.**	**Long**	**TD**
Dickie Post, San Diego	182	873	4.8	60	6
Jim Nance, Boston	193	750	3.9	43	6
Hoyle Granger, Houston	186	740	4.0	23	3
Mike Garrett, Kansas City	168	732	4.4	34t	6
Floyd Little, Denver	146	729	5.0	48t	6

LEADING PASSERS	**Att.**	**Comp.**	**Yards**	**TD**	**Int.**
Greg Cook, Cincinnati	197	106	1,854	15	11
Joe Namath, NY Jets	361	185	2,734	19	17
Daryle Lamonica, Oakland	426	221	3,302	34	25
Mike Livingston, Kansas City	161	84	1,123	4	6
John Hadl, San Diego	324	158	2,253	10	11

LEADING RECEIVERS	**No.**	**Yards**	**Avg.**	**Long**	**TD**
Lance Alworth, San Diego	64	1,003	15.7	76t	4
Fred Biletnikoff, Oakland	54	837	15.5	53t	12
Moses Denson, Denver	53	809	15.3	62t	10
Alvin Reed, Houston	51	664	13.0	43t	2
Warren Wells, Oakland	47	1,260	26.8	80t	14
Don Maynard, NY Jets	47	938	20.0	60t	6

LEADING SCORER	**TD**	**FG**	**PAT**	**TP**
Jim Turner, NY Jets	0	32	33	129

LEADING INTERCEPTOR	**No.**	**Yards**	**Avg.**	**Long**	**TD**
Emmitt Thomas, Kansas City	9	146	16.2	45t	1

LEADING PUNTER	**No.**	**Avg.**	**Long**
Dennis Partee, San Diego	71	44.6	62

LEADING PUNT RETURNER	**No.**	**Yards**	**Avg.**	**Long**	**TD**
Billy Thompson, Denver	25	288	11.5	40	0

LEADING KICKOFF RETURNER	**No.**	**Yards**	**Avg.**	**Long**	**TD**
Billy Thompson, Denver	18	513	28.5	63	0

SUPERLATIVES		
Rushing average	5.0	Carl Garrett, Boston
Receiving average	26.8	Warren Wells, Oakland
Completion percentage	59.0	Len Dawson, Kansas City
Touchdowns	14	Warren Wells, Oakland

LONGEST		
Run	83	Jess Phillips, Cincinnati
Pass	86t	Pete Beathard to Jerry LeVias, Houston
Interception	76t	Dave Grayson, Oakland
Punt	98	Steve O'Neal, NY Jets
Punt return	64	Noland Smith, Kansas City
Kickoff return	105t	Mercury Morris, Miami
Field goal	54	Jan Stenerud, Kansas City

1969 NFL STANDINGS

EASTERN CONFERENCE

Capitol Division	**W**	**L**	**T**	**Pct.**	**Pts.**	**OP**
Dallas	11	2	1	.846	369	223
Washington	7	5	2	.583	307	319
New Orleans	5	9	0	.357	311	393
Philadelphia	4	9	1	.308	279	377
Century Division	**W**	**L**	**T**	**Pct.**	**Pts.**	**OP**
Cleveland	10	3	1	.769	351	300
New York Giants	6	8	0	.429	264	298
St. Louis	4	9	1	.308	314	389
Pittsburgh	1	13	0	.071	218	404

WESTERN CONFERENCE

Coastal Division	**W**	**L**	**T**	**Pct.**	**Pts.**	**OP**
Los Angeles Rams	11	3	0	.786	320	243
Baltimore	8	5	1	.615	279	268
Atlanta	6	8	0	.429	276	268
San Francisco	4	8	2	.333	277	319
Central Division	**W**	**L**	**T**	**Pct.**	**Pts.**	**OP**
Minnesota	12	2	0	.857	379	133
Detroit	9	4	1	.692	259	188
Green Bay	8	6	0	.571	269	221
Chicago Bears	1	13	0	.071	210	339

Conference championships: Cleveland 38, Dallas 14; Minnesota 23, Los Angeles Rams 20

NFL championship: Minnesota 27, Cleveland 7

Super Bowl IV: Kansas City (AFL) 23, Minnesota (NFL) 7

LEADING RUSHERS	**Att.**	**Yards**	**Avg.**	**Long**	**TD**
Gale Sayers, Chi. Bears	236	1,032	4.4	28	8
Calvin Hill, Dallas	204	942	4.6	55	8
Tom Matte, Baltimore	235	909	3.9	26	11
Larry Brown, Washington	202	888	4.4	57	4
Tom Woodeshick, Philadelphia	186	831	4.5	21	4

LEADING PASSERS	**Att.**	**Comp.**	**Yards**	**TD**	**Int.**
Sonny Jurgensen, Washington	442	274	3,102	22	15
Bart Starr, Green Bay	148	92	1,161	9	6
Fran Tarkenton, NY Giants	409	220	2,918	23	8
Roman Gabriel, LA Rams	399	217	2,549	24	7
Craig Morton, Dallas	302	162	2,619	21	15

LEADING RECEIVERS	**No.**	**Yards**	**Avg.**	**Long**	**TD**
Dan Abramowicz, New Orleans	73	1,015	13.9	49t	7
Charley Taylor, Washington	71	883	12.4	88t	8
Roy Jefferson, Pittsburgh	67	1,079	16.1	63	9
Harold Jackson, Philadelphia	65	1,116	17.2	65t	9
Dave Williams, St. Louis	56	702	12.5	61	7

LEADING SCORER	**TD**	**FG**	**PAT**	**TP**
Fred Cox, Minnesota	0	26	43	121

LEADING INTERCEPTOR	**No.**	**Yards**	**Avg.**	**Long**	**TD**
Mel Renfro, Dallas	10	118	11.8	41	0

LEADING PUNTER	**No.**	**Avg.**	**Long**
David Lee, Baltimore	57	45.3	66

LEADING PUNT RETURNER	**No.**	**Yards**	**Avg.**	**Long**	**TD**
Alvin Haymond, LA Rams	33	435	13.2	52	0

LEADING KICKOFF RETURNER	**No.**	**Yards**	**Avg.**	**Long**	**TD**
Bobby Williams, Detroit	17	563	33.1	96t	1

SUPERLATIVES		
Rushing average	4.8	Tony Baker, New Orleans
Receiving average	22.3	Lance Rentzel, Dallas
Completion percentage	62.2	Bart Starr, Green Bay
Touchdowns	13	Tom Matte, Baltimore Lance Rentzel, Dallas

LONGEST		
Run	80t	Clint Jones, Minnesota
Pass	93t	Roman Gabriel to Wendell Tucker, LA Rams
Interception	85t	Doug Hart, Green Bay
Punt	81	Tom McNeill, New Orleans
Punt return	86t	Rickie Harris, Washington
Kickoff return	101t	Don McCall, Pittsburgh
Field goal	55	Tom Dempsey, New Orleans

1970 The merger agreement of 1966 was implemented, and the 26 teams of pro football were realigned into the American and National Football Conferences and began playing interleague regular-season games.

The AFC's make-up was rather easy after the three teams moving over from the NFL had been decided upon. The NFC realignment, however, was not arrived at until after months of discussion. Finally, one of five plans submitted by Commissioner Pete Rozelle was drawn in a lottery.

Each team was to play home-and-home with each other team in its division, three or five games with other teams of its own conference, and three interconference games. Because of the odd number of clubs in each conference, one would play four intersectional games.

Rozelle had to settle charges of tampering by the Miami Dolphins in their efforts to lure coach Don Shula from Baltimore. Shula was permitted to make the move, but in exchange Miami gave up its number-one draft choice in 1971. Don McCafferty replaced Shula as coach of the Colts.

Vince Lombardi, former coach of the Packers and Redskins, and Brian Piccolo, former running back for the Bears, died of cancer. Jimmy Conzelman, a prominent figure in the early days of pro football and a member of the Pro Football Hall of Fame, also died.

The Cincinnati Bengals moved into new 56,200-seat Riverfront Stadium and the Pittsburgh Steelers into new 50,350-seat Three Rivers Stadium.

Monday night football became a TV success as ABC began the first of a three-year contract.

There was the possibility of a strike by NFL players until early August. A new four-year agreement was signed between the owners and the NFL Players' Association.

The rules were changed requiring players' names on the backs of their jerseys, as they had been in the AFL, and making the stadium clock the official timer of the game, as had been the case in the AFL.

George Blanda, playing his twenty-first year of pro ball at the age of 43, engineered a series of dramatic finishes for Oakland. Blanda, backup to Daryle Lamonica as well as the Raiders' kicker, did this in a five-week span: threw two touchdown passes against Pittsburgh; kicked a 48-yard field goal with three seconds to go, tying Kansas City 17-17; kicked a 52-yard field goal with three seconds to play to beat Cleveland 23-20, drove the Raiders to a winning touchdown against Denver 24-19, and beat San Diego 20-17 on another field goal with four seconds left. Blanda was named the league's most valuable player and became a national folk hero. His performances helped the Raiders edge the Chiefs in the AFC West.

McCafferty's Colts won the AFC East at 11-2-1 and runner-up Miami's 10-4 record put Shula's Dolphins into the playoffs as the wild card team. Paul Brown's expansion team in Cincinnati won the AFC Central in its third season with an 8-6 record.

In the NFC East, Dallas (10-4) edged the Giants (9-5) behind the running of rookie of the year Duane Thomas. With new coach Bill Austin, the Redskins dropped to fourth place. John Brodie and Gene Washington of San Francisco emerged as the NFC's top passing combination while leading the 49ers to the Western Division title. Defense and Fred Cox's field goals were major factors in Minnesota's Central Division championship. The Vikings won despite losing quarterback Joe Kapp, who went to Boston, where he reported late and threw only 3 touchdown passes but 17 interceptions.

On November 8, Tom Dempsey of New Orleans set an NFL record with a 63-yard field goal on the game's last play to defeat Detroit 19-17. The Lions came back to edge the Rams 28-23 in the next-to-last game of the year, beating out the Los Angeles club for the NFC wild card berth.

Injuries crushed the hopes of two clubs. Gale Sayers of the Bears underwent surgery for a knee injury in midseason and never again regained his form. The Jets were handicapped when Joe Namath broke his wrist and Matt Snell tore his Achilles tendon.

The NFC won the competition with the AFC in the first season they played interconference games. There were 40 such games and the NFC won 27, the AFC 12, and there was one tie.

In the AFC playoffs, Baltimore blanked Cincinnati 17-0 and Oakland defeated Miami 21-14 in the first round. Dallas beat Detroit 5-0 on a field goal and safety and the 49ers surprised the Vikings at Minnesota 17-14 in the NFC.

Baltimore defeated Oakland 27-17 in the AFC Championship Game. Duane Thomas gained 143 yards and Walt Garrison 71 in Dallas's 17-10 NFC Championship Game win over San Francisco.

Super Bowl V was a battle of turnovers at the Orange Bowl. The Colts gave up three interceptions and four fumbles and the Cowboys had three passes intercepted and lost a fumble. Jim O'Brien's 32-yard field goal with five seconds to play won it for the Colts 16-13. Earl Morrall led Baltimore to victory after Johnny Unitas suffered damaged ribs.

The NFC won the first AFC-NFC Pro Bowl 27-6 as Mel Renfro of the Dallas Cowboys returned punts 82 and 56 yards for touchdowns. The game was played in Los Angeles.

1970 AFC STANDINGS

Eastern Division	W	L	T	Pct.	Pts.	OP
Baltimore	11	2	1	.846	321	234
Miami*	10	4	0	.714	297	228
New York Jets	4	10	0	.286	255	286
Buffalo	3	10	1	.231	204	337
Boston	2	12	0	.143	149	361
Central Division	**W**	**L**	**T**	**Pct.**	**Pts.**	**OP**
Cincinnati	8	6	0	.571	312	255
Cleveland	7	7	0	.500	286	265
Pittsburgh	5	9	0	.357	210	272
Houston	3	10	1	.231	217	352
Western Division	**W**	**L**	**T**	**Pct.**	**Pts.**	**OP**
Oakland	8	4	2	.667	300	293
Kansas City	7	5	2	.583	272	244
San Diego	5	6	3	.455	282	278
Denver	5	8	1	.385	253	264

**Wild Card qualifier for playoffs*

Divisional playoffs: Baltimore 17, Cincinnati 0; Oakland 21, Miami 14

AFC championship: Baltimore 27, Oakland 17

LEADING RUSHERS	**Att.**	**Yards**	**Avg.**	**Long**	**TD**
Floyd Little, Denver	209	901	4.3	80t	3
Larry Csonka, Miami	193	874	4.5	53	6
Hewritt Dixon, Oakland	197	861	4.4	39t	1
Ed Podolak, Kansas City	168	749	4.5	65t	3
Frenchy Fuqua, Pittsburgh	138	691	5.0	85t	7
LEADING PASSERS	**Att.**	**Comp.**	**Yards**	**TD**	**Int.**
Daryle Lamonica, Oakland	356	179	2,516	22	15
John Hadl, San Diego	327	162	2,388	22	15
Len Dawson, Kansas City	262	141	1,876	13	14
Bob Griese, Miami	245	142	2,019	12	17
Dennis Shaw, Buffalo	321	178	2,507	10	20
LEADING RECEIVERS	**No.**	**Yards**	**Avg.**	**Long**	**TD**
Marlin Briscoe, Buffalo	57	1,036	18.2	48	8
Eddie Hinton, Baltimore	47	733	15.6	40	5
Al Denson, Denver	47	646	13.7	42	2
Alvin Reed, Houston	47	604	12.9	34	2
Fred Biletnikoff, Oakland	45	768	17.1	51	7
LEADING SCORER	**TD**	**FG**	**PAT**		**TP**
Jan Stenerud, Kansas City	0	30	26		116
LEADING INTERCEPTOR	**No.**	**Yards**	**Avg.**	**Long**	**TD**
Johnny Robinson, Kansas City	10	155	15.5	57	0
LEADING PUNTER	**No.**		**Avg.**		**Long**
Dave Lewis, Cincinnati	79		46.2		63
LEADING PUNT RETURNER	**No.**	**Yards**	**Avg.**	**Long**	**TD**
Ed Podolak, Kansas City	23	311	13.5	60	0
LEADING KICKOFF RETURNER	**No.**	**Yards**	**Avg.**	**Long**	**TD**
Jim Duncan, Baltimore	20	707	35.4	99t	1

SUPERLATIVES

Rushing average	5.0	Frenchy Fuqua, Pittsburgh
Receiving average	22.9	Gary Garrison, San Diego
Completion percentage	58.0	Bob Griese, Miami
Touchdowns	12	Gary Garrison, San Diego

LONGEST

Run	85t	Frenchy Fuqua, Pittsburgh
Pass	87t	Terry Bradshaw to Dave Smith, Pittsburgh Jerry Rhome to Charlie Joiner, Houston
Interception	86	Dick Anderson, Miami
Punt	73	Spike Jones, Houston
Punt return	80t	Ron Gardin, Baltimore
Kickoff return	99t	Jim Duncan, Baltimore
Field goal	55	Jan Stenerud, Kansas City

1970 NFC STANDINGS

Eastern Division	W	L	T	Pct.	Pts.	OP
Dallas	10	4	0	.714	299	221
New York Giants	9	5	0	.643	301	270
St. Louis	8	5	1	.615	325	228
Washington	6	8	0	.429	297	314
Philadelphia	3	10	1	.231	241	332
Central Division	**W**	**L**	**T**	**Pct.**	**Pts.**	**OP**
Minnesota	12	2	0	.857	335	143
Detroit*	10	4	0	.714	347	202
Chicago Bears	6	8	0	.429	256	261
Green Bay	6	8	0	.429	196	293
Western Division	**W**	**L**	**T**	**Pct.**	**Pts.**	**OP**
San Francisco	10	3	1	.769	352	267
Los Angeles Rams	9	4	1	.692	325	202
Atlanta	4	8	2	.333	206	261
New Orleans	2	11	1	.154	172	347

**Wild Card qualifier for playoffs*

Divisional playoffs: Dallas 5, Detroit 0; San Francisco 17, Minnesota 14

NFC championship: Dallas 17, San Francisco 10

Super Bowl V: Baltimore (AFC) 16, Dallas (NFC) 13

LEADING RUSHERS	**Att.**	**Yards**	**Avg.**	**Long**	**TD**
Larry Brown, Washington	237	1,125	4.7	75t	5
Ron Johnson, NY Giants	263	1,027	3.9	68t	8
MacArthur Lane, St. Louis	206	977	4.7	75	11
Donny Anderson, Green Bay	222	853	3.8	54	5
Duane Thomas, Dallas	151	803	5.3	47t	5
LEADING PASSERS	**Att.**	**Comp.**	**Yards**	**TD**	**Int.**
John Brodie, San Francisco	378	223	2,941	24	10
Sonny Jurgensen, Washington	337	202	2,354	23	10
Fran Tarkenton, NY Giants	389	219	2,777	19	12
Bob Berry, Atlanta	269	156	1,806	16	13
Craig Morton, Dallas	207	102	1,819	15	7
LEADING RECEIVERS	**No.**	**Yards**	**Avg.**	**Long**	**TD**
Dick Gordon, Chi. Bears	71	1,026	14.5	69t	13
Dan Abramowicz, New Orleans	55	906	16.5	48	5
Gene Washington, San Francisco	53	1,100	20.8	79t	12
Jack Snow, LA Rams	51	859	16.8	71	7
Clifton McNeil, NY Giants	50	764	15.3	59	4
Lee Bougess, Philadelphia	50	401	8.0	34	2
LEADING SCORER	**TD**	**FG**	**PAT**		**TP**
Fred Cox, Minnesota	0	30	35		125
LEADING INTERCEPTOR	**No.**	**Yards**	**Avg.**	**Long**	**TD**
Dick LeBeau, Detroit	9	96	10.7	43	0
LEADING PUNTER	**No.**		**Avg.**		**Long**
Julian Fagan, New Orleans	77		42.5		64
LEADING PUNT RETURNER	**No.**	**Yards**	**Avg.**	**Long**	**TD**
Bruce Taylor, San Francisco	43	516	12.0	76	0
LEADING KICKOFF RETURNER	**No.**	**Yards**	**Avg.**	**Long**	**TD**
Cecil Turner, Chi. Bears	23	752	32.7	96t	4

SUPERLATIVES

Rushing average	5.3	Duane Thomas, Dallas
Receiving average	21.2	John Gilliam, St. Louis
Completion percentage	60.0	Sonny Jurgensen, Washington
Touchdowns	13	MacArthur Lane, St. Louis Dick Gordon, Chi. Bears

LONGEST

Run	76	Greg Landry, Detroit
Pass	89t	Don Horn to Carroll Dale, Green Bay Craig Morton to Bob Hayes, Dallas
Interception	76t	Doug Hart, Green Bay
Punt	68	Bill Johnson, NY Giants
Punt return	77t	Tom McCauley, Atlanta
Kickoff return	101t	Dave Hampton, Green Bay
Field goal	63	Tom Dempsey, New Orleans

1971 Five teams switched to new stadiums. The Dallas Cowboys left the Cotton Bowl, their home since 1960, to open the new 65,101-seat Texas Stadium at Irving, Texas, another suburban location. The Philadelphia Eagles occupied 66,052-seat Veterans Stadium and the San Francisco 49ers switched from Kezar Stadium to 61,246-seat Candlestick Park. The Chicago Bears, who had played at Wrigley Field (originally Cubs Park) since they had moved from Decatur, Illinois, in 1921, moved into Soldier Field. The huge stadium's seating capacity was reduced to 55,049.

The Boston Patriots had wandered from Boston University, to Fenway Park, to Boston College, and to Harvard Stadium. They finally got their own stadium in Foxboro, Massachusetts, when the 61,275-seat Schaefer Stadium was opened. The team then changed its name to the New England Patriots.

Quarterbacks were the first three selections in the college draft. All of them became starters. Stanford's Jim Plunkett was number one for the Patriots, throwing 19 touchdown passes. Santa Clara's Dan Pastorini took over at Houston. Mississippi's Archie Manning started strong with the Saints but injuries made him a part-time performer.

The number-one draft choice the Baltimore Colts had been awarded from Miami in exchange for coach Don Shula was used to draft running back Don McCauley of North Carolina.

George Blanda, Oakland's veteran kicker, moved into first place on the all-time scoring list with 1,647 points, topping Lou Groza, and Bob Tucker of the New York Giants became the first tight end to lead a conference in receiving with 59 catches in the NFC.

After many years of high-powered offenses, defenses seemed to catch up in 1971. The increasing use of zone defenses took away much of the passing game and returned emphasis on inside running and the kicking game. The four best defensive teams in the NFC and the three best defensive teams in the AFC all made the playoffs.

George Allen, insisting "the future is now," took over the Washington Redskins and made a series of trades that brought defensive tackle Diron Talbert, linebackers Myron Pottios and Jack Pardee, and a host of other former Los Angeles Rams to Washington in return mainly for future draft choices. Allen coached the Redskins into the NFC playoffs as the wild card team with a 9-4-1 record. It was the first time Washington reached the playoffs since 1945.

Dallas was the Eastern Division champion. Roger Staubach was given the starting nod over Craig Morton after the Cowboys got off to a slow start, and Staubach led the league in passing and guided the Cowboys to seven consecutive victories to end the season. Minnesota won the NFC Central in its usual manner—with defense. San Francisco barely won the West as the Rams, behind rookie coach Tommy Prothro, lost the lead with just a week to go.

Cleveland overcame a midseason slump and won the AFC Central with a 9-5 record in Nick Skorich's first year as coach. Kansas City's 10-3-1 topped Oakland's 8-4-2 in the AFC West.

Miami won 10 games and the AFC Eastern Division. Baltimore was the runner-up and wild card team.

The San Diego Chargers brought back Sid Gillman, who lasted until midseason, when general manager Harland Svare took over as coach. Lou Saban quit as coach of the Denver Broncos after nine games and assistant Jerry Smith took over.

In a divisional playoff, the Dolphins edged Kansas City 27-24 in the longest game ever played when Garo Yepremian kicked a 37-yard field goal after 22 minutes and 40 seconds of overtime on Christmas afternoon. Jan Stenerud of the Chiefs missed a 31-yard field-goal try with 35 seconds left in regulation time. Baltimore beat Cleveland 20-3 in the other playoff.

San Francisco defeated Washington 24-20 in an NFC Divisional Playoff Game. Dallas won the other first-round playoff 20-12 over Minnesota.

In the AFC Championship Game, safety Dick Anderson of Miami intercepted three passes by Johnny Unitas, and Miami defeated Baltimore 21-0. Dallas used a powerful running attack to grind down San Francisco 14-3 in the NFC Championship Game.

The NFC won the Super Bowl when Dallas beat Miami 24-3. The Cowboys played a near-flawless game and held the Dolphins to 80 yards rushing, while gaining 252 themselves.

1971 AFC STANDINGS

Eastern Division	W	L	T	Pct.	Pts.	OP
Miami	10	3	1	.769	315	174
Baltimore*	10	4	0	.714	313	140
New England	6	8	0	.429	238	325
New York Jets	6	8	0	.429	212	299
Buffalo	1	13	0	.071	184	394
Central Division	**W**	**L**	**T**	**Pct.**	**Pts.**	**OP**
Cleveland	9	5	0	.643	285	273
Pittsburgh	6	8	0	.429	246	292
Houston	4	9	1	.308	251	330
Cincinnati	4	10	0	.286	284	265
Western Division	**W**	**L**	**T**	**Pct.**	**Pts.**	**OP**
Kansas City	10	3	1	.769	302	208
Oakland	8	4	2	.667	344	278
San Diego	6	8	0	.429	311	341
Denver	4	9	1	.308	203	275

**Wild Card qualifier for playoffs*

Divisional playoffs: Miami 27, Kansas City 24, overtime; Baltimore 20, Cleveland 3

AFC championship: Miami 21, Baltimore 0

LEADING RUSHERS	**Att.**	**Yards**	**Avg.**	**Long**	**TD**
Floyd Little, Denver	284	1,133	4.0	40	6
Larry Csonka, Miami	195	1,051	5.4	28	7

Marv Hubbard, Oakland	181	867	4.8	20	5
Leroy Kelly, Cleveland	234	865	3.7	35	10
Carl Garrett, New England	181	784	4.3	38	1
LEADING PASSERS	**Att.**	**Comp.**	**Yards**	**TD**	**Int.**
Bob Griese, Miami	263	145	2,089	19	9
Len Dawson, Kansas City	301	167	2,504	15	13
Virgil Carter, Cincinnati	222	138	1,624	10	7
John Hadl, San Diego	431	233	3,075	21	25
Bill Nelsen, Cleveland	325	174	2,319	13	23
LEADING RECEIVERS	**No.**	**Yards**	**Avg.**	**Long**	**TD**
Fred Biletnikoff, Oakland	61	929	15.2	49	9
Otis Taylor, Kansas City	57	1,110	19.5	82	7
Randy Vataha, New England	51	872	17.1	88t	9
Ron Shanklin, Pittsburgh	49	652	13.3	42	6
Frenchy Fuqua, Pittsburgh	49	427	8.7	40t	1
LEADING SCORER	**TD**	**FG**	**PAT**		**TP**
Garo Yepremian, Miami	0	28	33		117
LEADING INTERCEPTOR	**No.**	**Yards**	**Avg.**	**Long**	**TD**
Ken Houston, Houston	9	220	24.4	48t	4
LEADING PUNTER	**No.**		**Avg.**		**Long**
Dave Lewis, Cincinnati	72		44.8		56
LEADING PUNT RETURNER	**No.**	**Yards**	**Avg.**	**Long**	**TD**
Leroy Kelly, Cleveland	30	292	9.7	74	0
LEADING KICKOFF RETURNER	**No.**	**Yards**	**Avg.**	**Long**	**TD**
Mercury Morris, Miami	15	423	28.2	94t	1

SUPERLATIVES

Rushing average	5.4	Larry Csonka, Miami
Receiving average	23.2	Paul Warfield, Miami
Completion percentage	62.2	Virgil Carter, Cincinnati
Touchdowns	12	Leroy Kelly, Cleveland

LONGEST

Run	86t	Essex Johnson, Cincinnati
Pass	90t	Virgil Carter to Speedy Thomas, Cincinnati
Interception	70t	John Rowser, Pittsburgh
Punt	76	David Lee, Baltimore
Punt return	74	Leroy Kelly, Cleveland
Kickoff return	94t	Mercury Morris, Miami
Field goal	54	Jan Stenerud, Kansas City

1971 NFC STANDINGS

Eastern Division	**W**	**L**	**T**	**Pct.**	**Pts.**	**OP**
Dallas	11	3	0	.786	406	222
Washington*	9	4	1	.692	276	190
Philadelphia	6	7	1	.462	221	302
St. Louis	4	9	1	.308	231	279
New York Giants	4	10	0	.286	228	362
Central Division	**W**	**L**	**T**	**Pct.**	**Pts.**	**OP**
Minnesota	11	3	0	.786	245	139
Detroit	7	6	1	.538	341	286
Chicago Bears	6	8	0	.429	185	276
Green Bay	4	8	2	.333	274	298
Western Division	**W**	**L**	**T**	**Pct.**	**Pts.**	**OP**
San Francisco	9	5	0	.643	300	216
Los Angeles Rams	8	5	1	.615	313	260
Atlanta	7	6	1	.538	274	277
New Orleans	4	8	2	.333	266	347

**Wild Card qualifier for playoffs*

Divisional playoffs: Dallas 20, Minnesota 12;
San Francisco 24, Washington 20

NFC championship: Dallas 14, San Francisco 3

Super Bowl VI: Dallas (NFC) 24, Miami (AFC) 3

LEADING RUSHERS	**Att.**	**Yards**	**Avg.**	**Long**	**TD**
John Brockington, Green Bay	216	1,105	5.1	52t	4
Steve Owens, Detroit	246	1,035	4.2	23	8
Willie Ellison, LA Rams	211	1,000	4.7	80t	4
Larry Brown, Washington	253	948	3.7	34	4
Ken Willard, San Francisco	216	855	4.0	49	4
LEADING PASSERS	**Att.**	**Comp.**	**Yards**	**TD**	**Int.**
Roger Staubach, Dallas	211	126	1,882	15	4
Greg Landry, Detroit	261	136	2,237	16	13
Billy Kilmer, Washington	306	166	2,221	13	13
Bob Berry, Atlanta	226	136	2,005	11	16
Roman Gabriel, LA Rams	352	180	2,238	17	10
LEADING RECEIVERS	**No.**	**Yards**	**Avg.**	**Long**	**TD**
Bob Tucker, NY Giants	59	791	13.4	63t	4
Ted Kwalick, San Francisco	52	664	12.8	42t	5
Harold Jackson, Philadelphia	47	716	15.2	69t	3
Roy Jefferson, Washington	47	701	14.9	70t	4
Gene Washington, San Francisco	46	884	19.2	71t	4
George Farmer, Chi. Bears	46	737	16.0	64	5
LEADING SCORER	**TD**	**FG**	**PAT**		**TP**
Curt Knight, Washington	0	29	27		114
LEADING INTERCEPTOR	**No.**	**Yards**	**Avg.**	**Long**	**TD**
Bill Bradley, Philadelphia	11	248	22.5	51	0
LEADING PUNTER	**No.**		**Avg.**		**Long**
Tom McNeill, Philadelphia	73		42.0		64
LEADING PUNT RETURNER	**No.**	**Yards**	**Avg.**	**Long**	**TD**
Speedy Duncan, Washington	22	233	10.6	33	0
LEADING KICKOFF RETURNER	**No.**	**Yards**	**Avg.**	**Long**	**TD**
Travis Williams, LA Rams	25	743	29.7	105t	1

SUPERLATIVES

Rushing average	5.1	John Brockington, Green Bay
Receiving average	24.0	Bob Hayes, Dallas
Completion percentage	60.2	Bob Berry, Atlanta
Touchdowns	13	Duane Thomas, Dallas

LONGEST

Run	80t	Willie Ellison, LA Rams
Pass	85t	Roger Staubach to Bob Hayes, Dallas
Interception	89	Charlie West, Minnesota
Punt	64	Julian Fagan, New Orleans; Tom McNeill, Philadelphia
Punt return	50	Bill Walik, Philadelphia
Kickoff return	105t	Travis Williams, LA Rams
Field goal	54	Tom Dempsey, Philadelphia

1972 Three teams had management changes. Robert Irsay bought the Los Angeles Rams from the estate of the late Dan Reeves, and traded the franchise to Carroll Rosenbloom, owner of the Baltimore Colts. Irsay wound up as owner of the Colts and Rosenbloom took control of the Rams. William Bidwill became the sole owner of the St. Louis Cardinals, buying out his brother, Charles (Stormy) Bidwill. Kansas City moved into 78,907-seat Arrowhead Stadium.

In hopes of increasing scoring and countering the zone defense, the owners adopted a new rule to move in the hashmarks or inbounds lines from 20 yards to 23 yards, 1 foot, 9 inches, leaving only 18 feet, 6 inches, the width of the goal-post crossbar, in the middle of the field. The method of determining won-lost percentage changed. Tie games, previously not counted in the standings, were made equal to a half-game won and a half-game lost.

A series of trades involved big name players in the league. Quarterback Fran Tarkenton, traded to the Giants by the Vikings in early 1967, went back to Minnesota in a swap that sent receiver Bob Grim and draft choices to New York. Running back Duane Thomas was shipped to San Diego by Dallas, and defensive end Fred Dryer went from the Giants to the Rams via the Patriots. Denver dealt with Houston to get quarterback Charley Johnson.

Jack Tatum of Oakland erased a 49-year-old record when he ran 104 yards with a recovered fumble, beating the old mark of 98 by George Halas of the Bears against the Oorang Indians in 1923.

The running backs responded to the rules changes with a record 10 players rushing for 1,000 yards or more. O.J. Simpson found the offensive style of the Buffalo Bills' new coach Lou Saban just what he wanted and led the league with 1,251 yards. Larry Csonka (1,117) and Eugene (Mercury) Morris (1,000) of Miami became the first teammates to rush for 1,000 yards the same season. Morris made it when the league found an error in the statistics in which Morris had been charged with a nine-yard loss that should have been listed as a fumble by Earl Morrall. Dave Hampton of Atlanta made it to 1,001 yards in the last game but was thrown for a six-yard loss and finished at 995 yards.

Don Maynard of the New York Jets topped the all-time pass receivers with 632 receptions, one more than the retired Raymond Berry. Bobby Douglass of the Bears ran for 968 yards, a record for a quarterback, and led the Bears in rushing.

Coach Don Shula's Dolphins breezed to a 14-0 record, seven full games ahead of the runner-up Jets (7-7) in the AFC East. Oakland regained control of the AFC West at 10-3-1 after a one-year lapse. Chuck Noll brought Pittsburgh its first division title at 11-3, helped by young quarterback Terry Bradshaw and rookie running back Franco Harris. Cleveland (10-4) qualified as the wild card team, behind Mike Phipps, who took over for quarterback Bill Nelsen.

In the NFC East, Washington edged Dallas for the title, although the Cowboys earned the wild card position. The Redskins had the NFC's best defense, rushing leader (Larry Brown), and most inspirational quarterback (Billy Kilmer). The Cowboys played the season without Roger Staubach, who was injured in the preseason. In the Central, a new Alabama quarterback, Scott Hunter, led the Packers back past the Vikings. The 49ers won their third consecutive West title due in part to a collapse by the Rams, who finished only 6-7-1.

Miami had to come from behind to beat Cleveland 20-14 in its first playoff game and Pittsburgh had to come up with a near-miraculous play to defeat Oakland 13-7. Terry Bradshaw threw a desperation pass on fourth and 10 with 22 seconds to play and the Raiders ahead 7-6. The ball, intended for John (Frenchy) Fuqua, bounced off Oakland safety Jack Tatum and was caught by Franco Harris just off his shoe tops. Harris ran 60 yards for the winning touchdown.

In the NFC divisional playoffs, Roger Staubach threw two touchdown passes in 38 seconds as Dallas rallied to beat the 49ers 30-28, and Washington defeated Green Bay 16-3.

Miami beat Pittsburgh 21-17 for the AFC championship and Washington advanced to the Super Bowl with a 26-3 victory over the Cowboys on four field goals by Curt Knight and two touchdown passes from Billy Kilmer to Charley Taylor.

The Dolphins made NFL history, climaxing an entire season without defeat (17-0), with a 14-7 victory over Washington in Super Bowl VII before a record Super Bowl crowd of 90,182 at the Los Angeles Memorial Coliseum. No team ever had gone all the way without a defeat or a tie.

Miami ended its perfect season by shutting out the Redskins until Garo Yepremian, trying to salvage something from an abortive field-goal try, attempted to pass and fumbled. Mike Bass grabbed the ball and ran 49 yards for the lone Washington score with 2:07 to play.

Running back Gale Sayers of Chicago, quarterback Bart Starr of Green Bay, and safety Larry Wilson of St. Louis retired at the end of the season.

1972 AFC STANDINGS

Eastern Division	**W**	**L**	**T**	**Pct.**	**Pts.**	**OP**
Miami	14	0	0	1.000	385	171
New York Jets	7	7	0	.500	367	324
Baltimore	5	9	0	.429	235	252
Buffalo	4	9	1	.321	257	377
New England	3	11	0	.214	192	446
Central Division	**W**	**L**	**T**	**Pct.**	**Pts.**	**OP**
Pittsburgh	11	3	0	.786	343	175
Cleveland*	10	4	0	.714	268	249
Cincinnati	8	6	0	.571	299	229
Houston	1	13	0	.071	164	380
Western Division	**W**	**L**	**T**	**Pct.**	**Pts.**	**OP**
Oakland	10	3	1	.750	365	248
Kansas City	8	6	0	.571	287	254
Denver	5	9	0	.357	325	350
San Diego	4	9	1	.321	264	344

**Wild Card qualifier for playoffs*

Divisional playoffs: Pittsburgh 13, Oakland 7;
Miami 20, Cleveland 14

AFC championship: Miami 21, Pittsburgh 17

LEADING RUSHERS	**Att.**	**Yards**	**Avg.**	**Long**	**TD**
O. J. Simpson, Buffalo	292	1,251	4.3	94t	6
Larry Csonka, Miami	213	1,117	5.2	45	6
Marv Hubbard, Oakland	219	1,100	5.0	39	4
Franco Harris, Pittsburgh	188	1,055	5.6	75t	10
Mike Garrett, San Diego	272	1,031	3.8	41t	6
LEADING PASSERS	**Att.**	**Comp.**	**Yards**	**TD**	**Int.**
Earl Morrall, Miami	150	83	1,360	11	7
Daryle Lamonica, Oakland	281	149	1,998	18	12
Charley Johnson, Denver	238	132	1,783	14	14
Johnny Unitas, Baltimore	157	88	1,111	4	6
Ken Anderson, Cincinnati	301	171	1,918	7	7
LEADING RECEIVERS	**No.**	**Yards**	**Avg.**	**Long**	**TD**
Fred Biletnikoff, Oakland	58	802	13.8	39t	7
Otis Taylor, Kansas City	57	821	14.4	44	6
Chip Myers, Cincinnati	57	792	13.9	42	3
J. D. Hill, Buffalo	52	754	14.5	58t	5
Gary Garrison, San Diego	52	744	14.3	52t	7
LEADING SCORER	**TD**	**FG**	**PAT**		**TP**
Bobby Howfield, NY Jets	0	27	40		121
LEADING INTERCEPTOR	**No.**	**Yards**	**Avg.**	**Long**	**TD**
Mike Sensibaugh, Kansas City	8	65	8.1	35	0
LEADING PUNTER	**No.**		**Avg.**		**Long**
Jerrel Wilson, Kansas City	66		44.8		69
LEADING PUNT RETURNER	**No.**	**Yards**	**Avg.**	**Long**	**TD**
Chris Farasopoulos, NY Jets	17	179	10.5	65t	1
LEADING KICKOFF RETURNER	**No.**	**Yards**	**Avg.**	**Long**	**TD**
Bruce Laird, Baltimore	29	843	29.1	73	0

SUPERLATIVES

Rushing average	5.6	Franco Harris, Pittsburgh
Receiving average	21.4	Rich Caster, NY Jets
Completion percentage	57.4	Len Dawson, Kansas City
Touchdowns	14	Emerson Boozer, NY Jets

LONGEST

Run	94t	O.J. Simpson, Buffalo
Pass	83t	Joe Namath to Eddie Bell, NY Jets
Interception	82t	Phil Villapiano, Oakland
Punt	72	Bobby Walden, Pittsburgh
Punt return	66t	Tommy Casanova, Cincinnati
Kickoff return	94t	Randy Montgomery, Denver
Field goal	57	Don Cockroft, Cleveland

1972 NFC STANDINGS

Eastern Division	W	L	T	Pct.	Pts.	OP
Washington	11	3	0	.786	336	218
Dallas*	10	4	0	.714	319	240
New York Giants	8	6	0	.571	331	247
St. Louis	4	9	1	.321	193	303
Philadelphia	2	11	1	.179	145	352
Central Division	**W**	**L**	**T**	**Pct.**	**Pts.**	**OP**
Green Bay	10	4	0	.714	304	226
Detroit	8	5	1	.607	339	290
Minnesota	7	7	0	.500	301	252
Chicago Bears	4	9	1	.321	225	275
Western Division	**W**	**L**	**T**	**Pct.**	**Pts.**	**OP**
San Francisco	8	5	1	.607	353	249
Atlanta	7	7	0	.500	269	274
Los Angeles Rams	6	7	1	.464	291	286
New Orleans	2	11	1	.179	215	361

**Wild Card qualifier for playoffs*

Divisional playoffs: Dallas 30, San Francisco 28;
Washington 16, Green Bay 3

NFC championship: Washington 26, Dallas 3

Super Bowl VII: Miami (AFC) 14, Washington (NFC) 7

LEADING RUSHERS	Att.	Yards	Avg.	Long	TD
Larry Brown, Washington	285	1,216	4.3	38t	8
Ron Johnson, NY Giants	298	1,182	4.0	35t	9
Calvin Hill, Dallas	245	1,036	4.2	26	6
John Brockington, Green Bay	274	1,027	3.7	30t	8
Dave Hampton, Atlanta	230	995	4.3	56t	6

LEADING PASSERS	Att.	Comp.	Yards	TD	Int.
Norm Snead, NY Giants	325	196	2,307	17	12
Bob Berry, Atlanta	277	154	2,158	13	12
Fran Tarkenton, Minnesota	378	215	2,651	18	13
Bill Kilmer, Washington	225	120	1,640	19	11
Steve Spurrier, San Francisco	269	147	1,983	18	16

LEADING RECEIVERS	No.	Yards	Avg.	Long	TD
Harold Jackson, Philadelphia	62	1,048	16.9	77t	4
Bob Tucker, NY Giants	55	764	13.9	39	4
Art Malone, Atlanta	50	585	11.7	57t	2
Charley Taylor, Washington	49	673	13.7	70t	7
John Gilliam, Minnesota	47	1,035	22.0	66t	7
Bob Newland, New Orleans	47	579	12.3	42t	2

LEADING SCORER	TD	FG	PAT	TP
Chester Marcol, Green Bay	0	33	29	128

LEADING INTERCEPTOR	No.	Yards	Avg.	Long	TD
Bill Bradley, Philadelphia	9	73	8.1	21	0

LEADING PUNTER	No.	Avg.	Long
Dave Chapple, LA Rams	53	44.2	70

LEADING PUNT RETURNER	No.	Yards	Avg.	Long	TD
Ken Ellis, Green Bay	14	215	15.4	80t	1

LEADING KICKOFF RETURNER	No.	Yards	Avg.	Long	TD
Ron Smith, Chi. Bears	30	924	30.8	94t	1

SUPERLATIVES

Rushing average	6.9	Bobby Douglass, Chi. Bears
Receiving average	22.0	John Gilliam, Minnesota
Completion percentage	60.3	Norm Snead, NY Giants
Touchdowns	14	Ron Johnson, NY Giants

LONGEST

Run	68	Larry Smith, LA Rams
Pass	98	Jim Hart to Bobby Moore, St. Louis
Interception	88t	Rudy Redmond, Detroit
Punt	71	Julian Fagan, New Orleans
Punt return	85t	Jon Staggers, Green Bay
Kickoff return	98t	Vic Washington, San Francisco
Field goal	54	Toni Fritsch, Dallas

1973 Congress passed a three-year bill that lifted the hometown TV blackouts on games sold out 72 hours before kickoff. The NFL opposed the legislation as a threat to the sale of season tickets and the first step toward a television studio-type game with empty seats at the stadiums. When the season actually was played, the ticket sales weren't affected, but large numbers of fans started not showing up for select games, causing the start of the term "no-show."

The league formed NFL Charities, a nonprofit foundation that would receive its revenue from licensing league and club trademarks, to meet educational and charitable needs and provide economic support for former players.

The New York Giants were forced to move out of Yankee Stadium, their home since 1956, due to stadium renovations, and played their last five games at the Yale Bowl in New Haven, Connecticut. Buffalo opened 80,020-seat Rich Stadium at suburban Orchard Park, New York.

The World Football League was formed in a meeting in Los Angeles in October and announced its plans to begin play in 1974.

O.J. Simpson of the Buffalo Bills broke the single-season rushing record with 2,003 yards. He had a record 250 yards against New England opening day. He passed midseason with 1,000 yards, the goal of most outstanding runners for a full season. At the end he had set records for most rushing attempts (332), most 100-yard games in a season (11), and most 200-yard games in a season (3). John Brockington of Green Bay also put his name in the record book as the only man to gain over 1,000 yards in each of his first three pro seasons.

Miami's bid for a second straight perfect season ended early. The Dolphins won their opener 21-13 over San Francisco for 18 straight, tying the record set by the 1933-34 Bears and equaled by the 1941-42 Bears. However, the Dolphins were tripped up by the Raiders 12-7 in their second game, which was played in Berkeley, California, on September 23.

Miami lost only one more game on the way to a 12-2 record and a third straight title in the AFC East with Bob Griese doing the passing, a three-pronged running attack of Larry Csonka, Mercury Morris, and Jim Kiick, and the "No Name Defense," so-called because of its lack of individual recognition.

Ken Anderson and Essex Johnson, aided by rookies Charles (Boobie) Clark and Isaac Curtis, brought Cincinnati the AFC Central title at 10-4, winning the division despite Pittsburgh's matching 10-4 because the Bengals had a better record in intraconference games. The Steelers qualified for the playoffs as the wild card team. Oakland took the West at 9-4-1 by beating runner-up Denver (7-5-2) in the final game 21-7.

Dallas (10-4) and George Allen's "Over the Hill Gang" at Washington (10-4) ruled the NFC East, with Dallas winning the division on an edge in total points for the two games the clubs split. Washington got the NFC wild card spot.

Rookie running back Chuck Foreman teamed with Fran Tarkenton and deep threat John Gilliam to help the Vikings to the NFC Central title. No other team in the division had a winning record.

Chuck Knox became the coach of the Los Angeles Rams and traded for San Diego quarterback John Hadl. Hadl led the league in passing for most of the year and combined with young running backs Lawrence McCutcheon and Jim Bertelsen to give the Rams an explosive offense. The Rams won the West easily, going 12-2. The acquisition of Hadl also allowed the Rams to trade quarterback Roman Gabriel, who went to the Eagles in exchange for star receiver Harold Jackson and a handful of high draft choices. The Chargers replaced Hadl by trading for Johnny Unitas, who retired at the end of the season after helping break in rookie Dan Fouts.

In the AFC playoffs Miami disposed of Cincinnati 34-16 and Oakland got even with Pittsburgh 33-14. Minnesota ousted Washington 27-20 and Roger Staubach's 83-yard pass to Drew Pearson helped Dallas beat Los Angeles 27-16 in the NFC playoffs.

The Dolphins won the AFC championship by defeating Oakland 27-10 on 117 yards and three touchdowns by Larry Csonka. The Vikings ran over the Cowboys 27-10 for the NFC title.

The Dolphins joined the Green Bay Packers as two-time Super Bowl winners by methodically beating the Vikings 24-7 with Csonka rushing for a record 145 yards at Rice Stadium in Houston.

1973 AFC STANDINGS

Eastern Division	W	L	T	Pct.	Pts.	OP
Miami	12	2	0	.857	343	150
Buffalo	9	5	0	.643	259	230
New England	5	9	0	.357	258	300
Baltimore	4	10	0	.286	226	341
New York Jets	4	10	0	.286	240	306
Central Division	**W**	**L**	**T**	**Pct.**	**Pts.**	**OP**
Cincinnati	10	4	0	.714	286	231
Pittsburgh*	10	4	0	.714	347	210
Cleveland	7	5	2	.571	234	255
Houston	1	13	0	.071	199	447
Western Division	**W**	**L**	**T**	**Pct.**	**Pts.**	**OP**
Oakland	9	4	1	.679	292	175
Denver	7	5	2	.571	354	296
Kansas City	7	5	2	.571	231	192
San Diego	2	11	1	.179	188	386

**Wild Card qualifier for playoffs*

Divisional playoffs: Oakland 33, Pittsburgh 14;
Miami 34, Cincinnati 16

AFC championship: Miami 27, Oakland 10

LEADING RUSHERS	Att.	Yards	Avg.	Long	TD
O. J. Simpson, Buffalo	332	2,003	6.0	80t	12
Larry Csonka, Miami	219	1,003	4.6	25	5
Essex Johnson, Cincinnati	195	997	5.1	46	4
Boobie Clark, Cincinnati	254	988	3.9	26	8
Floyd Little, Denver	256	979	3.8	47	12

LEADING PASSERS	Att.	Comp.	Yards	TD	Int.
Ken Stabler, Oakland	260	163	1,997	14	10
Bob Griese, Miami	218	116	1,422	17	8
Ken Anderson, Cincinnati	329	179	2,428	18	12
Charley Johnson, Denver	346	184	2,465	20	17
Al Woodall, NY Jets	201	101	1,228	9	8

LEADING RECEIVERS	No.	Yards	Avg.	Long	TD
Fred Willis, Houston	57	371	6.5	50	1
Ed Podolak, Kansas City	55	445	8.1	25	0
Reggie Rucker, New England	53	743	14.0	64	3
Fred Biletnikoff, Oakland	48	660	13.8	32	4
Isaac Curtis, Cincinnati	45	843	18.7	77t	9
Mike Siani, Oakland	45	742	16.5	80t	3
Boobie Clark, Cincinnati	45	347	7.7	39	0

LEADING SCORER	TD	FG	PAT	TP
Roy Gerela, Pittsburgh	0	29	36	123

LEADING INTERCEPTORS	No.	Yards	Avg.	Long	TD
Dick Anderson, Miami	8	163	20.4	38t	2
Mike Wagner, Pittsburgh	8	134	16.8	38	0

LEADING PUNTER	No.	Avg.	Long
Jerrel Wilson, Kansas City	80	45.5	68

LEADING PUNT RETURNER	No.	Yards	Avg.	Long	TD
Ron Smith, San Diego	27	352	13.0	84t	2

LEADING KICKOFF RETURNER	No.	Yards	Avg.	Long	TD
Wallace Francis, Buffalo	23	687	29.9	101t	2

SUPERLATIVES

Rushing average	6.4	Mercury Morris, Miami
Receiving average	18.7	Isaac Curtis, Cincinnati
Completion percentage	62.7	Ken Stabler, Oakland
Touchdowns	13	Floyd Little, Denver

LONGEST

Run	80t	O.J. Simpson, Buffalo
Pass	80t	Ken Stabler to Mike Siani, Oakland
Interception	87	Joe Blahak, Houston
Punt	78	Bill Van Heusen, Denver
Punt return	84t	Ron Smith, San Diego
Kickoff return	103t	Bob Gresham, Houston
Field goal	53	Garo Yepremian, Miami

1973 NFC STANDINGS

Eastern Division	W	L	T	Pct.	Pts.	OP
Dallas	10	4	0	.714	382	203
Washington*	10	4	0	.714	325	198
Philadelphia	5	8	1	.393	310	393
St. Louis	4	9	1	.321	286	365
New York Giants	2	11	1	.179	226	362
Central Division	**W**	**L**	**T**	**Pct.**	**Pts.**	**OP**
Minnesota	12	2	0	.857	296	168
Detroit	6	7	1	.464	271	247
Green Bay	5	7	2	.429	202	259
Chicago Bears	3	11	0	.214	195	334
Western Division	**W**	**L**	**T**	**Pct.**	**Pts.**	**OP**
Los Angeles Rams	12	2	0	.857	388	178
Atlanta	9	5	0	.643	318	224
New Orleans	5	9	0	.357	163	312
San Francisco	5	9	0	.357	262	319

**Wild Card qualifier for playoffs*

Divisional playoffs: Minnesota 27, Washington 20;
Dallas 27, Los Angeles Rams 16

NFC championship: Minnesota 27, Dallas 10

Super Bowl VIII: Miami (AFC) 24, Minnesota (NFC) 7

LEADING RUSHERS	Att.	Yards	Avg.	Long	TD
John Brockington, Green Bay	265	1,144	4.3	53	3
Calvin Hill, Dallas	273	1,142	4.2	21	6
L. McCutcheon, LA Rams	210	1,097	5.2	37	2
Dave Hampton, Atlanta	263	997	3.8	25	4
Tom Sullivan, Philadelphia	217	968	4.5	37	4

LEADING PASSERS	Att.	Comp.	Yards	TD	Int.
Roger Staubach, Dallas	286	179	2,428	23	15

1970s: A Photographic Portfolio

In 1970, John Brodie (12) led the NFL in passing and Gene Washington (18) in receiving yards as the 49ers won their first divisional title with a 10-3-1 record.

In 1970, his second season, Larry Brown of the Redskins led the NFL in rushing with 1,125 yards and also caught 37 passes. Two years later, Brown was the main performer in Washington's march to Super Bowl VII, leading the NFC with 1,216 yards, making 32 receptions, and scoring 12 touchdowns.

In 1970, Ron Johnson became the first Giants player to rush for 1,000 yards in a season (1,027).

Otis Taylor, one of the NFL's best receivers, first received deserved acclaim after Super Bowl IV.

Floyd Little led the AFC in rushing in 1970 and the NFL in 1971, with a Denver record 1,133 yards.

Two of the most valuable blockers of the 1970s were guard Dan Dierdorf (72), who played from 1971 to 1983 with St. Louis, and MacArthur Lane (36), who later blocked for Green Bay's John Brockington.

The Raiders' Fred Biletnikoff retired as the number-four receiver in NFL history with 589 catches.

One of the greatest individual performances ever was by Kansas City's Ed Podolak (with ball) in an AFC Divisional Playoff Game with Miami on Christmas Day, 1971. Podolak gained 350 all-purpose yards—85 rushing, 110 receiving, and 155 on kick returns, including this 78-yard return in the fourth quarter.

Earl Morrall led Baltimore to Super Bowl III, then produced a Colts victory in Super Bowl V.

On a snowy day in 1973, O.J. Simpson of Buffalo ran for 200 yards against the Jets to break Jim Brown's record of 1,863 yards and become the first back ever to rush for 2,000 yards in a season (2,003).

Miami's Larry Csonka rushed for more than 1,000 yards three times and was MVP of Super Bowl VIII.

John Brockington of Green Bay was the first player to rush for more than 1,000 yards in each of his first three years. As a rookie (1971), he led the NFC in rushing with 1,105 yards and a 5.1-yard average.

Oakland's Ken Stabler took over for Daryle Lamonica in 1973 and went on to lead the AFC in passing.

Obtained from the Rams in early 1973, Roman Gabriel led the NFL in yards passing (3,219).

Denver's Otis Armstrong interrupted O.J. Simpson's string of rushing titles, with 1,407 yards in 1974.

In the mid-1970s, the Rams possessed one of the best offenses in the NFL, with blockers Tom Mack (65) and Charlie Cowan (73), receiver Harold Jackson (29), and quarterback James Harris (12). Harris was the AFC-NFC Pro Bowl's most valuable player in 1975 and led the NFC in passing in 1976.

Chuck Foreman (44) was a major reason the Vikings dominated the NFC Central in the 1970s. In 1975, Foreman led the NFL in receiving, the NFC in scoring, and was second in the conference in rushing.

In 1975 and 1977, the Colts' Lydell Mitchell rushed for 1,000 yards and led the AFC in receiving.

Walter Payton of the Bears rushed for an NFL-record 275 yards against Minnesota, November 20, 1977.

In 1976, the Steelers became the second NFL team to have two 1,000-yard rushers in the same season. Behind the blocking of an outstanding line anchored by all-pro center Mike Webster, Franco Harris (32) rushed for 1,128 yards and Rocky Bleier (20) rushed for 1,036. The Steelers won four Super Bowls in the 1970s.

Defensive end Lee Roy Selmon (63) was the first player ever selected in the draft by Tampa Bay. He was named defensive player of the year in 1979.

Jim Zorn went from the bottom to the top—from being a free agent from Cal-Poly Pomona to being Seattle's first quarterback to being an all-pro in 1978.

Drew Pearson was Roger Staubach's target for miracles, such as the Hail Mary pass in 1975.

Archie Manning, 1978 NFC player of the year, may be the best quarterback never to play for a winner.

Ahmad Rashad is best remembered as a Viking, but he caught a 98-yard pass with St. Louis.

Terry Bradshaw, the most valuable player in Super Bowls XIII and XIV, quarterbacked Pittsburgh to four Super Bowl championships in the 1970s.

For his first three years (1978-80), Houston's Earl Campbell was as good a running back as ever played, leading the NFL in rushing three times.

Fran Tarkenton, Minnesota	274	169	2,113	15	7
John Hadl, LA Rams	258	135	2,008	22	11
Roman Gabriel, Philadelphia	460	270	3,219	23	12
Bill Kilmer, Washington	227	122	1,656	14	9
LEADING RECEIVERS	**No.**	**Yards**	**Avg.**	**Long**	**TD**
Harold Carmichael, Philadelphia	67	1,116	16.7	73	9
Charley Taylor, Washington	59	801	13.6	53	7
Charle Young, Philadelphia	55	854	15.5	80t	6
Bob Tucker, NY Giants	50	681	13.6	33	5
Tom Sullivan, Philadelphia	50	322	6.4	29	1
LEADING SCORER	**TD**	**FG**		**PAT**	**TP**
David Ray, LA Rams	0	30		40	130
LEADING INTERCEPTOR	**No.**	**Yards**	**Avg.**	**Long**	**TD**
Bobby Bryant, Minnesota	7	105	15.0	46t	1
LEADING PUNTER	**No.**		**Avg.**		**Long**
Tom Wittum, San Francisco	79		43.7		62
LEADING PUNT RETURNER	**No.**	**Yards**	**Avg.**	**Long**	**TD**
Bruce Taylor, San Francisco	15	207	13.8	61	0
LEADING KICKOFF RETURNER	**No.**	**Yards**	**Avg.**	**Long**	**TD**
Carl Garrett, Chi. Bears	16	486	30.4	67	0

SUPERLATIVES

Rushing average	5.2	Lawrence McCutcheon, LA Rams
Receiving average	21.9	Harold Jackson, LA Rams
Completion percentage	62.6	Roger Staubach, Dallas
Touchdowns	14	Larry Brown, Washington

LONGEST

Run	63	Tom Wittum, San Francisco
Pass	84t	Greg Landry to Ron Jessie, Detroit
Interception	95t	Dick Jauron, Detroit
Punt	72	John James, Atlanta
Punt return	72	Ike Hill, Chi. Bears
Kickoff return	97t	Herb Mul-Key, Washington Don Shy, St. Louis
Field goal	54	Bruce Gossett, San Francisco

1974 Significant rules changes were made. Sudden-death overtime was adopted for all preseason and regular-season games. The goal posts were moved back to the end line and kickoffs were to be made from the 35, not the 40. Missed field goals outside the 20 were to go back to the line of scrimmage instead of being touchbacks. Only two outside men on the kicking team were allowed downfield before the ball was punted. Defensive players were allowed to "chuck" or bump a pass receiver only once, and rolling blocks on wide receivers were made illegal. The holding penalty was reduced to 10 yards and receivers were prohibited from making crack-back blocks below the waist.

The Toronto Northmen of the World Football League made news in March when they announced that Larry Csonka, Paul Warfield, and Jim Kiick of the NFL champion Miami Dolphins would play out their options in 1974 and join the Northmen in 1975 in a reported three-year $3 million deal.

The NFL decided to expand to 28 clubs by adding Tampa Bay and Seattle to begin play in 1976. Commissioner Pete Rozelle was voted a new 10-year contract. A 47-man player limit was adopted.

Weeb Ewbank, coach of the New York Jets, retired and was replaced by his son-in-law, assistant coach Charley Winner. Coach Don McCafferty of the Detroit Lions died of a heart attack during the preseason and was replaced by Rick Forzano.

Owners and players were unable to agree on a new collective bargaining agreement as the old four-year pact expired. Rookies came to training camp but the veterans stayed out, many of them carrying picket signs. The annual Chicago All-Star Game was canceled. The annual Hall of Fame Game between Buffalo and St. Louis was played almost entirely with rookies. The veterans reported under provisions of a 14-day cooling off period and the strike ended August 28 in time for the final preseason games, most of which were played with rookie teams.

The results of the rules changes were a considerable increase in touchdowns, fewer field goals, fewer fair-catch signals, and longer punt and kickoff returns.

The Miami offense faltered a little, but the defense was as strong as ever. The Dolphins won the AFC East again, and the second-place Bills qualified for the wild card position. Baltimore had the poorest record in the NFL, but it had one of the brightest young stars in quarterback Bert Jones. Only a month after Ken Anderson of Cincinnati set a record by completing 16 consecutive passes against the Colts, Jones broke it with 17 in a row against the Jets. In the AFC Central, Anderson led the NFL in passing, but the Bengals finished second to Pittsburgh, which had the conference's best defense but couldn't decide between Terry Bradshaw and Joe Gilliam as its starting quarterback. In the West, the Raiders had the best record in the NFL (12-2), the Broncos had their second winning season behind quarterback Charley Johnson and league rushing leader Otis Armstrong, and the Chargers had a new coach (Tommy Prothro) and the league's top rushing rookie (Don Woods).

Coach Don Coryell put the St. Louis Cardinals in the playoffs for the first time since they left Chicago in 1960 by winning the NFC East. St. Louis and Washington finished 10-4 but the Cardinals beat the Redskins twice to win the division while the Redskins became the wild card entry. The Minnesota Vikings and Los Angeles Rams easily won the Central and Western Divisions in the NFC. The Rams traded their starting quarterback, John Hadl, to the Packers in October, but James Harris took over as the starter, finished second in the NFC in passing, and went on to be named most valuable player in the AFC-NFC Pro Bowl.

The Miami Dolphins' reign in the NFL ended when they were beaten by Oakland 28-26 on a sensational catch by Clarence Davis of Ken Stabler's pass with 26 seconds to play in the AFC Divisional Playoff Game. Pittsburgh beat Buffalo in the other AFC playoff. In the NFC, Minnesota defeated St. Louis 30-14 and Los Angeles won over Washington 19-10.

Pittsburgh reached the Super Bowl for the first time by defeating Oakland 24-13 in the AFC Championship Game. Pittsburgh gave up only 29 yards rushing. Minnesota returned to the Super Bowl for the third time by handing Los Angeles a 14-10 defeat for the NFC title. The key to the game was a Rams 98-yard drive, which didn't produce any points.

Owner Art Rooney finally came up with a winner in Pittsburgh after 42 years. Chuck Noll's Steelers went all the way to a Super Bowl championship. Running back Franco Harris broke a record with 158 yards rushing in the Steelers' 16-6 victory over the Vikings in Super Bowl IX at Tulane Stadium in New Orleans.

At the end of the season, Sonny Jurgensen of Washington and Jim Otto of Oakland retired.

1974 AFC STANDINGS

Eastern Division	**W**	**L**	**T**	**Pct.**	**Pts.**	**OP**
Miami	11	3	0	.786	327	216
Buffalo*	9	5	0	.643	264	244
New England	7	7	0	.500	348	289
New York Jets	7	7	0	.500	279	300
Baltimore	2	12	0	.143	190	329
Central Division	**W**	**L**	**T**	**Pct.**	**Pts.**	**OP**
Pittsburgh	10	3	1	.750	305	189
Cincinnati	7	7	0	.500	283	259
Houston	7	7	0	.500	236	282
Cleveland	4	10	0	.286	251	344
Western Division	**W**	**L**	**T**	**Pct.**	**Pts.**	**OP**
Oakland	12	2	0	.857	355	228
Denver	7	6	1	.536	302	294
Kansas City	5	9	0	.357	233	293
San Diego	5	9	0	.357	212	285

**Wild Card qualifier for playoffs*

Divisional playoffs: Oakland 28, Miami 26; Pittsburgh 32, Buffalo 14

AFC championship: Pittsburgh 24, Oakland 13

LEADING RUSHERS	**Att.**	**Yards**	**Avg.**	**Long**	**TD**
Otis Armstrong, Denver	263	1,407	5.3	43	9
Don Woods, San Diego	227	1,162	5.1	56t	7
O. J. Simpson, Buffalo	270	1,125	4.2	41t	3
Franco Harris, Pittsburgh	208	1,006	4.8	54	5
Marv Hubbard, Oakland	188	865	4.6	32	4
LEADING PASSERS	**Att.**	**Comp.**	**Yards**	**TD**	**Int.**
Ken Anderson, Cincinnati	328	213	2,667	18	10
Ken Stabler, Oakland	310	178	2,469	26	12
Charley Johnson, Denver	244	136	1,969	13	9
Bob Griese, Miami	253	152	1,968	16	15
Dan Pastorini, Houston	247	140	1,571	10	10
LEADING RECEIVERS	**No.**	**Yards**	**Avg.**	**Long**	**TD**
Lydell Mitchell, Baltimore	72	544	7.6	24	2
Cliff Branch, Oakland	60	1,092	18.2	67t	13
Ed Podolak, Kansas City	43	306	7.1	26	1
Riley Odoms, Denver	42	639	15.2	41	6
Fred Biletnikoff, Oakland	42	593	14.1	46	7
LEADING SCORER	**TD**	**FG**		**PAT**	**TP**
Roy Gerela, Pittsburgh	0	20		33	93
LEADING INTERCEPTOR	**No.**	**Yards**	**Avg.**	**Long**	**TD**
Emmitt Thomas, Kansas City	12	214	17.8	73t	2
LEADING PUNTER	**No.**		**Avg.**		**Long**
Ray Guy, Oakland	74		42.2		66
LEADING PUNT RETURNER	**No.**	**Yards**	**Avg.**	**Long**	**TD**
Lemar Parrish, Cincinnati	18	338	18.8	90t	2
LEADING KICKOFF RETURNER	**No.**	**Yards**	**Avg.**	**Long**	**TD**
Greg Pruitt, Cleveland	22	606	27.5	88t	1

SUPERLATIVES

Rushing average	5.3	Otis Armstrong, Denver
Receiving average	21.1	Isaac Curtis, Cincinnati
Completion percentage	64.9	Ken Anderson, Cincinnati
Touchdowns	13	Cliff Branch, Oakland

LONGEST

Run	75t	Sam Cunningham, New Orleans
Pass	89t	Joe Namath to Rich Caster, NY Jets
Interception	73t	Emmitt Thomas, Kansas City
Punt	69	David Beverly, Houston
Punt return	90t	Lemar Parrish, Cincinnati
Kickoff return	88t	Greg Pruitt, Cleveland
Field goal	50	Jan Stenerud, Kansas City

1974 NFC STANDINGS

Eastern Division	**W**	**L**	**T**	**Pct.**	**Pts.**	**OP**
St. Louis	10	4	0	.714	285	218
Washington*	10	4	0	.714	320	196
Dallas	8	6	0	.571	297	235
Philadelphia	7	7	0	.500	242	217
New York Giants	2	12	0	.143	195	299
Central Division	**W**	**L**	**T**	**Pct.**	**Pts.**	**OP**
Minnesota	10	4	0	.714	310	195
Detroit	7	7	0	.500	256	270
Green Bay	6	8	0	.429	210	206
Chicago Bears	4	10	0	.286	152	279
Western Division	**W**	**L**	**T**	**Pct.**	**Pts.**	**OP**
Los Angeles Rams	10	4	0	.714	263	181
San Francisco	6	8	0	.429	226	236
New Orleans	5	9	0	.357	166	263
Atlanta	3	11	0	.214	111	271

**Wild Card qualifier for playoffs*

Divisional playoffs: Minnesota 30, St. Louis 14; Los Angeles Rams 19, Washington 10

NFC championship: Minnesota 14, Los Angeles Rams 10

Super Bowl IX: Pittsburgh (AFC) 16, Minnesota (NFC) 6

LEADING RUSHERS	**Att.**	**Yards**	**Avg.**	**Long**	**TD**
L. McCutcheon, LA Rams	236	1,109	4.7	23t	3
John Brockington, Green Bay	266	883	3.3	33	5
Calvin Hill, Dallas	185	844	4.6	27	7
Chuck Foreman, Minnesota	199	777	3.9	32	9
Tom Sullivan, Philadelphia	244	760	3.1	28t	11
LEADING PASSERS	**Att.**	**Comp.**	**Yards**	**TD**	**Int.**
Sonny Jurgensen, Washington	167	107	1,185	11	5
James Harris, LA Rams	198	106	1,544	11	6
Billy Kilmer, Washington	234	137	1,632	10	6
Fran Tarkenton, Minnesota	351	199	2,598	17	12
Jim Hart, St. Louis	388	200	2,411	20	8
LEADING RECEIVERS	**No.**	**Yards**	**Avg.**	**Long**	**TD**
Charle Young, Philadelphia	63	696	11.0	29	3
Drew Pearson, Dallas	62	1,087	17.5	50t	2
Harold Carmichael, Philadelphia	56	649	11.6	39	8
Ron Jessie, Detroit	54	761	14.1	46	3
Charley Taylor, Washington	54	738	13.7	51	5
LEADING SCORER	**TD**	**FG**		**PAT**	**TP**
Chester Marcol, Green Bay	0	25		19	94
LEADING INTERCEPTOR	**No.**	**Yards**	**Avg.**	**Long**	**TD**
Ray Brown, Atlanta	8	164	20.5	59t	1
LEADING PUNTER	**No.**		**Avg.**		**Long**
Tom Blanchard, New Orleans	88		42.1		71
LEADING PUNT RETURNER	**No.**	**Yards**	**Avg.**	**Long**	**TD**
Dick Jauron, Detroit	17	286	16.8	58	0
LEADING KICKOFF RETURNER	**No.**	**Yards**	**Avg.**	**Long**	**TD**
Terry Metcalf, St. Louis	20	623	31.2	94t	1

SUPERLATIVES

Rushing average	4.7	Terry Metcalf, St. Louis
Receiving average	21.2	Gene Washington, San Francisco
Completion percentage	64.1	Sonny Jurgensen, Washington
Touchdowns	15	Chuck Foreman, Minnesota

LONGEST

Run	75t	Terry Metcalf, St. Louis
Pass	81	Gary Hammond to Jackie Smith, St. Louis
Interception	59t	Ray Brown, Atlanta
Punt	71	Tom Blanchard, New Orleans

Punt return	98t	Dennis Morgan, Dallas
Kickoff return	102t	Larry Jones, Washington
Field goal	52	Chester Marcol, Green Bay Bill McClard, New Orleans

1975 An interpretation of the rules made oversized huddles and "lingering on the field" illegal. The owners established a 43-man player limit and did away with taxi squads.

The playoff format was changed to reward the teams with the highest won-lost percentages by making them the hosts for the divisional playoffs. The ultimate survivors with the best records would host the championship games.

Legal problems plagued the owners. A court decision declaring the compensation rule, commonly known as the Rozelle Rule, illegal, was appealed.

A one-game strike during the preseason schedule preceded another year without an agreement between the NFL and the Players Association. The New England Patriots refused to play a preseason game with the Jets but all five striking teams agreed to open the regular season despite rejection of a contract offer by the NFL Management Council.

The New Orleans Saints left Tulane Stadium, their home since 1967, and moved into the 72,000-seat Louisiana Superdome. The Superdome was built on a 53-acre tract in downtown New Orleans and its huge dome rose 273 feet above the ground. It was equipped with five giant television screens to add to the fans' enjoyment of the games.

The Detroit Lions left Tiger Stadium, where they had played since 1937, and moved to the new suburban Pontiac Metropolitan Stadium in Pontiac, Michigan. An unusual feature of the stadium, which later was renamed the Pontiac Silverdome, was its roof, a tent of Teflon-coated fiberglass fabric fitting over the top, held up by steel cables, and inflated by compressed air.

Several successful players from the World Football League, including quarterback Tony Adams and tight end Greg Latta, jumped to the NFL. The WFL ended its operation in the twelfth week of its second season, putting 380 players out of work.

Last in the Eastern Division at 2-12 in 1974, Baltimore started with a 1-4 record under new coach Ted Marchibroda, then ran off nine straight victories. The Colts beat Miami twice, 33-17 and 10-7 on a 31-yard field goal by Toni Linhart after 12:44 of sudden-death overtime. Their success in those two games was the difference in the AFC East because Miami also was 10-4, but didn't even get a wild card berth. O.J. Simpson of Buffalo had 1,817 yards rushing, the third-most ever, and a record 23 touchdowns.

Chuck Noll's Steelers lost their second game of the season to Buffalo, then went on an 11-game winning streak before bowing to Los Angeles in the final game for a 12-2 season. Until the Rams game, the Steelers had won 10 in a row on the road and were 9-0 against the NFC since 1972. Despite the streaks, the Steelers had tough competition in the AFC Central with runner-up and wild card Cincinnati 11-3 and Houston 10-4. The Oilers lost two each to the Steelers and Bengals.

Oakland ran away with the AFC West for its fourth straight division title and eighth in nine years. George Blanda, 49, played his final season for Oakland and left a list of records including most active seasons (26), most games played (340), most consecutive games played (224), most points scored (2,002), most field goals (335), and most points after touchdown (943).

In the NFC East, St. Louis defeated Dallas 31-17 late in the season to win the title. The Cowboys earned the wild card position. Los Angeles won the West by a record seven games over second-place San Francisco. The Vikings were the only team in the NFC that didn't give up at least 125 points more than the league-leading Rams' defense. Behind Chuck Foreman, Fran Tarkenton, and the conference's second-best defense, Minnesota easily won the NFC Central. Foreman scored 22 touchdowns (the second-most ever), led the NFL with 73 receptions, and was second in the NFC with 1,070 yards rushing. Tarkenton finished the season with all-time records for career passing attempts, completions, and touchdown passes, all formerly held by Johnny Unitas.

The Colts' winning streak was snapped by Pittsburgh 28-10 in the first playoff game, one in which quarterback Bert Jones was injured. Oakland held on against a Cincinnati closing rush for a 31-28 victory in the other divisional playoff.

A last-minute, 50-yard pass from Roger Staubach to Drew Pearson gave Dallas a 17-14 playoff win over Minnesota. Los Angeles defeated St. Louis 35-23 behind reserve quarterback Ron Jaworski.

Pittsburgh outlasted the Raiders 16-10 on an icy field at Pittsburgh for the AFC championship when Jack Lambert recovered three fumbles. The Raiders had reached the Steelers' 15 when time ran out.

Dallas became the first wild card team to reach the Super Bowl (although second-place Kansas City of the AFC West in 1969 had won Super Bowl IV before the wild card system) when the Cowboys shocked the Rams 37-7 on four touchdown passes by Roger Staubach, three to Preston Pearson, to win the NFC title.

At Miami, Terry Bradshaw's 64-yard pass to Lynn Swann helped the Steelers win their second straight Super Bowl, 21-17 over the Cowboys. Dallas rallied and threatened until Glen Edwards made an interception in the end zone on the final play of the game.

1975 AFC STANDINGS

Eastern Division	**W**	**L**	**T**	**Pct.**	**Pts.**	**OP**
Baltimore	10	4	0	.714	395	269
Miami	10	4	0	.714	357	222
Buffalo	8	6	0	.571	420	355
New England	3	11	0	.214	258	358
New York Jets	3	11	0	.214	258	433
Central Division	**W**	**L**	**T**	**Pct.**	**Pts.**	**OP**
Pittsburgh	12	2	0	.857	373	162
Cincinnati*	11	3	0	.786	340	246
Houston	10	4	0	.714	293	226
Cleveland	3	11	0	.214	218	372
Western Division	**W**	**L**	**T**	**Pct.**	**Pts.**	**OP**
Oakland	11	3	0	.786	375	255
Denver	6	8	0	.429	254	307
Kansas City	5	9	0	.357	282	341
San Diego	2	12	0	.143	189	345

**Wild Card qualifier for playoffs*

Divisional playoffs: Pittsburgh 28, Baltimore 10;
Oakland 31, Cincinnati 28

AFC championship: Pittsburgh 16, Oakland 10

LEADING RUSHERS	**Att.**	**Yards**	**Avg.**	**Long**	**TD**
O. J. Simpson, Buffalo	329	1,817	5.5	88t	16
Franco Harris, Pittsburgh	262	1,246	4.8	36	10
Lydell Mitchell, Baltimore	289	1,193	4.1	70t	11
Greg Pruitt, Cleveland	217	1,067	4.9	50	8
John Riggins, NY Jets	238	1,005	4.2	42	8
LEADING PASSERS	**Att.**	**Comp.**	**Yards**	**TD**	**Int.**
Ken Anderson, Cincinnati	377	228	3,169	21	11
Len Dawson, Kansas City	140	93	1,095	5	4
Bert Jones, Baltimore	344	203	2,483	18	8
Terry Bradshaw, Pittsburgh	286	165	2,055	18	9
Bob Griese, Miami	191	118	1,693	14	13
LEADING RECEIVERS	**No.**	**Yards**	**Avg.**	**Long**	**TD**
Reggie Rucker, Cleveland	60	770	12.8	40t	3
Lydell Mitchell, Baltimore	60	544	9.1	35t	4
Bob Chandler, Buffalo	55	746	13.6	35	6
Ken Burrough, Houston	53	1,063	20.1	77t	8
Cliff Branch, Oakland	51	893	17.5	53	9
LEADING SCORER	**TD**	**FG**		**PAT**	**TP**
O.J. Simpson, Buffalo	23	0		0	138
LEADING INTERCEPTOR	**No.**	**Yards**	**Avg.**	**Long**	**TD**
Mel Blount, Pittsburgh	11	121	11.0	47	0
LEADING PUNTER	**No.**		**Avg.**		**Long**
Ray Guy, Oakland	68		43.8		64
LEADING PUNT RETURNER	**No.**	**Yards**	**Avg.**	**Long**	**TD**
Billy Johnson, Houston	40	612	15.3	83t	3
LEADING KICKOFF RETURNER	**No.**	**Yards**	**Avg.**	**Long**	**TD**
Harold Hart, Oakland	17	518	30.5	102t	1

SUPERLATIVES

Rushing average	5.5	O.J. Simpson, Buffalo
Receiving average	21.2	Isaac Curtis, Cincinnati
Completion percentage	66.4	Len Dawson, Kansas City
Touchdowns	23	O.J. Simpson, Buffalo

LONGEST

Run	88t	O.J. Simpson, Buffalo
Pass	91	Joe Namath to Rich Caster, NY Jets
Interception	74	Zeke Moore, Houston
Punt	74	Marv Bateman, Buffalo
Punt return	83t	Billy Johnson, Houston
Kickoff return	102t	Harold Hart, Oakland
Field goal	53	Jim Turner, Denver

1975 NFC STANDINGS

Eastern Division	**W**	**L**	**T**	**Pct.**	**Pts.**	**OP**
St. Louis	11	3	0	.786	356	276
Dallas*	10	4	0	.714	350	268
Washington	8	6	0	.571	325	276
New York Giants	5	9	0	.357	216	306
Philadelphia	4	10	0	.286	225	302
Central Division	**W**	**L**	**T**	**Pct.**	**Pts.**	**OP**
Minnesota	12	2	0	.857	377	180
Detroit	7	7	0	.500	245	262
Chicago Bears	4	10	0	.286	191	379
Green Bay	4	10	0	.286	226	285
Western Division	**W**	**L**	**T**	**Pct.**	**Pts.**	**OP**
Los Angeles Rams	12	2	0	.857	312	135
San Francisco	5	9	0	.357	255	286
Atlanta	4	10	0	.286	240	289
New Orleans	2	12	0	.143	165	360

**Wild Card qualifier for playoffs*

Divisional playoffs: Los Angeles Rams 35, St. Louis 23;
Dallas 17, Minnesota 14

NFC championship: Dallas 37, Los Angeles Rams 7

Super Bowl X: Pittsburgh (AFC) 21, Dallas (NFC) 17

LEADING RUSHERS	**Att.**	**Yards**	**Avg.**	**Long**	**TD**
Jim Otis, St. Louis	269	1,076	4.0	30	5
Chuck Foreman, Minnesota	280	1,070	3.8	31t	13
Dave Hampton, Atlanta	250	1,002	4.0	22	5
Robert Newhouse, Dallas	209	930	4.4	29	2
Mike Thomas, Washington	235	919	3.9	34	4
LEADING PASSERS	**Att.**	**Comp.**	**Yards**	**TD**	**Int.**
Fran Tarkenton, Minnesota	425	273	2,994	25	13
Roger Staubach, Dallas	348	198	2,666	17	16
Billy Kilmer, Washington	346	178	2,440	23	16
James Harris, LA Rams	285	157	2,148	14	15
Norm Snead, San Francisco	189	108	1,337	9	10
LEADING RECEIVERS	**No.**	**Yards**	**Avg.**	**Long**	**TD**
Chuck Foreman, Minnesota	73	691	9.5	33	9
Ken Payne, Green Bay	58	766	13.2	54	0
Ed Marinaro, Minnesota	54	462	8.6	25	3
Charley Taylor, Washington	53	744	14.0	64	6
John Gilliam, Minnesota	50	777	15.5	46	7
LEADING SCORER	**TD**	**FG**		**PAT**	**TP**
Chuck Foreman, Minnesota	22	0		0	132
LEADING INTERCEPTOR	**No.**	**Yards**	**Avg.**	**Long**	**TD**
Paul Krause, Minnesota	10	201	20.1	81	0
LEADING PUNTER	**No.**		**Avg.**		**Long**
Herman Weaver, Detroit	80		42.0		61
LEADING PUNT RETURNER	**No.**	**Yards**	**Avg.**	**Long**	**TD**
Terry Metcalf, St. Louis	23	285	12.4	69t	1
LEADING KICKOFF RETURNER	**No.**	**Yards**	**Avg.**	**Long**	**TD**
Walter Payton, Chi. Bears	14	444	31.7	70	0

SUPERLATIVES

Rushing average	5.4	Delvin Williams, San Francisco
Receiving average	20.2	Alfred Jenkins, Atlanta
Completion percentage	64.2	Fran Tarkenton, Minnesota
Touchdowns	22	Chuck Foreman, Minnesota

LONGEST

Run	57t	Jerry Latin, St. Louis
Pass	96t	Billy Kilmer to Frank Grant, Washington
Interception	89t	Frank LeMaster, Philadelphia
Punt	75	John James, Atlanta
Punt return	69t	Terry Metcalf, St. Louis
Kickoff return	97t	Thomas Henderson, Dallas
Field goal	55	Bob Thomas, Chi. Bears

1976 The NFL expanded to 28 teams with the addition of the Seattle Seahawks and the Tampa Bay Buccaneers. The Seahawks moved into the new 65,000-seat Kingdome and the Buccaneers took over Tampa Stadium, expanded to a capacity of 71,400. The New York Giants, who had been forced to play their home games in Yale Bowl and Shea Stadium since 1973, settled into new Giants Stadium with its 76,500 seats in East Rutherford, New Jersey.

Legal complications involving the process of allocating veteran players to Seattle and Tampa Bay delayed the process until March 30-31 with a resultant delay of the college draft until April 8-9. Tampa Bay had the first draft pick after winning a coin toss with Seattle and selected Oklahoma's Lee Roy Selmon, a defensive lineman.

The NFL operated without an agreement with the

Players Association for the third consecutive year although there were several meetings between the two groups. A court decision found the draft system in violation of the law in the absence of collective bargaining.

Thirty-second clocks were installed to make everyone aware of the time remaining between the ready-to-play signal and the snap of the ball.

Paul Brown stepped down at Cincinnati after coaching high school, college, military, and professional teams for 41 years. He picked a long-time assistant, Bill Johnson, as his successor and remained as general manager of the Bengals.

O.J. Simpson sought a trade to the Los Angeles Rams, and did not re-sign with the Buffalo Bills until just before their opening game. There were several important trades, however. New England sent Jim Plunkett to San Francisco and decided to go with Steve Grogan at quarterback. Green Bay traded John Hadl to Houston for Lynn Dickey, who had been a reserve behind Dan Pastorini.

Free agents Calvin Hill, Jean Fugett, and John Riggins wound up with Washington, Larry Csonka with the Giants, Paul Warfield with Cleveland, Jim Kiick with Denver, and John Gilliam with Atlanta.

Baltimore repeated in the AFC East, although New England also matched the 11-3 record. The Colts took the division on a better intradivision record, 7-1 to 6-2. The Patriots made the playoffs for the first time since the merger as the wild card entry. Pittsburgh came back after losing four of its first five, including blowing a 28-14 lead at Oakland in the final three minutes of the season's first game. The Steelers swept their last nine, five by shutouts, matching front-running Cincinnati's 10-4 record in the AFC Central. The Steelers advanced to the playoffs since they had beaten the Bengals twice. Oakland won the AFC West with a 10-game win streak despite injuries to the defensive unit that forced coach John Madden to use a three-man line.

In the NFC, Dallas won the East, and Washington, written off several times during the season, earned the wild card playoff berth by beating the Cowboys on the last day of the season. St. Louis had the same record as Washington, but missed out on the playoffs because of two losses to the Redskins. Minnesota was as stong as ever in the Central, with the addition of wide receivers Ahmad Rashad and Sammy White, the latter a rookie. The Vikings won the division with an 11-2-1 record. The Rams won the West despite an offense that had to adjust to three different starting quarterbacks—James Harris, Ron Jaworski, and Pat Haden—during the year.

The top individual accomplishment of the year occured on Thanksgiving Day, when O.J. Simpson of the Bills rushed for a record 273 yards against Detroit.

Pittsburgh rolled over Baltimore 40-14 in the AFC Divisional Playoffs while Oakland won a 24-21 victory over New England, which suffered a costly roughing-the-passer call on the Raiders' game-winning drive in the final minute.

Brent McClanahan and Chuck Foreman each rushed for more than 100 yards in Minnesota's first-round win over Washington 35-20, while Los Angeles edged Dallas 14-12 in the NFC Divisional Playoffs.

Pittsburgh's hopes for a possible third Super Bowl ended in the AFC Championship Game at Oakland. The Steelers lost 24-7 as both regular running backs, Franco Harris and Rocky Bleier, were out with injuries.

Minnesota shocked Los Angeles for the NFC championship as Bobby Bryant scooped up a blocked field-goal try and ran 90 yards for a touchdown that started them on the way to a 24-13 win.

The Raiders, who had lost six AFC Championship Games since being in their last Super Bowl, were in control all the way in a 32-14 rout of Minnesota in Super Bowl XI. The game was played January 9, at the Rose Bowl in Pasadena. Clarence Davis rushed for 137 yards to lead Oakland to a Super Bowl record 429 yards total offense.

At the end of the season, Merlin Olsen of the Rams, one of the greatest defensive linemen ever, retired.

1976 AFC STANDINGS

Eastern Division	W	L	T	Pct.	Pts.	OP
Baltimore	11	3	0	.786	417	246
New England*	11	3	0	.786	376	236
Miami	6	8	0	.429	263	264
New York Jets	3	11	0	.214	169	383
Buffalo	2	12	0	.143	245	363
Central Division	**W**	**L**	**T**	**Pct.**	**Pts.**	**OP**
Pittsburgh	10	4	0	.714	342	138
Cincinnati	10	4	0	.714	335	210
Cleveland	9	5	0	.643	267	287
Houston	5	9	0	.357	222	273
Western Division	**W**	**L**	**T**	**Pct.**	**Pts.**	**OP**
Oakland	13	1	0	.929	350	237
Denver	9	5	0	.643	315	206
San Diego	6	8	0	.429	248	285
Kansas City	5	9	0	.357	290	376
Tampa Bay	0	14	0	.000	125	412

**Wild Card qualifier for playoffs*

Divisional playoffs: Oakland 24, New England 21; Pittsburgh 40, Baltimore 14

AFC championship: Oakland 24, Pittsburgh 7

LEADING RUSHERS	Att.	Yards	Avg.	Long	TD
O. J. Simpson, Buffalo	290	1,503	5.2	75t	8
Lydell Mitchell, Baltimore	289	1,200	4.2	43	5
Franco Harris, Pittsburgh	289	1,128	3.9	30	14
Rocky Bleier, Pittsburgh	220	1,036	4.7	28	5
Mark van Eeghen, Oakland	233	1,012	4.3	21	3
LEADING PASSERS	**Att.**	**Comp.**	**Yards**	**TD**	**Int.**
Ken Stabler, Oakland	291	194	2,737	27	17
Bert Jones, Baltimore	343	207	3,104	24	9
Joe Ferguson, Buffalo	151	74	1,086	9	1
Bob Griese, Miami	272	162	2,097	11	12
Mike Livingston, Kansas City	338	189	2,682	12	13
LEADING RECEIVERS	**No.**	**Yards**	**Avg.**	**Long**	**TD**
MacArthur Lane, Kansas City	66	686	10.4	44	1
Bob Chandler, Buffalo	61	824	13.5	58t	10
Lydell Mitchell, Baltimore	60	555	9.3	40t	3
Dave Casper, Oakland	53	691	13.0	30t	10
Ken Burrough, Houston	51	932	18.3	69t	7
LEADING SCORER	**TD**	**FG**	**PAT**		**TP**
Toni Linhart, Baltimore	0	20	49		109
LEADING INTERCEPTOR	**No.**	**Yards**	**Avg.**	**Long**	**TD**
Ken Riley, Cincinnati	9	141	15.7	53t	1
LEADING PUNTER	**No.**		**Avg.**		**Long**
Marv Bateman, Buffalo	86		42.8		78
LEADING PUNT RETURNER	**No.**	**Yards**	**Avg.**	**Long**	**TD**
Rick Upchurch, Denver	39	536	13.7	92t	4
LEADING KICKOFF RETURNER	**No.**	**Yards**	**Avg.**	**Long**	**TD**
Duriel Harris, Miami	17	559	32.9	69	0

SUPERLATIVES

Rushing average	5.6	Don Calhoun, New England
Receiving average	25.9	Roger Carr, Baltimore
Completion percentage	66.7	Ken Stabler, Oakland
Touchdowns	14	Franco Harris, Pittsburgh

LONGEST

Run	77t	Archie Griffin, Cincinnati
Pass	88t	Ken Stabler to Cliff Branch, Oakland
Interception	101t	Tony Greene, Buffalo
Punt	78	Marv Bateman, Buffalo
Punt return	92t	Rick Upchurch, Denver
Kickoff return	97t	Willie Shelby, Cincinnati
Field goal	54	Skip Butler, Houston

1976 NFC STANDINGS

Eastern Division	W	L	T	Pct.	Pts.	OP
Dallas	11	3	0	.786	296	194
Washington*	10	4	0	.714	291	217
St. Louis	10	4	0	.714	309	267
Philadelphia	4	10	0	.286	165	286
New York Giants	3	11	0	.214	170	250
Central Division	**W**	**L**	**T**	**Pct.**	**Pts.**	**OP**
Minnesota	11	2	1	.821	305	176
Chicago Bears	7	7	0	.500	253	216
Detroit	6	8	0	.429	262	220
Green Bay	5	9	0	.357	218	299
Western Division	**W**	**L**	**T**	**Pct.**	**Pts.**	**OP**
Los Angeles Rams	10	3	1	.750	351	190
San Francisco	8	6	0	.571	270	190
Atlanta	4	10	0	.286	172	312
New Orleans	4	10	0	.286	253	346
Seattle	2	12	0	.143	229	429

**Wild Card qualifier for playoffs*

Divisional playoffs: Minnesota 35, Washington 20; Los Angeles Rams 14, Dallas 12

NFC championship: Minnesota 24, Los Angeles Rams 13

Super Bowl XI: Oakland (AFC) 32, Minnesota (NFC) 14

LEADING RUSHERS	Att.	Yards	Avg.	Long	TD
Walter Payton, Chi. Bears	311	1,390	4.5	60	13
Delvin Williams, San Francisco	248	1,203	4.9	80t	7
L. McCutcheon, LA Rams	291	1,168	4.0	40	9
Chuck Foreman, Minnesota	278	1,155	4.2	46	13
Mike Thomas, Washington	254	1,101	4.3	28	5
LEADING PASSERS	**Att.**	**Comp.**	**Yards**	**TD**	**Int.**
James Harris, LA Rams	158	91	1,460	8	6
Greg Landry, Detroit	291	168	2,191	17	8
Fran Tarkenton, Minnesota	412	255	2,961	17	8
Jim Hart, St. Louis	388	218	2,946	18	13
Roger Staubach, Dallas	369	208	2,715	14	11
LEADING RECEIVERS	**No.**	**Yards**	**Avg.**	**Long**	**TD**
Drew Pearson, Dallas	58	806	13.9	40t	6
Chuck Foreman, Minnesota	55	567	10.3	41t	1
Steve Largent, Seattle	54	705	13.1	45	4
Tony Galbreath, New Orleans	54	420	7.8	35	1
Ahmad Rashad, Minnesota	53	671	12.7	47	3
LEADING SCORER	**TD**	**FG**	**PAT**		**TP**
Mark Moseley, Washington	0	22	31		97
LEADING INTERCEPTOR	**No.**	**Yards**	**Avg.**	**Long**	**TD**
Monte Jackson, LA Rams	10	173	17.3	46t	3
LEADING PUNTER	**No.**		**Avg.**		**Long**
John James, Atlanta	101		42.1		67
LEADING PUNT RETURNER	**No.**	**Yards**	**Avg.**	**Long**	**TD**
Eddie Brown, Washington	48	646	13.5	71t	1
LEADING KICKOFF RETURNER	**No.**	**Yards**	**Avg.**	**Long**	**TD**
Cullen Bryant, LA Rams	16	459	28.7	90t	1

SUPERLATIVES

Rushing average	4.9	Delvin Williams, San Francisco
Receiving average	22.9	Ron Jessie, LA Rams
Completion percentage	61.9	Fran Tarkenton, Minnesota
Touchdowns	14	Chuck Foreman, Minnesota

LONGEST

Run	80t	Delvin Williams, San Francisco
Pass	85t	Jim Plunkett to Delvin Williams, San Francisco
Interception	83t	Jim Merlo, New Orleans
Punt	69	Herman Weaver, Detroit
Punt return	71t	Eddie Brown, Washington
Kickoff return	90t	Cullen Bryant, LA Rams
Field goal	50	Joe Danelo, NY Giants Rich Szaro, New Orleans

1977 The National Football League Players Association and the National Football League Management Council ratified a collective-bargaining agreement extending until July 15, 1982, covering five football seasons while continuing the pension plan—including the years 1974, 1975, and 1976—with contributions totaling more than $55 million. Total cost of the agreement was estimated at $107 million. The agreement called for a college draft at least through 1986, contained a no-strike, no-suit clause, established a 45-man player limit, reduced pension vesting to four years, and provided for increases in minimum salaries and preseason and postseason pay, improved insurance, medical, and dental benefits, and modified previous practices in player movement and control. The agreement reaffirmed the NFL Commissioner's disciplinary authority. Additionally, the agreement called for the NFL member clubs to make payments totaling $16 million over the next 10 years to settle various legal disputes.

Rules changes were adopted to open up the passing game and to cut down on injuries. Defenders were permitted to make contact with eligible receivers only once, the head slap was outlawed, and wide receivers were prohibited from clipping, even in the legal clipping zone.

Tampa Bay was permanently aligned in the NFC Central Division and Seattle in the AFC Western Division.

Before the season began, Edward J. DeBartolo, Jr. bought the San Francisco 49ers, and replaced coach Monte Clark with Ken Meyer.

Tampa Bay had the first draft choice and selected USC tailback Ricky Bell. Dallas traded with Seattle for the number-two pick and drafted running back Tony Dorsett, the Heisman Trophy winner from Pittsburgh.

The Denver Broncos, with new head coach Red Miller and new quarterback Craig Morton, made the playoffs for the first time ever, winning the AFC West with a 12-2 record. The Broncos' "Orange Crush" defense gave up the fewest points in the AFC. Oakland finished a game behind and earned the wild card berth. Baltimore won the AFC East for the third consecutive season, although the Colts had the same record (10-4) as Miami. The Colts won on the basis of a better record within the conference. Pittsburgh dropped to its poorest record (9-5) since 1971, but the Steelers still won the weak AFC Central, qualifying for the playoffs for the sixth year in a row.

In the NFC, Dallas won its first eight games on the way to a 12-2 record, Los Angeles was the only team in the West to have a winning record, and Minnesota and Chicago had the same record in the Central, 9-5. The Vikings won the title on the basis of more victories in games against common opponents. The Bears qualified for the playoffs as a wild card team.

Oakland defeated Baltimore 37-31 after 15:43 of overtime in the third-longest game in NFL history, and Denver topped Pittsburgh 34-21 in the AFC Divisional Playoffs. In the NFC, Minnesota beat Los Angeles 14-7 in a downpour in Los Angeles, and Dallas defeated Chicago 37-7.

Oakland's hopes for a second-consecutive Super Bowl were ended by Denver's combination of Craig Morton and Haven Moses, who connected for two touchdowns in a 20-17 Broncos victory. Dallas qualified for a record fourth Super Bowl on the strength of its defense, which shut down Minnesota 23-6.

The Cowboys evened their Super Bowl record at 2-2 on January 15 with a 27-10 victory over the Broncos in the Louisiana Superdome in New Orleans in Super Bowl XII. The Dallas defense dominated the game, forcing eight turnovers, holding the Broncos to only 156 yards, and allowing Denver to keep the ball just 21 minutes. The game was the first Super Bowl to be played indoors, and was viewed by more than 102 million people, making it the most-watched sports event in television history.

1977 AFC STANDINGS

Eastern Division	**W**	**L**	**T**	**Pct.**	**Pts.**	**OP**
Baltimore	10	4	0	.714	295	221
Miami	10	4	0	.714	313	197
New England	9	5	0	.643	278	217
New York Jets	3	11	0	.214	191	300
Buffalo	3	11	0	.214	160	313
Central Division	**W**	**L**	**T**	**Pct.**	**Pts.**	**OP**
Pittsburgh	9	5	0	.643	283	243
Houston	8	6	0	.571	299	230
Cincinnati	8	6	0	.571	238	235
Cleveland	6	8	0	.429	269	267
Western Division	**W**	**L**	**T**	**Pct.**	**Pts.**	**OP**
Denver	12	2	0	.857	274	148
Oakland*	11	3	0	.786	351	230
San Diego	7	7	0	.500	222	205
Seattle	5	9	0	.357	282	373
Kansas City	2	12	0	.143	225	349

**Wild Card qualifier for playoffs*

Divisional playoffs: Denver 34, Pittsburgh 21;
Oakland 37, Baltimore 31, overtime

AFC championship: Denver 20, Oakland 17

LEADING RUSHERS	**Att.**	**Yards**	**Avg.**	**Long**	**TD**
Mark van Eeghen, Oakland	324	1,273	3.9	27	7
Franco Harris, Pittsburgh	300	1,162	3.9	61t	11
Lydell Mitchell, Baltimore	301	1,159	3.9	64t	3
Greg Pruitt, Cleveland	236	1,086	4.6	78t	3
Sam Cunningham, New England	270	1,015	3.8	31t	4

LEADING PASSERS	**Att.**	**Comp.**	**Yards**	**TD**	**Int.**
Bob Griese, Miami	307	180	2,252	22	13
Craig Morton, Denver	254	131	1,929	14	8
Bert Jones, Baltimore	393	224	2,686	17	11
Ken Stabler, Oakland	294	169	2,176	20	20
Terry Bradshaw, Pittsburgh	314	162	2,523	17	19

LEADING RECEIVERS	**No.**	**Yards**	**Avg.**	**Long**	**TD**
Lydell Mitchell, Baltimore	71	620	8.7	38	4
Bob Chandler, Buffalo	60	745	12.4	31	4
Clark Gaines, NY Jets	55	469	8.5	31	1
Nat Moore, Miami	52	765	14.7	73t	12
Don McCauley, Baltimore	51	495	9.7	34t	2

LEADING SCORER	**TD**	**FG**	**PAT**	**TP**
Errol Mann, Oakland	0	20	39	99

LEADING INTERCEPTOR	**No.**	**Yards**	**Avg.**	**Long**	**TD**
Lyle Blackwood, Baltimore	10	163	16.3	37	0

LEADING PUNTER	**No.**	**Avg.**	**Long**
Ray Guy, Oakland	59	43.3	74

LEADING PUNT RETURNER	**No.**	**Yards**	**Avg.**	**Long**	**TD**
Billy Johnson, Houston	35	539	15.4	87t	2

LEADING KICKOFF RETURNER	**No.**	**Yards**	**Avg.**	**Long**	**TD**
Raymond Clayborn, New England	28	869	31.0	101t	3

SUPERLATIVES		
Rushing average	4.8	Benny Malone, Miami
Receiving average	21.1	Wesley Walker, NY Jets
Completion percentage	58.6	Bob Griese, Miami
Touchdowns	13	Nat Moore, Miami

LONGEST		
Run	78t	Greg Pruitt, Cleveland
Pass	94t	Ken Anderson to Billy Brooks, Cincinnati
Interception	102t	Gary Barbaro, Kansas City
Punt	75	Marv Bateman, Buffalo
Punt return	91t	Keith Moody, Buffalo
Kickoff return	101t	Raymond Clayborn, New England
Field goal	51	John Leypoldt, Seattle

1977 NFC STANDINGS

Eastern Division	**W**	**L**	**T**	**Pct.**	**Pts.**	**OP**
Dallas	12	2	0	.857	345	212
Washington	9	5	0	.643	196	189
St. Louis	7	7	0	.500	272	287
Philadelphia	5	9	0	.357	220	207
New York Giants	5	9	0	.357	181	265
Central Division	**W**	**L**	**T**	**Pct.**	**Pts.**	**OP**
Minnesota	9	5	0	.643	231	227
Chicago Bears*	9	5	0	.643	255	253
Detroit	6	8	0	.429	183	252
Green Bay	4	10	0	.286	134	219
Tampa Bay	2	12	0	.143	103	223
Western Division	**W**	**L**	**T**	**Pct.**	**Pts.**	**OP**
Los Angeles Rams	10	4	0	.714	302	146
Atlanta	7	7	0	.500	179	129
San Francisco	5	9	0	.357	220	260
New Orleans	3	11	0	.214	232	336

**Wild Card qualifier for playoffs*

Divisional playoffs: Dallas 37, Chicago Bears 7;
Minnesota 14, Los Angeles Rams 7

NFC championship: Dallas 23, Minnesota 6

Super Bowl XII: Dallas (NFC) 27, Denver (AFC) 10

LEADING RUSHERS	**Att.**	**Yards**	**Avg.**	**Long**	**TD**
Walter Payton, Chi. Bears	339	1,852	5.5	73	14
L. McCutcheon, LA Rams	294	1,238	4.2	48	7
Chuck Foreman, Minnesota	270	1,112	4.1	51	6
Tony Dorsett, Dallas	208	1,007	4.8	84t	12
Delvin Williams, San Francisco	268	931	3.5	40	7

LEADING PASSERS	**Att.**	**Comp.**	**Yards**	**TD**	**Int.**
Roger Staubach, Dallas	361	210	2,620	18	9
Pat Haden, LA Rams	216	122	1,551	11	6
Fran Tarkenton, Minnesota	258	155	1,734	9	14
Greg Landry, Detroit	240	135	1,359	6	7
Archie Manning, New Orleans	205	113	1,284	8	9

LEADING RECEIVERS	**No.**	**Yards**	**Avg.**	**Long**	**TD**
Ahmad Rashad, Minnesota	51	681	13.4	48t	2
James Scott, Chi. Bears	50	809	16.2	72t	3
Drew Pearson, Dallas	48	870	18.1	67	2
Harold Jackson, LA Rams	48	666	13.9	58	6
Harold Carmichael, Philadelphia	46	665	14.5	50t	7
Preston Pearson, Dallas	46	535	11.6	36t	4

LEADING SCORER	**TD**	**FG**	**PAT**	**TP**
Walter Payton, Chi. Bears	16	0	0	96

LEADING INTERCEPTOR	**No.**	**Yards**	**Avg.**	**Long**	**TD**
Rolland Lawrence, Atlanta	7	138	19.7	36	0

LEADING PUNTER	**No.**	**Avg.**	**Long**
Tom Blanchard, New Orleans	82	42.4	66

LEADING PUNT RETURNER	**No.**	**Yards**	**Avg.**	**Long**	**TD**
Larry Marshall, Philadelphia	46	489	10.6	48	0

LEADING KICKOFF RETURNER	**No.**	**Yards**	**Avg.**	**Long**	**TD**
Wilbert Montgomery, Philadelphia	23	619	26.9	99t	1

SUPERLATIVES		
Rushing average	5.5	Walter Payton, Chi. Bears
Receiving average	20.6	Mel Gray, St. Louis
Completion percentage	60.1	Fran Tarkenton, Minnesota
Touchdowns	16	Walter Payton, Chi. Bears

LONGEST		
Run	84t	Tony Dorsett, Dallas
Pass	95t	Lynn Dickey to Steve Odom, Green Bay
Interception	79t	Thomas Henderson, Dallas
		Mike Sensibaugh, St. Louis
Punt	70	Dave Green, Tampa Bay
Punt return	87t	Eddie Payton, Detroit
Kickoff return	99t	Wilbert Montgomery, Philadelphia
Field goal	54	Mark Moseley, Washington

1978 The Los Angeles Rams announced their intention to move from the Los Angeles Memorial Coliseum to Anaheim Stadium following the 1979 season. The Los Angeles Coliseum Commission filed an antitrust suit in federal court challenging NFL principles requiring league approval of transfers of team locations.

The NFL continued a trend toward opening up the offensive game. Rules changes permitted a defender to maintain contact with a receiver within five yards of the line of scrimmage, but restricted contact beyond that point. The pass-blocking rule was interpreted to permit the extending of arms and open hands.

There were a number of increases in the league. A seventh official, the side judge, was added to the game officiating crew; active team rosters were increased to 45 players; and the number of regular-season games was increased from 14 to 16, with the number of preseason games dropped to four.

Wild card teams were added to the playoffs in both conferences. The first week following the regular season would match wild card teams in both conferences.

The league signed a new television contract worth more than $5 million to each club. The contract included provisions for prime-time games on Thursday and Sunday nights.

There were 10 new head coaches at the beginning of training camp: Chuck Knox at Buffalo; George Allen, who had moved to Los Angeles to take Knox's old position; Jack Pardee, who moved from Chicago to Washington; Neill Armstrong, a Minnesota assistant who replaced Pardee; Bud Wilkinson, the legendary coach of the Oklahoma Sooners, at St. Louis, replacing Don Coryell; Sam Rutigliano, who took over at Cleveland; Marv Levy at Kansas City; Monte Clark at Detroit; Dick Nolan, who had replaced Hank Stram in New Orleans; and Pete McCulley at San Francisco. During the preseason, Allen was fired and replaced by offensive coordinator Ray Malavasi. San Diego coach Tommy Prothro resigned in the middle of the season and was replaced by Coryell. Homer Rice took over for Bill Johnson at Cincinnati after five games.

With one game left in the 1978 season, Chuck Fairbanks quit his position as New England head coach and general manager to take the head coaching position at the University of Colorado. Successful Oakland Raiders head coach John Madden retired at the end of the season due to a severe ulcer condition.

In the AFC Central, Pittsburgh won its first seven games en route to a 14-2 record, the best in the league. Houston finished 10-6 and earned one of the two wild card spots. The Oilers were led by rookie Earl Campbell, the former Heisman Trophy winner from Texas and the first pick in the NFL draft, who led the NFL with 1,450 yards rushing. New England and Miami each finished with 11-5 records. The Patriots were crowned the AFC East champion and the Dolphins the second wild card team. In the West, Denver won seven of eight games in the division to edge Oakland, Seattle, and San Diego by a game.

Dallas and Los Angeles ended with the best records (12-4) in the NFC, with their runners-up, Philadelphia and Atlanta, gaining the wild card spots. In the Central Division, Minnesota won despite an 8-7-1 record, the poorest ever to win a title in the NFL.

In the wild card games, Atlanta edged Philadelphia 14-13 and Houston surprised Miami 17-9.

The AFC Divisional Playoffs were one-sided games. Pittsburgh totally shut down Denver 33-10. Houston caught New England flat—perhaps from the announcement that their coach had quit—and won 31-14.

Dallas and Los Angeles were dominant in the NFC playoffs. The Cowboys came from behind with substitute quarterback Danny White to defeat Atlanta 27-20, and the Rams broke open a close game in the second half to defeat Minnesota 34-10.

The Cowboys earned the right to their second-consecutive Super Bowl, and a record fifth overall, with 28 points in the second half of a 28-0 win over the Rams in the NFC Championship Game.

Pittsburgh dominated the Oilers on a frozen field to win 34-5 in the AFC Championship Game, setting the stage for the first Super Bowl rematch.

Pittsburgh, behind Terry Bradshaw's four touchdown passes, defeated Dallas 35-31 in Super Bowl XIII to become the first team to win three Super Bowls. Playing in front of a sellout crowd in Miami's Orange Bowl and the largest audience ever to watch a televised event (35,090,000 homes), the Steelers built a big lead, then held off the Cowboys' late surge.

1978 AFC STANDINGS

Eastern Division	**W**	**L**	**T**	**Pct.**	**Pts.**	**OP**
New England	11	5	0	.688	358	286
Miami*	11	5	0	.688	372	254
New York Jets	8	8	0	.500	359	364
Buffalo	5	11	0	.313	302	354
Baltimore	5	11	0	.313	239	421
Central Division	**W**	**L**	**T**	**Pct.**	**Pts.**	**OP**
Pittsburgh	14	2	0	.875	356	195
Houston*	10	6	0	.625	283	298
Cleveland	8	8	0	.500	334	356
Cincinnati	4	12	0	.250	252	284
Western Division	**W**	**L**	**T**	**Pct.**	**Pts.**	**OP**
Denver	10	6	0	.625	282	198
Oakland	9	7	0	.563	311	283
Seattle	9	7	0	.563	345	358
San Diego	9	7	0	.563	355	309
Kansas City	4	12	0	.250	243	327

**Wild Card qualifiers for playoffs*

Wild Card game: Houston 17, Miami 9

Divisional playoffs: Pittsburgh 33, Denver 10; Houston 31, New England 14

AFC championship: Pittsburgh 34, Houston 5

LEADING RUSHERS	**Att.**	**Yards**	**Avg.**	**Long**	**TD**
Earl Campbell, Houston	302	1,450	4.8	81t	13
Delvin Williams, Miami	272	1,258	4.6	58	8
Franco Harris, Pittsburgh	310	1,082	3.5	37	8
Mark van Eeghen, Oakland	270	1,080	4.0	34	9
Terry Miller, Buffalo	238	1,060	4.5	60t	7
LEADING PASSERS	**Att.**	**Comp.**	**Yards**	**TD**	**Int.**
Terry Bradshaw, Pittsburgh	368	207	2,915	28	20
Dan Fouts, San Diego	381	224	2,999	24	20
Bob Griese, Miami	235	148	1,791	11	11
Brian Sipe, Cleveland	399	222	2,906	21	15
Craig Morton, Denver	267	146	1,802	11	8
LEADING RECEIVERS	**No.**	**Yards**	**Avg.**	**Long**	**TD**
Steve Largent, Seattle	71	1,168	16.5	57t	8
Dave Casper, Oakland	62	852	13.7	44	9
Lynn Swann, Pittsburgh	61	880	14.4	62	11
Lydell Mitchell, San Diego	57	500	8.8	55t	2
John Jefferson, San Diego	56	1,001	17.9	46t	13
LEADING SCORER	**TD**	**FG**	**PAT**	**TP**	
Pat Leahy, NY Jets	0	22	41	107	
LEADING INTERCEPTOR	**No.**	**Yards**	**Avg.**	**Long**	**TD**
Thom Darden, Cleveland	10	200	20.0	46	0
LEADING PUNTER	**No.**	**Avg.**	**Long**		
Pat McInally, Cincinnati	91	43.1	65		
LEADING PUNT RETURNER	**No.**	**Yards**	**Avg.**	**Long**	**TD**
Rick Upchurch, Denver	36	493	13.7	75t	1
LEADING KICKOFF RETURNER	**No.**	**Yards**	**Avg.**	**Long**	**TD**
Keith Wright, Cleveland	30	789	26.3	86	0

SUPERLATIVES

Rushing average	6.0	Ted McKnight, Kansas City
Receiving average	24.4	Wesley Walker, NY Jets
Completion percentage	63.0	Bob Griese, Miami
Touchdowns	15	David Sims, Seattle

LONGEST

Run	81t	Earl Campbell, Houston
Pass	92t	Joe Ferguson to Frank Lewis, Buffalo
Interception	85t	Charles Romes, Buffalo
Punt	79	Chuck Ramsey, NY Jets
Punt return	82t	Bruce Harper, NY Jets
		Keith Moody, Buffalo
Kickoff return	102t	Curtis Brown, Buffalo
Field goal	52	Chris Bahr, Cincinnati

1978 NFC STANDINGS

Eastern Division	**W**	**L**	**T**	**Pct.**	**Pts.**	**OP**
Dallas	12	4	0	.750	384	208
Philadelphia*	9	7	0	.563	270	250
Washington	8	8	0	.500	273	283
St. Louis	6	10	0	.375	248	296
New York Giants	6	10	0	.375	264	298
Central Division	**W**	**L**	**T**	**Pct.**	**Pts.**	**OP**
Minnesota	8	7	1	.531	294	306
Green Bay	8	7	1	.531	249	269
Detroit	7	9	0	.438	290	300
Chicago Bears	7	9	0	.438	253	274
Tampa Bay	5	11	0	.313	241	259
Western Division	**W**	**L**	**T**	**Pct.**	**Pts.**	**OP**
Los Angeles Rams	12	4	0	.750	316	245
Atlanta*	9	7	0	.563	240	290
New Orleans	7	9	0	.438	281	298
San Francisco	2	14	0	.125	219	350

**Wild Card qualifiers for playoffs*

Wild Card game: Atlanta 14, Philadelphia 13

Divisional playoffs: Dallas 27, Atlanta 20; Los Angeles Rams 34, Minnesota 10

NFC championship: Dallas 28, Los Angeles Rams 0

Super Bowl XIII: Pittsburgh (AFC) 35, Dallas (NFC) 31

LEADING RUSHERS	**Att.**	**Yards**	**Avg.**	**Long**	**TD**
Walter Payton, Chi. Bears	333	1,395	4.2	76	11
Tony Dorsett, Dallas	290	1,325	4.6	63	7
Wilbert Montgomery, Philadelphia	259	1,220	4.7	47	9
Terdell Middleton, Green Bay	284	1,116	3.9	76t	11
John Riggins, Washington	248	1,014	4.1	31	5
LEADING PASSERS	**Att.**	**Comp.**	**Yards**	**TD**	**Int.**
Roger Staubach, Dallas	413	231	3,190	25	16
Archie Manning, New Orleans	471	291	3,416	17	16
Gary Danielson, Detroit	351	199	2,294	18	17
Fran Tarkenton, Minnesota	572	345	3,468	25	32
Ron Jaworski, Philadelphia	398	206	2,487	16	16
LEADING RECEIVERS	**No.**	**Yards**	**Avg.**	**Long**	**TD**
Rickey Young, Minnesota	88	704	8.0	48	5
Tony Galbreath, New Orleans	74	582	7.9	35	2
Ahmad Rashad, Minnesota	66	769	11.7	58t	8
Pat Tilley, St. Louis	62	900	14.5	43	3
Chuck Foreman, Minnesota	61	396	6.5	20	2
LEADING SCORER	**TD**	**FG**	**PAT**	**TP**	
Frank Corral, LA Rams	0	29	31	118	
LEADING INTERCEPTORS	**No.**	**Yards**	**Avg.**	**Long**	**TD**
Ken Stone, St. Louis	9	139	15.4	33	0
Willie Buchanon, Green Bay	9	93	10.3	77t	1
LEADING PUNTER	**No.**	**Avg.**	**Long**		
Tom Skladany, Detroit	86	42.5	63		
LEADING PUNT RETURNER	**No.**	**Yards**	**Avg.**	**Long**	**TD**
Jackie Wallace, LA Rams	52	618	11.9	58	0
LEADING KICKOFF RETURNER	**No.**	**Yards**	**Avg.**	**Long**	**TD**
Steve Odom, Green Bay	25	677	27.1	95t	1

SUPERLATIVES

Rushing average	4.7	Wilbert Montgomery, Philadelphia
Receiving average	20.0	Morris Owens, Tampa Bay
Completion percentage	61.8	Archie Manning, New Orleans
Touchdowns	12	Terdell Middleton, Green Bay

LONGEST

Run	76t	Terdell Middleton, Green Bay
	76	Walter Payton, Chi. Bears
Pass	91t	Roger Staubach to Tony Dorsett, Dallas
Interception	97t	Tommy Myers, New Orleans
Punt	81	Mike Wood, St. Louis
Punt return	80t	Tony Green, Washington
Kickoff return	100t	Dennis Pearson, Atlanta
Field goal	52	Mark Moseley, Washington

1979 The NFL's rules changes emphasized additional player safety. The changes prohibited players on the receiving team from blocking below the waist during kickoffs, punts, and field-goal attempts; prohibited the wearing of torn or altered equipment and exposed pads that could be hazardous; extended the zone in which there could be no crack-back blocks; and instructed officials quickly to whistle a play dead when a quarterback was clearly in the grasp of a tackler.

The 1980 AFC-NFC Pro Bowl Game was awarded to Honolulu, Hawaii, marking the first time in the 30-year history of the game that it would be played in a non-NFL city.

Carroll Rosenbloom, the owner and the president of the Los Angeles Rams, drowned off the coast of Florida in the spring. His widow, Georgia, took over the operation of the club.

Buffalo made Ohio State All-America Tom Cousineau the first pick of the draft, but the rookie linebacker signed with Montreal of the Canadian Football League.

Pittsburgh won its sixth straight AFC Central title with a 12-4 record, the best in football, but just beat out the improved Oilers, who again featured Earl Campbell, the NFL's leading rusher with 1,697 yards. After losing to Pittsburgh 38-7 early in the season, Houston defeated the Steelers 20-17 at the end of the year to finish 11-5. San Diego used a record-breaking passing game to win the AFC West title; Dan Fouts passed for a record 4,082 yards. Denver, which was in the title hunt until losing its last two games of the year, earned one of the wild card spots. New England had a lead in the AFC East after 10 weeks, but lost four of its final six games to finish second to Miami.

In the NFC West, Los Angeles survived an injury-wracked season to win its seventh consecutive title, an NFL record. The Rams played four different quarterbacks during the season. They defeated the Saints on the last day of the season to clinch the title. Tampa Bay rode the best defense in the league to the NFC Central title in only the club's fourth year. Chicago finished second and gained a wild card berth. Minnesota, without Fran Tarkenton (who retired before the season began), dropped to third. In the East, Dallas held off a challenge from a new contender—Philadelphia. The Cowboys' 35-34 come-from-behind victory over Washington in the season finale clinched the title for Dallas, put Philadelphia into the playoffs as a wild card, and dropped the Redskins from the playoff picture.

In the AFC Wild Card Game, the Oilers overcame the loss of Campbell and quarterback Dan Pastorini to defeat the Broncos 13-7. Philadelphia defeated Chicago 27-17 in the NFC.

In the divisional playoffs, the Oilers, still without Campbell and Pastorini, surprised San Diego 17-14 behind four interceptions and a key return of a blocked field goal by rookie safety Vernon Perry. Pittsburgh thrashed Miami 34-14 to set up a rematch of the 1978 AFC Championship Game.

In the NFC, Tampa Bay defeated Philadelphia 24-17, and the Rams nipped the Cowboys 21-19 on a touchdown pass from Vince Ferragamo to Billy Waddy with two minutes left in the game.

Pittsburgh qualified for its fourth Super Bowl in six years with a 27-13 victory over the Oilers, who lost despite the return of Campbell and Pastorini.

Los Angeles ended Tampa Bay's Cinderella season with a 9-0 victory on three Frank Corral field goals, the first championship game ever in which a touchdown wasn't scored.

The Steelers won their fourth Super Bowl in as many attempts, with a 31-19 come-from-behind victory over the Rams at the Rose Bowl in Pasadena. Terry Bradshaw threw two fourth-quarter passes to John Stallworth to bring Pittsburgh from behind. A record number of television viewers (the game was seen in 35,330,000 homes) watched the game.

League attendance set a record, surpassing 12 million (12,771,800) for the first time.

1979 AFC STANDINGS

Eastern Division	**W**	**L**	**T**	**Pct.**	**Pts.**	**OP**
Miami	10	6	0	.625	341	257
New England	9	7	0	.563	411	326
New York Jets	8	8	0	.500	337	383
Buffalo	7	9	0	.438	268	279
Baltimore	5	11	0	.313	271	351
Central Division	**W**	**L**	**T**	**Pct.**	**Pts.**	**OP**
Pittsburgh	12	4	0	.750	416	262
Houston*	11	5	0	.688	362	331
Cleveland	9	7	0	.563	359	352
Cincinnati	4	12	0	.250	337	421
Western Division	**W**	**L**	**T**	**Pct.**	**Pts.**	**OP**
San Diego	12	4	0	.750	411	246
Denver*	10	6	0	.625	289	262
Seattle	9	7	0	.563	378	372
Oakland	9	7	0	.563	365	337
Kansas City	7	9	0	.438	238	262

**Wild Card qualifiers for playoffs*

Wild Card game: Houston 13, Denver 7

Divisional playoffs: Houston 17, San Diego 14; Pittsburgh 34, Miami 14

AFC championship: Pittsburgh 27, Houston 13

LEADING RUSHERS	**Att.**	**Yards**	**Avg.**	**Long**	**TD**
Earl Campbell, Houston	368	1,697	4.6	61t	19
Mike Pruitt, Cleveland	264	1,294	4.9	77t	9
Franco Harris, Pittsburgh	267	1,186	4.4	71t	11
Clark Gaines, NY Jets	186	905	4.9	52	0
Joe Washington, Baltimore	242	884	3.7	26	4
LEADING PASSERS	**Att.**	**Comp.**	**Yards**	**TD**	**Int.**
Dan Fouts, San Diego	530	332	4,082	24	24
Ken Stabler, Oakland	498	304	3,615	26	22
Ken Anderson, Cincinnati	339	189	2,340	16	10
Jim Zorn, Seattle	505	285	3,661	20	18
Steve Grogan, New England	423	206	3,286	28	20
LEADING RECEIVERS	**No.**	**Yards**	**Avg.**	**Long**	**TD**
Joe Washington, Baltimore	82	750	9.1	43t	3

Charlie Joiner, San Diego	72	1,008	14.0	39	4
John Stallworth, Pittsburgh	70	1,183	16.9	65t	8
Steve Largent, Seattle	66	1,237	18.7	55t	9
Rick Upchurch, Denver	64	937	14.6	47	7

LEADING SCORER	**TD**	**FG**	**PAT**	**TP**
John Smith, New England	0	23	46	115

LEADING INTERCEPTOR	**No.**	**Yards**	**Avg.**	**Long**	**TD**
Mike Reinfeldt, Houston	12	205	17.1	39	0

LEADING PUNTER	**No.**	**Avg.**	**Long**
Bob Grupp, Kansas City	89	43.6	74

LEADING PUNT RETURNER	**No.**	**Yards**	**Avg.**	**Long**	**TD**
Tony Nathan, Miami	28	306	10.9	86t	1

LEADING KICKOFF RETURNER	**No.**	**Yards**	**Avg.**	**Long**	**TD**
Larry Brunson, Oakland	17	441	25.9	89	0

SUPERLATIVES

Rushing average	5.0	Sidney Thornton, Pittsburgh
Receiving average	22.8	Stanley Morgan, New England
Completion percentage	62.6	Dan Fouts, San Diego
Touchdowns	19	Earl Campbell, Houston

LONGEST

Run	84t	Ted McKnight, Kansas City
Pass	84t	Joe Ferguson to Curtis Brown, Buffalo
Interception	96t	Ray Griffin, Cincinnati
Punt	74	Bob Grupp, Kansas City
Punt return	88t	J. T. Smith, Kansas City
Kickoff return	104t	Ira Matthews, Oakland
Field goal	55	Chris Bahr, Cincinnati

1979 NFC STANDINGS

Eastern Division	**W**	**L**	**T**	**Pct.**	**Pts.**	**OP**
Dallas	11	5	0	.688	371	313
Philadelphia*	11	5	0	.688	339	282
Washington	10	6	0	.625	348	295
New York Giants	6	10	0	.375	237	323
St. Louis	5	11	0	.313	307	358
Central Division	**W**	**L**	**T**	**Pct.**	**Pts.**	**OP**
Tampa Bay	10	6	0	.625	273	237
Chicago Bears*	10	6	0	.625	306	249
Minnesota	7	9	0	.438	259	337
Green Bay	5	11	0	.313	246	316
Detroit	2	14	0	.125	219	365
Western Division	**W**	**L**	**T**	**Pct.**	**Pts.**	**OP**
Los Angeles Rams	9	7	0	.563	323	309
New Orleans	8	8	0	.500	370	360
Atlanta	6	10	0	.375	300	388
San Francisco	2	14	0	.125	308	416

**Wild Card qualifiers for playoffs*

Wild Card game: Philadelphia 27, Chicago Bears 17

Divisional playoffs: Tampa Bay 24, Philadelphia 17; Los Angeles Rams 21, Dallas 19

NFC championship: Los Angeles Rams 9, Tampa Bay 0

Super Bowl XIV: Pittsburgh (AFC) 31, Los Angeles Rams (NFC) 19

LEADING RUSHERS	**Att.**	**Yards**	**Avg.**	**Long**	**TD**
Walter Payton, Chi. Bears	369	1,610	4.4	43t	14
Ottis Anderson, St. Louis	331	1,605	4.8	76t	8
Wilbert Montgomery, Philadelphia	338	1,512	4.5	62t	9
Ricky Bell, Tampa Bay	283	1,263	4.5	49	7
Chuck Muncie, New Orleans	238	1,198	5.0	69t	11

LEADING PASSERS	**Att.**	**Comp.**	**Yards**	**TD**	**Int.**
Roger Staubach, Dallas	461	267	3,586	27	11
Joe Theismann, Washington	395	233	2,797	20	13
Ron Jaworski, Philadelphia	374	190	2,669	18	12
Archie Manning, New Orleans	420	252	3,169	15	20
Steve DeBerg, San Francisco	578	347	3,652	17	21

LEADING RECEIVERS	**No.**	**Yards**	**Avg.**	**Long**	**TD**
Ahmad Rashad, Minnesota	80	1,156	14.5	52t	9
Wallace Francis, Atlanta	74	1,013	13.7	42	8
Rickey Young, Minnesota	72	519	7.2	18	4
Wes Chandler, New Orleans	65	1,069	16.4	85	6
Freddie Scott, Detroit	62	929	15.0	50	5

LEADING SCORER	**TD**	**FG**	**PAT**	**TP**
Mark Moseley, Washington	0	25	39	114

LEADING INTERCEPTOR	**No.**	**Yards**	**Avg.**	**Long**	**TD**
Lemar Parrish, Washington	9	65	7.2	23	0

LEADING PUNTER	**No.**	**Avg.**	**Long**
Dave Jennings, NY Giants	104	42.7	72

LEADING PUNT RETURNER	**No.**	**Yards**	**Avg.**	**Long**	**TD**
John Sciarra, Philadelphia	16	182	11.4	38	0

LEADING KICKOFF RETURNER	**No.**	**Yards**	**Avg.**	**Long**	**TD**
Jimmy Edwards, Minnesota	44	1,103	25.1	83	0

SUPERLATIVES

Rushing average	5.1	Wendell Tyler, LA Rams
Receiving average	18.7	Drew Pearson, Dallas
Completion percentage	60.0	Steve DeBerg, San Francisco
Touchdowns	16	Walter Payton, Chi. Bears

LONGEST

Run	80	Leroy Harris, Philadelphia
Pass	85	Archie Manning to Wes Chandler, New Orleans
Interception	78	Carl Allen, St. Louis
Punt	74	Mike Bragg, Washington
Punt return	77t	Steve Schubert, Chi. Bears
	77	Lee Nelson, St. Louis
Kickoff return	106t	Roy Green, St. Louis
Field goal	59	Tony Franklin, Philadelphia

1980 CBS, with a record bid of $12 million, won the national radio rights to 26 NFL regular-season games and all 10 postseason games for the 1980-83 seasons.

The Los Angeles Rams moved their offices to Anaheim, and started using Anaheim Stadium as their home field.

In March, the Oakland Raiders joined the Los Angeles Coliseum Commission's antitrust suit against the NFL. The suit contended the league violated antitrust laws in declining to approve a proposed move by the Raiders from Oakland to Los Angeles.

Five teams in the AFC finished with 11-5 records and qualified for the playoffs. Buffalo, the league's top defensive team, won the East, one game ahead of New England. Cleveland, with Brian Sipe leading the league in passing, won the Central over Houston, for whom Earl Campbell once again won the rushing title. The Browns won the title because of a better record in the conference than the Oilers. San Diego won the West over wild card Oakland on the basis of net points in division games. The Chargers featured the league's most productive passing game, in which Dan Fouts set a record with 4,715 yards while passing to the AFC's top three receivers—Kellen Winslow, John Jefferson, and Charlie Joiner. The Raiders had the league's top defensive player—Lester Hayes, who intercepted 13 passes in the regular season and then picked off 5 more in the playoffs—and the comeback story of the year—Jim Plunkett, who became the starter early in the year after not playing for several seasons.

In the NFC East, Philadelphia and Dallas each had 12-4 records, but the Eagles won the title on net points in the division. Dallas played without the retired Roger Staubach. Atlanta, with Steve Bartkowski leading the NFL with 31 touchdown passes, ran off nine wins in a row to edge the Rams, who were one game off pace with an 11-5 record. Minnesota and Detroit had 9-7 records, but the Vikings won the divisional title because of a better conference record. Detroit had the league's top rookie—running back Billy Sims, who had been the number-one pick in the draft.

In the wild card games, the home teams won handily. Oakland stopped the Oilers' offense and won 27-7, but the Rams couldn't stop the Cowboys and lost 34-13.

Mike Davis intercepted Sipe's pass in the end zone with 41 seconds left to preserve a 14-12 Oakland victory over Cleveland in the AFC divisional playoffs. Fouts hit Ron Smith with a 50-yard pass with two minutes left to lead San Diego to a 20-14 victory over Buffalo in the other AFC game.

In the NFC, Dallas scored three touchdowns in the fourth quarter to come from behind to defeat Atlanta 30-27. Philadelphia took advantage of eight Minnesota turnovers to defeat the Vikings 31-16.

In the AFC Championship Game, Oakland jumped to an early 28-7 lead and hung on to beat San Diego 34-27.

Philadelphia also won its rubber match with Dallas, dominating the Cowboys on the ground with 263 yards, while holding Dallas to only 90 yards. The Eagles outscored the Cowboys 13-0 in the second half to win 20-7.

Jim Plunkett threw three touchdown passes to lead the Oakland Raiders to a 27-10 victory over the Eagles in Super Bowl XV at the Louisiana Superdome in New Orleans. Linebacker Rod Martin intercepted three passes to shut down the Eagles' offense and help the Raiders become the first wild card team to win the Super Bowl.

1980 AFC STANDINGS

Eastern Division	**W**	**L**	**T**	**Pct.**	**Pts.**	**OP**
Buffalo	11	5	0	.688	320	260
New England	10	6	0	.625	441	325
Miami	8	8	0	.500	266	305
Baltimore	7	9	0	.438	355	387
New York Jets	4	12	0	.250	302	395
Central Division	**W**	**L**	**T**	**Pct.**	**Pts.**	**OP**
Cleveland	11	5	0	.688	357	310
Houston*	11	5	0	.688	295	251
Pittsburgh	9	7	0	.563	352	313
Cincinnati	6	10	0	.375	244	312
Western Division	**W**	**L**	**T**	**Pct.**	**Pts.**	**OP**
San Diego	11	5	0	.688	418	327
Oakland*	11	5	0	.688	364	306
Kansas City	8	8	0	.500	319	336
Denver	8	8	0	.500	310	323
Seattle	4	12	0	.250	291	408

**Wild Card qualifiers for playoffs*

Wild Card game: Oakland 27, Houston 7

Divisional playoffs: San Diego 20, Buffalo 14; Oakland 14, Cleveland 12

AFC championship: Oakland 34, San Diego 27

LEADING RUSHERS	**Att.**	**Yards**	**Avg.**	**Long**	**TD**
Earl Campbell, Houston	373	1,934	5.2	55t	13
Joe Cribbs, Buffalo	306	1,185	3.9	48	11
Mike Pruitt, Cleveland	249	1,034	4.2	56t	6
Mark van Eeghen, Oakland	222	838	3.8	34	5
C. Muncie, S. Diego-N. Orleans	175	827	4.7	53	6

LEADING PASSERS	**Att.**	**Comp.**	**Yards**	**TD**	**Int.**
Brian Sipe, Cleveland	554	337	4,132	30	14
Dan Fouts, San Diego	589	348	4,715	30	24
Craig Morton, Denver	301	183	2,150	12	13
Steve Fuller, Kansas City	320	193	2,250	10	12
Bert Jones, Baltimore	446	248	3,134	23	21

LEADING RECEIVERS	**No.**	**Yards**	**Avg.**	**Long**	**TD**
Kellen Winslow, San Diego	89	1,290	14.5	65	9
John Jefferson, San Diego	82	1,340	16.3	58t	13
Charlie Joiner, San Diego	71	1,132	15.9	51	4
Steve Largent, Seattle	66	1,064	16.1	67t	6
Mike Pruitt, Cleveland	63	471	7.5	28	0

LEADING SCORER	**TD**	**FG**	**PAT**	**TP**
John Smith, New England	0	26	51	129

LEADING INTERCEPTOR	**No.**	**Yards**	**Avg.**	**Long**	**TD**
Lester Hayes, Oakland	13	273	21.0	61	1

LEADING PUNTER	**No.**	**Avg.**	**Long**
Luke Prestridge, Denver	70	43.9	57

LEADING PUNT RETURNER	**No.**	**Yards**	**Avg.**	**Long**	**TD**
J. T. Smith, Kansas City	40	581	14.5	75t	2

LEADING KICKOFF RETURNER	**No.**	**Yards**	**Avg.**	**Long**	**TD**
Horace Ivory, New England	36	992	27.6	98t	1

SUPERLATIVES

Rushing average	5.2	Earl Campbell, Houston
Receiving average	22.0	Stanley Morgan, New England
Completion percentage	64.1	Ken Stabler, Houston
Touchdowns	13	Earl Campbell, Houston
		Curtis Dickey, Baltimore
		John Jefferson, San Diego

LONGEST

Run	89t	Kenny King, Oakland
Pass	86t	Jim Plunkett to Cliff Branch, Oakland
Interception	93t	Randy Gradishar, Denver
Punt	71	George Roberts, Miami
Punt return	75t	Roland James, New England
		Will Lewis, Seattle
		J. T. Smith, Kansas City
Kickoff return	98t	Horace Ivory, New England
Field goal	57	Nick Lowery, Kansas City
		Fred Steinfort, Denver

1980 NFC STANDINGS

Eastern Division	**W**	**L**	**T**	**Pct.**	**Pts.**	**OP**
Philadelphia	12	4	0	.750	384	222
Dallas*	12	4	0	.750	454	311
Washington	6	10	0	.375	261	293
St. Louis	5	11	0	.313	299	350
New York Giants	4	12	0	.250	249	425
Central Division	**W**	**L**	**T**	**Pct.**	**Pts.**	**OP**
Minnesota	9	7	0	.563	317	308
Detroit	9	7	0	.563	334	272
Chicago Bears	7	9	0	.438	304	264
Tampa Bay	5	10	1	.344	271	341
Green Bay	5	10	1	.344	231	371
Western Division	**W**	**L**	**T**	**Pct.**	**Pts.**	**OP**
Atlanta	12	4	0	.750	405	272
Los Angeles Rams*	11	5	0	.688	424	289
San Francisco	6	10	0	.375	320	415
New Orleans	1	15	0	.063	291	487

**Wild Card qualifiers for playoffs*

Wild Card game: Dallas 34, Los Angeles Rams 13

Divisional playoffs: Philadelphia 31, Minnesota 16; Dallas 30, Atlanta 27

NFC championship: Philadelphia 20, Dallas 7

Super Bowl XV: Oakland (AFC) 27, Philadelphia (NFC) 10

LEADING RUSHERS	**Att.**	**Yards**	**Avg.**	**Long**	**TD**
Walter Payton, Chi. Bears	317	1,460	4.6	69t	6
Ottis Anderson, St. Louis	301	1,352	4.5	52	9
William Andrews, Atlanta	265	1,308	4.9	33	4
Billy Sims, Detroit	313	1,303	4.2	52	13
Tony Dorsett, Dallas	278	1,185	4.3	56	11

LEADING PASSERS	**Att.**	**Comp.**	**Yards**	**TD**	**Int.**
Ron Jaworski, Philadelphia	451	257	3,529	27	12

	Att.	Comp.	Yards	TD	Int.
Vince Ferragamo, LA Rams	404	240	3,199	30	19
Steve Bartkowski, Atlanta	463	257	3,544	31	16
Joe Montana, San Francisco	273	176	1,795	15	9
Gary Danielson, Detroit	417	244	3,223	13	11
LEADING RECEIVERS	**No.**	**Yards**	**Avg.**	**Long**	**TD**
Earl Cooper, San Francisco	83	567	6.8	66t	4
Dwight Clark, San Francisco	82	991	12.1	71t	8
James Lofton, Green Bay	71	1,226	17.3	47	4
Ahmad Rashad, Minnesota	69	1,095	15.9	76t	5
Pat Tilley, St. Louis	68	966	14.2	60t	6
LEADING SCORER	**TD**	**FG**	**PAT**		**TP**
Ed Murray, Detroit	0	27	35		116
LEADING INTERCEPTOR	**No.**	**Yards**	**Avg.**	**Long**	**TD**
Nolan Cromwell, LA Rams	8	140	17.5	34	1
LEADING PUNTER	**No.**		**Avg.**		**Long**
Dave Jennings, NY Giants	94		44.8		63
LEADING PUNT RETURNER	**No.**	**Yards**	**Avg.**	**Long**	**TD**
Kenny Johnson, Atlanta	23	281	12.2	56	0
LEADING KICKOFF RETURNER	**No.**	**Yards**	**Avg.**	**Long**	**TD**
Rich Mauti, New Orleans	31	798	25.7	52	0

SUPERLATIVES

Rushing average	5.0	Dexter Bussey, Detroit
Receiving average	19.3	James Scott, Chi. Bears
Completion percentage	64.5	Joe Montana, San Francisco
Touchdowns	16	Billy Sims, Detroit

LONGEST

Run	72t	Wilbert Montgomery, Philadelphia
Pass	93t	Steve DeBerg to Freddie Solomon, San Francisco
Interception	99t	Johnnie Johnson, LA Rams
Punt	67	Tom Skladany, Detroit
Punt return	66	Alvin Garrett, NY Giants
Kickoff return	101t	James Owens, San Francisco
Field goal	52	Ed Murray, Detroit Mark Moseley, Washington Rafael Septien, Dallas

1981 Industrialist Edgar F. Kaiser purchased the Denver Broncos in February.

In August, the trial of the antitrust suit by the Los Angeles Coliseum Commission and the Oakland Raiders against the other 27 NFL clubs ended in a mistrial after three months. A retrial was scheduled for September, but later delayed to March, 1982.

Four teams named new head coaches before the season. Ed Biles replaced Bum Phillips at Houston, Phillips took over for Dick Stanfel at New Orleans, Joe Gibbs replaced Jack Pardee in Washington, and Dan Reeves succeeded Red Miller at Denver.

Running back George Rogers of South Carolina, the 1980 Heisman Trophy winner, was the first player chosen in the draft, by the New Orleans Saints. Rogers went on to lead the NFL in rushing with 1,674 yards and be voted rookie of the year.

For the first time, both wild card teams were from the same division, and it happened in both conferences. In the AFC East, Miami defeated Buffalo 16-6 in the season-ending showdown of the top two teams. The Dolphins won the division and the Bills dropped to third, but both made the playoffs, along with the second-place Jets. In the AFC Central, Houston crumbled without Bum Phillips, Cleveland reversed its record of the year before, and the surprising Bengals, coached by Forrest Gregg and led by NFL passing leader Ken Anderson, had the best record in the AFC. San Diego and Air Coryell again won the AFC West, although Denver had an identical 10-6 record. The Chargers won the division on the basis of a better division record, and then the Broncos lost a wild card spot to Buffalo as a result of the Bills' 9-7 win over the Broncos.

Dallas won the NFC East, but both Philadelphia and the New York Giants qualified for wild card positions. The Eagles still had the best defense in the league, but lost both games with the Cowboys. Tampa Bay won the NFC Central despite having only a 9-7 record by sweeping games with runners-up Detroit and Green Bay. The surprise team of the NFC was San Francisco, which finished with the best record in football (13-3) and won the NFC West by six games over Atlanta.

The state of New York had three teams in the wild card games, and two of them were still left after the games. The Giants built a quick lead on Eagles mistakes and held on to win 27-21. The Bills also built a big lead, 24-0 in the second quarter. A Jets' rally came too late, and the Bills won 31-27.

San Diego and Miami clashed in one of the most exciting games of all time, with the Chargers coming out on top 41-38 in overtime. The winning field goal was kicked by Rolf Benirschke after three potential game winners had been missed. Cincinnati stopped a late Buffalo drive and defeated the Bills 28-21 in the other AFC game.

In the NFC, Dallas crushed Tampa Bay 38-0 and San Francisco defeated a big-play Giants team 38-24.

Cincinnati dominated the AFC Championship Game at home in minus-nine-degree weather, with a wind-chill factor of minus 59. The Bengals and the weather stopped the Chargers' passing game in a 27-7 rout.

San Francisco drove 89 yards in the last five minutes to score the winning touchdown and defeat Dallas 28-27 in the NFC Championship Game.

Ray Wersching kicked four field goals to lead the 49ers to a 26-21 victory over the Bengals in Super Bowl XVI in the Pontiac Silverdome. Ken Anderson completed 25 of 34 passes for 300 yards and accounted for three second-half touchdowns, but the Bengals couldn't overcome a 20-0 halftime deficit in the first Super Bowl played in the north.

1981 AFC STANDINGS

Eastern Division	**W**	**L**	**T**	**Pct.**	**Pts.**	**OP**
Miami	11	4	1	.719	345	275
New York Jets*	10	5	1	.656	355	287
Buffalo*	10	6	0	.625	311	276
Baltimore	2	14	0	.125	259	533
New England	2	14	0	.125	322	370
Central Division	**W**	**L**	**T**	**Pct.**	**Pts.**	**OP**
Cincinnati	12	4	0	.750	421	304
Pittsburgh	8	8	0	.500	356	297
Houston	7	9	0	.438	281	355
Cleveland	5	11	0	.313	276	375
Western Division	**W**	**L**	**T**	**Pct.**	**Pts.**	**OP**
San Diego	10	6	0	.625	478	390
Denver	10	6	0	.625	321	289
Kansas City	9	7	0	.563	343	290
Oakland	7	9	0	.438	273	343
Seattle	6	10	0	.375	322	388

**Wild Card qualifiers for playoffs*

Wild Card game: Buffalo 31, New York Jets 27
Divisional playoffs: San Diego 41, Miami 38, overtime;
Cincinnati 28, Buffalo 21
AFC championship: Cincinnati 27, San Diego 7

LEADING RUSHERS	**Att.**	**Yards**	**Avg.**	**Long**	**TD**
Earl Campbell, Houston	361	1,376	3.8	43	10
Chuck Muncie, San Diego	251	1,144	4.6	73t	19
Joe Delaney, Kansas City	234	1,121	4.8	82t	3
Mike Pruitt, Cleveland	247	1,103	4.5	21	7
Joe Cribbs, Buffalo	257	1,097	4.3	35	3
LEADING PASSERS	**Att.**	**Comp.**	**Yards**	**TD**	**Int.**
Ken Anderson, Cincinnati	479	300	3,754	29	10
Craig Morton, Denver	376	225	3,195	21	14
Dan Fouts, San Diego	609	360	4,802	33	17
Terry Bradshaw, Pittsburgh	370	201	2,887	22	14
Jim Zorn, Seattle	397	236	2,788	13	9
LEADING RECEIVERS	**No.**	**Yards**	**Avg.**	**Long**	**TD**
Kellen Winslow, San Diego	88	1,075	12.2	67t	10
Steve Largent, Seattle	75	1,224	16.3	57t	9
Dan Ross, Cincinnati	71	910	12.8	37	5
Frank Lewis, Buffalo	70	1,244	17.8	33	4
Charlie Joiner, San Diego	70	1,188	17.0	57	7
LEADING SCORERS	**TD**	**FG**	**PAT**		**TP**
Jim Breech, Cincinnati	0	22	49		115
Nick Lowery, Kansas City	0	26	37		115
LEADING INTERCEPTOR	**No.**	**Yards**	**Avg.**	**Long**	**TD**
John Harris, Seattle	10	155	15.5	42t	2
LEADING PUNTER	**No.**		**Avg.**		**Long**
Pat McInally, Cincinnati	72		45.4		62
LEADING PUNT RETURNER	**No.**	**Yards**	**Avg.**	**Long**	**TD**
James Brooks, San Diego	22	290	13.2	42	0
LEADING KICKOFF RETURNER	**No.**	**Yards**	**Avg.**	**Long**	**TD**
Carl Roaches, Houston	28	769	27.5	96t	1

SUPERLATIVES

Rushing average	5.3	Tony Nathan, Miami
Receiving average	23.4	Stanley Morgan, New England
Completion percentage	62.6	Ken Anderson, Cincinnati
Touchdowns	19	Chuck Muncie, San Diego

LONGEST

Run	82t	Joe Delaney, Kansas City
Pass	95t	Craig Morton to Steve Watson, Denver
Interception	102t	Louis Breeden, Cincinnati
Punt	75	Rich Camarillo, New England
Punt return	87t	Tommy Vigorito, Miami
Kickoff return	96t	Carl Roaches, Houston
Field goal	54	Efren Herrera, Seattle

1981 NFC STANDINGS

Eastern Division	**W**	**L**	**T**	**Pct.**	**Pts.**	**OP**
Dallas	12	4	0	.750	367	277
Philadelphia*	10	6	0	.625	368	221
New York Giants*	9	7	0	.563	295	257
Washington	8	8	0	.500	347	349
St. Louis	7	9	0	.438	315	408
Central Division	**W**	**L**	**T**	**Pct.**	**Pts.**	**OP**
Tampa Bay	9	7	0	.563	315	268
Detroit	8	8	0	.500	397	322
Green Bay	8	8	0	.500	324	361
Minnesota	7	9	0	.438	325	369
Chicago Bears	6	10	0	.375	253	324
Western Division	**W**	**L**	**T**	**Pct.**	**Pts.**	**OP**
San Francisco	13	3	0	.813	357	250
Atlanta	7	9	0	.438	426	355
Los Angeles Rams	6	10	0	.375	303	351
New Orleans	4	12	0	.250	207	378

**Wild Card qualifiers for playoffs*

Wild Card game: New York Giants 27, Philadelphia 21
Divisional playoffs: Dallas 38, Tampa Bay 0;
San Francisco 38, New York Giants 24
NFC championship: San Francisco 28, Dallas 27
Super Bowl XVI: San Francisco (NFC) 26, Cincinnati (AFC) 21

LEADING RUSHERS	**Att.**	**Yards**	**Avg.**	**Long**	**TD**
George Rogers, New Orleans	378	1,674	4.4	79t	13
Tony Dorsett, Dallas	342	1,646	4.8	75t	4
Billy Sims, Detroit	296	1,437	4.9	51	13
W. Montgomery, Philadelphia	286	1,402	4.9	41	8
Ottis Anderson, St. Louis	328	1,376	4.2	28	9
LEADING PASSERS	**Att.**	**Comp.**	**Yards**	**TD**	**Int.**
Joe Montana, San Francisco	488	311	3,565	19	12
Danny White, Dallas	391	223	3,098	22	13
Steve Bartkowski, Atlanta	533	297	3,829	30	23
Lynn Dickey, Green Bay	354	204	2,593	17	15
Joe Theismann, Washington	496	293	3,568	19	20
LEADING RECEIVERS	**No.**	**Yards**	**Avg.**	**Long**	**TD**
Dwight Clark, San Francisco	85	1,105	13.0	78t	4
Ted Brown, Minnesota	83	694	8.4	63	2
William Andrews, Atlanta	81	735	9.1	70t	2
Joe Senser, Minnesota	79	1,004	12.7	53	8
James Lofton, Green Bay	71	1,294	18.2	75t	8
LEADING SCORERS	**TD**	**FG**	**PAT**		**TP**
Ed Murray, Detroit	0	25	46		121
Rafael Septien, Dallas	0	27	40		121
LEADING INTERCEPTOR	**No.**	**Yards**	**Avg.**	**Long**	**TD**
Everson Walls, Dallas	11	133	12.2	33	0
LEADING PUNTER	**No.**		**Avg.**		**Long**
Tom Skladany, Detroit	64		43.5		74
LEADING PUNT RETURNER	**No.**	**Yards**	**Avg.**	**Long**	**TD**
LeRoy Irvin, LA Rams	46	615	13.4	84t	3
LEADING KICKOFF RETURNER	**No.**	**Yards**	**Avg.**	**Long**	**TD**
Mike Nelms, Washington	37	1,099	29.7	84	0

SUPERLATIVES

Rushing average	4.9	Wilbert Montgomery, Philadelphia
Receiving average	21.0	Kevin House, Tampa Bay
Completion percentage	63.7	Joe Montana, San Francisco
Touchdowns	17	Wendell Tyler, LA Rams

LONGEST

Run	79t	George Rogers, New Orleans
Pass	94t	Eric Hipple to Leonard Thompson, Detroit
Interception	101t	Tom Pridemore, Atlanta
Punt	75	Carl Birdsong, St. Louis
Punt return	94t	Mark Lee, Green Bay
Kickoff return	99t	Eddie Payton, Minnesota
Field goal	55	Joe Danelo, NY Giants

1982 In March, the NFL announced a new contract with the three major television networks (ABC, CBS, and NBC) to televise all NFL regular season and postseason games. The five-year (1982-86) contract was for $2.1 billion.

On May 7, a United States Federal District Court jury ruled against the NFL in the trial of the antitrust suit brought by the Oakland Raiders and the Los Angeles Coliseum Commission. The verdict opened the way for the Raiders to move to Los Angeles, which they did before the 1982 season.

On May 11, the formation of the new United States Football League was announced at a press conference. The league planned to play a spring schedule, beginning in March, 1983.

The NFL season opened with three new head coaches, Mike Ditka with the Bears, Frank Kush with the Colts, and Ron Meyer with the Patriots.

After two weeks of games, on September 20, following the completion of a Monday night game between Green Bay and the New York Giants, the NFL Players Association called a strike, and the season temporarily ended. While negotiations between the Players Association and the NFL Management Council progressed slowly, the players attempted to stage their own games. Two all-star games, one in Washington and one in Los Angeles, were held, but both were played before sparse crowds.

After 57 days, the strike ended when a new Collective Bargaining Agreement, to run until 1987, was worked out by Ed Garvey, the executive director of the Players Association, and Jack Donlan, the executive director of the NFL Management Council. Paul Martha, a Pittsburgh attorney and former Steelers safety, served as an intermediary in bringing the two sides to the agreement. There were several major components to the collective bargaining agreement, which was officially ratified on December 11, more than three weeks after it originally was reached and after the season resumed.

Under the collective bargaining agreement, the NFL draft was extended through 1992, and the veteran free-agent system was left basically unchanged from the 1977 agreement. A minimum salary schedule for years of experience was established for the first time. Training camp and postseason pay were increased. A severance-pay system was introduced for the first time in professional sports. Players' medical, insurance, and retirement benefits were increased.

On November 21, the season resumed. It had a different format than that planned before it started, however. Eight games had been lost during the strike, and seven would not be made up. The schedule was to be picked up with the week 11 games. The season would progress through the week 16 games, with the last week of the regular season being one of the weeks that had been scheduled during the time lost to the strike.

The playoff field was expanded to a 16-team tournament, with 8 from each conference. For one year, teams made the playoffs based on their conference record, instead of their divisional standing. There was no formal recognition of divisions or divisional winners. The top-seeded team in each conference—the one with the best record—would play the number-eight seed, number-two would play number-seven, etc.

The larger playoff format allowed one team from each conference to make the playoffs with a losing record—the first time that had happened in NFL history.

In the AFC, the new Los Angeles Raiders had the best record (8-1), thanks in large part to rookie Marcus Allen, the former Heisman Trophy winner from USC, who led the league in scoring, was fourth in rushing, and led all AFC backs in receiving. San Diego, with Dan Fouts passing for more yards per game than any quarterback in NFL history and Wes Chandler leading the league in yards receiving per game, was the other representative from the teams that usually constitute the AFC West. Seattle just missed the playoffs; during the strike, the team fired its only head coach ever, Jack Patera, and replaced him with director of football operations Mike McCormack, who directed the Seahawks to four victories in seven games. Miami, New England, and the New York Jets—three teams normally in the East—made the playoffs, as did Cincinnati and Cleveland from the Central.

Miami and New England played the most memorable game of the season in the December snow of Schaefer Stadium. With 4:45 left in a scoreless tie, John Smith of New England kicked the winning field goal, but not until a patch of the field had been cleared for Smith's attempt by a tractor with a sweeping attachment, driven by an inmate from a prison on a work-release program. The Bengals, by comparison, rode the arm of Ken Anderson, who broke Sammy Baugh's 37-year-old record by completing 70.3 percent of his passes and Broncos quarterback Steve DeBerg's three-week-old record by hitting 20 in a row against Houston. Cleveland made the tournament with a 4-5 mark.

The top team in the NFC was Washington, which gave up the fewest points in the league and featured the fiery Joe Theismann at quarterback. Dallas and St. Louis also represented the NFC East. Atlanta was the only team from the NFC West, while Green Bay, Minnesota, Tampa Bay, and Detroit (4-5) made it from the NFC Central. Defending Super Bowl champion San Francisco dropped to a 3-6 record, good only for an eleventh-place finish.

In the first round of the AFC playoffs, the Raiders and Dolphins won easily, as expected (27-10 and 28-13), while the Jets upset the Bengals 44-17 behind 202 yards rushing from Freeman McNeil, and the Chargers scored twice on fourth-quarter passes from Fouts to Kellen Winslow to edge the Steelers 31-28.

The NFC also had several one-sided games. Lynn Dickey threw four touchdown passes to lead Green Bay to a 41-16 victory over St. Louis, and Theismann hit Alvin Garrett for three scores and John Riggins pounded the NFC's top rushing defense for 119 yards in Washington's 31-7 victory over Detroit. Minnesota scored late in the game to edge Atlanta 30-24, and Dallas knocked off Tampa Bay 30-17.

In the second round of the playoffs the Jets held on to upset the Raiders 17-14 with two late interceptions by Lance Mehl. The game was played before a record crowd of 90,038 at the Los Angeles Memorial Coliseum. Miami thrashed San Diego 34-13, gaining revenge for the overtime loss a year earlier. Washington and Dallas each won more convincingly than the scores would indicate (21-7 and 37-26).

In the NFC Championship Game, the Redskins knocked Dallas quarterback Danny White out of the game in the first half and won 31-17. On a muddy field in Miami, linebacker A.J. Duhe of the Dolphins intercepted three passes, returning one for a touchdown, to almost single-handedly defeat the Jets 14-0.

The Rose Bowl in Pasadena, California, was the site of Super Bowl XVII, where 103,667 saw John Riggins run for 166 yards to lead the Redskins to a 27-17 victory over the Dolphins.

1982 AFC STANDINGS

	W	L	T	Pct.	Pts.	OP
Los Angeles Raiders*	8	1	0	.889	260	200
Miami*	7	2	0	.778	198	131
Cincinnati*	7	2	0	.778	232	177
Pittsburgh*	6	3	0	.667	204	146
San Diego*	6	3	0	.667	288	221
New York Jets*	6	3	0	.667	245	166
New England*	5	4	0	.556	143	157
Cleveland*	4	5	0	.444	140	182
Buffalo	4	5	0	.444	150	154
Seattle	4	5	0	.444	127	147
Kansas City	3	6	0	.333	176	184
Denver	2	7	0	.222	148	226
Houston	1	8	0	.111	136	245
Baltimore	0	8	1	.056	113	236

**Qualifiers for playoffs*

First round playoffs: Los Angeles Raiders 27, Cleveland 10
Miami 28, New England 13
New York Jets 44, Cincinnati 17
San Diego 31, Pittsburgh 28
Second round playoffs: New York Jets 17, Los Angeles Raiders 14
Miami 34, San Diego 13
AFC championship: Miami 14, New York Jets 0

LEADING RUSHERS	**Att.**	**Yards**	**Avg.**	**Long**	**TD**
Freeman McNeil, NY Jets	151	786	5.2	48	6
Andra Franklin, Miami	177	701	4.0	25t	7
Marcus Allen, LA Raiders	160	697	4.4	53	11
Joe Cribbs, Buffalo	134	633	4.9	62t	3
Tony Collins, New England	164	632	3.9	54	1

LEADING PASSERS	**Att.**	**Comp.**	**Yards**	**TD**	**Int.**
Ken Anderson, Cincinnati	309	218	2,495	12	9
Dan Fouts, San Diego	330	204	2,883	17	11
Richard Todd, NY Jets	261	153	1,961	14	8
Steve Grogan, New England	122	66	930	7	4
Terry Bradshaw, Pittsburgh	240	127	1,768	17	11

LEADING RECEIVERS	**No.**	**Yards**	**Avg.**	**Long**	**TD**
Kellen Winslow, San Diego	54	721	13.4	40	6
Wes Chandler, San Diego	49	1,032	21.1	66t	9
Cris Collinsworth, Cincinnati	49	700	14.3	50	1
Ozzie Newsome, Cleveland	49	633	12.9	54	3
Dan Ross, Cincinnati	47	508	10.8	28	3

LEADING SCORER	**TD**	**FG**	**PAT**	**TP**
Marcus Allen, LA Raiders	14	0	0	84

LEADING INTERCEPTORS	**No.**	**Yards**	**Avg.**	**Long**	**TD**
Ken Riley, Cincinnati	5	88	17.6	56t	1
Bobby Jackson, NY Jets	5	84	16.8	77t	1
Dwayne Woodruff, Pittsburgh	5	53	10.6	30	0
Donnie Shell, Pittsburgh	5	27	5.4	18	0

LEADING PUNTER	**No.**	**Avg.**	**Long**
Luke Prestridge, Denver	45	45.0	65

LEADING PUNT RETURNER	**No.**	**Yards**	**Avg.**	**Long**	**TD**
Rick Upchurch, Denver	15	242	16.1	78t	2

LEADING KICKOFF RETURNER	**No.**	**Yards**	**Avg.**	**Long**	**TD**
Mike Mosley, Buffalo	18	487	27.1	66	0

SUPERLATIVES

Rushing average	5.2	Freeman McNeil, NY Jets
Receiving average	21.1	Wes Chandler, San Diego
Completion percentage	70.6	Ken Anderson, Cincinnati
Touchdowns	14	Marcus Allen, LA Raiders

LONGEST

Run	62t	Joe Cribbs, Buffalo
Pass	75t	Matt Cavanaugh to Stanley Morgan, New England
Interception	99t	Rick Sanford, New England
Punt	76	Rich Camarillo, New England
Punt return	78t	Rick Upchurch, Denver
Kickoff return	98t	Ricky Smith, New England
Field goal	58	Dan Miller, Baltimore

1982 NFC STANDINGS

	W	L	T	Pct.	Pts.	OP
Washington*	8	1	0	.889	190	128
Dallas*	6	3	0	.667	226	145
Green Bay*	5	3	1	.611	226	169
Minnesota*	5	4	0	.556	187	198
Atlanta*	5	4	0	.556	183	199
St. Louis*	5	4	0	.556	135	170
Tampa Bay*	5	4	0	.556	158	178
Detroit*	4	5	0	.444	181	176
New Orleans	4	5	0	.444	129	160
New York Giants	4	5	0	.444	164	160
San Francisco	3	6	0	.333	209	206
Chicago Bears	3	6	0	.333	141	174
Philadelphia	3	6	0	.333	191	195
Los Angeles Rams	2	7	0	.222	200	250

**Qualifiers for playoffs*

First round playoffs: Washington 31, Detroit 7
Green Bay 41, St. Louis 16
Dallas 30, Tampa Bay 17
Minnesota 30, Atlanta 24
Second round playoffs: Washington 21, Minnesota 7
Dallas 37, Green Bay 26
NFC championship: Washington 31, Dallas 17
Super Bowl XVII: Washington (NFC) 27, Miami (AFC) 17

LEADING RUSHERS	**Att.**	**Yards**	**Avg.**	**Long**	**TD**
Tony Dorsett, Dallas	177	745	4.2	99t	5
Billy Sims, Detroit	172	639	3.7	29	4
Walter Payton, Chi. Bears	148	596	4.0	26	1
Ottis Anderson, St. Louis	145	587	4.0	64	3
William Andrews, Atlanta	139	573	4.1	19t	5

LEADING PASSERS	**Att.**	**Comp.**	**Yards**	**TD**	**Int.**
Joe Theismann, Washington	252	161	2,033	13	9
Danny White, Dallas	247	156	2,079	16	12
Joe Montana, San Francisco	346	213	2,613	17	11
Jim McMahon, Chi. Bears	210	120	1,501	9	7
Steve Bartkowski, Atlanta	262	166	1,905	8	11

LEADING RECEIVERS	**No.**	**Yards**	**Avg.**	**Long**	**TD**
Dwight Clark, San Francisco	60	913	15.2	51	5
James Wilder, Tampa Bay	53	466	8.8	32	1
William Andrews, Atlanta	42	503	12.0	86t	2
Wendell Tyler, LA Rams	38	375	9.9	40	4
Jeff Moore, San Francisco	37	405	10.9	55	4

LEADING SCORER	**TD**	**FG**	**PAT**	**TP**
Wendell Tyler, LA Rams	13	0	0	78

LEADING INTERCEPTOR	**No.**	**Yards**	**Avg.**	**Long**	**TD**
Everson Walls, Dallas	7	61	8.7	37	0

LEADING PUNTER	**No.**	**Avg.**	**Long**
Carl Birdsong, St. Louis	54	43.8	65

LEADING PUNT RETURNER	**No.**	**Yards**	**Avg.**	**Long**	**TD**
Billy Johnson, Atlanta	24	273	11.4	71	0

LEADING KICKOFF RETURNER	**No.**	**Yards**	**Avg.**	**Long**	**TD**
Alvin Hall, Detroit	16	426	26.6	96t	1

SUPERLATIVES

Rushing average	4.5	Wilbert Montgomery, Philadelphia

1980s: A Photographic Portfolio

Joe Montana led the greatest comeback in NFL history in 1980, when the 49ers came from a 35-7 halftime deficit to beat New Orleans 38-35 in overtime.

Mark Gastineau of the New York Jets is the official NFL career leader in sacks (60½), a category that wasn't recorded until the 1980s.

Kellen Winslow of San Diego is perhaps the NFL's best-ever tight end. He led the NFL in receiving in 1980 and 1981, and the AFC in 1982.

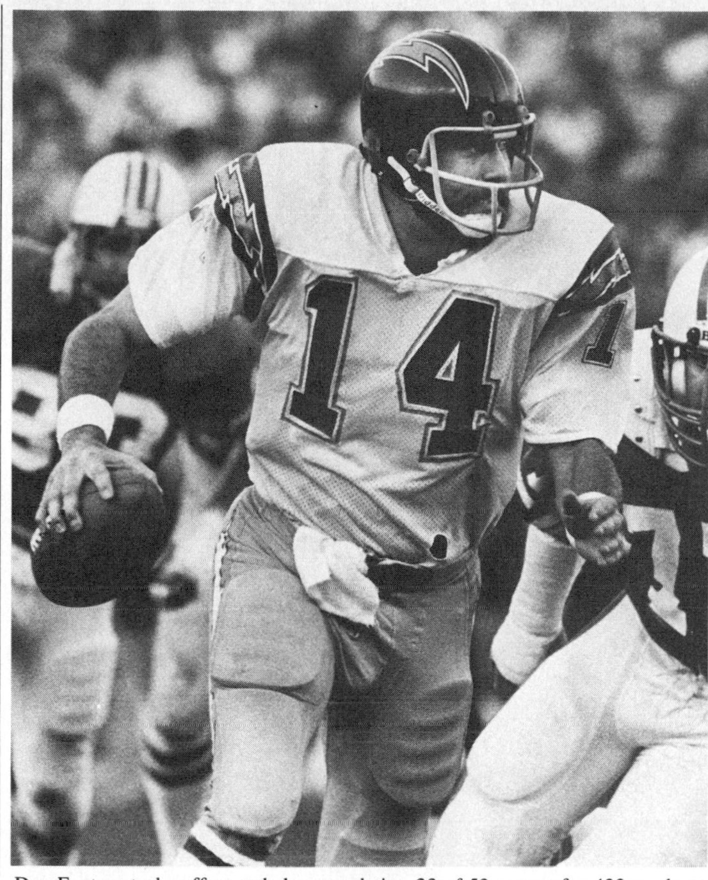

Dan Fouts set playoff records by completing 33 of 53 passes for 433 yards as San Diego beat Miami 41-38 in overtime in a 1980 playoff game.

Tony Dorsett of Dallas has run for more than 1,000 yards eight times in his career—every season except 1982—and has a career total of 10,832 yards.

Guard John Hannah (73) of the New England Patriots has been hailed as the greatest offensive lineman in the history of pro football.

The most productive running back in the history of the NFL, Walter Payton of the Chicago Bears has rushed for 14,860 yards and caught 422 passes.

Eric Dickerson of the Los Angeles Rams led the NFL in rushing with a rookie record 1,808 yards in 1983. The next year, he broke O.J. Simpson's NFL single-season record with 2,105 yards rushing.

In 1984, Miami's Dan Marino set NFL records with 5,084 yards passing and 48 touchdown passes.

Art Monk was almost unstoppable in 1984, setting the NFL record for receptions in a season, 106.

Seattle's Steve Largent has been one of the most consistent receivers in NFL history. Fifth in all-time receptions (624), he has caught 50 or more passes in a season a record eight times.

On this catch against Pittsburgh, November 25, 1984, San Diego's Charlie Joiner broke Charley Taylor's NFL record for career receptions (649).

Mark Clayton's third touchdown reception against Dallas, with 51 seconds remaining in the 1984 season, gave the Miami receiver an NFL record 18.

Running back Marcus Allen of the Los Angeles Raiders earned rookie of the year honors by leading the NFL in scoring in 1982. In each of his next three seasons, he rushed for more than 1,000 yards, including an NFL-high 1,759 in 1985, when he was selected the league's most valuable player.

Receiving average	21.6	Charlie Brown, Washington
Completion percentage	63.9	Joe Theismann, Washington
Touchdowns	13	Wendell Tyler, LA Rams

LONGEST

Run	99t	Tony Dorsett, Dallas
Pass	86t	Steve Bartkowski to William Andrews, Atlanta
Interception	97t	Lawrence Taylor, NY Giants
Punt	81	Bob Parsons, Chi. Bears
Punt return	93t	Dana McLemore, San Francisco
Kickoff return	96t	Alvin Hall, Detroit
Field goal	53	Rafael Septien, Dallas

1983 On April 13, a United States Federal District Court jury awarded the Los Angeles Raiders and the Los Angeles Coliseum Commission more than $47 million in damages from the NFL for antitrust violations. The league immediately appealed.

The NFL draft was one of the most productive ever. The first-round choices included running backs Eric Dickerson and Curt Warner; quarterbacks John Elway, Todd Blackledge, Tony Eason, Ken O'Brien, and Dan Marino; and linemen Chris Hinton, Jim Covert, Bruce Matthews, Dave Rimington, and Don Mosebar.

On June 29, Schaefer Stadium in Foxboro, Massachusetts, was renamed Sullivan Stadium in honor of Patriots owner William H. Sullivan and his family.

Commissioner Pete Rozelle took action against the growing threat of drug use on July 25. Rozelle suspended without pay through the fourth game of the season four players who had been involved with illicit drugs—Ross Browner and Pete Johnson of Cincinnati, E.J. Junior of St. Louis, and Greg Stemrick of Houston.

Almost one-third of the head coaches in the NFL were new at the beginning of the season. In the NFC, John Robinson joined the Rams, Dan Henning the Falcons, Marion Campbell the Eagles, and Bill Parcells the Giants. In the AFC, Chuck Knox moved to Seattle with Kay Stephenson replacing him in Buffalo, John Mackovic was hired in Kansas City, and Joe Walton took over the Jets.

The AFC season was dominated by the Dolphins and Raiders, who tied for the conference's best record (12-4). Miami started slowly, but won 9 of its last 10 games—and the AFC East—behind Marino, the league passing leader. The Raiders won the West with the top-scoring team in the conference. Two other Western Division teams, Seattle and Denver, also made the playoffs as wild cards. It was the first time ever for the Seahawks, who were led on the field by new quarterback Dave Krieg and AFC rookie of the year Warner. Denver also had a new quarterback in Elway. Pittsburgh got only one game out of Terry Bradshaw, a win over the Jets, but Cliff Stoudt took the Steelers to the AFC Central title.

In the NFC, Washington and Dallas were the top two teams, and the regular season came down to their meeting in week 15. The Redskins dominated the Cowboys 31-10 to win the East, and Dallas earned a wild card spot despite losing again the next week to San Francisco. The 49ers won the West, finishing a half game ahead of the Rams, who featured NFC rookie of the year Eric Dickerson. Detroit turned the conference's best defense into the NFC Central title.

On October 31, George Halas, the owner of the Bears, the winningest coach in pro football history, and the last survivor of the NFL's second organizational meeting in 1920, died at the age of 88.

In the AFC Wild Card Game, Seattle was flawless in ousting Denver 31-7. In the NFC, the Rams upset the Cowboys in Dallas 24-17.

The big upset in the divisional playoffs came in the AFC, where Seattle scored twice in the final two minutes to beat Miami 27-20. The Raiders had no such letdown, beating Pittsburgh 38-10.

Washington also was on top of its game. The Redskins ran up the most lopsided victory in the team's history, beating the Rams 51-7. San Francisco beat Detroit 24-23, but not until Lions kicker Ed Murray missed a field goal in the final 10 seconds of the game.

The Raiders ended Seattle's Cinderella season in the AFC Championship Game, running up a 27-0 lead in the third quarter and hanging on for a 30-14 victory. Another playoff record crowd—91,445—was on hand at the Coliseum.

In the NFC, the 49ers trailed 21-0 after three quarters, but San Francisco's Joe Montana threw three touchdown passes to tie the game. After a controversial penalty against the defense, Mark Moseley's field goal won it for Washington with just 40 seconds left, 24-21.

Super Bowl XVIII in Tampa, Florida, was supposed to be a repeat of the Redskins' 37-35 last-minute victory over the Raiders in the regular season. The Raiders held up their end of the scoring bargain, but the Redskins didn't, and Los Angeles won 38-9.

1983 AFC STANDINGS

Eastern Division	**W**	**L**	**T**	**Pct.**	**Pts.**	**OP**
Miami	12	4	0	.750	389	250
New England	8	8	0	.500	274	289
Buffalo	8	8	0	.500	283	351
Baltimore	7	9	0	.438	264	354
New York Jets	7	9	0	.438	313	331
Central Division	**W**	**L**	**T**	**Pct.**	**Pts.**	**OP**
Pittsburgh	10	6	0	.625	355	303
Cleveland	9	7	0	.563	356	342
Cincinnati	7	9	0	.438	346	302
Houston	2	14	0	.125	288	460
Western Division	**W**	**L**	**T**	**Pct.**	**Pts.**	**OP**
Los Angeles Raiders	12	4	0	.750	442	338
Seattle*	9	7	0	.563	403	397
Denver*	9	7	0	.563	302	327
San Diego	6	10	0	.375	358	462
Kansas City	6	10	0	.375	386	367

**Wild Card qualifiers for playoffs*

Wild Card game: Seattle 31, Denver 7

Divisional playoffs: Seattle 27, Miami 20
Los Angeles Raiders 38, Pittsburgh 10

AFC championship: Los Angeles Raiders 30, Seattle 14

LEADING RUSHERS	**Att.**	**Yards**	**Avg.**	**Long**	**TD**
Curt Warner, Seattle	335	1,449	4.3	60	13
Earl Campbell, Houston	322	1,301	4.0	42	12
Mike Pruitt, Cleveland	293	1,184	4.0	27	10
Joe Cribbs, Buffalo	263	1,131	4.3	45	3
Curtis Dickey, Baltimore	254	1,122	4.4	56	4

LEADING PASSERS	**Att.**	**Comp.**	**Yards**	**TD**	**Int.**
Dan Marino, Miami	296	173	2,210	20	6
Dave Krieg, Seattle	243	147	2,139	18	11
Dan Fouts, San Diego	340	215	2,975	20	15
Ken Anderson, Cincinnati	297	198	2,333	12	13
Jim Plunkett, LA Raiders	379	230	2,935	20	18

LEADING RECEIVERS	**No.**	**Yards**	**Avg.**	**Long**	**TD**
Todd Christensen, LA Raiders	92	1,247	13.6	45	12
Ozzie Newsome, Cleveland	89	970	10.9	66t	6
Kellen Winslow, San Diego	88	1,172	13.3	46	8
Tim Smith, Houston	83	1,176	14.2	47t	6
Carlos Carson, Kansas City	80	1,351	16.9	50t	7

LEADING SCORER	**TD**	**FG**	**PAT**	**TP**
Gary Anderson, Pittsburgh	0	27	38	199

LEADING INTERCEPTORS	**No.**	**Yards**	**Avg.**	**Long**	**TD**
Ken Riley, Cincinnati	8	89	11.1	42t	2
Vann McElroy, LA Raiders	8	68	8.5	28	0

LEADING PUNTER	**No.**	**Avg.**	**Long**
Rohn Stark, Baltimore	91	45.3	68

LEADING PUNT RETURNER	**No.**	**Yards**	**Avg.**	**Long**	**TD**
Kirk Springs, NY Jets	23	287	12.5	76t	1

LEADING KICKOFF RETURNER	**No.**	**Yards**	**Avg.**	**Long**	**TD**
Fulton Walker, Miami	36	962	26.7	78	0

SUPERLATIVES

Rushing average	5.5	Mosi Tatupu, New England
Receiving average	19.7	Mark Duper, Miami
Completion percentage	66.7	Ken Anderson, Cincinnati
Touchdowns	14	Pete Johnson, Cincinnati
		Curt Warner, Seattle

LONGEST

Run	80	Larry Moriarty, Houston
Pass	99t	Jim Plunkett to Cliff Branch, LA Raiders
Interception	73t	Jacob Green, Seattle
Punt	70	Rich Camarillo, New England
Punt return	97t	Greg Pruitt, LA Raiders
Kickoff return	97t	Carl Roaches, Houston
Field goal	58	Nick Lowery, Kansas City
		Steve Cox, Cleveland

1983 NFC STANDINGS

Eastern Division	**W**	**L**	**T**	**Pct.**	**Pts.**	**OP**
Washington	14	2	0	.875	541	332
Dallas*	12	4	0	.750	479	360
St. Louis	8	7	1	.531	374	428
Philadelphia	5	11	0	.313	233	322
New York Giants	3	12	1	.219	267	347
Central Division	**W**	**L**	**T**	**Pct.**	**Pts.**	**OP**
Detroit	9	7	0	.563	347	286
Green Bay	8	8	0	.500	429	439
Chicago Bears	8	8	0	.500	311	301
Minnesota	8	8	0	.500	316	348
Tampa Bay	2	14	0	.125	241	380
Western Division	**W**	**L**	**T**	**Pct.**	**Pts.**	**OP**
San Francisco	10	6	0	.625	432	293
Los Angeles Rams*	9	7	0	.563	361	344
New Orleans	8	8	0	.500	319	337
Atlanta	7	9	0	.438	370	389

**Wild Card qualifiers for playoffs*

Wild Card game: Los Angeles Rams 24, Dallas 17

Divisional playoffs: San Francisco 24, Detroit 23
Washington 51, Los Angeles Rams 7

NFC championship: Washington 24, San Francisco 21

Super Bowl XVIII: Los Angeles Raiders (AFC) 38, Washington (NFC) 9

LEADING RUSHERS	**Att.**	**Yards**	**Avg.**	**Long**	**TD**
Eric Dickerson, LA Rams	390	1,808	4.6	85t	18
William Andrews, Atlanta	331	1,567	4.7	27	7
Walter Payton, Chi. Bears	314	1,421	4.5	49t	6
John Riggins, Washington	375	1,347	3.6	44	24
Tony Dorsett, Dallas	289	1,321	4.6	77	8

LEADING PASSERS	**Att.**	**Comp.**	**Yards**	**TD**	**Int.**
Steve Bartkowski, Atlanta	432	274	3,167	22	5
Joe Theismann, Washington	459	276	3,714	29	11
Joe Montana, San Francisco	515	332	3,910	26	12
Neil Lomax, St. Louis	354	209	2,636	24	11
Lynn Dickey, Green Bay	484	289	4,458	32	29

LEADING RECEIVERS	**No.**	**Yards**	**Avg.**	**Long**	**TD**
Roy Green, St. Louis	78	1,227	15.7	71t	14
Charlie Brown, Washington	78	1,225	15.7	75t	8
Earnest Gray, NY Giants	78	1,139	14.6	62	5
Ron Springs, Dallas	73	589	8.1	80t	1
Dwight Clark, San Francisco	70	840	12.0	46t	8

LEADING SCORER	**TD**	**FG**	**PAT**	**TP**
Mark Moseley, Washington	0	33	62	161

LEADING INTERCEPTOR	**No.**	**Yards**	**Avg.**	**Long**	**TD**
Mark Murphy, Washington	9	127	14.1	48	0

LEADING PUNTER	**No.**	**Avg.**	**Long**
Frank Garcia, Tampa Bay	95	42.2	64

LEADING PUNT RETURNER	**No.**	**Yards**	**Avg.**	**Long**	**TD**
Henry Ellard, LA Rams	16	217	13.6	72t	1

LEADING KICKOFF RETURNER	**No.**	**Yards**	**Avg.**	**Long**	**TD**
Darrin Nelson, Minnesota	18	445	24.7	50	0

SUPERLATIVES

Rushing average	5.3	Joe Washington, Washington
Receiving average	22.4	James Lofton, Green Bay
Completion percentage	64.5	Joe Montana, San Francisco
Touchdowns	24	John Riggins, Washington

LONGEST

Run	85t	Eric Dickerson, LA Rams
Pass	87t	Jim McMahon to Willie Gault, Chi. Bears
Interception	70t	Bobby Johnson, New Orleans
		Mel Kaufman, Washington
	70	Roosevelt Barnes, Detroit
Punt	70	Bucky Scribner, Green Bay
Punt return	90t	Phillip Epps, Green Bay
Kickoff return	66	Stump Mitchell, St. Louis
Field goal	56	Ali Haji-Sheikh, NY Giants (twice)

1984 Three NFL franchises were sold before the season began. In March, an 11-man group headed by H.R. (Bum) Bright purchased the Dallas Cowboys from founder Clint Murchison. Club president Tex Schramm was designated as the managing general partner. One day later, Canadian businessman Patrick Bowlen purchased a majority interest in the Denver Broncos from Edgar Kaiser. In August, real estate developer Alex G. Spanos, already a minority stockholder, purchased a majority interest in the San Diego Chargers from Eugene Klein.

The Colts suddenly left Baltimore, their home since 1953, and moved to Indianapolis, Indiana, on March 28. The team's new stadium was the new, 60,127-seat Hoosier Dome.

The AFC season was dominated by one team and its star player. With Dan Marino setting NFL records with 362 completions, 5,084 yards, and 48 touchdown passes, Miami roared to a 14-2 record, the best in the conference. On the other end of many of Marino's strikes was Mark Clayton, who caught 18 touchdown passes. Second-place New England got a new coach at midseason when Ron Meyer was fired and replaced by Raymond Berry. In the AFC Central, Cincinnati, under new head coach Sam Wyche, made a strong, late-season run at Pittsburgh, but the Steelers upset the Raiders in their final game to win the division. The Raiders, meanwhile, dropped to third in the West, but still qualified for the playoffs, as did second-place Seattle, which won with a scrappy defense that set an NFL record with 63 takeaways. The winner of the West was Denver, which featured the league's toughest defense to score on and its own *wunderkind* quarterback, John Elway.

In the NFC, the dominant team was San Francisco. The 49ers ran up the most regular-season wins (15) in NFL history while winning the West. The Rams, with Eric Dickerson breaking O.J. Simpson's single-season rushing record with 2,105 yards, earned a wild card playoff berth. The other wild card spot went to the Giants, who finished at 9-7, as did two other non-qualifying NFC East teams, Dallas and St. Louis. Washington won the East at 11-5 by knocking off the Cardinals 29-27 in the season finale. In the Central Division, the Bears won the title with the stingiest defense in the NFL. The most honored individual on the Bears was Walter Payton, who broke Jim Brown's career rushing mark. Minnesota, playing without Bud Grant as its coach for the first time since 1966 (he had retired and been replaced by Les Steckel), had the poorest record in the NFC, 3-13. Green Bay also had a new head coach, former Browns and Bengals coach Forrest Gregg.

The wild card games featured two close contests. Seattle dominated the Raiders on the ground to win 13-7. The Giants stopped the Rams, after the Los Angeles club had a first-and-goal in the fourth quarter, to win 16-13.

Miami avenged its defeat of the previous year in an AFC Divisional Playoff Game with a 31-10 victory over Seattle, and Pittsburgh upset highly favored Denver 24-17.

In the NFC, Joe Montana's three touchdown passes led San Francisco to a 21-10 victory over the Giants, and the Bears won 23-19 to become the first team to beat the Redskins in a playoff game in Washington in 44 years.

The championship games were almost completely opposite. The Dolphins got four touchdown passes from Marino, and needed them to beat the Steelers 45-28. In the NFC, the 49ers' defense dominated the Bears in a 23-0 victory.

Super Bowl XIX in Palo Alto, California, showed the difference between a team with a great passing attack and a team with an arsenal of offensive and defensive weapons. Before 84,059 fans at Stanford Stadium, the balanced 49ers and quarterback Joe Montana whipped the Dolphins 38-16.

1984 AFC STANDINGS

Eastern Division	**W**	**L**	**T**	**Pct.**	**Pts.**	**OP**
Miami	14	2	0	.875	513	298
New England	9	7	0	.563	362	352
New York Jets	7	9	0	.438	332	364
Indianapolis	4	12	0	.250	239	414
Buffalo	2	14	0	.125	250	454
Central Division	**W**	**L**	**T**	**Pct.**	**Pts.**	**OP**
Pittsburgh	9	7	0	.563	387	310
Cincinnati	8	8	0	.500	339	339
Cleveland	5	11	0	.313	250	297
Houston	2	14	0	.125	240	437
Western Division	**W**	**L**	**T**	**Pct.**	**Pts.**	**OP**
Denver	13	3	0	.813	353	241
Seattle*	12	4	0	.750	418	282
Los Angeles Raiders*	11	5	0	.688	368	278
Kansas City	8	8	0	.500	314	324
San Diego	7	9	0	.438	394	413

**Wild Card qualifiers for playoffs*

Wild Card game: Seattle 13, Los Angeles Raiders 7
Divisional playoffs: Miami 31, Seattle 10
Pittsburgh 24, Denver 17
AFC championship: Miami 45, Pittsburgh 28

LEADING RUSHERS	**Att.**	**Yards**	**Avg.**	**Long**	**TD**
Earnest Jackson, San Diego	296	1,179	4.0	32t	8
Marcus Allen, LA Raiders	275	1,168	4.2	52t	13
Sammy Winder, Denver	296	1,153	3.9	24	4
Greg Bell, Buffalo	262	1,100	4.2	85t	7
Freeman McNeil, NY Jets	229	1,070	4.7	53	5

LEADING PASSERS	**Att.**	**Comp.**	**Yards**	**TD**	**Int.**
Dan Marino, Miami	564	362	5,084	48	17
Tony Eason, New England	431	259	3,228	23	8
Dan Fouts, San Diego	507	317	3,740	19	17
Dave Krieg, Seattle	480	276	3,671	32	24
Ken Anderson, Cincinnati	275	175	2,107	10	12

LEADING RECEIVERS	**No.**	**Yards**	**Avg.**	**Long**	**TD**
Ozzie Newsome, Cleveland	89	1,001	11.2	52	5
John Stallworth, Pittsburgh	80	1,395	17.4	51	11
Todd Christensen, LA Raiders	80	1,007	12.6	38	7
Steve Largent, Seattle	74	1,164	15.7	65	12
Mark Clayton, Miami	73	1,389	19.0	65t	18

LEADING SCORER	**TD**	**FG**	**PAT**	**TP**
Gary Anderson, Pittsburgh	0	24	45	117

LEADING INTERCEPTOR	**No.**	**Yards**	**Avg.**	**Long**	**TD**
Ken Easley, Seattle	10	126	12.6	58t	2

LEADING PUNTER	**No.**	**Avg.**	**Long**
Jim Arnold, Kansas City	98	44.9	63

LEADING PUNT RETURNER	**No.**	**Yards**	**Avg.**	**Long**	**TD**
Mike Martin, Cincinnati	24	376	15.7	55	0

LEADING KICKOFF RETURNER	**No.**	**Yards**	**Avg.**	**Long**	**TD**
Bobby Humphery, NY Jets	22	675	30.7	97t	1

SUPERLATIVES		
Rushing average	5.0	Joe Carter, Miami
Receiving average	20.4	Daryl Turner, Seattle
Completion percentage	64.2	Dan Marino, Miami
Touchdowns	18	Marcus Allen, LA Raiders Mark Clayton, Miami

LONGEST		
Run	85t	Greg Bell, Buffalo
Pass	92	Marc Wilson to Marcus Allen, LA Raiders
Interception	99t	Gill Byrd, San Diego
Punt	89	Luke Prestridge, New England
Punt return	76t	Louis Lipps, Pittsburgh
Kickoff return	97t	Bobby Humphery, NY Jets
Field goal	60	Steve Cox, Cleveland

1984 NFC STANDINGS

Eastern Division	**W**	**L**	**T**	**Pct.**	**Pts.**	**OP**
Washington	11	5	0	.688	426	310
New York Giants*	9	7	0	.563	299	301
St. Louis	9	7	0	.563	423	345
Dallas	9	7	0	.563	308	308
Philadelphia	6	9	1	.406	278	320
Central Division	**W**	**L**	**T**	**Pct.**	**Pts.**	**OP**
Chicago Bears	10	6	0	.625	325	248
Green Bay	8	8	0	.500	390	309
Tampa Bay	6	10	0	.375	335	380
Detroit	4	11	1	.281	283	408
Minnesota	3	13	0	.188	276	484
Western Division	**W**	**L**	**T**	**Pct.**	**Pts.**	**OP**
San Francisco	15	1	0	.938	475	227
Los Angeles Rams*	10	6	0	.625	346	316
New Orleans	7	9	0	.438	298	361
Atlanta	4	12	0	.250	281	382

**Wild Card qualifiers for playoffs*

Wild Card game: New York Giants 16, Los Angeles Rams 13
Divisional playoffs: San Francisco 21, New York Giants 10
Chicago Bears 23, Washington 10
NFC championship: San Francisco 23, Chicago Bears 0
Super Bowl XIX: San Francisco (NFC) 38, Miami (AFC) 16

LEADING RUSHERS	**Att.**	**Yards**	**Avg.**	**Long**	**TD**
Eric Dickerson, LA Rams	379	2,105	5.6	66	14
Walter Payton, Chi. Bears	381	1,684	4.4	72t	11
James Wilder, Tampa Bay	407	1,544	3.8	37	13
Gerald Riggs, Atlanta	353	1,486	4.2	57	13
Wendell Tyler, San Francisco	246	1,262	5.1	40	7

LEADING PASSERS	**Att.**	**Comp.**	**Yards**	**TD**	**Int.**
Joe Montana, San Francisco	432	279	3,630	28	10
Neil Lomax, St. Louis	560	345	4,614	28	16
Steve Bartkowski, Atlanta	269	181	2,158	11	10
Joe Theismann, Washington	477	283	3,391	24	13
Lynn Dickey, Green Bay	401	237	3,195	25	19

LEADING RECEIVERS	**No.**	**Yards**	**Avg.**	**Long**	**TD**
Art Monk, Washington	106	1,372	12.9	72	7
James Wilder, Tampa Bay	85	685	8.1	50	0
Roy Green, St. Louis	78	1,555	19.9	83t	12
James Jones, Detroit	77	662	8.6	39	5
Kevin House, Tampa Bay	76	1,005	13.2	55	5

LEADING SCORER	**TD**	**FG**	**PAT**	**TP**
Ray Wersching, San Francisco	0	25	56	131

LEADING INTERCEPTOR	**No.**	**Yards**	**Avg.**	**Long**	**TD**
Tom Flynn, Green Bay	9	106	11.8	31	0

LEADING PUNTER	**No.**	**Avg.**	**Long**
Brian Hansen, New Orleans	69	43.8	66

LEADING PUNT RETURNER	**No.**	**Yards**	**Avg.**	**Long**	**TD**
Henry Ellard, LA Rams	30	403	13.4	83t	2

LEADING KICKOFF RETURNER	**No.**	**Yards**	**Avg.**	**Long**	**TD**
Barry Redden, LA Rams	23	530	23.0	40	0

SUPERLATIVES		
Rushing average	6.0	Hokie Gajan, New Orleans
Receiving average	22.0	James Lofton, Green Bay
Completion percentage	67.3	Steve Bartkowski, Atlanta
Touchdowns	14	Eric Dickerson, LA Rams John Riggins, Washington

LONGEST		
Run	81	Billy Sims, Detroit
Pass	90t	Ron Jaworski to Mike Quick, Philadelphia
Interception	99t	Tim Lewis, Green Bay
Punt	87	David Finzer, Chi. Bears
Punt return	83t	Henry Ellard, LA Rams
Kickoff return	97t	Del Rodgers, Green Bay
Field goal	54	Jan Stenerud, Minnesota

1985 NBC Radio and the NFL entered into a two-year agreement granting NBC the radio rights to a 37-game package in each of the next two years, including all playoff games.

In April, Norman Braman, in partnership with Edward Leibowitz, bought the Philadelphia Eagles from Leonard Tose. Two months later, a group headed by Tom Benson, Jr., purchased the New Orleans Saints from John Mecom.

The regular season was dominated by one team, the Chicago Bears, and one player, Bears rookie defensive tackle William (The Refrigerator) Perry. The Bears, with the best defense in the NFL and an explosive offense, equaled the 49ers' record for most victories in a season, going 15-1 and winning the NFC Central. The 308-pound Perry became a national folk hero when he lined up at running back and not only blocked for Walter Payton's touchdowns, but scored three himself, including one on a pass reception. In the West, the Rams won their first seven games and then held off a late-season surge by San Francisco to win the title. The 49ers gained a wild card berth. Dallas won the East despite having the same record (10-6) as the Giants and Redskins. The Giants were the second wild card team. The Redskins' playoff hopes were damaged when Joe Theismann broke his leg on a Monday night game against the Giants.

Miami fought off challenges by New England and the New York Jets to win the AFC East. The Dolphins moved ahead in the next-to-last week by beating the Patriots 30-27, while the Jets lost to the Bears 19-6. All three teams made the playoffs. The Raiders beat the Broncos twice on field goals in overtime, and Los Angeles edged Denver for the AFC West title. The Broncos just missed out on a wild card spot. Cleveland won the AFC Central at 8-8.

The two New York teams hosted the wild card games, and they came away with a split. The Jets self-destructed with four turnovers in a 26-14 New England win. The Giants were aided in their 17-3 victory by 10 passes dropped by San Francisco receivers.

In one AFC Divisional Playoff Game, the Browns built a 21-3 lead in the fourth quarter, but the Dolphins came back to win 24-21. In the other game, the Patriots recovered a fumbled kickoff in the end zone for the winning touchdown in a 27-20 victory in Los Angeles.

Defenses dominated the NFC Divisional Playoff Games. Eric Dickerson broke open a 3-0 game with two long touchdown runs in the third quarter, and the Rams beat the Cowboys 20-0. Dickerson ran for 248 yards, an NFL playoff record. In Chicago, the Bears totally shut down the Giants 21-0.

Both championship games were one-sided. In the AFC, Tony Eason grabbed the spotlight from Dan Marino with three touchdown passes, and the Patriots earned a trip to their first Super Bowl 31-14. The Bears' defense held the Rams to 130 yards and scored the game's final touchdown in a 24-0 victory.

Super Bowl XX, at the Louisiana Superdome in New Orleans, was the most one-sided game in Super Bowl history. The Bears dominated the Patriots to win 46-10. The game was viewed by a United States television audience of 127 million, making it the most-watched televised event of all time.

1985 AFC STANDINGS

Eastern Division	**W**	**L**	**T**	**Pct.**	**Pts.**	**OP**
Miami	12	4	0	.750	428	320

	W	L	T	Pct.	Pts.	OP
New York Jets*	11	5	0	.688	393	264
New England*	11	5	0	.688	362	290
Indianapolis	5	11	0	.313	320	386
Buffalo	2	14	0	.125	200	381
Central Division	**W**	**L**	**T**	**Pct.**	**Pts.**	**OP**
Cleveland	8	8	0	.500	287	294
Cincinnati	7	9	0	.438	441	437
Pittsburgh	7	9	0	.438	379	355
Houston	5	11	0	.313	284	412
Western Division	**W**	**L**	**T**	**Pct.**	**Pts.**	**OP**
Los Angeles Raiders	12	4	0	.750	354	308
Denver	11	5	0	.688	380	329
Seattle	8	8	0	.500	349	303
San Diego	8	8	0	.500	467	435
Kansas City	6	10	0	.375	317	360

**Wild Card qualifiers for playoffs*

Wild Card game: New England 26, New York Jets 14

Divisional playoffs: Miami 24, Cleveland 21
New England 27, Los Angeles Raiders 20

AFC championship: New England 31, Miami 14

LEADING RUSHERS	**Att.**	**Yards**	**Avg.**	**Long**	**TD**
Marcus Allen, LA Raiders	380	1,759	4.6	61t	11
Freeman McNeil, NY Jets	294	1,331	4.5	69	3
Craig James, New England	263	1,227	4.7	65t	5
Kevin Mack, Cleveland	222	1,104	5.0	61	7
Curt Warner, Seattle	291	1,094	3.8	38	8

LEADING PASSERS	**Att.**	**Comp.**	**Yards**	**TD**	**Int.**
Ken O'Brien, NY Jets	488	297	3,888	25	8
Boomer Esiason, Cincinnati	431	251	3,443	27	12
Dan Fouts, San Diego	430	254	3,638	27	20
Dan Marino, Miami	567	336	4,137	30	21
Bill Kenney, Kansas City	338	181	2,536	17	9

LEADING RECEIVERS	**No.**	**Yards**	**Avg.**	**Long**	**TD**
Lionel James, San Diego	86	1,027	11.9	67t	6
Todd Christensen, LA Raiders	82	987	12.0	48	6
Butch Woolfolk, Houston	80	814	10.2	80t	4
Steve Largent, Seattle	79	1,287	16.3	43	6
Mickey Shuler, NY Jets	76	879	11.6	35	7

LEADING SCORER	**TD**	**FG**	**PAT**	**TP**
Gary Anderson, Pittsburgh	0	33	40	139

LEADING INTERCEPTORS	**No.**	**Yards**	**Avg.**	**Long**	**TD**
Albert Lewis, Kansas City	8	59	7.4	16	0
Eugene Daniel, Indianapolis	8	53	6.6	29	0

LEADING PUNTER	**No.**	**Avg.**	**Long**
Rohn Stark, Indianapolis	78	45.9	68

LEADING PUNT RETURNER	**No.**	**Yards**	**Avg.**	**Long**	**TD**
Irving Fryar, New England	37	520	14.1	85t	2

LEADING KICKOFF RETURNER	**No.**	**Yards**	**Avg.**	**Long**	**TD**
Glen Young, Cleveland	35	898	25.7	63	0

SUPERLATIVES		
Rushing average	5.2	George Wonsley, Indianapolis
Receiving average	21.9	Stephone Paige, Kansas City
Completion percentage	60.9	Ken O'Brien, NY Jets
Touchdowns	15	Louis Lipps, Pittsburgh

LONGEST		
Run	77t	Greg Bell, Buffalo
Pass	96t	Ken O'Brien to Wesley Walker, NY Jets
Interception	83	Fred Marion, New England
Punt	75	Rich Camarillo, New England
Punt return	85t	Irving Fryar, New England
Kickoff return	98t	Gary Anderson, San Diego
Field goal	58	Nick Lowery, Kansas City

1985 NFC STANDINGS

Eastern Division	**W**	**L**	**T**	**Pct.**	**Pts.**	**OP**
Dallas	10	6	0	.625	357	333
New York Giants*	10	6	0	.625	399	283
Washington	10	6	0	.625	297	312
Philadelphia	7	9	0	.438	286	310
St. Louis	5	11	0	.313	278	414
Central Division	**W**	**L**	**T**	**Pct.**	**Pts.**	**OP**
Chicago Bears	15	1	0	.938	456	198
Green Bay	8	8	0	.500	337	355
Minnesota	7	9	0	.438	346	359
Detroit	7	9	0	.438	307	366
Tampa Bay	2	14	0	.125	294	448
Western Division	**W**	**L**	**T**	**Pct.**	**Pts.**	**OP**
Los Angeles Rams	11	5	0	.688	340	277
San Francisco*	10	6	0	.625	411	263
New Orleans	5	11	0	.313	294	401
Atlanta	4	12	0	.250	282	452

**Wild Card qualifiers for playoffs*

Wild Card game: New York Giants 17, San Francisco 3

Divisional playoffs: Los Angeles Rams 20, Dallas 0
Chicago Bears 21, New York Giants 0

NFC championship: Chicago Bears 24, Los Angeles Rams 0

Super Bowl XX: Chicago Bears (NFC) 46, New England (AFC) 10

LEADING RUSHERS	**Att.**	**Yards**	**Avg.**	**Long**	**TD**
Gerald Riggs, Atlanta	397	1,719	4.3	50	10
Walter Payton, Chi. Bears	324	1,551	4.8	40t	9
Joe Morris, NY Giants	294	1,336	4.5	65t	21
Tony Dorsett, Dallas	305	1,307	4.3	60t	7
James Wilder, Tampa Bay	365	1,300	3.6	28	10

LEADING PASSERS	**Att.**	**Comp.**	**Yards**	**TD**	**Int.**
Joe Montana, San Francisco	494	303	3,653	27	13
Jim McMahon, Chi. Bears	318	178	2,392	15	11
Dieter Brock, LA Rams	365	218	2,658	16	13
Danny White, Dallas	450	267	3,157	21	17
Neil Lomax, St. Louis	471	265	3,214	18	12

LEADING RECEIVERS	**No.**	**Yards**	**Avg.**	**Long**	**TD**
Roger Craig, San Francisco	92	1,016	11.0	73	6
Art Monk, Washington	91	1,226	13.5	53	2
Tony Hill, Dallas	74	1,113	15.0	53t	7
Mike Quick, Philadelphia	73	1,247	17.1	99t	11
Gary Clark, Washington	72	926	12.9	55	5

LEADING SCORER	**TD**	**FG**	**PAT**	**TP**
Kevin Butler, Chi. Bears	0	31	51	144

LEADING INTERCEPTOR	**No.**	**Yards**	**Avg.**	**Long**	**TD**
Everson Walls, Dallas	9	31	3.4	19	0

LEADING PUNTER	**No.**	**Avg.**	**Long**
Dick Donnelly, Atlanta	59	43.6	68

LEADING PUNT RETURNER	**No.**	**Yards**	**Avg.**	**Long**	**TD**
Henry Ellard, LA Rams	37	501	13.5	80t	1

LEADING KICKOFF RETURNER	**No.**	**Yards**	**Avg.**	**Long**	**TD**
Ron Brown, LA Rams	28	918	32.8	98t	3

SUPERLATIVES		
Rushing average	5.5	Stump Mitchell, St. Louis
Receiving average	21.3	Willie Gault, Chi. Bears
Completion percentage	61.3	Joe Montana, San Francisco
Touchdowns	21	Joe Morris, NY Giants

LONGEST		
Run	80	Jessie Clark, Green Bay
Pass	99t	Ron Jaworski to Mike Quick, Philadelphia
Interception	90	Mike Richardson, Chi. Bears
Punt	75	Mike Horan, Philadelphia
Punt return	80t	Henry Ellard, LA Rams
Kickoff return	99t	Willie Gault, Chi. Bears
Field goal	55	Morten Andersen, New Orleans

1986 At the league meetings in March, the use of instant replay to help officials on possession calls was approved. The league also voted to play an annual preseason game on other continents, to be called the American Bowl.

During the meetings, Commissioner Pete Rozelle announced that he unilaterally would implement a new drug policy if one couldn't be worked out with the NFL Players Association. Shortly thereafter, the Players Association announced its plan for the new policy.

Extinct Leagues

THE THREE EARLY AFLs

There have been four American Football Leagues—in 1926, 1936-37, 1940-41, and 1960-69. Each entered into competition with the NFL seeking parity with it as an entity of American sport. The fourth succeeded and is now the American Football Conference. The first three failed.

Timothy J. Mara purchased an NFL franchise for New York City in 1925. The Giants' games at the Polo Grounds drew small crowds and the team was losing money until the arrival of Red Grange. But when Grange played in the Polo Grounds in New York, 70,000 attended. It made Mara see the potential of pro football.

Grange's personal manager, C.C. (Cash and Carry) Pyle, informed the Bears that Grange would not play for them in 1926 unless he was given a five-figure salary and one-third ownership of the team. George Halas and Dutch Sternaman, owners of the team, refused.

So Pyle went to New York, the site of Grange's conquests the year before, and leased Yankee Stadium from the baseball team. He then petitioned the NFL for a franchise.

Mara, whose Giants played just across the Harlem River at the Polo Grounds, would not agree to that. But he and the other NFL owners did agree that a second franchise could be located in New York City provided it was at Ebbets Field in Brooklyn. This compromise was rejected by Pyle, who wanted an NFL team at Yankee Stadium. If he did not get it, he said, he would start his own league, which he did.

The AFL was built around Grange and the Yankees. There were eight other teams, including a road team listed as the Los Angeles Wildcats and the Rock Island Independents, who left the NFL to join the AFL. Politician and former Princeton athlete Bill Edwards was hired by Pyle to be commissioner of the AFL at a salary of $25,000, 10 times the $2,500 salary paid NFL commissioner Joe Carr. But it is believed that Edwards and AFL coaches and players never received their salaries in full.

New York Giants' coach Bob Folwell left to join the Philadelphia Quakers and so did the Giants' star tackle, Century Milstead. Al Nesser played for a time with the Cleveland Panthers. Mike Michalske played for the Yankees and Ray Flaherty for the Los Angeles Wildcats; both were NFL stars later with the Packers and Giants, respectively. Joey Sternaman, brother of the Bears' co-owner, formed the Chicago Bulls, who leased Comiskey Park, forcing the NFL Cardinals to move to smaller Normal Park.

Support of the AFL was minimal outside New York City. At the end of October, Cleveland and Newark folded, and the Newark players sued for their salaries. In early November, the Brooklyn Horsemen folded and then merged with the NFL's Brooklyn franchise. Rock Island and Boston died of financial woes in mid-November. Only Philadelphia, New York, Chicago, and the travelling Los Angeles Wildcats remained in business at the season's end.

Mara of the Giants, who had suffered losses in the war with the AFL, wanted one more crack at it and challenged Pyle's Yankees to a game. Pyle agreed to it at first, then backed down. Mara turned to the Quakers, champions of the AFL. The Quakers, anxious to make a few extra dollars, agreed.

The first AFL thus achieved in one year what other challengers to the NFL would not in the years ahead—an interleague playoff. The game the Quakers and Giants played December 12, 1926, has been called "the first Super Bowl." But the fact remains that the Giants had finished seventh in the NFL that year.

Bad weather engulfed the Polo Grounds on the day of the game and snow obliterated the yard lines. Only 5,000 persons watched as the Quakers managed only one first down and the Giants won 31-0.

As a lone concession to the AFL, the NFL extended membership to the Yankees the following season and they remained in the league for two more years until they went out of business.

1926 AFL STANDINGS	W	L	T	Pct.
Philadelphia Quakers	7	2	0	.778
New York Yankees	9	5	0	.643
Cleveland Panthers	3	2	0	.600
Los Angeles Wildcats	6	6	2	.500
Chicago Bulls	5	6	3	.455
Boston Bulldogs	2	4	0	.333
Rock Island Independents	2	5	1	.286
Brooklyn Horsemen	1	3	0	.250
Newark Bears	0	4	2	.000

Ten years after the demise of the first AFL, another rival league appeared having the same name. It lasted two years and never had more than six teams.

The second AFL had a team in Yankee Stadium called the Yankees. This was an obligatory feature of every rival league to operate in the years before the Giants quit the Polo Grounds and moved to Yankee Stadium themselves in 1956.

An AFL team called the Brooklyn Tigers set up shop at Ebbets Field to play home games while the Dodgers were on the road. Dodgers' owner Dan Topping objected strongly to the arrangement. Dr. Harry March, former team physician of the Giants and a close friend of Tim Mara, was the AFL's president. March gave a curious explanation of the Brooklyn arrangement to the newspapers, saying that "continuous football at Ebbets Field . . . would work toward the benefit of both clubs, keeping football interest at a high pitch."

The AFL made the second abortive attempt to establish pro football in Cincinnati. This time the name Bengals was adopted, and, while the pros failed again to take hold in the Ohio city, the nickname would reappear 32 years later.

In 1936 two AFL teams played the first pro game in a then insignificant arena in Miami. Hank Soar scored two touchdowns to lead the Boston Shamrocks to a 14-6 victory over the New York Yankees. The Grange tour had stopped in Miami in 1925 during the Florida land boom, when the Bears and their opponents played in a ramshackle stadium that was thrown up overnight for the occasion and torn down the following day. This AFL game of 1936 played an important role in the history of a later and more permanent stadium. As sports editor Dinty Dennis of the *Miami Herald* wrote, "The game was the football 'swan song' for the wooden sports arena, stadium manager E.E. Seiler announcing the wrecking crews would go to work early this week to demolish the inadequate stands and make way for the new concrete Orange Bowl stadium."

Notable players were part of the second AFL. There were three well-known former New York Giants in the league. Ken Strong played for the Yankees, Harry Newman for Brooklyn and Rochester, and Morris (Red) Badgro was player-coach of Rochester in 1936. Sid Gillman, later a successful coach, played end for Cleveland.

Difficulty struck the Yankees' franchise when, after an estimated 26,000 fans had already arrived for a game against the Pittsburgh Americans, vandals cut the wires lighting the outside of Yankee Stadium. According to a newspaper report, "With no lights available, ticket sellers could not operate and the drastic act of closing all gates was the only alternative as a milling throng assailed two police emergency squads which were rushed to the gates."

No such problems beset the champion Boston Shamrocks. A Boston paper wrote of "the customary scant crowd at Fenway Park" for a Shamrocks' game. A championship game was scheduled at Cleveland, but the Boston players refused to go because they were owed pay for past games. Boston was the league champion, anyway, because it had the best won-lost record.

1936 AFL STANDINGS	W	L	T	Pct.
Boston Shamrocks	8	3	0	.727
Cleveland Rams	5	2	2	.714
New York Yankees	5	3	2	.625
Pittsburgh Americans	3	2	1	.600
Rochester Tigers	1	6	0	.143
Brooklyn Tigers	0	6	1	.000

The AFL of 1937 had the first genuine Los Angeles franchise, the first to actually operate in that city. It was hoped, as a press release distributed with the schedule explained, that "the powerful Los Angeles club will provide the intersectional tang which has done so much to inspirit collegiate football. . . ."

The Los Angeles Bulldogs had operated as an independent team the year before they joined the AFL and reportedly defeated three NFL teams in exhibition games. They had a former USC tailback named Bill Howard, another runner of note named Ed (Crazylegs) Stark, and a barefooted punter named Bob Miller. They strengthened themselves with new players for 1937 and even tried unsuccessfully to arrange a film contract for Sammy Baugh of TCU to convince him to sign a contract with them; he signed with the Washington Redskins of the NFL instead.

Gus Henderson was the coach of the Bulldogs. He had been head coach at USC for 6 years and at Tulsa for 11. He employed spread formations, something he called the "Befuddle Huddle," and details of coaching more often credited to coaches such as Paul Brown. They were described in a Rochester newspaper: "There is a set time for arising in the morning. Only special foods are allowed at the training table—at home and on the road. The players always travel in one group and never are allowed to separate without special permission from Henderson."

The Bulldogs gained the distinction of being the only pro team ever to play out the entire period of its membership in a league without being defeated. They won every game on their eastern swing and then defeated the teams that came to play them in Gilmore Stadium in Los Angeles. The league folded with the Bulldogs as its last champions.

Los Angeles was left with a championship in 1937—and no team. But the second American Football League had given birth to a team in Cleveland called the Rams, which, under new management, applied for and gained NFL membership in 1937. Nine years later, it was this Rams team that left Ohio and moved west to Los Angeles.

1937 AFL STANDINGS	W	L	T	Pct.
Los Angeles Bulldogs	8	0	0	1.000
Rochester Tigers	3	3	1	.500
New York Yankees	2	3	1	.400
Cincinnati Bengals	2	3	2	.400
Boston Shamrocks	2	5	0	.286
Pittsburgh Americans	0	3	0	.000

Of all the rival leagues in history, six have been accorded major league status. Of those six, none was smaller, more poorly timed, or appears to have had less meaning than the third American Football League, which operated in 1940-41.

Organized at a meeting in Buffalo, it immediately faced a challenge over its right to call itself the "American Football League" because there was another group by that name, which had formerly been known as the Mid-West Professional Football League.

That crisis passed when the other AFL went under. The new AFL set up headquarters in Columbus, the same city in which the NFL headquarters was located. W.D. Griffith, former publicity director at Ohio

State, became president of the new AFL. The Columbus Bullies won the league championship in both seasons the league operated.

1940 AFL STANDINGS	W	L	T	Pct.
Columbus Bullies	8	1	1	.889
Milwaukee Chiefs	7	2	0	.777
Boston Bears	5	4	1	.556
New York Yankees	4	5	0	.445
Buffalo Indians	2	8	0	.200
Cincinnati Bengals	1	7	0	.125

The New York Yankees changed their name to the Americans for the 1941 season. The third AFL failed to sign many big-name players but former college stars John Kimbrough of Texas A&M and Tom Harmon of Michigan made their pro football debuts with the Americans, October 19, 1941, in a 7-7 tie with Columbus. Kimbrough made the all-league team even though he played only half the season.

Center Lee Mulleneaux of Columbus previously had played with six different NFL teams and with the Cincinnati Bengals of the second AFL.

A game in Cincinnati was forfeited because the Bengals did not have enough players. The AFL's personnel troubles continued as Harmon and other players enlisted in the Armed Forces. As a Hall of Fame press release in later years explained, "World War II was undoubtedly the major reason why AFL number three met with failure, but there was nothing in its two-year existence to indicate any other eventual outcome."

1941 AFL STANDINGS	W	L	T	Pct.
Columbus Bullies	5	1	2	.833
New York Americans	5	2	1	.714
Milwaukee Chiefs	4	3	1	.571
Buffalo Indians	2	6	0	.250
Cincinnati Bengals	1	5	2	.167

THE AAFC

The All-America Football Conference of 1946-49 had a greater influence on professional football, reached more people, and made more inroads on the strength of the National Football League than any other now defunct rival league.

The AAFC produced the Baltimore Colts, Cleveland Browns, and San Francisco 49ers. It produced a host of players who went on to star in the NFL, such as Otto Graham, Elroy (Crazylegs) Hirsch, Joe Perry, and Y.A. Tittle. It placed the first permanent franchise in California, the 49ers (they and the Los Angeles Dons were in business by those names before the Rams arrived from Cleveland).

The AAFC was the first league to travel by air; it made charter arrangements with airlines while the NFL still rode trains. The AAFC occupied three big stadiums that no NFL team then used—Municipal Stadium in Cleveland, Memorial Coliseum in Los Angeles (which the Dons shared with the new Los Angeles Rams), and Yankee Stadium in New York—and with occasional big crowds in them the AAFC actually had a greater average attendance in the four years of its existence than the NFL—38,319 to 27,602.

Blacks had been part of pro football in the twenties, but they had not played in the NFL since 1933. Black AAFC stars included Marion Motley and Bill Willis of Cleveland, Len Ford of Los Angeles, Buddy Young of the New York Yankees, and Perry of San Francisco.

The AAFC probably spawned the widespread use of zone defenses in pro football. It willingly hired college coaches, who had been teaching that kind of pass defense for years, while man-for-man was the style in the NFL.

Finally, the AAFC hurt the NFL, signed many of its players, succeeded in getting college stars the NFL wanted, drained away fans and interest, and fought hard for its survival. It gave players an alternative, and NFL teams were forced to pay higher salaries. Those teams that did not became losers. That was how the AAFC influenced pro football.

World War II weakened the NFL. The Cleveland Rams dropped out of the league one year. Pittsburgh merged its team with Philadelphia one season and with the Chicago Cardinals the next. Players were at such a premium that Bronko Nagurski, who had not worn a football uniform since 1937, rejoined the Chicago Bears in 1943.

But there was a feeling that there would be prosperity as never before once the war ended. There was so much prosperity, in fact, that a second pro league seemed possible to many visionaries and there were men willing to finance it. Mickey McBride, owner of a taxicab company in Cleveland, had attempted unsuccessfully to buy the Rams. Oilman James F. Brueil, representing Buffalo, had deposited $25,000 with the NFL for a franchise. Anthony Morabito, owner of a lumber business in San Francisco, had been trying to arrange an NFL franchise for that city since 1940. Actor Don Ameche had asked his friend, sports editor Arch Ward of the *Chicago Tribune*, to help him get a team in the NFL.

The climate for sports seemed especially good in Chicago. The major commissioners of sport, Elmer Layden of football and Judge Kenesaw Mountain Landis of baseball, both had their offices there in the early forties. It was in Chicago that the great Bears' teams had first played their T-formation with man-in-motion and in 1940 stunned the nation by winning the NFL Championship Game 73-0. And it was there that Ward, a canny newspaperman, had organized the baseball all-star game and football Chicago College All-Star Game and established himself as a man with clout in the world of sport.

Ward's influence at his newspaper was considerable. The promotions he created convinced advertisers of the power of the *Tribune*. This won him the confidence of his publisher, Colonel Robert McCormick, and it was Ward who often represented the paper at *Associated Press* publishers conventions.

Ward was considered a possibility for the commissionership of the National Football League in 1940. He turned it down. His name came up again in 1941, and he again refused it. But he recommended Elmer Layden, coach and athletic director at Notre Dame, and Layden was hired by the NFL.

Ward still did business with the NFL each year as the director of the Chicago College All-Star Game between college players and the NFL champion. He wanted pro football to expand. He wanted to see an annual "world series of football." And he was frustrated that he could not get the NFL to admit Ameche as a club owner. For all these reasons, Ward decided to organize a new pro football league that would begin its operations as soon as World War II ended.

Two other groups, the Trans-America League and the United States Football League, also planned to begin play once the war ended. But they faded from view as the AAFC began to gain momentum. The first meeting of the league was held in St. Louis in June, 1944. People representing Buffalo, Chicago, Cleveland, Los Angeles, New York, and San Francisco were present. Miami entered the league a year later. The New York investor withdrew and each AAFC team paid $75,000, and promised $25,000 from its gate receipts, to Dan Topping to move his Brooklyn Dodgers team from the NFL to the new league. He purchased controlling interest in the baseball Yankees and his football team became the New York Yankees. A new franchise in Brooklyn secured Ebbets Field and took the name Dodgers.

The league chose to name itself the "All-America Football Conference" because "All-America" was a popular sports term and it reflected the fact that the league stretched from border to border. Jim Crowley became its commissioner. He had been a member—along with NFL commissioner Layden—of the Four Horsemen of Notre Dame.

Layden was present at the *Chicago Tribune's* annual pregame smoker the night before the All-Star Game in August, 1945. He learned that Ward was going to use the occasion to make an announcement about the All-America Football Conference. Layden decided to issue a statement about it through his press agent, George Strickler. Layden recalled later, "I reminded George that over the years there had always been talk about new professional leagues sprouting up and that as far as I was concerned the All-America Conference should 'first get a ball, then make a schedule, and then play a game.' "

The statement would be flung at Layden in print for the next four years. It is the thing that is most remembered from his commissionership, that (as expedient historians have simplified it) he said of the AAFC, "Tell them to get a football first."

Gerald Smith, vice president of the Street & Smith publishing house that put out a popular annual football magazine, was one of the owners of the Brooklyn team. It hired Dr. Mal Stevens, an orthopedic surgeon, as coach.

Brueil owned the Buffalo team, the Bisons. He hired Sam Cordovano, who was replaced by Lowell (Red) Dawson as coach before the season began, and rented Memorial Stadium.

John L. Keeshin, owner of a race track, headed the Chicago Rockets. He said their name was "inspired by the new speed age in which rocket travel, even to the moon, is predicted." Dick Hanley was hired as the Rockets' coach, and Soldier Field was secured for the team's games.

McBride, owner of a Cleveland cab company, became president of the team he later named the Browns. Seeking a coach, he asked John Dietrich of the *Cleveland Press,* "Who is the best football coach in America?"

Dietrich replied, "Paul Brown." McBride hired the former Ohio State coach. And the Browns' owner rented 80,000-seat Municipal Stadium although the Cleveland Rams, who had now departed for Los Angeles, had played their regular-season games in smaller League Park since 1942.

There were now two pro football teams in Los Angeles, where there had been none. Each scheduled its games at Memorial Coliseum. The AAFC Dons, owned by Ameche, Ben Lindheimer, and others, hired Dudley DeGroot as coach.

Miami Seahawks owner Harvey Hester hired Jack Meagher as coach and secured the Orange Bowl. Topping hired Ray Flaherty to coach his team at Yankee Stadium. And Morabito named Lawrence (Buck) Shaw his coach and rented Kezar Stadium.

The AAFC teams had no trouble finding players. There were scores of them leaving military service or coming out of college football. Brooklyn signed tackle Martin Ruby of Texas A&M, captain of the 1946 College All-Stars, and Glenn Dobbs of Tulsa. Buffalo got Steve Juzwik of Notre Dame. Chicago's coach, Hanley, its most celebrated player, Elroy (Crazylegs) Hirsch, and many of its other players had been together on the team at El Toro Marine Air Base in California and were signed by the Rockets as a group. As a result, it was predicted that the Rockets would be the best team in the league.

One-hundred former NFL players eventually signed with AAFC teams. Cleveland signed Chet Adams of the Rams, saying his contract was with the Cleveland, not the Los Angeles, Rams. A court upheld the Browns' claim. Cleveland also signed Otto Graham of Northwestern.

Los Angeles lured all-pro tackle Lee Artoe away from the Chicago Bears and won a legal dispute honoring the contract it had signed with Angelo Bertelli of Notre Dame, winner of the Heisman Trophy. Miami got Hamp Pool of the Chicago Bears.

Orban (Spec) Sanders had been only a substitute at Texas before World War II, but the New York Yankees, recognizing his potential, signed him to a three-year contract. New York also signed 1944 NFL most valuable player Frank Sinkwich of Detroit. "There is a strong possibility that this may form the basis of a little fight," said coach Gus Dorais of Detroit, but the Yankees kept Sinkwich. The New York team also received one player from each of the other teams in the league, in addition to the $75,000 each team paid owner Topping to move to the AAFC.

San Francisco landed Norm Standlee, who had been a star for the Chicago Bears before the war, and Frankie Albert of Stanford.

Forty of the 66 College All-Stars signed with the AAFC. Chicago, Los Angeles, New York, and San Francisco were heavily stocked with former service players.

There were enough players, commissioner Crowley said, "for a dozen leagues." The AAFC did not hold a draft its first year and the NFL held its draft in secret to avoid giving the AAFC a ready list of players to seek out and attempt to sign.

The Washington Redskins appeared to be the NFL team hardest hit by the AAFC signings. They lost their pre-war coach, Flaherty, to the New York Yankees; their 1945 coach, DeGroot, to Los Angeles; and a dozen of their players to various teams in the AAFC. They had been Eastern Division champions in 1945, but they did not win another championship for the next quarter of a century.

The AAFC's adoption of air travel was not so much an achievement as it was a necessity. No other league in any sport had ever attempted to play weekly games in cities as far flung as Los Angeles, San Francisco, and Miami. The charter contract with United Air Lines to carry AAFC clubs in DC-4 planes was called the largest such contract in history. And although there were suitable training camp sites nearby, the Dodgers trained in Bend, Oregon, the Chicago Rockets in Santa Rosa, California, and the Miami Seahawks in North Carolina.

The league schedule was a demanding one not only because of the unprecedented cross-country flights it entailed but also because it was a crazy quilt in which some teams played Sunday, others Friday night, and others at night in the middle of the week.

The Cleveland Browns won their first six games by a total score of 149-20. A crowd of 60,135 watched their opener, when they crushed Miami 44-0. Graham, the Browns' quarterback, led an attack that featured fullback Marion Motley and ends Dante Lavelli and Mac Speedie. The Browns won 12 of their 14 games and the league championship. Owner McBride promoted the team on his taxicabs, on billboards, and in radio advertising. He formed an all-girl band called the Musical Majorettes, who performed at halftime. The team drew 400,000 fans and made $200,000 in profits. Brown, who had signed as coach for $25,000 and 15 percent of the profits, made $55,000 for the year.

Brooklyn won only three games, but tailback Glenn Dobbs was a sensational performer, leading the league in passing and punting. He was named the AAFC's most valuable player.

In the Dodgers' opening game, Dobbs came out of the game with a chipped bone in his hand. His coach, Dr. Mal Stevens, applied a flexible splint to the hand. Dobbs then went back in and led the Dodgers to a 28-14 victory.

Troubles struck the Miami Seahawks and Chicago Rockets. The Seahawks played home games on Monday nights. They did not have a very good team, and, although they were in Miami, they became the first pro team to be rained out twice in one season. The largest crowd of the season at their games was 9,700 and the smallest was 2,250. Their coach, Jack Meagher, resigned after six games, and Hamp Pool was player-coach for the rest of the season. After the season, the AAFC paid $61,000 in salaries owed to Seahawks players, $19,000 owed to United Air Lines, and expelled the Seahawks from the league.

Instead of becoming one of the league's best teams as expected, the Chicago Rockets became one of its worst. Hanley could not exert the discipline he had practiced as a Marine colonel and coach of many of the same players at El Toro. Early in the Rockets' season, the players demanded that Hanley be fired, and he was replaced by a committee of players —Bob Dove, Ned Mathews, and Willie Wilkin. Hanley's former assistants, Pat Boland and Ernie Nevers, were left in limbo as the players' committee remained in charge for five games, two of which, in fact, the Rockets won. The *Chicago Tribune* covered a practice in which Nevers passed the time by stripping to the waist and taking a sun bath. With six games left, the team was placed in the hands of Boland, and it finished in last place.

Stevens, the Brooklyn coach, resigned before the seventh game, in which he was replaced by assistant Tom Scott. Cliff Battles finished the season as head coach.

The all-league team was made up of ends Alyn Beals of San Francisco and Dante Lavelli of Cleveland, tackles Martin Ruby of Brooklyn and Frank (Bruiser) Kinard of New York, guards Bruno Banducci of San Francisco and Bill Willis of Cleveland, center Bob Nelson of Los Angeles, quarterback Otto Graham of Cleveland, halfbacks Glenn Dobbs of Brooklyn and Spec Sanders of New York, and fullback Marion Motley of Cleveland.

Noting that costs were high, commissioner Crowley wrote in a magazine article that pro salaries had increased 100 to 200 percent. "Should the two leagues ever agree on a common draft and a hands-off policy, the figures will drop somewhat," he wrote. "But they will never go back to the days when a good lineman played for only $100 to $150 a game."

1946 AAFC STANDINGS

Eastern Division	**W**	**L**	**T**	**Pct.**	**Pts.**	**OP**
New York Yankees	10	3	1	.769	270	192
Brooklyn Dodgers	3	10	1	.231	226	339
Buffalo Bisons	3	10	1	.231	249	370
Miami Seahawks	3	11	0	.154	167	378
Western Division	**W**	**L**	**T**	**Pct.**	**Pts.**	**OP**
Cleveland Browns	12	2	0	.857	423	137
San Francisco 49ers	9	5	0	.643	307	189
Los Angeles Dons	7	5	2	.583	305	290
Chicago Rockets	5	6	3	.455	263	315

AAFC championship: Cleveland 14, New York Yankees 9

LEADING RUSHERS	**Att.**	**Yards**	**Avg.**	**TD**
Spec Sanders, NY Yankees	140	709	5.1	6
Norm Standlee, San Francisco	134	651	4.9	2
Vic Kulbitski, Buffalo	97	605	6.2	2
Marion Motley, Cleveland	73	601	8.2	5
Edgar Jones, Cleveland	77	539	7.0	4

LEADING PASSERS	**Att.**	**Comp.**	**Yards**	**TD**	**Int.**
Glenn Dobbs, Brooklyn	269	135	1,886	13	15
Otto Graham, Cleveland	174	95	1,834	17	5
Charlie O'Rourke, LA Dons	182	105	1,250	12	14
Frankie Albert, San Francisco	197	104	1,404	14	14
Bob Hoernschemeyer, Chi. Roc.	193	95	1,266	14	14

LEADING RECEIVERS	**No.**	**Yards**	**Avg.**	**TD**
Dante Lavelli, Cleveland	40	843	21.1	8
Alyn Beals, San Francisco	40	586	14.7	10
Saxon Judd, Brooklyn	34	443	13.0	4
Ed King, Buffalo	30	466	15.5	6
Elroy Hirsch, Chi. Rockets	27	347	12.9	3

The failure of the Seahawks and the uncertain launching of the Rockets had embarrassed the All-America Football Conference. In 1947 there were more administrative changes, coaching changes, and symptoms of an illness that could be fatal—imbalance, a widening gulf between the league's haves and its have-nots.

But 1947 was, nevertheless, the greatest year in the brief history of the AAFC. Cleveland won the championship again and appeared more unbeatable than ever. And the league's teams in New York City and Los Angeles were exciting ones that won more games and attracted more fans than their NFL rivals.

There was no larger manifestation of faith in the league's future than that made by its commissioner, Jim Crowley, who turned his back on the security of his five-year contract, resigned, and headed a group that purchased the struggling Rockets. In addition, Crowley became their coach.

There was another manifestation of faith in the league in New York. Larry MacPhail and Del Webb, co-owners with Dan Topping of the baseball Yankees, bought into his football team.

Crowley was replaced as commissioner by Admiral Jonas J. Ingram, former commander of the Atlantic fleet. Ingram moved the league offices to New York. The AAFC made a new charter agreement with Howard Hughes's Trans World Airlines and announced a more sensible schedule in which games were confined to Friday nights and Sunday afternoons, except that there would be two Thanksgiving Day games. The New York Yankees got a break in the schedule in that they played Los Angeles and San Francisco on successive dates whereas all other clubs had to cross the Rockies twice; the Dons had to fly to the East Coast three times.

Representatives seeking a franchise in Baltimore had attended early meetings of the AAFC in 1944 and 1945, but had been unable at first to rent a stadium for their games and missed being charter members of the league. Baltimore now entered the AAFC as its eighth city, replacing Miami. Robert H. Rodenberg was the principal owner of the Baltimore team, the Colts, and he hired Cecil Isbell to coach the team at Municipal Stadium.

The Bisons changed their name to the Bills.

National attention was focused on the San Francisco 49ers when owner Tony Morabito drafted Glenn Davis of Army and also traded for the rights to Davis's famous partner in Army's "Mr. Inside and Mr. Outside" backfield, Felix (Doc) Blanchard. Morabito wanted them to delay their 90-day furlough following their graduation from West Point and join the 49ers. There was a great national controversy about whether these men should pursue their army careers or sign professional football contracts. The War Department at last ordered them to abide by existing policy. Davis later played for the Los Angeles Rams, but Blanchard became a career Air Force officer.

Buddy Young of Illinois and George Ratterman of Notre Dame led the College All-Stars to a 16-0 victory over the Chicago Bears and then Young signed with the Yankees and Ratterman with the Bills.

The powerful Browns were the focus of widespread interest. When they opened their 1947 season by routing Buffalo 30-14, they were watched by the entire coaching staff of the Chicago Bears.

The most sensational AAFC trade occurred when the Dodgers sent most valuable player Glenn Dobbs to Los Angeles, which sent Angelo Bertelli to Chicago, which sent Bob (Hunchy) Hoernschemeyer to Brooklyn. Dodgers' coach Cliff Battles wanted Hoernschemeyer for his quarterback, and the Dons wanted an exciting back to compete for attention in Los Angeles with the Rams' Bob Waterfield.

Dobbs made the Los Angeles Dons an exciting team that played before 304,177 fans, including a professional record crowd of 82,576 that watched the Dons lose to the New York Yankees 30-14 September 12 at the Los Angeles Coliseum.

But by far the most sensational player of the year

was single-wing tailback Spec Sanders of the New York Yankees. He rushed for 1,432 yards, a figure that ranked as the best in history if the AAFC statistics had been accepted for the all-time pro football records. He also passed for 1,442 yards, gained 250 yards rushing in one game against Chicago, had 450 yards of total offense against San Francisco, punted for a 42.1-yard average, and scored 19 touchdowns.

The AAFC game that is remembered more than any other was played November 23, 1947, at Yankee Stadium. The Yankees (9-2) took the field against the Browns (10-1) before a crowd of 70,060. The Yankees stunned the Browns by going ahead 28-0 in the first half, but Graham brought Cleveland from behind in a stirring comeback that was climaxed when Lou Saban, who was playing in place of the injured Lou Groza, kicked the tying extra point. The game ended 28-28. The same two teams played three weeks later for the AAFC championship, and Cleveland won 14-3.

Graham was named most valuable player. The all-league team was made up of ends Dante Lavelli and Mac Speedie of Cleveland, tackles Nate Johnson of New York and Lou Rymkus of Cleveland, guards Bruno Banducci of San Francisco and Bill Willis of Cleveland, center Bob Nelson of Los Angeles, quarterback Otto Graham of Cleveland, halfbacks Chet Mutryn of Buffalo and Spec Sanders of New York, and fullback Marion Motley of Cleveland.

1947 AAFC STANDINGS

Eastern Division	W	L	T	Pct.	Pts.	OP
New York Yankees	11	2	1	.846	378	239
Buffalo Bills	8	4	2	.667	320	288
Brooklyn Dodgers	3	10	1	.231	181	340
Baltimore Colts	2	11	1	.154	167	377
Western Division	**W**	**L**	**T**	**Pct.**	**Pts.**	**OP**
Cleveland Browns	12	1	1	.923	410	185
San Francisco 49ers	8	4	2	.667	327	264
Los Angeles Dons	7	7	0	.500	328	256
Chicago Rockets	1	13	0	.071	263	425

AAFC championship: Cleveland 14, New York Yankees 3.

LEADING RUSHERS	Att.	Yards	Avg.	TD
Spec Sanders, NY Yankees	231	1,432	6.2	18
John Strzykalski, San Francisco	143	906	6.3	5
Marion Motley, Cleveland	146	889	6.0	8
Chet Mutryn, Buffalo	140	868	6.2	9
Buddy Young, NY Yankees	116	712	6.1	3

LEADING PASSERS	Att.	Comp.	Yards	TD	Int.
Otto Graham, Cleveland	269	163	2,753	25	11
Bud Schwenk, Baltimore	327	168	2,236	13	20
Frankie Albert, San Francisco	242	128	1,692	18	15
George Ratterman, Buffalo	244	124	1,840	22	20
Spec Sanders, NY Yankees	171	93	1,442	14	17

LEADING RECEIVERS	No.	Yards	Avg.	TD
Mac Speedie, Cleveland	67	1,146	17.1	6
Dante Lavelli, Cleveland	49	799	16.3	9
Alyn Beals, San Francisco	47	655	13.9	10
Lamar Davis, Baltimore	46	515	11.2	2
Billy Hillenbrand, Baltimore	39	702	18.0	7

The member teams of the AAFC began to see by 1948 that the optimistic predictions they had made earlier for their attendance, income, and success in competing against the NFL were not being realized. The outlook grew dimmer and dimmer for the league's weak teams. Wholesale ownership and coaching changes began, the commissioner made a novel and unsuccessful attempt to balance competition in the league, and for the first time there were public overtures made to the NFL for a merger.

New ownership headed by Robert C. Embry took over the Baltimore Colts. Branch Rickey, who ran baseball's Brooklyn Dodgers and Ebbets Field, took control of the struggling Dodgers football team. R. Edward Garn headed a Chicago civic group that purchased the Rockets.

The new coaches were Carl Voyles at Brooklyn, Ed McKeever at Chicago, Jimmy Phelan at Los Angeles, and Norman (Red) Strader for New York in midseason.

AAFC commissioner Ingram ordered the strongest teams in the league to distribute some of their players to the weakest clubs in order to create more balance. The Yankees were the only team to abide by both the letter and the spirit of the directive. They apparently were even more generous than they needed to be and, with many of their best players scattered to other cities, dropped to a 6-8 record in 1948. New York never had a strong AAFC team again. The Browns traded the rights to rookie quarterback Y. A. Tittle to Baltimore.

When committees from the two leagues met in December and issued a joint statement about their willingness to end the war, it was the first time the NFL officially recognized that the AAFC existed. In the talks, the NFL offered to take in Cleveland and San Francisco and let Ben Lindheimer of the Dons buy into the Rams. An AAFC concession came when Topping of the Yankees offered to cease operations and be satisfied to collect rent from another team for Yankee Stadium. The discussions ended, however, when the NFL adamantly refused to admit any teams other than the Browns and 49ers. The AAFC decided to prolong the struggle another year.

The league's two best teams were together in the same division. Cleveland went through an entire season without losing a game for the first time, and San Francisco was 12-2. When they met in a regular-season game at Cleveland, 82,769 were present. Quarterback Otto Graham of Cleveland passed for 25 touchdowns for the season and Frankie Albert of San Francisco had 29. In addition, the 49ers had a team rushing average of 6.1 yards per carry.

The Browns defeated the Yankees in New York on a Sunday, the Dons in Los Angeles the following Thursday (Thanksgiving Day), and the 49ers 31-28 in San Francisco three days later on Sunday—three victories in eight days.

Tailback Glenn Dobbs of the Dons passed for 405 yards in a game against the 49ers, but also threw seven interceptions, and the Dons lost. Tittle had 346 yards passing on 11 completions, a 31.5-yard average per completion, in a game against New York.

Two teams with .500 records, Baltimore and Buffalo, played off for the Eastern Division championship and the winner, Buffalo, lost the AAFC Championship Game to Cleveland 49-7.

Graham and Albert were named co-most valuable players. The all-league team was made up of ends Alyn Beals of San Francisco and Mac Speedie of Cleveland, tackles Bob Reinhard of Los Angeles and Lou Rymkus of Cleveland, guards Dick Barwegan of Baltimore and Bill Willis of Cleveland, center Bob Nelson of Los Angeles, quarterback Otto Graham of Cleveland, halfbacks Chet Mutryn of Buffalo and John Strzykalski of San Francisco, and fullback Marion Motley of Cleveland.

1948 AAFC STANDINGS

Eastern Division	W	L	T	Pct.	Pts.	OP
Buffalo Bills	7	7	0	.500	360	358
Baltimore Colts	7	7	0	.500	333	327
New York Yankees	6	8	0	.429	265	301
Brooklyn Dodgers	2	12	0	.143	253	387
Western Division	**W**	**L**	**T**	**Pct.**	**Pts.**	**OP**
Cleveland Browns	14	0	0	1.000	389	190
San Francisco 49ers	12	2	0	.857	495	248
Los Angeles Dons	7	7	0	.500	258	305
Chicago Rockets	1	13	0	.071	202	439

Eastern Division playoff: Buffalo 28, Baltimore 17
AAFC championship: Cleveland 49, Buffalo 7

LEADING RUSHERS	Att.	Yards	Avg.	TD
Marion Motley, Cleveland	157	964	6.1	5
John Strzykalski, San Francisco	141	915	6.5	4
Chet Mutryn, Buffalo	147	823	5.6	10
Spec Sanders, NY Yankees	169	759	4.5	9
Lou Tomasetti, Buffalo	134	716	5.3	7

LEADING PASSERS	Att.	Comp.	Yards	TD	Int.
Otto Graham, Cleveland	333	173	2,713	25	15
Glenn Dobbs, LA Dons	369	185	2,403	21	20
Y.A. Tittle, Baltimore	289	161	2,522	16	9
George Ratterman, Buffalo	335	168	2,577	16	22
Frankie Albert, San Francisco	246	154	1,990	29	10

LEADING RECEIVERS	No.	Yards	Avg.	TD
Mac Speedie, Cleveland	58	816	14.1	4
Al Baldwin, Buffalo	54	916	17.0	8
Billy Hillenbrand, Baltimore	50	970	19.4	6
Dolly King, Chi. Rockets	50	647	12.9	7
Alyn Beals, San Francisco	45	591	13.1	14

The AAFC was always fully covered in the pages of the *Chicago Tribune*. Arch Ward was the sports editor of the paper and the founder of the league. He was also the director of the Chicago College All-Star Game, which matched the NFL champion and the College All-Stars. In 1949 all three came together in a critical issue with Ward at its vortex.

Ward promised the AAFC he would get its champion into the all-star game. The contract with the NFL was up and Ward told NFL owners he wasn't going to renew. Suddenly, however, Ward reversed himself and signed a new contract with the NFL, shutting out the AAFC.

A gleeful NFL celebrated and some people concluded in print that Ward had lacked faith in the ability of the AAFC to keep the all-star game alive. But Ward actually had suffered a rare defeat at his newspaper. The NFL owners had gone over his head. Warned of Ward's influence with Robert McCormick, the publisher, the NFL went instead to managing editor J. Loy Maloney, who put the question before the paper's board of directors. The board renewed the NFL's contract.

Crushed, the AAFC staggered on. The Brooklyn Dodgers, "Branch Rickey's white elephant," merged with the New York Yankees. The Baltimore Colts acquired their third president in three years, Walter S. Driskill. James C. Thompson and others purchased the struggling Chicago Rockets and renamed them the Hornets.

Ben Lindheimer of the Dons, who apparently aided other clubs as well with outright payments, traded back Herman Wedemeyer to Baltimore, and, when the Colts said they could not handle his $12,000 contract, Lindheimer agreed to pay half of it.

The league's attendance dropped 30 percent from the previous year. Coaching shuffles were everywhere. Owner Driskill replaced Cecil Isbell as coach at Baltimore after four games; Driskill's record was 1-7. Clem Crowe became coach at Buffalo. Ray Flaherty, former Yankees coach, took over the Chicago Hornets. Of all AAFC coaches, only Paul Brown of Cleveland and Lawrence (Buck) Shaw of San Francisco coached their teams throughout the league's four-year existence.

Ingram resigned as commissioner and his former deputy, O.O. (Scrappy) Kessing, took over. He said, "Our league is not dead, not dying, and not going to die."

It died in December, 1949. The merger was instigated by Horace Stoneham, owner of the baseball Giants and the Polo Grounds, where the football Giants played and which was one of the stadiums suffering from the malaise of the pro football war. Stoneham arranged a meeting between George Weiss of the baseball and football Yankees and Bert Bell, Commissioner of the NFL, in New York City. Out of this came a meeting between Bell and J. Arthur Friedlund, a lawyer who represented the All-America Football Conference. "They talked for a while there in New York and then came to Philadelphia [to Bell's office] two days ago," the *New York Mirror* reported. "Three days of round-the-clock conferences came to an end shortly after noon today and the two men, tired but jubilant, summoned reporters to break the news."

The Cleveland Browns, "the one prize the National League wants," Gordon Cobbledick wrote in the *Cleveland Plain-Dealer,* joined the NFL.

So did the San Francisco 49ers, because they were an exciting winning team and because NFL teams on the East Coast could go west and play both Los Angeles and San Francisco for the same amount of plane fare, and receive two cash guarantees from gate receipts.

The Baltimore Colts won only one game in 1949 but they came into the NFL, too. Owner George Preston Marshall of the Washington Redskins, who had been a fiery opponent of the AAFC, became convinced that Baltimore could become a strong rival —and one with little travel costs—for the Redskins. The *New York Times* reported, "It was Marshall's willingness to let the Baltimore Colts into the NFL which reportedly dissolved the four-year feud . . . Marshall revealed he had cleared the way for Baltimore's admission by waiving his territorial rights for a nominal fee of $150,000.

"Puffing on an Indian peace pipe for the benefit of photographers, Marshall called league Commissioner Bert Bell in Philadelphia to try to clear up some points about the armistice.

" 'Hello, peace pipe,' he greeted Bell. 'What league am I supposed to be in?' "

The Redskins were placed in the new American Conference of the NFL.

Breuil, owner of the Buffalo Bills, received a 25 percent interest in the Cleveland Browns, and the Browns were awarded three Bills' players—Rex Bumgardner, John Kissell, and Abe Gibron.

Six Brooklyn-New York Yankees players were awarded to the New York Giants, including Tom Landry, Otto Schnellbacher, Harmon Rowe, and Arnie Weinmeister. Some called it "the greatest input of talent in the Giants' history."

Ted Collins, owner of the NFL New York Bulldogs, was given a 10-year lease on Yankee Stadium. He had moved his team from Boston to New York, expecting the AAFC to fold earlier, and when it did not he had had to share Stoneham's Polo Grounds with the New York Giants.

Collins's team took the name New York Yanks and acquired the star backs of the old AAFC Yankees, Spec Sanders and Buddy Young. In other notable player shifts, end Len Ford of the Dons joined Cleveland and back Bob (Hunchy) Hoernschemeyer of the Yankees joined the Detroit Lions.

The interests of the Chicago Hornets were purchased by the league and the franchise was disbanded.

The merger agreement was announced the day before the Browns and 49ers were to play for the last championship, December 11, 1949. Only 22,000 fans watched as Cleveland won 21-7. The Browns then agreed to play a team of AAFC all-stars in Houston. Only a small crowd attended and the all-stars won 12-7.

The AAFC never named a most valuable player for 1949. The all-star team was made up of ends Alyn Beals of San Francisco and Mac Speedie of Cleveland, tackles Bob Reinhard of Los Angeles and Arnie Weinmeister of Brooklyn-New York, guards Dick Barwegan of Baltimore and Visco Grgich of San Francisco, center (an accommodation because he actually played linebacker) Lou Saban of Cleveland, quarterback Otto Graham of Cleveland, halfbacks Frankie Albert of San Francisco (an accommodation because he actually played quarterback) and Chet Mutryn of Buffalo, and fullback Joe Perry of San Francisco.

The AAFC's all-time statistical champions were Marion Motley of Cleveland, rushing, 3,024 yards; Graham, passing, 592 completions, 10,085 yards, and 86 touchdowns; Speedie, receiving, 211 catches; and Beals, scoring, 46 touchdowns and two extra points for a total of 278 points.

For a period of about two months after the merger, the NFL in its press releases and in newspaper articles was called the "National-American Football League." That ended in March and the name National Football League was restored.

Many reasons have been given why the AAFC failed. The Cleveland Browns had a 51-4-3 record and were too good for the rest of the league. If Cleveland and New York had been in the same division, there would have been a tighter race in the East and strong competition in the West between Los Angeles and San Francisco.

The AAFC was in direct competition with the NFL in New York, Chicago, and Los Angeles. During 1946-49, there were three teams in Chicago—the Bears, Cardinals, and Hornets-Rockets.

Former player Buddy Young said, "The weakness of the AAFC was in overall coaching and player depth. Some of the coaches had never been associated with pro football and didn't realize the necessity of having more than eleven or fifteen good players. In college, you could get by that way but in the pros you had to have depth."

In a master stroke, NFL Commissioner Bell scheduled the AAFC champion Browns against the NFL champion Philadelphia Eagles on a Saturday night of the 1950 season, before the rest of the league's teams opened the following day. Cleveland won 35-10, lost only two games the entire season, and won the championship.

1949 AFC STANDINGS	W	L	T	Pct.	Pts.	OP
Cleveland Browns	9	1	2	.900	339	171
San Francisco 49ers	9	3	0	.750	416	227
Brooklyn-NY Yankees	8	4	0	.667	196	206
Buffalo Bills	5	5	2	.500	236	256
Chicago Hornets	4	8	0	.333	179	268
Los Angeles Dons	4	8	0	.333	253	322
Baltimore Colts	1	11	0	.083	172	341

Playoff: Cleveland 31, Buffalo 21
Playoff: San Francisco 17, Brooklyn-New York 7
Championship: Cleveland 21, San Francisco 7

LEADING RUSHERS	Att.	Yards	Avg.	TD
Joe Perry, San Francisco	115	783	6.8	8
Chet Mutryn, Buffalo	131	696	5.3	5
Marion Motley, Cleveland	113	570	5.0	8
Ollie Cline, Buffalo	125	518	4.1	3
Buddy Young, Brooklyn-NY	76	495	6.5	5
LEADING PASSERS	**Att.**	**Comp.**	**Yards**	**TD**
Otto Graham, Cleveland	285	161	2,785	19
Y. A. Tittle, Baltimore	289	148	2,209	14
George Ratterman, Buffalo	252	146	1,777	14
Frankie Albert, San Francisco	260	129	1,862	27
Bob Hoernschemeyer, Chi. Hornets	167	69	1,063	6
LEADING RECEIVERS	**No.**	**Yards**	**Avg.**	**TD**
Mac Speedie, Cleveland	62	1,028	16.6	7
Al Baldwin, Buffalo	53	719	13.6	7
Alyn Beals, San Francisco	44	678	15.4	12
Dan Edwards, Chi. Hornets	42	573	13.6	3
Lamar Davis, Baltimore	38	548	14.4	1

THE WFL

The overwhelming success of the American Football League of 1960-69 set off an era of expansion in sport. By merging with the NFL, the AFL increased professional football to 26 teams. Baseball grew to 24. Rival basketball and hockey leagues, the American Basketball Association and World Hockey Association, appeared.

The latter creations were the work of Dennis Murphy, a southern California public relations man, and Gary L. Davidson and Donald J. Regan, lawyers who had an office across the hall from Murphy in a building in Newport Beach. Davidson became the first president of each league, the ABA in 1967 and the WHA in 1971.

He resigned the presidency of the hockey league in October, 1973, and began laying plans for a third creation, the World Football League. He took the title of commissioner and pursued buyers for franchises in the league. It was announced that the league "would eventually encompass the entire world."

Its first meeting took place in Los Angeles in January, 1974. Twelve franchises existed at the time or grew from that meeting. Their locations, their names, and their ownership changed often. Sometimes the owners were from the enfranchised cities and sometimes they were not.

The Birmingham Americans franchise was headed by Bill Putnam, a former Navy underwater demolition expert, vice president of the J.P. Morgan Company in New York City, executive vice president of Jack Kent Cooke Enterprises, owner of the Philadelphia Flyers of the National Hockey League, and president of the group controlling the Atlanta Hawks of the National Basketball Association and Atlanta Flames of the NHL. A former secretary named Carol Tygart Stallworth became part-owner and president of the Americans. Jack Gotta was hired as coach and the team arranged to play at Legion Field.

Nick Mileti, part-owner of baseball's Cleveland Indians, purchased a franchise he in turn sold to Tom Origer, an owner of apartment buildings in Chicago. This franchise became the Chicago Fire. Origer was the first owner to sign a player, wide receiver Jim Seymour. He named Jim Spavital his coach and secured Soldier Field for the Fire's games.

The Detroit Wheels became the property of a large group of investors headed by Louis R. Lee, a 28-year-old Detroit lawyer and a former University of Michigan football player. The team's identity as a Detroit franchise was strained when it arranged to play at Rynearson Stadium on the campus of Eastern Michigan University, 37 miles away in Ypsilanti. Dan Boisture became the Wheels' coach.

The Florida Blazers had origins elsewhere. E. Joseph Wheeler, owner of a marine biology and engineering company, purchased a franchise he named variously as the Washington Capitals, the Washington-Baltimore Ambassadors, and the Washington Ambassadors. He was unable to lease RFK Stadium in Washington and moved the team to Norfolk, Virginia, in April. In May, he sold the team to a group headed by Rommie Loudd, who moved it to Orlando and named it the Florida Blazers. Jack Pardee had already been named coach of the team, which rented the Tangerine Bowl Stadium.

A franchise that became the Hawaiians, in Honolulu, was originally started by Danny Rogers, manager of a sales firm and a former basketball coach. Chris B. Hemmeter, developer of restaurants and building projects in Hawaii, and Sam D. Battistone, the president of Invest West, which owned Sambo's restaurants, became owners of the Hawaiians. Mike Giddings was hired as their coach, and Honolulu Stadium the site of their home games.

Steve Arnold, a San Franciscan who once was the player agent of Jim Brown, owned a franchise the WFL first intended for Memphis but which became the Houston Texans. The Astrodome was rented, and Jim Garrett became the Texans' coach.

Fran Monaco, operator of medical laboratories and co-owner of a restaurant in Deland, Florida, became the owner of the Jacksonville Sharks. He named his wife, Douglas, as the vice president and they hired Bud Asher, the coach of New Smyrna Beach (Florida) High School as coach. They were to play their games at the Gator Bowl Stadium.

The franchise of John Bassett, Jr., was originally the Toronto Northmen, but it became the Memphis Southmen. Bassett, a millionaire Canadian, had interests in a television station, a newspaper, a film company, and Toronto's Canadian Football League team and World Hockey Association team. But he had to move his WFL team because of opposition from the CFL, which enlisted the Canadian minister of health and welfare in its cause. Memphis investors joining Bassett in the team's ownership included entertainers Charlie Rich and Isaac Hayes. John McVay was named coach of the Southmen, and they rented Memphis Memorial Stadium.

The New York Stars had an active period of development. Howard Baldwin, 31-year-old president of the New England Whalers of the World Hockey Association, originally intended to form a team in Boston that was first called the Bulldogs, then the Bulls. It signed a player, wide receiver George Sauer, and hired a coach, Babe Parilli, while it was still the Bulldogs. Baldwin, however, could not find financial backing. Robert J. Schmertz, land developer and owner of the Boston Celtics of the NBA, emerged as the Bulldogs' principal owner and moved them to New York, where they became the Stars. The site they preferred, Yankee Stadium, was undergoing renovation, and the Stars found themselves at a serious disadvantage when they had to settle for aging Downing Stadium on Randall's Island.

The city of Philadelphia was represented at the first meeting of the WFL by Ken Bogdanoff, who once had been a lifeguard at an apartment complex in Philadelphia where Birmingham owner Bill Putnam lived. The two often talked sports at poolside. Bogdanoff later worked as assistant ticket manager of the Flyers, but he was unemployed at the time of the WFL meeting. He and a partner raised $50,000 to make a down payment on a WFL franchise priced by Davidson at $400,000. The partner dropped out with his $25,000, however, and so did Bogdanoff on the morning of the organizational meeting. But at the request of the founders, he stayed to answer the roll call for Philadelphia. Control of the team was later passed to John B. Kelly, Jr., a Philadelphia city councilman, and then to attorney John Bosacco. The team, which was called the Bell, rented JFK Stadium and named Ron Waller as its coach.

Grant Gelker, an Orange County, California, businessman and a friend of Davidson, headed a franchise originally intended for New York City but which finally was placed in Portland and became the Storm. Dick Coury became its coach and it leased Civic Stadium.

Larry G. Hatfield was, with Davidson, a member of the Balboa Bay Club at Newport Beach, California. Hatfield had become wealthy operating a computer and graphics company in Jackson, Mississippi, and then a trucking company in southern California. He formed the Southern California Sun. Al Lapin, head of the parent company of International House of Pancakes and Orange Julius chains, was also a Sun backer. The southern California team rented Anaheim Stadium and hired Tom Fears as coach.

Franchises in Tokyo and Mexico City were discussed but did not materialize.

The league held a draft of players and arranged a novel schedule in which each team would begin its season in July while the NFL teams were still in training camps, and the majority of the WFL's games would be played Wednesday nights. Each team would play 20 games and there would be no preseason. A contract was made with the independent TVS Television Network for one WFL game a week to be played Thursday night and shown on prime-time television. Never had pro football been played and televised nationally in midweek.

Making a schedule proved a difficult task. Hawaii adamantly insisted on Sunday games, saying midweek football would not go over in Honolulu. Detroit could not play a home game in a week when Eastern Michigan had a home game. Toronto moved to Memphis, and Washington moved to Virginia, then Florida. The problems were overcome, however, and a schedule was announced in May.

The schedule was not the WFL's only novelty. The league's singular instead of plural nicknames began with the Fire in Chicago; the Bell, Storm, and Sun followed. Changes in pro football rules were announced. The WFL voted to kick off from the 30-yard line instead of the 40; to move the goal posts from the goal lines to the end lines; to move in the hashmarks; to ban fair catches of punts; to allow men in motion toward the line of scrimmage before the snap; to play a fifth quarter in the event of a tie; to require receivers to have only one foot inbounds to make a legal catch; to prohibit bump-and-run against receivers once they were three yards past the line of scrimmage; to bring the ball back to the line of scrimmage instead of the 20-yard line after field goals missed from outside the 20 and fourth-down passes incomplete inside the 20; and to count touchdowns as seven instead of six points and have an "action point" counting one point, to be tried after a touchdown by either running or passing, not kicking. The WFL decided to use an invention called a "Dickerrod" instead of the orthodox chain unit for measuring down yardage. And the league at first intended to use a football with swirls painted on it, similar to the red, white, and blue basketball used in the ABA. It dropped the colored ball idea, however.

Despite its novelties, skepticism about the WFL prevailed until March 31, 1974, when Bassett announced he had signed Larry Csonka, Jim Kiick, and Paul Warfield of the Super Bowl champion Miami Dolphins to three-year contracts starting with the 1975 football season, a year away. What was described as a $3 million package for the three of them had iron-clad guarantees they would get the money whatever happened to the league.

Other signings followed, Bill Bergey of Cincinnati with Florida; John Gilliam of Minnesota, Calvin Hill of Dallas, and Ted Kwalick of San Francisco with the Hawaiians; and Curley Culp of Kansas City and Daryle Lamonica of Oakland with Southern California. By June 4, WFL teams claimed the signings of 59 NFL players who were playing out their options and would be ready to join the WFL, most of them in 1975. The NFL was stunned, and the Dallas Cowboys obtained a restraining order blocking the signing of other Cowboys players.

Big crowds were reported at opening games of the WFL in mid-July. There was a revelation from Philadelphia, however, that dealt the league a heavy blow. The Bell had announced an attendance of 55,534 for its opening game against Portland and 64,719 for a game 15 days later against the New York Stars. But an official of the team admitted the figures were inflated. He disclosed that for tax purposes the team had actually reported having sold 13,800 tickets for the first game and 6,200 for the second; the rest of the tickets had been given away. Credibility of the league suffered.

Four teams—one-third of the league—fell on hard times two months into the season. The league took over the operations of Detroit and Jacksonville, and then both teams folded. The Houston Texans were moved to Shreveport, Louisiana, and became the Steamer, and the New York Stars moved to Charlotte, North Carolina, and became the Hornets.

Detroit's former general manager had asserted in his team's media book that the Wheels "could make an honest, qualified run at the WFL title in our first year." It did not, losing its first 10 games and drawing no crowd larger than 10,631. The owners of the team reportedly borrowed $265,000 from the league. Troubles continued. The Wheels' trainer had to borrow athletic tape from other teams, the players had to bring their own towels, and the coach could not afford to have the games filmed. The team went bankrupt and listed debts of $2.5 million.

In Jacksonville, the owner reportedly borrowed $27,000 from his coach, Asher, and then fired him. Charlie Tate was named the new coach. Players went unpaid for several weeks and Commissioner Davidson visited them when they played in Southern California and handed out an estimated $65,000 in paychecks. The franchise was surrendered to the league October 8.

Difficulty in meeting the Astrodome rent contributed to the relocation of the Texans to Shreveport. In New York, the Stars averaged only 8,000 fans for six home games. On opening night, the keys to the ticket booths at Downing Stadium could not be located and the booths were broken open so tickets could be sold. Traffic in and out of the island stadium jammed often. Relocated in Charlotte, the team was taken over by a group led by Upton Bell, son of former NFL Commissioner Bert Bell and former general manager of the New England Patriots. Difficulties continued, and in November the operator of a cleaning service, J. Rodney Ryan, filed suit against the team for money he was owed. Immediately after a game, the Hornets had to surrender their jerseys, pants, and other equipment to sheriff's deputies bearing writs impounding it.

Davidson resigned the commissionership October 29. Origer and Bassett were said to have urged his resignation. Origer, who said he had lost $750,000 to $800,000, apparently threatened to fold his team if Davidson did not quit. A month later, Hemmeter of Hawaii was named the new commissioner.

The WFL playoff structure went through several changes in which the field grew from four teams to six to eight, the latter only two less than the league membership. The playoff field then was reduced to three, then increased to six. In the playoffs, Southern California players Booker Brown, Kermit Johnson, and James McAlister did not play following a dispute, and the Sun lost.

The "World Bowl" for the WFL championship December 5 at Birmingham matched two teams that reflected the league's troubles. The Birmingham Americans were supposed to have missed five payrolls in a row, the Florida Blazers fifteen. The Americans were hounded by creditors. Their players threatened to boycott the game and then changed their minds and agreed to play.

Florida was a sentimental favorite, *Sports Illustrated* wrote, "because of its greater deprivation." The team was under the operation of the league. A sale to a new owner had fallen through when, according to newspaper reports, it was learned the buyer was a convicted felon. Coach Jack Pardee and his assistants were providing the toilet paper for the locker room.

Alternate quarterbacks George Mira and Matthew Reed led the Americans to a narrow 22-21 victory for the championship. Mira was named the game's most valuable player. When it ended, a Florida player snatched the game ball and dashed away but Birmingham players caught up with him under the stands and, after a tussle, reclaimed the football.

The Americans' uniforms were repossessed after the game by sheriff's deputies. The equipment was later sold as souvenirs by a sporting goods store.

Quarterback Tony Adams of Southern California and running backs J.J. Jennings of Memphis and Tommy Reamon of Florida were named co-most valuable players in the league.

1974 WFL STANDINGS

Eastern Division	**W**	**L**	**T**	**Pct.**	**Pts.**	**OP**
Florida Blazers	14	6	0	.700	419	280
N.Y. Stars-Char. Hornets	10	10	0	.500	467	350
Philadelphia Bell	9	11	0	.421	493	413
Jacksonville Sharks	4	10	0	.286	258	358
Central Division	**W**	**L**	**T**	**Pct.**	**Pts.**	**OP**
Memphis Southmen	17	3	0	.850	629	365
Birmingham Americans	15	5	0	.750	503	394
Chicago Fire	7	13	0	.368	446	622
Detroit Wheels	1	13	0	.071	209	358
Western Division	**W**	**L**	**T**	**Pct.**	**Pts.**	**OP**
Southern California Sun	13	7	0	.650	486	441
Hawaiians	9	11	0	.450	413	425
Portland Storm	7	12	1	.375	264	426
Hou. Tex.-Shrev. Steamer	7	12	1	.375	240	415

First round playoffs: Florida 18, Philadelphia 3;
Hawaiians 34, Southern California 14

Semifinals: Florida, 18, Memphis 15;
Birmingham 22, Hawaiians 19
"World Bowl": Birmingham 22, Florida 21

LEADING RUSHERS	Att.	Yards	Avg.	Long	TD
Tommy Reamon, Florida	386	1,576	4.1	55	11
J.J. Jennings, Memphis	322	1,524	4.7	21	11
Jim Nance, Houston-Shreveport	300	1,240	4.1	27	8
John Land, Philadelphia	243	1,136	4.7	46	8
Rufus Ferguson, Portland	260	1,086	4.2	74	6
LEADING PASSERS	**Att.**	**Comp.**	**Yards**	**TD**	**Int.**
Tony Adams, So. California	510	276	3,905	23	18
King Corcoran, Philadelphia	545	280	3,631	31	24
Bob Davis, Florida	413	232	2,977	21	23
Virgil Carter, Chi. Fire	358	195	2,629	27	16
John Huarte, Memphis	296	154	2,416	24	16
LEADING RECEIVERS	**No.**	**Yards**	**Avg.**	**Long**	**TD**
Tim Delaney, Hawaiians	89	1,232	13.8	42	8
Rick Eber, Houston-Shreveport	66	771	11.7	63	5
James McAlister, So. California	65	772	11.9	70	4
Dennis Homan, Birmingham	61	930	15.3	73	8
Alfred Jenkins, Birmingham	60	1,326	22.1	95	12
Ed Marshall, Memphis	60	1,159	19.3	56	19

The World Football League returned in 1975 saying it was a different organization altogether; it was now the New World Football League. All the debts from the first year would be paid, the league said, but no deadline was given. The statistics and records from the first year appeared in the press manual "as a service to the media who may be interested in the continuity of such records.

"It should be noted, however, that last year's teams played for what is now legally known as the Football Creditor's Payment Plan, Inc., formerly known as the World Football League, and now in Chapter Eleven reorganizational proceedings. This year's World Football League is a completely separate and distinctive league, even though some players and franchise locations are the same as the 'old' World Football League of 1974."

Ten teams were in fact in the same place. Every franchise except the hapless Detroit Wheels was resurrected. All but three had new leadership; Bassett still controlled the Memphis franchise, Bosacco still owned the Philadelphia Bell, and Bell still led a group controlling the Charlotte team.

The Florida Blazers became the San Antonio Wings. Birmingham became the Vulcans, Chicago the Winds, Jacksonville the Express, and Portland the Thunder. Sometimes Memphis was called the Southmen and sometimes the Grizzlies.

Each ownership group was forbidden to sell for three years, and ordered to put $545,000 in escrow and make a $75,000 payment to league headquarters, which were relocated in New York. Each team was to adopt an austere budget and face inspection of its books every two weeks. Padding of attendance figures was strictly forbidden.

Hemmeter, the new commissioner, announced a profit-sharing concept that became known as the Hemmeter Plan. It called for players to share in the net income with their owners; if there was no income, the players would get the minimum salary, $500 a game. The Hemmeter Plan did not affect the large contracts such as the ones made between Bassett and Csonka, Kiick, and Warfield.

Two of a team's games would be exhibitions, for which players would get $200 a game. There would be no training-camp pay.

The WFL schedule for 1975 called for Saturday, not Wednesday, games, and had an oddity in that, because of a stadium conflict, there would be a regular-season game between Charlotte and San Antonio during the exhibition part of the schedule. TVS did not renew its contract to televise WFL games. An experiment in which linebackers wore red pants, running backs green pants, receivers orange pants, defensive backs yellow pants, offensive linemen white pants, and defensive linemen black pants in exhibition games was roundly criticized and abandoned. The Dickerrod was dropped. And the league decided that for economy reasons, only one game official, the referee, would travel; the other officials would be provided locally.

At last the league had well-known players. This was the year for Csonka, Kiick, Warfield, Hill, Gilliam, and Kwalick to begin playing. They appeared with Hemmeter at a press conference at the Waldorf-Astoria Hotel, to showcase the appeal and solidarity of the "new" WFL. Southern California signed running back Anthony Davis of USC.

There were troubles elsewhere, however. Bill Bergey, Curley Culp, L.C. Greenwood, and Ken Stabler were star players who broached WFL contracts that had been scheduled to begin in 1975 and returned to the NFL. Joe Namath of the New York Jets spurned a reputed $4 million contract from the Chicago Winds and their representative, Chicago real estate and insurance figure Eugene Pullano.

The "governors" of the teams, as the owners were called, were banker Ferd Weil of Birmingham; Bell of Charlotte; Pullano of Chicago; jewelry manufacturer Edward Sultan, Jr., of the Hawaiians; land developer Earl Knabb of Jacksonville; Bassett of Memphis; Bosacco of Philadelphia; attorney Richard V. Bayless of Portland; financial consultant Norm Bevan of San Antonio; oil and gas executive John B. Atkins, Jr., of Shreveport; and former Hawaiians part-owner Sam Battistone of Southern California.

Mike Giddings of Hawaii; Babe Parilli, who moved from Charlotte to Chicago; John McVay of Memphis; and Tom Fears of Southern California were the returning coaches. Newcomers were Marvin Bass of Birmingham, Bob Gibson of Charlotte, Charlie Tate of Jacksonville, Willie Wood of Philadelphia, Greg Barton of Portland, Perry Moss of San Antonio, and Marshall Taylor of Shreveport.

The Chicago Winds were the league's first casualty. They failed to sign Namath. Their season-ticket sale thereafter did not climb above 2,000. Parilli was hired as their coach and general manager and then fired before the end of July and replaced with two people, Abe Gibron as coach and Leo Cahill as general manager; a furious Parilli said he thought his contract had been "for life." Two of the Winds' investors, whom another member of the ownership group could remember only by their first names, withdrew $175,000 they had on deposit with the league. The WFL responded by booting the team out of the league September 2.

Profiles of the other teams show why they followed the Winds into extinction less than two months later. The Charlotte Hornets were evicted from a baseball park where they practiced because they owed rent on it. The Hawaiians wilted under the expense of flying a 50-man traveling party on a swing that carried them from Honolulu to Jacksonville, Philadelphia, and Portland over 18 days at a cost of $31,700 for the air fare alone.

The Hawaiians' payroll faltered and alternate quarterbacks Sonny Sixkiller and Rick Cassata quit the team. One of two quarterbacks hurriedly signed to replace them was Jim Fassel, who was reached in California, where he had been employed as the driver of a beer truck. The Hawaiians lost Calvin Hill early in the year with a knee injury.

The blocking dummies and a blocking sled owned by the Jacksonville Express were impounded.

Bosacco of Philadelphia moved his games from Kennedy Stadium to Franklin Field. The average attendance dipped to 3,222. On the road, the Bell arrived at Anaheim Stadium for a practice the day before a game with the Sun. The team drove up in a yellow school bus. The stadium guard did not believe they were a football team until one of the players opened his shirt and revealed a Bell T-shirt.

The next night the Bell and Sun played a wild game that went on for three hours and 32 minutes before Southern California won 58-39. The game was being televised back to Philadelphia on WTAF. At 1:30 A.M., when there still were 10 minutes left in the game, WTAF played the national anthem and signed off the air.

Portland's franchise encountered hard times and the league assessed the nine other teams more than $300,000 to keep the team going. Southern California faced financial shortages after the expensive contract signed with Anthony Davis. The Sun had quarterback troubles when Daryle Lamonica was sidelined with a injury and Pat Haden departed in September for his studies in England as a Rhodes scholar.

But two franchises approached being genuinely healthy. Birmingham drew good crowds. It always had; it was over-generous bonuses that had bankrupted the 1974 Americans. Memphis also drew well, but Csonka, its star attraction, went out with a torn tendon in his abdomen in August. Birmingham and Memphis were the only teams to exceed the 20,000 average attendance the WFL had said it needed to survive the year.

The World Football League died October 22, 1975, twelve weeks or a little more than halfway through its second season. At the league's offices in New York, Hemmeter read a statement to the press. He said the league might have made it if it could have held out a couple more years.

He defended the Hemmeter plan. "The plan worked beautifully," he said. "But it was never intended to develop a market. What we needed was a strong marketing plan. You can have an exciting product, but if it doesn't have customer appeal on the shelf, it's worthless."

Players from folded teams or players released from their contracts were allowed to join NFL teams immediately. Gilliam played a game with the Minnesota Vikings a week after the demise of the Chicago Winds. Kwalick signed with Oakland and played in six NFL games after 11 in the WFL.

The next season, Csonka signed with the New York Giants, Kiick with Denver, Warfield with Cleveland, and Hill with Washington.

A survey by the *Washington Post* in September, 1976, showed that among players who never played before in the NFL but did in the WFL, three were starting in the NFL. They were wide receiver J.K. McKay of Tampa Bay and punters Danny White of Dallas and Rusty Jackson of Los Angeles.

1975 WFL STANDINGS

Eastern Division	W	L	T	Pct.	Pts.	OP
Birmingham Vulcans	9	3	0	.750	257	186
Memphis Southmen	7	4	0	.636	254	206
Charlotte Hornets	6	5	0	.545	225	199
Jacksonville Express	6	5	0	.545	227	247
Philadelphia Bell	4	7	0	.364	195	237
Western Division	**W**	**L**	**T**	**Pct.**	**Pts.**	**OP**
Southern California Sun	7	5	0	.583	354	341
San Antonio Wings	7	6	0	.538	364	268
Shreveport Steamer	5	7	0	.417	276	313
Hawaiians	4	7	0	.364	210	281
Portland Thunder	4	7	0	.364	213	239
Chicago Winds	1	4	0	.200	67	124

LEADING RUSHERS	Att.	Yards	Avg.	Long	TD
Anthony Davis, So. California	239	1,200	5.0	33	16
Art Cantrelle, Birmingham	201	814	4.0	29	10
Rufus Ferguson, Portland	187	768	4.1	61	7
Jim Nance, Shreveport	190	767	4.0	35	7
Al Haywood, Jacksonville	131	687	5.2	25	4
LEADING PASSERS	**Att.**	**Comp.**	**Yards**	**TD**	**Int.**
John Walton, San Antonio	338	167	2,405	19	22
Edd Hargett, Shreveport	288	158	2,100	15	11
Pat Haden, So. California	163	98	1,404	11	9
Danny White, Memphis	195	104	1,445	10	8
George Mira, Jacksonville	254	123	1,675	12	12
LEADING RECEIVERS	**No.**	**Yards**	**Avg.**	**Long**	**TD**
Eddie Richardson, San Antonio	46	682	14.8	45	4
Terry Lindsey, So. California	43	669	15.6	76	4
Tim Delaney, Hawaii	44	594	13.5	31	5
Ed Marshall, Memphis	31	582	18.8	58	9
Dennis Hughes, Jacksonville	36	552	15.3	39	4

Teams of the NFL

ATLANTA FALCONS

1964 Atlanta was discussed by both the National and American Football Leagues as a possible location for a new pro football team. Baseball's Milwaukee Braves announced they intended to move and become the Atlanta Braves. Funding was worked out for a new stadium. Mayor Ivan Allen, Jr., broke ground for the $18 million Atlanta Stadium, "with money we didn't have, for teams that didn't exist," April 15.

1965 Rivalry began in earnest between the NFL and AFL to locate an expansion team in Atlanta. The AFL awarded a franchise for Atlanta to J. Leonard Reinsch of the Cox Broadcasting Corporation, June 8. NFL Commissioner Pete Rozelle, who earlier had said his league's next expansion was planned for 1967, two years hence, moved up the timetable. He sent public opinion pollster Lou Harris to Atlanta, and Harris conducted a poll showing that the citizens overwhelmingly favored an NFL team over an AFL team. Harris's poll had dealt the AFL a bitter defeat. Rankin M. Smith, 41-year-old executive vice president of the Life of Georgia Insurance Company, was awarded an NFL franchise for approximately $8.5 million, June 30. Smith's franchise was awarded a lease for the stadium under construction, and Reinsch's AFL franchise ceased to exist. Smith, asked why he bought the team, said, "Doesn't every adult male in America want to own his own football team?" Julia Elliott, a Griffin, Georgia, schoolteacher, won a radio station's contest to name the team; she suggested Falcons, August 29. Wayland Moore Studios of Atlanta designed the team's striking emblem. Halfback Bob Paremore and split end Gary Barnes, who had formerly been with the Cardinals and Bears, respectively, were the first players to sign with the Falcons, September 9. Tommy Nobis, the Outland Trophy-winning linebacker from Texas, was the first draft choice of Atlanta and of the entire NFL; the Falcons, who got an extra choice on each of the first five rounds, also selected quarterback Randy Johnson of Texas A&I on the first round, November 27. Season ticket sales set an NFL record when they reached 26,000 in November and were stopped when they reached 45,000.

1966 Norb Hecker, defensive backfield coach for Vince Lombardi of the Green Bay Packers, was named Falcons' head coach, January 26. Forty-two veteran players, three from each of the 14 established teams, were selected in an expansion draft, February 15. The best turned out to be fullback Junior Coffey, obtained from Green Bay. The Falcons' first training camp was at Blue Ridge Assembly, a YMCA camp at Black Mountain, North Carolina. On August 1, the Falcons lost their first preseason game, 9-7 to Philadelphia. They lost three more before defeating San Francisco 24-17 at Columbia, South Carolina, August 27. Atlanta lost its first regular-season game to Los Angeles 19-14 at Atlanta Stadium, September 11. Atlanta's first touchdown was a 53-yard pass from Johnson to Barnes. Nine more losses followed before Atlanta defeated the New York Giants 27-16 at Yankee Stadium for its first regular-season victory, November 20. Three weeks later, the Falcons earned their first Atlanta Stadium victory by defeating St. Louis 16-10, December 11. Coffey led the Falcons in rushing, with 722 yards, and Johnson in passing, with 1,795 yards.

1967 Frank E. Wall was named general manager, January 31. Atlanta traded its number-one draft choice for 1967 to San Francisco for wide receiver Bernie Casey, tackle Jim Wilson, and defensive end Jim Norton, March 14. In a preseason game, the Falcons defeated their AFL rivals, the Miami Dolphins, 27-17 to lay claim to the championship of the South. Training camp was moved to East Tennessee State in Johnson City, Tennessee. Nobis returned an interception 41 yards to lead Atlanta over Minnesota 21-20 for the team's only victory in its second season, October 30. Nobis was named Atlanta's first all-pro.

1968 Coffey suffered a knee injury in the preseason and missed the entire year. After three opening losses, Norb Hecker was dismissed as coach and replaced by Norm Van Brocklin, former head coach of the Minnesota Vikings, October 1. The Falcons lost to Green Bay 38-7 in Van Brocklin's first game as coach, October 6. Atlanta ended an 11-game losing streak by defeating the New York Giants 24-21 the following week. Van Brocklin placed five starting players on waivers, and replaced Johnson with Bob Berry, whom he had coached in Minnesota. Van Brocklin dismissed five assistant coaches the day after the season finale, a 14-12 loss to San Francisco.

1969 The Falcons used the second pick in the draft to select All-America tackle George Kunz of Notre Dame. Atlanta had its best season yet with six victories. It defeated San Francisco 24-12 in the season opener, September 21. Atlanta set a club record for most points by defeating Chicago 48-31, November 16. The Falcons ended Minnesota's 12-game winning streak with a 10-3 victory over the Vikings in the last game of the season, December 21. The last remaining Falcons' player from the expansion draft of 1966 left the team in the middle of the season: Coffey was traded to the New York Giants, October 29. The team's offensive star was flanker Paul Flatley, who made 45 receptions for 834 yards.

1970 Van Brocklin assumed the role of general manager in addition to being the head coach, and Frank Wall became president and Rankin M. Smith chairman of the board, January 6. The Falcons had their best preseason yet, a 4-1 record, but they won only four regular-season games.There were some quality players on the team, such as Nobis, Kunz, cornerback Ken Reaves, defensive end Claude Humphrey, and tight end Jim Mitchell, but they were too few for a winning record.

1971 The training camp site was changed again, moving to Furman University in Greenville, South Carolina. Atlanta defeated San Francisco in its home opener for the third straight year, this time winning 20-17, September 19. The Falcons went on to record their first winning season ever, 7-6-1. The winning record was assured when Ken Burrow caught the winning touchdown pass from Berry in a 24-20 victory over New Orleans, December 19.

1972 Van Brocklin made four trades during the NFL draft, sending six veterans to other teams for draft choices. He used one of the choices to draft Heisman Trophy winner Pat Sullivan, quarterback from Auburn, on the second round. Running back Dave Hampton gained a club record 161 yards in a 31-3 victory over Los Angeles, the team's first victory over the Rams in 11 meetings, October 1. Atlanta lost 17-14 to Kansas City in the final game of the season, missing a chance to finish above .500, and Hampton went over 1,000 yards rushing to 1,001 but then lost six yards to complete the year with 995, December 17. Atlanta's record ended at 7-7.

1973 Atlanta traded Berry and a number-one draft choice to Minnesota for quarterback Bob Lee and linebacker Lonnie Warwick. An eventful season began when Atlanta, quarterbacked by Dick Shiner, set 35 team records while overwhelming New Orleans 62-7 in the opening game, September 16. Three defeats followed, then the Falcons defeated Chicago 46-6. Atlanta stopped the unbeaten Minnesota Vikings 20-14 on Monday night television. Shiner was put on waivers, and Lee took over at quarterback. A 28-20 triumph over the New York Jets was Atlanta's seventh victory in a row, December 9. The Falcons missed the playoffs, however, when they lost two of their last three games. Hampton just missed 1,000 yards again, finishing with 997.

1974 The Falcons' hopes for their first playoff berth were shattered by three consecutive losses to open the season. Close victories over the Giants and the Bears were followed by three more losses. There was almost open rebellion among the players against the stern discipline of Van Brocklin. After the Falcons dropped to 2-6, Van Brocklin challenged a reporter to a fist fight. Van Brocklin subsequently was fired and replaced as head coach by defensive coordinator Marion Campbell, November 6. The Atlanta offense continued to stumble around the rest of the season, whether led by Lee, Sullivan, or rookie Kim McQuilken, and the team finished 3-11. McQuilken led the Falcons to a 10-3 victory over Green Bay in the final game of the season, but there were an NFL-record 48,830 no-shows at rain-swept Atlanta Stadium, December 15.

1975 Atlanta traded Kunz to Baltimore for the Colts' first- and sixth-round draft choices, January 27. The Falcons made California quarterback Steve Bartkowski the first choice of the entire NFL draft, January 28. Pat Peppler was named general manager, February 26. Atlanta Stadium was renamed Atlanta-Fulton County Stadium. The Falcons won only four games, but had some exciting performances. Bartkowski improved as the season progressed, but the most surprising newcomer was Alfred Jenkins, who caught 38 passes for 767 yards after being picked up from the defunct World Football League. Hampton reached 1,000 yards rushing, gaining 61 in the season finale to finish with 1,002.

1976 Former Minnesota wide receiver John Gilliam, who had played out his option, signed with the Falcons, May 5. Atlanta lost four of its first five games and Campbell was replaced as coach by general manager Peppler, October 12. A 17-10 upset of the defending NFC champion Dallas Cowboys was the Falcons' second straight victory and third in four games; quarterback Scott Hunter sneaked for the winning touchdown and Nobis made a key interception, November 21. Two weeks later, the Falcons were humiliated 59-0 at Los Angeles as the Rams made 30 first downs, 569 net yards, and a record eight touchdowns rushing.

1977 Eddie LeBaron, an attorney and a former quarterback for the Washington Redskins and Dallas Cowboys, was named general manager, replacing Peppler, February 1. Two days later, Los Angeles Rams assistant coach Leeman Bennett was named head coach. Nobis retired in the offseason. The Falcons upset the Rams 17-6 in the season opener. As the season progressed, the defense, known as the "Grits Blitz," emerged as the team's cornerstone and set a modern NFL record by allowing just 129 points in a 14-game season. The defense reached its peak against Tampa Bay, when it allowed just 78 yards in total offense en route to a 17-0 victory. For the first half of the season, Hunter was the starting quarterback, but he was replaced in midseason by Bartkowski. With a 6-6 record, the Falcons still had playoff aspirations, but, on December 11, the Rams ended them 23-7. A victory in the season finale against New Orleans gave the Falcons a 7-7 record.

1978 The Falcons opened their new training complex in Suwanee, Georgia. Despite a promising start, when Atlanta beat Houston 20-14 in the opener, the Falcons fell to the back of the pack with three straight losses. They appeared to be in big trouble when the mainstay of the defensive line, Humphrey, retired after four games. But, behind Bartkowski, who enjoyed his finest season with 2,489 yards passing, the

Falcons won five in a row to finish 9-7. The key games were a 14-0 defeat of Detroit, the Falcons' first shutout ever in Atlanta-Fulton County Stadium; a 15-7 Monday night victory over the Rams, when Tim Mazzetti kicked five field goals; and a victory over Washington, which clinched the Falcons' first playoff berth ever. On December 24, the Falcons fell behind early in the NFC Wild Card Game and trailed the Eagles 13-0 with eight minutes to play. But Bartkowski threw two touchdown passes to win the game, 14-13. A week later, the Falcons led Dallas 20-13 at halftime. Quarterback Danny White sparked a Cowboys rally that eliminated the Falcons 27-20.

1979 The draft brought in the backfield tandem of William Andrews and Lynn Cain. Andrews made his mark immediately, rushing for a record 167 yards in the opener against New Orleans, a 40-34 overtime victory. He went on to establish the Falcons' single-season rushing mark with 1,023 yards. Cain also set an Atlanta record on October 14 when he became the first Falcon to score three touchdowns in a game. The new rushing stars helped Bartkowski, who set single-game passing marks by hitting 20 of 29 for 326 yards against Denver, September 17. Bartkowski's top receiver was Wallace Francis, who set Atlanta records with 74 receptions for 1,013 yards. Despite 300 points by the offense, the defense broke down, allowing 388. After winning their first two games, the Falcons lost 9 of the next 11 to finish 6-10.

1980 When the season began, the Falcons started slowly, posting a 3-3 record after six weeks. But, with Bartkowski setting team passing records, the Falcons set a club record with a nine-game winning streak. On October 19, Bartkowski threw four touchdown passes against the Saints, and three weeks later he passed for a team-record 378 yards against St. Louis. The key victory in the streak occurred on October 26 against Los Angeles, when Bartkowski overcame a third-and-38 to throw a game-winning, 54-yard touchdown pass to Alfred Jackson in the waning moments of the game. Despite a loss to the Rams in the regular-season finale, the Falcons won their first NFC West title with a 12-4 record. Bartkowski passed for 3,544 yards and 31 touchdowns. The Falcons dominated the first three quarters of their divisional playoff game, but lost 30-27 when Dallas erupted for 20 points in the final period.

1981 The season began in awesome fashion, as the Falcons crushed New Orleans, Green Bay, and San Francisco behind seven touchdown passes by Bartkowski. But having suffered some key injuries, Atlanta lost three in a row, falling to 6-6 late in the season. A 31-27 victory over Houston on November 29 boosted the Falcons' playoff chances, but they lost the last three games of the year to finish 7-9. Despite the losing record, the Falcons led the NFC in scoring with 426 points; the team's weak point was the defense, which allowed 355 points. Bartkowski threw 30 touchdown passes, while Jenkins led the league with 1,358 yards receiving and 13 touchdown catches. Andrews had his third straight 1,000-yard rushing season (1,301) and set a team record by catching 81 passes.

1982 LeBaron was promoted to executive vice president, and director of pro personnel Tom Braatz became general manager, January 26. The Falcons chose Gerald Riggs, a running back from Arizona State, in the first round of the draft. The Falcons won their opener 16-14 over the New York Giants aided by a 91-yard fumble return for a touchdown by Bob Glazebrook. A three-game winning streak in the middle of the strike-shortened season gave the Falcons a 5-4 record and qualified them for the playoffs. Minnesota defeated Atlanta 30-24 in the first round of the playoffs. Andrews, who finished fifth in the NFC in rushing and third in receiving, was joined at the Pro Bowl by center Jeff Van Note, guard R.C. Thielemann, and tackle Mike Kenn.

1983 Leeman Bennett was dismissed as head coach and replaced by Dan Henning, an assistant coach with Washington. In Henning's debut, the Falcons defeated the Bears 20-17, but they lost five of their next six. A strong finish was highlighted by a 28-24 victory over San Francisco, November 20, attained on the last play of the game. Billy Johnson made a falling catch of a long pass from Bartkowski, got up, and scored. A week later, Kenny Johnson returned two interceptions for touchdowns, and the Falcons beat Green Bay in overtime 47-41. Bartkowski led the NFC in passing, while Andrews set a club record with 1,567 yards rushing.

1984 Andrews suffered a severe knee injury in training camp and missed the entire season. Riggs replaced him and rushed for a club record 202 yards in an opening 36-28 win at New Orleans, September 2. The Falcons won for the first time ever in Los Angeles, when Mick Luckhurst, who had become the club's career scoring leader earlier in the year, kicked a 37-yard field goal as time expired for a 30-28 victory. Atlanta then lost nine in a row on the way to a 4-12 finish. Riggs finished fourth in the NFC with 1,486 rushing yards, Stacey Bailey was fourth in receiving yards with 1,138, and the sore-kneed Bartkowski was fifth in passing.

1985 The Falcons selected Pittsburgh tackle Bill Fralic with the second pick in the draft. Despite Johnson surpassing Rick Upchurch to become the NFL's all-time leader in punt return yardage, Atlanta was edged by Detroit 28-27 in the opener. The Falcons went on to lose their first six, and, after five weeks, Bartkowski was replaced by David Archer. In Archer's second start, Atlanta beat New Orleans 31-24. The Falcons then lost six of their next seven before finishing with two victories. Riggs led the NFC in rushing with 1,719 yards.

1986 LeBaron was fired and Braatz become director of college scouting, leaving the day-to-day running of the team to Rankin Smith, Jr., and Taylor Smith. Bartkowski was released. The Falcons traded for Cincinnati quarterback Turk Schonert.

MEMBERS OF HALL OF FAME:
None

FALCONS RECORD, 1966-85

Year	Won	Lost	Tied	Pct.	Fin.	Pts.	OP
1966	3	11	0	.214	7	204	437
1967	1	12	1	.077	4	175	422
1968	2	12	0	.143	4	170	389
1969	6	8	0	.429	3	276	268
1970	4	8	2	.333	3	206	261
1971	7	6	1	.538	3	274	277
1972	7	7	0	.500	2	269	274
1973	9	5	0	.643	2	318	224
1974	3	11	0	.214	4	111	271
1975	4	10	0	.286	3	240	289
1976	4	10	0	.286	3	172	312
1977	7	7	0	.500	2	179	129
1978a	9	7	0	.563	2	240	290
1979	6	10	0	.375	3	300	388
1980b	12	4	0	.750	1	405	272
1981	7	9	0	.438	2	426	355
1982c	5	4	0	.556	5	183	199
1983	7	9	0	.438	4	370	389
1984	4	12	0	.250	4	281	382
1985	4	12	0	.250	4	282	452
20 Years	111	174	4	.391		5,081	6,280

aNFC Wild Card Qualifier for Playoffs; 1-1 in Playoffs
bNFC Western Division Champion; 0-1 in Playoffs
cNFC Qualifier for Playoffs; 0-1 in Playoffs

RECORD HOLDERS

CAREER

Rushing attempts	William Andrews, 1979-83	1,253
Rushing yards	William Andrews, 1979-83	5,772
Pass attempts	Steve Bartkowski, 1975-85	3,329
Pass completions	Steve Bartkowski, 1975-85	1,870
Passing yards	Steve Bartkowski, 1975-85	23,468
Touchdown passes	Steve Bartkowski, 1975-85	154
Receptions	Alfred Jenkins, 1975-83	359
Receiving yards	Alfred Jenkins, 1975-83	6,257
Interceptions	Rolland Lawrence, 1973-81	39
Punting average	Billy Lothridge, 1966-71	41.3
Punt return avg.	Al Dodd, 1973-74	11.8
Kickoff return avg.	Ron Smith, 1966-67	24.3
Field goals	Mick Luckhurst, 1981-85	92
Touchdowns	Alfred Jenkins, 1975-83	40
	William Andrews, 1979-83	40
Points	Mick Luckhurst, 1981-85	451

SEASON

Rushing attempts	Gerald Riggs, 1985	397
Rushing yards	Gerald Riggs, 1985	1,719
Pass attempts	Steve Bartkowski, 1981	533
Pass completions	Steve Bartkowski, 1981	297
Passing yards	Steve Bartkowski, 1981	3,830
Touchdown passes	Steve Bartkowski, 1980	31
Receptions	William Andrews, 1981	81
Receiving yards	Alfred Jenkins, 1981	1,358
Interceptions	Rolland Lawrence, 1975	9
Punting average	Billy Lothridge, 1968	44.3
Punt return avg.	Gerald Tinker, 1974	13.9
Kickoff return avg.	Dennis Pearson, 1978	26.7
Field goals	Nick Mike-Mayer, 1973	26
Touchdowns	Alfred Jenkins, 1981	13
	Gerald Riggs, 1984	13
Points	Mick Luckhurst, 1981	114

GAME

Rushing attempts	Gerald Riggs, 11-17-85	41
Rushing yards	Gerald Riggs, 9-2-84	202
Pass attempts	Steve Bartkowski, 9-19-82	56
Pass completions	Steve Bartkowski, 9-19-82	34
Passing yards	Steve Bartkowski, 11-15-81	416
Touchdown passes	Randy Johnson, 11-16-69	4
	Steve Bartkowski, 10-19-80	4
	Steve Bartkowski, 10-18-81	4
Receptions	William Andrews, 11-15-81	15
Receiving yards	Alfred Jackson, 12-2-84	193
Interceptions	31 times	2
Field goals	Nick Mike-Mayer, 11-4-73	5
	Tim Mazzetti, 10-30-78	5
Touchdowns	7 times	3
Points	7 times	18

COACHING HISTORY

1966-68	Norb Hecker*	4-26-1
1968-74	Norm Van Brocklin**	37-49-3
1974-76	Marion Campbell***	6-19-0
1976	Pat Peppler	3- 6-0
1977-82	Leeman Bennett	47-44-0
1983-85	Dan Henning	15-33-0

**Replaced after three games in 1968*
***Replaced after eight games in 1974*
****Replaced after five games in 1976*

FIRST PLAYER SELECTED

1966 Tommy Nobis, LB, Texas
1967 (2) Leo Carroll, DE, San Diego State
1968 Claude Humphrey, DE, Tennessee State
1969 George Kunz, T, Notre Dame
1970 John Small, LB, Citadel
1971 Joe Profit, RB, Northeast Louisiana
1972 Clarence Ellis, S, Notre Dame
1973 (2) Greg Marx, DT, Notre Dame
1974 (2) Gerald Tinker, WR, Kent State
1975 Steve Bartkowski, QB, California
1976 Bubba Bean, RB, Texas A&M
1977 Warren Bryant, T, Kentucky
1978 Mike Kenn, T, Michigan
1979 Don Smith, DE, Miami
1980 Junior Miller, TE, Nebraska
1981 Bobby Butler, CB, Florida State
1982 Gerald Riggs, RB, Arizona State
1983 Mike Pitts, DE, Alabama
1984 Rick Bryan, DT, Oklahoma
1984* Joey Jones, WR, Alabama
1985 Bill Fralic, T, Pittsburgh
1986 Tony Casillas, NT, Oklahoma
**Supplemental Draft*

FALCONS PLAYER OF THE YEAR

1966 Tommy Nobis, LB
1967 Junior Coffey, RB
1968 Tommy Nobis, LB
1969 Jim Butler, RB
1970 Jim Mitchell, TE
1971 Don Hansen, LB
1972 Dave Hampton, RB
1973 Bob Lee, QB
1974 Ray Brown, S
1975 Dave Hampton, RB
1976 Claude Humphrey, DE
1977 Rolland Lawrence, CB
1978 Greg Brezina, LB
1979 Wallace Francis, WR
1980 Steve Bartkowski, QB
1981 William Andrews, RB
1982 Fulton Kuykendall, LB
1983 William Andrews, RB
1984 Gerald Riggs, RB
1985 Gerald Riggs, RB

BUFFALO BILLS

1959 Ralph C. Wilson, Jr., a minority stockholder of the Detroit Lions who long had sought a team of his own, was granted an American Football League franchise for Buffalo. Wilson initially had wanted a franchise in Miami, but was unable to lease the Orange Bowl. Several friends convinced him he should investigate Buffalo, which enthusiastically had supported the Bills of the All-America Football Conference before that league folded. Wilson's former commanding officer in the Navy lived in Buffalo and introduced Wilson to Paul Neville, the managing editor of the *Buffalo Evening News*. Neville pledged full personal and civic support for a new team, leading Wilson to put up a $100,000 performance bond and sign a lease on War Memorial Stadium. The city voted to increase the seating capacity of the stadium by 14,000, from 22,500 to 36,500. Wilson named the team the Bills. Richie Lucas, an All-America quarterback from Penn State, was the team's first draft choice, and Joe Schaffer of Tennessee was the first player to sign a contract. Garrard (Buster) Ramsey was named head coach. Dick Gallagher, an assistant coach and director of player personnel with the Cleveland Browns, was selected as general manager.

1960 The club's first training camp was held in East Aurora, New York. On July 30, the Bills lost to Boston 28-7 at War Memorial Stadium in the AFL's first preseason game. The team's first victory came two weeks later, 31-14 over Denver at Rochester, New York. In Buffalo's first regular-season game, the Bills lost to the New York Titans 27-3, September 11. The Bills recorded their first regular-season victory, September 23, shutting out Boston 13-0. The Bills had one of the AFL's best defenses, but the offense finished last in total yards as neither former Browns star Tommy O'Connell nor Lucas could generate much of an attack. The most pleasant surprise in the 5-8-1 season was the play of rookie fullback Wray Carlton, who scored 11 touchdowns. The Bills had an average home attendance of 16,000.

1961 Denver ruined the Bills' home opener at War Memorial Stadium with a 22-10 victory. Lou Saban was replaced by Mike Holovak in Boston, and immediately was hired as Buffalo's new director of player personnel, amid rumors he would be the Bills' next head coach. Without any one quarterback who could take charge, the Bills finished the season with a 6-8 record.

1962 The rumors proved true. Ramsey was fired, and Saban was hired as head coach. The Bills signed 6-foot 2-inch, 243-pound Canadian Football League star fullback Cookie Gilchrist, who gained 1,099 yards, becoming the AFL's first 1,000-yard rusher. Quarterback Jack Kemp was claimed for the $100 waiver price from San Diego and proved to be a budding star. Houston ruined Saban's debut, beating the Bills 28-23. But after a slow start, Buffalo finished with seven wins and a tie in the last nine games for a 7-6-1 record.

1963 The Bills signed their first two "name" players, Dave Behrman, a center from Michigan State, and Jim Dunaway, a tackle from Mississippi. They also signed quarterback Daryle Lamonica of Notre Dame. The club moved its training camp to suburban Blasdell, New York. Gilchrist set an all-time pro rushing record, gaining 243 yards and scoring five touchdowns in a 45-14 victory over the New York Jets. After an 0-3-1 start, the Bills came on strong to tie the Patriots in the East, but Buffalo lost 26-8 to Boston in an Eastern Division playoff game in 24-degree weather.

1964 The Bills continued their fast finish of the year before, recording the league's best record (12-2) behind the stingiest defense and most productive offense in the AFL. The front four of Ron McDole, Jim Dunaway, Tom Sestak, and Tom Day turned into the league's best and held opponents to fewer than 65 yards rushing per game. Gilchrist led the league in rushing (as did the Bills) with 981 yards. Meanwhile, Kemp shared the quarterback job with Lamonica, who averaged better than 20 yards per completion. Flanker Elbert Dubenion caught 42 passes for 1,139 yards, a fantastic 27.1-yard average, and 10 touchdowns. Saban also unveiled pro football's first soccer-style kicker, Pete Gogolak, who scored 102 points. The Bills won their first nine before losing to Boston 36-28. They clinched the division title in the season finale with a 24-14 victory over the Patriots in the snow at Fenway Park, December 20. The next week, before a standing-room-only crowd at War Memorial Stadium, the Bills won the AFL Championship Game 20-7 over San Diego.

1965 Gilchrist, who had demanded extra money after the Bills won the championship, was traded to Denver for fullback Billy Joe. Despite the power of Carlton, the running went flat, and the passing game was hurt by injuries to Dubenion and split end Glenn Bass. Nevertheless, the defense remained the league's best, led by Sestak, linebacker Mike Stratton, and defensive backs George (Butch) Byrd and George Saimes, all of whom were named all-AFL. The defense was enough to carry the Bills to another title with a 10-3-1 record, winning the Eastern Division by five games over the New York Jets. The Bills had lost to San Diego 34-3 during the regular season, but in the AFL Championship Game, the defense shut down the Chargers 23-0.

1966 Saban announced he was resigning to accept a position as the head coach at the University of Maryland. Joe Collier, an assistant coach, was named head coach. The AFL All-Stars defeated the Bills 30-19, January 15. Collier's regular-season head coaching debut was unsuccessful. San Diego beat the Bills 27-7, September 4. Buffalo rallied to have another good season and defeated Denver in the last game of the year to win a third straight Eastern Division championship with a 9-4-1 record. Bobby Burnett, a halfback from Arkansas, rushed for 766 yards and was named rookie of the year. Kansas City ended the Bills' hold on the AFL championship, winning 31-7 in Buffalo before 42,080 at War Memorial Stadium, January 1.

1967 Lamonica and Bass were traded to Oakland for Tom Flores and Art Powell, neither of whom created an impact. Playing an NFL opponent for the first time in the preseason, the Bills lost 19-17 to Detroit. Although the defense remained one of the league's best, the offense was weakened by injuries and by Kemp's sub-par season. Keith Lincoln, who had been obtained from San Diego, led the team with 601 yards rushing and 41 receptions, but the Bills still dropped to 4-10 and third place.

1968 Kemp was injured and lost for the season, as was Flores. Former Bill Daryle Lamonica came to town and helped Oakland beat Buffalo 48-6 in the second game, following which Collier was fired and replaced by Harvey Johnson, the team's director of player personnel. Five quarterbacks shuffled through the lineup, and the Bills finished with the poorest record in football (1-12-1). Dubenion, the last of the original Bills, retired as a player and joined the team's scouting department.

1969 John Rauch resigned as Oakland head coach and agreed to a four-year contract to coach the Bills. In the most significant draft in the history of the franchise, O.J. Simpson was selected as the first choice. Four months of intense negotiations followed with the Heisman Trophy winner from USC and his agent. A month after training camp opened, O.J. signed a long-term contract with the Bills and reported for duty, August 9. Rauch got his first victory as a Buffalo coach, beating Denver 41-28, September 28 after losing two.

1970 In the first season of interleague play, the Bills began to show promise for the future. Quarterback Dennis Shaw was named NFL rookie of the year. Marlin Briscoe was the AFC's top receiver with 57 catches. The roster contained several other highly regarded players, such as cornerback Robert James and Haven Moses, another speedy pass catcher. But through it all, there was concern about O.J. Simpson, who was something of a disappointment even before missing the final seven games with injuries. Some felt Simpson simply wasn't as good as advertised. Others contended it was impossible to run on a team that couldn't block. Still more wondered why Rauch didn't find ways to get him the ball more often.

1971 Early in training camp, Rauch resigned. Harvey Johnson once again was named interim coach. The Bills defeated New England 27-20, November 28. It was significant because it was their first—and only—regular-season victory of the year. Simpson led the offense with 742 yards. Saban returned from his six-year exile to become vice president in charge of football and head coach, December 23.

1972 Convinced the Bills had to be built from the bottom up, Saban began by fortifying the trenches. His first pick—and the number-one choice in the NFL draft—was Walt Patulski, 6-foot 6-inch, 259-pound Notre Dame defensive end. His second pick was guard Reggie McKenzie, the All-America blocker from Michigan. Just before the season opened, he obtained tackle Dave Foley on waivers from the Jets. All were starters almost immediately. In April, ground was broken for the club's new 80,000-seat stadium in Orchard Park, New York. Saban won his first regular-season game in the second week, beating San Francisco 27-20. Getting the ball much more often, O.J. Simpson started to live up to his reputation. He led the NFL with 1,251 yards and was named all-pro.

1973 Continuing his search for capable linemen, Saban made Michigan tackle Paul Seymour and Michigan State guard Joe DeLamielleure his first two selections in the draft. The Bills' season-ticket sale for their first year in Orchard Park passed 46,206, the listed capacity of old War Memorial Stadium. A sellout crowd of 80,020 watched the first preseason game in Orchard Park, won by the Washington Redskins 37-21. O.J. Simpson set a single-game NFL record of 250 yards in Buffalo's 31-13 opening game win over New England in Foxboro. The Bills made their Monday night television debut, beating Kansas City 23-14 with Simpson going over 1,000 yards for the season, October 29. In a dramatic final game at Shea Stadium, Simpson ran for 200 yards and finished with 2,003 for the season, breaking Jim Brown's 10-year-old rushing record. The Bills became the first team in league history to run for more than 3,000 yards.

1974 The Bills participated in the Hall of Fame game in Canton, Ohio, losing to St. Louis 21-13. In the season opener, Buffalo edged Oakland 21-20 in the final minute. A 29-28 victory over New England was the Bills' sixth consecutive victory and gave them possession of first place in the AFC Eastern Division, November 3. A 6-0 shutout of Baltimore was their ninth win of the season and first shutout since 1965. O.J. Simpson went over 1,000 yards for the season in that game, the third consecutive year he surpassed that mark. Miami defeated Cincinnati, assuring the Bills their first appearance in a postseason playoff since 1966, December 12. Pittsburgh beat the

Bills 32-14 in a divisional playoff game in Pittsburgh, December 22.

1975 In the season opener, Buffalo warmed up its potent offense to bombard the New York Jets 42-14. In their first Monday night television loss, the Bills dropped a 17-14 decision to the New York Giants. O. J. Simpson led the NFL in rushing for the third time in four years, with 1,817 yards, the third-most ever. In the final game of the season, Simpson scored his twenty-third touchdown, setting another NFL record.

1976 The lingering story of the summer was O. J. Simpson's insistence on a trade to Los Angeles. On the day before the season opened, Simpson signed a three-year contract estimated at $2 million-plus to play in Buffalo. After three losses in the first five games, Lou Saban resigned "in the best interests of the team." Jim Ringo, the offensive line coach and former all-pro center with Vince Lombardi's Green Bay Packers, was signed as the new coach. Two games later, quarterback Joe Ferguson suffered some broken bones in his back and was out for the season. The Bills never recovered and did not win a game under Ringo. Simpson started slowly, gaining only 105 yards in the first three games, but he finished with 1,503 to lead the league.

1977 Seven games into the season a knee injury did what NFL defenses hadn't been able to do—stop O. J. Simpson. After rushing for more than 7,500 yards in the previous five seasons, Simpson missed the last half of the season and finished the year with only 557. The Bills won only once with Simpson and twice without him, and head coach Jim Ringo was dismissed at the end of the 3-11 season. Ferguson was one of the bright spots, leading the NFL in passing yardage (2,803).

1978 Buffalo hired former Rams head coach Chuck Knox as head coach and vice president in charge of football operations on January 12. Two months later, the Bills obtained a number of high draft choices for Simpson in a trade with San Francisco. To replace Simpson, Knox drafted running back Terry Miller, the Heisman Trophy runner-up from Oklahoma State. Miller led the Bills with 1,060 yards, including 97 in Knox's first victory at Buffalo, a 24-17 win over Baltimore on September 24. The Bills finished 5-11, but 7 of those losses were by a touchdown or less.

1979 The Bills' main concern was to shore up a weak defense. They were successful, giving up 75 fewer points than the season before. The leaders of the defense were rookie nose tackle Fred Smerlas, linebacker Jim Haslett, who was named defensive rookie of the year, and former Rams linebacker Isiah Robertson. The Bills used the first pick of the 1979 NFL draft on former Ohio State linebacker Tom Cousineau, but he signed with Montreal of the Canadian Football League. The defense continued to improve, but the Bills stalled late in the season due to an inconsistent offense that scored 21 touchdowns in five early games but only 9 the rest of the season. In fact, the offense did not score a touchdown the last three games of the year, all losses. Ferguson passed for a Bills' record 3,572 yards. Against the Jets on September 23, he hit NFL offensive rookie of the year Jerry Butler with 10 passes for 255 yards.

1980 Knox continued to build up the defense, obtaining linebacker Phil Villapiano from the Raiders and safety Bill Simpson from the Rams. The biggest draft choice was running back Joe Cribbs from Auburn, who ran for 1,185 yards and caught 52 passes. With some needed spark offensively and a defense that gave up the fewest yards in the NFL, the Bills went on to win their first division title since 1966. A 26-24 victory over San Diego on October 5 gave Buffalo a 5-0 record, the best in pro football, and the division lead. An 18-13 win over San Francisco on December 21 clinched the AFC East title. The Bills lost to San Diego 20-14 when Dan Fouts threw a 50-yard touchdown pass to Ron Smith with two minutes left in the AFC Divisional Playoff Game.

1981 Led by Cribbs, who again ran for more than 1,000 yards and also caught seven touchdown passes, Buffalo engaged in a season-long race with Miami and the New York Jets for the 1981 AFC East crown. On December 19, the Dolphins defeated the Bills 16-6 in the final game of the season to win the title. The loss dropped Buffalo to third behind the New York Jets, but all three teams made the playoffs. On December 26, the Bills took a 24-0 lead in the wild card game at Shea Stadium, then held off the Jets, 31-27. Trailing by a touchdown in the 1981 AFC Divisional Playoff Game on January 3, the Bills picked up a first down at the Cincinnati 14. But a delay-of-game penalty forced them to replay the down. They didn't make the first down the second time, and Cincinnati ran out the clock and won 28-21.

1982 After matching an offer sheet by the Houston Oilers, Buffalo traded former number-one draft pick Tom Cousineau, who had spent three seasons in the Canadian Football League, to Cleveland for three draft choices. In the strike-abbreviated season, the Bills missed the cutoff for the playoffs with a 4-5 record. McKenzie returned from a serious knee injury for his eleventh season, and he helped solidify a strong running game that led the NFL. Cribbs had the league's top rushing average with 90 yards per game, and fullback Roosevelt Leaks contributed 405 yards rushing. Ferguson slumped, however, and finished last in the NFL's quarterback ratings.

1983 On February 1, six days after Knox left to become head coach of the Seattle Seahawks, Buffalo announced he would be replaced by Kay Stephenson. Although a frustrating rash of injuries caused 22 players, including 10 starters, to miss at least one game, the Bills were 7-4 after 11 games, tied with Miami for first place in the AFC East standings. But Buffalo dropped four of its final five games to finish tied for second with New England at 8-8. On October 9 against Miami, Ferguson completed 38 of 55 passes for 419 yards—all team records—and passed for five touchdowns to tie another club mark. In all Ferguson set or tied eight Bills single-game passing records, and led Buffalo to a 38-35 overtime victory that ended a 16-year winless streak at the Orange Bowl for the Bills. In a 41-17 loss to the Los Angeles Rams on November 27, Ferguson passed for 233 yards to become the twentieth player in NFL history to top the 25,000-yard mark. Cribbs rushed for 185 yards in a 14-9 victory against Kansas City on December 4. He finished the season with 1,131 yards rushing, fourth-best in the AFC, and was selected to his third AFC-NFC Pro Bowl. Smerlas made the AFC Pro Bowl squad for the fourth time.

1984 A 2-14 nosedive gave Buffalo the NFL's poorest record. Just about everything went wrong as the team dropped its first 11 games. The Bills finally earned their first victory on November 18 by stunning Dallas 14-3 at Rich Stadium. Rookie running back Greg Bell, the Bills' first-round draft choice from Notre Dame, set the tone of the game on Buffalo's first play from scrimmage by running 85 yards for a touchdown. He finished with 205 yards rushing. Reality returned the following week in the form of a 41-14 loss to Washington. Bell finished the season with 1,100 yards and seven touchdowns rushing, and he was named to the AFC-NFC Pro Bowl. Byron Franklin led the team with 69 receptions. The offense was ranked twenty-seventh in the NFL, and the defense was twenty-seventh in points allowed.

1985 With the first pick in the NFL draft, the Bills selected Virginia Tech defensive end Bruce Smith, the 1984 Outland Trophy winner. The Bills had 16 draft picks in all, including 2 in each of the first four rounds. O. J. Simpson was inducted into the Pro Football Hall of Fame, August 3. After the Bills began the season with four consecutive losses, Wilson replaced Stephenson as head coach with defensive coordinator Hank Bullough. Bullough lost his NFL coaching debut 49-17 at Indianapolis, October 4. Cribbs returned to the Bills on October 13 after spending two seasons in the United States Football League. One week later, he was in the lineup as the Bills defeated the Colts 21-9. Though Cribbs gained just 41 yards rushing, he helped take the pressure off of Bell. The relief provided by Cribbs was temporary; the Bills continued to lose, and finished the season 2-14. To replace Ferguson, who was traded to Detroit before the season, the Bills acquired Bruce Mathison from the Chargers and Vince Ferragamo from the Rams. They shared the quarterback position, but finished at the bottom of the AFC rankings. Bell's season totals included 883 yards rushing and 58 catches, and he had a club-record 13-reception performance against San Diego, September 8.

MEMBER OF HALL OF FAME:
O. J. Simpson

BILLS RECORD, 1960-85

Year	Won	Lost	Tied	Pct.	Fin.	Pts.	OP
1960	5	8	1	.385	3	296	303
1961	6	8	0	.429	4	294	342
1962	7	6	1	.538	3	309	272
1963a	7	6	1	.538	2	304	291
1964b	12	2	0	.857	1	400	242
1965b	10	3	1	.769	1	313	226
1966c	9	4	1	.692	1	358	255
1967	4	10	0	.286	3	237	285
1968	1	12	1	.077	5	199	367
1969	4	10	0	.286	4	230	359
1970	3	10	1	.231	4	204	337
1971	1	13	0	.071	5	184	394
1972	4	9	1	.321	4	257	377
1973	9	5	0	.643	2	259	230
1974d	9	5	0	.643	2	264	244
1975	8	6	0	.571	3	420	355
1976	2	12	0	.143	5	245	363
1977	3	11	0	.214	5	160	313
1978	5	11	0	.313	4	302	354
1979	7	9	0	.438	4	268	279
1980e	11	5	0	.688	1	320	260
1981f	10	6	0	.625	3	311	276
1982	4	5	0	.444	9	150	154
1983	8	8	0	.500	3	283	351
1984	2	14	0	.125	5	250	454
1985	2	14	0	.125	5	200	381
26 Years	153	212	8	.421		7,017	8,064

a*AFL Eastern Division Runnerup; 0-1 in Playoffs*
b*AFL Champion; 1-0 in Playoffs*
c*AFL Eastern Division Champion; 0-1 in Playoffs*
d*AFC Wild Card Qualifier for Playoffs; 0-1 in Playoffs*
e*AFC Eastern Division Champion; 0-1 in Playoffs*
f*AFC Wild Card Qualifier for Playoffs; 1-1 in Playoffs*

RECORD HOLDERS

CAREER

Rushing attempts	O. J. Simpson, 1969-77	2,123
Rushing yards	O. J. Simpson, 1969-77	10,183
Pass attempts	Joe Ferguson, 1973-84	4,166
Pass completions	Joe Ferguson, 1973-84	2,188
Passing yards	Joe Ferguson, 1973-84	27,590
Touchdown passes	Joe Ferguson, 1973-84	181
Receptions	Elbert Dubenion, 1960-67	296
Receiving yards	Elbert Dubenion, 1960-67	5,304
Interceptions	George (Butch) Byrd, 1964-70	40
Punting average	Paul Maguire, 1964-70	42.1
Punt return avg.	Keith Moody, 1976-79	10.5
Kickoff return avg.	Wallace Francis, 1973-74	27.2
Field goals	John Leypodt, 1971-76	74
Touchdowns	OJ. Simpson, 1969-77	70
Points	O. J. Simpson, 1969-77	420

SEASON

Rushing attempts	O. J. Simpson, 1973	332
Rushing yards	O. J. Simpson, 1973	2,003
Pass attempts	Joe Ferguson, 1983	508
Pass completions	Joe Ferguson, 1983	281
Passing yards	Joe Ferguson, 1981	3,652
Touchdown passes	Joe Ferguson, 1983	26
Receptions	Frank Lewis, 1981	70
Receiving yards	Frank Lewis, 1981	1,244
Interceptions	Billy Atkins, 1961	10
	Tom Janik, 1967	10

Punting average	Billy Atkins, 1961	44.5
Punt return avg.	Keith Moody, 1977	13.1
Kickoff return avg.	Ed Rutkowski, 1963	30.2
Field goals	Pete Gogolak, 1965	28
Touchdowns	O.J. Simpson, 1975	23
Points	O.J. Simpson, 1975	138
GAME		
Rushing attempts	O.J. Simpson, 10-29-73	39
Rushing yards	O.J. Simpson, 11-25-76	273
Pass attempts	Joe Ferguson, 10-9-83	55
Pass completions	Joe Ferguson, 10-9-83	38
Passing yards	Joe Ferguson, 10-9-83	419
Touchdown passes	Joe Ferguson, 9-23-79	5
	Joe Ferguson, 10-9-83	5
Receptions	Greg Bell, 9-8-85	13
Receiving yards	Jerry Butler, 9-23-79	255
Interceptions	7 times	3
Field goals	Pete Gogolak, 12-5-65	5
Touchdowns	Cookie Gilchrist, 12-8-63	5
Points	Cookie Gilchrist, 12-8-63	30

COACHING HISTORY

1960-61	Garrard (Buster) Ramsey	11-16-1
1962-65	Lou Saban	38-18-3
1966-68	Joe Collier*	13-17-1
1968	Harvey Johnson	1-10-1
1969-70	John Rauch	7-20-1
1971	Harvey Johnson	1-13-0
1972-76	Lou Saban**	32-29-1
1976-77	Jim Ringo	3-20-0
1978-82	Chuck Knox	38-38-0
1983-85	Kay Stephenson***	10-26-0
1985	Hank Bullough	2-10-0

**Replaced after two games in 1968*
***Resigned after five games in 1976*
****Replaced after four games in 1985*

FIRST PLAYER SELECTED

1960	Richie Lucas, QB, Penn State
1961	Ken Rice, T, Auburn
1962	Ernie Davis, HB, Syracuse
1963	Dave Behrman, C, Michigan State
1964	Carl Eller, T, Minnesota
1965	Jim Davidson, T, Ohio State
1965†	Ken Ambrusko, HB, Maryland
1966	Mike Dennis, HB, Mississippi
1966†	Jack Gregory, E, Tennessee-Chattanooga
1967	John Pitts, S, Arizona State
1968	Haven Moses, SE, San Diego State
1969	O.J. Simpson, RB, USC
1970	Al Cowlings, DE, USC
1971	J.D. Hill, WR, Arizona State
1972	Walt Patulski, DE, Notre Dame
1973	Paul Seymour, T, Michigan
1974	Reuben Gant, TE, Oklahoma State
1975	Tom Ruud, LB, Nebraska
1976	Mario Clark, DB, Oregon
1977	(2) Phil Dokes, DT, Oklahoma State
1978	Terry Miller, RB, Oklahoma State
1979	Tom Cousineau, LB, Ohio State
1980	Jim Ritcher, C, North Carolina State
1981	Booker Moore, RB, Penn State
1982	Perry Tuttle, WR, Clemson
1983	Tony Hunter, TE, Notre Dame
1984	Greg Bell, RB, Notre Dame
1984*	Dwight Drane, DB, Oklahoma
1985	Bruce Smith, DE, Virginia Tech
1986	Ronnie Harmon, RB, Iowa

†Redshirt Draft
**Supplemental Draft*

BILLS SILVER ANNIVERSARY TEAM (1984)

OFFENSE		
WR	Bob Chandler	1971-79
WR	Elbert Dubenion	1960-68
TE	Ernie Warlick	1962-65
T	Joe Devlin	1976-82, 1984
T	Stew Barber	1961-69
G	Billy Shaw	1961-69
G	Reggie McKenzie	1972-82
C	Al Bemiller	1961-69
QB	Jack Kemp	1962-69
RB	O.J. Simpson	1969-77
RB	Cookie Gilchrist	1962-64
DEFENSE		
DE	Ron McDole	1963-70
DE	Ben Williams	1976-85
DT	Tom Sestak	1962-68
DT	Fred Smerlas	1979-85
LB	Mike Stratton	1962-72
LB	John Tracey	1962-67
LB	Jim Haslett	1979-85
CB	Robert James	1969-74
CB	George (Butch) Byrd	1964-70
S	George Saimes	1963-69
S	Steve Freeman	1975-85
SPECIALISTS		
P	Paul Maguire	1964-70
K	Pete Gogolak	1964-65

CHICAGO BEARS

1920 A. E. Staley, who owned the A. E. Staley Manufacturing Company in Decatur, Illinois, hired 25-year-old George Halas to work in his plant, play on his semipro baseball team, and organize a company football team. Staley promised Halas enough of a budget to attract top ballplayers, and he also agreed to let them practice on company time. Halas signed end Guy Chamberlin, halfback Jimmy Conzelman, halfback Ed (Dutch) Sternaman, center George Trafton, and quarterback Chuck Dressen. Halas himself played end and served as coach. Halas contacted Ralph Hay about playing the Canton Bulldogs, whom Hay managed. Hay told Halas of a plan to organize professional football in the Ohio-Illinois area, and invited him to a meeting on the subject. The meeting, which was the second organizational meeting of the American Pro Football Association, was attended by representatives of 10 teams, including Halas and Morgan O'Brien representing Staley's interests, September 17. The loosely organized league began play on September 26, and the next week, on October 3, the Staleys played their first game. A crowd of 1,500 watched as the Staleys defeated the non-APFA Moline Tractors 20-0 at Staley Field. Sternaman scored three touchdowns and Hugh Blacklock kicked two extra points. Unlike most teams, the Staleys didn't run the Single Wing, but lined up in the T-formation, which Halas had learned under Bob Zuppke at Illinois. After defeating the Kewanee Walworths, the Staleys played their first game against an APFA team, the Rock Island Independents, on October 17. Conzelman ran 43 yards for a touchdown, Blacklock added the extra point, and the Staleys won 7-0. The Staleys' first loss came on November 28, when Len Sachs of the Chicago Cardinals returned a fumble for a touchdown, Paddy Driscoll added the extra point, and the Cardinals held on for a 7-6 victory. The next week the Staleys avenged that loss with a 10-0 victory over the Cardinals. Needing a win over the Akron Pros in the last game of the year to gain the APFA championship, Halas hired Driscoll from the Cardinals for one game. Nevertheless, the Staleys managed only a 0-0 tie and finished the season with a 10-1-2 record. Akron was awarded the championship. Each member of the squad received $1,900 for his season's work.

1921 A business recession prompted Staley to withdraw the sponsorship of his football team. However, he suggested Halas take over the team and relocate it in Chicago. Halas accepted the offer and, for $5,000, agreed to call the team the Chicago Staleys for one year. Halas made Sternaman half owner of the team in order to cut his risks in half and avoid paying one more salary. Halas and Sternaman signed a lease with William Veeck, Sr., owner of the Chicago Cubs, to play at Cubs Park in exchange for 15 percent of each game's gross. They signed Chamberlin, Trafton, and Blacklock from the old Decatur team. The APFA race came down to the Staleys and the Buffalo All-Americans. On Thanksgiving Day, Buffalo beat the Staleys 7-6, but Halas's team won a rematch on December 4, 10-7. The All-Americans, who finished 9-1-2, claimed that the second game was merely an exhibition, noted that one of the Staleys' victories had been against a non-association team, and argued they had won the championship. Halas argued that the Staleys were 9-1-1 even without their 35-0 opening-day victory over independent Waukegan. NFL President Joe Carr ruled in favor of the Staleys, giving Halas his first championship.

1922 At the league meeting in June, Halas was responsible for two names officially being changed. The first was the renaming of the APFA the National Football League. The second, done in order to link his team in the public mind with the successful Cubs, was the changing of the Staleys to the Chicago Bears. Chamberlin left the Bears for Canton, where he became player-coach of the Bulldogs. His team defeated the Bears 7-6. The Bears later lost two games to the Cardinals, 6-0 and 9-0, in which all of the points were scored on dropkicks by Driscoll. The Bears finished second behind undefeated Canton with a 9-3 record. On November 27, Halas engineered the Bears' first player deal, paying the Rock Island Independents $100 for tackle Ed Healey.

1923 The Bears dropped two decisions in their first four games, including a 6-0 loss to Canton, and couldn't catch up with the Bulldogs, who finished 11-0-1 to the Bears' 9-2-1. Midway through the season, Sternaman's younger brother Joey, a quarterback, joined the team. On November 4, in a game against the Oorang Indians, Jim Thorpe fumbled at the Bears' 2, and Halas scooped up the ball and raced 98 yards for a touchdown. The return yardage remained a record until 1972.

1924 The Bears lost their first game of the season, 5-0 to Green Bay on September 21. However, the game didn't count in the league standings because it was played before the start of the official league season, which at the league meeting had been scheduled to run from September 27 to November 30. The first two official games were a scoreless tie with Rock Island and a 16-14 loss to the new Cleveland Bulldogs. Although the Bears didn't lose again the rest of the season, finishing at 6-1-4, they could manage only second place behind the Bulldogs, who went 7-1-1. After the end of the season, the Bears again played the Bulldogs, winning 23-0. Halas insisted that both teams had agreed that the game was to be played for the championship. But, ruling that the clubs didn't have the right to schedule games without league permission, Carr declared Cleveland the champion.

1925 Halas signed Red Grange, who had finished his collegiate career at Illinois one day earlier, November 22. In return for a significant share of the gate, Grange, through his agent, C.C. Pyle, agreed to play the rest of the season with the Bears. That proved to be 19 games: the two already-scheduled league games and a 17-game barnstorming tour that included five league teams (which could be scheduled through December 20) and 12 independent or all-star teams. On November 26, 36,000 people showed up for Grange's first game, but he gained only 40 yards in a 0-0 tie with the Cardinals. Nonetheless, Grange proved he was the first strong gate attraction in the NFL. More than 73,000 New Yorkers watched as Grange and the Bears defeated the Giants at the Polo Grounds 19-7, December 6. The Bears played the Los Angeles Tigers before 75,000 at the Los Angeles Coliseum, January 16. The Bears beat the Washington All-Stars in Seattle 34-0, to end the tour, January 31. The tour netted Pyle and Grange $100,000 each. The Bears had a 12-5 record on the tour. They finished the NFL season 9-5-3.

1926 Cubs Park was renamed Wrigley Field. Pyle asked the Bears for a five-figure salary and one-third ownership of the Bears for Grange. Halas refused, and Grange and Pyle started the American Football League, putting Grange with the New York Yankees. That left the Bears without a running star or a drawing card. The problem was solved when Halas acquired Paddy Driscoll from the financially depressed Cardinals for $3,500. Driscoll proved worth it, leading the NFL with 86 points. The Bears also obtained tackle Roy (Link) Lyman from Frankford. The Bears, the Pottsville Maroons, and the Frankford Yellow Jackets all fought for the league championship. The Bears were in contention until late in the season, when they played Frankford. Guy Chamberlin blocked Driscoll's extra-point attempt to give his team a 7-6 win. Frankford ended the season with a 14-1-1 record. The Bears were second at 12-1-3.

1927 The Bears started off 5-0, but lost three out of five games in midseason to drop out of the running for the championship. When the eventual champion Giants beat the Bears 13-7 on November 27, Joe Guyon knocked Halas out of the game with broken ribs. The Bears finished 9-3-2 and in third place.

1928 Friction between Halas and Dutch Sternaman over who was going to run the offense caused some problems, but not as many as the Packers and Lions caused. After an early-season tie in Green Bay, the Packers beat the Bears twice in Chicago. The Lions also knocked off the Bears twice. The Bears' 7-5-1 record was good for fifth in the league.

1929 Grange came out of retirement to play for the Bears. A knee injury affected his once peerless maneuverability, but he still was a sound all-purpose back. The Bears started off 4-1-1, but lost eight and tied one of their last nine games, finishing 4-9-2 for their first losing record. They were shut out three times during the season by the Packers, six times overall. The low point of the season was a 40-6 loss to the Cardinals on Thanksgiving Day, when Ernie Nevers scored six touchdowns and four extra points for all 40 points.

1930 Halas stepped down as coach and retired as a player. He and Sternaman compromised their disagreements by hiring former Illinois assistant Ralph Jones, who was the head coach at Lake Forest Academy. Jones promised Halas and Sternaman a championship in three years. He changed the Bears' T-formation. He moved the ends wide, spaced the halfbacks wider, and made one of the halfbacks a man-in-motion. This spiced up the plodding T-formation. Driscoll retired, and Trafton was not invited back. Trafton ignored the message, however. He reported and won back the center's job. The Bears signed 6-foot 2-inch, 230-pound fullback Bronko Nagurski from Minnesota. Carl Brumbaugh, a rookie from Florida, became the Bears' quarterback. Right after the completion of the college season, Halas signed Notre Dame fullback Joe Savoldi. President Carr fined the Bears $1,000 for signing a collegian before his class had graduated. Ironically, Savoldi lasted only four games; the competition with Nagurski was too great. The Bears won their last five games to finish third at 9-4-1.

1931 Jones continued to build toward a championship team by signing versatile halfback Keith Molesworth. The Bears lost their second game of the year to the Packers and then lost back-to-back games to Frankford and Green Bay to drop to 3-3. They could never get back into the championship race, although they did defeat the champion Packers 7-6 in the next-to-last game of the season. The Bears finished third at 8-5, and Grange was the only member of the team to make the NFL's first official all-league team.

1932 The Bears signed end Bill Hewitt from Michigan. A veteran from the 1929 club, Joe Kopcha, returned from retirement to play guard. The Bears started off slowly, with three scoreless ties and a 2-0 loss to Green Bay in the first four games. But they didn't lose the rest of the season. In the last game of the season, the Bears beat the Packers 9-0 on a 14-yard field goal by Paul (Tiny) Engebretsen and a 56-yard run by Nagurski. That gave Chicago a 6-1-6 record and forced a playoff between the Bears and the Portsmouth Spartans which was held in Chicago, December 18. Bad weather forced Halas to move the game indoors to Chicago Stadium, where the field was only 80 yards long. The Bears won 9-0 when Nagurski threw a touchdown pass to Grange, who was all alone in the end zone. Ralph Jones had kept his promise to deliver a championship within three years. The Bears, however, lost $18,000 for the year. As a result, Sternaman wanted out; he sold his half of the team to Halas for $38,000. Halas had to borrow the money, $5,000 from Charles Bidwill.

1933 The league aligned itself into Eastern and Western divisions; the Bears were named one of the five Western teams. Jones resigned as coach. Halas returned to the sidelines as his replacement. The Bears had their first out-of-town training camp, at Notre Dame. Three promising rookies joined the club—fullback-kicker Jack Manders, 260-pound tackle George Musso, and end Bill Karr. Despite two losses and a tie in a three-week stretch in midseason, the Bears won the Western Division with a 10-2-1 record. In the NFL Championship Game, 26,000 people watched at Wrigley Field as Manders kicked three field goals and two extra points, and the Bears defeated the Giants 23-21. The winning points were scored when Nagurski lobbed a short pass to Hewitt, who lateraled to Karr, who scored.

1934 The Bears held training camp at Lane Tech High School in Chicago. They played the best college players in the first Chicago College All-Star Game, before 79,432 at Soldier Field, August 31. The game ended in a scoreless tie. Chicago signed rookie halfback Beattie Feathers of Tennessee. The Bears won all 13 league contests. Feathers became the first pro back to gain 1,000 yards, totaling 1,004 yards. He also set an NFL record by averaging 9.94 yards per carry. Manders led the league in scoring with 79 points. The Bears met the Giants at the Polo Grounds for the NFL championship. The day was cold, and the field was frozen. The Bears led 13-3 after three quarters. But some of the Giants' players switched to tennis shoes and gained better traction. New York scored 27 points in the final period and won 30-13. The Bears dominated the all-pro selections, with Feathers, Nagurski, Hewitt, and Kopcha. Grange, a reserve during the season, retired.

1935 The Bears switched their training camp to St. John's Military Academy in Delafield, Wisconsin. Brumbaugh and Lyman retired before the season. Nagurski was out most of the year with a hip injury. Feathers was hurt off and on all season. The Bears struggled to a 6-4-2 record that included two losses and two ties in a four-week period.

1936 The NFL held its first draft of college seniors. On the advice of West Virginians Karr and Brumbaugh, Halas took lineman Joe Stydahar from that school on the first round. He also picked halfback Ray Nolting in a later round. On the ninth round, he chose guard Dan Fortmann. The Bears obtained the rights from Philadelphia for the NFL's very first draft pick, Jay Berwanger, but the University of Chicago star chose not to play pro football. Stydahar and Fortmann became starters. Nagurski came back strong from his injuries. Manders led the league in field goals for the third year. The Bears opened with a 30-3 win over Green Bay. Halas's team won five more before losing a rematch to the Packers 21-10. With two weeks left, both teams were 9-1, but the Bears lost their last two to finish 9-3 to Green Bay's 10-1-1.

1937 The Bears defeated the Packers 14-2 in the opener on their way to a 5-0 record. A tie with the Giants and a 24-14 loss to Green Bay brought back memories of the previous season's collapse. The Bears cut short any negative thoughts, winning their last four for a 9-1-1 record and the Western Division title. Manders again led the league in scoring. In the NFL Championship Game, the Bears lost 28-21 to Washington as Sammy Baugh passed for 347 yards. Each Chicago player received $127.78 as his share of the championship game purse. At the end of the season, Nagurski retired.

1938 Feathers was traded to Brooklyn, and Molesworth quit to coach at the U.S. Naval Academy. At mid-year, Halas purchased fullback Joe Maniaci from Brooklyn. After a 4-1 start, the Bears lost three in a row and finished in third place at 6-5. Despite a split with the champion Packers, the Bears lost twice each to second-place Detroit and fourth-place Cleveland. Their main weakness was in ball-handling, as they fumbled 56 times.

1939 The Bears' T-formation was growing more complex each year. New plays were drawn for it constantly by Halas and voluntary assistant Clark Shaughnessy, head coach of the University of Chicago. The offense acquired a complicated play-calling system. It also put emphasis on a quarterback who was a good ball handler. The Bears found their man when they drafted Sid Luckman, a Single-Wing tailback from Columbia. Luckman learned the formation slowly, but by the end of the season he had taken over the starting job. Also a starter as a rookie was fullback Bill Osmanski, who led the league in rushing with 699 yards. The Bears moved up to second in the Western Division with an 8-3 record.

1940 The Bears obtained Duke halfback George McAfee, who had been drafted by the Philadelphia Eagles in the first round, in exchange for three players. The Bears also drafted center Clyde (Bulldog) Turner, tackle Lee Artoe, tackle Ed Kolman, end Ken Kavanaugh, and halfback Ray (Scooter) McLean. McAfee ran 93 yards for a touchdown against the Green Bay Packers on the first kickoff he fielded in league competition, and the Bears went on to a 41-10 victory in the opener. With the league's leading rushing attack, the Bears won the Western Division with an 8-3 record. The Bears faced the Redskins in Washington, D.C., for the NFL championship, December 8. Ten different Bears scored touchdowns as Chicago smashed Washington 73-0. Chicago's defense intercepted eight passes and allowed only 22 yards rushing. The Bears got $873 per man as their championship share.

1941 The Bears drafted backs Norm Standlee and Hugh Gallarneau from Stanford's 1940 Rose Bowl team. They alternated with Osmanski and McAfee in a backfield that led the league in both rushing and passing. McAfee led the league in average yards per carry at 7.3. The Bears averaged more than 36 points a game on their way to tying Green Bay for the Western Division title. Both teams had 10-1-0 records, with the Bears having beaten the Packers 25-17 and the Packers having returned the favor 16-14. The two teams met in a playoff at Wrigley Field, before 43,425, December 14. Gallarneau returned a punt 81 yards for a touchdown in the first quarter, and the Bears went on to win 33-14. A crowd of 13,341 showed up at Wrigley Field to watch the Bears play the Giants for the NFL championship, December 21. Standlee scored two touchdowns and McAfee and Kavanaugh one each as the Bears won 37-9.

1942 McAfee, Standlee, Osmanski, Maniaci, Stydahar, Kavanaugh, and end Dick Plasman each missed at least part of the season while serving in the Armed Forces. With the top three fullbacks gone, Halas simply plugged in his fourth stringer, Gary Famiglietti, who led the team with 503 yards rushing and the league with eight touchdowns on the ground. After a 44-28 victory over Green Bay in the opener, the Bears weren't really tested again, finishing the season 11-0 and tops in the league in offense and defense. Even the loss of Halas, who joined the Navy on November 1, didn't matter, as assistants Hunk Anderson and Luke Johnsos kept the team winning. The Bears' winning streak came to an end in the NFL Championship Game, when Sammy Baugh and Andy Farkas led Washington to a 14-6 victory.

1943 Nagurski, 35, came out of retirement to play tackle for the Bears. Luckman became the first professional quarterback to pass for more than 400 yards in a game when he threw for 433 yards and seven touchdowns in a 56-7 win over the New York Giants, November 14. Needing a win over the Cardinals in the season finale to clinch the division title, the Bears trailed 24-14 at the end of three quarters. The coaches put Nagurski in at fullback, and he ran for 84 yards on 16 carries to lead the Bears to a 35-24 victory. In the NFL Championship Game, Luckman threw five touchdown passes and Nagurski scored his last touchdown as the Bears beat Washington 41-21. Nagurski then retired for the second and last time.

1944 Chicago set up training facilities at St. Joseph's College in Rensselaer, Indiana. Luckman was called into the Merchant Marine and was available to the team only on weekends. His understudy was 35-year-old Gene Ronzani. The Bears lost their first two games, to Green Bay and Cleveland, and never caught the Packers. They finished second with a 6-3-1 record. The individual highlight of the season came in a game against Card-Pitt. Several players were ejected for fighting, forcing all-pro center Turner to play fullback. The only time he carried the ball, Turner ran 48 yards for a touchdown.

1945 The war-depleted Bears lost seven of their first eight games. Halas came back from the Navy, November 22. Kavanaugh, Stydahar, McAfee, and Gallarneau all came back before the season ended. McAfee returned for the next-to-the-last game of the season. He made Halas promise to use him sparingly. Halas put him in for only 12 minutes, and in that time McAfee scored three touchdowns. The Bears won their last two games and finished fourth at 3-7. Luckman tied with Baugh for the NFL passing title.

1946 With the return of most of their pre-war team from the service, and with Halas as head coach for the full season, the Bears jumped right back to the top of the league. They won the Western Division by two games with an 8-2-1 record. In the championship game in New York, the Bears defeated the Giants 24-14. Luckman ran a quarterback keeper 19 yards for a fourth-quarter touchdown that broke a 14-14 tie.

1947 The Bears lost their first two games, including one to the crosstown rival Cardinals 31-7. But they won eight of their next nine and went into the season finale against the Cardinals tied with them at 8-3. The Cardinals scored on the first play of the game and went on to win 30-21. Despite a sluggish running attack, Luckman passed for 2,712 yards, Jim Keane led the league in receiving with 64 catches, and Kavanaugh led with 13 touchdown receptions.

1948 The Bears drafted quarterbacks Bobby Layne of Texas and Johnny Lujack of Notre Dame, and tackle George Connor, also of Notre Dame. The Bears beat the Cardinals 28-17 in the second game of the season, but a 12-7 loss to Philadelphia three weeks later dropped them back into a tie with the Cardinals. With both teams 10-1 going into their season-ending clash, the Cardinals won 24-21.

1949 Just before the season started, Halas sold Layne to the New York Bulldogs. Luckman contracted a thyroid condition that kept him out most of the season, and Lujack became the starting quarterback. Lujack didn't miss a beat, leading the NFL in attempts (312), completions (162), yards (2,658), and touchdowns (23). He also set an NFL record with 468 yards passing in a 52-21 victory over the Cardinals, in which he threw six touchdown passes. The Bears finished at 9-3, but lost the Western Division title to the 8-2-2 Los Angeles Rams on percentage points. The Rams had beaten the Bears both times they played during the season.

1950 The Bears became one of seven teams in the new National Conference. Lujack hurt his arm and his passing dropped off, but his outstanding running helped the Bears tie the Rams for the conference title at 9-3. The two teams played off in the Los Angeles Memorial Coliseum with the Rams' Tom Fears catching three touchdown passes in Los Angeles's 24-14 victory over Chicago, December 17.

1951 Luckman, McAfee, and Kavanaugh all retired. With Lujack's arm never having come all the way back, a weak passing game was offset by the league's best running attack, led by John Dottley and George Gulyanics. Despite a late-season slump, the Bears still had a chance to win the conference in the last game of the year, but the Cardinals beat them, dropping the Bears to fourth place.

1952 The Bears drafted end Bill McColl and linebacker Bill George. Lujack retired, and the Bears tried unsuccessfully to replace him, as three youngsters—George Blanda, Bob Williams, and Steve Romanik—were given a chance. With no passing game, the Bears' opponents could concentrate on stopping the running attack, and the Bears' offense ground to a halt. They didn't win more than one game in a row all year and finished with a 5-7 record.

1953 Turner, the last of the 1940-41 championship players, retired. Blanda led the league in attempts (362) and completions (169), but the offense couldn't generate many points, while the defense was the second-poorest in the league. The highlight of the 3-8-1 season was a 24-21 victory that knocked the Rams out of the playoffs.

1954 The Bears selected four immediate contributors in the draft—quarterback Zeke Bratkowski, end Harlon Hill, tackle Stan Jones, and center Larry Strickland. Bratkowski alternated with Blanda at quarterback, and between them they threw for more than 3,000 yards. Hill gained 1,124 yards on 45 receptions and led the league with 12 touchdown catches. George Connor was lost for the year with an injury. The Bears won their last four games to finish 8-4, and ended the season with a 28-24 victory over the Western champion Lions.

1955 Halas announced he would retire in favor of a younger coach after the 1955 season. Rookie backs Rick Casares and Bobby Watkins became starters. Both averaged more than five yards a carry. Bratkowski went into the service, and second-year quarterback Ed Brown took over the position. Hill caught 42 passes. The Bears lost their first three games, then won six in a row, including two over the Rams, before suffering a 53-14 upset by the Cardinals. The Bears won their last two, but finished 8-4, a half game behind the Rams (8-3-1).

1956 True to his promise, Halas gave way to a younger man. Long-time assistant Paddy Driscoll, who was two years younger than Halas, became the new head coach. Connor retired. The Bears lost their first game to Baltimore 28-21, then won or tied the next eight. In a rematch with the Colts, Chicago won 58-27. In the tenth game, the Bears lost 42-10 to Detroit. Going into the final game, again against Detroit, the Bears were 8-2-1, while the Lions were 9-2. Chicago won the rematch 38-21 and with it the National Conference title. The leader of the top ground game in the NFL was Casares, who led the league with 1,126 yards. At the same time, Brown led the league in passing. Hill ended the year with 47 catches for 1,128 yards. The NFL Championship Game was played on an icy field in Yankee Stadium. The Giants won 47-7.

1957 The Bears were supposed to be even better, with Bratkowski back from the service and rookie Willie Galimore paired with Casares. But the team lost its first three games of the year and never recovered on the way to a 5-7 record. The slumping offense was the problem; the defense gave up fewer points than in 1956.

1958 Halas returned as head coach. The Bears were in the title race most of the year. Eventual winner Baltimore beat them twice, and their only other losses were to Los Angeles and Pittsburgh. The Bears and Rams drew 90,833 to a game in the Los Angeles Memorial Coliseum. Chicago finished second, one game behind the Colts at 8-4.

1959 Chicago lost four of its first five games, then won seven in a row. On the last Sunday of the season, the Bears were tied with San Francisco for second place at 7-4. Baltimore was on top with an 8-3 record. San Francisco lost to Green Bay 36-14, and Chicago beat Detroit 25-14. But Baltimore beat the Rams 45-26 to clinch the Western Conference title.

1960 The Bears were one-half game out of first place in mid-November with a 5-3-1 record. But they lost to the Packers 41-13, the Browns 42-0, and the Lions 36-0. They finished fifth with a 5-6-1 record. It was only the sixth time the Bears had finished under .500 since 1920.

1961 In the first round of the draft, Chicago picked tight end Mike Ditka from Pittsburgh. Halas obtained veteran quarterback Bill Wade from the Rams. The Bears' defense continued to be potent; on October 22, it dismantled the 49ers' Shotgun offense 31-0. The offense also came back to life, as Galimore ran for 707 yards, Wade threw for 2,258 yards and 22 touchdowns, and Ditka caught 56 passes for 1,076 yards and 12 touchdowns. The Bears were in contention until a 31-28 loss to Green Bay, November 12. They finished with an 8-6 record.

1962 Injuries sidelined Casares and Galimore. Ronnie Bull won rookie-of-the-year honors at halfback. Wade set two team records by passing for 3,172 yards and by completing 225 passes. Ditka and fifth-year receiver Johnny Morris caught 58 passes each. Chicago had a 9-5 record, third-best in the Western Conference behind Green Bay (13-1) and Detroit (11-3). Although the Bears were blown out 49-0 and 38-7 by Green Bay, they beat Baltimore 35-15 and 57-0.

1963 Assistant coach George Allen installed a zone defense, and suddenly the Bears had the strongest defense in the NFL. Chicago won its first five games before losing to San Francisco. The Bears defeated Green Bay twice, 10-3 and 26-7. Chicago won the Western Conference with an 11-1-2 record, one-half game ahead of the Packers, 11-2-1. The Bears' defense allowed an average of only 10.3 points a game. The offense was led by Wade, who threw for 2,301 yards, and Ditka, who caught 59 passes. The NFL Championship Game with the Giants was played in eight-degree weather before 45,801 at Wrigley Field. The Bears intercepted five passes by Y.A. Tittle, Wade scored two touchdowns, and the Bears won 14-10. The winning share was $5,899 a player. It was Chicago's first NFL championship since 1946.

1964 Galimore and end John Farrington were killed in an automobile accident during training camp. Injuries to ends Doug Atkins and Ed O'Bradovich and linebacker Bill George handicapped the Bears' defense, and, with a sluggish offense, the team collapsed. One of the early-season embarrassments was a 52-0 loss to Baltimore. Wade and Rudy Bukich shared the quarterback position, and the lack of runners turned the offense almost entirely to a passing game. Morris set an NFL record with 93 receptions for 1,200 yards, while Ditka finished second in the league with 75 catches. The Bears finished 5-9.

1965 Linebacker Dick Butkus of Illinois and halfback Gale Sayers of Kansas were drafted on the first round. Butkus revitalized the defense and Sayers the offense. Sayers scored six touchdowns against the 49ers in a 61-20 Chicago win that avenged an earlier 52-24 loss to San Francisco. The Bears finished third in the Western Conference with a 9-5 record. Sayers set an NFL record with 22 touchdowns, while leading the league in scoring and finishing second in rushing, punt returns, and kickoff returns.

1966 Allen left to become head coach of the Rams,

but not until Halas had gone to court to keep him in Chicago. Morris was out for most of the year with an injured knee, and Ditka dropped to 32 receptions. Sayers had another record-setting year, gaining a combined 2,440 yards. He led the NFL in rushing with 1,231 yards, caught 34 passes, and led the league in kickoff returns. Chicago finished fifth with a 5-7-2 record.

1967 The Bears were aligned in the new Central Division of the Western Conference. Ditka was traded to Philadelphia for quarterback Jack Concannon, who became the starter. But the story once again was Butkus on defense and Sayers on offense. Despite being slowed with injuries, Sayers finished third in the NFL with 880 yards rushing and was second in kickoff returns, including returning three for touchdowns. After a slow start, the Bears went 5-1-1 to finish 7-6-1 and in second place.

1968 Halas, 73, retired as head coach of the Bears, May 27. After 40 seasons of pro coaching, his record was 325 wins, 151 defeats, and 31 ties. Jim Dooley, a player or coach with the Bears since 1952, was named head coach, May 28. The Bears lost their first two games before beating the Vikings. In the Minnesota game, Concannon fractured a collarbone, and his backup, Rudy Bukich, separated a shoulder. Virgil Carter, third-string quarterback, led the Bears to four straight wins at mid-year. The last game of the four was against San Francisco. In it, 49ers defensive back Kermit Alexander tackled Sayers low, and the impact tore ligaments and cartilage in Sayers's right knee, putting him out for the year. Carter broke his ankle a week later, against Atlanta. The Bears lost three of their last five games and finished second behind the Vikings at 7-7. Despite the injury, Sayers finished fifth in the NFL with 856 yards and a league-leading 6.2-yard average.

1969 Sayers came back from knee surgery to lead the league in rushing with 1,032 yards, and Butkus again was all-pro, but the Bears didn't offer much else. Concannon, Carter, and rookie Bobby Douglass alternated at quarterback for a team with the poorest passing attack in the NFL. The team also rated twelfth in scoring defense. The result of this combined failure was a 1-13 record.

1970 Halas, 75, was elected president of the National Football Conference, March 19. Running back Brian Piccolo, 26, died of cancer, June 16. Sayers hurt his right knee in preseason and missed most of the year. Ross Montgomery led the team in rushing with only 229 yards. The result was a strong emphasis on the passing game, which saw Dick Gordon lead the league with 71 receptions for 1,026 yards and 13 touchdowns. Douglass replaced Concannon and threw four touchdown passes against the Bills in his first start. But, late in the game, Douglass broke his wrist and was out for the rest of the season. The most exciting player on the team was rookie Cecil Turner, who tied an NFL record with four kickoff returns for touchdowns. The Bears finished third with a 6-8 record, but whipped Green Bay 35-17 in their last game in Wrigley Field, December 13.

1971 The Bears moved into Soldier Field. Chicago won five out of its first seven games. Then both the first- and second-string quarterbacks, Kent Nix and Concannon, got hurt. Douglass took over, but the Bears lost six of the last seven games. A bad knee kept Sayers immobilized most of the year. Butkus was again all-pro. Dooley, whose four-year record was 20-36, was dismissed as coach.

1972 Abe Gibron, an assistant coach since 1965, was named head coach, January 27. Sayers retired before the season began. Douglass was given the starting quarterback spot. He completed only 38 percent of his passes, last in the NFL in that category, but he gained a quarterback-rushing record of 968 yards. The Bears led the NFC in rushing yardage, but were last in passing. Chicago played .500 football the first half of the season, then dropped six of its last seven games to finish last in the NFC Central at 4-9-1.

1973 The Bears drafted defensive tackle Wally Chambers on the first round. Gibron kept Douglass at quarterback until midseason; rookie Gary Huff from Florida State was given the job, November 18. Huff threw four interceptions in his debut as the Lions beat the Bears 30-7. With the NFL's poorest offense, the Bears finished last again in the NFC Central at 3-11-0. After the season, Butkus retired.

1974 Halas named Jim Finks executive vice president, general manager, and chief operating officer. The Bears finished last for the third year in a row with a 4-10 record. The Bears finished twenty-sixth in offense as neither Douglass nor Huff could generate any consistent attack. Although the defense wasn't bad, the Bears were outscored by 127 points. After the last game, Abe Gibron, who compiled a three-year record of 11-30-1, was fired. Jack Pardee, former NFL linebacker, was named head coach.

1975 Chicago took Walter Payton, a running back from Jackson State, on the first round of the draft. The Bears opened their new training facility at Lake Forest Academy in Lake Forest, Illinois, May 1. A 26-yard field goal by Bob Thomas gave Pardee his first NFL coaching victory, 15-13 over Philadelphia, September 28. After Douglass was waived and Huff was unsuccessful, Bob Avellini, a rookie from Maryland, became the starter. Payton gained a combined total of 300 yards in a 42-17 victory over the Saints, December 21. For the season, he had 679 yards rushing and led the NFL in kickoff returns, but the Bears' defense allowed 379 points, most in the NFC. Chicago waived, traded, or released 76 players under contract in 1975. Chicago ended the season at 4-10, its seventh consecutive losing year.

1976 The Bears sprang back to 7-7 and second place, and Pardee was named coach of the year. Pardee's top weapon was Payton, who led the NFC in rushing with 1,390 yards and 13 touchdowns. Young Roland Harper added 625 yards, and Avellini showed flashes of brilliance. The Bears defeated two playoff teams —Minnesota and Washington—and lost by one point to Minnesota and Oakland. The secondary had two young members, Doug Plank and Gary Fencik.

1977 Quarterback Mike Phipps was obtained from Cleveland shortly before the season started. Payton got the Bears off to a fast start with 160 yards rushing in a season-opening 30-20 victory over Detroit, but the team stumbled to 3-5. The Bears appeared to be in total disarray following a 47-0 defeat by Houston, but the season turned around when the Bears overcame a 17-0 deficit to defeat Kansas City 28-27 on November 13. A week later, Payton rushed for 275 yards against Minnesota to establish an NFL single-game rushing record. The Bears carried a five-game winning streak into the final game, needing only a victory over the New York Giants to lock up a wild card spot in the playoffs. Despite bad game conditions, the Bears pulled out that game 12-9 when Bob Thomas kicked a 28-yard field goal with only nine seconds left in overtime. The magic ended on December 26, when the Bears were routed by Dallas 37-7 in the playoffs. Payton finished the season with a league-leading 1,852 yards rushing.

1978 Pardee resigned on January 19 to accept the head-coaching position with Washington. Neill Armstrong, the Vikings' defensive coordinator, replaced Pardee on February 16. Chicago opened the season with three victories, but dropped eight games in a row to fall out of playoff contention. After 10 weeks, Phipps replaced Avellini as the starting quarterback. Four victories in the last six games improved the Bears' record to 7-9. On October 12, defensive tackle Alan Page was acquired from the Vikings, and he proceeded to lead the team in sacks with 11½. Payton rushed for 1,395 yards and led the NFC for the third consecutive year.

1979 On September 3, the club moved into Halas Hall, a $1.6-million headquarters on the Lake Forest College campus. The Bears began the season by defeating divisional foes Green Bay and Minnesota. On September 16, they lost to the Cowboys 24-20, despite 134 yards rushing by Payton, who supplanted Rick Casares as the club's all-time rushing leader. A sputtering offense cost the Bears losses in four of the next five games; even more costly was the loss of quarterback Vince Evans for the season with a staph infection after he made only three starts. But Phipps, who replaced Avellini after three games, guided the Bears to seven victories in the last eight games, and they secured a wild card playoff position with a 10-6 record. The euphoria over the season-ending 42-6 rout of St. Louis was tempered by the death of club president George Halas, Jr., from a heart attack. On December 23, the Bears' season ended with a 27-17 loss to Philadelphia in the NFC Wild Card Game, after Chicago led at halftime 17-0. Payton rushed for 1,610 yards to again lead the NFC.

1980 Halas, the chairman of the board, assumed the role of club president. Fully recovered from his illness, Evans became the Bears' starting quarterback after the team began the season with a 2-4 record. Under their new quarterback, the Bears played .500 football and finished the season 7-9, including a 61-7 victory over the Packers on December 7. Payton led the NFC in rushing for the fifth consecutive year, with 1,460 yards. He also led the Bears in receiving and raised his combined yardage total to more than 10,000 yards, breaking Sayers's team record.

1981 The draft produced linebacker Mike Singletary, but the team suffered a blow before the season even started when top wide receiver James Scott signed with the Canadian Football League. The Bears lost six of their first seven games, but on October 25 they upset San Diego 20-17 in overtime. Three consecutive victories at the end of the season produced a final 6-10 record that included a 4-0 mark against AFC West teams. In his first full season as a starter, Evans passed for 2,354 yards. Payton rushed for 1,222 yards and led the Bears with 41 receptions. Second-year player Matt Suhey became the other running back and added 521 yards.

1982 Armstrong was released, January 4. Mike Ditka, a former star tight end and an assistant with Dallas, was named head coach, January 20. In the first round of the draft, the Bears selected BYU All-America quarterback Jim McMahon. The Bears started slowly, losing both games before the strike, but went 3-4 when the season continued. In McMahon's first start, he passed for 233 yards and two touchdowns as the Bears beat Detroit 20-17. On December 26, Payton rushed for 104 yards to become the fourth player in history to gain 10,000 in a career. That same day, Payton gained 102 yards on pass receptions to help the Bears beat the Rams 34-26 despite a 509-yard passing day by Rams quarterback Vince Ferragamo. For the season, Payton finished third in the NFC in rushing, McMahon fourth in passing, and Suhey tied for sixth in receiving.

1983 The Bears had one of their best drafts ever, selecting tackle Jim Covert, wide receiver Willie Gault, defensive backs Mike Richardson and Dave Duerson, and defensive end Richard Dent. Early in the season, Jerry Vainisi was named general manager. On October 31, Halas, the Bears' owner and founder, died. He was succeeded as club president by his grandson, Michael McCaskey. On the field, the Bears got off to a 3-7 start, then made a spirited run at the title, winning five of the last six to finish 8-8. The turning point was a 17-14 victory over Philadelphia in which Walter Payton ran for 131 yards. The next week Payton gained 106 yards to pass O.J. Simpson on the all-time rushing list in a 27-0 victory over Tampa Bay. Payton finished the season with 1,421 yards and 53 receptions, while Suhey had 681 yards.

1984 Chicago's "46" defense came together under defensive coordinator Buddy Ryan, and the Bears suddenly became the best defensive team in the league, finishing first in total and rushing defense and second in passing defense. The keys were a fabulous line, with Dent and tackles Dan Hampton and Steve McMichael, and the NFL's defensive player of the year, Singletary. The Bears won their first three, including a 27-0 whitewash of Denver. On October 7, the Bears beat New Orleans 20-7, with Payton running for 154 yards to break Jim Brown's career rushing record (12,312). On November 4, the bruising defense took charge, sacking Los Angeles Raiders quarterbacks nine times and intercepting three of their passes in a 17-6 victory. McMahon was injured against the Raiders and lost for the season. Steve Fuller guided the team to a 3-3 finish that gave the Bears their first NFC Central title, with a 10-6 record. Fuller threw two touchdown passes and the defense recorded seven sacks as the Bears beat Washington 23-19 in the playoffs. The next week, the season ended with a 23-0 loss to San Francisco in the NFC Championship Game. Payton finished the year with 1,684 yards (13,309 in his career) and also became the Bears' all-time receiving leader.

1985 The best defense in the league was joined by the best rushing attack and the result was the best team in the NFL. The Bears stormed to a 12-0 record before losing to Miami. In the opener, the Bears trailed 21-7 before McMahon passed for two touchdowns and ran for two more for a 38-28 victory over Tampa Bay. Two weeks later, with the Bears trailing Minnesota 17-9 in the third quarter, an injured McMahon came off the bench to throw touchdown bombs on his first two plays and first three possessions, to turn the game into a 33-24 Bears triumph. Against San Francisco, Ditka inserted rookie defensive tackle William (The Refrigerator) Perry into the lineup as a running back. When he did it again the next week against Green Bay in a Monday night game, a national hero was created. The Bears seemed to peak with back-to-back 44-0 and 36-0 victories over Dallas and Atlanta. The next week, Miami upset Chicago 38-24. Three victories to close out the regular season gave the Bears a 15-1 mark that equaled San Francisco's record for most wins in a regular season. Payton finished second in the NFC in rushing, with 1,551 yards to run his career total to a record 14,860. McMahon was second in passing. On defense, Dent, McMichael, and Singletary were named all-pro. The Bears cruised through the playoffs, seemingly more concerned about making video tapes than about opponents. They beat the Giants 21-0 and, in the NFC Championship Game, the Rams 24-0. In Super Bowl XX, they spotted New England a 3-0 lead, then produced six turnovers for a record 46-10 victory.

MEMBERS OF HALL OF FAME:
Doug Atkins, George Blanda, Dick Butkus, Guy Chamberlin, George Connor, Jimmy Conzelman, John (Paddy) Driscoll, Danny Fortmann, Bill George, Red Grange, George Halas, Ed Healey, Bill Hewitt, Walt Kiesling, Bobby Layne, Sid Luckman, Roy (Link) Lyman, George McAfee, George Musso, Bronko Nagurski, Gale Sayers, Joe Stydahar, George Trafton, Clyde (Bulldog) Turner

BEARS RECORD, 1920-85

Year	Won	Lost	Tied	Pct.	Fin.	Pts.	OP
Decatur Staleys							
1920	10	1	2	.909	2	164	21
Chicago Staleys							
1921a	9	1	1	.900	1	128	53
Chicago Bears							
1922	9	3	0	.750	2	123	44
1923	9	2	1	.818	2	123	35
1924	6	1	4	.857	2	122	44
1925	9	5	3	.643	7	158	96
1926	12	1	3	.923	2	216	63
1927	9	3	2	.750	3	149	98
1928	7	5	1	.583	5	175	85
1929	4	9	2	.308	9	119	227
1930	9	4	1	.692	3	169	71
1931	8	5	0	.615	3	145	92
1932b	6	1	6	.857	1	151	44
1933b	10	2	1	.833	1	133	82
1934c	13	0	0	1.000	1	286	86
1935	6	4	2	.600	3t	192	106
1936	9	3	0	.750	2	222	94
1937c	9	1	1	.900	1	201	100
1938	6	5	0	.545	3	194	148
1939	8	3	0	.727	2	298	157
1940b	8	3	0	.727	1	238	152
1941d	10	1	0	.909	1	396	147
1942c	11	0	0	1.000	1	376	84
1943b	8	1	1	.889	1	303	157
1944	6	3	1	.667	2t	258	172
1945	3	7	0	.300	4	192	235
1946b	8	2	1	.800	1	289	193
1947	8	4	0	.667	2	363	241
1948	10	2	0	.833	2	375	151
1949	9	3	0	.750	2	332	218
1950e	9	3	0	.750	2	279	207
1951	7	5	0	.583	4	286	282
1952	5	7	0	.417	5	245	326
1953	3	8	1	.273	4	218	262
1954	8	4	0	.667	2	301	279
1955	8	4	0	.667	2	294	251
1956f	9	2	1	.818	1	363	246
1957	5	7	0	.417	5	203	211
1958	8	4	0	.667	2t	298	230
1959	8	4	0	.667	2	252	196
1960	5	6	1	.455	5	194	299
1961	8	6	0	.571	3t	326	302
1962	9	5	0	.643	3	321	287
1963b	11	1	2	.917	1	301	144
1964	5	9	0	.357	6	260	379
1965	9	5	0	.643	3	409	275
1966	5	7	2	.417	5	234	272
1967	7	6	1	.538	2	239	218
1968	7	7	0	.500	2	250	333
1969	1	13	0	.071	4	210	339
1970	6	8	0	.429	3	256	261
1971	6	8	0	.429	3	185	276
1972	4	9	1	.321	4	225	275
1973	3	11	0	.214	4	195	334
1974	4	10	0	.286	4	152	279
1975	4	10	0	.286	3	191	379
1976	7	7	0	.500	2	253	216
1977g	9	5	0	.643	2	255	253
1978	7	9	0	.438	4	253	274
1979g	10	6	0	.625	2	306	249
1980	7	9	0	.438	3	304	264
1981	6	10	0	.375	5	253	324
1982	3	6	0	.333	12	141	174
1983	8	8	0	.500	3	311	301
1984h	10	6	0	.625	1	325	248
1985i	15	1	0	.938	1	456	198
66 Years	495	321	42	.601		16,134	13,139

aNFL Champion; No Playoffs
bNFL Champion; 1-0 in Playoffs
cNFL Western Division Champion; 0-1 in Playoffs
dNFL Champion; 2-0 in Playoffs
eNFL National Conference Runnerup; 0-1 in Playoffs
fNFL Western Conference Champion; 0-1 in Playoffs
gNFC Wild Card Qualifier for Playoffs; 0-1 in Playoffs
hNFC Central Division Champion; 1-1 in Playoffs
iSuper Bowl Champion; 3-0 in Playoffs

RECORD HOLDERS

CAREER

Rushing attempts	Walter Payton, 1975-85	3,371
Rushing yards	Walter Payton, 1975-85	14,860
Pass attempts	Sid Luckman, 1939-50	1,744
Pass completions	Sid Luckman, 1939-50	904
Passing yards	Sid Luckman, 1939-50	14,686
Touchdown passes	Sid Luckman, 1939-50	137
Receptions	Walter Payton, 1975-85	422
Receiving yards	Johnny Morris, 1958-67	5,059
Interceptions	Richie Petitbon, 1959-68	37
Punting average	George Gulyanics, 1947-52	44.5
Punt return avg.	Ray (Scooter) McLean, 1940-47	14.8
Kickoff return avg.	Gale Sayers, 1965-71	30.6
Field goals	Bob Thomas, 1975-84	128
Touchdowns	Walter Payton, 1975-85	109
Points	Walter Payton, 1975-85	654

SEASON

Rushing attempts	Walter Payton, 1984	381
Rushing yards	Walter Payton, 1977	1,852
Pass attempts	Vince Evans, 1981	436
Pass completions	Bill Wade, 1962	225
Passing yards	Bill Wade, 1962	3,172
Touchdown passes	Sid Luckman, 1943	28
Receptions	Johnny Morris, 1964	93
Receiving yards	Johnny Morris, 1964	1,200
Interceptions	Roosevelt Taylor, 1963	9
Punting average	Bobby Joe Greene, 1963	46.4
Punt return avg.	Harry Clark, 1943	15.8
Kickoff return avg.	Gale Sayers, 1967	37.7
Field goals	Kevin Butler, 1985	31
Touchdowns	Gale Sayers, 1965	22
Points	Kevin Butler, 1985	144

GAME

Rushing attempts	Walter Payton, 11-20-77	40
Rushing yards	Walter Payton, 11-20-77	275
Pass attempts	Bill Wade, 10-25-64	57
Pass completions	Bill Wade, 10-25-64	33
Passing yards	Johnny Lujack, 12-11-49	468
Touchdown passes	Sid Luckman, 11-14-43	7
Receptions	Jim Keane, 10-23-49	14
Receiving yards	Harlon Hill, 10-31-54	214
Interceptions	5 times	3
Field goals	Roger LeClerc, 12-3-61	5
	Mac Percival, 10-20-68	5
Touchdowns	Gale Sayers, 12-12-65	6
Points	Gale Sayers, 12-12-65	36

COACHING HISTORY

1920-29	George Halas	84-31-19
1930-32	Ralph Jones	24-10- 7
1933-42	George Halas*	89-24- 4
1942-45	Hunk Anderson, Luke Johnsos**	23-12- 2
1946-55	George Halas	76-43- 2
1956-57	John (Paddy) Driscoll	14-10- 1
1958-67	George Halas	76-53- 6
1968-71	Jim Dooley	20-36- 0
1972-74	Abe Gibron	11-30- 1
1975-77	Jack Pardee	20-23- 0
1978-81	Neill Armstrong	30-35- 0
1982-85	Mike Ditka	40-22- 0

**Resigned after six games in 1942 to enter U.S. Navy*
***Co-coaches*

FIRST PLAYER SELECTED

1936	Joe Stydahar, T, West Virginia
1937	Les McDonald, E, Nebraska
1938	Joe Gray, HB, Oregon State
1939	Sid Luckman, QB, Columbia
1940	Clyde (Bulldog) Turner, C, Hardin-Simmons
1941	Tom Harmon, HB, Michigan
1942	Frankie Albert, QB, Stanford
1943	Bob Steuber, HB, Missouri
1944	Ray Evans, HB, Kansas
1945	Don Lund, HB, Michigan
1946	Johnny Lujack, QB, Notre Dame
1947	Bob Fenimore, HB, Oklahoma State
1948	Bobby Layne, QB, Texas
1949	Dick Harris, C, Texas
1950	Chuck Hunsinger, HB, Florida
1951	Bob Williams, QB, Notre Dame
1952	Jim Dooley, HB, Miami
1953	Billy Anderson, HB, Compton J.C.
1954	Stan Wallace, HB, Illinois
1955	Ron Drzewiecki, HB, Marquette
1956	Menan (Tex) Schriewer, E, Texas
1957	Earl Leggett, T, LSU
1958	Chuck Howley, G, West Virginia
1959	Don Clark, HB, Ohio State
1960	Roger Davis, G, Syracuse
1961	Mike Ditka, E, Pittsburgh
1962	Ronnie Bull, FB, Baylor
1963	Dave Behrman, C, Michigan State
1964	Dick Evey, DT, Tennessee
1965	Dick Butkus, LB, Illinois
1966	George Rice, DT, LSU
1967	Loyd Phillips, DE, Arkansas
1968	Mike Hull, RB, USC
1969	Rufus Mayes, T, Ohio State
1970	(3) George Farmer, WR, UCLA
1971	Joe Moore, RB, Missouri
1972	Lionel Antoine, T, Southern Illinois
1973	Wally Chambers, DE, Eastern Kentucky
1974	Waymond Bryant, LB, Tennessee State
1975	Walter Payton, RB, Jackson State
1976	Dennis Lick, T, Wisconsin
1977	Ted Albrecht, G, California
1978	(3) Brad Shearer, DT, Texas
1979	Dan Hampton, DT, Arkansas
1980	Otis Wilson, LB, Louisville
1981	Keith Van Horne, T, USC
1982	Jim McMahon, QB, BYU
1983	Jim Covert, T, Pittsburgh
1984	Wilber Marshall, LB, Florida
1984*	None (all picks traded to Cleveland)
1985	William Perry, DT, Clemson
1986	Neal Anderson, RB, Florida

**Supplemental Draft*

CINCINNATI BENGALS

1965 Paul Brown had the urge to get back into football but he wasn't sure where an appropriate site was. His son, Mike, did a study on pro football expansion and recommended Cincinnati as a potential site. On December 14, Brown met with Governor James Rhodes and the two discussed a possible franchise before Cincinnati business and civic leaders.

1966 Fearful the Reds' baseball team would leave town and feeling pressure from local businessmen pushing for a pro football franchise, Cincinnati's City Council approved the construction of Riverfront Stadium, December 15. The stadium was granted a 48-acre downtown site, bounded by Second Street and the Ohio River.

1967 Brown's group was awarded an AFL expansion franchise, September 27. "I feel as if I'm breathing again," Brown said. Brown hired Al LoCasale as director of player personnel. Brown called the team the Bengals, the name of the 1937 Cincinnati AFL franchise. The Bengals acquired their first player, trading two draft choices to Miami for quarterback John Stofa, December 26.

1968 The Bengals selected 40 veteran players in an allocation draft. Brown's AFL rivals were not particularly generous. As UPI reported: "The owners made sure that Brown doesn't start another dynasty too soon [referring to Brown's success with the Cleveland Browns in the All-America Football Conference and then the NFL]." Nevertheless, Brown selected several older veterans who still had a few good years left—tackle Ernie Wright, linebacker Sherrill Headrick, and defensive back Bobby Hunt—and several talented, but relatively untested youngsters—flanker Rod Sherman and defensive lineman Willie Lee Jones. With additional choices in each round of the college draft, the Bengals fared well. The club's first selection was All-America center Bob Johnson of Tennessee. Other quality draftees included running backs Paul Robinson and Warren McVea, defensive backs Jess Phillips and Essex Johnson (each of whom later was moved to running back), linebacker Al Beauchamp, tackle Howard Fest, and, on the twelfth round, tight end Bob Trumpy. The Bengals opened their first training camp at Wilmington (Ohio) College on July 5. Cincinnati lost its first preseason game 38-14 to Kansas City before 21,682 at Nippert Stadium. The Bengals went the entire first half without a first down. Three weeks later, the new team recorded its first victory by defeating the Pittsburgh Steelers 19-3 in a preseason game at Morgantown, West Virginia. The Bengals lost their regular-season opener 29-13 to San Diego. They bounced back to win their first two home games, 24-10 over Denver and 34-23 over Buffalo. Injuries to top quarterbacks Stofa and Dewey Warren sent the Bengals into a seven-game losing streak in midseason, and a 3-11 final record. The brightest light for the team was the play of Robinson, who won the AFL rushing title with 1,023 yards and was named AFL rookie of the year. Trumpy led the team with 37 receptions for 639 yards.

1969 Brown selected quarterback Greg Cook of the University of Cincinnati in the first round of the draft, January 28. The same draft produced middle linebacker Bill Bergey and cornerback Ken Riley. Other AFL teams stopped referring to them as "the Baby Bengals" when they beat Miami 27-21 in the opener, September 14. It was Brown's three-hundredth coaching victory and an impressive debut for Cook, who threw two touchdown passes. The following week, Cook passed for three touchdowns and ran for another as Cincinnati surprised San Diego 34-20. Then the Bengals defeated Kansas City 24-19 to stretch their record to 3-0. However, Cook suffered a serious arm injury when he was hit by linebacker Willie Lanier and sat out the next four games. The Bengals lost all four games. Cook returned to spark a 31-17 win over Oakland and a 31-31 tie with Houston. Against the Oilers, Cook passed for four touchdowns. Brown was named AFL coach of the year. Bergey was honored as AFL defensive rookie of the year. Cook led the league in passing, throwing for 1,854 yards and 15 touchdowns and averaging 9.41 yards per attempt, still the highest figure ever for a rookie quarterback.

1970 The season opened gloomily as Cook's arm went dead at the Wilmington training camp. Brown put Cook on the injured list and enlisted Virgil Carter, a Chicago Bears' and Buffalo Bills' castoff, to play quarterback. On August 8, the Bengals defeated Washington 27-12 in a preseason game to open Riverfront Stadium. The Bengals beat Oakland in the opener 31-21 but lost the next six, falling to last place in the Central Division. Carter ended the skid, throwing three touchdown passes in a 43-14 rout of Buffalo, November 8. The following week, the biggest sports crowd in Cincinnati history (60,007) jammed Riverfront Stadium to watch Brown's Bengals upset his old Cleveland team 14-10. Key players in the win were rookie defensive tackles Mike Reid and Ron Carpenter. The Bengals staged a remarkable comeback, sweeping their last seven games to win the Central Division with an 8-6 record. They clinched their first division title with a 45-7 win over Boston before 60,157 fans at Riverfront, December 20. The inexperienced Bengals were no match for Baltimore in their AFC playoff game as the Colts won 17-0.

1971 The Bengals fared well in the draft, adding quarterback Ken Anderson in the third round. The Bengals looked invincible as they rolled through a 5-0-1 preseason and manhandled Philadelphia 37-14 in the league opener. Carter passed for 273 yards and three touchdowns against the Eagles. Reid sacked Philadelphia passer Pete Liske five times. The season disintegrated rapidly, however, as the Bengals lost their next seven games. The most damaging setback was a 20-17 loss in Green Bay in which Carter and safety Ken Dyer were injured. Dyer snapped a vertebra in his neck, and it was a year before he regained the use of his arms and legs. A 10-6 loss in Houston was the most humiliating game in Cincinnati's brief history. The Oilers scored on a 48-yard interception return on which no Bengals player gave chase. Although the Bengals lost 10 games, 6 were by four points or fewer.

1972 Brown went for defensive help in the college draft, February 1, and selected end Sherman White and safety Tommy Casanova. Anderson, rapidly gaining maturity, unseated Carter as Cincinnati's number-one quarterback. He found an outstanding receiver in Chip Myers, who made 57 receptions. The season unfolded in three stages: the fast start —four wins in five games; the midseason slump —four losses in five games; and the fast finish—winning three of the final four, including a 61-7 thrashing of Houston. But the Bengals couldn't catch Cleveland for the wild card berth.

1973 The Bengals started a number of rookies on their offense, including running back Boobie Clark and wide receiver Isaac Curtis. It took a while for the new players to blend as the Bengals started 4-4. But they swept their last six games and won their second Central Division title. Clark, with 988 yards, and veteran Essex Johnson, with 997, led a powerful ground attack. Meanwhile, Anderson set club records with 179 completions, 2,428 yards, and 18 touchdown passes. Curtis and Clark tied for the club lead with 45 receptions, on which Curtis gained 843 yards and scored nine touchdowns. In the playoffs, it was Miami that moved well on the ground, as the Dolphins stormed past the Bengals 34-16.

1974 Cincinnati traded Bergey to Philadelphia for two first-round draft choices and a third-round pick. The Bengals won four of their first five games to lead the Central Division but couldn't keep pace with Super Bowl-bound Pittsburgh. Brown derived some consolation from his first season series sweep of Cleveland. Curtis caught five passes for 117 yards and a touchdown in the Bengals' 33-7 win over the Browns in the opener, September 15. Four weeks later, Anderson threw three more scoring passes as Cincinnati beat the Browns 34-24. Anderson threw four touchdown passes in a 33-6 rout of Kansas City, November 24. Anderson won the NFL passing championship, completing a club record 64.9 percent of his attempts. Cornerback Lemar Parrish led the NFL in punt returns, including a 90-yard touchdown against Washington, October 6.

1975 Despite the premature retirement of Reid, the Bengals launched their season by winning the first six games. Linebacker Jim LeClair preserved a 21-19 victory over Houston, making all four tackles in a goal-line stand. Rookie Marvin Cobb raced 52 yards with his first pro interception to give Cincinnati a 14-10 win over Oakland. The Bengals won their eighth game in nine starts against Buffalo, 33-24, as Anderson completed 30 of 46 passes for 447 yards and two touchdowns, November 17. The yardage was the tenth-highest one-game total in NFL history. Anderson missed a game with an injury, but reserve quarterback John Reaves led the Bengals to a 23-19 win over Houston, November 30. Cincinnati scored 27 points in the first quarter to crush San Diego 47-14 and finish with its best regular-season record, 11-3. The Bengals qualified as the wild card team for the AFC playoffs but their losing postseason record continued with a 31-28 loss to Oakland, December 28. Anderson won his second NFL passing championship.

1976 Paul Brown announced his retirement after 41 seasons of coaching, January 1. Brown named Bill Johnson, his long-time line coach, to succeed him. Brown continued to serve as the club's general manager, vice president, and owner. The Bengals set a fast pace in the Central Division, winning 9 of their first 11 games. Anderson had his best game in a 45-21 win over Cleveland, passing for four touchdowns. Archie Griffin, who became a starter as a rookie, rushed for 139 yards and scored on a 77-yard run as Cincinnati rallied to beat Kansas City 27-24. The season came down to two games against Pittsburgh and Oakland and the Bengals lost both—7-3 to the Steelers, November 28, and 35-20 to the Raiders, December 6. Those defeats not only cost Cincinnati the Central Division title but the AFC wild card spot as well. Cornerback Ken Riley led the AFC with nine interceptions.

1977 Cincinnati drafted Pete Johnson in the second round. The Bengals started slowly, winning only two of their first six games. Then they turned their season around, going 6-1 and getting back into playoff contention. The last victory in that streak was 17-10 over the Steelers on December 10, a game that the Bengals won with 10 points in 18 seconds. Needing a victory in Houston in the final game of the season to clinch the division, the Bengals were defeated by the Oilers 21-16, as Billy (White Shoes) Johnson ran for 263 all-purpose (rushing, receiving, and return) yards. Tommy Casanova retired at the end of the season to pursue a medical career.

1978 Preseason injuries to Anderson kept him out for more than a month, and the Bengals lost their first eight games, at one point scoring only three points in a three-game span. After five losses, Bill Johnson resigned as head coach on October 2 and was replaced by Homer Rice. On October 29, Anderson was back in the lineup to throw bombs of 45 and 57 yards to lead Cincinnati to its first victory, 28-13 over Houston. The Bengals then lost four in a row, but closed with consecutive victories over Atlanta (37-7), the Los Angeles Rams (20-19), and Cleveland (48-16).

1979 After the fast finish the season before, Cincinnati expected big things, but got a repeat of the previous season's 4-12 record. The Bengals defeated two playoff-bound teams, Philadelphia and the Super Bowl champion Steelers. The defense gave up more points than any other NFL team, including 51 to Buffalo, 42 to Houston, and 38 to Dallas and Baltimore. Despite a 16-12 victory over Cleveland in the season finale on December 16, Rice was fired. Former Cleveland Browns coach Forrest Gregg was named head coach on December 28.

1980 Having already built a strong defensive line through the draft, the Bengals dramatically improved their offensive line with the addition of number-one pick Anthony Muñoz of USC. The Bengals' season got off to a bad start when Anderson was injured in preseason. Although he started 12 games, Anderson completed only 2 because of injuries and was limited to six touchdown passes all year. Despite two early victories over Pittsburgh, the Bengals entered the last month of the season with a 3-9 record. Consecutive victories over Kansas City, Baltimore, and Chicago brought the Bengals' final record to 6-10.

1981 The Bengals unveiled their new uniforms with tiger-striped helmets, jerseys, and pants on April 9. Three weeks later, in the second round of the draft, Cincinnati picked wide receiver Cris Collinsworth of Florida. The Bengals started off fast, winning their first two games. At midseason they still led the AFC Central with a 5-3 record, and they increased their lead thereafter, finishing the last half of the season 7-1, the only loss being to San Francisco. On December 6, Anderson threw two touchdown passes and the Bengals clinched the Central Division with a 17-10 victory over the Steelers. Anderson led the NFL in passing with a 98.5 rating. In the 1981 AFC Divisional Playoff Game against Buffalo on January 3, the Bengals jumped out to a 14-0 lead and won 28-21, for their first playoff victory ever. Playing in their first AFC Championship Game, the Bengals defeated the San Diego Chargers 27-7 on a day in which the weather gained as much attention as the teams. The temperature was nine degrees below zero at game time, with a wind-chill factor of minus 59. In Super Bowl XVI on January 24, a second-half rally couldn't make up a 20-0 halftime deficit, and San Francisco won 26-21.

1982 The Bengals finished 7-2 and qualified for a playoff berth in the NFL's restructured postseason format, due to the 57-day players strike. In a first-round game against the New York Jets, Cincinnati took a 14-3 first-quarter lead. But, led by Freeman McNeil's 202 yards rushing, the Jets rallied to win 44-17. Anderson had another brilliant season. He led the NFL in passing for the fourth time, completing 218 of 309 passes for 2,495 yards and 12 touchdowns. He also set an NFL record by completing 20 consecutive passes, and he erased Sammy Baugh's 37-year-old NFL single-season record for completion percentage, connecting on 70.55 percent. Collinsworth finished second in the AFC with 49 receptions, and tight end Dan Ross was close behind with 47. Cornerback Ken Riley intercepted five passes, placing him first among active players.

1983 Cincinnati drafted 6-foot 3-inch, 290-pound Nebraska center Dave Rimington, the first two-time winner of the Outland Trophy, in the first round of the NFL draft. Bothered by the early-season absence of running back Pete Johnson, the Bengals lost six of their first seven games. Johnson's return to the lineup helped Cincinnati finish with a 6-3 flourish, to wind up 7-9 overall. Collinsworth set a Bengals single-season record with 1,130 yards receiving, breaking his own record of 1,009 set in 1981. Riley finished the season with 8 interceptions, and retired as the number-four interceptor of all time with 65. On December 26, Gregg left the Bengals to replace Bart Starr as head coach of the Green Bay Packers, for whom he had starred as a tackle in the 1960s. Two days later, Paul Brown replaced Gregg with University of Indiana head coach Sam Wyche, formerly the quarterback coach for the San Francisco 49ers. Wyche was no stranger to Cincinnati; during his nine-year NFL career as a quarterback, Wyche played for the Bengals under Brown from 1968-1970. "We have the man we wanted," Brown said. "We sought him, he didn't seek us. He is an innovative man who will install a wide-open offense that our fans will really enjoy."

1984 On May 29, the Bengals traded Johnson to San Diego for running back James Brooks. It took the Bengals some time to become acclimated to the Wyche system; they lost their first five games of the season. Rookie Boomer Esiason made his first career start at quarterback against Houston on October 7 and scored the game's only touchdown as the Bengals won 13-3. "Has President Reagan called yet?" quipped Wyche. Linebacker Glenn Cameron had a more realistic comment. "At least now my dog won't bite me, and my wife won't lock the door on me." Five victories in their next eight games gave the Bengals a 6-8 record, just one game behind first-place Pittsburgh in the AFC Central. A four-touchdown performance by fullback Larry Kinnebrew sparked one victory against Houston, and, on November 11, Kinnebrew scored on a three-yard touchdown run in the final minute of play as the Bengals defeated Pittsburgh 22-20. Esiason, again filling in for injured Ken Anderson, threw a short touchdown pass to Muñoz on a tackle-eligible play to set up an overtime victory against Cleveland, and Anderson came off the bench to complete 18 of 26 passes for 191 yards and two touchdowns to key a victory over New Orleans in the next-to-last week of the season. When told he looked like the Anderson of old, the 35-year-old quarterback replied, "I am old." Needing a victory combined with a Pittsburgh loss on the final Sunday of the regular season, the Bengals did their part by defeating Buffalo 52-21, as Anderson fired three first-half touchdown passes. But the Steelers defeated the Los Angeles Raiders 13-7 to win the AFC Central title.

1985 Once again, the Bengals were slow out of the gate, and began the season with three consecutive losses before ripping Pittsburgh 37-24 for their first victory, September 30. Typical of the Bengals' unpredictable season was a four-week stretch beginning on November 17. In back-to-back losses to the Raiders and Browns, Cincinnati was held without a touchdown. Then in consecutive weeks they bombed Houston 45-27 and Dallas 50-24. The victory over the Cowboys gave the Bengals a 7-7 record and a share of first place in the AFC Central with Cleveland. But Cincinnati dropped its final two games, finishing 7-9 and out of the playoffs. Esiason, taking over full time for Anderson, was the AFC's number-two rated quarterback, and passed for 3,443 yards and 27 touchdowns. Brooks rushed for 929 yards and a 4.8 average.

MEMBER OF HALL OF FAME:
Paul Brown

BENGALS RECORD, 1968-85

Year	Won	Lost	Tied	Pct.	Fin.	Pts.	OP
1968	3	11	0	.214	5	215	329
1969	4	9	1	.308	5	280	367
1970a	8	6	0	.571	1	312	255
1971	4	10	0	.286	4	284	265
1972	8	6	0	.571	3	299	229
1973a	10	4	0	.714	1	286	231
1974	7	7	0	.500	2	283	259
1975b	11	3	0	.786	2	340	246
1976	10	4	0	.714	2	335	210
1977	8	6	0	.571	3	238	235
1978	4	12	0	.250	4	252	284
1979	4	12	0	.250	4	337	421
1980	6	10	0	.375	4	244	312
1981c	12	4	0	.750	1	421	304
1982d	7	2	0	.778	3	232	177
1983	7	9	0	.438	3	346	302
1984	8	8	0	.500	2	339	339
1985	7	9	0	.438	2	441	437
18 Years	128	132	1	.490		5,474	5,202

aAFC Central Division Champion; 0-1 in Playoffs
bAFC Wild Card Qualifier for Playoffs; 0-1 in Playoffs
cAFC Champion; 2-1 in Playoffs
dAFC Qualifier for Playoffs; 0-1 in Playoffs

RECORD HOLDERS

CAREER

Rushing attempts	Pete Johnson, 1977-83	1,402
Rushing yards	Pete Johnson, 1977-83	5,421
Pass attempts	Ken Anderson, 1971-85	4,452
Pass completions	Ken Anderson, 1971-85	2,643
Passing yards	Ken Anderson, 1971-85	32,667
Touchdown passes	Ken Anderson, 1971-85	196
Receptions	Isaac Curtis, 1973-84	420
Receiving yards	Isaac Curtis, 1973-84	7,106
Interceptions	Ken Riley, 1969-83	63
Punting average	Dave Lewis, 1970-73	43.9
Punt return avg.	Mike Martin, 1983-85	11.0
Kickoff return avg.	Lemar Parrish, 1970-78	24.7
Field goals	Horst Muhlmann, 1969-74	120
	Jim Breech, 1979-85	120
Touchdowns	Pete Johnson, 1977-83	70
Points	Jim Breech, 1979-85	610

SEASON

Rushing attempts	Pete Johnson, 1981	274
Rushing yards	Pete Johnson, 1981	1,077
Pass attempts	Ken Anderson, 1981	479
Pass completions	Ken Anderson, 1981	300
Passing yards	Ken Anderson, 1981	3,754
Touchdown passes	Ken Anderson, 1981	29
Receptions	Dan Ross, 1981	71
Receiving yards	Cris Collinsworth, 1983	1,130
Interceptions	Ken Riley, 1976	9
Punting average	Dave Lewis, 1970	46.2
Punt return avg.	Mike Martin, 1984	15.7
Kickoff return avg.	Lemar Parrish, 1980	30.2
Field goals	Horst Muhlmann, 1972	27
Touchdowns	Pete Johnson, 1981	16
Points	Jim Breech, 1985	120

GAME

Rushing attempts	Pete Johnson, 12-4-83	38
Rushing yards	Pete Johnson, 12-17-78	160
Pass attempts	Ken Anderson, 12-20-82	56
Pass completions	Ken Anderson, 12-20-82	40
Passing yards	Ken Anderson, 11-17-75	447
Touchdown passes	4 times	4
Receptions	6 times	10
Receiving yards	Cris Collinsworth, 10-2-83	216
Interceptions	4 times	3
Field goals	Horst Muhlmann, 11-8-70	5
	Horst Muhlmann, 9-24-72	5
Touchdowns	Larry Kinnebrew, 10-28-84	4
Points	Larry Kinnebrew, 10-28-84	24

COACHING HISTORY

1968-75	Paul Brown	55-59-1
1976-78	Bill Johnson*	18-15-0
1978-79	Homer Rice	8-19-0
1980-83	Forrest Gregg	34-27-0
1984-85	Sam Wyche	15-17-0

**Replaced after five games in 1978*

FIRST PLAYER SELECTED

1968	Bob Johnson, C, Tennessee
1969	Greg Cook, QB, Cincinnati
1970	Mike Reid, DT, Penn State
1971	Vernon Holland, T, Tennessee State
1972	Sherman White, DE, California
1973	Isaac Curtis, WR, San Diego State
1974	Bill Kollar, DT, Montana State
1975	Glenn Cameron, LB, Florida
1976	Billy Brooks, WR, Oklahoma
1977	Eddie Edwards, DT, Miami
1978	Ross Browner, DE, Notre Dame
1979	Jack Thompson, QB, Washington State
1980	Anthony Muñoz, T, USC
1981	David Verser, WR, Kansas
1982	Glen Collins, DE, Mississippi State
1983	Dave Rimington, C, Nebraska
1984	Ricky Hunley, LB, Arizona
1984*	Wayne Peace, QB, Florida
1985	Eddie Brown, WR, Miami
1986	Joe Kelly, LB, Washington

**Supplemental Draft*

CLEVELAND BROWNS

1946 Arthur (Mickey) McBride was one of six prospective owners who met with Arch Ward, *Chicago Tribune* sports editor, at a St. Louis hotel to thrash out plans for the All-America Football Conference, June 4, 1944. Taking the advice of Ward and another newspaperman, John Dietrich of the *Cleveland Plain Dealer,* McBride—who owned taxicab companies, a radio station, a printing company, a race-wire syndicate, and real-estate holdings—named Paul Brown as coach of the new Cleveland team. Brown had been a highly successful coach at Massillon (Ohio) High School, at Ohio State, and at Great Lakes Naval Training Station during World War II. McBride offered a $1,000 war bond to the fan coming up with a nickname for the team. The winner was a Navy man, John J. Harnett of Lawrence, Massachusetts, who was one of 36 entrants choosing "Panthers." But there had been an AFL team called the Cleveland Panthers in the 1920s. Brown vetoed the nickname. "I won't start out with anything associated with our enterprise that smacks of failure," he said. "That old Panther team failed. I want no part of that name." A number of contest entrants had suggested the name of the team be the Browns, some indicating it would be in honor of its head coach, and some in honor of boxing champion Joe Louis, the "Brown Bomber." Paul Brown had at first turned the suggestion down, but he relented. The team was named the Browns, although the controversy has continued over whom the honor was for. William E. Thompson received a $1,000 war bond as the man who officially made the suggestion for the new nickname. Brown personally selected the style and colors—brown, orange, and white—of the uniforms. Brown was also general manager and one of many players he signed while the war still was going was Otto Graham, a Single-Wing tailback from Northwestern, whom he would convert into one of the finest T-formation quarterbacks of all time. Brown filled out much of the rest of his roster with men who had played for him at Ohio State or Great Lakes—Lou Groza, Dante Lavelli, Marion Motley, Bill Willis—or against him—Mac Speedie and Ed (Special Delivery) Jones. Motley and Willis were the first two black players signed by an AAFC team. The Browns' training camp was held at Bowling Green in northwestern Ohio. The Browns played the first AAFC regular-season game, beating the Miami Seahawks 44-0 at Cleveland Stadium, September 6. The AAFC's first official touchdown was scored on a 19-yard pass from quarterback Cliff Lewis to Speedie. The Browns won seven in a row before losing back-to-back games to the San Francisco 49ers and the Los Angeles Dons. They wrapped up the Western Division title with a 42-17 win over the Buffalo Bills, then defeated the New York Yankees in the championship game 14-9. Lavelli led the AAFC in receiving, Groza in scoring, and Tom Colella in interceptions.

1947 Tony Adamle, whom Brown had coached at Ohio State, and Horace Gillom, whom Brown had coached against at Massillon, joined the team. En route to a second straight championship, Graham and Speedie combined on a screen pass that went for a 99-yard touchdown. The 49ers posed the big Western Division threat again, but the Browns beat them 14-7 and 37-14, while losing only to the Dons 13-10, and finishing at 12-1-1. In the season's most exciting game, on November 23, the Browns fell behind the New York Yankees 28-0, but came back to salvage a 28-28 tie. The Browns met the Yankees again in the AAFC Championship Game, and Motley rushed for 109 yards to lead Cleveland to a 14-3 victory. Graham, who was named the AAFC's most valuable player, led the league in passing, while Speedie led in receiving, and Colella in interceptions.

1948 Brown sent the rights to Michigan All-America Bob Chappuis to the Brooklyn Dodgers for halfback Dub Jones, who combined with Speedie and Lavelli to give the Browns three brilliant receivers. Brown also traded for linemen Alex Agase and Forrest (Chubby) Grigg, and drafted defensive backs Tommy James and Warren Lahr. Lavelli was out until midseason with a broken leg, but the Browns rolled on, this time to an unbeaten season. The two highlights of the season were games with San Francisco, which also was 10-0 until the Browns beat them 14-7. Two weeks later, the Browns clinched the division with a 31-28 win over the 49ers, who finished 12-2. With the 7-7 Buffalo Bills the Browns' opponent in the championship game, it promised to be anticlimactic, and it was, as the Browns won 49-7. Graham again led the legaue in passing, Speedie in receiving, and Motley in rushing, while the defense gave up the fewest points.

1949 Brown brought in quite a bit of new talent and the team sputtered a little, losing to the 49ers 56-28. Brown exploded in anger at his players after that loss and they responded with a 61-14 victory over the Dons in which Graham threw six touchdown passes, four to Lavelli. For the fourth year in a row, the Browns finished with the best record in the AAFC, 9-1-2. Graham and Speedie led the league in passing and receiving for the third consecutive year. In a playoff game, the Browns stopped the Bills 31-21. Then they won the AAFC's last title game 21-7 over the 49ers, before just 22,550 fans. Two days before, a merger with the National Football League had been announced. The AAFC's last order of business was a game between the Browns and a league all-star team. Led by quarterback George Ratterman, who would join Cleveland two years later, the All-Stars scored a 12-7 win. The Browns, ironically, helped kill the AAFC. "We were too good, if that sounds possible," Brown said. "Even in Cleveland, the fans stopped coming because they just assumed we'd go out and dominate the opposition so strongly, there would be no contest."

1950 Before starting play in the NFL, Brown picked up Abe Gibron, Rex Bumgardner, and John Kissell from the AAFC Bills and Len Ford from the Dons. The Browns played the Philadelphia Eagles, the defending NFL champions, in the season opener. Eagles coach Earle (Greasy) Neale had said his team was better, that all Cleveland did was throw the ball. The Browns won 35-10 as Graham threw three touchdown passes. But in the third game of the season, Steve Owen and the New York Giants used their Umbrella defense to shut out Cleveland 6-0. It was the first time the Browns ever had been shut out. The Giants beat the Browns again that season, and Cleveland needed a win over the Eagles to tie the Giants for first place in the American Conference. They got it 13-7 without Graham throwing a single pass. Lahr returned an interception for a touchdown, and Groza kicked two field goals. The Browns and Giants finished with 10-2 regular-season records. They had a playoff in 10-degree cold at Cleveland; Groza kicked two field goals in an 8-3 win over the Giants. Willis saved the game when he tackled New York's Gene (Choo-Choo) Roberts from behind at the Browns' 4-yard line in the fourth quarter. In the NFL Championship Game, the Browns got a field goal from Groza with 28 seconds to play to beat the Los Angeles Rams 30-28.

1951 There were some rumors Brown would leave pro football and take over again as Ohio State coach. But he stayed and, after an opening-day loss to San Francisco, the Browns won 11 in a row. This time, however, they failed to win the championship. In a title-game rematch, the Rams beat them 24-17 on a 73-yard pass-and-run play from Norm Van Brocklin to Tom Fears.

1952 The Browns, after a battle with Philadelphia and New York, won their third straight Eastern Conference title but three key players, Speedie (the league's leading receiver), Dub Jones, and Kissell, were lost with injuries in a victory over the Giants. None was ready for the NFL Championship Game two weeks later against the Detroit Lions. Graham, who had his poorest passing season as a pro, was working with two rookie receivers—Ray Renfro and Darrell (Pete) Brewster—and the Browns scored only on Harry (Chick) Jagade's run in a 17-7 loss.

1953 The Browns drafted Doug Atkins, the giant lineman from Tennessee, halfback Bill Reynolds, and guard Chuck Noll (on the twenty-third round), and Brown swung a 15-player trade with Baltimore that brought tackles Mike McCormack and Don Colo, linebacker Tom Catlin, defensive back John Petitbon, and guard Herschel Forester. They did lose Speedie and Kissell in a bidding war with the Canadian Football League, however. McBride sold the team to a group headed by David Jones, a Cleveland industrialist, for $600,000, the highest price ever paid for a pro football franchise at the time. The syndicate that owned the Browns took out a large life insurance policy on Paul Brown, figuring he was their primary asset. On the field, the Browns won every regular-season game until the last one, a 42-27 loss to Philadelphia. Graham led the NFL in passing. In the championship game, Cleveland took a 16-10 lead over Detroit on Groza's two fourth-quarter field goals. But a Bobby Layne touchdown pass to Jim Doran denied Cleveland the NFL title, 17-16. Graham announced he'd retire after the 1954 season.

1954 Willis, Lin Houston, and George Young, all from the original 1946 team, retired, and eight other players departed. The team started poorly, going 1-2 and losing 55-27 to Pittsburgh, then won eight straight. They met the Lions again in the last regular-season game, and Detroit won 14-10. But the game meant nothing, since both teams had already won division titles. The title game did, since Graham figured it would be his last. He threw three touchdown passes and scored three times himself as the Browns overwhelmed the Lions 56-10. Reynolds set up three scores with two kickoff returns and a punt return and Cleveland intercepted six passes.

1955 Four games into the preseason, it was obvious the old Browns magic was not there without Graham. Brown called Graham and asked if he would change his mind. "He came back without too much coaxing," Brown said. Graham suffered physically and mentally upon his return but he led the Browns into the NFL Championship Game again. The team scored its highest NFL total in the regular season, 349 points, as Graham again led the league in passing. Graham and other veterans told Brown they felt a spread, wide-open offense would work best in the title game against the Rams, and they were right. Cleveland rolled to a 38-14 victory. Graham passed for two touchdowns and ran for two more. When he came out of the game the 85,000 fans in the Los Angeles Coliseum gave him a long ovation. This time Graham retired for good.

1956 Lavelli and Dub Jones joined Graham in retirement. Missing three vital ingredients, the offense didn't respond. Brown vacillated between quarterbacks Babe Parilli and George Ratterman, who had sat on the bench as Graham's substitute for four years. Ratterman injured his knee in the fourth regular-season game and his Browns' career was over. Parilli then hurt a shoulder and Tommy O'Connell, who had been cut by the Bears, became the quarter-

back. The team had its first losing season, 5-7.
1957 Brown wanted to draft a quarterback but two coin tosses went against him and Cleveland was dropped to sixth in drafting order. It turned out to be an incredible stroke of luck. The Browns chose Jim Brown, who was to become perhaps the best runner in NFL history. "There was no doubt," said chief talent scout Dick Gallagher, "he could do a lot of work for us—that he was the man to make our system go." Brown drafted a quarterback, Milt Plum, on the second round. John Bayuk, a running back from Colorado, was assigned uniform number 32 in training camp. Jim Brown, reporting from the Chicago College All-Star game, wore number 45—for one game. Then Bayuk was released and Brown got number 32. Parilli was traded to Green Bay for Bobby Garrett, but Garrett was released, and O'Connell and Plum were named to run the offense. O'Connell led the NFL in passing. The Browns started four rookies, including Jim Brown. Four games into the season, Brown ran for an NFL-record 237 yards against the Rams, on his way to leading the NFL in rushing. The Browns won the Eastern Division title, but came up against the Lions again in the championship game. This time they were buried 59-14. Brown was named rookie of the year.
1958 Halfbacks Bobby Mitchell (seventh round) and Leroy Bolden were among the club's draft choices. O'Connell retired, leaving the job to Plum. Jim Brown and Mitchell led the team to a 5-0 start, then Mitchell was benched in favor of Bolden after fumbling three times against the Giants. It was the start of a deteriorating relationship between Paul Brown and several of his players—notably Jim Brown and Mitchell. Cleveland had only to beat New York in the final regular-season game to win the Eastern Division title but it lost 13-10 on Pat Summerall's field goal with two minutes to play, forcing a playoff, in which the Browns lost to the Giants 10-0 as Giants defensive coach Tom Landry devised a means to stop Jim Brown. Cleveland gained just 24 yards rushing and had only 86 yards total offense.
1959 With Brown and Mitchell the most productive pair of backs in the league, the Browns stayed tied with the Giants for first place through eight weeks. Then on successive weekends, they lost 21-20 to Pittsburgh and San Francisco. On the next-to-last week of the season, the Giants clinched the title by burying the Browns 48-7. Although Jim Brown gained 1,329 yards and earned his third NFL rushing title, fans began to openly wonder why Paul Brown couldn't keep winning titles.
1960 The Browns were at times one of the best—and at times one of the worst—teams in the NFL. They opened the season with a 41-24 rout of eventual champion Philadelphia, but later dropped a game to Pittsburgh. In November, the Giants held Jim Brown and Mitchell to a total of six yards rushing, while beating the Browns 17-13. The next month, the Browns' offense went crazy, clobbering the Giants 48-34. Brown again led the league in rushing, and Plum led the league in passing, but Paul Brown's relationship with his players continued to deteriorate.
1961 Arthur Modell, a former New York City advertising executive with much experience in television, bought the Browns for $3,925,000, January 25. The price was more than six times what the Jones syndicate had paid original owner McBride eight years before. Modell didn't claim to know a lot about football. "My expertise was in one area, television," he said. There was suspicion about Modell's role at first but he told Paul Brown he wanted him to run the football end of the business while he would handle administration and details. "We were entertainment," Modell said. "The first thing I wanted to be sure we did was put on a good show." It was innovative thinking for the time. Lou Groza returned to the team after a one-year retirement, Brown led the league in rushing, and Plum led in passing. The Browns were in the thick of the title hunt until a 1-2-1 finish.
1962 Mitchell was traded to Washington for the rights to Heisman Trophy winner Ernie Davis of Syracuse, the halfback Paul Brown wanted to team with Jim Brown. Plum was traded to Detroit, and quarterback Frank Ryan joined the team in a trade with the Rams. Davis wore his jersey only for publicity pictures. Tragically, he was dying of leukemia. The Browns won all their preseason games and their league opener, then Mitchell and the Redskins beat them and they began to slump. They finished third in the Eastern Division after never being in contention. Jim Brown didn't win the rushing title for the only time in his nine-year career, and threatened to retire unless he could play for a new coach.
1963 Modell called Paul Brown into his office and told him he was through as coach and general manager—after 17 years—even though he had six years remaining on his contract, January 5. Blanton Collier, 56, a Browns' assistant who had been the architect of the club's superb defenses and Paul Brown's most trusted associate, was named head coach. Collier was almost the antithesis of Brown—soft-spoken, openly warm, a man who didn't call plays from the sideline via messenger guards. Under Collier the team won six straight with Ryan firmly in control at quarterback, and receiver Gary Collins beginning to hit his stride. Jim Brown had his finest season as a pro, setting a record with 1,863 yards, and Ernie Green proved to be an excellent replacement for Mitchell. But a midseason slump saw the Browns lose three of four, and they finished one game behind New York in the Eastern Conference.
1964 Brown won his seventh rushing title, but the story of the team was the addition of Paul Warfield, a rookie from Ohio State who suddenly helped give the Browns one of the league's best passing games. The Browns roared to an 8-1-1 record and then held off the hard-charging St. Louis Cardinals for the Eastern Conference title, their first since 1957. With the title on the line, the Browns crushed the Giants 52-20 in the season finale. In a major upset, Cleveland dominated the Baltimore Colts 27-0 in the NFL Championship Game, as Ryan threw three touchdown passes to Collins.
1965 Otto Graham became the first member of the Browns—and the first player from the AAFC—to be inducted into the Pro Football Hall of Fame. Ryan suffered a severe shoulder injury in the Pro Bowl, had his arm in a cast much of the winter, and wasn't as effective during the season as he previously had been. Warfield broke his shoulder in the Chicago College All-Star game and was out for 10 weeks. The team had nagging injuries to several other players but didn't miss a step, thanks mostly to Brown, who led the league with 1,544 yards and was named the NFL's most valuable player. The Browns clinched the Eastern Conference title three games before the season's end with a 42-21 win over Pittsburgh. On a wet, snowy day on Lambeau Field in Green Bay, the Packers led only 13-12 at the half, but then dominated the championship game and won 23-12. After 12,312 yards rushing, 126 touchdowns, and eight rushing titles, Brown retired.
1966 Leroy Kelly, who had led the league in punt returns in 1965, took over for Brown and finished second in the NFL with 1,141 yards rushing, while scoring a league-high 16 touchdowns; Green finished seventh with 750 yards, and his 5.2-yard average was third behind Kelly (5.5) and Gale Sayers (5.4). Ryan led the league with 29 touchdown passes, 12 to Collins. The Browns lost two of their first three games but then made a run at the Cowboys for the Eastern Division title. A 33-21 loss to the Eagles in the next-to-last week eliminated the Browns from the race, and they finished second at 9-5.
1967 Paul Brown was inducted into the Pro Football Hall of Fame. The NFL was realigned and the Browns were placed in the Century Division. They won it with a 9-5 record achieved with the league's best rushing attack. Kelly led the NFL with 1,205 yards rushing, and Green finished ninth with 710 yards and a 4.9-yard average, second only to Kelly's 5.1 average. Cleveland met the Cowboys, Capitol Division winners, in the Eastern Conference championship. Devastated by Bob Hayes's pass catching and punt returning, the Browns lost 52-14.
1968 Ryan had begun to slip, so Collier obtained quarterback Bill Nelsen from Pittsburgh. Groza, who was in a preseason kicking battle with Don Cockroft, decided to retire again. This time he meant it and "the Toe's" jersey, number 76, was retired. Collins was out most of the year with a shoulder injury, but Nelsen ignited the team and it won the Century Division, edging the Cardinals by half a game. Kelly led the NFL in rushing with 1,239 yards and in scoring with 20 touchdowns. Cleveland beat Dallas 31-20 in the playoffs. But it was different against Baltimore in the NFL Championship Game. Tom Matte ran for three touchdowns and the Colts held the Browns to 56 yards rushing and won 34-0.
1969 The Browns went 10-3-1 and won their third straight Century Division title, led again by Nelsen, Kelly, Collins, and Warfield. The team led the NFL in touchdowns. Kelly and Bo Scott ran well as Cleveland beat Dallas 38-14 in the first round of the playoffs. Then the Browns lost to the Vikings 27-7 in eight-degree weather in Minnesota.
1970 The Browns became members of the American Football Conference Central Division as three old-line NFL teams joined American Football League teams in the realignment. The Browns traded Warfield to Miami to get the draft choice that enabled them to get a promising young quarterback, Mike Phipps of Purdue. But Phipps needed plenty more seasoning, and the passing game was unproductive, leading to a drop to second place behind Paul Brown's Bengals. At midseason, Collier announced his retirement effective at the end of the year.
1971 Nick Skorich, an aide to Collier, took over as the Browns' third head coach. After a 4-1 start, the Browns dropped four games in a row, but then won their last five for the AFC Central title, the only team in the division with a winning record. But the Browns lost to Baltimore in the first round of the playoffs 20-3.
1972 Phipps became the starting quarterback and led the Browns to a 10-4 record, good enough for a wild card berth in the playoffs. It was clinched with season-ending victories over the Bengals and Jets. Kelly led a tough running game, Cockroft was the most accurate kicker in the NFL, and the Browns' pass defense, led by youngsters Thom Darden and Clarence Scott, was tops in the AFC. In an AFC Divisional Playoff Game, the Browns almost upset the undefeated Dolphins, but lost 20-14.
1973 Age and the retirement of players such as Nelsen and guard Gene Hickerson combined with injuries and an ineffective Mike Phipps to drop the Browns to third place. Despite a struggling offense, the defense played well, and cornerback Clarence Scott and defensive tackle Jerry Sherk were selected to the Pro Bowl, as was kick returner Greg Pruitt.
1974 Cleveland lost five of its first six before it could put anything together, then lost its last two games. For the second time in their history, the Browns had a losing record, 4-10. For the first time, they finished in last place.
1975 Forrest Gregg, former star offensive tackle at

Green Bay and a Skorich assistant for one season, was named the Browns' fourth head coach. Blanton Collier returned as quarterbacks coach. The team moved its training quarters from Hiram College to Kent State. The team won just three games. "There was a definite turnaround in attitude and performance the last seven games," Gregg said. Greg Pruitt gained 1,067 yards, emerging as one of the NFL's top runners.

1976 Paul Warfield was back after a six-year absence to lead a rebuilt receiving corps. Gregg found a quarterback of the future in third-year man Brian Sipe. Sipe took over in the second half of the season opener with the Jets after Mike Phipps suffered a slight shoulder separation. The Browns won five of their last six to compile their finest record since 1972. They were in playoff contention until the final week. The Browns finished four games over .500 and just one game behind Pittsburgh and Cincinnati in the AFC Central Division. Greg Pruitt was handicapped by a badly sprained ankle for the last half of the season but he still managed to rush for 1,000 yards, seventh-best in the AFC. The other running back, free-agent Cleo Miller, earned a starting job with a great preseason effort and, despite a series of on and off the field injuries, gained 613 yards.

1977 The Browns' defense lost a stabilizing influence when tackle Jerry Sherk went out with a preseason knee injury. But Sipe and Pruitt led a powerful offensive attack that was at its best in a 44-7 defeat of Kansas City, in which the Browns rushed for 322 yards and gained a club record of 34 first downs. Halfway through the season, Cleveland had a 5-2 record, good for first place in the AFC Central Division. On November 6, the Browns lost to Cincinnati 10-7, despite a 20 for 28 passing performance by Sipe. The next week Sipe was lost for the season with an injury, and the Steelers defeated the Browns 35-31. With David Mays at quarterback, the Browns could win only one of their last five games and finished 6-8. With one game remaining in the season, Gregg resigned. Defensive assistant Dick Modzelewski took over for the season finale at Seattle, which Cleveland lost 20-19. Pruitt rushed for more than 1,000 yards (1,086) for the third straight year.

1978 Sam Rutigliano became the team's head coach. The Browns seemed to go as Pruitt went. With a healthy Pruitt, the Browns started 3-0, but when he was injured, the team lost four of its next five. Pruitt came back for the second half of the season, and the Browns finished with an 8-8 record, good for third in the AFC Central Division behind the Steelers and the rejuvenated Oilers. Sipe played his first full season as a starter and passed for 2,906 yards and 21 touchdowns. Darden led the NFL with 10 interceptions.

1979 Cleveland traded for defensive end Lyle Alzado on August 14. Alzado added much to the Browns' pass rush, but it wasn't enough to provide defensive balance to the high-powered offense. The Browns were the "Kardiac Kids" of the NFL: In 12 of their 16 games the outcome was in doubt until the final minute. They also played three overtime games. The Browns were in the playoff picture until the last two weeks of the season, when they lost at Oakland and Cincinnati. Mike Pruitt rushed for 1,294 yards in his first season as a full-time player, and Sipe passed for a club-record 3,793 yards and 28 touchdowns.

1980 The "Kardiac Kids" returned. Of their 16 games, 13 were decided by a touchdown or less. After losing their first two games, Cleveland came back behind Sipe, who became only the third player ever to pass for 4,000 yards in a season (4,132), on his way to leading the NFL in passing and earning NFL player-of-the-year honors. On November 30, the Browns defeated the Oilers 17-14 in a battle of AFC Central Division leaders, when Clarence Scott intercepted a pass with a little over a minute left. On December 14, the Vikings scored three times in the last five minutes to defeat the Browns 28-23. A week later Cleveland clinched its first division title in nine years with a 27-24 victory over the Bengals. The Browns' season of come-from-behind victories ended January 4, when Mike Davis of the Raiders intercepted Sipe's pass in the end zone with 41 seconds left for a 14-12 Oakland victory in the 1980 AFC Divisional Playoff Game.

1981 Mike Pruitt had his third straight 1,000-yard rushing year, and Sipe passed for 3,876 yards, but the Browns could not repeat their last-minute finishes and fell to 5-11, last in the division. They were blasted by San Diego 44-14 in the regular-season opener and never could get untracked. Cleveland never got above .500 during the season.

1982 Despite a slump by Sipe and a 4-5 record in the strike-shortened season, the Browns qualified for the eighth and final AFC playoff spot—the first time ever a losing record was good enough for the playoffs. "Everything considered, we did okay," said Rutigliano. "We made it to the playoffs after the dirt had already been delivered to Cleveland Stadium to bury us." The Browns lost to the Los Angeles Raiders in the first round 27-10. Linebacker Tom Cousineau, acquired before the season in a trade with Buffalo, led the Browns in unassisted tackles. Rookie linebacker Chip Banks, the Browns' number-one draft pick from USC, went to the AFC-NFC Pro Bowl. Tight end Ozzie Newsome tied for second in the AFC with 49 receptions for 633 yards.

1983 Paul Warfield, who played for the Browns from 1964-69 and from 1976-77, and Bobby Mitchell, who played for Cleveland from 1958-61, were inducted into the Pro Football Hall of Fame. The Browns won three of their first four games, then dropped three of their next four. With an 8-7 record going into their final game, the Browns needed a victory over Pittsburgh combined with a Seattle loss to qualify for a wild card playoff berth. The Browns won 30-17, but the Seahawks defeated New England to eliminate Cleveland. Sipe passed for 3,566 yards and 26 touchdowns. He moved past Frank Ryan into first place on the all-time Cleveland list for career touchdown passes with a four-touchdown performance against Detroit. Newsome moved past Milt Morin, Paul Warfield, Ray Renfro, Reggie Rucker, Greg Pruitt, and former leader Gary Collins into first place on the all-time Browns list for career receptions with 351.

1984 Long-time public relations director Nate Wallack died, January 16. Former Colts general manager Ernie Accorsi was named assistant to the president. The Browns selected UCLA safety Don Rogers in the first round of the NFL draft. When Sipe left the team for the USFL, Paul McDonald took over at quarterback and passed for 3,472 yards, but had 23 interceptions and only 14 touchdown passes. Newsome led the AFC with 89 receptions and was the Browns' only Pro Bowl selection. A knee injury to Mike Pruitt limited the productive running back to 506 yards rushing. Steve Cox kicked a 60-yard field goal, the second-longest in NFL history, against Cincinnati, October 21. Cleveland lost its first three games, defeated Pittsburgh, then lost three more in a row. "Now I know what it feels like to be in a gas chamber," said Rutigliano after a 24-20 loss to the Jets dropped the Browns to 1-6. "We were suffocated by our own mistakes." After another loss to Cincinnati, Modell fired Rutigliano and replaced him with defensive coordinator Marty Schottenheimer. On November 4, running back Earnest Byner scooped up a fumble by teammate Willis Adams midway through the fourth quarter and raced 55 yards for the winning points as the Browns defeated Buffalo 13-10 for Schottenheimer's first victory.

1985 Tackle Doug Dieken, a mainstay on the Browns' line for 14 years, retired. With nine new players on offense (compared to the 1984 opener), the Browns began the season with a 4-2 run, lost four straight, then went 4-2 over the final playoff stretch to finish 8-8 and win the AFC Central championship. The Browns threw a scare into Miami in a divisional playoff game, leading the Dolphins 21-3 in the third quarter. But Miami scored three touchdowns in the final 20 minutes for a 24-21 victory. Byner and Kevin Mack, a pair of 23-year-olds, became the third running-back tandem in NFL history to each rush for more than 1,000 yards in a season for the same team. Rookie Bernie Kosar shared the quarterback job with Gary Danielson, who was acquired from Detroit. Newsome moved past Jackie Smith to become the NFL's career reception leader for tight ends.

1986 Rogers died of a drug overdose.

MEMBERS OF HALL OF FAME:

Doug Atkins, Jim Brown, Paul Brown, Willie Davis, Len Ford, Frank Gatski, Otto Graham, Lou Groza, Dante Lavelli, Mike McCormack, Bobby Mitchell, Marion Motley, Paul Warfield, Bill Willis

BROWNS RECORD, 1946-85

Year	Won	Lost	Tied	Pct.	Fin.	Pts.	OP
1946a	12	2	0	.857	1	423	137
1947a	12	1	1	.923	1	410	185
1948a	14	0	0	1.000	1	389	190
1949b	9	1	2	.900	1	339	171
1950c	10	2	0	.833	1	310	144
1951d	11	1	0	.917	1	331	152
1952d	8	4	0	.667	1	310	213
1953e	11	1	0	.917	1	348	162
1954f	9	3	0	.750	1	336	162
1955f	9	2	1	.818	1	349	218
1956	5	7	0	.417	4t	167	177
1957e	9	2	1	.818	1	269	172
1958g	9	3	0	.750	2	302	217
1959	7	5	0	.583	2t	270	214
1960h	8	3	1	.727	2	362	217
1961	8	5	1	.615	3	319	270
1962	7	6	1	.538	3	291	257
1963h	10	4	0	.714	2	343	262
1964f	10	3	1	.769	1	415	293
1965e	11	3	0	.786	1	363	325
1966	9	5	0	.643	2t	403	259
1967i	9	5	0	.643	1	334	297
1968j	10	4	0	.714	1	394	273
1969j	10	3	1	.769	1	351	300
1970	7	7	0	.500	2	286	265
1971k	9	5	0	.643	1	285	273
1972l	10	4	0	.714	2	268	249
1973	7	5	2	.571	3	234	255
1974	4	10	0	.286	4	251	344
1975	3	11	0	.214	4	218	372
1976	9	5	0	.643	3	267	287
1977	6	8	0	.429	4	269	267
1978	8	8	0	.500	3	334	356
1979	9	7	0	.563	3	359	352
1980k	11	5	0	.688	1	357	310
1981	5	11	0	.313	4	276	375
1982m	4	5	0	.444	8	140	182
1983	9	7	0	.563	2	356	342
1984	5	11	0	.313	3	250	297
1985k	8	8	0	.500	1	287	294
4 AAFC Years	47	4	3	.898		1,561	683
36 NFL Years	294	188	9	.608		11,004	9,404
40 Pro Years	341	192	12	.637		12,565	10,087

a AAFC Champion; 1-0 in Playoffs
b AAFC Champion; 2-0 in Playoffs
c NFL Champion; 2-0 in Playoffs
d NFL American Conference Champion; 0-1 in Playoffs
e NFL Eastern Conference Champion; 0-1 in Playoffs
f NFL Champion; 1-0 in Playoffs
g NFL Eastern Conference Runnerup; 0-1 in Playoffs
h NFL Eastern Conference Runnerup; 0-1 in Playoff Bowl
i NFL Century Division Champion; 0-2 in Playoffs
j NFL Eastern Conference Champion; 1-1 in Playoffs
k AFC Central Division Champion; 0-1 in Playoffs
l AFC Wild Card Qualifier for Playoffs; 0-1 in Playoffs
m AFC Qualifier for Playoffs; 0-1 in Playoffs

RECORD HOLDERS

CAREER

Rushing attempts	Jim Brown, 1957-65	2,359
Rushing yards	Jim Brown, 1957-65	12,312
Pass attempts	Brian Sipe, 1974-83	3,439
Pass completions	Brian Sipe, 1974-83	1,944
Passing yards	Brian Sipe, 1974-83	23,713
Touchdown passes	Brian Sipe, 1974-83	154
Receptions	Ozzie Newsome, 1978-85	502

Receiving yards	Ozzie Newsome, 1978-85	6,281
Interceptions	Thom Darden, 1972-74, 1976-81	45
Punting average	Horace Gillom, 1950-56	43.8
Punt return avg.	Greg Pruitt, 1973-81	11.8
Kickoff return avg.	Greg Pruitt, 1973-81	26.3
Field goals	Lou Groza, 1950-59, 1961-67	234
Touchdowns	Jim Brown, 1957-65	126
Points	Lou Groza, 1950-59, 1961-67	1,349
SEASON		
Rushing attempts	Jim Brown, 1961	305
Rushing yards	Jim Brown,1963	1,863
Pass attempts	Brian Sipe, 1981	567
Pass completions	Brian Sipe, 1980	337
Passing yards	Brian Sipe, 1980	4,132
Touchdown passes	Brian Sipe, 1980	30
Receptions	Ozzie Newsome, 1983	89
	Ozzie Newsome, 1984	89
Receiving yards	Paul Warfield, 1968	1,067
Interceptions	Thom Darden, 1978	10
Punting average	Gary Collins, 1965	46.7
Punt return avg.	Leroy Kelly, 1965	15.6
Kickoff return avg.	Bo Scott, 1969	28.9
Field goals	Matt Bahr, 1984	24
Touchdowns	Jim Brown, 1965	21
Points	Jim Brown, 1965	126
GAME		
Rushing attempts	Jim Brown, 10-4-59	37
Rushing yards	Jim Brown, 11-24-57	237
	Jim Brown, 11-19-61	237
Pass attempts	Brian Sipe, 9-7-81	57
Pass completions	Brian Sipe, 12-5-82	33
Passing yards	Brian Sipe, 10-25-81	444
Touchdown passes	Frank Ryan, 12-12-64	5
	Bill Nelsen, 11-2-69	5
	Brian Sipe, 10-7-79	5
Receptions	Ozzie Newsome, 10-14-84	14
Receiving yards	Ozzie Newsome, 10-14-84	191
Interceptions	7 times	3
Field goals	Don Cockroft, 10-19-75	5
Touchdowns	Dub Jones, 11-25-51	6
Points	Dub Jones, 11-25-51	36

COACHING HISTORY

1946-62	Paul Brown	167-54-8
		NFL only: 115-50-5
1963-70	Blanton Collier	79-40-2
1971-74	Nick Skorich	30-26-2
1975-77	Forrest Gregg*	18-23-0
1977	Dick Modzelewski	0- 1-0
1978-84	Sam Rutigliano**	47-52-0
1984-85	Marty Schottenheimer	12-12-0

**Resigned after 13 games in 1977*
***Replaced after eight games in 1984*

FIRST PLAYER SELECTED

1947† Dick Hoerner, FB, Iowa
1948† Jeff Durkota, HB, Penn State
1949† Jack Mitchell, QB, Oklahoma
1950 Ken Carpenter, HB, Oregon State
1951 Kenny Konz, HB, LSU
1952 Bert Rechichar, DB, Tennessee
1953 Doug Atkins, DT, Tennessee
1954 Bobby Garrett, QB, Stanford
1955 Kent Burris, C, Oklahoma
1956 Preston Carpenter, HB, Arkansas
1957 Jim Brown, FB, Syracuse
1958 Jim Shofner, DB, TCU
1959 Rick Kreitling, E, Illinois
1960 Jim Houston, DE, Ohio State
1961 Bobby Crespino, E, Mississippi
1962 Gary Collins, E, Maryland
1963 Tom Hutchinson, E, Kentucky
1964 Paul Warfield, HB, Ohio State
1965 (2) Jim Garcia, T, Purdue
1966 Milt Morin, TE, Massachusetts
1967 Bob Matheson, LB, Duke
1968 Marvin Upshaw, DT-DE, Trinity (Texas)
1969 Ron Johnson, RB, Michigan
1970 Mike Phipps, QB, Purdue
1971 Clarence Scott, CB, Kansas State
1972 Thom Darden, DB, Michigan
1973 Steve Holden, WR, Arizona State
1974 (2) Billy Corbett, T, Johnson C. Smith
1975 Mack Mitchell, DE, Houston
1976 Mike Pruitt, RB, Purdue
1977 Robert L. Jackson, LB, Texas A&M
1978 Clay Matthews, LB, USC
1979 Willis Adams, WR, Houston
1980 Charles White, RB, USC
1981 Hanford Dixon, CB, Southern Mississippi
1982 Chip Banks, LB, USC
1983 (2) Ron Brown, WR, Arizona State
1984 Don Rogers, S, UCLA
1984* Kevin Mack, RB, Clemson
1985 (2) Greg Allen, RB, Florida State
1985* Bernie Kosar, QB, Miami
1986 (2) Webster Slaughter, WR, San Diego State
†AAFC Draft
**Supplemental Draft*

DALLAS COWBOYS

1959 The NFL had indicated an interest in an expansion team being placed in Dallas, and, as the new franchise was being approved, Clint Murchison, Jr., and Bedford Wynne were selected as the owners-to-be. Prior to the NFL draft, Murchison signed two outstanding college players, quarterback Don Meredith of SMU and fullback Don Perkins of New Mexico, to personal services contracts guaranteeing their playing for the new franchise, should it be granted. Although both players subsequently were drafted, Murchison retained their rights by trading future draft picks for them.

1960 Murchison and Wynne officially were awarded the Dallas franchise at the annual league meeting in Miami, January 28. The team was named the Rangers, but that name was changed to the Cowboys in March. Also in March, Dallas selected 36 players from the other 12 NFL teams in an expansion draft. Tex Schramm, who had spent 10 years in the Los Angeles Rams' front office and had worked for CBS Television as assistant director of sports, was named general manager. Tom Landry, a former fullback at Texas and defensive back with the New York Giants, and then the defensive coach of the Giants, was named head coach. The Cowboys were aligned in the Western Conference for their first season. Hoping to win the Dallas fans, Landry made his team offense-conscious. Dallas traded its first draft choice to Washington for Eddie LeBaron, the 5-foot 8-inch quarterback who had led the NFL in passing in 1958. LeBaron joined aging end Billy Howton and a young linebacker, Jerry Tubbs, as the best players on the team. The first training camp was held at Pacific University in Forest Grove, Oregon. On August 6, the Cowboys lost their first preseason game 16-10 to San Francisco. Two weeks later they lost their home opener in the Cotton Bowl to Baltimore 14-10. The Cowboys finally made the win column with a 14-3 victory over the Giants in Louisville, Kentucky, in which Frank Clarke caught touchdown passes of 73 yards from LeBaron and 74 yards from Meredith. In their first regular-season game, the Cowboys fell to Pittsburgh 35-28. They then lost nine more in a row before tying the Giants 31-31 on December 4. Attendance averaged 21,417.

1961 Talent scout Gil Brandt took charge of the Cowboys' college draft. His first pick was Bob Lilly, an All-America defensive tackle from TCU. Brandt also signed Amos Marsh, a fullback from Oregon State who was ignored by the other clubs. The Cowboys opened with two victories. They scored 10 points in the last 56 seconds to upset Pittsburgh 27-24 in the opener before 23,500 at the Cotton Bowl, September 17. The following week, Dallas knocked off Minnesota's expansion Vikings 21-7. The Cowboys scored their first shutout, 28-0 over the Vikings, and were tied for first place in the Eastern Conference with a 3-1 record, October 1. The euphoria died quickly as the Cowboys won just one of their last 10 games. The Cowboys were much improved, however, with a running attack generated by Perkins, who had missed all of 1960 with an injury, and a deep passing game with Clarke the main target.

1962 Landry introduced the shuttling quarterback offense. Rather than send in plays by alternating the guards, Paul Brown style, Landry let LeBaron and Meredith play alternate downs. The idea was an immediate success as the Cowboys bolted to a 4-3-1 start and stayed within a half-game of first place through midseason. A crowd of 45,668 fans was at the Cotton Bowl for the showdown between Dallas and the front-running New York Giants, November 15. The Giants routed the Cowboys 41-10 and LeBaron was injured, crippling the Dallas attack. The Cowboys won just one of their last six games, but their wide-open offense (398 points) was one of the best statistically. Perkins and Tubbs became the first Dallas players selected all-pro. Perkins ran for 945 yards, while Clarke caught 47 passes for 1,043 yards and a league-leading 14 touchdowns.

1963 The Cowboys opened the season at a new training camp, their fourth in four years. But this one, located at California Lutheran in Thousand Oaks, California, would remain the Cowboys' home every succeeding summer. The season started dismally as the Cowboys dropped six of their first seven games. The only bright spot came in a 21-17 loss to Washington when Howton broke Don Hutson's all-time career record for pass-receiving yardage, surpassing the 8,000-yard mark, September 29. Injuries took their toll on the diminutive LeBaron and he gave way to Meredith for the second half of the schedule. Following the season, LeBaron retired.

1964 With one year to go on his original contract, Landry was signed to a 10-year extension, giving him the longest coaching pact in the history of pro sports to that time. Howton joined LeBaron in retirement, and the Cowboys traded for two receivers, Buddy Dial of Pittsburgh and Tommy McDonald of Philadelphia. McDonald came through with 46 catches, but the price Dallas paid for his services —kicker Sam Baker—was steep. Landry turned the kicking duties over to Dick Van Raaphorst, whose erratic kicks were costly in several close games. Rookie Mel Renfro had a brilliant year, intercepting seven passes and leading the NFL in kick returns. Clarke set a club record with 65 receptions.

1965 Dallas had an extraordinary crop of rookies, including split end Bob Hayes, tackle Ralph Neely, halfback Dan Reeves, defensive tackle Jethro Pugh, and the number-one draft pick, quarterback Craig Morton. Hayes, the Olympic champion sprinter, had the most immediate impact, catching 46 passes, averaging 22 yards per catch, and scoring 13 touchdowns. Hayes's blazing speed forced defensive secondaries to abandon man-to-man coverage and adopt the zone. With receivers such as Hayes and Clarke at his disposal, Meredith had a great year, throwing 22 touchdown passes. The Cowboys were unpredictable and exciting. Following impressive victories over San Francisco and Pittsburgh, they attracted their first home sellout (76,251) to the Cotton Bowl for a game against Cleveland, September 21. The Browns won 24-17 but the Cowboys rallied to win three of their last four games to finish second and qualify for the Playoff Bowl. Dallas lost its first postseason game, 35-3 to Baltimore.

1966 Schramm was named president of the club by owner Clint Murchison, who retained the title of chairman of the board. On the field, the pieces finally fell into place. The already abundant talent was augmented by rookies John Niland, a guard, and Walt Garrison, a fullback. Dallas opened with four straight victories, including romps over the New York Giants (52-7), Atlanta (47-14), and Philadelphia (56-7). Meredith threw five touchdown passes in the opener against New York and five more against the Eagles. In the first seven weeks, the Cowboys averaged 39 points a game. In a 31-30 win over Washington, Hayes gained 246 yards on pass receptions, including a 95-yard touchdown. Dallas practically clinched its first Eastern Conference championship with a dramatic 26-14 win over the second-place Cleveland Browns before an overflow crowd of 80,259 at the Cotton Bowl, November 24. The stars of the offense were Meredith, who passed for 2,805 yards and 24 touchdowns; Hayes, who caught 64 passes for 1,232 yards and 13 touchdowns;

and Reeves, who, in his first year as a starter, led the NFL with 16 touchdowns. The Cowboys and the Green Bay Packers played one of the most thrilling championship games in NFL history, January 1. Green Bay won 34-27 when Tom Brown intercepted Meredith's pass in the end zone in the final moments.

1967 Early in the season, Meredith suffered severe rib injuries, a broken nose, and subsequent pneumonia. Morton, a rapidly maturing quarterback, filled in for Meredith in several key games. Reeves totaled over 1,100 yards and 11 touchdowns rushing and receiving. Hayes and Lance Rentzel, who was obtained from the Vikings, combined for 18 touchdown receptions. The defense featured five all-pros, Lilly and George Andrie on the line, linebacker Chuck Howley, and Renfro and Cornell Green in the secondary. In the Eastern Conference title game against Cleveland, Meredith completed 10 of 12 passes for two scores as Dallas roared to a 24-0 lead. Dallas won 52-14. "It was our greatest game ever," said Landry. The Cowboys and Packers played for the NFL championship on the coldest December 31 in Green Bay history—13 degrees below zero. Dallas overcame a 14-0 deficit for a 17-14 fourth-quarter lead on Reeves's 50-yard scoring pass to Rentzel. Starr's last-second quarterback sneak won the game for Green Bay 21-17.

1968 Late in the sluggish preseason, Landry held a closed-door meeting in which he blasted his players for a lack of pride and a poor attitude. The Cowboys responded by going unbeaten through their first six league games, including victories over Detroit (59-13) and Philadelphia (45-13). The Cowboys suffered a key loss in a 27-10 win over St. Louis when Reeves went down with torn knee ligaments. He was replaced by second-year back Craig Baynham. The Cowboys finished strong with five straight victories. Meredith finished second in the NFL in passing. Dallas was upset by Cleveland in the Eastern Conference championship game 31-20, December 21. The dejected Cowboys regrouped to beat Minnesota in the Playoff Bowl 17-13.

1969 Ground was broken for Texas Stadium, a lavish $30 million structure in suburban Irving with a seating capacity of 65,000, January 25. That set the tone for a season of change. Meredith, the last of the original Cowboys, announced his retirement, July 5. Less than two weeks later, Perkins, the team's leading rusher seven of the previous eight seasons, announced his retirement. Garrison replaced Perkins; Morton took over for Meredith. Roger Staubach, 27, joined the Cowboys as a rookie quarterback following four years of naval service. Calvin Hill, a rookie from Yale, replaced Reeves at halfback and rushed for 942 yards. When Hayes was injured, Rentzel took up the slack, and led the NFL with a 22.3-yard average and 12 touchdown receptions. The Cowboys rolled to the Capitol Division title with an 11-2-1 record. Renfro set a club record with 10 interceptions. The season closed on a low note as the Cowboys lost to Cleveland 38-14 in the Eastern Conference title game at the Cotton Bowl. In the Playoff Bowl, the Rams defeated the Cowboys 31-0.

1970 The Cowboys finished the preseason 1-5, and Landry named Staubach to start the league opener against Philadelphia. Dallas won 17-7 but Staubach was unimpressive. After a 54-13 rout at the hands of Minnesota, Landry went back to Morton. The low point came in a 38-0 loss to division-leading St. Louis. The defeat dropped Dallas to third place with a 5-4 record. The free-and-easy Cowboys swept their last five games and shot past the Cardinals and New York Giants, who faded in December. Duane Thomas, a rookie halfback from West Texas State, led the offense, replacing the injured Hill. The defense, bolstered by the addition of all-pro cornerback Herb Adderley, did not allow a touchdown in the last 17 quarters. Dallas clinched the division title by burying Houston 52-10 on Morton's five touchdown passes, December 20. The Cowboys edged Detroit 5-0 in an NFC Divisional Playoff Game as Thomas rushed for 135 yards. Thomas gained 143 yards to lead the Cowboys past San Francisco 17-10 in the NFC Championship Game at Kezar Stadium, January 3. The Cowboys committed five costly turnovers and lost Super Bowl V to Baltimore 16-13 on Jim O'Brien's last-second 32-yard field goal, January 17. Howley became the only member of a losing team ever to be named Super Bowl most valuable player.

1971 The Cowboys moved into their new home, Texas Stadium, October 24. Through the first half of the season, Landry alternated Morton and Staubach at quarterback with poor results (4-3). When the Cowboys lost to the Chicago Bears with Morton and Staubach alternating plays and throwing four interceptions, Landry made a decision. He picked Staubach as his number-one man because of Staubach's scrambling ability and flair for leadership. Staubach quickly established himself as the NFL's most accurate passer (60 percent completions) and a skillful runner (averaging 8.4 yards a carry). With Thomas, Hill, and Garrison in the backfield, Dallas had the best ground game in football. Under Staubach, the Cowboys won their last seven games and won the Eastern Division. The Dallas defense forced five turnovers to beat Minnesota 20-12 in the NFC playoffs. The Cowboys defeated San Francisco 14-3 in the NFC Championship Game as George Andrie returned an interception to the 1-yard line. With Staubach hitting 12 of 19 passes and Thomas rushing for 95 yards, Dallas rolled over Miami 24-3 in Super Bowl VI at New Orleans, January 16.

1972 Staubach suffered a shoulder separation in the final preseason game and was sidelined for three months. Thomas alienated Dallas management and was traded to San Diego. Andrie and Lilly were hampered much of the year with back injuries. With all these woes, the Cowboys struggled through an erratic season, slipping to second place in the Eastern Division behind Washington. They had a chance to tie for first the final week but lost 23-3 to the New York Giants. The one steady performer was Calvin Hill, who became the first Cowboys' player ever to rush for more than 1,000 yards, totaling 1,036. Hill also led Dallas receivers with 43 catches. Staubach came off the bench in the second half and threw two touchdown passes in the final 1:48 to spark Dallas to a dramatic 30-28 win over San Francisco in the NFC playoffs. In the NFC Championship Game, the Cowboys were thrashed 26-3 by the Redskins.

1973 The Cowboys and Landry recorded their one-hundredth NFL victory with a 40-3 win over New Orleans at Texas Stadium, September 24. After a 3-0 start, the Cowboys lost three of their next four games including a 14-7 affair in Washington in which Garrison was stopped on the goal line by Ken Houston as the gun sounded. Lee Roy Jordan, the veteran middle linebacker, turned the season around, intercepting three Ken Anderson passes in the first quarter to inspire a 38-10 win over Cincinnati, November 4. Drew Pearson, a free-agent wide receiver, made his first NFL start replacing injured Mike Montgomery in a 31-10 win over Philadelphia. Dallas gained revenge on the Redskins with a 27-7 win at Texas Stadium, December 9 as Dallas regained the Eastern Division crown. Staubach won his second NFL passing championship, hitting 63 percent of his attempts, 23 for touchdowns. Hill rushed for a club-record 1,142 yards. Dallas held off Los Angeles 27-16 in an NFC Divisional Playoff Game at Texas Stadium. Without the injured Hill and Lilly, the Cowboys were no match for Minnesota in the NFC Championship Game, losing 27-10 at Texas Stadium, December 30.

1974 For the first time, Dallas had the first pick overall in the NFL draft. Using a choice they acquired from Houston in exchange for Tody Smith and Billy Parks, Dallas selected Ed (Too Tall) Jones, a 6-foot 8-inch, 260-pound defensive end from Tennessee State. The Cowboys got off to their poorest start since 1963, losing four of their first five games and slipping into last place. Hill ended the slump, scoring three touchdowns in a 31-24 win over Philadelphia, October 20. The Cowboys surged back into contention, winning seven of their next eight, highlighted by a 24-23 win over Washington, November 28. Rookie quarterback Clint Longley, subbing for the injured Staubach, threw two touchdown passes including a 50-yarder to Pearson with 28 seconds left to win it. The strong finish fell short, however, as Dallas missed the playoffs for the first time in nine years.

1975 In the first round, the Cowboys chose defensive lineman Randy White of Maryland. With Hill signed by Hawaii of the World Football League and Garrison retired, Landry revamped his offense, installing the Shotgun formation with Staubach taking the snap eight yards behind center. The new look surprised Los Angeles, and the Cowboys upset the favored Rams 18-7 in the league opener, September 21. The following week, rookie linebacker Thomas Henderson returned a kickoff 97 yards for a touchdown as Dallas beat St. Louis in overtime 37-31. After a 4-0 start, the Cowboys hit the skids, slipping to third place at 5-3 before catching fire again. Bob Lilly, who had retired before the season, was honored at a game against Philadelphia as his uniform number 74 was retired, November 23. The Cowboys won five of their last six to finish second to St. Louis in the Eastern Division and secure the NFC wild card berth. Dallas pulled off a stunner in the playoff opener, upending Minnesota 17-14 on Staubach's 50-yard touchdown pass to Drew Pearson with 24 seconds left, December 27. Staubach was magnificent in the NFC Championship Game, throwing four touchdown passes, three to free-agent halfback Preston Pearson, as the underdog Cowboys embarrassed Los Angeles 37-7, January 4. In Super Bowl X in Miami, Dallas led most of the way but lost to Pittsburgh 21-17, January 18.

1976 Scott Laidlaw, a second-year running back from Stanford, gained 104 yards in his first NFL start as Dallas beat Philadelphia 27-7 in the opening game. Staubach had the best game of his career, passing for 339 yards and two touchdowns as Dallas outlasted Baltimore 30-27, September 26. The Cowboys won their first five games as Staubach completed a remarkable 73.5 percent of his passes. Dallas beat Chicago 31-21, but Staubach broke a finger on his passing hand, an injury that bothered him the remainder of the season, October 24. The Cowboys clinched their first Eastern Division title since 1973 by beating Philadelphia 26-7 December 5 at Philadelphia. The team's offensive star was Drew Pearson, who led the NFC in receiving. The Cowboys' sputtering offense proved their undoing in the NFC playoffs as they lost to Los Angeles in the first round 14-12, December 19. Lee Roy Jordan announced his retirement after 14 seasons with the Cowboys. Don Meredith and Don Perkins joined Bob Lilly in the Cowboys' Ring of Honor.

1977 The Cowboys traded four draft choices to Seattle for the second pick in the draft and then selected Heisman Trophy winner Tony Dorsett of Pittsburgh. Dallas also chose wide receiver Tony Hill and offensive lineman Jim Cooper. Chuck Howley became the fourth member of the Cowboys' Ring of Honor. The Cowboys won eight consecutive games for their best start ever, then suffered consecutive losses to St. Louis and Pittsburgh. In the Steelers game, Dorsett started for the first time. The Cowboys closed out their schedule with four victories, including a 14-6 win over Denver in the season finale. Despite being nurtured slowly, Dorsett finished the season with 1,007 yards and 13 touchdowns. The Cowboys' 12-2 record was the best in football, and it gave them the home-field advantage in the playoffs. On December 26, they opened the playoffs with a 37-7 victory over Chicago. Charlie Waters set a playoff record with three interceptions in the game. In the NFC Championship Game, the Cowboys limited the Vikings to only 66 yards rushing and won 23-6. Two weeks later, Dallas used eight Denver turnovers and a stifling defense to win Super Bowl XII 27-10.

1978 The Cowboys began 6-2, but the offense bogged down in losses to Minnesota and Miami and they slumped to 6-4. Then Staubach, Dorsett, and a defense that held six consecutive foes to an average of 10 points combined to close the year with six victories, a 12-4 record, and the club's tenth divisional championship. Staubach led the NFL in passing, and Dorsett set a club record with 1,325 yards rushing. In the playoff opener against Atlanta, the Cowboys trailed 20-13 at halftime and had lost Staubach to a first-half concussion. But backup Danny White rallied the team to a 27-20 victory. Dallas and the Rams battled to a scoreless tie in the first half of the NFC Championship Game. The Cowboys then used two interceptions by Charlie Waters to convert a close game into a 28-0 victory. Two weeks later, Staubach's last-minute heroics weren't enough, as he rallied the Cowboys from a 35-17 deficit, but the Steelers held on and won Super Bowl XIII 35-31.

1979 The Cowboys released their highlight film entitled "America's Team." The nickname stuck, and fans throughout the country began using the label. Jethro Pugh retired before the season, and Ed (Too Tall) Jones left football to pursue a career in professional boxing. To fill the resulting defensive gaps, John Dutton was acquired from Baltimore in early October. The Cowboys appeared invincible in winning seven of their first eight regular-season games in 1979, including romps over Minnesota and the Los Angeles Rams, but the defense collapsed in three consecutive losses, to Philadelphia, 31-21; Washington, 34-20; and Houston, 30-24. The team recovered to win its last three games and the NFC East title with an 11-5 record. Staubach led the league in passing for the fourth time. Playing in Texas Stadium on December 30, the Cowboys were ousted from the playoffs when Rams quarterback Vince Ferragamo threw a 50-yard touchdown pass to Billy Waddy with 2:06 remaining to win 21-19.

1980 The Cowboys lost two of their long-time leaders in the offseason when Staubach and safety Cliff Harris announced their retirements. But in July, the club welcomed back Jones, who returned after a year away as a boxer. Bob Lilly became the first player elected to the Pro Football Hall of Fame solely for his play as a Cowboy. Danny White replaced Staubach and guided the team to a league-leading 454 points and a 12-4 record. He threw four touchdown passes in a 59-14 victory over San Francisco on October 12 and duplicated that feat in a 35-27 win over Philadelphia in the season finale. But White's 3,287 yards and 28 touchdown passes and Dorsett's 1,185 yards rushing weren't enough, as Dallas finished second to Philadelphia. On December 28, the Cowboys crushed the Rams 34-13 in the NFC Wild Card Game. Trailing 24-10 after three periods, Dallas exploded in the fourth quarter to win 30-27 in a divisional playoff game against Atlanta on January 4. A week later, Dallas lost to Philadelphia 20-7, as the Eagles' defense throttled the Cowboys.

1981 The season opened with question marks in the defensive backfield, but rookies Michael Downs and Everson Walls successfully filled the holes; Walls finished the season with a league-leading 11 interceptions. The Cowboys started fast, with four straight victories. But a slump, which included a 45-14 pounding by San Francisco, dropped the Cowboys behind the Eagles, despite a 17-14 victory over Philadelphia. A four-game winning streak late in the year resulted in another NFC East championship, however, with the clinching victory coming on December 13, when Dallas defeated Philadelphia 21-10. The Cowboys finished with a 12-4 record and Dorsett enjoyed his finest season, rushing for 1,646 yards, second-best in the NFL. He also became the first NFL player ever to rush for 1,000 yards or more in each of his first five seasons. On January 2, the Doomsday II defense totally shut down Tampa Bay and the Cowboys easily won a divisional playoff game 38-0. But a week later, the defense fell victim to a game-winning, 89-yard drive mounted by San Francisco in the NFC Championship Game 28-27.

1982 The Cowboys lost their season opener for the first time since 1964 as the Steelers won 36-28, giving them five straight victories over Dallas, including Super Bowls X and XIII. The Cowboys did not lose again until December 26, beating St. Louis 24-7, then coming back after the strike layoff with five victories in a row, including a 24-10 win that gave Washington its only loss of the season. Losses in the final two games made the Cowboys 6-3, to establish an NFL record of 17 consecutive winning seasons. In the season finale against the Vikings, Dorsett ran 99 yards for a touchdown, the longest run from scrimmage in NFL history. Dorsett led the NFC in rushing, Danny White was second in passing, and Everson Walls tied an NFL record by leading the league in interceptions for the second year in a row. In the Super Bowl tournament, the Cowboys beat the Buccaneers 30-17 and the Packers 37-26 to advance to the NFC Championship Game for the third year in a row. But there they fell to the Redskins 31-17.

1983 In the first Monday night game of the year, the Cowboys defeated Washington 31-30. The Redskins led 23-3 at halftime, but Danny White threw three touchdown passes and ran for another for the victory. The Cowboys won their next six games, then lost to the Raiders 40-38 when Chris Bahr kicked a 26-yard field goal with 20 seconds left. On October 9, former quarterback Roger Staubach became the sixth member of the Cowboys' Ring of Honor. Ground was broken for the Cowboys' new headquarters and training facility at the Valley Ranch in northwest Dallas County. Losses in the final two games dropped the Cowboys to 12-4, but they still earned a playoff berth, their NFL-record ninth straight, as a wild card. The Los Angeles Rams defeated them in the NFC Wild Card Game 24-17. Danny White set team records with 533 attempts, 334 completions, 3,980 yards, and 29 touchdowns.

1984 Early in the Cowboys' Silver season, on March 19, the sale of the Cowboys from the Murchison family to an 11-member limited partnership headed by Dallas businessman H.R. (Bum) Bright was approved by the NFL owners; the sale was finalized May 18. On March 27, the Cowboys and Triland International announced plans to develop Cowboys Center, a multi-use complex adjacent to the team's new headquarters. The Dallas roster was shaken up by the retirements of DuPree, offensive tackle Pat Donovan, and defensive end Harvey Martin, and the offseason loss of wide receiver Drew Pearson, badly injured in an automobile accident. Landry couldn't decide on a quarterback, playing White and Gary Hogeboom throughout the season, and the offense suffered accordingly. Though the Cowboys extended their NFL record to 19 consecutive winning seasons with a 9-7 campaign, it was not good enough to make the playoffs—the first time in 10 years Dallas missed postseason play. The killer was a 28-21 loss to Miami in the season finale.

1985 Staubach was enshrined in the Pro Football Hall of Fame in his first year of eligibility, August 3. The season got off to a great start with a 44-14 shellacking of arch-rival Washington in the opener. Dallas went 7-3 through the first 10 weeks. Then the Cowboys met the Bears, and the eventual Super Bowl champions handed them their worst defeat ever, 44-0, ending the second-longest shutout-free streak in NFL history, 218 games. Dallas finished 10-6 to win its thirteenth division championship. The Rams played spoilers again in the playoffs, beating the Cowboys 20-0 in an NFC Divisional Playoff Game. Walls intercepted nine passes to become the only player ever to lead the NFL in interceptions three times. Danny White, again given the quarterback job, responded with 3,157 yards passing and a number-four ranking in the NFC. Dorsett led the ground game with 1,307 yards.

MEMBERS OF HALL OF FAME:
Herb Adderley, Lance Alworth, Forrest Gregg, Bob Lilly, Roger Staubach

COWBOYS RECORD, 1960-85

Year	Won	Lost	Tied	Pct.	Fin.	Pts.	OP
1960	0	11	1	.000	7	177	369
1961	4	9	1	.308	6	236	380
1962	5	8	1	.385	5	398	402
1963	4	10	0	.286	5	305	378
1964	5	8	1	.385	5	250	289
1965a	7	7	0	.500	2t	325	280
1966b	10	3	1	.769	1	445	239
1967c	9	5	0	.643	1	342	268
1968d	12	2	0	.857	1	431	186
1969e	11	2	1	.846	1	369	223
1970f	10	4	0	.714	1	299	221
1971g	11	3	0	.786	1	406	222
1972h	10	4	0	.714	2	319	240
1973i	10	4	0	.714	1	382	203
1974	8	6	0	.571	3	297	235
1975f	10	4	0	.714	2	350	268
1976j	11	3	0	.786	1	296	194
1977g	12	2	0	.857	1	345	212
1978f	12	4	0	.750	1	384	208
1979j	11	5	0	.688	1	371	313
1980k	12	4	0	.750	2	454	311
1981i	12	4	0	.750	1	367	277
1982l	6	3	0	.667	2	226	145
1983m	12	4	0	.750	2	479	360
1984	9	7	0	.563	4	308	308
1985j	10	6	0	.625	1	357	333
26 Years	233	132	6	.636		8,918	7,064

a*NFL Eastern Conference Runnerup; 0-1 in Playoff Bowl*
b*NFL Eastern Conference Champion; 0-1 in Playoffs*
c*NFL Eastern Conference Champion; 1-1 in Playoffs*
d*NFL Capitol Division Champion; 1-1 in Playoffs*
e*NFL Capitol Division Champion; 0-2 in Playoffs*
f*NFC Champion; 2-1 in Playoffs*
g*Super Bowl Champion; 3-0 in Playoffs*
h*NFC Wild Card Qualifier for Playoffs; 1-1 in Playoffs*
i*NFC Eastern Division Champion; 1-1 in Playoffs*
j*NFC Eastern Division Champion; 0-1 in Playoffs*
k*NFC Wild Card Qualifier for Playoffs; 2-1 in Playoffs*
l*NFC Qualifier for Playoffs; 2-1 in Playoffs*
m*NFC Wild Card Qualifier for Playoffs; 0-1 in Playoffs*

RECORD HOLDERS

CAREER

Rushing attempts	Tony Dorsett, 1977-85	2,441
Rushing yards	Tony Dorsett, 1977-85	10,832
Pass attempts	Roger Staubach, 1969-79	2,958
Pass completions	Roger Staubach, 1969-79	1,685
Passing yards	Roger Staubach, 1969-79	22,700
Touchdown passes	Roger Staubach, 1969-79	153
Receptions	Drew Pearson, 1973-83	489
Receiving yards	Drew Pearson, 1973-83	7,822
Interceptions	Mel Renfro, 1964-77	52
Punting average	Sam Baker, 1962-63	45.1
Punt return avg.	Bob Hayes, 1965-74	11.1
Kickoff return avg.	Mel Renfro, 1964-77	26.4
Field goals	Rafael Septien, 1978-85	147
Touchdowns	Tony Dorsett, 1977-85	79
Points	Rafael Septien, 1978-85	786

SEASON

Rushing attempts	Tony Dorsett, 1981	342
Rushing yards	Tony Dorsett, 1981	1,646
Pass attempts	Danny White, 1983	533
Pass completions	Danny White, 1983	334
Passing yards	Danny White, 1983	3,980

Touchdown passes	Danny White, 1983	29
Receptions	Tony Hill, 1985	74
Receiving yards	Bob Hayes, 1966	1,232
Interceptions	Everson Walls, 1981	11
Punting average	Sam Baker, 1962	45.4
Punt return avg.	Bob Hayes, 1968	20.8
Kickoff return avg.	Mel Renfro, 1965	30.0
Field goals	Rafael Septien, 1981	27
Touchdowns	Dan Reeves, 1966	16
Points	Rafael Septien, 1983	123
GAME		
Rushing attempts	Calvin Hill, 11-10-74	32
Rushing yards	Tony Dorsett, 12-4-77	206
Pass attempts	Roger Staubach, 10-26-75	49
	Gary Hogeboom, 12-22-85	49
Pass completions	Gary Hogeboom, 9-3-84	33
Passing yards	Don Meredith, 11-10-63	460
Touchdown passes	7 times	5
Receptions	Lance Rentzel, 11-19-67	13
Receiving yards	Bob Hayes, 11-13-66	246
Interceptions	Herb Adderley, 9-26-71	3
	Lee Roy Jordan, 11-4-73	3
	Dennis Thurman, 12-13-81	3
Field goals	4 times	4
Touchdowns	4 times	4
Points	4 times	24

COACHING HISTORY

1960-85 Tom Landry 254-150-6

FIRST PLAYER SELECTED

1960 None
1961 Bob Lilly, DT, TCU
1962 (2) Sonny Gibbs, QB, TCU
1963 Lee Roy Jordan, LB, Alabama
1964 Scott Appleton, DT, Texas
1965 Craig Morton, QB, California
1966 John Niland, G, Iowa
1967 (3) Phil Clark, DB, Northwestern
1968 Dennis Homan, FL, Alabama
1969 Calvin Hill, RB, Yale
1970 Duane Thomas, RB, West Texas State
1971 Tody Smith, DE, USC
1972 Bill Thomas, RB, Boston College
1973 Billy Joe DuPree, TE, Michigan State
1974 Ed (Too Tall) Jones, DE, Tennessee State
1975 Randy White, LB, Maryland
1976 Aaron Kyle, DB, Wyoming
1977 Tony Dorsett, RB, Pittsburgh
1978 Larry Bethea, DE, Michigan State
1979 Robert Shaw, C, Tennessee
1980 (3) Bill Roe, LB, Colorado
1981 Howard Richards, T, Missouri
1982 Rod Hill, CB, Kentucky State
1983 Jim Jeffcoat, DE, Arizona State
1984 Billy Cannon, LB, Texas A&M
1984* Todd Fowler, TE, Stephen F. Austin
1985 Kevin Brooks, DE, Michigan
1986 Mike Sherrard, WR, UCLA
Supplemental Draft

COWBOYS SILVER SEASON ALL-TIME TEAM (1984)

OFFENSE

WR	Drew Pearson	1973-83
WR	Bob Hayes	1965-74
TE	Billy Joe DuPree	1973-83
T	Ralph Neely	1965-77
T	Rayfield Wright	1967-79
G	John Niland	1966-74
G	Herb Scott	1975-84
C	John Fitzgerald	1971-80
QB	Roger Staubach	1969-79
QB	Don Meredith	1960-68
RB	Tony Dorsett	1977-85
RB	Walt Garrison	1966-74
RB	Don Perkins	1961-68
DEFENSE		
DE	Ed (Too Tall) Jones	1974-85
DE	Harvey Martin	1973-83
DT	Bob Lilly	1961-74
DT	Randy White	1975-85
LB	Lee Roy Jordan	1963-76
LB	Chuck Howley	1961-72
LB	D.D. Lewis	1968-81
CB	Mel Renfro	1964-77
CB	Everson Walls	1981-85
CB	Cornell Green	1962-74
S	Charlie Waters	1970-81
S	Cliff Harris	1970-79
SPECIALISTS		
P	Danny White	1976-85
K	Rafael Septien	1978-85

COWBOYS RING OF HONOR

Pos.	Player	Inducted
DT	Bob Lilly	1975
QB	Don Meredith	1976
RB	Don Perkins	1976
LB	Chuck Howley	1977
DB	Mel Renfro	1981
QB	Roger Staubach	1983

DENVER BRONCOS

1959 The Denver Broncos, with Bob Howsam as their principal owner, were named a charter member of the American Football League, August 14. Dean Griffing was named the team's first general manager. The Broncos' first selection in the AFL player draft was Roger LeClerc, a center from Trinity (Connecticut).
1960 Frank Filchock was named the first head coach of the Broncos, January 1. The team was placed in the AFL's Western Division with the Dallas Texans, Los Angeles Chargers, and Oakland Raiders. The Broncos' first training camp opened in July at Colorado School of Mines. The team played its games in Bears Stadium, primarily a baseball facility with limited seating capacity. After losing all five of their preseason games, on September 9 the Broncos won their first regular-season game, defeating the Patriots in Boston 13-10, before 21,597. In their first home game, 18,372 watched the Broncos beat Oakland 31-14. Attendance grew worse, dropping to 5,861 for the final home game, a 30-27 loss to the New York Titans. The Broncos finished the season 4-9-1.
1961 Bob Howsam and his father, Lee, sold their stock to a new syndicate headed by Cal Kunz and Gerry Phipps. Kunz was named president. With an offense built around the passing of quarterback Frank Tripucka, end Lionel Taylor, who had been cut from the Chicago Bears, developed into one of the AFL's premier receivers. He set a pro record with 100 pass receptions for the season. The team's record was only 3-11, and at the end of the year Filchock was released as head coach.
1962 Jack Faulkner, who had coached under Sid Gillman at the University of Cincinnati and with the Los Angeles and San Diego Chargers, was named head coach. He was also given the added assignment of general manager after Dean Griffing was dismissed. Faulkner changed the team's colors from brown and gold to orange, blue, and white. The team's vertically striped socks, objects of some ridicule, were burned at a public ceremony. In Faulkner's first regular-season game, the Broncos stunned the Chargers, a team they never had beaten, 30-21 before a crowd estimated at 28,000. When Denver defeated Houston 20-10 before a record crowd of 34,496 at Bears Stadium, it ran its record for the year to 6-1. The Broncos' weaknesses became apparent, however, particularly in the defensive secondary, and the team slumped badly the second half of the season, finishing with a 7-7 record. Taylor again led the league in receiving, with 77 catches. Faulkner was named AFL coach of the year by both wire services, and home attendance was up more than 100 percent over the previous year.
1963 Faulkner initiated a youth movement, managing to sign some top draft choices for the first time in the history of the franchise. Veteran Frank Tripucka retired, leaving Denver with a critical problem at quarterback. Mickey Slaughter, a rookie from Louisiana Tech, got the first crack at the job but soon was sidelined with a concussion. John McCormick, a rookie from Massachusetts, was next. He injured a knee and went out for the year, October 13. Don Breaux, formerly a taxi-squad player at San Diego, shared the job the rest of the season with Slaughter. Fourteen rookies played regularly on a team that finished the season 2-11-1. Fullback Billy Joe was named rookie of the year, and Taylor led the league in receiving for the fourth consecutive year.
1964 Faulkner, desperate for a quarterback, completed a trade with Houston for Jacky Lee, who came to the team on a two-year, lend-lease arrangement. To get him, the Broncos had to give up Bud McFadin, their all-league tackle, and a high draft choice. A nine-player trade with the New York Jets, designed to bolster Denver's sagging defense, didn't work out and pressure began to build. Speaking before a game against Boston, Faulkner, whose team was winless, said the game was "the most important of my career." He proved prophetic. Denver lost and Faulkner was fired. Mac Speedie, the team's receivers coach, was appointed to take over on an interim basis. The Broncos reacted by outscoring Kansas City 33-27 in a wild first game for Speedie. The Broncos then reverted to their losing ways and wound up 2-11-1.
1965 A serious split occurred at the ownership-management level as attendance began to drop. Kunz and his bloc of majority stockholders became convinced the Broncos were a losing proposition and attempted to sell. Cox Broadcasting Company tendered a reported $4 million offer and announced it planned to move the franchise to Atlanta. Gerry and Allan Phipps, owners of 42 percent of the club, made what turned out to be the most important decision in the history of the franchise. They decided they wanted the team to remain in Denver. They bought out the holdings of the others for $1.5 million. The brief threat of the team moving out of town triggered a tremendous response from the citizens of the city. Ticket sales boomed at an unprecedented rate. Two major trades—for Kansas City halfback Abner Haynes and Buffalo fullback Cookie Gilchrist—generated even more interest, and by May 1, the season-ticket figure reached 22,000, an all-time high. Allan Phipps was named president of Empire Sports. Gerry Phipps was redesignated chairman of the board. Jim Burris, general manager of the baseball franchise also held by Empire Sports, assumed duties as the Broncos' new general manager. Although Gilchrist and Haynes both helped, the team finished 4-10. Attendance, however, increased to an average of 31,398, a record for an AFL Western Division team. Six of the seven home crowds topped 30,000.
1966 Legislation was passed creating a Metropolitan Stadium district in Denver. Voters were informed a four-county metropolitan region would vote on building a multimillion-dollar all-purpose stadium before March, 1967. One of the major provisions of the bill was that the tenants—the football Broncos and baseball Bears—sign a 10-year lease. Internal problems, which seemed to follow Gilchrist as stubbornly as opposing linebackers, surfaced again, with Speedie and his top offensive player finally reaching a point of no return. Gilchrist, a holdout, was traded to Miami. The Broncos felt the effects of his absence in the first game of the season. Houston beat them 45-7 and the Broncos failed to generate even one first down. A week later, after a 24-10 loss to Boston, Speedie resigned. Ray Malavasi, the line coach, was named the interim head coach. Late in December, Lou Saban was signed to a 10-year contract as coach and general manager.
1967 Voters turned down the stadium bond issue, but Broncos fans immediately organized a fund-raising drive to improve Bears Stadium and keep the team in Denver. Floyd Little, the Syracuse All-America running back, became the first number-one draft choice ever to sign with the Broncos. Denver beat Detroit 13-7 in a preseason game; it was the first time an AFL team won a game over an NFL team. The Broncos gave up two number-one draft choices to San Diego for quarterback Steve Tensi. The season-ticket count reached a record 24,650. A single-game attendance record was set when 35,565 watched Denver lose to the New York Jets 38-24. Building toward the future, Saban started as many as 15 rookies during the season, which the Broncos finished at 3-11.
1968 The civic drive to raise $1.8 million ended successfully and the city of Denver received the stadium

as a gift after the purchase of the facility from Empire Sports by a non-profit group. Construction began on a 16,000-seat upper deck that would raise capacity to 50,000. Another new season ticket record of 27,348 was reached. The Broncos drew more than 50,000 for the first time when 50,002 watched Denver and Oakland play, November 10. Bears Stadium was officially renamed Denver Mile High Stadium. On the field, the Broncos won five games behind the play of Little and quarterback Marlin Briscoe, the first black to play regularly at quarterback in the AFL.

1969 The Broncos started the season with victories over Boston and the New York Jets. Little had a 166-yard rushing day, the top single-game yardage figure for an AFL back, October 19. But injuries slowed the Broncos. Tensi was bothered by a bad knee. Little missed five games with shoulder and knee problems. He finished fifth in the league in rushing (729 yards), after leading it before his injuries. A 13-0 win over San Diego at Mile High Stadium was the Broncos' first shutout ever. They finished the season 5-8-1.

1970 Bobby Anderson, the number-one draft choice from Colorado, joined Little to form one of the best running back tandems in the realigned NFL. In the first season in which he played in all 14 games, Little led the AFC with 901 yards rushing. The Broncos started off 4-1, but injuries to Tensi left the passing up to first Pete Liske and then rookie Al Pastrana. The Broncos again finished fourth, at 5-8-1.

1971 Tensi announced his retirement. Quarterback Don Horn was acquired from Green Bay for defensive end Alden Roche and an exchange of first-round draft positions. Season-ticket sales reached 47,500. In the first of seven sellouts at Mile High Stadium, the Broncos tied Miami 10-10. After an inconspicuous first half of the season, Horn went out with an injury and was replaced by inexperienced Steve Ramsey. After nine games, Saban resigned as head coach. A month later, he quit as general manager, too. Jerry Smith, one of his assistants, worked the final five games as interim head coach. Little became Denver's first 1,000-yard rusher and finished as pro football's top ground-gainer with 1,133 yards in a 4-9-1 season.

1972 John Ralston, successful coach at Stanford, was named new head coach and general manager. For the first time in the history of the franchise, there was no public sale of season tickets. More than 46,500 renewed their season tickets, however. Cal Poly-Pomona was chosen as the new Denver training-camp site. Charley Johnson was acquired from Houston for a third draft choice, giving Ralston the experienced quarterback he was seeking. Veteran defensive linemen Rich Jackson and Dave Costa were traded, but Ralston's new front four, featuring Paul Smith and Lyle Alzado, performed well, and Johnson and Little helped the team score enough points to propel the Broncos to five victories.

1973 Ralston added a rapidly improving defense to the AFC's top scoring offense, and the Broncos remained in the playoff hunt all season. Midway through the season, the Broncos first gained some respectability when they came from behind to tie Oakland 23-23 on a Monday night. In the season finale, with the Western Division title on the line, the Broncos played the Raiders. Trailing 14-10 in the fourth quarter, the Broncos gambled on a fake punt on fourth down, but Bill Van Heusen didn't pick up the necessary yards. The Raiders took over and scored to wrap up the win 21-17 and drop the Broncos (7-5-2) to second place.

1974 In a draft in which the plan was to fortify the team's defense, Ohio State linebacker Randy Gradishar became the top selection. Denver voters passed a $25-million bond issue to expand Mile High Stadium to more than 75,000 seats. The Broncos and Pittsburgh Steelers played the first regular-season overtime game. It finished in a 35-35 tie after neither team scored in the sudden-death period. Otis Armstrong ran for 1,407 yards and won the NFL rushing title as the Broncos again finished in second place.

1975 The expansion of Mile High Stadium officially began. The projection called for 63,500 capacity for 1976 and 75,000 in 1977. The Broncos defeated Green Bay 23-13 for their first victory ever on Monday night television. Playing before the largest crowd ever to witness a Denver game, the Broncos lost to Buffalo 38-14 before 79,864 in Buffalo. In his final home game as a Bronco, Little scored two touchdowns, one on a 66-yard pass play, in a 25-10 victory over Philadelphia. He wound up his career as the NFL's seventh all-time rusher with 6,323 yards, but the team's record fell to 6-8.

1976 Quarterback Charley Johnson announced his retirement, although he remained with the team as a scout and quarterback coach on a part-time basis. Season-ticket sales were cut off at 62,215, giving the team its seventh straight sellout season. With one of the most effective defenses in the league, the Broncos stayed in the fight for the playoffs all the way, just missing a wild card spot. Nevertheless, their 9-5 record was the best in team history. On December 18, assistant general manager Fred Gehrke replaced Ralston as general manager.

1977 John Ralston resigned as head coach on January 31 and was replaced the next day by New England Patriots assistant Robert (Red) Miller. Led by newly acquired (from the Giants) quarterback Craig Morton and the stingiest defense in the AFC, nicknamed the "Orange Crush," the Broncos swept to the best record in football, 12-2. They opened with six consecutive victories before losing to Oakland 24-14 on October 30. The Broncos bounced back to win six more and on December 4 clinched the AFC West title with a 24-14 win at Houston. Denver lost the season finale to Dallas 14-6 in a game in which Morton played only one series. Before the largest crowd ever to watch a sporting event in Colorado, 75,011, Morton threw two touchdown passes to lead the Broncos to a 34-21 victory over the Steelers in a divisional playoff game. On New Year's Day, the Broncos beat the Raiders 20-17 in the AFC Championship Game. The Broncos suffered eight turnovers in Super Bowl XII on January 15, and the Cowboys won easily 27-10.

1978 The Broncos again won the AFC West, with a 10-6 record nosing out Oakland, San Diego, and Seattle by one game each. Denver opened with a 14-6 victory over Oakland on September 3. The Broncos defeated the Raiders again on December 3, 21-6, and, a week later, clinched the division with a 24-3 win over Kansas City. On December 16, the Broncos lost the season finale 21-17 when the Steelers' defense held at its 1-yard line on the last play of the game. Two weeks later the Steelers again defeated the Broncos, this time in an AFC Divisional Playoff Game, 33-10.

1979 After two seasons as the best in the league, Denver's defense became erratic, giving up 42 points to Pittsburgh and 34 to Seattle. On its better days the defense shut out Cincinnati (10-0) and San Diego (7-0). With two weeks left the Broncos were tied with the Chargers for the AFC West lead, but they lost to Seattle 28-23 and to San Diego 17-7 in the last game of the regular season. On December 23, the Oilers overcame injuries to Earl Campbell and Dan Pastorini to defeat the Broncos in the AFC Wild Card Game 13-7.

1980 Matt Robinson won the starting quarterback job in the preseason over Morton. Despite an early 41-20 win over Dallas, the Broncos' offense sputtered behind Robinson and the team's record fell to 3-4. Morton started on October 26 and led a win over the New York Giants. Morton went on to have one of his most productive seasons, finishing third in the AFC in passing, with 2,150 yards and a 60.8 completion percentage. The Broncos managed an 8-8 final record, despite a combined 1-5 mark against San Diego, Oakland, and Kansas City.

1981 In March, the Broncos were purchased by Edgar F. Kaiser, Jr. On March 10, Grady Alderman was named general manager and Dan Reeves, formerly the offensive coordinator of the Cowboys, the new head coach. Reeves went with former Dallas teammate Morton at quarterback, and the Broncos started fast. On September 27, Morton completed 17 of 18 passes for 308 yards and four first-half touchdowns, as the Broncos defeated San Diego 42-24. Two weeks later they took sole possession of first place in the AFC West with a 27-21 victory over Detroit in which Morton hit wide receiver Steve Watson for a 95-yard touchdown. Although Denver's record trailed off as the season progressed, the Broncos remained in at least a tie for first place through the last week of the season. Denver's season-ending loss to Chicago, combined with San Diego's victory over Oakland, put the Chargers in the playoffs based on a tiebreaker. Both teams finished 10-6.

1982 The Broncos slipped to 2-7 in the strike-shortened season. One smoking gun was this figure: an NFL-high total of 36 turnovers, including 19 fumbles lost and 17 interceptions. With Morton injured, Steve DeBerg took over at quarterback, and set an NFL record by completing 18 consecutive passes in a two-game stretch against the Los Angeles Rams and Kansas City Chiefs. Rookie free agent Rich Karlis unexpectedly beat out incumbent Fred Steinfort in training camp, and kicked 15 of 16 extra points and 11 of 13 field goals, leading the AFC in the latter category with an .846 percentage. Punter Luke Prestridge was selected to the AFC Pro Bowl squad, along with kick returner Rick Upchurch and linebacker Randy Gradishar. Upchurch tied an NFL record with his eighth career punt return for a touchdown (78 yards) in a 37-16 loss to Kansas City, December 19, and led the NFL with a 16.1-yard average.

1983 In the biggest trade in franchise history, the Broncos acquired Stanford All-America quarterback John Elway, the first player selected in the NFL draft, from the Baltimore Colts in exchange for their own 1983 number-one pick (offensive lineman Chris Hinton), their 1984 first-round pick, and backup quarterback Mark Hermann. Elway started 10 games, but shared the position with DeBerg. After nine games, Denver was tied with the Los Angeles Raiders for first place in the AFC West with a 6-3 mark, but a 3-4 finish dropped the Broncos to 9-7. They qualified for a wild card playoff berth, but were defeated 31-7 in the first round by Seattle at the Kingdome. Steve Watson led Denver with 59 catches for 1,133 yards. With DeBerg injured and Elway ill, rookie Gary Kubiak quarterbacked the Broncos to a victory against Seattle, November 20.

1984 Gradishar and guard Tom Glassic retired. DeBerg was traded to the Tampa Bay Buccaneers. On March 23, 40-year-old Denver real estate magnate Patrick D. Bowlen became the new majority owner of the Broncos. Denver defeated Cincinnati 20-17 in its opener when Kubiak relieved the injured Elway in the second half and directed a decisive 75-yard fourth-quarter scoring march. The following week, the Chicago Bears shut out Denver 27-0, behind a 179-yard rushing performance from Walter Payton, but then the Broncos reeled off 10 victories in a row before losing back-to-back games to Seattle and Kansas City. Karlis's 28-yard field goal with 2:08 remaining gave the Broncos a 16-13 victory over San Diego and a share of the AFC West lead with Seattle, Denver's final regular-season opponent. In the Kingdome, Elway launched a 73-yard pass to Watson less than three minutes into the game, and Denver won 31-14 to clinch the AFC West championship. In the first postseason game at Mile High Stadium since 1977, Denver was upset in a divisional playoff game by Pittsburgh 24-17. Although the Broncos ranked twenty-second in the NFL in total offense, and twenty-fifth in total defense, they were remarkably opportunistic. A case in point: Denver's 28-7 victory against Detroit on October 7, when the Broncos had seven interceptions and three fumble recoveries. Elway showed marked improvement in his second season and began to fulfill some of his great promise. He passed for 2,598 yards and 18 touchdowns. Running back Sammy Winder topped the 1,000-yard plateau for the first time, rushing for 1,153 yards. Steve Busick replaced Gradishar and led the Broncos with 195 tackles.

1985 The Broncos finished 11-5, tied for the third-best record in the NFL, but missed the playoffs because of the tie-breaking formulas with two other 11-5 teams in the AFC, the New York Jets and New England Patriots. The Broncos thus became the first 11-5 team since the adoption of the wild-card format to be excluded from the playoffs. Two of the Broncos' five losses were to the Raiders within a three-week period late in the season. In the first game on November 24, Los Angeles placekicker Chris Bahr recovered his own onside kickoff in the third period to set up a go-ahead touchdown and later won the game with a field goal in overtime. Two weeks later, the Raiders overcame a 14-0 deficit to force another overtime—the third consecutive overtime game between the two teams—and again won on a field goal by Bahr. It was the fifth game in a row between the two AFC West rivals decided by three points or less. Elway had a banner season, setting club records for passing attempts (605), completions (327), and yards (3,891). Reeves became the winningest coach in Denver history with a five-season record of 45-28.

MEMBER OF HALL OF FAME:
Willie Brown

BRONCOS RECORD, 1960-85

Year	Won	Lost	Tied	Pct.	Fin.	Pts.	OP
1960	4	9	1	.308	4	309	393
1961	3	11	0	.214	3	251	432
1962	7	7	0	.500	2	353	334
1963	2	11	1	.154	4	301	473
1964	2	11	1	.154	4	240	438
1965	4	10	0	.286	4	303	392
1966	4	10	0	.286	4	196	381
1967	3	11	0	.214	4	256	409
1968	5	9	0	.357	4	255	404
1969	5	8	1	.385	4	297	344
1970	5	8	1	.385	4	253	264
1971	4	9	1	.308	4	203	275
1972	5	9	0	.357	3	325	350
1973	7	5	2	.571	2	354	296
1974	7	6	1	.536	2	302	294
1975	6	8	0	.429	2	254	307
1976	9	5	0	.643	2	315	206
1977a	12	2	0	.857	1	274	148
1978b	10	6	0	.625	1	282	198
1979c	10	6	0	.625	2	289	262
1980	8	8	0	.500	4	310	323
1981	10	6	0	.625	2	321	289
1982	2	7	0	.222	12	148	226
1983c	9	7	0	.563	3	302	327
1984b	13	3	0	.813	1	353	241
1985	11	5	0	.688	2	380	329
26 Years	167	197	9	.460		7,426	8,335

aAFC Champion; 2-1 in Playoffs
bAFC Western Division Champion; 0-1 in Playoffs
cAFC Wild Card Qualifier for Playoffs; 0-1 in Playoffs

RECORD HOLDERS

CAREER		
Rushing attempts	Floyd Little, 1967-75	1,641
Rushing yards	Floyd Little, 1967-75	6,323
Pass attempts	Craig Morton, 1977-82	1,594
Pass completions	Craig Morton, 1977-82	907
Passing yards	Craig Morton, 1977-82	11,895
Touchdown passes	Craig Morton, 1977-82	74
Receptions	Lionel Taylor, 1960-66	543
Receiving yards	Lionel Taylor, 1960-66	6,872
Interceptions	Goose Gonsoulin, 1960-66	43
Punting average	Jim Fraser, 1962-64	45.2
Punt return avg.	Rick Upchurch, 1975-83	12.1
Kickoff return avg.	Abner Haynes, 1965-66	26.3
Field goals	Jim Turner, 1971-79	151
Touchdowns	Floyd Little, 1967-75	54
Points	Jim Turner, 1971-79	742
SEASON		
Rushing attempts	Sammy Winder, 1984	296
Rushing yards	Otis Armstrong, 1974	1,407
Pass attempts	John Elway, 1985	605
Pass completions	John Elway, 1985	327
Passing yards	John Elway, 1985	3,891
Touchdown passes	Frank Tripucka, 1960	24
Receptions	Lionel Taylor, 1961	100
Receiving yards	Steve Watson, 1981	1,244
Interceptions	Goose Gonsoulin, 1960	11
Punting average	Jim Fraser, 1963	46.1
Punt return avg.	Floyd Little, 1967	16.9
Kickoff return avg.	Billy Thompson, 1969	28.5
Field goals	Gene Mingo, 1962	27
Touchdowns	Floyd Little, 1972	13
	Floyd Little, 1973	13
	Steve Watson, 1981	13
Points	Gene Mingo, 1962	137
GAME		
Rushing attempts	Sammy Winder, 10-28-84	34
Rushing yards	Otis Armstrong, 12-8-74	183
Pass attempts	Frank Tripucka, 9-15-62	56
Pass completions	Mickey Slaughter, 12-20-64	34
Passing yards	Frank Tripucka, 9-15-62	447
Touchdown passes	Frank Tripucka, 10-28-62	5
	John Elway, 11-18-84	5
Receptions	Lionel Taylor, 11-29-64	13
	Bobby Anderson, 9-30-73	13
Receiving yards	Lionel Taylor, 11-27-60	199
Interceptions	Goose Gonsoulin, 9-18-60	4
	Willie Brown, 11-15-64	4
Field goals	Gene Mingo, 10-6-63	5
	Rich Karlis, 11-20-83	5
Touchdowns	9 times	3
Points	Gene Mingo, 12-10-60	21

COACHING HISTORY

1960-61	Frank Filchock	7-20-1
1962-64	Jack Faulkner*	9-22-1
1964-66	Mac Speedie**	6-19-1
1966	Ray Malavasi	4- 8-0
1967-71	Lou Saban***	20-42-3
1971	Jerry Smith	2- 3-0
1972-76	John Ralston	34-33-3
1977-80	Red Miller	42-25-0
1981-85	Dan Reeves	45-30-0

**Replaced after four games in 1964*
***Replaced after two games in 1966*
****Resigned after nine games in 1971*

FIRST PLAYER SELECTED

1960	Roger LeClerc, C, Trinity (Connecticut)
1961	Bob Gaiters, HB, New Mexico State
1962	Merlin Olsen, DT, Utah State
1963	Kermit Alexander, HB, UCLA
1964	Bob Brown, T, Nebraska
1965	(2) Dick Butkus, LB, Illinois
1965†	Miller Farr, HB, Wichita State
1966	Jerry Shay, T, Purdue
1966†	Nick Eddy, HB, Notre Dame
1967	Floyd Little, HB, Syracuse
1968	(2) Curley Culp, DE, Arizona State
1969	(2) Grady Cavness, DB, Texas-El Paso
1970	Bobby Anderson, RB, Colorado
1971	Marv Montgomery, T, USC
1972	Riley Odoms, TE, Houston
1973	Otis Armstrong, RB, Purdue
1974	Randy Gradishar, LB, Ohio State
1975	Louis Wright, CB, San Jose State
1976	Tom Glassic, G, Virginia
1977	Steve Schindler, G, Boston College
1978	Don Latimer, DT, Miami
1979	Kelvin Clark, T, Nebraska
1980	(2) Rulon Jones, DE, Utah State
1981	Dennis Smith, S, USC
1982	Gerald Wilhite, RB, San Jose State
1983	Chris Hinton, G, Northwestern
1984	(2) Andre Townsend, NT-DE, Mississippi
1984*	Freddie Gilbert, DE, Georgia
1985	Steve Sewell, RB, Oklahoma
1986	(4) Jim Juriga, T, Illinois

†Redshirt Draft
**Supplemental Draft*

DETROIT LIONS

1930 The Portsmouth, Ohio, Spartans, an independent professional football team, entered the NFL. Portsmouth, a city on the Ohio River at the mouth of the Ohio Canal, had a population of 42,560. Harold Griffen, former player-coach for the Spartans, was one of the team's owners, along with Harry Doerr, Homer C. Shelby, and Harry Snyder. George (Potsy) Clark, the coach of Butler University, was named the Spartans' head coach. The top players on the team its first year in the league were tailback Chuck Bennett, fullback Mayes (Chief) McClain, and tackle Forrest (Jap) Douds, who was obtained in a trade with the Providence Steam Roller. The Spartans won their first game of the season 13-6 over the Newark Tornadoes, September 14. The highlight of the year was a 7-6 victory over the Chicago Bears. The Spartans finished the season at 5-6-3.

1931 The Spartans had an amazing influx of rookie talent, including backs Earl (Dutch) Clark from Colorado College and Glenn Presnell of Nebraska, and linemen George Christiansen of Oregon and Grover (Ox) Emerson of Texas. The Spartans won their first eight games to run neck and neck with Green Bay, before losing two in a row to the New York Giants and Chicago Bears. Two victories followed, but a 20-19 loss to the Chicago Cardinals virtually wrapped up the title for the Packers, who finished with a 12-2 record compared to Portsmouth's 11-3 mark, good for second place. The Spartans, Packers, and Bears each were fined $1,000 by the NFL for having players on their roster whose college classes had not graduated.

1932 Portsmouth was perhaps an even better team than in 1931, with the addition of rookie fullback Leroy (Ace) Gutowsky from Oklahoma City. The Spartans lost their third game of the year, to Green Bay, but came back to beat the Packers 19-0 in the season finale to finish 6-1-4 and tie for the best record in the league. The Bears finished 6-1-6, but ties didn't count in the standings, so both teams had winning percentages of .857. After the season, Dutch Clark left for his offseason job as the basketball coach at Colorado College. But when the Bears finished their season the next week, the league office quickly set up a game between the Bears and the Spartans for the championship, the first playoff game in league history. Clark couldn't make it back for the game, which was held indoors at Chicago Stadium due to inclement weather. Late in the game, Bronko Nagurski of the Bears threw a touchdown pass to Harold (Red) Grange. Potsy Clark complained that the pass wasn't thrown from five yards behind the line of scrimmage as the NFL rules dictated, but the score stood, and the Bears went on to win 9-0.

1933 Clark remained at Colorado College and retired from pro football. His replacement, Presnell, did an admirable job, leading the league in scoring, finishing second in passing, and ranking fourth in rushing. The Spartans started off with three straight wins and still were in the race for the championship with two games left. Both games were against the first-place Bears, and the Chicago team won 17-14 and 17-7. The Spartans finished a distant second.

1934 George Richards, a radio station owner, purchased the Spartans for $15,000, plus $6,500 to pay off the team's debts. He moved the club to Detroit June 30. Richards used his own radio station to conduct a contest to name the team; the winner was Lions. They signed an agreement to play their home games at the 25,000-seat University of Detroit Stadium. Dutch Clark rejoined the team. In their first game, the Lions beat the New York Giants 9-0 before

12,000 fans, September 23. They won their next nine games, including six more consecutive shutouts. Presnell kicked an NFL-record 54-yard field goal in a 3-0 victory over Green Bay. Green Bay snapped the streak 3-0 on Clark Hinkle's 47-yard field goal. The Lions closed with two games against the Chicago Bears, the first of which inaugurated the Lions' now-traditional Thanksgiving Day game. Richards decided a coast-to-coast radio broadcast of the game was a good idea, so he solicited 94 interested stations and hired Graham McNamee to handle the play-by-play. In Detroit, the game attracted unusual interest. All 26,000 tickets, including standing room, were sold out early. The undefeated Bears won both games by three points, 19-16 and 10-7, to drop the Lions into second place. Clark finished third in the league in rushing and fourth in passing.

1935 The Lions used an unstoppable rushing offense to win the Western Division championship with a 7-3-2 record. Three Lions finished in the top five in the league in rushing—wingback Ernie Caddel was second, Clark was fourth, and fullback Bill Shepherd, obtained from Boston, was fifth. Clark also led the league in scoring. In the NFL Championship Game, the Lions beat the New York Giants 26-7. Clark was the star of the title game, rushing for 80 yards, including a 42-yard touchdown. Other stars for Detroit were Raymond (Buddy) Parker, a rookie from Centenary who gained 70 yards and scored the Lions' final touchdown, and Caddel, who ran for 62 yards. The Lions sliced the covering off the ball and cut it into 26 pieces. Then those pieces were mounted on scrolls for team members.

1936 The league's best ground game set a yardage record (2,885) that wouldn't be broken until 1972 by the Miami Dolphins. Gutowsky finished second in the league in rushing, Clark third, and Caddel sixth (and with the best average). Nevertheless, two losses to the champion Packers helped drop the Lions into third place. At the end of the season, Potsy Clark quit as coach and moved to Brooklyn to coach the Dodgers. Richards hired Dutch Clark as head coach. The first draft of college players produced Sid Wagner, a guard from Michigan State.

1937 The highlight of the season was a 30-0 victory over Potsy Clark's Dodgers, October 17. Vern Huffman intercepted a pass and ran 100 yards to score in that game. Dutch Clark's team lost only to the Packers and the Bears and finished with a 7-4 record to tie for second in the West.

1938 Detroit drafted Alex Wojciechowicz, a center from Fordham's famed Seven Blocks of Granite, number one. The Lions moved their games to Briggs Stadium. They defeated Pittsburgh 16-7 before 50,000 fans in their first game there, September 9. Another 7-4 record secured undisputed second place. Dutch Clark accused Richards of meddling. The two disagreed over Byron (Whizzer) White of the Pittsburgh Steelers. Richards wanted White; Clark didn't. So White stayed in Pittsburgh. At the end of the season, Clark became coach of the Cleveland Rams. Richards appointed Elmer (Gus) Henderson the new coach of the Lions.

1939 The club won its first four games, but lost its final four to wind up 6-5 and third in Henderson's first—and last—year. The coach got into a hassle with Richards over Clyde (Bulldog) Turner, a center from Hardin-Simmons. Because Richards had paid Turner money while he was still in college, Henderson figured he was all set with the Lions, so he bypassed him on the first round of the draft, choosing Doyle Nave, a back from USC. That move wound up costing Henderson his job as the Chicago Bears grabbed Turner. Richards was fined $5,000 by NFL President Joe Carr for having tampered with Turner while he was in school. Nave never played a game for Detroit. Richards sold the Lions to Fred Mandel, a Chicago department store magnate. The sale price was reported at $225,000, a profit of more than $200,000 for Richards.

1940 Mandel's first action as owner was to bring back Potsy Clark as coach. Whizzer White, returning from his Rhodes scholar studies at Oxford, England, was lured to Detroit after Mandel paid Pittsburgh $15,000 for his rights. White led the NFL in rushing with 514 yards, but not even his play could turn the Lions into contenders. The Lions' record was 5-5-1, and Potsy Clark left for the second time.

1941 Bill Edwards from Case Western Reserve was hired as the Lions' fourth head coach in four years. Bill Jefferson returned a kickoff 101 yards for a touchdown, a club record, against the Bears, November 23, the only points the Lions scored in two games against the Bears. For the first time, Detroit suffered a losing season, going 4-6-1.

1942 World War II robbed the Lions of White and most of their top players. After three losses, Edwards quit and was replaced by John (Bull) Karcis, an assistant. The Lions became the first winless NFL team in nine years—since the Dayton Triangles of 1929—finishing the season with an 0-11 record. The Lions had the poorest offense in the league and the poorest defense—being outscored 263-38. At the end of the season, Karcis was fired.

1943 After a successful coaching career at the University of Detroit, Charles (Gus) Dorais was signed to a five-year contract as the Lions' head coach. The club received a lift from the signing of number-one draft pick Frank Sinkwich, the Heisman Trophy-winning tailback from Georgia. With Sinkwich running a revamped offense, the Lions won their first two games and finished 3-6-1. Late in the season, the Lions and Giants played a 0-0 tie, the last such game in NFL history.

1944 The Lions drafted Otto Graham of Northwestern number one, but he was called into military service before he could sign. He later said Detroit never even contacted him. Sinkwich, who had tried to join the service but had been rejected because of flat feet, wound up back with the Lions and enjoyed a brilliant season, running for 563 yards, throwing 12 touchdown passes, and scoring 66 points. After starting 1-3-1, the Lions became winners, finishing 6-3-1 and tied for second place in the Western Division. Sinkwich was voted the NFL's most valuable player.

1945 The Army Air Corps finally accepted Sinkwich and kept him on for service football after the war ended. The Lions had some other weapons by then, however, including Bob Westfall, Andy Farkas, and Chuck Fenenbock in the backfield, and built a five-game winning streak early and an overall record of 7-3, good for second place. It was the Lions' best record in 10 years.

1946 Sinkwich was discharged from the service but promptly jumped leagues and signed with the New York Yankees of the new All-America Football Conference. Fenenbock also jumped to the AAFC, and Graham signed with the new league's Browns. Farkas retired, and Wojciechowicz was traded to the Eagles. These moves depleted Dorais's roster of quality talents, and the Lions lost their first six before beating the Steelers 17-7. Then they closed with four more losses.

1947 Convinced something drastic was needed, Mandel signed Bill Dudley, after giving up Bob Cifers, Paul White, and a number-one draft choice to the Pittsburgh Steelers for the rights to Dudley. Mandel paid Dudley $20,000, the largest sum the Lions had ever given a player. The Lions also drafted Glenn Davis, Army's famed "Mr. Outside" in the Davis-Doc Blanchard years. They installed the T-formation. Davis didn't sign, the T-formation didn't work well, and Dudley couldn't do it alone as Detroit suffered through a 3-9 season.

1948 Mandel asked Dorais to resign. Dorais refused until a settlement paid him $100,000 on the remaining years of his contract. A week later, Mandel, who had become discouraged and disenchanted, sold the club for $185,000 to a syndicate of Detroit socialites and sportsmen headed by D. Lyle Fife and Edwin J. Anderson. Fife was elected president and Anderson vice president of the Lions. Their choice for a coach was Alvin (Bo) McMillin, coach at Indiana. They signed McMillin to a five-year contract as coach and general manager. The number-one draft choice was Y. A. Tittle, a quarterback from LSU, but he never signed, choosing to go with Baltimore of the AAFC. McMillin installed rookie Fred Enke as his quarterback. Enke passed for 1,328 yards and rushed for 365 more. The other top players were fullback Camp Wilson, who gained 612 yards, and end Bob Mann, the Lions' first black player, who caught 33 passes for 560 yards. The Lions finished last for the third year in a row.

1949 Fife and Anderson had problems in the front office. Anderson succeeded Fife as president. Nick Kerbawy, the club's publicity director, was appointed assistant to the general manager. McMillin shook up the club, bringing in a number of key new players. Defensively, rookie Don Doll finished second in the league in interceptions, and Bob Smith, fresh from the AAFC, finished fourth. Les Bingaman began to start at middle guard. On offense, quarterback Frank Tripucka and halfback Cloyce Box each saw action in his first year. The real stars of the team were Mann, who caught 66 passes for a league-leading 1,014 yards, and end John Greene, who had 42 receptions. For the first time since 1945, the Lions climbed out of last place, finishing fourth with a 4-8 record.

1950 The Lions acquired Bobby Layne from the New York Bulldogs for Mann. To go with their new passer, they also signed two of the most publicized college players of the decade and the last two Heisman Trophy winners, SMU halfback Doak Walker, and Notre Dame end Leon Hart. The Lions also drafted Thurman McGraw, a tackle from Colorado State, and Lou Creekmur, a tackle from William and Mary. Bob (Hunchy) Hoernschemeyer, a strong runner, also was obtained from the allocation draft of players left without teams by the demise of the AAFC. The improved Lions finished 6-6 and Walker became the NFL scoring champion with 128 points. Box was moved to end and caught 12 passes in a game against Baltimore, four for touchdowns. He gained 302 yards for the day, one short of the all-time record by Jim Benton of the Cleveland Rams. For the season, he had 50 receptions for 1,009 yards and 11 touchdowns. A player revolt resulted in the dismissal of McMillin. Two years remained on his contract, and the owners had to give McMillin $60,000. They vowed never again to give a coach a contract of more than one year. Buddy Parker was named head coach, December 20. Nick Kerbawy became general manager.

1951 Parker continued to build his team. The draft produced Jack Christiansen, a defensive back from Colorado State; Dorne Dibble, an end from Michigan State; and LaVern Torgeson, a center from Washington State. Just three weeks before the season opened, Parker got Pat Harder, the Chicago Cardinals' rugged fullback in their championship seasons, in exchange for John Panelli and the club's number-two draft choice in 1952. Attendance doubled at Briggs Stadium and the largest crowd in history, 50,567, saw the Lions lose to the Los Angeles Rams 27-21, October 14. They battled Los Angeles all the way, beating the Rams 24-22 in Los Angeles before narrowly losing out when San Francisco, behind Y.

A. Tittle, defeated Detroit 21-17 in the final game of the season. The Lions finished 7-4-1 to the Rams' 8-4.

1952 Despite no first- or second-round draft picks, Parker picked up Yale Lary, a back from Texas A&M, on the third round, and Jim David, a defensive back from Colorado State, on the twenty-second round. He also got Earl (Jug) Girard from the Packers to fill in for Doak Walker, who missed most of the preseason because of a severely cut arm suffered in a freak accident. Despite a poor start, Layne got his team moving again, beating Los Angeles twice in the first four games. He drove the Lions to five straight victories and into a tie with Los Angeles for the National Conference championship at 9-3, the Lions' best season since their first season in Detroit. The Lions had the second-most points in the league, while leading the NFL in defense. Smith, David, Lary, and Christiansen joined to become one of the best secondaries of all-time. Offensively, Layne had the second-most rushing-passing combined yards in the league (2,410), while Box, back from a year in the service, made 42 receptions for 924 yards and a league-high 15 touchdowns. In a playoff with Los Angeles, the Lions won the conference title 31-21. In the NFL Championship Game, Walker broke open a tight defensive battle with a 67-yard touchdown run, and the Lions defeated the Browns 17-7 for their first NFL championship in 17 years.

1953 The Lions drafted Harley Sewell, a guard from Texas, on the first round. They also signed linebacker Joe Schmidt from Pittsburgh and tackle Charlie Ane from USC. Layne continued to run the team in his raucous but effective way, and the club marched to another conference title with a 10-2 record, including six straight victories at the end of the regular season. Christiansen led the NFL with 12 interceptions. In the league championship game at Detroit, 54,577 watched Layne drive the Lions to a late touchdown. Then Walker kicked the extra point to give Detroit its second consecutive NFL championship, 17-16 over Cleveland.

1954 The Lions rolled to their third consecutive conference championship, despite the retirement of Harder and the loss of five players, including Lary, to military service. Layne missed parts of the season with injuries, but young Tom Dublinski replaced him and the Lions kept winning, finishing 9-2-1 with a 14-10 victory over Cleveland in the season finale. The Lions' mastery over the Browns ended in the NFL Championship Game. Otto Graham put on a spectacular show, passing for three touchdowns and running for three more, as the Browns whipped Detroit 56-10.

1955 Some offseason events started a disastrous slide in Detroit. Bingaman, Box, and McGraw all retired. Dublinski went to play in Canada. Layne's shoulder was separated in a riding accident in Texas. Layne played, but much of the zip was missing from his arm. The defense crumbled without Bingaman, although Creekmur eventually replaced him and did a remarkable job. Although Walker led the league in scoring, the Lions fell to last place in the Western Conference, losing their first six and finishing 3-9. Walker, Hoernschemeyer, and Girard announced their retirements after the final game.

1956 The club drafted Heisman Trophy-winning halfback Howard (Hopalong) Cassady, from Ohio State, number one. His addition, plus Layne's recovery from his shoulder injury, the emergence of Schmidt as one of football's best middle linebackers, and the return of Lary from the service turned Detroit back into a contender again. The Lions won their first six games, and a 42-10 victory over the Chicago Bears late in the season gave the Lions a half-game lead. In the season-ending rematch with the Bears, Chicago's Ed Meadows blindsided Layne, knocking him out of action with a concussion. The Bears won the game, and the conference title, 38-21.

1957 The Lions' draft choices included Terry Barr, a back from Michigan, and John Gordy, a guard from Tennessee. Parker finally won his battle for a longer contract, getting the directors to give him two years at $30,000 per season. Then, two days before the first preseason game, Parker made a dramatic and surprising announcement, August 12. He said he was resigning as head coach. "I am quitting," he told an audience at a "Meet the Lions" preseason banquet. "I can no longer control this team, and when I can't control it, I can't coach it. I don't want to get involved in another losing season, so I'm leaving Detroit." Perhaps a more reasonable explanation for his sudden resignation was a scene just prior to the banquet at a cocktail party. Parker had walked in to see some of his star players socializing with the owners, a practice Parker deplored. Assistant coach George Wilson took over the team. Wilson picked up another proven quarterback in Tobin Rote from Green Bay, and got fullback John Henry Johnson from San Francisco. Both acquisitions were important. Johnson led the Lions in rushing, and Rote took over at quarterback late in the season when Layne suffered a broken leg. The most valuable returning player was Christiansen, who again led the NFL in interceptions. The Lions battled into a tie with the 49ers for the Western Conference title. In the playoff game with the 49ers in San Francisco, the Lions trailed 27-7 in the third quarter, then roared back to win 31-27, scoring 24 points in 21 minutes. Rote led a 59-14 rout of Cleveland for the championship. He completed 12 of 19 passes for 280 yards, threw four touchdown passes, and scored once himself on a one-yard sneak.

1958 The champions picked up a prize rookie in number-one draft choice Alex Karras, a myopic defensive tackle from Iowa. The Lions lost to the College All-Stars in Chicago 35-19, then split their four preseason games. Two games into the regular season, Layne was traded to Pittsburgh. The team, deeply tied to the colorful quarterback emotionally, never seemed to recover from that loss. A slow start—the Lions were 0-3-1 after four games—and a stumbling finish—1-3—helped the Lions finish fifth in the Western Conference. Off the field, Edwin J. Anderson took over as general manager of the club, replacing Kerbawy. Christiansen retired, breaking up the secondary known as Chris's Crew.

1959 While age crept into vital positions, the Lions were trying to rebuild with an outstanding rookie fullback, Nick Pietrosante, the top draft choice from Notre Dame, and a defense that featured Schmidt, Lary, and Karras. Earl Morrall, obtained in the trade for Layne, shared the quarterback position with Rote. The Lions beat only the two last-place teams in the divisions—Los Angeles twice and the Chicago Cardinals—and finished 3-8-1.

1960 Rote played out his option and defected to the Canadian Football League. Jim Ninowski was obtained from Cleveland and took over at quarterback. The Lions lost their top draft choice, Johnny Robinson of LSU, to Kansas City of the new American Football League. A 300-pound rookie defensive tackle from Maryland-Eastern Shore, Roger Brown, and a wily, old defensive back, Dick (Night Train) Lane, arrived to further solidify a defense that was becoming one of the best in the league. David and Creekmur retired, and Jim Doran and Ane were lost in the draft to stock the new Dallas Cowboys. Coming fast the second half of the season, the Lions won six of their last seven games, including a 20-15 comeback victory over the Colts, to finish second behind Green Bay in the Western Conference. Pietrosante broke Gutkowsky's club rushing record with 872 yards, while rookie Gail Cogdill proved an outstanding receiving threat. The Lions beat the Browns 17-16 in the first Playoff Bowl.

1961 A bitter proxy fight for control of the club erupted, with D. Lyle Fife, the club's former president, trying to take over from the Edwin J. Anderson faction. The effort was unsuccessful. Anderson resigned as president, however, and was succeeded by William Clay Ford of the automotive family. Anderson remained as general manager. In a strange 8-5-1 season, the Lions lost five times at home, including a 49-0 embarrassment by San Francisco. But the Lions went undefeated on the road to once again finish second to the Packers in their division. The defense had become as good as any in the league, while the offense continued to be led by the powerful running of Pietrosante and the home-run threat of Cogdill, who caught 45 passes for 956 yards. The Lions beat the Eagles 38-10 in the Playoff Bowl. Because of the war with the AFL for talent, the NFL held its 1962 draft early and the Lions' top three picks were John Hadl, a quarterback from Kansas; Eddie Wilson, a quarterback from Arizona; and Bobby Thompson, a defensive back from Arizona State. Hadl and Wilson signed with the AFL and Thompson went to the Canadian Football League.

1962 Trying to quell open bitterness among the veterans for the failure in the draft, the Lions acquired quarterback Milt Plum, runner Tom Watkins, and linebacker Dave Lloyd from the Browns, sending Ninowski back to Cleveland along with Cassady and Bill Glass. Detroit won the most games in the franchise's history, 11, but it still wasn't good enough to beat out Vince Lombardi's powerful Green Bay champions. They had the Packers virtually beaten 7-6 in their first meeting, October 7. Then Plum inexplicably threw a third-down pass that was intercepted, and a Green Bay field goal with 27 seconds left to play beat the Lions 9-7. On Thanksgiving Day, however, the Lions pulled an upset, beating the Packers 26-14 in a memorable display of aggressive defensive football. The Lions sacked Bart Starr 11 times and deprived the Packers of a perfect season. The Lions made it three straight victories in the Playoff Bowl by beating Pittsburgh 17-10.

1963 The day following the Playoff Bowl, Commissioner Pete Rozelle announced the Lions, among others, were being investigated for alleged gambling on games. Karras and Green Bay's Paul Hornung were suspended a minimum of one year for betting on football games, April 17. The Lions' management was fined $4,000. Five Detroit players—Joe Schmidt, Wayne Walker, John Gordy, Gary Lowe, and Sam Williams—were fined $2,000 each. The Lions finally signed a number-one draft choice, Daryl Sanders, a tackle from Ohio State, but without Karras, and bothered by an abundance of injuries, the Lions plummeted to a 5-8-1 record and the middle of the division standings. Plum was replaced by Morrall, who passed for 2,621 yards and 24 touchdowns. Terry Barr and Cogdill were the most productive pair of receivers in the NFL; Barr caught 66 passes for 1,086 yards and a league-high 13 touchdowns, while Cogdill had 48 catches for 945 yards and 10 touchdowns.

1964 William Clay Ford took over as the Lions' sole owner after purchasing the remaining stock from 140 shareholders for $6.5 million. One of Ford's first moves was to restructure the front office. The key new figure was Russ Thomas, who was given the job of signing players and overseeing the draft. He was assigned the title of director of player personnel. Wilson was retained as coach, but some of his authority was removed. Again, the three top draft choices signed with AFL teams. Karras was reinstated, March 16. Detroit's brilliant defense was growing old, and the offense, torn by the controversy between Plum and Morrall at quarterback, couldn't get untracked in a 7-5-2 season. Ford fired all of Wilson's assistants, in a clear warning to the head coach. Wilson resigned, December 23.

1965 Harry Gilmer, assistant coach for the Minnesota Vikings, was named the Lions' head coach. The draft produced fullback Tom Nowatzke from Indiana, center Ed Flanagan from Purdue, defensive end Larry Hand from Appalachian State, and defensive back Tom Vaughn from Iowa State. Gilmer's first decision was to go with one quarterback, so he traded Morrall to New York in a three-way deal that brought linebacker Mike Lucci to the Lions from Cleveland. Gilmer gave Plum the quarterback job. But Plum had a poor year, as did most of the Lions, and the club regressed to 6-7-1. Schmidt, one of the best linebackers in football for 13 seasons, and Barr both retired after the final game.

1966 Resentment among the players surfaced over Gilmer, and the team continued to have problems. But Ford tried to soothe matters by adding Schmidt to the coaching staff and naming Karras captain. Just before the season, Pietrosante, the Lions' career rushing leader with 3,933 yards, was cut from the team. Plum started at quarterback again, but went down with a knee injury at midseason. Karl Sweetan, who was signed off the semipro Pontiac Arrows, was given the quarterback job. Flanker Pat Studstill suddenly developed into one of the best deep threats in the game, catching 67 passes for 1,266 yards, including a 99-yard touchdown pass from Sweetan against Baltimore, October 16. Garo Yepremian, a soccer-style placekicker from Cyprus, arrived at midseason and kicked an NFL-record six field goals in a game against Minnesota. The Lions and Vikings finished tied for last in the Western Conference.

1967 Gilmer was fired and paid off the final three years of his contract, January 5. Joe Schmidt became the new head coach. The NFL realigned and the Lions were placed in the Central Division of the Western Conference. The top draft choices included halfback Mel Farr from UCLA and defensive back Lem Barney from Jackson State. Russ Thomas was named general manager and Carl Brettschneider became the new director of player personnel. The Lions became the first NFL team to be beaten by an AFL team when Denver beat the Lions 13-7 in the first interleague preseason game. Roger Brown was traded to Los Angeles for the Rams' first, second, and third draft choices in 1968. Farr and Barney were named offensive and defensive rookies of the year in the NFL, but the Lions still finished 5-7-2. Farr rushed for 860 yards and led the Lions with 39 receptions, while Barney led the NFL with 10 interceptions, three of which he returned for touchdowns.

1968 Another good draft produced quarterback Greg Landry from Massachusetts, tight end Charlie Sanders from Minnesota, and wide receiver Earl McCullouch from USC. Bill Munson was obtained from the Rams for a number-one draft choice, Plum, Watkins, and Studstill. But Munson damaged his shoulder early, making Landry the starter in the season opener. Landry threw one touchdown pass and four interceptions in his first game. The offense never jelled and in one span the Lions went 16 successive quarters without producing a touchdown. In their last nine games, the Lions won only once.

1969 Brettschneider was dismissed, amid complaints that Thomas would not allow anyone else to have a voice in running the club. Thomas and Schmidt denied the charge publicly and vowed new unity. The Lions' defense finally started coming back to form, with the linebacking of Paul Naumoff, Mike Lucci, and Wayne Walker as its foundation. The offense struggled, however, with Farr injured and neither Munson nor Landry producing effectively. The defense carried the Lions to a 9-4-1 record.

1970 Running back Steve Owens, the Heisman Trophy winner from Oklahoma, was the number-one draft pick. Owens won a starting job, then injured a shoulder in the final preseason game and was out for most of the season. Although Munson played more at the beginning and Landry more at the end, the quarterback confusion continued. The rest of the offense improved, with Farr and Altie Taylor enjoying good years running. Sanders developed into an all-pro tight end, and the Lions made the playoffs as the wild card team with a stirring finish. They won five straight to finish with a 10-4 record. In the first round of the playoffs, the Dallas defense silenced the Lions 5-0, scoring on a safety and a field goal.

1971 The week before the season opened, Karras was released. Chuck Hughes, one of the Lions' wide receivers, died of a heart attack during a game against Chicago, collapsing on the field, October 24. Owens and Landry came into their own as full-fledged stars. Owens became the Lions' first 1,000-yard rusher with 1,035 yards. Landry set an NFL rushing record for his position with 530 yards and finished second in the NFC in passing. The Lions were in contention early in the season after a 4-1 start. But they lost their last three for a 7-6-1 record and placed second again.

1972 The Lions had one of the best offensive teams in the league, and finished second in scoring in the NFC. But the defense wasn't up to par, ranking tenth in the conference. Landry, Taylor, Owens, and Sanders all had outstanding years, but could only lead the team to a fourth consecutive second-place finish. At the end of the season, defensive stars Wayne Walker and Dick LeBeau retired. The citizens of Pontiac, Michigan, passed a bond issue for a domed stadium.

1973 After six seasons, Joe Schmidt announced his resignation as head coach, January 12. Don McCafferty, who had guided the Baltimore Colts to a victory in Super Bowl V, was named to replace him. Again, high hopes resulted in more disappointment, with the club finishing second behind Minnesota with a 6-7 record. "I don't think they want to win—at least it doesn't look like it," said Ford after the team started off 1-4-1. The Lions reversed that with a 5-3 finish behind Munson, who replaced Landry midway through the season. Construction began on a $55.7-million stadium in Pontiac, Michigan, in December.

1974 The Lions got a steal in the third round of the draft when they selected Dexter Bussey, a running back from Texas-Arlington. McCafferty died of a heart attack, July 28. Assistant coach Rick Forzano, a former head coach at the Naval Academy, was named the new head coach. The Lions lost their first four games, but came back to win seven of their last ten to finish second behind Minnesota's division champions. Forzano was given a three-year contract.

1975 The draft produced two future stars—defensive tackle Doug English of Texas in the second round and wide receiver Leonard Thompson of Oklahoma State in the eighth. The team opened 80,638-seat Pontiac Metropolitan Stadium, which featured an inflatable roof, with a 36-10 loss to Dallas before a record home crowd of 79,784. Detroit again won seven games and finished as the runner-up to Minnesota in the NFC Central. Both Munson and Landry went down with knee injuries. Joe Reed started most of the year at quarterback, completing 86 of 191 passes for 1,181 yards.

1976 The stadium's name was changed to the Pontiac Silverdome. Landry was healthy again and was the regular starter throughout the season, but the Lions picked up free agent Gary Danielson as a backup quarterback. The Lions won only one of their first four games. Forzano resigned, and Tommy Hudspeth, coordinator of personnel and scouting, was named coach. The Lions responded with a 30-10 victory over New England. Detroit won five of its last nine games under Hudspeth and placed third in the NFC Central, behind Minnesota and the Chicago Bears. The finish ended a seven-year streak for the Lions as a second-place team.

1977 Hudspeth was retained as head coach. The Lions employed a double-tight-end offense and won three of their first five games, to trail Minnesota by one game in the NFC Central. But the offense collapsed in consecutive losses to San Francisco, when the Lions gained only 119 yards, and in a 37-0 defeat to Dallas. Rookie running back Rick Kane lifted the offense when he rushed for 105 yards in a 20-0 victory over San Diego, the first shutout by Detroit in four seasons. But the team won just two of its final six games and finished 6-8. Despite the offensive disappointments, Danielson provided a glimmer of hope for the future when he started the final two games, including a 13-10 upset of Baltimore.

1978 Monte Clark, formerly the head coach of the San Francisco 49ers, was named head coach and director of football operations. The draft yielded defensive help, especially cornerback Luther Bradley and defensive end Al Baker. Baker led the NFL in sacks with 23, and the Lions finished second in the league with 55, including 15 in two victories over Tampa Bay. Baker and English both were selected to play in the Pro Bowl. The season began disastrously, with losses in six of the first seven games. But Clark's revamped offense began to jell in a 31-14 victory over San Diego on October 22. The Lions went 6-3 over the last nine weeks. Leading the resurgence was Danielson, who was installed at quarterback in October and set club records for pass attempts (351) and completions (199) while throwing for 2,294 yards. Danielson also set a club record with five touchdown passes in a 45-14 win over Minnesota on December 9. Bussey ran for 924 yards, the second-most in one season in team history.

1979 The Lions were crippled at quarterback when Danielson suffered a knee injury in the final preseason game and was lost for the season. His backup, Reed, was hurt in the opening loss to Tampa Bay and missed the next 10 weeks. The job was inherited by rookie Jeff Komlo, a ninth-round draft choice from Delaware. Komlo directed the Lions' first win, a 24-23 victory over Atlanta on September 23, and went on to start 14 games. The bright spots for the club were Freddie Scott, who had the best season by a Lions' receiver since 1966 (with 62 receptions for 929 yards), and Baker, who recorded 16 sacks. The Lions didn't win again until November 22, when they defeated the Bears 20-0. The 2-14 record was the poorest in the NFL.

1980 The Lions opened the draft by taking Billy Sims, the 1978 Heisman Trophy winner from Oklahoma. In the fourth round, they took quarterback Eric Hipple of Utah State, and, in the seventh round, kicker Ed Murray of Tulane. The defensive line was depleted before the season when English retired. Then John Woodcock left at midseason over a contract squabble. Sims got off to a blazing start, rushing for 153 yards and three touchdowns in a 41-20 romp over the Rams. The Lions followed with three easy victories that doubled the club's win total of the previous season. A loss to Atlanta was followed by a victory over New Orleans for a 5-1 record. But inconsistent offensive play stymied the Lions, and they won only twice in the next eight weeks. Season-ending victories over Tampa Bay and Green Bay gave Detroit a final record of 9-7. The Lions tied with Minnesota in the NFC Central, but the Vikings won the division with a superior conference record. Sims was voted rookie of the year after rushing for 1,303 yards, catching 51 passes, and scoring 16 touchdowns. Fellow rookie Murray led the NFC with 116 points, and Danielson had his finest season, passing for 3,233 yards.

1981 The defense got a big lift when English returned and had his best year, earning all-pro recognition. Six weeks into the new season, the Lions were a disappointing 2-4. The team suffered a blow in a 16-0 victory over Oakland on September 27, when Danielson was knocked out for 10 weeks with a dislocated wrist. Hipple became the starting quarterback on October 19 against the Chicago Bears after two starts by Komlo. Hipple threw for 336 yards and four touchdowns and also ran for two touchdowns in the 48-17 Monday night victory. Hipple followed that with a three-touchdown performance against Green Bay in a 31-27 victory. But consecutive losses to the Los Angeles Rams and Washington dropped the Lions to 4-6. On November 15, Detroit defeated Dallas 27-24 on Murray's 47-yard field goal as time expired. Controversy surfaced after the game; the Lions had 12 players on the field for the final play. The win stood. That victory inspired the Lions to three wins in the next four weeks, including a 45-7 romp over Minnesota on December 12. A week later, in a showdown for the division title, the Lions lost to Tampa Bay 20-17—suffering their first loss at home all year—and finished the season with an 8-8 record. Sims topped his rookie year with 1,437 yards rushing.

1982 The Lions seemed to be one of the teams hurt most by the 57-day players' strike, but they still regrouped to make the playoffs for the first time since 1970. The Lions won their first two games behind the running of Billy Sims, who had staged a six-week holdout during training camp. After the season resumed, the Lions alternated between Danielson and Hipple at quarterback, and, with a lack of consistency, they lost three in a row, including a 13-6 game to the Giants on Thanksgiving Day, when, with the score tied 6-6 in the fourth quarter, linebacker Lawrence Taylor intercepted a pass on the New York 3 and returned it 97 yards for the winning touchdown. In the final game of the regular season, third-string tight end Rob Rubick scored on a one-yard end-around with less than six minutes left, and the Lions defeated Green Bay 27-24 to make the playoffs with a 4-5 record. Sims finished as the number-two rusher in the NFC. The Lions were quickly ousted from the playoffs, losing 31-7 to Washington.

1983 English and end-tackle William Gay led the "Silver Rush" line on a defensive team that gave up the fewest points in the NFC. The Lions won their opener 11-0 over Tampa Bay as Gay made 5½ sacks and English recorded a safety. English also scored a safety the next week, but Cleveland won 31-26 to launch a 3-5 start for the Lions, which was to a great extent due to Sims suffering a broken hand. Sims returned in the second half of the season and rushed for 850 of his 1,040 yards, as the Lions went 6-2 to win the NFC Central with a 9-7 record. They clinched the title the final week when Ed Murray kicked three field goals in a 23-20 victory over Tampa Bay. The next week, Murray missed a field goal in the final seconds, and the Lions were knocked out of the playoffs by San Francisco 24-23.

1984 Danielson, who had played behind Hipple in 1983, won the starting job. A series of close losses started Detroit off on a down note, and the Lions never recovered. The Lions lost the opener 30-27 to San Francisco on a field goal with four seconds left. After an overtime win, they dropped three games by a total of eight points, including a 29-28 loss to Minnesota despite Danielson's four touchdown passes, three to Leonard Thompson. After rushing for 637 yards in the first half of the season, Sims, who had become the Lions' career rushing leader on his last carry, suffered ligament damage in his knee and missed the rest of the season. Five losses in their last six games dropped the Lions to 4-11-1. The high point of the year was a 31-28 victory over the Packers on Thanksgiving Day, in which the Lions rolled up 518 yards and virtually eliminated Green Bay from the playoffs. Second-year running back James Jones finished with 532 yards and a team-record 77 receptions. At the end of the season, Clark was fired.

1985 Darryl Rogers, coach at Arizona State, was named head coach, February 6. Danielson was traded to Cleveland, with Hipple becoming the starter for most of the season. Sims missed the entire season rehabilitating his knee, and the burden of the running game was placed on Jones, who gained 886 yards, but fell off dramatically in receiving. The Lions were inconsistent all season, beating the Cowboys (26-23, despite being outgained 554-200), the 49ers (23-21), and the Dolphins (31-21 the week after the Dallas game), but losing to Tampa Bay (19-16 in overtime). Nevertheless, the offense improved, with Hipple passing for 2,952 yards, and the defense pulled together after English was injured to give up 42 fewer points than in 1983.

1986 English, arguably the best Detroit defensive player since Joe Schmidt, retired.

MEMBERS OF HALL OF FAME:
Jack Christiansen, Earl (Dutch) Clark, Bill Dudley, Frank Gatski, Dick (Night Train) Lane, Yale Lary, Bobby Layne, Ollie Matson, Hugh McElhenny, Joe Schmidt, Doak Walker, Alex Wojciechowicz

LIONS RECORD, 1930-85

Year	Won	Lost	Tied	Pct.	Fin.	Pts.	OP
Portsmouth Spartans							
1930	5	6	3	.455	7t	176	161
1931	11	3	0	.786	2	175	77
1932a	6	1	4	.857	2	116	62
1933	6	5	0	.545	2	128	87
Detroit Lions							
1934	10	3	0	.769	2	238	59
1935b	7	3	2	.700	1	191	111
1936	8	4	0	.667	3	235	102
1937	7	4	0	.636	2t	180	105
1938	7	4	0	.636	2	119	108
1939	6	5	0	.545	3	145	150
1940	5	5	1	.500	3	138	153
1941	4	6	1	.400	3	121	195
1942	0	11	0	.000	5	38	263
1943	3	6	1	.333	3	178	218
1944	6	3	1	.667	2t	216	151
1945	7	3	0	.700	2	195	194
1946	1	10	0	.091	5	142	310
1947	3	9	0	.250	5	231	305
1948	2	10	0	.167	5	200	407
1949	4	8	0	.333	4	237	259
1950	6	6	0	.500	4	321	285
1951	7	4	1	.636	2t	336	259
1952c	9	3	0	.750	1	344	192
1953b	10	2	0	.833	1	271	205
1954d	9	2	1	.818	1	337	189
1955	3	9	0	.250	6	230	275
1956	9	3	0	.750	2	300	188
1957c	8	4	0	.667	1	251	231
1958	4	7	1	.364	5	261	276
1959	3	8	1	.273	5	203	275
1960e	7	5	0	.583	2t	239	212
1961e	8	5	1	.615	2	270	258
1962e	11	3	0	.786	2	315	177
1963	5	8	1	.385	4t	326	265
1964	7	5	2	.583	4	280	260
1965	6	7	1	.462	6	257	295
1966	4	9	1	.308	6t	206	317
1967	5	7	2	.417	3	260	259
1968	4	8	2	.333	4	207	241
1969	9	4	1	.692	2	259	188
1970f	10	4	0	.714	2	347	202
1971	7	6	1	.538	2	341	286
1972	8	5	1	.607	2	339	290
1973	6	7	1	.464	2	271	247
1974	7	7	0	.500	2	256	270
1975	7	7	0	.500	2	245	262
1976	6	8	0	.429	3	262	220
1977	6	8	0	.429	3	183	252
1978	7	9	0	.438	3	290	300
1979	2	14	0	.125	5	219	365
1980	9	7	0	.563	2	334	272
1981	8	8	0	.500	2	397	322
1982g	4	5	0	.444	8	181	176
1983h	9	7	0	.563	1	347	286
1984	4	11	1	.281	4	283	408
1985	7	9	0	.438	4	307	366
56 Years	349	336	32	.509		13,474	12,848

aNFL Runnerup; 0-1 in Playoffs
bNFL Champion; 1-0 in Playoffs
cNFL Champion; 2-0 in Playoffs
dNFL Western Conference Champion; 0-1 in Playoffs
eNFL Western Conference Runnerup; 1-0 in Playoff Bowl
fNFC Wild Card Qualifier for Playoffs; 0-1 in Playoffs
gNFC Qualifier for Playoffs; 0-1 in Playoffs
hNFC Central Division Champion; 0-1 in Playoffs

RECORD HOLDERS

CAREER

Rushing attempts	Dexter Bussey, 1974-84	1,203
Rushing yards	Billy Sims, 1980-84	5,106
Pass attempts	Bobby Layne, 1950-58	2,193
Pass completions	Bobby Layne, 1950-58	1,074
Passing yards	Bobby Layne, 1950-58	15,710
Touchdown passes	Bobby Layne, 1950-58	118
Receptions	Charlie Sanders, 1968-77	336
Receiving yards	Gail Cogdill, 1960-68	5,220
Interceptions	Dick LeBeau, 1959-72	62
Punting average	Yale Lary, 1952-53, 1956-64	44.3
Punt return avg.	Jack Christiansen, 1951-58	12.8
Kickoff return avg.	Pat Studstill, 1961-67	25.7
Field goals	Errol Mann, 1969-76	141
Touchdowns	Billy Sims, 1980-84	47
Points	Errol Mann, 1969-76	636

SEASON

Rushing attempts	Billy Sims, 1980	313
Rushing yards	Billy Sims, 1981	1,437
Pass attempts	Gary Danielson, 1980	417
Pass completions	Gary Danielson, 1984	252
Passing yards	Gary Danielson, 1980	3,223
Touchdown passes	Bobby Layne, 1951	26
Receptions	James Jones, 1984	77
Receiving yards	Pat Studstill, 1966	1,266
Interceptions	Don Doll, 1950	12
	Jack Christiansen, 1953	12
Punting average	Yale Lary, 1963	48.9
Punt return avg.	Jack Christiansen, 1952	21.5
Kickoff return avg.	Tom Watkins, 1965	34.4
Field goals	Ed Murray, 1980	27
Touchdowns	Billy Sims, 1980	16
Points	Doak Walker, 1950	128

GAME

Rushing attempts	Billy Sims, 11-20-83	36
	James Jones, 10-27-85	36
Rushing yards	Bob Hoernschemeyer, 11-23-50	198
Pass attempts	Harry Gilmer, 12-11-55	49
Pass completions	Gary Danielson, 12-14-80	29
Passing yards	Bobby Layne, 11-5-50	374
Touchdown passes	Gary Danielson, 12-9-78	5
Receptions	Cloyce Box, 12-3-50	12
Receiving yards	Cloyce Box, 12-3-50	302
Interceptions	Don Doll, 10-23-49	4
Field goals	Garo Yepremian, 11-13-66	6
Touchdowns	Cloyce Box, 12-3-50	4
Points	Cloyce Box, 12-3-50	24

COACHING HISTORY

1930-36	George (Potsy) Clark	54-26-9
1937-38	Earl (Dutch) Clark	14- 8-0
1939	Elmer (Gus) Henderson	6- 5-0
1940	George (Potsy) Clark	5- 5-1
1941-42	Bill Edwards*	4- 9-1
1942	John Karcis	0- 8-0
1943-47	Gus Dorais	20-31-2
1948-50	Alvin (Bo) McMillin	12-24-0
1951-56	Raymond (Buddy) Parker	50-24-2
1957-64	George Wilson	58-45-6
1965-66	Harry Gilmer	10-16-2
1967-72	Joe Schmidt	43-35-7
1973	Don McCafferty	6- 7-1
1974-76	Rick Forzano**	15-17-0
1976-77	Tommy Hudspeth	11-13-0
1978-84	Monte Clark	43-63-1
1985	Darryl Rogers	7- 9-0

**Replaced after three games in 1942*
***Resigned after four games in 1976*

FIRST PLAYER SELECTED

1936 Sid Wagner, G, Michigan State
1937 Lloyd Cardwell, HB, Nebraska
1938 Alex Wojciechowicz, C, Fordham
1939 John Pingel, HB, Michigan State
1940 Doyle Nave, QB, USC
1941 Jim Thomason, HB, Texas A&M
1942 Bob Westfall, FB, Michigan
1943 Frank Sinkwich, HB, Georgia
1944 Otto Graham, QB, Northwestern
1945 Frank Szymanski, C, Notre Dame
1946 Bill Dellastatious, HB, Missouri
1947 Glenn Davis, HB, Army
1948 Y.A. Tittle, QB, LSU
1949 John Rauch, QB, Georgia
1950 Leon Hart, E, Notre Dame

1951 (2) Dick Stanfel, G, San Francisco
1952 (3) Yale Lary, DB, Texas A&M
1953 Harley Sewell, G, Texas
1954 Dick Chapman, T, Rice
1955 Dave Middleton, HB, Auburn
1956 Howard (Hopalong) Cassady, HB, Ohio State
1957 Bill Glass, G, Baylor
1958 Alex Karras, T, Iowa
1959 Nick Pietrosante, FB, Notre Dame
1960 Johnny Robinson, S, LSU
1961 (2) Danny LaRose, T, Missouri
1962 John Hadl, QB, Kansas
1963 Daryl Sanders, T, Ohio State
1964 Pete Beathard, QB, USC
1965 Tom Nowatzke, FB, Indiana
1966 (2) Nick Eddy, HB, Notre Dame
1967 Mel Farr, HB, UCLA
1968 Greg Landry, QB, Massachusetts
1969 (2) Altie Taylor, RB, Utah State
1970 Steve Owens, RB, Oklahoma
1971 Bob Bell, DT, Cincinnati
1972 Herb Orvis, DE, Colorado
1973 Ernie Price, DE, Texas A&I
1974 Ed O'Neil, LB, Penn State
1975 Lynn Boden, G, South Dakota State
1976 James Hunter, DB, Grambling
1977 (2) Walt Williams, DB, New Mexico State
1978 Luther Bradley, DB, Notre Dame
1979 Keith Dorney, T, Penn State
1980 Billy Sims, RB, Oklahoma
1981 Mark Nichols WR, San Jose State
1982 Jimmy Williams, LB, Nebraska
1983 James Jones, RB, Florida
1984 David Lewis, TE, California
1984* Alphonso Williams, WR, Nevada-Reno
1985 Lomas Brown, T, Florida
1986 Chuck Long, QB, Iowa
Supplemental Draft

LIONS MOST VALUABLE PLAYER

1952 Jim Doran, E
1953 Dick Stanfel, G
1954 Bobby Layne, QB
1955 Joe Schmidt, LB
1956 Bobby Layne, QB
1957 Joe Schmidt, LB
1958 Joe Schmidt, LB
1959 Jim Martin, G
1960 Nick Pietrosante, FB
1961 Joe Schmidt, LB
1962 Gail Cogdill, E
1963 Earl Morrall, QB
1964 Jim Gibbons, TE
1965 Bruce Maher, S
1966 Pat Studstill, FL
1967 Mel Farr, FB
Lem Barney, CB
1968 Mel Farr, RB
Wayne Walker, LB
1969 Charlie Sanders, TE
Mike Lucci, LB
1970 Charlie Sanders, TE
Mike Lucci, LB
1971 Steve Owens, RB
Mike Lucci, LB
1972 Rockne Freitas, T
Larry Hand, DE
1973 Altie Taylor, RB
Herb Orvis, DT
1974 Bill Munson, QB
Levi Johnson, CB
1975 Dexter Bussey, RB
Paul Naumoff, LB
1976 Ray Jarvis, WR
Charlie Weaver, LB
1977 Jon Morris, C
Charlie Weaver, LB
1978 Gary Danielson, QB
Al Baker, DE
1979 Fred Scott, WR
Doug English, DT
1980 Billy Sims, RB
Dave Pureifory, DE
1981 Eric Hipple, QB
Stan White, LB
Ken Callicut, ST
1982 Billy Sims, RB
Al (Bubba) Baker, DE
Ken Callicut, ST
1983 Billy Sims, RB
William Gay, DE-DT
Roosevelt Barnes, ST
1984 James Jones, RB
Ken Fantetti, LB
Roosevelt Barnes, ST
1985 James Jones, RB
Jimmy Williams, LB
Alvin Hall, ST

GREEN BAY PACKERS

1919 On August 19, in the editorial room of the Green Bay *Press-Gazette,* Earl (Curly) Lambeau and George Calhoun met with a number of young men interested in playing football and organized a football team. Lambeau talked his employer at the Indian Packing Company into providing $500 for equipment for the team and allowing the team to use the company athletic field for practice. With these tie-ins, the name Packers was a natural. The Packers played their home games at Hagemeister Park, a large vacant lot. They went 10-1 their first year, outscoring their first 10 opponents 565 to 6 before losing to Beloit 6-0 in the season finale. At the end of the season, the players split the profits, each earning $16.75.

1920 A small bleacher with a capacity of a couple hundred was built at Hagemeister Park, and a fee was charged to sit there. The Packers went 9-1-1.

1921 After two years of successful operation as an independent team playing clubs from Wisconsin and Upper Michigan, the Packers joined the American Professional Football Association, predecessor to the National Football League. The franchise was awarded to John Clair of the Acme Packing Company, successor to the Indian Packing Company, August 27, 1921. A portable canvas fence was erected around Hagemeister Park, and a regular admission fee was charged. Lambeau continued to run the team as tailback, coach, general manager, publicity man, and ticket salesman. Howard (Cub) Buck, who had spent 1920 with the Canton Bulldogs, joined the Packers. Lambeau surrounded himself with Wisconsin players and signed a couple of his old Notre Dame buddies, Norm Barry and Grover Malone, for the backfield. The Packers won their first game against a league team October 23, beating Minneapolis 7-6. They finished the season 3-2-1 in league play. On November 27, they launched a series with the Chicago Staleys (the predecessors to the Bears), losing 20-0.

1922 John Clair was ordered to surrender the Packers' franchise to the league for using players who still were enrolled in college, January 28. When Lambeau learned the NFL planned a midsummer meeting, he made plans to rescue the Packers. With the $50 franchise fee in his pocket but lacking the means of traveling to the NFL meeting at Canton, Ohio, Lambeau asked a friend for help. The friend, Don Murphy, sold his Marmon Roadster automobile for $1,500 and accompanied Lambeau to Canton on the promise that Murphy would open the season in the Packers' lineup. Lambeau was awarded the franchise. Murphy played one minute of the opening game with Duluth. Lambeau changed the name of the team to the Blues, but local fans still referred to it as the Packers. Lambeau went with the flow and changed it back to Packers. The Packers signed tackle Francis (Jug) Earp and guard Howard (Whitey) Woodin. The weather turned against the Packers and it rained at almost every home game. The club bought rain insurance. One game was rained out, but the insurance company wouldn't pay because the official amount of rain was one one-hundredth of an inch short of that required in the policy. When it poured before a game with the Columbus Panhandles in November, the insurance had expired and Lambeau was ready to give up. Only the intervention of Andrew Turnbull, general manager of the *Press-Gazette,* saved the franchise. Turnbull told Lambeau to play the game and he'd work out the problems.

1923 Civic pride in the community of about 30,000, combined with a love of football, brought solid financial backing to the Packers. Turnbull organized a group known as the "Hungry Five," who paid the Packers' debts and started a campaign for civic support. The members were Turnbull; Lambeau; Lee Joannes, a grocery man; Dr. W. Webber Kelly, a physician; and Gerald Clifford, an attorney. At a meeting of 400 citizens at the local Elks club, the team was reorganized as the Green Bay Football Corporation, a public non-profit corporation, which retained Lambeau as coach and general manager. Stock was sold at $5 a share and every person who bought a share was assured a season ticket. Fifty leading citizens pledged to put up $100 each if the club needed additional money. Hagemeister Park was to be the site of a new high school, so the Packers moved to the outskirts of town to play in a new baseball park known as Bellevue Park. The Chicago Bears came to town for the first time and 5,000 people stormed the park to see the visitors from the big city score a 3-0 win. The Packers split a pair of games with the Racine Legion for the championship of Wisconsin. Green Bay improved its record to 7-2-1 and finished third.

1924 Verne Lewellen of Nebraska, one of the greatest punters of the era, joined the Packers and fit into the regular backfield with Oscar (Dutch) Hendrian, Charlie Mathys, and Lambeau. Green Bay beat the Bears for the first time in a bitterly fought opening game, 5-0, but the game didn't count in the standings because it was played the week before the season officially opened. The Packers shut out the Kansas City Cowboys, the Milwaukee Badgers, and the Minneapolis Marines in succession and followed with a 6-3 victory over Racine on a sensational catch of a 45-yard pass by Lambeau to Walter (Tillie) Voss. However, the Packers lost a rematch with the Bears 3-0 in Chicago in a game in which Voss and the Bears' Frank Hanny were ejected for fighting, and also bowed to Racine 7-0 in the season finale. The club was doing well at the gate and showed promise with a 7-4 record.

1925 Green Bay opened City Stadium barely in time to start the season. The stadium, with stands on each side of the field between the 30-yard lines, had a capacity of 6,000. In the second home game of the year, the Packers beat the Bears 14-10 for their first regular-season victory over their big-city neighbors. After a fast start, the Packers lost three of their last four to finish 8-5. Unfortunately for the Packers' treasury, they already had finished their season series with the Bears before Red Grange turned pro and started off on his whirlwind tour with the Bears that attracted record crowds at nearly every stop.

1926 In a year in which the NFL expanded to 22 teams, the Packers finished fifth with a 7-3-3 record. The Packers played the Bears three times, coming away with two ties and a 19-13 loss. On October 3, the Duluth Eskimoes with Ernie Nevers played to a 0-0 tie before a sellout crowd in Green Bay.

1927 Lambeau was putting in less time as a halfback and more time as a coach and general manager. Joe (Red) Dunn, who had played with Milwaukee and the Chicago Cardinals, arrived to take over at quarterback. Another top acquisition was Lavern Dilweg, a talented end who also had played with Milwaukee while finishing law school. With the help of this new talent the Packers finished second with a 7-2-1 record behind the 11-1-1 of the New York Giants, a team they never played. Both losses were to the Bears. The highlight of the season was a 13-0 victory over the Yankees in the Packers' first visit to New York.

1928 Although Green Bay tied the champion Providence Steam Roller 7-7 late in the season, two defeats by the Frankford Yellow Jackets doomed their title hopes. The Packers played the New York Giants for the first time, losing 6-0 at Milwaukee but winning 7-0 at the Polo Grounds. During the season Lambeau picked up fullback John (Bo) Molenda from the New York Yankees. Green Bay finished fourth. There was an unusual off-the-field competition when two players ran for the office of district attorney of Brown County. Lewellen won in the Republican primary and Dilweg lost in the Democratic primary. Lewellen won the general election and served until 1930.

1929 Lambeau made three master moves during the offseason, picking up halfback Johnny Blood (McNally), tackle-end Cal Hubbard, and guard Mike Michalske. Blood and Michalske were free agents, and Hubbard was traded by the Giants. The Packers engaged in a lively race for the title with the Giants. On November 24, when the two teams met at the Polo Grounds, the Packers were 9-0, the Giants 8-0-1. Green Bay won 20-6 while using only 12 players. Although the Packers were tied by the Frankford Yellow Jackets on Thanksgiving Day, they won the championship with a 12-0-1 record to New York's 13-1-1. The Packers were the first unbeaten team in the NFL since the Canton Bulldogs of 1922-23. When the Packers returned home after beating the Bears in Chicago in the final game, a crowd of 20,000 surged onto the tracks and forced the train carrying the team to halt. Green Bay's defense ended the season having given up only 22 points in 13 games, including eight shutouts.

1930 Lambeau retired as a player to devote all his time to coaching. Determined to improve the team, Lambeau brought in a new quarterback, Arnie Herber, who had played at Regis College in Denver. Although he didn't play regularly, Herber showed that he had a big future with the club. The Packers ran their three-year string to 22 games without defeat, beating the Bears and Minneapolis twice and the Cardinals, Giants, Frankford, and Portsmouth once each. Their winning streak finally was broken by the Cardinals 13-6 in a rematch at Comiskey Park. A 13-6 loss to the Giants threatened the Packers' plans for a second straight title but they rallied to beat Frankford and Staten Island. Despite a 21-0 defeat by the Bears, a 6-6 tie in the last game at Portsmouth enabled Green Bay at 10-3-1 to edge the Giants' 13-4-0 by .004 percentage points, .769 to .765. The second championship in a row touched off another rousing welcome home after a riotous trip by bus and train during which Blood crawled atop the train and rode home with the engineer and fireman.

1931 Lambeau picked up another excellent runner in Hank Bruder of Northwestern. Starting with a 26-0 victory over the new Cleveland Indians, the Packers burst out of the starting gate and raced to nine straight wins. The streak ended against the Chicago Cardinals when Nevers staged a spectacular performance in a 21-13 win, November 15. Green Bay headed east and defeated the Giants, Providence, and Brooklyn, and won an unprecedented third straight championship despite a 7-6 defeat by the Bears in the final game. The Packers' 12-2 record was one game better than the Portsmouth Spartans' 11-3. Although the Spartans, who never met the Packers, complained bitterly that a game had been tentatively scheduled, the game never was played.

1932 The best rookie to join the team was fullback Clarke Hinkle of Bucknell. Despite a loss to the Giants, who featured Benny Friedman, the Packers appeared to be on their way to their fourth consecutive title, as they started off 10-1-1. But, on December 4, Green Bay was beaten by Portsmouth 19-0 and the next week lost to the Bears 9-0. The Bears and Spartans tied for the title, forcing the first-ever NFL Championship Game, and the Packers dropped to third place. In the first official league statistics, Herber led the passers by completing 37 of 101 for 639 yards and nine touchdowns. At the end of the season the Packers were invited to play two games in Honolulu, where they scored victories before sell-out crowds. On the way home they stopped off in San Francisco to play Ernie Nevers's Pacific Coast All-Americans at Kezar Stadium, a charity game for the Knights of Columbus.

1933 A fan fell out of the temporary wooden bleachers at City Stadium and sued for $25,000, and the two firms carrying the Packers' insurance failed. The team went into receivership and once again the "Hungry Five" had to be called on to save the franchise, cutting front-office expenses and player personnel. Hinkle teamed with Bob Monnett, a rookie halfback from Michigan State, and Herber to lead the attack. Competing in the five-club Western Division of the newly divided NFL, the Packers dropped four of their last five and finished third at 5-7-1. After the season, Lee Joannes, president of the club from 1930 to 1947, invited 25 businessmen to a special meeting to start a fund-raising campaign. Housewives, high school students, firemen, policemen, and other citizens chipped in for a $15,000 "Save the Packers" fund. The club was incorporated by Dilweg, nearing the end of his career as an end, with 600 shares of common stock having no par value and a requirement that any profits be donated to the local American Legion post or other veterans' organization with no dividend or profit for the stockholders.

1934 With a new, sound financial base, the Packers were able to return their attention to the playing field where new opportunities for a passer like Herber had been opened up by the recent rules changes permitting forward passes anywhere behind the line of scrimmage. Herber led the league's passers for the second time in three seasons, and the Packers started on the way back with a third-place 7-6 record in a division dominated by the 13-0 Bears. Seating capacity at City Stadium was increased to 15,000.

1935 Don Hutson signed with Green Bay after having been pursued by both the Packers and Brooklyn Dodgers following a brilliant career at Alabama. The nimble sprinter played with the All Stars in the Chicago College All-Star Game against the Bears and saw brief action as a sub in the Packers' opener. By the time the club was ready for its second game, Hutson was ready to start. On the first play, Herber sent Blood down the right sideline and threw to Hutson up the middle for a stunning 83-yard touchdown play. Blood, returning after a year in Pittsburgh, was used primarily as a receiver. Although Hutson's catches beat the Bears twice, 7-0 and 17-14, the Packers lost three to the Cardinals and split with Detroit, the Western Division champion at 7-3-2 to the Packers' 8-4. The arrival of Hutson, who led the league with seven touchdowns while catching 18 passes for 420 yards, and the second-place finish filled the stands with paying customers. After the season, the Packers made another trip to San Francisco for a charity game with the Pacific All-Stars.

1936 In the first college draft, Green Bay selected guard Russ Letlow in the first round. Green Bay picked seventh, because its 1935 won-lost record was third-best in the league. The selection of Letlow was offset by the retirement of Michalske. The Packers absorbed their worst beating, 30-3 at the hands of the Bears in the second game of the season, but didn't lose again, squaring matters with the Bears later 21-10. Defeats by the Lions and Cardinals in their last two games cost the Bears their chance of catching Green Bay. For the first time since the NFL split into two divisions in 1933 the Packers won the championship, taking the Western Division with a 10-1-1 record and defeating the Boston Redskins 21-6 in a title game played at New York's Polo Grounds because of poor attendance for the Redskins in Boston. Hutson led the league with a record 34 pass receptions and Herber topped the passers for the third time by throwing for 1,239 yards and 11 touchdowns. In addition, other main components in the offense were backs Hinkle, George Sauer, and Bob Monnett, and end Milt Gantenbein.

1937 The success of 1936 was short-lived. The Packers not only lost the Chicago College All-Star Game 6-0 to the collegians, who were led by Sammy Baugh, but also dropped their first two regular-season games, bowing to both the Cardinals and Bears at City Stadium. They recovered in a seven-game winning streak, only to lose their last two games to the Giants and Redskins on the road, finishing at 7-4, one game behind the Bears. Herber was slowed by a hip injury, but he still could throw, and Hutson broke his own record with 41 receptions and seven touchdowns. The bulk of the running was done by Hinkle, who finished second in the league, and rookie Eddie Jankowski. Michalske, who had returned for one year, retired again, as did guard Lon Evans.

1938 The Packers selected tailback Cecil Isbell of Purdue and halfback Andy Uram of Minnesota in the draft. Lambeau frequently played Herber and Isbell in the same backfield, and both took turns throwing to Hutson, as did Monnett. Hutson dropped to second in the league in receiving, although he did lead the NFL with 548 yards and tied Blood's NFL record of nine touchdown receptions. Hinkle scored enough points on runs, pass receptions, conversions, and field goals to lead the league with 58 points. After clinching the Western Division title November 21, the Packers had to wait until December 12 to play the Giants for the league championship. Green Bay lost 23-17 in the title game with a limping Hutson seeing only part-time action because of a knee injury.

1939 Green Bay played a unique doubleheader with the Pittsburgh Steelers with 10-minute exhibition quarters. The Packers tied the first game and won the second 17-0 in a program that lasted from 7:30 P.M. to 11 P.M. Then the Packers went south to Dallas for an exhibition game with the Southwest College All-Stars at the Cotton Bowl, beating a team led by Davey O'Brien and Charles (Ki) Aldrich 31-20. The busy preseason didn't seem to bother the Packers, although they lost their third regular-season game in an upset by the Cleveland Rams. Uram set a record with a 97-yard touchdown run against the Cardinals, October 8. The Packers won seven of their last eight, beating out the Bears to win the Western Division for the second year in a row. Lambeau gave Hutson some relief on defense, switching him to safety while moving Larry Craig, a rookie from South Carolina, to defensive end and blocking back. Hutson responded with his best year as a long-distance receiver, leading the league with 34 catches and 846 yards, an average of 24.9 yards per reception. The championship game was shifted to the State Fair Park in Milwaukee, where 32,279 watched the Packers' defense take the Giants apart 27-0 for their fifth NFL title.

1940 Green Bay barely hung on 27-20 when passer Davey O'Brien of the Eagles threw 40 passes in the opening game at City Stadium. Then the Bears came in and won 41-10. "People are beginning to talk," warned Lambeau as he drove his Packers through heavy practice sessions. They responded by beating the Cardinals, but lost to Detroit, the New York Giants, and the Chicago Bears again for a second-place 6-4-1 finish. Although Isbell still kept his left arm taped to his side because of a shoulder separation in a college game, he did most of the passing. Hutson led the league in scoring with 57 points and also was first with six interceptions; his 45 receptions were more than anyone ever had caught before, but were a distant second to the record 58 caught by Don Looney of Philadelphia the same season. Hinkle's nine field goals were only one short of the record.

1941 Herber retired due to a leg injury, leaving Isbell to do most of the passing, although he was backed up by rookie Tony Canadeo. The Packers lost in the third game of the year to the Bears, but then won the rest of their games to finish 10-1. The most important victory was a 16-14 triumph over the Bears, which was Chicago's only loss of the season. Isbell led the league in passing, completing 117 of 206 for 1,479 yards and 15 touchdowns, all league highs. Hutson, the NFL's most valuable player, tied the league record by making 58 receptions for 738 yards and 10 touchdowns. He also set the NFL scoring record, with 95 points. In the first divisional playoff game ever, the Bears struck for 24 points in the second quarter to defeat the Packers 33-14.

1942 The Packers put together the most dominating passing attack in league history, and it carried them to an 8-2-1 record. Unfortunately, both losses were to the Bears, who went 11-0 to win the Western Division and drop the Packers into second place. Isbell led the NFL in passing, while setting league records with 146 completions, 2,021 yards, and 24 touchdown passes. Hutson, again the league's most valuable player, set records with 74 receptions for 1,211 yards and 17 touchdowns. He also scored a record 138 points, adding 33 extra points and a field goal to his touchdowns, and was second in the league with seven interceptions. Rookie fullback Ted Fritsch led the league in field-goal percentage after taking over for Hinkle, who went into the Coast Guard. Isbell surprised Packers' fans by retiring after the season. He explained, "I hadn't been up long when I saw Lambeau tell players like Herber, Gantenbein, and Bruder they were all done. I vowed I'd quit before they came around to tell me."

1943 The Packers opened with a 21-21 tie with the Bears, but a loss to Washington three weeks later dropped them from first place, and a 21-7 loss to the Bears ended Green Bay's hopes of a championship, even though the Redskins later knocked off the Bears. Chicago finished 8-1-1, to Green Bay's second-place 7-2-1. The Packers' passing game remained at a high level, even though Canadeo and Irv Comp replaced Isbell. Hutson led the league in receptions (47), receiving yards (776), and touchdown catches (11), as well as scoring (117 points) and field goals (3). He also finished third in interceptions and even threw a touchdown pass to Harry Jacunski.

1944 Green Bay, playing with veterans, servicemen on leave, and untried youngsters, opened with a six-game winning streak before running into a 21-0 shutout by the Bears. They were blanked again 24-0 by the Giants, but finished 8-2 to 6-3-1 for the Bears and the Lions in the West. Comp led the league with 1,159 yards passing and was second with 12 touchdowns, while Hutson again led the NFL in receiving, with 58 catches for 866 yards and nine touchdowns. Hutson was the league's leading scorer for the fifth consecutive year with 85 points. In the NFL Championship Game, the Packers went to New York and won their sixth league title, and first since 1939, by beating the Giants 14-7 in the Polo Grounds on two scores by Fritsch. Each Packers player took home $1,149, a record winning share, thanks to a crowd of 46,016.

1945 Hutson had been talking of retiring for years but Lambeau talked him into staying on as a player-coach for 1945. Hutson caught four touchdown passes and kicked five extra points for 29 points in the second quarter of a game against Detroit in which the Packers also set a record with 41 points in the same quarter en route to a 57-21 victory, October 7. Despite a strong start, the Packers' defense yielded 180 points and they lost four games, dropping to third place in the Western Division behind both the winning Cleveland Rams and the Lions. After winning his eighth pass-receiving title, a league record, with 47 receptions, Hutson retired after 11 seasons. He had caught at least one pass in 95 consecutive games, and held 33 league records, including being the all-time scorer (823 points) and pass receiver (488 receptions for 7,991 yards and 99 touchdowns).

1946 World War II was over and talent began flowing back to NFL clubs, but the retirement of Hutson left a void in the Packers' offense. The Bears and the newly located Los Angeles Rams each beat Green Bay twice, and the Packers also lost to the Chicago Cardinals for a 6-5 finish and third place. Without Hutson the passing became the poorest in the league, and the Packers tried to get by on the running of Canadeo, Fritsch, and rookie Walt Schlinkman. The offense was sluggish, scoring only 148 points. Fritsch accounted for most of the scoring. He led the league with 100 points on 10 touchdowns, 9 field goals, and 13 extra points. Roy Dale McKay topped NFL punters for the second straight year.

1947 Coach-general manager Lambeau was running into trouble from the front office. Some executive-committee members criticized his decision to buy Rockwood Lodge, a training base 15 miles north of Green Bay, for $25,000. On the field, Lambeau installed the T-formation, but quarterback Jack Jacobs was no Isbell, even though he threw 16 touchdown passes and led the league in punting. The running game suffered with the retirement of Letlow and tackle Bill Lee. The Packers finished third at 6-5-1 but four of the five defeats were by a total of only nine points.

1948 The war with the rival AAFC was beginning to hurt the Packers, who had limited resources to engage in bidding contests for players. Green Bay had lost first-round draft choices to the AAFC in 1946 and 1947 but signed Earl (Jug) Girard in 1948. After a 17-7 loss to the Cardinals dropped the Packers' record to 2-2, Lambeau fined the entire squad half a week's salary for "indifferent play." The Packers beat the Rams 16-0 the next week, but, when the players didn't get their money back, morale dropped to zero and they lost every game the rest of the way, finishing 3-9 for Green Bay's first losing record since 1933. The running of Canadeo and Schlinkman provided the only bright spots.

1949 The Bears shut out the Packers on opening day 17-0 and the Rams bombed them 48-7 the following week. Green Bay beat only the New York Bulldogs and the Lions en route to a last-place 2-10 season, their poorest in history. Attendance dropped and financial problems mounted. Matters became so desperate that an intrasquad game was played on Thanksgiving Day, with oldtimers such as Verne Lewellen, Arnie Herber, and Johnny Blood (McNally) raising $50,000. Despite Canadeo rushing for 1,052 yards to become the third runner in NFL history with more than 1,000, the Packers' offense scored only 114 points, while the defense gave up 329. The passing game was a disaster, with Girard, Jacobs, and rookie Stan Heath, the number-one draft pick, throwing 29 interceptions and five touchdowns.

1950 Lambeau, founder of the franchise, resigned under fire after a dispute with the citizen organization that ran the club, February 1. Lambeau criticized the system of operation by committee and was rebuffed in an effort to add Don Hutson to the executive committee. Adding to the problems, the Rockwood Lodge burned, January 24. New stock certificates were sold and $118,000 was raised. The committee hired Gene Ronzani, a former halfback with the Bears, to become the new head coach. Ronzani's team had a new look. The best lineman was rookie center Clayton Tonnemaker, while halfback Billy Grimes, picked up from the AAFC's Los Angeles Dons, replaced Canadeo as the top rusher. At quarterback, rookie Tobin Rote shared the job with former Cardinals star Paul Christman after Heath and Jacobs went to Canada and Girard was moved to defense. With all the changes, the offense improved dramatically, but the poorest defense in the league kept the Packers in fifth place with a 3-9 record.

1951 The Packers continued a modest improvement, winning three of their first five games before going into a seven-game tailspin that left them at 3-9 and in fifth place. Green Bay lost to the New York Yanks 31-28, the only game the Yanks won. Rote and second-year player Bobby Thomason shared the quarterback position and threw the ball more than any other team in the NFL. Unfortunately, they didn't throw it very successfully, and the Packers' ground game was non-existent, except for Rote, who set a record for quarterbacks with 523 yards rushing. The defense gave up a league-high 375 points.

1952 The draft brought in quarterback Vito (Babe) Parilli, end Billy Howton, defensive back Bobby Dillon, and tackle Dave (Hawg) Hanner, each of whom started and helped the Packers' fortunes turn around. Howton was particularly effective, catching 53 passes for two rookie records—1,231 yards and 13 touchdowns. Ronzani had the Packers in the thick of the race most of the way and was 6-3 with three games to go. One of the early-season successes was a 35-20 win over Washington, coached by Lambeau. However, the Packers lost the last three to Detroit, the Los Angeles Rams, and San Francisco and finished fourth behind those three teams.

1953 Among the rookies were Syracuse center Jim Ringo and linebacker Bill Forester of SMU. Despite the play of halfback Floyd (Breezy) Reid, who averaged 5.2 yards per carry, the offense collapsed, with Parilli and Rote throwing 34 interceptions and only nine touchdowns. With two games remaining, the executive committee fired Ronzani, saying he had resigned, and replaced him with assistants Hugh Devore and Ray (Scooter) McLean. The Packers' only victories in a 2-9-1 season were over the league's new entry, Baltimore.

1954 The 13-man executive committee realized a major change was in order, so they made Verne Lewellen, a former halfback, general manager, and hired Marquette's Lisle Blackbourn as coach. The Packers were competitive for the first half at 3-3. But they lost five of their last six, including two tight games against the eventual champion Lions, 21-17 and 28-24, and finished 4-8, barely ahead of the last-place Colts. With Parilli called into the service, the offense was led by Rote's 2,311 yards and 14 touchdowns passing, and his eight scores rushing. Howton caught 52 passes, while rookie end Max McGee caught 36 for nine touchdowns. Reid again averaged more than five yards per carry.

1955 The Packers won five of six home games, but lost five of six road games and settled for 6-6 and third place in the Western Conference, their best season since 1947. Howard Ferguson became a solid fullback with 859 yards, and Rote threw 17 touchdown passes, most of them to Howton and rookie Gary Knafelc. Fred Cone kicked 16 field goals. Attendance increased to 153,241 with East Stadium (formerly City Stadium) now at a capacity of more than 20,000. A home game at Milwaukee County Stadium drew a Wisconsin pro record of 40,199.

1956 The Packers were unbeaten in the preseason, including a win over the defending champion Browns. They lost their first two and were 2-6 before beating the Lions and Cardinals. Defeats by the Rams and 49ers on the road left them in fifth place at 4-8. The team continued to get good, young players, with three important rookies appearing—tackles Forrest Gregg and Bob Skoronski and quarterback Bart Starr. Rote led the league in passing yards (2,203) and touchdown passes (18), and Howton in receiving yards (1,188) and touchdowns (12), but the running game disappeared with an injury to Ferguson, and Rote again led the team, with 398 yards. Al Carmichael set an NFL record by returning a Bears' kickoff 106 yards for a touchdown, October 7.

1957 Heisman Trophy winner Paul Hornung was selected by the Packers as the bonus choice, but initially was a failure at quarterback and fullback, before being moved to halfback. Rote was traded to Detroit, and was succeeded by Starr and Parilli, who returned after a year in Canada. On September 29, the new City Stadium, a $1 million structure seating 32,150, was dedicated at a 21-7 opening-day victory over the Bears. Unfortunately, the club won only two more games the rest of the year. Blackbourn was fired with one more year to go on his contract.

1958 Assistant Ray (Scooter) McLean was named head coach. McLean had a nice-guy image, and the players quickly took advantage of it. The result was a 1-10-1 record, the poorest in Green Bay history. The lone victory, 38-35 over Philadelphia, almost turned into defeat when the Packers frittered away most of a 38-7 lead. Starr and Parilli shared the quarterback job, but neither was effective, as the offense scored the fewest points in the league, while the defense gave up the most. The rookie class included fullback Jim Taylor, guard Jerry Kramer, and linebacker Ray Nitschke.

1959 Green Bay's executive committee hired Vince Lombardi, an offensive assistant with the New York Giants, as head coach and general manager, January 28. Lombardi spent the winter looking at the films of the 1958 Packers and was convinced he had the basis for a contender. He selected Colorado quarterback Boyd Dowler in the draft, traded Howton to Cleveland for defensive end Bill Quinlan and defensive tackle Henry Jordan, acquired safety Emlen Tunnell from the Giants to solidify the defensive backfield, and picked up guard Fred (Fuzzy) Thurston from Baltimore. Lamar McHan, acquired from the Chicago Cardinals, started at quarterback, with Hornung and Taylor also in the backfield. When the Packers beat the Bears opening day, the players carried Lombardi off the field on their shoulders. Two more victories followed. Then came five straight defeats. Lombardi switched to Starr at quarterback, and the Packers swept their last four for a 7-5 record, their best since 1945. Hornung scored 94 points kicking and running to lead the NFL. Dowler, converted to flanker, led the team with 32 receptions.

1960 Lombardi drafted halfback Tom Moore, traded with Cleveland for defensive end Willie Davis, and signed free-agent safety Willie Wood. The Packers had a tough fight in the Western Conference. They wrapped it up by winning their last three on the road, clinching the title with a 35-21 victory at Los Angeles, where Starr threw a 91-yard touchdown pass to Dowler. The Packers came up short in the championship game in Philadelphia, where Norm Van Brocklin led the Eagles to a 17-13 victory. Chuck Bednarik tackled Taylor on the Eagles' 9-yard line at the final gun. During the season, the offensive stars were Taylor, who finished second in the league with 1,101 yards, and Hornung, who ran for 671 yards, caught 28 passes, and scored 15 touchdowns and an NFL record 176 points.

1961 The Packers added three important rookies —defensive tackle Ron Kostelnik, cornerback Herb Adderley, and halfback Elijah Pitts. Hornung, Dowler, and Nitschke were called into the service due to the Berlin crisis, but played most of the games on weekend passes. After an opening-day loss to Detroit, the Packers won six in a row, including a 45-7 victory over Baltimore when Hornung scored four touchdowns, a field goal, and six extra points for 33 points. The Packers clinched the Western Division title by beating the Giants 20-17 with two weeks left in the season. Hornung again led the league in scoring, with 146 points; Taylor finished second in rushing, with 1,307 yards; and Starr was third in passing. The Packers won their seventh NFL title with a 37-0 victory over the Giants, in which Hornung scored 19 points, a championship-game record.

1962 Lombardi made very few changes, and even the loss of Hornung with injuries didn't slow down the Packers. Moore took over his running and blocking chores, and Kramer became the new kicker. The Packers won their first 10 before losing 26-14 in Detroit on Thanksgiving Day. Three victories to close the season gave them a 13-1 record and the Western Division title. Taylor led the league in rushing with 1,474 yards, the only time in Jim Brown's career that the Cleveland star failed to win the rushing championship. Taylor scored an NFL record 19 touchdowns and led the league in scoring. Starr led the league in passing, and Wood in interceptions. Taylor pounded out 85 yards and Kramer kicked three field goals as the Packers beat the Giants 16-7 for the NFL title.

1963 NFL Commissioner Pete Rozelle suspended Hornung indefinitely for betting on NFL games, April 17. Four former Packers—Lambeau, Hutson, Blood, and Hubbard—were among the 17 charter members of the new Pro Football Hall of Fame at Canton, Ohio. Moore and Pitts filled in for Hornung in the backfield, and Kramer took over the placekicking job again. The Packers lost their opener to the Bears 10-3, then were battered by the Bears in a 26-7 rematch after winning eight straight. By the time of the second game against the Bears, Starr was out of action with a broken hand and had been replaced by Zeke Bratkowski. Another Thanksgiving Day visit to Detroit resulted in a 13-13 tie and the loss of Nitschke with a broken arm. Although Taylor ran for 1,018 yards, the Packers finished a half game behind the Bears, 11-1-2 to 11-2-1, and had to settle for a 40-23 Playoff Bowl victory over Cleveland.

1964 Hornung came back to play when his suspension was lifted, but he seemed to have lost his ability to kick under pressure. A missed extra point cost the Packers their first game with Baltimore, and another missed point and five missed field goals by Hornung accounted for a second 24-21 loss to the Colts. Kramer missed most of the season due to abdominal surgery, and Ringo was traded to Philadelphia. Taylor gained more than 1,000 yards for the fifth straight year with 1,169. Hornung contributed 415 yards and 107 points. Starr led the league in passing, and the defense allowed only 227 yards a game. An 8-5-1 finish left the Packers far behind the Colts' 12-2 record, and they suffered another jolt by losing the Playoff Bowl to St. Louis 24-17.

1965 In June, Lambeau died at age 67. After the kicking failures of 1964, Lombardi brought in Don Chandler from the Giants to handle both the punting and field-goal work. He also acquired flanker Carroll Dale from the Rams, and promoted tight end Marv Fleming and linebacker Dave Robinson to starting roles. The Packers trailed Pittsburgh 9-7 at halftime of their opening game, but scored 34 points in the second half for a 41-9 victory that started a six-game winning streak, including a 20-17 victory over the Colts in which Hornung, Taylor, and Starr were hurt. After losing three of five to drop into second place, the Packers beat the Colts 42-27 on a foggy December day, with Hornung scoring five touchdowns. A tie with San Francisco in the final game set up a playoff with Baltimore. Starr was injured early in the game, but Chandler's disputed field goal sent the game into overtime. Another field goal by Chandler won the game after 13:39 of sudden death. The injury-riddled Packers pulled themselves together to ruin Jim Brown's last playoff game by beating the Browns 23-12 in the snow at newly renamed Lambeau Field in Green Bay, January 2.

1966 The Packers signed top draft choices Donny Anderson and Jim Grabowski for a combined $1 million, but it was the veterans who kept Lombardi's machine running. Starr led the league in passing, and was intercepted only three times the entire season. Pitts took over for Hornung, who was injured. The defense led the NFL, giving up just 163 points. The Packers went 12-2, losing only to the 49ers and Vikings by a total of four points. In the NFL Championship Game, on January 1, Green Bay opened a 34-20 lead and held off a Dallas comeback to win 34-27. Tom Brown intercepted Don Meredith in the end zone to assure the victory. The first Super Bowl, pitting the champions of the AFL and NFL, was played at the Los Angeles Memorial Coliseum, January 15. After leading 14-10 at halftime, the Packers beat the Kansas City Chiefs 35-10. Starr was named the game's most valuable player.

1967 Taylor, who had played out his option, signed with the New Orleans Saints, who also selected Hornung in an expansion draft. The Packers were plagued by injuries, but no matter who Lombardi plugged into his team, it continued to win. When Grabowski and Pitts were hurt, Lombardi replaced them with Anderson, Ben Wilson, and Travis Williams, who also set NFL records by averaging 41.1 yards on kickoff returns and scoring on four of them. Starr also went down, but the Packers didn't slow a step under Bratkowski. In a 55-7 victory over Cleveland, the Packers scored a record 35 points in the first quarter. The Packers won the new NFL Central Division with a 9-4-1 record and then defeated the Rams 28-7 for the Western Conference title. The NFL Championship Game with Dallas was played in 13-below-zero weather with 15-mile-per-hour winds dropping the chill factor to minus-37. The Packers won what has come to be known as the "Ice Bowl" on Starr's third-down, one-yard quarterback sneak behind Jerry Kramer's block on Jethro Pugh with 13 seconds left. Super Bowl II was almost an anticlimax in the 68-degree heat of Miami's Orange Bowl. The Packers whipped the Oakland Raiders 33-14.

1968 Two weeks after his second Super Bowl triumph, Lombardi shocked the football world by announcing his retirement as coach. He remained at Green Bay as general manager and named Phil Bengtson, his long-time assistant, as his successor. Thurston, McGee, and Chandler retired. Starr's arm bothered him and he spent half the year on the bench watching Bratkowski play. The Packers desperately tried Mike Mercer, Errol Mann, Kramer, and Chuck Mercein as kickers, with little success. Thurston was replaced by Gale Gillingham. Minnesota, on the way to its first of four straight divisional titles, beat the Packers twice. Green Bay finished at 6-7-1.

1969 Lombardi left the Packers to become a part-owner, vice president, general manager, and coach of the Washington Redskins, February 5. Bengtson was given the additional job of general manager. It was a time of change at Green Bay. Bratkowski, Kramer, and Skoronski retired, Kostelnik went to Baltimore, and Tom Brown to Washington. Williams became the top rusher, and rookie Dave Hampton outgained Anderson and Grabowski. Shoulder trouble forced Starr out of the last four games, and young Don Horn threw 11 touchdown passes. Both Mercer and Booth Lusteg were inconsistent kickers. The Packers (5-2) were in the race at the halfway mark, but lost four of their next five and finished 8-6.

1970 Jordan, Willie Davis, and Dowler retired. The Packers traded Adderley to Dallas, Fleming to Miami, and Pitts, Bob Hyland, and Lee Roy Caffey to the Bears. Lombardi died of cancer, September 3. The Packers were shut out by the Lions on opening day, the first time they had been shut out since 1958, and the first at home since 1949. They won four of their next five, but then went into a slump that lasted the rest of the season, and saw them win only twice more, to finish 6-8 and in last place in the NFC Central. Starr was slowed by a sore arm, and injuries forced Anderson to be the heavy-duty ball carrier, leading the team in rushing (853 yards) and finishing second behind Dale in receiving. The defense, without the injured Robinson, finished tenth in the NFC. When the Packers were shut out 20-0 by the Lions in the final game, Bengtson resigned.

1971 Determined to make a complete break with the past, the Packers went into the college ranks to get a successor to Bengtson and signed Dan Devine of Missouri as head coach and general manager. Gregg moved to Dallas to wind up his career, and linebacker Nitschke, one of the last holdovers from the Lombardi days, was benched. On opening day, Devine was run over on the sidelines by Hyland (who had been traded from the Packers the year before) and suffered a broken leg while his team was losing to the Giants in a wild 42-40 game, which featured a 100-yard run by Ken Ellis with a missed field-goal attempt. Devine coached the rest of the year on crutches, watching a porous defense nullify the outstanding play of John Brockington, the top draft choice, who led the NFC with 1,105 yards. Starr threw only 45 passes, and Scott Hunter, a rookie from Alabama, had 17 passes intercepted. The Packers finished last again with a 4-8-2 record.

1972 Devine traded Anderson to the St. Louis Cardinals for MacArthur Lane. The pairing of Lane and Brockington proved effective, with Brockington gaining 1,027 yards and Lane 821. Starr retired as a player but remained as an assistant coach to call the plays for Hunter, whose favorite targets were Brockington and Lane. Wood also retired, but the new deep combination of Ken Ellis, Jim Hill, Al Matthews, and Willie Buchanon, the number-one draft choice, was a strong one. Kicker Chester Marcol, the team's third draft choice, led the league in scoring by hitting 33 of 48 field-goal attempts and 29 straight extra points for 128 points. The Packers won six of their last seven games and took their first division title since 1967 but lost 16-3 to Washington in the first round of the playoffs.

1973 The club was 2-1-1 after four games but won only one of the next seven and settled into third place at 5-7-2. Brockington had his third straight year of more than 1,000 yards as he gained 1,144 and led the NFC. Lane added 528 yards, but the passing game was not productive. Jerry Tagge, Hunter, and Jim Del Gaizo all were erratic and the bumper stickers proclaiming "The Pack is Back" were not true.

1974 Devine definitely was on the spot in his fourth year on the job. When Tagge floundered, Devine made a midseason deal with the Rams for 34-year-old quarterback John Hadl. The Packers gave up their first three draft choices for 1975 and their first two for 1976 in the deal. But Hadl didn't deliver and Brockington slumped to 3.3 yards per carry. Marcol kicked four field goals in a 21-19 win over Detroit and four more in a 19-7 win at Minnesota. Steve Odom raced 95 yards with a punt return against the Bears, November 10. The club was in the division race until it nosedived into a three-game losing streak to end the year at 6-8 in third place. Marcol led the league with 94 points on 25 field goals in 39 attempts and 19 consecutive extra points. At the end of the season, Devine resigned. Starr was given the job of trying to lead the Packers back to their former status. His only coaching experience had been one year as an assistant coach to Devine.

1975 Starr tried to piece together a team that was a shambles. The running game was a disaster, with Brockington dropping to 434 yards and a three-yard average. Hadl set a Packers record with 191 completions, but they netted only 2,095 yards and six touchdowns, as opposed to 21 interceptions. Unheralded Ken Payne had 12 receptions against Denver and finished second in the NFC with 58 for the year, good for 766 yards. Typically, he didn't score even once. Marcol missed the entire season with a torn leg muscle and was replaced by Joe Danelo. Green Bay lost its first four and eight of its first nine, but won three of the last five for a 4-10 record.

1976 Starr traded Hadl to Houston for quarterback Lynn Dickey in a deal that also cost Green Bay cornerback Ken Ellis and a fourth-round draft choice. It took Dickey time to get started after a long wait on the Houston bench, but he was coming on when he suffered a shoulder separation in the first Chicago game, November 14. He was lost for the year. Carlos Brown and Randy Johnson finished up, and the club lost four of its last five en route to a 5-9 finish and last place in the NFC Central Division.

1977 Gillingham, the last player from the Lombardi era, retired before the season. The club opened with a 24-20 victory over New Orleans, but staggered to nine losses in the next 10 weeks. Dickey was lost for the season when he broke his leg on the last play of a 24-6 loss to Los Angeles on November 13. Rookie David Whitehurst replaced him, starting the final five games. He guided the club to two victories in its last three games. Despite a 4-10 record, the defense allowed just 219 points. However, the offense was held to 16 points or less in every game after the opener. Dickey and wide receiver Steve Odom connected on the longest touchdown pass of the year—a 95-yard play against Minnesota on October 2.

1978 James Lofton, a wide receiver from Stanford, was the team's first draft choice. Whitehurst retained the starting quarterback job with Dickey still recovering from his broken leg. The rejuvenated offense sparked the Packers to a 6-1 start and first place in the NFC Central. Included in the fast start were a 28-17 victory over the Saints, in which Whitehurst and Lofton connected on three touchdown passes, and a 45-28 win over Seattle, which featured four rushing touchdowns by Terdell Middleton. Despite a six-week slump that produced only one victory and one tie, Green Bay moved within one victory of clinching the division with a 17-7 win over Tampa Bay on December 3. But the Packers lost back-to-back games to the Bears and the Rams, and Minnesota won the NFC Central with a better head-to-head record against Green Bay. Middleton became only the fourth Packers back to rush for more than 1,000 yards in a season, finishing with 1,116. Defensive tackle Ezra Johnson finished with 20½ sacks.

1979 Green Bay drafted running back Eddie Lee Ivery of Georgia Tech on the first round. With the offense performing erratically and the defense hampered by injuries, the club plunged to a 5-11 record. But the season included two memorable victories. In a Monday night game on October 1, the 1,000th game in Green Bay's history, the Packers upset heavily favored New England 27-14. The defense sparked the victory with five interceptions and five sacks. On November 11, Green Bay ended a five-year drought against Minnesota with a 19-7 victory at Milwaukee County Stadium. Dickey played the second half against Philadelphia on November 25, his first extended appearance in two years. Although he completed 14 of 22 passes for 144 yards, the Packers lost 21-10. Tight end Paul Coffman, a free agent in 1978, led the Packers with 56 receptions.

1980 Defensive tackle Bruce Clark of Penn State was the Packers' top draft choice, but he signed with the Canadian Football League. Kicker Chester Marcol became the unlikely running star in the season opener when he scooped up his own blocked field-goal attempt in overtime and ran for a 25-yard touchdown in a 12-6 victory over Chicago. The Packers then lost three straight games by big margins. Dickey, still rebounding from the inactivity of two previous seasons, regained his passing touch and directed a 14-9 victory over Cincinnati. In a tie with Tampa Bay on October 12, Dickey set Packers single-game passing records for attempts (51), completions (35), and yards (418). He also set season records with 478 attempts, 278 completions, and 3,529 yards. Dickey's favorite receiver was Lofton, who caught 71 passes for 1,226 yards. Lofton displayed his versatility when he filled in as a defensive back in a 23-16 victory over San Francisco on November 9. Two weeks later, Ivery and Gerry Ellis combined for 246 yards rushing, and the Packers defeated Minnesota 25-13, their first seasonal sweep of the Vikings since 1965. Green Bay finished 5-10-1.

1981 The Packers opened with a 16-9 victory over the Bears, but lost Eddie Lee Ivery for the season with a knee injury. A week later, the Packers lost to Atlanta 31-17 despite Lofton's eight catches for 179 yards. The slumping Packers reached the midseason mark with a 2-6 record. One high point in the first half of the season was the acquisition of wide receiver John Jefferson from San Diego for draft choices and Aundra Thompson. In his first start with the Packers, Jefferson caught seven passes for 121 yards in a loss to Minnesota. While Dickey sat out with a back injury, Whitehurst made his first start in nearly two years, and passed for 205 yards and three touchdowns in a 34-24 victory over Seattle. That win ignited the Packers, who won five of their next six games, the last three with Dickey back in the lineup. With a playoff berth riding on the final game, the Packers lost to the New York Jets 28-3, to finish 8-8.

1982 Judge Robert J. Parins was elected Packers president, May 3, succeeding Dominic Olejniczak, and becoming the first full-time executive in team history. Construction was completed on a 55,000-square-foot indoor-practice facility. The Packers started off hot, winning their first three. Trailing 19-7 in the third quarter of a Monday night game marred by two power blackouts and the fact that it was the last game before the players' strike, the Packers rallied for 20 points and a 27-19 victory over the Giants. The Packers clinched their first playoff berth since 1972 with a 38-7 victory over Atlanta in which Dickey threw two long touchdown passes to Lofton. Green Bay's 5-3-1 record was the third-best in the NFC, and they improved on it in the first round of the Super Bowl tournament by beating St. Louis 41-16. Dallas evened some old scores in the second round, defeating the Packers 37-26. All three starting receivers for the Packers—Lofton, Jefferson, and Coffman—were selected to the Pro Bowl, where Jefferson was co-most valuable player.

1983 Green Bay proved that it had the offense to win any game, and the defense to lose it, in a season-opening 41-38 victory over Houston. Dickey threw five touchdown passes, but it was Jan Stenerud's field goal in overtime that won the game. The Packers could get no offensive consistency, however, only twice winning two games in a row. They followed a 27-3 loss to the Giants with a 55-14 victory over the Buccaneers, in which they scored an NFL-record 49 points in the first half. Five of the Packers' games went into overtime, and six more were decided by no more than four points. The highlight of the season was a 48-47 victory over Washington, in which the lead changed hands five times in the fourth quarter before Stenerud won it with a 20-yard field goal with 54 seconds left. With a chance to win the Central Division, the Packers lost the last game of the year when Bob Thomas kicked a field goal with 10 seconds left to give the Bears a 23-21 victory. The next day, Starr was fired. Dickey completed the season with an NFC-record 4,458 yards passing and an NFL-leading 32 touchdown passes. On December 24, former Packers star tackle Forrest Gregg was hired as the team's new head coach.

1984 The Packers won their first game 24-23 over St. Louis, then lost seven in a row. They reversed their record in the second half of the season, running up a 7-1 mark that left them in second place with an 8-8 final record. The defense, with the addition of three rookies—defensive ends Alphonso Carreker and Donnie Humphrey and safety Tom Flynn, who led the NFC with nine interceptions—improved dramatically. The offense still was effective, with Dickey passing for 3,195 yards and 25 touchdowns, and Lofton catching 62 passes for 1,361 yards, a 22.0-yard average. The key for the Packers, though, was the return of the frequently injured Ivery, who gained 552 yards in the second half of the season after missing the first half.

1985 The Packers played musical quarterbacks all season, and the result was a second-place finish seven games behind the high-flying Bears. After several poor games, Dickey asked that he not start against St. Louis, September 29. Randy Wright started the game, but was ineffective and Dickey replaced him in the third quarter, throwing three touchdown passes in a 43-28 loss. The next week, with Dickey, Wright, and Jim Zorn all playing, the Packers beat the Lions 43-10. Zorn started against Minnesota on November 10, but Dickey replaced him and the Packers scored three touchdowns in a four-minute span of the fourth quarter to win 27-17. With Zorn at the helm, the Packers jelled late in the season, winning three of their last four to finish 8-8. Lofton, as usual, was the top receiver, catching 69 for 1,153 yards and breaking Don Hutson's team career-yardage record.

MEMBERS OF HALL OF FAME:
Herb Adderley, Johnny Blood (McNally), Tony Canadeo, Willie Davis, Len Ford, Forrest Gregg, Arnie Herber, Clarke Hinkle, Paul Hornung, Cal Hubbard, Don Hutson, Walt Kiesling, Earl (Curly) Lambeau, Vince Lombardi, Mike Michalske, Ray Nitschke, Jim Ringo, Bart Starr, Jim Taylor, Emlen Tunnell

PACKERS RECORD, 1921-85

Year	Won	Lost	Tied	Pct.	Fin.	Pts.	OP
1921	3	2	1	.600	6t	70	55
1922	4	3	3	.571	7	70	44
1923	7	2	1	.778	3t	85	34
1924	7	4	0	.636	6	102	38
1925	8	5	0	.615	9	151	110
1926	7	3	3	.700	5	151	60
1927	7	2	1	.778	2	113	43
1928	6	4	3	.600	4	120	92
1929a	12	0	1	1.000	1	198	24
1930a	10	3	1	.769	1	234	111
1931a	12	2	0	.857	1	291	94
1932	10	3	1	.769	3	152	63
1933	5	7	1	.417	3	170	107
1934	7	6	0	.538	3	156	112
1935	8	4	0	.667	2	181	96
1936b	10	1	1	.909	1	248	118
1937	7	4	0	.636	2t	220	122
1938c	8	3	0	.727	1	223	118
1939b	9	2	0	.818	1	233	153
1940	6	4	1	.600	2	238	155
1941d	10	1	0	.909	2	258	120
1942	8	2	1	.800	2	300	215
1943	7	2	1	.778	2	264	172
1944b	8	2	0	.800	1	238	141
1945	6	4	0	.600	3	258	173
1946	6	5	0	.545	3t	148	158
1947	6	5	1	.545	3	274	210
1948	3	9	0	.250	4	154	290
1949	2	10	0	.167	5	114	329
1950	3	9	0	.250	5t	244	406
1951	3	9	0	.250	5	254	375
1952	6	6	0	.500	4	295	312
1953	2	9	1	.182	6	200	338
1954	4	8	0	.333	5	234	251
1955	6	6	0	.500	3	258	276
1956	4	8	0	.333	5t	264	342
1957	3	9	0	.250	6	218	311
1958	1	10	1	.091	6	193	382
1959	7	5	0	.583	3t	248	246
1960e	8	4	0	.667	1	332	209
1961b	11	3	0	.786	1	391	223
1962b	13	1	0	.929	1	415	148
1963f	11	2	1	.846	2	369	206
1964g	8	5	1	.615	2t	342	245
1965h	10	3	1	.769	1	316	224
1966i	12	2	0	.857	1	335	163
1967j	9	4	1	.692	1	332	209
1968	6	7	1	.462	3	281	227
1969	8	6	0	.571	3	269	221
1970	6	8	0	.429	4	196	293
1971	4	8	2	.333	4	274	298
1972k	10	4	0	.714	1	304	226
1973	5	7	2	.429	3	202	259
1974	6	8	0	.429	3	210	206
1975	4	10	0	.286	4	226	285
1976	5	9	0	.357	4	218	299
1977	4	10	0	.286	3	134	219
1978	8	7	1	.531	2	249	269
1979	5	11	0	.313	4	246	316
1980	5	10	1	.344	5	231	371
1981	8	8	0	.500	3	324	361
1982l	5	3	1	.611	3	226	169
1983	8	8	0	.500	2	429	439
1984	8	8	0	.500	2	390	309
1985	8	8	0	.500	2	337	355
65 Years	443	347	35	.558		15,400	13,545

a*NFL Champion; No Playoffs*
b*NFL Champion; 1-0 in Playoffs*
c*NFL Western Division Champion; 0-1 in Playoffs*
d*NFL Western Division Runnerup; 0-1 in Playoffs*
e*NFL Western Conference Champion; 0-1 in Playoffs*
f*NFL Western Conference Runnerup; 1-0 in Playoff Bowl*
g*NFL Western Conference Runnerup; 0-1 in Playoff Bowl*
h*NFL Champion; 2-0 in Playoffs*
i*Super Bowl Champion; 2-0 in Playoffs*
j*Super Bowl Champion; 3-0 in Playoffs*
k*NFC Central Division Champion; 0-1 in Playoffs*
l*NFC Qualifier for Playoffs, 1-1 in Playoffs*

RECORD HOLDERS

CAREER

Rushing attempts	Jim Taylor, 1958-66	1,811
Rushing yards	Jim Taylor, 1958-66	8,207
Pass attempts	Bart Starr, 1956-71	3,149
Pass completions	Bart Starr, 1956-71	1,808
Passing yards	Bart Starr, 1956-71	23,718
Touchdown passes	Bart Starr, 1956-71	152
Receptions	Don Hutson, 1935-45	488
Receiving yards	James Lofton, 1978-85	8,816
Interceptions	Bobby Dillon, 1952-59	52
Punting average	Jerry Norton, 1963 64	43.4
Punt return avg.	Billy Grimes, 1950-52	13.2
Kickoff return avg.	Dave Hampton, 1970-71	28.9
Field goals	Chester Marcol, 1972-80	120
Touchdowns	Don Hutson, 1935-45	105
Points	Don Hutson, 1935-45	823

SEASON

Rushing attempts	Terdell Middleton, 1978	284
Rushing yards	Jim Taylor, 1962	1,407
Pass attempts	Lynn Dickey, 1983	484
Pass completions	Lynn Dickey, 1983	289
Passing yards	Lynn Dickey, 1983	4,458
Touchdown passes	Lynn Dickey, 1983	32
Receptions	Don Hutson, 1942	74
Receiving yards	James Lofton, 1984	1,361
Interceptions	Irv Comp, 1943	10
Punting average	Jerry Norton, 1963	44.7
Punt return avg.	Billy Grimes, 1950	19.1
Kickoff return avg.	Travis Williams, 1967	41.1
Field goals	Chester Marcol, 1972	33
Touchdowns	Jim Taylor, 1962	19
Points	Paul Hornung, 1960	176

GAME

Rushing attempts	Terdell Middleton, 11-26-78	39
Rushing yards	Jim Taylor, 12-3-61	186
Pass attempts	Lynn Dickey, 10-12-80	51
Pass completions	Lynn Dickey, 10-12-80	35
Passing yards	Lynn Dickey, 10-12-80	418
Touchdown passes	4 times	5
Receptions	Don Hutson, 11-22-42	14
Receiving yards	Billy Howton, 10-21-56	257
Interceptions	Bobby Dillon, 11-26-53	4
	Willie Buchanon, 9-24-78	4
Field goals	12 times	4
Touchdowns	Paul Hornung, 12-12-65	5
Points	Paul Hornung, 10-8-61	33

COACHING HISTORY

1921-49	Earl (Curly) Lambeau	212-106-21
1950-53	Gene Ronzani*	14- 31- 1
1953	Hugh Devore, Ray (Scooter) McLean**	0- 2- 0
1954-57	Lisle Blackbourn	17- 31- 0
1958	Ray (Scooter) McLean	1- 10- 1
1959-67	Vince Lombardi	99- 31- 4
1968-70	Phil Bengtson	20- 21- 1
1971-74	Dan Devine	25- 28- 4
1975-83	Bart Starr	53- 77- 3
1984-85	Forrest Gregg	16- 16- 0

**Replaced after 10 games in 1953*
***Co-coaches for last two games in 1953*

FIRST PLAYER SELECTED

1936	Russ Letlow, G, San Francisco
1937	Eddie Jankowski, FB, Wisconsin
1938	Cecil Isbell, HB, Purdue
1939	Larry Buhler, HB, Minnesota
1940	Hal Van Every, HB, Minnesota
1941	George Paskvan, FB, Wisconsin
1942	Urban Odson, T, Minnesota
1943	Dick Wildung, T, Minnesota
1944	Merv Pregulman, G, Michigan
1945	Walt Schlinkman, FB, Texas Tech
1946	Johnny (Strike) Strzykalski, HB, Marquette
1947	Ernie Case, QB, UCLA
1948	Earl (Jug) Girard, HB, Wisconsin
1949	Stan Heath, QB, Nevada-Reno
1950	Clayton Tonnemaker, C, Minnesota
1951	Bob Gain, T, Kentucky
1952	Vito (Babe) Parilli, QB, Kentucky
1953	Al Carmichael, HB, USC
1954	Art Hunter, T, Notre Dame
1955	Tom Bettis, G, Purdue
1956	Jack Losch, HB, Miami
1957	Paul Hornung, QB, Notre Dame
1958	Dan Currie, C, Michigan State
1959	Randy Duncan, QB, Iowa
1960	Tom Moore, HB, Vanderbilt
1961	Herb Adderley, HB, Michigan State
1962	Earl Gros, FB, LSU
1963	Dave Robinson, E, Penn State
1964	Lloyd Voss, DT, Nebraska
1965	Donny Anderson, HB, Texas Tech
1966	Jim Grabowski, FB, Illinois
1967	Bob Hyland, C, Boston College
1968	Fred Carr, LB, Texas-El Paso
1969	Rich Moore, DT, Villanova
1970	Mike McCoy, DT, Notre Dame
1971	John Brockington, RB, Ohio State
1972	Willie Buchanon, CB, San Diego State
1973	Barry Smith, WR, Florida State
1974	Barty Smith, RB, Richmond
1975	(2) Bill Bain, G, USC
1976	Mark Koncar, T, Colorado
1977	Mike Butler, DE, Kansas
1978	James Lofton, WR, Stanford
1979	Eddie Lee Ivery, RB, Georgia Tech
1980	Bruce Clark, DT, Penn State
1981	Rich Campbell, QB, California
1982	Ron Hallstrom, G, Iowa
1983	Tim Lewis, CB, Pittsburgh
1984	Alphonso Carreker, DE, Florida State
1984*	Buford Jordan, RB, McNeese State
1985	Ken Ruettgers, T, USC
1986	(2) Kenneth Davis, RB, TCU

**Supplemental Draft*

PACKERS IRON MAN ERA ALL-TIME TEAM (1976)

E	Don Hutson	1935-45
E	Milt Gantenbein	1931-40
T	Cal Hubbard	1929-35
T	Buford (Baby) Ray	1938-48
G	Mike Michalske	1929-37
G	Charles (Buckets) Goldenberg	1933-45
C	Charley Brock	1939-47
BB	Larry Craig	1939-49
HB	Johnny Blood (McNally)	1928-36
HB	Tony Canadeo	1941-43, 1946-52
FB	Clarke Hinkle	1932-41

PACKERS MODERN ERA ALL-TIME TEAM (1976)

OFFENSE

WR	Boyd Dowler	1959-69
WR	Max McGee	1954, 1957-67
TE	Ron Kramer	1957, 1959-64
T	Bob Skoronski	1956, 1959-68
T	Forrest Gregg	1956, 1958-70
G	Fred (Fuzzy) Thurston	1959-67
G	Jerry Kramer	1958-68
C	Jim Ringo	1953-63
QB	Bart Starr	1956-71
RB	Paul Hornung	1957-62, 1964-66
RB	Jim Taylor	1958-66

DEFENSE

DE	Willie Davis	1960-69
DE	Lionel Aldridge	1963-71
DT	Henry Jordan	1959-69
DT	Dave (Hawg) Hanner	1952-64
LB	Dave Robinson	1963-72
LB	Fred Carr	1968-77
MLB	Ray Nitschke	1958-72
CB	Herb Adderley	1961-69
CB	Bob Jeter	1963-70
S	Willie Wood	1960-71
S	Bobby Dillon	1952-59

SPECIALISTS

P	Dick Deschaine	1955-57
K	Don Chandler	1965-67

HOUSTON OILERS

1959 K.S. (Bud) Adams, Jr., an oilman, announced Houston's entry into the American Football League, joining five other franchises—Dallas, Denver, Los Angeles, Minneapolis, and New York. The AFL was to begin play in 1960. The name Oilers was selected for the team by Adams "for sentimental and social reasons." John Breen was hired as Oilers' player personnel director. Rice refused to allow professional football the use of its 70,000-seat stadium, which had been Adams's first choice. In the first AFL player draft, the Oilers made Billy Cannon, All-America halfback and Heisman Trophy winner from LSU, their first choice. The first players to sign with the team were Don Hitt and Tony Banfield, both of Oklahoma State.
1960 The Oilers signed Cannon, but later had to go to court to establish the validity of the contract because Cannon also signed with the Los Angeles Rams of the NFL. Lou Rymkus was named the Oilers' head coach and hired Wally Lemm to handle his defensive backfield. John Breen, searching for an experienced quarterback, decided on George Blanda, formerly of the Chicago Bears, and lured him out of a one-year retirement. "While he is not the greatest quarterback in the world in some departments, he really knows how to take a defense apart," said Breen. Adams leased Jeppesen Stadium, a high school facility, and spent $200,000 renovating it and increasing the seating capacity from 22,000 to 36,000. The team opened its first training camp at the University of Houston. The Oilers lost their first preseason game 27-10 to Dallas, but came back to beat Denver 42-3 before 18,500 in the home opener at Jeppesen. Houston won its regular-season opener 37-22 over Oakland. The Oilers went 10-4, scored 379 points, and clinched the AFL's Eastern Division title by beating Buffalo 31-23 in Houston. The Oilers won the first AFL championship 24-16 over the Los Angeles Chargers before 32,000 at Jeppesen Stadium, January 1. Cannon was named the game's most valuable player.
1961 Tight end Willard Dewveall, a former SMU star, became the first player to jump leagues, playing out his option with the Chicago Bears and signing with Houston. Harris County voters passed a $22 million bond issue to finance a new domed stadium designated to be the home of the Oilers. Adams announced the team would train in Honolulu. Don Suman was named the club's new vice president and general manager. Lemm resigned as an assistant and entered private business. Six months later, after just one victory in the Oilers' first five starts, Lemm was rehired to replace Rymkus as head coach. The Oilers ran off 10 victories in a row, became the first pro team in history to score more than 500 points in a season, and won the AFL title for the second year in a row by defeating the San Diego Chargers 10-3. Blanda, the AFL's most valuable player, led the league in passing, including a record 36 touchdown passes, and kicked a record 55-yard field goal. Cannon led the league in rushing and accounted for 331 yards and five touchdowns against the New York Titans on December 10, rushing for 215 and catching five passes for 116. Flanker Charley Hennigan set a pro record with 1,746 receiving yards, while split end Bill Groman caught 17 touchdown passes.
1962 Lemm resigned to become head coach of the St. Louis Cardinals of the NFL. Frank (Pop) Ivy was signed by Adams as his third head coach in three years. Adams moved the training camp to Ellington Air Force Base in Texas. Blanda enjoyed an up-and-down season, throwing for six touchdowns against the New York Titans, but being intercepted a pro record 42 times for the season. After a slow start, the Oilers caught fire behind squat fullback Charley Tolar, who ran for 1,012 yards and caught 30 passes. The Oilers went 11-3 and won their third consecutive Eastern Division title. But in the AFL title game, Houston lost for the first time, although it took an historic six-quarter, double-overtime 20-17 win by the Dallas Texans to do it.
1963 Ivy signed a new two-year contract as head coach and general manager. After eight weeks, the Oilers were in first place, but then they collapsed, losing five of their last six and finishing in third place with a 6-8 record. Although Blanda led the league with 224 completions and 3,003 yards, an injury held Cannon to 45 yards rushing for the season, and without him the offense lacked consistency. The defense also dissolved at the end of the season, giving up 45 or more points three times in the final six games.
1964 The Oilers signed number-one draft choice Scott Appleton. The club began construction of a new training facility in Houston. Sammy Baugh was named backfield coach. Less than a month later, June 2, Adams relieved Ivy as head coach, replacing him with Baugh and naming Carroll Martin the new general manager. Cannon, once the club's most distinguished player, was traded to Oakland. A 4-10 season ended with the final pro game in Jeppesen Stadium, a 34-15 Oilers' victory over Denver. Hennigan established a pro record in that game, finishing the season with 101 receptions. In still another coaching change, Baugh was relieved as head coach but stayed on to assist his successor, Hugh (Bones) Taylor. Rymkus also rejoined the staff as line coach.
1965 The club announced it would not play in the Astrodome, Houston's new domed stadium, because of "an unrealistic lease agreement." A five-year lease was completed with Rice for its 70,000-seat stadium. The Houston contract with tackle Ralph Neely was declared invalid by an Oklahoma City Federal Court after the Oklahoma All-America had signed with both the Oilers and the NFL Dallas Cowboys. The club made Tommy Nobis, All-America linebacker from Texas, its number-one draft choice, but lost him to Atlanta. For the third year in a row, Blanda led the AFL in pass attempts and completions, but the Oilers again finished 4-10.
1966 Bud Adams appointed Don Klosterman the club's new executive vice president and general manager. Shortly afterward, Wally Lemm was rehired as head coach. Ernie Ladd, the Chargers' giant tackle, signed with the Oilers. The league ruled that Willie Frazier and Pete Jaquess be awarded to San Diego as compensation. Despite winning their first two games 45-7 and 31-0, the Oilers dropped to a 3-11 final, due in great part to the poorest defense in the league. One bright point was the play of rookie fullback Hoyle Granger, who averaged 6.9 yards per carry.
1967 In the first common draft involving the two leagues, the Oilers chose George Webster, the Michigan State All-America linebacker, number one. Two of the stars of the early years in Houston, Blanda and Hennigan, were let go. The club announced still another new training camp site, this time at Schreiner Institute in Kerrville, Texas. The Oilers became the first team to go from the cellar to the division championship in one season, going 9-4-1 with a defense that suddenly was the best in the league and a ground attack powered by Granger, who finished second in the AFL with 1,194 yards, and rookie Woody Campbell. On January 1, Oakland routed the Oilers 40-7 in the AFL Championship Game.
1968 Adams announced the team would move into the new Astrodome, after all, beginning with the 1968 season. The Oilers opened in the Astrodome by defeating Washington 9-3 in a preseason game. The regular season started in the Astrodome, too, with Houston losing to Kansas City 26-21. Although 11 Oilers were named to various all-star teams, the club finished the season with a 7-7 record. George Webster was one of four AFL players named to the first combined all-pro team. Jim Norton, last of the original Oilers, retired and the club retired his jersey, number 43.
1969 It was a case of the playoffs making the Oilers rather than the other way around. Despite a fine defensive unit, the Oilers had only one offensive threat—Hoyle Granger—and staggered to a 6-6-2 record while beating no teams with winning marks. But that was good enough for second place in the East, which earned Houston a playoff game with Oakland. On December 21, Daryle Lamonica threw six touchdown passes and the Raiders ripped the Oilers 56-7. At the end of the season, Webster was named to the All-Time AFL Team.
1970 Don Klosterman resigned as general manager to accept the same position with the Baltimore Colts. Quarterback Pete Beathard and cornerback Miller Farr were traded to St. Louis for quarterback Charley Johnson and cornerback Bob Atkins. Club veterans joined the NFL Players Association strike and were barred from training camp, June 30. The strike ended and the veterans reported August 3. In one of the most emotional games in the history of the franchise, the Oilers defeated the Dallas Cowboys for the first time, 37-21 in a preseason game. Lemm announced late in the season he would retire when it was over. The Oilers finished with a 3-10-1 record, losing 52-10 to Dallas in the final game.
1971 Ed Hughes, backfield coach for the San Francisco 49ers, was named the sixth coach in Oilers' history. In a draft known for its quality quarterbacks, Houston selected Dan Pastorini of Santa Clara on the first round and Kansas State's Lynn Dickey on round three. Bob Brodhead was announced as the team's new general manager. He resigned after only one month on the job. John Breen, the first pro football employee ever hired by Bud Adams, was given back his old job as general manager. After a 1-9-1 start, during which Pastorini beat out Johnson as the starting quarterback, the Oilers pulled together and won their last three games. But it was too late to save Hughes, who was fired at the end of the season and replaced by Bill Peterson, the coach at Rice.
1972 Bud Adams campaigned for and won Super Bowl VIII (1974) for the city of Houston. Quarterback Charley Johnson was traded to Denver. Dickey injured his hip in a preseason game and was out for the season. In October, linebacker Ron Pritchard and wide receiver Charlie Joiner were traded to Cincinnati for running backs Paul Robinson and Fred Willis. In still another deal, Webster was traded to Pittsburgh for wide receiver Dave Smith. The trades didn't help. Houston finished 1-13.
1973 The Oilers made John Matuszak, a 6-foot 7-inch, 282-pound defensive end from Tampa, the first selection in the entire NFL draft. Veteran coach and front office executive Sid Gillman was announced as the new executive vice president and general manager, replacing John Breen, who retired. All-pro safety Ken Houston was shipped to Washington in return for five Redskins players. After Peterson's two-year record reached 1-18, he was fired and Gillman assumed a dual role of coach and general manager. With the poorest offense in the AFC, the Oilers finished their second consecutive 1-13 season defeating only Baltimore 31-27.
1974 Sid Gillman announced his decision to stay at least one more season as coach and general manager. O.A. (Bum) Phillips was hired as the club's new defensive coordinator. The Oilers moved their training camp to Sam Houston State in Huntsville, Texas.

Matuszak attempted to jump his contract to sign with Houston of the World Football League. He eventually was put on the Oilers' inactive list and was traded to Kansas City for defensive tackle Curley Culp. Culp became an immediate force in Houston's new three-four defensive alignment and the Oilers won four in a row and six of their last eight to finish 7-7, their best record since 1969.

1975 Phillips was named head coach by Gillman, who said he would remain as general manager, January 25. A few weeks later, Gillman left and Phillips was given the added duties of general manager. The draft yielded the best linebacker to join the Oilers since Webster—Robert Brazile of Jackson State. The Oilers started fast with six wins in their first seven starts, including their first ever over an NFC team, 13-10 against Washington. Pittsburgh stopped the streak 24-17 on November 10, but the Oilers came back to beat Miami 20-19 as Billy (White Shoes) Johnson tied an NFL record for touchdowns in one season on kick returns. He had three on punts and one on a kickoff, including 83 yards with a punt in the victory over the Dolphins. The club finished the season with a 10-4 record, setting a new Houston home attendance record (48,000 average), but missed the playoffs.

1976 Before the season, the Oilers traded Dickey to Green Bay for quarterback John Hadl, cornerback Ken Ellis, and several draft choices. But Pastorini retained the starting role and Hadl finished on the bench. After four wins in the first five games, the Oilers suffered a series of injuries and lost six in a row. They staggered home with a 5-9 record.

1977 The Oilers got off to a strong start and, after a 27-10 victory over the Steelers on October 9, led the AFC Central Division. Pastorini was injured in the Pittsburgh game, and the Oilers had to go with Hadl. By the time Pastorini had fully recovered, Houston had dropped three straight. Celebrating Pastorini's return, the Oilers blasted Chicago 47-0 on November 6, and then won four of their last five to finish 8-6 for the season.

1978 The Oilers obtained the player they thought would lead them to the top by trading tight end Jimmie Giles and four draft choices to Tampa Bay to obtain the number-one draft choice, which they used to select Heisman Trophy-winning running back Earl Campbell of Texas. Houston also drafted quarterback Gifford Nielsen and wide receiver Mike Renfro. On October 23, the Oilers defeated the Steelers 24-17 for their first victory ever in a Monday night game. Four weeks later, the Oilers won again on Monday night, 35-30 over Miami, as Campbell ran for 199 yards and four touchdowns. Houston clinched a wild card berth in the playoffs on December 10 with a 17-12 victory over New Orleans. Campbell finished the season as the NFL's leading rusher. The wild card game was a rematch with Miami, and the Oilers again defeated the Dolphins, 17-9, behind a 20-for-29 passing performance by Pastorini. On December 31, Pastorini did it again, leading the Oilers to a 31-14 victory over New England. Houston's Cinderella season came to a close on January 7, as the Steelers scored 17 points in a two-minute span and won the AFC Championship Game 34-5.

1979 Before the season began, the Oilers lost tackle Greg Sampson, who underwent brain surgery, but replaced him by trading for Leon Gray, a Pro Bowl player for New England. The Oilers were put into a hole early in their 1979 quest for the division championship: Pittsburgh defeated them 38-7 on September 9. But Houston won 9 of its next 11 games to carry a 10-3 record into December. Despite a 20-17 Monday night victory over Pittsburgh on December 10, the Oilers again finished second to the Steelers, with an 11-5 record. Campbell led the league in rushing with 1,697 yards and tied NFL records by rushing for 100 or more yards 11 times in the season, 7 in succession, and by scoring 19 rushing touchdowns. In the first playoff game in Houston since 1962, the Oilers overcame injuries to Campbell and Pastorini to defeat Denver 13-7 in the wild card game. Again without Campbell and Pastorini, the Oilers shut down the NFL's best passing attack with four interceptions by Vernon Perry in a 17-14 win over San Diego in the divisional playoffs. In a rematch of the 1978 AFC Championship Game, the Oilers lost 27-13 to the Steelers on January 6.

1980 The Oilers traded Pastorini for Oakland quarterback Ken Stabler on May 15. Houston started the 1980 season 3-3, including a 31-17 loss to Pittsburgh in the opener, but on October 14 they turned their year around by obtaining tight end Dave Casper from Oakland for three draft choices. Utilizing a two-tight-end offense, the Oilers went 8-2 and defeated the Steelers 6-0 on December 4. Campbell gained 1,934 yards rushing, the second-highest total in NFL history. Despite having the same record as the Browns, the Oilers qualified for the playoffs as an AFC wild card team. In the first round of the playoffs the Raiders shut down Stabler and Campbell and won 27-7 on December 28. It was the third consecutive year that the Oilers had been defeated by the eventual Super Bowl champions. Three days later, Phillips was relieved as head coach.

1981 On January 2, former defensive coordinator Ed Biles was named head coach and Ladd K. Herzeg became executive vice president-general manager. Biles discarded Phillips's two-tight-end system and put Rob Carpenter in the backfield with Campbell. After a slow start, Biles reinstated blocking back Tim Wilson as Campbell's backfield mate and Campbell responded with 182 yards against the Bengals and 186 against Seattle. Carpenter was traded to the New York Giants. Campbell didn't run for 100 yards in any other game the rest of the season and the Oilers finished 7-9. Late in the season, Biles replaced Stabler with Nielsen. Campbell, who finished the season with 1,376 yards, led the AFC in rushing for the fourth straight year.

1982 The Oilers opened a new $42.5-million training facility less than two miles from the Astrodome. With the first number-one draft pick the Oilers owned since they had drafted Campbell, they selected Penn State guard Mike Munchak. Gray was traded to New Orleans for quarterback Archie Manning, Sept. 17. The Oilers were 1-1 in the two games that preceded the 57-day players strike, but were winless in the seven post-strike games to finish 1-8. Houston gained the fewest—and allowed the most—yards in the AFC.

1983 Biles hired new offensive and defensive coordinators—Kay Dalton and Chuck Studley, respectively. Assistant general manager Mike Holovak was promoted to vice president for player personnel. Offensive tackle Bruce Matthews was drafted in the first round. A heartbreaking 41-38 overtime loss to Green Bay in the opener began a string of 10 consecutive losses. After the sixth loss, a 26-14 defeat by the Denver Broncos, Biles resigned, leaving with an 8-23 record since replacing Phillips. Studley was appointed interim head coach, October 11. Manning and Casper were traded to the Minnesota Vikings for future draft choices, October 20. In quarterback Oliver Luck's first NFL start, the Oilers won their first game of the season, defeating Detroit 27-17, November 13. The victory ended a 17-game losing streak. Wide receiver Tim Smith, who previously had a career total of four receptions in three years with the Oilers, caught 83 passes for 1,176 yards. Earl Campbell returned to form, rushing for 1,301 yards (second best in the AFC) and 12 touchdowns. Defensive end Elvin Bethea retired after an outstanding 16-year career, all with the Oilers.

1984 Hugh Campbell, who had had great success as head coach of the Canadian Football League's Edmonton Eskimos, was named head coach of the Oilers, January 3. One month later, Campbell was reunited with Warren Moon, the strong-armed quarterback who had helped Campbell's Edmonton teams win five consecutive Grey Cup titles (1978-1982). Moon had been a free agent, and the Oilers won a bidding war among several NFL teams to sign him. Offensive tackle Dean Steinkuhler, the Lombardi Award and Outland Trophy winner from Nebraska, was chosen in the first round of the NFL draft. Houston lost its first 10 games of the season, and in early October, Earl Campbell was traded to New Orleans. On November 11, the Oilers defeated Kansas City 17-16 for Hugh Campbell's first victory as an NFL coach. The win also snapped an NFL record 23-game losing streak on the road. Tim Smith started the season on the bench, but wound up leading the team with 69 receptions for 1,141 yards. Moon improved on a week-to-week basis, and finished with 3,338 yards passing.

1985 Former Heisman Trophy-winning running back Mike Rozier, a refugee from the USFL, was signed, and the Oilers traded for New York Giants running back Butch Woolfolk. Woolfolk set a club record for running backs with 80 catches, but the ground attack was inadequate all year, averaging just 98.1 yards rushing for the season. The season started with a surprising 26-23 victory over defending AFC champion Miami, as cornerback Steve Brown intercepted two passes and Moon passed for 270 yards. But the Oilers, who were the most-penalized team in the NFL, then lost their next five games, and wound up with a disappointing 5-11 record. With two weeks to go in the season, Campbell was replaced as head coach by assistant Jerry Glanville, who later was retained for the 1986 season.

1986 With the third selection in the draft, the Oilers chose Purdue quarterback Jim Everett.

MEMBERS OF HALL OF FAME:
George Blanda, Sid Gillman, Ken Houston

OILERS RECORD, 1960-85

Year	Won	Lost	Tied	Pct.	Fin.	Pts.	OP
1960a	10	4	0	.714	1	379	285
1961a	10	3	1	.769	1	513	242
1962b	11	3	0	.786	1	387	270
1963	6	8	0	.429	3	302	372
1964	4	10	0	.286	4	310	355
1965	4	10	0	.286	4	298	429
1966	3	11	0	.214	4t	335	396
1967b	9	4	1	.692	1	258	199
1968	7	7	0	.500	2	303	248
1969c	6	6	2	.500	2	278	279
1970	3	10	1	.231	4	217	352
1971	4	9	1	.308	3	251	330
1972	1	13	0	.071	4	164	380
1973	1	13	0	.071	4	199	447
1974	7	7	0	.500	3	236	282
1975	10	4	0	.714	3	293	226
1976	5	9	0	.357	4	222	273
1977	8	6	0	.571	2	299	230
1978d	10	6	0	.625	2	283	298
1979d	11	5	0	.688	2	362	331
1980e	11	5	0	.688	2	295	251
1981	7	9	0	.438	3	281	355
1982	1	8	0	.111	13	136	245
1983	2	14	0	.125	4	288	460
1984	3	13	0	.188	4	240	437
1985	5	11	0	.313	4	284	412
26 Years	159	208	6	.434		7,413	8,384

a*AFL Champion; 1-0 in Playoffs*
b*AFL Eastern Division Champion; 0-1 in Playoffs*
c*AFL Eastern Division Runnerup; 0-1 in Playoffs*
d*AFC Wild Card Qualifier for Playoffs; 2-1 in Playoffs*
e*AFC Wild Card Qualifier for Playoffs; 0-1 in Playoffs*

RECORD HOLDERS
CAREER

Rushing attempts	Earl Campbell, 1978-84	1,979
Rushing yards	Earl Campbell, 1978-84	8,574

Pass attempts	George Blanda, 1960-66	2,784
Pass completions	Dan Pastorini, 1971-79	1,426
Passing yards	George Blanda, 1960-66	19,149
Touchdown passes	George Blanda, 1960-66	165
Receptions	Charley Hennigan, 1960-66	410
Receiving yards	Ken Burrough, 1971-82	6,907
Interceptions	Jim Norton, 1960-68	45
Punting average	Jim Norton, 1960-68	42.3
Punt return avg.	Billy Johnson, 1974-80	13.2
Kickoff return avg.	Bobby Jancik, 1962-67	26.4
Field goals	George Blanda, 1960-66	91
Touchdowns	Earl Campbell, 1978-84	73
Points	George Blanda, 1960-66	596
SEASON		
Rushing attempts	Earl Campbell, 1980	373
Rushing yards	Earl Campbell, 1980	1,934
Pass attempts	George Blanda, 1964	505
Pass completions	Ken Stabler, 1980	293
Passing yards	Warren Moon, 1984	3,338
Touchdown passes	George Blanda, 1961	36
Receptions	Charley Hennigan, 1964	101
Receiving yards	Charley Hennigan, 1961	1,746
Interceptions	Fred Glick, 1963	12
	Mike Reinfeldt, 1979	12
Punting average	Jim Norton, 1965	44.2
Punt return avg.	Billy Johnson, 1977	15.4
Kickoff return avg.	Ken Hall, 1960	31.2
Field goals	Toni Fritsch, 1979	21
	Tony Zendejas, 1985	21
Touchdowns	Earl Campbell, 1979	19
Points	George Blanda, 1960	115
GAME		
Rushing attempts	Earl Campbell, 10-11-81	39
Rushing yards	Billy Cannon, 12-10-61	216
Pass attempts	George Blanda, 11-1-64	68
Pass completions	George Blanda, 11-1-64	37
Passing yards	George Blanda, 10-29-61	464
Touchdown passes	George Blanda, 11-19-61	7
Receptions	Charley Hennigan, 10-13-61	13
Receiving yards	Charley Hennigan, 10-13-61	272
Interceptions	5 times	3
Field goals	Skip Butler, 10-12-75	6
Touchdowns	Billy Cannon, 12-10-61	5
Points	Billy Cannon, 12-10-61	30

COACHING HISTORY

1960-61	Lou Rymkus*	12- 7-1
1961	Wally Lemm	10- 0-0
1962-63	Frank (Pop) Ivy	17-12-0
1964	Sammy Baugh	4-10-0
1965	Hugh (Bones) Taylor	4-10-0
1966-70	Wally Lemm	28-40-4
1971	Ed Hughes	4- 9-1
1972-73	Bill Peterson**	1-18-0
1973-74	Sid Gillman	8-15-0
1975-80	O. A. (Bum) Phillips	59-38-0
1981-83	Ed Biles***	8-23-0
1983	Chuck Studley	2- 8-0
1984-85	Hugh Campbell****	8-22-0
1985	Jerry Glanville	0- 2-0

**Replaced after five games in 1961*
***Replaced after five games in 1973*
****Resigned after six games in 1983*
*****Replaced after 14 games in 1985*

FIRST PLAYER SELECTED

1960 Billy Cannon, HB, LSU
1961 Mike Ditka, E, Pittsburgh
1962 Ray Jacobs, DT, Howard Payne
1963 Danny Brabham, LB, Arkansas
1964 Scott Appleton, DT, Texas
1965 Lawrence Elkins, FL, Baylor
1965† Donny Anderson, HB, Texas Tech
1966 Tommy Nobis, LB, Texas
1966† Tom Fisher, LB, Tennessee
1967 George Webster, LB, Michigan State
1968 (2) Mac Haik, SE, Mississippi
1969 Ron Pritchard, LB, Arizona State
1970 Doug Wilkerson, G, North Carolina Central
1971 Dan Pastorini, QB, Santa Clara
1972 Greg Sampson, DE, Stanford
1973 John Matuszak, DE, Tampa
1974 (4) Steve Manstedt, LB, Nebraska
1975 Robert Brazile, LB, Jackson State
1976 (2) Mike Barber, TE, Louisiana Tech
1977 Morris Towns, T, Missouri
1978 Earl Campbell, RB, Texas
1979 (2) Mike Stensrud, DE, Iowa State
1980 (2) Angelo Fields, T, Michigan State
1981 (3) Michael Holston, WR, Morgan State
1982 Mike Munchak, G, Penn State
1983 Bruce Matthews, T, USC
1984 Dean Steinkuhler, T, Nebraska
1984* Mike Rozier, RB, Nebraska
1985 Ray Childress, DE, Texas A&M
1986 Jim Everett, QB, Purdue
†Redshirt Draft
**Supplemental Draft*

INDIANAPOLIS COLTS

1952 A team called the Baltimore Colts had played in the All-America Football Conference from 1947-49 and in the National Football League in 1950, but that franchise was returned to the league on January 18, 1951. The citizens of Baltimore, however, continued to work to get another franchise. On December 3, 1952, NFL Commissioner Bert Bell, addressing the Advertising Club, agreed to grant Baltimore the NFL's twelfth franchise (the Dallas Texans had folded at the end of the 1951 season) if, within the next six weeks, the fans would buy 15,000 season tickets and a suitable owner was found. On December 8, the ticket drive officially began.

1953 The ticket drive reached its goal of having sold 15,000 season tickets, January 8, one month after it began. Three days later, an ownership group headed by Carroll Rosenbloom, a business executive who had played for Bell when he was coaching at the University of Pennsylvania in 1927, and who had been hand-picked as the owner by Bell, was approved by the NFL owners. Rosenbloom owned 52 percent of the franchise, with the rest divided among William Hilgenberg, Zanvyl Krieger, Thomas Mullan, and R. Bruce Livie. On January 23, the Baltimore franchise officially entered the NFL. The same day, at Bell's suggestion, Rosenbloom hired Donald S. Kellett, a television executive who had been a coach at Pennsylvania, as general manager, and Keith Molesworth was named head coach. The team set up training facilities at Western Maryland College in Westminster, and adopted the nickname Colts, the same as the earlier NFL team had had. Baltimore was placed in the NFL's Western Conference. The team adopted blue, silver, and white as its colors. The Colts, who received the assets (including the players) of the Dallas franchise, put together one of the biggest trades in history before ever assembling a team; the Colts acquired 10 players from the Browns in exchange for five players, March 25. Among the players with the Colts when they opened the season were defensive tackle Art Donovan, defensive end Gino Marchetti, and halfback Buddy Young (all of whom had been with the Texans), as well as defensive backs Don Shula, Bert Rechichar, and Carl Taseff, who had been obtained in the trade with the Browns. In their NFL opener, the Colts stunned the Chicago Bears 13-9, September 27. Baltimore ran its record to 3-2 before reality caught up, and the team finished 3-9. Despite the losing record, home crowds averaged more than 28,000.

1954 Molesworth was shifted to chief talent scout. Rosenbloom and Kellett tried to get Cleveland assistant Blanton Collier as their head coach but settled instead on Browns aide Wilbur C. (Weeb) Ewbank. The Colts won only three games under Ewbank, but he told Rosenbloom he would produce a champion within five years.

1955 Molesworth's scouting system began to pay off. Twelve rookies made the team, including quarterback George Shaw, fullback Alan Ameche, halfback L. G. Dupre, tackles Jack Patera and George Preas, and center Dick Szymanski. All became regulars. One of the rookies who was a reserve was end Raymond Berry. Behind the ball carrying of Ameche, who led the NFL in rushing, the Colts won five games and finished fourth in the Western Conference.

1956 Three more important additions were made. Gene (Big Daddy) Lipscomb was picked up on waivers from Los Angeles. Lenny Moore was a first-round draft choice from Penn State. And a lanky, bony-faced young man who had had a tryout with the Pittsburgh Steelers in 1955 responded to an 80-cent phone call from Kellett and joined the team to understudy Shaw. His name was Johnny Unitas. Shaw injured his knee in the fourth game, forcing Unitas into action. The Colts tried to pry former backup Gary Kerkorian away from law school to replace Shaw, but by the time he showed up, the quarterback was Unitas. The season was erratic. Late in the year the team lost three games in a row and Ewbank's job was reported to be in jeopardy. But in the last game, Unitas threw a 53-yard scoring pass to beat Washington 19-17. Ewbank kept his job.

1957 Rosenbloom was named the team's president, February 4. Most of the personnel who would carry the Colts to great heights had been assembled. With Unitas leading the NFL in passing yardage (2,550) and touchdown passes (24), Berry leading in receiving yards (800), and Moore in average per carry (5.0), the Colts challenged for the first time. They won their first three games before losing three in a row. Then, after regaining first place with two weeks to go, they blew a 13-10 lead with less than two minutes to go in the game in San Francisco. In the season finale, they lost to the Rams, dropping to third place.

1958 The Colts won their first six games. The sixth was a 56-0 rout of the Packers, the first shutout in team history, but Unitas suffered fractured ribs and a punctured lung. Although Shaw played well in relief, Baltimore lost to New York 24-21. The defense was instrumental in a 17-0 win over the Bears, November 16. Unitas wore a special harness to protect his ribs and came back the next week. He threw a 58-yard pass to Moore on the first play from scrimmage and Baltimore romped over the Rams 34-7. By the end of the tenth game, and before they had to make what had become a "jinx" trip to the West Coast, the Colts had clinched their first division championship. They then dropped the last two games of the year, before meeting New York in the NFL Championship Game, December 28. Baltimore led the Giants 14-3 at halftime. In the third quarter, the Colts threatened to break the game open, marching to the Giants' 1-yard line. But the New York defense held. It was the Giants' turn—for two touchdowns and a 17-14 lead with two minutes to play. Baltimore took over on its own 14. Unitas hit Berry on three short passes and, with seven seconds left, Steve Myhra kicked a 20-yard field goal that sent the game into sudden-death overtime, the first ever in league play. The Giants got the ball first but had to punt. Baltimore took over on its 21. Unitas put together a brilliant drive. Finally, from the Giants' 8, he threw to Jim Mutscheller for seven yards. Then Ameche ran through a gaping hole for the winning touchdown and a 23-17 victory after 8:15 of overtime.

1959 The Colts had a 4-3 record after losing to Washington 27-24, November 8. Baltimore regrouped in the last five games, however, scoring 28, 45, 35, 34, and 45 points in consecutive victories. In the final game, the Colts scored 21 points in the fourth quarter to come from behind to defeat the Rams 45-26 in the Los Angeles Memorial Coliseum, December 12. In the championship game, played before 57,545 in Baltimore, Unitas combined with Moore on a first-half touchdown, but New York led 9-7 in the fourth quarter. After that it was all Colts as Baltimore won 31-16, December 27.

1960 With some of the championship edge gone and the defense growing slower with age, the team collapsed when a series of injuries occurred. Unitas suffered a fractured vertebra high in his back early in the season, and, while he still could throw well enough to set a league record with 3,099 yards, he was forbidden to run. So teams mounted an all-out rush against him. Then, in midseason, Ameche suffered a torn Achilles tendon, which ended his career. Berry led the NFL in receiving for the third consecutive season, and Moore averaged 21 yards per catch, but a passing offense alone couldn't stop the Colts from losing their last four games and finishing 6-6. In the third of those four losses, Unitas's streak of 47 games with at least one touchdown pass was stopped in a 10-3 loss to the Rams, December 11.

1961 Running back Joe Perry was acquired in a trade with San Francisco and led the team with 675 rushing yards. A jammed finger on his throwing hand slowed Unitas for much of the season, but the real story was that the defense had become average. The highlight of a sporadic year was a 45-21 victory over eventual NFL champion Green Bay in Baltimore, November 5. The Colts finished with four victories in the last five games to tie for third place.

1962 The Colts lost two close games to the Packers, 17-6, October 28, and 17-13, November 18, and had to win their last two games to finish 7-7. Unitas had an injury-free season, but his pass protection was suspect. He passed for 2,967 yards and 23 touchdowns. Moore missed six games with a cracked kneecap. Perry gained only 359 yards.

1963 Rosenbloom changed coaches, signing a former Colts defensive back, Don Shula, to replace Weeb Ewbank, January 8. Shula, who had been a defensive coach with the Detroit Lions, was only 33, but Rosenbloom said, "Football is a young man's game." Two Baltimore playing greats, defensive end Gino Marchetti and linebacker Bill Pellington, became player-coaches. A good nucleus was back in Unitas, Berry, Jim Parker, and leading receiver Jimmy Orr, but the Colts looked more to youth than they had in years, with such players as tight end John Mackey, fullback Jerry Hill, tackles Bob Vogel and Fred Miller, and safety Jerry Logan earning starting jobs, as did young Tom Matte, who replaced Moore. The team got off to a stumbling, injury-marred start but finished with five victories in its last six games and placed third.

1964 Rosenbloom purchased all remaining stock to gain full ownership, January 20. After an opening loss, the Colts won 11 games in a row, clinching their third Western Conference title by beating the Rams 24-7 in Los Angeles behind a surprisingly strong defense, November 22. Baltimore scored a team high 428 points. Moore regained his starting job and scored an NFL record 20 touchdowns. The defense forced opponents into 41 turnovers. The season was a huge success except for the NFL Championship Game with Cleveland, December 27. Neither team scored in the first half, but the Browns got 17 points in the third quarter and won 27-0.

1965 Marchetti and Pellington retired as players. But the Colts still were a young team and players such as Dennis Gaubatz and Steve Stonebreaker filled in well. The Colts raced to a 9-1-1 record, and held first place in the Western Division. Then Unitas injured his leg and number-two quarterback Gary Cuozzo suffered a shoulder separation. Shula had to make running back Tom Matte his quarterback. Matte responded with a dramatic performance that led the Colts past the Rams 20-17. He led the game's ball carriers with 99 yards, set up the deciding field goal, and handled the ball flawlessly. That victory got Baltimore into a Western Conference playoff with Green Bay. The undermanned Colts played courageously, taking the Packers into sudden death, but they were beaten 13-10 by a Don Chandler field goal, December 26. The Colts then defeated the Cowboys 35-3 in the Playoff Bowl, January 9.

1966 Baltimore won seven of its first nine games. Unitas injured his shoulder, and the team collapsed in the stretch run. The Colts continued to have trouble with the Packers—Vince Lombardi maintaining an apparent jinx over Shula—and two more losses to Green Bay (in five seasons Baltimore's record against the Packers was 2-9) helped consign the Colts to second place, three games behind Green Bay. On January 8, the Colts defeated Philadelphia 20-14 in the Playoff Bowl.

1967 Shula and newly named general manager Joe Campanella were made vice presidents, January 23. Campanella died, February 15. Publicity director Harry Hulmes was selected to become general manager. The top draft choices were defensive lineman Bubba Smith and safety Rick Volk. Under an NFL realignment, the Colts were moved into the Coastal Division. In a match of unbeaten Coastal Division teams, the Colts and Rams battled to a 24-24 tie in Baltimore, October 15. It all came down to a rematch in Los Angeles in the final game of the season, December 17. Baltimore had an 11-0-2 record; Los Angeles was 10-1-2. The winner would advance to the playoffs. Rams quarterback Roman Gabriel threw touchdown passes to Jack Snow, Bernie Casey, and Billy Truax as the Rams won 34-10. Baltimore finished 11-1-2, and both its offense and defense finished second in the NFL (behind the Rams), but the Colts did not make the playoffs because of the loss to the Rams. Shula was named NFL co-coach of the year with the Rams' George Allen.

1968 Art Donovan became the first Colt to be enshrined in the Pro Football Hall of Fame, August 3. The Colts began the season by winning five games, before losing 30-20 to Cleveland, October 20. The Colts then put together an eight-game winning streak, highlighted by two victories over Los Angeles and one over Green Bay. Baltimore ran its winning streak to nine by trouncing Minnesota 24-14 in the first round of the playoffs, December 22. The streak became 10 in the NFL Championship Game as Matte rushed for three touchdowns and Baltimore routed Cleveland 34-0, December 27. Some observers were comparing Baltimore with the finest NFL teams of all time. Earl Morrall, the Colts' quarterback most of the season with Unitas sidelined by injury, led the NFL in passing and was named the most valuable player. The Colts were heavily favored over the New York Jets, champions of the American Football League, in Super Bowl III in Miami, January 12. But the Jets posted a shocking 16-7 victory.

1969 Szymanski, Ordell Braase, and Bobby Boyd all retired, but Unitas was around, along with veterans such as Matte and Billy Ray Smith. Mike Curtis was switched from outside linebacker to middle linebacker in the seventh game and Ted Hendricks and Bob Grant started outside. The Colts had an erratic season, struggling to a 8-5-1 record and finishing two-and-one-half games behind the Rams.

1970 Don Klosterman was named general manager, January 6. Amid protests by Rosenbloom that started a long-standing feud, Shula moved to Miami to coach the Dolphins, February 18. Don McCafferty, an 11-year Colts assistant, was named head coach, April 3. At the start of the season, the Colts found themselves with a new set of opponents in the AFC East, having moved along with Pittsburgh and Cleveland from the NFC. The Colts lost only two games—one to Shula and Miami—in the regular season and won the AFC East. Baltimore defeated Cincinnati 17-0 in the AFC Divisional Playoffs, December 26. Behind Unitas's passing and rookie Norm Bulaich's running, the Colts powered past the Oakland Raiders 27-17 for their first AFC championship, January 3. The Colts were matched against the Dallas Cowboys in Super Bowl V at the Orange Bowl in Miami, January 17. There were 11 turnovers in a brutal defensive struggle. Baltimore, behind 13-6, tied the game midway through the fourth quarter. After Mike Curtis intercepted a Craig Morton pass in the final minute and returned it to the Dallas 28, rookie Jim O'Brien kicked a field goal with five seconds left for a 16-13 victory.

1971 Carroll Rosenbloom was elevated to chairman of the board, March 18. His son, Steve, took over as president. The Colts, with an inconsistent offense but the conference's best defense, finished half a game behind Miami in the AFC East but qualified for the playoffs as the AFC wild card team. The Colts began in the playoffs with a 20-3 victory over Cleveland as Don Nottingham rushed for 92 yards and two touchdowns and the defense intercepted three passes, December 26. Rosenbloom and the Colts were matched against Shula and the Dolphins in the AFC Championship Game, at the Orange Bowl, January 2. The Colts, playing without injured backs Bulaich and Matte, outgained the Dolphins 302 yards to 286 but were burned on big plays by Bob Griese, Paul Warfield, and Dick Anderson and lost 21-0. It was the Colts' first shutout defeat since 1965.

1972 Running back Lydell Mitchell was chosen in the second round of the draft. Robert Irsay, a 49-year-old businessman from Winnetka, Illinois, took control of the Colts in a unique transaction, July 13. Irsay first purchased the Los Angeles Rams from the estate of the late Dan Reeves, then traded the Rams to Rosenbloom for the Colts. Joe Thomas, 49, who had helped turn the Minnesota Vikings and Miami Dolphins into Super Bowl teams, was named vice president and general manager. Gino Marchetti was inducted into the Pro Football Hall of Fame, July 29. The Colts moved their major training facilities to the University of South Florida in Tampa. After five games, four of them losses, McCafferty was replaced as head coach by long-time assistant John Sandusky, October 16. The Colts were just 4-5 the rest of the way, losing their last two and missing the playoffs.

1973 An era ended when Johnny Unitas was traded to San Diego for future considerations, January 22. The Colts chose quarterback Bert Jones in the first round of the draft. Howard Schnellenberger, who had been Shula's top offensive coach for three years in Miami, was named head coach, February 14. The team again switched training sites, to McDonogh School in suburban Baltimore County. Raymond Berry and Jim Parker were inducted into the Hall of Fame. The Colts won their fewest games since 1954, finishing in a tie for last in the division at 4-10.

1974 Thomas set about to rebuild the Colts through the draft, selecting Roger Carr, Fred Cook, John Dutton, and Freddie Scott. After the team lost its first three games, Thomas assumed the coaching duties from Schnellenberger, September 29. The Colts won just two games and placed last in their division. But they were competitive toward the end, never losing by more than 11 points in their last eight games. Mitchell set a one-game record of 40 rushes, October 20. Jones set an NFL record of 17 consecutive pass completions, December 15. Mitchell won the league pass-receiving title with 72 receptions, the most ever by a running back.

1975 Ted Marchibroda, a former NFL quarterback and long-time assistant to George Allen at Los Angeles and Washington, was named head coach, January 15. "I'm a low-key coach who believes in the basics of football—execution, balance, and consistency," he said. Lenny Moore was inducted into the Pro Football Hall of Fame, August 2. The team switched training sites again, to Goucher College in suburban Baltimore. After losing four of their first five games, the Colts made one of the most startling turnarounds in NFL history, winning nine straight and taking the AFC East title. The Colts lost to the Pittsburgh Steelers 28-10 in the first round of the playoffs, December 27. Marchibroda was named NFL coach of the year. Mitchell became the Colts' first back to rush for more than 1,000 yards in a season, gaining 1,193.

1976 After the team lost four of its six preseason games, Irsay stormed into the locker room and said, "I've got to make some changes," September 2. He lashed out at Colts players and Marchibroda. Marchibroda resigned, September 5. "I can't tolerate this kind of interference," he said. The Colts' players offered a statement, read by Bert Jones, that charged Irsay and Thomas "have completely destroyed this team," September 6. Marchibroda agreed to return, with increased responsibilities, September 7. "I will have complete control over football matters," he said. The team had a brilliant season, finishing 11-3 and winning the Eastern Division championship. Jones threw for 3,104 yards, Mitchell ran for 1,200 and caught 60 passes, and Toni Linhart led the NFL with 109 points. But the Colts were rocked by Pittsburgh in an AFC Divisional Playoff Game 40-14.
1977 Joe Thomas resigned from the Colts' front office. Dick Szymanski was named general manager and Ernie Accorsi was named assistant general manager. In May, Johnny Unitas rejoined the Colts as a special consultant. The Colts opened the season with five consecutive wins and had a 9-1 record after 10 weeks. Then they dropped three straight, including a 13-10 loss to Detroit in which the Lions scored on a blocked punt with nine seconds left. Needing a win in New England in the season finale on December 18 to win a third-straight AFC East title, the Colts came from behind to win 30-24 on Jones's three touchdown passes. Mitchell's 1,159 yards rushing was third-best in the AFC and his 71 pass receptions were tops in the NFL. On December 24, Ken Stabler of the Oakland Raiders threw a 10-yard touchdown pass to Dave Casper after 15:43 of sudden-death overtime to end the third-longest playoff game in NFL history, and the Colts' season, 37-31.
1978 Former head coach Weeb Ewbank was inducted into the Pro Football Hall of Fame. Injuries to Jones and a sagging defense helped reverse Baltimore's record, which dropped from 10-4 to 5-11, good for only a last-place finish in the AFC East. Jones and both offensive tackles, George Kunz and David Taylor, were injured in preseason, and, before the Colts could adjust to the losses, they had been shut out in the first two regular-season games, 38-0 by Dallas and 42-0 by Miami. When Jones's backup Bill Troup was injured, untested Mike Kirkland had to take over. Jones came back in November to lead successive victories over Washington (on Monday night) and Seattle, but he was reinjured against the Seahawks and missed the rest of the season. The Colts dropped their last five games.
1979 Johnny Unitas was inducted into the Pro Football Hall of Fame in the summer, and Greg Landry broke some of Unitas's single-season passing records in the fall. The Colts' repeat of a 5-11 record bore no resemblance to the way things had been during the glory years under Unitas. Again, Baltimore showed that it needed Jones; when he was healthy the Colts went 3-1, without him they were 2-10. The high point of the season was a 31-26 victory over New England; the low point was a 50-21 loss to the Patriots three weeks later. Running back Joe Washington set a club record with 82 receptions, best in the NFL.
1980 Mike McCormack was named head coach on January 16, replacing Marchibroda. The Colts' new training complex opened in late February. World-class sprinter Curtis Dickey of Texas A&M was drafted on the first round in April. The changes initially seemed to add new life to the Colts, who started off with a 4-2 record. But the turning point came on October 19, when Baltimore blew an early lead against New England and lost 37-21. The Colts won only three games the rest of the season, finishing 7-9. The offensive line play was indicative of the Colts' team breakdown at midseason. After allowing Jones to be sacked only nine times in the first seven games, the line gave up a record 12 sacks to St. Louis in a 17-10 defeat.
1981 The Colts drafted fullback Randy McMillan of Pittsburgh in the first round and he began his NFL career by rushing for 146 yards and two touchdowns in a 29-28 victory over New England. But then both the Colts and McMillan cooled off; the team lost 14 straight and McMillan ran for only 403 yards and one touchdown in that period. However, McMillan wound up with 597 yards rushing and led the team with 50 receptions. The Colts redeemed their pride by defeating the Patriots again, 23-21 on December 20 to close out the season. For the year, the Colts gave up 533 points and an NFL record 424.6 yards per game. On December 22, McCormack was replaced as head coach by Frank Kush, who had coached for Hamilton of the Canadian Football League and at Arizona State.
1982 In a season shortened by the players strike, the Colts endured their first winless campaign ever, finishing 0-8-1. A 20-20 tie against Green Bay in the season's seventh week was the team's only relief from losing. The Colts had 31 new faces on the roster, including 21 rookies or first-year players. Fourth-round draft choice Mike Pagel from Arizona State beat out top draft pick Art Schlichter of Ohio State for the starting quarterback job. But the offense struggled and was the NFL's second-worst unit. The defense took several strides forward from its forgettable 1981 showing. Defensive end Donnell Thompson, nose tackle Leo Wisniewski, and linebacker Johnie Cooks all displayed promise. One bright spot was the punting of rookie Rohn Stark, a second-round draft choice from Florida State whose 44.4-yard average ranked second in the NFL.
1983 The NFL's youngest team, with an average of 24.2 years of age and just 1.6 years of experience, improved to 7-9—the greatest about-face for a winless team in the history of the NFL. The jump from zero to seven victories also ranked as the league's fourth-best overall upgrade. When number-one draft pick John Elway, an All-America quarterback from Stanford who was the number-one player selected in the NFL draft, balked at playing in Baltimore and threatened to pursue a professional baseball career if he couldn't play for another NFL team—preferably on the West Coast—the Colts traded him six days after the draft to Denver for lineman Chris Hinton, backup quarterback Mark Herrmann, and the Broncos' 1984 number-one draft choice. Hinton played well enough as a rookie to be selected to the AFC-NFC Pro Bowl as a guard, and was the first rookie offensive lineman to start for the AFC squad since the game began in 1970. The left side of the line, anchored by Hinton, became the Colts' strength in the AFC's leading ground attack. Running back Curtis Dickey rushed for 1,122 yards, and McMillan added 802 yards rushing. Another Colts rookie who made an immediate impact was linebacker Vernon Maxwell, who starred in the Colts' revitalized defense and was named NFL defensive rookie of the year. Stark led the NFL in punting with a 45.3 average and was named all-pro. Rookie placekicker Raul Allegre also had an outstanding season, kicking 30 field goals to set a new Colts single-season record. On December 18, the Colts defeated Houston 20-10 in their final game at Baltimore's Memorial Stadium.
1984 Irsay loaded his team's belongings onto a fleet of moving vans in the middle of the night of March 28-29, and transferred the Colts to Indianapolis. The bitterness of loyal Colts fans in Baltimore may have been equaled by the enthusiasm of the new Colts fans in Indianapolis. "The greatest thrill I've had in football was on April 2, 1984, when I walked into the Hoosier Dome with Mayor [Bill] Hudnut in front of all those fans," said Irsay of the 20,000 people who showed up to welcome the Colts to Indianapolis. "It is my intention for the Colts to be a vital contributing member of the greater Indianapolis community." The 61,000-seat Hoosier Dome, part of an $82-million downtown stadium and convention center, was the primary attraction for Irsay, who had grown disenchanted with Baltimore's Memorial Stadium. Jim Irsay, son of the owner, was named general manager, April 26. Two weeks after Indianapolis Colts tickets were put on sale, the club had received 143,000 season-ticket requests. The Colts lost their first regular-season game at the Hoosier Dome 23-14 to the New York Jets, September 2. The Colts' first victory in their new facility came on September 30, when they defeated the Buffalo Bills 31-17. Overall the Colts finished 4-12 and placed fourth in the AFC East standings. The offense ranked last in the NFL in passing, total offense, and scoring. With one game left in the season, Kush resigned and was replaced by assistant Hal Hunter, who oversaw the final game loss to New England.
1985 Rod Dowhower replaced Hunter as head coach, January 28. The Colts finished 4-4 at home, but that was offset by a 1-7 record on the road. The offense ranked first in the AFC in rushing, but last in the AFC and twenty-sixth in the league in passing. Stark, the NFL's leading punter, was the only Colts player selected to the AFC-NFC Pro Bowl.
1986 In April, the Colts obtained quarterback Gary Hogeboom from Dallas.

MEMBERS OF HALL OF FAME:
Raymond Berry, George Blanda, Art Donovan, Weeb Ewbank, Gino Marchetti, Lenny Moore, Jim Parker, Joe Perry, Y. A. Tittle, Johnny Unitas

COLTS RECORD, 1953-85

Year	Won	Lost	Tied	Pct.	Fin.	Pts.	OP
Baltimore Colts							
1953	3	9	0	.250	5	182	350
1954	3	9	0	.250	6	131	279
1955	5	6	1	.455	4	214	239
1956	5	7	0	.417	4	270	322
1957	7	5	0	.583	3	303	235
1958a	9	3	0	.750	1	381	203
1959a	9	3	0	.750	1	374	251
1960	6	6	0	.500	4	288	234
1961	8	6	0	.571	3t	302	307
1962	7	7	0	.500	4	293	288
1963	8	6	0	.571	3	316	285
1964b	12	2	0	.857	1	428	225
1965c	10	3	1	.769	2	389	284
1966d	9	5	0	.643	2	314	226
1967	11	1	2	.917	2	394	198
1968e	13	1	0	.929	1	402	144
1969	8	5	1	.615	2	279	268
1970f	11	2	1	.846	1	321	234
1971g	10	4	0	.714	2	313	140
1972	5	9	0	.357	3	235	252
1973	4	10	0	.286	4	226	341
1974	2	12	0	.143	5	190	329
1975h	10	4	0	.714	1	395	269
1976h	11	3	0	.786	1	417	246
1977h	10	4	0	.714	1	295	221
1978	5	11	0	.313	5	239	421
1979	5	11	0	.313	5	271	351
1980	7	9	0	.438	4	355	387
1981	2	14	0	.125	4	259	533
1982	0	8	1	.056	14	113	236
1983	7	9	0	.438	4	264	354
Indianapolis Colts							
1984	4	12	0	.250	4	239	414
1985	5	11	0	.313	4	320	386
33 Years	231	217	7	.515		9,712	9,452

a*NFL Champion; 1-0 in Playoffs*
b*NFL Western Conference Champion; 0-1 in Playoffs*
c*NFL Western Conference Runnerup; 1-1 in Playoffs*
d*NFL Western Conference Runnerup; 1-0 in Playoff Bowl*
e*NFL Champion; 2-1 in Playoffs*
f*Super Bowl Champion; 3-0 in Playoffs*
g*AFC Wild Card Qualifier for Playoffs; 1-1 in Playoffs*
h*Eastern Division Champion; 0-1 in Playoffs*

RECORD HOLDERS
CAREER

Rushing attempts	Lydell Mitchell, 1972-77	1,391
Rushing yards	Lydell Mitchell, 1972-77	5,487

Pass attempts	Johnny Unitas, 1956-72	5,110
Pass completions	Johnny Unitas, 1956-72	2,796
Passing yards	Johnny Unitas, 1956-72	39,768
Touchdown passes	Johnny Unitas, 1956-72	287
Receptions	Raymond Berry, 1955-67	631
Receiving yards	Raymond Berry, 1955-67	9,275
Interceptions	Bob Boyd, 1960-68	57
Punting average	Rohn Stark, 1982-85	45.2
Punt return avg.	Ron Gardin, 1970-71	11.8
Kickoff return avg.	Jim Duncan, 1969-71	32.5
Field goals	Lou Michaels, 1964-69	107
Touchdowns	Lenny Moore, 1956-67	113
Points	Lenny Moore, 1956-67	678
SEASON		
Rushing attempts	Lydell Mitchell, 1977	301
Rushing yards	Lydell Mitchell, 1976	1,200
Pass attempts	Greg Landry, 1979	459
Pass completions	Greg Landry, 1979	270
Passing yards	Johnny Unitas, 1963	3,481
Touchdown passes	Johnny Unitas, 1959	32
Receptions	Joe Washington, 1979	82
Receiving yards	Raymond Berry, 1960	1,298
Interceptions	Tom Keane, 1953	11
Punting average	Rohn Stark, 1985	45.9
Punt return avg.	Wendell Harris, 1964	12.6
Kickoff return avg.	Jim Duncan, 1970	35.4
Field goals	Raul Allegre, 1983	30
Touchdowns	Lenny Moore, 1964	20
Points	Lenny Moore, 1964	120
GAME		
Rushing attempts	Lydell Mitchell, 10-20-74	40
Rushing yards	Norm Bulaich, 9-19-71	198
Pass attempts	Bert Jones, 12-15-74	53
Pass completions	Bert Jones, 12-15-74	36
Passing yards	Johnny Unitas, 9-17-67	401
Touchdown passes	Gary Cuozzo, 11-14-65	5
Receptions	Lydell Mitchell, 12-15-74	13
	Joe Washington, 9-2-79	13
Receiving yards	Raymond Berry, 11-10-57	224
Interceptions	7 times	3
Field goals	Raul Allegre, 10-30-83	5
Touchdowns	4 times	4
Points	4 times	24

COACHING HISTORY

1953	Keith Molesworth	3- 9-0
1954-62	Weeb Ewbank	61-52-1
1963-69	Don Shula	75-26-4
1970-72	Don McCafferty*	26-11-1
1972	John Sandusky	4- 5-0
1973-74	Howard Schnellenberger**	4-13-0
1974	Joe Thomas	2- 9-0
1975-79	Ted Marchibroda	41-36-0
1980-81	Mike McCormack	9-23-0
1982-84	Frank Kush***	11-28-1
1984	Hal Hunter	0- 1-0
1985	Rod Dowhower	5-11-0

**Replaced after five games in 1972*
***Replaced after three games in 1974*
****Resigned after 15 games in 1984*

FIRST PLAYER SELECTED

1953	Billy Vessels, HB, Oklahoma
1954	Cotton Davidson, QB, Baylor
1955	George Shaw, QB, Oregon
1956	Lenny Moore, HB, Penn State
1957	Jim Parker, G, Ohio State
1958	Lenny Lyles; HB, Louisville
1959	Jackie Burkett, C, Auburn
1960	Ron Mix, T, USC
1961	Tom Matte, HB, Ohio State
1962	Wendell Harris, S, LSU
1963	Bob Vogel, T, Ohio State
1964	Marv Woodson, CB, Indiana
1965	Mike Curtis, LB, Duke
1966	Sam Ball, T, Kentucky
1967	Bubba Smith, DE, Michigan State
1968	John Williams, T, Minnesota
1969	Eddie Hinton, FL, Oklahoma
1970	Norm Bulaich, RB, TCU
1971	Don McCauley, RB, North Carolina
1972	Tom Drougas, T, Oregon
1973	Bert Jones, QB, LSU
1974	John Dutton, DE, Nebraska
1975	Ken Huff, G, North Carolina
1976	Ken Novak, DT, Purdue
1977	Randy Burke, WR, Kentucky
1978	Reese McCall, TE, Auburn
1979	Barry Krauss, LB, Alabama
1980	Curtis Dickey, RB, Texas A&M
1981	Randy McMillan, RB, Pittsburgh
1982	Johnie Cooks, LB, Mississippi State
1983	John Elway, QB, Stanford
1984	Leonard Coleman, CB, Vanderbilt
1984*	Paul Bergmann, TE, UCLA
1985	Duane Bickett, LB, USC
1986	Jon Hand, DE, Alabama

**Supplemental Draft*

KANSAS CITY CHIEFS

1959 Unsuccessful in his attempts to acquire a National Football League franchise for Dallas, millionaire Lamar Hunt founded and organized the American Football League with six original cities—New York, Houston, Denver, Los Angeles, Minneapolis, and Hunt's home, Dallas. Buffalo and Boston were added, and Oakland replaced Minneapolis. "Before there was a player, coach, or general manager in the league, there was Lamar Hunt," was the way Boston's Billy Sullivan put it. "Hunt was the cornerstone, the integrity of the league. Without him, there would have been no AFL." Not long after the Dallas Texans went into business, the NFL announced it would establish a team in Dallas. The other Dallas franchise was awarded to Clint Murchison, Jr. and Bedford Wynne, both oil millionaires. Hunt hired an unknown assistant at Miami named Hank Stram as his head coach. A self-styled disciplinarian, Stram was a short, barrel-chested man who said, "Show me a good loser, and I'll show you a loser—period." The Texans' first draft choice was a local hero, Don Meredith of SMU. But the All-America quarterback signed with the rival NFL Cowboys.

1960 Hunt was named the first president of the AFL, January 26. For their inaugural season in the Cotton Bowl, the Texans had a strong home-state identity. The quarterback was Cotton Davidson from Baylor. Fullback Jack Spikes had been an outstanding player at TCU, and halfback Abner Haynes had played at North Texas State. After winning five straight preseason games, the Texans drew 51,000 people for the final preseason game against Houston, a 24-3 victory. Haynes led the new league in rushing with 875 yards and was named the AFL's first most valuable player. The Texans had a flashy, high-scoring club, and only three losses by a total of four points kept them from winning the division championship. They did beat the Western Division champion Los Angeles Chargers 17-0 and the AFL champion Oilers 24-0, however. A variety of promotional ploys helped the Texans average 24,500 for their home games, highest in the new league.

1961 E.J. Holub, the Texas Tech All-America center described as "the best football player in America" by many scouts, was drafted first by both Dallas teams. Hunt considered it a major victory when Holub decided to play for his club. Hunt also signed three more quality rookies, SMU's Jerry Mays, Michigan State's Fred Arbanas, and Ohio State's Jim Tyrer. The revitalized Texans won four of their five preseason games and three of their first four in the regular season. But during that period, Spikes was injured, and his absence from the running attack put even more pressure on Davidson's already erratic passing. The team fell into a six-game losing streak, then rallied to win three of its last four and finished second in the Western Division at 6-8.

1962 Don Klosterman was named the club's player personnel director. Stram made his most important acquisition when he invited Len Dawson, a quarterback he once coached at Purdue, to join Dallas. Dawson had been cut by the Cleveland Browns of the NFL, but he moved in to star for the Texans. Another key addition was Curtis McClinton, a 6-foot 3-inch, 227-pound fullback who had enough speed to run the high hurdles at Kansas. With Dawson directing Haynes and McClinton, the Texans clinched the Western Division championship in November. They finished with an 11-3 record. Arbanas, fully recovered from a back injury that had kept him out of the 1961 season, was instrumental in the Texans' turnabout both as a receiver and an excellent blocker. His contribution to the ground game helped Haynes to his greatest year, which included 1,049 yards and a record 13 touchdowns rushing, 19 overall. AFL writers voted Dawson, who threw 29 touchdown passes, player of the year, McClinton rookie of the year, and Stram coach of the year. Frequently overlooked was the defense, which gave up the fewest points in the league and featured all-AFL performances by Holub and Sherrill Headrick at linebacker and Mays and Mel Branch on the line. Dallas won the AFL championship in the second overtime period when rookie Tommy Brooker kicked a 25-yard field goal to make the final score 20-17 over Houston, December 23.

1963 With the first pick in the AFL draft, the Texans chose Buck Buchanan, a defensive tackle from Grambling. H. Roe Bartle, the mayor of Kansas City, invited Hunt to move his team to Missouri. Bartle promised to enlarge Kansas City's Municipal Stadium and guaranteed Hunt three times as many season-ticket sales as the Texans had in Dallas. Impressed with the inducements and the fact the nearest pro football rival was 250 miles away, Hunt announced he was shifting the franchise to Kansas City and renaming it the Chiefs (after Bartle's nickname—the Chief), May 14. Rookie Stone Johnson suffered a fatal injury in a preseason game. Kansas City opened the regular season with a 59-7 victory over Denver, but the new-look Chiefs managed only one win and two ties in their next 10 games. Appropriately, the victory was in their home opener in Municipal Stadium, where they defeated Houston 27-7 before 27,801 fans. A three-game winning streak at the end of the season gave the Chiefs some measure of respectability, and the play of rookies Buchanan, linebacker Bobby Bell, and guard Ed Budde gave them hope for the future.

1964 Ten regulars were hurt at one time or another during the season. Curtis McClinton broke a hand in training camp. It bothered him all year. E.J. Holub tore a knee and missed the last five games. Johnny Robinson, the outstanding safety, suffered a rib injury in November and was out for the season. Arbanas, the tight end, was mugged on a Kansas City street and blinded in his left eye. Burdened with such ill fortune, the Chiefs played erratically. They beat the Chargers 49-6 and the Raiders 42-7, but they lost to Denver 33-27. Even the performances of Dawson, who led the league in passing with 2,879 yards and 30 touchdowns, and rookie Mack Lee Hill, who averaged a league-high 5.5 yards per carry, couldn't make the Chiefs a regular threat. Attendance was as disappointing as the final 7-7 record. Seven home games at Municipal Stadium drew only 126,881, and when AFL owners' meetings were held, there was discussion about the Chiefs' future in Kansas City.

1965 Gale Sayers, the spectacular breakaway runner from Kansas, was the club's number-one draft choice, but the Chicago Bears also made him their first selection and finally won him in a bidding duel. Otis Taylor, a wide receiver from Prairie View, joined the team. Haynes was traded to Denver for linebacker-punter Jim Fraser and cash. In a relatively routine knee surgery late in the season, Hill died on the operating table. The Chiefs finished 7-5-2; two of the losses were by three points or less.

1966 Halfback Mike Garrett, the Heisman Trophy winner from USC, was drafted in the twentieth round. Garrett also was drafted by his hometown Los Angeles Rams, but the Chiefs signed the swift runner for $400,000. "In the past we ground out yardage inch by inch. We moved by bus; now we travel by jet," said Stram. A crowd of 43,885, largest ever to see a sports event in Kansas City, turned out for the home opener against Buffalo. The Chiefs lost 29-14, but after the game, in the middle of the field, Stram and Bills' coach Joe Collier negotiated a trade. Kansas City got field goal kicker Mike Mercer for a fifth-round draft pick. The deal solidified the one weak link in the Chiefs' attack. Mercer proved his worth in a title-clinching 32-24 win over New York in late November, hitting from 32, 15, 47, and 33 yards. Garrett's lateral swiftness gave the Chiefs an outside threat. Garrett was second in AFL rushing with 801 yards, and his 5.45 yards per carry was the league's top average. Dawson led the league in passing, and Taylor and Chris Burford tied for third in pass receiving. The Chiefs finished three games ahead of Oakland. Using a flashy I-formation offense and an assortment of defenses, the Chiefs confused and outplayed Buffalo to win the AFL championship 31-7 and gain a berth in the first AFL-NFL World Championship Game. Kansas City went wild, with Chiefs boosters mobbing the airport to greet the team upon its return. In Super Bowl I, in Los Angeles, the Chiefs played Vince Lombardi's Green Bay Packers close for a half, trailing 14-10. But the Packers took charge in the final two periods for a 35-10 victory, January 15.

1967 The loss to Green Bay prompted an emphasis on defense in the Chiefs' draft. They got linebacking strength in Maxwell Trophy winner Jim Lynch from Notre Dame and Little All-America Willie Lanier from Morgan State. Specialists Jan Stenerud and Noland (Super Gnat) Smith also joined the team. Interest in the team skyrocketed. Season-ticket sales went over 30,000, and seating capacity for Municipal Stadium was increased from 40,000 to 47,000. In June, the voters in Jackson County approved a $43 million general obligation bond issue for construction of a sports complex that would feature both a football and baseball stadium. A two-thirds approval was required, and the bond carried with 67 percent of the vote. The Chiefs started well, but injuries to center Jon Gilliam and linebackers Holub and Lanier weakened the middle of the offensive and defensive teams. The Chiefs had to scramble for three consecutive wins at the end of the year, finishing second with a 9-5 mark. Stenerud, from Norway via Montana State, led the league in field goals with 21. Smith, a 5-foot 6-inch, 154-pound sprinter from Tennessee State, topped the AFL in kickoff-return yardage.

1968 The Chiefs' offensive firepower was depleted early in the season by injuries to backs Garrett, McClinton, and Bert Coan, and receivers Taylor and Gloster Richardson. Kansas City's offense scored no touchdowns (all were by the defense) in a 20-19 loss to the Jets. Stram improvised, bringing quarterback Jacky Lee and running back Robert Holmes off the bench, and both were outstanding in a 34-2 win over Denver in the third game. Dawson returned the next week to direct a 48-3 bombing of Miami. The Chiefs ran the winning streak to six en route to a 12-2 finish and a tie with Oakland for the Western Division championship. Dawson finished as the league's top passer for the fourth time, Holmes was the number-two rusher in the AFL, and the defense gave up the fewest points in the league. But in the playoff game, the Raiders built a 21-0 lead in the first quarter and advanced to the championship with a 41-6 victory, behind five touchdown passes by Daryle Lamonica. All the Chiefs' scoring came in the second quarter, when they ran 10 plays inside the Raiders' 10-yard line and netted just two field goals.

1969 The Chiefs posted a 6-0 preseason mark and kept the string going with comfortable victories over San Diego and Boston at the outset of the regular schedule. But in the 31-0 drubbing of the Patriots, Dawson injured a knee; he was replaced by Jacky Lee against Cincinnati. The Chiefs lost the game 24-19, and lost Lee with a cracked bone in his ankle. Mike Livingston became the third quarterback in as many weeks, and helped turn things around in a 26-13 victory over Denver that began a seven-game winning streak. Behind the running of "mini-backs" Garrett, Holmes, and Warren McVea, the Chiefs established the best ground game in the AFL. Two months into the season, Dawson returned to action. The Chiefs finished with an 11-3 record, second to Oakland's 12-1-1. But this was the first year of the new playoff system that pitted first- and second-place finishers in the opposite divisions against each other in the opening round. Kansas City relied on strong defensive play, which, during the season, had seen them lead the league against scoring, passing yards, and rushing yards, to turn back the defending Super Bowl champion New York Jets 13-6 in round one. The Chiefs, who had lost to Oakland twice in the regular season, rallied from an early 7-0 deficit to win 17-7 over the Raiders in the AFC Championship Game. Their opponents in Super Bowl IV in New Orleans were the Minnesota Vikings, and the Chiefs used the game as a crusade for the AFL. They wore patches on their jerseys saying "AFL-10," which referred to the 10-year existence of the AFL, which would become extinct in the new NFL setup. Oddsmakers had established the Vikings two-touchdown favorites, but the Chiefs came out with three Stenerud field goals and a second-quarter fumble recovery on the Minnesota 19-yard line that led to Mike Garrett's five-yard touchdown and a 16-0 halftime lead. A 46-yard pass from Dawson to Otis Taylor in the third quarter sealed Kansas City's first Super Bowl championship, 23-7.

1970 Relations soured between Stram and Garrett, and Garrett was traded to San Diego. The Chiefs seemed to miss the spark of the year before, despite the presence of multi-talented Ed Podolak, who replaced Garrett. Key injuries also contributed to the Chiefs' record dropping to 7-3-2 after 12 games. With a chance to still win the division, the Chiefs traveled to Oakland and lost 20-6, then dropped the final game to San Diego 31-13 as Garrett haunted them with his best game of the year, 95 yards.

1971 Stram opened up the offense again with the help of receivers such as rookie Elmo Wright and Morris Stroud. Taylor showed he still was one of the best pass catchers in football, leading the NFL in yards gained on receptions. Although the defense was hurt when Mays retired, the linebacking trio of Lanier, Bell, and Lynch was among the league's best. After an opening loss to San Diego, the Chiefs won five straight. In the next-to-last game with Oakland, a late field goal by Stenerud gave the Chiefs a 16-14 victory and the Western Division title. Stram awarded game balls to all 40 squad members. The team finished with a 10-3-1 record. But in the AFC playoff against Eastern Division champion Miami, Kansas City dropped a 27-24 double-overtime decision to the Dolphins, December 25. The game was the longest ever played, going 82:40.

1972 Hunt became the first person associated with the Chiefs to be elected to the Pro Football Hall of Fame. All-star safety Johnny Robinson retired, but Dawson ended speculation that he would do the same by signing a two-year contract in April. Kansas City fans were introduced to their new, modernistic Arrowhead Stadium, one of the most impressive facilities in pro football. With a seating capacity of 78,097, it was formally opened for a preseason game with the St. Louis Cardinals, August 12. The Chiefs opened the regular season with a loss to Miami but eventually rose to 5-3 with a 27-14 win over Oakland in the eighth week. Consecutive losses to Pittsburgh, San Diego, and Oakland put them out of contention, however, and they finished 8-6, second in the West.

1973 The defense continued to play with its customary vigor, but new holes began appearing in the Chiefs' offense. Dawson was hurt much of the time and had to give way to backup quarterback Pete Beathard, who had returned for his second tour of duty under Stram. Beathard could not get the club moving, so Mike Livingston got the next chance and generated some excitement by leading the club into first place in late November. But a 14-10 loss to Denver and a 37-7 loss to the division-leading Raiders took the Chiefs out of title contention and dropped them to third place.

1974 The Chiefs were 3-4 at the midway point of the season, but then lost consecutive games to the New York Giants and San Diego. The Chiefs' age was beginning to show. Dawson was 39. The offensive linemen were older, slower, and ready to be replaced. The defensive front four had to be overhauled. The result was the first losing record in Kansas City in 11 years. The Chiefs finished 5-9, and Stram, the only coach in the history of the franchise, was dismissed at the end of the season. Jack Steadman, the club's general manager, was appointed by Lamar Hunt to revamp the organization. Statistically, the highlight of the year was Emmitt Thomas's 12 interceptions, best in the NFL.

1975 Paul Wiggin, an assistant coach with the San Francisco 49ers, was named Chiefs' head coach. Wiggin directed his young, inexperienced club to four victories in five games at one point early in the season, including a 34-31 upset of Dallas on Monday night television. Injuries handicapped the Chiefs, and by the end of the year, they barely had enough able bodies. A 24-21 victory over the Detroit Lions was the only bright spot in the final six games, and Kansas City again finished 5-9 and third in the Western Division. After 19 memorable seasons, 14 with the Texans-Chiefs, Dawson announced his retirement.

1976 Continuing what he hoped was a rebuilding program, Wiggin suffered through four straight losses at the start of the season before getting his club turned around. Livingston, who had seemed on the verge of becoming the regular quarterback several times in previous seasons, finally took over the position and improved noticeably as the season progressed. The team finished with two victories in its last three games, including an impressive 39-14 smashing of Cleveland.

1977 The poorest season in the franchise's history cost both Wiggin and his successor, Tom Bettis, their jobs. Kansas City lost its first five games before winning on October 23. In that game, the Chiefs took advantage of San Diego fumbles to score twice in 31 seconds for a 21-16 win. The next week Cleveland defeated the Chiefs 44-7, and Wiggin was fired. Bettis was promoted to head coach. The Chiefs dedicated the next game to Wiggin and defeated Green Bay 20-10. But six straight losses closed out the season, and Bettis's contract was not renewed. The heart of the Chiefs' defense also departed, as 11-year veterans Lynch and Lanier retired after the season.

1978 Marv Levy, the former head coach of the Montreal Alouettes of the Canadian Football League, was named head coach. He drafted for defense, starting with defensive end Art Still in the first round. Levy installed the Wing-T as his offense. Although the Chiefs passed for only seven touchdowns, they had the second-most productive ground game in the league: A record five backs ran for at least 100 yards in a game. The highlight of the season came in a 23-0 victory over the Chargers on November 26, when the Chiefs intercepted five San Diego passes. Nevertheless, the Chiefs finished five games behind any other AFC West team.

1979 Quarterback Steve Fuller of Clemson was a first-round draft choice. Early in the season he replaced Livingston as the starter. With Fuller, the Chiefs improved from their 1-3 start to 7-9. Despite a gradual shift from the Wing-T, the running game remained effective. The passing game, however, was a disappointment, again producing only seven touchdowns. Late in the season, the Chiefs' defense began to make noticeable improvement, holding Baltimore to seven points and Tampa Bay to only a field goal.

1980 Despite injuries to some key starters, Kansas City continued to improve its record. It came back from an 0-4 start to finish 8-8. The defense came of age, with Still, Gary Barbaro, and Gary Green playing leading roles. When Fuller suffered a knee injury late in the season, Bill Kenney took over at quarterback and led the Chiefs to two victories in their last three games.

1981 With Kenney at quarterback, the Chiefs ignored their recent history of slow starts and came out winning. Linebacker Thomas Howard returned a fumble 65 yards for a touchdown with less than 2:00 remaining in the opener, and the Chiefs defeated the Steelers 37-33. On October 11, the Chiefs routed Oakland 27-0 on Kenney's 287 yards passing. Two weeks later the Chiefs defeated the Raiders again to take over first place in the AFC West with a 6-2 record. Two losses followed, but wins over Houston and Seattle put the Chiefs back in first place again. Three more losses eliminated the Chiefs from the playoffs, but a season-ending 10-6 victory over the Vikings gave the Chiefs their first winning season since 1973. Rookie Joe Delaney rushed for 1,121 yards and was voted AFC rookie of the year.

1982 Lack of offensive punch was the chief reason Kansas City finished 3-6 in the strike-shortened season. Delaney, plagued by injuries and an eye problem, dropped to 380 yards rushing. The defense, ranked fourth in the AFC, provided some bright spots. A blocked punt by cornerback Gary Green that was recovered in the Rams' end zone helped the Chiefs win their first game of the season, September 19. And in a 37-16 victory against Denver later in the season Barbaro and cornerback Eric Harris each returned interceptions for touchdowns. Jack Rudnay, a solid center for the Chiefs since 1969, retired.

1983 Delaney was the victim of a tragic drowning accident. He died while trying to save three children from the same fate. Todd Blackledge, the quarterback for Penn State's national championship team, was the Chiefs' top draft choice. Bobby Bell became the first Kansas City player to be inducted into the Pro Football Hall of Fame. Levy was fired, and the Chiefs named John Mackovic, the Dallas Cowboys' quarterback coach, to replace him. Mackovic promised the Chiefs would feature a wide-open attack that "could throw the ball 40 times a game." Mackovic kept his word; the Chiefs' offense improved dramatically. Kenney won the duel with Fuller for the starting quarterback position and had a terrific season, passing for a team-record 4,348 yards and 24 touchdowns. He had seven 300-yard games, and also set Kansas City records with 603 attempts and 346 completions. In a 38-17 victory over the New York Giants on October 16, Kenney passed for a career-high 342 yards and four touchdowns. He topped that figure two weeks later with 365 yards passing in a 27-24 loss to Denver, and, in a wild shootout with Seattle on November 27, he passed for 311 yards and four touchdowns. The Seahawks won that game, the third-highest scoring game ever, 51-48 in overtime. Despite the offensive fireworks, the Chiefs finished 6-10. But six of the losses came by five points or less. Wide receiver Carlos Carson set club records with 80 receptions for 1,351 yards. Placekicker Nick Lowery finished second in the AFC in scoring with 116 points, and, against the Washington Redskins, he tied an AFC record with a 58-yard field goal. Deron Cherry earned the starting free safety job when Barbaro didn't sign with the team. Cherry had seven interceptions to rank third in the AFC and was chosen for the Pro Bowl.

1984 The Chiefs drafted Pittsburgh nose tackle Bill Maas in the first round. Green was traded to the Los Angeles Rams. The Chiefs started quickly, defeating Pittsburgh and Cincinnati on the road in their first two games. But they won only 3 of their next 11 games before closing fast with three consecutive victories over AFC West rivals to finish the season with an 8-8 record. Kenney missed half the season with injuries, but he still passed for 2,098 yards and 15 touchdowns. The running game was the AFC's poorest, averaging just 95.4 yards per game. In a 24-20 victory against Tampa Bay, Kenney threw 46 passes and combined with Buccaneers quarterback Steve DeBerg to set an NFL single-game record with a total of 100 passing attempts. In a 17-16 loss to the Jets on October 7, Lowery converted all three of his field-goal attempts to become the NFL's career accuracy leader with 100 field goals in 131 tries, for a percentage of .736.

1985 Running back Theotis Brown suffered a heart attack in February and was uanable to play during the season. Nevertheless, the Chiefs got off to a quick start. After four games they had a 3-1 record and sole possession of first place in the AFC West. Then they lost seven straight games before finishing with a 3-2 flourish, winding up with a 6-10 record. Kenney started 10 games, but injuries reduced his role to limited duty and curtailed his effectiveness. Blackledge started the final five games. Cornerback Albert Lewis led the AFC with eight interceptions, and in an early-season victory against Seattle, Cherry tied an NFL record by intercepting four passes. The Chiefs' most prolific individual performance of the year came in the team's final game, a 38-34 victory against San Diego. Wide receiver Stephone Paige broke a 40-year-old NFL record with 309 yards receiving on eight catches, including touchdown receptions of 56 and 84 yards.

MEMBERS OF HALL OF FAME:
Bobby Bell, Lamar Hunt, Willie Lanier

CHIEFS RECORD, 1960-85

Year	Won	Lost	Tied	Pct.	Fin.	Pts.	OP
Dallas Texans							
1960	8	6	0	.571	2	362	253
1961	6	8	0	.429	2	334	343
1962a	11	3	0	.786	1	389	233
Kansas City Chiefs							
1963	5	7	2	.417	3	347	263
1964	7	7	0	.500	2	366	306
1965	7	5	2	.583	3	322	285
1966b	11	2	1	.846	1	448	276
1967	9	5	0	.643	2	408	254
1968c	12	2	0	.857	2	371	170
1969d	11	3	0	.786	2	359	177
1970	7	5	2	.583	2	272	244
1971e	10	3	1	.769	1	302	208
1972	8	6	0	.571	2	287	254
1973	7	5	2	.571	3	231	192
1974	5	9	0	.357	3	233	293
1975	5	9	0	.357	3	282	341
1976	5	9	0	.357	4	290	376
1977	2	12	0	.143	5	225	349
1978	4	12	0	.250	5	243	327
1979	7	9	0	.438	5	238	262
1980	8	8	0	.500	3	319	336
1981	9	7	0	.563	3	343	290
1982	3	6	0	.333	11	176	184
1983	6	10	0	.375	5	386	367
1984	8	8	0	.500	4	314	324
1985	6	10	0	.375	5	317	360
26 Years	187	176	10	.515		8,164	7,267

aAFL Champion; 1-0 in Playoffs
bAFL Champion; 1-1 in Playoffs
cAFL Western Division Runnerup; 0-1 in Playoffs
dSuper Bowl Champion; 3-0 in Playoffs
eAFC Western Division Champion; 0-1 in Playoffs

RECORD HOLDERS

CAREER		
Rushing attempts	Ed Podolak, 1969-77	1,158
Rushing yards	Ed Podolak, 1969-77	4,451
Pass attempts	Len Dawson, 1962-75	3,696
Pass completions	Len Dawson, 1962-75	2,115
Passing yards	Len Dawson, 1962-75	28,507
Touchdown passes	Len Dawson, 1962-75	237
Receptions	Otis Taylor, 1965-75	410
Receiving yards	Otis Taylor, 1965-75	7,306
Interceptions	Emmitt Thomas, 1966-78	58
Punting average	Jerrel Wilson, 1963-77	43.5
Punt return avg.	J. T. Smith, 1979-84	10.6
Kickoff return avg.	Noland Smith, 1967-69	26.8
Field goals	Jan Stenerud, 1967-79	279
Touchdowns	Otis Taylor, 1965-75	60
Points	Jan Stenerud, 1967-79	1,231
SEASON		
Rushing attempts	Mike Garrett, 1967	236
Rushing yards	Joe Delaney, 1981	1,121
Pass attempts	Bill Kenney, 1983	603
Pass completions	Bill Kenney, 1983	346
Passing yards	Bill Kenney, 1983	4,348
Touchdown passes	Len Dawson, 1964	30
Receptions	Carlos Carson, 1983	80
Receiving yards	Carlos Carson, 1983	1,351
Interceptions	Emmitt Thomas, 1974	12
Punting average	Jerrel Wilson, 1965	46.0
Punt return avg.	Abner Haynes, 1960	15.4
Kickoff return avg.	Dave Grayson, 1963	29.7
Field goals	Jan Stenerud, 1968	30
	Jan Stenerud, 1970	30
Touchdowns	Abner Haynes, 1962	19
Points	Jan Stenerud, 1968	129
GAME		
Rushing attempts	Woody Green, 11-3-74	30
Rushing yards	Joe Delaney, 11-15-81	193
Pass attempts	Bill Kenney, 10-30-83	52
Pass completions	Bill Kenney, 12-11-83	31
Passing yards	Len Dawson, 11-1-64	435
Touchdown passes	Len Dawson, 11-1-64	6
Receptions	Ed Podolak, 10-7-73	12
Receiving yards	Stephone Paige, 12-22-85	309
Interceptions	Bobby Ply, 12-16-62	4
	Bobby Hunt, 12-4-64	4
	Deron Cherry, 9-29-85	4
Field goals	Jan Stenerud, 11-2-69	5
	Jan Stenerud, 12-7-69	5
	Jan Stenerud, 12-19-71	5
	Nick Lowery, 9-12-85	5
Touchdowns	Abner Haynes, 11-26-61	5
Points	Abner Haynes, 11-26-61	30

COACHING HISTORY

1960-74	Hank Stram	129-79-10
1975-77	Paul Wiggin*	11-24- 0
1977	Tom Bettis	1- 6- 0
1978-82	Marv Levy	31-42- 0
1983-85	John Mackovic	20-28- 0

**Replaced after seven games in 1977*

FIRST PLAYER SELECTED

1960 Don Meredith, QB, SMU
1961 E. J. Holub, C, Texas Tech
1962 Ronnie Bull, HB, Baylor
1963 Buck Buchanan, DT, Grambling
1964 Pete Beathard, QB, USC
1965 Gale Sayers, HB, Kansas
1965† Alphonse Dotson, DT, Grambling
1966 Aaron Brown, DE, Minnesota
1966† George Youngblood, DB, Cal State-Los Angeles
1967 Gene Trosch, DE-DT, Miami
1968 Mo Moorman, G, Texas A&M
1969 Jim Marsalis, CB, Tennessee State
1970 Sid Smith, T, USC
1971 Elmo Wright, WR, Houston
1972 Jeff Kinney, RB, Nebraska
1973 (2) Gary Butler, TE, Rice
1974 Woody Green, RB, Arizona State
1975 (2) Elmore Stephens, TE, Kentucky
1976 Rod Walters, G, Iowa
1977 Gary Green, CB, Baylor
1978 Art Still, DE, Kentucky
1979 Mike Bell, DE, Colorado State
1980 Brad Budde, G, USC
1981 Willie Scott, TE, South Carolina
1982 Anthony Hancock, WR, Tennessee
1983 Todd Blackledge, QB, Penn State
1984 Bill Maas, NT, Pittsburgh
1984* Mark Adickes, T, Baylor
1985 Ethan Horton, RB, North Carolina
1986 Brian Jozwiak, T, West Virginia
†Redshirt Draft
**Supplemental Draft*

CHIEFS MOST VALUABLE PLAYER

1979 Gary Barbaro, S
1980 Art Still, DE
1981 Joe Delaney, RB
1982 Gary Green, CB
1983 Bill Kenney, QB
1984 Art Still, DE
1985 Lloyd Burruss, S

LOS ANGELES RAIDERS

1959 The American Football League was organized, August 14. It held its first player draft, November 22, and another draft, completing 53 rounds in all, December 2. The first choice of the Minneapolis franchise was quarterback Dale Hackbart of Wisconsin.
1960 The Minneapolis franchise of the AFL withdrew and elected to play in the National Football League instead. Barron Hilton, owner of the Los Angeles Chargers of the AFL, gave the league an ultimatum that unless it placed another franchise on the West Coast, he would withdraw from the AFL. Oakland became the eighth city to gain an AFL franchise, January 30. The franchise was owned by an eight-man syndicate headed by Y.C. (Chet) Soda and including Ed McGah, Robert Osborne, and Wayne Valley. Oakland inherited the Minneapolis draft list, but, because of the lateness of its entry into the league, also was allowed to select five players from each other AFL team. Dons and Señors each were given consideration as the team name, which ultimately became Raiders. Eddie Erdelatz of Navy was named the team's head coach. The regents of the University of California would not approve the use of its stadium for the Raiders' games, which were played at Kezar Stadium in San Francisco, the home of the rival 49ers of the NFL. Only 12,703 fans watched the Raiders lose to the Houston Oilers 37-22 in their first game. They had two good quarterbacks—Tom Flores and Babe Parilli—two hard runners—Tony Teresa and Billy Lott—and center Jim Otto and guard Wayne Hawkins were solid, but the Raiders had little else and finished with a 6-8 record.
1961 The Raiders' home games were moved to Candlestick Park in San Francisco. McGah, Osborne, and Valley bought out their five partners, and McGah was named president of the club. The team lost its first two games to Houston 55-0 and San Diego 44-0. "I don't know what to do about it," Erdelatz said. He was fired as coach. Marty Feldman, one of Erdelatz's assistants, was given the job, but he didn't fare much better. The Raiders scored the fewest points in the league, allowed the most points, played before mostly empty seats, and won only two games. The only bright spot was the play of Flores, Otto, and cornerback Fred Williamson. Osborne, discouraged by the turn of events, sold his interest in the club.
1962 Valley told Oakland city officials, "Either build us a stadium or we move." A much-discussed Oakland-Alameda County Coliseum complex was still in the planning stages, so until further action could be taken on it, Frank Youell Field was designated for the Raiders. It was a small high-school facility. Temporary stands were built and boosted its seating capacity to 20,000. It was still so small that even if the Raiders sold out every game, they would have lost money had it not been for the league's television contract. Before the season began, a special draft of veteran players was held to help Oakland and Denver. But with Flores out with a lung infection, the Raiders were still in bad shape and continued to struggle for victories. Feldman was replaced by Bill (Red) Conkright after two games. On the final day of the season, after having lost 19 in a row over two years, the Raiders finally won, beating Boston 20-0.
1963 After refusing their offers on several occasions, Al Davis, an assistant coach for the San Diego Chargers, accepted a three-year contract as the Raiders' head coach and general manager. "What I want is enough time and money to build the Raiders into a professional football team," Davis told Valley and McGah. Davis immediately began reorganizing the franchise. He hired a new business manager, director of player personnel, and ticket manager. He signed split end Art Powell, who had played out his option with the Titans, got quarterback Tom Flores back from his extended illness, and coaxed several useful players away from other teams. Halfback Clem Daniels, a former tight end, rushed for 1,099 yards, an AFL record. The Oakland defense also prospered under Davis. After a 2-4 start, the Raiders rallied to win their last eight games and finish one game behind San Diego. The last three games, in particular, established Oakland in its wide-open style. Trailing 27-10, the Raiders rallied in the fourth quarter to beat the Chargers 41-27. Then they edged Denver 35-31 and outscored Houston 52-49 in the highest-scoring game in AFL history.
1964 Tony Lorick, the number-one draft choice from Arizona State, signed with Oakland. He also signed with Baltimore of the NFL and, after a long hassle, wound up playing for the Colts. Davis's team slumped at the start, losing five straight, but came back to score four wins and a tie in the final five games, including victories over Buffalo and San Diego, the teams headed for the AFL title game. Two new acquisitions, 6-foot 7-inch, 265-pound end Ben Davidson and middle linebacker Dan Conners helped fortify Oakland's defense.
1965 Construction officially started on Oakland-Alameda County Coliseum. Davis continued to stockpile talent, acquiring such rookies as flanker Fred Biletnikoff, defensive back Kent McCloughan, linebacker Gus Otto, and tackles Harry Schuh and Bob Svihus. But an inability to beat Buffalo and San Diego—the Raiders lost all four of those games—killed the Raiders' title chances and they finished second to the Chargers in their division again, with an 8-5-1 record.
1966 Davis was named commissioner of the American Football League, succeeding Joe Foss, in April. Johnny Rauch was named Raiders head coach. The AFL and NFL agreed to a merger, June 8. Davis resigned as AFL commissioner and returned to Oakland as managing general partner. Oakland-Alameda County Coliseum opened, and in the first game there the Kansas City Chiefs defeated the Raiders 32-10 before 50,746, September 18. The Raiders slipped to a 1-3 mark but late-season victories over Kansas City, Houston, and San Diego helped produce an 8-5-1 season, again good for second place.
1967 Davis traded Flores and Powell to Buffalo for quarterback Daryle Lamonica and split end Glenn Bass. The Raiders also acquired split end Bill Miller from Buffalo, cornerback Willie Brown from Denver, and quarterback-kicker George Blanda, who had been released by Houston. Rookie guard Gene Upshaw from Texas A&I immediately established himself as one of the league's best blockers, and fullback Hewritt Dixon as one of the most efficient runners. The Raiders smashed Denver 51-0 in the season opener, and, after a 27-14 loss to New York in the fourth week, they won 10 straight games to capture the Western Division title with a 13-1 mark. Blanda won the AFL scoring championship, Lamonica led the league in passing, and the defense gave up the second-fewest points in the league. Lamonica also was named AFL player of the year, having thrown for 3,228 yards and 30 touchdowns. In the AFL Championship Game at Oakland, the Raiders stormed by Houston 40-7 for the right to meet Green Bay in the second AFL-NFL World Championship Game. Oakland was too young and too inexperienced, and the Packers won 33-14.
1968 The Raiders were hit with an unusual number of injuries, but found two new stars on offense, split end Warren Wells and running back Charlie Smith. Wells averaged 21.5 yards per catch, and Smith 5.3 yards per carry. The Raiders played the New York Jets at Oakland and trailed 32-29 with one minute, five seconds to play. The NBC television network switched from the game to begin the movie, "Heidi." The network's switchboard lit up with angry protests; the viewers never saw the Raiders come back with two late touchdowns to win what was later called the "Heidi Game," 43-32. Oakland rolled to a 12-2 record, but it wasn't enough for undisputed first place in the Western Division; they were tied with the Kansas City Chiefs. Oakland crushed the Chiefs 41-6 in a playoff, as Lamonica threw five touchdown passes. In the AFL title game in New York, the Raiders and Jets played a dramatic game with Joe Namath finally pulling it out for New York 27-23.
1969 Rauch became head coach of the Buffalo Bills. John Madden, a 32-year-old Raiders assistant, replaced him, becoming the youngest head coach in pro football. Lamonica continued as one of the game's most effective passers, again leading the AFL in that category. He threw six touchdown passes in the first half on the way to a 50-21 win over Buffalo, October 19. One week later, the Raiders beat San Diego to equal the AFL record for consecutive unbeaten games at 15. The streak ended the following week with a 31-17 loss to Cincinnati, but Oakland won its six remaining games and finished first in the Western Division with a 12-1-1 mark. Lamonica ended the season with 34 touchdown passes. Oakland routed Houston 56-7 in the first round of the playoffs. Kansas City, the second-place team in the division, upset Oakland 17-7 in the AFC Championship Game at Oakland.
1970 The Raiders were placed in the AFC Western Division as realignment of pro football took place. Blanda, 43, produced four victories and a tie in the final seconds of five consecutive games. Blanda threw two touchdown passes in a 31-14 victory over Pittsburgh. The following week he kicked a 48-yard field goal with three seconds remaining to tie Kansas City 17-17. A week later, again with three seconds left, he kicked a 52-yard field goal that gave the Raiders a 23-20 victory over Cleveland. In the next game, with Denver, Blanda came off the bench to ignite a late rally that beat the Broncos 24-19. Then he kicked a field goal with four seconds left to defeat San Diego 20-17. Thanks to Blanda, Oakland became the first AFC team to win four consecutive divisional championships. In the first round of the playoffs, the Raiders beat Miami 21-14. In the AFC Championship Game with Baltimore, Blanda, in for an injured Lamonica, completed 17 of 32 passes for 271 yards, but the Colts made three key interceptions. Baltimore won 27-17.
1971 The Raiders lost to the New England Patriots 20-6 in the opening game but went undefeated for the next nine weeks. The team's two best running backs, Smith and Dixon, both were sidelined with injuries, and Wells missed the whole season with legal problems, but Madden found the replacements—Pete Banaszak, Marv Hubbard, and Rod Sherman—to keep on winning. But then a 37-14 loss to Baltimore started a three-game losing streak, which included a 16-14 loss to Kansas City in the next-to-last game. Oakland finished with an 8-4-2 record. It was the first time in five years the Raiders failed to win the Western Division title.
1972 Davis and Madden continued to rebuild the Raiders and maintain the same remarkable winning percentage. Youngsters such as Horace Jones, Otis Sistrunk, Art Thoms, and Tony Cline were starting in the defensive line, and Phil Villapiano and Gerald Irons were new linebackers. Offensively, Hubbard gained 1,100 yards, while the flashy new addition was Cliff Branch, the world-class sprinter from Colorado who was developing into a new deep threat. Branch caught a key 19-yard pass in a last-

minute, 21-19 victory over San Diego. The win was the fourth in a six-game streak that closed out the Raiders' 10-3-1 season. After winning the Western Division title, Oakland traveled to Pittsburgh and was defeated 13-7 when Franco Harris scored the winning touchdown on a shoe-top catch of a deflected pass in the final seconds, a play that was nicknamed "The Immaculate Reception."

1973 The largest crowd ever to see a pro football game in the Bay Area, 74,121 at the University of California, watched Oakland end Miami's winning streak at 18 games with a 12-7 victory. After failing to score a touchdown in the first three games, Lamonica was benched in favor of Ken Stabler at quarterback. A mid-November slump cost the team a 17-9 loss to Pittsburgh and a 7-3 upset at the hands of Cleveland. The Raiders rallied for three consecutive victories, and entered the final game against Denver only a half-game in front of the vastly improved Broncos. The Raiders won 21-17, finishing at 9-4-1 for their sixth division championship in seven years. In the first round of the AFC playoffs, Oakland defeated Pittsburgh 33-14. Miami's defending Super Bowl champions were too strong in the AFC title game, however, and the Raiders fell 27-10.

1974 A 27-7 victory over Kansas City began a nine-game winning streak for the Raiders, September 22. The following week, Oakland shut out Pittsburgh 17-0. The streak ended with a 20-17 loss to Denver in the eleventh game, but the Raiders won the next three and finished 12-2 for another Western Division championship. In the first round of the AFC playoffs, against Miami, Stabler took the Raiders on a pressure drive late in the fourth quarter, then threw a clutch touchdown pass to Clarence Davis in the final minute for a 28-26 victory. Oakland's bid for the Super Bowl was shut off by Pittsburgh, 24-13, in the AFC title game at Oakland, December 29.

1975 Jim Otto, last of the original Raiders and the only all-AFL center ever, retired after 15 years as the team's starting center. In a nationally televised Monday night game, Oakland opened the season with a 31-21 victory over Miami, ending the Dolphins' 31-game winning streak in the Orange Bowl. The Raiders won their next two games but were jolted 42-10 by Kansas City and lost to Cincinnati 14-10. They rebounded to win seven straight, clinching the division title with a 37-34 overtime victory over Atlanta, November 30. In the first round of the playoffs, the Raiders edged Cincinnati 31-28. In the AFC title game, Pittsburgh ended the Raiders' hopes again, hanging on for a 16-10 victory at snow-coated Three Rivers Stadium, January 4. Oakland trailed Pittsburgh 16-7 with 1:38 to play and the Steelers in possession on the Raiders' 36-yard line. But a fumble recovery, a 41-yard George Blanda field goal, and a recovered onside kick gave the Raiders a shot at the conference championship with seven seconds left. The game ended as Branch took a pass from Stabler and was tackled at the Pittsburgh 15-yard line. Following the season, Blanda retired after 26 years in professional football.

1976 The Raiders opened the regular season with a turnabout, upending the Steelers 31-28 on Fred Steinfort's field goal with 18 seconds left. The following Monday night, Stabler completed 22 of 28 passing attempts in a 24-21 triumph over Kansas City. The Raiders got by Houston 14-13 on October 3. The following week their injury-riddled defense caved in and allowed New England seven touchdowns in a 48-17 loss. Oakland regrouped to win its last 10 games to finish 13-1 and claim another division championship. The main driving force was Stabler, who led the league in passing, completing 66.7 percent of his passes. Stabler dived in for the winning touchdown with time running out as the Raiders beat New England 24-21 in round one of the playoffs. In the AFC title game, Oakland ground out an impressive 24-7 victory over the defending champion Steelers. Oakland beat Minnesota decisively 32-14 in Super Bowl XI in Pasadena's Rose Bowl, January 9. Fred Biletnikoff was named the game's most valuable player after three clutch catches to set up Oakland touchdowns.

1977 The Raiders came into the regular season with a 13-game winning streak. Relying on the passing of Stabler and the running of Mark van Eeghen, who would lead the AFC in rushing, they increased it to 17 before losing 30-7 to the Broncos, who intercepted Stabler seven times. Oakland bounced back with a 28-27 victory over the Jets, then handed the Broncos their first defeat of the season, 24-14. On November 20, Stabler was injured in the first quarter and the Raiders lost to San Diego 12-7. The Raiders lost their third game of the season on December 4, 20-14 to the Los Angeles Rams. An 11-3 record earned a wild card spot in the playoffs. On December 24, Stabler threw three touchdowns to Dave Casper, the last after 15:43 of overtime, and the Raiders defeated the Colts 37-31 in the AFC Divisional Playoff Game. The Raiders lost to the Broncos 20-17 on January 1 in the AFC Championship Game.

1978 The season opened against the Broncos, who won 14-6. On September 10, Oakland evened its record at 1-1 when Stabler fumbled at the San Diego 24 on the last play of the game, Banaszak bobbled the ball forward, and Casper grabbed it in the end zone for the winning touchdown in a 21-20 victory. Oakland was inconsistent throughout the season, with Stabler hitting 58 percent of his passes, but throwing 30 interceptions. The Raiders finished only 3-5 in the AFC West and 9-7 overall, missing the playoffs for the first time since 1971.

1979 After 10 years as head coach, Madden retired on January 4. One month later, former quarterback Tom Flores was named as Madden's successor. Injuries forced Flores to install a two-tight-end offense, and Dave Casper and Raymond Chester became the first pair of tight ends from the same team to make the Pro Bowl. Although the passing game flourished, the running attack was a disappointment, finishing twenty-fourth in the league. The Raiders opened with a 24-17 victory over the Rams, then lost three games in a row. Battling back all year, the Raiders still were in the playoff picture until the last week of the season when a 29-24 Seattle victory gave Oakland its second straight 9-7 record and non-playoff season.

1980 Former center Jim Otto became the first Raider elected to the Pro Football Hall of Fame. Wanting a quarterback with better range, the Raiders traded Stabler to Houston for Dan Pastorini in the offseason. Van Eeghen broke the Raiders' career rushing yardage mark September 28 against Buffalo. After a 2-2 start, Pastorini was injured in a loss to Kansas City on October 5. Jim Plunkett, whose on-again, off-again career had him sitting on the Raiders' bench, took over and quarterbacked Oakland to six straight victories, a final record of 11-5, and into the AFC Wild Card Game. The defensive star for Oakland was Lester Hayes, who intercepted 13 passes, the second-most in a single season in NFL history. On December 28, Plunkett threw two touchdown passes, Hayes returned an interception for a touchdown, and the Raiders defeated Houston in the AFC Wild Card Game 27-7. The defense won one, the offense won one, and they shared in the glory in the third, as the Raiders swept to a victory in the Super Bowl. In the AFC Divisional Playoff Game, the Raiders intercepted Cleveland's Brian Sipe three times, including a game-clincher in the end zone by safety Mike Davis in the fourth quarter, leading to a 14-12 victory. Plunkett passed for 261 yards to help the Raiders defeat the Chargers 34-27 in the AFC Championship Game. Super Bowl XV was all Raiders, as they dominated the Eagles in a 27-10 victory. Plunkett was named the game's most valuable player.

1981 George Blanda became the second Raider elected to the Pro Football Hall of Fame. The Raiders' and the Los Angeles Coliseum Commission's antitrust suit against the NFL went to trial in Federal District Court in Los Angeles, May 11. The suit contended the league violated anti-monopoly statutes in blocking a proposed move by the Raiders from Oakland to the L.A. Coliseum to replace the Rams, who had moved to Anaheim Stadium. A mistrial was declared when the jury was unable to reach a verdict, August 13. The Cinderella season for Plunkett and the Raiders did not continue in 1981. Oakland fell to fourth place with a 7-9 record. The Raiders didn't win more than two games in a row at any point, and midway through the season Plunkett, center Dave Dalby, tight end Raymond Chester, and guard Gene Upshaw all were replaced by younger players. Van Eeghen and wide receiver Bobby Chandler spent most of the season on injured reserve.

1982 The Raiders selected Heisman Trophy winner Marcus Allen of USC in the draft. On May 7, a Federal District Court ruled in favor of the Raiders in their antitrust suit against the league, paving the way for their move to Los Angeles. The Raiders played their first home preseason game at the Los Angeles Memorial Coliseum on August 29, defeating Green Bay 24-3. On November 22, following the 57-day players strike, the Raiders finally played their first regular-season home game at the Coliseum, rallying from a 24-0 deficit to defeat San Diego 28-24. On December 12, the Raiders defeated the Kansas City Chiefs in the final seconds to earn their two-hundredth league victory and clinch their seventeenth winning season in 18 years. The Raiders earned the first $1 million home gate in history on December 18 while downing the Los Angeles Rams 37-31 in the regular-season finale. After defeating Cleveland 27-10 in a first-round playoff game, the Raiders lost to the Jets 17-14 in front of a paid crowd of 90,688 at the Coliseum. Allen finished fourth in the league in rushing, led the league in scoring, and caught more passes than any other AFC running back. Defensive end Lyle Alzado, acquired for a ninth-round draft choice in a preseason deal with Cleveland, finished with eight sacks and was voted comeback player of the year in the NFL. Art Shell retired after the season.

1983 E.W. McGah, the club's only remaining original partner, died at age 84, September 17. With a 27-14 victory over Miami on September 19, the Raiders improved their overall record on Monday night to an NFL-best 20-2-1. The Raiders won the AFC West with a 12-4 record, and then defeated Pittsburgh 38-10 in a divisional playoff game before an AFC record playoff crowd of 92,434 at the Coliseum. A week later, Los Angeles defeated Seattle 30-14 in front of the largest championship game crowd in AFC history, 92,335. The Raiders won the Super Bowl for the third time in eight years by defeating the Washington Redskins 38-9 in Game XVIII at Tampa Stadium. Allen had a career-high and Super Bowl-record 191 yards against the Redskins, including a dazzling 74-yard touchdown run on a broken play in the third quarter. In the regular season, tight end Todd Christensen set a Raiders record and led the NFL with 92 receptions for 1,247 yards and 12 touchdowns. Linebacker Ted Hendricks's twenty-fifth career kick block of a field-goal attempt by Kansas City's Nick Lowery with nine seconds left preserved a 21-20 Raiders victory. Free safety Vann McElroy tied for the AFC lead with eight interceptions.

1984 Former cornerback Willie Brown became the

third Raider inducted into the Pro Football Hall of Fame, July 28. The Raiders finished the regular season with an 11-5 record, but that was good for only third place in the tough AFC West. In the AFC Wild Card Game, Seattle surprised the Raiders with a game plan geared around the run, and defeated Los Angeles 13-7 at the Kingdome. Christensen had another productive season, catching 80 passes for 1,007 yards. Allen was the AFC's second-leading rusher with 1,168 yards, and tied for the league lead in touchdowns with 18. Defensive end Howie Long had 12 sacks, linebacker Rod Martin had 11, and the Raiders led the NFL in that category with 64.

1985 The Raiders opened the season impressively, recording 10 sacks in a 31-0 victory over the New York Jets. At the midway point of the season they were 6-2, tied with Denver for first place in the AFC West. After back-to-back losses to Seattle and San Diego dropped the Raiders a game behind the Broncos, Los Angeles regrouped to win its final six games. The Raiders won the division title with an AFC-best 12-4 record, one game ahead of Denver. The Raiders won two critical showdowns with the Broncos, both in overtime. In the first game, Allen ran 24 times for a regular-season career-high 173 yards, including 61 yards for the Raiders' first touchdown. In the second game at Denver, the Raiders rallied from a 14-0 deficit to win 17-14 on Chris Bahr's field goal at 4:55 of the extra period. The Raiders were favored to win their AFC Divisional Playoff Game against the Patriots, but in a 14-second span late in the third quarter, New England placekicker Tony Franklin tied the score at 20-20 with his second field goal, kicked off, then watched teammate Jim Bowman recover a fumble by the Raiders' Sam Seale in the end zone for a touchdown. The Raiders had three more attempts at the tying touchdown, but couldn't get past the Patriots' 41. Allen became the first Raider to lead the NFL in rushing, with 1,759 yards, and in the regular-season finale against the Rams on Monday night, he tied Walter Payton's NFL record with his ninth consecutive 100-yard rushing game. The Raiders' 16-6 victory over the Rams in that game improved their record on Monday night to 24-3-1. After the season, Alzado retired.

MEMBERS OF HALL OF FAME:
George Blanda, Willie Brown, Ron Mix, Jim Otto

RAIDERS RECORD, 1960-85

Year	Won	Lost	Tied	Pct.	Fin.	Pts.	OP
Oakland Raiders							
1960	6	8	0	.429	3	319	388
1961	2	12	0	.143	4	237	458
1962	1	13	0	.071	4	213	370
1963	10	4	0	.714	2	363	282
1964	5	7	2	.417	3	303	350
1965	8	5	1	.615	2	298	239
1966	8	5	1	.615	2	315	288
1967a	13	1	0	.929	1	468	233
1968b	12	2	0	.857	1	453	233
1969b	12	1	1	.923	1	377	242
1970c	8	4	2	.667	1	300	293
1971	8	4	2	.667	2	344	278
1972d	10	3	1	.750	1	365	248
1973c	9	4	1	.679	1	292	175
1974c	12	2	0	.857	1	355	228
1975c	11	3	0	.786	1	375	255
1976e	13	1	0	.929	1	350	237
1977f	11	3	0	.786	2	351	230
1978	9	7	0	.563	2	311	283
1979	9	7	0	.563	4	365	337
1980g	11	5	0	.688	2	364	306
1981	7	9	0	.438	4	273	343
Los Angeles Raiders							
1982h	8	1	0	.889	1	260	200
1983e	12	4	0	.750	1	442	338
1984i	11	5	0	.688	3	368	278
1985d	12	4	0	.750	1	354	308
26 Years	238	124	11	.653		8,815	7,420

a*AFL Champion; 1-1 in Playoffs*
b*AFL Western Division Champion; 1-1 in Playoffs*
c*AFC Western Division Champion; 1-1 in Playoffs*
d*AFC Western Division Champion; 0-1 in Playoffs*
e*Super Bowl Champion; 3-0 in Playoffs*
f*AFC Wild Card Qualifier for Playoffs; 1-1 in Playoffs*
g*Super Bowl Champion; 4-0 in Playoffs*
h*AFC Qualifier for Playoffs; 1-1 in Playoffs*
i*AFC Wild Card Qualifier for Playoffs; 0-1 in Playoffs*

RECORD HOLDERS

CAREER		
Rushing attempts	Mark van Eeghen, 1974-81	1,475
Rushing yards	Mark van Eeghen, 1974-81	5,907
Pass attempts	Ken Stabler, 1970-79	2,481
Pass completions	Ken Stabler, 1970-79	1,486
Passing yards	Ken Stabler, 1970-79	19,078
Touchdown passes	Ken Stabler, 1970-79	150
Receptions	Fred Biletnikoff, 1965-78	589
Receiving yards	Fred Biletnikoff, 1965-78	8,974
Interceptions	Willie Brown, 1967-78	39
Punting average	Ray Guy, 1973-85	42.6
Punt return avg.	Claude Gibson, 1963-65	12.6
Kickoff return avg.	Jack Larscheid, 1960-61	28.4
Field goals	George Blanda, 1967-75	156
Touchdowns	Fred Biletnikoff, 1967-78	77
Points	George Blanda, 1967-75	863
SEASON		
Rushing attempts	Marcus Allen, 1985	380
Rushing yards	Marcus Allen, 1985	1,759
Pass attempts	Ken Stabler, 1979	498
Pass completions	Ken Stabler, 1979	304
Passing yards	Ken Stabler, 1979	3,615
Touchdown passes	Daryle Lamonica, 1969	34
Receptions	Todd Christensen, 1983	92
Receiving yards	Art Powell, 1964	1,361
Interceptions	Lester Hayes, 1980	13
Punting average	Ray Guy, 1973	45.3
Punt return avg.	Claude Gibson, 1963	14.4
Kickoff return avg.	Harold Hart, 1975	30.5
Field goals	George Blanda, 1973	23
Touchdowns	Marcus Allen, 1984	18
Points	George Blanda, 1968	117
GAME		
Rushing attempts	Mark van Eeghen, 10-23-77	36
Rushing yards	Clem Daniels, 10-20-63	200
Pass attempts	Jim Plunkett, 10-5-80	52
Pass completions	Jim Plunkett, 9-12-85	34
Passing yards	Cotton Davidson, 10-25-64	427
Touchdown passes	Tom Flores, 12-22-63	6
	Daryle Lamonica, 10-19-69	6
Receptions	Dave Casper, 10-3-76	12
Receiving yards	Art Powell, 12-22-63	247
Interceptions	5 times	3
Field goals	9 times	4
Touchdowns	Art Powell, 12-22-63	4
	Marcus Allen, 9-24-84	4
Points	Art Powell, 12-22-63	24
	Marcus Allen, 9-24-84	24

COACHING HISTORY

1960-61	Eddie Erdelatz*	6-10-0
1961-62	Marty Feldman**	2-15-0
1962	William (Red) Conkright	1- 8-0
1963-65	Al Davis	23-16-3
1966-68	John Rauch	35-10-1
1969-78	John Madden	112-39-7
1979-85	Tom Flores	78-38-0

**Replaced after two games in 1961*
***Replaced after five games in 1962*

FIRST PLAYER SELECTED

1960 Dale Hackbart, QB, Wisconsin
1961 Joe Rutgens, T, Illinois
1962 Roman Gabriel, QB, North Carolina State
1963 (6) Butch Wilson, HB, Alabama
1964 Tony Lorick, HB, Arizona State
1965 Harry Schuh, T, Memphis State
1965† Larry Todd, HB, Arizona State
1966 Rodger Bird, HB, Kentucky
1966† Rod Sherman, HB, USC
1967 Gene Upshaw, G, Texas A&I
1968 Eldridge Dickey, QB, Tennessee State
1969 Art Thoms, DT, Syracuse
1970 Raymond Chester, TE, Morgan State
1971 Jack Tatum, S, Ohio State
1972 Mike Siani, WR, Villanova
1973 Ray Guy, P-K, Southern Mississippi
1974 Henry Lawrence, T, Florida A&M
1975 Neal Colzie, DB, Ohio State
1976 (2) Charles Philyaw, DT, Texas Southern
1977 (2) Mike Davis, DB, Colorado
1978 (2) Dave Browning, DE, Washington
1979 (2) Willie Jones, DE, Florida State
1980 Marc Wilson, QB, BYU
1981 Ted Watts, DB, Texas Tech
1982 Marcus Allen, RB, USC
1983 Don Mosebar, T, USC
1984 (2) Sean Jones, DE, Northeastern
1984* Chris Woods, WR, Auburn
1985 Jessie Hester, WR, Florida State
1986 Bob Buczkowski, DE, Pittsburgh
†Redshirt Draft
**Supplemental Draft*

LOS ANGELES RAMS

1937 The National Football League granted a Cleveland franchise to a syndicate headed by Homer Marshman, February 13. The franchise, which was the NFL's tenth, was given the draft choices that the league had made in case such a franchise was granted. Hugo Bezdek, the only man to manage a major league baseball team and an NFL team, was named head coach. Bob Kelley was named radio play-by-play announcer. The Rams lost their home opener to Detroit 28-0. The next week, they defeated the Eagles in Philadelphia 21-3, but they then lost nine straight to close the season at 1-10-0. The top players were two rookies, fullback Johnny Drake and center Chuck Cherundolo; two players picked up from the Chicago Bears, center Charles (Ookie) Miller and tackle Ted Rosequist; and a tailback from the second American Football League, Bob Snyder.

1938 When the Rams started 0-3, Bezdek resigned. He was replaced by assistant Art Lewis, who took the team to three straight victories, over the Lions, the Bears, and the Bears again. Although the Rams dropped four of their last five, they discovered an outstanding passing attack with Snyder throwing to rookie end Jim Benton.

1939 Earl (Dutch) Clark, former star player for Portsmouth and Detroit, replaced Lewis as head coach, but Lewis remained with the Rams as an assistant. The club made it to .500 for the first time, finishing 5-5-1. Parker Hall, a rookie tailback who was the team's first draft choice, won the Joe Carr Trophy awarded to the NFL's official most valuable player. Hall led the league in passing, was second in passing yardage, and finished fifth in rushing.

1940 The Rams raised the hopes of their fans with a season-opening victory over the Eagles. But three consecutive losses shut down the flow of paying customers and assured the Rams of being a losing financial proposition. Even Hall, who finished third in passing yards, and Drake, who was second in the league in rushing, couldn't help the Rams at the gate.

1941 Marshman and his associates sold the Rams to Daniel F. Reeves and Fred Levy, Jr., in June, 1941. The price was $100,000. Reeves, 29, whose older brother, Ed, had owned a part of the Washington Redskins, became the youngest owner in pro football. Billy Evans, former sports columnist, American Baseball League umpire, and Cleveland Indians general manager, was hired as the Rams' new general manager. The team won its first two games but lost its next nine to finish in last place.

1942 Evans resigned before the season, and the front office was thrown into disarray when both Reeves and Levy were called into the service. Even without Drake, who retired, the Rams still had one of the best backs in the league in Dante Magnani, who finished third in receiving and eighth in rushing.

1943 Levy sold out to Reeves, who obtained league permission to suspend operations in 1943. Clark resigned and Charles (Chile) Walsh was named head coach. The Rams' players were distributed throughout the league.

1944 Walsh became general manager and appointed Aldo (Buff) Donelli, the former Pittsburgh Steelers and Duquesne coach, as new head coach. The team, comprised mostly of pickup players, won its first three and finished with a 4-6 record. UCLA quarterback Bob Waterfield was drafted as a future.

1945 Donelli entered the service and was replaced by Chile Walsh's brother Adam, who inherited a team bursting with talent and immediately switched to the T-formation. Waterfield joined the club and demonstrated he was a brilliant all-around player and consummate leader. He passed for 1,609 yards, intercepted six passes, averaged more than 40 yards per punt, and led the league in kicking extra points. On November 22, Waterfield hit end Jim Benton 10 times for 303 yards, a yardage mark that would be the NFL record for 40 years. Waterfield was joined in the backfield by a brilliant halfback who had been a rookie in 1940 but then missed four years during the war—Fred Gehrke. Waterfield was named the NFL's most valuable player and led the Rams to a 9-1-0 season to win the team's first division title. Then, on an icy field, Waterfield led the Rams to a 15-14 victory over the Washington Redskins for the NFL championship. Despite the championship, Reeves lost $50,000. Reeves, who long had been dreaming of a shift to the West Coast, had to get a place to play. He coveted the Los Angeles Memorial Coliseum. By making a deal with George Preston Marshall to play a preseason game with Marshall's Redskins for *Los Angeles Times* Charities, Reeves secured the 101,296-seat Coliseum for his home field.

1946 Reeves petitioned the other owners at the league meeting to move his franchise from Cleveland to Los Angeles. He was refused, and he vowed he would sell the club and get out of football. The other owners reconsidered, and allowed the move. The new Los Angeles Rams had to compete with the Los Angeles Dons of the AAFC. In their first year in Los Angeles, the Rams had Tom Harmon, the former Heisman Trophy winner from Michigan who had returned from the Army; Kenny Washington, the former UCLA All-America; and Woody Strode. Washington and Strode were the first black players in the NFL since 1933. They also had Gehrke at halfback, Jim Hardy as a backup quarterback, and Fred Naumetz, a center and linebacker. Waterfield led the NFL in passing, and Benton led the league receivers with 63 catches for 981 yards. The Rams finished 6-4-1 but still lost money. Chile Walsh fired his brother Adam as head coach. Then Reeves fired Chile.

1947 Reeves assumed the duties of the general manager and hired Bob Snyder as head coach, with Joe Stydahar as an assistant. Financial losses mounted and Reeves decided he needed some partners. He recruited Ed Levy, his former partner, Ed and Harold Pauley, and Hal Seley. In the process, they got one of the best bargains in sports history. For one dollar, Pauley bought 30 percent of the stock. The Rams drafted All-America halfback Herman Wedemeyer of St. Mary's (California), but he chose to play for the Dons. The preseason game with the Washington Redskins drew a pro football record 80,889 to the Coliseum. The Rams had an exciting team with Waterfield, Benton, and Washington, who led the NFL with a 7.4-yard rushing average. But they were inconsistent and matched victories over Pittsburgh and the champion Cardinals with a loss to the beleaguered Boston Yanks.

1948 Snyder resigned, and Clark Shaughnessy was named head coach, September 3. In the second game of the season, trailing the Eagles 28-0 with 16 minutes to play, Waterfield threw four touchdown passes and kicked four extra points for a 28-28 tie. The Rams lost four of their next five games before rebounding to win four of their last five. With Waterfield injured, Hardy gained a club-record 406 yards passing against the Chicago Cardinals in a 27-24 loss. Hardy completed 28 of 53 attempts. The team finished 6-5-1. Rookie receiver Tom Fears, who got a chance to play due to Benton's retirement, led the league in receiving with 51 catches for 698 yards. Linebacker Don Paul of UCLA was another prominent rookie. The Rams lost approximately $250,000. Only the new partners kept the franchise alive by helping to absorb the losses. The AAFC Dons were the top pro team in Los Angeles, averaging 41,096 spectators to fewer than 34,000 for the Rams.

1949 Reeves's scouting system, one of the most innovative in pro sports, began to produce some of its best results, and players started turning up from little-known colleges. The rookie crop included quarterback Norm Van Brocklin from Oregon; Elroy (Crazylegs) Hirsch, a back from Wisconsin who had played three seasons for the Chicago Rockets of the AAFC; and backs Verda (Vitamin T) Smith of Abilene Christian and Paul (Tank) Younger from Grambling. Shaughnessy molded them into an exciting team with a wide-open offense, and they began with six straight victories. The acquisition of Van Brocklin provided depth, but began a quarterback controversy between Waterfield and Van Brocklin, the first of many in Los Angeles. Although the Rams slumped near season's end, winning two and losing two with two ties, they hung on to win their first Western Division title since moving from Cleveland. Fears repeated as the top pass catcher in the NFL with 77 for 1,013 yards. Philadelphia, long a jinx team for the Rams, beat Los Angeles again, 14-0 in a mud-covered championship game in Los Angeles. A heavy rainstorm that had ruined the field kept the crowd to 27,980.

1950 The NFL absorbed three members of the All-America Football Conference, and the Rams were left as the only pro team in Los Angeles. Shaughnessy was fired because of "internal friction" within the organization. Stydahar, 39, became the new head coach. Stydahar appointed Hampton Pool, Mel Hein, and Howard (Red) Hickey as assistants. Another good group of rookies joined the Rams, players such as end Bob Boyd, halfback Glenn Davis, defensive back Woodley Lewis, fullback (Deacon) Dan Towler, and middle guard Stan West. The Rams ran up 70 points in one game against Baltimore and 65 in another against Detroit. Against Green Bay, Fears caught 18 passes, an NFL single-game record. With a magnificent passing attack, the Rams recorded six straight victories and finished with a 9-3 record to tie the Chicago Bears for first place. They set 22 league records, scoring 466 points and 64 touchdowns. Fears led NFL receivers for the third straight year with 84 catches for 1,116 yards and seven touchdowns. Van Brocklin led NFL passers with 127 completions in 223 attempts for a club-record 2,061 yards and 18 touchdowns. The Rams beat the Bears 24-14 in a playoff, as Fears caught three touchdown passes. In a classic league championship game, Cleveland used a field goal in the closing seconds to win 30-28 in Cleveland. Davis, the former Heisman Trophy winner at Army, raced 82 yards to a touchdown on a pass from Waterfield on the Rams' first play.

1951 With Stydahar keeping the players happy and Pool devising ways to tap the great offensive resources, the Rams continued to win. The team drafted Bud McFadin, a 245-pound tackle from Texas, number one, and also picked up Dick Daugherty, a linebacker from Oregon; Andy Robustelli, a defensive end from Arnold College; and Charley Toogood, a tackle from Nebraska. A preseason game with the Redskins drew 95,985 to the Coliseum. Towler and Younger, two big, fast backs, joined Hoerner in what was known as the "Bull Elephant" backfield. Towler weighed 225 and Younger and Hoerner 220. Each of the three averaged more than six yards per carry, with Towler finishing third in the league with 854 yards. Waterfield and Van Brocklin were still throwing passes to Hirsch and Fears. Van Brocklin passed for an NFL record 554 yards in a 54-14 win over the New York Yanks, September 28. Hirsch caught four touchdown passes from Van Brocklin against the Yanks. Later, against the Packers, he caught three scoring passes from Waterfield. He led NFL receivers with 66 catches for a record 1,495 yards, while tying Don Hutson's record of 17 touchdown receptions. Waterfield took over the NFL passing leadership from Van Brocklin with 88 completions in 176 attempts for 1,566 yards and 13 touchdowns. Van Brocklin finished second. The Rams amassed more total yards, 5,506, than any previous club in NFL history. The Rams won the division with an 8-4 record, finishing a half-game ahead of Detroit and San Francisco. In the NFL Championship Game, Los Angeles defeated Cleveland 24-17 on a 73-yard pass from Van Brocklin to Fears. Hoerner and Towler also scored on one-yard bursts, and Waterfield kicked a 17-yard field goal. It was the Rams' first NFL championship in Los Angeles.

1952 Bill Wade, a quarterback from Vanderbilt, was the bonus draft choice, but he had to go into the service for two years before joining the club. Other top rookies were guard Duane Putnam, halfback Volney (Skeet) Quinlan, and free agent defensive back Dick (Night Train) Lane, who earned a starting job and then set an NFL record with 14 interceptions. The Rams traded 11 players to the Dallas Texans, including Hoerner, for linebacker Les Richter, who then entered the Army for two years. A serious rift began to develop between Stydahar and his top assistant, Pool. After a season-opening loss to Cleveland, 37-7, Stydahar brought his problems with Pool to Reeves and when the dust had settled, Stydahar had resigned and Pool, 37, was named new head coach. The Rams lost three of their first four games. Their lone victory in that stretch was a 30-28 win over Green Bay in the third game of the season; trailing 28-6 in the last quarter, Waterfield rallied the Rams to 24 points for the victory, climaxing with a 92-yard drive in the last two minutes that took seven plays, including three Waterfield pass completions for gains of 20, 30, and 26 yards. Then the Rams won eight straight to tie the Detroit Lions for first place in the National Conference. The Rams lost 31-21 to Detroit in the playoff game. Van Brocklin led the NFL in passing by completing 113 of 205 attempts for 1,736 yards and 14 touchdowns. Towler became the first Ram to lead the NFL in rushing, with 894 yards. At the end of the season, Waterfield announced his retirement. Pete Rozelle, the sports information director at the University of San Francisco, was hired as a member of the Rams' public relations staff.

1953 Club co-owner Harold Pauley died. The number-one draft choice was Donn Moomaw, an All-America linebacker from UCLA, but he chose to go into the ministry instead of playing pro football. Rookies included Rudy Bukich, a quarterback from USC; Gene (Big Daddy) Lipscomb, a defensive tackle who had not attended college; and Harland Svare, a linebacker from Washington State. Los Angeles defeated eventual champion Detroit twice, 31-19 and 37-24. The Rams finished 8-3-1, losing three games by a total of eight points and placing third in the Western Conference. Nevertheless, the Rams still had the most explosive offense in the NFL, with Van Brocklin finishing second in the league in passing, Hirsch third in receiving, and Towler and Quinlan second and third in rushing.

1954 Wade and Richter joined the team following military service. Richter moved in to start at linebacker, while Wade backed up Van Brocklin. Amid rumors of dissension, the Rams were no longer as consistent on offense and the defense began to deteriorate. They skidded to fourth place at 6-5-1 and all of Pool's assistant coaches resigned. Van Brocklin won the NFL passing title for the third time in five years, by completing 139 of 260 passes for 2,637 yards, third-best yardage figure in NFL history. Boyd caught 53 passes for an NFL-leading 1,212 yards. Hirsch announced his retirement at the end of the season.

1955 Pool resigned. Then began a long, well-publicized search for a new Rams' coach. When the announcement finally came, January 26, many people were disappointed. Sid Gillman was the selection. Although he was well respected by football people and had been highly successful at the University of Cincinnati, the general Los Angeles public reaction was skeptical. As usual, Reeves saw that the Rams had one of the most productive drafts. The outstanding rookies were Ron Waller, a halfback from Maryland; Don Burroughs, a defensive back from Colorado State; and Larry Morris, a linebacker and the number-one draft choice from Georgia Tech. Hirsch was talked out of his retirement just before the start of the regular season. After trying him on defense, Gillman switched Waller to offense, and the rookie had an outstanding season, rushing for 716 yards and being named to the all-pro team. The Rams lost two games to the Chicago Bears, but still finished a half game in front of Chicago in the Western Conference. In the league championship game, before a record crowd of 85,693 in Los Angeles, the Rams were no match for the Cleveland Browns, losing 38-14. Cleveland intercepted seven Los Angeles passes—six from Van Brocklin. Some problems developed among the feuding Rams' owners. Reeves's old friend, Fred Levy, switched his vote, and Reeves was relieved of the directorship of the team. Deacon Dan Towler retired with a club record 3,493 yards rushing, a career average of 5.2 yards per carry.

1956 The championship game loss to Cleveland convinced Gillman to make major changes. Veterans such as Robustelli and Ed Hughes were traded for draft choices. Lipscomb was picked up by Baltimore for the $100 waiver price. Gillman soon found he was not compatible with Van Brocklin. Wade began to get more playing time. Many veterans on the club were angered over Van Brocklin's benching. The fans, disgruntled over a team that won only four games, split into Van Brocklin and Wade factions. Fears, Quinlan, and Toogood retired.

1957 McFadin, who was seriously wounded in an offseason shooting incident, retired. The Rams' owners signed a five-year operational contract and named Rozelle general manager. The club itself still was in the midst of a major rebuilding program. New faces included halfback Jon Arnett, who was the number-one draft choice from USC; George Strugar, a hulking defensive tackle from Washington State; Jesse Whittenton, a defensive back from Texas-El Paso; and Del Shofner, a defensive back from Baylor. In a game in the Coliseum, the Rams drew 102,368—a pro football record—to see a 37-24 victory over San Francisco. Van Brocklin earned back the starting job, but Gillman changed the focus of the offense to a running game that led the NFL in yards. With second-year men Tommy Wilson and Joe Marconi, veteran Younger, and Arnett pounding out yardage, the Rams pulled together to win four of their last six games for a break-even record. Hirsch retired again. When he left the field for the last time after the Rams' season-ending victory over the Colts, the fans stormed him and ripped his clothes off for souvenirs. A disgruntled Van Brocklin also announced his retirement.

1958 Van Brocklin was traded to Philadelphia in the preseason for guard Buck Lansford, defensive back Jimmy Harris, and a 1959 first-round draft pick that the Rams used to select Dick Bass. That move made Wade the number-one quarterback for Los Angeles, but as a backup the Rams drafted Frank Ryan of Rice. Gillman made other moves to improve the Rams' offense. He put Arnett in the starting backfield and shifted Shofner from defensive back to split end. A crowd of 100,470 saw the Rams defeat the Chicago Bears 41-35 on Arnett's biggest day as a Ram. He ran a screen pass from Wade for 72 yards to the Chicago 3 to set up a touchdown; returned punts for 36 and 58 yards to set up touchdowns, and ran 52 yards from scrimmage to the Bears' 4 to set up another score. He finished the day with 298 total yards, yet never scored. A crowd of 100,202 showed up as the Rams defeated Baltimore's championship-bound Colts 30-28. Wade hit Shofner on a pass play covering 92 yards against the Bears, October 19. Wade and Red Phillips combined on a 93-yard pass play against Green Bay, November 16. Wade set several team passing records, including most yardage in a season—2,875 yards, just 63 yards short of the all-time NFL single-season record for yards gained passing, set by Sammy Baugh. Wade hit 181 of 341 passes for 18 touchdowns, and the Rams improved to an 8-4 record. Shofner caught 51 passes for an NFL-high 1,097 yards, averaging 21.5 yards per catch.

1959 Rozelle traded the rights to nine players to the Chicago Cardinals for halfback Ollie Matson. Included in the Rams' package to the Cardinals were Frank Fuller, a defensive tackle, and Ken Panfil, an offensive tackle. Later, Rozelle acquired defensive end Gene Brito from Washington. The best of the draft was little (5-11, 185), tough defensive back Eddie Meador, who had been a running back at Arkansas Tech. The New York Giants defeated the Rams 23-21 in the opening game. San Francisco shut Los Angeles out the next week 34-0. The Rams lost their last eight games to finish last in the Western Conference with a 2-10 record. Matson gained 863 yards in his first season. Reeves reportedly still had confidence in his head coach, but some of the other owners didn't. Gillman and his entire staff resigned on the last day of the season.

1960 The Rams drafted Billy Cannon, the Heisman Trophy-winning halfback from LSU, number one. He also was picked number one by Houston of the new American Football League. His case went to court, which ruled he was property of the Houston club. Following the death of Commissioner Bert Bell in November, 1959, a search for a successor began—and Rozelle was the compromise selection of the owners. Reeves hired one of his all-time favorites, Hirsch, as the new general manager. Another all-time Ram, Waterfield, was named head coach; Waterfield chose his old coach, Pool, and former teammates Fears and Paul to be among his assistants. The Rams lost their first four games, and Waterfield made massive changes to try to find the right combinations for his team. Ryan replaced Wade at quarterback. Shofner was moved back to defense, and rookie Carroll Dale became the starting split end. Matson was moved to flanker, where he caught only 15 passes. The one bright spot was the overall play of Bass, who showed that he was going to be a great back. Although the Rams won four of their final six games to finish 4-7-1, there had been so much change the season still seemed to finish in a shambles.

1961 The Rams got three outstanding linemen in the draft—USC end Marlin McKeever, Notre Dame guard Joe Scibelli, and New Mexico Highlands offensive tackle Charlie Cowan. The Rams' quarterback controversy combined with the rebuilding drive in a series of complicated trades on March 2. The Rams traded Wade to the Chicago Bears for defensive back Erich Barnes and quarterback Zeke Bratkowski. Then the Rams traded Barnes and linebacker John Guzick to the New York Giants for defensive back Lindon Crow plus a first draft choice—which turned out to be North Carolina State's prized quarterback Roman Gabriel. On the field, Bratkowski eventually beat out Ryan, but neither one generated any consistent offense. They did combine with Jim (Red) Phillips often enough, however, for the fourth-year end to lead the NFL with 78 receptions. Bass teamed with Arnett to give Los Angeles a dynamic, but small, running combination. But the defense, which boasted a promising rookie defensive end named David (Deacon) Jones, Meador, Lamar Lundy, and others, had its problems and the Rams wound up 4-10, ahead of only Minnesota, the expansion team.

1962 The Rams continued rebuilding through the draft. Besides Gabriel, Los Angeles also drafted defensive tackle Merlin Olsen from Utah State and Joe Carollo, a tackle from Notre Dame. Svare, 32, replaced Paul as defensive line coach. The new, promising rookies were unable to get the job done, however, and, eight games into the season, Svare took over from Waterfield as head coach, and the Rams finished a dismal 1-12-1, the only victory 28-14 over San Francisco. Bass became the first Ram to gain 1,000 yards rushing in a season, picking up 1,033 on 196 carries. In a sealed-bid auction among Reeves, Pauley, Levy, Seley, and comedian Bob Hope, Reeves came up with the high bid of $7.1 million and reacquired control of the franchise, December 27. It cost Reeves $4.8 million to purchase the shares his partners had gotten for one dollar and a share of the liabilities.

1963 Reeves sold 49 percent interest in the Rams to Gene Autry, Bob Reynolds, Leonard Firestone, Paul A. O'Bryan, Robert Lehman, J.D. Stetson Coleman, and Joseph A. Thomas. Richter retired before the season. Defensive tackle Roosevelt Grier was obtained in a trade with the New York Giants. Torn by another quarterback controversy involving Bratkowski, Gabriel, and Terry Baker, the Heisman Trophy winner and number-one draft choice from Oregon State, the team lost its first five games. Svare installed Gabriel at quarterback and the team won five of its last nine games. A new defensive front four of Jones, Olsen, Lamar Lundy, and Grier began to make its presence felt. It became known as the Fearsome Foursome.

1964 The Rams signed a 10-year contract to play in the Coliseum's new, scaled-down stadium of 65,000 seats. Fourteen rookies made the team, including tight end Billy Truax from LSU, but the team produced the same total of wins, five. Another quarterback, Bill Munson of Utah State, entered the picture as the number-one draft choice. Munson took over when Gabriel was injured. The surprise of the season was rookie Bucky Pope, who caught 25 passes for 786 yards, an amazing 31.4-yard average, and 10 touchdowns. Another rookie, Les Josephson, spelled the sore-kneed Bass for 451 yards.

1965 After the Coliseum installed theater-type seats, Reeves cracked, "We want to be sure our fans suffer in comfort." In a trade with Minnesota, the Rams picked up Notre Dame receiver Jack Snow, the Vikings' number-one choice, for Phillips and defensive tackle Gary Larsen. The Rams won only four games, but three came in the last four games—against Green Bay's NFL champions, St. Louis, and Cleveland—with Gabriel at quarterback after Munson injured his knee. Svare was fired as coach.

1966 The merger of the NFL and AFL was consummated, but no peace came to the Rams. It took a court battle to get Chicago Bears' assistant coach George Allen released from a contract with George Halas to become the Rams' new head coach. Allen had coached with the Rams as an assistant on Gillman's staff in 1957. The top draft choice was Tom Mack, a guard from Michigan. Bob Kelley, the radio voice of the Rams since 1937 and a vital force in their success in California, died. Allen made Gabriel the number-one quarterback. With Bass rushing for 1,090 yards and Allen magically shoring up the defense, the Rams had a chance to finish second in the Western

Conference until the final game, a 27-23 loss to champion Green Bay, and finished 8-6.

1967 After five years at Chapman College, the club moved its training camp to Cal State-Fullerton. Allen, who was just the opposite of Reeves in that he put little faith in draft choices, started his policy of trading them for established veterans, including defensive tackle Roger Brown from Detroit, who took over when Grier was injured. With the defense suddenly the best in the NFL, and the offense leading the league in scoring behind Gabriel and Josephson, the Rams swept to the best record in the NFL, 11-1-2. After a 3-1-2 start, the Rams won their last eight in a row to win the new Coastal Division title. Trailing the Colts by one game with two to go, the Rams beat the Packers 27-24. Trailing 24-20 with 54 seconds to play, Tony Guillory blocked a Packers' punt and Claude Crabb returned it to the Green Bay 5. Ten seconds later, Gabriel threw the winning touchdown pass to Bernie Casey. The next week, Gabriel combined with Snow to bomb the Colts 34-10 for the title. In the first round of the playoffs, the Packers dominated the Rams 28-7, but the Rams came back to defeat Cleveland 30-6 in the Playoff Bowl.

1968 Los Angeles had another outstanding season (10-3-1), but Baltimore won 13 of 14 games to finish first in the Coastal Division. The Rams' defense set a 14-game record for fewest yards allowed, 3,118. Offensively, the Rams lost Josephson for the season with a torn Achilles tendon, but young Willie Ellison filled in well. A strong personality difference surfaced between Reeves and Allen, and Reeves fired the head coach, December 26. Rams players immediately raised an outcry in defense of Allen. A dozen players appeared with Allen in a televised press conference.

1969 Reeves called Allen and asked him to come back as coach, January 1. Allen did not give an answer immediately. Then, at a press conference, Reeves announced that Allen had been retained as coach, January 6. Hirsch left his job as assistant to Reeves to become athletic director at his alma mater, Wisconsin. He was replaced by Jack Teele. John Sanders became assistant general manager. The Rams had three draft choices on the first round and they used them to pick running back Larry Smith from Florida, wide receiver Jim Seymour from Notre Dame, and tight end Bob Klein from USC. Behind the always-strong defense; the short passing game of Gabriel throwing to Snow, Truax, and Wendell Tucker; and a running attack led by Josephson and Smith, the Rams won their first 11 games, including victories over the Colts and Cowboys. The streak ended at the Coliseum when Minnesota scored a 20-13 victory, which was the first game of a three-game losing streak. Minnesota defeated the Rams 23-20 in the Western Conference title game in Bloomington, overcoming the Rams' 17-7 lead. The Rams bounced back in the Playoff Bowl, whipping the Cowboys 31-0. Gabriel was named the league's most valuable player. He completed 217 of 399 passes for 2,549 yards and 24 touchdowns. He set Rams records for both attempts and completions. Bass retired with 5,417 yards, tops in team history.

1970 The Rams picked a linebacker, Jack Reynolds from Tennessee, number one in the draft. They also got center Rich Saul of Michigan State. The Rams compiled a 9-4-1 record, good for second place in the new NFC Western Division. The team drew a record 904,979 for 14 regular-season games. At the end of the season, it was announced that George Allen's contract would not be renewed. Allen had lasted five years, tying him with Sid Gillman for the Rams' longevity record. Allen's teams had gone 51-19-4.

1971 Tommy Prothro, head coach of UCLA, was named the new Rams coach. Dan Reeves died of cancer in New York, April 15. William A. Barnes, Reeves's long-time friend and business associate, became president and general manager. Prothro made a trade with George Allen, who had become coach of the Washington Redskins. Prothro sent linebackers Jack Pardee, Myron Pottios, and Maxie Baughan, and defensive tackle Diron Talbert to Washington for linebacker Marlin McKeever and a host of draft choices. The Rams used one of the draft choices to choose Isiah Robertson, a linebacker from Southern. The Rams also drafted Jack Youngblood, a defensive end from Florida, and Dave Elmendorf, a defensive back from Texas A&M. The Rams traded for Lance Rentzel, a controversial wide receiver from Dallas, and Travis Williams, a running back-kick returner from Green Bay. Faced with one of the toughest schedules in the league, the Rams went 8-5-1 and finished second to San Francisco in the NFC West. The Rams lost to George Allen and the Redskins 38-24 in a Monday night game. The star of the season was Ellison, who set an NFL record with 247 yards rushing against New Orleans, December 5. For the season, he gained an even 1,000 yards.

1972 Robert Irsay, a Chicago-based industrialist, purchased the Rams from the Reeves estate for $19 million. Irsay then traded the franchise to Carroll Rosenbloom in exchange for the Baltimore Colts and $3 million. Rosenbloom named Don Klosterman as executive vice president and general manager and moved the training camp from Fullerton to Long Beach State. The Rams drafted Jim Bertelsen, a running back from Texas, on the second round, and Lawrence McCutcheon, a running back from Colorado State, on the third. Larry Brooks, a defensive tackle from Virginia State, came on the fourteenth round. Fred Dryer, a defensive end, was obtained in a trade with New England. The season was marred by injuries, particularly a mysterious ailment in Gabriel's right arm. The Rams were in contention in the first half of the season, then lost five of their last six and finished 6-7-1. Prothro and his coaching staff were dismissed.

1973 Chuck Knox, a Detroit Lions' assistant, was named head coach. The team returned to the colorful blue and gold uniforms of the 1950s after years of playing in blue and white. Klosterman traded defensive tackle Coy Bacon and running back Bob Thomas to San Diego for quarterback John Hadl. Ron Jaworski, a quick, strong-armed quarterback from Youngstown State, was drafted on the second round. Hadl moved in as the Rams' offensive leader and Gabriel asked to be traded. Gabriel was traded to Philadelphia for wide receiver Harold Jackson, plus first-round draft picks in 1974 and 1975. After a year in Long Beach, the team switched back to Cal State-Fullerton for training. The Rams won 12 of 14 games, the most victories in the team's history. Dallas upset the Rams 27-16 in the divisional playoffs. Hadl was named the NFC's most valuable player, and Knox was chosen coach of the year. In his first year on the active team, after a season on the taxi squad, McCutcheon gained 1,097 yards (a team record) and led the NFL with a 5.2-yard average per carry. McCutcheon and Bertelsen both were selected to the Pro Bowl, as were Jackson (who had 13 touchdown receptions), Hadl, and Mack on offense and Olsen, Robertson, and Youngblood on defense.

1974 Rosenbloom's son Steve was named assistant to the president. John Cappelletti, the Heisman Trophy-winning running back from Penn State, was selected in the first round of the draft. Hadl was traded to Green Bay after the Rams began the year with a 3-2 record, and Los Angeles got five draft choices in return. Backup quarterback James Harris helped the Rams to a 10-4 record and another division title. Harris was the first black player to quarterback a pro team to a championship. But the Rams were ousted once again in the playoffs. They beat Washington 19-10 in the divisional playoff, the Rams' first playoff victory since the 1951 championship. Then they lost 14-10 to Minnesota in the NFC title game at Minnesota. McCutcheon set a Rams' single-season rushing record by leading the conference with 1,109 yards on 236 carries. Harris was selected to the Pro Bowl as an alternate, then threw two touchdown passes and was named the game's most valuable player.

1975 The Rams had three first-round choices in the draft and they used them to select Mike Fanning, a defensive tackle from Notre Dame; Dennis Harrah, a guard from Miami; and Doug France, a tackle from Ohio State. The Rams lost 18-7 to Dallas in the opener, and then won six in a row. After a 24-23 loss to San Francisco, the Rams won six straight to close the regular season. Harris injured his shoulder in a late game against New Orleans, and Ron Jaworski took over to lead victories over Green Bay and defending Super Bowl champion Pittsburgh. Led by the front four of Olsen, Youngblood, Larry Brooks (who was forced out with a knee injury the last six games), and Dryer, the Rams allowed the second-fewest number of points, 135, in NFL history over a 14-game season. The Rams defeated St. Louis 35-23 in a divisional playoff game with Jaworski again filling in for Harris. McCutcheon broke an NFC playoff record with 202 yards on 37 carries. Dallas hammered the Rams 37-7 in the NFC Championship Game. Scibelli, Cowan, and Snow retired.

1976 Knox was given a five-year contract. Then Knox was presented with that age-old problem for Rams head coaches: a quarterback controversy. Harris won the job in the preseason, then was injured before the first game. Jaworski led the opening victory over Atlanta, but he, too, was injured. In the second game of the year, rookie quarterback Pat Haden—a product of USC, a former starter for the Southern California Sun of the WFL, and a local favorite—led the Rams to a 10-10 tie with Minnesota while outplaying Fran Tarkenton. When Harris returned, the position looked like a revolving door, with all three playing. Against Miami, Harris produced the Rams' best single-game passing day in 25 years, completing 17 of 29 passes for 436 yards. But then he was sacked mercilessly in a Monday night loss to Cincinnati, and Knox decided to go the last five games with Haden. Four of them were victories, and the Rams won their fourth consecutive championship. Ironically, Harris finished as the NFC's leading passer. McCutcheon broke his own record by rushing for 1,168 yards. Los Angeles edged Dallas 14-12 in the first round of the playoffs. But there was frustration again in Minnesota. On their first drive in the NFC Championship Game, the Rams stalled inside the Vikings' 1-yard line and elected to allow Tom Dempsey to try a field goal. It was blocked and returned for a 90-yard touchdown by the Vikings' Bobby Bryant. The Vikings went on to score a 24-13 victory. Olsen, perhaps the best defensive lineman of all time, retired.

1977 Knox refuted rumors that he would accept the head coaching job in Detroit and announced his intention to remain in Los Angeles for the duration of his contract. Jaworski, who had played out his option, was traded to Philadelphia for tight end Charle Young. An extraordinary draft reaped linebacker Bob Brudzinski, safety Nolan Cromwell, wide receiver Billy Waddy, running back Wendell Tyler, and quarterback Vince Ferragamo. On May 12, the club announced the signing of Joe Namath, the former New York Jets quarterback. Namath led the Rams to two wins in the first three weeks, but in a Monday night game against Chicago he completed only 16 of 40 passes with four interceptions before being forced out with injuries. The Rams lost 24-23. Haden became the starter for the rest of the season. The club rolled to eight victories in the next nine weeks behind Haden and McCutcheon, who rushed for 1,238 yards to establish a team record of 5,523 yards in a career. A 20-14 victory over Oakland on December 4 clinched their fifth-straight NFC West title. On December 26, the Rams lost to Minnesota 14-7 in an NFC Divisional Playoff Game in a rare rain-and-mud game in the Coliseum.

1978 Knox resigned to become head coach of the Buffalo Bills. A coaching merry-go-round began when Rosenbloom hired George Allen to return to Los Angeles. After two preseason losses, Allen was released and replaced by Ray Malavasi, a Rams assistant coach since 1973. All-pro cornerback Monte Jackson, unhappy with the Rams, was traded to Oakland before the season. The Rams opened the year with seven consecutive victories, then slumped offensively in losses to New Orleans and Atlanta. But the team regrouped and won five of its last seven games for a 12-4 record and its sixth straight NFC West title. Haden, in his first full year as a starter, set team records for pass attempts (444), completions (229), and yardage (2,995). During the season, the club announced its move to Anaheim, scheduled to take place after the 1979 season. On December 31 in an NFC Divisional Playoff Game, the Rams trounced longtime nemesis Minnesota 34-10, outscoring the Vikings 24-0 in the second half. In the NFC Championship Game on January 7, the Rams lost to Dallas 28-0 after a scoreless tie at halftime. The Rams were hampered by the absence of McCutcheon and injuries to fullback John Cappelletti and Haden.

1979 On April 2, Rosenbloom drowned while swimming off the Florida coast; his widow Georgia became majority owner of the team. Rosenbloom's son Steve was named executive vice president in charge of day-to-day operations, but soon was replaced by Don Klosterman and left the organization. The club's administrative offices were moved to Rams Park in Anaheim. Mack, who played in eight AFC-NFC Pro Bowls, retired before the season. The team lost its opener to Oakland, then improved its record to 4-2. But a devastating string of injuries took its toll and the Rams lost four games in five weeks. Despite the injuries, the defense turned in a powerful performance on November 4, holding Seattle to minus seven yards in a 24-0 victory. Haden set a club record by completing 13 consecutive passes against the Seahawks, but was lost for the year with a broken finger. With Ferragamo at quarterback, the Rams won four straight to clinch their seventh-straight NFC West title with a 9-7 record. On December 30, Ferragamo threw three touchdown passes, the last with 2:06 left, and the Rams defeated the Cowboys in an NFC Divisional Playoff Game 21-19. In the NFC Championship Game January 6, the Rams earned their first trip to the Super Bowl with a 9-0 shutout of Tampa Bay. Jack Youngblood played with a broken leg, a feat he would duplicate in the Super Bowl and Pro Bowl. On January 20, the Rams lost to Pittsburgh 31-19 in Super Bowl XIV, as the Steelers came from behind in the fourth quarter.

1980 The Rams drafted two-time All-America defensive back Johnnie Johnson of Texas in the first round of the draft. Tyler injured his hip in an automobile accident in the offseason and missed 12 games. Brooks, Brudzinski, Harrah, and Youngblood staged holdouts during training camp. The four players rejoined the team for the regular season, but Brudzinski walked out for good in midseason. The quarterback controversy now involved Haden and Ferragamo and wasn't resolved until Haden, who had won the job in the preseason, was injured in the opener and knocked out for the year. Ferragamo led the offense, setting records for completions (240), yards (3,199), and touchdowns (30). He quarterbacked the Rams to an 11-5 record, good for second place in the NFC West. Cromwell was named the NFC's defensive player of the year. The season ended on a disappointing note when the Rams were routed 34-13 by Dallas in the NFC Wild Card Game.

1981 Brudzinski was traded to Miami, Reynolds signed with San Francisco, and Dryer was released. The offense also was hurt by the loss of Ferragamo, who signed with Montreal of the Canadian Football League. A four-game winning streak early in the season pushed the Rams into first place with a 4-2 record. A key figure was Jeff Rutledge, who replaced Haden to lead victories over Green Bay and Atlanta. LeRoy Irvin also played a vital role in a 37-35 victory over the Falcons on October 11, when he returned two punts for touchdowns and set an NFL record for punt-return yardage in a game (207). But injuries to Haden and Rutledge contributed to a collapse that resulted in seven losses in the next eight games, and the Rams ended the season with Dan Pastorini, a free-agent acquisition, at quarterback. One of the few bright spots in the 6-10 season was Tyler, who came back from the previous season's injuries to lead the NFC with 17 touchdowns.

1982 On draft day, the Rams obtained quarterback Bert Jones from Baltimore. Haden retired, and Ferragamo rejoined the team. The Rams lost their first three games in the strike-shortened season. Jones led his first and last victory as a Ram in a 20-14 win over Kansas City, in which Tyler rushed for 138 yards and two touchdowns. A neck injury ended Jones's career, and he was replaced by Ferragamo, who finished the season with 1,609 yards in only five starts. Against the Bears, he passed for 509 yards, the second-most in NFL history, but the Rams still lost 34-26. Ferragamo had the Rams ahead of the Raiders until Marcus Allen scored with 29 seconds left for a 37-31 win. In the season finale, the Rams finally got their second victory of the year when Ivory Sully blocked a San Francisco field-goal attempt in the last two minutes to preserve a 21-20 lead. Tyler led the team in both rushing (564 yards) and receiving (38 catches), while topping the NFC with 13 touchdowns and 78 points. Following the season, Malavasi was fired.

1983 In February, John Robinson, the popular former coach at USC, was named head coach. The Rams traded Tyler to San Francisco, and, with the second selection in the draft, the Rams chose SMU running back Eric Dickerson, whom Robinson installed in his new one-back offense. Robinson's revamped 3-4 defense shut down the Giants 16-6 in the opener. Then Dickerson began to assert himself, scoring three touchdowns as the Rams beat the Saints 30-27. Against the Jets and the Lions, Dickerson put together back-to-back games with 192 and 199 yards rushing. The Rams ran neck and neck with the 49ers for the division lead most of the season, and even took over first place on November 27 with a 41-17 victory over Buffalo in which Ferragamo threw three touchdown passes. Losses to Philadelphia and New England gave the lead back to the 49ers, but the Rams still qualified for a wild card berth. Dickerson finished the season leading the league in rushing with a rookie record 1,808 yards, while Ferragamo set a club record with 3,276 yards passing. Ferragamo threw three touchdown passes to beat Dallas 24-17 in the NFC Wild Card Game, but the next week, the Rams were dismantled 51-7 by Washington.

1984 Ferragamo got off to a miserable start in a 20-13 loss to Dallas. A hand injury sidelined him two weeks later, and he never returned, being replaced by young Jeff Kemp. With the inexperienced Kemp running the team, the Rams turned more than ever to their ground game, and Dickerson responded, running for more than 100 yards a record 12 times, including 208 and 215 yards in victories over St. Louis and Houston. In the Houston game, on December 9, Dickerson broke O.J. Simpson's single-season rushing record of 2,003 yards. He finished the season with 2,105 yards; the Rams finished 10-6 and in second place in the NFC West. In the NFC Wild Card Game, the Rams hosted the first playoff game ever in Anaheim Stadium, but the Giants won 16-13.

1985 In the offseason, the Rams signed Dieter Brock, the Canadian Football League's all-time passer. Youngblood, who had set a club record for most consecutive games played (201), retired. Ferragamo was traded to Buffalo. Dickerson staged a holdout that didn't end until the third week of the season. The Rams won their first two games behind the running of Charles White, who had joined the club as a free agent. Then Dickerson returned and ran for 150 yards and three touchdowns on Monday night, as the Rams beat Seattle 35-24. Despite the fact that neither Brock nor Dickerson was consistently effective, the Rams extended their winning streak to seven games before being brought to earth by San Francisco, 28-14. Three losses in four games dropped the Rams to only a one-game lead over San Francisco, but on December 9, the Rams scored touchdowns on a kickoff return by Ron Brown and an interception return by Gary Green to beat the 49ers and virtually lock up the division title they won at 11-5. Dickerson finished the season with 1,234 yards, Brock ended up third in the NFC in passing, and Henry Ellard became the leading punt returner in NFL history. In an NFC Divisional Playoff Game, Dickerson ran for a record 248 yards, and the Rams beat the Cowboys 20-0. In the NFC Championship Game, the Rams were stopped by the Bears 24-0.

MEMBERS OF HALL OF FAME:
Tom Fears, Bill George, Sid Gillman, Elroy (Crazylegs) Hirsch, David (Deacon) Jones, Dick (Night Train) Lane, Ollie Matson, Joe Namath, Merlin Olsen, Dan Reeves, Andy Robustelli, Norm Van Brocklin, Bob Waterfield

RAMS RECORD, 1937-85

Year	Won	Lost	Tied	Pct.	Fin.	Pts.	OP
Cleveland Rams							
1937	1	10	0	.091	5	75	207
1938	4	7	0	.364	4	131	215
1939	5	5	1	.500	4	195	164
1940	4	6	1	.400	4	171	191
1941	2	9	0	.182	5	116	244
1942	5	6	0	.455	3	150	207
1943	The Rams suspended operations						
1944	4	6	0	.400	4	188	224
1945a	9	1	0	.900	1	244	136
Los Angeles Rams							
1946	6	4	1	.600	2	277	257
1947	6	6	0	.500	4	259	214
1948	6	5	1	.545	3	327	269
1949b	8	2	2	.800	1	360	239
1950c	9	3	0	.750	1	466	309
1951a	8	4	0	.667	1	392	261
1952d	9	3	0	.750	2	349	234
1953	8	3	1	.727	3	366	236
1954	6	5	1	.545	4	314	285
1955e	8	3	1	.727	1	260	231
1956	4	8	0	.333	5t	291	307
1957	6	6	0	.500	4	307	278
1958	8	4	0	.667	2t	344	278
1959	2	10	0	.167	6	242	315
1960	4	7	1	.364	6	265	297
1961	4	10	0	.286	6	263	333
1962	1	12	1	.077	7	220	334
1963	5	9	0	.357	6	210	350
1964	5	7	2	.417	5	283	339
1965	4	10	0	.286	7	269	328
1966	8	6	0	.571	3	289	212
1967f	11	1	2	.917	1	398	196
1968	10	3	1	.769	2	312	200
1969f	11	3	0	.786	1	320	243
1970	9	4	1	.692	2	325	202
1971	8	5	1	.615	2	313	260
1972	6	7	1	.464	3	291	286
1973g	12	2	0	.857	1	388	178
1974h	10	4	0	.714	1	263	181
1975h	12	2	0	.857	1	312	135
1976h	10	3	1	.750	1	351	190
1977g	10	4	0	.714	1	302	146
1978h	12	4	0	.750	1	316	245

Year	Won	Lost	Tied	Pct.	Fin.	Pts.	OP
1979i	9	7	0	.563	1	323	309
1980j	11	5	0	.688	2	424	289
1981	6	10	0	.375	3	303	351
1982	2	7	0	.222	14	200	250
1983k	9	7	0	.563	2	361	344
1984j	10	6	0	.625	2	346	316
1985h	11	5	0	.688	1	340	277
48 Years	338	267	20	.557		13,811	12,092

aNFL Champion; 1-0 in Playoffs
bNFL Western Division Champion; 0-1 in Playoffs
cNFL National Conference Champion; 1-1 in Playoffs
dNFL National Conference Runnerup; 0-1 in Playoffs
eNFL Western Conference Champion; 0-1 in Playoffs
fNFL Coastal Division Champion; 1-1 in Playoffs
gNFC Western Division Champion; 0-1 in Playoffs
hNFC Western Division Champion; 1-1 in Playoffs
iNFC Champion; 2-1 in Playoffs
jNFC Wild Card Qualifier for Playoffs; 0-1 in Playoffs
kNFC Wild Card Qualifier for Playoffs; 1-1 in Playoffs

RECORD HOLDERS

CAREER

Rushing attempts	Lawrence McCutcheon, 1973-79	1,435
Rushing yards	Lawrence McCutcheon, 1973-79	6,186
Pass attempts	Roman Gabriel, 1962-72	3,313
Pass completions	Roman Gabriel, 1962-72	1,705
Passing yards	Roman Gabriel, 1962-72	22,223
Touchdown passes	Roman Gabriel, 1962-72	154
Receptions	Tom Fears, 1948-56	400
Receiving yards	Elroy (Crazylegs) Hirsch, 1949-57	6,289
Interceptions	Eddie Meador, 1959-70	46
Punting average	Danny Villanueva, 1960-64	44.2
Punt return avg.	Henry Ellard, 1983-85	13.5
Kickoff return avg.	Ron Brown, 1984-85	27.4
Field goals	Bruce Gossett, 1964-69	120
Touchdowns	Elroy (Crazylegs) Hirsch, 1949-57	55
Points	Bob Waterfield, 1946-52	573

SEASON

Rushing attempts	Eric Dickerson, 1983	390
Rushing yards	Eric Dickerson, 1984	2,105
Pass attempts	Vince Ferragamo, 1983	464
Pass completions	Vince Ferragamo, 1983	274
Passing yards	Vince Ferragamo, 1983	3,276
Touchdown passes	Vince Ferragamo, 1980	30
Receptions	Tom Fears, 1950	84
Receiving yards	Elroy (Crazylegs) Hirsch, 1951	1,425
Interceptions	Dick (Night Train) Lane, 1952	14
Punting average	Danny Villanueva, 1962	45.5
Punt return avg.	Woodley Lewis, 1952	18.5
Kickoff return avg.	Verda (Vitamin T) Smith, 1950	33.7
Field goals	David Ray, 1973	30
Touchdowns	Eric Dickerson, 1983	20
Points	David Ray, 1973	130

GAME

Rushing attempts	Charles White, 9-15-85	36
Rushing yards	Willie Ellison, 12-5-71	247
Pass attempts	Jim Hardy, 10-31-48	53
Pass completions	Dieter Brock, 10-27-85	35
Passing yards	Norm Van Brocklin, 9-28-51	554
Touchdown passes	6 times	5
Receptions	Tom Fears, 12-3-50	18
Receiving yards	Jim Benton, 11-22-45	303
Interceptions	15 times	3
Field goals	Bob Waterfield, 12-9-51	5
Touchdowns	Bob Shaw, 12-11-49	4
	Elroy (Crazylegs) Hirsch, 9-28-51	4
	Harold Jackson, 10-14-73	4
Points	Bob Shaw, 12-11-49	24
	Elroy (Crazylegs) Hirsch, 9-28-51	24
	Harold Jackson, 10-14-73	24

COACHING HISTORY

1937-38	Hugo Bezdek*	1-13-0
1938	Art Lewis	4- 4-0
1939-42	Earl (Dutch) Clark	16-26-2
1943	The Rams suspended operations	
1944	Aldo (Buff) Donelli	4- 6-0
1945-46	Adam Walsh	16- 5-1
1947	Bob Snyder	6- 6-0
1948-49	Clark Shaughnessy	14- 8-3
1950-52	Joe Stydahar**	19- 9-0
1952-54	Hampton Pool	23-11-2
1955-59	Sid Gillman	28-32-1
1960-62	Bob Waterfield***	9-24-1
1962-65	Harland Svare	14-31-3
1966-70	George Allen	51-19-4
1971-72	Tommy Prothro	14-12-2
1973-77	Chuck Knox	57-20-1
1978-82	Ray Malavasi	43-36-0
1983-85	John Robinson	32-21-0

**Replaced after three games in 1938*
***Resigned after one game in 1952*
****Resigned after eight games in 1962*

FIRST PLAYER SELECTED

1937	Johnny Drake, HB, Purdue
1938	Corbett Davis, HB, Indiana
1939	Parker Hall, HB, Mississippi
1940	Ollie Cordill, HB, Rice
1941	Rudy Mucha, C, Washington
1942	Jack Wilson, HB, Baylor
1943	Mike Holovak, HB, Boston College
1944	Tony Butkovich, FB, Illinois
1945	Elroy (Crazylegs) Hirsch, HB, Wisconsin
1946	Emil Sitko, HB, Notre Dame
1947	Herman Wedemeyer, HB, St. Mary's (California)
1948	(2) Tom Keane, HB, West Virginia
1949	Bobby Thomason, QB, Virginia Military
1950	Ralph Pasquariello, FB, Villanova
1951	Bud McFadin, G, Texas
1952	Bill Wade, QB, Vanderbilt
1953	Donn Moomaw, LB, UCLA
1954	Ed Beatty, C, Mississippi
1955	Larry Morris, C, Georgia Tech
1956	Joe Marconi, FB, West Virginia
1957	Jon Arnett, HB, USC
1958	Lou Michaels, T, Kentucky
1959	Dick Bass, HB, Pacific
1960	Billy Cannon, HB, LSU
1961	Marlin McKeever, LB, USC
1962	Roman Gabriel, QB, North Carolina State
1963	Terry Baker, QB, Oregon State
1964	Bill Munson, QB, Utah State
1965	Clancy Williams, HB, Washington State
1966	Tom Mack, G, Michigan
1967	(2) Willie Ellison, HB, Texas Southern
1968	(2) Gary Beban, QB, UCLA
1969	Larry Smith, RB, Florida
1970	Jack Reynolds, LB, Tennessee
1971	Isiah Robertson, LB, Southern
1972	(2) Jim Bertelsen, RB, Texas
1973	(2) Cullen Bryant, DB, Colorado
1974	John Cappelletti, RB, Penn State
1975	Mike Fanning, DT, Notre Dame
1976	Kevin McLain, LB, Colorado State
1977	Bob Brudzinski, LB, Ohio State
1978	Elvis Peacock, RB, Oklahoma
1979	George Andrews, LB, Nebraska
1980	Johnnie Johnson, S, Texas
1981	Mel Owens, LB, Michigan
1982	Barry Redden, RB, Richmond
1983	Eric Dickerson, RB, SMU
1984	(5) Hal Stephens, DE, East Carolina
1984*	William Fuller, DE, North Carolina
1985	Jerry Gray, DB, Texas
1986	Mike Schad, T, Queen's

**Supplemental Draft*

DANIEL F. REEVES MEMORIAL AWARD

(Rams Most Valuable Player)

1969	Roman Gabriel, QB
1970	Merlin Olsen, DT
1971	Marlin McKeever, TE
1972	Merlin Olsen, DT
1973	John Hadl, QB
1974	Lawrence McCutcheon, RB
1975	Jack Youngblood, DE
1976	Jack Youngblood, DE
1977	Lawrence McCutcheon, RB
1978	Jim Youngblood, LB
1979	Jack Youngblood, DE
1980	Vince Ferragamo, QB
1981	Nolan Cromwell, S
1982	Vince Ferragamo, QB
1983	Eric Dickerson, RB
1984	Eric Dickerson, RB
1985	LeRoy Irvin, CB

RAMS ALL-TIME TEAM (1985)

OFFENSE

WR	Elroy (Crazylegs) Hirsch, 1949-57
WR	Tom Fears, 1948-56
TE	Bob Klein, 1969-76
OL	Tom Mack, 1966-78
OL	Charlie Cowan, 1961-75
OL	Joe Scibelli, 1961-75
OL	Dennis Harrah, 1975-85
C	Rich Saul, 1970-81
QB	Bob Waterfield, 1945-52
RB	Eric Dickerson, 1983-85
RB	Dick Bass, 1960-69
RB	Lawrence McCutcheon, 1972-79
K	Bob Waterfield, 1945-52

DEFENSE

DE	David (Deacon) Jones, 1961-71
DE	Jack Youngblood, 1971-84
DT	Merlin Olsen, 1962-76
DT	Roosevelt Grier, 1963-66
LB	Jack Reynolds, 1970-80
LB	Jack Pardee, 1957-64, 1966-70
LB	Les Richter, 1954-62
DB	Nolan Cromwell, 1977-85
DB	Eddie Meador, 1959-70
DB	Dave Elmendorf, 1971-79
DB	Dick (Night Train) Lane, 1952-53
P	Bob Waterfield, 1945-52
PR	LeRoy Irvin, 1980-85
KR	Jon Arnett, 1957-63

MIAMI DOLPHINS

1965 Joseph Robbie, a Minneapolis lawyer who owned a house in Miami, met AFL Commissioner Joe Foss in Washington, March 3. Robbie, a former classmate of Foss's at the University of South Dakota, was representing a friend who sought an AFL expansion franchise for Philadelphia. Foss rejected Philadelphia as a site, noting the Eagles had exclusive rights to Franklin Field. Foss suggested Robbie apply for the franchise in Miami. "With the population growth and climate, it'll be the best franchise in the league," Foss said. Seeking financial backing, Robbie went to entertainer Danny Thomas, a co-worker on the board of St. Jude's Hospital. Thomas, who earlier sought to buy the Chicago White Sox, agreed to become a partner. Thanks to the influence of United States Vice President Hubert Humphrey, Robbie's friend from Minnesota, Miami Mayor Robert King High agreed to invite the AFL to Miami, with the assurance that the team could play in the Orange Bowl. The AFL Executive Committee voted to expand in 1966 at a meeting in Monmouth Park, New Jersey, June 7. The league awarded its first expansion franchise to Robbie and Thomas for $7.5 million, August 16. Joe Thomas of the Minnesota Vikings was named director of player personnel, September 21. Mrs. Robert Swanson of West Miami won two lifetime passes in a contest to pick a team nickname. Her suggestion, Dolphins, was chosen from more than 20,000 entries. In the first round of the draft, the Dolphins selected Illinois fullback Jim Grabowski and Kentucky quarterback Rick Norton.

1966 In the expansion draft, Miami picked 31 players. The player selected fourteenth, tackle Norm Evans of the Houston Oilers, was destined to be a 10-year regular with the Dolphins. George Wilson was hired as head coach, January 29. Wilson had coached the Detroit Lions for eight seasons. The Dolphins opened their first training camp with 83 players in St. Petersburg, Florida, July 5. Grumbling began immediately as the players complained about the gravel practice field and the dormitory that was next to Sea World. "We couldn't sleep," Evans said. "The seals kept barking all night." The Dolphins' first preseason game was a 38-10 loss to San Diego, August 5, and Wilson accused Chargers coach Sid Gillman of running up the score. Training camp was moved to St. Andrews School in Boca Raton, Florida, August 7. A crowd of 36,366 fans came to the Orange Bowl to see the Dolphins lose to Kansas City 33-0. The Dolphins opened the regular season at the Orange Bowl against Oakland, September 2. Joe Auer thrilled the 26,776 fans by returning the opening kickoff 95 yards for a touchdown. The Raiders rallied to win 23-14. When injuries sidelined Norton and Dick Wood, Wilson installed his son, George, Jr., at quarterback. Wilson led the Dolphins to their first AFL victory, passing 67 yards to Billy Joe for a touchdown in a 24-7 win over Denver, October 16. The following week, Wilson injured his shoulder in a 20-13 win at Houston, and his father signed John Stofa from a semipro league in Lakeland, Florida, to finish the season at quarterback. Stofa threw four touchdown passes, one to Auer with 38 seconds left, to give the Miami team its third victory, a 29-28 surprise of Houston, December 18.

1967 It was a year of reorganization—on the field and in the front office. W.H. Keland of Racine, Wisconsin, purchased the interests of Martin Decker, George Hamid, Sr., and George Hamid, Jr., March 23. Robbie and Keland bought out Danny Thomas, June 1. In the first round of the first AFL-NFL draft, Miami drafted Purdue quarterback Bob Griese. Joe

Thomas completed a seven-man trade, acquiring halfback Abner Haynes from Denver. In the regular-season opener against Denver, Stofa broke his ankle, leaving Griese to run the offense. Haynes rushed for 151 yards in the 35-21 Miami victory. Hard times followed as the Dolphins lost their next eight, scoring just seven touchdowns. They ended the losing streak by beating Buffalo 17-14 on a fourth-down, 31-yard touchdown pass from Griese to Howard Twilley, November 26. The Dolphins defeated San Diego 41-24 and Boston 41-32 and lost to Houston 41-10 to close out their schedule. Cornerback Dick Westmoreland intercepted his AFL-leading tenth pass of the season against the Patriots. Griese finished the season fifth among AFL passers.

1968 The draft brought a fresh supply of talent to Miami. Thomas selected running backs Larry Csonka and Jim Kiick, tackle Doug Crusan, and safety Dick Anderson. All were starters in 1968. The Dolphins won their first interleague victory, beating the Eagles 23-7 in a preseason game, August 17. Two weeks later, Griese's favorite receiver, Jack Clancy, suffered a broken leg in a 22-13 loss to Baltimore. In the regular season, Miami recovered from a 0-3 start to win five games. Griese set club passing records of 2,473 yards, 186 completions, and 21 touchdowns.

1969 Thomas continued to upgrade Miami's personnel, drafting defensive linemen Bill Stanfill and Bob Heinz, running back Eugene (Mercury) Morris, and cornerback Lloyd Mumphord and trading for linebacker Nick Buoniconti and guard Larry Little. In all, 20 players missed seven games or more due to injury. Robbie became the Dolphins' majority owner when he purchased the interests of Keland with five other Miami businessmen. Griese passed for four touchdowns in a 34-31 loss to the New York Jets, November 2. One week later, Griese injured his right knee in a Boston downpour and missed the final five games. Wracked by injuries, the Dolphins slipped back into last place (3-10-1) and Wilson was relieved of his coaching duties.

1970 A new era began for the Dolphins when 40-year-old Don Shula left Baltimore to become head coach and vice president, February 18. Commissioner Pete Rozelle ordered Miami to give Baltimore its first-round draft pick in 1971 as compensation. "I'm not a miracle worker," Shula said. "I have no magic formulas. The only way I know is hard work." Shula put the Dolphins through a grueling training camp at Biscayne College in North Miami. The regimen paid off as the Dolphins won four straight preseason games and four of their first five league games. On October 3, Miami beat Oakland for the first time, 20-13, as newly acquired receiver Paul Warfield caught two touchdown passes. One week later, the Dolphins scored their first victory over the New York Jets, 20-6. The Dolphins went into a brief tailspin, losing three in a row, before closing the season with six consecutive wins. They avenged a 35-0 loss by beating Baltimore 34-17 as rookie safety Jake Scott scored on a 77-yard punt return. The Dolphins beat Buffalo 45-7 to clinch the AFC wild card spot, December 20. The Dolphins lost their first playoff game, 21-14 to the Raiders.

1971 Miami got off to a slow start, tying Denver and losing to the New York Jets. Angered, Shula cracked down on his players and they responded. The Dolphins won eight in a row, including Miami's first shutout ever, a 34-0 romp over Buffalo, November 7. Griese had matured into a poised pro quarterback. In a 41-3 win over New England, Griese set a record by throwing three consecutive passes for touchdowns. He rallied Miami from a 21-3 deficit to a 24-21 victory over Pittsburgh, November 14. The Dolphins clinched first place in the AFC Eastern Division on the final day of the season, beating Green Bay 27-6 before a record crowd of 74,215 at the Orange Bowl, December 19. Csonka became the club's first 1,000-yard rusher with 1,051 yards, placekicker Garo Yepremian led the NFL with 117 points, and Griese led the AFC in passing. The Dolphins won the longest game in NFL history (82 minutes, 40 seconds) as Yepremian kicked a 37-yard field goal in the second overtime to beat Kansas City 27-24 in an AFC Divisional Playoff Game, December 25. Miami dethroned the Colts, the defending champions, in the AFC title game 21-0. It was the first shutout against the Colts in 97 games. The Dolphins fell to Dallas 24-3 in Super Bowl VI, January 16.

1972 Joe Thomas left the Dolphins' front office. The Dolphins became the first team in NFL history to go through an entire season, including postseason games, unbeaten and untied. They opened the year with a 20-10 win over Kansas City, September 17. Griese hit Jim Mandich with a last-minute touchdown pass to upset the Vikings in Minnesota 16-14, October 1. Two weeks later, Griese suffered a broken right leg and dislocated ankle when he was hit by San Diego's Ron East. He was replaced by Earl Morrall, a 38-year-old backup quarterback who had been claimed on waivers from Baltimore. Yepremian kicked the longest field goal of his career (54 yards) to beat Buffalo 24-23 in the Orange Bowl. Shula became the first NFL coach to win 100 games in 10 seasons as Miami crushed New England with 501 yards 52-0. The Dolphins closed the regular season with a 16-0 win over Baltimore. Csonka and Morris each rushed for 1,000 yards as Miami set a league rushing record, 2,960 yards. Miami slipped past Cleveland 20-14 in an AFC Divisional Playoff Game, December 23. Griese came off the bench in the second half to spark the Dolphins to a 21-17 win over Pittsburgh in the AFC Championship Game, December 31. Miami capped its perfect season in Super Bowl VII at Los Angeles, defeating Washington for the world championship 14-7, January 14.

1973 The Dolphins' hopes for another perfect season were dashed in the second week when they fell to Oakland 12-7, September 23. Miami bounced back the following week to crush New England 44-23 as Morris scored three touchdowns and set a team record with 197 yards rushing. Miami shut out Baltimore for the fourth consecutive time 44-0 as cornerback Tim Foley returned two blocked punts for touchdowns, an NFL first, November 11. The next week, the Dolphins recorded their second consecutive shutout, beating Buffalo 17-0 to clinch their third successive AFC East championship. Warfield caught four touchdown passes from Griese in the first half to pace a 34-7 rout of Detroit. The win concluded the regular season, giving Miami the best two-year record in NFL history, 26-2. Miami defeated Cincinnati 34-16 in the AFC playoff, December 23. The Dolphins rushed for 266 yards to dominate Oakland 27-10 and win an unprecedented third straight AFC championship, December 30. Miami defeated Minnesota 24-7 in Super Bowl VIII at Houston's Rice Stadium, January 13. Csonka set Super Bowl records with 145 yards rushing on 33 carries.

1974 The organization was jolted by an announcement that Csonka, Kiick, and Warfield had signed a $3.3-million package deal to play for Toronto of the World Football League in 1975, March 31. The season began dismally as the Dolphins lost the opener in New England 34-24, September 15; Miami had not lost to the Patriots since 1971. The Dolphins struggled through the next six weeks, winning five lackluster games and losing to Washington 20-17. The offense finally exploded in a 42-7 rout of Atlanta, November 3. Two weeks later, Don Nottingham scored on a 23-yard run with 19 seconds left to beat Buffalo 35-28, the third time the Dolphins scored the winning points in the final 20 seconds. Miami rallied from a 24-point deficit to beat New England 34-27 in the regular-season finale. It was the Dolphins' thirty-first consecutive win at the Orange Bowl. A last-second desperation pass from Ken Stabler to Clarence Davis provided the winning touchdown as Oakland ended Miami's two-year domination of pro football with a dramatic 28-26 win in the playoffs.

1975 The departure of Csonka, Kiick, and Warfield weakened Miami. The Dolphins' Orange Bowl winning streak ended in their regular-season opener as Oakland won 31-21, despite three interceptions by safety Charlie Babb. The following week, the Dolphins rallied from a 14-0 halftime deficit to beat New England 22-14 and begin a seven-game winning streak. The Dolphins scored two touchdowns in the final two minutes to beat Buffalo 35-30 and reclaim first place in the AFC Eastern Division, October 26. In a showdown for the division lead, Baltimore beat Miami 33-17 at the Orange Bowl. Griese tore tendons in his toe and was sidelined for the rest of the season. Morrall was lost with torn knee ligaments the following week, but Don Strock guided Miami to two straight victories. Baltimore beat the Dolphins 10-7 in overtime to knock the Dolphins out of the playoffs for the first time since 1970.

1976 Scott, the club's all-time interception leader, was suspended in a dispute with Shula, then traded to Washington. Miami was hampered by injuries that sidelined 18 players during the season. Bill Arnsparger, former assistant coach, rejoined the Dolphins at midseason after being released as head coach by the Giants; his return inspired the Dolphins' defense to its finest effort of the year, a 10-3 win over New England. Wide receiver Freddie Solomon had an electrifying game against Buffalo, scoring on a 79-yard punt return, a 59-yard run, and a 53-yard pass play. Shula suffered his first losing season in 14 years as an NFL coach as the Dolphins fell to 6-8.

1977 Morrall retired on May 2 after a 21-year NFL career. Griese, who began wearing glasses on the field, led the league in passing, helping Miami bounce back to respectability in a strong but frustrating season. The Dolphins won their first three games and were 7-2 after nine games. Then, they lost 23-17 to Cincinnati on November 20 when the Bengals scored on a triple-reverse in the last minute. The Dolphins came back on Thanksgiving to roll up 503 yards and beat St. Louis 55-14, as Griese threw six touchdown passes. A 17-6 victory over Baltimore put Miami in a three-way tie for first place with two weeks to go. Despite a closing victory over Buffalo, the Dolphins missed the playoffs on a tiebreaker.

1978 The Dolphins lost Griese in the preseason when he suffered torn ligaments in his left knee. The team didn't miss a beat with Don Strock at the controls, going 5-2. His best game was against Baltimore when he passed for three touchdowns in a 42-0 victory. Griese returned for his first start of the season on October 22, but the Dolphins were defeated by the Patriots 33-24, knocking them out of first place. Miami came back to win three in a row but was defeated almost single-handedly by Houston's Earl Campbell, who ran for 199 yards and four touchdowns, in a Monday night game 35-30. The Dolphins earned the right to host the wild card game with a 23-3 victory over New England on December 18. Miami's 11 victories were the most since 1974. A big day by Houston's Dan Pastorini led to a 17-9 Oilers win in the AFC Wild Card Game on December 24.

1979 Larry Csonka rejoined the Dolphins after four years on February 22. Miami opened with four straight wins, highlighted by Csonka's three touchdowns against the Bears in a 31-16 victory. Consecutive losses to the Raiders and the Jets started Miami on a slump in which they went 3-5. With Griese benched in favor of Strock, the Dolphins defeated the Colts 28-24 on November 25. Two weeks later, Griese was back to complete 17 of 22 passes in a title-clinching victory at Detroit. On December 30, the Dolphins were overwhelmed by Pittsburgh in the AFC Divisional Playoff Game 34-14.

1980 The Dolphins lost their debut 17-7 to Buffalo. The loss ended the Dolphins' 20-game winning streak over the Bills. Miami played musical quarterbacks much of the season, with Griese, Strock, and rookie David Woodley all seeing action. Griese passed for 222 yards in the first half of a 30-17 loss to Baltimore on October 5, but suffered a shoulder injury that ended his career. Woodley finished the season as the starter, with his best day coming on November 9 when he ran for two touchdowns and threw for three more in a 35-14 win over the Rams.

1981 The offseason proved to be a tough time for the Dolphins. Little retired on February 5; Griese retired on June 25. Shula settled on Woodley at quarterback, and the second-year veteran got the Dolphins off to a 4-0 start before suffering a cracked rib against the Jets. Strock came in to salvage a 28-28 tie, but the Dolphins lost the next week to the Bills. With Woodley back in charge again, Miami got back on the winning track with a 13-10 victory over Washington. The Dolphins lost back-to-back games but managed to remain in a first-place tie with the Jets. A four-game win streak ended the season with Miami in first place with an 11-4-1 record. The Dolphins were involved in another of the classic overtime confrontations in pro football playoff history. They lost to San Diego 41-38 in the 1981 divisional playoffs.

1982 Shula guided a team averaging less than four years of NFL experience to a 7-2 record and the Dolphins' fourth Super Bowl appearance. Miami's "Killer Bees" defense, so named because six defensive starters had last names beginning with the letter "B," took center stage in the AFC playoffs, when the Dolphins defeated New England 28-13, San Diego 34-13, and the New York Jets 14-0 in the AFC Championship Game. In the victory against the Jets, linebacker A.J. Duhe set an AFC playoff record with three interceptions. In Super Bowl XVII at the Rose Bowl in Pasadena, California, Miami led the Washington Redskins with 10 minutes left to play before losing 27-17 in front of a sellout crowd of 103,667 and a television audience of nearly 115 million. Fulton Walker set a Super Bowl record with a 98-yard kickoff return for a touchdown.

1983 Quarterback Dan Marino of Pittsburgh was drafted with the twenty-seventh pick of the NFL draft. Linebacker Larry Gordon, 28, died of a rare heart disease while jogging in Arizona, June 25. In his first NFL start, a 38-35 overtime loss to Buffalo, Marino passed for 322 yards. Another rookie making his first start for the Dolphins in that game, wide receiver Mark Duper, caught seven passes for 202 yards. After six games, the Dolphins were 3-3. They finished with a 9-1 surge to win the AFC East title and make the playoffs for the tenth time in 14 years. Seattle upset Miami 27-20 in an AFC Divisional Playoff Game. Defensive coordinator Bill Arnsparger resigned to become head coach of LSU. Marino was the first rookie ever chosen to start at quarterback in the AFC-NFC Pro Bowl.

1984 Bob Kuechenberg, the last playing link to the Super Bowl VII team and a six-time Pro Bowl guard who played in more regular-season games than any other Dolphin, retired. On March 5, Robbie announced a plan to build a new stadium in North Dade County. Running back David Overstreet was killed in an automobile accident in Winona, Texas, June 24. Beginning with an opening-game 35-17 victory over the Washington Redskins, in which Marino completed 21 of 28 passes for 311 yards and five touchdowns, the Dolphins won 11 consecutive games. San Diego, which halted Miami's winning streak with a 34-28 victory on November 18, and the Los Angeles Raiders, who won a 45-34 shootout at the Orange Bowl on December 2, were the only teams to stop the Dolphins in the regular season. Miami finished 14-2 and won the AFC East by a five-game margin. Directing the most prolific offense in NFL history, Marino set league records for completions (362), yards passing (5,084), and touchdown passes (48). Wide receiver Mark Clayton caught 73 passes for 1,389 yards and an NFL-record 18 touchdowns, and Duper added 71 receptions for 1,306 yards. Miami avenged its 1983 playoff loss to Seattle with a 31-10 divisional playoff game victory at the Orange Bowl, and then defeated Pittsburgh 45-28 in the AFC Championship Game, as Marino shredded the Steelers for 421 yards and four touchdowns. Playing in a record-tying fifth Super Bowl (and Shula's record sixth as a head coach), Miami held a brief 10-3 lead against the San Francisco 49ers in Game XIX at Stanford Stadium. But the 49ers scored three consecutive touchdowns in the second quarter, and went on to win 38-16.

1985 Marino missed most of training camp because of a 37-day contract holdout, and was benched in the first quarter of Miami's opener against Houston after throwing two interceptions. The Oilers shocked the Dolphins 26-23. But Marino found his rhythm the next week against the Colts, passing for 329 yards and two touchdowns in a 30-13 Miami victory. Miami once again ruled the AFC East by winning its final seven games to ward off season-long challenges by both the Patriots and the Jets. Safety Glenn Blackwood knocked down four passes and intercepted two others to help Miami defeat New England 30-27 in a critical showdown at the Orange Bowl in the next-to-last Monday night game of the season. It was the Dolphins' eighteenth consecutive victory over the Patriots at the Orange Bowl. After trailing 21-3 in the third quarter of a divisional playoff game against Cleveland, the Dolphins scored three touchdowns in the final 20 minutes to pull out a 24-21 victory. But in the AFC Championship Game against the Patriots, the hex was finally dismantled, and New England defeated Miami at the Orange Bowl 31-14.

MEMBER OF HALL OF FAME:
Paul Warfield

DOLPHINS RECORD, 1966-85

Year	Won	Lost	Tied	Pct.	Fin.	Pts.	OP
1966	3	11	0	.214	5	213	362
1967	4	10	0	.286	3t	219	407
1968	5	8	1	.385	3	276	355
1969	3	10	1	.231	5	233	332
1970a	10	4	0	.714	2	297	228
1971b	10	3	1	.769	1	315	174
1972c	14	0	0	1.000	1	385	171
1973c	12	2	0	.857	1	343	150
1974d	11	3	0	.786	1	327	216
1975	10	4	0	.714	2	357	222
1976	6	8	0	.429	3	263	264
1977	10	4	0	.714	2	313	197
1978a	11	5	0	.688	2	372	254
1979d	10	6	0	.625	1	341	257
1980	8	8	0	.500	3	266	305
1981d	11	4	1	.719	1	345	275
1982e	7	2	0	.778	2	198	131
1983d	12	4	0	.750	1	389	250
1984b	14	2	0	.875	1	513	298
1985f	12	4	0	.750	1	428	320
20 Years	183	102	4	.640		6,393	5,168

aAFC Wild Card Qualifier for Playoffs; 0-1 in Playoffs
bAFC Champion; 2-1 in Playoffs
cSuper Bowl Champion; 3-0 in Playoffs
dAFC Eastern Division Champion; 0-1 in Playoffs
eAFC Champion; 3-1 in Playoffs
fAFC Eastern Division Champion; 1-1 in Playoffs

RECORD HOLDERS

CAREER

Rushing attempts	Larry Csonka, 1968-74, 1979	1,506
Rushing yards	Larry Csonka, 1968-74, 1979	6,737
Pass attempts	Bob Griese, 1967-80	3,429
Pass completions	Bob Griese, 1967-80	1,926
Passing yards	Bob Griese, 1967-80	25,092
Touchdown passes	Bob Griese, 1967-80	192
Receptions	Nat Moore, 1974-85	472
Receiving yards	Nat Moore, 1974-85	7,116
Interceptions	Jake Scott, 1970-75	35
Punting average	Reggie Roby, 1983-85	43.7
Punt return avg.	Freddie Solomon, 1975-77	11.4
Kickoff return avg.	Mercury Morris, 1969-75	26.5
Field goals	Garo Yepremian, 1970-78	165
Touchdowns	Nat Moore, 1974-85	68
Points	Garo Yepremian, 1970-78	830

SEASON

Rushing attempts	Delvin Williams, 1978	272
Rushing yards	Delvin Williams, 1978	1,258
Pass attempts	Dan Marino, 1985	567
Pass completions	Dan Marino, 1984	362
Passing yards	Dan Marino, 1984	5,084
Touchdown passes	Dan Marino, 1984	48
Receptions	Mark Clayton, 1984	73
Receiving yards	Mark Clayton, 1984	1,389
Interceptions	Dick Westmoreland, 1967	10
Punting average	Reggie Roby, 1984	44.7
Punt return avg.	Freddie Solomon, 1975	12.3
Kickoff return avg.	Duriel Harris, 1976	32.9
Field goals	Garo Yepremian, 1971	28
Touchdowns	Mark Clayton, 1984	18
Points	Garo Yepremian, 1971	117

GAME

Rushing attempts	Mercury Morris, 10-5-75	31
Rushing yards	Mercury Morris, 9-30-73	197
Pass attempts	Dan Marino, 12-2-84	57
Pass completions	Dan Marino, 12-2-84	35
Passing yards	Dan Marino, 12-2-84	470
Touchdown passes	Bob Griese, 11-24-77	6
Receptions	Duriel Harris, 10-28-79	10
	Tony Nathan, 9-29-85	10
Receiving yards	Mark Duper, 11-10-85	217
Interceptions	Dick Anderson, 12-3-73	4
Field goals	Garo Yepremian, 9-26-71	5
Touchdowns	Paul Warfield, 12-15-73	4
Points	Paul Warfield, 12-15-73	24

COACHING HISTORY

1966-69	George Wilson	15-39-2
1970-85	Don Shula	182-73-2

FIRST PLAYER SELECTED

1966 Jim Grabowski, FB, Illinois
1966† John Roderick, SE, SMU
1967 Bob Griese, QB, Purdue
1968 Larry Csonka, RB, Syracuse
1969 Bill Stanfill, DE, Georgia
1970 (2) Jim Mandich, TE, Michigan
1971 (2) Otto Stowe, WR, Iowa State
1972 Mike Kadish, DT, Notre Dame
1973 (2) Chuck Bradley, C, Oregon
1974 Don Reese, DE, Jackson State
1975 Darryl Carlton, T, Tampa
1976 Larry Gordon, LB, Arizona State
1977 A. J. Duhe, DE, LSU
1978 (2) Guy Benjamin, QB, Stanford
1979 Jon Giesler, T, Michigan
1980 Don McNeal, CB, Alabama
1981 David Overstreet, RB, Oklahoma
1982 Roy Foster, G, USC
1983 Dan Marino, QB, Pittsburgh
1984 Jackie Shipp, LB, Oklahoma
1984* Danny Knight, WR, Mississippi State
1985 Lorenzo Hampton, RB, Florida
1986 John Offerdahl, LB, Western Michigan

†Redshirt Draft
**Supplemental Draft*

DOLPHINS MOST VALUABLE PLAYER

1966 Joe Auer, HB
1967 Bob Griese, QB
1968 Bob Griese, QB
1969 Nick Buoniconti, LB
1970 Bob Griese, QB
Paul Warfield, WR
1971 Bob Griese, QB
1972 Earl Morrall, QB
1973 Larry Csonka, RB
1974 Bob Griese, QB
1975 Jim Langer, C
1976 Steve Towle, LB
1977 Bob Griese, QB
1978 Delvin Williams, RB
1979 Larry Csonka, RB
1980 David Woodley, QB
1981 Tony Nathan, RB
1982 Andra Franklin, RB
1983 Dan Marino, QB
1984 Dan Marino, QB
1985 Dan Marino, QB

MINNESOTA VIKINGS

1959 A group of investors headed by Bill Boyer, a Minneapolis auto dealer, and Max Winter, the former owner of the Minneapolis Lakers of the National Basketball Association, attempted to lure the Chicago Cardinals to Metropolitan Stadium in Bloomington, a suburb of Minneapolis. Failing that, the group applied for an expansion franchise for the NFL, but again was turned down. On August 14, a Minneapolis franchise, owned by Boyer and Winter, was named as one of the founding teams in the new American Football League.
1960 The Minneapolis franchise withdrew from the AFL on January 27, stating that problems obtaining a stadium prevented its membership. The next day, a franchise representing Minnesota (in order to avoid any conflicts between Minneapolis and St. Paul) was granted to Boyer, Winter, Ole Haugsurd, Bernard Ridder, Jr., and H.P. Skoglund, to begin play in the 1961 season. Winter became the first team president, Bert Rose was named general manager, and Joe Thomas was hired as the talent scout.
1961 Rose came up with a nickname, Vikings, and a head coach, Norm Van Brocklin. Van Brocklin had quarterbacked the Philadelphia Eagles to the NFL championship in 1960. The Vikings were stocked with 36 veteran players in the expansion draft. Most were castoffs and retreads, but one was Hugh McElhenny, a former all-pro halfback, from San Francisco. The Vikings traded a future draft choice to New York for quarterback George Shaw. The draft yielded Tommy Mason, a talented halfback from Tulane; Fran Tarkenton, a daring quarterback from Georgia; and Ed Sharockman, a cornerback from Pittsburgh. Defensive end Jim Marshall, who would start in every game through 1979, was acquired in a trade with Cleveland. Most observers predicted Minnesota, like Dallas in 1960, would go winless in its first season. The Vikings pulled a stunning upset in their first league game, embarrassing the Chicago Bears 37-13 at Metropolitan Stadium. Tarkenton replaced Shaw in the second quarter, threw four touchdown passes, and ran for the final score himself. The Vikings lost their next seven games but finished with a respectable 3-11 record.
1962 Van Brocklin made significant progress improving his personnel. With Tarkenton entrenched as the quarterback, Van Brocklin traded Shaw. He phased out the aging McElhenny in favor of Mason, who had back-to-back 100-yard games against Detroit and Baltimore. He added free-agent center Mick Tingelhoff. The highlight of a 2-11-1 season was a 31-21 win over Philadelphia, sweet revenge for Van Brocklin, who had resented not being named Eagles head coach following his retirement as a player.
1963 The Vikings began outgrowing their expansion image by beating San Francisco twice in the first three weeks as Bill Brown, a Chicago Bears reject, established himself at fullback. The Vikings won three more games and just barely missed upsets of Green Bay and Baltimore. Minnesota played the Bears, the eventual world champions, to a 17-17 tie at Wrigley Field late in the season. Paul Flatley, a surehanded receiver from Northwestern, led the team with 51 catches, and was voted the NFL rookie of the year. Mason became the team's first all-pro.
1964 Prior to the season, Rose was dismissed as general manager and replaced by former Pittsburgh quarterback Jim Finks. The top draft choice was Carl Eller, a towering defensive end from Minnesota. The Vikings won all five preseason games and beat Baltimore in the league opener. Minnesota beat Green Bay for the first time 24-23 as Tarkenton completed a 44-yard pass to Gordie Smith on fourth and 22 to set up Fred Cox's winning field goal. Marshall gained fame by picking up a San Francisco fumble and returning it 66 yards the wrong way for a safety, October 26. The Vikings won the game 27-22. Minnesota went unbeaten in the final four weeks of the season, tying Detroit and beating the Rams, the Giants, and the Bears by lopsided scores. Their strong stretch run enabled the Vikings to tie Green Bay for second place in the Western Conference at 8-5-1.
1965 With his strong veteran nucleus, plus additions such as defensive tackle Gary Larsen, linebacker Lonnie Warwick, halfback Dave Osborn, and flanker Lance Rentzel, Van Brocklin expected to win the Western Conference. The Vikings staggered to a 2-3 start, with the defense allowing an average of 35 points a game. They rallied from a 35-14 deficit to beat San Francisco 42-41 and ignite a three-game win streak. Their title hopes were buried the following week when Baltimore beat them 41-21 on substitute Gary Cuozzo's five touchdown passes. The next morning Van Brocklin told reporters he was resigning as head coach. By late afternoon he changed his mind. Not surprisingly, the disillusioned Vikings lost their next three games and finished 7-7.
1966 The unhealthy climate between Van Brocklin and his players was never more apparent than during the 1966 season. Van Brocklin and Tarkenton were hardly on speaking terms most of the year. After several seasons of contention, the Vikings were never a factor in the Western Conference, managing just one win in their first six games. Mason, the once-brilliant runner, was limping toward the end of his career on shattered knees. Brown was Minnesota's main offensive threat, rushing for 829 yards and catching 37 passes. Late in the season, Van Brocklin started Bob Berry ahead of Tarkenton. "I think he's trying to tell me something," Tarkenton said.
1967 Tarkenton issued a statement suggesting that either he or Van Brocklin be sent to another NFL team, February 9. A few days later, Van Brocklin resigned. In March, Tarkenton was traded to the New York Giants for two first- and two second-round draft choices. The trade helped ensure a bountiful rookie crop, which included Alan Page, Gene Washington, Clint Jones, Bobby Bryant, John Beasley, and Bob Grim. Finks signed Harry (Bud) Grant to a three-year contract as head coach. Grant had been a candidate for the original Vikings job in 1961 but chose to remain with Winnipeg of the Canadian Football League. Finks also imported a quarterback from Canada, Joe Kapp, a brawling, charismatic figure who quickly became Minnesota's team leader. The 3-8-3 season was highlighted by a 10-7 upset of Green Bay, the eventual Super Bowl champion. Dave Osborn ran for 972 yards, second-most in the NFL, and led the Vikings with 34 receptions.
1968 With the addition of top draft pick Ron Yary at offensive tackle and trade acquisition Paul Krause at free safety, Minnesota finally had the makings of a champion. The front four—Eller, Page, Larsen, and Marshall—emerged as one of the NFL's premier defensive lines. The offense, led by the reckless, free-wheeling Kapp, was explosive and unpredictable. The Vikings pulled out of a midseason slump to win their last two games and move past the Bears and Green Bay for their first NFL Central Division championship. With Osborn sidelined with injuries, Brown rushed for 805 yards and scored 14 touchdowns. Minnesota lost its first playoff game to Baltimore 24-14, December 22.
1969 The Vikings opened the season with a 24-23 loss to the lowly New York Giants and Tarkenton. The following week, Kapp tied an NFL record by throwing seven touchdown passes in a 52-14 rout of Baltimore. The Vikings won their next 11 games. They clinched the Central Division title with a 27-0 win over Detroit on Thanksgiving Day. The Vikings trailed the Rams by 10 points at the half but came back to win their Western Conference playoff game 23-20, December 27. Eller sacked Roman Gabriel in the end zone for a safety to clinch it. Minnesota had little trouble with Cleveland in the NFC Championship Game, burying the Browns in 8-degree cold 27-7, January 4. The Vikings played their poorest game of the season in Super Bowl IV, losing to Kansas City 23-7 in New Orleans, January 11.
1970 The Vikings lost their leader when Kapp sat out the early games over a contract dispute and then was sold to the Boston Patriots. Gary Cuozzo took over at quarterback and did a capable, if unspectacular, job. Minnesota continued to win on the strength of its outstanding defense, which allowed just 14 touchdowns in 14 regular-season games. The Vikings opened the season with a 27-10 win over Kansas City in a rematch of Super Bowl IV teams. Following a 13-10 loss to Green Bay, the Vikings won 10 of their last 11 games to run away with the Central Division for the third straight year. The offense plodded along without Kapp's leadership, but the defense still was the best in the league. Cornerback Ed Sharockman intercepted seven passes, and scored three touchdowns. Minnesota was shocked in the first round of the NFC playoffs, losing to San Francisco 17-14, December 27. The Vikings gave the game away on two interceptions and two fumbles, one of which the 49ers converted into the decisive field goal.
1971 Feeling they needed a more experienced quarterback, the Vikings traded offensive tackle Steve Smith and two high draft choices to Philadelphia for 31-year-old Norm Snead, January 22. Snead was a preseason disappointment and fell to third-string behind Cuozzo and Bob Lee. Injuries hampered Minnesota, sidelining receivers Washington and Beasley and middle linebacker Lonnie Warwick. Defense again carried the Vikings as they allowed just 12 touchdowns (2 rushing, 10 passing) during the regular season. Upset by the Bears in their second game 20-17, the Vikings allowed only two touchdowns in the next five weeks, shutting out Buffalo and Philadelphia. The season was typified by a 3-0 win over Green Bay in which the Vikings' defense stopped the Packers on the 1-yard line. Minnesota won its fourth consecutive Central Division title despite the quarterback problems. Lee, a three-year veteran, was given the starting assignment in the NFC playoff against Dallas, December 25. He threw two interceptions and was replaced by Cuozzo, who threw two more as the Vikings lost 20-12. Page was named the NFL's most valuable player, the first time a defensive lineman ever received the honor.
1972 Minnesota solidified its quarterback situation by trading Snead, Bob Grim, Vince Clements, and first- and second-round draft picks to the Giants for Tarkenton, whose return to the Vikings generated great hope for the 1972 season. The hope turned to frustration as the Vikings stumbled to a 7-7 finish. The defense, weakened by injuries to Page and Eller, was generally ineffective, allowing 252 points. The Vikings lost five games by four or fewer points. Tarkenton had an outstanding year, however, as did newly acquired receiver John Gilliam.
1973 A strong draft heralded a return to power for the Vikings. In the first round, Minnesota selected Chuck Foreman, a big, slashing runner from Miami. In the fifth round, they added Brent McClanahan, a halfback from Arizona State. Foreman gave the offense the game-breaking backfield punch it had lacked since the decline of Tommy Mason. In his second regular-season game, Foreman carried the ball 16 times for 116 yards in a 22-13 win over the Bears, September 23. Two weeks later, Foreman rushed for

114 yards in a 23-9 win over Detroit. He went on to earn rookie-of-the-year honors. The defense, healthy once again, returned to form, permitting just 15 touchdowns and 168 points, both NFC lows. The Vikings (12-2) were the only Central Division team to finish with a winning record. Tarkenton hit Gilliam with two second-half touchdown passes to beat Washington in an NFC playoff game 27-20, December 22. The Vikings won their second NFC championship by defeating Dallas 27-10 in Texas Stadium, December 30. The Vikings were crushed by Miami 24-7 in Super Bowl VIII at Rice Stadium in Houston, January 13.

1974 Jim Finks resigned in May. Mike Lynn was hired as assistant to president Max Winter, August 15, and became general manager shortly thereafter. Six rookies made the team from another productive draft. Foreman tied a club record by rushing for three touchdowns in a 32-17 win over Green Bay in the opener, September 15. Cox kicked a 27-yard field goal at the gun to beat Dallas 23-21, October 6. The Vikings won their fifth in a row as Tarkenton passed for 274 yards to rout Houston 51-10, October 13. Minnesota lost four of its next six, and the Central Division lead dwindled to one game over Detroit and Green Bay. Tarkenton ended the slump, passing for 319 yards and three touchdowns in a 29-9 win over New Orleans. Foreman set a club record with his fifty-third pass reception in a 23-10 win over Atlanta, December 7. In the NFC playoffs, the Vikings turned two St. Louis turnovers into touchdowns and a 30-14 victory, December 21. Minnesota's defense provided the key to a 14-10 win over the Los Angeles Rams in the NFC Championship Game at Metropolitan Stadium, December 29. Wally Hilgenberg's end-zone interception ended one threat, and two sacks by Page in the fourth quarter preserved the scant lead. Once again, the Vikings lost in the Super Bowl, this time to Pittsburgh 16-6 in New Orleans, January 12. A magnificent Pittsburgh defense limited the Vikings to just nine first downs and 17 yards rushing.

1975 The Vikings got off to their fastest start ever, winning their first 10 games. Joe Blahak, a reserve cornerback, blocked a punt for a safety in a 29-21 win over the New York Jets, October 12. The following week, Marshall set an NFL record with his twenty-fifth career fumble recovery in a 25-19 win over Detroit. Safety Paul Krause intercepted two passes in a 28-17 win over Green Bay to move into second place among the NFL's all-time pass interceptors with 69. Foreman rushed for more than 100 yards for the third straight game and the fifth in six weeks as the Vikings pounded San Diego 28-13, November 23. Foreman finished the season with 1,070 yards rushing, 73 pass receptions (a record for a running back), and an NFC-high 22 touchdowns. Tarkenton surpassed three of Johnny Unitas's career passing records: most attempts (5,225), most completions (2,931), and most touchdowns (291). The Vikings were eliminated in the NFC divisional playoffs, 17-14 by Dallas at Metropolitan Stadium, December 28. Minnesota had the game won until Roger Staubach hit Drew Pearson with a dramatic 50-yard touchdown pass with just 24 seconds left. Tarkenton was named the NFL's most valuable player.

1976 Minnesota won its eighth Central Division title in nine years. The defense stopped Los Angeles twice at the 1-yard line to preserve a 10-10 overtime tie, September 19. Cornerback Nate Allen, acquired in a trade with the 49ers, intercepted a pass and recovered a fumble to set up two Foreman touchdowns in a 17-6 upset of Pittsburgh, October 4. Tarkenton continued to make history, becoming the first man to reach 3,000 career completions in a 24-7 win over the New York Giants, October 17. He surpassed 40,000 yards passing in a 31-12 win over Philadelphia as Minnesota ran its unbeaten string to seven, October 24. And he threw his three-hundredth touchdown pass in a 27-21 win over Seattle, November 14. Foreman set a Vikings record with 200 yards rushing against the Eagles. Sammy White, a rookie receiver from Grambling, caught nine passes, three for touchdowns, in a 29-7 win over Miami, December 11. White was named NFC rookie of the year. Foreman and McClanahan combined for 215 yards rushing as Minnesota defeated Washington 35-20 in the NFC divisional playoffs, December 18. In the NFC Championship Game, Allen blocked a field-goal attempt by Tom Dempsey of the Rams, and Bryant returned the loose ball 90 yards for a touchdown. Bryant also intercepted two passes to preserve Minnesota's 24-13 triumph. The Vikings lost their fourth Super Bowl when they were defeated by Oakland 32-14 in Super Bowl XI on January 9.

1977 In the draft, Minnesota selected Rice quarterback Tommy Kramer in the first round. The team lost the 1977 opener to Dallas, but followed with four successive victories over NFC Central rivals. The Vikings displayed a knack for winning close games; they outscored opponents only 231-227. On November 13, Minnesota ran its record to 6-3 with a 42-10 drubbing of Cincinnati, but Tarkenton was lost for the season with a broken leg. Bob Lee started the next three games, but was relieved by Kramer when the Vikings dropped behind San Francisco 24-0. Kramer threw three touchdowns to spark a stunning 28-27 victory. Lee directed a 30-21 victory over Detroit in the season finale that clinched the NFC Central title with a 9-5 record. On December 26, Lee and the Vikings opened the playoffs in the rain in Los Angeles and shocked the favored Rams 14-7. The Vikings lost to the Cowboys 23-6 in the NFC Championship Game on January 1.

1978 A mediocre record (3-4, the slowest start since 1972) resulted in a shakeup of the defense early in the season. Eller lost his starting job to Mark Mullaney, and Page was released after starting the first six games. Tarkenton shouldered the offensive load and guided the team to a 5-1-1 record over the next seven weeks. Despite a pair of losses that ended the season, the Vikings won their sixth straight NFC Central title with an 8-7-1 record. Tarkenton established NFL records for most pass attempts (572) and completions (345), and his 25 touchdowns and 3,468 yards were team records. Rickey Young caught 88 passes to set an NFL record for running backs. In December, ground was broken for the Hubert H. Humphrey Metrodome, which was scheduled to become the team's new home in 1982. On December 31, the Rams broke a streak of four straight playoff losses to the Vikings with a 34-10 victory in a divisional playoff game.

1979 The Vikings experienced major changes when Tarkenton, Tingelhoff, and Marshall retired, and Eller was traded to Seattle. Ted Brown, a running back from North Carolina State, was the first draft choice. The Vikings' passing offense remained potent as Kramer became the starting quarterback and threw for 3,397 yards and 23 touchdowns. But the team started slowly at 4-4, then lost four of its next six games. The Vikings ended the year 7-9, their first losing season since 1967. Wide receiver Ahmad Rashad, who was obtained by the Vikings prior to the 1976 season in a trade with Seattle, set a club record with 1,156 yards receiving (on 80 catches).

1980 The Vikings opened the season by winning a shootout with Atlanta 24-23, but then stumbled to 3-5 at midseason. Particularly troublesome was the rushing offense, which exceeded 100 yards only twice in the first eight weeks. On November 2, the offense awoke in a 39-14 victory over Washington. That win was a portent of things to come, as the Vikings rolled to six victories in the final eight weeks. Kramer was the catalyst, throwing for a club-record 3,582 yards. Brown rushed for 912 yards and caught 62 passes for 623 yards. The Vikings clinched the NFC Central with a wild comeback against Cleveland on December 14, in which Kramer threw three touchdown passes in the fourth quarter to win 28-23. The last score was a 46-yard pass that Rashad caught in the end zone after it had been deflected by a defender. The Vikings finished at 9-7. Minnesota led Philadelphia 16-14 in the third quarter of a divisional playoff game, but eight second-half turnovers by the Vikings gave the Eagles a 31-16 victory.

1981 The team moved to its new facilities in Eden Prairie. With Kramer sidelined by a knee injury, the Vikings opened the 1981 season with two losses. Kramer returned to spark five victories in a row, including a 33-31 win over San Diego on October 11, when he passed for 444 yards. The performance was the best by an NFC quarterback in 1981. A 20-10 victory over New Orleans on November 15 gave the Vikings a 7-4 record and a two-game lead in the NFC Central. But Minnesota lost its last five games and finished in fourth place with a 7-9 record. Brown finished with 1,063 yards rushing and 83 pass receptions. Rashad caught 69 passes for 1,095 yards, his fifth-straight season with 50 or more catches.

1982 In a season shortened by the players' strike, the Vikings qualified for the Super Bowl tournament as the fourth-place team in the NFC with a 5-4 record. Kramer, as usual, led the way, compiling a career-best quarterback rating of 77.3 while passing for 2,037 yards and 15 touchdowns. In a 35-7 victory over the Bears, he threw five touchdown passes, his all-time NFL high, and completed 26 of 36 passes for 342 yards. Minnesota needed to defeat Dallas in the final regular-season game to clinch a first-round playoff game at home—and the Vikings did just that, 31-27, despite Tony Dorsett's 99-yard touchdown run, the longest run from scrimmage in NFL history. The Vikings then beat Altanta 30-24 in the first round before a 21-7 loss in Washington ended their season. Linebacker Matt Blair made his sixth consecutive Pro Bowl appearance.

1983 The Vikings started off as if they were on the way to the playoffs for the thirteenth time in 16 years, winning six of their first eight. Minnesota's playoff hopes were given a severe jolt when Kramer tore a ligament in his right knee and was lost for the season. Three days later, the Vikings acquired quarterback Archie Manning and tight end Dave Casper from Houston. However, Steve Dils took over at quarterback, while Manning participated in only two plays for the Vikings. Dils finished the season with 2,840 yards but only 11 touchdown passes. A streak in which the Vikings won only one of seven games dropped Minnesota into a three-team logjam for second place behind the Lions. The season ended on a winning note as the Vikings scored 13 points in the fourth quarter for a 20-14 come-from-behind victory over Cincinnati. Running back Darrin Nelson led Minnesota in rushing (642 yards), receiving (51 catches for 618 yards), and kickoff-return average (24.7 yards, which also ranked first in the NFC).

1984 Grant announced his retirement on January 28, at the age of 56. He was replaced the next day by 37-year-old assistant coach Les Steckel. It was Steckel's first-ever head-coaching assignment, and the inexperience showed as the Vikings finished last in the NFC Central with a 3-13 record. Once again Minnesota played a good part of its season without Kramer, who separated his right shoulder when hit from behind in a game against Detroit. The Vikings did get an unexpected boost from running back Alfred Anderson, a third-round draft choice from Baylor whose 773 rushing yards led all NFC rookies. Placekicker Jan Stenerud, an offseason acquisition from Green Bay who turned 42 during the season, made 20 of 23 field goals, including a club-record 54-yarder against Atlanta. Two days after the season's final game, it was announced that Grant would replace Steckel and come back as head coach.

1985 Grant's return couldn't have been scripted any better as the Vikings began their silver-anniversary season by taking advantage of seven turnovers for a stirring 28-21 come-from-behind victory over defending Super Bowl-champion San Francisco. The Vikings' season-long curse was playing in the same division with the indestructible Chicago Bears. Minnesota improved dramatically from 1984, however, finishing with a 7-9 record and cutting its points-allowed by 125 points. The Vikings even had a 17-9 lead over Chicago before Jim McMahon came off the bench to rally the Bears to a 33-24 victory. Kramer was impressive that night, completing 28 of 55 passes for 436 yards and three touchdowns. For the season, he passed for 3,522 yards; Steve Jordan caught a total of 68 passes, tops among NFC tight ends; and newcomer Anthony Carter made 43 catches for 821 yards and eight touchdowns. Safety Joey Browner was chosen to play in the Pro Bowl as a special-teams player. When the season ended, two old pros retired—Grant (with a career record of 168-109-5), to be replaced by Jerry Burns, a Vikings assistant since 1968, and Stenerud, who left after 19 seasons with more field goals (373) than anyone in pro football history.

MEMBERS OF HALL OF FAME:
Hugh McElhenny, Fran Tarkenton

VIKINGS RECORD, 1961-85

Year	Won	Lost	Tied	Pct.	Fin.	Pts.	OP
1961	3	11	0	.214	7	285	407
1962	2	11	1	.154	6	254	410
1963	5	8	1	.385	4t	309	390
1964	8	5	1	.615	2t	355	296
1965	7	7	0	.500	5	383	403
1966	4	9	1	.308	6t	292	304
1967	3	8	3	.273	4	233	294
1968a	8	6	0	.571	1	282	242
1969b	12	2	0	.857	1	379	133
1970c	12	2	0	.857	1	335	143
1971c	11	3	0	.786	1	245	139
1972	7	7	0	.500	3	301	252
1973d	12	2	0	.857	1	296	168
1974d	10	4	0	.714	1	310	195
1975c	12	2	0	.857	1	377	180
1976d	11	2	1	.821	1	305	176
1977e	9	5	0	.643	1	231	227
1978c	8	7	1	.531	1	294	306
1979	7	9	0	.438	3	259	337
1980c	9	7	0	.563	1	317	308
1981	7	9	0	.438	4	325	369
1982f	5	4	0	.556	4	187	198
1983	8	8	0	.500	4	316	348
1984	3	13	0	.188	5	276	484
1985	7	9	0	.438	3	346	359
25 Years	190	160	9	.542		7,492	7,068

aNFL Central Division Champion; 0-2 in Playoffs
bNFL Champion; 2-1 in Playoffs
cNFC Central Division Champion; 0-1 in Playoffs
dNFC Champion; 2-1 in Playoffs
eNFC Central Division Champion; 1-1 in Playoffs
fNFC Qualifier for Playoffs; 1-1 in Playoffs

RECORD HOLDERS

CAREER

Rushing attempts	Bill Brown, 1962-74	1,627
Rushing yards	Chuck Foreman, 1973-79	5,879
Pass attempts	Fran Tarkenton, 1961-66, 1972-78	4,569
Pass completions	Fran Tarkenton, 1961-66, 1972-78	2,635
Passing yards	Fran Tarkenton, 1961-66, 1972-78	33,098
Touchdown passes	Fran Tarkenton, 1961-66, 1972-78	239
Receptions	Ahmad Rashad, 1976-82	400
Receiving yards	Sammy White, 1976-85	6,001
Interceptions	Paul Krause, 1968-79	53
Punting average	Bobby Walden, 1964-67	42.9
Punt return avg.	Tommy Mason, 1961-66	10.5
Kickoff return avg.	Bob Reed, 1962-63	27.1
Field goals	Fred Cox, 1963-77	282
Touchdowns	Bill Brown, 1962-74	76
Points	Fred Cox, 1963-77	1,365

SEASON

Rushing attempts	Chuck Foreman, 1975	280
Rushing yards	Chuck Foreman, 1976	1,155
Pass attempts	Tommy Kramer, 1981	593
Pass completions	Fran Tarkenton, 1978	345
Passing yards	Tommy Kramer, 1981	3,912
Touchdown passes	Tommy Kramer, 1981	26
Receptions	Rickey Young, 1978	88
Receiving yards	Ahmad Rashad, 1979	1,156
Interceptions	Paul Krause, 1975	10
Punting average	Bobby Walden, 1964	46.4
Punt return avg.	Bill Butler, 1963	10.5
Kickoff return avg.	John Gilliam, 1972	26.3
Field goals	Fred Cox, 1970	30
Touchdowns	Chuck Foreman, 1975	22
Points	Chuck Foreman, 1975	132

GAME

Rushing attempts	Chuck Foreman, 11-23-75	33
	Chuck Foreman, 12-18-77	33
Rushing yards	Chuck Foreman, 10-24-76	200
Pass attempts	Steve Dils, 9-5-81	62
Pass completions	Tommy Kramer, 12-14-80	38
	Tommy Kramer, 11-29-81	38
Passing yards	Tommy Kramer, 12-14-80	456
Touchdown passes	Joe Kapp, 9-28-69	7
Receptions	Rickey Young, 12-16-79	15
Receiving yards	Sammy White, 11-7-76	210
Interceptions	Many times	3
Field goals	Fred Cox, 9-23-73	5
	Jan Stenerud, 9-23-84	5
Touchdowns	Chuck Foreman, 12-20-75	4
	Ahmad Rashad, 9-2-79	4
Points	Chuck Foreman, 12-20-75	24
	Ahmad Rashad, 9-2-79	24

COACHING HISTORY

1961-66	Norm Van Brocklin	29- 51-4
1967-83	Harry (Bud) Grant	161-100-5
1984	Les Steckel	3- 13-0
1985	Harry (Bud) Grant	7- 9-0
1986	Jerry Burns	

FIRST PLAYER SELECTED

1961	Tommy Mason, HB, Tulane
1962	(3) Bill Miller, SE, Miami
1963	Jim Dunaway, T, Mississippi
1964	Carl Eller, T, Minnesota
1965	Jack Snow, SE, Notre Dame
1966	Jerry Shay, DT, Purdue
1967	Clint Jones, HB, Michigan State
1968	Ron Yary, T, USC
1969	(2) Ed White, G, California
1970	John Ward, DT, Oklahoma State
1971	Leo Hayden, RB, Ohio State
1972	Jeff Siemon, LB, Stanford
1973	Chuck Foreman, RB, Miami
1974	Fred McNeill, LB, UCLA
1975	Mark Mullaney, DE, Colorado State
1976	James White, DT, Oklahoma State
1977	Tommy Kramer, QB, Rice
1978	Randy Holloway, DE, Pittsburgh
1979	Ted Brown, RB, North Carolina State
1980	Doug Martin, DT, Washington
1981	(2) Mardye McDole, WR, Mississippi State
1982	Darrin Nelson, RB, Stanford
1983	Joey Browner, DB, USC
1984	Keith Millard, DE, Washington State
1984*	Allanda Smith, CB, TCU
1985	Chris Doleman, LB, Pittsburgh
1986	Gerald Robinson, DE, Auburn

**Supplemental Draft*

VIKINGS ALL-TIME TEAM (1985)

OFFENSE

WR	Ahmad Rashad	1976-82
WR	Sammy White	1976-85
TE	Stu Voigt	1970-80
T	Ron Yary	1968-81
T	Grady Alderman	1961-74
G	Ed White	1969-77
G	Milt Sunde	1964-74
C	Mick Tingelhoff	1962-78
QB	Fran Tarkenton	1961-66, 1972-78
RB	Bill Brown	1962-74
RB	Chuck Foreman	1973-79
K	Fred Cox	1963-77

DEFENSE

DE	Jim Marshall	1961-79
DE	Carl Eller	1964-78
DT	Alan Page	1967-78
DT	Gary Larsen	1965-74
OLB	Matt Blair	1974-85
OLB	Roy Winston	1962-76
ILB	Jeff Siemon	1972-82
ILB	Scott Studwell	1977-85
CB	Bobby Bryant	1967-80
CB	Ed Sharockman	1962-72
S	Paul Krause	1968-79
S	Karl Kassulke	1963-72
P	Greg Coleman	1978-85

HEAD COACH

Harry (Bud) Grant	1967-83, 1985

NEW ENGLAND PATRIOTS

1959 The American Football League's eighth franchise was awarded to a group of 10 New England industrialists and sportsmen headed by William H. Sullivan, Jr., who was the club's president. The other nine individuals were John Ames, Jr., Dean Boylan, Dan Marr, Dom DiMaggio, Ed McMann, George Sargent, Paul Sonnabend, Joseph Sullivan, and Edgar Turner. The franchise, representing Boston, entered the league the day of the first draft (November 22), when the Patriots made halfback Gerhard Schwedes of Syracuse their first selection. Mike Holovak, the head coach at Boston College, was named director of player personnel. Ed McKeever was the club's first general manager. The first player to sign was Clemson quarterback Harvey White.

1960 Lou Saban, little-known coach at Western Illinois, was signed as the team's first head coach. "He's a Paul Brown with heart," said McKeever. A local newspaper held a contest to name the team. Patriots, suggested by 74 people, was the winner. The team adopted the colors red, white, and blue. Sullivan's biggest problem was finding a facility where his team could play. Fenway Park was unavailable. So were the stadiums of Boston College and Harvard. Boston University Field was chosen. The club opened its first training camp at the University of Massachusetts in Amherst. Some 350 players showed up. One was Ed (Butch) Songin, a former Boston College star who had quit Canadian football and was working as a probation officer near Boston. It became evident early in camp that Songin would be the club's best passer. In the first pro sports event ever staged in Harvard Stadium, the Patriots lost a preseason game to the Dallas Texans 24-14, August 14. A crowd of 21,597 was present for the regular-season opener at Boston University Field and welcomed pro football back to Boston. But the Patriots lost the game to Denver 13-10. A week later, the Patriots defeated the New York Titans 28-24 for their first victory, when Chuck Shonta picked up a fumble on the last play of the game and returned it for a touchdown. Financially, it was a rocky season for Sullivan. The team lost approximately $350,000, although the average home attendance of 16,500 provided some hope. In the final game of the season, a 37-21 loss to Houston, Saban moved defensive back Gino Cappelletti to flanker; the Patriots' best receiver of the 1960s had found a home.

1961 In a five-player trade with Oakland, Boston acquired Vito (Babe) Parilli, the experienced quarterback it felt it needed to build a winning team. But Sullivan, who was hoping for 10,000 season ticket sales, sold barely one-third that amount, and the team was not on solid footing as it began its second year. When the record fell to 2-3 and fan interest waned, Sullivan fired Saban and named Holovak head coach, October 19. Holovak stressed defense and the turnaround was almost immediate. The Patriots were 7-1-1 with Holovak as coach, leading the division for awhile. Cappelletti not only led the team with 45 receptions, he set the AFL record with 147 points on eight touchdowns, 17 field goals, and 48 extra points. Attendance improved, averaging more than 19,000. The club still lost money, but less than half the amount lost the previous year.

1962 Holovak made two acquisitions through the draft. Nick Buoniconti became the new middle linebacker and the key to the defense, and Billy Neighbors, an All-America blocker from Alabama, turned into the stabilizing force on the Patriots' offensive line. A victory over Houston 34-21 in the second game of the season stamped Boston as a strong contender. But in their next meeting later in the year, Parilli, now solidly entrenched as the quarterback, was hit just after throwing a pass in the second quarter. His collarbone was broken and he was lost for the season. The Patriots lost the game and their chance at the championship, finishing with a 9-4-1 record.

1963 The Patriots announced their new playing site of Fenway Park, home of the baseball Red Sox, with 38,000 seats. A severe back injury sidelined halfback Ron Burton and a pinched nerve inhibited Parilli. The team played erratically. The collapse of Houston, a regrouping in New York, a poor start by Buffalo, and the play of Cappelletti (who again led the league in scoring) kept the Patriots in the race, eventually allowing them to tie for first place in their division with a 7-6-1 record. Boston defeated Buffalo 26-8 in a playoff game dominated by heavy snow and Cappelletti's clutch field-goal kicking. In the AFL Championship Game with San Diego, the patched-up Patriots were no match for the Chargers. Keith Lincoln ran for 206 yards and San Diego scored an easy 51-10 victory.

1964 The Patriots drafted Jack Concannon, the All-America quarterback from Boston College, number one. But after a wild bidding war, Concannon decided to sign with the Philadelphia Eagles. Although there was some criticism of Holovak's "old folks" roster, he managed to get a lot out of it, closing with a rush that fell just short of a repeat division championship. The keys to the season were Parilli, who threw for 3,465 yards and 31 touchdowns, and Cappelletti, who caught 49 passes and scored seven touchdowns and a record 155 points. After setting a club attendance record of 199,707, the Patriots announced they had finished in the black for the first time.

1965 Jim Nance, a powerful fullback from Syracuse, was drafted in the nineteenth round. Joe Bellino, the former Heisman Trophy winner from Navy who spent four years in the service, also joined the team. Already weakened by age, the Patriots were further crippled by a series of injuries. Burton, fullback Larry Garron, and Cappelletti were a few of the top players who were injured. Parilli completed only 41 percent of his passes and threw 26 interceptions, and the kicking of Cappelletti, who again led the league with 132 points, had to carry the Patriots. It didn't carry them very far; although they won their last three games, they finished only 4-8-2.

1966 Plans for a mammoth year-round sports complex, were revealed for downtown Boston. The price tag, however, was estimated at $80 million, and the method of financing such a project remained a major stumbling block. The key to the Patriots' season turned out to be Nance, who finished with 1,458 yards rushing, an AFL record. Nance's presence helped Parilli enjoy an excellent season. The Patriots battled Buffalo for first place all season, and a late 14-3 victory over the Bills had Boston fans thinking championship. But in the final game of the year, Joe Namath and the Jets knocked them out of the lead and cost them the title 38-28.

1967 Although Nance continued to gain big yardage, the Patriots slipped badly, falling to last place. Parilli showed signs of age, there was little outside speed, and the defense couldn't carry the team. Nance still gained 1,216 yards, tops in the league, but no one else had more than 163 yards.

1968 In an attempt to trade some of the age for youth and enthusiasm, Holovak dealt Parilli to the New York Jets for quarterback Mike Taliaferro. But Taliaferro completed less than 40 percent of his passes and eventually lost his job to rookie Tom Sherman. Few of the other Patriots responded with good seasons. Nance injured an ankle that limited his effectiveness. Bad knees knocked defensive end Larry Eisenhauer and middle linebacker Buoniconti out of the lineup for a considerable time. Only tight end Jim Whalen, who made 47 receptions, was a real threat.

1969 Holovak was replaced as head coach by Clive Rush, and the Patriots lost the first seven games of the season. Buoniconti was traded to Miami. The Patriots rallied to win four of five games before losing their last two. Key new contributors included running back Carl Garrett, wide receiver Ron Sellers, and tackle Mike Montler, all rookies. Garrett led the AFL in rushing average; led the Patriots in receiving, punt returns, and kickoff returns; and was voted rookie of the year. All home games were played at Boston College Alumni Stadium.

1970 A large sum of money was spent to pick up Joe Kapp from Minnesota. But the quarterback who had taken the Vikings to Super Bowl IV wasn't the same one who showed up in Boston. He was out of shape and unfamiliar with the Patriots' system. He finished the season with three touchdown passes and 17 interceptions. His year was indicative of the entire team's performance. By midseason, Rush was fired and John Mazur was named head coach. Foxboro, Massachusetts, was officially selected as the new site for the team's home, and ground was broken for Schaefer Stadium. In the meantime, the Patriots played their home games at Harvard Stadium.

1971 Because it had moved out of Boston and would now represent a wider population area, the team's name was changed to the New England Patriots. Schaefer Stadium was dedicated in a 20-14 preseason win over the Giants before 60,423 fans. The biggest new name in town was rookie Jim Plunkett, Heisman Trophy-winning quarterback from Stanford. In his regular-season debut, Plunkett threw two touchdown passes to lead the Patriots to a 20-6 surprise of Oakland. Plunkett finished the season with 2,158 yards and 19 touchdowns and with rookie-of-the-year honors. His former Stanford teammate, Randy Vataha, became Plunkett's favorite target, catching 51 passes. Other newcomers included defensive lineman Julius Adams and linebacker Steve Kiner.

1972 A major difference of opinion erupted between general manager Upton Bell and Mazur on how the club should be built. The Patriots managed only three victories. Plunkett, with an inexperienced offensive line, was exposed to severe physical punishment. The defense also was young and ineffective. Several veterans, including Nance, Sellers, and Houston Antwine, were dealt off as part of the rebuilding program. Both Bell and Mazur became victims of their own debates. Mazur quit before the season was over and Bell was dispatched soon thereafter. Phil Bengtson, who was scouting for San Diego, was lent to the Patriots as interim coach.

1973 Chuck Fairbanks, the successful coach at the University of Oklahoma, was signed to a long-term contract as head coach and general manager. He immediately implemented a youth program. Rookies such as guard John Hannah, running back Sam Cunningham, and wide receiver Darryl Stingley and running back Mack Herron, from the Canadian Football League, all enjoyed outstanding seasons.

1974 Fairbanks put in a three-four defense and it became an immediate boost, with Ray (Sugar Bear) Hamilton playing the key nose tackle position. New England opened the season by shocking defending Super Bowl champion Miami 34-24. The Patriots used that win as impetus to run off four more in a row before Buffalo beat them 30-28, October 20. An unusual siege of injuries ruined what might have been a great season for the Patriots. A 6-1 start deteriorated into a 1-6 finish and a 7-7 overall record. Herron, a 5-foot 5-inch, 170-pounder, set a league record for combined offensive yardage (2,444). Cunningham gained 811 yards before he broke his leg. Plunkett passed for 2,457 yards and 19 touchdowns.

1975 Plunkett's recurring injuries kept both the quarterback situation and the team unstable. Plunkett separated his shoulder in a preseason game, then reseparated it against San Francisco, October 26. Neil Graff was Plunkett's first replacement, but Fairbanks eventually settled on Steve Grogan, a big, fifth-round draft choice from Kansas State, as his new passer. By the time Plunkett returned, a full-fledged quarterback controversy was underway. The team and the town were debating Plunkett versus Grogan. The fact that the club finished with a 3-11 record didn't help. Sullivan became the first majority owner of the team, purchasing additional voting stock to give him 88 percent of the franchise.

1976 In the biggest trade in Patriots' history, Plunkett was sent to San Francisco for quarterback Tom Owen and four draft choices. With Grogan as the new quarterback and help from youngsters such as running back Andy Johnson and cornerback Mike Haynes, the Patriots took off after an opening loss to Baltimore and won three games in a row, including a 48-17 victory over Oakland. The Patriots stayed in the AFC East race all year, won their last six, and eventually landed the wild card spot in the AFC playoffs, meeting Oakland in the first round. Though leading 21-10 going into the fourth quarter, the Patriots lost 24-21 when the eventual Super Bowl champion Raiders scored with 10 seconds remaining.

1977 Johnson was hurt in the preseason and offensive linemen John Hannah and Leon Gray held out due to salary disputes. The Patriots lost two of their first three games—both in the last minute of play and by scores of 30-27. New England then had four victories in a row, including a 17-3 game in which they held Baltimore to 86 yards. Another four-game winning streak followed defeats by Buffalo and Miami. On the final day of the season, although they had no chance of winning the AFC East, the Patriots led the Colts 21-3 before losing 30-24.

1978 Tragedy struck the Patriots in the third preseason game. In Oakland, Stingley was hit with a vicious tackle by Raiders safety Jack Tatum. The contact left Stingley permanently paralyzed. A 1-2 regular-season start was followed by seven straight victories as the Patriots established themselves as one of the dominant teams in the AFC. The streak was highlighted by a 529-yard offensive display in a 55-21 defeat of the Jets on October 29. Two weeks later, the winning streak ended when the Oilers roared back from a 23-0 second-quarter deficit to win 26-23. Three victories surrounding a loss to Dallas clinched the AFC East—the first outright championship in the club's history. Before the season-ending game with Miami, Fairbanks announced that he was resigning as head coach to take a similar position at Colorado. Assistants Ron Erhardt and Hank Bullough took over for the final game, but the disoriented Patriots lost to the Dolphins, 23-3. With Fairbanks on the sidelines at Sullivan's insistence, New England lost in the playoffs to Houston 31-14.

1979 Fairbanks was released from his contract on April 2. Four days later Erhardt was named head coach and Frank (Bucko) Kilroy general manager. The Patriots traded Gray to Houston. Stingley was named executive director of player personnel. Inconsistency was the trademark of the season. The Patriots scored 50 points twice, including a 56-3 drubbing of the Jets on September 9. The Jets came back to defeat the Patriots 27-26 exactly three months later, knocking them out of the playoffs. The running game suffered due to injuries to Johnson and Cunningham. Grogan threw a league-leading 28 touchdown passes, but was intercepted 20 times.

1980 The Patriots again came up a game short, despite leading the AFC in scoring, having the fourth-best defense, and sacking opposing quarterbacks 44 times. Grogan was leading the league in passing after seven games, and the Patriots were 6-1. But chronic knee problems cut down on Grogan's effectiveness, and inexperienced Matt Cavanaugh picked up. New England lost five of its next seven. Two victories to close out the season came too late and New England had to settle for second place.

1981 The Patriots suffered an inexplicable collapse, finishing with the poorest record in the NFL. Grogan and Cavanaugh shared time, but the Patriots seemed unable to find any stability. After four losses to open the season, the Patriots defeated Kansas City 33-17 on October 4 on the passing of Cavanaugh. Two weeks later Grogan accounted for three touchdowns and New England defeated Houston 38-10. Neither quarterback could spark the team the rest of the season, and the Patriots finished 2-14. Erhardt was fired on December 22.

1982 Ron Meyer, coach at SMU, was named the eighth head coach in Patriots history, January 15. With the number-one pick in the NFL draft, New England selected Texas All-America defensive tackle Ken Sims. With additional draft choices acquired in trades involving Russ Francis, Tim Fox, and Rod Shoate, the Patriots drafted a league-high 17 players. With the second-youngest team in the NFL, the Patriots finished 5-4 in the strike-shortened season. In the fourth game, Meyer replaced Cavanaugh with Grogan. In a 26-13 loss to Chicago on December 5, Grogan completed 13 of 28 passes for 231 yards to break Parilli's club records for career completions (1,140) and career passing yardage (16,911). In a bizarre episode against Miami on December 12, a work-release parolee behind the wheel of a tractor cleared a space on the snow-frozen turf of Schaefer Stadium to help placekicker John Smith kick a 33-yard field goal late in the fourth quarter. Smith's field goal broke a scoreless tie, and the Patriots won 3-0. The Patriots met the Dolphins again in the first round of the playoffs, but this time Miami won 28-13.

1983 Kilroy was named vice-president, and Patrick Sullivan was named general manager, February 16. The Patriots chose Illinois quarterback Tony Eason in the first round of the draft. On May 23, Schaefer Stadium was renamed Sullivan Stadium, in honor of the founder of the franchise, William H. (Billy) Sullivan. After opening the season with two losses, the Patriots hovered around the .500 mark the entire year, and finished with an 8-8 record. On October 30, Grogan completed a sweep of breaking every major club career-passing record held by Parilli, in a 24-13 loss to Atlanta. In a 30-0 loss to Cleveland on November 20, defensive end Adams set a new club record for most games played, 160, breaking the record held by tackle Tom Neville. In November, Haynes was traded to the Los Angeles Raiders. After rushing for just 543 yards in his first five NFL seasons, Mosi Tatupu ran for 578, while leading the NFL with a 5.5 average.

1984 The Patriots used the number-one selection in the NFL draft to select Nebraska wide receiver Irving Fryar. After a 44-24 loss to Miami, Meyer fired defensive coordinator Rod Rust, without the permission of Sullivan. On October 25, Sullivan fired Meyer, replaced him as head coach with Hall of Fame receiver Raymond Berry, and rehired Rust as defensive coordinator. The Patriots, 5-3 at the time, won three of their next four games for Berry. Three consecutive losses ended New England's playoff chances. The highlight of the season was a dramatic comeback victory over Seattle. Trailing 23-0 just before halftime, Eason replaced Grogan and ran for a touchdown on his first series. The Patriots then scored 31 unanswered points in the second half to win 38-23. Eason kept the job as starting quarterback and finished the season as the number-two ranked passer in the AFC, throwing for 3,228 yards, 23 touchdowns, and just eight interceptions. Running back Craig James, used more by Berry in the second half of the season, finished with 790 yards rushing on a 4.9 average. Linebacker Andre Tippett had 18½ quarterback sacks.

1985 The Patriots began the season with a 2-3 record. But then the team caught fire, and won six consecutive games. Included in that string were victories over each of the Patriots' AFC East opponents. Heading into the next-to-last game of the season against Miami at the Orange Bowl, the Patriots, Dolphins, and Jets all were tied for first place. In the showdown with Miami, New England rallied to tie the score at 27-27 with two fourth-quarter touchdowns, but lost for the eighteenth consecutive time at the Orange Bowl, 30-27. The Patriots earned a wild card berth the next week by defeating Cincinnati 34-23. Against the Jets at Giants Stadium, Tony Franklin kicked four field goals and Johnny Rembert scored on a fumble recovery to help the Patriots win their first playoff game since 1963, 26-14. New England also cashed in on a fumble recovery against the Raiders in a divisional playoff game in Los Angeles a week later when Jim Bowman fell on a fumble by the Raiders' Sam Seale in the end zone to give the Patriots the winning points in a 27-20 victory. In their third consecutive playoff game on the road, the Patriots capitalized on six Miami turnovers, snapping the Orange Bowl hex 31-14. New England punished the Dolphins on the ground with 255 yards rushing, and Eason passed just often enough to keep the Dolphins off balance, throwing three touchdowns. Franklin's 36-yard field goal in the second minute of play gave New England a brief 3-0 lead over the Chicago Bears in Super Bowl XX at the Louisiana Superdome in New Orleans. But the Bears won 46-10.

1986 In June, Hannah retired.

MEMBERS OF HALL OF FAME:
None

PATRIOTS RECORD, 1960-85

Year	Won	Lost	Tied	Pct.	Fin.	Pts.	OP
Boston Patriots							
1960	5	9	0	.357	4	286	349
1961	9	4	1	.692	2	413	313
1962	9	4	1	.692	2	346	295
1963a	7	6	1	.538	1	317	257
1964	10	3	1	.769	2	365	297
1965	4	8	2	.333	3	244	302
1966	8	4	2	.667	2	315	283
1967	3	10	1	.231	5	280	389
1968	4	10	0	.286	4	229	406
1969	4	10	0	.286	3t	266	316
1970	2	12	0	.143	5	149	361
New England Patriots							
1971	6	8	0	.429	3	238	325
1972	3	11	0	.214	5	192	446
1973	5	9	0	.357	3	258	300
1974	7	7	0	.500	3	348	289
1975	3	11	0	.214	4	258	358
1976b	11	3	0	.786	2	376	236
1977	9	5	0	.643	3	278	217
1978c	11	5	0	.688	1	358	286
1979	9	7	0	.563	2	411	326
1980	10	6	0	.625	2	441	325
1981	2	14	0	.125	5	322	370
1982d	5	4	0	.556	7	143	157
1983	8	8	0	.500	2	274	289
1984	9	7	0	.563	2	362	352
1985e	11	5	0	.688	3	362	290
26 Years	174	190	9	.479		7,831	8,134

a*AFL Eastern Division Champion; 1-1 in Playoffs*
b*AFC Wild Card Qualifier for Playoffs; 0-1 in Playoffs*
c*AFC Eastern Division Champion; 0-1 in Playoffs*
d*AFC Qualifier for Playoffs; 0-1 in Playoffs*
e*AFC Champion; 3-1 in Playoffs*

RECORD HOLDERS

CAREER

Rushing attempts	Sam Cunningham, 1973-79, 1981-82	1,385
Rushing yards	Sam Cunningham, 1973-79, 1981-82	5,453
Pass attempts	Steve Grogan, 1975-84	2,681
Pass completions	Steve Grogan, 1975-84	1,389
Passing yards	Steve Grogan, 1975-84	20,270
Touchdown passes	Steve Grogan, 1975-84	139
Receptions	Stanley Morgan, 1977-84	312
Receiving yards	Stanley Morgan, 1977-84	6,441
Interceptions	Ron Hall, 1961-67	29
Punting average	Rich Camarillo, 1981-84	43.3
Punt return avg.	Mack Herron, 1973-75	12.0
Kickoff return avg.	Horace Ivory, 1977-81	27.6
Field goals	Gino Cappelletti, 1960-70	176
Touchdowns	Sam Cunningham, 1973-79, 1981-82	49
Points	Gino Cappelletti, 1960-70	1,130

SEASON

Rushing attempts	Jim Nance, 1966	299
Rushing yards	Jim Nance, 1966	1,458
Pass attempts	Vito (Babe) Parilli, 1964	473
Pass completions	Tony Eason, 1984	259
Passing yards	Vito (Babe) Parilli, 1964	3,465
Touchdown passes	Vito (Babe) Parilli, 1964	31
Receptions	Derrick Ramsey, 1984	66
Receiving yards	Stanley Morgan, 1981	1,029
Interceptions	Ron Hall, 1964	11
Punting average	Rich Camarillo, 1983	44.6
Punt return avg.	Mack Herron, 1974	14.8
Kickoff return avg.	Raymond Clayborn, 1977	31.0
Field goals	John Smith, 1980	26
Touchdowns	Steve Grogan, 1976	13
	Stanley Morgan, 1979	13
Points	Gino Cappelletti, 1964	115

GAME

Rushing attempts	Jim Nance, 10-30-66	38
Rushing yards	Tony Collins, 9-18-83	212
Pass attempts	Vito (Babe) Parilli, 11-14-65	50
Pass completions	Tony Eason, 11-18-84	29
Passing yards	Vito (Babe) Parilli, 10-16-64	422
Touchdown passes	Vito (Babe) Parilli, 11-15-64	5
	Vito (Babe) Parilli, 10-15-67	5
	Steve Grogan, 9-9-79	5
Receptions	Art Graham, 11-20-66	11
Receiving yards	Stanley Morgan, 11-8-81	182
Interceptions	6 times	3
Field goals	Gino Cappelletti, 10-4-64	6
Touchdowns	13 times	3
Points	Gino Cappelletti, 12-18-65	28

COACHING HISTORY

1960-61	Lou Saban*	7-12-0
1961-68	Mike Holovak	53-47-9
1969-70	Clive Rush**	5-16-0
1970-72	John Mazur***	9-21-0
1972	Phil Bengtson	1- 4-0
1973-78	Chuck Fairbanks****	46-41-0
1978	Ron Erhardt, Hank Bullough*****	0- 1-0
1979-81	Ron Erhardt	21-27-0
1982-84	Ron Meyer******	18-16-0
1984-85	Raymond Berry	18-10-0

**Replaced after five games in 1961*
***Replaced after seven games in 1970*
****Resigned after nine games in 1972*
*****Replaced after 15 games in 1978*
******Co-coaches for one game in 1978*
*******Replaced after eight games in 1984*

FIRST PLAYER SELECTED

1960	Gerhard Schwedes, HB, Syracuse
1961	Tommy Mason, HB, Tulane
1962	Gary Collins, E, Maryland
1963	Art Graham, E, Boston College
1964	Jack Concannon, QB, Boston College
1965	Jerry Rush, T, Michigan State
1965†	David McCormick, T, LSU
1966	Karl Singer, T, Purdue
1966†	Willie Townes, DT, Tulsa
1967	John Charles, S, Purdue
1968	Dennis Byrd, DT, North Carolina State
1969	Ron Sellers, SE, Florida State
1970	Phil Olsen, DT, Utah State
1971	Jim Plunkett, QB, Stanford
1972	(2) Tom Reynolds, WR, San Diego State
1973	John Hannah, G, Alabama
1974	(2) Steve Corbett, G, Boston College
1975	Russ Francis, TE, Oregon
1976	Mike Haynes, CB, Arizona State
1977	Raymond Clayborn, CB, Texas
1978	Bob Cryder, G, Alabama
1979	Rick Sanford, DB, South Carolina
1980	Roland James, DB, Tennessee
1981	Brian Holloway, T, Stanford
1982	Ken Sims, DE, Texas
1983	Tony Eason, QB, Illinois
1984	Irving Fryar, WR, Nebraska
1984*	Ricky Sanders, WR, Southwest Texas State
1985	Trevor Matich, C, BYU
1986	Reggie Dupard, RB, SMU

†Redshirt Draft
**Supplemental Draft*

NEW ORLEANS SAINTS

1966 The National Football League, long impressed by the support New Orleans fans displayed for preseason games at Tulane Stadium, awarded an expansion franchise to the Crescent City, November 1. John W. Mecom, Jr., a millionaire sportsman, was designated majority stockholder and president of the franchise, December 15. Among his limited partners was Al Hirt, the Bourbon Street trumpet player. Vic Schwenk became the first major employee hired by the New Orleans franchise, when he was appointed director of player personnel, December 22.
1967 The team was named the Saints in honor of the Dixieland classic "When the Saints Go Marchin' In," which became the team's fight song. Mecom hired Tom Fears, a former end for the Los Angeles Rams and an assistant coach for Green Bay under Vince Lombardi, as head coach, January 27. The same day, former Rams kicker Paige Cothren became the first player to sign a Saints contract. On March 9, the Saints selected 42 players in an expansion draft, and a month later they made Les Kelley, a fullback from Alabama, their first pick in the regular draft. Fears chose to go with veteran players and assembled a cast of former NFL stars: Jim Taylor, Paul Hornung, Doug Atkins, Earl Leggett, and Lou Cordileone. The Saints traded their first draft choice to Baltimore for reserve quarterback Gary Cuozzo. New Orleans fans responded frantically to the Saints' arrival, purchasing 20,000 season tickets the day the box office opened and 33,400 before the season started. The Saints' first training camp was held at California Western University in San Diego. The Saints lost their first preseason game 16-7 to the Los Angeles Rams, August 2, but scored their first victory 10 days later by beating St. Louis 23-14 in Shreveport, Louisiana. On September 9, the Saints defeated Atlanta 27-14, giving them their first victory in New Orleans and a 5-1 preseason record, the best ever for an expansion team. When rookie John Gilliam returned the opening kickoff 94 yards for a touchdown in their regular-season debut against Los Angeles, the 80,789 fans in Tulane Stadium nearly went berserk. The Rams rallied to win 27-13 but the Saints made a strong first impression, September 17. New Orleans went winless through the first seven games before beating Philadelphia 31-24 at Tulane Stadium, November 5, as Walter Roberts scored three touchdowns. The Saints finished with three victories, tying a record for an expansion team. The team leaders the Saints' first year were an interesting collection: Taylor led them in rushing in his last NFL season; Dave Whitsell led the team and league in interceptions on the way to comeback-player-of-the-year honors and being the first Saint selected to the Pro Bowl; seventeenth-round draft choice Dan Abramowicz led them in receiving (50 catches); and former 49ers quarterback Billy Kilmer shared the position with Cuozzo.
1968 Schwenk was promoted to general manager, March 29. Fears improved his offense by signing end Dave Parks, who had played out his option in San Francisco, July 17. He had to pay a steep price, however, as Commissioner Pete Rozelle made New Orleans part with its top draft choice, defensive tackle Kevin Hardy of Notre Dame, and its number-one pick in the 1969 draft as compensation. Following a painful preseason, Taylor announced his retirement as a player, September 10. New Orleans played competitive football in almost every game, beating Pittsburgh 24-14 in its final game to finish third in the Century Division. The Saints' two-year record of 7-20-1 was the best to date for an expansion team.
1969 Fears added several exciting offensive players, including running backs Andy Livingston and Tony Baker and placekicker Tom Dempsey. After an 0-6 start, the Saints rebounded. The turning point was a wild 51-42 win over St. Louis, November 2. Kilmer passed for 354 yards and six touchdowns in the victory. Dempsey set a club record with four field goals, including one with 11 seconds left to pull out a 25-24 win over the New York Giants, November 16. The Saints closed the season with a 27-24 win over Pittsburgh and finished in third place at 5-9 in the Capitol Division. Abramowicz led the NFL with 73 pass receptions for 1,015 yards, and Baker led the league with a 4.8-yard rushing average. Atkins, 39, retired after 17 seasons in the NFL.
1970 In the realignment of the NFL, New Orleans joined the NFC West, January 16. The Saints won only one of their first seven games. Mecom fired Fears and hired J.D. Roberts, formerly of the Richmond team of the Atlantic Coast Football League, as head coach, November 3. In Roberts's first game, the Saints scored a memorable 19-17 upset of Detroit at Tulane Stadium, November 8. The winning points came on the final play—a record-setting, 63-yard field goal by Dempsey, the free-agent kicker who was born without a right hand and without toes on his right foot. But without the injured Livingston, Abramowicz was the only offensive threat on the team, and the Saints dropped their final six games.
1971 In the first round of the draft, the Saints selected Mississippi quarterback Archie Manning. Manning, a long-time favorite with football fans in the South, received a hero's welcome in New Orleans. In his pro debut, Manning scored the winning touchdown on the last play of the game to upset the Los Angeles Rams 24-20 at Tulane Stadium. It was the Saints' first win ever over the Rams. Manning's fourth-quarter heroics also led to a 24-14 victory over Dallas. Foot and leg injuries sidelined Manning late in the season, and New Orleans slipped to last place in the Western Division of the NFC. Jim Strong, acquired from the 49ers, led the Saints with 404 yards rushing.
1972 The Saints appointed former astronaut Richard F. Gordon, Jr., executive vice president, January 7. The Saints equaled their poorest season record, achieved in 1970, at 2-11-1. The Saints' defense took a step forward, when safety Tommy Myers of Syracuse was selected in the college draft. Manning netted more than 3,000 yards running and passing and accounted for 20 of the team's 26 touchdowns but took a terrible beating behind the Saints' porous offensive line.
1973 Mecom fired J.D. Roberts and appointed John North head coach, August 26. North, an ex-Marine, learned his football as an assistant under Blanton Collier at Kentucky. After a scoreless first quarter, Atlanta erupted to embarrass New Orleans in the league opener 62-7 at Tulane Stadium, September 16. The following week, the Saints were humiliated 40-3 by Dallas at Texas Stadium. But the Saints won four of their next six games, including a 19-3 surprise of Washington, October 28. Bill McClard, acquired on waivers earlier in the week, kicked four field goals to beat the Redskins. As the season progressed, North built the defense into a respectable unit, with players such as Myers, defensive end Billy Newsome, linebacker Joe Federspiel, and defensive back Ernie Jackson. In the middle of the season, the Saints traded Abramowicz, their all-time receiving leader, to San Francisco.
1974 The Saints snapped a 19-game winless streak on the road with a 13-3 decision over Atlanta, October 20. The Saints rushed for a club-record 232 yards in the game, and reserve quarterback Bobby Scott threw the first touchdown pass of his NFL career. New Orleans upset Philadelphia 14-10 the following week at Tulane Stadium. The Saints won their fifth game, equaling their best record, as rookie quarterback Larry Cipa, a fifteenth-round draft choice, led a 14-10 victory over St. Louis, December 8.
1975 New Orleans moved into the world's largest indoor stadium, the Louisiana Superdome, to open the preseason against Houston, August 9. The move culminated years of controversy surrounding the construction of the gigantic arena, which had a football seating capacity of 72,000. In the first regular-season game in the Superdome, the Saints lost to Cincinnati 21-0. Rich Szaro, a free agent from Harvard, kicked a 20-yard field goal to give the Saints a last-second, 20-19 victory over Green Bay, October 12. Following a 38-14 loss to the Rams, North was fired as head coach and replaced by Ernie Hefferle, the Saints' director of pro personnel, October 25. The Saints won their first game under Hefferle, 23-7 over Atlanta, but lost the last seven to finish 2-12.
1976 The Saints hired Hank Stram, the man who coached Kansas City to the Super Bowl IV championship, as their fifth head coach, January 20. Stram traded linebacker Rick Middleton to San Diego for quarterback Bobby Douglass and a third-round draft choice, April 2. The Saints' first two draft choices were Chuck Muncie, All-America running back from California, and Tony Galbreath, running back from Missouri. The offense missed Manning, who sat out the entire season following surgery on his right arm and was replaced by Douglass. Stram's first victory was sweet personal revenge as his Saints defeated the Chiefs in Kansas City 27-17, September 26. In that game, Galbreath rushed for 146 yards and two touchdowns, Muncie for 126 yards. The Saints scored the most one-sided win in their history, a 30-0 rout of Atlanta, October 10. They also beat Seattle 51-27, November 21.
1977 The Saints opened with two close losses, then pounded Chicago 42-24, as Manning ran for three touchdowns and passed for a fourth. The defense proved unreliable during the season and gave up 336 points, the most in the NFC. New Orleans won only two more games the rest of the year and finished 3-11. One of those victories came against the Rams (27-26) on October 30 on a pass from Tom Blanchard to Elois Grooms on a fake field goal. A low point occurred on December 11 when the Saints became the first team in the NFL to lose to Tampa Bay. The Buccaneers returned three interceptions for touchdowns in the 33-14 victory.
1978 All-pro guard Conrad Dobler and wide receiver Ike Harris were obtained from St. Louis. Dick Nolan was named to replace Hank Stram as head coach on February 6. Eddie Jones became the new executive vice president, and Harry Hulmes was named vice president of player personnel. For only the second time in their 12-year history, the Saints won a season opener, defeating Minnesota 31-24. At 2-4 the Saints embarked on a three-game winning streak for the first time in their history, including a 10-3 victory over the Rams—the team's first win in the Los Angeles Memorial Coliseum. The Saints won only two more games, but both were landmarks. On December 3, a 24-13 victory over San Francisco made this the first Saints team to win six games in a season. In the season finale, the Saints gained revenge and a seventh victory with a 17-10 decision over Tampa Bay. The team's most valuable player, and the NFC player of the year, was Manning, who completed 291 of 471 passes (62 percent) for 3,416 yards and 17 touchdowns. Galbreath not only led the team in rushing (635 yards), he broke Abramowicz's club record by catching 74 passes.
1979 Russell Erxleben, an All-America kicker from Texas, was the Saints' first draft pick. The choice

was a disaster, as Erxleben had kicking problems almost immediately and was replaced by Garo Yepremian. New Orleans opened with three consecutive losses and was 2-4 after six weeks. But against Tampa Bay on October 14, the Saints enjoyed the biggest second half in club history with 42 points, resulting in a 42-14 victory. Consecutive wins over Detroit and Washington ignited a serious run at the NFC West title, and on six occasions in October and November the Saints were first or tied for first in the division as their record rose to 7-6. A loss to Oakland on December 3 crippled the team's title chances, and a week later San Diego eliminated the Saints from the division race. New Orleans closed out the season by defeating Los Angeles in the last game at the Los Angeles Coliseum. Finishing 8-8, the Saints ranked second in the NFC in points with 370. Chuck Muncie became the first Saint to top the 1,000-yard rushing total in a season with 1,198, second-year wide receiver Wes Chandler broke Abramowicz's receiving-yardage mark, with 65 catches for 1,069 yards, and Manning passed for 3,169 yards and 20 touchdowns. On December 20, Steve Rosenbloom was named executive vice president and general manager.

1980 Dick Steinberg, formerly with the Los Angeles Rams, was named vice president of player personnel on June 25. A disastrous season unfolded as the Saints lost their first 14 games and finished 1-15. Muncie was traded to San Diego after the fourth game. Nolan was relieved of his coaching duties November 25, the day after the club's twelfth loss. Dick Stanfel was appointed interim head coach. The Saints opened up a 35-7 lead at halftime over the 49ers on December 7, but still lost 38-35. A week later they finally won when Tony Galbreath scored on a one-yard run in the fourth quarter to beat the New York Jets 21-20. Ironically, Manning compiled the best statistics of his career: 309 completions, 3,716 yards, and 23 touchdowns. But the defense allowed a whopping 487 points.

1981 Rosenbloom and Steinberg resigned January 20. Two days later, O. A. (Bum) Phillips, formerly with Houston, was named head coach. Fred Williams was appointed chief administrator. With the first choice in the draft, the Saints selected running back George Rogers, the Heisman Trophy winner from South Carolina. Galbreath was traded to Minnesota. After losing the opener to Atlanta, the Saints defeated Los Angeles 23-17, as Rogers rushed for 162 yards. Although they won only three more times, those included victories over AFC champion Cincinnati, a second win over the Rams, and a poignant 27-24 victory against Phillips's former team, the Oilers. Rogers set an NFL rookie rushing record, and led the league in rushing with 1,674 yards.

1982 Eddie Jones rejoined the Saints as president, while head coach Bum Phillips added the title of general manager. Veteran quarterback Ken Stabler signed with the Saints as a free agent during the preseason. He became the regular quarterback when Manning, the heart of the franchise since his rookie season of 1971, was traded to Houston on September 17 for tackle Leon Gray. In a season cut short by a prolonged players' strike, the Saints barely missed qualifying for the playoffs for the first time in their history. They finished the season with a 4-5 record, just one game out of the postseason tournament, after soundly defeating Atlanta 35-6. Rogers again led the Saints in rushing. His 166 yards against Dallas was the NFL's top rushing performance of the season and a New Orleans record.

1983 Only Mike Lansford's 42-yard field goal with six seconds to play, which gave the Rams a 26-24 victory in the season's final game, kept the Saints out of the playoffs. A regular-season record of 8-8 equaled the best mark in franchise history. New Orleans finished with the top-ranked defense in the NFC, and the number-one pass defense in the NFL. Outside linebacker Rickey Jackson led all NFL linebackers with 12. Rogers led the Saints in rushing (1,144 yards) for the third year in a row, and set a team single-game record when he picked up 206 yards in the season opener, a 28-17 victory over St. Louis. On September 18, the Saints defeated the Bears 34-31 for their first overtime victory ever.

1984 Mindful that Stabler was close to retiring, the Saints made an offseason trade for New York Jets quarterback Richard Todd. Stabler made it official when he announced his retirement on October 22, one day after completing 2 of 9 passes for 34 yards in a 30-27 overtime loss in Dallas. Phillips was reunited with running back Earl Campbell, whom he coached in Houston, when the Saints acquired Campbell from the Oilers on October 9. New Orleans again finished third with a 7-9 record. Jackson, defensive end Bruce Clark, and rookie punter Brian Hansen all were selected for the Pro Bowl.

1985 New Orleans car dealer Tom Benson became the Saints' managing general partner when he bought the team from John Mecom, Jr., for $70.2 million. The purchase officially was completed on June 3, the same day the Saints announced a commitment to continue playing in the Superdome for the next 21 years. Just prior to the NFL draft, the Saints traded Rogers to Washington. Decimated by injuries, New Orleans slumped to 5-11, good for third place. Included among the victories was a 20-17 upset over defending Super Bowl-champion San Francisco on Phillips's sixty-second birthday. Eight weeks later, after a 30-23 victory in Minnesota that featured Campbell's first 100-yard game (160) in two years, Phillips resigned and was replaced by his son Wade, the Saints' defensive coordinator. The Saints scored 20 points in less than six minutes to beat the Rams 29-3 in the first game under Wade Phillips, then they lost their last three. Morten Andersen led the NFC in field-goal percentage (31 of 35, .886) and converted his last 14 in a row. He was chosen for the Pro Bowl along with Jackson, who made it for the third consecutive year.

1986 Veteran NFL executive Jim Finks became the Saints' new president and general manager, replacing Jones, who was fired. Jim Mora, a former NFL assistant who coached two USFL championship teams, was hired as the new head coach.

MEMBERS OF HALL OF FAME:
Doug Atkins, Jim Taylor

SAINTS RECORD, 1967-85

Year	Won	Lost	Tied	Pct.	Fin.	Pts.	OP
1967	3	11	0	.214	4	233	379
1968	4	9	1	.308	3	246	327
1969	5	9	0	.357	3	311	393
1970	2	11	1	.154	4	172	347
1971	4	8	2	.333	4	266	347
1972	2	11	1	.179	4	215	361
1973	5	9	0	.357	3	163	312
1974	5	9	0	.357	3	166	263
1975	2	12	0	.143	4	165	360
1976	4	10	0	.286	4	253	346
1977	3	11	0	.214	4	232	336
1978	7	9	0	.438	3	281	298
1979	8	8	0	.500	2	370	360
1980	1	15	0	.063	4	291	487
1981	4	12	0	.250	4	207	378
1982	4	5	0	.444	10	129	160
1983	8	8	0	.500	3	319	337
1984	7	9	0	.438	3	298	361
1985	5	11	0	.313	3	294	401
19 Years	83	187	5	.311		4,611	6,553

RECORD HOLDERS

CAREER

Rushing attempts	George Rogers, 1981-84	995
Rushing yards	George Rogers, 1981-84	4,267
Pass attempts	Archie Manning, 1971-82	3,335
Pass completions	Archie Manning, 1971-82	1,849
Passing yards	Archie Manning, 1971-82	21,734
Touchdown passes	Archie Manning, 1971-82	115
Receptions	Dan Abramowicz, 1967-73	309
Receiving yards	Dan Abramowicz, 1967-73	4,875
Interceptions	Tommy Myers, 1972-82	36
Punting average	Brian Hansen, 1984-85	42.9
Punt return avg.	Gil Chapman, 1975	12.2
Kickoff return avg.	Walter (The Flea) Roberts, 1967	26.3
Field goals	Morten Andersen, 1982-85	71
Touchdowns	Dan Abramowicz, 1967-73	37
Points	Morten Andersen, 1982-85	317

SEASON

Rushing attempts	George Rogers, 1981	378
Rushing yards	George Rogers, 1981	1,674
Pass attempts	Archie Manning, 1980	509
Pass completions	Archie Manning, 1980	309
Passing yards	Archie Manning, 1980	3,716
Touchdown passes	Archie Manning, 1980	23
Receptions	Tony Galbreath, 1978	74
Receiving yards	Wes Chandler, 1979	1,069
Interceptions	Dave Whitsell, 1967	10
Punting average	Brian Hansen, 1984	43.8
Punt return avg.	Gil Chapman, 1975	12.2
Kickoff return avg.	Don Shy, 1969	27.9
Field goals	Morten Andersen, 1985	31
Touchdowns	George Rogers, 1981	13
Points	Morten Andersen, 1985	120

GAME

Rushing attempts	Earl Campbell, 11-24-85	35
Rushing yards	George Rogers, 9-4-83	206
Pass attempts	Archie Manning, 9-10-78	53
Pass completions	Archie Manning, 9-10-78	33
Passing yards	Archie Manning, 12-7-80	377
Touchdown passes	Billy Kilmer, 11-2-69	6
Receptions	Tony Galbreath, 9-10-78	14
Receiving yards	Wes Chandler, 9-2-79	205
Interceptions	Tommy Myers, 9-3-78	3
	Dave Waymer, 10-6-85	3
Field goals	Garo Yepremian, 10-14-79	6
Touchdowns	6 times	3
Points	6 times	18

COACHING HISTORY

1967-70	Tom Fears*	13-34-2
1970-72	J. D. Roberts	7-25-3
1973-75	John North**	11-23-0
1975	Ernie Hefferle	1- 7-0
1976-77	Hank Stram	7-21-0
1978-80	Dick Nolan***	15-29-0
1980	Dick Stanfel	1- 3-0
1981-85	Bum Phillips****	27-42-0
1985	Wade Phillips	1- 3-0
1986	Jim Mora	

**Replaced after seven games in 1970*
***Replaced after six games in 1975*
****Replaced after 12 games in 1980*
*****Resigned after 12 games in 1985*

FIRST PLAYER SELECTED

1967 Les Kelley, FB, Alabama
1968 Kevin Hardy, DE, Notre Dame
1969 John Shinners, G, Xavier
1970 Ken Burrough, WR, Texas Southern
1971 Archie Manning, QB, Mississippi
1972 Royce Smith, G, Georgia
1973 (2) Derland Moore, DE, Oklahoma
1974 Rick Middleton, LB, Ohio State
1975 Larry Burton, WR, Purdue
1976 Chuck Muncie, RB, California
1977 Joe Campbell, DE, Maryland
1978 Wes Chandler, WR, Florida
1979 Russell Erxleben, P-K, Texas
1980 Stan Brock, T, Colorado
1981 George Rogers, RB, South Carolina
1981* Dave Wilson, QB, Illinois
1982 Lindsay Scott, WR, Georgia
1983 (2) Steve Korte, G, Arkansas
1984 (2) James Geathers, DT, Wichita State
1984* Vaughan Johnson, LB, North Carolina State
1985 Alvin Toles, LB, Tennessee
1986 Jim Dombrowski, T, Virginia
**Supplemental Draft*

SAINTS MOST VALUABLE PLAYER

1967 Dave Whitsell, S
1968 Doug Atkins, DE
1969 Dan Abramowicz, WR
1970 Mike Tilleman, DT
1971 Jake Kupp, G
1972 Archie Manning, QB
1973 Billy Newsome, DE
1974 John Didion, C
1975 Mike Strachan, RB
1976 Tony Galbreath, RB
1977 Chuck Crist, S
1978 Archie Manning, QB
1979 Chuck Muncie, RB
1980 Archie Manning, QB
1981 George Rogers, RB
1982 Ken Stabler, QB
1983 Wayne Wilson, RB
1984 Hokie Gajan, RB
1985 Morten Andersen, K

NEW YORK GIANTS

1925 Tim Mara went to see Billy Gibson in hopes of buying an interest in heavyweight boxer Gene Tunney and wound up becoming the owner of an NFL franchise for New York for $500, August 1. Mara named the team Giants, after the baseball team with which it would share the Polo Grounds. He hired Bob Folwell, formerly of Navy, as coach and Dr. Harry March to recruit talent. Among the first Giants were old pros such as Jim Thorpe and Bob Nash and collegians such as Jack McBride of Syracuse, Hinkey Haines of Penn State, Century Milstead of Yale, and Lynn Bomar of Vanderbilt. The Giants won their first exhibition over Ducky Pond's All-Stars at New Britain, Connecticut. New York lost its first two regular-season games, both on the road. With the help of at least 5,000 free tickets, they drew about 25,000 to watch the home opener, a 14-0 loss to the Frankford Yellow Jackets, October 18. The Giants regrouped to win seven in a row, but Mara was $40,000 in the red when the Chicago Bears signed Red Grange and brought him to New York, December 6. A record crowd of 73,000 jammed the Polo Grounds, turning a negative cash flow into a financial bonanza. New York finished tied for fourth at 8-4.

1926 Grange's business manager, C. C. Pyle, tried to force his way into the NFL with a franchise at Yankee Stadium, but Mara objected. Pyle organized the rival American Football League. Folwell left the Giants to coach the Philadelphia entry in the AFL. Milstead also quit the team to go to the AFL. Dr. Joe Alexander was named the Giants' new coach, in a league that expanded to 22 clubs. The Giants had a bitter war with the Yankees and Grange. Alexander signed first-year players such as Jack Hagerty of Georgetown, Glenn Killinger of Penn State, and Walter Koppisch of Columbia, while Mara bought tackle Steve Owen from the Kansas City Cowboys. The team trained at Lake Ariel, Pennsylvania. The Giants beat Hartford and Providence to begin the season, then were shut out three games in a row. The Giants won five of their last six, but finished tied for sixth at 8-4-1. After the season, the Giants defeated coach Folwell's Philadelphia Quakers of the AFL 31-0. Despite free tickets, preliminary high school doubleheaders, and special entertainment, attendance was poor. Mara lost $40,000. Pyle's Yankees lost $100,000, however, and the AFL folded.

1927 Pyle's Yankees were admitted to the NFL after appeasing Mara's contention that he had the territorial rights to New York by agreeing to play 13 of their 16 games on the road and the other 3 when the Giants were out of town. Mara made a coaching change, promoting Earl Potteiger from assistant to succeed Alexander, who was too busy with his medical chores. The Giants signed Cal Hubbard, a 250-pound tackle from Geneva, re-signed Milstead, and added Faye (Mule) Wilson and Joe Guyon. The new players helped make the Giants the strongest team in the NFL. New York had its problems with Cleveland—in two games, the Giants battled Cleveland to a scoreless tie and lost 6-0—but not with the rest of the league. The team's 11-1-1 record was good for their first NFL championship. They scored 197 points and gave up only 20.

1928 Overconfidence led to bickering and there was unrest in the club, despite its 4-2-2 record in midseason. The Giants lost their last five, including two to Pyle's Yankees. Instead of an expected second straight title, Mara lost $40,000.

1929 Mara wanted Benny Friedman, an all-pro quarterback with Detroit, as a drawing card in the Polo Grounds, but he couldn't work out a trade. So Mara purchased the Detroit franchise, bringing Friedman, five other players, and its coach, LeRoy Andrews, to New York. Friedman signed the largest annual contract in league history—$10,000. After a 0-0 tie with Orange, the Giants won eight in a row, including two each over 1928 champion Providence and the Chicago Bears. Unbeaten Green Bay challenged the unbeaten Giants in a showdown game in the Polo Grounds on November 24, and the Packers emerged with a 20-6 victory. The Giants won their last five for a 13-1-1 record, but the Packers were champions at 12-0-1. Attendance averaged 25,000 and the Giants made a small profit.

1930 Ownership of the club was turned over to Jack and Wellington Mara, the two sons of the founder. Andrews remained as coach, with Friedman commuting between his pro job and his part-time work with the Yale coaching staff. The arrival of Chris (Red) Cagle, former All-America back at Army, brought huge crowds to the Polo Grounds when the Giants and Packers met in another important game late in the season. The Giants won 13-6 and moved into first place. New York lost its next two games, to the Staten Island Stapletons and Brooklyn Dodgers. Green Bay finished on top with 10-3-1 and a .769 percentage to the Giants' 13-4 and .765. After the season, the Giants played Knute Rockne's Notre Dame All-Stars in a charity game and raised $115,153 for the New York Unemployment Fund as 55,000 saw the Giants win 22-0.

1931 Center Mel Hein was signed by the Giants. Owen was named head coach. Friedman decided to quit pro ball and take a full-time job at Yale until the Giants rescheduled practice for a morning hour to ease their quarterback's commuting problems. The Giants were 3-3 when Friedman returned to the team. With Friedman in the lineup, the team scored four straight shutout victories. They collapsed in the final four weeks, however, and finished fifth at 7-6-1.

1932 The NFL was down to eight teams in the middle of the Depression, and the Giants were beginning to show their age. Friedman left to join Brooklyn as a player-coach and Owen signed ex-Giant Jack McBride, who had been released by the Dodgers, to do the passing. McBride helped Owen score a 6-0 upset of Green Bay, winner of three straight NFL titles and unbeaten in nine games. The Giants wound up tied for fourth at 4-6-2, losing the final game to the Bears, who clinched the championship. Ray Flaherty was the league's first official pass-receiving champion with 21 catches.

1933 New rules that opened up the game prompted the Giants to sign Harry Newman, a talented tailback from Michigan, and Ken Strong, a versatile back who was available because Staten Island went out of business. Training camp was at Pompton Lakes, New Jersey. Owen was back on the active list as a player for the last time as the Giants easily won the Eastern Division of the newly divided NFL with an 11-3 record. Philadelphia and Pittsburgh, new to the league, were in the same division, and the Giants ran up a 56-0 victory against the Eagles. In the first NFL Championship Game that had been planned, the Giants lost to the Bears 23-21 at Wrigley Field in a thriller in which the lead changed hands six times. Newman led the league in passing, and Strong tied for the scoring lead with 64 points.

1934 Tailback Ed Danowski and guard John Dell Isola, both of Fordham, were the most important newcomers. Newman set a league record with 34 carries in a game with Green Bay, November 11. Newman suffered two broken bones in his back in a late-season game against the Bears. Danowski took over in a backfield that also included Strong, Bo Molenda, and Dale Burnett. The Giants won the Eastern Division again and moved into a title game with the Bears at the Polo Grounds, December 9. That game came to be known as the Sneakers Game when the New York equipment manager made a hurried trip to Manhattan College and returned with basketball shoes for some of the Giants to wear in the second half on the icy turf. The Giants scored 27 points in the last quarter for a 30-13 victory and their first championship since 1927. Morris (Red) Badgro had 16 pass receptions to share the league lead with Joe Carter of Philadelphia.

1935 Danowski beat out Newman and took over as the starting quarterback. The Giants put together three straight shutouts in late season, beating the Bears 3-0, the Eagles 10-0, and the Dodgers 21-0. The new 24-man player limit helped Owen alternate a second team with his regulars, and they outclassed the opposition in the Eastern Division with a 9-3 record. In the NFL Championship Game, Detroit ground out a 26-7 victory over New York in the rain and snow at the University of Detroit Stadium. Danowski led the league's passers and helped his rookie receiver, Tod Goodwin, lead the league with 26 receptions. Elvin (Kink) Richards was third in rushing with 449 yards.

1936 Another rival AFL was organized and Newman, Badgro, and Strong left the Giants for the new league. Tackle Art Lewis of Ohio University and fullback Alphonse (Tuffy) Leemans of George Washington were the Giants' top choices in the first draft. The Giants even talked Cal Hubbard out of retirement for a few games. A promising 4-2-1 start deteriorated into a 5-5-1 record with one game left. But the record was good enough for the Giants still to be contenders. A victory over Boston would give them the title, while a loss meant third place. In a game in which the Giants' offense was totally shut down, the Redskins won 14-0, depriving New York of the title for the first time since divisions were formed in 1933. Leemans led the NFL in rushing with 830 yards.

1937 It was a year of change for the Giants, with 17 rookies on the 25-man squad, new uniforms with blue jerseys and silver pants, and a new Owen development, the A-formation. In the new offense, the line was unbalanced to one side and the backs overbalanced on the other side. Among the newcomers were tackle Ed Widseth of Minnesota, backs Hank Soar of Providence and Ward Cuff of Marquette, and ends Jim Lee Howell of Arkansas and Jim Poole of Mississippi. The A-formation was unveiled in Washington, in the first home game for the newly relocated Redskins; the Giants lost 13-3. New York was 6-1-2 in its next nine games. The Giants had a chance at the Eastern Division title in a rematch with the Redskins. More than 10,000 Redskins fans made the trip, marched up Broadway behind their band, and stormed the Polo Grounds to see Washington blast the Giants 49-14.

1938 Only five members of the 1934 championship team still were around—Danowski, Hein, Richards, Burnett, and Dell Isola. Owen alternated complete units by quarters in a most successful season climaxed by the Giants' third NFL title. After losing two of their first three games, the Giants won six and tied one in their next seven games for a 7-2-1 record. The Redskins (6-2-2) had kept pace and it all came down to a final game at the Polo Grounds with another big delegation of fans following the Redskins' band up Broadway. The Giants won 36-0 this time, then went on to defeat Green Bay 23-17 in the NFL Championship Game. Danowski led the league's passers, and Cuff had the most field goals, five. Hein was voted the NFL's most valuable player. The Giants wound up the year with a $200,000 profit.

1939 The Giants strayed far from home in preseason for the first time, switching their training camp to Superior, Wisconsin, to prepare for the Chicago College All-Star Game. The Giants beat the All-Stars 9-0 on two field goals by Strong and one by Cuff. The Giants were unbeaten until they ventured into Detroit's new home at Briggs Stadium for the first time and lost 18-14, November 5. For the third year in a row, it came down to a final game with Washington at the Polo Grounds. Both teams had 8-1-1 records. The Giants won 9-7 despite a hotly disputed field-goal attempt by the Redskins' Torrance (Bo) Russell. The Giants intercepted 35 passes during the season but in the championship game at the State Fair Grounds in Milwaukee, Green Bay picked off six New York passes and won 27-0.

1940 Danowski and John (Bull) Karcis retired. Leemans was injured in a midseason game with Pittsburgh, and Eddie Miller, the quarterback, was sidelined in a 13-0 loss to Cleveland. Center Hein called the plays as the Giants beat Green Bay and Washington. However, they lost to the Dodgers 14-6 on Mel Hein Day, the last game of a 6-4-1 season.

1941 The draft produced backs Len Eshmont of Fordham, George Franck of Minnesota, and Frank Reagan of Pennsylvania. The Giants came out of their Superior, Wisconsin, camp with 15 rookies on the squad. New York won its first five games. The Giants clinched their third Eastern Division title in four years by beating Washington 20-13 a week before they were beaten by the Dodgers for the second time, December 7, Pearl Harbor Day. With war declared, few people were interested in the league championship game with the Bears at Chicago, and only 13,341 saw Chicago capture a second consecutive title, 37-9, December 21.

1942 The military draft was beginning to cut into the pro rosters, and the Giants had 20 rookies on the squad. Eshmont, Reagan, and Poole were among those in military service. The top rookies were fullback Merle Hapes of Mississippi and tackle Al Blozis of Georgetown. The Giants lost two games to Pittsburgh, a team they had dominated 14-2-1 since it joined the league in 1933. Owen tried a bit of everything, including some T-formation, but the Giants sagged to 5-5-1 and third place.

1943 Steve Filipowicz was drafted first, but wasn't able to report until 1945. Wartime football produced a patchwork Giants team. Leemans, in his last year, saw limited action as a player-coach. After a 56-7 rout by the Bears in which Sid Luckman threw seven touchdown passes, November 14, the Giants rallied and gained a tie for first place in the Eastern Division by beating the Redskins in back-to-back games on the last two Sundays. Led by the passing of Sammy Baugh and the running of Andy Farkas, Washington won 28-0 over New York in a playoff game at the Polo Grounds, December 19. Bill Paschal, a rookie back from Georgia Tech, led the league by rushing for 572 yards. Cuff finished fourth with 523 yards and led in average per carry, at 6.5 yards.

1944 The Giants convinced 34-year-old Arnie Herber, retired since 1940, and kicker Ken Strong, retired since 1939, to take another try at pro ball. Paschal and Blozis played on weekend passes from the Army. The Giants scored five shutouts en route to the Eastern title, despite tying and losing to second-place Philadelphia. The Giants whipped the Packers 24-0 as Herber had a big day against his old teammates. Paschal led the league in rushing with 737 yards, and Strong's six field goals topped the league. Green Bay won the championship game with a 14-7 victory over the Giants at the Polo Grounds, December 17.

1945 Six weeks after he had played tackle in the 1944 title game, Blozis was killed in his first military action in France, January 31. World War II ended in late summer and the Giants' players began coming back. Paschal returned for half a year and gained 247 yards. Filipowicz, the top draft choice in 1943, reported and finished third on the team in rushing. Herber had the last great moment of his career against the Eagles, when he threw three touchdown passes in less than five minutes to bring the Giants to a 28-21 victory. After the Giants lost 17-0 to the Redskins in the season finale, Herber retired. The 3-6-1 season was the Giants' poorest ever.

1946 The Giants got a competitor for New York's football attention when Dan Topping put the New York Yankees in Yankee Stadium in the newly organized All-America Football Conference. Before the season, Hein retired and Cuff was traded to the Chicago Cardinals. Frank Filchock's days as an understudy to Sammy Baugh at Washington ended when he signed with the Giants for a reported $35,000 salary. He proved worth the price; Filchock passed for the fifth-most yards in the league (1,262) and led the Giants in rushing with 371 yards. The Giants won the Eastern Division with a 7-3-1 record. On the eve of the championship game against the Bears at the Polo Grounds, Filchock and Hapes were questioned about an attempt by a New York gambler to fix the game. Hapes was suspended for not reporting the contact, but Filchock played the game and played well in a 24-14 defeat. Both Filchock and Hapes were suspended indefinitely after the game.

1947 The loss of Filchock left the Giants without a quarterback until they acquired Paul Governali, a former Columbia All-America, from the Boston Yanks in a trade for Paschal and the draft rights to Notre Dame tackle George Connor. The Giants gained the rights to tackle DeWitt (Tex) Coulter of Army in an unusual transaction. Coulter quit the U.S. Military Academy in 1946 and was permitted to play with the Giants with the stipulation he had to go into the 1947 draft because his original class had not graduated. The Chicago Cardinals drafted Coulter in the first round and then traded him to the Giants for the rights to Vic Schwall, New York's first-round draft pick. The Giants were 0-7-2 after nine games and finished last for the first time with a 2-8-2 record. One victory was 35-31 over the Chicago Cardinals, who won the championship. Governali finished fourth in the league with 1,775 yards passing. The other bright spots were rookies Gene (Choo-Choo) Roberts, who led the team in rushing, and end Ray Poole, the top receiver.

1948 Charlie Conerly, a rangy passer who reminded Owen and Mara of Sammy Baugh, arrived on the scene from Mississippi. Washington had drafted Conerly in 1945 but he chose to return to college after serving in the Marines. The Giants obtained the rights to Conerly in a trade with the Redskins. Emlen Tunnell, Bill Swiacki, and Tony (Skippy) Minisi were among the 20 other rookies on the 35-man roster. The Giants' leaky defense allowed 388 points, losing to the Redskins 41-10, the Eagles 45-0, and the Cardinals 63-35. Midway through the season, Owen installed the T-formation as his primary offense. Conerly set an NFL record with 36 completions in a losing game against Pittsburgh, December 5. Conerly threw 22 touchdown passes in the 4-8 season, 10 to Swiacki, who caught 39 passes for 550 yards.

1949 Ted Collins moved his Boston Yanks franchise to New York and changed the name to New York Bulldogs. The Bulldogs shared the Polo Grounds with the Giants. Owen brought in Allie Sherman to help teach Conerly, who had always played the Single Wing, the T-formation. Rookies Bill Austin and Al DeRogatis made the squad. Consecutive losses to Philadelphia in the final two games dropped the Giants to 6-6 and third place in the East. Roberts tied for the scoring lead with 102 points on 17 touchdowns, nine while rushing for 634 yards and eight while catching 35 passes for 711 yards. Swiacki caught 47 passes and Poole 25. Conerly completed 152 passes for 2,138 yards and 17 touchdowns. Tunnell intercepted 10 passes, two for touchdowns.

1950 The realigned NFL admitted Cleveland, Baltimore, and San Francisco from the AAFC, and the Giants were placed in the American Conference with the Browns, four-time champions of the AAFC. Coach Owen devised a new "Umbrella" defense. Tom Landry, Otto Schnellbacher, and Harmon Rowe, three of five men assigned the Giants from the defunct Yankees, teamed with Tunnell in the four-man zone secondary. Ends Jim Duncan and Ray Poole sometimes dropped back in pass coverage. Arnie Weinmeister, another former Yankees player, anchored the defensive line at tackle. Roberts set a Giants record with 218 yards rushing against the Cardinals, November 12. Conerly played with a shoulder separation, and quarterback Travis Tidwell, the number-one draft choice from Auburn, saw a lot of action. The Giants defeated Cleveland twice, 6-0 and 17-13, and tied the Browns for the conference title at 10-2. The Giants lost the playoff 8-3 to Cleveland. Rookie Eddie Price ran for 703 yards.

1951 The Giants selected Kyle Rote of SMU as the bonus pick in the draft. Rote was injured in preseason and saw limited action. Coulter was lured out of a one-year retirement. After an opening-day tie with Pittsburgh, the Giants won all the rest except for two losses to Cleveland. The Browns beat the Giants 14-13 and 10-0 and repeated as conference champions (11-1), with the Giants in second place at 9-2-1. Price led the league in rushing with 971 yards and set an NFL record with 271 carries. Schnellbacher led the league with 11 interceptions, and Tunnell had a record four touchdowns on kick returns.

1952 Frank Gifford, a back from USC, was the team's first draft choice. Owen still was using much of the old A-formation, mixed occasionally with the T-formation, and Polo Grounds crowds vented their frustration on the coach throughout the season. The booing reached a zenith after the Giants returned home from a 63-7 drubbing by Pittsburgh. Conerly's shoulder was injured again, and Owen had to use both Landry and rookie Fred Benners at quarterback. Price again led the league in rushing attempts (183), and finished second in yards gained (748). Rote began to come into his own, as he ran for 421 yards and caught 21 passes for 240 more. Gifford was used mostly at defensive back, carrying the ball only 38 times for 116 yards. Tunnell gained more yardage on kick returns and interceptions (a total of 924 yards) than the league's rushing leader (Dan Towler of the Los Angeles Rams with 894 yards).

1953 Offensive linemen Rosey Brown, Ray Wietecha, and Jack Stroud joined the team. Injuries to Conerly and Price contributed to another season of frustration, climaxed by a 62-14 loss to Cleveland in the next-to-last week of the season. Owen's coaching career ended uncharacteristically—with a 27-16 defeat by Detroit and a 3-9 record. The Giants' head coach for 23 years, he was fired after the season, finishing with a career record of 153-108-17. Owen's teams won two NFL championships and finished first in their division six times.

1954 Jim Lee Howell, an end with the Giants from 1937 to 1948, was promoted from assistant coach to head coach. Allie Sherman left his assistant-coaching position to become a head coach in Canada. Howell hired Vince Lombardi from Army to become his offensive coach, and made Landry a player-coach with defensive responsibilities. Not only did Landry refine the Giants' 4-3-4 defense, he was named all-pro. Conerly announced his retirement, but Howell traveled to Conerly's home in Mississippi and talked him out of the decision. The Giants obtained end Bob Schnelker from Philadelphia, and another end, Ken MacAfee, joined the team after duty in the service.

Other new faces on the team included Dick Nolan, a defensive back from Maryland; Don Heinrich, quarterback from Washington; and Bobby Clatterbuck, another quarterback from Houston. The Giants lost two games to the conference champion Browns but improved to a 7-5 record. Gifford became an offensive halfback and gained 368 yards. Schnelker caught 30 passes, MacAfee 24; each man scored eight touchdowns. Conerly missed time with injuries but still threw 17 touchdown passes.

1955 Mel Triplett, a fullback from Toledo; Jimmy Patton, a defensive back from Mississippi; and Rosey Grier, a defensive tackle from Penn State, were among the draft choices signed. The Giants also signed Alex Webster, a halfback who had been the Canadian Football League's most valuable player in 1954. The Giants started slowly, losing five of their first seven games, but they were 4-0-1 in their last five games to finish third in the Eastern Conference. Webster rushed for 634 yards, while Gifford gained 351 yards and caught 33 passes.

1956 The Giants moved to Yankee Stadium. Sam Huff, a linebacker from West Virginia; Don Chandler, a kicker from Florida; and Jim Katcavage, a defensive end from Dayton, were obtained in the draft. Defensive end Andy Robustelli, defensive tackle Dick Modzelewski, and defensive back Ed Hughes were obtained in trades. Landry retired as a player to become the full-time defensive coordinator. Under Landry's tutelage, the newcomers joined with Tunnell, Grier, and linebacker Bill Svoboda to form the league's stingiest defense. Huff was named the NFL rookie of the year. Offensively, Gifford blossomed into the best all-around back in the NFL, finishing fifth in rushing and third in receiving. The Giants proved their fast finish of 1955 was not a fluke by winning six of their first seven games. Their final 8-3-1 record unseated the Browns as conference champions for the first time in Cleveland's seven seasons in the NFL. The Giants routed the Chicago Bears 47-7 in the NFL title game.

1957 Grier joined the Army. The Giants and the Browns were the primary contenders for the Eastern Conference title, and Cleveland gained a big edge by winning both games between the two teams, 6-3 and 34-28. A three-game losing streak at the end of the season dropped the Giants to 7-5. Gifford and Webster were the one-two punch again, with Gifford rushing for 528 yards and catching 41 passes, while Webster rushed for 478 yards and caught 30 passes. Chandler led the league in punting.

1958 The Giants made their living on the best defense in the league and a tough running game led by Gifford, Webster, Triplett, and rookie Phil King. The team was in the running with the Browns all season, and on November 9 defeated Baltimore 24-21 before a record Yankee Stadium crowd of 71,163. Despite an early-season victory over the Browns, the Giants still trailed Cleveland going into the season finale against Paul Brown's team. A 49-yard field goal by Pat Summerall in the snow gave the Giants a 13-10 victory in the final minute, enabling New York to tie for first place in the Eastern Conference. In a playoff game between the two teams, the Giants played a dazzling defensive game, holding Cleveland's Jim Brown to 18 yards and gaining a 10-0 victory, December 21. The Giants met Baltimore for the NFL championship in Yankee Stadium, December 28. The Colts tied the game 17-17 in the final seconds on a field goal by Steve Myrha. The Giants started with the ball in sudden-death overtime, but a drive fell inches short of a first down at midfield, and Baltimore took over after a punt. Led by quarterback Johnny Unitas, the Colts moved to the winning touchdown on a one-yard run by Alan Ameche after 8:15 of overtime. The 23-17 victory was seen by millions of people on NBC television and generally was credited with pushing interest in pro football to new heights.

1959 Tim Mara, founder of the Giants, died, February 16. Lombardi left the Giants to become head coach at Green Bay. Sherman returned from Canada to succeed Lombardi. Gifford failed in a brief preseason try at quarterback and returned to halfback. Conerly responded to the early challenge by having his best season and leading the NFL in passing. Gifford, meanwhile, averaged 5.1 yards per carry and 18.3 yards per reception, both among the best in the league. The Giants led from start to finish, despite losing their second game of the season to Philadelphia. After that, they bounced back to win five in a row, and closed out the season with four more consecutive victories. They eliminated their long-time nemesis, the Cleveland Browns, with a 48-7 romp, December 6. New York's 10-2 record was the best in the NFL. The Giants and the Colts were matched in the title game for the second consecutive year. New York led 9-7 after three quarters but Baltimore exploded for 24 points in the final 15 minutes for a 31-16 victory.

1960 Howell announced he would retire as coach after the 1960 season. Landry left the Giants to become head coach of the expansion Dallas Cowboys. The Giants had a new rival for New York's football attentions, the New York Titans, who played at the Polo Grounds. Webster suffered a serious knee injury in a preseason game. Conerly labored much of the season with a sore arm. Nevertheless, the Giants remained in contention until back-to-back losses to the Eagles. In the first game, Gifford suffered a concussion when he was knocked unconscious by a vicious tackle by Chuck Bednarik, November 20. Without Gifford for the rest of the season, the Giants won only one of their last four games and finished third.

1961 The Giants' first offer for a coach to succeed Howell was to Lombardi, who had coached two years in Green Bay after leaving New York. When that bid failed, the Giants signed Sherman as the new head coach. Gifford announced his retirement, the result of his concussion the season before. The Giants made a number of significant trades, getting quarterback Y. A. Tittle from San Francisco, ends Del Shofner from the Los Angeles Rams and Joe Walton from Philadelphia, and cornerback Erich Barnes from the Chicago Bears. Sherman began the season with Conerly at quarterback, but he shifted to Tittle in the second game and Tittle played the position the rest of the way. Barnes intercepted a Dallas pass and ran 102 yards for a touchdown, October 22. The Giants tied Philadelphia for first place in the Eastern Conference with a 38-21 victory in New York. The Giants won the rematch 28-24 in December and claimed undisputed first place. The Giants needed a tie in their final game against Cleveland to clinch the title and that's just what they got, 7-7. The Giants were no match for Lombardi's Green Bay team in the title game in Green Bay, December 31. The Packers won 37-0. Shofner caught 68 passes for 1,125 yards and 11 touchdowns. Webster rushed for 928 yards. Dick Lynch led the league with nine interceptions.

1962 Conerly, Rote, and Summerall retired. Gifford made a comeback after a one-year retirement and was moved to flanker in training camp. After a rocky start, the Giants won their last nine in a row to finish 12-2 and win the Eastern Conference by three games over Pittsburgh. In the second game of that streak, Tittle threw for 505 yards and seven touchdowns in a 49-34 victory over Washington, October 28. Shofner's 11 receptions totaled 269 yards in that game. For the season, Tittle and his receiving corps were equally impressive. Tittle passed for 3,224 yards and an NFL record 33 touchdowns. Shofner had 53 receptions for 1,133 yards and 12 touchdowns, Gifford had 39 for 796 yards and seven touchdowns, and Walton had 33 for 406 yards and nine touchdowns. Webster had 743 yards rushing and 47 receptions. The Giants met the Packers in the NFL title game for the second consecutive year, this time in Yankee Stadium. The Packers won 16-7 on a day on which the temperature was 20 degrees and 40-mile-an-hour winds whipped the turf. Huff and Packers' running back Jim Taylor had a spectacular individual duel in the Green Bay victory.

1963 The Giants had 10 starters who were age 30 or older. New York had an unimpressive 3-2 record after five weeks, but the team rebounded to win eight of its final nine games. A 33-17 victory over Pittsburgh in the final game of the season enabled the Giants to win their third consecutive Eastern Conference title. Tittle led the league in passing with 3,145 yards and 36 touchdown passes, breaking his own record. Shofner had 64 receptions for 1,181 yards and nine touchdowns. Lynch again led the NFL in interceptions. Chandler led the league in scoring with 106 points on 18 field goals and 52 extra points. The Giants had to play in another championship game on a cold winter day, this time in Chicago with the temperature at 8 degrees, December 29. Tittle was injured in the second quarter. He later returned to play, but the Giants' offense never got going. Chicago won 14-10.

1964 Before the season, Sherman traded away two of the team's most notable players—Huff to Washington and Modzelewski to Cleveland. Many of the players who had been so effective the previous year suddenly seemed to be over the hill—Tittle, Webster, Shofner, Gifford, and Robustelli. Tittle was injured in a 27-24 loss to Pittsburgh and was ineffective after he returned. Gary Wood was given the quarterback's spot but the rookie could not reverse the Giants' slide. New York closed with a 2-10-2 record and finished in last place for the first time since 1947. Webster and Gifford retired after the season.

1965 The draft brought the Giants running backs Tucker Fredrickson from Auburn (the number-one selection in the entire draft) and Ernie Koy from Texas and cornerbacks Carl (Spider) Lockhart from North Texas State and Willie Williams from Grambling. Tittle and Robustelli retired. Chandler was traded to Green Bay. Quarterback Earl Morrall was acquired from Detroit. Jack Mara, the club president for 31 years, died in June and his brother Wellington assumed the club president's duties. Fredrickson was teamed with Steve Thurlow and Koy in what was called the "Baby Bull" backfield. Morrall's passing to young speedster Homer Jones helped the Giants to a 7-7 record.

1966 New York signed soccer-style kicker Pete Gogolak after he played out his option with Buffalo of the American Football League, May 17. Less than a month later, the NFL and AFL agreed to merge, June 8. Morrall and Jones collaborated on a 98-yard touchdown pass on opening day, September 11, but the Giants could manage only a 34-34 tie with Pittsburgh. Then the Giants lost four in a row before beating Washington 13-10 for their only victory of the season. The Giants lost their last eight in a row to finish with their poorest record ever. The low point of the season was when the Redskins evened the score by bombarding them 72-41 in a game that set regular-season league highs for most points scored by one team (72) and by both teams (113), November 27. Morrall was injured late in the season in practice, and Sherman had to make due with quarterbacks Wood and Tom Kennedy. Jones caught 48 passes for 1,044 yards and eight touchdowns. The Giants' defense gave up a league-record 501 points and the team plunged to last place with a 1-12-1 record.

1967 The Giants obtained quarterback Fran Tarkenton from Minnesota in exchange for four high draft choices. New York also acquired middle linebacker Vince Costello from Cleveland. The Giants rebounded from their poor 1966 season by posting a 7-7 record. Tarkenton passed for 3,088 yards and 29 touchdowns. Tight end Aaron Thomas caught 51 passes for nine scores, while Jones added 49 for 1,209 yards and a league-high 13 touchdowns.

1968 The Tarkenton trade of 1967 virtually depleted the Giants of draft opportunities and they fared poorly in the draft. New York won its first four games. After 10 games, the team was 7-3 and only one game behind Dallas (whom they had beaten 27-21) in the NFL's Capitol Division. The Giants lost their last four games to finish second again. Tarkenton passed for 2,555 yards and 21 touchdowns. Jones averaged 23.5 yards on 46 receptions. Williams led the league with 10 interceptions.

1969 The Giants obtained running back Junior Coffey in a trade with Atlanta. In their first game ever against an AFL team, the Giants lost 37-14 to the New York Jets in a preseason game at the Yale Bowl, August 17. When the Giants dropped a preseason game to Pittsburgh the following week, Sherman was fired. Webster, an assistant coach and former star, was named head coach a week before the regular season began. The Giants won three of their first four games but a seven-game losing streak dropped the team out of contention. New York won its last three outings for a 6-8 record. Tarkenton passed for 2,918 yards and 23 touchdowns. Jones caught 42 passes but scored only once.

1970 Wide receiver Clifton McNeil was obtained from San Francisco. The Giants traded Jones to Cleveland for running back Ron Johnson and defensive tackle Jim Kanicki. New York lost its first three games, then won 9 of its next 10 to tie Dallas for first place with one week left in the season. On the season's final Sunday, the Giants lost 31-3 to the Los Angeles Rams while Dallas defeated Houston. Johnson became the Giants' first 1,000-yard rusher, totaling 1,027 yards. He also caught 48 passes. McNeil caught 50 passes. Tarkenton passed for 2,777 yards and 19 touchdowns.

1971 The Giants announced that they planned to move to a new stadium in East Rutherford, New Jersey, hopefully by 1975. The team lost all six preseason games, including a 27-14 loss to the Jets. The Giants defeated Green Bay 42-40 in the opening game. Johnson missed most of the season with a thigh injury. Fredrickson suffered an injured knee. The Giants, with the poorest defense in the NFC, had losing streaks of four and five games. Tarkenton, who led the league in completions, but threw only 11 touchdown passes, was benched in favor of Randy Johnson in the final game. Against Philadelphia, Johnson threw for 372 yards in a 41-28 loss. It was more yards in a game than Tarkenton had ever passed for. Bob Tucker became the first tight end to lead the NFL in pass receiving with 59 receptions for 791 yards.

1972 The Giants traded Tarkenton back to Minnesota in exchange for quarterback Norm Snead, wide receiver Bob Grim, running back Vince Clements, and two draft choices. Defensive end Jack Gregory was obtained from Cleveland. The draft produced defensive tackle John Mendenhall. The Giants lost their first two games, then won four in a row. The highlights of the season were a 62-10 victory over Philadelphia (a club record for most points), and a 23-3 win over Dallas in the season finale. The Giants' 8-6 finish was good for third in the NFC East. Snead led the league in passing, completing 60.3 percent of his passes. Tucker had 55 receptions. Johnson rushed for 1,182 yards, led the league with 14 touchdowns, and caught 45 passes.

1973 The Giants had a 6-0 record in the preseason and won their opening game against Houston 34-14. A week later, New York tied Philadelphia 23-23 in the final game played at old Yankee Stadium, September 23. The Giants played the rest of their home schedule at the Yale Bowl in New Haven, Connecticut, and practiced in New Jersey. The team won only one of its last 12 games. Webster announced his resignation as coach before the final game, a 31-7 loss to Minnesota in New Haven. Johnson rushed for 902 yards. Tucker caught 50 passes. The defense surrendered 362 points in the 2-11-1 season.

1974 Bill Arnsparger, the assistant coach who helped guide Miami to two Super Bowl championships, was named the Giants' ninth head coach. Andy Robustelli was named director of operations. The team continued to play its games at the Yale Bowl. New York scored a 14-6 upset victory in Dallas, September 29. In a pair of midseason transactions, Arnsparger traded quarterback Snead to San Francisco and obtained quarterback Craig Morton from Dallas. The Giants posted a 33-27 victory over Kansas City, November 3. New York lost all seven home games and ended with a 2-12 record.

1975 The new stadium in New Jersey wasn't ready yet, so the Giants shared Shea Stadium with the Jets. Two Giants home games had to be scheduled on Saturday afternoons to avoid conflict with the Jets' schedule. The Giants won their first four preseason games and began the regular season with a 23-14 victory over Philadelphia. A series of close defeats followed, including 13-7 and 14-3 losses to Dallas and a 13-10 loss to Philadelphia. The Giants surprised Buffalo 17-14 in a Monday night game, October 20. New York finished 5-9.

1976 The draft produced defensive end Troy Archer from Colorado and linebacker Harry Carson from South Carolina State. Larry Csonka, the former Miami running back who had played in the World Football League, signed as a free agent for a reported $1 million. Snead was re-acquired from San Francisco, September 1. After three seasons without a permanent home, the Giants moved into the new 76,000-seat Giants Stadium in East Rutherford, New Jersey, October 10. In the stadium's inaugural game, the Giants lost 24-14 to Dallas, their fifth consecutive loss. When the losing streak reached seven the following week, Arnsparger was fired and an assistant coach, John McVay, was given the job. The losing streak reached nine before the Giants defeated Washington 12-9, November 14. The victory ended a 14-game winless streak against George Allen-coached teams. The Giants won two of their final three games for a 3-11 record. Csonka was injured much of the year and gained 569 yards; he underwent knee surgery after the season. Doug Kotar led the club in rushing with 731 yards. Tucker caught 42 passes. McVay was signed to a long-term coaching contract.

1977 Morton was traded to Denver for quarterback Steve Ramsey, but Joe Pisarcik signed as a free agent after three years in the Canadian Football League and became the club's starting quarterback. The defense, led by all-pro linebacker Brad Van Pelt, remained tough throughout the season and ranked third in the NFC against the rush. The only runner to gain more than 100 yards against the unit was Herb Lusk of the Eagles. But the offense sputtered and the Giants won only four games after an opening victory over Washington. The club entered the final two weeks with a 5-7 record, then lost to Philadelphia in the final 20 seconds and to the Chicago Bears with 9 seconds left in overtime.

1978 Gordon King, an offensive tackle from Stanford, was the first draft pick. The Giants won the season opener 19-13 over Tampa Bay when Pisarcik completed nine of 15 passes and threw a 67-yard touchdown pass to Johnny Perkins. Pisarcik kept a hot hand through the first half of the season as the Giants rolled to a 5-3 record. The biggest victory came on October 22 when New York defeated first-place Washington 17-6 before the largest home crowd in the club's history, 76,192. The win was the Giants' fourth straight over the Redskins. However, the second half of the season was a washout as the Giants lost six straight and seven of their last eight to finish 6-10. The low point of the season came against Philadelphia, November 19. With less than 30 seconds left, the Giants had a 17-12 lead and the ball. But instead of falling on the ball to end the game, Pisarcik muffed a handoff to Larry Csonka, and Eagles safety Herman Edwards picked up the ball and ran 26 yards for the winning touchdown. The next day, offensive coordinator Bob Gibson, who had called the play, was fired.

1979 Ray Perkins, the San Diego Chargers' offensive coordinator, was named head coach in February. He set out to improve the Giants' passing offense by drafting Phil Simms, a quarterback from Morehead State, and Earnest Gray, a wide receiver from Memphis State, in the first two rounds. The team was shaken when Archer, a starting defensive tackle, was killed in an automobile accident one month before the opening of training camp. The Giants started with five consecutive losses before Simms and Billy Taylor, a second-year running back, made their first starts and led the club to a 17-14 victory over Tampa Bay on October 7. In the following game, Simms and Gray connected on eight pass completions for 169 yards and two touchdowns in a 32-16 win over San Francisco. Victories over Kansas City, the Los Angeles Rams, and Atlanta added up to five New York victories in six weeks, but the team won only once more, finishing the season 6-10.

1980 The Giants opened the season with an exciting 41-35 victory over St. Louis, in which Simms threw five touchdown passes, including four to Gray. But eight successive defeats scuttled the season. The collapse was prompted by a disastrous injury siege that put a total of 35 players on the injured-reserve list. By season's end, Van Pelt was the only one of six initial linebackers still on the active roster. The victory drought ended on November 9 with a 38-35 win over Dallas. The Giants won twice more to go 4-12. The injury-decimated defense permitted 55 touchdowns and 425 points, second most in the NFL.

1981 With the second selection in the draft, New York chose linebacker Lawrence Taylor of North Carolina. The Giants started slowly, going 2-3 the first five weeks, but then they obtained running back Rob Carpenter in a trade with Houston. Carpenter rushed for 103 yards and a touchdown in his first start, a 34-14 victory over St. Louis, and sparked a three-game winning streak. However, a three-game losing streak reversed the club's momentum. Then, on November 15, Simms suffered a separated shoulder against Washington. Second-year quarterback Scott Brunner became the starter and the team responded with four wins in the final five weeks, including a 13-10 overtime victory in the season finale against Dallas that sent the Giants into the playoffs as a wild card team. On December 27, the Giants posted a 27-21 victory in the NFC Wild Card Game against the Eagles. The ants opened a 20-0 first-quarter lead and then held off a late Eagles rally. The season ended for the Giants on January 3 when they were defeated 38-24 by the San Francisco 49ers in a divisional playoff game. Brunner passed for 290 yards and three touchdowns, but it wasn't quite enough against the eventual Super Bowl XVI champions.

1982 The Giants' offense was seriously hurt when Simms was lost for the season with a knee injury and Carpenter held out until the final five weeks. Three lost fumbles cost the Giants in an opening day 16-14 loss to Atlanta. The next week, in the first Monday night game ever played at Giants Stadium, turnovers again were the key in a 27-19 loss to Green Bay. The NFL Players Association had announced a players strike prior to the game and a pair of power shortages delayed the game 24 minutes. After the eight-week strike, the Giants ran into eventual Super Bowl champion Washington and suffered their third straight loss. They evened their record with three consecutive victories, but on December 15 Perkins stunned the team when he announced he was leaving after the regular season to become the head coach at Alabama. Defensive coordinator Bill Parcells was immediately named as his successor. The Redskins eked out a 15-14 win to slow New York's momentum. In the last week of the season, and with still-flickering playoff hopes, the Giants beat Philadelphia for the fourth straight time when Joe Danelo kicked a 25-yard field goal with two seconds left to play. New York lost its playoff bid, however.

1983 Turnovers and injuries plagued the Giants, making Parcells's first season as head coach less than auspicious. The team's 58 turnovers, including 27 lost fumbles and 31 interceptions, was the league's highest total. New York placed 25 players on the injured reserve list over the course of the season, making them the most physically debilitated team in the NFL. Oft-injured Simms came in to replace Brunner in the sixth week, and fractured his thumb to again end his season early. Despite the final 3-12-1 record, there were bright spots. Led by Pro Bowl linebackers Taylor and Harry Carson and cornerback Mark Haynes, the Giants ranked second in the NFC in total defense. On offense, team records were set for total yards (5,285) and first downs (296). And Gray tied for first in the NFC with 78 receptions, while rookie kicker Ali Haji-Sheikh set an all-time NFL record with 35 field goals and a team mark with 127 points. Butch Woolfolk not only led the team with 857 yards rushing, he set an NFL record with 43 carries in a 23-0 victory over Philadelphia.

1984 Thanks in part to Simms's first full, healthy season in four years, New York dramatically improved its record to 9-7. Simms broke Y. A. Tittle's club record for a season with 4,044 yards passing. Despite losing their last two games, the Giants got into the playoffs as a wild card team. They defeated the Rams 16-13 in the NFC Wild Card Game, but lost to the eventual Super Bowl champion 49ers 21-10 in an NFC Divisional Playoff Game.

1985 Woolfolk was traded to Houston in the offseason. Haynes held out for part of the season in a contract dispute, then came back and was injured. For the first time in 22 years, New York had consecutive winning seasons, finishing 10-6, the most victories since 1963. The Giants, whose six losses were by a total of 20 points, also repeated as an NFC wild card team. New York won the NFC Wild Card Game 17-3 over San Francisco, but lost to the eventual Super Bowl champion Chicago Bears 21-0. Five Giants were voted to the Pro Bowl, the most since 1963: Simms, Taylor, Carson, defensive end Leonard Marshall, and running back Joe Morris. Morris led the league with 21 touchdowns, and was third in the NFC with 1,336 yards, a club record. Simms topped the NFC with 3,829 yards and was the Pro Bowl's most valuable player.

1986 Haynes was traded to Denver.

MEMBERS OF HALL OF FAME:

Morris (Red) Badgro, Roosevelt Brown, Ray Flaherty, Frank Gifford, Joe Guyon, Mel Hein, Wilbur (Pete) Henry, Arnie Herber, Cal Hubbard, Sam Huff, Alphonse (Tuffy) Leemans, Vince Lombardi, Tim Mara, Hugh McElhenny, Steve Owen, Andy Robustelli, Ken Strong, Fran Tarkenton, Jim Thorpe, Y. A. Tittle, Emlen Tunnell, Arnie Weinmeister

GIANTS RECORD, 1925-85

Year	Won	Lost	Tied	Pct.	Fin.	Pts.	OP
1925	8	4	0	.667	4t	122	67
1926	8	4	1	.667	6t	147	51
1927a	11	1	1	.917	1	197	20
1928	4	7	2	.364	6	79	136
1929	13	1	1	.929	2	312	86
1930	13	4	0	.765	2	308	98
1931	7	6	1	.538	5	164	100
1932	4	6	2	.400	5	93	113
1933b	11	3	0	.786	1	244	101
1934c	8	5	0	.615	1	147	107
1935b	9	3	0	.750	1	180	96
1936	5	6	1	.455	3	115	163
1937	6	3	2	.667	2	128	109
1938c	8	2	1	.800	1	194	79
1939b	9	1	1	.900	1	168	85
1940	6	4	1	.600	3	131	133
1941b	8	3	0	.727	1	238	114
1942	5	5	1	.500	3	155	139
1943d	6	3	1	.667	2	197	170
1944b	8	1	1	.889	1	206	75
1945	3	6	1	.333	3t	179	198
1946b	7	3	1	.700	1	236	162
1947	2	8	2	.200	5	190	309
1948	4	8	0	.333	3t	297	388
1949	6	6	0	.500	3	287	298
1950e	10	2	0	.833	2	268	150
1951	9	2	1	.818	2	254	161
1952	7	5	0	.583	2t	234	231
1953	3	9	0	.250	5	179	277
1954	7	5	0	.583	3	293	184
1955	6	5	1	.545	3	267	223
1956c	8	3	1	.727	1	264	197
1957	7	5	0	.583	2	254	211
1958f	9	3	0	.750	1	246	183
1959f	10	2	0	.833	1	284	170
1960	6	4	2	.600	3	271	261
1961f	10	3	1	.769	1	368	220
1962f	12	2	0	.857	1	398	283
1963f	11	3	0	.786	1	448	280
1964	2	10	2	.167	7	241	399
1965	7	7	0	.500	2t	270	338
1966	1	12	1	.077	8	263	501
1967	7	7	0	.500	2	369	379
1968	7	7	0	.500	2	294	325
1969	6	8	0	.429	2	264	298
1970	9	5	0	.643	2	301	270
1971	4	10	0	.286	5	228	362
1972	8	6	0	.571	3	331	247
1973	2	11	1	.179	5	226	362
1974	2	12	0	.143	5	195	299
1975	5	9	0	.357	4	216	306
1976	3	11	0	.214	5	170	250
1977	5	9	0	.357	5	181	265
1978	6	10	0	.375	5	264	298
1979	6	10	0	.375	4	237	323
1980	4	12	0	.250	5	249	425
1981g	9	7	0	.563	3	295	257
1982	4	5	0	.444	10	164	160
1983	3	12	1	.219	5	267	347
1984g	9	7	0	.563	2	299	301
1985g	10	6	0	.625	2	399	283
61 Years	413	349	32	.540		14,465	13,423

aNFL Champion; No Playoffs
bNFL Eastern Division Champion; 0-1 in Playoffs
cNFL Champion; 1-0 in Playoffs
dNFL Eastern Division Runnerup; 0-1 in Playoffs
eNFL American Conference Runnerup; 0-1 in Playoffs
fNFL Eastern Conference Champion; 0-1 in Playoffs
gNFC Wild Card Qualifier for Playoffs; 1-1 in Playoffs

RECORD HOLDERS

CAREER

Rushing attempts	Alex Webster, 1955-64	1,196
Rushing yards	Alex Webster, 1955-64	4,638
Pass attempts	Charlie Conerly, 1948-61	2,833
Pass completions	Charlie Conerly, 1948-61	1,418
Passing yards	Charlie Conerly, 1948-61	19,488
Touchdown passes	Charlie Conerly, 1948-61	173
Receptions	Joe Morrison, 1959-72	395
Receiving yards	Frank Gifford, 1952-60, 1962-64	5,434
Interceptions	Emlen Tunnell, 1948-58	74
Punting average	Don Chandler, 1956-64	43.8
Punt return avg.	Bobby Hammond, 1976-78	9.1
Kickoff return avg.	Rocky Thompson, 1971-72	27.2
Field goals	Pete Gogolak, 1966-74	126
Touchdowns	Frank Gifford, 1952-60, 1962-64	78
Points	Pete Gogolak, 1966-74	646

SEASON

Rushing attempts	Ron Johnson, 1972	298
Rushing yards	Joe Morris, 1985	1,336
Pass attempts	Phil Simms, 1984	533
Pass completions	Phil Simms, 1984	286
Passing yards	Phil Simms, 1984	4,044
Touchdown passes	Y. A. Tittle, 1963	36
Receptions	Earnest Gray, 1983	78
Receiving yards	Homer Jones, 1967	1,209
Interceptions	Otto Schnellbacher, 1951	11
	Jim Patton, 1958	11
Punting average	Don Chandler, 1959	46.6
Punt return avg.	Merle Hapes, 1942	15.5
Kickoff return avg.	John Salscheider, 1949	31.6
Field goals	Ali Haji-Sheikh, 1983	35
Touchdowns	Joe Morris, 1985	21
Points	Ali Haji-Sheikh, 1983	127

GAME

Rushing attempts	Butch Woolfolk, 11-20-83	43
Rushing yards	Gene Roberts, 11-12-50	218
Pass attempts	Phil Simms, 10-13-85	62
Pass completions	Phil Simms, 10-13-85	40
Passing yards	Phil Simms, 10-13-85	513
Touchdown passes	Y. A. Tittle, 10-28-62	7
Receptions	Mark Bavaro, 10-13-85	12
Receiving yards	Del Shofner, 10-28-62	269
Interceptions	17 times	3
Field goals	Joe Danelo, 10-18-81	6
Touchdowns	Ron Johnson, 10-2-72	4
	Earnest Gray, 9-7-80	4
Points	Ron Johnson, 10-2-72	24
	Earnest Gray, 9-7-80	24

COACHING HISTORY

1925	Bob Folwell	8- 4- 0
1926	Joe Alexander	8- 4- 1
1927-28	Earl Potteiger	15- 8- 3
1929-30	LeRoy Andrews	26- 5- 1
1931-53	Steve Owen	153-108-17
1954-60	Jim Lee Howell	54- 29- 4
1961-68	Allie Sherman	57- 54- 4
1969-73	Alex Webster	29- 40- 1
1974-76	Bill Arnsparger*	7- 28- 0
1976-78	John McVay	14- 23- 0
1979-82	Ray Perkins	24- 35- 0
1983-85	Bill Parcells	24- 27- 1

**Replaced after seven games in 1976*

FIRST PLAYER SELECTED

1936	Art Lewis, T, Ohio U
1937	Ed Widseth, T, Minnesota
1938	George Karamatic, HB, Gonzaga
1939	Walt Nielson, FB, Arizona
1940	Grenny Lansdell, HB, USC
1941	George Franck, HB, Minnesota
1942	Merle Hapes, HB, Mississippi
1943	Steve Filipowicz, FB, Fordham
1944	Billy Hillenbrand, HB, Indiana
1945	Elmer Barbour, HB, Wake Forest
1946	George Connor, T, Notre Dame
1947	Vic Schwall, HB, Northwestern
1948	Tony Minisi, HB, Pennsylvania
1949	Paul Page, HB, SMU
1950	Travis Tidwell, QB, Auburn
1951	Kyle Rote, HB, SMU
1952	Frank Gifford, HB, USC
1953	Bobby Marlow, HB, Alabama
1954	(2) Ken Buck, E, Pacific
1955	Joe Heap, HB, Notre Dame
1956	(2) Henry Moore, FB, Arkansas
1957	(2) Sam DeLuca, T, South Carolina
1958	Phil King, FB, Vanderbilt
1959	Lee Grosscup, QB, Utah
1960	Lou Cordileone, G, Clemson
1961	(2) Bob Gaiters, B, New Mexico State
1962	Jerry Hillebrand, LB, Colorado
1963	(2) Frank Lasky, T, Florida
1964	Joe Don Looney, HB, Oklahoma
1965	Tucker Frederickson, HB, Auburn
1966	Francis Peay, T, Missouri
1967	(4) Louis Thompson, DT, Alabama
1968	(2) Dick Buzin, T, Penn State
1969	Fred Dryer, DE, San Diego State
1970	Jim Files, LB, Oklahoma
1971	Rocky Thompson, RB, West Texas State
1972	Eldridge Small, DB, Texas A&I
1973	(2) Brad Van Pelt, LB, Michigan State
1974	John Hicks, G, Ohio State
1975	(2) Al Simpson, T, Colorado State
1976	Troy Archer, DE, Colorado
1977	Gary Jeter, DT, USC
1978	Gordon King, T, Stanford
1979	Phil Simms, QB, Morehead State
1980	Mark Haynes, DB, Colorado
1981	Lawrence Taylor, LB, North Carolina
1982	Butch Woolfolk, RB, Michigan
1983	Terry Kinard, DB, Clemson
1984	Carl Banks, LB, Michigan State
1984*	Gary Zimmerman, G, Oregon
1985	George Adams, RB, Kentucky
1986	Eric Dorsey, DE, Notre Dame

**Supplemental Draft*

NEW YORK JETS

1959 Harry Wismer was granted the New York franchise in the American Football League's first organizational meeting in Chicago, August 14. The franchise was to be called the Titans. Notre Dame quarterback George Izo was the first player selected by New York in the draft. Sammy Baugh was hired as the club's head coach, December 18.

1960 Penn football coach Steve Sebo was hired as the Titans' general manager. Don Maynard, a free agent from Canada, became the first player to sign with the Titans. Wismer leased the Polo Grounds for his team's home games. The team, whose colors were blue and gold, opened training camp at the University of New Hampshire and more than 100 players reported. In the club's first preseason game, the Titans lost to the Los Angeles Chargers 27-7 before 27,778 at the Coliseum. The Titans finally won for the first time 52-31 over Buffalo in the last preseason game. Wismer's team drew just 9,607—5,727 paid—in the home opener, a 27-3 victory over Buffalo. Although the Titans' running game struggled and the defense was almost non-existent, the team did have an exciting passing game, with Al Dorow throwing to Maynard and young Art Powell. In 14 games, the second-place Titans were 7-7 and attracted 221,285 people for the season, home and away.

1961 Bear Mountain Inn in New York State was chosen as the new headquarters for training camp. Off the field, the Titans were in the news constantly. Wismer first feuded with Baugh, then with AFL Commissioner Joe Foss. Then he announced the team had lost $1.2 million in two years, and the press had a field day. On the field, Dorow, Maynard, and Powell were joined with good performances by fullback Bill Mathis, who rushed for 846 yards, but the Titans compiled their second consecutive 7-7 record, finishing third.

1962 Sebo quit as general manager to become athletic director at Virginia. Wismer announced Clyde (Bulldog) Turner would succeed Baugh as coach. The club moved to East Stroudsburg University for training camp. Just before the opening league game, quarterback Lee Grosscup was signed and he directed a 28-17 victory over Oakland. But part way through the season, Grosscup joined Mathis on the sidelines with injuries, and the Titans fell to last place. In November, Wismer could not meet his payroll and the AFL announced it would assume the costs of running the club until the end of the season. In seven home games, the Titans drew just 36,161.

1963 A five-man syndicate composed of David (Sonny) Werblin, Townsend B. Martin, Leon Hess, Donald Lillis, and Phil Iselin purchased the franchise for $1 million, March 28. Weeb Ewbank was named the new head coach and the owners changed the name of the team from Titans to Jets, April 15. The new training camp site was Peekskill, New York. Although finishing only 5-8-1 in the first year under the new ownership and coaching, the attendance improved to 103,550 in seven games. The highlight of the season occurred on December 1, when the Jets recorded the first shutout in team history, 17-0 over Kansas City.

1964 The Jets signed Matt Snell, a fullback from Ohio State, who was the first number-one pick to sign with the club. Snell went on to gain 948 yards, catch 56 passes, and be named the AFL's rookie of the year. The team moved to Shea Stadium and set an AFL record when a crowd of 45,665 watched New York beat Denver 30-6 in the opener. Two months later, 60,300 showed up to see Buffalo defeat the Jets 20-7. In the most significant trade in the history of the franchise, if not the AFL, the Jets dealt the draft rights to quarterback Jerry Rhome to Houston for a number-one draft choice. They used that choice to select quarterback Joe Namath of Alabama.

1965 One day after the Orange Bowl game, Namath signed a Jets' contract reported to be worth $427,000. Heisman Trophy winner John Huarte of Notre Dame agreed to a $200,000 contract one week later, giving the Jets over a half-million dollars worth of rookie quarterback talent. Three weeks after signing, Namath underwent surgery for cartilage and ligament damage in his right knee, injured while he was playing for Alabama. Namath recovered in time to throw his first official pass for the Jets against Kansas City, September 18. He started for the first time and passed for 287 yards, but the Jets lost to Buffalo 33-21, September 26. Namath finished the year as the AFL's rookie of the year in both wire-service polls, gaining 2,220 yards through the air and throwing 18 touchdown passes. Other rookies made valuable contributions, including George Sauer, Verlon Biggs, Al Atkinson, and Jim Hudson. Namath was named most valuable player in the AFL All-Star Game.

1966 The Jets opened the season by burying Houston 52-13, establishing a club record for points scored. They made an early run at the Eastern Division title, but four consecutive losses in the middle of the season ended any hopes. For the season, Namath passed for 3,379 yards, Sauer caught 63 passes, and rookie halfback Emerson Boozer netted 1,247 all-purpose yards. Namath closed the season by beating the Patriots 38-28 to knock them out of the Eastern Division championship. Eleven days later, he reported to the hospital for a tendon transfer and cartilage removal in his right knee.

1967 Boozer, enjoying an outstanding season, went down with torn ligaments in his knee and was lost for the season against Kansas City, November 5. A victory over Boston clinched the Jets' first winning season in history, November 19. But a loss to Oakland cost them a chance for the championship. Namath finished the season with 4,007 yards passing, the first pro quarterback ever to throw for 4,000 yards. Sauer and Maynard were one-two in AFL receiving. The Jets sold out all home games and established an AFL attendance record with 437,036 tickets sold for seven games.

1968 Namath entered the hospital and underwent surgery for the repair of a small tear in the tendon of his left knee. Sonny Werblin's partners, Don Lillis, Leon Hess, Townsend Martin, and Phil Iselin, bought him out. Lillis took over the presidency of the club, May 21. The team relocated its training camp at Hofstra University on Long Island. Lillis died, July 23. Iselin was appointed the new club president. In the season opener, Namath controlled the ball the final six minutes as the Jets defeated Kansas City 20-19. "Heidi" became the center of a nationwide controversy, when the decisive final minutes of a game between the Jets and Oakland were interrupted so the children's television special could begin on time. Much of the football audience didn't see the Raiders score twice in the final seconds to win 43-32. A 35-17 victory over Miami was the team's ninth of the year, a club record, and it finished at 11-3. In the AFL Championship Game, Namath and Don Maynard combined on the big plays in the fourth quarter to beat Oakland 27-23. Namath, in a prediction that would make him a legend, "guaranteed" the Jets would beat Baltimore in Super Bowl III. His sharp passing, combined with Snell's running and a marvelous defensive performance, made the Jets the first AFL team to win a Super Bowl, 16-7. It also gave Ewbank the distinction of becoming the only coach to win the world title in both leagues.

1969 In June, Namath announced he was retiring as the result of a dispute over his ownership of a Manhattan night spot, Bachelors III. The Jets reported to training camp without Namath, July 8. Ten days later, Namath said he was selling his night club and reporting to work. The Jets beat the College All-Stars 26-24, then blitzed the Giants 37-14 in the first meeting between the two New York teams. Ewbank celebrated his one-hundredth coaching win in the Jets' first victory at Buffalo. Two months later, another success over the Bills extended the club's record winning streak to six. The Jets defeated Houston 34-26 to win their second straight Eastern Division title, December 6. But in the playoffs, Kansas City knocked the Jets out of the running 13-6. Ewbank was named the all-time coach of the AFL and Namath, Maynard, and Gerry Philbin were chosen to the all-time AFL team.

1970 In the first Monday night television game, the Jets were beaten by new AFC rival Cleveland 31-21. Snell was lost for the season with a ruptured Achilles tendon suffered in the Buffalo game, October 4. Namath fractured his right wrist against Baltimore and was out for the year, October 18. In the first regular-season game between intracity rivals, the Giants came from behind to beat the Jets 22-10. Behind reserve quarterback Al Woodall, the Jets pulled off two upsets, stunning both the Los Angeles Rams and Minnesota, to finish 4-10.

1971 John Riggins, a running back from Kansas, was the team's number-one draft choice. Sauer announced his early retirement from football. Namath, trying to make a tackle after his fullback fumbled, injured his knee, had to undergo surgery again, and was lost for three and a half months. After spending 19 straight regular-season games on the sidelines, Namath returned to throw three touchdown passes and almost beat the 49ers, who won 24-21. The Jets set a one-season home attendance record of 441,099.

1972 Namath signed the contract that made him the highest-paid player in the game at a reported $250,000 a year. In the best day of his career statistically, Namath passed for 496 yards and six touchdowns to defeat Baltimore 44-34. Riggins ran for 168 yards, Boozer for 150 in a 41-13 win over New England, marking only the second time two backs from the same team ever rushed for 150 yards in a game. Maynard became pro football's all-time receiving leader with career catch number 632 in a game with Oakland, December 11. Ewbank announced 1973 would be his last as head coach of the Jets.

1973 Charley Winner, the former head coach of the St. Louis Cardinals, was named to succeed Ewbank in 1974 and serve as an assistant coach for one season. Baltimore linebacker Stan White tackled Namath on a blitz, separating the quarterback's shoulder and putting him out for two months. Ewbank closed a 4-10 season, overshadowed on his last day by Buffalo's O.J. Simpson, whose 200-yard afternoon pushed him to an NFL record 2,003 yards rushing for the season.

1974 Winner took over as coach as the NFL Players Association strike began. The Jets moved into a new training center in Hempstead, New York, with facilities for coaches, office personnel, and players, plus a huge practice area. After a 1-7 start, Namath snapped the slump with an emotional 26-20 victory over the Giants in overtime at Yale Bowl. Ewbank announced he would retire as vice president of the club at the end of the season. Six straight late-season victories included surprise victories over two playoff teams, Miami and Buffalo.

1975 The number-one pick in the draft was traded to New Orleans for defensive lineman Billy Newsome. Al Ward, a vice president with the Dallas Cowboys, was named general manager to succeed Ewbank. Namath turned down a reported multimillion-dollar offer from the World Football League and signed a new two-year agreement with the Jets. The Jets' players walked out of camp the week of the opening game in support of the New England players' strike. The players returned two days later and the strike was settled. After six losses in a row and a 2-7 record, Winner was fired and Ken Shipp, the offensive coordinator, was named interim head coach. Riggins, one of the few bright spots in a disappointing season, ran for 1,005 yards, the first player in the history of the club to reach 1,000 yards.

1976 Lou Holtz, coach at North Carolina State, signed a five-year contract to coach the Jets. Richard Todd, another quarterback from Alabama, was the Jets' first choice in the draft. Holtz couldn't make up his mind between Namath and Todd, and as a result neither was effective. The only real offensive threat was rookie running back Clark Gaines, who ran for 724 yards and caught 41 passes. Holtz resigned to become head coach at Arkansas prior to the final game, and Mike Holovak served as interim coach while the Jets were bombed 42-3 by the Bengals to fall to 3-11. Iselin died in his office, December 28. Leon Hess subsequently was appointed acting president.

1977 Defensive coach Walt Michaels was named head coach on January 5. Jim Kensil was named club president and chief operating officer. In April, an era ended when Namath was waived. USC tackle Marvin Powell was the number-one draft choice, and game-breaking wide receiver Wesley Walker number two. Michaels used Todd at quarterback and he led the Jets to two wins in the first four games. The Jets then lost seven in a row, including a 28-27 defeat in Oakland in which Todd threw for 396 yards and four touchdowns. Todd missed three of the losses with an injury suffered against Miami. On December 4, the Jets defeated New Orleans for their third win with Todd at quarterback, but closed out the season with two more losses for a 3-11. mark. On December 30, general manager Ward resigned.

1978 In February, the Jets adopted a new logo and a new uniform. Ewbank was inducted into the Hall of Fame. Todd got the team off to a fast start with three touchdown passes in a 33-20 win over Miami in the opener. Three weeks later, Todd was injured against Washington in a game that dropped the Jets' record to 2-2. With Matt Robinson replacing Todd, the Jets won four of their next six, including a 31-28 come-from-behind victory over Denver on November 5. Four losses in the last six weeks dropped the Jets to an 8-8 record, but Michaels was voted NFL coach of the year. Walker led the NFL with 1,169 receiving yards and a 24.4-yard average.

1979 Robinson won the starting job in the preseason, but made only one start. An injured thumb cost him the job after an initial overtime loss to Cleveland. After losing to New England 56-3 in the second game, the Jets came back under Todd to win four of the next six. Another overtime loss, this time 27-24 to Houston, started a slide in which New York lost four of five. Three consecutive victories to end the season earned the Jets their second straight 8-8 season. Included in that late streak was a 27-26 victory over the Patriots. The Jets finished with the most productive ground game in the NFL.

1980 The Jets ended any speculation over whom their quarterback was by trading Robinson to Denver. The Jets chose Johnny (Lam) Jones of Texas on the first round of the draft, hoping to have a receiver to complement Walker. Todd set an NFL record of 42 completions against San Francisco on September 21, including 17 to Gaines. But Walker was injured, and Jones didn't play up to expectations. The running attack dropped to tenth in the AFC, and the Jets fell to last place in the AFC Eastern Division with a 4-12 record. New York defeated Miami twice, but couldn't beat another AFC East team.

1981 Leon Hess acquired another 25 percent interest in the team, bringing his total to 75 percent of the club. Attempting to improve their ground game, the Jets drafted Freeman McNeil of UCLA in the first round. New York started 0-3, including a 31-0 beating by the Bills in the opener. A 33-17 victory over Houston on September 27 turned the team around, and it won 8 of its next 10 games, including a 33-14 victory over Buffalo. On November 22, Todd threw an 11-yard scoring pass to Jerome Barkum with 16 seconds remaining to defeat Miami 16-15, and the Jets moved into a tie for first place in the AFC East. A 27-23 loss to Seattle knocked the Jets out of first place, but they still finished 10-5-1 and qualified for the wild card game. The defense, led by ends Joe Klecko and Mark Gastineau, became known as the New York Sack Exchange. It accumulated 66 sacks, a league-leading total that was one short of the record. Klecko (20½) and Gastineau (20) were one-two in the league in individual sacks. In the AFC Wild Card Game, the Bills jumped out to a second-quarter lead of 24-0, then held on as the Jets stormed back to cut the margin to 31-27. Bill Simpson intercepted Todd's pass at the Buffalo 2-yard line in the last minute to preserve the victory for Buffalo. Todd passed for 3,231 yards and 25 touchdowns.

1982 Klecko suffered a knee injury in a 31-7 victory against the New England Patriots on September 19, and was lost for 14 weeks. The Jets finished 6-3 in the strike-abbreviated season, losing twice to Miami. McNeil became the first Jet to lead the NFL in rushing, with 786 yards on a 5.2 average, and rushed for 202 yards in a 44-17 first-round playoff victory against Cincinnati the Jets' first postseason win in 14 years. Aided by linebacker Lance Mehl's two interceptions in the final three minutes, the Jets advanced to the AFC Championship Game with a 17-14 victory over the Raiders at the Los Angeles Memorial Coliseum. The Jets and Miami combined for a total of 12 turnovers on a muddy field at the Orange Bowl, but Miami won 14-0 to win the AFC title and a berth in the Super Bowl. Todd was the third-ranked passer in the AFC.

1983 Michaels resigned, February 9. The next day offensive coordinator Joe Walton was named head coach. In an NFL draft rich with "name" quarterbacks, the Jets surprised everyone by selecting Cal-Davis quarterback Ken O'Brien with their first-round pick. In a 27-24 overtime victory against the Rams, McNeil suffered a separated shoulder that sidelined him for seven weeks. On October 6, citing Shea Stadium as "run down, neglected, and the NFL's poorest facility for athletes and spectators alike," the Jets announced their plans to move to the Meadowlands in East Rutherford, New Jersey, for the 1984 season. The club pledged to return to New York City if a "first-class, professional stadium" would be ready for occupancy starting in 1989 under a lease equitable to New York City and the Jets. The Jets dropped a 34-7 decision to the Pittsburgh Steelers in their final home game at Shea Stadium, December 10, and the following week lost the final game of the season 34-14 at Miami to finish with a 7-9 record. Klecko, who returned strongly from his knee injury, was named to the AFC-NFC Pro Bowl as a defensive tackle, as was Gastineau, who led the NFL with 19 quarterback sacks.

1984 Hess assumed full ownership of the club as Helen Dillon, a partner since 1968, sold her 25 percent interest in the club, February 9. The Jets lost their first regular-season home game at Giants Stadium 23-17 to the Pittsburgh Steelers, but with Pat Ryan at quarterback, they jumped to a 6-2 start. An injury to Ryan and six consecutive losses dashed the Jets' playoff hopes, and they finished 7-9 for the second year in a row. McNeil rushed for a club-record 1,070 yards.

1985 Joe Namath was inducted into the Pro Football Hall of Fame. The Jets lost their opener 31-0 to the Los Angeles Raiders, surrendering 10 quarterback sacks. But they rebounded to win seven of their next eight games, and finished with an 11-5 record and a wild card berth. The improvement from 7-9 to 11-5 represented the greatest turnaround for an AFC club, and the 11 victories equaled the club's single-season record. Much of the credit for the improvement went to the defense, which allowed the fewest points in the AFC (264) and the lowest average in club history (16.5 per game). In the AFC Wild Card Game against the Patriots, the Jets committed four turnovers, lost O'Brien to an injury late in the first half, and were stung by Tony Franklin's four field goals. The Patriots won 26-14. O'Brien was the NFL's top-rated quarterback, and passed for 3,888 yards and 25 touchdowns, while being intercepted just eight times. McNeil missed two entire games and parts of two others, but still set a club record with 1,331 yards rushing. Tight end Mickey Shuler had 76 receptions to break George Sauer's club record of 75.

MEMBERS OF HALL OF FAME:
Weeb Ewbank, Joe Namath

JETS RECORD, 1960-85

Year	Won	Lost	Tied	Pct.		Pts.	OP
New York Titans							
1960	7	7	0	.500	2	382	399
1961	7	7	0	.500	3	301	390
1962	5	9	0	.357	4	278	423
New York Jets							
1963	5	8	1	.385	4	249	399
1964	5	8	1	.385	3	278	315
1965	5	8	1	.385	2	285	303
1966	6	6	2	.500	3	322	312
1967	8	5	1	.615	2	371	329
1968a	11	3	0	.786	1	419	280
1969b	10	4	0	.714	1	353	269
1970	4	10	0	.286	3	255	286
1971	6	8	0	.429	4	212	299
1972	7	7	0	.500	2	367	324
1973	4	10	0	.286	5	240	306
1974	7	7	0	.500	4	279	300
1975	3	11	0	.214	5	256	433
1976	3	11	0	.214	4	169	383
1977	3	11	0	.214	4	191	300
1978	8	8	0	.500	3	359	364
1979	8	8	0	.500	3	337	383
1980	4	12	0	.250	5	302	395
1981c	10	5	1	.656	2	355	287
1982	6	3	0	.667	6	245	166
1983	7	9	0	.438	5	313	331
1984	7	9	0	.438	3	332	364
1985c	11	5	0	.688	2	393	264
26 Years	167	199	7	.457		7,843	8,604

a*Super Bowl Champion; 2-0 in Playoffs*
b*AFL Eastern Division Champion; 0-1 in Playoffs*
c*AFC Wild Card Qualifier for Playoffs; 0-1 in Playoffs*
d*AFC Qualifier for Playoffs; 2-1 in Playoffs*

RECORD HOLDERS

CAREER

Rushing attempts	Emerson Boozer, 1966-75	1,291
Rushing yards	Emerson Boozer, 1966-75	5,104
Pass attempts	Joe Namath, 1965-76	3,655
Pass completions	Joe Namath, 1965-76	1,836
Passing yards	Joe Namath, 1965-76	27,057
Touchdown passes	Joe Namath, 1965-76	170
Receptions	Don Maynard, 1960-72	627
Receiving yards	Don Maynard, 1960-72	11,732
Interceptions	Bill Baird, 1963-69	34
Punting average	Curley Johnson, 1961-68	42.8
Punt return avg.	Dick Christy, 1961-63	16.2
Kickoff return avg.	Bobby Humphery, 1984-85	26.6
Field goals	Pat Leahy, 1974-85	184
Touchdowns	Don Maynard, 1960-72	88
Points	Pat Leahy, 1974-85	901

SEASON

Rushing attempts	Freeman McNeil, 1985	294
Rushing yards	Freeman McNeil, 1985	1,331
Pass attempts	Richard Todd, 1983	518
Pass completions	Richard Todd, 1983	308
Passing yards	Joe Namath, 1967	4,007
Touchdown passes	Al Dorow, 1960	26
	Joe Namath, 1967	26
Receptions	Mickey Shuler, 1985	76
Receiving yards	Don Maynard, 1967	1,434
Interceptions	Dainard Paulson, 1964	12

Punting average	Curley Johnson, 1965	45.3
Punt return avg.	Dick Christy, 1961	21.3
Kickoff return avg	Bobby Humphery, 1984	30.7
Field goals	Jim Turner, 1968	34
Touchdowns	Art Powell, 1960	14
	Don Maynard, 1965	14
	Emerson Boozer, 1972	14
Points	Jim Turner, 1968	145
GAME		
Rushing attempts	George Nock, 11-29-70	32
	John Riggins, 10-15-72	32
Rushing yards	Freeman McNeil, 9-15-85	192
Pass attempts	Joe Namath, 10-18-70	62
Pass completions	Richard Todd, 9-21-80	42
Passing yards	Joe Namath, 9-24-72	496
Touchdown passes	Joe Namath, 9-24-72	6
Receptions	Clark Gaines, 9-21-80	17
Receiving yards	Don Maynard, 11-17-68	228
Interceptions	Dainard Paulson, 9-28-63	3
	Bill Baird, 10-31-64	3
	Rich Sowells, 9-23-73	3
Field goals	Jim Turner, 11-3-68	6
	Bobby Howfield, 12-3-72	6
Touchdowns	8 times	3
Points	Jim Turner, 11-3-68	19
	Pat Leahy, 9-16-84	19

COACHING HISTORY

1960-61	Sammy Baugh	14-14-0
1962	Clyde (Bulldog) Turner	5- 9-0
1963-73	Weeb Ewbank	73-78-6
1974-75	Charley Winner*	9-14-0
1975	Ken Shipp	1- 4-0
1976	Lou Holtz**	3-10-0
1976	Mike Holovak	0- 1-0
1977-82	Walt Michaels	41-49-1
1983-85	Joe Walton	25-24-0

**Replaced after nine games in 1975*
***Resigned after 13 games in 1976*

FIRST PLAYER SELECTED

1960	George Izo, QB, Notre Dame
1961	Tom Brown, G, Minnesota
1962	Sandy Stephens, QB, Minnesota
1963	Jerry Stovall, S, LSU
1964	Matt Snell, FB, Ohio State
1965	Joe Namath, QB, Alabama
1965†	Johnny Roland, HB, Missouri
1966	Bill Yearby, T, Michigan
1966†	Don Parker, E, Virginia
1967	Paul Seller, G, Notre Dame
1968	Lee White, RB, Weber State
1969	Dave Foley, T, Ohio State
1970	Steve Tannen, CB, Florida
1971	John Riggins, RB, Kansas
1972	Jerome Barkum, WR, Jackson State
1973	Burgess Owens, DB, Miami
1974	Carl Barzilauskas, DT, Indiana
1975	(2) Anthony Davis, RB, USC
1976	Richard Todd, QB, Alabama
1977	Marvin Powell, T, USC
1978	Chris Ward, T, Ohio State
1979	Marty Lyons, DE-DT, Alabama
1980	Johnny (Lam) Jones, WR, Texas
1981	Freeman McNeil, RB, UCLA
1982	Bob Crable, LB, Notre Dame
1983	Ken O'Brien, QB, Cal-Davis
1984	Russell Carter, DB, SMU
1984*	Ken Hobart, QB, Idaho
1985	Al Toon, WR, Wisconsin
1986	Mike Haight, T, Iowa

†Redshirt Draft
**Supplemental Draft*

JETS MOST VALUABLE PLAYER

1961	Bill Mathis, FB
1962	Dick Christy, HB
1963	Bake Turner, SE
1964	Dainard Paulson, S
1965	Matt Snell, FB
1966	George Sauer, SE
1967	Don Maynard, FL
1968	Joe Namath, QB
1969	Joe Namath, QB
1970	John Elliott, DT
1971	Larry Grantham, LB
1972	John Riggins, RB
1973	Emerson Boozer, RB
1974	Joe Namath, QB
1975	John Riggins, RB
1976	Clark Gaines, RB
1977	Randy Rasmussen, G
1978	Wesley Walker, WR
1979	Marvin Powell, T
1980	Bruce Harper, RB-KR
1981	Richard Todd, QB
1982	Freeman McNeil, RB
1983	Lance Mehl, LB
1984	Freeman McNeil, RB
1985	Ken O'Brien, QB

PHILADELPHIA EAGLES

1933 Knowing a state law banning sports on Sunday was about to be repealed, Bert Bell and Lud Wray applied for an NFL franchise. The league approved their bid, but made a stipulation that Bell and Wray pay 25 percent of the outstanding liens against the former Frankford Yellow Jackets club, which had been forfeited to the league with large debts. Bell named the team in honor of the eagle, symbol of the National Recovery Administration of the New Deal. Bell was the team's general manager and ticket salesman, Wray the coach. The Eagles opened with a 56-0 loss to the New York Giants, followed by losses of 25-0 and 35-9. Remarkably, the rookie-laden Eagles regrouped and went four weeks without a loss. They even tied the powerful Chicago Bears 3-3 at Baker Bowl, November 12. The Eagles' top player was Tom (Swede) Hanson, a 6-foot 1-inch, 190-pound halfback from Temple who rushed for 494 yards.

1934 The Eagles became known for their inconsistency in their second season. In one stretch, they were shut out in three consecutive games. The following week, they blasted the Cincinnati Reds 64-0 at Baker Bowl. Hanson led the team with 805 yards rushing, second-most in the league. Joe Carter, an end from SMU, caught 16 passes for 238 yards and four touchdowns to lead the NFL.

1935 Realizing he was losing all the good college players to the top NFL teams, Bell proposed a draft, with the weakest clubs getting first shot at the All-America players. Bell's idea, considered the ideal way of balancing power in the league, was ratified by the owners, May 19. It didn't solve Bell's immediate problems, however. His Eagles continued to lose both games and money. Hanson was slowed by injuries and the offense almost ground to a halt. The Eagles did pick up one new player who contributed, however—rookie end Edgar (Eggs) Manske, who caught four touchdown passes. Another player not as successful was Edwin (Alabama) Pitts, the legendary prison halfback who had been a star not at a college but while serving time at Sing Sing federal penitentiary.

1936 In the first three seasons, the Eagles had lost more than $80,000 and Wray was losing interest in his investment. Bell purchased sole ownership for $4,000, disposed of Wray as head coach, and took the job himself. The first college draft was held and the Eagles, with the first pick, chose Jay Berwanger, the Heisman Trophy-winning halfback from the University of Chicago. The Eagles traded the rights for him to the Chicago Bears, however, and he never played pro football. The Eagles' home games were moved from Baker Bowl to Municipal Stadium. They won their opener, then lost 11 straight games. They were shut out six times, and their leading scorer was center Hank Reese, who made nine points on two field goals and three extra points.

1937 The Eagles improved, but only slightly, winning two games. Bell traded the league's first draft choice, Nebraska fullback Sam Francis, to the Chicago Bears for Bill Hewitt, an all-pro end. Hewitt led the team with 16 pass receptions, five for touchdowns. Bell uncovered an effective backfield pairing, Emmett Mortell of Wisconsin and Dave Smukler of Temple. Mortell led the Eagles with 312 yards rushing, and Smukler had 432 passing.

1938 Bell's blend of youth and experience finally began to mesh as the Eagles won five games and climbed past Pittsburgh into fourth place in the Eastern Division. The Eagles finished the year with victories over Pittsburgh and Detroit. The offensive star was Smukler, a versatile 6-foot 1-inch, 226-pounder with deceptive speed and agility. Smukler rushed for 313 yards, passed for 524 more, accounted for 10 touchdowns and was six-for-six kicking extra points. The receivers, Carter and Hewitt, also had good seasons, combining to catch 45 passes for 623 yards and 11 touchdowns.

1939 Bell signed Davey O'Brien, the 5-foot 7-inch, 150-pound Heisman Trophy-winning quarterback from TCU. O'Brien signed for $12,000, plus a percentage of the gate. Bell had the tiny quarterback insured with Lloyds of London. The policy called for Lloyds to pay the Eagles $1,500 for every game O'Brien missed due to injury. O'Brien not only stayed intact, he also set an NFL record for the most passing yardage in one season (1,324) and most completions in a game (21 in a 27-14 loss to the Chicago Bears). The Eagles finished with a 1-9-1 record.

1940 The Eagles switched their home field from Municipal Stadium to Shibe Park in north Philadelphia. O'Brien was brilliant but he could not lift the Eagles out of the Eastern Division cellar. Philadelphia lost its first nine games before beating Pittsburgh 7-0. The following week, O'Brien and Washington's great Sammy Baugh hooked up in a spectacular passing exhibition. Inspired by playing against his TCU predecessor, O'Brien threw a record 60 passes and completed 33 with no interceptions. He won his personal duel with Baugh, but the Eagles lost 13-6. Don Looney, a rookie receiver also from TCU, led the NFL with 58 catches, breaking Don Hutson's league record by 17 receptions. Following the season, O'Brien retired to join the FBI.

1941 Bell gave up the Eagles in a complicated piece of front-office maneuvering. Bell sold half the franchise to Art Rooney, who had sold his Pittsburgh franchise to Alexis Thompson of New York. Before the teams took the field, Rooney and Bell swapped Thompson their Philadelphia franchise for his Pittsburgh franchise. One of Thompson's first moves was to hire Earle (Greasy) Neale as his head coach, and two of Neale's initial steps were to install the T-formation and to obtain as his quarterback Tommy Thompson, a former Tulsa star who had been a reserve in Pittsburgh in 1940. Although blind in one eye, Thompson was an outstanding passer, and he adapted to Neale's system immediately. Unfortunately, he had no receiver of equal ability, because Looney had gone to Pittsburgh in exchange for Thompson.

1942 Most NFL teams lost their quarterbacks to the Armed Forces as World War II encompassed the United States. Not the Eagles, however, because Thompson was passed over due to his bad eye. The military depleted the Eagles in other areas, however, taking the three top runners—Jim Castiglia, Dan DeSantis, and Terry Fox—as well as Bob Suffridge, Neale's best lineman. The Eagles won their opener over Pittsburgh 24-14, then lost eight in a row.

1943 Faced with financial and manpower problems, the Eagles and Steelers joined forces. The hybrid team officially was named Phil-Pitt, although it popularly was called the Steagles. It was coached jointly by Neale and Pittsburgh's Walt Kiesling. The top player with each team, Thompson of the Eagles and Bill Dudley of the Steelers, missed the season, but Phil-Pitt uncovered surprising talent from the college ranks. Rookie tackles Al Wistert from Michigan and Frank (Bucko) Kilroy from Temple excelled on the line. Free agent Jack Hinkle rushed for 571 yards and scored four touchdowns. Even end Bill Hewitt came out of retirement, wearing a helmet for the first time in his career. Roy Zimmerman, obtained from Washington to replace Thompson, was the starting quarterback. His backup was 20-year-old rookie Allie Sherman. The Steagles won five games and finished just one game back.

1944 The Eagles and Steelers separated. The Eagles selected halfback Steve Van Buren of LSU in the first round of the draft. Philadelphia went unbeaten through seven games before losing to the Chicago Bears 28-7 at Shibe Park. Although the Eagles administered the only defeat of the year to the Giants, and tied them the other time the two teams met, the Giants won the division by half a game due to the Eagles' loss to the Bears and an earlier tie with the Redskins. Nevertheless, Philadelphia finished in second place with its best-ever record of 7-1-2. Van Buren, a 6-foot, 205-pound power runner with speed, bowled over the NFL's defenses. He joined with Hinkle and Mel Bleeker to give the Eagles the NFL's most productive ground game.

1945 The Eagles finished second to Washington with a 7-3 record. Van Buren led the NFL in rushing, with 832 yards and a 5.8-yard average; scoring, with 110 points (18 touchdowns, two extra points); and kickoff returns, with a 28.7-yard average. Van Buren scored on a 69-yard run against Detroit and returned a kickoff 98 yards for a touchdown against the New York Giants. The Eagles' top receiver was Jack Ferrante, a product of the Philadelphia sandlots who had never attended college. Ferrante caught 21 passes for 474 yards and seven touchdowns. Kilroy, a hard-hitting 6-foot 2-inch, 240-pounder, played middle guard in the defensive line.

1946 Neale added impressive talent to the Eagles' roster, trading for Alex Wojciechowicz, an outstanding center and linebacker, and Joe Muha, a rugged rookie fullback and punter. The Eagles also signed Bosh Pritchard, a quick, breakaway halfback who was just completing his military duty, and 5-foot 9-inch, 175-pound Russ Craft, a defensive back from Alabama. An injury to Van Buren slowed the offense, and the Eagles' record slipped to 6-5. Van Buren rushed for 529 yards, third in the league. Thompson, starting ahead of Zimmerman again, led the league with a 55.3 completion percentage.

1947 The last piece fit into Neale's offensive puzzle when the Eagles signed Pete Pihos, a 6-foot 1-inch, 215-pound rookie fullback from Indiana. The Eagles didn't need a fullback, so Neale made Pihos an end. The threat of Pihos caused defenses to spread out, opening more holes for Van Buren and Pritchard. Van Buren set a league record by rushing for 1,008 yards and 13 touchdowns. Thompson completed 53 percent of his passes for 16 touchdowns. Meanwhile, Neale's defense caused havoc. He stacked the middle of his line with the likes of Kilroy and Vic Sears and used his linebackers outside to hold up and intimidate the offensive ends. It was a 5-2-4 alignment, extremely physical, with the four deep backs playing up close. It was called the Eagle defense. Philadelphia split two games with the suddenly emerging Pittsburgh Steelers, and the two teams tied for first place. In a playoff for the Eastern Division title, the Eagles ran over the Steelers 21-0 in Pittsburgh, December 21. The Chicago Cardinals defeated the Eagles in the NFL Championship Game 28-21 at frozen Comiskey Park, December 28. The Eagles filed their cleats before the game to get better traction, but were discovered doing it and prohibited from wearing the sharpened cleats. Van Buren, slipping on the ice in flat-soled shoes, gained just 26 yards in 18 carries.

1948 The Eagles were winless in their first two games, losing 21-14 to the Chicago Cardinals and tying the Los Angeles Rams 28-28. They caught fire with back-to-back 45-0 victories over the New York Giants and Washington Redskins, and Neale's team was unstoppable the rest of the year. Thompson ran the T-formation to perfection, completed 57 percent of his passes, and threw for 25 touchdowns, while leading the league in passing. Van Buren led the league's rushers for the third time with 945 yards. Pritchard added seven touchdowns, four on runs, two on passes, and one on a punt return. Pihos caught 46 passes, 11 for touchdowns. Muha led the league with a 47.2-yard punting average. Neale even had the NFL's best kicker, Cliff (Automatic) Patton, who converted 50 of 50 extra points and 8 of 12 field-goal attempts. Captain Al Wistert, a tenacious 6-foot 1-inch, 215-pounder, was an all-pro tackle. The Eagles won their second Eastern Division title with a 9-2-1 record. They won their first world championship with a 7-0 victory over the Chicago Cardinals at Shibe Park, December 19. The game was played in a blinding snowstorm. Van Buren woke up that morning, saw the snow, and went back to bed, assuming the game would be postponed. He was awakened by a phone call from Neale, rode to the stadium in a trolley car, and scored the game's only touchdown on a five-yard run in the fourth quarter.

1949 Thompson sold the Eagles to a syndicate of 100 local businessmen, organized by James P. Clark, for $250,000, January 15. Vince McNally was named general manager. With the bonus pick of the draft, the Eagles selected Chuck Bednarik, All-America center-linebacker from Pennsylvania. The Eagles rolled through the regular season, winning 11 games and losing only one. The Eagles won the Eastern Division for the third straight year. Van Buren set another league record, rushing for 1,146 yards. Pritchard led the league in average per carry (6.0), while gaining 506 yards. Thompson was second in the NFL in passing, while Pihos, Ferrante, and young Neill Armstrong gave the Eagles one of the league's best sets of receivers. The Eagles' most impressive victory was a 38-14 trouncing of the previously unbeaten Los Angeles Rams at Shibe Park. The Rams and Eagles met again in the NFL Championship Game in Los Angeles Memorial Coliseum, December 18. A heavy rain turned the field into a quagmire but it didn't slow the Eagles' punishing running attack, which rolled up 274 yards to the Rams' 21. Van Buren carried the ball 31 times for 196 yards to lead the Eagles' 14-0 championship triumph. The Eagles scored on Thompson's 31-yard pass to Pihos and a blocked punt by rookie end Leo Skladany.

1950 In the first week of the season, the defending NFL champion Eagles were matched against the Browns, the upstart newcomers from the All-America Football Conference, before a record 71,237 at Philadelphia's Municipal Stadium. The Browns pulled a stunning 35-10 upset, foreshadowing the Eagles' decline. The Eagles won six of their next seven but Van Buren was sidelined with a foot injury and the team lacked the power to handle the top opponents. They lost their last four games to fall to third place in the Eastern Division. A feud between Neale and owner Clark erupted late in the season; the players had to pull Neale off Clark after an altercation in the Polo Grounds' locker room. Neale was fired following the season.

1951 The Eagles named Alvin (Bo) McMillin head coach in February. McMillin, a successful college coach at Indiana, directed the Eagles to victories in their first two games, but stomach cancer forced him to resign. Wayne Millner succeeded McMillin, and the team sagged to 4-8. Van Buren played on the bad foot and gained just 327 yards on 112 carries. Adrian Burk succeeded Thompson, who had retired, at quarterback and threw a league-high 23 interceptions. One bright note was the addition of Bobby Walston, a 6-foot, 190-pound end and placekicker from Georgia. Walston caught 31 passes, scored eight touchdowns, and added 46 points kicking. He was named NFL rookie of the year.

1952 Van Buren suffered a serious knee injury at training camp and retired. The club fired Millner and named Jim Trimble head coach, September 9. Trimble acquired Bobby Thomason from Green Bay and made him the starting quarterback. Trimble also moved Harry (Bud) Grant, a defensive end as a rookie in 1951, ahead of Pihos at offensive end. Trimble felt Pihos would be more effective as a defensive end. The move paid off as Pihos was named all-pro on defense, while Grant finished second in the league in pass receiving with 56 catches for 997 yards. With Van Buren gone, most of the ball carrying was done by John Huzvar, a plodding 6-foot 4-inch, 240-pound fullback from North Carolina State.

1953 Clark retired as president and was named chairman of the board. Frank L. McNamee was elected club president. Trimble kept the Eagles in contention despite the loss of Grant, who jumped to the Canadian Football League. Trimble switched Pihos back to offense and he responded by catching 63 passes for 1,049 yards and 10 touchdowns to lead the NFL. Walston caught 41 passes as Thomason and Burk combined to pass for a league-high 3,250 yards. The Eagles had good balance in their running game with three backs—Don Johnson, Jerry Williams, and Frank Ziegler—totaling more than 1,100 yards. Rookie defensive back Tom Brookshier of Colorado led the club with eight interceptions. The highlight of the year came the final week, when the Eagles upset Cleveland 42-27 to spoil the Browns' hopes for a perfect season.

1954 The Eagles beat Cleveland 28-10 in the opener at Shibe Park, stirring hopes of a return to glory. The Eagles won their first four games, including a 49-21 rout of Washington in which Burk threw seven touchdown passes, to take the early lead in the Eastern Division. The Eagles then lost four of five games, including a rematch with the Browns, 6-0. For the third straight year, the Eagles finished second with seven victories. Pihos caught 60 passes to share the NFL receiving title with the 49ers' Billy Wilson. Walston caught 11 touchdown passes and led the league in scoring with 114 points. Burk led the league with 23 touchdown passes.

1955 The Eagles overcame a 10-point deficit to defeat the New York Giants 27-17 in the league opener at Shibe Park, but the victory was costly. Bucko Kilroy, the all-pro middle guard starting his one-hundred-first consecutive game, tore ligaments in his knee and never played again. The defense recovered gradually as Norman (Wildman) Willey and Tom Scott developed into a pair of top-flight pass-rushing ends. Young Jess Richardson, who played at Alabama, was groomed to replace Kilroy. Bednarik had another great season at linebacker. Pihos continued to show the way on offense, leading the NFL in pass receiving for the third straight year with 62 catches. The Eagles were plagued by an ineffective running game and suffered through a 4-7-1 season.

1956 Trimble was dismissed after four seasons as head coach. Hugh Devore, a Notre Dame graduate, was named to succeed him. The Eagles' veteran nucleus disappeared. Kilroy, Pihos, and defensive tackle Mike Jarmoluk all retired, leaving Devore with the weakest team in the Eastern Division. The Eagles' best runner was Ken Keller, a rookie from North Carolina who gained 433 yards. The passing attack slipped badly due to the loss of Pihos, and Thomason and Burk finished with 5 touchdown passes and 27 interceptions. The strength of the team was a good defensive secondary, which included Brookshier, Ed (Bibbles) Bawel, Jerry Norton, and Eddie Bell.

1957 The Eagles had their best college draft, selecting Michigan State fullback Clarence Peaks, halfbacks Billy Ray Barnes of Wake Forest, and Tommy McDonald of Oklahoma, and quarterback Sonny Jurgensen of Duke. Assistant coach Charlie Gauer convinced Devore to use McDonald at wide receiver, and, against Washington, the 5-foot 10-inch, 180-

pound speedster caught two touchdown passes in a 21-12 win. Jurgensen split time with Thomason at quarterback and led the Eagles to a 17-7 upset of Cleveland. Barnes and Peaks combined for more than 1,000 yards rushing. The Eagles won only four games but they had promise for the future.

1958 Devore was fired and Buck Shaw hired as head coach. Shaw saw long-range potential in Jurgensen, but felt the Eagles needed an experienced quarterback to win in the next few years. He traded tackle Buck Lansford, defensive back Jimmy Harris, and a first-round draft choice to Los Angeles for 32-year-old Norm Van Brocklin. Shaw put together an exciting passing attack, employing McDonald at flanker and moving Pete Retzlaff, a 6-foot 1-inch, 210-pound fullback, to split end. Retzlaff, who was cut by Detroit in 1956, was virtually a clone of Pihos, with superb hands and an uncanny ability for running patterns. In his first year as a regular, Retzlaff caught 56 passes to tie Baltimore's Raymond Berry for the NFL receiving title. McDonald caught just 29 passes but nine went for touchdowns. Van Brocklin passed more than any other quarterback (374 attempts, 198 completions, and 2,409 yards). Although the Eagles finished the year in last place (2-9-1), Van Brocklin predicted major improvement for next season. The Eagles moved their home site from Connie Mack Stadium to the University of Pennsylvania's Franklin Field and attendance almost doubled despite the record.

1959 Led by Bednarik at center, the Eagles' offensive line gave Van Brocklin time to find his receivers. Given time, the Dutchman could pick apart almost any defense, as he proved in a stunning 49-21 upset of the New York Giants, September 22. The victory gave the younger Eagles confidence, and they swept six of eight games to challenge New York and Cleveland for the Eastern Conference lead. McDonald was virtually unstoppable as he caught 47 passes and scored 11 touchdowns, one on an 81-yard punt return, the longest in Eagles history. Bert Bell, the one-time Eagles owner and now the NFL Commissioner, died, October 11. Bell suffered a fatal heart attack while watching the Eagles beat Pittsburgh 28-24 at Franklin Field. The Eagles had a chance to finish alone in second place but they lost to Cleveland 28-21 in the final week. The Eagles and Browns finished tied at 7-5.

1960 The Eagles were jolted 41-24 by the Cleveland Browns in the league opener at Franklin Field. But, under the fierce leadership of Van Brocklin and Bednarik, they regrouped to win their next nine games and clinch their first Eastern Division title in 11 years. The key victory was a 31-29 thriller over Cleveland in which Bobby Walston kicked a 39-yard field goal with two seconds left. The Eagles wrapped up the division with back-to-back wins over the New York Giants, 17-10 and 31-23. Peaks broke his leg at midseason and was replaced by Ted Dean, a rookie from Wichita State who also was the club's leading kick returner. A touchdown by Dean broke open the second victory over New York. When injuries depleted the defense, Bednarik, who was 35, began playing at both center and outside linebacker. The Eagles' running game was weak—only the expansion Dallas Cowboys rushed for fewer yards—but Van Brocklin had a great season, passing for 2,471 yards and 24 touchdowns and finishing second in the league in passing. Retzlaff, McDonald, and Walston caught a total of 115 passes for 22 touchdowns. The Eagles won their third NFL championship, defeating Green Bay 17-13 before 67,325 fans at Franklin Field, December 26. The Eagles won the title in typical fashion, coming from behind in the fourth quarter on a Van Brocklin-engineered drive, culminated by Dean's five-yard end sweep. After the championship game, Shaw retired as head coach. Van Brocklin was the overwhelming choice as the NFL's most valuable player.

1961 The year began with unexpected turmoil as Shaw's top assistant, Nick Skorich, was named head coach. Van Brocklin was outraged, claiming the Eagles' management had promised he would succeed Shaw. Van Brocklin was asked to stay on as player-coach but he refused, saying "That stuff went out with Johnny Blood." Van Brocklin retired and became head coach of the new Minnesota Vikings. Few people expected the Eagles to repeat as Eastern Conference champions with the unproved Jurgensen taking over at quarterback. But Jurgensen bombed every secondary he faced, and the Eagles won seven of their first eight games, holding onto first place. The Eagles' title hopes collapsed, however, when Brookshier suffered a broken leg in a 16-14 win over Chicago. Skorich inserted a rookie, Glen Amerson, in Brookshier's spot and New York and Cleveland picked on him while routing the Eagles 38-21 and 45-24. The Eagles still had a chance to catch the Giants late in the season, but a controversial roughing-the-kicker penalty against Leo Sugar helped New York beat Philadelphia again, 28-24. The Eagles lost to Detroit in the Playoff Bowl 38-10 as Jurgensen suffered a shoulder separation and tackle J. D. Smith broke his leg. Jurgensen had emerged as the best passer in the NFL, setting two league records—235 completions and 3,723 yards—and tying a third—32 touchdowns. McDonald finished second in the league in receptions, with 64, but led with 1,144 yards and 13 touchdowns.

1962 James P. Clark, former president and chairman of the board of the Eagles, died, April 17. Injuries continued to haunt the Eagles. Jurgensen never fully recovered from his shoulder injury, then went down with loose knee cartilage. Retzlaff, Walston, and reserve tight end Dick Lucas all suffered broken arms. Peaks and Dean were sidelined with broken bones in their feet. Reserve fullback Theron Sapp was lost with a shoulder separation. Howard (Hopalong) Cassady played only four games before breaking his leg. Don (The Blade) Burroughs, the team's leading pass interceptor, suffered cracked ribs. Only Tommy McDonald, the smallest man on the team, stayed healthy, catching 58 passes for 1,146 yards and scoring 10 touchdowns. The Eagles struggled through a bleak 3-10-1 season, but Jurgensen provided some thrills, completing 33 of 57 passes against New York and throwing for five touchdowns at St. Louis. Even with a bad shoulder, he led the league with 3,261 yards. Timmy Brown, who had been picked up from the Packers several years earlier, suddenly blossomed. He led the team in rushing, punt returns, kickoff returns, and scoring, and finished second in receiving. He gave great promise of things to come when he amassed 341 all-purpose yards in the finale against the Cardinals.

1963 Problems began in training camp as Jurgensen and backup quarterback King Hill left camp to dramatize their demands for more money. Management gave in and the quarterbacks returned. The loss of Bednarik, who retired after 14 brilliant NFL seasons, left a leadership void in the defense. The club also was hit with more injuries as Jurgensen reinjured his arm. McDonald separated his shoulder, Peaks dislocated his elbow, linebacker Maxie Baughan broke his thumb, and tackle Frank Fuller broke his leg. The only bright spot was Brown, who set an NFL record for most all-purpose yards in a season, 2,428. Jerry Wolman, an energetic young building tycoon, purchased the sagging franchise for $5.5 million, December 5.

1964 Wolman signed Joe Kuharich, former coach of the Chicago Cardinals and Washington Redskins, to succeed Skorich, February 27. Kuharich, who also was named general manager, quickly dismantled the team, trading McDonald to Dallas, Jurgensen and safety Jim Carr to Washington, Lee Roy Caffey and a first-round draft pick to Green Bay, Dean to Minnesota, and Peaks to Pittsburgh. In return, Kuharich received quarterback Norm Snead, halfback Ollie Matson, fullback Earl Gros, center Jim Ringo, defensive tackle Floyd Peters, and kicker Sam Baker. Three outstanding rookies also helped the club—tackle Bob Brown, linebacker Mike Morgan, and defensive back Joe Scarpati. The Eagles opened with a 38-7 victory over the New York Giants as they successfully employed Burroughs on safety blitzes to harass the immobile Y. A. Tittle. They won four of their first seven games to quiet the grumbling fans, who missed the electrifying Jurgensen-to-McDonald combination. Baker set a club record with 16 field goals.

1965 The Eagles' record slipped to 5-9 but the team showed encouraging progress, particularly on the offensive line, where Brown, the 6-foot 4-inch, 280-pound former Nebraska All-America, asserted himself. Ed Blaine, a former Green Bay Packer, matured into a solid guard, as did Jim Skaggs. This youthful group was balanced by Ringo, the 34-year-old former all-pro center. With the revamped line clearing the way, Timmy Brown rushed for 861 yards, third-best in the NFL, while leading the league with a 5.4-yard average and catching 50 passes. Retzlaff, switched to tight end at age 34, caught 66 passes for 1,190 yards and 10 touchdowns.

1966 Kuharich traded away two more popular players, shipping Baughan and cornerback Irv Cross to Los Angeles for tackle Frank Molden, linebacker Fred Brown, cornerback Aaron Martin, and flanker Willie Brown. After a sluggish start, the Eagles got their offense going with the running of Brown, Gros, and two promising fullbacks, Tom Woodeshick and Izzy Lang. The potent running game offset a dismal season by Snead. With Kuharich rotating his quarterback position among Snead, Hill, and Jack Concannon, a young scrambler from Boston College, the Eagles won seven of their last nine to tie Cleveland for second place. Typical of the helter-skelter season was a 24-23 upset of division-champion Dallas in which Brown returned two kickoffs for touchdowns and Martin scored on a punt return. The Eagles were beaten 20-14 by Baltimore in the Playoff Bowl.

1967 Inspired by the Eagles' first winning season in five years, Wolman rewarded Kuharich with a 15-year contract as coach and general manager. Kuharich traded Concannon to the Chicago Bears for all-pro tight end Mike Ditka and sent Gros to Pittsburgh for split end Gary Ballman. Snead made a strong comeback, climbing to fifth in NFL passing with a club-record 3,399 yards and 29 touchdowns. When injuries slowed Ditka and Ballman, Snead turned to Ben Hawkins and the second-year flanker from Arizona State responded, catching 59 passes for 1,265 yards (a club record) and 10 touchdowns. The running game was ably handled by Woodeshick, who gained 670 yards after Brown was hurt, but the defense collapsed, allowing 409 points. Even though the Eagles finished in second place, their 6-7-1 record had fans calling for Kuharich's head by the end of the season.

1968 After 17 years of training at Hershey, Pennsylvania, the Eagles moved to Albright College in Reading, Pennsylvania. The tone for the year was established in the preseason opener, when Snead suffered a broken leg on the first play from scrimmage. Brown was traded to Baltimore for defensive back and kick-return specialist Alvin Haymond. The Eagles lost their first 11 league games, inspiring hope among Eagles' fans that the team would go winless and earn the right to select USC All-America running back O.J. Simpson in the draft. When the Eagles won two of their last three games, Buffalo (1-12-1) moved past them in the drafting position. The only bright spot in the season was the play of Woodeshick, who finished third in the league in rushing, with 947 yards. Fans organized a "Joe [Kuharich] Must Go" movement, distributing buttons and even paying a skywriter to spread their message above Franklin Field as the Eagles lost to Minnesota 24-17. The season ended with Wolman desperately trying to avoid bankruptcy.

1969 The beleaguered Wolman was forced to sell the franchise to Leonard Tose, a Norristown, Pennsylvania, trucking magnate, for $16.1 million. Tose fired Kuharich, agreeing to pay him for the duration of his contract, and hired Retzlaff, the former all-pro receiver, as general manager. Retzlaff hired Jerry Williams, former Eagles halfback and assistant, as head coach. Retzlaff traded Bob Brown and Izzy Lang to Los Angeles for defensive halfback Irv Cross, tackle Joe Carollo, guard Don Chuy, and receiver Harold Jackson. The Eagles drafted Leroy Keyes, the versatile Purdue halfback. Due to a lengthy contract dispute, Keyes did not join the Eagles until September and was slow rounding into shape. Williams used Keyes on offense but he was a disappointment, averaging just three yards per carry, while Woodeshick again was forced to carry the heavy work load. The real steal of the draft was defensive back Bill Bradley, whom the Eagles selected on the third round. Jackson blossomed with playing time and caught 65 passes for a league-high 1,116 yards. Jackson and Hawkins combined to give the Eagles scoring punch, catching 17 touchdown passes between them.

1970 Williams planned to switch Keyes to cornerback, but a torn Achilles tendon sidelined the versatile Keyes. Woodeshick injured his knee in preseason training and carried the ball just 52 times. Bradley suffered torn knee ligaments in the preseason opener and was lost for the year. Tim Rossovich, a defensive end converted to middle linebacker, tore ligaments in his ankle during the preseason but refused to undergo surgery. Rossovich started all 14 league games and led the team with 174 tackles. The Eagles lost their first seven games and spent the season in last place in the Eastern Division. The highlight of the year was a 23-20 upset of the New York Giants in a Monday night game.

1971 The Eagles moved to Veterans Stadium with a seating capacity of 66,052. After suffering crushing defeats in the first three league games, Tose fired Williams and promoted defensive line coach Ed Khayat to head coach. Williams called a press conference and bitterly denounced Tose as "a man of little character." The players drafted a statement supporting Williams, and the franchise bordered on anarchy for a week. Khayat, an admirer of General George Patton, ordered all players to cut their hair and shave off their mustaches. Several players, led by Rossovich, resisted before giving in. Snead was traded to Minnesota. The Eagles won six and tied one of their final nine games. Bradley set a team record and led the NFL with 11 pass interceptions.

1972 Khayat's stern discipline backfired the second year. Keyes, running back Lee Bouggess, and linebacker Steve Zabel all suffered serious injuries in a training camp where contact drills were long and punishing. Bradley and Rossovich staged a joint contract holdout that degenerated into a power struggle between Retzlaff and the two players. Retzlaff settled the matter by trading Rossovich to San Diego, and Bradley later signed his contract. Pete Liske performed erratically at quarterback and was replaced by John Reaves, the number-one draft pick from Florida. Reaves displayed a strong arm and courage working behind the Eagles' blockers, but his inexperience led to costly mistakes. Jackson led the NFL with 62 receptions for 1,048 yards. The franchise hit an all-time low when the New York Giants buried the Eagles 62-10 at Yankee Stadium. The morning following the season finale, Tose accepted Retzlaff's resignation and fired the entire coaching staff. Bradley became the first player in NFL history to win the interception title two consecutive years; he had nine.

1973 Tose hired Mike McCormack, long-time assistant in Washington, as head coach. An excellent draft yielded Texas tackle Jerry Sisemore, USC tight end Charle Young, TCU center Guy Morriss, Michigan safety Randy Logan, and San Diego State cornerback Joe Lavender. McCormack traded a draft choice to Baltimore for fullback Norm Bulaich, then dealt Harold Jackson plus two number-one draft picks to the Rams for Roman Gabriel, a 33-year-old quarterback. Gabriel became the NFL's comeback player of the year as he led the league in four passing categories, including 3,219 yards and 23 touchdowns. Young teamed with 6-foot 8-inch Harold Carmichael to give the Eagles the best pair of receivers in football. Carmichael led the NFL with 67 pass receptions and 1,116 yards. Young led all tight ends with 55 catches. Tom Sullivan emerged as a quality halfback, rushing for 968 yards. The Eagles won five games, including a 30-16 upset of Dallas.

1974 Hoping to patch up a porous defense, McCormack traded two first-round draft picks and one second to Cincinnati for middle linebacker Bill Bergey. After a disappointing 7-3 loss to St. Louis in the opener, the Eagles won four straight and surged into contention for the first time since 1961. A 31-24 loss in Dallas broke the momentum and the Eagles lost six straight games, forcing McCormack to bench Gabriel and start rookie Mike Boryla at quarterback for the final three weeks. Boryla, a former Stanford star, displayed remarkable poise in his first NFL exposure, directing victories over Green Bay, the New York Giants, and Detroit. Young caught 63 passes to lead all NFC receivers. Bergey, an all-pro, made 160 tackles and led the team with five interceptions. After the season, Tose appointed Jim Murray, the team's administrative assistant, general manager.

1975 The Eagles lost their first two games to opponents they were favored to beat—the Giants (23-14) and the Bears (15-13). Following the Chicago loss McCormack remarked that there were two "dogs" on his roster. The statement came to haunt McCormack as the entire squad seethed at the label. With the team floundering at 2-8, McCormack benched Gabriel and went back to Boryla. Boryla won two of his four starts as the Eagles finished 4-10. Three of the losses came on last-second field goals. The Eagles defeated Washington twice, their first series sweep of the Redskins since 1961. Following the season, Tose announced he would not renew McCormack's contract.

1976 Tose hired Dick Vermeil to become the Eagles' fifth head coach in nine years, February 8. Vermeil had gained national prominence a month earlier when his underdog UCLA team upset top-ranked Ohio State 23-10 in the Rose Bowl. Gabriel was slow recovering from offseason knee surgery and did not rejoin the team until mid-October. Given the starting spot, Boryla threw eight interceptions in the first three games. Vermeil won his first game as an NFL coach when the Eagles beat the New York Giants 20-7 at Veterans Stadium, September 19. Vermeil uncovered a potential star runner in rookie Mike Hogan, a ninth-round draft pick from Tennessee-Chattanooga. Hogan missed half the season with a dislocated shoulder but led the team with 561 yards rushing. The Eagles went through a prolonged slump, losing eight of nine, as the offense scored just two touchdowns in four weeks. The Eagles didn't score more than two touchdowns in a game until the final week, when they trounced Seattle 27-10.

1977 Ron Jaworski was obtained from the Los Angeles Rams for tight end Charle Young. The club was without a draft choice for the first four rounds but selected Wilbert Montgomery, a running back from Abilene Christian, in the sixth round. Jaworski, a full-time, starting quarterback for the first time in his career, led the club to a 13-3 victory over Tampa Bay in the season opener. However, the Eagles were haunted by a series of close defeats and lost 9 of the next 11 games. One bright spot was the defense, which recorded 47 sacks and 21 interceptions, while permitting just 207 points. After going 3-9, the Eagles finished the season with back-to-back victories over the Giants and the Jets. In the season finale, Montgomery made his first start and rushed for 103 yards and two touchdowns. Jaworski finished the season with 18 touchdown passes.

1978 The season opened with a heartbreaking 16-14 loss to Los Angeles when the Rams scored on a 46-yard field goal with seven seconds left. Following another close loss to Washington, Montgomery rushed for 104 yards to key a 24-17 victory over New Orleans. But the club struggled to a 4-5 record after nine weeks. Then the newly installed 3-4 defense, led by Bergey, asserted itself and helped deliver a four-game winning streak. With an 8-7 record, the Eagles entered the final contest against the Giants requiring a victory to make the playoffs for the first time since 1960. Montgomery rushed for 130 yards to lead a 20-3 win and clinch a winning record for the first time since 1966. In the Wild Card Game on December 24, the Eagles jumped to a 13-0 lead over Atlanta midway through the fourth quarter, but Steve Bartkowski threw two touchdown passes, and the Falcons came back to win 14-13. Montgomery finished the season with 1,220 yards rushing to break a 29-year-old club record set by Steve Van Buren. Jaworski passed for 2,487 yards and 16 touchdowns, and Carmichael caught 55 passes for 1,072 yards.

1979 The Eagles used their first number-one draft choice since 1973 to select UCLA linebacker Jerry Robinson. Defensive end Claude Humphrey was obtained from Atlanta prior to the season. The Eagles opened the season by defeating the New York Giants, and had a 6-1 record after seven weeks. But a midseason slump produced three successive defeats. In one of those lossses, a 24-19 defeat by Cleveland on November 4, Carmichael broke an NFL record by catching a pass in his one-hundred-sixth consecutive game. The following week, the rest of the club awoke in a 31-21 victory over Dallas, which included a 59-yard field goal, the second-longest in NFL history, by rookie Tony Franklin. The win launched a four-game winning streak, including a 44-7 romp over Detroit that insured a wild card berth in the playoffs. However, the Eagles lost a chance to win the NFC East when they were defeated by Dallas 24-17. Nonetheless, they finished with an 11-5 mark. Montgomery rushed for 1,512 yards to break his own club record. On December 23, a second-half rally led by Jaworski defeated the Bears in the NFC Wild Card Game 27-17. A week later the Eagles fell to Tampa Bay 24-17 in an NFC Divisional Playoff Game. Vermeil was chosen as the NFL coach of the year.

1980 The Eagles got off to a fast start when they crushed Denver (27-6), Minnesota (42-7), and the New York Giants (35-3). After a loss to St. Louis, they embarked on a new eight-game winning streak, including a 17-10 victory over Dallas on October 19. On November 23, the Eagles defeated Oakland 10-7, as the defense recorded eight sacks against their eventual opponent in the Super Bowl. Despite three losses in four games to close out the season, the Eagles won the NFC East on tiebreaking procedures with a 12-4 record. The defense allowed fewer points (222) than any other team in the league, and held 10 opponents to under 100 yards rushing. The offense overcame the loss of Montgomery for part of the season, thanks to a big-play season by Jaworski, who passed for 3,529 yards and 27 touchdowns. The Eagles converted eight Minnesota turnovers into a 31-16 victory in an NFC Divisional Playoff Game on January 3. The defense then shut down Dallas to win the NFC Championship Game 20-7 on January 11. But the defense broke down and the offense sputtered in Super Bowl XV; the Raiders won 27-10.

1981 Injuries struck early in the season as the Eagles lost both fullbacks, Leroy Harris and Perry Harrington, with broken legs. The team still raced to a 6-0 mark as the defense limited each opponent to 14 points or less. On November 1, the Eagles lost to the Cowboys 17-14 and fell into a first-place tie with Dallas at 7-2. Consecutive routs of St. Louis (52-10) and Baltimore (38-13) enabled Philadelphia to regain first place, but the offense slumped and the Eagles suffered four successive defeats. The team ended the regular season with a 38-0 pounding of St. Louis, which gave the Eagles a 10-6 record, second place in the NFC East, and the home field in the NFC Wild Card Game. On December 27, the other wild card team, the New York Giants, jumped to a 20-0 first-quarter lead and hung on to win 27-21. During the regular season, the Eagles could again point to their defense as one of the dominant forces in the NFL; it gave up only 221 points, fewest in the league.

1982 The Eagles split their first two games of the season, one a victory over Cleveland and the other an overtime loss to the eventual Super Bowl champion Washington Redskins. Following the eight-week strike layoff, the Eagles lost four games in a row, eventually finishing 3-6 and missing the playoffs for the first time since 1977. A 24-20 victory at Dallas on December 26 was the last win for Vermeil, who resigned shortly after the season, citing "burnout" as his reason. Despite the short season, Jaworski still passed for 2,076 yards. Defensive end Dennis Harrison, whose 10½ sacks were second-best in the NFL, was the Eagles' lone representative in the AFC-NFC Pro Bowl.

1983 Marion Campbell, the team's defensive coordinator for six years, was named to replace Vermeil. Campbell got the Eagles off to a fast start, winning four of the first six games. But the Eagles were beaten 37-7 by the Cowboys and slumped into a seven-game losing streak to finish 5-11, fourth in the NFC East. Injuries to tight end John Spagnola and Montgomery severely hurt the offense. The highlight of the season was the blossoming of wide receiver Mike Quick, drafted in the first round out of North Carolina State in 1982. Quick led the league and set a club record with 1,409 yards receiving on 69 receptions, good for 13 touchdowns. Jaworski threw for 3,315 yards to surpass the 20,000-yard mark in his career.

1984 The Eagles couldn't overcome a 1-4 start, though they mounted a serious effort over the last 11 games. Their 6-9-1 record, though, put them at the bottom of the increasingly competitive division. A club-record 60 sacks signaled improvement on defense. Montgomery ran for 789 yards and set Eagles career-rushing records for yards (6,538) and attempts (1,465), surpassing the marks set by Steve Van Buren. Rookie kicker Paul McFadden, taken on the twelfth round, became the season's surprise when he set a team scoring record of 116 points. Jaworski broke his leg, ending his streak of 116 consecutive starts. Joe Pisarcik started the last three games at quarterback. Quick made his second Pro Bowl appearance after catching 61 passes for 1,052 yards.

1985 On March 12, Tose announced the sale of the team to Florida automobile dealers Norman Braman and Ed Leibowitz; it became official on April 29. Braman immediately elevated Harry Gamble to vice president-general manager, overseeing day-to-day operations of the club. Running back Wilbert Montgomery was traded to Detroit, and Earnest Jackson was picked up from San Diego to replace him. The team had its moments, splitting with division rivals Washington and Dallas and defeating St. Louis twice. Beginning with a 30-7 victory over the Cardinals, the Eagles won five of six games, including a 23-17 overtime game with Atlanta in which the winning score was a 99-yard touchdown pass from Jaworski to Quick. But Philadelphia lost four in a row, and Campbell's firing was announced before the season finale, which the Eagles won 37-35 over Minnesota. Quick set a team record with 73 catches, and Jackson ran for 1,028 yards. The leader of the improving defense, safety Wes Hopkins, was named all-pro.

1986 Buddy Ryan, architect of Chicago's "46" defense, was named head coach shortly after the Bears' Super Bowl XX victory.

MEMBERS OF HALL OF FAME:
Chuck Bednarik, Bert Bell, Bill Hewitt, Sonny Jurgensen, Ollie Matson, Earle (Greasy) Neale, Pete Pihos, Jim Ringo, Norm Van Brocklin, Steve Van Buren, Alex Wojciechowicz

EAGLES RECORD, 1933-85

Year	Won	Lost	Tied	Pct.	Fin.	Pts.	OP
1933	3	5	1	.375	4	77	158
1934	4	7	0	.364	3t	127	85
1935	2	9	0	.182	5	60	179
1936	1	11	0	.083	5	51	206
1937	2	8	1	.200	5	86	177
1938	5	6	0	.455	4	154	164
1939	1	9	1	.100	4t	105	200
1940	1	10	0	.091	5	111	211
1941	2	8	1	.200	4	119	218
1942	2	9	0	.182	5	134	239
1943 (Phil-Pitt)	5	4	1	.556	3	225	230
1944	7	1	2	.875	2	267	131
1945	7	3	0	.700	2	272	133
1946	6	5	0	.545	2	231	220
1947a	8	4	0	.667	1	308	242
1948b	9	2	1	.818	1	376	156
1949b	11	1	0	.917	1	364	134
1950	6	6	0	.500	3t	254	141
1951	4	8	0	.333	5	234	264
1952	7	5	0	.583	2t	252	271
1953	7	4	1	.636	2	352	215
1954	7	4	1	.636	2	284	230
1955	4	7	1	.364	4t	248	231
1956	3	8	1	.273	6	143	215
1957	4	8	0	.333	5	173	230
1958	2	9	1	.182	5t	235	306
1959	7	5	0	.583	2t	268	278
1960b	10	2	0	.833	1	321	246
1961c	10	4	0	.714	2	361	297
1962	3	10	1	.231	7	282	356
1963	2	10	2	.167	7	242	381
1964	6	8	0	.429	3	312	313
1965	5	9	0	.357	5t	363	359
1966c	9	5	0	.643	2t	326	340
1967	6	7	1	.462	2	351	409
1968	2	12	0	.143	4	202	351
1969	4	9	1	.308	4	279	377
1970	3	10	1	.231	4	241	332
1971	6	7	1	.462	3	221	302
1972	2	11	1	.179	5	145	352
1973	5	8	1	.393	3	310	393
1974	7	7	0	.500	4	242	217
1975	4	10	0	.286	5	225	302
1976	4	10	0	.286	4	165	286
1977	5	9	0	.357	4	220	207
1978d	9	7	0	.563	2	270	250
1979e	11	5	0	.688	2	339	282
1980f	12	4	0	.750	1	384	222
1981d	10	6	0	.625	2	368	221
1982	3	6	0	.333	13	191	195
1983	5	11	0	.313	4	233	322
1984	6	9	1	.406	5	278	320
1985	7	9	0	.438	4	286	310
53 Years	283	371	23	.435		12,667	13,406

a*NFL Eastern Division Champion; 1-1 in Playoffs*
b*NFL Champion; 1-0 in Playoffs*
c*NFL Eastern Conference Runnerup; 0-1 in Playoff Bowl*
d*NFC Wild Card Qualifier for Playoffs; 0-1 in Playoffs*
e*NFC Wild Card Qualifier for Playoffs; 1-1 in Playoffs*
f*NFC Champion; 2-1 in Playoffs*

RECORD HOLDERS

CAREER

Rushing attempts	Wilbert Montgomery, 1977-84	1,465
Rushing yards	Wilbert Montgomery, 1977-84	6,538
Pass attempts	Ron Jaworski, 1977-85	3,673
Pass completions	Ron Jaworski, 1977-85	1,960
Passing yards	Ron Jaworski, 1977-85	25,558
Touchdown passes	Ron Jaworski, 1977-85	167
Receptions	Harold Carmichael, 1971-83	589
Receiving yards	Harold Carmichael, 1971-83	8,978
Interceptions	Bill Bradley, 1969-76	34
Punt return avg.	Bosh Pritchard, 1942, 1946-51	11.3
Kickoff return avg.	Steve Van Buren, 1944-51	26.7
Field goals	Sam Baker, 1964-69	90
Touchdowns	Harold Carmichael, 1971-83	79
Points	Bobby Walston, 1951-62	881

SEASON

Rushing attempts	Wilbert Montgomery, 1979	338
Rushing yards	Wilbert Montgomery, 1979	1,512
Pass attempts	Ron Jaworski, 1985	484
Pass completions	Roman Gabriel, 1973	270
Passing yards	Sonny Jurgensen, 1961	3,723
Touchdown passes	Sonny Jurgensen, 1961	32
Receptions	Mike Quick, 1985	73
Receiving yards	Mike Quick, 1983	1,409
Interceptions	Bill Bradley, 1971	11
Punting average	Joe Muha, 1948	47.3
Punt return avg.	Steve Van Buren, 1944	15.3
Kickoff return avg.	Steve Van Buren, 1945	28.7
Field goals	Paul McFadden, 1984	30
Touchdowns	Steve Van Buren, 1945	18
Points	Paul McFadden, 1984	116

GAME

Rushing attempts	Steve Van Buren, 11-20-49	35
Rushing yards	Steve Van Buren, 11-27-49	205
Pass attempts	Davey O'Brien, 12-1-40	60
Pass completions	Davey O'Brien, 12-1-40	33
Passing yards	Bobby Thomason, 1-18-53	437
Touchdown passes	Adrian Burk, 10-17-54	7
Receptions	Don Looney, 12-1-40	14
Receiving yards	Tommy McDonald, 12-10-60	237
Interceptions	Russ Craft, 9-24-50	4
Field goals	Tom Dempsey, 11-12-72	6
Touchdowns	5 times	4
Points	Bobby Walston, 10-17-54	25

COACHING HISTORY

1933-35	Lud Wray	9-21-1
1936-40	Bert Bell	10-44-2
1941-50	Earle (Greasy) Neale*	66-44-5
1951	Alvin (Bo) McMillin**	2- 0-0
1951	Wayne Millner	2- 8-0
1952-55	Jim Trimble	25-20-3
1956-57	Hugh Devore	7-16-1
1958-60	Lawrence (Buck) Shaw	20-16-1
1961-63	Nick Skorich	15-25-3
1964-68	Joe Kuharich	28-42-1
1969-71	Jerry Williams***	7-22-2
1971-72	Ed Khayat	8-15-2
1973-75	Mike McCormack	16-25-1
1976-82	Dick Vermeil	57-51-0
1983-85	Marion Campbell****	17-29-1
1985	Fred Bruney	1- 0-0
1986	Buddy Ryan	

**Co-coach with Walt Kiesling of 1943 Philadelphia-Pittsburgh merged team*
***Retired after two games in 1951*
****Replaced after three games in 1971*
*****Replaced after 15 games in 1985*

FIRST PLAYER SELECTED

1936	Jay Berwanger, HB, Chicago
1937	Sam Francis, FB, Nebraska
1938	Jim McDonald, HB, Ohio State
1939	Davey O'Brien, QB, TCU
1940	George McAfee, HB, Duke
1941	Art Jones, HB, Richmond
1942	Pete Kmetovic, HB, Stanford
1943	Joe Muha, FB, Virginia Military
1944	Steve Van Buren, HB, LSU
1945	John Yonaker, E, Notre Dame
1946	Leo Riggs, HB, USC
1947	Neill Armstrong, E, Oklahoma State
1948	Clyde (Smackover) Scott, HB, Arkansas, Navy
1949	Chuck Bednarik, C, Pennsylvania
1950	Harry (Bud) Grant, E, Minnesota
1951	Ebert Van Buren, FB, LSU
1952	Johnny Bright, FB, Drake
1953	(2) Al Conway, HB, Army
1954	Neil Worden, FB, Notre Dame
1955	Dick Bielski, FB, Maryland
1956	Bob Pellegrini, C, Maryland
1957	Clarence Peaks, FB, Michigan State
1958	Walt Kowalczyk, FB, Michigan State
1959	(2) J. D. Smith, T, Rice
1960	Ron Burton, HB, Northwestern
1961	Art Baker, FB, Syracuse
1962	(2) Pete Case, T, Georgia

1963 Ed Budde, T, Michigan State
1964 Bob Brown, T, Nebraska
1965 (2) Ray Rissmiller, T, Georgia
1966 Randy Beisler, T, Indiana
1967 Harry Jones, HB, Arkansas
1968 Tim Rossovich, DE, USC
1969 Leroy Keyes, RB, Purdue
1970 Steve Zabel, TE-LB, Oklahoma
1971 Richard Harris, DE, Grambling
1972 John Reaves, QB, Florida
1973 Jerry Sisemore, T, Texas
1974 (3) Mitch Sutton, DT, Kansas
1975 (7) Bill Capraun, T, Miami
1976 (4) Mike Smith, DE, Florida
1977 (5) Skip Sharp, CB, Kansas
1978 (3) Reggie Wilkes, LB, Georgia Tech
1979 Jerry Robinson, LB, UCLA
1980 Roynell Young, CB, Alcorn State
1981 Leonard Mitchell, DE, Houston
1982 Mike Quick, WR, North Carolina State
1983 Michael Haddix, RB, Mississippi State
1984 Kenny Jackson, WR, Penn State
1984* Reggie White, DE, Tennessee
1985 Kevin Allen, T, Indiana
1986 Keith Byars, RB, Ohio State
Supplemental Draft

EAGLES MOST VALUABLE PLAYER
1949 Bosh Pritchard, HB
1950 Jack Myers, HB
1951 Chuck Bednarik, C
1952 Russ Craft, DB
1953 Pete Pihos, E
1954 Frank (Bucko) Kilroy, T
1955 Jess Richardson, T
1956 Bobby Walston, E
1957 Jerry Norton, S-P
1958 Lum Snyder, T
1959 Norm Van Brocklin, QB
1960 Bobby Walston, E
Chuck Bednarik, C
1961 Sonny Jurgensen, QB
Tom Brookshier, DB
1962 Tim Brown, HB
Riley Gunnels, DT
1963 Pete Retzlaff, E
Dave Lloyd, LB
1964 Jim Ringo, C
Maxie Baughan, LB
1965 Pete Retzlaff, E
Floyd Peters, DT
1966 Bob Brown, T
Joe Scarpati, DB
1967 Ben Hawkins, FL
Harold Wells, LB
1968 Tom Woodeshick, RB
Mel Tom, DE
1969 Norm Snead, QB
Tim Rossovich, LB
1970 Jim Skaggs, G
Gary Pettigrew, DT
1971 Mike Evans, C
Ernie Calloway, DT
1972 Harold Jackson, WR
Bill Bradley, S-P
1973 Harold Carmichael, WR
Roman Gabriel, QB
Randy Logan, DB
1974 Ron (Po) James, RB
Bill Bergey, LB
1975 Charle Young, TE
Bill Bradley, S-P
1976 Jerry Sisemore, T
Frank LeMaster, LB
1977 Harold Carmichael, WR
Bill Bergey, LB
1978 Wilbert Montgomery, RB
Carl Hairston, DE
Dennis Franks, ST
1979 Ron Jaworski, QB
John Bunting, LB
John Sciarra, ST
1980 Ron Jaworski, QB
Carl Hairston, DE
John Sciarra, ST
1981 Wilbert Montgomery, RB
Carl Hairston, DE
Ray Phillips, ST
1982 None selected
1983 Mike Quick, WR
Jerry Robinson, LB
Bill Cowher, ST
1984 John Spagnola, TE
Ken Clarke, NT
Paul McFadden, ST
1985 Ron Jaworski, QB
Wes Hopkins, S
Paul McFadden, ST

PITTSBURGH STEELERS

1933 With the announced legalization of Sunday professional sports in Pennsylvania, 32-year-old Art Rooney, a former boxer and semipro football player and owner, purchased an NFL franchise for $2,500 with his winnings from a good day at the racetrack. Rooney named the team the Pirates after Pittsburgh's National League baseball team, and scheduled his home games for Forbes Field. Rooney named Forrest (Jap) Douds as head coach. A few days before the opener, Rooney learned that the new laws didn't go into effect until the Tuesday after the game. He circumvented the problem by giving the superintendent of police free box seats to the game, which the New York Giants won 23-2. The next week the Pirates recorded their first win, 14-13 over the Chicago Cardinals. After a 3-3-2 start, the Pirates lost three straight games to end the season.

1934 Rooney appointed Luby DiMelio head coach and acquired Johnny Blood (McNally), the eccentric but gifted halfback, in a trade with Green Bay. Blood was injured and missed most of the season as the Pirates finished in last place for the second straight year. Their best player was rookie tailback Warren Heller from the University of Pittsburgh, who led the team in rushing (528 yards) and passing (112 attempts, 31 completions, 511 yards).

1935 Rooney sent Blood back to Green Bay and tried his third head coach in three years, hiring Joe Bach, the successful Duquesne coach. The Pirates defeated Philadelphia 17-7 in the first game, but lost their next four games. The losing streak ended with a 17-13 upset of the undefeated Chicago Cardinals. The Pirates had a good defense against the rush but were vulnerable to the pass. Their top lineman was Joe (Tiny) Wiehl, a 5-foot 11-inch, 255-pound tackle.

1936 Bach installed an unbalanced line offense that helped the Pirates win their first three games and take the lead in the Eastern Division. Behind the passing of Ed Matesic, with one game left in the season, the Pirates were in first place and needed only to beat the Boston Redskins to clinch the division title. However, Rooney had already promised a friend that his team would play an exhibition game on the West Coast. The Pirates were forced to travel by train from Pittsburgh to California and then back to Boston for the big game. Exhausted by the journey, the Pirates lost 30-0 to the Redskins and finished second.

1937 Bach returned to his first love, college coaching, and Rooney was forced to look for another head coach. He signed Blood, 32, as a player-coach and appointed tackle Walt Kiesling as his assistant. The unpredictable Blood ignored curfews and encouraged his players to do the same. "He would vanish for days at a time," Rooney said, "and show up, claiming he had been at the library." In his first game, Blood returned the opening kickoff for a touchdown against the Eagles, turned to his players and said: "Boys, that's the way it should be done." The Pirates, inspired by their extraordinary coach, won their first two games, upset the title-bound Washington Redskins and finished third in the Eastern Division. Blood was the leading receiver and number-three passer.

1938 Rooney signed Byron (Whizzer) White for $15,800, the largest contract in pro football history to that date. White, an All-America halfback at Colorado University, agreed to play for the Pirates only after learning he could postpone his acceptance of a Rhodes scholarship. White, a 6-foot 1-inch, 195-pound power runner, rushed for a league-leading 567 yards. The Pirates won two in a row in midseason, but, unknown to Blood, Rooney sold tailback Frank Filchock to Washington. Without the threat of Filchock's passes, defenses ganged up to stop White, and the Pirates lost their last six games, scoring only three touchdowns.

1939 White left for Oxford University in England and his studies as a Rhodes scholar, suggesting he might never return to pro football. Rooney sold the rights to him to the Detroit Lions. Blood tried everything but could not lift the team's sagging spirit. When the Bears clobbered the Pirates 32-0, Blood resigned. Kiesling took over as head coach and began enforcing curfew and bedchecks. The Pirates averted a winless season by defeating Philadelphia 24-12 in their final game to go 1-9-1.

1940 Kiesling obtained Chicago Bears tailback Billy Patterson, but he was a disappointment, rushing for just 171 yards and throwing 15 interceptions. The Steelers never got their offense untracked, but a rugged defense enabled them to go unbeaten through their first three games—one win and two ties. The Steelers managed just one touchdown in the next five weeks and lost all five games. Pittsburgh never scored more than 10 points in any game and finished 2-7-2. The showing left Rooney so discouraged he sold the franchise to Alexis Thompson.

1941 Rooney bought into the Philadelphia Eagles with Bert Bell. By April, Thompson was yearning to get back to Philadelphia and Rooney was homesick for Pittsburgh, so they swapped franchises. The Pirates were renamed the Steelers. Bell opened the season as head coach but stepped down after the Steelers lost two games. Rooney hired Aldo (Buff) Donelli, who tried to coach the Steelers and Duquesne at the same time. After five games (all losses), Commissioner Elmer Layden ordered Donelli replaced, declaring his dual coaching interests inappropriate. Kiesling took over for the final four games and the Steelers finished the year with just one victory, an upset of second-place Brooklyn.

1942 Thanks to a remarkable rookie season by tailback Bill Dudley, the Steelers rocketed to their first winning record (7-4) and second place in the Eastern Division. Dudley, a 5-foot 10-inch, 175-pound All-America at Virginia, had little speed and a weak arm, but he achieved astonishing success due to his desire. Dudley led the NFL in rushing with 696 yards, scored six touchdowns and passed for two more, returned punts and kickoffs, punted, and played defense. With Dudley winning rookie-of-the-year honors, Pittsburgh won seven of its last nine games.

1943 World War II depleted the Pittsburgh roster and the Steelers merged with the Philadelphia Eagles to form Phil-Pitt, which was popularly known as the Steagles. They lost their top offensive threat when Dudley enlisted in the Army Air Corps and went to the Pacific as a bomber pilot. Kiesling and the Eagles' Earle (Greasy) Neale shared the coaching duties. The Steagles finished a competitive third in the East with a 5-4-1 record, just one game out of first place. Roy Zimmerman, purchased from Washington, was the starting quarterback, and the club's top rusher was free agent Jack Hinkle, a 6-foot, 215-pounder who gained 571 yards.

1944 The Steelers merged with the weak Chicago Cardinals, forming Card-Pitt. This hybrid outfit was so bad it became known as the Carpets. Coached by Kiesling and Phil Handler, Card-Pitt went 0-10 and was outscored 328-108. After the third loss, a 34-7 rout by the Bears, three Card-Pitt players were fined for what management termed "indifferent play." One of those cited was fullback Johnny Grigas, one of the team's few decent players. Grigas rushed for 610 yards to rank second in the NFL, passed for 690 yards, and accounted for 9 of the 16 Card-Pitt touchdowns. Grigas became so disgusted with the beating he absorbed each week that he packed his gear and left minutes before the season finale against the Chicago Bears. Without Grigas, the team lost 49-7.

1945 The Steelers were once again the exclusive property of Pittsburgh. Jim Leonard took over as head coach. The Steelers won just two games, scored only 79 points, and allowed a division-high 220. The Pittsburgh offense managed eight touchdowns (none by passing) in 10 league games. Dudley returned from the service for the last four games and scored three touchdowns to lead the Steelers.

1946 Rooney hired Dr. John B. (Jock) Sutherland as head coach. In 25 years of coaching, most of them at the University of Pittsburgh, Sutherland never had a losing team. He was a stern disciplinarian and he put the Steelers through a tough training camp. Sutherland and Dudley disliked each other from the start and their hostility was a source of friction on the team. Dudley's differences with the coach did not interfere with his performance. He led the NFL in rushing (604 yards), interceptions (10), and punt returns (14.3-yard average). He also led the Steelers in passing, kickoff returns, punting, and scoring. With Dudley leading the way, Pittsburgh jumped off to a 4-2-1 start. Dudley injured his ribs in a 14-7 win over Washington and Sutherland forced him to play hurt in the remaining four games. Dudley was so enraged he told Rooney he would quit football unless the Steelers traded him after the season. Reluctantly, Rooney dealt Dudley to Detroit for Bob Cifers, Paul White, and a number-one draft choice.

1947 Sutherland moved Johnny Clement to tailback to replace Dudley, and the Steelers' Single Wing kept rolling. Clement finished second in the league in rushing (670 yards), passed for 1,004 yards, and accounted for 11 touchdowns. The team started poorly, losing two of the first three games, then won six straight. The key victory was a 35-24 win over the Eagles in which the Steelers overcame a 10-point halftime deficit. Pittsburgh appeared certain to win its first division title, but the team lost 49-7 to the Chicago Bears, then dropped a rematch with the Eagles 21-0. That enabled Philadelphia to tie Pittsburgh for first place and force a playoff for the Eastern Division championship. The week before the playoff game, the Steelers' players went on strike for a day, insisting they be paid extra for the additional week of practice. Sutherland was outraged, and the discontent tore the club apart. In the playoff game, without the injured Clement, the Steelers were dominated by Philadelphia 21-0 at Forbes Field.

1948 Sutherland died of a stroke in April and Rooney appointed his top assistant, John Michelosen, to succeed him. Michelosen, 32, had quarterbacked Sutherland's Pittsburgh team to a 1937 Rose Bowl victory over Washington. Michelosen, like Sutherland, believed in stern discipline and the Single Wing. He lacked Sutherland's shrewdness, however, and the Steelers slipped back into their losing ways. They won two of their first three games, then went into a tailspin, losing six of the next seven. Clement slumped to 261 yards and was replaced as the main passer by Ray Evans. Fullback Jerry Shipkey (eight touchdowns) and halfback-receiver Joe Glamp (56 points) did most of the scoring.

1949 Every other NFL club had adopted the T-formation, but Michelosen stayed with the Single Wing. Rookie Joe Geri of Clemson was Pittsburgh's top offensive player, rushing for 543 yards, passing for 554, accounting for 10 scores, kicking 12 extra points, and averaging over 43 yards per punt. At 5 feet 10 inches and 180 pounds, however, Geri lacked size, and the constant pounding wore him down. Pittsburgh won only two of its last seven games, but still finished in second place. The top defensive player was Bill McPeak, a 6-foot 1-inch, 200-pound rookie defensive end from the University of Pittsburgh. Another rookie was Jim Finks, a record-setting passer at Tulsa who was switched to defensive back by Michelosen.

1950 Geri had another fine season, rushing for 705 yards, passing for 866, accounting for nine scores, and adding 46 points kicking. However, the Steelers' Single-Wing attack just didn't work anymore. In half their games, the Steelers managed one touchdown or none. They won games on the strength of a stubborn defense led by McPeak and Ernie Stautner, a rookie defensive tackle from Boston College. They upset the New York Giants 17-6 and outlasted the Eagles 9-7 on three field goals by Geri. Pittsburgh finished 6-6, tied with Philadelphia for third place.

1951 The offense grew stagnant and Pittsburgh fans became restless in Michelosen's fourth year as head coach. Six times the Steelers' rugged defense held its opponents to two touchdowns or less, yet Pittsburgh was able to win only four games. The Steelers lost their first three games before beating the Chicago Cardinals 28-14. The next day, the local paper ran a banner headline: "Steelers Win, So What?" The fans wanted Michelosen to put Finks on offense and let him throw the ball. Michelosen kept Finks on defense. In the season finale, Michelosen lost both tailbacks, Geri and Chuck Ortmann, with injuries and was forced to use Finks. Finks completed 13 of 20 passes to beat Washington 20-10. Michelosen was fired a few days later.

1952 Rooney rehired Joe Bach, the man who coached the Steelers in 1935-36. "That bull-headed Irishman was the best organizer I ever had," Rooney said. Bach junked the Single Wing (which was never seen regularly again in the NFL) and installed the T-formation. It took the Pittsburgh players time to adjust and they lost their first four games. As Finks gained confidence at quarterback, the Steelers turned the corner with wins over Washington and the Chicago Cardinals. The highlight of the season was a 63-7 rout of the New York Giants at Forbes Field, November 20. Lynn Chandnois returned the opening kickoff 91 yards for a touchdown and Finks threw four touchdown passes. For the season, Finks threw 20 touchdown passes to tie Otto Graham for the NFL lead, and passed for 2,307 yards. Chandnois topped the league in kickoff returns, and Elbie Nickel made 55 pass receptions, nine for touchdowns.

1953 Finks suffered a preseason knee injury that hampered him, and his passing yardage dropped to 1,484. His touchdown output dwindled to eight and he began splitting time with Bill Mackrides, a former backup quarterback with the Eagles. With Finks struggling, the Pittsburgh offense slipped badly. The Steelers started the season as darkhorse contenders in the East but needed wins in their last two games to finish 6-6. Nickel's 62 pass receptions ranked second in the NFL. Chandnois had another fine season, accounting for over 1,500 yards in total offense. Pittsburgh's top defender was safety Jack Butler with nine interceptions and three touchdowns.

1954 Illness forced Bach to resign during the preseason, and Rooney named Walt Kiesling head coach for the third time. The Steelers started impressively, winning four of their first five games, including their first win ever over the Packers at Green Bay 21-20. Their only defeat in the first month was a 24-22 loss to the Eagles in Philadelphia. Two weeks later, the Steelers gained revenge with a bloody 17-7 win over the Eagles before a standing-room-only crowd at Forbes Field, October 23. Nickel was the star, scoring on a 53-yard touchdown pass from Finks. Pittsburgh came out of the game so battered it won only one of its remaining games. Pittsburgh's top offensive performer was Ray Mathews, a 6-foot, 185-pound halfback who led the club with 44 pass receptions, 242 yards rushing, and eight touchdowns.

1955 Kiesling cut a rookie quarterback named Johnny Unitas in training camp. The Steelers jumped off to another promising start, winning four of their first five. Their only loss was a controversial 27-26 decision to Los Angeles. Pittsburgh's title dreams were crushed when the offense hit a lengthy dry spell starting with a 24-0 loss to the Eagles. Finks drew the fans' ire by throwing 26 interceptions, but he also led the league with 344 attempts, 165 completions, and 2,270 yards. The Steelers lost their last seven games and fell to last place for the first time since 1945.

1956 Finks, 28, retired and went to Notre Dame as an assistant coach. Kiesling gave the quarterback job to Ted Marchibroda, a 5-foot 10-inch, 180-pound second-year man from St. Bonaventure. Marchibroda played respectably, completing 45 percent of his passes, 12 for touchdowns. Kiesling made way for several impressive young players—linemen Joe Krupa, Frank Varrichione, and Willie McClung, linebacker John Reger, and safety Gary Glick. The best of the young runners was Lowell Perry of Michigan State, but a fractured pelvis ended his career at midseason. Fran Rogel, a fullback from Penn State, led the Steelers in rushing for the fourth year.

1957 In the college draft, Kiesling passed over Syracuse fullback Jim Brown in favor of Purdue quarterback Len Dawson. Kiesling called Dawson "my quarterback of the future." Kiesling's future ran out in August when Rooney replaced him with Buddy Parker, who had unexpectedly walked out on his job as head coach in Detroit. Never one to build slowly, Parker made several quick trades for offensive help. He sent two number-one draft picks and linebacker Marv Matuszak to San Francisco for quarterback Earl Morrall and rookie lineman Mike Sandusky, then acquired halfback Billy Wells from Washington. Morrall passed for 1,900 yards and 11 touchdowns. Wells, a 5-foot 9-inch, 170-pounder from Michigan State, led Pittsburgh in rushing, punt returns, and kickoff returns. Jack (Goose) McClairen, a rangy 6-foot 4-inch, 215-pound receiver, caught 46 passes to rank third in the NFL. Butler tied a team record with 10 pass interceptions.

1958 Parker won three divisional championships in Detroit with Bobby Layne at quarterback, so he jumped at the chance to trade for Layne two weeks into the season. Parker gave up Morrall and two draft choices for the 31-year-old Layne, a colorful, swashbuckling figure who took over the 0-2 Steelers and pulled off a 24-3 upset of Philadelphia in his debut. After losses to New York and Cleveland, Layne put the Pittsburgh offense in gear, winning six and tying one of the last seven games. The strong finish enabled the Steelers to climb to third place with a 7-4-1 record, their best record since 1947. Parker had assembled a veteran team, led by Layne, ex-Lions halfback Tom Tracy, and ex-Rams fullback Paul (Tank) Younger. Layne ranked second in the NFL in passing with 2,510 yards and 14 touchdowns. Tracy led the team with 714 yards rushing and nine touchdowns. Jimmy Orr was a standout rookie flanker, catching 33 passes for 910 yards and seven touchdowns.

1959 The Steelers opened the season with a 17-7 upset of Cleveland, stretching their unbeaten streak to eight games, but they lacked the consistency to stay with the top Eastern clubs. Parker claimed Buddy Dial, a rookie receiver from Rice who was cut by the New York Giants. Pittsburgh struggled early in the season but finished strong, losing just one of the last six games. Tracy rushed for 794 yards and scored eight touchdowns. Layne was plagued by 21 interceptions and slipped to eighth in passing.

1960 Veteran safety Butler retired. A series of injuries slowed key members of the offense—Layne (bruised hand), fullback John Henry Johnson (bruised leg), Orr (pulled muscle), and Sandusky (bad knee). With an unsettled roster, Parker had difficulty early in the season, winning just two of the first eight games and dropping from contention. The Steelers managed another late rally, winning their final three home games, including a 14-10 upset of Cleveland and a snowy 27-21 win over the NFL title-bound Eagles. Dial, one of the few regulars to stay healthy, had another outstanding season, catching 40 passes for 972 yards and nine touchdowns. The defense, led by 33-year-old Ernie Stautner and end George Tarasovic, remained formidable.

1961 Another poor start put Pittsburgh out of the race early. The Steelers lost their first four games while Layne was sidelined with an injured shoulder. Rudy Bukich, a 30-year-old journeyman, took over at quarterback and displayed a strong but erratic arm. Johnson, a hard-running veteran of the Canadian Football League, took charge of the Pittsburgh offense, rushing for 787 yards. Dial led the Steelers' receivers for the second year in a row, catching 53 passes for 1,047 yards and a club-record 12 touchdowns. Parker made a number of key acquisitions to strengthen the team, adding tackle Charlie Bradshaw from the Los Angeles Rams, and going to Baltimore for four players—center Buzz Nutter, defensive end-kicker Lou Michaels, defensive tackle Gene (Big Daddy) Lipscomb, and young cornerback Johnny Sample. Sample led the team in interceptions (eight), punt returns, and kickoff returns.

1962 Layne made a stirring comeback and the Steelers had the best season in their history, winning nine games and finishing second in the Eastern Conference. The defense was hurt when linebacker Myron Pottios went out with a broken arm in the preseason, but a trade for safety Clendon Thomas and the development of young Willie Daniel helped shore up the secondary. On offense, Johnson became the first Steeler to rush for more than 1,000 yards, gaining 1,141. Rookie Joe Womack and young Dick Hoak gave the Steelers more depth than they previously had had in the backfield. Layne was injured late in the season and Parker turned the quarterbacking duties over to Ed Brown, a 33-year-old veteran who had just been acquired from the Bears. Brown led the Steelers to three straight victories and a berth in the Playoff Bowl, where they lost 17-10 to Detroit.

1963 Layne retired with the NFL career record for touchdown passes. Bert Bell, Johnny Blood (McNally), and Cal Hubbard each was selected to the charter class of the Hall of Fame. Lipscomb died of a drug overdose, May 10. Parker installed Brown as the Steelers' number-one quarterback and put rookie Frank Atkinson of Stanford in Lipscomb's tackle spot. Pittsburgh displayed surprising early-season strength, routing the New York Giants 31-0 at Pitt Stadium. The Steelers blew a 13-point lead in the final four minutes to lose to St. Louis 24-23 and fell from first place, October 13. Parker was outraged, telling his players: "You disgraced me, you disgraced yourselves." Fearing Parker's wrath, the Steelers regrouped quickly, losing just one of their next eight games to make a serious run at the Eastern Conference crown. Most of their victories were close ones. They beat Washington when safety Dick Haley returned a fourth-quarter interception for a touchdown. They beat Dallas when Brown hit flanker Bill (Red) Mack with an 85-yard touchdown pass in the last three minutes, October 27. They beat Cleveland 9-7 on Brown's late scoring pass to split end Gary Ballman, November 10. They beat Washington 34-28 as Ballman scored two touchdowns and amassed 320 yards on kick returns, November 17. They tied the Eagles 20-20 on Michaels's 24-yard field goal at the gun. They beat Dallas 24-19 on reserve fullback Theron Sapp's 24-yard touchdown run with 1:50 to go. The Steelers had a chance to win the conference title by beating the Giants in the season finale at Yankee Stadium, December 15. On a cold, windy day, the Giants took a 16-0 lead and won 33-17 as Joe Morrison scored three touchdowns. Dial set a Steelers' club record with 1,295 yards on pass receptions. Stautner retired after 14 seasons.

1964 Rooney was inducted into the Pro Football Hall of Fame. Parker sent Dial to Dallas for the NFL draft rights to Scott Appleton, the Texas lineman. Appleton signed with the AFL Houston Oilers, leaving the Steelers with nothing to show for the deal. Many of Parker's veteran players faded into mediocrity, particularly Brown, who floundered at quarterback. The only steady performers were Johnson, who rushed for 1,048 yards, and Ballman, who caught 47 passes. The defense, which allowed 30 points or more in five straight games, was a major factor in the Steelers' fall to sixth place.

1965 Two weeks before the league opener, Parker walked out on the Steelers, informing Art Rooney: "I can't win with this bunch of stiffs." Rooney turned the team over to Mike Nixon, a long-time assistant. The Steelers lost their opener 41-9 to Green Bay and stumbled through a 2-12 season, their poorest in two decades. Brown was traded to Baltimore, and Bill Nelsen, in his third season from USC, took over at quarterback. Johnson carried the ball just three times before being injured.

1966 Rooney hired Bill Austin, line coach under Vince Lombardi at Green Bay, to succeed Nixon. Austin played the Lombardi role, conducting brutal practices and administering frequent verbal lashings, but he lacked Lombardi's magic. The players chafed under Austin's stern methods. Nelsen hurt his knee in the second game and was replaced by Ron Smith, a 22-year-old quarterback waived earlier by the Packers. The club sputtered under Smith and offered no signs of life until Nelsen returned for the final three games. Under Nelsen, Pittsburgh beat the New York Giants 47-28 and Atlanta 57-33 to finish 5-8-1. The Steelers' leading rusher was rookie Willie Ashbury, who gained 544 yards.

1967 Nelsen's bad knees put him on the bench much of the season and Austin signed Kent Nix, a former Green Bay taxi-squad quarterback, to fill in. Nix had his troubles, throwing 19 interceptions. The Steelers won just 2 of their first 11 games and discontent with Austin grew among the players. Two young prospects displayed potential—outside linebacker Andy Russell, who rejoined the team after two seasons in the Army, and J. R. Wilburn, a sure-handed wide receiver from the University of South Carolina, who led the team with 51 pass receptions.

1968 Austin traded Nelsen (following a dispute with offensive coach Don Heinrich) to Cleveland for Dick Shiner. The Steelers lost their first six games before winning the infamous "O.J. Bowl" 6-3 over the Eagles on Booth Lusteg's last-second field goal. The two teams were vying with Buffalo for the poorest record and the right to draft O.J. Simpson. The only noteworthy performers in the season were halfback Dick Hoak, who rushed for 858 yards, and flanker Roy Jefferson, who caught 58 passes for 1,074 yards and scored 12 touchdowns. Austin was fired after the 2-11-1 year had ended.

1969 Rooney hired Chuck Noll, a 36-year-old assistant with the Baltimore Colts, to replace Austin as head coach. Noll, once a messenger guard under Paul Brown, was considered a defensive expert. In his first season, the Steelers won only one game but they added some promising players. The best of the bunch was Mean Joe Greene, 6-foot 4-inch, 275-pound defensive tackle from North Texas State. Greene started all 14 games and was named NFL defensive rookie of the year. "We're gonna build a championship team in Pittsburgh," Noll promised, "and Joe Greene will be the cornerstone." Jefferson caught 67 passes for 1,079 yards and nine touchdowns.

1970 The Steelers were one of the three NFL clubs (joining Baltimore and Cleveland) to move to the American Football Conference following the merger. Pittsburgh had first pick in the college draft and selected Terry Bradshaw, a quarterback from Louisiana Tech. Bradshaw's wide-eyed enthusiasm reflected a new spirit on the team, which heightened as the Steelers moved into their new home, Three Rivers Stadium. The Steelers had a young, unpredictable team that was cold (losing three), hot (winning four of five), and cold (losing five of six) during the season. Although the Steelers won just five games, they were clearly on the way up. The defense began to solidify behind Greene and Russell. John (Frenchy) Fuqua set a team rushing record by gaining 218 yards in the finale against Philadelphia, December 20. The rookie crop included Bradshaw, receiver Ron Shanklin, and defensive back Mel Blount.

1971 Another good draft bolstered the Pittsburgh roster with receiver Frank Lewis, linebacker Jack Ham, tight end Larry Brown, guard Gerry Mullins, defensive linemen Dwight White and Ernie Holmes, and safeties Mike Wagner and Glen Edwards. With those rookies surrounding proven veterans such as Greene, Russell, L.C. Greenwood, Ray Mansfield, and Bruce Van Dyke, the Steelers grew up in a hurry. In their third game, they beat San Diego 21-17 as the defense twice turned the Chargers back at the goal line. "It's a sign we're coming of age," Russell said. "Two years ago, we would have lost this game." With just four weeks left in the season, Pittsburgh was tied with Cleveland for first place in the Central Division with a 5-5 record. The Browns won their four remaining games, while the Steelers lost three of four. But Noll saw hope for the future. "The experience will prove valuable to our younger players," Noll said. "I expect us to come back stronger than ever next year."

1972 The catalyst for the club's rise was number-one draft choice Franco Harris, a 6-foot 2-inch, 230-pound rookie fullback from Penn State. Harris rushed for 1,055 yards, caught 21 passes, scored 11 touchdowns, and was named rookie of the year. With Harris trampling would-be tacklers and Bradshaw maturing rapidly at quarterback, the Pittsburgh offense scored a team-record 343 points. With Greene emerging as the NFL's premier lineman, Pittsburgh's defense allowed just 175 points, second only to unbeaten Miami. Two key wins during the regular season were a 40-17 pounding of Cincinnati and a 30-0 shutout of Cleveland, both at Three Rivers Stadium. Against the Browns, Harris rushed for 102 yards. It was the sixth straight 100-yard game for Harris, tying Jim Brown's NFL record. The Steelers clinched their first division title in the 40-year history of the franchise with a 24-2 win over San Diego, December 17. The club's 11-3 record was the best ever. In their first playoff game since 1947, the Steelers edged Oakland 13-7 at Three Rivers Stadium, December 23. The finish was one of the most stunning in NFL history as the Steelers trailed 7-6 with 22 seconds remaining, fourth and 10 on their own 40-yard line. Bradshaw threw a pass to Fuqua but Oakland safety Jack Tatum deflected the ball. Harris caught the pass at his shoe tops in full stride and carried it in for the winning touchdown. The following week, the Dolphins ended Pittsburgh's miracle season with a 21-17 win in the AFC Championship Game.

1973 Joe Gilliam, a young black quarterback from Tennessee State, took over when Bradshaw and Terry Hanratty were injured. Gilliam was prone to interceptions. He started a key game against Miami, and threw three interceptions in the first quarter en route to a 30-26 defeat. The Steelers lost three of their last five games, and as the wild card team had little momentum going into the playoffs. Injuries hampered the Steelers most of the season, sidelining Bradshaw (shoulder separation), Harris (bad knee), Fuqua (broken collarbone), and Hanratty (broken ribs). Considering their medical condition, the Steelers did well to finish 10-4 and make the AFC playoffs. Oakland trounced them 33-14 in the first round.

1974 The season started in turmoil as Noll named Gilliam his starting quarterback prior to the opener. Gilliam led the Steelers to four wins and a tie in six starts but his wide-open, pass-on-every-down style conflicted with Noll's ideas of percentage football. After Gilliam completed 5 of 18 passes against Cleveland, Noll reinstated Bradshaw at quarterback. In Bradshaw's first start, Harris rushed for a career-high 141 yards in a 24-17 win over Atlanta, October 28. The Steelers clinched their second AFC Central Division title December 8 when Harris rushed for 136 yards and rookie wide receiver Lynn Swann made a spectacular touchdown catch in a 21-17 win over New England. The real strength of the team was the defense, which developed into the best in the NFL. The key addition was rookie linebacker Jack Lambert. A key offensive addition was Rocky Bleier, a running back who recovered from leg injuries suffered in Vietnam and became a starter. Another was a little-known center from Wisconsin who would become one of the best in the history of the NFL—Mike Webster. Harris rushed for three touchdowns and the Steelers rolled up 438 yards total offense to crush Buffalo 32-14 in the first round of the AFC playoffs at Three Rivers Stadium, December 22. The Steelers played near-perfect football to upset Oakland 24-13 in the AFC Championship Game at Oakland, December 29. Harris was the offensive star, rushing for 111 yards and two touchdowns. Pittsburgh's Steel Curtain defense was superb, limiting the Raiders to just 29 yards rushing. Against Minnesota, in Super Bowl IX in New Orleans, Harris rushed for 158 yards (a Super Bowl record) and the Steelers' defense limited the Vikings to just 17 yards on the ground in a 16-6 victory, January 12.

1975 After an upset loss to Buffalo the second week, the Steelers won 11 straight in an awesome display of offensive and defensive power. Bleier rushed for 163 yards in a 16-13 win over Green Bay, October 26. Although Greene was sidelined with a back injury, the Steelers brushed aside Cincinnati (30-24) and Houston twice within four weeks to take command in the Central Division. Harris became only the seventh runner in NFL history to surpass 1,000 yards three times, in a 31-17 win over Cleveland, December 7. Harris finished with 1,246 yards (a club record) and scored 11 touchdowns. Bradshaw had his best season, completing 58 percent of his passes, 18 for touchdowns. Swann caught more touchdown passes (11) than anyone in the AFC. Blount led the league with 11 interceptions. The Steelers won the Central Division with a 12-2 record with Cincinnati (11-3) and Houston (10-4) breathing down their necks. The Steelers rolled over Baltimore in their AFC playoff, 28-10. The Steelers nailed down their second straight AFC championship with a 16-10 win over Oakland at Three Rivers Stadium, January 4. The game was played in zero-degree weather resulting in 13 turnovers. The Steelers upended Dallas 21-17 in Super Bowl X, January 18. Swann won the game's most valuable player award, catching four passes for 161 yards, including the game-winning 64-yard scoring bomb from Bradshaw.

1976 The Steelers lost four of their first five games and did not escape last place until the ninth week. After that start, however, Pittsburgh recovered to win nine straight games and clinch its fourth Central Division crown since 1972. The turnabout began with a 23-6 win over Cincinnati in Three Rivers Stadium, October 17. Rookie quarterback Mike Kruczek subbed for the injured Bradshaw and handed off to Harris 41 times (an NFL record) in the game. With people dismissing their playoff chances as hopeless, the Steelers' defense put together its most astounding display of football ever, not permitting a touchdown for 22 quarters, recording three consecutive shutouts, not allowing a touchdown in eight of the last nine league games and totally blanking five of its final eight opponents. The key game in the comeback was a 7-3 win over Cincinnati that pulled the Steelers within one game of the lead with two to play, November 28. The following week, Pittsburgh moved into a tie for first with a 42-0 win over Tampa Bay as Harris surpassed 1,000 yards for the fourth time. The Steelers clinched the division title with a 21-0 win over Houston in the finale. The Steelers hit their peak in a 40-14 rout of Baltimore in the first round of the AFC playoffs in Baltimore, December 19. Harris gained 132 yards on 18 carries (giving him 958 yards in 10 postseason games) and Bradshaw completed 14 of 18 passes for 264 yards and three touchdowns. Without the injured Harris (ribs) and Bleier (foot), the Steelers lost 24-7 to Oakland in the AFC Championship Game in Oakland, December 26.

1977 The Steelers started off 2-1, but in a 27-10 loss to Houston on October 9, Bradshaw suffered a broken wrist and backup Mike Kruczek went out for the season with a shoulder separation. Bradshaw came back with his wrist in a cast and led the Steelers to victories over Cincinnati and Houston, but he threw five interceptions in a 31-21 loss to Baltimore. The Steelers won five of their last six to clinch their fourth straight division title. The newest Pittsburgh star was young wide receiver John Stallworth. On December 24, the Broncos defeated Pittsburgh in the AFC Divisional Playoff Game 34-21.

1978 The Steelers were victims of injuries to key players, but still had the best record in the NFL. Bradshaw had his best season, throwing 28 touchdown passes and leading the AFC in passing. His success throwing to Swann and Stallworth compensated for injuries to tight end Bennie Cunningham and tackle Larry Brown. The defense, also overcoming injuries, gave up an NFL-low 195 points. The Steelers streaked to seven victories before losing to Houston 24-17. After a loss to the Rams, the Steelers won five straight, including a victory over the Oilers. On December 30, Bradshaw connected with Stallworth 10 times (a playoff record) and the Steelers defeated Denver 33-10 in an AFC Divisional Playoff Game. On January 7, a 17-point outburst in 48 seconds late in the first half led Pittsburgh to a 34-5 victory over Houston for the AFC championship. Two weeks later, Bradshaw threw four touchdowns as Pittsburgh built a 35-17 lead over Dallas and hung on to win 35-31 in Super Bowl XIII. Bradshaw was named most valuable player.

1979 The season was a repeat of 1978, as the Steelers shared the best record in the NFL (12-4) with San Diego, won their sixth straight AFC Central Division title, and led the league in scoring. Four consecutive victories opened the season. Two losses in the next three weeks preceded impressive victories over Denver, Dallas, and Washington. A loss to Houston in a Monday night game was the last blemish on the Steelers' record. Franco Harris had his seventh 1,000-yard rushing season, tying Jim Brown's NFL record. On December 30, the Steelers beat the Dolphins 34-14 in the AFC Divisional Playoff Game. In a rematch of 1978's AFC Championship Game, the Steelers defeated the Oilers 27-13. Two long passes to Stallworth—one for a touchdown—in the fourth quarter brought the Steelers from behind in Super Bowl XIV, and they defeated the Los Angeles Rams 31-19 for their fourth NFL title of the 1970s. Bradshaw was named the game's most valuable player for the second straight year.

1980 Injuries to key players slowed the Steelers' defense of their Super Bowl title. They fell to 9-7 and missed the playoffs for the first time since 1971. Bradshaw, Swann, Stallworth, Lambert, and Ham all suffered injuries and had to miss parts of the season. The Steelers started off 4-1 but couldn't play consistently with frequent lineup changes, going 5-6 the rest of the season. The Steel Curtain defense dropped from the previous season's 49 sacks to 18.

1981 The Steelers rebuilt following the offseason retirements of Bleier, Mike Wagner, and Dwight White. They lost their first two games, but came back to win four straight. On October 18, the Bengals totally shut down Pittsburgh's offense and dropped them out of first place with a 34-7 defeat. The Steelers managed to stay in the race most of the season, but on December 7 Bradshaw broke his hand in a 30-27 loss to Oakland. The next week young Mark Malone, the first-round draft choice in 1980, replaced Bradshaw, and the Steelers lost the rematch with Cincinnati 17-10. A loss to Houston in the last game of the year dropped Pittsburgh to 8-8, the club's poorest record since 1971.

1982 Bradshaw threw three touchdown passes and Harris rushed for 103 yards as the Steelers opened with a 36-28 victory at Dallas to end two Cowboys streaks: a string of 17 consecutive opening-day victories and an 18-game home winning streak. The following week the Steelers defeated Cincinnati for the first time since 1979 as Bradshaw threw three more touchdown passes, including the game-winner at 1:08 in overtime. In the final game of the strike-shortened season, Pittsburgh clinched home-field advantage in the opening round of the playoffs by defeating Cleveland 37-21. In a first-round game against San Diego at Three Rivers Stadium, Bradshaw's 14-yard touchdown pass to Stallworth gave the Steelers a 28-17 fourth-quarter lead, but the Chargers rallied for a 31-28 victory. Bradshaw threw for a league-high 17 touchdown passes. The Steelers switched from a 4-3 defense to a heavy-blitzing 3-4, and wound up with 34 quarterback sacks and the top rushing defense in the league. After the season, Swann and Ham retired. Lambert led the team in tackles for the ninth consecutive season.

1983 Harris passed the 11,000-yard rushing plateau with a 118-yard performance in a 25-21 victory against Green Bay, September 11. Two weeks later he rushed 106 yards to move past O.J. Simpson into the number-two position on the NFL's all-time rushing list. Quarterback Cliff Stoudt, playing because of an elbow injury to Bradshaw, tied Bill Nelsen's club record with 13 consecutive completions to help the Steelers beat the Browns for the fourteenth time in a row at Three Rivers Stadium, 44-17. Donnie Shell's thirty-fifth career interception set up a clinching touchdown against Baltimore on November 13 as the Steelers won their seventh straight for a 9-2 record. Three consecutive losses shaved their AFC Central lead to one game. But Bradshaw, making his first appearance of the season, directed two long scoring drives before reinjuring his elbow in the first half to help Pittsburgh defeat the New York Jets 34-7 and clinch the division title. Mel Blount's fifty-seventh career interception and Harris's forty-seventh 100-yard game were other highlights of the victory. The Steelers were eliminated from the playoffs in the first round for the second year in a row, this time by the Los Angeles Raiders, 38-10.

1984 The Steelers continued to be a team in transition, with a number of new starters replacing long-time veterans. Blount and Bradshaw retired, and Harris, after holding out the entire preseason in a contract dispute, was traded to Seattle before the second game of the regular season. David Woodley, who had been acquired from Miami, took over at quarterback, but when he was injured, Mark Malone got the call. Malone finished the season strongly, completing 54 percent of his passes for 2,137 yards and 16 touchdowns. Stallworth had his best season, catching 80 passes for 1,395 yards and 11 touchdowns. Rookie of the year Louis Lipps added 45 receptions and finished second in the AFC in punt returns. Malone directed the offense efficiently in a 24-17 divisional playoff victory against Denver. The Steelers' gambling defense kept the Broncos off balance, and Pittsburgh dominated the line of scrimmage with effective trap blocking, which helped Frank Pollard rush for 99 yards and Walter Abercrombie rush for 75. In the AFC Championship Game against Miami, the Steelers were unable to successfully blitz Dolphins quarterback Dan Marino, who passed for 421 yards and four touchdowns. Miami won 45-28.

1985 For the first time since 1971, the Steelers finished with a losing record, 7-9. They opened the season with a 45-3 victory against Indianapolis, in which Malone tied Bradshaw's club record by passing for five touchdowns. A 71-yard punt return for a touchdown by Lipps helped the Steelers defeat Kansas City 36-28 on November 10 to even their record at 5-5. The following week, Pollard rushed for 123 yards and Abercrombie added 107 in a 30-7 victory over Houston, the first time in nine years Pittsburgh had two 100-yard performances from running backs in one game. But four losses in their final five games, all to non-division opponents, kept the Steelers out of the playoffs for only the third time in 14 years. Lipps caught 59 passes for 1,134 yards, ranked third in the NFL in punt returns, and led the AFC with 15 touchdowns.

MEMBERS OF HALL OF FAME:
Bert Bell, Johnny Blood (McNally), Bill Dudley, Cal Hubbard, Walt Kiesling, Bobby Layne, Marion Motley, Art Rooney, Ernie Stautner

STEELERS RECORD, 1933-85

Year	Won	Lost	Tied	Pct.	Fin.	Pts.	OP
Pittsburgh Pirates							
1933	3	6	2	.333	5	67	208
1934	2	10	0	.167	5	51	206
1935	4	8	0	.333	3	100	209
1936	6	6	0	.500	2	98	187
1937	4	7	0	.364	3	122	145
1938	2	9	0	.182	5	79	169
1939	1	9	1	.100	4t	114	216
1940	2	7	2	.222	4	60	178
Pittsburgh Steelers							
1941	1	9	1	.100	5	103	276
1942	7	4	0	.636	2	167	119
1943 (Phil-Pitt)	5	4	1	.556	3	225	230
1944 (Card-Pitt)	0	10	0	.000	5	108	328
1945	2	8	0	.200	5	79	220
1946	5	5	1	.500	3t	136	117
1947a	8	4	0	.667	2	240	259
1948	4	8	0	.333	3t	200	243
1949	6	5	1	.545	2	224	214
1950	6	6	0	.500	3t	180	195
1951	4	7	1	.364	4	183	235
1952	5	7	0	.417	4	300	273
1953	6	6	0	.500	4	211	263
1954	5	7	0	.417	4	219	263
1955	4	8	0	.333	6	195	285
1956	5	7	0	.417	4t	217	250
1957	6	6	0	.500	3	161	178
1958	7	4	1	.636	3	261	230
1959	6	5	1	.545	4	257	216
1960	5	6	1	.455	5	240	275
1961	6	8	0	.429	5	295	287
1962b	9	5	0	.643	2	312	363
1963	7	4	3	.636	4	321	295
1964	5	9	0	.357	6	253	315
1965	2	12	0	.143	7	202	397
1966	5	8	1	.385	6	316	347
1967	4	9	1	.308	4	281	320
1968	2	11	1	.154	4	244	397
1969	1	13	0	.071	4	218	404
1970	5	9	0	.357	3	210	272
1971	6	8	0	.429	2	246	292
1972c	11	3	0	.786	1	343	175
1973d	10	4	0	.714	2	347	210
1974e	10	3	1	.750	1	305	189
1975e	12	2	0	.857	1	373	162
1976c	10	4	0	.714	1	342	138
1977f	9	5	0	.643	1	283	243
1978e	14	2	0	.875	1	356	195
1979e	12	4	0	.750	1	416	262
1980	9	7	0	.563	3	352	313
1981	8	8	0	.500	2	356	297
1982g	6	3	0	.667	4	204	146
1983f	10	6	0	.625	1	355	303
1984c	9	7	0	.563	1	387	310
1985	7	9	0	.438	3	379	355
53 Years	310	352	20	.469		12,293	13,174

aNFL Eastern Division Runnerup; 0-1 in Playoffs
bNFL Eastern Conference Runnerup; 0-1 in Playoff Bowl
cAFC Central Division Champion; 1-1 in Playoffs
dAFC Wild Card Qualifier for Playoffs; 0-1 in Playoffs
eSuper Bowl Champion; 3-0 in Playoffs
fAFC Central Division Champion; 0-1 in Playoffs
gAFC Qualifier for Playoffs; 0-1 in Playoffs

RECORD HOLDERS

CAREER		
Rushing attempts	Franco Harris, 1972-83	2,881
Rushing yards	Franco Harris, 1972-83	11,950
Pass attempts	Terry Bradshaw, 1970-83	3,901
Pass completions	Terry Bradshaw, 1970-83	2,025
Passing yards	Terry Bradshaw, 1970-83	27,989
Touchdown passes	Terry Bradshaw, 1970-83	212
Receptions	John Stallworth, 1974-85	462
Receiving yards	John Stallworth, 1974-85	7,736
Interceptions	Mel Blount, 1971-83	57
Punting average	Bobby Joe Green, 1960-61	45.7
Punt return avg.	Bobby Gage, 1949-50	14.9
Kickoff return avg.	Lynn Chandnois, 1950-56	29.6
Field goals	Roy Gerela, 1971-78	146
Touchdowns	Franco Harris, 1972-83	100
Points	Roy Gerela, 1971-78	731
SEASON		
Rushing attempts	Franco Harris, 1978	310
Rushing yards	Franco Harris, 1975	1,246
Pass attempts	Terry Bradshaw, 1979	472
Pass completions	Terry Bradshaw, 1979	259
Passing yards	Terry Bradshaw, 1979	3,724
Touchdown passes	Terry Bradshaw, 1978	28
Receptions	John Stallworth, 1984	80
Receiving yards	John Stallworth, 1984	1,395
Interceptions	Mel Blount, 1975	11
Punting average	Bobby Joe Green, 1961	47.0
Punt return avg.	Bobby Gage, 1949	16.0
Kickoff return avg.	Lynn Chandnois, 1952	35.2
Field goals	Gary Anderson, 1985	33
Touchdowns	Louis Lipps, 1985	15
Points	Gary Anderson, 1985	139
GAME		
Rushing attempts	Franco Harris, 10-17-76	41
Rushing yards	John Fuqua, 12-20-70	218
Pass attempts	Joe Gilliam, 9-22-74	50
Pass completions	Joe Gilliam, 9-22-74	31
Passing yards	Bobby Layne, 12-3-58	409
Touchdown passes	Terry Bradshaw, 11-15-81	5
	Mark Malone, 9-8-85	5
Receptions	J.R. Wilburn, 10-22-67	12
Receiving yards	Buddy Dial, 10-22-61	235
Interceptions	Jack Butler, 12-13-53	4
Field goals	Gary Anderson, 11-10-85	5
Touchdowns	Ray Mathews, 10-17-54	4
	Roy Jefferson, 11-3-68	4
Points	Ray Mathews, 10-17-54	24
	Roy Jefferson, 11-3-68	24

COACHING HISTORY

1933	Forrest (Jap) Douds	3- 6-2
1934	Luby DiMelio	2- 10-0
1935-36	Joe Bach	10- 14-0
1937-39	Johnny Blood (McNally)*	6- 19-0
1939-40	Walt Kiesling	3- 13-3
1941	Bert Bell**	0- 2-0
1941	Aldo (Buff) Donelli***	0- 5-0
1941-44	Walt Kiesling****	13- 20-2
1945	Jim Leonard	2- 8-0
1946-47	Jock Sutherland	13- 10-1
1948-51	John Michelosen	20- 26-2
1952-53	Joe Bach	11- 13-0
1954-56	Walt Kiesling	14- 22-0
1957-64	Raymond (Buddy) Parker	51- 48-6
1965	Mike Nixon	2- 12-0
1966-68	Bill Austin	11- 28-3
1969-85	Chuck Noll	164-104-1

**Replaced after three games in 1939*
***Resigned after two games in 1941*
****Replaced after five games in 1941*
*****Co-coach with Earle (Greasy) Neale of 1943 Philadelphia-Pittsburgh merged team and with Phil Handler of 1944 Chicago Cardinals-Pittsburgh merged team*

FIRST PLAYER SELECTED

1936 Bill Shakespeare, HB, Notre Dame
1937 Mike Basrak, C, Duquesne
1938 Byron (Whizzer) White, HB, Colorado
1939 (3) Bill Patterson, QB, Baylor
1940 Kay Eakin, QB, Arkansas
1941 Chet Gladchuk, C, Boston College
1942 Bill Dudley, HB, Virginia
1943 Bill Daley, HB, Minnesota
1944 Johnny Podesto, HB, St. Mary's (California)
1945 Paul Duhart, HB, Florida
1946 Felix (Doc) Blanchard, FB, Army
1947 Hub Bechtol, E, Texas
1948 Dan Edwards, E, Georgia
1949 Bobby Gage, HB, Clemson
1950 Lynn Chandnois, HB, Michigan State
1951 Clarence (Butch) Avinger, FB, Alabama
1952 Ed Modzelewski, FB, Maryland
1953 Ted Marchibroda, QB, Detroit
1954 Johnny Lattner, HB, Notre Dame
1955 Frank Varrichione, T, Notre Dame
1956 Gary Glick, QB, Colorado State
1957 Len Dawson, QB, Purdue
1958 (2) Larry Krutko, FB, West Virginia
1959 (8) Tom Barnett, HB, Purdue
1960 Jack Spikes, FB, TCU
1961 (2) Myron Pottios, LB, Notre Dame
1962 Bob Ferguson, FB, Ohio State
1963 (8) Frank Atkinson, T, Stanford
1964 Paul Martha, HB, Pittsburgh
1965 (2) Roy Jefferson, HB, Utah
1966 Dick Leftridge, FB, West Virginia
1967 (2) Don Shy, HB, San Diego State
1968 Mike Taylor, T, USC
1969 Joe Greene, DT, North Texas State
1970 Terry Bradshaw, QB, Louisiana Tech
1971 Frank Lewis, WR, Grambling
1972 Franco Harris, RB, Penn State
1973 J. T. Thomas, CB, Florida State
1974 Lynn Swann, WR, USC
1975 Dave Brown, DB, Michigan
1976 Bennie Cunningham, TE, Clemson
1977 Robin Cole, LB, New Mexico
1978 Ron Johnson, CB, Eastern Michigan
1979 Greg Hawthorne, RB, Baylor
1980 Mark Malone, QB, Arizona State
1981 Keith Gary, DE, Oklahoma
1982 Walter Abercrombie, RB, Baylor
1983 Gabe Rivera, NT-DE, Texas Tech
1984 Louis Lipps, WR, Southern Mississippi
1984* Duane Gunn, WR, Indiana
1985 Darryl Sims, DE, Wisconsin
1986 John Rienstra, G, Temple
**Supplemental Draft*

STEELERS MOST VALUABLE PLAYERS

1969 Roy Jefferson, WR
1970 Joe Greene, DT
1971 Andy Russell, LB
1972 Franco Harris, RB
1973 Ron Shanklin, WR
1974 Glen Edwards, S
1975 Mel Blount, CB
1976 Jack Lambert, LB
1977 Terry Bradshaw, QB
1978 Terry Bradshaw, QB
1979 John Stallworth, WR
1980 Donnie Shell, S
1981 Jack Lambert, LB
1982 Dwayne Woodruff, CB
1983 Gary Anderson, K
1984 John Stallworth, WR
1985 Louis Lipps, WR

STEELERS ALL-TIME TEAM (1982)

OFFENSE
WR John Stallworth, 1974-85
WR Lynn Swann, 1974-82
TE Elbie Nickel, 1947-57
T Larry Brown, 1971-84
T Jon Kolb, 1969-81
G Sam Davis, 1967-79
G Gerry Mullins, 1971-79
C Mike Webster, 1974-85
QB Terry Bradshaw, 1970-83
RB Franco Harris, 1972-83
RB Rocky Bleier, 1968, 1970-80
K Roy Gerela, 1971-78

DEFENSE
DE L.C. Greenwood, 1969-81
DE Dwight White, 1971-80
DT Joe Greene, 1969-81
DT Ernie Stautner, 1950-63
LB Jack Ham, 1971-82
LB Jack Lambert, 1978-84
LB Andy Russell, 1963, 1966-76
CB Mel Blount, 1970-83
CB Jack Butler, 1951-59
S Donnie Shell, 1974-85
S Mike Wagner, 1971-80
P Pat Brady, 1952-54

COACH
Chuck Noll

ST. LOUIS CARDINALS

1899-1919 The Cardinals were organized in 1899 by a painting and decorating contractor named Chris O'Brien. He formed a neighborhood team in a predominantly Irish area of Chicago's south side, and it played under the name Morgan Athletic Club. The team soon changed its playing site to Normal Field (on the corner of Normal Boulevard and Racine Avenue) and began to call itself the Normals. In 1901, O'Brien found a bargain in second-hand jerseys discarded by the University of Chicago. They were faded maroon in color; O'Brien labeled them "cardinal." The jersey color plus the location of the field led to a new and obvious nickname: the Racine Cardinals. In Chicago at the time, football competition was exclusively amateur, but such opposition became increasingly hard to find, and in 1906 the team had to disband. In 1913 O'Brien reorganized the Cardinals. By 1917 they were able to buy new uniforms and hire a coach, Marston Smith. That year they lost only two games and were champions of the Chicago Football League. The war in Europe and a flu epidemic in this country forced the team to suspend operations once again in 1918. Following Armistice Day, O'Brien organized the Cardinals for a third time. From then on, the Cardinals were a permanent part of professional football.

1920 The Racine Cardinals became a charter member of the American Professional Football Association, the forerunner of the NFL. Immediately after joining the league, O'Brien lured a great halfback, John (Paddy) Driscoll, to the Cardinals for a $300 per game contract. It was a price considered outlandish for the times, but Driscoll was an authentic superstar, a superior runner, blocker, punter, and maybe the best dropkicker ever to play football. Driscoll also served as the coach for the Cardinals. In the Cardinals' first game against another team in the APFA, they played the Chicago Tigers to a 0-0 tie, October 10. Although they continued to play their games at Normal Field, by early in the season, the Racine Cardinals generally had come to be known as the Chicago Cardinals. A rematch against the Chicago Tigers on November 7 spawned a legend that makes fascinating telling, but, unfortunately, isn't true. The story goes that O'Brien bet the APFA franchise rights to Chicago on the game, with the loser being forced to fold. When Driscoll ran 40 yards for the game's only touchdown and the Cardinals won 6-3, they had the rights to the city, and the Tigers ceased to exist at the end of the season. In reality, the APFA had no such franchise rights at that time. The game was actually for the pro championship of Chicago, a title with more prestige than anything the little-known APFA could offer. However, the Cardinals' victory did help push the Tigers into the history books. After the game, both the media and the fans jumped on the Cardinals' bandwagon, and the Tigers, with dwindling attendance, folded because they lost too much money. Late in the season, the Cardinals played their first games against the Decatur Staleys, with Chicago winning 7-6 and Decatur winning 10-0. The Cardinals finished with a 6-2-2 record.

1921 Despite the addition of several outstanding players—rookie halfback Pete Steger and guard Garland Buckeye, who had played with the Tigers in 1920—the Cardinals had an erratic season. A 20-0 victory over Minneapolis preceded a 23-0 loss to Akron. The Cardinals finished tied for eighth with a 3-3-2 record, but still held the league champion Staleys, now located in Chicago, to a 0-0 tie. They also played their first game against new league member Green Bay, a 3-3 tie.

1922 The Cardinals moved their playing site to Comiskey Park. With Arnold Horween (who played under the alias Arnold McMahon) balancing the attack with Driscoll, the Cardinals became one of the league's powers, winning their first six games to set up a crucial back-to-back series with the 5-0-2 Canton Bulldogs. The Bulldogs won 7-0 in Chicago and then, after trailing 3-0 in the fourth quarter, 20-3 in Canton. Bulldogs player-coach Guy Chamberlin scored on two interceptions and blocked a punt to set up the third touchdown in the second game. The Cardinals then knocked the Bears out of the championship picture. The margin of victory in both contests was Driscoll's dropkicking; he scored all 15 points in 6-0 and 9-0 victories. The Cardinals finished in third place with an 8-3 record.

1923 Although he remained the team's—and the league's—leading scorer, Driscoll handed the duties of player-coach to Horween. The Cardinals won their first five, while giving up only three points. Included was a 60-0 victory over the Rochester Jeffersons. On November 4, the Cardinals played undefeated Canton, and led 3-0 late in the game on Driscoll's 47-yard dropkick field goal. Then the Bulldogs scored a touchdown for a 7-3 victory. After two more shutout victories, the Cardinals swooned, losing three of their last four, to finish 8-4.

1924 Again the Cardinals started off quickly, winning their first three. But then a 6-0 loss to the Bears started a three-game losing streak. Another loss to the Bears, 21-0 in the season finale, dropped the Cardinals to eighth place with a 5-4-1 record.

1925 The Cardinals had a new coach, former halfback Norm Barry. After an opening-day loss to Hammond, the Cardinals, with Driscoll still providing most of the punch, won eight in a row, including a 9-0 win over the Bears. On Thanksgiving Day, more than 36,000 people—the largest crowd in pro football history—turned out to see the Cardinals play the Bears, who featured halfback Red Grange in his first pro game. The Cardinals held Grange to 40 yards rushing, and Driscoll's punting kept the Bears pinned deep in their territory in a scoreless tie. On December 6, the first-place Cardinals lost 21-7 to the second-place Pottsville Maroons in the last regularly scheduled game of the year. However, league rules allowed games to be scheduled until December 20, so, hoping to enhance his chances of getting another game against the Bears and Grange, O'Brien scheduled games against Milwaukee and Hammond for the next week. Playing two teams that had been disbanded and then pulled back together on short notice, the Cardinals won easily, 59-0 and 13-0. Meanwhile, Pottsville scheduled a game at Shibe Park in Philadelphia against a team of Notre Dame All-Stars. Despite repeated warnings by NFL Commissioner Joe Carr that the game violated Frankford's territorial rights and couldn't be played, the Maroons played it and won 9-7. Carr suspended Pottsville from all NFL rights, including the right to compete for the championship. Shortly thereafter, he fined the Cardinals $1,000 and banned halfback Art Folz from the NFL for life when it was learned that Milwaukee had used high school players procured by Folz for its late-season encounter with the Cardinals. Nevertheless, the Cardinals finished with the best record, 11-2-1 compared to 10-2 for Pottsville and 8-2-2 for Detroit. When the league awarded the championship in February, however, O'Brien, embarrassed over the fiasco about the Milwaukee game, refused to accept it.

1926 Despite being defending champions, the Cardinals had problems before the season even began. The Chicago Bulls of the new AFL leased Comiskey Park, forcing the Cardinals back to Normal Field. The Bulls also made an offer to Driscoll to jump leagues. O'Brien couldn't match the deal, so he sold Driscoll to the Bears, because George Halas could. Without Driscoll, the Cardinals fell out of contention. After a 4-0 start, they scored only 12 points in their last eight games and finished in tenth place, with a 5-6-1 record.

1927 O'Brien signed the great Guy Chamberlin as player-coach, but the Cardinals gave Chamberlin the only losing season of his career, going 3-7-1 despite a 2-1 start. The high point of the season was a 3-0 victory over the Bears that knocked Driscoll's team out of championship contention.

1928 Chamberlin left the team and was replaced by Fred Gillies, who could do nothing to stop the Cardinals' slide, as they finished 1-5. The Cardinals beat Dayton 7-0, but didn't score a point the rest of the season. Jim Thorpe joined the team briefly, before retiring from pro football.

1929 O'Brien sold the Cardinals to a Chicago dentist named David Jones for $25,000. Jones wasted little time in his attempts to restore the team. He returned them to Comiskey Park. He replaced Gillies with Dewey Scanlon, formerly the head coach of Duluth. When Scanlon joined the Cardinals, so did Ernie Nevers, who had played for Scanlon before a one-year retirement in 1928. Still in his prime at 26, Nevers had lost none of his great skill. On Thanksgiving Day against the Bears, he scored 40 points on six touchdowns and four extra points, all the points in a 40-6 win. As a team, however, the Cardinals improved only slightly, finishing with a 6-6-1 record.

1930 Nevers became player-coach, and the Cardinals finished seventh with a 5-6-2 record. They did their part for Depression relief, however, playing an exhibition game against the Bears with the proceeds going to the unemployed. The game was notable because it was played indoors, in Chicago Stadium, and the field was only 80 yards long.

1931 LeRoy Andrews became the head coach, but he resigned after the Cardinals lost their first two games. Nevers took over once again, and the team responded with a 5-2 record the rest of the way. Nevers played nearly every minute of the season, and was the star when the Cardinals upset the champion Packers 21-13.

1932 The twin ravages of aggressive play and 60-minute games finally caught up with Nevers, and he retired. Jack Chevigny replaced him as coach, but nobody could take Nevers's place on the field. The Cardinals also were hurt by the retirement of tackle Duke Slater. Without Nevers, the Cardinals were hapless. They won only two games and finished next to last.

1933 Jones had seen his team deteriorate in the four years he had owned it. As a result, he was primed for a sale. He got the opportunity while at a dinner party aboard a yacht owned by Chicago tycoon Charles W. Bidwill, Sr., who was a vice president of the Chicago Bears. In an offhand remark, somebody suggested to Jones that he sell the Cardinals to Bidwill. Jones replied that the team could be had for a price; he named $50,000 as that sum. Bidwill took $2,000 out of his pocket and secured the deal. Bidwill divested himself of his Bears' holdings. Bidwill's regime brought some immediate changes. His business associate, Ray Bennigsen, became chief assistant in football matters. Paul Schissler was appointed coach. The league had changed, too, dividing into divisions. The new arrangement did not help the Cardinals. They finished last in the Western Division and lost to Pittsburgh and Cincinnati, two expansion teams.

1934 The ineptitude of the 1933 team was not lost on Charles Bidwill. Only six veterans were kept, and the 1934 squad contained 17 rookies, including halfback Doug Russell. The youngsters responded well enough, as the Cardinals won five games, all by shutout.

1935 Milan Creighton, a 27-year-old end, took over as player-coach. The young Cardinals started the season with three consecutive wins, but then their one-dimensional offense caught up with them and they finished 6-4-2. The attack was built around Russell, who led the NFL with 499 yards rushing. The defense was one of the strongest in the league, and was built around three all-pros—linebacker Mike Mikulak, end Bill Smith, and rookie tackle Tony Blazine. The Cardinals knocked the Packers out of the championship by beating them three times.

1936 The Cardinals defeated the Bears for the first time since Nevers scored 40 points in 1929. Otherwise it was a dismal season. The Cardinals' offense was not strong to begin with, and Russell went out for the season with an injury. The Cardinals were helped immensely when they obtained George Grosvenor from the Bears to replace Russell.

1937 The Cardinals made good use of the college draft. They selected an entire passing attack from LSU in tailback Pat Coffee and end Gaynell Tinsley. Tinsley finished second behind Don Hutson of Green Bay with 36 receptions, and set an NFL record with 675 yards receiving. The Cardinals' best players, Russell and Smith, were slowed by injuries for most of the year. Chicago finished fourth at 5-5-1.

1938 Chicago repeated a pattern of backsliding after a promising season. The Cardinals managed only two victories and finished last. Tinsley provided the bulk of excitement. He led the league in receptions with 41 and caught a 98-yard touchdown pass against Cleveland.

1939 Bidwill fired Creighton and brought back Nevers as coach. Any chance for improvement was lost, however, when Tinsley held out for more money than Bidwill was willing to pay. Tinsley retired to coach high school football. Two fine rookies showed promise, 195-pound center Charles (Ki) Aldrich and fullback Marshall Goldberg. But neither they nor Nevers could revive the Cardinals after Tinsley left. The Cardinals finished in last place at 1-10.

1940 Bidwill replaced Nevers with former Bears quarterback Jimmy Conzelman. Conzelman was acknowledged as an offensive genius, but that was not enough to restore the talent-thin Cardinals. The year's only bright spot was a 21-7 victory over the Bears in the third game of the year. It was one of only two victories.

1941 For the first time in four years, the Cardinals did not finish last. They won three games including a 10-7 upset of the Eastern Division champion Giants. Two young players—Goldberg and guard Joe Kuharich—blossomed and became among the best in the league.

1942 The war hit the team heavily. The Cardinals' top passer, receiver, and lineman—Johnny Clement, Bill Dewell, and Kuharich—all went into the service. The new passer, Bud Schwenk, threw the ball more than any player in the league, but finished with 27 interceptions and only six touchdown passes. After winning their first two games, the Cardinals dropped eight of their last nine to finish in fourth place. Conzelman quit to work in the front office of the St. Louis Browns baseball team.

1943 Long-time assistant Phil Handler was named coach. For the second season in a row, the top passer and receiver went into the service. Handler had only rookie Ronnie Cahill to replace Schwenk at tailback. But he replaced Frank (Pop) Ivy at end with Eddie Rucinski, who went on to be named all-pro. The Cardinals lost all 10 games.

1944 As a wartime emergency measure, the Cardinals combined with the Pittsburgh Steelers to play as one team. The team's official name was Card-Pitt, but it was known throughout the league as the Carpets. Former Cardinals guard Walt Kiesling was Pittsburgh's coach, and he combined with Handler as co-coach. The team split its home games between Comiskey Park and Forbes Field in Pittsburgh and failed to win a game in 10 tries, despite the presence of John Grigas, who finished second in the league in rushing.

1945 The Card-Pitt union dissolved. Although the Cardinals finished last again, they made some major changes. They converted to the T-formation when Bidwill found a quarterback, Paul Christman of Missouri. Christman was an ungainly runner, but was a natural passer and a fine leader. Kuharich and Dewell came back from the service to fortify the line and the passing game. The Cardinals won only one game, but that was against the Bears, 16-7.

1946 In one series of offseason moves, Bidwill turned the Cardinals from a last-place team to one that would very soon be NFL champions. First, he lured Conzelman back as head coach. Then, he put together a marvelous set of rookies, including fullback Pat Harder (the first-round draft choice), halfback Elmer Angsman, end Mal Kutner, guard Buster Ramsey, and tackle Stan Mauldin. Suddenly, the Cardinals had an outstanding passing attack, with both Dewell and Mauldin averaging more than 23 yards per catch, and a tough ground attack, with Harder and Angsman joining Goldberg. The Cardinals improved to 6-5, and, in the last game of the year, beat the Bears 35-28 when Christman threw a touchdown pass to Kutner on the final play.

1947 Bidwill signed Georgia All-America Charley Trippi to the biggest contract in league history, $100,000 spread over four years, January 16. Trippi turned down an offer from baseball's New York Yankees for twice that much. Halfback Trippi immediately became a member of what Bidwill called "my million-dollar backfield," which also included Christman, who threw for 2,191 yards; Harder, who led the NFL in scoring with 102 points; and Goldberg, who, by the time the season rolled around, was relegated mainly to defense, with Angsman playing offensively. Those five plus Kutner, who caught 43 passes for a league-leading 944 yards, and Conzelman's offensive ingenuity led the Cardinals to their greatest glory. But Bidwill was not around to see it. He died, April 19. His widow, Violet, authorized Ray Bennigsen to carry on; she took no part in football operations in 1947. The Cardinals opened with three straight wins, including one over the Bears. They lost to the Los Angeles Rams, then ran off four more victories. They won the Western Division title with a 30-21 victory over the Bears in the last game of the regular season. The championship game against the Eagles was played on a frozen field at Comiskey Park. With Trippi and Angsman running virtually at will, the Cardinals won 28-21.

1948 The Cardinals routed the College All-Stars 28-0, then carried the momentum into the season opener with Philadelphia, which they won 21-14. Mauldin, an all-pro, collapsed in the dressing room after the game and died of a heart attack. The Cardinals lost their only game of the regular season the following week, against the Bears. Then they posted 10 victories in a row to finish first in the Western Division for the second year in a row. The team once again was unstoppable offensively during the regular season. Harder led the league in scoring with 110 points; Trippi, Angsman, and Harder finished in the top six in the league in rushing; and Kutner again led the league in receiving yardage, with 41 catches for 943 yards, a 23-yard average and an NFL-high 14 touchdowns. Once again, they faced the Eagles for the NFL championship. The game was played in miserable weather. The field was covered with snow, and the yard lines were obliterated. Christman had a fractured finger and couldn't play. Philadelphia's Steve Van Buren broke a scoreless tie with a fourth-quarter touchdown, and the Eagles won 7-0. Conzelman resigned after the game.

1949 Violet Bidwill married St. Louis businessman Walter Wolfner, and they became involved in team operations. Bennigsen, still nominally in charge of operations, thought assistant coach Raymond (Buddy) Parker should be elevated to head coach. The Wolfners favored Phil Handler. They compromised by naming the two men co-coaches. Chicago lost four of its first six games before Handler was moved into the front office and Parker made the coach. Under Parker, the team finished respectably, winning or tying five of the last six games. Harder led the league in scoring for the third consecutive season, with 102 points.

1950 Parker resigned. Earl (Curly) Lambeau, the long-time coach of Green Bay, was hired. Bennigsen resigned. The Cardinals were placed in the American Conference of the newly aligned NFL. Lambeau traded Christman to Green Bay just before the season and promoted second-string quarterback Jim Hardy. Hardy had talent but he was inconsistent. He made the Cardinals' record book twice—throwing eight interceptions against Philadelphia, September 24, and throwing six touchdown passes against Baltimore, October 2. An NFL record five of those touchdowns were caught by end Bob Shaw. With many of the players from the glory years injured, retired, or aging, the Cardinals finished fifth with a 5-7 record.

1951 The Cardinals' front office was reorganized. Violet Bidwill Wolfner was named chairman of the board; Walter Wolfner was named managing director; and Bidwill's two sons, Charles, Jr. (Stormy) and Bill, were named president and vice president, respectively. The control of the team lay with Walter Wolfner. Lambeau made Trippi his new quarterback. Lambeau quarreled with Wolfner all year, and he quit with two games left to play. Assistant coaches Cecil Isbell and Phil Handler ran the team for the rest of the year. The season's only solace was two victories over the Bears, the last of which spoiled that team's chances for a conference title. The Cardinals fell into last place with a 3-9 record.

1952 The Cardinals drafted Ollie Matson in the first round. Matson was an Olympic medalist and a spectacular halfback from the University of San Francisco. Wolfner hired former Cardinals guard Joe Kuharich, who had coached Matson at San Francisco, as coach. The Cardinals won three of their first four games, but despite a valiant effort by Trippi and an outstanding receiver in Don Stonesifer, they dropped seven of the last eight games to finish fifth with a 4-8 record. Kuharich quit after the season.

1953 Wolfner hired Joe Stydahar, former coach of the Los Angeles Rams. Matson went into the Army just before the season. Trippi was moved back to halfback, leaving the quarterback job to Jim Root and Steve Romanik. With little offense, the Cardinals won only once all year, a season-ending 24-17 victory over the Bears.

1954 Matson was sensational upon his return from the service, but the Cardinals' offense floundered under the direction of rookie Lamar McHan. Dick (Night Train) Lane was acquired from the Rams and led the NFL with 10 interceptions, but the defense still gave up the second-most points in the league. Stydahar was fired after the 2-10 season and replaced by assistant Ray Richards.

1955 The team had its best record in five years, 4-7-1, including a shocking 53-14 thrashing of the Bears that kept Halas's team from winning the Western Conference. The individual highlights were the play of Matson and Lane's brief appearance on offense, when he caught a 97-yard touchdown pass from Ogden Compton.

1956 The Cardinals continued to improve under Richards. Matson gained 924 yards to set a team record, and fourth-year fullback Johnny Olszewski added 598 yards. Lane got some help in the defensive backfield from second-year man Lindon Crow. Midseason injuries to linemen Chuck Ulrich and Tony Pasquesi hurt the defense. The Cardinals were in contention until the next-to-the-last game of the year against the Bears. Matson had touchdown runs of 83 and 65 yards against the Bears called back because of penalties, and the Cardinals lost 10-3. They finished second behind the Giants with a 7-5 record.

1957 The Cardinals dropped to a 3-9 record with virtually the same team that finished second in 1956. No one but Matson played up to the previous year's level, however, and the offense scored 40 fewer points while the defense gave up 117 more. Richards was fired as head coach.

1958 Frank (Pop) Ivy, a Cardinals star of the 1940s, was brought in to coach the team. Ivy had been coaching in Canada, and in the CFL he was known for his complicated offenses. After joining the Cardinals, he installed a Double-Wing formation. The team drafted halfbacks John David Crow and Bobby Joe Conrad of Texas A&M and quarterback King Hill of Rice. The Cardinals tied Philadelphia for last place at 2-9-1.

1959 The Cardinals rebuilt their offensive and defensive lines through trades. Dick (Night Train) Lane went to Detroit for defensive end Perry Richards. Linebacker Bill Koman was acquired from Philadelphia for Chuck Weber. The Cardinals traded Matson to the Rams for eight players and a draft choice. Despite Crow and Hill maturing into starting roles, and Conrad moving to offense, where he scored 84 points, the Cardinals finished last at 2-10.

1960 Studies done by the league office had found St. Louis to be a desirable city for an NFL franchise. On March 13, the league owners voted to let the financially troubled Cardinals relocate there. The Cardinals had to share 34,000-seat Busch Stadium with the baseball Cardinals. Season-ticket sales fell well below the 25,000 some city fathers had promised the league. The Cardinals quickly won over the town, however, when they beat the Rams in the season opener 43-21. They had their best year since 1956 and finished fourth with a 6-5-1 record. Crow broke Matson's team rushing record by gaining 1,071 yards. Included were 203 yards against Pittsburgh the last week of the year. Young end Sonny Randle caught 62 passes for 893 yards and an NFL-leading 15 touchdown receptions. On defense, rookie Larry Wilson earned a starting job at cornerback.

1961 Ivy signed Sam Etcheverry, the top passer in the Canadian Football League. He also picked up halfback Prentice Gautt from Cleveland. Gautt led the Cardinals in rushing when Crow broke his ankle, but Etcheverry hurt an arm in training camp and never regained his form. Other injuries, such as tackle Ken Panfill's dislocated kneecap, and inconsistent performances by both the offense and the defense so frustrated Ivy that he resigned with two games to play despite having just defeated Washington 38-24. Assistant coaches Chuck Drulis, Ray Prochaska, and Ray Willsey took over for the final two games, and the Cardinals won them both to finish 7-7.

1962 Violet Bidwill Wolfner died, January 29. Under the terms of Mrs. Wolfner's will, all her property reverted to her sons upon death. She had owned 90 percent of the Cardinals, 10 percent having been bought by St. Louis beer magnate Joseph Griesedieck. Walter Wolfner contested the will, but a probate court in Chicago ruled it valid, March 28. With that, Charles and Bill Bidwill became legal owners of the Cardinals. The two men retained their titles of president (Charles) and vice president (Bill), but each took a more active role in operations. The Bidwills selected Wally Lemm, who had been an assistant under both Richards and Ivy, as coach. Charley Johnson, a little-used rookie in 1961, became the starting quarterback in the fourth game and passed for 2,440 yards. Lemm switched Conrad to flanker, and Conrad responded by catching 62 passes. Randle led the club with 63 receptions for 1,158 yards, and Crow returned to rush for 751 yards. Despite the offensive totals, the club couldn't generate a consistent attack, and a lack of defense helped drop the Cardinals to 4-9-1.

1963 The Cardinals had an exceptional draft, selecting tight end Jackie Smith, split end Billy Gambrell, defensive end Don Brumm, linebackers Larry Stallings and Dave Meggyesy, and defensive back Jerry Stovall. Crow and Gautt both were lost with injuries, but they were replaced by former defensive back Bill Triplett and reserve Joe Childress, each of whom finished in the top 10 rushers in the league. Johnson had a fabulous year, throwing for 3,280 yards and 28 touchdowns, while Conrad led the NFL in receiving with 73 catches for 967 yards and 10 touchdowns, and Randle turned 51 receptions into 1,014 yards and 12 touchdowns. The offensive explosion led the Cardinals to a 9-5 record, good for third place. Meanwhile, ground was broken for a new all-sports stadium in St. Louis.

1964 The completion date of 1965 for St. Louis's new stadium was obviously not going to be met. In July, a group from Atlanta approached the Bidwills about moving the team to that city. Atlanta was building a new stadium. The stadium authority in St. Louis matched Atlanta's terms; that, plus renewed civic support for the team, convinced the Bidwills to stay in St. Louis. The Cardinals had another successful year, stumbling only at midseason when they lost to Baltimore, Dallas, and New York in a four-week period. The team's 9-3-2 record was only one-half game behind Cleveland's 10-3-1. In two games against the Browns, the Cardinals got a tie and a victory. Johnson led the NFL in attempts (420), completions (223), and passing yards (3,045), while passing for 21 touchdowns. The Cardinals defeated Green Bay 24-17 in the Playoff Bowl in Miami.

1965 The Cardinals drafted quarterback Joe Namath of Alabama in the first round but couldn't sign him. Crow was traded to the 49ers for kick returner Abe Woodson. The Cardinals won four of their first five games, but Johnson injured his shoulder in the fourth game and was not effective for the rest of the season. Gautt and Joe Childress missed most of the season with injuries, and Wilson and Stovall also were hurt. The Cardinals lost eight of their last nine games and tied Philadelphia for fifth place in the Eastern Conference with a 5-9 record. Lemm announced after the last game that he would not return as coach.

1966 Charley Winner was named coach. The Cardinals took three quarterbacks in the draft, but rookie free agent Jim Hart beat out all of them to make the team. The Cardinals moved into Busch Memorial Stadium, which seated 51,392. They made their debut in Busch with a 20-10 preseason victory over the Atlanta Falcons, August 6. The team started fast under Winner, going 7-1-1 in its first nine games. Then Johnson was injured and lost for the year. A succession of injuries followed. Key players such as Randle, cornerback Pat Fischer, and offensive linemen Bob DeMarco, Ken Gray, and Irv Goode also were lost for varying lengths of time with injuries. Backup quarterback Terry Nofsinger couldn't carry the load, and, despite help from rookie fullback Johnny Roland, who led the team with 695 yards, the Cardinals scored only 52 points in their last five games. They lost four of them and finished fourth at 8-5-1.

1967 The Cardinals were realigned in the Century Division. Randle was traded to San Francisco, and Johnson and Stallings missed much of the season in the Army. Hart became the quarterback and passed for 3,008 yards but also threw 30 interceptions. Smith had an exceptional year, catching 56 passes for 1,205 yards. Roland finished fourth in the league with 876 yards rushing. Jim Bakken led the league in scoring with 117 points, including a record seven field goals in a 28-14 victory over Pittsburgh. All the offensive effort was offset by a leaky defense, however, and, after a 5-3 start, the Cardinals won only once more and finished 6-7-1.

1968 Gautt and linebackers Dale Meinert and Bill Koman retired, and it took the Cardinals a while to adjust, as they dropped three of their first four games. But a 27-21 victory over Cleveland turned the season around, and the Cardinals finished 8-1-1, including a season-ending 27-16 defeat of the Browns, who nevertheless finished 10-4, a half game ahead of the Cardinals (9-4-1). Hart kept the quarterback job despite the return of Johnson; fullback Willis Crenshaw gained 813 yards rushing; and Smith continued to demonstrate that there wasn't a better tight end in football.

1969 Injuries decimated the Cardinals as 11 members of the team underwent surgery. The defense was particularly affected. By mid-year Wilson was the only healthy veteran defensive back. The team became highly vulnerable to the pass, and it gave up an average of 27.7 points a game. Despite the presence of three outstanding receivers—Dave Williams, John Gilliam, and Smith—the offense was erratic with Johnson and Hart sharing the quarterback job. The Cardinals dropped to third place in the Century Division with a 4-9-1 record.

1970 Johnson was traded to Houston for quarterback Pete Beathard in January, but Hart kept the starting job. After an opening loss to the Rams, the Cardinals won eight of their next 10, including 20-7 and 38-0 victories over Dallas. St. Louis entered December in first place with an 8-2-1 record, but then collapsed, losing its last three and dropping to third place. Hart, Smith, Gilliam, and running back MacArthur Lane kept things exciting, and young Roger Wehrli joined Wilson and Stovall as stars in an outstanding secondary. But the individual stars weren't enough, and, at the end of the season, Winner was fired.

1971 Bob Hollway, an assistant with Minnesota, was named head coach. Two promising rookies were tackle Dan Dierdorf and wide receiver Mel Gray, but not enough of the veterans performed well enough for a winning season. Hart and Beathard shared the quarterback job, but neither was effective. The offense scored only 231 points, and the Cardinals finished 4-9-1 and in fourth place.

1972 Bill Bidwill bought his brother Charles's share of the team, September 12. Assistant coach Chuck Drulis collapsed on the airplane carrying the team home from a preseason game in Houston; by the time the plane made an emergency landing in Little Rock, Arkansas, Drulis was dead of a heart attack. The Cardinals traded wide receiver John Gilliam to Minnesota for quarterback Gary Cuozzo. Tim Van Galder, who had been on the taxi squad since 1967, outplayed both Cuozzo and Hart in the preseason, and became the number-one quarterback. Van Galder was injured in the fourth game of the season, and Cuozzo and Hart shared the position the rest of the year. The offense showed its confusion, scoring only 193 points. The season was typified by a pass from Hart to rookie wide receiver Bobby Moore (who changed his name to Ahmad Rashad the next year), which went for a Cardinals record 98 yards against the Rams. Incredibly, Moore didn't score. Two weeks before the season ended, Wilson announced the end of his 13-year playing career. For the second year in a row, the Cardinals had a 4-9-1 record. Despite winning the last two games, Hollway was fired.

1973 Bidwill named Don Coryell, coach of San Diego State, as the twenty-sixth head coach in the Cardinals' history, January 18. Coryell drafted running back Terry Metcalf and defensive lineman Dave Butz, both of whom played, and helped, immediately. Coryell named Hart his quarterback, and Hart responded with one of his best seasons. But late-season injuries crippled both the offense and defense and led to a third successive 4-9-1 season.

1974 A surprisingly tough defense joined with Coryell's revamped offense, and the Cardinals won their first seven games and, after a slump, edged Washington for the Eastern Division title with a 10-4 record. Hart led the league with 20 touchdown passes, and journeyman fullback Jim Otis rushed for 664 yards, but the real story was Metcalf, who led the team and finished in the top seven in the NFC in rushing, receiving, and punt returns, while leading the league in kickoff returns. In their first postseason championship competition of any kind since 1948, the Cardinals lost to Minnesota 30-14 in an NFC Divisional Playoff Game.

1975 The Cardinals clinched their second consecutive Eastern Division title in the thirteenth week of the season when they beat the Chicago Bears 34-20. They finished with an 11-3 record, their best since the 1948 team went 11-1. Otis led the NFC in rushing with 1,076 yards. Metcalf set an NFL record for total yardage by gaining 2,462 with his running, receiving, and returning. The offensive line, with four eventual all-pros—tackle Dierdorf, guards Conrad Dobler and Bob Young, and center Tom Banks—allowed Hart to be sacked a record-low eight times all year. In the first round of the playoffs, the Rams' Lawrence McCutcheon gained 202 yards on 37 carries and Los Angeles returned two interceptions for touchdowns. The Cardinals lost 35-23.

1976 The top offense in the league kept the Cardinals in contention until the end, but late-season losses to Washington and Dallas first gave the Cowboys the championship and then gave the Redskins the wild card berth due to a tiebreaker. Hart passed for 2,946 yards and led the NFC with 18 touchdown passes, while Otis ran for 891 yards.

1977 Held scoreless for the first time since 1974, the Cardinals lost their opener to Denver 7-0. A week later, Hart led the way to the first victory of the season by completing 12 consecutive passes, a club record, in a 16-13 win over the Bears. After two more losses, Hart got hot in a 21-17 victory over Philadelphia, and the Cardinals launched a six-game winning streak. Included in that streak was a 49-31 win over New Orleans, when Metcalf accounted for 268 yards in offense. Against Dallas, Hart threw two touchdowns passes in the final quarter to beat the Cowboys 24-17. But the winning streak ended abruptly when the Cardinals were demolished by Miami 55-14. The Cardinals never recovered and lost their final three games to fall out of playoff contention. The team finished 7-7, and Coryell resigned as head coach.

1978 After a 15-year absence from coaching, 62-year-old Bud Wilkinson, a legendary coach at Oklahoma, accepted the job as head coach of the Cardinals on March 2. He faced a rebuilding job with the offense, because Metcalf signed with the Canadian Football League, and Ike Harris, the leading receiver in 1977, was traded to New Orleans along with Dobler. As the offense floundered, the Cardinals went winless through the first eight weeks of the season. Complicating matters was a shoulder injury to Hart. However, Hart regained his health and passed for 260 yards in a 16-10 win over Philadelphia. Wilkinson's first pro coaching victory was followed by three in succession and five in the final seven weeks, which gave the Cardinals a final record of 6-10. Hart enjoyed an outstanding season: 240 completions for 3,121 yards and 16 touchdowns. Pat Tilley made 62 receptions. Following the season, Bakken retired after 17 years with the Cardinals.

1979 Tight end J. V. Cain, a former number-one draft choice, died of heart failure in training camp. The club's top draft choice was Ottis Anderson of Miami, who rushed for 193 yards in an opening loss to Dallas and had the greatest season of any rookie running back in NFL history. Anderson rushed for 1,605 yards and had nine 100-yard games, both league records for a rookie. However, the Cardinals won only twice in the first nine weeks. In a 37-7 victory over Minnesota on November 4, Anderson ran for 164 yards to reach the 1,000-yard barrier. When the club plummeted to 3-10 and Bidwill and Wilkinson argued over who the starting quarterback should be—Hart or young Steve Pisarkiewicz—Wilkinson was released. Former safety Larry Wilson stepped in as interim coach. Pisarkiewicz started in a victory over San Francisco, and the club won two of its final three games to finish 5-11.

1980 Jim Hanifan, a former assistant coach for the Cardinals, was named head coach January 30. After an 0-3 start, the Cardinals upset Philadelphia 24-14 as Anderson rushed for 151 yards and two touchdowns. A 40-7 rout of New Orleans followed, but the Cardinals didn't win successive games again until the end of the season and finished the year at 5-11. Tilley enjoyed his best season with 68 catches for 966 yards. Anderson rushed for 1,352 yards.

1981 E.J. Junior, a linebacker, and Neil Lomax, a quarterback, were selected in the first two rounds of the draft. The club lost its first two games, then defeated Washington 40-30 on September 20. The star of the game was Roy Green, who doubled as a wide receiver and a safety and contributed a touchdown catch and a key interception. Green continued his double duty throughout the season and finished with 33 pass receptions and three interceptions. Despite victories over Dallas, when Neil O'Donoghue kicked a 37-yard field goal with 23 seconds left, and Minnesota, when Hart threw the two-hundredth touchdown pass of his career, the Cardinals fell to 3-7 after 10 weeks. On November 15, Lomax was given a start, and he guided the Cardinals to a 24-0 victory over Buffalo. Lomax then started in consecutive victories over Baltimore, New England, and New Orleans that improved the Cardinals' record to 7-7 and moved them into contention for a wild card berth in the playoffs. But, on December 13, the Cardinals lost to the New York Giants 20-10 to end their hopes.

1982 With Lomax taking over as the starter, the Cardinals got out of the gate slowly in the strike-shortened season, losing two of their first three. But a 23-20 victory over Atlanta got the Cardinals rolling, and they won four of their last six, qualifying for the expanded Super Bowl tournament. The highlights of the season were a 23-20 victory over Philadelphia in which Stump Mitchell replaced Anderson and rushed for 145 yards, and a 24-21 win over the Giants in which Wehrli, who had announced his retirement earlier in the week, scored a touchdown on a fake field goal. The low point was the first round of the playoffs, when the Cardinals were never a threat in a 41-16 loss to Green Bay. Anderson finished fourth in the NFC in rushing with 587 yards.

1983 Dierdorf retired, and Hart was released. The Cardinals got off to a miserable start, going 1-5. But a 34-27 victory over Tampa Bay, in which Lomax threw three touchdown passes, turned the season around. The Cardinals raced to a 7-2-1 finish. On December 11, after trailing 17-0, the Cardinals beat the eventual Super Bowl champion Raiders 34-24. A 31-7 victory over Philadelphia concluded the season with St. Louis just missing the playoffs. The big offensive year was led by Lomax, who finished fourth in the NFC in passing; Green, who led the conference with 78 receptions for 1,227 yards and an NFL-high 14 touchdowns; and Anderson, with 1,270 yards rushing. The resurgent defense was led by ends Curtis Greer and Al (Bubba) Baker.

1984 The league's third-best offense kept the Cardinals in contention down to the wire. Lomax set an NFC record with 4,614 yards passing, Green led the NFL with 1,555 receiving yards on 78 receptions, and Anderson rushed for 1,174 yards and caught 70 passes. The Cardinals moved into a tie for first place on October 21 when they defeated first-place Washington. O'Donoghue, who had missed a field goal and an extra point earlier in the game, kicked a 21-yarder with three seconds left. A 24-17 loss to the Cowboys on November 11 dropped the Cardinals to fourth place in the tight NFC East, but they still had a chance to win the division with a victory over the Redskins in the season finale. Washington's Mark Moseley kicked a field goal late in the game, and O'Donoghue missed one on the last play, to end the Cardinals' season 29-27. Lomax set team records with 37 completions in 46 attempts for 478 yards.

1985 The Cardinals won three of their first four, but then went to pieces. Eight losses in nine weeks doomed them to last place with a 5-11 final record. In the Cardinals' only victory in the last seven weeks, the team showed up in knee-length maroon socks to replace the normal red and white ones. Whether the win could be attributed to the socks or to Mitchell's 158 yards and three touchdowns, the next week the league office condemned the socks to oblivion. For much of the season, Lomax lost both his effectiveness and his confidence, despite passing for 3,214 yards. Injuries to Green and Anderson doomed the offense, although Mitchell replaced Anderson and ran for 1,006 yards and an NFL-high 5.5-yard average. After the last game, Hanifan, who had coached more games than any other Cardinals coach, was fired.

1986 Gene Stallings, an assistant with the Dallas Cowboys, was named head coach.

MEMBERS OF HALL OF FAME:

Charles Bidwill, Sr., Guy Chamberlin, Jimmy Conzelman, John (Paddy) Driscoll, Walt Kiesling, Earl (Curly) Lambeau, Dick (Night Train) Lane, Ollie Matson, Ernie Nevers, Jim Thorpe, Charley Trippi, Larry Wilson

CARDINALS RECORD, 1920-85

Year	Won	Lost	Tied	Pct.	Fin.	Pts.	OP
Chicago Cardinals							
1920	6	2	2	.750	4t	115	43
1921	3	3	2	.500	8t	54	53
1922	8	3	0	.727	3	96	50
1923	8	4	0	.667	6	161	56
1924	5	4	1	.556	9	90	67
1925a	11	2	1	.846	1	230	65
1926	5	6	1	.455	10	74	98
1927	3	7	1	.300	9	69	134
1928	1	5	0	.167	9	7	107
1929	6	6	1	.500	4t	154	83
1930	5	6	2	.455	7t	128	132
1931	5	4	0	.556	4	120	128
1932	2	6	2	.250	6t	72	114
1933	1	9	1	.100	5	52	101
1934	5	6	0	.455	4	80	84
1935	6	4	2	.600	3t	99	97
1936	3	8	1	.273	4	74	143
1937	5	5	1	.500	4	135	165
1938	2	9	0	.182	5	111	168
1939	1	10	0	.091	5	84	254
1940	2	7	2	.222	5	139	222
1941	3	7	1	.300	4	127	197
1942	3	8	0	.273	4	98	209
1943	0	10	0	.000	4	95	238
1944 (Card-Pitt)	0	10	0	.000	5	108	328
1945	1	9	0	.100	5	98	228
1946	6	5	0	.545	3t	260	198
1947b	9	3	0	.750	1	306	231
1948c	11	1	0	.917	1	395	226
1949	6	5	1	.545	3	360	301
1950	5	7	0	.417	5	233	287

Year	Won	Lost	Tied	Pct.	Fin.	Pts.	OP
1951	3	9	0	.250	6	210	287
1952	4	8	0	.333	5t	172	221
1953	1	10	1	.091	6	190	337
1954	2	10	0	.167	6	183	347
1955	4	7	1	.364	4t	224	252
1956	7	5	0	.583	2	240	182
1957	3	9	0	.250	6	200	299
1958	2	9	1	.182	5t	261	356
1959	2	10	0	.167	6	234	324
St. Louis Cardinals							
1960	6	5	1	.545	4	288	230
1961	7	7	0	.500	4	279	267
1962	4	9	1	.308	6	287	361
1963	9	5	0	.643	3	341	283
1964d	9	3	2	.750	2	357	331
1965	5	9	0	.357	5t	296	309
1966	8	5	1	.615	4	264	265
1967	6	7	1	.462	3	333	356
1968	9	4	1	.692	2	325	289
1969	4	9	1	.308	3	314	389
1970	8	5	1	.615	3	325	228
1971	4	9	1	.308	4	231	279
1972	4	9	1	.321	4	193	303
1973	4	9	1	.321	4	286	365
1974e	10	4	0	.714	1	285	218
1975e	11	3	0	.786	1	356	276
1976	10	4	0	.714	3	309	267
1977	7	7	0	.500	3	272	287
1978	6	10	0	.375	4	248	296
1979	5	11	0	.313	5	307	358
1980	5	11	0	.313	4	299	350
1981	7	9	0	.438	5	315	408
1982f	5	4	0	.556	6	135	170
1983	8	7	1	.531	3	374	428
1984	9	7	0	.563	3	423	345
1985	5	11	0	.313	5	278	414
66 Years	340	441	38	.438		13,858	15,484

a*NFL Champion; No Playoffs*
b*NFL Champion; 1-0 in Playoffs*
c*NFL Western Division Champion; 0-1 in Playoffs*
d*NFL Eastern Conference Runnerup; 1-0 in Playoff Bowl*
e*NFC Eastern Division Champion; 0-1 in Playoffs*
f*NFC Qualifier for Playoffs; 0-1 in Playoffs*

RECORD HOLDERS

CAREER

Rushing attempts	Ottis Anderson, 1979-85	1,808
Rushing yards	Ottis Anderson, 1979-85	7,845
Pass attempts	Jim Hart, 1966-83	5,096
Pass completions	Jim Hart, 1966-83	2,590
Passing yards	Jim Hart, 1966-83	34,639
Touchdown passes	Jim Hart, 1966-83	209
Receptions	Jackie Smith, 1963-77	480
Receiving yards	Jackie Smith, 1963-77	7,918
Interceptions	Larry Wilson, 1960-72	52
Punting average	Jerry Norton, 1959-61	44.9
Punt return avg.	Charley Trippi, 1947-55	13.7
Kickoff return avg.	Ollie Matson, 1952, 1954-58	28.5
Field goals	Jim Bakken, 1962-78	282
Touchdowns	Sonny Randle, 1959-66	60
Points	Jim Bakken, 1962-78	1,380

SEASON

Rushing attempts	Ottis Anderson, 1979	331
Rushing yards	Ottis Anderson, 1979	1,605
Pass attempts	Neil Lomax, 1984	560
Pass complotions	Neil Lomax, 1984	345
Passing yards	Neil Lomax, 1984	4,619
Touchdown passes	Charley Johnson, 1963	28
	Neil Lomax, 1984	28
Receptions	Roy Green, 1983	78
	Roy Green, 1984	78
Receiving yards	Roy Green, 1984	1,555
Interceptions	Bob Nussbaumer, 1949	12
Punting average	Jerry Norton, 1960	45.6
Punt return avg.	John (Red) Cochran, 1949	20.9
Kickoff return avg.	Ollie Matson, 1958	35.5
Field goals	Jim Bakken, 1967	27
Touchdowns	John David Crow, 1962	17
Points	Jim Bakken, 1967	117
	Neil O'Donoghue, 1984	117

GAME

Rushing attempts	Wayne Morris, 11-19-78	36
Rushing yards	John David Crow, 12-18-60	203
Pass attempts	Neil Lomax, 11-4-84	52
	Neil Lomax, 11-11-84	52
Pass completions	Neil Lomax, 12-16-84	37
Passing yards	Neil Lomax, 12-16-84	468
Touchdown passes	Jim Hardy, 10-2-50	6
	Charley Johnson, 9-26-65	6
	Charley Johnson, 11-2-69	6
Receptions	Sonny Randle, 11-4-62	16
Receiving yards	Sonny Randle, 11-4-62	256
Interceptions	Bob Nussbaumer, 11-13-49	4
	Jerry Norton, 11-20-60	4
Field goals	Jim Bakken, 9-24-67	7
Touchdowns	Ernie Nevers, 11-28-29	6
Points	Ernie Nevers, 11-28-29	40

COACHING HISTORY

1920-22	John (Paddy) Driscoll	17- 8-4
1923-24	Arnold Horween	13- 8-1
1925-26	Norman Barry	16- 8-2
1927	Guy Chamberlin	3- 7-1
1928	Fred Gillies	1- 5-0
1929	Dewey Scanlon	6- 6-1
1930	Ernie Nevers	5- 6-2
1931	LeRoy Andrews*	0- 2-0
1931	Ernie Nevers	5- 2-0
1932	Jack Chevigny	2- 6-2
1933-34	Paul Schissler	6-15-1
1935-38	Milan Creighton	16-26-4
1939	Ernie Nevers	1-10-0
1940-42	Jimmy Conzelman	8-22-3
1943-45	Phil Handler**	1-29-0
1946-48	Jimmy Conzelman	27-10-0
1949	Phil Handler, Raymond (Buddy) Parker***	2- 4-0
1949	Raymond (Buddy) Parker	4- 1-1
1950-51	Earl (Curly) Lambeau****	7-15-0
1951	Phil Handler, Cecil Isbell *****	1- 1-0
1952	Joe Kuharich	4- 8-0
1953-54	Joe Stydahar	3-20-1
1955-57	Ray Richards	14-21-1
1958-61	Frank (Pop) Ivy******	17-29-2
1961	Chuck Drulis, Ray Prochaska, Ray Willsey*******	2- 0-0
1962-65	Wally Lemm	28-26-3
1966-70	Charley Winner	35-30-5
1971-72	Bob Hollway	8-18-2
1973-77	Don Coryell	42-29-1
1978-79	Bud Wilkinson********	9-20-0
1979	Larry Wilson	2- 1-0
1980-85	Jim Hanifan	39-50-1
1986	Gene Stallings	

**Resigned after two games in 1931*
***Co-coach with Walt Kiesling of 1944 Chicago Cardinals-Pittsburgh merged team*
****Co-coaches for first six games in 1949*
*****Resigned after 10 games in 1951*
******Co-coaches for last two games in 1951*
*******Resigned after 12 games in 1961*
********Co-coaches for last two games in 1961*
*********Replaced after 13 games in 1979*

FIRST PLAYER SELECTED

1936	Jim Lawrence, HB, TCU
1937	Ray Buivid, HB, Marquette
1938	Jack Robbins, QB, Arkansas
1939	Ki Aldrich, C, TCU
1940	George Cafego, QB, Tennessee
1941	John Kimbrough, FB, Texas A&M
1942	Steve Lach, FB, Duke
1943	Glenn Dobbs, QB, Tulsa
1944	Pat Harder, FB, Wisconsin
1945	Charley Trippi, HB, Georgia
1946	Dub Jones, HB, Tulane
1947	DeWitt (Tex) Coulter, T, Army
1948	Jim Spavital, FB, Oklahoma State
1949	Bill Fischer, G, Notre Dame
1950	(2) Jack Jennings, T, Ohio State
1951	Jerry Groom, C, Notre Dame
1952	Ollie Matson, HB, San Francisco
1953	Johnny Olszewski, HB, California
1954	Lamar McHan, QB, Arkansas
1955	Max Boydston, E, Oklahoma
1956	Joe Childress, FB, Auburn
1957	Jerry Tubbs, C, Oklahoma
1958	King Hill, QB, Rice
1959	Billy Stacy, HB, Mississippi State
1960	George Izo, QB, Notre Dame
1961	Ken Rice, T, Auburn
1962	Fate Echols, DT, Northwestern
1963	Jerry Stovall, S, LSU
1964	Ken Kortas, T, Louisville
1965	Joe Namath, QB, Alabama
1966	Carl McAdams, LB, Oklahoma
1967	Dave Williams, FL, Washington
1968	MacArthur Lane, RB, Utah State
1969	Roger Wehrli, CB, Missouri
1970	Larry Stegent, RB, Texas A&M
1971	Norm Thompson, CB, Utah
1972	Bobby Moore, RB-WR, Oregon
1973	Dave Butz, DT, Purdue
1974	J. V. Cain, TE, Colorado
1975	Tim Gray, CB, Texas A&M
1976	Mike Dawson, DT, Arizona
1977	Steve Pisarkiewicz, QB, Missouri
1978	Steve Little, P-K, Arkansas
1979	Ottis Anderson, RB, Miami
1980	Curtis Greer, DE, Michigan
1981	E. J. Junior, LB, Alabama
1982	Luis Sharpe, T, UCLA
1983	Leonard Smith, CB, McNeese State
1984	Clyde Duncan, WR, Tennessee
1984*	Mike Ruether, C, Texas
1985	Freddie Joe Nunn, LB, Mississippi
1986	Anthony Bell, LB, Michigan State

**Supplemental Draft*

SAN DIEGO CHARGERS

1959 The Los Angeles Chargers were founded by hotel magnate Barron Hilton as one of the original six teams of the American Football League, August 14. The Chargers were scheduled to play their games in the Los Angeles Memorial Coliseum, which also was the home of the NFL's Los Angeles Rams. Frank Leahy, former coach at Boston College and Notre Dame, became general manager, October 14. Gerald Courtney of Hollywood won a trip to Mexico after submitting the name Chargers in a name-the-team contest. Hilton liked the name because it had three different implications—an electrical charge (later indicated by lightning bolts on the Chargers' helmets and pants), a horse charging (which was the symbol on the club's stationery), and the new Hilton Carte Blanche charge card. At the first AFL draft, on November 22, the Chargers' first selection was Notre Dame end Monty Stickles.

1960 Sid Gillman, who had coached the Rams for five years, was signed to a three-year contract as the first coach of the Chargers, January 7. A special tryout camp was conducted in Burbank, and 207 candidates showed up, April 9. Leahy resigned due to ill health, July 1. Gillman took over the additional duties of general manager, July 9. The team's first training camp opened at Chapman College in Orange, 30 miles southeast of Los Angeles. In the team's first preseason game, Paul Lowe, who had called the club and offered his services, returned the opening kickoff 105 yards for a touchdown, August 6. The Chargers won the game 27-7 over the New York Titans, before 27,778 in the Coliseum. On September 10, the Chargers came back from a 20-7 deficit in the fourth quarter to edge the Dallas Texans 21-20 in the AFL regular-season opener for both teams. With Gillman choreographing a flashy offense featuring Lowe, NFL castoff Jack Kemp at quarterback, and ends Dave Kocourek and Ralph Anderson (who died of diabetes on November 26), the Chargers won the Western Division with a 10-4 record. However, only 9,928 people showed up to watch them defeat Denver 41-33 to clinch the title. In the first AFL Championship Game, the Chargers were beaten 24-16 by the Houston Oilers, January 1.

1961 Five days after the first AFL Championship Game, the Greater San Diego Sports Association was formed to attract major sports—namely the Chargers—to San Diego. On February 10, Hilton, who had lost more than $900,000 the year before, was given approval by the AFL to move his franchise to San Diego, where it would play in an enlarged, 34,000-seat Balboa Stadium. On a 93-degree August afternoon, the Chargers made their debut in their new home, beating Houston 27-14 before 12,304. They continued to celebrate their new home by winning 11 games in a row. Three defensive rookies—end Earl Faison, tackle Ernie Ladd, and linebacker Chuck Allen—joined the Chargers' offensive stars to make the race for the Western Division title a runaway. The fans began to appreciate the team more as it won more. A crowd of 33,788 turned out to see the Chargers defeat the Dallas Texans 24-14 to run their record to 11-0, before a late-season slump dropped their final mark to 12-2. The slump continued in the AFL Championship Game, when the offense couldn't generate many points, and the Houston Oilers again won 10-3 before 29,556 in Balboa Stadium.

1962 Perhaps the most important draft in the history of the franchise brought in two players who would have a profound effect on this team, flanker Lance Alworth from Arkansas and quarterback John Hadl from Kansas. The season degenerated into a series of losses as the Chargers suffered one injury after another. Lowe missed the entire season with a broken arm, linebacker Bob Laraba was killed in an offseason automobile accident, and 11 starters missed at least half the season, including Alworth, Allen, center Wayne Frazier, and defensive back Charley McNeil. The hardest loss to take occurred when Kemp suffered a broken hand in the preseason and Gillman tried to slip him through waivers to the reserve list. Buffalo claimed him for the $100 waivers fee. In the absence of established stars, Hadl and second-year fullback Keith Lincoln both made impressive starting debuts.

1963 Gillman convinced Tobin Rote, the former quarterback with Green Bay and Detroit, to sign with the Chargers after he quit Toronto of the Canadian Football League. Hilton and his father, Conrad, decided to sell one-third interest in the team to San Diego businessmen John Mabee, George Pernicano, Kenneth Swanson, and James Copley and M.L. Bengston of Los Angeles. Gillman moved the club's training camp to Rough Acres, a desert outpost 40 miles out of town. The Chargers came out of that camp fit and healthy, and, with Rote leading the league in passing, Alworth averaging 20 yards per reception, and Lowe and Lincoln sporting the best two averages per carry in the league, the Chargers showed the best offense in the AFL. San Diego ran up an 11-3 record, clinching the Western Division title the last day of the season with a 58-20 victory over Denver. The Chargers climaxed the best season in their history by burying Boston 51-10 before 30,127 in Balboa Stadium to win the AFL championship, January 5. Lincoln rushed for 206 yards on 13 carries, caught seven passes for 123 yards, completed a 20-yard pass, and scored two touchdowns. He was voted the player of the game. Afterward, Otto Graham, the former Cleveland Browns' star and NFL coach, said, "If the Chargers could play the best in the NFL, I'd have to pick the Chargers."

1964 The Chargers opened the regular season by beating Houston, then lost two of three. Rote had a sore arm, so Gillman moved Hadl in to start his first game in Boston. Hadl responded by completing 17 of 29 passes for 229 yards and three touchdowns in a 26-17 victory. The club established a San Diego attendance record when 34,865 saw the Chargers lose to Buffalo 27-24, November 26. A 38-3 rout of the New York Jets made it eight wins for the year and clinched a fourth Western Division championship. Alworth, who already was considered the best pass receiver in pro football, was injured and missed the AFL title game in Buffalo. And after he sparked the first San Diego scoring drive in that game, Lincoln also went down. Without two of their most prominent weapons, the Chargers were beaten 20-7 by the Bills at War Memorial Stadium, December 26.

1965 Gillman suddenly began to have troubles at the bargaining table. Lincoln and linebacker Frank Buncom became stubborn holdouts. Faison and Ladd both announced their intentions of playing out their options. Ladd was fined, suspended, and finally reinstated. Construction of a $28 million San Diego Stadium in the heart of Mission Valley was authorized by a 73 percent vote in a special municipal election. Lowe and Alworth both had big years, finishing one-two in the balloting by AFL players for player of the year. Lowe set a league record with 1,121 rushing yards. Alworth caught 69 passes for an incredible 1,602 yards, a 23.2-yard average, and 14 touchdowns. Seemingly unnoticed in comparison were Hadl, who led the league in passing, and the two best linemen in the league, Ron Mix and Walt Sweeney. The Chargers led the division from opening day, although Oakland and Kansas City made it interesting. A 9-2-3 record was enough, however. Buffalo was there to spoil things again in the AFL title game, this time 23-0 at Balboa Stadium, December 26.

1966 A group of 21 business executives, headed by Eugene Klein and Sam Schulman of Beverly Hills, purchased the Chargers for $10 million. Klein and Schulman became general partners with Klein replacing Hilton as club president and Schulman taking over as chairman of the board. Barron and Conrad Hilton retained a substantial interest in the team. Copley and Pernicano retained limited interests. Gillman was signed to a new five-year contract as coach and general manager. Hadl had his best season, passing for 2,846 yards and 23 touchdowns, and Alworth made 73 receptions for 1,383 yards and 13 scores. The defense fell apart, however, and the Chargers finished 7-6-1, failing to win the Western Division for the first time since 1962.

1967 San Diego Stadium was dedicated as 45,988 fans looked on, August 20. Playing their first NFL opponent that night, the Chargers were beaten 38-17 by Detroit in a preseason game. A week later, in their first confrontation with their southern California rivals, the Rams, the Chargers were whipped 50-7. San Diego opened the regular season with a flourish, however, going 5-0-1 and eventually ran its record to 8-1-1. But four straight losses dropped the Chargers to third place for the second year in a row. Hadl and Alworth had their usual phenomenal seasons, and Gary Garrison emerged as one of the league's best receivers on the side opposite Alworth, but the team's real story was a pair of rookies who finished in the top five in the league in rushing—halfback Dickie Post and fullback Brad Hubbert.

1968 In a memorable preseason game, the Chargers beat the Rams 35-13 behind John Hadl's two touchdown passes and 302 yards, August 24. Getting off to another fast start, San Diego upset Oakland, the defending AFL champion, 23-14. Alworth caught nine passes for 182 yards to hand the Raiders their first loss at home in three years. Once again, an 8-2 start was spoiled by three losses in the final four games as the Chargers finished third in the AFL Western Division. Hadl led the league in passing yards (3,473) and touchdowns (27), Alworth in receiving (68 for 1,312 yards), Post in average per carry (5.0), and Garrison had 52 catches for 1,103 yards, but the defense began to crumble.

1969 The club moved its training camp facilities from Escondido to Cal-Irvine, 40 miles north of San Diego. The Chargers opened the regular season with two losses on the road, but when they returned home a record crowd of 54,042 was in San Diego Stadium to see them play the New York Jets. The Chargers won 34-27 as Garrison caught 10 passes for 188 yards and two touchdowns. Gillman announced his retirement from coaching because of a stomach ulcer and chest hernia, November 10. He continued as general manager. Assistant Charlie Waller was appointed head coach and the team finished 8-6 and in third place for the fourth consecutive year. In the final week against Buffalo, Alworth caught a pass in his ninety-sixth consecutive game to break the pro record of Don Hutson. Alworth led the AFL in pass receptions with 64, and Post led the league in rushing with 873 yards.

1970 The highlight of the Chargers' season was a 27-10 win over the Browns at Cleveland before 80,047, the largest crowd ever to see San Diego play, November 1. Garrison had an outstanding season, but Alworth and Post were injured and the team struggled through its first losing season in eight years, although, once again, it finished third in its division. After the 5-6-3 finish, a reorganization was announced, with Gillman coming back as head coach and Waller staying on as offensive coach.

1971 Harland Svare was named general manager. Alworth was traded to Dallas. After a slow start, Klein announced Gillman's resignation "by mutual consent," November 22. Svare, who formerly coached the Rams, was named coach. The team finished with two wins and two losses under Svare, who kept an emphasis on the passing game with Hadl and Garrison, but also made excellent use of Mike Garrett, who had been obtained from the Chiefs in the midseason of 1970. The Chargers finished 6-8.

1972 Svare began a series of major trades by dealing for defensive end David (Deacon) Jones of the Rams. Svare changed the complexion of the club in a 12-hour trading session, acquiring running back Duane Thomas from Dallas, linebacker Tim Rossovich from Philadelphia, and defensive tackle Dave Costa from Denver, July 30. After much controversy, Thomas never played for the Chargers. Following a 2-1-1 start, the Chargers lost 8 of their last 10 games to finish 4-9-1 and in last place in the AFC West. Garrett finished with 1,031 yards and became the first pro player to gain 1,000 with two different teams.

1973 Heisman Trophy winner Johnny Rodgers was the Chargers' top draft choice, but the Nebraska running back decided to sign with Montreal of the Canadian Football League. Klein announced the acquisition of quarterback Johnny Unitas. In the second part of a three-team deal, San Diego sent Hadl to Los Angeles for defensive lineman Coy Bacon and running back Bob Thomas. Against Pittsburgh, in the fourth game of the year, a back injury that had plagued Unitas was aggravated and he was rendered almost immobile. The Steelers built a 38-0 halftime lead and rookie Dan Fouts took over at quarterback in the third quarter. Fouts remained there for the rest of the season, with Unitas playing in a total of five games and ending his long pro career. Svare announced his resignation as head coach but said he would remain as general manager, November 5. Ron Waller, special teams coach, was appointed interim head coach.

1974 Tommy Prothro, formerly of UCLA and the Los Angeles Rams, was appointed the Chargers' new coach. Prothro began overhauling the team, trading Jones and Sweeney to Washington. The Chargers, Klein, and Svare were implicated in a drug scandal, with NFL Commissioner Pete Rozelle fining the owner, general manager, and several players and placing them on probation. Prothro's first Chargers training camp at the new United States International University site was interrupted by picketing veterans who were striking as members of the NFL Players Association. A little-known rookie, Don Woods, was picked up on waivers from Green Bay. Woods established a rookie rushing record, gaining 1,162 yards and winning rookie of the year honors.

1975 Johnny Sanders, a long-time Los Angeles Rams' executive, was named assistant to the president for player personnel, February 21. Paul (Tank) Younger, another ex-Rams player and scout, was appointed assistant general manager, June 17. Despite improvement by Fouts, the team struggled during the season, losing twice in overtime and dropping its first 11 games in a row, before rallying to win two of its final three games. A loss in Cincinnati on the final Sunday made the record 2-12.

1976 Svare was released as general manager and replaced by Sanders, February 16. Joe Washington, the All-America runner from Oklahoma, was the team's top draft choice. The Chargers played the first NFL game outside of North America against the St. Louis Cardinals in Tokyo, August 16; St. Louis won 20-10. Washington injured a knee playing a preseason game in his old college stadium at Norman, Oklahoma, and had to undergo surgery. The club opened with its best record in years, 3-0, after beating St. Louis 43-24. But a porous pass defense finally caught up with

San Diego and it finished the season 6-8. Charlie Joiner, who had been obtained in a trade with Cincinnati, led the Chargers with 50 receptions.

1977 Before the season began, the Chargers gained one quarterback and lost another. On July 12, they sent a draft choice to the Los Angeles Rams for James Harris. A 125-day retirement by Fouts made Harris the starter. Harris led the Chargers to three straight victories at one point, and on October 30 he rolled out and bulled his way into the end zone on the final play of the game for a 14-13 victory over Miami. An ankle injury ended his season on November 13 in a 17-14 loss to Denver, a game in which backup Bill Munson broke his leg. The next week, rookie Cliff Olander, drafted primarily as a punter, was the quarterback in a 12-7 surprise of the Raiders. Fouts returned to lead the Chargers to two wins and two close losses in the last four games. San Diego's 7-7 record was its best since 1969.

1978 Lance Alworth became the first player from the AFL to be named to the Pro Football Hall of Fame. The season got off to a disappointing 1-3 start, and Prothro resigned after four games. On September 25, former San Diego State and St. Louis Cardinals coach Don Coryell was named head coach. The team finished 7-1 for an overall record of 9-7. Fouts threw 24 touchdown passes, 13 to wide receiver John Jefferson, the first-round draft choice from Arizona State who was voted AFC rookie of the year.

1979 The Chargers drafted tight end Kellen Winslow of Missouri on the first round. A record-setting passing attack led San Diego to the championship of the AFC West and a 12-4 record, the best since 1963. Fouts broke Joe Namath's single-season passing record by throwing for 4,082 yards. Fouts tied an NFL record with three consecutive 300-yard passing performances. San Diego completed its sweep of the teams that would play in Super Bowl XIV with a 35-7 defeat of Pittsburgh that was highlighted by a 77-yard interception return by linebacker Woodrow Lowe. On December 17, San Diego won the division with a 17-7 victory over Denver. Vernon Perry intercepted four of Fouts's passes to help Houston to a 17-14 victory in the AFC Divisional Playoff Game.

1980 The Chargers won their second straight AFC West title with a passing attack that broke the records it set the year before. Fouts passed for an all-time high of 4,715 yards; Winslow led the league in receptions; and Winslow, Jefferson, and Charlie Joiner each had more than 1,000 yards on receptions. The Chargers also improved their ground game with the acquisition of Chuck Muncie from New Orleans on September 29. The Chargers started off 4-0, then, after a slump, finished 5-1 for an 11-5 record. On October 19, Fouts passed for a club record 444 yards in a 44-7 defeat of the New York Giants. A 26-17 victory over Pittsburgh in the season finale gave the Chargers the AFC West championship. Fouts hit Ron Smith with a 50-yard touchdown pass with 2:08 to go to lead the Chargers to a 20-14 victory over Buffalo in the 1980 AFC Divisional Playoff Game on January 3. A week later the Chargers couldn't overcome a 28-7 second-quarter deficit and lost 34-27 to the Raiders in the 1980 AFC Championship Game.

1981 A prolonged holdout by Jefferson from the start of training camp ended with his trade to Green Bay. The Chargers then obtained Wes Chandler from New Orleans. Fouts again broke his own single-season record by passing for 4,802 yards; Winslow again led the league in receiving; and Joiner and Chandler joined Winslow with more than 1,000 yards receiving. Despite lapses by the defense, which allowed the second-most points in the AFC, the Chargers were still very much in the playoff race late in the year. A 23-10 victory over Oakland in the final Monday night game, coupled with Denver's loss to Chicago the day before, gave the Chargers a 10-6 record and the AFC West championship for the third straight year. The Chargers-Dolphins matchup in the divisional playoffs on January 2 was a game to remember. The Chargers mounted a 24-0 first-quarter lead. They fell behind 38-31 in the fourth period, tied the score in the last minute, and finally won 41-38 after 13:52 of overtime on Rolf Benirschke's 29-yard field goal. Fouts passed for 433 yards. Winslow caught a postseason record 13 passes for 166 yards and blocked a Miami field-goal attempt late in the fourth quarter. A week later, drained by the preceding game and facing sub-zero weather (minus-59 wind-chill factor) as well as a strong Cincinnati team, the Chargers lost in the AFC Championship Game 27-7.

1982 For the first time since 1979, the defense held an opponent without a touchdown as the Chargers won their opener 23-3 against Denver. In the first Monday night game following the 57-day players strike, the Chargers zoomed to a 24-0 lead over the Los Angeles Raiders before the Raiders rallied to win 28-24. San Diego posted a 6-3 record and qualified for a playoff berth in the expanded postseason format. In a first-round game against Pittsburgh, Fouts completed 27 of 42 passes for 333 yards and three touchdowns, including the game-winner to Winslow with one minute left to give the Chargers a 31-28 victory. It was a different story in round two, as Miami won 34-13. For the season, Fouts averaged a staggering total of 320.3 yards passing per game, and completed a league-high 17 touchdown passes. In a memorable duel with San Francisco, Fouts completed 33 of 48 passes for 450 yards and five touchdowns to give the Chargers a 41-37 victory. In an aerial contest with Cincinnati quarterback Ken Anderson, Fouts passed for 435 yards as the Chargers outgunned the Bengals 50-34. Winslow led the AFC in receiving for the third consecutive year with 54 receptions. Chandler added 49 catches for 1,032 yards in eight games, and his average of 129 yards per game set an NFL record.

1983 The Chargers signed a new 20-year lease to play their home games at San Diego Jack Murphy Stadium. With three picks in the first round of the draft, the Chargers selected linebacker Billy Ray Smith, running back Gary Anderson, and defensive back Gill Byrd. Sid Gillman was inducted into the Hall of Fame. San Diego finished 6-10, the club's poorest record since 1975. On October 2, Fouts injured his throwing shoulder in a 41-34 victory against the New York Giants and missed six weeks. He was replaced by Ed Luther. Winslow caught 14 passes to set a club record in a 41-38 victory over Kansas City. He finished the season with 88 receptions for 1,172 yards. Benirschke became the most accurate field-goal kicker in the history of the NFL on September 12, when his 51-yard field goal, the one-hundredth of his career, gave him a career percentage of .720 to surpass the mark held by Toni Fritsch.

1984 On August 1, Alex G. Spanos purchased the majority interest in the Chargers from Klein. The Chargers hovered around .500 all year, then dipped two games under that figure with losses in their final two games to finish in last place in the AFC West with a 7-9 record. The ranks were again thinned by injuries. Fouts missed four games, and Winslow, after catching 55 passes in the team's first eight games, tore knee ligaments in a 44-37 loss to the Los Angeles Raiders on October 21, and was lost for the season. On the brighter side, first-year running back Earnest Jackson led the AFC in rushing with 1,179 yards. Joiner caught pass number 650 against Pittsburgh, November 25, to become the leading receiver in pro football history.

1985 In an 8-8 season, the Chargers finished 3-5 against the AFC West, ending an 11-game losing streak agaist division opponents that extended back to 1983. San Diego led the NFL in total offense for the sixth time in seven years, and also led the league in passing offense. But the Chargers again finished last in the league in both total and pass defense. They lost their last six games on the road, and won their last six games at home. Lionel James set an NFL record for running backs with 1,027 yards receiving, and set another NFL mark with 2,535 combined net yards. His 86 receptions led the AFC. Fouts moved into second place on the NFL's all-time completion list with 2,839, behind Fran Tarkenton's total of 3,686. Guard Ed White surpassed Mick Tingelhoff's record for most games played by an offensive lineman when he appeared in game number 241, against Kansas City, December 22.

MEMBERS OF HALL OF FAME:
Lance Alworth, Sid Gillman, David (Deacon) Jones, Ron Mix, Johnny Unitas

CHARGERS RECORD, 1960-85

Year	Won	Lost	Tied	Pct.	Fin.	Pts.	OP
Los Angeles Chargers							
1960a	10	4	0	.714	1	373	336
San Diego Chargers							
1961a	12	2	0	.857	1	396	219
1962	4	10	0	.286	3	314	392
1963b	11	3	0	.786	1	399	256
1964a	8	5	1	.615	1	341	300
1965a	9	2	3	.818	1	340	227
1966	7	6	1	.538	3	335	284
1967	8	5	1	.615	3	360	352
1968	9	5	0	.643	3	382	310
1969	8	6	0	.571	3	288	276
1970	5	6	3	.455	3	282	278
1971	6	8	0	.429	3	311	341
1972	4	9	1	.321	4	264	344
1973	2	11	1	.179	4	188	386
1974	5	9	0	.357	4	212	285
1975	2	12	0	.143	4	189	345
1976	6	8	0	.429	3	248	285
1977	7	7	0	.500	3	222	205
1978	9	7	0	.563	4	355	309
1979c	12	4	0	.750	1	411	246
1980d	11	5	0	.688	1	418	327
1981d	10	6	0	.625	1	478	390
1982e	6	3	0	.667	5	288	221
1983	6	10	0	.375	4	358	462
1984	7	9	0	.438	5	394	413
1985	8	8	0	.500	4	467	435
26 Years	192	170	11	.529		8,613	8,224

a*AFL Western Conference Champion; 0-1 in Playoffs*
b*AFL Champion; 1-0 in Playoffs*
c*AFC Western Division Champion; 0-1 in Playoffs*
d*AFC Western Division Champion; 1-1 in Playoffs*
e*AFC Qualifier for Playoffs; 1-1 in Playoffs*

RECORD HOLDERS

CAREER

Rushing attempts	Paul Lowe, 1960-67	1,014
Rushing yards	Paul Lowe, 1960-67	4,963
Pass attempts	Dan Fouts, 1973-85	4,810
Pass completions	Dan Fouts, 1973-85	2,839
Passing yards	Dan Fouts, 1973-85	37,492
Touchdown passes	Dan Fouts, 1973-85	228
Receptions	Charlie Joiner, 1976-85	552
Receiving yards	Lance Alworth, 1962-70	9,585
Interceptions	Dick Harris, 1960-65	29
Punting average	Dennis Partee, 1968-75	41.2
Punt return avg.	Leslie (Speedy) Duncan, 1964-70	12.3
Kickoff return avg.	Leslie (Speedy) Duncan, 1964-70	25.2
Field goals	Rolf Benirschke, 1977-85	130
Touchdowns	Lance Alworth, 1962-70	83
Points	Rolf Benirschke, 1977-85	679

SEASON

Rushing attempts	Earnest Jackson, 1984	296
Rushing yards	Earnest Jackson, 1984	1,179
Pass attempts	Dan Fouts, 1981	609
Pass completions	Dan Fouts, 1981	360
Passing yards	Dan Fouts, 1981	4,802
Touchdown passes	Dan Fouts, 1981	33
Receptions	Kellen Winslow, 1980	89
Receiving yards	Lance Alworth, 1965	1,602
Interceptions	Charlie McNeil, 1961	9
Punting average	Dennis Partee, 1969	44.6
Punt return avg.	Leslie (Speedy) Duncan, 1965	15.5
Kickoff return avg.	Keith Lincoln, 1962	28.4
Field goals	Rolf Benirschke, 1980	24
Touchdowns	Chuck Muncie, 1981	19
Points	Rolf Benirschke, 1980	118

GAME

Rushing attempts	Earnest Jackson, 10-7-84	33

Rushing yards	Brad Hubbert, 12-24-67	189
Pass attempts	Mark Herrmann, 12-22-85	58
Pass completions	Dan Fouts, 11-18-84	37
	Mark Herrmann, 12-22-85	37
Passing yards	Dan Fouts, 10-19-80	444
	Dan Fouts, 12-11-82	444
Touchdown passes	Dan Fouts, 11-22-81	6
Receptions	Kellen Winslow, 10-7-84	15
Receiving yards	Wes Chandler, 12-20-82	260
Interceptions	9 times	3
Field goals	5 times	4
Touchdowns	Kellen Winslow, 11-22-81	5
Points	Kellen Winslow, 11-22-81	30

COACHING HISTORY

1960-69	Sid Gillman*	83-51-6
1969-70	Charlie Waller	9- 7-3
1971	Sid Gillman**	4- 6-0
1971-73	Harland Svare***	7-17-2
1973	Ron Waller	1- 5-0
1974-78	Tommy Prothro****	21-39-0
1978-85	Don Coryell	71-53-0

*Retired after nine games in 1969
**Resigned after 10 games in 1971
***Resigned after eight games in 1973
****Resigned after four games in 1978

FIRST PLAYER SELECTED

1960 Monty Stickles, E, Notre Dame
1961 Earl Faison, DE, Indiana
1962 Bob Ferguson, FB, Ohio State
1963 Walt Sweeney, E, Syracuse
1964 Ted Davis, E, Georgia Tech
1965 Steve DeLong, G, Tennessee
1965† Gary Garrison, E, San Diego State
1966 Don Davis, T, Cal State-Los Angeles
1966† Bob Windsor, E, Kentucky
1967 Ron Billingsley, DT, Wyoming
1968 Russ Washington, T, Missouri
1969 Marty Domres, QB, Columbia
1970 Walker Gillette, WR, Richmond
1971 Leon Burns, RB, Long Beach State
1972 (2) Pete Lazetich, DE, Stanford
1973 Johnny Rodgers, WR, Nebraska
1974 Bo Matthews, RB, Colorado
1975 Gary Johnson, DT, Grambling
1976 Joe Washington, RB, Oklahoma
1977 Bob Rush, C, Memphis State
1978 John Jefferson, WR, Arizona State
1979 Kellen Winslow, TE, Missouri
1980 (4) Ed Luther, QB, San Jose State
1981 James Brooks, RB-KR, Auburn
1982 (7) Hollis Hall, CB, Clemson
1983 Billy Ray Smith, LB, Arkansas
1984 Mossy Cade, CB, Texas
1984* Lee Williams, DE, Bethune-Cookman
1985 Jim Lachey, T, Ohio State
1986 Leslie O'Neal, DE, Oklahoma State
†Redshirt Draft
*Supplemental Draft

CHARGERS MOST VALUABLE PLAYER

1961 Earl Faison, DE
1962 Ron Mix, T
1963 Tobin Rote, QB
1964 Keith Lincoln, FB
1965 Lance Alworth, FL
1966 Lance Alworth, FL
1967 John Hadl, QB
1968 John Hadl, QB
1969 Steve DeLong, DE
1970 Gary Garrison, WR
1971 John Hadl, QB
1972 Cid Edwards, RB
1973 Russ Washington, T
1974 Don Woods, RB
1975 Pat Curran, TE
1976 Charlie Joiner, WR
1977 Louie Kelcher, DT
1978 John Jefferson, WR
1979 Don Fouts, QB
1980 John Jefferson, WR
1981 Dan Fouts, QB
1982 Dan Fouts, QB
1983 Charlie Joiner, WR
1984 Earnest Jackson, RB
1985 Lionel James, RB

CHARGERS HALL OF FAME

1977 Lance Alworth, FL, 1962-70
1978 Ron Mix, T, 1960-69
1979 Paul Lowe, HB, 1960-68
1980 Keith Lincoln, FB, 1961-66, 1968
Barron Hilton, Majority Owner, 1960-66
1981 Ernie Ladd, DT, 1961-65
Walt Sweeney, G, 1963-73
1983 John Hadl, QB, 1962-72
1984 Chuck Allen, CB, 1961-69
1985 Sid Gillman, Head Coach, 1960-69, 1971
Gary Garrison, WR, 1966-76

SAN FRANCISCO 49ERS

1946 Anthony J. (Tony) Morabito, a partner in a San Francisco lumber firm, formed the 49ers as a charter member of the All-America Football Conference. Morabito had tried but failed to get a franchise in the National Football League. One of Morabito's partners in Lumber Terminals of San Francisco, Allen E. Sorrell or E.J. Turre, selected the team's nickname; each has been given credit for it at one time or another. John Blackinger was named general manager of the 49ers. Their original emblem showed a booted prospector in a lumberjack's shirt and checkered pants, his hat blown off and his hair askew, his feet splayed apart, and in his hands two six-shooters firing. Morabito raided NFL teams, signing 12 of their players, and signed notable Bay Area college players such as quarterback Frankie Albert and fullback Norm Standlee of Stanford. Lawrence (Buck) Shaw of Santa Clara was named 49ers' head coach. The team rented Kezar Stadium for its games. It finished second to the Cleveland Browns in the AAFC's Western Division in its first season and won one of its two games against Cleveland, 34-20. Forty-Niners end Alyn Beals tied for the AAFC lead in pass receiving with 40 catches for 586 yards. Standlee finished second in the AAFC in rushing, and Albert fourth in passing. Beals and guard Bruno Banducci were named to the all-league team.

1947 Before the season started, Morabito caused quite a stir nationally by trying to sign Glenn Davis and Felix (Doc) Blanchard, the Army All America backs, to five-year contracts that would let them play with the 49ers on their yearly furloughs. Davis and Blanchard wanted to join the 49ers, but they were not allowed to by the War Department. The 49ers again finished second to the Browns in the Western Division. Their offense again was led by Albert, who finished third in passing; Beals, who was third in receiving; and halfback Johnny Strzykalski, who was second in rushing. Morabito borrowed $100,000, bought out his original partners, and divided the ownership of the 49ers on a 75-25 basis with his brother Vic. "There's this nut with a hearing aid in San Francisco who is putting his own money into this damn team," said Harry Wismer, Washington Redskins broadcaster.

1948 The 49ers put together the best rushing attack in the history of professional football (3,663 yards), led by Strzykalski, again second in the league in rushing, and rookie Joe Perry. The passing game didn't suffer either, as Albert threw 29 touchdown passes and was named co-most valuable player of the AAFC. Nevertheless, San Francisco finished second behind the Browns again, with a 12-2 record to Cleveland's 14-0. A crowd of 82,769 in Cleveland watched the Browns' first victory over the 49ers, 14-7. The rematch in San Francisco drew 59,785 to see Cleveland win 31-28.

1949 San Francisco gave the Cleveland Browns the worst beating (56-28) in their history, as Albert threw five touchdown passes in a game at Kezar Stadium, October 9. The victory moved San Francisco into first place in the AAFC, but successive losses to the Brooklyn-New York Yankees (24-3) and the Browns (30-28) dropped the 49ers into their accustomed second-place finish. Again the 49ers had the best offense in the league, with Perry leading in rushing, Beals in touchdown receptions, and Albert in touchdown passes and punting. There was no division play and there was a playoff of the top four teams for the championship. In the first round, the 49ers defeated the third-place Yankees 17-7. The Browns and 49ers played for the championship in Cleveland and only 22,550 fans watched as Cleveland won 21-7. Shaw, coach of the 49ers, said, "Four years ago, I'd never even met Paul Brown [the Cleveland coach]. Now I scheme to beat him, dream of beating him, and wind up screaming because I haven't beaten him." A merger was arranged between the NFL and AAFC, and, by its terms, Cleveland, San Francisco, and the Baltimore Colts would enter the NFL, December 9.

1950 The 49ers struggled through their first season in the NFL, winning only three games. The rushing game still was potent with Perry and Strzykalski, but Albert developed a tendency to throw interceptions. A rival coach said they were "not big enough or tough enough." Tackle Leo Nomellini started his career with San Francisco, playing both offense and defense. Gordy Soltau was another star rookie.

1951 Quarterback Y. A. Tittle was acquired in the draft from the extinct 1950 Baltimore Colts franchise to play behind Albert. Albert, however, suffered a shoulder injury and Tittle was pressed into service late in the season. The team became a contender, winning its last three games and finishing third in the NFL's National Conference. Soltau finished second in the league in receiving, while rookie Billy Wilson earned the other end spot. Rookie linebacker Hardy Brown joined Nomellini and defensive backs Jim Cason and Lowell Wagner as the heart of the defense.

1952 Lou Spadia was named general manager of the 49ers. Standlee was stricken with polio and never played football again. The 49ers got off to the best start in the league, winning their first five games. But then they lost to the Bears 20-17 when Albert ran for a first down from punt formation, didn't make it, and the Bears scored shortly thereafter. The play soured the relationship between Shaw and Albert, contributing to a second-half collapse that saw the 49ers lose four of six. The bright spots in the season were Soltau, who led the league in scoring; Perry, who ran for 725 yards; and rookie halfback Hugh McElhenny, who led the league with a 7.0-yard rushing average. At the end of the season, Albert and Strzykalski retired.

1953 Bob St. Clair, a 6-foot 9-inch, 260-pound tackle, joined the team. The 49ers had their best season to date in the NFL, losing only three games by a total of nine points. Two of the three losses came with Tittle on the sidelines due to a severe facial injury. Perry led the league in rushing with 1,018 yards. His 10 rushing touchdowns were the most in the league, as were Wilson's 10 receiving touchdowns. Soltau again led the NFL in overall scoring with 114 points.

1954 San Francisco acquired halfback John Henry Johnson, who had been in the Canadian Football League, and he joined Tittle, Perry, and McElhenny in one of the best backfields in pro football history. Undefeated after five games, the 49ers and the season came apart, however, when McElhenny, leading the league with 515 yards and an 8.0-yard average, suffered a shoulder separation in the sixth game, a 31-27 loss to the Chicago Bears. The 49ers lost four of their last seven to finish 7-4-1, despite Perry and Johnson finishing first and second in rushing, and McElhenny managing to finish eighth in his half season. Perry, by gaining 1,049 yards, became the first back in history to gain more than 1,000 yards in consecutive seasons. At the end of the season, Shaw was fired as head coach.

1955 Shaw was replaced by Norman (Red) Strader, a strict disciplinarian who was unpopular with the players. Strader moved Johnson to defense and tried to replace him with rookie Dickie Moegle, but neither move worked. When McElhenny again was injured, the rushing load fell entirely on Perry, who couldn't carry the entire offense. Unable to score as they had in the past, the 49ers fell to 4-8.

1956 Strader was replaced as coach by former 49ers quarterback Frankie Albert. Albert went with rookie

Earl Morrall at quarterback initially, but a miserable start made him switch back to Tittle. McElhenny finally had a healthy season and responded with 916 yards, third in the NFL. The 49ers went 4-0-1 in their last five games to pull themselves into third place. San Francisco drew 522,339 fans for 12 games, an NFL record at the time.

1957 Tittle and 6-foot 5-inch rookie end R.C. Owens devised the Alley-Oop pass in which Tittle threw the ball in a high arc, and Owens ran to the point of reception and outjumped the defensive backs for the ball. But while Owens got the publicity, a lot of the work was done by Wilson, who led the league in receptions for the second year in a row. Founder Tony Morabito suffered a fatal heart attack during a game against the Chicago Bears at Kezar Stadium, October 27. Albert told his players of Morabito's death during halftime, and they made an emotional comeback to beat the Bears 21-17. Tittle suffered pulled muscles in both his legs in the next-to-last regular-season game, but rookie quarterback John Brodie came in and threw a touchdown pass to McElhenny as the 49ers defeated Baltimore 17-13. Tittle limped in the next week, and the 49ers came from behind to defeat Green Bay 27-20 and tie the Detroit Lions for the Western Conference championship. The two teams met in a playoff and San Francisco took a 24-7 halftime lead, only to see Detroit come from behind and win 31-27, December 22.

1958 Vic Morabito took over the team's operation. Although Perry and Wilson still were each at the top of his game, many of their teammates had lost some effectiveness. Tittle shared his job with rookie John Brodie, and McElhenny began to be replaced by J.D. Smith. An up-and-down season ended at 6-6, and Albert resigned at the end of the year.

1959 Assistant coach Howard (Red) Hickey was promoted to head coach. A revamped rushing attack, featuring 1,036 yards by Smith, and a suddenly stronger defense led the 49ers to first place midway through the season with a 6-1 record. But then they collapsed, winning only one of the last five games, and dropped to third place. Other than Smith, the brightest spot was the play of rookie defensive tackle Charlie Krueger.

1960 The 49ers suddenly became the least scored-upon team in the NFL, but the offense faltered and the team slipped into mediocrity. With the more mobile Brodie beating out Tittle, Hickey salvaged a frustrating season when he installed the Shotgun formation with the quarterback standing three to five yards back and taking a long snap from center, then passing or handing off. The 49ers won four of their last five games and tied for second place in the Western Conference.

1961 Tittle, who was better suited to the T-formation, was traded to the New York Giants for guard Lou Cordileone. There were still three 49ers quarterbacks to operate the Shotgun—Brodie, Bobby Waters, and rookie Billy Kilmer. Brodie was a passer, and Kilmer and Waters each were outstanding runners. With the three alternating, the 49ers thrashed four teams on the way to a 4-1 record. However, the Chicago Bears stopped the 49ers with middle linebacker Bill George playing on the line of scrimmage and often stunting and moving back into the backfield; Chicago won by a shocking 31-0 score. The 49ers went back to the T-formation, but Hickey said he could have continued to play the Shotgun if his players had not lost confidence in it. San Francisco lost to Baltimore 27-24 on the final day of the season and missed a chance to finish in a tie for second place.

1962 San Francisco started as one of the favorites in the Western Conference, but the 49ers lost their first two games and four in a row in the middle of the season to finish 6-8, including 2-5 at Kezar. The offense had real potential, however. Brodie continued to improve, young Bernie Casey made 53 receptions, Smith rushed for 907 yards, and Kilmer averaged 5.1 yards as a halfback before breaking his leg in an automobile accident.

1963 Injuries destroyed the season, with Kilmer missing the entire year, Brodie breaking an arm early, and defensive stalwarts Krueger, Walt Rock, and Floyd Dean all suffering knee or leg injuries. With the aging Lamar McHan running the offense, all the team featured was Casey and return man Abe Woodson, who returned three kickoffs for touchdowns. After three games of the poorest season in club history, Hickey resigned and was replaced by Jack Christiansen. At the end of the season, Nomellini retired holding the record for consecutive games, 174.

1964 Owner Vic Morabito died of a heart attack at age 44. Josephine and Jane Morabito, widows of the late brothers, kept control and gave Lou Spadia authority to run the team. The 49ers' running backs were decimated by injuries. The passing game was effective, though, with Brodie throwing to Casey, tight end Monty Stickles, and rookie Dave Parks. The defense featured two bright newcomers—linebacker Dave Wilcox and defensive back Jimmy Johnson, converted after three years at flanker.

1965 The 49ers blossomed into the NFL's most exciting offensive team. Rookie Ken Willard and John David Crow, obtained from St. Louis, gave the team a solid running game, while Brodie led the league in pass attempts (391), completions (242), yards (3,112), and touchdowns (30). Parks led in receiving, with 80 catches for 1,344 yards and 12 touchdowns. The highlight of a pleasing 7-6-1 season was a 52-24 opening-game victory over the Bears, the most points ever scored against George Halas's team.

1966 San Francisco played another respectable, but still disappointing, season, finishing 6-6-2. The 49ers had all the offensive tools, but they played in spurts, destroying Detroit and the Chicago Bears by identical 41-14 scores, while losing to last-place Minnesota 28-3.

1967 The 49ers got off to a fast start, winning five out of six games, including administering the only defeat of the year to the Rams. Hit by injuries to Willard, Crow, Parks, and others, however, they lost six straight. The fans were yelling for a new quarterback, and rookie Steve Spurrier saw some action, as did young George Mira, who led the team to victories in its last two games. At the end of the season, Christiansen was fired.

1968 Spadia took the title of president, and Jack White was named general manager. Dallas Cowboys' assistant coach Dick Nolan was named 49ers head coach. The 49ers went 0-3-1 against the Rams and Colts, but 7-3 against the rest of the league. The offensive stars were Brodie, who led the league with 3,020 yards passing after Nolan decided he was the starter; Willard, who finished second in the NFL in rushing with 967 yards; and flanker Clifton McNeil, who led the league in pass receptions (71) after being obtained from Cleveland to replace Parks, who had signed with New Orleans. Krueger, Wilcox, and cornerback Kermit Alexander continued to shine on defense.

1969 The best successive drafts in team history—with Ted Kwalick, Gene Washington, and Forrest Blue on offense and Skip Vanderbundt, Tommy Hart, Jim Sniadecki, and Earl Edwards on defense—couldn't offset a devastating run of injuries. The 49ers didn't win a game until the sixth week of the season and finished 4-8-2 with Spurrier at quarterback.

1970 The 49ers surged to a 10-3-1 record and the Western Division championship. The offense was the best in the NFL, and Brodie led the league in passing and Washington in receiving yards (1,100) and touchdowns (12). Cornerback Bruce Taylor was the top punt returner. In the season finale, the 49ers beat Oakland 38-7. In an NFC Divisional Playoff Game, they defeated the Minnesota Vikings 17-14 on two touchdown passes by Brodie in the fourth quarter, the last to wide receiver Dick Witcher with less than a minute to play. In the NFC Championship Game, the 49ers lost to the Dallas Cowboys 17-10. Nolan was named NFC coach of the year, Brodie player of the year, and Taylor rookie of the year. The NFC Western Division championship was the first title of any kind for the 49ers in their 25-year history.

1971 The 49ers left Kezar Stadium and moved their home games to Candlestick Park. Their offense was as strong as ever, with Brodie leading the conference in passing yards (2,642) and touchdowns (18), Gene Washington tops in receiving yards (884), and Kwalick second in receptions. Willard joined with rookie Vic Washington to form one of the most productive running combinations in the league. The 49ers finished 9-5, half a game ahead of the Rams. They clinched their second consecutive division championship with a 31-27 victory over the Detroit Lions on the last day of the season. San Francisco defeated the Washington Redskins 24-20 but again faced Dallas in the championship game and again lost, this time 14-3.

1972 When Brodie was injured early in the season, Spurrier took over a team that was struggling. Under Spurrier, the 49ers won five of their last six, clinching their third consecutive Western Division title with a 20-17 victory over Minnesota in the season finale. In that game, Brodie returned to throw two touchdown passes in the fourth quarter, the second one with 19 seconds left. Other than the quarterbacks, the stars of the NFC's top-scoring team were Gene Washington, who led the league with 12 touchdown receptions, and Vic Washington, who led the team in rushing and was second in receiving. The other story was a defensive line that was the equal of any in the league, with Cedrick Hardman, Krueger, Hart, and Edwards. San Francisco met its nemesis, Dallas, in an NFC Divisional Playoff Game and, despite leading 28-13, lost 30-28 as Cowboys' quarterback Roger Staubach led a sensational comeback.

1973 The 49ers slumped to 5-9 as neither the offense nor the defense played up to previous standards. Brodie was benched after a slow start, and Spurrier and Joe Reed shared the job. The offense did receive a lift when it picked up Dan Abramowicz from New Orleans, but both Washingtons suffered through subpar seasons, and Willard was benched. At the end of the season, Brodie and Krueger retired.

1974 Quarterback Steve Spurrier was injured the week before the regular season began and was sidelined for most of the year. The 49ers used five different quarterbacks and lost a team-record seven games in a row at one point. The bright spots were the play of rookie quarterback Tom Owen and rookie running back Wilbur Jackson, and a hot finish in which the 49ers won four of their last five. Wilcox retired at the end of the year.

1975 The 49ers started slowly, going 2-5, but a hot spell brought their record up to 5-5. Included was a 24-23 victory over the Rams, ending a string of 10 consecutive losses to Los Angeles. Four losses to end the season cost Nolan his job. Spurrier shared the quarterback job with Norm Snead, young Delvin Williams averaged 5.4 yards per carry, and Gene Washington looked like his old self again.

1976 Miami assistant Monte Clark became head coach. Quarterback Jim Plunkett was acquired in a trade with the New England Patriots. San Francisco won six of its first seven games but lost a 23-20 overtime game at St. Louis, slumped, and finished second in the division behind the Rams. Hardman, Hart,

Jimmy Webb, and Cleveland Elam became one of the best defensive lines in the league. Williams ran for 1,203 yards and led the NFC with a 4.9-yard average. The team's 8-6 record was its first winning season in four years.

1977 A new era began for the 49ers on March 31 when the team became the property of 31-year-old Edward J. DeBartolo, Jr., the youngest owner in the NFL. Joe Thomas was appointed vice president and general manager, and Ken Meyer, the former offensive coordinator with the Rams, became head coach. The 49ers went 0-5 to begin the season, including two losses by shutouts. On October 23, Jim Plunkett called his own plays for the first time all season, and the 49ers defeated Detroit 28-7. The defense also took part and registered 22 sacks in four consecutive victories, in which each opponent scored 10 points or less. On November 27, the 49ers defeated the Saints 20-17 to improve their record to 5-6. But the team was stunned the following week when Minnesota rallied from a 27-7 deficit in the fourth quarter to win 28-27. The erratic 49ers lost their final three games and finished 5-9.

1978 Pete McCulley replaced Meyer as head coach. Thomas shuffled the team with a series of player-personnel maneuvers. After nine seasons with Buffalo, O. J. Simpson was obtained for draft choices; wide receiver Freddie Solomon was acquired from Miami for Williams; Hart was traded to the Bears; and Plunkett was released before the season. Steve DeBerg became the starting quarterback. San Francisco lost its first four games, then defeated Cincinnati 28-12. But the 49ers won only one more game in a disastrous season and finished 2-14, the poorest record in club history. Simpson gained only 593 yards in nine games, then was lost for the season with a shoulder injury. DeBerg completed only 45 percent of his passes and threw 22 interceptions. After a 1-8 start, McCulley was replaced by Fred O'Connor, who was released at the end of the season.

1979 Bill Walsh, the head coach at Stanford, was appointed head coach and general manager January 9; Thomas was released. Quarterback Joe Montana was selected in the third round of the draft, and wide receiver Dwight Clark was chosen in the tenth round. The 49ers didn't win their first game until October 21 against Atlanta, 20-15, and again suffered a 2-14 season. But the offense displayed marked improvement by scoring 308 points. Walsh's innovative passing offense produced a big year, as DeBerg completed 347 of 578 passes for 3,652 yards. Simpson rushed for 460 yards, then retired after the season.

1980 With two choices in the first round, the 49ers selected running back Earl Cooper and defensive end Jim Stuckey. The 49ers won the season opener over New Orleans 26-23 when Ray Wersching kicked a 37-yard field goal in the final seconds. They followed with consecutive victories over St. Louis and the New York Jets. DeBerg and Montana split playing time during most of the season, but Montana, favored by Walsh because of his mobility, started the last five games. After a 3-0 start, the 49ers lost their next eight games. In a 59-14 loss to Dallas on October 12, running back Paul Hofer was lost for the year with a knee injury. On November 23, the 49ers blanked the New York Giants 12-0 and launched another three-game winning streak. Two weeks later, the 49ers overcame a 35-7 halftime deficit against New Orleans to win 38-35. The 49ers finished 6-10. Cooper led the NFC with 83 receptions; Clark had 82.

1981 A remarkable draft yielded Ronnie Lott, Eric Wright, and Carlton Williamson, all of whom earned starting positions in the defensive secondary. Jack Reynolds, released by the Rams, was signed and installed as an inside linebacker. DeBerg was traded to Denver before the season, allowing Montana to become the full-time starter. The club lost two of its first three games but then exploded for a seven-game winning streak to open up a three-game lead in the NFC West. Defensive end Fred Dean was obtained from San Diego before the Dallas game on October 11, and he became one of the leaders of the new defense. The 49ers routed the Cowboys 45-14. After a loss to Cleveland on November 15, the 49ers won their final five games, and clinched the NFC West championship November 29 with a 17-10 victory over the Giants. San Francisco finished 13-3, the best record in the NFL. Montana threw for 3,565 yards and was the top-rated passer in the NFC. Clark led NFC receivers with 85 catches for 1,105 yards. The defense allowed just 250 points, the second-lowest total in the conference. The 49ers beat the Giants 38-24 in a playoff game on January 3. In the NFC Championship Game on January 10, Montana directed an 89-yard scoring drive in the closing minutes to defeat Dallas 28-27. Clark climaxed the drive with a leaping catch in the end zone for a six-yard touchdown. In Super Bowl XVI in Pontiac, Michigan, January 24, the 49ers defeated Cincinnati 26-21 for San Francisco's first NFL championship.

1982 The 49ers did not enjoy the strike-shortened season, losing the two games prior to the strike and playing inconsistently afterwards to finish with a 3-6 mark that wasn't good enough to get into the expanded playoffs. The two stars of the season were Montana and Clark. Montana set an NFL record by passing for more than 300 yards in five consecutive games, including a team-record 408 yards in a 31-20 victory over St. Louis. Clark led the NFL in receiving with 60 catches for 913 yards.

1983 Without a first-round selection, the 49ers still managed to pluck running back Roger Craig in the draft. They also picked up running back Wendell Tyler in a trade with the Rams. The 49ers lost the opener 22-17 to Philadelphia when Montana was injured, but he came back the next Thursday night to throw four touchdown passes while Wright intercepted three Minnesota passes, and the 49ers won 48-17, launching a four-game winning streak. After a midseason slump when they lost four of five games, the 49ers won their last three to take the division with a 10-6 record. On offense, Montana set a team record with 3,910 passing yards, Ray Wersching scored a record 126 points, and Tyler and Craig rushed for 856 and 725 yards, respectively. On defense, Fred Dean led the NFL with 17½ sacks. In an NFC Divisional Playoff Game, Detroit's Ed Murray missed a field goal with 11 seconds left, and the 49ers won 24-23. In the NFC Championship Game, the 49ers, trailing Washington 21-0 in the fourth quarter, forged a 21-21 tie, before losing 24-21.

1984 The 49ers fielded one of the greatest teams in NFL history, winning a record 15 regular-season games. Montana entered the season as the top career passer in league history. San Francisco started with six consecutive victories, including a 21-9 defeat of Philadelphia when, with Montana missing the game, reserve Matt Cavanaugh threw three touchdown passes. The 49ers lost to Pittsburgh 20-17 on Gary Anderson's field goal with less than two minutes left, October 14. They won nine in a row to finish 15-1. The two key games were against the second-place Rams, a 33-0 blowout and a 19-16 season-ending victory. Wersching led the league in scoring, Montana led the NFC in passing, Tyler set a team record with 1,262 yards rushing, and the defense gave up the fewest points in the league. Montana threw three touchdown passes to sink the New York Giants in the divisional playoffs. The defense then took over, shutting down Walter Payton and the Bears in a 23-0 victory in the NFC Championship Game. In Super Bowl XIX, Craig scored three touchdowns, Montana accounted for 390 yards, the defense shut down Miami quarterback Dan Marino, and the 49ers won 38-16.

1985 The season started on a bad note, when the Vikings took advantage of seven San Francisco turnovers to win 28-21. After that, plagued by injuries, the 49ers never could catch up with the quick-starting Rams and even dropped to 3-4 after seven games. A win over the Rams got San Francisco back on the right track, and the 49ers won five of the next six. In the only loss, 17-16 to Denver, the 49ers couldn't convert on a short field-goal attempt as holder Cavanaugh bobbled a snap when he was distracted by a snowball thrown from the stands. Late in the season, the Rams knocked the 49ers into the wild card playoff berth with a 27-20 victory in which they scored on a kickoff return, an interception return, and a bobbled 49ers interception. Montana again led the NFC in passing, and Craig became the first player in history to gain 1,000 yards both rushing (1,050) and receiving (1,016), while leading the NFL with 92 receptions, a record for running backs. In the NFC Wild Card Game, the Giants' defense controlled the ailing 49ers, and New York won 17-3.

MEMBERS OF HALL OF FAME:
Hugh McElhenny, Leo Nomellini, Joe Perry, O. J. Simpson, Y. A. Tittle

49ERS RECORD, 1946-85

Year	Won	Lost	Tied	Pct.	Fin.	Pts.	OP
1946	9	5	0	.643	2	307	189
1947	8	4	2	.667	2	327	264
1948	12	2	0	.857	2	495	248
1949a	9	3	0	.750	2	416	227
1950	3	9	0	.250	5t	213	300
1951	7	4	1	.636	2t	255	205
1952	7	5	0	.583	3	285	221
1953	9	3	0	.750	2	372	237
1954	7	4	1	.636	3	313	251
1955	4	8	0	.333	5	216	298
1956	5	6	1	.455	3	233	284
1957b	8	4	0	.667	2	260	264
1958	6	6	0	.500	4	257	324
1959	7	5	0	.583	3t	255	237
1960	7	5	0	.583	2t	208	205
1961	7	6	1	.538	5	346	272
1962	6	8	0	.429	5	282	331
1963	2	12	0	.143	7	198	391
1964	4	10	0	.286	7	236	330
1965	7	6	1	.538	4	421	402
1966	6	6	2	.500	4	320	325
1967	7	7	0	.500	3	273	337
1968	7	6	1	.538	3	303	310
1969	4	8	2	.333	4	277	319
1970c	10	3	1	.769	1	352	267
1971c	9	5	0	.643	1	300	216
1972d	8	5	1	.607	1	353	249
1973	5	9	0	.357	4	262	319
1974	6	8	0	.429	2	226	236
1975	5	9	0	.357	2	255	286
1976	8	6	0	.571	2	270	190
1977	5	9	0	.357	3	220	260
1978	2	14	0	.125	4	219	350
1979	2	14	0	.125	4	308	416
1980	6	10	0	.375	3	320	415
1981e	13	3	0	.813	1	357	250
1982	3	6	0	.333	11	209	206
1983c	10	6	0	.625	1	432	293
1984e	15	1	0	.938	1	475	227
1985f	10	6	0	.625	2	411	263
4 AAFC Years	38	14	2	.722		1,545	928
36 NFL Years	237	242	12	.495		10,492	10,286
40 Pro Years	275	256	14	.517		12,037	11,214

a*AAFC Runnerup; 1-1 in Playoffs*
b*NFL Western Conference Runnerup; 0-1 in Playoffs*
c*NFC Western Division Champion; 1-1 in Playoffs*
d*NFC Western Division Champion; 0-1 in Playoffs*
e*Super Bowl Champion; 3-0 in Playoffs*
f*Wild Card Qualifier for Playoffs; 0-1 in Playoffs*

RECORD HOLDERS

CAREER

Rushing attempts	Ken Willard, 1965-73	1,582
Rushing yards	Joe Perry, 1950-60, 1963	7,344
Pass attempts	John Brodie, 1957-73	4,491
Pass completions	John Brodie, 1957-73	2,469
Passing yards	John Brodie, 1957-73	31,548
Touchdown passes	John Brodie, 1957-73	214
Receptions	Dwight Clark, 1979-85	421
Receiving yards	Gene Washington, 1969-77	6,664
Interceptions	Jimmy Johnson, 1961-76	47
Punting average	Tommy Davis, 1959-69	44.7

Punt return avg.	Dana McLemore, 1982-85	10.5
Kickoff return avg.	Abe Woodson, 1958-64	29.4
Field goals	Ray Wersching, 1977-85	152
Touchdowns	Ken Willard, 1965-73	61
Points	Ray Wersching, 1977-85	780
SEASON		
Rushing attempts	Delvin Williams, 1977	268
Rushing yards	Wendell Tyler, 1984	1,262
Pass attempts	Steve DeBerg, 1979	578
Pass completions	Steve DeBerg, 1979	347
Passing yards	Joe Montana, 1983	3,910
Touchdown passes	John Brodie, 1965	30
Receptions	Roger Craig, 1985	92
Receiving yards	Dave Parks, 1965	1,344
Interceptions	Dave Baker, 1960	10
Punting average	Tommy Davis, 1965	45.8
Punt return avg.	Dana McLemore, 1982	22.3
Kickoff return avg.	Joe Arenas, 1953	34.4
Field goals	Bruce Gossett, 1973	26
Touchdowns	Roger Craig, 1985	15
Points	Ray Wersching, 1984	131
GAME		
Rushing attempts	Delvin Williams, 10-31-76	34
Rushing yards	Delvin Williams, 10-31-76	194
Pass attempts	Joe Montana, 10-6-85	57
Pass completions	Joe Montana, 10-6-85	37
Passing yards	Joe Montana, 10-6-85	429
Touchdown passes	John Brodie, 11-23-65	5
	Steve Spurrier, 11-19-72	5
	Joe Montana, 10-6-85	5
Receptions	Bernie Casey, 11-13-66	12
	Dwight Clark, 12-11-82	12
	Roger Craig, 10-6-85	12
Receiving yards	Jerry Rice, 12-9-85	241
Interceptions	Dave Baker, 12-4-60	4
Field goals	Ray Wersching, 10-16-83	6
Touchdowns	Billy Kilmer, 10-15-61	4
Points	Gordy Soltau, 10-27-51	26

COACHING HISTORY

1946-54	Lawrence (Buck) Shaw	72-40-4
	NFL only:	33-25-2
1955	Norman (Red) Strader	4- 8-0
1956-58	Frankie Albert	19-17-1
1959-63	Howard (Red) Hickey*	27-27-1
1963-67	Jack Christiansen	26-38-3
1968-75	Dick Nolan	56-56-5
1976	Monte Clark	8- 6-0
1977	Ken Meyer	5- 9-0
1978	Pete McCulley**	1- 8-0
1978	Fred O'Connor	1- 6-0
1979-85	Bill Walsh	66-48-0

**Resigned after three games in 1963*
***Replaced after nine games in 1978*

FIRST PLAYER SELECTED

1947†	Glenn Davis, B, Army
1948†	Joe Scott, HB, San Francisco
1949†	Chester Fritz, T, Missouri
1950	Leo Nomellini, T, Minnesota
1951	Y. A. Tittle, QB, LSU
1952	Hugh McElhenny, HB, Washington
1953	Harry Babcock, E, Georgia
1954	Bernie Faloney, QB, Maryland
1955	Dickie Moegle, HB, Rice
1956	Earl Morrall, QB, Michigan State
1957	John Brodie, QB, Stanford
1958	Jim Pace, HB, Michigan
1959	Dave Baker, QB, Oklahoma
1960	Monty Stickles, E, Notre Dame
1961	Jimmy Johnson, HB, UCLA
1962	Lance Alworth, HB, Arkansas
1963	Kermit Alexander, HB, UCLA
1964	Dave Parks, E, Texas Tech
1965	Ken Willard, FB, North Carolina
1966	Stan Hindman, DE, Mississippi
1967	Steve Spurrier, QB, Florida
1968	Forrest Blue, C, Auburn
1969	Ted Kwalick, TE, Penn State
1970	Cedrick Hardman, DE, North Texas State
1971	Tim Anderson, S, Ohio State
1972	Terry Beasley, WR, Auburn
1973	Mike Holmes, DB, Texas Southern
1974	Wilbur Jackson, RB, Alabama
1975	Jimmy Webb, DT, Mississippi State
1976	(2) Randy Cross, C, UCLA
1977	(3) Elmo Boyd, WR, Eastern Kentucky
1978	Ken MacAfee, TE, Notre Dame
1979	(2) James Owens, WR-RB, UCLA
1980	Earl Cooper, RB, Rice
1981	Ronnie Lott, DB, USC
1982	(2) Bubba Paris, T, Michigan
1983	(2) Roger Craig, RB, Nebraska
1984	Todd Shell, LB, BYU
1984*	Derrick Crawford, WR, Memphis State
1985	Jerry Rice, WR, Mississippi Valley State
1986	(2) Larry Roberts, DE, Alabama

† AAFC Draft
**Supplemental Draft*

SEATTLE SEAHAWKS

1972 Seattle Professional Football, Inc., a group of business and community leaders, announced its intention to bid for an NFL franchise for the city of Seattle, June 15. Herman Sarkowsky, principal owner of the National Basketball Association's Portland Trail Blazers, was spokesman for the group. He was joined by D. E. (Ned) Skinner, Howard S. Wright, M. Lamont Bean, Lynn P. Himmelman, and Lloyd W. Nordstrom. In November, construction began on the $67 million Kingdome with a seating capacity of 65,000 for football.

1974 The National Football League awarded a franchise to Seattle Professional Football, Inc. for $16 million, December 5. Nordstrom was the majority owner, with Sarkowsky, Skinner, Himmelman, Wright, and Bean partners.

1975 John Thompson, executive director of the NFL Management Council, was named general manager of the Seattle franchise, March 6. In April, Mark Duncan was named assistant general manager and Dick Mansperger, director of player personnel with the Dallas Cowboys, was appointed to a similar post in Seattle. A contest to name the team drew 20,365 entries; "Seahawks" was selected, June 17. Season ticket applications were accepted and 24,168 requests arrived the first day, July 28. The season ticket sale closed 27 days later with 59,000 purchased. "We anticipated a good sale," Thompson said, "but no one in his right mind would have predicted this." The Seahawks adopted blue, green, and silver as their official colors. The team signed a 20-year lease to play all home games in the Kingdome.

1976 Jack Patera, an assistant coach with the Minnesota Vikings, was named first head coach of the Seahawks, January 3. Lloyd Nordstrom, spokesman for the majority owners, died of a heart attack while vacationing in Mexico, January 20. The Seahawks selected 39 NFL veterans in the allocation draft, March 30. Among the top veterans chosen were tackle Norm Evans of Miami and linebacker Mike Curtis of Baltimore, both former members of Super Bowl champions. The Seahawks selected 25 rookies in their first college draft, April 8. Steve Niehaus, a 6-foot 4-inch, 270-pound defensive tackle from Notre Dame, was the number-one choice. The Seahawks opened their first training camp at Eastern Washington University in Cheney. On August 1, the Seahawks played their first game before 60,825 in the Kingdome, with the 49ers defeating them 27-20. Four weeks later, the Seahawks won their first preseason game, 17-16 over San Diego, when rookie quarterback Jim Zorn threw a touchdown pass to Ron Howard with 13 seconds left. The Seahawks won two regular-season games in their first season, when they were part of the NFC Western Division. In their league opener, they battled St. Louis furiously before losing 30-24 in the Kingdome. Zorn passed for two touchdowns and ran for another. After losing five games, the Seahawks recorded their first victory, beating Tampa Bay 13-10, October 17. Seattle scored its first win over an established team as Sherman Smith, converted from quarterback to running back, rushed for 124 yards and scored two touchdowns in a 30-13 rout of Atlanta, November 7. The following week, Zorn passed for two touchdowns and ran for a third as the Seahawks pushed Minnesota before losing 27-21. Steve Largent, a rookie wide receiver from Tulsa, caught 54 passes to rank third in the NFC. Zorn passed for 2,571 yards, the most ever by a first-year NFL quarterback.

1977 Seattle was permanently aligned in the AFC Western Division. The Seahawks traded their first-round draft choice to Dallas for the Cowboys' first-round pick and three second-round picks. The Cowboys chose Tony Dorsett; Seattle chose tackle Steve August on the first round. The Seahawks opened with four consecutive losses. Zorn was injured in the second game, a 42-20 loss to Cincinnati. On October 16, backup quarterback Steve Myer threw four touchdowns to lead Seattle to its first victory of the season, 30-23 over Tampa Bay. Two weeks later, Zorn made his first start in a month and threw for four touchdowns as Seattle set 15 club records in a 56-17 win over Buffalo. On November 13, the Seahawks registered their first shutout ever, 17-0 against the Jets. Victories in the last two games gave Seattle a 5-9 record, the best ever for a second-year expansion team.

1978 The Seahawks shed their expansion team tag. They finished 9-7 and only one game out of first place. The offense, led by Zorn, proved one of the most explosive in the NFL, but the defense lagged behind. On October 8, Efren Herrera kicked a 19-yard field goal on the final play of the game for a 29-28 victory over Minnesota. Two weeks later, the defense came alive and intercepted Ken Stabler four times, leading to a 27-7 surprise of Oakland. An overtime loss to Denver was followed by four victories in five weeks. A 17-16 win in Oakland made the Seahawks the first team since 1965 to defeat the Raiders twice in the regular season. Although playoff hopes were dimmed by a loss to San Diego on December 10, the Seahawks closed out with a winning season in only their third year. Running back David Sims led the league with 15 touchdowns, and Steve Largent made 71 receptions to lead the AFC. Patera was named NFL coach of the year.

1979 In a move to bolster the defense, Seattle made UCLA defensive tackle Manu Tuiasosopo its first choice in the draft. Sims was forced into early retirement with a neck injury. The Seahawks started slowly, winning only twice in their first seven games. A 34-14 victory over the Oilers turned the season around and Seattle finished with a rush, going 7-2 and ending with victories over Denver and Oakland (their fourth straight against the Raiders). Zorn passed for a club-record 3,661 yards, and Largent, who was selected to his second straight Pro Bowl, led the NFL with 1,237 yards receiving.

1980 The Seahawks were thinking playoffs after a 4-3 start that included a victory in Houston (26-7) and a 14-0 shutout of the Redskins in Washington. But the loss of Smith with a knee injury and the breakdown of the offensive line (which allowed 51 sacks) sent the Seahawks into a tailspin. They lost their last nine games and finished 4-12. Included in the disappointing record were eight straight losses in the Kingdome. Zorn again threw for over 3,000 yards (3,346), and Largent (66) and Sam McCullum (62) combined to catch 128 passes. The defense gave up 408 points, the most in the AFC.

1981 The Seahawks tried to shore up one of their weakest areas by drafting three-time UCLA All-America defensive back Kenny Easley. Seattle didn't get out of the cellar of the AFC West for one week in a disappointing season that saw the team start off 1-6. A strong finish brought the final record to 6-10, which included victories over Denver, San Diego, and the New York Jets. The Seahawks defeated the Jets twice, giving them victories in all six meetings between the clubs since Seattle entered the NFL. Largent was second in the AFC in receptions with a club-record 75 and was chosen for his third AFC-NFC Pro Bowl appearance.

1982 Sarkowsky stepped down as managing general partner and was replaced by John Nordstrom. Mike McCormack, former head coach of the Philadelphia Eagles and Baltimore Colts, was named director of football operations, March 11. During the 57-day players strike, head coach Jack Patera and general manager John Thompson were fired. McCormack was named interim head coach, October 13. When the season resumed on November 21, Zorn's 34-yard touchdown pass to Largent with 49 seconds left gave McCormack and the Seahawks a 17-10 victory against Denver. Seattle finished 4-5.

1983 McCormack was named president and general manager, January 3. Chuck Knox, former head coach of the Los Angeles Rams and Buffalo Bills, was named head coach, January 26. With Knox a proponent of a strong, dominant running game, the Seahawks used eight of their nine draft picks to select offensive players, including Penn State All-America running back Curt Warner. While setting a club record with 57 rushing attempts, the Seahawks defeated the New York Jets 17-10 to give Knox his first victory as Seattle's head coach, September 11. Midway through the season, Dave Krieg replaced Zorn at quarterback and finished as the second-ranked AFC passer with 2,139 yards and 18 touchdowns. Warner led the AFC in rushing, and helped Seattle clinch its first playoff berth with a 9-7 record. Krieg's three touchdown passes led the Seahawks past Denver 31-7 in the AFC Wild Card Game before 60,752 at the Kingdome, December 24. A week later, Seattle drove 66 yards in five plays late in the fourth quarter to upset Miami 27-20 in a divisional playoff game at the Orange Bowl. In the AFC Championship Game, the Los Angeles Raiders, who had lost to Seattle twice in the regular season, shut down Warner and dashed the Seahawks' Super Bowl hopes 30-14.

1984 Seattle defeated Cleveland 33-0 on September 3 to win its regular-season opener for the first time ever. But the enthusiasm was dampened because of a season-ending knee injury to Warner. Knox revamped the offense and Krieg, in his first full season as the starting quarterback, passed for 3,671 yards and 32 touchdowns. On October 29, Seattle posted its second shutout of the season with a 24-0 victory over San Diego, as Largent caught three touchdown passes and Easley intercepted a club-record three passes. On November 4, the Seahawks set an NFL record by returning four interceptions for touchdowns, including two by cornerback Dave Brown, in a 45-0 victory over Kansas City. In a 27-24 victory at Denver on November 25, Krieg passed for 406 yards and three touchdowns, including an 80-yard scoring strike to rookie speedster Daryl Turner on the game's first play, as the Seahawks gained a share of first place with the Broncos. In the final regular-season game, Denver won a rematch with Seattle 31-14 to clinch the AFC West title. Seattle, which finished with a best-ever record of 12-4, eliminated the defending Super Bowl champion Raiders in the AFC Wild Card Game with a 13-7 victory. But the Seahawks lost to Miami 31-10 in a divisional playoff game at the Orange Bowl the following week. For the season, the defense gave up the fewest points (282) and had the most sacks (55) in club history. The Seahawks also forced 63 turnovers, second-most in NFL history. Easley led the league with 10 interceptions and Largent caught 74 passes.

1985 Despite the return of Warner, who rushed for 1,094 yards, Seattle slipped to 8-8 and missed the playoffs. Largent set club records for catches and yards in a season, breaking his own marks with totals of 79 receptions and a league-high 1,287 yards. He also extended his consecutive-game receiving streak to 123 and became the first player in NFL history to record eight 50-catch seasons. Defensive end Jacob Green led the Seahawks with 13½ sacks. The team finished with 61, eclipsing their one-year club-record by 6. In a 49-35 come-from-behind victory over San Diego on September 15, Krieg tied his own club record by throwing five touchdown passes. Four of them went to Turner, including three in a furious second-half rally. In a 17-14 loss to the New York Jets on October 27, Krieg extended his streak of consecutive games with at least one touchdown pass to 26, moving past Daryle Lamonica into second place in NFL history behind Johnny Unitas.

MEMBERS OF HALL OF FAME:
None

SEAHAWKS RECORD, 1976-85

Year	Won	Lost	Tied	Pct.	Fin.	Pts.	OP
1976	2	12	0	.143	5	229	429
1977	5	9	0	.357	4	282	373
1978	9	7	0	.563	3	345	358
1979	9	7	0	.563	3	378	372
1980	4	12	0	.250	5	291	408
1981	6	10	0	.375	5	322	388
1982	4	5	0	.444	10	127	147
1983a	9	7	0	.563	2	403	397
1984b	12	4	0	.750	2	418	282
1985	8	8	0	.500	3	349	303
10 Years	68	81	0	.456		3,144	3,457

aAFC Wild Card Qualifier for Playoffs; 2-1 in Playoffs
bAFC Wild Card Qualifier for Playoffs; 1-1 in Playoffs

RECORD HOLDERS

CAREER

Rushing attempts	Sherman Smith, 1976-82	810
Rushing yards	Sherman Smith, 1976-82	3,429
Pass attempts	Jim Zorn, 1976-84	2,992
Pass completions	Jim Zorn, 1976-84	1,593
Passing yards	Jim Zorn, 1976-84	20,042
Touchdown passes	Jim Zorn, 1976-84	107
Receptions	Steve Largent, 1976-85	624
Receiving yards	Steve Largent, 1976-85	9,059
Interceptions	Dave Brown, 1976-85	45
Punting average	Herman Weaver, 1977-80	40.0
Punt return avg.	Paul Johns, 1981-84	11.2
Kickoff return avg.	Al Hunter, 1977-80	22.0
Field goals	Efren Herrera, 1978-81	64
Touchdowns	Steve Largent, 1976-85	79
Points	Steve Largent, 1976-85	475

SEASON

Rushing attempts	Curt Warner, 1983	335
Rushing yards	Curt Warner, 1983	1,449
Pass attempts	Dave Krieg, 1985	532
Pass completions	Jim Zorn, 1979	285
	Dave Krieg, 1985	285
Passing yards	Dave Krieg, 1984	3,671
Touchdown passes	Dave Krieg, 1984	32
Receptions	Steve Largent, 1985	79
Receiving yards	Steve Largent, 1985	1,287
Interceptions	John Harris, 1981	10
Punting average	Herman Weaver, 1980	41.8
Punt return avg.	Kenny Easley, 1984	12.1
Kickoff return avg.	Al Hunter, 1978	24.1
Field goals	Efren Herrera, 1980	20
	Norm Johnson, 1984	20
Touchdowns	David Sims, 1978	15
	Sherman Smith, 1979	15
Points	Norm Johnson, 1984	110

GAME

Rushing attempts	Curt Warner, 11-27-83	32
Rushing yards	Curt Warner, 11-27-83	207
Pass attempts	Dave Krieg, 10-13-85	51
Pass completions	Dave Krieg, 10-13-85	33
Passing yards	Dave Krieg, 11-20-83	418
Touchdown passes	Dave Krieg, 12-2-84	5
	Dave Krieg, 9-15-85	5
Receptions	David Hughes, 9-27-81	12
	Steve Largent, 11-25-84	12
Receiving yards	Steve Largent, 11-25-84	191
Interceptions	Kenny Easley, 9-3-84	3
Field goals	Norm Johnson, 9-3-84	5
Touchdowns	Daryl Turner, 9-15-85	4
Points	Daryl Turner, 9-15-85	24

COACHING HISTORY

1976-82	Jack Patera*	35-59-0
1982	Mike McCormack	4- 3-0
1983-85	Chuck Knox	32-21-0

**Replaced after two games in 1982*

FIRST PLAYER SELECTED

1976	Steve Niehaus, DT, Notre Dame
1977	Steve August, G, Tulsa
1978	Keith Simpson, DB, Memphis State
1979	Manu Tuiasosopo, DT, UCLA
1980	Jacob Green, DE, Texas A&M
1981	Kenny Easley, S, UCLA
1982	Jeff Bryant, DE, Clemson
1983	Curt Warner, RB, Penn State
1984	Terry Taylor, CB, Southern Illinois
1984*	Gordon Hudson, TE, BYU
1985	(2) Owen Gill, RB, Iowa
1986	John L. Williams, RB, Florida

**Supplemental Draft*

TAMPA BAY BUCCANEERS

1974 Commissioner Pete Rozelle awarded a National Football League franchise to Tampa Bay in a press conference at New York's Drake Hotel, April 24. Rozelle said the league long had been impressed by Tampa Bay's strong support of NFL preseason games over the years. Overall, 13 preseason contests had been held at Tampa Stadium with an average attendance of 41,000. Philadelphia construction tycoon Tom McCloskey was awarded the franchise, October 30, but he withdrew two weeks later. The franchise was awarded to Hugh F. Culverhouse, a Jacksonville attorney and real-estate investor, for $16 million, December 5. Culverhouse previously had attempted to purchase the Los Angeles Rams.

1975 More than 400 nicknames for the team were submitted to an advisory board and Culverhouse selected Buccaneers, February 15. The Tampa City Council voted to approve expansion of Tampa Stadium from 46,500 to 72,000 seats, making it the seventh-largest stadium in the NFL. The Buccaneers adopted the colors of orange and white with red trim and approved the symbol of a swashbuckling buccaneer. Culverhouse signed John McKay of USC to a five-year contract as head coach, October 31.

1976 Tampa Bay selected 39 players (20 defensive, 19 offensive) in the veteran-allocation draft in New York, March 30. The Buccaneers made their first trade, sending two players and a draft choice to San Francisco for quarterback Steve Spurrier, the former Heisman Trophy winner from Florida, April 2. A week later, Tampa Bay had the first pick in the college draft and selected Lee Roy Selmon, the All-America middle guard from Oklahoma. The Buccaneers drafted his brother, Dewey, a defensive tackle, on the second round. The Buccaneers played their first preseason game on July 31, losing 26-3 to the Los Angeles Rams. Two weeks later, they defeated Atlanta 17-3 for the franchise's first victory. The Buccaneers, the fifth team in the AFC West, became the first 0-14 team in NFL history, and the first team to go winless since the 1960 Dallas Cowboys. They failed to score a touchdown in their first three league games and were shut out five times. They opened with a 20-0 loss in Houston, September 12. A week later, San Diego spoiled Tampa Bay's home opener, 23-0. While some of the defeats were one-sided, others were frustratingly close, such as a 23-20 final-minute setback to Miami on October 24. Tampa Bay's leading rusher was Louis Carter, who gained 521 yards. Spurrier, who alternated with rookie Parnell Dickinson, was the leading passer.

1977 With the first selection in the draft, the Buccaneers picked Ricky Bell, a running back from USC. The Buccaneers were realigned into the Central Division of the NFC. A unique schedule permitted the team to play one game against every team in its new conference. With McKay emphasizing defense, Tampa Bay ranked ninth in the NFC in defensive statistics. However, the offense scored a league-low 103 points and finished last in the NFL in every major offensive category. The troubles began in the preseason when quarterback Mike Boryla suffered a knee injury and was lost for the season. With Gary Huff also unavailable, the quarterbacking chores fell to untested Randy Hedberg and Jeb Blount. The Buccaneers lost their first 12 games of the season, including six by shutouts, and extended their winless streak to 26 games. But on December 11 in New Orleans, the defense became offensive and scored three touchdowns on interceptions, leading the Buccaneers to their first NFL victory 33-14. More than 8,000 fans were on hand to greet the team when it returned to

Tampa. A week later, Tampa Bay made it two in a row with a 17-7 victory over St. Louis in Tampa.

1978 Tampa Bay traded the first choice in the draft to Houston for tight end Jimmie Giles and four draft choices. The Oilers selected Earl Campbell; one of the Buccaneers' choices was Doug Williams, a quarterback from Grambling. After two close losses to open the season, the Buccaneers defeated Minnesota 16-10. Lee Roy Selmon sparked the victory by recording three sacks. The team followed with a 14-9 victory over Atlanta on September 24. With an improving offense, the Buccaneers won three more games during the season and finished 5-11. Williams had his best game on October 8 when he threw for 226 yards in a 30-13 victory over Kansas City. In a loss to the New York Giants on October 15, Jimmy DuBose became the first Buccaneers running back to exceed 100 yards rushing in a game.

1979 The Buccaneers opened the season with a convincing 31-16 victory over Detroit. A blossoming offense then sparked consecutive victories over Baltimore, Green Bay, and Los Angeles. On September 30, rookie Jerry Eckwood scored on the longest touchdown run in team history—61 yards—to lead the Buccaneers to a 17-13 win over the Chicago Bears. That victory preserved Tampa Bay's status as the lone unbeaten club in the NFL. Following a loss to the New York Giants, the team won four times in the next six weeks to move within one victory of clinching the divisional crown. On November 25, Bell rushed for 101 yards to become the first Tampa Bay runner to surpass the 1,000-yard mark in a season, but Minnesota blocked two extra points, a punt, and a field goal to win 23-22. The defeat was the first of three in a row for the Buccaneers, and forced a must-win situation in the season finale against Kansas City. Playing in a downpour, the Buccaneers won 3-0 on a 19-yard field goal in the fourth quarter. Tampa Bay finished 10-6 to tie the Bears for first place in the NFC Central. But the Buccaneers won the division on a tiebreaker. Lee Roy Selmon was named the NFC's defensive player of the year. Bell finished with 1,263 yards rushing. The Buccaneers defeated Philadelphia in a divisional playoff game 24-17. In the NFC Championship Game on January 6, the Buccaneers were shut out by the Rams 9-0.

1980 The Buccaneers posted a 17-12 victory over Cincinnati in the season opener. On September 11, they avenged their loss in the title game by defeating Los Angeles 10-9. But Tampa Bay then stumbled to four losses and a tie in the next five games. Consecutive victories over San Francisco and the New York Giants improved their record to 4-4-1, but the Buccaneers won just one game in the final seven weeks and finished 5-10-1. The team's biggest failure was in its own division, where it went 1-6-1. Despite the decline, Williams had his best season, throwing for 3,396 yards and 20 touchdowns.

1981 Linebacker Hugh Green of Pittsburgh was Tampa Bay's top draft pick and became an immediate starter. Second-round pick James Wilder, a running back from Missouri, also started. The Buccaneers opened the season with a 21-13 victory over Minnesota. With Williams on a tear, the club improved its record to 4-2 after consecutive victories over Detroit and Green Bay. But a midseason slump produced four defeats in five weeks, and Tampa Bay fell to 5-6. Trailing Minnesota by two games, on November 22, the offense jelled to lead a 37-3 rout of Green Bay. The Buccaneers followed with back-to-back victories over New Orleans and Atlanta and assumed first place in the division. But a loss to San Diego dropped the team into a first-place tie with Detroit, setting up a battle for the division championship with the Lions. In the season finale, the Buccaneers became the first visiting team in 1981 to win in the Pontiac Silverdome by defeating the Lions 20-17. David Logan, a nose tackle, scored the winning touchdown on a 21-yard run with a recovered fumble. Tampa Bay won the division with a 9-7 record. Williams passed for a career-high 3,563 yards, and Kevin House caught 56 passes for 1,176 yards. The Buccaneers' revitalized defense was led by Cedric Brown's club-record nine interceptions. In a divisional playoff game in Dallas on January 2, the Buccaneers were beaten by the Cowboys 38-0.

1982 Bell, Dewey Selmon, and linebacker David Lewis were traded to San Diego. The strike-shortened regular season started with three straight losses, but a 23-17 victory over Miami turned it around, November 29. The Buccaneers won five of their last six games, including a dramatic comeback in the season finale to beat the Chicago Bears 26-23 in overtime and qualify as one of the 16 teams in the Super Bowl tournament. A 33-yard field goal by Bill Capece 3:14 into overtime won the game after a 40-yard field goal by Capece with 26 seconds left in regulation had tied it and capped the greatest comeback in Tampa Bay history (17 points in 22 minutes). However, the season ended on a familiar note a week later as Dallas eliminated the Buccaneers for the second consecutive season with a first-round victory at Texas Stadium, 30-17. Wilder started to develop into one of the most productive backs in the NFL, gaining 324 yards rushing and finishing third in the league with 53 receptions. Lee Roy Selmon and Green led the NFC's top-ranked defense.

1983 The Buccaneers lost their first nine games and finished 2-14 and in last place in the Central Division. Most of the Buccaneers' problems were on offense, where they ranked last in the NFL. After Williams signed with the USFL during the offseason, Tampa Bay traded a 1984 first-round draft choice to Cincinnati for quarterback Jack Thompson, who threw for 2,906 yards and 18 touchdowns but couldn't generate a consistent attack. Wilder led the team in rushing (640 yards) and receiving (57 catches), despite missing six games with injuries. He gained a team-record 219 yards, the most by an NFL running back since 1977, in a 17-12 victory at Minnesota, November 6.

1984 In the offseason, Tampa Bay acquired quarterback Steve DeBerg from Denver. After two losses, DeBerg relieved Thompson against Detroit and led a 21-17 come-from-behind victory. DeBerg started the last 13 games and passed for 3,554 yards to lead Tampa Bay to a 6-10 record, good for third place. McKay announced his resignation as head coach on November 5, one day after a 27-24 loss at Minnesota that marked the Buccaneers' fourth consecutive defeat. The resignation became effective at the end of the season, when McKay would assume a new role as president of the club. Tampa Bay got a remarkable season from Wilder, who set team records for rushing (1,544 yards) and receiving (85 catches for 685 yards), and an NFL record for carries in a season (407). In the season finale against the New York Jets, McKay ordered the defense to let the Jets score, thus giving Wilder a chance to break O.J. Simpson's NFL record of 2,243 yards from scrimmage. Wilder still fell short, Eric Dickerson of the Rams broke the record, and the Buccaneers received a fine for the move. Selmon was chosen a Pro Bowl starter for the sixth consecutive season.

1985 Former Atlanta Falcons coach Leeman Bennett became just the second head coach in Tampa Bay history when he was chosen to succeed McKay, January 23. The Buccaneers had to play the entire season without Selmon, who sustained a herniated disc prior to the start of training camp. In addition, Green was traded to Miami. The Buccaneers lost their first nine games before shutting out St. Louis 16-0. They also lost their final four to finish with a 2-14 record. Wilder again was the team leader, with 1,300 yards rushing, 53 receptions, and 10 touchdowns.

1986 Selmon retired, April 23. The Buccaneers chose Auburn's Heisman Trophy-winning running back Bo Jackson with the first pick in the draft.

MEMBERS OF HALL OF FAME:
None

BUCCANEERS RECORD, 1976-85

Year	Won	Lost	Tied	Pct.	Fin.	Pts.	OP
1976	0	14	0	.000	5	125	412
1977	2	12	0	.143	5	103	223
1978	5	11	0	.313	5	241	259
1979a	10	6	0	.625	1	273	237
1980	5	10	1	.344	4	271	341
1981b	9	7	0	.563	1	315	268
1982c	5	4	0	.556	7	158	178
1983	2	14	0	.125	5	241	380
1984	6	10	0	.375	3	335	380
1985	2	14	0	.125	5	294	448
10 Years	46	102	1	.312		2,356	3,126

aNFC Central Division Champion; 1-1 in Playoffs
bNFC Central Division Champion; 0-1 in Playoffs
cNFC Qualifier for Playoffs; 0-1 in Playoffs

RECORD HOLDERS

CAREER

Rushing attempts	James Wilder, 1981-85	1,123
Rushing yards	James Wilder, 1981-85	4,178
Pass attempts	Doug Williams, 1978-82	1,890
Pass completions	Doug Williams, 1978-82	895
Passing yards	Doug Williams, 1978-82	12,648
Touchdown passes	Doug Williams, 1978-82	73
Receptions	James Wilder, 1981-85	296
Receiving yards	Kevin House, 1980-85	4,722
Interceptions	Cedric Brown, 1977-84	29
Punting average	Frank Garcia, 1983-85	42.0
Punt return avg.	Leon Bright, 1984-85	8.5
Kickoff return avg.	Phil Freeman, 1985	22.6
Field goals	Bill Capece, 1981-83	43
Touchdowns	James Wilder, 1981-85	38
Points	James Wilder, 1981-85	228

SEASON

Rushing attempts	James Wilder, 1984	407
Rushing yards	James Wilder, 1984	1,544
Pass attempts	Doug Williams, 1980	521
Pass completions	Steve DeBerg, 1984	308
Passing yards	Doug Williams, 1981	3,563
Touchdown passes	Doug Williams, 1980	20
Receptions	James Wilder, 1984	85
Receiving yards	Kevin House, 1981	1,176
Interceptions	Cedric Brown, 1981	9
Punting average	Larry Swider, 1981	42.7
Punt return avg.	Danny Reece, 1978	8.9
Kickoff return avg.	Isaac Hagins, 1977	23.5
Field goals	Donald Igwebuike, 1985	22
Touchdowns	James Wilder, 1984	13
Points	Donald Igwebuike, 1985	96

GAME

Rushing attempts	James Wilder, 9-30-84	43
Rushing yards	James Wilder, 11-6-83	219
Pass attempts	Doug Williams, 9-28-80	56
Pass completions	Doug Williams, 9-28-80	30
	Doug Williams, 11-16-80	30
	Jack Thompson, 9-25-83	30
Passing yards	Doug Williams, 11-16-80	486
Touchdown passes	Doug Williams, 11-16-80	4
	Doug Williams, 10-4-81	4
	Jack Thompson, 11-27-83	4
	Steve DeBerg, 10-20-85	4
Receptions	James Wilder, 9-15-85	13
Receiving yards	Kevin House, 10-18-81	178
Interceptions	16 times	2
Field goals	Bill Capece, 10-30-83	4
	Bill Capece, 1-2-83	4
	Donald Igwebuike, 11-24-85	4
Touchdowns	Jimmie Giles, 10-20-85	4
Points	Jimmie Giles, 10-20-85	24

COACHING HISTORY

1976-84	John McKay	45-91-1
1985	Leeman Bennett	2-14-0

FIRST PLAYER SELECTED

1976 Lee Roy Selmon, DE, Oklahoma
1977 Ricky Bell, RB, USC
1978 Doug Williams, QB, Grambling
1979 (2) Greg Roberts, G, Oklahoma
1980 Ray Snell, G, Wisconsin
1981 Hugh Green, LB, Pittsburgh
1982 Sean Farrell, G, Penn State
1983 (2) Randy Grimes, C, Baylor
1984 (2) Keith Browner, LB, USC
1984* Steve Young, QB, BYU
1985 Ron Holmes, DE, Washington
1986 Bo Jackson, RB, Auburn
**Supplemental Draft*

WASHINGTON REDSKINS

1932 George Preston Marshall of Washington, D.C., the head of a four-man syndicate that included Vincent Bendix, Jay O'Brien, and M. Dorland Doyle, was granted a National Football League franchise for Boston. The owners contracted to play at Braves Field, home of the National League baseball team, and decided to call their team the Braves, as well. Lud Wray was hired as the first coach. The Braves lost their first game 14-0 to Brooklyn, but defeated the New York Giants the next week 14-6. Led by three rookies—tailback Cliff Battles, the NFL's leading rusher with 576 yards, fullback Jim Musick, and tackle Glen (Turk) Edwards—the Braves went 4-4-2, including tying the champion Bears and winning their last two games. Despite their success, by the end of the season, the Braves had lost $46,000. Marshall's three partners pulled out, leaving him as sole owner of the team.

1933 Marshall moved the club to Fenway Park, home of baseball's American League Red Sox. He changed the name of the team to Redskins. Wray quit to coach Philadelphia. Marshall hired a full-blooded Indian as the team's coach, William (Lone Star) Dietz. On opening day of practice, the entire club was lined up for the team picture in war paint, feathers, and full headdress. Despite the presence of Musick and Battles, who finished first and second in the league in rushing, the team stayed at .500, going 5-5-2. The Redskins beat both division champions, the Bears and the Giants, but they lost to the fifth-place Steelers and tied the Cardinals, the team with the poorest record in the league. Part of the problem was Dietz's love for trick plays, even when they didn't work. By the end of the season, he occasionally was paying Battles extra to call them. Edwards missed the first three minutes of the first game of the season, and the last seven minutes of the last, but played every minute in between—710 out of a possible 720 minutes. Money was so tight that when the ball was kicked into the stands, Marshall would run to the spot and personally ask that it be returned.

1934 The Redskins had a good crop of rookies and hoped to win their first championship, but only Battles and Edwards played up to expectations. The team finished second—again at .500 with a 6-6 record. Marshall, however, was encouraged by the improved attendance and felt the franchise soon would turn into a money maker.

1935 In an attempt to draw more fans, Marshall dismissed Dietz and hired hometown hero Eddie Casey, a former Harvard player, as his new coach. But the Redskins made the mistake of sending their most productive back—Bill Shepherd—to Detroit for ineffective Doug Nott. With only Battles to carry the load, and with Marshall constantly interfering with Casey's sideline instructions, the Redskins scored more than a touchdown only three times and finished 2-8-1.

1936 Ray Flaherty was signed as the new head coach, and made his position clear from the outset. He insisted that Marshall stay off the field and in the stands. With Flaherty's leadership and outstanding performances by Battles and young fullback Ernest (Pug) Rentner, the Redskins won the Eastern Division championship. They clinched the title on the last day of the season, beating the second-place Giants 14-0. Despite the title, the Redskins hadn't drawn well, especially after the press had blasted Marshall, who, in the midst of the stretch drive, had raised ticket prices on the day of a game without any advance notice. When the Boston fans failed to get excited enough for Marshall, he moved the championship game to New York, where nearly 30,000 people watched Green Bay beat the Redskins 21-6.

1937 The NFL approved the transfer of the Boston franchise to Washington, D.C., February 13. Marshall's showman instincts seemed to blossom in the nation's capital. He organized the Redskins' band and he produced elaborate halftime shows. The Redskins drafted Sammy Baugh, All-America tailback from TCU, then signed him for $8,000 a year. Washington opened its season in Griffith Stadium on a Thursday night, and drew 19,941 to see the Redskins beat the Giants 13-3. Baugh completed 11 of 16 passes in the victory. New York was the victim again in the game that decided the Eastern Division championship. The Redskins won 49-14 in a game that attracted 10,000 Washington fans to New York. A week later, Baugh threw for 335 yards as the Redskins defeated the Chicago Bears 28-21 in the NFL Championship Game. For the season, Baugh led the league in passing, and Battles in rushing with 874 yards.

1938 Battles quit over a salary dispute. Baugh separated his shoulder in the opener, and, when he returned, was not as effective as in his rookie year. Rookies Andy Farkas, a fullback, and Bill Hartman, a tailback, combined with tailback Frank Filchock, who was obtained from Pittsburgh, to keep the Redskins in contention throughout the season. They were eliminated in the final game, a 36-0 loss to the champion Giants.

1939 The Redskins trained at Cheyney, Washington. Flaherty decided to try to keep Baugh healthy by alternating him with Filchock by quarters. The plan was especially beneficial to Filchock, who led the league in touchdown passes and finished second in combined rushing-passing yardage. The Redskins played their first scoreless tie since 1935 against the Giants, October 1. Filchock and Farkas teamed on a record 99-yard touchdown pass play against Pittsburgh, October 15. The Eastern Division title came down to the final game—in fact, the final 45 seconds. But the Redskins' Bo Russell missed a disputed field-goal attempt, and New York won 9-7. Most of the players thought the kick was good, but the referee ruled the kick had sailed to the right of the goal post. On the train ride home, Marshall called Russell to his compartment and, before newsmen, signed him to a 1940 contract.

1940 The Redskins trained at Gonzaga University in Washington. Farkas was lost with a knee injury that required surgery three weeks before the start of the season. A healthy Baugh led the league in passing, set an NFL record with a 51.4-yard punting average, and took the club to a 9-2 record and the Eastern Division championship, beating the Chicago Bears 7-3 along the way. The Bears complained about the officiating, and Marshall ripped them in the newspapers. "The Bears are front-runners," he said. "Quitters. They're not a second-half team, just a bunch of crybabies." Those remarks may have had something to do with what happened in the rematch with the Bears in the NFL Championship Game. For the first time, an NFL game was broadcast coast-to-coast. Chicago, using the T-formation with man-in-motion to perfection, embarrassed the Redskins 73-0. Baugh was asked if an early Washington pass for a touchdown that was dropped would have made any difference. "Sure," drawled Baugh, "the game would have wound up 73-7."

1941 Farkas was back at full strength, all-pro center Charles (Ki) Aldrich joined the team from the Chicago Cardinals, and the Redskins looked better than ever while running up a 5-1 record. Then the roof caved in, and the team lost four in a row to finish 6-5. The killer was a 20-13 loss in which the Giants scored 10 points in the final 50 seconds to knock Washington out of the total picture. During the season finale on December 7, various high-ranking government and military personnel were paged over the public-address system as the Redskins beat Philadelphia 20-14, but it wasn't until after the game most of the fans learned that World War II had begun for the United States.

1942 In the second game of the season, the Giants failed to make one first down, gained only one yard rushing, and completed just one pass, but it was good for a touchdown. Another score on an interception gave New York a 14-7 victory. It was Washington's only loss en route to a 10-1 record. Baugh finished second in the league in passing, but the real story of the season was a suddenly dominant defense. In Flaherty's last game as coach before entering the Navy, he was able to avenge the 73-0 defeat to the Bears. To motivate the team, he simply wrote "73-0" in large figures on the blackboard in the Washington dressing room the day of the NFL Championship Game. That was enough as Baugh threw for one touchdown and Farkas ran for another for a 14-6 triumph that stopped the Bears' undefeated string at 18.

1943 Arthur (Dutch) Bergman took over as head coach. With Baugh dominating the league, the Redskins went 6-0-1 to start the season. They then lost their last three games, including back-to-back contests with the Giants, which forced a divisional playoff in New York. On December 19, Baugh threw three touchdown passes to lead the Redskins to a 28-0 victory over the Giants. The next week, Baugh was injured in the NFL Championship Game, and the Bears beat the Redskins 41-21. For the season, Baugh led the NFL in passing, punting, and interceptions, setting a league record with 11 interceptions.

1944 Dudley DeGroot was the new head coach, and the new weapon in Washington was the T-formation. Marshall hired Clark Shaughnessy, who had been a voluntary assistant coach for the Bears, to teach it to Baugh and company. Baugh, who had always been a tailback, didn't care for it at first, but then slowly made the adjustment. Filchock, just out of the Coast Guard, adapted to it immediately and split time with Baugh. Filchock led the league in passing, and Baugh was second. Just as in the previous year, the Redskins faded after a 5-0-1 start, finishing 6-3-1 and in third place.

1945 Baugh, who had to do some running while operating the Single Wing, said he could "operate the T in a top hat and tails." He made it look almost that easy in a 24-14 win over the Giants in which he completed 20 of 24 passes for 265 yards and two touchdowns. The four misses were "throwaways," Baugh said. Baugh completed 70.3 percent of his passes to set an NFL record, while leading the league in passing. He got unexpected help from fullback Frank Akins, who finished second in the league in rushing with 797 yards. The Redskins won the Eastern Division title with an 8-2 record. They lost the NFL Championship Game to the Cleveland Rams 15-14 in sub-zero weather when Baugh's pass hit the goal post for a safety and Bob Waterfield's try for a Rams extra point hit the crossbar and bounced over for the margin of victory.

1946 Cal Rossi, a back from UCLA, was the top draftee but his selection was voided because he still had college eligibility remaining. Marshall refused to compete with the new All-America Football Conference, and lost some key players, such as tackle Willie Wilkin, placekicker Joe Aguirre, and even the coach, DeGroot. Turk Edwards took over as the new coach. Marshall traded Filchock to the New York Giants, a deal that backfired when Baugh was injured. Filchock led the Giants to the Eastern Division championship. The Redskins turned from near-champions to a 5-5-1 team.

1947 Cal Rossi was the number-one choice again. Rossi met with Marshall and Edwards, voiced his appreciation of their offer, and then returned to California to become a schoolteacher and small businessman. The Redskins lost 45-42 to Philadelphia on opening day and that set the tone for the season. Baugh had his biggest year, leading the league in passing while setting NFL records for attempts (354), completions (210), and passing yardage (2,938). Baugh connected with halfbacks Bob Nussbaumer and Eddie Saenz and end Hugh (Bones) Taylor enough to make the Redskins one of the top offensive teams in the league. But the NFL's poorest defense helped drop the Redskins to a 4-8 record and fourth place.

1948 Impressed with Alabama's Harry Gilmer, and worried about grooming a successor to Baugh, Marshall sold the draft rights to Mississippi quarterback Charlie Conerly and signed Gilmer as the top draft choice. Baugh proved there still was some life in his arm, however, as he passed for an NFL record 446 yards in beating Boston 59-21, October 31. Despite a record 13 interceptions by rookie safety Dan Sandifer, the Redskins' erratic defense kept them away from the championship and in second place with a 7-5 record. Baugh threw for 2,599 yards and 22 touchdowns.

1949 Edwards was moved to the front office, and Admiral John (Billick) Whelchel, former Naval Academy coach, was brought in to take over as coach. He signed a five-year contract, but was gone three games before the end of the season and replaced by Herman Ball, a team scout. The team finished 4-7-1, despite Baugh's leading the league in passing for the sixth time. There was considerable discontent in the media over Marshall's failure to sign black players.

1950 The Redskins became one of the first two pro teams to have all of their games televised. Taylor and fullback Rob Goode had good seasons, but there wasn't much more help for the aging Baugh. Gilmer and rookie halfback Charlie (Choo-Choo) Justice both were major disappointments, as was the final 3-9 record.

1951 Three lopsided losses into the season, Ball was fired. Marshall wanted to hire Heartley (Hunk) Anderson, a Bears assistant coach, but George Halas wouldn't allow it unless the Redskins threw tackle Paul Lipscomb into the deal. Marshall refused and decided instead to hire former Redskins halfback Dick Todd. The team responded by winning its first two games for Todd and finished third at 5-7. Goode finished second in the league in rushing with 951 yards, but the passing game, led by the aging Baugh and the journeyman Gilmer, was weak.

1952 Todd signed for another year as coach, but resigned before September. He said he had to have respect to stay as coach, and, although he liked Marshall, he didn't "agree with the way he runs the Redskins." Earl (Curly) Lambeau, the former coach of the Green Bay Packers, took over. Baugh broke his hand in a preseason game and was limited to holding for kicks and teaching rookie Eddie LeBaron the nuances of quarterbacking in the pros. Gilmer backed up LeBaron. After a 2-2 start, the Redskins lost six in a row before Baugh returned to the starting lineup. He led the Redskins to two victories, 27-17 over the Giants and 27-21 over the Eagles, and then retired after 16 years in Washington.

1953 After a slow start, the Redskins turned their season around and won four of their last six to finish 6-5-1 and in third place. Justice finally contributed as had been expected, and Taylor had another good year, but the key to the surge was strong defense built around end Gene Brito, rookie tackle Dick Modzelewski, linebacker Chuck Drazenovich and defensive back Don Doll. A 10-0 shutout of Philadelphia was Lambeau's two hundred and thirtieth—and last—NFL victory.

1954 Marshall hired Joe Kuharich, former coach at the University of San Francisco, as head coach. But the team was devastated before the season when LeBaron and Brito jumped to the Canadian Football League and Doll was traded to the Rams. With the defense giving up the most points in the league and the offense struggling behind rookie quarterback Al Dorow, the Redskins fell to 3-9. Tragedy struck near the end of the season when guard Dave Sparks died of a heart attack following a 34-14 loss to Cleveland.

1955 LeBaron and Brito returned from Canada and were joined on the new-look Redskins by halfback Vic Janowicz, the former Heisman Trophy winner from Ohio State who abandoned a pro baseball career to try the NFL. The Redskins scored 21 points in 137 seconds in a game with Philadelphia, October 1. Trailing 16-0 in the third quarter, LeBaron passed to Janowicz for a touchdown. Ralph Thomas recovered the kickoff in the end zone for another touchdown. LaVern Torgeson recovered a fumble on the Eagles' 13. Janowicz scored immediately, and the Redskins won 31-30. Janowicz wound up as the second-leading scorer in the league, and the rejuvenated Redskins finished second in the Eastern Conference with an 8-4 record.

1956 In a tragic training camp accident, Janowicz was thrown from a car and struck a tree, suffering brain damage, which ended his football career. Sam Baker joined the Redskins following a stint in the Canadian Football League and assumed Janowicz's punting and placekicking duties. Baker led the league with 17 field goals in 25 attempts and was the Redskins' top scorer with 67 points. But the team, demoralized by Janowicz's tragedy and ineffective due to injuries to LeBaron and Dorow, staggered to a 6-6-0 third-place finish.

1957 Defensive back Roy Barni was shot to death in a barroom brawl during training camp. Despite a fine performance by rookie fullback Don Bosseler, the team struggled through most of the season. With three games left, the defense jelled and held Chicago, Philadelphia, and Pittsburgh to a combined total of 13 points. But the Redskins remained under .500 at 5-6-1.

1958 The club continued to have problems keeping pace with NFL contenders. And the pressure on Marshall to begin signing black players was building again. Fullback Johnny Olszewski averaged 5.2 yards per carry after being obtained from the Cardinals, Bosseler was a tough runner, and LeBaron led the league in passing, but the Redskins still couldn't score regularly, and they offered even less defensively. In the season finale, the Redskins had their most impressive performance—a 20-0 victory over Philadelphia—but it wasn't enough to save Kuharich.

1959 Assistant coach Mike Nixon was promoted to the top job, but nothing changed. Bosseler and Olszewski performed well, the defense gave up the most points in the league, and, after two early victories, the Redskins lost eight of nine to finish 3-9. The highlight of the season was Sam Baker's 46-yard field goal that allowed Washington to upset the defending world champion Baltimore Colts 27-24, November 8. The club signed a 30-year lease to play in the proposed D.C. Stadium. Congress gave approval for construction of the stadium.

1960 Still seeking a quarterback after using four number-one choices in seven years in an attempt to solve the problem, the Redskins tried again with Richie Lucas of Penn State, who signed with Buffalo of the new American Football League. Ralph Guglielmi kept the quarterback job, but he had to run for his life much of the season. The club scored 16 or fewer points in eight of its nine losses in a 1-9-2 season, defeating only the first-year Dallas Cowboys.

1961 Nixon was replaced by Bill McPeak, a rookie coach who opened with a rookie quarterback, Norm Snead of Wake Forest, the number-one draft choice. The pair suffered through a frightful season in their first year in new 55,004-seat D.C. Stadium, which opened October 1. The Redskins went 0-12-1 before beating Dallas 34-24 in the final game to avert a winless season. Still, Snead passed for 2,337 yards and 11 touchdowns, the most passing yardage since Baugh's 2,599 in 1948.

1962 Marshall made history in Washington by drafting the Redskins' first black player, Heisman Trophy winner Ernie Davis from Syracuse. Then he traded Davis to Cleveland for Bobby Mitchell and Cleveland's first-round pick Leroy Jackson, two black halfbacks. Guard John Nisby and defensive back Ron Hatcher joined Mitchell and Jackson as the first black players on the Redskins' roster. McPeak's team showed immediate improvement, going 5-7-2. Mitchell was moved to flanker and led the NFL in receiving, with 72 catches for 1,384 yards and 11 touchdowns. Snead showed flashes of brilliance, passing for 2,926 yards and 22 touchdowns.

1963 The Redskins were exciting on offense, with Snead passing to Mitchell and an assortment of good receivers. Snead threw for a team record 3,043 yards. Mitchell again led the NFL in receiving yards, with 1,436 on 69 receptions. But a weak rushing attack and a weaker defense kept the Redskins in sixth place with a 3-11 record.

1964 Snead was traded to Philadelphia for quarterback Sonny Jurgensen. Another controversial deal sent halfback Dick James to the Giants for Sam Huff, the celebrated middle linebacker. Charley Taylor, a halfback from Arizona State, was the number-one draft choice and he joined with Mitchell to inject speed into the Washington offense. Taylor rushed for 755 yards, caught 53 passes, and was voted the NFL's rookie of the year. Huff and rookie defensive back Paul Krause from Iowa put some muscle into the defense. The Redskins won six of eight games in the middle of the season for a 6-8 record. All home games were sellouts. Jurgensen passed for 2,934 yards and 24 touchdowns.

1965 Without a running game to balance it, the Washington offense slipped considerably and the team lost its first five games. But then the club played its greatest comeback game in history, rallying from a 21-point deficit for a 34-31 win over Dallas as Jurgensen passed for more than 400 yards and three touchdowns, November 28. The defense, bolstered by rookie linebacker Chris Hanburger, was better until cornerback Johnny Sample was suspended late in the season for insubordination. The Redskins again finished 6-8.

1966 McPeak was released, and Otto Graham, the former Cleveland Browns quarterback, was named coach and general manager. Graham emphasized the passing game even more than McPeak, and Jurgensen set NFL records with 436 attempts and 254 completions, while passing for 3,209 yards and 28 touchdowns. Midway through the season, Taylor was moved to split end; he led the NFL with 72 receptions for 1,119 yards and 12 touchdowns. Graham also overhauled the defense—putting in seven new starters—but the results weren't as successful, and the team finished 7-7.

1967 Jurgensen won the league passing title, setting league records for attempts (508), completions (288), and yards (3,747). He also passed for 31 touchdowns, a club record. Three Redskins receivers were among the top four in the league. Taylor led the league with 70 catches, tight end Jerry Smith had 67, and Mitchell had 60. But the running threat was still missing, the kicking game deteriorated, and Washington finished in third place in the four-team Capitol Division.

1968 Middle linebacker Huff announced his retirement. Graham sent a future first-round draft pick to Los Angeles for quarterback Gary Beban, the Heisman Trophy winner from UCLA. Beban, after signing a lucrative contract, flopped in training camp, spent most of the year on the taxi squad, and was even tried unsuccessfully as a running back late in the season. Safety Paul Krause was traded to Minnesota. After a disappointing 5-9 season, due in part to injuries that cut Jurgensen's passing yardage to 1,980, Graham was fired.

1969 Vince Lombardi left Green Bay to become part-owner, executive vice president, and head coach of the Redskins. Marshall died at age 72, August 9. Lombardi constructed what the other Washington coaches seemingly had ignored—a strong running game. Rookie halfback Larry Brown of Kansas State (888 yards) and fullback Charley Harraway (428 yards) formed a new backfield combination, while Jurgensen led the NFL in passing with 3,102 yards. The defense tightened considerably, led by defensive backs Pat Fischer and Brig Owens, and linebackers Hanburger and Huff, who came out of retirement to play for Lombardi for one year. Washington had its first winning season since 1955, 7-5-2.

1970 Two weeks before the start of the season, on September 3, Lombardi died of cancer. Assistant coach Bill Austin took over, but the team didn't play with the same precision. Only Brown, coming into his own as an all-pro, had an outstanding year, becoming the first Redskin ever to gain 1,000 yards rushing. He ran for 1,125 on 237 carries, a 4.8 average. Jurgensen threw for 2,354 yards and finished second in the NFC in passing.

1971 Former Los Angeles Rams coach George Allen was named the new head coach and general manager of the Redskins. Allen immediately implemented the plan he made so successful as the Rams' coach. He started trading for as many veteran players as possible. They included quarterback Billy Kilmer, who came from New Orleans; wide receiver Roy Jefferson from Baltimore; defensive tackle Diron Talbert and linebacker Jack Pardee from the Rams; defensive end Ron McDole from Buffalo; defensive end Verlon Biggs from the New York Jets; and others, who collectively became known as the Over the Hill Gang. Construction began on Redskin Park, the team's new practice and training-camp facility near Dulles Airport. Washington finished with a 9-4-1 record, the most Redskins' victories in 29 years, and got into its first playoff game in 26 years. Kilmer took over for the injured Jurgensen and passed for 2,221 yards, Brown rushed for 948 yards, and the defense gave up the second-fewest points in the NFC. After leading at halftime, the Redskins, the NFC wild card team, lost to San Francisco 24-20 in an NFC divisional playoff. Allen was named NFC coach of the year.

1972 Led by an outstanding defensive unit, the Redskins beat out Dallas for the division title. It was the Redskins' first championship in 30 years. Although Jurgensen again was injured much of the time, the Washington offense operated efficiently, with Kilmer (1,648 yards and 19 touchdowns) and Brown maintaining ball control. Although he missed two games with injuries, Brown gained 1,216 yards to lead the NFC in rushing and set a Redskins' record. In the first round of the playoffs, the Redskins defeated Green Bay 16-3. Then, in the NFC Championship Game, the Redskins defeated the Cowboys 26-3 to gain their first Super Bowl. The Miami Dolphins, at the peak of their efficiency, downed the Redskins 14-7 in Super Bowl VII in the Los Angeles Memorial Coliseum, January 14.

1973 Allen added more old names—defensive back Ken Houston and linebacker Dave Robinson—to his Over the Hill Gang. Led again by the NFC's number-two defense, the Redskins finished 10-4 and earned a wild card playoff berth. Jurgensen and Kilmer shared playing time at quarterback. Kilmer passed for 1,656 yards and Jurgensen for 904. Brown gained 860 yards rushing, but his average dipped to 3.2 yards as he began to slow down from heavy usage in his first five years. In an NFC Divisional Playoff Game, the Minnesota Vikings exploded in the fourth quarter to beat the Redskins 27-20.

1974 Jack Kent Cooke became the majority stockholder of the Redskins. The Over the Hill Gang proved it wasn't over the hill, compiling another 10-4 season and making it to the playoffs for the fourth straight season. Jurgensen celebrated his fortieth birthday and led the NFC in passing. Brown was slowed with knee injuries, gaining only 430 yards. Some signs of age began to show up front in the Redskins' units. In the first round of the playoffs, the Redskins, again the wild card team, were beaten by the Los Angeles Rams 19-10.

1975 After 18 seasons in the league, 11 as a Redskin, Jurgensen retired. Allen, who rarely employed first-year players, came up with an outstanding rookie in running back Mike Thomas of Nevada-Las Vegas. Thomas rushed for 919 yards to lead the team. Kilmer passed for 2,440 yards, but overall, the Redskins were sluggish on offense and played the poorest defense of the Allen years to miss the playoffs for the first time since he took over as coach. The Redskins got off to a 6-2 start, but dropped to 8-6. With the wild card berth on the line late in the season, they were thrashed by Dallas 31-10. Taylor became the NFL's all-time leading receiver, catching 53 passes for a career total of 635.

1976 The number-one draft choice was traded to Miami for the rights to quarterback Joe Theismann, the eighth straight year the team had gone without a pick in the first round. Allen signed free-agent running backs John Riggins and Calvin Hill. Again, the reports of the Redskins' collapse proved exaggerated. A new quarterback controversy developed between Kilmer and Theismann. The offense got 1,101 yards from Thomas. Dallas won the Eastern Division title, but Washington's 10-4 record was good for the wild card berth again. In the first round of the playoffs, the Redskins were beaten 35-20 by Minnesota.

1977 Cornerback Lemar Parrish and defensive end Coy Bacon were acquired in a trade with Cincinnati in June. Billy Kilmer opened the year as the starting quarterback, but later split time with Joe Theismann. The Redskins lost the opener when the Giants staged a late rally to win 20-17. The defeat was the first for an Allen-coached team in a season opener. Led by the defense, the Redskins rebounded with consecutive victories over Atlanta, St. Louis, and Tampa Bay. On October 16, Riggins suffered a knee injury and was lost for the season, joining Hanburger and Fischer on injured reserve. On December 10, Kilmer made his first start in six weeks and guided the team to successive wins over St. Louis and Los Angeles. Despite a 9-5 record, the Redskins were edged out of the wild card spot for the playoffs by Chicago. The defense allowed only 189 points, a team record.

1978 Allen left to coach the Rams and was replaced by Jack Pardee, the former head coach of the Bears and a linebacker with the Redskins. Two 13-year veterans, tight end Jerry Smith and Charley Taylor, the NFL's all-time leading receiver, retired. Theismann won the job as starting quarterback and guided the team to six successive victories to open the season. The victory string included an offensive shootout with Philadelphia (35-30) and a defensive struggle with Dallas (9-5). The start was the club's best in 35 years. However, the offense settled into a prolonged slump, and the Redskins won only two games in the final 10 weeks to drop to 8-8. Riggins returned to lead the team in rushing with 1,014 yards.

1979 The Redskins opened the year with a narrow loss to Houston, then rolled to six victories in the next seven weeks. The defense posted one shutout in the streak and held four other opponents to nine points or less. The lone defeat, to Philadelphia, was avenged on October 21 with a 17-7 Redskins victory. Two more losses dropped the Redskins' record to 6-4, but then they won four games in the next five weeks. This time the spark was provided by the offense, which scored 30 or more points in all four games. Requiring a victory to advance to the playoffs, the Redskins ended the season with a divisional showdown in Dallas. Despite building a 34-21 lead, the Redskins couldn't stop Roger Staubach, who passed for two late touchdowns and a 35-34 Dallas victory. The Redskins finished 10-6, and Theismann ended the season with 2,797 yards passing and 20 touchdowns. The defense finished with 47 sacks, 26 interceptions, and 34 fumble recoveries. Pardee was named NFL coach of the year.

1980 With its first number-one draft choice since 1968, Washington selected Art Monk, a wide receiver from Syracuse. Monk proceeded to lead the team in pass receptions with 58 for 797 yards. But the offense was hurt when Riggins sat out the season due to a contract dispute. The Redskins won their first game on September 14 with a 23-21 victory over the Giants, but won only twice more in the next 11 weeks. On December 7, the Redskins shut off San Diego's passing attack and defeated the Chargers 40-17. The victory preceded season-closing victories over the Giants and St. Louis for a 6-10 final record. Despite the losing record, the Redskins' pass defense was rated best in the NFL, permitting an average of only 135.7 yards per game and a completion rate of 47 percent by opposing quarterbacks. Theismann threw for a personal high 2,962 yards. Safety Ken Houston retired after the season.

1981 Pardee was released as head coach and replaced on January 13 by Joe Gibbs, the San Diego Chargers' offensive coordinator. The offense received an apparent boost when Riggins rejoined the team, Joe Washington was acquired from Baltimore, and Terry Metcalf was acquired from St. Louis. Still, the Redskins opened the year with five straight losses, as the offense was slow to get untracked. Washington won its first game on October 11 with a 24-7 victory over Chicago. Two weeks later, Theismann converted a broken play into a one-yard touchdown run and a 24-22 victory over New England. The victory sparked the dormant offense and was the first of four in a row, including a 42-21 win over St. Louis on November 1 in which Riggins ran for three touchdowns. Following two losses, the Redskins closed out their season by defeating Philadelphia, Baltimore, and the Los Angeles Rams to finish 8-8. Washington led the club with 916 yards rushing and 70 pass receptions, while Theismann passed for 3,568 yards on a club-record 293 completions.

1982 With an 0-4 preseason giving concern about another slow start, Mark Moseley kicked a 26-yard field goal in overtime to give the Redskins a 37-34 victory over the Eagles in the opener. Moseley was the big story for the Redskins all during the strike-shortened season. He kicked a record 21 consecutive field goals, was named the NFL's most valuable player, and continually was the difference for the Redskins. He kicked four field goals as Washington defeated St. Louis 12-7 and three field goals to beat the Giants 15-14. Despite a midseason loss to Dallas, the Redskins finished 8-1, the best record in the NFL. Although the top offensive performer during the regular season was Theismann, who led the NFC in passing, Riggins became the main man in the playoffs. In the first round of the Super Bowl tournament, Washington beat Detroit 31-7. The next week, Riggins pounded for 185 yards, and Washington beat Minnesota 21-7. In the NFC Championship Game, Riggins ran for 140 yards as the Redskins defeated the Cowboys 31-17. Washington won Super Bowl XVII 27-17 over Miami as Riggins ran for a record 166 yards, including the winning 43-yard touchdown in the fourth quarter.

1983 After an opening-day 31-30 loss to Dallas, Washington took up where it left off in 1982. The Redskins won five in a row, including a dramatic 37-35 victory over the Los Angeles Raiders October 2, in which Washington trailed 35-20 midway through the fourth quarter. The Redskins finished with nine consecutive victories and clinched the title on December 11 with a 31-10 victory over the Cowboys. Washington had the best record in the NFL, 14-2. The Redskins set an NFL record by scoring 541 points; Moseley led the NFL with 161 points, the most ever by a kicker; Theismann passed for 3,714 yards and 29 touchdowns; wide receiver Charlie Brown tied for the NFC lead with 78 receptions; and Riggins set a team record with 1,347 yards rushing and an NFL record with 24 touchdowns. The juggernaut continued in the playoffs, where the Redskins defeated the Rams 51-7. In the NFC Championship Game, Washington jumped to a 21-0 lead over San Francisco but needed a last-minute field goal by Moseley to win 24-21. The dream season came to an end in Super Bowl XVIII in Tampa, Florida, when the Raiders defeated the Redskins 38-9.

1984 The Redskins came out of the gate slowly, losing their first two. They won five games by convincing margins before a midseason slump. Four victories to end the season gave them a final 11-5 record. On December 9, Dallas jumped to a 21-6 halftime lead, but the Redskins came back to win 30-28 for their first-ever sweep of the Cowboys. The next week, Moseley kicked a 37-yard field goal at the end of the game to give the Redskins a 29-27 victory over the Cardinals and Washington's third consecutive NFC East title. Monk caught 11 passes against the Cardinals to finish the season with an NFL record 106 receptions, breaking a 20-year-old mark. Theismann passed for 3,391 yards, and Riggins gained 1,239. In an NFC Divisional Playoff Game, the Bears sacked Theismann seven times and controlled Riggins to beat the Redskins 23-19.

1985 Majority owner Jack Kent Cooke purchased the team's remaining stock on February 28. A 44-14 loss to Dallas in the season opener initiated a 1-3 start that put Washington in last place, from where the Redskins never could catch up. Washington overcame the loss of Theismann, who suffered a compound fracture of his right leg on a sack, and beat the Giants 23-21, November 18. Rookie Jay Schroeder threw the winning touchdown pass to tight end Clint Didier after the Redskins had recovered an onside kick. George Rogers, obtained in the offseason, rushed for 206 yards, a team record, in a 27-16 victory over St. Louis in the season finale. The Redskins finished 10-6, the same record as the Cowboys and the Giants, but missed out on the playoffs due to a tiebreaker. Monk finished second in the NFL with 91 receptions.

1986 In April, the Redskins released Riggins, the club's all-time rushing leader.

MEMBERS OF HALL OF FAME:

Cliff Battles, Sammy Baugh, Bill Dudley, Glen (Turk) Edwards, Ray Flaherty, Ken Houston, Sam Huff, David (Deacon) Jones, Sonny Jurgensen, Earl (Curly) Lambeau, Vince Lombardi, George Preston Marshall, Wayne Millner, Bobby Mitchell, Charley Taylor

REDSKINS RECORD, 1932-85

Year	Won	Lost	Tied	Pct.	Fin.	Pts.	OP
Boston Braves							
1932	4	4	2	.500	4	55	79
Boston Redskins							
1933	5	5	2	.500	3	103	97
1934	6	6	0	.500	2	107	94
1935	2	8	1	.200	4	65	123
1936a	7	5	0	.583	1	149	110
Washington Redskins							
1937b	8	3	0	.727	1	195	120
1938	6	3	2	.667	2	148	154
1939	8	2	1	.800	2	242	94
1940a	9	2	0	.818	1	245	142
1941	6	5	0	.545	3	176	174
1942b	10	1	0	.909	1	227	102
1943c	6	3	1	.667	1	229	137
1944	6	3	1	.667	3	169	180
1945a	8	2	0	.800	1	209	121
1946	5	5	1	.500	3t	171	191
1947	4	8	0	.333	4	295	367
1948	7	5	0	.583	2	291	287
1949	4	7	1	.364	4	268	339
1950	3	9	0	.250	6	232	326
1951	5	7	0	.417	3	183	296
1952	4	8	0	.333	5t	240	287
1953	6	5	1	.545	3	208	215
1954	3	9	0	.250	5	207	432
1955	8	4	0	.667	2	246	222
1956	6	6	0	.500	3	183	225
1957	5	6	1	.455	4	251	230
1958	4	7	1	.364	4	214	268
1959	3	9	0	.250	5	185	350
1960	1	9	2	.100	6	178	309
1961	1	12	1	.077	7	174	392
1962	5	7	2	.417	4	305	376
1963	3	11	0	.214	6	279	398
1964	6	8	0	.429	3t	307	305
1965	6	8	0	.429	4	257	301
1966	7	7	0	.500	5	351	355
1967	5	6	3	.455	3	347	353
1968	5	9	0	.357	3	249	358
1969	7	5	2	.583	2	307	319
1970	6	8	0	.429	4	297	314
1971d	9	4	1	.692	2	276	190
1972e	11	3	0	.786	1	336	218
1973d	10	4	0	.714	2	325	198
1974d	10	4	0	.714	2	320	196
1975	8	6	0	.571	3	325	276
1976d	10	4	0	.714	2	291	217
1977	9	5	0	.643	2	196	189
1978	8	8	0	.500	3	273	283
1979	10	6	0	.625	3	348	295
1980	6	10	0	.375	3	261	293
1981	8	8	0	.500	4	347	349
1982f	8	1	0	.889	1	190	128
1983e	14	2	0	.875	1	541	332
1984g	11	5	0	.688	1	426	310
1985	10	6	0	.625	3	297	312
54 Years	352	313	26	.528		13,296	13,328

aNFL Eastern Division Champion; 0-1 in Playoffs
bNFL Champion; 1-0 in Playoffs
cNFL Eastern Division Champion; 1-1 in Playoffs
dNFC Wild Card Qualifier for Playoffs; 0-1 in Playoffs
eNFC Champion; 2-1 in Playoffs
fSuper Bowl Champion; 4-0 in Playoffs
gNFC Eastern Division Champion; 0-1 in Playoffs

RECORD HOLDERS

CAREER

Rushing attempts	John Riggins, 1976-79, 1981-85	1,988
Rushing yards	John Riggins, 1976-79, 1981-85	7,472
Pass attempts	Joe Theismann, 1974-85	3,602
Pass completions	Joe Theismann, 1974-85	2,044
Passing yards	Joe Theismann, 1974-85	25,206
Touchdown passes	Sonny Jurgensen, 1964-74	209
Receptions	Charley Taylor, 1964-77	649
Receiving yards	Charley Taylor, 1964-77	9,140
Interceptions	Brig Owens, 1966-77	36
Punting average	Sammy Baugh, 1937-52	45.1
Punt return avg.	Johnny Williams, 1952-53	12.8
Kickoff return avg.	Bobby Mitchell, 1962-68	28.5
Field goals	Mark Moseley, 1974-85	257
Touchdowns	Charley Taylor, 1964-77	90
Points	Mark Moseley, 1974-85	1,176

SEASON

Rushing attempts	John Riggins, 1983	375
Rushing yards	John Riggins, 1983	1,347
Pass attempts	Sonny Jurgensen, 1967	508
Pass completions	Joe Theismann, 1981	293
Passing yards	Sonny Jurgensen, 1967	3,747
Touchdown passes	Sonny Jurgensen, 1967	31
Receptions	Art Monk, 1984	106
Receiving yards	Bobby Mitchell, 1963	1,436
Interceptions	Dan Sandifer, 1948	13
Punting average	Sammy Baugh, 1940	51.4
Punt return avg.	Johnny Williams, 1952	15.3
Kickoff return avg.	Mike Nelms, 1981	29.7
Field goals	Mark Moseley, 1983	33
Touchdowns	John Riggins, 1983	24
Points	Mark Moseley, 1983	161

GAME

Rushing attempts	George Rogers, 12-8-85	36
Rushing yards	George Rogers, 12-21-85	206
Pass attempts	Jay Schroeder, 12-1-85	58
Pass completions	Sonny Jurgensen, 11-26-67	32
Passing yards	Sammy Baugh, 10-31-48	446
Touchdown passes	Sammy Baugh, 10-31-43	6
	Sammy Baugh, 11-23-47	6
Receptions	Art Monk, 12-15-85	13
Receiving yards	Art Monk, 12-15-85	230
Interceptions	Sammy Baugh, 11-14-43	4
	Dan Sandifer, 10-31-48	4
Field goals	4 times	5
Touchdowns	Dick James, 12-17-61	4
	Larry Brown, 12-4-73	4
Points	Dick James, 12-17-61	24
	Larry Brown, 12-4-73	24

COACHING HISTORY

1932	Lud Wray	4- 4-2
1933-34	William (Lone Star) Dietz	11-11-2
1935	Eddie Casey	2- 8-1
1936-42	Ray Flaherty	56-23-3
1943	Arthur (Dutch) Bergman	7- 4-1
1944-45	Dudley DeGroot	14- 6-1
1946-48	Glen (Turk) Edwards	16-18-1
1949	John Whelchel*	3- 3-1
1949-51	Herman Ball**	4-16-0
1951	Dick Todd	5- 4-0
1952-53	Earl (Curly) Lambeau	10-13-1
1954-58	Joe Kuharich	26-32-2
1959-60	Mike Nixon	4-18-2
1961-65	Bill McPeak	21-46-3
1966-68	Otto Graham	17-22-3
1969	Vince Lombardi	7- 5-2
1970	Bill Austin	6- 8-0
1971-77	George Allen	69-35-1
1978-80	Jack Pardee	24-24-0
1981-85	Joe Gibbs	57-24-0

**Replaced after seven games in 1949*
***Replaced after three games in 1951*

FIRST PLAYER SELECTED

1936 Riley Smith, QB, Alabama
1937 Sammy Baugh, QB, TCU
1938 Andy Farkas, FB, Detroit
1939 I. B. Hale, T, TCU
1940 Ed Boell, HB, NYU
1941 Forest Evashevski, QB, Michigan
1942 Orban (Spec) Sanders, HB, Texas
1943 Jack Jenkins, FB, Missouri
1944 Mike Micka, HB, Colgate
1945 Jim Hardy, QB, USC
1946 Cal Rossi, HB, UCLA†
1947 Cal Rossi, HB, UCLA
1948 Harry Gilmer, QB, Alabama
1949 Rob Goode, FB, Texas A&M
1950 George Thomas, HB, Oklahoma
1951 Leon Heath, FB, Oklahoma
1952 Larry Isbell, QB, Baylor
1953 Jack Scarbath, QB, Maryland
1954 Steve Meilinger, E, Kentucky
1955 Ralph Guglielmi, QB, Notre Dame
1956 Ed Vereb, HB, Maryland
1957 Don Bosseler, FB, Miami
1958 (2) Mike Sommer, HB, George Washington
1959 Don Allard, QB, Boston College
1960 Richie Lucas, QB, Penn State
1961 Norm Snead, QB, Wake Forest
1962 Ernie Davis, HB, Syracuse
1963 Pat Richter, TE, Wisconsin
1964 Charley Taylor, HB, Arizona State
1965 (2) Bob Breitenstein, T, Tulsa
1966 Charlie Gogolak, K, Princeton
1967 Ray McDonald, FB, Idaho
1968 Jim Smith, DB, Oregon
1969 (2) Eugene Epps, DB, Texas-El Paso
1970 (2) Bill Brundige, DE, Colorado
1971 (2) Cotton Speyrer, WR, Texas
1972 (8) Moses Denson, RB, Maryland-Eastern Shore
1973 (5) Charles Cantrell, G, Lamar
1974 (6) Jon Keyworth, TE, Colorado
1975 (5) Mike Thomas, RB, Nevada-Las Vegas
1976 (5) Mike Hughes, G, Baylor
1977 (4) Duncan McColl, DE, Stanford
1978 (6) Tony Green, RB, Florida
1979 (4) Don Warren, TE, San Diego State
1980 Art Monk, WR, Syracuse
1981 Mark May, T, Pittsburgh
1982 (2) Vernon Dean, CB, San Diego State
1983 Darrell Green, CB, Texas A&I
1984 (2) Bob Slater, DT, Oklahoma
1984* Tony Zendejas, K, Nevada-Reno
1985 (2) Tory Nixon, CB, San Diego State
1986 (2) Markus Koch, DE, Boise State

†Choice voided due to ineligibility
**Supplemental Draft*

All-Time Roster

The roster includes players in the National Football League (1920-85), the fourth American Football League (1960-69), and the All-America Football Conference (1946-49). To qualify, a player need not have played in a game, but must have been on an active roster during the regular season or the playoffs.

The position at which a player is listed is that at which he spent most of his career. Only players who played major portions of their careers at different positions are listed at more than one position. Modern players are divided into offensive and defensive teams. Those who were in professional football when virtually everyone played both ways are listed simply by their offensive positions, as was the style of the day. Similarly, those players who kicked or punted when that was part of a player's regular duty are not listed as a kicker or punter; those who kicked as their sole job, or who kicked in addition to playing another position when that was not a common occurrence, are listed as kickers or punters, however.

The pre-modern-era back frequently lined up at more than one backfield position in the same game, and often also played from more than one formation, so that similar positions could have different names. For example, in some teams' designations a Single-Wing blocking back was called a quarterback; the Portsmouth Spartans/Detroit Lions, however, listed Earl (Dutch) Clark as a quarterback, although he played what most NFL teams would have called tailback. To avoid confusion, a back from the pre-modern era is listed at the position he officially played, even if he played many. The positions also have been modernized, so that blocking backs have been listed as quarterbacks, and tailbacks and wingbacks as halfbacks, although there are exceptions, such as Clark and Sammy Baugh, who played half his career as a tailback and half as a T-formation quarterback; both are listed HB-QB.

A player's school generally is that at which he finished his career. During World War II, a number of college players were forced to transfer from one school to another in order to receive training required by the Armed Forces. If a player contributed significantly at both schools, each is listed. The schools are listed by their current names, rather than by what they were known as when the players attended them. For example, Don Maynard is shown as attending Texas-El Paso, the current name for what was then known as Texas Western.

In the early days of the NFL, players frequently would bounce from team to team, sometimes playing for the same team two or three separate times in one season. To avoid confusion, such players are shown as having played for any one team in any one season only once.

A

Abbey, Joe, E, North Texas State, Chi. Bears 1948-49; NY Bulldogs 1949
Abbott, Lafayette, HB, Syracuse, Dayton 1921-29
Abbruzzi, Lou, HB, Rhode Island State, Boston 1946
Abell, Bud, LB, Missouri, Kansas City 1966-68
Abercrombie, Walter, RB, Baylor, Pittsburgh 1982-85
Aberson, Cliff, HB, Green Bay 1946
Able, Fred, HB, Washington, Milwaukee 1926
Abraham, Robert, LB, North Carolina State, Houston 1982-85
Abramowicz, Dan, WR, Xavier, New Orleans 1967-73; San Francisco 1973-74; Buffalo 1975
Abramowitz, Sid, T, Tulsa, Baltimore 1983; Seattle 1984; NY Jets 1985
Abrams, Nate, E, Green Bay 1921
Abramson, George, T, Minnesota, Green Bay 1925
Abrell, Dick, QB, Purdue, Dayton, 1920
Abruzzese, Ray, DB, Alabama, Buffalo 1962-64
Abruzzino, Frank, E, Colgate, Brooklyn 1931; Cincinnati 1933
Absher, Dick, LB-K, Maryland, Washington 1967; Atlanta 1967-68; New Orleans 1969-71; Philadelphia 1972
Achica, George, NT, USC, Indianapolis 1985
Achui, Walter (Sneeze), HB, Dayton, Dayton 1927-28
Acker, Bill, DT, Texas, St. Louis 1980-81; Kansas City 1982; Cincinnati 1983; Buffalo 1984
Ackerman, Rick, DT, Memphis State, San Diego 1982-84; LA Raiders 1984
Acks, Ron, LB, Illinois, Atlanta 1968-71; New England 1972-73; Green Bay 1974-76
Acorn, Fred, CB, Texas, Tampa Bay 1984
Adamchik, Ed, C, Pittsburgh, NY Giants 1965; Pittsburgh 1965
Adamle, Mike, RB, Northwestern, Kansas City 1971-72; NY Jets 1973-74; Chi. Bears 1975-76
Adamle, Tony, LB, Ohio State, Cleveland 1947-51, 1954
Adams, Bill, G, Holy Cross, Buffalo 1972-78
Adams, Bob, TE, Pacific, Pittsburgh 1969-71; New England 1973-74; Denver 1975; Atlanta 1976
Adams, Brent, T, Tennessee-Chattanooga, Atlanta 1975-77
Adams, Chet, T, Ohio U., Cleveland 1939-42; Green Bay 1943; Cleveland (AAFC) 1946-48; Buffalo (AAFC) 1949; NY Yanks 1950
Adams, Curtis, RB, Central Michigan, San Diego 1985
Adams, Doug, LB, Ohio State, Cincinnati 1971-74
Adams, George, RB, Kentucky, NY Giants 1985
Adams, Henry, C, Pittsburgh, Chi. Cardinals 1939
Adams, Joe, T, DePaul, Rochester 1924
Adams, John (Tree), T, Notre Dame, Washington 1945-49
Adams, John, FB-TE, Cal State-Los Angeles, Chi. Bears 1959-62; LA Rams 1963
Adams, Julius, DE, Texas Southern, New England 1971-85
Adams, O'Neal, E, Arkansas, NY Giants 1942-44; Brooklyn (AAFC) 1946-47
Adams, Pete, G, USC, Cleveland 1974, 1976
Adams, Sam, G, Prairie View A&M, New England 1972-80; New Orleans 1981
Adams, Stanley, LB, Memphis State, LA Raiders 1984
Adams, Tom, SE, Minnesota-Duluth, Minnesota 1962
Adams, Tony, QB, Utah State, Kansas City 1975-78
Adams, Verlin, E, Morris Harvey, NY Giants 1943-45
Adams, Willie, LB, New Mexico State, Washington 1965-66
Adams, Willis, WR, Houston, Cleveland 1979-85
Adamson, Ken, G, Notre Dame, Denver 1960-62
Addams, Abe, E, Indiana, Detroit 1949
Adderley, Herb, CB, Michigan State, Green Bay 1961-69; Dallas 1970-72
Addison, Tom, LB, South Carolina, Boston 1960-67
Adducci, Nick, FB, Nebraska, Washington 1954-55
Adkins, Bob, E, Marshall, Green Bay 1940-41, 1945
Adkins, Margene, WR, Henderson J.C., Dallas 1970-71; New Orleans 1972; NY Jets 1973
Adkins, Roy, G, Millikin, Decatur 1920; Chi. Staleys 1921
Adkins, Sam, QB, Wichita State, Seattle 1977-82
Afflis, Dick (The Bruiser), G, Nevada-Reno, Green Bay 1951-54
Agajanian, Ben, K, New Mexico, Pittsburgh 1945; Philadelphia 1945; LA Dons (AAFC) 1947-48; NY Giants 1949, 1954-57; LA Rams 1953; LA Chargers 1960; Dallas Texans 1961; Green Bay 1961; Oakland 1962; San Diego 1964
Agase, Alex, G, Purdue, Illinois, LA Dons (AAFC) 1947; Chi. Rockets (AAFC) 1947; Cleveland 1948-51; Baltimore 1953
Agee, Sam, FB, Vanderbilt, Chi. Cardinals 1938-39
Agler, Bob, FB, Otterbein, LA Rams 1948-49
Aguirre, Joe, E, St. Mary's (California), Washington 1941, 1943-45; LA Dons (AAFC) 1946-49
Ahrens, Dave, LB, Wisconsin, St. Louis 1981-84; Indianapolis 1985
Aiello, Tony, HB, Youngstown State, Detroit 1944; Brooklyn 1944
Ailinger, Jim, G, Buffalo, Buffalo 1924
Aiu, Charlie, G, Hawaii, San Diego 1976-78; Seattle 1978
Akin, Harold, T, Oklahoma State, San Diego 1967-68
Akin, Len, G, Baylor, Chi. Bears 1942
Akins, Al, HB, Washington State, Cleveland (AAFC) 1946; Brooklyn (AAFC) 1947-48; Buffalo (AAFC) 1948
Akins, Frank, FB, Washington State, Washington 1943-46; Baltimore (AAFC) 1947
Akiu, Mike, WR, Hawaii, Houston 1985
Alban, Dick, DB, Northwestern, Washington 1952-55; Pittsburgh 1956-59
Albanese, Don, E, Columbus 1925
Albanese, Vannie, HB, Syracuse, Brooklyn 1937-38
Alberghini, Tom, G, Holy Cross, Pittsburgh 1945
Albert, Frankie, QB, Stanford, San Francisco 1946-52
Albert, Sergio, K, U.S. International, St. Louis 1974
Albrecht, Art, T, Wisconsin, Pittsburgh 1942; Chi. Cardinals 1943; Boston 1944
Albrecht, Ted, T, California, Chi. Bears 1977-81
Albright, Bill, G, Wisconsin, NY Giants 1951-54
Albritton, Vince, S-LB, Washington, Dallas 1984-85
Alderman, Grady, G-T, Detroit, Detroit 1960; Minnesota 1961-74
Alderton, John, DE, Maryland, Pittsburgh 1953
Aldrich, Ki, C, TCU, Chi. Cardinals 1939-40; Washington 1941-42, 1945-47
Aldridge, Allen, DE, Prairie View A&M, Houston 1971-72; Cleveland 1974
Aldridge, Ben, HB, Oklahoma State, NY Yanks 1950-51; San Francisco 1952; Green Bay 1953
Aldridge, Jerry, RB, Angelo State, San Francisco 1980
Aldridge, Lionel, DE, Utah State, Green Bay 1963-71; San Diego 1972-73
Alexakos, Steve, G, San Diego State, Denver 1970; NY Giants 1971
Alexander, Charles, RB, LSU, Cincinnati 1979-85
Alexander, Dan, G, LSU, NY Jets 1977-85
Alexander, Glenn, WR, Grambling, Buffalo 1970
Alexander, Joe, C, Syracuse, Rochester 1921-22, 1924; NY Giants 1925-27
Alexander, John, T, Rutgers, Milwaukee 1922; NY Giants 1926
Alexander, John, DE, Rutgers, Miami 1977-78
Alexander, Kermit, DB, UCLA, San Francisco 1963-69; LA Rams 1970-71; Philadelphia 1972-73
Alexander, Ray, WR, Florida A&M, Denver 1984
Alexander, Robert, RB, West Virginia, LA Rams 1982-83
Alexander, Willie, CB, Alcorn State, Houston 1971-79
Alflen, Ted, RB, Springfield, Denver 1969
Alfonse, Julie, QB, Minnesota, Cleveland 1937-38
Alford, Bruce, E, TCU, NY Yankees (AAFC) 1946-49; NY Yanks 1950-51
Alford, Bruce, K, TCU, Washington 1967; Buffalo 1968-69
Alford, Gene, HB, Texas Tech, Portsmouth 1931-33; St. Louis 1934; Cincinnati 1934
Alford, Mike, C, Auburn, St. Louis 1965; Detroit 1966
Alfson, Warren, G, Nebraska, Brooklyn 1941
Allard, Don, QB, Boston College, NY Titans 1961; Boston 1962
Allegre, Raul, K, Texas, Baltimore 1983; Indianapolis 1984-85
Allen, Anthony, WR, Washington, Atlanta 1985
Allen, Buddy, HB, Utah State, Denver 1961
Allen, Carl, HB, Ouachita Baptist, Brooklyn (AAFC) 1948
Allen, Carl, CB, Southern Mississippi, St. Louis 1977-81
Allen, Chuck, LB, Washington, San Diego 1961-69; Pittsburgh 1970-71; Philadelphia 1972
Allen, Dalva, DE, Houston, Houston 1960-61; Oakland 1962-64
Allen, Don, FB, Texas, Denver 1960
Allen, Doug, LB, Penn State, Buffalo 1974-75
Allen, Duane, TE, Santa Ana J.C., LA Rams 1961-64; Pittsburgh 1965; Baltimore 1965; Chi. Bears 1966-67
Allen, Ed, E, Creighton, Chi. Cardinals 1928
Allen, Eddie, HB, Pennsylvania, Chi. Bears 1947
Allen, Ermal, QB, Kentucky, Cleveland (AAFC) 1947
Allen, Frank, E, Indiana, Muncie 1921
Allen, Gary, RB, Hawaii, Houston 1982-83; Dallas 1983-84
Allen, George, DT, West Texas State, Houston 1966
Allen, Gerry, RB, Nebraska-Omaha, Baltimore 1966; Washington 1967-69
Allen, Grady, LB, Texas A&M, Atlanta 1968-72
Allen, Greg, RB, Florida State, Cleveland 1985
Allen, Jackie, DB, Baylor, Oakland 1969; Buffalo 1970-71; Philadelphia 1972
Allen, Jeff, DB, Iowa State, St. Louis 1971
Allen, Jeff, CB, Cal-Davis, Miami 1980; San Diego 1982
Allen, Jimmy, DB, UCLA, Pittsburgh 1974-77
Allen, John, C, Purdue, Washington 1955-58
Allen, Kevin, T, Indiana, Philadelphia 1985
Allen, Lou, T, Duke, Pittsburgh 1950-51
Allen, Lynn, HB, Detroit 1920
Allen, Marcus, RB, USC, LA Raiders 1982-85
Allen, Nate, CB, Texas Southern, Kansas City 1971-74; San Francisco 1975; Minnesota 1976-78
Allen, Patrick, CB, Utah State, Houston 1984-85
Allerman, Kurt, LB, Penn State, St. Louis 1977-79, 1982-84; Green Bay 1980-81; Detroit 1985
Alley, Don, FL, Adams State, Baltimore 1967; Pittsburgh 1969
Allison, Butch, T, Missouri, Baltimore 1966
Allison, Henry, G, San Diego State, Philadelphia 1971-72; St. Louis 1975-77; Denver 1977
Allison, Jim, RB, San Diego State, San Diego 1965-68
Allison, Neely, E, Texas A&M, Buffalo 1926-27; NY Giants 1928
Alliston, Buddy, LB, Mississippi, Denver 1960
Allman, Bob, E, Michigan State, Chi. Bears 1936
Allton, Joe, T, Oklahoma, Chi. Cardinals 1942
Alston, Mack, TE, Maryland-Eastern Shore, Washington 1970-72; Houston 1973-76; Baltimore 1977-80
Alt, John, T, Iowa, Kansas City 1984-85
Alvarez, Wilson, K, Southeastern Louisiana, Seattle 1981
Alvers, Steve, TE-C, Miami, Buffalo 1981; NY Jets 1982
Alward, Tom, G, Nebraska, Tampa Bay 1976
Alworth, Lance, FL, Arkansas, San Diego 1962-70; Dallas 1971-72
Alzado, Lyle, DE, Yankton, Denver 1971-78; Cleveland 1979-81; LA Raiders 1982-1985
Amberg, John, DB, Kansas, NY Giants 1951-52
Ambrose, Dick, LB, Virginia, Cleveland 1975-83
Ambrose, John, C, Catholic, Brooklyn 1932
Ambrose, Walt, G, Carroll (Wisconsin), Portsmouth 1930
Ameche, Alan (The Horse), FB, Wisconsin, Baltimore 1955-60
Amerson, Glen, DB, Texas Tech, Philadelphia 1961
Ames, Dave, HB, Richmond, NY Titans 1961; Denver 1961
Amman, Richard, DE, Florida State, Baltimore 1972-73
Amsler, Marty, DE, Evansville, Chi. Bears 1967-69; Cincinnati 1970; Green Bay 1970
Amstutz, Joe, C, Indiana, Cleveland 1957
Amundsen, Norm, G, Wisconsin, Green Bay 1957
Amundson, George, RB, Iowa State, Houston 1973-74; Philadelphia 1975
Ananis, Vito, HB, Boston College, Washington 1945
Andabaker, Rudy, G, Pittsburgh, Pittsburgh 1952, 1954
Andersen, Morten, K, Michigan State, New Orleans 1982-85
Andersen, Stan, T, Stanford, Cleveland 1940-41; Detroit 1941

Anderson, Alfred, RB, Baylor, Minnesota 1984-85
Anderson, Anthony, RB, Temple, Pittsburgh 1979; Atlanta 1980
Anderson, Art, DT, Idaho, Chi. Bears 1961-62; Pittsburgh 1963
Anderson, Bill, E, West Virginia, Boston 1945
Anderson, Bill, SE, Tennessee, Washington 1958-63; Green Bay 1965-66
Anderson, Billy, HB, Compton J.C., Chi. Bears 1953-54
Anderson, Billy Guy, QB, Tulsa, Houston 1967
Anderson, Bob, HB, Army, NY Giants 1963
Anderson, Bobby, RB, Colorado, Denver 1970-73; New England 1975; Washington 1975
Anderson, Brad, WR, Arizona, Chi. Bears 1984-85
Anderson, Bruce, DE, Willamette, LA Rams 1966; NY Giants 1967-69; Washington 1970
Anderson, Charlie, E, Louisiana Tech, Chi. Cardinals 1956
Anderson, Chet, T, Louisville 1923
Anderson, Chet, TE, Minnesota, Pittsburgh 1967
Anderson, Cliff, E, Indiana, Chi. Cardinals 1952-53; NY Giants 1953
Anderson, Curtis, DE, Central State (Ohio), Kansas City 1979
Anderson, Dick, T, Ohio State, New Orleans 1967
Anderson, Dick, S, Colorado, Miami 1968-77
Anderson, Don, CB, Purdue, Indianapolis 1985
Anderson, Donny, RB-P, Texas Tech, Green Bay 1966-71; St. Louis 1972-74
Anderson, Eddie, E, Notre Dame, Rochester 1922; Chi. Cardinals 1922-25; Chi. Bears 1923
Anderson, Ezzret, E, Kentucky State, LA Dons (AAFC) 1947
Anderson, Fred, DE, Prairie View A&M, Pittsburgh 1978; Seattle 1980-82
Anderson, Gary, G, Stanford, Detroit 1977-78; New Orleans 1978
Anderson, Gary, K, Syracuse, Pittsburgh 1982-85
Anderson, Gary, RB, Arkansas, San Diego 1985
Anderson, Hunk, G, Notre Dame, Chi. Bears 1922-25
Anderson, Jerry, DB, Oklahoma, Cincinnati 1977; Tampa Bay 1978
Anderson, John, LB, Michigan, Green Bay 1978-85
Anderson, Ken, QB, Augustana (Illinois), Cincinnati 1971-85
Anderson, Kim, CB, Arizona State, Baltimore 1980-83; Indianapolis 1984
Anderson, Larry, DB-KR, Louisiana Tech, Pittsburgh 1978-81; Baltimore 1982-83; Indianapolis 1984
Anderson, Marcus, WR, Tulane, Chi. Bears 1981
Anderson, (Mini) Max, RB, Arizona State, Buffalo 1968-69
Anderson, Ockie, HB, Colgate, Buffalo 1920-22
Anderson, Ottis, RB, Miami, St. Louis 1979-85
Anderson, Preston, S, Rice, Cleveland 1974
Anderson, Ralph, TE, Cal State-Los Angeles, Chi. Bears 1958; LA Chargers 1960
Anderson, Ralph (Sticks), S, West Texas State, Pittsburgh 1971-72; New England 1973
Anderson, Ricky, RB, South Carolina State, San Diego 1978
Anderson, Roger, DT, Virginia Union, NY Giants 1964-65, 1967-68
Anderson, Scott, C, Missouri, Minnesota 1974, 1976
Anderson, Stuart, LB, Virginia, Washington 1982-85; Cleveland 1984
Anderson, Taz, SE, Georgia Tech, St. Louis 1961-64; Atlanta 1966-67
Anderson, Terry, WR, Bethune-Cookman, Miami 1977-78; Washington 1978
Anderson, Tim, S, Ohio State, San Francisco 1975; Buffalo 1976
Anderson, Tom, HB, Haskell, Kansas City 1924
Anderson, Vickey Ray, RB, Oklahoma, Green Bay 1980
Anderson, Warren, WR, West Virginia State, Houston 1977; St. Louis 1978
Anderson, Will, HB, Syracuse, Cleveland 1923; Rochester 1924
Anderson, Winnie, E, Colgate, NY Giants 1936
Andrako, Steve, C, Ohio State, Washington 1940
Andrews, Al, LB, New Mexico State, Buffalo 1970-71
Andrews, Billy, LB, Southeastern Louisiana, Cleveland 1967-74; San Diego 1975; Kansas City 1976-77
Andrews, George, LB, Nebraska, LA Rams 1979-84
Andrews, Jabby, HB, Texas, St. Louis 1934
Andrews, John, TE, Indiana, San Diego 1972; Baltimore 1973-74
Andrews, John, DE, Morgan State, Miami 1975-76
Andrews, LeRoy, G, Pittsburg State, St. Louis 1923; Kansas City 1924-26; Cleveland 1927; Detroit 1928
Andrews, Tom, C, Louisville, Chi. Bears 1984-85
Andrews, William, RB, Auburn, Atlanta 1979-83
Andrie, George, DE, Marquette, Dallas 1962-72
Andros, Plato, G, Oklahoma, Chi. Cardinals 1947-50
Andrulewicz, Ted, HB, Villanova, Newark 1930
Andrus, Lou, LB, BYU, Denver 1967
Andrusking, Sig, G, Detroit, Brooklyn 1937
Andrusyshyn, Zenon, P-K, UCLA, Kansas City 1978
Ane, Charlie, C, USC, Detroit 1953-59
Ane, Charlie, C, Michigan State, Kansas City 1975-80
Angle, Bob, HB, Iowa State, Chi. Cardinals 1950
Angsman, Elmer, HB, Notre Dame, Chi. Cardinals 1946-52
Annan, Dunc, QB, Chicago, Chi. Tigers 1920; Toledo 1922; Hammond 1923-26; Kenosha 1924; Akron 1925-26
Anthony, Charles, LB, USC, San Diego 1974
Anthony, Tyrone, RB, North Carolina, New Orleans 1984-85
Antoine, Lionel, T, Southern Illinois, Chi. Bears 1972-76, 1978
Antwine, Houston, DT, Southern Illinois, Boston, 1961-70; New England 1971; Philadelphia 1972
Apolskis, Chuck, E, DePaul, Chi. Bears 1938-39
Apolskis, Ray, G, Marquette, Chi. Cardinals 1941-42, 1945-50
Apple, Jim, HB, Upsala, NY Titans 1961
Applegran, Clarence, G, Illinois, Detroit 1920
Appleton, Scott, DE, Texas, Houston 1964-66; San Diego 1967-68
Aspit, Marger, HB, USC, Frankford 1931; Brooklyn 1931; Green Bay 1932; Boston 1933
Apuna, Ben, LB, Arizona State, NY Giants 1980
Arbanas, Fred, TE, Michigan State, Dallas Texans 1962; Kansas City 1963-70
Arbubakrr, Hasson, DE, Texas Tech, Tampa Bay 1983; Minnesota 1984
Archer, Dan, G-T, Oregon, Oakland 1967; Cincinnati 1968
Archer, David, QB, Iowa State, Atlanta 1984-85
Archer, Troy, DT, Colorado, NY Giants 1976-78
Archoska, Julie, E, Syracuse, Staten Island 1930
Ard, Billy, G, Wake Forest, NY Giants 1981-85
Ardizzone, Tony, C, Northwestern, Chi. Bears 1979
Arena, Tony, C, Michigan State, Detroit 1942
Arenas, Joe, HB, Nebraska-Omaha, San Francisco 1951-57
Arenz, Arnie, QB, St. Louis, Boston 1934
Argus, Bob, FB, Rochester 1920-25
Ariail, Dave, E, Auburn, Brooklyn 1934; Cincinnati 1934
Ariri, Obed, K, Clemson, Tampa Bay 1984
Arms, Lloyd, G, Oklahoma State, Chi. Cardinals 1946-48
Armstrong, Adger, RB, Texas A&M, Houston 1980-82; Tampa Bay 1983-85
Armstrong, Bill, G, UCLA, Brooklyn 1943
Armstrong, Bob, T, Missouri, Portsmouth 1931-32
Armstrong, Charlie, HB, Mississippi College, Brooklyn (AAFC) 1946
Armstrong, Graham, T, John Carroll, Cleveland 1941, 1945; Buffalo (AAFC) 1947-48
Armstrong, Harvey, NT, Oklahoma State, Philadelphia 1982-84
Armstrong, Johnny, QB, Dubuque, Rock Island 1923-25
Armstrong, Neill, E, Oklahoma State, Philadelphia 1947-51
Armstrong, Norris, HB, Centre, Milwaukee 1922
Armstrong, Otis, RB, Purdue, Denver 1973-80
Armstrong, Ray, DT, TCU, Oakland 1960
Arndt, Al, G, South Dakota State, Pittsburgh 1935
Arndt, Dick, DT, Idaho, Pittsburgh 1967-70
Arneson, Jim, G-C, Arizona, Dallas 1973-74; Washington 1975
Arneson, Mark, LB, Arizona, St. Louis 1972-80
Arnett, Jon, HB, USC, LA Rams 1957-63; Chi. Bears 1964-66
Arnold, Jay, QB, Texas, Philadelphia 1937-40; Pittsburgh 1941
Arnold, Jim, P, Vanderbilt, Kansas City 1983-85
Arnold, John, WR, Wyoming, Detroit 1979-80
Arnold, LeFrancis, G, Oregon, Denver 1974
Arnold, Walt, TE, New Mexico, LA Rams 1980-81; Houston 1982-83; Washington 1984; Kansas City 1984-85
Arrington, Rick, QB, Tulsa, Philadelphia 1970-72
Arrobio, Chuck, T, USC, Minnesota 1966
Arrowhead, E, Miami (Ohio), Oorang 1922-23
Arterburn, Elmer, DB, Texas Tech, Chi. Cardinals 1954
Arthur, Gary, TE, Miami (Ohio), NY Jets 1970-71
Artman, Corwan (Chang), T, Stanford, NY Giants 1931; Boston 1932; Pittsburgh 1933
Artoe, Lee, T, Santa Clara, California, Chi. Bears 1940-42, 1945; LA Dons (AAFC) 1946-47; Baltimore (AAFC) 1948
Asad, Doug, E, Northwestern, Oakland 1960-61
Asbury, Willie, RB, Kent State, Pittsburgh 1966-68
Aschbacher, Darrell, G, Oregon, Philadelphia 1959
Aschenbrenner, Frank, FB, Northwestern, Chi. Hornets (AAFC) 1949
Ash, Julian, G, Oregon State, LA Buccaneers 1926
Ashbaugh, Bill, FB, Pittsburgh, Rock Island 1924; Kansas City 1924-25
Ashburn, Cliff, G, Nebraska, NY Giants 1929; Chi. Bears 1930
Asher, Bob, T, Vanderbilt, Dallas 1970; Chi. Bears 1972-75
Ashley, Walker Lee, LB, Penn State, Green Bay 1983; Minnesota 1984
Ashmore, Roger, T, Gonzaga, Milwaukee 1926; Duluth 1927; Chi. Bears 1927; Green Bay 1928-29
Ashton, Josh, RB, Tulsa, New England 1972-74; St. Louis 1975
Askea, Mike, T, Stanford, Denver 1973
Askson, Burt, DE, Texas Southern, Pittsburgh 1971; New Orleans 1973; Green Bay 1975-77
Aspatore, Ed, T, Marquette, Cincinnati 1934; Chi. Bears 1934
Atchason, Jack, TE, Western Illinois, Boston 1960; Houston 1960
Atcherson, John, E, Columbus 1922
Atessis, Bill, DE, Texas, New England 1971
Athas, Pete, S, Tennessee, NY Giants 1971-74; Cleveland 1975; Minnesota 1975; New Orleans 1976
Atkeson, Dale, HB, Washington 1954-56
Atkins, Billy, DB-P, Auburn, San Francisco 1958-59; Buffalo 1960-61, 1963; NY Titans 1962; NY Jets 1963; Denver 1964
Atkins, Bob, CB, Grambling, St. Louis 1968-69; Houston 1970-76
Atkins, Dave, RB, Texas-El Paso, San Francisco 1973-74; San Diego 1975
Atkins, Doug, DE, Tennessee, Cleveland 1953-54; Chi. Bears 1955-66; New Orleans 1967-69
Atkins, George, G, Auburn, Detroit 1955
Atkins, Kevin, LB, Illinois, Chi. Bears 1983
Atkins, Pervis, HB-FL, New Mexico State, LA Rams 1961-63; Washington 1964-65; Oakland 1965-66
Atkins, Steve, RB, Maryland, Green Bay 1979-81
Atkinson, Al, LB, Villanova, NY Jets 1965-74
Atkinson, Frank, DT, Stanford, Pittsburgh 1963; Denver 1964
Atkinson, George, DB, Morris Brown, Oakland 1966-77
Atkinson, Jess, K, Maryland, NY Giants 1985; St. Louis 1985
Attache, Reginald, HB, Oorang 1922
Atty, Alex, G, West Virginia, Cleveland 1939
Atwood, John, HB, Wisconsin, NY Giants 1948
Audet, Earl, T, USC, Washington 1945; LA Dons (AAFC) 1946-48
Audick, Dan, G-T, Hawaii, St. Louis 1977, 1983-84; San Diego 1978-80; San Francisco 1981-82
Auer, Howie, T, Michigan, Chi. Cardinals 1933; Philadelphia 1933
Auer, Joe, RB, Georgia Tech, Buffalo 1964-65; Miami 1966-67; Atlanta 1968
Auer, Scott, G-T, Michigan State, Kansas City 1984-85
Aughtman, Dowe, G, Auburn, Dallas 1984
August, Ed, HB, Villanova, Providence 1931
August, Steve, T, Tulsa, Seattle 1977-84; Pittsburgh 1984
Augusterfer, Gene, QB, Catholic, Pittsburgh 1935
Augustyniak, Mike, RB, Purdue, NY Jets 1981-83
Ault, Chalmers, G, West Virginia Wesleyan, Cleveland 1924-25
Austin, Bill, G, Oregon State, NY Giants 1949-50, 1953-57
Austin, Cliff, RB, Clemson, New Orleans 1983; Atlanta 1984-85
Austin, Darrell, T-G-C, South Carolina, NY Jets 1975-78; Tampa Bay 1979-80
Austin, Hise, CB, Prairie View A&M, Green Bay 1973, Kansas City 1975
Austin, Jim, E, St. Mary's (California), Brooklyn 1937-38; Detroit 1939
Austin, Ocie, DB, Utah State, Baltimore 1968-69; Pittsburgh 1970-71
Autrey, Billy, C, Stephen F. Austin, Chi. Bears 1953
Autry, Hank, C, Southern Mississippi, Houston 1969-70
Avedisian, Chuck, G, Providence, NY Giants 1942-44
Avellini, Bob, QB, Maryland, Chi. Bears 1975-84; NY Jets 1984
Aveni, John, K, Indiana, Chi. Bears 1959-60; Washington 1961
Averno, Sisto, G, Muhlenberg, Baltimore 1950, 1953-54; NY Yanks 1951; Dallas 1952
Avery, Don, T, USC, Washington 1946-47; LA Dons (AAFC) 1948
Avery, Jim, TE, Northern Illinois, Washington 1966
Avery, Ken, LB, Southern Mississippi, NY Giants 1967-68; Cincinnati 1969-74; Kansas City 1975
Avezzano, Joe, C, Florida State, Boston 1966
Avinger, Clarence (Butch), HB, Alabama, NY Giants 1953
Aydelette, Buddy, T, Alabama, Green Bay 1980
Ayers, John, G, West Texas State, San Francisco 1977-85
Azelby, Joe, LB, Harvard, Buffalo 1984

B

Baab, Mike, C, Texas, Cleveland 1982-85
Baack, Steve, T, Oregon, Detroit 1984-85
Babartsky, Al, T, Fordham, Chi. Cardinals 1938-39, 1941-42; Chi. Bears 1943-45
Babb, Charlie, S, Memphis State, Miami 1972-79
Babb, Gene, FB-LB, Austin, San Francisco 1957-58; Dallas Cowboys 1960-61; Houston 1962-63
Babcock, Harry, E, Georgia, San Francisco 1953-55
Babich, Bob, LB, Miami (Ohio), San Diego 1970-72; Cleveland 1973-78
Babinecz, John, LB, Villanova, Dallas 1972-73; Chi. Bears 1975
Baccaglio, Martin, DE, San Jose State, San Diego 1968; Cincinnati 1968-70
Bacchus, Carl, E, Missouri, Cleveland 1927; Detroit 1928
Bachmaier, Joe, C-G, Rochester 1920-24
Bachman, Jay, C, Cincinnati, Denver 1968-71
Bachman, Ted, CB, New Mexico State, Seattle 1976; Miami 1976
Bachor, Ludwig, T, Detroit, Detroit 1928
Bacon, Coy, DE, Jackson State, LA Rams 1968-72; San Diego 1973-75; Cincinnati 1976-77; Washington 1978-81
Bacon, Frank, HB, Wabash, Dayton 1920-26; Akron 1923
Badaczewski, John, G, Case Western Reserve, Boston 1946-48; Chi. Cardinals 1948; Washington 1949-51; Chi. Bears 1953
Badar, Rich, QB, Indiana, Pittsburgh 1967
Badgro, Morris (Red), E, USC, NY Yankees 1927; NY Giants 1930-35; Brooklyn 1936
Bagarus, Steve, HB, Notre Dame, Washington 1945-46, 1948; LA Rams 1947
Bagby, Herm, HB, Arkansas, Brooklyn 1926; Kansas City 1926; Cleveland 1927
Bagdon, Eddie, G, Michigan State, Chi. Cardinals 1950-51; Washington 1952
Baggett, Billy, HB, LSU, Dallas 1952
Bahan, Pete, HB, Notre Dame, Cleveland 1923
Bahnsen, Ken, FB, North Texas State, San Francisco 1953
Bahr, Chris, K, Penn State, Cincinnati 1976-79; Oakland 1980-81; LA Raiders 1982-85
Bahr, Matt, K, Penn State, Pittsburgh 1979-1980; San Francisco 1981; Cleveland 1981-1985

Bailey, Bill, E, Duke, Brooklyn 1940-41
Bailey, Byron, HB, Washington State, Detroit 1952-53; Green Bay 1953
Bailey, Don, C, Miami, Tampa Bay 1983; Indianapolis 1984-85
Bailey, Edwin, G, South Carolina State, Seattle 1981-85
Bailey, Elmer, WR, Minnesota, Miami 1980-81; Baltimore 1982
Bailey, Harold, QB-WR, Oklahoma State, Houston 1981-82
Bailey, Howard, T, Tennessee, Philadelphia 1935
Bailey, Jim, G, West Virginia, Chi. Rockets (AAFC) 1949
Bailey, Jim, DT-DE, Kansas, Baltimore 1970-74; NY Jets 1975; Atlanta 1976-78
Bailey, Larry, DT, Pacific, Atlanta 1974
Bailey, Mark, RB, Long Beach State, Kansas City 1977-78
Bailey, Monk, DB, Utah, St. Louis 1964-65
Bailey, Russ, C, West Virginia, Akron 1920-21
Bailey, Sam, E, Georgia, Boston 1946
Bailey, Stacey, WR, San Jose State, Atlanta 1982-85
Bailey, Teddy, FB, Cincinnati, Buffalo 1967; Boston 1969
Bailey, Tom, RB, Florida State, Philadelphia 1971-74
Bain, Bill, T, USC, Green Bay 1975; Denver 1976, 1978; NY Giants 1978; LA Rams 1979-1985
Baird, Bill, S, Cal State-San Francisco, NY Jets 1963-69
Baisi, Al, G, West Virginia, Chi. Bears 1940-41, 1946; Philadelphia 1947
Baker, Al (Bubba), DE, Colorado State, Detroit 1978-82; St. Louis 1983-85
Baker, Art, FB, Syracuse, Buffalo 1961-62
Baker, Charlie, LB, New Mexico, St. Louis 1980-85
Baker, Conway, T, Centenary, Chi. Cardinals 1936-43, 1945; Card-Pitt 1944
Baker, Dave, DB, Oklahoma, San Francisco 1959-61
Baker, Ed, QB, Lafayette, Houston 1972
Baker, Frank, E, Northwestern, Green Bay 1931
Baker, Jerry, T, Tulane, Denver 1983
Baker, Jesse, DE, Jacksonville State, Houston 1979-85
Baker, John, DE, North Carolina Central, LA Rams 1958-61; Philadelphia 1962; Pittsburgh 1963-67; Detroit 1968
Baker, John, DE, Norfolk State, NY Giants 1970
Baker, Johnny, LB, Mississippi State, Houston 1963-66; San Diego 1967
Baker, Jon, G-LB, California, NY Giants 1949-52
Baker, Keith, WR, Texas Southern, Philadelphia 1985
Baker, Larry, T, Bowling Green, NY Titans 1960
Baker, Leo, LB, New Mexico State, Cincinnati 1984
Baker, Mel, WR, Texas Southern, Miami 1974; New Orleans 1975; New England 1975; San Diego 1975; Houston 1976
Baker, Ralph, LB, Penn State, NY Jets 1964-74
Baker, Ron, G, Oklahoma State, Baltimore 1978-79; Philadelphia 1980-85
Baker, Roy (Bullet), QB, USC, NY Yankees 1927; Green Bay 1928-29; Chi. Cardinals 1929-30; Staten Island 1931
Baker, Sam, K-FB, Oregon State, Washington 1953, 1956-59; Cleveland 1960-61; Dallas 1962-63: Philadelphia 1964-69
Baker, Terry, QB-HB, Oregon State, LA Rams 1963-65
Baker, Tony, RB, Iowa State, New Orleans 1968-71; Philadelphia 1971-72; LA Rams 1973-74; San Diego 1975
Baker, Wayne, DT, BYU, San Francisco 1975
Bakken, Jim, K, Wisconsin, St. Louis 1962-78
Balacz, Frank, FB, Iowa, Green Bay 1939-41; Chi. Cardinals 1941, 1945
Balatti, Ed, E, San Francisco (AAFC) 1946-48; NY Yankees (AAFC) 1948; Buffalo (AAFC) 1948
Baldacci, Lou, HB, Michigan, Pittsburgh 1956
Baldassin, Mike, LB, Washington, San Francisco 1977-78
Baldinger, Brian, C-G, Duke, Dallas 1982-84
Baldinger, Rich, T, Wake Forest, NY Giants 1982-83; Kansas City 1983-85
Baldischwiler, Karl, T, Oklahoma, Detroit 1978-82; Baltimore 1983; Indianapolis 1985
Baldwin, Al, E, Arkansas, Buffalo (AAFC) 1947-49; Green Bay 1950
Baldwin, Bob, RB, Clemson, Baltimore 1966
Baldwin, Burr, E, UCLA, LA Dons (AAFC) 1947-49
Baldwin, Cliff, HB, Muncie 1920-21
Baldwin, George, E, Virginia, Canton 1925
Baldwin, Jack, C, Centenary, NY Yankees (AAFC) 1946-47; San Francisco (AAFC) 1947; Buffalo (AAFC) 1948
Baldwin, Keith, DE, Texas A&M, Cleveland 1982-85
Baldwin, Tom, DT, Tulsa, NY Jets 1984-85
Ball, Larry, LB, Louisville, Miami 1972-74, 1977-78; Detroit 1975; Tampa Bay 1976
Ball, Sam, T, Kentucky, Baltimore 1966-70
Ballard, Quinton, DT, Elon, Baltimore 1983
Ballman, Gary, FL-TE, Michigan State, Pittsburgh 1962-66; Philadelphia 1967-72; NY Giants 1973; Minnesota 1973
Ballou, Mike, LB, UCLA, Boston 1970
Balog, Bob, C, Denver, Pittsburgh, 1949-50
Baltzell, Vic, HB, Southwestern (Kansas), Boston 1935
Banas, Steve, QB, Notre Dame, Detroit 1935; Philadelphia 1935
Banaszak, John, DE, Eastern Michigan, Pittsburgh 1975-81
Banaszak, Pete, RB, Miami, Oakland 1966-78
Banaszek, Cas, T, Northwestern, San Francisco 1968-76
Bancroft, Hugh, E, Alfred, Rochester 1923
Banducci, Bruno, G, Stanford, Philadelphia 1944-45; San Francisco 1946-54
Bandura, John, E, Southwestern Louisiana, Brooklyn 1943
Bandy, Don, G, Tulsa, Washington 1967-68
Banet, Herb, HB, Manchester, Green Bay 1937
Banfield, Tony, DB, Oklahoma State, Houston 1960-63, 1965
Bangs, Ben, HB, Washington State, LA Buccaneers 1926
Banjavcic, Emil, HB, Arizona, Detroit 1942
Banker, Ted, G-C, Southeast Missouri State, NY Jets 1984-85
Banks, Carl, LB, Michigan State, NY Giants 1984-85
Banks, Chip, LB, USC, Cleveland 1982-85
Banks, Estes, RB, Colorado, Oakland 1967; Cincinnati 1968
Banks, Fred, WR-KR, Liberty Baptist, Cleveland 1985
Banks, Gordon, WR, Stanford, New Orleans 1980-81; Dallas 1985
Banks, Tom, C, Auburn, St. Louis 1971-80
Banks, Willie, G, Alcorn State, Washington 1968-69; NY Giants 1970; New England 1973
Bankston, Warren, RB-TE, Tulane, Pittsburgh 1969-72; Oakland 1973-78
Bannon, Bruce, LB, Penn State, Miami 1973-74
Banonis, Vince, C, Detroit, Chi. Cardinals 1942; 1946-50; Card-Pitt 1944; Detroit 1951-53
Bansavage, Al, LB, USC, LA Chargers 1960; Oakland 1961
Banta, Jack, FB, USC, Washington 1941; Philadelphia 1941, 1944-45; LA Rams 1946-48
Barbaro, Gary, S, Nicholls State, Kansas City 1976-82
Barbee, Joe, DT, Kent State, Oakland 1960
Barber, Ben, T, Virginia Military, Buffalo 1925
Barber, Bob, DE, Grambling, Green Bay 1976-79
Barber, Ernie, C, San Francisco, Washington 1945
Barber, Jim, T, San Francisco, Boston 1935-36; Washington 1937-41
Barber, Marion, RB, Minnesota, NY Jets 1982-85
Barber, Mark, FB, South Dakota State, Cleveland 1937
Barber, Mike, TE, Louisiana Tech, Houston 1976-81; LA Rams 1982-85; Denver 1985
Barber, Rudy, LB, Bethune-Cookman, Miami 1968
Barber, Stew, T, Penn State, Buffalo 1961-69
Barbolak, Pete, T, Purdue, Pittsburgh 1949
Barbour, Elmer, QB, Wake Forest, NY Giants 1945
Barefield, John, LB, Texas A&I, St. Louis 1978-80
Barefoot, Ken, TE, Virginia Tech, Washington 1968
Barfield, Ken, G, Mississippi, Washington 1954
Baril, Adrian, T, St. Thomas (Minnesota), Minneapolis 1923-24; Milwaukee 1925
Barisich, Carl, DT, Princeton, Cleveland 1973-75; Seattle 1976; Miami 1977-80
Barker, Dick, G, Iowa State, Chi. Staleys 1921; Rock Island 1921
Barker, Ed, E, Washington State, Pittsburgh 1953; Washington 1954
Barker, Hub, QB, Arkansas, NY Giants 1943-45
Barker, Leo, LB, New Mexico State, Cincinnati 1984-85
Barkman, Ralph, QB, Albright, Orange 1929; Newark 1930
Barkum, Jerome, WR-TE, Jackson State, NY Jets 1972-83
Barle, Lou, QB, Minnesota-Duluth, Detroit 1938; Cleveland 1939
Barna, George, E, Hobart, Frankford 1929
Barnard, Charles (Hap), E, Central State (Oklahoma), NY Giants 1938
Barnes, Al, WR, New Mexico State, Detroit 1972-73
Barnes, Benny, DB, Stanford, Dallas 1972-82
Barnes, Billy Ray, HB, Wake Forest, Philadelphia 1957-61; Washington 1962-63; Minnesota 1965-66
Barnes, Bruce, P, UCLA, New England 1973-74
Barnes, Charley, TE, Northeast Louisiana, Dallas Texans 1961
Barnes, Earnest, NT, Mississippi State, Baltimore 1983
Barnes, Emery, DE, Oregon, Green Bay 1956
Barnes, Erich, DB, Purdue, Chi. Bears 1958-60; NY Giants 1961-64; Cleveland 1965-71
Barnes, Ernie, G, North Carolina Central, NY Titans 1960; San Diego 1961-62; Denver 1963-64
Barnes, Gary, SE, Clemson, Green Bay 1962; Dallas 1963; Chi. Bears 1964; Atlanta 1966-67
Barnes, Jeff, LB, California, Oakland 1977-81; LA Raiders 1982-85
Barnes, Joe, QB, Texas Tech, Chi. Bears 1974
Barnes, Larry, FB, Colorado State, San Francisco 1957; Oakland 1960
Barnes, Larry, RB, Tennessee State, San Diego 1977-78; St. Louis 1978; Philadelphia 1978-79
Barnes, Mike, DB, Texas-Arlington, St. Louis 1967-68
Barnes, Mike, DE, Miami, Baltimore 1973-81
Barnes, Pete, LB, Southern, Houston 1967-68; San Diego 1969-72; St. Louis 1973-75; New England 1976-77
Barnes, Rodrigo, LB, Rice, Dallas 1973-74; New England 1974-75; Miami 1975; Oakland 1976
Barnes, Roosevelt, LB, Purdue, Detroit 1982-85
Barnes, Walter (Piggy), G, LSU, Philadelphia 1948-51
Barnes, Walter, DT-DE, Nebraska, Washington 1966-68; Denver 1969-71
Barnett, Bill, DE, Nebraska, Miami 1980-85
Barnett, Buster, TE, Jackson State, Buffalo 1981-84
Barnett, Dean, TE, Nevada-Las Vegas, Denver 1983
Barnett, Doug, DE, Azusa Pacific, LA Rams 1982-83; Washington 1985
Barnett, Solon, T, Baylor, Green Bay 1945-46
Barnett, Steve, Oregon, Chi. Bears 1963; Washington 1964
Barnett, Tom, HB, Purdue, Pittsburgh 1959-60
Barney, Eppie, FL, Iowa State, Cleveland 1967-68
Barney, Lem, CB-KR, Jackson State, Detroit 1967-77
Barnhart, Dan, HB, Centenary, Philadelphia 1934
Barni, Roy, DB, San Francisco, Chi. Cardinals 1952-53; Philadelphia 1954-55; Washington 1955-56
Barnikow, Ed, HB, Hartford 1926
Barnum, Len (Feets), QB-FB, West Virginia Wesleyan, NY Giants 1938-40; Philadelphia 1941-42
Barnum, Pete, FB, West Virginia, Columbus 1926
Barnwell, Malcolm, WR, Virginia Union, Oakland 1981; LA Raiders 1982-84; Washington 1985; New Orleans 1985
Barr, Terry, DB-WR, Michigan, Detroit 1957-65
Barr, Wallace (Shorty), HB, Wisconsin, Racine 1923-24, 1926; Milwaukee 1925
Barrabee, Bob, E, NYU, Staten Island 1931
Barrager, Nate, C, USC, Minneapolis 1930; Frankford 1930-31; Green Bay 1931-32, 1934-35
Barrel, C, Carlisle, Oorang 1922-23
Barrett, Bob, E, Baldwin-Wallace, Buffalo 1960
Barrett, David, RB, Houston, Tampa Bay 1982
Barrett, Emmett, C, Portland, NY Giants 1942
Barrett, Jan, SE, Fresno State, Green Bay 1963; Oakland 1963-64
Barrett, Jean, T, Tulsa, San Francisco 1973-80
Barrett, Jeff, E, LSU, Brooklyn 1936-38
Barrett, John, T, Detroit, Akron 1924-25; Detroit 1926, 1928; Pottsville 1927
Barrett, Johnny, HB, Washington & Lee, Chi. Tigers 1920; Hammond 1922-23
Barrington, Tom, RB, Ohio State, Washington 1966; New Orleans 1967
Barron, Jim, T, Georgetown (Washington D.C.), Rochester 1921
Barry, Al, G, USC, Green Bay 1954, 1957; NY Giants 1958-59; LA Chargers 1960
Barry, Fred, DB, Boston U., Pittsburgh 1970
Barry, Norm, QB, Notre Dame, Chi. Cardinals 1921; Green Bay 1921
Barry, Odell, SE, Findlay, Denver 1964-65
Barry, Paul, FB, Tulsa, LA Rams 1950, 1952; Washington 1953; Chi. Cardinals 1954
Barsha, John, FB, Syracuse, Rochester 1920
Bartholomew, Sam, FB, Tennessee, Philadelphia 1941
Bartkowski, Steve, QB, California, Atlanta 1975-85; Washington 1985
Bartlett, Earl, HB, Centre, Pittsburgh 1939
Barton, Don, HB, Texas, Green Bay 1953
Barton, Greg, QB, Tulsa, Detroit 1969
Barton, Jim, C, Marshall, Dallas Texans 1960; Denver 1961-62
Bartos, Hank, G, North Carolina, Washington 1938
Bartos, Joe, HB, Navy, Washington 1950
Barwegan, Dick, G, Purdue, NY Yankees (AAFC) 1947; Baltimore (AAFC) 1948-49; Chi. Bears 1950-52; Baltimore 1953-54
Barzilauskas, Carl, DT, Indiana, NY Jets 1974-77; Green Bay 1978-79
Barzilauskas, Fritz, G, Yale, Boston 1947-48; NY Bulldogs 1949; NY Giants 1951
Basca, Mike, HB, Villanova, Philadelphia 1941
Baschnagel, Brian, WR, Ohio State, Chi. Bears 1976-84
Basing, Myrt, E-HB, Lawrence, Green Bay 1923-27
Basinger, Mike, T, Cal-Riverside, Green Bay 1974
Baska, Rich, LB, UCLA, Denver 1976-77
Basrak, Mike, C, Duquesne, Pittsburgh 1937-38
Bass, Bill, HB, Nevada-Reno, Chi. Rockets (AAFC) 1947
Bass, Dick, RB, Pacific, LA Rams 1960-69
Bass, Don, TE, Houston, Cincinnati 1978-81; New Orleans 1982
Bass, Glenn, SE, East Carolina, Buffalo 1961-66; Houston 1967-68
Bass, Mike, CB, Michigan, Detroit 1967; Washington 1969-75
Bass, Norm, DB, Pacific, Denver 1964
Bassett, Henry, T, Nebraska, Kansas City 1924
Bassett, Maurice, FB, Langston, Cleveland 1954-56
Bassi, Dick, G, Santa Clara, Washington 1937; Chi. Bears 1938-39; Philadelphia 1940; Pittsburgh 1941; San Francisco 1946-47
Bassman, Herman (Reds), HB, Ursinus, Philadelphia 1936
Baston, Bert, E, Minnesota, Cleveland 1920-21
Batchellor, Don, T, Grove City, Canton 1922; Toledo 1923
Bateman, Marv, P, Utah, Dallas 1972-74; Buffalo 1974-77
Bates, Bill, S, Tennessee, Dallas 1983-85
Bates, Ted, LB, Oregon State, Chi. Cardinals 1959; St. Louis 1960-62; NY Jets 1963
Batinski, Stan, G, Temple, Detroit 1941, 1943-47; Boston 1948; NY Bulldogs 1949
Batorski, John, E, Colgate, Buffalo (AAFC) 1946
Batten, Pat, FB, Hardin-Simmons, Detroit 1964
Battle, Jim, G, Southern Illinois, Minnesota 1963
Battle, Jim, T, Southern, Cleveland 1966
Battle, Mike, S-KR, USC, NY Jets 1969-70
Battle, Ralph, S, Jacksonville State, Cincinnati 1984
Battle, Ron, TE, North Texas State, LA Rams 1981-82
Battles, Cliff, HB, West Virginia Wesleyan, Boston 1932-36; Washington 1937
Batton, Bobby Joe, RB, Nevada-Las Vegas, NY Jets 1980
Bauer, Hank, RB, California Lutheran, San Diego 1977-82
Bauer, Herb, T, Baldwin-Wallace, Cleveland 1925
Bauer, John, G, Illinois, NY Giants 1954
Baugh, Sammy, QB, TCU, Washington 1937-52

Baughan, Maxie, LB, Georgia Tech, Philadelphia 1960-65; LA Rams 1966-70; Washington 1971-74
Baujan, Harry, E, Notre Dame, Cleveland 1920-21
Baumann, Alf, T, Northwestern, Chi. Rockets (AAFC) 1947; Philadelphia 1947; Chi. Bears 1948-50
Baumgardner, Max, E, Texas, Detroit 1948
Baumgartner, Bill, E, Minnesota, Baltimore (AAFC) 1947
Baumgartner, Steve, DE, Purdue, New Orleans 1973-77; Houston 1977-79
Baumhower, Bob, NT, Alabama, Miami 1977-84
Bausch, Frank, C, Kansas, Boston 1934-36; Chi. Bears 1937-40; Philadelphia 1941
Bausch, Jim, FB, Kansas, Cincinnati 1933; Chi. Cardinals 1933
Bavaro, Mark, TE, Notre Dame, NY Giants 1985
Bawel, Ed (Bibbles), DB, Evansville, Philadelphia 1952, 1955-56
Baxter, Ernie, HB, Centre, Racine 1923; Kenosha 1924
Baxter, Lloyd, C, SMU, Green Bay 1948
Bayless, Martin, S, Bowling Green, St. Louis 1984; Buffalo 1984-85
Bayless, Tom, G, Purdue, NY Jets 1970
Bayley, John, T, Syracuse, NY Yankees 1927
Baylor, Raymond, DE, Texas Southern, San Diego 1974
Baylor, Tim, S, Morgan State, Baltimore 1976-78; Minnesota 1979
Baynham, Craig, RB, Georgia Tech, Dallas 1967-69; Chi. Bears 1970; St. Louis 1972
Baysinger, Reeves, T, Syracuse, Rochester 1924
Baze, Winnie, HB, Texas Tech, Philadelphia 1937
Beach, Fred, G, California, LA Buccaneers 1926
Beach, Pat, TE, Washington State, Baltimore 1982-83; Indianapolis 1985
Beach, Walter, DB, Central Michigan, Boston 1960-61; Cleveland 1963-66
Beal, Norm, DB, Missouri, St. Louis 1962
Beals, Alyn, E, Santa Clara, San Francisco 1946-51
Beamer, Tim, S, Johnson C. Smith, Buffalo 1971
Beamon, Autry, S, East Texas State, Minnesota 1975-76; Seattle 1977-79; Cleveland 1980-81
Beams, Byron, T, Notre Dame, Pittsburgh 1959-60; Houston 1961
Bean, Bubba, RB, Texas A&M, Atlanta 1976, 1978-79
Beard, Ed, LB, Tennessee, San Francisco 1965-72
Beard, Tom, C, Michigan State, Buffalo 1972
Beasley, John, G, Earlham, Dayton 1923
Beasley, John, HB, South Dakota, Green Bay 1924
Beasley, John, TE, California, Minnesota 1967-73; New Orleans 1973-74
Beasley, Terry, WR, Auburn, San Francisco 1972, 1974-75
Beasley, Tom, DE-DT, Virginia Tech, Pittsburgh 1978-83; Washington 1984-85
Beathard, Pete, QB, USC, Kansas City 1964-67, 1973; Houston 1967-69; St. Louis 1970-71; LA Rams 1972
Beattie, Bob, T, Princeton, NY Yankees 1927; Orange 1929; Newark 1930
Beatty, Charles, DB, North Texas State, Pittsburgh 1969-72; St. Louis 1972
Beatty, Ed, C, Mississippi, San Francisco 1955-56; Pittsburgh 1957-61; Washington 1961
Beauchamp, Al, LB, Southern, Cincinnati 1968-75; St. Louis 1976
Beauchamp, Joe, CB, Iowa State, San Diego 1966-75
Beaudoin, Doug, S, Minnesota, New England 1976-79; Miami 1980; San Diego 1981
Beaver, Jim, DT, Florida, Philadelphia 1962
Beban, Gary, QB-FL, UCLA, Washington 1968-69
Bebout, Nick, T, Wyoming, Atlanta 1973-75; Seattle 1976-79
Bechtol, Hub, E, Texas, Baltimore (AAFC) 1947-49
Beck, Braden, LB, Stanford, Houston 1971
Beck, Carl, FB, West Virginia, Buffalo 1921
Beck, Clarence, T, Penn State, Pottsville 1925
Beck, Ken, DT, Texas A&M, Green Bay 1959-60
Beck, Marty, HB, Fordham, Akron 1921-22, 1924, 1926
Beck, Ray, G, Georgia Tech, NY Giants 1952, 1955-57
Becker, Dave, S, Iowa, Chi. Bears 1980
Becker, Doug, LB, Notre Dame, Chi. Bears 1978; Buffalo 1978
Becker, John, T, Denison, Dayton 1926-29
Becker, Kurt, G, Michigan, Chi. Bears 1982-85
Becker, Wayland, E, Marquette, Chi. Bears 1934; Brooklyn 1934-35; Green Bay 1936-38; Pittsburgh 1939
Beckett, Jack, T, Oregon, Buffalo 1920
Beckley, Art, HB, Michigan State, Dayton 1926
Beckman, Ed, TE, Florida State, Kansas City 1977-84
Beckman, Tom, DE, Michigan, St. Louis 1972
Bedford, Bill, E, SMU, Rochester 1925
Bednar, Al, G, Lafayette, Frankford 1924-25; NY Giants 1925-26
Bednarik, Chuck, C-LB, Pennsylvania, Philadelphia 1949-62
Bedore, Tom, G, Washington 1944
Bedsole, Hal, TE, USC, Minnesota 1964-66
Beebe, Keith, HB, Occidental, NY Giants 1944
Beekley, Bruce, LB, Oregon, Green Bay 1980
Beekley, Ferris, G, Miami (Ohio), Cincinnati 1921
Beer, Tom, TE-G, Houston, Denver 1967-69; Boston 1970; New England 1971-72
Beeson, Terry, LB, Kansas, Seattle 1977-81, San Francisco 1982
Behan, Charlie, E, Northern Illinois, Detroit 1942
Behman, Russell (Bull), T, Dickinson, Frankford 1924-25, 1927-31
Behrman, Dave, T, Michigan State, Buffalo 1963, 1965; Denver 1967
Beier, Tom, DB, Miami, Miami 1967, 1969
Beil, Larry, T, Portland, NY Giants 1948
Beinor, Ed, T, Notre Dame, Chi. Cardinals 1940-41; Washington 1941-42
Beirne, Jim, WR, Purdue, Houston 1968-73, 1975-76; San Diego 1974
Beisler, Randy, DE-G, Indiana, Philadelphia 1966-68; San Francisco 1969-74; Kansas City 1975
Belanich, Bill, T, Dayton, Dayton 1927-29
Belcher, Kevin, G, Texas-El Paso, NY Giants 1983-84
Belcher, Kevin, T, Wisconsin, LA Raiders 1985
Belden, Bob, QB, Notre Dame, Dallas 1969-70
Belden, Charles (Bunny), HB, St. Mary's (California), Duluth 1927; Chi. Cardinals 1929-31
Belding, Les, E, Iowa, Rock Island 1925
Belichick, Steve, FB, Case Western Reserve, Detroit 1941
Belk, Bill, DE, Maryland-Eastern Shore, San Francisco 1968-74
Belk, Rocky, WR, Miami, Cleveland 1983
Bell, Bill, K, Kansas, Atlanta 1971-72; New England 1973
Bell, Bob, DT, Cincinnati, Detroit 1971-73; St. Louis 1974-78
Bell, Bobby, LB, Minnesota, Kansas City 1963-74
Bell, Bobby, LB, Missouri, NY Jets 1984
Bell, Carlos, TE, Houston, New Orleans 1971
Bell, Ed, G, Indiana, Miami (AAFC) 1946; Green Bay 1947-49
Bell, Eddie, LB, Pennsylvania, Philadelphia 1955-58; NY Titans 1960
Bell, Eddie (The Flea), WR, Idaho State, NY Jets 1970-75
Bell, Gordon, RB, Michigan, NY Giants 1976-77; St. Louis 1978-79
Bell, Greg, RB, Notre Dame, Buffalo 1984-85
Bell, Henry, RB, Denver 1960
Bell, Jerry, TE, Arizona State, Tampa Bay 1982-85
Bell, Joe, DE, Norfolk State, Oakland 1979
Bell, Kay, T, Washington State, Chi. Bears 1937; NY Giants 1942
Bell, Kevin, WR, Lamar, NY Jets 1978
Bell, Mark, TE, Colorado State, Seattle 1979-80, 1982; Baltimore 1983; Indianapolis 1984
Bell, Mark, WR, Colorado State, St. Louis 1981
Bell, Mike, DE, Colorado State, Kansas City 1979-85
Bell, Rick, RB, St. John's (Minnesota), Minnesota 1983
Bell, Ricky, RB, USC, Tampa Bay 1977-81, San Diego 1982
Bell, Theo, WR, Arizona, Pittsburgh 1976, 1978-80; Tampa Bay 1981-85
Bell, Todd, S, Ohio State, Chi. Bears 1981-84
Bellinger, Bob, G, Gonzaga, NY Giants 1934-35
Bellinger, Rodney, CB, Miami, Buffalo 1984-85
Bellino, Joe, RB-KR, Navy, Boston 1965-67
Belotti, George, C, USC, Houston 1960-61; San Diego 1961
Belser, Caeser, DB, Arkansas-Pine Bluff, Kansas City 1968-71; San Francisco 1974
Belton, Horace, RB, Southeastern Louisiana, Kansas City 1978-80
Belton, Willie, RB, Maryland-Eastern Shore, Atlanta 1971-72; St. Louis 1973-74
Bemiller, Al, C, Syracuse, Buffalo 1961-69
Bendross, Jesse, WR, Alabama, San Diego 1984-85
Benirschke, Rolf, K, Cal-Davis, San Diego 1977-85
Benish, Dan, DT, Clemson, Atlanta 1983-85
Benjamin, Guy, QB, Stanford, Miami 1978-79; New Orleans 1980; San Francisco 1981-83
Benjamin, Tony, RB, Duke, Seattle 1977-79
Benkert, Heinie, HB, Rutgers, NY Giants 1925; Pottsville 1926; Orange 1929; Newark 1930
Benners, Fred, QB, SMU, NY Giants 1952
Bennett, Barry, NT, Concordia, (Minnesota) New Orleans 1978-81; NY Jets 1982-85
Bennett, Chuck, HB, Indiana, Portsmouth 1930; Chi. Cardinals 1933
Bennett, Earl, G, Hardin-Simmons, Green Bay 1946
Bennett, Joe, T, Marquette, Chi. Tigers 1920; Milwaukee 1922
Bennett, Monte, NT, Kansas State, New Orleans 1981
Bennett, Phil, LB, Miami, Boston 1960
Bennett, Woody, RB, Miami, NY Jets 1979-80; Miami 1980-85
Benson, Brad, C-T, Penn State, NY Giants 1977-85
Benson, Charles, DE, Baylor, Miami 1983-84; Indianapolis 1985
Benson, Cliff, TE, Purdue, Atlanta 1984-85
Benson, Duane, LB, Hamline, Oakland 1967-71; Atlanta 1972-73; Houston 1974-76
Benson, George, HB, Northwestern, Brooklyn (AAFC) 1947
Benson, Harry, G, Western Maryland, Philadelphia 1935
Benson, Thomas, LB, Oklahoma, Atlanta 1984-85
Bentley, Albert, RB, Miami, Indianapolis 1985
Benton, Jim, E, Arkansas, Cleveland 1938-40, 1942, 1944-45; Chi. Bears 1943; LA Rams 1946-47
Bentz, Ed, E, Rochester 1922
Bentz, Roman, T, Tulane, NY Yankees (AAFC) 1946-48; San Francisco (AAFC) 1948
Bentzien, Al, G, Marquette, Racine 1924
Benz, Larry, S, Northwestern, Cleveland 1963-65
Bercich, Bob, DB, Michigan State, Dallas Cowboys 1960-61
Berezney, Paul, T, Fordham, Green Bay 1942-44; Miami (AAFC) 1946
Berezney, Pete, T, Notre Dame, LA Dons (AAFC) 1947; Baltimore (AAFC) 1948
Bergen, Bill, HB, Marquette, Milwaukee 1926
Berger, Ron, DE, Wayne State, Boston 1969-70; New England 1971-72
Berger, Wally, T, Iowa State, Milwaukee 1924
Bergerson, Gil, T, Oregon State, Chi. Bears 1932-33; Chi. Cardinals 1933; Brooklyn 1935-36
Bergey, Bill, LB, Arkansas State, Cincinnati 1969-73; Philadelphia 1974-80
Bergey, Bruce, DE, UCLA, Kansas City 1971
Bergold, Scott, T, Wisconsin, St. Louis 1985
Bernard, Chuck, C, Michigan, Detroit 1934
Bernard, Dave, QB, Mississippi, Cleveland 1944-45
Bernard, George, G, DePauw, Racine 1926
Bernardi, Frank, HB, Colorado, Chi. Cardinals 1955-57; Denver 1960
Berner, Mil, C, Syracuse, Cincinnati 1933
Bernet, Ed, E, Pittsburgh 1955; Dallas Texans 1960
Bernet, Lee, T, Wisconsin, Denver 1955-56
Bernhardt, George, G, Illinois, Brooklyn (AAFC) 1946-48; Chi. Rockets (AAFC) 1948
Bernhardt, Roger, G, Kansas, NY Jets 1974; Kansas City 1975
Bernich, Ken, LB, Auburn, NY Jets 1975
Bernoske, Dan, G, Indiana, Louisville 1926
Berns, Bill (Bobby), G-T, Purdue, Muncie 1920; Dayton 1922-24
Berns, Rick, RB, Nebraska, Tampa Bay 1979-80; LA Raiders 1982-83
Berquist, Jay, G, Nebraska, Kansas City 1924, 1926; Chi. Cardinals 1927
Berra, Tim, WR, Massachusetts, Baltimore 1974
Berrang, Ed, DE, Villanova, Washington 1949-52; Detroit 1951
Berrehsen, Bill, T, Washington & Jefferson, Columbus 1926
Berry, Bob, QB, Oregon, Minnesota 1965-67, 1973-76; Atlanta 1968-72
Berry, Charlie, E, Lafayette, Pottsville 1925-26
Berry, Connie Mack, E, North Carolina State, Detroit 1939; Cleveland 1940; Chi. Bears 1942-46; Chi. Rockets (AAFC) 1947
Berry, Dan, HB, California, Philadelphia 1967
Berry, George, G, Beloit, Racine 1922; Hammond 1922-24, 1926; Akron 1924-26
Berry, Gil, HB, Illinois, Chi. Cardinals 1935
Berry, Howard, HB, Pennsylvania, Rochester 1921-22
Berry, Raymond, SE, SMU, Baltimore 1955-67
Berry, Reggie, DB, Long Beach State, San Diego 1972-74
Berry, Rex, HB, BYU, San Francisco 1951-56
Berry, Royce, DE, Houston, Cincinnati 1969-74; Chi. Bears 1976
Berry, Wayne, HB, Washington State, NY Giants 1954
Berryman, Robert (Punk), HB, Penn State, Frankford 1924
Berschet, Marv, G, Illinois, Washington 1954-55
Bertagnolli, Libero, G, Washington (St. Louis), Chi. Cardinals 1942, 1945
Bertelli, Angelo, QB, Notre Dame, LA Dons (AAFC) 1946; Chi. Rockets (AAFC) 1947-48
Bertelsen, Jim, RB, Texas, LA Rams 1972-76
Bertoglio, Jim, HB, Creighton, Columbus 1926
Bertuca, Tony, LB, Cal State-Chico, Baltimore 1974
Berwick, Ed, C, Loyola (Chicago), Louisville 1926
Berzinski, Willie, HB, Wisconsin-LaCrosse, Philadelphia 1956
Besana, Fred, QB, California, Buffalo 1977; NY Giants 1978
Beson, Warren, C, Minnesota, Baltimore (AAFC) 1949
Bess, Rufus, CB, South Carolina State, Oakland 1979; Buffalo 1980-81; Minnesota 1982-85
Bessillieu, Don, S, Georgia Tech, Miami 1979-81; St. Louis 1982; LA Raiders 1983, 1985
Best, Art, RB, Kent State, Chi. Bears 1977-78; NY Giants 1980
Best, Greg, S, Kansas State, Pittsburgh 1983; Cleveland 1984
Best, Keith, LB, Kansas State, Kansas City 1972
Bethea, Elvin, DE, North Carolina A&T, Houston 1968-83
Bethea, Larry, DT, Michigan State, Dallas 1978-1983
Bethune, Bobby, DB, Mississippi State, San Diego 1962
Bettencourt, Larry, C, St. Mary's (California), Green Bay 1933
Betters, Doug, DE, Nevada-Reno, Miami 1978-85
Betterson, James, RB, North Carolina, Philadelphia 1977-79
Bettiga, Mike, WR, Cal State-Humboldt, San Francisco 1973-74
Bettis, Tom, LB, Purdue, Green Bay 1955-61; Pittsburgh 1962; Chi. Bears 1963
Bettridge, Ed, LB, Bowling Green, Cleveland 1964
Bettridge, John, FB, Ohio State, Cleveland 1937; Chi. Bears 1937
Beuthel, Lloyd, G, Colgate, Buffalo 1927
Beutler, Tom, LB, Toledo, Cleveland 1970; Baltimore 1971
Beverly, David, P, Auburn, Houston 1974-75; Green Bay 1975-80
Beverly, Ed, WR, Arizona State, San Francisco 1973
Beverly, Randy, S, Colorado State, NY Jets 1967-69; Boston 1970; New England 1971
Biancone, John, HB, Oregon State, Brooklyn 1936
Biasucci, Dean, K, Western Carolina, Indianapolis 1984
Bickett, Duane, LB, USC, Indianapolis 1985
Bieberstein, Adolph, G, Wisconsin, Racine 1926
Biedermann, Leo, T, California, Cleveland 1978
Bielski, Dick, FB-TE-K, Maryland, Philadelphia 1955-59; Dallas Cowboys 1960-61; Baltimore 1962-63
Bienemann, Tom, DE, Drake, Chi. Cardinals 1951-56
Bierce, Bruce (Scotty), E, Akron, Akron 1920-22, 1925; Cleveland 1923-24
Big Bear, T, Oorang 1923
Biggs, Riley, C, Baylor, NY Giants 1926-27

Biggs, Verlon, DE, Jackson State, NY Jets 1965-70; Washington 1971-74
Bighead, Jack, E, Pepperdine, Baltimore 1954; LA Rams 1955
Bihl, Vic, T, Bucknell, Pottsville 1925
Bilbo, Jon, T, Mississippi, Chi. Cardinals 1938-39
Bilda, Dick, HB, Marquette, Green Bay 1944
Biletnikoff, Fred, WR, Florida State, Oakland 1965-78
Billingsley, Ron, DT, Wyoming, San Diego 1967-70; Houston 1971-72
Billman, John, G, Minnesota, Brooklyn (AAFC) 1946; Chi. Rockets (AAFC) 1947
Billock, Frank, G, St. Mary's (California), Pittsburgh 1937
Bingaman, Les, G, Illinois, Detroit 1948-54
Bingham, Craig, LB, Syracuse, Pittsburgh 1982-84; San Diego 1985
Bingham, Don, HB, Sul Ross, Chi. Bears 1956
Bingham, Gregg, LB, Purdue, Houston 1973-84
Bingham, Guy, G-C-T, Montana, NY Jets 1980-85
Binotto, John, HB, Duquesne, Pittsburgh 1942; Philadelphia 1942
Biodrowski, Denny, G, Memphis State, Kansas City 1963-67
Bird, Rodger, DB, Kentucky, Oakland 1966-68
Bird, Steve, WR, Eastern Kentucky, St. Louis 1983-84; San Diego 1984
Birdsong, Carl, P, Oklahoma State, St. Louis 1981-85
Birdwell, Dan, DT, Houston, Oakland 1962-69
Birk, Ferdinand, HB, Purdue, Hammond 1922
Birlem, Keith, HB, San Jose State, Chi. Cardinals 1939; Washington 1939
Birney, Tom, K, Michigan, Green Bay 1979-80
Bisbee, Bert, HB, Minnesota, Milwaukee 1922
Biscaha, Joe, SE, Richmond, NY Giants 1959; Boston 1960
Bishop, Bill, DT, North Texas State, Chi. Bears 1952-60; Minnesota 1961
Bishop, Don, CB, Los Angeles C.C., Pittsburgh 1958-59; Chi. Bears 1959; Dallas 1960-65
Bishop, Keith, C, Baylor, Denver 1980, 1982-85
Bishop, Richard, NT, Louisville, New England 1976-81; Miami 1982; LA Rams 1983
Bishop, Sonny, G, Fresno State, Dallas Texans 1962; Oakland 1963; Houston 1964-69
Bissell, Fred, E, Fordham, Akron 1925-26
Bitterlich, Don, K, Temple, Seattle 1976
Bivins, Charlie, HB, Morris Brown, Chi. Bears 1960-66; Pittsburgh 1967; Buffalo 1967
Bizer, Herb, E, John Carroll, Buffalo 1929
Bjork, Del, T, Oregon, Chi. Bears 1937-38
Bjorklund, Bob, C, Minnesota, Philadelphia 1941
Bjorklund, Hank, RB, Princeton, NY Jets 1972-74
Black, Blondy, HB, Mississippi State, Buffalo (AAFC) 1946; Baltimore (AAFC) 1947
Black, Charlie, E, Kansas, Duluth 1925
Black, James, RB, Akron, Cleveland 1984
Black, Mike, P, Arizona State, Detroit 1983-85
Black, Stan, DB, Mississippi State, San Francisco 1977
Black, Tim, LB, Baylor, St. Louis 1977
Black Bear, E, Oorang 1922-23
Blackburn, Bill, C, Rice, Chi. Cardinals 1946-50
Blackledge, Todd, QB, Penn State, Kansas City 1983-85
Blacklock, Hugh, T, Michigan State, Decatur 1920; Chi. Staleys 1921; Chi. Bears 1922-25; Brooklyn 1925
Blackman, Lennon, FB, Tulsa, Chi. Bears 1930
Blackmon, Don, LB, Tulsa, New England 1981-85
Blackmore, Richard, CB, Mississippi State, Philadelphia 1979-82; San Francisco 1983
Blackwell, Alois, RB, Houston, Dallas 1978-79
Blackwell, Hal, HB, South Carolina, Chi. Cardinals 1945
Blackwood, Glenn, S, Texas, Miami 1979-85
Blackwood, Lyle, S, TCU, Cincinnati 1973-75; Seattle 1976; Baltimore 1977-80; Miami 1981-85
Blados, Brian, G, North Carolina, Cincinnati 1984-85
Blahak, Joe, DB, Nebraska, Houston 1973; Minnesota 1974-75, 1977; Tampa Bay 1976; New England 1976
Blailock, Russ, T, Baylor, Milwaukee 1923; Akron 1925
Blaine, Ed, G, Missouri, Green Bay 1962; Philadelphia 1963-66
Blair, George, DB, Mississippi, San Diego 1961-64
Blair, Matt, LB, Iowa State, Minnesota 1974-85
Blair, T.C., TE, Tulsa, Detroit 1974
Blake, Tom, T, Cincinnati, NY Bulldogs 1949
Blanchard, Dick, LB, Tulsa, New England 1972
Blanchard, Tom, P, Oregon, NY Giants 1971-73; New Orleans 1974-78
Bland, Carl, WR, Virginia Union, Detroit 1984-85
Blanda, George, QB-K, Kentucky, Chi. Bears 1949-58; Baltimore 1950; Houston 1960-66; Oakland 1967-75
Blandin, Ernie, T, Tulane, Cleveland (AAFC) 1946-47; Baltimore (AAFC) 1948-49; Baltimore 1950, 1953
Blankenship, Greg, LB, Cal State-Hayward, Oakland 1976; Pittsburgh 1976
Blanks, Sid, RB, Texas A&I, Houston 1964, 1966-68; Boston 1969-70
Blanton, Jerry, LB, Kentucky, Kansas City 1979-85
Blazer, Phil, G, North Carolina, Buffalo 1960
Blazine, Tony, T, Illinois Wesleyan, Chi. Cardinals 1935-40; NY Giants 1941
Bleamer, Jeff, T, Penn State, Philadelphia 1975-76; NY Jets 1977
Bledsoe, Curtis, RB, San Diego State, Kansas City 1981-82
Bleeker, Mal, G, Columbia, Brooklyn 1930
Bleeker, Mel, HB, USC, Philadelphia 1944-46; LA Rams 1947
Bleick, Tom, DB, Georgia Tech, Baltimore 1966; Atlanta 1967
Bleier, Rocky, RB, Notre Dame, Pittsburgh 1968, 1971-80
Blessing, Paul, E, Kearney State, Detroit 1944
Bligen, Dennis, RB, St. John's (New York), NY Jets 1984-85
Blinka, Stan, LB, Sam Houston State, NY Jets 1979-83
Bliss, Harry, HB, Ohio State, Columbus 1921
Bliss, Homer, G, Washington & Jefferson, Chi. Cardinals 1928
Blocker, Frank, C, Purdue, Hammond 1920
Blondin, Tom, G, West Virginia Wesleyan, Cincinnati 1933
Blood (McNally), Johnny, HB, St. John's (Minnesota), Milwaukee 1925-26; Duluth 1926-27; Pottsville 1928; Green Bay 1929-33, 1935-36; Pittsburgh 1934, 1937-39
Bloodgood, Elbert, QB, Nebraska, Kansas City 1925-26; Cleveland 1927; NY Giants 1928; Green Bay 1930
Blount, Jeb, QB, Tulsa, Tampa Bay 1977
Blount, Lamar, E, Mississippi State, Miami (AAFC) 1946; Buffalo (AAFC) 1947; Baltimore (AAFC) 1947
Blount, Mel, CB, Southern, Pittsburgh 1970-83
Blount, Tony, S, Virginia, NY Giants 1980
Blozis, Al, T, Georgetown (Washington D.C.), NY Giants 1942-44
Blue, Forrest, C, Auburn, San Francisco 1968-74; Baltimore 1975-78
Blue, Luther, WR, Iowa State, Detroit 1977-79
Blumenstock, Jim, FB, Fordham, NY Giants 1947
Blumenthal, Morris, HB, Northwestern, Chi. Cardinals 1925
Blumer, Herb, T, Missouri, Chi. Cardinals 1925-30, 1933
Blye, Ronnie, RB, Florida A&M, NY Giants 1968; Philadelphia 1969
Board, Dwaine, DE, North Carolina A&T, San Francisco 1979-85
Boatwright, Bon, DT, Oklahoma State, San Diego 1974
Bobo, Hubert, LB, Ohio State, LA Chargers 1960; NY Titans 1960
Bock, Wayne, DT, Illinois, Chi. Cardinals 1957
Boden, Lynn, G, South Dakota State, Detroit 1975-78; Chi. Bears 1979
Bodenger, Maury, G, Tulane, Portsmouth 1931-33; Detroit 1934
Boedecker, Bill, HB, DePaul, Chi. Rockets (AAFC) 1946; Cleveland (AAFC) 1947-49; Green Bay 1950; Philadelphia 1950
Boeke, Jim, T, Heidelberg, LA Rams 1960-63; Dallas 1964-67; New Orleans 1968
Boensch, Fred, G, Stanford, Washington 1947-48
Boettcher, Ray, FB, Lawrence, Racine 1926
Boggan, Rex, DT, Mississippi, NY Giants 1955
Bogue, George, HB, Stanford, Chi. Cardinals 1930; Newark 1930
Bohannon, Fred, CB-KR, Mississippi Valley State, Pittsburgh 1982
Bohling, Dewey, HB, Hardin-Simmons, NY Titans 1960-61; Buffalo 1961
Bohlmann, Frank, G, Marquette, Chi. Cardinals 1942
Bohovich, Reed, G, Lehigh, NY Giants 1962
Bohren, Karl, HB, Pittsburgh, Buffalo 1927
Bojovic, Novo, K, Central Michigan, St. Louis 1985
Bokamper, Kim, LB-DE, San Jose State, Miami 1977-85
Bolan, George, FB, Purdue, Chi. Staleys 1921; Chi. Bears 1922-24
Bolan, Joe, T, Purdue, Louisville 1926
Bolden, Leroy, HB, Michigan State, Cleveland 1958-59
Bolden, Rickey, TE-T, SMU, Cleveland 1984-85
Boldt, Chase, E, Louisville 1921-23
Bolin, Bookie, G, Mississippi, NY Giants 1962-67; Minnesota 1968-69
Bolinger, Russ, T, Long Beach State, Detroit 1976-82; LA Rams 1983-85
Bolkovac, Nick, DT, Pittsburgh, Pittsburgh 1953-54
Boll, Don, T, Nebraska, Washington 1953-59; NY Giants 1960
Bollinger, Eddie, G, Bucknell, Frankford 1930
Bolton, Andy, RB, Fisk, Seattle 1976; Detroit 1976-78
Bolton, Ron, CB, Norfolk State, New England 1972-75; Cleveland 1976-82
Bolzan, Scott, T, Northern Illinois, Cleveland 1985
Bomar, Lynn, E, Vanderbilt, NY Giants 1925-26
Bonadies, Jack, G, Hartford 1926
Bond, Chuck, T, Washington, Washington 1937-38
Bond, Jim, G, Pittsburgh, Brooklyn 1926
Bond, Randall (Rink), FB, Washington, Washington 1938; Pittsburgh 1939
Bondurant, Bourbon, G, DePauw, Muncie 1921; Evansville 1922; Chi. Bears 1922
Bonelli, Ernie, HB, Pittsburgh, Chi. Cardinals 1945; Pittsburgh 1946
Bonner, Glen, RB, Washington, San Diego 1974-75
Bonness, Rik, LB, Nebraska, Oakland 1976; Tampa Bay 1977-79
Bono, Steve, QB, UCLA, Minnesota 1985
Bonowitz, Elliott, G, Wilmington, Columbus 1922-23; Dayton 1924-26
Bookman, Johnny, DB, Miami, NY Giants 1957; Dallas Texans 1960; NY Titans 1961
Bookout, Billy, DB, Austin, Green Bay 1955-56
Books, Bob, HB, Dickinson, Frankford 1926
Boone, Dave, DE, Eastern Michigan, Minnesota 1974
Boone, Jack, HB, Elon, Cleveland 1942
Boone, J.R., HB, Tulsa, Chi. Bears 1948-51; San Francisco 1952; Green Bay 1953
Booth, Clarence, T, SMU, Chi. Cardinals 1943; Card-Pitt 1944
Booth, Dick, HB, Case Western Reserve, Detroit 1941, 1945
Boozer, Emerson, RB, Maryland-Eastern Shore, NY Jets 1966-75
Borak, Tony, E, Creighton, Green Bay 1938
Borchardt, Jon, G-T, Montana State, Buffalo 1979-84; Seattle 1985
Bordelon, Ken, LB, LSU, New Orleans 1976-77; 1979-83
Borden, Les, E, Fordham, NY Giants 1935
Borden, Nate, DE, Indiana, Green Bay 1955-59; Dallas Cowboys 1960-61; Buffalo 1962
Borelli, Nick, HB, Muhlenberg, Newark 1930
Borntraeger, Bill, QB, Louisville 1923
Borton, John, QB, Ohio State, Cleveland 1957
Bortz, Mark, G, Iowa, Chi. Bears 1983-85
Boryla, Mike, QB, Stanford, Philadelphia 1974-76; Tampa Bay 1978
Bosarge, Wade, S, Tulsa, Miami 1977; New Orleans 1977
Bosch, Frank, DT, Colorado, Washington 1968
Bosdett, John, E, Chi. Tigers 1920
Bosley, Bruce, C, West Virginia, San Francisco 1956-68; Atlanta 1969
Bosseler, Don, FB, Miami, Washington 1957-64
Bostic, Jeff, C-G, Clemson, Washington 1980-85
Bostic, Joe, G, Clemson, St. Louis 1979-85
Bostic, Jonathan, CB, Bethune-Cookman, Detroit 1985
Bostic, Keith, S, Michigan, Houston 1983-85
Bostick, Lew, G, Alabama, Cleveland 1939
Boston, McKinley, LB, Minnesota, NY Giants 1968-69
Boswell, Ben, T, TCU, Portsmouth 1933; Boston 1934
Botchan, Ron, LB, Occidental, LA Chargers 1960; Houston 1962
Boudreaux, Jim, DE, Louisiana Tech, Boston 1966-68
Bouggess, Lee, RB, Louisville, Philadelphia 1970-71, 1973
Bouley, Gil, T, Boston College, Cleveland 1945; LA Rams 1946-50
Boures, Emil, C-G, Pittsburgh, Pittsburgh 1982-85
Boutwell, Leon, QB, Carlisle, Oorang 1922-23
Boutwell, Tommy, QB, Southern Mississippi, Miami 1969
Bouza, Matt, WR, California, San Francisco 1981; Baltimore 1982-83; Indianapolis 1984-85
Bova, Tony, E, St. Francis, Pittsburgh 1942, 1945-47; Phil-Pitt 1943; Card-Pitt 1944
Bove, Pete, G, Holy Cross, Newark 1930
Bowdell, Gordon, WR, Michigan, Denver 1971
Bowdoin, Jim, G, Alabama, Green Bay 1928-31; NY Giants 1932; Brooklyn 1932, 1934; Portsmouth 1933
Bower, Phil, HB, Dartmouth, Cleveland 1921
Bowers, Bill, DB, USC, LA Rams 1954
Bowie, Larry, G, Purdue, Minnesota 1962-68
Bowling, Andy, LB, Virginia Tech, Atlanta 1967
Bowman, Bill, FB, William & Mary, Detroit 1954, 1956; Pittsburgh 1957
Bowman, Jim, S, Central Michigan, New England 1985
Bowman, Ken, C, Wisconsin, Green Bay 1964-73
Bowman, Steve, RB, Alabama, NY Giants 1966
Bowser, Arda, HB, Bucknell, Canton 1922; Cleveland 1923
Bowser, Charles, LB, Duke, Miami 1982-85
Bowyer, Walt, DE, Arizona State, Denver 1983-84
Box, Cloyce, E, West Texas State, Detroit 1949-50, 1952-54
Boyarsky, Jerry, NT, Pittsburgh, New Orleans 1981; Cincinnati 1982-85
Boyd, Bill, HB, Westminster (Missouri), Chi. Cardinals 1930-31
Boyd, Bob, E-DB, Loyola (Los Angeles), LA Rams 1950-51, 1953-57
Boyd, Bobby, CB, Oklahoma, Baltimore 1960-68
Boyd, Brent, G, UCLA, Minnesota 1980-83, 1985
Boyd, Dennis, DT, Oregon State, Seattle 1977-82
Boyd, Elmo, WR, Eastern Kentucky, San Francisco 1978; Green Bay 1978
Boyd, Greg, S, Arizona, New England 1973; New Orleans 1974
Boyd, Greg, DE-NT, San Diego State, New England 1977-78; Denver 1980-82; Green Bay 1983; LA Raiders 1984; San Francisco 1984
Boyd, Sam, E, Baylor, Pittsburgh 1939-40
Boyda, Mike, FB, Washington & Lee, NY Bulldogs 1949
Boydston, Max, E, Oklahoma, Chi. Cardinals 1955-58; Dallas Texans 1960-61; Oakland 1962
Boyer, Mark, TE, USC, Indianapolis 1985
Boyer, Verdi, G, UCLA, Brooklyn 1936
Boyett, Lon, TE, Cal State-Northridge, San Francisco 1978
Boyette, Garland, LB, Grambling, St. Louis 1962-63; Houston 1966-72
Boykin, Greg, RB, Northwestern, New Orleans 1977; San Francisco 1978
Boylan, Jim, FL, Washington State, Minnesota 1963
Boyle, Bill (Knuckles), T, NY Giants 1934
Boynton, Ben Lee, QB, Williams, Washington 1921; Rochester 1921-22; Buffalo 1924
Boynton, George, DB, East Texas State, Oakland 1962
Boynton, John, T, Tennessee, Miami 1969
Braase, Ordell, DE, South Dakota, Baltimore 1957-68
Braatz, Tom, DE, Marquette, Washington 1957-59; LA Rams 1958; Dallas Cowboys 1960
Brabham, Danny, LB, Arkansas, Houston 1963-67; Cincinnati 1968

Brace, Bill, G, Brown, Buffalo 1920-22
Bracelin, Greg, LB, California, Denver 1980; Oakland 1981; Baltimore 1982-83; Indianapolis 1984
Bracken, Don, P, Michigan, Green Bay 1985
Brackett, M.L., DT, Auburn, Chi. Bears 1956-57; NY Giants 1958
Brackins, Charlie (Choo-Choo), QB, Prairie View A&M, Green Bay 1955
Braden, Dave, G, Marquette, Chi. Cardinals 1945
Bradfute, Byron, T, Southern Mississippi, Dallas Cowboys 1960-61
Bradley, Bill, S-P, Texas, Philadelphia 1969-76; St. Louis 1977
Bradley, Carlos, LB, Wake Forest, San Diego 1981-85
Bradley, Chuck, TE, Oregon, San Diego 1975-77; Chi. Bears 1977
Bradley, Dave, T, Penn State, Green Bay 1969-71; St. Louis 1972
Bradley, Ed, DE, Wake Forest, Chi. Bears 1950, 1952
Bradley, Ed, LB, Wake Forest, Pittsburgh 1972-75; Seattle 1976; San Francisco 1977-78
Bradley, Hal, E, Elon, Chi. Cardinals 1938-39; Washington 1938-39
Bradley, Harold, G, Iowa, Chi. Cardinals 1928
Bradley, Harold, G, Iowa, Cleveland 1954-56; Philadelphia 1958
Bradley, Henry, DT, Alcorn State, Cleveland 1979-82
Bradley, Luther, CB, Notre Dame, Detroit 1978-81
Bradshaw, Charlie, T, Baylor, LA Rams 1958-60; Pittsburgh 1961-66; Detroit 1967-68
Bradshaw, Craig, QB, Utah State, Houston 1980
Bradshaw, Jim, HB, Nevada-Reno, Kansas City 1924
Bradshaw, Jim, DB, Tennessee-Chattanooga, Pittsburgh 1963-67
Bradshaw, Morris, WR, Ohio State, Oakland 1974-78
Bradshaw, Terry, QB, Louisiana Tech, Pittsburgh 1970-83
Bradshaw, Wes, QB, Baylor, Rock Island 1924
Brady, Ed, LB, Illinois, LA Rams 1984-85
Brady, Pat, P, Nevada-Reno, Pittsburgh 1952-54
Brady, Phil, DB, BYU, Denver 1969
Bragg, Mike, P, Richmond, Washington 1968-79
Braggs, Byron, NT, Alabama, Green Bay 1981-83; Tampa Bay 1984
Bragonier, Dennis, DB, Stanford, San Francisco 1974
Brahaney, Tom, C, Oklahoma, St. Louis 1973-78
Brahm, Larry, G, Temple, Cleveland 1942
Braidwood, Chuck, E, Tennessee-Chattanooga, Portsmouth 1930; Cleveland 1931; Chi. Cardinals 1932; Cincinnati 1933
Braman, Bill, T, Racine 1922-23
Bramlett, John (Bull), LB, Memphis State, Denver 1965-66; Miami 1967-68; Boston 1969-70; Atlanta 1971
Brammer, Mark, TE, Michigan State, Buffalo 1980-84
Brancato, George, HB, LSU, Chi. Cardinals 1954
Branch, Cliff, WR, Colorado, Oakland 1972-81; LA Raiders 1982-85
Branch, Mel, DE, LSU, Dallas Texans 1960-62; Kansas City 1963-65; Miami 1966-68
Branch, Reggie, RB, East Carolina, Washington 1985
Brandau, Art, C, Tennessee, Pittsburgh 1945-46
Brandt, Jim (Popcorn), HB, St. Thomas (Minnesota), Pittsburgh 1952-54
Braney, John (Speed), G, Syracuse, Providence 1925-26
Brannon, Phil, E, Holy Cross, Cleveland 1925
Brannon, Solomon, DB, Morris Brown, Kansas City 1965-66
Branstetter, Kent, T, Houston, Green Bay 1973
Brantley, Scot, LB, Florida, Tampa Bay 1980-85
Branton, Gene, WR, Texas Southern, Tampa Bay 1983, 1985
Bratkowski, Zeke, QB, Georgia, Chi. Bears 1954, 1957-60; LA Rams 1961-63; Green Bay 1963-68, 1971
Bratt, Joe, E, Wisconsin-Superior, Duluth 1924
Bravo, Alex, DB, Cal Poly-SLO, LA Rams 1957-58; Oakland 1960-61
Brawley, Ed, G, Holy Cross, Cleveland 1921
Braxton, Hezekiah, RB, Virginia Union, San Diego 1962; Buffalo 1963
Braxton, Jim, RB, West Virginia, Buffalo 1971-78; Miami 1978
Bray, Maurice (Mule), T, SMU, Pittsburgh 1935-36
Bray, Ray, G, Western Michigan, Chi. Bears 1939-42, 1946-51; Green Bay 1952
Brazell, Carl, QB, Baylor, Cleveland 1938
Braziel, Larry, CB, USC, Baltimore 1979-81; Cleveland 1982-85
Brazile, Robert, LB, Jackson State, Houston 1975-84
Brazinsky, Sam, C, Villanova, Buffalo (AAFC) 1946
Breaux, Don, QB, McNeese State, Denver 1963; San Diego 1965
Bredde, Bill, HB, Oklahoma State, Chi. Cardinals 1954
Bredice, John, E, Boston U., Philadelphia 1956
Breding, Ed, LB, Texas A&M, Washington 1967-68
Breech, Jim, K, California, Oakland 1979; Cincinnati 1980-85
Breeden, Louis, CB, North Carolina Central, Cincinnati 1978-85
Breedlove, Rod, LB, Maryland, Washington 1960-64; Pittsburgh 1965-67
Breedon, Bill, HB, Oklahoma, Pittsburgh 1937
Breen, Gene, LB, Virginia Tech, Green Bay 1964; Pittsburgh 1965-66; LA Rams 1967-68
Breitenstein, Bob, T, Tulsa, Denver 1965-67; Minnesota 1967; Atlanta 1969-70
Brenkert, Wayne, HB, Washington & Jefferson, Akron 1923-24
Brennan, Brian, WR, Boston College, Cleveland 1984-85
Brennan, John, G, Michigan, Green Bay 1939
Brennan, Leo, T, Holy Cross, Philadelphia 1942
Brennan, Matt, HB, Lafayette, NY Giants 1925; Brooklyn 1926
Brennan, Willis, G, Chi. Cardinals 1920-27
Brenner, Al, DB, Michigan State, NY Giants 1969
Brenner, Hoby, TE, USC, New Orleans 1981-85
Brenner, Ray, HB, Canton 1925
Brethauer, Monte, E, Oregon, Baltimore 1953, 1955
Brett, Ed, E, Washington State, Chi. Cardinals 1936; Pittsburgh 1936-37
Brettschneider, Carl, LB, Iowa State, Chi. Cardinals 1956-59; Detroit 1960-63
Breunig, Bob, LB, Arizona State, Dallas 1975-84
Brewer, Brooke, HB, Maryland, Cleveland 1921; Akron 1922
Brewer, Billy, DB, Mississippi, Washington 1960
Brewer, Chris, RB, Arizona, Denver 1984
Brewer, John, HB, Georgia Tech, Dayton 1929
Brewer, John, FB, Louisville, Philadelphia 1952-53
Brewer, Johnny, LB-TE, Mississippi, Cleveland 1961-67; New Orleans 1968
Brewington, Jim, T, North Carolina Central, Oakland 1961
Brewster, Darrell (Pete), SE, Purdue, Cleveland 1952-58; Pittsburgh 1959-60
Brewster, Walt, T, West Virginia, Buffalo 1929
Brezina, Bobby, HB, Houston, Houston 1963
Brezina, Greg, LB, Houston, Atlanta 1968-69, 1971-79
Brian, Bill, T, Gonzaga, Philadelphia 1935-36
Brian, Harry, HB, Grove City, Hartford 1926
Briante, Frank, FB, NYU, Staten Island 1929; Newark 1930
Brick, Shirley, E, Rice, Buffalo 1920
Brickley, George, HB, Trinity (Connecticut), Cleveland 1920; NY Giants 1921
Bridgeford, Lane, HB, Knox, Rock Island 1921-22
Briehl, Tom, LB, Stanford, Houston 1985
Briggs, Bill, DE, Iowa, Washington 1966-67
Briggs, Bob, FB, Central State (Oklahoma), Washington 1965
Briggs, Bob, DT, Heidelberg, San Diego 1968-70; Cleveland 1971-73; Kansas City 1974
Brigham, Haven, G, Ohio State, Columbus 1920
Bright, Greg, S, Morehead State, Cincinnati 1980-81
Bright, Leon, RB-KR, Florida State, NY Giants 1981-83; Tampa Bay 1984-85
Brill, Hal, HB, Wichita State, Detroit 1939
Brindley, Walt, FB, Drake, Rock Island 1921-22
Brink, Larry, DE, Northern Illinois, LA Rams 1948-53; Chi. Bears 1954
Brinson, Larry, RB, Florida, Dallas 1977-79; Seattle 1980
Briscoe, Marlin, WR-QB, Nebraska-Omaha, Denver 1968; Buffalo 1969-71; Miami 1972-74; San Diego 1975; Detroit 1975; New England 1976
Brister, Willie, TE, Southern, NY Jets 1974-75
Bristor, John, CB, Waynesburg, San Francisco 1979
Bristow, Obie, HB, Kansas City 1924-26
Brito, Gene, E-DE, Loyola (Los Angeles), Washington 1951-53; 1955-58; LA Rams 1959-60
Britt, Charley, DB, Georgia, LA Rams 1960-63; Minnesota 1964; San Francisco 1964
Britt, Eddie, FB, Holy Cross, Boston 1936; Washington 1937; Brooklyn 1938
Britt, James, CB, LSU, Atlanta 1983-85
Britt, Maurice, E, Arkansas, Detroit 1941
Britt, Oscar, G, Mississippi, Washington 1946
Britt, Rankin, E, Texas A&M, Philadelphia 1939
Brittenum, Jon, QB, Arkansas, San Diego 1967-68
Britton, Earl, FB, Illinois, Chi. Bears 1925; Brooklyn 1926; Frankford 1927; Dayton 1927-28; Chi. Cardinals 1929
Broadley, Karl, G, Bethany (West Virginia), Cleveland 1925
Broadnax, Jerry, TE, Southern, Houston 1974
Broadstone, Marion, T, Nebraska, NY Giants 1931
Brock, Charley, C, Nebraska, Green Bay 1939-47
Brock, Clyde, DT, Utah State, Dallas 1962-63; San Francisco 1963
Brock, Dieter, QB, Jacksonville State, LA Rams 1985
Brock, Lou, QB, Purdue, Green Bay 1940-45
Brock, Pete, C, Colorado, New England 1976-85
Brock, Stan, T, Colorado, New Orleans 1980-85
Brock, Willie, C, Colorado, Detroit 1978
Brockington, John, RB, Ohio State, Green Bay 1971-77; Kansas City 1977
Broda, Hal, E, Brown, Cleveland 1927
Broderick, Ted, HB, Louisville 1923
Brodhead, Bob, QB, Duke, Buffalo 1960
Brodie, John, QB, Stanford, San Francisco 1957-73
Brodnax, J.W., FB, LSU, Denver 1960
Brodnicki, Chuck, C, Villanova, Philadelphia 1934; Brooklyn 1934
Broker, Ed, T, Carlisle, Oorang 1922
Broker, Hippo, QB, Carlisle, Oorang 1922
Brooker, Tommy, TE-K, Alabama, Dallas Texans 1962; Kansas City 1963-66
Brookins, Mitchell, WR, Illinois, Buffalo 1984-85
Brooks, Billy, WR, Oklahoma, Cincinnati 1976-79; San Diego 1981; Houston 1981
Brooks, Bob, FB, Ohio U., NY Titans 1961
Brooks, Bobby, DB, Bishop, NY Giants 1974-76
Brooks, Clifford, CB, Tennessee State, Cleveland 1972-74; Philadelphia 1975-76; NY Jets 1976; Buffalo 1976
Brooks, James, RB, Auburn, San Diego 1981-83; Cincinnati 1984-85
Brooks, Jon, LB, Clemson, Detroit 1979; Atlanta 1980; St. Louis 1980
Brooks, Kevin, DE, Michigan, Dallas 1985
Brooks, Larry, DT, Virginia State, LA Rams 1972-82
Brooks, Leo, DT, Texas, Houston 1970-72; St. Louis 1973-76
Brooks, Perry, DT, Southern, Washington 1978-84
Brookshier, Tom, DB, Colorado, Philadelphia 1953, 1956-61
Brophy, Jay, LB, Miami, Miami 1984-85
Brosky, Al, DB, Illinois, Chi. Cardinals 1954
Broughton, Willie, DE, Miami, Indianapolis 1985
Broussard, Fred, C, Texas A&M, Pittsburgh 1955; NY Giants 1955
Broussard, Steve, P, SMU, Green Bay 1975
Brovelli, Angelo, QB, St. Mary's (California), Pittsburgh 1933-34
Brown, Aaron, DE, Minnesota, Kansas City 1966, 1968-72; Green Bay 1973-74
Brown, Aaron, LB, Ohio State, Tampa Bay 1978-80; Philadelphia 1985
Brown, Allen, TE, Mississippi, Green Bay 1966-67
Brown, Arnold, CB, North Carolina Central, Detroit 1985
Brown, Barry, LB, Florida, Baltimore 1966-67; NY Giants 1968; Boston 1969-70
Brown, Bill, QB, Texas Tech, Brooklyn 1943-44; Pittsburgh 1945
Brown, Bill, LB, Syracuse, Boston 1960
Brown, Bill, FB, Illinois, Chi. Bears 1961; Minnesota 1962-74
Brown, Bob, T, Nebraska, Philadelphia 1964-68; LA Rams 1969-70; Oakland 1971-73
Brown, Bob, DE, Arkansas-Pine Bluff, Green Bay 1966-73; San Diego 1974; Cincinnati 1975-76
Brown, Bob, TE, Alcorn State, St. Louis 1969; Minnesota 1971; New Orleans 1972-73
Brown, Booker, T, USC, San Diego 1975, 1977
Brown, Boyd, TE, Alcorn State, Denver 1974-76; NY Giants 1977
Brown, Bud, S, Southern Mississippi, Miami 1984-85
Brown, Buddy, G, Arkansas, Washington 1951-52; Green Bay 1953-56
Brown, Carlos, QB, Pacific, Green Bay 1975-76
Brown, Cedric, S, Kent State, Tampa Bay 1976-84
Brown, Charley, T, Houston, Oakland 1962
Brown, Charlie, DB, Syracuse, Chi. Bears 1966-67; Buffalo 1968
Brown, Charlie, RB, Missouri, New Orleans 1967-68
Brown, Charlie, WR, Northern Arizona, Detroit 1970
Brown, Charlie, WR, South Carolina College, Washington 1982-84; Atlanta 1985
Brown, Chris, DB, Notre Dame, Pittsburgh 1984-85
Brown, Chuck, C-G, Houston, St. Louis 1979-80
Brown, Clay, TE, BYU, Atlanta 1982; Denver 1983
Brown, Curtis, RB, Missouri, Buffalo 1977-82; Houston 1983
Brown, Dan, DE, Villanova, Washington 1950
Brown, Dave, HB, Alabama, NY Giants 1943, 1946-47
Brown, Dave, CB, Michigan, Pittsburgh 1975; Seattle 1976-85
Brown, Dean, DB, Fort Valley State, Cleveland 1969; Miami 1970
Brown, Dick, G, Iowa, Portsmouth 1930
Brown, Don, HB, Houston, Houston 1960
Brown, Don, T, Santa Clara, San Diego 1983
Brown, Doug, DT, Fresno State, Oakland 1964
Brown, Ed, HB, Syracuse, Milwaukee 1922
Brown, Ed, QB, San Francisco, Chi. Bears 1954-61; Pittsburgh 1962-65; Baltimore 1965
Brown, Eddie, S-KR, Tennessee, Cleveland 1974-75; Washington 1975-77; LA Rams 1978-79
Brown, Eddie, WR, Miami, Cincinnati 1985
Brown, Fred, G, NYU, Staten Island 1930
Brown, Fred, HB, Georgia, Buffalo 1961, 1963
Brown, Fred, LB-DE, Miami, LA Rams 1965; Philadelphia 1967-69
Brown, George, G, Carnegie-Mellon, Akron 1923
Brown, George, G, TCU, NY Yankees (AAFC) 1949; NY Yanks 1950
Brown, Greg, DE, Kansas State, Philadelphia 1981-85
Brown, Guy, LB, Houston, Dallas 1977-82
Brown, Hardy (Thumper), LB, Tulsa, Brooklyn (AAFC) 1948; Chi. Hornets (AAFC) 1949; Baltimore 1950; Washington 1950; San Francisco 1951-56; Chi. Cardinals 1956; Denver 1960
Brown, Howard, G, Indiana, Detroit 1948-50
Brown, Jack, C, Dayton, Dayton 1926-29
Brown, Jesse, HB, Pittsburgh, Pottsville 1926
Brown, Jim, FB, Syracuse, Cleveland 1957-65
Brown, John, C, North Carolina Central, LA Dons 1947-49
Brown, John, T, Syracuse, Cleveland 1962-66; Pittsburgh 1967-71
Brown, Ken, RB, Cleveland 1970-75
Brown, Ken, C, New Mexico, Denver 1979; Green Bay 1980
Brown, Larry, RB, Kansas State, Washington 1969-76
Brown, Larry, TE-T, Kansas, Pittsburgh 1971-84
Brown, Larry, T, Miami, Kansas City 1978-79
Brown, Lomas, T, Florida, Detroit 1985
Brown, Mark, LB, Purdue, Miami 1983-85
Brown, Marv, HB, East Texas State, Detroit 1957
Brown, Matt, HB, Syracuse, Akron 1920
Brown, Norris, TE, Georgia, Minnesota 1983
Brown, Otto, DB, Prairie View A&M, Dallas 1969; NY Giants

1970-73
Brown, Pete, C, Georgia Tech, San Francisco 1953-54
Brown, Preston, WR-KR, Vanderbilt, New England 1980, 1982; NY Jets 1983; Cleveland 1984
Brown, Ray, DB, Mississippi, Baltimore 1958-60
Brown, Ray, S, West Texas State, Atlanta 1971-77; New Orleans 1978-80
Brown, Reggie, RB, Oregon, Atlanta 1982-83
Brown, Robert, LB, Virginia Tech, Green Bay 1982-85
Brown, Roger, DT, Maryland-Eastern Shore, Detroit 1960-66; LA Rams 1967-69
Brown, Ron, WR, Arizona State, LA Rams 1984-85
Brown, Roosevelt, T, Morgan State, NY Giants 1953-65
Brown, Rush, DT, Ball State, St. Louis 1980-83
Brown, Sidney, DB, Oklahoma, New England 1978
Brown, Stan, WR, Purdue, Cleveland 1971
Brown, Steve, CB-KR, Oregon, Houston 1983-85
Brown, Ted, RB, North Carolina State, Minnesota 1979-85
Brown, Terry, DB, Oklahoma State, St. Louis 1969-70; Minnesota 1972-75; Cleveland 1976
Brown, Theotis, RB, UCLA, St. Louis 1979-81; Seattle 1981-83; Kansas City 1983-84
Brown, Thomas, DE, Baylor, Philadelphia 1980; Cleveland 1981, 1983
Brown, Tim, RB-KR, Ball State, Green Bay 1959; Philadelphia 1960-67; Baltimore 1968
Brown, Tom, E, William & Mary, Pittsburgh 1942
Brown, Tom, S, Maryland, Green Bay 1964-68; Washington 1969
Brown, Willie, CB, Grambling, Denver 1963-66; Oakland 1967-78
Brown, Willie, FL, USC, LA Rams 1964-65; Philadelphia 1966
Browne, Gordie, T, Boston College, NY Jets 1974-75
Browner, Jim, S, Notre Dame, Cincinnati 1979-80
Browner, Joey, S, USC, Minnesota 1983-85
Browner, Keith, LB, USC, Tampa Bay 1984-85
Browner, Ross, DE, Notre Dame, Cincinnati 1978-85
Browning, Bob, QB, William Jewell, Kansas City 1925
Browning, Charley, RB, Washington, NY Jets 1965
Browning, Dave, DE, Washington, Oakland 1978-81; LA Raiders 1982; New England 1983
Browning, Greg, E, Denver, NY Giants 1947
Brownlee, Claude, DT, Benedictine, Miami 1967
Brubaker, Dick, SE, Ohio State, Chi. Cardinals 1955, 1957; Buffalo 1960
Bruce, Gail, E, Washington, San Francisco 1948-51
Bruckner, Les, FB, Michigan State, Chi. Cardinals 1945
Bruckner, Nick, WR, Syracuse, NY Jets 1983-85
Bruder, Hank, QB, Northwestern, Green Bay 1931-39; Pittsburgh 1940
Bruder, Woodruff (Doc), FB, West Virginia, Buffalo 1925; Frankford 1925-26
Brudzinski, Bob, LB, Ohio State, LA Rams 1977-80; Miami 1980-85
Brueckman, Charlie, C, Pittsburgh, Washington 1958; LA Chargers 1960
Bruer, Bob, TE, Mankato State, Chi. Bears 1976; San Francisco 1979-80; Minnesota 1980-83
Bruggers, Bob, LB, Minnesota, Miami 1967-68; San Diego 1968-71
Brumbaugh, Boyd, HB, Duquesne, Brooklyn 1938-39; Pittsburgh 1939-41
Brumbaugh, Carl, QB, Florida, Chi. Bears 1930-34, 1936, 1938; Brooklyn 1937; Cleveland 1937
Brumbaugh, Justin, FB, Bucknell, Frankford 1931
Brumfield, Jack, DE, Southern Mississippi, San Francisco 1954
Brumfield, Jim, RB-KR, Indiana State, Pittsburgh 1971
Brumley, Bob, HB, Rice, Detroit 1945
Brumm, Don, DE, Purdue, St. Louis 1963-69, 1972; Philadelphia 1970-71
Brumm, Roman, G, Wisconsin, Racine 1922, 1924, 1926; Milwaukee 1925
Brundage, Dewey, DE, BYU, Pittsburgh 1954
Brundige, Bill, DT, Colorado, Washington 1970-77
Brune, Larry, S, Rice, Minnesota 1980
Brunelli, Sam, T, Colorado State, Denver 1966-71
Brunet, Bob, RB, Louisiana Tech, Washington 1968, 1970-73, 1975-77
Bruney, Fred, DB, Ohio State, San Francisco 1953, 1956; Pittsburgh 1956-57; LA Rams 1958; Boston 1960-62
Brunklacher, Austin, G, Alabama, Louisville 1921-23
Brunner, Scott, QB, Delaware, NY Giants 1980-83; St. Louis 1985
Brunson, Larry, WR, Colorado, Kansas City 1974-77; Oakland 1978-79; Denver 1980
Brunson, Mike, WR-RB, Arizona State, Atlanta 1970
Brupbacher, Ross, LB, Texas A&M, Chi. Bears 1970-72, 1976
Brutz, Jim, T, Notre Dame, Chi. Rockets (AAFC) 1946, 1948
Bryan, Billy, C-G, Duke, Denver 1977-85
Bryan, John, HB, Chicago, Chi. Cardinals 1922, 1926; Chi. Bears 1923-25; Milwaukee 1925-26
Bryan, Rick, DT, Oklahoma, Atlanta 1984-85
Bryant, Bill, DB, Grambling, NY Giants 1976-78
Bryant, Bob, T, Texas Tech, San Francisco (AAFC) 1946-49
Bryant, Bob, TE, Texas, Dallas Texans 1960
Bryant, Bobby, CB, South Carolina, Minnesota 1968-80
Bryant, Charlie, RB, Allen, St. Louis 1966-67; Atlanta 1968-69
Bryant, Chuck, TE, Ohio State, St. Louis 1962
Bryant, Cullen, S-RB, Colorado, LA Rams 1973-82; Seattle 1983-84
Bryant, Hubie, WR, Minnesota, Pittsburgh 1970; New England 1971-72
Bryant, Jeff, DE, Clemson, Seattle 1982-85
Bryant, Jim, QB, Pennsylvania, Cleveland 1920
Bryant, Steve, WR, Purdue, Houston 1982-85
Bryant, Trent, CB, Arkansas, Washington 1981; Kansas City 1982-83
Bryant, Walter, HB, Texas Tech, Baltimore 1955
Bryant, Warren, T, Kentucky, Atlanta 1977-84; LA Raiders 1984
Bryant, Waymond, LB, Tennessee State, Chi. Bears 1974-77
Buben, Mark, NT, Tufts, New England 1979, 1981; Cleveland 1982
Bucchianeri, Amadeo, G, Indiana, Green Bay 1941, 1944-45
Bucek, Felix, G, Texas A&M, Pittsburgh 1946
Buchanan, Buck, DT, Grambling, Kansas City 1963-75
Buchanan, Steve, QB, Miami (Ohio), Dayton 1929
Buchanan, Tim, LB, Hawaii, Cincinnati 1969
Buchanon, Willie, CB, San Diego State, Green Bay 1972-78; San Diego 1979-82
Bucher, Frank, E, Detroit, Detroit 1925; Pottsville 1925-26
Buck, Howard (Cub), T, Wisconsin, Canton 1920; Green Bay 1921-25
Buckey, Don, WR, North Carolina State, NY Jets 1976
Buckeye, Garland, G, Chi. Tigers 1920; Chi. Cardinals 1921-24
Buckler, Bill, G, Alabama, Chi. Bears 1926-28, 1931-33
Bucklew, Phil, E, Xavier, Cleveland 1937
Buckley, Ed, QB, NYU, Staten Island 1930
Bucklin, Tom, G, Idaho, Chi. Cardinals 1927; NY Giants 1931
Buckman, Tom, TE, Texas A&M, Denver 1969
Buda, Carl, G, Tulsa, Pittsburgh 1945
Budd, Frank, FL, Villanova, Philadelphia 1962; Washington 1963
Budd, Johnny, T, Lafayette, Frankford 1926; Pottsville 1927-28
Budde, Brad, G, USC, Kansas City 1980-85
Budde, Ed, G, Michigan State, Kansas City 1963-76
Budka, Frank, DB, Notre Dame, LA Rams 1964
Budness, Bill, LB, Boston U., Oakland 1964-70
Budrewicz, Tom, G, Brown, NY Titans 1961
Buehler, George, G, Stanford, Oakland 1969-78; Cleveland 1978-79
Buetow, Bart, DT, Minnesota, NY Giants 1973; Minnesota 1976
Buffalo, G, Haskell, Oorang 1922-23
Buffington, Harry, G, Oklahoma State, NY Giants 1942; Brooklyn (AAFC) 1946-48
Buffone, Doug, LB, Louisville, Chi. Bears 1966-79
Buford, Maury, P, Texas Tech, San Diego 1982-84; Chi. Bears 1985
Bugenhagen, Gary, G, Syracuse, Buffalo 1967; Boston 1970
Buggs, Danny (Lightning), WR, West Virginia, NY Giants 1975-76; Washington 1976-79
Buhler, Larry, FB, Minnesota, Green Bay 1939-41
Buie, Drew, WR, Catawba, Oakland 1969-71; Cincinnati 1972
Buivid, Ray (Buzz), HB, Marquette, Chi. Bears 1937-38
Bujnoch, Glenn, G, Texas A&M, Cincinnati 1976-82; Tampa Bay 1983-84
Bukant, Joe, HB, Washington (St. Louis), Philadelphia 1938-40; Chi. Cardinals 1942-43
Bukaty, Fred, FB, Kansas, Denver 1961
Bukich, Rudy, QB, USC, LA Rams 1953, 1956; Washington 1957-58; Chi. Bears 1958-59, 1962-68; Pittsburgh 1960-61
Buksar, George, LB, Purdue, Chi. Hornets (AAFC) 1949; Baltimore 1950; Washington 1951-52
Bulaich, Norm, RB, TCU, Baltimore 1970-72; Philadelphia 1973-74; Miami 1975-79
Buland, Walt, T, Rock Island 1920-21, 1924; Green Bay 1924; Duluth 1926
Bulger, Chet, T, Auburn, Chi. Cardinals 1942-43, 1945-49; Card-Pitt 1944; Detroit 1950
Bull, Ronnie, RB, Baylor, Chi. Bears 1962-70; Philadelphia 1971
Bull, Scott, QB, Arkansas, San Francisco 1976-78
Bullard, Louis, T, Jackson State, Seattle 1978-80
Bullman, Gale, E, West Virginia Wesleyan, Columbus 1925
Bullocks, Amos, RB, Southern Illinois, Dallas 1962-64; Pittsburgh 1966
Bullough, Hank, G, Michigan State, Green Bay 1955, 1958
Bultman, Arthur (Red), C, Marquette, Brooklyn 1931; Green Bay 1932-34
Bumgardner, Rex, HB, West Virginia, Buffalo (AAFC) 1948-49; Cleveland 1950-52
Buncom, Frank, LB, USC, San Diego 1962-67; Cincinnati 1968
Bundra, Mike, DT, USC, Detroit 1962-63; Minnesota 1964; Cleveland 1964; NY Giants 1965; Baltimore 1965
Bungarda, Ken, T, Missouri, San Francisco 1980
Bunting, John, LB, North Carolina, Philadelphia 1972-82
Bunyan, John, G, NYU, Staten Island 1929-30, 1932; Brooklyn 1932
Bunz, Dan, LB, Long Beach State, San Francisco 1978-84; Detroit 1985
Buoniconti, Nick, LB, Notre Dame, Boston 1962-68; Miami 1969-74, 1976
Burch, Jerry, E, Georgia Tech, Oakland 1961
Burchfield, Don, TE, Ball State, New Orleans 1971
Burdick, Lloyd, T, Illinois, Chi. Bears 1931-32; Cincinnati 1933
Burford, Chris, SE, Stanford, Dallas Texans 1960-62; Kansas City 1963-67
Burgeis, Glen, T, Tulsa, Chi. Bears 1945
Burgess, Fernanza, DB, Morris Brown, Miami 1984; NY Jets 1984
Burgess, Ronnie, CB, Wake Forest, Green Bay 1985
Burgin, Al, G, Toledo 1922
Burgmeier, Ted, S, Notre Dame, Kansas City 1978
Burgner, Earl (Puss), QB, Wittenberg, Dayton 1923
Burk, Adrian, QB, Baylor, Baltimore 1950; Philadelphia 1951-56
Burk, Scott, S, Oklahoma State, Cincinnati 1979
Burke, Charlie, HB, Dartmouth, Providence 1925-26
Burke, Don, LB, USC, San Francisco 1950-54
Burke, Mark, DB, West Virginia, Philadelphia 1976
Burke, Mike, P, Miami, LA Rams 1974
Burke, Randy, WR, Kentucky, Baltimore 1978-81
Burke, Vern, SE, Oregon State, San Francisco 1965; Atlanta 1966; New Orleans 1967
Burkett, Chris, WR, Jackson State, Buffalo 1985
Burkett, Jeff, E, LSU, Chi. Cardinals 1947
Burkett, Jackie, LB, Auburn, Baltimore 1961-66; New Orleans 1967, 1970; Dallas 1968-69
Burks, Joe, C, Washington State, Milwaukee 1926
Burks, Randy, WR, Southeastern Oklahoma, Chi. Bears 1976
Burks, Ray, LB, UCLA, Kansas City 1977
Burks, Steve, WR, Arkansas State, New England 1975-77
Burl, Alex, HB, Colorado State, Chi. Cardinals 1956
Burleson, John, G, SMU, Pittsburgh 1933; Cincinnati 1933; Portsmouth 1933
Burley, Gary, DT-NT, Pittsburgh, Cincinnati 1976-83; Atlanta 1984
Burman, George, C, Northwestern, Chi. Bears 1964; LA Rams 1967; Washington 1971-72
Burmeister, Forrest, G, Purdue, Cleveland 1937
Burnell, Max, HB, Notre Dame, Chi. Bears 1944
Burnett, Bobby, RB, Arkansas, Buffalo 1966-67; Denver 1969
Burnett, Dale, HB, Emporia State, NY Giants 1930-39
Burnett, Len, DB, Oregon, Pittsburgh 1961
Burnett, Ray, HB, Chi. Cardinals 1938
Burnette, Tom, FB, North Carolina, Pittsburgh 1938; Philadelphia 1938
Burnham, Len, DE, U.S. International, Philadelphia 1977-80
Burnham, Stan, HB, Harvard, Frankford 1925
Burnine, Hank, SE, Missouri, NY Giants 1956; Philadelphia 1956-57
Burns, Bob, RB, Georgia, NY Jets 1974
Burns, Ed, QB, Nebraska, New Orleans 1978-79
Burns, Leon, RB, Long Beach State, San Diego 1971
Burns, Mike, DB, USC, San Francisco 1977
Burnsite, George, Wisconsin, Racine 1926
Burrell, Clinton, CB, LSU, Cleveland 1979-84
Burrell, George, DB, Pennsylvania, Denver 1969
Burrell, John, SE, Rice, Pittsburgh 1962-64; Washington 1966-67
Burrell, Ode, RB, Mississippi State, Houston 1964-69
Burris, Bo, DB, Houston, New Orleans 1967-69
Burris, Paul (Buddy), G, Oklahoma, Green Bay 1949-51
Burrough, Ken, WR, Texas Southern, New Orleans 1970; Houston 1971-81
Burroughs, Derrick, CB, Memphis State, Buffalo 1985
Burroughs, Don (Blade), DB, Colorado State, LA Rams 1955-59; Philadelphia 1960-64
Burroughs, James, CB, Michigan State, Baltimore 1982-83; Indianapolis 1984
Burrow, Jim, DB, Nebraska, Green Bay 1976
Burrow, Ken, WR, San Diego State, Atlanta 1971-75
Burrus, Harry, E, Hardin-Simmons, NY Yankees (AAFC) 1946-47
Burruss, Lloyd, S, Maryland, Kansas City 1981-85
Burson, Jimmy, DB, Auburn, St. Louis 1963-67; Atlanta 1968
Burt, Hal, G, Kansas, Cleveland 1924
Burt, Jim, NT, Miami, NY Giants 1981-85
Burt, Russ, HB, Canisius, Buffalo 1925
Burton, Albert, DE, Bethune-Cookman, Houston 1976-77; NY Jets 1977
Burton, Larry, WR, Purdue, New Orleans 1975-77; San Diego 1978-79
Burton, Leon, HB, Arizona State, NY Titans 1960
Burton, Lyle, G, DePauw, Rock Island 1924-25
Burton, Ron, HB, Northwestern, Boston 1960-65
Busby, Sherrill, E, Troy State, Brooklyn 1940
Busch, Elmer, G, Carlisle, Oorang 1922-23
Busch, Nick, G, Gonzaga, LA Buccaneers 1926
Bush, Blair, C, Washington, Cincinnati 1978-82; Seattle 1983-85
Bush, Frank, LB, North Carolina State, Houston 1985
Bush, Ray, E, Loyola (Chicago), Louisville 1926
Bushby, Tom, HB, Kansas State, Cincinnati 1934; Philadelphia 1934
Busich, Sam, E, Ohio State, Boston 1936; Cleveland 1937; Detroit 1943
Busick, Steve, LB, USC, Denver 1981-85
Busler, Ray, T, Marquette, Chi. Cardinals 1940-41, 1945
Buss, Art, T, Michigan State, Chi. Bears 1934-35; Philadelphia 1936-37
Busse, Ellis, HB, Chicago, Chi. Cardinals 1929
Bussell, Gerry, DB, Georgia Tech, Denver 1965
Bussey, Dexter, RB, Texas-Arlington, Detroit 1974-84
Bussey, Young, QB, LSU, Chi. Bears 1940-41
Butcher, Wendell, HB, Gustavus Adolphus, Brooklyn 1939-42

Butkus, Carl, T, George Washington, Washington 1948; NY Yankees (AAFC) 1948; NY Giants 1949
Butkus, Dick, LB, Illinois, Chi. Bears 1965-73
Butler, Bill, DB-RB, Tennessee-Chattanooga, Green Bay 1959; Dallas Cowboys 1960; Pittsburgh 1961; Minnesota 1962-64
Butler, Bill, LB, Cal State-Northridge, Denver 1970
Butler, Bill, RB, Kansas State, New Orleans 1972-74
Butler, Bob, G, Kentucky, Philadelphia 1962; NY Jets 1963
Butler, Bobby, CB, Florida State, Atlanta 1981-85
Butler, Chuck, LB, Boise State, Seattle 1984
Butler, Frank, C, Michigan State, Green Bay 1934-36, 1938
Butler, Gary, TE, Rice, Kansas City 1973; Chi. Bears 1975-76; Tampa Bay 1977
Butler, Gerald, WR, Nicholls State, Kansas City 1977
Butler, Jack, DB, St. Bonaventure, Pittsburgh 1951-59
Butler, Jerry, WR, Clemson, Buffalo 1979-83, 1985
Butler, Jim (Cannonball), RB, Edward Waters, Pittsburgh 1965-67; Atlanta 1968-71; St. Louis 1972
Butler, Jim, TE, Tulsa, Houston 1972
Butler, Johnny, HB, Tennessee, Phil-Pitt 1943; Card-Pitt 1944; Brooklyn 1944; Philadelphia 1945
Butler, Keith, LB, Memphis State, Seattle 1978-85
Butler, Kevin, K, Georgia, Chi. Bears 1985
Butler, Mike, DE, Kansas, Green Bay 1977-82, 1985
Butler, Ray, WR, USC, Baltimore 1980-83; Indianapolis 1984-85; Seattle 1985
Butler, Skip, K, Texas-Arlington, New Orleans 1971; NY Giants 1971; Houston 1972-77
Butsko, Harry, LB, Maryland, Washington 1963
Buttle, Greg, LB, Penn State, NY Jets 1976-84
Butts, Eddie, HB-FB, Cal State-Chico, Chi. Cardinals 1929
Butz, Dave, DE-DT, Purdue, St. Louis 1973-74; Washington 1975-85
Buzin, Rich, T, Penn State, NY Giants 1968-70; LA Rams 1971; Chi. Bears 1972
Buzynski, Bernie, LB, Holy Cross, Buffalo 1960
Byas, Rick, DB, Wayne State, Atlanta 1974-80
Byers, Ken, G, Cincinnati, NY Giants 1962-64; Minnesota 1964-65
Byers, Scott, S, Long Beach State, San Diego 1984
Bykowski, Frank, G, Purdue, Pittsburgh 1940
Byler, Joe, T, Nebraska, NY Giants 1946
Byner, Earnest, RB, East Carolina, Cleveland 1984-85
Byrd, Darryl, LB, Illinois, LA Raiders 1983-84
Byrd, Dennis, DE, North Carolina State, Boston 1968
Byrd, George (Butch), DB, Boston U., Buffalo 1964-70; Denver 1971
Byrd, Gill, CB, San Jose State, San Diego 1983-85
Byrd, Mac, LB, USC, LA Rams 1965
Byrd, Richard, NT-DE, Southern Mississippi, Houston 1985
Byrne, Bill, G, Boston College, Philadelphia 1963

C

Cabral, Brian, LB, Colorado, Atlanta 1979; Green Bay 1980; Chi. Bears 1981-85
Cabrelli, Larry, E, Colgate, Philadelphia 1941-42, 1944-47; Phil-Pitt 1943
Cabrinha, Gus, HB, Dayton, Dayton 1927
Caddel, Ernie, HB, Stanford, Portsmouth 1933; Detroit 1934-38
Cade, Mossy, DB, Texas, Green Bay 1985
Cadile, Jim, G, San Jose State, Chi. Bears 1962-72
Cadwell, John, G, Oregon State, Dallas Texans 1961
Cafego, George (Bad News), QB, Tennessee, Brooklyn 1940, 1943; Washington 1943; Boston 1944-45
Caffey, Lee Roy, LB, Texas A&M, Philadelphia 1963; Green Bay 1964-69; Chi. Bears 1970; Dallas 1971; San Diego 1972
Cagle, Chris (Red), HB, Army, NY Giants 1930-32; Brooklyn 1933-34
Cagle, Jim, DT, Georgia, Philadelphia 1974
Cagle, Johnny, LB, Clemson, Boston 1969
Cahill, Bill, S, Washington, Buffalo 1973-74
Cahill, Dave, DT, Arizona State, Philadelphia 1966; LA Rams 1967; Atlanta 1969
Cahill, Ronnie, HB, Holy Cross, Chi. Cardinals 1943
Cahoon, Ivan (Tiny), T, Gonzaga, Green Bay 1926-29
Cain, J.V., TE, Colorado, St. Louis 1974-77
Cain, Jim, DE, Alabama, Chi. Cardinals 1949; Detroit 1950, 1953-55
Cain, Lynn, RB, USC, Atlanta 1979-84; LA Rams 1985
Calac, Pete, FB, Carlisle, Canton 1920, 1925-26; Cleveland 1921; Washington 1921; Oorang 1922-23; Buffalo 1924
Calcagni, Ralph, T, Pennsylvania, Boston 1946; Pittsburgh 1947
Caldwell, Alan, CB, North Carolina, NY Giants 1979
Caldwell, Bruce, HB, Yale, NY Giants 1928
Caldwell, Bryan, DE, Arizona State, Houston 1984
Caldwell, Cy, T, Baldwin-Wallace, Akron 1925-26
Caldwell, Darryl, T, Tennessee State, Buffalo 1983
Caldwell, Tony, LB, Washington, LA Raiders 1983-85
Caleb, Jamie, RB, Grambling, Cleveland 1960, 1965; Minnesota 1961
Calhoun, Don, RB, Kansas State, Buffalo 1974-75; New England 1975-81; Philadelphia 1982
Calhoun, Eric, T, Denison, Dayton 1926
Calhoun, Mike, DT, Notre Dame, San Francisco 1980; Tampa Bay 1980
Call, Jack, HB, Colgate, Baltimore 1957-58; Pittsburgh 1959
Call, Kevin, T, Colorado State, Indianapolis 1984-85
Callahan, Bob, C, Michigan, Buffalo (AAFC) 1948
Callahan, Dan, G, Wooster, NY Titans 1960
Callahan, Jim, HB, Texas, Detroit 1946
Calland, Lee, DB, Louisville, Minnesota 1963-65; Atlanta 1966-68; Chi. Bears 1969; Pittsburgh 1969-72
Callicut, Ken, RB, Clemson, Detroit 1978-82
Calligaro, Len, QB, Wisconsin, NY Giants 1944
Callihan, Bill, QB, Nebraska, Detroit 1940-45
Calloway, Ernie, DT, Texas Southern, Philadelphia 1969-72
Calvelli, Tony, C, Stanford, Detroit 1939-40; San Francisco (AAFC) 1947
Calvin, Tom, FB, Alabama, Pittsburgh 1953-54
Camarillo, Rich, P, Washington, New England 1981-85
Cambal, Dennis, TE, William & Mary, NY Jets 1973
Cameron, Ed, G, Washington & Lee, Detroit 1926
Cameron, Glenn, LB, Florida, Cincinnati 1975-85
Cameron, Jack, WR, Winston-Salem State, Chi. Bears 1984
Cameron, Paul, HB, UCLA, Pittsburgh 1954
Camp, Jim, HB, North Carolina, Brooklyn (AAFC) 1948
Camp, Reggie, DE, California, Cleveland 1983-85
Campana, Al, HB, Youngstown State, Chi. Bears 1950-52; Chi. Cardinals 1953
Campanella, Joe, DT, Ohio State, Dallas 1952; Baltimore 1953-57
Campbell, Bill, G, Oklahoma, Chi. Cardinals 1945-49; NY Bulldogs 1949
Campbell, Bobby, RB, Penn State, Pittsburgh 1969
Campbell, Carter, LB-DE, Weber State, San Francisco 1970; Denver 1971; NY Giants 1972-73
Campbell, Don, T, Carnegie-Mellon, Pittsburgh 1939-40
Campbell, Earl, RB, Texas, Houston 1978-84; New Orleans 1984-85
Campbell, Gary, LB, Colorado, Chi. Bears 1977-83
Campbell, Glenn, E, Emporia State, NY Giants 1929-33; Pittsburgh 1935
Campbell, Jack, T, Utah, Seattle 1982
Campbell, Jim, LB, West Texas State, San Diego 1969
Campbell, Joe, DE, Maryland, New Orleans 1977-78; Oakland 1979-81
Campbell, John, LB, Minnesota 1963-64; Pittsburgh 1965-69; Baltimore 1969
Campbell, Ken, E, West Chester, NY Titans 1960
Campbell, Leon (Muscles), HB, Arkansas, Baltimore 1950; Chi. Bears 1952-54; Pittsburgh 1955
Campbell, Marion, DT, Georgia, San Francisco 1954-55; Philadelphia 1956-61
Campbell, Mike, RB, Lenoir-Rhyne, Detroit 1968
Campbell, Milt, HB, Indiana, Cleveland 1957
Campbell, Ray, LB, Marquette, Pittsburgh 1958-60
Campbell, Rich, QB, California, Green Bay 1981-84
Campbell, Scott, QB, Purdue, Pittsburgh 1984-85
Campbell, Sonny, RB, Northern Arizona, Atlanta 1970-71
Campbell, Stan, G, Iowa State, Detroit 1952, 1955-58; Philadelphia 1959-61; Oakland 1962
Campbell, Tommy, DB, Iowa State, Philadelphia 1976
Campbell, Woody, RB, Northwestern, Houston 1967-71
Campfield, Billy, RB-KR, Kansas, Philadelphia 1978-82; NY Giants 1983
Campiglio, Bob, HB, West Liberty State, Staten Island 1932; Boston 1933
Campion, Tom, T, Southeastern Louisiana, Philadelphia 1947
Campofreda, Nick, C, Western Maryland, Washington 1944
Campora, Don, DT, Pacific, San Francisco 1950, 1952; Washington 1953
Canada, Larry, RB, Wisconsin, Denver 1978-79, 1981
Canadeo, Tony, HB, Gonzaga, Green Bay, 1941-44, 1946-52
Canady, Jim, HB, Texas, Chi. Bears 1948-49; NY Bulldogs 1949
Canale, John, DE, Tennessee, Miami 1966; Boston 1968
Canale, Justin, G, Mississippi State, Boston 1965-68; Cincinnati 1969
Canale, Rocco, G, Boston College, Phil-Pitt 1943; Philadelphia 1944-45; Boston 1946-47
Cancik, Phil, LB, Northern Arizona, NY Giants 1980; Kansas City 1981
Cannady, John, LB, Indiana, NY Giants 1947-54
Cannamela, Pat, LB, USC, Dallas 1952
Cannava, Tony, HB, Boston College, Green Bay 1950
Cannavino, Joe, DB, Ohio State, Oakland 1960-61; Buffalo 1962
Cannella, John, T, Fordham, NY Giants 1933-34; Brooklyn 1934
Cannon, Billy, RB-TE, LSU, Houston 1960-63; Oakland 1964-69; Kansas City 1970
Cannon, Billy, LB, Texas A&M, Dallas 1984
Cannon, John, DE, William & Mary, Tampa Bay 1982-85
Cannon, Mark, C, Texas-Arlington, Green Bay 1984-85
Cantor, Leo, FB, UCLA, NY Giants 1942; Chi. Cardinals 1945
Capatelli, Jerry, G, Iowa, Pittsburgh 1937
Capece, Bill, K, Florida State, Tampa Bay 1981-83
Capers, Wayne, WR, Kansas, Pittsburgh 1983-84; Indianapolis 1985
Capone, Warren, LB, LSU, Dallas 1975; New Orleans 1976
Capp, Dick, TE, Boston College, Green Bay 1967; Pittsburgh 1968
Cappadonna, Bob, FB, Northeastern, Boston 1966-67; Buffalo 1968
Cappelletti, Gino, FL-K, Minnesota, Boston 1960-70
Cappelletti, John, RB, Penn State, LA Rams 1974-78; San Diego 1980-83
Cappelman, Bill, QB, Florida State, Minnesota 1970; Detroit 1973
Capps, Wilbur, T, East Central (Oklahoma), Frankford 1929-30; Minneapolis 1930
Capria, Carl, S, Purdue, Detroit 1974; NY Jets 1975
Capron, Ralph, HB, Minnesota, Chi. Tigers 1920
Capuzzi, Jim, QB, Cincinnati, Green Bay 1955-56
Cara, Dom (Mac), E, North Carolina State, Pittsburgh, 1937-38
Caranci, Roland, T, Colorado, NY Giants 1944
Carano, Glenn, QB, Nevada-Las Vegas, Dallas 1978-83
Carapella, Al, T, Miami, San Francisco 1951-55
Carberry, Glen, E, Notre Dame, Buffalo 1923-24; Cleveland 1925
Card, Harper, T, Louisville 1921-22
Cardarelli, Carl, C, Akron 1924; Cleveland 1925
Cardinal, Fred, LB, Baldwin-Wallace, NY Yankees (AAFC) 1947
Cardwell, Joe, T, Duke, Pittsburgh 1937-38
Cardwell, John, HB, St. Louis 1923
Cardwell, Lloyd, HB, Nebraska, Detroit 1937-43
Carey, Bob, E, Michigan State, LA Rams 1952, 1954, 1956; Chi. Bears 1958
Carey, Joe, G, Chi. Cardinals 1920; Green Bay 1921
Carl, Harland, HB, Wisconsin, Chi. Bears 1956
Carlson, Clarence, E, Beloit, Louisville 1926
Carlson, Dean, QB, Iowa State, Kansas City 1974
Carlson, Hal, T, DePaul, Chi. Cardinals 1937
Carlson, Irv, G, St. John's (Minnesota), Kenosha 1924
Carlson, Jules (Zuck), G, Oregon State, Chi. Bears 1929-36; Chi. Cardinals 1937
Carlson, Okie, G, Iowa State, Duluth 1924-27
Carlson, Roy, E, Bradley, Chi. Bears 1928; Dayton 1929
Carlson, Wes, G, Detroit, Green Bay 1926; Detroit 1926
Carlton, Darryl, T, Tampa, Miami 1975-76; Tampa Bay 1977-79
Carlton, Wray, FB, Duke, Buffalo 1960-67
Carman, Charlie, T, Vanderbilt, Detroit 1920-21
Carman, Ed, T, Purdue, Hammond 1922, 1925; Buffalo 1925
Carmichael, Al, HB, USC, Green Bay 1953-58; Denver 1960-61
Carmichael, Harold, WR, Southern, Philadelphia 1971-83; Dallas 1984
Carmichael, Paul, RB, El Camino J.C., Denver 1965
Carnelly, Ray, QB, Carnegie-Mellon, Brooklyn 1939
Carney, Art, G, Navy, NY Giants 1925-26
Carolan, Reg, TE, Idaho, San Diego 1962-63; Kansas City 1964-68
Caroline, J.C., DB, Illinois, Chi. Bears 1956-65
Carollo, Joe, T, Notre Dame, LA Rams 1962-68, 1971; Philadelphia 1969; Cleveland 1972-73
Caron, Roger, T, Harvard, Indianapolis 1985
Carothers, Don, E, Bradley, Denver 1960
Carpe, Joe, T, Millikin, Frankford 1926-27; Pottsville 1928; Boston 1929; Philadelphia 1933
Carpenter, Brian, CB, Michigan, NY Giants 1982; Washington 1983-84; Buffalo 1984
Carpenter, Jack, T, Missouri, Michigan, Buffalo (AAFC) 1947-49; San Francisco (AAFC) 1949
Carpenter, Ken, HB, Oregon State, Cleveland 1950-53; Denver 1960
Carpenter, Lew, HB, Arkansas, Detroit 1953-55; Cleveland 1957-58; Green Bay 1959-63
Carpenter, Preston, HB-TE, Arkansas, Cleveland 1956-59; Pittsburgh 1960-63; Washington 1964-66; Minnesota 1966; Miami 1967
Carpenter, Rob, RB, Miami (Ohio), Houston 1977-81; NY Giants 1981-85
Carpenter, Ron, LB, Texas A&M, San Diego 1964-65
Carpenter, Ron, DE, North Carolina State, Cincinnati 1970-76
Carpenter, Steve, S, Western Illinois, NY Jets 1980; St. Louis 1981
Carr, Earl, RB, Florida, San Francisco 1978
Carr, Eddie, HB, San Francisco (AAFC) 1947-49
Carr, Fred, LB, Texas-El Paso, Green Bay 1968-77
Carr, Gregg, LB, Auburn, Pittsburgh 1985
Carr, Harlan, QB, Syracuse, Buffalo 1927; Pottsville 1927
Carr, Henry, DB, Arizona State, NY Giants 1965-67
Carr, Jimmy, DB, Morris Harvey, Chi. Cardinals 1955, 1957; Philadelphia 1959-63; Washington 1964-65
Carr, Lee, HB, Hammond 1926
Carr, Levert, T, North Central (Illinois), San Diego 1969; Buffalo 1970-71; Houston 1972-73
Carr, Paul, LB, Houston, San Francisco 1955-57
Carr, Roger, WR, Louisiana Tech, Baltimore 1974-81; Seattle 1982; San Diego 1983
Carr, Tom, DT, Morgan State, New Orleans 1968
Carreker, Alphonso, DE, Florida State, Green Bay 1984-85
Carrell, Duane, P, Florida State, Dallas 1974; LA Rams 1975; NY Jets 1976-77; St. Louis 1977
Carrell, John, LB, Texas Tech, Houston 1966
Carrington, Ed, TE, Virginia, NY Giants 1954-55; Philadelphia 1955
Carroll, Bart, C, Colgate, Rochester 1920, 1923
Carroll, Elmer (Bird), E, Washington & Jefferson, Canton 1921-23, 1925
Carroll, Jay, TE, Minnesota, Tampa Bay 1984-85
Carroll, Jim, LB, Notre Dame, NY Giants 1965-66; Washington 1966-68; NY Jets 1969
Carroll, Joe, LB, Pittsburgh, Oakland 1972-73
Carroll, Leo, DE, San Diego State, Green Bay 1968; Wash-

ington 1969
Carroll, Ronnie, G, Sam Houston State, Houston 1974
Carroll, Vic, T, Nevada-Reno, Boston 1936; Washington 1937-42; NY Giants 1943-47
Carson, Carlos, WR, LSU, Kansas City 1980-85
Carson, Harry, LB, South Carolina State, NY Giants 1976-85
Carson, Howard, LB, Howard Payne, LA Rams 1981-83
Carson, Howie, HB, Illinois, Cleveland 1937
Carson, Johnny, SE, Georgia, Washington 1954-59; Houston 1960
Carson, Kern, RB, San Diego State, San Diego 1965; NY Jets 1965
Carson, Malcolm, G, Tennessee-Chattanooga, Minnesota 1984
Carter, Allen, RB, USC, New England 1975-76; NY Giants 1976
Carter, Anthony, WR, Michigan, Minnesota 1985
Carter, Blanchard, G, Nevada-Las Vegas, Tampa Bay 1977
Carter, David, G-C, Western Kentucky, Houston 1977-84; New Orleans 1984-85
Carter, Gerald, WR, Texas A&M, Tampa Bay 1980, 1985; NY Jets 1980-84
Carter, Jim, LB, Minnesota, Green Bay 1970-75, 1977-78
Carter, Joe, E, SMU, Philadelphia 1933-40; Green Bay 1942; Brooklyn 1944; Chi. Cardinals 1945
Carter, Joe, RB, Alabama, Miami 1984-85
Carter, Kent, LB, USC, New England 1974
Carter, Louis, RB, Maryland, Oakland 1975; Tampa Bay 1976-78
Carter, M.L., CB, Cal State-Fullerton, Kansas City 1979-81
Carter, Michael, NT, SMU, San Francisco 1984-85
Carter, Mike, WR, Cal State-Sacramento, Green Bay 1970; San Diego 1972
Carter, Ross, G, Oregon, Chi. Cardinals 1936-39
Carter, Rubin, NT, Miami, Denver 1975-85
Carter, Russell, DB, SMU, NY Jets 1984-85
Carter, Virgil, QB, BYU, Chi. Bears 1968-69, 1976; Cincinnati 1970-72; San Diego 1975
Carter, Willie, HB, Tennessee State, Chi. Cardinals 1953
Carthon, Maurice, RB, Arkansas State, NY Giants 1985
Cartin, Charlie, T, Holy Cross, Frankford 1925
Carver, Dale, LB, Georgia, Cleveland 1983
Carver, Melvin, RB, Nevada-Las Vegas, Tampa Bay 1982-85
Carwell, Larry, DB, Iowa State, Houston 1967-68; Boston 1969-70; New England 1971-72
Casanega, Ken, HB, Santa Clara, San Francisco (AAFC) 1946, 1948
Casanova, Tommy, S-KR, LSU, Cincinnati 1972-77
Casares, Rick, FB, Florida, Chi. Bears 1954-64; Washington 1965; Miami 1966
Case, Ernie, QB, UCLA, Baltimore (AAFC) 1947
Case, Frank, DE, Penn State, Kansas City 1981
Case, Pete, G, Georgia, Philadelphia 1962-64; NY Giants 1965-70
Case, Scott, S, Oklahoma, Atlanta 1984-85
Casey, Al, HB, Arkansas, St. Louis 1923
Casey, Bernie, FL, Bowling Green, San Francisco 1961-66; LA Rams 1967-68
Casey, Eddie, HB, Harvard, Buffalo 1920
Casey, Tim, LB, Oregon, Chi. Bears 1969; Denver 1969
Casey, Tom, HB, Hampton, NY Yankees (AAFC) 1948
Cash, John, DE, Allen, Denver 1961-62
Cash, Rick, DE, Northeast Missouri State, Atlanta 1968; LA Rams 1969; New England 1972-73
Casner, Ken, T, Baylor, LA Rams 1952
Cason, Jim, DB, LSU, San Francisco 1948-52, 1954; LA Rams 1955-56
Cason, Wendell, CB, Oregon, Atlanta 1985
Casper, Cy, QB, TCU, St. Louis 1934; Green Bay 1934; Pittsburgh 1935
Casper, Dave, TE, Notre Dame, Oakland 1974-80; Houston 1980-83; Minnesota 1983; LA Raiders 1984
Cassady, Craig, S, Ohio State, New Orleans 1977
Cassady, Howard (Hopalong), HB-FL, Ohio State, Detroit 1956-61, 1963; Cleveland 1962; Philadelphia 1962
Cassara, Frank, LB, St. Mary's (California), San Francisco 1954
Cassese, Tom, RB, C.W. Post, Denver 1967
Cassiano, Dick, HB, Pittsburgh, Brooklyn 1940
Cassidy, Bill, E, Detroit, Kenosha 1924
Cassidy, Joe, HB, St. Mary's (California), Pittsburgh 1937
Cassidy, Ron, WR, Utah State, Green Bay 1979-81, 1983-84
Casteel, Mike, HB, Western Michigan, Rock Island 1922
Caster, Richard, WR-TE, Jackson State, NY Jets 1970-77; Houston 1978-80; New Orleans 1981; Washington 1981-82
Castete, Jess, DB, McNeese State, Chi. Bears 1956; LA Rams 1956-57
Castiglia, Jim, FB, Georgetown (Washington D.C.), Philadelphia 1941, 1945-46; Baltimore (AAFC) 1947; Washington 1947-48
Castille, Jeremiah, CB, Alabama, Tampa Bay 1983-85
Castor, Chris, WR, Duke, Seattle 1983-84
Catano, Mark, DE, Valdosta State, Pittsburgh 1984-85
Cater, Greg, P, Tennessee-Chattanooga, Buffalo 1980-83
Cathcart, Royal, HB, Cal-Santa Barbara, San Francisco 1950
Cathcart, Sam, HB, Cal-Santa Barbara, San Francisco 1949-50, 1952
Catlin, Tom, LB, Oklahoma, Cleveland 1953-54, 1957-58; Philadelphia 1959
Cato, Daryl, C, Arkansas, Miami (AAFC) 1946
Cavalli, Carmen, SE, Richmond, Oakland 1960
Cavanaugh, Matt, QB, Pittsburgh, New England 1978-82; San Francisco 1983-85
Caveness, Ronnie, LB, Arkansas, Kansas City 1965; Houston 1966-68
Caver, James, WR, Missouri, Detroit 1983
Cavness, Grady, DB, Texas-El Paso, Denver 1969; Atlanta 1970
Cavosie, John, HB, Butler, Portsmouth 1931-33
Caylor, Lowell, DB, Miami (Ohio), Cleveland 1964
Caywood, Les, G, St. John's (New York), Kansas City 1926; Buffalo 1926; NY Giants 1927, 1929-32; Cleveland 1927; Pottsville 1927; Detroit 1928; Chi. Cardinals 1931; Brooklyn 1932; Cincinnati 1933-34
Cearing, Lloyd, HB, Valparaiso, Hammond 1922-23
Cefalo, Jimmy, WR, Penn State, Miami 1978-84
Celeri, Bob, QB, California, NY Yanks 1951; Dallas 1952
Celotto, Mario, LB, USC, Buffalo 1978; Oakland 1980-81; LA Rams 1981
Cemore, Tony, G, Creighton, Philadelphia 1941
Cenci, John, C, Pittsburgh, Pittsburgh 1956
Cephous, Frank, RB, UCLA, NY Giants 1984
Ceppetelli, Gene, C, Villanova, Philadelphia 1968-69; NY Giants 1969
Cerne, Joe, C, Northwestern, San Francisco 1965-67; Atlanta 1968
Cesare, Billy, DB-KR, Miami, Tampa Bay 1978-79, 1981; Detroit 1982
Chadwick, Jeff, WR, Grand Valley State, Detroit 1983-85
Chalmers, George, G, NYU, Brooklyn 1933
Chamberlain, Dan, SE, Cal State-Sacramento, Buffalo 1960-61
Chamberlain, Garth, G, BYU, Pittsburgh 1945
Chamberlin, Guy, E, Nebraska, Decatur 1920; Chi. Staleys 1921; Canton 1922-23; Cleveland 1924; Frankford 1925-26; Chi. Cardinals 1927
Chambers, Rusty, LB, Tulane, New Orleans 1975-76; Miami 1976-80
Chambers, Wally, DT, Eastern Kentucky, Chi. Bears 1973-77; Tampa Bay 1978-79
Champagne, Ed, T, LSU, LA Rams 1947-50
Champion, Jim, G, Mississippi State, NY Yanks 1950-51
Chandler, Al, TE, Oklahoma, Cincinnati 1973-74; New England 1976-79; St. Louis 1978-79
Chandler, Bob, WR, USC, Buffalo 1971-79; Oakland 1980-81; LA Raiders 1982
Chandler, Don, K-P, Florida, NY Giants 1956-64; Green Bay 1965-67
Chandler, Edgar, LB, Georgia, Buffalo 1968-72; New England 1973
Chandler, Karl, G-C, Princeton, NY Giants 1974-77; Detroit 1978
Chandler, Wes, WR-KR, Florida, New Orleans 1978-81; San Diego 1981-85
Chandnois, Lynn, HB, Michigan State, Pittsburgh 1950-56
Chapman, Clarence, CB, Eastern Michigan, New Orleans 1976-80; Cincinnati 1980-81; Detroit 1985
Chapman, Gil, WR, Michigan, New Orleans 1975
Chapman, Mike, C-G, Texas, Atlanta 1984
Chapple, Dave, P, Cal-Santa Barbara, Buffalo 1971; LA Rams 1972-74; New England 1974
Chapple, John, LB, Stanford, San Francisco 1965
Chappius, Bob, HB, Michigan, Brooklyn (AAFC) 1948; Chi. Hornets (AAFC) 1949
Charles, John, DB, Purdue, Boston 1967-69; Minnesota 1970; Houston 1971-74
Charles, Win, HB, William & Mary, Dayton 1928
Charon, Carl, DB, Michigan State, Buffalo 1962-63
Charpier, Len, FB, Illinois, Chi. Cardinals 1920
Charles, Mike, NT, Syracuse, Miami 1983-85
Chase, Ben, G, Navy, Detroit 1947
Chase, Ralph, T, Pittsburgh, Akron 1926
Chatman, Cliff, RB, Central State (Oklahoma), NY Giants 1982
Chavous, Barney, DE, South Carolina State, Denver 1973-85
Cheatham, Ernie, T, Loyola (Los Angeles), Pittsburgh 1954; Baltimore 1954
Cheatham, Lloyd, QB, Auburn, Chi. Cardinals 1942; NY Yankees (AAFC) 1946-48
Checkaye, Severin (Cooney), QB, Carlisle, Muncie 1920-21
Cheek, Richard, G, Auburn, Buffalo 1970
Cheeks, B.W., RB, Texas Southern, Houston 1965
Chelf, Don, G, Iowa, Buffalo 1960-61
Chenoweth, George (Red), HB, Louisville 1921
Cherne, Hal, T, DePaul, Boston 1933
Cheroke, George, G, Ohio State, Cleveland (AAFC) 1946
Cherry, Deron, S, Rutgers, Kansas City 1981-85
Cherry, Ed, HB, Hardin-Simmons, Chi. Cardinals 1938-39; Pittsburgh 1939
Cherry, Raphel, S, Hawaii, Washington 1985
Cherry, Stan, LB, Morgan State, Baltimore 1973
Cherundolo, Chuck, C, Penn State, Cleveland 1937-39; Philadelphia 1940; Pittsburgh 1941-42, 1945-48
Chesbro, Marcel (Red), G, Colgate, Cleveland 1938
Chesley, Al, LB, Pittsburgh, Philadelphia 1979-82; Chi. Bears 1982
Chesley, Francis, LB, Wyoming, Green Bay 1978
Chesley, John, TE, Oklahoma State, Miami 1984
Chesney, Chet, C, DePaul, Chi. Bears 1939-40
Chesser, George, RB, Delta State, Miami 1966-67
Chesson, Wes, WR, Duke, Atlanta 1971-73; Philadelphia 1973-74
Chester, Raymond, TE, Morgan State, Oakland 1970-72, 1978-81; Baltimore 1973-77
Cheverko, George, HB, Fordham, NY Giants 1947-48; Washington 1948
Cheyunski, Jim, LB, Syracuse, Boston 1968-70; New England 1971-72; Buffalo 1973-74; Baltimore 1975-76; Green Bay 1977
Chicken, Fred, HB, St. Thomas (Minnesota), Rock Island 1920-21; Minneapolis 1922-24
Chickerneo, John (Chick), QB, Pittsburgh, NY Giants 1942
Chickillo, Nick, G, Miami, Chi. Cardinals 1953
Chickillo, Tony, NT, Miami, San Diego 1984-85
Childress, Joe, FB, Auburn, Chi. Cardinals 1956-59; St. Louis 1960, 1962-65
Childress, Ray, DE, Texas A&M, Houston 1985
Childs, Clarence, DB-KR, Florida A&M, NY Giants 1964-67; Chi. Bears 1968
Childs, Henry, TE, Kansas State, Atlanta 1974; New Orleans 1974-80; LA Rams 1981; Green Bay 1984
Childs, Jim, WR, Cal Poly-SLO, St. Louis 1978-80
Chipley, Bill, E, Washington & Lee, Boston 1947-48; NY Bulldogs 1949
Chisick, Andy, C, Villanova, Chi. Cardinals 1940-41
Chlebek, Ed, QB, Western Michigan, NY Jets 1963
Choate, G, Haskell, Kansas City 1924
Choboian, Max, QB, Cal State-Northridge, Denver 1966
Choma, John, G, Virginia, San Francisco 1981-83
Chomyszak, Steve, DT, Syracuse, NY Jets 1966; Cincinnati 1968-73
Chorovich, Dick, T, Miami (Ohio), Baltimore 1955-56; LA Chargers 1960
Chrape, Joe, G, Hibbing J.C., Minneapolis 1929
Christensen, Erik, E, Richmond, Washington 1956
Christensen, Frank (Little Chris), FB, Utah, Detroit 1934-37
Christensen, George (Big Chris), T, Oregon, Portsmouth 1931-33; Detroit 1934-38
Christensen, Jeff, QB, Eastern Illinois, Philadelphia 1983-85
Christensen, Koester, E, Michigan State, Portsmouth 1930
Christensen, Todd, TE, BYU, NY Giants 1979; Oakland 1979-81; LA Raiders 1982-85
Christenson, Marty, FB, Minnesota, Chi. Cardinals 1940
Christiansen, Bob, TE, UCLA, Buffalo 1972
Christiansen, Jack, DB-KR, Colorado State, Detroit 1951-58
Christianson, Oscar (Bully), E, Minneapolis 1921-24
Christman, Floyd, FB, Theil, Buffalo 1925
Christman, Paul, QB, Missouri, Chi. Cardinals 1945-49; Green Bay 1950
Christopher, Herb, S, Morris Brown, Kansas City 1979-82
Christopherson, Jim, LB, Concordia (Minnesota), Minnesota 1962
Christy, Dick, HB-KR, North Carolina State, Pittsburgh 1958; Boston 1960; NY Titans 1961-62; NY Jets 1963
Christy, Earl, DB, Maryland-Eastern Shore, NY Jets 1966-68
Christy, Greg, T, Pittsburgh, Buffalo 1985
Churchman, Charlie, HB, Virginia, Columbus 1925
Churchman, Ricky, S, Texas, San Francisco 1980-81
Churchwell, Don, G, Mississippi, Washington 1959; Oakland 1960
Chuy, Don, G, Clemson, LA Rams 1963-68; Philadelphia 1969
Cibulas, Joe, T, Duquesne, Pittsburgh 1945
Ciccolella, Mike, LB, Dayton, NY Giants 1966-68
Ciccone, Ben, C, Duquesne, Pittsburgh 1934-35; Chi. Cardinals 1942
Cichowski, Gene, DB, Indiana, Pittsburgh 1957; Washington 1958-59
Cichowski, Tom, T, Maryland, Denver 1967-68
Cifelli, Gus, T, Notre Dame, Detroit 1950-52; Green Bay 1953; Philadelphia 1954; Pittsburgh 1954
Cifers, Bob, QB, Tennessee, Detroit 1946; Pittsburgh 1947-48; Green Bay 1949
Cifers, Ed, E, Tennessee, Washington 1941-42, 1946; Chi. Bears 1947-48
Cindrich, Ralph, LB, Pittsburgh, New England 1972; Houston 1973-75; Denver 1974
Cipa, Larry, QB, Michigan, New Orleans 1974-75
Civiletto, Frank, HB, Springfield, Cleveland 1923
Clabo, Neil, P, Tennessee, Minnesota 1975-77
Clack, Jim, C-G, Wake Forest, Pittsburgh 1971-77; NY Giants 1978-81
Clago, Walt, E, Detroit, Detroit 1921; Rock Island 1922
Clair, Frank, E, Ohio State, Washington 1941
Claitt, Rickey, RB, Bethune-Cookman, Washington 1980-81
Clancy, Jack, WR, Michigan, Miami 1967-69; Green Bay 1970
Clancy, Sam, DE, Pittsburgh, Seattle 1983; Cleveland 1985
Clancy, Sean, LB, Amherst, Miami 1978; St. Louis 1979-80
Clancy, Stu, QB, Holy Cross, Newark 1930; Staten Island 1931-32; NY Giants 1932-35
Clanton, Chuck, DB, Auburn, Green Bay 1985
Claphan, Sam, T, Oklahoma, San Diego 1981-85
Claridge, Dennis, QB, Nebraska, Green Bay 1964-65; Atlanta 1966
Clark, Al, CB, Eastern Michigan, Detroit 1971; LA Rams 1972-75; Philadelphia 1976
Clark, Allan, RB, Northern Arizona, New England 1979-80;

Buffalo 1982; Green Bay 1982
Clark, Art, HB, Nevada-Reno, Frankford 1927; Duluth 1927
Clark, Beryl, HB, Oklahoma, Chi. Cardinals 1940
Clark, Bill, G-C, Dayton 1920; Chi. Cardinals 1920
Clark, Boobie, RB, Bethune-Cookman, Cincinnati 1973-78; Houston 1979-80
Clark, Brian, T, Clemson, Denver 1982
Clark, Brian, K, Florida, Tampa Bay 1982
Clark, Bruce, DE, Penn State, New Orleans 1982-85
Clark, Bryan, QB, Michigan State, San Francisco 1982, 1984; Cincinnati 1984
Clark, Charlie, G, Harvard, Chi. Cardinals 1924
Clark, Don, G, USC, San Francisco (AAFC) 1948-49
Clark, Dwight, WR, Clemson, San Francisco 1979-85
Clark, Earl (Dutch), HB-QB, Colorado College, Portsmouth 1931-32; Detroit 1934-38
Clark, Ernie, LB, Michigan State, Detroit 1963-67; St. Louis 1968
Clark, Gail, LB, Michigan State, Chi. Bears 1973; New England 1974
Clark, Gary, WR, James Madison, Washington 1985
Clark, Harold (Babe), E, Cathedral, Dayton 1920; Rochester 1920-25
Clark, Harry, HB, West Virginia, Chi. Bears 1940-43; LA Dons (AAFC) 1946-48; Chi. Rockets (AAFC) 1948
Clark, Herman, G, Oregon State, Chi. Bears 1952, 1954-57
Clark, Howard, DE, Tennessee-Chattanooga, LA Chargers 1960; San Diego 1961
Clark, Jessie, RB, Arkansas, Green Bay 1983-85
Clark, Jim, T, Oregon State, Washington 1953-54
Clark, Jimmy, HB, Pittsburgh, Pittsburgh 1933-34
Clark, Kelvin, T, Nebraska, Denver 1979-81; New Orleans 1982-85
Clark, Ken, P, St. Mary's (Nova Scotia), LA Rams 1979
Clark, Leroy, K, Prairie View A&M, Houston 1976
Clark, Mario, CB, Oregon, Buffalo 1976-83; San Francisco 1984
Clark, Mike, K, Texas A&M, Philadelphia 1963; Pittsburgh 1964-67; Dallas 1968-71, 1973
Clark, Mike, DE, Florida, Washington 1981; San Francisco 1982
Clark, Monte, T, USC, San Francisco 1959-61; Dallas Cowboys 1962; Cleveland 1963-69
Clark, Myers (Algy), QB, Ohio State, Brooklyn 1930; Cleveland 1931; Boston 1932; Cincinnati 1933-34; Philadelphia 1934
Clark, Phil, CB, Northwestern, Dallas 1967-69; Chi. Bears 1970; New England 1971
Clark, Randy, G-C, Northern Illinois, St. Louis 1980-85
Clark, Randy, S, Florida, Tampa Bay 1984
Clark, Steve, DE, Kansas State, New England 1981
Clark, Steve, G, Utah, Miami 1982-85
Clark, Wayne, E, Utah, Detroit 1944-45
Clark, Wayne, QB, U.S. International, San Diego 1970, 1972-73; Cincinnati 1974
Clarke, Frank, FL, Colorado, Cleveland 1957-59; Dallas 1960-67
Clarke, Hagood, DB, Florida, Buffalo 1964-68
Clarke, Ken, NT, Syracuse, Philadelphia 1978-85
Clarke, Leon, TE, USC, LA Rams 1956-59; Cleveland 1960-62; Minnesota 1963
Clarke, Pearl, HB, Oorang 1922
Clarkin, Bill, T, Benedictine, Orange 1929
Clarkson, Stu, C, Texas A&I, Chi. Bears 1942, 1946-51
Clatt, Corwin, FB, Notre Dame, Chi. Cardinals 1948-49
Clatterbuck, Bobby, QB, Houston, NY Giants 1954-57; LA Chargers 1960
Clay, Billy, DB, Mississippi, Washington 1966
Clay, Boyd, T, Tennessee, Cleveland 1940-42, 1944
Clay, Ozzie, FL, Iowa State, Washington 1964
Clay, Randy, HB, Texas, NY Giants 1950-53
Clay, Roy, HB, Colorado State, NY Giants 1944
Clay, Walt, HB, Colorado, Chi. Rockets (AAFC) 1946-47; LA Dons (AAFC) 1947-49
Clayborn, Raymond, CB, Texas, New England 1977-85
Claypool, Ralph, C, Purdue, Chi. Cardinals 1925-26, 1928
Clayton, Harvey, CB, Florida State, Pittsburgh 1983-85
Clayton, Mark, WR, Louisville, Miami 1983-85
Clayton, Ralph, WR, Michigan, St. Louis 1981
Cleary, Paul, E, USC, NY Yankees (AAFC) 1948; Chi. Hornets (AAFC) 1949
Clemens, Bob, HB, Georgia, Green Bay 1955
Clemens, Bob, HB, Pittsburgh, Baltimore 1962
Clemens, Cal, QB, USC, Green Bay 1936
Clement, Alex, HB, Williams, Frankford 1925
Clement, Henry, E, North Carolina, Pittsburgh 1961
Clement, Johnny (Zero), HB, SMU, Chi. Cardinals 1941; Pittsburgh 1946-48; Chi. Hornets (AAFC) 1949
Clements, Chase, T, Washington & Jefferson, Akron 1925
Clements, Vince, RB, Connecticut, NY Giants 1972-73
Clemons, Craig, CB, Iowa, Chi. Bears 1972-77
Clemons, Ray, G, St. Mary's (California), Green Bay 1947
Clemons, Raymond, G, Central State (Oklahoma), Detroit 1939
Cleve, Einar, FB, St. Olaf, Minneapolis 1922-24
Clifton, Kyle, LB, TCU, NY Jets 1984-85
Clime, Ben, T, Swarthmore, Rochester 1920
Cline, Doug, LB, Clemson, Houston 1960-66; San Diego 1966
Cline, Ollie, FB, Ohio State, Cleveland (AAFC) 1948; Buffalo (AAFC) 1949; Detroit 1950-53
Cline, Tony, DE, Miami, Oakland 1970-75; San Francisco 1976-77
Clinkscale, Dextor, S, South Carolina State, Dallas 1980-85
Cloud, Jack, FB, William & Mary, Green Bay 1950-51; Washington 1952-53
Cloutier, Dave, DB, Maine, Boston 1964
Clow, Herb, QB, Duluth 1924
Clowes, John, T, William & Mary, Brooklyn (AAFC) 1948; Chi. Hornets (AAFC) 1949; NY Yanks 1950-51; Detroit 1951
Clune, Don, WR, Pennsylvania, NY Giants 1974-75; Seattle 1976
Coady, Rich, C, Memphis State, Chi. Bears 1970-74
Coaker, John, T, Rochester 1924
Coan, Bert, RB, Kansas, San Diego 1962; Kansas City 1963-68
Coates, Ray, HB, LSU, NY Giants 1948-49
Cobb, Alf, G, Syracuse, Akron 1920-22; Cleveland 1923-25
Cobb, Bill, T, Kansas State, T, Duluth 1924-26
Cobb, Bob, DE, Arizona, LA Rams 1981; Tampa Bay 1982; Minnesota 1984
Cobb, Garry, LB, USC, Detroit 1979-84; Philadelphia 1985
Cobb, Marvin, CB, USC, Cincinnati 1975-79; Pittsburgh 1980; Minnesota 1980
Cobb, Mike, TE, Michigan State, Cincinnati 1977; Chi. Bears 1978-81
Cobb, Tom, T, Arkansas, Kansas City 1926; Cleveland 1927; Detroit 1928; Chi. Cardinals 1931
Cochran, John (Red), DB, Wake Forest, Chi. Cardinals 1947-50
Cochran, Tom, FB, Auburn, Washington 1949
Cockrell, Gene, T, Hardin-Simmons, NY Titans 1960-62
Cockroft, Don, K, Adams State, Cleveland 1968-80
Cocroft, Sherman, S, San Jose State, Kansas City 1985
Coder, Ron, G, Penn State, Seattle 1976-77, 1979; St. Louis 1980
Cody, Bill, LB, Auburn, Detroit 1966; New Orleans 1967-70; Philadelphia 1972
Cody, Ed, FB, Purdue, Green Bay 1947-48; Chi. Bears 1949-50
Cofall, Stanley, HB, Notre Dame, Cleveland 1920; NY Giants 1921
Cofer, Mike, DE, Tennessee, Detroit 1983-85
Coffee, Pat, HB, LSU, Chi. Cardinals 1937-38
Coffey, Don, FL, Memphis State, Denver 1963
Coffey, Junior, RB, Washington, Green Bay 1965; Atlanta 1966-67, 1969; NY Giants 1969, 1971
Coffey, Ken, S, Southwest Texas State, Washington 1983-84
Coffield, Randy, LB, Florida State, Seattle 1976; NY Giants 1978-79
Coffman, Paul, TE, Kansas State, Green Bay 1978-85
Cogdill, Gail, SE, Detroit 1960-68; Baltimore 1968; Atlanta 1969-70
Cohen, Abe, G, Tennessee-Chattanooga, Boston 1960
Coia, Angelo, SE, USC, Chi. Bears 1960-63; Washington 1964-65; Atlanta 1966
Colahan, John, G, Colorado Mines, NY Yankees 1928
Colavito, Steve, LB, Wake Forest, Philadelphia 1975
Colbert, Danny, CB, Tulsa, San Diego 1974-76
Colbert, Rondy, DB, Lamar, NY Giants 1975-76; St. Louis 1977
Colchico, Dan, DE, San Jose State, San Francisco 1960-65; New Orleans 1969
Colclough, Jim, SE, Boston College, Boston 1960-68
Cole, Eddie, LB, Mississippi, Detroit 1979-80
Cole, Emerson, FB, Toledo, Cleveland 1950-52; Chi. Bears 1952
Cole, Fred, G, Maryland, LA Chargers 1960
Cole, John (King), HB, St. Joseph's (Pennsylvania), Philadelphia 1938, 1940
Cole, Larry, DE-DT, Hawaii, Dallas 1968-80
Cole, Linzy, WR-KR, TCU, Chi. Bears 1970; Houston 1971-72; Buffalo 1972
Cole, Mike, E, Hammond 1920, 1922
Cole, Pete, G, Trinity (Texas), NY Giants 1937-40
Cole, Robin, DE-LB, New Mexico, Pittsburgh 1977-85
Cole, Terry, RB, Indiana, Baltimore 1968-69; Pittsburgh 1970; Miami 1971
Colella, Tommy, HB, Canisius, Detroit 1942-43; Cleveland 1944-45; Cleveland (AAFC) 1946-48; Buffalo (AAFC) 1949
Coleman, Al, DB, Tennessee State, Minnesota 1967; Cincinnati 1969-71; Philadelphia 1972-73
Coleman, Dennis, LB, Mississippi, New England 1971
Coleman, Don, LB, Michigan, New Orleans 1974-75
Coleman, Fred, TE, Northeast Louisiana, Buffalo 1976
Coleman, Greg, P, Florida A&M, Cleveland 1977; Minnesota 1978-85
Coleman, Herb, C, Notre Dame, Chi. Rockets (AAFC) 1946-48; Baltimore (AAFC) 1948
Coleman, Leonard, CB, Vanderbilt, Indianapolis 1985
Coleman, Monte, LB, Central Arkansas, Washington 1979-85
Coleman, Ralph, LB, North Carolina A&T, Dallas 1972
Coleman, Ronnie, RB, Alabama A&M, Houston 1974-81
Coleman, Steve, DE, Delaware State, Denver 1974
Colhouer, Jake, G, Oklahoma State, Chi. Cardinals 1946-48; NY Giants 1949
Collett, Elmer, G, Cal State-San Francisco, San Francisco 1967-72; Baltimore 1973-77
Collie, Bruce, T, Texas-Arlington, San Francisco 1985
Collier, Bob, T, SMU, LA Rams 1951
Collier, Floyd, T, San Jose State, San Francisco (AAFC) 1948
Collier, Jim, TE, Arkansas, NY Giants 1962; Washington 1963
Collier, Mike, RB, Morgan State, Pittsburgh 1975; Buffalo 1977-79
Collier, Tim, CB, East Texas State, Kansas City 1976-79; St. Louis 1980-82; San Francisco 1982-83
Collins, Albin (Rip), HB, LSU, Chi. Hornets (AAFC) 1949; Baltimore 1950; Green Bay 1951
Collins, Dwight, WR, Pittsburgh, Minnesota 1984
Collins, Gary, FL-P, Maryland, Cleveland 1962-71
Collins, George, G, Georgia, St. Louis 1978-82
Collins, Glen, DE, Mississippi State, Cincinnati 1982-85
Collins, Greg, LB, Notre Dame, San Francisco 1975; Seattle 1976; Buffalo 1977
Collins, Harry, G, Canisius, Buffalo 1924
Collins, Jerald, LB, Western Michigan, Buffalo 1969-71
Collins, Jim, LB, Syracuse, LA Rams 1981-85
Collins, Kirk, S, Baylor, LA Rams 1981-83
Collins, Larry, RB, Texas A&I, Cleveland 1978
Collins, Paul (Rip), E, Pittsburgh, Boston 1932-35
Collins, Paul, QB, Missouri, Chi. Cardinals 1945
Collins, Ray, T, LSU, San Francisco 1950-52; NY Giants 1954; Dallas Texans 1960-61
Collins, Sonny, RB, Kentucky, Atlanta 1976
Collins, Tony, RB, East Carolina, New England 1981-85
Collinsworth, Cris, WR, Florida, Cincinnati 1981-85
Colman, Wayne, LB, Temple, Philadelphia 1968-69; New Orleans 1969-74, 1976
Colmer, Mickey, HB, Miramonte J.C., Brooklyn (AAFC) 1946-48; NY Yankees (AAFC) 1949
Colo, Don, DT, Brown, Baltimore 1950; NY Yanks 1951; Dallas 1952; Cleveland 1953-58
Colquitt, Craig, P, Tennessee, Pittsburgh 1978-81, 1983-84
Colquitt, Jimmy, P, Tennessee, Seattle 1985
Colter, Jeff, DB, Kansas, Minnesota 1984
Colteryahn, Lloyd, E, Maryland, Baltimore 1954-56
Colvin, Jim (Rocky), DT, Houston, Baltimore 1960-63; Dallas 1964-66; NY Giants 1967
Colzie, Neal, S-KR, Ohio State, Oakland 1975-78; Miami 1979; Tampa Bay 1980-83
Comber, John (Hook), HB, Toronto, Canton 1926
Combs, Bill, E, Purdue, Philadelphia 1942
Combs, Chris, TE, New Mexico, St. Louis 1980-81
Comeaux, Darren, LB, Arizona State, Denver 1982-85
Comer, Marty, E, Tulane, Buffalo (AAFC) 1946-48
Commisa, Vince, G, Notre Dame, Boston 1944
Comp, Irv, HB, Benedictine, Green Bay 1943-49
Compagno, Tony, FB, St. Mary's (California), Pittsburgh 1946-48
Compton, Dick, FL, McMurray, Detroit 1962-64; Houston 1965; Pittsburgh 1966-68
Compton, Ogden, QB, Hardin-Simmons, Chi. Cardinals 1955
Comstock, Ed, G, Washington (St. Louis), Buffalo 1929; Brooklyn 1930; Staten Island 1931
Comstock, Rudy, G, Georgetown (Washington D.C.), Canton 1923, 1925; Cleveland 1924; Frankford 1926-29, NY Giants 1930; Green Bay 1931-33
Concannon, Ernie, G, NYU, Staten Island 1932; Boston 1934-36
Concannon, Jack, QB, Boston College, Philadelphia 1964-66; Chi. Bears 1967-71; Dallas 1973; Green Bay 1974; Detroit 1975
Condit, Merl, HB, Carnegie-Mellon, Pittsburgh 1940, 1946; Brooklyn 1941-43; Washington 1945
Condon, Tom, G, Boston College, Kansas City 1974-84; New England 1985
Condren, Glen, DT, Oklahoma, NY Giants 1965-67; Atlanta 1969-72
Cone, Fred, FB-K, Clemson, Green Bay 1951-57; Dallas Cowboys 1960
Conerly, Charlie, QB, Mississippi, NY Giants 1948-61
Conger, Mel, E, Georgia, NY Yankees (AAFC) 1946; Brooklyn (AAFC) 1947
Conjar, Larry, RB, Notre Dame, Cleveland 1967; Philadelphia 1968; Baltimore 1969-70
Conkright, Bill (Red), C, Oklahoma, Chi. Bears 1937-38; Cleveland 1939-42, 1944; Washington 1943; Brooklyn 1943
Conlee, Gerry, C, St. Mary's (California), Cleveland 1938; Detroit 1943; San Francisco (AAFC) 1946-47
Conley, John, T, Ohio Northern, Columbus 1922, 1926
Conley, Steve, LB, Kansas, Cincinnati 1972; St. Louis 1972
Conn, Dick, S, Georgia, Pittsburgh 1974; New England 1975-79
Conn, George (Tuffy), HB, Oregon State, Akron 1920; Cleveland 1920
Connaughton, Harry (Babe), G, Georgetown (Washington D.C.), Frankford 1927
Connell, Mike, P, Cincinnati, San Francisco 1978; Washington 1980-81
Connelly, Mike, G, Utah State, Dallas 1960-67; Pittsburgh 1968
Conner, Clyde, SE, Pacific, San Francisco 1956-63
Conners, Dan, LB, Miami, Oakland 1964-74
Connolly, Harry, HB, Boston College, Brooklyn (AAFC) 1946
Connolly, Ted, G, Santa Clara, San Francisco 1954, 1956-62; Cleveland 1963
Connor, Bill, T, Catholic, Boston, 1929; Newark 1930
Connor, George (Moose), T-DT-LB, Notre Dame, Chi. Bears 1948-55
Connors, Ham, E, Rochester 1925

Connors, Stafford, HB, New Hampshire, Providence 1925; Brooklyn 1926
Conoly, Bill, G, Texas, Chi. Cardinals 1946
Conover, Larry, C, Penn State, Canton 1921-23; Cleveland 1925; Frankford 1926
Conrad, Bobby Joe, FL-K, Texas A&M, Chi. Cardinals 1958-59; St. Louis 1960-68; Dallas 1969
Conrad, Marty, C, Western Illinois, Toledo 1922-23; Kenosha 1924; Akron 1925
Constantine, Irv, HB, Syracuse, Staten Island 1931
Conti, Enio, G, Bucknell, Philadelphia 1941-42, 1944-45; Phil-Pitt 1943
Contoulis, John, DT, Connecticut, NY Giants 1964
Contz, Bill, T, Penn State, Cleveland 1983-85
Conway, David, K, Texas, Green Bay 1971
Conzelman, Jimmy, HB-QB, Washington (St. Louis), Decatur 1920; Rock Island 1921-22; Milwaukee 1923-24; Detroit 1925-26; Providence 1927-29
Cook, Charles, NT, Miami, NY Giants 1983
Cook, Clair, HB, Dayton 1928
Cook, Dave, HB, Illinois, Chi. Cardinals 1934-36; Brooklyn 1936
Cook, Ed, T, Notre Dame, Chi. Cardinals 1958-59; St. Louis 1960-65; Atlanta 1966-67
Cook, Fred, DE, Southern Mississippi, Baltimore 1974-80
Cook, Gene, SE, Toledo, Detroit 1959
Cook, Greg, QB, Cincinnati, Cincinnati 1969, 1973
Cook, Jim, G, Green Bay 1921
Cook, Leon, T, Northwestern, Philadelphia 1942
Cook, Ted, E, Alabama, Detroit 1947; Green Bay 1948-50
Cooke, Bill, DT, Massachusetts, Green Bay 1975; San Francisco 1976-77; Detroit 1978; Seattle 1978-80
Cooke, Ed, DE, Maryland, Chi. Bears 1958; Philadelphia 1958; Baltimore 1959; NY Titans 1960-62; NY Jets 1963; Denver 1964-65; Miami 1966-67
Cooks, Johnie, LB, Mississippi State, Baltimore 1982-83; Indianapolis 1984-85
Coolbaugh, Bob, SE, Richmond, Oakland 1961
Coombs, Larry, C, Idaho, New Orleans 1980
Coombs, Tom, TE, Idaho, NY Jets 1982-83
Coomer, Joe, T, Austin, Pittsburgh 1941, 1945-46; Chi. Cardinals 1947-49
Coon, Ed (Ty), G, North Carolina State, Brooklyn 1940
Cooney, Mark, DE, Colorado, Green Bay 1974
Cooper, Bert, LB, Florida State, Tampa Bay 1976
Cooper, Bill (Bud), QB, Penn State, Cleveland 1937
Cooper, Bill (Cannonball), LB, Muskingum, San Francisco 1961-64
Cooper, Earl, RB-TE, Rice, San Francisco 1980-85
Cooper, Evan, CB, Michigan, Philadelphia 1984-85
Cooper, Hal, G, Detroit, Detroit 1937
Cooper, Jim, C, North Texas State, Brooklyn (AAFC) 1948
Cooper, Jim, G, Temple, Dallas 1977-85
Cooper, Joe, K, California, Houston 1984
Cooper, Ken, G, Vanderbilt, Baltimore (AAFC) 1949; Baltimore 1950
Cooper, Louis, LB, Western Carolina, Kansas City 1985
Cooper, Mark, G, Miami, Denver 1983-85
Cooper, Norm, C, Howard, Brooklyn 1937-38
Cooper, Sam, T, Geneva, Pittsburgh 1933
Cooper, Taylor, C, Muncie 1921
Cooper, Thurlow, DE, Maine, NY Titans 1960-62
Cope, Frank, T, Santa Clara, NY Giants 1938-47
Cope, Jim, LB, Ohio State, Atlanta 1976
Copeland, Jim, G-C, Virginia, Cleveland 1967-74
Copeland, Ron, WR, UCLA, Chi. Bears 1969
Copley, Charlie, T, Missouri-Rolla, Akron 1920-22; Milwaukee 1922
Coppage, Alton, E, Oklahoma, Chi. Cardinals 1940-42; Cleveland (AAFC) 1946; Buffalo (AAFC) 1947
Coppens, Gus, T, UCLA, NY Giants 1979
Corbett, George, QB, Millikin, Chi. Bears 1932-38
Corbett, Jim, TE, Pittsburgh, Cincinnati 1977-81
Corbett, Steve, G, Boston College, New England 1975
Corbitt, Don, C, Arizona, Washington 1948
Corbo, Tom, G, Duquesne, Cleveland 1944
Corcoran, Art, E, Georgetown (Washington D.C.), Canton 1920-21; Cleveland 1921; Akron 1922; Milwaukee 1922; Buffalo 1923
Corcoran, Jim (King), QB, Maryland, Boston 1968
Corcoran, John, C, St. Louis, Minneapolis 1930
Cordileone, Lou, DT, Clemson, NY Giants 1960; San Francisco 1961; LA Rams 1962; Pittsburgh 1962-63; New Orleans 1967-68
Cordill, Ollie, HB, Rice, Cleveland 1940
Cordill, Ollie, P, Memphis State, San Diego 1967; Atlanta 1968; New Orleans 1969
Cordovano, Sam, G, Georgetown (Washington D.C.), Newark 1930
Corey, Walt, LB, Miami, Dallas Texans 1960, 1962; Kansas City 1963-66
Corgan, Chuck, E, Arkansas, Kansas City 1924-26; Hartford 1926; NY Giants 1927
Corgan, Mike, FB, Notre Dame, Detroit 1943
Corker, John, LB, Oklahoma State, Houston 1980-82
Corley, Anthony, RB, Nevada-Reno, Pittsburgh 1984; San Diego 1985
Corley, Bert, C, Mississippi State, Buffalo (AAFC) 1947; Baltimore (AAFC) 1948
Corn, Joe, HB, LA Rams 1948
Cornelison, Jerry, T, SMU, Dallas Texans 1960-62; Kansas City 1964-65
Cornelius, Charles, CB, Bethune-Cookman, Miami 1977-78; San Francisco 1979-80
Cornell, Bo, RB, Washington, Cleveland 1971-72; Buffalo 1973-77
Cornish, Frank, DT, Grambling, Chi. Bears 1966; Miami 1970-71; Buffalo 1972
Cornsweet, Al, FB, Brown, Cleveland 1931
Cornwell, Fred, TE, USC, Dallas 1984-85
Coronado, Bob, SE, Pacific, Pittsburgh 1961
Corral, Frank, K-P, UCLA, LA Rams 1978-81
Correal, Chuck, C, Penn State, Atlanta 1979-80; Cleveland 1981
Cortemeglia, Chris, HB, SMU, Frankford 1927
Cortez, Bruce, CB, Parsons, New Orleans 1967
Corzine, Les (Red), FB, Davis & Elkins, Cincinnati 1933-34; St. Louis 1934; NY Giants 1935-37; Chi. Bears 1938
Cosbie, Doug, TE, Santa Clara, Dallas 1979-85
Coslet, Bruce, TE, Pacific, Cincinnati 1969-76
Cosner, Don, HB, Montana State, Chi. Cardinals 1939
Costa, Dave, DT, Utah, Oakland 1963-65; Buffalo 1966, 1974; Denver 1967-71; San Diego 1972-73
Costa, Paul, TE-T, Notre Dame, Buffalo 1965-72
Costello, Rory, C, Cincinnati 1921
Costello, Tom, LB, Dayton, NY Giants 1964-65
Costello, Vince, LB, Ohio U., Cleveland 1957-66; NY Giants 1967-68
Costict, Ray, LB, Mississippi State, New England 1977-79
Coston, Fred, C, Texas A&M, Philadelphia 1939
Cothren, Paige, FB-K, Mississippi, LA Rams 1957-58; Philadelphia 1959
Cotney, Mark, S, Cameron State, Houston 1975; Tampa Bay 1976-84
Cotton, Barney, G, Nebraska, Cincinnati 1979; St. Louis 1980-81
Cotton, Craig, TE, Youngstown State, Detroit 1969-72; Chi. Bears 1973; San Diego 1975
Cotton, Forrest (Fod), T, Notre Dame, Rock Island 1923-25
Cotton, Russ, QB, Texas-El Paso, Brooklyn 1941; Pittsburgh 1942
Cottrell, Bill, G-C-T, Delaware Valley, Detroit 1967-70; Denver 1972
Cottrell, Ted, LB, Delaware Valley, Atlanta 1969
Coughlin, Danny, HB, Notre Dame, Minneapolis 1923
Coughlin, Frank, T, Notre Dame, Detroit 1921; Green Bay 1921; Rock Island 1921
Coulter, DeWitt (Tex), T, Army, NY Giants 1946-49, 1951-52
Coumier, Ulysses, HB, Louisiana College, Buffalo 1929
Counts, Johnny, DB-KR, Illinois, NY Giants 1962-63
Couppee, Al, FB-G, Iowa, Washington 1946
Courson, Steve, G, South Carolina, 1978-83; Tampa Bay 1984-85
Courtney, Gerry, HB, Syracuse, Brooklyn 1942
Cousineau, Tom, LB, Ohio State, Cleveland 1982-85
Cousino, Brad, LB, Miami (Ohio), Cincinnati 1975; NY Giants 1976; Pittsburgh 1977
Coutre, Larry, HB, Notre Dame, Green Bay 1950, 1953; Baltimore 1953
Covert, Jim, T, Pittsburgh, Chi. Bears 1983-85
Cowan, Bob, HB, Indiana, Cleveland (AAFC) 1947-48; Baltimore (AAFC) 1949
Cowan, Charlie, T, New Mexico Highlands, LA Rams 1961-75
Cowan, Larry, RB, Jackson State, Miami 1982; New England 1982
Cowan, Les, T, McMurray, Chi. Bears 1951
Cowher, Bill, LB, North Carolina State, Cleveland 1980, 1982; Philadelphia 1983-84
Cowhig, Jerry, FB, Notre Dame, LA Rams 1947-49; Chi. Cardinals 1950; Philadelphia 1951
Cowins, Ben, RB, Arkansas, Kansas City 1979
Cowlings, Al, DE, USC, Buffalo 1970-72; Houston 1973-74; LA Rams 1975; Seattle 1976; San Francisco 1979
Cox, Arthur, TE, Texas Southern, Atlanta 1983-85
Cox, Billy, HB, Duke, Washington 1951-52, 1955
Cox, Fred, K, Pittsburgh, Minnesota 1963-77
Cox, Jim, G, Stanford, San Francisco (AAFC) 1948
Cox, Jim, TE, Miami, Miami 1968
Cox, Larry, DT, Abilene Christian, Denver 1966-68
Cox, Norm, HB, TCU, Chi. Rockets (AAFC) 1946-47
Cox, Steve, P-K, Arkansas, Cleveland 1981-84; Washington 1985
Coyle, Frank, E, Detroit, Milwaukee 1924; Rock Island 1924-25
Coyle, Ross, DB, Oklahoma, LA Rams 1961
Crabb, Claude, DB, Colorado, Washington 1962-63; Philadelphia 1964-65; LA Rams 1966-68
Crable, Bob, LB, Notre Dame, NY Jets 1982-85
Crabtree, Clem, T, Wake Forest, Detroit 1940-41
Crabtree, Clyde, QB, Florida, Frankford 1930; Minneapolis 1930
Crabtree, Eric, WR, Pittsburgh, Denver 1966-68; Cincinnati 1969-71; New England 1971
Craddock, Nate, RB, Parsons, Baltimore 1963
Craft, Donnie, RB, Louisville, Houston 1982-84
Craft, Russ, DB, Alabama, Philadelphia 1946-53; Pittsburgh 1954
Craig, Clark, E, Pennsylvania, Frankford 1925
Craig, Dobie, FL, Howard Payne, Oakland 1962-63; Houston 1964
Craig, Larry, QB, South Carolina, Green Bay 1939-49
Craig, Neal, CB, Fisk, Cincinnati 1971-73; Buffalo 1974; Cleveland 1975-76
Craig, Reggie, WR, Arkansas, Kansas City 1975-76; Cleveland 1977; Buffalo 1977
Craig, Roger, RB, Nebraska, San Francisco 1983-85
Craig, Steve, TE, Northwestern, Minnesota 1974-78
Crain, Milt, FB, Baylor, Boston 1944
Crakes, Joe, E, South Dakota, Cincinnati 1933
Cramer, Carl, HB, Hamline, Cleveland 1920; Akron 1921-26
Crane, Dennis, DT, USC, Washington 1968-69; NY Giants 1970
Crane, Gary, LB, Arkansas State, Denver 1969
Crane, Paul, LB, Alabama, NY Jets 1966-72
Crangle, Jack, FB, Illinois, Chi. Cardinals 1923
Crangle, Mike, DE, Tennessee-Martin, New Orleans 1972
Crass, Bill, HB, LSU, Chi. Cardinals 1937
Craven, Bill, S, Harvard, Cleveland 1976
Crawford, Bill, G, British Columbia, NY Giants 1960
Crawford, Denver, T, Tennessee, NY Yankees (AAFC) 1948
Crawford, Ed, HB, Mississippi, NY Giants 1957
Crawford, Fred, T, Duke, Chi. Bears 1935
Crawford, Hilton, DB, Grambling, Buffalo 1969
Crawford, Jim, HB, Wyoming, Boston 1960-64
Crawford, Ken, FB-HB-C, Miami (Ohio), Akron 1920; Cincinnati 1921; Dayton 1923; Hammond 1925
Crawford, Rufus, RB, Virginia State, Seattle 1978
Crawford, Walter (Mush), T, Illinois, Chi. Bears 1925; NY Yankees 1927
Crayne, Dick, FB, Iowa, Brooklyn 1936-37
Creech, Bob, LB, TCU, Philadelphia 1971-72; New Orleans 1973
Creekmur, Lou, T, William & Mary, Detroit 1950-59
Cregar, Bill, G, Holy Cross, Pittsburgh 1947-48
Creighton, Milan, E, Arkansas, Chi. Cardinals 1931-37
Cremer, Ted, E, Auburn, Detroit 1946-47; Green Bay 1948
Crennel, Carl, LB, West Virginia, Pittsburgh 1970
Crenshaw, Leon, DT, Tuskegee, Green Bay 1968
Crenshaw, Willis, RB, Kansas State, St. Louis 1964-69; Denver 1970
Crespino, Bobby, TE, Mississippi, Cleveland 1961-63; NY Giants 1964-68
Creswell, Smiley, DE, Michigan State, Philadelphia 1985; New England 1985
Crews, Ron, DT, Nevada-Las Vegas, Cleveland 1980
Cribbs, Joe, RB, Auburn, Buffalo 1980-83, 1985
Crimmins, Bernie, G, Notre Dame, Green Bay 1945
Crisler, Hal, E, San Jose State, Boston 1946-47; Washington 1948-49; Baltimore 1950
Crissy, Cris, WR, Princeton, Washington 1981
Crist, Chuck, DB, Penn State, NY Giants 1972-74; New Orleans 1975-77; San Francisco 1978
Criswell, Kirby, LB-DE, Kansas, St. Louis 1980-81
Critchfield, Hank, C, Wooster, Cleveland 1931
Critchfield, Larry, G, Grove City, Pittsburgh 1933
Criter, Ken, LB, Wisconsin, Denver 1969-74
Crittendon, Jack, E, Wayne State (Nebraska), Chi. Cardinals 1954
Crockett, Bobby, WR, Arkansas, Buffalo 1966, 1968-69
Crockett, Monte, New Mexico Highlands, Buffalo 1960-62
Croft, Abe, E, SMU, Chi. Bears 1944-45
Croft, Don, DT, Texas-El Paso, Buffalo 1972, 1974-75; Detroit 1976
Croft, Jack, G, Utah State, Racine 1924
Croft, Milburn (Tiny), Ripon, Green Bay 1942-47
Croft, Win, G, Utah, Brooklyn 1935; Pittsburgh 1936
Croftcheck, Don, G, Indiana, Washington 1965-66; Chi. Bears 1967
Cromwell, Nolan, S, Kansas, LA Rams 1977-85
Cronan, Pete, LB, Boston College, Seattle 1977-79, 1981; Washington 1981-85
Cronin, Bill, HB, Boston College, Providence 1927-29
Cronin, Bill, TE, Boston College, Philadelphia 1965; Miami 1966
Cronin, Frank, E, St. Mary's (Minnesota), Duluth 1927
Cronin, Gene, DE, Pacific, Detroit 1956-59; Dallas Cowboys 1960; Washington 1961-62
Cronin, Jack, HB, Boston College, Providence 1927-30
Cronin, Jerry, E, Rutgers, Brooklyn 1932
Cronin, Tom, HB, Marquette, Green Bay 1922
Cronkhite, Henry (Doc), E, Kansas State, Brooklyn 1934
Crook, Al, C, Washington & Jefferson, Detroit 1925-26; Kansas City 1926
Croom, Sylvester, C, Alabama, New Orleans 1975
Cropper, Marshall, WR, Maryland-Eastern Shore, Pittsburgh 1967-69
Crosby, Cleveland, DE, Arizona, Cleveland 1980; Baltimore 1982
Crosby, Ron, LB, Penn State, New Orleans 1978; NY Jets 1979-83
Crosby, Steve, RB, Fort Hays State, NY Giants 1974-76
Cross, Billy, HB, West Texas State, Chi. Cardinals 1951-53
Cross, Bobby, T, Stephen F. Austin, Chi. Bears 1952; LA Rams 1954-55; San Francisco 1956-57; Chi. Cardinals 1958-59; Boston 1960
Cross, Irv, DB, Northwestern, Philadelphia 1961-65, 1969; LA Rams 1966-68
Cross, Justin, T, Western State (Colorado), Buffalo 1982-85
Cross, Randy, G-C, UCLA, San Francisco 1976-85
Crossan, Dave, C, Maryland, Washington 1965-69
Crosswhite, Leon, RB, Oklahoma, Detroit 1973-74

Crotty, Jim, DB, Notre Dame, Washington 1960-61; Buffalo 1961-62
Crouch, Terry, G, Oklahoma, Baltimore 1982
Croudip, David, DB, San Diego State, LA Rams 1984; San Diego 1985; Atlanta 1985
Crouse, Ray, RB, Nevada-Las Vegas, Green Bay 1984
Crouthamel, Jake, RB, Dartmouth, Boston 1960
Crow, Al, DT, William & Mary, Boston 1960
Crow, John David, FB-TE, Texas A&M, Chi. Cardinals 1958-59; St. Louis 1960-64; San Francisco 1965-68
Crow, Lindon, DB, USC, Chi. Cardinals 1955-57; NY Giants 1958-60; LA Rams 1961-64
Crow, Orien, C, Haskell, Boston 1933-34
Crow, Wayne, HB, California, Oakland 1960-61; Buffalo 1962-63
Crowder, Earl, QB, Oklahoma, Chi. Cardinals 1939; Cleveland 1940
Crowder, Randy, DT, Penn State, Miami 1974-76; Tampa Bay 1978-80
Crowe, Larry, RB, Texas Southern, Philadelphia 1972; Atlanta 1975
Crowe, Paul, HB, St. Mary's (California), San Francisco (AAFC) 1948-49; LA Dons (AAFC) 1949; NY Yanks 1951
Crowell, Odis, T, Hardin-Simmons, San Francisco 1947
Crowl, Dick, C, Rutgers, Brooklyn 1930
Crowley, Jim, HB, Notre Dame, Green Bay 1925; Providence 1925
Crowley, Joe, E, Dartmouth, Boston 1944-45
Crowther, Rae, E, Colgate, Frankford 1925-26
Crowther, Saville, G, Colgate, Frankford 1925
Croyle, Phil, LB, California, Houston 1971-73; Buffalo 1973
Crum, Bob, DE, Arizona, St. Louis 1974
Crump, Dwayne, DB, Fresno State, St. Louis 1973-76
Crump, George, DE, East Carolina, New England 1982-83
Crump, Harry, FB, Boston College, Boston 1963
Crusan, Doug, T, Indiana, Miami 1968-74
Crutcher, Tommy, LB, TCU, Green Bay 1964-67, 1971-72; NY Giants 1968-69
Crutchfield, Dwayne, RB, Iowa State, NY Jets 1982-83; Houston 1983; LA Rams 1984
Cryder, Bob, T, Alabama, New England 1978-83; Seattle 1984-85
Csonka, Larry, FB, Syracuse, Miami 1968-74, 1979; NY Giants 1976-78
Cuba, Paul, T, Pittsburgh, Philadelphia 1933-35
Cudzik, Walt, C, Purdue, Washington 1954; Boston 1960-63; Buffalo 1964
Cuff, Ward, HB, Marquette, NY Giants 1937-45; Chi. Cardinals 1946; Green Bay 1947
Culbreath, Jim, RB, Oklahoma, Green Bay 1977-79; Philadelphia 1980
Cullars, Willie, DE, Kansas State, Philadelphia 1974
Cullen, Dave, G, Geneva, Cleveland 1931
Cullen, Ron, T, Oklahoma, Milwaukee 1922
Cullom, Jim, G, California, NY Yanks 1951
Culp, Curley, DT-NT, Arizona State, Kansas City 1968-74; Houston 1974-80
Culpepper, Ed, T, Alabama, Chi. Cardinals 1958-59; St. Louis 1960; Minnesota 1961; Houston 1962-63
Culver, Al, T, Notre Dame, Chi. Bears 1932; Geen Bay 1932
Culver, Frank, C, Syracuse, Buffalo 1923-24; Canton 1923, 1925; Rochester 1924
Cumby, George, LB, Oklahoma, Green Bay 1980-85
Cumiskey, Frank, E, Ohio State, Brooklyn 1937
Cummings, Ed, LB, Stanford, NY Jets 1964; Denver 1965
Cuneo, Ed, G, Columbia, Orange 1929; Brooklyn 1930
Cunningham, Bennie, TE, Clemson, Pittsburgh 1976-85
Cunningham, Carl, LB, Houston, Denver 1967-70; New Orleans 1971
Cunningham, Dick, LB, Arkansas, Buffalo 1967-72; Philadelphia 1973; Houston 1973
Cunningham, Doug, RB, Mississippi, San Francisco 1967-73; Washington 1974
Cunningham, Doug, WR, Rice, Minnesota 1979
Cunningham, Eric, G, Penn State, NY Jets 1979-80
Cunningham, Harold (Cookie), E, Ohio State, Cleveland 1927; Chi. Bears 1929; Staten Island 1931
Cunningham, Jay, DB, Bowling Green, Boston 1965-67
Cunningham, Jim, HB, Pittsburgh, Washington 1961-63
Cunningham, Leon, C, South Carolina, Detroit 1955
Cunningham, Randall, QB, Nevada-Las Vegas, Philadelphia 1985
Cunningham, Sam (Bam), RB, USC, New England 1973-79, 1981-82
Cuozzo, Gary, QB, Virginia, Baltimore 1963-66; New Orleans 1967; Minnesota 1968-71; St. Louis 1972
Cuppoletti, Bree, G, Oregon, Chi. Cardinals 1934-38; Philadelphia 1939
Curchin, Jeff, T, Florida State, Chi. Bears 1970-71; Buffalo 1972
Curcillo, Tony, FB, Ohio State, Chi. Cardinals 1953
Curcio, Mike, LB, Temple, Philadelphia 1981; NY Giants 1982; Green Bay 1983
Cure, Armand, HB, Rhode Island, Baltimore (AAFC) 1947
Cureton, Will, QB, East Texas State, Cleveland 1975
Curley, August, LB, USC, Detroit 1983-85
Curran, Harry, HB, Boston College, Chi. Cardinals 1920-21
Curran, Pat, TE, Lakeland, LA Rams 1969-74; San Diego 1975-78
Curran, Willie, WR, UCLA, Atlanta 1982-84
Current, Mike, T, Ohio State, Miami 1967, 1977-78; Denver 1967-75; Tampa Bay 1976
Currie, Dan, LB, Michigan State, Green Bay 1958-64; LA Rams 1965-66
Currier, Bill, DB, South Carolina, Houston 1977-79; New England 1980; NY Giants 1981-85
Currivan, Dan, E, Boston College, Chi. Cardinals 1943; Card-Pitt 1944; Boston 1945-48; LA Rams 1948-49
Curry, Bill, C, Georgia Tech, Green Bay 1965-66; Baltimore 1967-72; Houston 1973; LA Rams 1974
Curry, Buddy, LB, North Carolina, Atlanta 1980-85
Curry, Craig, S, Texas, Tampa Bay 1984-85
Curry, Roy, FL, Jackson State, Pittsburgh 1963
Curtin, Don, QB, Marquette, Racine 1926; Milwaukee 1926
Curtis, Isaac, WR, San Diego State, Cincinnati 1973-84
Curtis, Mike, LB, Duke, Baltimore 1965-75; Seattle 1976; Washington 1977-78
Curtis, Tom, S, Michigan, Baltimore 1970-71
Curzon, Harry, HB, Buffalo 1925; Hammond 1925-26; Louisville 1926; Chi. Cardinals 1928
Cusick, Pete, T, Ohio State, New England 1975
Cutler, Harry, T, Dayton 1920
Cutsinger, Gary, DE, Oklahoma State, Houston 1962-68
Cvercko, Andy, G, Northwestern, Green Bay 1960; Dallas Cowboys 1961-62; Cleveland 1963; Washington 1963
Cyre, Hec, T, Gonzaga, Green Bay 1926-27; NY Yankees 1928
Czarobski, Ziggy, G, Notre Dame, Chi. Rockets (AAFC) 1948, Chi. Hornets (AAFC) 1949

D

Daanen, Jerry, WR, Miami, St. Louis 1968
Dabney, Carlton, DT, Morgan State, Atlanta 1968
Daddio, Bill, E, Pittsburgh, Chi. Cardinals 1941-42; Buffalo (AAFC) 1946
D'Addio, Dave, RB, Maryland, Detroit 1984
Dadmun, Harry, G, Harvard, Canton 1920; NY Giants 1921
Daffer, Ted, DE, Tennessee, Chi. Bears 1954
Dagata, Fred, FB, Providence, Providence 1931
D'Agostino, Frank, G, Auburn, Philadelphia 1956; NY Titans 1960
Dahlgren, George (Swede), G, Beloit, Kenosha 1924; Hammond 1925-26
Dahms, Tom, T, San Diego State, LA Rams 1951-54; Green Bay 1955; Chi. Cardinals 1956; San Francisco 1957
Dailey, Ted, E, Pittsburgh, Pittsburgh 1933
Dalby, Dave, C, UCLA, Oakland 1972-81; LA Raiders 1982-85
Dale, Carroll, WR, Virginia Tech, LA Rams 1960-64; Green Bay 1965-72; Minnesota 1973
Dale, Jeffery, S, LSU, San Diego 1985
Dale, Roland, DE, Mississippi, Washington 1950
Daley, Bill, FB, Minnesota, Michigan, Miami (AAFC) 1946, Brooklyn (AAFC) 1946; Chi. Rockets (AAFC) 1947; NY Yankees (AAFC) 1948
Dallafior, Ken, G, Minnesota, San Diego 1985
Dally, Dilly, G, Hartford 1926
D'Alonzo, Pete, FB, Villanova, Detroit 1951-52
Dalrymple, Bob (Slats), C, Wabash, Evansville 1922
Dalton, Leather, FB, Carroll (Wisconsin), Racine 1922
Dalton, Oakley, DT, Jackson State, New Orleans 1977
D'Amato, Mike, DB, Hofstra, NY Jets 1968
Damiani, Frank, T, Manhattan, NY Giants 1944
Damkroger, Maury, LB, Nebraska, New England 1974-75
Damore, John, G, Northwestern, Chi. Bears 1957, 1959
Danahe, Dick, T, USC, LA Dons (AAFC) 1947-48
Dancewicz, Frank (Boley), QB, Notre Dame, Boston 1946-48
Danelo, Joe, K, Washington State, Green Bay 1975; NY Giants 1976-82; Buffalo 1983-84
Danenhauer, Bill, DE, Emporia State, Denver 1960; Boston 1960
Danenhauer, Eldon, T, Pittsburg State, Denver 1960-65
Daney, George, G, Texas-El Paso, Kansas City 1968-74
Daniel, Eugene, CB, LSU, Indianapolis 1984-85
Daniel, Kenny, DB, San Jose State, NY Giants 1984
Daniel, Willie, DB, Mississippi State, Pittsburgh 1961-66; LA Rams 1967-69
Daniell, Ave, T, Pittsburgh, Green Bay 1937; Brooklyn 1937
Daniell, Jim, T, Ohio State, Chi. Bears 1945; Cleveland 1946
Daniels, Calvin, LB, North Carolina, Kansas City 1982-85
Daniels, Clem, FB, Prairie View A&M, Dallas Texans 1960; Oakland 1961-67; San Francisco 1968
Daniels, Dave, DT, Florida A&M, Oakland 1966
Daniels, Dick, DB, Pacific (Oregon), Dallas 1966-68; Chi. Bears 1969
Danielson, Gary, QB, Purdue, Detroit 1976-84; Cleveland 1985
Danjean, Ernie, G, Auburn, Green Bay 1957
Danmeier, Rick, K, Sioux Falls, Minnesota 1978-82
Danowski, Eddie, QB, Fordham, NY Giants 1934-39, 1941
Danziger, Fred, FB, Michigan State, Cleveland 1931
DaPrato, Neno, FB, Michigan State, Detroit 1921
Darby, Alvis, TE, Florida, Seattle 1976; Houston 1976; Tampa Bay 1978
Darby, Byron, DE, USC, Philadelphia 1983-85
Darby, Paul, WR, Southwest Texas State, NY Jets 1979-80
Dardar, Ramsey, DT, LSU, St. Louis 1984
Darden, Thom, S, Michigan, Cleveland 1972-74, 1976-81
Darling, Bernard (Boob), C, Beloit, Green Bay 1927-31
Darnall, Bill, WR, North Carolina, Miami 1968-69
Darns, Phil, DE, Mississippi Valley State, Tampa Bay 1984
Darragh, Dan, QB, William & Mary, Buffalo 1968-70
Darre, Bernie, G, Tulane, Washington 1961
Darrow, Barry, T, Montana, Cleveland 1974-78
Dasstling, Dane, T, Marietta, Cincinnati 1921
Daugherty, Bob, RB, Tulsa, San Francisco 1966
Daugherty, Dick, LB-G, Oregon, LA Rams 1951-53, 1956-58
Daugherty, Russ, HB, Illinois, Frankford 1927
Daukas, Lou, C, Cornell, Brooklyn (AAFC) 1947
Daukas, Nick, T, Dartmouth, Brooklyn (AAFC) 1946-47
Daum, Carl (Red), E, Akron, Akron 1922-26
Davenport, Ron, RB, Louisville, Miami 1985
Davenport, Wayne, HB, Hardin-Simmons, Green Bay 1931
David, Bob, G, Villanova, LA Rams 1947-48; Chi. Rockets (AAFC) 1948
David, Jim, DB, Colorado State, Detroit 1952-59
David, Stan, LB, Texas Tech, Buffalo 1984
Davidson, Ben, DE, Washington, Green Bay 1961; Washington 1962-63; Oakland 1964-71
Davidson, Bill, HB, Temple, Pittsburgh 1937-39
Davidson, Chy, WR, Rhode Island, NY Jets 1984-85
Davidson, Cotton, QB, Baylor, Baltimore 1954, 1957; Dallas Texans 1960-62; Oakland 1962-66, 1968
Davidson, Greg, C, North Texas State, Houston 1980-82
Davidson, Joe, G, Colgate, Chi. Cardinals 1928; Newark 1930
Davidson, Pete, DT, Citadel, Houston 1960
Davies, Tommy, HB, Pittsburgh, Hammond 1922
Davis, Al, RB, Tennessee State, Philadelphia 1971-72
Davis, Andy, HB, George Washington, Washington 1952
Davis, Anthony, RB, USC, Tampa Bay 1977; Houston 1978; LA Rams 1978
Davis, Arch, HB, Notre Dame, Columbus 1925-26
Davis, Art, T, Alabama State, Chi. Bears 1953
Davis, Art, HB, Mississippi State, Pittsburgh 1956
Davis, Ben, DB, Defiance, Cleveland 1967-68, 1970-73; Detroit 1974-76
Davis, Bill, T, Texas Tech, Chi. Cardinals 1940-41; Brooklyn 1943; Miami (AAFC) 1946
Davis, Billy, LB, Clemson, St. Louis 1984
Davis, Bob, QB, Kentucky, Cleveland 1938; Philadelphia 1942; Boston 1944-46
Davis, Bob, E, Penn State, Pittsburgh 1946-50
Davis, Bob, T, Georgia Tech, Boston 1948
Davis, Bob, QB, Virginia, Houston 1967-69; NY Jets 1970-72; New Orleans 1973
Davis, Brad, RB, LSU, Atlanta 1975-76
Davis, Bruce, T, UCLA, Oakland 1979-81; LA Raiders 1982-85
Davis, Bruce, WR, Baylor, Cleveland 1984
Davis, Butch, DB, Missouri, Chi. Bears 1970
Davis, Carl, T, West Virginia, Akron 1926; Frankford 1927
Davis, Charlie, RB, Colorado, Cincinnati 1974; Tampa Bay 1976
Davis, Charlie, DT, TCU, Pittsburgh 1974; St. Louis 1975-79; Houston 1980
Davis, Clarence, RB, USC, Oakland 1971-78
Davis, Corbett, HB, Indiana, Cleveland 1938-39, 1941-42
Davis, Dave, WR, Tennessee State, Green Bay 1971-72; Pittsburgh 1973; New Orleans 1974
Davis, Dick, T, Kansas, Dallas Texans 1960
Davis, Dick, RB, Nebraska, Denver 1970; New Orleans 1970
Davis, Don, DT, Cal State-Los Angeles, NY Giants 1966
Davis, Donnie, WR-TE, Southern, Dallas Cowboys 1962; Houston 1970
Davis, Doug, T, Kentucky, Minnesota 1966-72
Davis, Ed (Doc), G, Indiana, Muncie 1920; Dayton 1920-21; Columbus 1921-22
Davis, Fred, T-DT, Alabama, Washington 1941-42, 1945; Chi. Bears 1946-51
Davis, Gaines, G, Texas Tech, NY Giants 1936
Davis, Gary, RB, Cal Poly-SLO, Miami 1976-79; Tampa Bay 1980-81; Cleveland 1981
Davis, Glenn, HB, Army, LA Rams 1950-51
Davis, Glenn, SE, Ohio State, Detroit 1960-61
Davis, Harper, HB, Mississippi State, LA Dons (AAFC) 1949; Chi. Bears 1950; Green Bay 1951
Davis, Harrison, WR, Virginia, San Diego 1974
Davis, Henry, LB, Grambling, NY Giants 1968-69; Pittsburgh 1970-73
Davis, Jack, G, Arizona, Denver 1960
Davis, Jack, G, Maryland, Boston 1960
Davis, James, CB, Southern, LA Raiders 1982-85
Davis, Jeff, LB, Clemson, Tampa Bay 1982-85
Davis, Jerry, HB, Southeastern Louisiana, Chi. Cardinals 1948-51; Dallas 1952
Davis, Jerry, DB, Morris Brown, NY Jets 1975
Davis, Joe, E, USC, Brooklyn (AAFC) 1946
Davis, John, HB, Columbus 1920
Davis, Johnny, RB, Alabama, Tampa Bay 1978-80; San Francisco 1981; Cleveland 1982-85
Davis, Kyle, C, Oklahoma, Dallas 1975; San Francisco 1978
Davis, Lamar (Racehorse), E, Georgia, Miami (AAFC) 1946; Baltimore (AAFC) 1947-49
Davis, Lee, CB, Mississippi, Cincinnati 1985
Davis, Marvin, DE, Wichita State, Denver 1966
Davis, Marvin, LB, Southern, Houston 1974
Davis, Mike, S, Colorado, Oakland 1978-81; LA Raiders 1982-85
Davis, Milt, DB, UCLA, Baltimore 1957-60
Davis, Norman, G, Grambling, Baltimore 1967; New Orleans

1969; Philadelphia 1970
Davis, Oliver, DB, Tennessee State, Cleveland 1977-80; Cincinnati 1981-82
Davis, Pahl, G, Marquette, Green Bay 1922
Davis, Paul, QB, Otterbein, Pittsburgh 1947-48
Davis, Paul, LB, North Carolina, Atlanta 1981-82; NY Giants 1983; St. Louis 1983
Davis, Preston, CB, Baylor, Indianapolis 1984-85
Davis, Ralph, G, Wisconsin, Green Bay 1947-48
Davis, Ray, G, Samford, Portsmouth 1932-33; Chi. Cardinals 1935
Davis, Ricky, S, Alabama, Cincinnati 1975; Tampa Bay 1976; Kansas City 1977
Davis, Roger, G, Syracuse, Chi. Bears 1960-63; LA Rams 1964; NY Giants 1965-66
Davis, Ron, DE, Virginia State, St. Louis 1973
Davis, Roosevelt, DE, Tennessee State, NY Giants 1965-67
Davis, Russell, RB, Michigan, Pittsburgh 1980-83
Davis, Sam, G, Allen, Pittsburgh 1967-79
Davis, Sonny, LB, Baylor, Dallas Cowboys 1961
Davis, Stan, WR, Memphis State, Philadelphia 1973
Davis, Steve, RB, Delaware State, Pittsburgh 1972-74; NY Jets 1975-76
Davis, Sylvester (Red), HB, Geneva, Portsmouth 1933; Philadelphia 1933
Davis, Ted, LB, Georgia Tech, Baltimore 1964-66; New Orleans 1967-69; Miami 1970
Davis, Tommy, K, LSU, San Francisco 1959-69
Davis, Tony, RB, Nebraska, Cincinnati 1976-78; Tampa Bay 1979-81
Davis, Tyrone, CB, Clemson, NY Giants 1985
Davis, Van, E, Georgia, NY Yankees (AAFC) 1947-49
Davis, Vern, DB, Western Michigan, Philadelphia 1971
Davis, Wayne, CB, Indiana State, San Diego 1985
Davis, Willie, T-DE, Grambling, Cleveland 1958-59; Green Bay 1960-69
Davlin, Mike, T, San Francisco, Washington 1955
Dawkins, Joe, RB, Wisconsin, Houston 1970-71; Denver 1971-73, 1976; NY Giants 1974-75
Dawkins, Julius, WR, Pittsburgh, Buffalo 1983-84
Dawley, Fred, FB, Michigan, Detroit 1944
Dawson, Bill, DE, Florida State, Boston 1965
Dawson, Doug, G, Texas, St. Louis 1984-85
Dawson, Gib, HB, Texas, Green Bay 1953
Dawson, Len, QB, Purdue, Pittsburgh 1957-59; Cleveland 1960-61; Dallas Texans 1962; Kansas City 1963-75
Dawson, Lin, TE, North Carolina State, New England 1981-85
Dawson, Mike, DT, Arizona, St. Louis 1976-82; Detroit 1983; Kansas City 1984
Dawson, Rhett, WR, Florida State, Houston 1972; Minnesota 1973
Day, Al, LB, Eastern Michigan, Denver 1960
Day, Eagle, QB, Mississippi, Washington 1959-60
Day, Tom, DE, North Carolina A&T, St. Louis 1960; Buffalo 1961-66, 1968; San Diego 1967
Dayhoff, Harry, HB, Bucknell, Frankford 1924; Pottsville 1925
Daykin, Tony, LB, Georgia Tech, Detroit 1977-78; Atlanta 1979-81
Deadeye (Jack Thorpe), T, Oorang 1922-23
Deal, Rufus, FB, Auburn, Washington 1942
Dean, Floyd, LB, Florida, San Francisco 1964-65
Dean, Fred, DE, Louisiana Tech, San Diego 1975-81; San Francisco 1981-85
Dean, Fred, G, Texas Southern, Chi. Bears 1977; Washington 1978-82
Dean, Hal, G, Ohio State, LA Rams 1947-49
Dean, Jimmy, DE, Texas A&M, Houston 1978
Dean, Randy, QB, Northwestern, NY Giants 1977-79
Dean, Ted, FB, Wichita State, Philadelphia 1960-63; Minnesota 1964
Dean, Tom, T, SMU, Boston 1946-47
Dean, Vernon, CB, San Diego State, Washington 1982-85
DeBerg, Steve, QB, San Jose State, San Francisco 1978-80; Denver 1981-83; Tampa Bay 1984-85
DeBernardi, Fred, DE, Texas-El Paso, Kansas City 1974
deBruijn, Case, P, Idaho State, Kansas City 1982
DeCarbo, Nick, G, Duquesne, Pittsburgh 1933
DeCarlo, Art, HB-SE-DB, Georgia, Pittsburgh 1953; Washington 1956-57; Baltimore 1957-60
DeClerk, Frank, C, St. Ambrose, Rock Island 1921-25
deCorrevont, Bill, HB, Northwestern, Washington 1945; Detroit 1946; Chi. Cardinals 1947-48; Chi. Bears 1948-49
Dee, Bob, DE, Holy Cross, Washington 1957-58; Boston 1960-67
Deeks, Don, T, Washington, Boston 1945-47; Washington 1947; Green Bay 1948
Deer Slayer, E, Oorang 1922
Dees, Bob, G, Southwest Missouri State, Green Bay 1952
DeFelice, Nick, T, Southern Connecticut State, NY Jets 1965-66
DeFilippo, Lou, C, Fordham, NY Giants 1941, 1945-47
DeFrance, Chris, WR, Arizona State, Washington 1979
DeFruiter, Bob, HB, Nebraska, Washington 1945-47; Detroit 1947; LA Rams 1948
Degen, Dick, LB, Long Beach State, San Diego 1965-66
DeGree, Cy, G, Notre Dame, Detroit 1921
DeGrenier, Jack, RB, Texas-Arlington, New Orleans 1974
Degrate, Tony, DT, Texas, Green Bay 1985
Deibel, Art, T, Lafayette, Canton 1926
DeJurnett, Charles, DT-NT, San Jose State, San Diego 1976-80; LA Rams 1982-85
Dekdebrun, Al, QB, Cornell, Buffalo (AAFC) 1946; Chi. Rockets (AAFC) 1947; NY Yankees (AAFC) 1948; Boston 1948
Dekker, Paul, E, Michigan State, Washington 1953
DeLamielleure, Joe, G, Michigan State, Buffalo 1973-79, 1985; Cleveland 1980-84
Delaney, Jeff, S, Pittsburgh, LA Rams 1980; Detroit 1981; Tampa Bay 1981; Baltimore 1982-83
Delaney, Joe, RB, Northwestern State (Louisiana), Kansas City 1981-82
DeLaPorte, Darol, FB, Milwaukee 1925
deLauer, Bob, C, USC, Cleveland 1945; LA Rams 1946
Del Bello, Jack, QB, Miami, Baltimore 1953
DeLeone, Tom, C-G, Ohio State, Cincinnati 1972-73; Cleveland 1974-84
Delevan, Burt, T, Pacific, Chi. Cardinals 1955-56
Del Gaizo, Jim, QB, Tampa, Miami 1972; Green Bay 1973; NY Giants 1974
Del Greco, Al, K, Auburn, Green Bay 1984-85
DeLisle, Jim, DT, Wisconsin, Green Bay 1971
Dellenbach, Jeff, T, Wisconsin, Miami 1985
Dell Isola, John, G, Fordham, NY Giants 1934-40
Dellerba, Spiro, FB, Ohio State, Cleveland (AAFC) 1947; Baltimore (AAFC) 1948-49
Dellinger, Larry, G, St. Mary's (Ohio), Dayton 1920-23
DeLoach, Ralph, DE, California, NY Jets 1981
DeLong, Steve, DE, Tennessee, San Diego 1965-71; Chi. Bears 1972
Deloplaine, Jack, RB, Salem (West Virginia), Pittsburgh 1976-79; Washington 1978; Chi. Bears 1979
Del Rio, Jack, LB, USC, New Orleans 1985
DeLuca, Sam, T, South Carolina, LA Chargers 1960; San Diego 1961, 1963; NY Jets 1964-66
DeLuca, Tony, NT, Rhode Island, Green Bay 1984
DeLucca, Jerry, T, Tennessee, Philadelphia 1959; Boston 1960-61, 1963-64; Buffalo 1962-63
DeMao, Al, C, Duquesne, Washingon 1945-53
DeMarco, Bob, C, Dayton, St. Louis 1961-69; Miami 1970-71; Cleveland 1972-74; LA Rams 1975
DeMarco, Mario, G, Miami, Detroit 1949
Demarie, John, G, LSU, Cleveland 1967-75; Seattle 1976
Demas, George, G, Washington & Jefferson, Staten Island 1932; Brooklyn 1934
Demery, Calvin, WR, Arizona State, Minnesota 1972
Demko, George, DE, Appalachian State, Pittsburgh 1961
Demmy (Demyanovich), Joe,T, Staten Island 1930-31
DeMoe, Gus, E, Green Bay 1921
Demory, Bill, QB, Arizona, NY Jets 1973-74
DeMoss, Bob, QB, Purdue, NY Bulldogs 1949
Dempsey, Frank, E, Florida, Chi. Bears 1950-53
Dempsey, John, T, Bucknell, Pittsburgh 1934; Philadelphia 1934, 1937
Dempsey, Tom, K, Palomar J.C., New Orleans 1969-70; Philadelphia 1971-74; LA Rams 1975-76; Houston 1977; Buffalo 1978-79
Denfield, Fred, G, Navy, Rock Island 1920; Duluth 1925
Den Herder, Vern, DE, Central Iowa, Miami 1971-82
Dennard, Mark, C, Texas A&M, Miami 1979-83; Philadelphia 1984-85
Dennard, Preston, WR, New Mexico, LA Rams 1978-83; Buffalo 1984; Green Bay 1985
Dennerlein, Jerry, T, St. Mary's (California), NY Giants 1937, 1940
Dennery, Mike, LB, Southern Mississippi, Oakland 1974-75; Miami 1976
Dennery, Vince, E, Fordham, NY Giants 1941
Denney, Austin, TE, Tennessee, Chi. Bears 1967-69; Buffalo 1970-71
Dennis, Al, G, Grambling, San Diego 1973; Cleveland 1976-77
Dennis, Guy, G, Florida, Cincinnati 1969-72; Detroit 1973-75
Dennis, Mike, RB, Mississippi, LA Rams 1968-69
Dennis, Mike, DB, Wyoming, NY Giants 1980-83; San Diego 1984; NY Jets 1984
Dennison, Doug, RB-KR, Kutztown, Dallas 1974-78
Dennison, Glenn, TE, Miami, NY Jets 1984
Dennison, Rick, LB, Colorado State, Denver 1982-85
Denny, Earl, RB, Missouri, Minnesota 1967-68
Denson, Al, WR, Florida A&M, Denver 1964-70; Minnesota 1971
Denson, Keith, WR-KR, San Diego State, NY Jets 1976
Denson, Moses, RB, Maryland Eastern Shore, Washington 1974-75
Dent, Richard, DE, Tennessee State, Chi. Bears 1983-85
Denton, Bob, DT, Pacific, Cleveland 1960; Minnesota 1961-64
Denton, Winnie, G, Harvard, Evansville 1922
Denvir, John, G, Colorado, Denver 1962
DeOssie, Steve, LB, Boston College, Dallas 1984-85
DePascal, Carmine, E, Wichita State, Pittsburgh 1945
DePaso, Tom, LB, Penn State, Cincinnati 1978-79
DePaul, Henry, G, Duquesne, Pittsburgh 1945
Depler, John, C, Illinois, Orange 1929; Dayton 1929; Newark 1930
DePoyster, Jerry, P, Wyoming, Detroit 1968; Oakland 1971-72
DeRatt, Jimmy, DB, North Carolina, New Orleans 1975
Derby, Dean, DB, Washington, Pittsburgh 1957-61; Minnesota 1961-62
Deremer, Art, C, Niagara, Brooklyn 1942
DeRogatis, Al, DT, Duke, NY Giants 1949-52
DeRoo, Brian, WR, Redlands, Baltimore 1979-81
Derr, Ben, HB, Pennsylvania, Chi. Tigers 1920
DeSantis, Dan, HB, Niagara, Philadelphia 1941
Deschaine, Dick, P, Green Bay 1955-57; Cleveland 1958
DeShane, Chuck, HB, Alabama, Detroit 1945-49
DeSimone, Rick, TE, Cal State-Northridge, San Francisco 1978
DesJardien, Paul (Shorty), C-G, Chicago, Chi. Tigers 1920; Rock Island 1921
Deskin, Versil, E, Drake, Chi. Cardinals 1935-39
Deskins, Don, G, Michigan, Oakland 1960
Dess, Darrell, G, North Carolina State, Pittsburgh 1958; NY Giants 1959-64, 1966-69; Washington 1965-66
DeStefano, Fred, FB, Northwestern, Chi. Cardinals 1924-25
DeSutter, Wayne, T, Western Illinois, Buffalo 1966
Deters, Harold, K, North Carolina State, Dallas 1967
Detwiler, Chuck, RB, Utah State, San Diego 1970-72; St. Louis 1973
Detwiler, John, HB, Kansas, Hammond 1923-24
DeVaughn, Dennis, DB, Bishop, Philadelphia 1982-83
Devlin, Chris, LB, Penn State, Cincinnati 1975-76, 1978; Chi. Bears 1978
Devlin, Joe, T, Iowa, Buffalo 1976-82, 1984-85
Devlin, Mark, HB, Holy Cross, Cleveland 1920; Rock Island 1920
DeVleigher, Chuck, DT, Memphis State, Buffalo 1969
Devrow, Billy, DB, Southern Mississippi, Cleveland 1967
Dewar, Jim, HB, Indiana, Cleveland (AAFC)1947; Brooklyn (AAFC) 1948
DeWeese, Everett (Ebby), G, Dayton 1927-28; Portsmouth 1930
Dewell, Bill, E, SMU, Chi. Cardinals 1940-41, 1945-49
Dewveall, Willard, TE, SMU, Chi. Bears 1959-60; Houston 1961-64
DeWitz, Herb, HB, Nebraska, Cleveland 1927
DeWitz, Rufe, HB, Nebraska, Kansas City 1924-26
Dial, Benjy, QB, Eastern New Mexico, Philadelphia 1967
Dial, Buddy, SE, Rice, Pittsburgh 1959-63; Dallas 1964-66
Diamond, Bill, G, Miami, Kansas City 1963
Diamond, Charley, T, Miami, Dallas Texans 1960-62; Kansas City 1963
Diana, Rich, RB, Yale, Miami 1982
Dibb, John, T, Army, Newark 1930
Dibble, Dorne, SE-DB, Michigan State, Detroit 1951, 1953-57
Dickel, Dan, LB, Iowa, Baltimore 1974-77; Detroit 1978
Dickerson, Anthony, LB, SMU, Dallas 1980-84; Buffalo 1985
Dickerson, Eric, RB, SMU, LA Rams 1983-85
Dickey, Curtis, RB, Texas A&M, Baltimore 1980-83; Indianapolis 1984-85; Cleveland 1985
Dickey, Eldridge, QB-WR, Tennessee State, Oakland 1968, 1971
Dickey, Lynn, QB, Kansas State, Houston 1971, 1973-75; Green Bay 1976-77, 1979-85
Dickey, Wallace, T, Southwest Texas State, Denver 1968-69
Dickinson, Bo, FB, Southern Mississippi, Dallas Texans 1960-61, Denver 1962-63; Houston 1963; Oakland 1964
Dickinson, Parnell, QB, Mississippi Valley State, Tampa Bay 1976
Dickinson, Tom, E, Syracuse, Detroit 1920
Dickson, Paul, DT, Baylor, LA Rams 1959; Dallas Cowboys 1960; Minnesota 1961-70; St. Louis 1971
Dicus, Chuck, WR, Arkansas, San Diego 1971-72; Pittsburgh 1973
Didier, Clint, TE, Portland State, Washington 1982-85
Didion, John, C, Oregon State, Washington 1969; New Orleans 1971-74
Diehl, Charlie, G, Idaho, Chi. Cardinals 1930-31; St. Louis 1934
Diehl, Dave, E, Michigan State, Detroit 1939-40, 1944-45
Diehl, John, DT, Virginia, Baltimore 1961-64, Dallas 1965
Diehl, Wally, FB, Bucknell, Frankford 1928-30
Dieken, Doug, T, Illinois, Cleveland 1971-84
Dierdorf, Dan, T-C, Michigan, St. Louis 1971-83
Dierking, Scott, RB, Purdue, NY Jets 1977-83; Tampa Bay 1984
Dieter, Herb, G-T, Pennsylvania, Buffalo 1922
Dieterich, Chris, G, North Carolina State, Detroit 1980-85
Dietz, Joe, G, Hammond 1920
diFilippo, Dave, G, Villanova, Philadelphia 1941
Diggs, Shelton, WR, USC, NY Jets 1977
Digris, Bernie, T, Holy Cross, Chi. Bears 1943
Dillon, Bobby, DB, Texas, Green Bay 1952-59
Dillon, Terry, DB, Montana, Minnesota 1963
Dils, Steve, QB, Stanford, Minnesota 1979-84; LA Rams 1984-85
Dilts, Bucky, P, Georgia, Denver 1977-78; Baltimore 1979
Dilweg, LaVern, E, Marquette, Milwaukee 1926; Green Bay 1927-34
Dimancheff, Boris (Babe), HB, Purdue, Boston 1945-46; Chi. Cardinals 1947-50; Chi. Bears 1952
DiMidio, Tony, T, West Chester, Kansas City 1966-67
Dimitroff, Tom, QB, Miami (Ohio), Boston 1960
Dimmick, Don, HB, Hobart, Buffalo 1926-27
Dimmick, Tom, G, Houston, Philadelphia 1956; Dallas Texans 1960
Dimler, Rich, DT, USC, Cleveland 1979; Green Bay 1980
Dinkel, Tom, LB, Kansas, Cincinnati 1978-83, 1985
Dion, Terry, DE, Oregon, Seattle 1980

DiPierro, Ray, G, Ohio State, Green Bay 1950-51
Dirden, Johnnie, WR-KR, Sam Houston State, Houston 1978-79; Pittsburgh 1981
Dirks, Mike, G-T, Wyoming, Philadelphia 1968-71
Discend, Leo, T, Albright, Brooklyn 1938-39; Green Bay 1940
Discenzo, Tony, T, Michigan State, Buffalo 1960; Boston 1960
Ditka, Mike, TE, Pittsburgh, Chi. Bears 1961-66; Philadelphia 1967-68; Dallas 1969-72
Dittrich, John, G, Wisconsin, Chi. Cardinals 1956; Green Bay 1959; Oakland 1960; Buffalo 1961
DiVito, Joe, QB, Boston College, Denver 1968
Dixon, Al, TE, Iowa State, NY Giants 1977-79; Kansas City 1979-82; Philadelphia 1983; San Diego 1984; San Francisco 1984
Dixon, Dwayne, WR, Florida, Tampa Bay 1984
Dixon, Hanford, CB, Southern Mississippi, Cleveland 1981-85
Dixon, Hewritt, FB-TE, Florida A&M, Denver 1963-65; Oakland 1966-70
Dixon, Rich, LB, California, Atlanta 1983
Dixon, Zachary, RB-KR, Temple, Denver 1979; NY Giants 1979; Philadelphia 1980; Baltimore 1980-83; Seattle 1983-84
Doane, Earling (Dinger), FB-T, Tufts, Cleveland 1920; NY Giants 1921; Milwaukee 1922-24; Detroit 1925-26; Pottsville 1927; Providence 1927
Dobbins, Herb, T, San Diego State, Philadelphia 1974
Dobbins, Ollie, DB, Morgan State, Buffalo 1964
Dobbs, Glenn, HB, Tulsa, Brooklyn (AAFC) 1946-47; LA Dons (AAFC) 1948-49
Dobeleit, Dick, HB, Ohio State, Dayton 1925-26
Dobelstein, Bob, G, Tennessee, NY Giants 1946-48; LA Dons (AAFC) 1949
Dobler, Conrad, G, Wyoming, St. Louis 1972-77; New Orleans 1978-79; Buffalo 1980-81
Dobrus, Pete, T, Carnegie-Mellon, Brooklyn 1941
Dockery, John, DB, Harvard, NY Jets 1968-71; Pittsburgh 1972-73
Dodd, Al, WR, Northwestern State (Louisiana), Chi. Bears 1967; New Orleans 1969-71; Atlanta 1973-74
Dodge, Kirk, LB, Nevada-Las Vegas, Detroit 1984
Dodrill, Dale, MG, Colorado State, Pittsburgh 1951-59
Dodson, Les, HB, Mississippi, Pittsburgh 1941
Doehring, John (Bull), FB, Chi. Bears 1932-34, 1936-37; Pittsburgh 1935
Doell, Walt, T, Texas, Cincinnati 1933
Doelling, Fred, HB, Pennsylvania, Dallas Cowboys 1960
Doerger, Jerry, T, Wisconsin, Chi. Bears 1982; San Diego 1985
Doherty, Bill, C, Marietta, Cincinnati 1921
Doherty, George, G, Louisiana Tech, Brooklyn 1944; Boston 1945; NY Yankees (AAFC) 1946; Buffalo (AAFC) 1946-47
Doig, Steve, LB, New Hampshire, Detroit 1982-84
Dokes, Phil, DE, Oklahoma State, Buffalo 1977-78
Dolbin, Jack, WR, Wake Forest, Denver 1975-79
Doleman, Chris, LB, Pittsburgh, Minnesota 1985
Doll, Don, DB, USC, Detroit 1949-52; Washington 1953; LA Rams 1954
Dolly, Dick, E, West Virginia, Pittsburgh 1941, 1945
Doloway, Cliff, E, Carnegie-Mellon, Pittsburgh 1935
Dombroski, Paul, CB, Linfield, Kansas City 1980-81; New England 1981-84; Tampa Bay 1985
Dombrowski, Leon, LB, Delaware, NY Titans 1960
Domnanovich, Joe, C, Alabama, Boston 1946-48; NY Bulldogs 1949; NY Yanks 1950-51
Domres, Marty, QB, Columbia, San Diego 1969-71; Baltimore 1972-75; San Francisco 1976; NY Jets 1977
Domres, Tom, T, Wisconsin, Houston 1968-71; Denver 1971-72
Donahue, John, T, Boston College, Providence 1926-27
Donahue, Mark, G, Michigan, Cincinnati 1978-79
Donahue, Oscar, FL, San Jose State, Minnesota 1962
Donaldson, Gene, G, Kentucky, Cleveland 1953
Donaldson, Gene, FB, Purdue, Buffalo 1967
Donaldson, Jeff, S, Colorado, Houston 1984-85
Donaldson, John, HB, Georgia, Chi. Hornets (AAFC) 1949; LA Dons (AAFC) 1949
Donaldson, Ray, C, Georgia, Baltimore 1980-83; Indianapolis 1984-85
Don Carlos, Waldo, C, Drake, Green Bay 1931
Donchez, Tom, RB, Penn State, Chi. Bears 1975
Donckers, Bill, QB, San Diego State, St. Louis 1976-77
Donelli, Allan, HB, Duquesne, Pittsburgh 1941-42; Philadelphia 1942
Donlan, Jim, G, Hammond 1926
Donley, Doug, WR, Ohio State, Dallas 1981-84
Donnahoo, Roger, LB, Michigan State, NY Titans 1960
Donnalley, Kevin, S, North Dakota State, New England 1981
Donnalley, Rick, C-G, North Carolina, Pittsburgh 1982-83; Washington 1984-85
Donnell, Ben, DE, Vanderbilt, LA Chargers 1960
Donnelly, George, DB, Illinois, San Francisco 1965-67
Donnelly, Rick, P, Wyoming, Atlanta 1985
Donohue, Bill, QB, Carnegie-Mellon, Frankford 1927
Donohue, Leon,T, San Jose State, San Francisco 1962-64; Dallas 1965-67
Donohue, Mike, TE, San Francisco, Atlanta 1968, 1970-71; Green Bay 1973-74
Donovan, Art, DT, Boston College, Baltimore 1950, 1953-61; NY Yanks 1951; Dallas 1952
Donovan, Pat, T, Stanford, Dallas 1975-83
Donovan, Tom, WR, Penn State, New Orleans 1980
Doolan, George, C, Racine 1922
Doolan, John, HB, Georgetown (Washington D.C.), Washington 1945; NY Giants 1945-46; Chi. Cardinals 1947-48
Dooley, Jim, FL, Miami, Chi. Bears 1952-54, 1956-57, 1959-62
Dooley, John, G, Syracuse, Rochester 1922-25; Milwaukee 1923
Doornink, Dan, RB, Washington State, NY Giants 1978; Seattle 1979-85
Doran, Jim, DE-SE, Iowa State, Detroit 1951-59; Dallas Cowboys 1960-62
D'Orazio, Joe, T, Ithaca, Detroit 1944
Dorfman, Art, G, Boston U., Buffalo 1929
Dornbrook, Thom, G-T, Kentucky, Pittsburgh 1979; Miami 1980
Dorney, Keith, T, Penn State, Detroit 1979-85
Dorow, Al, QB, Michigan State, Washington 1954-56; Philadelphia 1957; NY Titans 1960-61; Buffalo 1962
Dorris, Andy, DE, New Mexico State, St. Louis 1973; New Orleans 1973-76; Seattle 1977; Houston 1977-81
Dorsett, Tony, RB, Pittsburgh, Dallas 1977-85
Dorsey, Dick, FL, USC, Oakland 1962
Dorsey, John, LB, Connecticut, Green Bay 1984-85
Dorsey, Larry, WR, Tennessee State, San Diego 1976-77; Kansas City 1978
Dorsey, Nate, DE, Mississippi Valley State, New England 1973
Doss, Noble, HB, Texas, Philadelphia 1947-48; NY Yankees (AAFC) 1949
Doss, Reggie, DE, Hampton, LA Rams 1978-85
Dotson, Alphonse, DT, Grambling, Kansas City 1965; Miami 1966; Oakland 1968-70
Dottley, John (Kayo), FB, Mississippi, Chi. Bears 1951-53
Douds, Forrest (Jap), T, Washington & Jefferson, Providence 1930
Dougherty, Bob, LB, Kentucky, LA Rams 1957; Pittsburgh 1958; Oakland 1960-63
Dougherty, Phil, C, Santa Clara, Chi. Cardinals 1938
Doughty, Glenn, WR, Michigan, Baltimore 1972-79
Douglas, Ben, HB, Grinnell, Brooklyn 1933
Douglas, Bob, HB, Kansas State, Pittsburgh 1938
Douglas, Everett, T, Florida, NY Giants 1953
Douglas, Freddie, WR, Arkansas, Tampa Bay 1976
Douglas, George, C, Marquette, Green Bay 1921
Douglas, Jay, C, Memphis State, San Diego 1973-74
Douglas, John, CB, Texas Southern, New Orleans 1967-68; Houston 1969
Douglas, John, LB, Missouri, NY Giants 1970-73
Douglas, Merrill, FB, Utah, Chi. Bears 1958-60; Dallas Cowboys 1961; Philadelphia 1962
Douglas, Otis, T, William & Mary, Philadelphia 1946-49
Douglass, Bobby, QB, Kansas, Chi. Bears 1969-75; San Diego 1975; New Orleans 1976-77; Green Bay 1978
Douglass, Mike, LB, San Diego State, Green Bay 1978-85
Douthitt, Earl, S, Iowa, Chi. Bears 1975
Dove, Bob, E-DE, Notre Dame, Chi. Rockets (AAFC) 1946-47; Chi. Cardinals 1948-53; Detroit 1953-54
Dove, Eddie, DB, Colorado, San Francisco 1959-63; NY Giants 1963
Dove, Jerome, CB, Colorado State, San Diego 1977-80
Dow, Harley, G, San Jose State, San Francisco 1950
Dow, Ken, HB, Oregon State, Washington 1941
Dow, Woody, QB, West Texas State, Philadelphia 1938-40
Dowd, Gerry, C, St. Mary's (California), Cleveland 1939
Dowda, Harry, HB-DB, Wake Forest, Washington 1949-53; Philadelphia 1954-55
Dowden, Steve, T, Baylor, Green Bay 1952
Dowdle, Mike, LB, Texas, Dallas Cowboys 1960-62; San Francisco 1963-64
Dowell, Gwyn (Mule), FB, Texas Tech, Chi. Cardinals 1935-36
Dowler, Boyd, FL, Colorado, Green Bay 1959-69; Washington 1971
Dowler, Tom, HB, Colgate, Brooklyn 1931
Dowling, Brian, QB, Yale, New England 1972-73; Green Bay 1977
Dowling, Pat, E, DePaul, Chi. Cardinals 1929
Downing, Walt, G, Michigan, San Francisco 1978-83
Downs, Bob, G, USC, San Francisco 1951
Downs, Michael, S, Rice, Dallas 1981-85
Downwind, Xavier, HB, Oorang 1922
Doyle, Dick (Skip), HB, Ohio State, Pittsburgh 1955; Denver 1960
Doyle, Ed, G, Canisius, Buffalo 1927
Doyle, Eddie, E, Army, Frankford 1924; Pottsville 1925
Doyle, Ted, T, Nebraska, Pittsburgh 1938-42, 1945; Phil-Pitt 1943; Card-Pitt 1944
Dragon, Oscar, RB, Arizona State, San Diego 1972
Drake, Bill, DB, Oregon, LA Rams 1973-74
Drake, Joe, NT, Arizona, Philadelphia 1985
Drake, Johnny, HB, Purdue, Cleveland 1937-41
Draveling, Leo, T, Michigan, Cincinnati 1933
Drayer, Clarence, T, Illinois, Dayton 1925-26
Drazenovich, Chuck, LB, Penn State, Washington 1950-59
Drechsler, Dave, G, North Carolina, Green Bay 1983-84
Dreher, Fred, E, Denver, Chi. Bears 1938
Dressel, Chris, TE, Stanford, Houston 1983-85
Dressen, Chuck, QB, Decatur 1920; Racine 1922-23
Dressler, Doug, RB, Cal State-Chico, Cincinnati 1970-72, 1974; New England 1975; Kansas City 1975
Drewrey, Willie, WR, West Virginia, Houston 1985
Drews, Ted, E, Princeton, Brooklyn 1926; Chi. Bears 1928
Dreyer, Wally, HB, Wisconsin, Chi. Bears 1949; Green Bay 1950
Driscoll, John (Paddy), HB-QB, Northwestern, Chi. Cardinals 1920-25; Decatur 1920; Chi. Bears 1926-29
Driskill, Joe, DB, Northeast Louisiana, St. Louis 1960-61
Drougas, Tom, T, Oregon, Baltimore 1972-73; Denver 1974; Kansas City 1974; Miami 1975-76
Druehl, Bill, HB, Colby, Boston 1929
Drulis, Al, FB, Temple, Chi. Cardinals 1945-46; Pittsburgh 1947
Drulis, Chuck, G, Temple, Chi. Bears 1942, 1945-49; Green Bay 1950
Drumstead, John, G, Hammond 1925
Drungo, Elbert, T, Tennessee State, Houston 1969-71, 1973-77; Buffalo 1978
Drury, Lyle (Hoot), E, St. Louis, Chi. Bears 1930-31
Druschel, Rick, G-T, North Carolina State, Pittsburgh 1974
Druze, Johnny, E, Fordham, Brooklyn 1938
Dryden, John, HB, Staten Island 1930
Dryer, Fred, DE, San Diego State, NY Giants 1969-71; LA Rams 1972-81
Drzewiecki, Ron, HB, Marquette, Chi. Bears 1955, 1957
Dubenion, Elbert (Golden Wheels), WR, Bluffton, Buffalo 1960-68
Dubenitz, Greg, G, Yale, Washington 1979
Dublinski, Tom, QB, Utah, Detroit 1952-54; NY Giants 1958; Denver 1960
Dubofsky, Maurice (Mush), G, Georgetown (Washington D.C.), NY Giants 1932
DuBois, Phil, TE, San Diego State, Washington 1979-80; LA Rams 1981
DuBose, Jimmy, RB, Florida, Tampa Bay 1976-78
Dubzinski, Walt, G, Boston College, NY Giants 1943; Boston 1944
Duckett, Kenny, WR, Wake Forest, New Orleans 1982-85; Dallas 1985
Duckworth, Bobby, WR, Arkansas, San Diego 1982-84; LA Rams 1985
Duckworth, Joe, E, Colgate, Washington 1947
Ducote, Richard (Moon), HB, Auburn, Cleveland 1920
Duda, Mark, DT, Maryland, St. Louis 1983-85
Dudek, Mitch, G, Xavier, NY Jets 1966
Duden, Dick, E, Navy, NY Giants 1949
Dudish, Andy, HB, Georgia, Buffalo (AAFC) 1946; Baltimore (AAFC) 1947; Brooklyn (AAFC) 1948; Detroit 1948
Dudley, (Bullet) Bill, HB, Virginia, Pittsburgh 1942, 1945-46; Detroit 1947-49; Washington 1950-51, 1953
Dudley, Paul, HB, Arkansas, NY Giants 1962; Philadelphia 1963
Duerson, Dave, S, Notre Dame, Chi. Bears 1983-85
Dufek, Don, S, Michigan, Seattle 1976-77, 1979-84
Dufek, Joe, QB, Yale, Buffalo 1983-85; San Diego 1985
Dufft, Jim, G, Rutgers, Rochester 1921; Milwaukee 1922
Duffy, Pat, HB, Dayton, Dayton 1929
Duford, Wilfred, HB, Marquette, Green Bay 1924
Dufour, Dan, G-C, UCLA, Atlanta 1983-84
Dugan, Bill, G, Penn State, Seattle 1981-83; Minnesota 1984
Dugan, Fred, SE, Dayton, San Francisco 1958-59; Dallas Cowboys 1960; Washington 1961-63
Dugan, Len, C, Wichita State, NY Giants 1936; Chi. Cardinals 1937-39; Pittsburgh 1939
Duggan, Ed, HB, Notre Dame, Rock Island 1921
Duggan, Gil, T, Oklahoma, NY Giants 1940; Chi. Cardinals 1942-43, 1945; Card-Pitt 1944; LA Dons (AAFC) 1946; Buffalo (AAFC) 1947
Dugger, Jack, E, Ohio State, Buffalo (AAFC) 1946; Detroit 1947-48; Chi. Bears 1949
Duggins, George, E, Purdue, Chi. Cardinals 1934
Duhart, Paul, HB, Florida, Green Bay 1944; Pittsburgh 1945; Boston 1945
Duhe, A.J., DE-LB, LSU, Miami 1977-84
Duhon, Bobby, RB, Tulane, NY Giants 1968, 1970-72
Duich, Steve, G-T, San Diego State, Atlanta 1968; Washington 1969
Duke, Paul, C, Georgia Tech, NY Yankees (AAFC) 1947
Dukes, Mike, LB, Clemson, Houston 1960-63; Boston 1964-65; NY Jets 1965
DuLac, Bill, G, Eastern Michigan, New England 1974-75
Dumler, Doug, C, Nebraska, New England 1973-75; Minnesota 1976-77
DuMoe, Joe, E, Syracuse, Rochester 1920-21
Dumont, Jim, LB, Rutgers, Cleveland 1984
Dunaway, Craig, TE, Michigan, Pittsburgh 1983
Dunaway, Dave, SE, Duke, Green Bay 1968; Atlanta 1968; NY Giants 1969
Dunaway, Jim, DT, Mississippi, Buffalo 1963-71; Miami 1972
Dunbar, Jubilee, WR, Southern, New Orleans 1973; Cleveland 1974
Duncan, Brian, RB-KR, SMU, Cleveland 1976-77; Houston 1978
Duncan, Clyde, WR, Tennessee, St. Louis 1984-85
Duncan, Frank, S, Cal State-San Francisco, San Diego 1979-81
Duncan, Jim, DE, Wake Forest, NY Giants 1950-53
Duncan, Jimmy, DB-KR, Maryland-Eastern Shore, Baltimore 1969-71

Duncan, Ken, K, Tulsa, Green Bay 1971
Duncan, Leslie (Speedy), S-KR, Jackson State, San Diego 1964-70; Washington 1971-74
Duncan, Maury, QB, Cal State-San Francisco, San Francisco 1954-55
Duncan, Randy, QB, Iowa, Dallas Texans 1960
Duncan, Rick, K, East Montana State, Denver 1967; Philadelphia 1968; Detroit 1969
Duncan, Ron, TE, Wittenberg, Cleveland 1967
Duncum, Bobby, T, West Texas State, St. Louis 1968
Dunek, Ken, TE, Memphis State, Philadelphia 1980
Dungy, Tony, DB-QB, Minnesota, Pittsburgh 1977-78; San Francisco 1979
Duniven, Tommy, QB, Texas Tech, Houston 1977-78
Dunlap, Bob, QB, Oklahoma, Chi. Bears 1935; NY Giants 1936
Dunlap, Leonard, CB, North Texas State, Baltimore 1971; San Diego 1972-74; Detroit 1975
Dunn, Bob, C, NYU, Staten Island 1929
Dunn, Coye, HB, USC, Washington 1943
Dunn, Gary, NT, Miami, Pittsburgh 1976, 1978-85
Dunn, Joseph (Red), QB, Marquette, Milwaukee 1924-25; Chi. Cardinals 1925-26; Green Bay 1927-31
Dunn, K.D., TE, Clemson, Tampa Bay 1985
Dunn, Pat, FB, Detroit 1920-21
Dunn, Paul, RB-WR, U.S. International, Cincinnati 1970
Dunn, Perry Lee, RB, Mississippi, Dallas 1964-65; Atlanta 1966-68; Baltimore 1969
Dunn, Rodney, G, Duluth 1923
Dunnigan, Mert, T, Minnesota, Minneapolis 1924; Milwaukee 1925-26
Dunnigan, Walt, E, Minnesota, Green Bay 1922
Dunsmore, Pat, TE, Drake, Chi. Bears 1983-84
Dunstan, Bill, DT, Utah State, Philadelphia 1973-76; Buffalo 1977; LA Rams 1979
Dunstan, Elwyn, T, Portland, Chi. Cardinals 1938-39; Cleveland 1939-41
Duper, Mark, WR, Northwestern State (Louisiana), Miami 1982-85
Dupre, Charlie, DB, Baylor, NY Titans 1960
Dupre, L.G. (Long Gone), HB, Baylor, Baltimore 1955-59; Dallas Cowboys 1960-61
DuPree, Billy Joe, TE, Michigan State, Dallas 1973-83
Dupree, Myron, CB, North Carolina Central, Denver 1983
Duranko, Pete, DE-LB, Notre Dame, Denver 1967-70, 1972-74
Durdan, Don, HB, Oregon State, San Francisco 1946-47
Duren, Clarence, CB, California, St. Louis 1973-76; San Diego 1977
Durham, Darius, WR, San Diego State, San Francisco 1983
Durham, Steve, DE, Clemson, Baltimore 1982
Durishan, Jack, T, Pittsburgh, NY Yankees (AAFC) 1947
Durkee, Charlie, K, Oklahoma State, New Orleans 1967-68, 1971-72
Durko, John, E, Albright, Philadelphia 1944; Chi. Cardinals 1945
Durko, Sandy, S, USC, Cincinnati 1970-71; New England 1973-74
Durkota, Jeff, FB, Penn State, LA Dons (AAFC) 1948
Dusek, Brad, LB, Texas A&M, Washington 1974-81
Dusenberry, Bill, RB, Johnson C. Smith, New Orleans 1970
Dutton, Bill, HB, Pittsburgh, Pittsburgh 1946
Dutton, John, DE-DT, Nebraska, Baltimore 1974-78; Dallas 1979-85
Duvall, Earl, G-T, Ohio U., Columbus 1924-26
Dvorak, Ben, HB, Minnesota, Minneapolis 1921-22
Dvorak, Rick, DE, Wichita State, NY Giants 1974-77; Miami 1977
Dworsky, Dan, FB, Michigan, LA Dons (AAFC) 1949
Dwyer, Bob, HB, Georgetown (Washington D.C.), Orange 1929
Dwyer, Jack, HB, Loyola (Los Angeles), Washington 1951; LA Rams 1952-54
Dye, Les, E, Syracuse, Washington 1944-45
Dyer, Henry, RB, Grambling, LA Rams 1966, 1968; Washington 1969
Dyer, Ken, S, Arizona State, San Diego 1968; Cincinnati 1969-71
Dykes, Donald, CB, Southeastern Louisiana, NY Jets 1979-81; San Diego 1982

E

Eagle, Alex, T, Oregon, Brooklyn 1935
Eagle Feather, HB, Carlisle, Oorang 1922-23
Eaglin, Larry, CB, Stephen F. Austin, Houston 1973
Earhart, Ralph, HB, Texas Tech, Green Bay 1948-49
Earl, Robin, RB-TE, Washington, Chi. Bears 1977-82
Early, Guy, G, Miami (Ohio), Dayton 1920; Cincinnati 1921
Early, Jim, RB, Michigan State, NY Jets 1978
Earon, Blaine, DE, Duke, Detroit 1952-53
Earpe, Francis (Jug), G, Monmouth, Rock Island 1921-22, 1924; Green Bay 1922-23; NY Yankees 1927
Easley, Kenny, S, UCLA, Seattle 1981-85
Easley, Walt, RB, West Virginia, San Francisco 1981-82
Easman, Ricky, LB-CB, Florida, Dallas 1985; Tampa Bay 1985
Eason, Bo, S, Cal-Davis, Houston 1984-85
Eason, John, WR, Florida A&M, Oakland 1968
Eason, Roger, T, Oklahoma, Cleveland 1945; LA Rams 1946-48; Green Bay 1949
Eason, Tony, QB, Illinois, New England 1983-85
East, Ron, DE-DT, Montana State, Dallas 1967-70; San Diego 1971-73; Cleveland 1975; Atlanta 1976; Seattle 1977
Easterling, Ray, S, Richmond, Atlanta 1972-79
Easton, Lou, T, California, NY Giants 1945
Eaton, Scott, FL, Oregon State, NY Giants 1967-71
Eaton, Vic, QB, Missouri, Pittsburgh 1955
Ebding, Harry, E, St. Mary's (California), Portsmouth 1931-33; Detroit 1934-37
Eber, Rick, WR, Tulsa, Atlanta 1968; San Diego 1969-70
Eberdt, Jess, C, Alabama, Brooklyn 1932
Ebersole, Hal, G, Cornell, Cleveland 1923
Ebersole, John, LB-DE, Penn State, NY Jets 1970-77
Eberts, Bernie, G, Catholic, Minneapolis 1924
Ebli, Ray, E, Notre Dame, Chi. Cardinals 1942; Buffalo (AAFC) 1946; Chi. Rockets (AAFC) 1947
Eby, Byron, HB, Ohio State, Portsmouth 1930
Echols, Fate, T, Northwestern, St. Louis 1962-63; Philadelphia 1963
Echols, Terry, LB, Marshall, Pittsburgh 1984
Eck, Keith, C, UCLA, NY Giants 1979
Eckberg, Gus, HB, West Virginia, Cleveland 1925
Ecker, Ed, T, John Carroll, Chi. Bears 1947; Chi. Rockets (AAFC) 1948; Green Bay 1950-51; Washington 1952
Eckhardt, Oscar (Ox), FB-HB, Texas, NY Giants 1928
Eckl, Bob, T, Wisconsin, Chi. Cardinals 1945
Ecklund, Brad (Whitey), C, Oregon, NY Yankees (AAFC) 1949; NY Yanks 1950-51; Dallas 1952; Baltimore 1953
Eckstein, Dolph, C, Brown, Providence 1925-26
Eckwood, Jerry, RB, Arkansas, Tampa Bay 1979-81
Eddings, Floyd, WR, California, NY Giants 1982-83
Eddy, Nick, RB, Notre Dame, Detroit 1968, 1972
Edelman, Brad, G, Missouri, New Orleans 1982-85
Edgar, Alex, HB, Bucknell, Buffalo 1923; Akron 1923
Edgerson, Booker, CB, Western Illinois, Buffalo 1962-69; Denver 1970
Edler, Bob, HB, Ohio Wesleyan, Cleveland 1923
Edmondson, Van, C, Oklahoma, Buffalo 1926
Edmunds, Randall, LB, Georgia Tech, Miami 1968-69; New England 1971; Baltimore 1972
Edwards, Bill, HB, Hartford 1926
Edwards, Bill (Monk), G, Baylor, NY Giants 1940-42, 1946
Edwards, Charles (Bud), FB, Brown, Providence 1930-31; Chi. Bears 1931
Edwards, Cid, RB, Tennessee State, St. Louis 1968-71; San Diego 1972-74; Chi. Bears 1975
Edwards, Dan, E, Georgia, Brooklyn (AAFC) 1948; Chi. Hornets (AAFC) 1949; NY Yanks 1950-51; Dallas 1952; Baltimore 1953-54
Edwards, Dave, LB, Auburn, Dallas 1963-75
Edwards, David, S, Illinois, Pittsburgh 1985
Edwards, Earl, DE-DT, Wichita State, San Francisco 1969-72; Buffalo 1973-75; Cleveland 1976-78
Edwards, Eddie, DE, Miami, Cincinnati 1977-85
Edwards, Emmett, WR, Kansas, Houston 1975-76; Buffalo 1976
Edwards, Gene (Horse), G, Notre Dame, Canton 1920-21; Toledo 1922; Cleveland 1923-25
Edwards, Glen (Turk), T, Washington State, Boston 1932-36; Washington 1937-40
Edwards, Glen, S, Florida A&M, Pittsburgh 1971-77; San Diego 1978-81
Edwards, Herman, CB, San Diego State, Philadelphia 1977-85
Edwards, Jimmy, RB, Northeast Louisiana, Minnesota 1979
Edwards, Lloyd, TE, San Diego State, Oakland 1969
Edwards, Marshall, HB, Wake Forest, Brooklyn 1943
Edwards, Randy, DE, Alabama, Seattle 1984-85
Edwards, Stan, RB, Michigan, Houston 1982-85
Edwards, Tom, T, Michigan, Detroit 1926
Edwards, Weldon, T, TCU, Washington 1948
Egan, Dick, E-HB, Wilmington, Chi. Cardinals 1920-23; Kenosha 1924; Dayton 1924
Eggers, Doug, LB, South Dakota State, Baltimore 1954-57; Chi. Cardinals 1958
Egloff, Ron, TE, Wisconsin, Denver 1977-83; San Diego 1984
Ehin, Chuck, DE, BYU, San Diego 1983-85
Ehlers, Tom, LB, Kentucky, Philadelphia 1975-77; Buffalo 1978
Ehrhardt, Clyde, C, Georgia, Washington 1946, 1948-49
Ehrmann, Joe, DT, Syracuse, Baltimore 1973-80; Detroit 1981-82
Eibner, John, T, Kentucky, Philadelphia 1941-42, 1946
Eichenlaub, Ray, FB, Notre Dame, Columbus 1925; Cleveland 1925
Eiden, Ed, HB, Scranton, Philadelphia 1944; Detroit 1944
Eiden, Jim, T, Louisville 1926
Eidson, Jim, G-C, Mississippi State, Dallas 1976
Eifrid, Jim, LB, Colorado State, Denver 1961
Eikenberg, Charley, QB, Rice, Chi. Cardinals 1948
Eischeid, Mike, K, Upper Iowa, Oakland 1966-71; Minnesota 1972-74
Eisenhauer, Larry, DE, Boston College, Boston 1961-69
Ekberg, Gus, E, Minnesota, Minneapolis 1921
Ekern, Carl, LB, San Jose State, LA Rams 1976-78, 1980-85
Elam, Cleveland, DE, Tennessee State, San Francisco 1975-78; Detroit 1979
Elder, Donnie, CB, Memphis State, NY Jets 1985
Eley, Monroe, RB, Arizona State, Atlanta 1975, 1977-78
Elia, Bruce, LB, Ohio State, Miami 1975; San Francisco 1976-78
Elias, Homer, G, Tennessee State, Detroit 1978-84
Eliason, Don, E, Hamline, Brooklyn 1942; Boston 1946
Eliopulos, Jim, LB, Wyoming, St. Louis 1983; NY Jets 1983-85
Elkins, Fait (Chief), FB, Haskell, Frankford 1928-29; Chi. Cardinals 1929; Cincinnati 1933
Elkins, Lawrence, WR, Baylor, Houston 1966-67
Elko, Bill, NT, LSU, San Diego 1983-84
Ellard, Henry, WR-KR, Fresno State, LA Rams 1983-85
Ellena, Jack, G, UCLA, LA Rams 1955-56
Ellenbogen, Bill, G, Virginia Tech, NY Giants 1976-77
Ellender, Richard, WR, McNeese State, Houston 1979
Ellenson, Gene, T, Georgia, Miami (AAFC) 1946
Eller, Carl, DE, Minnesota, Minnesota 1964-78; Seattle 1979
Ellersick, Don, DB, Washington State, LA Rams 1960
Ellerson, Gary, RB, Wisconsin, Green Bay 1985
Elliott, Al (Rowdy), HB, Wisconsin, Racine 1922-24; Rock Island 1925
Elliott, Burt, HB, Green Bay 1921
Elliott, Carlton, E, Virginia, Green Bay 1951-54
Elliott, Charlie, T, Oregon, NY Yankees (AAFC) 1947; Chi. Rockets (AAFC) 1948; San Francisco (AAFC) 1948
Elliott, Doc, FB, Lafayette, Canton 1922-23; Cleveland 1924-25, 1931
Elliott, Jim, P, Presbyterian, Pittsburgh 1967
Elliott, John, DT, Texas, NY Jets 1967-73
Elliott, Lenvil, RB, Northeast Missouri State, Cincinnati 1973-78; San Francisco 1979-81
Elliott, Tony, NT, North Texas State, New Orleans 1982-85
Ellis, Allan, CB, UCLA, Chi. Bears 1973-77, 1979-80
Ellis, Clarence, CB, Notre Dame, Atlanta 1972-74
Ellis, Drew, T, TCU, Philadelphia 1938-39
Ellis, Gerry, RB, Missouri, Green Bay 1980-85
Ellis, Herb, C, Texas A&M, NY Bulldogs 1949
Ellis, John, G, Vanderbilt, Brooklyn 1944
Ellis, Ken, CB, Southern, Green Bay 1970-75; Houston 1976; Miami 1976; Cleveland 1977; Detroit 1979; LA Rams 1979
Ellis, Larry, LB, Syracuse, Detroit 1948
Ellis, Ray, S, Ohio State, Philadelphia 1981-85
Ellis, Roger, LB, Maine, NY Titans 1960-62; NY Jets 1963
Ellis, Walt (Speed), T, Detroit, Columbus 1924-25; Detroit 1925-26; Chi. Cardinals 1926-27
Ellison, Glenn, RB, Arkansas, Oakland 1971
Ellison, Mark, G, Dayton, NY Giants 1972-73
Ellison, Riki, LB, USC, San Francisco 1983-85
Ellison, Willie, RB, Texas Southern, LA Rams 1967-72; Kansas City 1973-74
Ellor, Albert (Bud), G, Bucknell, Newark 1930
Ellstrom, Marvin (Swede), HB-FB, Oklahoma, Boston 1934; Philadelphia 1934; Pittsburgh 1935; Chi. Cardinals 1936
Ellzey, Charley, LB, Southern Mississippi, St. Louis 1960-61
Elmendorf, Dave, S, Texas A&M, LA Rams 1971-79
Elmore, Doug, DB, Mississippi, Washington 1962
Elness, Leland (Shorty), QB, Bradley, Chi. Bears 1929
Elrod, Jimbo, LB, Oklahoma, Kansas City 1976-78
Elser, Earl, T, Butler, Portsmouth 1933; Cincinnati 1934; St. Louis 1934
Elsey, Earl, HB, Loyola (Los Angeles), LA Dons (AAFC) 1946
Elshire, Neil, DE, Oregon, Minnesota 1981-85
Elston, Arthur (Dutch), QB, South Carolina, Cleveland 1942; San Francisco (AAFC) 1946-48
Elter, Leo, FB, Villanova, Pittsburgh 1953-54, 1958-59; Washington 1955-57
Elway, John, QB, Stanford, Denver 1983-85
Elwell, Jack, SE, Purdue, St. Louis 1962
Ely, Harold, T, Iowa, Chi. Bears 1932; Brooklyn 1932-34
Ely, Larry, LB, Iowa, Cincinnati 1970-71; Chi. Bears 1975
Elzey, Paul, LB, Toledo, Cincinnati 1968
Emanuel, Frank, LB, Tennessee, Miami 1966-69; New Orleans 1970
Embree, John, WR, Compton J.C., Denver 1969-70
Embree, Mel, E, Pepperdine, Baltimore 1953; Chi. Cardinals 1954
Emelianchick, Pete, TE, Richmond, Philadelphia 1967
Emerick, Bob, T, Miami (Ohio), Detroit 1934; Cleveland 1937
Emerson, Grover (Ox), G, Texas, Portsmouth 1931-33; Detroit 1934-37; Brooklyn 1938
Emerson, Vern, T, Minnesota-Duluth, St. Louis 1969-71
Emmons, Frank, HB, Oregon, Philadelphia 1940
Enderle, Dick, G, Minnesota, Atlanta 1969-71; NY Giants 1972-75; San Francisco 1976; Green Bay 1976
Endress, John, HB, Evansville 1922
Endriss, Al, E, Cal State-San Francisco, San Francisco 1952
Engebretsen, Paul (Tiny), G, Northwestern, Chi. Bears 1932; Pittsburgh 1933; Chi. Cardinals 1933; Brooklyn 1934; Green Bay 1934-41
Engel, Steve, RB, Colorado, Cleveland 1970
Engelhard, Joe, HB, Rose-Hulman Tech, Louisville 1921-22
Engelmann, Wuert, HB, South Dakota State, Green Bay 1930-33
Engels, Rick, P, Tulsa, Seattle 1976; Pittsburgh 1977; Philadelphia 1978
English, Doug, DT, Texas, Detroit 1975-79, 1981-85
Englund, Harry, E, Decatur 1920; Chi. Staleys 1921; Chi. Bears 1922, 1924
Engstrom, George, G, Wisconsin-Superior, Duluth 1924
Enich, Steve, G, Marquette, Chi. Cardinals 1945
Enis, Hunter, QB, TCU, Dallas Texans 1960; San Diego 1961; Denver 1962; Oakland 1962

Enke, Fred, QB, Arizona, Detroit 1948-51; Philadelphia 1952; Baltimore 1953-54
Enright, Rex, FB, Notre Dame, Green Bay 1926-27
Enyart, Bill (Earthquake), FB-LB, Oregon State, Buffalo 1969-70; Oakland 1971
Epperson, Pat, TE, Adams State, Denver 1960
Epps, Bobby, HB, Pittsburgh, NY Giants 1954-55, 1957
Epps, Phillip, WR-KR, TCU, Green Bay 1982-85
Erdlitz, Dick, HB, Northwestern, Philadelphia 1942, 1945; Miami (AAFC) 1946
Erehart, Arch, HB, Indiana, Muncie 1920-21
Erenberg, Rich, RB-KR, Colgate, Pittsburgh 1984-85
Erickson, Bernard, LB, Abilene Christian, San Diego 1967-68; Cincinnati 1968
Erickson, Bill, G, Mississippi, NY Giants 1948; NY Yankees (AAFC) 1949
Erickson, Carleton (Bud), C, Washington, Washington 1938-39
Erickson, Hal (Swede), HB, Washington & Jefferson, Green Bay 1923; Milwaukee 1923-24; Chi. Cardinals 1925-28; Minneapolis 1929-30
Erickson, Harold, E, Minneapolis 1921-22
Erickson, Mickey, C, Northwestern, Chi. Cardinals 1930-31; Boston 1932
Erickson, Walden, T, Washington, Pottsville 1927
Ericson, Swede, HB, Kenosha 1924
Erlandson, Tom, LB, Washington State, Denver 1962-65; Miami 1966-67; San Diego 1968
Ernst, Jack, QB, Lafayette, Frankford 1925, 1930; Pottsville 1925-28; NY Yankees 1928; Boston 1929
Ernst, Mike, QB, Cal State Fullerton, Denver 1972; Cincinnati 1973
Erwig, Bill, T, Syracuse, Rochester 1920-21
Erwin, Terry, RB, Boston College, Denver 1968
Erxleben, Russell, P, Texas, New Orleans 1980-83
Eschbach, Herb, C, Penn State, Providence 1930-31
Eshmont, Len, HB, Fordham, NY Giants 1941; San Francisco (AAFC) 1946-49
Esiason, Boomer, QB, Maryland, Cincinnati 1984-85
Espie, Al, T, Louisville 1923
Esposito, Mike, FB, Boston College, Atlanta 1976-79
Esser, Clarence, DE, Wisconsin, Chi. Cardinals 1947
Essink, Ron, T, Grand Valley State, Seattle 1980-85
Essman, Charlie, G, Dayton, Columbus 1920
Estes, Don, G, LSU, San Diego 1966
Estes, Lawrence, DE, Alcorn State, New Orleans 1970-71; Philadelphia 1972; Kansas City 1975-77
Estes, Roy, HB, Georgia, Green Bay 1928
Etcheverry, Sam, QB, Denver, St. Louis 1961-62
Etelman, Carl, HB, Tufts, Providence 1926
Ethridge, Joe, T, SMU, Green Bay 1949
Ettenhaus, John, T, Rochester 1921
Etter, Bob, K, Georgia, Atlanta 1968-69
Ettinger, Don (Red Dog), G-LB, Kansas, NY Giants 1948-50
Evans, Charlie, RB, USC, NY Giants 1971-73; Washington 1974
Evans, Chuck, LB, Stanford, New Orleans 1980-81
Evans, Dale, HB, Kansas State, Denver 1961
Evans, Dick, E, Iowa, Green Bay 1940, 1943; Chi. Cardinals 1941-42
Evans, Earl (Buck), G, Harvard, Chi. Cardinals 1925; Chi. Bears 1926-29
Evans, Fred (Dippy), HB, Notre Dame, Cleveland (AAFC) 1946; Buffalo (AAFC) 1947; Chi. Rockets (AAFC) 1947-48; Chi. Bears 1948
Evans, Jack, HB, California, Green Bay 1929
Evans, Jim, WR, Texas-El Paso, NY Jets 1964-65
Evans, Joe, SE, Oklahoma State, Pittsburgh 1958
Evans, Johnny, QB-P, North Carolina State, Cleveland 1978-80
Evans, Jon, G, TCU, Green Bay 1933-37
Evans, Larry, LB, Mississippi, Denver 1976-82; San Diego 1983
Evans, Leon, DE, Miami, Detroit 1985
Evans, Mike, C, Boston College, Philadelphia 1968-73
Evans, Murray, QB, Hardin-Simmons, Detroit 1942-43
Evans, Norm, T, TCU, Houston 1965; Miami 1966-75; Seattle 1976-78
Evans, Ray, HB, Kansas, Pittsburgh 1948
Evans, Ray, T, Texas-El Paso, San Francisco 1949-50
Evans, Reggie, RB, Richmond, Washington 1983
Evans, Robert, DE, Texas A&M, Houston 1965
Evans, Vince, QB-KR, USC, Chi. Bears 1977-83
Evansen, Paul, G, Oregon State, San Francisco (AAFC) 1948
Everett, Major, RB, Mississippi College, Philadelphia 1983-85
Evey, Dick, DE, Tennessee, Chi. Bears 1964-69; LA Rams 1970; Detroit 1971
Ewald, George, HB, Louisville, Louisville 1921
Eyre, Nick, T, BYU, Houston 1981
Ezerins, Vilnis, RB, Wisconsin-Whitewater, LA Rams 1968

F

Fada, Rob, G, Pittsburgh, Chi. Bears 1983-84; Kansas City 1985
Fagan, Julian, P, Mississippi, New Orleans 1970-72; NY Jets 1973
Fagiolo, Carl, G, Philadelphia 1944
Fahay, John, E, Marquette, Racine 1926; Chi. Bears 1926; Minneapolis 1929
Fahnhorst, Jim, LB, Minnesota, San Francisco 1984-85
Fahnhorst, Keith, T, Minnesota, San Francisco 1974-85
Failing, Fred, G, Central J.C. (Kansas), Chi. Cardinals 1930
Fairband, Bill, LB, Colorado, Oakland 1967-68
Fairchild, Greg, G-T, Tulsa, Cincinnati 1976-77; Cleveland 1978
Fairchild, Paul, G, Kansas, New England 1984-85
Faircloth, Art, HB, North Carolina State, NY Giants 1947-48
Fairley, Leonard, S, Alcorn State, Houston 1974; Buffalo 1974
Faison, Earl, DE, Indiana, San Diego 1961-66; Miami 1966
Falaschi, Nello, QB, Santa Clara, NY Giants 1938-41
Falcon, Dick, G-C, Chi. Tigers 1920
Falcon, Gil, FB, Wabash, Hammond 1920, 1924-25; Chi. Tigers 1920; Canton 1921; Toledo 1922-23; Akron 1925
Falcon, Terry, G, Montana, New England 1978-79; NY Giants 1980
Falkenstein, Tony, FB, St. Mary's (California), Green Bay 1943; Brooklyn 1944; Boston 1944
Fallon, Mickey, G, Syracuse, Milwaukee 1922
Falls, Mike, G, Minnesota, Dallas Cowboys 1960-61
Famiglietti, Gary, FB, Boston U., Chi. Bears 1938-45; Boston 1946
Fanning, Mike, DE-DT, Notre Dame, LA Rams 1975-82; Detroit 1983; Seattle 1984
Fanning, Stan, DT, Idaho, Chi. Bears 1960-62; LA Rams 1963; Houston 1964; Denver 1964
Fantetti, Ken, LB, Wyoming, Detroit 1979-85
Fanucchi, Ledio, T, Fresno State, Chi. Cardinals 1954
Fanucci, Mike, DE, Arizona State, Washington 1972; Houston 1973; Green Bay 1974
Farasopoulos, Chris, S-KR, BYU, NY Jets 1971-73; New Orleans 1974
Farber, Hap, LB, Mississippi, Minnesota 1970; New Orleans 1970
Farina, Nick, C, Villanova, Pottsville 1927
Farkas, Andy, HB, Detroit, Washington 1938-44; Detroit 1945
Farley, Dale, LB, West Virginia, Miami 1971; Buffalo 1972-73
Farley, Dick, DB, Boston U., San Diego 1968-69
Farley, John, RB, Cal State-Sacramento, Cincinnati 1984
Farman, Dick, G, Washington State, Washington 1939-43
Farmer, Dave, RB, USC, Tampa Bay 1978
Farmer, George, WR, UCLA, Chi. Bears 1970-75; Detroit 1975
Farmer, George, WR, Southern, LA Rams 1982-84
Farmer, Karl, WR, Pittsburgh, Atlanta 1976-77; Tampa Bay 1978
Farmer, Lonnie, LB, Tennessee-Chattanooga, Boston 1964-66
Farmer, Roger, WR, Baker, NY Jets 1979
Farmer, Ted, RB, Oregon, St. Louis 1978
Farmer, Tom, HB, Iowa, LA Rams 1946; Washington 1947-48
Farr, Mel, RB, UCLA, Detroit 1967-73
Farr, Miller, CB, Wichita State, Denver 1965; San Diego 1965-66; Houston 1967-69; St. Louis 1970-72; Detroit 1973
Farragut, Ken, C, Mississippi, Philadelphia 1951-54
Farrar, Vinnie, QB-G, North Carolina State, Pittsburgh 1939
Farrell, Ed (Scrap Iron), FB, Muhlenberg, Pittsburgh 1938; Brooklyn 1938-39
Farrell, Sean, G, Penn State, Tampa Bay 1982-85
Farren, Paul, G-T, Boston U., Cleveland 1983-85
Farrior, Curt, DT, Montana State, Kansas City 1963-65
Farrington, John (Bo), SE, Prairie View A&M, Chi. Bears 1960-63
Farris, John, G, San Diego State, San Diego 1965-66
Farris, Tom, QB, Wisconsin, Chi. Bears 1946-47; Chi. Rockets (AAFC) 1948
Farroh, Shipley, G, Iowa, Pittsburgh 1938
Faulkner, Chris, TE, Florida, LA Rams 1984; San Diego 1985
Faulkner, Staley, T, Texas, Houston 1964
Faumuina, Wilson, DT, San Jose State, Atlanta 1977-81
Faurot, Ron, DT-DE, Arkansas, NY Jets 1984-85
Fausch, Frank, HB, Western Michigan, Evansville 1921-22
Faust, Dick, T, Otterbein, Dayton 1924, 1928-29
Faust, George, QB, Minnesota, Chi. Cardinals 1939
Faust, Paul, LB, Minnesota, Minnesota 1967
Faverty, Hal, C, Wisconsin, Green Bay 1952
Favron, Calvin, LB, Southeastern Louisiana, St. Louis 1979-82
Fawcett, Jake, T, SMU, Cleveland 1942, 1944; Brooklyn 1943; LA Rams 1946
Fay, Jim, HB, Canisius, Buffalo 1926
Faye, Allen, E, Marquette, Green Bay 1922
Feacher, Ricky, WR, Mississippi Valley State, New England 1976; Cleveland 1976-84
Feagin, Wiley, G, Houston, Baltimore, 1961-62; Washington 1963
Feamster, Tom, DE, Florida State, Baltimore 1956
Fears, Tom, E, UCLA, LA Rams 1948-56
Feasel, Grant, C, Abilene Christian, Baltimore 1983; Indianapolis 1984; Minnesota 1984
Feather, Elvin (Tiny), FB-HB, Kansas State, Cleveland 1927; Detroit 1928; NY Giants 1929-33; Staten Island 1931; Cincinnati 1934
Feathers, Beattie, HB, Tennessee, Chi. Bears 1934-37; Brooklyn 1938-39; Green Bay 1940
Federovich, John (Ace), T, Davis & Elkins, Chi. Bears 1941, 1946
Federspiel, Joe, LB, Kentucky, New Orleans 1972-80; Baltimore 1981
Fedora, Walt, FB, George Washington, Brooklyn 1942
Feehery, Gerry, C, Syracuse, Philadelphia 1983-85
Feeney, Al, C, Notre Dame, Canton 1920-21
Feher, Nick, G, Georgia, San Francisco 1951-54; Pittsburgh 1955
Feibish, Bernie, C, NYU, Philadelphia 1941
Feist, Lou, T, Canisius, Buffalo 1924-26
Feitchtinger, Andy, E, Decatur 1920; Chi. Staleys 1921
Fekete, Gene, FB, Ohio State, Cleveland (AAFC) 1946
Fekete, John, HB, Ohio U., Buffalo (AAFC) 1946
Felber, Fred, E, North Dakota, Boston 1932
Feldhaus, Bill, T, Cincinnati, Detroit 1937-40
Feldhausen, Paul, T, Northland, Boston 1968
Felker, Art, E, Marquette, Green Bay 1951
Felker, Gene, E, Wisconsin, Dallas 1952
Feller, Happy, K, Texas, Philadelphia 1971; New Orleans 1972-73
Fellows, Mark, LB, Montana State, San Diego 1985
Fellows, Ron, CB, Missouri, Dallas 1981-85
Felt, Dick, DB, BYU, NY Titans 1960-61; Boston 1962-66
Felton, Eric, CB, Texas Tech, New Orleans 1978-80
Felton, Ralph, LB, Maryland, Washington 1954-60; Buffalo 1961-62
Felts, Bobby, RB, Florida A&M, Baltimore 1965; Detroit 1965-67
Fena, Tom, G, Denver, Detroit 1937
Fencik, Gary, S, Yale, Chi. Bears 1976-85
Fencil, Dick, E, Northwestern, Philadelphia 1933
Fenenbock, Chuck, HB, UCLA, Detroit 1943, 1945; LA Dons (AAFC) 1946-48; Chi. Rockets (AAFC) 1948
Fenimore, Bob, HB, Oklahoma State, Chi. Bears 1947
Fennema, Carl, C, Washington, NY Giants 1948-49
Fenner, Lane, WR, Florida State, San Diego 1968
Fenner, Lee, E, St. Mary's (Ohio), Dayton 1920-29; Portsmouth 1930
Fergerson, Duke, WR, San Diego State, Seattle 1977-79; Buffalo 1980
Ferguson, Bill, LB, San Diego State, NY Jets 1973-74
Ferguson, Bob, FB, Ohio State, Pittsburgh 1962-63; Minnesota 1963
Ferguson, Charley, SE-TE, Tennessee State, Cleveland 1961; Minnesota 1962; Buffalo 1963, 1965-66, 1969
Ferguson, Gene, T, Norfolk State, San Diego 1969-70; Houston 1971-72
Ferguson, Howie, FB, Green Bay 1953-58; LA Chargers 1960
Ferguson, Jim, C, USC, New Orleans 1968; Atlanta 1969; Chi. Bears 1969
Ferguson, Joe, QB, Arkansas, Buffalo 1973-84; Detroit 1985
Ferguson, Keith, DE-LB, Ohio State, San Diego 1981-85; Detroit 1985
Ferguson, Larry, HB, Iowa, Detroit 1963
Ferguson, Tom, T, Louisville 1921
Ferguson, Vagas, RB, Notre Dame, New England 1980-82; Houston 1983; Cleveland 1983
Ferko, John (Fritz), G, West Chester, Philadelphia 1937-38
Fernandes, Ron, DE, Eastern Michigan, Baltimore 1976-79
Fernandez, Manny, DT, Utah, Miami 1968-75
Ferragamo, Vince, QB, Nebraska, LA Rams 1977-80, 1982-84; Buffalo 1985; Green Bay 1985
Ferrante, Jack, E, Philadelphia 1941, 1944-50
Ferrante, Orlando, G, USC, LA Chargers 1960; San Diego 1961
Ferrari, Ron, LB, Illinois, San Francisco 1982-85
Ferrell, Bobby, RB, UCLA, San Francisco 1976-80
Ferrell, Earl, RB, East Tennessee State, St. Louis 1982-85
Ferris, Neil, HB, Loyola (Los Angeles), Washington 1951-52; Philadelphia 1952; LA Rams 1953
Ferry, Lou, T, Villanova, Green Bay 1949; Chi. Cardinals 1951; Pittsburgh 1952-55
Fersen, Paul, T, Georgia, New Orleans 1973-74
Fest, Howard, G-C-T, Texas, Cincinnati 1968-75; Tampa Bay 1976
Fetherston, Jim, LB, California, San Diego 1968-69
Fetz, Gus, HB, Chi. Bears 1923
Ficca, Dan, G, USC, Oakland 1962; NY Jets 1963-66
Fichman, Leon, T, Alabama, Detroit 1946-47
Fichtner, Ross, S, Purdue, Cleveland 1960-67; New Orleans 1968
Fiedler, Bill, G, Pennsylvania, Philadelphia 1938
Field, Doak, LB, Baylor, St. Louis 1981
Field, Harry, T, Oregon State, Chi. Cardinals 1934-36
Fielder, Don, DE, Kentucky, Tampa Bay 1985
Fields, Angelo, T, Michigan State, Houston 1980-81; Green Bay 1982
Fields, Edgar, DE-DT, Texas A&M, Atlanta 1977-80; Detroit 1981
Fields, George, DE, Bakersfield J.C., Oakland 1960-61
Fields, Greg, DE, Grambling, Baltimore 1979-80
Fields, Jerry, LB, Ohio State, NY Titans 1961-62
Fields, Jitter, CB-KR, Texas, New Orleans 1984
Fields, Joe, C, Widener, NY Jets 1975-85
Fife, Ralph, G, Pittsburgh, Chi. Cardinals 1942, 1945; Pittsburgh 1946
Fifer, Bill, G, West Texas State, Detroit 1978; New Orleans 1978; Seattle 1979
Figner, George, DB, Colorado, Chi. Bears 1953
Fike, Dan, G-T, Florida, Cleveland 1985
Filak, Jack, T, Penn State, Frankford 1927-29
Filchock, Frank, QB, Indiana, Pittsburgh 1938; Washington 1938-41, 1944-45; NY Giants 1946; Baltimore 1950
Files, Jim, LB, Oklahoma, NY Giants 1970-73
Filipowicz, Steve, FB, Fordham, NY Giants 1945-46

Filipski, Gene, HB, Army, Villanova, NY Giants 1956-57
Finch, Karl, SE, Cal Poly-Pomona, LA Rams 1962
Finch, Olin (Bull), HB, Whittier, LA Buccaneers 1926
Fink, Mike, S, Missouri, New Orleans 1973
Finks, Jim, QB, Tulsa, Pittsburgh 1949-55
Finlay, Jack, G, UCLA, LA Rams 1947-51
Finn, Bernie, HB, Holy Cross, Newark 1930; Staten Island 1930, 1932; Chi. Cardinals 1932
Finn, John, HB-FB, Villanova, Frankford 1924
Finnegan, Jim, E, St. Louis, St. Louis 1923
Finneran, Gary, DT, USC, LA Chargers 1960; San Diego 1961
Finnie, Roger, G-T, Florida A&M, NY Jets 1969-72; St. Louis 1973-78; New Orleans 1979
Finnin, Tom, DT, Detroit, Baltimore 1953-56; Chi. Cardinals 1957
Finsterwald, Russ, HB, Syracuse, Detroit 1920
Finzer, Dave, P, DePauw, Chi. Bears 1984; Seattle 1985
Fiorentino, Al, G, Boston College, Washington 1943-44; Boston 1945
Fiorentino, Ed, E, Boston College, Boston 1947
Fischer, Bill (Moose), T, Notre Dame, Chi. Cardinals 1949-53
Fischer, Clark, HB, Marquette, Milwaukee 1926
Fischer, Cletis, HB, Nebraska, NY Giants 1949
Fischer, Pat, CB, Nebraska, St. Louis 1961-67; Washington 1968-77
Fishel, Dick, QB, Syracuse, Brooklyn 1933
Fisher, Bob, HB, Ohio Northern, Canton 1925
Fisher, Bob, T, USC, Washington 1940
Fisher, Bob, TE, SMU, Chi. Bears 1980-81
Fisher, Darrell, HB, Iowa, Buffalo 1925
Fisher, Doug, LB, San Diego State, Pittsburgh 1969-70
Fisher, Ed, G, Arizona State, Houston 1974-82
Fisher, Eddie, G, Columbia, Buffalo 1925
Fisher, Ev, QB-E, Santa Clara, Chi. Cardinals 1938-39; Pittsburgh 1940
Fisher, George, T, Indiana, Hammond 1926
Fisher, Jeff, CB-KR, USC, Chi. Bears 1981-84
Fisher, Mike, WR, Baylor, St. Louis 1981
Fisher, Ray, T-G, Eastern Illinois, Pittsburgh 1959
Fishman, Abe, G, Evansville 1921-22
Fishman, Alex, T, Evansville, 1921-22
Fisk, Bill, E, USC, Detroit 1940-43; San Francisco (AAFC) 1946-47; LA Dons (AAFC) 1948
Fiske, Max, HB, DePaul, Pittsburgh 1936-39; Chi. Cardinals 1937
Fiss, Galen, LB, Kansas, Cleveland 1956-66
Fitzgerald, Don, C, Holy Cross, Staten Island 1930-31
Fitzgerald, Francis, HB, Detroit, Toledo 1923
Fitzgerald, Freeman, C, Notre Dame; Rock Island 1920-21
Fitzgerald, John, C, Boston College, Dallas 1971-80
Fitzgerald, Mickey, RB, Virginia Tech, Atlanta 1981; Philadelphia 1981
Fitzgerald, Mike, DB, Iowa State, Minnesota 1966-67; NY Giants 1967; Atlanta 1967
Fitzgibbon, Paul, QB, Creighton, Duluth 1926; Frankford 1927; Chi. Cardinals 1928; Green Bay 1930-32
Fitzke, Bob, HB, Idaho, Frankford 1925
Fitzkee, Scott, WR, Penn State, Philadelphia 1979-80; San Diego 1981-82
Fivaz, Bill, G, Syracuse, Rochester 1925; Milwaukee 1925
Flagerman, Jack, C, St. Mary's (California), LA Dons (AAFC) 1948
Flaherty, Dick, E, Marquette, Green Bay 1926
Flaherty, Jim, E, Georgetown (Washington D.C.), Chi. Bears 1923
Flaherty, Ray, E, Gonzaga, NY Yankees 1927-28; NY Giants 1928-29, 1931-35
Flanagan, Dick, G, Ohio State, Chi. Bears 1948-49; Detroit 1950-52; Pittsburgh 1953-54
Flanagan, Ed, C, Purdue, Detroit 1965-74; San Diego 1975-76
Flanagan, Latham, E, Carnegie-Mellon, Chi. Bears 1931; Chi. Cardinals 1931
Flanagan, William (Hoot), HB, Pittsburgh, Pottsville 1925-26
Flanigan, Jim, LB, Pittsburgh, Green Bay 1967-70; New Orleans 1971
Flannigan, Bill, T, Beloit, Louisville 1926
Flatley, Paul, SE, Northwestern, Minnesota 1963-67; Atlanta 1968
Flattery, Wilson, G, Wooster, Canton 1925-26
Flavin, Jack, HB, Georgetown (Washington D.C.), Buffalo 1923-24
Fleckenstein, Bill, C, Iowa, Chi. Bears 1925-30; Portsmouth 1930; Frankford 1931; Brooklyn 1931
Fleischman, Godfrey (Jack), G, Purdue, Detroit 1925-26; Providence 1927-29
Fleming, Don, DB, Florida, Cleveland 1960-62
Fleming, George, HB, Washington, Oakland 1961
Fleming, Marv, TE, Utah, Green Bay 1963-69; Miami 1970-74
Fleming, Wilmer, HB, Mt. Union, Canton 1925
Flenniken, Max, HB, Geneva, Chi. Cardinals 1930; NY Giants 1931
Fletcher, Andy, FB, Maryland, Buffalo 1920
Fletcher, Billy Ray, DB, Memphis State, Denver 1966
Fletcher, Chris, S, Temple, San Diego 1970-76
Fletcher, Ollie, G, USC, LA Dons (AAFC) 1949; Baltimore 1950
Fletcher, Simon, DE, Houston, Denver 1985
Flick, Tom, QB, Washington, Washington 1981; New England 1982; Cleveland 1984
Flint, George, DT, Arizona State, Buffalo 1962-65, 1968-69
Flint, Judson, CB, Memphis State, Cleveland 1980-82; Buffalo 1983
Flohr, Les, C, Bethany (Kansas), Cleveland 1927
Flones, Brian, LB, Washington State, Seattle 1981-82
Flora, Bill, HB, Michigan, Chi. Cardinals 1928
Florence, Paul, E, Loyola (Chicago), Chi. Cardinals 1920
Flores, Tom, QB, Pacific, Oakland 1960-61, 1963-66; Buffalo 1967-69; Kansas City 1969
Flower, Jim, T-E, Ohio State, Columbus 1920; Akron 1921-24
Flowers, Bernie, E, Purdue, Baltimore 1956
Flowers, Bob, C, Texas Tech, Green Bay 1942-49
Flowers, Charlie, FB, Mississippi, LA Chargers 1960; San Diego 1961; NY Titans 1962
Flowers, Dick, QB, Northwestern, Baltimore 1953
Flowers, Keith, C, TCU, Dallas 1952
Flowers, Larry, S, Texas Tech, NY Giants 1981-85; NY Jets 1985
Flowers, Richmond, DB-WR-KR, Tennessee, Dallas 1969-71; NY Giants 1971-73
Floyd, Bobby Jack, FB, TCU, Green Bay 1952; Chi. Bears 1953
Floyd, Don, DE, TCU, Houston 1960-67
Floyd, George, DB, Eastern Kentucky, NY Jets 1982, 1984
Floyd, John, WR, Northeast Louisiana, San Diego 1979-80; St. Louis 1981
Flynn, Don, DB, Houston, Dallas Texans 1960-61; NY Titans 1961
Flynn, Furlong, T, Cornell, Hartford 1926
Flynn, Paul, E, Minnesota, Minneapolis 1922-23
Flynn, Tom, S, Pittsburgh, Green Bay 1984-85
Foldberg, Hank, E, Army, Brooklyn (AAFC) 1948; Chi. Hornets (AAFC) 1949
Foley, Dave, T, Ohio State, NY Jets 1970-71; Buffalo 1972-77
Foley, Jim, HB-FB, Syracuse, Hartford 1926
Foley, Steve, DB, Tulane, Denver 1976-85
Foley, Tim, CB, Purdue, Miami 1970-80
Foley, Tim, T, Notre Dame, Baltimore 1981
Folk, Dick, FB, Illinois Wesleyan, Brooklyn 1939
Folkins, Lee, TE, Washington, Green Bay 1961; Dallas 1962-64; Pittsburgh 1965
Follet, Beryl, QB, NYU, Staten Island 1930-31
Folsom, Steve, TE, Utah, Philadelphia 1981; NY Giants 1982
Foltz, Vern, C, St. Vincent, Washington 1944; Pittsburgh 1945
Fontenot, Herman, WR, LSU, Cleveland 1985
Fontes, Wayne, DB, Michigan State, NY Titans 1962
Foote, Chris, C, USC, Baltimore 1980-81; NY Giants 1982-83
Foote, Jim, QB, Delaware Valley, Houston 1974, 1976
Ford, Adrian, HB, Lafayette, Frankford 1927; Pottsville 1927
Ford, Charlie, CB, Houston, Chi. Bears 1971-73; Philadelphia 1974; Buffalo 1975; NY Giants 1975
Ford, Fred, HB, Cal Poly-SLO, Buffalo 1960; LA Chargers 1960
Ford, Garrett, RB, West Virginia, Denver 1968
Ford, Henry, DB, Pittsburgh, Cleveland 1955; Pittsburgh 1956
Ford, Jim, RB, Texas Southern, New Orleans 1971-72
Ford, Len, E-DE, Michigan, LA Dons (AAFC) 1948-49; Cleveland 1950-57; Green Bay 1958
Ford, Mike, QB, SMU, Tampa Bay 1981
Ford, Salem, HB, Louisville, Louisville 1922-23
Fordham, Jim, FB, Georgia, Chi. Bears 1944-45
Foreman, Chuck, RB, Miami, Minnesota 1973-79; New England 1980
Forester, Bill, LB, SMU, Green Bay 1953-63
Forester, Herschel, G, SMU, Cleveland 1954-57
Forkovitch, Nick, FB, William & Mary, Brooklyn (AAFC) 1948
Forrest, Eddie, C, Santa Clara, San Francisco (AAFC) 1946-47
Forrest, Tom, G, Cincinnati, Chi. Bears 1974
Forsberg, Fred, LB, Washington, Denver 1968, 1970-73; Buffalo 1973; San Diego 1974
Forst, Art (Dutch), HB, Villanova, Providence 1926
Forsythe, Ben, C, Syracuse, Rochester 1920
Forte, Aldo, G, Montana, Chi. Bears 1939-41, 1946; Detroit 1946; Green Bay 1947
Forte, Bob, HB, Arkansas, Green Bay 1946-50, 1952-53
Forte, Ike, RB, Arkansas, New England 1976-77; Washington 1978-80; NY Giants 1981
Fortmann, Dan, G, Colgate, Chi. Bears 1936-43
Fortmeyer, Al, HB, Cincinnati 1921
Fortner, Larry, QB, Miami (Ohio), Atlanta 1979-80
Fortunato, Joe, LB, Mississippi State, Chi. Bears 1955-56
Fortune, Burnell, G, DePauw, Minneapolis 1923; Kenosha 1924; Hammond 1924-25
Fortune, Hosea, WR, Rice, San Diego 1983
Foruria, John, DB, Idaho, Pittsburgh 1967-68
Fosdick, Bob, G, Iowa, Minneapolis 1923-24; Rock Island 1924
Foster, Bob, HB, Racine 1922-23; Milwaukee 1924
Foster, Eddie, WR, Houston, Houston 1977-78
Foster, Fred, HB, Syracuse, Buffalo 1923; Rochester 1923-24
Foster, Gene, RB, Arizona State, San Diego 1965-70
Foster, Jerome, DE, Ohio State, Houston 1983-84
Foster, Jim, QB, Bucknell, Buffalo 1925
Foster, Ralph, T, Oklahoma State, Chi. Cardinals 1945-46
Foster, Roy, G-T, USC, Miami 1982-85
Foster, Will, LB, Eastern Michigan, New England 1973-74
Foules, Elbert, CB, Alcorn State, Philadelphia 1983-85
Fournet, Sid, G, LSU, LA Rams 1955-56; Pittsburgh 1957; Dallas Texans 1960-61; NY Titans 1962; NY Jets 1963
Fouts, Dan, QB, Oregon, San Diego 1973-85
Fowler, Amos, G, Southern Mississippi, Detroit 1978-84
Fowler, Aubrey, HB, Arkansas, Baltimore (AAFC) 1948
Fowler, Bobby, FB, Tennessee-Martin, NY Titans 1962
Fowler, Bobby, TE, Louisiana Tech, New Orleans 1985
Fowler, Charlie, G, Houston, Miami 1967-68
Fowler, Dan, G, Kentucky, NY Giants 1979
Fowler, Jerry, G, Northwestern State (Louisiana), Houston 1964
Fowler, Todd, RB, Stephen F. Austin, Dallas 1985
Fowler, Wayne, C, Richmond, Buffalo 1970
Fowler, Willmer, HB, Northwestern, Buffalo 1960-61
Fowlkes, Dennis, LB, West Virginia, Minnesota 1983-85
Fox, Sam, E, Ohio State, NY Giants 1945
Fox, Terry, FB, Miami, Philadelphia 1941, 1945; Miami (AAFC) 1946
Fox, Tim, S, Ohio State, New England 1976-81; San Diego 1982-84; LA Rams 1985
Frahm, Herald (Dick), HB, Nebraska, Staten Island 1932; Philadelphia 1935
Fralic, Bill, T, Pittsburgh, Atlanta 1985
France, Doug, T, Ohio State, LA Rams 1975-81; Houston 1983
Franchesi, Pete, HB, San Francisco, San Francisco (AAFC) 1946
Franci, Jason, SE, Cal-Santa Barbara, Denver 1966
Francis, Dave, FB, Ohio State, Washington 1963
Francis, Gene, FB, Chicago, Chi. Cardinals 1926
Francis, Joe, QB, Oregon State, Green Bay 1958-59
Francis, Phil, RB, Stanford, San Francisco 1979-80
Francis, Russ, TE, Oregon, New England 1975-80; San Francisco 1982-85
Francis, Sam, FB-HB, Nebraska, Chi. Bears 1937-38; Pittsburgh 1939; Brooklyn 1939-40
Francis, Wallace, WR, Arkansas-Pine Bluff, Buffalo 1973-74; Atlanta 1975-81
Franck, George, FB, Minnesota, NY Giants 1941, 1945-47
Franckhauser, Tom, DB, Purdue, LA Rams 1959; Dallas Cowboys 1960-61; Minnesota 1962-63
Franckowiak, Mike, RB, Central Michigan, Denver 1975-76; Buffalo 1977-78
Franco, Ed, G, Fordham, Boston 1944
Frank, Bill, T, Colorado, Dallas 1964
Frank, Joe, T, Georgetown (Washington D.C.), Philadelphia 1941-42; Phil-Pitt 1943
Frank, John, TE, Ohio State, San Francisco 1984-85
Frank, Paul, QB, Waynesburg, Newark 1930
Frankian, Ike, E, St. Mary's (California), Boston 1933; NY Giants 1934-35
Franklin, Andra, RB, Nebraska, Miami 1981-84
Franklin, Bobby, S, Mississippi, Cleveland 1960-66
Franklin, Byron, WR, Auburn, Buffalo 1981, 1983-84; Seattle 1985
Franklin, Cleveland, RB, Baylor, Philadelphia 1977-78; Baltimore 1979-82
Franklin, Dennis, WR, Michigan, Detroit 1975-76
Franklin, George, RB, Texas A&I, Atlanta 1978; NY Giants 1979
Franklin, Larry, WR, Jackson State, Tampa Bay 1978
Franklin, Norm (Red), HB, Oregon State, Brooklyn 1935-37
Franklin, Paul, FB, Franklin, Chi. Bears 1931-33
Franklin, Tony, K, Texas A&M, Philadelphia 1979-83; New England 1984-85
Franklin, Willie, WR, Oklahoma, Baltimore 1972
Frankowski, Ray, G, Washington, Green Bay 1945; LA Dons (AAFC) 1946-48
Franks, Dennis, C, Michigan, Philadelphia 1976-78; Detroit 1979
Franks, Elvis, DE, Morgan State, Cleveland 1980-84; LA Raiders 1985
Franta, Herb, T, St. Thomas (Minnesota), Minneapolis 1929-30; Green Bay 1930
Frantz, Jack, LB, California, Buffalo 1968
Fraser, Jim, LB-P, Wisconsin, Denver 1962-64; Kansas City 1965; Boston 1966; New Orleans 1968
Frazier, Al, FL, Florida A&M, Denver 1961-63
Frazier, Charley, SE, Texas Southern, Houston 1962-68; Boston 1969-70
Frazier, Cliff, DT, UCLA, Kansas City 1977
Frazier, Curt, DB, Fresno State, Cincinnati 1968
Frazier, Guy, LB, Wyoming, Cincinnati 1981-84; Buffalo 1985
Frazier, Leslie, CB, Alcorn State, Chi. Bears 1981-85
Frazier, Wayne, C, Auburn, San Diego 1962; Houston 1965; Kansas City 1966-67; Buffalo 1967
Frazier, Willie, TE, Arkansas-Pine Bluff, Houston 1964-65, 1971, 1975; San Diego 1966-70; Kansas City 1971-72
Frederick, Andy, DT, New Mexico, Dallas 1977-81; Cleveland 1982; Chi. Bears 1983-85
Frederickson, Tucker, RB, Auburn, NY Giants 1965, 1967-71
Freelon, Solomon, G, Grambling, Houston 1972-74
Freeman, Bobby, DB, Auburn, Cleveland 1957-58; Green Bay 1959; Philadelphia 1960-61; Washington 1962
Freeman, Jack, G, Texas, Brooklyn (AAFC) 1946
Freeman, Mike, DB, Fresno State, Atlanta 1968-70
Freeman, Mike, G, Arizona, Denver 1984
Freeman, Phil, WR, Arizona, Tampa Bay 1985
Freeman, Steve, S, Mississippi State, Buffalo 1975-85
Freitas, Jesse, QB, Santa Clara, San Francisco (AAFC) 1946-47; Chi. Rockets (AAFC) 1948; Buffalo (AAFC) 1949
Freitas, Jesse, QB, San Diego State, San Diego 1974-75

Freitas, Rockne (Rocky), T, Oregon State, Detroit 1968-77; Tampa Bay 1978
French, Barry (Bear), G, Purdue, Baltimore (AAFC) 1947-49; Baltimore 1950; Detroit 1951
French, Ernest, S, Alabama A&M, Pittsburgh 1982
French, Walter, HB, Army, Rochester 1922; Pottsville 1925
Frey, Dick, DE-G, Texas A&M, Dallas Texans 1960; Houston 1961
Frey, Glenn, QB, Temple, Philadelphia 1937-38
Frick, Ray, C, Pennsylvania, Brooklyn 1941
Frickey, Walter, E, Rochester 1920
Friede, Mike, WR, Indiana, Detroit 1980; NY Giants 1980-81
Friedlund, Bob, E, Michigan State, Philadelphia 1946
Friedman, Benny, QB, Michigan, Kansas City 1926; Cleveland 1927; Detroit 1928; NY Giants 1929-31; Brooklyn 1932-34
Friedman, Bob, G, Washington, Philadelphia 1944
Friedman, Jake, E, Hartford 1926
Friend, Ben, T, LSU, Cleveland 1939
Fries, Sherwood, G, Colorado State, Green Bay 1943
Fritsch, Ernie, C, Detroit, St. Louis 1960
Fritsch, Lou, HB, Evansville 1921
Fritsch, Ted, FB, Wisconsin-Stevens Point, Green Bay 1942-50
Fritsch, Ted, C, St. Norbert, Atlanta 1972-74; Washington 1976-79
Fritsch, Toni, K, Dallas 1971-73, 1975; San Diego 1976; Houston 1977-81; New Orleans 1982
Fritts, George, T, Clemson, Philadelphia 1945
Fritts, Stan, RB, North Carolina State, Cincinnati 1975-76
Fritz, Ralph, G, Michigan, Philadelphia 1941
Fritzsche, Jim, T-G, Purdue, Philadelphia 1983
Frizzell, William, CB, North Carolina Central, Detroit 1984-85
Frketich, Len, T, Penn State, Pittsburgh 1945
Frohbose, Bill, DB, Miami, Detroit 1974
Fronczek, Andy, T, Richmond, Brooklyn 1941
Frongillo, John, C, Baylor, Houston 1962-66
Frost, Ken, DT, Tennessee, Dallas Cowboys 1961-62
Frugone, Jim (Babe), HB, Syracuse, NY Giants 1925
Frump, Milton (Babe), G, Ohio Wesleyan, Chi. Bears 1930
Frutig, Ed, E, Michigan, Green Bay 1941, 1945; Detroit 1945-46
Fry, Bob, T, Kentucky, LA Rams 1953, 1956-59; Dallas 1960-64
Fry, Harry, E, Bucknell, Staten Island 1932
Fry, Wes, FB-HB-QB, Iowa, NY Yankees 1927
Fryar, Irving, WR-KR, Nebraska, New England 1984-85
Frye, David, LB, Purdue, Atlanta 1983-85
Fryer, Brian, WR, Alberta, Washington 1976
Fryer, Kenny, HB, West Virginia, Brooklyn 1944
Fucci, Dom, DB, Kentucky, Detroit 1955
Fugett, Jean, TE, Amherst, Dallas 1972-75; Washington 1976-79
Fugler, Dick, T, Tulane, Pittsburgh 1952; Chi. Cardinals 1954
Fulcher, Bill, LB, Georgia Tech, Washington 1956-58
Fuller, Charley, RB, Cal State-San Francisco, Oakland 1961-62
Fuller, Frank, DT, Kentucky, LA Rams 1953, 1955, 1957-58; Chi. Cardinals 1959; St. Louis 1960-62; Philadelphia 1963
Fuller, Jeff, S, Texas A&M, San Francisco 1984-85
Fuller, Johnny, DB, Lamar, San Francisco 1968-73; New Orleans 1974-75
Fuller, Larry, HB, Washington 1944-45; Chi. Cardinals 1945
Fuller, Mike, CB-KR, Auburn, San Diego 1975-80; Cincinnati 1981-82
Fuller, Steve, QB, Clemson, Kansas City 1979-82; LA Rams 1983; Chi. Bears 1984-85
Fullerton, Ed, DB, Maryland, Pittsburgh 1953
Fulton, Dan, WR, Nebraska-Omaha, Buffalo 1979; Cleveland 1981-82
Fulton, Ed, G, Maryland, LA Rams 1978; Buffalo 1979
Fulton, Ted (Curley), G, Oglethorpe, Brooklyn 1931-32
Fultz, Mike, DT, Nebraska, New Orleans 1977-80; Miami 1981; Baltimore 1981
Funchess, Tom, T, Jackson State, Boston 1968-70; Houston 1971-73; Miami 1974
Fuqua, John (Frenchy), RB, Morgan State, NY Giants 1969; Pittsburgh 1970-76
Fuqua, Ray, E, SMU, Brooklyn 1935-36
Furey, James, LB, Kansas State, NY Titans 1960
Furman, John, QB, Texas-El Paso, Cleveland 1962
Furness, Steve, DE-DT, Rhode Island, Pittsburgh 1972-80; Detroit 1981
Furst, Tony, T, Dayton, Detroit 1940-41, 1944
Fusina, Chuck, QB, Penn State, Tampa Bay 1979-81
Fussell, Tom, DE, LSU, Boston 1967

G

Gabler, John, C, West Virginia, Dayton 1925-26
Gabriel, Roman, QB, North Carolina State, LA Rams 1962-72; Philadelphia 1973-77
Gaddis, Bob, WR, Mississippi Valley State, Buffalo 1976
Gaechter, Mike, S, Oregon, Dallas 1962-69
Gaffney, Derrick, WR, Florida, NY Jets 1978-84
Gaffney, Jim, HB, Tennessee, Washington 1945-46
Gafford, Monk, HB, Auburn, Miami (AAFC) 1946; Brooklyn (AAFC) 1946-48
Gage, Bobby, HB, Clemson, Pittsburgh 1949-50
Gagliano, Bob, QB, Utah State, Kansas City 1981-83
Gagner, Larry, G, Florida, Pittsburgh 1966-69; Kansas City 1972
Gagnon, Dave, RB, Ferris State, Chi. Bears 1974
Gagnon, Roy, G, Oregon, Detroit 1935
Gain, Bob, DT, Kentucky, Cleveland 1952, 1954-64
Gaines, Clark, RB, Wake Forest, NY Jets 1976-80; Kansas City 1981-82
Gaines, Greg, LB, Tennessee, Seattle 1981, 1983-85
Gaines, Lawrence, RB, Wyoming, Detroit 1976, 1978-79
Gaines, Wentford, DB, Cincinnati, Pittsburgh 1978; Chi. Bears 1978-80
Gainor, Charlie, E, North Dakota, Chi. Cardinals 1939
Gaiser, George, T, SMU, Denver 1968
Gaison, Blane, S, Hawaii, Atlanta 1981-84
Gaiters, Bob, HB, New Mexico State, NY Giants 1961-62; San Francisco 1962; Denver 1963
Gajan, Hokie, RB, LSU, New Orleans 1982-85
Galbreath, Tony, RB, Missouri, New Orleans 1976-80; Minnesota 1981-83; NY Giants 1984-85
Galiffa, Arnold, QB, Army, NY Giants 1953; San Francisco 1954
Galigher, Ed, DE-DT, UCLA, NY Jets 1972-76; San Francisco 1977-79
Galimore, Willie, HB, Florida A&M, Chi. Bears 1957-63
Galitzin, Stan, C, Villanova, NY Giants 1937-39
Gallagher, Allen, T, USC, New England 1974
Gallagher, Bernie, G, Pennsylvania, LA Dons (AAFC) 1947
Gallagher, Dave, DE, Michigan, Chi. Bears 1974; NY Giants 1975-76; Detroit 1978-79
Gallagher, Ed, T, Washington & Jefferson, NY Yankees 1928
Gallagher, Frank, G, North Carolina, Detroit 1967-72; Atlanta 1973; Minnesota 1973
Gallarneau, Hugh, HB, Stanford, Chi. Bears 1941-42, 1945-47
Gallegos, Chon, QB, San Jose State, Oakland 1962
Gallovich, Tony, HB, Wake Forest, Cleveland 1941
Galloway, David, DT, Florida, St. Louis 1982-85
Galloway, Duane, LB, Arizona State, Detroit 1985
Galvin, John, QB, Purdue, Baltimore (AAFC) 1947
Gambino, Lu, HB, Maryland, Baltimore (AAFC) 1948-49
Gamble, R.C., RB, South Carolina State, Boston 1968-69
Gambold, Bob, QB, Washington State, Philadelphia 1953
Gambrell, Billy, WR, South Carolina, St. Louis 1963-67; Detroit 1968
Ganas, Rusty, DT, South Carolina, Baltimore 1971
Gandee, Sherwin (Sonny), DE, Ohio State, Dallas 1952; Detroit 1952-56
Gann, Mike, DE, Notre Dame, Atlanta 1985
Gansberg, Al, E-T, Miami (Ohio), Louisville 1926
Gant, Earl, RB, Missouri, Kansas City 1979-80
Gant, Reuben, TE, Oklahoma State, Buffalo 1974-80
Gantenbein, Milt, E, Wisconsin, Green Bay 1931-40
Gantt, Greg, P-K, Alabama, NY Jets 1974-75
Gantt, Jerry, T, North Carolina Central, Buffalo 1970
Gaona, Bob, T, Wake Forest, Pittsburgh 1953-56; Philadelphia 1957
Garcia, Bubba, WR, Texas-El Paso, Kansas City 1980-81
Garcia, Eddie, K, SMU, Green Bay 1983-84
Garcia, Frank, P, Arizona State, Seattle 1981; Tampa Bay 1983-85
Garcia, Jim, DE, Purdue, Cleveland 1965; NY Giants 1966; New Orleans 1967; Atlanta 1968
Gardella, Gus, FB, Holy Cross, Green Bay 1922
Gardin, Ron, DB-KR, Arizona, Baltimore 1970-71; New England 1971
Gardner, Ellis, G-T, Georgia Tech, Kansas City 1983; Houston 1984; Indianapolis 1984
Gardner, Frank, E, Carlisle, Rock Island 1920
Gardner, George, E, Carlisle, Cleveland 1923
Gardner, Milt, G, Wisconsin, Detroit 1920-21; Buffalo 1921; Green Bay 1922-26; Kenosha 1924
Garlich, Chris, LB, Missouri, St. Louis 1979
Garlin, Don, HB, USC, San Francisco 1949-50
Garlington, John, LB, LSU, Cleveland 1968-77
Garnaas, Bill, HB, Minnesota, Pittsburgh 1946-48
Garner, Bob, G, NY Giants 1945
Garner, Bob, DB, Fresno State, LA Chargers 1960; Oakland 1961-63
Garner, Hal, LB, Utah State, Buffalo 1985
Garnett, Scott, NT, Washington, Denver 1984; San Francisco 1985; San Diego 1985
Garnjost, Don, G, Evansville 1921
Garrett, Al, G, Rutgers, Akron 1920; Cleveland 1920; Milwaukee 1922
Garrett, Alvin, RB-WR, Angelo State, NY Giants 1980-81; Washington 1981-84
Garrett, Bobby, QB, Stanford, Green Bay 1954
Garrett, Carl, RB, New Mexico Highlands, Boston 1969-70; New England 1971-72; Chi. Bears 1973-74; NY Jets 1975; Oakland 1976-77
Garrett, Drake, DB, Michigan State, Denver 1968, 1970
Garrett, Dub, G, Mississippi State, Baltimore (AAFC) 1948-49; Chi. Bears 1950
Garrett, J.D., HB, Grambling, Boston 1964-67
Garrett, Len, TE, New Mexico Highlands, Green Bay 1971-73; New Orleans 1973-75; San Francisco 1975
Garrett, Mike, RB, USC, Kansas City 1966-70; San Diego 1970-73
Garrett, Mike, P, Georgia, Baltimore 1981
Garrett, Reggie, WR, Eastern Michigan, Pittsburgh 1974-75
Garrett, Thurman, C, Oklahoma State, Chi. Bears 1947-48
Garrison, Gary, WR, San Diego State, San Diego 1966-76; Houston 1977
Garrison, Walt, FB, Oklahoma State, Dallas 1966-74
Garrity, Greg, WR, Penn State, Pittsburgh 1983-84; Philadelphia 1984-85
Garron, Larry, HB, Western Illinois, Boston 1960-68
Garror, Leon, S, Alcorn State, Buffalo 1972-73
Garry, Ben, RB, Southern Mississippi, Baltimore 1979-80
Gartner, Chris, K, Indiana, Cleveland 1974
Garvey, Frank, E, Holy Cross, Providence 1925-26
Garvey, Hec, T, Notre Dame, Chi. Bears 1922-25; Hartford 1926; Brooklyn 1926, 1930; NY Giants 1927-28; Providence 1929; Staten Island 1931
Gary, Keith, DE, Oklahoma, Pittsburgh 1983-85
Gary, Russell, S, Nebraska, New Orleans 1981-85
Garza, Dan, E, Oregon, NY Yankees (AAFC) 1949; NY Yanks 1951
Garzoni, Mike, G, USC, Washington 1947; NY Giants 1948; NY Yankees (AAFC) 1948
Gasparella, Joe, QB-LB, Notre Dame, Pittsburgh 1948, 1950-51; Chi. Cardinals 1951
Gassert, Ron, DT, Virginia, Green Bay 1962
Gastineau, Mark, DE, East Central (Oklahoma), NY Jets 1979-85
Gatewood, Les, C, Baylor, Green Bay 1946-47
Gatewood, Tom, WR, Notre Dame, NY Giants 1972-73
Gatski, Frank (Gunner), C, Auburn, Cleveland 1946-56; Detroit 1957
Gaubatz, Dennis, LB, LSU, Detroit, 1963-64; Baltimore 1965-69
Gaudio, Bob, G, Ohio State, Cleveland 1947-49, 1951
Gauer, Charlie, E, Colgate, Phil-Pitt 1943; Philadelphia 1944-45
Gaul, Frank, T, Notre Dame, NY Bulldogs 1949
Gaulke, Hal, QB-E, Columbus 1920-22
Gault, Billy, DB, TCU, Minnesota 1961
Gault, Don, QB, Hofstra, Cleveland 1970
Gault, Willie, WR-KR, Tennessee, Chi. Bears 1983-85
Gaunty, Steve, WR, Northern Colorado, Kansas City 1979
Gaustad, Art, G, Minneapolis 1921-23
Gautt, Prentice, RB, Oklahoma, Cleveland 1960; St. Louis 1961-67
Gavigan, Mike, HB, St. Bonaventure, Rochester 1923
Gavin, Chuck, DE, Tennessee State, Denver 1960-63
Gavin, Fritz, E, Green Bay 1921, 1923
Gavin, Patrick (Buck), FB-HB, Buffalo 1920, 1922; Detroit 1921; Rock Island 1921-22, 1924-25; Hammond 1926
Gavric, Momcilo, K, San Francisco 1969
Gay, Billy, HB, Notre Dame, Chi. Cardinals 1951-52
Gay, Blenda, DE, Fayetteville State, San Diego 1974; Philadelphia 1975-76
Gay, Chet, G-T, Minnesota, Buffalo 1925; Racine 1926; Milwaukee 1926
Gay, William, TE-DE, USC, Detroit 1978-85
Gaydos, Kent, WR, Florida State, Green Bay 1975
Gayer, Walt, T, Creighton, Duluth 1926
Gayle, Shaun, CB, Ohio State, Chi. Bears 1984-85
Gaziano, Frank, G, Holy Cross, Boston 1944
Geathers, James, DE, Wichita State, New Orleans 1984-85
Geddes, Bob, LB, UCLA, Denver 1972; New England 1973-75
Geddes, Ken, LB, Nebraska, LA Rams 1971-75; Seattle 1976-78
Gedman, Gene, HB, Indiana, Detroit 1953, 1956-58
Gehrke, Bruce, E, Columbia, NY Giants 1948
Gehrke, Fred, HB, Utah, Cleveland 1940, 1945; LA Rams 1946-49; San Francisco 1950; Chi. Cardinals 1950
Gehrke, Jack, WR, Utah, Kansas City 1968; Cincinnati 1969; Denver 1971
Gelatka, Chuck, E, Mississippi State, NY Giants 1937-40
Gent, Pete, FL-TE, Michigan State, Dallas 1964-68
Gentry, Byron, G, USC, Pittsburgh 1937-39
Gentry, Curtis, DB, Maryland-Eastern Shore, Chi. Bears 1966-68
Gentry, Dale, E, Washington State, LA Dons (AAFC) 1946-48
Gentry, Dennis, RB, Baylor, Chi. Bears 1982-85
Gentry, Lee, FB, Tulsa, Washington 1941
Gentry, Weldon, G, Oklahoma, Providence 1930-31
George, Bill, LB, Wake Forest, Chi. Bears 1952-65; LA Rams 1966
George, Ed, DT, Wake Forest, Baltimore 1975; Philadelphia 1976-78
George, Karl, C, Carroll (Wisconsin), Racine 1922
George, Ray, T, USC, Detroit 1939; Philadelphia 1940
George, Steve, DE, Houston, St. Louis 1974; Atlanta 1976
George, Tim, WR, Carson-Newman, Cincinnati 1973; Cleveland 1974
Gepford, Sid, HB, Millikin, Decatur 1920
Gerber, Woody, G, Alabama, Philadelphia 1941-42
Geredine, Thomas, WR, Northeast Missouri State, Atlanta 1973-74; LA Rams 1976
Gerela, Roy, K, New Mexico State, Houston 1969-70; Pittsburgh 1971-78; San Diego 1979
Geri, Joe, HB, Georgia, Pittsburgh 1949-51; Chi. Cardinals 1952
German, Jim, HB, Centre, Washington 1939; Chi. Cardinals 1940
Germany, Willie, S, Morgan State, Atlanta 1972; Detroit 1973;

Houston 1975; New England 1976
Gersbach, Carl, LB, West Chester, Philadelphia 1970; Minnesota 1971-72; San Diego 1973-74; Chi. Bears 1975; St. Louis 1976
Gervais, Rick, S, Stanford, San Francisco 1981-83
Getchell, Gorham, E, Temple, Baltimore (AAFC) 1947
Getty, Charlie, T, Penn State, Kansas City 1974-83
Getz, Fred, E, Tennessee-Chattanooga, Brooklyn 1930
Geyer, Bill, HB, Colgate, Chi. Bears 1942-43, 1946
Ghecas, Lou, HB, Georgetown (Washington D.C.), Philadelphia 1941
Ghee, Milt, QB, Dartmouth, Chi. Tigers 1920; Cleveland 1921; Hammond 1922-23
Ghersanich, Vern, G, Auburn, Chi. Cardinals 1943
Giacomarro, Ralph, P, Penn State, Atlanta 1983-85
Giammona, Louie, RB-KR, Utah State, NY Jets 1976; Philadelphia 1978-82
Giancanelli, Skip, HB, Loyola (Los Angeles), Philadelphia 1953-56
Gianelli, Mario (Yo Yo), G, Boston College, Philadelphia 1948-51
Giannoni, Jack, E, St. Mary's (California), Cleveland 1938
Giaquinto, Nick, RB, Connecticut, Miami 1980-81; Washington 1981-83
Giaver, Bill, HB, Georgia Tech, Hammond 1922, 1925; Rock Island 1923; Racine 1924; Louisville 1926
Gibbons, Austin, C, DePaul, Chi. Cardinals 1929
Gibbons, Jim, SE-TE, Iowa, Detroit 1958-68
Gibbons, Mike, T, Southwestern Oklahoma, NY Giants 1976-77
Gibbs, Donnie, P, TCU, New Orleans 1974
Gibbs, Pat, DB, Lamar, Philadelphia 1972
Gibbs, Sonny, QB, TCU, Dallas, 1963; Detroit 1964
Gibler, Andy, TE, Missouri, Cincinnati 1983
Giblin, Robert, DB, Houston, NY Giants 1975; St. Louis 1977
Gibron, Abe, G, Purdue, Buffalo (AAFC) 1949; Cleveland 1950-56; Philadelphia 1956-57; Chi. Bears 1958-59
Gibson, Billy Joe, HB, Tulsa, Cleveland 1942, 1944; Washington 1943; Brooklyn (AAFC) 1946-47
Gibson, Claude (Hoot), DB, North Carolina State, San Diego 1961-62; Oakland 1963-65
Gibson, Denver (Butch), G, Grove City, Newark 1930; NY Giants 1930-34
Gibson, Dick, G, Centre, Louisville 1922-23
Gibson, Ernest, CB, Furman, New England 1984-85
Gibson, George, G, Minnesota, Frankford 1930; Minneapolis 1930
Gibson, Paul, E, North Carolina State, Buffalo (AAFC) 1947-49
Gibson, Paul, DB, Texas-El Paso, Green Bay 1972
Gibson, Reuben, RB, Memphis State, Buffalo 1977
Giddens, Frank, T, New Mexico, Philadelphia 1981-82
Giddens, Herschel, T, Louisiana Tech, Philadelphia 1938; Boston 1944
Giesler, Jon, T, Michigan, Miami 1979-85
Gifford, Bob, QB, Denver, Brooklyn 1942
Gifford, Frank, HB-FL-DB, USC, NY Giants 1952-60, 1962-64
Gift, Wayne, QB, Purdue, Cleveland 1937
Gilbert, Daren, T, Cal State-Fullerton, New Orleans 1985
Gilbert, Gale, QB, California, Seattle 1985
Gilbert, Kline, T, Mississippi, Chi. Bears 1953-57
Gilbert, Lewis, TE, Florida, Atlanta 1978
Gilbert, Wally, HB, Valparaiso, Duluth 1923-27
Gilburg, Tom, T-P, Syracuse, Baltimore 1961-65
Gilchrist, Cookie, FB, Buffalo 1962-64; Denver 1965, 1967; Miami 1966
Gilchrist, George, T, Tennessee State, Chi. Cardinals 1953
Gildea, Denny, C, Holy Cross, Hartford 1926
Gildea, Johnny, QB, St. Bonaventure, Pittsburgh 1935-37; NY Giants 1938
Giles, Jimmie, TE, Alcorn State, Houston 1977; Tampa Bay 1978-85
Gill, Owen, RB, Iowa, Indianapolis 1985
Gill, Randy, LB, San Jose State, St. Louis 1978; Tampa Bay 1978
Gill, Roger, RB, Texas Tech, Philadelphia 1964-65
Gill, Sloko, G, Youngstown State, Detroit 1942
Gillard, Larry, DT, Mississippi State, NY Giants 1978
Gillen, John, LB, Illinois, St. Louis 1981-82; New England 1983
Gillespie, Scoop, RB, William Jewell, Pittsburgh 1984
Gillett, Fred, LB, Cal State-Los Angeles, San Diego 1962; Oakland 1964
Gillette, Jim, HB, Virginia, Cleveland 1940, 1944-45; Boston 1946, Washington 1947; Green Bay 1947; Detroit 1948
Gillette, Walker, WR, Richmond, San Diego 1970-71; St. Louis 1972-73; NY Giants 1974-76
Gilliam, Joe, QB, Tennessee State, Pittsburgh 1972-75
Gilliam, John, WR-KR, South Carolina State, New Orleans 1967-68, 1977; St. Louis 1969-1971; Minnesota 1972-75; Atlanta 1976; Chi. Bears 1977
Gilliam, Jon, C, East Texas State, Dallas Texans 1961-62; Kansas City 1963-67
Gillies, Fred, T, Cornell, Chi. Cardinals 1920-28
Gillingham, Gale, G, Minnesota, Green Bay 1966-74, 1976
Gillis, Don, C, Rice, Chi. Cardinals 1958-59; St. Louis 1960-61
Gillis, Joe, T, Detroit, Toledo 1923
Gillo, Hank, HB-FB, Colgate, Hammond 1920-21; Racine 1922-24, 1926; Milwaukee 1925
Gillom, Horace, E-P, Nevada-Reno, Cleveland 1947-56
Gillson, Bob, G, Colgate, Brooklyn 1930-31
Gilmer, Harry, QB-DB, Alabama, Washington 1948-52, 1954; Detroit 1955-56
Gilroy, John, G, NY Giants 1930
Gilroy, Johnny, QB, Georgetown (Washington D.C.), Canton 1920; Cleveland 1920; Washington 1921
Ginn, Hubert, RB, Florida A&M, Miami 1970-75; Baltimore 1973; Oakland 1976-77
Ginn, Tommie, G, Arkansas, Detroit 1980-81
Ginney, Jerry, G, Santa Clara, Philadelphia 1940
Gipson, Paul, RB, Houston, Atlanta 1969; Detroit 1971; New England 1973
Gipson, Tom, DT, Texas-El Paso, Oakland 1971
Girard, Earl (Jug), HB, Wisconsin, Green Bay 1948-51; Detroit 1952-56; Pittsburgh 1957
Gissinger, Andrew, T, Syracuse, San Diego 1982-84
Glacken, Scotty, QB, Duke, Denver 1966-67
Gladchuk, Chet, C, Boston College, NY Giants 1941, 1946-47
Gladden, Mack, E, Missouri, St. Louis 1934
Gladieux, Bob, RB, Notre Dame, Boston 1969; New England 1970-72; Buffalo 1970
Gladstone, Bill, G, Evansville 1922
Glamp, Joe, HB, LSU, Pittsburgh 1947-49
Glasgow, Nesby, S, Washington, Baltimore 1979-83, Indianapolis 1984-85
Glass, Bill, DE, Baylor, Detroit 1958-61; Cleveland 1962-68
Glass, Bill, G, Baylor, Cincinnati 1980-81
Glass, Chip, TE, Florida State, Cleveland 1969-73; NY Giants 1974
Glass, Glenn, DB, Tennessee, Pittsburgh 1962-63; Philadelphia 1964-65; Atlanta 1966; Denver 1966
Glass, Leland, WR, Oregon, Green Bay 1972-73
Glassgow, Bill, HB, Iowa, Portsmouth 1930; Chi. Cardinals 1931
Glassic, Tom, G, Virginia, Denver 1976-83
Glassman, Frank, G, Wilmington, Buffalo 1929
Glassman, Morris, E, Columbus 1921-22
Glatz, Fred, DE, Pittsburgh, Pittsburgh 1956
Glazebrook, Bob, S, Fresno State, Atlanta 1978-83
Glenn, Bill, QB, Eastern Illinois, Chi. Bears 1944
Glenn, Howard, G, Linfield, NY Titans 1960
Glenn, Kerry, LB, Minnesota, NY Jets 1985
Glennie, George, G, Colgate, Racine 1926
Glick, Ed, HB, Green Bay 1921-22
Glick, Freddie, S, Colorado State, Chi. Cardinals 1959; St. Louis 1960; Houston 1961-66
Glick, Gary, DB, Colorado State, Pittsburgh 1956-59; Washington 1959-61; Baltimore 1961; San Diego 1963
Gloden, Fred, HB, Tulane, Philadelphia 1941; Miami (AAFC) 1946
Glosson, Clyde, WR, Texas-El Paso, Buffalo 1970
Glover, Kevin, C, Maryland, Detroit 1985
Glover, Rich, DT, Nebraska, NY Giants 1973; Philadelphia 1975
Glueck, Larry, DB, Villanova, Chi. Bears 1963-65
Goad, Paul, FB, Abilene Christian, San Francisco 1956
Gob, Art, SE, Pittsburgh, Washington 1959-60; LA Chargers 1960
Goble, Les, HB, Alfred, Chi. Cardinals 1954-55
Goddard, Ed, QB, Washington State, Brooklyn 1937; Cleveland 1937-38
Godfrey, Chris, G, Michigan, NY Jets 1980; NY Giants 1984-85
Godfrey, Herb, E, Washington State, Cleveland 1942
Godwin, Bill, C, Georgia, Boston 1947-48
Godwin, Walt, G, Georgia Tech, Staten Island 1929
Goebel, Paul, E, Michigan, Columbus 1923-25
Goeddeke, George, G-C, Notre Dame, Denver 1967-72
Goetz, Angus, T, Michigan, Buffalo 1920, 1922; Columbus 1923
Goff, Clark, T, Florida, Pittsburgh 1940
Goff, Willard, DT, West Texas State, Atlanta 1985
Gofourth, Derrel, C-G, Oklahoma State, Green Bay 1977-82; San Diego 1983-84
Gogolak, Charlie, K, Princeton, Washington 1966-68; Boston 1970; New England 1971-72
Gogolak, Pete, K, Cornell, Buffalo 1964-65; NY Giants 1966-74
Goich, Dan, DT, California, Detroit 1969; New Orleans 1971; NY Giants 1972-73
Goldberg, Marshall (Biggie), HB-DB, Pittsburgh, Chi. Cardinals 1939-43, 1946-48
Golden, Tim, LB, Florida, New England 1982-84; Philadelphia 1985
Goldenberg, Charles (Buckets), G, Wisconsin, Green Bay 1933-45
Goldfein, Jersey, HB, Wisconsin-Superior, Duluth 1927
Golding, Joe, HB, Oklahoma, Boston 1947-48; NY Bulldogs 1949; NY Yanks 1950-51
Goldman, Sam, E, Howard, Boston 1944, 1946-47; Chi. Cardinals 1948; Detroit 1949
Goldsberry, John, T, Indiana, Chi. Cardinals 1949-50
Goldsmith, Earl, E, Evansville 1921-22
Goldsmith, Wendell, C, Emporia State, NY Giants 1940
Goldstein, Al, SE, North Carolina, Oakland 1961
Goldston, Ralph, HB, Youngstown State, Philadelphia 1952, 1954-55
Golembeski, Tony, E, Holy Cross, Providence 1925-26, 1929
Golic, Bob, LB-NT, Notre Dame, New England 1979-82; Cleveland 1983-85
Golomb, Rudy, G, Carroll (Wisconsin), Philadelphia 1936
Golsen, Gene, FB, Georgetown (Washington D.C.), Louisville 1926
Golsen, Tom, G, Georgetown (Washington D.C.), Louisville 1926
Golsteyn, Jerry, QB, Northern Illinois, NY Giants 1977-78; Detroit 1979; Baltimore 1979; Tampa Bay 1982-83; LA Raiders 1984
Golub, Chris, S, Kansas, Kansas City 1977
Gompers, Bill, HB, Notre Dame, Buffalo (AAFC) 1948
Gonda, George, HB, Duquesne, Pittsburgh 1942
Gonsoulin, Austin (Goose), DB, Baylor, Denver 1960-66; San Francisco 1967
Gonya, Bob, T, Northwestern, Philadelphia 1933-34
Gonzaga, John, T, San Francisco 1956-59; Dallas Cowboys 1960; Detroit 1961-65; Denver 1966
Gonzalez, Leon, WR, Bethune-Cookman, Dallas 1985
Gonzalez, Noe, RB, Southwest Texas State, New England 1974
Good, Tom, LB, Marshall, San Diego 1966
Goodbread, Royce, HB, Florida, Frankford 1930; Minneapolis 1930; Providence 1931
Goode, Conrad, T-C, Missouri, NY Giants 1984-85
Goode, Don, LB, Kansas, San Diego 1974-79; Cleveland 1980-81
Goode, Irv, G-C, Kentucky, St. Louis 1962-71; Miami 1973-74
Goode, John, TE, Youngstown State, St. Louis 1984; Philadelphia 1985
Goode, Rob, FB, Texas A&M, Washington 1949-51, 1954-55; Philadelphia 1955
Goode, Tom, LB-C, Mississippi, Houston 1962-65; Miami 1966-69; Baltimore 1970
Goodlow, Eugene, WR, Kansas State, New Orleans 1983-85
Goodman, Aubrey, T, Chicago, Chi. Cardinals 1927
Goodman, Brian, G, UCLA, Houston 1973-74
Goodman, Hank, T, West Virginia, Detroit 1942
Goodman, Harvey, G, Miami, Denver 1976
Goodman, John, DE-NT-LB, Oklahoma, Pittsburgh 1981-85
Goodman, Les, RB, Yankton, Green Bay 1973-74
Goodnight, Clyde, E, Tulsa, Green Bay 1945-48; Washington 1949-50
Goodnight, Owen, HB, Hardin-Simmons, Cleveland 1941
Goodridge, Bob, WR, Vanderbilt, Minnesota 1968
Goodrum, Charles, G-T, Florida A&M, Minnesota 1972-78
Goodson, John, P, Texas, Pittsburgh 1982
Goodspeed, Mark, T, Nebraska, St. Louis 1980
Goodwin, Doug, RB, Maryland-Eastern Shore, Buffalo 1966; Atlanta 1968
Goodwin, Earl, E, Bucknell, Pottsville 1928
Goodwin, Myrl, QB-HB, Bucknell, Pottsville 1928
Goodwin, Ronnie, SE, Baylor, Philadelphia 1963-68
Goodwin, Tod, E, West Virginia, NY Giants 1935-36
Goodyear, John, HB, Marquette, Washington 1942
Goolsby, Jim, C, Mississippi State, Cleveland 1940
Goosby, Tom, G, Baldwin-Wallace, Cleveland 1963; Washington 1966
Goovert, Ron, LB, Michigan State, Detroit 1967
Gordon, Bobby, DB, Tennessee, Chi. Cardinals 1958; Houston 1960
Gordon, Cornell, DB, North Carolina A&T, NY Jets 1965-69; Denver 1970-72
Gordon, Dick, WR, Michigan State, Chi. Bears 1965-71; LA Rams 1972-73; Green Bay 1973; San Diego 1974
Gordon, Ira, G-T, Kansas State, San Diego 1970-75
Gordon, John, DT, Hawaii, Detroit 1972
Gordon, Larry, LB, Arizona State, Miami 1976-82
Gordon, Lou, T, Illinois, Chi. Cardinals 1930-35; Brooklyn 1931; Green Bay 1936-37; Chi. Bears 1938
Gordon, Ralph, HB, Cleveland 1920
Gordy, John, T, Tennessee, Detroit 1957, 1959-67
Gore, Gordon, HB, Southwestern Oklahoma, Detroit 1939
Gorgal, Alex, HB, Rock Island 1923
Gorgal, Ken, HB, Purdue, Cleveland 1950, 1953-54; Chi. Bears 1955-56; Green Bay 1956
Gorgone, Pete, QB, Muhlenberg, NY Giants 1946
Gorinski, Walt, FB, LSU, Pittsburgh 1946
Gorman, Earl (Bud), G, Evansville 1921-22; Racine 1922-23; Kenosha 1924
Gormley, Tom, T, Georgetown (Washington D.C.), Canton 1920; Cleveland 1920; NY Giants 1921
Gorrill, Charley, E, Ohio State, Columbus 1926
Goss, Don, T, SMU, Cleveland 1956
Gossage, Gene, T, Northwestern, Philadelphia 1960-62
Gossett, Bruce, K-P, Richmond, LA Rams 1964-69; San Francisco 1970-74
Gossett, Jeff, P, Eastern Illinois, Kansas City 1981-82; Cleveland 1983, 1985
Gothard, Preston, TE, Alabama, Pittsburgh 1985
Gotshalk, Len, T, Cal State-Humboldt, Atlanta 1972-76
Governali, Paul, QB, Columbia, Boston 1946-47; NY Giants 1947-48
Gozdowski, Casimir (Hippo), FB-G, Toledo 1922
Grabfelder, Earl, HB, Kentucky, Louisville 1923
Grabinski, Ted, C, Duquesne, Pittsburgh 1939-40
Grabosky, Gene, DT, Syracuse, Buffalo 1960
Grabowski, Jim, FB, Illinois, Green Bay 1966-70; Chi. Bears 1971
Grace, Les, E, Temple, Newark 1930
Gradishar, Randy, LB, Ohio State, Denver 1974-83
Grady, Garry, DB, Eastern Michigan, Miami 1969

Graf, Dave, LB, Penn State, Cleveland 1975-79; Washington 1981
Graff, Neil, QB, Wisconsin, New England 1974-75; Seattle 1976; Pittsburgh 1976-77; Green Bay 1978
Graham, Al, G, Dayton 1925-29; Portsmouth 1930; Providence 1930-31; Chi. Cardinals 1932-33
Graham, Art, SE, Boston College, Boston 1963-68
Graham, Clarence, QB, Dayton 1928
Graham, Dave, T, Virginia, Philadelphia 1963-66, 1968-69
Graham, David, DE, Morehouse, Seattle 1982
Graham, Fred, E, West Virginia, Frankford 1926
Graham, Kenny, DB, Washington State, San Diego 1964-69; Cincinnati 1970; Pittsburgh 1970
Graham, Les, G, Tulsa, Detroit 1938
Graham, Lyle, C, Richmond, Philadelphia 1941
Graham, Mike, FB, Cincinnati, LA Dons (AAFC) 1948
Graham, Milt, T-DT, Colgate, Boston 1961-63
Graham, Otto, QB, Northwestern, Cleveland 1946-55
Graham, Tom, G, Temple, Philadelphia 1935
Graham, Tom, LB, Oregon, Denver 1972-74; Kansas City 1974; San Diego 1975-77; Buffalo 1978
Graham, William, S, Texas, Detroit 1982-85
Grain, Ed, G, Pennsylvania, NY Yankees (AAFC) 1947; Baltimore (AAFC) 1947-48
Grandberry, Ken, RB, Washington State, Chi. Bears 1974
Grandelius, Sonny, HB, Michigan State, NY Giants 1953
Granderson, Rufus, DT, Prairie View A&M, Dallas Texans 1960
Grandinette, George, G, Fordham, Brooklyn 1943
Grange, Garland, E, Illinois, Chi. Bears 1929-31
Grange, Harold (Red), HB, Illinois, Chi. Bears 1925, 1929-34; NY Yankees 1927
Granger, Charlie, T, Southern, Dallas Cowboys 1961; St. Louis 1961
Granger, Hoyle, FB, Mississippi State, Houston 1966-70, 1972; New Orleans 1971
Granger, Norm, RB, Iowa, Dallas 1984
Grannell, Dave, TE, Arizona State, San Diego 1974
Grant, Aaron, C, Tennessee-Chattanooga, Portsmouth 1930
Grant, Bob, LB, Wake Forest, Baltimore 1968; Washington 1971
Grant, Darryl, DT, Rice, Washington 1981-85
Grant, Frank, WR, South Colorado State, Washington 1973-78; Tampa Bay 1978
Grant, Harry (Bud), E-DE, Minnesota, Philadelphia 1951-52
Grant, Hugh (Ducky), QB, St. Mary's (California), Chi. Cardinals 1928
Grant, John, DE, USC, Denver 1973-79
Grant, Len, T, NYU, NY Giants 1930-37
Grant, Otis, WR, Michigan State, LA Rams 1983-84
Grant, Reggie, CB, Oregon, NY Jets 1978
Grant, Ross, G, NYU, Staten Island 1932; Cincinnati 1933-34
Grant, Wes, DE-DT, UCLA, Buffalo 1971; San Diego 1971; Cleveland 1972; Houston 1973
Grant, Will, C, Kentucky, Buffalo 1978-85
Grantham, Larry, LB, Mississippi, NY Titans 1960-62; NY Jets 1963-72
Grate, Carl, G, Georgia, NY Giants 1945
Grate, Willie, TE, South Carolina State, Buffalo 1969-70
Gravelle, Gordon, T, BYU, Pittsburgh 1972-76; NY Giants 1977-79; LA Rams 1979
Graves, Marsharne, T, Arizona, Denver 1984
Graves, Ray, C, Tennessee, Philadelphia 1942, 1946; Phil-Pitt 1943
Graves, Tom, LB, Michigan State, Pittsburgh 1979
Graves, White, DB, LSU, Boston 1965-67; Cincinnati 1968
Gray, Bill, G, Oregon State, Washington 1947-48
Gray, Dan, DE, Rutgers, Detroit 1978
Gray, Earnest, WR, Memphis State, NY Giants 1979-84; St. Louis 1985
Gray, Hector, CB, Florida State, Detroit 1981-83
Gray, Jack, E, Princeton, Green Bay 1923
Gray, Jerry, CB, Texas, LA Rams 1985
Gray, Jim, DB, Toledo, NY Jets 1966; Philadelphia 1967
Gray, Johnnie, S, Cal State-Fullerton, Green Bay 1975-84
Gray, Ken, G, Howard Payne, Chi. Cardinals 1958-59; St. Louis 1960-69; Houston 1970
Gray, Kevin, S, Eastern Illinois, New Orleans 1982
Gray, Leon, T, Jackson State, New England 1973-78; Houston 1979-81; New Orleans 1982-83
Gray, Mel, WR, Missouri, St. Louis 1971-82
Gray, Moses, T, Indiana, NY Titans 1961-62
Gray, Sam, E, Tulsa, Pittsburgh 1946-47
Gray, Tim, DB, Texas A&M, St. Louis 1975; Kansas City 1976-78; San Francisco 1979
Gray Horse, HB, Oorang 1923
Grayson, Dave, S, Oregon, Dallas Texans 1961-62; Kansas City 1963-64; Oakland 1965-70
Greaves, Gary, G, Miami, Houston 1960
Grecni, Dick, LB, Ohio U., Minnesota 1961
Greco, Don, G, Western Illinois, Detroit 1982-85
Green, Allen, K, Mississippi, Dallas Cowboys 1961
Green, Arthur, RB, Albany State, New Orleans 1972
Green, Bobby Joe, P, Florida, Pittsburgh 1960-61; Chi. Bears 1963-73
Green, Boyce, RB, Carson-Newman, Cleveland 1983-85
Green, Bubba, DT, North Carolina State, Baltimore 1981
Green, Charlie, QB, Wittenberg, Oakland 1966
Green, Cleveland, T, Southern, Miami 1979-85
Green, Cornell, CB, Utah State, Dallas 1962-74
Green, Curtis, DT-DE, Alabama State, Detroit 1981-85
Green, Darrell, CB, Texas A&I, Washington 1983-85
Green, Dave, P, Ohio U., Houston 1973; Cincinnati 1973-75; Tampa Bay 1976-78
Green, David, RB, Edinboro, Cleveland 1982
Green, Donnie, T, Purdue, Buffalo 1971-76; Philadelphia 1977; Detroit 1978
Green, Ernie, FB, Louisville, Cleveland 1962-68
Green, Gary, CB, Baylor, Kansas City 1977-83; LA Rams 1984-85
Green, Hugh, LB, Pittsburgh, Tampa Bay 1981-85; Miami 1985
Green, J.B.H., T, Louisville 1926
Green, Jacob, DE, Texas A&M, Seattle 1980-85
Green, Jerry, HB, Georgia Tech, Boston 1960
Green, Jessie, WR, Tulsa, Seattle 1979-80
Green, Joe, DB, Bowling Green, NY Giants 1970-71
Green, John, HB, Holy Cross, Milwaukee 1922
Green, Johnny, DE, Tulsa, Philadelphia 1947-51
Green, Johnny, QB, Tennessee-Chattanooga, Buffalo 1960-61; NY Titans 1962; NY Jets 1963
Green, Larry, E-G, Georgetown (Washington D.C.), Canton 1920
Green, Mike, LB, Oklahoma State, San Diego 1983-85
Green, Nelson, T, Tulsa, NY Yankees (AAFC) 1948
Green, Ron, FL, North Dakota, Cleveland 1967-68
Green, Roy, S-WR, Henderson State, St. Louis 1979-85
Green, Sammy, LB, Florida, Seattle 1976-79; Houston 1980
Green, Tony, KR-RB, Florida, Washington 1978; NY Giants 1979; Seattle 1979
Green, Van, DB, Shaw, Cleveland 1973-76; Buffalo 1976
Green, Woody, RB, Arizona State, Kansas City 1974-76
Greenberg, Ben, FB, Rutgers, Brooklyn 1930
Greene, Danny, WR, Washington, Seattle 1985
Greene, Doug, DB, Texas A&I, St. Louis 1978; Buffalo 1979-80
Greene, Ed, E, Loyola (Chicago), Chi. Cardinals 1926-27
Greene, Frank, QB, Tulsa, Chi. Cardinals 1934
Greene, George (Tiger), CB, Western Carolina, Atlanta 1985
Greene, Joe, DT, North Texas State, Pittsburgh 1969-81
Greene, John, E, Michigan, Detroit 1944-50
Greene, Ken, S, Washington State, St. Louis 1978-82; San Diego 1983-84
Greene, Kevin, LB, Auburn, LA Rams 1985
Greene, Marcellus, CB, Arizona, Minnesota 1984
Greene, Ted, LB, Tampa, Dallas Texans 1960-62
Greene, Tom, QB, Holy Cross, Boston 1960; Dallas Texans 1961
Greene, Tony, CB, Maryland, Buffalo 1971-79
Greeney, Norm, G, Notre Dame, Green Bay 1933; Pittsburgh 1934-35
Greenfield, Tom, C, Arizona, Green Bay 1939-41
Greenhalgh, Bob, FB, San Francisco, NY Giants 1949
Greenich, Harley, HB, Mississippi, Chi. Bears 1944
Greenlee, Fritz, LB, Arizona State, San Francisco 1969
Greenshields, Donn, T, Penn State, Brooklyn 1932-33
Greenwood, David, S, Wisconsin, Tampa Bay 1985
Greenwood, Don, QB, Missouri, Illinois, Cleveland 1945; Cleveland (AAFC) 1946-47
Greenwood, Glenn, HB-FB, Iowa, Chi. Bears 1924; Louisville 1926
Greenwood, L.C., DE, Arkansas-Pine Bluff, Pittsburgh 1969-81
Greer, Al, SE, Jackson State, Detroit 1963
Greer, Charlie, DB, Colorado, Denver 1968-74
Greer, Curtis, DE, Michigan, St. Louis 1980-85
Greer, Jim, SE, Elizabeth City State, Denver 1960
Grefe, Ted, E, Northwestern, Detroit 1945
Gregg, Ed, E, Kentucky, Louisville 1922
Gregg, Forrest, T-G, SMU, Green Bay 1956, 1958-70; Dallas 1971
Gregor, Bob, S, Washington State, San Diego 1981-84
Gregory, Ben, RB, Nebraska, Buffalo 1968
Gregory, Bill, DT-DE, Wisconsin, Dallas 1971-77; Seattle 1978-80
Gregory, Bruce, HB, Michigan, Detroit 1926
Gregory, Frank, HB-FB, Williams, Buffalo 1923-24
Gregory, Garland, G, Louisiana Tech, San Francisco (AAFC) 1946-47
Gregory, Glynn, SE, SMU, Dallas Cowboys 1961-62
Gregory, Jack, DE, Delta State, Cleveland 1967-71, 1979; NY Giants 1971-78
Gregory, John, G, Tennessee-Chattanooga, Cleveland 1941
Gregory, Ken, SE, Whittier, Baltimore 1961; Philadelphia 1962; NY Jets 1963
Gregory, Mike, G, Denison, Cleveland 1931
Gremminger, Henry, DB, Baylor, Green Bay 1956-65; LA Rams 1966
Gresham, Bob, RB, West Virginia, New Orleans 1971-72; Houston 1973-74; NY Jets 1975-76
Grgich, Visco, G-LB, Santa Clara, San Francisco 1946-52
Grier, Roosevelt (Rosey), DT, Penn State, NY Giants 1955-56, 1958-62; LA Rams 1963-66
Griese, Bob, QB, Purdue, Miami 1967-80
Griffen, Harold (Tubby), C, Iowa, Green Bay 1928; Portsmouth 1930, 1932
Griffin, Archie, RB, Ohio State, Cincinnati 1976-83
Griffin, Bob, G, Arkansas, LA Rams 1953-57; Denver 1961; St. Louis 1961
Griffin, Bobby, HB, Baylor, NY Yanks 1951
Griffin, Don, HB, Illinois, Chi. Rockets (AAFC) 1946
Griffin, James, S, Middle Tennessee State, Cincinnati 1983-85
Griffin, Jeff, CB, Utah, St. Louis 1981-85
Griffin, Jim, DE, Grambling, San Diego 1966-67; Cincinnati 1968
Griffin, John, DB, Memphis State, LA Rams 1963; Denver 1964-66
Griffin, Keith, RB-KR, Miami, Washington 1984-85
Griffin, Ray, CB, Ohio State, Cincinnati 1978-84
Griffin, Wade, T, Mississippi, Baltimore 1977-81
Griffing, Glynn, QB, Mississippi, NY Giants 1963
Griffith, Forrest, HB, Kansas, NY Giants 1950-51
Griffith, Homer, HB, USC, Chi. Cardinals 1934
Griffiths, Paul, G, Penn State, Canton 1921
Grigas, Johnny, HB, Holy Cross, Chi. Cardinals 1943; Card-Pitt 1944; Boston 1945-47
Grigg, Cecil (Tex), QB, Austin, Canton 1920-23; Rochester 1924-25; NY Giants 1926; Frankford 1927
Grigg, Forrest (Chubby), DT, Tulsa, Buffalo (AAFC) 1946; Chi. Rockets (AAFC) 1947; Cleveland 1948-51; Dallas 1952
Griggs, Anthony, LB, Ohio State, Philadelphia 1982-85
Griggs, Billy, TE, Virginia, NY Jets 1985
Griggs, Haldane, HB, Butler, Akron 1926
Griggs, Perry, KR, Troy State, Baltimore 1977
Grigonis, Frank, FB, Tennessee-Chattanooga, Detroit 1942
Grim, Bob, WR, Oregon, Minnesota 1967-71, 1976-77; NY Giants 1972-74; Chi. Bears 1975
Grimes, Billy, HB, Oklahoma State, LA Dons (AAFC) 1949; Green Bay 1950-52
Grimes, George, HB, Virginia, Detroit 1948
Grimes, Randy, C-G, Baylor, Tampa Bay 1983-85
Grimm, Dan, G, Colorado, Green Bay 1963, 1965; Atlanta 1966-68; Baltimore 1969; Washington 1969
Grimm, Russ, G, Pittsburgh, Washington 1981-85
Grimsley, John, LB, Kentucky, Houston 1984-85
Groce, Ron, RB, Macalester, Minnesota 1976
Grogan, Steve, QB, Kansas State, New England 1975-85
Groman, Bill, SE, Heidelberg, Houston 1960-62; Denver 1963; Buffalo 1964-65
Groom, Jerry, C, Notre Dame, Chi. Cardinals 1951-55
Groomes, Mel, HB, Indiana, Detroit 1948-49
Grooms, Elois, DE, Tennessee Tech, New Orleans 1975-81; St. Louis 1982-85
Gros, Earl, FB, LSU, Green Bay 1962-63; Philadelphia 1964-66; Pittsburgh 1967-69; New Orleans 1970
Gross, Al, S, Arizona, Cleveland 1983-85
Gross, Andy, G, Auburn, NY Giants 1967-68
Gross, George, DT, Auburn, San Diego 1963-67
Gross, Lee, C, Auburn, New Orleans 1975-77; Baltimore 1979
Grossart, Kyle, QB, Oregon State, NY Jets 1981
Grosscup, Lee, QB, Utah, NY Giants 1960-61; NY Titans 1962
Grossman, Jack, HB-FB, Rutgers, Brooklyn 1932, 1934-36
Grossman, Randy, TE, Temple, Pittsburgh 1974-81
Grossman, Rex, HB-K, Indiana, Baltimore (AAFC) 1948-49; Baltimore 1950; Detroit 1950
Grosvenor, George, HB, Colorado, Chi. Bears 1935-36; Chi. Cardinals 1936-37
Groth, Jeff, WR, Bowling Green, Miami 1979; Houston 1979-80; New Orleans 1981-85
Grottkau, Bob, G, Oregon, Detroit 1959-60; Dallas Cowboys 1961
Grove, Roger, HB, Michigan State, Green Bay 1931-35
Groves, George, G, Marquette, Buffalo (AAFC) 1947; Baltimore (AAFC) 1948
Groza, Lou (The Toe), T-K, Ohio State, Cleveland 1946-59, 1961-67
Grube, Charlie, E, Michigan, Detroit 1926
Grube, Frank, E, Lafayette, NY Yankees 1928
Gruber, Herb, E, Louisville 1921-23
Gruneisen, Sam, C, Villanova, San Diego 1962-72; Houston 1973
Grupp, Bob, P, Duke, Kansas City 1979-81
Gryco, Al, HB, South Carolina, Chi. Bears 1944-45
Guarnieri, Al, E, Canisius, Buffalo 1924; Canton 1925
Gucciardo, Pat, DB, Kent State, NY Jets 1966
Gudauskas, Pete (The Toe), G-K, Murray State, Cleveland 1940; Chi. Bears 1943-45
Gude, Henry, C-G, Vanderbilt, Philadelphia 1946
Gudmundson, Scott, QB, George Washington, Boston 1944-45
Guendling, Mike, LB, Northwestern, San Diego 1985
Gueno, Jim, LB, Tulane, Green Bay 1976-80
Guesman, Dick, DT, West Virginia, NY Titans 1960-62; NY Jets 1963; Denver 1964
Guffey, Roy, E, Oklahoma, Buffalo 1926
Guglielmi, Ralph, QB, Notre Dame, Washington 1955, 1958-60; St. Louis 1961; NY Giants 1962-63; Philadelphia 1963
Guidry, Paul, LB, McNeese State, Buffalo 1966-72; Houston 1973
Guigliano, Patsy, QB, Louisville 1923
Guilbeau, Rusty, LB, McNeese State, NY Jets 1982-85
Guillory, John, DB, Stanford, Cincinnati 1969-70
Guillory, Tony, LB-DE, Lamar, LA Rams 1965, 1967-69
Gulian, Mike, T, Brown, Buffalo 1923; Frankford 1924; Providence 1925-27
Gulseth, Don, LB, North Dakota, Denver 1966
Gulyanics, George, HB-P, Ellisville J.C., Chi. Bears 1947-52
Guman, Mike, RB, Penn State, LA Rams 1980-85
Gunderman, Bob, E, Virginia, Pittsburgh 1957

Gunderson, Hal, C, Rock Island 1920-21; Minneapolis 1921-23
Gundlach, Herman, G, Harvard, Boston 1935
Gunn, Jimmy, LB, USC, Chi. Bears 1970-75; NY Giants 1975; Tampa Bay 1976
Gunnels, Riley, DT, Georgia, Philadelphia 1960-64; Pittsburgh 1965-66
Gunner, Harry, DE, Oregon State, Cincinnati 1968-69; Chi. Bears 1970
Gunter, Greg, C, Nassau C.C., NY Jets 1985
Gunter, Michael, RB, Tulsa, Kansas City 1984
Gursky, Al, LB, Penn State, NY Giants 1963
Gussie, Mike, G, West Virginia, Brooklyn 1940
Gustafson, Ed, C, George Washington, Brooklyn (AAFC) 1947-48
Guthrie, Grant, K, Florida State, Buffalo 1970-71
Guthrie, Keith, NT, Texas A&M, San Diego 1984
Gutknecht, Al, G, Niagara, Brooklyn 1943; Cleveland 1944
Gutowsky, Leroy (Ace), FB, Oklahoma City, Portsmouth 1932-33; Detroit 1934-38; Brooklyn 1939
Gutteron, Bill, QB, Nevada-Reno, LA Buccaneers 1926
Guy, Buzz, G, Duke, NY Giants 1958-59; Dallas Cowboys 1960; Houston 1961; Denver 1961
Guy, Charlie, C-G-QB, Washington & Jefferson, Detroit 1920-21; Buffalo 1921-22; Cleveland 1923; Columbus 1925; Dayton 1925-26
Guy, Lou, DB-FL, Mississippi, NY Giants 1963; Oakland 1964
Guy, Ray, P, Southern Mississippi, Oakland 1973-81; LA Raiders 1982-85
Guyon, Joe, HB, Carlisle, Georgia Tech, Canton 1920; Cleveland 1921; Washington 1921; Oorang 1922-23; Rock Island 1924; Kansas City 1924-25; NY Giants 1927
Guzik, John, LB, Pittsburgh, LA Rams 1959-60; Houston 1961
Gwinn, Ross, G, Northwestern State (Louisiana), New Orleans 1968
Gwosden, Milo, E, Pittsburgh, Buffalo 1925

H

Haak, Bob, T, Indiana, Brooklyn 1939
Haas, Bob, HB, Purdue, Dayton 1929
Haas, Bruno, HB, Worcester, Cleveland 1921; Akron 1921
Hachten, Bill, G, Stanford, NY Giants 1947
Hackbart, Dale, S, Wisconsin, Green Bay 1960; Washington 1961-63; Minnesota 1966-70; St. Louis 1971-72; Denver 1973
Hackenbruck, Johnny, T, Oregon State, Detroit 1940
Hackney, Elmer, FB, Kansas State, Philadelphia 1940; Pittsburgh 1941; Detroit 1942-46
Hadden, Al, HB-FB, Washington & Jefferson, Cleveland 1925; Detroit 1925-26; Providence 1927-30; Chi. Bears 1928
Haddix, Michael, RB, Mississippi State, Philadelphia 1983-85
Haden, Jack, T, Arkansas, NY Giants 1936-38
Haden, Pat, QB-P, USC, LA Rams 1976-81
Hadl, John, QB-P, Kansas, San Diego 1962-72; LA Rams 1973-74; Green Bay 1974-75; Houston 1976-77
Hadley, David, CB, Alcorn State, Kansas City 1970-72
Hadnot, James, RB, Texas Tech, Kansas City 1980-83
Hafen, Barney, E, Utah, Detroit 1949-50
Haffner, George, QB, McNeese State, Baltimore 1965
Haffner, Mike, WR, UCLA, Denver 1968-70; Cincinnati 1971
Hagberg, Roger, FB, Minnesota, Oakland 1965-69
Hagberg, Rudolph (Swede), C, West Virginia, Buffalo 1929; Brooklyn 1930
Hageman, Fred, C, Kansas, Washington 1961-64
Hagen, Halvor, G, Weber State, Dallas 1969; New England 1971-72; Buffalo 1973-75
Hagenbuckle, Vern, E, Dartmouth, Providence 1926
Hagerty, Jack, HB-FB, Georgetown (Washington D.C.), NY Giants 1926-30, 1932
Hagerty, Loris (Horse), FB, Iowa, Brooklyn 1930
Haggerty, John, G, Tufts, Cleveland 1920; Canton 1920; NY Giants 1921
Haggerty, Mike, T, Miami, Pittsburgh 1967-70; New England 1971; Detroit 1973
Haggerty, Steve, DB, Nevada-Las Vegas, Denver 1975
Hagins, Isaac, WR, Southern, Tampa Bay 1976-80
Hagood, Rickey, NT, South Carolina, San Diego 1984
Hahn, Ray, E, Kansas State, Hammond 1926
Haik, Mac, WR, Mississippi, Houston 1968-71
Haines, By, HB, Washington, Pittsburgh 1937
Haines, Harry (Hoot), T, Colgate, Brooklyn 1930-31; Staten Island 1931
Haines, Hinkey, QB, Penn State, NY Giants 1925-28; Staten Island 1929, 1931
Haines, John, NT, Texas, Minnesota 1984
Haines, Kris, WR, Notre Dame, Washington 1979; Chi. Bears 1979-81
Hairston, Carl, DE, Maryland-Eastern Shore, Philadelphia 1976-83; Cleveland 1984-85
Hajek, Chuck, C, Northwestern, Philadelphia 1934
Haji-Sheikh, Ali, K, Michigan, NY Giants 1983-85
Halas, George, E, Illinois, Decatur 1920; Chi. Staleys 1921; Chi. Bears 1922-29
Hale, Dave, DE-DT, Ottawa (Kansas), Chi. Bears 1969-71
Haley, Art, HB, Akron, Canton 1920; Akron 1923
Haley, Darryl, T, Utah, New England 1982-84
Haley, Dick, DB, Pittsburgh, Washington 1959-60; Minnesota 1961; Pittsburgh 1961-64
Halicki, Eddie, HB-FB, Bucknell, Frankford 1929-30; Minneapolis 1930
Hall, Alvin, DB, LA Rams 1961-63
Hall, Alvin, CB-KR, Miami (Ohio), Detroit 1981-85
Hall, Charlie, LB, Houston, Cleveland 1971-80
Hall, Charlie, DB, Pittsburgh, Green Bay 1971-76
Hall, Dino, RB-KR, Glassboro State, Cleveland 1979-83
Hall, Forrest, HB, San Francisco, San Francisco (AAFC) 1948
Hall, Galen, QB, Penn State, Washington 1962; NY Jets 1963
Hall, Harold, C, Springfield, NY Giants 1942
Hall, Irv, HB, Brown, Philadelphia 1942
Hall, John, HB, TCU, Chi. Cardinals 1940-41, 1943; Detroit 1942
Hall, John, E, Iowa, NY Giants 1955
Hall, Ken, HB-KR, Texas A&M, Chi. Cardinals 1959; Houston 1960-61; St. Louis 1961
Hall, Parker, HB, Mississippi, Cleveland 1939-42; San Francisco (AAFC) 1946
Hall, Pete, E, Marquette, NY Giants 1961
Hall, Randy, CB, Idaho, Baltimore 1974, 1976
Hall, Ray, T, Illinois, NY Yankees 1927
Hall, Ron, DB, Missouri Valley, Pittsburgh 1959; Boston 1961-67
Hall, Tom, SE, Minnesota, Detroit 1962-63; Minnesota 1964-66, 1968-69; New Orleans 1967
Hall, Willie, LB, USC, New Orleans 1972-73; Oakland 1975-78
Hall, Windlan, S, Arizona State, San Francisco 1972-75; Minnesota 1976-77; Washington 1977
Halladay, Dick, E, Chicago, Racine 1922-24
Halleck, Neil, HB, Columbus 1924
Halliday, Jack, T, SMU, LA Rams 1951
Halloran, Clarence (Dimp), HB, Fordham, Hartford 1926
Hallquist, Stone, QB-G, Middlebury, Milwaukee 1926
Hallstrom, Ron, T-G, Iowa, Green Bay 1982-85
Halperin, Robert (Buck), QB, Notre Dame, Brooklyn 1932
Halpern, Willie, G-T, CCNY, Staten Island 1930
Halstrom, Bernie, HB-FB, Illinois, Chi. Cardinals 1920-21
Haluska, Jim, QB, Wisconsin, Chi. Bears 1956
Halverson, Bill, T, Oregon State, Philadelphia 1942
Halverson, Dean, LB, Washington, LA Rams 1968, 1971-72; Atlanta 1970; Philadelphia 1973-75
Ham, Jack, LB, Penn State, Pittsburgh 1971-82
Haman, Jack, C, Northwestern, Cleveland 1940-41
Hamas, Steve, FB-HB, Penn State, Orange 1929
Hambacher, Carl, HB, Bucknell, Orange 1929
Hamel, Dean, DT, Tulsa, Washington 1985
Hamer, Ernest (Tex), FB-HB-QB, Pennsylvania, Frankford 1924-28
Hamill, Ching, QB, Central Connecticut State, Providence 1925
Hamilton, Andy, WR, LSU, Kansas City 1973-74; New Orleans 1975
Hamilton, Harry, S, Penn State, NY Jets 1984-85
Hamilton, Ray (Sugar Bear), DT-NT, Oklahoma, New England 1973-81
Hamilton, Raymond, E, Arkansas, Cleveland 1938, 1944-45; Detroit 1939; LA Rams 1946-47
Hamilton, Steve, DE, East Carolina, Washington 1985
Hamilton, Wes, G, Tulsa, Minnesota 1976-84
Hamity, Lew, HB, Chicago, Chi. Bears 1941
Hamlin, Gene, C, Western Michigan, Washington 1970; Chi. Bears 1971; Detroit 1972
Hamm, Bob, DE, Nevada-Reno, Houston 1983-84; Kansas City 1985
Hammack, Mal, FB, Florida, Chi. Cardinals 1955, 1957-59; St. Louis 1960-66
Hammond, Bobby, RB-KR, Morgan State, NY Giants 1976-79; Washington 1979-80
Hammond, Gary, WR-KR, SMU, St. Louis 1973-76
Hammond, Henry, E, Southwestern (Memphis), Chi. Bears 1937
Hammond, Kim, QB, Florida State, Miami 1969; Boston 1969
Hammond, Wayne, DT, Montana State, Denver 1976
Hampton, Dan, DE-DT, Arkansas, Chi. Bears 1979-85
Hampton, Dave, RB, Wyoming, Green Bay 1969-71; Atlanta 1972-76; Philadelphia 1976
Hampton, Lorenzo, RB, Florida, Miami 1985
Hanburger, Chris, LB, North Carolina, Washington 1965-78
Hancock, Anthony, WR-KR, Tennessee, Kansas City 1982-85
Hancock, Mike, TE, Idaho State, Washington 1973-74
Hand, Larry, DE, Appalachian State, Detroit 1965-77
Handler, Phil, TCU, G, Chi. Cardinals 1930-36
Handley, Dick, C, Fresno State, Baltimore (AAFC) 1947
Hanke, Carl, E, Minnesota, Hammond 1921-23; Chi. Bears 1922; Chi. Cardinals 1924
Hanken, Ray, E, George Washington, NY Giants 1937-38
Hanley, Dick, HB, Washington State, Racine 1924
Hanley, Ed, HB, Case Western Reserve, Detroit 1920-21
Hanlon, Bob, HB, Loras, Chi. Cardinals 1948; Pittsburgh 1949
Hanna, Elzaphan (Zip), G, South Carolina, Washington 1945
Hannah, Charley, DE-T, Alabama, Tampa Bay 1977-82; LA Raiders 1983-85
Hannah, Herb, T, Alabama, NY Giants 1951
Hannah, John, G, Alabama, New England 1973-85
Hanneman, Chuck, E, Eastern Michigan, Detroit 1937-41; Cleveland 1941
Hanneman, Craig, DE-DT, Oregon State, Pittsburgh 1972-73; New England 1974-75
Hanner, Dave (Hawg), DT, Arkansas, Green Bay 1952-64
Hannon, Tommy, S, Michigan State, Minnesota 1977-84
Hannula, Jim, T, Northern Illinois, Cincinnati 1982-83
Hanny, Frank (Duke), E, Indiana, Chi. Bears 1923-27; Providence 1928-29; Portsmouth 1930; Green Bay 1930
Hanratty, Terry, QB, Notre Dame, Pittsburgh 1969-75; Tampa Bay 1976
Hanricus, Ralph, HB, Rochester 1922
Hansen, Brian, P, Sioux Falls, New Orleans 1984-85
Hansen, Cliff, HB, Luther, Chi. Cardinals 1933
Hansen, Dale, T, Michigan State, Detroit 1944, 1948-49
Hansen, Don, LB, Illinois, Minnesota 1966-67; Atlanta 1969-75; Seattle 1976; Green Bay 1976-77
Hansen, Ron, G, Minnesota, Washington 1954
Hansen, Roscoe, T, North Carolina, Philadelphia 1951
Hansen, Wayne, G, Texas-El Paso, Chi. Bears 1950-58; Dallas Cowboys 1960
Hanson, Dick, T, North Dakota State, NY Giants 1971
Hanson, Hal, G-T, South Dakota, Rock Island 1921
Hanson, Hal, G, Minnesota, Frankford 1928-30; Minneapolis 1930
Hanson, Homer, G, Kansas State, Cincinnati 1934; Philadelphia 1935; Chi. Cardinals 1935-36
Hanson, Ray, G-T, Ohio Wesleyan, Columbus 1923-24
Hanson, Roy, HB-QB, Rock Island 1921; Minneapolis 1923; Green Bay 1923
Hanson, Steve, E, Kansas City 1925; Louisville 1926
Hanson, Tom (Swede), FB-HB, Temple, Brooklyn 1931; Staten Island 1932; Philadelphia 1933-37; Pittsburgh 1938
Hantla, Bob, G, Kansas, San Francisco 1954-55
Hanulak, Chet (The Jet), HB, Maryland, Cleveland 1954, 1957
Hapes, Merle, HB, Mississippi, NY Giants 1942, 1946
Hardaway, Milton, T, Oklahoma State, San Diego 1978
Hardee, Billy, DB, Virginia Tech, Denver 1976; NY Jets 1977
Hardeman, Buddy, RB-KR, Iowa State, Washington 1979-80
Hardeman, Don, RB, Texas A&I, Houston 1975-77; Baltimore 1978-79
Harden, Lee, DB, Texas-El Paso, Green Bay 1970
Harden, Mike, S, Michigan, Denver 1980-85
Harder, Pat, FB-K, Wisconsin, Chi. Cardinals 1946-50; Detroit 1951-53
Harding, Greg, S, Nicholls State, New Orleans 1984
Harding, Roger, C, California, Cleveland 1945; LA Rams 1946; Philadelphia 1947; Detroit 1948; Green Bay 1949; NY Bulldogs 1949
Hardison, Dee, DT, North Carolina, Buffalo 1978-80; NY Giants 1981-85
Hardman, Cedrick, DE, North Texas State, San Francisco 1970-79; Oakland 1980-81
Hardy, Andre, RB-KR, St. Mary's (California), Philadelphia 1984; Seattle 1985
Hardy, Bruce, TE, Arizona State, Miami 1978-85
Hardy, Carroll, HB, Colorado, San Francisco 1955
Hardy, Charley, SE, San Jose State, Oakland 1960-62
Hardy, Cliff, CB, Michigan State, Chi. Bears 1971
Hardy, Dick, T, Boston College, Racine 1926
Hardy, Edgar, G, Jackson State, San Francisco 1973
Hardy, Isham, G, William & Mary, Akron 1923
Hardy, Jim, QB, USC, LA Rams 1946-48; Chi. Cardinals 1949-51; Detroit 1952
Hardy, John, FB, Haskell, Akron 1926
Hardy, Kevin, DE-DT, Notre Dame, San Francisco 1968; Green Bay 1970; San Diego 1971-72
Hardy, Larry, TE, Jackson State, New Orleans 1978-85
Hardy, Robert, DT, Jackson State, Seattle 1979-82
Hare, Cecil, HB, Gonzaga, Washington 1941-42, 1945; NY Giants 1946
Hare, Eddie, P, Tulsa, New England 1979
Hare, Ray, QB, Gonzaga, Washington 1940-43; Brooklyn 1944; NY Yankees (AAFC) 1946
Hargett, Edd, QB, Texas A&M, New Orleans 1969-72
Hargrove, Jim, LB, Howard Payne, Minnesota 1967, 1969-70; St. Louis 1971-72
Hargrove, Jim, RB, Wake Forest, Cincinnati 1981
Harkey, Lem, FB, Emporia State, San Francisco 1955; Pittsburgh 1955
Harkey, Steve, RB, Georgia Tech, NY Jets 1971-72
Harlan, Jim, T-C, Howard Payne, Washington 1978
Harlan, Julian, HB, Hammond 1922
Harley, Chick, HB, Ohio State, Chi. Staleys 1921
Harmon, Clarence, RB, Mississippi State, Washington 1977-82
Harmon, Derrick, RB, Cornell, San Francisco 1984-85
Harmon, Ed, LB, Louisville, Cincinnati 1969
Harmon, Ham, C, Tulsa, Chi. Cardinals 1937
Harmon, Mike, WR-KR, Mississippi, NY Jets 1983
Harmon, Tom, HB, Michigan, LA Rams 1946-47
Harmon, Tom, G, Gustavus Adolphus, Atlanta 1967
Harms, Art, T, Vermont, Frankford 1925; NY Giants 1926
Harness, Jim, DB, Mississippi State, Baltimore 1956
Harold, George, DB, Allen, Baltimore 1966-67; Washington 1968
Harper, Bruce, RB-KR, Kutztown, NY Jets 1977-84
Harper, Charlie, G-T, Oklahoma State, NY Giants 1966-72
Harper, Darrell, HB, Michigan State, Buffalo 1960
Harper, Jack, HB, Florida, Miami 1967-68
Harper, John, LB, Southern Illinois, Atlanta 1983
Harper, Maurice (Moose), C, Austin, Philadelphia 1937-40; Pittsburgh 1940
Harper, Ray, HB, Indiana, Louisville 1921

Harper, Roland, RB, Louisiana Tech, Chi. Bears 1975-78, 1980-82
Harper, Willie, LB, Nebraska, San Francisco 1973-77, 1979-83
Harrah, Dennis, G, Miami, LA Rams 1975-85
Harraway, Charley, RB, San Jose State, Cleveland 1966-68; Washington 1969-73
Harrell, James, LB, Florida, Detroit 1979-83, 1985
Harrell, Rick, C, Clemson, NY Jets 1973
Harrell, Sam, RB, East Carolina, Minnesota 1981-82
Harrell, Willard, RB-KR, Pacific, Green Bay 1975-77; St. Louis 1978-84
Harrington, John, E, Marquette, Cleveland (AAFC) 1946; Chi. Rockets (AAFC) 1947
Harrington, LaRue, RB, Norfolk State, San Diego 1980
Harrington, Perry, RB, Jackson State, Philadelphia 1980-83; St. Louis 1984-85
Harris, Al, DE-LB, Arizona State, Chi. Bears 1979-84
Harris, Amos, G, Mississippi State, Brooklyn (AAFC) 1947-48
Harris, Bill, E, Hardin-Simmons, Pittsburgh 1937
Harris, Bill, RB, Colorado, Atlanta 1968; Minnesota 1969; New Orleans 1971
Harris, Bo, LB, LSU, Cincinnati 1975-82
Harris, Bob, LB, Auburn, St. Louis 1983-85
Harris, Cliff, S, Ouachita Baptist, Dallas 1970-79
Harris, Dick, S, McNeese State, LA Chargers 1960; San Diego 1961-65
Harris, Don, DB, Rutgers, Washington 1978-79; NY Giants 1980
Harris, Dud, T, Marietta, Portsmouth 1930; Brooklyn 1930
Harris, Duriel, WR, New Mexico State, Miami 1976-83, 1985; Dallas 1984; Cleveland 1984
Harris, Elmore, HB, Morgan State, Brooklyn (AAFC) 1947
Harris, Eric, CB, Memphis State, Kansas City 1980-82; LA Rams 1983-85
Harris, Franco, RB, Penn State, Pittsburgh 1972-83; Seattle 1984
Harris, George, T, Louisville, Louisville 1921
Harris, Hank, G, Texas, Washington 1947-48
Harris, Harry, QB, West Virginia, Akron 1920
Harris, Ike, WR, Iowa State, St. Louis 1975-77; New Orleans 1978-81
Harris, James, QB, Grambling, Buffalo 1969-71; LA Rams 1973-76; San Diego 1977-81
Harris, Jim, DT, Utah State, NY Jets 1965-67
Harris, Jim, DB, Howard Payne, Washington 1970
Harris, Jimmy, DB, Oklahoma, Philadelphia 1957, LA Rams 1958; Dallas Texans 1960; Dallas Cowboys 1961
Harris, Joe, LB, Georgia Tech, Washington 1977; San Francisco 1978; Minnesota 1979; LA Rams 1979-81; Baltimore 1982
Harris, John (Soldier), FB, Hartford 1926
Harris, John, DB, Santa Monica J.C., Oakland 1960-61
Harris, John, S, Arizona State, Seattle 1978-85
Harris, Ken (Bunk), FB, Syracuse, Duluth 1923-24
Harris, Larry, T, Oklahoma State, Houston 1978
Harris, Leotis, G, Arkansas, Green Bay 1978-83
Harris, Leroy, RB, Arkansas State, Miami 1977-78; Philadelphia 1979-82
Harris, Lou, DB, Kent State, Pittsburgh 1968
Harris, M.L., TE, Kansas State, Cincinnati 1980-85
Harris, Marshall, DE-NT, TCU, Cleveland 1980-82; New England 1983
Harris, Marv, LB, Stanford, LA Rams 1964
Harris, Ollie, E, Geneva, NY Giants 1926
Harris, Paul, LB, Alabama, Tampa Bay 1977-78; Minnesota 1978
Harris, Phil, DB, Texas, NY Giants 1966
Harris, Richard, DE, Grambling, Philadelphia 1971-73; Chi. Bears 1974-75; Seattle 1976-77
Harris, Rickie, DB-KR, Arizona, Washington 1965-70; New England 1971-72
Harris, Roy, DT, Florida, Atlanta 1984-85
Harris, Tim, RB-KR, Washington State, Pittsburgh 1983
Harris, Tony, WR, Toledo, San Francisco 1971
Harris, Welton (Jack), FB-E, Wisconsin, Green Bay 1925-26
Harris, Wendell, DB, LSU, Baltimore 1962-65; NY Giants 1966-67
Harrison, Bob, LB, Oklahoma, San Francisco 1959-61, 1965-67; Philadelphia 1962-63; Pittsburgh 1964
Harrison, Bob, DB, Ohio U., Baltimore 1961
Harrison, Dennis, DE, Vanderbilt, Philadelphia 1978-84; LA Rams 1985
Harrison, Dick, E, Boston College, Boston 1944
Harrison, Dwight, WR-DB, Texas A&I, Denver 1971-72; Buffalo 1972-77; Baltimore 1978; Oakland 1979-80
Harrison, Ed, E, Boston College, Brooklyn 1926
Harrison, Glynn, RB, Georgia, Kansas City 1976
Harrison, Granville, E, Mississippi State, Philadelphia 1941; Detroit 1942
Harrison, Jim, FB, Missouri, Chi. Bears 1971-74
Harrison, Kenny, WR, SMU, San Francisco 1976-79; Washington 1980
Harrison, Max, E, Auburn, NY Giants 1940
Harrison, Pat, T, Howard (Alabama), Brooklyn 1937
Harrison, Reggie, RB, Cincinnati, St. Louis 1974; Pittsburgh 1974-77; Green Bay 1978
Hart, Ben, DB, Oklahoma, New Orleans 1967
Hart, Dick, G, Philadelphia 1967-70; Buffalo 1972
Hart, Doug, DB, Texas-Arlington, Green Bay 1964-71
Hart, Harold, DB-KR, Texas Southern, Oakland 1974-75, 1978; NY Giants 1977
Hart, Jeff, T, Oregon State, San Francisco 1975; New Orleans 1976; Baltimore 1979-83
Hart, Jim, QB, Southern Illinois, St. Louis 1966-83; Washington 1984
Hart, Leo, QB, Duke, Atlanta 1971; Buffalo 1972
Hart, Leon, E-FB, Notre Dame, Detroit 1950-57
Hart, Les, QB, Colgate, Staten Island 1931
Hart, Pete, FB, Hardin-Simmons, NY Titans 1960
Hart, Tommy, DE, Morris Brown, San Francisco 1968-77; Chi. Bears 1978-79
Hartenstine, Mike, DE, Penn State, Chi. Bears 1975-85
Hartle, Greg, LB, Newberry, St. Louis 1974-76
Hartley, Howard, DB, Duke, Washington 1948; Pittsburgh 1949-52
Hartley, Ken, P, Catawba, New England 1981
Hartman, Bill, QB, Georgia, Washington 1938
Hartman, Fred, T, Rice, Chi. Bears 1947; Philadelphia 1948
Hartman, Jim, E, Colorado State, Brooklyn 1938
Hartnett, Perry, G, SMU, Chi. Bears 1982-83
Hartong, George, G-T, Chicago, Hammond 1921; Racine 1923; Chi. Cardinals 1924
Hartshorn, Larry, G, Kansas State, Chi. Cardinals 1955
Hartwig, Carter, S, USC, Houston 1979-84
Hartwig, Keith, WR, Arizona, Minnesota 1977; Green Bay 1977
Harty, John, NT-DE, Iowa, San Francisco 1981-83, 1985
Hartzog, Howard (Bug), T, Baylor, NY Giants 1928
Harvey, Claude, LB, Prairie View A&M, Houston 1970
Harvey, George, G, Kansas, New Orleans 1967
Harvey, Jim, T-G, Mississippi, Oakland 1966-71
Harvey, Marvin, TE, Southern Mississippi, Kansas City 1981
Harvey, Maurice, S, Ball State, Denver 1978, 1980; Green Bay 1981-83; Detroit 1983; Tampa Bay 1984
Harvey, Norm, T-E, Detroit, Buffalo 1925, 1927; Detroit 1926; NY Yankees 1927; Providence 1928-29
Harvey, Richard, DB, Jackson State, Philadelphia 1970; New Orleans 1971
Harvey, Waddy, T, Virginia Tech, Buffalo 1969-70
Hasbrouck, John (Ziggy), FB-HB, Rutgers, Rock Island 1921; Rochester 1921
Hasenohrl, George, T, Ohio State, NY Giants 1974
Haslerig, Clint, RB, Michigan, Chi. Bears 1974; Buffalo 1975; Minnesota 1975; NY Jets 1976
Haslett, Jim, LB, Indiana (Pennsylvania), Buffalo 1979-85
Haslip, Wilbert, RB, Hawaii, Kansas City 1979
Hasselbeck, Don, TE, Colorado, New England 1977-83; LA Raiders 1983; Minnesota 1984; NY Giants 1985
Hastings, Bill, T, Ohio U., Portsmouth 1930-31
Hastings, Charlie, HB, Pittsburgh, Cleveland 1920
Hatcher, Dale, P, Clemson, LA Rams 1985
Hatcher, Ron, FB, Michigan State, Washington 1962
Hatchett, Derrick, CB, Texas, Baltimore 1980-83; Houston 1983
Hathaway, Russ, T, Indiana, Muncie 1920, Dayton 1920-24, Canton 1922; Pottsville 1925-26; Buffalo 1927
Hathaway, Steve, LB, West Virginia, Indianapolis 1984
Hathcock, Dave, DB, Memphis State, Green Bay 1966; NY Giants 1967
Hatley, Johnny Ray, G, Sul Ross, Chi. Bears 1953; Chi. Cardinals 1954-55; Denver 1960
Hauptly, Joe, G, Pottsville 1925
Hauser, Art, G, Xavier, LA Rams 1954-57; Chi Cardinals 1959; NY Giants 1959; Boston 1960; Denver 1961
Hauser, Earl, T-E, Miami (Ohio), Dayton 1920; Cincinnati 1921; Louisville 1921
Hauser, Ken, FB, Washington & Jefferson, Buffalo 1927; Newark 1930
Hauss, Len, C, Georgia, Washington 1964-77
Haven, John, E, Hamline, Duluth 1923
Havens, Charlie, C, Western Maryland, Frankford 1930
Haverdick, Dave, DT, Morehead State, Detroit 1970
Havig, Dennis, G, Colorado, Atlanta 1972-75; Houston 1976; Green Bay 1977
Havrilak, Sam, QB-RB-WR, Bucknell, Baltimore 1969-73; New Orleans 1974
Hawk, Joe, G, Columbus 1920
Hawkins, Alex, SE-HB, South Carolina, Baltimore 1956-65, 1967-68; Atlanta 1966-67
Hawkins, Andy, LB, Texas A&I, Tampa Bay 1980-83
Hawkins, Ben, WR, Arizona State, Philadelphia 1966-73; Cleveland 1974
Hawkins, Clarence, RB, Florida A&M, Oakland 1979
Hawkins, Frank, RB, Nevada-Reno, Oakland 1981; LA Raiders 1982-85
Hawkins, John, T, USC, LA Buccaneers 1926
Hawkins, Mike, LB, Texas A&I, New England 1978-81; LA Raiders 1982
Hawkins, Nate, WR, Nevada-Las Vegas, Houston 1975
Hawkins, Rip, LB, North Carolina, Minnesota 1961-65
Hawkins, Wayne, G, Pacific, Oakland 1960-69
Haworth, Steve, S, Oklahoma, Atlanta 1983-84
Haws, Harvey, QB, Dartmouth, Frankford 1924-25
Hawthorne, Greg, RB-WR, Pittsburgh 1979-83; New England 1984-85
Hayden, Ken, C, Arkansas, Philadelphia 1942; Washington 1943
Hayden, Leo, RB, Ohio State, Minnesota 1971; St. Louis 1972-73
Hayduk, Henry, G, Washington State, Pittsburgh 1935; Brooklyn 1935
Hayes, Billie, CB, San Diego State, New Orleans 1972
Hayes, Bob, WR-KR, Florida A&M, Dallas 1965-74; San Francisco 1975
Hayes, Dave, E, Notre Dame, Green Bay 1921-22
Hayes, Dick, LB, Clemson, Pittsburgh 1959-60, 1962
Hayes, Ed, DB, Morgan State, Philadelphia 1970
Hayes, Gary, CB, Fresno State, Green Bay 1984-85
Hayes, Jeff, P, North Carolina, Washington 1982-85
Hayes, Jerry, E, Notre Dame, Rock Island 1921
Hayes, Jim, DT, Jackson State, Houston 1965-66
Hayes, Joe, WR-KR, Central State (Oklahoma), Philadelphia 1984
Hayes, Jonathon, TE, Iowa, Kansas City 1985
Hayes, Larry, LB, Vanderbilt, NY Giants 1961; LA Rams 1962-63
Hayes, Lester, CB, Texas A&M, Oakland 1977-81; LA Raiders 1982-85
Hayes, Luther, DE, USC, San Diego 1961
Hayes, Norb, E, Marquette, Racine 1922; Green Bay 1923
Hayes, Ray, FB, Central State (Oklahoma), Minnesota 1961
Hayes, Ray, DT, Toledo, NY Jets 1968
Hayes, Rudy, LB, Clemson, Pittsburgh 1959-60, 1962
Hayes, Tom, CB, San Diego State, Atlanta 1971-75; San Diego 1976
Hayes, Wendell, RB, Cal State-Humboldt, Dallas 1963; Denver 1965-67; Kansas City 1968-74
Hayhoe, Bill, T, USC, Green Bay 1969-73
Hayman, Conway, G, Delaware, Houston 1975-80
Hayman, Gary, RB, Penn State, Buffalo 1974-75
Haymond, Alvin, DB-KR, Southern, Baltimore 1964-67; Philadelphia 1968; LA Rams 1969-71; Washington 1972; Houston 1973
Haynes, Abner, HB-FL, North Texas State, Dallas Texans 1960-62; Kansas City 1963-64; Denver 1965-66; Miami 1967; NY Jets 1967
Haynes, Hall, HB, Santa Clara, Washington 1950, 1953; LA Rams 1954-55
Haynes, James, Mississippi Valley State, New Orleans 1984-85
Haynes, Joe, C-G, Tulsa, Buffalo (AAFC) 1947
Haynes, Louis, LB, North Texas State, Kansas City 1982-83
Haynes, Mark, CB, Colorado, NY Giants 1980-85
Haynes, Mike, CB, Arizona State, New England 1976-82; LA Raiders 1983-85
Haynes, Reggie, TE, Nevada-Las Vegas, Washington 1978
Hays, George, DE, St. Bonaventure, Pittsburgh 1950-52; Green Bay 1953
Hays, Harold, LB, Southern Mississippi, Dallas 1963-67; San Francisco 1968-69
Haywood, Al, RB, Bethune-Cookman, Denver 1975
Hazelhurst, Bob, HB, Denver, Boston 1948
Hazeltine, Matt, LB, California, San Francisco 1955-68; NY Giants 1970
Hazelton, Major, DB, Florida A&M, Chi. Bears 1968-69; New Orleans 1970
Hazelwood, Ted, T, North Carolina, Chi. Hornets (AAFC) 1949; Washington 1953
Headen, Andy, LB, Clemson, NY Giants 1983-85
Headrick, Sherrill, LB, TCU, Dallas Texans 1960-62; Kansas City 1963-67; Cincinnati 1968
Healy, Chip, LB, Vanderbilt, St. Louis 1969
Healy, Don, T, Maryland, Chi. Bears 1958-59; Dallas Cowboys 1960-61; Buffalo 1962
Healy, Ed, T, Dartmouth, Rock Island 1920-22; Chi. Bears 1922-27
Heap, Joe, HB, Notre Dame, NY Giants 1955
Heap, Walt, HB, Texas, LA Dons (AAFC) 1947-48
Heard, Herman, RB, Southern Colorado, Kansas City 1984-85
Hearden, Len, HB, Ripon, Green Bay 1924
Hearden, Tom (Red), HB, Notre Dame, Green Bay 1927-28; Chi. Bears 1929
Heater, Don, RB, Montana Tech, St. Louis 1972
Heater, Larry, RB, Arizona, NY Giants 1980-83
Heater, William (Red), T, Syracuse, Brooklyn 1940
Heath, Clayton, RB, Wake Forest, Buffalo 1976; Miami 1976
Heath, Jo Jo, CB, Pittsburgh, Cincinnati 1980; Philadelphia 1981
Heath, Stan, QB, Nevada-Reno, Green Bay 1949
Hebert, Bobby, QB, Northwestern State (Louisiana), New Orleans 1985
Hebert, Bud, S, Oklahoma, NY Giants 1980
Hebert, Ken, P, Houston, Pittsburgh 1968
Hecht, Al, G, Alabama, Chi. Rockets (AAFC) 1947
Heck, Bob, E, Purdue, Chi. Hornets (AAFC) 1949
Heck, Ralph, LB, Colorado, Philadelphia 1963-65; Atlanta 1966-68; NY Giants 1969-71
Heckard, Steve, SE, Davidson, LA Rams 1965-66
Hecker, Norb, DB, Baldwin-Wallace, LA Rams 1951-53; Washington 1955-57
Hector, Johnny, RB, Texas A&M, NY Jets 1983-85
Hector, Willie, T, Pacific, LA Rams 1961
Hedberg, Randy, QB, Minot State, Tampa Bay 1977
Heenan, Pat, SE-DB, Notre Dame, Washington 1960
Heeter, Gene, TE, West Virginia, NY Jets 1963-65
Heflin, Victor, CB, Delaware State, St. Louis 1982-84
Heflin, Vince, WR, Central State (Ohio), Miami 1982-85
Hefner, Larry, LB, Clemson, Green Bay 1972-75
Hegarty, Bill, T, Villanova, Pittsburgh 1953; Washington 1953

Hegman, Mike, LB, Tennessee State, Dallas 1976-85
Heidel, Jimmy, DB, Mississippi, St. Louis 1966; New Orleans 1967
Heikkenen, Ralph, G, Michigan, Brooklyn 1939
Heileman, Charlie, E, Iowa State, Chi. Bears 1939
Heimkreiter, Steve, LB, Notre Dame, Baltimore 1980
Heimsch, John, FB, Marquette, Milwaukee 1926
Hein, Bob, E, Kent State, Brooklyn (AAFC) 1947
Hein, Mel, C, Washington State, NY Giants 1931-45
Heineman, Ken, HB, Texas-El Paso, Cleveland 1940-41; Brooklyn 1943
Heinisch, Fred, QB, Loras, Racine 1923-24, 1926; Kenosha 1924
Heinlein, Pete, G, Rochester 1920
Heinrich, Don, QB, Washington, NY Giants 1954-59; Dallas Cowboys 1960; Oakland 1962
Heinz, Bob, DT, Pacific, Miami 1969-74, 1976-77; Washington 1978
Hekkers, George, T, Wisconsin, Miami (AAFC) 1946; Baltimore (AAFC) 1947; Detroit 1947-49
Held, Paul, QB, San Jose State, Pittsburgh 1954; Green Bay 1955
Heldt, Carl, T, Purdue, Brooklyn 1935-36
Heldt, John, C, Iowa, Columbus 1923, 1926
Heller, Ron, T, Penn State, Tampa Bay 1984-85
Heller, Warren, HB, Pittsburgh, Pittsburgh 1934-36
Hellestrae, Dale, T, SMU, Buffalo 1985
Hellium, Jerry, DT, Tulane, Cleveland 1952-53; Green Bay 1954-57; Houston 1960
Helms, Jack, E, Georgia Tech, Detroit 1946
Helton, Darius, G, North Carolina Central, Kansas City 1977
Helvie, Chuck, E, Purdue, Muncie 1920-21; Dayton 1920
Helwig, John, G, Notre Dame, Chi. Bears 1953-56
Hempel, Bill, T, Carroll (Wisconsin), Chi. Bears 1942
Hemphill, Darryl, S, West Texas State, Baltimore 1982
Hendershot, Larry, LB, Arizona State, Washington 1967
Henderson, Herb, FB, Ohio State, Evansville 1921-22
Henderson, John, WR, Michigan, Detroit 1965-67; Minnesota 1968-72
Henderson, Jon, WR, Colorado State, Pittsburgh 1968-69; Washington 1970
Henderson, Reuben, CB, San Diego State, Chi. Bears 1981-82; San Diego 1983-84
Henderson, Thomas (Hollywood), LB, Langston, Dallas 1975-79; San Francisco 1980; Houston 1980
Henderson, Wyatt, WR, Fresno State, San Diego 1981
Henderson, Zac, S, Oklahoma, Philadelphia 1980
Hendley, Dick, QB, Clemson, Pittsburgh 1951
Hendren, Bob, T, USC, Washington 1949-51
Hendren, Jerry, WR, Idaho, Denver 1970
Hendren, John, FB, Bucknell, Canton 1920; Cleveland 1921
Hendrian, Oscar (Dutch), QB, Detroit, Canton 1922; Akron 1923; Green Bay 1924; Rock Island 1925; NY Giants 1925
Hendricks, Ted, LB, Miami, Baltimore 1969-73; Green Bay 1974; Oakland 1975-81; LA Raiders 1982-83
Hendy, John, CB, Long Beach State, San Diego 1985
Henke, Ed, DE, USC, LA Dons (AAFC) 1949; San Francisco 1951-53, 1956-60; St. Louis 1961-63
Henke, Karl, DT, Tulsa, NY Jets 1968; Boston 1969
Henley, Carey, RB, Tennessee-Chattanooga, Buffalo 1962
Hennessey, Jerry, DE, Santa Clara, Chi. Cardinals 1950-51; Washington 1952-53
Hennessey, Tom, DB, Holy Cross, Boston 1965-66
Hennessy, John, DE-LB, Michigan, NY Jets 1977-78
Hennigan, Charley, SE, Northwestern State (Louisiana), Houston 1960-66
Hennigan, Mike, LB, Tennessee Tech, Detroit 1973-75; NY Jets 1976-78
Henning, Dan, QB, William & Mary, San Diego 1966
Henry, Bernard, WR, Arizona State, Baltimore 1982-83; Indianapolis 1984-85
Henry, Fritz, G, Akron 1925
Henry, Jack, T, Staten Island 1932
Henry, Mike (Tarzan), LB, USC, Pittsburgh 1959-61; LA Rams 1962-64
Henry, Steve, DB, Emporia State, St. Louis 1979-80; Baltimore 1981
Henry, Tom, HB, Rock Island 1920
Henry, Urban, DT, Georgia Tech, LA Rams 1961; Green Bay 1963; Pittsburgh 1964
Henry, Wally, WR-KR, UCLA, Philadelphia 1977-82
Henry, Wilbur (Pete), T, Washington & Jefferson, Canton 1920-23, 1925-26; NY Giants 1927; Pottsville 1927-28
Hensley, Dick, E, Kentucky, NY Giants 1949; Pittsburgh 1952; Chi. Bears 1953
Henson, Gary, DE, Colorado, Philadelphia 1963
Henson, Harold (Champ), RB, Ohio State, Cincinnati 1975
Henson, Ken, C, TCU, Pittsburgh 1965
Henson, Luther, NT, Ohio State, New England 1982-84
Hepburn, Lonnie, CB, Texas Southern, Baltimore 1971-72; Denver 1974
Herber, Arnie, HB-QB, Regis, Green Bay 1930-40; NY Giants 1944-45
Herchman, Bill, DT, Texas Tech, San Francisco 1956-59; Dallas Cowboys 1960-61; Houston 1962
Hergert, Joe, LB, Florida, Buffalo 1960-61
Herkenhoff, Matt, T, Minnesota, Kansas City 1976-85
Herman, B.L., QB, West Chester, Philadelphia 1951
Herman, Chuck, G, Arkansas, Atlanta 1980
Herman, Dave, G, Michigan State, NY Jets 1964-73
Herman, Dick, LB, Florida State, Oakland 1965
Herman, Ed, Northwestern, Rock Island 1925
Hermann, John, DB, UCLA, NY Giants 1956; Baltimore 1956
Hermeling, Terry, T, Nevada-Reno, Washington 1970-73, 1975-80
Hernandez, Joe, FL, Arizona, Washington 1964
Hernandez, Matt, T, Purdue, Seattle 1983; Minnesota 1984
Herndon, Don, HB, Tampa, NY Titans 1960
Herock, Ken, TE, West Virginia, Oakland 1963-67; Cincinnati 1968; Boston 1969
Heron, Fred, DT, San Jose State, St. Louis 1966-72
Herosian, Brian, S, Connecticut, Baltimore 1973
Herrera, Efren, K, UCLA, Dallas, 1974, 1976-77; Seattle 1978-81; Buffalo 1982
Herrin, Houston, G, St. Mary's (California), Cleveland 1931
Herring, George, QB, Southern Mississippi, Denver 1960-61
Herring, Hal, C, Auburn, Buffalo (AAFC) 1949; Cleveland 1950-52
Herrmann, Don, WR, Waynesburg, NY Giants 1969-74; New Orleans 1975-77
Herrmann, Mark, QB, Purdue, Denver 1981-82; Baltimore 1983; Indianapolis 1984; San Diego 1985
Herron, Bruce, LB, New Mexico, Chi. Bears 1978-82
Herron, Mack, RB-KR, Kansas State, New England 1973-75; Atlanta 1975
Herron, Pat, E, Pittsburgh, Cleveland 1920
Hershey, Kirk, E, Cornell, Philadelphia 1941; Cleveland 1941
Hertel, Rob, QB, USC, Cincinnati 1978; Philadelphia 1980
Hertwig, Craig, T, Georgia, Detroit 1975-77
Hertz, Frank, E, Carroll (Wisconsin), Milwaukee 1926
Hess, Wally, FB, Indiana, Hammond 1920-25; Kenosha 1924
Hester, Jessie, WR, Florida State, LA Raiders 1985
Hester, Jim, TE, North Dakota, New Orleans 1967-69; Chi. Bears 1970
Hester, Ray, LB, Tulane, New Orleans 1971-73
Hester, Ron, LB, Florida State, Miami 1982
Hettema, Dave, T, New Mexico, San Francisco 1967; Atlanta 1970
Hewitt, Bill, E, Michigan, Chi. Bears 1932-36; Philadelphia 1937-39; Phil-Pitt 1943
Hewko, Bob, QB, Florida, Tampa Bay 1983
Hews, Bob, T, Princeton, Buffalo 1971
Heywood, Ralph, E, USC, Chi. Rockets (AAFC) 1946; Detroit 1947; Boston 1948; NY Bulldogs 1949
Hibbs, Jesse, T, USC, Chi. Bears 1931
Hibler, Mike, LB, Stanford, Cincinnati 1968
Hickerson, Gene, G, Mississippi, Cleveland 1959-60, 1962-73
Hickey, Bo, RB, Maryland, Denver 1967
Hickey, Howard (Red), E, Arkansas, Pittsburgh 1941; Cleveland 1942, 1945; LA Rams 1946-48
Hickl, Ray, LB, Texas A&I, NY Giants 1969
Hickman, Dallas, DE, California, Washington 1976-81; Baltimore 1981
Hickman, Donnie, G, USC, Washington 1978; Detroit 1978
Hickman, Herman, G, Tennessee, Brooklyn 1932-34
Hickman, Larry, FB, Baylor, Chi. Cardinals 1959; Green Bay 1960
Hicks, Bryan, S, McNeese State, Cincinnati 1980-82
Hicks, Dwight, S, Michigan, San Francisco 1979-85
Hicks, Eddie, RB, East Carolina, NY Giants 1979-80
Hicks, John, G, Ohio State, NY Giants 1974-77
Hicks, Mark, LB, Arizona State, Seattle 1983
Hicks, R.W., C, Cal State-Humboldt, Detroit 1975
Hicks, Sylvester, DT, Tennessee State, Kansas City 1978-81
Hicks, Tom, LB, Illinois, Chi. Bears 1976-80
Hicks, Victor, TE, Oklahoma, LA Rams 1980
Hicks, W.K., DB, Texas Southern, Houston 1964-69; NY Jets 1970-72
Hiemstra, Ed, G, Sterling, NY Giants 1942
Higgins, Austin, C, Louisville 1921-23
Higgins, Bob, E, Penn State, Canton 1920-21
Higgins, Jim, G, Xavier, Miami 1966
Higgins, John, G, Trinity (Texas), Chi. Cardinals 1941
Higgins, Luke, G, Notre Dame, Baltimore (AAFC) 1947
Higgins, Paul, HB, Brown, Providence 1925
Higgins, Tom, T, North Carolina, Chi. Cardinals 1953; Philadelphia 1954-55
Higgins, Tom, LB, North Carolina State, Buffalo 1979
High, Len, E, Decatur 1920
Highsmith, Don, RB, Michigan State, Oakland 1970-72; Green Bay 1973
Highsmith, Walt, G-T, Florida A&M, Denver 1968-69; Houston 1972
Hightower, Ben, E, Sam Houston State, Cleveland 1942; Detroit 1943
Hilgenberg, Jay, C, Iowa, Chi. Bears 1981-85
Hilgenberg, Joel, C-G, Iowa, New Orleans 1984-85
Hilgenberg, Wally, LB, Iowa, Detroit 1964-66; Minnesota 1968-79
Hilger, Rusty, QB, Oklahoma State, LA Raiders 1985
Hill, Barry, S, Iowa State, Miami 1975-76
Hill, Bob, G, Haskell, Oorang 1922
Hill, Calvin, RB, Yale, Dallas 1969-74; Washington 1976-77; Cleveland 1978-81
Hill, Charlie, HB, Baker, Kansas City 1924-26
Hill, Dave, T, Auburn, Kansas City 1963-74
Hill, David, TE, Texas A&I, Detroit 1976-82; LA Rams 1983-85
Hill, Don, HB, Stanford, Green Bay 1929; Chi. Cardinals 1929
Hill, Drew, WR-KR, Georgia Tech, LA Rams 1979-82, 1984; Houston 1985
Hill, Eddie, RB, Memphis State, LA Rams 1979-80; Miami 1981-84
Hill, Fred, TE, USC, Philadelphia 1965-71
Hill, Gary, DB, USC, Minnesota 1965
Hill, Greg, CB, Oklahoma State, Houston 1983; Kansas City 1984-85
Hill, Harlon, SE, North Alabama, Chi. Bears 1954-61; Pittsburgh 1962; Detroit 1962
Hill, Harold, E, Samford, Brooklyn 1938-40
Hill, Harry (Cowboy), HB, Oklahoma, Toledo 1923; Kansas City 1924-26; NY Giants 1926
Hill, Ike, WR, Catawba, Buffalo 1970-71; Chi. Bears 1973-74; Miami 1976
Hill, Irv, QB, Trinity (Texas), Chi. Cardinals 1931-32
Hill, J.D., WR, Arizona State, Buffalo 1971-75; Detroit 1976-77
Hill, Jack, HB, Utah State, Denver 1961
Hill, Jerry, FB, Wyoming, Baltimore 1961, 1963-70
Hill, Jim, DB, Tennessee, Detroit 1951-52; Pittsburgh 1955
Hill, Jim, S, Texas A&I, San Diego 1969-71; Green Bay 1972-74; Cleveland 1975
Hill, Jimmy, DB, Sam Houston State, Chi. Cardinals 1955-57, 1959; St. Louis 1960-64; Detroit 1965; Kansas City 1966
Hill, John (Kid), T, Amherst, NY Giants 1926
Hill, John, C, Lehigh, NY Giants 1972-74; New Orleans 1975-84; San Francisco 1985
Hill, Kenny, S, Yale, Oakland 1981; LA Raiders 1982-83; NY Giants 1984-85
Hill, Kent, G, Georgia Tech, LA Rams 1979-85
Hill, King, QB-P, Rice, Chi. Cardinals 1958-59; St. Louis 1960, 1969; Philadelphia 1961-68; Minnesota 1968
Hill, Mack Lee, FB, Southern, Kansas City 1964-65
Hill, Ralph, C, Florida A&M, NY Giants 1976-77
Hill, Rod, CB-KR, Kentucky State, Dallas 1982-83; Buffalo 1984-85
Hill, Tony, WR, Stanford, Dallas 1977-85
Hill, Winston, T, Texas Southern, NY Jets 1963-76; LA Rams 1977
Hillebrand, Jerry, LB, Colorado, NY Giants 1963-66; St. Louis 1967; Pittsburgh 1968-70
Hillenbrand, Billy, HB, Indiana, Chi. Rockets (AAFC) 1946; Baltimore (AAFC) 1947-48
Hillhouse, Andy, HB, Brown, Buffalo 1920-21
Hillman, Bill, FB, Tennessee, Detroit 1947
Hilpert, Hal, HB, Oklahoma City, NY Giants 1930; Cincinnati 1933
Hilton, John, TE, Richmond, Pittsburgh 1965-69; Green Bay 1970; Minnesota 1971; Detroit 1972-73
Hilton, Roy, DE, Jackson State, Baltimore 1965-73; NY Giants 1974; Atlanta 1975
Hilton, Scott, DE-LB, San Francisco 1979-80
Himes, Dick, T, Ohio State, Green Bay 1968-77
Hinchman, Hubert (Curly), HB, Butler, Chi. Cardinals 1933-34; Detroit 1934
Hindman, Stan, DE-DT, Mississippi, San Francisco 1966-71, 1973-74
Hines, Andre, T, Stanford, Seattle 1980
Hines, Glen Ray, T, Arkansas, Houston 1966-70; New Orleans 1971-72; Pittsburgh 1973
Hines, Jimmy, WR, Texas Southern, Miami 1969
Hinkle, Bryan, LB, Oregon, Pittsburgh 1982-85
Hinkle, Clarke, FB, Bucknell, Green Bay 1932-41
Hinkle, Jack, HB, Syracuse, NY Giants 1940; Phil-Pitt 1943; Philadelphia 1944-47
Hinte, Harold (Tex), E, Pittsburgh, Green Bay 1942; Pittsburgh 1942
Hinton, Chris, G, Northwestern, Baltimore 1983; Indianapolis 1984-85
Hinton, Chuck, DE-DT, North Carolina Central, Pittsburgh 1964-71; NY Jets 1971; Baltimore 1972
Hinton, Chuck, C, Mississippi, NY Giants 1967-69
Hinton, Eddie, WR, Oklahoma, Baltimore 1969-72; Houston 1973; New England 1974
Hinton, J.W., QB, TCU, Staten Island 1932
Hipp, I.M., RB, Nebraska, Oakland 1981
Hippa, Sam, E, Dayton, Dayton 1927-28
Hipple, Eric, QB, Utah State, Detroit 1980-85
Hipps, Claude, HB, Georgia, Pittsburgh 1952-53
Hirsch, Ed (Buckets), FB, Northwestern, Buffalo (AAFC) 1947-49
Hirsch, Elroy (Crazylegs), HB-FL, Michigan, Wisconsin, Chi. Rockets (AAFC) 1946-48; LA Rams 1949-57
Hitt, Joel, E, Mississippi College, Cleveland 1939
Hix, Billy, E, Arkansas, Philadelphia 1950
Hoage, Terry, S, Georgia, New Orleans 1984-85
Hoaglin, Fred, C, Pittsburgh, Cleveland 1966-72; Baltimore 1973; Houston 1974-75; Seattle 1976
Hoague, Joe, HB, Colgate, Pittsburgh 1941-42; Boston 1946
Hoak, Dick, RB, Penn State, Pittsburgh 1961-70
Hoban, Mike, G, Michigan, Chi. Bears 1974
Hobbs, Bill, LB, Texas A&M, Philadelphia 1969-71; New Orleans 1972
Hobbs, Homer, G, Georgia, San Francisco 1949-50
Hobley, Liffort, S, LSU, St. Louis 1985
Hobscheid, Frank, G, Chicago, Racine 1926; Chi. Bears 1927

Hobson, Ben, HB, St. Louis, Buffalo 1926-27
Hock, John, T, Santa Clara, Chi. Cardinals 1950; LA Rams 1953, 1955-57
Hodel, Merwin, FB, Colorado, NY Giants 1953
Hodge, Floyd, WR, Utah, Atlanta 1982-84
Hodges, Herman, E, Samford, Brooklyn 1939-42
Hodgins, Norm, S, LSU, Chi. Bears 1974
Hodgson, Pat, SE, Georgia, Washington 1966
Hoel, Bob, G, Pittsburgh, Pittsburgh 1935; Chi. Cardinals 1937-38
Hoerner, Dick, FB, Iowa, LA Rams 1947-51; Dallas 1952
Hoernschemeyer, Bob (Hunchy), HB, Indiana, Chi. Rockets (AAFC) 1946-47; Brooklyn (AAFC) 1947-48; Chi. Hornets (AAFC) 1949; Detroit 1950-55
Hoey, George, LB, Michigan, St. Louis 1971; New England 1972-73; San Diego 1974; Denver 1975; NY Jets 1975
Hofer, Paul, RB, Mississippi, San Francisco 1976-80
Hoffman, Bob, FB-QB, USC, Washington 1940-41; LA Rams 1946-48; LA Dons (AAFC) 1949
Hoffman, Dalton, RB, Baylor, Houston 1965-66
Hoffman, Gary, T, Santa Clara, Green Bay 1984
Hoffman, Jack, E, Xavier, Chi. Bears 1952, 1955-58
Hoffman, Jake, HB, Syracuse, Rochester 1925
Hoffman, John, FB, Arkansas, Chi. Bears 1949-56
Hoffman, John, DE, Hawaii, Washington 1969; Chi. Bears 1971; St. Louis 1972; Denver 1972
Hoffman, Will, G, Lehigh, Frankford 1924-26; Pottsville 1927
Hogan, Darrell, G, Trinity (Texas), Pittsburgh 1949-53
Hogan, Mike, RB, Tennessee-Chattanooga, Philadelphia 1976-78, 1980; San Francisco 1979; NY Giants 1980
Hogan, Paul, HB, Washington & Jefferson, Akron 1924; Canton 1925; NY Giants 1926; Frankford 1926; Chi. Cardinals 1927
Hogan, Tom, T, Detroit, Detroit 1925; Chi. Cardinals 1926
Hogeboom, Gary, QB, Central Michigan, Dallas 1980-85
Hoggard, D.D., CB, North Carolina State, Cleveland 1985
Hogland, Doug, G, Oregon State, San Francisco 1953-55; Chi. Cardinals 1956-58; Detroit 1958
Hogue, Frank, HB, Akron 1924
Hogue, Murrell, G, Centenary, NY Yankees 1928; Chi. Cardinals 1929-30; Minneapolis 1930
Hohman, Jon, G, Wisconsin, Denver 1965-66
Hohn, Bobby, DB, Nebraska, Pittsburgh 1965-69
Hoisington, Al, SE, Pasadena C.C., Oakland 1960; Buffalo 1900
Hoke, Jonathan, CB, Ball State, Chi. Bears 1980
Hokuf, Steve, QB, Nebraska, Boston 1933-35
Holcomb, Bill, T, Texas Tech, Pittsburgh 1937; Philadelphia 1937
Holden, Sam, T, Grambling, New Orleans 1971
Holden, Steve, WR-KR, Arizona State, Cleveland 1973-76; Cincinnati 1977
Holder, Lew, E, Texas, LA Dons (AAFC) 1949
Hole, Ernie, T, Muncie 1920-21
Hole, Mickey, HB, Muncie 1920-21
Holifield, Jimmy, DB, Jackson State, NY Giants 1968-69
Holladay, Bob, DB, Tulsa, LA Rams 1956; San Francisco 1956-57
Holland, John, WR, Tennessee State, Minnesota 1974; Buffalo 1975-77
Holland, Vernon, T, Tennessee State, Cincinnati 1971-79; Detroit 1980; NY Giants 1980
Hollar, John, FB, Appalachian State, Washington 1948-49; Detroit 1949
Hollas, Hugo, S, Rice, New Orleans 1970-72; San Francisco 1974
Holle, Eric, DE-NT, Texas, Kansas City 1984-85
Holler, Ed, LB, South Carolina, Green Bay 1963; Pittsburgh 1964
Holleran, Tom, FB, Pittsburgh, Toledo 1922; Buffalo 1923
Holley, Ken, HB, Holy Cross, Miami (AAFC) 1946
Holliday, Ron, WR, Pittsburgh, San Diego 1973
Hollingsworth, Joe, FB, Eastern Kentucky, Pittsburgh 1949-51
Hollingsworth, Shawn, T, Angelo State, Denver 1983
Holloman, Gus, S, Houston, Denver 1968-69; NY Jets 1970-72
Holloway, Brian, T, Stanford, New England 1981-85
Holloway, Glen, G, North Texas State, Chi. Bears 1970-73; Cleveland 1974
Holloway, Randy, DE, Pittsburgh, Minnesota 1978-84; St. Louis 1984
Holloway, Stan, LB, California, New Orleans 1980
Holly, Bob, QB, Princeton, Washington 1982-83; Philadelphia 1984; Atlanta 1984-85
Holm, Tony, FB, Alabama, Providence 1930; Portsmouth 1931; Chi. Cardinals 1932; Pittsburgh 1933
Holman, Danny, QB, San Jose State, Pittsburgh 1968
Holman, Rodney, TE, Tulane, Cincinnati 1982-85
Holman, Willie, DE-DT, South Carolina State, Chi. Bears 1968-73; Washington 1973
Holmer, Walt, FB, Northwestern, Chi. Bears 1929-30; Chi. Cardinals 1931-32; Boston 1933; Pittsburgh 1933
Holmes, Ernie, DT, Texas Southern, Pittsburgh 1972-77; New England 1978
Holmes, Jack, RB, Texas Southern, New Orleans 1978-82
Holmes, Jerry, CB, West Virginia, NY Jets 1980-83
Holmes, John, DE, Florida A&M, Miami 1966
Holmes, Mel, G-T, North Carolina A&T, Pittsburgh 1971-73
Holmes, Mike, DB, Texas Southern, San Francisco 1974-75; Buffalo 1976; Miami 1976
Holmes, Pat, DE, Texas Tech, Houston 1966-72; Kansas City 1973
Holmes, Robert (Tank), RB, Southern, Kansas City 1968-71; Houston 1971-72, 1975; San Diego 1973
Holmes, Ron, DE, Washington, Tampa Bay 1985
Holmes, Rudy, DB, Drake, Atlanta 1974
Holmoe, Tom, S, BYU, San Francisco 1983-84
Holohan, Pete, TE, Notre Dame, San Diego 1981-85
Holovak, Mike, FB, Boston College, LA Rams 1946; Chi. Bears 1947-48
Holston, Michael, WR, Morgan State, Houston 1981-85; Kansas City 1985
Holt, Harry, TE, Arizona, Cleveland 1983-85
Holt, Issiac, CB, Alcorn State, Minnesota 1985
Holt, John, CB-KR, West Texas State, Tampa Bay 1981-85
Holt, Robert, WR, Baylor, Buffalo 1982
Holtzman, Glen, DT, North Texas State, LA Rams 1955-58
Holub, E.J., C-LB, Texas Tech, Dallas Texans 1961-62; Kansas City 1963-70
Holz, Gordy, T, Minnesota, Denver 1960-63; NY Jets 1964
Holzer, Tom, DE, Louisville, San Francisco 1967
Homan, Dennis, WR, Alabama, Dallas 1968-70; Kansas City 1971-72
Homan, Henry (Two Bits), QB, Lebanon Valley, Frankford 1925-30
Honaker, Charlie, E, Ohio State, Cleveland 1924
Hood, Estus, CB, Illinois State, Green Bay 1978-84
Hood, Frank, HB, Pittsburgh, Pittsburgh 1933
Hood, Winford, G, Georgia, Denver 1984-85
Hooker, Fair, WR, Arizona State, Cleveland 1969-74
Hooks, Alvin, WR, Cal State-Northridge, Philadelphia 1981
Hooks, Jim, RB, Central State (Oklahoma), Detroit 1973-76
Hooks, Roland, RB, North Carolina State, Buffalo 1976-82
Hooligan, Henry, RB, Bishop, Houston 1965
Hoopes, Mitch, P, Arizona, Dallas 1975; San Diego 1976; Houston 1976; Detroit 1977; Philadelphia 1978
Hoover, Melvin, WR, Arizona State, Philadelphia 1982-84
Hopkins, Andy, RB, Stephen F. Austin, Houston 1971
Hopkins, Jerry, LB, Texas A&M, Denver 1963-66; Miami 1967; Oakland 1968
Hopkins, Roy, RB, Texas Southern, Houston 1967-70
Hopkins, Ted, E, Columbus 1921-22
Hopkins, Thomas, T, Alabama A&M, Cleveland 1983
Hopkins, Wes, S, SMU, Philadelphia 1983-85
Hopp, Harry, HB, Nebraska, Detroit 1941-43; Miami (AAFC) 1946; Buffalo (AAFC) 1946; LA Dons (AAFC) 1947
Hoptowit, Al, T, Washington State, Chi. Bears 1942-45
Horan, Michael, P, Long Beach State, Philadelphia 1984-85
Hord, Roy, G, Duke, LA Rams 1960-62; Philadelphia 1962; NY Jets 1963
Horn, Bob, LB, Oregon State, San Diego 1976-81; San Francisco 1982-83
Horn, Dick, QB-P, Stanford, Baltimore 1958
Horn, Don, QB, San Diego State, Green Bay 1967-70; Denver 1971-72; Cleveland 1973; San Diego 1974
Horn, Rod, NT, Nebraska, Cincinnati 1980-81
Hornbeak, Jay, HB, Washington, Brooklyn 1935
Horne, Dick, E, Oregon, NY Giants 1941; Miami (AAFC) 1946; San Francisco (AAFC) 1947
Horner, Sam, HB, VMI, Washington 1960-61; NY Giants 1962
Hornick, Bill, T, Tulane, Pittsburgh 1947
Horning, Clarence (Steamer), T, Colgate, Detroit 1920-21; Buffalo 1921; Toledo 1922-23
Hornsby, Ron, LB, Southeastern Louisiana, NY Giants 1971-74
Hornung, Paul, HB-K, Notre Dame, Green Bay 1957-62, 1964-66
Horrell, Bill, G, Michigan State, Philadelphia 1952
Horstmann, Roy, FB, Purdue, Boston 1933; Chi. Cardinals 1934
Horton, Bob, LB, Boston U., San Diego 1964-65
Horton, Ethan, RB, North Carolina, Kansas City 1985
Horton, Greg, G, Colorado, LA Rams 1976-78, 1980; Tampa Bay 1978-79
Horton, Larry, DT, Iowa, Chi. Bears 1972
Horton, Les, FB, Rutgers, Newark 1930
Horton, Ray, CB, Washington, Cincinnati 1983-85
Horvath, Les, HB, Ohio State, LA Rams 1947-48; Cleveland (AAFC) 1949
Horween (McMahon), Arnold, QB, Harvard, Chi. Cardinals 1921-24
Horween (McMahon), Ralph, FB, Harvard, Chi. Cardinals 1921-23
Hoskins, Bob, DT-G, Wichita State, San Francisco 1970-75
Hoss, Clark, TE, Oregon State, Philadelphia 1972
Hostetler, Jeff, QB, West Virginia, NY Giants 1984-85
Houck, Joe, G, Columbus 1920-21
Hough, Jim, G, Utah State, Minnesota 1978-85
Houghton, Jerry, DT, Washington State, Washington 1950; Chi. Cardinals 1951
Houle, Wilfred, QB, St. Thomas (Minnesota), Minneapolis 1924
House, Kevin, WR, Southern Illinois, Tampa Bay 1980-85
Houser, John, G, Redlands, LA Rams 1957-59; Dallas Cowboys 1960-61; St. Louis 1963
Houston, Bill, WR, Jackson State, Dallas 1974
Houston, Jim, DE-LB, Ohio State, Cleveland 1960-72
Houston, Ken, S, Prairie View A&M, Houston, 1967-72; Washington 1973-80
Houston, Lin, G, Ohio State, Cleveland 1946-53
Houston, Rich, WR, East Texas State, NY Giants 1969-73
Houston, Walt, G, Purdue, Washington 1955
Hover, Don, LB, Washington State, Washington 1978-79
Hovious, Junie, QB, Mississippi, NY Giants 1945
Howard, Al (Red), G, Princeton, Brooklyn 1926; NY Giants 1927
Howard, Billy, DT, Alcorn State, Detroit 1974-76
Howard, Bob, G, Marietta, Kansas City 1924-26; Cleveland 1927; Detroit 1928; NY Giants 1929-30
Howard, Bobby, CB, San Diego State, San Diego 1967-74; New England 1974-75; Philadelphia 1978-79
Howard, Bryan, S, Tennessee State, Minnesota 1982
Howard, Carl, CB, Rutgers, Dallas 1984; Tampa Bay 1985; NY Jets 1985
Howard, Davie, LB, Long Beach State, Minnesota 1985
Howard, Gene, DB, Langston, New Orleans 1968-70; LA Rams 1971-72
Howard, Harry, DB, Ohio State, NY Jets 1976
Howard, Leroy, DB, Bishop, Houston 1971
Howard, Lynn (Tubby), HB, Indiana, Green Bay 1921-22
Howard, Paul, G, BYU, Denver 1973-75, 1977-85
Howard, Percy, WR, Austin Peay, Dallas 1975
Howard, Ron, TE, Seattle, Dallas 1974-75; Seattle 1976-78; Buffalo 1979
Howard, Sherman, HB, Nevada-Reno, NY Yankees (AAFC) 1949; NY Yanks 1950-51; Cleveland 1952-53
Howard, Thomas, LB, Texas Tech, Kansas City 1977-83; St. Louis 1984-85
Howe, Glen, T, Southern Mississippi, Pittsburgh 1985; Atlanta 1985
Howell, Clarence, E, Texas A&M, San Francisco (AAFC) 1948
Howell, Delles, CB, Grambling, New Orleans 1970-72; NY Jets 1973-75
Howell, Earl, HB, Mississippi, LA Dons (AAFC) 1949
Howell, Foster, T, TCU, Cincinnati 1934
Howell, Jim Lee, E, Arkansas, NY Giants 1937-42, 1946-48
Howell, John, QB, Nebraska, Green Bay 1938
Howell, Lane, T, Grambling, NY Giants 1963-64; Philadelphia 1965-69
Howell, Leroy, DE, Appalachian State, Buffalo 1984
Howell, Mike, CB, Grambling, Cleveland 1965-72; Miami 1972
Howell, Millard (Dixie), QB, Alabama, Boston 1937
Howell, Pat, G, USC, Atlanta 1979-83; Houston 1983-85
Howell, Steve, RB-TE, Baylor, Miami 1979-81
Howell, Wilfred, E, Catholic, Boston 1929
Hower, Charlie, HB, Louisville 1921
Howfield, Bobby, K, Denver 1968-70; NY Jets 1971-74
Howley, Chuck, LB, West Virginia, Chi. Bears 1958-59, Dallas 1961-73
Howser, Jim, T, Louisville 1921
Howton, Billy, SE, Rice, Green Bay 1952-58; Cleveland 1959; Dallas 1960-63
Hoyem, Lynn, G-C, Long Beach State, Dallas 1962-63, Philadelphia 1964-67
Hrabetin, Frank, T, Loyola (Los Angeles), Philadelphia 1942; Miami (AAFC) 1946; Brooklyn (AAFC) 1946
Hrivnak, Gary, DE-DT, Purdue, Chi. Bears 1973-75
Huard, John, LB, Maine, Denver 1967-69; New Orleans 1971
Huarte, John, QB, Notre Dame, Boston 1966-67; Philadelphia 1968; Kansas City 1970-71; Chi. Bears 1972
Hubach, Mike, P, Kansas, New England 1980-81
Hubbard, Cal, T-E, Centenary, Geneva, NY Giants 1927-28, 1936; Green Bay 1929-33, 1935; Pittsburgh 1936
Hubbard, Dave, T, BYU, New Orleans 1977
Hubbard, Marv, FB, Colgate, Oakland 1969-75; Detroit 1977
Hubbard, Wesley (Bud), E, San Jose State, Brooklyn 1935
Hubbell, Frank, E, Tennessee, LA Rams 1947-49
Hubbert, Brad, FB, Arizona, San Diego 1967-70
Hubka, Gene, HB, Bucknell, Pittsburgh 1947
Huckleby, Harlan, RB, Michigan, Green Bay 1980-85
Huddleston, John, LB, Utah, Oakland 1978-79
Hudlow, Floyd, SE, Arizona, Buffalo 1965; Atlanta 1967-68
Hudock, Mike, C, Miami, NY Titans 1960-62; NY Jets 1963-65; Miami 1966; Kansas City 1967
Hudson, Bill, DT, Clemson, San Diego 1961-62; Boston 1963
Hudson, Bob, DB-LB, Clemson, NY Giants 1951-52; Philadelphia 1953-55, 1957-58; Washington 1959; Dallas Texans 1960; Denver 1960-61
Hudson, Bob, RB, Northeastern Oklahoma, Green Bay 1972; Oakland 1973-74
Hudson, Dick, FB, Washington 1921; Minneapolis 1923; Hammond 1925-26
Hudson, Dick, G, Memphis State, San Diego 1962; Buffalo 1963-67
Hudson, Jim, S, Texas, NY Jets 1965-70
Hudson, Nat, G, Georgia, New Orleans 1981-82
Hueller, Jack, G, Racine 1922-24
Huey, Gene, DB, Wyoming, San Diego 1969
Huff, Gary, QB, Florida State, Chi.Bears 1973-76; Tampa Bay 1977-78; San Francisco 1980
Huff, Ken, G, North Carolina, Baltimore 1975-82; Washington 1983-85
Huff, Marty, LB, Michigan, San Francisco 1972
Huff, Sam, LB, West Virginia, NY Giants 1956-63; Washington 1964-67, 1969
Huffine, Ken, FB, Purdue, Muncie 1921; Chi. Staleys 1921; Dayton 1922-26
Huffman, Dave, C-G-T, Notre Dame, Minnesota 1979-83, 1985
Huffman, Dick, DT,Tennessee, LA Rams 1947-50
Huffman, Frank, G, Marshall, Chi. Cardinals 1939-41

Huffman, Iolas, T, Ohio State, Cleveland 1923; Buffalo 1924
Huffman, Tim, G-T, Notre Dame, Green Bay 1981-85
Huffman, Vern, QB, Indiana, Detroit 1937-38
Hufford, Darrell, E, California, LA Buccaneers 1926
Hufnagel, John, QB, Penn State, Denver 1974-75
Hugasian, Harry, HB, Stanford, Chi. Bears 1955; Baltimore 1955
Hugger, Keith, WR, Connecticut, NY Giants 1983
Huggins, Roy, FB, Vanderbilt, Cleveland 1944
Hughes, Bernie, C, Oregon, Chi. Cardinals 1934-36
Hughes, Bill (Hoss), C, Texas, Philadelphia 1937-40; Chi. Bears 1941
Hughes, Bob, DE, Jackson State, Atlanta 1967, 1969
Hughes, Chuck, WR, Texas-El Paso, Philadelphia 1967-69; Detroit 1970-71
Hughes, David, RB, Boise State, Seattle 1981-85
Hughes, Dennis (Country), TE, Georgia, Pittsburgh 1970-71
Hughes, Denny, C, George Washington, Pottsville 1925
Hughes, Dick, HB, Tulsa, Pittsburgh 1957
Hughes, Ed, DB, Tulsa, LA Rams 1954-55; NY Giants 1956-58
Hughes, Ernie, G, Notre Dame, San Francisco 1978, 1980; NY Giants 1981-83
Hughes, George, G, William & Mary, Pittsburgh 1950-54
Hughes, Henry (Honolulu), QB-FB, Oregon State, Boston 1932
Hughes, Pat, LB, Boston U., NY Giants 1970-76; New Orleans 1977-79
Hughes, Randy, S, Oklahoma, Dallas 1975-80
Hughitt, Tommy, QB, Michigan, Buffalo 1920-24
Hughley, George, FB, Central State (Oklahoma), Washington 1965
Hugret, Joe, E, NYU, Brooklyn 1934
Hull, Bill, DE, Wake Forest, Dallas Texans 1962
Hull, Mike, TE-RB, USC, Chi. Bears 1968; Washington 1971-74
Hull, Tom, LB, Penn State, San Francisco 1974; Green Bay 1975
Hultman, Vivian, E, Michigan State, Detroit 1925-26; Pottsville 1927
Hultz, Don, DE-DT, Southern Mississippi, Minnesota 1963; Philadelphia 1964-73; Chi. Bears 1974
Hultz, George, DT, Southern Mississippi, St. Louis 1962
Humbert, Dick, E, Richmond, Philadelphia 1941, 1945-49
Humble, Weldon, G, Rice, Cleveland 1947-50; Dallas 1952
Humiston, Mike, LB, Weber State, Buffalo 1981; Baltimore 1982; Indianapolis 1984
Humm, David, QB, Nebraska, Oakland 1975-79; Buffalo 1980; Baltimore 1981-82; LA Raiders 1983-84
Hummel, Arnie, FB-G, Lombard, Kansas City 1926; Chi. Cardinals 1927
Hummell, Swede, HB, Drake, Providence 1926
Hummon, Mack, E, Wittenberg, Dayton 1926-28
Humphery, Bobby, WR-KR, New Mexico State, NY Jets 1984-85
Humphrey, Buddy, QB, Baylor, LA Rams 1959-60; Dallas Cowboys 1961-62; St. Louis 1963-65; Houston 1966
Humphrey, Claude, DE, Tennessee State, Atlanta 1968-74, 1976-78; Philadelphia 1979-81
Humphrey, Donnie, DE, Auburn, Green Bay 1984-85
Humphrey, Paul, C, Purdue, Brooklyn 1939
Humphrey, Tom, C, Abilene Christian, Kansas City 1974
Humphreys, Bob, K, Wichita State, Denver 1967-68
Humphries, Stefan, G, Michigan, Chi. Bears 1984-85
Huneke, Charlie, T, Benedictine, Chi. Rockets (AAFC) 1946-47; Brooklyn (AAFC) 1947-48
Hunley, La Monte, LB, Arizona, Indianapolis 1985
Hunley, Rickey, LB, Arizona, Denver 1984-85
Hunt, Ben, T, Alabama, Toledo 1923
Hunt, Bob, RB, Heidelberg, Cleveland 1974
Hunt, Bobby, DB, Auburn, Dallas Texans 1962; Kansas City 1963-67; Cincinnati 1968-69
Hunt, Byron, LB, SMU, NY Giants 1981-85
Hunt, Calvin, C, Baylor, Philadelphia 1970; Houston 1972-73
Hunt, Charlie, LB, Florida State, San Francisco 1973; Tampa Bay 1976
Hunt, Daryl, LB, Oklahoma, Houston 1979-84
Hunt, Ervin, DB, Fresno State, Green Bay 1970
Hunt, George, K, Tennessee, Baltimore 1973; NY Giants 1975
Hunt, Jim (Earthquake), DE-DT, Prairie View A&M, Boston 1960-70
Hunt, John, HB, Marshall, Chi. Bears 1945
Hunt, John, G, Florida, Dallas 1984
Hunt, Kevin, T-G, Doane, Green Bay 1972; Houston 1973-77; New Orleans 1978
Hunt, Mike, LB, Minnesota, Green Bay 1978-80
Hunt, Ron, T, Oregon, Cincinnati 1976-78
Hunt, Sam, LB, Stephen F. Austin, New England 1974-80
Hunter, Al, RB, Notre Dame, Seattle 1977-80
Hunter, Art, C, Notre Dame, Green Bay 1954; Cleveland 1956-59; LA Rams 1960-64; Pittsburgh 1965
Hunter, Billy, FL, Syracuse, Washington 1965; Miami 1966
Hunter, Daniel, CB, Henderson State, Denver 1985
Hunter, Herman, RB-KR, Tennessee State, Philadelphia 1985
Hunter, James, DB, Grambling, Detroit 1976-82
Hunter, James, NT, USC, Baltimore 1982
Hunter, Merle, G, Ashland, Hammond 1925-26
Hunter, Monty, S, Salem (West Virginia), Dallas 1982; St. Louis 1983
Hunter, Romney, E, Marshall, Portsmouth 1933
Hunter, Scott, QB, Alabama, Green Bay 1971-73; Buffalo 1974; Atlanta 1976-78; Detroit 1979
Hunter, Tony, TE, Notre Dame, Buffalo 1983-84; LA Rams 1985
Hupke, Tom, G, Alabama, Detroit 1934-37; Cleveland 1938-39
Hurlburt, John, HB, Chicago, Chi. Cardinals 1924-25
Hurley, Bill, S, Syracuse, New Orleans 1982-83; Buffalo 1983
Hurley, George, G, Washington State, Boston 1932-33
Hurley, John, E, Washington State, Cleveland 1931
Hurst, Bill, G, Oregon, Chi. Bears 1924; Kenosha 1924
Hurston, Chuck, DE-LB, Auburn, Kansas City 1965-70; Buffalo 1971
Hurt, Eric, CB, San Jose State, Dallas 1980
Husmann, Ed, DT, Nebraska, Chi. Cardinals 1953, 1956-59; Dallas Cowboys 1960; Houston 1961-65
Hust, Al, E, Tennessee, Chi. Cardinals 1946
Hutcherson, Ken, LB, Livingston, Dallas 1974; San Diego 1975
Hutchinson, Bill, QB, Dartmouth, NY Giants 1942
Hutchinson, Elvin, HB, Whittier, Detroit 1939
Hutchinson, Ralph, T, Tennessee-Chattanooga, NY Giants 1949
Hutchinson, Scott, DE, Florida, Buffalo 1978-80; Tampa Bay 1981
Hutchinson, Tom, SE, Kentucky, Cleveland 1963-65; Atlanta 1966
Hutchison, Anthony, RB, Texas Tech, Chi. Bears 1983-84; Buffalo 1985
Hutchison, Chuck, G, Ohio State, St. Louis 1970-72; Cleveland 1973-75
Huth, Gerry, G, Wake Forest, NY Giants 1956; Philadelphia 1959-60; Minnesota 1961-63
Huther, Bruce, LB, New Hampshire, Dallas 1977-80, 1983; Cleveland 1981; Chi. Bears 1982
Hutson, Don, E, Alabama, Green Bay 1935-45
Hutson, Merle, G, Heidelberg, Cleveland 1931
Hutton, Jack, HB, Purdue, Frankford 1930
Huxhold, Ken, G, Wisconsin, Philadelphia 1954-58
Huzvar, John, FB, North Carolina State, Philadelphia 1952; Baltimore 1953-54
Hyatt, Freddie, WR, Auburn, St. Louis 1968-72; New Orleans 1973; Washington 1973
Hyde, Glenn, T-C, Pittsburgh, Denver 1976-81, 1985; Baltimore 1982
Hyland, Bob, T-G-C, Boston College, Green Bay 1967-69, 1976; Chi. Bears 1970; NY Giants 1971-75; New England 1977
Hynes, Paul, DB, Louisiana Tech, Dallas Texans 1961; NY Titans 1961-62
Hynoski, Henry, RB, Temple, Cleveland 1975

I

Iacavazzi, Cosmo, RB, Princeton, NY Jets 1965
Ieremia, Mekeli, DT, BYU, Buffalo 1978
Iglehart, Floyd, DB, Wiley, LA Rams 1958
Igwebuike, Donald, K, Clemson, Tampa Bay 1985
Ilg, Ray, LB, Colgate, Boston 1967-68
Ilgenfritz, Mark, DE, Vanderbilt, Cleveland 1974
Ilkin, Tunch, T, Indiana State, Pittsburgh 1980-85
Illman, Ed, QB, Montana, Chi. Cardinals 1928
Illowit, Roy, T, CCNY, Brooklyn 1937
Iman, Ken, C, Southeast Missouri State, Green Bay 1960-63; LA Rams 1965-74
Imhof, Martin, DE, San Diego State, St. Louis 1972; Washington 1974; New England 1975; Denver 1976
Imlay, Tut, HB, California, LA Buccaneers 1926; NY Giants 1927
Ingalls, Bob, C, Michigan, Green Bay 1942
Ingle, John, HB, Evansville 1921
Ingram, Brian, LB, Tennessee, New England 1982-85
Ingwerson, Burt, T, Illinois, Decatur 1920; Chi. Staleys 1921
Inman, Jerry, DT, Oregon, Denver 1968-71, 1973
Inmon, Earl, LB, Bethune-Cookman, Tampa Bay 1978
Intrieri, Marne, G-FB, Loyola (Baltimore), Staten Island 1932; Boston 1933-34
Ippolito, Tony, G, Purdue, Chi. Bears 1943
Irgens, Einar, E, Minneapolis 1921-24
Irgens, Newman, HB, Minneapolis 1922
Irons, Gerald, LB, Maryland-Eastern Shore, Oakland 1970-75; Cleveland 1976-79
Irvin, Barlow, G, Texas A&M, Buffalo 1926-27
Irvin, Cecil (Tex), T-FB, Davis & Elkins, Providence 1931; NY Giants 1932-35
Irvin, Darrell, DE, Oklahoma, Buffalo 1980-83
Irvin, LeRoy, CB-KR, Kansas, LA Rams 1980-85
Irwin, Don, FB, Colgate, Boston 1936; Washington 1937-39
Irwin, Harry, (Dutch) QB-E, Merced, Rochester 1920
Irwin, Jim, HB, Louisville 1921-23
Irwin, Tim, T, Tennessee, Minnesota 1981-85
Irwin, Willie, E, Florida A&M, Philadelphia 1953
Isaacson, Ted, T, Washington, Chi. Cardinals 1934-35
Isabel, Wilmer, HB, Ohio State, Columbus 1923-24
Isbell, Cecil, QB-HB, Purdue, Green Bay 1938-42
Isbell, Joe Bob, G, Houston, Dallas 1962-64; Cleveland 1966
Isenbarger, John, RB-WR, Indiana, San Francisco 1970-73
Isselhardt, Ralph, G, Franklin, Detroit 1937; Cleveland 1937
Itzel, John, HB, Pittsburgh, Pittsburgh 1945
Iverson, Chris (Duke), HB, Oregon, NY Giants 1947; NY Yankees (AAFC) 1948-49; NY Yanks 1950-51
Ivery, Eddie Lee, RB, Georgia Tech, Green Bay 1979-85
Ivory, Bob, G, Detroit, Detroit 1947
Ivory, Horace, RB, Oklahoma, New England 1977-81; Seattle 1981-82
Ivy, Frank (Pop), E, Oklahoma, Pittsburgh 1940; Chi. Cardinals 1940-42, 1945-47
Iwanowski, Mark, TE, Pennsylvania, NY Jets 1978
Izo, George, QB, Notre Dame, St. Louis 1960; Washington 1961-64; Detroit 1965; Pittsburgh 1966

J

Jackson, Alfred, WR, Texas, Atlanta 1978-84
Jackson, Bernard, DB, Washington State, Cincinnati 1972-76; Denver 1977-80; San Diego 1980
Jackson, Bill, S, North Carolina, Cleveland 1982
Jackson, Billy, RB, Alabama, Kansas City 1981-84
Jackson, Bob (Stonewall), FB, North Carolina A&T, NY Giants 1950-51
Jackson, Bob, RB, New Mexico State, San Diego 1962-63; Houston Oilers 1964-65; Oakland 1964
Jackson, Bobby, DB, Alabama, Philadelphia 1960; Chi. Bears 1961
Jackson, Bobby, CB, Florida State, NY Jets 1978-85
Jackson, Charles, LB, Washington, Kansas City 1978-84; NY Jets 1985
Jackson, Charlie, DB, SMU, Chi. Cardinals 1958; Dallas Texans 1960
Jackson, Cleveland, TE, Nevada-Las Vegas, NY Giants 1979
Jackson, Colville, T, Chicago, Evansville 1921; Hammond 1921
Jackson, Don, HB, North Carolina, Philadelphia 1936
Jackson, Earnest, RB, Texas A&M, San Diego 1983-84; Philadelphia 1985
Jackson, Ernie, CB, Duke, New Orleans 1972-77; Atlanta 1978
Jackson, Ernie, CB, Jackson State, Detroit 1979
Jackson, Frank, FL, SMU, Dallas Texans 1961-62; Kansas City 1963-65; Miami 1966-67
Jackson, Gerald, S, Mississippi State, Kansas City 1979
Jackson, Harold, WR, Jackson State, LA Rams 1968, 1973-77; Philadelphia 1969-72; New England 1978-81; Minnesota 1982; Seattle 1983
Jackson, Henry, FB, Missouri, Detroit 1928
Jackson, Honor, DB, Pacific, New England 1972-73; NY Giants 1973-74
Jackson, Jazz, RB, Western Kentucky, NY Jets 1974-76
Jackson, Jeff, LB, Auburn, Atlanta 1984-85
Jackson, Jim, RB, Western Illinois, San Francisco 1966-67
Jackson, Joey, DE-DT, New Mexico State, NY Jets 1972-73; Minnesota 1977
Jackson, Johnny, DE, Southern, Philadelphia 1977
Jackson, Ken, T, Texas, Dallas 1952; Baltimore 1953-57
Jackson, Kenny, WR, Penn State, Philadelphia 1984-85
Jackson, Larron, G-T, Missouri, Denver 1971-74; Atlanta 1975-76
Jackson, Larry, C, Loyola (Chicago), Louisville 1926
Jackson, Leroy, HB, Western Illinois, Washington 1962-63
Jackson, Louis, RB, Cal Poly-SLO, NY Giants 1981
Jackson, Mel, G, USC, Green Bay 1976-80
Jackson, Michael, LB, Washington, Seattle 1979-85
Jackson, Monte, CB, San Diego State, LA Rams 1975-77, 1983; Oakland 1979-81; LA Raiders 1982
Jackson, Noah, G, Tampa, Chi. Bears 1975-83; Tampa Bay 1984
Jackson, Perry (Arnold Shockley), T, Southwestern Oklahoma, Providence 1928-30
Jackson, Randy, T, Florida, Chi. Bears 1967-74
Jackson, Randy, RB, Wichita State, Buffalo 1972; San Francisco 1973; Philadelphia 1974
Jackson, Rich, LB-DE, Southern, Oakland 1966; Denver 1967-72; Cleveland 1972
Jackson, Rickey, LB, Pittsburgh, New Orleans 1981-85
Jackson, Robert, T-G, Duke, Cleveland 1975-85
Jackson, Robert, LB, Texas A&M, Cleveland 1978-81; Atlanta 1982
Jackson, Robert, S, Central Michigan, Cincinnati 1982-85
Jackson, Roger, S, Bethune-Cookman, Denver 1982-85
Jackson, Roland, LB, Rice, St. Louis 1962
Jackson, Rusty, P, LSU, LA Rams 1976; Buffalo 1978
Jackson, Steve, LB, Texas-Arlington, Washington 1966-67
Jackson, Steve, DB, LSU, Oakland 1977
Jackson, Terry, CB, San Diego State, NY Giants 1978-83; Seattle 1984-85
Jackson, Tom, LB, Louisville, Denver 1973-85
Jackson, Trent, RB, Illinois, Philadelphia 1966; Washington 1967
Jackson, Wilbur, RB, Alabama, San Francisco 1974-79; Washington 1980-82
Jackunas, Frank, C, Detroit, Buffalo 1962; Denver 1963
Jacobs, Allen, RB, Utah, Green Bay 1965; NY Giants 1966-67
Jacobs, Dave, K, Syracuse, NY Jets 1979; Cleveland 1981
Jacobs, Harry, LB, Bradley, Boston 1960-62; Buffalo 1963-69; New Orleans 1970
Jacobs, (Indian) Jack, QB, Oklahoma, Cleveland 1942, 1945; Washington 1946; Green Bay 1947-49
Jacobs, Marv, T, Chi. Cardinals 1948
Jacobs, Proverb, T, California, Philadelphia 1958; NY Giants 1960; NY Titans 1961-62; Oakland 1963-64
Jacobs, Ray, DT, Howard Payne, Denver 1963-66; Miami 1967-68; Boston 1969

Jacobs, Stan, HB, Illinois, Detroit 1920
Jacobson, Jack, DB, Oklahoma State, San Diego 1965
Jacobson, Larry, DE-DT, Nebraska, NY Giants 1972-74
Jacoby, Joe, T, Louisville, Washington 1981-85
Jacquith, Jim, QB, Kansas City 1926
Jacunski, Harry, E, Fordham, Green Bay 1939-44
Jaffurs, Johnny, G, Penn State, Washington 1946
Jagade, Harry (Chick), FB, Indiana, Baltimore (AAFC) 1949; Cleveland 1951-53; Chi. Bears 1954-55
Jagielski, Harry, G, Indiana, Chi. Cardinals 1956; Washington 1956; Boston 1960-61; Oakland 1961
Jakes, Van, CB, Kent State, Kansas City 1983-84
Jakowenko, George, K, Syracuse, Oakland 1974; Buffalo 1976
Jamerson, Charles (Lefty), E, Arkansas, Hartford 1926
James, Claudis, WR, Jackson State, Green Bay 1967-68
James, Craig, RB, SMU, New England 1984-85
James, Dan, T, Ohio State, Pittsburgh 1960-66; Chi. Bears 1967
James, Dick, HB-DB, Oregon, Washington 1956-63; NY Giants 1964; Minnesota 1965
James, John, P, Florida, Atlanta 1972-81; Detroit 1982; Houston 1982-84
James, June, LB, Texas, Detroit 1985
James, Lionel (Little Train), RB-KR, Auburn, San Diego 1984-85
James, Nathaniel, CB, Florida A&M, Cleveland 1968
James, Robert, CB, Fisk, Buffalo 1969-74
James, Roland, S-KR, Tennessee, New England 1980-85
James, Ron (Po), RB, New Mexico State, Philadelphia 1972-75
James, Ted, C-G, Nebraska, Frankford 1929
James, Tommy, DB, Ohio State, Detroit 1947; Cleveland 1948-55; Baltimore 1956
Jameson, Larry, DT, Indiana, Tampa Bay 1976
Jamieson, Bob, C, Franklin & Marshall, Frankford 1924
Jamieson, Dick, QB, Bradley, NY Titans 1960-61
Jamison, Al, T, Colgate, Houston 1960-62
Janata, John, T, Illinois, Chi. Bears 1983
Jancik, Bobby, S, Lamar, Houston 1962-67
Janecek, Clarence, G, Purdue, Pittsburgh 1933
Janerette, Charlie, G, Penn State, LA Rams 1960; NY Giants 1961-62; NY Jets 1963; Denver Broncos 1964-65
Janet, Ernie, G-C, Washington, Chi. Bears 1972-74; Green Bay 1975; Philadelphia 1975
Janiak, Len, HB, Ohio U., Brooklyn 1939; Cleveland 1940-42
Janik, Tommy, DB-P, Texas A&I, Denver 1963-64; Buffalo 1965-68; Boston 1969-70; New England 1971
Jankovich, Keever, LB, Pacific, Dallas 1952; Chi. Cardinals 1953
Jankowski, Bruce, WR, Ohio State, Kansas City 1971-72
Jankowski, Eddie, HB, Wisconsin, Green Bay 1937-41
Janowicz, Vic, HB-K, Ohio State, Washington 1954-55
Jansante, Val, E, Duquesne, Pittsburgh 1946-51; Green Bay 1951
Jansing, Lou, FB, Louisville 1922
Jappe, Paul, E, Syracuse, NY Giants 1925, 1927-28; Brooklyn 1926
Jaqua, Jon, DB, Lewis & Clark, Washington 1970-72
Jaquess, Pete, DB, Eastern New Mexico, Houston 1964-65; Miami 1966-67; Denver 1967-70
Jarmoluk, Mike, T, Temple, Chi. Bears 1946-47; Boston 1948; NY Bulldogs 1949; Philadelphia 1949-55
Jarvi, Toimi, HB, Northern Illinois, Philadelphia 1944; Pittsburgh 1945
Jarvis, Bruce, C, Washington, Buffalo 1971-74
Jarvis, Ray, WR, Norfolk State, Atlanta 1971-72; Buffalo 1973; Detroit 1974-78
Jaszewski, Floyd, T, Minnesota, Detroit 1950-51
Jauron, Dick, S-KR, Yale, Detroit 1973-77; Cincinnati 1978-81
Jawish, Henry (Heinie), G, Georgetown (Washington D.C.), Pottsville 1926
Jaworski, Ron, QB, Youngstown State, LA Rams 1974-76; Philadelphia 1977-85
Jaynes, David, QB, Kansas, Kansas City 1974
Jecha, Ralph, G, Northwestern, Chi. Bears 1955; Pittsburgh 1956
Jeffcoat, Jim, DE, Arizona State, Dallas 1983-85
Jeffers, Ed, G, Oklahoma State, Brooklyn (AAFC) 1947
Jefferson, Billy, HB, Mississippi State, Detroit 1941; Brooklyn 1942; Philadelphia 1942
Jefferson, Charles, CB, McNeese State, Houston 1979-80
Jefferson, John, WR, Arizona State, San Diego 1978-80; Green Bay 1981-84; Cleveland 1985
Jefferson, Roy, WR, Utah, Pittsburgh 1965-69; Baltimore 1970; Washington 1971-76
Jeffrey, Neal, QB, Baylor, San Diego 1976-77
Jeffries, Bob, G, Missouri, Brooklyn 1942
Jelacic, Jon, DE, Minnesota, NY Giants 1958; Oakland 1961-64
Jelesky, Tom, T, Purdue, Philadelphia 1985
Jelley, Tom, E, Miami, Pittsburgh 1951
Jencks, Bob, TE-K, Miami (Ohio), Chi. Bears 1963-64; Washington 1965
Jenison, Ray, T, South Dakota State, Green Bay 1931
Jenke, Noel, LB, Minnesota, Minnesota 1971; Atlanta 1972; Green Bay 1973-74
Jenkins, Al, T-G, Tulsa, Cleveland 1969-70; Miami 1972; Houston 1973
Jenkins, Alfred, WR, Morris Brown, Atlanta 1975-83
Jenkins, Eddie, RB, Holy Cross, Miami 1972; NY Giants 1974; Buffalo 1974; New England 1974
Jenkins, Fletcher, DE, Washington, Baltimore 1982
Jenkins, Jacque, HB, Vanderbilt, Washington 1943, 1946-47
Jenkins, Jonathan, T, Dartmouth, Baltimore (AAFC) 1949; Baltimore 1950; NY Yanks 1950
Jenkins, Ken, RB-KR, Bucknell, Detroit 1983-84; Washington 1985
Jenkins, Leon, DB, West Virginia, Detroit 1972
Jenkins, Walt, DE-DT, Wayne State, Detroit 1955
Jennings, Dave, P, St. Lawrence, NY Giants 1974-84; NY Jets 1985
Jennings, Jack, T, Ohio State, Chi. Cardinals 1950-57
Jennings, Jim, E, Missouri, Green Bay 1955
Jennings, Lou, E, Haskell, Providence 1929; Portsmouth 1930
Jennings, Rick, WR, Maryland, Oakland 1976-77; Tampa Bay 1977; San Francisco 1977
Jennings, Stanford, RB-KR, Furman, Cincinnati 1984-85
Jensen, Bob, E, Iowa State, Chi. Rockets (AAFC) 1948; Chi. Hornets (AAFC) 1949; Baltimore 1950
Jensen, Derrick, RB-TE, Texas-Arlington, Oakland 1979-81; LA Raiders 1982-85
Jensen, Jim, RB-TE, Iowa, Dallas 1976; Denver 1977, 1979-80; Green Bay 1981-82
Jensen, Jim, QB-WR, Boston U., Miami 1981-85
Jensen, Russ, QB, California Lutheran, LA Raiders 1985
Jensvold, Leo, QB, Iowa, Chi. Bears 1931; Cleveland 1931
Jeralds, Luther, DE, North Carolina Central, Dallas Texans 1961
Jerome, Jim, LB, Syracuse, NY Jets 1977
Jerue, Mark, LB, Washington, LA Rams 1983-85
Jessen, Ernie, T, Iowa, Cleveland 1931
Jessie, Ron, WR, Kansas, Detroit 1971-74; LA Rams 1975-79; Buffalo 1980-81
Jessup, Bill, HB-FL, USC, San Francisco 1951-52, 1954, 1956-58; Denver 1960
Jeter, Bob, CB, Iowa, Green Bay 1963-70; Chi. Bears 1971-73
Jeter, Gary, DT-DE, USC, NY Giants 1977-82; LA Rams 1983-85
Jeter, Gene, LB, Arkansas-Pine Bluff, Denver 1965-67
Jeter, Perry (Jet), HB, Cal Poly-SLO, Chi. Bears 1956-57
Jeter, Tony, TE, Nebraska, Pittsburgh 1966, 1968
Jett, John, E, Wake Forest, Detroit 1941
Jewett, Bob, SE, Michigan State, Chi. Bears 1958
Jiggetts, Dan, T, Harvard, Chi. Bears 1976-82
Jilek, Dan, LB, Michigan, Buffalo 1978-79
Jiles, Dwayne, LB, Texas Tech, Philadelphia 1985
Joachim, Steve, QB, Temple, NY Jets 1976
Jobko, Bill, LB, Ohio State, LA Rams 1958-62; Minnesota 1963-65; Atlanta 1966
Jocher, Art, G, Manhattan, Brooklyn 1940, 1942
Jodat, Jim, RB, Carthage, LA Rams 1977-79; Seattle 1980-81
Joe, Billy, FB, Villanova, Denver 1963-64; Buffalo 1965; Miami 1966; NY Jets 1967-68
Joe, Larry, HB, Penn State, Buffalo (AAFC) 1949
Joesting, Herb, FB, Minnesota, Minneapolis 1929-30; Frankford 1930-31; Chi. Bears 1931-32
Johansson, Ove, K, Abilene Christian, Philadelphia 1977
Johns, Freeman, WR, SMU, LA Rams 1976-77
Johns, Jim, G, Michigan, Cleveland 1923-24; Minneapolis 1924
Johns, Paul, WR, Tulsa, Seattle 1981-84
Johns, Pete, S, Tulane, Houston 1967-68
Johnson, Al, HB, Hardin-Simmons, Philadelphia 1948
Johnson, Al, S, Cincinnati, Houston 1972-74, 1976-78
Johnson, Andy, RB, Georgia, New England 1974-76, 1978-81
Johnson, Art, T, Fordham, Duluth 1923-27
Johnson, Benny, CB, Johnson C. Smith, Houston 1970-73; New Orleans 1976
Johnson, Bert (Warhorse), HB, Kentucky, Brooklyn 1937; Chi. Bears 1938-39; Chi. Cardinals 1939-41; Philadelphia 1942
Johnson, Bill, E, Minnesota, Green Bay 1941
Johnson, Bill (Tiger), Tyler J.C., San Francisco 1946-56
Johnson, Bill, G, SMU, Chi. Bears 1947
Johnson, Bill, P, Livingston, NY Giants 1970
Johnson, Bill, RB, Arkansas State, Cincinnati 1985
Johnson, Billy, DB, Nebraska, Boston 1966-68
Johnson, Billy (White Shoes), WR-KR, Widener, Houston 1974-80; Atlanta 1982-85
Johnson, Bob, T, Tennessee-Chattanooga, Portsmouth 1930
Johnson, Bob, C, Tennessee, Cincinnati 1968-79
Johnson, Bobby, DB, Texas, New Orleans 1983-84; St. Louis 1985
Johnson, Bobby, WR, Kansas, NY Giants 1984-85
Johnson, Butch, WR-KR, Cal-Riverside, Dallas 1976-83; Denver 1984-85
Johnson, C.E., E-T, Northwestern, Hammond 1920
Johnson, Carl, T-G, Nebraska, New Orleans 1972-73
Johnson, Cecil, HB, East Texas State, Brooklyn 1943-44
Johnson, Cecil, LB, Pittsburgh, Tampa Bay 1977-85
Johnson, Charles, CB, Grambling, San Francisco 1979-80; St. Louis 1981
Johnson, Charles, NT, Maryland, Green Bay 1979-80, 1983
Johnson, Charley, QB, New Mexico State, St. Louis 1961-69; Houston 1970-71; Denver 1972-75
Johnson, Charlie, DT, Louisville, San Francisco 1966-68
Johnson, Charlie, DT-NT, Colorado, Philadelphia 1977-81; Minnesota 1982-84
Johnson, Clyde, T, Kentucky, LA Rams 1946-47; LA Dons (AAFC) 1948
Johnson, Cornelius, G, Virginia Union, Baltimore 1968-73
Johnson, Curley, TE-RB-P, Houston, Dallas Texans 1960; NY Titans 1961-62; NY Jets 1963-68; NY Giants 1969
Johnson, Curtis, CB, Toledo, Miami 1970-78
Johnson, Dan, TE, Iowa State, Miami 1983-85
Johnson, Danny, LB, Tennessee State, Green Bay 1978
Johnson, Darryl, DB, Morgan State, Boston 1968-70
Johnson, Demetrious, S, Missouri, Detroit 1983-85
Johnson, Dennis, DT, Delaware, Washington 1974-77; Buffalo 1978
Johnson, Dennis, RB-TE, Mississippi State, Buffalo 1978-79; NY Giants 1980
Johnson, Dennis, LB, USC, Minnesota 1980-85; Tampa Bay 1985
Johnson, Dick, TE, Minnesota, Kansas City 1963
Johnson, Don, C, Northwestern, Cleveland 1942
Johnson, Don, HB, California, Philadelphia 1953-55
Johnson, Earl, CB, South Carolina, New Orleans 1985
Johnson, Eddie, LB, Louisville, Cleveland 1981-85
Johnson, Ellis, RB, Southeastern Louisiana, Boston 1965-66
Johnson, Eric, S, Washington State, Philadelphia 1977-78; San Francisco 1979
Johnson, Essex, RB, Grambling, Cincinnati 1968-75; Tampa Bay 1976
Johnson, Ezra, DE, Morris Brown, Green Bay 1977-85
Johnson, Farnham, E, Michigan, Wisconsin, Chi. Rockets (AAFC) 1948
Johnson, Frank (Pike), T, Washington & Lee, Akron 1920-21
Johnson, Gary (Big Hands), DT, Grambling, San Diego 1975-84; San Francisco 1984-85
Johnson, Gary Don, DT, Baylor, Baltimore 1980
Johnson, Gene, DB, Cincinnati, Philadelphia 1959-60; Minnesota 1961; NY Giants 1961
Johnson, George, HB, Drake, Racine 1922
Johnson, Gil, QB, SMU, NY Yankees (AAFC) 1949
Johnson, Glenn, T, Arizona State, NY Yankees (AAFC) 1948; Green Bay 1949
Johnson, Greg, DT-DE, Florida State, Baltimore 1977; Chi. Bears 1977; Tampa Bay 1977
Johnson, Greggory, DB, Oklahoma State, Seattle 1981-83
Johnson, Harvey, QB-K, William & Mary, NY Yankees (AAFC) 1946-49; NY Yanks 1951
Johnson, Henry, LB, Georgia Tech, Minnesota 1980-83
Johnson, Herb, HB, Washington (St. Louis), NY Giants 1954
Johnson, Howard (Smiley), G, Georgia, Green Bay 1940-41
Johnson, Jack, T, Utah, Detroit 1934-40
Johnson, Jack, DB, Miami, Chi. Bears 1957-59; Buffalo 1960-61; Dallas Texans 1961
Johnson, Jay, LB, East Texas State, Philadelphia 1969-70
Johnson, Jerry, HB, Morningside, Rock Island 1921-22
Johnson, Jesse, S, Colorado, NY Jets 1980-83
Johnson, Jimmy, WR-CB, UCLA, San Francisco 1961-76
Johnson, Joe, HB, Mississippi, NY Giants 1948
Johnson, Joe, HB-FL, Boston College, Green Bay 1954-58; Boston 1960-61
Johnson, John, DT, Indiana, Chi. Bears 1963-68
Johnson, John Henry, FB, Arizona State, San Francisco 1954-56; Detroit 1957-59; Pittsburgh 1960-65; Houston 1966
Johnson, Johnnie, S, Texas, LA Rams 1980-85
Johnson, Ken, DT, Indiana, Cincinnati 1971-77
Johnson, Ken, QB, Colorado, Buffalo 1977
Johnson, Ken, DE, Knoxville, Buffalo 1979-84
Johnson, Ken, RB, Miami, NY Giants 1979
Johnson, Kenny, CB-KR, Mississippi State, Atlanta 1980-85
Johnson, Kermit, RB, UCLA, San Francisco 1975-76
Johnson, Larry (Chief), C, Haskell, Boston 1933-35; NY Giants 1936-39; Washington 1944
Johnson, Lawrence, CB, Wisconsin, Cleveland 1979-84; Buffalo 1984-85
Johnson, Lee, P, BYU, Houston 1985
Johnson, Len, G-C, Wisconsin-St. Cloud, NY Giants 1970
Johnson, Leo, HB, Millikin, Decatur 1920
Johnson, Leo, WR, Tennessee State, San Francisco 1969-70
Johnson, Leon, E, Columbia, Orange 1929
Johnson, Levi, CB, Texas A&I, Detroit 1973-77
Johnson, Lorne, FB, Temple, Philadelphia 1934
Johnson, Mark, LB, Missouri, Buffalo 1975-76; Cleveland 1977
Johnson, Marshall, WR, Houston, Baltimore 1975, 1977-78
Johnson, Marv, DB, San Jose State, LA Rams 1950-51; Green Bay 1952-53
Johnson, Mike, CB, Kansas, Dallas 1966-69
Johnson, Mike, DE, Illinois, Houston 1984
Johnson, Mitch, G-T, UCLA, Dallas 1965; Washington 1966-67, 1972; LA Rams 1969-70; Cleveland 1971
Johnson, Monte, LB, Nebraska, Oakland 1973-79
Johnson, Nate, T, Illinois, NY Yankees (AAFC) 1946-47; Chi. Rockets (AAFC) 1948; Chi. Hornets (AAFC) 1949; NY Yanks 1950
Johnson, Nate, WR, Hillsdale, NY Giants 1980
Johnson, Norm, K, UCLA, Seattle 1982-85
Johnson, O.G., FB, Chi. Bears 1924
Johnson, Oscar, HB, Vermont, Boston 1929
Johnson, Pete, DB, Virginia Military, Chi. Bears 1959
Johnson, Pete, FB, Ohio State, Cincinnati 1977-83; San Diego 1984; Miami 1984
Johnson, Preston, RB, Florida A&M, Boston 1968

Johnson, Randy, QB, Texas A&I, Atlanta 1966-70; NY Giants 1971-73; Washington 1975; Green Bay 1976
Johnson, Randy, G, Georgia, Tampa Bay 1977-78
Johnson, Ray, HB, Denver, Cleveland 1937-38; Chi. Cardinals 1940
Johnson, Rich, RB, Illinois, Houston 1969
Johnson, Richard, CB, Wisconsin, Houston 1985
Johnson, Ron, HB, Michigan, Cleveland 1969; NY Giants 1970-75
Johnson, Ron, DB, Eastern Michigan, Pittsburgh 1978-84
Johnson, Ron, WR, Long Beach State, Philadelphia 1985
Johnson, Rudy, HB, Nebraska, San Francisco 1964-65; Atlanta 1966
Johnson, Sammy, RB, North Carolina, San Francisco 1974-76; Minnesota 1976-78; Philadelphia 1979; Green Bay 1979
Johnson, Stan, DT, Tennessee State, Kansas City 1978
Johnson, Tom, DT, Michigan, Green Bay 1952
Johnson, Trumaine, WR, Grambling, San Diego 1985
Johnson, Vance, WR, Arizona, Denver 1985
Johnson, Walter, DT, Cal State-Los Angeles, Cleveland 1965-76; Cincinnati 1977
Johnson, Walter, DE, Tuskegee, San Francisco 1967
Johnsos, Luke, E, Northwestern, Chi. Bears 1929-36, 1938
Johnston, Art, HB, Lawrence, Green Bay 1931
Johnston, Chester (Swede), HB, Marquette, St. Louis 1934; Green Bay 1934-38; Pittsburgh 1939-40
Johnston, Jimmy, HB, Washington, Washington 1939-40; Chi. Cardinals 1946
Johnston, Mark, CB, Northwestern, Houston 1960-63; Oakland 1964; NY Jets 1964
Johnston, Preston, HB, SMU, Miami (AAFC) 1946; Buffalo (AAFC) 1946
Johnston, Rex, HB, USC, Pittsburgh 1960
Joiner, Charlie, WR, Grambling, Houston 1969-72; Cincinnati 1972-75; San Diego 1976-85
Joiner, Tim, LB, LSU, Houston 1983-84
Jolitz, Evan, LB, Cincinnati, Cincinnati 1974
Jolley, Al, T, Kansas State, Akron 1922; Dayton 1923; Oorang 1923; Buffalo 1929; Brooklyn 1930; Cleveland 1931
Jolley, Gordon, T, Utah, Detroit 1972-75; Seattle 1976-77
Jolley, Lewis, RB, North Carolina, Houston 1972-73
Jolly, Ken, LB, Mid-American Nazerene, Kansas City 1984-85
Jolly, Mike, S, Michigan, Green Bay 1980, 1982-83
Jonas, Don, HB, Penn State, Philadelphia 1962
Jonas, Marv, C, Utah, Brooklyn 1931
Jonasen, Charlie, E, Minneapolis 1921-23
Jones, A.J. (Jam), RB, Texas, LA Rams 1982-85; Detroit 1985
Jones, Andrew, RB, Washington State, New Orleans 1975-76
Jones, Anthony, TE, Wichita State, Washington 1984-85
Jones, Arrington, RB, Winston-Salem, San Francisco 1981
Jones, Art, HB, Richmond, Pittsburgh 1941, 1945
Jones, Ben, FB, Grove City, Canton 1923, 1925; Dayton 1924; Cleveland 1924-25; Frankford 1925-26; Chi. Cardinals 1927-28
Jones, Bert, QB, LSU, Baltimore 1973-81; LA Rams 1982
Jones, Billy, G, West Virginia Wesleyan, Brooklyn (AAFC) 1947
Jones, Bob, G, Indiana, Green Bay 1934
Jones, Bob, SE, San Diego State, Chi. Bears 1967-69
Jones, Bob, S, Virginia Union, Cincinnati 1973-74; Atlanta 1975-76
Jones, Bobby, WR, NY Jets 1978-82; Cleveland 1983
Jones, Boyd, T, Texas Southern, Green Bay 1984
Jones, Buck, T, Oorang 1922
Jones, Calvin, CB, Washington, Denver 1973-76
Jones, Casey, HB, Union (Tennessee), Detroit 1946
Jones, Cedric, WR, Duke, New England 1982-85
Jones, Charlie, E, George Washington, Washington 1955
Jones, Clint, RB, Michigan State, Minnesota 1967-72; San Diego 1973
Jones, Cody, DE-DT, San Jose State, LA Rams 1974-78, 1980-82
Jones, Curtis, G, Missouri, San Diego 1968
Jones, Daryll, S, Georgia, Green Bay 1984-85
Jones, Dave, WR, Kansas State, Cleveland 1969-71
Jones, David (Deacon), DE, Mississippi Valley State, LA Rams 1961-71; San Diego 1972-73; Washington 1974
Jones, David, C, Texas, Detroit 1984-85
Jones, Doug, DB, Cal State-Northridge, Kansas City 1973-74; Buffalo 1976-78
Jones, Dub, HB-FL, Tulane, Miami (AAFC) 1946; Brooklyn (AAFC) 1946-48; Cleveland 1948-55
Jones, E.J., RB, Kansas, Kansas City 1985
Jones, Earl, CB, Norfolk State, Atlanta 1980-83
Jones, Ed (Too Tall), DE, Tennessee State, Dallas 1974-78, 1980-85
Jones, Ed, DB, Rutgers, Buffalo 1975
Jones, Edgar (Special Delivery), HB, Pittsburgh, Chi. Bears 1945; Cleveland (AAFC) 1946-49
Jones, Ellis, G, Tulsa, Boston 1945
Jones, Elmer, G, Wake Forest, Buffalo (AAFC) 1946; Detroit 1947-48
Jones, Ernie, DB, Miami, Seattle 1976; NY Giants 1977-79
Jones, Ezell, T, Minnesota, Boston 1969-70
Jones, Gene, DB, Rice, Houston 1961
Jones, Gordon, WR, Pittsburgh, Tampa Bay 1979-82; LA Raiders 1983-84
Jones, Greg, RB, UCLA, Buffalo 1970-71
Jones, Harris, G, Johnson C. Smith, San Diego 1971; Houston 1973-74
Jones, Harry, RB, Arkansas, Philadelphia 1967-70
Jones, Harvey, HB, Baylor, Cleveland 1944-45; Washington 1947
Jones, Henry, RB, Grambling, Denver 1969
Jones, Homer, SE-KR, Texas Southern, NY Giants 1964-69; Cleveland 1970
Jones, Horace, DE, Louisville, Oakland 1971-75; Seattle 1977
Jones, J.J., QB, Fisk, NY Jets 1975
Jones, James, RB-KR, Mississippi State, Dallas 1980-82, 1984-85
Jones, James, FB, Florida, Detroit 1983-85
Jones, Jerry, G, Notre Dame, Decatur 1920; Rock Island 1922; Cleveland 1924
Jones, Jerry, T, Bowling Green, Atlanta 1966; New Orleans 1967-69
Jones, Jimmie, DE, Wichita State, NY Jets 1969-70; Washington 1971-73
Jones, Jimmie, RB, UCLA, Detroit 1974
Jones, Jimmy, RB, Washington, LA Rams 1958; Oakland 1961
Jones, Jimmy, SE, Wisconsin, Chi. Bears 1965-67; Denver 1968
Jones, Joe (Turkey), DE, Tennessee State, Cleveland 1970-71, 1973, 1975-78; Philadelphia 1974-75; Washington 1979-80
Jones, Johnny (Lam), WR, Texas, NY Jets 1980-84
Jones, June, QB, Portland State, Atlanta 1977-79, 1981
Jones, Ken, HB, Franklin & Marshall, Buffalo 1924
Jones, Ken, DE, Arkansas State, Buffalo 1976-85
Jones, Kim, RB, Colorado, New Orleans 1976-79
Jones, Larry, WR-KR, Northeast Missouri State, Washington 1974-77; San Francisco 1978
Jones, Leroy, DE, Norfolk State, San Diego 1976-83
Jones, Lew, G, Weatherford J.C., Brooklyn 1943
Jones, Marchall (Deacon), HB, North Dakota, Hammond 1920; Detroit 1920; Akron 1921
Jones, Melvin, G, Houston, Washington 1981
Jones, Mike, LB, Jackson State, Seattle 1977
Jones, Mike, WR, Tennessee State, Minnesota 1983-85
Jones, Quinn, RB, Tulsa, Atlanta 1980
Jones, Ralph, E, Alabama, Detroit 1946; Baltimore (AAFC) 1947
Jones, Ray, DB, Southern, Philadelphia 1970; Miami 1971; San Diego 1972; New Orleans 1973
Jones, Ricky, DB, Tuskegee, Cleveland 1977-79; Baltimore 1980-83
Jones, Robbie, LB, Alabama, NY Giants 1984-85
Jones, Ron, TE, Texas-El Paso, Green Bay 1969
Jones, Rulon, DE, Utah State, Denver 1980-85
Jones, Sean, DE, Northwestern, LA Raiders 1984-85
Jones, Spike, P, Georgia, Houston 1970; Buffalo 1971-74; Philadelphia 1975-77
Jones, Stan, G-T-DT, Maryland, Chi. Bears 1954-65; Washington 1966
Jones, Steve, RB, Duke, Buffalo 1973-74; St. Louis 1974-78
Jones, Terry, DT, Alabama, Green Bay 1978-84
Jones, Thurman, FB, Abilene Christian, Brooklyn 1941-42
Jones, Tom (Pottsville), G, Bucknell, Minneapolis 1930; Frankford 1930-31; NY Giants 1932-36; Green Bay 1938
Jones, Tom, T, Miami (Ohio), Cleveland 1955
Jones, Willie, DB, Purdue, Buffalo 1962
Jones, Willie, DE, Florida State, Oakland 1979-81
Jones, Willie Lee, DE-DT, Kansas State, Houston 1967; Cincinnati 1968, 1970-71
Jordan, Curtis, S, Texas Tech, Tampa Bay 1976-80; Washington 1981-85
Jordan, David, G, Auburn, NY Giants 1984-85
Jordan, Don, RB, Houston, Chi. Bears 1984
Jordan, Frank, HB, Rock Island 1920
Jordan, Henry, DT, Virginia, Cleveland 1957-58; Green Bay 1959-69
Jordan, Jeff, DB, Tulsa, Minnesota 1965-67
Jordan, Jeff, RB, Washington, LA Rams 1970; Washington 1971-72
Jordan, Jimmy, RB, Florida, New Orleans 1967
Jordan, Larry, LB-DE, Youngstown State, Denver 1962, 1964
Jordan, Lee Roy, LB, Alabama, Dallas 1963-76
Jordan, Shelby, T, Washington (St. Louis), New England 1975, 1977-82; LA Raiders 1983-85
Jordan, Steve, TE, Brown, Minnesota 1982-85
Jorgensen, Carl, T, St. Mary's (California), Green Bay 1934; Philadelphia 1935
Jorgensen, Wagner, C, St. Mary's (California), Brooklyn 1936-37
Joseph, Chalmers (Red), E, Miami (Ohio), Dayton 1927; Portsmouth 1930; Cleveland 1931
Joseph, Zern, T, Miami (Ohio), Dayton 1925, 1927
Josephson, Les, RB, Augustana (South Dakota), LA Rams 1964-67, 1969-74
Joswick, Bob, DE-DT, Tulsa, Miami 1968-69
Joyce, Don, DT, Tulane, Chi. Cardinals 1951-53; Baltimore 1954-60; Minnesota 1961; Denver 1962
Joyce, Terry, TE-P, Southern State (Missouri), St. Louis 1976-77
Joyner, L.C., DB, Oakland 1960
Joyner, Willie, RB, Maryland, Houston 1984
Judd, Saxon, E, Tulsa, Brooklyn (AAFC) 1946-48
Judie, Ed, LB, Northern Arizona, San Francisco 1982-83; Tampa Bay 1983; Miami 1984
Judson, William, CB, South Carolina State, Miami 1982-85
Juenger, Dave, WR, Ohio U., Chi. Bears 1973
Julian, Fred, HB, Michigan, NY Titans 1960
Jungmichel, Buddy, G, Texas, Miami (AAFC) 1946
Junior, E.J., LB, Alabama, St. Louis 1981-85
Junker, Steve, TE, Xavier, Detroit 1957, 1959-60; Washington 1961-62
Junkin, Trey, LB-TE, Louisiana Tech, Buffalo 1983-84; Washington 1984; LA Raiders 1985
Jurgensen, Sonny, QB, Duke, Philadelphia 1957-63; Washington 1964-74
Jurich, Mike, T, Denver, Brooklyn 1941-42
Jurich, Tom, K, Northern Arizona, New Orleans 1978
Jurkiewicz, Walt, C, Indiana, Detroit 1946
Jury, Bob, S, Pittsburgh, San Francisco 1978
Juster, Rube, T, Minnesota, Boston 1946
Justice, Charlie (Choo-Choo), HB, North Carolina, Washington 1950, 1952-54
Justice, Ed, HB, Gonzaga, Washington 1936-42
Justin, Kerry, CB, Oregon State, Seattle 1978-83
Justin, Sid, DB, Long Beach State, LA Rams 1979; Baltimore 1982
Juzwik, Steve, HB, Notre Dame, Washington 1942; Buffalo (AAFC) 1946-47; Chi. Rockets (AAFC) 1948

K

Kab, Vyto, TE, Penn State, Philadelphia 1982-85; NY Giants 1985
Kabealo, Mike, HB, Ohio State, Cleveland 1944
Kaczmarek, Mike, LB, Southern Illinois, Baltimore 1973
Kadesky, Max, E, Iowa, Rock Island 1923
Kadish, Mike, DT, Notre Dame, Buffalo 1973-81
Kadziel, Ron, LB, Stanford, New England 1972
Kaer, Mort, QB, USC, Frankford 1931
Kafentzis, Mark, S, Hawaii, Cleveland 1982; Baltimore 1983; Indianapolis 1984
Kahl, Cy, QB-FB, North Dakota, Portsmouth 1930-31
Kahler, Bob, HB, Nebraska, Green Bay 1942-44
Kahler, Royal, T, Nebraska, Pittsburgh 1941; Green Bay 1942
Kahn, Ed, G, North Carolina, Boston 1935-36; Washington 1937
Kaimer, Karl, DE, Boston U., NY Titans 1962
Kaiser, John, LB, Arizona, Seattle 1984-85
Kakasic, George, G, Duquesne, Pittsburgh 1936-39
Kakela, Wayne, C, Minnesota, Minneapolis 1930
Kalina, Dave, WR, Miami, Pittsburgh 1970
Kalmanir, Tommy (Cricket), HB, Nevada-Reno, LA Rams 1949-51; Baltimore 1953
Kalsu, Bob, G, Oklahoma, Buffalo 1968
Kamana, John, RB, USC, LA Rams 1984
Kamanu, Lew, DE, Weber State, Detroit 1967-68
Kaminski, Larry, C, Purdue, Denver 1966-73
Kammerer, Carl, DE-LB, Pacific, San Francisco 1961-62; Washington 1963-69
Kamp, Jim, G, Oklahoma City, T, Staten Island 1932; Boston 1933
Kampa, Bob, DE, California, Buffalo 1973-74; Denver 1974
Kane, Carl, HB, St. Louis, Philadelphia 1936
Kane, Herb, T, East Central (Oklahoma), NY Giants 1944-45
Kane, Jim, G, Rochester 1920; NY Giants 1921
Kane, Rick, RB, San Jose State, Detroit 1977-83, 1985; Washington 1984
Kanicki, Jim, DT, Michigan State, Cleveland 1963-69; NY Giants 1970-71
Kantor, Joe, RB, Notre Dame, Washington 1966
Kanya, Al, T, Syracuse, Staten Island 1931-32
Kapele, John, DT, BYU, Pittsburgh 1960-62; Philadelphia 1962
Kapitansky, Bernie, G, Long Island, Brooklyn 1942
Kaplan, Bernie, G, Western Maryland, NY Giants 1935-36; Philadelphia 1942
Kaplan, Ken, T, New Hampshire, Tampa Bay 1984-85
Kaplan, Sid, QB-HB, Hamline, Minneapolis 1923
Kaplanoff, Karl, T, Ohio State, Brooklyn 1939
Kaporch, Al, T, St. Bonaventure, Detroit 1943-45
Kapp, Joe, QB, California, Minnesota 1967-69; Boston 1970
Kapter, Alex, G, Northwestern, Cleveland (AAFC) 1946-47
Karamatic, George (Automatic), FB, Gonzaga, Washington 1938
Karas, Emil, LB, Dayton, Washington 1959; LA Chargers 1960; San Diego 1961-64, 1966
Karch, Bob, T, Ohio State, Columbus 1921-22; Louisville 1923
Karcher, Jim, G, Ohio State, Boston 1936; Washington 1937-39
Karcis, John (Bull), FB, Carnegie-Mellon, Brooklyn 1932-35; Pittsburgh 1936-38; NY Giants 1938-39, 1943
Karilivacz, Carl, DB, Syracuse, Detroit 1953-57; NY Giants 1958; LA Rams 1959-60
Karlis, Rich, K, Cincinnati, Denver 1982-85
Karmazin, Mike, G, Duke, NY Yankees (AAFC) 1946
Karnofsky, Abe (Sonny), HB, Arizona, Philadelphia 1945; Boston 1946
Karpowich, Ed, T, Catholic, Pittsburgh 1936-39
Karr, Bill, E, West Virginia, Chi. Bears 1933-38
Karras, Alex, DT, Iowa, Detroit 1958-62, 1964-70
Karras, Johnny, HB, Illinois, Chi. Cardinals 1952

Karras, Lou, T, Purdue, Washington 1950-51
Karras, Ted, T, Indiana, Pittsburgh 1958-59; Chi. Bears 1960-64; Detroit 1965; LA Rams 1966
Karrs, John, QB, Duquesne, Cleveland 1944
Karstens, George, C, Indiana, Detroit 1949
Karwales, Jack, E, Michigan, Chi. Cardinals 1947
Kasap, Mike, T, Illinois, Purdue, Baltimore (AAFC) 1947
Kaska, Tony, FB-QB, Illinois Wesleyan, Detroit 1935; Brooklyn 1936-38
Kasky, Ed, T, Villanova, Philadelphia 1942
Kasper, Tom, HB, Notre Dame, Rochester 1923
Kasperek, Dick, C, Iowa State, St. Louis 1966-68
Kassel, Chuck, E, Illinois, Chi. Bears 1927; Frankford 1927-28; Chi. Cardinals 1929-33
Kassulke, Karl, S, Drake, Minnesota 1963-72
Katalinas, Leo, T, Catholic, Green Bay 1938
Katcavage, Jim, DE, Dayton, NY Giants 1956-68
Katcik, Joe, DT, Notre Dame, NY Titans 1960
Katrishen, Mike, T, Southern Mississippi, Washington 1948-49
Kauahi, Kani, C, Hawaii, Seattle 1982-85
Kauffman, John, T, Dayton 1929
Kaufman, Mel, LB, Cal Poly-SLO, Washington 1981-85
Kavanaugh, Ken, E, LSU, Chi. Bears 1940-41, 1945-50
Kavel, George, HB, Carnegie-Mellon, Philadelphia 1934; Pittsburgh 1934
Kaw, Ed, HB, Cornell, Buffalo 1924
Kawal, Ed, C, Illinois, Chi. Bears 1931, 1934-36; Washington 1937
Kay, Bill, CB, Purdue, Houston 1981-83; St. Louis 1984; San Diego 1984
Kay, Clarence, TE, Georgia, Denver 1984-85
Kay, Rick, LB, Colorado, LA Rams 1973, 1975-77; Atlanta 1977
Keahey, Eulis (Duce), T, George Washington, NY Giants 1942; Brooklyn 1942
Keane, Jim, E, Iowa, Chi. Bears 1946-51; Green Bay 1952
Keane, Tom, DB, West Virginia, LA Rams 1948-51; Dallas 1952; Baltimore 1953-54; Chi. Cardinals 1955
Kearney, Jim, CB, Prairie View A&M, Detroit 1965-66; Kansas City 1967-75; New Orleans 1976
Kearney, Tim, LB, Northern Michigan, Cincinnati 1972-74; Kansas City 1975; St. Louis 1976-81
Kearns, Tom, T, Miami, NY Giants 1945; Chi. Cardinals 1946
Keating, Bill, G, Michigan, Denver 1966-67; Miami 1967
Keating, Chris, LB, Maine, Buffalo 1979-84; Washington 1985
Keating, Tom, DT, Michigan, Buffalo 1964-65; Oakland 1966-67, 1969-72; Pittsburgh 1973; Kansas City 1974-75
Keck, Stan, T, Princeton, Cleveland 1923; Rochester 1923
Keckin, Val, QB, Southern Mississippi, San Diego 1962
Keeble, Joe, QB, UCLA, Pittsburgh 1936; Cleveland 1937
Keete, Emmett, G, Notre Dame, Chi. Tigers 1920; Green Bay 1921; Rock Island 1921-22; Milwaukee 1922
Keefe, Jerry, G, Decatur 1920
Keefer, Jack, HB, Brown, Providence 1926; Dayton 1928
Keeling, Ray, T, Texas, Philadelphia 1938-39
Keeling, Rex, P, Samford, Cincinnati 1968
Keen, Allen (Rabbit), HB, Arkansas, Philadelphia 1937-38
Keenan, Ed, G, Washington (Maryland), Hartford 1926
Keenan, Jack, G-T, South Carolina, Washington 1944-45
Keene, Bob, HB, Detroit, Detroit 1943-45
Keeton, Durwood, S, Oklahoma, New England 1975
Keithley, Gary, QB, Texas-El Paso, St. Louis 1973-75
Kekeris, Jim, T, Missouri, Philadelphia 1947; Green Bay 1948
Kelcher, Louie, DT, SMU, San Diego 1975-83; San Francisco 1984
Kell, Paul, T, Notre Dame, Green Bay 1939-40
Kellagher, Bill, HB, Fordham, Chi. Rockets (AAFC) 1946-48
Kellar, Bill, WR, Stanford, Kansas City 1978
Kellar, Mark, RB, Northern Illinois, Minnesota 1976-78
Keller, Ken, HB, North Carolina, Philadelphia 1956-57
Keller, Larry, LB, Houston, NY Jets 1976-78
Keller, Mike, LB, Michigan, Dallas 1972
Kellermann, Ernie, S, Miami (Ohio), Cleveland 1966-71; Cincinnati 1972; Buffalo 1973
Kelley, Bill, E, Texas Tech, Green Bay 1949
Kelley, Bob, C, West Texas State, Philadelphia 1955-56
Kelley, Brian, LB, California Lutheran, NY Giants 1978-83
Kelley, Ed, T, Texas, LA Dons (AAFC) 1949
Kelley, Ed, DB, Texas, Dallas Texans 1961-62
Kelley, Frank, HB, South Dakota State, Cleveland 1927
Kelley, Gordon, LB, Georgia, San Francisco 1960-61; Washington 1962-63
Kelley, Ike, LB, Ohio State, Philadelphia 1966-67, 1969-71
Kelley, Les, FB-LB, Alabama, New Orleans 1967-69
Kelley, Mike, T-G, Notre Dame, Houston 1985
Kellison, John, G, West Virginia Wesleyan, Canton 1920-21; Toledo 1922
Kellogg, Bill, FB-HB, Syracuse, Frankford 1924; Rochester 1925; Chi. Cardinals 1926
Kellogg, Bob, HB, Tulane, Chi. Cardinals 1940
Kellogg, Clarence, FB, St. Mary's (California), Chi. Cardinals 1936
Kellogg, Mike, RB, Santa Clara, Denver 1966-67
Kellum, Marv, LB, Wichita State, Pittsburgh 1974-76; St. Louis 1977
Kelly, Bob, HB, Notre Dame, LA Dons (AAFC) 1947-48; Baltimore (AAFC) 1949
Kelly, Bob, DT, New Mexico State, Houston 1961-64; Kansas City 1967; Cincinnati 1968; Atlanta 1969
Kelly, Charles (Doc), HB, Northwestern, Duluth 1923-26
Kelly, Clancy, G, Olympia, Toledo 1922; Buffalo 1923, 1926; Rochester 1925
Kelly, Ellison, G, Michigan State, NY Giants 1959
Kelly, Elmo, E, Wichita State, Chi. Bears 1944
Kelly, Jim, HB, Detroit, Detroit 1920
Kelly, Jim, TE, Notre Dame, Pittsburgh 1963; Philadelphia 1965, 1967
Kelly, Jim, TE, Tennessee State, Chi. Bears 1974
Kelly, John (Shipwreck), HB, Kentucky, NY Giants 1932; Brooklyn 1933-34, 1937
Kelly, John, T, Florida A&M, Washington 1966-67
Kelly, Leroy, RB, Morgan State, Cleveland 1964-73
Kelly, Mike, TE, Davidson, Cincinnati 1970-72; New Orleans 1973
Kelly, William (Wild Bill), QB, Montana, NY Yankees 1927-28; Frankford 1929; Brooklyn 1930
Kelsch, Christian (Mose), HB, Pittsburgh 1933-34
Kelsch, Matt, E, Iowa, Brooklyn 1930
Kemp, Bobby, S, Cal State-Fullerton, Cincinnati 1981-85
Kemp, Jack, QB, Occidental, Pittsburgh 1957; LA Chargers 1960; San Diego 1961-62; Buffalo 1962-67, 1969
Kemp, Jeff, QB, Dartmouth, LA Rams 1981-85
Kemp, Ray, T, Duquesne, Pittsburgh 1933
Kempf, Florian, K, Pennsylvania, Houston 1982-84
Kempinski, Charlie, G, Mississippi, LA Chargers 1960
Kempton, Herbert (Fido), HB, Yale, Canton 1921
Kendall, Charlie, DB, UCLA, Houston 1960
Kendrick, Jim, E-QB, Texas A&M, Toledo 1922; Canton 1922; Louisville 1923; Chi. Bears 1924; Hammond 1925; Buffalo 1925-26; NY Giants 1927
Kendrick, Vince, RB, Florida, Atlanta 1974; Tampa Bay 1976
Kenerson, John, G, Kentucky State, LA Rams 1960; Pittsburgh 1962; NY Titans 1962
Kenn, Mike, T, Michigan, Atlanta 1978-85
Kennard, George, G, Kansas, NY Giants 1952-54
Kennard, Ken, DT, Angelo State, Houston 1977-83
Kenneally, George, E, St. Bonaventure, Pottsville 1926-28; Boston 1929, 1932; Chi. Cardinals 1930; Philadelphia 1933-35
Kennedy, Allan, T, Washington State, San Francisco 1981, 1983-84
Kennedy, Bill, E-G, Michigan State, Detroit 1942; Boston 1947
Kennedy, Bob, HB-FB, Washington State, NY Yankees (AAFC) 1946-49; NY Yanks 1950
Kennedy, Bob, HB, North Carolina, LA Dons (AAFC) 1949
Kennedy, Jimmie, TE, Colorado State, Baltimore 1975-77
Kennedy, Joe, FB, Columbia, Buffalo 1925
Kennedy, Mike, S, Toledo, Buffalo 1983; Houston 1984
Kennedy, Tom, T, Wayne State (Nebraska), Detroit 1944
Kennedy, Tom, QB, Cal State-Los Angeles, NY Giants 1966
Kenney, Bill, QB, Northern Colorado, Kansas City 1979-85
Kenney, Charlie, G, San Francisco, San Francisco (AAFC) 1947
Kenney, Steve, G, Clemson, Philadelphia 1980-85
Kent, Greg, T, Utah, Oakland 1966; Detroit 1968
Kenyon, Bill, HB, Georgetown (Washington D.C.), NY Giants 1925
Kenyon, Crowell, G, Ripon, Green Bay 1923
Ker, Crawford, G, Florida, Dallas 1985
Kerbow, Randy, FL, Rice, Houston 1963
Kercher, Bob, E, Georgetown (Washington D.C.), Green Bay 1944
Kercher, Dick, HB, Tulsa, Detroit 1954
Kercheval, Ralph, HB, Kentucky, Brooklyn 1934-40
Keriasotis, Nick, G, St. Ambrose, Chi. Bears 1942, 1945
Kerkorian, Gary, QB, Stanford, Pittsburgh 1952; Baltimore 1954-56
Kern, Bill, T, Pittsburgh, Green Bay 1929-30
Kern, Don, TE, Arizona State, Cincinnati 1984-85
Kern, Rex, S, Ohio State, Baltimore 1971-73; Buffalo 1974
Kerns, John, T, Ohio U., Buffalo (AAFC) 1947-49
Kernwein, Graham, HB, Chicago, Racine 1926
Kerr, Bill, E, Notre Dame, LA Dons (AAFC) 1946
Kerr, George, T-HB, Catholic, Cleveland 1920
Kerr, Jim, DB, Penn State, Washington 1961-62
Kerrigan, Mike, QB, Northwestern, New England 1983-84
Kerrigan, Tom, G, Columbia, Orange 1929; Newark 1930
Kersey, Merritt, P, West Chester, Philadelphia 1974-75
Kershaw, George, E, Colgate, NY Giants 1949
Kersten, Wally, T, Minnesota, LA Rams 1982; Tampa Bay 1985
Ketzko, Alex, T, Michigan State, Detroit 1943
Keuper, Ken, HB, Georgia, Green Bay 1945-47; NY Giants 1948
Key, Wade, G, Southwest Texas State, Philadelphia 1970-78
Keyes, Bob, HB, San Diego, Oakland 1960
Keyes, Jimmy, LB, Mississippi, Miami 1968-69
Keyes, Leroy, RB-DB, Purdue, Philadelphia 1969-72; Kansas City 1973
Keys, Brady, DB, Colorado State, Pittsburgh 1961-67; Minnesota 1967; St. Louis 1968
Keys, Howard, C-T, Oklahoma State, Philadelphia 1960-63
Keys, Tyrone, DE, Mississippi State, Chi. Bears 1983-85
Keyworth, Jon, FB, Colorado, Denver 1974-80
Khayat, Bob, G-K, Mississippi, Washington 1960, 1962-63
Khayat, Eddie, DE, Tulane, Washington 1957, 1962-63; Philadelphia 1958-61, 1964-65; Boston 1966
Kibler, Bill, HB, Buffalo 1922
Kichefski, Walt, E, Miami, Pittsburgh 1940-42; Card-Pitt 1944
Kidd, John, P, Northwestern, Buffalo 1984-85
Kiel, Blair, QB, Notre Dame, Tampa Bay 1984
Kielbasa, Max, HB, Duquesne, Pittsburgh 1946
Kieley, Howard, T-G, Duluth 1923-25; Chi. Cardinals 1926
Kiesling, Walt, G, St. Thomas (Minnesota), Duluth 1926-27; Pottsville 1928; Chi. Cardinals 1929-33; Chi. Bears 1934; Green Bay 1935-36; Pittsburgh 1937-38
Kiewel, Jeff, G, Arizona, Atlanta 1985
Kiick, George, HB, Bucknell, Pittsburgh 1940, 1945
Kiick, Jim, RB, Wyoming, Miami 1966-74; Denver 1976-77; Washington 1977
Kilbourne, Wally, T, Minnesota, Green Bay 1939
Kilcullen, Bob, DT, Texas Tech, Chi. Bears 1957-58, 1960-66
Kiley, Roger, E, Notre Dame, Chi. Cardinals 1923
Kilgore, Jon, P, Auburn, LA Rams 1965-67; Chi. Bears 1968; San Francisco 1969
Killett, Charlie, RB, Memphis State, NY Giants 1963
Killian, Gene, G, Tennessee, Dallas 1974
Killiher, Lou, G, Chi. Cardinals 1928
Killinger, Glenn, QB, Penn State, Canton 1921; NY Giants 1926
Killorin, Pat, C, Syracuse, Pittsburgh 1966
Kilmer, Billy, QB-HB, UCLA, San Francisco 1961-62, 1964, 1966; New Orleans 1967-70; Washington 1971-78
Kilroy, Frank (Bucko), G, Temple, Phil-Pitt 1943; Philadelphia 1944-55
Kilson, David, CB, Nevada-Reno, Buffalo 1983
Kimball, Bobby, WR, Oklahoma, Green Bay 1979-80
Kimball, Bruce, G, Massachusetts, NY Giants 1982; Washington 1983-84
Kimber, Bill, SE, Florida State, NY Giants 1959-60; Boston 1961
Kimble, Frank, E, West Virginia, Pittsburgh 1945
Kimbrough, Elbert, DB, Northwestern, LA Rams 1961; San Francisco 1962-66; New Orleans 1968
Kimbrough, John (Jarrin' John), FB, Texas A&M, LA Dons (AAFC) 1946-48
Kimbrough, John, WR, Wisconsin-St. Cloud, Buffalo 1977
Kimmel, J.D., DT, Army, Houston, Washington 1955-56; Green Bay 1958
Kimmel, Jon, CB, Colgate, Philadelphia 1985
Kinard, Billy, DB, Mississippi, Cleveland 1956; Green Bay 1957-58; Buffalo 1960
Kinard, Frank (Bruiser), T, Mississippi, Brooklyn 1938-44; NY Yankees (AAFC) 1946-47
Kinard, George, G, Mississippi, Brooklyn 1941-42; NY Yankees (AAFC) 1946
Kinard, Terry, S, Clemson, NY Giants 1983-85
Kincaid, Jim, DB, South Carolina, Washington 1954
Kinderdine, George, C, Dayton 1920-29
Kinderdine, Jim, G, Dayton 1924
Kinderdine, Walt, HB-FB, Dayton 1923-25
Kinderman, Keith, RB, Florida State, San Diego 1963-64, Houston 1965
Kindig, Howard, C-T, Cal State-Los Angeles, San Diego 1965-67; Buffalo 1967-71; Miami 1972; NY Jets 1974
Kindle, Greg, T-G, Tennessee State,St. Louis 1974-75; Atlanta 1976-77
Kindricks, Bill, DT, Alabama A&M, Cincinnati 1968
Kindt, Don, HB-DB, Wisconsin, Chi. Bears 1947-55
Kinek, George, DB, Tulane, Chi. Cardinals 1954
Kinek, Mike, E, Michigan State, Cleveland 1940
Kiner, Steve, LB, Tennessee, Dallas 1970; New England 1971, 1973; Houston 1974-78
King, Angelo, LB, South Carolina State, Dallas 1981-83; Detroit 1984-85
King, Bruce, RB, Purdue, Kansas City 1985
King, Charley, DB, Purdue, Buffalo 1966-67; Cincinnati 1968-69
King, Claude, HB, Houston, Houston 1961; Boston 1962
King, David, CB, Auburn, San Diego 1985
King, Dick, HB, Harvard, Hammond 1921; Rochester 1922; Milwaukee 1922; St. Louis 1923
King, Don, DT, Kentucky, Cleveland 1954; Philadelphia 1956; Green Bay 1956; Denver 1960
King, Eddie, G, Boston College, Buffalo (AAFC) 1948-49; Baltimore 1950
King, Emanuel, LB, Alabama, Cincinnati 1985
King, Emmett, HB, Chi. Cardinals 1954
King, Fred, FB, Hobart, Brooklyn 1937
King, Gordon, T, Stanford, NY Giants 1978-83, 1985
King, Henry, DB, Utah State, NY Jets 1967
King, Horace, RB, Georgia, Detroit 1975-83
King, Jerome, CB, Purdue, Atlanta 1979-80; NY Giants 1980
King, Kenny, RB, Oklahoma, Houston 1979; Oakland 1980-81; LA Raiders 1982-85
King, Lafayette (Dolly), E, Georgia, Buffalo (AAFC) 1946-47; Chi. Rockets (AAFC) 1948; Chi. Hornets (AAFC) 1949
King, Linden, S-LB, Colorado State, San Diego 1978-85
King, Paul (Gus), HB, Centre, Dayton 1921; Cincinnati 1921; Toledo 1922
King, Phil (Chief), FB, Vanderbilt, NY Giants 1958-63; Pittsburgh 1964; Minnesota 1965-66
King, Ralph, T, Chicago, Racine 1924; Chi. Bears 1925
King, Rip, FB-HB, West Virginia, Akron 1920-22; Chi. Cardinals 1923-24; Hammond 1925
King, Steve, LB, Tulsa, New England 1973-81
King, Tony, FL, Findlay, Buffalo 1967
Kingery, Ellsworth, DB, Tulane, Chi. Cardinals 1954

Kingery, Wayne, HB, LSU, Baltimore (AAFC) 1949
Kingrea, Rick, LB, Tulane, Cleveland 1971-72; Buffalo 1973; New Orleans 1973-78
Kingsriter, Doug, TE, Minnesota, Minnesota 1973-75
Kinlaw, Reggie, DT-NT, Oklahoma, Oakland 1979-81; LA Raiders 1982-84; Seattle 1985
Kinnebrew, Larry, FB, Tennessee State, Cincinnati 1983-85
Kinney, George, DE, Wiley, Houston 1965
Kinney, Jeff, RB, Nebraska, Kansas City 1972-76; Buffalo 1976
Kinney, Steve, T, Utah State, Chi. Bears 1973-74
Kinney, Vince, WR, Maryland, Denver 1978-79
Kinscherf, Carl, HB, Colgate, NY Giants 1943-44
Kirby, John, LB, Nebraska, Minnesota 1964-69; NY Giants 1969-70
Kirchbaum, Kelly, LB, Kentucky, Kansas City 1980
Kirchiro, Bill, G, Maryland, Baltimore 1962
Kirchner, Dolph, T, Louisville 1926
Kirchner, Mark, T, Baylor, Pittsburgh 1983; Kansas City 1983; Indianapolis 1984
Kirk, Ernest, DE, Howard Payne, Houston 1977
Kirk, George, C, Baylor, Buffalo 1926
Kirk, Ken, LB, Mississippi, Chi. Bears 1960-61; Pittsburgh 1962; LA Rams 1963
Kirkgard, Harry, HB, Waynesburg, Toledo 1923
Kirkland, B'ho, G, Alabama, Brooklyn 1935-36
Kirkland, Mike, QB, Arkansas, Baltimore 1976-78
Kirkman, Roger (Reds), QB, Washington & Jefferson, Philadelphia 1933-35
Kirksey, Roy, G, Maryland-Eastern Shore, NY Jets 1971-72; Philadelphia 1973-74
Kirleski, Frank, HB, Lafayette, Pottsville 1927-28; Orange 1929; Newark 1930; Brooklyn 1931
Kirner, Gary, T, USC, San Diego 1964-69
Kirouac, Lou, DE-K, Boston College, NY Giants 1963; Baltimore 1964; Atlanta 1966-67
Kish, Ben, FB, Pittsburgh, Brooklyn 1940-41; Phil-Pitt 1943; Philadelphia 1944-49
Kisiday, George, E, Columbia, Buffalo (AAFC) 1946
Kissell, Dolph, HB, Boston College, Chi. Bears 1942
Kissell, Ed, DB, Wake Forest, Pittsburgh 1952, 1954
Kissell, John, DT, Boston College, Buffalo (AAFC) 1948-49; Cleveland 1950-52, 1954-56
Kissell, Vito, FB, Holy Cross, Buffalo (AAFC) 1948; Baltimore 1950; NY Yanks 1951
Kitson, Syd, G, Wake Forest, Green Bay 1980-81, 1983-84; Dallas 1984
Kittredge, Paul, HB, Holy Cross, Boston 1929
Kitzmiller, John (Dutch), FB, Oregon, NY Giants 1931
Kizzire, Lee, FB, Wyoming, Detroit 1937
Klapstein, Earl, T, Pacific, Pittsburgh 1946
Klasoskus, Al, T, Holy Cross, NY Giants 1942
Klasnic, John, HB, Brooklyn (AAFC) 1948
Klaus, Fee, C, Green Bay 1921
Klawitter, Dick, C, South Dakota State, Chi. Bears 1956
Klecko, Joe, DE-DT, Temple, NY Jets 1977-85
Klein, Bob, TE, USC, LA Rams 1969-76; San Diego 1977-80
Klein, Dick, T, Iowa, Chi. Bears 1958-59; Dallas Cowboys 1960; Pittsburgh 1961; Boston 1961-62; Oakland 1963-64
Klenk, Quentin, E, USC, Buffalo (AAFC) 1946; Chi. Rockets (AAFC) 1946
Klever, Rocky, TE, Montana, NY Jets 1983-85
Klewicki, Ed, E, Michigan State, Detroit 1935-38
Klieban, Roger, HB, Wisconsin-Milwaukee, Green Bay 1921
Klimek, Tony, DE, Illinois, Chi. Cardinals 1951-52
Kline, Harry (Jiggs), E, Emporia State, NY Giants 1939-40, 1942
Kloppenberg, Harry, E, Fordham, Staten Island 1930; Brooklyn 1931, 1933-34
Klosterman, Don, QB, Loyola (Los Angeles), LA Rams 1952
Klotovich, Mike, HB, St. Mary's (California), NY Giants 1945
Klotz, Jack, T, Widener, NY Titans 1960-62; San Diego 1962; NY Jets 1963; Houston 1964
Klug, Al, T, Marquette, Buffalo (AAFC) 1946; Baltimore (AAFC) 1947-48
Klug, Dave, LB, Concordia, Kansas City 1981-83
Klumb, John, E, Washington State, Chi. Cardinals 1939-40; Pittsburgh 1940
Klutka, Nick, E, Florida, Buffalo (AAFC) 1946
Kmetovic, Pete, HB, Stanford, Philadelphia 1946; Detroit 1947
Knabb, Chet, HB-FB, Cincinnati 1921
Knafelc, Gary, FL-TE, Colorado, Chi. Cardinals 1954; Green Bay 1954-62; San Francisco 1963
Knafelc, Greg, QB, Notre Dame, New Orleans 1983
Knapper, Joe, FB, Ottawa (Kansas), Philadelphia 1934
Knapple, Jeff, QB, Northern Colorado, Denver 1980
Knecht, Bill, T, Xavier, Dayton 1925-26
Knief, Gayle, WR, Morningside, Boston 1970
Knight, Charlie, C, Chi. Cardinals 1920-21
Knight, Curt, K, Coast Guard, Washington 1969-73
Knight, David, WR, William & Mary, NY Jets 1973-77
Knight, Pat, LB, SMU, NY Giants 1952, 1954-55
Knoff, Kurt, S, Kansas, Houston 1977-78; Minnesota 1979-82
Knolla, John, HB, Creighton, Chi. Cardinals 1942, 1945
Knop, Oscar, FB-E, Illinois, Chi. Tigers 1920; Hammond 1920, 1922-23; Chi. Bears 1923-28
Knorr, Larry, C, Dayton, Detroit 1942, 1945
Knox, Bill, DB, Purdue, Chi. Bears 1974-76
Knox, Charlie, T, St. Edmonds, Philadelphia 1937
Knox, Ronnie, QB, UCLA, Chi. Bears 1957
Knox, Sam, G, New Hampshire, Detroit 1934-36
Knutson, Gene, E, Michigan, Green Bay 1954, 1956
Knutson, Steve, G, USC, Green Bay 1976-77; San Francisco 1978
Kober, Matt, G, Villanova, Brooklyn 1940
Kobolinski, Stan, C, Boston College, Brooklyn 1926; Pottsville 1926
Kobrosky, Mickey, QB, Trinity (Connecticut), NY Giants 1937
Koch, George, HB, St. Mary's (Texas), Cleveland 1945; Buffalo (AAFC) 1947
Koch, Greg, T, Arkansas, Green Bay 1977-85
Koch, Pete, DE, Maryland, Cincinnati 1984; Kansas City 1985
Koch, Polly, G-T, Rock Island 1920
Kochel, Mike, G, Fordham, Chi. Cardinals 1939
Kochman, Roger, HB-KR, Penn State, Buffalo 1963
Kocourek, Dave, TE, Wisconsin, LA Chargers 1960; San Diego 1961-65; Miami 1966; Oakland 1967-68
Kodba, Joe, C, Purdue, Baltimore (AAFC) 1947
Koegel, Vic, LB, Ohio State, Cincinnati 1974
Koegel, Warren, C, Penn State, Oakland 1971; St. Louis 1973; NY Jets 1974
Koehler, Bob, FB, Northwestern, Decatur 1920; Chi. Cardinals 1921-26
Koeninger, Art, C, Tennessee-Chattanooga, Frankford 1931; Staten Island 1932; Philadelphia 1933
Koeper, Rich, T, Oregon State, Atlanta 1966
Koepfer, Karl, G, Bowling Green, Detroit 1958
Kofler, Matt, QB, San Diego State, Buffalo 1982-84; Indianapolis 1985
Kohlbrand, Joe, DE, Miami, New Orleans 1985
Kohrs, Bob, LB-DE, Arizona State, Pittsburgh 1981-85
Koken, Mike, HB, Notre Dame, Chi. Cardinals 1933
Kolb, Jon, C-T, Oklahoma State, Pittsburgh 1969-81
Kolberg, Elmer, E-HB, Oregon State, Philadelphia 1939-40; Pittsburgh 1941
Kolen, Mike, LB, Auburn, Miami 1970-75, 1977
Kolesar, Bob, G, Michigan, Cleveland (AAFC) 1946
Kollar, Bill, DT, Montana State, Cincinnati 1974-76; Tampa Bay 1977-81
Kolls, Louis, C-G, St. Ambrose, Chi. Cardinals 1920; Hammond 1920; Rock Island 1922-25; NY Yankees 1927
Kolman, Ed, T, Temple, Chi. Bears 1940-42, 1946-47; NY Giants 1949
Kolodziejski, Chris, TE, Wyoming, Pittsburgh 1984
Koman, Bill, LB, North Carolina, Baltimore 1956; Philadelphia 1957-58; Chi. Cardinals 1959; St. Louis 1960-67
Komlo, Jeff, QB, Delaware, Detroit 1979-81; Atlanta 1982; Tampa Bay 1983
Kompara, John, DT, South Carolina, LA Chargers 1960
Koncar, Mark, T, Colorado, Green Bay 1976-77, 1979-81; Houston 1982
Kondria, John, T, St. Vincent, Pittsburgh 1945
Konetsky, Floyd, E, Florida, Cleveland 1944-45; Baltimore (AAFC) 1947
Koniszewski, John, T, George Washington, Washington 1945-46, 1948
Konovsky, Bob, G, Wisconsin, Chi. Cardinals 1958-59; Chi. Bears 1960; Denver 1961
Konz, Kenny, DB, LSU, Cleveland 1953-59
Koons, Joe, C, Scranton, Brooklyn 1941
Koontz, Ed, LB, Catawba, Boston 1968
Koontz, Joe, SE, Cal State-San Francisco, NY Giants 1968
Kopay, Dave, RB, Washington, San Francisco 1964-67; Detroit 1968; Washington 1969-70; New Orleans 1971; Green Bay 1972
Kopcha, Joe, G, Tennessee-Chattanooga, Chi. Bears 1929, 1932-35; Detroit 1936
Koplow, Joe, T, Boston U., Providence 1926; Boston 1929
Koppisch, Walter, HB-FB, Columbia, Buffalo 1925; NY Giants 1926
Korisky, Ed, C, Villanova, Boston 1944
Kortas, Ken, DT, Louisville, St. Louis 1964; Pittsburgh 1965-68; Chi. Bears 1969
Korte, Steve, C, Arkansas, New Orleans 1983-85
Korver, Kelvin, DT, Northwestern (Iowa), Oakland 1973-75
Kosar, Bernie, QB, Miami, Cleveland 1985
Kosel, Stan, HB, Albright, Brooklyn 1938-39
Kosens, Terry, DB, Hofstra, Minnesota 1963
Koshlap, Julie, HB, Georgetown (Washington D.C.), Pittsburgh 1945
Kosikowski, Frank, E, Notre Dame, Cleveland (AAFC) 1948; Buffalo (AAFC) 1948
Kosins, Gary, RB, Dayton, Chi. Bears 1972-74
Koslowski, Stan, FB, Holy Cross, Miami (AAFC) 1946
Kostelnik, Ron, DT, Cincinnati, Green Bay 1961-68; Baltimore 1969
Kostiuk, Mike, T, Detroit Tech, Cleveland 1941; Detroit 1945; Buffalo (AAFC) 1946
Kostka, Stan, FB, Minnesota, Brooklyn 1935
Kostos, Marty, E, Albright, Frankford 1929
Kostos, Tony, E, Bucknell, Frankford 1927-31; Minneapolis 1930
Kotal, Eddie, QB-HB, Lawrence, Green Bay 1925-29
Kotar, Doug, RB, Kentucky, NY Giants 1974-80
Kotite, Rich, TE, Wagner, NY Giants 1967, 1969, 1971-72; Pittsburgh 1968
Kottler, Marty, FB, Centre, Pittsburgh 1933
Kovac, Ed, FB, Cincinnati, Baltimore 1960; NY Titans 1962
Kovach, Jim, LB, Kentucky, New Orleans 1979-85; San Francisco 1985
Kovascy, Bill, T, Illinois, Hammond 1923
Kovatch, John, E, Notre Dame, Washington 1942, 1946; Green Bay 1947
Kovatch, Johnny, E, Northwestern, Cleveland 1938
Kowalczyk, Walt, FB, Michigan State, Philadelphia 1958-59; Dallas Cowboys 1960; Oakland 1961
Kowalkowski, Bob, G, Virginia, Detroit 1966-76; Green Bay 1977
Kowalski, Adolph, QB, Tulsa, Brooklyn (AAFC) 1947
Kowalski, Andy, E, Mississippi State, Brooklyn 1943-44; Boston 1945; Miami (AAFC) 1946
Kowalski, Gary, T, Boston College, LA Rams 1983; San Diego 1985
Koy, Ernie, RB-P, Texas, NY Giants 1965-70
Koy, Ted, RB-TE-LB, Texas, Oakland 1970; Buffalo 1971-74
Kozel, Chet, G-T, Mississippi, Buffalo (AAFC) 1947-48; Chi. Rockets (AAFC) 1948
Kozerski, Bruce, T-C, Holy Cross, Cincinnati 1984-85
Koziak, Mike, G, Notre Dame, Duluth 1924-25
Kozlowski, Mike, S, Colorado, Miami 1979, 1981-85
Kozlowsky, Joe, T, Boston College, Providence 1925-27, 1930; Boston 1929
Kraayeveld, Dave, DE-DT, Milton, Seattle 1978
Kracum, George, FB, Pittsburgh, Brooklyn 1941
Kraehe, Ollie, G-E, Washington (St. Louis), Rock Island 1922; St. Louis 1923
Kraemer, Eldred, G, Pittsburgh, San Francisco 1955
Kraft, Reynolds, E, Illinois, Minneapolis 1922
Kragen, Greg, NT, Utah State, Denver 1985
Krahl, Jim, DT, Texas Tech, NY Giants 1978; Baltimore 1979; San Francisco 1980
Krakau, Merv, LB, Iowa State, Buffalo 1973-78; New England 1978
Kraker, Joe, T, Saskatchewan, Rock Island 1924
Krakowski, Joe, DB, Illinois, Washington 1961; Oakland 1963-66
Krall, Gerry, HB, Ohio State, Detroit 1950
Kramer, Fritz, G, Washington State, NY Yankees 1927
Kramer, George, G, Minneapolis 1921-24
Kramer, Jack, T, Marquette, Buffalo (AAFC) 1946
Kramer, Jerry, G-K, Idaho, Green Bay 1958-68
Kramer, Kent, TE, Minnesota, San Francisco 1966; New Orleans 1967; Minnesota 1969-70; Philadelphia 1971-74
Kramer, Ron, E-TE, Michigan, Green Bay 1957, 1959-65; Detroit 1965-67
Kramer, Tommy, QB, Rice, Minnesota 1977-85
Kranz, Ken, DB, Wisconsin-Milwaukee, Green Bay 1949
Kratzer, Danny, WR, Missouri Valley, Kansas City 1973
Kraus, Frank, T-G, Hobart, Buffalo 1924
Krause, Bill, G, Baldwin-Wallace, Cleveland 1938
Krause, Henry (Reds), C, St. Louis, Brooklyn 1936-37; Washington 1937-38
Krause, Larry, RB-KR, St. Norbert, Green Bay 1970-71, 1973-74
Krause, Max, QB-FB, Gonzaga, NY Giants 1933-36; Washington 1937-40
Krause, Paul, S, Iowa, Washington 1964-67; Minnesota 1968-79
Krauss, Barry, LB, Alabama, Baltimore 1979-83; Indianapolis 1984-85
Krayenbuhl, Craig, HB, Louisville 1922
Kraynak, Rich, LB, Pittsburgh, Philadelphia 1983-85
Kreamcheck, John, DT, William & Mary, Chi. Bears 1953-55
Kreider, Steve, WR, Lehigh, Cincinnati 1979-85
Kreinheder, Walt, G-QB, Michigan, Akron 1922; St. Louis 1923; Cleveland 1925
Kreitling, Rich, SE, Illinois, Cleveland 1959-63; Chi. Bears 1964
Krejci, Joe, E, Peru State, Chi. Cardinals 1934
Kremer, Ken, NT, Ball State, Kansas City 1979-84
Kremser, Karl, K, Tennessee, Miami 1969-70
Krenk, Mitch, TE, Nebraska, Chi. Bears 1984
Krentler, Ty, FB, Detroit, Detroit 1920
Krepfle, Keith, TE, Iowa State, Philadelphia 1975-81; Atlanta 1982
Kreriwicz, Mark, G, Ohio State, Cleveland 1985
Kresky, Joe, G, Wisconsin, Boston 1932; Philadelphia 1933-35; Pittsburgh 1935
Krevis, Al, T, Boston College, Cincinnati 1975; NY Jets 1976
Krieg, Dave, QB, Milton, Seattle 1980-85
Krieg, Jim, WR, Washington, Denver 1972
Krieger, Bob, E, Dartmouth, Philadelphia 1941, 1946
Krieger, Earl, HB-E, Ohio U., Detroit 1921; Columbus 1922
Kriel, Emmett, G, Baylor, Philadelphia 1939
Kriewald, Doug, G, West Texas State, Chi. Bears 1967-68
Krimm, John, S, Notre Dame, New Orleans 1982
Kring, Frank, HB, TCU, Detroit 1945
Krisher, Bill, G, Oklahoma, Pittsburgh 1958; Dallas Texans 1960-61
Kriss, Howard, HB, Ohio State, Cleveland 1931
Kristufek, Frank, T, Pittsburgh, Brooklyn 1940-41
Krivonak, Joe, G, South Carolina, Miami (AAFC) 1946
Krol, Joe, HB, West Ontario, Detroit 1945
Kroll, Alex, C, Rutgers, NY Titans 1962
Kroll, Bob, DB, Northern Michigan, Green Bay 1972-73
Kroner, Gary, K, Wisconsin, Denver 1965-67
Krouse, Ray, DT, Maryland, NY Giants 1951-55; Detroit

1956-57; Baltimore 1958-59; Washington 1960
Kruczek, Mike, QB, Boston College, Pittsburgh 1976-79; Washington 1980
Krueck, Ed, E, Indiana Central, Cincinnati 1921
Krueger, Al, T, Drake, Kansas City 1924
Krueger, Al, E, USC, Washington 1941-42; LA Dons (AAFC) 1946
Krueger, Charlie, DT, Texas A&M, San Francisco 1959-73
Krueger, Rolf, DE, Texas A&M, St. Louis 1969-71; San Francisco 1972-74
Krumrie, Tim, NT, Wisconsin, Cincinnati 1983-85
Krupa, Joe, DT, Purdue, Pittsburgh 1956-64
Kruse, Bob, G, Wayne State (Nebraska), Oakland 1967-68; Buffalo 1969
Krutko, Larry, FB, West Virginia, Pittsburgh 1959-60
Krysl, Jerry, T, Kansas State, Cleveland 1927
Ksionzyk, John, QB, St. Bonaventure, LA Rams 1947
Kubiak, Gary, QB, Texas A&M, Denver 1983-85
Kubin, Larry, LB, Penn State, Washington 1982-84; Buffalo 1985; Tampa Bay 1985
Kubula, Ray, C, Texas A&M, Denver 1964-67
Kucharski, Ted, E, Holy Cross, Providence 1930
Kuchta, Frank, C, Notre Dame, Washington 1958-59; Denver 1960
Kuczinski, Bernie, E, Pennsylvania, Detroit 1943; Philadelphia 1946
Kuczo, Paul, HB, Villanova, Staten Island 1929
Kuechenberg, Bob, G-T, Notre Dame, Miami 1970-83
Kuechenberg, Rudy, LB, Indiana, Chi. Bears 1967-69; Cleveland 1970; Green Bay 1970; Atlanta 1971
Kuehl, Walter (Waddy), HB, Dubuque, Rock Island 1920, 1923; Detroit 1921; Buffalo 1921-22; Dayton 1924
Kuehn, Art, C, UCLA, Seattle 1976-82; New England 1983
Kuehner, Oscar, T-G, Columbus 1920-21
Kuffel, Ray, E, Marquette, Buffalo (AAFC) 1947; Chi. Rockets (AAFC) 1948; Chi. Hornets (AAFC) 1949
Kugler, Pete, NT, Penn State, San Francisco 1981-83
Kuharich, Joe, G, Notre Dame, Chi. Cardinals 1940-41, 1945
Kuick, Stan, G, Beloit, Green Bay 1926; Milwaukee 1926
Kulbacki, Joe, HB, Purdue, Buffalo 1960
Kulbitski, Vic, FB, Notre Dame, Buffalo (AAFC) 1946-48
Kunz, George, T, Notre Dame, Atlanta 1969-74; Baltimore 1975-77, 1980
Kunz, Lee, LB, Nebraska, Chi. Bears 1979-81
Kunz, Terry, RB, Colorado, Oakland 1976
Kupcinet, Irv, QB, North Dakota, Philadelphia 1935
Kupp, Jake, G, Washington, Dallas 1964-66; Washington 1966; Atlanta 1967; New Orleans 1967-75
Kurek, Ralph, FB, Wisconsin, Chi. Bears 1965-70
Kurnick, Howie, LB, Cincinnati, Cincinnati 1979
Kurrasch, Roy, E, UCLA, NY Yankees (AAFC) 1947; Pittsburgh 1948
Kurth, Joe, T, Notre Dame, Green Bay 1933-34
Kush, Rod, S, Nebraska-Omaha, Buffalo 1980-84; Houston 1985
Kusko, John, FB-HB, Temple, Philadelphia 1936-38
Kusserow, Lou, HB, Columbia, NY Yankees (AAFC) 1949; NY Yanks 1950
Kutler, Rudy, E, Ohio State, Cleveland 1925
Kutner, Mal, E, Texas, Chi. Cardinals 1946-50
Kuusisto, Bill, G, Minnesota, Green Bay 1941-46
Kuykendall, Fulton, LB, UCLA, Atlanta 1975-84; San Francisco 1985
Kuziel, Bob, C, Pittsburgh, New Orleans 1972; Washington 1975-80
Kuzman, John, T, Fordham, Chi. Cardinals 1941; San Francisco (AAFC) 1946; Chi. Rockets (AAFC) 1947
Kvaternick, Zonie, G, Kansas, Pittsburgh 1934
Kwalick, Ted, TE, Penn State, San Francisco 1969-74; Oakland 1975-77
Kyle, Aaron, CB, Wyoming, Dallas 1976-79; Denver 1980-82
Kyle, James (Rip), G, Gettysburg, Canton 1925-26
Kyle, John, FB, Indiana, Cleveland 1923

L

Laabs, Kermit, HB, Beloit, Green Bay 1929
Laack, Galen, G, Pacific, Philadelphia 1958
Laakso, Eric, T, Tulane, Miami 1978-84
Laaveg, Paul, T-G, Iowa, Washington 1970-75
LaBissoniere, Joe, C, St. Thomas (Minnesota), Hammond 1922
Lacey, Bob, SE, North Carolina, Minnesota 1964; NY Giants 1965
Lach, Steve, HB, Duke, Chi. Cardinals 1942; Pittsburgh 1946-47
Lachey, Jim, T, Ohio State, San Diego 1985
Lachman, Dick, HB, Philadelphia 1933-35
LaCrosse, Dave, LB, Wake Forest, Pittsburgh 1977
Lacy, Ken, RB, Tulsa, Kansas City 1984-85
Ladd, Ernie, DT, Grambling, San Diego 1961-65; Houston 1966-67; Kansas City 1967-68
Ladd, Jim, E, Bowling Green, Chi. Cardinals 1954
Ladrow, Walt, HB, Green Bay 1921
Ladygo, Pete, G, Maryland, Pittsburgh 1952, 1954
Lafary, Dave, T, Purdue, New Orleans 1977-85
LaFitte, Bill, E, Ouachita Baptist, Brooklyn 1944
LaFleur, Greg, TE, LSU, St. Louis 1981-85
LaFleur, Joe (Frenchy), G, Marquette, Chi. Bears 1922-24
Lage, Dick, TE, Lenoir-Rhyne, St. Louis 1961
Lagod, Chet, G, Tennessee-Chattanooga, NY Giants 1953
LaGrand, Morris, RB, Tampa, Kansas City 1975; New Orleans 1975
Lahar, Hal, G, Oklahoma, Chi. Bears 1941; Buffalo (AAFC) 1946-48
Lahey, Tom, E, John Carroll, Chi. Rockets 1946-47
LaHood, Mike, G, Wyoming, LA Rams 1969, 1971-72; St. Louis 1970
Lahr, Warren, S, Case Western Reserve, Cleveland 1949-59
Laidlaw, Scott, RB, Stanford, Dallas 1975-79; NY Giants 1980
Lainhart, Porter, FB, Washington State, Chi. Cardinals 1933; Philadelphia 1933
Laird, Bruce, S-KR, American International, Baltimore 1972-81; San Diego 1982-83
Laird, Jim, G-FB, Colgate, Rochester 1920-21; Buffalo 1920-22; Providence 1925-28; Staten Island 1931
Lajousky, Bill, G, Catholic, Pittsburgh 1936
Lakes, Roland, DT, Wichita State, San Francisco 1961-70; NY Giants 1971
Lally, Bob, LB, Cornell, Green Bay 1976
LaLonde, Roger, DT, Muskingum, Detroit 1964; NY Giants 1965
Lamana, Pete, C, Boston College, Chi. Rockets (AAFC) 1946-48
Lamas, Joe, G, Mount St. Mary's, Pittsburgh 1942
Lamb, Mack, CB, Tennessee State, Miami 1967-68
Lamb, Roddy, HB, Lombard, Rock Island 1925; Chi. Cardinals 1926-27, 1933
Lamb, Ron, RB, South Carolina, Denver 1968; Cincinnati 1968-71; Atlanta 1972
Lamb, Walt, E, Oklahoma, Chi. Bears 1946
Lambeau, Earl (Curly), HB, Notre Dame, Green Bay 1921-29
Lambert, Frank, P, Mississippi, Pittsburgh 1965-66
Lambert, Gordon, LB, Tennessee-Martin, Denver 1968-69
Lambert, Jack, LB, Kent State, Pittsburgh 1974-84
Lamberti, Pat, LB, Richmond, NY Titans 1961; Denver 1961
Lamme, Emerald (Buck), E, Ohio Wesleyan, Cleveland 1931
Lammons, Pete, TE, Texas, NY Jets 1966-71; Green Bay 1972
Lamonica, Daryle, QB, Notre Dame, Buffalo 1963-66; Oakland 1967-74
Lamson, Chuck, DB, Wyoming, Minnesota 1962-63; LA Rams 1965-67
Land, Fred, T, LSU, San Francisco (AAFC) 1948
Land, Mel, LB, Michigan State, Miami 1979; San Francisco 1980
Lande, Cliff, E, Carroll (Wisconsin), Green Bay 1921
Lander, Lowell, DB, Westminster, Chi. Cardinals 1958
Landers, Walt, RB, Clark, Green Bay 1978-79
Landeta, Sean, P, Towson State, NY Giants 1985
Landrigan, Jim, T, Dartmouth, Baltimore (AAFC) 1947
Landrum, Mike, TE, Southern Mississippi, Atlanta 1984
Landry, Greg, QB, Massachusetts, Detroit 1968-78; Baltimore 1979-81; Chi. Bears 1984
Landry, Tom, DB, Texas, NY Yankees (AAFC) 1949; NY Giants 1950-55
Landsberg, Mort, HB, Cornell, Philadelphia 1941; LA Dons (AAFC) 1947
Lane, Bob, LB, Baylor, San Diego 1963-64
Lane, Clayton, T, New Hampshire, NY Yankees (AAFC) 1948
Lane, Dick (Night Train), CB, Scottsbluff J.C., LA Rams 1952-53; Chi. Cardinals 1954-59; Detroit 1960-65
Lane, Eric, RB-KR, BYU, Seattle 1981-85
Lane, Francis (Ox), T, Marquette, Milwaukee 1926
Lane, Garcia, CB, Ohio State, Kansas City 1985
Lane, Gary, QB, Missouri, Cleveland 1966-67; NY Giants 1968
Lane, Les, T, South Dakota, Brooklyn 1939
Lane, Lew, QB, St. Mary's of the Plains, Kansas City 1924
Lane, MacArthur, RB, Utah State, St. Louis 1968-71; Green Bay 1972-74; Kansas City 1975-78
Lane, Skip, DB, Mississippi, NY Jets 1984; Kansas City 1984
Lang, Gene, RB-KR, LSU, Denver 1984-85
Lang, Izzy, FB, Tennessee State, Philadelphia 1964-68; LA Rams 1969
Lang, Tex, T, Duluth 1927
Langas, Bob, DE, Wayne State (Nebraska), Detroit 1954
Lange, Bill, G, Dayton, LA Rams 1951-52; Baltimore 1953; Chi. Cardinals 1954-55
Lange, Jim, E, Montana State, Chi. Cardinals 1929
Langer, Jim, C, South Dakota State, Miami 1970-79; Minnesota 1980-81
Langhoff, Irv, HB, Marquette, Racine 1923-24
Langhorne, Reginald, WR, Elizabeth City State, Cleveland 1985
Lanham, Charlie, T, Louisville 1922-23
Lanier, Ken, T, Florida State, Denver 1981-85
Lanier, Willie, LB, Morgan State, Kansas City 1967-77
Lankas, Jim, FB, St. Mary's (California), Philadelphia 1942; Green Bay 1943
Lankford, Paul, CB, Penn State, Miami 1982-85
Lanphear, Dan, DE, Wisconsin, Houston 1960, 1962
Lansdell, Grenny, QB, USC, NY Giants 1940
Lansford, Buck, T-G, Texas, Philadelphia 1955-57; LA Rams 1958-60
Lansford, Jim, T, Texas, Dallas 1952
Lansford, Mike, K, Washington, LA Rams 1982-85
Lantz, Monty, C, Grove City, Pittsburgh 1933
Lanum, Ralph, HB-FB, Illinois, Decatur 1920; Chi. Staleys 1921; Chi. Bears 1922-24
Lapham, Bill, C, Iowa, Philadelphia 1960; Minnesota 1961
Lapham, Dave, T-C, Syracuse, Cincinnati 1974-83
Lapka, Myron, DT-NT, USC, NY Giants 1980; LA Rams 1982-83
Lapka, Ted, E, St. Ambrose, Washington 1943-44, 1946
LaPointe, Ron, TE, Penn State, Baltimore 1980
LaPorta, Phil, T, Penn State, New Orleans 1974-75
LaPresta, Benny, QB, St. Louis, Boston 1933; St. Louis 1934
Laraba, Bob, LB, Texas-El Paso, LA Chargers 1960; San Diego 1961
Laraway, Jack, LB, Purdue, Buffalo 1960; Houston 1961
Largent, Steve, WR, Tulsa, Seattle 1976-85
LaRosa, Paul, E, Chi. Cardinals 1920-21
LaRose, Danny, T, Missouri, Detroit 1961-63; Pittsburgh 1964; San Francisco 1965; Denver 1966
Larpenter, Carl, T-G, Texas, Denver 1960-61; Dallas Texans 1962
Larscheid, Jack, HB-KR, Pacific, Oakland 1960-61
Larsen, Gary, DT, Concordia (Minnesota), LA Rams 1964; Minnesota 1965-74
Larsen, Swede, HB, Hammond 1923
Larson, Bill, FB, Illinois Wesleyan, Boston 1960
Larson, Bill, TE, Colorado State, San Francisco 1975; Detroit 1977; Philadelphia 1978; Denver 1980; Green Bay 1980
Larson, Fred, C, Notre Dame, Chi. Bears 1922; Milwaukee 1923-24; Green Bay 1925; Chi. Cardinals 1929
Larson, Greg, C-T-G, Minnesota, NY Giants 1961-73
Larson, Louie, FB, Minnesota, Duluth 1926; Chi. Cardinals 1929
Larson, Lynn, T, Kansas State, Baltimore 1971
Larson, Paul, QB, California, Chi. Cardinals 1957; Oakland 1960
Larson, Pete, RB, Cornell, Washington 1967-68
Lary, Yale, DB-P, Texas A&M, Detroit 1952-53, 1956-64
Lascari, John, E, Georgetown (Washington D.C.), NY Giants 1942
Lash, Jim, TE, Northwestern, Minnesota 1973-76; San Francisco 1976-77
Laskey, Bill, LB, Michigan, Buffalo 1965; Oakland 1966-67, 1969-70; Baltimore 1971-72; Denver 1973-74
Laski, M.K., E, Northwestern, Chi. Bears 1958
Lasky, Frank, T, Florida, NY Giants 1964-65
Laslavic, Jim, LB, Penn State, Detroit 1973-77; San Diego 1978-81; Green Bay 1982
Lassahn, Lou, E, Western Maryland, Pittsburgh 1938
Lasse, Dick, LB, Syracuse, Pittsburgh 1958-59; Washington 1960-61; NY Giants 1962
Lassiter, Ike, DE-DT, St. Augustine, Denver 1962-64; Oakland 1965-69; Boston 1970
Laster, Art, T, Maryland-Eastern Shore, Buffalo 1970; New England 1971
Laster, Donald, T, Tennessee State, Washington 1982; Detroit 1984
Lathrop, Kit, DT, Arizona State, Denver 1979; Green Bay 1979-80
Latimer, Al, CB, Clemson, Philadelphia 1979; San Francisco 1980; Detroit 1982-84
Latimer, Don, NT, Miami, Denver 1978-83
Latin, Jerry, RB, Northern Illinois, St. Louis 1975-78; LA Rams 1978
Latone, Tony, FB, Pottsville 1925-28; Boston 1929; Provi-Providence 1930
Latourette, Chuck, WR-P, Rice, St. Louis 1967-68, 1970-71
Latta, Greg, TE, Morgan State, Chi. Bears 1975-80
Lattner, Johnny, HB, Notre Dame, Pittsburgh 1954
Latzke, Paul, C, Pacific, San Diego 1966-68
Lauer, Al, HB, Iowa, Evansville 1922
Lauer, Hal (Dutch), HB, Detroit, Rock Island 1922; Green Bay 1922; Toledo 1923; Detroit 1925-26
Lauer, Larry, C, Alabama, Green Bay 1956-57
Laufenberg, Babe, QB, Indiana, Washington 1983, 1985; San Diego 1985
Laughing Gas, HB, Oorang 1922
Laughlin, Bud, FB, Kansas, San Francisco 1955
Laughlin, Jim, LB, Ohio State, Atlanta 1980-82; Green Bay 1983; LA Rams 1984-85
Lauricella, Hank, HB, Tennessee, Dallas 1952
Laurinaitis, Frank, C, Richmond, Brooklyn (AAFC) 1947
Lauro, Lindy, DB, Pittsburgh, Chi. Cardinals 1951
Laux, Ted, HB, St. Joseph's (Pennsylvania), Phil-Pitt 1943; Philadelphia 1944
Lavan, Al, DB, Colorado State, Atlanta 1969
Lavelli, Dante, E, Ohio State, Cleveland 1946-56
Lavender, Joe, CB, San Diego State, Philadelphia 1973-75; Washington 1976-82
Lavette, Robert, RB, Georgia Tech, Dallas 1985
Law, Dennis, WR, East Tennessee State, Cincinnati 1978; Washington 1979
Law, Hubbard, G, Sam Houston State, Pittsburgh 1942, 1945
Law, John, T, Notre Dame, Newark 1930
Lawler, Al, HB, Texas, Chi. Bears 1948
Lawless, Burton, G, Florida, Dallas 1975-79; Detroit 1980; Miami 1981
Lawrence, Amos, RB-KR, North Carolina, San Francisco

1981-82
Lawrence, Don, T, Notre Dame, Washington 1959-61
Lawrence, Ed, HB-FB, Brown, Boston 1929; Staten Island 1930
Lawrence, Henry, T, Florida A&M, Oakland 1974-81; LA Raiders 1982-85
Lawrence, Jimmy, HB, TCU, Chi. Cardinals 1936-39; Green Bay 1939
Lawrence, Kent, WR, Georgia, Philadelphia 1969; Atlanta 1970
Lawrence, Larry, QB, Iowa, Oakland 1974-75; Tampa Bay 1976
Lawrence, Rolland, CB, Tabor, Atlanta 1973-80
Laws, Joe, HB, Iowa, Green Bay 1934-45
Lawson, Alphonso, FL, Delaware State, NY Jets 1964
Lawson, Jerome, DB, Utah, Buffalo 1968
Lawson, Jim, E, Stanford, NY Yankees 1927
Lawson, Odell, RB, Langston, Boston 1970; New England 1971; New Orleans 1973-74
Lawson, Roger, RB, Western Michigan, Chi. Bears 1972-73
Lawson, Steve, G, Kansas, Cincinnati 1971-72; Minnesota 1973-75; San Francisco 1976-77
Lay, Russ, G, Michigan State, Detroit 1934; St. Louis 1934; Cincinnati 1934
Layden, Bob, E, Southwestern (Kansas), Detroit 1943
Layden, Pete, FB, Texas, NY Yankees (AAFC) 1948-49; NY Yanks 1950
Layne, Bobby, QB-K, Texas, Chi. Bears 1948; NY Bulldogs 1949; Detroit 1950-58; Pittsburgh 1958-62
Layport, John, G, Wooster, Columbus 1924; Dayton 1925-26
Lazetich, Bill, HB, Montana, Cleveland 1939, 1942
Lazetich, Milan, G, Michigan, Cleveland 1945; LA Rams 1946-50
Lazetich, Pete, DT, Stanford, San Diego 1972-74; Philadelphia 1976-77
Lea, Paul, T, Tulane, Pittsburgh 1951
Leaf, Garland, T, Syracuse, Louisville 1926
Leahy, Bernie, HB, Notre Dame, Chi. Bears 1932
Leahy, Bob, QB, Emporia State, Pittsburgh 1971
Leahy, Jerry, T, Colorado, Pittsburgh 1957
Leahy, Pat, K, St. Louis, NY Jets 1974-85
Leaks, Roosevelt, RB, Texas, Baltimore 1975-79; Buffalo 1980-83
Leaper, Wes, E, Wisconsin, Green Bay 1921, 1923
Lear, Les, G, Manitoba, Cleveland 1944-45; LA Rams 1946; Detroit 1947
Leary, Tom, E, Fordham, Frankford 1927-28, 1931; Staten Island 1929; Newark 1930
Leatherman, Paul, E, Illinois, Hammond 1922
Leathers, Milt, G, Georgia, Philadelphia 1933
Leavitt, Allan, K, Georgia, Atlanta 1977; Tampa Bay 1977
LeBaron, Eddie, QB, Pacific, Washington 1952-53, 1955-59; Dallas 1960-63
LeBeau, Dick, DB, Ohio State, Detroit 1959-72
Lebengood, Howard (Fungy), HB, Villanova, Pottsville 1925
Leberman, Bob, DB, Syracuse, Baltimore 1954
Lechner, Ed, G-T, Minnesota, NY Giants 1942
Lechthaler, Roy, G, Lebanon Valley, Philadelphia 1933
Leckonby, Bill, HB, St. Lawrence, Brooklyn 1939-41
LeClair, Jim, QB, C.W. Post, Denver 1967-68
LeClair, Jim, LB, North Dakota, Cincinnati 1972-83
LeClerc, Roger, LB-K, Trinity (Connecticut), Chi. Bears 1960-66; Denver 1967
LeCount, Terry, WR, Florida, San Francisco 1978-79; Minnesota 1979-84
Lecture, Jim, G, Northwestern, Buffalo (AAFC) 1946
Ledbetter, Homer (Doc), HB-QB, Arkansas, Staten Island 1932; Chi. Cardinals 1932-33
Ledbetter, Monte, FL, Northwestern State (Louisiana), Houston 1967; Buffalo 1967-69; Atlanta 1969
Ledbetter, Toy, HB, Oklahoma State, Philadelphia 1950, 1953-55
Ledyard, Hal, QB, Tennessee-Chattanooga, San Francisco 1953
Lee, Bernie, QB, Villanova, Philadelphia 1938; Pittsburgh 1938
Lee, Bill, T, Alabama, Brooklyn 1935-37; Green Bay 1937-42, 1946
Lee, Bivian, DB, Prairie View A&M, New Orleans 1971-75
Lee, Bob, G, Missouri, Boston 1960
Lee, Bob, WR, Minnesota, St. Louis 1969; Atlanta 1969
Lee, Bob, QB-P, Pacific, Minnesota 1969-72, 1975-78; Atlanta 1973-74; LA Rams 1979-80
Lee, Carl, S, Marshall, Minnesota 1983-85
Lee, David, P, Louisiana Tech, Baltimore 1966-78
Lee, Dwight, RB, Michigan State, San Francisco 1968; Atlanta 1968
Lee, Gene, C, Florida, Boston 1946
Lee, Herman, T, Florida A&M, Pittsburgh 1957; Chi. Bears 1958-66
Lee, Hilary (Biff), G, Oklahoma, Cleveland 1931; Portsmouth 1931; Cincinnati 1933-34
Lee, Jack, HB, Carnegie-Mellon, Pittsburgh 1939
Lee, Jacky, QB, Cincinnati, Houston 1960-63, 1966-67; Denver 1964-65; Kansas City 1967-69
Lee, Jeff, WR, Nebraska, St. Louis 1980
Lee, John, DE, Nebraska, San Diego 1976-80; New England 1981
Lee, Keith, DB, Colorado State, New England 1981-84; Indianapolis 1985
Lee, Ken, LB, Washington, Detroit 1971; Buffalo 1972
Lee, Larry, G-C, UCLA, Detroit 1981-85; Miami 1985
Lee, Mark, CB-KR, Washington, Green Bay 1980-85
Lee, Mike, LB, Nevada-Las Vegas, San Diego 1974
Lee, Monte, LB, Texas, St. Louis 1961; Detroit 1963-64; Baltimore 1965
Lee, Oudious, DT, Nebraska, St. Louis 1980
Lee, Ron, FB, West Virginia, Baltimore 1976-78
Lee, Ronnie, TE-G, Baylor, Miami 1979-82, 1984-85; Atlanta 1983
Lee, Willie, DT, Bethune-Cookman, Kansas City 1976-77
Leemans, Alphonse (Tuffy), HB, George Washington, NY Giants 1936-43
Leetzow, Max, DE, Idaho, Denver 1965-66
Leeuwenberg, Dick, T, Stanford, Chi. Bears 1965
Lefear, Billy, WR-KR, Henderson State, Cleveland 1972-75
LeFebvre, Gil, HB, Cincinnati 1933-34; Detroit 1935
LeForce, Clyde, QB, Tulsa, Detroit 1947-49
Leftridge, Dick, FB, West Virginia, Pittsburgh 1966
Leggett, Dave, QB, Ohio State, Chi. Cardinals 1955
Leggett, Earl, DT, LSU, Chi. Bears 1957-60, 1962-65; LA Rams 1966; New Orleans 1967-68
Lehrer, Chris, HB, Auburn, Rochester 1922
Leicht, Jake, HB, Oregon, Baltimore (AAFC) 1948-49
Leigh, Charlie, RB, Cleveland 1968-69; Miami 1971-74; Green Bay 1974
Leisk, Wardell, G, LSU, Brooklyn 1937
Leith, Al, HB, Pennsylvania, Brooklyn 1926
LeJeune (Jean), Walt, T-FB, Bethany (Kansas), Akron 1922-23; Milwaukee 1924; Green Bay 1925-26; Pottsville 1927
LeMaster, Frank, LB, Kentucky, Philadelphia 1974-82
Lemek, Ray, G, Notre Dame, Washington 1957-61; Pittsburgh 1962-65
Lemmerman, Bruce, QB, Cal State-Northridge, Atlanta 1968-69
LeMoine, Jim, T-G, Utah State, Buffalo 1967; Houston 1968-69
Lemon, Cliff, E, Centre, Chi. Bears 1926
Lemon, Mike, LB, Kansas, New Orleans 1975; Denver 1975; Tampa Bay 1976-77
Lenc, George, E, Augustana (Illinois), Brooklyn 1939
Lenkaitis, Bill, C-G, Penn State, San Diego 1968-70; New England 1971-81
Lennan, Reid, G, Washington 1945; LA Dons (AAFC) 1947
Lens, Greg, DT, Trinity (Texas), Atlanta 1970-71
Lensing, Vince, T-G, Notre Dame, Evansville 1921
Lentz, Jack, S, Holy Cross, Denver 1967-68
Lentz, Pesky, HB-FB, Wittenberg, Dayton 1920
Leo, Bobby, RB-KR, Harvard, Boston 1967-68
Leo, Charlie, G, Indiana, Boston 1960-62; Buffalo 1963
Leo, Jim, DE-LB, Cincinnati, NY Giants 1960; Minnesota 1961-62
Leon, Tony, G, Alabama, Washington 1943; Brooklyn 1944; Boston 1945-46
Leonard, Bill, E, Notre Dame, Baltimore (AAFC) 1949
Leonard, Cecil, DB, Tuskegee, NY Jets 1969-70
Leonard, Jim, G, Colgate, Rochester 1923; Chi. Bears 1924
Leonard, Jim, FB-QB, Notre Dame, Philadelphia 1934-37
Leonard, Jim, C-G, Santa Clara, Tampa Bay 1980-83; San Francisco 1985; San Diego 1985
Leonard, John, G, Indiana, Chi. Cardinals 1922-23
Leonard, Tony, DB, Virginia Union, San Francisco 1976-77
Leonetti, Bob, G, Wake Forest, Buffalo (AAFC) 1948; Brooklyn (AAFC) 1948
Leopold, Bobby, LB, Notre Dame, San Francisco 1980-83
Lepper, Barney, T, Buffalo 1920
Lesane, Jimmy, HB, Virginia, Chi. Bears 1952, 1954; Baltimore 1954
Lester, Darrell, C, TCU, Green Bay 1937-38
Lester, Darrell, RB, McNeese State, Minnesota 1964; Denver 1965-66
Lester, Harold (Pinky), E, Providence 1926
Letlow, Russ, G, San Francisco, Green Bay 1939-42, 1946
Letner, Bob (Cotton), LB, Tennessee, Buffalo 1961
Letsinger, Jim, G, Purdue, Pittsburgh 1933
Levanitis, Steve, T, Boston College, Philadelphia 1942
Levanti, Lou, G, Illinois, Pittsburgh 1951-52
LeVeck, Jack, LB, Ohio U., St. Louis 1973-74; Cleveland 1975
Levenick, Dave, LB, Wisconsin, Atlanta 1983-84
Levenseller, Mike, WR, Washington State, Buffalo 1978; Tampa Bay 1978; Cincinnati 1979-82
Levey, Jim, HB, Pittsburgh 1934-36
LeVias, Jerry, WR-KR, SMU, Houston 1969-70; San Diego 1971-74
Levy, Harvey, G, Syracuse, NY Yankees 1928
Levy, Len, G, Minnesota, Cleveland 1945; LA Rams 1946; LA Dons (AAFC) 1947-48
Lewellen, Verne, HB-FB, Nebraska, Green Bay 1924-32; NY Yankees 1927
Lewis, Albert, CB, Grambling, Kansas City 1983-85
Lewis, Art, T, West Virginia, Cincinnati 1921
Lewis, Art (Pappy), T, Ohio U., NY Giants 1936; Cleveland 1938-39
Lewis, Bill, HB, TCU, Cincinnati 1934
Lewis, Cliff, QB-DB, Duke, Cleveland 1946-51
Lewis, Cliff, LB, Southern Mississippi, Green Bay 1981-84
Lewis, D.D., LB, Mississippi State, Dallas 1968, 1970-81
Lewis, Danny, FB, Wisconsin, Detroit 1958-64; Washington 1965; NY Giants 1966
Lewis, Daryl, TE, Texas-Arlington, Cleveland 1984
Lewis, Dave, P-QB, Stanford, Cincinnati 1970-73
Lewis, David, LB, USC, Tampa Bay 1977-81; San Diego 1982
Lewis, David, TE, California, Detroit 1984-85
Lewis, Eddie, DB, Kansas, San Francisco 1976-79; Detroit 1979-80
Lewis, Ernie, FB, Colorado, Chi. Rockets (AAFC) 1946-48; Chi. Hornets (AAFC) 1949
Lewis, Frank, WR, Grambling, Pittsburgh 1971-77; Buffalo 1978-83
Lewis, Gary, FB, Arizona State, San Francisco 1964-69; New Orleans 1970
Lewis, Gary, TE, Texas-Arlington, Green Bay 1981-84
Lewis, Gary, NT, Oklahoma State, New Orleans 1983
Lewis, Hal, DB, Arizona State, Denver 1968
Lewis, Harold, HB, Houston, Baltimore 1959; Buffalo 1960
Lewis, Herman, DE, Virginia Union, Denver 1968
Lewis, Jess, LB, Oregon State, Houston 1970
Lewis, Joe, DT, Compton J.C., Pittsburgh 1959-60; Baltimore 1961; Philadelphia 1962
Lewis, Kenny, RB, Virginia Tech, NY Jets 1980-81, 1983
Lewis, Leland (Tiny), FB, Northwestern, Portsmouth 1930; Cleveland 1931
Lewis, Leo, WR-KR, Missouri, Minnesota 1981-85
Lewis, Mark, TE, Texas A&M, Green Bay 1985
Lewis, Mac, T, Iowa, Chi. Cardinals 1959
Lewis, Mike, DT-DE, Arkansas-Pine Bluff, Atlanta 1971-79; Green Bay 1980
Lewis, Ray, G, Louisville 1921
Lewis, Reggie, DE-NT, North Texas State, Tampa Bay 1979-80
Lewis, Reggie, DE, San Diego State, New Orleans 1982-84
Lewis, Richard, LB, Portland State, Houston 1972; Buffalo 1973-74; New Orleans 1974-75
Lewis, Rodney, CB, Nebraska, New Orleans 1982-84
Lewis, Scott, DE, Grambling, Houston 1971
Lewis, Sherman, DB-KR, Michigan State, NY Jets 1966-67
Lewis, Stan, DE, Wayne State (Nebraska), Cleveland 1975
Lewis, Terry, CB, Michigan State, San Diego 1985
Lewis, Tim, DB-KR, Pittsburgh, Green Bay 1983-85
Lewis, Will, CB-KR, Millersville, Seattle 1980-81; Kansas City 1981
Lewis, Woodley, DB-SE, Oregon, LA Rams 1950-55; Chi. Cardinals 1956-59; Dallas Cowboys 1960
Leypoldt, John, K, Buffalo 1971-76; Seattle 1976-78; New Orleans 1978
Lick, Dennis, T, Wisconsin, Chi. Bears 1976-82
Lidberg, Carl (Cully), FB, Minnesota, Green Bay 1926, 1929-30
Liddick, Dave, DT, George Washington, Pittsburgh 1957
Liebel, Frank, E, Norwich, NY Giants 1942-47; Chi. Cardinals 1948
Liebenstein, Todd, DE, Nevada-Las Vegas, Washington 1982-85
Liebrum, Don, HB, Manchester, NY Giants 1942
Liggett, Bob, DT, Nebraska, Kansas City 1970
Liles, Alva, DT, Boise State, Detroit 1980; Oakland 1980
Liles, Elvin (Sonny), G, Oklahoma State, Detroit 1943-45; Cleveland 1945
Lilja, George, G-C, Michigan, LA Rams 1982-83; NY Jets 1983-84; Cleveland 1984-85
Lillard, Joe, HB, Oregon State, Chi. Cardinals 1932-33
Lilly, Bob, DT, TCU, Dallas 1961-74
Lilly, Tony, S, Florida, Denver 1984-85
Lillywhite, Verl, FB, USC, San Francisco 1948-51
Lince, Dave, TE, North Dakota, Philadelphia 1966-67
Lincoln, Keith, FB, Washington State, San Diego 1961-66; Buffalo 1967-68; San Francisco 1968
Lind, Al, C, Northwestern, Chi. Cardinals 1936
Lind, Mike, FB, Notre Dame, San Francisco 1963-64; Pitts-Pittsburgh 1965-66
Lindahl, Virgil, G, Wayne State (Nebraska), NY Giants 1945
Linden, Errol, T, Houston, Cleveland 1961; Minnesota 1962-65; Atlanta 1966-68; New Orleans 1969
Lindon, Luther, T, Kentucky, Detroit 1944-45
Lindow, Al, HB, Washington (St. Louis), Chi. Cardinals 1945
Lindquist, Paul, DT, New Hampshire, Boston 1961
Lindsey, Dale, LB, Western Kentucky, Cleveland 1965-73; New Orleans 1973
Lindsey, Hub, RB, Wyoming, Denver 1968
Lindsey, Jim, RB, Arkansas, Minnesota 1966-72
Lindsey, Menzies, QB, Wabash, Evansville 1921-22
Lindskog, Vic, C, Stanford, Philadelphia 1944-51
Lindstrom, Chris, NT-DE, Boston U., Cincinnati 1983; San Francisco 1983; Tampa Bay 1985
Lindstrom, Dave, DE, Boston U., Kansas City 1978-85
Line, Bill, DT, SMU, Chi. Bears 1972
Lingenfelter, Bob, T, Nebraska, Cleveland 1977; Minnesota 1978
Lingner, Adam, C-G, Illinois, Kansas City 1983-85
Linhart, Toni, K, Austria Tech, New Orleans 1972; Baltimore 1974-79; NY Jets 1979

Lininger, Ray, C, Ohio State, Detroit 1950-51
Linnan, Frank, T, Marquette, Racine 1922, 1926
Linne, Aubrey, TE, TCU, Baltimore 1961
Linnin, Chris, DT, Washington, NY Giants 1980
Lintzenich, Joe, HB-FB, St. Louis, Chi. Bears 1930-31
Lio, Augie, G, Georgetown (Washington D.C.), Detroit 1941-43; Boston 1944-45; Philadelphia 1946; Baltimore (AAFC) 1947
Lipinski, Jim, T, Fairmont State, Chi. Cardinals 1950
Lipostad, Ed, G, Wake Forest, Chi. Cardinals 1952
Lippett, Ronnie, CB, Miami, New England 1983-85
Lipps, Louis, WR-KR, Southern Mississippi, Pittsburgh 1984-85
Lipscomb, Eugene (Big Daddy), DT, LA Rams 1953-55; Baltimore 1956-60; Pittsburgh 1961-62
Lipscomb, Paul, DT-T, Tennessee, Green Bay 1945-49; Washington 1950-54; Chi. Bears 1954
Lipski, John (Bull), C, Temple, Philadelphia 1933-34
Lisbon, Don, RB, Bowling Green, San Francisco 1963-64
Lisch, Rusty, QB-S, Notre Dame, St. Louis 1980-83; Chi. Bears 1984
Liscio, Tony, T, Tulsa, Dallas 1963-64, 1966-71
Liske, Pete, QB, Penn State, NY Jets 1964; Denver 1969-70; Philadelphia 1971-72
Liston, Paul, T, Georgetown (Washington D.C.), Newark 1930
Little, Dave, TE, Tennessee State, Kansas City 1984; Philadelphia 1985
Little, David, LB, Florida, Pittsburgh 1981-85
Little, Everett, G, Houston, Tampa Bay 1976; Oakland 1977
Little, Floyd, RB, Syracuse, Denver 1967-75
Little, George, DT, Iowa, Miami 1985
Little, Jack, T, Texas A&M, Baltimore 1953-54
Little, John, DE-DT, Oklahoma State, NY Jets 1970-74; Houston 1975-76; Buffalo 1977
Little, Larry, G, Bethune-Cookman, San Diego 1967-68; Miami 1969-80
Little, Lou, T, Pennsylvania, Buffalo 1920-21
Little, Steve, K, Arkansas, St. Louis 1978-80
Littlefield, Carl, HB-FB, Washington State, Cleveland 1938; Pittsburgh 1939
Little Twig, Joe, E, Carlisle, Oorang 1922-23; Rock Island 1924-25; Canton 1926; Akron 1926
Livers, Virgil, CB-KR, Western Kentucky, Chi. Bears 1975-79
Livingston, Andy, FB, Phoenix J.C., Chi. Bears 1964-65, 1967-68; New Orleans 1969
Livingston, Bob, HB, Notre Dame, Chi. Rockets (AAFC) 1948; Chi. Hornets (AAFC) 1949; Buffalo (AAFC) 1949; Baltimore 1950
Livingston, Cliff, LB, UCLA, NY Giants 1954-61; Minnesota 1961; LA Rams 1963-65
Livingston, Dale, P, Western Michigan, Cincinnati 1968-69; Green Bay 1970
Livingston, Howie, HB-DB, Fullerton J.C., NY Giants 1944-47; Washington 1948-50; San Francisco 1950; Chi. Bears 1953
Livingston, Mike, QB, SMU, Kansas City 1968-79; Minnesota 1980
Livingston, Ted, T, Indiana, Cleveland 1937-40
Livingston, Walt, HB, Heidelberg, Boston 1960
Livingston, Warren, DB, Arizona, Dallas 1961-66
Lloyd, Dan, LB, Washington, NY Giants 1976-79
Lloyd, Dave, LB-K, Georgia, Cleveland 1959-61; Detroit 1962; Philadelphia 1963-70
Lloyd, Jeff, NT, West Texas State, Buffalo 1976; Kansas City 1978
Lockett, Frank, WR, Nebraska, Miami 1985
Lockett, J.W., RB, Central State (Oklahoma), Dallas Cowboys 1961-62; Baltimore 1963; Washington 1964
Lockhart, Carl (Spider), S-KR, North Texas State, NY Giants 1965-75
Lockhart, Eugene, LB, Houston, Dallas 1984-85
Locklin, Billy, LB, New Mexico State, Oakland 1960
Locklin, Kerry, TE, New Mexico State, LA Rams 1982
Loepfe, Dick, T, Wisconsin, Chi. Cardinals 1948-49
Loewen, Chuck, T-G, South Dakota State, San Diego 1980-82, 1984
Lofton, James, WR, Stanford, Green Bay 1978-85
Lofton, Oscar, SE, Southeastern Louisiana, Boston 1960
Logan (Wyhowanec), Andy, T, Case Western Reserve, Detroit 1941
Logan, Chuck, TE, Northwestern, Pittsburgh 1964; St. Louis 1967-68
Logan, Dave, WR, Colorado, Cleveland 1976-83; Denver 1984
Logan, David, NT, Pittsburgh, Tampa Bay 1979-85
Logan, Dick, G, Ohio State, Green Bay 1952-53
Logan, Jim, G, Indiana, Chi. Bears 1943
Logan, Jerry, S, West Texas State, Baltimore 1963-72
Logan, Obert, S, Trinity (Texas), Dallas 1965-66; New Orleans 1967
Logan, Randy, S, Michigan, Philadelphia 1973-83
Logel, Bob, DE, Buffalo (AAFC) 1949
Lohmeyer, John, DE-DT, Emporia State, Kansas City 1973, 1975-77
Lokanc, Joe, G, Northwestern, Chi. Cardinals 1941
Lollar, George, FB, Howard, Green Bay 1928
Lolotai, Al, G, Weber State, Washington 1945; LA Dons (AAFC) 1946-49
Lomakoski, John, DT, Western Michigan, Detroit 1962
Lomas, Mark, DE-DT, Northern Arizona, NY Jets 1970-74
Lomasney, Tom, E-QB, Villanova, Staten Island 1929
Lomax, Neil, QB, Portland State, St. Louis 1981-85
London, Mike, LB, Wisconsin, San Diego 1966
London, Tom, DB, North Carolina State, Cleveland 1978; New Orleans 1980
Lone Star, G-T, Carlisle, Columbus 1920
Lone Wolf, G, Carlisle, Oorang 1922-23
Long, Bill, E, Oklahoma State, Pittsburgh 1949-50
Long, Bob, HB, Tennessee, Boston 1947
Long, Bob, LB, UCLA, Detroit 1955-59; LA Rams 1960-61; Dallas Cowboys 1962
Long, Bob, SE, Wichita State, Green Bay 1964-67; Atlanta 1968; Washington 1969; LA Rams 1970
Long, Buford, HB, Florida, NY Giants 1953-55
Long, Carson, K, Pittsburgh, Buffalo 1977
Long, Charlie, G, Tennessee-Chattanooga, Boston 1961-69
Long, Dave, DE, Iowa, St. Louis 1966-68; New Orleans 1969-72
Long, Doug, S, Whitworth, Seattle 1977-78
Long, Harvey, G-T, Detroit, Chi. Bears 1929; Frankford 1930
Long, Howie, DE, Villanova, Oakland 1981; LA Raiders 1982-85
Long, John, QB, Colgate, Chi. Bears 1944-45
Long, Ken, G, Purdue, Detroit 1976
Long, Kevin, RB, South Carolina, NY Jets 1977-81
Long, Louie, E, SMU, Portsmouth 1931
Long, Mel, LB, Toledo, Cleveland 1972-74
Long, Mike, SE, Brandeis, Boston 1960
Long, Terry, G, East Carolina, Pittsburgh 1984-85
Long, Tom, G, Ohio State, Columbus 1925
Longenecker, Ken, DT, Lebanon Valley, Pittsburgh 1960
Longley, Clint, QB, Abilene Christian, Dallas 1974-75; San Diego 1976
Longmire, Sam, DB, Purdue, Kansas City 1967-68
Longo, Tom, DB, Notre Dame, NY Giants 1969; St. Louis 1971
Longo, Tony, G, Connecticut, Providence 1928
Longstreet, Roy, C, Iowa State, Racine 1926
Long Time Sleep (Nick Lassa), T, Carlisle, Oorang 1922-23
Longua, Paul, E, Villanova, Orange 1929; Newark 1930
Look, Dean, QB, Michigan State, NY Titans 1962
Lookabaugh, John, E, Maryland, Washington 1946-47
Loomis, Ace, HB, Wisconsin-LaCrosse, Green Bay 1951-53
Looney, Don, E, TCU, Philadelphia 1940; Pittsburgh 1941-42
Looney, Jim, LB, Purdue, San Francisco 1981
Looney, Joe Don, RB-P, Oklahoma, Baltimore 1964; Detroit 1965-66; Washington 1966-67; New Orleans 1969
Lopasky, Bill, G-T, West Virginia, San Francisco 1961
Lorch, Karl, DE, USC, Washington 1976-81
Lord, Jack, G, Rutgers, Staten Island 1929
Lorick, Tony, RB, Arizona State, Baltimore 1964-67; New Orleans 1968-69
Losch, Jack, HB, Miami, Green Bay 1956
Lothamer, Ed, DT, Michigan State, Kansas City 1964-72
Lothridge, Billy, QB-P, Georgia Tech, Dallas 1964; LA Rams 1965; Atlanta 1966-71; Miami 1972
Lott, Billy, HB-DB, Mississippi, NY Giants 1958; Oakland 1960; Boston 1961-63
Lott, John, T, Bucknell, Orange 1929; Brooklyn 1930
Lott, Ronnie, DB, USC, San Francisco 1981-85
Lott, Thomas, RB, Oklahoma, St. Louis 1979
Lou, Ron, C, Arizona State, Houston 1973, 1976; Philadelphia 1975
Loucks, Alvin, G, Michigan, Detroit 1920
Loucks, Ed, E, Washington & Jefferson, Cleveland 1925
Loudd, Rommie, LB, UCLA, LA Chargers 1960; Boston 1961-62
Louderback, Tom, LB, San Jose State, Philadelphia 1958-59; Oakland 1960-61; Buffalo 1962
Loukas, Angelo, G, Northwestern, Buffalo 1969; Boston 1970
Love, Duval, G, UCLA, LA Rams 1985
Love, John, FL-KR, North Texas State, Washington 1967; LA Rams 1972
Love, Walter, WR, Westminister (Utah), NY Giants 1973
LoVetere, John, DT, Compton J.C., LA Rams 1959-62; NY Giants 1963-65
Lovin, Fritz, G, Minneapolis 1929
LoVuolo, Frank, E, St. Bonaventure, NY Giants 1949
Lowdermilk, Kirk, C, Ohio State, Minnesota 1985
Lowe, Gary, DB, Michigan State, Washington 1956-57; Detroit 1957-64
Lowe, George (Bull), E-T, Lafayette, Canton 1920; Cleveland 1921; Buffalo 1922; Rock Island 1923; Frankford 1924-26; Providence 1925, 1927
Lowe, Lloyd, HB, North Texas State, Chi. Bears 1953-54
Lowe, Paul, RB, Oregon State, LA Chargers 1960; San Diego 1961, 1963-68; Kansas City 1968-69
Lowe, Woodrow, LB, Alabama, San Diego 1976-85
Lowery, Darby, T-E, Ursinus, Rochester 1920-25
Lowery, Nick, K, Dartmouth, New England 1978; Kansas City 1980-85
Lowry, Orlando, LB, Ohio State, Indianapolis 1985
Lowry, Quentin, LB, Youngstown State, Washington 1981-83; Tampa Bay 1983
Lowther, Russ, HB, Detroit, Detroit 1944; Pittsburgh 1945
Loyd, Alex, E, Oklahoma State, San Francisco 1950
Loyd, Mike, QB, Missouri Southern State, St. Louis 1979-80
Lubratovich, Milo, T, Wisconsin, Brooklyn 1931-37
Lucas, Dick, TE, Boston College, Philadelphia 1960-63
Lucas, Richie, QB, Penn State, Buffalo 1960-61
Lucci, Mike, LB, Tennessee, Cleveland 1962-64; Detroit 1965-73
Luce, Derrel, LB, Baylor, Baltimore 1975-78; Minnesota 1979-80; Detroit 1980
Luce, Lew, HB, Penn State, Washington 1961
Lucente, John, FB, West Virginia, Pittsburgh 1945
Luck, Oliver, QB, West Virginia, Houston 1982-85
Luck, Terry, QB, Nebraska, Cleveland 1977
Luckhurst, Mick, K, California, Atlanta 1981-85
Luckman, Sid, QB, Columbia, Chi. Bears 1939-50
Lucky, Bill, DT, Baylor, Green Bay 1955
Ludtke, Norm, G, Carroll (Wisconsin) , Green Bay 1924
Lueck, Bill, G, Arizona, Green Bay 1968-74; Philadelphia 1975
Luft, Don, DE, Indiana, Philadelphia 1954
Luhn, Nolan, E, Tulsa, Green Bay 1945-49
Lujack, Johnny, QB-DB, Notre Dame, Chi. Bears 1948-51
Luke, Steve, S, Ohio State, Green Bay 1975-80
Luke, Tommy, DB, Mississippi, Denver 1968
Luken, Tom, G, Purdue, Philadelphia 1972-75, 1977-78
Lukens, Jim, E, Washington & Lee, Buffalo (AAFC) 1949
Lummus, Jack, E, Baylor, NY Giants 1941
Lumpkin, Joey, LB, Arizona State, Buffalo 1982-83
Lumpkin, Ron, DB, Arizona State, NY Giants 1973
Lumpkin, Roy (Father), QB, Georgia Tech, Portsmouth 1930-33; Detroit 1934; Brooklyn 1935-37
Luna, Bobby, DB-P, Alabama, San Francisco 1955; Pittsburgh 1959
Lunceford, Dave, T, Baylor, Chi. Cardinals 1957
Lund, Bill, HB, Case Western Reserve, Cleveland (AAFC) 1946-47
Lunday, Kenneth (Kayo), C, Arkansas, NY Giants 1937-41, 1946-47
Lunde, Les, G, Ripon, Racine 1922-24
Lundell, Bob, E, Gustavus Adolphus, Minneapolis 1929-30; Staten Island 1930
Lundy, Lamar, DE-TE, Purdue, LA Rams 1957-69
Lungren, Charlie, HB, Swarthmore, Rock Island 1923
Lunsford, Mel, DE-DT, Central State (Ohio), New England 1973-80
Lunz, Gerry, T-G, Marquette, Chi. Cardinals 1925-26; Frankford 1930
Lurtsema, Bob, DT-DE, Western Michigan, NY Giants 1967-71; Minnesota 1972-76; Seattle 1976-77
Lusby, Vaughn, CB, Arkansas, Cincinnati 1979; Chi. Bears 1980
Luscinski, Jim, T-G, Norwich, NY Jets 1982
Lusk, Bob, C, William & Mary, Detroit 1956
Lusk, Herb, RB, Long Beach State, Philadelphia 1976-78
Lusteg, Booth, K, Connecticut, Buffalo 1966; Miami 1967; NY Jets 1967; Pittsburgh 1968; Green Bay 1969
Luther, Ed, QB, San Jose State, San Diego 1980-84
Lutz, David, T, Georgia Tech, Kansas City 1983-85
Lyday, Allen, DB, Nebraska, Houston 1984-85
Lyle, Dewey, G, Rock Island 1920-22, 1924-25; Green Bay 1922-23
Lyle, Garry, DB, George Washington, Chi. Bears 1968-74
Lyles, Lenny, DB-KR, Louisville, Baltimore 1958, 1961-69; San Francisco 1959-60
Lyles, Lester, S, Virginia, NY Jets 1985
Lyles, Robert, LB, TCU, Houston 1984-85
Lyman, Del, T, UCLA, Green Bay 1941; Cleveland 1941, 1944
Lyman, Jeff, LB, BYU, St. Louis 1972; Buffalo 1972
Lyman, Roy (Link), T-G, Nebraska, Canton 1922-23, 1925; Cleveland 1924; Frankford 1925; Chi. Bears 1926-28, 1930-31, 1933-34
Lynch, Dick, DB, Notre Dame, Washington 1958; NY Giants 1959-66
Lynch, Ed, E, Catholic, Rochester 1925; Detroit 1926; Hartford 1926; Providence 1927
Lynch, Fran, RB, Hofstra, Denver 1967-75
Lynch, Jim, LB, Notre Dame, Kansas City 1967-77
Lynch, Lynn, G, Illinois, Chi. Cardinals 1951
Lynch, Paul, HB, Ohio Northern, Columbus 1925
Lynch, Tom, G, Boston College, Seattle 1977-80; Buffalo 1981-84
Lynn, Johnny, DB, UCLA, NY Jets 1979, 1981-85
Lyon, George (Babe), T, Kansas State, NY Giants 1929; Portsmouth 1930; Chi. Bears 1931; Cleveland 1931; Brooklyn 1932; St. Louis 1934
Lyons, Dicky, DB, Kentucky, New Orleans 1970
Lyons, John, E, Tulsa, Brooklyn 1933
Lyons, Leo, E, Rochester 1920
Lyons, Marty, DE-DT, Alabama, NY Jets 1979-85
Lyons, Tommy, G-C, Georgia, Denver 1971-78
Lytle, Rob, RB, Michigan, Denver 1977-83

M

Maack, Herb, T, Columbia, Brooklyn (AAFC) 1946
Maas, Bill, NT, Pittsburgh, Kansas City 1984-85
Mabra, Ron, DB, Howard (Washington D.C.), Atlanta 1975-76; NY Jets 1977
MacAfee, Ken, E, Alabama, NY Giants 1954-58; Philadelphia

1959; Washington 1959
MacAfee, Ken, TE, Notre Dame, San Francisco 1978-79
Macaulay, John, C, Stanford, San Francisco 1984
MacAuliffe, Jack, HB, Beloit, Green Bay 1926
MacCollum, Max, E, Centre, Louisville 1922
MacDonald, Mark, G, Boston College, Minnesota 1985
MacDowell, Jay, T-DT, Washington, Philadelphia 1946-51
Maceau, Mel, C, Marquette, Cleveland (AAFC) 1946-48
Macek, Don, C-G, Boston College, San Diego 1976-85
Macerelli, John, G, St. Vincent, Cleveland 1956
Machurek, Mike, QB, Idaho State, Detroit 1982-84
Macioszczyk, Art, FB, Western Michigan, Philadelphia 1944, 1947; Washington 1948
Mack, Bill (Red), FL, Notre Dame, Pittsburgh 1961-63, 1965; Philadelphia 1964; Atlanta 1966; Green Bay 1966
Mack, Cedric, CB-WR, Baylor, St. Louis 1983-85
Mack, Kevin, RB, Clemson, Cleveland 1985
Mack, Tom, G, Michigan, LA Rams 1966-78
Mackbee, Earsell, DB, Utah State, Minnesota 1965-69
Mackenroth, Jack, C, North Dakota, Detroit 1938
Mackert, Bob, T, West Virginia, Rochester 1925
Mackey, Dee, TE, East Texas State, San Francisco 1960; Baltimore 1961-62; NY Jets 1963-65
Mackey, John, TE, Syracuse, Baltimore 1963-71; San Diego 1972
Mackey, Kyle, QB, East Texas State, St. Louis 1984
MacKinnon, Jacque, TE-FB, Colgate, San Diego 1961-69; Oakland 1970
Mackorell, John, HB, Davidson, NY Giants 1935
Mackrides, Bill, QB, Nevada-Reno, Philadelphia 1948-51; Pittsburgh 1953; NY Giants 1953
MacLean, Stu, HB, Indiana, Louisville 1921
MacLeod, Bob, HB, Dartmouth, Chi. Bears 1939
MacLeod, Tom, LB, Minnesota, Green Bay 1973; Baltimore 1974-75, 1977-78
MacMillan, Stew, C, North Dakota, Cleveland 1931
MacMurdo, Jim, T, Pittsburgh, Boston 1932-33; Philadelphia 1934-37
Macon, Eddie, HB, Pacific, Chi. Bears 1952-53; Oakland 1960
MacPhee, Walter (Waddy), HB, Princeton, Providence 1925-26
MacWherter, Kyle, FB, Millikin, Decatur 1920
Maczuzak, John, DT, Pittsburgh, Kansas City 1964
Madar, Elmer, E, Michigan, Baltimore (AAFC) 1947
Madarik, Elmer (Tippy), HB, Detroit, Detroit 1945-47; Washington 1948
Madden, Lloyd, HB, Colorado Mines, Chi. Cardinals 1940
Maddock, Bob, G, Notre Dame, Chi. Cardinals 1942, 1946
Maddox, Bob, DE, Frostburg State, Cincinnati 1974; Kansas City 1975-76
Maddox, George (Buster), T, Kansas State, Green Bay 1935
Maderos, George, DB, Cal State-Chico, San Francisco 1955-56
Madigan, John, C, St. Mary's (Minnesota), Minneapolis 1922, 1924; Duluth 1923
Maeda, Chet, HB, Colorado State, Chi. Cardinals 1945
Maeder, Al, T, Minnesota, Minneapolis 1929
Magac, Mike, G, Missouri, San Francisco 1960-64; Pittsburgh 1965-66
Magee, Calvin, TE, Southern, Tampa Bay 1985
Magee, Jim, C, Villanova, Boston 1944-46
Magee, Johnny, G, Rice, Philadelphia 1948-55
Maggiolo, Achille (Chick), HB, Notre Dame, Buffalo (AAFC) 1948; Detroit 1949; Baltimore 1950
Magliolo, Joe, FB, Texas, NY Yankees (AAFC) 1948
Maglisceau, Al, T, Geneva, Frankford 1929
Magnani, Dante, HB, St. Mary's (California), Cleveland 1940-42; Chi. Bears 1943, 1946, 1949; LA Rams 1947-48; Detroit 1950
Magner, Jim, HB, North Carolina, Frankford 1931
Magnuson, Glen, C, Northwestern, Hammond 1925
Maguire, Paul, LB-P, Citadel, LA Chargers 1960; San Diego 1961-63; Buffalo 1964-70
Magulick, George, HB, St. Francis (Pennsylvania), Card-Pitt 1944
Mahalic, Drew, LB, Notre Dame, San Diego 1975; Philadelphia 1976-78
Mahan, Bob, FB, Washington (St. Louis), Buffalo 1929; Brooklyn 1930
Mahan, Walter (Red), G, West Virginia, Frankford 1926
Maher, Bernie, E, Detroit, Detroit 1920
Maher, Bruce, DB, Detroit, Detroit 1960-67; NY Giants 1968-69
Maher, Frank, HB, Toledo, Pittsburgh 1941; Cleveland 1941
Mahoney, Ike, HB, Creighton, Chi. Cardinals 1925-28, 1931
Mahoney, John, HB, Canisius, Buffalo 1923
Mahoney, Roger, C, Penn State, Frankford 1928-30; Minneapolis 1930
Mahrt, Al, QB, St. Mary's (Ohio), Dayton 1920-22
Mahrt, Armin, HB, West Virginia, Dayton 1924-26; Pottsville 1925
Mahrt, John, E, Dayton, Dayton 1925
Mahrt, Lou, QB, Dayton, Dayton 1926-27
Maidlow, Steve, LB, Michigan State, Cincinnati 1983-84; Buffalo 1985
Maillard, Ralph, T, Creighton, Chi. Bears 1929
Mains, Gil, DT, Murray State, Detroit 1954-61
Maitland, Jack, RB, Williams, Baltimore 1970; New England 1971-72
Majors, Billy, DB, Tennessee, Buffalo 1961
Majors, Bobby, DB-KR, Tennessee, Cleveland 1972
Malancon, Rydell, LB, LSU, Atlanta 1984
Malcolm, Harry, T, Washington & Jefferson, Frankford 1929
Maley, Howard (Red), HB, SMU, Boston 1946-47
Malinchak, Bill, WR, Indiana, Detroit 1966-69; Washington 1970-74, 1976
Malinowski, Gene, HB, Detroit, Boston 1948
Malkovich, Joe, C, Duquesne, Pittsburgh 1935
Mallick, Francis, DT, Pittsburgh 1965
Mallory, Irvin, DB, Virginia Union, New England 1971
Mallory, John, DB, West Virginia, Philadelphia 1968; Atlanta 1969-71
Mallory, Larry, S, Tennessee State, NY Giants 1976-78
Mallory, Rick, G, Washington, Tampa Bay 1985
Mallouf, Ray, QB, SMU, Chi. Cardinals 1941, 1946-48; NY Giants 1949
Malloy, Les, QB, Loyola (Chicago), Chi. Cardinals 1931-33
Malone, Art, RB, Arizona State, Atlanta 1970-74; Philadelphia 1975-76
Malone, Benny, RB, Arizona State, Miami 1974-78; Washington 1978-79
Malone, Charley, E, Texas A&M, Boston 1934-36; Washington 1937-40, 1942
Malone, Grover (Molly), HB, Notre Dame, Chi. Tigers 1920; Green Bay 1921; Rock Island 1921; Akron 1923
Malone, Mark, QB-WR, Arizona State, Pittsburgh 1980-85
Maloney, Gerald (Red), E, Dartmouth, Providence 1925; NY Yankees 1927; Boston 1929
Maloney, Norm, E, Purdue, San Francisco (AAFC) 1948-49
Mancha, Vaughn, C, Alabama, Boston 1948
Mandarino, Mike, C-G, La Salle, Philadelphia 1944-45
Manders, Clarence (Pug), FB-QB, Drake, Brooklyn 1939-44; Boston 1945; NY Yankees (AAFC) 1946; Buffalo (AAFC) 1947
Manders, Dave, C, Michigan State, Dallas 1964-66, 1968-74
Manders, Jack (Automatic), FB, Minnesota, Chi. Bears 1933-40
Mandich, Jim, TE, Michigan, Miami 1970-77; Pittsburgh 1978
Mandley, Pete, WR-KR, Northern Arizona, Detroit 1984-85
Maness, James, WR, TCU, Chi. Bears 1985
Manfreda, Tony, HB, Holy Cross, Newark 1930
Manges, Mark, QB, Maryland, St. Louis 1978
Mangiero, Dino, NT, Rutgers, Kansas City 1980-83; Seattle 1984
Mangum, John, DT, Southern Mississippi, Boston 1966-67
Mangum, Pete, LB, Mississippi, NY Giants 1954; Denver 1960
Maniaci, Joe, FB, Fordham, Brooklyn 1936-38; Chi. Bears 1938-41
Manion, Jim, G, St. Thomas (Minnesota), Duluth 1926-27
Mankat, Carl, G-T, Colgate, Dayton 1928-29
Mankins, Jim, RB, Florida State, Atlanta 1967
Manley, Dexter, DE, Oklahoma State, Washington 1981-85
Manley, Joe, LB, Mississippi State, San Francisco 1953
Manley, Leon, G, Oklahoma, Green Bay 1950-52
Mann, Bob, E, Michigan, Detroit 1948-49; Green Bay 1950-53
Mann, Charles, DE, Nevada-Reno, Washington 1983-85
Mann, Dave, HB-P, Oregon State, Chi. Cardinals 1955-57
Mann, Errol, K, North Dakota, Green Bay 1968; Detroit 1969-76; Oakland 1976-78
Manning, Archie, QB, Mississippi, New Orleans 1971-75, 1977-82; Houston 1982-83; Minnesota 1983-84
Manning, Jim, HB, Fordham, Hartford 1926; Providence 1926
Manning, Pete, SE-DB, Wake Forest, Chi. Bears 1960-61
Manning, Roosevelt, DT, Northeastern Oklahoma, Atlanta 1972-75; Philadelphia 1975
Manning, Wade, WR-KR, Ohio State, Dallas 1979; Denver 1981-82
Manor, Brison, DE, Arkansas, Denver 1977-84; Tampa Bay 1984
Manoukian, Don, G, Stanford, Oakland 1960
Mansfield, Jerry, FB-E, Rock Island 1920-21
Mansfield, Ray, C-DT, Washington, Philadelphia 1963; Pittsburgh 1964-76
Mansfield, Von, DB, Wisconsin, Philadelphia 1982
Manske, Edgar (Eggs), E, Northwestern, Philadelphia 1935-36; Chi. Bears 1937-40; Pittsburgh 1938
Mantell, Joe, G, Columbus 1924
Manton, Tillie, HB, TCU, NY Giants 1936-38; Washington 1938; Brooklyn 1943
Manucci, Dan, QB, Kansas State, Buffalo 1979-80
Manuel, Lionel, WR-KR, Pacific, NY Giants 1984-85
Manumaleuga, Frank, LB, San Jose State, Kansas City 1979-81
Manzini, Bap, C, St. Vincent, Philadelphia 1944-45, 1948
Manzo, Joe, T, Boston College, Detroit 1945
Maple, Howie, HB, Oregon State, Chi. Cardinals 1930
Maples, Bobby, C, Baylor, Houston 1965-70; Pittsburgh 1971; Denver 1972-78
Maples, James (Butch), LB, Baylor, Baltimore 1963
Maples, Tal, C, Tennessee, Cincinnati 1934
Marangi, Gary, QB, Boston College, Buffalo 1974-76; Cleveland 1977
Maras, Joe, C, Duquesne, Pittsburgh 1938-40
Marchetti, Gino, T-DE, San Francisco, Dallas 1952; Baltimore 1953-64, 1966
Marchi, Basilio, C, NYU, Pittsburgh 1934; Philadelphia 1941-42
Marchibroda, Ted, QB, St. Bonaventure, Detroit, Pittsburgh 1953, 1955-56; Chi. Cardinals 1957
Marchlewski, Frank, C, Minnesota, LA Rams 1965, 1968-69; Atlanta 1966-68; Buffalo 1970
Marciniak, Ron, G, Kansas State, Washington 1955
Marcol, Chester, K, Hillsdale, Green Bay 1972-80; Houston 1980
Marcolini, Hugo, HB, St. Bonaventure, Brooklyn (AAFC) 1948
Marconi, Joe, FB, West Virginia, LA Rams 1956-61; Chi. Bears 1962-66
Marcontelli, Ed, G, Lamar, St. Louis 1967; Houston 1967
Marcus, Pete, E, Kentucky, Washington 1944
Marderian, Greg, DT, USC, Atlanta 1976
Marefos, Andy, FB, St. Mary's (California), NY Giants 1941-42; LA Dons (AAFC) 1946
Marek, Joey, FB, Texas Tech, Brooklyn 1943
Marelli, Ray, G, Notre Dame, Chi. Cardinals 1928
Margarita, Henry (Bob), FB, Brown, Chi. Bears 1944-46
Margerum, Ken, WR, Stanford, Chi. Bears 1981-83, 1985
Margucci, Joe, HB, USC, Detroit 1947-48
Marinaro, Ed, RB, Cornell, Minnesota 1972-75; NY Jets 1976; Seattle 1977
Marino, Dan, QB, Pittsburgh, Miami 1983-85
Marino, Vic, G, Ohio State, Baltimore (AAFC) 1947
Marinovich, Marv, LB, USC, Oakland 1965
Marion, Frank, LB, Florida A&M, NY Giants 1977-83
Marion, Fred, S, Miami, New England 1982-85
Marion, Jerry, FL, Wyoming, Pittsburgh 1967
Marion, Phil, FB, Michigan, Detroit 1925-26
Mark, Lou, E, North Carolina State, Brooklyn 1938-40; Boston 1945
Marker, Cliff, HB, Washington State, Canton 1926; Frankford 1927; NY Giants 1927
Marker, Henry, QB, West Virginia, Pittsburgh 1934
Markham, Dale, DE-T, North Dakota, NY Giants 1980; St. Louis 1981
Marko, Steve, HB, Brooklyn 1944; Boston 1945
Markov, Vic, T, Washington, Cleveland 1938
Markovich, Mark, G, Penn State, San Diego 1974-75; Detroit 1976-77
Marks, Larry, QB, Indiana, Akron 1926; NY Yankees 1927; Green Bay 1928
Marone, Sal, G, Manhattan, NY Giants 1943
Maronic, Duke, G, Philadelphia 1944-50; NY Giants 1951
Maronic, Steve, G, North Carolina, Detroit 1939-40
Marotti, Lou, G, Toledo, Chi. Cardinals 1943, 1945; Card-Pitt 1944
Marquardt, John, E, Illinois, Chi. Cardinals 1921
Marques, Bob, LB, Boston U., NY Titans 1960
Marsalis, Jim, CB, Tennessee State, Kansas City 1969-75; New Orleans 1977
Marsh, Aaron, WR, Eastern Kentucky, Boston 1968-69
Marsh, Amos, HB-FB, Oregon State, Dallas 1961-64; Detroit 1965-67
Marsh, Curt, C-G, Washington, Oakland 1981; LA Raiders 1982, 1984-85
Marsh, Doug, TE, Michigan, St. Louis 1980-85
Marsh, Frank, DB, Oregon State, San Diego 1967
Marshall, Al, WR, Boise State, New England 1974
Marshall, Bobby (Rube), T-E, Minnesota, Rock Island 1920-21; Minneapolis 1922-24; Duluth 1923
Marshall, Charles (Tank), DT, Texas A&M, NY Jets 1977
Marshall, Charley, E, NYU, Staten Island 1931-32
Marshall, Chuck, DB, Oregon State, Denver 1962
Marshall, David, LB, Eastern Michigan, Cleveland 1984
Marshall, Ed, WR, Cameron State, Cincinnati 1971; NY Jets 1976; NY Giants 1976-77
Marshall, Greg, DT, Oregon State, Baltimore 1978
Marshall, Henry, WR, Missouri, Kansas City 1976-85
Marshall, James, CB, Jackson State, New Orleans 1980
Marshall, Jim, DE, Ohio State, Cleveland 1960; Minnesota 1961-79
Marshall, Larry, KR-DB, Maryland, Kansas City 1972-73, 1978; Minnesota 1974; Philadelphia 1974-77; LA Rams 1978
Marshall, Leonard, DE, LSU, NY Giants 1983-85
Marshall, Pete, E, Carnegie-Mellon, Cleveland 1920
Marshall, Randy, DE, Linfield, Atlanta 1970-71
Marshall, Richard (Bud), DT, Stephen F. Austin, Green Bay 1965; Washington 1966; Atlanta 1966; Houston 1967-68
Marshall, Wilber, LB, Florida, Chi. Bears 1984-85
Marston, Ralph, QB, Boston U., Boston 1929
Martell, Herm, E, Green Bay 1921
Martha, Paul, S, Pittsburgh, Pittsburgh 1964-69; Denver 1970
Martin, Aaron, DB-KR, North Carolina College, LA Rams 1964-65; Philadelphia 1966-67; Washington 1968
Martin, Amos, LB, Louisville, Minnesota 1972-76; Seattle 1977
Martin, Billy, HB, Minnesota, Chi. Bears 1962-64
Martin, Billy, TE, Georgia Tech, Chi. Bears 1964-65; Atlanta 1966-67; Minnesota 1968
Martin, Blanche, HB, Michigan State, NY Titans 1960; LA Chargers 1960
Martin, Bob, LB, Nebraska, NY Jets 1976-79; San Francisco 1979
Martin, Caleb, T, Louisiana Tech, Chi. Cardinals 1947
Martin, Charles, DT, Livingston, Green Bay 1984-85
Martin, Chris, LB, Auburn, New Orleans 1983; Minnesota 1984-85
Martin, D'Artagnan, DB, Kentucky State, New Orleans 1971
Martin, Dave, LB, Notre Dame, Kansas City 1968; Chi. Bears 1969
Martin, Don, DB, Yale, New England 1973; Kansas City 1975; Tampa Bay 1976

Martin, Doug, DE, Washington, Minnesota 1980-85
Martin, Eric, WR, LSU, New Orleans 1985
Martin, Frank, HB, Alabama, Brooklyn 1943-44; NY Giants 1945; Boston 1945
Martin, George, DE, Oregon, NY Giants 1975-85
Martin, Glen, HB, Southern Illinois, Chi. Cardinals 1932
Martin, Harvey, DE, East Texas State, Dallas 1973-83
Martin, Hersh, HB, Missouri, Staten Island 1929; Newark 1930
Martin, Ike, HB, William Jewell, Canton 1920
Martin, Jim, LB-K, Notre Dame, Cleveland 1950; Detroit 1951-61; Baltimore 1963; Washington 1964
Martin, Jack, C, Navy, LA Rams 1947-49
Martin, Joe, HB, Louisville 1921
Martin, John, HB, Oklahoma, Chi. Cardinals 1941-43; Card-Pitt 1944; Boston 1944-45
Martin, Larry, DT, San Diego State, San Diego 1966
Martin, Mike, WR, Illinois, Cincinnati 1983-85
Martin, Robbie, KR-WR, Cal Poly-SLO, Detroit 1981-84; Indianapolis 1985
Martin, Rod, LB, USC, Oakland 1977-81; LA Raiders 1982-85
Martin, Saladin, CB, San Diego State, NY Jets 1980; San Francisco 1981
Martin, Vern, QB, Texas, Pittsburgh 1942
Martineau, Roy, G, Syracuse, Buffalo 1923; Rochester 1924-25
Martinelli, Jim, C, Scranton, Buffalo (AAFC) 1946
Martini, Rich, WR, Cal-Davis, Oakland 1979-80; New Orleans 1981
Martinkovich, John, DE, Xavier, Green Bay 1951-56; NY Giants 1957
Martinovich, Phil, G, Pacific, Detroit 1939; Chi. Bears 1940; Brooklyn (AAFC) 1946-47
Marvaso, Tommy, DB, Cincinnati, NY Jets 1976-77
Marve, Eugene, LB, Saginaw Valley State, Buffalo 1982-85
Marvin, Mickey, G, Tennessee, Oakland 1977-81; LA Raiders 1982-85
Marx, Greg, DE, Notre Dame, Atlanta 1973
Masini, Len, FB-LB, Fresno State, San Francisco (AAFC) 1947-48; LA Dons (AAFC) 1948
Maskas, John, G, Virginia Tech, Buffalo (AAFC) 1947, 1949
Maslowski, Matt, WR, San Diego, LA Rams 1971; Chi. Bears 1972
Mason, Dave, DB, Nebraska, New England 1973; Green Bay 1974
Mason, Joel, E, Western Michigan, Chi. Cardinals 1939; Green Bay 1942-45
Mason, Lindsey, T, Kansas, Oakland 1978, 1980-81; San Francisco 1982; Indianapolis 1983
Mason, Sam, FB, Virginia Military, Minneapolis 1922; Milwaukee 1925
Mason, Tommy, HB-KR, Tulane, Minnesota 1961-66; LA Rams 1967-70; Washington 1971-72
Mass, Wayne, DT, Clemson, Chi. Bears 1968-70; Miami 1971; New England 1972; Philadelphia 1972
Massey, Carleton, DE, Texas, Cleveland 1954-56; Green Bay 1957-58
Massey, Jim, DB, Linfield, New England 1974-75
Masters, Billy, TE, LSU, Buffalo 1967-69; Denver 1970-74; Kansas City 1975-76
Masters, Bob, HB, Baylor, Philadelphia 1937-38, 1942; Pittsburgh 1939; Phil-Pitt 1943; Chi. Bears 1943-44
Masters, Norm, T, Michigan State, Green Bay 1957-64
Masters, Walt, QB, Pennsylvania, Philadelphia 1936; Chi. Cardinals 1943; Card-Pitt 1944
Masterson, Bernie, QB, Nebraska, Chi. Bears 1934-40
Masterson, Bob, E, Miami, Washington 1938-43; Brooklyn 1944; Boston 1945; Brooklyn (AAFC) 1946
Masterson, Forest, C, Iowa, Chi. Bears 1945
Mastrangelo, John, G, Notre Dame, Pittsburgh 1947-48; NY Yankees (AAFC) 1949; NY Giants 1950
Mastrogany, Gus, E, Iowa, Chi. Bears 1931
Matan, Bill, DE, Kansas State, NY Giants 1966
Matesic, Ed, HB, Pittsburgh, Philadelphia 1934-35; Pittsburgh 1936
Matesic, Joe, DT, Arizona State, Pittsburgh 1954
Matheson, Bob, DE-LB, Duke, Cleveland 1967-70; Miami 1971-79
Matheson, Jack, E, Western Michigan, Detroit 1943-46; Chi. Bears 1947
Matheson, Riley (Rattler), G, Texas-El Paso, Cleveland 1939-42, 1944-45; Detroit 1943; LA Rams 1946-47; San Francisco (AAFC) 1948
Mathews, Frank, E, Northwestern, Racine 1926
Mathews, Ned, HB, UCLA, Detroit 1941-43; Boston 1945; Chi. Rockets (AAFC) 1946; San Francisco (AAFC) 1946-47
Mathews, Neil, T, Pennsylvania, Chi. Tigers 1920
Mathews, Ray, HB-FL, Clemson, Pittsburgh 1951-59; Dallas Cowboys 1960
Mathis, Bill, FB, Clemson, NY Titans 1960-62; NY Jets 1963-69
Mathis, Reggie, LB, Oklahoma, New Orleans 1979-80
Mathison, Bruce, QB, Nebraska, San Diego 1983-84; Buffalo 1985
Mathys, Charlie, QB, Indiana, Hammond 1921; Green Bay 1922-26
Matich, Trevor, C, BYU, New England 1985
Matisi, John, T, Duquesne, Brooklyn 1943; Buffalo (AAFC) 1946
Matisi, Tony, T, Pittsburgh, Detroit 1938
Matlock, John, C, Miami, NY Jets 1967; Cincinnati 1968; Atlanta 1970-71; Buffalo 1972
Matson, Ollie, HB, San Francisco, Chi. Cardinals 1952, 1954-58; LA Rams 1959-62; Detroit 1963; Philadelphia 1964-66
Matson, Pat, G, Oregon, Denver 1966-67; Cincinnati 1968-74; Green Bay 1975
Matsos, Archie, LB, Michigan State, Buffalo 1960-62; Oakland 1963-65; Denver 1966; San Diego 1966
Matsu, Art, QB, William & Mary, Dayton 1928
Matte, Tom, RB-QB, Ohio State, Baltimore 1961-72
Matteo, Frank, T, Syracuse, Rochester 1922-25
Mattern, Joe, HB, Minnesota, Cleveland 1920; Minneapolis 1922
Matthews, Al, CB, Texas A&I, Green Bay 1970-75; Seattle 1976; San Francisco 1977
Matthews, Allama, TE, Vanderbilt, Atlanta 1983-85
Matthews, Bill, LB, South Dakota State, New England 1979-81
Matthews, Bo, RB, Colorado, San Diego 1974-79; NY Giants 1980-81; Miami 1981
Matthews, Bruce, T-C, USC, Houston 1983-85
Matthews, Clay, DE, Georgia Tech, San Francisco 1950, 1953-55
Matthews, Clay, LB, USC, Cleveland 1978-85
Matthews, Henry, RB, Michigan State, New England 1972; New Orleans 1973; Atlanta 1973
Matthews, Ira, KR-RB, Wisconsin, Oakland 1979-81
Matthews, Wes, SE, Northeastern Oklahoma, Miami 1966
Mattiford, John, G, Marshall, Detroit 1941
Mattingly, Fran, G, Texas A&I, Chi. Rockets (AAFC) 1947
Mattioli, Frank, G, Pittsburgh, Pittsburgh 1946
Mattison, Ralph, G, Davis & Elkins, Brooklyn 1930
Mattos, Harry, HB, St. Mary's (California), Green Bay 1936; Cleveland 1937
Mattox, Jack, DT, Fresno State, Denver 1961-62
Mattox, Marv, HB, Washington & Lee, Milwaukee 1923
Mattson, Riley, T, Oregon, Washington 1961-64; Chi. Bears 1966
Matuszak, John, DE-DT, Tampa, Houston 1973; Kansas City 1974-75; Oakland 1976-81
Matuszak, Marv, LB, Tulsa, Pittsburgh 1953, 1955-56; San Francisco 1957-58; Green Bay 1958; Baltimore 1959-61; Buffalo 1962-63; Denver 1964
Matuza, Al, C, Georgetown (Washington D.C.), Chi. Bears 1941-43
Mauck, Carl, C, Southern Illinois, Baltimore 1969; Miami 1970; San Diego 1971-74; Houston 1975-81
Mauer, Jake, G, Racine 1923
Maul, Elmo (Tuffy), FB, St. Mary's (California), LA Buccaneers 1926
Mauldin, Stan, T, Texas, Chi. Cardinals 1946-48
Maurer, Andy, G, Oregon, Atlanta 1970-73; New Orleans 1974; Minnesota 1974-75; San Francisco 1976; Denver 1977
Mauti, Rich, WR-KR, Penn State, New Orleans 1977-83; Washington 1984
Maves, Earl, HB, Wisconsin, Detroit 1948; Baltimore (AAFC) 1948
Mavraides, Menil (Minnie), G, Notre Dame, Philadelphia 1954, 1957
Maxie, Brett, CB, Texas Southern, New Orleans 1985
Maxson, Alvin, RB, SMU, New Orleans 1974-76; Pittsburgh 1977-78; Tampa Bay 1978; Houston 1978; NY Giants 1978
Maxwell, Bruce, RB, Arkansas, Detroit 1970
Maxwell, Joey, E, Notre Dame, Frankford 1927-29
Maxwell, Tom, S, Texas A&M, Baltimore 1969-70; Oakland 1971-73; Houston 1974
Maxwell, Vernon, LB, Arizona State, Baltimore 1983; Indianapolis 1984; Detroit 1985
May, Art, DE-DT, Tuskegee, New England 1971
May, Bill, QB, LSU, Chi. Cardinals 1937-38
May, Dean, QB, Louisville, Philadelphia 1984
May, Jack, C, Centenary, Cleveland 1938
May, Mark, T-G, Pittsburgh, Washington 1981-85
May, Ray, LB, USC, Pittsburgh 1967-69; Baltimore 1970-73; Denver 1973-75
May, Walt, G, Decatur 1920
Mayberry, Doug, FB, Utah State, Minnesota 1961-62; Oakland 1963
Mayberry, James, RB, Colorado, Atlanta 1979-81
Mayer, Emil, E, Catholic, Pottsville 1927; Portsmouth 1930
Mayer, Frank, G, Notre Dame, Green Bay 1927
Mayes, Ben, DT, Drake, Houston 1969
Mayes, Carl, HB, Texas, LA Rams 1952
Mayes, Rufus, T, Ohio State, Chi. Bears 1969; Cincinnati 1970-78; Philadelphia 1979
Mayhew, Hayden (Tex), G, Texas-El Paso, Pittsburgh 1936-38
Mayl, Gene, E, Notre Dame, Dayton 1925-26
Maynard, Don, WR, Texas-El Paso, NY Giants 1958; NY Titans 1960-62; NY Jets 1963-72; St. Louis 1973
Maynard, Les, HB, Rider, Staten Island 1932; Philadelphia 1933
Maynaugh, Roland, G, St. Thomas (Minnesota), Minneapolis 1924
Mayne, Mickey, HB, Texas, Brooklyn (AAFC) 1946; Cleveland (AAFC) 1947; Baltimore (AAFC) 1948
Mayo, Ron, TE, Morgan State, Houston 1973; Baltimore 1974
Mayock, Mike, S, Boston College, NY Giants 1982-83
Mays, Dave, QB, Texas Southern, Cleveland 1976-77; Buffalo 1978
Mays, Jerry, DE, SMU, Dallas Texans 1961-62; Kansas City 1963-70
Mays, Stafford, DE, Washington, St. Louis 1980-85
Maznicki, Frank, HB, Boston College, Chi. Bears 1942, 1946; Boston 1947
Mazurek, Ed, T, Xavier, NY Giants 1960
Mazurek, Fred, FL, Pittsburgh, Washington 1965-66
Mazza, Vince, E, Detroit 1945-46; Buffalo (AAFC) 1947-49
Mazzanti, Gino, HB, Arkansas, Baltimore 1950
Mazzanti, Jerry, DE, Arkansas, Philadelphia 1963; Detroit 1966; Pittsburgh 1967
Mazzetti, Tim, K, Pennsylvania, Atlanta 1978-80
McAdams, Bob, DT, North Carolina Central, NY Jets 1963-64
McAdams, Carl, LB, Oklahoma, NY Jets 1967-69
McAdams, Dean, HB, Washington, Brooklyn 1941-43
McAfee, George, HB-DB, Duke, Chi. Bears 1940-41, 1945-50
McAfee, Wes, HB, Duke, Philadelphia 1941
McAleney, Ed, DE, Massachusetts, Atlanta 1976; Tampa Bay 1976
McAlister, James, RB, UCLA, Philadelphia 1975-76; New England 1978
McAlister, Ken, LB, San Francisco, Seattle 1982-83; San Francisco 1983; Kansas City 1984
McArthur, Jack, C, Santa Clara, LA Buccaneers 1926; Buffalo 1927; NY Yankees 1927-28; Orange 1929; Newark 1930; Brooklyn 1930; Frankford 1930; Providence 1930-31
McBath, Mike, DE, Penn State, Buffalo 1968-72
McBride, Charlie, QB, Washington State, Chi. Cardinals 1936
McBride, Jack, HB, Syracuse, NY Giants 1925-28, 1932-34; Providence 1929; Brooklyn 1930-32
McBride, Norm, DE, Utah, Miami 1969-70
McBride, Ron, RB, Missouri, Green Bay 1973
McCabe, Richie, DB, Pittsburgh, Pittsburgh 1955, 1957-58; Washington 1959; Buffalo 1960-61
McCafferty, Don, E, Ohio State, NY Giants 1946
McCaffray, Art, T, Pacific, Pittsburgh 1946
McCaffrey, Mike, LB, California, Buffalo 1970
McCaffrey, Robert, C, USC, Green Bay 1975
McCain, Bob, E, Mississippi, Brooklyn (AAFC) 1946
McCall, Bob, RB, Arizona, New England 1973
McCall, Don, RB, USC, New Orleans 1967-68, 1970; Pittsburgh 1969
McCall, Ed, DB, Miles, Cincinnati 1968
McCall, Joe, RB, Pittsburgh, LA Raiders 1984
McCall, Reese, TE, Auburn, Baltimore 1978-82; Detroit 1983-85
McCall, Ron, LB, Weber State, San Diego 1967-68
McCambridge, John, DE, Northwestern, Detroit 1967
McCann, Jim, P, Arizona State, San Francisco 1971-72; NY Giants 1973; Kansas City 1975
McCann, Ernie, T, Penn State, Hartford 1926
McCann, Tim, DT, Princeton, NY Giants 1969
McCarren, Larry, C, Illinois, Green Bay 1973-84
McCarthy, Brendan, RB, Boston College, Atlanta 1968; Denver 1968-69
McCarthy, Jim, T, California, Duluth 1927
McCarthy, Jim, E, Illinois, Brooklyn (AAFC) 1946-47; Chi. Rockets (AAFC) 1948; Chi. Hornets (AAFC) 1949
McCarthy, John, QB, St. Francis, Card-Pitt 1944
McCarthy, Vince, QB, St. Viator, Rock Island 1924-25
McCartney, Ron, LB, Tennessee, Atlanta 1977-79
McCarty, Mickey, TE, TCU, Kansas City 1969
McCauley, Don, RB, North Carolina, Baltimore 1971-81
McCauley, Tom, S, Wisconsin, Atlanta 1969-71
McCausland, Leo, C-T, Detroit, Akron 1922
McCaw, Bill, E, Indiana, Racine 1923
McCaw, Bill, G, Loyola (Chicago), Louisville 1926
McChesney, Bob, E, UCLA, Boston 1936; Washington 1937-42
McChesney, Bob, E, Hardin-Simmons, NY Giants 1950-52
McClain, Clifford, RB, South Carolina State, NY Jets 1970-73
McClain, Clinton (Red), FB, SMU, NY Giants 1941
McClain, Dewey, LB, East Central (Oklahoma), Atlanta 1976-80
McClain, Joe, G, St. John's (New York), NY Yankees 1928
McClain, Mayes, HB, Haskell, Portsmouth 1930-31; Staten Island 1931
McClairen, Jack (Goose), SE, Bethune-Cookman, Pittsburgh 1955-60
McClanahan, Brent, RB, Arizona State, Minnesota 1973-79
McClanahan, Randy, LB, Southwestern Louisiana, Oakland 1977, 1980-81; Buffalo 1978; LA Raiders 1982
McClard, Bill, K, Arkansas, San Diego 1972; New Orleans 1973-75
McClellan, Mike, DB, Oklahoma, Philadelphia 1962-63
McClendon, Willie, RB-KR, Georgia, Chi. Bears 1979-82
McClinton, Curtis, FB, Kansas, Dallas Texans 1962; Kansas City 1963-69
McCloskey, Mike, TE, Penn State, Houston 1983-85
McCloughan, Kent, CB, Nebraska, Oakland 1965-70
McClung, Willie, T, Florida A&M, Pittsburgh 1955-57; Cleveland 1958-59; Detroit 1960-61
McClure, Robert (Buster), G, Nevada-Reno, Boston 1947-48
McClure, Wayne, LB, Mississippi, Cincinnati 1968, 1970
McColl, Bill, FL, Stanford, Chi. Bears 1952-59
McColl, Milt, LB, Stanford, San Francisco 1981-85
McCollum, Harley, T, Tulane, NY Yankees (AAFC) 1946; Chi. Rockets (AAFC) 1947
McCollum, James (Bubba), DT, Kentucky, Houston 1974
McComb, Don, DE, Villanova, Boston 1960

McCombs, Nat (Big Twig), T, Haskell, Akron 1926; Buffalo 1929
McConkey, Phil, WR-KR, Navy, NY Giants 1984-85
McConnell, Brian, LB, Michigan State, Buffalo 1973; Houston 1973
McConnell, Dewey, E, Wyoming, Pittsburgh 1954
McConnell, Felton, G, Georgia Tech, Buffalo 1927
McCord, Darris, DE, Tennessee, Detroit 1955-67
McCormack, Mike, T-DT, Kansas, NY Yanks 1951; Cleveland 1954-62
McCormick, Dave, T, LSU, San Francisco 1966; New Orleans 1967-68
McCormick, Elmer, G, Buffalo 1923-25; Frankford 1925; Hartford 1926
McCormick, Felix, FB, Bucknell, Orange 1929; Newark 1930
McCormick, Frank, HB, South Dakota, Akron 1920-21
McCormick, John, QB, Massachusetts, Minnesota 1962; Denver 1963, 1965-66, 1968
McCormick, Len (Tuffy), C-LB, Baylor, Baltimore (AAFC) 1948
McCormick, Tom, HB, Pacific, LA Rams 1953-55; San Francisco 1956
McCormick, Walt, C, USC, San Francisco (AAFC) 1948
McCoy, Joel, HB, Alabama, Detroit 1946
McCoy, Larry, LB, Lamar, LA Raiders 1984
McCoy, Lloyd, G, San Diego State, San Diego 1964
McCoy, Mike, DT, Notre Dame, Green Bay 1970-76; Oakland 1977-78; NY Giants 1979-80; Detroit 1980
McCoy, Mike, CB-KR, Colorado, Green Bay 1976-83
McCrary, Greg, TE, Clark, Atlanta 1975, 1977; Washington 1978; San Diego 1978
McCrary, Hurdis, HB-FB, Georgia, Green Bay 1929-33
McCray, Prentice, CB, Arizona State, New England 1974-80; Detroit 1980
McCray, Willie, DE, Troy State, San Francisco 1978
McCreary, Bob, T, Wake Forest, Dallas Cowboys 1961
McCreary, Loaird, TE, Tennessee State, Miami 1976-78; NY Giants 1979
McCrillis, Ed, G, Brown, Providence 1926; Boston 1929
McCrohan, John, T, Princeton, Rochester 1920
McCrumbly, John, LB, Texas A&M, Buffalo 1975
McCullers, Dale, LB, Florida State, Miami 1969
McCullouch, Earl, WR, USC, Detroit 1968-73
McCullough, Bob, G, Colorado, Denver 1962-65
McCullough, Harold, HB, Cornell, Brooklyn 1942
McCullough, Hugh, HB, Oklahoma, Pittsburgh 1939; Chi. Cardinals 1940-41; Phil-Pitt 1943; Boston 1945
McCullough, Jim, G, Holy Cross, Brooklyn 1926
McCullum, Sam, WR, Montana State, Minnesota 1974-75, 1982-83; Seattle 1976-81
McCurry, Dave, DB, Iowa State, New England 1974
McCusker, Jim, T, Pittsburgh, Chi. Cardinals 1958; Philadelphia 1959-62; Cleveland 1963; NY Jets 1964
McCutcheon, Lawrence, RB, Colorado State, LA Rams 1972-79; Denver 1980; Seattle 1980; Buffalo 1981
McDade, Karl, C, Portland, Pittsburgh 1938
McDaniel, Edward (Wahoo), LB, Oklahoma, Houston 1960; Denver 1961-63; NY Jets 1964-65; Miami 1966-68
McDaniel, John, WR, Lincoln (Missouri), Cincinnati 1974-77; Washington 1978-80
McDaniel, LeCharles, CB, Cal Poly-SLO, Washington 1981-82; NY Giants 1983-84
McDaniel, Orlando, WR, LSU, Denver 1982
McDaniels, Dave, WR, Mississippi Valley State, Dallas 1968
McDermott, Gary, RB, Tulsa, Buffalo 1968; Atlanta 1969
McDermott, Lloyd, DT, Kentucky, Detroit 1950; Chi. Cardinals 1950-51
McDole, Mardye, WR-KR, Mississippi State, Minnesota 1981-83
McDole, Ron, DE, Nebraska, St. Louis 1961; Houston 1962; Buffalo 1963-70; Washington 1971-78
McDonald, Don (Flip), E, Oklahoma, Brooklyn 1944; Philadelphia 1944-46; NY Yankees (AAFC) 1948
McDonald, Don, DB, Houston, Buffalo 1961
McDonald, Dwight, WR, San Diego State, San Diego 1975-78
McDonald, Ed, HB, Duquesne, Pittsburgh 1936
McDonald, James, TE, USC, LA Rams 1983-85; Detroit 1985
McDonald, Jim, QB, Ohio State, Detroit 1938-39
McDonald, John, T, Lawrence, Evansville 1921; Louisville 1926
McDonald, Les, E, Nebraska, Chi. Bears 1937-39; Philadelphia 1940; Detroit 1940
McDonald, Mike, LB, Catawba, St. Louis 1976
McDonald, Mike, LB, USC, LA Rams 1983-84
McDonald, Paul, QB, USC, Cleveland 1980-85
McDonald, Ray, FB, Idaho, Washington 1967-68
McDonald, Tommy, FL, Oklahoma, Philadelphia 1957-63; Dallas 1964; LA Rams 1965-66; Atlanta 1967; Cleveland 1968
McDonald, Walt, C, Utah, Brooklyn 1935
McDonald, Walt, QB, Tulane, Miami (AAFC) 1946; Brooklyn (AAFC) 1946-48; Chi. Hornets (AAFC) 1949
McDonnell, Mickey, HB, Duluth 1923-25; Chi. Cardinals 1925-30; Frankford 1931
McDonough, Bob, G, Duke, Philadelphia 1946
McDonough, Coley, QB, Dayton, Chi. Cardinals 1939; Pittsburgh 1939-41; Card-Pitt 1944
McDonough, Paul, E, Utah, Pittsburgh 1938; Cleveland 1939-41
McDougald, Doug, DE, Virginia Tech, New England 1980
McDougall, Gerry, FB, UCLA, San Diego 1962-64, 1968
McDowell, John, T, St. John's (Minnesota), Green Bay 1964; NY Giants 1965; St. Louis 1966
McElhenny, Hugh (The King), HB-KR, Washington, San Francisco 1952-60; Minnesota 1961-62; NY Giants 1963; Detroit 1964
McElroy, Bucky, HB, Southern Mississippi, Chi. Bears 1954
McElroy, Reggie, G-T, West Texas State, NY Jets 1983-85
McElroy, Vann, S, Baylor, LA Raiders 1982-85
McElwain, Bill, HB, Northwestern, Chi. Cardinals 1924, 1926; Chi. Bears 1925
McEnulty, Doug, HB, Wichita State, Chi. Bears 1943-44
McEvoy, Ed, HB, Spring Hill, Hartford 1926
McFadden, Banks, HB, Clemson, Brooklyn 1940
McFadden, Marv, G, Michigan State, Pittsburgh 1953, 1956
McFadden, Paul, K, Youngstown State, Philadelphia 1984-85
McFadin, Bud, G-DT, Texas, LA Rams 1952-56; Denver 1960-63; Houston 1964-65
McFarland, Jim, TE, Nebraska, St. Louis 1970-74; Miami 1975
McFarland, Kay, FL, Colorado State, San Francisco 1962-66, 1968
McFarlane, Nyle, HB, BYU, Oakland 1960
McGarry, Barney, G, Utah, Cleveland 1939-42
McGaw, Walt, G, Beloit, Green Bay 1926
McGeary, Clarence (Clink), T, North Dakota State, Green Bay 1950
McGee, Ben, DE-DT, Jackson State, Pittsburgh 1964-72
McGee, Bob, T, Santa Clara, Chi. Cardinals 1938
McGee, Buford, RB, Mississippi, San Diego 1984-85
McGee, Carl, LB, Duke, San Diego 1980
McGee, Ed, T, Temple, NY Giants 1940; Boston 1944-46
McGee, George, T, Southern, Boston 1960
McGee, Harry, C, Kansas State, Cleveland 1927; Staten Island 1929, 1932; Newark 1930
McGee, Max, SE-P, Tulane, Green Bay 1954, 1957-67
McGee, Mike, G, Duke, St. Louis 1960-62
McGee, Molly, RB, Rhode Island, Atlanta 1974
McGee, Tony, DE-NT, Bishop, Chi. Bears 1971-73; New England 1974-81; Washington 1982-84
McGee, Willie, WR-KR, Alcorn State, San Diego 1973; LA Rams 1974-75; San Francisco 1976-77; Detroit 1978
McGeever, John, DB, Auburn, Denver 1962-65; Miami 1966
McGehean, Bob, HB, Louisville 1923
McGeorge, Rich, TE, Elon, Green Bay 1970-78
McGibbony, Charlie, HB, Arkansas State, Brooklyn 1944
McGilbra, Sandy, T, Redlands, Buffalo 1926
McGill, Eddie, TE, Western Carolina, St. Louis 1982-83
McGill, George, C, Racine 1922
McGill, Mike, LB, Notre Dame, Minnesota 1968-70; St. Louis 1971-72
McGill, Ralph, CB, Tulsa, San Francisco 1972-77; New Orleans 1978
McGinley, Eddie, T, Pennsylvania, NY Giants 1925
McGinnis, A.B., C, Lehigh, Canton 1920
McGinnis, Larry, E, Marquette, Milwaukee 1923-24
McGirl, Len, G, Missouri, St. Louis 1934
McGlasson, Ed, C, Youngstown State, NY Jets 1979; LA Rams 1980; NY Giants 1981
McGlone, Joe, QB, Harvard, Providence 1926
McGoldrick, Hugh, T, Lehigh, Providence 1925
McGrath, Brian, G, NYU, Louisville 1922
McGrath, Dick, T, Holy Cross, Brooklyn 1926
McGrath, Frank, E, Georgetown (Washington D.C.), Frankford 1927; NY Yankees 1928
McGrath, Mark, WR, Montana State, Seattle 1981; Washington 1983-85
McGraw, Mike, LB, Wyoming, St. Louis 1976; Detroit 1977
McGraw, Thurman (Fum), DT, Colorado State, Detroit 1950-54
McGregor, Keli, TE, Colorado State, Denver 1985; Indianapolis 1985
McGrew, Dan, C, Purdue, Buffalo 1960
McGrew, Larry, LB, USC, New England 1980, 1982-85
McGriff, Curtis, DE, Alabama, NY Giants 1980-85
McGriff, Lee, WR, Florida, Tampa Bay 1976
McGriff, Tyrone, G, Florida A&M, Pittsburgh 1980-82
McGuirk, Warren, T, Boston College, Providence 1929-30
McHan, Lamar, QB, Arkansas, Chi. Cardinals 1954-58; Green Bay 1959-60; Baltimore 1961-63; San Francisco 1963
McHugh, Pat, HB-DB, Georgia Tech, Philadelphia 1947-51
McIlany, Dan, RB, Texas A&M, LA Rams 1965
McIlhenny, Don, HB, SMU, Detroit 1956; Green Bay 1957-59; Dallas Cowboys 1960; San Francisco 1961
McIllwain, Wally, HB, Illinois, Racine 1926
McInally, Pat, P-WR, Harvard, Cincinnati 1976-85
McInerny, Arnie, C-FB, Notre Dame, Chi. Cardinals 1920-27
McInnis, Hugh, TE, Southern Mississippi, St. Louis 1960-62; Detroit 1964; Atlanta 1966
McIntosh, Ira, HB, Rhode Island State, Providence 1925-26
McIntyre, Guy, G-RB, Georgia, San Francisco 1984-85
McIntyre, Jeff, LB, Arizona State, San Francisco 1979; St. Louis 1980
McIntyre, Secdrick, RB, Auburn, Atlanta 1977
McIvor, Rick, QB, Texas, St. Louis 1984-85
McKalip, Bill, E, Oregon State, Portsmouth 1931-32; Detroit 1934, 1936
McKay, Bob, T, Texas, Cleveland 1970-75; New England 1976-78
McKay, John (J.K.), WR, USC, Tampa Bay 1976-78
McKay, Roy Dale, HB-P, Texas, Green Bay 1944-47
McKee, Paul, E, Syracuse, Washington 1947-48
McKeever, Marlin, TE-LB, USC, LA Rams 1961-66, 1971-72; Minnesota 1967; Washington 1968-70; Philadelphia 1973
McKenzie, Raleigh, G, Tennessee, Washington 1985
McKenzie, Reggie, G, Michigan, Buffalo 1972-82; Seattle 1983-84
McKenzie, Reggie, LB, Tennessee, LA Raiders 1985
McKetes, Jack, HB, Hammond 1926
McKibben, Mike, LB, Kent State, NY Jets 1979-80
McKinley, Bill, DE-LB, Arizona, Buffalo 1971
McKinnely, Phil, T, UCLA, Atlanta 1976-80; LA Rams 1981
McKinney, Bill, LB, West Texas State, Chi. Bears 1972
McKinney, Odis, S, Colorado, NY Giants 1978-79; Oakland 1980-81; LA Raiders 1982-85; Kansas City 1985
McKinney, Royce, DB, Kentucky State, Buffalo 1975
McKinney, Zion, WR, South Carolina, Washington 1980
McKinnis, Hugh, RB, Arizona State, Cleveland 1973-75; Seattle 1976
McKinnon, Dennis, WR, Florida State, Chi. Bears 1983-85
McKinnon, Don, LB, Dartmouth, Boston 1963-64
McKissack, Dick, FB, SMU, Dallas 1952
McKnight, Dennis, G, Drake, San Diego 1982-85
McKnight, Ted, RB, Minnesota-Duluth, Kansas City 1977-81
McKoy, Bill, LB, Purdue, Denver 1970-72; San Francisco 1974
McLain, Kevin, LB, Colorado State, LA Rams 1976-79
McLaughlin, Charlie, FB, Wichita State, St. Louis 1934
McLaughlin, Joe, LB, Massachusetts, Green Bay 1979; NY Giants 1980-84
McLaughlin, Lee, G, Virginia, Green Bay 1941
McLaughlin, Leon, C, UCLA, LA Rams 1951-55
McLaughry, John, QB, Brown, NY Giants 1940
McLean, Ray (Toody), FB, Green Bay 1921
McLean, Ray (Scooter), HB, St. Anselm, Chi. Bears 1940-47
McLean, Scott, LB, Florida State, Dallas 1983
McLemore, Dana, KR-CB, Hawaii, San Francisco 1982-85
McLemore, Emmett, QB, Haskell, Oorang 1922-23; Kansas City 1924
McLenna, Bruce, FB, Hillsdale, Detroit 1966
McLeod, Bob, TE, Abilene Christian, Houston 1961-66
McLeod, Mike, DB, Montana State, Green Bay 1984-85
McLeod, Russ, C, St. Louis, St. Louis 1934
McLinton, Harold (Tank), LB, Southern, Washington 1969-78
McMahan, Jack, HB, Heidelberg, Cincinnati 1921
McMahon, Art, DB, North Carolina State, Boston 1968-70; New England 1972
McMahon, Byron, G, Cornell, Chi. Cardinals 1923
McMahon, Harry (Shorty), HB-QB, Holy Cross, Hartford 1926
McMahon, Jim, QB, BYU, Chi. Bears 1982-85
McMakin, John, TE, Clemson, Pittsburgh 1972-74; Detroit 1975; Seattle 1976
McMath, Herb, DE, Morningside, Oakland 1976; Green Bay 1977
McMichael, Steve, DT, Texas, New England 1980; Chi. Bears 1981-85
McMichaels, John, HB, Birmingham Southern, Brooklyn 1944
McMillan, Chuck, HB, John Carroll, Baltimore 1954
McMillan, Eddie, S, Florida State, LA Rams 1973-75; Seattle 1976-77; Buffalo 1978
McMillan, Ernie, T, Illinois, St. Louis 1961-74; Green Bay 1975
McMillan, Randy, RB, Pittsburgh, Baltimore 1981-83; Indianapolis 1984-85
McMillen, Jim, G, Illinois, Chi. Bears 1924-28
McMillian, Audrey, DB, Houston, Houston 1985
McMillin, Alvin (Bo), QB, Centre, Milwaukee 1922-23; Cleveland 1923
McMillin, Jim, DB, Colorado State, Denver 1961-62, 1964-65; Oakland 1963-64
McMullan, John, G, Notre Dame, NY Titans 1960-61
McMullen, Danny, G, Nebraska, NY Giants 1929; Chi. Bears 1930-31; Portsmouth 1932
McMurtry, Chuck, T, Whittier, Buffalo 1960-61; Oakland 1962-63
McNally, Frank, C, St. Mary's (California), Chi. Cardinals 1931-34
McNamara, Bob, E, NYU, Boston 1934
McNamara, Bob, DB, Minnesota, Denver 1960-61
McNamara, Ed, T, Holy Cross, Pittsburgh 1945
McNamara, Tom, G, Detroit, Toledo 1923; Detroit 1925-26
McNanie, Sean, DE, San Diego State, Buffalo 1984-85
McNeal, Don, CB, Alabama, Miami 1980-82, 1984-85
McNeil, Charlie, DB, Compton J.C., LA Chargers 1960; San Diego 1961-64
McNeil, Clifton, WR-KR, Grambling, Cleveland 1964-67; San Francisco 1968-69; NY Giants 1970-71; Washington 1971-72; Houston 1973
McNeil, Frank, E, Washington & Jefferson, Brooklyn 1932
McNeil, Freeman, RB, UCLA, NY Jets 1981-85
McNeil, Pat, RB, Baylor, Kansas City 1976-77
McNeill, Fred, LB, UCLA, Minnesota 1974-85
McNeill, Rod, RB, USC, New Orleans 1974-75; Tampa Bay 1976
McNeill, Tom, P, Stephen F. Austin, New Orleans 1967-69; Minnesota 1970; Philadelphia 1971-73
McNellis, Bill, HB, St. Mary's (Minnesota), Duluth 1927
McNorton, Bruce, CB, Georgetown (Kentucky), Detroit 1982-85
McNulty, Paul, E, Notre Dame, Chi. Cardinals 1924-25
McPeak, Bill, DE, Pittsburgh, Pittsburgh 1949-57
McPhail, Buck, FB-K, Oklahoma, Baltimore 1953

McPhail, Hal, HB, Xavier, Boston 1934-35
McPhee, Frank, DE, Princeton, Chi. Cardinals 1955
McPherson, Forrest (Amy), T, Nebraska, Chi. Bears 1935; Philadelphia 1935-37; Green Bay 1943-45
McPherson, Miles, S, New Haven, San Diego 1982-85
McQuade, Johnny, HB, Georgetown (Washington D.C.), Canton 1922
McQuaid, Dan, T, Nevada-Las Vegas, Washington 1985
McQuarters, Ed, DT, Oklahoma, St. Louis 1965
McQuay, Leon, RB-KR, Tampa, NY Giants 1974; New England 1975; New Orleans 1976
McQuilken, Kim, QB, Lehigh, Atlanta 1974-77; Washington 1978-80
McRae, Bennie, CB, Michigan, Chi. Bears 1962-70; NY Giants 1970
McRae, Franklin, DT, Tennessee State, Chi. Bears 1967
McRae, Jerrold, WR, Tennessee State, Kansas City 1978; Philadelphia 1979
McRae, Stan, E, Michigan, Washington 1945
McRaven, Bill, HB, Murray State, Cleveland 1939
McRoberts, Bob, HB, Wisconsin-Stout, Boston 1944
McRoberts, Wade, C, Westminster, Canton 1925-26
McShane, Charles, LB, California Lutheran, Seattle 1977-79
McShea, Joe, G, Rochester, Rochester 1923
McSwain, Chuck, RB-KR, Clemson, Dallas 1983-84
McSwain, Rod, CB, Clemson, New England 1984-85
McVea, Warren, RB-WR-KR, Houston, Cincinnati 1968; Kansas City 1969-71, 1973
McWatters, Bill, FB, North Texas State, Minnesota 1964
McWilliams, Bill, HB, Jordan, Detroit 1934
McWilliams, Tom (Shorty), HB, Army, Mississippi State, LA Dons (AAFC) 1949; Pittsburgh 1950
Mead, Jack, E, Wisconsin, NY Giants 1946-47
Meade, Jim, FB, Maryland, Washington 1939-40
Meade, Mike, RB, Penn State, Green Bay 1982-83; Detroit 1984-85
Meador, Eddie, S, Arkansas Tech, LA Rams 1959-70
Meadow, Ralph, E, California, Canton 1920
Meadows, Darryl, S, Toledo, Houston 1982-84
Meadows, Ed, DE, Duke, Chi. Bears 1954, 1956-57; Pittsburgh 1955; Philadelphia 1958; Washington 1959
Meadows, Eric, HB, Pittsburgh, Milwaukee 1923
Meadows, Joe, E, Canton 1920
Meads, Johnny, LB, Nicholls State, Houston 1984-85
Meagher, Jack, E, Notre Dame, Chi. Tigers 1920
Meamber, Tim, LB, Washington, Minnesota 1985
Means, Dave, DE, Southeast Missouri State, Buffalo 1974
Mecham, Curt, HB, Oregon, Brooklyn 1942
Mecklenburg, Karl, DE-LB, Minnesota, Denver 1983-85
Medlin, Dan, G, North Carolina State, Oakland 1974-76, 1979; Tampa Bay 1977-78
Medved, Ron, S, Washington, Philadelphia 1966-70
Meeker, Herbert (Butch), HB, Washington State, Providence 1930-31
Meeks, Bryant (Meatball), C, South Carolina, Pittsburgh 1947-48
Meeks, Ed, HB, Louisville, Louisville 1922
Meese, Ward, E, Wabash, Evansville 1922; Milwaukee 1922; St. Louis 1923; Kenosha 1924; Hammond 1925
Meggysey, Dave, LB, Syracuse, St. Louis 1963-69
Mehelich, Chuck, E-DE, Duquesne, Pittsburgh 1946-51
Mehelich, Tom, G, St. Thomas (Minnesota), Minneapolis 1929
Mehl, Lance, LB, Penn State, NY Jets 1980-85
Mehre, Harry, C, Notre Dame, Minneapolis 1923-24
Mehringer, Pete, T, Kansas, Chi. Cardinals 1934-36
Meilinger, Steve, E-TE, Kentucky, Washington 1956-57; Green Bay 1958, 1960; Pittsburgh 1961; St. Louis 1961
Meinert, Dale, LB, Oklahoma State, Chi. Cardinals 1958-59; St. Louis 1960-67
Meinhardt, George, G, St. Louis, St. Louis 1923
Meisenheimer, Darrell, LB, Oklahoma State, NY Yanks 1951
Meisner, Greg, NT, Pittsburgh, LA Rams 1981-85
Meixler, Ed, LB, Boston U., Boston 1965
Melinkovich, Mike, DE, Gray Harbor J.C., St. Louis 1965-66; Detroit 1967
Mellekas, John, T-C, Arizona, Chi. Bears 1956, 1958-61; San Francisco 1962; Philadelphia 1963
Mello, Jim, FB, Notre Dame, Boston 1947; LA Rams 1948; Chi. Rockets (AAFC) 1948; Detroit 1949
Mellody, Dutch, HB-FB, Rochester 1921
Mellus, John, T, Villanova, NY Giants 1938-41; San Francisco (AAFC) 1946; Baltimore (AAFC) 1947-49
Melontree, Andrew, LB, Baylor, Cincinnati 1980
Melville, Dan, P, California, San Francisco 1979
Melvin, Tom, E, Marietta, Cincinnati 1921
Memmelaar, Dale, G, Wyoming, Chi. Cardinals 1959; St. Louis 1960-61; Dallas 1962-63; Cleveland 1964-65; Baltimore 1966-67
Menasco, Don, DB, Texas, NY Giants 1952-53; Washington 1954
Mendenhall, John, DT, Grambling, NY Giants 1972-79; Detroit 1980
Mendenhall, Ken, C, Oklahoma, Baltimore 1971-80
Mendenhall, Mat, DE, BYU, Washington 1981-82
Mendenhall, Terry, LB, San Diego State, Oakland 1971-72
Mendez, Mario, HB, San Diego State, San Diego 1964
Menefee, Hartwell (Pep), FL, New Mexico State, NY Giants 1966
Menefee, Vic, E, Morningside, Rock Island 1921
Mercein, Chuck, FB, Yale, NY Giants 1965-67; Green Bay 1967-68; Washington 1969; NY Jets 1970
Mercer, Ken, QB, Simpson, Frankford 1927-29
Mercer, Mike, K, Arizona State, Minnesota 1961-62; Oakland 1963-66; Kansas City 1966; Buffalo 1967-68; Green Bay 1968-69; San Diego 1970
Meredith, Don, QB, SMU, Dallas 1960-68
Meredith, Dudley, DT, Lamar, Houston 1963, 1968; Buffalo 1964-68
Meredith, Russ, G, West Virginia, Louisville 1923; Cleveland 1925
Mergen, Mike, T, San Francisco, Chi. Cardinals 1952
Mergenthal, Art, G, Notre Dame, Cleveland 1945; LA Rams 1946
Merillat, Lou, E, Army, Canton 1925
Merkel, Monte, G, Kansas, Chi. Bears 1943
Merkins, Guido, WR-QB-KR-DB, Sam Houston State, Houston 1978-80; New Orleans 1980-85
Merkle, Ed, G, Oklahoma State, Washington 1944
Merkovsky, Elmer, T, Pittsburgh, Card-Pitt 1944; Pittsburgh 1945-46
Merlin, Ed, G, Vanderbilt, Brooklyn 1938-39
Merlo, Jim, LB, Stanford, New Orleans 1973-74, 1976-79
Merrill, Casey, DE, Cal-Davis, Green Bay 1979-83; NY Giants 1983-85
Merrill, Mark, LB, Minnesota, NY Jets 1978-79; Chi. Bears 1979; Denver 1981-82; Buffalo 1983-84; LA Raiders 1984
Merrill, Walt, T, Alabama, Brooklyn 1940-42
Merriman, Sam, LB, Idaho, Seattle 1983-85
Merriweather, Mike, LB, Pacific, Pittsburgh 1982-85
Merrow, Jeff, DT, West Virginia, Atlanta 1975-83
Mertens, Jerry, DB, Drake, San Francisco 1958-62, 1964-65
Mertens, Jim, TE, Fairmont State, Miami 1969
Mertes, Bus, HB-FB, Iowa, Chi. Cardinals 1946; LA Dons (AAFC) 1946; Baltimore (AAFC) 1947-48; NY Giants 1949
Merz, Curt, G, Iowa, Dallas Texans 1962; Kansas City 1963-68
Mesak, Dick, T, St. Mary's (California), Detroit 1945
Meseroll, Mark, T, Florida State, New Orleans 1978
Messer, Dale, FL, Fresno State, San Francisco 1961-65
Messner, Max, LB, Cincinnati, Detroit 1960-63; NY Giants 1964; Pittsburgh 1964-65
Mestnik, Frank, FB, Marquette, St. Louis 1960-61; Green Bay 1963
Metcalf, Bo Scott, DB, Baylor, Kansas City 1983; Indianapolis 1984
Metcalf, Terry, RB-KR, Long Beach State, St. Louis 1973-77; Washington 1981
Method, Russ, HB, Duluth 1923-27; Chi. Cardinals 1929
Metzelaars, Pete, TE, Wabash, Seattle 1982-84; Buffalo 1985
Metzger, Lou, HB, Georgetown (Washington D.C.), Louisville 1926
Meyer, Dennis, S, Arkansas State, Pittsburgh 1973
Meyer, Ed, T, West Texas State, Buffalo 1960
Meyer, Ernie, G, Geneva, Portsmouth 1930
Meyer, Fred, E, Stanford, Philadelphia 1942, 1945
Meyer, Gil, E, Wake Forest, Baltimore (AAFC) 1947
Meyer, John, LB, Notre Dame, Houston 1966
Meyer, Ron, QB, South Dakota State, Pittsburgh 1966
Meyers, Bob, FB, Stanford, San Francisco 1952
Meyers, Jerry, DT, Northern Illinois, Chi. Bears 1976-79; Kansas City 1980
Meyers, John, DT, Washington, Dallas 1962-63; Philadelphia 1964-67
Meyers, Paul, E, Wisconsin, Hammond 1920; NY Giants 1921; Racine 1923
Meylan, Wayne, LB, Nebraska, Cleveland 1968-69; Minnesota 1970
Mialik, Larry, DE, Nebraska, Atlanta 1972-74; San Diego 1976
Miano, Rich, S, Hawaii, NY Jets 1985
Michael, Bill, G, Ohio State, Pittsburgh 1957
Michael, Rich, T, Ohio State, Houston 1960-63, 1965-66
Michaels, Al, HB, Heidelberg, Akron 1923-24; Cleveland 1925
Michaels, Eddie, G, Villanova, Chi. Bears 1936; Washington 1937; Phil-Pitt 1943; Philadelphia 1944-46
Michaels, Lou, DE-K, Kentucky, LA Rams 1958-60; Pittsburgh 1961-63; Baltimore 1964-69; Green Bay 1971
Michaels, Walt, LB, Washington & Lee, Green Bay 1951; Cleveland 1952-61; NY Jets 1963
Michalik, Art (Automatic), G-K, St. Ambrose, San Francisco 1953-54; Pittsburgh 1955-56
Michalske, Mike, G, Penn State, NY Yankees 1927-28; Green Bay 1929-35, 1937
Michel, Mike, K-P, Stanford, Miami 1977; Philadelphia 1978
Michel, Tom, HB, East Carolina, Minnesota 1964
Michels, Johnny, G, Tennessee, Philadelphia 1953
Micho, Bobby, TE, Texas, San Diego 1984
Micka, Mike, HB, Colgate, Washington 1944-45; Boston 1945-48
Middendorf, Dave, G, Washington State, Cincinnati 1968-69; NY Jets 1970
Middlebrook, Oren, WR, Arkansas State, Philadelphia 1978
Middleton, Dave, SE, Auburn, Detroit 1955-60; Minnesota 1961
Middleton, Frank, RB, Florida A&M, Indianapolis 1984-85
Middleton, Rick, LB, Ohio State, New Orleans 1974-75; San Diego 1976-78
Middleton, Terdell, RB, Memphis State, Green Bay 1977-81; Tampa Bay 1982-83
Midler, Lou, G, Minnesota, Pittsburgh 1939; Green Bay 1940
Mielziner, Saul, C, Carnegie-Mellon, NY Giants 1929-30; Brooklyn 1931-34
Mieszkowski, Ed, T, Notre Dame, Brooklyn (AAFC) 1946-47
Mihajlovich, Lou, E, Indiana, LA Dons (AAFC) 1948
Mihal, Joe, T, Purdue, Chi. Bears 1940-41; LA Dons (AAFC) 1946; Chi. Rockets (AAFC) 1947
Mike, Bob, T, UCLA, San Francisco (AAFC) 1948-49
Mike-Mayer, Nick, K, Temple, Atlanta 1973-77; Philadelphia 1977-78; Buffalo 1979-82
Mike-Mayer, Steve, K, Maryland, San Francisco 1975-76; Detroit 1977; New Orleans 1978; Baltimore 1979-80
Mikeska, Russ, TE, Texas A&M, Atlanta 1979-82
Miketa, Andy, C, North Carolina, Detroit 1954-55
Miklich, Bill, QB-G, Idaho, NY Giants 1947-48; Detroit 1948
Mikolajczyk, Ron, G, Tampa, NY Giants 1976-79
Mikula, Tom, FB, William & Mary, Brooklyn (AAFC) 1948
Mikulak, Mike, FB, Oregon, Chi. Cardinals 1934-36
Milam, Barnes, G, Austin, Philadelphia 1934
Milan, Don, QB, Cal Poly-SLO, Green Bay 1975
Milan, Joe, E-T, Phillips, Kansas City 1924-25
Milano, Arch, E, St. Francis, Detroit 1945
Mildren, Jack, S, Oklahoma, Baltimore 1972-73; New England 1974
Miles, Leo, DB, Virginia State, NY Giants 1953
Miles, Mark, HB, Washington & Lee, Akron 1920
Milks, Jack, LB, San Diego State, San Diego 1966
Millard, Bryan, T, Texas, Seattle 1984-85
Millard, Keith, DE, Washington State, Minnesota 1985
Millen, Matt, LB, Penn State, Oakland 1980-81; LA Raiders 1982-85
Miller, Al, QB, Harvard, Boston 1929
Miller, Alan, FB, Boston College, Boston 1960; Oakland 1961-63, 1965
Miller, Allen, LB, Ohio U., Washington 1962-63
Miller, Bill, SE, Miami, Dallas Texans 1962; Buffalo 1963; Oakland 1964, 1966-68
Miller, Bill, DT, New Mexico Highlands, Houston 1962
Miller, Blake, E, Michigan State, Detroit 1920-21
Miller, Bob (Dutch), C, Wittenberg, Portsmouth 1931
Miller, Bob, DT, Virginia, Detroit 1952-58
Miller, Brett, T, Iowa, Atlanta 1983-85
Miller, Calvin, DT, Oklahoma State, NY Giants 1979; Atlanta 1980
Miller, Charles (Ookie), C, Purdue, Chi. Bears 1932-36; Cleveland 1937; Green Bay 1938
Miller, Clark, DE, Utah State, San Francisco 1962-68; Washington 1969; LA Rams 1970
Miller, Cleo, RB, Arkansas-Pine Bluff, Kansas City 1974-75; Cleveland 1975-82
Miller, Danny, K, Miami, New England 1982; Baltimore 1982; Washington 1982
Miller, Don, HB, Notre Dame, Providence 1925
Miller, Don, DB, SMU, Philadelphia 1954; Green Bay 1954
Miller, Eddie, QB, New Mexico State, NY Giants 1939-40
Miller, Fred, T, Pacific, Washington 1955
Miller, Fred, DT, LSU, Baltimore 1963-72
Miller, Hal, T, Georgia Tech, San Francisco 1953
Miller, Henry (Heinie), E, Pennsylvania, Buffalo 1920-21; Frankford 1924; Milwaukee 1925
Miller, Jim, HB, West Virginia Wesleyan, Brooklyn 1930
Miller, Jim, G, Iowa, Atlanta 1971-72, 1974
Miller, Jim, P, Mississippi, San Francisco 1980-82; Dallas 1983-84
Miller, John (Bing), T, NYU, Staten Island 1929-31
Miller, Johnny, T, Boston College, Washington 1956, 1958-59; Green Bay 1960
Miller, Johnny, G, Livingstone, San Francisco 1977-78
Miller, Junior, TE, Nebraska, Atlanta 1980-83; New Orleans 1984
Miller, Kevin, WR, Louisville, Minnesota 1978-80
Miller, Lloyd, T, Dartmouth, Louisville 1921-23
Miller, Mark, QB, Bowling Green, Cleveland 1978-79; Green Bay 1980
Miller, Matt, T, Colorado, Cleveland 1979-82
Miller, Mike, WR, Tennessee, NY Giants 1983; New Orleans 1985
Miller, Milford (Dub), G, Chadron State, Chi. Bears 1935; Chi. Cardinals 1936-37
Miller, Paul, HB, South Dakota State, Green Bay 1936-38
Miller, Paul, DE, LSU, LA Rams 1954-57; Dallas Texans 1960-61; San Diego 1962
Miller, Ralph (Primo), T, Rice, Cleveland 1937-38
Miller, Ralph, G, Alabama State, Houston 1972-73
Miller, Ray (Candy), E, Purdue, Dayton 1921; Canton 1922; Racine 1922-23
Miller, Robert, RB, Kansas, Minnesota 1975-80
Miller, Ron, TE, USC, LA Rams 1956
Miller, Ron, QB, Wisconsin, LA Rams 1962
Miller, Shawn, NT, Utah State, LA Rams 1984-85
Miller, Terry, LB, Illinois, Detroit 1970; St. Louis 1971-74
Miller, Terry, RB, Oklahoma State, Buffalo 1978-80; Seattle 1981
Miller, Tom, E, Hampden-Sydney, Phil-Pitt 1943; Philadelphia 1944; Washington 1945; Green Bay 1946
Miller, Verne, HB, St. Mary's (Minnesota), Minneapolis 1930
Miller, Willie, WR, Colorado State, Cleveland 1975-76; LA Rams 1978-82

Milling, Al, G, Richmond, Philadelphia 1942
Millman, Bob, HB, Lafayette, Pottsville 1926-27
Millner, Wayne, E, Notre Dame, Boston 1936; Washington 1937-41, 1945
Mills, Charlie, FB, Maryland, Buffalo 1920
Mills, Dick, G, Pittsburgh, Detroit 1961-62
Mills, Jim, T, Hawaii, Baltimore 1983; Indianapolis 1984
Mills, Joe, C-T, Carnegie-Mellon, Akron 1922-26
Mills, Pete, FL-DB, Wichita State, Buffalo 1965-66
Mills, Stan, HB-E, Maryland, Akron 1924
Mills, Tom, HB-FB, Green Bay 1922-23
Milner, Bill, G, Duke, Chi. Bears 1947-49; NY Giants 1950
Milo, Ray, S, New Mexico State, Kansas City 1978
Milot, Rich, LB, Penn State, Washington 1979-85
Milstead, Century, T, Yale, NY Giants 1925, 1927-28
Milstead, Charlie, QB-DB, Texas A&M, Miami 1968-69
Milton, Gene, WR, Florida A&M, Miami 1968-69
Milton, Jack, E, USC, St. Louis 1923; Kansas City 1924
Milton, Tom, E, Lake Forest, Milwaukee 1923; St. Louis 1923; Green Bay 1924
Minarik, Hank, E, Michigan State, Pittsburgh 1951
Miner, Tom, E-K, Tulsa, Pittsburgh 1958
Mingo, Gene, HB-K, Denver 1960-64; Oakland 1964-65; Miami 1966-67; Washington 1967; New Orleans 1967; Pittsburgh 1969-70
Minick, Paul, G, Iowa, Buffalo 1927; Green Bay 1928-29
Minini, Frank, HB, San Jose State, Chi. Bears 1947-48; Pittsburgh 1949
Minisi, Tony (Skippy), HB, Pennsylvania, NY Giants 1948
Minniear, Randy, RB, Purdue, NY Giants 1967-69; Cleveland 1970
Minnifield, Frank, CB, Louisville, Cleveland 1984-85
Minor, Claudie, T, San Diego State, Denver 1974-82
Minor, Lincoln, RB, New Mexico State, New Orleans 1973
Minor, Vic, S, Northeast Louisiana, Seattle 1980-81
Minter, Cedric, RB, Boise State, NY Jets 1984-85
Minter, Tom, DB, Baylor, Denver 1962; Buffalo 1962
Mintun, Jake, C, Decatur 1920; Chi. Staleys 1921; Chi. Bears 1922; Racine 1922-24, 1926; Kansas City 1925
Mioduszewski, Ed, HB, William & Mary, Baltimore 1953
Mira, George, QB, Miami, San Francisco 1964-68; Philadelphia 1969; Miami 1971
Miraldi, Dean, T-G, Utah, Philadelphia 1982-84; Denver 1985
Mirich, Rex, DT, Arizona State, Oakland 1964-66; Denver 1967-69; Boston 1970
Mischak, Bob, G, Army, NY Giants 1958; NY Titans 1960-62; Oakland 1963-65
Mishel, Dave, HB, Brown, Providence 1927; Cleveland 1931
Misko, John, P, Oregon State, LA Rams 1982-84
Mistler, John, WR, Arizona State, NY Giants 1981-84; Buffalo 1984
Mitcham, Gene, SE, Arizona State, Philadelphia 1958
Mitchell, Aaron, CB, Nevada-Las Vegas, Dallas 1979-80; Tampa Bay 1981
Mitchell, Al, T, Thiel, Buffalo 1924
Mitchell, Alvin, DB, Morgan State, Cleveland 1968-69; Denver 1970
Mitchell, Bob, HB, Stanford, LA Dons (AAFC) 1946-48
Mitchell, Bobby, HB-FL, Illinois, Cleveland 1958-61; Washington 1962-68
Mitchell, Charley, DB, Washington, Denver 1963-67; Buffalo 1968
Mitchell, Charlie, HB, Tulsa, Chi. Bears 1945; Green Bay 1946
Mitchell, Dale, LB, USC, San Francisco 1976-77
Mitchell, Ed, G, Southern, San Diego 1965-67
Mitchell, Fondren, HB, Florida, Miami (AAFC) 1946
Mitchell, Granville (Buster), E, Davis & Elkins, Portsmouth 1931-33; Detroit 1934-35; NY Giants 1935-36; Brooklyn 1937
Mitchell, Hal, T, UCLA, NY Giants 1952
Mitchell, Jim, TE, Prairie View A&M, Atlanta 1969-79
Mitchell, Jim, DE-DT, Virginia State, Detroit 1970-77
Mitchell, Ken, LB, Nevada-Las Vegas, Atlanta 1973-74
Mitchell, Leonard, DE-T, Houston, Philadelphia 1981-85
Mitchell, Leroy, DB, Texas Southern, Boston 1967-69; Houston 1970; Denver 1971-73
Mitchell, Lydell, RB, Penn State, Baltimore 1972-77; San Diego 1978-79; LA Rams 1980
Mitchell, Mack, DE, Houston, Cleveland 1975-78; Cincinnati 1979
Mitchell, Martin, CB, Tulane, Philadelphia 1977
Mitchell, Melvin, G-C, Tennessee State, Miami 1976-78; Detroit 1977; Minnesota 1980
Mitchell, Paul, T, Minnesota, LA Dons (AAFC) 1946-48
Mitchell, Stan, RB, Tennessee, Miami 1966-70
Mitchell, Stump, RB-KR, Citadel, St. Louis 1981-85
Mitchell, Ted, C, Bucknell, Orange 1929; Newark 1930
Mitchell, Tom, TE, Bucknell, Oakland 1966; Baltimore 1968-73; San Francisco 1974-77
Mitchell, Willie, DB, Tennessee State, Kansas City 1964-70
Mitinger, Bob, LB, Penn State, San Diego 1962-64, 1966, 1968
Mix, Ron, T, USC, LA Chargers 1960; San Diego 1961-69; Oakland 1970
Mixon, Billy, HB, Georgia, San Francisco 1953-54
Mizell, Warner, HB, Georgia Tech, Brooklyn 1931; Frankford 1931
Moan, Kelly, HB, West Virginia, Cleveland 1939
Mobley, Rudy, HB, Hardin-Simmons, Baltimore (AAFC) 1947
Mock, Mike, LB, Texas Tech, NY Jets 1978
Mockmore, Charlie, G, Iowa, Rock Island 1920
Modzelewski, Dick (Little Mo), DT, Maryland, Washington 1953-54; Pittsburgh 1955; NY Giants 1956-63; Cleveland 1964-66
Modzelewski, Ed (Big Mo), FB, Maryland, Pittsburgh 1952; Cleveland 1955-59
Moe, Hal, HB, Oregon State, Chi. Cardinals 1933
Moegle, Dickie, DB-KR, Rice, San Francisco 1955-59; Pittsburgh 1960; Dallas Cowboys 1961
Moegle, Ed, HB, Detroit, Detroit 1920-21
Moffett, Tim, WR, Mississippi, LA Raiders 1985
Mohardt, Johnny, HB, Notre Dame, Chi. Cardinals 1922-23; Racine 1924; Chi. Bears 1925
Mohring, John, LB, C.W. Post, Cleveland 1980; Detroit 1980
Mohs, Louie, E, St. Thomas (Minnesota), Minneapolis 1923-24
Moje, Dick, E, Loyola (Los Angeles), Green Bay 1951
Mojsiejenko, Ralf, P-K, Michigan State, San Diego 1985
Molden, Frank, DT, Jackson State, LA Rams 1965; Philadelphia 1968; NY Giants 1969
Molenda, Bo, FB, Michigan, NY Yankees 1927-28; Green Bay 1929-32; NY Giants 1931-35
Molesworth, Keith, QB, Monmouth, Chi. Bears 1931-37
Molinet, Lou, FB, Cornell, Frankford 1927
Momsen, Bob, G, Ohio State, Detroit 1951; San Francisco 1952
Momsen, Tony, C, Michigan, Pittsburgh 1951; Washington 1952
Monachino, Jim, HB, California, San Francisco 1951, 1953; Washington 1955
Monaco, Bob, C, Vanderbilt, St. Louis 1985
Monaco, Ray, G, Holy Cross, Washington 1944; Cleveland 1945
Monahan, Regis, G, Ohio State, Detroit 1935-38; Chi. Cardinals 1939
Monds, Wonder, S, Nebraska, San Francisco 1978
Monelie, Bill, HB, St. Mary's (Minnesota), Duluth 1927
Monfort, Avery, HB, New Mexico, Chi. Cardinals 1941
Monger, Matt, LB, Oklahoma State, NY Jets 1985
Monk, Art, WR, Syracuse, Washington 1980-85
Monnett, Bob, HB, Michigan State, Green Bay 1933-38
Monroe, Carl, KR-RB, Utah, San Francisco 1983-85
Monroe, Henry, CB, Mississippi State, Philadelphia 1979
Mont, Tommy, QB, Maryland, Washington 1947-49
Montalbo, Mel, DB, Utah State, Oakland 1962
Montana, Joe, QB, Notre Dame, San Francisco 1979-85
Montgomery, Bill, T, St. Louis, St. Louis 1934
Montgomery, Bill, FB, LSU, Chi. Cardinals 1946
Montgomery, Blanchard, LB, UCLA, San Francisco 1983-84
Montgomery, Cle, KR-WR, Abilene Christian, Cincinnati 1980; Cleveland 1981; Oakland 1981; LA Raiders 1982-85
Montgomery, Cliff, QB, Columbia, Brooklyn 1934
Montgomery, Jim, T, Texas A&M, Detroit 1946
Montgomery, Marv, T, USC, Denver 1971-76; New Orleans 1976-77; Atlanta 1978
Montgomery, Mike, RB-WR, Kansas State, San Diego 1971; Dallas 1972-73; New Orleans 1974
Montgomery, Ralph, T, Centre, Chi. Cardinals 1923; Frankford 1927
Montgomery, Randy, S, Weber State, Denver 1971-73; Chi. Bears 1974
Montgomery, Ross, RB, TCU, Chi. Bears 1969-70
Montgomery, Wilbert, RB, Abilene Christian, Philadelphia 1977-84; Detroit 1985
Montler, Mike, G-C, Colorado, Boston 1969-70; New England 1971-72; Buffalo 1973-76; Denver 1977; Detroit 1978
Montoya, Max, G, UCLA, Cincinnati 1979-85
Moody, Keith, DB, Syracuse, Buffalo 1976-79; Oakland 1980
Moody, Wilkie, FB-HB, Denison, Columbus 1920, 1924-25
Mooers, Doug, DE-DT, Whittier, New Orleans 1971-72
Moon, Warren, QB, Washington, Houston 1984-85
Mooney, Bow Tipp, HB, Abilene Christian, Chi. Bears 1944-45
Mooney, Ed, LB, Texas Tech, Detroit 1968-71; Baltimore 1973
Mooney, George, HB, Milwaukee 1922-24
Mooney, Jim, E-T, Georgetown (Washington D.C.), Newark 1930; Brooklyn 1930-31; Cincinnati 1933-34; Chi. Cardinals 1935; Chi. Bears 1935
Mooney, Tex (O.T. Schupbach), T, West Texas State, Cleveland 1942; Brooklyn 1943
Moore, Al, HB, Northwestern, Chi. Bears 1932
Moore, Al, E, Texas A&M, Green Bay 1939
Moore, Alex, DB, Norfolk State, Denver 1968
Moore, Alvin, RB, Arizona State, Baltimore 1983; Indianapolis 1984; Detroit 1985
Moore, Arthur, DT, Tulsa, New England 1973-74, 1976-77
Moore, Bill (Bucky), HB, Loyola (New Orleans), Chi. Cardinals 1932; Pittsburgh 1933
Moore, Bill, E, North Carolina, Detroit 1939
Moore, Bill (Red), G, Penn State, Pittsburgh 1947-49
Moore, Blake, C-G, Wooster, Cincinnati 1980-83; Green Bay 1984-85
Moore, Bob, TE, Stanford, Oakland 1971-75; Tampa Bay 1976-77; Denver 1978
Moore, Booker, RB, Penn State, Buffalo 1982-85
Moore, Chuck, G, Arkansas, Washington 1962
Moore, Cliff, HB, Penn State, Cincinnati 1934
Moore, Dean, LB, Iowa, San Francisco 1978
Moore, Denis, DE-DT, USC, Detroit 1967-69
Moore, Derland, DE-NT, Oklahoma, New Orleans 1973-85
Moore, Eugene, RB, Occidental, San Francisco 1969
Moore, Fred, DT, Memphis State, San Diego 1964-66
Moore, Gene, C, Colorado, Brooklyn 1938
Moore, Henry, DB, Arkansas, NY Giants 1956; Baltimore 1957
Moore, Jeff, RB, Jackson State, Seattle 1979-81; San Francisco 1982-83; Washington 1984
Moore, Jeff, WR, Tennessee, LA Rams 1980-81
Moore, Jerry, DB, Arkansas, Chi. Bears 1971-72; New Orleans 1973-74
Moore, Jimmy, G, Ohio State, Baltimore 1981
Moore, Joe, RB, Missouri, Chi. Bears 1971, 1973
Moore, Ken, G, West Virginia Wesleyan, NY Giants 1940
Moore, Ken, TE, Northern Illinois, Atlanta 1978
Moore, Lenny, HB-FL, Penn State, Baltimore 1956-67
Moore, Leroy, DE, Fort Valley State, Buffalo 1960, 1962-63; Boston 1961-62; Denver 1964-65
Moore, Mack, DE, Texas A&M, Miami 1985
Moore, Manfred, RB-KR, USC, San Francisco 1974-75; Tampa Bay 1976; Oakland 1976; Minnesota 1977
Moore, Maulty, DT, Bethune-Cookman, Miami 1972-74; Cincinnati 1975; Tampa Bay 1976
Moore, McNeill, DB, Sam Houston State, Chi. Bears 1954, 1956-57
Moore, Nat, WR-KR, Florida, Miami 1974-85
Moore, Paul, HB, Presbyterian, Detroit 1940-41
Moore, Randy, DT, Arizona State, Denver 1976
Moore, Reynaud, CB, UCLA, New Orleans 1971
Moore, Rich, DT, Villanova, Green Bay 1969
Moore, Rocco, G-T, Western Michigan, Chi. Bears 1980
Moore, Steve, G-T, Tennessee State, New England 1983-85
Moore, Tom, HB-FB, Vanderbilt, Green Bay 1960-65; LA Rams 1966; Atlanta 1967
Moore, Walt, HB, Lafayette, Pottsville 1927
Moore, Wayne, T, Lamar, Miami 1970-78
Moore, Wilbur, HB, Minnesota, Washington 1939-46
Moore, Zeke, CB, Lincoln (Missouri), Houston 1967-77
Moorehead, Emery, TE-WR, Colorado, NY Giants 1977-79; Denver 1980; Chi. Bears 1981-85
Mooring, John, T-G, Tampa, NY Jets 1971-73; New Orleans 1974
Moorman, Mo, G, Texas A&M, Kansas City 1968-73
Mooty, Jim, DB, Arkansas, Dallas Cowboys 1960
Morales, Gonzales, HB, St. Mary's (California), Pittsburgh 1947-48
Moran, Art, T, Marquette, Milwaukee 1926
Moran, Eric, T, Washington, Houston 1984-85
Moran, Francis (Hap), HB-FB, Carnegie-Mellon, Frankford 1925-27; Chi. Cardinals 1927; Pottsville 1928; NY Giants 1928-33
Moran, Frank, C-T, Akron 1920; Hammond 1920
Moran, Jim, G, Holy Cross, Boston 1935-36
Moran, Jim, DT, Idaho, NY Giants 1964, 1966-67
Moran, Rich, C-G, San Diego State, Green Bay 1985
Moran, Tom, QB, Centre, NY Giants 1925
Moreau, Doug, TE-P, LSU, Miami 1966-69
Moreino, Joe, T, Idaho State, NY Jets 197878
Morelli, Fran, T, Colgate, NY Titans 1962
Morelli, John, G, Georgetown (Washington D.C.), Boston 1944-45
Moresco, Tim, S, Syracuse, Green Bay 1977; NY Jets 1978-80
Morgado, Arnold, RB, Hawaii, Kansas City 1977-80
Morgan, Bill, T, Oregon, NY Giants 1933-36
Morgan, Bob (Bubber), T, Maryland, Chi. Cardinals 1954; Washington 1954
Morgan, Bobby, DB, New Mexico, Pittsburgh 1967
Morgan, Boyd (Red), HB, USC, Washington 1939-40
Morgan, Dennis, RB, Western Illinois, Dallas 1974; Philadelphia 1975
Morgan, Joe, T, Southern Mississippi, San Francisco (AAFC) 1949
Morgan, Karl, NT, UCLA, Tampa Bay 1984-85
Morgan, Melvin, DB, Mississippi Valley State, Cincinnati 1976-78; San Francisco 1979-80
Morgan, Mike, LB, LSU, Philadelphia 1964-67; Washington 1968; New Orleans 1969-70
Morgan, Mike, RB, Wisconsin, Chi. Bears 1978
Morgan, Stanley, WR-KR, Tennessee, New England 1977-85
Moriarty, Larry, RB, Notre Dame, Houston 1983-85
Moriarty, Pat, RB, Georgia Tech, Cleveland 1979
Moriarty, Tom, S, Bowling Green, Atlanta 1977-79, 1981; Pittsburgh 1980
Morin, Milt, TE, Massachusetts, Cleveland 1966-75
Moritz, Brett, G, Nebraska, Tampa Bay 1978
Morley, Sam, E, Stanford, Washington 1954
Morlock, Jack, HB, Marshall, Detroit 1940
Moroski, Mike, QB, Cal-Davis, Atlanta 1979-84; Houston 1985
Morrall, Earl, QB-P, Michigan State, San Francisco 1956; Pittsburgh 1957-58; Detroit 1958-64; NY Giants 1965-67; Baltimore 1968-71; Miami 1972-76
Morris, Bob, G, Cornell, Brooklyn 1926
Morris, Chris, T, Indiana, Cleveland 1972-73; New Orleans 1975
Morris, Dennit, LB, Oklahoma, San Francisco 1958; Houston 1960-61
Morris, Donnie Joe, RB, North Texas State, Kansas City 1974
Morris, Dwaine, NT-DE, Southeastern Louisiana, Philadelphia 1985
Morris, Eugene (Mercury), RB, West Texas State, Miami 1969-75; San Diego 1976

Morris, Frank, FB, Boston U., Chi. Bears 1942
Morris, George, HB, Baldwin-Wallace, Cleveland 1941-42
Morris, George, LB, Georgia Tech, San Francisco 1956
Morris, Glen, E, Colorado State, Detroit 1940
Morris, Jack, DB, Oregon, LA Rams 1958-60; Pittsburgh 1960; Minnesota 1961
Morris, Joe, RB, Syracuse, NY Giants 1982-85
Morris, Johnny, FL-HB, Cal-Santa Barbara, Chi. Bears 1958-67
Morris, Jon, C, Holy Cross, Boston 1964-70; New England 1971-74; Detroit 1975-77; Chi. Bears 1978
Morris, Larry, LB, Georgia Tech, LA Rams 1955-57; Chi. Bears 1959-65; Atlanta 1966
Morris, Randall, RB, Tennessee, Seattle 1984-85
Morris, Riley, LB, Florida A&M, Oakland 1960-62
Morris, Thomas, S-CB, Michigan State, Tampa Bay 1982-83
Morris, Wayne, RB-KR, SMU, St. Louis 1976-83; San Diego 1984
Morrison, Bill, HB, Evansville 1921
Morrison, Charlie, G-E, Rochester 1920
Morrison, Dennis, QB, Kansas State, San Francisco 1974
Morrison, Don, T, Texas-Arlington, New Orleans 1971-77; Baltimore 1978; Detroit 1979
Morrison, Ed, HB, West Virginia, Frankford 1927
Morrison, Fred (Curly), FB-P, Ohio State, Chi. Bears 1950-53; Cleveland 1954-56
Morrison, Joe, RB-FL-DB, Cincinnati, NY Giants 1959-72
Morrison, Maynard, C, Michigan, Brooklyn 1933-34
Morrison, Reece, RB, Southwest Texas State, Cleveland 1968-72; Cincinnati 1972-73
Morriss, Guy, C-G, TCU, Philadelphia 1973-83; New England 1984-85
Morrissey, Frank, T, Boston College, Rochester 1921
Morrissey, Jim, LB, Michigan State, Chi. Bears 1985
Morrow, Bob, HB, Illinois Wesleyan, Chi. Cardinals 1941-43
Morrow, Jim, HB, Pittsburgh, Canton 1921; Buffalo 1922
Morrow, John, G, Kearney State, Chi. Cardinals 1937-38
Morrow, John, C, Michigan, LA Rams 1956, 1958-59; Cleveland 1960-66
Morrow, Tommy, DB, Southern Mississippi, Oakland 1962-64
Morse, Raymond (Butch), E, Oregon, Detroit 1935-38, 1940
Morse, Steve, RB, Virginia, Pittsburgh 1985
Morse, William (Red), G, Duluth 1923
Mortell, Emmett, QB, Wisconsin, Philadelphia 1937-39
Mortensen, Fred, QB, Arizona State, Washington 1979
Morton, Craig, QB, California, Dallas 1965-74; NY Giants 1974-76; Denver 1977-82
Morton, Dave, LB, UCLA, San Francisco 1979
Morton, Greg, DE, Michigan, Buffalo 1977
Morton, John, E-DB, Missouri, Purdue, Chi. Bears 1945; LA Dons (AAFC) 1946; Buffalo (AAFC) 1947
Morton, John, LB, TCU, San Francisco 1953
Morton, Michael, KR-RB, Nevada-Las Vegas, Tampa Bay 1982-84; Washington 1985
Morze, Frank, C, Boston College, San Francisco 1957-61, 1964; Cleveland 1962-63
Moscrip, Jim (Monk), E, Stanford, Detroit 1938-39
Mosebar, Don, T-C-G, USC, LA Raiders 1983-85
Moseley, Mark, K, Stephen F. Austin, Philadelphia 1970; Houston 1971-72; Washington 1974-85
Moselle, Dom, HB, Wisconsin-Superior, Cleveland 1950; Green Bay 1951-52; Philadelphia 1954
Moser, Bob, C, Pacific, Chi. Bears 1951-53
Moser, Rick, RB-KR, Rhode Island, Pittsburgh 1978-79, 1981-82; Miami 1980; Kansas City 1981; Tampa Bay 1982
Moser, Ted, G, Louisville 1921
Moses, Don, QB, USC, Cincinnati 1933
Moses, Haven, WR, San Diego State, Buffalo 1968-72; Denver 1972-81
Mosher, Clure, C, Louisville, Pittsburgh 1942
Mosier, John, TE, Kansas, Denver 1971; Baltimore 1972; New England 1973
Mosley, Henry, HB, Morris-Brown, Chi. Bears 1955
Mosley, Mike, WR-KR, Texas A&M, Buffalo 1982-84
Mosley, Norm, HB, Alabama, Pittsburgh 1948
Mosley, Russ, HB, Alabama, Green Bay 1945-46
Mosley, Wayne, RB, Alabama A&M, Buffalo 1974
Moss, Eddie, RB, Southeast Missouri State, St. Louis 1973-76; Washington 1977
Moss, Joe, T, Maryland, Washington 1952
Moss, Martin, DT, UCLA, Detroit 1982-85
Moss, Paul, E, Purdue, Pittsburgh 1933; St. Louis 1934
Moss, Perry, QB, Illinois, Green Bay 1948
Moss, Roland, TE-RB, Toledo, Baltimore 1969; San Diego 1970; Buffalo 1970; New England 1971
Mostardi, Rich, DB, Kent State, Cleveland 1960; Minnesota 1961; Oakland 1962
Mote, Kelly, E-DB, Duke, Detroit 1947-49; NY Giants 1950-52
Moten, Bobby, WR, Bishop, Denver 1968
Moten, Gary, LB, SMU, San Francisco 1983
Motl, Bob, E, Northwestern, Chi. Rockets (AAFC) 1946
Motley, Marion, FB-LB, Nevada-Reno, Cleveland 1946-53; Pittsburgh 1954
Mott, Norm (Buster), HB, Georgia, Green Bay 1933; Cincinnati 1934; Pittsburgh 1934
Mott, Steve, C, Alabama, Detroit 1983-85
Mowatt, Zeke, TE, Florida State, NY Giants 1983-84
Moyer, Alex, LB, Northwestern, Miami 1985
Moyer, Paul, S, Arizona State, Seattle 1983-85
Moynihan, Dick, QB, Villanova, Frankford 1927
Moynihan, Tim, C, Notre Dame, Chi. Cardinals 1932-33
Mrkonic, George, G, Kansas, Philadelphia 1953
Mucha, Rudy, HB, Washington, Cleveland 1941, 1945; Chi. Bears 1945-46
Muckensturm, Jerry, LB, Arkansas State, Chi. Bears 1976-83
Mucker, Larry, WR, Arizona State, Tampa Bay 1977-80
Mudd, Howard, G, Hillsdale, San Francisco 1964-69; Chi. Bears 1969-70
Muehlheuser, Frank, FB, Colgate, Boston 1948; NY Bulldogs 1949
Muelhaupt, Ed, G, Iowa State, Buffalo 1960-61
Muellner, Bill, E, DePaul, Chi. Cardinals 1937
Mugg, Garvin, T, North Texas State, Detroit 1945
Muha, Joe, FB-LB, Virginia Military, Philadelphia 1946-50
Muhammad, Calvin, WR, Texas Southern, LA Raiders 1982-83; Washington 1984-85
Muhlmann, Horst, K, Cincinnati 1969-74; Philadelphia 1975-77
Muirhead, Stan, G, Michigan, Dayton 1924; Cleveland 1924
Mularkey, Mike, TE, Florida, Minnesota 1983-85
Mulbarger, Joe, T, Alderson-Broaddus, Columbus 1920-26
Muldoon, Matt, T, St. Mary's (California), Rochester 1922
Mul-Key, Herb, KR-RB, Washington 1972-74
Mullady, Tom, TE, Southwestern (Memphis), NY Giants 1979-84
Mullaney, Mark, DE, Colorado State, Minnesota 1975-85
Mullen, Davlin, CB-KR, Western Kentucky, NY Jets 1983-85
Mullen, Tom, G, Southwest Missouri State, NY Giants 1974-77; St. Louis 1978
Mullen, Verne, E, Illinois, Evansville 1922; Canton 1923; Chi. Bears 1924-26; Chi. Cardinals 1927; Pottsville 1927-28
Mulleneaux, Carl, E, Utah State, Green Bay 1938-41, 1945-46
Mulleneaux, Lee (Moose), C, Arizona, NY Giants 1932; Cincinnati 1933-34; St. Louis 1934; Pittsburgh 1935-36; Green Bay 1938; Chi. Cardinals 1938
Muller, Harold (Brick), E, California, LA Buccaneers 1926
Mulligan, George, E, Catholic, Philadelphia 1936
Mulligan, Wayne, C, Clemson, St. Louis 1969-73; NY Jets 1974-75
Mullins, Don, DB, Houston, Chi. Bears 1961-62
Mullins, Eric, WR, Stanford, Houston 1984
Mullins, Gerry (Moon), G-T-TE, USC, Pittsburgh 1971-79
Mullins, Noah (Moon), HB, Kentucky, Chi. Bears 1948-49; NY Giants 1949
Mulready, Jerry, E, North Dakota State, Chi. Rockets (AAFC) 1947
Mulvey, Vince, FB, Syracuse, Buffalo 1923
Mumford, Tony, RB, Penn State, St. Louis 1985
Mumgavin, Jock, E, Wisconsin, Chi. Tigers 1920
Mumley, Nick, DE, Purdue, NY Titans 1960-62
Mumphord, Lloyd, CB, Texas Southern, Miami 1969-74; Baltimore 1975-78
Munchak, Mike, G, Penn State, Houston 1982-85
Muncie, Chuck, RB-KR, California, New Orleans 1976-80; San Diego 1980-84
Munday, George, T, Emporia State, Cleveland 1931; NY Giants 1931-32; Cincinnati 1933-34; St. Louis 1934
Mundee, Fred, C, Notre Dame, Chi. Bears 1943-45
Munn, Lyle, E, Kansas State, Kansas City 1925-26; Cleveland 1927; Detroit 1928; NY Giants 1929
Munns, George, QB, Miami (Ohio), Cincinnati 1921
Muñoz, Anthony, T, USC, Cincinnati 1980-85
Munsey, Nelson, CB, Wyoming, Baltimore 1972-77; Minnesota 1978
Munson, Bill, QB, Utah State, LA Rams 1964-67; Detroit 1968-75; Seattle 1976; San Diego 1977; Buffalo 1978-79
Murakowski, Art, FB, Northwestern, Detroit 1951
Muransky, Ed, T, Michigan, LA Raiders 1982-84
Murchison, Ola Lee, SE, Pacific, Dallas Cowboys 1961
Murdock, Guy, C, Michigan, Houston 1972
Murdock, Jesse, RB, California Western, Oakland 1963; Buffalo 1963
Murdock, Les, K, Florida State, NY Giants 1967
Murley, Dick, T, Purdue, Pittsburgh 1956; Philadelphia 1956
Murphy, Bill, G, Washington (St. Louis), Chi. Cardinals 1940-41
Murphy, Bill, SE, Cornell, Boston 1960
Murphy, Dennis, DT, Florida, Chi. Bears 1965
Murphy, Don, B, Green Bay 1922
Murphy, Fred, SE, Georgia Tech, Cleveland 1960; Minnesota 1961
Murphy, George, QB, USC, LA Dons (AAFC) 1949
Murphy, Harvey, E, Mississippi, Cleveland 1940
Murphy, J.T., G, Dartmouth, Canton 1920; Cleveland 1921
Murphy, Jack, HB, Hammond 1922
Murphy, James, WR, Utah State, Kansas City 1981
Murphy, Jim, HB, St. Thomas (Minnesota), Racine 1926; Chi. Cardinals 1928
Murphy, Mark, S, Colgate, Washington 1977-84
Murphy, Mark, S, West Liberty State, Green Bay 1980-85
Murphy, Mike, LB, Southwest Missouri State, Houston 1979
Murphy, Phil, C, Marquette, Duluth 1926
Murphy, Phil, DT, South Carolina State, LA Rams 1980-81
Murphy, Tom, HB, Wisconsin-Superior, Milwaukee 1926
Murphy, Tom, HB, St. Mary's of the Plains, Kansas City 1926; Columbus 1926
Murphy, Tom, HB, Arkansas, Chi. Cardinals 1934
Murrah, Bill, T, Texas A&M, Canton 1922; St. Louis 1923
Murray, Calvin, RB, Ohio State, Philadelphia 1981-82
Murray, Dick (Jab), T, Marquette, Green Bay 1921-24; Racine 1922
Murray, Earl, G, Purdue, Baltimore 1950; NY Giants 1951; Pittsburgh 1952
Murray, Ed, K, Tulane, Detroit 1980-85
Murray, Franny, HB, Pennsylvania, Philadelphia 1939-40
Murray, John (Jock), E, St. Thomas (Minnesota), Duluth 1926
Murrell, Bill, TE, Winston-Salem State, St. Louis 1979
Murry, Don, T, Wisconsin, Racine 1922-24; Chi. Bears 1925-32
Murtagh, George, C, Georgetown (Washington D.C.), NY Giants 1926-32
Murtha, Greg, T, Minnesota, Baltimore 1982
Murtha, Paul, HB, Columbus 1921
Musgrove, Spain, DT, Utah State, Washington 1967-69; Houston 1970
Musick, Jim, HB, USC, Boston 1932-33, 1935-36
Musser, Neal, LB, North Carolina State, Atlanta 1981-82
Musso, George (Moose), T-G, Millikin, Chi. Bears 1933-44
Musso, Johnny, RB, Alabama, Chi. Bears 1975-77
Mutryn, Chet, HB, Xavier, Buffalo (AAFC) 1946-49; Baltimore 1950
Mutscheller, Jim, E-TE, Notre Dame, Baltimore 1954-61
Myer, Steve, QB, New Mexico, Seattle 1976-79
Myers, Bob, DT, Ohio State, Baltimore 1955
Myers, Brad, HB, Bucknell, LA Rams 1953, 1956; Philadelphia 1958
Myers, Chip, WR, Northeastern Oklahoma, San Francisco 1967; Cincinnati 1969-76
Myers, Cyril, E, Ohio State, Toledo 1922; Cleveland 1923, 1925
Myers, Dave, G, NYU, Staten Island 1930
Myers, Denny, G, Iowa, Brooklyn 1931; Chi. Bears 1931
Myers, Frank, T, Texas A&M, Minnesota 1978-79
Myers, Jack (Moose), FB, UCLA, Philadelphia 1948-50; LA Rams 1952
Myers, Jerry, DE, Northern Illinois, Kansas City 1980
Myers, Tom, HB, Fordham, NY Giants 1925; Brooklyn 1926
Myers, Tommy, QB, Northwestern, Detroit 1965-66
Myers, Tommy, S, Syracuse, New Orleans 1972-81
Myers, Wilbur, S, Delta State, Denver 1983
Myhra, Steve, K-LB, North Dakota, Baltimore 1957-61
Myles, Harry, E, West Virginia, Buffalo 1929
Myles, Henry, E, Hampden-Sydney, Newark 1930
Myrtle, Chip, LB, Maryland, Denver 1967-72; San Diego 1974

N

Nabors, Roland, C, Texas Tech, NY Yankees (AAFC) 1948
Nacrelli, Andy, SE, Fordham, Philadelphia 1958
Nadolney, Romanus (Peaches), G, Notre Dame, Green Bay 1922; Milwaukee 1923-25
Nafziger, Dana, TE-LB, Cal Poly-SLO, Tampa Bay 1977-79, 1981-82
Nagel, Ray, HB, UCLA, Chi. Cardinals 1953
Nagel, Ross, T, St. Louis, Chi. Cardinals 1942
Nagler, Gern, SE, Santa Clara, Chi. Cardinals 1953, 1955-58; Pittsburgh 1959; Cleveland 1960-61
Nagurski, Bronko, FB-T, Minnesota, Chi. Bears 1930-37, 1943
Naiota, John, HB, St. Francis, Pittsburgh 1942, 1945
Nairan, Ralph, E, Trinity (Texas), Buffalo 1926
Nairn, Harvey, WR, Southern, NY Jets 1968
Nairne, Rob, LB, Oregon State, Denver 1977-80; New Orleans 1981-83
Namath, Joe, QB, Alabama, NY Jets 1965-76; LA Rams 1977
Nance, Jim, FB, Syracuse, Boston 1965-70; New England 1971; NY Jets 1973
Naponic, Bob, QB, Illinois, Houston 1970
Napier, Walter (Buffalo), DT, Paul Quinn, Dallas Texans 1960-61
Nardacci, Nick, HB, West Virginia, Cleveland 1925
Nardi, Dick, HB, Ohio State, Detroit 1938; Brooklyn 1939; Pittsburgh 1939
Nash, Bob (Nasty), T, Rutgers, Akron 1920; Buffalo 1921-23; Rochester 1924; NY Giants 1925
Nash, Joe, NT, Boston College, Seattle 1982-85
Nash, Tom, E, Georgia, Green Bay 1929-32; Brooklyn 1933-34
Nason, Ed, HB, Oorang 1922
Nathan, Tony, RB-KR, Alabama, Miami 1979-85
Natowich, Andy, HB, Holy Cross, Washington 1944
Naumetz, Fred, C-LB, Boston College, LA Rams 1946-50
Naumoff, Paul, LB, Tennessee, Detroit 1967-78
Naumu, John, HB, USC, LA Dons (AAFC) 1948
Neacy, Clem, E, Colgate, Milwaukee 1924-26; Duluth 1927; Chi. Bears 1927; Chi. Cardinals 1928
Neal, Dan, C, Kentucky, Baltimore 1973-74; Chi. Bears 1975-83
Neal, Ed, G-DT, Tulane, Green Bay 1945-51; Chi. Bears 1951
Neal, Louis, WR, Prairie View A&M, Atlanta 1973-74
Neal, Ray, G, Washington & Jefferson, Akron 1922; Hammond 1924-26
Neal, Richard, DE-DT, Southern, New Orleans 1969-72, 1978; NY Jets 1973-77
Neal, Robert (Speedy), RB, Miami, Buffalo 1984
Neck, Tommy, DB, LSU, Chi. Bears 1962
Neely, Ralph, T, Oklahoma, Dallas 1965-77
Neff, Bob, DB, Stephen F. Austin, Miami 1966-68
Negus, Fred, C, Wisconsin, Chi. Rockets (AAFC) 1947-48; Chi. Hornets (AAFC) 1949

Nehemiah, Renaldo (Skeets), WR, Maryland, San Francisco 1982-84
Neidert, John, LB, Louisville, Cincinnati 1968; NY Jets 1968-69; Chi. Bears 1970
Neighbors, Billy, G, Alabama, Boston 1962-65; Miami 1966-69
Neihaus, Frank, HB, Washington & Jefferson, Akron 1925; Pottsville 1926
Neihaus, Ralph, T, Dayton, Cleveland 1939
Neil, Kenny, DE, Iowa State, NY Jets 1981-83
Neill, Bill, NT, Pittsburgh, NY Giants 1981-83; Green Bay 1984
Neill, Jim, HB, Texas Tech, NY Giants 1937; Chi. Cardinals 1939
Neils, Steve, LB, Minnesota, St. Louis 1974-80
Nelms, Mike, KR-DB-WR, Baylor, Washington 1980-84
Nelsen, Bill, QB, USC, Pittsburgh 1963-67; Cleveland 1968-72
Nelson, Al, S-KR, Cincinnati, Philadelphia 1965-73
Nelson, Andy, S, Memphis State, Baltimore 1957-63; NY Giants 1964
Nelson, Benny, DB, Alabama, Houston 1964
Nelson, Bill, T, Oregon State, LA Rams 1971-75
Nelson, Bob, C, Baylor, Detroit 1941, 1945; LA Dons (AAFC) 1946-49; Baltimore 1950
Nelson, Bob, LB, Nebraska, Buffalo 1975-77; San Francisco 1979; Oakland 1980; LA Raiders 1982-84
Nelson, Chuck, K, Washington, LA Rams 1983; Buffalo 1984
Nelson, Darrell, TE, Memphis State, Pittsburgh 1984-85
Nelson, Darrin, RB-KR, Stanford, Minnesota 1982-85
Nelson, David, RB, Heidelberg, Minnesota 1984
Nelson, Dennis, T, Illinois State, Baltimore 1970-74; Philadelphia 1976-77
Nelson, Derrie, LB, Nebraska, San Diego 1983-85
Nelson, Don, C, Ohio Wesleyan, Canton 1926
Nelson, Don, G, Iowa, Brooklyn 1937
Nelson, Edmund, NT, Auburn, Pittsburgh 1982-85
Nelson, Everett (Packie), T, Illinois, Chi. Bears 1929
Nelson, Frank, HB, Utah, Boston 1948; NY Bulldogs 1949
Nelson, Herb, E, Pennsylvania, Buffalo (AAFC) 1946; Brooklyn (AAFC) 1947-48
Nelson, Jimmy, HB, Alabama, Miami (AAFC) 1946
Nelson, Karl, T, Iowa State, NY Giants 1984-85
Nelson, Lee, S, Florida State, St. Louis 1976-85
Nelson, Ralph, RB, Washington 1975; Seattle 1976
Nelson, Reed, C, BYU, Detroit 1947
Nelson, Shane, LB, Baylor, Buffalo 1977-82
Nelson, Steve, LB, North Dakota State, New England 1974-85
Nelson, Terry, TE, Arkansas-Pine Bluff, LA Rams 1973-80
Nemecek, Andy, G, Ohio State, Columbus 1923-25
Nemecek, Jerry, E, NYU, Brooklyn 1931
Nemeth, Steve, HB-QB, Notre Dame, Cleveland 1945; Chi. Rockets (AAFC) 1946; Baltimore (AAFC) 1947
Nemzek, Ted, G, Moorhead State, Minneapolis 1930
Nery, Carl, G, Duquesne, Pittsburgh 1940-42
Nery, Ron, DE, Kansas State, LA Chargers 1960; San Diego 1961-62; Denver 1963; Houston 1963
Nesbitt, Dick, HB-FB, Drake, Chi. Bears 1930-33; Chi. Cardinals 1933; Brooklyn 1934
Ness, Val, G, Minneapolis 1922
Nesser, Al (Nappy), G, Akron 1920-26; Cleveland Bulldogs 1925; NY Giants 1926-28; Cleveland Indians 1931
Nesser, Charlie, HB, Columbus 1921
Nesser, Frank, FB-G-T, Columbus 1920-22, 1925-26
Nesser, Fred, T, Columbus 1921
Nesser, John, QB-G, Columbus 1921
Nesser, Phil, G-T, Columbus 1920-21
Nesser, Ted, G-C, Columbus 1920-21
Netherton, Bill, E, Louisville 1921-22
Nettles, Doug, CB, Vanderbilt, Baltimore 1974-75, 1977-79; NY Giants 1980
Nettles, Jim, S, Wisconsin, Philadelphia 1965-68; LA Rams 1969-72
Neuman, Bob, E, Illinois Wesleyan, Chi. Cardinals 1934-36
Neumann, Tom, HB, Northern Michigan, Boston 1960
Nevers, Ernie, FB, Stanford, Duluth 1926-27; Chi. Cardinals 1929-31
Nevett, Elijah, DB, Clark, New Orleans 1967-70
Neville, Tom, T, Mississippi State, Boston 1965-70; New England 1971-74, 1976-77; Denver 1978; NY Giants 1979
Newashe, T, Carlisle, Oorang 1922
Newell, Steve, WR, Long Beach State, San Diego 1967
Newhouse, Robert, RB, Houston, Dallas 1972-83
Newland, Bob, WR, Oregon, New Orleans 1971-74
Newland, Howard, T, Detroit, Louisville 1921
Newman, Ed, G, Duke, Miami 1973-84
Newman, Harry, QB, Michigan, NY Giants 1933-35
Newman, Howard, T, Ohio U., Akron 1924
Newman, Olin, E-HB, Carnegie-Mellon, Akron 1925-26
Newmeyer, Don, T, California, LA Buccaneers 1926
Newsome, Billy, DE, Grambling, Baltimore 1970-72; New Orleans 1973-74; NY Jets 1975-76; Chi. Bears 1977
Newsome, Harry, P, Wake Forest, Pittsburgh 1985
Newsome, Ozzie, TE, Alabama, Cleveland 1978-85
Newsome, Timmy, RB-KR, Winston-Salem State, Dallas 1980-85
Newsome, Vince, S, Washington, LA Rams 1983-85
Newton, Bob, T, Nebraska, Chi. Bears 1971-75; Seattle 1976-81
Newton, Chuck, HB-FB, Washington, Philadelphia 1939-40
Newton, Tim, NT, Florida, Minnesota 1985
Newton, Tom, RB, California, NY Jets 1977-82
Niccolai, Armand, T, Duquesne, Pittsburgh 1934-42
Nicely, Joe, T, Staten Island 1930
Nichelini, Al, HB, St. Mary's (California), Chi. Cardinals 1935-36
Nichols, Al, FB, Temple, Pittsburgh 1945
Nichols, Bob, T, Stanford, Pittsburgh 1965; LA Rams 1966-67
Nichols, Bobby, TE, Boston U., Boston 1967-68
Nichols, Ham, G, Rice, Chi. Cardinals 1947-49; Green Bay 1951
Nichols, John, G, Ohio State, Canton 1926
Nichols, Mark, LB, Colorado State, San Francisco 1978
Nichols, Mark, WR, San Jose State, Detroit 1981-85
Nichols, Mike, C, Arkansas-Monticello, Denver 1960-61
Nichols, Ralph, T, Kansas State, Hartford 1926
Nichols, Ricky, WR, East Carolina, Indianapolis 1985
Nichols, Robbie, LB, Tulsa, Baltimore 1970-71
Nichols, Sid, HB-QB, Illinois, Rock Island 1920-21
Nicholson, Jim, T, Michigan State, Kansas City 1974-79; San Francisco 1981
Nickel, Elbie, E, Cincinnati, Pittsburgh 1947-57
Nickla, Ed, G, Maryland, Chi. Bears 1959
Nicklas, Pete, T, Baylor, Oakland 1962
Nicksich, George, G, St. Bonaventure, Pittsburgh 1950
Nicolas, Scott, LB, Miami, Cleveland 1982-85
Niedziela, Bruno, T, Iowa, Chi. Rockets (AAFC) 1947
Niehaus, Steve, DT, Notre Dame, Seattle 1976-78; Minnesota 1979
Nielsen, Gifford, QB, BYU, Houston 1978-83
Nielsen, Hans, K, Michigan State, Chi. Bears 1981
Nielsen, Walt, FB, Arizona, NY Giants 1940
Niemann, Walt, C, Michigan, Green Bay 1922-24
Niemi, Laurie, DT, Washington State, Washington 1949-53
Nighswander, Nick, C, Morehead State, Buffalo 1974
Niland, John, G, Iowa, Dallas 1966-74; Philadelphia 1975
Niles, Jerry, QB, Iowa, NY Giants 1947
Ninowski, Jim, QB, Michigan State, Cleveland 1958-59, 1962-66; Detroit 1960-61; Washington 1967-68; New Orleans 1969
Nipp, Maury, G, Loyola (Los Angeles), Philadelphia 1952-53, 1956
Nisbet, Dave, E, Washington, Chi. Cardinals 1933
Nisby, John, G, Pacific, Pittsburgh 1957-61; Washington 1962-64
Nitschke, Ray, LB, Illinois, Green Bay 1958-72
Nix, Doyle, DB, SMU, Green Bay 1955; Washington 1958-59; LA Chargers 1960; Dallas Texans 1961
Nix, Emery, QB, TCU, NY Giants 1943, 1946
Nix, George, T, Haskell, Buffalo 1926
Nix, Jack, HB, Mississippi State, Cleveland 1940
Nix, Jack, E, USC, San Francisco 1950
Nix, Kent, QB, TCU, Pittsburgh 1967-69; Chi. Bears 1970-71; Houston 1972
Nixon, Fred, WR, Oklahoma, Green Bay 1980-81
Nixon, Jeff, S, Richmond, Buffalo 1979-82
Nixon (Nicksick), Mike, HB, Pittsburgh, Pittsburgh 1935; Brooklyn 1942
Nixon, Tory, CB, San Diego State, San Francisco 1985
Niziolek, Bob, TE, Colorado, Detroit 1981
Nobile, Leo, G, Penn State, Washington 1947; Pittsburgh 1948-49
Nobis, Tommy, LB, Texas, Atlanta 1966-76
Noble, Brian, LB, Arizona State, Green Bay 1985
Noble, Dave, HB, Nebraska, Cleveland 1924-25
Noble, Dick, G, Trinity (Connecticut), Hartford 1926
Noble, Jim, E, Syracuse, Buffalo 1925
Nocera, John, LB, Iowa, Philadelphia 1959-62; Denver 1963
Nock, George, RB, Morgan State, NY Jets 1969-71; Washington 1972
Nofsinger, Terry, QB, Utah, Pittsburgh 1961-64; St. Louis 1965-66; Atlanta 1967
Noga, Niko, LB, Hawaii, St. Louis 1984-85
Nolan, Dick, DB, Maryland, NY Giants 1954-57, 1959-61; Chi. Cardinals 1958; Dallas Cowboys 1962
Nolan, Earl, T, Arizona, Chi. Cardinals 1937-38
Nolan, Jack, G, Santa Clara, LA Buccaneers 1926
Nolan, John, T, Penn State, Boston 1948; NY Bulldogs 1949; NY Yanks 1950
Nolander, Don, C, Minnesota, LA Dons (AAFC) 1946
Noll, Chuck, G-LB, Dayton, Cleveland 1953-59
Nolting, Ray, HB, Cincinnati, Chi. Bears 1936-43
Nomellini, Leo, T-DT, Minnesota, San Francisco 1950-63
Nomina, Tom, DT, Miami (Ohio), Denver 1963-65; Miami 1966-68
Nonnemaker, Ike, E, Wittenberg, Columbus 1926
Noonan, Jerry, HB, Fordham, NY Giants 1921; Rochester 1921-24; Hammond 1923
Noonan, Karl, SE, Iowa, Miami 1966-71
Noppenberg, John, HB-FB, Miami, Pittsburgh 1940-41; Detroit 1941
Norberg, Hank, E, Stanford, San Francisco (AAFC) 1946-47; Chi. Bears 1948
Norby, John, HB, Idaho, St. Louis 1934; Philadelphia 1934; NY Giants 1934; Brooklyn 1935
Nord, Keith, S, St. Cloud State, Minnesota 1979-83, 1985
Nordquist, Mark, G-C, Pacific, Philadelphia 1968-74; Chi. Bears 1975-76; San Francisco 1976
Nordstrom, Harry, G, Trinity (Connecticut), NY Giants 1925; Brooklyn 1926
Noreene, Olaf, HB, Minnesota, Evansville 1921
Norgard, Al, E, Stanford, Green Bay 1934
Nori, Reino, QB-HB, Northern Illinois, Brooklyn 1937; Chi. Bears 1938
Norman, Ben, RB, Colorado State, Denver 1980
Norman, Bob, C, Chi. Cardinals 1945
Norman, Chris, P, South Carolina, Denver 1984-85
Norman, Dick, QB, Stanford, Chi. Bears 1961
Norman, Jim, G, Washington 1955
Norman, Joe, LB, Indiana, Seattle 1979-81, 1983
Norman, Pettis, TE, Johnson C. Smith, Dallas 1962-70; San Diego 1971-73
Norman, Tim, G, Illinois, Chi. Bears 1983
Norman, Will, HB-FB, Washington & Jefferson, Pottsville 1928; Newark 1929
Norris, Hal, LB, California, Washington 1955-56
Norris, Jack, E, Maryland, Staten Island 1932
Norris, Jim, DT, Houston, Oakland 1962-64
Norris, Trusse, E, UCLA, LA Chargers 1960
Norris, Ulysses, TE, Georgia, Detroit 1979-83; Buffalo 1984-85
North, Jim, T, Central Washington, Washington 1944
North, Johnny, E, Vanderbilt, Baltimore (AAFC) 1948-49; Baltimore 1950
Norton, Don, SE, Iowa, LA Chargers 1960; San Diego 1961-66
Norton, Jerry, S-P, SMU, Philadelphia 1954-58; Chi. Cardinals 1959; St. Louis 1960-61; Dallas Cowboys 1962; Green Bay 1963-64
Norton, Jim, DB, Idaho, Houston 1960-68
Norton, Jim, T, Washington, San Francisco 1965-66; Atlanta 1967-68; Philadelphia 1968; Washington 1969; NY Giants 1970
Norton, Marty, HB, Carleton, Minneapolis 1922, 1924; Green Bay 1925-28
Norton, Ray, HB, Cleveland 1925
Norton, Ray, FL-KR, San Jose State, San Francisco 1960-61
Norton, Rick, QB, Kentucky, Miami 1966-69; Green Bay 1970
Norwood, Scott, K, James Madison, Buffalo 1985
Nosich, John, T, Duquesne, Pittsburgh 1938
Nott, Doug, QB, Detroit, Detroit 1935; Boston 1935
Nott, Mike, QB, Santa Clara, Kansas City 1976
Nottingham, Don, RB, Kent State, Baltimore 1971-73; Miami 1973-77
Novacek, Jay, WR, Wyoming, St. Louis 1985
Novak, Eddie, FB, Rock Island 1920-22, 1925; Minneapolis 1924
Novak, Jack, TE, Wisconsin, Cincinnati 1975; Tampa Bay 1976-77
Novak, Ken, DT, Purdue, Baltimore 1976-77
Novotny, Ray, HB, Ashland, Portsmouth 1930; Cleveland 1931; Brooklyn 1932
Novsek, Joe, DE, Tulsa, Oakland 1962
Nowak, Gary, T, Michigan State, San Diego 1971
Nowak, Walt, E, Villanova, Philadelphia 1944
Nowaskey, Bob, E, George Washington, Chi. Bears 1940-42; LA Dons (AAFC) 1946-47; Baltimore (AAFC) 1948-49; Baltimore 1950
Nowatzke, Tom, FB, Indiana, Detroit 1965-69; Baltimore 1970-72
Noyes, Len, T, Montana, Brooklyn 1938
Nugent, Clem, HB, Iowa, Rochester 1924
Nugent, Dan, G, Auburn, Washington 1976-78, 1980
Nugent, Phil, DB, Tulane, Denver 1961
Nugent, Terry, QB, Colorado State, Cleveland 1984
Nunamaker, Julian, G, Tennessee-Martin, Buffalo 1969-70
Nunley, Frank (Fudgehammer), LB, Michigan, San Francisco 1967-76
Nunn, Freddie Joe, LB, Mississippi, St. Louis 1985
Nunnery, R.B., T, LSU, Dallas Texans 1960
Nussbaumer, Bob, HB-DB, Michigan, Green Bay 1946, 1951; Washington 1947-48; Chi. Cardinals 1949-50
Nutter, Madison (Buzz), C, Virginia Tech, Baltimore 1954-60, 1965; Pittsburgh 1961-64
Nutting, Ed, T, Georgia Tech, Cleveland 1961; Dallas 1963
Nuzum, Jerry, HB, New Mexico State, Pittsburgh 1948-51
Nuzum, Rick, C, Kentucky, LA Rams 1977; Green Bay 1978
Nydall, Mally, FB-QB, Minnesota, Minneapolis 1929-30; Frankford 1930-31
Nye, Blaine, G, Stanford, Dallas 1968-76
Nyers, Dick, HB, Indiana Central, Baltimore 1956-57
Nygren, Bernie, HB, San Jose State, LA Dons (AAFC) 1946; Brooklyn (AAFC) 1947
Nystrom, Lee, T, Macalester, Green Bay 1973-74
Nyvall, Vic, RB, Northwestern State (Louisiana), New Orleans 1970

O

Oakes, Bill, T, Haskell, Green Bay 1921
Oakes, Don, T, Virginia Tech, Philadelphia 1961-62; Boston 1963-68
Oakley, Charley, DB, LSU, Chi. Cardinals 1954
Oas, Ben, C, St. Mary's (Minnesota), Minneapolis 1929-30
Oates, Bart, C, BYU, NY Giants 1985
Oates, Brad, T, BYU, St. Louis 1976-77, 1979-80; Detroit 1978; Kansas City 1980; Cincinnati 1981; Green Bay 1981
Oatis, Victor, WR, Northwestern State (Louisiana), Baltimore

1983
Oats, Carleton, DE-DT, Florida A&M, Oakland 1965-72; Green Bay 1973
O'Bard, Ron, CB, BYU, San Diego 1985
Obeck, Vic, G, Springfield, Chi. Cardinals 1945; Brooklyn (AAFC) 1946
Obee, Duncan, C, Dayton, Detroit 1941
Oberbroekling, Ray, T, Columbia College, Kenosha 1924
Oberg, Tom, DB, Portland State, Denver 1968-69
O'Boyle, Harry, HB, Notre Dame, Green Bay 1928-29, 1932; Philadelphia 1933
O'Bradovich, Ed, DE, Illinois, Chi. Bears 1961-72
Obradovich, Jim, TE, USC, NY Giants 1975; San Francisco 1976-77; Tampa Bay 1978-83
O'Brien, Bill, HB, Detroit 1947
O'Brien, Charlie, E, Carleton, Duluth 1926
O'Brien, Dave, T, Boston College, Minnesota 1963-64; NY Giants 1965; St. Louis 1966-67
O'Brien, Davey, QB, TCU, Philadelphia 1939-40
O'Brien, Fran, T, Michigan State, Cleveland 1959; Washington 1960-66; Pittsburgh 1966-68
O'Brien, Gail, T, Nebraska, Boston 1934-36
O'Brien, Jack, E, Florida, Pittsburgh 1954-56
O'Brien, Jim, K-WR, Cincinnati, Baltimore 1970-72; Detroit 1973
O'Brien, John, HB, Minnesota, Minneapolis 1929
O'Brien, Ken, QB, Cal-Davis, NY Jets 1983-85
Obrovac, Mike, T, Bowling Green, Cincinnati 1981-83
Obst, Henry, G, Syracuse, Staten Island 1931; Philadelphia 1933
O'Connell, Grattan, E, Boston College, Hartford 1926; Providence 1927
O'Connell, Harry, C, Chi. Bears 1924
O'Connell, Milt, E, Lafayette, Frankford 1924-25
O'Connell, Tommy, QB, Illinois, Chi. Bears 1953; Cleveland 1956-57; Buffalo 1960-61
O'Connor, Bill (Zeke), E, Notre Dame, Buffalo (AAFC) 1948; Cleveland (AAFC) 1949; NY Yanks 1951
O'Connor, Bob, G-QB, Stanford, Green Bay 1935
O'Connor, Dan, G, Georgetown (Washington D.C.), Canton 1920; Cleveland 1921
O'Connor, Frank, T, Holy Cross, Hartford 1926
O'Dell, Stu, LB, Indiana, Washington 1974, 1976-77; Baltimore 1978
O'Delli, Mel, HB, Duquesne, Pittsburgh 1945
Oden, McDonald, TE, Tennessee State, Cleveland 1980-82
Oden, Olaf (Curly), QB, Brown, Providence 1925-31; Boston 1932
Odle, Phil, WR, BYU, Detroit 1968-70
Odom, Cliff, LB, Texas-Arlington, Cleveland 1980; Baltimore 1982-83; Indianapolis 1984-85
Odom, Henry, RB-KR, South Carolina State, Pittsburgh 1983
Odom, Ricky, S, USC, Kansas City 1978; San Francisco 1978
Odom, Sammy, LB, Northwestern State (Louisiana), Houston 1964
Odom, Steve, WR, Utah, Green Bay 1974-79; NY Giants 1979
Odoms, Riley, TE, Houston, Denver 1972-83
O'Donahue, Pat, DE, Wisconsin, San Francisco 1952; Green Bay 1955
O'Donnell, Dick, E, Minnesota, Duluth 1923; Green Bay 1924-30; Brooklyn 1931
O'Donnell, Joe, G, Michigan, Buffalo 1964-67, 1969-71
O'Donoghue, Neil, K, Auburn, Buffalo 1977; Tampa Bay 1978-79; St. Louis 1980-85
Odson, Urban, T, Minnesota, Green Bay 1946-49
Oech, Vern, T, Minnesota, Chi. Bears 1936
Oehler, John, C, Purdue, Pittsburgh 1933-34; Brooklyn 1935-36
Oehlrich, Arnie, HB, Nebraska, Frankford 1928-29
Oehlrich, John, HB, St. Ambrose, Pittsburgh 1938; Chi. Bears 1938
Ogas, Dave, LB, San Diego State, Oakland 1968; Buffalo 1969
Ogden, Ray, TE-SE, Alabama, St. Louis 1965-66; New Orleans 1967; Atlanta 1967-68; Chi. Bears 1969-71
Ogle, Rick, LB, Colorado, St. Louis 1971; Detroit 1972
Oglesby, Paul, DT, UCLA, Oakland 1960
Ogrin, Pat, DT, Wyoming, Washington 1981-82
O'Hanley, Ross, DB, Boston College, Boston 1960-65
O'Hearn, Jack, G-T, Cornell, Cleveland 1920; NY Giants 1921; Buffalo 1921
Ohlgren, Earl, E, Minnesota, Green Bay 1942
Okoniewski, Steve, DT-DE, Montana, Buffalo 1972-73; Green Bay 1974-75; St. Louis 1976
Olander, Cliff, QB, New Mexico State, San Diego 1977-79; NY Giants 1980
Olderman, Bob, G, Virginia, Kansas City 1985
Oldershaw, Doug, G, Cal-Santa Barbara, NY Giants 1939-41
Oldham, Ray, S, Middle Tennessee State, Baltimore 1973-78; Pittsburgh 1978; NY Giants 1979; Detroit 1980-82
Oldham, Jim, E-HB, Arizona, Racine 1926
Olds, Bill, RB, Nebraska, Baltimore 1973-75; Seattle 1976; Philadelphia 1976
Olenchalk, John, C-LB, Stanford, Kansas City 1981-82
Olenjiniczak, Stan, T, Pittsburgh, Pittsburgh 1935
Olenski, Mitch, T, Alabama, Miami (AAFC) 1946; Detroit 1947
Olerich, Dave, LB, San Francisco, San Francisco 1967-68, 1972-73; St. Louis 1969; Houston 1971
Oliker, Aaron, E, West Virginia, Pottsville 1926
Oliphant, Elmer, HB, Purdue, Army, Rochester 1920; Buffalo 1921
Oliver, Bill, G, Alabama, NY Yankees 1927
Oliver, Bob, T, Abilene Christian, Cleveland 1969
Oliver, Clancy, S, San Diego State, Pittsburgh 1969-70
Oliver, Frank, DB, Kentucky State, Buffalo 1975; Tampa Bay 1976
Oliver, Greg, RB, Trinity (Texas), Philadelphia 1973-74
Oliver, Hubie, FB, Arizona, Philadelphia 1981-85
Oliver, Ralph (Chip), LB, USC, Oakland 1968-69
Oliver, Vince, QB, Indiana, Chi. Cardinals 1945
Olkewicz, Neal, LB, Maryland, Washington 1979-85
Olmstead, Larry, G, Purdue, Louisville 1922-23
Olsen, Merlin, DT, Utah State, LA Rams 1962-76
Olsen, Norm, T, Alabama, Cleveland 1944
Olsen, Orrin, C, BYU, Kansas City 1976
Olsen, Phil, T-C, Utah State, LA Rams 1971-74; Denver 1975-76
Olsen, Ralph, DE, Utah, Green Bay 1949
Olson, Carl, T, UCLA, Chi. Cardinals 1942
Olson, Forrest (Tiny), G, Iowa, NY Yankees 1927
Olson, Glenn, HB, Iowa, Cleveland 1940
Olson, Hal, T, Clemson, Buffalo 1960-62; Denver 1963-64
Olsonoski, Larry, G, Minnesota, Green Bay 1948-49; NY Bulldogs 1949
Olsson, Lance, T, Purdue, San Francisco 1968-69
Olsson, Les, G, Mercer, Boston 1934-36; Washington 1937-38
Olszewski, Al, E, Pittsburgh, Pittsburgh 1945
Olszewski, John (Johnny O), FB, California, Chi. Cardinals 1953-57; Washington 1958-60; Detroit 1961; Denver 1962
Oltz, Russ, T-G, Washington & Jefferson, Hammond 1920-21, 1923-25; Kenosha 1924
O'Mahoney, Jim, LB, Miami, NY Jets 1965-66
O'Malley, Jim, LB, Notre Dame, Denver 1973-75
O'Malley, Joe, E, Georgia, Pittsburgh 1955-56
O'Malley, Tom, QB, Cincinnati, Green Bay 1950
O'Neal, Calvin, LB, Michigan, Baltimore 1978
O'Neal, Jim, G, TCU, Chi. Rockets (AAFC) 1946-47
O'Neal, Steve, P, Texas A&M, NY Jets 1969-72; New Orleans 1973
O'Neil, Bill, E, Marquette, Evansville 1921-22
O'Neil, Bob, G, Notre Dame, Pittsburgh 1956-57; NY Titans 1961
O'Neil, Charles (Red), C, Connecticut, Hartford 1926
O'Neil, Ed, LB, Penn State, Detroit 1974-79; Green Bay 1980
O'Neil, Gerald (Tip), HB-FB, Detroit, Dayton 1922; Toledo 1922-23
O'Neill, Bill, HB, Detroit, Detroit 1935; Cleveland 1937
O'Neill, Tom, E, St. Mary's (Minnesota), Duluth 1925
Onesti, Larry, LB, Northwestern, Houston 1962-65
Oniskey, Dick, G, Tennessee-Chattanooga, Pittsburgh 1955
Onkotz, Dennis, LB, Penn State, NY Jets 1970
Opalewski, Ed, T, Eastern Michigan, Detroit 1943-44
Opperman, Jim, LB, Colorado State, Philadelphia 1975
O'Quinn, John (Red), E, Wake Forest, Chi. Bears 1950-51; Philadelphia 1951
Orduna, Joe, RB, Nebraska, NY Giants 1972-73; Baltimore 1974
Oriard, Mike, C, Notre Dame, Kansas City 1970-73
Oristaglio, Bob, DE, Pennsylvania, Buffalo (AAFC) 1949; Baltimore 1950; Cleveland 1951; Philadelphia 1952
Orlich, Dan, E-DE, Nevada-Reno, Green Bay 1949-51
Ormsbee, Elliott, HB, Bradley, Philadelphia 1946
O'Rourke, Charlie, QB, Boston College, Chi. Bears 1942; LA Dons (AAFC) 1946-47; Baltimore (AAFC) 1948-49
Orosz, Tom, P, Ohio State, Miami 1981-82; San Francisco 1983-84
Orr, Jimmy, FL, Georgia, Pittsburgh 1958-60; Baltimore 1961-70
Ortega, Ralph, LB, Florida, Atlanta 1975-78; Miami 1979-80
Ortego, Keith, WR, McNeese State, Chi. Bears 1985
Orth, Henry, G, Miami (Ohio), Cincinnati 1921
Ortman, Chuck, HB-QB, Michigan, Pittsburgh 1951; Dallas 1952
Orvis, Herb, DE-DT, Colorado, Detroit 1972-77; Baltimore 1978-81
Orwoll, Ossie, HB, Luther, Milwaukee 1926
Osborn, Dave, RB, North Dakota, Minnesota 1965-75; Green Bay 1976
Osborn, Mike, LB, Kansas State, Philadelphia 1978
Osborn, Robert (Duke), G, Penn State, Canton 1921-23; Cleveland 1924; Pottsville 1925-28
Osborne, Clancy, LB, Arizona State, San Francisco 1959-60; Minnesota 1961-62; Oakland 1963-64
Osborne, Jim, DT, Southern, Chi. Bears 1972-84
Osborne, Richard, TE, Texas A&M, Philadelphia 1976-78; NY Jets 1976
Osborne, Tom, SE, Hastings, Washington 1960-61
Osby, Vince, LB, Illinois, San Diego 1984-85
Osiecki, Sandy, QB, Arizona State, Kansas City 1984
Osley, Willie, CB, Illinois, New England 1974; Kansas City 1974
Osmanski, Bill, FB, Holy Cross, Chi. Bears 1939-43, 1946-47
Osmanski, Joe, FB, Holy Cross, Chi. Bears 1946-49; NY Bulldogs 1949
Ossowski, Ted, T, Oregon State, NY Yankees (AAFC) 1947
O'Steen, Dwayne, CB, San Jose State, LA Rams 1978-79; Oakland 1980-81; Baltimore 1982; Tampa Bay 1982-83; Green Bay 1983-84
Ostendarp, Jim (Smokey), HB, Bucknell, NY Giants 1950-51
Ostrowski, Chet, DE, Notre Dame, Washington 1954-59
O'Toole, Bill, G, St. Mary's (Minnesota), Duluth 1924
Otte, Lowell, E, Iowa, Buffalo 1927
Ottele, Dick, QB, Washington, LA Dons (AAFC) 1948
Otis, Jim, FB, Ohio State, New Orleans 1970; Kansas City 1971-72; St. Louis 1973-78
Otto, Al, C-T, Louisville 1922-23
Otto, Gus, LB, Missouri, Oakland 1965-73
Otto, Jim, C, Miami, Oakland 1960-74
Oubre, Louis, T, Oklahoma, New Orleans 1982-84
Outlaw, Johnny, CB, Jackson State, Boston 1969-70; New England 1971-72; Philadelphia 1973-78
Overmyer, Bill, LB, Ashland, Philadelphia 1972
Overstreet, David, RB, Oklahoma, Miami 1983
Overton, Jerry, DB, Utah, Dallas 1963
Owen, Alton, QB, Mercer, NY Giants 1939-40, 1942
Owen, Bill, T, Oklahoma State, Kansas City 1926; Cleveland 1927; Detroit 1928; NY Giants 1929-36
Owen, Steve, T, Phillips, Kansas City 1924-26; NY Giants 1926-31, 1933
Owen, Tom, QB, Wichita State, San Francisco 1974-75; New England 1976, 1978-81; Washington 1982; NY Giants 1983
Owens, Artie, WR, West Virginia, San Diego 1976-79; Buffalo 1980; New Orleans 1980
Owens, Brig, S, Cincinnati, Washington 1966-77
Owens, Burgess, S, Miami, NY Jets 1973-79; Oakland 1980-81; LA Raiders 1982
Owens, Dennis, NT, North Carolina State, New England 1982-85
Owens, Don, DT, Southern Mississippi, Washington 1957; Philadelphia 1958-60; St. Louis 1960-63
Owens, Harry (Brick), G, Lawrence, Green Bay 1922
Owens, Ike, E, Illinois, Chi. Rockets (AAFC) 1948
Owens, James, RB-WR-KR, UCLA, San Francisco 1979-80; Tampa Bay 1981-84
Owens, Jim, E, Oklahoma, Baltimore 1950
Owens, Joe, DE, Alcorn State, San Diego 1970; New Orleans 1971-75; Houston 1976
Owens, Luke, DT, Kent State, Baltimore 1957; Chi. Cardinals 1958-59; St. Louis 1960-65
Owens, Marv, WR, San Diego State, St. Louis 1973; NY Jets 1974
Owens, Mel, LB, Michigan, LA Rams 1981-85
Owens, Morris, WR, Arizona State, Miami 1975-76; Tampa Bay 1976-79
Owens, R.C., SE, College of Idaho, San Francisco 1957-61; Baltimore 1962-63; NY Giants 1964
Owens, Steve, RB, Oklahoma, Detroit 1970-74
Owens, Terry, T, Jacksonville State, San Diego 1966-75
Owens, Tinker, WR-KR, Oklahoma, New Orleans 1976, 1978-80
Owens, Truet (Pete), C-G, Texas Tech, Brooklyn 1943
Ozdowski, Mike, DE, Virginia, Baltimore 1978-81

P

Pace, Jim, HB, Michigan, San Francisco 1958
Pacella, Dave, G-C, Maryland, Philadelphia 1984
Pacewicz, Vince, QB, San Francisco, Washington 1947
Packer, Walter, CB-RB-KR, Mississippi State, Seattle 1977; Tampa Bay 1977
Padan, Bob, HB, Ohio State, Louisville 1922
Padgen, Gary, LB, Arizona State, Baltimore 1982-83; Indianapolis 1984
Padlow, Max, E, Ohio State, Philadelphia 1935-36
Paffrath, Bob, HB, Minnesota, Miami (AAFC) 1946; Brooklyn (AAFC) 1946
Pagac, Fred, TE, Ohio State, Chi. Bears 1974; Tampa Bay 1976
Page, Alan, DT, Notre Dame, Minnesota 1967-78; Chi. Bears 1978-81
Page, Paul, HB, SMU, Baltimore (AAFC) 1949
Pagel, Mike, QB, Arizona State, Baltimore 1982-83; Indianapolis 1984-85
Pagliei, Joe, FB, Clemson, Philadelphia 1959; NY Titans 1960
Pahl, Lou, FB, St. Thomas (Minnesota), Minneapolis 1923-24
Paige, Stephone, WR, Fresno State, Kansas City 1983-85
Paige, Tony, FB, Virginia Tech, NY Jets 1984-85
Paine, Homer, T, Oklahoma, Chi. Hornets (AAFC) 1949
Paine, Jeff, LB, Texas A&M, Kansas City 1984-85
Palatella, Lou, G, Pittsburgh, San Francisco 1955-58
Palazzi, Lou, C, Penn State, NY Giants 1946-47
Palewicz, Al, Miami, Kansas City 1973-75; NY Jets 1977
Palm, Mike, QB, Penn State, NY Giants 1925-26; Cincinnati 1933
Palmer, Chuck, QB-HB, Northwestern, Racine 1924; Louisville 1926
Palmer, Darrell, T-DT, TCU, NY Yankees (AAFC) 1946-48; Cleveland 1949-53
Palmer, Dick, LB, Kentucky, Miami 1970; Buffalo 1972; New Orleans 1972-73; Atlanta 1974

Palmer, Gery, T, Kansas, Kansas City 1975
Palmer, Les, HB, North Carolina State, Philadelphia 1948
Palmer, Mike, T, Minneapolis 1922
Palmer, Scott, DT, Texas, NY Jets 1971; St. Louis 1972
Palmer, Tom, DT, Wake Forest, Pittsburgh 1953-54
Paluck, John, DE, Pittsburgh, Washington 1956, 1959-65
Palumbo, Sam, LB, Notre Dame, Cleveland 1955-56; Green Bay 1957; Buffalo 1960
Panaccion, Tony, T, Penn State, Frankford 1930
Panciera, Don, QB, San Francisco, NY Yankees (AAFC) 1949; Detroit 1950; Chi. Cardinals 1952
Pane, Chris, DB-KR, Cal State-Chico, Denver 1978-79
Panelli, John (Pep), FB-LB, Notre Dame, Detroit 1949-50; Chi. Cardinals 1951-53
Panfil, Ken, DT, Purdue, LA Rams 1956-58; Chi. Cardinals 1959; St. Louis 1960-62
Pangle, Hal, FB-HB, Oregon State, Chi. Cardinals 1935-38
Pankey, Irv, T, Penn State, LA Rams 1980-82, 1984-85
Pannell, Ernie, T, Texas A&M, Green Bay 1941-42, 1945
Paolucci, Ben, DT, Wayne State, Detroit 1959
Papac, Nick, QB, Fresno State, Oakland 1961
Papach, George, FB-DB, Purdue, Pittsburgh 1948-49
Papale, Vince, WR, St. Joseph's (Pennsylvania), Philadelphia 1976-78
Pape, Oran, HB, Iowa, Green Bay 1930; Minneapolis 1930; Providence 1931; Boston 1932; Staten Island 1932
Papit, Johnny, HB, Virginia, Washington 1951-53; Green Bay 1953
Pappio, Joe, E-FB, Haskell, Chi. Cardinals 1930
Pardee, Jack, LB, Texas A&M, LA Rams 1957-64, 1966-70; Washington 1971-72
Pardonner, Paul, QB, Purdue, Chi. Cardinals 1934-35
Paremore, Bob, RB, Florida A&M, St. Louis 1963-64
Parilli, Vito (Babe), QB, Kentucky, Green Bay 1952-53, 1957-58; Cleveland 1956; Oakland 1960; Boston 1961-67; NY Jets 1968-69
Paris, Bubba, T, Michigan, San Francisco 1983-85
Parish, Don, LB, Stanford, St. Louis 1970-72; LA Rams 1971; Denver 1972
Park, Ernie, G-T, McMurray, San Diego 1963-65; Miami 1966; Denver 1967; Cincinnati 1969
Parker, Andy, TE, Utah, LA Raiders 1984-85
Parker, Artimus, S, USC, Philadelphia 1974-76; NY Jets 1977
Parker, Charlie, G, Southern Mississippi, Denver 1965
Parker, Clarence (Ace), HB-QB, Duke, Brooklyn 1937-41; Boston 1945; NY Yankees (AAFC) 1946
Parker, Dave, E, Hardin-Simmons, Brooklyn 1941
Parker, Don, G, Virginia, San Francisco 1967
Parker, Ervin, LB, South Carolina State, Buffalo 1980-83
Parker, Frank, DT, Oklahoma State, Cleveland 1962-64, 1966-67; Pittsburgh 1968; NY Giants 1969
Parker, Howard, QB-LB, SMU, NY Yankees (AAFC) 1948
Parker, Jim, T-G, Ohio State, Baltimore 1957-67
Parker, Joe, E, Texas, Chi. Cardinals 1946-47
Parker, Joel, WR, Florida, New Orleans 1974-75, 1977
Parker, Kenny, DB, Fordham, NY Giants 1970
Parker, Kerry, CB, Grambling, Kansas City 1984
Parker, Raymond (Buddy), FB, Centenary, Detroit 1935-36; Chi. Cardinals 1937-43
Parker, Rodney, WR, Tennessee State, Philadelphia 1980-81
Parker, Steve, DE, Idaho, New Orleans 1980
Parker, Steve, DE, East Tennessee State, Baltimore 1983; Indianapolis 1984
Parker, Willie, DT, Arkansas-Pine Bluff, Houston 1967-70
Parker, Willie, C-G, North Texas State, Buffalo 1973-78
Parkin, Dave, S, Utah State, Detroit 1979
Parkinson, Tom (Doc), FB, Pittsburgh, Staten Island 1931
Parks, Billy, WR, Long Beach State, San Diego 1971; Dallas 1972; Houston 1973-75
Parks, Dave, SE-TE, Texas Tech, San Francisco 1964-67; New Orleans 1968-72
Parks, Mickey, C, Oklahoma, Washington 1938-40; Chi. Rockets (AAFC) 1946
Parlavecchio, Chet, LB, Penn State, Green Bay 1983; St. Louis 1983
Parmer, Jim, FB, Oklahoma State, Philadelphia 1948-56
Parnell, Fred (Babe), T, Colgate, NY Giants 1925-27
Parriott, Bill, FB, West Virginia, Cincinnati 1934
Parris, Gary, TE, Florida State, San Diego 1973-74; Cleveland 1975-78; St. Louis 1979-80
Parrish, Bernie, S, Florida, Cleveland, 1959-66; Houston 1966
Parrish, Don, DE, Pittsburgh, Kansas City 1978
Parrish, Lemar, CB-KR, Lincoln (Missouri), Cincinnati 1970-77; Washington 1978-81; Buffalo 1982
Parros, Rick, RB, Utah State, Denver 1981-84; Seattle 1985
Parry, Owen (Ox), T, Baylor, NY Giants 1937-39
Parseghian, Ara, HB, Miami (Ohio), Cleveland (AAFC) 1948-49
Parsley, Cliff, P, Oklahoma State, Houston 1977-82
Parson, Ray, T, Minnesota, Detroit 1971
Parsons, Bob, P-TE, Penn State, Chi. Bears 1972-83
Parsons, Earle, HB, USC, San Francisco (AAFC) 1946-47
Parsons, Lloyd, FB, Gustavus Adolphus, Detroit 1941
Partee, Dennis, K-P, SMU, San Diego 1968-75
Partlow, Gene, FB, Cleveland 1923
Partlow, Lou, FB, Dayton 1920-27, 1929
Partridge, Rick, P, Utah, New Orleans 1979; San Diego 1980
Paschal, Bill, HB, Georgia Tech, NY Giants 1943-47; Boston 1947-48
Paschal, Doug, RB, North Carolina, Minnesota 1980
Paschka, Gordon, FB-G, Minnesota, Phil-Pitt 1943; NY Giants 1947
Pashe, Bill, DB, George Washington, NY Jets 1964
Paskvan, George, FB, Wisconsin, Green Bay 1941
Pasqua, Joe, T, SMU, Cleveland 1942; Washington 1943; LA Rams 1946
Pasquariello, Ralph, FB, Villanova, LA Rams 1950; Chi. Cardinals 1951-52
Paquesi, Tony, DT, Notre Dame, Chi. Cardinals 1955-57
Pass, Randy, G, Georgia Tech, Green Bay 1978
Passuelo, Bill, G, Columbus 1923
Pastin, Frank, G, Waynesburg, Pittsburgh 1942
Pastorini, Dan, QB-P, Santa Clara, Houston 1971-79; Oakland 1980; LA Rams 1981; Philadelphia 1982-83
Pastrana, Al, QB, Maryland, Denver 1969-70
Patanelli, Mike, E, Ball State, Brooklyn (AAFC) 1947
Pate, Lloyd, RB, Cincinnati, Buffalo 1970
Pate, Rupert, G, Wake Forest, Chi. Cardinals 1940; Philadelphia 1942
Patera, Dennis, K, BYU, San Francisco 1968
Patera, Jack, G-LB, Oregon, Baltimore 1955-57; Chi. Cardinals 1958-59; Dallas Cowboys 1960-61
Paternoster, Angelo, G, Georgetown (Washington D.C.), Washington 1943
Patrick, Frank, FB, Pittsburgh, Chi. Cardinals 1938-39
Patrick, Frank, QB, Nebraska, Green Bay 1970-72
Patrick, John, FB, Penn State, Pittsburgh 1941, 1945-46
Patrick, Mike, P, Mississippi State, New England 1975-78
Patrick, Wayne, RB, Louisville, Buffalo 1968-72
Patt, Maurice (Babe), E, Carnegie-Mellon, Detroit 1938; Cleveland 1939-42
Patten, Joel, T, Duke, Cleveland 1980
Pattera, Herb, LB, Michigan State, Buffalo 1963
Patterson, Billy, QB, Baylor, Chi. Bears 1939; Pittsburgh 1940
Patterson, Don, CB, Georgia Tech, Detroit 1979; NY Giants 1980
Patterson, Elvis, CB, Kansas, NY Giants 1984-85
Patterson, Paul, HB, Illinois, Chi. Hornets (AAFC) 1949
Pattillo, Darrell, CB, Long Beach State, San Diego 1983
Pattison, Roger, G, Minnesota, Kenosha 1924
Patton, Bob, T, Clemson, NY Giants 1952
Patton, Bob, C, Delaware, Buffalo 1976
Patton, Cliff, G-K, TCU, Philadelphia 1946-50; Chi. Cardinals 1951
Patton, Jerry, DT, Nebraska, Buffalo 1972-73; Philadelphia 1974; New England 1975
Patton, Jimmy, S, Mississippi, NY Giants 1955-66
Patton, Ricky, RB, Jackson State, Atlanta 1978-79; Green Bay 1979; San Francisco 1980-82
Patulski, Walt, DE, Notre Dame, Buffalo 1972-75; St. Louis 1977
Paul, Don, LB, UCLA, LA Rams 1948-55
Paul, Don, DB, Washington State, Chi. Cardinals 1950-53; Cleveland 1954-58
Paul, Harold, T, Oklahoma, San Diego 1974
Paul, Whitney, LB, Colorado, Kansas City 1976-81; New Orleans 1982-85
Paulekas, Tony, C, Washington & Jefferson, Green Bay 1936
Pauley, Frank (Heavy), T, Washington & Jefferson, Chi. Bears 1930
Paulson, Dainard, S, Oregon State, NY Titans 1961-62; NY Jets 1963-66
Pavelec, Ted, G, Detroit, Detroit 1941-43
Pavkov, Stonko, G, Idaho, Pittsburgh 1939-40
Pavlich, Charlie, G, San Francisco (AAFC) 1946
Payn, Marshall, C, Franklin & Marshall, Rochester 1925
Payne, Charley, HB, Detroit, Detroit 1937
Payne, Ken, WR, Langston, Green Bay 1974-77; Philadelphia 1978
Payton, Eddie, RB-KR, Jackson State, Cleveland 1977; Detroit 1977; Kansas City 1978; Minnesota 1980-82
Payton, Walter, RB-KR, Jackson State, Chi. Bears 1975-85
Peabody, Dwight, E, Ohio State, Columbus 1920; Toledo 1922
Peace, Larry, HB, Pittsburgh, Brooklyn 1941
Peacock, Elvis, RB, Oklahoma, LA Rams 1979-80; Cincinnati 1981
Peacock, Johnny, DB, Houston, Houston 1969-70
Peaks, Clarence, FB, Michigan State, Philadelphia 1957-63; Pittsburgh 1964-65
Pear, Dave, DT-NT, Washington, Baltimore 1975; Tampa Bay 1976-78; Oakland 1979-80
Pearce, Harley, E-HB, Ohio Wesleyan, Columbus 1926
Pearce, Walter (Pard), QB, Pennsylvania, Decatur 1920; Chi. Staleys 1921; Chi. Bears 1922; Kenosha 1924; Providence 1925
Pearcy, Jim, G, Marshall, Chi. Rockets (AAFC) 1946-48; Chi. Hornets (AAFC) 1949
Pearlman, Red, G-T, Pittsburgh, Cleveland 1920-21
Pearson, Barry, WR, Northwestern, Pittsburgh 1972-73; Kansas City 1974-76
Pearson, Bert, C, Kansas State, Chi. Bears 1929-34
Pearson, Dennis, WR, San Diego State, Atlanta, 1978-79
Pearson, Drew, WR, Tulsa, Dallas 1973-83
Pearson, Dud, QB, Notre Dame, Racine 1922
Pearson, Lindell, HB, Oklahoma, Detroit 1950-52; Green Bay 1952
Pearson, Preston, RB-DB-KR, Illinois, Baltimore 1967-69; Pittsburgh 1970-74; Dallas 1975-80
Pearson, Willie, DB, North Carolina A&T, Miami 1969
Pease, George, QB, Columbia, Orange 1929
Peay, Francis, T, Missouri, NY Giants 1966-67; Green Bay 1968-72; Kansas City 1973-74
Pederson, Jim, E, Augsburg, Minneapolis 1930; Frankford 1930-31; Chi. Bears 1932
Pederson, Winfield, T, Minnesota, NY Giants 1941, 1945; Boston 1946
Peebles, Jim, E, Vanderbilt, Washington 1946-49, 1951
Peery, Gordon (Skeet), QB, Oklahoma State, Cleveland 1927
Peets, Brian, TE, Pacific, Seattle 1978-79; San Francisco 1981
Peiffer, Dan, C, Southeast Missouri State, Chi. Bears 1975-77; Washington 1980
Pelfrey, Ray, E-HB-P, Eastern Kentucky State, Green Bay 1951; Dallas 1952; Chi. Cardinals 1952; NY Giants 1953
Pellegrini, Bob, LB, Maryland, Philadelphia 1956, 1958-61; Washington 1962-65
Pellegrini, Joe, DT-NT, Idaho, NY Jets 1978-79
Pellegrini, Joe, G-C, Harvard, NY Jets 1982-83; Atlanta 1984-85
Pellington, Bill, LB, Rutgers, Baltimore 1953-64
Pelluer, Scott, LB, Washington, New Orleans 1981-85
Pelluer, Steve, QB, Washington, Dallas 1984-85
Pena, Bubba, G, Massachusetts, Cleveland 1972
Penaranda, Jairo, RB, UCLA, LA Rams 1981; Philadelphia 1985
Penchion, Robert, G-T, Alcorn State, Buffalo 1972-73; San Francisco 1974-75; Seattle 1976
Penn, Jesse, LB, Virginia Tech, Dallas 1985
Pennington, Durwood, K, Georgia, Dallas Texans 1962
Pennywell, Carlos, WR, Grambling, New England 1978-81
Pennywell, Robert, LB, Grambling, Atlanta 1977-80
Penrose, Craig, QB, San Diego State, Denver 1976-79; NY Jets 1980
Pense, Leon, QB, Arkansas, Pittsburgh 1945
Pentecost, John, G, UCLA, Minnesota 1967
Peoples, George, RB, Auburn, Dallas 1982; New England 1983; Tampa Bay 1984-85
Peoples, Woody, G, Grambling, San Francisco 1968-75, 1977; Philadelphia 1978-80
Pepper, Gene, G, Missouri, Washington 1950-53; Baltimore 1954
Peratoni, Frank, C, Princeton, NY Yankees (AAFC) 1948-49
Percival, Mac, K, Texas Tech, Chi. Bears 1967-73; Dallas 1974
Perdue, Willard (Bolo), E, Duke, NY Giants 1940; Brooklyn (AAFC) 1946
Perez, Pete, G, Illinois, Chi. Bears 1945
Pergine, John, LB, Notre Dame, LA Rams 1969-72; Washington 1973-75
Perina, Bob, HB, Princeton, NY Yankees (AAFC) 1946; Brooklyn (AAFC) 1947; Chi. Rockets (AAFC) 1948; Chi. Bears 1949; Baltimore 1950
Perini, Evo (Pete), LB-FB, Ohio State, Chi. Bears 1954-55; Cleveland 1955
Perkins, Art, FB, North Texas State, LA Rams 1962-63
Perkins, Bill, RB, Iowa, NY Jets 1963
Perkins, Don, FB, Wisconsin-Platteville, Green Bay 1943-45; Chi. Bears 1945-46
Perkins, Don, FB, New Mexico, Dallas 1961-68
Perkins, Horace, CB, Colorado, Kansas City 1979
Perkins, Jim, T, Colorado, Denver 1962-64
Perkins, Johnny, WR, Abilene Christian, NY Giants 1977-83
Perkins, Ray, WR, Alabama, Baltimore 1967-71
Perkins, Willis, G, Texas Southern, Boston 1961; Houston 1961-63
Perko, John, G, Duquesne, Pittsburgh 1937-40, 1945-47; Card-Pitt 1944
Perko, John, G, Minnesota, Buffalo (AAFC) 1946
Perko, Mike, NT, Utah State, Atlanta 1982
Perko, Tom, LB, Pittsburgh, Green Bay 1976
Perlo, Phil, LB, Maryland, Houston 1960
Perot, Petey, G, Northwestern State (Louisiana), Philadelphia 1979-82, 1984; New Orleans 1985
Perpich, George, T, Georgetown (Washington D.C.), Brooklyn (AAFC) 1946; Baltimore (AAFC) 1947
Perreault, Pete, T-G, Boston U., NY Jets 1963-67, 1969-70; Cincinnati 1968; Minnesota 1971
Perretta, Ralph, G, Purdue, San Diego 1975-80; NY Giants 1980
Perrie, Mike, HB, St. Mary's (California), Cleveland 1939
Perrin, Benny, S, Alabama, St. Louis 1982-85
Perrin, John, QB, Chicago, Hartford 1926
Perrin, Lonnie, RB, Illinois, Denver 1976-78; Washington 1979; Chi. Bears 1979
Perrotti, Mike, T, Cincinnati, LA Dons (AAFC) 1948-49
Perry, Claude, T, Alabama, Green Bay 1927-35; Brooklyn 1931
Perry, Gerry, T-K, California, Detroit 1954, 1956-59; St. Louis 1960-62
Perry, Joe (The Jet), FB, Compton J.C., San Francisco 1948-60, 1963; Baltimore 1961-62
Perry, Leon, RB, Mississippi, NY Giants 1980-82
Perry, Lowell, E-DB, Michigan, Pittsburgh 1956
Perry, Mike, QB, St. Mary's (California), Cleveland 1939
Perry, Rod, CB, Colorado, LA Rams 1975-82; Cleveland 1983-84
Perry, Scott, S, Williams, Cincinnati 1976-79; San Francisco

1980; San Diego 1980
Perry, Vernon, S, Jackson State, Houston 1979-82; New Orleans 1983
Perry, William (The Refrigerator), DT-RB, Clemson, Chi. Bears 1985
Perryman, Jim, S, Millikin, Buffalo 1985
Person, Ara (Sonny), TE, Morgan State, St. Louis 1972
Peshmalyan, Baruyr, E, Yale, Chi. Tigers 1920
Pesonen, Dick, DB, Minnesota-Duluth, Green Bay 1960; Minnesota 1961; NY Giants 1962-64
Pessalano, Lou, T, Villanova, Staten Island 1929
Pesuit, Wally, T, Kentucky, Atlanta 1976; Miami 1976-78; Detroit 1979-80
Petchel, John, QB, Duquesne, Cleveland 1942, 1944; Pittsburgh 1945
Petcoff, Boni, T, Ohio State, Columbus 1924-26
Peters, Anton, T, Florida, Denver 1963
Peters, Floyd, DT, Cal State-San Francisco, Cleveland 1959-62; Detroit 1963; Philadelphia 1964-69; Washington 1970
Peters, Frank, T, Ohio U., Cincinnati 1969
Peters, Frosty, QB-HB, Illinois, Portsmouth 1930; Providence 1930; Brooklyn 1931; Chi. Cardinals 1932
Peters, Tony, S, Oklahoma, Cleveland 1975-78; Washington 1979-82, 1984-85
Peters, Volney, DT, USC, Chi. Cardinals 1952-53; Washington 1954-57; Philadelphia 1958; LA Chargers 1960; Oakland 1961
Petersen, Kurt, G, Missouri, Dallas 1980-85
Petersen, Ted, T-C, Eastern Illinois, Pittsburgh 1977-83; Cleveland 1984; Indianapolis 1984
Peterson, Bill, LB, San Jose State, Cincinnati 1968-72; Kansas City 1975
Peterson, Cal, LB, UCLA, Dallas 1974-75; Tampa Bay 1976; Kansas City 1979-81; LA Raiders 1982
Peterson, Jerry, T, Texas, Baltimore 1956
Peterson, Jim, LB, San Diego State, LA Rams 1974-75; Tampa Bay 1976
Peterson, Ken, G, Utah, Minnesota 1961
Peterson, Kenneth (Ike), HB, Gonzaga, Chi. Cardinals 1935; Detroit 1936
Peterson, Len, E, Kansas City 1924
Peterson, Les (Tex), Texas, E-T, Portsmouth 1931; Staten Island 1932; Green Bay 1932-34; Brooklyn 1933
Peterson, Nelson, HB, West Virginia Wesleyan, Washington 1937; Cleveland 1938
Peterson, Phil, HB, Wisconsin, Brooklyn 1934
Peterson, Ray, HB, San Francisco, Green Bay 1937
Petitbon, John, HB, Notre Dame, Dallas 1952; Cleveland 1955-56; Green Bay 1957
Petitbon, Richie, S, Tulane, Chi. Bears 1959-68; LA Rams 1969-70; Washington 1971-72
Petrella, Bob, DB, Tennessee, Miami 1966-71
Petrella, John, HB, Penn State, Pittsburgh 1945
Petrich, Bob, DE, West Texas State, San Diego 1963-66; Buffalo 1967
Petrie, Elmer, FB, Cleveland 1920; Toledo 1922
Petrilas, Bill, HB, NY Giants 1944-45
Petro, Steve, G, Pittsburgh, Brooklyn 1940-41
Petrovich, George, T, Texas, Chi. Cardinals 1949-50
Petties, Neal, SE, San Diego State, Baltimore 1964-66
Pettigrew, Gary, DT, Stanford, Philadelphia 1966-74; NY Giants 1974
Petty, John, FB, Purdue, Chi. Bears 1942
Petty, Larry, G, Illinois, Canton 1920
Petty, Ross, G, Illinois, Decatur 1920
Petway, David, S, Northern Illinois, Green Bay 1981
Peviani, Bob, G, USC, NY Giants 1953
Peyton, Leo, FB, St. Lawrence, Rochester 1923-24
Pfohl, Bob, HB, Purdue, Baltimore (AAFC) 1948-49
Pharmer, Art, FB, Minnesota, Minneapolis 1930; Frankford 1930-31
Pharr, Tommy, S, Mississippi State, Buffalo 1970
Phelan, Bob, HB, Notre Dame, Toledo 1922; Rock Island 1923-24
Phelps, Don (Dopey), HB, Kentucky, Cleveland 1950-52
Philbin, Gerry, DE, Buffalo, NY Jets 1964-72; Philadelphia 1973
Phillips, Charles, S, USC, Oakland 1975-79
Phillips, Ewell, G, Oklahoma Baptist, NY Giants 1936
Phillips, George, FB, UCLA, Cleveland 1945
Phillips, Irvin, CB, Arkansas Tech, San Diego 1981; LA Raiders 1983
Phillips, Jess, RB-KR, Michigan State, Cincinnati 1968-73; New Orleans 1974; Oakland 1975; New England 1976-77
Phillips, Jim (Red), SE-TE, Auburn, LA Rams 1958-64; Minnesota 1965-67
Phillips, Joe, WR, Kentucky, Washington 1985
Phillips, Kirk, WR, Tulsa, Dallas 1984
Phillips, Loyd, DE, Arkansas, Chi. Bears 1967-69
Phillips, Mel, S, North Carolina A&T, San Francisco 1966-77
Phillips, Mike, C, Western Maryland, Baltimore (AAFC) 1947
Phillips, Ray, LB, Nebraska, Cincinnati 1977-78; Philadelphia 1978-81
Phillips, Reggie, CB, SMU, Chi. Bears 1985
Phillips, Rod, RB, Jackson State, LA Rams 1975-78; St. Louis 1979-80
Philpott, Dean, DB, Fresno State, Chi. Cardinals 1958
Philpott, Ed, LB, Miami (Ohio), Boston 1967-70; New England 1971
Philyaw, Charles, DE, Texas Southern, Oakland 1976-79
Phipps, Mike, QB, Purdue, Cleveland 1970-76; Chi. Bears 1977-81
Piasecky, Al, E, Duke, Washington 1943-45
Picard, Bob, WR, Eastern Washington State, Philadelphia 1973-76; Detroit 1976
Piccolo, Bill, C, Canisius, NY Giants 1943-45
Piccolo, Brian, RB, Wake Forest, Chi. Bears 1966-69
Piccone, Lou, WR-KR, West Liberty State, NY Jets 1974-76; Buffalo 1977-82
Pickard, Bob, WR, Xavier, Detroit 1974
Pickel, Bill, DE, Rutgers, LA Raiders 1983-85
Pickens, Bob, T, Nebraska, Chi. Bears 1967-69
Pickering, Clay, WR, Maine, Cincinnati 1984-85
Piepul, Milt, FB, Notre Dame, Detroit 1941
Pierce, Bemus, FB, Carlisle, Akron 1920; Oorang 1922-23
Pierce, Danny, RB, Memphis State, Washington 1970
Pierce, Don, C, Kansas, Brooklyn 1942; Chi. Cardinals 1943
Pierce, George, G-T, Michigan, Chi. Tigers 1920
Pierotti, Al, C, Washington & Lee, Akron 1920; Cleveland 1920; NY Giants 1921; Milwaukee 1922-24; Providence 1927; Boston 1929
Pierre, John, E, Pittsburgh, Pittsburgh 1945
Pierson, Reggie, DB, Oklahoma State, Tampa Bay 1976; Detroit 1976
Pietrosante, Nick, FB, Notre Dame, Detroit 1959-65; Cleveland 1966-67
Pietrzak, Jim, T-C, Eastern Michigan, NY Giants 1974-75, 1977-79; New Orleans 1979-84
Pifferini, Bob, C, San Jose State, Detroit 1949
Pifferini, Bob, LB, UCLA, Chi. Bears 1972-75; LA Rams 1977
Piggott, Bert, HB, Illinois, LA Dons (AAFC) 1947
Pignatelli, Carl, FB, Iowa, Cleveland 1931
Pihos, Pete, E-DE, Indiana, Philadelphia 1947-55
Pilconis, Joe, E, Temple, Philadelphia 1934, 1936-37
Pillath, Roger, T, Wisconsin, LA Rams 1965; Pittsburgh 1966
Pillers, Lawrence, DE-DT, Alcorn State, NY Jets 1976-80; San Francisco 1980-84; Atlanta 1985
Pillman, Brian, LB, Miami (Ohio), Cincinnati 1984
Pinckert, Erny, HB, USC, Boston 1932-36; Washington 1937-40
Pincura, Stan, QB, Ohio State, Cleveland 1937-38
Pinder, Cyril, RB, Illinois, Philadelphia 1968, Chi. Bears 1971-72; Dallas 1973
Pine, Eddie, LB, Utah, San Francisco 1962-64; Pittsburgh 1965
Pingel, Johnny, HB, Michigan State, Detroit 1939
Pinkney, Reggie, S, East Carolina, Detroit 1977-78, Baltimore 1979-81
Pinney, Ray, C-T, Washington, Pittsburgh 1976-78, 1980-82, 1985
Piper, Scott, WR, Arizona, Atlanta 1976
Pipkin, Joyce, E, Arkansas, NY Giants 1948; LA Dons (AAFC) 1949
Piro, Hank, E, Syracuse, Philadelphia 1941
Pirro, Rocco, G, Catholic, Pittsburgh 1940-41; Buffalo (AAFC) 1946-49
Pisarcik, Joe, QB, New Mexico State, NY Giants 1977-79; Philadelphia 1980-84
Pisarkiewicz, Steve, QB, Missouri, St. Louis 1978-79; Green Bay 1980
Piskor, Roman, T, Niagara, NY Yankees (AAFC) 1946; Cleveland (AAFC) 1947; Chi. Rockets (AAFC) 1948
Pitcock, Chuck, C-G, Tulane, New Orleans 1985
Pittman, Charlie, RB, Penn State, St. Louis 1970; Baltimore 1971
Pittman, Danny, WR-KR, Wyoming, NY Giants 1980-83; St. Louis 1983-84
Pittman, Mel, C, Hardin-Simmons, Pittsburgh 1935
Pitts, Edwin (Alabama), HB, Philadelphia 1935
Pitts, Elijah, RB, Philander Smith, Green Bay 1961-69, 1971; LA Rams 1970; New Orleans 1970
Pitts, Frank, WR, Southern, Kansas City 1965-70; Cleveland 1971-73; Oakland 1974
Pitts, Hugh, LB, TCU, LA Rams 1956; Houston 1960
Pitts, John, S, Arizona State, Buffalo 1967-73; Denver 1973-75; Cleveland 1975
Pitts, Mike, DE, Alabama, Atlanta 1983-85
Pivarnik, Joe, G, Notre Dame, Philadelphia 1936
Pivec, Dave, TE, Notre Dame, LA Rams 1966-68; Denver 1969
Plank, Doug, S, Ohio State, Chi. Bears 1975-82
Plank, Earl, E, Columbus 1926; Buffalo 1929; Brooklyn 1930
Plansky, Tony, FB-HB, Georgetown (Washington D.C.), NY Giants 1928-29; Boston 1932
Planutis, Jerry, FB, Michigan State, Washington 1956
Plasman, Dick, E, Vanderbilt, Chi. Bears 1937-41, 1946; Chi. Cardinals 1946-47
Platukas, George, E, Duquesne, Pittsburgh 1938-41; Cleveland 1942
Pleasant, Mike, WR, Oklahoma, LA Rams 1984
Pleasant, Reggie, CB, Clemson, Atlanta 1985
Pliska, Joe, HB, Notre Dame, Hammond 1920-21
Plum, Milt, QB, Penn State, Cleveland 1957-61; Detroit 1962-67; LA Rams 1968; NY Giants 1969
Plummer, Tony, S, Pacific, St. Louis 1970; Atlanta 1971-73; LA Rams 1974
Plump, Dave, DB, Fresno State, San Diego 1966
Plumridge, Ted, C, St. John's (New York), Brooklyn 1926
Plunkett, Art, T, Nevada-Las Vegas, St. Louis 1981-84; New England 1985
Plunkett, Jim, QB, Stanford, New England 1971-75; San Francisco 1976-77; Oakland 1978-81; LA Raiders 1982-85
Plunkett, Sherman, T, Maryland-Eastern Shore, Baltimore 1958-60; NY Titans 1961-62; NY Jets 1963-67
Plunkett, Warren, QB, Minnesota, Cleveland 1942
Ply, Bobby, DB, Baylor, Dallas Texans 1962; Kansas City 1963-67; Buffalo 1967; Denver 1967
Poage, Ray, TE, Texas, Minnesota 1963; Philadelphia 1964-65; New Orleans 1967-70; Atlanta 1971
Podmajerski, Paul, G, Illinois, Chi. Bears 1944
Podolak, Ed, RB-KR, Iowa, Kansas City 1969-77
Podoley, Jim, HB, Central Michigan, Washington 1957-60
Poe, Johnnie, CB, Missouri, New Orleans 1981-85
Pohlman, John, FB, Brown, Providence 1925
Poillon, Dick, HB, Canisius, Washington 1942, 1946-49
Poimbeouf, Lance, G, Southwestern Louisiana, Dallas 1963
Pokorny, Frank, WR, Youngstown State, Pittsburgh 1985
Polanski, John, FB, Wake Forest, Detroit 1942; LA Dons (AAFC) 1946
Pollard, Al, HB, Army, NY Yanks 1951; Philadelphia 1951-53
Pollard, Bob, DT, Weber State, New Orleans 1971-77; St. Louis 1978-81
Pollard, Frank, RB, Baylor, Pittsburgh 1980-85
Pollard, Fritz, HB, Brown, Akron 1920-21, 1925-26; Milwaukee 1922; Hammond 1923-25; Providence 1925
Polley, Tom, LB, Nevada-Las Vegas, Philadelphia 1985
Pollock, Bill (Red), HB, Widener, Chi. Bears 1935-36
Polofsky, Gordon, LB, Tennessee, Chi. Cardinals 1952-54
Polowski, Larry, LB, Boise State, Seattle 1979
Polsfoot, Fran, E, Washington State, Chi. Cardinals 1950-52; Washington 1953
Poltl, Randy, S, Stanford, Minnesota 1974; Denver 1975-77
Ponder, David, DT, Florida State, Dallas 1985
Pool, Hampton, E, Stanford, Chi. Bears 1940-43; Miami (AAFC) 1946
Poole, Barney, E-DE, Army, Mississippi, NY Yankees (AAFC) 1949; NY Yanks 1950-51; Dallas 1952; Baltimore 1953; NY Giants 1954
Poole, Bob, TE, Clemson, San Francisco 1964-65; Houston 1966-67
Poole, Jim, E, Mississippi, NY Giants 1937-41, 1945-46; Chi. Cardinals 1945
Poole, Ken, DE, Northeast Louisiana, Miami 1981
Poole, Larry, RB, Kent State, Cleveland 1975-77; Houston 1978
Poole, Nathan, RB, Louisville, Cincinnati 1979-80; Denver 1982-83, 1985
Poole, Oliver, E, Mississippi, NY Yankees (AAFC) 1947; Baltimore (AAFC) 1948; Detroit 1949
Poole, Ray, E, Mississippi, NY Giants 1947-52
Poole, Steve, LB, Tennessee, NY Jets 1976
Popa, Eli, LB, Illinois, Chi. Cardinals 1952
Pope, Bucky, SE, Catawba, LA Rams 1964, 1966-67; Green Bay 1968
Pope, Ken, DB, Oklahoma, New England 1974
Pope, Lew, FB, Purdue, Providence 1931; Cincinnati 1933-34
Popovich, John, HB, St. Vincent, Card-Pitt 1944; Pittsburgh 1945
Popovich, Milt, FB, Montana, Chi. Cardinals 1938-42
Porter, Lewis, DB, Southern, Kansas City 1970
Porter, Ricky, RB, Slippery Rock, Detroit 1982; Baltimore 1983
Porter, Ron, LB, Idaho, Baltimore 1967-69; Philadelphia 1969-72; Minnesota 1973
Porter, Tracy, WR, LSU, Detroit 1981-82; Baltimore 1983; Indianapolis 1984
Porter, Willie, DB, Texas Southern, Boston 1968
Porterfield, Garry, TE, Tulsa, Dallas 1965
Posey, David, K, Florida, New England 1978
Post, Bobby, DB, Merchant Marine, NY Giants 1967
Post, Dickie, HB, Houston, San Diego 1967-70; Denver 1971; Houston 1971
Postus, Al, HB, Villanova, Pittsburgh 1945
Poth, Phil, G, Gonzaga, Philadelphia 1934
Poto, John, HB, Boston 1947-48
Potteiger, Earl, QB, Ursinus, Buffalo 1920; Chi. Cardinals 1921; Milwaukee 1922; Kenosha 1924; NY Giants 1925-28
Potter, Kevin, S, Missouri, Houston 1983; Chi. Bears 1983-84
Potter, Steve, LB, Virginia, Miami 1981-82; Kansas City 1983; Buffalo 1984
Pottios, Myron, LB, Notre Dame, Pittsburgh 1961, 1963-65; LA Rams 1966-70; Washington 1971-74
Potts, Bill, HB, Villanova, Pittsburgh 1934
Potts, Bob (Daddy), T, Clemson, Frankford 1926
Potts, Charles, DB, Purdue, Detroit 1972
Pough, Ernie, WR, Texas Southern, Pittsburgh 1976-77; NY Giants 1978
Powe, Karl, WR, Alabama State, Dallas 1985
Powell, Art, SE, San Jose State, Philadelphia 1959; NY Titans 1960-62; Oakland 1963-66; Buffalo 1967; Minnesota 1968
Powell, Charley, DE, San Francisco 1952-53, 1955-57; Oakland 1960-61
Powell, Darnell, RB, Tennessee-Chattanooga, Buffalo 1976; NY Jets 1978
Powell, Dick (Tiny), E, Davis & Elkins, NY Giants 1932; Cincinnati 1933
Powell, Jesse, LB, West Texas State, Miami 1969-73

Powell, Marvin, T, USC, NY Jets 1977-85
Powell, Preston, FB, Grambling, Cleveland 1961
Powell, Roger, E, Texas A&M, Buffalo 1926
Powell, Steve, RB, Northeast Missouri State, Buffalo 1978-79
Powell, Tim, DE, Northwestern, LA Rams 1965; Pittsburgh 1966
Powers, Clyde, S, Oklahoma, NY Giants 1974-77
Powers, Jim, QB, USC, San Francisco 1950-53
Powers, John, SE, Notre Dame, Pittsburgh 1962-66
Powers, Sam, G, Northern Michigan, Green Bay 1921
Powers, Warren, DB, Nebraska, Oakland 1963-68
Pozderac, Phil, T, Notre Dame, Dallas 1982-85
Prater, Dean, DE, Oklahoma State, Kansas City 1982-83; Buffalo 1984-85
Prather, Dale, E, George Washington, Cleveland 1937-38
Prather, Guy, LB, Grambling, Green Bay 1981-85
Pratt, Robert, G, North Carolina, Baltimore 1974-81; Seattle 1982-85
Prchlik, John, T, Yale, Detroit 1949-53
Preas, George, T, Virginia Tech, Baltimore 1955-65
Prebola, Gene, SE, Boston U., Oakland 1960; Denver 1961-63
Preece, Steve, S, Oregon State, New Orleans 1969; Philadelphia 1970-72; Denver 1972; LA Rams 1973-76; Seattle 1977
Pregulman, Merv, G, Michigan, Green Bay 1946; Detroit 1947-48; NY Bulldogs 1949
Prescott, Harold (Ace), E, Hardin-Simmons, Green Bay 1946; Philadelphia 1947-49; NY Bulldogs 1949
Presnell, Glenn, QB, Nebraska, Portsmouth 1931-33; Detroit 1934-36
Pressley, Lee, C, Oklahoma, Washington 1945
Prestel, Jim, DT, Idaho, Cleveland 1960; Minnesota 1961-65; NY Giants 1966; Washington 1967
Preston, Dave, RB, Bowling Green, Denver 1978-83
Preston, Pat, G, Wake Forest, Chi. Bears 1946-49
Preston, Ray, LB, Syracuse, San Diego 1976-84
Prestridge, Luke, P, Baylor, Denver 1979-83; New England 1984
Prewitt, Felton, C, Tulsa, Buffalo (AAFC) 1946-48; Baltimore (AAFC) 1949
Priatko, Bill, LB, Pittsburgh, Pittsburgh 1957
Price, Charles (Cotton), QB, Texas A&M, Detroit 1940-41, 1945; Miami (AAFC) 1946
Price, Eddie, FB, Tulane, NY Giants 1950-55
Price, Elex, DT, Alcorn State, New Orleans 1973-80
Price, Ernie, DE-DT, Texas A&I, Detroit 1973-78; Seattle 1978-79; Cleveland 1979
Price, Jim, LB, Auburn, NY Jets 1963; Denver 1964
Price, Sam, RB, Illinois, Miami 1966-68
Pricer, Billy, FB, Oklahoma, Baltimore 1957-60; Dallas Texans 1961
Pride, Dan, LB, Jackson State, Chi. Bears 1968-69
Pridemore, Tom, S, West Virginia, Atlanta 1978-85
Priestley, Bob, E, Brown, Philadelphia 1942
Principe, Dom, FB, Fordham, NY Giants 1940-42; Brooklyn (AAFC) 1946
Pringle, Alan, K, Rice, Detroit 1975
Print, Bob, LB, Dayton, San Diego 1967-68
Prior, Mike, S, Illinois State, Tampa Bay 1985
Prisby, Errol, DB, Cincinnati, Denver 1967
Prisco, Nick, HB, Rutgers, Philadelphia 1933
Pritchard, Bill, FB-HB, Penn State, Providence 1927; NY Yankees 1928
Pritchard, Bosh, HB, Virginia Military, Cleveland 1942; Philadelphia 1942, 1946-49, 1951; NY Giants 1951
Pritchard, Ron, LB, Arizona State, Houston 1969-72; Cincinnati 1972-77
Pritchett, Billy, FB, West Texas State, Cleveland 1975; Atlanta 1976-77
Pritko, Steve, E, Villanova, NY Giants 1943; Cleveland 1944-45; LA Rams 1946-47; Boston 1948; NY Bulldogs 1949; Green Bay 1949-50
Prochaska, Ray, E, Nebraska, Cleveland 1941
Proctor, Dewey, HB, Furman, NY Yankees (AAFC) 1946-47, 1949; Chi. Rockets (AAFC) 1948
Proctor, Rex, DB, Rice, Chi. Bears 1953
Profit, Joe, RB, Northeast Louisiana, Atlanta 1971-73; New Orleans 1973
Prokop, Eddie, FB, Georgia Tech, NY Yankees (AAFC) 1946-47, 1949; Chi. Rockets (AAFC) 1948
Prokop, Joe, HB, Bradley, Chi. Rockets (AAFC) 1948
Prokop, Joe, P, Cal Poly-Pomona, Green Bay 1985
Promuto, Vince, G, Holy Cross, Washington 1960-70
Protz, Jack, LB, Syracuse, San Diego 1970
Prout, Bob, DB, Knox, Oakland 1974; NY Jets 1975
Provence, Andrew, NT, South Carolina, Atlanta 1983-85
Provo, Fred, HB, Washington, Green Bay 1948
Provost, Ted, DB, Ohio State, Minnesota 1970; St. Louis 1971
Prudhomme, Remi, G-C, LSU, Buffalo 1966-67, 1972; Kansas City 1968-69; New Orleans 1971-72
Pruett, Perry, DB, North Texas State, New England 1971
Pruitt, Greg, RB-KR, Oklahoma, Cleveland 1973-81; LA Raiders 1982-84
Pruitt, Mike, RB, Purdue, Cleveland 1976-84; Buffalo 1985; Kansas City 1985
Pryor, Barry, RB, Boston U., Miami 1969-70
Psaltis, Jim, HB, USC, Chi. Cardinals 1953-54; Green Bay 1955
Ptacek, Bob, QB, Michigan, Cleveland 1959
Pucci, Ben, T-DT, Buffalo (AAFC) 1946; Chi. Rockets (AAFC) 1947; Cleveland (AAFC) 1948
Puddy, Hal, T, Oregon State, San Francisco (AAFC) 1948
Pudloski, Chet, T, Villanova, Cleveland 1944
Puetz, Garry, G-T, Valparaiso, NY Jets 1973-78; Tampa Bay 1978; Philadelphia 1979; New England 1979-81; Washington 1982
Pugh, Howard, T, Toledo, Milwaukee 1922
Pugh, Jethro, DT, Elizabeth City State, Dallas 1965-78
Pugh, Marion, QB, Texas A&M, NY Giants 1941-45; Miami (AAFC) 1946
Puki, Craig, LB, Tennessee, San Francisco 1980-81; St. Louis 1982
Puplis, Andy, HB, Notre Dame, Chi. Cardinals 1943
Purdin, Cal, HB, Tulsa, Chi. Cardinals 1943; Miami (AAFC) 1946; Brooklyn (AAFC) 1946
Purdy, Clair, HB, Brown, Rochester 1920; NY Giants 1921; Milwaukee 1922
Purdy, Everette (Pid), QB, Beloit, Green Bay 1926-27
Pureifory, Dave, DE-DT, Eastern Michigan, Green Bay 1972-77; Cincinnati 1978; Detroit 1978-82
Purnell, Frank, FB, Alcorn State, Green Bay 1957
Purnell, Jim, LB, Wisconsin, Chi. Bears 1964, 1966-68; LA Rams 1969-72
Purvis, Vic, DB, Southern Mississippi, Boston 1966-67
Putman, Earl, C, Arizona State, Chi. Cardinals 1957
Putnam, Duane, G, Pacific, LA Rams 1952-59, 1962; Dallas Cowboys 1960; Cleveland 1961
Putzier, Fred, HB, St. Olaf, Minneapolis 1924
Puzzouli, Dave, NT, Pittsburgh, Cleveland 1983-85
Pyburn, Jack, T, Texas A&M, Miami 1967-68
Pyeatt, John, DB, Denver 1960-61
Pyle, Mike, C, Yale, Chi. Bears 1961-69
Pyle, Palmer, G, Michigan State, Baltimore 1960-63; Minnesota 1964; Oakland 1966
Pylman, Bob, T, South Dakota State, Philadelphia 1938-39
Pyne, George, T, Holy Cross, Providence 1931
Pyne, George, DT, Olivet, Boston 1965

Q

Quam, Charles (Red), HB, Duluth 1926
Quast, John, E, Purdue, Louisville 1923
Quatse, Jess, T, Pittsburgh, Green Bay 1933; Pittsburgh 1933-34; NY Giants 1935
Quayle, Frank, RB, Virginia, Denver 1969
Queen, Jeff, RB-TE, Morgan State, San Diego 1969-71; Oakland 1972-73; Houston 1974
Quick, Mike, WR, North Carolina State, Philadelphia 1982-85
Quigley, Gerald (Red), QB, Rochester 1920
Quillan, Fred, C, Oregon, San Francisco 1978-85
Quillen, Frank, E, Pennsylvania, Chi. Rockets (AAFC) 1946-47
Quilter, Charley, T, Tyler J.C., San Francisco 1949-50
Quinlan, Billy, DE, Michigan State, Cleveland 1957-58; Green Bay 1959-62; Philadelphia 1963; Detroit 1964; Washington 1965
Quinlan, Volney (Skeet), HB, San Diego State, LA Rams 1952-56; Cleveland 1956
Quinn, George (Paddy), HB, Rock Island 1920-21
Quinn, Ivan, G, Carroll (Wisconsin), Kansas City 1924
Quinn, Jeff, QB, Nebraska, Pittsburgh 1982; Tampa Bay 1982
Quinn, Steve, C, Notre Dame, Houston 1968
Quirk, Ed, FB-C, Missouri, Washington 1948-51

R

Raba, Bob, TE, Maryland, NY Jets 1977-79; Baltimore 1980; Washington 1981
Rabb, Warren, QB, LSU, Detroit 1960; Buffalo 1961-62
Rabold, Mike, G, Indiana, Detroit 1959; St. Louis 1960; Minnesota 1961-62; Chi. Bears 1964-67
Raborn, Carroll (Buster), C, SMU, Pittsburgh 1936-37
Racis, Frankie, G, Pottsville 1925-28; NY Yankees 1928; Boston 1929; Providence 1930; Frankford 1931
Rackley, David, CB, Texas Southern, New Orleans 1985
Radachowsky, George, S, Boston College, Indianapolis 1984-85
Rade, John, LB, Boise State, Atlanta 1983-85
Radecic, Scott, LB, Penn State, Kansas City 1984-85
Rademacher, Bill, SE, Northern Michigan, NY Jets 1964-68; Boston 1969-70
Rader, Dave, QB, Tulsa, NY Giants 1979
Radford, Bruce, DE, Grambling, Denver 1979; Tampa Bay 1980; St. Louis 1981
Radick, Ken, E, Marquette, Green Bay 1930-31; Brooklyn 1931
Radloff, Wayne, C, Georgia, Atlanta 1985
Rado, Alex (Moose), HB, New River State, Pittsburgh 1934
Rado, George, G, Duquesne, Pittsburgh 1935-37; Philadelphia 1937-38
Radosevich, George, C, Pittsburgh, Baltimore 1954-56
Radovich, Bill (Squato), G, USC, Detroit 1938-41, 1945; LA Dons (AAFC) 1946-47
Radzievich, Vic, QB-G, Connecticut, Hartford 1926
Rae, Mike, QB, USC, Oakland 1976-77; Tampa Bay 1978-80; Washington 1981
Raffel, Bill, E, Pennsylvania, Brooklyn 1932
Rafferty, Tom, G-C, Penn State, Dallas 1976-85
Rafter, Bill, FB, Syracuse, Rochester 1924
Ragazzo, Phil, T, Case Western Reserve, Cleveland 1939-40; Philadelphia 1940-41; NY Giants 1945-47
Ragsdale, George, RB-KR, North Carolina A&T, Tampa Bay 1977-79
Ragunas, Vince, LB, Virginia Military, Pittsburgh 1949
Raible, Steve, WR, Georgia Tech, Seattle 1976-81
Raiff, Jim, G, Dayton, Baltimore 1954
Raimey, Dave, DB, Michigan, Cleveland 1964
Raimondi, Ben, QB, Indiana, NY Yankees (AAFC) 1947
Rains, Dan, LB, Cincinnati, Chi. Bears 1982-84
Raines, Mike, DE-DT, Alabama, San Francisco 1974
Rajkovich, Pete, FB, Detroit, Pittsburgh 1934
Rakestraw, Larry, QB, Georgia, Chi. Bears 1964, 1966-68
Ralph, Dan, DT, Oregon, St. Louis 1984
Ramey, Jim, DE, Kentucky, St. Louis 1979
Ramona, Joe, G-LB, Santa Clara, NY Giants 1953
Ramsey, Chuck, P, Wake Forest, NY Jets 1977-84
Ramsey, Derrick, TE, Kentucky, Oakland 1978-81; LA Raiders 1982-83; New England 1983-85
Ramsey, Frank, T, Oregon State, Chi. Bears 1945
Ramsey, Garrard (Buster), G, William & Mary, Chi. Cardinals 1946-51
Ramsey, Herschel (Red), E, Texas Tech, Philadelphia 1938-40, 1945
Ramsey, Knox, G, William & Mary, LA Dons (AAFC) 1948-49; Chi. Cardinals 1950-51; Philadelphia 1952; Washington 1952-53
Ramsey, Nate, S, Indiana, Philadelphia 1963-72; New Orleans 1973
Ramsey, Ray, HB-DB, Bradley, Chi. Rockets (AAFC) 1947; Brooklyn (AAFC) 1948; Chi. Hornets (AAFC) 1949; Chi. Cardinals 1950-53
Ramsey, Steve, QB, North Texas State, New Orleans 1970; Denver 1971-76
Ramsey, Tom, QB, UCLA, New England 1985
Ramson, Eason, TE, Washington State, St. Louis 1978; San Francisco 1979-83; Buffalo 1985
Randall, Dennis, DE, Oklahoma State, NY Jets 1967; Cincinnati 1968
Randall, Tom, G, Iowa State, Dallas 1978; Houston 1979
Randels, Horace (Proc), E, Kansas State, Kansas City 1926; Cleveland 1927; Detroit 1928
Randle, Ervin, LB, Baylor, Tampa Bay 1985
Randle, Sonny, SE, Virginia, Chi. Cardinals 1959; St. Louis 1960-66; San Francisco 1967-68; Dallas 1968
Randle, Tate, S, Texas Tech, Houston 1982-83; Baltimore 1983; Indianapolis 1984-85
Randolph, Al, S, Iowa, San Francisco 1966-70, 1974; Green Bay 1971; Cincinnati 1972; Detroit 1972; Minnesota 1973; Buffalo 1974
Randolph, Clare, C, Indiana, Chi. Cardinals 1930; Portsmouth 1931-33; Detroit 1934-36
Randolph, Harry, HB, Bethany (West Virginia), Columbus 1923
Randolph, Terry, S, American International, Green Bay 1977
Rankin, Walt, FB-LB, Texas Tech, Chi. Cardinals 1941, 1943, 1945-47; Card-Pitt 1944
Ransom, Brian, QB, Tennessee State, Houston 1983-85
Ranspot, Keith, E, SMU, Chi. Cardinals 1940; Green Bay 1942; Detroit 1942; Brooklyn 1943; Boston 1944-45
Rapacz, John, C, Oklahoma, Chi. Rockets (AAFC) 1948; Chi. Hornets (AAFC) 1949; NY Giants 1950-54
Rapp, Bob, HB, Columbus 1922-26; Buffalo 1929
Rapp, Herb, C, Xavier, Staten Island 1930-31
Rapp, Manny, HB, St. Louis, St. Louis 1934
Rascher, Amby, T, Indiana, Portsmouth 1932
Rash, Lou, CB-S, Mississippi Valley State, Philadelphia 1984
Rashad, Ahmad (Bobby Moore), WR, Oregon, St. Louis 1972-73; Buffalo 1974; Minnesota 1976-82
Raskowski, Leon, T, Ohio State, Staten Island 1932; Brooklyn 1933; Pittsburgh 1933; Philadelphia 1935
Rasley, Rocky, G, Oregon State, Detroit 1969-70, 1972 73; New Orleans 1974; Kansas City 1975
Rasmussen, Randy, G, Kearney State, NY Jets 1967-81
Rasmussen, Randy, C-G, Minnesota, Pittsburgh 1984-85
Rasmussen, Wayne, S, South Dakota State, Detroit 1964-72
Rassas, Nick, DB, Notre Dame, Atlanta 1966-68
Rate, Ed, HB, Purdue, Milwaukee 1923
Ratekin, Roy, T, Colorado State, Akron 1921
Rather, Bo, WR, Michigan, Miami 1973, 1978; Chi. Bears 1974-78
Ratica, Joe, C, St. Vincent, Brooklyn 1939
Ratkowski, Ray, HB, Notre Dame, Boston 1961
Ratliff, Don, DE, Maryland, Philadelphia 1975
Ratterman, George, QB, Notre Dame, Buffalo (AAFC) 1947-49; NY Yankees 1950-51; Cleveland 1952-56
Rauch, Dick, G, Penn State, Toledo 1922; Pottsville 1925; NY Yankees 1928
Rauch, Johnny, QB, Georgia, NY Bulldogs 1949; NY Yanks 1950-51; Philadelphia 1951
Ravensburg, Bob, E, Indiana, Chi. Cardinals 1948-49
Rawlings, Bob, FB, Georgetown (Washington D.C.), Buffalo 1922
Ray, Art, G, Holy Cross, Buffalo 1926
Ray, Buford (Baby), T, Vanderbilt, Green Bay 1938-48
Ray, David, K, Alabama, LA Rams 1969-74
Ray, Darrol, S, Oklahoma, NY Jets 1980-84
Ray, Eddie, FB, LSU, Boston 1970; San Diego 1971; Atlanta 1972-74; Buffalo 1976
Ray, Ricky, CB, Norfolk State, New Orleans 1979-81; Miami 1981-82
Rayburn, Van, E, Tennessee, Brooklyn 1933

Raye, Jimmy, DB, Michigan State, Philadelphia 1969
Rayhle, Fred, TE, Tennessee-Chattanooga, Seattle 1977
Razzano, Rick, LB, Virginia Tech, Cincinnati 1980-84
Read, Jack, G, Akron 1921
Reader, Russ, HB, Michigan State, Chi. Bears 1947
Reagan, Frankie, HB, Pennsylvania, NY Giants 1941, 1946-48; Philadelphia 1949-51
Reagen, Ed, T, Brooklyn 1926
Ream, Chuck, T, Ohio State, Cleveland 1938
Reamon, Tommy, RB, Missouri, Kansas City 1976
Reardon, Kerry, S, Iowa, Kansas City 1971-76
Reasons, Gary, LB, Northwestern State (Louisiana), NY Giants 1984-85
Reaves, John, QB, Florida, Philadelphia 1972-74; Cincinnati 1975-78; Minnesota 1979; Houston 1981
Reaves, Ken, CB, Norfolk State, Atlanta 1966-73; New Orleans 1974; St. Louis 1974-77
Reavis, Dave, T, Arkansas, Pittsburgh 1974-75; Tampa Bay 1976-83
Rebowe, Rusty, LB, Nicholls State, New Orleans 1978
Rebseaman, Paul, C, Centenary, Pottsville 1927
Recher, Dave, C, Iowa, Philadelphia 1965-68
Rechichar, Bert, LB-DB-K, Tennessee, Cleveland 1952; Baltimore 1953-59; Pittsburgh 1960; NY Titans 1961
Reckmack, Ray, QB, Syracuse, Detroit 1937; Brooklyn 1937
Rector, Ron, RB, Northwestern, Washington 1966; Atlanta 1966-67
Recutt, Ray, E, Virginia Military, Phil-Pitt 1943
Red Fang, T, Oorang 1922-23
Red Foot, E, Oorang 1923
Red Fox, HB, Oorang 1922-23
Redd, Glen, LB, BYU, New Orleans 1981, 1983-85
Redden, Barry, RB-KR, Richmond, LA Rams 1982-85
Redinger, Otis, HB, Penn State, Canton 1925
Redman, Rick, LB-P, Washington, San Diego 1965-73
Redmond, Gus, HB, Dayton 1920-22, 1924
Redmond, Rudy, CB, Pacific, Atlanta 1969-71; Detroit 1971-73
Redmond, Tom, DE, Vanderbilt, St. Louis 1960-65
Redwine, Jarvis, RB-KR, Nebraska, Minnesota 1981-83
Reeberg, Lucien, T, Hampton, Detroit 1963
Reece, Beasley, S, North Texas State, Dallas 1976; NY Giants 1977-83; Tampa Bay 1983-84
Reece, Danny, DB-KR, USC, Tampa Bay 1976-80
Reece, Don, T-FB, Missouri, Miami (AAFC) 1946
Reece, Geoff, C, Washington State, LA Rams 1976; Seattle 1977; Baltimore 1978
Reed, Andre, WR, Kutztown, Buffalo 1985
Reed, Alvin, TE, Prairie View A&M, Houston 1967-72; Washington 1973-75
Reed, Bob, HB, Pacific, Minnesota 1962-63
Reed, Doug, DE, San Diego State, LA Rams 1984-85
Reed, Frank, DB, Washington, Atlanta 1976-80
Reed, Henry, LB-DE, Weber State, NY Giants 1971-74
Reed, James, LB, California, Philadelphia 1977
Reed, Joe, HB, LSU, Chi. Cardinals 1937, 1939
Reed, Joe, QB, Mississippi State, San Francisco 1972-74; Detroit 1975-79
Reed, Leo, G, Colorado State, Houston 1961; Denver 1961
Reed, Mark, QB, Moorhead State, NY Giants 1982
Reed, Oscar, RB, Colorado State, Minnesota 1964-74; Atlanta 1975
Reed, Robert, G, Tennessee State, Washington 1965
Reed, Smith, RB, Alcorn State, NY Giants 1965-66
Reed, Taft, RB, Jackson State, Philadelphia 1967
Reed, Tony, RB, Colorado, Kansas City 1977-80; Denver 1981
Reese, Archie, DT-NT, Clemson, San Francisco 1978-81; LA Raiders 1982-83
Reese, Booker, DE, Bethune-Cookman, Tampa Bay 1982-84; LA Rams 1984-85
Reese, Dave, E, Denison, Dayton 1920-23
Reese, Don, DE-DT, Jackson State, Miami 1974-76; New Orleans 1978-80; San Diego 1981
Reese, Guy, T, SMU, Dallas 1962-63; Baltimore 1964-65; Atlanta 1966
Reese, Hank, C, Temple, NY Giants 1933-34; Philadelphia 1935-39
Reese, Jerry, S, Oklahoma, Kansas City 1979-80
Reese, Ken, HB, Alabama, Detroit 1947
Reese, Lloyd, FB, Tennessee, Chi. Bears 1946
Reese, Steve, LB, Louisville, NY Jets 1974-75; Tampa Bay 1976
Reeve, Lew, T, Iowa State, Chi. Tigers 1920
Reeves, Dan, RB, South Carolina, Dallas 1965-72
Reeves, Ken, G-T, Texas A&M, Philadelphia 1985
Reeves, Marion, DB, Clemson, Philadelphia 1974
Reeves, Roy, WR, South Carolina, Buffalo 1969
Regan, Jim, QB, Still, Columbus 1925
Reger, John, LB, Pittsburgh, Pittsburgh 1955-63; Washington 1964-66
Regner, Tom, G-T, Notre Dame, Houston 1967-72
Regnier, Pete, HB, Minnesota, Minneapolis 1921-22; Green Bay 1922
Rehnquist, Milt, G, Bethany (Kansas), Kansas City 1924-26; Cleveland 1925, 1927; Providence 1928-31; NY Giants 1931; Boston 1932
Reich, Frank, QB, Maryland, Buffalo 1985
Reichardt, Bill, FB, Iowa, Green Bay 1952
Reichenbach, Mike, LB, East Stroudsburg, Philadelphia 1984-85
Reichle, Dick, E, Illinois, Milwaukee 1923
Reichle, Lou, C, Butler, Columbus 1926
Reichow, Charlie, HB, St. Thomas (Minnesota), Racine 1926
Reichow, Jerry, FL-TE, Iowa, Detroit 1956-57, 1959; Philadelphia 1960; Minnesota 1961-64
Reid, Andy, RB, Georgia, Buffalo 1976
Reid, Bill, C, Stanford, San Francisco 1975
Reid, Floyd (Breezy), HB, Georgia, Chi. Bears 1950; Green Bay 1950-56
Reid, Joe, C, LSU, LA Rams 1951; Dallas 1952
Reid, Mike, DT, Penn State, Cincinnati 1970-74
Reifsnyder, Bob, DE, Navy, NY Titans 1960-61
Reihner, George, G, Penn State, Houston 1977-79, 1982
Reilly, Jim, G, Notre Dame, Buffalo 1970-71
Reilly, Kevin, LB, Villanova, Philadelphia 1973-74; New England 1975
Reilly, Mike, LB, Iowa, Chi. Bears 1964-68; Minnesota 1969
Reilly, Mike, LB, Oklahoma, LA Rams 1982
Reimers, Bruce, T, Iowa State, Cincinnati 1984-85
Reinfeldt, Mike, S, Wisconsin-Milwaukee, Oakland 1976; Houston 1976-83
Reinhard, Bill, HB, California, LA Dons (AAFC) 1947-48
Reinhard, Bob, T-DT, California, LA Dons (AAFC) 1946-49; LA Rams 1950
Reiser, Earl, HB, Louisville 1923
Reissig, Bill, QB, Fort Hays State, Brooklyn 1938-39
Reisz, Al, HB-QB, Southeastern Louisiana, Cleveland 1944-45; LA Rams 1946; Buffalo (AAFC) 1947
Reiter, Wilbur, G, West Virginia Wesleyan, Dayton 1926-27
Rembert, Johnny, LB, Clemson, New England 1983-85
Remington, Bill, C, Washington State, San Francisco (AAFC) 1946
Remmert, Dennis, LB, Iowa State, Buffalo 1960
Renfro, Dean, HB, North Texas State, Baltimore 1955
Renfro, Dick, FB, Washington State, San Francisco (AAFC) 1946
Renfro, Mel, DB-KR, Oregon, Dallas 1964-77
Renfro, Mike, WR, TCU, Houston 1978-83; Dallas 1984-85
Renfro, Ray, HB-FL, North Texas State, Cleveland 1952-63
Renfro, Will, DT, Memphis State, Washington 1957-59; Pittsburgh 1960; Philadelphia 1961
Rengel, Mike, DT, Hawaii, New Orleans 1969
Renn, Bob, HB, Florida State, NY Titans 1961
Rennaker, Terry, LB, Stanford, Seattle 1980
Rentner, Ernest (Pug), FB, Northwestern, Boston 1934-36; Chi. Bears 1937
Rentz, Larry, WR, Florida, San Diego 1969
Rentzel, Lance, WR, Oklahoma, Minnesota 1965-66; Dallas 1967-70; LA Rams 1971-72, 1974
Repko, Joe, T, Boston College, Pittsburgh 1946-47, LA Rams 1948-49
Reppond, Mike, WR, Arkansas, Chi. Bears 1973
Ressler, Glenn, G-T, Penn State, Baltimore 1965-74
Restic, Joe, DB, Villanova, Philadelphia 1952
Retzlaff, Pete, SE-TE, South Dakota State, Philadelphia 1956-66
Reuter, Vic, C, Lafayette, Staten Island 1932
Reutershan, Randy, WR, Pittsburgh, Pittsburgh 1978
Ruett, Ray, E, Virginia Military, Phil-Pitt 1943
Reveiz, Fuad, K, Tennessee, Miami 1985
Rexer, Freeman, E, Tulane, Chi. Cardinals 1943, 1945; Detroit 1944; Boston 1944
Reynolds, Al, G, Tarkio, Dallas Texans 1960-62; Kansas City 1963-67
Reynolds, Bill, HB, Mississippi, Brooklyn 1944; Chi. Cardinals 1945
Reynolds, Billy, HB, Pittsburgh, Cleveland 1953-54, 1957; Pittsburgh 1958; Oakland 1960
Reynolds, Bob, T, Stanford, Detroit 1937-38
Reynolds, Bob, T, Bowling Green, St. Louis 1963-71, 1973; New England 1972-73
Reynolds, Chuck, C-G, Tulsa, Cleveland 1969-70
Reynolds, Ed, LB, Virginia, New England 1983-85
Reynolds, Homer, G, Tulsa, St. Louis 1934
Reynolds, Jack (Hacksaw), LB, Tennessee, LA Rams 1970-80; San Francisco 1981-84
Reynolds, Jim, FB, Oklahoma State, Pittsburgh 1946
Reynolds, Jim, HB, Auburn, Miami (AAFC) 1946
Reynolds, John, C, Baylor, Chi. Cardinals 1937
Reynolds, M.C. (Mack), QB, LSU, Chi. Cardinals 1958-59; Washington 1960; Buffalo 1961; Oakland 1962
Reynolds, Owen, E-FB, Georgia, NY Giants 1925; Brooklyn 1926
Reynolds, Quentin, T, Brown, Brooklyn 1926
Reynolds, Tom, WR, San Diego State, New England 1972; Chi. Bears 1973
Rhea, Floyd, G, Oregon, Chi. Cardinals 1943; Brooklyn 1944; Boston 1945; Detroit 1947
Rhea, Hugh, G, Nebraska, Brooklyn 1933
Rhenstrom, Elmer, E, Beloit, Racine 1922
Rhodemyre, Jay, C, Kentucky, Green Bay 1948-49, 1951-52
Rhodes, Bruce, S-KR, Cal State-San Francisco, San Francisco 1976; Detroit 1978
Rhodes, Danny, LB, Arkansas, Baltimore 1974
Rhodes, Don, T, Washington & Jefferson, Pittsburgh 1933
Rhodes, Ray, DB-WR, Tulsa, NY Giants 1974-79; San Francisco 1980
Rhome, Jerry, QB, Tulsa, Dallas 1965-67; Cleveland 1969; Houston 1970; LA Rams 1971
Rhone, Earnie, LB, Henderson State, Miami 1975, 1977-84
Rhymes, Buster, WR, Oklahoma, Minnesota 1985
Ribar, Frank, G, Duke, Washington 1943
Ribble, Loran (Babe), G, Hardin-Simmons, Portsmouth 1932; Chi. Cardinals 1933; Pittsburgh 1934-35
Riblett, Paul, E, Pennsylvania, Brooklyn 1932-36
Ricardo, Benny, K, San Diego State, Buffalo 1976; Detroit 1976, 1978-79; New Orleans 1980-81; Minnesota 1983; San Diego 1984
Ricca, Jim, DT, Georgetown (Washington D.C.), Washington 1951-54; Detroit 1955; Philadelphia 1955-56
Rice, Allen, RB-S, Baylor, Minnesota 1984-85
Rice, Andy, DT, Texas Southern, Kansas City 1966-67; Houston 1967; Cincinnati 1968-69; San Diego 1970-71; Chi. Bears 1972-73
Rice, Bill, C-QB, NY Giants 1929
Rice, Floyd, LB-TE, Alcorn State, Houston 1971-73; San Diego 1973-75; Oakland 1976-77; New Orleans 1978
Rice, George, DT, LSU, Houston 1966-69
Rice, Harold, DE, Tennessee State, Oakland 1971
Rice, Jerry, WR, Mississippi Valley State, San Francisco 1985
Rice, Ken, T, Auburn, Buffalo 1961, 1963; Oakland 1964-65; Miami 1966-67
Rich, Herb, DB, Vanderbilt, Baltimore 1950; LA Rams 1951-53; NY Giants 1954-56
Rich, Randy, S, New Mexico, Denver 1977; Detroit 1977; Oakland 1978; Cleveland 1978-79
Richards, Bobby, DE, LSU, Philadelphia 1962-65; Atlanta 1966-67
Richards, Dick, HB, Kentucky, Brooklyn 1933
Richards, Elvin (Kink), FB-HB, Simpson, NY Giants 1933-39
Richards, Golden, WR, Hawaii, Dallas 1973-78; Chi. Bears 1978-79
Richards, Howard, T, Missouri, Dallas 1981-85
Richards, Jim, DB, Virginia Tech, NY Jets 1968-69
Richards, Perry, SE, Detroit, Pittsburgh 1957; Detroit 1958; Chi. Cardinals 1959; St. Louis 1960; Buffalo 1961; NY Titans 1962
Richards, Pete, C, Swarthmore, Frankford 1927
Richards, Ray, G, Nebraska, Frankford 1930; Chi. Bears 1933, 1935; Detroit 1934
Richardson, Al, LB, Georgia Tech, Atlanta 1980-85
Richardson, Alvin, DE, Grambling, Boston 1960
Richardson, Bob (Red), DB, UCLA, Denver 1966
Richardson, Charlie, QB, Milwaukee 1925
Richardson, Eric, WR, San Jose State, Buffalo 1985
Richardson, Gloster, WR, Jackson State, Kansas City 1967-70; Dallas 1971; Cleveland 1972-74
Richardson, Grady, TE, Cal State-Fullerton, Washington 1979-80
Richardson, Jeff, T-C, Michigan State, NY Jets 1967-68; Miami 1969
Richardson, Jerry, FL, Wofford, Baltimore 1959-60
Richardson, Jerry, DB, West Texas State, LA Rams 1964-65; Atlanta 1966-67
Richardson, Jess, DT, Alabama, Philadelphia 1953-56, 1958-61; Boston 1962-64
Richardson, John, DT, UCLA, Miami 1967-71; St. Louis 1972-73
Richardson, Mike, RB, SMU, Houston 1969-71
Richardson, Mike, CB, Arizona State, Chi. Bears 1983-85
Richardson, Pete, DB, Dayton, Buffalo 1969-71
Richardson, Tom, WR, Jackson State, Boston 1969-70
Richardson, Willie, WR, Jackson State, Baltimore 1963-69, 1971; Miami 1970
Richeson, Ray, G, Alabama, Chi. Hornets (AAFC) 1949
Richey, Mike, T, North Carolina, Buffalo 1969; New Orleans 1970
Richins, Al, HB, Utah, Detroit 1953
Richter, Frank, LB, Georgia, Denver 1967-69
Richter, Hal, T, Otterbein, Louisville 1926; Columbus 1926
Richter, Les, LB, California, LA Rams 1954-62
Richter, Pat, TE-P, Wisconsin, Washington 1963-70
Rickards, Paul, QB, Pittsburgh, LA Rams 1948
Ricks, Lawrence, RB, Michigan, Kansas City 1983-84
Riddell, Speed, E, Nebraska, Rock Island 1920
Riddick, Ray, E, Fordham, Green Bay 1940-42, 1946
Riddick, Robb, RB-KR, Millersville, Buffalo 1981, 1983-84
Ridge, Houston, DE, San Diego State, San Diego 1966-69
Ridgway, Colin, P, Lamar, Dallas 1965
Ridlehuber, Preston, RB, Georgia, Atlanta 1966; Oakland 1968; Buffalo 1969
Ridler, Don, T, Michigan State, Cleveland 1931
Ridlon, Jim, DB, Syracuse, San Francisco 1957-62; Dallas 1963-64
Rieth, Bill, C, Carnegie-Mellon, Cleveland 1941-42, 1944-45
Rieves, Charley, LB, Houston, Oakland 1962-63; Houston 1964-65
Rifenburg, Dick, E, Michigan, Detroit 1950
Riffle, Charley, G, Notre Dame, Cleveland 1944; NY Yankees (AAFC) 1946-48
Riffle, Dick, HB, Albright, Philadelphia 1938-40; Pittsburgh 1941-42
Riggins, John, RB, Kansas, NY Jets 1971-75; Washington 1976-79, 1981-85
Riggle, Bobby, DB, Penn State, Atlanta 1966-67

Riggs, Gerald, RB, Arizona State, Atlanta 1982-85
Riggs, Thron, T, Washington, Boston 1944
Righetti, Joe, DT, Waynesburg, Cleveland 1969-70
Riley, Avon, LB, UCLA, Houston 1981-85
Riley, Butch, LB, Texas A&I, Baltimore 1969
Riley, Jack, T, Northwestern, Boston 1933
Riley, Jim, DE, Oklahoma, Miami 1967-71
Riley, Ken (Rattler), CB, Florida A&M, Cincinnati 1969-83
Riley, Larry, DB, Salem (West Virginia), Denver 1977; NY Jets 1978
Riley, Lee, DB, Detroit, Detroit 1955; Philadelphia 1956, 1958-59; NY Giants 1960; NY Titans 1961-62
Riley, Preston, WR, Memphis State, San Francisco 1970-72; New Orleans 1973
Riley, Steve, T, USC, Minnesota 1974-84
Rimington, Dave, C, Nebraska, Cincinnati 1983-85
Ring, Bill, RB, BYU, San Francisco 1981-85
Ringo, Jim, C, Syracuse, Green Bay 1953-63; Philadelphia 1964-67
Ringwalt, Carroll, C, Indiana, Portsmouth 1930; Frankford 1931
Riopel, Al, HB, Holy Cross, Providence 1925
Riordan, Charlie, E, NYU, Staten Island 1929
Risher, Alan, QB, LSU, Tampa Bay 1985
Risien, Cody, T, Texas A&M, Cleveland 1979-83, 1985
Risk, Ed, FB, Purdue, Chi. Cardinals 1932
Risley, Elliott, T, Indiana, Hammond 1921-23
Rissmiller, Ray, T, Georgia, Philadelphia 1966; New Orleans 1967; Buffalo 1968
Risvold, Ray, HB, St. Edward's (Texas), Chi. Cardinals 1927-28
Ritchart, Del, C, Colorado, Detroit 1936-37
Ritcher, Jim, G-C, North Carolina State, Buffalo 1980-85
Rivera, Gabe, DT, Texas Tech, Pittsburgh 1983
Rivera, Henry, DB, Oregon State, Oakland 1962; Buffalo 1963
Rivera, Ron, LB, California, Chi. Bears 1984-85
Rivera, Steve, WR, California, San Francisco 1976-77; Chi. Bears 1977
Rivers, Jamie, LB, Bowling Green, St. Louis 1968-73; NY Jets 1974-75
Rivers, Nate, RB, South Carolina State, NY Giants 1980
Rives, Don, LB, Texas Tech, Chi. Bears 1973-78
Rizzo, Jack, S, Lehigh, NY Giants 1973
Rizzo, Joe, LB, Merchant Marine, Denver 1974-80
Roach, Jackie, G, Louisville 1921
Roach, John, QB, SMU, Chi. Cardinals 1956, 1959; St. Louis 1960; Green Bay 1961-63; Dallas 1964
Roach, Rollin, HB, TCU, Chi. Cardinals 1927
Roach, Travis, G, Texas, NY Jets 1974
Roaches, Carl, KR-WR, Texas A&M, Houston 1980-84; New Orleans 1985
Roan, Oscar, TE, SMU, Cleveland 1975-78
Robb, Harry, QB, Penn State, Washington 1921; Canton 1921-23, 1925-26
Robb, Joe, DE, TCU, Philadelphia 1959-60; St. Louis 1961-67; Detroit 1968-71
Robb, Loyal, T, Rock Island 1920
Robb, Stan, E-HB, Centre, Canton 1926
Robbins, Jack, QB, Arkansas, Chi. Cardinals 1938-39
Robbins, Randy, CB, Arizona, Denver 1984-85
Robbins, Tootie, T, East Carolina, St. Louis 1982-85
Roberson, Bo, FL, Cornell, San Diego 1961; Oakland 1962-65; Buffalo 1965; Miami 1966
Roberson, Vern, S, Grambling, Miami 1977; San Francisco 1978
Roberts, Archie, QB, Columbia, Miami 1967
Roberts, Bill, HB, Dartmouth, Green Bay 1956
Roberts, C.R., FB, USC, San Francisco 1959-62
Roberts, Cliff, T, Illinois, Oakland 1961
Roberts, Fred, T, Iowa, Portsmouth 1930-32
Roberts, Gary, G, Purdue, Atlanta 1970
Roberts, Gene (Choo-Choo), HB, Tennessee-Chattanooga, NY Giants 1947-50
Roberts, George, P, Virginia Tech, Miami 1978-80; San Diego 1981; Atlanta 1982
Roberts, Greg, G, Oklahoma, Tampa Bay 1979-82
Roberts, Guy, HB, Iowa State, Canton 1926; Pottsville 1927
Roberts, Guy, LB, Maryland, Houston 1972-75; Atlanta 1976; Miami 1977
Roberts, Hal, P, Houston, St. Louis 1974
Roberts, Jack, HB-FB, Georgia, Boston 1932; Staten Island 1932; Philadelphia 1933-34; Pittsburgh 1934
Roberts, Jim (Red), E, Centre, Toledo 1922; Akron 1923
Roberts, Mace, E, Hammond 1920-22, 1924
Roberts, Tom, T, DePaul, NY Giants 1943; Chi. Bears 1944-45
Roberts, Walcott (Wooky), QB-HB, Navy, Canton 1922-23; Cleveland 1924-25; Frankford 1926
Roberts, Walter (The Flea), WR-KR, San Jose State, Cleveland 1964-66; New Orleans 1967; Washington 1969-70
Roberts, Wesley, DE, TCU, NY Jets 1980
Roberts, William, T, Ohio State, NY Giants 1984
Roberts, Willie, CB, Houston, Chi. Bears 1973
Robertson, Bob, C, Illinois, Houston 1968
Robertson, Bobby, HB, USC, Brooklyn 1942
Robertson, Harry, T, Syracuse, Rochester 1922
Robertson, Isiah (Butch), LB, Southern, LA Rams 1971-78; Buffalo 1979-82
Robertson, Jim, QB, Carnegie-Mellon, Akron 1924-25
Robertson, Lake, E, Mississippi, Detroit 1945
Robertson, Tom, C, Tulsa, Brooklyn 1941-42; NY Yankees (AAFC) 1946
Robeson, Paul, E, Rutgers, Hammond 1920; Akron 1921; Milwaukee 1922
Robinson, Bill, HB, Lincoln (Missouri), Green Bay 1952
Robinson, Bo, RB-TE, West Texas State, Detroit 1979-80; Atlanta 1981-83; New England 1984
Robinson, Charley, G-LB, Morgan State, Baltimore 1954
Robinson, Craig, T, Houston, New Orleans 1972-73
Robinson, Dave, LB, Penn State, Green Bay 1963-72; Washington 1973-74
Robinson, Ed, HB, Northwestern, Hammond 1923-26; Kenosha 1925-26; Louisville 1926
Robinson, Eugene, CB, Colgate, Seattle 1985
Robinson, Fred, G, Washington, Cleveland 1957
Robinson, Fred, DE, Miami, San Diego 1984-85
Robinson, Gil, E, Catawba, Pittsburgh 1933
Robinson, Glenn, DE, Oklahoma State, Baltimore 1975; Tampa Bay 1976-77
Robinson, Gregg, DE, Dartmouth, NY Jets 1978
Robinson, Jack, T, Northeast Missouri State, Brooklyn 1935-36; Chi. Cardinals 1936-37; Cleveland 1938; Pittsburgh 1938
Robinson, Jerry, SE, Grambling, San Diego 1962-64; NY Jets 1965
Robinson, Jerry, LB, UCLA, Philadelphia 1979-84; LA Raiders 1985
Robinson, Jimmy, WR, Georgia Tech, NY Giants 1976-79; San Francisco 1980
Robinson, Johnnie, DB, Tennessee State, Detroit 1966-67
Robinson, Johnny, HB-S, LSU, Dallas Texans 1960-62; Kansas City 1963-71
Robinson, Johnny, NT, Louisiana Tech, Oakland 1981; LA Raiders 1982-83
Robinson, Larry, RB, Tennessee, Dallas 1973
Robinson, Mark, S, Penn State, Kansas City 1984-85
Robinson, Matt, QB, Georgia, NY Jets 1977-79; Denver 1980; Buffalo 1981-82
Robinson, Mike, DE, Arizona, Cleveland 1981-82
Robinson, Paul, RB, Arizona, Cincinnati 1968-72; Houston 1972-73
Robinson, Rex, K, Georgia, New England 1982
Robinson, Shelton, LB, North Carolina, Seattle 1982-85
Robinson, Stacy, WR, North Dakota State, NY Giants 1985
Robinson, Virgil, RB, Grambling, New Orleans 1971-72
Robinson, Wayne, LB, Minnesota, Philadelphia 1952-56
Robiskie, Terry, RB, LSU, Oakland 1977-79; Miami 1980-81
Robison, Burle, E, BYU, Philadelphia 1935
Robison, George, G, Virginia Military, Dallas 1952
Robl, Hal, FB, Wisconsin-Oshkosh, Chi. Cardinals 1945
Robnett, Ed, FB, Texas Tech, San Francisco (AAFC) 1947
Robnett, Marshall, C, Texas A&M, Chi. Cardinals 1943, 1945; Card-Pitt 1944
Robotti, Frank, LB, Boston College, Boston 1961
Robustelli, Andy, E-DE, Arnold, LA Rams 1951-55; NY Giants 1956-64
Roby, Doug, HB, Michigan, Cleveland 1923
Roby, Reggie, P, Iowa, Miami 1983-85
Roche, Alden, DE-DT, Southern, Denver 1970; Green Bay 1971-76; Seattle 1976-78
Rochester, Paul (Rocky), DT, Michigan State, Dallas Texans 1960-62; Kansas City 1963; NY Jets 1963-69
Rock, Walter, T, Maryland, San Francisco 1963-67; Washington 1968-73
Rockenbach, Lyle, G, Michigan State, Detroit 1943
Rockford, Jim, DB, Oklahoma, San Diego 1985
Rockins, Chris, S, Oklahoma State, Cleveland 1984-85
Rockwell, Hank, C, Arizona State, Cleveland 1940-42; LA Dons (AAFC) 1946-48
Rodak, Mike, QB, Case Western Reserve, Cleveland 1939-40; Pittsburgh 1942
Roder, Mirro, K, Chi. Bears 1973-74; Tampa Bay 1976
Roderick, Ben, Columbia, HB, Buffalo 1923, 1927; Canton 1923, 1926
Roderick, John, FL, SMU, Miami 1966-67; Oakland 1968
Rodgers, Del, RB, Utah, Green Bay 1982, 1984
Rodgers, Hosea, FB, North Carolina, LA Dons (AAFC) 1949
Rodgers, John, TE, Louisiana Tech, Pittsburgh 1982-84
Rodgers, Johnny, WR-KR, Nebraska, San Diego 1977-78
Rodgers, Tom, T, Bucknell, Boston 1947
Rodgers, Willie, RB, Kentucky, Houston 1972, 1974-75
Rodriguez, Jess, HB, Salem (West Virginia), Buffalo 1929
Rodriguez, Kelly, HB, West Virginia Wesleyan, Frankford 1930; Minneapolis 1930
Roe, Bill, LB, Colorado, Dallas 1980
Roedel, Herb, G, Marquette, Oakland 1961
Roehnelt, Bill, LB, Bradley, Chi. Bears 1958-59; Washington 1960; Denver 1961-62
Roepke, John, HB, Penn State, Frankford 1928
Roessler, Fritz, E, Marquette, Racine 1922-24; Milwaukee 1925
Roffler, William (Bud), DB, Washington State, Philadelphia 1954
Rogalla, John, FB, Scranton, Philadelphia 1945
Rogas, Dan, G, Tulane, Detroit 1951; Philadelphia 1952
Rogel, Fran, FB, Penn State, Pittsburgh 1950-57
Rogers, Bill, T, Villanova, Detroit 1938-40, 1944
Rogers, Charley, QB, Pennsylvania, Frankford 1927-29
Rogers, Cullen, HB, Texas A&M, Pittsburgh 1946
Rogers, Don, C, South Carolina, LA Chargers 1960; San Diego 1961-64
Rogers, Don, S, UCLA, Cleveland 1984-85
Rogers, Doug, DE, Stanford, Atlanta 1982-83; New England 1983-84
Rogers, George, RB, South Carolina, New Orleans 1981-84; Washington 1985
Rogers, Glynn, G, TCU, Chi. Cardinals 1939
Rogers, Jimmy, RB, Oklahoma, New Orleans 1980-84
Rogers, John, C, Notre Dame, Cincinnati 1933-34
Rogers, Mel, LB, Florida A&M, San Diego 1971, 1973-74; LA Rams 1976; Chi. Bears 1977
Rogers, Stan, T, Maryland, Denver 1975
Rogers, Steve, RB, LSU, New Orleans 1975; NY Jets 1976
Rogers, Walt, HB, Ohio U., Columbus 1921-22
Rogge, George, E, Iowa, Chi. Cardinals 1931-33; St. Louis 1934
Roggeman, Tom, G, Purdue, Chi. Bears 1956-57
Rohde, Len, T, Utah State, San Francisco 1960-74
Rohleder, George, E-T, Wittenberg, Columbus 1925; Akron 1926
Rohrer, Jeff, LB, Yale, Dallas 1982-85
Rohrig, Herman, FB, Nebraska, Green Bay 1941, 1946-47
Rokisky, John, E, Duquesne, Cleveland (AAFC) 1946; Chi. Rockets (AAFC) 1947; NY Yankees (AAFC) 1948
Roland, Johnny, RB, Missouri, St. Louis 1966-72; NY Giants 1973
Roll, Clayton, E, Miami (Ohio), Dayton 1927
Rolle, Dave, FB, Oklahoma, Denver 1960
Roller, Dave, DT, Kentucky, NY Giants 1971; Green Bay 1975-78; Minnesota 1979-80
Roman, George, T, Case Western Reserve, Boston 1948; NY Bulldogs 1949; NY Giants 1950
Roman, John, T, Idaho State, NY Jets 1976-78
Roman, Nick, DE, Ohio State, Cincinnati 1970-71; Cleveland 1972-74
Romanik, Steve, QB, Villanova, Chi. Bears 1950-53; Chi. Cardinals 1953-54
Romaniszyn, Jim, LB, Edinboro, Cleveland 1973-74; New England 1976
Romano, Jim, C, Penn State, LA Raiders 1982-84; Houston 1984-85
Romboli, Rudy, FB, Boston 1946-48
Rome, Stan, WR, Clemson, Kansas City 1979-82
Romeo, Tony, SE, Florida State, Dallas Texans 1961; Boston 1962-67
Romero, Ray, G, Kansas State, Philadelphia 1951
Romes, Charles, CB, North Carolina Central, Buffalo 1977-85
Romine, Al, HB, North Alabama, Green Bay 1955, 1958
Romney, Milt, QB, Chicago, Racine 1923-24; Chi. Bears 1924-28
Ronzani, Gene, QB, Marquette, Chi. Bears 1933-38, 1944-45
Rooney, Bill, HB-FB, Duluth 1923-25, 1927; NY Giants 1925; Brooklyn 1926; Chi. Cardinals 1929
Rooney, Cobb, QB, Duluth 1924-27; NY Yankees 1928; Chi. Cardinals 1929-30
Rooney, Joe, E, Duluth 1923-24, 1926-27; Rock Island 1924-25; Pottsville 1928
Roopenian, Mark, NT, Boston College, Buffalo 1982-83
Root, Jim, QB, Miami (Ohio), Chi. Cardinals 1953, 1956
Roquemore, Durwood, S, Texas A&I, Kansas City 1982-83
Rorison, Jim (Red), T, USC, Pittsburgh 1938
Rosato, Sal, FB, Villanova, Washington 1945-47
Rosatti, Roman (Rosey), T, Michigan, Cleveland 1923; Green Bay 1924, 1926-27; NY Giants 1928
Rosdahl, Harrison (Hatch), G-DE, Penn State, Buffalo 1964; Kansas City 1964-67
Rose, Al, E, Texas, Providence 1930-31; Green Bay 1932-36
Rose, Bob, C, Ripon, Green Bay 1926
Rose, Donovan, CB, Hampton, Kansas City 1980
Rose, Gene, HB, Wisconsin, Chi. Cardinals 1929-32
Rose, George, DB, Auburn, Minnesota 1964-66; New Orleans 1967
Rose, Joe, TE, California, Miami 1980-85
Rose, Roy, E, Tennessee, NY Giants 1936
Rose, Tam, QB, Syracuse, Tonawanda 1921
Rosecrans, Jim, LB, Penn State, NY Jets 1976
Rosema, Rocky, LB, Michigan, St. Louis 1969-71
Rosen, Stan, HB, Rutgers, Buffalo 1929
Rosenberger, Tubby, T, Evansville 1921
Rosenow, Gus, HB, Ripon, Green Bay 1921
Rosequist, Ted, T, Ohio State, Chi. Bears 1934-36; Cleveland 1937
Roskie, Ken, FB, South Carolina, San Francisco (AAFC) 1946; Detroit 1948; Green Bay 1948
Rosnagle, Ted, S, Portland State, Minnesota 1985
Ross, Dan, TE-WR, Northeastern, Cincinnati 1979-83, 1985; Seattle 1985
Ross, Dave, SE, Cal State-Los Angeles, NY Titans 1960
Ross, Kevin, CB, Temple, Kansas City 1984-85
Ross, Louis, DE, South Carolina State, Buffalo 1971-72; Kansas City 1975
Ross, Oliver, RB, Alabama A&M, Denver 1973-75; Seattle 1976
Ross, Willie, FB, Nebraska, Buffalo 1964
Rosso, George, DB, Ohio State, Washington 1954
Rossovich, Tim, DE-LB, USC, Philadelphia 1968-71; San Diego 1972-73; Houston 1976

Rosteck, Ernie, C, Detroit 1943-44
Rostosky, Pete, T, Connecticut, Pittsburgh 1984-85
Rote, Kyle, HB-FL, SMU, NY Giants 1951-61
Rote, Tobin, QB, Rice, Green Bay 1950-56; Detroit 1957-59; San Diego 1963-64; Denver 1966
Rothrock, Cliff, C, North Dakota State, Chi. Rockets (AAFC) 1947
Rothwell, Fred, C, Kansas State, Detroit 1974
Roton, Herb, E, Auburn, Philadelphia 1937
Rotunno, Tony, HB, St. Ambrose, Chi. Rockets (AAFC) 1947
Roudebush, George, HB, Denison, Dayton 1920-21
Rourke, Jim, T-G, Boston College, Kansas City 1980-84; New Orleans 1985
Rouse, Curtis, G-T, Tennessee-Chattanooga, Minnesota 1982-85
Rouse, Stillman, E, Missouri, Detroit 1940
Rouson, Lee, RB, Colorado, NY Giants 1985
Roussel, Tom, LB, Southern Mississippi, Washington 1968-70; New Orleans 1971-72; Philadelphia 1973
Roussos, Mike, T, Pittsburgh, Washington 1948-49; Detroit 1949
Roveto, John, K, Southwestern Louisiana, Chi. Bears 1981-82
Rovinski, Tony, E, Holy Cross, NY Giants 1933
Rowan, Ev, E, Ohio State, Brooklyn 1930, 1932; Philadelphia 1933
Rowan, John, HB, Tennessee, Louisville 1923
Rowden, Larry, LB, Houston, Chi. Bears 1971-72
Rowe, Bob, FB, Colgate, Detroit 1934; Philadelphia 1935
Rowe, Bob, DT-DE, Western Michigan, St. Louis 1967-75
Rowe, Dave, DT-DE, Penn State, New Orleans 1967-70; New England 1971-73, San Diego 1974-75, Oakland 1975-78, Baltimore 1978
Rowe, Harmon, DB, San Francisco, NY Yankees (AAFC) 1947-49; NY Giants 1950-52
Rowland, Brad, HB, McMurry, Chi. Bears 1951
Rowland, Justin, DB, TCU, Chi. Bears 1960; Minnesota 1961; Denver 1962
Rowley, Bob, LB, Virginia, Pittsburgh 1963; NY Jets 1964
Rowser, John, CB, Michigan, Green Bay 1967-69; Pittsburgh 1970-73; Denver 1974-76
Roy, Elmer, E, Rochester 1921-25; Buffalo 1927
Roy, Frank, G, Utah, St. Louis 1966
Royston, Ed, G, Wake Forest, NY Giants 1948-49
Rozelle, Aubrey, LB, Delta State, Pittsburgh 1957
Rozier, Bob, DE, California, St. Louis 1979
Rozier, Mike, RB, Nebraska, Houston 1985
Rozumek, Dave, LB, New Hampshire, Kansas City 1976-79
Rubens, Larry, C, Montana State, Green Bay 1982-83
Rubick, Rob, TE, Grand Valley State, Detroit 1982-85
Rubino, Tony, G, Wake Forest, Detroit 1943, 1946
Rubke, Karl, LB, USC, San Francisco 1957-60, 1962-65; Minnesota 1961; Atlanta 1966-67; Oakland 1968
Ruby, Martin, T-DT, Texas A&M, Brooklyn (AAFC) 1946-48; NY Yankees (AAFC) 1949; NY Yanks 1950
Rucinzki, Eddie, E, Indiana, Brooklyn 1941-42; Chi. Cardinals 1943, 1945-46; Card-Pitt 1944
Rucka, Leo, C, Rice, San Francisco 1956
Rucker, Conrad, TE, Southern, Houston 1978-79; Tampa Bay 1980; LA Rams 1980
Rucker, Reggie, WR, Boston U., Dallas 1970-71; NY Giants 1971; New England 1971-74; Cleveland 1975-81
Rudnay, Jack, C, Northwestern, Kansas City 1970-82
Rudnick, Tim, S, Notre Dame, Baltimore 1974
Rudolph, Ben, DT-DE, Long Beach State, NY Jets 1981-85
Rudolph, Council, DE, Kentucky State, Houston 1972; St. Louis 1973-75; Tampa Bay 1976-77
Rudolph, Jack, LB, Georgia Tech, Boston 1960, 1962-65; Miami 1966
Rudzinski, Paul, LB, Michigan State, Green Bay 1978-80
Ruettgers, Ken, T, USC, Green Bay 1985
Ruetz, Howie, DT, Loras, Green Bay 1951-53
Ruetz, Joe, G, Notre Dame, Chi. Rockets (AAFC) 1946, 1948
Ruff, Guy, LB, Syracuse, Pittsburgh 1982
Ruh, Emmett, FB-HB, Davis & Elkins, Columbus 1921-22
Ruh, Homer, E, Columbus 1920-25
Rukas, Justin, G, LSU, Brooklyn 1936
Rule, Gordon, DB, Dartmouth, Green Bay 1968-69
Runager, Max, P, South Carolina, Philadelphia 1978-83; San Francisco 1984-85
Rundquist, Elmer, T, Illinois, Chi. Cardinals 1922
Rundquist, Harry (Porky), T, North Dakota, Duluth 1923-26
Runkle, Gil, C, Detroit 1920
Runnels, Tom, HB, North Texas State, Washington 1956-57
Running Deer, E-HB, Haskell, Oorang 1922-23
Running Wolf, (H. Casey), T, Haskell, Akron 1926
Runsey, Roy, T, Evansville 1921
Ruple, Ernie, T, Arkansas, Pittsburgh 1968
Rupp, John, G, Buffalo 1920
Rupp, Nelson, QB, Denison, Chi. Staleys 1921; Dayton 1921
Rush, Bob, C, Memphis State, San Diego 1977, 1979-82; Kansas City 1983-85
Rush, Clive, E, Miami (Ohio), Green Bay 1953
Rush, Jerry, DT, Michigan State, Detroit 1965-71
Rush, Jim, HB, Minnesota, Minneapolis 1922
Rushing, Marion, LB, Southern Illinois, Chi. Cardinals 1959; St. Louis 1960-65; Atlanta 1966-68; Houston 1968
Ruskusky, Ray, E, St. Mary's (California), NY Yankees (AAFC) 1947
Russ, Carl, LB, Michigan, Atlanta 1975; NY Jets 1976-77
Russ, Pat, DT, Purdue, Minnesota 1963
Russas, Al, T, Tennessee, Detroit 1949
Russell, Andy, LB, Missouri, Pittsburgh 1963, 1966-76
Russell, Benny, QB, Louisville, Buffalo 1968
Russell, Bo, T, Auburn, Washington 1939-40
Russell, Booker, RB, Southwest Texas State, Oakland 1978-79; San Diego 1980; Philadelphia 1981
Russell, Doug, HB, Kansas State, Chi. Cardinals 1934-39; Cleveland 1939
Russell, Jack, E, Baylor, NY Yankees (AAFC) 1946-49; NY Yanks 1950
Russell, Jim, T, Temple, Philadelphia 1936-37
Russell, Ken, T, Bowling Green, Detroit 1957-59
Russell, Lafayette (Reb), HB, Northwestern, NY Giants 1933; Philadelphia 1933
Russell, Reggie, E, NYU, Chi. Bears 1928
Russell, Rusty, T, South Carolina, Philadelphia 1984
Rust, Reggy, FB, Oregon State, Boston 1932
Rutgens, Joe, DT, Illinois, Washington 1961-69
Ruthstrom, Ralph, FB, SMU, Cleveland 1945; LA Rams 1946; Washington 1947; Baltimore (AAFC) 1949
Rutkowski, Charlie, DE, Ripon, Buffalo 1960
Rutkowski, Ed, HB-FL-QB, Notre Dame, Buffalo 1963-68
Rutledge, Jeff, QB, Alabama, LA Rams 1979-81; NY Giants 1982-85
Ruud, Tom, LB, Nebraska, Buffalo 1975-77, Cincinnati 1978-79
Ruzich, Steve, G, Ohio State, Green Bay 1952-54
Ryan, Clarence, HB, West Virginia, Buffalo 1929
Ryan, Dave, HB, Hardin-Simmons, Detroit 1945-46; Boston 1948
Ryan, Ed, E, St. Mary's (California), Pittsburgh 1948
Ryan, Frank, QB, Rice, LA Rams 1958-61; Cleveland 1962-68; Washington 1969-70
Ryan, Jim, HB, Notre Dame, Rock Island 1924; Chi. Cardinals 1924
Ryan, Jim, LB, William & Mary, Denver 1979-85
Ryan, Joe, DE, Villanova, NY Titans 1960
Ryan, John, T, Detroit, Chi. Bears 1929; Portsmouth 1930
Ryan, Kent (Rip), HB, Utah State, Detroit 1938-40
Ryan, Pat, QB, Tennessee, NY Jets 1978-85
Ryan, Rocky, HB, Illinois, Philadelphia 1956-58; Chi. Bears 1958
Rychlec, Tom, TE, American International, Detroit 1958; Buffalo 1960-62; Denver 1963
Ryckman, Billy, WR-KR, Louisiana Tech, Atlanta 1977-79
Ryczek, Dan, C, Virginia, Washington 1973-75; Tampa Bay 1976-77; LA Rams 1978-79
Ryczek, Paul, C, Virginia, Atlanta 1974-79; New Orleans 1981
Rydalch, Ron, DT, Utah, Chi. Bears 1975-80
Ryder, Nick, FB, Miami, Detroit 1963-64
Rydzewski, Frank, T, Notre Dame, Cleveland 1920; Chi. Tigers 1920; Hammond 1920, 1922-26; Chi. Cardinals 1921; Chi. Bears 1923; Milwaukee 1925
Rykovich, Julie, HB, Illinois, Buffalo (AAFC) 1947-48; Chi. Rockets (AAFC) 1948; Chi. Bears 1949-51; Washington 1952-53
Rymkus, Lou, T, Notre Dame, Washington 1943; Cleveland 1946-51
Rzempoluch, Ted, DB, Virginia, Washington 1963

S

Sabados, Andy, G, Citadel, Chi. Cardinals 1939-40
Sabal, Ron, T, Purdue, Oakland 1960-61
Saban, Lou, FB-LB, Indiana, Cleveland (AAFC) 1946-49
Sabasteanski, Joe, C, Fordham, Boston 1947-48; NY Bulldogs 1949
Sabatino, Bill, DT, Colorado, Cleveland 1968; Atlanta 1969
Sabucco, Tino, C, San Francisco, San Francisco (AAFC) 1949
Sachese, Frank, HB, Texas Tech, Brooklyn 1943-44; Boston 1945
Sachese, Jack, C, Texas, Boston 1945
Sachs, Len, E, Loyola (Chicago), Chi. Cardinals 1920-22, 1925; Milwaukee 1923-24; Hammond 1924-25; Louisville 1926
Sack, John, G, Pittsburgh, Columbus 1923, 1925; Canton 1926
Sacksteder, Norb, HB, St. Mary's (Minnesota), Dayton 1920, 1925; Detroit 1921; Canton 1922, 1925
Sacrinty, Nick, QB, Wake Forest, Chi. Bears 1947
Sader, Steve, FB, Phil-Pitt 1943
Saenz, Eddie, HB, USC, Washington 1946-51
Safford, Saint (St.), WR, San Jose State, Cincinnati 1968
Sagely, Floyd, E, Arkansas, San Francisco 1954, 1956; Chi. Cardinals 1957
Saidock, Tom, DT, Michigan State, Philadelphia 1957; NY Titans 1960-61; Buffalo 1962
Saimes, George, S, Michigan State, Buffalo 1963-69; Denver 1970-72
St. Clair, Bob, T, San Francisco, Tulsa, San Francisco 1953-63
St. Clair, Mike, DE, Grambling, Cleveland 1976-79; Cincinnati 1980-82
St. Germaine, Tom, G, Carlisle, Oorang 1922
St. Jean, Len, G, Northern Michigan, Boston 1964-70; New England 1971-73
St. John, Herb, G, Georgia, Brooklyn (AAFC) 1948; Chi. Hornets (AAFC) 1949
Salaam, Abdul, (Larry Faulk), DE-DT, Kent State, NY Jets 1976-83
Salata, Andy, G, Pittsburgh, Orange 1929; Newark 1930
Salata, Paul, E, USC, San Francisco 1949-50; Baltimore 1950
Saldi, Jay, TE, South Carolina, Dallas 1976-82; Chi. Bears 1983-84
Salem, Eddie, HB, Alabama, Washington 1951
Salem, Harvey, T, California, Houston 1983-85
Salemi, Sam, HB, St. John's (New York), NY Yankees 1928
Sally, Jerome, NT, Missouri, NY Giants 1982-85
Salonen, Brian, TE-LB, Montana, Dallas 1984-85
Salsbury, Jim, G, UCLA, Detroit 1955-56; Green Bay 1957-58
Salschneider, Jack, HB, St. Thomas (Minnesota), NY Giants 1949
Salter, Bryant, S, Pittsburgh, San Diego 1971-73; Washington 1974-75; Miami 1976; Baltimore 1976
Sample, Charlie, FB, Toledo, Green Bay 1942, 1945
Sample, Johnny, CB, Maryland-Eastern Shore, Baltimore 1958-60; Pittsburgh 1961-62; Washington 1963-65; NY Jets 1966-68
Sampleton, Lawrence, TE, Texas, Philadelphia 1982-84
Sampson, Art, G, Dayton 1921
Sampson, Clint, WR, San Diego State, Denver 1983-85
Sampson, Greg, T-DT, Stanford, Houston 1972-78
Sampson, Howard, DB, Arkansas, Green Bay 1978-79
Sampson, Seneca, HB, Brown, Providence 1926
Sams, Ron, G, Pittsburgh, Green Bay 1983; Minnesota 1984
Samuel, Don, HB, Oregon State, Pittsburgh 1949-50
Samuels, Tony, TE, Bethune-Cookman, Kansas City 1977-80; Tampa Bay 1980
Samuelson, Carl, T-DT, Nebraska, Pittsburgh 1948-51
Sanchez, John, T, San Francisco, Chi. Rockets (AAFC) 1947; Detroit 1947; Washington 1947-49; NY Giants 1949-50
Sandberg, Arnie, HB, Minnesota, LA Buccaneers 1926
Sandberg, Carl, HB, Minneapolis 1929
Sandberg, Sig, T, Iowa Wesleyan, St. Louis 1934; Pittsburgh 1935-37; Brooklyn 1937
Sandefur, Wayne, FB, Purdue, Pittsburgh 1936-37
Sandeman, Bill, DT, Pacific, Dallas 1966; New Orleans 1967; Atlanta 1967-73
Sanders, Bob, LB, North Texas State, Atlanta 1967
Sanders, Charlie, TE, Minnesota, Detroit 1968-77
Sanders, Clarence, LB, Cincinnati, Kansas City 1978, 1980
Sanders, Daryl, T, Ohio State, Detroit 1963-66
Sanders, Eric, T, Nevada-Reno, Atlanta 1981-85
Sanders, Gene, T-DE, Texas A&M, Tampa Bay 1979-85
Sanders, Jack, G, SMU, Pittsburgh 1940-42; Philadelphia 1945
Sanders, John (Deac), DB, South Dakota, New England 1974-76; Philadelphia 1977-79
Sanders, Ken, DE, Howard Payne, Detroit 1972-79; Minnesota 1980-81
Sanders, Lonnie, DB, Michigan State, Washington 1963-67; St. Louis 1968-69
Sanders, Orban (Spec), HB-DB, Texas, NY Yankees (AAFC) 1946-48; NY Yanks 1950
Sanders, Paul, HB, Utah State, Boston 1944
Sanders, Thomas, RB, Texas A&M, Chi. Bears 1985
Sanderson, Reggie, RB, Stanford, Chi. Bears 1973
Sandifer, Bill, DT, UCLA, San Francisco 1974-76; Seattle 1977-78
Sandifer, Dan, DB, LSU, Washington 1948-49; Detroit 1950; San Francisco 1950; Philadelphia 1950-51; Green Bay 1952-53; Chi. Cardinals 1953
Sandig, Curt, HB, St. Mary's (Texas), Pittsburgh 1942; Buffalo (AAFC) 1946
Sandusky, Alex, G, Clarion, Baltimore 1954-66
Sandusky, John, DT, Villanova, Cleveland 1950-55; Green Bay 1956
Sandusky, Mike, T-G, Maryland, Pittsburgh 1957-65
Sanford, Hayward (Sandy), E, Alabama, Washington 1940
Sanford, Jim, T, Lehigh, Duluth 1924
Sanford, Leo, LB, Louisiana Tech, Chi. Cardinals 1951-57; Baltimore 1958
Sanford, Lucius, LB, Georgia Tech, Buffalo 1978-85
Sanford, Rick, DB-KR, South Carolina, New England 1979-84; Seattle 1985
Sanooke, Stilwell, E, Carlisle, Oorang 1922
Sansen, Ollie, FB, Iowa, Brooklyn 1932-35
Santone, Al, G, Georgia Tech, Hartford 1926
Sanzotta, Dominic (Mickey), HB, Case Western Reserve, Detroit 1942, 1946
Sapienza, Americo (Rick), DB, Villanova, NY Titans 1960
Sapolu, Jesse, G, Hawaii, San Francisco 1983-84
Sapp, Theron, FB, Georgia, Philadelphia 1959-63; Pittsburgh 1963-65
Sarafiny, Al, C, St. Edward's, Green Bay 1933
Sarausky, Tony, FB, Fordham, NY Giants 1935-37; Brooklyn 1938
Sarboe, Phil, HB, Washington State, Boston 1934; Chi. Cardinals 1934-36; Brooklyn 1936
Sardisco, Tony, G, Tulane, Washington 1956; San Francisco 1956; Boston 1960-62
Sark, Harvey, G, Phillips, NY Giants 1931; Cincinnati 1934
Sarratt, Charley, QB, Oklahoma, Detroit 1948
Sarringhaus, Paul, HB, Ohio State, Chi. Cardinals 1946; Detroit 1948
Sartin, Dan, DT, Mississippi, San Diego 1969
Sartori, Larry, G, Fordham, Detroit 1942, 1945
Satcher, Doug, LB, Southern Mississippi, Boston 1966-68
Satenstein, Bernie, G, NYU, Staten Island 1929-32; NY Giants

1933
Satterfield, Al, T, Vanderbilt, San Francisco (AAFC) 1947
Satterwhite, Howard, WR, Sam Houston State, NY Jets 1976; Washington 1977; Baltimore 1977
Sauer, Ed (Tubby), T-G, Miami (Ohio), Dayton 1920-26; Canton 1921; Akron 1922; Pottsville 1925
Sauer, George, FB, Nebraska, Green Bay 1935-37
Sauer, George, SE, Texas, NY Jets 1965-70
Saul, Bill, LB, Penn State, Baltimore 1962-63; Pittsburgh 1964, 1966-68; New Orleans 1969; Detroit 1970
Saul, Rich, G-C, Michigan State, LA Rams 1970-81
Saul, Ron, G, Michigan State, Houston 1970-75; Washington 1976-81
Sauls, Mac, DB, Southwest Texas State, St. Louis 1968-69
Saumer, Syl, HB, St. Olaf, Cincinnati 1934; Pittsburgh 1934
Saunders, John, DB, Toledo, Buffalo 1972; San Francisco 1974-75
Saunders, Russ, FB, USC, Green Bay 1931
Saunders, Tom, HB, Evansville 1922; Toledo 1922
Savatsky, Ollie, E, Miami (Ohio), Cleveland 1937
Savitsky, George, T, Pennsylvania, Philadelphia 1948-49
Savoldi, Joe, FB, Notre Dame, Chi. Bears 1930
Sawyer, Herm, T, Syracuse, Rochester 1922
Sawyer, John, TE, SMU, Houston 1975-76; Seattle 1977-78, 1980-82; Washington 1983; Denver 1983-84
Sawyer, Ken, S, Syracuse, Cincinnati 1974
Saxon, Mike, P, San Diego State, Dallas 1985
Saxton, James, HB, Texas, Dallas Texans 1962
Sayers, Gale, HB-KR, Kansas, Chi. Bears 1965-71
Sayers, Ron, HB-KR, Nebraska-Omaha, San Diego 1969
Sazio, Ralph, T, William & Mary, Brooklyn (AAFC) 1948
Sbranti, Ron, LB, Utah State, Denver 1966
Scafide, John, T, Tulane, Boston 1933
Scales, Charlie, FB, Indiana, Pittsburgh 1960-61; Cleveland 1962-65; Atlanta 1966
Scales, Dwight, WR, Grambling, LA Rams 1976-78; NY Giants 1979; San Diego 1981-83
Scales, Hurles, CB, North Texas State, Chi. Bears 1974; St. Louis 1974; Green Bay 1975
Scalissi, Ted, HB, Ripon, Chi. Rockets (AAFC) 1947
Scalzi, Johnny, HB, Georgetown (Washington D.C.), Brooklyn 1931
Scanlan, Jerry, T-G, Hawaii, Washington 1980-81
Scanlon, Dewey, HB, Valparaiso, Duluth 1926
Scanlon, John, HB, DePaul, Chi. Cardinals 1921; Louisville 1926
Scarbath, Jack, QB, Maryland, Washington 1953-54; Pittsburgh 1956
Scarber, Sam, RB, New Mexico, San Diego 1975-76
Scardine, Carmen, HB, Chi. Cardinals 1932
Scarpati, Joe, S, North Carolina State, Philadelphia 1964-69; New Orleans 1970
Scarpitto, Bob, FL-P, Notre Dame, San Diego 1961; Denver 1962-67; Boston 1968
Scarry, Mike (Mo), C, Waynesburg, Cleveland 1944-45; Cleveland (AAFC) 1946-47
Schaake, Elmer, FB, Kansas, Portsmouth 1933
Schabarum, Pete, HB, California, San Francisco 1951, 1953-54
Schaefer, Don, FB, Notre Dame, Philadelphia 1956
Schaffer, Joe, LB, Tennessee, Buffalo 1960
Schaffnit, Pete, E, California, LA Buccaneers 1926
Schafrath, Dick, T, Ohio State, Cleveland 1959-71
Schammell, Fran, G, Iowa, Green Bay 1937
Scharer, Eddie, QB, Notre Dame, Detroit 1926, 1928; Pottsville 1927
Schaukowitch, Carl, G, Penn State, Denver 1975
Schaum, Greg, DE, Michigan State, Dallas 1976; New England 1978
Schein, Joe, T, Brown, Providence 1931
Schell, Herb, HB, Columbus 1924
Schenker, Nate, T, Samford, Cleveland 1939
Scherer, Bernie, E, Nebraska, Green Bay 1936-38; Pittsburgh 1939
Scheuer, Abraham (Babe), T, NYU, NY Giants 1934
Schibanoff, Alex, T, Franklin & Marshall, Detroit 1941-42
Schichtle, Henry, QB, Wichita State, NY Giants 1964
Schick, Doyle, DB, Kansas, Washington 1961
Schieb, Lee (Skippy), C, Washington (St. Louis), Brooklyn 1930
Schiechl, John, C, Santa Clara, Pittsburgh 1941-42; Detroit 1942; Chi. Bears 1945-46; San Francisco (AAFC) 1947
Schilling, Ralph, E, Oklahoma City, Washington 1946; Buffalo (AAFC) 1946
Schindler, Steve, G, Boston College, Denver 1977-78
Schleich, Vic, T, Nebraska, NY Yankees (AAFC) 1947
Schleicher, Maury, LB, Penn State, Chi. Cardinals 1959; LA Chargers 1960; San Diego 1961-62
Schleusner, Vin, T, Iowa, Portsmouth 1930-31
Schlichter, Art, QB, Ohio State, Baltimore 1982; Indianapolis 1984-85
Schlinkman, Walt, FB, Texas Tech, Green Bay 1946-49
Schmaar, Herm, E, Catholic, Brooklyn 1943
Schmaehl, Art, FB, Green Bay 1921
Schmautz, Ray, LB, San Diego State, Oakland 1966
Schmedding, Jim, G, Weber State, San Diego 1968-70
Schmidt, Bob, T-C, Minnesota, NY Giants 1959-60; Houston 1961-63; Boston 1964-65; Buffalo 1966-67
Schmidt, George, C, Lewis, Green Bay 1952; Chi. Cardinals 1953
Schmidt, Henry, DT, USC, San Francisco 1959-60; San Diego 1961-64; Buffalo 1965; NY Jets 1966
Schmidt, John, C, Carnegie-Mellon, Pittsburgh 1940
Schmidt, Joe, LB, Pittsburgh, Detroit 1953-65
Schmidt, Kermit (Dutch), E, Cal Poly-SLO, Boston 1932; Cincinnati 1933
Schmidt, Roy, G, Long Beach State, New Orleans 1967-68; Atlanta 1969; Washington 1970; Minnesota 1971
Schmidt, Terry, CB, Ball State, New Orleans 1974-75; Chi. Bears 1976-84
Schmiesing, Joe, DE-DT, New Mexico State, St. Louis 1968-71; Detroit 1972; Baltimore 1973; NY Jets 1974
Schmit, Bob, LB, Nebraska, NY Giants 1975-76
Schmitt, George, S, Delaware, St. Louis 1983
Schmitt, John, C, Hofstra, NY Jets 1964-73; Green Bay 1974
Schmitt, Ted, C, Pittsburgh, Philadelphia 1938-40
Schmitz, Bob, LB, Montana State, Pittsburgh 1961-66; Minnesota 1966
Schnarr, Steve, RB, Otterbein, Buffalo 1975
Schneider, Don, HB, Pennsylvania, Buffalo (AAFC) 1948
Schneider, John, HB, Columbus 1920
Schneider, Roy, T, Tulane, Brooklyn (AAFC) 1947
Schneidman, Herm (Biff), QB, Iowa, Green Bay 1935-38; Chi. Cardinals 1940
Schnelker, Bob, E-SE, Bowling Green, Philadelphia 1953; NY Giants 1954-60; Minnesota 1961; Pittsburgh 1961
Schnellbacher, Otto, DB, Kansas, NY Yankees (AAFC) 1948-49; NY Giants 1950-51
Schneller, John, E, Wisconsin, Portsmouth 1933; Detroit 1934-36
Schnitker, Mike, G, Colorado, Denver 1969-74
Schoemann, Roy, C, Marquette, Green Bay 1938
Schoen, Tom, S, Notre Dame, Cleveland 1970
Schoenke, Ray, G-T, SMU, Dallas 1963-64; Washington 1966-75
Scholl, Roy, G, Lehigh, Boston 1929
Scholtz, Bob, C, Notre Dame, Detroit 1960-64; NY Giants 1965-66
Scholtz, Bruce, LB, Texas, Seattle 1982-85
Scholtz, Chris, T, Arizona, Dallas 1983
Schonert, Turk, QB, Stanford, Cincinnati 1980-85
Schottel, Ivan, HB, Northwest Missouri State, Detroit 1946, 1948
Schottenheimer, Marty, LB, Pittsburgh, Buffalo 1965-68; Boston 1969-70
Schrader, Jim, C, Notre Dame, Washington 1954, 1956-61; Philadelphia 1962-64
Schreiber, Adam, G, Texas, Seattle 1984; New Orleans 1985
Schreiber, Larry, RB, Tennessee Tech, San Francisco 1971-75; Chi. Bears 1976
Schroeder, Bill, HB, Wisconsin, Chi. Rockets (AAFC) 1946-47
Schroeder, Gene (Flash), E-SE, Virginia, Chi. Bears 1951-52, 1954-57
Schroeder, Jay, QB, UCLA, Washington 1984-85
Schroll, Bill, FB, LSU, Buffalo (AAFC) 1949; Detroit 1950; Green Bay 1951
Schroy, Ken, S, Maryland, NY Jets 1977-84
Schuber, Jim, QB, Navy, Brooklyn 1930
Schubert, Eric, K, Pittsburgh, NY Giants 1985
Schubert, Steve, WR-KR, Massachusetts, New England 1974; Chi. Bears 1975-79
Schuehle, Jake, FB, Rice, Philadelphia 1939
Schuelke, Karl, FB, Wisconsin, Pittsburgh 1939
Schuessler, Erwin, T, Cincinnati 1921
Schuette, Carl, C-LB, Marquette, Buffalo (AAFC) 1948-49; Green Bay 1950-51
Schuette, Paul, G, Wisconsin, NY Giants 1928; Chi. Bears 1930-32; Boston 1932
Schuh, Harry, T, Memphis State, Oakland 1965-70; LA Rams 1971-73; Green Bay 1974
Schuh, Jeff, LB, Minnesota, Cincinnati 1981-85
Schuhmacher, John, G, USC, Houston 1978, 1981-85
Schuler, Bill, T, Yale, NY Giants 1947-48
Schultz, Charlie, T, Minnesota, Green Bay 1939-41
Schultz, Chris, T, Arizona, Dallas 1983, 1985
Schultz, Eberle, T-G, Oregon State, Philadelphia 1940; Pittsburgh 1941-42; Phil-Pitt 1943; Card-Pitt 1944; Cleveland 1945; LA Rams 1946-47
Schultz, John, WR, Maryland, Denver 1976-78
Schultz, Randy, RB, Iowa State, Cleveland 1966; New Orleans 1967-68
Schulz, Jody, LB, East Carolina, Philadelphia 1983-84
Schumacher, Gregg, DE, Illinois, LA Rams 1967-68
Schumacher, Kurt, T, Ohio State, New Orleans 1975-77; Tampa Bay 1978
Schupp, Walt, T, Miami (Ohio), Cincinnati 1921
Schuster, Dick, G, Penn State, Canton 1925
Schwab, Ray, QB, Oklahoma City, NY Giants 1931; Staten Island 1932
Schwall, Vic, HB, Northwestern, Chi. Cardinals 1947-50
Schwammel, Ade, T, Oregon State, Green Bay 1934-36, 1943-44
Schwartz, Don, S, Washington State, New Orleans 1978-80; St. Louis 1981
Schwartz, Elmer, FB, Washington State, Portsmouth 1931; Chi. Cardinals 1932; Pittsburgh 1933
Schwartz, Perry, E, California, Brooklyn 1938-42; NY Yankees (AAFC) 1946
Schwarzer, Ted, G, Centenary, Buffalo 1926
Schweda, Brian, DE, Kansas, Chi. Bears 1966; New Orleans 1967-68
Schweder, John (Bull), G, Pennsylvania, Baltimore 1950; Pittsburgh 1951-55
Schwedes, Gerhard, HB, Syracuse, Boston 1960-61
Schweickert, Bob, QB, Virginia Tech, NY Jets 1965, 1967
Schweidler, Dick, HB, St. Louis, Chi. Bears 1938-39, 1946
Schwenk, Wilson (Bud), QB, Washington (St. Louis), Chi. Cardinals 1942; Cleveland (AAFC) 1946; Baltimore (AAFC) 1947; NY Yankees (AAFC) 1948
Sciarra, John, S-KR, UCLA, Philadelphia 1978-83
Scibelli, Joe, G, Notre Dame, LA Rams 1961-75
Scoggins, Eric, LB, USC, San Francisco 1982
Scollard, Nick, E, St. Joseph's (Indiana), Boston 1946-48; NY Bulldogs 1949
Scolnick, Glenn, WR, Indiana, Pittsburgh 1973
Scott, Bill, DB, Idaho, Cincinnati 1968
Scott, Bo, RB, Ohio State, Cleveland 1969-74
Scott, Bobby, QB, Tennessee, New Orleans 1973-82
Scott, Carlos, C, Texas-El Paso, St. Loius 1983-85
Scott, Charlie, T, Auburn, Providence 1926
Scott, Chris, DE, Purdue, Indianapolis 1984-85
Scott, Clarence, DB, Morgan State, Boston 1969-70; New England 1971-72
Scott, Clarence, DB, Kansas State, Cleveland 1971-83
Scott, Clyde (Smackover), HB, Arkansas, Philadelphia 1949-52; Detroit 1952
Scott, Dave, T, Kansas, Atlanta 1976-82
Scott, Ed, G, Monmouth, Rock Island 1924
Scott, Freddie, WR, Amherst, Baltimore 1974-77; Detroit 1978-83
Scott, Gene, G, Hamline, Akron 1923; Minneapolis 1924
Scott, George, HB, Miami (Ohio), NY Giants 1959
Scott, Herbert, G, Virginia Union, Dallas 1975-84
Scott, Jake, S-KR, Georgia, Miami 1970-75; Washington 1976-78
Scott, James, WR, Henderson J.C., Chi. Bears 1976-80, 1982-83
Scott, Joe, HB, San Francisco, NY Giants 1948-53
Scott, John, DT, Ohio State, Buffalo 1960-61
Scott, Johnny, HB, Lafayette, Buffalo 1920-23; Frankford 1924
Scott, Lew, DB, Oregon State, Denver 1966
Scott, Lindsay, WR, Georgia, New Orleans 1982-85
Scott, Malcolm, TE, LSU, NY Giants 1983
Scott, Perry, E, Muhlenberg, Detroit 1942
Scott, Phil, E, Nebraska, Orange 1929
Scott, Prince, E, Texas Tech, Miami (AAFC) 1946
Scott, Ralph, T, Wisconsin, Chi. Staleys 1921; Chi. Bears 1922-25; NY Yankees 1927
Scott, Randy, LB, Alabama, Green Bay 1981-85
Scott, Tom, DE-LB, Virginia, Philadelphia 1953-58; NY Giants 1959-64
Scott, Victor, CB, Colorado, Dallas 1984-85
Scott, Vince, G, Notre Dame, Buffalo (AAFC) 1947-48
Scott, Wilbert, LB, Indiana, Pittsburgh 1961
Scott, Willie, TE, South Carolina, Kansas City 1981-85
Scotti, Ben, DB, Maryland, Washington 1959-61; Philadelphia 1962-63; San Francisco 1964
Scrabis, Bob, QB, Penn State, NY Titans 1960-62
Scribner, Bucky, P, Kansas, Green Bay 1983-84
Scribner, Rob, RB, UCLA, LA Rams 1973-76
Scruggs, Ted, E, Rice, Brooklyn (AAFC) 1947-48
Scrutchins, Ed, DE, Toledo, Houston 1966
Scudero, Joe (Scooter), DB, San Francisco, Washington 1954-58; Pittsburgh 1960
Scully, John, G-C, Notre Dame, Atlanta 1981-85
Sczurek, Stan, LB, Purdue, Cleveland 1963-65; NY Giants 1966
Seabaugh, Todd, LB, San Diego State, Pittsburgh 1984
Seabright, Charlie (Goose), QB, West Virginia, Cleveland 1941; Pittsburgh 1946-50
Seabron, Thomas, LB, Michigan, San Francisco 1979-80; St. Louis 1980
Seal, Paul, TE, Michigan, New Orleans 1974-76; San Francisco 1977-79
Seale, Sam, WR-CB, Western State (Colorado), LA Raiders 1984-85
Seals, George, G-DT, Missouri, Washington 1964; Chi. Bears 1965-71; Kansas City 1972-73
Searcey, Bill, G, Alabama, San Diego 1985
Sears, Dick, HB, Kansas State, Kansas City 1924
Sears, Jim, HB, USC, Chi. Cardinals 1954, 1957-58; LA Chargers 1960; Denver 1961
Sears, Vic, T-DT, Oregon State, Philadelphia 1941-42, 1945-53; Phil-Pitt 1943
Seasholtz, George, HB-FB, Lafayette, Milwaukee 1922; Kenosha 1924
Seay, Virgil, WR-KR, Troy State, Washington 1981-84; Atlanta 1984
Sebastian, Mike, HB, Pittsburgh, Philadelphia 1935; Pittsburgh 1935; Boston 1935
Sebek, Nick, QB, Indiana, Washington 1950
Sebo, Sam, FB, Syracuse, Newark 1930
Seborg, Henry, QB, Western Michigan, Minneapolis 1930; Frankford 1930-31

Sebro, Bob, G, Colorado, St. Louis 1982
Sechrist, Walt, G, West Virginia, Hammond 1920; Akron 1924; Cleveland 1925; Frankford 1925; Hammond 1926; Louisville 1926
Secord, Joe, C, Green Bay 1922
Sedbrook, Len, HB, Phillips, Detroit 1928; NY Giants 1929-31
Sedlock, Bob, T, Georgia, Buffalo 1960
Seedborg, John, K, Arizona State, Washington 1965
Seeds, Frank, HB, Iowa, Canton 1926
Seeman, George, E, Nebraska, Green Bay 1940
Segal, Maury, E, Cleveland 1925
Segretta, Rocco (Rocky), E, Hartford 1926
Seibert, Ed, G, West Virginia Wesleyan, Hammond 1923
Seibert, Ed, G, Otterbein, Dayton 1927-28
Seibold, Champ, T, Wisconsin, Green Bay 1934-38, 1940; Chi. Cardinals 1942
Seick, Earl (Red), G, Manhattan, NY Giants 1942
Seidel, Fred, G, Pittsburgh, Canton 1921
Seidelson, Harry, G, Pittsburgh, Frankford 1925; Akron 1926
Seifert, Mike, DE, Wisconsin, Cleveland 1974
Seiler, Paul, T-C, Notre Dame, NY Jets 1967, 1969; Oakland 1971-73
Seiple, Larry, TE-P, Kentucky, Miami 1967-77
Selawski, Gene, T, Purdue, LA Rams 1959; Cleveland 1960; San Diego 1961
Self, Clarence, HB-DB, Wisconsin, Chi. Cardinals 1949; Detroit 1950-51; Green Bay 1952, 1954-55
Selfridge, Andy, LB, Virginia, Buffalo 1972; NY Giants 1974-75, 1977; Miami 1976
Seliger, Frank, T, Hammond 1920-21
Sellers, Goldie, DB-KR, Grambling, Denver 1966-67; Kansas City 1968-69
Sellers, Ron, WR, Florida State, Boston 1969-70; New England 1971; Dallas 1972; Miami 1973
Selmon, Dewey, DT-LB, Oklahoma, Tampa Bay 1976-80; San Diego 1982
Selmon, Lee Roy, DE, Oklahoma, Tampa Bay 1976-84
Seltzer, Harry, FB, Morris-Harvey, Detroit 1942
Semes, Bernie, HB, Duquesne, Card-Pitt 1944
Sendlein, Robin, LB, Texas, Minnesota 1981-84; Miami 1985
Senn, Bill, HB, Knox, Chi. Bears 1926-31; Brooklyn 1931; Cincinnati 1933; St. Louis 1934
Seno, Frank, HB-DB, George Washington, Washington 1943-44, 1949; Chi. Cardinals 1945-46; Boston 1946-48
Sensenbaugher, Dean, HB, Ohio State, Cleveland (AAFC) 1948; NY Bulldogs 1949
Senser, Joe, TE, West Chester, Minnesota 1980-84
Sensibaugh, Mike, S, Ohio State, Kansas City 1971-75; St. Louis 1976-78
Septien, Rafael, K, Southwestern Louisiana, LA Rams 1977; Dallas 1978-85
Sergienko, George, T, American International, Brooklyn 1943-44; Boston 1945; Brooklyn (AAFC) 1946
Serini, Washington, G, Kentucky, Chi. Bears 1948-51; Green Bay 1952
Sermon, Ray, HB, Central State (Missouri), Kansas City 1925
Sestak, Tom, DT, McNeese State, Buffalo 1962-68
Setcavage, Joe, HB, Duquesne, Brooklyn 1943
Setron, Joe, G, West Virginia, Cleveland 1923
Severson, Jeff, S, Long Beach State, Washington 1972; Houston 1973-74; Denver 1975; St. Louis 1976-77; LA Rams 1978
Sevy, Jeff, T, California, Chi. Bears 1975-78; Seattle 1979-80
Sewell, Harley, G, Texas, Detroit 1953-62; LA Rams 1963
Sewell, Steve, RB, Oklahoma, Denver 1985
Sexton, Brent, S, Elon, Pittsburgh 1977
Sexton, Lin, HB, Wichita State, LA Dons (AAFC) 1948
Seyfrit, Mike (Si), E, Notre Dame, Toledo 1923; Hammond 1924
Seymour, Bob, HB, Oklahoma, Washington 1940-45; LA Dons (AAFC) 1946
Seymour, Jim, WR, Notre Dame, Chi. Bears 1970-72
Seymour, Paul, TE-T, Michigan, Buffalo 1973-77
Shackleford, Don, G, Pacific, Denver 1964
Shaffer, Craig, LB, Indiana State, St. Louis 1982-84
Shaffer, George, QB, Washington & Jefferson, Pittsburgh 1933
Shaffer, Leland, QB, Kansas State, NY Giants 1935-43, 1945
Shank, Henry, HB, Decatur 1920
Shanklin, Ron, WR, North Texas State, Pittsburgh 1970-74; Chi. Bears 1975-76
Shanley, Jim, HB, Oregon, Green Bay 1958
Shann, Bobby, DB, Boston College, Philadelphia 1965, 1967
Shannon, Carver, DB, Southern Illinois, LA Rams 1962-64
Shapiro, Jack, HB, NYU, Staten Island 1929
Share, Nate, G, Tufts, Providence 1925-26
Sharkey, Ed, G-LB, Duke, NY Yankees (AAFC) 1947-49; NY Yanks 1950; Cleveland 1952; Baltimore 1953; Philadelphia 1954-55; San Francisco 1955-56
Sharockman, Ed, CB, Pittsburgh, Minnesota 1962-72
Sharp, Ev, T, Cal Poly-SLO, Washington 1944-45
Sharp, Rick, T-DT, Washington, Pittsburgh 1970-71; Denver 1972
Sharpe, Luis, T, UCLA, St. Louis 1982-85
Shaub, Harry, G, Cornell, Philadelphia 1935
Shaw, Billy, G, Georgia Tech, Buffalo 1961-69
Shaw, Bob, E, Ohio State, Cleveland 1945; LA Rams 1946, 1949; Chi. Cardinals 1950
Shaw, Bob, WR, Winston-Salem State, New Orleans 1970
Shaw, Charlie, G, Oklahoma State, San Francisco 1950
Shaw, Dennis, QB, San Diego State, Buffalo 1970-73; St. Louis 1974-75; NY Giants 1976; Kansas City 1978
Shaw, Ed, FB-T, Nebraska, Rock Island 1920; Canton 1922-23; Akron 1923
Shaw, George, QB, Oregon, Baltimore 1955-58; NY Giants 1959-60; Minnesota 1961; Denver 1962
Shaw, Glen, FB, Kentucky, Chi. Bears 1960; LA Rams 1962; Oakland 1963-64
Shaw, Jesse, G, USC, Chi. Cardinals 1931
Shaw, Nate, DB, USC, LA Rams 1969-70
Shaw, Pete, S, Northwestern, San Diego 1977-81; NY Giants 1982-84
Shaw, Robert, C, Tennessee, Dallas 1979-81
Shay, Jerry, DT, Purdue, Minnesota 1966-67; Atlanta 1968-69; NY Giants 1970-71
Shea, Pat, G, USC, San Diego 1962-65
Sheard, Al (Shag), HB, St. Lawrence, Rochester 1923-25
Shearer, Brad, DT, Texas, Chi. Bears 1978, 1980-81
Shearer, Ron, T, Drake, Portsmouth 1930
Shearin, Joe, G, Texas, LA Rams 1983-84; Tampa Bay 1985
Shears, Larry, CB, Lincoln (Missouri), Atlanta 1971-72
Shedlosky, Ed, HB, Fordham, NY Giants 1945
Sheehan, John, G, Boston College, Providence 1925
Sheeks, Paul, QB, South Dakota, Akron 1921-22
Shekleton, Vin, G, Marquette, Racine 1922
Shelbourne, John, FB, Dartmouth, Hammond 1922
Shelby, Willie, RB-KR, Alabama, Cincinnati 1976-77; St. Louis 1978
Sheldon, Jim, E, Brown, Brooklyn 1926
Shell, Art, T, Maryland-Eastern Shore, Oakland 1968-81, LA Raiders 1982
Shell, Donnie, S, South Carolina State, Pittsburgh 1974-85
Shell, Todd, LB, BYU, San Francisco 1984-85
Shelley, Dexter (Deck), HB, Texas, Providence 1931; Portsmouth 1931; Chi. Cardinals 1932; Green Bay 1932
Shellog, Alec, T, Notre Dame, Brooklyn 1939; Chi. Bears 1939
Shelton, Murray, E, Cornell, Buffalo 1920
Shenefelt, Paul, T, Manchester, Chi. Cardinals 1934-35
Shepard, Charlie, HB, North Texas State, Pittsburgh 1956
Shepherd, Bill, FB, Western Maryland, Boston 1935; Detroit 1935-40
Sheppard, Henry, T-G, SMU, Cleveland 1976-81
Sherer, Dave, SE, SMU, Baltimore 1959; Dallas Cowboys 1960
Sheriff, Stan, LB, Cal Poly-SLO, Pittsburgh 1954; San Francisco 1955-57; Cleveland 1957
Sherk, Jerry, DT, Oklahoma State, Cleveland 1970-81
Sherlag, Bob, WR, Memphis State, Atlanta 1966
Sherman, Allie, QB, Brooklyn, Phil-Pitt 1943, Philadelphia 1944-47
Sherman, Bob, DB, Iowa, Pittsburgh 1964-65
Sherman, Rod, WR, USC, Oakland 1967, 1969-71; Cincinnati 1968; Denver 1972; LA Rams 1973
Sherman, Saul (Solly), QB, Chicago, Chi. Bears 1939-40
Sherman, Tom, QB, Penn State, Boston 1968-69; Buffalo 1969
Sherman, Will, DB, St. Mary's (California), Dallas 1952; LA Rams 1954-60; Minnesota 1961
Sherrod, Horace (Bud), DE, Tennessee, NY Giants 1952
Sherwin, Tim, TE, Boston College, Baltimore 1981-83; Indianapolis 1984-85
Shetley, Rhoten, QB-FB, Furman, Brooklyn 1940-42; Brooklyn (AAFC) 1946
Shield, Joe, QB, Trinity (Connecticut), Green Bay 1985
Shields, Billy, T, Georgia Tech, San Diego 1975-83; San Francisco 1984; NY Jets 1985; Kansas City 1985
Shields, Burrell, HB-DB, John Carroll, Pittsburgh 1954; Baltimore 1955
Shields, Lebron, T, Tennessee, Baltimore 1960; Minnesota 1961
Shiner, Dick, QB, Maryland, Washington 1964-66; Cleveland 1967; Pittsburgh 1968-69; NY Giants 1970; Atlanta 1971, 1973; New England 1973-74
Shinners, John, G, Xavier, New Orleans 1969-71; Baltimore 1972; Cincinnati 1973-77
Shinnick, Don, LB, UCLA, Baltimore 1957-68
Shipkey, Jerry, FB-LB, UCLA, Pittsburgh 1948-52; Chi. Bears 1953
Shipp, Billy, DT, Alabama, NY Giants 1954
Shipp, Jackie, LB, Oklahoma, Miami 1984-85
Shipp, Joe, TE, USC, Buffalo 1979
Shires, Marshall, T, Tennessee, Philadelphia 1945
Shirey, Fred, T, Nebraska, Green Bay 1940; Cleveland 1940-41
Shirk, Gary, TE, Morehead State, NY Giants 1976-82
Shirk, Jack, E, Oklahoma, Chi. Cardinals 1940
Shirkey, George, DT, Stephen F. Austin, Houston 1960-61; Oakland 1962
Shirley, Marion, T, Oklahoma City, NY Yankees (AAFC) 1948-49
Shiver, Raymond (Rex), DB, Miami, LA Rams 1956
Shiver, Sanders, LB, Carson-Newman, Baltimore 1976-83; Miami 1984-85
Shivers, Roy, RB-KR, Utah State, St. Louis 1966-72
Shlapak, Boris, K, Michigan State, Baltimore 1972
Shoals, Roger, T, Maryland, Cleveland 1963-64; Detroit 1965-70; Denver 1971
Shoate, Rod, LB, Oklahoma, New England 1975, 1977-81
Shockley, Arnold, (Perry Jackson), G, Southwestern Oklahoma, Providence 1928-29; Boston 1929
Shockley, Bill, HB-K, West Chester, NY Titans 1960-62; Buffalo 1961; Pittsburgh 1968
Shoemake, Hub, G, Illinois, Decatur 1920; Chi. Staleys 1921
Shoener, Hal, E, Iowa, San Francisco 1948-50
Shoener, Herb, E, Iowa, Washington 1948-49
Shofner, Del, DB-SE, Baylor, LA Rams 1957-60; NY Giants 1961-67
Shofner, Jim, DB, TCU, Cleveland 1958-63
Shonk, John, E, West Virginia, Philadelphia 1941
Shonta, Chuck, DB, Eastern Michigan, Boston 1960-67
Shook, Fred, C, TCU, Chi. Cardinals 1941
Short, Laval, NT, Colorado, Denver 1980; Tampa Bay 1981
Shorter, Jim, DB, Detroit, Cleveland 1962-63; Washington 1964-67; Pittsburgh 1969
Shorthose, George, WR, Missouri, Kansas City 1985
Shoults, Paul, HB, Miami (Ohio), NY Bulldogs 1949
Shugart, Clyde, G, Iowa State, Washington 1939-44
Shula, David, WR, Dartmouth, Baltimore 1981
Shula, Don, DB, John Carroll, Cleveland 1951-52; Baltimore 1953-56; Washington 1957
Shuler, Mickey, TE, Penn State, NY Jets 1978-85
Shull, Steve, LB, William & Mary, Miami 1980-82
Shultz, John, FB, Temple, Frankford 1930
Shumann, Mike, WR, Florida State, San Francisco 1978-79, 1981; Tampa Bay 1980; St. Louis 1982
Shumate, Mark, T, Wisconsin, NY Jets 1985; Green Bay 1985
Shumon, Ron, LB, Wichita State, Cincinnati 1978; San Francisco 1979
Shurnas, Marshall, E, Missouri, Cleveland (AAFC) 1947
Shurtcliffe, Charlie, HB, Marietta, Buffalo 1929
Shurtleff, Bert, T, Brown, Providence 1925-26, Boston 1929
Shurtz, Hubert, T, LSU, Pittsburgh 1948
Shy, Don, RB, San Diego State, Pittsburgh 1967-68; New Orleans 1969; Chi. Bears 1970-72; St. Louis 1973
Shy, Les, RB, Long Beach State, Dallas 1966-69; NY Giants 1970
Siani, Mike, WR, Villanova, Oakland 1972-77; Baltimore 1978-80
Siano, Tony, C, Fordham, Boston 1932; Brooklyn 1934
Sidle, Jimmy, RB, Auburn, Atlanta 1966
Sidorik, Alex, T, Mississippi, Boston 1947; Baltimore (AAFC) 1948-49
Sieb, Wally, HB, Ripon, Racine 1922
Siegal, Johnny, E, Columbia, Chi. Bears 1939-43
Siegert, Herb, G, Illinois, Washington 1949-51
Siegert, Wayne, G, Illinois, NY Yanks 1951
Siegfried, Orville, HB, Washington & Jefferson, St. Louis 1923
Siegle, Jules, FB, Northwestern, NY Giants 1948
Siemering, Larry, C, San Francisco, Boston 1935-36
Sieminski, Chuck, DT, Penn State, San Francisco 1963-65, Detroit 1966; Atlanta 1966-67
Siemon, Jeff, LB, Stanford, Minnesota 1972-82
Sieracki, Stan, T, Pennsylvania, Frankford 1927
Sieradzki, Steve, HB, Michigan State, NY Yankees (AAFC) 1948; Brooklyn (AAFC) 1948
Sierocinski, Steve, T, Boston 1946
Sies, Dale, G-QB, Pittsburgh, Cleveland 1920; Dayton 1921-22, 1924; Rock Island 1923; Kenosha 1924
Sievers, Eric, TE, Maryland, San Diego 1981-85
Sigillo, Dom, T, Xavier, Chi. Bears 1943-44; Detroit 1945
Sigmund, Art, G, Chi. Bears 1923
Signaigo, Joe, G, Notre Dame, NY Yankees (AAFC) 1948-49; NY Yanks 1950
Sigurdson, Sig, E, Pacific Lutheran, Baltimore (AAFC) 1947
Sikich, Mike, G, Northwestern, Cleveland 1971
Sikich, Rudy, T, Minnesota, Cleveland 1945
Sikora, Mike, G, Oregon, Chi. Cardinals 1952
Sikora, Robert, T, Indiana, Cleveland 1984
Silas, Sam, DT-DE, Southern Illinois, St. Louis 1963-67; NY Giants 1968; San Francisco 1969-70
Sillin, Frank, HB, Western Maryland, Dayton 1927-29
Silvestri, Carl, DB, Wisconsin, St. Louis 1965; Atlanta 1966
Simas, Bill, HB, St. Mary's (California), Chi. Cardinals 1932-33
Simendinger, Ken, HB, Holy Cross, Hartford 1926
Simensen, Don, T, St. Thomas (Minnesota), LA Rams 1951-52
Simerson, John, C-T, Purdue, Philadelphia 1957-58; Pittsburgh 1958; Houston 1960; Boston 1961
Simington, Milt, G, Arkansas, Cleveland 1941; Pittsburgh 1942
Simkus, Arnie, T, Michigan, NY Jets 1965; Minnesota 1967
Simmons, Bob, G-T, Texas, Kansas City 1977-83
Simmons, Cleo, TE, Jackson State, Dallas 1983
Simmons, Dave, LB, Georgia Tech, St. Louis 1965-66; New Orleans 1967; Dallas 1968
Simmons, Davie, LB, North Carolina, Green Bay 1979; Detroit 1980
Simmons, Floyd, HB, Notre Dame, Chi. Rockets (AAFC) 1948
Simmons, Jack, C, Detroit, Baltimore (AAFC) 1948; Detroit 1949-50; Chi. Cardinals 1951-56
Simmons, Jeff, WR, USC, LA Rams 1983
Simmons, Jerry, WR, Bethune-Cookman, Pittsburgh 1965-66; New Orleans 1967; Atlanta 1967-69; Chi. Bears 1969; Denver 1971-74
Simmons, Jim (Jinks), HB, Southwestern Oklahoma, Cleveland 1927; Providence 1928
Simmons, John, CB-KR, SMU, Cincinnati 1981-85
Simmons, Leon, LB, Grambling, Denver 1983

Simmons, Roy, G, Georgia Tech, NY Giants 1979-81
Simmons, Tony, DE, Tennessee, San Diego 1985
Simms, Bob, LB, Rutgers, NY Giants 1960-62; Pittsburgh 1962
Simms, Phil, QB, Morehead State, NY Giants 1979-81, 1983-85
Simon, Bobby, T, Grambling, Houston 1976
Simon, Jim, G, Miami, Detroit 1963-65; Atlanta 1966-68
Simon, John, E, Hamline, Minneapolis 1924
Simone, Mike, LB, Stanford, Denver 1972-74
Simonetti, Len (Meatball), T, Tennessee, Cleveland (AAFC) 1947-48
Simonini, Ed, LB, Texas A&M, Baltimore 1976-81
Simons, Keith, NT, Minnesota, Kansas City 1976-77; St. Louis 1978-79
Simonson, Dave, T, Minnesota, Baltimore 1974; NY Giants 1975; Houston 1976; Seattle 1976; Detroit 1977
Simpkins, Ron, LB, Michigan, Cincinnati 1980-85
Simpson, Al, T, Colorado State, NY Giants 1975-76
Simpson, Bill, S, Michigan State, LA Rams 1974-78; Buffalo 1980-82
Simpson, Bob, DE, Colorado, Miami 1978
Simpson, Eber, HB, Wisconsin, Minneapolis 1921-24; St. Louis 1923
Simpson, Howard, DT, Auburn, Minnesota 1964
Simpson, Jackie, DB, Florida, Baltimore 1958-60; Pittsburgh 1961-62
Simpson, Jackie, LB, Mississippi, Denver 1961; Oakland 1962-64
Simpson, Jimmy, HB, Detroit, Toledo 1922; St. Louis 1923; Kenosha 1924
Simpson, Keith, CB, Memphis State, Seattle 1978-85
Simpson, Mike, DB, Houston, San Francisco 1970-72
Simpson, Nate, RB, Tennessee State, Green Bay 1977-79
Simpson, O.J. (Juice), RB, USC, Buffalo 1969-77; San Francisco 1978-79
Simpson, Willie, FB, Cal State-San Francisco, Oakland 1962
Sims, Billy, RB, Oklahoma, Detroit 1980-84
Sims, Darryl, DE-DT, Wisconsin, Pittsburgh 1985
Sims, David, RB, Georgia Tech, Seattle 1977-79
Sims, George, DB, Baylor, LA Rams 1949-50
Sims, Jimmy, LB, USC, Tampa Bay 1976
Sims, Ken, DE, Texas, New England 1982-85
Sims, Marvin, RB, Clemson, Baltimore 1980-81
Sims, Mickey, DT, South Carolina State, Cleveland 1977-79
Singer, Karl, T, Purdue, Boston 1966-68
Singer, Walt, E, Syracuse, NY Giants 1935-36
Singletary, Bill, LB, Temple, NY Giants 1974
Singletary, Mike, LB, Baylor, Chi. Bears 1981-85
Singleton, Bill, G, Hammond 1922
Singleton, John, HB, Dayton 1929
Singleton, Ron, T, Grambling, San Diego 1976; San Francisco 1977-80
Sinko, Steve, T, Duquesne, Boston 1934-36
Sinkovitz, Frank, C, Duke, Pittsburgh 1947-52
Sinkwich, Frankie, HB, Georgia, Detroit 1943-44; NY Yankees (AAFC) 1946-47; Baltimore (AAFC) 1947
Sinnott, John, T, Brown, NY Giants 1980; Baltimore 1982
Sipe, Brian, QB, San Diego State, Cleveland 1974-83
Sirochman, George, G, Duquesne, Pittsburgh 1942; Detroit 1944
Sisemore, Jerry, T, Texas, Philadelphia 1973-84
Sisk, Johnny (Big Train), HB, Marquette, Chi. Bears 1932-36
Sisk, Johnny, DB, Miami, Chi. Bears 1964
Sistrunk, Manny, DT, Arkansas-Pine Bluff, Washington 1970-75; Philadelphia 1976-79
Sistrunk, Otis, DE-DT, Oakland 1972-78
Sites, Vinnie, E, Pittsburgh, Pittsburgh 1936-37
Sitko, Emil (Red), HB, Notre Dame, San Francisco 1950; Chi. Cardinals 1951-52
Sivell, Jim (Happy), G, Auburn, Brooklyn 1938-42, 1944; NY Giants 1944-45; Miami (AAFC) 1946
Siwek, Mike, DT, Western Michigan, St. Louis 1970
Skaggs, Jim, G, Washington, Philadelphia 1963-67, 1969-72
Skansi, Paul, WR-KR, Washington, Pittsburgh 1983; Seattle 1984-85
Skaugstad, Daryle, NT, California, Houston 1981-82; San Francisco 1983; Green Bay 1983
Skeate, Gil, FB, Gonzaga, Green Bay 1927
Skibinski, Joe, G, Purdue, Cleveland 1952; Green Bay 1955-56
Skibinski, John, RB, Purdue, Chi. Bears 1978-81
Skinner, Gerald, T, Arkansas, Green Bay 1978
Skladany, Joe (Muggsy), E, Pittsburgh, Pittsburgh 1934
Skladany, Leo, DE, Pittsburgh, Philadelphia 1949; NY Giants 1950
Skladany, Tom, P, Ohio State, Detroit 1978-82; Philadelphia 1983
Sklopan, John, DB, Southern Mississippi, Denver 1963
Skoczen, Stan, HB, Case Western Reserve, Cleveland 1944
Skoglund, Bob, E, Notre Dame, Green Bay 1947
Skorich, Nick, G, Cincinnati, Pittsburgh 1946-48
Skoronski, Bob, T, Indiana, Green Bay 1956, 1959-68
Skoronski, Ed, E, Purdue, Pittsburgh 1935-36; Brooklyn 1937; Cleveland 1937
Skorupan, John, LB, Penn State, Buffalo 1973-77; NY Giants 1978-80
Skudin, Dave, G, NYU, Staten Island 1929
Slaby, Lou, LB, Pittsburgh, NY Giants 1964-65; Detroit 1966
Slackford, Fred, FB, Notre Dame, Dayton 1920; Canton 1921
Slagle, George, T, Louisville 1926
Slater, Fred (Duke), T, Iowa, Milwaukee 1922; Rock Island 1922-25; Chi. Cardinals 1926-31
Slater, Howie, FB, Washington State, Milwaukee 1926
Slater, Jackie, T, Jackson State, LA Rams 1976-85
Slater, Mark, C, Minnesota, San Diego 1978; Philadelphia 1979-83
Slater, Walt, HB, Tennessee, Pittsburgh 1947
Slaton, Tony, C, USC, LA Rams 1984-85
Slaughter, Chuck, T, South Carolina, New Orleans 1982
Slaughter, Mickey, QB, Louisiana Tech, Denver 1963-66
Sledge, Leroy, RB, Bakersfield J.C., Houston 1971
Sleight, Elmer (Red), T, Purdue, Green Bay 1930-31
Sligh, Richard, DT, North Carolina Central, Oakland 1967
Slivinski, Steve, G, Washington, Washington 1939-43
Sloan, Bonnie, DT, Austin Peay, St. Louis 1973
Sloan, Dwight, QB, Arkansas, Chi. Cardinals 1938; Detroit 1939-40
Sloan, Steve, QB, Alabama, Atlanta 1966-67
Slone, Pete, E, Muncie 1921
Slosburg, Phil, HB, Temple, Boston 1948; NY Bulldogs 1949
Slough, Elmer, HB, Oklahoma, Buffalo 1926
Slough, Greg, LB, USC, Oakland 1971-72
Slovak, Marty, HB, Toledo, Cleveland 1938-41
Slyker, Bill, E, Ohio State, Evansville 1922
Small, Eldridge, WR-DB, Texas A&I, NY Giants 1972-74
Small, Fred, LB, Washington, Pittsburgh 1985
Small, George, NT, North Carolina A&T, NY Giants 1980
Small, Gerald, CB, San Jose State, Miami 1978-83; Atlanta 1984
Small, John, DT-C, Citadel, Atlanta 1970-72; Detroit 1973-74
Smeja, Rudy, E, Michigan, Chi. Bears 1944-45; Philadelphia 1946
Smerek, Don, DT, Nevada-Reno, Dallas 1981-85
Smerlas, Fred, NT, Boston College, Buffalo 1979-85
Smigelsky, Dave, P, Virginia Tech, Atlanta 1982
Smilanich, Bronko, HB, Arizona, Cleveland 1939
Smiley, Tom, RB, Lamar, Cincinnati 1968; Denver 1969; Houston 1970
Smith, Aaron, LB, Utah State, Denver 1984
Smith, Allen, E, Mississippi, Chi. Bears 1947-48
Smith, Allen, RB, Fort Valley State, Buffalo 1966-67
Smith, Allen, RB, Findlay, NY Jets 1966
Smith, Art, LB, Hawaii, Denver 1980
Smith, Barry, WR, Florida State, Green Bay 1973-75; Tampa Bay 1976
Smith, Barty, RB, Richmond, Green Bay 1974-80
Smith, Ben, E, Alabama, Green Bay 1933; Pittsburgh 1934-35; Washington 1937
Smith, Bill, E, Washington, Chi. Cardinals 1934-39
Smith, Bill, T, North Carolina, Chi. Rockets (AAFC) 1948; LA Dons (AAFC) 1948
Smith, Billy Ray, DT, Arkansas, LA Rams 1957; Pittsburgh 1958-60; Baltimore 1961-62, 1964-70
Smith, Billy Ray, LB, Arkansas, San Diego 1983-85
Smith, Blane, LB, Purdue, Green Bay 1977
Smith, Bob, DB, Iowa, Buffalo (AAFC) 1948; Brooklyn (AAFC) 1948; Chi. Hornets 1949; Detroit 1949-53
Smith, Bob, FB, Texas A&M, Detroit 1953-54
Smith, Bob, HB, Nebraska, Cleveland 1955-56; Philadelphia 1956
Smith, Bob, S, Miami (Ohio), Houston 1968
Smith, Bobby, DB, UCLA, LA Rams 1962-65; Detroit 1965-66
Smith, Bobby, RB, North Texas State, Buffalo 1964-65; Pittsburgh 1966
Smith, Bruce, HB, Minnesota, Green Bay 1945-48; LA Rams 1948
Smith, Bruce, DE, Virginia Tech, Buffalo 1985
Smith, Bubba, DE-DT, Michigan State, Baltimore 1967-71; Oakland 1973-74; Houston 1975-76
Smith, Byron, DE, California, Indianapolis 1984-85
Smith, Carl, FB, Tennessee, Buffalo 1960
Smith, Charles (Homeboy), WR, Grambling, Philadelphia 1974-81
Smith, Charles (Rabbit), HB, Georgia, Chi. Cardinals 1947
Smith, Charlie, DE, Abilene Christian, San Francisco 1956
Smith, Charlie, RB, Utah, Oakland 1968-74; San Diego 1975
Smith, Clyde, C, Missouri, Kansas City 1926; Cleveland 1927; Providence 1928-29
Smith, Dan, DB, Northeastern Oklahoma, Denver 1961
Smith, Dave, FB, Ripon, Houston 1960-64
Smith, Dave, WR, Indiana (Pennsylvania), Pittsburgh 1970-72; Houston 1972; Kansas City 1973
Smith, Dave, RB, Utah, San Diego 1970
Smith, Dennis, S, USC, Denver 1981-85
Smith, Dick (Red), QB, Notre Dame, Green Bay 1927, 1929; NY Yankees 1928; Newark 1930; NY Giants 1931
Smith, Dick, C, Ohio State, Philadelphia 1933; Chi. Bears 1933
Smith, Dick, DB, Northwestern, Washington 1967-68
Smith, Don, G, Orange 1929; Newark 1930
Smith, Don, G, Florida A&M, Denver 1967
Smith, Don, DE, Miami, Atlanta 1979-84; Buffalo 1985
Smith, Donnell, DE, Southern, Green Bay 1971; New England 1973-74
Smith, Doug, C, Bowling Green, LA Rams 1978-85
Smith, Doug, NT, Auburn, Houston 1985
Smith, Earl, T, Ripon, Green Bay 1922; Rock Island 1923
Smith, Ed, HB, NYU, Boston 1936; Green Bay 1937
Smith, Ed, DE, Colorado College, Denver 1973-74
Smith, Ed, LB, Vanderbilt, Baltimore 1980-81
Smith, Ernie, T, USC, Green Bay 1935-37, 1939
Smith, Ernie, DB, Compton J.C., San Francisco 1955-56
Smith, Fletcher, DB, Tennessee State, Kansas City 1966-67; Cincinnati 1968-71
Smith, Franky, T, Alabama A&M, Kansas City 1980
Smith, Gary, G, Virginia Tech, Cincinnati 1984
Smith, Gaylon, HB, Southwestern (Memphis), Cleveland 1939-42; Cleveland (AAFC) 1946
Smith, Gene, G, Georgia, Portsmouth 1930; Frankford 1930
Smith, George, C, California, Washington 1937, 1941-43; Brooklyn 1944; Boston 1945; San Francisco (AAFC) 1947
Smith, George (Locomotive), FB, Villanova, Chi. Cardinals 1943
Smith, Gordon, SE, Missouri, Minnesota 1961-65
Smith, Greg, NT, Kansas, Minnesota 1984
Smith, Hal, DT, UCLA, Boston 1960; Denver 1960; Oakland 1961
Smith, Hank, G-T, Rochester 1920-25
Smith, Harry, T, USC, Detroit 1940
Smith, Holden, WR, California, Baltimore 1982
Smith, Hugh, SE, Kansas, Washington 1962; Denver 1962
Smith, J.D., FB-DB, North Carolina A&T, Chi. Bears 1956; San Francisco 1956-64; Dallas 1965-66
Smith, J.D., T, Rice, Philadelphia 1959-63; Detroit 1964, 1966
Smith, J.T., WR-KR, North Texas State, Washington 1978; Kansas City 1978-84; St. Louis 1985
Smith, Jack, E, Stanford, Philadelphia 1942; Washington 1943
Smith, Jack, T, Florida, Philadelphia 1945
Smith, Jackie, TE, Northwestern State (Louisiana), St. Louis 1963-77; Dallas 1978
Smith, Jackie, DB, Troy State, Philadelphia 1971
Smith, James (Jetstream), HB, Compton J.C., Oakland 1960; Chi. Bears 1961
Smith, Jeff, LB, USC, NY Giants 1966
Smith, Jeff, RB, Nebraska, Kansas City 1985
Smith, Jerry, G, Wisconsin, San Francisco 1952-53, 1956; Green Bay 1956
Smith, Jerry, TE, Arizona State, Washington 1965-77
Smith, Jim, T, Colorado, LA Dons (AAFC) 1947
Smith, Jim (Yazoo), DB, Oregon, Washington 1968
Smith, Jim, WR, Michigan, Pittsburgh 1977-82; LA Raiders 1985
Smith, Jimmy, S, Utah State, Denver 1969
Smith, Jimmy, RB, Elon, Green Bay 1984; LA Raiders 1984; Washington 1984
Smith, Jim Ray, G, Baylor, Cleveland 1956-62; Dallas 1963-64
Smith, Joe, E, Texas Tech, Baltimore (AAFC) 1948
Smith, John, K, Southampton, New England 1974-83
Smith, John, WR, North Texas State, Washington 1978
Smith, John, WR, Tennessee State, Cleveland 1979
Smith, Johnny Ray, CB-KR, Lamar, Tampa Bay 1982-83; San Diego 1984
Smith, Ken, TE, New Mexico, Cleveland 1977
Smith, Lance, G, LSU, St. Louis 1985
Smith, Larry, RB, Florida, LA Rams 1969-73; Washington 1974
Smith, Laverne, RB, Kansas, Pittsburgh 1977
Smith, Len, T, Wisconsin, Racine 1923-24
Smith, Leo, E, Providence, Providence 1928
Smith, Leonard, S, McNeese State, St. Louis 1983-85
Smith, Lucious, CB, Cal State-Fullerton, LA Rams 1980-82; Kansas City 1983; Buffalo 1984; San Diego 1984-85
Smith, Lyman, DT, Duke, Minnesota 1978
Smith, Marty, DT, Louisville, Buffalo 1976
Smith, Mike, WR, Grambling, Atlanta 1980
Smith, Mike, CB, Texas-El Paso, Miami 1985
Smith, Milt, E, UCLA, Philadelphia 1945
Smith, Noland (Super Gnat), KR-WR, Tennessee State, Kansas City 1967-69; San Francisco 1969
Smith, Oke, E, Drake, Rock Island 1920-21
Smith, Olin, T, Ohio Wesleyan, Cleveland 1924
Smith, Ollie, WR, Tennessee State, Baltimore 1973-74; Green Bay 1976-77
Smith, Orland, T, Brown, Providence 1927-29
Smith, Oscar, HB, Texas-El Paso, Green Bay 1948-49; NY Bulldogs 1949
Smith, Pat, FB, Michigan, Buffalo 1920-21, 1923
Smith, Paul, DT-DE, New Mexico, Denver 1968-78; Washington 1979-80
Smith, Perry, CB, Colorado State, Green Bay 1973-76; St. Louis 1977-79; Denver 1980-81
Smith, Phil, WR, San Diego State, Baltimore 1983; Indianapolis 1984
Smith, Ralph (Catfish), SE, Mississippi, Philadelphia 1962-64; Cleveland 1965-68; Atlanta 1969
Smith, Ray, C, Missouri, Portsmouth 1930; Providence 1930-31; Philadelphia 1933
Smith, Ray Gene, HB, Midwestern State (Texas), Chi. Bears 1954-57
Smith, Reggie, KR-WR, North Carolina Central, Atlanta 1980-81
Smith, Rex, E, Wisconsin-LaCrosse, Green Bay 1922
Smith, Ricky, DB, Alabama State, New England 1982-84; Washington 1984
Smith, Riley, QB, Alabama, Boston 1936; Washington 1937-38
Smith, Robert, DE, Grambling, Minnesota 1985
Smith, Ron, QB, Richmond, LA Rams 1965; Pittsburgh 1966
Smith, Ron, KR-DB, Wisconsin, Chi. Bears 1965, 1970-72; Atlanta 1966-67; LA Rams 1968-69; San Diego 1973;

Oakland 1974
Smith, Ron, WR, San Diego State, LA Rams 1978-79; San Diego 1980-81; Philadelphia 1981-83
Smith, Royce, G, Georgia, New Orleans 1972-73; Atlanta 1974-76
Smith, Russ, C, Illinois, Chi. Staleys 1921; Chi. Bears 1922, 1925; Canton 1923; Milwaukee 1923-24; Cleveland 1924; Detroit 1925; Hammond 1926
Smith, Russ, RB, Miami, San Diego 1969-70
Smith, Sherman, RB, Miami (Ohio), Seattle 1976-82; San Diego 1983
Smith, Sid, T, USC, Kansas City 1970-72; Houston 1974
Smith, Steve, DT-DE, Michigan, Pittsburgh 1966; Minnesota 1968-70; Philadelphia 1971-73
Smith, Stu, QB, Bucknell, Pittsburgh 1937-38
Smith, Tim, WR, Nebraska, Houston 1980-85
Smith, Tody, DE, USC, Dallas 1971-72; Houston 1973-76; Buffalo 1976
Smith, Tom, RB, Miami, Miami 1973
Smith, Tommie, WR, San Jose State, Cincinnati 1969
Smith, Truett, QB, Mississippi State, Pittsburgh 1950-51
Smith, Verda (Vitamin T), HB-FL, Abilene Christian, LA Rams 1949-53
Smith, Waddell, WR, Kansas, Dallas 1984
Smith, Warren, C, Carlton, Green Bay 1921
Smith, Wayne, CB, Purdue, Detroit 1980-82; St. Louis 1982-85
Smith, Wilfred, T-G, DePauw, Muncie 1920-21; Louisville 1922; Chi. Cardinals 1923-25
Smith, Willie, T, Michigan, Denver 1960; Oakland 1961
Smith, Willis (Wee Willie), HB, Idaho, NY Giants 1934
Smith, Zeke, G, Auburn, Baltimore 1960; NY Giants 1961
Smolinski, Mark, FB, Wyoming, Baltimore 1961-62; NY Jets 1963-68
Smukler, Dave, FB, Temple, Philadelphia 1936-39; Boston 1944
Smyth, Bill, T, Cincinnati, LA Rams 1947-50
Smythe, Lou, FB, Texas, Canton 1920-23; Rochester 1924-25; Frankford 1925-26, Providence 1926, Hartford 1926
Snead, Norm, QB, Wake Forest, Washington 1961-63; Philadelphia 1964-70; Minnesota 1971; NY Giants 1972-74, 1976; San Francisco 1974-75
Sneddon, Bob, HB, St. Mary's (California), Washington 1944; Detroit 1945; LA Dons (AAFC) 1946
Snell, George, FB, Penn State, Brooklyn 1926, Buffalo 1927
Snell, Matt, FB, Ohio State, NY Jets 1964-72
Snell, Ray, G-T, Wisconsin, Tampa Bay 1980-83; Pittsburgh 1984-85; Detroit 1985
Snelling, Ken, FB, UCLA, Green Bay 1945
Sniadecki, Jim, LB, Indiana, San Francisco 1969-73
Snider, Malcolm, G-T, Stanford, Atlanta 1969-71; Green Bay 1972-74
Snidow, Ron, DE, Oregon, Washington 1963-67; Cleveland 1968-72
Snoots, Lee, HB-FB, Columbus 1920-25
Snorton, Matt, DE, Michigan State, Denver 1965
Snow, Jack, SE, Notre Dame, LA Rams 1965-75
Snowden, Cal, DE, Indiana, St. Louis 1969-70; Buffalo 1971; San Diego 1972-73
Snowden, Jim, T-DE, Notre Dame, Washington 1965-71
Snyder, Al, FL, Holy Cross, Boston 1964; Baltimore 1966
Snyder, Bill (Bull), G, Ohio U., Pittsburgh 1934-35
Snyder, Bob, QB, Ohio U., Cleveland 1937-38; Chi. Bears 1939-41, 1943
Snyder, Jerry, HB, Maryland, NY Giants 1929; Staten Island 1930
Snyder, Lum, T, Georgia Tech, Philadelphia 1952-55, 1958
Snyder, Todd, WR, Ohio U., Atlanta 1970-72
Soar, Hank, HB, Providence, NY Giants 1937-44, 1946
Sobocinski, Phil, C, Wisconsin, Atlanta 1968
Soboleski, Joe, DT, Michigan, Chi. Hornets (AAFC) 1949; Washington 1949; Detroit 1950; NY Yanks 1951; Dallas 1952
Sochia, Brian, NT, Northwestern Oklahoma, Houston 1983-85
Sodaski, John, DB-LB, Villanova, Pittsburgh 1970; Philadelphia 1972-73
Sofish, Alec, G, Grove City, Providence 1931
Sohn, Ben, FB, Washington, Cincinnati 1934
Sohn, Ben, G, USC, NY Giants 1941
Sohn, Kurt, KR-WR, Fordham, NY Jets 1981-82, 1984-85
Sokolosky, John, C, Wayne State, Detroit 1978
Soleau, Bob, LB, William & Mary, Pittsburgh 1964
Solomon, Freddie, WR-KR, Tampa, Miami 1975-77; San Francisco 1978-85
Solomon, Roland, CB, Utah, Dallas 1980; Buffalo 1981; Denver 1981
Solon, Lorin, HB, Cleveland 1920
Solt, Ron, G, Maryland, Indianapolis 1984-85
Soltau, Gordy, SE-K, Minnesota, San Francisco 1950-58
Soltis, Bob, DB, Minnesota, Boston 1960-61
Somers, George, T, La Salle, Philadelphia 1939-40; Pittsburgh 1941-42
Sommer, Mike, HB, George Washington, Washington 1958-59, 1961; Baltimore 1959-61; Oakland 1963
Songin, Eddie (Butch), QB, Boston College, Boston 1960-61; NY Titans 1962
Sonnenberg, Gus, G, Dartmouth, Columbus 1923; Detroit 1925-26; Providence 1927-28, 1930
Sorce, Ross, T, Georgetown (Washington D.C.), Pittsburgh 1945
Sorenson, Glen, G, Utah State, Green Bay 1943-45
Sorey, Jim, G, Texas Southern, Buffalo 1960-62
Sorey, Revie, G, Illinois, Chi. Bears 1975-81, 1983
Sorrell, Henry, LB, Tennessee-Chattanooga, Denver 1967
Sortet, Wilbur, E, West Virginia, Pittsburgh 1933-40
Sortun, Rick, G, Washington, St. Louis 1964-69
Sossamon, Lou, C-LB, South Carolina, NY Yankees (AAFC) 1946-48
Souchak, Frank, E, Pittsburgh, Pittsburgh 1939
Souders, Cecil (Cy), E, Ohio State, Detroit 1947-49
South, Ronnie, QB, Arkansas, New Orleans 1968
Southard, Tommy, WR, Furman, St. Louis 1978; Houston 1978
Sovio, Henry, TE, Hawaii, Atlanta 1973
Sowell, Robert, CB, Howard (Washington D.C.), Miami 1983-85
Sowells, Rich, CB, Alcorn State, NY Jets 1971-76; Houston 1977
Spadaccini, Vic, QB, Minnesota, Cleveland 1938-40
Spagna, Joe, T-G, Lehigh, Cleveland 1920; Buffalo 1920-21; Frankford 1924-25
Spagnola, John, TE, Yale, Philadelphia 1979-82, 1984-85
Spain, Dick, C-T, Army, Evansville 1921-22
Spangler, Gene, HB, Tulsa, Detroit 1946
Spani, Gary, LB, Kansas State, Kansas City 1978-85
Spaniel, Frank, HB, Notre Dame, Baltimore 1950; Washington 1950
Sparkman, Al, T, Texas A&M, LA Rams 1948-49
Sparks, Dave, G-T, South Carolina, San Francisco 1951; Washington 1954
Sparlis, Al, G, UCLA, Green Bay 1946
Spavital, Jim, FB, Oklahoma State, LA Dons (AAFC) 1949; Baltimore 1950
Spear, Glen, FB, Drake, Kansas City 1926
Spears, Ron, DE, San Diego State, New England 1982-83; Green Bay 1983
Speck, Norman (Dutch), G, Canton 1920-23, 1925-26; Hammond 1920; Evansville 1921; Akron 1924
Speedie, Mac, E, Utah, Cleveland 1946-52
Speegle, Cliff, C, Oklahoma, Chi. Cardinals 1945
Speelman, Harry, G, Michigan State, Detroit 1940
Speights, Dick, WR, Wyoming, San Diego 1968
Spellman, John, E, Brown, Providence 1925-31; Boston 1932
Spence, Julian, DB, Sam Houston State, Chi. Cardinals 1956; San Francisco 1957; Houston 1960-61
Spencer, Jim, G, Dayton, Dayton 1928-29
Spencer, Joe, T, Oklahoma State, Brooklyn (AAFC) 1948; Cleveland (AAFC) 1949; Green Bay 1950-51
Spencer, Maurice, CB, North Carolina Central, St. Louis 1974; LA Rams 1974; New Orleans 1974-76, 1978
Spencer, Tim, RB, Ohio State, San Diego 1985
Spencer, Todd, RB-KR, USC, Pittsburgh 1984-85
Spencer, Willie, RB, Minnesota 1976; NY Giants 1977-78
Speth, George, T, Murray State, Detroit 1942
Speyrer, Cotton, WR, Texas, Baltimore 1972-74; Miami 1975
Spicer, Rob, LB, Indiana, NY Jets 1973
Spiegel, Clarence, T-G, Wisconsin, Evansville 1921-22
Spiers, Bob, T, Ohio State, Akron 1922; Cleveland 1925
Spikes, Jack, FB, TCU, Dallas Texans 1960-62; Kansas City 1963-64, San Diego 1964; Houston 1965; Buffalo 1966-67
Spilis, John, WR, Northern Illinois, Green Bay 1969-71
Spiller, Phil, DB, Cal State-Los Angeles, St. Louis 1967; Atlanta 1968; Cincinnati 1968
Spillers, Raymond, T, Arkansas, Philadelphia 1937
Spinks, Jack, G, Alcorn State, Pittsburgh 1952; Chi. Cardinals 1953; Green Bay 1955-56; NY Giants 1956-57
Spinney, Art, G, Boston College, Baltimore 1950, 1953-60
Spirida, John, E, St. Anselm, Washington 1939
Spiva, Andy, LB, Tennessee, Atlanta 1977
Spivey, Mike, CB, Colorado, Chi. Bears 1977-79; Oakland 1980; New Orleans 1980-81
Sponaugle, Bob, E, Pennsylvania, NY Bulldogs 1949
Spradlin, Danny, LB, Tennessee, Dallas 1981-82; Tampa Bay 1983-84; St. Louis 1985
Springer, Hal, E, Central State (Oklahoma), NY Giants 1945
Springs, Kirk, KR-DB, Miami (Ohio), NY Jets 1981-85
Springs, Ron, RB, Ohio State, Dallas 1979-84; Tampa Bay 1985
Springsteen, Bill, C, Lehigh, Frankford 1925-26; Chi. Cardinals 1927-28
Sprinkle, Ed, E-DE, Hardin-Simmons, Chi. Bears 1944-55
Sprinkle, Hubert, T, Carnegie-Mellon, Akron 1923-24; Cleveland 1925
Sproul, Dennis, QB, Arizona State, Green Bay 1978
Spruill, Jim, T, Rice, Baltimore (AAFC) 1948-49
Spurrier, Steve, QB-P, Florida, San Francisco 1967-75; Tampa Bay 1976
Squirek, Jack, LB, Illinois, LA Raiders 1982-85
Squyres, Seaman, HB, Rice, Cincinnati 1933
Stabler, Ken (Snake), QB, Alabama, Oakland 1970-79; Houston 1980-81; New Orleans 1982-84
Stacco, Ed, T, Colgate, Detroit 1947; Washington 1948
Stachowicz, Ray, P, Michigan State, Green Bay 1981-82; Chi. Bears 1983
Stachowski, Rich, NT, California, Denver 1983
Stackpool, Jack, HB, Washington, Philadelphia 1942
Stacy, Billy, DB, Mississippi State, Chi. Cardinals 1959; St. Louis 1960-63
Stacy, Jim (Red), T, Oklahoma, Detroit 1935-37
Stafford, Dick, DE, Texas Tech, Philadelphia 1962-63
Stafford, Harry, HB, Texas, NY Giants 1934
Staggers, Jon, WR-KR, Missouri, Pittsburgh 1970-71; Green Bay 1972-74; Detroit 1975
Staggs, Jeff, LB, San Diego State, San Diego 1967-71; St. Louis 1972-73
Stahl, Ed, G, Pittsburgh, Cleveland 1920; Dayton 1921
Stahlman, Dick, T, Northwestern, Hammond 1924; Kenosha 1924; Akron 1924-25; NY Giants 1927-28, 1930; Green Bay 1931-32; Chi. Bears 1933
Stalcup, Jerry, LB, Wisconsin, LA Rams 1960; Denver 1961-62
Staley, Bill, DT, Utah State, Cincinnati 1968-69; Chi. Bears 1970-72
Stallings, Don, DT, North Carolina, Washington 1960
Stallings, Larry, LB, Georgia Tech, St. Louis 1963-76
Stalls, Dave, DT-DE, Northern Colorado, Dallas 1977-79; Tampa Bay 1980-83; LA Raiders 1983, 1985
Stallworth, John, WR, Alabama A&M, Pittsburgh 1974-85
Stamps, Sylvester, WR-KR, Jackson State, Atlanta 1984-85
Stanback, Harry, DE, North Carolina, Baltimore 1982
Stanback, Haskel, RB, Tennessee, Atlanta 1974-79
Stanciel, Jeff, RB, Mississippi Valley State, Atlanta 1969
Standlee, Norm, FB-LB, Stanford, Chi. Bears 1941; San Francisco 1946-52
Stanfel, Dick, G, San Francisco, Detroit 1952-55; Washington 1956-58
Stanfill, Bill, DE, Georgia, Miami 1969-76
Stankavage, Scott, QB, North Carolina, Denver 1984
Stanley, C.B., T, Tulsa, Buffalo (AAFC) 1946
Stanley, Walter, WR-KR, Mesa, Green Bay 1985
Stansauk, Don, DT, Denver, Green Bay 1950-51
Stanton, Bill, E, North Carolina State, Buffalo (AAFC) 1949
Stanton, Henry, E, Arizona, NY Yankees (AAFC) 1946-47
Stanton, Jack, HB, North Carolina State, Pittsburgh 1961
Starch, Ken, RB, Wisconsin, Green Bay 1976
Stark, Howie, T, Wisconsin, Racine 1926
Stark, Rohn, P, Florida State, Baltimore 1982-83; Indianapolis 1984-85
Starke, George, T, Columbia, Washington 1973-84
Starks, Marshall, DB, Illinois, NY Jets 1963-64
Starling, Bruce, DB, Florida, Denver 1963-64
Staroba, Paul, WR, Michigan, Cleveland 1972; Green Bay 1973
Starr, Bart, QB, Alabama, Green Bay 1956-71
Starret, Ben, QB, St. Mary's (California), Pittsburgh 1941; Green Bay 1942-45
Starring, Stephen, WR, McNeese State, New England 1983-85
Stasica, Leo, HB, Colorado, Brooklyn 1941; Philadelphia 1941; Washington 1943; Boston 1944
Stasica, Stan, HB, South Carolina, Miami (AAFC) 1946
Staten, Randy, DE, Minnesota, NY Giants 1967
Staton, Jim, DT, Wake Forest, Washington 1951
Statuto, Art, C, Notre Dame, Buffalo (AAFC) 1948-49; LA Rams 1950
Staubach, Roger, QB, Navy, Dallas 1969-79
Stauch, Scott, RB, UCLA, New Orleans 1981
Stautberg, Jerry, G, Cincinnati, Chi. Bears 1951
Stautner, Ernie, DT, Boston College, Pittsburgh 1950-63
Stautzenberger, Odell, G, Texas A&M, Buffalo (AAFC) 1949
Steber, John, G, Georgia Tech, Washington 1946-50
Steele, Cliff, QB, Syracuse, Rochester 1921-22; Akron 1922
Steele, Ernie, HB, Washington, Philadelphia 1942, 1944-48; Phil-Pitt 1943
Steele, Larry, P, Santa Rosa J.C., Denver 1974
Steele, Percy (Red), E, Harvard, Canton 1921
Steele, Robert, WR, North Alabama, Dallas 1978; Minnesota 1979
Steels, Anthony, RB-KR, Nebraska, San Diego 1985; Buffalo 1985
Steen, Frank, E, Rice, Green Bay 1939
Steen, Jim, T, Syracuse, Detroit 1935-36
Steere, Dick, G, Drake, Philadelphia 1951
Steffen, Jim, DB, UCLA, Detroit 1959-61; Washington 1961-65
Stefik, Bob, E, Niagara, Buffalo (AAFC) 1948
Stegent, Larry, RB, Texas A&M, St. Louis 1971
Steger, Pete, HB, Chi. Cardinals 1921
Stehouwer, Ron, G, Colorado State, Pittsburgh 1960-64
Stein, Bill, G, Fordham, Duluth 1923-27; Chi. Cardinals 1927-28
Stein, Bob, LB, Minnesota, Kansas City 1969-72; LA Rams 1973-74; San Diego 1975; Minnesota 1975
Stein, Herb, C, Pittsburgh, Buffalo 1921; Toledo 1922; Frankford 1924; Pottsville 1925-26, 1928
Stein, Russ, T, Washington & Jefferson, Toledo 1922; Frankford 1924; Pottsville 1925; Canton 1926
Stein, Sammy, E, Staten Island 1929-30; NY Giants 1931; Brooklyn 1932
Steinbach, Larry, T, St. Thomas (Minnesota), Chi. Bears 1930-31; Chi. Cardinals 1931-33; Philadelphia 1933
Steinbrunner, Don, DT, Washington State, Cleveland 1953
Steiner, Roy (Rebel), E, Alabama, Green Bay 1950-51
Steinfeld, Al, C-T, C.W. Post, Kansas City 1982; Houston 1983; NY Giants 1983
Steinfort, Fred, K, Boston College, Oakland 1976; Atlanta 1977-78; Denver 1979-81; Buffalo 1983; New England 1983
Steinke, Gil, HB, Texas A&I, Philadelphia 1945-48
Steinkemper, Bill, T, Notre Dame, Chi. Bears 1943

Steinkuhler, Dean, G, Nebraska, Houston 1984-85
Steinmetz, Ken, FB, Boston 1944-45
Stemrick, Greg, CB, Colorado State, Houston 1975-82; New Orleans 1983
Stenerud, Jan, K, Montana State, Kansas City 1967-79; Green Bay 1980-83; Minnesota 1984-85
Stenger, Brian, LB, Notre Dame, Pittsburgh 1969-72; New England 1973
Stenn (Stenko), Paul, T, Villanova, NY Giants 1942; Washington 1946; Pittsburgh 1947; Chi. Bears 1948-51
Stennett, Fred, FB, St. Mary's (California), Portsmouth 1931; Chi. Cardinals 1932
Stensrud, Mike, NT, Iowa, Houston , 1979-85
Stephens, Bill, C, Brown, Brooklyn 1926
Stephens, Bruce, WR, Columbia, NY Jets 1978
Stephens, Hal, T, East Carolina, Detroit 1985; Kansas City 1985
Stephens, Harold, QB, Hardin-Simmons, NY Titans 1962
Stephens, Johnny, E, Marshall, Cleveland 1938
Stephens, Larry, DE, Texas, Cleveland 1960-61; LA Rams 1962; Dallas 1963-67
Stephens, Louis (Red), G, San Francisco, Washington 1955-60
Stephens, Ray, C, Idaho, NY Yankees 1927
Stephens, Steve, TE, Oklahoma State, NY Jets 1981
Stephens, Tom, SE-DB, Syracuse, Boston 1960-64
Stephenson, Davidson (Trapper), G, West Virginia, LA Rams 1950; Green Bay 1951-55
Stephenson, Dwight, C, Alabama, Miami 1980-85
Stephenson, Kay, QB, Florida, San Diego 1967; Buffalo 1968
Steponovich, Mike, G, St. Mary's (California), Boston 1933
Steponovich, Tony, G, USC, Minneapolis 1930; Frankford 1930
Steptoe, Jack, WR, Utah, San Francisco 1978
Sterling, Ernest, DE, Grambling, Dallas 1969
Sternaman, Ed (Dutch), HB, Illinois, Decatur 1920; Chi. Staleys 1921; Chi. Bears 1922-27
Sternaman, Joey, QB, Illinois, Chi. Bears 1922-25, 1927-30; Duluth 1923
Sterr, Gil, QB, Carroll (Wisconsin), Racine 1926
Stetz, Bill, G, Boston College, Philadelphia 1967
Steuber, Bob, HB, Missouri, Chi. Bears 1943; Cleveland (AAFC) 1946; LA Dons (AAFC) 1947; Buffalo (AAFC) 1948
Stevens, Billy, QB, Texas-El Paso, Green Bay 1968-69
Stevens, Dick, T-G, Baylor, Philadelphia 1970-74
Stevens, Don, HB-DB, Illinois, Philadelphia 1952, 1954
Stevens, Howard, RB-KR, Louisville, New Orleans 1973-74; Baltimore 1975-77
Stevens, Pete, C, Temple, Philadelphia 1936
Stevenson, Art, G, Fordham, NY Giants 1926; Brooklyn 1926; NY Yankees 1928
Stevenson, Mark, G, Notre Dame, Columbus 1922
Stevenson, Mark, C-G, Western Illinois, Detroit 1985
Stevenson, Ralph, G, Oklahoma, Cleveland 1940
Stevenson, Ricky, DB, Arizona, Cleveland 1970
Steverson, Norris, QB-HB, Arizona State, Cincinnati 1934
Steward, Dean, HB, Ursinus, Phil-Pitt 1943
Stewart, Charlie, G, Colgate, Akron 1923
Stewart, Jimmy, DB, Tulsa, New Orleans 1977; Detroit 1979
Stewart, Joe, WR, Missouri, Oakland 1978-79
Stewart, Mark, LB, Washington, Minnesota 1984
Stewart, Ralph, C, Notre Dame, NY Yankees (AAFC) 1947-48; Baltimore (AAFC) 1948
Stewart, Steve, LB, Minnesota, Atlanta 1978; Green Bay 1979
Stewart, Vaughn, C, Alabama, Chi. Cardinals 1943; Brooklyn 1943-44
Stewart, Wayne, TE, California, NY Jets 1969-72; San Diego 1974
Stickel, Walt, T-DT, Pennsylvania, Chi. Bears 1946-49; Philadelphia 1950-51
Stickles, Monty, TE, Notre Dame, San Francisco 1960-67; New Orleans 1968
Stidham, Howard, LB, Tennessee Tech, San Francisco 1977
Stief, Dave, WR, Portland State, St. Louis 1978-82; Washington 1983
Stienke, Jim, DB, Southwest Texas State, Cleveland 1973; NY Giants 1974-77; Atlanta 1978
Stieve, Terry, G, Wisconsin, New Orleans 1976-77; St. Louis 1978-79, 1981-84
Stifler, Jim, E-HB, Brown, Providence 1926-27
Stiger, Jim, FB, Washington, Dallas 1963-65; LA Rams 1965-67
Still, Art, DE, Kentucky, Kansas City 1978-85
Still, Jim, QB-DB, Georgia Tech, Buffalo (AAFC) 1948-49
Stills, Ken, S, Wisconsin, Green Bay 1985
Stillwell, Roger, DT, Stanford, Chi. Bears 1975-77
Stinchcomb, Gaylord (Pete), QB, Ohio State, Chi. Staleys 1921; Chi. Bears 1922; Columbus 1923; Cleveland 1923; Louisville 1926
Stincic, Tom, LB, Michigan, Dallas 1969-71; New Orleans 1972
Stingley, Darryl, WR, Purdue, New England 1973-77
Stinnette, Jim, FB, Oregon State, Denver 1961-62
Stith, Carel, DT, Nebraska, Houston 1967-69
Stith, Howard, G, Louisville 1921
Stits, Bill, DB, UCLA, Detroit 1954-56; San Francisco 1957-58; Washington 1959; NY Giants 1959-61
Stobbs, Bill, FB, Washington & Jefferson, Detroit 1921
Stock, Herb, FB, Kenyon, Columbus 1924-25
Stock, John, SE, Pittsburgh, Pittsburgh 1956
Stockton, Herschel (Mule), G, McMurray, Philadelphia 1937-38
Stockton, Houston, FB, Gonzaga, Frankford 1925-26, 1928; Providence 1929; Boston 1929
Stoecklein, Earl, G, Dayton 1920
Stoepel, Terry, TE, Tulsa, Chi. Bears 1967; Houston 1970
Stofa, John, QB, Buffalo, Miami 1966-67, 1969-70; Cincinnati 1968-69
Stofer, Ken, QB, Cornell, Buffalo (AAFC) 1946
Stofko, Ed, HB, St. Francis (Pennsylvania), Pittsburgh 1945
Stojack, Frank (Toughie), G, Washington State, Brooklyn 1935-36
Stokes, Jesse, DB, Corpus Christi, Denver 1968
Stokes, Lee (Dixie), C, Centenary, Detroit 1937-39; Chi. Cardinals 1943
Stokes, Sim, WR, Northern Arizona, Dallas 1967
Stokes, Tim, T, Oregon, LA Rams 1974; Washington 1975-77; Green Bay 1978-82; NY Giants 1981
Stolberg, Eric, WR, Indiana, New England 1971
Stolfa, Alton, QB, Luther, Chi. Bears 1939
Stolhandske, Tom, DE, Texas, San Francisco 1955
Stone, Avatus, HB-P, Syracuse, Baltimore 1958
Stone, Billy, HB, Bradley, Baltimore (AAFC) 1949; Baltimore 1950; Chi. Bears 1951-54
Stone, Donnie, FB, Arkansas, Denver 1961-64; Buffalo 1965; Houston 1966
Stone, Jack, T, Oregon, Dallas Texans 1960; Oakland 1961-62
Stone, Ken, S, Vanderbilt, Buffalo 1973; Washington 1973-75; Tampa Bay 1976; St. Louis 1977-80
Stonebraker, John, E, USC, Green Bay 1942
Stonebreaker, Steve, TE-LB, Detroit, Minnesota 1962-63; Baltimore 1964-66; New Orleans 1967-68
Stonesifer, Don, E, Northwestern, Chi. Cardinals 1951-56
Storer, John, HB, Lehigh, Frankford 1924
Storm, Ed, HB, Santa Clara, Philadelphia 1934-35
Story, Bill, T, Southern Illinois, Kansas City 1975
Stotsberry, Harold, T, Xavier, Brooklyn 1930
Stotter, Rich, LB, Houston, Houston 1968
Stough, Glen, T, Duke, Pittsburgh 1945
Stoudt, Cliff, QB, Youngstown State, Pittsburgh 1977-83
Stout, Pete, FB, TCU, Washington 1949-50
Stovall, Dick, C, Abilene Christian, Detroit 1947-48; Washington 1949
Stovall, Jerry, S, LSU, St. Louis 1963-71
Stover, Jeff, NT, Oregon, San Francisco 1982-85
Stover, Stewart (Smokey), LB, Northeast Louisiana, Dallas Texans 1960-62; Kansas City 1963-66
Stowe, Otto, WR, Iowa State, Miami 1971-72; Dallas 1973; Denver 1974
Strachan, Mike, RB, Iowa State, New Orleans 1975-80
Strachan, Steve, RB, Boston College, LA Raiders 1985
Strack, Charlie, G, Colgate, Chi. Cardinals 1928
Stracka, Tim, TE, Wisconsin, Cleveland 1983-84
Strada, John, TE, William Jewell, NY Giants 1974; Kansas City 1974
Strader, Norman (Red), QB, St. Mary's (California), Chi. Cardinals 1927
Strahan, Art, DT, Texas Southern, Atlanta 1968
Strahan, Ray, DE, Texas Southern, Houston 1965
Stralka, Clem, G, Georgetown (Washington D.C.), Washington 1938-42, 1945-46
Stramiello, Mike, E, Colgate, Brooklyn 1930-32, 1934; Staten Island 1932
Strand, Eli, G, Iowa State, Pittsburgh 1966; New Orleans 1967
Strand, Lief, C, Fordham, Duluth 1924
Stransky, Bob, HB, Colorado, Denver 1960
Strasser, Clarence, E, Findlay, Canton 1925
Stratton, Mike, LB, Tennessee, Buffalo 1962-72; San Diego 1973
Strausbaugh, Jim, HB, Ohio State, Chi. Cardinals 1946
Strauss, Art (Dutch), FB-E, Phillips, Toledo 1923; Kansas City 1924
Strauthers, Tom, DE, Jackson State, Philadelphia 1983-85
Straw, Don, G, Washington & Jefferson, Detroit 1920
Strayhorn, Les, RB-KR, East Carolina, Dallas 1973-74
Strenger, Rich, T, Michigan, Detroit 1983-85
Stribling, Bill, E, Mississippi, NY Giants 1951-53; Philadelphia 1955-57
Stricker, Tony, DB, Colorado, NY Jets 1963
Strickland, Bill, G, Lombard, Milwaukee 1923; Racine 1923
Strickland, Bishop, FB, South Carolina, San Francisco 1951
Strickland, Dave, G, Memphis State, Denver 1960
Strickland, Larry, C, North Texas State, Chi. Bears 1954-59
Striegel, Bill, G, Pacific, Philadelphia 1959; Boston 1960; Oakland 1960
Stringer, Art, LB, Ball State, Houston 1977-81
Stringer, Bob, FB, Tulsa, Philadelphia 1952-53
Stringer, Gene, FB-HB, John Carroll, Cleveland 1925
Stringer, Scott, DB, California, St. Louis 1974
Stringert, Hal, CB, Hawaii, San Diego 1975-80
Stringfellow, Joe, E, Southern Mississippi, Detroit 1942
Strock, Don, QB, Virginia Tech, Miami 1974-85
Strode, Woody, E, UCLA, LA Rams 1946
Strofolino, Mike, LB, Villanova, LA Rams 1965; Baltimore 1965; St. Louis 1966-68
Strohmeyer, George, C, Notre Dame, Brooklyn (AAFC) 1948; Chi. Hornets (AAFC) 1949
Strom, Frank, T, Claremore J.C., Brooklyn 1944
Stromberg, Mike, LB, Temple, NY Jets 1968
Strong, Jim, RB, Houston, San Francisco 1970; New Orleans 1971-72
Strong, Ken, FB-K, NYU, Staten Island 1929-32; NY Giants 1933-35, 1939, 1944-47
Strong, Ray, RB, Nevada-Las Vegas, Atlanta 1978-82
Stroschein, Breck, E, UCLA, NY Yanks 1951
Strosnider, Aubrey, G, Dayton, Dayton 1928
Stroth, Vince, G-C, BYU, San Francisco 1985
Stroud, Jack, G-T, Tennessee, NY Giants 1953-64
Stroud, Morris, TE, Clark, Kansas City 1969-74
Strozier, Art, TE, Kansas State, San Diego 1970-71
Strugar, George, DT, Washington, LA Rams 1957-61; Pittsburgh 1962; NY Titans 1962; NY Jets 1963
Strutt, Art, HB, Duquesne, Pittsburgh 1935-36
Strzykalski, Johnny (Strike), HB, Marquette, San Francisco 1946-52
Stuart, Jim, T, Oregon, Washington 1941
Stuart, Roy, G, Tulsa, Cleveland 1942; Detroit 1943; Buffalo (AAFC) 1946
Stuckey, Bill, HB, Loyola (Chicago), Louisville 1926
Stuckey, Henry, CB, Missouri, Miami 1973-74; NY Giants 1975-76
Stuckey, Jim, DE, Clemson, San Francisco 1980-85
Studaway, Mark, DE, Tennessee, Houston 1984; Tampa Bay 1985
Studdard, Dave, T, Texas, Denver 1979-85
Studdard, Les, T, Texas, Kansas City 1982; Houston 1983
Studdard, Vern, WR-KR, Mississippi, NY Jets 1971
Studstill, Pat, WR-P, Houston, Detroit 1961-62, 1964-67; LA Rams 1968-71; New England 1972
Studwell, Scott, LB, Illinois, Minnesota 1977-85
Stuessy, Mel, T, St. Edward's (Texas), Chi. Cardinals 1926
Stuhldreher, Harry, QB, Notre Dame, Brooklyn 1926
Stukes, Charlie, S, Maryland-Eastern Shore, Baltimore 1967-72; LA Rams 1973-74
Sturgeon, Cecil, T, North Dakota State, Philadelphia 1941
Sturgeon, Lyle, T, North Dakota State, Green Bay 1937
Sturm, Jerry, C, Illinois, Denver 1961-66; New Orleans 1967-70; Houston 1971; Philadelphia 1972
Sturt, Fred, G, Bowling Green, Washington 1974; New England 1976-78; New Orleans 1978-81
Sturtridge, Dick, HB, DePauw, Chi. Bears 1928-29
Stydahar, Joe, T, West Virginia, Chi. Bears 1936-42, 1945-46
Stynchula, Andy, DE, Penn State, Washington 1960-63; NY Giants 1964-65; Baltimore 1966-67; Dallas 1968
Suchy, Larry, DB, Mississippi College, Atlanta 1968
Suchy, Paul, E, Cleveland 1925
Suci, Bob, DB, Michigan State, Houston 1962; Boston 1963
Sucic, Steve, FB, Illinois, LA Rams 1946; Boston 1947; Detroit 1947-48
Suess, Ray, T, Villanova, Duluth 1926-27
Suffridge, Bob, G, Tennessee, Philadelphia 1941, 1945
Sugar, Leo, DE, Purdue, Chi. Cardinals 1954-59; St. Louis 1960; Philadelphia 1961; Detroit 1962
Suggs, Shafer, S, Ball State, NY Jets 1976-80; Cincinnati 1980
Suggs, Walt, T-C, Mississippi State, Houston 1962-71
Suhey, Matt, RB, Penn State, Chi. Bears 1980-85
Suhey, Steve, G, Penn State, Pittsburgh 1948-49
Sulatis, Joe, HB-FB, NY Giants 1943-45, 1947-53; Boston 1946
Sulima, George, E, Boston U., Pittsburgh 1952-54
Sullivan, Bob, HB, Iowa, Pittsburgh 1947; Brooklyn (AAFC) 1948
Sullivan, Bob, HB, Holy Cross, San Francisco (AAFC) 1948
Sullivan, Dan, G-T, Boston College, Baltimore 1962-72
Sullivan, Dave, WR, Virginia, Cleveland 1973-74
Sullivan, Frank, C, Loyola (New Orleans), Chi. Bears 1935-39; Pittsburgh 1940
Sullivan, George, HB, Pennsylvania, Frankford 1924-25
Sullivan, George, E, Notre Dame, Boston 1948
Sullivan, Gerry, T, Illinois, Cleveland 1974-81
Sullivan, Hew (Red), G-T, Duluth 1926
Sullivan, Jim, DT, Lincoln (Missouri), Atlanta 1970
Sullivan, John, E, Buffalo 1921
Sullivan, John, LB, Illinois, NY Jets 1979-80
Sullivan, Pat, QB, Auburn, Atlanta 1972-75
Sullivan, Steve, QB, Montana, Milwaukee 1922; Evansville 1922; Hammond 1922-23; Kansas City 1924
Sullivan, Tom, RB, Miami, Philadelphia 1972-77; Cleveland 1978
Sullivan, Walter, QB, Beloit, Green Bay 1921
Sully, Ivory, S-KR, Delaware, LA Rams 1979-84; Tampa Bay 1985
Suminski, Dave, G, Wisconsin, Washington 1953; Chi. Cardinals 1953
Sumler, Tony, DB, Wichita State, Detroit 1978
Summerall, Pat, E-DE-K, Arkansas, Detroit 1952; Chi. Cardinals 1953-57; NY Giants 1957-61
Summerell, Carl, QB, East Carolina, NY Giants 1974-75
Summerhays, Bob, FB-LB, Utah, Green Bay 1949-51
Summers, Don, TE, Boise State, Denver 1984-85
Summers, Freddie, DB, Wake Forest, Cleveland 1969-71
Summers, Jim, DB, Michigan State, Denver 1967
Summers, Wilbur, P, Louisville, Detroit 1977
Sumner, Charlie, DB, William & Mary, Chi. Bears 1955, 1958-60; Minnesota 1961-62
Sumner, Walt, DB, Florida State, Cleveland 1969-74
Sumpter, Tony, G, Cameron State, Chi. Rockets (AAFC) 1946-47

Sunde, Milt, G, Minnesota, Minnesota 1964-74
Sunter, Ian, K, Detroit 1976; Cincinnati 1980
Supulski, Len, E, Dickinson, Philadelphia 1942
Surabian, Zareh, T, Williams, Providence 1927; Boston 1929
Susoeff, Nick, E, Washington State, San Francisco (AAFC) 1946-49
Susteric, Ed, HB, Findlay, Cleveland (AAFC) 1949
Sutch, George, FB, Temple, Chi. Cardinals 1946
Sutherin, Don, DB, Ohio State, NY Giants 1959; Pittsburgh 1959-60
Sutherland, Doug, DT, Wisconsin-Superior, New Orleans 1970; Minnesota 1971-81
Sutro, John, T, San Jose State, San Francisco 1962
Sutton, Archie, T, Illinois, Minnesota 1965-67
Sutton, Eddie, HB, North Carolina, Washington 1957-59; NY Giants 1960
Sutton, Joseph (Bud), HB-DB, Temple, Buffalo (AAFC) 1949; Philadelphia 1950-52
Sutton, Mickey, DB, Auburn, Houston 1966
Sutton, Mitch, DT, Kansas, Philadelphia 1974-75
Svare, Harland, LB, Washington State, LA Rams 1953-54; NY Giants 1955-60
Svendsen, Earl (Bud), G, Minnesota, Green Bay 1937, 1939; Brooklyn 1940-43
Svendsen, George, C, Minnesota, Green Bay 1935-37, 1940-41
Sverchek, Paul, NT, Cal Poly-SLO, Minnesota 1984
Svihus, Bob, T, USC, Oakland 1964-70; NY Jets 1971-73
Svoboda, Bill, LB, Tulane, Chi. Cardinals 1950-53; NY Giants 1954-58
Swain, Alton, E, Trinity (Texas), Buffalo 1926
Swain, Bill, LB, Oregon, LA Rams 1963; Minnesota 1964; NY Giants 1965, 1967; Detroit 1968-69
Swain, John, CB, Miami, Minnesota 1981-84; Miami 1985; Pittsburgh 1985
Swanke, Karl, T-C, Boston College, Green Bay 1980-85
Swann, Lynn, WR-KR, USC, Pittsburgh 1974-82
Swanson, Evar, E, Lombard, Milwaukee 1924; Rock Island 1925; Chi. Cardinals 1926-27
Swanson, Terry, P, Massachusetts, Boston 1967-68; Cincinnati 1969
Swatland, Dick, G, Notre Dame, Houston 1968
Sweeney, Calvin, WR, USC, Pittsburgh 1980-85
Sweeney, Jake, T, Cincinnati, Chi. Bears 1944
Sweeney, Jim, G-C, Pittsburgh, NY Jets 1984-85
Sweeney, Neal, SE, Tulsa, Denver 1967
Sweeney, Steve, WR, California, Oakland 1973
Sweeney, Walt, G-T, Syracuse, San Diego 1963-73; Washington 1974-75
Sweet, Fred, HB, Brown, Providence 1925-26
Sweet, Joe, WR, Tennessee State, LA Rams 1972-73; New England 1974; San Diego 1975
Sweetan, Karl, QB, Wake Forest, Detroit 1966-67; New Orleans 1968; LA Rams 1969-70
Sweetland, Fred, FB, Washington & Lee, Akron 1920; NY Giants 1921
Sweiger, Bob, HB, Minnesota, NY Yankees (AAFC) 1946-48; Chi. Hornets (AAFC) 1949
Swenson, Bob, LB, California, Denver 1975-79, 1981-83
Swiacki, Bill, E, Columbia, NY Giants 1948-50; Detroit 1951-52
Swiadon, Phil, G, NYU, Brooklyn 1943
Swider, Larry, P, Pittsburgh, Detroit 1979; St. Loius 1980; Tampa Bay 1981-82
Swift, Doug, LB, Amherst, Miami 1970-75
Swilley, Dennis, G-C, Texas A&M, Minnesota 1977-83, 1985
Swinford, Wayne, DB, Georgia, San Francisco 1965-67
Swink, Jim, HB, TCU, Dallas Texans 1960
Swinney, Clovis, DE-DT, Arkansas State, New Orleans 1970; NY Jets 1971
Swisher, Bob, HB, Northwestern, Chi. Bears 1938-41, 1945
Switowicz, Mike, FB, Notre Dame, NY Yanks 1950; Chi. Cardinals 1950
Switzer, Marvin, S, Kansas State, Buffalo 1978
Switzer, Veryl, HB, Kansas State, Green Bay 1954-55
Sydnor, Willie, WR-KR, Syracuse, Pittsburgh 1982
Sykes, Alfred, WR, Florida A&M, New England 1971
Sykes, Bob, FB, San Jose State, Washington 1952
Sykes, Gene, DB, LSU, Buffalo 1963-65; Denver 1967
Sykes, John, RB, Morgan State, San Diego 1972
Sylvester, John, HB, Temple, NY Yankees (AAFC) 1947; Baltimore (AAFC) 1948
Sylvester, Steve, G-T-C, Notre Dame, Oakland 1975-81; LA Raiders 1982-83
Symank, John, DB, Florida, Green Bay 1957-62; St. Louis 1963
Synhorst, John, T, Iowa, Rock Island 1920
Sytsma, Stan, LB, Minnesota, Atlanta 1980
Szafaryn, Len, T, North Carolina, Washington 1949; Green Bay 1950, 1953-56; Philadelphia 1957-58
Szakash, Paul, HB, Montana, Detroit 1938-39, 1941-42
Szaro, Rich, K, Harvard, New Orleans 1975-78; NY Jets 1979
Szczecko, Joe, DT, Northwestern, Atlanta 1966-68; NY Giants 1969
Szot, Walt, T, Bucknell, Chi. Cardinals 1946-48; Pittsburgh 1949-50
Szymakowski, Dave, FL, West Texas State, New Orleans 1968
Szymanski, Dick, C-LB, Notre Dame, Baltimore 1955, 1957-68
Szymanski, Frank, C-LB, Notre Dame, Detroit 1945-47; Philadelphia 1948; Chi. Bears 1949

T

Tabor, Paul, C-G, Oklahoma, Chi. Bears 1980
Tabor, Phil, DE-DT, Oklahoma, NY Giants 1979-82
Tackett, Doyle, QB, Brooklyn (AAFC) 1946-48
Tackwell, Charles (Cookie), E, Kansas State, Minneapolis 1930; Frankford 1930-31; Chi. Bears 1931-33; Cincinnati 1933-34
Taffoni, Joe, T, Tennessee-Martin, Cleveland 1967-70; NY Giants 1972-73
Taft, Merrill, HB, Wisconsin, Chi. Bears 1924
Tagge, Jerry, QB, Nebraska, Green Bay 1972-74
Tait, Art, DE, Mississippi State, NY Yanks 1951; Dallas 1952
Talamini, Bob, G, Kentucky, Houston 1960-67; NY Jets 1968
Talbert, Diron, DE-DT, Texas, LA Rams 1967-70; Washington 1971-80
Talbert, Don, T, Texas, Dallas 1962-65, 1971; Atlanta 1966-68; New Orleans 1969-70
Talbot, John, E, Brown, Providence 1926
Talcott, Don, T, Nevada-Reno, Philadelphia 1947
Taliaferro, George, HB-QB, Indiana, LA Dons (AAFC) 1949; NY Yanks 1950-51; Dallas 1952; Baltimore 1953-54; Philadelphia 1955
Taliaferro, Mike, QB, Illinois, NY Jets 1964-67; Boston 1968-70
Tallant, Dave, T, Grove City, Hammond 1921-25
Talley, Darryl, LB, West Virginia, Buffalo 1983-85
Talton, Ken, RB, Cornell, Kansas City 1980
Tamburo, Sam, E, Penn State, NY Bulldogs 1949
Tandy, George, C, North Carolina, Cleveland 1921
Tanguay, Jim, HB, NYU, Pittsburgh 1933
Tannen, Steve, S, Florida, NY Jets 1970-74
Tanner, Bob, E, Minnesota, Frankford 1930
Tanner, Hamp, T, Georgia, San Francisco 1951; Dallas 1952
Tanner, John, E-HB, Centre, Toledo 1922; Cleveland 1923-24
Tanner, John, LB, Tennessee Tech, San Diego 1971; New England 1973-74
Tarasovic, George, DE, LSU, Pittsburgh 1952-53, 1956-63; Philadelphia 1963-65; Denver 1966
Tarbox, Bruce, G, Syracuse, LA Rams 1961
Tarkenton, Fran, QB, Georgia, Minnesota 1961-66, 1972-78; NY Giants 1967-71
Tarr, Jerry, FL, Oregon, Denver 1962
Tarr, Jim, E, Missouri, Cleveland 1931
Tarrant, Bob, E, Pittsburgh State, NY Giants 1936
Tarrant, Jim, HB, Tennessee, Miami (AAFC) 1946
Tarver, John, RB, Colorado, New England 1972-74; Philadelphia 1975
Taseff, Carl, DB-KR, John Carroll, Cleveland 1951; Baltimore 1953-61; Philadelphia 1961; Buffalo 1962
Tasker, Steve, WR, Northwestern, Houston 1985
Tassos, Damon, G, Texas A&M, Detroit 1945-46; Green Bay 1947-49
Tatarek, Bob, DT, Miami, Buffalo 1968-72; Detroit 1972
Tate, Frank, LB, North Carolina Central, San Diego 1975
Tate, John, LB, Jackson State, NY Giants 1976
Tate, Rodney, RB-KR, Texas, Cincinnati 1982-83; Atlanta 1984
Tatman, Pete, HB, Nebraska, Minnestoa 1967
Tatum, Jack, S, Ohio State, Oakland 1971-79; Houston 1980
Tatum, Jess, E, North Carolina State, Pittsburgh 1938
Tatupu, Mosi, RB, USC, New England 1978-85
Taugher, Claude (Biff), HB, Marquette, Green Bay 1922
Tausch, Terry, G-T, Texas, Minnesota 1982-85
Tautolo, John, G, UCLA, NY Giants 1982-83
Tautolo, Terry, LB, UCLA, Philadelphia 1976-79; San Francisco 1980-81; Detroit 1981-82, 1984; Miami 1983
Tavenor, John, C, Indiana, Miami (AAFC) 1946
Taylor, Altie, RB, Utah State, Detroit 1969-75; Houston 1976
Taylor, Billy, RB, Texas Tech, NY Giants 1978-81; NY Jets 1981
Taylor, Bob, DT, Maryland-Eastern Shore, NY Giants 1963-64
Taylor, Bruce, CB-KR, Boston U., San Francisco 1970-77
Taylor, Charley, WR-HB, Arizona State, Washington 1964-75, 1977
Taylor, Charlie, HB, Ouachita Baptist, Brooklyn 1944
Taylor, Chuck, G, Stanford, Miami (AAFC) 1946
Taylor, Clifton, RB, Memphis State, Chi. Bears 1974; Green Bay 1976
Taylor, Corky, DB, Kansas State, LA Rams 1955, 1957
Taylor, David, T, Catawba, Baltimore 1973-77
Taylor, Ed, CB, Memphis State, NY Jets 1975-79; Miami 1979-82
Taylor, Erquiet (Babe), G, Albright, Staten Island 1931
Taylor, Greg, RB, Virginia, New England 1982
Taylor, Hosea, DE, Houston, Baltimore 1981; 1983
Taylor, Hugh (Bones), E, Oklahoma City, Washington 1947-54
Taylor, J.T., T, Missouri, New Orleans 1978-81
Taylor, Jesse, RB, Cincinnati, San Diego 1972
Taylor, Jim, FB, LSU, Green Bay 1958-66; New Orleans 1967
Taylor, Jim Bob, QB, Georgia Tech, Baltimore 1983
Taylor, Joe, DB, North Carolina A&T, Chi. Bears 1967-74
Taylor, John (Tarzan), T, Ohio State, Decatur 1920; Chi. Staleys 1921; Canton 1922; Brooklyn 1926
Taylor, Johnny, LB, Hawaii, Atlanta 1984-85
Taylor, Kenny, CB, Oregon State, Chi. Bears 1985
Taylor, Lawrence, LB, North Carolina, NY Giants 1981-85
Taylor, Lenny, WR, Tennessee, Green Bay 1984
Taylor, Lionel, WR, New Mexico Highlands, Chi. Bears 1959; Denver 1960-66; Houston 1967-68
Taylor, Malcolm, DE, Tennessee State, Houston 1982-83
Taylor, Mike, T, USC, Pittsburgh 1968-69; New Orleans 1969-70; Washington 1971; St. Louis 1973
Taylor, Mike, LB, Michigan, NY Jets 1972-73
Taylor, Otis, WR, Prairie View A&M, Kansas City 1965-75
Taylor, Roger, T, Oklahoma State, Kansas City 1981
Taylor, Roosevelt, DB, Grambling, Chi. Bears 1961-69; San Diego 1969; San Francisco 1970-71; Washington 1972
Taylor, Sammy, FL, Grambling, San Diego 1965
Taylor, Steve, S, Kansas, Kansas City 1976
Taylor, Terry, CB, Southern Illinois, Seattle 1984-85
Taylor, Willie, WR, Pittsburgh, Green Bay 1978
Tays, Jim, HB, Penn State, Kansas City 1924; Chi. Cardinals 1925; Dayton 1927; Newark 1930; Staten Island 1930
Teague, Matthew, DE, Prairie View A&M, Atlanta 1980-81
Teal, Jimmy, WR, Texas A&M, Buffalo 1985
Teal, Willie, CB, LSU, Minnesota 1980-85
Tearry, Larry, C, Wake Forest, Detroit 1978-79
Tebell, Gus, E, Wisconsin, Columbus 1923-24
Teel, Jim, LB, Purdue, Detroit 1973
Teerlinck, John, DT, Western Illinois, San Diego 1974-75
Teeter, Al, E, Minnesota, Staten Island 1932
Teeuws, Len, T-DT, Tulane, LA Rams 1952-53; Chi. Cardinals 1954-57
Temp, Jim, DE, Wisconsin, Green Bay 1957-60
Ten Napel, Garth, LB, Texas A&M, Detroit 1976-77; Atlanta 1978
Tenner, Bob, E, Minnesota, Green Bay 1935
Tensi, Steve, QB, Florida State, San Diego 1965-66; Denver 1967-70
Tepe, Lou, C, Duke, Pittsburgh 1953-55
Teresa, Tony, HB, San Jose State, San Francisco 1958; Oakland 1960
Tereshinski, Joe, E-DE, Georgia, Washington 1947-54
Terlep, George, QB, Notre Dame, Buffalo (AAFC) 1946-48; Cleveland (AAFC)1948
Terrell, Marvin (Bo), G, Mississippi, Dallas Texans 1960-62; Kansas City 1963
Terrell, Ray, HB, Mississippi, Cleveland (AAFC) 1946-47; Baltimore (AAFC) 1947
Terry, Nat, CB, Florida State, Pittsburgh 1978; Detroit 1978
Tersch, Rudy, T, Minneapolis 1921-23
Tesser, Ray, E, Carnegie-Mellon, Pittsburgh 1933-34
Testerman, Don, RB, Clemson, Seattle 1976-78, 1980
Teteak, Deral, G, Wisconsin, Green Bay 1952-56
Tevis, Lee, HB, Miami (Ohio), Brooklyn (AAFC) 1947-48
Tew, Lowell, FB, Alabama, NY Yankees (AAFC) 1948-49
Thacker, Al, HB, Morris Harvey, Philadelphia 1942
Tharp, Corky, DB, Alabama, NY Titans 1960
Thaxton, James, TE, Tennessee State, San Diego 1973-74; Cleveland 1974; New Orleans 1976-77; St. Louis 1978
Thayer, Harry, T, Tennessee, Portsmouth 1933
Thayer, Tom, G-C, Notre Dame, Chi. Bears 1985
Theismann, Joe, QB-KR, Notre Dame, Washington 1974-85
Theofiledes, Harry, QB, Waynesburg, Washington 1968
Thibaut, Jim, FB, Tulane, Buffalo (AAFC) 1946
Thibert, Jim, LB, Toledo, Denver 1965
Thiele, Carl (Dutch), E, Denison, Dayton 1920-23
Thielemann, R.C., G, Arkansas, Atlanta 1977-84; Washington 1985
Thielscher, Karl, FB, Dartmouth, Buffalo 1920
Thomas, Aaron, SE-TE, Oregon State, San Francisco 1961-62; NY Giants 1962-70
Thomas, Alonzo (Skip), S, USC, Oakland 1972-77
Thomas, Ben, NT, Auburn, New England 1985
Thomas, Bill, HB, Penn State, Frankford 1924
Thomas, Bill, RB, Boston College, Dallas 1972; Houston 1973; Kansas City 1974
Thomas, Bob, RB, Arizona State, LA Rams 1971-72; San Diego 1973-74
Thomas, Bob, K, Notre Dame, Chi. Bears 1975-84; Detroit 1982; San Diego 1985
Thomas, Cal, G, Tulsa, Detroit 1939-40
Thomas, Calvin, RB, Illinois, Chi. Bears 1982-85
Thomas, Carl, T, Pennsylvania, Rochester 1920-21; Buffalo 1922-23
Thomas, Charlie, RB, Tennessee State, Kansas City 1975
Thomas, Chuck, C-G, Oklahoma, Atlanta 1985
Thomas, Clendon, DB-WR, Oklahoma, LA Rams 1958-61; Pittsburgh 1962-68
Thomas, Donnie, LB, Indiana, New England 1976
Thomas, Duane, RB, West Texas State, Dallas 1970-71; Washington 1973-74
Thomas, Earl, WR-TE, Houston, Chi. Bears 1971-73; St. Louis 1974-75; Houston 1976
Thomas, Earlie, CB, Colorado State, NY Jets 1970-74; Denver 1975
Thomas, Emmitt, CB, Bishop, Kansas City 1966-78
Thomas, Enid, HB, Pennsylvania, Hartford 1926
Thomas, Gene, RB, Florida A&M, Kansas City 1966-67
Thomas, George, HB, Oklahoma, Washington 1950-51; NY Giants 1952
Thomas, Ike, WR-DB, Bishop, Dallas 1971; Green Bay 1972-73; Buffalo 1975
Thomas, J.T., DB, Florida State, Pittsburgh 1973-77, 1979-81;

Denver 1982
Thomas, Jesse, DB, Michigan State, Baltimore 1955-57; LA Chargers 1960
Thomas, Jewerl, RB, San Jose State, LA Rams 1980-82; Kansas City 1983; San Diego 1984
Thomas, Jim, G, Oklahoma, Chi. Cardinals 1939
Thomas, Jimmy, RB-WR, Texas-Arlington, San Francisco 1969-73
Thomas, John, G, Pacific, San Francisco 1958-67
Thomas, Kelly, T, USC, Tampa Bay 1983-84
Thomas, Ken, RB, San Jose State, Kansas City 1983
Thomas, Lee, DE, Jackson State, San Diego 1971-72; Cincinnati 1973
Thomas, Lynn, CB, Pittsburgh, San Francisco 1981-82
Thomas, Mike, RB, Nevada-Las Vegas, Washington 1975-78; San Diego 1979-80
Thomas, Norris, CB, Southern Mississippi, Tampa Bay 1980-84
Thomas, Pat, CB, Texas A&M, LA Rams 1976-82
Thomas, Ralph, E-HB, San Francisco, Chi. Cardinals 1952; Washington 1955-56
Thomas, Rex, HB, St. John's (New York), Brooklyn 1926, 1930-31; Cleveland 1927; Detroit 1928
Thomas, Rodell, LB, Alabama State, Miami 1981, 1983 84; Seattle 1981-82
Thomas, Russ, T, Ohio State, Detroit 1946-49
Thomas, Sean, CB, TCU, Cincinnati 1985; Atlanta 1985
Thomas, Speedy, WR, Utah, Cincinnati 1969-72; New Orleans 1973-74
Thomas, Spencer, S, Washburn, Washington 1975; Baltimore 1976
Thomas, Todd, C, North Dakota, Kansas City 1981
Thomas, V.P., E-HB, Rochester 1920
Thomas, Zack, WR-KR, South Carolina State, Denver 1983-84; Tampa Bay 1984
Thomaselli, Rich, RB, West Virginia Wesleyan, Houston 1981-82
Thomason, Bobby, QB, Virginia Military, LA Rams 1949; Green Bay 1951; Philadelphia 1952-57
Thomason, Jim, HB, Texas A&M, Detroit 1945
Thomason, John (Stumpy), QB, Georgia Tech, Brooklyn 1930-35; Philadelphia 1935-36
Thompson, Alvie, G-T, Lombard, Rock Island 1923; Kansas City 1924-26
Thompson, Arland, G, Baylor, Denver 1980; Green Bay 1981; Baltimore 1982
Thompson, Aundra, WR-KR, East Texas State, Green Bay 1977-81; San Diego 1981; New Orleans 1981-82; Baltimore 1983
Thompson, Billy, CB-KR, Maryland-Eastern Shore, Denver 1969-81
Thompson, Bobby, DB, Arizona State, Detroit 1964-68; New Orleans 1969
Thompson, Bobby, RB, Oklahoma, Detroit 1975-76
Thompson, Broderick, T, Kansas, Dallas 1985
Thompson, Bryant, G, Syracuse, Rochester 1922
Thompson, Clarence (Tuffy), HB, Minnesota, Pittsburgh 1937-38; Green Bay 1939
Thompson, Dave, HB, Denison, Cincinnati 1921
Thompson, Dave, T-G, Clemson, Detroit 1971-73; New Orleans 1974-75
Thompson, Del, RB, Texas-El Paso, Kansas City 1982
Thompson, Don, G, Redlands, LA Buccaneers 1926
Thompson, Don, LB, Richmond, Baltimore 1962-63; Philadelphia 1964
Thompson, Donnell, DE, North Carolina, Baltimore 1981-83; Indianapolis 1984-85
Thompson, Fred, E, Nebraska, Rock Island 1924
Thompson, Gary, CB, San Jose State, Buffalo 1983-84
Thompson, George, G, Iowa, Rock Island 1923-25
Thompson, Hal, E, Delaware, Brooklyn (AAFC) 1947-48
Thompson, Harry, G, UCLA, LA Rams 1950-54; Chi. Cardinals 1955
Thompson, Jack, QB, Washington State, Cincinnati 1979-82; Tampa Bay 1983-84
Thompson, James, WR, Memphis State, NY Giants 1978
Thompson, Jesse, WR, California, Detroit 1978, 1980
Thompson, Jim, DT, Southern Mississippi, Denver 1965
Thompson, John, T, Lafayette, Frankford 1929
Thompson, John, TE, Utah State, Green Bay 1979-82
Thompson, Kenny, WR, Utah State, St. Louis 1982-83
Thompson, Leonard, WR-KR, Oklahoma State, Detroit 1975-85
Thompson, Norm, CB, Utah, St. Louis 1971-76; Baltimore 1977-79
Thompson, Ralph (Rocky), KR-RB, West Texas State, NY Giants 1971-73
Thompson, Ricky, WR, Baylor, Baltimore 1976-77; Washington 1978-81; St. Louis 1982
Thompson, Robert, LB, Michigan, Tampa Bay 1983-84
Thompson, Russ, T, Nebraska, Chi. Bears 1936-39; Philadelphia 1940
Thompson, Steve, DE-DT, Washington, NY Jets 1968-70, 1972-73
Thompson, Ted, LB, SMU, Houston 1975-84
Thompson, Tommy, QB, Tulsa, Pittsburgh 1940; Philadelphia 1941-42, 1945-50
Thompson, Tommy, LB, William & Mary, Cleveland 1949-53
Thompson, Tommy, RB, Southern Illinois, San Diego 1974
Thompson, Vince, RB, Villanova, Detroit 1981, 1983
Thompson, Weegie, WR, Florida State, Pittsburgh 1984-85
Thompson, Woody, RB, Miami, Atlanta 1975-77
Thoms, Art, DT, Syracuse, Oakland 1969-75; Philadelphia 1977
Thornbladh, Bob, LB, Michigan, Kansas City 1974
Thornhill, Claude (Tiny), T, Pittsburgh, Cleveland 1920; Buffalo 1920
Thornton, Bill (Thunder), FB, Nebraska, St. Louis 1963-65, 1967
Thornton, Bob, G, Santa Clara, San Francisco (AAFC) 1946-47
Thornton, Bruce, DT-DE, Illinois, Dallas 1979-81; St. Louis 1982
Thornton, Bubba, WR, TCU, Buffalo 1969
Thornton, Dick, HB, Missouri-Rolla, Philadelphia 1933
Thornton, Jack, LB, Auburn, Miami 1966
Thornton, Sidney, RB, Northwestern State (Louisiana), Pittsburgh 1978-82
Thorp, Don, NT, Illinois, New Orleans 1984
Thorpe, Jim, HB, Carlisle, Canton 1920, 1926; Cleveland 1921; Oorang 1922-23; Toledo 1923; Rock Island 1924; NY Giants 1925; Chi. Cardinals 1928
Thorpe, Wilred, G, Arkansas, Cleveland 1941-42
Threadgill, Bruce, S, Mississippi State, San Francisco 1978
Thrift, Cliff, LB, East Central (Oklahoma), San Diego 1979-84; Chi. Bears 1985
Thrower, Jim, CB, East Texas State, Philadelphia 1970-72; Detroit 1973-74
Thrower, Willie, QB, Michigan State, Chi. Bears 1953
Thunder, Baptiste, G, Carlisle, Oorang 1922
Thurbon, Bob, HB, Pittsburgh, Phil-Pitt 1943; Card-Pitt 1944; Buffalo (AAFC) 1946
Thurlow, Steve, FB, Stanford, NY Giants 1964-66; Washington 1966-68
Thurman, Dennis, DB, USC, Dallas 1978-85
Thurman, John, T, Pennsylvania, LA Buccaneers 1926
Thurston, Fred (Fuzzy), G, Valparaiso, Baltimore 1958; Green Bay 1959-67
Tice, John, TE, Maryland, New Orleans 1983-85
Tice, Mike, TE, Maryland, Seattle 1981-85
Tidd, Glenn, T-G, Dayton 1920-24
Tidmore, Sam, LB, Ohio State, Cleveland 1962-63
Tidwell, Billy, HB, Texas A&M, San Francisco 1954
Tidwell, Travis, QB, Auburn, NY Giants 1950-51
Tierney, Festus, G, Minnesota, Hammond 1922; Minneapolis 1923-24; Milwaukee 1925
Tierney, Leo, C, Georgia Tech, Cleveland 1978; NY Giants 1978
Tilleman, Mike, DT, Montana, Minnesota 1966; New Orleans 1967-70; Houston 1971-72; Atlanta 1973-76
Tiller, Jim, HB-KR, Purdue, NY Titans 1962
Tiller, Morgan, E, Denver, Boston 1944; Pittsburgh 1945
Tilley, Emmett, LB, Duke, Miami 1983
Tilley, Pat, WR-KR, Louisiana Tech, St. Louis 1976-85
Tillman, Al, C, Oklahoma, Baltimore (AAFC) 1949
Tillman, Andre, TE, Texas Tech, Miami 1975-78
Tillman, Faddie, DT, Boise State, New Orleans 1972
Tillman, Rusty, LB, Northern Arizona, Washington 1970-77
Timberlake, Bob, QB, Michigan, NY Giants 1965
Timberlake, George, G-LB, USC, Green Bay 1955
Times, Ken, DT, Southern, San Francisco 1980; St. Louis 1981
Timmons, Charlie, FB, Clemson, Brooklyn (AAFC) 1946
Tingelhoff, Mick, C, Nebraska, Minnesota 1962-78
Tinker, Gerald, WR-KR, Kent State, Atlanta 1974-75; Green Bay 1975
Tinsley, Buddy, T, Baylor, LA Dons (AAFC) 1949
Tinsley, Gaynell, E, LSU, Chi. Cardinals 1937-38, 1940
Tinsley, Jess, T, LSU, Chi. Cardinals 1929-33
Tinsley, Pete, G, Georgia, Green Bay 1938-45
Tinsley, Sid, HB, Clemson, Pittsburgh 1945
Tippett, Andre, LB, Iowa, New England 1982-85
Tipton, Dave, DE, Stanford, NY Giants 1971-73; San Diego 1974-75; Seattle 1976
Tipton, Dave, DT-NT, Western Illinois, New England 1975-76; San Diego 1975
Tipton, Howie, QB-HB, USC, Chi. Cardinals 1933-37
Titchenal, Bob, E, San Jose State, Washington 1940-42; San Francisco (AAFC) 1946; LA Dons (AAFC) 1947
Titensor, Glen, G, BYU, Dallas 1981-85
Titmas, Herb, QB, Syracuse, Providence 1931
Tittle, Y.A., QB, LSU, Baltimore 1948-50; San Francisco 1951-60; NY Giants 1961-64
Titus, George, C, Holy Cross, Pittsburgh 1946
Titus, Si, E, Holy Cross, Brooklyn 1940-42; Pittsburgh 1945
Tobey, Dave, LB, Oregon, Minnesota 1966-67; Denver 1968
Tobin, Bill, HB, Missouri, Houston 1963
Tobin, Elgie, QB, Penn State, Akron 1920-21
Tobin, George, G, Notre Dame, NY Giants 1947
Tobin, Leo, G, Grove City, Akron 1921
Tobin, Rex, E, Minnesota, Duluth 1925
Tobin, Steve, C, Minnesota, NY Giants 1980
Toburen, Nelson, LB, Wichita State, Green Bay 1961-62
Todd, Dick, HB, Texas A&M, Washington 1939-42, 1945-48
Todd, Jim, RB, Ball State, Detroit 1966
Todd, Larry, RB, Arizona State, Oakland 1965-69
Todd, Richard, QB, Alabama, NY Jets 1976-83; New Orleans 1984-85
Toews, Jeff, G-C, Washington, Miami 1979-85
Toews, Loren, LB, California, Pittsburgh 1973-83
Tofil, Joe, E, Indiana, Brooklyn 1942
Tolar, Charley, FB, Northwestern State (Louisiana), Houston 1960-66
Tolbert, Jim, DB, Lincoln (Missouri), San Diego 1966-71, 1976; Houston 1972; St. Louis 1973-75
Toler, Ken, WR, Mississippi, New England 1981-82
Toles, Alvin, LB, Tennessee, New Orleans 1985
Tollefson, Charlie, G, Iowa, Green Bay 1944-46
Tolleson, Tommy, DB, Alabama, Atlanta 1966
Tolley, Ed, G, Dayton 1929
Toloumu, David, RB, Hawaii, Atlanta 1982
Tom, Mel, DE-LB, San Jose State, Philadelphia 1967-73; Chi. Bears 1973-75
Tomahawk, HB, Carlisle, Oorang 1923
Tomaini, Army, T, Catawba, NY Giants 1945
Tomaini, John, E, Georgetown (Washington D.C.), Orange 1929; Newark 1930; Brooklyn 1930-31
Tomaselli, Carl, E, Scranton, NY Giants 1940
Tomasetti, Lou, HB, Bucknell, Pittsburgh 1939-40; Detroit 1941; Philadelphia 1941-42; Buffalo (AAFC) 1946-49
Tomasic, Andy, HB, Temple, Pittsburgh 1942, 1946
Tomczak, Mike, QB, Ohio State, Chi. Bears 1985
Tomlin, Brad, G, Syracuse, Akron 1920 21; Milwaukee 1922; NY Giants 1925-26
Tomlin, J.T., G, Hammond 1921
Tomlinson, Dick, G, Kansas, Pittsburgh 1950-51
Tommerson, Clarence, HB, Wisconsin, Pittsburgh 1938-39
Toneff, Bob, DT, Notre Dame, San Francisco 1952, 1954-58; Washington 1959-64
Tonelli, Amerigo (Tony), C, USC, Detroit 1939
Tonelli, Mario, HB, Notre Dame, Chi. Cardinals 1940, 1945
Toner, Ed, DT, Massachusetts, Boston 1967-69
Toner, Tom, LB, Idaho State, Green Bay 1973, 1975-77
Tongue, Marco, DB, Bowie State, Baltimore 1983
Tonnemaker, Clayton, C-LB, Minnesota, Green Bay 1950, 1953-54
Toogood, Charley, T-DT, Nebraska, LA Rams 1951-56; Chi. Cardinals 1957
Toomay, Pat, DE, Vanderbilt, Dallas 1970-74; Buffalo 1975; Tampa Bay 1976; Oakland 1977-79
Toon, Al, WR, Wisconsin, NY Jets 1985
Topor, Ted, LB, Michigan, Detroit 1955
Topp, Bob, E, Michigan, NY Giants 1954
Toran, Stacey, S, Notre Dame, LA Raiders 1984-85
Torczon, Laverne, DE, Nebraska, Buffalo 1960-62; NY Titans 1962; NY Jets 1963-65; Miami 1966
Torgeson, LaVern (Torgy), LB, Washington State, Detroit 1951-54; Washington 1955-57
Torkelson, Eric, RB, Connecticut, Green Bay 1974-79, 1981
Torrance, Jack, T, LSU, Chi. Bears 1939-40
Torrey, Bob, RB, Penn State, NY Giants 1979; Miami 1979; Philadelphia 1980
Toscani, Francis (Bud), HB, St. Mary's (California), Brooklyn 1932; Chi. Cardinals 1932
Tosi, Flavio (Bull), E, Boston College, Boston 1934-36
Tosi, John, G, Niagara, Pittsburgh 1939; Brooklyn 1939
Toth, Zollie, FB, LSU, NY Yanks 1950-51; Dallas 1952; Baltimore 1954
Towle, Steve, LB, Kansas, Miami 1975-80
Towle, Thurston, E, Brown, Boston 1929
Towler, (Deacon) Dan, FB, Washington & Jefferson, LA Rams 1950-55
Townes, Willie, DE, Tulsa, Dallas 1966-68; New Orleans 1970
Towns, Bobby, DB-HB, Georgia, St. Louis 1960; Boston 1960
Towns, Morris (Mo), T, Missouri, Houston 1977-83; Washington 1984
Townsell, Jo Jo, WR, UCLA, NY Jets 1985
Townsend, Andre, DE-NT, Mississippi, Denver 1984-85
Townsend, Curtis, LB, Arkansas, St. Louis 1978
Townsend, Greg, DE, TCU, LA Raiders 1983-85
Townsend, Otto, G, Minneapolis 1922
Tracey, John, LB, Texas A&M, Chi. Cardinals 1959; St. Louis 1960; Philadelphia 1961; Buffalo 1962-67
Tracy, Tom (The Bomb), FB-HB, Tennessee, Detroit 1956-57; Pittsburgh 1958-63; Washington 1963-64
Trafton, George, C, Notre Dame, Decatur 1920; Chi. Staleys 1921; Chi. Bears 1922-32
Trammel, Allen, DB, Florida, Houston 1966
Trapp, Richard, SE, Florida, Buffalo 1968; San Diego 1969
Trask, Orville, DT, Rice, Houston 1960-61; Oakland 1962
Travenio, Herb, K, San Diego 1964-65
Travis, Ed, T, Missouri, Rock Island 1921; St. Louis 1923
Travis, John, FB, San Diego State, San Diego 1966
Traynham, Jerry, HB, USC, Denver 1961
Traynham, Wade, K, Frederick, Atlanta 1966-67
Traynor, Barney, C, Colgate, Milwaukee 1925
Traynor, Mike, HB, Canisius, Buffalo 1923-24
Traynowicz, Mark, G, Nebraska, Buffalo 1985
Treadway, John, T, Hardin-Simmons, NY Giants 1948; Detroit 1949
Trebotich, Ivan (Buzz), HB, St. Mary's (California), Detroit 1944-45; Baltimore (AAFC) 1947
Triggs, John, FB, Providence, Providence 1926
Trigilio, Frank, FB, Vermont, Miami (AAFC) 1946
Trimble, Steve, DB, Maryland, Denver 1981-83
Trimble, Wayne, DB, Alabama, San Francisco 1967
Triplett, Bill, HB, Miami (Ohio), St. Louis 1962-63, 1965-66;

NY Giants 1967; Detroit 1968-72
Triplett, Mel, FB, Toledo, NY Giants 1955-60; Minnesota1961-62
Triplett, Wally, HB, Penn State, Detroit 1949-50; Chi. Cardinals 1952-53
Trippi, Charley, HB-QB-DB, Georgia, Chi. Cardinals 1947-55
Tripson, John, T, Mississippi State, Detroit 1941
Tripucka, Frank, QB, Notre Dame, Philadelphia 1949; Detroit 1949; Chi. Cardinals 1950-52; Dallas 1952; Denver 1960-63
Trocano, Rick, QB-S, Pittsburgh, Cleveland 1981-83
Trocolor, Bob, QB-HB, Alabama, NY Giants 1942-43; Brooklyn 1944
Trosch, Gene, DE-DT, Miami, Kansas City 1967, 1969
Trost, Milt, T, Marquette, Chi. Bears 1935-39; Philadelphia 1940
Troup, Bill, QB, South Carolina, Baltimore 1974, 1976-79; Philadelphia 1975; Green Bay 1980
Trout, David, K, Pittsburgh, Pittsburgh 1981
Trowbridge, Ray, E, Boston College, Cleveland 1920; NY Giants 1921
Truax, Billy, TE, LSU, LA Rams 1964-69; Dallas 1970-74
Truax, Dalton, T, Tulane, Oakland 1960
Truesdell, Hal, T, Hamline, Minneapolis 1930
Trull, Don, QB, Baylor, Houston 1964-69; Boston 1967
Trumpy, Bob, TE, Utah, Cincinnati 1968-77
Tryon, Eddie, HB, Colgate, NY Yankees 1927
Tschappatt, Chalmers, T, West Virginia Wesleyan, Dayton 1921
Tsoutsouvas, Lou, C, Stanford, Pittsburgh 1938
Tsoutsouvas, Sam, C, Oregon State, Detroit 1940
Tubbs, Jerry, LB, Oklahoma, Chi. Cardinals 1957-58; San Francisco 1958-59; Dallas 1960-67
Tucker, Bill, RB, Tennessee State, San Francisco 1967-70; Chi. Bears 1971
Tucker, Bob, TE, Bloomsburg, NY Giants 1970-77; Minnesota 1977-80
Tucker, Gary, HB, Tennessee-Chattanooga, Miami 1968
Tucker, Travis, TE, Southern Connecticut, Cleveland 1985
Tucker, Wendell, WR, South Carolina State, LA Rams 1967-70
Tuckett, Phil, WR, Weber State, San Diego 1968
Tuckey, Dick, HB, Manhattan, Washington 1938; Cleveland 1938
Tuggle, Anthony, CB, Nicholls State, Pittsburgh 1985
Tuggle, John, RB-KR, California, NY Giants 1983
Tuiasosopo, Manu, DT-NT, UCLA, Seattle 1979-83; San Francisco 1984-85
Tuinei, Mark, DT-C, Hawaii, Dallas 1983-85
Tuinei, Tom, DT, Hawaii, Detroit 1980
Tullis, Walter, WR, Delaware State, Green Bay 1978-79
Tullis, Willie, CB-KR, Troy State, Houston 1981-84; New Orleans 1985
Tully, Darrell, HB, East Texas State, Detroit 1939
Tully, George, E, Dartmouth, Frankford 1927
Tunnell, Emlen, S-KR, Iowa, NY Giants 1948-58; Green Bay 1959-61
Turbert, Frank, QB, Morris Harvey, Boston 1944
Turk, Dan, C, Wisconsin, Pittsburgh 1985
Turk, Godwin, LB, Southern, NY Jets 1975; Denver 1976-78
Turley, Doug, E, Scranton, Washington 1944-48
Turley, John, QB, Ohio Wesleyan, Pittsburgh 1935-36
Turnbow, Guy, T, Mississippi, Philadelphia 1933-34
Turnbow, Jesse, DT, Tennessee, Cleveland 1978
Turner, Bake, FL, Texas Tech, Baltimore 1962; NY Jets 1963-69; Boston 1970
Turner, Cecil, WR-KR, Cal Poly-SLO, Chi. Bears 1968-73
Turner, Clem, RB, Cincinnati, Cincinnati 1969; Denver 1970-72
Turner, Clyde (Bulldog), C-LB, Hardin-Simmons, Chi. Bears 1940-52
Turner, Daryl, WR, Michigan State, Seattle 1984-85
Turner, David (Deacon), RB, San Diego State, Cincinnati 1978-80
Turner, Hal, DE, Tennessee State, Detroit 1954
Turner, Herschel, G, Kentucky, St. Louis 1964-65
Turner, J.T., G-T-DT, Duke, NY Giants 1977-83; Washington 1984
Turner, Jay, QB, George Washington, Washington 1938-39
Turner, Jim, HB, Northwestern, Milwaukee 1923
Turner, Jim, C, Oklahoma State, Cleveland 1937
Turner, Jim, K, Utah State, NY Jets 1964-70; Denver 1971-79
Turner, Jimmie, LB, Presbyterian, Dallas 1984
Turner, Jimmy, CB, UCLA, Cincinnati 1983-85
Turner, John, G, Ohio State, Dayton 1920
Turner, John, DB, Miami, Minnesota 1978-83, 1985; San Diego 1984
Turner, Keena, LB, Purdue, San Francisco 1980-85
Turner, Kevin, LB, Pacific, NY Giants 1980; Washington 1981; Seattle 1981
Turner, Maurice, RB, Utah State, Minnesota 1984-85; Green Bay 1985
Turner, Rich, DT, Oklahoma, Green Bay 1981-83
Turner, Robert, RB, Oklahoma State, Houston 1978
Turner, Rocky, WR-DB, Tennessee-Chattanooga, NY Jets 1972-73
Turner, Vince, DB, Missouri, NY Jets 1964
Turner, Wylie, DB, Angelo State, Green Bay 1979-80
Turnure, Tom, C, Washington, Detroit 1980-83, 1985
Tutson, Tom, CB, South Carolina State, Atlanta 1983
Tuttle, George, E, Minnesota, Green Bay 1927
Tuttle, Orville, G, Oklahoma City, NY Giants 1937-41, 1946
Tuttle, Perry, WR, Clemson, Buffalo 1982-83; Tampa Bay 1984; Atlanta 1984
Twedell, Fred, G, Minnesota, Green Bay 1939
Twilley, Howard, WR, Tulsa, Miami 1966-76
Tyler, Andre, WR-KR, Stanford, Tampa Bay 1982-83
Tyler, Maurice, DB, Morgan State, Buffalo 1972; Denver 1973-74; San Diego 1975; Detroit 1976; NY Jets 1977; NY Giants 1978
Tyler, Pete, QB, Hardin-Simmons, Chi. Cardinals 1937-38
Tyler, Toussaint, RB, Washington, New Orleans 1981-82
Tyler, Wendell, RB-KR, UCLA, LA Rams 1977-82; San Francisco 1983-85
Tynes, Dave, FB-HB, Texas, Columbus 1924-25
Tyree, Jim, E, Oklahoma, Boston 1948
Tyrer, Jim, T, Ohio State, Dallas Texans 1961-62; Kansas City 1963-73; Washington 1974
Tyrrell, Joe, G, Temple, Philadelphia 1952
Tyrrell, Tim, RB, Northern Illinois, Atlanta 1984-85
Tyson, Dick, G, Tulsa, Oakland 1966; Denver 1967

U

Ucovich, Mitch, T, San Jose State, Washington 1944; Chi. Cardinals 1945
Uecker, Keith, T, Auburn, Denver 1982-83; Green Bay 1984-85
Uguccioni, Enrico (Rocky), E, Murray State, Brooklyn 1944
Uhrinyak, Steve, G, Franklin & Marshall, Washington 1939
Ulinski, Eddie, G, Marshall, Cleveland (AAFC) 1946-49
Ulinski, Harry, C, Kentucky, Washington 1950-51, 1953-56
Ullery, Bill, HB, Penn State, Dayton 1922
Ulmer, Mike, CB, Doane, Chi. Bears 1980
Ulrich, Chuck, DT, Illinois, Chi. Cardinals 1954-58
Ulrich, Hub, E, Kansas, Miami (AAFC) 1946
Umont, Frank, T, NY Giants 1943-45
Umphrey, Rich, C, Colorado, NY Giants 1982-84; San Diego 1985
Underwood, Jack, G, Duluth 1924-27; Pottsville 1927; Buffalo 1927; Chi. Cardinals 1929
Underwood, John, G, Rice, Milwaukee 1923
Underwood, Olen, LB, Texas, NY Giants 1965; Houston 1966-70; Denver 1971
Underwood, Wayne, T, Davis & Elkins, Cleveland 1937
Ungerer, Joe, T, Fordham, Washington 1944-45
Unitas, Johnny, QB, Louisville, Baltimore 1955-72; San Diego 1973
Upchurch, Rick, WR-KR, Minnesota, Denver 1975-83
Uperesa, Tuufuli, G-T, Montana, Philadelphia 1971
Upshaw, Gene, G, Texas A&I, Oakland 1967-81
Upshaw, Marvin, DE, Trinity (Texas), Cleveland 1968-69; Kansas City 1970-75; St. Louis 1976
Uram, Andy, HB, Minnesota, Green Bay 1938-43
Urban, Alex, E, South Carolina, Green Bay 1941, 1944-45
Urban, Gasper, G, Notre Dame, Chi. Rockets (AAFC) 1948
Urban, Lou, E, Boston College, Buffalo 1921-24
Urbanek, Jim, DT, Mississippi, Miami 1968
Uremovich, Emil, T, Indiana, Detroit 1941-42, 1945-46; Chi. Rockets (AAFC) 1948
Urenda, Herman, DB, Pacific, Oakland 1963
Ursella, Rube, QB, Minnesota, Rock Island 1920, 1924-25; Minneapolis 1921; Akron 1926; Hammond 1926
Usher, Eddie, QB, Michigan, Buffalo 1921; Rock Island 1922; Green Bay 1922; Kansas City 1924
Usher, Lou, T, Syracuse, Rochester 1920-21; Chi. Staleys 1921; Hammond 1921, 1923-24, 1926; Chi. Bears 1923; Milwaukee 1924; Kenosha 1924
Utt, Ben, G, Georgia Tech, Baltimore 1982-83; Indianapolis 1984-85
Uzdavinis, Walt, E, Fordham, Cleveland 1937

V

Vacanti, Sam, QB, Nebraska, Chi. Rockets (AAFC) 1947-48; Baltimore (AAFC) 1948-49
Vactor, Ted, DB, Nebraska, Washington 1969-73; Chi. Bears 1975
Vainowski, Pete, G, Louisville 1926
Vairo, Dom, E, Notre Dame, Green Bay 1935
Valdez, Vernon, DB, San Diego State, LA Rams 1960; Buffalo 1961; Oakland 1962
Valentine, Zack, LB, East Carolina, Pittsburgh 1979-81; Philadelphia 1982
Vallez, Emilio, TE, New Mexico, Chi. Bears 1968-69
Van Brocklin, Norm, QB-P, Oregon, LA Rams 1949-57; Philadelphia 1958-60
Van Buren, Ebert, HB-LB, LSU, Philadelphia 1951-53
Van Buren, Steve, HB, LSU, Philadelphia 1944-51
Vance, Bob, HB, CCNY, Staten Island 1932
Vance, Joe, HB, Southwest Texas State, Brooklyn 1931
Vanderbundt, Skip, LB, Oregon State, San Francisco 1969-77; New Orleans 1978
VanderKelen, Ron, QB, Wisconsin, Minnesota 1963-67
Vanderloo, George, FB, Iowa State, Rock Island 1921
Vandersea, Phil, LB, Massachusetts, Green Bay 1966, 1968-69; New Orleans 1967
Vandeweghe, Al, E, William & Mary, Buffalo (AAFC) 1946
Van Divier, Randy, T, Washington, Baltimore 1981; LA Raiders 1982
Van Doren, Bob, DE, USC, San Francisco 1953
Van Duyne, Bob, G, Idaho, Baltimore 1974-80
Van Dyke, Bruce, G, Missouri, Philadelphia 1966; Pittsburgh 1967-73; Green Bay 1974-76
Van Dyke, Jim, HB, Louisville 1922-23
Van Dyne, Charlie, T, Missouri, Buffalo 1925
van Eeghen, Mark, RB, Colgate, Oakland 1974-81; New England 1982-83
Van Every, Hal, HB, Minnesota, Green Bay 1940-41
Van Galder, Tim, QB, Iowa State, St. Louis 1972
Van Heusen, Billy, SE-P, Maryland, Denver 1968-76
Van Horn, Doug, T, Ohio State, Detroit 1966; NY Giants 1968-79
Van Horne, Charlie, HB, Washington & Lee, Buffalo 1927; Orange 1929
Van Horne, Keith, T, USC, Chi. Bears 1981-85
Vann, Norwood, LB, East Carolina, LA Rams 1984-85
Van Note, Jeff, C, Kentucky, Atlanta 1969-85
Vanoy, Vernon, DE, Kansas, NY Giants 1971; Green Bay 1972; Houston 1973
Van Pelt, Brad, LB, Michigan State, NY Giants 1973-83; LA Raiders 1984-85
Van Raaphorst, Dick, K, Ohio State, Dallas 1964; San Diego 1966-67
Van Sickle, Clyde, T, Arkansas, Frankford 1930; Green Bay 1932-33
Vant Hull, Fred, G, Minnesota, Green Bay 1942
Van Tone, Art, HB, Southern Mississippi, Detroit 1943-45; Brooklyn (AAFC) 1946
Van Valkenberg, Pete, RB, BYU, Buffalo 1973; Green Bay 1974; Chi. Bears 1974
Van Wagner, Jim, RB, Michigan Tech, New Orleans 1978
Vanzo, Fred, QB, Northwestern, Detroit 1938-41; Chi. Cardinals 1941
Vardian, John, HB, Miami (AAFC) 1946; Baltimore (AAFC) 1947-48
Vargo, Larry, DB-LB, Detroit, Detroit 1962-63; Minnesota 1964-65; NY Giants 1966
Varrichione, Frank, T, Notre Dame, Pittsburgh 1955-60; LA Rams 1961-65
Varty, Mike, LB, Northwestern, Washington 1974; Baltimore 1975
Vasicek, Vic, LB, Texas, Buffalo (AAFC) 1949; LA Rams 1950
Vassau, Roy, T, St. Thomas (Minnesota), Milwaukee 1923
Vasys, Arunas, LB, Notre Dame, Philadelphia 1966-68
Vataha, Randy, WR, Stanford, New England 1971-76; Green Bay 1977
Vaughan, Charles (Pug), HB, Tennessee, Detroit 1935; Chi. Cardinals 1936
Vaughan, Harp, HB, Indiana U. (Pennsylvania), Pittsburgh 1933-34
Vaughan, Ruben, DE-DT, Colorado, San Francisco 1979; LA Raiders 1982; Minnesota 1984
Vaughn, Bill, HB, SMU, Buffalo 1926
Vaughn, Bob, G, Mississippi, Denver 1968
Vaughn, Tommy, DB, Iowa State, Detroit 1965-71
Vaught, Ted, E, TCU, San Francisco 1955
Veach, Walter, HB, Decatur 1920
Veals, Elton, RB, Tulane, Pittsburgh 1984
Vedder, Norton, HB, Buffalo 1927
Vella, John, T, USC, Oakland 1972-79; Minnesota 1980
Vellone, Jim, G, USC, Minnesota 1966-70
Venturelli, Fred, T, Chi. Bears 1948
Venuto, Sam, HB, Guilford, Washington 1952
Vereb, Ed, HB, Maryland, Washington 1960
Vereen, Carl, T, Georgia Tech, Green Bay 1957
Vergara, George, E, Notre Dame, Green Bay 1925
Veris, Garin, DE, Stanford, New England 1985
Verry, Norm, T, USC, Chi. Rockets (AAFC) 1946-47
Verser, David, WR, Kansas, Cincinnati 1981-84; Tampa Bay 1985
Vertefeuille, Brian, G, Idaho State, San Diego 1974
Vessels, Billy, HB, Oklahoma, Baltimore 1956
Vesser, John, E, Idaho, Chi. Cardinals 1927, 1930-31
Vetrano, Joe, HB-K, Southern Mississippi, San Francisco (AAFC) 1946-49
Vetter, Jack, HB, McPherson, Brooklyn 1942
Vexall, Roy, FB, Duluth 1923-25
Vezmar, Walt, G, Michigan State, Detroit 1946-47
Vick, Dick, QB, Washington & Jefferson, Kenosha 1924; Detroit 1925-26; Canton 1926
Vick, Ernie, C, Michigan, Detroit Panthers 1925; Chi. Bears 1927-28; Detroit Wolverines 1928
Vidal, Eugene, FB, Army, Washington 1921
Vidoni, Vic, E, Duquesne, Pittsburgh 1935-36
Vigorito, Tommy, RB-KR, Virginia, Miami 1981-83, 1985
Villanueva, Danny, K-P, New Mexico State, LA Rams 1960-64; Dallas 1965-67
Villapiano, Phil, LB, Bowling Green, Oakland 1971-79; Buffalo 1980-83
Viltz, Theo, CB, USC, Houston 1966
Vince, Ralph, G, Washington & Jefferson, Cleveland 1923-25
Vincent, Ted, DT, Wichita State, Cincinnati 1978; San Francisco 1979-80
Vinnola, Paul, HB, Santa Clara, LA Dons (AAFC) 1946
Vinyard, Kenny, K, Texas Tech, Atlanta 1970
Virkus, Scott, DE, San Francisco C.C., Buffalo 1983-84; New England 1984; Indianapolis 1984-85
Visger, George, DT, Colorado, San Francisco 1980
Visnic, Larry, G, Benedictine, NY Giants 1943-45
Vitali, Mark, QB, Purdue, Kansas City 1977
Vitiello, Sandro, K, Massachusetts, Cincinnati 1980

Vodicka, Joe, HB, Chi. Bears 1943, 1945; Chi. Cardinals 1945
Vogds, Evan, G, Wisconsin, Chi. Rockets (AAFC) 1946-47; Green Bay 1948-49
Vogel, Bob, T, Ohio State, Baltimore 1963-72
Vogelaar, Carroll, T, San Francisco, Boston 1947-48; NY Bulldogs 1949; NY Yanks 1950
Vogler, Tim, C, Ohio State, Buffalo 1979-85
Voight, Bob, DT, Cal State-Los Angeles, Oakland 1961
Voight, Mike, RB, North Carolina, Houston 1977
Voigt, Stu, TE, Wisconsin, Minnesota 1970-80
Vokaty, Otto, HB, Heidelberg, Cleveland 1931; NY Giants 1932; Chi. Cardinals 1933; Cincinnati 1934
Volk, Rick, S, Michigan, Baltimore 1967-75; NY Giants 1976; Miami 1977-78
Vollenweider, Jim, RB, Miami, San Francisco 1962-63
Volok, Bill, T-G, Tulsa, Chi. Cardinals 1934-39
Volz, Pete, E, Brown, Chi. Tigers 1920; Cincinnati 1921
Volz, Wilbur, HB, Missouri, Buffalo (AAFC) 1949
von Schamann, Uwe, K, Oklahoma, Miami 1979-84
Von Sonn, Andy, LB, UCLA, LA Rams 1964
Vosberg, Don, E, Marquette, NY Giants 1941
Voss, Lloyd, DE-DT, Nebraska, Green Bay 1964-65; Pittsburgh 1966-71; Denver 1972
Voss, Walter (Tillie), E, Detroit, Detroit 1921, 1925; Buffalo 1921, 1929; Rock Island 1922; Akron 1922; Toledo 1923; Green Bay 1924; NY Giants 1926; Chi. Bears 1927-28; Dayton 1929
Voytek, Ed, G, Purdue, Washington 1957-58
Vucinich, Milt, C, Stanford, Chi. Bears 1945

W

Waddell, Charles, TE, North Carolina, Tampa Bay 1977
Waddy, Billy, WR-KR, Colorado, LA Rams 1977-82; Minnesota 1984
Waddy, Ray, CB, Texas A&I, Washington 1979-80
Wade, Bill, QB, Vanderbilt, LA Rams 1954-60; Chi. Bears 1961-66
Wade, Bob, DB, Morgan State, Pittsburgh 1968; Washington 1969; Denver 1970
Wade, Charlie, WR, Tennessee State, Chi. Bears 1974; Green Bay 1975; Kansas City 1977
Wade, Jim, HB, Oklahoma City, NY Bulldogs 1949
Wade, Tommy, QB, Texas, Pittsburgh 1964-65
Waechter, Henry, DE-DT, Nebraska, Chi. Bears 1982, 1984-85; Baltimore 1983; Indianapolis 1984
Wafer, Carl, DE-DT, Tennessee State, Green Bay 1974; NY Giants 1974
Wager, Clint, E, St. Mary's (Minnesota), Chi. Bears 1942; Chi. Cardinals 1943, 1945; Card-Pitt 1944
Wager, John (Red), C, Carthage, Portsmouth 1931-33
Wages, Harmon, RB, Florida, Atlanta 1968-71, 1973
Wagner, Buff, HB, Northern Michigan, Green Bay 1921
Wagner, Lowell, HB, USC, NY Yankees (AAFC) 1946-48; San Francisco 1949-53, 1955
Wagner, Mike, S, Western Illinois, Pittsburgh 1971-80
Wagner, Ray, E, Columbia, Newark 1930; Brooklyn 1931
Wagner, Ray, T, Kent State, Cincinnati 1982
Wagner, Sid, G, Michigan State, Detroit 1936-38
Wagner, Steve, S, Wisconsin, Green Bay 1976-79; Philadelphia 1980-81
Wagner, Vince, K, Northwestern (Minnesota), Seattle 1981
Wagoner, Danny, DB, Kansas, Detroit 1982-84; Minnesota 1984; Atlanta 1985
Wagstaff, Jim, DB, Idaho State, Chi. Cardinals 1959; Buffalo 1960-61
Wainscott, Loyd, LB, Texas, Houston 1969-70
Waite, Carl, E-HB, Georgetown (Washington D.C.), Frankford 1928; Orange 1929; Newark 1930
Waite, Will, C, Fordham, Columbus 1920-21
Walbridge, Larry, C, NY Giants 1925
Waldemore, Stan, G-T, Nebraska, NY Jets 1978-84
Walden, Bobby, P, Georgia, Minnesota 1964-67; Pittsburgh 1968-77
Waldron, Austin, G, Gonzaga, Chi. Cardinals 1927
Waldsmith, Ralph (Fat), G, Akron, Cleveland 1921; Canton 1922
Walik, Billy, WR-KR, Villanova, Philadelphia 1970-72
Walker, Bill, G, Kentucky, Columbus 1922
Walker, Bill, G, Virginia Military, Boston 1944-45
Walker, Byron, WR, Citadel, Seattle 1982-85
Walker, Chuck, DT-DE, Duke, St. Louis 1964-72; Atlanta 1972-75
Walker, Clarence, RB, Southern Illinois, Denver 1963
Walker, Cleo, LB-C, Louisville, Green Bay 1970; Atlanta 1971
Walker, Doak, HB-K, SMU, Detroit 1950-55
Walker, Donnie, S, Central State (Ohio), Buffalo 1973-74; NY Jets 1975
Walker, Dwight, WR-KR, Nicholls State, Cleveland 1982-84
Walker, Elliott, RB, Pittsburgh, San Francisco 1978
Walker, Fulton, CB-KR, West Virginia, Miami 1981-85; LA Raiders 1985
Walker, Glen, P, USC, LA Rams 1977-78
Walker, James, LB, Kansas State, Kansas City 1982-83
Walker, Louie, LB, Colorado State, Dallas 1974
Walker, Malcolm, C, Rice, Dallas 1966-69; Green Bay 1970
Walker, Mickey, G, Michigan State, NY Giants 1961-65
Walker, Mike, DE, Tulane, New Orleans 1971
Walker, Mike, K, New England 1972
Walker, Paul, E, Yale, NY Giants 1948
Walker, Quentin, WR, Virginia, St. Louis 1984
Walker, Randy, P, Northwestern State (Louisiana), Green Bay 1974
Walker, Rick, TE, UCLA, Cincinnati 1977-79; Washington 1980-85
Walker, Tim, LB, Savannah State, Seattle 1980
Walker, Val Joe, DB, SMU, Green Bay 1953-56; San Francisco 1957
Walker, Wayne, LB-K, Idaho, Detroit 1958-72
Walker, Wayne, LB-P, Northwestern State (Louisiana), Kansas City 1967; Houston 1968
Walker, Wesley, WR, California, NY Jets 1977-85
Walker, Willie, FL, Tennessee State, Detroit 1966
Wallace, Bev, QB, Compton J.C., San Francisco (AAFC) 1947-49; NY Yanks 1951
Wallace, Bob, TE, Texas-El Paso, Chi. Bears 1968-72
Wallace, Fred (Dutch), C-G, Virginia, Akron 1923-24, 1926; Cleveland 1925; Canton 1926
Wallace, Gordon, HB, Rochester, Rochester 1923
Wallace, Henry, DB, Pacific, LA Chargers 1960
Wallace, Jackie, S, Arizona, Minnesota 1974; Baltimore 1975-76; LA Rams 1977-79
Wallace, John, E, Notre Dame, Chi. Bears 1928; Dayton 1929
Wallace, Rodney, G-T, New Mexico, Dallas 1971-73
Wallace, Roger, WR, Bowling Green, NY Giants 1976
Wallace, Stan, LB, Illinois, Chi. Bears 1954, 1956-58
Waller, Bill, E, Illinois, Brooklyn 1938
Waller, Ron, HB-KR, Maryland, LA Rams 1955-58; LA Chargers 1960
Wallner, Fred, G, Notre Dame, Chi. Cardinals 1951-52, 1954-55; Houston 1960
Walls, Everson, CB, Grambling, Dallas 1981-85
Walls, Herkie, KR-WR, Texas, Houston 1983-85
Walls, Will, E, TCU, NY Giants 1937-39, 1941-43
Walquist, Laurie, QB, Illinois, Chi. Bears 1922-31
Walsh, Bill, C, Notre Dame, Pittsburgh 1949-54
Walsh, Ed, T, Widener, NY Titans 1961
Walsh, Jim, RB, San Jose State, Seattle 1980
Walsh, Ward, RB, Colorado, Houston 1971-72; Green Bay 1972
Walston, Bobby, E-TE-K, Georgia, Philadelphia 1951-62
Walter, Joe, T, Texas Tech, Cincinnati 1985
Walter, Mike, LB, Oregon, Dallas 1983; San Francisco 1984-85
Walters, Danny, CB, Arkansas, San Diego 1983-85
Walters, Les, SE, Penn State, Washington 1958
Walters, Rod, G, Iowa, Kansas City 1976, 1978-80; Miami 1980; Detroit 1980
Walters, Stan, T, Syracuse, Cincinnati 1972-74; Philadelphia 1975-83
Walters, Tom, DB, Southern Mississippi, Washington 1964-67
Walterscheid, Lennie, S-KR, Southern Utah State, Chi. Bears 1977-82; Buffalo 1983-84
Walton, Bruce, T, UCLA, Dallas 1973-75
Walton, Chuck, G, Iowa, Detroit 1967-74
Walton, Frank (Tiger), G, Pittsburgh, Boston 1934; Washington 1944-45
Walton, Joe, TE, Pittsburgh, Washington 1957-60; NY Giants 1962-63
Walton, Johnnie, QB, Elizabeth City State, Philadelphia 1976-79
Walton, Larry, WR, Arizona State, Detroit 1969-74, 1976; Buffalo 1978
Walton, Sam, T, East Texas State, NY Jets 1968-69; New Orleans 1971
Walton, Wayne, G-T, Abilene Christian, NY Giants 1971; Kansas City 1973-74
Walton, Whip, LB, San Diego State, NY Giants 1980
Wanless, George, HB-E, Louisville 1922-23
Wantland, Hal, DB, Tennessee, Miami 1966
Ward, Bill, T, Pennsylvania, Buffalo 1921
Ward, Bill, G, Washington State, Washington 1946-47; Detroit 1947-49
Ward, Carl, DB, Michigan, Cleveland 1967-68; New Orleans 1969
Ward, Chris, T, Ohio State, NY Jets 1978-83; New Orleans 1984
Ward, Dave, T, New Mexico, Boston 1933
Ward, Elmer, C, Utah State, Detroit 1935
Ward, Gillie, T, Notre Dame, Dayton 1923
Ward, Jimmy, QB, Gettysburg, Baltimore 1967-68; Philadelphia 1971
Ward, John, T, USC, Frankford 1930; Minneapolis 1930
Ward, John Henry, DE-G, Oklahoma State, Minnesota 1970-73, 1975; Tampa Bay 1976; Chi. Bears 1976
Ward, Paul, DT, Whitworth, Detroit 1961-62
Wardlow, Duane, SE, Washington, LA Rams 1954, 1956
Ware, Charlie, T, Birmingham Southern, Brooklyn 1944
War Eagle, T-G, Oorang 1922
Warfield, Paul, WR, Ohio State, Cleveland 1964-69, 1976-77; Miami 1970-74
Warlick, Ernie, TE, North Carolina Central, Buffalo 1962-65
Warner, Bob, HB, Duluth 1927
Warner, Charley, DB, Prairie View A&M, Kansas City 1963-64; Buffalo 1964-66
Warner, Curt, RB, Penn State, Seattle 1983-85
Warnke, Dave, K, Augsburg, Tampa Bay 1983
Warren, Buist, HB, Tennessee, Philadelphia 1945; Pittsburgh 1945
Warren, Dewey, QB, Tennessee, Cincinnati 1968
Warren, Don, TE, San Diego State, Washington 1979-85
Warren, Frank, DE, Auburn, New Orleans 1981-85
Warren, Jimmy, DB, Illinois, San Diego 1964-65; Miami 1966-69; Oakland 1970-74, 1977
Warren, John, P, Tennessee, Dallas 1983-84
Warren, Morrie, FB, Arizona State, Brooklyn (AAFC) 1948
Warrington, Caleb (Tex), C, Auburn, Brooklyn (AAFC) 1946-48
Warweg, Earl, QB, Evansville 1921
Warwick, Lonnie, LB, Tennessee Tech, Minnesota 1965-72; Atlanta 1973-74
Warzeka, Ron, DT, Montana State, Oakland 1960
Washington, Al, LB, Ohio State, NY Jets 1981
Washington, Anthony, CB, Fresno State, Pittsburgh 1981-82; Washington 1983-84
Washington, Chris, LB, Iowa State, Tampa Bay 1984-85
Washington, Clarence, DT, Arkansas-Pine Bluff, Pittsburgh 1969-70
Washington, Clyde, DB, Purdue, Boston 1960-61; NY Jets 1963-65
Washington, Dave, TE, USC, Denver 1968
Washington, Dave, LB, Alcorn State, Denver 1970-71; Buffalo 1972-74; San Francisco 1975-77; Detroit 1978-79; New Orleans 1980
Washington, Dick, DB, Bethune-Cookman, Miami 1968
Washington, Eric, DB, Texas-El Paso, St. Louis 1972-73
Washington, Fred, T, North Texas State, Washington 1968
Washington, Gene, WR, Michigan State, Minnesota 1967-72; Denver 1973
Washington, Gene, WR, Stanford, San Francisco 1969-77; Detroit 1979
Washington, Gene, WR, Georgia, NY Giants 1979
Washington, Harry, WR, Colorado State, Minnesota 1978; Chi. Bears 1979
Washington, Joe, RB, Illinois State, Atlanta 1973
Washington, Joe, RB-KR, Oklahoma, San Diego 1977; Baltimore 1978-80; Washington 1981-84; Atlanta 1985
Washington, Kenny, HB, UCLA, LA Rams 1946-48
Washington, Lionel, CB, Tulane, St. Louis 1983-85
Washington, Mark, CB, Morgan State, Dallas 1970-78; New England 1979
Washington, Mike, CB, Alabama, Tampa Bay 1976-84
Washington, Ronnie, LB, Northeast Louisiana, Atlanta 1985
Washington, Russ, T, Missouri, San Diego 1968-82
Washington, Sam, CB, Mississippi Valley State, Pittsburgh 1982-85; Cincinnati 1985
Washington, Ted, RB, San Diego State, Cincinnati 1968
Washington, Ted, LB, Mississippi Valley State, Houston 1973-82
Washington, Tim, CB, Fresno State, San Francisco 1982; Kansas City 1982
Washington, Vic, DB-RB, Wyoming, San Francisco 1971-73; Houston 1974; Buffalo 1975-76
Waskiewicz, Jim, LB, Wichita State, NY Jets 1966-67; Atlanta 1969
Wasserbach, Lloyd, T, Wisconsin, Chi. Rockets (AAFC) 1946-47
Waterfield, Bob, QB-K-P, UCLA, Cleveland 1945; LA Rams 1946-52
Waters, Andre, KR-CB, Cheyney State, Philadelphia 1984-85
Waters, Bobby, QB, Presbyterian, San Francisco 1960-64
Waters, Charlie, DB, Clemson, Dallas 1970-78, 1980-81
Waters, Dale, E, Florida, Cleveland 1931; Portsmouth 1931; Boston 1932-33
Watford, Jerry, DE, Alabama, Chi. Cardinals 1953-54
Watkins, Bobby, HB, Ohio State, Chi. Bears 1955-57; Chi. Cardinals 1958
Watkins, Bobby, CB, Southwest Texas State, Detroit 1982-85
Watkins, Foster, QB, West Texas State, Philadelphia 1940-41
Watkins, Gordon, T, Georgia Tech, Minneapolis 1930; Frankford 1930; Brooklyn 1931
Watkins, Larry, RB, Alcorn State, Detroit 1969; Philadelphia 1970-72; Buffalo 1973-74; NY Giants 1975-77
Watkins, Tom, HB, Iowa State, Cleveland 1961; Detroit 1962-65, 1967; Pittsburgh 1968
Watson, Allen, K, Newport (Wales), Pittsburgh 1970
Watson, Dave, G, Georgia Tech, Boston 1963-64
Watson, Ed, LB, Grambling, Houston 1969
Watson, Grady (Rat), HB, Texas, Toledo 1922-23; Kenosha 1924; Hammond 1924-25; Buffalo 1927
Watson, Jim, C, Pacific, Washington 1945
Watson, Joe, C, Rice, Detroit 1950
Watson, John, T-G, Oklahoma, San Francisco 1971-76; New Orleans 1977-79
Watson, Mike, T, Miami (Ohio), New Orleans 1977
Watson, Pete, TE, Tufts, Cincinnati 1972
Watson, Sid, HB, Northeastern, Pittsburgh 1955-57; Washington 1958
Watson, Steve, WR, Temple, Denver 1979-85
Watt, Joe, HB-DB, Syracuse, Boston 1947; Detroit 1947-48; NY Bulldogs 1949
Watt, Walt, HB, Miami, Chi. Cardinals 1945
Wattelet, Frank, S, Kansas, New Orleans 1981-85
Watters, Bob, DE, Lincoln (Missouri), NY Titans 1962; NY Jets 1963-64
Watters, Len, E, Springfield, Buffalo 1924

Watts, George, T, Appalachian State, Washington 1942
Watts, Rickey, WR, Tulsa, Chi. Bears 1979-83
Watts, Robert, LB, Boston College, Oakland 1978
Watts, Ted, CB, Texas Tech, Oakland 1981; LA Raiders 1982-84; NY Giants 1985
Way, Charlie, HB, Penn State, Canton 1921; Frankford 1924
Waymer, Dave, CB, Notre Dame, New Orleans 1980-85
Wayt, Russell, LB, Rice, Dallas 1965
Wear, Bob, C, Penn State, Philadelphia 1942
Weatherall, Jim, DT, Oklahoma, Philadelphia 1955-57; Washington 1958; Detroit 1959-60
Weatherford, Jim, DB, Tennessee, Atlanta 1969
Weatherly, Gerry (Bones), C, Rice, Chi. Bears 1950, 1952-54
Weatherly, Jim, C, Atlanta 1976
Weathers, Carl, LB-DE, San Diego State, Oakland 1970-71
Weathers, Clarence, WR, Delaware State, New England 1983-84; Cleveland 1985
Weathers, Curtis, LB, Mississippi, Cleveland 1979-85
Weathers, Guy, G, Baylor, Buffalo 1926
Weathers, Robert, RB, Arizona State, New England 1982-85
Weatherspoon, Cephus, WR, Fort Lewis, New Orleans 1972
Weatherwax, Jim, DE-DT, Cal State-Los Angeles, Green Bay 1966-67, 1969
Weaver, Charles (Buck), G, Chicago, Chi. Cardinals 1930; Portsmouth 1930
Weaver, Charlie, LB, USC, Detroit 1971-80; Washington 1981
Weaver, Emanuel, NT, South Carolina, Cincinnati 1982
Weaver, Gary, LB, Fresno State, Oakland 1973-74; Green Bay 1975-79
Weaver, Herman (Thunderfoot), P, Tennessee, Detroit 1970-76; Seattle 1977-80
Weaver, Jim (Red), C, Centre, Columbus 1923
Weaver, John, G, Miami (Ohio), NY Bulldogs 1949
Weaver, Larrye, HB, Fullerton J.C., NY Giants 1955
Webb, Allen, HB-DB, Arnold, NY Giants 1961-65
Webb, Art, G, Geneseo Wesleyan, Rochester 1920; Milwaukee 1922
Webb, Don, DB, Iowa State, Boston 1961-62, 1964-70; New England 1971
Webb, George, E, Texas Tech, Brooklyn 1943
Webb, Jimmy, DT, Mississippi State, San Francisco 1975-80; San Diego 1981
Webb, Ken, HB, Presbyterian, Detroit 1958-62; Cleveland 1963
Webber, Harry, E, Morningside, Rock Island 1920, 1923
Webber, Howard (Cowboy), E, Kansas State, Kansas City 1924-26; Cleveland 1925, 1927; Hartford 1926; NY Giants 1926; Green Bay 1928; Providence 1930; Newark 1930
Weber, Charlie, C, Colgate, Brooklyn 1926
Weber, Chuck, LB, West Chester, Cleveland 1955-56; Chi. Cardinals 1956-58; Philadelphia 1959-61
Weber, Dick, HB, St. Louis, Detroit 1945
Webster, Alex, FB, North Carolina State, NY Giants 1955-64
Webster, Cornell, CB, Tulsa, Seattle 1977-80
Webster, Dave, DB, Prairie View A&M, Dallas Texans 1960-61
Webster, Fred, HB, Colgate, Racine 1924
Webster, George, LB, Michigan State, Houston 1967-72; Pittsburgh 1972-73; New England 1974-76
Webster, Mike, C, Wisconsin, Pittsburgh 1974-85
Webster, Tim, K, Arkansas, Green Bay 1971
Wedel, Dick, G, Wake Forest, Chi. Cardinals 1948
Wedemeyer, Herman, HB, St. Mary's (California), LA Dons (AAFC) 1948; Baltimore (AAFC) 1949
Weed, Tad, K, Ohio State, Pittsburgh 1955
Weedon, Don, G, Texas, Philadelphia 1947
Weeks, George, E, Alabama, Brooklyn 1944
Weese, Norris, QB, Mississippi, Denver 1976-79
Wegener, Bill, G, Missouri, Houston 1962-63
Weger, Mike, S, Bowling Green, Detroit 1967-73, 1975; Houston 1976-77
Wegert, Ted, FB, Philadelphia 1955-56; NY Titans 1960; Denver 1960; Buffalo 1960
Wehba, Ray, E, USC, Brooklyn 1943; Green Bay 1944
Wehrli, Roger, CB, Missouri, St. Louis 1969-82
Weimer, Chuck, HB, Wilmington, Buffalo 1929; Brooklyn 1930; Cleveland 1931
Weinberg, Henry, G, Duquesne, Pittsburgh 1934
Weinberg, Saul, T, Case Western Reserve, Cleveland 1923
Weiner, Al (Reds), HB, Muhlenberg, Philadelphia 1934
Weiner, Art, E, North Carolina, NY Yanks 1950
Weiner, Bernie, T, Kansas State, Brooklyn 1942
Weinmeister, Arnie, DT, Washington, NY Yankees (AAFC) 1948-49; NY Giants 1950-53
Weinstock, Izzy, QB, Pittsburgh, Philadelphia 1935; Pittsburgh 1937-38
Weir, Ed, T, Nebraska, Frankford 1926-28
Weir, Joe, E, Nebraska, Frankford 1927
Weir, Sammy, FL, Arkansas State, Houston 1965; NY Jets 1966
Weisacosky, Ed, LB, Miami, NY Giants 1967; Miami 1968-70; New England 1971-72
Weisenbaugh, Henry, HB, Pittsburgh, Pittsburgh 1935; Boston 1935-36
Weisgerber, Dick, QB, Villanova, Green Bay 1938-40, 1942
Weishuhn, Clayton, LB, Angelo State, New England 1982-84
Weiss, Howie, HB, Wisconsin, Detroit 1939-40
Weiss, John, E, NY Giants 1944-47
Welch, Claxton, RB, Oregon, Dallas 1969-71; New England 1973
Welch, Gibby, HB, Pittsburgh, NY Yankees 1928; Providence 1929
Welch, Herb, DB, UCLA, NY Giants 1985
Welch, Jim, DB-HB, SMU, Baltimore 1960-67; Detroit 1968
Weldin, Hal, C, Northwestern, St. Louis 1934
Weldon, John (Bodie), HB, Lafayette, Buffalo 1920-22
Weldon, Larry, QB, Presbyterian, Washington 1944-45
Wellborn, Joe, C, Texas A&M, NY Giants 1966
Weller, Louis (Rabbit), HB, Haskell, Boston 1933
Weller, Ray, T, Nebraska, St. Louis 1923; Milwaukee 1924; Chi. Cardinals 1925-27; Frankford 1928
Wellman, Mike, C, Kansas, Green Bay 1979-80
Wells, Billy, HB-KR, Michigan State, Washington 1954, 1956-57; Pittsburgh 1957; Philadelphia 1958; Boston 1960
Wells, Don, E, Georgia, Green Bay 1946-49
Wells, Harold, LB, Purdue, Philadelphia 1965-68; NY Giants 1969
Wells, Joel, HB, Clemson, NY Giants 1961
Wells, Mike, QB, Illinois, NY Giants 1975; Cincinnati 1977
Wells, Norm, G, Northwestern, Dallas 1980
Wells, Robert, T, Johnson C. Smith, San Diego 1968-70
Wells, Terry, RB, Southern Mississippi, Houston 1974; Green Bay 1975
Wells, Warren, SE, Texas Southern, Detroit 1964; Oakland 1967-70
Welmus, Woodchuck, E, Carlisle, Oorang 1923
Welsh, Jim, G, Colgate, Frankford 1924-25; Pottsville 1926
Weltman, Larry, HB, Syracuse, Rochester 1922
Wemple, Don, E, Colgate, Brooklyn 1941
Wendell, Marty, G, Notre Dame, Chi. Hornets (AAFC) 1949
Wender, Jack, RB, Fresno State, Tampa Bay 1977
Wendler, Hal, HB, Ohio State, Akron 1926
Wendlick, Joe, E, Oregon State, Philadelphia 1940; Pittsburgh 1941
Wendryhoski, Joe, C, Illinois, LA Rams 1964-66; New Orleans 1967-68
Wendt, Ken, G, Marquette, Chi. Cardinals 1932
Wenglikowski, Al, LB, Pittsburgh, Buffalo 1984
Wenig, Obe, E, Morningside, Rock Island 1920-22
Wenke, Adolph, T, Nebraska, Milwaukee 1923
Wentworth, Shirley (Cy), HB, New Hampshire, Providence 1925-26; Boston 1929
Wentz, Barney, HB, Penn State, Pottsville 1925-28
Wenzel, Ralph, E, Tulane, Pittsburgh 1942
Wenzel, Ralph, G, San Diego State, Pittsburgh 1966-70; San Diego 1972-73
Werder, Bus, G, Georgetown (Washington D.C.), NY Yankees (AAFC) 1948
Werder, Gerry, C-T, Penn State, Buffalo 1920; Tonawanda 1921
Werl, Bob, DE, Miami, NY Jets 1966
Werner, Clyde, LB, Washington, Kansas City 1970, 1972-74, 1976
Werner, Sox, HB, Central Missouri State, St. Louis 1923
Wersching, Ray, K, California, San Diego 1973-76; San Francisco 1977-85
Werwaiss, Elbert (Mule), T, Dean J.C., Hartford 1926
Wesbecher, Al, C, Washington & Jefferson, Cleveland 1920
Wesley, Cecil (Bull), C-FB, Alabama, Providence 1926-27; NY Giants 1928; Portsmouth 1930
Wesson, Ricky, CB, SMU, Kansas City 1977
West, Belf, T, Colgate, Canton 1921
West, Bill, DB, Tennessee State, Denver 1972
West, Charlie, DB-KR, Texas-El Paso, Minnesota 1968-73; Detroit 1974-77; Denver 1978-79
West, David, DB, Central State (Ohio), NY Jets 1963
West, Ed, TE, Auburn, Green Bay 1984-85
West, Hodges, T, Tennessee, Philadelphia 1941
West, Jeff, P, Cincinnati, St. Louis 1975; San Diego 1976-79; Seattle 1981-85
West, Mel, HB-KR, Missouri, Boston 1961; NY Titans 1961-62
West, Pat, FB, USC, Cleveland 1945; LA Rams 1946-48; Green Bay 1948
West, Robert, WR, San Diego State, Kansas City 1972-73; San Francisco 1974
West, Stan, G, Oklahoma, LA Rams 1950-54; NY Giants 1955; Chi. Cardinals 1956-57
West, Walt, QB, Pittsburgh, Cleveland 1944
West, Willie, DB, Oregon, St. Louis 1960-61; Buffalo 1962-63; Denver 1964; NY Jets 1964-65; Miami 1966-68
Westbrook, Don, WR, Nebraska, New England 1977-81
Westbrooks, Greg, LB, Colorado, New Orleans 1975-77; St. Louis 1978; Oakland 1978-81; LA Rams 1979-80
Westfall, Bob, FB, Michigan, Detroit 1944-47
Westfall, Ed, HB, Ohio Wesleyan, Boston 1932-33; Pittsburgh 1933
Westmoreland, Dick, DB, North Carolina A&T, San Diego 1963-65; Miami 1966-69
Weston, Jeff, DT, Notre Dame, NY Giants 1979-82
Westoupal, Joe, C, Nebraska, Kansas City 1926; Detroit 1928; NY Giants 1929-30
Wetoska, Bob, T, Notre Dame, Chi. Bears 1960-69
Wetterlund, Chet, HB, Illinois Wesleyan, Detroit 1942
Wettstein, Max, TE, Florida State, Denver 1966
Wetz, Harlan, T, Texas, Brooklyn (AAFC) 1947
Wetzel, Damon (Buzz), FB, Ohio State, Chi. Bears 1935; Pittsburgh 1935
Wetzel, Marty, LB, Tulane, NY Jets 1981
Wetzel, Ron, TE, Arizona State, Kansas City 1983
Wexler, Bill, C, NYU, Staten Island 1930
Whalen, Bill, C-G, Chi. Cardinals 1920, 1922-24
Whalen, Jim, WR, Boston College, Boston 1965-69; Denver 1970-71; Philadelphia 1971
Whalen, Jerry, C, Canisius, Buffalo (AAFC) 1948
Whalen, Tom, QB, Catholic, Pittsburgh 1933
Whaley, Ben, G, Virginia State, LA Dons (AAFC) 1949
Wham, Tom, E, Furman, Chi. Cardinals 1949-51
Wharton, Hogan, G, Houston, Houston 1960-63
Whatley, Jim, T, Alabama, Brooklyn 1936-38
Wheeler, Dwight, T-C, Tennessee State, New England 1978-83; LA Raiders 1984
Wheeler, Ernie, HB, North Dakota State, Pittsburgh 1939
Wheeler, Kyle, E, Ripon, Green Bay 1921-23
Wheeler, Manch, QB, Maine, Buffalo 1962
Wheeler, Ted, G-TE, West Texas State, St. Louis 1967-68; Chi. Bears 1970
Wheeler, Wayne, WR, Alabama, Chi. Bears 1974
Wheelright, Ernie, FB, Southern Illinois, NY Giants 1964-65; Atlanta 1966-67; New Orleans 1967-70
Whelen, Tom, E, Georgetown (Washington D.C.), Canton 1920; Cleveland 1921
Whipple, Ray, E, Notre Dame, Detroit 1920
Whire, John, FB, Georgia, Philadelphia 1933
Whisenhunt, Ken, TE, Georgia Tech, Atlanta 1985
Whitaker, Bill, S, Missouri, Green Bay 1981-82; St. Louis 1983-84
Whitaker, Creston, WR, North Texas State, New Orleans 1972
Whitcomb, Frank, G, Syracuse, Rochester 1920-21
White, Allie, T, TCU, Philadelphia 1939
White, Andre, TE, Florida A&M, Denver 1967; Cincinnati 1968; San Diego 1968
White, Arthur (Tarzan), G, Alabama, NY Giants 1937-39, 1945; Chi. Cardinals 1940-41
White, Bob, E, Louisville 1923
White, Bob, DB, Stanford, San Francisco 1951-52; Cleveland 1955, Baltimore 1955
White, Bob, FB, Ohio State, Houston 1960
White, Brad, DT, Tennessee, Tampa Bay 1981-83; Indianapolis 1984-85
White, Buck, FB, Valparaiso, Chi. Bears 1924-25, 1927-29
White, Byron (Whizzer), HB, Colorado, Pittsburgh 1938; Detroit 1940-41
White, Charles, RB, USC, Cleveland 1980-82, 1984; LA Rams 1985
White, Charlie, RB, Bethune-Cookman, NY Jets 1977; Tampa Bay 1978
White, Craig, WR, Missouri, Buffalo 1984
White, Danny, QB-P, Arizona State, Dallas 1976-85
White, Daryl, G, Nebraska, Detroit 1974
White, Dwight, DE, East Texas State, Pittsburgh 1971-80
White, Ed, G-T, California, Minnesota 1969-77; San Diego 1978-85
White, Ellery, HB, Minnesota, LA Buccaneers 1926
White, Freeman, TE, Nebraska, NY Giants 1966-69
White, Gene, G, Indiana, Buffalo (AAFC) 1946
White, Gene, DE, Georgia, Green Bay 1954
White, Gene, RB, Florida A&M, Oakland 1962
White, Harvey, QB, Clemson, Boston 1960
White, James (Duck), DT-NT, Oklahoma State, Minnesota 1976-84
White, James, DE, LSU, Cleveland 1985
White, Jan, TE, Ohio State, Buffalo 1971-72
White, Jeff, P, Texas-El Paso, New England 1973
White, Jeris, CB, Hawaii, Miami 1974-76; Tampa Bay 1977-79; Washington 1980-82
White, Jim, T, Notre Dame, NY Giants 1946-50
White, Jim, DE, Colorado State, New England 1972; Houston 1974-75; Seattle 1976; Denver 1976
White, John, TE, Texas Southern, Houston 1960-61; Oakland 1962
White, Lee, RB, Weber State, NY Jets 1968-70; LA Rams 1971; San Diego 1972
White, Lyman, LB, LSU, Atlanta 1981-82
White, Mac, E, Marietta, Toledo 1922-23
White, Marsh, RB, Arkansas, NY Giants 1975-76
White, Mike, DT, Albany State, Cincinnati 1979-80; Seattle 1981-82
White, Paul, HB, Michigan, Pittsburgh 1947
White, Paul, RB, Texas-El Paso, St. Louis 1970-71
White, Phil, FB, Oklahoma, Kansas City 1924-25; NY Giants 1925, 1927
White, Randy, DT-LB, Maryland, Dallas 1975-85
White, Ray, LB, Syracuse, San Diego 1971-72; St. Louis 1975-76
White, Reggie, DE, Tennessee, Philadelphia 1985
White, Roy, E, NYU, Buffalo 1927
White, Sammy, WR, Grambling, Minnesota 1976-84
White, Sherman, DE, California, Cincinnati 1972-75; Buffalo 1976-83
White, Stan, LB, Ohio State, Baltimore 1972-79; Detroit 1980-82
White, Walter, TE, Maryland, Kansas City 1975-79
White, Wilbur (Red), HB, Colorado State, Brooklyn 1935; Detroit 1936
White, Wilford (Whizzer), HB, Arizona State, Chi. Bears

1951-52
White Cloud, E, Haskell, Oorang 1922
Whited, Mike, T, Pacific, Detroit 1980
Whited, Marv, QB, Oklahoma, Washington 1942, 1945
Whitehead, Rubin (Bud), DB, Florida State, San Diego 1961-68
Whitehead, Walker, HB, Evansville 1921-22
Whitehurst, David, QB, Furman, Green Bay 1977-83; Kansas City 1984
Whitfield, A.D., RB, North Texas State, Dallas 1965; Washington 1966-68
Whitlatch, Blake, LB, LSU, NY Jets 1978
Whitley, Hall, LB, Texas A&I, NY Titans 1960
Whitley, Wilson, DT-NT, Houston, Cincinnati 1977-82; Houston 1983
Whitlow, Bob, C, Arizona, Washington 1960-61; Detroit 1961-65; Atlanta 1966; Cleveland 1968
Whitlow, Ken, C, Rice, Miami (AAFC) 1946
Whitman, S.J., DB, Tulsa, Chi. Cardinals 1951-53; Chi. Bears 1953-54
Whitmyer, Nat, DB, Washington, LA Rams 1963; San Diego 1966
Whitsell, Dave, DB, Indiana, Detroit 1958-60; Chi. Bears 1961-66; New Orleans 1967-69
Whitten, Bobby, T, Kansas, Cincinnati 1981
Whittenton, Jesse, DB, Texas-El Paso, LA Rams 1956-57; Green Bay 1958-64
Whittingham, Fred, LB, Cal Poly-SLO, LA Rams 1964; Philadelphia 1966, 1971; New Orleans 1967-68; Dallas 1969; Boston 1970
Whittington, Arthur, RB-KR, SMU, Oakland 1978-81; Buffalo 1982
Whittington, C.L., S, Prairie View A&M, Houston 1974-76, 1978
Whittington, Mike, LB, Notre Dame, NY Giants 1980-83
Whitwell, Mike, S, Texas A&M, Cleveland 1982-83
Wiatrak, John, C, Washington, Detroit 1939
Wiberg, Ossie, HB, Nebraska Wesleyan, Cleveland 1927; Detroit 1928; NY Giants 1930; Brooklyn 1932; Cincinnati 1933
Wickert, Tom, T, Washington State, Miami 1974; New Orleans 1975-76; Detroit 1977; Kansas City 1977
Wickett, Lloyd, T, Oregon State, Detroit 1943, 1946
Wicks, Bob, WR, Utah State, St. Louis 1972; New Orleans 1974
Widby, Ron, P, Tennessee, Dallas 1968-71; Green Bay 1972-73
Widerquist, Chet, T, Washington & Jefferson, Milwaukee 1923-24; Rock Island 1925; Chi. Cardinals 1926, 1928; Detroit 1928; Minneapolis 1929
Widseth, Ed, T, Minnesota, NY Giants 1937-40
Wiedich, Ralph, T, Emporia State, Kansas City 1924
Wiehl, Joe (Tiny), T, Duquesne, Pittsburgh 1935
Wiese, Bob, HB, Michigan, Detroit 1947-48
Wietecha, Ray, C, Northwestern, NY Giants 1953-62
Wiethe, John (Socko), G, Xavier, Detroit 1939-42
Wiggin, Paul, DE, Stanford, Cleveland 1957-67
Wiggs, Gene, G, Louisville 1921
Wiggs, Hubert, FB, Vanderbilt, Louisville 1921-23
Wightkin, Bill, T-DE, Notre Dame, Chi. Bears 1950-57
Wilbur, John, G, Stanford, Dallas 1966-69; LA Rams 1970; Washington 1971-73
Wilburn, Barry, CB, Mississippi, Washington 1985
Wilburn, J.R., WR-TE, South Carolina, Pittsburgh 1966-70
Wilcher, Mike, LB, North Carolina, LA Rams 1983-85
Wilcox, Dave, LB, Oregon, San Francisco 1964-74
Wilcox, John, T, Oklahoma, Buffalo 1926; Staten Island 1930
Wilcox, John, T, Oregon, Philadelphia 1960
Wilcox, Ned, HB, Swarthmore, Frankford 1926-27
Wilde, George, HB, Texas A&M, Washington 1947
Wilder, Bert, DE, North Carolina State, NY Jets 1964-67
Wilder, Hal, G, Nebraska, St. Louis 1923
Wilder, James, RB, Missouri, Tampa Bay 1981-85
Wildung, Dick, G, Minnesota, Green Bay 1946-51, 1953
Wiley, Jack, T, Waynesburg, Pittsburgh 1946-50
Wilging, Cole, T, Xavier, Cincinnati 1934
Wilkerson, Basil, E, Oklahoma City, Staten Island 1932; Boston 1932; Cincinnati 1934
Wilkerson, Daryl, DT, Houston, Baltimore 1981
Wilkerson, Doug, G, North Carolina Central, Houston 1970; San Diego 1971-84
Wilkerson, Jerry, DE, Oregon State, LA Rams 1979; Cleveland 1980; San Francisco 1980
Wilkes, Reggie, LB, Georgia Tech, Philadelphia 1978-85
Wilkin, Wilbur (Wee Willie), T, St. Mary's (California), Washington 1938-43; Chi. Rockets (AAFC) 1946
Wilkins, Dick, E, Oregon, LA Dons (AAFC) 1949; Dallas 1952; NY Giants 1954
Wilkins, Roy, DE-LB, Georgia, LA Rams 1958-59; Washington 1960-61
Wilkins, Ted, E, Indiana, Green Bay 1925
Wilkinson, Bob, E, UCLA, NY Giants 1951-52
Wilks, Jim, LB, San Diego State, New Orleans 1981-85
Will, Erwin, DT, Dayton, Philadelphia 1965
Willard, Ken, FB, North Carolina, San Francisco 1965-73; St. Louis 1974
Willegalle, Henry, HB, Carleton, Minneapolis 1929
Willey, Norm (Wildman), DE, Marshall, Philadelphia 1950-57
Willhite, Gerald, RB-KR, San Jose State, Denver 1982-85
Williams, A.D., DE, Pacific, Green Bay 1959; Cleveland 1960; Minnesota 1961
Williams, Al, G, Vanderbilt, Detroit 1921
Williams, Arthur (Pop), FB, Central Connecticut State, Providence 1928-31; Brooklyn 1932
Williams, Ben, DT, Mississippi, Buffalo 1976-85
Williams, Bob, QB, Notre Dame, Chi. Bears 1951-52, 1955
Williams, Bobby, DB-KR, Central State (Oklahoma), St. Louis 1966-67; Detroit 1969-71
Williams, Boyd, C, Syracuse, Philadelphia 1947
Williams, Brian, TE, Southern, New England 1982
Williams, Brooks, TE, North Carolina, New Orleans 1978-81; Chi. Bears 1981-82
Williams, Broughton, T, Florida, Chi. Bears 1947
Williams, Byron, WR, Texas-Arlington, Philadelphia 1983; NY Giants 1983-85
Williams, Charlie, WR, Prairie View A&M, LA Rams 1970
Williams, Charlie, CB, Jackson State, Philadelphia 1978
Williams, Chris, CB, LSU, Buffalo 1982-83
Williams, Clancy, CB, Washington State, LA Rams 1965-72
Williams, Clarence, DE, Prairie View A&M, Green Bay 1970-77
Williams, Clarence, RB, South Carolina, San Diego 1978-81; Washington 1982
Williams, Clyde, T, Georgia Tech, Philadelphia 1935
Williams, Clyde, T, Southern, St. Louis 1967-71
Williams, Cy, G, Florida, Staten Island 1929-30; Brooklyn 1932
Williams, Daniel (Doc), G, Wisconsin-St. Cloud, Duluth 1923-27
Williams, Dave, WR, Washington, St. Louis 1967-71; San Diego 1972-73; Pittsburgh 1973
Williams, Dave, RB-KR, Colorado, San Francisco 1977-78; Chi. Bears 1979-81
Williams, Del, G-T, Florida State, New Orleans 1967-73
Williams, Delvin, RB, Kansas, San Francisco 1974-77; Miami 1978-80; Green Bay 1981
Williams, Derwin, WR, New Mexico, New England 1985
Williams, Dokie, WR-KR, UCLA, LA Raiders 1983-85
Williams, Don, G, Texas, Pittsburgh 1941
Williams, Doug, QB, Grambling, Tampa Bay 1978-82
Williams, Ed, RB, Langston, Cincinnati 1974-75; Tampa Bay 1976-77
Williams, Ed, LB, Texas, New England 1984-85
Williams, Ellery, E, Santa Clara, NY Giants 1950
Williams, Eric, LB, USC, St. Louis 1977-82; LA Rams 1982-83; Pittsburgh 1983
Williams, Eric, S, North Carolina State, Pittsburgh 1983-85
Williams, Eric, DE-DT, Washington State, Detroit 1984-85
Williams, Erwin, WR, Maryland-Eastern Shore, Pittsburgh 1969
Williams, Eugene, LB, Tulsa, Seattle 1982-83
Williams, Frank, FB, Utah State, NY Giants 1948
Williams, Frank, FB, Pepperdine, LA Rams 1961
Williams, Fred, DT, Arkansas, Chi. Bears 1952-63; Washington 1964-65
Williams, Gardner, DB, St. Mary's (California), Detroit 1984
Williams, Garland, T, Georgia, Brooklyn (AAFC) 1947-48; Chi. Hornets (AAFC) 1949
Williams, Gary, WR, Ohio State, Cincinnati 1984
Williams, Gerard, CB, Langston, Washington 1976-78; San Francisco 1979-80; St. Louis 1980
Williams, Greg, S, Mississippi State, Washington 1982-85
Williams, Henry, DB, San Diego State, Oakland 1979; LA Rams 1983; San Diego 1983
Williams, Herb, DB, Southern, San Francisco 1980; St. Louis 1981-82
Williams, Howie, DB, Howard J.C., Green Bay 1962-63; San Francisco 1963; Oakland 1964-69
Williams, Ike, HB, Georgia Tech, Staten Island 1929
Williams, Jake, T, TCU, Chi. Cardinals 1929-33
Williams, Jamie, TE, Nebraska, St. Louis 1983; Houston 1984-85
Williams, Jay (Inky), E, Brown, Canton 1921; Hammond 1921-26; Kenosha 1924; Dayton 1924; Cleveland 1925
Williams, Jeff, RB, Oklahoma State, Minnesota 1966
Williams, Jeff, T, Rhode Island, LA Rams 1977; Washington 1978-80; San Diego 1981; Chi. Bears 1982
Williams, Jerry, HB-DB, Washington State, LA Rams 1949-52; Philadelphia 1953-54
Williams, Jim, DB, Alcorn State, Cincinnati 1968
Williams, Jimmy, LB, Nebraska, Detroit 1982-85
Williams, Joe, G, Lafayette, Canton 1923; NY Giants 1925-26
Williams, Joe, HB, Ohio State, Cleveland 1937; Pittsburgh 1939
Williams, Joe, RB, Wyoming, Dallas 1971; New Orleans 1972
Williams, Joel, C, Texas, San Francisco (AAFC) 1948; Baltimore 1950
Williams, Joel, LB, Wisconsin-La Crosse, Atlanta 1979-82; Philadelphia 1983-85
Williams, John (Tex), C, Auburn, Philadelphia 1942; Miami (AAFC) 1946
Williams, John, T, Minnesota, Baltimore 1968-71; LA Rams 1972-79
Williams, John, RB, Wisconsin, Dallas 1985; Seattle 1985
Williams, Johnny, DB, USC, Washington 1952-53; San Francisco 1954
Williams, Jon, RB-KR, Penn State, New England 1984
Williams, Kendall, CB, Arizona State, Baltimore 1983
Williams, Kevin, WR-KR, USC, Baltimore 1981
Williams, Kevin, CB, Iowa State, Washington 1985
Williams, Lawrence, WR, Texas Tech, Kansas City 1976-77; Cleveland 1977
Williams, Lee, DE, Bethune-Cookman, San Diego 1984-85
Williams, Lester, NT, Miami, New England 1982-85
Williams, Maxie, T-G, Southeastern Louisiana, Houston 1965; Miami 1966-70
Williams, Mike, CB, LSU, San Diego 1975-82; LA Rams 1983
Williams, Mike, RB, New Mexico, Kansas City 1979-81
Williams, Mike, TE, Alabama A&M, Washington 1982-84
Williams, Mike, RB, Mississippi College, Philadelphia 1983-84
Williams, Monk, DB-KR, Arkansas-Pine Bluff, Cincinnati 1968
Williams, Newton, RB, Arizona State, San Francisco 1982; Baltimore 1983
Williams, Oliver, WR, Illinois, Indianapolis 1985
Williams, Perry, RB, Purdue, Green Bay 1969-73; Chi. Bears 1974
Williams, Perry, CB, North Carolina State, NY Giants 1984-85
Williams, Ralph, G-T, Southern, Houston 1982-83; New Orleans 1985
Williams, Ray, WR-KR, Washington State, Detroit 1980
Williams, Reggie, LB, Dartmouth, Cincinnati 1976-85
Williams, Rex, C, Texas Tech, Chi. Cardinals 1940; Detroit 1945
Williams, Richard, WR, Abilene Christian, New Orleans 1974
Williams, Richard, RB, Memphis State, Atlanta 1983-84
Williams, Ricky, CB, Langston, LA Raiders 1985
Williams, Robert, S, Eastern Illinois, Pittsburgh 1984
Williams, Roger, DB, Grambling, LA Rams 1971-72
Williams, Rolland, HB, Wisconsin, Minneapolis 1923; Racine 1923
Williams, Roy, DT, Pacific, San Francisco 1963
Williams, Sam, S, California, San Diego 1974-75; Houston 1976
Williams, Sammie, DE, Michigan State, LA Rams 1959; Detroit 1960-65; Atlanta 1966-67
Williams, Sid, LB, Southern, Cleveland 1964-66; Washington 1967; Baltimore 1968; Pittsburgh 1969
Williams, Stan, E-DB, Baylor, Dallas 1952
Williams, Steve, DE, Western Carolina, Baltimore 1974
Williams, Ted, HB, Boston College, Philadelphia 1942; Boston 1944
Williams, Toby, DE, Nebraska, New England 1983-85
Williams, Tom, DT, Cal-Davis, San Diego 1970-71
Williams, Travis, HB, Indiana, Evansville 1921-22
Williams, Travis, RB-KR, Arizona State, Green Bay 1967-70; LA Rams 1971
Williams, Van, RB-KR, Carson-Newman, Buffalo 1983-85
Williams, Vaughn, DB, Stanford, Indianapolis 1984
Williams, Vince, RB, Oregon, San Francisco 1982-83
Williams, Walt, HB, Boston U., Chi. Rockets (AAFC) 1946; Boston 1947
Williams, Walt, CB, New Mexico State, Detroit 1977-80; Green Bay 1981; Minnesota 1982; Chi. Bears 1982-83
Williams, Wandy, RB, Hofstra, Denver 1969-70
Williams, Willie, CB, Grambling, NY Giants 1965, 1967-73; Oakland 1966
Williams, Windell, E, Rice, Baltimore (AAFC) 1948-49
Williamson, Carlton, S, Pittsburgh, San Francisco 1981-85
Williamson, Ernie, T, North Carolina, Washington 1947; NY Giants 1948; LA Dons (AAFC) 1949
Williamson, Fred (The Hammer), DB, Northwestern, Pittsburgh 1960; Oakland 1961-64; Kansas City 1965-67
Williamson, J.R., LB-C, Louisiana Tech, Oakland 1964-67; Boston 1968-70
Willingham, Larry, DB-KR, Auburn, St. Louis 1971-72
Willis, Bill, G, Ohio State, Cleveland 1946-53
Willis, Chester, RB, Auburn, Oakland 1981; LA Raiders 1982-84
Willis, Fred, RB, Boston College, Cincinnati 1971-72; Houston 1972-76
Willis, Keith, DE, Northwestern, Pittsburgh 1982-85
Willis, Larry, DB, Texas-El Paso, Washington 1973
Willis, Leonard, WR-KR, Ohio State, Minnesota 1976; New Orleans 1977; Buffalo 1977-79
Willis, Mitch, NT, SMU, LA Raiders 1985
Willson, Joe, G, Pennsylvania, Buffalo 1926-27
Willson, Osborne (Diddle), G, Pennsylvania, Philadelphia 1933-35
Wilmer, Ray, S, Louisiana Tech, Seattle 1984
Wilson, Abe, G, Washington, Providence 1927-29
Wilson, Ben, FB, USC, LA Rams 1963-65; Green Bay 1967
Wilson, Bill, E, Gonzaga, Chi. Cardinals 1935-37
Wilson, Billy, SE, San Jose State, San Francisco 1951-60
Wilson, Bobby, HB, SMU, Brooklyn 1936
Wilson, Brenard, S, Vanderbilt, Philadelphia 1979-85
Wilson, Butch, TE, Alabama, Baltimore 1963-67; NY Giants 1968-69
Wilson, Camp, HB, Tulsa, Detroit 1946-49
Wilson, Darrell, CB, Connecticut, New England 1981
Wilson, Darryal, WR, Tennessee, New England 1983
Wilson, Dave, QB, Illinois, New Orleans 1981, 1983-85
Wilson, Don, KR-S, North Carolina State, Buffalo 1984-85
Wilson, Drip, C, Cleveland 1931
Wilson, Earl, DE, Kentucky, San Diego 1985
Wilson, Eddie, QB, Arizona, Dallas Texans 1962; Kansas City 1963-64; Boston 1965
Wilson, Eric, LB, Maryland, Buffalo 1985
Wilson, Faye (Mule), FB-HB, Texas A&M, Buffalo 1926; Kansas City 1926; NY Giants 1927-30; Staten Island 1930
Wilson, Gene, E, SMU, Green Bay 1947-48

Wilson, George (Wildcat), HB, Washington, Providence 1927-29
Wilson, George, E, Northwestern, Chi. Bears 1937-46
Wilson, George, Jr., QB, Xavier, Miami 1966
Wilson, Gordon, G, Texas-El Paso, Cleveland 1941; Chi. Cardinals 1942-43, 1945; Brooklyn 1944; Boston 1944
Wilson, Harry, RB, Nebraska, Philadelphia 1967, 1969
Wilson, J.C., CB, Pittsburgh, Houston 1978-83
Wilson, Jack, HB, Baylor, LA Rams 1946-47
Wilson, Jerrel, P-TE, Southern Mississippi, Kansas City 1963-77; New England 1978
Wilson, Jim, G, Georgia, San Francisco 1965-66; Atlanta 1967; LA Rams 1968
Wilson, Joe, RB, Holy Cross, Cincinnati 1973; New England 1974
Wilson, Johnny, E, Case Western Reserve, Cleveland 1939-42
Wilson, Larry, S, Utah, St. Louis 1960-73
Wilson, Lee, E, Cornell (Iowa), Minneapolis 1929-30; Frankford 1930-31
Wilson, Marc, QB, BYU, Oakland 1980-81; LA Raiders 1982-85
Wilson, Mike, E, Lehigh, Rock Island 1923-25
Wilson, Mike, G-T, Dayton, Cincinnati 1969-70; Buffalo 1971; Kansas City 1975
Wilson, Mike, DB, Western Illinois, St. Louis 1969
Wilson, Mike, T, Georgia, Cincinnati 1979-85
Wilson, Mike, WR, Washington State, San Francisco 1981-85
Wilson, Milt, T, Wisconsin-Oshkosh, Green Bay 1921; Akron 1923-24
Wilson, Nemiah, CB, Grambling, Denver 1965-67; Oakland 1968-74; Chi. Bears 1975
Wilson, Otis, LB, Louisville, Chi. Bears 1980-85
Wilson, Percy, QB, Detroit 1920
Wilson, Stanley, RB, Oklahoma, Cincinnati 1983-84
Wilson, Steve, C-T, Georgia, Tampa Bay 1976-85
Wilson, Steve, CB-WR, Howard, Dallas 1979-81; Denver 1982-85
Wilson, Stu, E, Washington & Jefferson, Staten Island 1932
Wilson, Tim, RB-TE, Maryland, Houston 1977-82; New Orleans 1983-84
Wilson, (Touchdown) Tommy, HB, LA Rams 1956-61; Cleveland 1962; Minnesota 1963
Wilson, Wade, QB, East Texas State, Minnesota 1981-85
Wilson, Wayne, RB-KR, Shepherd, New Orleans 1979-85
Wilton, Ed, E, Georgia Tech, Pottsville 1926
Wimberly, Abner, E, LSU, LA Dons (AAFC) 1949; Green Bay 1950-52
Wimberly, By, G, Washington & Jefferson, Detroit 1925
Wimmer, Gary, LB, Stanford, Seattle 1983
Winans, Jeff, DT-DE, USC, Buffalo 1973, 1975; New Orleans 1976; Oakland 1976; Tampa Bay 1977-78
Windauer, Bill, DT, Iowa, Baltimore 1973-74; Miami 1975; NY Giants 1975; Atlanta 1976
Windbiele, Joe, C, Evansville 1921-22
Windburn, Ernie, E, Central Missouri State, St. Louis 1923
Winder, Sammy, RB, Southern Mississippi, Denver 1982-85
Windsor, Bob, TE, Kentucky, San Francisco 1967-71; New England 1972-75
Winfield, Vern, G, Minnesota, Philadelphia 1972-73
Winfrey, Carl, LB, Wisconsin, Minnesota 1971; Pittsburgh 1972
Winfrey, Stan, RB, Arkansas State, Miami 1975-79; Tampa Bay 1977; Buffalo 1977
Wingate, Elmer, DE, Maryland, Baltimore 1953
Wingate, Heath, C, Bowling Green, Washington 1967
Wingle, Blake, G, UCLA, Pittsburgh 1983-85; Green Bay 1985
Wingo, Rich, LB, Alabama, Green Bay 1979, 1981-84
Wink, Dean, DE, Yankton, Philadelphia 1967-68
Winkel, Bob, DE-DT, Kentucky, NY Jets 1979-80
Winkelman, Ben, E, Arkansas, Milwaukee 1922-24
Winkler, Bernie, T, Texas Tech, LA Dons (AAFC) 1948
Winkler, Francis, DE, Memphis State, Green Bay 1968-69
Winkler, Jim, G-DT, Texas A&M, LA Rams 1951-52; Baltimore 1953
Winkler, Joe, C, Purdue, Cleveland 1945
Winkler, Randy, T-G, Tarleton State, Detroit 1967; Atlanta 1968; Green Bay 1971
Winneshek, Bill, C, Carlisle, Oorang 1922
Winslow, Bob, E, USC, Detroit 1940; Brooklyn 1940
Winslow, Doug, WR, Drake, New Orleans 1973; Washington 1976
Winslow, Kellen, TE, Missouri, San Diego 1979-85
Winslow, Paul, HB, North Carolina Central, Green Bay 1960
Winston, Charlie, G, Purdue, Dayton 1920
Winston, Dennis (Dirt), LB, Arkansas, Pittsburgh 1977-81, 1985; New Orleans 1982-85
Winston, Kelton, DB, Wiley, LA Rams 1967-68
Winston, Lloyd, FB, USC, San Francisco 1962-63
Winston, Roy, LB, LSU, Minnesota 1962-76
Winter, Bill, LB, St. Olaf, NY Giants 1962-64
Winter, Blaise, DE, Syracuse, Indianapolis 1984
Winterheimer, Leon, T, Evansville 1922
Winters, Arnold, T, Green Bay 1941
Winters, Chet, RB, Oklahoma, Green Bay 1983
Winters, Lin, QB, Ohio Wesleyan, Columbus 1923-24
Winther, Richard (Wimpy), C, Mississippi, Green Bay 1971; New Orleans 1972
Wiper, Don, QB, Ohio State, Columbus 1922
Wirgowski, Dennis, DE-DT, Purdue, Boston 1970; New England 1971-72; Philadelphia 1973
Wise, Phil, S, Nebraska-Omaha, NY Jets 1971-76; Minnesota 1977-79
Wisener, Gary, SE-DB, Baylor, Dallas Cowboys 1960; Houston 1961
Wisniewski, Leo, NT, Penn State, Baltimore 1982-83; Indianapolis 1984
Wissinger, Zonar, G, Pittsburgh, Pottsville 1926
Wissman, Pete, C-LB, St. Louis, San Francisco 1949-52, 1954
Wistert, Al (Whitey), T, Michigan, Phil-Pitt 1943; Philadelphia 1944-51
Witcher, Al, SE, Baylor, Houston 1960
Witcher, Dick, WR, UCLA, San Francisco 1966-73
Withrow, Cal, C, Kentucky, San Diego 1970; Green Bay 1971-73; St. Louis 1974
Witkowski, John, QB, Columbia, Detroit 1984
Witt, Mel, DE, Texas-Arlington, Boston 1967-70
Witte, Earl, QB, Gustavus-Adolphus, Green Bay 1934
Witte, Mark, TE, North Texas State, Tampa Bay 1983-85
Wittenborn, John, G-K, Southeast Missouri State, San Francisco 1958-60; Philadelphia 1960-62; Houston 1964-68
Witter, Bob, HB, Alfred, Rochester 1920
Witter, Ray, FB, Syracuse, Rochester 1921, 1923
Wittum, Tom, P, Northern Illinois, San Francisco 1973-77
Witucki, Casimir (Slug), G, Indiana, Washington 1950-51, 1953-56
Wizbicki, Alex, HB, Holy Cross, Buffalo (AAFC) 1947-49; Green Bay 1950
Woerner, Ernie, T, Bucknell, Newark 1930
Woerner, Scott, S-KR, Georgia, Atlanta 1981
Woit, Dick, DB, Arkansas State, Detroit 1955
Woitt, John, DB, Mississippi State, San Francisco 1968-69
Wojciechowicz, Alex, C-LB, Fordham, Detroit 1938-46; Philadelphia 1946-50
Wojcik, Greg, DT, USC, LA Rams 1971; San Diego 1972-73, 1975
Wolf, Dick, QB-HB, Miami (Ohio), Cleveland 1923-25, 1927
Wolf, Jim, DE, Prairie View A&M, Pittsburgh 1974; Kansas City 1976
Wolfe, Hugh (Red), FB, Texas, NY Giants 1938
Wolff, Wayne, G, Wake Forest, Buffalo 1961
Wolfley, Craig, G, Syracuse, Pittsburgh 1980-85
Wolfley, Ron, RB, West Virginia, St. Louis 1985
Wolford, Oscar, G, Columbus 1920-22, 1924
Wolski, Bill, HB, Notre Dame, Atlanta 1966
Woltman, Clem, T, Purdue, Philadelphia 1938-40
Womack, Bruce, G, West Texas State, Detroit 1951
Womack, Joe, HB, Cal State-Los Angeles, Pittsburgh 1962
Womble, Royce, HB, North Texas State, Baltimore 1954-57; LA Chargers 1960
Wondolowski, Bill, WR, Eastern Montana, San Francisco 1969
Wonsley, George, RB, Mississippi State, Indianapolis 1984-85
Wonsley, Otis, RB-KR, Alcorn State, Washington 1981-85
Wood, Bill, DB, West Virginia Wesleyan, NY Jets 1963
Wood, Bo, DE, North Carolina, Atlanta 1967
Wood, Bob, T, Alabama, Chi. Cardinals 1940
Wood, Dick, QB, Auburn, San Diego 1962; Denver 1962; NY Jets 1963-64; Oakland 1965; Miami 1966
Wood, Duane, DB, Oklahoma State, Dallas Texans 1960-62; Kansas City 1963-64
Wood, Gary, QB, Cornell, NY Giants 1964-66, 1968; New Orleans 1967
Wood, Jim, G, Rochester 1921, 1923-24
Wood, Marv, G, California, Kenosha 1924
Wood, Mike, K, Southeast Missouri State, Minnesota 1978; St. Louis 1978-79; San Diego 1979-80; Baltimore 1981-82
Wood, Richard, LB, USC, NY Jets 1975; Tampa Bay 1976-84
Wood, Willie, S-KR, USC, Green Bay 1960-71
Woodall, Al, QB, Duke, NY Jets 1969-74
Woodard, Ken, LB, Tuskegee, Denver 1982-85
Woodcock, John, DT-LB, Hawaii, Detroit 1976-80; San Diego 1981-82
Woodeshick, Tom, FB, West Virginia, Philadelphia 1963-71; St. Louis 1972
Woodin, Howard (Whitey), G, Marquette, Racine 1922; Green Bay 1922-31
Woodley, David, QB, LSU, Miami 1980-83; Pittsburgh 1984-85
Woodlief, Doug, LB, Memphis State, LA Rams 1965-69
Woodring, John, LB, Brown, NY Jets 1981-85
Woodruff, Dwayne, CB, Louisville, Pittsburgh 1979-85
Woodruff, Jim, E, Pittsburgh, Chi. Cardinals 1926; Buffalo 1929
Woodruff, Lee (Cowboy), HB, Mississippi, Providence 1931; Boston 1932; Philadelphia 1933
Woodruff, Tony, WR, Fresno State, Philadelphia 1982-84
Woods, Don, RB, New Mexico Highlands, San Diego 1974-80; San Francisco 1980
Woods, Gerry, HB, Butler, Columbus 1926
Woods, Glenn, DT, Prairie View A&M, Houston 1969
Woods, Larry, T, Tennessee State, Detroit 1971-72; Miami 1973; NY Jets 1974-75; Seattle 1976
Woods, Mike, LB, Cincinnati, Baltimore 1978-81
Woods, Rick, S-KR, Boise State, Pittsburgh 1982-85
Woods, Robert, T, Tennessee State, NY Jets 1973-77; New Orleans 1977-80; Washington 1981
Woods, Robert, WR-KR, Grambling, Houston 1978; Detroit 1979
Woodson, Abe, DB-KR, Illinois, San Francisco 1958-64; St. Louis 1965-66
Woodson, Freddie, DE-DT, Florida A&M, Miami 1967-69
Woodson, Marv, DB-KR, Indiana, Pittsburgh 1964-69; New Orleans 1969
Woodward, Dick, C, Iowa, LA Dons (AAFC) 1949; NY Giants 1950-51, 1953; Washington 1952
Woolfolk, Butch, RB-KR, Michigan, NY Giants 1982-84; Houston 1985
Woolford, Gary, S, Florida State, NY Giants 1980
Woolsey, Rolly, S-KR, Boise State, Dallas 1975; Seattle 1976; Cleveland 1977; St. Louis 1978
Wooten, John, G, Colorado, Cleveland 1959-67; Washington 1968
Wooten, Ron, G, North Carolina, New England 1982-85
Word, Roscoe, DB-KR, Jackson State, NY Jets 1974-76; Buffalo 1976; NY Giants 1976; Tampa Bay 1976
Worden, Jim, HB, Waynesburg, Cleveland 1945
Worden, Neil (Bull), FB, Notre Dame, Philadelphia 1954, 1957
Worden, Stu, G, Hampden-Sydney, Brooklyn 1930, 1932-34
Work, Joe, HB, Miami (Ohio), Cleveland 1923-25
Workman, Blake, HB, Tulsa, Cincinnati 1933; St. Louis 1934
Workman, Harry, HB, Ohio State, Cleveland 1924-25, 1931; NY Giants 1932
Wortman, Keith, T-G, Nebraska, Green Bay 1972-75; St. Louis 1976-81
Woudenberg, John, T, Denver, Pittsburgh 1940-42; San Francisco (AAFC) 1946-49
Woulfe, Mike, LB, Colorado, Philadelphia 1962
Wozniak, John, G, Alabama, Brooklyn (AAFC) 1948; NY Yankees (AAFC) 1949; NY Yanks 1950-51; Dallas 1952
Wray, Lud, C, Pennsylvania, Buffalo 1920-21; Rochester 1922
Wren, Lowe (Junior), DB, Missouri, Cleveland 1956-59; Pittsburgh 1960; NY Titans 1961
Wright, Al, HB, Oklahoma State, Frankford 1930
Wright, Brad, QB, New Mexico, Dallas 1982
Wright, Elmo, WR, Houston, Kansas City 1971-74; Houston 1975; New England 1975
Wright, Eric, CB, Missouri, San Francisco 1981-85
Wright, Ernie, T, Ohio State, LA Chargers 1960; San Diego 1961-67, 1972; Cincinnati 1968-71
Wright, Felix, DB, Drake, Cleveland 1985
Wright, George, DT, Sam Houston State, Baltimore 1970-71; Cleveland 1972
Wright, Gordon, G, Delaware State, Philadelphia 1967; NY Jets 1969
Wright, James Earl, HB, Memphis State, Denver 1964
Wright, Jeff, DB, Minnesota, Minnesota 1971-77
Wright, Jim, G, SMU, Boston 1947
Wright, Jim, TE, TCU, Atlanta 1978; Denver 1980-85
Wright, John, FB, Maryland, Baltimore (AAFC) 1947
Wright, John, WR, Illinois, Atlanta 1968; Detroit 1969
Wright, Johnnie, RB, South Carolina, Baltimore 1982
Wright, Keith, WR-KR, Memphis State, Cleveland 1978-80
Wright, Lonnie, DB, Colorado State, Denver 1966-67
Wright, Louis, CB, San Jose State, Denver 1975-85
Wright, Nate, CB, San Diego State, Atlanta 1969; St. Louis 1969-70; Minnesota 1971-80
Wright, Ralph, T, Kentucky, Brooklyn 1933
Wright, Randy, QB, Wisconsin, Green Bay 1984-85
Wright, Rayfield, T-TE, Fort Valley State, Dallas 1967-79
Wright, Steve, T, Alabama, Green Bay 1964-67; NY Giants 1968-69; Washington 1970; Chi. Bears 1971; St. Louis 1972
Wright, Steve, T-G, Northern Iowa, Dallas 1981-82; Baltimore 1983; Indianapolis 1984
Wright, Ted, HB-FB, North Texas State, Boston 1934-35; Brooklyn 1935
Wrightman, Tim, TE, UCLA, Chi. Bears 1985
Wrinkle Meat (Stancil Powell), G, Carlisle, Oorang 1922
Wukits, Al (Buckets), C, Duquesne, Phil-Pitt 1943; Card-Pitt 1944; Pittsburgh 1945; Miami (AAFC) 1946; Buffalo (AAFC) 1946
Wulff, Jim, DB, Michigan State, Washington 1960-61
Wunsch, Harry, G, Notre Dame, Green Bay 1934
Wyant, Fred, QB, West Virginia, Washington 1956
Wyatt, Alvin, CB, Bethune-Cookman, Oakland 1970; Buffalo 1971-72; Houston 1973
Wyatt, Doug, S, Tulsa, New Orleans 1970-72; Detroit 1973-74
Wyatt, Kervin, LB, Maryland, NY Giants 1980
Wyche, Sam, QB, Furman, Cincinnati 1968-70; Washington 1971-72; Detroit 1974; St. Louis 1976; Buffalo 1976
Wycinsky, Craig, G, Michigan, Cleveland 1972
Wycoff, Doug, QB, Georgia Tech, NY Giants 1927, 1931; Staten Island 1929-30, 1932; Boston 1934
Wycoff, Lee, HB-FB, Washburn, St. Louis 1923
Wydo, Frank, T, Cornell, Pittsburgh 1947-51; Philadelphia 1952-57
Wyhonic, John, G, Alabama, Philadelphia 1946-47; Buffalo (AAFC) 1948-49
Wyland, Guido (Pudge), G, Iowa, Rock Island 1920
Wyman, Arnie, FB, Minnesota, Rock Island 1920
Wynn, William, DE, Tennessee State, Philadelphia 1973-76; Washington 1977
Wynne, Chet, FB, Notre Dame, Rochester 1922
Wynne, Elmer, FB, Notre Dame, Chi. Bears 1928; Dayton 1929
Wynne, Harry, E, Arkansas, Boston 1944; NY Giants 1945
Wysocki, Pete, LB, Western Michigan, Washington 1975-80

Y

Yablok, Julius (Izzy), QB, Colgate, Brooklyn 1930-31; Staten

Island 1931
Yablonski, Venton, FB, Columbia, Chi. Cardinals 1948-51
Yaccino, John, DB, Pittsburgh, Buffalo 1962
Yackanich, Joe, G, Fordham, NY Yankees (AAFC) 1946-48
Yagiello, Ray, G, Catawba, LA Rams 1948-49
Yakavonis, Ray, DE-NT, East Stroudsburg, Minnesota 1981-83; Kansas City 1983
Yanchar, Bill, DT, Purdue, Cleveland 1970
Yankowski, Ron, DE, Kansas State, St. Louis 1971-80
Yarbrough, Jim, T, Florida, Detroit 1969-77
Yarno, George, G-T, Washington State, Tampa Bay 1979-83, 1985
Yarno, John, C, Idaho, Seattle 1977-82
Yarr, Tom, C, Notre Dame, Chi. Cardinals 1933
Yary, Ron, T, USC, Minnesota 1968-81; LA Rams 1982
Yates, Bob, T, Syracuse, Boston 1960-65
Yeager, Howie, HB, Cal-Santa Barbara, NY Giants 1941
Yeager, Jim, T, Lehigh, Brooklyn 1926; Orange 1929
Yearby, Bill, DE, Michigan, NY Jets 1966
Yeates, Jeff, DE, Boston College, Buffalo 1974-76; Atlanta 1976-84
Yeisley, Paul, E, Chi. Cardinals 1927-28
Yelverton, Billy, DE, Mississippi, Denver 1960
Yelvington, Dick, T, Georgia, NY Giants 1952-57
Yepremian, Garo, K, Detroit 1966-67; Miami 1970-78; New Orleans 1979; Tampa Bay 1980-81
Yerger, Howie, HB, Penn State, Louisville 1921
Yerges, Howard (Littleboy), HB, Ohio State, Columbus 1920
Yewcic, Tom, QB-P, Michigan State, Boston 1961-66
Yezerski, John, T, St. Mary's (California), Brooklyn 1936
Yohn, John David, LB, Gettysburg, Baltimore 1962; NY Jets 1963
Yoho, Mack, DE, Miami (Ohio), Buffalo 1960-63
Yokas, Frank, G, LA Dons (AAFC) 1946; Baltimore (AAFC) 1947
Yonaker, John, E-DE, Notre Dame, Cleveland (AAFC) 1946-49; NY Yanks 1950; Washington 1952
Yonamine, Wally, HB, San Francisco (AAFC) 1947
Youel, Jim, QB, Iowa, Washington 1946-48; Boston 1948
Youmans, Maury, DE, Syracuse, Chi. Bears 1960-62; Dallas 1964-65
Younce, Len, G, Oregon State, NY Giants 1941, 1943-44, 1946-48
Young, Adrian, LB, USC, Philadelphia 1968-72; Detroit 1972; Chi. Bears 1973
Young, Al, HB, California, LA Buccaneers 1926
Young, Al, WR, South Carolina State, Pittsburgh 1971-72
Young, Andre, S, Louisiana Tech, San Diego 1982-84
Young, Anthony, S, Temple, Indianapolis 1985
Young, Ben, TE, Texas-Arlington, Atlanta 1983
Young, Bill, T, Alabama, Washington 1937-42, 1946
Young, Billy, G, Ohio State, Green Bay 1929
Young, Bob, G, Howard Payne, Denver 1966-70; Houston 1971, 1980; St. Louis 1972-79; New Orleans 1981
Young, Buddy, HB, Illinois, NY Yankees (AAFC) 1947-49; NY Yanks 1950-51; Dallas 1952; Baltimore 1953-55
Young, Charle, TE, USC, Philadelphia 1973-76; LA Rams 1977-79; San Francisco 1980-82; Seattle 1983-85
Young, Charles, RB, North Carolina State, Dallas 1974-76
Young, Dave, TE, Purdue, NY Giants 1981
Young, Dick, FB-HB, Tennessee-Chattanooga, Baltimore 1955-56; Pittsburgh 1957
Young, Fredd, LB, New Mexico State, Seattle 1984-85
Young, George, DE, Georgia, Cleveland 1946-53
Young, Glen, WR, Mississippi State, Philadelphia 1983; St. Louis 1984; Cleveland 1984-85
Young, Glenn, DB, Purdue, Green Bay 1956
Young, Herm, E, Detroit, Providence 1930
Young, James, DE, Texas Southern, Houston 1977-79
Young, Jim, RB, Queens, Minnesota 1965-66
Young, Joe, DE, Arizona, Denver 1960-61
Young, Les, FB, Macalester, Providence 1927
Young, Lonnie, S, Michigan State, St. Louis 1985
Young, Mike, WR, UCLA, LA Rams 1985
Young, Paul, C, Oklahoma, Green Bay 1933
Young, Randy, E, Millikin, Decatur 1920
Young, Randy, T, Iowa State, Tampa Bay 1976
Young, Rickey, RB, Jackson State, San Diego 1975-77; Minnesota 1978-83
Young, Roy, T, Texas A&M, Washington 1938
Young, Roynell, CB, Alcorn State, Philadelphia 1980-85
Young, Russ, FB, Dayton 1925-26
Young, Sam, G-T, Brown, Providence 1925-27; Minneapolis 1929-30
Young, Steve, T, Colorado, Tampa Bay 1976; Miami 1977; Green Bay 1979
Young, Steve, QB, BYU, Tampa Bay 1985
Young, Tyrone, WR, Florida, New Orleans 1983-84
Young, Waddy, E, Oklahoma, Brooklyn 1939-40
Young, Wilbur, DE, William Penn, Kansas City 1971-77; San Diego 1978-82; Washington 1981
Young, Willie, T-G, Grambling, NY Giants 1966-75
Young, Willie, T, Alcorn State, Buffalo 1971; Miami 1973
Youngblood, George, DB, Cal State-Los Angeles, LA Rams 1966; Cleveland 1967; New Orleans 1967-68; Chi. Bears 1969
Youngblood, Jack, DE, Florida, LA Rams 1971-84
Youngblood, Jim, LB, Tennessee Tech, LA Rams 1973-84; Washington 1984
Youngelman, Sid, DT, Alabama, San Francisco 1955; Philadelphia 1956-58; Cleveland 1959; NY Titans 1960-61; Buffalo 1962-63
Younger, Paul (Tank), FB-LB, Grambling, LA Rams 1949-57; Pittsburgh 1958
Youngfleish, Francis (Yank), C, Villanova, Pottsville 1926-27
Youngstrom, Adolph (Swede), G, Dartmouth, Buffalo 1920-25; Canton 1921; Frankford 1926-27
Youso, Frank, T, Minnesota, NY Giants 1958-60; Minnesota 1961-62; Oakland 1963-65
Yovicsin, Johnny, E, Gettysburg, Philadelphia 1944
Yowarsky, Walt, DE, Kentucky, Washington 1951, 1954; Detroit 1955; NY Giants 1955-57; San Francisco 1958
Yurchey, John, HB, Duquesne, Pittsburgh 1940

Z

Zabel, Steve, LB-TE, Oklahoma, Philadelphia 1970-74; New England 1975-78
Zadworney, Frank, FB, Ohio State, Brooklyn 1940
Zaeske, Paul, WR, North Park, Houston 1969-70
Zagers, Bert, HB, Michigan State, Washington 1955, 1957-58
Zalejski, Ernie, HB, Notre Dame, Baltimore 1950
Zamberlin, John, LB, Pacific Lutheran, New England 1979-82; Kansas City 1983-84
Zamlynsky, Ziggy, HB, Villanova, San Francisco (AAFC) 1946
Zander, Carl, LB, Tennessee, Cincinnati 1985
Zanders, Emanuel, G, Jackson State, New Orleans 1974-80; Chicago 1981
Zaninelli, Silvio, FB, Duquesne, Pittsburgh 1934-37
Zapalac, Bill, LB-DE, Texas, NY Jets 1971-73
Zapustus, Joe, E, Fordham, NY Giants 1933
Zarnas, Gust, G, Ohio State, Chi. Bears 1938; Brooklyn 1939; Green Bay 1939-40
Zaruba, Carroll, DB, Nebraska, Dallas Texans 1960
Zatkoff, Roger, LB, Michigan, Green Bay 1953-56; Detroit 1957-58
Zaunbrecher, Godfrey, C, LSU, Minnesota 1971-73
Zawadzkas, Jerry, TE, Columbia, Detroit 1967
Zecher, Rich, DT, Utah State, Oakland 1965; Miami 1966-67; Buffalo 1967
Zehrer, Henry, HB, Hartford 1926
Zele, Mike, DT, Kent State, Atlanta 1979-83
Zelencik, Connie, C, Purdue, Buffalo 1977
Zelencik, Frank, T, Oglethorpe, Chi. Cardinals 1939
Zeller, Jerry, HB, Evansville 1921-22
Zeller, Joe, G, Indiana, Green Bay 1932; Chi. Bears 1933-38
Zeman, Bob, DB, Wisconsin, LA Chargers 1960; San Diego 1961, 1965-66; Denver 1962-63
Zendejas, Tony, K, Nevada-Reno, Houston 1985
Zeno, Coleman, WR, Grambling, NY Giants 1971
Zeno, Joe, G, Holy Cross, Washington 1942-44; Boston 1946-47
Zerbe, Harold, E, Canton 1926
Ziegler, Frank, HB, Georgia Tech, Philadelphia 1949-53
Ziff, Dave, E, Syracuse, Rochester 1925; Brooklyn 1926
Zilly, Jack, E, Notre Dame, LA Rams 1947-51; Philadelphia 1952
Zimmerman, Carl, G, Mount Union, Dayton 1927-29
Zimmerman, Don, WR, Northeast Louisiana, Philadelphia 1973-76; Green Bay 1976
Zimmerman, Giff, HB, Syracuse, Akron 1924; Canton 1925
Zimmerman, Leroy, QB, San Jose State, Washington 1940-42; Philadelphia 1943-46; Detroit 1947; Boston 1948
Zimny, Bob, T, Indiana, Chi. Cardinals 1945-49
Zirinsky, Walt, HB, Lafayette, Cleveland 1945
Zizak, Vince, T, Villanova, Chi. Bears 1934; Philadelphia 1934-37
Zofko, Mickey, RB, Auburn, Detroit 1971-74; NY Giants 1974
Zoia, Clyde, G, Notre Dame, Chi. Cardinals 1920-23
Zoll, Carl, G, Green Bay 1921-22
Zoll, Dick, G, Indiana, Cleveland 1937-38
Zoll, Marty, G, Green Bay 1921
Zombek, Joe, DE, Pittsburgh, Pittsburgh 1954
Zontini, Lou, HB, Notre Dame, Chi. Cardinals 1940-41; Cleveland 1944; Buffalo (AAFC) 1946
Zook, John, DE, Kansas, Atlanta 1969-75; St. Louis 1976-80
Zopetti, Frank, HB, Duquesne, Pittsburgh 1941
Zorich, George, G, Northwestern, Chi. Bears 1944-45; Miami (AAFC) 1946; Baltimore (AAFC) 1947
Zorn, Jim, QB, Cal Poly-Pomona, Seattle 1976-84; Green Bay 1985
Zucco, Vic, DB, Michigan State, Chi. Bears 1957-60
Zuidmulder, Dave, HB, St. Ambrose, Green Bay 1929-31
Zunker, Charlie, T, Southwest Texas State, Cincinnati 1934
Zupek, Al, QB, Lawrence, Green Bay 1946
Zuver, Merle, C, Nebraska, Green Bay 1930
Zuzzio, Tony, G, Muhlenberg, Detroit 1942
Zyntell, Jim, G, Holy Cross, NY Giants 1933; Philadelphia 1933-35

All-Time Team vs. Team

The all-time team vs. team includes all games between NFL teams, whether current or extinct, that have been in the league since 1933. All teams from the 1960-69 American Football League also are included. The scores of early games between current teams that were in the league prior to 1933 also are included.

Philadelphia and Pittsburgh merged in 1943, and the Chicago Cardinals and Pittsburgh merged in 1944. The scores of the Phil-Pitt team are under both Philadelphia and Pittsburgh, and the scores of the Card-Pitt team are under both the St. Louis Cardinals and Pittsburgh.

A number of teams have moved from one city to another or have changed their team names. Those changes are indicated in notes at the end of the relevant series. The notes also indicate which games, if any, were playoff games.

The sites of each game are abbreviated in parentheses after the score. Overtime games are indicated by (OT). Extinct teams are indicated by asterisks.

ATLANTA vs. BUFFALO
Series tied, 2-2
1973—Bills, 17-6 (A)
1977—Bills, 3-0 (B)
1980—Falcons, 30-14 (B)
1983—Falcons, 31-14 (A)
(Points—Falcons 67, Bills 48)

ATLANTA vs. CHI. BEARS
Falcons lead series, 9-5
1966—Bears, 23-6 (C)
1967—Bears, 23-14 (A)
1968—Falcons, 16-13 (C)
1969—Falcons, 48-31 (A)
1970—Bears, 23-14 (A)
1972—Falcons, 37-21 (C)
1973—Falcons, 46-6 (A)
1974—Falcons, 13-10 (A)
1976—Falcons, 10-0 (C)
1977—Falcons, 16-10 (C)
1978—Bears, 13-7 (C)
1980—Falcons, 28-17 (A)
1983—Falcons, 20-17 (C)
1985—Bears, 36-0 (C)
(Points—Falcons 275, Bears 243)

ATLANTA vs. CINCINNATI
Bengals lead series, 4-1
1971—Falcons, 9-6 (C)
1975—Bengals, 21-14 (A)
1978—Bengals, 37-7 (C)
1981—Bengals, 30-28 (A)
1984—Bengals, 35-14 (C)
(Points—Bengals 129, Falcons 72)

ATLANTA vs. CLEVELAND
Browns lead series, 6-1
1966—Browns, 49-17 (A)
1968—Browns, 30-7 (C)
1971—Falcons, 31-14 (C)
1976—Browns, 20-17 (A)
1978—Browns, 24-16 (A)
1981—Browns, 28-17 (C)
1984—Browns, 23-7 (A)
(Points—Browns 188, Falcons 112)

ATLANTA vs. DALLAS
Cowboys lead series, 8-1
1966—Cowboys, 47-14 (A)
1967—Cowboys, 37-7 (D)
1969—Cowboys, 24-17 (A)
1970—Cowboys, 13-0 (D)
1974—Cowboys, 24-0 (A)
1976—Falcons, 17-10 (A)
1978—*Cowboys, 27-20 (D)
1980—*Cowboys, 30-27 (A)
1985—Cowboys, 24-10 (D)
(Points—Cowboys 236, Falcons 112)
**NFC Divisional Playoff*

ATLANTA vs. DENVER
Series tied, 3-3
1970—Broncos, 24-10 (D)
1972—Falcons, 23-20 (A)
1975—Falcons, 35-21 (A)
1979—Broncos, 20-17 (A) OT
1982—Falcons, 34-27 (D)
1985—Broncos, 44-28 (A)
(Points—Broncos 156, Falcons 147)

ATLANTA vs. DETROIT
Lions lead series, 12-4
1966—Lions, 28-10 (D)
1967—Lions, 24-3 (D)
1968—Lions, 24-7 (A)
1969—Lions, 27-21 (D)
1971—Lions, 41-38 (D)
1972—Lions, 26-23 (A)
1973—Lions, 31-6 (D)
1975—Lions, 17-14 (A)
1976—Lions, 24-10 (D)
1977—Falcons, 17-6 (A)
1978—Falcons, 14-0 (A)
1979—Lions, 24-23 (D)
1980—Falcons, 43-28 (A)
1983—Falcons, 30-14 (D)
1984—Lions, 27-24 (A) OT
1985—Lions, 28-27 (A)
(Points—Lions 369, Falcons 310)

ATLANTA vs. GREEN BAY
Packers lead series, 8-6
1966—Packers, 56-3 (Mil)
1967—Packers, 23-0 (Mil)
1968—Packers, 38-7 (A)
1969—Packers, 28-10 (GB)
1970—Packers, 27-24 (GB)
1971—Falcons, 28-21 (A)
1972—Falcons, 10-9 (Mil)
1974—Falcons, 10-3 (A)
1975—Packers, 22-13 (GB)
1976—Packers, 24-20 (A)
1979—Falcons, 25-7 (A)
1981—Falcons, 31-17 (GB)
1982—Packers, 38-7 (A)
1983—Falcons, 47-41 (A) OT
(Points—Packers 354, Falcons 235)

ATLANTA vs. HOUSTON
Falcons lead series, 4-1
1972—Falcons, 20-10 (A)
1976—Oilers, 20-14 (H)
1978—Falcons, 20-14 (A)
1981—Falcons, 31-27 (H)
1984—Falcons, 42-10 (A)
(Points—Falcons 127, Oilers 81)

ATLANTA vs. *INDIANAPOLIS
Colts lead series, 8-0
1966—Colts, 19-7 (A)
1967—Colts, 38-31 (B)
Colts, 49-7 (A)
1968—Colts, 28-20 (A)
Colts, 44-0 (B)
1969—Colts, 21-14 (A)
Colts, 13-6 (B)
1974—Colts, 17-7 (A)
(Points—Colts 229, Falcons 92)
**Franchise in Baltimore prior to 1984*

ATLANTA vs. KANSAS CITY
Chiefs lead series, 2-0
1972—Chiefs, 17-14 (A)
1985—Chiefs, 38-10 (KC)
(Points—Chiefs 55, Falcons 24)

ATLANTA vs. *LA RAIDERS
Raiders lead series, 4-1
1971—Falcons, 24-13 (A)
1975—Raiders, 37-34 (O) OT
1979—Raiders, 50-19 (O)
1982—Raiders, 38-14 (A)
1985—Raiders, 34-24 (A)
(Points—Raiders 172, Falcons 115)
**Franchise in Oakland prior to 1982*

ATLANTA vs. LA RAMS
Rams lead series, 28-8-2
1966—Rams, 19-14 (A)
1967—Rams, 31-3 (A)
Rams, 20-3 (LA)
1968—Rams, 27-14 (LA)
Rams, 17-10 (A)
1969—Rams, 17-7 (LA)
Rams, 38-6 (A)
1970—Tie, 10-10 (LA)
Rams, 17-7 (A)
1971—Tie, 20-20 (LA)
Rams, 24-16 (A)
1972—Falcons, 31-3 (A)
Rams, 20-7 (LA)
1973—Rams, 31-0 (LA)
Falcons, 15-13 (A)
1974—Rams, 21-0 (LA)
Rams, 30-7 (A)
1975—Rams, 22-7 (LA)
Rams, 16-7 (A)
1976—Rams, 30-14 (A)
Rams, 59-0 (LA)
1977—Falcons, 17-6 (A)
Rams, 23-7 (LA)
1978—Rams, 10-0 (LA)
Falcons, 15-7 (A)
1979—Rams, 20-14 (LA)
Rams, 34-13 (A)
1980—Falcons, 13-10 (A)
Rams, 20-17 (LA) OT
1981—Rams, 37-35 (A)
Rams, 21-16 (LA)
1982—Falcons, 34-17 (A)
1983—Rams, 27-21 (LA)
Rams, 36-13 (A)
1984—Falcons, 30-28 (LA)
Rams, 24-10 (A)
1985—Rams, 17-6 (LA)
Falcons, 30-14 (A)
(Points—Rams 836, Falcons 489)

ATLANTA vs. MIAMI
Dolphins lead series, 4-0
1970—Dolphins, 20-7 (A)
1974—Dolphins, 42-7 (M)
1980—Dolphins, 20-17 (A)
1983—Dolphins, 31-24 (M)
(Points—Dolphins 113, Falcons 55)

ATLANTA vs. MINNESOTA
Vikings lead series, 9-6
1966—Falcons, 20-13 (M)
1967—Falcons, 21-20 (A)
1968—Vikings, 47-7 (M)
1969—Falcons, 10-3 (A)
1970—Vikings, 37-7 (A)
1971—Vikings, 24-7 (M)
1973—Falcons, 20-14 (A)
1974—Vikings, 23-10 (M)
1975—Vikings, 38-0 (M)
1977—Vikings, 14-7 (A)
1980—Vikings, 24-23 (M)
1981—Falcons, 31-30 (A)
1982—*Vikings, 30-24 (M)
1984—Vikings, 27-20 (M)
1985—Falcons, 14-13 (A)
(Points—Vikings 357, Falcons 221)
**NFC First Round Playoff*

ATLANTA vs. NEW ENGLAND
Series tied, 2-2
1972—Patriots, 21-20 (NE)
1977—Patriots, 16-10 (A)
1980—Falcons, 37-21 (NE)
1983—Falcons, 24-13 (A)
(Points—Falcons 91, Patriots 71)

ATLANTA vs. NEW ORLEANS
Falcons lead series, 23-11
1967—Saints, 27-24 (NO)
1969—Falcons, 45-17 (A)
1970—Falcons, 14-3 (NO)
Falcons, 32-14 (A)
1971—Falcons, 28-6 (A)
Falcons, 24-20 (NO)
1972—Falcons, 21-14 (NO)
Falcons, 36-20 (A)
1973—Falcons, 62-7 (NO)
Falcons, 14-10 (A)
1974—Saints, 14-13 (NO)
Saints, 13-3 (A)
1975—Falcons, 14-7 (A)
Saints, 23-7 (NO)
1976—Saints, 30-0 (NO)
Falcons, 23-20 (A)
1977—Saints, 21-20 (NO)
Falcons, 35-7 (A)
1978—Falcons, 20-17 (NO)
Falcons, 20-17 (A)
1979—Falcons, 40-34 (NO) OT
Saints, 37-6 (A)
1980—Falcons, 41-14 (NO)
Falcons, 31-13 (A)
1981—Falcons, 27-0 (A)
Falcons, 41-10 (NO)
1982—Falcons, 35-0 (A)
Saints, 35-6 (NO)
1983—Saints, 19-17 (A)
Saints, 27-10 (NO)
1984—Falcons, 36-28 (NO)
Saints, 17-13 (A)
1985—Falcons, 31-24 (A)
Falcons, 16-10 (NO)
(Points—Falcons 805, Saints 575)

ATLANTA vs. NY GIANTS
Falcons lead series, 6-5
1966—Falcons, 27-16 (NY)
1968—Falcons, 24-21 (A)
1971—Giants, 21-17 (A)
1974—Falcons, 14-7 (New Haven)
1977—Falcons, 17-3 (A)
1978—Falcons, 23-20 (A)
1979—Giants, 24-3 (NY)
1981—Giants, 27-24 (A) OT
1982—Falcons, 16-14 (NY)
1983—Giants, 16-13 (A) OT
1984—Giants, 19-7 (A)
(Points—Giants 188, Falcons 185)

ATLANTA vs. NY JETS
Falcons lead series, 2-1
1973—Falcons, 28-20 (NY)
1980—Jets, 14-7 (A)
1983—Falcons, 27-21 (NY)
(Points—Falcons 62, Jets 55)

ATLANTA vs. PHILADELPHIA
Series tied, 6-6-1
1966—Eagles, 23-10 (P)
1967—Eagles, 38-7 (A)
1969—Falcons, 27-3 (P)
1970—Tie, 13-13 (P)
1973—Falcons, 44-27 (P)
1976—Eagles, 14-13 (A)
1978—*Falcons, 14-13 (A)
1979—Falcons, 14-10 (P)
1980—Falcons, 20-17 (P)
1981—Eagles, 16-13 (P)
1983—Eagles, 28-24 (A)
1984—Falcons, 26-10 (A)
1985—Eagles, 23-17 (P) OT
(Points—Falcons 242, Eagles 235)
**NFC Wild Card Game*

ATLANTA vs. PITTSBURGH
Steelers lead series, 6-1
1966—Steelers, 57-33 (A)
1968—Steelers, 41-21 (A)
1970—Falcons, 27-16 (A)
1974—Steelers, 24-17 (P)
1978—Steelers, 31-7 (P)
1981—Steelers, 34-20 (A)
1984—Steelers, 35-10 (P)
(Points—Steelers 238, Falcons 135)

ATLANTA vs. ST. LOUIS
Cardinals lead series, 6-3
1966—Falcons, 16-10 (A)
1968—Cardinals, 17-12 (StL)
1971—Cardinals, 26-9 (A)
1973—Cardinals, 32-10 (A)
1975—Cardinals, 23-20 (StL)
1978—Cardinals, 42-21 (StL)
1980—Falcons, 33-27 (StL) OT
1981—Falcons, 41-20 (A)
1982—Cardinals, 23-20 (A)
(Points—Cardinals 220, Falcons 182)

ATLANTA vs. SAN DIEGO
Falcons lead series, 2-0
1973—Falcons, 41-0 (SD)
1979—Falcons, 28-26 (SD)
(Points—Falcons 69, Chargers 26)

ATLANTA vs. SAN FRANCISCO
49ers lead series, 21-17
1966—49ers, 44-7 (A)
1967—49ers, 38-7 (SF)
49ers, 34-28 (A)
1968—49ers, 28-13 (SF)
49ers, 14-12 (A)
1969—Falcons, 24-12 (A)
Falcons, 21-7 (SF)
1970—Falcons, 21-20 (A)
49ers, 24-20 (SF)
1971—Falcons, 20-17 (A)
49ers, 24-3 (SF)
1972—49ers, 49-14 (A)
49ers, 20-0 (SF)
1973—49ers, 13-9 (A)
Falcons, 17-3 (SF)
1974—49ers, 16-10 (A)
49ers, 27-0 (SF)
1975—Falcons, 17-3 (SF)
Falcons, 31-9 (A)
1976—49ers, 15-0 (SF)
Falcons, 21-16 (A)
1977—Falcons, 7-0 (SF)
49ers, 10-3 (A)
1978—Falcons, 20-17 (SF)
Falcons, 21-10 (A)
1979—49ers, 20-15 (SF)
Falcons, 31-21 (A)
1980—Falcons, 20-17 (SF)
Falcons, 35-10 (A)
1981—Falcons, 34-17 (A)
49ers, 17-14 (SF)
1982—Falcons, 17-7 (SF)
1983—49ers, 24-20 (SF)
Falcons, 28-24 (A)
1984—49ers, 14-5 (SF)
49ers, 35-17 (A)
1985—49ers, 35-16 (SF)
49ers, 38-17 (A)
(Points—49ers 749, Falcons 615)

ATLANTA vs. SEATTLE
Seahawks lead series, 3-0
1976—Seahawks, 30-13 (S)
1979—Seahawks, 31-28 (A)
1985—Seahawks, 30-26 (S)
(Points—Seahawks 91, Falcons 67)

ATLANTA vs. TAMPA BAY
Buccaneers lead series, 3-2
1977—Falcons, 17-0 (TB)
1978—Buccaneers, 14-9 (TB)
1979—Falcons, 17-14 (A)
1981—Buccaneers, 24-23 (TB)
1984—Buccaneers, 23-6 (TB)
(Points—Buccaneers 75, Falcons 72)

ATLANTA vs. WASHINGTON
Redskins lead series, 9-2-1
1966—Redskins, 33-20 (W)
1967—Tie, 20-20 (A)
1969—Redskins, 27-20 (W)
1972—Redskins, 24-13 (W)
1975—Redskins, 30-27 (A)
1977—Redskins, 10-6 (W)
1978—Falcons, 20-17 (A)
1979—Redskins, 16-7 (A)
1980—Falcons, 10-6 (A)
1983—Redskins, 37-21 (W)
1984—Redskins, 27-14 (W)
1985—Redskins, 44-10 (A)
(Points—Redskins 291, Falcons 188)

***1950 BALTIMORE vs **CHI. CARDINALS**
Cardinals won series, 1-0
1950—Cardinals 55-13 (C)
**Extinct team*
***Franchise moved to St. Louis in 1960*

***1950 BALTIMORE vs. CLEVELAND**
Browns won series, 1-0
1950—Browns, 31-0 (B)
Extinct team

***1950 BALTIMORE vs. DETROIT**
Lions won series, 1-0
1950—Lions, 45-21 (B)

***1950 BALTIMORE vs. GREEN BAY**
Colts won series, 1-0
1950—Colts, 41-21 (B)
**Extinct team*

***1950 BALTIMORE vs. LA RAMS**
Rams won series, 1-0
1950—Rams, 70-27 (LA)
**Extinct team*

***1950 BALTIMORE vs. NY GIANTS**
Giants won series, 1-0
1950—Giants, 55-20 (B)
**Extinct team*

***1950 BALTIMORE vs. *NY YANKS**
Yanks won series, 1-0
1950—Yanks, 51-14 (NY)
**Extinct team*

***1950 BALTIMORE vs. PHILADELPHIA**
Eagles won series, 1-0
1950—Eagles, 24-14 (B)
**Extinct team*

***1950 BALTIMORE vs. PITTSBURGH**
Steelers won series, 1-0
1950—Steelers, 17-7 (P)
**Extinct team*

***1950 BALTIMORE vs. SAN FRANCISCO**
49ers won series, 1-0
1950—49ers, 17-14 (SF)
**Extinct team*

***1950 BALTIMORE vs. WASHINGTON**
Redskins won series, 2-0
1950—Redskins, 34-14 (B)

Redskins, 38-28 (W)
(Points—Redskins 76, Colts 42)
*Extinct team

***BOSTON YANKS vs. *BROOKLYN TIGERS**
Yanks won series, 2-0
1944—Yanks, 17-14 (Brook)
Yanks 13-6 (Bos)
(Points—Yanks 30, Tigers 20)
*Extinct team

***BOSTON YANKS vs. CHI. BEARS**
Bears won series, 3-0
1944—Bears, 21-7 (C)
1947—Bears, 28-24 (B)
1946—Bears, 51-17 (B)
(Points—Bears 100, Yanks 48)
*Extinct team

***BOSTON YANKS vs. **CHI. CARDINALS**
Cardinals won series, 3-0
1946—Cardinals, 28-14 (B)
1947—Cardinals, 27-7 (C)
1948—Cardinals, 49-27 (C)
(Points—Cardinals 104, Yanks 48)
*Extinct team
**Franchise moved to St. Louis in 1960

***BOSTON YANKS vs. DETROIT**
Lions won series, 3-2
1944—Lions, 38-7 (D)
1945—Lions, 10-9 (B)
1946—Yanks, 34-10 (D)
1947—Lions, 21-7 (B)
1948—Yanks, 17-14 (D)
(Points—Lions 93, Yanks 74)
*Extinct team

***BOSTON YANKS vs. GREEN BAY**
Packers won series, 2-0
1945—Packers, 38-14 (GB)
Packers, 28-0 (B)
(Points—Packers 66, Yanks 14)
*Extinct team

***BOSTON YANKS vs. **LA RAMS**
Yanks won series, 2-1
1945—Rams, 20-7 (C)
1946—Yanks, 40-21 (B)
1947—Yanks, 27-16 (LA)
(Points—Yanks 74, Rams 57)
*Extinct team
**Franchise in Cleveland prior to 1946

***BOSTON YANKS vs. NY GIANTS**
Giants won series, 5-1-3
1944—Giants, 22-10 (B)
Giants, 31-0 (NY)
1945—Tie, 13-13 (B)
1946—Giants, 17-0 (B)
Tie, 28-28 (NY)
1947—Tie, 7-7 (B)
Yanks, 14-0 (NY)
1948—Giants, 27-7 (B)
Giants, 28-14 (NY)
(Points—Giants 173, Yanks 93)
*Extinct team

***BOSTON YANKS vs. PHILADELPHIA**
Eagles won series, 7-2
1944—Eagles, 28-7 (B)
Eagles, 38-0 (P)
1945—Eagles, 35-7 (P)
1946—Eagles, 49-25 (B)
Eagles, 40-14 (P)
1947—Eagles, 32-0 (P)
Yanks, 21-14 (B)
1948—Eagles, 45-0 (P)
Yanks, 37-14 (B)
(Points—Eagles 295, Yanks 111)
*Extinct team

***BOSTON YANKS vs. PITTSBURGH**
Steelers won series, 5-3
1945—Yanks, 28-7 (B)
Yanks, 10-6 (P)
1946—Steelers, 16-7 (P)
Steelers, 33-7 (B)
1947—Steelers, 30-14 (B)
Steelers, 17-7 (P)
1948—Steelers, 24-14 (P)
Yanks, 13-7 (B)
(Points—Steelers 140, Yanks 100)
*Extinct team

***BOSTON YANKS vs. WASHINGTON**
Redskins won series, 8-2
1944—Redskins, 21-14 (B)
Redskins, 14-7 (W)
1945—Yanks, 28-20 (B)
Redskins, 34-7 (W)
1946—Redskins, 14-6 (B)
Redskins, 17-14 (W)
1947—Yanks, 27-24 (B)
Redskins, 40-13 (W)
1948—Redskins 59-21 (W)
Redskins, 23-7 (B)
(Points—Redskins 266, Yanks 144)
*Extinct team

***BROOKLYN DODGERS vs. CHI. BEARS**
Bears won series, 10-0-1
1930—Tie, 0-0 (C)
1931—Bears, 26-0 (B)
1932—Bears, 20-0 (C)
1933—Bears, 10-0 (B)
1934—Bears, 21-7 (B)
1935—Bears, 24-14 (C)
1937—Bears, 29-7 (C)
1938—Bears, 24-6 (B)
1940—Bears, 16-7 (C)
1942—Bears, 35-0 (B)
1943—Bears, 33-21 (C)
(Points—Bears 238, Dodgers 62)
*Extinct team

***BROOKLYN DODGERS vs. **CHI. CARDINALS**
Dodgers won series, 8-4
1931—Cardinals, 14-7 (B)
1932—Cardinals, 27-7 (C)
Dodgers, 3-0 (B)
1933—Dodgers, 7-0 (B)
Dodgers, 3-0 (C)
1934—Cardinals, 21-0 (B)
1935—Dodgers, 14-12 (B)
1936—Dodgers, 9-0 (B)
1938—Dodgers, 13-0 (B)
1940—Dodgers, 14-9 (B)
1941—Cardinals, 20-6 (B)
1943—Dodgers, 7-0 (B)
(Points—Cardinals 103, Dodgers 90)
*Extinct team
**Franchise moved to St. Louis in 1960

***BROOKLYN DODGERS vs. *CINCINNATI REDS**
Series tied, 1-1
1933—Dodgers, 27-0 (B)
Reds, 10-0 (C)
(Points—Dodgers 27, Red, 10)
*Extinct team

***BROOKLYN DODGERS vs. **CLEVELAND RAMS**
Dodgers won series, 3-1
1937—Dodgers, 9-7 (B)
1939—Dodgers, 23-12 (B)
1940—Dodgers, 29-14 (B)
1942—Rams, 17-0 (B)
(Points—Dodgers 61, Rams 50)
*Extinct team
**Franchise moved to Los Angeles in 1946

***BROOKLYN DODGERS vs. **DETROIT**
Lions won series, 12-3
1930—Spartans, 12-0 (B)
1931—Spartans, 14-0 (P)
Spartans, 19-0 (B)
1932—Spartans, 17-7 (B)
1934—Lions, 28-0 (D)
1935—Dodgers, 12-10 (D)
Lions, 28-0 (B)
1936—Lions, 14-7 (B)
Lions, 14-6 (D)
1937—Lions, 30-0 (D)
1939—Lions, 27-7 (D)
1941—Dodgers, 14-7 (B)
1942—Dodgers, 28-7 (D)
1943—Lions, 27-0 (D)
1944—Lions, 19-14 (D)
(Points—Lions 273, Dodgers 95)
*Extinct team known as Tigers in 1944
**Franchise in Portsmouth prior to 1934 and known as the Spartans.

***BROOKLYN DODGERS vs. GREEN BAY**
Packers won series, 10-0
1931—Packers, 32-6 (GB)
Packers, 7-0 (B)
1932—Packers, 13-0 (GB)
Packers, 7-0 (B)
1936—Packers, 38-7 (B)
1938—Packers, 35-7 (GB)
1939—Packers, 28-0 (B)
1941—Packers, 30-7 (GB)
1943—Packers, 31-7 (B)
1944—Packers, 14-7 (GB)
(Points—Packers 235, Dodgers 41)
*Extinct team known as Tigers in 1944

***BROOKLYN DODGERS vs. NY GIANTS**
Giants won series, 22-5-3
1930—Dodgers, 7-6 (NY)
Giants, 13-0 (B)
1931—Giants, 27-0 (NY)
Giants, 19-6 (B)
1932—Giants, 20-12 (NY)
Giants, 13-7 (B)
1933—Giants, 21-7 (NY)
Giants, 10-0 (B)
1934—Giants, 14-0 (NY)
Giants, 27-0 (B)
1935—Giants, 10-7 (NY)
Giants, 21-0 (B)
1936—Tie, 10-10 (NY)
Giants, 14-0 (B)
1937—Giants, 21-0 (B)
Tie, 13-13 (NY)
1938—Giants, 28-14 (NY)
Tie, 7-7 (B)
1939—Giants, 7-6 (B)
Giants, 28-7 (NY)
1940—Giants, 10-7 (B)
Dodgers, 14-6 (NY)
1941—Dodgers, 16-13 (B)
Dodgers, 21-7 (NY)
1942—Dodgers, 17-7 (B)
Giants, 10-0 (NY)
1943—Giants, 20-0 (B)
Giants, 24-7 (NY)
1944—Giants, 14-7 (B)
Giants, 7-0 (NY)
(Points—Giants 447, Dodgers 192)
*Extinct team known as Tigers in 1944

***BROOKLYN DODGERS vs. **PHILADELPHIA**
Dodgers won series, 15-6-1
1934—Dodgers, 10-7 (P)
Eagles, 13-0 (B)
1935—Dodgers, 17-6 (B)
Dodgers, 3-0 (P)
1936—Dodgers, 18-0 (B)
Dodgers, 13-7 (P)
1937—Dodgers, 13-7 (P)
Eagles, 14-10 (B)
1938—Dodgers, 10-7 (P)
Dodgers, 32-14 (B)
1939—Tie, 0-0 (P)
Dodgers, 23-14 (B)
1940—Dodgers, 30-17 (B)
Dodgers, 21-7 (P)
1941—Dodgers, 24-13 (P)
Dodgers, 15-6 (B)
1942—Dodgers, 35-14 (P)
Eagles, 14-7 (B)
1943—Phil-Pitt, 17-0 (P)
Dodgers, 13-7 (B)
1944—Eagles, 21-7 (B)
Eagles, 34-0 (P)
(Points—Dodgers 301, Eagles 239
*Extinct team known as Tigers in 1944
**Eagles known as Phil-Pitt in 1943

***BROOKLYN DODGERS vs. **PITTSBURGH**
Dodgers won series, 12-9-1
1933—Tie, 3-3 (B)
Dodgers, 32-0 (P)
1934—Dodgers, 21-3 (B)
Dodgers, 10-0 (P)
1935—Dodgers, 13-7 (P)
Pirates, 16-7 (B)
1936—Pirates, 10-6 (B)
Pirates, 10-7 (P)
1937—Pirates, 21-0 (B)
Dodgers, 23-0 (P)
1938—Pirates, 17-3 (B)
Dodgers, 17-7 (P)
1939—Dodgers, 12-7 (B)
Dodgers, 17-13 (P)
1940—Dodgers, 10-3 (P)
Dodgers, 21-0 (B)
1941—Steelers, 14-7 (P)
Dodgers, 35-7 (B)
1942—Steelers, 7-0 (B)
Steelers, 13-0 (P)
1943—Phil-Pitt, 17-0 (Phil)
Dodgers, 13-7 (B)
(Points—Dodgers 257, Steelers 182)
*Extinct team
**Steelers known as Pirates prior to 1941 and as Phil-Pitt in 1943

***BROOKLYN DODGERS vs. **WASHINGTON**
Redskins won series, 17-5-3
1932—Dodgers, 14-0 (Bos)
Braves, 7-0 (Brook)
1933—Dodgers, 14-0 (Brook)
1934—Dodgers, 10-6 (Brook)
Redskins, 13-3 (Bos)
1935—Redskins, 7-0 (Bos)
Tie, 0-0 (Brook)
1936—Redskins, 14-3 (Brook)
Redskins 30-3 (Bos)
1937—Redskins, 11-7 (W)
Redskins, 21-0 (B)
1938—Tie, 16-16 (W)
Tie, 6-6 (B)
1939—Redskins, 41-13 (W)
Redskins, 42-0 (B)
1940—Redskins, 24-17 (W)
Dodgers, 16-14 (B)
1941—Redskins, 3-0 (W)
Dodgers, 13-7 (B)
1942—Redskins, 21-10 (B)
Redskins, 23-3 (W)
1943—Redskins, 27-0 (W)
Redskins, 48-10 (B)
1944—Redskins, 17-14 (W)
Redskins, 10-0 (B)
(Points—Redskins 408, Dodgers 175)
*Extinct team known as Tigers in 1944
**Franchise in Boston prior to 1937 and known as the Braves prior to 1933

***BROOKLYN TIGERS vs. BOSTON YANKS**
Yanks won series, 2-0
See *Boston Yanks vs. *Brooklyn Tigers
*Extinct team

BUFFALO vs. ATLANTA
Series tied, 2-2,
See Atlanta vs. Buffalo

BUFFALO vs. CHICAGO
Bears lead series, 2-1
1970—Bears, 31-13 (C)
1974—Bills, 16-6 (B)
1979—Bears, 7-0 (B)
(Points—Bears 44, Bills 29)

BUFFALO vs. CINCINNATI
Bengals lead series, 8-5
1968—Bengals, 34-23 (C)
1969—Bills, 16-13 (B)
1970—Bengals, 43-14 (B)
1973—Bengals, 16-13 (B)
1975—Bengals, 33-24 (C)
1978—Bills, 5-0 (B)
1979—Bills, 51-24 (B)
1980—Bills, 14-0 (C)
1981—Bengals, 27-24 (C) OT
*Bengals, 28-21 (C)
1983—Bills, 10-6 (C)
1984—Bengals, 52-21 (C)
1985—Bengals, 23-17 (B)
(Points—Bengals 299, Bills 253)
*AFC Divisional Playoff

BUFFALO vs. CLEVELAND
Browns lead series, 5-2
1972—Browns, 27-10 (C)
1974—Bills, 15-10 (C)
1977—Browns, 27-16 (B)
1978—Browns, 41-20 (C)
1981—Bills, 22-13 (B)
1984—Browns, 13-10 (B)
1985—Browns, 17-7 (C)
(Points—Browns 148, Bills 100)

BUFFALO vs. DALLAS
Cowboys lead series, 3-1
1971—Cowboys, 49-37 (B)
1976—Cowboys, 17-10 (D)
1981—Cowboys, 27-14 (D)
1984—Bills, 14-3 (B)
(Points—Cowboys 96, Bills 75)

BUFFALO vs. DENVER
Bills lead series, 13-9-1
1960—Broncos, 27-21 (B)
Tie, 38-38 (D)
1961—Broncos, 22-10 (B)
Bills, 23-10 (D)
1962—Broncos, 23-20 (B)
Bills, 45-38 (D)
1963—Bills, 30-28 (D)
Bills, 27-17 (B)
1964—Bills, 30-13 (B)
Bills, 30-19 (D)
1965—Bills, 30-15 (D)
Bills, 31-13 (B)
1966—Bills, 38-21 (B)
1967—Bills, 17-16 (D)
Broncos, 21-20 (B)
1968—Broncos, 34-32 (D)
1969—Bills, 41-28 (B)
1970—Broncos, 25-10 (B)
1975—Bills, 38-14 (B)
1977—Broncos, 26-6 (D)
1979—Broncos, 19-16 (B)
1981—Bills, 9-7 (B)
1984—Broncos, 37-7 (B)
(Points—Bills 569, Broncos 511)

BUFFALO vs. DETROIT
Series tied, 1-1-1
1972—Tie, 21-21 (B)
1976—Lions, 27-14 (D)
1979—Bills, 20-17 (D)
(Points—Lions 65, Bills 55)

BUFFALO vs. GREEN BAY
Bills lead series, 2-1
1974—Bills, 27-7 (GB)
1979—Bills, 19-12 (B)
1982—Packers, 33-21 (Mil)
(Points—Bills 67, Packers 52)

BUFFALO vs. HOUSTON
Oilers lead series, 17-9
1960—Bills, 25-24 (B)
Oilers, 31-23 (H)
1961—Bills, 22-12 (H)
Oilers, 28-16 (B)
1962—Oilers, 28-23 (B)
Oilers, 17-14 (H)
1963—Oilers, 31-20 (B)
Oilers, 28-14 (H)
1964—Bills, 48-17 (H)
Bills, 24-10 (B)
1965—Oilers, 19-17 (B)
Bills, 29-18 (H)
1966—Bills, 27-20 (B)
Bills, 42-20 (H)
1967—Oilers, 20-3 (B)
Oilers, 10-3 (H)
1968—Oilers, 30-7 (B)
Oilers, 35-6 (H)
1969—Oilers, 17-3 (B)
Oilers, 28-14 (H)
1971—Oilers, 20-14 (B)
1974—Oilers, 21-9 (B)
1976—Oilers, 13-3 (B)
1978—Oilers, 17-10 (H)
1983—Bills, 30-13 (B)
1985—Bills, 20-0 (B)
(Points—Oilers 527, Bills 466)

BUFFALO vs. *INDIANAPOLIS
Series tied, 15-15-1
1970—Tie, 17-17 (Balt)
Colts, 20-14 (Buff)
1971—Colts, 43-0 (Buff)
Colts, 24-0 (Balt)
1972—Colts, 17-0 (Buff)
Colts, 35-7 (Balt)
1973—Bills, 31-13 (Buff)
Bills, 24-17 (Balt)
1974—Bills, 27-14 (Balt)
Bills, 6-0 (Buff)
1975—Bills, 38-31 (Balt)
Colts, 42-35 (Buff)
1976—Colts, 31-13 (Buff)
Colts, 58-20 (Balt)
1977—Colts, 17-14 (Balt)
Colts, 31-13 (Buff)
1978—Bills, 24-17 (Buff)
Bills, 21-14 (Balt)
1979—Bills, 31-13 (Balt)
Colts, 14-13 (Buff)
1980—Colts, 17-12 (Buff)
Colts, 28-24 (Balt)
1981—Bills, 35-3 (Balt)
Bills, 23-17 (Buff)
1982—Bills, 20-0 (Buff)
1983—Bills, 28-23 (Buff)
Bills, 30-7 (Balt)
1984—Colts, 31-17 (I)
Bills, 21-15 (Buff)
1985—Colts, 49-17 (I)
Bills, 21-9 (Buff)
(Points—Colts 667, Bills 596)
*Franchise in Baltimore prior to 1984

BUFFALO vs. *KANSAS CITY
Bills lead series, 14-11-1
1960—Texans, 45-28 (B)
Texans, 24-7 (D)

1961—Bills, 27-24 (B)
Bills, 30-20 (D)
1962—Texans, 41-21 (D)
Bills, 23-14 (B)
1963—Tie, 27-27 (B)
Bills, 35-26 (KC)
1964—Bills, 34-17 (B)
Bills, 35-22 (KC)
1965—Bills, 23-7 (KC)
Bills, 34-25 (B)
1966—Chiefs, 42-20 (B)
Bills, 29-14 (KC)
**Chiefs, 31-7 (B)
1967—Chiefs, 23-13 (KC)
1968—Chiefs, 18-7 (B)
1969—Chiefs, 29-7 (B)
Chiefs, 22-19 (KC)
1971—Chiefs, 22-9 (KC)
1973—Bills, 23-14 (B)
1976—Bills, 50-17 (B)
1978—Bills, 28-13 (B)
Chiefs, 14-10 (KC)
1982—Bills, 14-9 (B)
1983—Bills, 14-9 (KC)
(Points—Chiefs 574, Bills 569)
*Franchise in Dallas prior to 1963 and known as Texans
**AFL Championship

BUFFALO vs. *LA RAIDERS
Raiders lead series, 12-11
1960—Bills, 38-9 (B)
Raiders, 20-7 (O)
1961—Raiders, 31-22 (B)
Bills, 26-21 (O)
1962—Bills, 14-6 (B)
Bills, 10-6 (O)
1963—Raiders, 35-17 (O)
Bills, 12-0 (B)
1964—Bills, 23-20 (B)
Raiders, 16-13 (O)
1965—Bills, 17-12 (B)
Bills, 17-14 (O)
1966—Bills, 31-10 (O)
1967—Raiders, 24-20 (B)
Raiders, 28-21 (O)
1968—Raiders, 48-6 (B)
Raiders, 13-10 (O)
1969—Raiders, 50-21 (O)
1972—Raiders, 28-16 (O)
1974—Bills, 21-20 (B)
1977—Raiders, 34-13 (O)
1980—Bills, 24-7 (B)
1983—Raiders, 27-24 (B)
(Points—Raiders 479, Bills 423)
*Franchise in Oakland prior to 1982

BUFFALO vs. LA RAMS
Rams lead series, 3-1
1970—Rams, 19-0 (B)
1974—Rams, 19-14 (LA)
1980—Bills, 10-7 (B) OT
1983—Rams, 41-17 (LA)
(Points—Rams 86, Bills 41)

BUFFALO vs. MIAMI
Dolphins lead series, 32-7-1
1966—Bills, 58-24 (B)
Bills, 29-0 (M)
1967—Bills, 35-13 (B)
Dolphins, 17-14 (M)
1968—Tie, 14-14 (M)
Dolphins, 21-17 (B)
1969—Dolphins, 24-6 (M)
Bills, 28-3 (B)
1970—Dolphins, 33-14 (B)
Dolphins, 45-7 (M)
1971—Dolphins, 29-14 (B)
Dolphins, 34-0 (M)
1972—Dolphins, 24-23 (M)
Dolphins, 30-16 (B)
1973—Dolphins, 27-6 (M)
Dolphins, 17-0 (B)
1974—Dolphins, 24-16 (B)
Dolphins, 35-28 (M)
1975—Dolphins, 35-30 (B)
Dolphins, 31-21 (M)
1976—Dolphins, 30-21 (B)
Dolphins, 45-27 (M)
1977—Dolphins, 13-0 (B)
Dolphins, 31-14 (M)
1978—Dolphins, 31-24 (M)
Dolphins, 25-24 (B)
1979—Dolphins, 9-7 (B)
Dolphins, 17-7 (M)
1980—Bills, 17-7 (B)
Dolphins, 17-14 (M)
1981—Bills, 31-21 (B)
Dolphins, 16-6 (M)
1982—Dolphins, 9-7 (B)
Dolphins, 27-10 (M)
1983—Dolphins, 12-0 (B)
Bills, 38-35 (M) OT
1984—Dolphins, 21-17 (B)
Dolphins, 38-7 (M)
1985—Dolphins, 23-14 (B)
Dolphins, 28-0 (M)
(Points—Dolphins 935, Bills 661)

BUFFALO vs. MINNESOTA
Vikings lead series, 4-1
1971—Vikings, 19-0 (M)
1975—Vikings, 35-13 (B)
1979—Vikings, 10-3 (M)
1982—Bills, 23-22 (B)
1985—Vikings, 27-20 (B)
(Points—Vikings 113, Bills 59)

BUFFALO vs. *NEW ENGLAND
Patriots lead series, 28-23-1
1960—Bills, 13-0 (B)
Bills, 38-14 (Buff)
1961—Patriots, 23-21 (Buff)
Patriots, 52-21 (B)
1962—Tie, 28-28 (Buff)
Patriots, 21-10 (B)
1963—Bills, 28-21 (Buff)
Patriots, 17-7 (B)
**Patriots, 26-8 (Buff)
1964—Patriots, 36-28 (Buff)
Bills, 24-14 (B)
1965—Bills, 24-7 (Buff)
Bills, 23-7 (B)
1966—Patriots, 20-10 (Buff)
Patriots, 14-3 (B)
1967—Patriots, 23-0 (Buff)
Bills, 44-16 (B)
1968—Patriots, 16-7 (Buff)
Patriots, 23-6 (B)
1969—Bills, 23-16 (Buff)
Patriots, 35-21 (B)
1970—Bills, 45-10 (B)
Patriots, 14-10 (Buff)
1971—Patriots, 38-33 (NE)
Bills, 27-20 (Buff)
1972—Bills, 38-14 (Buff)
Bills, 27-24 (NE)
1973—Bills, 31-13 (NE)
Bills, 37-13 (Buff)
1974—Bills, 30-28 (Buff)
Bills, 29-28 (NE)
1975—Bills, 45-31 (Buff)
Bills, 34-14 (NE)
1976—Patriots, 26-22 (Buff)
Patriots, 20-10 (NE)
1977—Bills, 24-14 (NE)
Patriots, 20-7 (Buff)
1978—Patriots, 14-10 (Buff)
Patriots, 26-24 (NE)
1979—Patriots, 26-6 (Buff)
Bills, 16-13 (NE) OT
1980—Bills, 31-13 (Buff)
Patriots, 24-2 (NE)
1981—Bills, 20-17 (Buff)
Bills, 19-10 (NE)
1982—Patriots, 30-19 (NE)
1983—Patriots, 31-0 (Buff)
Patriots, 21-7 (NE)
1984—Patriots, 21-17 (Buff)
Patriots, 38-10 (NE)
1985—Patriots, 17-14 (Buff)
Patriots, 14-3 (NE)
(Points—Patriots 1,071, Bills 1,034)
*Franchise in Boston prior to 1971
**Divisional Playoff

BUFFALO vs. NEW ORLEANS
Bills lead series, 2-1
1973—Saints, 13-0 (NO)
1980—Bills, 35-26 (NO)
1983—Bills, 27-21 (B)
(Points—Bills 62, Saints 60)

BUFFALO vs. NY GIANTS
Giants lead series, 2-1
1970—Giants, 20-6 (NY)
1975—Giants, 17-14 (B)
1978—Bills, 41-17 (B)
(Points—Bills 61, Giants 54)

BUFFALO vs. *NY JETS
Bills lead series, 26-25
1960—Titans, 27-3 (NY)
Titans, 17-13 (B)
1961—Bills, 41-31 (B)
Titans, 21-14 (NY)
1962—Titans, 17-6 (B)
Bills, 20-3 (NY)
1963—Bills, 45-14 (B)
Bills, 19-10 (NY)
1964—Bills, 34-24 (B)
Bills, 20-7 (NY)
1965—Bills, 33-21 (B)
Jets, 14-12 (NY)
1966—Bills, 33-23 (NY)
Bills, 14-3 (B)
1967—Bills, 20-17 (B)
Jets, 20-10 (NY)
1968—Bills, 37-35 (B)
Jets, 25-21 (NY)
1969—Jets, 33-19 (B)
Jets, 16-6 (NY)
1970—Bills, 34-31 (B)
Bills, 10-6 (NY)
1971—Jets, 28-17 (NY)
Jets, 20-7 (B)
1972—Jets, 41-24 (B)
Jets, 41-3 (NY)
1973—Bills, 9-7 (B)
Bills, 34-14 (NY)
1974—Bills, 16-12 (B)
Jets, 20-10 (NY)
1975—Bills, 42-14 (B)
Bills, 24-23 (NY)
1976—Jets, 17-14 (NY)
Jets, 19-14 (B)
1977—Jets, 24-19 (B)
Bills, 14-10 (NY)
1978—Jets, 21-20 (B)
Jets, 45-14 (NY)
1979—Bills, 46-31 (B)
Bills, 14-12 (NY)
1980—Bills, 20-10 (B)
Bills, 31-24 (NY)
1981—Bills, 31-0 (B)
Jets, 33-14 (NY)
**Bills, 31-27 (NY)
1983—Jets, 34-10 (B)
Bills, 24-17 (NY)
1984—Jets, 28-26 (B)
Jets, 21-17 (NY)
1985—Jets, 42-3 (NY)
Jets, 27-7 (B)
(Points—Jets 1,077, Bills 1,019)
*Jets known as Titans prior to 1963
**AFC Wild Card Game

BUFFALO vs. PHILADELPHIA
Eagles lead series, 3-1
1973—Bills, 27-26 (B)
1981—Eagles, 20-14 (B)
1984—Eagles, 27-17 (B)
1985—Eagles, 21-17 (P)
(Points—Eagles 94, Bills 75)

BUFFALO vs. PITTSBURGH
Steelers lead series, 6-3
1970—Steelers, 23-10 (P)
1972—Steelers, 38-21 (B)
1974—*Steelers, 32-14 (P)
1975—Bills, 30-21 (P)
1978—Steelers, 28-17 (B)
1979—Steelers, 28-0 (P)
1980—Bills, 28-13 (B)
1982—Bills, 13-0 (B)
1985—Steelers, 30-24 (P)
(Points—Steelers 213, Bills 157)
*AFC Divisional Playoff

BUFFALO vs. ST. LOUIS
Cardinals lead series, 3-1
1971—Cardinals, 28-23 (B)
1975—Bills, 32-14 (StL)
1981—Cardinals, 24-0 (StL)
1984—Cardinals, 37-7 (StL)
(Points—Cardinals 103, Bills 62)

BUFFALO vs. *SAN DIEGO
Chargers lead series, 17-9-2
1960—Chargers, 24-10 (B)
Bills, 32-3 (LA)
1961—Chargers, 19-11 (B)
Chargers, 28-10 (SD)
1962—Bills, 35-10 (B)
Bills, 40-20 (SD)
1963—Chargers, 14-10 (SD)
Chargers, 23-13 (B)
1964—Bills, 30-3 (B)
Bills, 27-24 (SD)
**Bills, 20-7 (B)
1965—Chargers, 34-3 (B)
Tie, 20-20 (SD)
**Bills, 23-0 (SD)
1966—Chargers, 27-7 (SD)
Tie, 17-17 (B)
1967—Chargers, 37-17 (B)
1968—Chargers, 21-6 (B)
1969—Chargers, 45-6 (SD)
1971—Chargers, 20-3 (SD)
1973—Chargers, 34-7 (SD)
1976—Chargers, 34-13 (B)
1979—Chargers, 27-19 (SD)
1980—Bills, 26-24 (SD)
***Chargers, 20-14 (SD)
1981—Bills, 28-27 (SD)
1985—Chargers, 14-9 (B)
Chargers, 40-7 (SD)
(Points—Chargers 616, Bills 463)
*Franchise in Los Angeles prior to 1961
**AFL Championship
***AFC Divisional Playoff

BUFFALO vs. SAN FRANCISCO
Bills lead series, 2-1
1972—Bills, 27-20 (B)
1980—Bills, 18-13 (SF)
1983—49ers, 23-10 (B)
(Points—49ers 56, Bills 55)

BUFFALO vs. SEATTLE
Seahawks lead series, 2-0
1977—Seahawks, 56-17 (S)
1984—Seahawks, 31-28 (S)
(Points—Seahawks 87, Bills 45)

BUFFALO vs. TAMPA BAY
Buccaneers lead series, 2-1
1976—Bills, 14-9 (TB)
1978—Buccaneers, 31-10 (TB)
1982—Buccaneers, 24-23 (TB)
(Points—Buccaneers 64, Bills 47)

BUFFALO vs. WASHINGTON
Series tied 2-2
1972—Bills, 24-17 (W)
1977—Redskins, 10-0 (B)
1981—Bills, 21-14 (B)
1984—Redskins, 41-14 (W)
(Points—Redskins 82, Bills 59)

CHI. BEARS vs. ATLANTA
Falcons lead series, 9-5;
See Atlanta vs. Chi. Bears

CHI. BEARS vs. *BOSTON YANKS
Bears won series, 3-0
See *Boston Yanks vs. Chi. Bears
*Extinct team

CHI. BEARS vs. *BROOKLYN DODGERS
Bears won series, 10-0-1
See *Brooklyn Dodgers vs. Chi. Bears
*Extinct team

CHI. BEARS vs. BUFFALO
Bears lead series, 2-1;
See Buffalo vs. Chi. Bears

CHI. BEARS vs. CINCINNATI
Bengals lead series, 2-0;
1972—Bengals, 13-3 (Chi)
1980—Bengals, 17-14 (Chi) OT
(Points—Bengals 30, Bears 17)

CHI. BEARS vs *CINCINNATI REDS
Bears won series, 2-0
1934—Bears, 21-3 (Cin)
Bears, 41-7 (Chi)
(Points—Bears 62, Reds 10
*Extinct team

CHI. BEARS vs. CLEVELAND
Browns lead series, 6-2
1951—Browns, 42-21 (Cle)
1954—Browns, 39-10 (Chi)
1960—Browns, 42-0 (Cle)
1961—Bears, 17-14 (Chi)
1967—Browns, 24-0 (Cle)
1969—Browns, 28-24 (Chi)
1972—Bears, 17-0 (Cle)
1980—Browns, 27-21 (Cle)
(Points—Browns 216, Bears 110)

CHI. BEARS vs. DALLAS
Cowboys lead series, 8-4
1960—Bears, 17-7 (C)
1962—Bears, 34-33 (D)
1964—Cowboys, 24-10 (C)
1968—Cowboys, 34-3 (C)
1971—Bears, 23-19 (C)
1973—Cowboys, 20-17 (C)
1976—Cowboys, 31-21 (D)
1977—*Cowboys, 37-7 (D)
1979—Cowboys, 24-20 (D)
1981—Cowboys, 10-9 (D)
1984—Cowboys, 23-14 (C)
1985—Bears, 44-0 (D)
(Points—Cowboys 262, Bears 219)
*NFC Divisional Playoff

CHI. BEARS vs. *DALLAS TEXANS
Series tied, 1-1
1952—Bears, 38-20 (C)
Texans, 27-23 (D)
(Points—Bears 61, Texans 47)
*Extinct team

CHI. BEARS vs. DENVER
Bears lead series, 4-3
1971—Broncos, 6-3 (D)
1973—Bears, 33-14 (D)
1976—Broncos, 28-14 (C)
1978—Broncos, 16-7 (D)
1981—Bears, 35-24 (C)
1983—Bears, 31-14 (C)
1984—Bears, 27-0 (C)
(Points—Bears 150, Broncos 102)

CHI. BEARS vs. *DETROIT
Bears lead series, 64-44-5
1930—Spartans, 7-6 (P)
Bears, 14-6 (C)
1931—Bears, 9-6 (C)
Spartans, 3-0 (P)
1932—Tie, 13-13 (C)
Tie, 7-7 (P)
**Bears, 9-0 (C)
1933—Bears, 17-14 (C)
Bears, 17-7 (P)
1934—Bears, 19-16 (D)
Bears, 10-7 (C)
1935—Tie, 20-20 (C)
Lions, 14-2 (D)
1936—Bears, 12-10 (C)
Lions, 13-7 (D)
1937—Bears, 28-20 (C)
Bears, 13-0 (D)
1938—Lions, 13-7 (C)
Lions, 14-7 (D)
1939—Lions, 10-0 (C)
Bears, 23-13 (D)
1940—Bears, 7-0 (C)
Lions, 17-14 (D)
1941—Bears, 49-0 (C)
Bears, 24-7 (D)
1942—Bears, 16-0 (C)
Bears, 42-0 (D)
1943—Bears, 27-21 (D)
Bears, 35-14 (C)
1944—Tie, 21-21 (C)
Lions, 41-21 (D)
1945—Lions, 16-10 (D)
Lions, 35-28 (C)
1946—Bears, 42-6 (C)
Bears, 45-24 (D)
1947—Bears, 33-24 (C)
Bears, 34-14 (D)
1948—Bears, 28-0 (C)
Bears, 42-14 (D)
1949—Bears, 27-24 (C)
Bears, 28-7 (D)
1950—Bears, 35-21 (D)
Bears, 6-3 (C)
1951—Bears, 28-23 (D)
Lions, 41-28 (C)
1952—Bears, 24-23 (C)
Lions, 45-21 (D)
1953—Lions, 20-16 (C)
Lions, 13-7 (D)
1954—Lions, 48-23 (D)
Bears, 28-24 (C)
1955—Bears, 24-14 (D)
Bears, 21-20 (C)
1956—Lions, 42-10 (D)
Bears, 38-21 (C)
1957—Bears, 27-7 (D)
Lions, 21-13 (C)
1958—Bears, 20-7 (D)
Bears, 21-16 (C)
1959—Bears, 24-14 (D)
Bears, 25-14 (C)
1960—Bears, 28-7 (C)
Lions, 36-0 (D)
1961—Bears, 31-17 (D)
Lions, 16-15 (C)
1962—Lions, 11-3 (D)
Bears, 3-0 (C)
1963—Bears, 37-21 (D)
Bears, 24-14 (C)
1964—Lions, 10-0 (C)
Bears, 27-24 (D)
1965—Bears, 38-10 (C)
Bears, 17-10 (D)
1966—Lions, 14-3 (D)
Tie, 10-10 (C)
1967—Bears, 14-3 (C)
Bears, 27-13 (D)
1968—Lions, 42-0 (D)
Lions, 28-10 (C)
1969—Lions, 13-7 (D)
Lions, 20-3 (C)
1970—Lions, 28-14 (D)
Lions, 16-10 (C)
1971—Bears, 28-23 (D)
Lions, 28-3 (C)
1972—Lions, 38-24 (C)
Lions, 14-0 (D)
1973—Lions, 30-7 (C)
Lions, 40-7 (D)
1974—Bears, 17-9 (C)

Lions, 34-17 (D)
1975—Lions, 27-7 (D)
Bears, 25-21 (C)
1976—Bears, 10-3 (C)
Lions, 14-10 (D)
1977—Bears, 30-20 (C)
Bears, 31-14 (D)
1978—Bears, 19-0 (D)
Lions, 21-17 (C)
1979—Bears, 35-7 (C)
Lions, 20-0 (D)
1980—Bears, 24-7 (C)
Bears, 23-17 (D) OT
1981—Lions, 48-17 (D)
Lions, 23-7 (C)
1982—Lions, 17-10 (D)
Bears, 20-17 (C)
1983—Lions, 31-17 (D)
Lions, 38-17 (C)
1984—Bears, 16-14 (C)
Bears, 30-13 (D)
1985—Bears, 24-3 (C)
Bears, 37-17 (D)
(Points—Bears 2,102, Lions 1,906)
Franchise in Portsmouth prior to 1934 and known as the Spartans
***NFL Championship*

***CHI. BEARS vs. GREEN BAY**
Bears lead series, 70-55-6
1921—Staleys, 20-0 (C)
1923—Bears, 3-0 (GB)
1924—Bears, 3-0 (C)
1925—Packers, 14-10 (GB)
Bears, 21-0 (C)
1926—Tie, 6-6 (GB)
Bears, 19-13 (C)
Tie, 3-3 (C)
1927—Bears, 7-6 (GB)
Bears, 14-6 (C)
1928—Tie, 12-12 (GB)
Packers, 16-6 (C)
Packers, 6-0 (C)
1929—Packers, 23-0 (GB)
Packers, 14-0 (C)
Packers, 25-0 (C)
1930—Packers, 7-0 (GB)
Packers, 13-12 (C)
Bears, 21-0 (C)
1931—Packers, 7-0 (GB)
Packers, 6-2 (C)
Bears, 7-6 (C)
1932—Tie, 0-0 (GB)
Packers, 2-0 (C)
Bears, 9-0 (C)
1933—Bears, 14-7 (GB)
Bears, 10-7 (C)
Bears, 7-6 (C)
1934—Bears, 24-10 (GB)
Bears, 27-14 (C)
1935—Packers, 7-0 (GB)
Packers, 17-14 (C)
1936—Bears, 30-3 (GB)
Packers, 21-10 (C)
1937—Bears, 14-2 (GB)
Packers, 24-14 (C)
1938—Bears, 2-0 (GB)
Packers, 24-17 (C)
1939—Packers, 21-16 (GB)
Bears, 30-27 (C)
1940—Bears, 41-10 (GB)
Bears, 14-7 (C)
1941—Bears, 25-17 (GB)
Packers, 16-14 (C)
**Bears, 33-14 (C)
1942—Bears, 44-28 (GB)
Bears, 38-7 (C)
1943—Tie, 21-21 (GB)
Bears, 21-7 (C)
1944—Packers, 42-28 (GB)
Bears, 21-0 (C)
1945—Packers, 31-21 (GB)
Bears, 28-24 (C)
1946—Bears, 30-7 (GB)
Bears, 10-7 (C)
1947—Packers, 29-20 (GB)
Bears, 20-17 (C)
1948—Bears, 45-7 (GB)
Bears, 7-6 (C)
1949—Bears, 17-0 (GB)
Bears, 24-3 (C)
1950—Packers, 31-21 (GB)
Bears, 28-14 (C)
1951—Bears, 31-20 (GB)
Bears, 24-13 (C)
1952—Bears, 24-14 (GB)
Packers, 41-28 (C)
1953—Bears, 17-13 (GB)
Tie, 21-21 (C)
1954—Bears, 10-3 (GB)
Bears, 28-23 (C)
1955—Packers, 24-3 (GB)
Bears, 52-31 (C)
1956—Bears, 37-21 (GB)
Bears, 38-14 (C)
1957—Packers, 21-17 (GB)
Bears, 21-14 (C)
1958—Bears, 34-20 (GB)
Bears, 24-10 (C)
1959—Packers, 9-6 (GB)
Bears, 28-17 (C)
1960—Bears, 17-14 (GB)
Packers, 41-13 (C)
1961—Packers, 24-0 (GB)
Packers, 31-28 (C)
1962—Packers, 49-0 (GB)
Packers, 38-7 (C)
1963—Bears, 10-3 (GB)
Bears, 26-7 (C)
1964—Packers, 23-12 (GB)
Packers, 17-3 (C)
1965—Packers, 23-14 (GB)
Bears, 31-10 (C)
1966—Packers, 17-0 (C)
Packers, 13-6 (GB)
1967—Packers, 13-10 (GB)
Packers, 17-13 (C)
1968—Bears, 13-10 (GB)
Packers, 28-27 (C)
1969—Packers, 17-0 (GB)
Packers, 21-3 (C)
1970—Packers, 20-19 (GB)
Bears, 35-17 (C)
1971—Packers, 17-14 (C)
Packers, 31-10 (GB)
1972—Packers, 20-17 (GB)
Packers, 23-17 (C)
1973—Bears, 31-17 (GB)
Packers, 21-0 (C)
1974—Bears, 10-9 (C)
Packers, 20-3 (Mil)
1975—Bears, 27-14 (C)
Packers, 28-7 (GB)
1976—Bears, 24-13 (C)
Bears, 16-10 (GB)
1977—Bears, 26-0 (GB)
Bears, 21-10 (C)
1978—Packers, 24-14 (GB)
Bears, 14-0 (C)
1979—Bears, 6-3 (C)
Bears, 15-14 (GB)
1980—Packers, 12-6 (GB) OT
Bears, 61-7 (C)
1981—Packers, 16-9 (C)
Packers, 21-17 (GB)
1983—Packers, 31-28 (GB)
Bears, 23-21 (C)
1984—Bears, 9-7 (GB)
Packers, 20-14 (C)
1985—Bears, 23-7 (C)
Bears, 16-10 (GB)
(Points—Bears 2,183, Packers 1,928)
**Bears known as Staleys prior to 1922*
***Division Playoff*

CHI. BEARS vs. HOUSTON
Oilers lead series, 2-1
1973—Bears, 35-14 (C)
1977—Oilers, 47-0 (H)
1980—Oilers, 10-6 (C)
(Points—Oilers 71, Bears 41)

CHI. BEARS vs. *INDIANAPOLIS
Colts lead series, 21-14
1953—Colts, 13-9 (B)
Colts, 16-14 (C)
1954—Bears, 28-9 (C)
Bears, 28-13 (B)
1955—Colts, 23-17 (B)
Bears, 38-10 (C)
1956—Colts, 28-21 (B)
Bears, 58-27 (C)
1957—Colts, 21-10 (B)
Colts, 29-14 (C)
1958—Colts, 51-38 (B)
Colts, 17-0 (C)
1959—Bears, 26-21 (B)
Colts, 21-7 (C)
1960—Colts, 42-7 (B)
Colts, 24-20 (C)
1961—Bears, 24-10 (C)
Bears, 21-20 (B)
1962—Bears, 35-15 (C)
Bears, 57-0 (B)
1963—Bears, 10-3 (C)
Bears, 17-7 (B)
1964—Colts, 52-0 (B)
Colts, 40-24 (C)
1965—Colts, 26-21 (C)
Bears, 13-0 (B)
1966—Bears, 27-17 (C)
Colts, 21-16 (B)
1967—Colts, 24-3 (C)
1968—Colts, 28-7 (B)
1969—Colts, 24-21 (C)
1970—Colts, 21-20 (B)
1975—Colts, 35-7 (C)
1983—Colts, 22-19 (B) OT
1985—Bears, 17-10 (C)
(Points—Colts 740, Bears 694)
**Franchise in Baltimore prior to 1984*

CHI. BEARS vs. KANSAS CITY
Bears lead series, 2-1
1973—Chiefs, 19-7 (KC)
1977—Bears, 28-27 (C)
1981—Bears, 16-13 (KC) OT
(Points—Chiefs 59, Bears 51)

CHI. BEARS vs. *LA RAIDERS
Raiders lead series, 3-2
1972—Raiders, 28-21 (O)
1976—Raiders, 28-27 (C)
1978—Raiders, 25-19 (C) OT
1981—Bears, 23-6 (O)
1984—Bears, 17-6 (C)
(Points—Bears 107, Raiders 93)
**Franchise in Oakland prior to 1982*

CHI. BEARS vs. *LA RAMS
Bears lead series, 43-27-3
1937—Bears, 20-2 (Clev)
Bears, 15-7 (C)
1938—Rams, 14-7 (C)
Rams, 23-21 (Clev)
1939—Bears, 30-21 (Clev)
Bears, 35-21 (C)
1940—Bears, 21-14 (Clev)
Bears, 47-25 (C)
1941—Bears, 48-21 (Clev)
Bears, 31-13 (C)
1942—Bears, 21-7 (Clev)
Bears, 47-0 (C)
1944—Rams, 19-7 (Clev)
Bears, 28-21 (C)
1945—Rams, 17-0 (Clev)
Rams, 41-21 (C)
1946—Tie, 28-28 (C)
Bears, 27-21 (LA)
1947—Bears, 41-21 (LA)
Rams, 17-14 (C)
1948—Bears, 42-21 (C)
Bears, 21-6 (LA)
1949—Rams, 31-16 (C)
Rams, 27-24 (LA)
1950—Bears, 24-20 (LA)
Bears, 24-14 (C)
**Rams, 24-14 (LA)
1951—Rams, 42-17 (C)
1952—Rams, 31-7 (LA)
Rams, 40-24 (C)
1953—Rams, 38-24 (LA)
Bears, 24-21 (C)
1954—Rams, 42-38 (LA)
Bears, 24-13 (C)
1955—Bears, 31-20 (LA)
Bears, 24-3 (C)
1956—Bears, 35-24 (LA)
Bears, 30-21 (C)
1957—Bears, 34-26 (C)
Bears, 16-10 (LA)
1958—Bears, 31-10 (C)
Rams, 41-35 (LA)
1959—Rams, 28-21 (C)
Bears, 26-21 (LA)
1960—Bears, 34-27 (C)
Tie, 24-24 (LA)
1961—Bears, 21-17 (LA)
Bears, 28-24 (C)
1962—Bears, 27-23 (LA)
Bears, 30-14 (C)
1963—Bears, 52-14 (LA)
Bears, 6-0 (C)
1964—Bears, 38-17 (C)
Bears, 34-24 (LA)
1965—Rams, 30-28 (LA)
Bears, 31-6 (C)
1966—Rams, 31-17 (LA)
Bears, 17-10 (C)
1967—Rams, 28-17 (C)
1968—Bears, 17-16 (LA)
1969—Rams, 9-7 (C)
1971—Rams, 17-3 (LA)
1972—Tie, 13-13 (C)
1973—Rams, 26-0 (C)
1975—Rams, 38-10 (LA)
1976—Rams, 20-12 (LA)
1977—Bears, 24-23 (C)
1979—Bears, 27-23 (C)
1981—Rams, 24-7 (C)
1982—Bears, 34-26 (LA)
1983—Rams, 21-14 (LA)
1984—Rams, 29-13 (LA)
1985—***Bears, 24-0 (C)
(Points—Bears 1,724, Rams 1,501)
**Franchise in Cleveland prior to 1946*
***Conference Playoff*
****NFC Championship*

CHI. BEARS vs. MIAMI
Dolphins lead series, 4-0
1971—Dolphins, 34-3 (M)
1975—Dolphins, 46-13 (C)
1979—Dolphins, 31-16 (M)
1985—Dolphins, 38-24 (M)
(Points—Dolphins 149, Bears 56)

CHI. BEARS vs. MINNESOTA
Vikings lead series, 25-22-2
1961—Vikings, 37-13 (M)
Bears, 52-35 (C)
1962—Bears, 13-0 (M)
Bears, 31-30 (C)
1963—Bears, 28-7 (M)
Tie, 17-17 (C)
1964—Bears, 34-28 (M)
Vikings, 41-14 (C)
1965—Bears, 45-37 (M)
Vikings, 24-17 (C)
1966—Bears, 13-10 (M)
Bears, 41-28 (C)
1967—Bears, 17-7 (M)
Tie, 10-10 (C)
1968—Bears, 27-17 (M)
Bears, 26-24 (C)
1969—Vikings, 31-0 (C)
Vikings, 31-14 (M)
1970—Vikings, 24-0 (C)
Vikings, 16-13 (M)
1971—Bears, 20-17 (M)
Vikings, 27-10 (C)
1972—Bears, 13-10 (C)
Vikings, 23-10 (M)
1973—Vikings, 22-13 (C)
Vikings, 31-13 (M)
1974—Vikings, 11-7 (M)
Vikings, 17-0 (C)
1975—Vikings, 28-3 (M)
Vikings, 13-9 (C)
1976—Vikings, 20-19 (M)
Bears, 14-13 (C)
1977—Vikings, 22-16 (M) OT
Bears, 10-7 (C)
1978—Vikings, 24-20 (C)
Vikings, 17-14 (M)
1979—Bears, 26-7 (C)
Vikings, 30-27 (M)
1980—Vikings, 34-14 (C)
Vikings, 13-7 (M)
1981—Vikings, 24-21 (M)
Bears, 10-9 (C)
1982—Vikings, 35-7 (M)
1983—Vikings, 23-14 (C)
Bears, 19-13 (M)
1984—Bears, 16-7 (C)
Bears, 34-3 (M)
1985—Bears, 33-24 (M)
Bears, 27-9 (C)
(Points—Vikings 987, Bears 871)

CHI. BEARS vs. NEW ENGLAND
Bears lead series, 3-2
1973—Patriots, 13-10 (C)
1979—Patriots, 27-7 (C)
1982—Bears, 26-13 (C)
1985—Bears, 20-7 (C)
*Bears, 46-10 (New Orleans)
(Points—Bears 109, Patriots 70)
**Super Bowl XX*

CHI. BEARS vs. NEW ORLEANS
Bears lead series, 7-4
1968—Bears, 23-17 (NO)
1970—Bears, 24-3 (NO)
1971—Bears, 35-14 (C)
1973—Saints, 21-16 (NO)
1974—Bears, 24-10 (C)
1975—Bears, 42-17 (NO)
1977—Saints, 42-24 (C)
1980—Bears, 22-3 (C)
1982—Saints, 10-0 (C)
1983—Saints, 34-31 (NO) OT
1984—Bears, 20-7 (C)
(Points—Bears 261, Saints 178)

CHI. BEARS vs. NY GIANTS
Bears lead series, 27-16-2
1925—Bears, 19-7 (NY)
Giants, 9-0 (C)
1926—Bears, 7-0 (C)
1927—Giants, 13-7 (NY)
1928—Bears, 13-0 (C)
1929—Giants, 26-14 (C)
Giants, 34-0 (NY)
Giants, 14-9 (C)
1930—Giants, 12-0 (C)
Bears, 12-0 (NY)
1931—Bears, 6-0 (C)
Bears, 12-6 (NY)
Giants, 25-6 (C)
1932—Bears, 28-8 (NY)
Bears, 6-0 (C)
1933—Bears, 14-10 (C)
Giants, 3-0 (NY)
*Bears, 23-21 (C)
1934—Bears, 27-7 (C)
Bears, 10-9 (NY)
*Giants, 30-13 (NY)
1935—Bears, 20-3 (NY)
Giants, 3-0 (C)
1936—Bears, 25-7 (NY)
1937—Tie, 3-3 (NY)
1939—Giants, 16-13 (NY)
1940—Bears, 37-21 (NY)
1941—*Bears, 37-9 (C)
1942—Bears, 26-7 (NY)
1943—Bears, 56-7 (NY)
1946—Giants, 14-0 (NY)
*Bears, 24-14 (NY)
1948—Bears, 35-14 (C)
1949—Giants, 35-28 (NY)
1956—Tie, 17-17 (NY)
*Giants, 47-7 (NY)
1962—Giants, 26-24 (C)
1963—*Bears, 14-10 (C)
1965—Bears, 35-14 (NY)
1967—Bears, 34-7 (C)
1969—Giants, 28-24 (NY)
1970—Bears, 24-16 (NY)
1974—Bears, 16-13 (C)
1977—Bears, 12-9 (NY) OT
1985—**Bears, 21-0 (C)
(Points—Bears 758, Giants 574)
**NFL Championship*
***NFC Divisional Playoff*

CHI. BEARS vs. NY JETS
Bears lead series, 2-1
1974—Jets, 23-21 (C)
1979—Bears, 23-13 (C)
1985—Bears, 19-6 (NY)
(Points—Bears 63, Jets 42)

CHI. BEARS vs. *NY YANKS
Bears won series, 3-1
1950—Yanks, 38-27 (NY)
Bears, 28-20 (C)
1951—Bears, 24-21 (C)
Bears, 45-21 (NY)
(Points—Bears, 124, Yanks 100)
**Extinct team*

CHI. BEARS vs. *PHILADELPHIA
Bears lead series, 20-4-1
1933—Tie, 3-3 (P)
1935—Bears, 39-0 (P)
1936—Bears, 17-0 (P)
Bears, 28-7 (P)
1938—Bears, 28-6 (P)
1939—Bears, 27-14 (C)
1941—Bears, 49-14 (P)
1942—Bears, 45-14 (C)
1943—Bears, 48-21 (C)
1944—Bears, 28-7 (P)
1946—Bears, 21-14 (C)
1947—Bears, 40-7 (C)
1948—Eagles, 12-7 (P)
1949—Bears, 38-21 (C)
1955—Bears, 17-10 (C)
1961—Eagles, 16-14 (P)
1963—Bears, 16-7 (C)
1968—Bears, 29-16 (P)
1970—Bears, 20-16 (C)
1972—Bears, 21-12 (P)
1975—Bears, 15-13 (C)
1979—**Eagles, 27-17 (P)
1980—Eagles, 17-14 (P)
1983—Bears, 7-6 (P)
Bears, 17-14 (C)
(Points—Bears 605, Eagles 294)
*Eagles known as Phil-Pitt in 1943
***NFC Wild Card Game*

CHI. BEARS vs. *PITTSBURGH
Bears lead series, 16-4-1
1934—Bears, 28-0 (P)
1935—Bears, 23-7 (P)
1936—Bears, 27-9 (P)
Bears, 26-6 (C)
1937—Bears, 7-0 (P)

1939—Bears, 32-0 (P)
1941—Bears, 34-7 (C)
1943—Bears, 48-21 (C)
1944—Bears, 34-7 (C)
Bears, 49-7 (P)
1945—Bears, 28-7 (P)
1947—Bears, 49-7 (C)
1949—Bears, 30-21 (C)
1958—Steelers, 24-10 (P)
1959—Bears, 27-21 (C)
1963—Tie, 17-17 (P)
1967—Steelers, 41-13 (P)
1969—Bears, 38-7 (C)
1971—Bears, 17-15 (C)
1975—Steelers, 34-3 (P)
1980—Steelers, 38-3 (P)
(Points—Bears 543, Steelers 296)
Steelers known as Pirates prior to 1941, as Phil-Pitt in 1943, and as Card-Pitt in 1944

***CHI. BEARS vs. **ST. LOUIS**
Bears lead series, 52-25-6
(NP denotes Normal Park;
Wr denotes Wrigley Field;
Co denotes Comiskey Park;
So denotes Soldier Field;
all Chicago)
1920—Cardinals, 7-6 (NP)
Staleys, 10-0 (Wr)
1921—Tie, 0-0 (Wr)
1922—Cardinals, 6-0 (Co)
Cardinals, 9-0 (Co)
1923—Bears, 3-0 (Wr)
1924—Bears, 6-0 (Wr)
Bears, 21-0 (Co)
1925—Cardinals, 9-0 (Co)
Tie, 0-0 (Wr)
1926—Bears, 16-0 (Wr)
Bears, 10-0 (So)
Tie, 0-0 (Wr)
1927—Bears, 9-0 (NP)
Cardinals, 3-0 (Wr)
1928—Bears, 15-0 (NP)
Bears, 34-0 (Wr)
1929—Tie, 0-0 (Wr)
Cardinals, 40-6 (Co)
1930—Bears, 32-6 (Co)
Bears, 6-0 (Wr)
1931—Bears, 26-13 (Wr)
Bears, 18-7 (Wr)
1932—Tie, 0-0 (Wr)
Bears, 34-0 (Wr)
1933—Bears, 12-9 (Wr)
Bears, 22-6 (Wr)
1934—Bears, 20-0 (Wr)
Bears, 17-6 (Wr)
1935—Tie, 7-7 (Wr)
Bears, 13-0 (Wr)
1936—Bears, 7-3 (Wr)
Cardinals, 14-7 (Wr)
1937—Bears, 16-7 (Wr)
Bears, 42-28 (Wr)
1938—Bears, 16-13 (So)
Bears, 34-28 (Wr)
1939—Bears, 44-7 (Wr)
Bears, 48-7 (Co)
1940—Cardinals, 21-7 (Co)
Bears, 31-23 (Wr)
1941—Bears, 53-7 (Wr)
Bears, 34-24 (Co)
1942—Bears, 41-14 (Wr)
Bears, 21-7 (Co)
1943—Bears, 20-0 (Wr)
Bears, 35-24 (Co)
1944—Bears, 34-7 (Wr)
Bears, 49-7 (Pitt)
1945—Cardinals, 16-7 (Wr)
Bears, 28-20 (Co)
1946—Bears, 34-17 (Co)
Cardinals, 35-28 (Wr)
1947—Cardinals, 31-7 (Co)
Cardinals, 30-21 (Wr)
1948—Bears, 28-17 (Co)
Cardinals, 24-21 (Wr)
1949—Bears, 17-7 (Co)
Bears, 52-21 (Wr)
1950—Bears, 27-6 (Wr)
Cardinals, 20-10 (Co)
1951—Cardinals, 28-14 (Co)
Cardinals, 24-14 (Wr)
1952—Cardinals, 21-10 (Co)
Bears, 10-7 (Wr)
1953—Cardinals, 24-17 (Wr)
1954—Bears, 29-7 (Co)
1955—Cardinals, 53-14 (Co)
1956—Bears, 10-3 (Wr)
1957—Bears, 14-6 (Co)
1958—Bears, 30-14 (Wr)
1959—Bears, 31-7 (So)
1965—Bears, 34-13 (Wr)
1966—Cardinals, 24-17 (StL)
1967—Bears, 30-3 (Wr)
1969—Cardinals, 20-17 (StL)
1972—Bears, 27-10 (StL)
1975—Cardinals, 34-20 (So)
1977—Cardinals, 16-13 (StL)
1978—Bears, 17-10 (So)
1979—Bears, 42-6 (So)
1982—Cardinals, 10-7 (So)
1984—Cardinals, 38-21 (StL)
(Points—Bears 1,600, Cardinals 991)
**Franchise in Decatur prior to 1921; Bears known as Staleys prior to 1922*
***Franchise in Chicago prior to 1960; Cardinals known as Card-Pitt in 1944*

CHI. BEARS vs. SAN DIEGO
Chargers lead series, 4-1
1970—Chargers, 20-7 (C)
1974—Chargers, 28-21 (SD)
1978—Chargers, 40-7 (SD)
1981—Bears, 20-17 (C) OT
1984—Chargers, 20-7 (SD)
(Points—Chargers 125, Bears 62)

CHI. BEARS vs. SAN FRANCISCO
Bears lead series, 24-23-1
1950—Bears, 32-20 (SF)
Bears, 17-0 (C)
1951—Bears, 13-7 (C)
1952—49ers, 40-16 (C)
Bears, 20-17 (SF)
1953—49ers, 35-28 (C)
49ers, 24-14 (SF)
1954—49ers, 31-24 (C)
Bears, 31-27 (SF)
1955—49ers, 20-19 (C)
Bears, 34-23 (SF)
1956—Bears, 31-7 (C)
Bears, 38-21 (SF)
1957—49ers, 21-17 (C)
49ers, 21-17 (SF)
1958—Bears, 28-6 (C)
Bears, 27-14 (SF)
1959—49ers, 20-17 (SF)
Bears, 14-3 (C)
1960—Bears, 27-10 (C)
49ers, 25-7 (SF)
1961—Bears, 31-0 (C)
49ers, 41-31 (SF)
1962—Bears, 30-14 (SF)
49ers, 34-27 (C)
1963—49ers, 20-14 (SF)
Bears, 27-7 (C)
1964—49ers, 31-21 (SF)
Bears, 23-21 (C)
1965—49ers, 52-24 (SF)
Bears, 61-20 (C)
1966—Tie, 30-30 (C)
49ers, 41-14 (SF)
1967—Bears, 28-14 (SF)
1968—Bears, 27-19 (C)
1969—49ers, 42-21 (SF)
1970—49ers, 37-16 (C)
1971—49ers, 13-0 (SF)
1972—49ers, 34-21 (C)
1974—49ers, 34-0 (C)
1975—49ers, 31-3 (SF)
1976—Bears, 19-12 (SF)
1978—Bears, 16-13 (SF)
1979—Bears, 28-27 (SF)
1981—49ers, 28-17 (SF)
1983—Bears, 13-3 (C)
1984—*49ers, 23-0 (SF)
1985—Bears, 26-10 (SF)
(Points—49ers 1,043, Bears 1,039)
**NFC Championship*

CHI. BEARS vs. SEATTLE
Seahawks lead series, 3-1
1976—Bears, 34-7 (S)
1978—Seahawks, 31-29 (C)
1982—Seahawks, 20-14 (S)
1984—Seahawks, 38-9 (S)
(Points—Seahawks 96, Bears 86)

CHI. BEARS vs. TAMPA BAY
Bears lead series, 12-4
1977—Bears, 10-0 (TB)
1978—Buccaneers, 33-19 (TB)
Bears, 14-3 (C)
1979—Buccaneers, 17-13 (C)
Bears, 14-0 (TB)
1980—Bears, 23-0 (C)
Bears, 14-13 (TB)
1981—Bears, 28-17 (C)
Buccaneers, 20-10 (TB)
1982—Buccaneers, 26-23 (TB) OT
1983—Bears, 17-10 (C)
Bears, 27-0 (TB)
1984—Bears, 34-14 (C)
Bears, 44-9 (TB)
1985—Bears, 38-28 (C)
Bears, 27-19 (TB)
(Points—Bears 355, Buccaneers 209)

CHI. BEARS vs. *WASHINGTON
Bears lead series, 20-11-1
1932—Tie, 7-7 (B)
1933—Bears, 7-0 (C)
Redskins, 10-0 (B)
1934—Bears, 21-0 (B)
1935—Bears, 30-14 (B)
1936—Bears, 26-0 (B)
1937—**Redskins, 28-21 (C)
1938—Bears, 31-7 (C)
1940—Redskins, 7-3 (W)
**Bears, 73-0 (W)
1941—Bears, 35-21 (C)
1942—**Redskins, 14-6 (W)
1943—Redskins, 21-7 (W)
**Bears, 41-21 (C)
1945—Redskins, 28-21 (W)
1946—Bears, 24-20 (C)
1947—Bears, 56-20 (W)
1948—Bears, 48-13 (C)
1949—Bears, 31-21 (W)
1951—Bears, 27-0 (W)
1953—Bears, 27-24 (W)
1957—Redskins, 14-3 (C)
1964—Redskins, 27-20 (W)
1968—Redskins, 38-28 (C)
1971—Bears, 16-15 (C)
1974—Redskins, 42-0 (W)
1976—Bears, 33-7 (C)
1978—Bears, 14-10 (W)
1980—Bears, 35-21 (C)
1981—Redskins, 24-7 (C)
1984—***Bears, 23-19 (W)
1985—Bears, 45-10 (C)
(Points—Bears 766, Redskins 503)
**Franchise in Boston prior to 1937 and known as Braves prior to 1933*
***NFL Championship*
****NFC Divisional Playoff*

CINCINNATI vs. ATLANTA
Bengals lead series, 4-1;
See Atlanta vs. Cincinnati

CINCINNATI vs. BUFFALO
Bengals lead series, 8-5;
See Buffalo vs. Cincinnati

CINCINNATI vs. CHI. BEARS
Bengals lead series, 2-0;
See Chi. Bears vs. Cincinnati

CINCINNATI vs. CLEVELAND
Bengals lead series, 16-15
1970—Browns, 30-27 (Cle)
Bengals, 14-10 (Cin)
1971—Browns, 27-24 (Cin)
Browns, 31-27 (Cle)
1972—Browns, 27-6 (Cle)
Browns, 27-24 (Cin)
1973—Browns, 17-10 (Cle)
Bengals, 34-17 (Cin)
1974—Bengals, 33-7 (Cin)
Bengals, 34-24 (Cle)
1975—Bengals, 24-17 (Cin)
Browns, 35-23 (Cle)
1976—Bengals, 45-24 (Cle)
Bengals, 21-6 (Cin)
1977—Browns, 13-3 (Cin)
Bengals, 10-7 (Cle)
1978—Browns, 13-10 (Cle) OT
Bengals, 48-16 (Cin)
1979—Browns, 28-27 (Cle)
Bengals, 16-12 (Cin)
1980—Browns, 31-7 (Cle)
Browns, 27-24 (Cin)
1981—Browns, 20-17 (Cin)
Bengals, 41-21 (Cle)
1982—Bengals, 23-10 (Cin)
1983—Browns, 17-7 (Clev)
Bengals, 28-21 (Cin)
1984—Bengals, 12-9 (Cin)
Bengals, 20-17 (Clev) OT
1985—Bengals, 27-10 (Cin)
Browns, 24-6 (Clev)
(Points—Bengals 672, Browns 595)

CINCINNATI vs. DALLAS
Cowboys lead series, 2-1
1973—Cowboys, 38-10 (D)
1979—Cowboys, 38-13 (D)
1985—Bengals, 50-24 (C)
(Points—Cowboys 100, Bengals 73)

CINCINNATI vs. DENVER
Broncos lead series, 8-6
1968—Bengals, 24-10 (C)
Broncos, 10-7 (D)
1969—Broncos, 30-23 (C)
Broncos, 27-16 (D)
1971—Bengals, 24-10 (D)
1972—Bengals, 21-10 (C)
1973—Broncos, 28-10 (D)
1975—Bengals, 17-16 (D)
1976—Bengals, 17-7 (C)
1977—Broncos, 24-13 (C)
1979—Broncos, 10-0 (D)
1981—Bengals, 38-21 (C)
1983—Broncos, 24-17 (D)
1984—Broncos, 20-17 (D)
(Points—Broncos 247, Bengals 244)

CINCINNATI vs. DETROIT
Lions lead series, 2-1
1970—Lions, 38-3 (D)
1974—Lions, 23-19 (C)
1983—Bengals, 17-9 (C)
(Points—Lions 70, Bengals 39)

CINCINNATI vs. GREEN BAY
Bengals lead series, 3-2
1971—Packers, 20-17 (GB)
1976—Bengals, 28-7 (C)
1977—Bengals, 17-7 (Mil)
1980—Packers, 14-9 (GB)
1983—Bengals, 34-14 (C)
(Points—Bengals 105, Packers 62)

CINCINNATI vs. HOUSTON
Bengals lead series, 20-13-1
1968—Oilers, 27-17 (C)
1969—Tie, 31-31 (H)
1970—Oilers, 20-13 (C)
Bengals, 30-20 (H)
1971—Oilers, 10-6 (H)
Bengals, 28-13 (C)
1972—Bengals, 30-7 (C)
Bengals, 61-17 (H)
1973—Bengals, 24-10 (C)
Bengals, 27-24 (H)
1974—Oilers, 34-21 (C)
Oilers, 20-3 (H)
1975—Bengals, 21-19 (H)
Bengals, 23-19 (C)
1976—Bengals, 27-7 (H)
Bengals, 31-27 (C)
1977—Bengals, 13-10 (C) OT
Oilers, 21-16 (H)
1978—Bengals, 28-13 (C)
Oilers, 17-10 (H)
1979—Oilers, 30-27 (C) OT
Oilers, 42-21 (H)
1980—Oilers, 13-10 (C)
Oilers, 23-3 (H)
1981—Oilers, 17-10 (H)
Bengals, 34-21 (C)
1982—Bengals, 27-6 (C)
Bengals, 35-27 (H)
1983—Bengals, 55-14 (H)
Bengals, 38-10 (C)
1984—Bengals, 13-3 (C)
Bengals, 31-13 (H)
1985—Oilers, 44-27 (H)
Bengals, 45-27 (C)
(Points—Bengals 836, Oilers 656)

CINCINNATI vs.*INDIANAPOLIS
Colts lead series, 5-4
1970—**Colts, 17-0 (B)
1972—Colts, 20-19 (C)
1974—Bengals, 24-14 (B)
1976—Colts, 28-27 (B)
1979—Colts, 38-28 (B)
1980—Bengals, 34-33 (C)
1981—Bengals, 41-19 (B)
1982—Bengals, 20-17 (B)
1983—Colts, 34-31 (C)
(Points—Bengals 224, Colts 220)
**Franchise in Baltimore prior to 1984*
***AFC Divisional Playoff*

CINCINNATI vs. KANSAS CITY
Chiefs lead series, 8-7
1968—Chiefs, 13-3 (KC)
Chiefs, 16-9 (C)
1969—Bengals, 24-19 (C)
Chiefs, 42-22 (KC)
1970—Chiefs, 27-19 (C)
1972—Bengals, 23-16 (KC)
1973—Bengals, 14-6 (C)
1974—Bengals, 33-6 (C)
1976—Bengals, 27-24 (KC)
1977—Bengals, 27-7 (KC)
1978—Chiefs, 24-23 (C)
1979—Chiefs, 10-7 (C)
1980—Bengals, 20-6 (KC)
1983—Chiefs, 20-15 (KC)
1984—Chiefs, 27-22 (C)
(Points—Bengals 288, Chiefs 263)

CINCINNATI vs. *LA RAIDERS
Raiders lead series, 12-4
1968—Raiders, 31-10 (O)
Raiders, 34-0 (C)
1969—Bengals, 31-17 (C)
Raiders, 37-17 (O)
1970—Bengals, 31-21 (C)
1971—Raiders, 31-27 (O)
1972—Raiders, 20-14 (C)
1974—Raiders, 30-27 (O)
1975—Bengals, 14-10 (C)
**Raiders, 31-28 (O)
1976—Raiders, 35-20 (O)
1978—Raiders, 34-21 (C)
1980—Raiders, 28-17 (O)
1982—Bengals, 31-17 (C)
1983—Raiders, 20-10 (C)
1985—Raiders, 13-6 (LA)
(Points—Raiders 409, Bengals 304)
**Franchise in Oakland prior to 1982*
***AFC Divisional Playoff*

CINCINNATI vs. LA RAMS
Bengals lead series, 3-2
1972—Rams, 15-12 (LA)
1976—Bengals, 20-12 (C)
1978—Bengals, 20-19 (LA)
1981—Bengals, 24-10 (C)
1984—Rams, 24-14 (C)
(Points—Bengals 90, Rams 80)

CINCINNATI vs. MIAMI
Dolphins lead series, 7-3
1968—Dolphins, 24-22 (C)
Bengals, 38-21 (M)
1969—Bengals, 27-21 (C)
1971—Dolphins, 23-13 (C)
1973—*Dolphins, 34-16 (M)
1974—Dolphins, 24-3 (M)
1977—Bengals, 23-17 (C)
1978—Dolphins, 21-0 (M)
1980—Dolphins, 17-16 (M)
1983—Dolphins, 38-14 (M)
(Points—Dolphins 240, Bengals 172)
**AFC Divisional Playoff*

CINCINNATI vs. MINNESOTA
Series tied, 2-2
1973—Bengals, 27-0 (C)
1977—Vikings, 42-10 (M)
1980—Bengals, 14-0 (C)
1983—Vikings, 20-14 (M)
(Points—Bengals 65, Vikings 62)

CINCINNATI vs. *NEW ENGLAND
Patriots lead series, 6-3
1968—Patriots, 33-14 (B)
1969—Patriots, 25-14 (C)
1970—Bengals, 45-7 (C)
1972—Bengals, 31-7 (NE)
1975—Bengals, 27-10 (C)
1978—Patriots, 10-3 (C)
1979—Patriots, 20-14 (C)
1984—Patriots, 20-14 (NE)
1985—Patriots, 34-23 (NE)
(Points—Bengals 185, Patriots 166)
**Franchise in Boston prior to 1971*

CINCINNATI vs. NEW ORLEANS
Bengals lead series 3-2
1970—Bengals, 26-6 (C)
1975—Bengals, 21-0 (NO)
1978—Saints, 20-18 (C)
1981—Saints, 17-7 (NO)
1984—Bengals, 24-21 (NO)
(Points—Bengals 96, Saints 64)

CINCINNATI vs. NY GIANTS
Bengals lead series, 3-0
1972—Bengals, 13-10 (C)
1977—Bengals, 30-13 (C)
1985—Bengals, 35-30 (C)
(Points—Bengals 78, Giants 53)

CINCINNATI vs. NY JETS
Jets lead series, 7-3
1968—Jets, 27-14 (NY)
1969—Jets, 21-7 (C)
Jets, 40-7 (NY)
1971—Jets, 35-21 (NY)
1973—Bengals, 20-14 (C)
1976—Bengals, 42-3 (NY)
1981—Bengals, 31-30 (NY)
1982—*Jets, 44-17 (C)
1984—Jets, 43-23 (NY)
1985—Jets, 29-20 (C)

(Points—Jets 286, Bengals 202)
**AFC First Round Playoff*
CINCINNATI vs. PHILADELPHIA
Bengals lead series, 4-0
1971—Bengals, 37-14 (C)
1975—Bengals, 31-0 (P)
1979—Bengals, 37-13 (C)
1982—Bengals, 18-14 (P)
(Points—Bengals 123, Eagles 41)
CINCINNATI vs. PITTSBURGH
Steelers lead series, 17-14
1970—Steelers, 21-10 (P)
Bengals, 34-7 (C)
1971—Steelers, 21-10 (P)
Steelers, 21-13 (C)
1972—Bengals, 15-10 (C)
Steelers, 40-17 (P)
1973—Bengals, 19-7 (C)
Steelers, 20-13 (P)
1974—Bengals, 17-10 (C)
Steelers, 27-3 (P)
1975—Steelers, 30-24 (C)
Steelers, 35-14 (P)
1976—Steelers, 23-6 (P)
Steelers, 7-3 (C)
1977—Steelers, 20-14 (P)
Bengals, 17-10 (C)
1978—Steelers, 28-3 (C)
Steelers, 7-6 (P)
1979—Bengals, 34-10 (C)
Steelers, 37-17 (P)
1980—Bengals, 30-28 (C)
Bengals, 17-16 (P)
1981—Bengals, 34-7 (C)
Bengals, 17-10 (P)
1982—Steelers, 26-20 (P) OT
1983—Steelers, 24-14 (C)
Bengals, 23-10 (P)
1984—Steelers, 38-17 (P)
Bengals, 22-20 (C)
1985—Bengals, 37-24 (P)
Bengals, 26-21 (C)
(Points—Steelers 615, Bengals 546)
CINCINNATI vs. ST. LOUIS
Bengals lead series, 2-1
1973—Bengals, 42-24 (C)
1979—Bengals, 34-28 (C)
1985—Cardinals, 41-27 (StL)
(Points—Bengals 103, Cardinals 93)
CINCINNATI vs. SAN DIEGO
Chargers lead series, 10-7
1968—Chargers, 29-13 (SD)
Chargers, 31-10 (C)
1969—Bengals, 34-20 (C)
Chargers, 21-14 (SD)
1970—Bengals, 17-14 (SD)
1971—Bengals, 31-0 (C)
1973—Bengals, 20-13 (SD)
1974—Chargers, 20-17 (C)
1975—Bengals, 47-17 (C)
1977—Chargers, 24-3 (SD)
1978—Chargers, 22-13 (SD)
1979—Chargers, 26-24 (C)
1980—Chargers, 31-14 (C)
1981—Bengals, 40-17 (SD)
*Bengals, 27-7 (C)
1982—Chargers, 50-34 (SD)
1985—Chargers, 44-41 (C)
(Points—Bengals 399, Chargers 386)
**AFC Championship*
CINCINNATI vs. SAN FRANCISCO
49ers lead series, 4-1
1974—Bengals, 21-3 (SF)
1978—49ers, 28-12 (SF)
1981—49ers, 21-3 (C)
*49ers, 26-21 (Detroit)
1984—49ers, 23-17 (SF)
(Points—49ers 101, Bengals 74)
**Super Bowl XVI*
CINCINNATI vs. SEATTLE
Bengals lead series, 3-2
1977—Bengals, 42-20 (C)
1981—Bengals, 27-21 (C)
1982—Bengals, 24-10 (C)
1984—Seahawks, 26-6 (C)
1985—Seahawks, 28-24 (C)
(Points—Bengals 123, Seahawks 105)
CINCINNATI vs. TAMPA BAY
Bengals lead series, 2-1
1976—Bengals, 21-0 (C)
1980—Buccaneers, 17-12 (C)
1983—Bengals, 23-17 (TB)
(Points—Bengals 56, Buccaneers 34)

CINCINNATI vs. WASHINGTON
Redskins lead series, 3-1
1970—Redskins, 20-0 (W)
1974—Bengals, 28-17 (C)
1979—Redskins, 28-14 (W)
1985—Redskins, 27-24 (W)
(Points—Redskins 92, Bengals 66)

***CINCINNATI REDS vs. *BROOKLYN DODGERS**
Series tied, 1-1; See *Brooklyn Dodgers vs. *Cincinnati Reds
**Extinct teams*
***CINCINNATI REDS vs. CHI. BEARS**
Bears won series, 2-0
See Chi. Bears vs. *Cincinnati Reds
**Extinct team*
***CINCINNATI REDS vs. **CHI. CARDINALS**
Cardinals won series, 3-1
1933—Cardinals, 3-0 (Cin)
Reds, 12-9 (Chi)
1934—Cardinals, 9-0 (Dayton)
Cardinals, 16-0 (Cin)
(Points—Cardinals 37, Reds 12)
**Extinct team*
***Franchise moved to St. Louis in 1960*
***CINCINNATI REDS vs. **DETROIT**
Lions won series, 2-1
1933—Spartans, 21-0 (P)
Reds, 10-7 (C)
1934—Lions, 38-0 (C)
(Points—Lions 66, Reds 10)
**Extinct team*
***Franchise in Portsmouth prior to 1934 and known as the Spartans*
***CINCINNATI REDS vs. GREEN BAY**
Packers won series, 1-0
1934—Packers, 41-0 (GB)
Extinct team
***CINCINNATI REDS vs. PHILADELPHIA**
Eagles won series, 3-0
1933—Eagles, 6-0 (C)
Eagles, 20-3 (P)
1934—Eagles, 64-0 (P)
(Points—Eagles 90, Reds 3)
**Extinct team*
***CINCINNATI REDS vs. **PITTSBURGH**
Steelers won series, 2-0-1
1933—Pirates, 17-3 (P)
Tie, 0-0 (C)
1934—Pirates, 13-0 (P)
(Points—Steelers 30, Reds 3)
**Extinct team*
***Steelers known as Pirates prior to 1941*
CLEVELAND vs. ATLANTA
Browns lead series, 6-1;
See Atlanta vs. Cleveland
CLEVELAND vs. *1950 BALTIMORE
Browns won series, 1-0
See *1950 Baltimore vs. Cleveland
**Extinct team*
CLEVELAND vs. BUFFALO
Browns lead series, 5-2;
See Buffalo vs. Cleveland
CLEVELAND vs. CHI. BEARS
Browns lead series, 6-2;
See Chi. Bears vs. Cleveland
CLEVELAND vs. CINCINNATI
Bengals lead series, 16-15;
See Cincinnati vs. Cleveland
CLEVELAND vs. DALLAS
Browns lead series, 15-9
1960—Browns, 48-7 (D)
1961—Browns, 25-7 (C)
Browns, 38-17 (D)
1962—Browns, 19-10 (C)
Cowboys, 45-21 (D)
1963—Browns, 41-24 (D)
Browns, 27-17 (C)
1964—Browns, 27-6 (C)
Browns, 20-16 (D)
1965—Browns, 23-17 (C)
Browns, 24-17 (D)
1966—Browns, 30-21 (C)
Cowboys, 26-14 (D)
1967—Cowboys, 21-14 (C)
*Cowboys, 52-14 (D)
1968—Cowboys, 28-7 (C)
*Browns, 31-20 (C)
1969—Browns, 42-10 (C)
*Browns, 38-14 (D)
1970—Cowboys, 6-2 (C)
1974—Cowboys, 41-17 (D)
1979—Browns, 26-7 (C)
1982—Cowboys, 31-14 (D)
1985—Cowboys, 20-7 (D)
(Points—Browns 569, Cowboys 480)
**Conference Championship*
CLEVELAND vs. DENVER
Broncos lead series, 8-3
1970—Browns, 27-13 (D)
1971—Broncos, 27-0 (C)
1972—Browns, 27-20 (D)
1974—Browns, 23-21 (C)
1975—Broncos, 16-15 (D)
1976—Broncos, 44-13 (D)
1978—Broncos, 19-7 (C)
1980—Broncos, 19-16 (C)
1981—Broncos, 23-20 (D) OT
1983—Broncos, 27-6 (D)
1984—Broncos, 24-14 (C)
(Points—Broncos 253, Browns 168)
CLEVELAND vs. DETROIT
Lions lead series, 13-3
1952—Lions, 17-6 (D)
*Lions, 17-7 (C)
1953—*Lions, 17-16 (D)
1954—Lions, 14-10 (C)
*Browns, 56-10 (C)
1957—Lions, 20-7 (D)
*Lions, 59-14 (D)
1958—Lions, 30-10 (C)
1960—**Lions, 17-16 (M)
1963—Lions, 38-10 (D)
1964—Browns, 37-21 (C)
1967—Lions, 31-14 (D)
1969—Lions, 28-21 (C)
1970—Lions, 41-24 (C)
1975—Lions, 21-10 (D)
1983—Browns, 31-26 (D)
(Points—Lions 407, Browns 289)
**NFL Championship*
***Miami Playoff Bowl*
CLEVELAND vs. GREEN BAY
Packers lead series, 8-5
1953—Browns, 27-0 (Mil)
1955—Browns, 41-10 (C)
1956—Browns, 24-7 (Mil)
1961—Packers, 49-17 (C)
1963—*Packers, 40-23 (M)
1964—Packers, 28-21 (Mil)
1965—**Packers, 23-12 (GB)
1966—Packers, 21-20 (C)
1967—Packers, 55-7 (Mil)
1969—Browns, 20-7 (C)
1972—Packers, 26-10 (C)
1980—Browns, 26-21 (C)
1983—Packers, 35-21 (Mil)
(Points—Packers 322, Browns 269)
**Miami Playoff Bowl*
***NFL Championship*
CLEVELAND vs. HOUSTON
Browns lead series, 20-11
1970—Browns, 28-14 (C)
Browns, 21-10 (H)
1971—Browns, 31-0 (C)
Browns, 37-24 (H)
1972—Browns, 23-17 (H)
Browns, 20-0 (C)
1973—Browns, 42-13 (C)
Browns, 23-13 (H)
1974—Browns, 20-7 (C)
Oilers, 28-24 (H)
1975—Oilers, 40-10 (C)
Oilers, 21-10 (H)
1976—Browns, 21-7 (H)
Browns, 13-10 (C)
1977—Browns, 24-23 (H)
Oilers, 19-15 (C)
1978—Oilers, 16-13 (C)
Oilers, 14-10 (H)
1979—Oilers, 31-10 (H)
Browns, 14-7 (C)
1980—Oilers, 16-7 (C)
Browns, 17-14 (H)
1981—Oilers, 9-3 (C)
Oilers, 17-13 (H)
1982—Browns, 20-14 (H)
1983—Browns, 25-19 (C) OT
Oilers, 34-27 (H)
1984—Browns, 27-10 (C)
Browns, 27-20 (H)
1985—Browns, 21-6 (H)
Browns, 28-21 (C)
(Points—Browns 624, Oilers 494)
CLEVELAND vs. *INDIANAPOLIS
Browns lead series, 10-5
1956—Colts, 21-7 (C)
1959—Browns, 38-31 (B)
1962—Colts, 36-14 (C)
1964—**Browns, 27-0 (C)
1968—Browns, 30-20 (B)
**Colts, 34-0 (C)
1971—Browns, 14-13 (B)
***Colts, 20-3 (C)
1973—Browns, 24-14 (C)
1975—Colts, 21-7 (B)
1978—Browns, 45-24 (B)
1979—Browns, 13-10 (C)
1980—Browns, 28-27 (B)
1981—Browns, 42-28 (C)
1983—Browns, 41-23 (C)
(Points—Browns 333, Colts 322)
**Franchise in Baltimore prior to 1984*
***NFL Championship*
****AFC Divisional Playoff*
CLEVELAND vs. KANSAS CITY
Chiefs lead series, 5-4-1
1971—Chiefs, 13-7 (KC)
1972—Chiefs, 31-7 (C)
1973—Tie, 20-20 (KC)
1975—Browns, 40-14 (C)
1976—Chiefs, 39-14 (KC)
1977—Browns, 44-7 (C)
1978—Chiefs, 17-3 (KC)
1979—Browns, 27-24 (KC)
1980—Browns, 20-13 (C)
1984—Chiefs, 10-6 (KC)
(Points—Browns 188, Chiefs 188)
CLEVELAND vs. *LA RAIDERS
Raiders lead series, 9-1
1970—Raiders, 23-20 (O)
1971—Raiders, 34-20 (C)
1973—Browns, 7-3 (O)
1974—Raiders, 40-24 (C)
1975—Raiders, 38-17 (O)
1977—Raiders, 26-10 (C)
1979—Raiders, 19-14 (O)
1980—**Raiders, 14-12 (C)
1982—***Raiders, 27-10 (LA)
1985—Raiders, 21-20 (C)
(Points—Raiders 245, Browns 154)
**Franchise in Oakland prior to 1982*
***AFC Divisional Playoff*
****AFC First Round Playoff*
CLEVELAND vs. LA RAMS
Series tied, 8-8
1950—*Browns, 30-28 (C)
1951—Browns, 38-23 (LA)
*Rams, 24-17 (LA)
1952—Browns, 37-7 (C)
1955—*Browns, 38-14 (LA)
1957—Browns, 45-31 (C)
1958—Browns, 30-27 (LA)
1963—Browns, 20-6 (C)
1965—Rams, 42-7 (LA)
1967—**Rams, 30-6 (M)
1968—Rams, 24-6 (C)
1973—Rams, 30-17 (LA)
1977—Rams, 9-0 (C)
1978—Browns, 30-19 (C)
1981—Rams, 27-16 (LA)
1984—Rams, 20-17 (LA)
(Points—Rams 361, Browns 354)
**NFL Championship*
***Miami Playoff Bowl*
CLEVELAND vs. MIAMI
Series tied, 3-3
1970—Browns, 28-0 (M)
1972—*Dolphins, 20-14 (M)
1973—Dolphins, 17-9 (C)
1976—Browns, 17-13 (C)
1979—Browns, 30-24 (C) OT
1985—*Dolphins, 24-21 (M)
(Points—Browns 119, Dolphins 98)
**AFC Divisional Playoff*
CLEVELAND vs. MINNESOTA
Vikings lead series, 7-1
1965—Vikings, 27-17 (C)
1967—Browns, 14-10 (C)
1969—Vikings, 51-3 (M)
*Vikings, 27-7 (M)
1973—Vikings, 26-3 (M)
1975—Vikings, 42-10 (C)
1980—Vikings, 28-23 (M)
1983—Vikings, 27-21 (C)
(Points—Vikings 238, Browns 98)
**NFL Championship*
CLEVELAND vs. NEW ENGLAND
Browns lead series, 6-2
1971—Browns, 27-7 (C)
1974—Browns, 21-14 (NE)
1977—Browns, 30-27 (C) OT
1980—Patriots, 34-17 (NE)
1982—Browns, 10-7 (C)
1983—Browns, 30-0 (NE)
1984—Patriots, 17-16 (C)
1985—Browns, 24-20 (C)
(Points—Browns 175, Patriots 126)
CLEVELAND vs. NEW ORLEANS
Browns lead series, 8-1
1967—Browns, 42-7 (NO)
1968—Browns, 24-10 (NO)
Browns, 35-17 (C)
1969—Browns, 27-17 (NO)
1971—Browns, 21-17 (NO)
1975—Browns, 17-16 (C)
1978—Browns, 24-16 (NO)
1981—Browns, 20-17 (C)
1984—Saints 16-14 (C)
(Points—Browns 224, Saints 133)
CLEVELAND vs. NY GIANTS
Browns lead series, 26-16-2
1950—Giants, 6-0 (C)
Giants, 17-13 (NY)
*Browns, 8-3 (C)
1951—Browns, 14-13 (C)
Browns, 10-0 (NY)
1952—Giants, 17-9 (C)
Giants, 37-34 (NY)
1953—Browns, 7-0 (NY)
Browns, 62-14 (C)
1954—Browns, 24-14 (C)
Browns, 16-7 (NY)
1955—Browns, 24-14 (C)
Tie, 35-35 (NY)
1956—Giants, 21-9 (C)
Browns, 24-7 (NY)
1957—Browns, 6-3 (C)
Browns, 34-28 (NY)
1958—Giants, 21-17 (C)
Giants, 13-10 (NY)
*Giants, 10-0 (NY)
1959—Giants, 10-6 (C)
Giants, 48-7 (NY)
1960—Giants, 17-13 (C)
Browns, 48-34 (NY)
1961—Giants, 37-21 (C)
Tie, 7-7 (NY)
1962—Browns, 17-7 (C)
Giants, 17-13 (NY)
1963—Browns, 35-24 (NY)
Giants, 33-6 (C)
1964—Browns, 42-20 (C)
Browns, 52-20 (NY)
1965—Browns, 38-14 (NY)
Browns, 34-21 (C)
1966—Browns, 28-7 (NY)
Browns, 49-40 (C)
1967—Giants, 38-34 (NY)
Browns, 24-14 (C)
1968—Browns, 45-10 (C)
1969—Browns, 28-17 (C)
Giants, 27-14 (NY)
1973—Browns, 12-10 (C)
1977—Browns, 21-7 (NY)
1985—Browns, 35-33 (NY)
(Points—Browns 985, Giants 792)
**Conference Playoff*
CLEVELAND vs. NY JETS
Browns lead series, 7-3
1970—Browns, 31-21 (C)
1972—Browns, 26-10 (NY)
1976—Browns, 38-17 (C)
1978—Browns, 37-34 (C) OT
1979—Browns, 25-22 (NY) OT
1980—Browns, 17-14 (C)
1981—Jets, 14-13 (C)
1983—Browns, 10-7 (C)
1984—Jets, 24-20 (C)
1985—Jets, 37-10 (NY)
(Points—Browns 227, Jets 200)
CLEVELAND vs. PHILADELPHIA
Browns lead series, 29-11-1
1950—Browns, 35-10 (P)
Browns, 13-7 (C)
1951—Browns, 20-17 (C)
Browns, 24-9 (NY)
1952—Browns, 49-7 (P)
Eagles, 28-20 (C)
1953—Browns, 37-13 (C)
Eagles, 42-27 (P)
1954—Eagles, 28-10 (P)
Browns, 6-0 (C)
1955—Browns, 21-17 (C)
Eagles, 33-17 (P)
1956—Browns, 16-0 (P)
Browns, 17-14 (C)
1957—Browns, 24-7 (C)
Eagles, 17-7 (P)
1958—Browns, 28-14 (C)

Browns, 21-14 (P)
1959—Browns, 28-7 (C)
Browns, 28-21 (P)
1960—Browns, 41-24 (P)
Eagles, 31-29 (C)
1961—Eagles, 27-20 (P)
Browns, 45-24 (C)
1962—Eagles, 35-7 (P)
Tie, 14-14 (C)
1963—Browns, 37-7 (C)
Browns, 23-17 (P)
1964—Browns, 28-20 (P)
Browns, 38-24 (C)
1965—Browns, 35-17 (P)
Browns, 38-34 (C)
1966—Browns, 27-7 (C)
Eagles, 33-21 (P)
1967—Eagles, 28-24 (P)
1968—Browns, 47-13 (C)
1969—Browns, 27-20 (P)
1972—Browns, 27-17 (P)
1976—Browns, 24-3 (C)
1979—Browns, 24-19 (P)
1982—Eagles, 24-21 (C)
(Points—Browns 1,045, Eagles 743)

CLEVELAND vs. PITTSBURGH
Browns lead series, 41-31
1950—Browns, 30-17 (P)
Browns, 45-7 (C)
1951—Browns, 17-0 (C)
Browns, 28-0 (P)
1952—Browns, 21-20 (P)
Browns, 29-28 (C)
1953—Browns, 34-16 (C)
Browns, 20-16 (P)
1954—Steelers, 55-27 (P)
Browns, 42-7 (C)
1955—Browns, 41-14 (C)
Browns, 30-7 (P)
1956—Browns, 14-10 (P)
Steelers, 24-16 (C)
1957—Browns, 23-12 (P)
Browns, 24-0 (C)
1958—Browns, 45-12 (P)
Browns, 27-10 (C)
1959—Steelers, 17-7 (P)
Steelers, 21-20 (C)
1960—Browns, 28-20 (C)
Steelers, 14-10 (P)
1961—Browns, 30-28 (P)
Steelers, 17-13 (C)
1962—Browns, 41-14 (P)
Browns, 35-14 (C)
1963—Browns, 35-23 (C)
Steelers, 9-7 (P)
1964—Steelers, 23-7 (C)
Browns, 30-17 (P)
1965—Browns, 24-19 (C)
Browns, 42-21 (P)
1966—Browns, 41-10 (C)
Steelers, 16-6 (P)
1967—Browns, 21-10 (C)
Browns, 34-14 (P)
1968—Browns, 31-24 (C)
Browns, 45-24 (P)
1969—Browns, 42-31 (C)
Browns, 24-3 (P)
1970—Browns, 15-7 (C)
Steelers, 28-9 (P)
1971—Browns, 27-17 (C)
Steelers, 26-9 (P)
1972—Browns, 26-24 (C)
Steelers, 30-0 (P)
1973—Steelers, 33-6 (P)
Browns, 21-16 (C)
1974—Steelers, 20-16 (P)
Steelers, 26-16 (C)
1975—Steelers, 42-6 (C)
Steelers, 31-17 (P)
1976—Steelers, 31-14 (P)
Browns, 18-16 (C)
1977—Steelers, 28-14 (C)
Steelers, 35-31 (P)
1978—Steelers, 15-9 (P) OT
Steelers, 34-14 (C)
1979—Steelers, 51-35 (C)
Steelers, 33-30 (P) OT
1980—Browns, 27-26 (C)
Steelers, 16-13 (P)
1981—Steelers, 13-7 (P)
Steelers, 32-10 (C)
1982—Browns, 10-9 (C)
Steelers, 37-21 (P)
1983—Steelers, 44-17 (P)
Browns, 30-17 (C)
1984—Browns, 20-10 (C)
Steelers, 23-20 (P)
1985—Browns, 17-7 (C)
Steelers, 10-9 (P)
(Points—Browns 1,620, Steelers 1,431)

CLEVELAND vs. *ST. LOUIS
Browns lead series, 30-10-3
1950—Browns, 34-24 (Cle)
Browns, 10-7 (Chi)
1951—Browns, 34-17 (Chi)
Browns, 49-28 (Cle)
1952—Browns, 28-13 (Cle)
Browns, 10-0 (Chi)
1953—Browns, 27-7 (Chi)
Browns, 27-16 (Cle)
1954—Browns, 31-7 (Cle)
Browns, 35-3 (Chi)
1955—Browns, 26-20 (Chi)
Browns, 35-24 (Cle)
1956—Cardinals, 9-7 (Chi)
Cardinals, 24-7 (Cle)
1957—Browns, 17-7 (Chi)
Browns, 31-0 (Cle)
1958—Browns, 35-28 (Cle)
Browns, 38-24 (Chi)
1959—Browns, 34-7 (Chi)
Browns, 17-7 (Cle)
1960—Browns, 28-27 (C)
Tie, 17-17 (StL)
1961—Browns, 20-17 (C)
Browns, 21-10 (StL)
1962—Browns, 34-7 (StL)
Browns, 38-14 (C)
1963—Cardinals, 20-14 (C)
Browns, 24-10 (StL)
1964—Tie, 33-33 (C)
Cardinals, 28-19 (StL)
1965—Cardinals, 49-13 (C)
Browns, 27-24 (StL)
1966—Cardinals, 34-28 (C)
Browns, 38-10 (StL)
1967—Browns, 20-16 (C)
Browns, 20-16 (StL)
1968—Cardinals, 27-21 (C)
Cardinals, 27-16 (StL)
1969—Tie, 21-21 (C)
Browns, 27-21 (StL)
1974—Cardinals, 29-7 (StL)
1979—Browns, 38-20 (StL)
1985—Cardinals, 27-24 (C) OT
(Points—Browns 1,080, Cardinals 776)
**Franchise in Chicago (Chi) prior to 1960*

CLEVELAND vs. SAN DIEGO
Chargers lead series, 5-4-1
1970—Chargers, 27-10 (C)
1972—Browns, 21-17 (SD)
1973—Tie, 16-16 (C)
1974—Chargers, 36-35 (SD)
1976—Browns, 21-17 (C)
1977—Chargers, 37-14 (SD)
1981—Chargers, 44-14 (C)
1982—Chargers, 30-13 (C)
1983—Browns, 30-24 (SD) OT
1985—Browns, 21-7 (SD)
(Points—Chargers 255, Browns 195)

CLEVELAND vs. SAN FRANCISCO
Browns lead series, 8-4
1950—Browns, 34-14 (C)
1951—49ers, 24-10 (SF)
1953—Browns, 23-21 (C)
1955—Browns, 38-3 (SF)
1959—49ers, 21-20 (C)
1962—Browns, 13-10 (SF)
1968—Browns, 33-21 (SF)
1970—49ers, 34-31 (SF)
1974—Browns, 7-0 (C)
1978—Browns, 24-7 (C)
1981—Browns, 15-12 (SF)
1984—49ers, 41-7 (C)
(Points—Browns 255, 49ers 208)

CLEVELAND vs. SEATTLE
Seahawks lead series, 7-2
1977—Seahawks, 20-19 (S)
1978—Seahawks, 47-24 (S)
1979—Seahawks, 29-24 (C)
1980—Browns, 27-3 (S)
1981—Seahawks, 42-21 (S)
1982—Browns, 21-7 (S)
1983—Seahawks, 24-9 (C)
1984—Seahawks, 33-0 (S)
1985—Seahawks, 31-13 (S)
(Points—Seahawks 236, Browns 158)

CLEVELAND vs. TAMPA BAY
Browns lead series, 3-0
1976—Browns, 24-7 (TB)
1980—Browns, 34-27 (TB)
1983—Browns, 20-0 (C)
(Points—Browns 78, Buccaneers 34)

CLEVELAND vs. WASHINGTON
Browns lead series, 31-8-1
1950—Browns, 20-14 (C)
Browns, 45-21 (W)
1951—Browns, 45-0 (C)
1952—Browns, 19-15 (C)
Browns, 48-24 (W)
1953—Browns, 30-14 (W)
Browns, 27-3 (C)
1954—Browns, 62-3 (C)
Browns, 34-14 (W)
1955—Redskins, 27-17 (C)
Browns, 24-14 (W)
1956—Redskins, 20-9 (W)
Redskins, 20-17 (C)
1957—Browns, 21-17 (C)
Tie, 30-30 (W)
1958—Browns, 20-10 (W)
Browns, 21-14 (C)
1959—Browns, 34-7 (C)
Browns, 31-17 (W)
1960—Browns, 31-10 (W)
Browns, 27-16 (C)
1961—Browns, 31-7 (C)
Browns, 17-6 (W)
1962—Redskins, 17-16 (C)
Redskins, 17-9 (W)
1963—Browns, 37-14 (C)
Browns, 27-20 (W)
1964—Browns, 27-13 (W)
Browns, 34-24 (C)
1965—Browns, 17-7 (W)
Browns, 24-16 (C)
1966—Browns, 38-14 (W)
Browns, 14-3 (C)
1967—Browns, 42-37 (C)
1968—Browns, 24-21 (W)
1969—Browns, 27-23 (C)
1971—Browns, 20-13 (W)
1975—Redskins, 23-7 (C)
1979—Redskins, 13-9 (C)
1985—Redskins, 14-7 (C)
(Points—Browns 1,039, Redskins 612)

DALLAS vs. ATLANTA
Cowboys lead series, 8-1;
See Atlanta vs. Dallas

DALLAS vs. BUFFALO
Cowboys lead series, 3-1;
See Buffalo vs. Dallas

DALLAS vs. CHI. BEARS
Cowboys lead series, 8-4;
See Chi. Bears vs. Dallas

DALLAS vs. CINCINNATI
Cowboys lead series, 2-1;
See Cincinnati vs. Dallas

DALLAS vs. CLEVELAND
Browns lead series, 15-9;
See Cleveland vs. Dallas

DALLAS vs. DENVER
Cowboys lead series, 3-1
1973—Cowboys, 22-10 (Den)
1977—Cowboys, 14-6 (Dal)
*Cowboys, 27-10 (New Orleans)
1980—Broncos, 41-20 (Den)
(Points—Cowboys 83, Broncos 67)
**Super Bowl XII*

DALLAS vs. DETROIT
Cowboys lead series, 6-3
1960—Lions, 23-14 (Det)
1963—Cowboys, 17-14 (Dal)
1968—Cowboys, 59-13 (Dal)
1970—*Cowboys, 5-0 (Dal)
1972—Cowboys, 28-24 (Dal)
1975—Cowboys, 36-10 (Det)
1977—Cowboys, 37-0 (Dal)
1981—Lions, 27-24 (Det)
1985—Lions, 26-21 (Det)
(Points—Cowboys 241, Lions 137)
**NFC Divisional Playoff*

DALLAS vs. GREEN BAY
Packers lead series, 8-5
1960—Packers, 41-7 (GB)
1964—Packers, 45-21 (D)
1965—Packers, 13-3 (Mil)
1966—*Packers, 34-27 (D)
1967—*Packers, 21-17 (GB)
1968—Packers, 28-17 (D)
1970—Cowboys, 16-3 (D)
1972—Packers, 16-13 (Mil)
1975—Packers, 19-17 (D)
1978—Cowboys, 42-14 (Mil)
1980—Cowboys, 28-7 (Mil)
1982—**Cowboys, 37-26 (D)
1984—Cowboys, 20-6 (D)
(Points—Packers 273, Cowboys 265)
**NFL Championship*
***NFC Second Round Playoff*

DALLAS vs. HOUSTON
Cowboys lead series, 4-1
1970—Cowboys, 52-10 (D)
1974—Cowboys, 10-0 (H)
1979—Oilers, 30-24 (D)
1982—Cowboys, 37-7 (H)
1985—Cowboys, 17-10 (H)
(Points—Cowboys 140, Oilers 57)

DALLAS vs. *INDIANAPOLIS
Cowboys lead series, 6-4
1960—Colts, 45-7 (D)
1965—**Colts, 35-3 (M)
1967—Colts, 23-17 (B)
1969—Cowboys, 27-10 (D)
1970—***Colts, 16-13 (Miami)
1972—Cowboys, 21-0 (B)
1976—Cowboys, 30-27 (D)
1978—Cowboys, 38-0 (D)
1981—Cowboys, 37-13 (B)
1984—Cowboys, 22-3 (D)
(Points—Cowboys 215, Colts 172)
**Franchise in Baltimore prior to 1984*
***Miami Playoff Bowl*
****Super Bowl V*

DALLAS vs. KANSAS CITY
Cowboys lead series, 2-1
1970—Cowboys, 27-16 (KC)
1975—Chiefs, 34-31 (D)
1983—Cowboys, 41-21 (D)
(Points—Cowboys 99, Chiefs 71)

DALLAS vs. *LA RAIDERS
Raiders lead series, 2-1
1974—Raiders, 27-23 (O)
1980—Cowboys, 19-13 (O)
1983—Raiders, 40-38 (D)
(Points—Raiders 80, Cowboys 80)
**Franchise in Oakland prior to 1982*

DALLAS vs. LA RAMS
Rams lead series, 11-10
1960—Rams, 38-13 (D)
1962—Cowboys, 27-17 (LA)
1967—Rams, 35-13 (D)
1969—Rams, 24-23 (LA)
*Rams, 31-0 (M)
1971—Cowboys, 28-21 (D)
1973—Rams, 37-31 (LA)
**Cowboys, 27-16 (D)
1975—Cowboys, 18-7 (D)
***Cowboys, 37-7 (LA)
1976—**Rams, 14-12 (D)
1978—Rams, 27-14 (LA)
***Cowboys, 28-0 (LA)
1979—Cowboys, 30-6 (D)
**Rams, 21-19 (D)
1980—Rams, 38-14 (LA)
****Cowboys, 34-13 (D)
1981—Cowboys, 29-17 (D)
1983—****Rams, 24-17 (D)
1984—Cowboys, 20-13 (LA)
1985—**Rams, 20-0 (LA)
(Points—Cowboys 434, Rams 426)
**Miami Playoff Bowl*
***NFC Divisional Playoff*
****NFC Championship*
*****NFC Wild Card Game*

DALLAS vs. MIAMI
Dolphins lead series, 3-2
1971—*Cowboys, 24-3 (New Orleans)
1973—Dolphins, 14-7 (D)
1978—Dolphins, 23-16 (M)
1981—Cowboys, 28-27 (D)
1984—Dolphins, 28-21 (M)
(Points—Cowboys 96, Dolphins 95)
**Super Bowl VI*

DALLAS vs. MINNESOTA
Cowboys lead series, 11-5
1961—Cowboys, 21-7 (D)
Cowboys, 28-0 (M)
1966—Cowboys, 28-17 (D)
1968—Cowboys, 20-7 (M)
*Cowboys, 17-13 (Miami)
1970—Vikings, 54-13 (M)
1971—**Cowboys, 20-12 (M)
1973—***Vikings, 27-10 (D)
1974—Vikings, 23-21 (D)
1975—**Cowboys, 17-14 (M)
1977—Cowboys, 16-10 (M) OT
***Cowboys, 23-6 (D)
1978—Vikings, 21-10 (D)
1979—Cowboys, 36-20 (M)
1982—Vikings, 31-27 (M)
1983—Cowboys, 37-24 (M)
(Points—Cowboys 344, Vikings 286)
**Miami Playoff Bowl*
***NFC Divisional Playoff*
****NFC Championship*

DALLAS vs. NEW ENGLAND
Cowboys lead series, 5-0
1971—Cowboys, 44-21 (D)
1975—Cowboys, 34-31 (NE)
1978—Cowboys, 17-10 (D)
1981—Cowboys, 35-21 (NE)
1984—Cowboys, 20-17 (D)
(Points—Cowboys 150, Patriots 100)

DALLAS vs. NEW ORLEANS
Cowboys lead series, 11-1
1967—Cowboys, 14-10 (D)
Cowboys, 27-10 (NO)
1968—Cowboys, 17-3 (NO)
1969—Cowboys, 21-17 (NO)
Cowboys, 33-17 (D)
1971—Saints, 24-14 (NO)
1973—Cowboys, 40-3 (D)
1976—Cowboys, 24-6 (NO)
1978—Cowboys, 27-7 (D)
1982—Cowboys, 21-7 (D)
1983—Cowboys, 21-20 (D)
1984—Cowboys, 30-27 (D) OT
(Points—Cowboys 289, Saints 151)

DALLAS vs. NY GIANTS
Cowboys lead series, 32-13-2
1960—Tie, 31-31 (NY)
1961—Giants, 31-10 (D)
Cowboys, 17-16 (NY)
1962—Giants, 41-10 (D)
Giants, 41-31 (NY)
1963—Giants, 37-21 (NY)
Giants, 34-27 (D)
1964—Tie, 13-13 (D)
Cowboys, 31-21 (NY)
1965—Cowboys, 31-2 (D)
Cowboys, 38-20 (NY)
1966—Cowboys, 52-7 (D)
Cowboys, 17-7 (NY)
1967—Cowboys, 38-24 (D)
1968—Giants, 27-21 (D)
Cowboys, 28-10 (NY)
1969—Cowboys, 25-3 (D)
1970—Cowboys, 28-10 (D)
Giants, 23-20 (NY)
1971—Cowboys, 20-13 (D)
Cowboys, 42-14 (NY)
1972—Cowboys, 23-14 (NY)
Giants, 23-3 (D)
1973—Cowboys, 45-28 (D)
Cowboys, 23-10 (New Haven)
1974—Giants, 14-6 (D)
Cowboys, 21-7 (New Haven)
1975—Cowboys, 13-7 (NY)
Cowboys, 14-3 (D)
1976—Cowboys, 24-14 (NY)
Cowboys, 9-3 (D)
1977—Cowboys, 41-21 (D)
Cowboys, 24-10 (NY)
1978—Cowboys, 34-24 (NY)
Cowboys, 24-3 (D)
1979—Cowboys, 16-14 (NY)
Cowboys, 28-7 (D)
1980—Cowboys, 24-3 (D)
Giants, 38-35 (NY)
1981—Cowboys, 18-10 (D)
Giants, 13-10 (NY) OT
1983—Cowboys, 28-13 (D)
Cowboys, 38-20 (NY)
1984—Giants, 28-7 (NY)
Giants, 19-7 (D)
1985—Cowboys, 30-29 (NY)
Cowboys, 28-21 (D)
(Points—Cowboys 1,124, Giants 821)

DALLAS vs. NY JETS
Cowboys lead series, 3-0
1971—Cowboys, 52-10 (D)
1975—Cowboys, 31-21 (NY)
1978—Cowboys, 30-7 (NY)
(Points—Cowboys 113, Jets 38)

DALLAS vs. PHILADELPHIA
Cowboys lead series, 34-17
1960—Eagles, 27-25 (D)
1961—Eagles, 43-7 (D)
Eagles, 35-13 (P)

1962—Cowboys, 41-19 (D)
Eagles, 28-14 (P)
1963—Eagles, 24-21 (P)
Cowboys, 27-20 (D)
1964—Eagles, 17-14 (D)
Eagles, 24-14 (P)
1965—Eagles, 35-24 (D)
Cowboys, 21-19 (P)
1966—Cowboys, 56-7 (D)
Eagles, 24-23 (P)
1967—Eagles, 21-14 (P)
Cowboys, 38-17 (D)
1968—Cowboys, 45-13 (P)
Cowboys, 34-14 (D)
1969—Cowboys, 38-7 (P)
Cowboys, 49-14 (D)
1970—Cowboys, 17-7 (P)
Cowboys, 21-17 (D)
1971—Cowboys, 42-7 (P)
Cowboys, 20-7 (D)
1972—Cowboys, 28-6 (D)
Cowboys, 28-7 (P)
1973—Eagles, 30-16 (P)
Cowboys, 31-10 (D)
1974—Eagles, 13-10 (P)
Cowboys, 31-24 (D)
1975—Cowboys, 20-17 (P)
Cowboys, 27-17 (D)
1976—Cowboys, 27-7 (D)
Cowboys, 26-7 (P)
1977—Cowboys, 16-10 (P)
Cowboys, 24-14 (D)
1978—Cowboys, 14-7 (D)
Cowboys, 31-13 (P)
1979—Eagles, 31-21 (D)
Cowboys, 24-17 (P)
1980—Eagles, 17-10 (P)
Cowboys, 35-27 (D)
*Eagles, 20-7 (P)
1981—Cowboys, 17-14 (P)
Cowboys, 21-10 (D)
1982—Eagles, 24-20 (D)
1983—Cowboys, 37-7 (D)
Cowboys, 27-20 (P)
1984—Cowboys, 23-17 (D)
Cowboys, 26-10 (P)
1985—Eagles, 16-14 (P)
Cowboys, 34-17 (D)
(Points—Cowboys 1,263, Eagles 875)
NFC Championship

DALLAS vs. PITTSBURGH
Steelers lead series, 12-11
1960—Steelers, 35-28 (D)
1961—Cowboys, 27-24 (D)
Steelers, 37-7 (P)
1962—Steelers, 30-28 (D)
Cowboys, 42-27 (P)
1963—Steelers, 27-21 (P)
Steelers, 24-19 (D)
1964—Steelers, 23-17 (P)
Cowboys, 17-14 (D)
1965—Steelers, 22-13 (P)
Cowboys, 24-17 (D)
1966—Cowboys, 52-21 (D)
Cowboys, 20-7 (P)
1967—Cowboys, 24-21 (P)
1968—Cowboys, 28-7 (D)
1969—Cowboys, 10-7 (P)
1972—Cowboys, 17-13 (D)
1975—*Steelers, 21-17 (Miami)
1977—Steelers, 28-13 (P)
1978—**Steelers, 35-31 (Miami)
1979—Steelers, 14-3 (P)
1982—Steelers, 36-28 (D)
1985—Cowboys, 27-13 (D)
(Points—Cowboys 513, Steelers 503)
Super Bowl X
***Super Bowl XIII*

DALLAS vs. ST. LOUIS
Cowboys lead series, 29-17-1
1960—Cardinals, 12-10 (StL)
1961—Cardinals, 31-17 (D)
Cardinals, 31-13 (StL)
1962—Cardinals, 28-24 (D)
Cardinals, 52-20 (StL)
1963—Cardinals, 34-7 (D)
Cowboys, 28-24 (StL)
1964—Cardinals, 16-6 (D)
Cowboys, 31-13 (StL)
1965—Cardinals, 20-13 (StL)
Cowboys, 27-13 (D)
1966—Tie, 10-10 (StL)
Cowboys, 31-17 (D)
1967—Cowboys, 46-21 (D)
1968—Cowboys, 27-10 (StL)
1969—Cowboys, 24-3 (D)
1970—Cardinals, 20-7 (StL)
Cardinals, 38-0 (D)
1971—Cowboys, 16-13 (StL)
Cowboys, 31-12 (D)
1972—Cowboys, 33-24 (D)
Cowboys, 27-6 (StL)
1973—Cowboys, 45-10 (D)
Cowboys, 30-3 (StL)
1974—Cardinals, 31-28 (StL)
Cowboys, 17-14 (D)
1975—Cowboys, 37-31 (D) OT
Cardinals, 31-17 (StL)
1976—Cardinals, 21-17 (StL)
Cowboys, 19-14 (D)
1977—Cowboys, 30-24 (StL)
Cardinals, 24-17 (D)
1978—Cowboys, 21-12 (D)
Cowboys, 24-21 (StL) OT
1979—Cowboys, 22-21 (StL)
Cowboys, 22-13 (D)
1980—Cowboys, 27-24 (StL)
Cowboys, 31-21 (D)
1981—Cowboys, 30-17 (D)
Cardinals, 20-17 (StL)
1982—Cowboys, 24-7 (StL)
1983—Cowboys, 34-17 (StL)
Cowboys, 35-17 (D)
1984—Cardinals, 31-20 (D)
Cowboys, 24-17 (StL)
1985—Cardinals, 21-10 (StL)
Cowboys, 35-17 (D)
(Points—Cowboys 1,081, Cardinals 927)

DALLAS vs. SAN DIEGO
Cowboys lead series, 2-1
1972—Cowboys, 34-28 (SD)
1980—Cowboys, 42-31 (D)
1983—Chargers, 24-23 (SD)
(Points—Cowboys 99, Chargers 83)

DALLAS vs. SAN FRANCISCO
Series tied, 8-8-1
1960—49ers, 26-14 (D)
1963—49ers, 31-24 (SF)
1965—Cowboys, 39-31 (D)
1967—49ers, 24-16 (SF)
1969—Tie, 24-24 (D)
1970—*Cowboys, 17-10 (SF)
1971—*Cowboys, 14-3 (D)
1972—49ers, 31-10 (D)
**Cowboys, 30-28 (SF)
1974—Cowboys, 20-14 (D)
1977—Cowboys, 42-35 (SF)
1979—Cowboys, 21-13 (SF)
1980—Cowboys, 59-14 (D)
1981—49ers, 42-14 (SF)
*49ers, 28-27 (SF)
1983—49ers, 42-17 (SF)
1985—49ers, 31-16 (SF)
(Points—49ers 430, Cowboys 404)
NFC Championship
***NFC Divisional Playoff*

DALLAS vs. SEATTLE
Cowboys lead series, 3-0
1976—Cowboys, 28-13 (S)
1980—Cowboys, 51-7 (D)
1983—Cowboys, 35-10 (S)
(Points—Cowboys 114, Seahawks 30)

DALLAS vs. TAMPA BAY
Cowboys lead series, 6-0
1977—Cowboys, 23-7 (D)
1980—Cowboys, 28-17 (D)
1981—*Cowboys, 38-0 (D)
1982—Cowboys, 14-9 (D)
**Cowboys, 30-17 (D)
1983—Cowboys, 27-24 (D) OT
(Points—Cowboys 160, Buccaneers 74)
NFC Divisional Playoff
***NFC First Round Playoff*

DALLAS vs. WASHINGTON
Cowboys lead series, 30-20-2
1960—Redskins, 26-14 (W)
1961—Tie, 28-28 (D)
Redskins, 34-24 (W)
1962—Tie, 35-35 (D)
Cowboys, 38-10 (W)
1963—Redskins, 21-17 (W)
Cowboys, 35-20 (D)
1964—Cowboys, 24-18 (D)
Redskins, 28-16 (W)
1965—Cowboys, 27-7 (D)
Redskins, 34-31 (W)
1966—Cowboys, 31-30 (W)
Redskins, 34-31 (D)
1967—Cowboys, 17-14 (W)
Redskins, 27-20 (D)
1968—Cowboys, 44-24 (W)
Cowboys, 29-20 (D)
1969—Cowboys, 41-28 (W)
Cowboys, 20-10 (D)
1970—Cowboys, 45-21 (W)
Cowboys, 34-0 (D)
1971—Redskins, 20-16 (D)
Cowboys, 13-0 (W)
1972—Redskins, 24-20 (W)
Cowboys, 34-24 (D)
*Redskins, 26-3 (W)
1973—Redskins, 14-7 (W)
Cowboys, 27-7 (D)
1974—Redskins, 28-21 (W)
Cowboys, 24-23 (D)
1975—Redskins, 30-24 (W) OT
Cowboys, 31-10 (D)
1976—Cowboys, 20-7 (W)
Redskins, 27-14 (D)
1977—Cowboys, 34-16 (D)
Cowboys, 14-7 (W)
1978—Redskins, 9-5 (W)
Cowboys, 37-10 (D)
1979—Redskins, 34-20 (W)
Cowboys, 35-34 (D)
1980—Cowboys, 17-3 (W)
Cowboys, 14-10 (D)
1981—Cowboys, 26-10 (W)
Cowboys, 24-10 (D)
1982—Cowboys, 24-10 (W)
*Redskins, 31-17 (W)
1983—Cowboys, 31-30 (W)
Redskins, 31-10 (D)
1984—Redskins, 34-14 (W)
Redskins, 30-28 (D)
1985—Cowboys, 44-14 (D)
Cowboys, 13-7 (W)
(Points—Cowboys 1,262, Redskins 1,039)
NFC Championship

***DALLAS TEXANS vs. CHI. BEARS**
Series tied, 1-1
See Chi. Bears vs. *Dallas Texans
Extinct team

***DALLAS TEXANS vs. DETROIT**
Lions won series, 2-0
1952—Lions, 43-13 (Det)
Lions, 41-6 (Dal)
(Points—Lions 84, Texans 19)
Extinct team

***DALLAS TEXANS vs. GREEN BAY**
Packers won series, 2-0
1952—Packers, 24-14 (D)
Packers, 42-14 (GB)
(Points—Packers 66, Texans 28)
Extinct team

***DALLAS TEXANS vs. LA RAMS**
Rams won series, 2-0
1952—Rams, 42-20 (LA)
Rams, 27-6 (D)
(Points—Rams 69, Texans 26)
Extinct team

***DALLAS TEXANS vs. NY GIANTS**
Giants won series, 1-0
1952—Giants, 24-6 (D)
Extinct team

***DALLAS TEXANS vs. PHILADELPHIA**
Eagles won series, 1-0
1952—Eagles, 38-21 (P)
Extinct team

***DALLAS TEXANS vs. SAN FRANCISCO**
49ers won series, 2-0
1952—49ers, 37-14 (D)
49ers, 48-21 (SF)
(Points—49ers 85, Texans 35)
Extinct team

DENVER vs. ATLANTA
Series tied, 3-3;
See Atlanta vs. Denver

DENVER vs. BUFFALO
Bills lead series, 13-9-1;
See Buffalo vs. Denver

DENVER vs. CHI. BEARS
Bears lead series, 4-3;
See Chi. Bears vs. Denver

DENVER vs. CINCINNATI
Broncos lead series, 8-6;
See Cincinnati vs. Denver

DENVER vs. CLEVELAND
Broncos lead series, 8-3;
See Cleveland vs. Denver

DENVER vs. DALLAS
Cowboys lead series, 3-1;
See Dallas vs. Denver

DENVER vs. DETROIT
Broncos lead series, 3-2
1971—Lions, 24-20 (Den)
1974—Broncos, 31-27 (Det)
1978—Lions, 17-14 (Det)
1981—Broncos, 27-21 (Den)
1984—Broncos, 28-7 (Det)
(Points—Broncos 120, Lions 96)

DENVER vs. GREEN BAY
Broncos lead series, 3-1
1971—Packers, 34-13 (Mil)
1975—Broncos, 23-13 (D)
1978—Broncos, 16-3 (D)
1984—Broncos, 17-14 (D)
(Points—Broncos 69, Packers 64)

DENVER vs. HOUSTON
Oilers lead series, 18-10-1
1960—Oilers, 45-25 (D)
Oilers, 20-10 (H)
1961—Oilers, 55-14 (D)
Oilers, 45-14 (H)
1962—Broncos, 20-10 (D)
Oilers, 34-17 (H)
1963—Oilers, 20-14 (D)
Oilers, 33-24 (D)
1964—Oilers, 38-17 (D)
Oilers, 34-15 (H)
1965—Broncos, 28-17 (D)
Broncos, 31-21 (H)
1966—Oilers, 45-7 (H)
Broncos, 40-38 (D)
1967—Oilers, 10-6 (H)
Oilers, 20-18 (D)
1968—Oilers, 38-17 (H)
1969—Oilers, 24-21 (H)
Tie, 20-20 (D)
1970—Oilers, 31-21 (H)
1972—Broncos, 30-17 (D)
1973—Broncos, 48-20 (H)
1974—Broncos, 37-14 (D)
1976—Oilers, 17-3 (H)
1977—Broncos, 24-14 (H)
1979—*Oilers, 13-7 (H)
1980—Oilers, 20-16 (D)
1983—Broncos, 26-14 (H)
1985—Broncos, 31-20 (D)
(Points—Oilers 747, Broncos 601)
AFC Wild Card Game

DENVER vs. *INDIANAPOLIS
Broncos lead series, 6-1
1974—Broncos, 17-6 (B)
1977—Broncos, 27-13 (D)
1978—Colts, 7-6 (B)
1981—Broncos, 28-10 (D)
1983—Broncos, 17-10 (B)
Broncos, 21-19 (D)
1985—Broncos, 15-10 (I)
(Points—Broncos 131, Colts 75)
Franchise in Baltimore prior to 1984

DENVER vs. *KANSAS CITY
Chiefs lead series, 33-18
1960—Texans, 17-14 (D)
Texans, 34-7 (Da)
1961—Texans, 19-12 (D)
Texans, 49-21 (Da)
1962—Texans, 24-3 (D)
Texans, 17-10 (Da)
1963—Chiefs, 59-7 (D)
Chiefs, 52-21 (KC)
1964—Broncos, 33-27 (D)
Chiefs, 49-39 (KC)
1965—Chiefs, 31-23 (D)
Chiefs, 45-35 (KC)
1966—Chiefs, 37-10 (KC)
Chiefs, 56-10 (D)
1967—Chiefs, 52-9 (KC)
Chiefs, 38-24 (D)
1968—Chiefs, 34-2 (KC)
Chiefs, 30-7 (D)
1969—Chiefs, 26-13 (D)
Chiefs, 31-17 (KC)
1970—Broncos, 26-13 (D)
Chiefs, 16-0 (KC)
1971—Chiefs, 16-3 (D)
Chiefs, 28-10 (KC)
1972—Chiefs, 45-24 (D)
Chiefs, 24-21 (KC)
1973—Chiefs, 16-14 (KC)
Broncos, 14-10 (D)
1974—Broncos, 17-14 (KC)
Chiefs, 42-34 (D)
1975—Broncos, 37-33 (D)
Chiefs, 26-13 (KC)
1976—Broncos, 35-26 (KC)
Broncos, 17-16 (D)
1977—Broncos, 23-7 (D)
Broncos, 14-7 (KC)
1978—Broncos, 23-17 (KC) OT
Broncos, 24-3 (D)
1979—Broncos, 24-10 (KC)
Broncos, 20-3 (D)
1980—Chiefs, 23-17 (D)
Chiefs, 31-14 (KC)
1981—Chiefs, 28-14 (KC)
Broncos, 16-13 (D)
1982—Chiefs, 37-16 (D)
1983—Broncos, 27-24 (D)
Chiefs, 48-17 (KC)
1984—Broncos, 21-0 (D)
Chiefs, 16-13 (KC)
1985—Broncos, 30-10 (KC)
Broncos, 14-13 (D)
(Points—Chiefs 1,342, Broncos 909)
Franchise in Dallas prior to 1963 and known as Texans

DENVER vs. *LA RAIDERS
Raiders lead series, 36-14-2
1960—Broncos, 31-14 (D)
Raiders, 48-10 (O)
1961—Raiders, 33-19 (O)
Broncos, 27-24 (D)
1962—Broncos, 44-7 (D)
Broncos, 23-6 (O)
1963—Raiders, 26-10 (D)
Raiders, 35-31 (O)
1964—Raiders, 40-7 (O)
Tie, 20-20 (D)
1965—Raiders, 28-20 (D)
Raiders, 24-13 (O)
1966—Raiders, 17-3 (D)
Raiders, 28-10 (O)
1967—Raiders, 51-0 (O)
Raiders, 21-17 (D)
1968—Raiders, 43-7 (D)
Raiders, 33-27 (O)
1969—Raiders, 24-14 (D)
Raiders, 41-10 (O)
1970—Raiders, 35-23 (O)
Raiders, 24-19 (D)
1971—Raiders, 27-16 (D)
Raiders, 21-13 (O)
1972—Broncos, 30-23 (O)
Raiders, 37-20 (D)
1973—Tie, 23-23 (D)
Raiders, 21-17 (O)
1974—Raiders, 28-17 (D)
Broncos, 20-17 (O)
1975—Raiders, 42-17 (D)
Raiders, 17-10 (O)
1976—Raiders, 17-10 (D)
Raiders, 19-6 (O)
1977—Broncos, 30-7 (O)
Raiders, 24-14 (D)
**Broncos, 20-17 (D)
1978—Broncos, 14-6 (D)
Broncos, 21-6 (O)
1979—Raiders, 27-3 (O)
Raiders, 14-10 (D)
1980—Raiders, 9-3 (O)
Raiders, 24-21 (D)
1981—Broncos, 9-7 (D)
Broncos, 17-0 (O)
1982—Raiders, 27-10 (LA)
1983—Raiders, 22-7 (D)
Raiders, 22-20 (LA)
1984—Broncos, 16-13 (D)
Broncos, 22-19 (LA) OT
1985—Raiders, 31-28 (LA) OT
Raiders, 17-14 (D) OT
(Points—Raiders 1,206, Broncos 863)
Franchise in Oakland prior to 1982
***AFC Championship*

DENVER vs. LA RAMS
Rams lead series, 3-2
1972—Broncos, 16-10 (LA)
1974—Rams, 17-10 (D)
1979—Rams, 13-9 (D)
1982—Broncos, 27-24 (LA)
1985—Rams, 20-16 (LA)
(Points—Rams 84, Broncos 78)

DENVER vs. MIAMI
Dolphins lead series, 5-2-1
1966—Dolphins, 24-7 (M)
Broncos, 17-7 (D)
1967—Dolphins, 35-21 (M)
1968—Broncos, 21-14 (D)
1969—Dolphins, 27-24 (M)
1971—Tie, 10-10 (D)
1975—Dolphins, 14-13 (M)
1985—Dolphins, 30-26 (D)

(Points—Dolphins 161, Broncos 139)

DENVER vs. MINNESOTA
Series tied, 2-2
1972—Vikings, 23-20 (D)
1978—Vikings, 12-9 (M) OT
1981—Broncos, 19-17 (D)
1984—Broncos, 42-21 (D)
(Points—Broncos 90, Vikings 73)

DENVER vs. *NEW ENGLAND
Patriots lead series, 12-11
1960—Broncos, 13-10 (B)
Broncos, 31-24 (D)
1961—Patriots, 45-17 (B)
Patriots, 28-24 (D)
1962—Patriots, 41-16 (B)
Patriots, 33-29 (D)
1963—Broncos, 14-10 (D)
Patriots, 40-21 (B)
1964—Patriots, 39-10 (D)
Patriots, 12-7 (B)
1965—Broncos, 27-10 (B)
Patriots, 28-20 (D)
1966—Patriots, 24-10 (D)
Broncos, 17-10 (B)
1967—Broncos, 26-21 (D)
1968—Patriots, 20-17 (D)
Broncos, 35-14 (B)
1969—Broncos, 35-7 (D)
1972—Broncos, 45-21 (D)
1976—Patriots, 38-14 (NE)
1979—Broncos, 45-10 (D)
1980—Patriots, 23-14 (NE)
1984—Broncos, 26-19 (D)
(Points—Patriots 527, Broncos 513)
Franchise in Boston prior to 1971

DENVER vs. NEW ORLEANS
Broncos lead series, 4-0
1970—Broncos, 31-6 (NO)
1974—Broncos, 33-17 (D)
1979—Broncos, 10-3 (D)
1985—Broncos, 34-23 (D)
(Points—Broncos 108, Saints 49)

DENVER vs. NY GIANTS
Broncos lead series, 2-1
1972—Giants, 29-17 (NY)
1976—Broncos, 14-13 (D)
1980—Broncos, 14-9 (NY)
(Points—Giants 51, Broncos 45)

DENVER vs. *NY JETS
Series tied, 10-10-1
1960—Titans, 28-24 (NY)
Titans, 30-27 (D)
1961—Titans, 35-28 (NY)
Broncos, 27-10 (D)
1962—Broncos, 32-10 (NY)
Titans, 46-45 (D)
1963—Tie, 35-35 (NY)
Jets, 14-9 (D)
1964—Jets, 30-6 (NY)
Broncos, 20-16 (D)
1965—Broncos, 16-13 (D)
Jets, 45-10 (NY)
1966—Jets, 16-7 (D)
1967—Jets, 38-24 (D)
Broncos, 33-24 (NY)
1968—Broncos, 21-13 (NY)
1969—Broncos, 21-19 (D)
1973—Broncos, 40-28 (NY)
1976—Broncos, 46-3 (D)
1978—Jets, 31-28 (D)
1980—Broncos, 31-24 (D)
(Points—Broncos 530, Jets 508)
Jets known as Titans prior to 1963

DENVER vs. PHILADELPHIA
Eagles lead series, 3-1
1971—Eagles, 17-16 (P)
1975—Broncos, 25-10 (D)
1980—Eagles, 27-6 (P)
1983—Eagles, 13-10 (D)
(Points—Eagles 67, Broncos 57)

DENVER vs. PITTSBURGH
Broncos lead series, 7-5-1
1970—Broncos, 16-13 (D)
1971—Broncos, 22-10 (P)
1973—Broncos, 23-13 (P)
1974—Tie, 35-35 (D) OT
1975—Steelers, 20-9 (P)
1977—Broncos, 21-7 (D)
*Broncos, 34-21 (D)
1978—Steelers, 21-17 (D)
*Steelers, 33-10 (P)
1979—Steelers, 42-7 (P)
1983—Broncos, 14-10 (P)
1984—*Steelers, 24-17 (D)
1985—Broncos, 31-23 (P)
(Points—Steelers 272, Broncos 256)
AFC Divisional Playoff

DENVER vs. ST. LOUIS
Broncos lead series, 1-0-1
1973—Tie, 17-17 (StL)
1977—Broncos, 7-0 (D)
(Points—Broncos 24, Cardinals 17)

DENVER vs. *SAN DIEGO
Chargers lead series, 27-24-1
1960—Chargers, 23-19 (D)
Chargers, 41-33 (LA)
1961—Chargers, 37-0 (SD)
Chargers, 19-16 (D)
1962—Broncos, 30-21 (D)
Broncos, 23-20 (SD)
1963—Broncos, 50-34 (D)
Chargers, 58-20 (SD)
1964—Chargers, 42-14 (SD)
Chargers, 31-20 (D)
1965—Chargers, 34-31 (SD)
Chargers, 33-21 (D)
1966—Chargers, 24-17 (SD)
Broncos, 20-17 (D)
1967—Chargers, 38-21 (D)
Chargers, 24-20 (SD)
1968—Chargers, 55-24 (SD)
Chargers, 47-23 (D)
1969—Broncos, 13-0 (D)
Chargers, 45-24 (SD)
1970—Chargers, 24-21 (SD)
Tie, 17-17 (D)
1971—Broncos, 20-16 (D)
Chargers, 45-17 (SD)
1972—Chargers, 37-14 (SD)
Broncos, 38-13 (D)
1973—Broncos, 30-19 (D)
Broncos, 42-28 (SD)
1974—Broncos, 27-7 (D)
Chargers, 17-0 (SD)
1975—Broncos, 27-17 (SD)
Broncos, 13-10 (D) OT
1976—Broncos, 26-0 (D)
Broncos, 17-0 (SD)
1977—Broncos, 17-14 (SD)
Broncos, 17-9 (D)
1978—Broncos, 27-14 (D)
Chargers, 23-0 (SD)
1979—Broncos, 7-0 (D)
Chargers, 17-7 (SD)
1980—Chargers, 30-13 (D)
Broncos, 20-13 (SD)
1981—Broncos, 42-24 (D)
Chargers, 34-17 (SD)
1982—Chargers, 23-3 (D)
Chargers, 30-20 (SD)
1983—Broncos, 14-6 (D)
Chargers, 31-7 (SD)
1984—Broncos, 16-13 (SD)
Broncos, 16-13 (D)
1985—Chargers, 30-10 (SD)
Broncos, 30-24 (D) OT
(Points—Chargers 1,241, Broncos 1,031)
Franchise in Los Angeles prior to 1961

DENVER vs. SAN FRANCISCO
Broncos lead series, 3-2
1970—49ers, 19-14 (SF)
1973—49ers, 36-34 (D)
1979—Broncos, 38-28 (SF)
1982—Broncos, 24-21 (D)
1985—Broncos, 17-16 (D)
(Points—Broncos 127, 49ers 120)

DENVER vs. SEATTLE
Broncos lead series, 11-7
1977—Broncos, 24-13 (S)
1978—Broncos, 28-7 (D)
Broncos, 20-17 (S) OT
1979—Broncos, 37-34 (D)
Seahawks, 28-23 (S)
1980—Broncos, 36-20 (D)
Broncos, 25-17 (S)
1981—Seahawks, 13-10 (S)
Broncos, 23-13 (D)
1982—Seahawks, 17-10 (D)
Seahawks, 13-11 (S)
1983—Seahawks, 27-19 (S)
Broncos, 38-27 (D)
*Seahawks, 31-7 (S)
1984—Seahawks, 27-24 (D)
Broncos, 31-14 (S)
1985—Broncos, 13-10 (D) OT
Broncos, 27-24 (S)
(Points—Broncos 406, Seahawks 352)
AFC Wild Card Game

DENVER vs. TAMPA BAY
Broncos lead series, 2-0
1976—Broncos, 48-13 (D)
1981—Broncos, 24-7 (TB)
(Points—Broncos 72, Buccaneers 20)

DENVER vs. WASHINGTON
Redskins lead series, 2-1
1970—Redskins, 19-3 (D)
1974—Redskins, 30-3 (W)
1980—Broncos, 20-17 (D)
(Points—Redskins 66, Broncos 26)

DETROIT vs. ATLANTA
Lions lead series, 12-4;
See Atlanta vs. Detroit

DETROIT vs. *1950 BALTIMORE
Lions won series, 1-0
See *1950 Baltimore vs. Detroit
Extinct team

DETROIT vs. *BOSTON YANKS
Lions won series, 3-2
See *Boston Yanks vs. Detroit
Extinct team

DETROIT vs. *BROOKLYN DODGERS
Lions won series, 12-3
See *Brooklyn Dodgers vs. Detroit
Extinct team

DETROIT vs. BUFFALO
Series tied, 1-1-1;
See Buffalo vs. Detroit

DETROIT vs. CHI. BEARS
Bears lead series, 64-44-5;
See Chi. Bears vs. Detroit

DETROIT vs. CINCINNATI
Lions lead series, 2-1;
See Cincinnati vs. Detroit

DETROIT vs. *CINCINNATI REDS
Lions won series, 2-1
See *Cincinnati Reds vs. Detroit
Extinct team

DETROIT vs. CLEVELAND
Lions lead series, 13-3;
See Cleveland vs. Detroit

DETROIT vs. DALLAS
Cowboys lead series, 6-3;
See Dallas vs. Detroit

DETROIT vs. *DALLAS TEXANS
Lions won series, 2-0
See *Dallas Texans vs. Detroit
Extinct team

DETROIT vs. DENVER
Broncos lead series, 3-2;
See Denver vs. Detroit

***DETROIT vs. GREEN BAY**
Packers lead series, 57-47-7
1930—Packers, 47-13 (GB)
Tie, 6-6 (P)
1932—Packers, 15-10 (GB)
Spartans, 19-0 (P)
1933—Packers, 17-0 (GB)
Spartans, 7-0 (P)
1934—Lions, 3-0 (GB)
Packers, 3-0 (D)
1935—Packers, 13-9 (GB)
Packers, 31-7 (GB)
Lions, 20-10 (D)
1936—Packers, 20-18 (GB)
Packers, 26-17 (D)
1937—Packers, 26-6 (GB)
Packers, 14-13 (D)
1938—Lions, 17-7 (GB)
Packers, 28-7 (D)
1939—Packers, 26-7 (GB)
Packers, 12-7 (D)
1940—Lions, 23-14 (GB)
Packers, 50-7 (D)
1941—Packers, 23-0 (GB)
Packers, 24-7 (D)
1942—Packers, 38-7 (Mil)
Packers, 28-7 (D)
1943—Packers, 35-14 (GB)
Packers, 27-6 (D)
1944—Packers, 27-6 (GB)
Packers, 14-0 (D)
1945—Packers, 57-21 (Mil)
Lions, 14-3 (D)
1946—Packers, 10-7 (Mil)
Packers, 9-0 (D)
1947—Packers, 34-17 (GB)
Packers, 35-14 (D)
1948—Packers, 33-21 (GB)
Lions, 24-20 (D)
1949—Packers, 16-14 (GB)
Lions, 21-7 (D)
1950—Lions, 45-7 (GB)
Lions, 24-21 (D)
1951—Lions, 24-17 (GB)
Lions, 52-35 (D)
1952—Lions, 52-17 (GB)
Lions, 48-24 (D)
1953—Lions, 14-7 (GB)
Lions, 34-15 (D)
1954—Lions, 21-17 (GB)
Lions, 28-24 (D)
1955—Packers, 20-17 (GB)
Lions, 24-10 (D)
1956—Lions, 20-16 (GB)
Packers, 24-20 (D)
1957—Lions, 24-14 (GB)
Lions, 18-6 (D)
1958—Tie, 13-13 (GB)
Lions, 24-14 (D)
1959—Packers, 28-10 (GB)
Packers, 24-17 (D)
1960—Packers, 28-9 (GB)
Lions, 23-10 (D)
1961—Lions, 17-13 (Mil)
Packers, 17-9 (D)
1962—Packers, 9-7 (GB)
Lions, 26-14 (D)
1963—Packers, 31-10 (Mil)
Tie, 13-13 (D)
1964—Packers, 14-10 (D)
Packers, 30-7 (GB)
1965—Packers, 31-21 (D)
Lions, 12-7 (GB)
1966—Packers, 23-14 (GB)
Packers, 31-7 (D)
1967—Tie, 17-17 (GB)
Packers, 27-17 (D)
1968—Lions, 23-17 (GB)
Tie, 14-14 (D)
1969—Packers, 28-17 (D)
Lions, 16-10 (GB)
1970—Lions, 40-0 (GB)
Lions, 20-0 (D)
1971—Lions, 31-28 (D)
Tie, 14-14 (Mil)
1972—Packers, 24-23 (D)
Packers, 33-7 (GB)
1973—Tie, 13-13 (GB)
Lions, 34-0 (D)
1974—Packers, 21-19 (Mil)
Lions, 19-17 (D)
1975—Lions, 30-16 (Mil)
Lions, 13-10 (D)
1976—Packers, 24-14 (GB)
Lions, 27-6 (D)
1977—Lions, 10-6 (D)
Packers, 10-9 (GB)
1978—Packers, 13-7 (D)
Packers, 35-14 (Mil)
1979—Packers, 24-16 (Mil)
Packers, 18-13 (D)
1980—Lions, 29-7 (Mil)
Lions, 24-3 (D)
1981—Lions, 31-27 (D)
Packers, 31-17 (GB)
1982—Lions, 30-10 (GB)
Lions, 27-24 (D)
1983—Lions, 38-14 (D)
Lions, 23-20 (Mil) OT
1984—Packers, [illegible]1-9 (GB)
Lions, 31-28 (D)
1985—Packers, 43-10 (GB)
Packers, 26-23 (D)
(Points—Packers 2,128, Lions 1,899)
Franchise in Portsmouth prior to 1934 and known as the Spartans

DETROIT vs. HOUSTON
Oilers lead series, 2-1
1971—Lions, 31-7 (H)
1975—Oilers, 24-8 (H)
1983—Oilers, 27-17 (H)
(Points—Oilers 58, Lions 56)

DETROIT vs. *INDIANAPOLIS
Colts lead series, 17-16-2
1953—Lions, 27-17 (B)
Lions, 17-7 (D)
1954—Lions, 35-0 (D)
Lions, 27-3 (B)
1955—Colts, 28-13 (B)
Lions, 24-14 (D)
1956—Lions, 31-14 (B)
Lions, 27-3 (D)
1957—Colts, 34-14 (B)
Lions, 31-27 (D)
1958—Colts, 28-15 (B)
Colts, 40-14 (D)
1959—Colts, 21-9 (B)
Colts, 31-24 (D)
1960—Lions, 30-17 (D)
Lions, 20-15 (B)
1961—Lions, 16-15 (B)
Colts, 17-14 (D)
1962—Lions, 29-20 (B)
Lions, 21-14 (D)
1963—Colts, 25-21 (D)
Colts, 24-21 (B)
1964—Colts, 34-0 (D)
Lions, 31-14 (B)
1965—Colts, 31-7 (B)
Tie, 24-24 (D)
1966—Colts, 45-14 (B)
Lions, 20-14 (D)
1967—Colts, 41-7 (B)
1968—Colts, 27-10 (D)
1969—Tie, 17-17 (B)
1973—Colts, 29-27 (D)
1977—Lions, 13-10 (B)
1980—Colts, 10-9 (D)
1985—Colts, 14-6 (I)
(Points—Colts 724, Lions 665)
Franchise in Baltimore prior to 1984

DETROIT vs. KANSAS CITY
Series tied, 2-2
1971—Lions, 32-21 (D)
1975—Chiefs, 24-21 (KC) OT
1980—Chiefs, 20-17 (KC)
1981—Lions, 27-10 (D)
(Points—Lions 97, Chiefs 75)

DETROIT vs. *LA RAIDERS
Raiders lead series, 3-2
1970—Lions, 28-14 (D)
1974—Raiders, 35-13 (O)
1978—Raiders, 29-17 (O)
1981—Lions, 16-0 (D)
1984—Raiders, 24-3 (D)
(Points—Raiders 102, Lions 77)
Franchise in Oakland prior to 1982

DETROIT vs. *LA RAMS
Rams lead series, 36-34-1
1937—Lions, 28-0 (C)
Lions, 27-7 (D)
1938—Rams, 21-17 (C)
Lions, 6-0 (D)
1939—Lions, 15-7 (D)
Rams, 14-3 (C)
1940—Lions, 6-0 (D)
Rams, 24-0 (C)
1941—Lions, 17-7 (D)
Lions, 14-0 (C)
1942—Rams, 14-0 (D)
Rams, 27-7 (C)
1944—Rams, 20-17 (D)
Lions, 26-14 (C)
1945—Rams, 28-21 (D)
1946—Rams, 35-14 (LA)
Rams, 41-20 (D)
1947—Rams, 27-13 (D)
Rams, 28-17 (LA)
1948—Rams, 44-7 (LA)
Rams, 34-27 (D)
1949—Rams, 27-24 (LA)
Rams, 21-10 (D)
1950—Rams, 30-28 (D)
Rams, 65-24 (LA)
1951—Rams, 27-21 (D)
Lions, 24-22 (LA)
1952—Lions, 17-14 (LA)
Lions, 24-16 (D)
**Lions, 31-21 (D)
1953—Rams, 31-19 (D)
Rams, 37-24 (LA)
1954—Lions, 21-3 (D)
Lions, 27-24 (LA)
1955—Rams, 17-10 (D)
Rams, 24-13 (LA)
1956—Lions, 24-21 (D)
Lions, 16-7 (LA)
1957—Lions, 10-7 (D)
Rams, 35-17 (LA)
1958—Rams, 42-28 (D)
Lions, 41-24 (LA)
1959—Lions, 17-7 (LA)
Lions, 23-17 (D)
1960—Rams, 48-35 (LA)
Lions, 12-10 (D)
1961—Lions, 14-13 (D)
Lions, 28-10 (LA)
1962—Lions, 13-10 (D)
Lions, 12-3 (LA)
1963—Lions, 23-2 (LA)
Rams, 28-21 (D)
1964—Tie, 17-17 (LA)
Lions, 37-17 (D)
1965—Lions, 20-0 (D)
Lions, 31-7 (LA)
1966—Rams, 14-7 (D)
Rams, 23-3 (LA)
1967—Rams, 31-7 (D)
1968—Rams, 10-7 (LA)
1969—Lions, 28-0 (D)

1970—Lions, 28-23 (LA)
1971—Rams, 21-13 (D)
1972—Lions, 34-17 (LA)
1974—Rams, 16-13 (LA)
1975—Rams, 20-0 (D)
1976—Rams, 20-17 (D)
1980—Lions, 41-20 (LA)
1981—Rams, 20-13 (LA)
1982—Lions, 19-14 (LA)
1983—Rams, 21-10 (LA)
(Points—Rams 1,366, Lions 1,298)
Franchise in Cleveland prior to 1946
***Conference Playoff*

DETROIT vs. MIAMI
Dolphins lead series, 2-1
1973—Dolphins, 34-7 (M)
1979—Dolphins, 28-10 (D)
1985—Lions, 31-21 (D)
(Points—Dolphins 83, Lions 48)

DETROIT vs. MINNESOTA
Vikings lead series, 30-17-2
1961—Lions, 37-10 (M)
Lions, 13-7 (D)
1962—Lions, 17-6 (M)
Lions, 37-23 (D)
1963—Lions, 28-10 (D)
Vikings, 34-31 (M)
1964—Lions, 24-20 (M)
Tie, 23-23 (D)
1965—Lions, 31-29 (M)
Vikings, 29-7 (D)
1966—Lions, 32-31 (M)
Vikings, 28-16 (D)
1967—Tie, 10-10 (M)
Lions, 14-3 (D)
1968—Vikings, 24-10 (M)
Vikings, 13-6 (D)
1969—Vikings, 24-10 (M)
Vikings, 27-0 (D)
1970—Vikings, 30-17 (D)
Vikings, 24-20 (M)
1971—Vikings, 16-13 (D)
Vikings, 29-10 (M)
1972—Vikings, 34-10 (D)
Vikings, 16-14 (M)
1973—Vikings, 23-9 (D)
Vikings, 28-7 (M)
1974—Vikings, 7-6 (D)
Lions, 20-16 (M)
1975—Vikings, 25-19 (M)
Lions, 17-10 (D)
1976—Vikings, 10-9 (D)
Vikings, 31-23 (M)
1977—Vikings, 14-7 (M)
Vikings, 30-21 (D)
1978—Vikings, 17-7 (M)
Lions, 45-14 (D)
1979—Vikings, 13-10 (D)
Vikings, 14-7 (M)
1980—Lions, 27-7 (D)
Vikings, 34-0 (M)
1981—Vikings, 26-24 (M)
Lions, 45-7 (D)
1982—Vikings, 34-31 (D)
1983—Vikings, 20-17 (M)
Lions, 13-2 (D)
1984—Vikings, 29-28 (D)
Lions, 16-14 (M)
1985—Vikings, 16-13 (M)
Lions, 41-21 (D)
(Points—Vikings 962, Lions 892)

DETROIT vs. NEW ENGLAND
Series tied, 2-2
1971—Lions, 34-7 (NE)
1976—Lions, 30-10 (D)
1979—Patriots, 24-17 (NE)
1985—Patriots, 23-6 (NE)
(Points—Lions 87, Patriots 64)

DETROIT vs. NEW ORLEANS
Series tied, 4-4-1
1968—Tie, 20-20 (D)
1970—Saints, 19-17 (NO)
1972—Lions, 27-14 (D)
1973—Saints, 20-13 (NO)
1974—Lions, 19-14 (D)
1976—Saints, 17-16 (NO)
1977—Lions, 23-19 (D)
1979—Saints, 17-7 (NO)
1980—Lions, 24-13 (D)
(Points—Lions 166, Saints 153)

DETROIT vs. *NY BULLDOGS
Lions won series, 1-0
1949—Lions, 28-27 (D)
**Extinct team*

***DETROIT vs. NY GIANTS**
Lions lead series, 18-11-1
1930—Giants, 19-6 (P)
1931—Spartans, 14-6 (P)
Giants, 14-0 (NY)
1932—Spartans, 7-0 (P)
Spartans, 6-0 (NY)
1933—Spartans, 17-7 (P)
Giants, 13-10 (NY)
1934—Lions, 9-0 (D)
1935—**Lions, 26-7 (D)
1936—Giants, 14-7 (NY)
Lions, 38-0 (D)
1937—Lions, 17-0 (NY)
1939—Lions, 18-14 (D)
1941—Giants, 20-13 (NY)
1943—Tie, 0-0 (D)
1945—Giants, 35-14 (NY)
1947—Lions, 35-7 (D)
1949—Lions, 45-21 (NY)
1953—Lions, 27-16 (NY)
1955—Giants, 24-19 (D)
1958—Giants, 19-17 (D)
1962—Giants, 17-14 (NY)
1964—Lions, 26-3 (D)
1967—Lions, 30-7 (NY)
1969—Lions, 24-0 (D)
1972—Lions, 30-16 (D)
1974—Lions, 20-19 (D)
1976—Giants, 24-10 (NY)
1982—Giants, 13-6 (D)
1983—Lions, 15-9 (D)
(Points—Lions 520, Giants 344)
**Franchise in Portsmouth prior to 1934 and known as the Spartans*
***NFL Championship*

DETROIT vs. NY JETS
Series tied, 2-2
1972—Lions, 37-20 (D)
1979—Jets, 31-10 (NY)
1982—Jets, 28-13 (D)
1985—Lions, 31-20 (D)
(Points—Jets 99, Lions 91)

DETROIT vs. *NY YANKS
Lions won series, 2-1-1
1950—Yanks, 44-21 (NY)
Lions, 49-14 (D)
1951—Lions, 37-10 (NY)
Tie, 24-24 (D)
(Points—Lions 131, Yanks 92)
**Extinct team*

***DETROIT vs. **PHILADELPHIA**
Lions lead series, 12-10-2
1933—Spartans, 25-0 (P)
1934—Lions, 10-0 (P)
1935—Lions, 35-0 (D)
1936—Lions, 23-0 (P)
1938—Eagles, 21-7 (D)
1940—Lions, 21-0 (P)
1941—Lions, 21-17 (D)
1943—Phil-Pitt, 35-34 (Pitt)
1945—Lions, 28-24 (D)
1948—Eagles, 45-21 (P)
1949—Eagles, 22-14 (D)
1951—Lions, 28-10 (P)
1954—Tie, 13-13 (D)
1957—Lions, 27-16 (P)
1960—Eagles, 28-10 (P)
1961—Eagles, 27-24 (D)
***Lions, 28-10 (M)
1965—Lions, 35-28 (P)
1968—Eagles, 12-0 (D)
1971—Eagles, 23-20 (D)
1974—Eagles, 28-17 (P)
1977—Lions, 17-13 (D)
1979—Eagles, 44-7 (P)
1984—Tie, 23-23 (D) OT
(Points—Lions 488, Eagles 439)
**Franchise in Portsmouth prior to 1934 and known as the Spartans*
***Eagles known as Phil-Pitt in 1943*
****Miami Playoff Bowl*

DETROIT vs. *PITTSBURGH
Lions lead series, 16-9-1
1934—Lions, 40-7 (D)
1936—Lions, 28-3 (D)
1937—Lions, 7-3 (D)
1938—Lions, 16-7 (D)
1940—Pirates, 10-7 (D)
1942—Steelers, 35-7 (D)
1943—Phil-Pitt, 35-34 (P)
1944—Lions, 27-6 (P)
Lions, 21-7 (D)
1946—Lions, 17-7 (D)
1947—Steelers, 17-10 (P)
1948—Lions, 17-14 (D)
1949—Steelers, 14-7 (P)
1950—Lions, 10-7 (D)
1952—Lions, 31-6 (P)
1953—Lions, 38-21 (D)
1955—Lions, 31-28 (P)
1956—Lions, 45-7 (D)
1959—Tie, 10-10 (P)
1962—Lions, 45-7 (D)
**Lions, 17-10 (M)
1966—Steelers, 17-3 (P)
1967—Steelers, 24-14 (D)
1969—Steelers, 16-13 (P)
1973—Steelers, 24-10 (P)
1983—Lions, 45-3 (D)
(Points—Lions 550, Steelers 345)
**Steelers known as Pirates prior to 1941, as Phil-Pitt in 1943, and as Card-Pitt in 1944*
***Miami Playoff Bowl*

***DETROIT vs. **ST. LOUIS**
Lions lead series, 27-15-5
1930—Tie, 0-0 (P)
Cardinals, 23-0 (C)
1931—Cardinals, 20-19 (C)
1932—Tie, 7-7 (P)
1933—Spartans, 7-6 (P)
1934—Lions, 6-0 (D)
Lions, 17-13 (C)
1935—Tie, 10-10 (D)
Lions, 7-6 (C)
1936—Lions, 39-0 (D)
Lions, 14-7 (C)
1937—Lions, 16-7 (C)
Lions, 16-7 (D)
1938—Lions, 10-0 (D)
Lions, 7-3 (C)
1939—Lions, 21-3 (D)
Lions, 17-3 (C)
1940—Tie, 0-0 (Buffalo)
Lions, 43-14 (C)
1941—Tie, 14-14 (C)
Lions, 21-3 (D)
1942—Cardinals, 13-0 (C)
Cardinals, 7-0 (D)
1943—Lions, 35-17 (D)
Lions, 7-0 (C)
1944—Lions, 27-6 (Pitt)
Lions, 21-7 (D)
1945—Lions, 10-0 (C)
Lions, 26-0 (D)
1946—Cardinals, 34-14 (C)
Cardinals, 36-14 (D)
1947—Cardinals, 45-21 (C)
Cardinals, 17-7 (D)
1948—Cardinals, 56-20 (C)
Cardinals, 28-14 (D)
1949—Lions, 24-7 (C)
Cardinals, 42-19 (D)
1959—Lions, 45-21 (D)
1961—Lions, 45-14 (StL)
1967—Cardinals, 38-28 (StL)
1969—Lions, 20-0 (D)
1970—Lions, 16-3 (D)
1973—Lions, 20-16 (StL)
1975—Cardinals, 24-13 (D)
1978—Cardinals, 21-14 (StL)
1980—Lions, 20-7 (D)
Cardinals, 24-23 (StL)
(Points—Lions 794, Cardinals 639)
**Franchise in Portsmouth prior to 1934 and known as the Spartans*
***Franchise in Chicago prior to 1960 and known as Card-Pitt in 1944*

DETROIT vs. *ST. LOUIS GUNNERS
Lions won series, 1-0
1934—Lions, 40-7 (D)
**Extinct team*

DETROIT vs. SAN DIEGO
Lions lead series, 3-2
1972—Lions, 34-20 (D)
1977—Lions, 20-0 (D)
1978—Lions, 31-14 (D)
1981—Chargers, 28-23 (SD)
1984—Chargers, 27-24 (SD)
(Points—Lions 132, Chargers 89)

DETROIT vs. SAN FRANCISCO
Lions lead series, 26-23-1
1950—Lions, 24-7 (D)
49ers, 28-27 (SF)
1951—49ers, 20-10 (D)
49ers, 21-17 (SF)
1952—49ers, 17-3 (SF)
49ers, 28-0 (D)
1953—Lions, 24-21 (D)
Lions, 14-10 (SF)
1954—49ers, 37-31 (SF)
Lions, 48-7 (D)
1955—49ers, 27-24 (D)
49ers, 38-21 (SF)
1956—Lions, 20-17 (D)
Lions, 17-13 (SF)
1957—49ers, 35-31 (SF)
Lions, 31-10 (D)
*Lions, 31-27 (SF)
1958—49ers, 24-21 (SF)
Lions, 35-21 (D)
1959—49ers, 34-13 (D)
49ers, 33-7 (SF)
1960—49ers, 14-10 (D)
Lions, 24-0 (SF)
1961—49ers, 49-0 (D)
Tie, 20-20 (SF)
1962—Lions, 45-24 (D)
Lions, 38-24 (SF)
1963—Lions, 26-3 (D)
Lions, 45-7 (SF)
1964—Lions, 26-17 (SF)
Lions, 24-7 (D)
1965—49ers, 27-21 (D)
49ers, 17-14 (SF)
1966—49ers, 27-24 (SF)
49ers, 41-14 (D)
1967—Lions, 45-3 (SF)
1968—49ers, 14-7 (D)
1969—Lions, 26-14 (SF)
1970—Lions, 28-7 (D)
1971—49ers, 31-27 (SF)
1973—Lions, 30-20 (D)
1974—Lions, 17-13 (D)
1975—Lions, 28-17 (SF)
1977—49ers, 28-7 (SF)
1978—Lions, 33-14 (D)
1980—Lions, 17-13 (D)
1981—Lions, 24-17 (D)
1983—**49ers, 24-23 (SF)
1984—49ers, 30-27 (D)
1985—Lions, 23-21 (D)
(Points—Lions 1,142, 49ers 1,018)
**Conference Playoff*
***NFC Divisional Playoff*

DETROIT vs. SEATTLE
Seahawks lead series, 2-1
1976—Lions, 41-14 (S)
1978—Seahawks, 28-16 (S)
1984—Seahawks, 38-17 (S)
(Points—Seahawks 80, Lions 74)

DETROIT vs. TAMPA BAY
Lions lead series, 9-7
1977—Lions, 16-7 (D)
1978—Lions, 15-7 (TB)
Lions, 34-23 (D)
1979—Buccaneers, 31-16 (TB)
Buccaneers, 16-14 (D)
1980—Lions, 24-10 (TB)
Lions, 27-14 (D)
1981—Buccaneers, 28-10 (TB)
Buccaneers, 20-17 (D)
1982—Buccaneers, 23-21 (TB)
1983—Lions, 11-0 (TB)
Lions, 23-20 (D)
1984—Buccaneers, 21-17 (TB)
Lions, 13-7 (D) OT
1985—Lions, 30-9 (D)
Buccaneers, 19-16 (TB) OT
(Points—Lions 304, Buccaneers 255)

***DETROIT vs. **WASHINGTON**
Redskins lead series, 19-8
1932—Spartans, 10-0 (P)
1933—Spartans, 13-0 (B)
1934—Lions, 24-0 (D)
1935—Lions, 17-7 (B)
Lions, 14-0 (D)
1938—Redskins, 7-5 (D)
1939—Redskins, 31-7 (W)
1940—Redskins, 20-14 (D)
1942—Redskins, 15-3 (D)
1943—Redskins, 42-20 (W)
1946—Redskins, 17-16 (W)
1947—Lions, 38-21 (D)
1948—Redskins, 46-21 (W)
1951—Lions, 35-17 (D)
1956—Redskins, 18-17 (W)
1965—Lions, 14-10 (D)
1968—Redskins, 14-3 (W)
1970—Redskins, 31-10 (W)
1973—Redskins, 20-0 (D)
1976—Redskins, 20-7 (W)
1978—Redskins, 21-19 (D)
1979—Redskins, 27-24 (D)
1981—Redskins, 33-31 (W)
1982—***Redskins, 31-7 (W)
1983—Redskins, 38-17 (W)
1984—Redskins, 28-14 (W)
1985—Redskins, 24-3 (W)
(Points—Redskins 538, Lions 403)
**Franchise in Portsmouth prior to 1934 and known as the Spartans.*
***Franchise in Boston prior to 1937*
****NFC First Round Playoff*

GREEN BAY vs. ATLANTA
Packers lead series, 8-6;
See Atlanta vs. Green Bay

GREEN BAY vs. *1950 BALTIMORE
Colts won series, 1-0
See *1950 Baltimore vs. Green Bay
**Extinct team*

GREEN BAY vs. *BOSTON YANKS
Packers won series, 2-0
See *Boston Yanks vs. Green Bay
**Extinct team*

GREEN BAY vs. *BROOKLYN DODGERS
Packers won series, 10-0
See *Brooklyn Dodgers vs. Green Bay
**Extinct team*

GREEN BAY vs. BUFFALO
Bills lead series, 2-1;
See Buffalo vs. Green Bay

GREEN BAY vs. CHI. BEARS
Bears lead series, 70-55-6;
See Chi. Bears vs. Green Bay

GREEN BAY vs. CINCINNATI
Bengals lead series, 3-2;
See Cincinnati vs. Green Bay

GREEN BAY vs. *CINCINNATI REDS
Packers won series, 1-0
See *Cincinnati Reds vs. Green Bay
**Extinct team*

GREEN BAY vs. CLEVELAND
Packers lead series, 8-5;
See Cleveland vs. Green Bay

GREEN BAY vs. DALLAS
Packers lead series, 8-5;
See Dallas vs. Green Bay

GREEN BAY vs. *DALLAS TEXANS
Packers won series, 2-0
See *Dallas Texans vs. Green Bay
**Extinct team*

GREEN BAY vs. DENVER
Broncos lead series, 3-1;
See Denver vs. Green Bay

GREEN BAY vs. DETROIT
Packers lead series, 57-47-7;
See Detroit vs. Green Bay

GREEN BAY vs. HOUSTON
Series tied, 2-2
1972—Packers, 23-10 (H)
1977—Oilers, 16-10 (GB)
1980—Oilers, 22-3 (GB)
1983—Packers, 41-38 (H) OT

GREEN BAY vs. *INDIANAPOLIS
Packers lead series, 18-17-1
1953—Packers, 37-14 (GB)
Packers, 35-24 (B)
1954—Packers, 7-6 (B)
Packers, 24-13 (Mil)
1955—Colts, 24-20 (Mil)
Colts, 14-10 (B)
1956—Packers, 38-33 (Mil)
Colts, 28-21 (B)
1957—Colts, 45-17 (Mil)
Packers, 24-21 (B)
1958—Colts, 24-17 (Mil)
Colts, 56-0 (B)
1959—Colts, 38-21 (B)
Colts, 28-24 (Mil)
1960—Packers, 35-21 (GB)
Colts, 38-24 (B)
1961—Packers, 45-7 (GB)
Colts, 45-21 (B)
1962—Packers, 17-6 (B)
Packers, 17-13 (GB)
1963—Packers, 31-20 (GB)
Packers, 34-20 (B)
1964—Colts, 21-20 (GB)
Colts, 24-21 (B)
1965—Packers, 20-17 (Mil)
Packers, 42-27 (B)
**Packers, 13-10 (GB) OT
1966—Packers, 24-3 (Mil)
Packers, 14-10 (B)
1967—Colts, 13-10 (B)
1968—Colts, 16-3 (GB)
1969—Colts, 14-6 (B)
1970—Colts, 13-10 (Mil)
1974—Packers, 20-13 (B)
1982—Tie, 20-20 (B) OT
1985—Colts, 37-10 (I)
(Points—Colts 776, Packers 752)

*Franchise in Baltimore prior to 1984
**Conference Playoff

GREEN BAY vs. KANSAS CITY
Series tied, 1-1-1
1966—*Packers, 35-10 (Los Angeles)
1973—Tie, 10-10 (Mil)
1977—Chiefs, 20-10 (KC)
(Points—Packers 55, Chiefs 40)
*Super Bowl I

GREEN BAY vs. *LA RAIDERS
Raiders lead series, 4-1
1967—**Packers, 33-14 (Miami)
1972—Raiders, 20-14 (GB)
1976—Raiders, 18-14 (O)
1978—Raiders, 28-3 (GB)
1984—Raiders, 28-7 (LA)
(Points—Raiders 108, Packers 71)
*Franchise in Oakland prior to 1982
**Super Bowl II

GREEN BAY vs. *LA RAMS
Rams lead series, 39-34-2
1937—Packers, 35-10 (C)
Packers, 35-7 (GB)
1938—Packers, 26-17 (GB)
Packers, 28-7 (C)
1939—Rams, 27-24 (GB)
Packers, 7-6 (C)
1940—Packers, 31-14 (GB)
Tie, 13-13 (C)
1941—Packers, 24-7 (Mil)
Packers, 17-14 (C)
1942—Packers, 45-28 (GB)
Packers, 30-12 (C)
1944—Packers, 30-21 (GB)
Packers, 42-7 (C)
1945—Rams, 27-14 (GB)
Rams, 20-7 (C)
1946—Rams, 21-17 (Mil)
Rams, 38-17 (LA)
1947—Packers, 17-14 (Mil)
Packers, 30-10 (LA)
1948—Packers, 16-0 (GB)
Rams, 24-10 (LA)
1949—Rams, 48-7 (GB)
Rams, 35-7 (LA)
1950—Rams, 45-14 (Mil)
Rams, 51-14 (LA)
1951—Rams, 28-0 (Mil)
Rams, 42-14 (LA)
1952—Rams, 30-28 (Mil)
Rams, 45-27 (LA)
1953—Rams, 38-20 (Mil)
Rams, 33-17 (LA)
1954—Packers, 35-17 (Mil)
Rams, 35-27 (LA)
1955—Packers, 30-28 (Mil)
Rams, 31-17 (LA)
1956—Packers, 42-17 (Mil)
Rams, 49-21 (LA)
1957—Rams, 31-27 (Mil)
Rams, 42-17 (LA)
1958—Rams, 20-7 (GB)
Rams, 34-20 (LA)
1959—Rams, 45-6 (Mil)
Packers, 38-20 (LA)
1960—Rams, 33-31 (Mil)
Packers, 35-2 (LA)
1961—Packers, 35-17 (GB)
Packers, 24-17 (LA)
1962—Packers, 41-10 (Mil)
Packers, 20-17 (LA)
1963—Packers, 42-10 (GB)
Packers, 31-14 (LA)
1964—Rams, 27-17 (Mil)
Tie, 24-24 (LA)
1965—Packers, 6-3 (Mil)
Rams, 21-10 (LA)
1966—Packers, 24-13 (GB)
Packers, 27-23 (LA)
1967—Rams, 27-24 (LA)
**Packers, 28-7 (Mil)
1968—Rams, 16-14 (Mil)
1969—Rams, 34-21 (LA)
1970—Rams, 31-21 (GB)
1971—Rams, 30-13 (LA)
1973—Rams, 24-7 (LA)
1974—Packers, 17-6 (Mil)
1975—Rams, 22-5 (LA)
1977—Rams, 24-6 (Mil)
1978—Rams, 31-14 (LA)
1980—Rams, 51-21 (LA)
1981—Rams, 35-23 (LA)
1982—Packers, 35-23 (Mil)
1983—Packers, 27-24 (Mil)
1984—Packers, 31-6 (Mil)
1985—Rams, 34-17 (LA)
(Points—Rams 1,783, Packers 1,641)
*Franchise in Cleveland prior to 1946
**Conference Championship

GREEN BAY vs. MIAMI
Dolphins lead series, 4-0
1971—Dolphins, 27-6 (Mia)
1975—Dolphins, 31-7 (GB)
1979—Dolphins, 27-7 (Mia)
1985—Dolphins, 34-24 (GB)
(Points—Dolphins 119, Packers 44)

GREEN BAY vs. MINNESOTA
Series tied, 24-24-1
1961—Packers, 33-7 (Minn)
Packers, 28-10 (Mil)
1962—Packers, 34-7 (GB)
Packers, 48-21 (Minn)
1963—Packers, 37-28 (Minn)
Packers, 28-7 (GB)
1964—Vikings, 24-23 (GB)
Packers, 42-13 (Minn)
1965—Packers, 38-13 (Minn)
Packers, 24-19 (GB)
1966—Vikings, 20-17 (GB)
Packers, 28-16 (Minn)
1967—Vikings, 10-7 (Mil)
Packers, 30-27 (Minn)
1968—Vikings, 26-13 (Mil)
Vikings, 14-10 (Minn)
1969—Vikings, 19-7 (Minn)
Vikings, 9-7 (Mil)
1970—Packers, 13-10 (Mil)
Vikings, 10-3 (Minn)
1971—Vikings, 24-13 (GB)
Vikings, 3-0 (Minn)
1972—Vikings, 27-13 (GB)
Packers, 23-7 (Minn)
1973—Vikings, 11-3 (Minn)
Vikings, 31-7 (GB)
1974—Vikings, 32-17 (GB)
Packers, 19-7 (Minn)
1975—Vikings, 28-17 (GB)
Vikings, 24-3 (Minn)
1976—Vikings, 17-10 (Mil)
Vikings, 20-9 (Minn)
1977—Vikings, 19-7 (Minn)
Vikings, 13-6 (GB)
1978—Vikings, 21-7 (Minn)
Tie, 10-10 (GB) OT
1979—Vikings, 27-21 (Minn) OT
Packers, 19-7 (Mil)
1980—Packers, 16-3 (GB)
Packers, 25-13 (Minn)
1981—Vikings, 30-13 (Mil)
Packers, 35-23 (Minn)
1982—Packers, 26-7 (Mil)
1983—Vikings, 20-17 (GB) OT
Packers, 29-21 (Minn)
1984—Packers, 45-17 (Mil)
Packers, 38-14 (Minn)
1985—Packers, 20-17 (Mil)
Packers, 27-17 (Minn)
(Points—Packers 965, Vikings 820)

GREEN BAY vs. NEW ENGLAND
Patriots lead series, 2-1
1973—Patriots, 33-24 (NE)
1979—Packers, 27-14 (GB)
1985—Patriots, 26-20 (NE)
(Points—Patriots 73, Packers 71)

GREEN BAY vs. NEW ORLEANS
Packers lead series, 10-2
1968—Packers, 29-7 (Mil)
1971—Saints, 29-21 (Mil)
1972—Packers, 30-20 (NO)
1973—Packers, 30-10 (Mil)
1975—Saints, 20-19 (NO)
1976—Packers, 32-27 (Mil)
1977—Packers, 24-20 (NO)
1978—Packers, 28-17 (Mil)
1979—Packers, 28-19 (Mil)
1981—Packers, 35-7 (NO)
1984—Packers, 23-13 (NO)
1985—Packers, 38-14 (Mil)
(Points—Packers 337, Saints 203)

GREEN BAY vs. *NY BULLDOGS
Packers won series, 1-0
1949—Packers, 19-0 (NY)
*Extinct team

GREEN BAY vs. NY GIANTS
Packers lead series, 25-18-2
1928—Giants, 6-0 (GB)
Packers, 7-0 (NY)
1929—Packers, 20-6 (NY)
1930—Packers, 14-7 (GB)
Giants, 13-6 (NY)
1931—Packers, 27-7 (GB)
Packers, 14-10 (NY)
1932—Packers, 13-0 (GB)
Giants, 6-0 (NY)
1933—Giants, 10-7 (Mil)
Giants, 17-6 (NY)
1934—Packers, 20-6 (Mil)
Giants, 17-3 (NY)
1935—Packers, 16-7 (GB)
1936—Packers, 26-14 (NY)
1937—Giants, 10-0 (NY)
1938—Giants, 15-3 (NY)
*Giants, 23-17 (NY)
1939—*Packers, 27-0 (Mil)
1940—Giants, 7-3 (NY)
1942—Tie, 21-21 (NY)
1943—Packers, 35-21 (NY)
1944—Giants, 24-0 (NY)
*Packers, 14-7 (NY)
1945—Packers, 23-14 (NY)
1947—Tie, 24-24 (NY)
1948—Giants, 49-3 (Mil)
1949—Giants, 30-10 (GB)
1952—Packers, 17-3 (NY)
1957—Giants, 31-17 (GB)
1959—Giants, 20-3 (NY)
1961—Packers, 20-17 (Mil)
*Packers, 37-0 (GB)
1962—*Packers, 16-7 (NY)
1967—Packers, 48-21 (NY)
1969—Packers, 20-10 (Mil)
1971—Giants, 42-40 (GB)
1973—Packers, 16-14 (New Haven)
1975—Packers, 40-14 (Mil)
1980—Giants, 27-21 (NY)
1981—Packers, 27-14 (NY)
Packers, 26-24 (Mil)
1982—Packers, 27-19 (NY)
1983—Giants, 27-3 (NY)
1985—Packers, 23-20 (GB)
(Points—Packers 760, Giants 681)
*NFL Championship

GREEN BAY vs. NY JETS
Jets lead series, 4-1
1973—Packers, 23-7 (Mil)
1979—Jets, 27-22 (GB)
1981—Jets, 28-3 (NY)
1982—Jets, 15-13 (NY)
1985—Jets, 24-3 (Mil)
(Points—Jets 101, Packers 64)

GREEN BAY vs. *NY YANKS
Yanks won series, 3-1
1950—Yanks, 44-31 (GB)
Yanks, 35-17 (NY)
1951—Packers, 29-27 (NY)
Yanks, 31-28 (GB)
(Points—Yanks 137, Packers 105)
*Extinct team

GREEN BAY vs. *PHILADELPHIA
Packers lead series, 18-5
1933—Packers, 35-9 (GB)
Packers, 10-0 (P)
1934—Packers, 19-6 (GB)
1935—Packers, 13-6 (P)
1937—Packers, 37-7 (Mil)
1939—Packers, 23-16 (P)
1940—Packers, 27-20 (GB)
1942—Packers, 7-0 (P)
1943—Packers, 38-28 (P)
1946—Packers, 19-7 (P)
1947—Eagles, 28-14 (P)
1951—Packers, 37-24 (GB)
1952—Packers, 12-10 (Mil)
1954—Packers, 37-14 (P)
1958—Packers, 38-35 (GB)
1960—**Eagles, 17-13 (P)
1962—Packers, 49-0 (P)
1968—Packers, 30-13 (GB)
1970—Packers, 30-17 (Mil)
1974—Eagles, 36-14 (P)
1976—Packers, 28-13 (GB)
1978—Eagles, 10-3 (P)
1979—Eagles, 21-10 (GB)
(Points—Packers 543, Eagles 337)
*Eagles known as Phil-Pitt in 1943
**NFL Championship

GREEN BAY vs. *PITTSBURGH
Packers lead series, 19-10
1933—Packers, 47-0 (GB)
1935—Packers, 27-0 (GB)
Packers, 34-14 (P)
1936—Packers, 42-10 (Mil)
1938—Packers, 20-0 (GB)
1940—Packers, 24-3 (Mil)
1941—Packers, 54-7 (P)
1942—Packers, 24-21 (Mil)
1943—Packers, 38-28 (Phil)
1944—Packers, 34-7 (GB)
Packers, 35-20 (Chi)
1946—Packers, 17-7 (GB)
1947—Steelers, 18-17 (Mil)
1948—Steelers, 38-7 (P)
1949—Steelers, 30-7 (Mil)
1951—Packers, 35-33 (Mil)
Steelers, 28-7 (P)
1953—Steelers, 31-14 (P)
1954—Steelers, 21-20 (GB)
1957—Packers, 27-10 (P)
1960—Packers, 19-13 (P)
1963—Packers, 33-14 (Mil)
1965—Packers, 41-9 (P)
1967—Steelers, 24-17 (GB)
1969—Packers, 38-34 (P)
1970—Packers, 20-12 (P)
1975—Packers, 16-13 (Mil)
1980—Steelers, 22-20 (P)
1983—Steelers, 25-21 (GB)
(Points—Packers 752, Steelers 495)

*Steelers known as Pirates prior to 1941, as Phil-Pitt in 1943, and as Card-Pitt in 1944

GREEN BAY vs. *ST. LOUIS
Packers lead series, 40-22-4
1921—Tie, 3-3 (C)
1922—Cardinals, 16-3 (C)
1924—Cardinals, 3-0 (C)
1925—Cardinals, 9-6 (C)
1926—Cardinals, 13-7 (GB)
Packers, 3-0 (C)
1927—Packers, 13-0 (GB)
Tie, 6-6 (C)
1928—Packers, 20-0 (GB)
1929—Packers, 9-2 (GB)
Packers, 7-6 (C)
Packers, 12-0 (C)
1930—Packers, 14-0 (GB)
Cardinals, 13-6 (C)
1931—Packers, 26-7 (GB)
Cardinals, 21-13 (C)
1932—Packers, 15-7 (GB)
Packers, 19-9 (C)
1933—Packers, 14-6 (C)
1934—Packers, 15-0 (GB)
Cardinals, 9-0 (Mil)
Cardinals, 6-0 (C)
1935—Cardinals, 7-6 (GB)
Cardinals, 3-0 (Mil)
Cardinals, 9-7 (C)
1936—Packers, 10-7 (GB)
Packers, 24-0 (Mil)
Tie, 0-0 (C)
1937—Cardinals, 14-7 (GB)
Packers, 34-13 (Mil)
1938—Packers, 28-7 (Mil)
Packers, 24-22 (Buffalo)
1939—Packers, 14-10 (GB)
Packers, 27-20 (Mil)
1940—Packers, 31-6 (Mil)
Packers, 28-7 (C)
1941—Packers, 14-13 (Mil)
Packers, 17-9 (GB)
1942—Packers, 17-13 (C)
Packers, 55-24 (GB)
1943—Packers, 28-7 (C)
Packers, 35-14 (Mil)
1944—Packers, 34-7 (GB)
Packers, 35-20 (C)
1945—Packers, 33-14 (GB)
1946—Packers, 19-7 (C)
Cardinals, 24-6 (GB)
1947—Cardinals, 14-10 (GB)
Cardinals, 21-20 (C)
1948—Cardinals, 17-7 (Mil)
Cardinals, 42-7 (C)
1949—Cardinals, 39-17 (Mil)
Cardinals, 41-21 (C)
1955—Packers, 31-14 (GB)
1956—Packers, 24-21 (C)
1962—Packers, 17-0 (Mil)
1963—Packers, 30-7 (StL)
1964—**Cardinals, 24-17 (M)
1967—Packers, 31-23 (StL)
1969—Packers, 45-28 (GB)
1971—Tie, 16-16 (StL)
1973—Packers, 25-21 (GB)
1976—Cardinals, 29-0 (StL)
1982—***Packers, 41-16 (GB)
1984—Packers, 24-23 (GB)
1985—Cardinals, 43-28 (StL)
(Points—Packers 1,155, Cardinals 852)

*Franchise in Chicago prior to 1960 and known as Card-Pitt in 1944
**Miami Playoff Bowl
***NFC First Round Playoff

GREEN BAY vs. *ST. LOUIS GUNNERS
Packers won series, 1-0
1934—Packers, 21-14 (StL)
*Extinct team

GREEN BAY vs. SAN DIEGO
Packers lead series, 3-1
1970—Packers, 22-20 (SD)
1974—Packers, 34-0 (GB)
1978—Packers, 24-3 (SD)
1984—Chargers, 34-28 (GB)
(Points—Packers 108, Chargers 57)

GREEN BAY vs. SAN FRANCISCO
49ers lead series, 22-20-1
1950—Packers, 25-21 (GB)
49ers, 30-14 (SF)
1951—49ers, 31-19 (SF)
1952—49ers, 24-14 (SF)
1953—49ers, 37-7 (Mil)
49ers, 48-14 (SF)
1954—49ers, 23-17 (Mil)
49ers, 35-0 (SF)
1955—Packers, 27-21 (Mil)
Packers, 28-7 (SF)
1956—49ers, 17-16 (GB)
49ers, 38-20 (SF)
1957—49ers, 24-14 (Mil)
49ers, 27-20 (SF)
1958—49ers, 33-12 (Mil)
49ers, 48-21 (SF)
1959—Packers, 21-20 (GB)
Packers, 36-14 (SF)
1960—Packers, 41-14 (Mil)
Packers, 13-0 (SF)
1961—Packers, 30-10 (GB)
49ers, 22-21 (SF)
1962—Packers, 31-13 (Mil)
Packers, 31-21 (SF)
1963—Packers, 28-10 (Mil)
Packers, 21-17 (SF)
1964—Packers, 24-14 (Mil)
49ers, 24-14 (SF)
1965—Packers, 27-10 (GB)
Tie, 24-24 (SF)
1966—49ers, 21-20 (SF)
Packers, 20-7 (Mil)
1967—Packers, 13-0 (GB)
1968—49ers, 27-20 (SF)
1969—Packers, 14-7 (Mil)
1970—49ers, 26-10 (SF)
1972—Packers, 34-24 (Mil)
1973—49ers, 20-6 (SF)
1974—49ers, 7-6 (SF)
1976—49ers, 26-14 (GB)
1977—Packers, 16-14 (Mil)
1980—Packers, 23-16 (Mil)
1981—49ers, 13-3 (Mil)
(Points—49ers 885, Packers 829)

GREEN BAY vs. SEATTLE
Packers lead series, 3-1
1976—Packers, 27-20 (Mil)
1978—Packers, 45-28 (Mil)
1981—Packers, 34-24 (GB)
1984—Seahawks, 30-24 (Mil)
(Points—Packers 130, Seahawks 102)

GREEN BAY vs. TAMPA BAY
Packers lead series, 8-6-1
1977—Packers, 13-0 (TB)
1978—Packers, 9-7 (GB)
Packers, 17-7 (TB)
1979—Buccaneers, 21-10 (GB)
Buccaneers, 21-3 (TB)
1980—Tie, 14-14 (TB) OT
Buccaneers, 20-17 (Mil)
1981—Buccaneers, 21-10 (GB)
Buccaneers, 37-3 (TB)
1983—Packers, 55-14 (GB)
Packers, 12-9 (TB) OT
1984—Buccaneers, 30-27 (TB) OT
Packers, 27-14 (GB)
1985—Packers, 21-0 (GB)
Packers, 20-17 (TB)
(Points—Packers 258, Buccaneers 232)

GREEN BAY vs. *WASHINGTON
Packers lead series, 14-11-1
1932—Packers, 21-0 (B)
1933—Tie, 7-7 (GB)
Redskins, 20-7 (B)
1934—Packers, 10-0 (B)
1936—Packers, 31-2 (GB)
Packers, 7-3 (B)
**Packers, 21-6 (New York)
1937—Redskins, 14-6 (W)
1939—Packers, 24-14 (Mil)

1941—Packers, 22-17 (W)
1943—Redskins, 33-7 (Mil)
1946—Packers, 20-7 (W)
1947—Packers, 27-10 (Mil)
1948—Redskins, 23-7 (Mil)
1949—Redskins, 30-0 (W)
1950—Packers, 35-21 (Mil)
1952—Packers, 35-20 (Mil)
1958—Redskins, 37-21 (W)
1959—Packers, 21-0 (GB)
1968—Packers, 27-7 (W)
1972—Redskins, 21-16 (W)
***Redskins, 16-3 (W)
1974—Redskins, 17-6 (GB)
1977—Redskins, 10-9 (W)
1979—Redskins, 38-21 (W)
1983—Packers, 48-47 (GB)
(Points—Packers 459, Redskins 420)
Franchise in Boston prior to 1937 and known as Braves prior to 1933
***NFL Championship*
****NFC Divisional Playoff*

HOUSTON vs. ATLANTA
Falcons lead series, 4-1;
See Atlanta vs. Houston
HOUSTON vs. BUFFALO
Oilers lead series, 17-9;
See Buffalo vs. Houston
HOUSTON vs. CHI. BEARS
Oilers lead series, 2-1;
See Chi. Bears vs. Houston
HOUSTON vs. CINCINNATI
Bengals lead series, 20-13-1;
See Cincinnati vs. Houston
HOUSTON vs. CLEVELAND
Browns lead series, 20-11;
See Cleveland vs. Houston
HOUSTON vs. DALLAS
Cowboys lead series, 4-1;
See Dallas vs. Houston
HOUSTON vs. DENVER
Oilers lead series, 18-10-1;
See Denver vs. Houston
HOUSTON vs. DETROIT
Oilers lead series, 2-1;
See Detroit vs. Houston
HOUSTON vs. GREEN BAY
Series tied, 2-2;
See Green Bay vs. Houston
HOUSTON vs. *INDIANAPOLIS
Colts lead series, 5-3
1970—Colts, 24-20 (H)
1973—Oilers, 31-27 (B)
1976—Colts, 38-14 (B)
1979—Oilers, 28-16 (B)
1980—Oilers, 21-16 (H)
1983—Colts, 20-10 (B)
1984—Colts, 35-21 (H)
1985—Colts, 34-16 (I)
(Points—Colts 210, Oilers 161)
Franchise in Baltimore prior to 1984
HOUSTON vs. *KANSAS CITY
Chiefs lead series, 20-12
1960—Oilers, 20-10 (H)
Texans, 24-0 (D)
1961—Texans, 26-21 (D)
Oilers, 38-7 (H)
1962—Texans, 31-7 (H)
Oilers, 14-6 (D)
**Texans, 20-17 (H) OT
1963—Chiefs, 28-7 (KC)
Oilers, 28-7 (H)
1964—Chiefs, 28-7 (KC)
Chiefs, 28-19 (H)
1965—Chiefs, 52-21 (KC)
Oilers, 38-36 (H)
1966—Chiefs, 48-23 (KC)
1967—Chiefs, 25-20 (H)
Oilers, 24-19 (KC)
1968—Chiefs, 26-21 (H)
Chiefs, 24-10 (KC)
1969—Chiefs, 24-0 (KC)
1970—Chiefs, 24-9 (KC)
1971—Chiefs, 20-16 (H)
1973—Chiefs, 38-14 (KC)
1974—Chiefs, 17-7 (H)
1975—Oilers, 17-13 (KC)
1977—Oilers, 34-20 (H)
1978—Oilers, 20-17 (KC)
1979—Oilers, 20-6 (H)
1980—Chiefs, 21-20 (KC)
1981—Chiefs, 23-10 (KC)
1983—Chiefs, 13-10 (H) OT
1984—Oilers, 17-16 (KC)
1985—Oilers, 23-20 (H)
(Points—Chiefs 717, Oilers 552)
Franchise in Dallas prior to 1963 and known as Texans
***AFL Championship*
HOUSTON vs. *LA RAIDERS
Raiders lead series, 21-10
1960—Oilers, 37-22 (O)
Raiders, 14-13 (H)
1961—Oilers, 55-0 (H)
Oilers, 47-16 (O)
1962—Oilers, 28-20 (O)
Oilers, 32-17 (H)
1963—Raiders, 24-13 (H)
Raiders, 52-49 (O)
1964—Oilers, 42-28 (H)
Raiders, 20-10 (O)
1965—Raiders, 21-17 (O)
Raiders, 33-21 (H)
1966—Oilers, 31-0 (H)
Raiders, 38-23 (O)
1967—Raiders, 19-7 (H)
**Raiders, 40-7 (O)
1968—Raiders, 24-15 (H)
1969—Raiders, 21-17 (O)
***Raiders, 56-7 (O)
1971—Raiders, 41-21 (O)
1972—Raiders, 34-0 (H)
1973—Raiders, 17-6 (H)
1975—Oilers, 27-26 (O)
1976—Raiders, 14-13 (H)
1977—Raiders, 34-29 (O)
1978—Raiders, 21-17 (O)
1979—Oilers, 31-17 (H)
1980—****Raiders, 27-7 (O)
1981—Oilers, 17-16 (H)
1983—Raiders, 20-6 (LA)
1984—Raiders, 24-14 (H)
(Points—Raiders 756, Oilers 659)
Franchise in Oakland prior to 1982
***AFL Championship*
****Inter-Divisional Playoff*
*****AFC Wild Card Game*
HOUSTON vs. LA RAMS
Rams lead series, 3-1
1973—Rams, 31-26 (H)
1978—Rams, 10-6 (H)
1981—Oilers, 27-20 (LA)
1984—Rams, 27-16 (LA)
(Points—Rams 88, Oilers 75)
HOUSTON vs. MIAMI
Oilers lead series, 10-9
1966—Dolphins, 20-13 (H)
Dolphins, 29-28 (M)
1967—Oilers, 17-14 (H)
Oilers, 41-10 (M)
1968—Oilers, 24-10 (M)
Dolphins, 24-7 (H)
1969—Oilers, 22-10 (H)
Oilers, 32-7 (M)
1970—Dolphins, 20-10 (H)
1972—Dolphins, 34-13 (M)
1975—Oilers, 20-19 (H)
1977—Dolphins, 27-7 (M)
1978—Oilers, 35-30 (H)
*Oilers, 17-9 (M)
1979—Oilers, 9-6 (M)
1981—Dolphins, 16-10 (H)
1983—Dolphins, 24-17 (H)
1984—Dolphins, 28-10 (M)
1985—Oilers, 26-23 (H)
(Points—Dolphins 360, Oilers 358)
AFC Wild Card Game
HOUSTON vs. MINNESOTA
Vikings lead series, 2-1
1974—Vikings, 51-10 (M)
1980—Oilers, 20-16 (H)
1983—Vikings, 34-14 (M)
(Points—Vikings 101, Oilers 44)
HOUSTON vs. *NEW ENGLAND
Patriots lead series 14-13-1
1960—Oilers, 24-10 (B)
Oilers, 37-21 (H)
1961—Tie, 31-31 (B)
Oilers, 27-15 (H)
1962—Patriots, 34-21 (B)
Oilers, 21-17 (H)
1963—Patriots, 45-3 (B)
Patriots, 46-28 (H)
1964—Patriots, 25-24 (B)
Patriots, 34-17 (H)
1965—Oilers, 31-10 (H)
Patriots, 42-14 (B)
1966—Patriots, 27-21 (B)
Patriots, 38-14 (H)
1967—Patriots, 18-7 (B)
Oilers, 27-6 (H)
1968—Oilers, 16-0 (B)
Oilers, 45-17 (H)
1969—Patriots, 24-0 (B)
Oilers, 27-23 (H)
1971—Patriots, 28-20 (NE)
1973—Patriots, 32-0 (H)
1975—Oilers, 7-0 (NE)
1978—Oilers, 26-23 (NE)
**Oilers, 31-14 (NE)
1980—Oilers, 38-34 (H)
1981—Patriots, 38-10 (NE)
1982—Patriots, 29-21 (NE)
(Points—Patriots 681, Oilers 588)
Franchise in Boston prior to 1971
***AFC Divisional Playoff*
HOUSTON vs. NEW ORLEANS
Series tied, 2-2-1
1971—Tie, 13-13 (H)
1976—Oilers, 31-26 (NO)
1978—Oilers, 17-12 (NO)
1981—Saints, 27-24 (H)
1984—Saints, 27-10 (H)
(Points—Saints 105, Oilers 95)
HOUSTON vs. NY GIANTS
Giants lead series, 3-0
1973—Giants, 34-14 (NY)
1982—Giants, 17-14 (NY)
1985—Giants, 35-14 (H)
(Points—Giants 86, Oilers 42)
HOUSTON vs. *NY JETS
Oilers lead series, 15-10-1
1960—Oilers, 27-21 (H)
Oilers, 42-28 (NY)
1961—Oilers, 49-13 (H)
Oilers, 48-21 (NY)
1962—Oilers, 56-17 (H)
Oilers, 44-10 (NY)
1963—Jets, 24-17 (NY)
Oilers, 31-27 (H)
1964—Jets, 24-21 (NY)
Oilers, 33-17 (H)
1965—Oilers, 27-21 (H)
Jets, 41-14 (NY)
1966—Jets, 52-13 (NY)
Oilers, 24-0 (H)
1967—Tie, 28-28 (NY)
1968—Jets, 20-14 (H)
Jets, 26-7 (NY)
1969—Jets, 26-17 (NY)
Jets, 34-26 (H)
1972—Oilers, 26-20 (H)
1974—Oilers, 27-22 (NY)
1977—Oilers, 20-0 (H)
1979—Oilers, 27-24 (H) OT
1980—Jets, 31-28 (NY) OT
1981—Jets, 33-17 (NY)
1984—Oilers, 31-20 (H)
(Points—Oilers 714, Jets 600)
Jets known as Titans prior to 1963
HOUSTON vs. PHILADELPHIA
Eagles lead series, 3-0
1972—Eagles, 18-17 (H)
1979—Eagles, 26-20 (H)
1982—Eagles, 35-14 (P)
(Points—Eagles 79, Oilers 51)
HOUSTON vs. PITTSBURGH
Steelers lead series, 24-9
1970—Oilers, 19-7 (P)
Steelers, 7-3 (H)
1971—Steelers, 23-16 (P)
Oilers, 29-3 (H)
1972—Steelers, 24-7 (P)
Steelers, 9-3 (H)
1973—Steelers, 36-7 (H)
Steelers, 33-7 (P)
1974—Steelers, 13-7 (H)
Oilers, 13-10 (P)
1975—Steelers, 24-17 (P)
Steelers, 32-9 (H)
1976—Steelers, 32-16 (P)
Steelers, 21-0 (H)
1977—Oilers, 27-10 (H)
Steelers, 27-10 (P)
1978—Oilers, 24-17 (P)
Steelers, 13-3 (H)
*Steelers, 34-5 (P)
1979—Steelers, 38-7 (P)
Oilers, 20-17 (H)
*Steelers, 27-13 (P)
1980—Steelers, 31-17 (P)
Oilers, 6-0 (H)
1981—Steelers, 26-13 (P)
Oilers, 21-20 (H)
1982—Steelers, 24-10 (H)
1983—Steelers, 40-28 (H)
Steelers, 17-10 (P)
1984—Steelers, 35-7 (P)
Oilers, 23-20 (H) OT
1985—Steelers, 20-0 (P)
Steelers, 30-7 (H)
(Points—Steelers 720, Oilers 404)
AFC Championship
HOUSTON vs. ST. LOUIS
Cardinals lead series, 3-1
1970—Cardinals, 44-0 (StL)
1974—Cardinals, 31-27 (H)
1979—Cardinals, 24-17 (H)
1985—Oilers, 20-10 (StL)
(Points—Cardinals 109, Oilers 64)
HOUSTON vs. *SAN DIEGO
Chargers lead series, 16-12-1
1960—Oilers, 38-28 (H)
Chargers, 24-21 (LA)
**Oilers, 24-16 (H)
1961—Chargers, 34-24 (SD)
Oilers, 33-13 (H)
**Oilers, 10-3 (SD)
1962—Oilers, 42-17 (SD)
Oilers, 33-27 (H)
1963—Chargers, 27-0 (SD)
Chargers 20-14 (H)
1964—Chargers, 27-21 (SD)
Chargers, 20-17 (H)
1965—Chargers, 31-14 (SD)
Chargers, 37-26 (H)
1966—Chargers, 28-22 (H)
1967—Chargers, 13-3 (SD)
Oilers, 24-17 (H)
1968—Chargers, 30-14 (SD)
1969—Chargers, 21-17 (H)
1970—Tie, 31-31 (SD)
1971—Oilers, 49-33 (H)
1972—Chargers, 34-20 (SD)
1974—Oilers, 21-14 (H)
1975—Oilers, 33-17 (H)
1976—Chargers, 30-27 (SD)
1978—Chargers, 45-24 (H)
1979—***Oilers, 17-14 (SD)
1984—Chargers, 31-14 (SD)
1985—Oilers, 37-35 (H)
(Points—Chargers 717, Oilers 670)
Franchise in Los Angeles prior to 1961
***AFL Championship*
****AFC Divisional Playoff*
HOUSTON vs. SAN FRANCISCO
49ers lead series, 3-2
1970—49ers, 30-20 (H)
1975—Oilers, 27-13 (SF)
1978—Oilers, 20-19 (H)
1981—49ers, 28-6 (SF)
1984—49ers, 34-21 (H)
(Points—49ers 124, Oilers 94)
HOUSTON vs. SEATTLE
Oilers lead series, 3-2
1977—Oilers, 22-10 (S)
1979—Seahawks, 34-14 (S)
1980—Seahawks, 26-7 (H)
1981—Oilers, 35-17 (H)
1982—Oilers, 23-21 (H)
(Points—Seahawks 108, Oilers 101)
HOUSTON vs. TAMPA BAY
Oilers lead series, 2-1
1976—Oilers, 20-0 (H)
1980—Oilers, 20-14 (H)
1983—Buccaneers, 33-24 (TB)
(Points—Oilers 64, Buccaneers 47)
HOUSTON vs. WASHINGTON
Series tied, 2-2
1971—Redskins, 22-13 (W)
1975—Oilers, 13-10 (H)
1979—Oilers, 29-27 (W)
1985—Redskins, 16-13 (W)
(Points—Redskins 75, Oilers 68)

INDIANAPOLIS vs. ATLANTA
Colts lead series, 8-0;
See Atlanta vs. Indianapolis
INDIANAPOLIS vs. BUFFALO
Series tied, 15-15-1;
See Buffalo vs. Indianapolis
INDIANAPOLIS vs. CHI. BEARS
Colts lead series, 21-14;
See Chi. Bears vs. Indianapolis
INDIANAPOLIS vs. CINCINNATI
Colts lead series, 5-4;
See Cincinnati vs. Indianapolis
INDIANAPOLIS vs. CLEVELAND
Browns lead series, 10-5;
See Cleveland vs. Indianapolis
INDIANAPOLIS vs. DALLAS
Cowboys lead series, 6-4;
See Dallas vs. Indianapolis
INDIANAPOLIS vs. DENVER
Broncos lead series, 6-1;
See Denver vs. Indianapolis
INDIANAPOLIS vs. DETROIT
Colts lead series, 17-16-2;
See Detroit vs. Indianapolis
INDIANAPOLIS vs. GREEN BAY
Packers lead series, 18-17-1;
See Green Bay vs. Indianapolis
INDIANAPOLIS vs. HOUSTON
Colts lead series, 5-3;
See Houston vs. Indianapolis
***INDIANAPOLIS vs. KANSAS CITY**
Chiefs lead series, 6-3
1970—Chiefs, 44-24 (B)
1972—Chiefs, 24-10 (KC)
1975—Colts, 28-14 (B)
1977—Colts, 17-6 (KC)
1979—Chiefs, 14-0 (KC)
Chiefs, 10-7 (B)
1980—Colts, 31-24 (KC)
Chiefs, 38-28 (B)
1985—Chiefs, 20-7 (KC)
(Points—Chiefs 194, Colts 152)
Franchise in Baltimore prior to 1984
***INDIANAPOLIS vs. **LA RAIDERS**
Raiders lead series, 4-2
1970—***Colts, 27-17 (B)
1971—Colts, 37-14 (O)
1973—Raiders, 34-21 (B)
1975—Raiders, 31-20 (B)
1977—****Raiders, 37-31 (B) OT
1984—Raiders, 21-7 (LA)
(Points—Raiders 154, Colts 143)
Franchise in Baltimore prior to 1984
***Franchise in Oakland prior to 1982*
****AFC Championship*
*****AFC Divisional Playoff*
***INDIANAPOLIS vs. LA RAMS**
Colts lead series, 20-14-2
1953—Rams, 21-13 (B)
Rams, 45-2 (LA)
1954—Rams, 48-0 (B)
Colts, 22-21 (LA)
1955—Tie, 17-17 (B)
Rams, 20-14 (LA)
1956—Colts, 56-21 (B)
Rams, 31-7 (LA)
1957—Colts, 31-14 (B)
Rams, 37-21 (LA)
1958—Colts, 34-7 (B)
Rams, 30-28 (LA)
1959—Colts, 35-21 (B)
Colts, 45-26 (LA)
1960—Colts, 31-17 (B)
Rams, 10-3 (LA)
1961—Colts, 27-24 (B)
Rams, 34-17 (LA)
1962—Colts, 30-27 (B)
Colts, 14-2 (LA)
1963—Rams, 17-16 (LA)
Colts, 19-16 (B)
1964—Colts, 35-20 (B)
Colts, 24-7 (LA)
1965—Colts, 35-20 (B)
Colts, 20-17 (LA)
1966—Colts, 17-3 (LA)
Rams, 23-7 (B)
1967—Tie, 24-24 (B)
Rams, 34-10 (LA)
1968—Colts, 27-10 (B)
Colts, 28-24 (LA)
1969—Rams, 27-20 (B)
Colts, 13-7 (LA)
1971—Colts, 24-17 (B)
1975—Rams, 24-13 (LA)
(Points—Colts 779, Rams 763)
Franchise in Baltimore prior to 1984
***INDIANAPOLIS vs. MIAMI**
Dolphins lead series, 24-9
1970—Colts, 35-0 (B)
Dolphins, 34-17 (M)
1971—Dolphins, 17-14 (M)
Colts, 14-3 (B)
**Dolphins, 21-0 (M)
1972—Dolphins, 23-0 (B)
Dolphins, 16-0 (M)
1973—Dolphins, 44-0 (M)
Colts, 16-3 (B)
1974—Dolphins, 17-7 (M)
Dolphins, 17-16 (B)
1975—Colts, 33-17 (M)
Colts, 10-7 (B) OT
1976—Colts, 28-14 (B)
Colts, 17-16 (M)
1977—Colts, 45-28 (B)
Dolphins, 17-6 (M)

1978—Dolphins, 42-0 (B)
Dolphins, 26-8 (M)
1979—Dolphins, 19-0 (M)
Dolphins, 28-24 (B)
1980—Colts, 30-17 (M)
Dolphins, 24-14 (B)
1981—Dolphins, 31-28 (B)
Dolphins, 27-10 (M)
1982—Dolphins, 24-20 (M)
Dolphins, 34-7 (B)
1983—Dolphins, 21-7 (B)
Dolphins, 37-0 (M)
1984—Dolphins, 44-7 (M)
Dolphins, 35-17 (I)
1985—Dolphins, 30-13 (M)
Dolphins, 34-20 (I)
(Points—Dolphins 767, Colts 463)
Franchise in Baltimore prior to 1984
**AFC Championship*

***INDIANAPOLIS vs. MINNESOTA**
Colts lead series, 12-5-1
1961—Colts, 34-33 (B)
Vikings, 28-20 (M)
1962—Colts, 34-7 (M)
Colts, 42-17 (B)
1963—Colts, 37-34 (M)
Colts, 41-10 (B)
1964—Vikings, 34-24 (M)
Colts, 17-14 (B)
1965—Colts, 35-16 (B)
Colts, 41-21 (M)
1966—Colts, 38-23 (M)
Colts, 20-17 (B)
1967—Tie, 20-20 (M)
1968—Colts, 21-9 (B)
**Colts, 24-14 (B)
1969—Vikings, 52-14 (M)
1971—Vikings, 10-3 (M)
1982—Vikings, 13-10 (M)
(Points—Colts 475, Vikings 372)
Franchise in Baltimore prior to 1984
Conference Championship

***INDIANAPOLIS vs. **NEW ENGLAND**
Patriots lead series, 16-15
1970—Colts, 14-6 (Bos)
Colts, 27-3 (Balt)
1971—Colts, 23-3 (NE)
Patriots, 21-17 (Balt)
1972—Colts, 24-17 (NE)
Colts, 31-0 (Balt)
1973—Patriots, 24-16 (NE)
Colts, 18-13 (Balt)
1974—Patriots, 42-3 (NE)
Patriots, 27-17 (Balt)
1975—Patriots, 21-10 (NE)
Colts, 34-21 (Balt)
1976—Colts, 27-13 (NE)
Patriots, 21-14 (Balt)
1977—Patriots, 17-3 (NE)
Colts, 30-24 (Balt)
1978—Colts, 34-27 (NE)
Patriots, 35-14 (Balt)
1979—Colts, 31-26 (Balt)
Patriots, 50-21 (NE)
1980—Patriots, 37-21 (Balt)
Patriots, 47-21 (NE)
1981—Colts, 29-28 (NE)
Colts, 23-21 (Balt)
1982—Patriots, 24-13 (Balt)
1983—Colts, 29-23 (NE) OT
Colts, 12-7 (B)
1984—Patriots, 50-17 (I)
Patriots, 16-10 (NE)
1985—Patriots, 34-15 (NE)
Patriots, 38-31 (I)
(Points—Patriots 736, Colts 629)
Franchise in Baltimore prior to 1984
**Franchise in Boston prior to 1971*

***INDIANAPOLIS vs. NEW ORLEANS**
Colts lead series, 3-0
1967—Colts, 30-10 (B)
1969—Colts, 30-10 (NO)
1973—Colts, 14-10 (B)
(Points—Colts 74, Saints 30)
Franchise in Baltimore prior to 1984

***INDIANAPOLIS vs. NY GIANTS**
Colts lead series, 7-3
1954—Colts, 20-14 (B)
1955—Giants, 17-7 (NY)
1958—Giants, 24-21 (NY)
**Colts, 23-17 (NY) OT
1959—**Colts, 31-16 (B)
1963—Giants, 37-28 (B)
1968—Colts, 26-0 (NY)
1971—Colts, 31-7 (NY)
1975—Colts, 21-0 (NY)
1979—Colts, 31-7 (NY)
(Points—Colts 239, Giants 139)
Franchise in Baltimore prior to 1984
**NFL Championship*

***INDIANAPOLIS vs. NY JETS**
Series tied, 16-16
1968—**Jets 16-7 (Miami)
1970—Colts, 29-22 (NY)
Colts, 35-20 (B)
1971—Colts, 22-0 (B)
Colts, 14-13 (NY)
1972—Jets, 44-34 (B)
Jets, 24-20 (NY)
1973—Jets, 34-10 (B)
Jets, 20-17 (NY)
1974—Colts, 35-20 (NY)
Jets, 45-38 (B)
1975—Colts, 45-28 (NY)
Colts, 52-19 (B)
1976—Colts, 20-0 (NY)
Colts, 33-16 (B)
1977—Colts, 20-12 (NY)
Colts, 33-12 (B)
1978—Jets, 33-10 (B)
Jets, 24-16 (NY)
1979—Colts, 10-8 (B)
Jets, 30-17 (NY)
1980—Colts, 17-14 (NY)
Colts, 35-21 (B)
1981—Jets, 41-14 (B)
Jets, 25-0 (NY)
1982—Jets, 37-0 (NY)
1983—Colts, 17-14 (NY)
Jets, 10-6 (B)
1984—Jets, 23-14 (I)
Colts, 9-5 (NY)
1985—Jets, 25-20 (NY)
Jets, 35-17 (I)
(Points—Jets 690, Colts 666)
Franchise in Baltimore prior to 1984
**Super Bowl III*

***INDIANAPOLIS vs. PHILADELPHIA**
Colts lead series, 6-5
1953—Eagles, 45-14 (P)
1965—Colts, 34-24 (B)
1966—**Colts, 20-14 (M)
1967—Colts, 38-6 (P)
1969—Colts, 24-20 (B)
1970—Colts, 29-10 (B)
1974—Eagles, 30-10 (P)
1978—Eagles, 17-14 (B)
1981—Eagles, 38-13 (P)
1983—Colts, 22-21 (P)
1984—Eagles, 16-7 (P)
(Points—Eagles 241, Colts 225)
Franchise in Baltimore prior to 1984
**Miami Playoff Bowl*

***INDIANAPOLIS vs. PITTSBURGH**
Steelers lead series, 9-4
1957—Steelers, 19-13 (B)
1968—Colts, 41-7 (P)
1971—Colts, 34-21 (B)
1974—Steelers, 30-0 (B)
1975—**Steelers, 28-10 (P)
1976—**Steelers, 40-14 (B)
1977—Colts, 31-21 (B)
1978—Steelers, 35-13 (P)
1979—Steelers, 17-13 (P)
1980—Steelers, 20-17 (B)
1983—Steelers, 24-13 (B)
1984—Colts, 17-16 (I)
1985—Steelers, 45-3 (P)
(Points—Steelers 323, Colts 219)
Franchise in Baltimore prior to 1984
**AFC Divisional Playoff*

***INDIANAPOLIS vs. ST. LOUIS**
Cardinals lead series 5-4
1961—Colts, 16-0 (B)
1964—Colts, 47-27 (B)
1968—Colts, 27-0 (B)
1972—Cardinals, 10-3 (B)
1976—Cardinals, 24-17 (StL)
1978—Colts, 30-17 (StL)
1980—Cardinals, 17-10 (B)
1981—Cardinals, 35-24 (B)
1984—Cardinals, 34-33 (I)
(Points—Colts 207, Cardinals 164)
Franchise in Baltimore prior to 1984

***INDIANAPOLIS vs. SAN DIEGO**
Chargers lead series, 4-2
1970—Colts, 16-14 (SD)
1972—Chargers, 23-20 (B)
1976—Colts, 37-21 (SD)
1981—Chargers, 43-14 (B)
1982—Chargers, 44-26 (SD)
1984—Chargers, 38-10 (I)
(Points—Chargers 183, Colts 123)
Franchise in Baltimore prior to 1984

***INDIANAPOLIS vs. SAN FRANCISCO**
Colts lead series, 21-14
1953—49ers, 38-21 (B)
49ers, 45-14 (SF)
1954—Colts, 17-13 (B)
49ers, 10-7 (SF)
1955—Colts, 26-14 (B)
49ers, 35-24 (SF)
1956—49ers, 20-17 (B)
49ers, 30-17 (SF)
1957—Colts, 27-21 (B)
49ers, 17-13 (SF)
1958—Colts, 35-27 (B)
49ers, 21-12 (SF)
1959—Colts, 45-14 (B)
Colts, 34-14 (SF)
1960—49ers, 30-22 (B)
49ers, 34-10 (SF)
1961—Colts, 20-17 (B)
Colts, 27-24 (SF)
1962—49ers, 21-13 (B)
Colts, 22-3 (SF)
1963—Colts, 20-14 (SF)
Colts, 20-3 (B)
1964—Colts, 37-7 (B)
Colts, 14-3 (SF)
1965—Colts, 27-24 (B)
Colts, 34-28 (SF)
1966—Colts, 36-14 (B)
Colts, 30-14 (SF)
1967—Colts, 41-7 (B)
Colts, 26-9 (SF)
1968—Colts, 27-10 (B)
Colts, 42-14 (SF)
1969—49ers, 24-21 (B)
49ers, 20-17 (SF)
1972—49ers, 24-21 (SF)
(Points—Colts 836, 49ers 663)
Franchise in Baltimore prior to 1984

***INDIANAPOLIS vs. SEATTLE**
Colts lead series, 2-0
1977—Colts, 29-14 (S)
1978—Colts, 17-14 (S)
(Points—Colts 46, Seahawks 28)
Franchise in Baltimore prior to 1984

***INDIANAPOLIS vs. TAMPA BAY**
Colts lead series, 2-1
1976—Colts, 42-17 (B)
1979—Buccaneers, 29-26 (B) OT
1985—Colts, 31-23 (TB)
(Points—Colts 99, Buccaneers 69)
Franchise in Baltimore prior to 1984

***INDIANAPOLIS vs. WASHINGTON**
Colts lead series, 15-6
1953—Colts, 27-17 (B)
1954—Redskins, 24-21 (W)
1955—Redskins, 14-13 (B)
1956—Colts, 19-17 (B)
1957—Colts, 21-17 (W)
1958—Colts, 35-10 (B)
1959—Redskins, 27-24 (W)
1960—Colts, 20-0 (B)
1961—Colts, 27-6 (W)
1962—Colts, 34-21 (B)
1963—Colts, 36-20 (W)
1964—Colts, 45-17 (B)
1965—Colts, 38-7 (W)
1966—Colts, 37-10 (B)
1967—Colts, 17-13 (W)
1969—Colts, 41-17 (B)
1973—Redskins, 22-14 (W)
1977—Colts, 10-3 (B)
1978—Colts, 21-17 (B)
1981—Redskins, 38-14 (W)
1984—Redskins, 35-7 (I)
(Points—Colts 521, Redskins 352)
Franchise in Baltimore prior to 1984

KANSAS CITY vs. ATLANTA
Chiefs lead series, 2-0;
See Atlanta vs. Kansas City

KANSAS CITY vs. BUFFALO
Bills lead series, 14-11-1;
See Buffalo vs. Kansas City

KANSAS CITY vs. CHI. BEARS
Bears lead series, 2-1;
See Chi. Bears vs. Kansas City

KANSAS CITY vs. CINCINNATI
Chiefs lead series, 8-7;
See Cincinnati vs. Kansas City

KANSAS CITY vs. CLEVELAND
Chiefs lead series, 5-4-1;
See Cleveland vs. Kansas City

KANSAS CITY vs. DALLAS
Cowboys lead series, 2-1;
See Dallas vs. Kansas City

KANSAS CITY vs. DENVER
Chiefs lead series, 33-18;
See Denver vs. Kansas City

KANSAS CITY vs. DETROIT
Series tied, 2-2;
See Detroit vs. Kansas City

KANSAS CITY vs. GREEN BAY
Series tied, 1-1-1;
See Green Bay vs. Kansas City

KANSAS CITY vs. HOUSTON
Chiefs lead series, 20-12;
See Houston vs. Kansas City

KANSAS CITY vs. INDIANAPOLIS
Chiefs lead series, 6-3;
See Indianapolis vs. Kansas City

***KANSAS CITY vs. **LA RAIDERS**
Raiders lead series, 30-21-2
1960—Texans, 34-16 (O)
Raiders, 20-19 (D)
1961—Texans, 42-35 (O)
Texans, 43-11 (D)
1962—Texans, 26-16 (O)
Texans, 35-7 (D)
1963—Raiders, 10-7 (O)
Raiders, 22-7 (KC)
1964—Chiefs, 21-9 (O)
Chiefs, 42-7 (KC)
1965—Raiders, 37-10 (O)
Chiefs, 14-7 (KC)
1966—Chiefs, 32-10 (O)
Raiders, 34-13 (KC)
1967—Raiders, 23-21 (O)
Raiders, 44-22 (KC)
1968—Chiefs, 24-10 (KC)
Raiders, 38-21 (O)
***Raiders, 41-6 (O)
1969—Raiders, 27-24 (KC)
Raiders, 10-6 (O)
****Chiefs, 17-7 (O)
1970—Tie, 17-17 (KC)
Raiders, 20-6 (O)
1971—Tie, 20-20 (O)
Chiefs, 16-14 (KC)
1972—Chiefs, 27-14 (KC)
Raiders, 26-3 (O)
1973—Chiefs, 16-3 (KC)
Raiders, 37-7 (O)
1974—Raiders, 27-7 (O)
Raiders, 7-6 (KC)
1975—Chiefs, 42-10 (KC)
Raiders, 28-20 (O)
1976—Raiders, 24-21 (KC)
Raiders, 21-10 (O)
1977—Raiders, 37-28 (KC)
Raiders, 21-20 (O)
1978—Raiders, 28-6 (O)
Raiders, 20-10 (KC)
1979—Chiefs, 35-7 (KC)
Chiefs, 24-21 (O)
1980—Raiders, 27-14 (KC)
Chiefs, 31-17 (O)
1981—Chiefs, 27-0 (KC)
Chiefs, 28-17 (O)
1982—Raiders, 21-16 (KC)
1983—Raiders, 21-20 (LA)
Raiders, 28-20 (KC)
1984—Raiders, 22-20 (KC)
Raiders, 17-7 (LA)
1985—Chiefs, 36-20 (KC)
Raiders, 19-10 (LA)
(Points—Chiefs 1,056, Raiders 1,052)
Franchise in Dallas prior to 1963 and known as Texans
**Franchise in Oakland prior to 1982*
***Division Playoff*
****AFL Championship*

KANSAS CITY vs. LA RAMS
Rams lead series, 3-0
1973—Rams, 23-13 (KC)
1982—Rams, 20-14 (LA)
1985—Rams, 16-0 (KC)
(Points—Rams 59, Chiefs 27)

KANSAS CITY vs. MIAMI
Chiefs lead series, 7-6
1966—Chiefs, 34-16 (KC)
Chiefs, 19-18 (M)
1967—Chiefs, 24-0 (M)
Chiefs, 41-0 (KC)
1968—Chiefs, 48-3 (M)
1969—Chiefs, 17-10 (KC)
1971—*Dolphins, 27-24 (KC) OT
1972—Dolphins, 20-10 (KC)
1974—Dolphins, 9-3 (M)
1976—Chiefs, 20-17 (M) OT
1981—Dolphins, 17-7 (KC)
1983—Dolphins, 14-6 (M)
1985—Dolphins, 31-0 (M)
(Points—Chiefs 253, Dolphins 182)
AFC Divisional Playoff

KANSAS CITY vs. MINNESOTA
Series tied, 2-2
1969—*Chiefs, 23-7 (New Orleans)
1970—Vikings, 27-10 (M)
1974—Vikings, 35-15 (KC)
1981—Chiefs, 10-6 (M)
(Points—Vikings 75, Chiefs 58)
Super Bowl IV

***KANSAS CITY vs. **NEW ENGLAND**
Chiefs lead series, 11-7-3
1960—Patriots, 42-14 (B)
Texans, 34-0 (D)
1961—Patriots, 18-17 (D)
Patriots, 28-21 (B)
1962—Texans, 42-28 (D)
Texans, 27-7 (B)
1963—Tie, 24-24 (B)
Chiefs, 35-3 (KC)
1964—Patriots, 24-7 (B)
Patriots, 31-24 (KC)
1965—Chiefs, 27-17 (KC)
Tie, 10-10 (B)
1966—Chiefs, 43-24 (B)
Tie, 27-27 (KC)
1967—Chiefs, 33-10 (B)
1968—Chiefs, 31-17 (KC)
1969—Chiefs, 31-0 (B)
1970—Chiefs, 23-10 (KC)
1973—Chiefs, 10-7 (NE)
1977—Patriots, 21-17 (NE)
1981—Patriots, 33-17 (NE)
(Points—Chiefs 514, Patriots 381)
Franchise located in Dallas prior to 1963 and known as Texans
**Franchise in Boston prior to 1971*

KANSAS CITY vs. NEW ORLEANS
Series tied, 2-2
1972—Chiefs, 20-17 (NO)
1976—Saints, 27-17 (KC)
1982—Saints, 27-17 (NO)
1985—Chiefs, 47-27 (NO)
(Points—Chiefs 101, Saints 98)

KANSAS CITY vs. NY GIANTS
Giants lead series, 4-1
1974—Giants, 33-27 (KC)
1978—Giants, 26-10 (NY)
1979—Giants, 21-17 (KC)
1983—Chiefs, 38-17 (KC)
1984—Giants, 28-27 (NY)
(Points—Giants 125, Chiefs 119)

***KANSAS CITY vs. **NY JETS**
Chiefs lead series, 13-11
1960—Titans, 37-35 (D)
Titans, 41-35 (NY)
1961—Titans, 28-7 (NY)
Texans, 35-24 (D)
1962—Texans, 20-17 (D)
Texans, 52-31 (NY)
1963—Jets, 17-0 (NY)
Chiefs, 48-0 (KC)
1964—Jets, 27-14 (NY)
Chiefs, 24-7 (KC)
1965—Chiefs, 14-10 (NY)
Jets, 13-10 (KC)
1966—Chiefs, 32-24 (NY)
1967—Chiefs, 42-18 (KC)
Chiefs, 21-7 (NY)
1968—Jets, 20-19 (KC)
1969—Chiefs, 34-16 (NY)
***Chiefs, 13-6 (NY)
1971—Jets, 13-10 (NY)
1974—Chiefs, 24-16 (KC)
1975—Jets, 30-24 (KC)
1982—Chiefs, 37-13 (KC)
1984—Jets, 17-16 (KC)
Jets, 28-7 (NY)
(Points—Chiefs 573, Jets 460)

*Franchise in Dallas prior to 1963 and known as Texans
**Jets known as Titans prior to 1963
***Inter-Divisional Playoff

KANSAS CITY vs. PHILADELPHIA
Eagles lead series, 1-0
1972—Eagles, 21-20 (KC)

KANSAS CITY vs. PITTSBURGH
Steelers lead series, 9-4
1970—Chiefs, 31-14 (P)
1971—Chiefs, 38-16 (KC)
1972—Steelers, 16-7 (P)
1974—Steelers, 34-24 (KC)
1975—Steelers, 28-3 (P)
1976—Steelers, 45-0 (KC)
1978—Steelers, 27-24 (P)
1979—Steelers, 30-3 (KC)
1980—Steelers, 21-16 (P)
1981—Chiefs, 37-33 (P)
1982—Steelers, 35-14 (P)
1984—Chiefs, 37-27 (P)
1985—Steelers, 36-28 (KC)
(Points—Steelers 362, Chiefs 262)

KANSAS CITY vs. ST. LOUIS
Chiefs lead series, 3-0-1
1970—Tie, 6-6 (KC)
1974—Chiefs, 17-13 (StL)
1980—Chiefs, 21-13 (StL)
1983—Chiefs, 38-14 (KC)
(Points—Chiefs 82, Cardinals 46)

***KANSAS CITY vs. **SAN DIEGO**
Chargers lead series, 26-24-1
1960—Chargers, 21-20 (LA)
Texans, 17-0 (D)
1961—Chargers, 26-10 (D)
Chargers, 24-14 (SD)
1962—Chargers, 32-28 (SD)
Texans, 26-17 (D)
1963—Chargers, 24-10 (SD)
Chargers, 38-17 (KC)
1964—Chargers, 28-14 (KC)
Chiefs, 49-6 (SD)
1965—Tie, 10-10 (SD)
Chiefs, 31-7 (KC)
1966—Chiefs, 24-14 (KC)
Chiefs, 27-17 (SD)
1967—Chargers, 45-31 (SD)
Chargers, 17-16 (KC)
1968—Chiefs, 27-20 (KC)
Chiefs, 40-3 (SD)
1969—Chiefs, 27-9 (SD)
Chiefs, 27-3 (KC)
1970—Chiefs, 26-14 (KC)
Chargers, 31-13 (SD)
1971—Chargers, 21-14 (SD)
Chiefs, 31-10 (KC)
1972—Chiefs, 26-14 (SD)
Chargers, 27-17 (KC)
1973—Chiefs, 19-0 (SD)
Chiefs, 33-6 (KC)
1974—Chiefs, 24-14 (SD)
Chargers, 14-7 (KC)
1975—Chiefs, 12-10 (SD)
Chargers, 28-20 (KC)
1976—Chargers, 30-16 (KC)
Chiefs, 23-20 (SD)
1977—Chargers, 23-7 (KC)
Chiefs, 21-16 (SD)
1978—Chargers, 29-23 (SD) OT
Chiefs, 23-0 (KC)
1979—Chargers, 20-14 (KC)
Chargers, 28-7 (SD)
1980—Chargers, 24-7 (KC)
Chargers, 20-7 (SD)
1981—Chargers, 42-31 (KC)
Chargers, 22-20 (SD)
1982—Chiefs, 19-12 (KC)
1983—Chargers, 17-14 (KC)
Chargers, 41-38 (SD)
1984—Chiefs, 31-13 (KC)
Chiefs, 42-21 (SD)
1985—Chargers, 31-20 (SD)
Chiefs, 38-34 (KC)
(Points—Chiefs 1,108, Chargers 993)
*Franchise in Dallas prior to 1963 and known as Texans
**Franchise in Los Angeles prior to 1961

KANSAS CITY vs. SAN FRANCISCO
49ers lead series, 3-1
1971—Chiefs, 26-17 (SF)
1975—49ers, 20-3 (KC)
1982—49ers, 26-13 (KC)
1985—49ers, 31-3 (SF)
(Points—49ers 94, Chiefs 45)

KANSAS CITY vs. SEATTLE
Chiefs lead series, 8-7
1977—Seahawks, 34-31 (KC)
1978—Seahawks, 13-10 (KC)
Seahawks, 23-19 (S)
1979—Chiefs, 24-6 (S)
Chiefs, 37-21 (KC)
1980—Seahawks, 17-16 (KC)
Chiefs, 31-30 (S)
1981—Chiefs, 20-14 (S)
Chiefs, 40-13 (KC)
1983—Chiefs, 17-13 (KC)
Seahawks, 51-48 (S) OT
1984—Seahawks, 45-0 (S)
Chiefs, 34-7 (KC)
1985—Chiefs, 28-7 (KC)
Seahawks, 24-6 (S)
(Points—Chiefs 361, Seahawks 318)

KANSAS CITY vs. TAMPA BAY
Chiefs lead series, 3-2
1976—Chiefs, 28-19 (TB)
1978—Buccaneers, 30-13 (KC)
1979—Buccaneers, 3-0 (TB)
1981—Chiefs, 19-10 (KC)
1984—Chiefs, 24-20 (KC)
(Points—Chiefs 84, Buccaneers 82)

KANSAS CITY vs. WASHINGTON
Chiefs lead series, 2-1
1971—Chiefs, 27-20 (KC)
1976—Chiefs, 33-30 (W)
1983—Redskins, 27-12 (W)
(Points—Redskins 77, Chiefs 72)

LA RAIDERS vs. ATLANTA
Raiders lead series, 4-1;
See Atlanta vs. LA Raiders

LA RAIDERS vs. BUFFALO
Raiders lead series, 12-11;
See Buffalo vs. LA Raiders

LA RAIDERS vs. CHI. BEARS
Raiders lead series, 3-2;
See Chi. Bears vs. LA Raiders

LA RAIDERS vs. CINCINNATI
Raiders lead series, 12-4;
See Cincinnati vs. LA Raiders

LA RAIDERS vs. CLEVELAND
Raiders lead series, 9-1;
See Cleveland vs. LA Raiders

LA RAIDERS vs. DALLAS
Raiders lead series, 2-1;
See Dallas vs. LA Raiders

LA RAIDERS vs. DENVER
Raiders lead series, 36-14-2;
See Denver vs. LA Raiders

LA RAIDERS vs. DETROIT
Raiders lead series, 3-2;
See Detroit vs. LA Raiders

LA RAIDERS vs. GREEN BAY
Raiders lead series, 4-1;
See Green Bay vs. LA Raiders

LA RAIDERS vs. HOUSTON
Raiders lead series, 21-10;
See Houston vs. LA Raiders

LA RAIDERS vs. INDIANAPOLIS
Raiders lead series, 4-2;
See Indianapolis vs. LA Raiders

LA RAIDERS vs. KANSAS CITY
Raiders lead series, 30-21-2;
See Kansas City vs. LA Raiders

***LA RAIDERS vs. LA RAMS**
Raiders lead series, 4-1
1972—Raiders, 45-17 (O)
1977—Rams, 20-14 (LA)
1979—Raiders, 24-17 (LA)
1982—Raiders, 37-31 (LA Raiders)
1985—Raiders, 16-6 (LA Rams)
(Points—Raiders 136, Rams 91)
*Franchise in Oakland prior to 1982

***LA RAIDERS vs. MIAMI**
Raiders lead series, 14-3-1
1966—Raiders, 23-14 (M)
Raiders, 21-10 (O)
1967—Raiders, 31-17 (O)
1968—Raiders, 47-21 (M)
1969—Raiders, 20-17 (O)
Tie, 20-20 (M)
1970—Dolphins, 20-13 (M)
**Raiders, 21-14 (O)
1973—Raiders, 12-7 (O)
***Dolphins, 27-10 (M)
1974—**Raiders, 28-26 (O)
1975—Raiders, 31-21 (M)
1978—Dolphins, 23-6 (M)
1979—Raiders, 13-3 (O)
1980—Raiders, 16-10 (O)
1981—Raiders, 33-17 (M)
1983—Raiders, 27-14 (LA)
1984—Raiders, 45-34 (M)
(Points—Raiders 417, Dolphins 315)
*Franchise in Oakland prior to 1982
**AFC Divisional Playoff
***AFC Championship

***LA RAIDERS vs. MINNESOTA**
Raiders lead series, 5-1
1973—Vikings, 24-16 (M)
1976—**Raiders, 32-14 (Pasadena)
1977—Raiders, 35-13 (O)
1978—Raiders, 27-20 (O)
1981—Raiders, 36-10 (M)
1984—Raiders, 23-20 (LA)
(Points—Raiders 169, Vikings 101)
*Franchise in Oakland prior to 1982
**Super Bowl XI

***LA RAIDERS vs. **NEW ENGLAND**
Series tied, 12-12-1
1960—Raiders, 27-14 (O)
Patriots, 34-28 (B)
1961—Patriots, 20-17 (B)
Patriots, 35-21 (O)
1962—Patriots, 26-16 (B)
Raiders, 20-0 (O)
1963—Patriots, 20-14 (O)
Patriots, 20-14 (B)
1964—Patriots, 17-14 (O)
Tie, 43-43 (B)
1965—Raiders, 24-10 (B)
Raiders, 30-21 (O)
1966—Patriots, 24-21 (B)
1967—Raiders, 35-7 (O)
Raiders, 48-14 (B)
1968—Raiders, 41-10 (O)
1969—Raiders, 38-23 (B)
1971—Patriots, 20-6 (NE)
1974—Raiders, 41-26 (O)
1976—Patriots, 48-17 (NE)
***Raiders, 24-21 (O)
1978—Patriots, 21-14 (O)
1981—Raiders, 27-17 (O)
1985—Raiders, 35-20 (NE)
***Patriots, 27-20 (LA)
(Points—Raiders 635, Patriots 538)
*Franchise in Oakland prior to 1982
**Franchise in Boston prior to 1971
***AFC Divisional Playoff

***LA RAIDERS vs. NEW ORLEANS**
Raiders lead series, 3-0-1
1971—Tie, 21-21 (NO)
1975—Raiders, 48-10 (O)
1979—Raiders, 42-35 (NO)
1985—Raiders, 23-13 (LA)
(Points—Raiders 134, Saints 79)
*Franchise in Oakland prior to 1982

***LA RAIDERS vs. NY GIANTS**
Raiders lead series, 3-0
1973—Raiders, 42-0 (O)
1980—Raiders, 33-17 (NY)
1983—Raiders, 27-12 (LA)
(Points—Raiders 102, Giants 29)
*Franchise in Oakland prior to 1982

***LA RAIDERS vs. **NY JETS**
Raiders lead series, 12-11-2
1960—Raiders, 28-27 (NY)
Titans, 31-28 (O)
1961—Titans, 14-6 (O)
Titans, 23-12 (NY)
1962—Titans, 28-17 (O)
Titans, 31-21 (NY)
1963—Jets, 10-7 (NY)
Raiders, 49-26 (O)
1964—Jets, 35-13 (NY)
Raiders, 35-26 (O)
1965—Tie, 24-24 (NY)
Raiders, 24-14 (O)
1966—Raiders, 24-21 (NY)
Tie, 28-28 (O)
1967—Jets, 27-14 (NY)
Raiders, 38-29 (O)
1968—Raiders, 43-32 (O)
***Jets, 27-23 (NY)
1969—Raiders, 27-14 (NY)
1970—Raiders, 14-13 (NY)
1972—Raiders, 24-16 (O)
1977—Raiders, 28-27 (NY)
1979—Jets, 28-19 (NY)
1982—****Jets, 17-14 (LA)
1985—Raiders, 31-0 (LA)
(Points—Raiders 591, Jets 568)
*Franchise in Oakland prior to 1982
**Jets known as Titans prior to 1963
***AFL Championship
****AFC Second Round Playoff

***LA RAIDERS vs. PHILADELPHIA**
Raiders lead series, 3-1
1971—Raiders, 34-10 (O)
1976—Raiders, 26-7 (P)
1980—Eagles, 10-7 (P)
**Raiders, 27-10 (NO)
(Points—Raiders 94, Eagles 37)
*Franchise in Oakland prior to 1982
**Super Bowl XV

***LA RAIDERS vs. PITTSBURGH**
Raiders lead series, 9-6
1970—Raiders, 31-14 (O)
1972—Steelers, 34-28 (P)
**Steelers, 13-7 (P)
1973—Steelers, 17-9 (O)
**Raiders, 33-14 (O)
1974—Raiders, 17-0 (P)
***Steelers, 24-13 (O)
1975—***Steelers, 16-10 (P)
1976—Raiders, 31-28 (O)
***Raiders, 24-7 (O)
1977—Raiders, 16-7 (P)
1980—Raiders, 45-34 (P)
1981—Raiders, 30-27 (O)
1983—**Raiders, 38-10 (LA)
1984—Steelers, 13-7 (LA)
(Points—Raiders 339, Steelers 258)
*Franchise in Oakland prior to 1982
**AFC Divisional Playoff
***AFC Championship

***LA RAIDERS vs. ST. LOUIS**
Series tied, 1-1
1973—Raiders, 17-10 (StL)
1983—Cardinals, 34-24 (LA)
(Points—Cardinals 44, Raiders 41)
*Franchise in Oakland prior to 1982

***LA RAIDERS vs. **SAN DIEGO**
Raiders lead series, 33-18-2
1960—Chargers, 52-28 (LA)
Chargers, 41-17 (O)
1961—Chargers, 44-0 (SD)
Chargers, 41-10 (O)
1962—Chargers, 42-33 (O)
Chargers, 31-21 (SD)
1963—Raiders, 34-33 (SD)
Raiders, 41-27 (O)
1964—Chargers, 31-17 (O)
Raiders, 21-20 (SD)
1965—Chargers, 17-6 (O)
Chargers, 24-14 (SD)
1966—Chargers, 29-20 (O)
Raiders, 41-19 (SD)
1967—Raiders, 51-10 (O)
Raiders, 41-21 (SD)
1968—Chargers, 23-14 (O)
Raiders, 34-27 (SD)
1969—Raiders, 24-12 (SD)
Raiders, 21-16 (O)
1970—Tie, 27-27 (SD)
Raiders, 20-17 (O)
1971—Raiders, 34-0 (SD)
Raiders, 34-33 (O)
1972—Tie, 17-17 (O)
Raiders, 21-19 (SD)
1973—Raiders, 27-17 (SD)
Raiders, 31-3 (O)
1974—Raiders, 14-10 (SD)
Raiders, 17-10 (O)
1975—Raiders, 6-0 (SD)
Raiders, 25-0 (O)
1976—Raiders, 27-17 (SD)
Raiders, 24-0 (O)
1977—Raiders, 24-0 (O)
Chargers, 12-7 (SD)
1978—Raiders, 21-20 (SD)
Chargers, 27-23 (O)
1979—Chargers, 30-10 (SD)
Raiders, 45-22 (O)
1980—Chargers, 30-24 (SD) OT
Raiders, 38-24 (O)
***Raiders, 34-27 (SD)
1981—Chargers, 55-21 (O)
Chargers, 23-10 (SD)
1982—Raiders, 28-24 (LA)
Raiders, 41-34 (SD)
1983—Raiders, 42-10 (SD)
Raiders, 30-14 (LA)
1984—Raiders, 33-30 (LA)
Raiders, 44-37 (SD)
1985—Raiders, 34-21 (LA)
Chargers, 40-34 (SD) OT
(Points—Raiders 1,355, Chargers 1,210)
*Franchise in Oakland prior to 1982
**Franchise in Los Angeles prior to 1961
***AFC Championship

***LA RAIDERS vs. SAN FRANCISCO**
Raiders lead series, 3-2
1970—49ers, 38-7 (O)
1974—Raiders, 35-24 (SF)
1979—Raiders, 23-10 (O)
1982—Raiders, 23-17 (SF)
1985—49ers, 34-10 (LA)
(Points—49ers 123, Raiders 98)
*Franchise in Oakland prior to 1982

***LA RAIDERS vs. SEATTLE**
Series tied, 9-9
1977—Raiders, 44-7 (O)
1978—Seahawks, 27-7 (S)
Seahawks, 17-16 (O)
1979—Seahawks, 27-10 (S)
Seahawks, 29-24 (O)
1980—Raiders, 33-14 (O)
Raiders, 19-17 (S)
1981—Raiders, 20-10 (O)
Raiders, 32-31 (S)
1982—Raiders, 28-23 (LA)
1983—Seahawks, 38-36 (S)
Seahawks, 34-21 (LA)
**Raiders, 30-14 (LA)
1984—Raiders, 28-14 (LA)
Seahawks, 17-14 (S)
***Seahawks, 13-7 (S)
1985—Seahawks, 33-3 (S)
Raiders, 13-3 (LA)
(Points—Raiders 385, Seahawks 368)
*Franchise in Oakland prior to 1982
**AFC Championship
***AFC Wild Card Game

***LA RAIDERS vs. TAMPA BAY**
Raiders lead series, 2-0
1976—Raiders, 49-16 (O)
1981—Raiders, 18-16 (O)
(Points—Raiders 67, Buccaneers 32)
*Franchise in Oakland prior to 1982

***LA RAIDERS vs. WASHINGTON**
Raiders lead series, 4-1
1970—Raiders, 34-20 (O)
1975—Raiders, 26-23 (W) OT
1980—Raiders, 24-21 (O)
1983—Redskins, 37-35 (W)
**Raiders, 38-9 (Tampa)
(Points—Raiders 157, Redskins 110)
*Franchise in Oakland prior to 1982
**Super Bowl XVIII

LA RAMS vs. ATLANTA
Rams lead series, 28-8-2;
See Atlanta vs. LA Rams

LA RAMS vs. *1950 BALTIMORE
Rams won series, 1-0
See *1950 Baltimore vs. LA Rams
*Extinct team

LA RAMS vs. *BOSTON YANKS
Yanks won series, 2-1
See *Boston Yanks vs. LA Rams
*Extinct team

LA RAMS vs. *BROOKLYN DODGERS
Dodgers won series, 3-1
See *Brooklyn Dodgers vs. Cleveland Rams
*Extinct team

LA RAMS vs. BUFFALO
Rams lead series, 3-1;
See Buffalo vs. LA Rams

LA RAMS vs. CHI. BEARS
Bears lead series, 43-27-3;
See Chi. Bears vs. LA Rams

LA RAMS vs. CINCINNATI
Bengals lead series, 3-2;
See Cincinnati vs. LA Rams

LA RAMS vs. CLEVELAND
Series tied, 8-8;
See Cleveland vs. LA Rams

LA RAMS vs. DALLAS
Rams lead series, 11-10;
See Dallas vs. LA Rams

LA RAMS vs. *DALLAS TEXANS
Rams won series, 2-0
See *Dallas Texans vs. LA Rams
*Extinct team

LA RAMS vs. DENVER
Rams lead series, 3-2;
See Denver vs. LA Rams

LA RAMS vs. DETROIT
Rams lead series, 36-34-1;
See Detroit vs. LA Rams

LA RAMS vs. GREEN BAY
Rams lead series, 39-34-2;

See Green Bay vs. LA. Rams
LA RAMS vs. HOUSTON
Rams lead series, 3-1;
See Houston vs. LA Rams
LA RAMS vs. INDIANAPOLIS
Colts lead series, 20-14-2;
See Indianapolis vs. LA Rams
LA RAMS vs. KANSAS CITY
Rams lead series, 3-0;
See Kansas City vs. LA Rams
LA RAMS VS. LA RAIDERS
Raiders lead series, 4-1;
See LA Raiders vs. LA Rams
LA RAMS vs. MIAMI
Dolphins lead series, 3-1
1971—Dolphins, 20-14 (LA)
1976—Rams, 31-28 (M)
1980—Dolphins, 35-14 (LA)
1983—Dolphins, 30-14 (M)
(Points—Dolphins 113, Rams 73)
LA RAMS vs. MINNESOTA
Vikings lead series, 15-12-2
1961—Rams, 31-17 (LA)
Vikings, 42-21 (M)
1962—Vikings, 38-14 (LA)
Tie, 24-24 (M)
1963—Rams, 27-24 (LA)
Vikings, 21-13 (M)
1964—Rams, 22-13 (LA)
Vikings, 34-13 (M)
1965—Vikings, 38-35 (LA)
Vikings, 24-13 (M)
1966—Vikings, 35-7 (M)
Rams, 21-6 (LA)
1967—Rams, 39-3 (LA)
1968—Rams, 31-3 (M)
1969—Vikings, 20-13 (LA)
*Vikings, 23-20 (M)
1970—Vikings, 13-3 (M)
1972—Vikings, 45-41 (LA)
1973—Vikings, 10-9 (M)
1974—Rams, 20-17 (LA)
**Vikings, 14-10 (M)
1976—Tie, 10-10 (M) OT
**Vikings, 24-13 (M)
1977—Rams, 35-3 (LA)
***Vikings, 14-7 (LA)
1978—Rams, 34-17 (M)
***Rams, 34-10 (LA)
1979—Rams, 27-21 (LA) OT
1985—Rams, 13-10 (LA)
(Points—Rams 600, Vikings 573)
Conference Championship
***NFC Championship*
****NFC Divisional Playoff*
LA RAMS vs. NEW ENGLAND
Patriots lead series, 2-1
1974—Patriots, 20-14 (NE)
1980—Rams, 17-14 (NE)
1983—Patriots, 21-7 (LA)
(Points—Patriots 55, Rams 38)
LA RAMS vs. NEW ORLEANS
Rams lead series, 23-9
1967—Rams 27-13 (NO)
1969—Rams, 36-17 (LA)
1970—Rams, 30-17 (NO)
Rams, 34-16 (LA)
1971—Saints, 24-20 (NO)
Rams, 45-28 (LA)
1972—Rams, 34-14 (LA)
Saints, 19-16 (NO)
1973—Rams, 29-7 (LA)
Rams, 24-13 (NO)
1974—Rams, 24-0 (LA)
Saints, 20-7 (NO)
1975—Rams, 38-14 (LA)
Rams, 14-7 (NO)
1976—Rams, 16-10 (NO)
Rams, 33-14 (LA)
1977—Rams, 14-7 (LA)
Saints, 27-26 (NO)
1978—Rams, 26-20 (NO)
Saints, 10-3 (LA)
1979—Rams, 35-17 (NO)
Saints, 29-14 (LA)
1980—Rams, 45-31 (LA)
Rams, 27-7 (NO)
1981—Saints, 23-17 (NO)
Saints, 21-13 (LA)
1983—Rams, 30-27 (LA)
Rams, 26-24 (NO)
1984—Rams, 28-10 (NO)
Rams, 34-21 (LA)
1985—Rams, 28-10 (LA)
Saints, 29-3 (NO)
(Points—Rams 796, Saints 546)
LA RAMS vs. *NY BULLDOGS
Rams won series, 1-0
1949—Rams, 42-20 (LA)
Extinct team
***LA RAMS vs. NY GIANTS**
Rams lead series, 16-8
1938—Giants, 28-0 (NY)
1940—Rams, 13-0 (NY)
1941—Giants, 49-14 (NY)
1945—Rams, 21-17 (NY)
1946—Rams, 31-21 (NY)
1947—Rams, 34-10 (LA)
1948—Rams, 52-37 (NY)
1953—Rams, 21-7 (LA)
1954—Rams, 17-16 (NY)
1959—Giants, 23-21 (LA)
1961—Giants, 24-14 (NY)
1966—Rams, 55-14 (LA)
1968—Rams, 24-21 (LA)
1970—Rams, 31-3 (NY)
1973—Rams, 40-6 (LA)
1976—Rams, 24-10 (LA)
1978—Rams, 20-17 (NY)
1979—Giants, 20-14 (LA)
1980—Rams, 28-7 (NY)
1981—Giants, 10-7 (NY)
1983—Rams, 16-6 (NY)
1984—Rams, 33-12 (LA)
**Giants, 16-13 (LA)
1985—Giants, 24-19 (NY)
(Points—Rams 562, Giants 398)
**Franchise in Cleveland prior to 1946*
***NFC Wild Card Game*
LA RAMS vs. NY JETS
Series tied, 2-2
1970—Jets, 31-20 (LA)
1974—Rams, 20-13 (NY)
1980—Rams, 38-13 (LA)
1983—Jets, 27-24 (NY) OT
(Points—Rams 102, Jets 84)
LA RAMS vs. *NY YANKS
Rams won series, 4-0
1950—Rams, 45-28 (LA)
Rams, 43-35 (NY)
1951—Rams, 54-14 (LA)
Rams, 48-21 (LA)
(Points—Rams 190, Yanks 98)
***LA RAMS vs. PHILADELPHIA**
Rams lead series, 15-9-1
1937—Rams, 21-3 (P)
1939—Rams, 35-13 (Colorado Springs)
1940—Rams, 21-13 (C)
1942—Rams, 24-14 (Akron)
1944—Eagles, 26-13 (P)
1945—Eagles, 28-14 (P)
1946—Eagles, 25-14 (LA)
1947—Eagles, 14-7 (P)
1948—Tie, 28-28 (LA)
1949—Eagles, 38-14 (P)
**Eagles, 14-0 (LA)
1950—Eagles, 56-20 (P)
1955—Rams, 23-21 (P)
1956—Rams, 27-7 (LA)
1957—Rams, 17-13 (LA)
1959—Eagles, 23-20 (P)
1964—Rams, 20-10 (LA)
1967—Rams, 33-17 (LA)
1969—Rams, 23-17 (P)
1972—Rams, 34-3 (P)
1975—Rams, 42-3 (P)
1977—Rams, 20-0 (LA)
1978—Rams, 16-14 (P)
1983—Eagles, 13-9 (P)
1985—Rams, 17-6 (P)
(Points—Rams 512, Eagles 419)
**Franchise in Cleveland prior to 1946*
***NFL Championship*
***LA RAMS vs. **PITTSBURGH**
Rams lead series, 14-4-2
1938—Rams, 13-7 (New Orleans)
1939—Tie, 14-14 (C)
1941—Rams, 17-14 (Akron)
1944—Rams, 30-28 (P)
Rams, 33-6 (Chi)
1947—Rams, 48-7 (P)
1948—Rams, 31-14 (LA)
1949—Tie, 7-7 (P)
1952—Rams, 28-14 (LA)
1955—Rams, 27-26 (LA)
1956—Steelers, 30-13 (P)
1961—Rams, 24-14 (LA)
1964—Rams, 26-14 (P)
1968—Rams, 45-10 (LA)
1971—Rams, 23-14 (P)
1975—Rams, 10-3 (LA)
1978—Rams, 10-7 (LA)
1979—***Steelers, 31-19 (Pasadena)
1981—Steelers, 24-0 (P)
1984—Steelers, 24-14 (P)
(Points—Rams 432, Steelers 308)
**Franchise in Cleveland prior to 1946*
***Steelers known as Pirates prior to 1941 and as Card-Pitt in 1944*
****Super Bowl XIV*
***LA RAMS vs. **ST. LOUIS**
Rams lead series, 22-15-2
1937—Cardinals, 6-0 (Clev)
Cardinals, 13-7 (Chi)
1938—Cardinals, 7-6 (Clev)
Cardinals, 31-17 (Chi)
1939—Rams, 24-0 (Chi)
Rams, 14-0 (Clev)
1940—Rams, 26-14 (Clev)
Cardinals, 17-7 (Chi)
1941—Rams, 10-6 (Clev)
Cardinals, 7-0 (Chi)
1942—Cardinals, 7-0 (Chi)
Rams, 7-3 (Clev)
1944—Rams, 30-28 (Pitt)
Rams, 33-6 (Chi)
1945—Rams, 21-0 (Clev)
Rams, 35-21 (Chi)
1946—Cardinals, 34-10 (Chi)
Rams, 17-14 (LA)
1947—Rams, 27-7 (LA)
Cardinals, 17-10 (Chi)
1948—Cardinals, 27-22 (LA)
Cardinals, 27-24 (Chi)
1949—Tie, 28-28 (Chi)
Cardinals, 31-27 (LA)
1951—Rams, 45-21 (LA)
1953—Tie, 24-24 (Chi)
1954—Rams, 28-17 (LA)
1958—Rams, 20-14 (Chi)
1960—Cardinals, 43-21 (LA)
1965—Rams, 27-3 (StL)
1968—Rams, 24-13 (StL)
1970—Rams, 34-13 (LA)
1972—Cardinals, 24-14 (StL)
1975—***Rams, 35-23 (LA)
1976—Cardinals, 30-28 (LA)
1979—Rams, 21-0 (LA)
1980—Rams, 21-13 (StL)
1984—Rams, 16-13 (StL)
1985—Rams, 46-14 (LA)
(Points—Rams 806, Cardinals 616)
**Franchise in Cleveland prior to 1946*
***Franchise in Chicago prior to 1960 and known as Card-Pitt in 1944*
****NFC Divisional Playoff*
LA RAMS vs. SAN DIEGO
Rams lead series, 2-1
1970—Rams, 37-10 (LA)
1975—Rams, 13-10 (SD) OT
1979—Chargers, 40-16 (LA)
(Points—Rams 66, Chargers 60)
LA RAMS vs. SAN FRANCISCO
Rams lead series, 44-26-2
1950—Rams, 35-14 (SF)
Rams, 28-21 (LA)
1951—49ers, 44-17 (SF)
Rams, 23-16 (LA)
1952—Rams, 35-9 (LA)
Rams, 34-21 (SF)
1953—49ers, 31-30 (SF)
49ers, 31-27 (LA)
1954—Tie, 24-24 (LA)
Rams, 42-34 (SF)
1955—Rams, 23-14 (SF)
Rams, 27-14 (LA)
1956—49ers, 33-30 (SF)
Rams, 30-6 (LA)
1957—49ers, 23-20 (SF)
Rams, 37-24 (LA)
1958—Rams, 33-3 (SF)
Rams, 56-7 (LA)
1959—49ers, 34-0 (SF)
49ers, 24-16 (LA)
1960—49ers, 13-9 (SF)
49ers, 23-7 (LA)
1961—49ers, 35-0 (SF)
Rams, 17-7 (LA)
1962—Rams, 28-14 (SF)
49ers, 24-17 (LA)
1963—Rams, 28-21 (LA)
Rams, 21-17 (SF)
1964—Rams, 42-14 (LA)
49ers, 28-7 (SF)
1965—49ers, 45-21 (LA)
49ers, 30-27 (SF)
1966—Rams, 34-3 (LA)
49ers, 21-13 (SF)
1967—49ers, 27-24 (LA)
Rams, 17-7 (SF)
1968—Rams, 24-10 (LA)
Tie, 20-20 (SF)
1969—Rams, 27-21 (SF)
Rams, 41-30 (LA)
1970—49ers, 20-6 (LA)
Rams, 30-13 (SF)
1971—Rams, 20-13 (SF)
Rams, 17-6 (LA)
1972—Rams, 31-7 (LA)
Rams, 26-16 (SF)
1973—Rams, 40-20 (SF)
Rams, 31-13 (LA)
1974—Rams, 37-14 (LA)
Rams, 15-13 (SF)
1975—Rams, 23-14 (SF)
49ers, 24-23 (LA)
1976—49ers, 16-0 (LA)
Rams, 23-3 (SF)
1977—Rams, 34-14 (LA)
Rams, 23-10 (SF)
1978—Rams, 27-10 (LA)
Rams, 31-28 (SF)
1979—Rams, 27-24 (LA)
Rams, 26-20 (SF)
1980—Rams, 48-26 (LA)
Rams, 31-17 (SF)
1981—49ers, 20-17 (SF)
49ers, 33-31 (LA)
1982—49ers, 30-24 (LA)
Rams, 21-20 (SF)
1983—Rams, 10-7 (SF)
49ers, 45-35 (LA)
1984—49ers, 33-0 (LA)
49ers, 19-16 (SF)
1985—49ers, 28-14 (LA)
Rams, 27-20 (SF)
(Points—Rams 1,755, 49ers 1,433)
LA RAMS vs. SEATTLE
Rams lead series, 3-0
1976—Rams, 45-6 (LA)
1979—Rams, 24-0 (S)
1985—Rams, 35-24 (S)
(Points—Rams 104, Seahawks 30)
LA RAMS vs. TAMPA BAY
Rams lead series, 5-2
1977—Rams, 31-0 (LA)
1978—Rams, 26-23 (LA)
1979—Buccaneers, 21-6 (TB)
*Rams, 9-0 (TB)
1980—Buccaneers, 10-9 (TB)
1984—Rams, 34-33 (TB)
1985—Rams, 31-27 (TB)
(Points—Rams 146, Buccaneers 114)
**NFC Championship*
***LA RAMS vs. WASHINGTON**
Redskins lead series, 14-5-1
1937—Redskins, 16-7 (C)
1938—Redskins, 37-13 (W)
1941—Redskins, 17-13 (W)
1942—Redskins, 33-14 (W)
1944—Redskins, 14-10 (W)
1945—**Rams, 15-14 (C)
1948—Rams, 41-13 (W)
1949—Rams, 53-27 (LA)
1951—Redskins, 31-21 (W)
1962—Redskins, 20-14 (W)
1963—Redskins, 37-14 (LA)
1967—Tie, 28-28 (LA)
1969—Rams, 24-13 (W)
1971—Redskins, 38-24 (LA)
1974—Redskins, 23-17 (LA)
***Rams, 19-10 (LA)
1977—Redskins, 17-14 (W)
1981—Redskins, 30-7 (LA)
1983—Redskins, 42-20 (LA)
***Redskins, 51-7 (W)
(Points—Redskins 511, Rams 375)
**Franchise in Cleveland prior to 1946*
***NFL Championship*
****NFC Divisional Playoff*

MIAMI vs. ATLANTA
Dolphins lead series, 4-0;
See Atlanta vs. Miami
MIAMI vs. BUFFALO
Dolphins lead series, 32-7-1;
See Buffalo vs. Miami
MIAMI vs. CHI. BEARS
Dolphins lead series, 4-0;
See Chi. Bears vs. Miami
MIAMI vs. CINCINNATI
Dolphins lead series, 7-3;
See Cincinnati vs. Miami
MIAMI vs. CLEVELAND
Series tied, 3-3;
See Cleveland vs. Miami
MIAMI vs. DALLAS
Dolphins lead series, 3-2;
See Dallas vs. Miami
MIAMI vs. DENVER
Dolphins lead series, 5-2-1;
See Denver vs. Miami
MIAMI vs. DETROIT
Dolphins lead series, 2-1;
See Detroit vs. Miami
MIAMI vs. GREEN BAY
Dolphins lead series, 4-0;
See Green Bay vs. Miami
MIAMI vs. HOUSTON
Oilers lead series, 10-9;
See Houston vs. Miami
MIAMI vs. INDIANAPOLIS
Dolphins lead series, 24-9;
See Indianapolis vs. Miami
MIAMI vs. KANSAS CITY
Chiefs lead series, 7-6;
See Kansas City vs. Miami
MIAMI vs. LA RAIDERS
Raiders lead series, 14-3-1;
See LA Raiders vs. Miami
MIAMI vs. LA RAMS
Dolphins lead series, 3-1;
See LA Rams vs. Miami
MIAMI vs. MINNESOTA
Dolphins lead series, 4-1
1972—Dolphins, 16-14 (Minn)
1973—*Dolphins, 24-7 (Houston)
1976—Vikings, 29-7 (Mia)
1979—Dolphins, 27-12 (Minn)
1982—Dolphins, 22-14 (Mia)
(Points—Dolphins 96, Vikings 76)
**Super Bowl VIII*
MIAMI vs. *NEW ENGLAND
Dolphins lead series, 25-15
1966—Patriots, 20-14 (M)
1967—Patriots, 41-10 (B)
Dolphins, 41-32 (M)
1968—Dolphins, 34-10 (B)
Dolphins, 38-7 (M)
1969—Dolphins, 17-16 (B)
Patriots, 38-23 (Tampa)
1970—Patriots, 27-14 (B)
Dolphins, 37-20 (M)
1971—Dolphins, 41-3 (M)
Patriots, 34-13 (NE)
1972—Dolphins, 52-0 (M)
Dolphins, 37-21 (NE)
1973—Dolphins, 44-23 (M)
Dolphins, 30-14 (NE)
1974—Patriots, 34-24 (NE)
Dolphins, 34-27 (M)
1975—Dolphins, 22-14 (NE)
Dolphins, 20-7 (M)
1976—Patriots, 30-14 (NE)
Dolphins, 10-3 (M)
1977—Dolphins, 17-5 (M)
Patriots, 14-10 (NE)
1978—Patriots, 33-24 (NE)
Dolphins, 23-3 (M)
1979—Patriots, 28-13 (NE)
Dolphins, 39-24 (M)
1980—Patriots, 34-0 (NE)
Dolphins, 16-13 (M) OT
1981—Dolphins, 30-27 (NE) OT
Dolphins, 24-14 (M)
1982—Patriots, 3-0 (NE)
**Dolphins, 28-13 (M)
1983—Dolphins, 34-24 (M)
Patriots, 17-6 (NE)
1984—Dolphins, 28-7 (M)
Dolphins, 44-24 (NE)
1985—Patriots, 17-13 (NE)
Dolphins, 30-27 (M)
***Patriots, 31-14 (M)
(Points—Dolphins 962, Patriots 779)
**Franchise in Boston prior to 1971*
***AFC First Round Playoff*
****AFC Championship*
MIAMI vs. NEW ORLEANS
Dolphins lead series, 3-1
1970—Dolphins, 21-10 (M)
1974—Dolphins, 21-0 (NO)
1980—Dolphins, 21-16 (M)
1983—Saints, 17-7 (NO)
(Points—Dolphins 70, Saints 43)
MIAMI vs. NY GIANTS
Dolphins lead series, 1-0
1972—Dolphins, 23-13 (NY)
MIAMI vs. NY JETS
Dolphins lead series, 22-18-1

1966—Jets, 19-14 (M)
Jets, 30-13 (NY)
1967—Jets, 29-7 (NY)
Jets, 33-14 (M)
1968—Jets, 35-17 (NY)
Jets, 31-7 (M)
1969—Jets, 34-31 (NY)
Jets, 27-9 (M)
1970—Dolphins, 20-6 (NY)
Dolphins, 16-10 (M)
1971—Jets, 14-10 (M)
Dolphins, 30-14 (NY)
1972—Dolphins, 27-17 (NY)
Dolphins, 28-24 (M)
1973—Dolphins, 31-3 (M)
Dolphins, 24-14 (NY)
1974—Dolphins, 21-17 (M)
Jets, 17-14 (NY)
1975—Dolphins, 43-0 (NY)
Dolphins, 27-7 (M)
1976—Dolphins, 16-0 (M)
Dolphins, 27-7 (NY)
1977—Dolphins, 21-17 (M)
Dolphins, 14-10 (NY)
1978—Jets, 33-20 (NY)
Jets, 24-13 (M)
1979—Jets, 33-27 (NY)
Jets, 27-24 (M)
1980—Jets, 17-14 (NY)
Jets, 24-17 (M)
1981—Tie, 28-28 (M) OT
Jets, 16-15 (NY)
1982—Dolphins, 45-28 (NY)
Dolphins, 20-19 (M)
*Dolphins, 14-0 (M)
1983—Dolphins, 32-14 (NY)
Dolphins, 34-14 (M)
1984—Dolphins, 31-17 (NY)
Dolphins, 28-17 (M)
1985—Jets, 23-7 (NY)
Dolphins, 21-17 (M)
(Points—Dolphins 871, Jets 766)
AFC Championship

MIAMI vs. PHILADELPHIA
Dolphins lead series, 3-2
1970—Eagles, 24-17 (P)
1975—Dolphins, 24-16 (M)
1978—Eagles, 17-3 (P)
1981—Dolphins, 13-10 (M)
1984—Dolphins, 24-23 (M)
(Points—Eagles 90, Dolphins 81)

MIAMI vs. PITTSBURGH
Dolphins lead series, 7-3
1971—Dolphins, 24-21 (M)
1972—*Dolphins, 21-17 (P)
1973—Dolphins, 30-26 (M)
1976—Steelers, 14-3 (P)
1979—**Steelers, 34-14 (P)
1980—Steelers, 23-10 (P)
1981—Dolphins, 30-10 (M)
1984—Dolphins, 31-7 (P)
*Dolphins, 45-28 (M)
1985—Dolphins, 24-20 (M)
(Points—Dolphins 232, Steelers 200)
**AFC Championship*
***AFC Divisional Playoff*

MIAMI vs. ST. LOUIS
Dolphins lead series, 5-0
1972—Dolphins, 31-10 (M)
1977—Dolphins, 55-14 (StL)
1978—Dolphins, 24-10 (M)
1981—Dolphins, 20-7 (StL)
1984—Dolphins, 36-28 (StL)
(Points—Dolphins 166, Cardinals 69)

MIAMI vs. SAN DIEGO
Chargers lead series, 8-5
1966—Chargers, 44-10 (SD)
1967—Chargers, 24-0 (SD)
Dolphins, 41-24 (M)
1968—Chargers, 34-28 (SD)
1969—Chargers, 21-14 (M)
1972—Dolphins, 24-10 (M)
1974—Dolphins, 28-21 (SD)
1977—Chargers, 14-13 (M)
1978—Dolphins, 28-21 (SD)
1980—Chargers, 27-24 (M) OT
1981—*Chargers, 41-38 (M) OT
1982—**Dolphins, 34-13 (M)
1984—Chargers, 34-28 (SD) OT
(Points—Chargers 328, Dolphins 310)
**AFC Divisional Playoff*
***AFC Second Round Playoff*

MIAMI vs. SAN FRANCISCO
Dolphins lead series, 4-1
1973—Dolphins, 21-13 (M)
1977—Dolphins, 19-15 (SF)
1980—Dolphins, 17-13 (M)
1983—Dolphins, 20-17 (SF)
1984—*49ers, 38-16 (Stanford)
(Points—49ers 96, Dolphins 93)
**Super Bowl XIX*

MIAMI vs. SEATTLE
Dolphins lead series, 3-1
1977—Dolphins, 31-13 (M)
1979—Dolphins, 19-10 (M)
1983—*Seahawks, 27-20 (M)
1984—*Dolphins, 31-10 (M)
(Points—Dolphins 101, Seahawks 60)
**AFC Divisional Playoff*

MIAMI vs. TAMPA BAY
Dolphins lead series, 2-1
1976—Dolphins, 23-20 (TB)
1982—Buccaneers, 23-17 (TB)
1985—Dolphins, 41-38 (M)
(Points—Dolphins 81, Buccaneers 81)

MIAMI vs. WASHINGTON
Dolphins lead series, 4-2
1972—*Dolphins, 14-7 (Los Angeles)
1974—Redskins, 20-17 (W)
1978—Dolphins, 16-0 (W)
1981—Dolphins, 13-10 (M)
1982—**Redskins, 27-17 (Pasadena)
1984—Dolphins, 35-17 (W)
(Points—Dolphins 112, Redskins 81)
**Super Bowl VII*
***Super Bowl XVII*

MINNESOTA vs. ATLANTA
Vikings lead series, 9-6;
See Atlanta vs. Minnesota

MINNESOTA vs. BUFFALO
Vikings lead series, 4-1;
See Buffalo vs. Minnesota

MINNESOTA vs. CHI. BEARS
Vikings lead series, 25-22-2;
See Chi. Bears vs. Minnesota

MINNESOTA vs. CINCINNATI
Series tied, 2-2;
See Cincinnati vs. Minnesota

MINNESOTA vs. CLEVELAND
Vikings lead series, 7-1;
See Cleveland vs. Minnesota

MINNESOTA vs. DALLAS
Cowboys lead series, 11-5;
See Dallas vs. Minnesota

MINNESOTA vs. DENVER
Series tied, 2-2;
See Denver vs. Minnesota

MINNESOTA vs. DETROIT
Vikings lead series, 30-17-2;
See Detroit vs. Minnesota

MINNESOTA vs. GREEN BAY
Series tied, 24-24-1;
See Green Bay vs. Minnesota

MINNESOTA vs. HOUSTON
Vikings lead series, 2-1;
See Houston vs. Minnesota

MINNESOTA vs. INDIANAPOLIS
Colts lead series, 12-5-1;
See Indianapolis vs. Minnesota

MINNESOTA vs. KANSAS CITY
Series tied, 2-2;
See Kansas City vs. Minnesota

MINNESOTA vs. LA RAIDERS
Raiders lead series, 5-1;
See LA Raiders vs. Minnesota

MINNESOTA vs. LA RAMS
Vikings lead series, 15-12-2;
See LA Rams vs. Minnesota

MINNESOTA vs. MIAMI
Dolphins lead series, 4-1;
See Miami vs. Minnesota

MINNESOTA vs. *NEW ENGLAND
Patriots lead series, 2-1
1970—Vikings, 35-14 (B)
1974—Patriots, 17-14 (M)
1979—Patriots, 27-23 (NE)
(Points—Vikings 72, Patriots 58)
**Franchise in Boston prior to 1971*

MINNESOTA vs. NEW ORLEANS
Vikings lead series, 8-4
1968—Saints, 20-17 (NO)
1970—Vikings, 26-0 (M)
1971—Vikings, 23-10 (NO)
1972—Vikings, 37-6 (M)
1974—Vikings, 29-9 (M)
1975—Vikings, 20-7 (NO)
1976—Vikings, 40-9 (NO)
1978—Saints, 31-24 (NO)
1980—Vikings, 23-20 (NO)
1981—Vikings, 20-10 (M)
1983—Saints, 17-16 (NO)
1985—Saints, 30-23 (M)
(Points—Vikings 298, Saints 169)

MINNESOTA vs. NY GIANTS
Vikings lead series, 6-1
1964—Vikings, 30-21 (NY)
1965—Vikings, 40-14 (M)
1967—Vikings, 27-24 (M)
1969—Giants, 24-23 (NY)
1971—Vikings, 17-10 (NY)
1973—Vikings, 31-7 (New Haven)
1976—Vikings, 24-7 (M)
(Points—Vikings 192, Giants 107)

MINNESOTA vs. NY JETS
Jets lead series, 3-1
1970—Jets, 20-10 (NY)
1975—Vikings, 29-21 (M)
1979—Jets, 14-7 (NY)
1982—Jets 42-14 (M)
(Points—Jets 97, Vikings 60)

MINNESOTA vs. PHILADELPHIA
Vikings lead series, 9-4
1962—Vikings, 31-21 (M)
1963—Vikings, 34-13 (P)
1968—Vikings, 24-17 (P)
1971—Vikings, 13-0 (P)
1973—Vikings, 28-21 (M)
1976—Vikings, 31-12 (P)
1978—Vikings, 28-27 (M)
1980—Eagles, 42-7 (M)
*Eagles, 31-16 (P)
1981—Vikings, 35-23 (M)
1984—Eagles, 19-17 (P)
1985—Vikings, 28-23 (P)
Eagles, 37-35 (M)
(Points—Vikings 327, Eagles 286)
**NFC Divisional Playoff*

MINNESOTA vs. PITTSBURGH
Vikings lead series, 5-4
1962—Steelers, 39-31 (P)
1964—Vikings, 30-10 (M)
1967—Vikings, 41-27 (P)
1969—Vikings, 52-14 (M)
1972—Steelers, 23-10 (P)
1974—*Steelers, 16-6 (New Orleans)
1976—Vikings, 17-6 (M)
1980—Steelers, 23-17 (M)
1983—Vikings, 17-14 (P)
(Points—Vikings 221, Steelers 172)
**Super Bowl IX*

MINNESOTA vs. ST. LOUIS
Cardinals lead series, 7-3
1963—Cardinals, 56-14 (M)
1967—Cardinals, 34-24 (M)
1969—Vikings, 27-10 (StL)
1972—Cardinals, 19-17 (M)
1974—Vikings, 28-24 (StL)
*Vikings, 30-14 (M)
1977—Cardinals, 27-7 (M)
1979—Cardinals, 37-7 (StL)
1981—Cardinals, 30-17 (StL)
1983—Cardinals, 41-31 (StL)
(Points—Cardinals 292, Vikings 202)
**NFC Divisional Playoff*

MINNESOTA vs. SAN DIEGO
Series tied, 3-3
1971—Chargers, 30-14 (SD)
1975—Vikings, 28-13 (M)
1978—Chargers, 13-7 (M)
1981—Vikings, 33-31 (SD)
1984—Chargers, 42-13 (M)
1985—Vikings, 21-17 (M)
(Points—Chargers 146, Vikings 116)

MINNESOTA vs. SAN FRANCISCO
Vikings lead series, 13-12-1
1961—49ers, 38-24 (M)
49ers, 38-28 (SF)
1962—49ers, 21-7 (SF)
49ers, 35-12 (M)
1963—Vikings, 24-20 (SF)
Vikings, 45-14 (M)
1964—Vikings, 27-22 (SF)
Vikings, 24-7 (M)
1965—Vikings, 42-41 (SF)
49ers, 45-24 (M)
1966—Tie, 20-20 (SF)
Vikings, 28-3 (SF)
1967—49ers, 27-21 (M)
1968—Vikings, 30-20 (SF)
1969—Vikings, 10-7 (M)
1970—*49ers, 17-14 (M)
1971—49ers, 13-9 (M)
1972—49ers, 20-17 (SF)
1973—Vikings, 17-13 (SF)
1975—Vikings, 27-17 (M)
1976—49ers, 20-16 (SF)
1977—Vikings, 28-27 (M)
1979—Vikings, 28-22 (M)
1983—49ers, 48-17 (M)
1984—49ers, 51-7 (SF)
1985—Vikings, 28-21 (M)
(Points—49ers 627, Vikings 574)
**NFC Divisional Playoff*

MINNESOTA vs. SEATTLE
Seahawks lead series, 2-1
1976—Vikings, 27-21 (M)
1978—Seahawks, 29-28 (S)
1984—Seahawks, 20-12 (M)
(Points—Seahawks 70, Vikings 67)

MINNESOTA vs. TAMPA BAY
Vikings lead series, 11-5
1977—Vikings, 9-3 (TB)
1978—Buccaneers, 16-10 (M)
Vikings, 24-7 (TB)
1979—Buccaneers, 12-10 (M)
Vikings, 23-22 (TB)
1980—Vikings, 38-30 (M)
Vikings, 21-10 (TB)
1981—Buccaneers, 21-13 (TB)
Vikings, 25-10 (M)
1982—Vikings, 17-10 (M)
1983—Vikings, 19-16 (TB) OT
Buccaneers, 17-12 (M)
1984—Buccaneers, 35-31 (TB)
Vikings, 27-24 (M)
1985—Vikings, 31-16 (TB)
Vikings, 26-7 (M)
(Points—Vikings 336, Buccaneers 256)

MINNESOTA vs. WASHINGTON
Vikings lead series, 5-4
1968—Vikings, 27-14 (M)
1970—Vikings, 19-10 (W)
1972—Redskins, 24-21 (M)
1973—*Vikings, 27-20 (M)
1975—Redskins, 31-30 (W)
1976—*Vikings 35-20 (M)
1980—Vikings, 39-14 (W)
1982—**Redskins, 21-7 (W)
1984—Redskins, 31-17 (M)
(Points—Vikings 222, Redskins 185)
**NFC Divisional Playoff*
***NFC Second Round Playoff*

NEW ENGLAND vs. ATLANTA
Series tied, 2-2;
See Atlanta vs. New England

NEW ENGLAND vs. BUFFALO
Patriots lead series, 28-23-1;
See Buffalo vs. New England

NEW ENGLAND vs. CHI. BEARS
Bears lead series, 3-2;
See Chi. Bears vs. New England

NEW ENGLAND vs. CINCINNATI
Patriots lead series, 6-3;
See Cincinnati vs. New England

NEW ENGLAND vs. CLEVELAND
Browns lead series, 6-2;
See Cleveland vs. New England

NEW ENGLAND vs. DALLAS
Cowboys lead series, 5-0;
See Dallas vs. New England

NEW ENGLAND vs. DENVER
Patriots lead series, 12-11;
See Denver vs. New England

NEW ENGLAND vs. DETROIT
Series tied, 2-2;
See Detroit vs. New England

NEW ENGLAND vs. GREEN BAY
Patriots lead series, 2-1;
See Green Bay vs. New England

NEW ENGLAND vs. HOUSTON
Patriots lead series, 14-13-1;
See Houston vs. New England

NEW ENGLAND vs. INDIANAPOLIS
Patriots lead series, 16-15;
See Indianapolis vs. New England

NEW ENGLAND vs. KANSAS CITY
Chiefs lead series, 11-7-3;
See Kansas City vs. New England

NEW ENGLAND vs. LA RAIDERS
Series tied, 12-12-1;
See LA Raiders vs. New England

NEW ENGLAND vs. LA RAMS
Patriots lead series, 2-1;
See LA Rams vs. New England

NEW ENGLAND vs. MIAMI
Dolphins lead series, 25-15;
See Miami vs. New England

NEW ENGLAND vs. MINNESOTA
Patriots lead series, 2-1;
See Minnesota vs. New England

NEW ENGLAND vs. NEW ORLEANS
Patriots lead series, 4-0
1972—Patriots, 17-10 (NO)
1976—Patriots, 27-6 (NE)
1980—Patriots, 38-27 (NO)
1983—Patriots, 7-0 (NE)
(Points—Patriots 89, Saints 43)

***NEW ENGLAND vs. NY GIANTS**
Series tied, 1-1
1970—Giants, 16-0 (B)
1974—Patriots, 28-20 (New Haven)
(Points—Giants 36, Patriots 28)
**Franchise in Boston prior to 1971*

***NEW ENGLAND vs. **NY JETS**
Jets lead series, 29-22-1
1960—Patriots, 28-24 (NY)
Patriots, 38-21 (B)
1961—Titans, 21-20 (B)
Titans, 37-30 (NY)
1962—Patriots, 43-14 (NY)
Patriots, 24-17 (B)
1963—Patriots, 38-14 (B)
Jets, 31-24 (NY)
1964—Patriots, 26-10 (B)
Jets, 35-14 (NY)
1965—Jets, 30-20 (B)
Patriots, 27-23 (NY)
1966—Tie, 24-24 (B)
Jets, 38-28 (NY)
1967—Jets, 30-23 (NY)
Jets, 29-24 (B)
1968—Jets, 47-31 (Birmingham)
Jets, 48-14 (NY)
1969—Jets, 23-14 (B)
Jets, 23-17 (NY)
1970—Jets, 31-21 (B)
Jets, 17-3 (NY)
1971—Patriots, 20-0 (NE)
Jets, 13-6 (NY)
1972—Jets, 41-13 (NE)
Jets, 34-10 (NY)
1973—Jets, 9-7 (NE)
Jets, 33-13 (NY)
1974—Patriots, 24-0 (NY)
Jets, 21-16 (NE)
1975—Jets, 36-7 (NY)
Jets, 30-28 (NE)
1976—Patriots, 41-7 (NE)
Patriots, 38-24 (NY)
1977—Jets, 30-27 (NY)
Patriots, 24-13 (NE)
1978—Patriots, 55-21 (NE)
Patriots, 19-17 (NY)
1979—Patriots, 56-3 (NE)
Jets, 27-26 (NY)
1980—Patriots, 21-11 (NY)
Patriots, 34-21 (NE)
1981—Jets, 28-24 (NY)
Jets, 17-6 (NE)
1982—Jets, 31-7 (NE)
1983—Patriots, 23-13 (NE)
Jets, 26-3 (NY)
1984—Patriots, 28-21 (NY)
Patriots, 30-20 (NE)
1985—Patriots, 20-13 (NE)
Jets, 16-13 (NY) OT
***Patriots, 26-14 (NY)
(Points—Patriots 1,196, Jets 1,177)
**Franchise in Boston prior to 1971*
***Jets known as Titans prior to 1963*
****AFC Wild Card Game*

NEW ENGLAND vs. PHILADELPHIA
Eagles lead series, 3-2
1973—Eagles, 24-23 (P)
1977—Patriots, 14-6 (NE)
1978—Patriots, 24-14 (NE)
1981—Eagles, 13-3 (P)
1984—Eagles, 27-17 (P)
(Points—Eagles 84, Patriots 81)

NEW ENGLAND vs. PITTSBURGH
Steelers lead series, 5-2
1972—Steelers, 33-3 (P)
1974—Steelers, 21-17 (NE)
1976—Patriots, 30-27 (P)
1979—Steelers, 16-13 (NE) OT
1981—Steelers, 27-21 (P) OT
1982—Steelers, 37-14 (P)
1983—Patriots, 28-23 (P)
(Points—Steelers 184, Patriots 126)

***NEW ENGLAND vs. ST. LOUIS**
Cardinals lead series, 4-1
1970—Cardinals, 31-0 (StL)
1975—Cardinals, 24-17 (StL)
1978—Patriots, 16-6 (StL)
1981—Cardinals, 27-20 (NE)
1984—Cardinals, 33-10 (NE)
(Points—Cardinals 121, Patriots 63)
**Franchise in Boston prior to 1971*
***NEW ENGLAND vs. **SAN DIEGO**
Patriots lead series, 13-12-2
1960—Patriots, 35-0 (LA)
Chargers, 45-16 (B)
1961—Chargers, 38-27 (B)
Patriots, 41-0 (SD)
1962—Patriots, 24-20 (B)
Patriots, 20-14 (SD)
1963—Chargers, 17-13 (SD)
Chargers, 7-6 (B)
***Chargers, 51-10 (SD)
1964—Patriots, 33-28 (SD)
Chargers, 26-17 (B)
1965—Tie, 10-10 (B)
Patriots, 22-6 (SD)
1966—Chargers, 24-0 (SD)
Patriots, 35-17 (B)
1967—Chargers, 28-14 (SD)
Tie, 31-31 (SD)
1968—Chargers, 27-17 (B)
1969—Chargers, 13-10 (B)
Chargers, 28-18 (SD)
1970—Chargers, 16-14 (B)
1973—Patriots, 30-14 (NE)
1975—Patriots, 33-19 (SD)
1977—Patriots, 24-20 (SD)
1978—Patriots, 28-23 (NE)
1979—Patriots, 27-21 (NE)
1983—Patriots, 37-21 (NE)
(Points—Patriots 592, Chargers 564)
**Franchise in Boston prior to 1971*
***Franchise in Los Angeles prior to 1961*
****AFL Championship*
NEW ENGLAND vs. SAN FRANCISCO
49ers lead series, 3-1
1971—49ers, 27-10 (SF)
1975—Patriots, 24-16 (NE)
1980—49ers, 21-17 (SF)
1983—49ers, 33-13 (NE)
(Points—49ers 97, Patriots 64)
NEW ENGLAND vs. SEATTLE
Patriots lead series, 5-1
1977—Patriots, 31-0 (NE)
1980—Patriots, 37-31 (S)
1982—Patriots, 16-0 (S)
1983—Seahawks, 24-6 (S)
1984—Patriots, 38-23 (NE)
1985—Patriots, 20-13 (S)
(Points—Patriots 148, Seahawks 91)
NEW ENGLAND vs. TAMPA BAY
Patriots lead series, 2-0
1976—Patriots, 31-14 (TB)
1985—Patriots, 32-14 (TB)
(Points—Patriots 63, Buccaneers 28)
NEW ENGLAND vs. WASHINGTON
Redskins lead series, 3-1
1972—Patriots, 24-23 (NE)
1978—Redskins, 16-14 (NE)
1981—Redskins, 24-22 (W)
1984—Redskins, 26-10 (NE)
(Points—Redskins 89, Patriots 70)

NEW ORLEANS vs. ATLANTA
Falcons lead series, 23-11;
See Atlanta vs. New Orleans
NEW ORLEANS vs. BUFFALO
Bills lead series, 2-1;
See Buffalo vs. New Orleans
NEW ORLEANS vs. CHI. BEARS
Bears lead series, 7-4;
See Chi. Bears vs. New Orleans
NEW ORLEANS vs. CINCINNATI
Bengals lead series, 3-2;
See Cincinnati vs. New Orleans
NEW ORLEANS vs. CLEVELAND
Browns lead series, 8-1;
See Cleveland vs. New Orleans
NEW ORLEANS vs. DALLAS
Cowboys lead series, 11-1;
See Dallas vs. New Orleans
NEW ORLEANS vs. DENVER
Broncos lead series, 4-0;
See Denver vs. New Orleans
NEW ORLEANS vs. DETROIT
Series tied, 4-4-1;
See Detroit vs. New Orleans
NEW ORLEANS vs. GREEN BAY
Packers lead series, 10-2;
See Green Bay vs. New Orleans
NEW ORLEANS vs. HOUSTON
Series tied, 2-2-1;
See Houston vs. New Orleans
NEW ORLEANS vs. INDIANAPOLIS
Colts lead series, 3-0;
See Indianapolis vs. New Orleans
NEW ORLEANS vs. KANSAS CITY
Series tied, 2-2;
See Kansas City vs. New Orleans
NEW ORLEANS vs. LA RAIDERS
Raiders lead series, 3-0-1;
See LA Raiders vs. New Orleans
NEW ORLEANS vs. LA RAMS
Rams lead series, 23-9;
See LA Rams vs. New Orleans
NEW ORLEANS vs. MIAMI
Dolphins lead series, 3-1;
See Miami vs. New Orleans
NEW ORLEANS vs. MINNESOTA
Vikings lead series, 8-4;
See Minnesota vs. New Orleans
NEW ORLEANS vs. NEW ENGLAND
Patriots lead series, 4-0;
See New England vs. New Orleans
NEW ORLEANS vs. NY GIANTS
Giants lead series, 6-5
1967—Giants, 27-21 (NY)
1968—Giants, 38-21 (NY)
1969—Saints, 25-24 (NY)
1970—Saints, 14-10 (NO)
1972—Giants, 45-21 (NY)
1975—Giants, 28-14 (NY)
1978—Saints, 28-17 (NO)
1979—Saints, 24-14 (NO)
1981—Giants, 20-7 (NY)
1984—Saints, 10-3 (NY)
1985—Giants, 21-13 (NO)
(Points—Giants 247, Saints 198)
NEW ORLEANS vs. NY JETS
Jets lead series, 3-1
1972—Jets, 18-17 (NY)
1977—Jets, 16-13 (NO)
1980—Saints, 21-20 (NY)
1983—Jets, 31-28 (NO)
(Points—Jets 85, Saints 79)
NEW ORLEANS vs. PHILADELPHIA
Eagles lead series, 8-6
1967—Saints, 31-24 (NO)
Eagles, 48-21 (P)
1968—Eagles, 29-17 (P)
1969—Eagles, 13-10 (P)
Saints, 26-17 (NO)
1972—Saints, 21-3 (NO)
1974—Saints, 14-10 (NO)
1977—Eagles, 28-7 (P)
1978—Eagles, 24-17 (NO)
1979—Eagles, 26-14 (NO)
1980—Eagles, 34-21 (NO)
1981—Eagles, 31-14 (NO)
1983—Saints, 20-17 (P) OT
1985—Saints, 23-21 (NO)
(Points—Eagles 325, Saints 256)
NEW ORLEANS vs. PITTSBURGH
Series tied, 4-4
1967—Steelers, 14-10 (NO)
1968—Saints, 16-12 (P)
Saints, 24-14 (NO)
1969—Saints, 27-24 (NO)
1974—Steelers, 28-7 (NO)
1978—Steelers, 20-14 (P)
1981—Steelers, 20-6 (NO)
1984—Saints, 27-24 (NO)
(Points—Steelers 156, Saints 131)
NEW ORLEANS vs. ST. LOUIS
Cardinals lead series, 9-4
1967—Cardinals, 31-20 (StL)
1968—Cardinals, 21-20 (NO)
Cardinals, 31-17 (StL)
1969—Saints, 51-42 (StL)
1970—Cardinals, 24-17 (StL)
1974—Saints, 14-0 (NO)
1977—Cardinals, 49-31 (StL)
1980—Cardinals, 40-7 (NO)
1981—Cardinals, 30-3 (StL)
1982—Cardinals, 21-7 (NO)
1983—Saints, 28-17 (NO)
1984—Saints, 34-24 (NO)
1985—Cardinals, 28-16 (StL)
(Points—Cardinals 358, Saints 265)
NEW ORLEANS vs. SAN DIEGO
Chargers lead series, 3-0
1973—Chargers, 17-14 (SD)
1977—Chargers, 14-0 (NO)
1979—Chargers, 35-0 (NO)
(Points—Chargers 66, Saints 14)
NEW ORLEANS vs. SAN FRANCISCO
49ers lead series, 22-9-2
1967—49ers, 27-13 (SF)
1969—Saints, 43-38 (NO)
1970—Tie, 20-20 (SF)
49ers, 38-27 (NO)
1971—49ers, 38-20 (NO)
Saints, 26-20 (SF)
1972—49ers, 37-2 (NO)
Tie, 20-20 (SF)
1973—49ers, 40-0 (SF)
Saints, 16-10 (NO)
1974—49ers, 17-13 (NO)
49ers, 35-21 (SF)
1975—49ers, 35-21 (SF)
49ers, 16-6 (NO)
1976—49ers, 33-3 (SF)
49ers, 27-7 (NO)
1977—49ers, 10-7 (NO) OT
49ers, 20-17 (SF)
1978—Saints, 14-7 (SF)
Saints, 24-13 (NO)
1979—Saints, 30-21 (SF)
Saints, 31-20 (NO)
1980—49ers, 26-23 (NO)
49ers, 38-35 (SF) OT
1981—49ers, 21-14 (SF)
49ers, 21-17 (NO)
1982—Saints, 23-20 (SF)
1983—49ers, 32-13 (NO)
49ers, 27-0 (SF)
1984—49ers, 30-20 (SF)
49ers, 35-3 (NO)
1985—Saints, 20-17 (SF)
49ers, 31-19 (NO)
(Points—49ers 840, Saints 568)
NEW ORLEANS vs. SEATTLE
Seahawks lead series, 2-1
1976—Saints, 51-27 (S)
1979—Seahawks, 38-24 (S)
1985—Seahawks, 27-3 (NO)
(Points—Seahawks, 92, Saints 78)
NEW ORLEANS vs. TAMPA BAY
Saints lead series, 5-3
1977—Buccaneers, 33-14 (NO)
1978—Saints, 17-10 (TB)
1979—Saints, 42-14 (TB)
1981—Buccaneers, 31-14 (NO)
1982—Buccaneers, 13-10 (NO)
1983—Saints, 24-21 (TB)
1984—Saints, 17-13 (NO)
1985—Saints, 20-13 (NO)
(Points—Saints 158, Buccaneers 148)
NEW ORLEANS vs. WASHINGTON
Redskins lead series, 7-4
1967—Redskins, 30-10 (NO)
Saints, 30-14 (W)
1968—Saints, 37-17 (NO)
1969—Redskins, 26-20 (NO)
Redskins, 17-14 (W)
1971—Redskins, 24-14 (W)
1973—Saints, 19-3 (NO)
1975—Redskins, 41-3 (W)
1979—Saints, 14-10 (W)
1980—Redskins, 22-14 (W)
1982—Redskins, 27-10 (NO)
(Points—Redskins 231, Saints 185)

***NY BULLDOGS vs. **CHI. CARDINALS**
Cardinals won series, 1-0
1949—Cardinals, 65-20 (NY)
**Extinct team*
***Franchise moved to St. Louis in 1960*
***NY BULLDOGS vs. DETROIT**
Lions won series, 1-0
See Detroit vs. *NY Bulldogs
**Extinct team*
***NY BULLDOGS vs. GREEN BAY**
Packers won series, 1-0
See Green Bay vs. *NY Bulldogs
**Extinct team*
***NY BULLDOGS vs. LA RAMS**
Rams won series, 1-0
See LA Rams vs. *NY Bulldogs
**Extinct team*
***NY BULLDOGS vs. NY GIANTS**
Series tied, 1-1
1949—Giants, 38-14 (NYB)
Bulldogs, 31-24 (NYG)
(Points—Giants 62, Bulldogs 45)
**Extinct team*
***NY BULLDOGS vs. PHILADELPHIA**
Eagles won series, 2-0
1949—Eagles, 7-0 (NY)
Eagles, 42-0 (P)
(Points—Eagles 49, Bulldogs 0)
**Extinct team*
***NY BULLDOGS vs. PITTSBURGH**
Steelers won series, 2-0
1949—Steelers, 24-13 (P)
Steelers, 27-0 (NY)
(Points—Steelers 51, Bulldogs 13)
**Extinct team*
***NY BULLDOGS vs. WASHINGTON**
Redskins won series, 1-0-1
1949—Redskins 38-14 (W)
Tie, 14-14 (NY)
**Extinct team*
NY GIANTS vs. ATLANTA
Falcons lead series, 6-5;
See Atlanta vs. NY Giants
NY GIANTS vs. *1950 BALTIMORE
Giants won series, 1-0
See *1950 Baltimore vs. NY Giants
**Extinct team*
NY GIANTS vs. *BOSTON YANKS
Giants won series, 5-1-3;
See *Boston Yanks vs. NY Giants
**Extinct team*
NY GIANTS vs. *BROOKLYN DODGERS
Giants won series, 22-5-3;
See *Brooklyn Dodgers vs. NY Giants
**Extinct team*
NY GIANTS vs. BUFFALO
Giants lead series, 2-1;
See Buffalo vs. NY Giants
NY GIANTS vs. CHI. BEARS
Bears lead series, 27-16-2;
See Chi. Bears vs. NY Giants
NY GIANTS vs. CINCINNATI
Bengals lead series, 3-0;
See Cincinnati vs. NY Giants
NY GIANTS vs. CLEVELAND
Browns lead series, 26-16-2;
See Cleveland vs. NY Giants
NY GIANTS vs. DALLAS
Cowboys lead series, 32-13-2;
See Dallas vs. NY Giants
NY GIANTS vs. *DALLAS TEXANS
Giants won series, 1-0;
See *Dallas Texans vs. NY Giants
**Extinct team*
NY GIANTS vs. DENVER
Broncos lead series, 2-1;
See Denver vs. NY Giants
NY GIANTS vs. DETROIT
Lions lead series, 18-11-1;
See Detroit vs. NY Giants
NY GIANTS vs. GREEN BAY
Packers lead series, 25-18-2;
See Green Bay vs. NY Giants
NY GIANTS vs. HOUSTON
Giants lead series, 3-0;
See Houston vs. NY Giants
NY GIANTS vs. INDIANAPOLIS
Colts lead series, 7-3;
See Indianapolis vs. NY Giants
NY GIANTS vs. KANSAS CITY
Giants lead series, 4-1;
See Kansas City vs. NY Giants
NY GIANTS vs. LA RAIDERS
Raiders lead series, 3-0;
See LA Raiders vs. NY Giants
NY GIANTS vs. LA RAMS
Rams lead series, 16-8;
See LA Rams vs. NY Giants
NY GIANTS vs. MIAMI
Dolphins lead series, 1-0;
See Miami vs. NY Giants
NY GIANTS vs. MINNESOTA
Vikings lead series, 6-1;
See Minnesota vs. NY Giants
NY GIANTS vs. NEW ENGLAND
Series tied, 1-1;
See New England vs. NY Giants
NY GIANTS vs. NEW ORLEANS
Giants lead series, 6-5;
See New Orleans vs. NY Giants
NY GIANTS vs. NY JETS
Series tied, 2-2
1970—Giants, 22-10 (NYJ)
1974—Jets, 26-20 (New Haven) OT
1981—Jets, 26-7 (NYG)
1984—Giants, 20-10 (NYJ)
(Points—Jets 72, Giants 69)
NY GIANTS vs. NY YANKS
Giants won series, 3-0
1950—Giants, 51-7 (NYG)
1951—Giants, 37-31 (NYG)
Giants, 27-17 (NYG)
(Points—Giants 115, Yanks 55)
**Extinct team*
NY GIANTS vs. *PHILADELPHIA
Giants lead series, 57-46-2
1933—Giants, 56-0 (NY)
Giants, 20-14 (P)
1934—Giants, 17-0 (NY)
Eagles, 6-0 (P)
1935—Giants, 10-0 (NY)
Giants, 21-14 (P)
1936—Eagles, 10-7 (P)
Giants, 21-17 (NY)
1937—Giants, 16-7 (P)
Giants, 21-0 (NY)
1938—Eagles, 14-10 (P)
Giants, 17-7 (NY)
1939—Giants, 13-3 (P)
Giants, 27-10 (NY)
1940—Giants, 20-14 (P)
Giants, 17-7 (NY)
1941—Giants, 24-0 (P)
Giants, 16-0 (NY)
1942—Giants, 35-17 (NY)
Giants, 14-0 (P)
1943—Phil-Pitt, 28-14 (P)
Giants, 42-14 (NY)
1944—Eagles, 24-17 (NY)
Tie, 21-21 (P)
1945—Eagles, 38-17 (P)
Giants, 28-21 (NY)
1946—Eagles, 24-14 (P)
Giants, 45-17 (NY)
1947—Eagles, 23-0 (P)
Eagles, 41-24 (NY)
1948—Eagles, 45-0 (P)
Eagles, 35-14 (NY)
1949—Eagles, 24-3 (NY)
Eagles, 17-3 (P)
1950—Giants, 7-3 (NY)
Giants, 9-7 (P)
1951—Giants, 26-24 (NY)
Giants, 23-7 (P)
1952—Giants, 31-7 (P)
Eagles, 14-10 (NY)
1953—Eagles, 30-7 (P)
Giants, 37-28 (NY)
1954—Giants, 27-14 (NY)
Eagles, 29-14 (P)
1955—Eagles, 27-17 (P)
Giants, 31-7 (NY)
1956—Giants, 20-3 (NY)
Giants, 21-7 (P)
1957—Giants, 24-20 (P)
Giants, 13-0 (NY)
1958—Eagles, 27-24 (P)
Giants, 24-10 (NY)
1959—Eagles, 49-21 (P)
Giants, 24-7 (NY)
1960—Eagles, 17-10 (NY)
Eagles, 31-23 (P)
1961—Giants, 38-21 (NY)
Giants, 28-24 (P)
1962—Giants, 29-13 (P)
Giants, 19-14 (NY)
1963—Giants, 37-14 (P)
Giants, 42-14 (NY)
1964—Eagles, 38-7 (P)
Eagles, 23-17 (NY)
1965—Giants, 16-14 (P)
Giants, 35-27 (NY)
1966—Eagles, 35-17 (P)
Eagles, 31-3 (NY)
1967—Giants, 44-7 (NY)
1968—Giants, 34-25 (P)
Giants, 7-6 (NY)
1969—Eagles, 23-20 (NY)
1970—Giants, 30-23 (NY)
Eagles, 23-20 (P)
1971—Eagles, 23-7 (P)
Eagles, 41-28 (NY)
1972—Giants, 27-12 (P)
Giants, 62-10 (NY)

1973—Tie, 23-23 (NY)
Eagles, 20-16 (P)
1974—Eagles, 35-7 (P)
Eagles, 20-7 (New Haven)
1975—Giants, 23-14 (P)
Eagles, 13-10 (NY)
1976—Eagles, 20-7 (P)
Eagles, 10-0 (NY)
1977—Eagles, 28-10 (NY)
Eagles, 17-14 (P)
1978—Eagles, 19-17 (NY)
Eagles, 20-3 (P)
1979—Eagles, 23-17 (P)
Eagles, 17-13 (NY)
1980—Eagles, 35-3 (P)
Eagles, 31-16 (NY)
1981—Eagles, 24-10 (NY)
Giants, 20-10 (P)
**Giants, 27-21 (P)
1982—Giants, 23-7 (NY)
Giants, 26-24 (P)
1983—Eagles, 17-13 (NY)
Giants, 23-0 (P)
1984—Giants, 28-27 (NY)
Eagles, 24-10 (P)
1985—Giants, 21-0 (NY)
Giants, 16-10 (P) OT
(Points—Giants 2,037, Eagles 1,850)
*Eagles known as Phil-Pitt in 1943
**NFC Wild Card Game*

NY GIANTS vs. *PITTSBURGH
Giants lead series, 43-27-3
1933—Giants, 23-2 (P)
Giants, 27-3 (NY)
1934—Giants, 14-12 (P)
Giants, 17-7 (NY)
1935—Giants, 42-7 (P)
Giants, 13-0 (NY)
1936—Pirates, 10-7 (P)
1937—Giants, 10-7 (P)
Giants, 17-0 (NY)
1938—Giants, 27-14 (P)
Pirates, 13-10 (NY)
1939—Giants, 14-7 (P)
Giants, 23-7 (NY)
1940—Tie, 10-10 (P)
Giants, 12-0 (NY)
1941—Giants, 37-10 (P)
Giants, 28-7 (NY)
1942—Steelers, 13-10 (P)
Steelers, 17-9 (NY)
1943—Phil-Pitt, 28-14 (Phil)
Giants, 42-14 (NY)
1944—Giants, 23-0 (NY)
1945—Giants, 34-6 (P)
Steelers, 21-7 (NY)
1946—Giants, 17-14 (P)
Giants, 7-0 (NY)
1947—Steelers, 38-21 (NY)
Steelers, 24-7 (P)
1948—Giants, 34-27 (NY)
Steelers, 38-28 (P)
1949—Steelers, 28-7 (P)
Steelers, 21-17 (NY)
1950—Giants, 18-7 (P)
Steelers, 17-6 (NY)
1951—Tie, 13-13 (P)
Giants, 14-0 (NY)
1952—Steelers, 63-7 (P)
1953—Steelers, 24-14 (P)
Steelers, 14-10 (NY)
1954—Giants, 30-6 (P)
Giants, 24-3 (NY)
1955—Steelers, 30-23 (P)
Steelers, 19-17 (NY)
1956—Giants, 38-10 (NY)
Giants, 17-14 (P)
1957—Giants, 35-0 (NY)
Steelers, 21-10 (P)
1958—Giants, 17-6 (NY)
Steelers, 31-10 (P)
1959—Giants, 21-16 (P)
Steelers, 14-9 (NY)
1960—Giants, 19-17 (P)
Giants, 27-24 (NY)
1961—Giants, 17-14 (P)
Giants, 42-21 (NY)
1962—Giants, 31-27 (P)
Steelers, 20-17 (NY)
1963—Steelers, 31-0 (P)
Giants, 33-17 (NY)
1964—Steelers, 27-24 (P)
Steelers, 44-17 (NY)
1965—Giants, 23-13 (P)
Giants, 35-10 (NY)
1966—Tie, 34-34 (P)
Steelers, 47-28 (NY)
1967—Giants, 27-24 (P)
Giants, 28-20 (NY)
1968—Giants, 34-20 (P)
1969—Giants, 10-7 (NY)
Giants, 21-17 (P)
1971—Steelers, 17-13 (P)
1976—Steelers, 27-0 (NY)
1985—Giants, 28-10 (NY)
(Points—Giants 1,449, Steelers 1,201)
**Steelers known as Pirates prior to 1941, as Phil-Pitt in 1943, and as Card-Pitt in 1944*

NY GIANTS vs. *ST. LOUIS
Giants lead series, 54-31-2
1926—Giants, 20-0 (NY)
1927—Giants, 28-7 (NY)
1929—Giants, 24-21 (NY)
1930—Giants, 25-12 (NY)
Giants, 13-7 (C)
1935—Cardinals, 14-13 (NY)
1936—Giants, 14-6 (NY)
1938—Giants, 6-0 (NY)
1939—Giants, 17-7 (NY)
1941—Cardinals, 10-7 (NY)
1942—Giants, 21-7 (NY)
1943—Giants, 24-13 (NY)
1944—Giants, 23-0 (NY)
1946—Giants, 28-24 (NY)
1947—Giants, 35-31 (NY)
1948—Cardinals, 63-35 (NY)
1949—Giants, 41-38 (C)
1950—Cardinals, 17-3 (C)
Giants, 51-21 (NY)
1951—Giants, 28-17 (NY)
Giants, 10-0 (C)
1952—Cardinals, 24-23 (NY)
Giants, 28-6 (C)
1953—Giants, 21-7 (NY)
Giants, 23-20 (C)
1954—Giants, 41-10 (C)
Giants, 31-17 (NY)
1955—Cardinals, 28-17 (C)
Giants, 10-0 (NY)
1956—Cardinals, 35-27 (C)
Giants, 23-10 (NY)
1957—Giants, 27-14 (NY)
Giants, 28-21 (C)
1958—Giants, 37-7 (Buffalo)
Cardinals, 23-6 (NY)
1959—Giants, 9-3 (NY)
Giants, 30-20 (Minn)
1960—Giants, 35-14 (StL)
Cardinals, 20-13 (NY)
1961—Cardinals, 21-10 (NY)
Giants, 24-9 (StL)
1962—Giants, 31-14 (StL)
Giants, 31-28 (NY)
1963—Giants, 38-21 (StL)
Cardinals, 24-17 (NY)
1964—Giants, 34-17 (NY)
Tie, 10-10 (StL)
1965—Giants, 14-10 (NY)
Giants, 28-15 (StL)
1966—Cardinals, 24-19 (StL)
Cardinals, 20-17 (NY)
1967—Giants, 37-20 (StL)
Giants, 37-14 (NY)
1968—Cardinals, 28-21 (NY)
1969—Cardinals, 42-17 (StL)
Giants, 49-6 (NY)
1970—Giants, 35-17 (NY)
Giants, 34-17 (StL)
1971—Giants, 21-20 (StL)
Cardinals, 24-7 (NY)
1972—Giants, 27-21 (NY)
Giants, 13-7 (StL)
1973—Cardinals, 35-27 (StL)
Giants, 24-13 (New Haven)
1974—Cardinals, 23-21 (New Haven)
Cardinals, 26-14 (StL)
1975—Cardinals, 26-14 (StL)
Cardinals, 20-13 (NY)
1976—Cardinals, 27-21 (StL)
Cardinals, 17-14 (NY)
1977—Cardinals, 28-0 (StL)
Giants, 27-7 (NY)
1978—Cardinals, 20-10 (StL)
Giants, 17-0 (NY)
1979—Cardinals, 27-14 (NY)
Cardinals, 29-20 (StL)
1980—Giants, 41-35 (StL)
Cardinals, 23-7 (NY)
1981—Giants, 34-14 (NY)
Giants, 20-10 (StL)
1982—Cardinals, 24-21 (StL)
1983—Tie, 20-20 (StL) OT
Cardinals, 10-6 (NY)
1984—Giants, 16-10 (NY)
Cardinals, 31-21 (StL)
1985—Giants, 27-17 (NY)
Giants, 34-3 (StL)
(Points—Giants 1,949, Cardinals 1,518)
**Franchise in Chicago prior to 1960 and known as Card-Pitt in 1944*

NY GIANTS vs. SAN DIEGO
Series tied, 2-2
1971—Giants, 35-17 (NY)
1975—Giants, 35-24 (NY)
1980—Chargers, 44-7 (SD)
1983—Chargers, 41-34 (NY)
(Points—Chargers 126, Giants 111)

NY GIANTS vs. SAN FRANCISCO
Giants lead series, 10-7
1952—Giants, 23-14 (NY)
1956—Giants, 38-21 (SF)
1957—49ers, 27-17 (NY)
1960—Giants, 21-19 (SF)
1963—Giants, 48-14 (NY)
1968—49ers, 26-10 (NY)
1972—Giants, 23-17 (SF)
1975—Giants, 26-23 (SF)
1977—Giants, 20-17 (NY)
1978—Giants, 27-10 (NY)
1979—Giants, 32-16 (NY)
1980—49ers, 12-0 (SF)
1981—49ers, 17-10 (SF)
*49ers, 38-24 (SF)
1984—49ers, 31-10 (NY)
*49ers, 21-10 (SF)
1985—**Giants, 17-3 (NY)
(Points—Giants 356, 49ers 326)
**NFC Divisional Playoff*
***NFC Wild Card Game*

NY GIANTS vs. SEATTLE
Giants lead series, 3-1
1976—Giants, 28-16 (NY)
1980—Giants, 27-21 (S)
1981—Giants, 32-0 (S)
1983—Seahawks, 17-12 (NY)
(Points—Giants 99, Seahawks 54)

NY GIANTS vs. TAMPA BAY
Giants lead series, 6-3
1977—Giants, 10-0 (TB)
1978—Giants, 19-13 (TB)
Giants, 17-14 (NY)
1979—Giants, 17-14 (NY)
Buccaneers, 31-3 (TB)
1980—Buccaneers, 30-13 (TB)
1984—Giants, 17-14 (NY)
Buccaneers, 20-17 (TB)
1985—Giants, 22-20 (NY)
(Points—Buccaneers 156, Giants 135)

NY GIANTS vs. *WASHINGTON
Giants lead series, 58-46-3
1932—Braves, 14-6 (B)
Tie, 0-0 (NY)
1933—Redskins, 21-20 (B)
Giants, 7-0 (NY)
1934—Giants, 16-13 (B)
Giants, 3-0 (NY)
1935—Giants, 20-12 (B)
Giants, 17-6 (NY)
1936—Giants, 7-0 (B)
Redskins, 14-0 (NY)
1937—Redskins, 13-3 (W)
Redskins, 49-14 (NY)
1938—Giants, 10-7 (W)
Giants, 36-0 (NY)
1939—Tie, 0-0 (W)
Giants, 9-7 (NY)
1940—Redskins, 21-7 (W)
Giants, 21-7 (NY)
1941—Giants, 17-10 (W)
Giants, 20-13 (NY)
1942—Giants, 14-7 (W)
Redskins, 14-7 (NY)
1943—Giants, 14-10 (NY)
Giants, 31-7 (W)
**Redskins, 28-0 (NY)
1944—Giants, 16-13 (NY)
Giants, 31-0 (W)
1945—Redskins, 24-14 (NY)
Redskins, 17-0 (W)
1946—Redskins, 24-14 (W)
Giants, 31-0 (NY)
1947—Redskins, 28-20 (W)
Giants, 35-10 (NY)
1948—Redskins, 41-10 (W)
Redskins, 28-21 (NY)
1949—Giants, 45-35 (W)
Giants, 23-7 (NY)
1950—Giants, 21-17 (W)
Giants, 24-21 (NY)
1951—Giants, 35-14 (W)
Giants, 28-14 (NY)
1952—Giants, 14-10 (W)
Redskins, 27-17 (NY)
1953—Redskins, 13-9 (W)
Redskins, 24-21 (NY)
1954—Giants, 51-21 (W)
Giants, 24-7 (NY)
1955—Giants, 35-7 (NY)
Giants, 27-20 (W)
1956—Redskins, 33-7 (W)
Giants, 28-14 (NY)
1957—Giants, 24-20 (W)
Redskins, 31-14 (NY)
1958—Giants, 21-14 (W)
Giants, 30-0 (NY)
1959—Giants, 45-14 (NY)
Giants, 24-10 (W)
1960—Tie, 24-24 (NY)
Giants, 17-3 (W)
1961—Giants, 24-21 (W)
Giants, 53-0 (NY)
1962—Giants, 49-34 (NY)
Giants, 42-24 (NY)
1963—Giants, 24-14 (W)
Giants, 44-14 (NY)
1964—Giants, 13-10 (NY)
Redskins, 36-21 (W)
1965—Redskins, 23-7 (NY)
Giants, 27-10 (W)
1966—Giants, 13-10 (NY)
Redskins, 72-41 (W)
1967—Redskins, 38-34 (W)
1968—Giants, 48-21 (NY)
Giants, 13-10 (W)
1969—Redskins, 20-14 (W)
1970—Giants, 35-33 (NY)
Giants, 27-24 (W)
1971—Redskins, 30-3 (NY)
Redskins, 23-7 (W)
1972—Redskins, 23-16 (NY)
Redskins, 27-13 (W)
1973—Redskins, 21-3 (New Haven)
Redskins, 27-24 (W)
1974—Redskins, 13-10 (New Haven)
Redskins, 24-3 (W)
1975—Redskins, 49-13 (W)
Redskins, 21-13 (NY)
1976—Redskins, 19-17 (W)
Giants, 12-9 (NY)
1977—Giants, 20-17 (NY)
Giants, 17-6 (W)
1978—Giants, 17-6 (NY)
Redskins, 16-13 (W) OT
1979—Redskins, 27-0 (W)
Giants, 14-6 (NY)
1980—Redskins, 23-21 (NY)
Redskins, 16-13 (W)
1981—Giants, 17-7 (W)
Redskins, 30-27 (NY) OT
1982—Redskins, 27-17 (NY)
Redskins, 15-14 (W)
1983—Redskins, 33-17 (NY)
Redskins, 31-22 (W)
1984—Redskins, 30-14 (W)
Giants, 37-13 (NY)
1985—Giants, 17-3 (NY)
Redskins, 23-21 (W)
(Points—Giants 2,080, Redskins 1,887)
**Franchise in Boston prior to 1937 and known as Braves prior to 1933*
***Divisional Playoff*

NY JETS vs. ATLANTA
Falcons lead series, 2-1;
See Atlanta vs. NY Jets

NY JETS vs. BUFFALO
Bills lead series, 26-25;
See Buffalo vs. NY Jets

NY JETS vs. CHI. BEARS
Bears lead series, 2-1;
See Chi. Bears vs. NY Jets

NY JETS vs. CINCINNATI
Jets lead series, 7-3;
See Cincinnati vs. NY Jets

NY JETS vs. CLEVELAND
Browns lead series, 7-3;
See Cleveland vs. NY Jets

NY JETS vs. DALLAS
Cowboys lead series, 3-0;
See Dallas vs. NY Jets

NY JETS vs. DENVER
Series tied, 10-10-1;
See Denver vs. NY Jets

NY JETS vs. DETROIT
Series tied, 2-2;
See Detroit vs. NY Jets

NY JETS vs. GREEN BAY
Jets lead series, 4-1;
See Green Bay vs. NY Jets

NY JETS vs. HOUSTON
Oilers lead series, 15-10-1;
See Houston vs. NY Jets

NY JETS vs. INDIANAPOLIS
Series tied, 16-16;
See Indianapolis vs. NY Jets

NY JETS vs. KANSAS CITY
Chiefs lead series, 13-11;
See Kansas City vs. NY Jets

NY JETS vs. LA RAIDERS
Raiders lead series, 12-11-2;
See LA Raiders vs. NY Jets

NY JETS vs. LA RAMS
Series tied, 2-2;
See LA Rams vs. NY Jets

NY JETS vs. MIAMI
Dolphins lead series, 22-18-1;
See Miami vs. NY Jets

NY JETS vs. MINNESOTA
Jets lead series, 3-1;
See Minnesota vs. NY Jets

NY JETS vs. NEW ENGLAND
Jets lead series, 29-22-1;
See New England vs. NY Jets

NY JETS vs. NEW ORLEANS
Jets lead series, 3-1;
See New Orleans vs. NY Jets

NY JETS vs. NY GIANTS
Series tied, 2-2;
See NY Giants vs. NY Jets

NY JETS vs. PHILADELPHIA
Eagles lead series, 3-0
1973—Eagles, 24-23 (P)
1977—Eagles, 27-0 (P)
1978—Eagles, 17-9 (P)
(Points—Eagles 68, Jets 32)

NY JETS vs. PITTSBURGH
Steelers lead series, 8-0
1970—Steelers, 21-17 (P)
1973—Steelers, 26-14 (P)
1975—Steelers, 20-7 (NY)
1977—Steelers, 23-20 (NY)
1978—Steelers, 28-17 (NY)
1981—Steelers, 38-10 (P)
1983—Steelers, 34-7 (NY)
1984—Steelers, 23-17 (NY)
(Points—Steelers 213, Jets 109)

NY JETS vs. ST. LOUIS
Cardinals lead series, 2-1
1971—Cardinals, 17-10 (StL)
1975—Cardinals 37-6 (NY)
1978—Jets, 23-10 (NY)
(Points—Cardinals 64, Jets 39)

***NY JETS vs. **SAN DIEGO**
Chargers lead series, 14-7-1
1960—Chargers, 21-7 (NY)
Chargers, 50-43 (LA)
1961—Chargers, 25-10 (NY)
Chargers, 48-13 (SD)
1962—Chargers, 40-14 (SD)
Titans, 23-3 (NY)
1963—Chargers, 24-20 (SD)
Chargers, 53-7 (NY)
1964—Tie, 17-17 (NY)
Chargers, 38-3 (SD)
1965—Chargers, 34-9 (NY)
Chargers, 38-7 (SD)
1966—Jets, 17-16 (NY)
Chargers, 42-27 (SD)
1967—Jets, 42-31 (SD)
1968—Jets, 23-20 (NY)
Jets, 37-15 (SD)
1969—Chargers, 34-27 (SD)
1971—Chargers, 49-21 (SD)
1974—Jets, 27-14 (NY)
1975—Chargers, 24-16 (SD)
1983—Jets, 41-29 (SD)
(Points—Chargers 665, Jets 451)
**Jets known as Titans prior to 1963*
***Franchise in Los Angeles prior to 1961*

NY JETS vs. SAN FRANCISCO
49ers lead series, 3-1
1971—49ers, 24-21 (NY)
1976—49ers, 17-6 (SF)
1980—49ers, 37-27 (NY)
1983—Jets, 27-13 (SF)
(Points—49ers 91, Jets 81)

NY JETS vs. SEATTLE
Seahawks lead series, 7-1
1977—Seahawks, 17-0 (NY)
1978—Seahawks, 24-17 (NY)

1979—Seahawks, 30-7 (S)
1980—Seahawks, 27-17 (NY)
1981—Seahawks, 19-3 (NY)
Seahawks, 27-23 (S)
1983—Seahawks, 17-10 (NY)
1985—Jets, 17-14 (NY)
(Points—Seahawks 175, Jets 94)
NY JETS vs. TAMPA BAY
Jets lead series, 3-1
1976—Jets, 34-0 (NY)
1982—Jets, 32-17 (NY)
1984—Buccaneers, 41-21 (TB)
1985—Jets, 62-28 (NY)
(Points—Jets 149, Buccaneers 86)
NY JETS vs. WASHINGTON
Redskins lead series, 3-0
1972—Redskins, 35-17 (NY)
1976—Redskins, 37-16 (NY)
1978—Redskins, 23-3 (W)
(Points—Redskins 95, Jets 36)

PHILADELPHIA vs. ATLANTA
Series tied, 6-6-1;
See Atlanta vs. Philadelphia
PHILADELPHIA vs. *1950 BALTIMORE
Eagles won series, 1-0;
See *1950 Baltimore vs. Philadelphia
Extinct team
PHILADELPHIA vs. *BOSTON YANKS
Eagles won series, 7-2;
See *Boston Yanks vs. Philadelphia
Extinct team
PHILADELPHIA vs. *BROOKLYN DODGERS
Dodgers won series, 15-6-1;
See *Brooklyn Dodgers vs. Philadelphia
Extinct team
PHILADELPHIA vs. BUFFALO
Eagles lead series, 3-1;
See Buffalo vs. Philadelphia
PHILADELPHIA vs. CHI. BEARS
Bears lead series, 20-4-1;
See Chi. Bears vs. Philadelphia
PHILADELPHIA vs. CINCINNATI
Bengals lead series, 4-0;
See Cincinnati vs. Philadelphia
PHILADELPHIA vs. *CINCINNATI REDS
Eagles won series, 2-1;
See *Cincinnati Reds vs. Philadelphia
Extinct team
PHILADELPHIA vs. CLEVELAND
Browns lead series, 29-11-1;
See Cleveland vs. Philadelphia
PHILADELPHIA vs. DALLAS
Cowboys lead series, 34-17;
See Dallas vs. Philadelphia
PHILADELPHIA vs. *DALLAS TEXANS
Eagles won series, 1-0;
See *Dallas Texans vs. Philadelphia
Extinct team
PHILADELPHIA vs. DENVER
Eagles lead series, 3-1;
See Denver vs. Philadelphia
PHILADELPHIA vs. DETROIT
Lions lead series, 12-10-2;
See Detroit vs. Philadelphia
PHILADELPHIA vs. GREEN BAY
Packers lead series, 18-5;
See Green Bay vs. Philadelphia
PHILADELPHIA vs. HOUSTON
Eagles lead series, 3-0;
See Houston vs. Philadelphia
PHILADELPHIA vs. INDIANAPOLIS
Colts lead series, 6-5;
See Indianapolis vs. Philadelphia
PHILADELPHIA vs. KANSAS CITY
Eagles lead series, 1-0;
See Kansas City vs. Philadelphia
PHILADELPHIA vs. LA RAIDERS
Raiders lead series, 3-1;
See LA Raiders vs. Philadelphia
PHILADELPHIA vs. LA RAMS
Rams lead series, 15-9-1;
See LA Rams vs. Philadelphia
PHILADELPHIA vs. MIAMI
Dolphins lead series, 3-2;
See Miami vs. Philadelphia
PHILADELPHIA vs. MINNESOTA
Vikings lead series, 9-4;
See Minnesota vs. Philadelphia
PHILADELPHIA vs. NEW ENGLAND
Eagles lead series, 3-2;
See New England vs. Philadelphia
PHILADELPHIA vs. NEW ORLEANS
Eagles lead series, 8-6;
See New Orleans vs. Philadelphia
PHILADELPHIA vs. *NY BULLDOGS
Eagles won series, 2-0;
See *NY Bulldogs vs. Philadelphia
Extinct team
PHILADELPHIA vs. NY GIANTS
Giants lead series, 57-46-2;
See NY Giants vs. Philadelphia
PHILADELPHIA vs. NY JETS
Eagles lead series, 3-0;
See NY Jets vs. Philadelphia
PHILADELPHIA vs. *PITTSBURGH
Eagles lead series, 42-25-3
1933—Eagles, 25-6 (Phil)
1934—Eagles, 17-0 (Pitt)
Pirates, 9-7 (Phil)
1935—Pirates, 17-7 (Phil)
Eagles, 17-6 (Pitt)
1936—Pirates, 17-0 (Pitt)
Pirates, 6-0 (Johnstown, Pa.)
1937—Pirates, 27-14 (Pitt)
Pirates, 16-7 (Pitt)
1938—Eagles, 27-7 (Buffalo)
Eagles, 14-7 (Charleston, W. Va.)
1939—Eagles, 17-14 (Phil)
Pirates, 24-12 (Pitt)
1940—Pirates, 7-3 (Pitt)
Eagles, 7-0 (Phil)
1941—Eagles, 10-7 (Pitt)
Tie, 7-7 (Phil)
1942—Eagles, 24-14 (Pitt)
Steelers, 14-0 (Phil)
1945—Eagles, 45-3 (Pitt)
Eagles, 30-6 (Phil)
1946—Steelers, 10-7 (Pitt)
Eagles, 10-7 (Phil)
1947—Steelers, 35-24 (Pitt)
Eagles, 21-0 (Phil)
**Eagles, 21-0 (Pitt)
1948—Eagles, 34-7 (Pitt)
Eagles, 17-0 (Phil)
1949—Eagles, 38-7 (Pitt)
Eagles, 34-17 (Phil)
1950—Eagles, 17-10 (Pitt)
Steelers, 9-7 (Phil)
1951—Eagles, 34-13 (Pitt)
Steelers, 17-13 (Phil)
1952—Eagles, 31-25 (Pitt)
Eagles, 26-21 (Phil)
1953—Eagles, 23-17 (Phil)
Eagles, 35-7 (Pitt)
1954—Eagles, 24-22 (Phil)
Steelers, 17-7 (Pitt)
1955—Steelers, 13-7 (Pitt)
Eagles, 24-0 (Phil)
1956—Eagles, 35-21 (Pitt)
Eagles, 14-7 (Phil)
1957—Steelers, 6-0 (Pitt)
Eagles, 7-6 (Phil)
1958—Steelers, 24-3 (Pitt)
Steelers, 31-24 (Phil)
1959—Eagles, 28-24 (Phil)
Steelers, 31-0 (Pitt)
1960—Eagles, 34-7 (Phil)
Steelers, 27-21 (Pitt)
1961—Eagles, 21-16 (Phil)
Eagles, 35-24 (Pitt)
1962—Steelers, 13-7 (Pitt)
Steelers, 26-17 (Phil)
1963—Tie, 21-21 (Phil)
Tie, 20-20 (Pitt)
1964—Eagles, 21-7 (Phil)
Eagles, 34-10 (Pitt)
1965—Steelers, 20-14 (Phil)
Eagles, 47-13 (Pitt)
1966—Eagles, 31-14 (Pitt)
Eagles, 27-23 (Phil)
1967—Eagles, 34-24 (Phil)
1968—Steelers, 6-3 (Pitt)
1969—Eagles, 41-27 (Phil)
1970—Eagles, 30-20 (Phil)
1974—Steelers, 27-0 (Pitt)
1979—Eagles, 17-14 (Phil)
(Points—Eagles 1,330, Steelers 967)
**Steelers known as Pirates prior to 1941*
***Division Playoff*
***PHILADELPHIA vs. **ST. LOUIS**
Cardinals lead series, 40-35-4
1935—Cardinals, 12-3 (C)
1936—Cardinals, 13-0 (C)
1937—Tie, 6-6 (P)
1938—Eagles, 7-0 (Erie, Pa.)
1941—Eagles, 21-14 (P)
1943—Phil-Pitt, 34-13 (Pitt)
1945—Eagles, 21-6 (P)
1947—Cardinals, 45-21 (P)
***Cardinals, 28-21 (C)
1948—Cardinals, 21-14 (C)
***Eagles, 7-0 (P)
1949—Eagles, 28-3 (P)
1950—Eagles, 45-7 (C)
Cardinals, 14-10 (P)
1951—Eagles, 17-14 (C)
1952—Eagles, 10-7 (P)
Cardinals, 28-22 (C)
1953—Eagles, 56-17 (C)
Eagles, 38-0 (P)
1954—Eagles, 35-16 (C)
Eagles, 30-14 (P)
1955—Tie, 24-24 (C)
Eagles, 27-3 (P)
1956—Cardinals, 20-6 (P)
Cardinals, 28-17 (C)
1957—Eagles, 38-21 (C)
Cardinals, 31-27 (P)
1958—Tie, 21-21 (C)
Eagles, 49-21 (P)
1959—Eagles, 28-24 (Minn)
Eagles, 27-17 (P)
1960—Eagles, 31-27 (P)
Eagles, 20-6 (StL)
1961—Cardinals, 30-27 (P)
Eagles, 20-7 (StL)
1962—Cardinals, 27-21 (P)
Cardinals, 45-35 (StL)
1963—Cardinals, 28-24 (P)
Cardinals, 38-14 (StL)
1964—Cardinals, 38-13 (P)
Cardinals, 36-34 (StL)
1965—Eagles, 34-27 (P)
Eagles, 28-24 (StL)
1966—Cardinals, 16-13 (StL)
Cardinals, 41-10 (P)
1967—Cardinals, 48-14 (StL)
1968—Cardinals, 45-17 (P)
1969—Eagles, 34-30 (StL)
1970—Cardinals, 35-20 (P)
Cardinals, 23-14 (StL)
1971—Eagles, 37-20 (StL)
Eagles, 19-7 (P)
1972—Tie, 6-6 (P)
Cardinals, 24-23 (StL)
1973—Cardinals, 34-23 (P)
Eagles, 27-24 (StL)
1974—Cardinals, 7-3 (StL)
Cardinals, 13-3 (P)
1975—Cardinals, 31-20 (StL)
Cardinals, 24-23 (P)
1976—Cardinals, 33-14 (StL)
Cardinals, 17-14 (P)
1977—Cardinals, 21-17 (P)
Cardinals, 21-16 (StL)
1978—Cardinals, 16-10 (P)
Eagles, 14-10 (StL)
1979—Eagles, 24-20 (StL)
Eagles, 16-13 (P)
1980—Cardinals, 24-14 (StL)
Eagles, 17-3 (P)
1981—Eagles, 52-10 (StL)
Eagles, 38-0 (P)
1982—Cardinals, 23-20 (P)
1983—Cardinals, 14-11 (P)
Cardinals, 31-7 (StL)
1984—Cardinals, 34-14 (P)
Cardinals, 17-16 (StL)
1985—Eagles, 30-7 (P)
Eagles, 24-14 (StL)
(Points—Eagles 1,685, Cardinals 1,577)
**Eagles known as Phil-Pitt in 1943*
***Franchise in Chicago prior to 1960*
****NFL Championship*
PHILADELPHIA vs. SAN DIEGO
Chargers lead series, 2-1
1974—Eagles, 13-7 (SD)
1980—Chargers, 22-21 (SD)
1985—Chargers, 20-14 (SD)
(Points—Chargers 49, Eagles 48)
PHILADELPHIA vs. SAN FRANCISCO
49ers lead series, 10-4-1
1951—Eagles, 21-14 (P)
1953—49ers, 31-21 (SF)
1956—Tie, 10-10 (P)
1958—49ers, 30-24 (P)
1959—49ers, 24-14 (SF)
1964—49ers, 28-24 (P)
1966—Eagles, 35-34 (SF)
1967—49ers, 28-27 (P)
1969—49ers, 14-13 (SF)
1971—49ers, 31-3 (P)
1973—49ers, 38-28 (SF)
1975—Eagles, 27-17 (P)
1983—Eagles, 22-17 (SF)
1984—49ers, 21-9 (P)
1985—49ers, 24-13 (SF)
(Points—49ers 361, Eagles 291)
PHILADELPHIA vs. SEATTLE
Eagles lead series, 2-0
1976—Eagles, 27-10 (P)
1980—Eagles, 27-20 (S)
(Points—Eagles 54, Seahawks 30)
PHILADELPHIA vs. TAMPA BAY
Eagles lead series, 2-1
1977—Eagles, 13-3 (P)
1979—*Buccaneers, 24-17 (TB)
1981—Eagles, 20-10 (P)
(Points—Eagles 50, Buccaneers 37)
**NFC Divisional Playoff*
***PHILADELPHIA vs. **WASHINGTON**
Redskins lead series, 57-40-6
1934—Redskins, 6-0 (B)
Redskins, 14-7 (P)
1935—Eagles, 7-6 (B)
1936—Redskins, 26-3 (P)
Redskins, 17-7 (B)
1937—Eagles, 14-0 (W)
Redskins, 10-7 (P)
1938—Redskins, 26-23 (P)
Redskins, 20-14 (W)
1939—Redskins, 7-0 (P)
Redskins, 7-6 (W)
1940—Redskins, 34-17 (P)
Redskins, 13-6 (W)
1941—Redskins, 21-17 (P)
Redskins, 20-14 (W)
1942—Redskins, 14-10 (P)
Redskins, 30-27 (W)
1943—Tie, 14-14 (P)
Phil-Pitt, 27-14 (W)
1944—Tie, 31-31 (P)
Eagles, 37-7 (W)
1945—Redskins, 24-14 (W)
Eagles, 16-0 (P)
1946—Eagles, 28-24 (W)
Redskins, 27-10 (P)
1947—Eagles, 45-42 (P)
Eagles, 38-14 (W)
1948—Eagles, 45-0 (W)
Eagles, 42-21 (P)
1949—Eagles, 49-14 (P)
Eagles, 44-21 (W)
1950—Eagles, 35-3 (P)
Eagles, 33-0 (W)
1951—Redskins, 27-23 (P)
Eagles, 35-21 (W)
1952—Eagles, 38-20 (P)
Redskins, 27-21 (W)
1953—Tie, 21-21 (P)
Redskins, 10-0 (W)
1954—Eagles, 49-21 (W)
Eagles, 41-33 (P)
1955—Redskins, 31-30 (P)
Redskins, 34-21 (W)
1956—Eagles, 13-9 (P)
Redskins, 19-17 (W)
1957—Eagles, 21-12 (P)
Redskins, 42-7 (W)
1958—Redskins, 24-14 (P)
Redskins, 20-0 (W)
1959—Eagles, 30-23 (P)
Eagles, 34-14 (W)
1960—Eagles, 19-13 (P)
Eagles, 38-28 (W)
1961—Eagles, 14-7 (P)
Eagles, 27-24 (W)
1962—Redskins, 27-21 (P)
Eagles, 37-14 (W)
1963—Eagles, 37-24 (W)
Redskins, 13-10 (P)
1964—Redskins, 35-20 (W)
Redskins, 21-10 (P)
1965—Redskins, 23-21 (W)
Eagles, 21-14 (P)
1966—Redskins, 27-13 (P)
Eagles, 37-28 (W)
1967—Eagles, 35-24 (P)
Tie, 35-35 (W)
1968—Redskins, 17-14 (W)
Redskins, 16-10 (P)
1969—Tie, 28-28 (W)
Redskins, 34-29 (P)
1970—Redskins, 33-21 (P)
Redskins, 24-6 (W)
1971—Tie, 7-7 (W)
Redskins, 20-13 (P)
1972—Redskins, 14-0 (W)
Redskins, 23-7 (P)
1973—Redskins, 28-7 (P)
Redskins, 38-20 (W)
1974—Redskins, 27-20 (P)
Redskins, 26-7 (W)
1975—Eagles, 26-10 (P)
Eagles, 26-3 (W)
1976—Redskins, 20-17 (P) OT
Redskins, 24-0 (W)
1977—Redskins, 23-17 (W)
Redskins, 17-14 (P)
1978—Redskins, 35-30 (W)
Eagles, 17-10 (P)
1979—Eagles, 28-17 (P)
Redskins, 17-7 (W)
1980—Eagles, 24-14 (P)
Eagles, 24-0 (W)
1981—Eagles, 36-13 (P)
Redskins, 15-13 (W)
1982—Redskins, 37-34 (P) OT
Redskins, 13-9 (W)
1983—Redskins, 23-13 (P)
Redskins, 28-24 (W)
1984—Redskins, 20-0 (W)
Eagles, 16-10 (P)
1985—Eagles, 19-6 (W)
Redskins, 17-12 (P)
(Points—Eagles 2,092, Redskins 1,999)
**Eagles known as Phil-Pitt in 1943*
***Franchise in Boston prior to 1937*

PITTSBURGH vs. ATLANTA
Steelers lead series, 6-1;
See Atlanta vs. Pittsburgh
PITTSBURGH vs. *1950 BALTIMORE
Steelers won series, 1-0;
See *1950 Baltimore vs. Pittsburgh
Extinct team
PITTSBURGH vs. *BOSTON YANKS
Steelers won series, 5-3;
See *Boston Yanks vs. Pittsburgh
Extinct team
PITTSBURGH vs. *BROOKLYN DODGERS
Dodgers won series, 12-9-1;
See *Brooklyn Dodgers vs. Pittsburgh
Extinct team
PITTSBURGH vs. BUFFALO
Steelers lead series, 6-3;
See Buffalo vs. Pittsburgh
PITTSBURGH vs. CHI. BEARS
Bears lead series, 16-4-1;
See Chi. Bears vs. Pittsburgh
PITTSBURGH vs. CINCINNATI
Steelers lead series, 17-14;
See Cincinnati vs. Pittsburgh
PITTSBURGH vs. CINCINNATI REDS
Steelers won series, 2-0-1;
See *Cincinnati Reds vs. Pittsburgh
Extinct team
PITTSBURGH vs. CLEVELAND
Browns lead series, 41-31;
See Cleveland vs. Pittsburgh
PITTSBURGH vs. DALLAS
Steelers lead series, 12-11;
See Dallas vs. Pittsburgh
PITTSBURGH vs. DENVER
Broncos lead series, 7-5-1;
See Denver vs. Pittsburgh
PITTSBURGH vs. DETROIT
Lions lead series, 16-9-1;
See Detroit vs. Pittsburgh
PITTSBURGH vs. GREEN BAY
Packers lead series, 19-10;
See Green Bay vs. Pittsburgh
PITTSBURGH vs. HOUSTON
Steelers lead series, 24-9;
See Houston vs. Pittsburgh
PITTSBURGH vs. INDIANAPOLIS
Steelers lead series, 9-4;
See Indianapolis vs. Pittsburgh
PITTSBURGH vs. KANSAS CITY
Steelers lead series, 9-4;

See Kansas City vs. Pittsburgh
PITTSBURGH vs. LA RAIDERS
Raiders lead series, 9-6;
See LA Raiders vs. Pittsburgh
PITTSBURGH vs. LA RAMS
Rams lead series, 14-4-2;
See LA Rams vs. Pittsburgh
PITTSBURGH vs. MIAMI
Dolphins lead series, 7-3;
See Miami vs. Pittsburgh
PITTSBURGH vs. MINNESOTA
Vikings lead series, 5-4;
See Minnesota vs. Pittsburgh
PITTSBURGH vs. NEW ENGLAND
Steelers lead series, 5-2;
See New England vs. Pittsburgh
PITTSBURGH vs. NEW ORLEANS
Series tied, 4-4;
See New Orleans vs. Pittsburgh
PITTSBURGH vs. *NY BULLDOGS
Steelers won series, 2-0;
See *NY Bulldogs vs. Pittsburgh
**Extinct team*
PITTSBURGH vs. NY GIANTS
Giants lead series, 43-27-3;
See NY Giants vs. Pittsburgh
PITTSBURGH vs. NY JETS
Steelers lead series, 8-0;
See NY Jets vs. Pittsburgh
PITTSBURGH vs. PHILADELPHIA
Eagles lead series, 42-25-3;
See Philadelphia vs. Pittsburgh
***PITTSBURGH vs. **ST. LOUIS**
Steelers lead series, 30-20-3
1933—Pirates, 14-13 (C)
1935—Pirates, 17-13 (P)
1936—Cardinals, 14-6 (C)
1937—Cardinals, 13-7 (P)
1939—Cardinals, 10-0 (P)
1940—Tie, 7-7 (P)
1942—Steelers, 19-3 (P)
1943—Phil-Pitt, 34-13 (P)
1945—Steelers, 23-0 (P)
1946—Steelers, 14-7 (P)
1948—Cardinals, 24-7 (P)
1950—Steelers, 28-17 (C)
Steelers, 28-7 (P)
1951—Steelers, 28-14 (C)
1952—Steelers, 34-28 (C)
Steelers, 17-14 (P)
1953—Steelers, 31-28 (P)
Steelers, 21-17 (C)
1954—Cardinals, 17-14 (C)
Steelers, 20-17 (P)
1955—Steelers, 14-7 (P)
Cardinals, 27-13 (C)
1956—Steelers, 14-7 (P)
Cardinals, 38-27 (C)
1957—Steelers, 29-20 (P)
Steelers, 27-2 (C)
1958—Steelers, 27-20 (C)
Steelers, 38-21 (P)
1959—Cardinals, 45-24 (C)
Steelers, 35-20 (P)
1960—Steelers, 27-14 (P)
Cardinals, 38-7 (StL)
1961—Steelers, 30-27 (P)
Cardinals, 20-0 (StL)
1962—Steelers, 26-17 (StL)
Steelers, 19-7 (P)
1963—Steelers, 23-10 (P)
Cardinals, 24-23 (StL)
1964—Cardinals, 34-30 (StL)
Cardinals, 21-20 (P)
1965—Cardinals, 20-7 (P)
Cardinals, 21-17 (P)
1966—Steelers, 30-9 (P)
Cardinals, 6-3 (StL)
1967—Cardinals, 28-14 (P)
Tie, 14-14 (StL)
1968—Tie, 28-28 (StL)
Cardinals, 20-10 (P)
1969—Cardinals, 27-14 (P)
Cardinals, 47-10 (StL)
1972—Steelers, 25-19 (StL)
1979—Steelers, 24-21 (StL)
1985—Steelers, 23-10 (P)
(Points—Steelers 1,041, Cardinals 965)
**Steelers known as Pirates prior to 1941 and as Phil-Pitt in 1943*
***Franchise in Chicago prior to 1960*
PITTSBURGH vs. *ST. LOUIS GUNNERS
Gunners won series, 1-0;
1934—Gunners, 6-0 (StL)
**Extinct team*
PITTSBURGH vs. SAN DIEGO
Steelers lead series, 8-4
1971—Steelers, 21-17 (P)
1972—Steelers, 24-2 (SD)
1973—Steelers, 38-21 (P)
1975—Steelers, 37-0 (SD)
1976—Steelers, 23-0 (P)
1977—Steelers, 10-9 (SD)
1979—Chargers, 35-7 (SD)
1980—Chargers, 26-17 (SD)
1982—*Chargers, 31-28 (P)
1983—Steelers, 26-3 (P)
1984—Steelers, 52-24 (P)
1985—Chargers, 54-44 (SD)
(Points—Steelers 327, Chargers 222)
**AFC First Round Playoff*
PITTSBURGH vs. SAN FRANCISCO
Series tied, 6-6
1951—49ers, 28-24 (P)
1952—Steelers, 24-7 (SF)
1954—49ers, 31-3 (SF)
1958—49ers, 23-20 (SF)
1961—Steelers, 20-10 (P)
1965—49ers, 27-17 (SF)
1968—49ers, 45-28 (P)
1973—Steelers, 37-14 (SF)
1977—Steelers, 27-0 (P)
1978—Steelers, 24-7 (SF)
1981—49ers, 17-14 (P)
1984—Steelers, 20-17 (SF)
(Points—Steelers 258, 49ers 226)
PITTSBURGH vs. SEATTLE
Steelers lead series, 3-2
1977—Steelers, 30-20 (P)
1978—Steelers, 21-10 (P)
1981—Seahawks, 24-21 (S)
1982—Seahawks, 16-0 (S)
1983—Steelers, 27-21 (S)
(Points—Steelers 99, Seahawks 91)
PITTSBURGH vs. TAMPA BAY
Steelers lead series, 3-0
1976—Steelers, 42-0 (P)
1980—Steelers, 24-21 (TB)
1983—Steelers, 17-12 (P)
(Points—Steelers 83, Buccaneers 33)
***PITTSBURGH vs. **WASHINGTON**
Redskins lead series, 41-28-4
1933—Redskins, 21-6 (P)
Pirates, 16-14 (B)
1934—Redskins, 7-0 (P)
Redskins, 39-0 (B)
1935—Pirates, 6-0 (P)
Redskins, 13-3 (B)
1936—Pirates, 10-0 (P)
Redskins, 30-0 (B)
1937—Redskins, 34-20 (W)
Pirates, 21-13 (P)
1938—Redskins, 7-0 (P)
Redskins, 15-0 (W)
1939—Redskins, 44-14 (W)
Redskins, 21-14 (P)
1940—Redskins, 40-10 (P)
Redskins, 37-10 (W)
1941—Redskins, 24-20 (P)
Redskins, 23-3 (W)
1942—Redskins, 28-14 (W)
Redskins, 14-0 (P)
1943—Tie, 14-14 (Phil)
Phil-Pitt, 27-14 (W)
1944—Redskins, 42-20 (W)
1945—Redskins, 14-0 (P)
Redskins, 24-0 (W)
1946—Tie, 14-14 (W)
Steelers, 14-7 (P)
1947—Redskins, 27-26 (W)
Steelers, 21-14 (P)
1948—Redskins, 17-14 (W)
Steelers, 10-7 (P)
1949—Redskins, 27-14 (P)
Redskins, 27-14 (W)
1950—Steelers, 26-7 (W)
Redskins, 24-7 (P)
1951—Redskins, 22-7 (P)
Steelers, 20-10 (W)
1952—Redskins, 28-24 (P)
Steelers, 24-23 (W)
1953—Redskins, 17-9 (P)
Steelers, 14-13 (W)
1954—Steelers, 37-7 (P)
Redskins, 17-14 (W)
1955—Redskins, 23-14 (P)
Redskins, 28-17 (W)
1956—Steelers, 30-13 (P)
Steelers, 23-0 (W)
1957—Steelers, 28-7 (P)
Redskins, 10-3 (W)
1958—Steelers, 24-16 (P)
Tie, 14-14 (W)
1959—Redskins, 23-17 (P)
Steelers, 27-6 (W)
1960—Tie, 27-27 (W)
Steelers, 22-10 (P)
1961—Steelers, 20-0 (P)
Steelers, 30-14 (P)
1962—Steelers, 23-21 (P)
Steelers, 27-24 (W)
1963—Steelers, 38-27 (P)
Steelers, 34-28 (W)
1964—Redskins, 30-0 (P)
Steelers, 14-7 (W)
1965—Redskins, 31-3 (P)
Redskins, 35-14 (W)
1966—Redskins, 33-27 (P)
Redskins, 24-10 (W)
1967—Redskins, 15-10 (P)
1968—Redskins, 16-13 (W)
1969—Redskins, 14-7 (P)
1973—Steelers, 21-16 (P)
1979—Steelers, 38-7 (P)
1985—Redskins, 30-23 (P)
(Points—Redskins 1,389, Steelers 1,135)
**Steelers known as Pirates prior to 1941, as Phil-Pitt in 1943, and as Card-Pitt in 1944*
***Franchise in Boston prior to 1937*

ST. LOUIS vs. ATLANTA
Cardinals lead series, 6-3;
See Atlanta vs. St. Louis
ST. LOUIS vs. *1950 BALTIMORE
Cardinals won series, 1-0;
See *1950 Baltimore vs. Chi. Cardinals
**Extinct team*
ST. LOUIS vs. *BOSTON YANKS
Cardinals won series, 3-0;
See *Boston Yanks vs. Chi. Cardinals
**Extinct team*
ST. LOUIS vs. *BROOKLYN DODGERS
Dodgers won series, 8-4
See *Brooklyn Dodgers vs. Chi. Cardinals
**Extinct team*
ST. LOUIS vs. BUFFALO
Cardinals lead series, 3-1;
See Buffalo vs. St. Louis
ST. LOUIS vs. CHI. BEARS
Bears lead series, 52-25-6;
See Chi. Bears vs. St. Louis
ST. LOUIS vs. CINCINNATI
Bengals lead series, 2-1;
See Cincinnati vs. St. Louis
ST. LOUIS vs. *CINCINNATI REDS
Cardinals won series, 3-1;
See *Cincinnati Reds vs. Chi. Cardinals
**Extinct team*
ST. LOUIS vs. CLEVELAND
Browns lead series, 30-10-3;
See Cleveland vs. St. Louis
ST. LOUIS vs. DALLAS
Cowboys lead series, 29-17-1;
See Dallas vs. St. Louis
ST. LOUIS vs. DENVER
Broncos lead series, 1-0-1;
See Denver vs. St. Louis
ST. LOUIS vs. DETROIT
Lions lead series, 27-15-5;
See Detroit vs. St. Louis
ST. LOUIS vs. GREEN BAY
Packers lead series, 40-22-4;
See Green Bay vs. St. Louis
ST. LOUIS vs. HOUSTON
Cardinals lead series, 3-1;
See Houston vs. St. Louis
ST. LOUIS vs. INDIANAPOLIS
Cardinals lead series, 5-4;
See Indianapolis vs. St. Louis
ST. LOUIS vs. KANSAS CITY
Chiefs lead series, 3-0-1;
See Kansas City vs. St. Louis
ST. LOUIS vs. LA RAIDERS
Series tied, 1-1;
See LA Raiders vs. St. Louis
ST. LOUIS vs. LA RAMS
Rams lead series, 22-15-2;
See LA Rams vs. St. Louis
ST. LOUIS vs. MIAMI
Dolphins lead series, 5-0;
See Miami vs. St. Louis
ST. LOUIS vs. MINNESOTA
Cardinals lead series, 7-3;
See Minnesota vs. St. Louis
ST. LOUIS vs. NEW ENGLAND
Cardinals lead series, 4-1;
See New England vs. St. Louis
ST. LOUIS vs. NEW ORLEANS
Cardinals lead series, 9-4;
See New Orleans vs. St. Louis
ST. LOUIS vs. *NY BULLDOGS
Cardinals won series, 1-0;
See *NY Bulldogs vs. Chi. Cardinals
**Extinct team*
ST. LOUIS vs. NY GIANTS
Giants lead series, 54-31-2;
See NY Giants vs. St. Louis
ST. LOUIS vs. NY JETS
Cardinals lead series, 2-1;
See NY Jets vs. St. Louis
ST. LOUIS vs. PHILADELPHIA
Cardinals lead series, 40-35-4;
See Philadelphia vs. St. Louis
ST. LOUIS vs. PITTSBURGH
Steelers lead series, 30-20-3;
See Pittsburgh vs. St. Louis
ST. LOUIS vs. SAN DIEGO
Chargers lead series, 2-1;
1971—Chargers, 20-17 (SD)
1976—Chargers, 43-24 (SD)
1983—Cardinals, 44-14 (StL)
(Points—Cardinals 85, Chargers 77)
***ST. LOUIS vs. SAN FRANCISCO**
Cardinals lead series, 7-6
1951—Cardinals, 27-21 (SF)
1957—Cardinals, 20-10 (SF)
1962—49ers, 24-17 (StL)
1964—Cardinals, 23-13 (SF)
1968—49ers, 35-17 (SF)
1971—49ers, 26-14 (StL)
1974—Cardinals, 34-9 (SF)
1976—Cardinals, 23-20 (StL) OT
1978—Cardinals, 16-10 (SF)
1979—Cardinals, 13-10 (StL)
1980—49ers, 24-21 (SF) OT
1982—49ers, 31-20 (StL)
1983—49ers, 42-27 (StL)
(Points—49ers 275, Cardinals 272)
**Team in Chicago prior to 1960*
ST. LOUIS vs. SEATTLE
Cardinals lead series, 2-0
1976—Cardinals, 30-24 (S)
1983—Cardinals, 33-28 (StL)
(Points—Cardinals 63, Seahawks 52)
ST. LOUIS vs. TAMPA BAY
Buccaneers lead series, 3-1
1977—Buccaneers, 17-7 (TB)
1981—Buccaneers, 20-10 (TB)
1983—Cardinals, 34-27 (TB)
1985—Buccaneers, 16-0 (TB)
(Points—Buccaneers 80, Cardinals 51)
***ST. LOUIS vs. **WASHINGTON**
Redskins lead series, 50-32-2
1932—Cardinals, 9-0 (B)
Braves, 8-6 (C)
1933—Redskins, 10-0 (C)
Tie, 0-0 (B)
1934—Redskins, 9-0 (B)
1935—Cardinals, 6-0 (B)
1936—Redskins, 13-10 (B)
1937—Cardinals, 21-14 (W)
1939—Redskins, 28-7 (W)
1940—Redskins, 28-21 (W)
1942—Redskins, 28-0 (W)
1943—Redskins, 13-7 (W)
1944—Redskins, 42-20 (W)
1945—Redskins, 24-21 (W)
1947—Redskins, 45-21 (W)
1949—Cardinals, 38-7 (C)
1950—Cardinals, 38-28 (W)
1951—Redskins, 7-3 (C)
Redskins, 20-17 (W)
1952—Redskins, 23-7 (C)
Cardinals, 17-6 (W)
1953—Redskins, 24-13 (C)
Redskins, 28-17 (W)
1954—Cardinals, 38-16 (C)
Redskins, 37-20 (W)
1955—Cardinals, 24-10 (W)
Redskins, 31-0 (C)
1956—Cardinals, 31-3 (W)
Redskins, 17-14 (C)
1957—Redskins, 37-14 (C)
Cardinals, 44-14 (W)
1958—Cardinals, 37-10 (C)
Redskins, 45-31 (W)
1959—Cardinals, 49-21 (C)
Redskins, 23-14 (W)
1960—Cardinals, 44-7 (StL)
Cardinals, 26-14 (W)
1961—Cardinals, 24-0 (W)
Cardinals, 38-24 (StL)
1962—Redskins, 24-14 (W)
Tie, 17-17 (StL)
1963—Cardinals, 21-7 (W)
Cardinals, 24-20 (StL)
1964—Cardinals, 23-17 (W)
Cardinals, 38-24 (StL)
1965—Cardinals, 37-16 (W)
Redskins, 24-20 (StL)
1966—Cardinals, 23-7 (StL)
Redskins, 26-20 (W)
1967—Cardinals, 27-21 (W)
1968—Cardinals, 41-14 (StL)
1969—Redskins, 33-17 (W)
1970—Cardinals, 27-17 (StL)
Redskins, 28-27 (W)
1971—Redskins, 24-17 (StL)
Redskins, 20-0 (W)
1972—Redskins, 24-10 (W)
Redskins, 33-3 (StL)
1973—Cardinals, 34-27 (StL)
Redskins, 31-13 (W)
1974—Cardinals, 17-10 (W)
Cardinals, 23-20 (StL)
1975—Redskins, 27-17 (W)
Cardinals, 20-17 (StL) OT
1976—Redskins, 20-10 (W)
Redskins, 16-10 (StL)
1977—Redskins, 24-14 (W)
Redskins, 26-20 (StL)
1978—Redskins, 28-10 (StL)
Cardinals, 27-17 (W)
1979—Redskins, 17-7 (StL)
Redskins, 30-28 (W)
1980—Redskins, 23-0 (W)
Redskins, 31-7 (StL)
1981—Cardinals, 40-30 (StL)
Redskins, 42-21 (W)
1982—Redskins, 12-7 (StL)
Redskins, 28-0 (W)
1983—Redskins, 38-14 (StL)
Redskins, 45-7 (W)
1984—Cardinals, 26-24 (StL)
Redskins, 29-27 (W)
1985—Redskins, 27-10 (W)
Redskins, 27-16 (StL)
(Points—Redskins 1,776, Cardinals 1,578)
**Team in Chicago prior to 1960 and known as Card-Pitt in 1944*
***Team in Boston prior to 1937 and known as Braves prior to 1933*

***ST. LOUIS GUNNERS vs. DETROIT**
Lions won series, 1-0;
See Detroit vs. *St. Louis Gunners
**Extinct team*
***ST. LOUIS GUNNERS vs. GREEN BAY**
Packers won series, 1-0;
See Green Bay vs. *St. Louis Gunners
**Extinct team*
***ST. LOUIS GUNNERS vs. PITTSBURGH**
Gunners won series, 1-0;
See Pittsburgh vs. *St. Louis Gunners
**Extinct team*

SAN DIEGO vs. ATLANTA
Falcons lead series, 2-0;
See Atlanta vs. San Diego
SAN DIEGO vs. BUFFALO
Chargers lead series, 17-9-2;
See Buffalo vs. San Diego
SAN DIEGO vs. CHI. BEARS
Chargers lead series, 4-1;
See Chi. Bears vs. San Diego
SAN DIEGO vs. CINCINNATI
Chargers lead series, 10-7;
See Cincinnati vs. San Diego
SAN DIEGO vs. CLEVELAND
Chargers lead series, 5-4-1;
See Cleveland vs. San Diego
SAN DIEGO vs. DALLAS
Cowboys lead series, 2-1;

See Dallas vs. San Diego
SAN DIEGO vs. DENVER
Chargers lead series, 27-24-1;
See Denver vs. San Diego
SAN DIEGO vs. DETROIT
Lions lead series, 3-2;
See Detroit vs. San Diego
SAN DIEGO vs. GREEN BAY
Packers lead series, 3-1;
See Green Bay vs. San Diego
SAN DIEGO vs. HOUSTON
Chargers lead series, 16-12-1;
See Houston vs. San Diego
SAN DIEGO vs. INDIANAPOLIS
Chargers lead series, 4-2;
See Indianapolis vs. San Diego
SAN DIEGO vs. KANSAS CITY
Chargers lead series, 26-24-1;
See Kansas City vs. San Diego
SAN DIEGO vs. LA RAIDERS
Raiders lead series, 33-18-2;
See LA Raiders vs. San Diego
SAN DIEGO vs. LA RAMS
Rams lead series, 2-1;
See LA Rams vs. San Diego
SAN DIEGO vs. MIAMI
Chargers lead series, 8-5;
See Miami vs. San Diego
SAN DIEGO vs. MINNESOTA
Series tied, 3-3;
See Minnesota vs. San Diego
SAN DIEGO vs. NEW ENGLAND
Patriots lead series, 13-12-2;
See New England vs. San Diego
SAN DIEGO vs. NEW ORLEANS
Chargers lead series, 3-0;
See New Orleans vs. San Diego
SAN DIEGO vs. NY GIANTS
Series tied, 2-2;
See NY Giants vs. San Diego
SAN DIEGO vs. NY JETS
Chargers lead series, 14-7-1;
See NY Jets vs. San Diego
SAN DIEGO vs. PHILADELPHIA
Chargers lead series, 2-1;
See Philadelphia vs. San Diego
SAN DIEGO vs. PITTSBURGH
Steelers lead series, 8-4;
See Pittsburgh vs. San Diego
SAN DIEGO vs. ST. LOUIS
Chargers lead series, 2-1;
See St. Louis vs. San Diego
SAN DIEGO vs. SAN FRANCISCO
Chargers lead series, 3-1
1972—49ers, 34-3 (SF)
1976—Chargers, 13-7 (SD) OT
1979—Chargers, 31-9 (SD)
1982—Chargers, 41-37 (SF)
(Points—Chargers, 88, 49ers 87)
SAN DIEGO vs. SEATTLE
Chargers lead series, 9-6
1977—Chargers, 30-28 (S)
1978—Chargers, 24-20 (S)
Chargers, 37-10 (SD)
1979—Chargers, 33-16 (S)
Chargers, 20-10 (SD)
1980—Chargers, 34-13 (S)
Chargers, 21-14 (SD)
1981—Chargers, 24-10 (SD)
Seahawks, 44-23 (S)
1983—Seahawks, 34-31 (S)
Chargers, 28-21 (SD)
1984—Seahawks, 31-17 (S)
Seahawks, 24-0 (SD)
1985—Seahawks, 49-35 (SD)
Seahawks, 26-21 (S)
(Points—Chargers 378, Seahawks 350)
SAN DIEGO vs. TAMPA BAY
Chargers lead series, 2-0
1976—Chargers, 23-0 (TB)
1981—Chargers, 24-23 (TB)
(Points—Chargers 47, Buccaneers 23)
SAN DIEGO vs. WASHINGTON
Redskins lead series, 3-0
1973—Redskins, 38-0 (W)
1980—Redskins, 40-17 (W)
1983—Redskins, 27-24 (SD)
(Points—Redskins 105, Chargers 41)

SAN FRANCISCO vs. ATLANTA
49ers lead series, 21-17;
See Atlanta vs. San Francisco
SAN FRANCISCO vs. *1950 BALTIMORE
49ers won series, 1-0;
See *1950 Baltimore vs. San Francisco
**Extinct team*
SAN FRANCISCO vs. BUFFALO
Bills lead series, 2-1;
See Buffalo vs. San Francisco
SAN FRANCISCO vs. CHI. BEARS
Bears lead series, 24-23-1;
See Chi. Bears vs. San Francisco
SAN FRANCISCO vs. CINCINNATI
49ers lead series, 4-1;
See Cincinnati vs. San Francisco
SAN FRANCISCO vs. CLEVELAND
Browns lead series, 8-4;
See Cleveland vs. San Francisco
SAN FRANCISCO vs. DALLAS
Series tied, 8-8-1;
See Dallas vs. San Francisco
SAN FRANCISCO vs. *DALLAS TEXANS
49ers won series, 2-0;
See *Dallas Texans vs. San Francisco
**Extinct team*
SAN FRANCISCO vs. DENVER
Broncos lead series, 3-2;
See Denver vs. San Francisco
SAN FRANCISCO vs. DETROIT
Lions lead series, 26-23-1;
See Detroit vs. San Francisco
SAN FRANCISCO vs. GREEN BAY
49ers lead series, 22-20-1;
See Green Bay vs. San Francisco
SAN FRANCISCO vs. HOUSTON
49ers lead series, 3-2;
See Houston vs. San Francisco
SAN FRANCISCO vs. INDIANAPOLIS
Colts lead series, 21-14;
See Indianapolis vs. San Francisco
SAN FRANCISCO vs. KANSAS CITY
49ers lead series, 3-1;
See Kansas City vs. San Francisco
SAN FRANCISCO vs. LA RAIDERS
Raiders lead series, 3-2;
See LA Raiders vs. San Francisco
SAN FRANCISCO vs. LA RAMS
Rams lead series, 44-26-2;
See LA Rams vs. San Francisco
SAN FRANCISCO vs. MIAMI
Dolphins lead series, 4-1;
See Miami vs. San Francisco
SAN FRANCISCO vs. MINNESOTA
Vikings lead series, 13-12-1;
See Minnesota vs. San Francisco
SAN FRANCISCO vs. NEW ENGLAND
49ers lead series, 3-1;
See New England vs. San Francisco
SAN FRANCISCO vs. NEW ORLEANS
49ers lead series, 22-9-2;
See New Orleans vs. San Francisco
SAN FRANCISCO vs. NY GIANTS
Giants lead series, 10-7;
See NY Giants vs. San Francisco
SAN FRANCISCO vs. NY JETS
49ers lead series, 3-1;
See NY Jets vs. San Francisco
SAN FRANCISCO vs. *NY YANKS
Yanks won series, 2-1-1;
See *NY Yanks vs. San Francisco
**Extinct team*
SAN FRANCISCO vs. PHILADELPHIA
49ers lead series, 10-4-1;
See Philadelphia vs. San Francisco
SAN FRANCISCO vs. PITTSBURGH
Series tied, 6-6;
See Pittsburgh vs. San Francisco
SAN FRANCISCO vs. ST. LOUIS
Cardinals lead series, 7-6;
See St. Louis vs. San Francisco
SAN FRANCISCO vs. SAN DIEGO
Chargers lead series, 3-1;
See San Diego vs. San Francisco
SAN FRANCISCO vs. SEATTLE
49ers lead series, 2-1
1976—49ers, 37-21 (S)
1979—Seahawks, 35-24 (SF)
1985—49ers, 19-6 (SF)
(Points—49ers 80, Seahawks 62)
SAN FRANCISCO vs. TAMPA BAY
49ers lead series, 5-1
1977—49ers, 20-10 (SF)
1978—49ers, 6-3 (SF)
1979—49ers, 23-7 (SF)
1980—Buccaneers, 24-23 (SF)
1983—49ers, 35-21 (SF)
1984—49ers, 24-17 (SF)
(Points—49ers 131, Buccaneers 82)
SAN FRANCISCO vs. WASHINGTON
49ers lead series, 8-6-1
1952—49ers, 23-17 (W)
1954—49ers, 41-7 (SF)
1955—Redskins, 7-0 (W)
1961—49ers, 35-3 (SF)
1967—Redskins, 31-28 (W)
1969—Tie, 17-17 (SF)
1970—49ers, 26-17 (SF)
1971—*49ers, 24-20 (SF)
1973—Redskins, 33-9 (W)
1976—Redskins, 24-21 (SF)
1978—Redskins, 38-20 (W)
1981—49ers, 30-17 (W)
1983—**Redskins, 24-21 (W)
1984—49ers, 37-31 (SF)
1985—49ers, 35-8 (W)
(Points—49ers 367, Redskins 294)
**NFC Divisional Playoff*
***NFC Championship*

SEATTLE vs. ATLANTA
Seahawks lead series, 3-0;
See Atlanta vs. Seattle
SEATTLE vs. BUFFALO
Seahawks lead series, 2-0;
See Buffalo vs. Seattle
SEATTLE vs. CHI. BEARS
Seahawks lead series, 3-1;
See Chi. Bears vs. Seattle
SEATTLE vs. CINCINNATI
Bengals lead series, 3-2;
See Cincinnati vs. Seattle
SEATTLE vs. CLEVELAND
Seahawks lead series, 7-2;
See Cleveland vs. Seattle
SEATTLE vs. DALLAS
Cowboys lead series, 3-0;
See Dallas vs. Seattle
SEATTLE vs. DENVER
Broncos lead series, 11-7;
See Denver vs. Seattle
SEATTLE vs. DETROIT
Seahawks lead series, 2-1;
See Detroit vs. Seattle
SEATTLE vs. GREEN BAY
Packers lead series, 3-1;
See Green Bay vs. Seattle
SEATTLE vs. HOUSTON
Oilers lead series, 3-2;
See Houston vs. Seattle
SEATTLE vs. INDIANAPOLIS
Colts lead series, 2-0;
See Indianapolis vs. Seattle
SEATTLE vs. KANSAS CITY
Chiefs lead series, 8-7;
See Kansas City vs. Seattle
SEATTLE vs. LA RAIDERS
Series tied, 9-9;
See LA Raiders vs. Seattle
SEATTLE vs. LA RAMS
Rams lead series, 3-0;
See LA Rams vs. Seattle
SEATTLE vs. MIAMI
Dolphins lead series, 3-1;
See Miami vs. Seattle
SEATTLE vs. MINNESOTA
Seahawks lead series, 2-1;
See Minnesota vs. Seattle
SEATTLE vs. NEW ENGLAND
Patriots lead series, 5-1;
See New England vs. Seattle
SEATTLE vs. NEW ORLEANS
Seahawks lead series, 2-1;
See New Orleans vs. Seattle
SEATTLE vs. NY GIANTS
Giants lead series, 3-1;
See NY Giants vs. Seattle
SEATTLE vs. NY JETS
Seahawks lead series, 7-1;
See NY Jets vs. Seattle
SEATTLE vs. PHILADELPHIA
Eagles lead series, 2-0;
See Philadelphia vs. Seattle
SEATTLE vs. PITTSBURGH
Steelers lead series, 3-2;
See Pittsburgh vs. Seattle
SEATTLE vs. ST. LOUIS
Cardinals lead series, 2-0;
See St. Louis vs. Seattle
SEATTLE vs. SAN DIEGO
Chargers lead series, 9-6;
See San Diego vs. Seattle
SEATTLE vs. SAN FRANCISCO
49ers lead series, 2-1;
See San Francisco vs. Seattle
SEATTLE vs. TAMPA BAY
Seahawks lead series, 2-0
1976—Seahawks, 13-10 (TB)
1977—Seahawks, 30-23 (S)
(Points—Seahawks 43, Buccaneers 33)
SEATTLE vs. WASHINGTON
Redskins lead series, 2-1
1976—Redskins, 31-7 (W)
1980—Seahawks, 14-0 (W)
1983—Redskins, 27-17 (S)
(Points—Redskins 58, Seahawks 38)

TAMPA BAY vs. ATLANTA
Buccaneers lead series, 3-2;
See Atlanta vs. Tampa Bay
TAMPA BAY vs. BUFFALO
Buccaneers lead series, 2-1;
See Buffalo vs. Tampa Bay
TAMPA BAY vs. CHI. BEARS
Bears lead series, 12-4;
See Chi. Bears vs. Tampa Bay
TAMPA BAY vs. CINCINNATI
Bengals lead series, 2-1;
See Cincinnati vs. Tampa Bay
TAMPA BAY vs. CLEVELAND
Browns lead series, 3-0;
See Cleveland vs. Tampa Bay
TAMPA BAY vs. DALLAS
Cowboys lead series, 6-0;
See Dallas vs. Tampa Bay
TAMPA BAY vs. DENVER
Broncos lead series, 2-0;
See Denver vs. Tampa Bay
TAMPA BAY vs. DETROIT
Lions lead series, 9-7;
See Detroit vs. Tampa Bay
TAMPA BAY vs. GREEN BAY
Packers lead series, 8-6-1;
See Green Bay vs. Tampa Bay
TAMPA BAY vs. HOUSTON
Oilers lead series, 2-1;
See Houston vs. Tampa Bay
TAMPA BAY vs. INDIANAPOLIS
Colts lead series, 2-1;
See Indianapolis vs. Tampa Bay
TAMPA BAY vs. KANSAS CITY
Chiefs lead series, 3-2;
See Kansas City vs. Tampa Bay
TAMPA BAY vs. LA RAIDERS
Raiders lead series, 2-0;
See LA Raiders vs. Tampa Bay
TAMPA BAY vs. LA RAMS
Rams lead series, 5-2;
See LA Rams vs. Tampa Bay
TAMPA BAY vs. MIAMI
Dolphins lead series, 2-1;
See Miami vs. Tampa Bay
TAMPA BAY vs. MINNESOTA
Vikings lead series, 11-5;
See Minnesota vs. Tampa Bay
TAMPA BAY vs. NEW ENGLAND
Patriots lead series, 2-0;
See New England vs. Tampa Bay
TAMPA BAY vs. NEW ORLEANS
Saints lead series, 5-3;
See New Orleans vs. Tampa Bay
TAMPA BAY vs. NY GIANTS
Giants lead series, 6-3;
See NY Giants vs. Tampa Bay
TAMPA BAY vs. NY JETS
Jets lead series, 3-1;
See NY Jets vs. Tampa Bay
TAMPA BAY vs. PHILADELPHIA
Eagles lead series, 2-1;
See Philadelphia vs. Tampa Bay
TAMPA BAY vs. PITTSBURGH
Steelers lead series, 3-0;
See Pittsburgh vs. Tampa Bay
TAMPA BAY vs. ST. LOUIS
Buccaneers lead series, 3-1;
See St. Louis vs. Tampa Bay
TAMPA BAY vs. SAN DIEGO
Chargers lead series, 2-0;
See San Diego vs. Tampa Bay
TAMPA BAY vs. SAN FRANCISCO
49ers lead series, 5-1;
See San Francisco vs. Tampa Bay
TAMPA BAY vs. SEATTLE
Seahawks lead series, 2-0;
See Seattle vs. Tampa Bay
TAMPA BAY vs. WASHINGTON
Redskins lead series, 2-0
1977—Redskins, 10-0 (TB)
1982—Redskins, 21-13 (TB)
(Points—Redskins 31, Buccaneers 13)

WASHINGTON vs. ATLANTA
Redskins lead series, 9-2-1;
See Atlanta vs. Washington
WASHINGTON vs. *1950 BALTIMORE
Redskins won series, 2-0;
See *1950 Baltimore vs. Washington
**Extinct team*
WASHINGTON vs. *BOSTON YANKS
Redskins won series, 8-2;
See *Boston Yanks vs. Washington
**Extinct team*
WASHINGTON vs. *BROOKLYN DODGERS
Redskins won series, 17-5-3;
See *Brooklyn Dodgers vs Washington
**Extinct team*
WASHINGTON vs. BUFFALO
Series tied 2-2;
See Buffalo vs. Washington
WASHINGTON vs. CHI. BEARS
Bears lead series, 20-11-1;
See Chi. Bears vs. Washington
WASHINGTON vs. CINCINNATI
Redskins lead series, 3-1;
See Cincinnati vs. Washington
WASHINGTON vs. CLEVELAND
Browns lead series, 31-8-1;
See Cleveland vs. Washington
WASHINGTON vs. DALLAS
Cowboys lead series, 30-20-2;
See Dallas vs. Washington
WASHINGTON vs. DENVER
Redskins lead series, 2-1;
See Denver vs. Washington
WASHINGTON vs. DETROIT
Redskins lead series, 19-8;
See Detroit vs. Washington
WASHINGTON vs. GREEN BAY
Packers lead series, 14-11-1;
See Green Bay vs. Washington
WASHINGTON vs. HOUSTON
Series tied, 2-2;
See Houston vs. Washington
WASHINGTON vs. INDIANAPOLIS
Colts lead series, 15-6;
See Indianapolis vs. Washington
WASHINGTON vs. KANSAS CITY
Chiefs lead series, 2-1;
See Kansas City vs. Washington
WASHINGTON vs. LA RAIDERS
Raiders lead series, 4-1;
See LA Raiders vs. Washington
WASHINGTON vs. LA RAMS
Redskins lead series, 14-5-1;
See LA Rams vs. Washington
WASHINGTON vs. MIAMI
Dolphins lead series, 4-2;
See Miami vs. Washington
WASHINGTON vs. MINNESOTA
Vikings lead series, 5-4;
See Minnesota vs. Washington
WASHINGTON vs. NEW ENGLAND
Redskins lead series, 3-1;
See New England vs. Washington
WASHINGTON vs. NEW ORLEANS
Redskins lead series, 7-4;
See New Orleans vs. Washington
WASHINGTON vs. *NY BULLDOGS
Redskins won series, 1-0-1;
See *NY Bulldogs vs. Washington
**Extinct team*
WASHINGTON vs. NY GIANTS
Giants lead series, 58-46-3;
See NY Giants vs. Washington
WASHINGTON vs. NY JETS
Redskins lead series, 3-0;
See NY Jets vs. Washington
WASHINGTON vs. PHILADELPHIA

Redskins lead series, 57-40-6;
See Philadelphia vs. Washington

WASHINGTON vs. PITTSBURGH
Redskins lead series, 41-28-4;
See Pittsburgh vs. Washington

WASHINGTON vs. ST. LOUIS
Redskins lead series, 50-32-2;
See St. Louis vs. Washington

WASHINGTON vs. SAN DIEGO
Redskins lead series, 3-0;
See San Diego vs. Washington

WASHINGTON vs. SAN FRANCISCO
49ers lead series, 8-6-1;
See San Francisco vs. Washington

WASHINGTON vs. SEATTLE
Redskins lead series, 2-1;
See Seattle vs. Washington

WASHINGTON vs. TAMPA BAY
Redskins lead series, 2-0;
See Tampa Bay vs. Washington

The Super Bowl

SUPER BOWL I

GREEN BAY 35, KANSAS CITY 10

The Green Bay Packers, leading 14-10 at halftime, scored two third-quarter touchdowns and advanced to a 35-10 victory over the Kansas City Chiefs in the first Super Bowl, officially designated as the AFL-NFL World Championship Game.

The Super Bowl was the result of the 1966 merger between the American Football League and National Football League. The game matched champions from each league in the Los Angeles Memorial Coliseum. Green Bay of the NFL was a 13½-point favorite but the game was in doubt after Kansas City of the AFL outgained the Packers 181-164 and led 11-9 in first downs in the first half.

Green Bay was the first team to score, after nine minutes of the first quarter. The Packers marched 43 yards in five plays to the Chiefs' 37-yard line after an exchange of punts. On the sixth play, quarterback Bart Starr froze the Chiefs' secondary with a play-action fake at the line of scrimmage, then passed to end Max McGee. The ball was thrown slightly behind McGee, who caught the pass with one hand, balanced the ball on his hip, and outran the Chiefs the remaining 19 yards to the end zone.

The 34-year-old McGee, who caught four passes for 91 yards and one touchdown during the regular season, replaced Boyd Dowler on the second play of the game. Dowler reinjured a shoulder blocking linebacker E. J. Holub on a sweep to the left side.

Kansas City tied the score 7-7 in the second quarter with a six-play, 66-yard drive. Quarterback Len Dawson threw a pass from the 7-yard line to fullback Curtis McClinton, who caught the ball in the end zone. The Packers went ahead 14-7 on their next possession. A 64-yard pass play, Starr to Carroll Dale for a touchdown, was called back because left tackle Bob Skoronski was in motion before the snap of the ball. The Packers recovered from the setback to score 11 plays later. Fullback Jim Taylor, behind blocks from guards Fred (Fuzzy) Thurston and Jerry Kramer, swept left end for 14 yards, concluding a 73-yard drive that took 14 plays. The Packers kept the drive going by converting four third downs.

The Chiefs started from their 26 on the next series. After Dawson was dropped for an eight-yard loss on first down, Kansas City moved 50 yards in five plays. On third and 10 from Green Bay's 32, Dawson connected with running back Mike Garrett for an eight-yard gain. Mike Mercer then kicked a 31-yard field goal with 54 seconds remaining in the half, cutting the Packers' lead to 14-10.

The Chiefs marched 20 yards in three plays after taking the kickoff for the third quarter. On third and five from Kansas City's 49, Dawson received a heavy rush from tackle Henry Jordan and end Willie Davis. Jordan hit Dawson's arm as he followed through on a pass and Willie Wood intercepted. Wood returned the ball 50 yards to the Chiefs' 5-yard line. Elijah Pitts went through left tackle on the next play for a touchdown that made it 21-10.

The Chiefs did not threaten again. They had the ball for six more series and punted each time—from the 50-yard line and their 18, 2, 39, 40, and 16.

Packers coach Vince Lombardi, whose team converted 10 of 14 third-down situations, was asked to compare the Chiefs with teams of the NFL, a question many sports fans had been asking.

"In my opinion, the Chiefs don't rate with the top names in the NFL," he said. "They are a good football team with fine speed, but I'd have to say NFL football is better. Dallas is a better team and so are several others. That's what you wanted me to say, wasn't it?"

Date—January 15, 1967
Site—Memorial Coliseum, Los Angeles
Time—1:05 P.M. PST
Conditions—72 degrees, sunny
Playing Surface—Grass
Television and Radio—National Broadcasting Company (NBC) and Columbia Broadcasting System (CBS)
Regular Season Records—Green Bay, 12-2; Kansas City, 11-2-1
League Championships—Green Bay defeated the Dallas Cowboys 34-27 for the NFL title; Kansas City defeated the Buffalo Bills 31-7 for the AFL title
Players' Shares—$15,000 to each member of the winning team; $7,500 to each member of the losing team
Attendance—61,946
Gross Receipts—$2,768,211.64
Officials—Referee, Norm Schacter, NFL; umpire, George Young, AFL; line judge, Al Sabato, AFL; head linesman, Bernie Ulman, NFL; back judge, Jack Reader, AFL; field judge, Mike Lisetski, NFL
Coaches—Hank Stram, Kansas City; Vince Lombardi, Green Bay

Kansas City	Starters, Offense	Green Bay
Chris Burford	SE	Boyd Dowler
Jim Tyrer	LT	Bob Skoronski
Ed Budde	LG	Fred (Fuzzy) Thurston
Wayne Frazier	C	Bill Curry
Curt Merz	RG	Jerry Kramer
Dave Hill	RT	Forrest Gregg
Fred Arbanas	TE	Marv Fleming
Otis Taylor	FL	Carroll Dale
Len Dawson	QB	Bart Starr
Curtis McClinton	FB	Jim Taylor
Mike Garrett	HB	Elijah Pitts
	Starters, Defense	
Jerry Mays	LE	Willie Davis
Andy Rice	LT	Ron Kostelnik
Buck Buchanan	RT	Henry Jordan
Chuck Hurston	RE	Lionel Aldridge
Bobby Bell	LLB	Dave Robinson
Sherrill Headrick	MLB	Ray Nitschke
E. J. Holub	RLB	Lee Roy Caffey
Fred Williamson	LCB	Herb Adderley
Willie Mitchell	RCB	Bob Jeter
Bobby Hunt	SS	Tom Brown
Johnny Robinson	FS	Willie Wood

Kansas City	0	10	0	0	—	10
Green Bay	7	7	14	7	—	35

GB—McGee 37 pass from Starr (Chandler kick)
KC—McClinton 7 pass from Dawson (Mercer kick)
GB—Taylor 14 run (Chandler kick)
KC—FG Mercer 31
GB—Pitts 5 run (Chandler kick)
GB—McGee 13 pass from Starr (Chandler kick)
GB—Pitts 1 run (Chandler kick)

TEAM STATISTICS	KC	GB
First downs	17	21
Rushing	4	10
Passing	12	11
By penalty	1	0
Total yardage	239	358
Net rushing yardage	72	130
Net passing yardage	167	228
Passes att.-comp.-had int.	32-17-1	24-16-1

RUSHING
Kansas City—Dawson, 3 for 24; Garrett, 6 for 17; McClinton, 6 for 16; Beathard, 1 for 14; Coan, 3 for 1.
Green Bay—J. Taylor, 16 for 53, 1 TD; Pitts, 11 for 45, 2 TDs; D. Anderson, 4 for 30; Grabowski, 2 for 2.
PASSING
Kansas City—Dawson, 16 of 27 for 211, 1 TD, 1 int.; Beathard, 1 of 5 for 17.
Green Bay—Starr, 16 of 23 for 250, 2 TDs, 1 int.; Bratkowski, 0 of 1.
RECEIVING
Kansas City—Burford, 4 for 67; O. Taylor, 4 for 57; Garrett, 3 for 28; McClinton, 2 for 34, 1 TD; Arbanas, 2 for 30; Carolan, 1 for 7; Coan, 1 for 5.
Green Bay—McGee, 7 for 138, 2 TDs; Dale, 4 for 59; Pitts, 2 for 32; Fleming, 2 for 22; J. Taylor, 1 for −1.
PUNTING
Kansas City—Wilson, 7 for 317, 45.3 average.
Green Bay—Chandler, 3 for 130, 43.3 average; D. Anderson, 1 for 43.
PUNT RETURNS
Kansas City—Garrett, 2 for 17; E. Thomas, 1 for 2.
Green Bay—D. Anderson, 3 for 25; Wood, 1 for −2, 1 fair catch.
KICKOFF RETURNS
Kansas City—Coan, 4 for 87; Garrett, 2 for 23.
Green Bay—Adderley, 2 for 40; D. Anderson, 1 for 25.
INTERCEPTIONS
Kansas City—Mitchell, 1 for 0.
Green Bay—Wood, 1 for 50.

KANSAS CITY CHIEFS

No.	Name	Pos.	Ht.	Wt.	Year
52	Abell, Bud	LB	6-3	220	R
84	Arbanas, Fred	TE	6-3	240	5
10	Beathard, Pete	QB	6-2	210	3
78	Bell, Bobby	LB	6-4	228	4
61	Biodrowski, Denny	G	6-1	225	4
87	Brown, Aaron	DE	6-5	265	R
86	Buchanan, Buck	DT	6-7	287	4
71	Budde, Ed	G	6-5	260	4
88	Burford, Chris	SE	6-3	220	7
80	Carolan, Reg	TE	6-6	238	5
23	Coan, Bert	FB	6-4	220	5
56	Corey, Walt	LB	6-1	233	6
16	Dawson, Len	QB	6-0	190	10
72	DiMidio, Tony	T	6-3	250	R
66	Frazier, Wayne	C	6-3	245	3
21	Garrett, Mike	HB	5-9	195	R
69	Headrick, Sherrill	LB	6-2	240	8
73	Hill, Dave	T	6-5	264	4
55	Holub, E. J.	LB	6-4	236	6
20	Hunt, Bobby	S	6-1	193	5
85	Hurston, Chuck	DE	6-6	240	2
75	Mays, Jerry	DE	6-4	252	6
32	McClinton, Curtis	FB	6-3	227	5
15	Mercer, Mike	K	6-0	210	6
64	Merz, Curt	G	6-4	267	7
22	Mitchell, Willie	CB	6-1	185	3
25	Pitts, Frank	SE	6-2	190	2
14	Ply, Bobby	S	6-1	196	5
60	Reynolds, Al	G	6-3	250	7
58	Rice, Andy	DT	6-2	260	R
42	Robinson, Johnny	S	6-1	205	7
17	Smith, Fletcher	S	6-2	188	R
35	Stover, Smokey	LB	6-0	227	7
89	Taylor, Otis	FL	6-2	211	2
18	Thomas, Emmitt	CB	6-2	189	R
45	Thomas, Gene	HB	6-1	210	R
77	Tyrer, Jim	T	6-6	292	6
24	Williamson, Fred	CB	6-3	209	7
44	Wilson, Jerrel	P	6-4	222	4

GREEN BAY PACKERS

No.	Name	Pos.	Ht.	Wt.	Year
26	Adderley, Herb	CB	6-0	210	6
82	Aldridge, Lionel	DE	6-4	245	4
88	Anderson, Bill	TE	6-3	216	8
44	Anderson, Donny	HB	6-2	210	R
57	Bowman, Ken	C	6-3	230	3
12	Bratkowski, Zeke	QB	6-3	200	11
78	Brown, Bob	DE	6-5	270	R
40	Brown, Tom	S	6-1	190	3
60	Caffey, Lee Roy	LB	6-3	250	4
34	Chandler, Don	P-K	6-2	210	11
56	Crutcher, Tommy	LB	6-3	230	3
50	Curry, Bill	C	6-2	235	2
84	Dale, Carroll	FL	6-2	200	7
87	Davis, Willie	DE	6-3	245	9
86	Dowler, Boyd	SE	6-5	225	8
81	Fleming, Marv	TE	6-4	235	4
68	Gillingham, Gale	G	6-3	250	R
33	Grabowski, Jim	FB	6-2	215	R
75	Gregg, Forrest	T	6-4	250	10
43	Hart, Doug	S	6-0	190	3
45	Hathcock, Dave	CB	6-0	190	R
5	Hornung, Paul	HB	6-2	215	9
21	Jeter, Bob	CB	6-1	205	4
74	Jordan, Henry	DT	6-3	250	10
77	Kostelnik, Ron	DT	6-4	260	6
64	Kramer, Jerry	G	6-3	245	9
80	Long, Bob	FL	6-3	190	3
27	Mack, Bill (Red)	FL	5-10	185	6
85	McGee, Max	SE	6-3	205	11
66	Nitschke, Ray	LB	6-3	240	9
22	Pitts, Elijah	HB	6-1	205	6
89	Robinson, Dave	LB	6-3	245	4
76	Skoronski, Bob	DT	6-3	250	9
15	Starr, Bart	QB	6-1	200	11
31	Taylor, Jim	FB	6-0	215	9
63	Thurston, Fred (Fuzzy)	G	6-1	245	9
37	Vandersea, Phil	FB	6-3	225	R
73	Weatherwax, Jim	DT	6-7	275	R
24	Wood, Willie	S	5-10	190	7
72	Wright, Steve	T	6-6	250	3

SUPER BOWL II

GREEN BAY 33, OAKLAND 14

The Green Bay Packers, 14-point favorites at the start of the game, defeated the Oakland Raiders 33-14 for their second straight Super Bowl victory. Packers quarterback Bart Starr completed 13 of 24 passes for 202 yards and one touchdown and helped the Packers convert 6 of 11 third-down situations.

The Packers moved 34 yards in 11 plays the first time they had the ball. On fourth and 11 from Oakland's 32, Don Chandler kicked a 39-yard field goal, his first of four. The Packers then held the ball for 8:40 during their second possession, moving 84 yards, from their 3 to the Raiders' 13, in 17 plays. Chandler kicked a 20-yard field goal for a 6-0 lead.

Green Bay increased its lead to 13-0 moments later, after holding Oakland without a first down. On the first play from the Packers' 38-yard line, Starr passed to Boyd Dowler, who ran inside of cornerback Kent McCloughan and was beyond the last defender when he caught the ball and completed a 62-yard touchdown. "I just bulled by McCloughan," Dowler explained. "He was playing me tight and bumped me and I ran through him. There was no one left to stop me." Carroll Dale had been the primary receiver, but when the Raiders blitzed, Starr sensed that Dowler would be open.

Oakland closed to 13-7 on the following series. The Raiders moved 78 yards in nine plays, scoring on Daryle Lamonica's 23-yard pass to end Bill Miller. The drive took 4:20 as Lamonica completed four of five passes for 58 yards. Miller got behind defensive backs Herb Adderley and Tom Brown in the end zone. "I was supposed to take Miller deep, but I played him too soft," said Brown. "[Linebacker] Dave Robinson dropped back with him as far as he could, and I should have taken him, but I didn't."

Green Bay led 16-7 at halftime after Oakland's Rodger Bird fumbled a fair catch on a punt at the Raiders' 45-yard line. Dick Capp, who had been activated by Green Bay the day before, made the recovery. Starr completed a pass to Dowler for a nine-yard gain to the 36 with six seconds left in the half. Chandler then kicked a 43-yard field goal.

The Packers broke open the game in the third quarter, just as they had done in defeating the Kansas City Chiefs 35-10 in Super Bowl I. They went 82 yards in 11 plays on their second possession. Donny Anderson scored a touchdown from the 2-yard line to make the score 23-7. Starr converted two third-down situations during that drive, once passing to Max McGee for a 35-yard gain on third and one and passing 11 yards to Dale on third and nine.

Chandler's 31-yard field goal gave Green Bay a 26-7 lead at the end of the quarter. Early in the fourth period, defensive back Herb Adderley intercepted a pass by Lamonica and ran 60 yards for Green Bay's final touchdown. "Lamonica was trying to hit Fred Biletnikoff on a slant-in," said Adderley. "I played the ball and cut in front of him. It was no gamble."

Oakland scored the final touchdown with 9:13 remaining in the game. The Raiders went 74 yards in four plays, Lamonica throwing to Miller again for 23 yards and the touchdown. Miller beat Brown once more after a pass play from Lamonica to Pete Banaszak covered 41 yards and set up the play.

"It wasn't our best," said Packers coach Vince Lombardi of his team's effort. "All year it seemed like as soon as we got a couple touchdowns ahead we let up. Maybe that's the sign of a veteran team, such as ours. I don't know."

Several days after the game Lombardi announced that he was retiring as the Packers' coach to devote full time to his job as general manager.

Date—January 14, 1968
Site—Orange Bowl, Miami
Time—3:05 P.M. EST
Conditions—86, partly cloudy
Playing Surface—Grass
Television and Radio—Columbia Broadcasting System (CBS)
Regular Season Records—Green Bay, 9-4-1, Oakland, 13-1
League Championships—Green Bay defeated the Dallas Cowboys 21-17 for the NFL title; Oakland defeated the Houston Oilers 40-7 for the AFL title
Players' Shares—$15,000 to each member of the winning team; $7,500 to each member of the losing team
Attendance—75,546
Gross Receipts—$3,349,106.89
Officials—Referee, Jack Vest, AFL; umpire, Ralph Morcroft, NFL; line judge, Bruce Alford, NFL; head linesman, Tony Veteri, AFL; back judge, Stan Javie, NFL; field judge, Bob Bauer, AFL
Coaches—Vince Lombardi, Green Bay; John Rauch, Oakland

Green Bay	Starters, Offense	Oakland
Boyd Dowler	SE	Bill Miller
Bob Skoronski	LT	Bob Svihus
Gale Gillingham	LG	Gene Upshaw
Ken Bowman	C	Jim Otto
Jerry Kramer	RG	Wayne Hawkins
Forrest Gregg	RT	Harry Schuh
Marv Fleming	TE	Billy Cannon
Carroll Dale	FL	Fred Biletnikoff
Bart Starr	QB	Daryle Lamonica
Ben Wilson	RB	Hewritt Dixon
Donny Anderson	RB	Pete Banaszak
	Starters, Defense	
Willie Davis	LE	Isaac Lassiter
Ron Kostelnik	LT	Dan Birdwell
Henry Jordan	RT	Tom Keating
Lionel Aldridge	RE	Ben Davidson
Dave Robinson	LLB	Bill Laskey
Ray Nitschke	MLB	Dan Conners
Lee Roy Caffey	RLB	Gus Otto
Herb Adderley	LCB	Kent McCloughan
Bob Jeter	RCB	Willie Brown
Tom Brown	SS	Warren Powers
Willie Wood	FS	Howie Williams

Green Bay	3	13	10	7	—	33
Oakland	0	7	0	7	—	14

GB —FG Chandler 39
GB —FG Chandler 20
GB —Dowler 62 pass from Starr (Chandler kick)
Oak—Miller 23 pass from Lamonica (Blanda kick)
GB —FG Chandler 43
GB —Anderson 2 run (Chandler kick)
GB —FG Chandler 31
GB —Adderley 60 interception (Chandler kick)
Oak—Miller 23 pass from Lamonica (Blanda kick)

TEAM STATISTICS	GB	Oak
First downs	19	16
Rushing	11	5
Passing	7	10
By penalty	1	1
Total yardage	322	293
Net rushing yardage	160	107
Net passing yardage	162	186
Passes att.-comp.-had int.	24-13-0	34-15-1

RUSHING
Green Bay—Wilson, 17 for 62; Anderson, 14 for 48, 1 TD; Williams, 8 for 36; Starr, 1 for 14; Mercein, 1 for 0.
Oakland—Dixon, 12 for 54; Todd, 2 for 37; Banaszak, 6 for 16.
PASSING
Green Bay—Starr, 13 of 24 for 202, 1 TD.
Oakland—Lamonica, 15 of 34 for 208, 2 TDs, 1 int.
RECEIVING
Green Bay—Dale, 4 for 43; Fleming, 4 for 35; Dowler, 2 for 71, 1 TD; Anderson, 2 for 18; McGee, 1 for 35.
Oakland—Miller, 5 for 84, 2 TDs; Banaszak, 4 for 69; Cannon, 2 for 25; Biletnikoff, 2 for 10; Wells, 1 for 17; Dixon, 1 for 3.
PUNTING
Green Bay—Anderson, 6 for 234, 39.0 average.
Oakland—Eischeid, 6 for 264, 44.0 average.
PUNT RETURNS
Green Bay—Wood, 3 for 35.
Oakland—Bird, 2 for 12, 1 fair catch; Wells, 1 for 0.
KICKOFF RETURNS
Green Bay—Adderley, 1 for 24; Williams, 1 for 18; Crutcher, 1 for 7.
Oakland—Todd, 3 for 63; Grayson, 2 for 61; Hawkins, 1 for 3; Kocourek, 1 for 0, Kocourek lateraled to Grayson, who returned 11 yards.
INTERCEPTIONS
Green Bay—Adderley, 1 for 60, 1 TD.
Oakland—None.

GREEN BAY PACKERS

No.	Name	Pos.	Ht.	Wt.	Year
26	Adderley, Herb	CB	6-0	200	7
82	Aldridge, Lionel	DE	6-4	245	5
44	Anderson, Donny	HB-P	6-3	210	2
57	Bowman, Ken	C	6-3	230	4
12	Bratkowski, Zeke	QB	6-3	210	12
78	Brown, Bob	DE	6-5	260	2
40	Brown, Tom	S	6-1	195	4
60	Caffey, Lee Roy	LB	6-3	250	5
88	Capp, Dick	TE-LB	6-3	235	R
34	Chandler, Don	K	6-2	210	12
56	Crutcher, Tommy	LB	6-3	230	4
84	Dale, Carroll	FL	6-2	200	8
87	Davis, Willie	DE	6-3	245	10
86	Dowler, Boyd	SE	6-5	225	9
55	Flanigan, Jim	LB	6-3	240	R
81	Fleming, Marv	TE	6-4	235	5
68	Gillingham, Gale	G	6-3	255	2
33	Grabowski, Jim	FB	6-2	220	2
75	Gregg, Forrest	T	6-4	250	11
43	Hart, Doug	S	6-0	190	4
13	Horn, Don	QB	6-2	195	R
50	Hyland, Bob	C-G	6-5	250	R
21	Jeter, Bob	CB	6-1	205	5
74	Jordan, Henry	DT	6-3	250	11
77	Kostelnik, Ron	DT	6-4	260	7
64	Kramer, Jerry	G	6-3	245	10
80	Long, Bob	FL	6-3	205	4
85	McGee, Max	SE	6-3	210	12
30	Mercein, Chuck	FB	6-2	225	4
66	Nitschke, Ray	LB	6-3	235	10
89	Robinson, Dave	LB	6-3	240	5
45	Rowser, John	CB	6-1	180	R
76	Skoronski, Bob	T	6-3	245	10
15	Starr, Bart	QB	6-1	190	12
63	Thurston, Fred (Fuzzy)	G	6-1	245	10
73	Weatherwax, Jim	DT	6-7	260	2
23	Williams, Travis	HB	6-1	210	R
36	Wilson, Ben	FB	6-1	230	4
24	Wood, Willie	S	5-10	190	8
72	Wright, Steve	T	6-6	250	4

OAKLAND RAIDERS

No.	Name	Pos.	Ht.	Wt.	Year
78	Archer, Dan	G-T	6-5	245	R
40	Banaszak, Pete	HB	5-11	200	2
50	Benson, Duane	LB	6-2	215	R
25	Biletnikoff, Fred	FL	6-1	190	3
21	Bird, Rodger	S	5-11	195	2
53	Birdwell, Dan	DT	6-4	250	6
16	Blanda, George	K-QB	6-3	215	18
24	Brown, Willie	CB	6-1	190	5
48	Budness, Bill	LB	6-2	215	4
33	Cannon, Billy	TE	6-1	215	8
55	Conners, Dan	LB	6-1	230	4
83	Davidson, Ben	DE	6-7	265	7
35	Dixon, Hewritt	FB	6-1	220	5
11	Eischeid, Mike	P	6-0	190	2
45	Grayson, Dave	S	5-10	185	7
30	Hagberg, Roger	FB	6-1	215	6
70	Harvey, Jim	G	6-5	245	2
65	Hawkins, Wayne	G	6-0	240	8
84	Herock, Ken	TE	6-2	230	4
74	Keating, Tom	DT	6-2	247	4
88	Kocourek, Dave	TE	6-5	240	9
62	Kruse, Bob	G	6-2	250	R
3	Lamonica, Daryle	QB	6-3	215	5
42	Laskey, Bill	LB	6-3	235	3
77	Lassiter, Isaac	DE	6-5	270	6
47	McCloughan, Kent	CB	6-1	190	3
89	Miller, Bill	SE	6-0	190	6
85	Oats, Carleton	DE	6-2	235	3
34	Otto, Gus	LB	6-2	220	3
00	Otto, Jim	C	6-2	240	8
20	Powers, Warren	S	6-0	190	5
79	Schuh, Harry	T	6-2	260	3
23	Sherman, Rod	FL	6-0	190	R
73	Sligh, Richard	DT-DE	7-0	300	R
76	Svihus, Bob	T	6-4	245	3
22	Todd, Larry	HB	6-1	185	3
63	Upshaw, Gene	G	6-5	255	R
81	Wells, Warren	SE	6-1	190	2
29	Williams, Howie	CB	6-1	186	6
52	Williamson, John	LB	6-2	220	4

SUPER BOWL III

NY JETS 16, BALTIMORE 7

The New York Jets defeated the Baltimore Colts 16-7 to become the first American Football League team to defeat a National Football League team in the Super Bowl. The game was the first to officially have that title. Quarterback Joe Namath "guaranteed" a victory by the Jets, although the Colts were favored by three touchdowns and were considered one of the greatest teams in the 49-year history of the NFL.

Namath appeared at the Miami Touchdown Club dinner at Miami Springs Villa to receive an award three days before the game. "This isn't an award for me," he said of a player-of-the-year honor presented by the AFL President, Milt Woodard. "Had it not been for my high school coach, Larry Bruno, and my college coach at Alabama, Paul Bryant, and many other people—including all my teammates—I wouldn't be here. This should be a most valuable player award for the entire team. You can be the greatest athlete in the entire world, but if you don't win those football games, it doesn't mean anything.

"And we're going to win Sunday, I'll guarantee you."

Namath's remarks made national headlines and caused widespread comment among other Jets and Colts. It created more interest in a game that many thought would be more one-sided than the Green Bay Packers' victories in Super Bowls I and II. One sportswriter predicted the Colts would win 55-0; another forecast a 48-0 Baltimore victory.

The Jets took the opening kickoff. On the first play fullback Matt Snell gained three yards at left tackle. On the second play, Snell gained nine yards before he was tackled by safety Rick Volk. When the players unpiled after the tackle Snell returned to the Jets' huddle. But Volk remained on the ground. Volk had been knocked momentarily unconscious by the impact of the collision. The Jets had established a running game in which Snell would set Super Bowl records with 30 carries for 121 yards.

The Jets took a 7-0 lead in the second quarter when Snell ran four yards off left tackle, ending an 80-yard, 12-play drive. Snell gained 35 yards in six carries during the drive and Namath completed four of five passes for 43 yards, including one of 12 yards to Snell.

Field goals of 32, 30, and 9 yards by Jim Turner gave the Jets a 16-0 lead in the fourth quarter.

Baltimore moved 80 yards in 15 plays to score its touchdown, a one-yard run by fullback Jerry Hill with 3:19 left in the game. The Colts' Tom Mitchell recovered Lou Michaels's onside kick after the touchdown and Baltimore moved to New York's 19, but Johnny Unitas's fourth-down pass to Jimmy Orr was overthrown and New York took over with 2:21 remaining.

Unitas, who missed most of the season with an elbow injury, replaced Earl Morrall in the third quarter. Morrall, the NFL's most valuable player in 1968, missed an open receiver, Orr, in the end zone near the end of the half; Morrall's pass to Jerry Hill was intercepted by Jim Hudson on the play, which began with Morrall handing off to Tom Matte, who passed back to Morrall. The quarterback did not see Orr. Morrall also was intercepted in the end zone and on the 2 in the second quarter.

"We didn't make the big plays we have all season," said Baltimore coach Don Shula. "We just didn't do it . . . . They deserved the victory."

Namath at first refused to talk to writers from cities with teams in the NFL when the Jets opened their dressing room to the media. "If you had seen us all year, you wouldn't have been surprised," he said.

Date—January 12, 1969
Site—Orange Bowl, Miami
Time—3:05 P.M. EST
Conditions—73 degrees, overcast, threat of rain
Playing Surface—Grass
Television and Radio—National Broadcasting Company (NBC)
Regular Season Records—New York, 11-3; Baltimore, 13-1
League Championships—New York defeated the Oakland Raiders 27-23 for the AFL title; Baltimore defeated the Cleveland Browns 34-0 for the NFL title
Players' Shares—$15,000 to each member of the winning team; $7,500 to each member of the losing team
Attendance—75,377
Gross Receipts—$3,374,985.64
Officials—Referee, Tommy Bell, NFL; umpire, Walt Parker, AFL; line judge, Cal LePore, AFL; head linesman, George Murphy, NFL; back judge, Jack Reader, AFL; field judge, Joe Gonzales, NFL
Coaches—Weeb Ewbank, NY Jets; Don Shula, Baltimore

NY Jets	Starters, Offense	Baltimore
George Sauer	SE	Jimmy Orr
Winston Hill	LT	Bob Vogel
Bob Talamini	LG	Glenn Ressler
John Schmitt	C	Bill Curry
Randy Rasmussen	RG	Dan Sullivan
Dave Herman	RT	Sam Ball
Pete Lammons	TE	John Mackey
Don Maynard	FL	Willie Richardson
Joe Namath	QB	Earl Morrall
Matt Snell	RB	Jerry Hill
Emerson Boozer	RB	Tom Matte
	Starters, Defense	
Gerry Philbin	LE	Bubba Smith
Paul Rochester	LT	Billy Ray Smith
John Elliott	RT	Fred Miller
Verlon Biggs	RE	Ordell Braase
Ralph Baker	LLB	Mike Curtis
Al Atkinson	MLB	Dennis Gaubatz
Larry Grantham	RLB	Don Shinnick
Johnny Sample	LCB	Bobby Boyd
Randy Beverly	RCB	Lenny Lyles
Jim Hudson	SS	Jerry Logan
Bill Baird	FS	Rick Volk

NY Jets	0	7	6	3	—	16
Baltimore	0	0	0	7	—	7

NYJ—Snell 4 run (J. Turner kick)
NYJ—FG J. Turner 32
NYJ—FG J. Turner 30
NYJ—FG J. Turner 9
Balt—Hill 1 run (Michaels kick)

TEAM STATISTICS	NYJ	Balt
First downs	21	18
Rushing	10	7
Passing	10	9
By penalty	1	2
Total yardage	337	324
Net rushing yardage	142	143
Net passing yardage	195	181
Passes att.-comp.-had int.	29-17-0	41-17-4

RUSHING
NY Jets—Snell, 30 for 121, 1 TD; Boozer, 10 for 19; Mathis, 3 for 2.
Baltimore—Matte, 11 for 116; Hill, 9 for 29, 1 TD; Unitas, 1 for 0; Morrall, 2 for −2.
PASSING
NY Jets—Namath, 17 of 28 for 206; Parilli, 0 of 1.
Baltimore—Unitas, 11 of 24 for 110, 1 int; Morrall, 6 of 17 for 71, 3 int.
RECEIVING
NY Jets—Sauer, 8 for 133; Snell, 4 for 40; Mathis, 3 for 20; Lammons, 2 for 13.
Baltimore—Richardson, 6 for 58; Orr, 3 for 42; Mackey, 3 for 35; Matte, 2 for 30; Hill, 2 for 1; Mitchell, 1 for 15.
PUNTING
NY Jets—Johnson, 4 for 155, 38.8 average.
Baltimore—Lee, 3 for 133, 44.3 average.
PUNT RETURNS
NY Jets—Baird, 1 for 0, 1 fair catch.
Baltimore—Brown, 4 for 34.
KICKOFF RETURNS
NY Jets—Christy, 1 for 25.
Baltimore—Pearson, 2 for 59; Brown, 2 for 46.
INTERCEPTIONS
NY Jets—Beverly, 2 for 0; Hudson, 1 for 9; Sample, 1 for 0.
Baltimore—None.

NEW YORK JETS

No.	Name	Pos.	Ht.	Wt.	Year
62	Atkinson, Al	LB	6-2	230	4
46	Baird, Bill	S	5-10	180	6
51	Baker, Ralph	LB	6-3	235	5
42	Beverly, Randy	CB	5-11	198	2
86	Biggs, Verlon	DE	6-4	268	4
32	Boozer, Emerson	RB	5-11	202	3
45	Christy, Earl	CB	5-11	195	3
56	Crane, Paul	LB-C	6-2	205	3
47	D'Amato, Mike	S	6-2	204	R
43	Dockery, John	CB	6-0	186	R
80	Elliott, John	DT	6-4	249	2
48	Gordon, Cornell	S	6-0	187	4
60	Grantham, Larry	LB	6-0	212	9
67	Herman, Dave	T	6-1	255	5
75	Hill, Winston	T	6-4	280	6
22	Hudson, Jim	S	6-2	210	4
33	Johnson, Curley	P-TE	6-0	215	11
87	Lammons, Pete	TE	6-3	233	3
31	Mathis, Bill	RB	6-1	220	9
13	Maynard, Don	FL	6-1	179	11
50	McAdams, Carl	DT-LB	6-3	245	2
12	Namath, Joe	QB	6-2	195	4
63	Neidert, John	LB	6-2	230	R
15	Parilli, Babe	QB	6-0	190	15
81	Philbin, Gerry	DE	6-2	245	5
23	Rademacher, Bill	SE	6-1	190	5
66	Rasmussen, Randy	G	6-2	255	2
26	Richards, Jim	S	6-1	180	R
74	Richardson, Jeff	T-C	6-3	250	2
72	Rochester, Paul	DT	6-2	250	9
24	Sample, John	CB	6-1	204	11
83	Sauer, George	SE	6-2	195	4
52	Schmitt, John	C	6-4	245	5
30	Smolinski, Mark	RB	6-1	215	8
41	Snell, Matt	RB	6-2	219	5
61	Talamini, Bob	G	6-1	255	9
85	Thompson, Steve	DE	6-5	240	R
29	Turner, Bake	FL	6-1	179	7
11	Turner, Jim	K-QB	6-2	205	5
71	Walton, Sam	T	6-5	276	R

BALTIMORE COLTS

No.	Name	Pos.	Ht.	Wt.	Year
37	Austin, Ocie	S	6-3	200	R
73	Ball, Sam	T	6-4	240	3
40	Boyd, Bobby	CB	5-10	192	9
81	Braase, Ordell	DE	6-4	245	12
2	Brown, Timmy	RB	5-11	200	10
34	Cole, Terry	RB	6-1	220	R
50	Curry, Bill	C	6-2	235	4
32	Curtis, Mike	LB	6-2	232	4
53	Gaubatz, Dennis	LB	6-2	232	6
25	Hawkins, Alex	FL	6-1	186	10
45	Hill, Jerry	RB	5-11	215	7
85	Hilton, Roy	DE	6-6	240	4
61	Johnson, Cornelius	G	6-2	245	R
49	Lee, David	P	6-4	215	3
20	Logan, Jerry	S	6-1	190	6
43	Lyles, Lenny	CB	6-2	204	11
88	Mackey, John	TE	6-2	224	6
41	Matte, Tom	RB	6-0	214	8
79	Michaels, Lou	DE-K	6-2	250	11
76	Miller, Fred	DT	6-3	250	6
84	Mitchell, Tom	TE	6-2	235	R
15	Morrall, Earl	QB	6-2	206	13
28	Orr, Jimmy	SE	5-11	185	11
26	Pearson, Preston	RB	6-1	190	2
27	Perkins, Ray	SE	6-0	183	2
55	Porter, Ron	LB	6-3	232	2
62	Ressler, Glenn	G	6-3	250	4
87	Richardson, Willie	FL	6-2	198	6
66	Shinnick, Don	LB	6-0	228	12
74	Smith, Billy Ray	DT	6-4	250	10
78	Smith, Bubba	DE	6-7	295	2
47	Stukes, Charlie	CB	6-3	212	2
71	Sullivan, Dan	G	6-3	250	7
52	Szymanski, Dick	C	6-3	235	13
19	Unitas, Johnny	QB	6-1	196	13
72	Vogel, Bob	T	6-5	250	6
21	Volk, Rick	S	6-3	195	2
16	Ward, Jim	QB	6-2	195	2
75	Williams, John	G	6-3	256	R
64	Williams, Sidney	LB	6-2	235	5

SUPER BOWL IV

KANSAS CITY 23, MINNESOTA 7

Quarterback Len Dawson, who missed six regular-season games because of a knee injury and whose name had been linked to a federal gambling investigation in Detroit five days before the Super Bowl, completed 12 of 17 passes for 142 yards and one touchdown as the Kansas City Chiefs defeated the Minnesota Vikings 23-7.

The Chiefs' victory was the second in a row by an AFL team over a heavily favored NFL team. The New York Jets were three-touchdown underdogs before they defeated Baltimore; the Chiefs were two-touchdown underdogs.

Dawson was eventually cleared of impropriety in the gambling investigation. The attention made him the focal point in the game; an added burden was what many considered a poor performance by Dawson in Super Bowl I.

Whereas the Chiefs never led in Super Bowl I, they never trailed in Super Bowl IV. They marched 42 yards to Jan Stenerud's 48-yard field goal the first time they had the ball. They moved 55 yards to Stenerud's 32-yard field goal on their second possession, and they went 27 yards to Stenerud's 25-yard field goal the third time.

This gave Kansas City a 9-0 lead with 7:52 left in the half. Charlie West fumbled Stenerud's kickoff after the third field goal and Remi Prudhomme recovered for the Chiefs at Minnesota's 19-yard line. Dawson was tackled for a loss of eight yards by Jim Marshall on the first play. Fullback Wendell Hayes ran 13 yards on the second play, and Dawson passed 10 yards to Otis Taylor for a first down. Halfback Mike Garrett lost a yard to the 5 on the following play. Dawson kept the ball for no gain, and it was third down. On the next play, the Chiefs' line pulled in one direction; the Vikings gave pursuit, and Garrett went back against the grain and scored a five-yard touchdown for a 16-0 lead.

The Vikings forced the Chiefs to punt on the first series of the third quarter and took possession on their 31-yard line. They moved 69 yards in 10 plays, including 47 yards passing by Joe Kapp, who went four of four. Dave Osborn's four-yard run with 4:32 left in the quarter made the score 16-7.

"Let's put out that fire, Leonard," Chiefs coach Hank Stram said to Dawson. "Let's make sure they don't get any closer." The Chiefs started from their 18-yard line. In five plays they had reached their 32; it was third down and seven yards for a first down.

Dawson had handed the ball to receiver Frank Pitts on reverses twice in the first half. Pitts had gained 19 yards the first time and 11 yards the second time. Dawson called for the reverse a third time and Pitts gained seven yards, enough for another first down.

Two plays later, from the Minnesota 46, Dawson threw a short pass to Taylor, who caught the ball on the 41 in front of Earsell Mackbee. Taylor ran through Mackbee, who had suffered a pinched nerve in his neck earlier and whose arm was numb. The last person with a chance to catch Taylor was Vikings safety Karl Kassulke. Taylor faked Kassulke, who fell down at the 10-yard line.

The touchdown gave Kansas City a 23-7 lead with 1:22 remaining in the third quarter. The Vikings had the ball three times in the fourth quarter, giving it up at Kansas City's 46 and their own 38 and 48, each time on interceptions.

"The best thing about this game is that we don't have to answer for it the next three years, like we did last time," said Dawson after the victory. Then Dawson went to answer a telephone call. It was President Richard Nixon, offering his congratulations.

Date—January 11, 1970
Site—Tulane Stadium, New Orleans
Time—2:35 P.M. CST
Conditions—61, heavy overcast, wet field
Playing Surface—Grass
Television and Radio—Columbia Broadcasting System (CBS)
Regular Season Records—Kansas City, 11-3; Minnesota, 12-2
League Championships—Kansas City defeated the Oakland Raiders 17-7 for the AFL title; Minnesota defeated the Cleveland Browns 27-7 for the NFL title
Players' Shares—$15,000 to each member of the winning team; $7,500 to each member of the losing team
Attendance—80,562
Gross Receipts—$3,817,872.69
Officials—Referee, John McDonough, NFL; umpire, Lou Palazzi, AFL; line judge, Bill Schleibaum, NFL; head linesman, Harry Kessel, NFL; back judge, Tom Kelleher, NFL; field judge, Charlie Musser, AFL
Coaches—Bud Grant, Minnesota; Hank Stram, Kansas City

Minnesota	**Starters, Offense**	**Kansas City**
Gene Washington	WR	Frank Pitts
Grady Alderman	LT	Jim Tyrer
Jim Vellone	LG	Ed Budde
Mick Tingelhoff	C	E. J. Holub
Milt Sunde	RG	Mo Moorman
Ron Yary	RT	Dave Hill
John Beasley	TE	Fred Arbanas
John Henderson	WR	Otis Taylor
Joe Kapp	QB	Len Dawson
Bill Brown	RB	Robert Holmes
Dave Osborn	RB	Mike Garrett
	Starters, Defense	
Carl Eller	LE	Jerry Mays
Gary Larsen	LT	Curley Culp
Alan Page	RT	Buck Buchanan
Jim Marshall	RE	Aaron Brown
Roy Winston	LLB	Bobby Bell
Lonnie Warwick	MLB	Willie Lanier
Wally Hilgenberg	RLB	Jim Lynch
Earsell Mackbee	LCB	Jim Marsalis
Ed Sharockman	RCB	Emmitt Thomas
Karl Kassulke	LS-SS	Jim Kearney
Paul Krause	RS-FS	Johnny Robinson

Minnesota	0	0	7	0	—	7
Kansas City	3	13	7	0	—	23

KC —FG Stenerud 48
KC —FG Stenerud 32
KC —FG Stenerud 25
KC —Garrett 5 run (Stenerud kick)
Minn—Osborn 4 run (Cox kick)
KC —Taylor 46 pass from Dawson (Stenerud kick)

TEAM STATISTICS	**Minn**	**KC**
First downs	13	18
Rushing	2	8
Passing	10	7
By penalty	1	3
Total yardage	239	273
Net rushing yardage	67	151
Net passing yardage	172	122
Passes att.-comp.-had int.	28-17-3	17-12-1

RUSHING
Minnesota—Brown, 6 for 26; Reed, 4 for 17; Osborn, 7 for 15, 1 TD; Kapp, 2 for 9.
Kansas City—Garrett, 11 for 39, 1 TD; Pitts, 3 for 37; Hayes, 8 for 31; McVea, 12 for 26; Dawson, 3 for 11; Holmes, 5 for 7.
PASSING
Minnesota—Kapp, 16 of 25 for 183, 2 int.; Cuozzo, 1 of 3 for 16, 1 int.
Kansas City—Dawson, 12 of 17 for 142, 1 TD, 1 int.
RECEIVING
Minnesota—Henderson, 7 for 111; Brown, 3 for 11; Beasley, 2 for 41; Reed, 2 for 16; Osborn, 2 for 11; Washington, 1 for 9.
Kansas City—Taylor, 6 for 81, 1 TD; Pitts, 3 for 33; Garrett, 2 for 25; Hayes, 1 for 3.
PUNTING
Minnesota—Lee, 3 for 111, 37.0 average.
Kansas City—Wilson, 4 for 194, 48.5 average.
PUNT RETURNS
Minnesota—West, 2 for 18.
Kansas City—Garrett, 1 for 0.
KICKOFF RETURNS
Minnesota—West, 3 for 46; Jones, 1 for 33.
Kansas City—Hayes, 2 for 36.
INTERCEPTIONS
Minnesota—Krause, 1 for 0.
Kansas City—Lanier, 1 for 9; Robinson, 1 for 9; Thomas, 1 for 6.

MINNESOTA VIKINGS

No.	Name	Pos.	Ht.	Wt.	Year
67	Alderman, Grady	T	6-2	245	10
87	Beasley, John	TE	6-3	230	3
30	Brown, Bill	RB	5-11	230	9
14	Cox, Fred	K	5-10	200	7
15	Cuozzo, Gary	QB	6-1	195	7
71	Davis, Doug	T	6-4	255	4
76	Dickson, Paul	DT	6-5	250	11
81	Eller, Carl	DE	6-6	250	6
27	Grim, Bob	WR	6-0	195	3
49	Hackbart, Dale	S	6-3	205	8
50	Hargrove, Jim	LB	6-3	233	2
35	Harris, Bill	RB	6-0	204	2
80	Henderson, John	WR	6-3	190	5
58	Hilgenberg, Wally	LB	6-3	231	5
26	Jones, Clinton	RB	6-0	200	3
11	Kapp, Joe	QB	6-3	208	3
29	Kassulke, Karl	S	6-0	195	7
89	Kramer, Kent	TE	6-4	235	3
22	Krause, Paul	S	6-3	188	6
77	Larsen, Gary	DT	6-5	255	6
19	Lee, Bob	QB-P	6-3	195	R
21	Lindsey, Jim	RB	6-2	210	4
46	Mackbee, Earsell	CB	6-0	195	5
70	Marshall, Jim	DE	6-3	247	10
55	McGill, Mike	LB	6-2	235	2
41	Osborn, Dave	RB	6-0	205	5
88	Page, Alan	DT	6-4	245	3
32	Reed, Oscar	RB	6-0	220	2
57	Reilly, Mike	LB	6-2	240	6
45	Sharockman, Ed	CB	6-0	200	8
74	Smith, Steve	DE	6-5	250	3
64	Sunde, Milt	G	6-2	250	6
53	Tingelhoff, Mick	C	6-2	237	8
63	Vellone, Jim	G	6-3	255	4
59	Warwick, Lonnie	LB	6-3	235	5
84	Washington, Gene	WR	6-3	208	3
40	West, Charlie	S	6-1	190	2
62	White, Ed	G	6-3	260	R
60	Winston, Roy	LB	5-11	226	8
73	Yary, Ron	T	6-5	265	2

KANSAS CITY CHIEFS

No.	Name	Pos.	Ht.	Wt.	Year
84	Arbanas, Fred	TE	6-3	240	8
78	Bell, Bobby	LB	6-4	228	7
24	Belser, Ceaser	S	6-0	212	2
87	Brown, Aaron	DE	6-5	265	3
86	Buchanan, Buck	DT	6-7	287	7
71	Budde, Ed	G	6-5	260	7
61	Culp, Curley	DT	6-1	265	2
60	Daney, George	G	6-4	240	2
16	Dawson, Len	QB	6-0	190	13
12	Flores, Tom	QB	6-1	202	9
21	Garrett, Mike	RB	5-9	190	4
38	Hayes, Wendell	RB	6-1	220	5
73	Hill, Dave	T	6-5	260	7
45	Holmes, Robert	RB	5-9	220	2
55	Holub, E. J.	C	6-4	236	9
85	Hurston, Chuck	LB	6-6	240	5
46	Kearney, Jim	S	6-2	206	5
63	Lanier, Willie	LB	6-1	245	3
10	Livingston, Mike	QB	6-3	205	2
82	Lothamer, Ed	DT	6-5	270	6
51	Lynch, Jim	LB	6-1	235	3
40	Marsalis, Jim	CB	5-11	194	R
75	Mays, Jerry	DE	6-4	252	9
32	McClinton, Curtis	TE	6-3	227	8
6	McVea, Warren	RB	5-10	182	2
22	Mitchell, Willie	CB	6-0	185	6
76	Moorman, Mo	G	6-5	252	2
25	Pitts, Frank	WR	6-2	199	5
14	Podolak, Ed	RB	6-1	204	R
65	Prudhomme, Remi	C	6-4	250	4
30	Richardson, Gloster	WR	6-0	200	3
42	Robinson, Johnny	S	6-1	205	10
20	Sellers, Goldie	CB	6-2	198	4
66	Stein, Bob	LB	6-3	235	R
3	Stenerud, Jan	K	6-2	187	3
89	Taylor, Otis	WR	6-3	215	5
18	Thomas, Emmitt	CB	6-2	192	4
74	Trosch, Gene	DE	6-7	277	2
77	Tyrer, Jim	T	6-6	275	9
44	Wilson, Jerrel	P	6-4	222	7

SUPER BOWL V

BALTIMORE 16, DALLAS 13

Jim O'Brien's 32-yard field goal with five seconds remaining in the game gave Baltimore a 16-13 victory over the Dallas Cowboys in Super Bowl V, a game marked by 11 fumbles and interceptions and 14 penalties. The Colts led in turnovers 7-4; Dallas led in penalties 9-5.

Dallas opened the scoring. Mike Clark kicked a 14-yard field goal for a 3-0 lead with 5:32 left in the first quarter after Cliff Harris recovered Ron Gardin's fumble on a punt return at the Baltimore 9. The Cowboys went 57 yards in eight plays to Clark's 30-yard field goal and a 6-0 advantage eight seconds into the second quarter.

Baltimore tied the score 42 seconds later. On the third play after the kickoff, quarterback Johnny Unitas threw a medium-deep pass to Eddie Hinton. Hinton tipped the ball; Cowboys defensive back Mel Renfro also tipped the ball. Colts tight end John Mackey, who was running free behind the defense, caught the pass at Dallas's 45-yard line. Mackey ran untouched to the end zone, completing a 75-yard touchdown play. O'Brien's point after touchdown was blocked by Mark Washington.

The Cowboys moved in front 13-6 with 7:53 remaining in the half. Unitas, back to pass, scrambled under pressure and fumbled when he was hit by middle linebacker Lee Roy Jordan. Tackle Jethro Pugh recovered at Baltimore's 28-yard line. Three plays later quarterback Craig Morton threw a seven-yard scoring pass to rookie running back Duane Thomas.

Dallas had a chance to score another touchdown early in the third quarter, but Thomas fumbled on the 1-yard line when he was hit by safety Jerry Logan; Jim Duncan recovered for the Colts. A pass from Morton to running back Walt Garrison in the fourth quarter was intercepted by Colts safety Rick Volk, who returned the ball 30 yards to the Cowboys' 3. Fullback Tom Nowatzke scored on the second play and O'Brien's point after touchdown made the score 13-13 with 7:35 left in the game.

Dallas took over on Baltimore's 48-yard line with 1:52 remaining after a punt. Thomas lost a yard on the first play, and Fred Miller sacked Morton for a loss of nine on the second play. Dallas was penalized for holding on the same play and was pushed back to its 27-yard line with 1:09 remaining. Morton's high pass to running back Dan Reeves bounced off Reeves's hands and was intercepted by middle linebacker Mike Curtis, who ran 13 yards to Dallas's 28.

Two running plays gained three yards and used 50 of the remaining 59 seconds. The ball was on the Cowboys' 25-yard line when O'Brien entered the game. The Cowboys called time.

When play resumed, the Cowboys attempted to take time again but were informed by referee Norm Schachter that they could not call successive time outs without a play being run. The Cowboys were trying to unnerve O'Brien. When Earl Morrall, who had replaced the injured Unitas midway through the game, kneeled to take the snap, O'Brien whispered, "The wind . . . the wind?" "There is no wind," said Morrall. "Just kick the ball straight."

O'Brien's kick went end over end, curved toward the right goal post, then veered back to the middle and through the uprights.

When it was suggested the Colts were lucky to have won, tackle Bob Vogel said, "So what? I've had luck decide against us so many times I'm sick of it. I quit being proud years ago when we lost games we should have won. The way I look at it, we're going to get the Super Bowl ring because we won the games that counted this year. We deserve it."

Date—January 17, 1971
Site—Orange Bowl, Miami
Time—2:00 P.M. EST
Conditions—70 degrees, clear skies
Playing Surface—Poly-Turf
Television and Radio—National Broadcasting Company (NBC)
Regular Season Records—Baltimore, 11-2-1; Dallas, 10-4
Conference Championships—Baltimore defeated the Oakland Raiders 27-17 for the AFC title; Dallas defeated the San Francisco 49ers 17-10 for the NFC title
Players' Shares—$15,000 to each member of the winning team; $7,500 to each member of the losing team
Attendance—79,204
Gross Receipts—$3,992,280.01
Officials—Referee, Norm Schacter; umpire, Paul Trepinski; line judge, Jack Fette; head linesman, Ed Marion; back judge, Hugh Gamber; field judge, Fritz Graf
Coaches—Don McCafferty, Baltimore; Tom Landry, Dallas

Baltimore	Starters, Offense	Dallas
Eddie Hinton	WR	Bob Hayes
Bob Vogel	LT	Ralph Neely
Glenn Ressler	LG	John Niland
Bill Curry	C	Dave Manders
John Williams	RG	Blaine Nye
Dan Sullivan	RT	Rayfield Wright
John Mackey	TE	Pettis Norman
Roy Jefferson	WR	Reggie Rucker
Johnny Unitas	QB	Craig Morton
Tom Nowatzke	RB	Walt Garrison
Norm Bulaich	RB	Duane Thomas
	Starters, Defense	
Bubba Smith	LE	Larry Cole
Billy Ray Smith	LT	Jethro Pugh
Fred Miller	RT	Bob Lilly
Roy Hilton	RE	George Andrie
Ray May	LLB	Dave Edwards
Mike Curtis	MLB	Lee Roy Jordan
Ted Hendricks	RLB	Chuck Howley
Charlie Stukes	LCB	Herb Adderley
Jim Duncan	RCB	Mel Renfro
Jerry Logan	SS	Cornell Green
Rick Volk	FS	Charlie Waters

Baltimore	0	6	0	10	—	16
Dallas	3	10	0	0	—	13

Dall—FG Clark 14
Dall—FG Clark 30
Balt—Mackey 75 pass from Unitas (kick blocked)
Dall—Thomas 7 pass from Morton (Clark kick)
Balt—Nowatzke 2 run (O'Brien kick)
Balt—FG O'Brien 32

TEAM STATISTICS	Balt	Dall
First downs	14	10
Rushing	4	4
Passing	6	5
By penalty	4	1
Total yardage	329	215
Net rushing yardage	69	102
Net passing yardage	260	113
Passes att.-comp.-had int.	25-11-3	26-12-3

RUSHING
Baltimore—Nowatzke, 10 for 33, 1 TD; Bulaich, 18 for 28; Unitas, 1 for 4; Havrilak, 1 for 3; Morrall, 1 for 1.
Dallas—Garrison, 12 for 65; Thomas, 18 for 35; Morton, 1 for 2.
PASSING
Baltimore—Morrall, 7 of 15 for 147, 1 int; Unitas, 3 of 9 for 88, 1 TD, 2 int; Havrilak, 1 of 1 for 25.
Dallas—Morton, 12 of 26 for 127, 1 TD, 3 int.
RECEIVING
Baltimore—Jefferson, 3 for 52; Mackey, 2 for 80, 1 TD; Hinton, 2 for 51; Havrilak, 2 for 27; Nowatzke, 1 for 45; Bulaich, 1 for 5.
Dallas—Reeves, 5 for 46; Thomas, 4 for 21, 1 TD; Garrison, 2 for 19; Hayes, 1 for 41.
PUNTING
Baltimore—Lee, 4 for 166, 41.5 average.
Dallas—Widby, 9 for 377, 41.9 average.
PUNT RETURNS
Baltimore—Gardin, 4 for 4, 3 fair catches; Logan, 1 for 8.
Dallas—Hayes, 3 for 9.
KICKOFF RETURNS
Baltimore—Duncan, 4 for 90.
Dallas—Harris, 1 for 18; Hill, 1 for 14; Kiner, 1 for 2.
INTERCEPTIONS
Baltimore—Volk, 1 for 30; Logan, 1 for 14; Curtis, 1 for 13.
Dallas—Howley, 2 for 22; Renfro, 1 for 0.

BALTIMORE COLTS

No.	Name	Pos.	Ht.	Wt.	Year
73	Ball, Sam	T	6-4	240	5
36	Bulaich, Norm	RB	6-1	218	R
50	Curry, Bill	C	6-2	235	6
32	Curtis, Mike	LB	6-2	232	6
35	Duncan, Jim	CB	6-2	200	2
30	Gardin, Ron	CB	5-11	180	R
53	Goode, Tom	C	6-3	245	9
51	Grant, Bob	LB	6-2	225	3
17	Havrilak, Sam	RB	6-2	195	2
83	Hendricks, Ted	LB	6-7	215	2
45	Hill, Jerry	RB	5-11	217	10
85	Hilton, Roy	DE	6-6	240	6
33	Hinton, Eddie	WR	6-0	200	2
87	Jefferson, Roy	WR	6-2	195	6
61	Johnson, Cornelius	G	6-2	245	3
49	Lee, David	P	6-4	230	5
20	Logan, Jerry	S	6-1	190	8
88	Mackey, John	TE	6-2	224	8
40	Maitland, Jack	RB	6-1	210	R
42	Maxwell, Tom	CB	6-2	195	2
56	May, Ray	LB	6-1	230	4
76	Miller, Fred	DT	6-3	250	8
84	Mitchell, Tom	TE	6-2	215	4
15	Morrall, Earl	QB	6-2	206	15
81	Newsome, Billy	DE	6-4	240	R
52	Nichols, Robbie	LB	6-3	220	R
34	Nowatzke, Tom	RB	6-3	230	6
80	O'Brien, Jim	K-WR	6-0	195	R
28	Orr, Jimmy	WR	5-11	185	13
27	Perkins, Ray	WR	6-0	183	4
62	Ressler, Glenn	G	6-3	250	6
74	Smith, Billy Ray	DT	6-4	250	12
78	Smith, Bubba	DE	6-7	295	4
47	Stukes, Charlie	CB	6-3	212	4
71	Sullivan, Dan	G	6-3	250	9
19	Unitas, Johnny	QB	6-1	196	15
72	Vogel, Bob	T	6-5	250	8
21	Volk, Rick	S	6-3	195	4
75	Williams, John	G	6-3	256	3
60	Wright, George	DT	6-3	260	R

DALLAS COWBOYS

No.	Name	Pos.	Ht.	Wt.	Year
26	Adderley, Herb	CB	6-1	200	10
66	Andrie, George	DE	6-6	250	9
78	Asher, Bob	T	6-5	250	R
83	Clark, Mike	K	6-1	205	8
63	Cole, Larry	DE	6-4	225	3
89	Ditka, Mike	TE	6-3	225	10
77	East, Ron	DT	6-4	242	4
52	Edwards, Dave	LB	6-1	225	8
45	Flowers, Richmond	S	6-0	180	2
32	Garrison, Walt	RB	6-0	205	5
34	Green, Cornell	S	6-3	208	9
43	Harris, Cliff	S	6-0	184	R
22	Hayes, Bob	WR	5-11	185	6
35	Hill, Calvin	RB	6-4	227	2
24	Homan, Dennis	WR	6-1	181	3
54	Howley, Chuck	LB	6-2	225	12
55	Jordan, Lee Roy	LB	6-1	221	8
60	Kiner, Steve	LB	6-0	218	R
50	Lewis, D. D.	LB	6-1	225	2
74	Lilly, Bob	DT	6-5	260	10
72	Liscio, Tony	T	6-5	255	7
51	Manders, Dave	C	6-2	250	6
14	Morton, Craig	QB	6-4	214	6
73	Neely, Ralph	G	6-6	255	6
76	Niland, John	G	6-3	245	5
84	Norman, Pettis	TE	6-3	220	9
61	Nye, Blaine	G	6-4	251	3
75	Pugh, Jethro	DT	6-6	260	6
30	Reeves, Dan	RB	6-1	220	6
20	Renfro, Mel	S	6-0	190	7
88	Rucker, Reggie	WR	6-2	190	R
12	Staubach, Roger	QB	6-3	197	2
56	Stincic, Tom	LB	6-4	230	2
33	Thomas, Duane	RB	6-1	220	R
67	Toomay, Pat	DE	6-5	244	R
46	Washington, Mark	CB	5-10	188	R
41	Waters, Charlie	S	6-1	193	R
42	Welch, Claxton	RB	5-11	203	2
10	Widby, Ron	P	6-4	210	3
70	Wright, Rayfield	T	6-6	255	4

SUPER BOWL VI

DALLAS 24, MIAMI 3

The Dallas Cowboys defeated the Miami Dolphins 24-3 in Super Bowl VI, setting a Super Bowl team rushing record of 252 yards and controlling the ball for 69 plays to Miami's 44.

Mike Clark kicked a nine-yard field goal with 1:23 left in the first quarter to give Dallas a 3-0 lead. The Cowboys had moved 50 yards in 11 plays after linebacker Chuck Howley recovered a fumble by Larry Csonka on Dallas's 48-yard line. It was Csonka's first fumble of the season.

The Cowboys' defense was evident on the next series. On third and nine at Miami's 38, Dolphins quarterback Bob Griese went back to pass; with no receivers open, Griese scrambled, trying to avoid tackle Bob Lilly, who finally ran him down for a 29-yard loss as the quarter ended.

Dallas moved ahead 10-0 with a 76-yard, 10-play drive that culminated with a seven-yard touchdown pass from Roger Staubach to Lance Alworth in the corner of the end zone with 1:15 remaining in the half. The drive had only one play that gained fewer than five yards.

Miami drove 44 yards in five plays to position Garo Yepremian for a 31-yard field goal with four seconds left in the half that made the score 10-3.

The Cowboys took the second-half kickoff and went 71 yards in eight plays, scoring a touchdown on Duane Thomas's three-yard run to raise their lead to 17-3. Calvin Hill, playing in relief of Thomas, caught one pass for 12 yards, but the other seven plays on the drive were runs. Walt Garrison ran wide for three, Thomas wide for four and seven, then through the right side for 23. Wide receiver Bob Hayes ran a reverse for 16, and Garrison set up the touchdown by going three yards around the left side.

After the touchdown, Dallas gained 16 yards in nine plays the remainder of the quarter. Miami had the ball for 10 plays during the quarter and gained 13 yards. The Dolphins had the ball on their 49-yard line on the fourth play of the fourth quarter. Griese's pass intended for Jim Kiick was intercepted by Howley, who ran 41 yards to the Dolphins' 9. Three plays later Staubach passed seven yards to Mike Ditka for a touchdown.

The Dolphins then entered Dallas territory for the only time in the second half, driving to the 16 before Griese fumbled, with Larry Cole recovering for the Cowboys. Dallas moved 79 yards, from its 20 to Miami's 1, in 11 plays, controlling the ball for six minutes and 40 seconds. On first down, Calvin Hill fumbled and Manny Fernandez recovered on the 4 for Miami. The Dolphins had advanced to their 24 when the game ended.

"My biggest disappointment was that we never challenged," said Miami coach Don Shula, a loser in the Super Bowl for the second time. "They completely dominated."

The Cowboys also shut off a play that had been suggested to Shula by President Richard Nixon. Shula had received a telephone call from the President after the Dolphins qualified for the Super Bowl. "The Cowboys are a good defensive team," Nixon told Shula, "but I think you can hit Paul Warfield on that down-and-in pattern."

Warfield, the Dolphins' star wide receiver, had raced downfield and veered toward the middle of the field to catch a pass that went for a 50-yard gain against Baltimore in the AFC Championship Game. But the Cowboys double-teamed Warfield, and he was unsuccessful running the pattern.

"We made sure they didn't complete that pass on us," said Cowboys coach Tom Landry.

Date—January 16, 1972
Site—Tulane Stadium, New Orleans
Time—1:35 P.M. CST
Conditions—39 degrees, sunny
Playing Surface—Poly-Turf
Television and Radio—Columbia Broadcasting System (CBS)
Regular Season Records—Dallas, 11-3; Miami, 10-3-1
Conference Championships—Dallas defeated the San Francisco 49ers 14-3 for the NFC title; Miami defeated the Baltimore Colts 21-0 for the AFC title
Players' Shares—$15,000 to each member of the winning team; $7,500 to each member of the losing team
Attendance—81,023
Gross Receipts—$4,041,527.89
Officials—Referee, Jim Tunney; umpire, Joe Connell; line judge, Art Holst; head linesman, Al Sabato; back judge, Ralph Vandenberg; field judge, Bob Wortman
Coaches—Tom Landry, Dallas; Don Shula, Miami

Dallas	**Starters, Offense**	**Miami**
Bob Hayes	WR	Paul Warfield
Tony Liscio	LT	Doug Crusan
John Niland	LG	Bob Kuechenberg
Dave Manders	C	Bob DeMarco
Blaine Nye	RG	Larry Little
Rayfield Wright	RT	Norm Evans
Mike Ditka	TE	Marv Fleming
Lance Alworth	WR	Howard Twilley
Roger Staubach	QB	Bob Griese
Walt Garrison	RB	Larry Csonka
Duane Thomas	RB	Jim Kiick
	Starters, Defense	
Larry Cole	LE	Jim Riley
Jethro Pugh	LT	Manny Fernandez
Bob Lilly	RT	Bob Heinz
George Andrie	RE	Bill Stanfill
Dave Edwards	LLB	Doug Swift
Lee Roy Jordan	MLB	Nick Buoniconti
Chuck Howley	RLB	Mike Kolen
Herb Adderley	LCB	Tim Foley
Mel Renfro	RCB	Curtis Johnson
Cornell Green	SS	Dick Anderson
Cliff Harris	FS	Jake Scott

Dallas	3	7	7	7	—	24
Miami	0	3	0	0	—	3

Dall—FG Clark 9
Dall—Alworth 7 pass from Staubach (Clark kick)
Mia—FG Yepremian 31
Dall—D. Thomas 3 run (Clark kick)
Dall—Ditka 7 pass from Staubach (Clark kick)

TEAM STATISTICS	**Dall**	**Mia**
First downs	23	10
Rushing	15	3
Passing	8	7
By penalty	0	0
Total yardage	352	185
Net rushing yardage	252	80
Net passing yardage	100	105
Passes att.-comp.-had int.	19-12-0	23-12-1

RUSHING
Dallas—D. Thomas, 19 for 95, 1 TD; Garrison, 14 for 74; Hill, 7 for 25; Staubach, 5 for 18; Ditka, 1 for 17; Hayes, 1 for 16; Reeves, 1 for 7.
Miami—Csonka, 9 for 40; Kiick, 10 for 40; Griese, 1 for 0.

PASSING
Dallas—Staubach, 12 of 19 for 119, 2 TDs.
Miami—Griese, 12 of 23 for 134, 1 int.

RECEIVING
Dallas—D. Thomas, 3 for 17; Alworth, 2 for 28, 1 TD; Ditka, 2 for 28, 1 TD; Hayes, 2 for 23; Garrison, 2 for 11; Hill, 1 for 12.
Miami—Warfield, 4 for 39; Kiick, 3 for 21; Csonka, 2 for 18; Fleming, 1 for 27; Twilley, 1 for 20; Mandich, 1 for 9.

PUNTING
Dallas—Widby, 5 for 186, 37.2 average.
Miami—Seiple, 5 for 200, 40.0 average.

PUNT RETURNS
Dallas—Hayes, 1 for -1, 1 fair catch; Harris, 2 fair catches.
Miami—Scott, 1 for 21.

KICKOFF RETURNS
Dallas—I. Thomas, 1 for 23; Waters, 1 for 11.
Miami—Morris, 4 for 90; Ginn, 1 for 32.

INTERCEPTIONS
Dallas—Howley, 1 for 41.
Miami—None.

DALLAS COWBOYS

No.	**Name**	**Pos.**	**Ht.**	**Wt.**	**Year**
26	Adderley, Herb	CB	6-1	200	11
19	Alworth, Lance	WR	6-0	180	10
66	Andrie, George	DE	6-6	250	10
60	Caffey, Lee Roy	LB	6-3	240	9
83	Clark, Mike	K	6-1	205	9
63	Cole, Larry	DE	6-4	250	4
89	Ditka, Mike	TE	6-3	213	11
52	Edwards, Dave	LB	6-1	225	9
62	Fitzgerald, John	C	6-5	250	R
32	Garrison, Walt	RB	6-0	205	6
34	Green, Cornell	S	6-3	208	10
79	Gregg, Forrest	G	6-4	250	15
77	Gregory, Bill	DT	6-5	255	R
43	Harris, Cliff	S	6-0	184	2
22	Hayes, Bob	WR	5-11	185	7
35	Hill, Calvin	RB	6-4	227	3
54	Howley, Chuck	LB	6-2	225	13
55	Jordan, Lee Roy	LB	6-1	221	9
50	Lewis, D. D.	LB	6-1	225	3
74	Lilly, Bob	DT	6-5	260	11
64	Liscio, Tony	T	6-5	255	8
51	Manders, Dave	C	6-2	250	7
14	Morton, Craig	QB	6-4	214	7
76	Niland, John	G	6-3	245	6
61	Nye, Blaine	G	6-4	251	4
75	Pugh, Jethro	DT	6-6	260	7
30	Reeves, Dan	RB	6-1	200	7
20	Renfro, Mel	CB	6-0	190	8
31	Richardson, Gloster	WR	6-2	200	5
85	Smith, Tody	DE	6-5	245	R
12	Staubach, Roger	QB	6-3	197	3
33	Thomas, Duane	RB	6-1	205	2
37	Thomas, Ike	CB	6-2	193	R
67	Toomay, Pat	DE	6-5	244	2
87	Truax, Billy	TE	6-5	240	8
71	Wallace, Rodney	G	6-5	255	R
41	Waters, Charlie	S	6-1	193	2
42	Welch, Claxton	RB	5-11	203	3
10	Widby, Ron	P	6-4	210	4
70	Wright, Rayfield	T	6-6	255	5

MIAMI DOLPHINS

No.	**Name**	**Pos.**	**Ht.**	**Wt.**	**Year**
40	Anderson, Dick	S	6-2	196	4
85	Buoniconti, Nick	LB	5-11	220	10
31	Cole, Terry	RB	6-1	220	4
77	Crusan, Doug	T	6-4	250	4
39	Csonka, Larry	RB	6-2	237	4
61	DeMarco, Bob	C	6-2	250	11
86	Den Herder, Vern	DE	6-6	250	R
73	Evans, Norm	T	6-5	252	7
75	Fernandez, Manny	DT	6-2	248	4
80	Fleming, Marv	TE	6-4	235	9
25	Foley, Tim	CB	6-0	194	2
32	Ginn, Hubert	RB	5-10	188	2
12	Griese, Bob	QB	6-1	190	5
72	Heinz, Bob	DT	6-6	280	3
45	Johnson, Curtis	CB	6-1	196	2
71	Cornish, Frank	DT	6-3	285	6
21	Kiick, Jim	RB	5-11	215	4
57	Kolen, Mike	LB	6-2	220	2
67	Kuechenberg, Bob	G	6-2	247	2
62	Langer, Jim	G	6-2	250	2
15	Leigh, Charles	RB	5-11	205	3
66	Little, Larry	G	6-1	265	5
88	Mandich, Jim	TE	6-2	224	2
53	Matheson, Bob	LB	6-4	240	5
10	Mira, George	QB	5-11	192	7
79	Moore, Wayne	T	6-6	265	2
22	Morris, Eugene (Mercury)	RB	5-10	190	3
26	Mumphord, Lloyd	CB	5-10	180	3
89	Noonan, Karl	WR	6-2	198	6
48	Petrella, Bob	S	5-11	190	6
56	Powell, Jesse	LB	6-2	215	3
70	Riley, Jim	DE	6-4	250	5
13	Scott, Jake	S	6-0	188	2
20	Seiple, Larry	P	6-0	215	5
84	Stanfill, Bill	DE	6-5	250	3
82	Stowe, Otto	WR	6-2	188	R
59	Swift, Doug	LB	6-3	228	2
81	Twilley, Howard	WR	5-10	185	6
42	Warfield, Paul	WR	6-0	185	8
1	Yepremian, Garo	K	5-8	172	4

SUPER BOWL VII

MIAMI 14, WASHINGTON 7

The Miami Dolphins defeated the Washington Redskins 14-7 in Super Bowl VII and completed a season in which they won all of their 17 games, to become the first perfect-record team in NFL history.

The Dolphins, who entered the game as two-point underdogs, outgained the Redskins 253-228 in total yardage, shut down NFL rushing leader Larry Brown, and never were seriously threatened.

The Dolphins took a 7-0 lead the third time they had the ball, moving 63 yards in six plays and scoring on a 28-yard pass play—quarterback Bob Griese to wide receiver Howard Twilley—on the next-to-last play of the first quarter. Twilley ran inside then outside on his pattern, turning Redskins cornerback Pat Fischer completely around.

The Dolphins scored in the second quarter when Griese passed 37 yards to Paul Warfield, who caught the ball on the Redskins' 10 and completed a 47-yard play, but Marlin Briscoe, the wide receiver opposite Warfield, had moved forward before the snap of the ball, and the touchdown was nullified.

Washington forced the Dolphins to punt and began a drive from its own 17-yard line. On third down from the Dolphins' 48-yard line, Redskins quarterback Billy Kilmer threw a pass that was intercepted by middle linebacker Nick Buoniconti, who returned the ball 32 yards to Washington's 27.

The Dolphins scored with 18 seconds left in the half on the fifth play after the interception. Jim Kiick went across from the 1-yard line behind right guard Larry Little.

Miami missed an opportunity to go ahead 21-0 in the third quarter. The Dolphins moved 78 yards from their 17 to the Redskins' 5, but on the eighth play of the drive Griese's pass for tight end Marv Fleming was intercepted in the end zone by Brig Owens.

Washington moved from its 11-yard line to the Dolphins' 10 in the fourth quarter, a 79-yard advance that took 14 plays and consumed more than seven minutes. Kilmer's third-down pass to Charley Taylor was intercepted in the end zone by Jake Scott, who returned the ball 55 yards to the Redskins' 48.

Miami advanced 14 yards in five plays to position Garo Yepremian for a 42-yard field-goal attempt. The snap from center Howard Kindig was low. Holder Earl Morrall had to place the ball quickly. Yepremian's kick was low and Bill Brundige blocked the attempt. Yepremian picked up the ball and attempted to pass. The ball slipped out of his hand and into the air. Washington's Mike Bass caught the ball and ran 49 yards for a touchdown with 2:07 remaining.

Leading 14-7, Miami controlled the ball for six plays before punting to Washington, which took over on its 30-yard line with 1:14 left. Kilmer's first two passes were incomplete. His third, to Larry Brown, resulted in a four-yard loss. Kilmer was thrown for a loss of nine yards on fourth down. There were 33 seconds remaining in the game. Game officials stopped the clock to clear the field of fans; the clock started again, and time ran out before Miami could launch a play.

"This is the first time the goat of the game is in the winners' locker room," Yepremian said. "I should have fallen on the ball, but my mind went blank."

"We were never really in the game . . . and we were never really out of it," said Jack Pardee, linebacker and co-captain of the Redskins.

"The pressure's off," said Miami coach Don Shula, whose teams had been beaten in two previous Super Bowls. "I was aware of the reputation I had gotten . . . the losses were there; you couldn't hide them. But that's all in the past."

Date—January 14, 1973
Site—Memorial Coliseum, Los Angeles
Time—12:30 P.M. PST
Conditions—84 degrees, sunny, hazy
Playing Surface—Grass
Television and Radio—National Broadcasting Company (NBC)
Regular Season Records—Miami, 14-0; Washington, 11-3
Conference Championships—Miami defeated the Pittsburgh Steelers 21-17 for the AFC title; Washington defeated the Dallas Cowboys 26-3 for the NFC title
Players' Shares—$15,000 to each member of the winning team; $7,500 to each member of the losing team
Attendance—90,182
Gross Receipts—$4,180,086.53
Officials—Referee, Tom Bell; umpire, Lou Palazzi; line judge, Bruce Alford; head linesman, Tony Veteri; back judge, Tom Kelleher; field judge, Tony Skover
Coaches—Don Shula, Miami; George Allen, Washington

Miami	Starters, Offense	Washington
Paul Warfield	WR	Charley Taylor
Wayne Moore	LT	Terry Hermeling
Bob Kuechenberg	LG	Paul Laaveg
Jim Langer	C	Len Hauss
Larry Little	RG	John Wilbur
Norm Evans	RT	Walter Rock
Marv Fleming	TE	Jerry Smith
Howard Twilley	WR	Roy Jefferson
Bob Griese	QB	Billy Kilmer
Larry Csonka	RB	Charley Harraway
Jim Kiick	RB	Larry Brown
	Starters, Defense	
Vern Den Herder	LE	Ron McDole
Manny Fernandez	LT	Bill Brundige
Bob Heinz	RT	Diron Talbert
Bill Stanfill	RE	Verlon Biggs
Doug Swift	LLB	Jack Pardee
Nick Buoniconti	MLB	Myron Pottios
Mike Kolen	RLB	Chris Hanburger
Lloyd Mumphord	LCB	Pat Fischer
Curtis Johnson	RCB	Mike Bass
Dick Anderson	SS	Brig Owens
Jake Scott	FS	Roosevelt Taylor

Miami	7	7	0	0	—	14
Washington	0	0	0	7	—	7

Mia —Twilley 28 pass from Griese (Yepremian kick)
Mia —Kiick 1 run (Yepremian kick)
Wash—Bass 49 fumble return (Knight kick)

TEAM STATISTICS	Mia	Wash
First downs	12	16
Rushing	7	9
Passing	5	7
By penalty	0	0
Total yardage	253	228
Net rushing yardage	184	141
Net passing yardage	69	87
Passes att.-comp.-had int.	11-8-1	28-14-3

RUSHING
Miami—Csonka, 15 for 112; Kiick, 12 for 38, 1 TD; Morris, 10 for 34.
Washington—Brown, 22 for 72; Harraway, 10 for 37; Kilmer, 2 for 18; C. Taylor, 1 for 8; Smith, 1 for 6.

PASSSING
Miami—Griese, 8 of 11 for 88, 1 TD, 1 int.
Washington—Kilmer, 14 of 28 for 104, 3 int.

RECEIVING
Miami—Warfield, 3 for 36; Kiick, 2 for 6; Twilley, 1 for 28, 1 TD; Mandich, 1 for 19; Csonka, 1 for -1.
Washington—Jefferson, 5 for 50; Brown, 5 for 26; C. Taylor, 2 for 20; Smith, 1 for 11; Harraway, 1 for -3.

PUNTING
Miami—Seiple, 7 for 301, 43.0 average.
Washington—Bragg, 5 for 156, 31.2 average.

PUNT RETURNS
Miami—Scott, 2 for 4, 2 fair catches; Anderson, 1 fair catch.
Washington—Haymond, 4 for 9; Vactor, 2 fair catches.

KICKOFF RETURNS
Miami—Morris, 2 for 33.
Washington—Haymond, 2 for 30; Mul-Key, 1 for 15.

INTERCEPTIONS
Miami—Scott, 2 for 63; Buoniconti, 1 for 32.
Washington—Owens, 1 for 0.

MIAMI DOLPHINS

No.	Name	Pos.	Ht.	Wt.	Year
40	Anderson, Dick	S	6-2	196	5
49	Babb, Charlie	S	6-0	190	R
51	Ball, Larry	LB	6-6	225	R
86	Briscoe, Marlin	WR	5-11	178	4
85	Buoniconti, Nick	LB	5-11	220	11
77	Crusan, Doug	T	6-4	250	5
39	Csonka, Larry	RB	6-2	237	5
11	Del Gaizo, Jim	QB	6-1	198	R
83	Den Herder, Vern	DE	6-6	250	2
78	Dunaway, Jim	DT	6-4	277	10
73	Evans, Norm	T	6-5	250	8
75	Fernandez, Manny	DT	6-2	250	5
80	Fleming, Marv	TE	6-4	232	10
25	Foley, Tim	CB	6-0	194	3
32	Ginn, Hubert	RB	5-10	185	3
12	Griese, Bob	QB	6-1	190	6
72	Heinz, Bob	DT	6-6	265	4
60	Jenkins, Al	G-T	6-2	245	3
28	Jenkins, Ed	RB	6-2	210	R
45	Johnson, Curtis	CB	6-1	196	3
68	Kadish, Mike	DT	6-5	265	R
21	Kiick, Jim	RB	5-11	214	5
54	Kindig, Howard	T-C	6-6	260	6
57	Kolen, Mike	LB	6-2	220	3
67	Kuechenberg, Bob	G	6-2	248	3
62	Langer, Jim	C	6-2	250	3
23	Leigh, Charles	RB	5-11	206	4
66	Little, Larry	G	6-1	265	6
7	Lothridge, Billy	P	6-1	200	9
88	Mandich, Jim	TE	6-2	224	3
53	Matheson, Bob	LB	6-4	235	6
65	Moore, Maulty	DT	6-5	265	R
79	Moore, Wayne	T	6-6	265	3
15	Morrall, Earl	QB	6-2	210	17
22	Morris, Eugene (Mercury)	RB	5-10	190	4
26	Mumphord, Lloyd	CB	5-10	176	4
89	Noonan, Karl	WR	6-2	198	7
56	Powell, Jesse	LB	6-2	220	4
13	Scott, Jake	S	6-0	188	3
20	Seiple, Larry	P	6-0	214	6
84	Stanfill, Bill	DE	6-5	250	4
82	Stowe, Otto	WR	6-2	188	2
47	Stuckey, Henry	CB	6-0	180	R
59	Swift, Doug	LB	6-3	226	3
81	Twilley, Howard	WR	5-10	185	7
42	Warfield, Paul	WR	6-0	188	9
1	Yepremian, Garo	K	5-8	175	5

WASHINGTON REDSKINS

No.	Name	Pos.	Ht.	Wt.	Year
81	Alston, Mack	TE	6-2	230	3
41	Bass, Mike	CB	6-0	190	5
89	Biggs, Verlon	DE	6-4	275	8
4	Bragg, Mike	P	5-11	186	5
43	Brown, Larry	RB	5-11	195	4
77	Brundige, Bill	DT	6-5	270	3
26	Brunet, Bob	RB	6-1	205	4
58	Burman, George	C-G	6-3	255	7
45	Duncan, Leslie (Speedy)	S	5-10	180	9
68	Fanucci, Mike	DE	6-4	225	R
37	Fischer, Pat	CB	5-9	170	12
55	Hanburger, Chris	LB	6-2	218	8
31	Harraway, Charley	RB	6-2	215	7
56	Hauss, Len	C	6-2	235	9
13	Haymond, Alvin	S	6-0	194	9
75	Hermeling, Terry	T	6-5	255	3
25	Hull, Mike	RB	6-3	220	5
48	Jaqua, Jon	S	6-0	190	3
80	Jefferson, Roy	WR	6-2	195	8
63	Johnson, Mitch	T	6-4	250	7
82	Jones, Jimmie	DE	6-5	215	4
17	Kilmer, Billy	QB	6-0	204	11
50	Kiner, Steve	LB	6-1	220	3
5	Knight, Curt	K	6-2	190	4
73	Laaveg, Paul	G	6-4	250	3
79	McDole, Ron	DE	6-4	265	12
53	McLinton, Harold	LB	6-2	235	4
85	McNeil, Clifton	WR	6-2	187	9
28	Mul-Key, Herb	RB	6-0	190	R
40	Nock, George	RB	5-10	205	4
23	Owens, Brig	S	5-11	190	7
32	Pardee, Jack	LB	6-2	225	15
16	Petitbon, Richie	S	6-3	208	14
66	Pottios, Myron	LB	6-2	232	12
76	Rock, Walter	T	6-5	255	10
62	Schoenke, Ray	T	6-4	250	9
44	Severson, Jeff	S	6-1	180	R
64	Sistrunk, Manny	DT	6-5	265	3
87	Smith, Jerry	TE	6-3	208	8
72	Talbert, Diron	DT	6-5	255	6
19	Taliaferro, Mike	QB	6-2	202	9
42	Taylor, Charley	WR	6-2	210	9
22	Taylor, Roosevelt	S	5-11	186	12
67	Tillman, Rusty	LB	6-2	230	3
29	Vactor, Ted	CB	6-0	185	4
60	Wilbur, John	G	6-3	251	7
18	Wyche, Sam	QB	6-4	218	5

SUPER BOWL VIII

MIAMI 24, MINNESOTA 7

The Miami Dolphins defeated the Minnesota Vikings 24-7 in Super Bowl VIII, a game in which the Dolphins took control on the first series of offensive plays.

Following the opening kickoff, Miami moved 62 yards in 10 plays, scoring on Larry Csonka's five-yard run. After Minnesota ran three plays and punted, Miami marched 56 yards in 10 plays, scoring on Jim Kiick's one-yard run.

At the end of the first quarter, Miami had run 20 plays and gained 118 yards. Minnesota had run six plays and gained 25 yards. The Dolphins had eight first downs, the Vikings one.

The Dolphins marched 44 yards in seven plays to Garo Yepremian's 28-yard field goal that made the score 17-0 with 6:02 left in the half. Minnesota took the following kickoff and drove 74 yards to the Dolphins' 6-yard line. On the drive, Fran Tarkenton completed four of six passes for 66 yards. On fourth and one, Oscar Reed fumbled when hit by linebacker Nick Buoniconti, and Miami safety Jake Scott recovered on the 6.

Minnesota lost a chance to get back into the game at the beginning of the third quarter. John Gilliam returned Yepremian's kickoff 65 yards to Miami's 34-yard line, but Minnesota's Stu Voigt was penalized for clipping and the ball was returned to the Vikings' 11-yard line. The Vikings punted four plays later, and Miami began from Minnesota's 43. On the eighth play (four of which were runs by Csonka), the Dolphins scored on Csonka's two-yard run up the middle.

Csonka was confused on the play on which he scored his second touchdown, which punctuated a performance in which he set Super Bowl records with 33 carries and 145 yards rushing. Quarterback Bob Griese forgot the number on which the ball was supposed to be snapped by center Jim Langer. "What's the count?" Griese asked Csonka. The running back thought for a moment. "What's the count?" Griese demanded. "It's on two, isn't it?" said Csonka, "No, no . . . it's on one," said Kiick, the other running back. Griese finally agreed with Csonka. But Langer snapped the ball to the startled quarterback on one; Griese juggled the ball and handed off to Csonka, who followed Kiick, Langer, guard Larry Little, and tackle Norm Evans into the end zone.

"Bob had that wide-eyed look when he gave me the ball," said Csonka. "I'm just happy I didn't cause him to drop the ball."

Minnesota scored its touchdown after a drive that began on the Vikings' 43-yard line with 1:34 left in the third quarter and concluded with quarterback Fran Tarkenton's four-yard touchdown run 1:35 into the final quarter.

The Vikings moved from their 3-yard line to Miami's 32 later in the quarter but Tarkenton's pass to Jim Lash was intercepted on the goal line by Curtis Johnson. Miami took possession with 6:24 remaining in the game and moved 61 yards in 13 plays before the clock ran out and the game ended.

The victory was Miami's second in a row in the Super Bowl, equalling Green Bay's achievement in Super Bowls I and II. Csonka was asked if he thought Miami was stronger than the Packers' teams.

"I don't know about legends or statistics," said Csonka. "Football is a 'now' game; that's all that matters."

Miami also set a record by making its third appearance in the game. Minnesota set a record by losing for the second time.

Date—January 13, 1974
Site—Rice Stadium, Houston
Time—2:30 P.M. CST
Conditions—50 degrees, overcast
Playing Surface—AstroTurf
Television and Radio—Columbia Broadcasting System (CBS)
Regular Season Records—Miami, 12-2; Minnesota, 12-2
League Championships—Miami defeated the Oakland Raiders 27-10 for the AFC title; Minnesota defeated the Dallas Cowboys 27-10 for the NFC title
Players' Shares—$15,000 to each member of the winning team; $7,500 to each member of the losing team
Attendance—68,142
Gross Receipts—$3,953,641.22
Officials—Referee, Ben Dreith; umpire, Ralph Morcroft; line judge, Jack Fette; head linesman, Leo Miles; back judge, Stan Javie; field judge, Fritz Graf
Coaches—Bud Grant, Minnesota; Don Shula, Miami

Minnesota	Starters, Offense	Miami
Carroll Dale	WR	Paul Warfield
Grady Alderman	LT	Wayne Moore
Ed White	LG	Bob Kuechenberg
Mick Tingelhoff	C	Jim Langer
Frank Gallagher	RG	Larry Little
Ron Yary	RT	Norm Evans
Stu Voigt	TE	Jim Mandich
John Gilliam	WR	Marlin Briscoe
Fran Tarkenton	QB	Bob Griese
Oscar Reed	RB	Larry Csonka
Chuck Foreman	RB	Eugene (Mercury) Morris
	Starters, Defense	
Carl Eller	LE	Vern Den Herder
Gary Larsen	LT	Manny Fernandez
Alan Page	RT	Bob Heinz
Jim Marshall	RE	Bill Stanfill
Roy Winston	LLB	Doug Swift
Jeff Siemon	MLB	Nick Buoniconti
Wally Hilgenberg	RLB	Mike Kolen
Nate Wright	LCB	Lloyd Mumphord
Bob Bryant	RCB	Curtis Johnson
Jeff Wright	LS-SS	Dick Anderson
Paul Krause	RS-FS	Jake Scott

Minnesota	0	0	0	7	—	7
Miami	14	3	7	0	—	24

Mia —Csonka 5 run (Yepremian kick)
Mia —Kiick 1 run (Yepremian kick)
Mia —FG Yepremian 28
Mia —Csonka 2 run (Yepremian kick)
Minn—Tarkenton 4 run (Cox kick)

TEAM STATISTICS	Minn	Mia
First downs	14	21
Rushing	5	13
Passing	8	4
By penalty	1	4
Total yardage	238	259
Net rushing yardage	72	196
Net passing yardage	166	63
Passes att.-comp.-had int.	28-18-1	7-6-0

RUSHING
Minnesota—Reed, 11 for 32; Foreman, 7 for 18; Tarkenton, 4 for 17, 1 TD; Marinaro, 1 for 3; B. Brown, 1 for 2.
Miami—Csonka, 33 for 145, 2 TDs; Morris, 11 for 34; Kiick, 7 for 10, 1 TD; Griese, 2 for 7.

PASSING
Minnesota—Tarkenton, 18 of 28 for 182, 1 int.
Miami—Griese, 6 of 7 for 73.

RECEIVING
Minnesota—Foreman, 5 for 27; Gilliam, 4 for 44; Voigt, 3 for 46; Marinaro, 2 for 39; B. Brown, 1 for 9; Kingsriter, 1 for 9; Lash, 1 for 9; Reed, 1 for -1.
Miami—Warfield, 2 for 33; Mandich, 2 for 21; Briscoe, 2 for 19.

PUNTING
Minnesota—Eischeid, 5 for 211, 42.2 average.
Miami—Seiple, 3 for 119, 39.7 average.

PUNT RETURNS
Minnesota—Bryant, 1 fair catch.
Miami—Scott, 3 for 20, 1 fair catch.

KICKOFF RETURNS
Minnesota—Gilliam, 2 for 41; West, 2 for 28.
Miami—Scott, 2 for 47.

INTERCEPTIONS
Minnesota—None.
Miami—Johnson, 1 for 10.

MINNESOTA VIKINGS

No.	Name	Pos.	Ht.	Wt.	Year
67	Alderman, Grady	T	6-2	247	14
85	Ballman, Gary	TE	6-1	215	12
17	Berry, Bob	QB	5-11	185	9
30	Brown, Bill	RB	5-11	222	13
24	Brown, Terry	S	6-2	205	4
20	Bryant, Bob	CB	6-1	170	6
14	Cox, Fred	K	5-10	200	11
84	Dale, Carroll	WR	6-2	200	14
86	Dawson, Rhett	WR	6-1	182	2
11	Eischeid, Mike	P	6-0	190	7
81	Eller, Carl	DE	6-6	247	10
44	Foreman, Chuck	RB	6-2	216	R
66	Gallagher, Frank	G	6-2	245	7
42	Gilliam, John	WR	6-1	195	7
68	Goodrum, Charles	T-G	6-3	256	R
58	Hilgenberg, Wally	LB	6-3	229	10
89	Kingsriter, Doug	TE	6-2	222	R
22	Krause, Paul	S	6-3	200	10
77	Larsen, Gary	DT	6-5	255	10
82	Lash, Jim	WR	6-2	199	R
65	Lawson, Steve	G	6-3	265	3
75	Lurtsema, Bob	DT-DE	6-6	250	7
49	Marinaro, Ed	RB	6-2	212	2
70	Marshall, Jim	DE	6-4	240	14
55	Martin, Amos	LB	6-3	228	2
33	McClanahan, Brent	RB	5-10	202	R
41	Osborn, Dave	RB	6-0	208	9
88	Page, Alan	DT	6-4	245	7
52	Porter, Ron	LB	6-3	232	7
34	Randolph, Al	S	6-2	205	7
32	Reed, Oscar	RB	6-0	222	6
50	Siemon, Jeff	LB	6-2	230	2
74	Smiley, Larry	DT	6-5	248	R
64	Sunde, Milt	G	6-2	250	10
69	Sutherland, Doug	DT	6-3	250	4
10	Tarkenton, Fran	QB	6-0	190	13
53	Tingelhoff, Mick	C	6-2	237	12
83	Voigt, Stu	TE	6-1	225	4
25	Wallace, Jackie	CB	6-2	203	R
15	Wells, Mike	QB	6-5	229	R
40	West, Charlie	CB	6-1	197	6
62	White, Ed	G	6-3	262	5
60	Winston, Roy	LB	5-11	222	12
23	Wright, Jeff	S	5-11	190	3
43	Wright, Nate	CB	5-11	180	5
73	Yary, Ron	T	6-6	255	6
51	Zaunbrecher, Godfrey	C	6-2	240	3

MIAMI DOLPHINS

No.	Name	Pos.	Ht.	Wt.	Year
40	Anderson, Dick	S	6-2	196	6
49	Babb, Charles	S	6-0	190	2
51	Ball, Larry	LB	6-6	235	2
58	Bannon, Bruce	LB	6-3	225	R
86	Briscoe, Marlin	WR	5-11	175	6
85	Buoniconti, Nick	LB	5-11	220	12
77	Crusan, Doug	T	6-4	250	6
39	Csonka, Larry	RB	6-2	237	6
83	Den Herder, Vern	DE	6-6	252	3
73	Evans, Norm	T	6-5	250	9
75	Fernandez, Manny	DT	6-2	250	6
80	Fleming, Marv	TE	6-4	230	11
25	Foley, Tim	CB	6-0	194	4
55	Goode, Irv	C-G	6-5	262	11
12	Griese, Bob	QB	6-1	190	7
72	Heinz, Bob	DT-DE	6-6	265	5
45	Johnson, Curtis	CB	6-1	196	4
21	Kiick, Jim	RB	5-11	214	6
57	Kolen, Mike	LB	6-2	222	4
67	Kuechenberg, Bob	G	6-2	252	4
62	Langer, Jim	C	6-2	253	4
23	Leigh, Charles	RB	5-11	206	5
66	Little, Larry	G	6-1	265	7
88	Mandich, Jim	TE	6-2	224	4
53	Matheson, Bob	LB	6-4	235	7
65	Moore, Maulty	DT	6-5	265	2
79	Moore, Wayne	T	6-6	265	4
15	Morrall, Earl	QB	6-2	210	18
22	Morris, Eugene (Mercury)	RB	5-10	192	5
26	Mumphord, Lloyd	CB	5-10	176	5
64	Newman, Ed	G	6-2	245	R
36	Nottingham, Don	RB	5-10	210	3
82	Rather, Bo	WR	6-1	182	R
13	Scott, Jake	S	6-0	188	4
20	Seiple, Larry	P-TE	6-0	214	7
34	Sellers, Ron	WR	6-4	204	5
29	Smith, Tom	RB	6-1	218	R
84	Stanfill, Bill	DE	6-5	252	5
10	Strock, Don	QB	6-5	216	R
48	Stuckey, Henry	CB	6-1	180	R
59	Swift, Doug	LB	6-3	226	4
81	Twilley, Howard	WR	5-10	185	8
89	Wade, Charley	WR	5-10	170	R
42	Warfield, Paul	WR	6-0	188	10
70	Woods, Larry	DT	6-6	260	3
1	Yepremian, Garo	K	5-8	175	7
76	Young, Willie	T	6-5	262	4

SUPER BOWL IX

PITTSBURGH 16, MINNESOTA 6

Fullback Franco Harris set Super Bowl records by rushing 34 times for 158 yards, and the Pittsburgh Steelers outrushed the Minnesota Vikings 249-17 and won Super Bowl IX 16-6, the club's first championship in its 42-year history. The loss was the Vikings' third without a victory in the Super Bowl.

The Steelers led 2-0 at halftime after each team squandered several scoring opportunities. With 7:11 left in the second quarter, Minnesota quarterback Fran Tarkenton fumbled a handoff to running back Dave Osborn. Attempting to regain possession of the ball, Tarkenton slid into the end zone where he was downed by Dwight White for a safety.

Bill Brown of the Vikings fumbled the second-half kickoff, and Pittsburgh's Marv Kellum recovered at the Minnesota 30. Four plays later, Harris, who gained 97 yards in 22 carries in the second half, scored on a nine-yard run to increase Pittsburgh's lead to 9-0.

The score remained 9-0 until early in the fourth quarter. Minnesota linebacker Matt Blair blocked Bobby Walden's punt at the 15-yard line, and the ball was recovered in the end zone by the Vikings' Terry Brown for a touchdown with 10:33 remaining in the game. Fred Cox's extra point hit the left upright and the score was 9-6.

The Steelers began their next series on the 34-yard line. At the 42, quarterback Terry Bradshaw faced third and two. Disdaining the run or short pass, Bradshaw threw a 30-yard completion to tight end Larry Brown. After Harris and Rocky Bleier moved the ball from the Vikings' 28 to the 4, Bradshaw faced another third-down situation. He rolled to his right, searched for a receiver, and found Brown for a touchdown that resulted in a 16-6 lead.

"I looked first to pass to the halfback [Rocky Bleier]," said Bradshaw. "It depended on what their cornerbacks did. If they had come up, I would have passed; if they had laid back, I would have run. They laid back, so I started to run, but I knew I couldn't run the ball in for a touchdown."

Bradshaw said Brown made a smart move. "He stopped after running toward the corner of the end zone, then started again. That made the middle linebacker [Jeff Siemon] commit himself, and I drilled the ball to Larry." The Steelers had driven 66 yards in 12 plays and controlled the ball for seven minutes and two seconds.

Minnesota took over on its 39-yard line with 3:20 remaining. Tarkenton threw a pass intended for John Gilliam, down the middle of the field on first down. Free safety Mike Wagner intercepted the pass on Pittsburgh's 33 and returned the ball 26 yards to Minnesota's 41. Pittsburgh held possession for seven more plays, surrendering the ball on downs to the Vikings at their 23 with 37 seconds left.

Throughout the game, the Steelers appeared to confuse the Vikings with misdirection running plays as they outgained Minnesota 333-119 in total offense. Harris and Bleier (who gained 65 yards on 17 carries) repeatedly found holes in the defense that were opened when Vikings linemen followed the flow of pulling Steelers linemen. On defense, the Steelers put a man directly over center Mick Tingelhoff. Tackle Ernie Holmes sometimes would attack Tingelhoff directly after the snap of the ball; sometimes Holmes would loop around Joe Greene to the outside and participate in double-teaming action with Greene. Tarkenton was the objective. He completed just 11 of 26 passes for 102 yards with three interceptions. Four attempts were deflected and many others were thrown under severe pressure.

Date—January 12, 1975
Site—Tulane Stadium, New Orleans
Time—2:00 P.M. CST
Conditions—46 degrees, cloudy
Playing Surface—Poly-Turf
Television and Radio—National Broadcasting Company (NBC)
Regular Season Records—Pittsburgh, 10-3-1; Minnesota, 10-4
Conference Championships—Pittsburgh defeated the Oakland Raiders 24-13 for the AFC title; Minnesota defeated the Los Angeles Rams 14-10 for the NFC title
Players' Shares—$15,000 to each member of the winning team; $7,500 to each member of the losing team
Attendance—80,997
Gross Receipts—$5,126,000.00
Officials—Referee, Bernie Ulman; umpire, Al Conway; line judge, Bruce Alford; head linesman, Ed Marion; back judge, Ray Douglas; field judge, Dick Dolack
Coaches—Chuck Noll, Pittsburgh; Bud Grant, Minnesota

Pittsburgh	Starters, Offense	Minnesota
Frank Lewis	WR	Jim Lash
Jon Kolb	LT	Charles Goodrum
Jim Clack	LG	Andy Maurer
Ray Mansfield	C	Mick Tingelhoff
Gerry Mullins	RG	Ed White
Gordon Gravelle	RT	Ron Yary
Larry Brown	TE	Stu Voigt
Ron Shanklin	WR	John Gilliam
Terry Bradshaw	QB	Fran Tarkenton
Rocky Bleier	RB	Dave Osborn
Franco Harris	RB	Chuck Foreman
	Starters, Defense	
L.C. Greenwood	LE	Carl Eller
Joe Greene	LT	Doug Sutherland
Ernie Holmes	RT	Alan Page
Dwight White	RE	Jim Marshall
Jack Ham	LLB	Roy Winston
Jack Lambert	MLB	Jeff Siemon
Andy Russell	RLB	Wally Hilgenberg
J.T. Thomas	LCB	Nate Wright
Mel Blount	RCB	Jackie Wallace
Mike Wagner	SS-LS	Jeff Wright
Glen Edwards	FS-RS	Paul Krause

Pittsburgh	0	2	7	7	—	16
Minnesota	0	0	0	6	—	6

Pitt —Safety, White downed Tarkenton in end zone
Pitt —Harris 9 run (Gerela kick)
Minn—T. Brown recovered blocked punt in end zone (kick failed)
Pitt —L. Brown 4 pass from Bradshaw (Gerela kick)

TEAM STATISTICS	Pitt	Minn
First downs	17	9
Rushing	11	2
Passing	5	5
By penalty	1	2
Total yardage	333	119
Net rushing yardage	249	17
Net passing yardage	84	102
Passes att.-comp.-had int.	14-9-0	26-11-3

RUSHING
Pittsburgh—Harris, 34 for 158, 1 TD; Bleier, 17 for 65; Bradshaw, 5 for 33; Swann, 1 for -7.
Minnesota—Foreman, 12 for 18; Tarkenton, 1 for 0; Osborn, 8 for -1.

PASSING
Pittsburgh—Bradshaw, 9 of 14 for 96, 1 TD.
Minnesota—Tarkenton, 11 of 26 for 102, 3 int.

RECEIVING
Pittsburgh—Brown, 3 for 49, 1 TD; Stallworth, 3 for 24; Bleier, 2 for 11; Lewis, 1 for 12.
Minnesota—Foreman, 5 for 50; Voigt, 2 for 31; Osborn, 2 for 7; Gilliam, 1 for 16; Reed, 1 for -2.

PUNTING
Pittsburgh—Walden, 7 for 243, 34.7 average.
Minnesota—Eischeid, 6 for 223, 37.2 average.

PUNT RETURNS
Pittsburgh—Swann, 3 for 34; Edwards, 2 for 2.
Minnesota—McCullum, 3 for 11; N. Wright, 1 for 1; Wallace, 1 fair catch.

KICKOFF RETURNS
Pittsburgh—Harrison, 2 for 17; Pearson, 1 for 15.
Minnesota—McCullum, 1 for 26; McClanahan, 1 for 22; B. Brown, 1 for 2.

INTERCEPTIONS
Pittsburgh—Wagner, 1 for 26; Blount, 1 for 10; Greene, 1 for 10.
Minnesota—None.

PITTSBURGH STEELERS

No.	Name	Pos.	Ht.	Wt.	Year
45	Allen, Jim	CB	6-2	194	R
20	Bleier, Rocky	RB	5-11	210	6
47	Blount, Mel	CB	6-3	205	5
38	Bradley, Ed	LB	6-2	239	3
12	Bradshaw, Terry	QB	6-3	218	5
87	Brown, Larry	TE	6-4	229	4
50	Clack, Jim	G-C	6-3	250	4
22	Conn, Richard	S	6-0	185	R
77	Davis, Charlie	DT	6-1	265	R
57	Davis, Sam	G	6-1	255	8
35	Davis, Steve	RB	6-1	218	3
73	Druschel, Rick	G-T	6-2	248	R
27	Edwards, Glen	S	6-0	185	4
64	Furness, Steve	DT-DE	6-4	255	3
86	Garrett, Reggie	WR	6-1	172	R
10	Gerela, Roy	K	5-10	185	6
17	Gilliam, Joe	QB	6-2	187	3
71	Gravelle, Gordon	T-G	6-5	250	3
75	Greene, Joe	DT	6-4	275	6
68	Greenwood, L. C.	DE	6-6	245	6
84	Grossman, Randy	TE	6-1	215	R
59	Ham, Jack	LB	6-1	225	4
5	Hanratty, Terry	QB	6-1	210	6
32	Harris, Franco	RB	6-2	230	3
46	Harrison, Reggie	RB	5-11	215	R
63	Holmes, Ernie	DT	6-3	260	3
54	Kellum, Marv	LB	6-2	225	R
55	Kolb, Jon	T	6-3	262	6
58	Lambert, Jack	LB	6-4	215	R
43	Lewis, Frank	WR	6-1	196	4
56	Mansfield, Ray	C	6-3	260	12
89	McMakin, John	TE	6-3	232	3
72	Mullins, Gerry	G-T	6-3	244	4
26	Pearson, Preston	RB	6-1	205	8
74	Reavis, Dave	T	6-5	250	1
34	Russell, Andy	LB	6-2	225	10
25	Shanklin, Ron	WR	6-1	190	5
31	Shell, Donnie	S-CB	5-11	190	R
82	Stallworth, John	WR	6-2	183	R
88	Swann, Lynn	WR	5-10	178	R
24	Thomas, J. T.	CB	6-2	196	2
51	Toews, Loren	LB	6-3	212	2
23	Wagner, Mike	S	6-1	210	4
39	Walden, Bobby	P	6-0	190	11
52	Webster, Mike	C-G	6-1	232	R
78	White, Dwight	DE	6-4	255	4
62	Wolf, Jim	DE	6-2	230	R

MINNESOTA VIKINGS

No.	Name	Pos.	Ht.	Wt.	Year
67	Alderman, Grady	T	6-2	247	15
56	Anderson, Scott	C	6-4	234	R
17	Berry, Bob	QB	5-11	185	10
21	Blahak, Joe	CB-S	5-10	188	2
59	Blair, Matt	LB	6-5	229	R
71	Boone, Dave	DE	6-3	248	R
30	Brown, Bill	RB	5-11	222	14
24	Brown, Terry	S	6-2	205	5
14	Cox, Fred	K	5-10	200	12
84	Craig, Steve	TE	6-3	231	R
11	Eischeid, Mike	P	6-0	190	8
81	Eller, Carl	DE	6-6	247	11
44	Foreman, Chuck	RB	6-2	207	2
42	Gilliam, John	WR	6-1	195	8
68	Goodrum, Charles	T-G	6-3	256	2
58	Hilgenberg, Wally	LB	6-3	229	11
85	Holland, John	WR	6-0	190	R
89	Kingsriter, Doug	TE	6-2	222	2
22	Krause, Paul	S	6-3	200	11
77	Larsen, Gary	DT	6-5	255	11
82	Lash, Jim	WR	6-2	199	2
65	Lawson, Steve	G	6-3	265	4
75	Lurtsema, Bob	DE-DT	6-6	250	8
49	Marinaro, Ed	RB	6-2	212	3
70	Marshall, Jim	DE	6-4	240	15
55	Martin, Amos	LB	6-3	228	3
66	Maurer, Andy	G	6-3	247	5
33	McClanahan, Brent	RB	5-10	202	2
80	McCullum, Sam	WR	6-2	203	R
54	McNeill, Fred	LB	6-2	229	R
41	Osborn, Dave	RB	6-0	208	10
88	Page, Alan	DT	6-4	245	8
29	Poltl, Randy	CB	6-3	190	R
32	Reed, Oscar	RB	6-0	222	7
78	Riley, Steve	T	6-6	258	R
50	Siemon, Jeff	LB	6-2	230	3
64	Sunde, Milt	G	6-2	250	11
69	Sutherland, Doug	DT	6-3	250	5
10	Tarkenton, Fran	QB	6-0	190	14
53	Tingelhoff, Mick	C	6-2	240	13
83	Voigt, Stu	TE	6-1	225	5
25	Wallace, Jackie	CB	6-3	197	2
62	White, Ed	G	6-3	268	6
60	Winston, Roy	LB	5-11	222	13
23	Wright, Jeff	S	5-11	190	4
43	Wright, Nate	CB	5-11	180	6
73	Yary, Ron	T	6-6	255	7

SUPER BOWL X

PITTSBURGH 21, DALLAS 17

Quarterback Terry Bradshaw threw a pass that covered 59 yards to wide receiver Lynn Swann, who carried the ball the final five yards for a 64-yard touchdown that proved to be the crucial points in the Steelers' 21-17 victory over the Dallas Cowboys in Super Bowl X. Bradshaw was knocked unconscious when he was hit by safety Cliff Harris and did not see Swann make the catch.

The touchdown gave Pittsburgh a 21-10 lead with 3:02 remaining in the game. Dallas took over on its 20-yard line with 2:54 remaining and went 80 yards in five plays, scoring with 1:48 left on Roger Staubach's 34-yard pass to Percy Howard.

Pittsburgh began the next series on Dallas's 42 after guard Gerry Mullins of Pittsburgh recovered Toni Fritsch's onside kick. On fourth down and nine at the Cowboys' 41, the Steelers did not punt, and Rocky Bleier was stopped after a two-yard gain. Dallas moved to the Steelers' 38-yard line before Staubach's pass to Drew Pearson was intercepted by Glen Edwards in the end zone. Edwards returned the ball 30 yards as the game came to an end.

In a game that generally was acclaimed the best and most exciting of the Super Bowls to that point, the Steelers outgained Dallas 339-270 but did not take the lead until the fourth quarter.

At the end of the Steelers' first offensive series, punter Bobby Walden bobbled the snap from center and recovered at his 29-yard line, where he was tackled by Billy Joe DuPree.

On the next play, Staubach threw a pass to Drew Pearson, who was alone on a crossing pattern in the middle of the field at the 15-yard line; Pearson scored the game's first touchdown after 4:36 of play.

The Steelers answered on the next series, moving 67 yards in eight plays and scoring on a seven-yard pass from Bradshaw to tight end Randy Grossman. The big play of the drive was a 32-yard pass from Bradshaw to Lynn Swann. Dallas went ahead 10-7 on the next series by marching 46 yards in 11 plays to Fritsch's 36-yard field goal.

Dallas held its three-point lead for the rest of the second quarter, all of the third quarter, and for the first 3:32 of the fourth quarter. But a play in that scoreless third quarter changed the complexion of the game. After Pittsburgh's Roy Gerela missed his second field-goal attempt of the game, Cliff Harris mockingly patted him on the helmet. Pittsburgh linebacker Jack Lambert was incensed, and he flung Harris to the ground. Lambert played the rest of the game at tornado strength. He delivered crushing tackles (14 in all) and gave his teammates a spark.

"I felt we were intimidated a little in the first half," Lambert said. "The Pittsburgh Steelers aren't supposed to be intimidated. We're supposed to do the intimidating. I decided to do something about it."

Pittsburgh's Reggie Harrison also did something. Early in the fourth quarter, he blocked a punt by Mitch Hoopes, and the ball rolled out of the end zone for a safety and two points for the Steelers.

After Hoopes punted on the ensuing free kick, the Steelers moved 25 yards in six plays to position Gerela for a 36-yard field goal. Pittsburgh led 12-10 with 8:41 left. On the first play after the kickoff, Mike Wagner of the Steelers intercepted a pass from Staubach that was intended for Drew Pearson, who ran the same pattern on which he scored in the first quarter. Wagner's 19-yard return set up an 18-yard field goal by Gerela, and Pittsburgh led 15-10 with 6:37 remaining.

Pittsburgh took over again with 4:25 left, and it was time for Bradshaw's heroics.

Date—January 18, 1976
Site—Orange Bowl, Miami
Time—2:00 P.M. EST
Conditions—57 degrees, clear
Playing Surface—Poly-Turf
Television and Radio—Columbia Broadcasting System (CBS)
Regular Season Records—Pittsburgh, 12-2; Dallas, 10-4
Conference Championships—Pittsburgh defeated the Oakland Raiders 16-10 for the AFC title; Dallas defeated the Los Angeles Rams 37-7 for the NFC title
Players' Shares—$15,000 to each member of the winning team; $7,500 to each member of the losing team
Attendance—80,187
Gross Receipts—$5,242,641.25
Officials—Referee, Norm Schachter; umpire, Joe Connell; line judge, Jack Fette; head linesman, Leo Miles; back judge, Stan Javie; field judge, Bill O'Brien
Coaches—Tom Landry, Dallas; Chuck Noll, Pittsburgh

Dallas	Starters, Offense	Pittsburgh
Golden Richards	WR	John Stallworth
Ralph Neely	LT	Jon Kolb
Burton Lawless	LG	Jim Clack
John Fitzgerald	C	Ray Mansfield
Blaine Nye	RG	Gerry Mullins
Rayfield Wright	RT	Gordon Gravelle
Jean Fugett	TE	Larry Brown
Drew Pearson	WR	Lynn Swann
Roger Staubach	QB	Terry Bradshaw
Robert Newhouse	RB	Rocky Bleier
Preston Pearson	RB	Franco Harris
	Starters, Defense	
Ed Jones	LE	L. C. Greenwood
Jethro Pugh	LT	Joe Greene
Larry Cole	RT	Ernie Holmes
Harvey Martin	RE	Dwight White
Dave Edwards	LLB	Jack Ham
Lee Roy Jordan	MLB	Jack Lambert
D. D. Lewis	RLB	Andy Russell
Mark Washington	LCB	J. T. Thomas
Mel Renfro	RCB	Mel Blount
Charlie Waters	SS	Mike Wagner
Cliff Harris	FS	Glen Edwards

Dallas	7	3	0	7	—	17
Pittsburgh	7	0	0	14	—	21

Dall—D. Pearson 29 pass from Staubach (Fritsch kick)
Pitt—Grossman 7 pass from Bradshaw (Gerela kick)
Dall—FG Fritsch 36
Pitt—Safety, Harrison blocked Hoopes' punt through end zone
Pitt—FG Gerela 36
Pitt—FG Gerela 18
Pitt—Swann 64 pass from Bradshaw (kick failed)
Dall—P. Howard 34 pass from Staubach (Fritsch kick)

TEAM STATISTICS	Dall	Pitt
First downs	14	13
Rushing	6	7
Passing	8	6
By penalty	0	0
Total yardage	270	339
Net rushing yardage	108	149
Net passing yardage	162	190
Passes att.-comp.-had int.	24-15-3	19-9-0

RUSHING
Dallas—Newhouse, 16 for 56; Staubach, 5 for 22; Dennison, 5 for 16; P. Pearson, 5 for 14.
Pittsburgh—Harris, 27 for 82; Bleier, 15 for 51; Bradshaw, 4 for 16.

PASSING
Dallas—Staubach, 15 of 24 for 204, 2 TDs, 3 int.
Pittsburgh—Bradshaw, 9 of 19 for 209, 2 TDs.

RECEIVING
Dallas—P. Pearson, 5 for 53; Young, 3 for 31; D. Pearson, 2 for 59, 1 TD; Newhouse, 2 for 12; P. Howard, 1 for 34, 1 TD; Fugett, 1 for 9; Dennison, 1 for 6.
Pittsburgh—Swann, 4 for 161, 1 TD; Stallworth, 2 for 8; Harris, 1 for 26; Grossman, 1 for 7, 1 TD; L. Brown, 1 for 7.

PUNTING
Dallas—Hoopes, 7 for 245, 35.0 average.
Pittsburgh—Walden, 4 for 159, 39.8 average.

PUNT RETURNS
Dallas—Richards, 1 for 5, 3 fair catches.
Pittsburgh—D. Brown, 3 for 14; Edwards, 2 for 17.

KICKOFF RETURNS
Dallas—T. Henderson, 48 after a lateral; P. Pearson, 4 for 48.
Pittsburgh—Blount, 3 for 64; Collier, 1 for 25.

INTERCEPTIONS
Dallas—None.
Pittsburgh—Edwards, 1 for 35; Thomas, 1 for 35; Wagner, 1 for 19.

DALLAS COWBOYS

No.	Name	Pos.	Ht.	Wt.	Year
31	Barnes, Benny	CB	6-1	185	4
53	Breunig, Bob	LB	6-2	227	R
59	Capone, Warren	LB	6-1	218	1
63	Cole, Larry	DT	6-5	250	8
57	Davis, Kyle	C	6-4	240	R
21	Dennison, Doug	RB	6-0	195	2
67	Donovan, Pat	T	6-4	250	R
89	DuPree, Billy Joe	TE	6-4	228	3
52	Edwards, Dave	LB	6-1	225	13
62	Fitzgerald, John	C	6-5	255	5
15	Fritsch, Toni	K	5-7	195	4
84	Fugett, Jean	TE-WR	6-3	226	4
77	Gregory, Bill	DT	6-5	252	5
43	Harris, Cliff	S	6-1	190	6
56	Henderson, Thomas	LB	6-2	220	R
9	Hoopes, Mitch	P	6-1	210	R
81	Howard, Percy	WR	6-4	210	R
87	Howard, Ron	TE	6-4	225	2
42	Hughes, Randy	S	6-4	200	R
72	Jones, Ed	DE	6-9	260	2
55	Jordan, Lee Roy	LB	6-1	221	13
66	Lawless, Burton	G	6-4	250	R
50	Lewis, D.D.	LB	6-1	218	7
19	Longley, Clint	QB	6-1	193	2
79	Martin, Harvey	DE	6-5	250	3
73	Neely, Ralph	T	6-6	260	11
44	Newhouse, Robert	RB	5-10	200	4
61	Nye, Blaine	G	6-4	255	8
88	Pearson, Drew	WR	6-0	180	3
26	Pearson, Preston	RB	6-1	205	9
58	Peterson, Calvin	LB	6-3	220	2
75	Pugh, Jethro	DT	6-6	250	11
20	Renfro, Mel	CB	6-0	190	12
83	Richards, Golden	WR	6-0	183	3
68	Scott, Herbert	G	6-2	250	R
12	Staubach, Roger	QB	6-3	197	7
78	Walton, Bruce	T	6-6	252	3
46	Washington, Mark	CB	5-11	186	6
41	Waters, Charlie	S	6-2	193	6
54	White, Randy	LB	6-4	245	R
45	Woolsey, Roland	CB-S	6-1	182	R
70	Wright, Rayfield	T	6-6	260	9
30	Young, Charles	RB	6-1	210	2

PITTSBURGH STEELERS

No.	Name	Pos.	Ht.	Wt.	Year
45	Allen, Jim	CB	6-2	194	2
76	Banaszak, John	DE	6-3	232	R
20	Bleier, Rocky	RB	5-11	210	7
47	Blount, Mel	CB	6-3	200	6
38	Bradley, Ed	LB	6-2	232	4
12	Bradshaw, Terry	QB	6-3	210	6
36	Brown, Dave	CB	6-1	200	R
87	Brown, Larry	TE	6-4	230	5
50	Clack, Jim	G	6-3	250	5
44	Collier, Mike	RB	5-11	200	R
57	Davis, Sam	G	6-1	250	9
27	Edwards, Glen	S	6-0	185	5
33	Fuqua, John	RB	5-11	200	7
64	Furness, Steve	DT	6-4	255	4
86	Garrett, Reggie	WR	6-1	175	2
10	Gerela, Roy	K	5-10	190	7
17	Gilliam, Joe	QB	6-2	187	4
71	Gravelle, Gordon	T	6-5	255	4
75	Greene, Joe	DT	6-4	275	7
68	Greenwood, L.C.	DE	6-6	245	7
84	Grossman, Randy	TE	6-1	215	2
59	Ham, Jack	LB	6-1	225	5
5	Hanratty, Terry	QB	6-1	205	7
32	Harris, Franco	RB	6-2	230	4
46	Harrison, Reggie	RB	5-11	215	2
63	Holmes, Ernie	DT	6-3	260	4
54	Kellum, Marv	LB	6-2	225	2
55	Kolb, Jon	T	6-3	262	7
58	Lambert, Jack	LB	6-4	220	2
43	Lewis, Frank	WR	6-1	196	5
56	Mansfield, Ray	C	6-3	260	13
72	Mullins, Gerry	G-T	6-3	240	5
74	Reavis, Dave	T	6-5	254	2
34	Russell, Andy	LB	6-2	220	11
31	Shell, Donnie	S	5-11	195	2
82	Stallworth, John	WR	6-2	185	2
88	Swann, Lynn	WR	6-0	180	2
24	Thomas, J. T.	CB	6-2	196	3
51	Toews, Loren	LB	6-3	222	3
23	Wagner, Mike	S	6-1	210	5
39	Walden, Bobby	P	6-0	197	12
52	Webster, Mike	C	6-1	245	2
78	White, Dwight	DE	6-4	255	5

SUPER BOWL XI

OAKLAND 32, MINNESOTA 14

The Oakland Raiders, making their first appearance in the Super Bowl in nine years, defeated the Minnesota Vikings 32-14 to score the most decisive victory in the series since Dallas beat Miami by 21 points in Super Bowl VI. Minnesota lost in the Super Bowl for the fourth time in four appearances.

Oakland took the ball after the opening kickoff and went from its 34 to the Vikings' 11 in eight plays. On fourth down, Errol Mann attempted a 29-yard field goal, but the ball hit the left upright. Raiders quarterback Ken Stabler summed up the confidence of his team when he conferred with head coach John Madden after the missed field goal. "Don't worry," said Stabler. "There's more where that came from."

Late in the first quarter, Oakland's Ray Guy sustained the first blocked punt of his four-season NFL career. Minnesota's Fred McNeill blocked the ball at Oakland's 28. Guy finally tackled McNeill at the 3 after a wild scramble for the ball. But the Vikings' Brent McClanahan fumbled on the second play after the recovery, and Oakland's Willie Hall recovered. Using the last 4:35 of the first quarter and the first 48 seconds of the second quarter, the Raiders then drove 90 yards in 12 plays. Mann's 24-yard field goal put Oakland on top 3-0.

Minnesota gave up the ball without gaining a first down on its next possession. Beginning at its 36, Oakland moved 64 yards in 10 plays, scoring on Stabler's one-yard pass to Dave Casper, who was alone in the end zone. The Vikings again could not gain a first down on their next series and, after a 25-yard punt return by Neal Colzie, Oakland went 35 yards in five plays, Pete Banaszak getting the touchdown for a 16-0 halftime lead.

After 30 minutes of play, Oakland had gained 288 yards, Minnesota 86. Oakland had 16 first downs, Minnesota 4. Clarence Davis of Oakland had gained 86 yards (his game total 137 yards, in 16 carries, represented a high for his eight-year pro career).

The Raiders, who were directing most of their attack over the left side of their line—behind tackle Art Shell and guard Gene Upshaw—moved 31 yards in five plays to Mann's 40-yard field goal with 5:16 left in the third quarter.

Minnesota scored on the next series. Fran Tarkenton's eight-yard pass to Sammy White with 47 seconds remaining in the quarter concluded a 12-play, 68-yard advance in which Tarkenton completed four of eight passes for 54 yards.

Tarkenton moved the Vikings again in the fourth period. He drove them from their 22 to Oakland's 37, but his pass intended for Chuck Foreman at the 30 was intercepted by Hall, who brought the ball back 16 yards. That served as the catalyst for a 54-yard march that ended with Banaszak scoring from the 2. The big play of the series was a 48-yard pass from Stabler to Fred Biletnikoff, who was named the game's most valuable player. Oakland led 26-7 with 7:39 remaining.

The Vikings' next thrust reached the Minnesota 47. On first down, Tarkenton threw a sideline pass to White. Willie Brown intercepted at the 25 and outraced Tarkenton, the final defender, on a 75-yard touchdown return that made it 32-7.

Minnesota scored the final touchdown on an 86-yard drive that culminated with an eight-yard pass from Bob Lee, who had replaced Tarkenton, to Stu Voigt with 25 seconds left.

"When you've got the horses, you ride them," said Stabler, referring to Shell and Upshaw. "We're not a fancy team. We just line up and try to knock you out of there. Nobody's better at it than those two guys."

Date—January 9, 1977
Site—Rose Bowl, Pasadena
Time—12:30 P.M. PST
Conditions—58 degrees, clear and sunny
Playing Surface—Grass
Television and Radio—National Broadcasting Company (NBC)
Regular Season Records—Oakland, 13-1; Minnesota, 11-2-1
Conference Championships—Oakland defeated the Pittsburgh Steelers 24-7 for the AFC title; Minnesota defeated the Los Angeles Rams 24-13 for the NFC title
Players' Shares—$15,000 to each member of the winning team; $7,500 to each member of the losing team
Attendance—100,421
Gross Receipts—$5,768,772.73
Officials—Referee, Jim Tunney; umpire, Lou Palazzi; line judge, Bill Swanson; head linesman, Ed Marion; back judge, Tom Kelleher; field judge, Armen Terzian
Coaches—John Madden, Oakland; Bud Grant, Minnesota

Oakland	Starters, Offense	Minnesota
Cliff Branch	WR	Ahmad Rashad
Art Shell	LT	Steve Riley
Gene Upshaw	LG	Charles Goodrum
Dave Dalby	C	Mick Tingelhoff
George Buehler	RG	Ed White
John Vella	RT	Ron Yary
Dave Casper	TE	Stu Voigt
Fred Biletnikoff	WR	Sammy White
Ken Stabler	QB	Fran Tarkenton
Mark van Eeghen	RB	Brent McClanahan
Clarence Davis	RB	Chuck Foreman
	Starters, Defense	
John Matuszak	LE	Carl Eller
Dave Rowe	NT-LT	Doug Sutherland
Otis Sistrunk	RE-RT	Alan Page
Phil Villapiano	LOLB-RE	Jim Marshall
Monte Johnson	LILB-LLB	Matt Blair
Willie Hall	RILB-MLB	Jeff Siemon
Ted Hendricks	ROLB-RLB	Wally Hilgenberg
Alonzo (Skip) Thomas	LCB	Nate Wright
Willie Brown	RCB	Bobby Bryant
George Atkinson	FS-LS	Jeff Wright
Jack Tatum	SS-RS	Paul Krause

Oakland	0	16	3	13	—	32
Minnesota	0	0	7	7	—	14

Oak —FG Mann 24
Oak —Casper 1 pass from Stabler (Mann kick)
Oak —Banaszak 1 run (kick failed)
Oak —FG Mann 40
Minn—S. White 8 pass from Tarkenton (Cox kick)
Oak —Banaszak 2 run (Mann kick)
Oak —Brown 75 interception return (kick failed)
Minn—Voigt 13 pass from Lee (Cox kick)

TEAM STATISTICS	Oak	Minn
First downs	21	20
Rushing	13	2
Passing	8	15
By penalty	0	3
Total yardage	429	353
Net rushing yardage	266	71
Net passing yardage	163	282
Passes att.-comp.-had int.	19-12-0	44-24-2

RUSHING
Oakland—Davis, 16 for 137; van Eeghen, 18 for 73; Garrett, 4 for 19; Banaszak, 10 for 19, 2 TDs; Ginn, 2 for 9; Rae, 2 for 9.
Minnesota—Foreman, 17 for 44; Johnson, 2 for 9; S. White, 1 for 7; Lee, 1 for 4; Miller, 2 for 4; McClanahan, 3 for 3.
PASSING
Oakland—Stabler, 12 of 19 for 180, 1 TD.
Minnesota—Tarkenton, 17 of 35 for 205, 1 TD, 2 int.; Lee, 7 of 9 for 81, 1 TD.
RECEIVING
Oakland—Biletnikoff, 4 for 79; Casper, 4 for 70, 1 TD; Branch, 3 for 20; Garrett, 1 for 11.
Minnesota—S. White, 5 for 77, 1 TD; Foreman, 5 for 62; Voigt, 4 for 49, 1 TD; Miller, 4 for 19; Rashad, 3 for 53; Johnson, 3 for 26.
PUNTING
Oakland—Guy, 4 for 162, 40.5 average.
Minnesota—Clabo, 7 for 265, 37.9 average.
PUNT RETURNS
Oakland—Colzie, 4 for 43.
Minnesota—Willis, 3 for 14.
KICKOFF RETURNS
Oakland—Garrett, 2 for 47; Siani, 1 for 0.
Minnesota—S. White, 4 for 79; Willis, 3 for 57.
INTERCEPTIONS
Oakland—Brown, 1 for 75, 1 TD; Hall, 1 for 16.
Minnesota—None.

OAKLAND RAIDERS

No.	Name	Pos.	Ht.	Wt.	Year
43	Atkinson, George	S	6-0	185	9
40	Banaszak, Pete	RB	6-0	210	11
46	Bankston, Warren	RB-TE	6-4	235	8
51	Barnes, Rodrigo	LB	6-1	215	4
25	Biletnikoff, Fred	WR	6-1	190	12
54	Bonness, Rik	LB	6-3	220	R
81	Bradshaw, Morris	WR	6-1	195	3
21	Branch, Cliff	WR	5-11	170	5
24	Brown, Willie	CB	6-1	210	14
64	Buehler, George	G	6-2	270	8
87	Casper, Dave	TE	6-4	228	3
20	Colzie, Neal	CB	6-2	205	2
50	Dalby, Dave	C	6-3	250	5
28	Davis, Clarence	RB	5-10	195	6
31	Garrett, Carl	RB	5-10	205	8
29	Ginn, Hubert	RB	5-9	185	7
8	Guy, Ray	P	6-3	195	4
39	Hall, Willie	LB	6-2	225	4
83	Hendricks, Ted	LB	6-7	220	8
11	Humm, David	QB	6-2	184	2
58	Johnson, Monte	LB	6-5	240	4
70	Lawrence, Henry	T	6-4	273	3
14	Mann, Errol	K	6-0	205	9
72	Matuszak, John	DE	6-7	270	4
61	McMath, Herb	DE	6-4	245	R
79	Medlin, Dan	G	6-4	252	3
36	Moore, Manfred	RB	6-0	200	3
47	Phillips, Charles	S	6-2	215	2
77	Philyaw, Charles	DE	6-9	270	R
15	Rae, Mike	QB	6-1	190	R
52	Rice, Floyd	LB	6-3	225	6
74	Rowe, Dave	NT	6-7	271	10
78	Shell, Art	T	6-5	265	9
49	Siani, Mike	WR	6-2	195	5
60	Sistrunk, Otis	DE	6-3	273	5
12	Stabler, Ken	QB	6-3	215	7
66	Sylvester, Steve	C	6-4	262	2
32	Tatum, Jack	S	5-11	206	5
26	Thomas, Alonzo (Skip)	CB	6-1	205	5
63	Upshaw, Gene	G	6-5	255	10
30	van Eeghen, Mark	RB	6-2	225	3
75	Vella, John	T	6-4	260	5
41	Villapiano, Phil	LB	6-2	225	6

MINNESOTA VIKINGS

No.	Name	Pos.	Ht.	Wt.	Year
20	Allen, Nate	CB	5-11	174	6
27	Beamon, Autry	S	6-1	190	2
17	Berry, Bob	QB	5-11	185	12
59	Blair, Matt	LB	6-5	229	3
20	Bryant, Bobby	CB	6-1	170	8
74	Buetow, Bart	T	6-5	250	3
12	Clabo, Neil	P	6-2	200	2
14	Cox, Fred	K	5-10	200	14
84	Craig, Steve	TE	6-3	231	3
57	Dumler, Doug	C	6-3	245	4
81	Eller, Carl	DE	6-6	247	13
44	Foreman, Chuck	RB	6-2	207	4
68	Goodrum, Charles	G	6-3	256	4
26	Grim, Bob	WR	6-0	188	10
47	Groce, Ron	RB	6-2	211	R
40	Hall, Windlan	S	5-11	175	5
61	Hamilton, Wes	G	6-3	255	R
58	Hilgenberg, Wally	LB	6-3	229	13
48	Johnson, Sammy	RB	6-1	226	3
22	Krause, Paul	S	6-3	200	13
19	Lee, Bob	QB	6-2	195	8
70	Marshall, Jim	DE	6-4	240	17
55	Martin, Amos	LB	6-3	228	5
33	McClanahan, Brent	RB	5-10	202	4
54	McNeill, Fred	LB	6-2	229	3
35	Miller, Robert	RB	5-11	204	2
77	Mullaney, Mark	DE	6-6	242	2
88	Page, Alan	DT	6-4	245	10
28	Rashad, Ahmad	WR	6-2	200	4
78	Riley, Steve	T	6-5	258	5
50	Siemon, Jeff	LB	6-3	237	5
69	Sutherland, Doug	DT	6-3	250	7
10	Tarkenton, Fran	QB	6-0	190	16
53	Tingelhoff, Mick	C	6-2	240	15
83	Voigt, Stu	TE	6-1	225	7
62	White, Ed	G	6-2	270	8
72	White, James	DT	6-3	263	R
85	White, Sammy	WR	5-11	189	R
80	Willis, Leonard	WR	5-10	180	R
60	Winston, Roy	LB	5-11	222	15
23	Wright, Jeff	S	5-11	190	6
42	Wright, Nate	CB	5-11	180	8
73	Yary, Ron	T	6-5	255	9

SUPER BOWL XII

DALLAS 27, DENVER 10

The Dallas Cowboys' defense totally controlled the first half of the game, intercepting four passes and recovering three fumbles. The Cowboys converted two of the interceptions into 10 points on the way to building a 13-0 halftime lead and went on to even their Super Bowl record at 2-2 with a 27-10 victory.

The game started slowly; there were three punts—two by the Cowboys—in the first 7:35. Midway through the first quarter, with Denver on its own 29-yard line, Dallas safety Randy Hughes intercepted a pass by Craig Morton to set the Cowboys up at the Broncos' 25. Five plays later Tony Dorsett scored from three yards out.

Denver's John Schultz returned the ensuing Dallas kickoff to the Broncos' 40. Two plays later Aaron Kyle intercepted Morton again and returned the ball to the Denver 35. Two Dallas runs gave the Cowboys a first and goal at the Denver 8. The Broncos' defense stiffened and the Cowboys were forced to settle for a 35-yard field goal by Efren Herrera.

Denver punted to start the second quarter. The Cowboys drove 32 yards to set up a 43-yard field goal by Herrera, which gave Dallas a 13-0 lead.

The last five times the Broncos had possession of the ball in the second quarter, they turned it over to the Cowboys. The Cowboys came up empty, however. Denver linebacker Tom Jackson recovered Billy Joe DuPree's fumble and Herrera missed three field goals.

Denver drove 35 yards to set up Jim Turner's field goal to start the second half. After an exchange of punts, the Cowboys marched 58 yards in only six plays to take a 20-3 lead. On third and 10, Roger Staubach threw a 45-yard touchdown pass to Butch Johnson, who made a spectacular diving catch in the end zone.

Denver gained some momentum with a 67-yard kickoff return to the Dallas 26 by Rick Upchurch. After his first pass was almost intercepted, Morton was relieved at quarterback by Norris Weese. Four plays later, Weese sent Rob Lytle off the left side of the line for a one-yard touchdown that cut the Cowboys' lead to 20-10.

With less than eight minutes remaining, the Cowboys' defense set up the final touchdown of the game. Weese fumbled while trying to pass, and defensive end Harvey Martin recovered on the Denver 29. On the next play, running back Robert Newhouse took a hand-off, went wide left, stopped, and threw a pass to wide receiver Golden Richards, who was alone in the end zone. It was the first touchdown pass Newhouse had thrown since the regular season of 1975.

The Broncos only had one more possession, which ended on the Dallas 24 when Weese's fourth-down pass went through Upchurch's hands. The Cowboys ran off the last three minutes of the game, helped by a roughing-the-kicker penalty.

The Cowboys dominated the statistics as well as the score, running up 325 yards to 156 for the Broncos. Staubach completed 17 of 25 for 183 yards and one touchdown. The Cowboys' defense held Morton to 19 net yards passing and intercepted four passes in all. Weese didn't fare much better than Morton; he ended with 16 net yards passing.

"They played the kind of game we usually play," said Morton. "They beat us at our own game—taking turnovers. So many times this season other teams gave us all those turnovers. Today it was just our turn."

Martin and defensive tackle Randy White were named the game's co-most valuable players.

Date—January 15, 1978
Site—Louisiana Superdome, New Orleans
Time—5:15 P.M. CST
Conditions—70 degrees, indoors
Playing Surface—AstroTurf
Television and Radio—Columbia Broadcasting System (CBS)
Regular Season Records—Denver, 12-2; Dallas, 12-2
Conference Championships—Denver defeated the Oakland Raiders 20-17 for the AFC title; Dallas defeated the Minnesota Vikings 23-6 for the NFC title
Players' Shares—$18,000 to each member of the winning team; $9,000 to each member of the losing team
Attendance—75,583
Gross Receipts—$6,923,141.50
Officials—Referee, Jim Tunney; umpire, Joe Connell; line judge, Art Holst; head linesman, Tony Veteri; back judge, Ray Douglas; field judge, Bob Wortman
Coaches—Tom Landry, Dallas; Red Miller, Denver

Dallas	Starters, Offense	Denver
Butch Johnson	WR	Jack Dolbin
Ralph Neely	LT	Andy Maurer
Herbert Scott	LG	Tom Glassic
John Fitzgerald	C	Mike Montler
Tom Rafferty	RG	Paul Howard
Pat Donovan	RT	Claudie Minor
Billy Joe DuPree	TE	Riley Odoms
Drew Pearson	WR	Haven Moses
Roger Staubach	QB	Craig Morton
Robert Newhouse	RB	Jon Keyworth
Tony Dorsett	RB	Otis Armstrong
	Starters, Defense	
Ed Jones	LE	Barney Chavous
Jethro Pugh	LT-NT	Rubin Carter
Randy White	RT-RE	Lyle Alzado
Harvey Martin	RE-LOLB	Bob Swenson
Thomas Henderson	LLB-LILB	Joe Rizzo
Bob Breunig	MLB-RILB	Randy Gradishar
D. D. Lewis	RLB-ROLB	Tom Jackson
Benny Barnes	LCB	Louis Wright
Aaron Kyle	RCB	Steve Foley
Charlie Waters	SS	Billy Thompson
Cliff Harris	FS	Bernard Jackson

Dallas	10	3	7	7	—	27
Denver	0	0	10	0	—	10

Dall—Dorsett 3 run (Herrera kick)
Dall—FG Herrera 35
Dall—FG Herrera 43
Den—FG Turner 47
Dall—Johnson 45 pass from Staubach (Herrera kick)
Den—Lytle 1 run (Turner kick)
Dall—Richards 29 pass from Newhouse (Herrera kick)

TEAM STATISTICS	Dall	Den
First downs	17	11
Rushing	8	8
Passing	8	1
By penalty	1	2
Total yardage	325	156
Net rushing yardage	143	121
Net passing yardage	182	35
Passes att.-comp.-had int.	28-19-0	25-8-4

RUSHING
Dallas—Dorsett, 15 for 66, 1 TD; Newhouse, 14 for 55; White, 1 for 13; P. Pearson, 3 for 11; Staubach, 3 for 6; Laidlaw, 1 for 1; Johnson, 1 for -9.
Denver—Lytle, 10 for 35, 1 TD; Armstrong, 7 for 27; Weese, 3 for 26; Jensen, 1 for 16; Keyworth, 5 for 9; Perrin, 3 for 8.
PASSING
Dallas—Staubach, 17 of 25 for 183, 1 TD; Newhouse, 1 of 1 for 29, 1 TD; D. White, 1 of 2 for 5.
Denver—Morton, 4 of 15 for 39, 4 int.; Weese, 4 of 10 for 22.
RECEIVING
Dallas—P. Pearson, 5 for 37; DuPree, 4 for 66; Newhouse, 3 for -1; Johnson, 2 for 53, 1 TD; Richards, 2 for 38, 1 TD; Dorsett, 2 for 11; D. Pearson, 1 for 13.
Denver—Dolbin, 2 for 24; Odoms, 2 for 9; Moses, 1 for 21; Upchurch, 1 for 9; Jensen, 1 for 5; Perrin, 1 for -7.
PUNTING
Dallas—D. White, 5 for 208, 41.6 average.
Denver—Dilts, 4 for 153, 38.3 average.
PUNT RETURNS
Dallas—Hill, 1 for 0, 1 fair catch.
Denver—Upchurch, 3 for 22; Schultz, 1 for 0.
KICKOFF RETURNS
Dallas—Johnson, 2 for 29; Brinson, 1 for 22.
Denver—Upchurch, 3 for 94; Schultz, 2 for 62; Jensen, 1 for 17.
INTERCEPTIONS
Dallas—Washington, 1 for 27; Kyle, 1 for 19; Barnes, 1 for 0; Hughes, 1 for 0.
Denver—None.

DALLAS COWBOYS

No.	Name	Pos.	Ht.	Wt.	Year
31	Barnes, Benny	CB	6-1	195	6
53	Breunig, Bob	LB	6-2	227	3
36	Brinson, Larry	RB	6-0	214	R
59	Brown, Guy	LB	6-4	215	R
18	Carano, Glenn	QB	6-3	195	R
63	Cole, Larry	DT	6-5	260	10
61	Cooper, Jim	T-G	6-5	252	R
21	Dennison, Doug	RB	6-0	204	4
67	Donovan, Pat	T	6-4	255	3
33	Dorsett, Tony	RB	5-11	192	R
89	DuPree, Billy Joe	TE	6-4	226	5
62	Fitzgerald, John	C	6-5	260	7
71	Frederick, Andy	T	6-6	241	R
77	Gregory, Bill	DT	6-5	260	7
43	Harris, Cliff	S	6-1	192	8
58	Hegman, Mike	LB	6-1	225	2
56	Henderson, Thomas	LB	6-2	220	3
1	Herrera, Efren	K	5-9	190	3
80	Hill, Tony	WR	6-2	196	R
42	Hughes, Randy	S	6-4	208	3
57	Huther, Bruce	LB	6-1	217	R
86	Johnson, Butch	WR	6-1	191	2
72	Jones, Ed	DE	6-9	265	4
25	Kyle, Aaron	CB	5-10	185	2
35	Laidlaw, Scott	RB	6-0	205	3
66	Lawless, Burton	G	6-4	250	3
50	Lewis, D. D.	LB	6-1	215	9
79	Martin, Harvey	DE	6-5	252	5
73	Neely, Ralph	T	6-6	255	13
44	Newhouse, Robert	RB	5-10	205	6
88	Pearson, Drew	WR	6-0	183	5
26	Pearson, Preston	RB	6-1	206	11
75	Pugh, Jethro	DT	6-6	250	13
64	Rafferty, Tom	G-C	6-3	250	2
20	Renfro, Mel	CB	6-0	192	14
83	Richards, Golden	WR	6-0	180	5
87	Saldi, Jay	TE	6-3	224	2
68	Scott, Herbert	G	6-2	250	3
65	Stalls, David	DT	6-4	236	R
12	Staubach, Roger	QB	6-3	202	9
46	Washington, Mark	CB	5-11	187	8
41	Waters, Charlie	S	6-2	198	8
11	White, Danny	QB-P	6-2	192	3
54	White, Randy	DT	6-4	245	3
70	Wright, Rayfield	T	6-6	260	11

DENVER BRONCOS

No.	Name	Pos.	Ht.	Wt.	Year
77	Alzado, Lyle	DE	6-3	250	7
73	Allison, Henry	T	6-3	263	5
24	Armstrong, Otis	RB	5-10	197	5
68	Carter, Rubin	NT	6-0	254	3
79	Chavous, Barney	DE	6-3	250	5
10	Dilts, Bucky	P	5-9	190	R
82	Dolbin, Jack	WR	5-10	183	3
85	Egloff, Ron	TE	6-5	227	R
56	Evans, Larry	LB	6-2	218	2
43	Foley, Steve	CB	6-2	190	2
62	Glassic, Tom	G	6-4	248	2
53	Gradishar, Randy	LB	6-3	231	4
63	Grant, John	NT	6-3	246	5
60	Howard, Paul	G	6-3	260	4
65	Hyde, Glenn	T	6-3	255	4
29	Jackson, Bernard	S	6-0	181	6
57	Jackson, Tom	LB	5-11	224	5
30	Jensen, Jim	RB	6-3	240	2
32	Keyworth, Jon	RB	6-3	234	4
41	Lytle, Rob	RB	6-1	198	R
66	Manor, Brison	DE	6-4	247	1
50	Maples, Bobby	C	6-3	250	13
74	Maurer, Andy	T	6-3	265	8
71	Minor, Claudie	T	6-4	280	4
52	Montler, Mike	C	6-4	250	9
7	Morton, Craig	QB	6-4	213	13
25	Moses, Haven	WR	6-2	200	10
58	Nairne, Rob	LB	6-4	220	R
88	Odoms, Riley	TE	6-4	232	6
12	Penrose, Craig	QB	6-3	205	2
35	Perrin, Lonnie	RB	6-1	224	2
21	Poltl, Randy	S	6-3	188	4
40	Rich, Randy	S	5-10	181	R
26	Riley, Larry	CB	5-10	189	R
59	Rizzo, Joe	LB	6-1	223	4
67	Schindler, Steve	G	6-3	252	R
86	Schultz, John	WR-KR	5-10	183	2
70	Smith, Paul	NT	6-3	250	10
51	Swenson, Bob	LB	6-3	225	3
36	Thompson, Billy	S	6-1	200	9
55	Turk, Godwin	LB	6-2	230	4
15	Turner, Jim	K	6-2	212	14
80	Upchurch, Rick	WR-KR	5-10	180	3
14	Weese, Norris	QB	6-1	193	2
20	Wright, Louis	CB	6-2	195	3

SUPER BOWL XIII

PITTSBURGH 35, DALLAS 31

In the first Super Bowl rematch, Pittsburgh quarterback Terry Bradshaw threw four touchdown passes to lead the Steelers to a 35-31 victory over the Dallas Cowboys. The Steelers became the first team to win three Super Bowls.

In the highest-scoring Super Bowl of all, Bradshaw threw for a personal-high 318 yards. He broke Bart Starr's passing yardage record by halftime, throwing for 253 yards and three touchdowns on his 11 first-half completions. He was voted the game's most valuable player.

Pittsburgh opened the scoring on its first possession. Bradshaw capped a 53-yard drive with a 28-yard pass to John Stallworth.

The Cowboys scored on the last play of the first quarter to tie the score at 7-7. Roger Staubach found Tony Hill alone on the 26, and Hill ran in for the touchdown to complete a 39-yard play.

Dallas took its only lead of the game when linebacker Mike Hegmen wrestled the ball away from Bradshaw early in the second quarter and ran 37 yards for a touchdown. Three plays later the score was tied again. Bradshaw threw a 75-yard touchdown pass to Stallworth, who caught it on the Dallas 35 and eluded Aaron Kyle en route to the end zone.

Pittsburgh's final score of the first half came with only 26 seconds left. With the Cowboys deep in Steelers territory, Mel Blount intercepted Staubach and returned it to the Pittsburgh 29. A personal foul penalty against Dallas took the ball to the 44. Bradshaw passed to wide receiver Lynn Swann for 29 yards, to Swann again for 21, and then to Rocky Bleier for 7 yards and a touchdown.

Dallas cut the Pittsburgh margin to only four points midway through the third quarter, but Rafael Septien's 27-yard field goal represented a moral victory for the Steelers. A short punt and a 12-yard return by Butch Johnson had set the Cowboys up on the Pittsburgh 42. With a third and three at the 10, Staubach passed to tight end Jackie Smith, who was alone in the end zone—and dropped the pass. Dallas settled for the field goal and the Steelers seemed in control thereafter.

Another major play occurred in the fourth quarter. Dallas cornerback Benny Barnes was called for pass interference on Swann, setting up the Steelers on the Dallas 23 after the 33-yard penalty. Three plays later, Franco Harris scored on a 22-yard run. The Steelers scored again following a fumble recovery on the ensuing kickoff. Bradshaw threw an 18-yard touchdown pass to Swann for the second Pittsburgh touchdown within 19 seconds.

Staubach got the Cowboys on the move late in the game. With only 2:23 left, he threw a seven-yard touchdown to Billy Joe DuPree, capping an eight-play, 89-yard drive. Dennis Thurman recovered Septien's onside kick at the Dallas 48, and Staubach led the Cowboys to another score. Passing on every down, Staubach completed a nine-play, 52-yard drive with a four-yard touchdown to Johnson with only 22 seconds left. A second onside kickoff attempt was recovered by Bleier to seal the victory.

"We were coming back until the Smith play," said Dallas coach Tom Landry. "That play really swung the momentum. You can tell how much it hurt us by looking at the difference in the score. Then at the end of the game there was just too much to make up in too little time—our offense couldn't quite do it."

The Dallas offense had nothing to be ashamed of—it netted 330 yards, only 27 less than the Steelers. The defenses each came up with big plays; there were six turnovers and nine sacks in the game.

Date—January 21, 1979
Site—Orange Bowl, Miami
Time—4:15 P.M. EST
Conditions—71 degrees, cloudy
Playing surface—Grass
Television—National Broadcasting Company (NBC)
Radio—Columbia Broadcasting System (CBS)
Regular Season Records—Pittsburgh, 14-2; Dallas, 12-4
Conference Championships—Pittsburgh defeated the Houston Oilers 34-5 for the AFC title; Dallas defeated the Los Angeles Rams 28-0 for the NFC title
Players' Shares—$18,000 to each member of the winning team; $9,000 to each member of the losing team
Attendance—79,484
Gross Receipts—$8,833,185.26
Officials—Referee, Pat Haggerty; umpire, Art Demmas; line judge, Jack Fette; head linesman, Jerry Bergman; back judge, Pat Knight; side judge, Dean Look; field judge, Fred Swearingen
Coaches—Chuck Noll, Pittsburgh; Tom Landry, Dallas

Pittsburgh	Starters, Offense	Dallas
John Stallworth	WR	Tony Hill
Jon Kolb	LT	Pat Donovan
Sam Davis	LG	Herbert Scott
Mike Webster	C	John Fitzgerald
Gerry Mullins	RG	Tom Rafferty
Ray Pinney	RT	Rayfield Wright
Randy Grossman	TE	Billy Joe DuPree
Lynn Swann	WR	Drew Pearson
Terry Bradshaw	QB	Roger Staubach
Rocky Bleier	RB	Robert Newhouse
Franco Harris	RB	Tony Dorsett
	Starters, Defense	
L. C. Greenwood	LE	Ed Jones
Joe Greene	LT	Larry Cole
Steve Furness	RT	Randy White
John Banaszak	RE	Harvey Martin
Jack Ham	LLB	Thomas Henderson
Jack Lambert	MLB	Bob Breunig
Loren Toews	RLB	D. D. Lewis
Ron Johnson	LCB	Benny Barnes
Mel Blount	RCB	Aaron Kyle
Donnie Shell	SS	Charlie Waters
Mike Wagner	FS	Cliff Harris

Pittsburgh	7	14	0	14	—	35
Dallas	7	7	3	14	—	31

Pitt —Stallworth 28 pass from Bradshaw (Gerela kick)
Dall—Hill 39 pass from Staubach (Septien kick)
Dall—Hegman 37 fumble return (Septien kick)
Pitt —Stallworth 75 pass from Bradshaw (Gerela kick)
Pitt —Bleier 7 pass from Bradshaw (Gerela kick)
Dall—FG Septien 27
Pitt —Harris 22 run (Gerela kick)
Pitt —Swann 18 pass from Bradshaw (Gerela kick)
Dall—DuPree 7 pass from Staubach (Septien kick)
Dall—B. Johnson 4 pass from Staubach (Septien kick)

TEAM STATISTICS	Pitt	Dall
First downs	19	21
Rushing	2	6
Passing	15	13
By penalty	2	2
Total yardage	357	330
Net rushing yardage	66	154
Net passing yardage	291	176
Passes att.-comp.-had int.	30-17-1	30-17-1

RUSHING
Pittsburgh—Harris, 20 for 68, 1 TD; Bleier, 2 for 3; Bradshaw, 2 for -5.
Dallas—Dorsett, 16 for 96; Staubach, 4 for 37; Laidlaw, 3 for 12; P. Pearson, 1 for 6; Newhouse, 8 for 3.

PASSING
Pittsburgh—Bradshaw, 17 of 30 for 318, 4 TDs, 1 int.
Dallas—Staubach, 17 of 30 for 228, 3 TDs, 1 int.

RECEIVING
Pittsburgh—Swann, 7 for 124, 1 TD; Stallworth, 3 for 115, 2 TDs; Grossman, 3 for 29; Bell, 2 for 21; Harris, 1 for 22; Bleier, 1 for 7, 1 TD.
Dallas—Dorsett, 5 for 44; D. Pearson, 4 for 73; Hill, 2 for 49, 1 TD; Johnson, 2 for 30, 1 TD; DuPree, 2 for 17, 1 TD; P. Pearson, 2 for 15.

PUNTING
Pittsburgh—Colquitt, 3 for 129, 43.0 average.
Dallas—D. White, 5 for 198, 39.6 average.

PUNT RETURNS
Pittsburgh—Bell, 4 for 27.
Dallas—Johnson, 2 for 33, 1 fair catch.

KICKOFF RETURNS
Pittsburgh—L. Anderson, 3 for 45.
Dallas—Johnson, 3 for 63; Brinson, 2 for 41; R. White, 1 for 0.

INTERCEPTIONS
Pittsburgh—Blount, 1 for 13.
Dallas—Lewis, 1 for 21.

PITTSBURGH STEELERS

No.	Name	Pos.	Ht.	Wt.	Year
69	Anderson, Fred	DE-DT	6-5	235	R
30	Anderson, Larry	CB-KR	5-11	177	R
76	Banaszak, John	DT-DE	6-3	244	4
65	Beasley, Tom	DT	6-5	253	1
83	Bell, Theo	WR-KR	6-0	180	2
20	Bleier, Rocky	RB	5-11	210	10
47	Blount, Mel	CB	6-3	205	9
12	Bradshaw, Terry	QB	6-3	215	9
79	Brown, Larry	T	6-4	245	8
56	Cole, Robin	LB	6-2	220	2
5	Colquitt, Craig	P	6-2	182	R
77	Courson, Steve	G	6-1	260	1
89	Cunningham, Bennie	TE	6-5	247	3
57	Davis, Sam	G	6-1	255	12
35	Deloplaine, Jack	RB-KR	5-10	205	3
21	Dungy, Tony	S	6-0	190	2
67	Dunn, Gary	DT	6-3	247	2
64	Furness, Steve	DT-DE	6-4	255	7
10	Gerela, Roy	K	5-10	185	10
75	Greene, Joe	DT	6-4	260	10
68	Greenwood, L.C.	DE	6-7	250	10
84	Grossman, Randy	TE	6-1	215	5
59	Ham, Jack	LB	6-1	225	8
32	Harris, Franco	RB	6-2	225	7
29	Johnson, Ron	CB	5-10	200	R
55	Kolb, Jon	T	6-2	262	10
15	Kruczek, Mike	QB	6-1	205	3
58	Lambert, Jack	LB	6-4	220	5
87	Mandich, Jim	TE	6-2	214	8
39	Moser, Rick	RB-KR	6-0	218	R
72	Mullins, Gerry	G	6-3	244	8
25	Oldham, Ray	S	5-11	192	6
66	Petersen, Ted	C-T	6-5	244	2
74	Pinney, Ray	T-C	6-4	240	3
31	Shell, Donnie	S	5-11	190	5
86	Smith, Jim	WR-KR	6-2	205	2
82	Stallworth, John	WR	6-2	183	5
18	Stoudt, Cliff	QB	6-4	210	2
88	Swann, Lynn	WR	6-0	180	5
38	Thornton, Sidney	RB	5-11	230	2
51	Toews, Loren	LB	6-3	222	6
23	Wagner, Mike	S	6-2	200	8
52	Webster, Mike	C	6-2	250	5
78	White, Dwight	DE	6-4	255	8
53	Winston, Dennis	LB	6-0	228	2

DALLAS COWBOYS

No.	Name	Pos.	Ht.	Wt.	Year
31	Barnes, Benny	CB	6-1	195	7
76	Bethea, Larry	DT	6-5	254	R
24	Blackwell, Alois	RB	5-10	195	R
53	Breunig, Bob	LB	6-2	225	4
36	Brinson, Larry	RB	6-0	214	2
59	Brown, Guy	LB	6-4	228	2
18	Carano, Glenn	QB	6-3	202	2
63	Cole, Larry	DT	6-5	252	11
61	Cooper, Jim	C-G-T	6-5	260	2
67	Donovan, Pat	T	6-4	250	4
33	Dorsett, Tony	RB	5-11	190	2
89	DuPree, Billy Joe	TE	6-4	229	6
62	Fitzgerald, John	C	6-5	260	8
71	Frederick, Andy	T	6-6	255	2
43	Harris, Cliff	S	6-1	192	9
58	Hegman, Mike	LB	6-1	225	3
56	Henderson, Thomas	LB	6-2	220	4
80	Hill, Tony	WR	6-2	198	2
42	Hughes, Randy	S	6-4	207	4
57	Huther, Bruce	LB	6-1	220	2
86	Johnson, Butch	WR	6-1	192	3
72	Jones, Ed	DE	6-9	270	5
25	Kyle, Aaron	CB	5-10	185	3
35	Laidlaw, Scott	RB	6-0	205	4
66	Lawless, Burton	G	6-4	255	4
50	Lewis, D. D.	LB	6-1	215	10
79	Martin, Harvey	DE	6-5	250	6
44	Newhouse, Robert	RB	5-10	215	7
88	Pearson, Drew	WR	6-0	183	6
26	Pearson, Preston	RB	6-1	206	12
75	Pugh, Jethro	DT	6-6	255	14
64	Rafferty, Tom	G	6-3	250	3
60	Randall, Tom	G	6-5	245	R
68	Scott, Herbert	G	6-2	252	4
1	Septien, Rafael	K	5-9	171	2
81	Smith, Jackie	TE	6-4	230	16
65	Stalls, Dave	DT-DE	6-4	245	2
12	Staubach, Roger	QB	6-3	202	10
82	Steele, Robert	WR	6-4	196	R
32	Thurman, Dennis	CB	5-11	170	R
46	Washington, Mark	CB	5-11	187	9
41	Waters, Charlie	S	6-2	200	9
11	White, Danny	QB-P	6-2	192	3
54	White, Randy	DT	6-4	250	4
70	Wright, Rayfield	T	6-6	260	12

SUPER BOWL XIV

PITTSBURGH 31, LA RAMS 19

Quarterback Terry Bradshaw threw a 73-yard touchdown pass to John Stallworth to bring the Pittsburgh Steelers from behind early in the fourth quarter, and then hit Stallworth again, with a 45-yard pass, to set up an insurance touchdown, as the Steelers won their fourth Super Bowl in as many appearances, a 31-19 victory over the Los Angeles Rams.

The first of the two long passes came with 2:56 gone in the fourth quarter and the Steelers trailing 19-17. On third and eight at the Pittsburgh 27, Bradshaw called a "60 Prevent Slot Hook and Go." Stallworth got behind Rams defensive backs Rod Perry and Dave Elmendorf, took the pass in stride at the Rams' 32-yard line, and ran in for the score.

Two series later, Stallworth ran the same pattern and Bradshaw found him for a first down at the Rams' 22. Franco Harris scored four plays later after a pass interference penalty on Pat Thomas gave the Steelers the ball on the 1-yard line.

In a game that ranks as one of the most exciting Super Bowls, the Rams' defense stopped the Steelers' running game, but was exploited by the poised Bradshaw. He overcame three interceptions to complete 14 of 21 passes for 309 yards and two touchdowns, and be voted the most valuable player.

The Steelers scored first, driving 55 yards the first time they had the ball to set up a 41-yard field goal by rookie Matt Bahr. Harris and Rocky Bleier ran the ball on 8 of the 10 plays in the drive.

A short kickoff gave the ball to the Rams at their 41. From there, they went 59 yards in eight plays to take the lead 7-3. After a short Vince Ferragamo to Wendell Tyler pass, the Rams ran on seven straight plays, culminating in a one-yard run by Cullen Bryant for the score.

A 45-yard kickoff return by Larry Anderson set Pittsburgh up on its own 47. Nine plays later Harris scored his first touchdown of the day on a one-yard run. Bradshaw passed twice on first down during the drive, picking up 12 yards to wide receiver Lynn Swann and 13 to tight end Bennie Cunningham.

Again, the Rams came back to score immediately. They drove 67 yards to the Pittsburgh 14, before settling for a 31-yard Frank Corral field goal that tied the game 10-10.

Two series later, Elmendorf intercepted Bradshaw and returned the ball to the Pittsburgh 39. Eight plays netted only 12 yards, and with 14 seconds left in the half Corral kicked a 45-yard field goal to send the Rams to the locker room with a 13-10 lead.

The statistics were close at halftime. The Rams led in total yards 130 to 127, each team had nine first downs, and the only turnover was Elmendorf's interception.

The Steelers wasted little time in the second half getting back on top. A 37-yard kickoff return by Anderson put them on their own 39, and, five plays later, Bradshaw threw a 47-yard touchdown pass to Swann.

But the Rams again matched the Steelers' score, this time in only four plays. A 50-yard pass from Ferragamo to Billy Waddy put the Rams on the 24. On the next play Ferragamo handed off to Lawrence McCutcheon, who swept right, stopped, and threw a 24-yard touchdown pass to Ron Smith, who had eluded defensive back Ron Johnson downfield.

The Rams still led 19-17 after Corral missed the extra point, but Bradshaw's two long passes put the Steelers ahead. Linebacker Jack Lambert intercepted Ferragamo at the Pittsburgh 14 to end one Rams' threat, and the Steelers held on downs to stop the last Los Angeles drive late in the game.

Date—January 20, 1980
Site—Rose Bowl, Pasadena
Time—3:15 P.M. PST
Conditions—67 degrees, sunny
Playing surface—Grass
Television and Radio—Columbia Broadcasting System (CBS)
Regular Season Records—Pittsburgh, 12-4; Los Angeles 9-7
Conference Championships—Pittsburgh defeated the Houston Oilers 27-13 for the AFC title; Los Angeles defeated the Tampa Bay Buccaneers 9-0 for the NFC title
Players' Shares—$18,000 to each member of the winning team; $9,000 to each member of the losing team
Attendance—103,985
Gross Receipts—$9,489,274.00
Officials—Referee, Fred Silva; umpire, Al Conway; line judge, Bob Beeks; head linesman, Burl Toler; back judge, Stan Javie; side judge, Ben Tompkins; field judge, Charley Musser
Coaches—Ray Malavasi, LA Rams; Chuck Noll, Pittsburgh

LA Rams	Starters, Offense	Pittsburgh
Billy Waddy	WR	John Stallworth
Doug France	LT	Jon Kolb
Kent Hill	LG	Sam Davis
Rich Saul	C	Mike Webster
Dennis Harrah	RG	Gerry Mullins
Jackie Slater	RT	Larry Brown
Terry Nelson	TE	Bennie Cunningham
Preston Dennard	WR	Lynn Swann
Vince Ferragamo	QB	Terry Bradshaw
Cullen Bryant	RB	Rocky Bleier
Wendell Tyler	RB	Franco Harris
	Starters, Defense	
Jack Youngblood	LE	L. C. Greenwood
Mike Fanning	LT	Joe Greene
Larry Brooks	RT	Gary Dunn
Fred Dryer	RE	John Banaszak
Jim Youngblood	LLB	Dennis Winston
Jack Reynolds	MLB	Jack Lambert
Bob Brudzinski	RLB	Robin Cole
Pat Thomas	LCB	Ron Johnson
Rod Perry	RCB	Mel Blount
Dave Elmendorf	SS	Donnie Shell
Nolan Cromwell	FS	J. T. Thomas

LA Rams	7	6	6	0	—	19
Pittsburgh	3	7	7	14	—	31

Pitt —FG Bahr 41
Rams—Bryant 1 run (Corral kick)
Pitt —Harris 1 run (Bahr kick)
Rams—FG Corral 31
Rams—FG Corral 45
Pitt —Swann 47 pass from Bradshaw (Bahr kick)
Rams—R. Smith 24 pass from McCutcheon (kick failed)
Pitt —Stallworth 73 pass from Bradshaw (Bahr kick)
Pitt —Harris 1 run (Bahr kick)

TEAM STATISTICS	Rams	Pitt
First downs	16	19
Rushing	6	8
Passing	9	10
By penalty	1	1
Total yardage	301	393
Net rushing yardage	107	84
Net passing yardage	194	309
Passes att.-comp.-had int.	26-16-1	21-14-3

RUSHING
LA Rams—Tyler, 17 for 60; Bryant, 6 for 30, 1 TD; McCutcheon, 5 for 10; Ferragamo, 1 for 7.
Pittsburgh—Harris, 20 for 46, 2 TDs; Bleier, 10 for 25; Bradshaw, 3 for 9; Thornton, 4 for 4.

PASSING
LA Rams—Ferragamo, 15 of 25 for 212, 1 int.; McCutcheon, 1 of 1 for 24, 1 TD.
Pittsburgh—Bradshaw, 14 of 21 for 309, 2 TDs, 3 int.

RECEIVING
LA Rams—Waddy, 3 for 75; Bryant, 3 for 21; Tyler, 3 for 20; Dennard, 2 for 32; Nelson, 2 for 20; D. Hill, 1 for 28; Smith, 1 for 24, 1 TD; McCutcheon, 1 for 16.
Pittsburgh—Swann, 5 for 79, 1 TD; Stallworth, 3 for 121, 1 TD; Harris, 3 for 66; Cunningham, 2 for 21; Thornton, 1 for 22.

PUNTING
LA Rams—Clark, 5 for 220, 44.0 average.
Pittsburgh—Colquitt, 2 for 85, 42.5 average.

PUNT RETURNS
LA Rams—Brown, 1 for 4.
Pittsburgh—Bell, 2 for 17; Smith, 2 for 14.

KICKOFF RETURNS
LA Rams—E. Hill, 3 for 47; Jodat, 2 for 32; Andrews, 1 for 0.
Pittsburgh—L. Anderson, 5 for 162.

INTERCEPTIONS
LA Rams—Elmendorf, 1 for 10; Brown, 1 for 6; Perry, 1 for -1; Thomas, 0 for 6.
Pittsburgh—Lambert, 1 for 16.

LOS ANGELES RAMS

No.	Name	Pos.	Ht.	Wt.	Year
52	Andrews, George	LB	6-3	226	R
62	Bain, Bill	G	6-4	270	5
90	Brooks, Larry	DT	6-3	254	8
25	Brown, Eddie	S-KR	5-11	190	5
59	Brudzinski, Bob	LB	6-4	231	3
32	Bryant, Cullen	RB	6-1	234	7
13	Clark, Ken	P	6-2	197	1
3	Corral, Frank	K	6-2	220	2
21	Cromwell, Nolan	S	6-1	197	3
88	Dennard, Preston	WR	6-1	185	2
71	Doss, Reggie	DE	6-4	267	2
89	Dryer, Fred	DE	6-6	230	11
28	Ellis, Ken	CB	5-11	180	10
42	Elmendorf, Dave	S	6-1	196	9
79	Fanning, Mike	DT	6-6	248	5
15	Ferragamo, Vince	QB	6-3	207	3
77	France, Doug	T	6-5	268	5
73	Gravelle, Gordon	T	6-5	252	8
60	Harrah, Dennis	G	6-5	251	5
51	Harris, Joe	LB	6-1	225	3
87	Hill, Drew	WR-KR	5-9	170	R
24	Hill, Eddie	RB-KR	6-2	197	R
72	Hill, Kent	G	6-5	260	R
43	Jodat, Jim	RB	5-11	207	3
19	Lee, Bob	QB	6-2	195	11
30	McCutcheon, Lawrence	RB	6-1	205	7
83	Nelson, Terry	TE	6-2	241	6
33	O'Steen, Dwayne	CB	6-1	190	2
49	Perry, Rod	CB	5-9	177	5
64	Reynolds, Jack	LB	6-1	231	10
8	Rutledge, Jeff	QB	6-2	200	R
54	Ryczek, Dan	C-G	6-3	245	7
61	Saul, Rich	C	6-3	243	10
78	Slater, Jackie	T	6-4	269	4
84	Smith, Ron	WR	6-0	185	2
37	Sully, Ivory	S-CB	6-0	193	R
27	Thomas, Pat	CB	5-9	184	4
26	Tyler, Wendell	RB	5-10	188	2
80	Waddy, Billy	WR	5-11	180	3
20	Wallace, Jackie	S	6-3	196	6
57	Westbrooks, Greg	LB	6-3	215	5
70	Wilkinson, Jerry	DE	6-9	255	R
86	Young, Charle	TE	6-4	234	7
85	Youngblood, Jack	DE	6-4	243	9
53	Youngblood, Jim	LB	6-3	231	7

PITTSBURGH STEELERS

No.	Name	Pos.	Ht.	Wt.	Year
33	Anderson, Anthony	RB	6-0	197	R
30	Anderson, Larry	CB-KR	5-11	177	2
9	Bahr, Matt	K	5-10	165	R
76	Banaszak, John	DE-DT	6-3	244	5
65	Beasley, Tom	DT	6-5	253	2
83	Bell, Theo	WR-KR	6-0	180	3
20	Bleier, Rocky	RB	5-11	210	11
47	Blount, Mel	CB	6-3	205	10
12	Bradshaw, Terry	QB	6-2	215	10
79	Brown, Larry	T	6-4	255	9
56	Cole, Robin	LB	6-2	220	3
5	Colquitt, Craig	P	6-2	182	2
77	Courson, Steve	G	6-1	260	2
89	Cunningham, Bennie	TE	6-5	247	4
57	Davis, Sam	G	6-1	255	13
63	Dornbrook, Thom	C-G	6-2	240	1
67	Dunn, Gary	DT	6-3	247	3
64	Furness, Steve	DT-DE	6-4	255	8
50	Graves, Tom	LB	6-3	228	R
75	Greene, Joe	DT	6-4	260	11
68	Greenwood, L. C.	DE	6-7	250	11
84	Grossman, Randy	TE	6-1	215	6
59	Ham, Jack	LB	6-1	225	9
32	Harris, Franco	RB	6-2	225	8
27	Hawthorne, Greg	RB	6-3	225	R
29	Johnson, Ron	CB	5-10	200	2
55	Kolb, Jon	T	6-2	262	11
15	Kruczek, Mike	QB	6-1	205	4
58	Lambert, Jack	LB	6-4	220	6
39	Moser, Rick	RB	6-0	210	2
72	Mullins, Gerry	G	6-3	244	9
66	Petersen, Ted	T-C	6-5	244	3
31	Shell, Donnie	S	5-11	190	6
86	Smith, Jim	WR-KR	6-2	205	3
82	Stallworth, John	WR	6-2	183	6
18	Stoudt, Cliff	QB	6-4	218	3
88	Swann, Lynn	WR	6-0	180	6
24	Thomas, J. T.	S	6-2	196	6
38	Thornton, Sidney	RB	5-11	230	3
51	Toews, Loren	LB	6-3	222	7
54	Valentine, Zack	LB	6-2	220	R
52	Webster, Mike	C	6-2	250	6
78	White, Dwight	DE	6-4	255	9
53	Winston, Dennis	LB	6-0	228	3
49	Woodruff, Dwayne	CB	5-11	189	R

SUPER BOWL XV

OAKLAND 27, PHILADELPHIA 10

The Oakland Raiders' defense, led by linebacker Rod Martin's game-record three interceptions, set up 10 points and controlled the tempo of the game as the Raiders defeated the Philadelphia Eagles 27-10. The win was the second in three Super Bowl appearances for the Raiders and marked the first time that a wild card team had won a Super Bowl.

Oakland took control of the game early. On the third play of the game, Martin intercepted Ron Jaworski's pass on the Philadelphia 47-yard line and returned it to the 30. Seven plays later, Raiders quarterback Jim Plunkett threw the first of his three touchdown passes of the day, a two-yarder to Cliff Branch.

The Eagles could gain only two first downs on the next two series, but after their second punt, the Raiders were pinned back on their own 14-yard line. With a third and four from the 20-yard line, Plunkett passed to running back Kenny King, who gathered the ball in at the Oakland 39 and raced down the left sideline 61 yards, completing an 80-yard touchdown, then the longest play in Super Bowl history.

The Eagles sustained a drive to score as the second quarter opened. Jaworski hit John Spagnola for 22 yards on the left side, and then came back to halfback Wilbert Montgomery for 25 yards over the middle to move the Eagles inside the Oakland 20. The Raiders held, and Philadelphia settled for a 30-yard field goal by Tony Franklin.

Neither team could score for the rest of the half. Raiders kicker Chris Bahr missed a 45-yard field goal attempt with less than four minutes in the half. Then, after the Eagles drove 62 yards to the Oakland 11-yard line with less than a minute left in the half, Franklin's short field goal attempt was blocked by linebacker Ted Hendricks and recovered by rookie linebacker Matt Millen.

After 30 minutes of play, each team had netted 164 yards, but the Raiders had dominated play and the scoreboard. Jaworski had completed only 9 of 22 passes and had the one big interception.

Behind Plunkett's passing, the Raiders applied the knockout punch to the Eagles early in the third quarter. Plunkett passed to King for 13 yards and a first down, to Bob Chandler for 32 yards and another first down, and to Branch for 29 yards and a touchdown. The scoring drive covered 76 yards in only five plays and took only 2:36 off the clock.

When the Eagles tried to get back into the game on Jaworski's arm, Martin intercepted his second pass of the game, setting up a 46-yard field goal by Bahr, which increased the Oakland lead to 24-3.

Jaworski led the Eagles to their only touchdown of the day to start the fourth quarter. He capped a 12-play, 88-yard drive with an eight-yard pass to tight end Keith Krepfle for the touchdown.

Any comeback hopes the Eagles had died when Oakland took the ensuing kickoff and marched 72 yards to Bahr's 35-yard field goal.

The last two Philadelphia thrusts each reached Oakland territory, but Willie Jones recovered Jaworski's fumble on the Oakland 42, and Martin intercepted his third pass of the day at the Raiders' 37. Oakland ran out the clock deep in the Eagles' territory.

"All Jim [Plunkett] needed was for someone to believe in him," said Raiders coach Tom Flores of his quarterback who was voted the most valuable player in the game, after completing 13 of 21 for 261 yards and three touchdowns. "Out there today he could accomplish almost anything he wanted. He was the key for us the whole way."

Date—January 25, 1981
Site—Louisiana Superdome, New Orleans
Time—5:15 P.M. CST
Conditions—72 degrees, indoors
Playing surface—AstroTurf
Television—National Broadcasting Company (NBC)
Radio—Columbia Broadcasting System (CBS)
Regular Season Records—Oakland, 11-5; Philadelphia, 12-4
Conference Championships—Oakland defeated the San Diego Chargers 34-27 for the AFC title; Philadelphia defeated the Dallas Cowboys 20-7 for the NFC title
Players' Shares—$18,000 to each member of the winning team; $9,000 to each member of the losing team
Attendance—76,135
Gross Receipts—$10,328,664.57
Officials—Referee, Ben Dreith; umpire, Frank Sinkovitz; line judge, Tom Dooley; head linesman, Tony Veteri; back judge, Tom Kelleher; side judge, Dean Look; field judge, Fritz Graf
Coaches—Tom Flores, Oakland; Dick Vermeil, Philadelphia

Oakland	Starters, Offense	Philadelphia
Cliff Branch	WR	Harold Carmichael
Art Shell	LT	Stan Walters
Gene Upshaw	LG	Petey Perot
Dave Dalby	C	Guy Morriss
Mickey Marvin	RG	Woody Peoples
Henry Lawrence	RT	Jerry Sisemore
Raymond Chester	TE	Keith Krepfle
Bob Chandler	WR-TE	John Spagnola
Jim Plunkett	QB	Ron Jaworski
Mark van Eeghen	RB	Leroy Harris
Kenny King	RB	Wilbert Montgomery
	Starters, Defense	
John Matuszak	LE	Dennis Harrison
Reggie Kinlaw	NT	Charlie Johnson
Dave Browning	RE	Carl Hairston
Ted Hendricks	LOLB	John Bunting
Matt Millen	LILB	Bill Bergey
Bob Nelson	RILB	Frank LeMaster
Rod Martin	ROLB	Jerry Robinson
Lester Hayes	LCB	Roynell Young
Dwayne O'Steen	RCB	Herman Edwards
Mike Davis	SS	Randy Logan
Burgess Owens	FS	Brenard Wilson

Oakland	14	0	10	3	—	27
Philadelphia	0	3	0	7	—	10

Oak—Branch 2 pass from Plunkett (Bahr kick)
Oak—King 80 pass from Plunkett (Bahr kick)
Phil—FG Franklin 30
Oak—Branch 29 pass from Plunkett (Bahr kick)
Oak—FG Bahr 46
Phil—Krepfle 8 pass from Jaworski (Franklin kick)
Oak—FG Bahr 35

TEAM STATISTICS	Oak	Phil
First downs	17	19
Rushing	6	3
Passing	10	14
By penalty	1	2
Total yardage	377	360
Net rushing yardage	117	69
Net passing yardage	260	291
Passes att.-comp.-had int.	21-13-0	38-18-3

RUSHING
Oakland—van Eeghen, 19 for 80; King, 6 for 18; Jensen, 3 for 12; Plunkett, 3 for 9; Whittington, 3 for −2.
Philadelphia—Montgomery, 16 for 44; Harris, 7 for 14; Giammona, 1 for 7; Harrington, 1 for 4; Jaworski, 1 for 0.

PASSING
Oakland—Plunkett, 13 of 21 for 261, 3 TDs.
Philadelphia—Jaworski, 18 of 38 for 291, 1 TD, 3 int.

RECEIVING
Oakland—Branch, 5 for 67, 2 TDs; Chandler, 4 for 77; King, 2 for 93, 1 TD; Chester, 2 for 24.
Philadelphia—Montgomery, 6 for 91; Carmichael, 5 for 83; Smith, 2 for 59; Krepfle, 2 for 16, 1 TD; Spagnola, 1 for 22; Parker, 1 for 19; Harris, 1 for 1.

PUNTING
Oakland—Guy, 3 for 126, 42.0 average.
Philadelphia—Runager, 3 for 110, 36.7 average.

PUNT RETURNS
Oakland—Matthews, 2 for 1, 1 fair catch.
Philadelphia—Sciarra, 2 for 18; Henry, 1 for 2.

KICKOFF RETURNS
Oakland—Matthews, 2 for 29; Moody, 1 for 19.
Philadelphia—Campfield, 5 for 87; Harrington, 1 for 0.

INTERCEPTIONS
Oakland—Martin, 3 for 44.
Philadelphia—None.

OAKLAND RAIDERS

No.	Name	Pos.	Ht.	Wt.	Year
10	Bahr, Chris	K	5-10	175	5
56	Barnes, Jeff	LB	6-2	215	4
81	Bradshaw, Morris	WR	6-1	195	7
21	Branch, Cliff	WR	5-11	170	9
73	Browning, Dave	DE	6-5	245	3
77	Campbell, Joe	DE-NT	6-6	250	4
52	Celotto, Mario	LB	6-3	225	2
85	Chandler, Bob	WR	6-1	180	10
88	Chester, Raymond	TE	6-4	235	11
46	Christensen, Todd	TE-RB	6-3	230	2
50	Dalby, Dave	C	6-3	250	9
79	Davis, Bruce	G-T	6-6	280	2
36	Davis, Mike	S	6-3	200	3
8	Guy, Ray	P	6-3	190	8
86	Hardman, Cedrick	DE	6-4	245	11
37	Hayes, Lester	CB	6-0	195	4
83	Hendricks, Ted	LB	6-7	225	12
42	Jackson, Monte	CB	5-11	200	6
31	Jensen, Derrick	RB	6-1	225	2
90	Jones, Willie	DE	6-4	245	2
33	King, Kenny	RB	5-11	205	2
62	Kinlaw, Reggie	NT	6-2	240	2
70	Lawrence, Henry	T	6-4	270	7
53	Martin, Rod	LB	6-2	210	4
89	Martini, Rich	WR	6-2	185	2
65	Marvin, Mickey	G	6-4	270	4
71	Mason, Lindsey	T-G	6-5	265	2
43	Matthews, Ira	KR-WR-RB	5-8	175	2
72	Matuszak, John	DE	6-8	280	8
57	McClanahan, Randy	LB	6-5	225	3
23	McKinney, Odis	CB	6-2	190	3
55	Millen, Matt	LB	6-2	260	R
26	Moody, Keith	CB-KR	5-11	175	5
51	Nelson, Bob	LB	6-4	230	5
35	O'Steen, Dwayne	CB	6-1	195	3
44	Owens, Burgess	S	6-2	200	8
74	Pear, Dave	NT	6-2	250	6
16	Plunkett, Jim	QB	6-2	205	10
84	Ramsey, Derrick	TE	6-4	225	3
78	Shell, Art	T	6-5	280	13
66	Sylvester, Steve	G-C	6-4	260	6
63	Upshaw, Gene	G	6-5	255	14
30	van Eeghen, Mark	RB	6-2	225	7
22	Whittington, Arthur	RB	5-11	180	3
6	Wilson, Marc	QB	6-5	205	R

PHILADELPHIA EAGLES

No.	Name	Pos.	Ht.	Wt.	Year
63	Baker, Ron	G	6-4	250	3
66	Bergey, Bill	LB	6-3	245	12
27	Blackmore, Richard	CB	5-10	174	2
97	Brown, Thomas	DE	6-4	240	R
95	Bunting, John	LB	6-1	220	9
37	Campfield, Billy	RB	6-0	205	3
17	Carmichael, Harold	WR	6-8	225	10
59	Chesley, Al	LB	6-3	240	2
71	Clarke, Ken	NT	6-2	260	3
46	Edwards, Herman	CB	6-0	190	4
1	Franklin, Tony	K	5-8	182	2
33	Giammona, Louie	RB-KR	5-9	180	4
78	Hairston, Carl	DE	6-3	260	5
35	Harrington, Perry	RB	5-11	210	R
20	Harris, Leroy	RB	5-9	230	4
68	Harrison, Dennis	DE	6-8	275	3
24	Henderson, Zac	S	6-1	190	R
89	Henry, Wally	WR-KR	5-8	170	4
16	Hertel, Rob	QB	6-2	198	2
87	Humphrey, Claude	DE	6-5	258	13
7	Jaworski, Ron	QB	6-2	196	6
65	Johnson, Charlie	NT	6-3	262	4
73	Kenney, Steve	T	6-4	262	1
84	Krepfle, Keith	TE	6-3	230	6
55	LeMaster, Frank	LB	6-2	238	7
41	Logan, Randy	S	6-1	195	8
31	Montgomery, Wilbert	RB	5-10	195	4
50	Morriss, Guy	C	6-4	255	8
83	Parker, Rodney	WR	6-1	190	1
69	Peoples, Woody	G	6-2	260	12
62	Perot, Petey	G	6-2	261	2
52	Phillips, Ray	LB	6-4	230	4
9	Pisarcik, Joe	QB	6-4	220	4
56	Robinson, Jerry	LB	6-2	218	2
4	Runager, Max	P	6-1	189	2
21	Sciarra, John	S-KR	5-11	185	3
76	Sisemore, Jerry	T	6-4	265	8
61	Slater, Mark	C	6-2	257	3
85	Smith, Charles	WR	6-1	185	7
88	Spagnola, John	TE	6-4	240	2
39	Torrey, Bob	RB	6-2	232	3
75	Walters, Stan	T	6-6	275	9
51	Wilkes, Reggie	LB	6-4	230	3
22	Wilson, Brenard	S	6-0	175	2
43	Young, Roynell	CB	6-1	181	R

SUPER BOWL XVI

SAN FRANCISCO 26, CINCINNATI 21

The San Francisco defense came up with big plays throughout the game, including a four-play goal-line stand late in the third quarter, to stave off Cincinnati's explosive offense and record a 26-21 victory in Super Bowl XVI at the Pontiac Silverdome.

The 49ers' defense set the tone of the game early in the first quarter. Amos Lawrence fumbled the opening kickoff and the Bengals recovered at the 49ers' 26-yard line. Six plays later, free safety Dwight Hicks intercepted Ken Anderson's pass, which was intended for Isaac Curtis, at the 5-yard line and returned it 27 yards.

The 49ers then drove 68 yards on 11 plays for a touchdown. The key play in the drive was a 14-yard "gadget" pass from Joe Montana to tight end Charle Young on third-and-one at the Cincinnati 47. On the play, Montana handed off to Ricky Patton, who gave the ball to Freddie Solomon, who pitched back to Montana, who threw to Young. The drive culminated in a one-yard run by Montana that gave San Francisco a 7-0 lead.

Early in the second quarter, the 49ers' defense thwarted another Cincinnati drive when Eric Wright stripped the ball loose from Cris Collinsworth at the San Francisco 8. Lynn Thomas recovered for the 49ers. Twelve plays and 92 yards later, Montana threw an 11-yard touchdown pass to running back Earl Cooper to complete the longest drive in Super Bowl history.

David Verser's fumble of the ensuing kickoff and a penalty for an illegal block pinned the Bengals at their 2. Six plays later, they were forced to punt.

Ray Wersching's 22-yard field goal with 15 seconds left in the half was followed 13 seconds later by three more points, set up by a San Francisco recovery of Archie Griffin's fumbled kickoff return.

Cincinnati marched to a touchdown to start the third quarter, driving 83 yards in nine plays. Anderson scored on a five-yard run.

An exchange of punts—one by the Bengals, two by the 49ers—gave Cincinnati the ball at midfield with 6:53 left in the quarter. Two big plays in the drive—a 49-yard pass from Anderson to Collinsworth on third and 23 and Pete Johnson's two-yard run on fourth and one at the San Francisco 5—put the Bengals in a first-and-goal situation at the 3. Johnson gained two on first down, but the 49ers rose to the occasion and stopped three successive plays from the 1 and took over with 1:17 left in the period.

The Cincinnati defense forced a punt, giving the Bengals possession at their 47. Eight plays later, Anderson threw a four-yard touchdown pass to tight end Dan Ross, cutting the 49ers' lead to 20-14 with 10:06 left in the game.

Montana then moved the 49ers 50 yards on a drive that ended in a 40-yard field goal by Wersching. Moments later, Anderson was intercepted by Wright, who returned it to the Cincinnati 22. Wersching kicked his fourth field goal, tying the Super Bowl record, with 1:57 left in the game.

Cincinnati took over at its own 26, and Anderson threw six consecutive completions, the last a three-yard touchdown pass to Ross with 16 seconds left. The Bengals' onside kick attempt was recovered by the 49ers, who ran out the clock.

Despite the 49ers' victory, the Bengals dominated the statistics, holding a 356-275 yardage edge. Anderson completed a record 25 (of 34) passes for 300 yards and two touchdowns, both to Ross, who set a Super Bowl mark with 11 receptions. Montana, the game's most valuable player, threw for 157 yards and one touchdown, completing 14 of 22 passes.

Date—January 24, 1982
Site—Pontiac Silverdome, Pontiac
Time—4:00 P.M. EST
Conditions—70 degrees, indoors
Playing Surface—AstroTurf
Television and Radio—Columbia Broadcasting System (CBS)
Regular Season Records—Cincinnati, 12-4; San Francisco, 13-3
Conference Championships—Cincinnati defeated the San Diego Chargers 27-7 for the AFC title; San Francisco defeated the Dallas Cowboys 28-27 for the NFC title
Players' Shares—$18,000 to each member of the winning team; $9,000 to each member of the losing team
Attendance—81,270
Gross Receipts—$10,641,034.083
Officials—Referee, Pat Haggerty; umpire, Al Conway; line judge, Bob Beeks; head linesman, Jerry Bergman; back judge, Bill Swanson; side judge, Bob Rice; field judge, Don Hakes
Coaches—Bill Walsh, San Francisco; Forrest Gregg, Cincinnati

San Francisco	Starters, Offense	Cincinnati
Dwight Clark	WR	Cris Collinsworth
Dan Audick	LT	Anthony Munoz
John Ayers	LG	Dave Lapham
Fred Quillan	C	Blair Bush
Randy Cross	RG	Max Montoya
Keith Fahnhorst	RT	Mike Wilson
Charle Young	TE	Dan Ross
Freddie Solomon	WR	Isaac Curtis
Joe Montana	QB	Ken Anderson
Ricky Patton	RB	Pete Johnson
Earl Cooper	RB	Charles Alexander
	Starters, Defense	
Jim Stuckey	LE	Eddie Edwards
Archie Reese	NT	Wilson Whitley
Dwaine Board	RE	Ross Browner
Willie Harper	LOLB	Bo Harris
Jack Reynolds	LILB	Jim LeClair
Craig Puki	RILB	Glenn Cameron
Keena Turner	ROLB	Reggie Williams
Ronnie Lott	LCB	Louis Breeden
Eric Wright	RCB	Ken Riley
Carlton Williamson	SS	Bobby Kemp
Dwight Hicks	FS	Bryan Hicks

San Francisco	7	13	0	6	—	26
Cincinnati	0	0	7	14	—	21

SF —Montana 1 run (Wersching kick)
SF —Cooper 11 pass from Montana (Wersching kick)
SF —FG Wersching 22
SF —FG Wersching 26
Cin—Anderson 5 run (Breech kick)
Cin—Ross 4 pass from Anderson (Breech kick)
SF —FG Wersching 40
SF —FG Wersching 23
Cin—Ross 3 pass from Anderson (Breech kick)

TEAM STATISTICS	SF	Cin
First downs	20	24
Rushing	9	7
Passing	9	13
By penalty	2	4
Total yardage	275	356
Net rushing yardage	127	72
Net passing yardage	148	284
Passes att.-comp.-had int.	22-14-0	34-25-2

RUSHING
San Francisco—Patton, 17 for 55; Cooper, 9 for 34; Montana, 6 for 18, 1 TD; Ring, 5 for 17; Davis, 2 for 5; Clark, 1 for −2.
Cincinnati—Johnson, 14 for 36; Alexander, 5 for 17; Anderson, 4 for 15, 1 TD; A. Griffin, 1 for 4.

PASSING
San Francisco—Montana, 14 of 22 for 157, 1 TD.
Cincinnati—Anderson, 25 of 34 for 300, 2 TDs, 2 int.

RECEIVING
San Francisco—Solomon, 4 for 52; Clark, 4 for 45; Cooper, 2 for 15, 1 TD; Wilson, 1 for 22; Young, 1 for 14; Patton, 1 for 6; Ring, 1 for 3.
Cincinnati—Ross, 11 for 104, 2 TDs; Collinsworth, 5 for 107; Curtis, 3 for 42; Kreider, 2 for 36; Johnson, 2 for 8; Alexander, 2 for 3.

PUNTING
San Francisco—Miller, 4 for 185, 46.3 average.
Cincinnati—McInally, 3 for 131, 43.7 average.

PUNT RETURNS
San Francisco—Hicks, 1 for 6; Solomon, 1 fair catch.
Cincinnati—Fuller, 4 for 35.

KICKOFF RETURNS
San Francisco—Hicks, 1 for 23; Lawrence, 1 for 17.
Cincinnati—Verser, 5 for 52; A. Griffin, 1 for 0; Frazier, 1 for 0.

INTERCEPTIONS
San Francisco—Hicks, 1 for 27; Wright, 1 for 25.
Cincinnati—None.

SAN FRANCISCO 49ERS

No.	Name	Pos.	Ht.	Wt.	Year
61	Audick, Dan	T	6-3	253	4
68	Ayers, John	G	6-5	260	5
7	Benjamin, Guy	QB	6-3	210	4
76	Board, Dwaine	DE	6-5	250	3
57	Bunz, Dan	LB	6-4	225	4
60	Choma, John	G-T	6-6	261	1
87	Clark, Dwight	WR	6-4	210	3
49	Cooper, Earl	RB	6-2	227	2
51	Cross, Randy	G	6-3	250	6
38	Davis, Johnny	RB	6-1	235	4
74	Dean, Fred	DE	6-2	230	7
62	Downing, Walt	C-G	6-3	254	4
31	Easley, Walt	RB	6-1	226	R
35	Elliott, Lenvil	RB	6-0	210	9
71	Fahnhorst, Keith	T	6-6	263	8
24	Gervais, Rick	S	5-11	190	R
59	Harper, Willie	LB	6-2	215	8
75	Harty, John	NT	6-4	253	R
22	Hicks, Dwight	S	6-1	189	3
66	Kennedy, Allan	T	6-7	245	R
20	Lawrence, Amos	RB	5-10	179	R
52	Leopold, Bobby	LB	6-1	215	2
42	Lott, Ronnie	CB	6-0	199	R
29	Martin, Saladin	CB	6-1	180	2
53	McColl, Milt	LB	6-6	220	R
3	Miller, Jim	P	5-11	183	2
16	Montana, Joe	QB	6-2	200	3
32	Patton, Ricky	RB	5-11	192	4
65	Pillers, Lawrence	DE	6-4	260	6
54	Puki, Craig	LB	6-1	231	2
56	Quillan, Fred	C	6-5	260	4
80	Ramson, Eason	TE	6-2	234	3
78	Reese, Archie	NT	6-3	262	4
64	Reynolds, Jack	LB	6-1	232	12
30	Ring, Bill	RB-KR	5-10	215	1
84	Shumann, Mike	WR	6-0	175	4
88	Solomon, Freddie	WR-KR	5-11	185	7
79	Stuckey, Jim	DE	6-4	251	2
28	Thomas, Lynn	CB	5-11	181	R
58	Turner, Keena	LB	6-2	219	2
14	Wersching, Ray	K	5-11	210	9
27	Williamson, Carlton	S	6-0	204	R
85	Wilson, Mike	WR	6-3	210	R
21	Wright, Eric	CB	6-1	180	R
86	Young, Charle	TE	6-4	234	9

CINCINNATI BENGALS

No.	Name	Pos.	Ht.	Wt.	Year
40	Alexander, Charles	RB	6-1	221	3
14	Anderson, Ken	QB	6-3	212	11
84	Bass, Don	WR-TE	6-2	220	4
10	Breech, Jim	K	5-6	161	3
34	Breeden, Louis	CB	5-11	185	4
79	Browner, Ross	DE	6-3	261	4
74	Bujnoch, Glenn	G	6-6	258	6
67	Burley, Gary	DE	6-3	274	6
58	Bush, Blair	C	6-3	252	4
50	Cameron, Glenn	LB	6-2	228	7
80	Collinsworth, Cris	WR	6-5	192	R
85	Curtis, Isaac	WR	6-1	192	9
21	Davis, Oliver	S	6-1	205	5
52	Dinkel, Tom	LB	6-3	237	4
73	Edwards, Eddie	DE	6-5	256	5
49	Frazier, Guy	LB	6-2	215	R
42	Fuller, Mike	S	5-10	182	7
45	Griffin, Archie	RB	5-9	184	6
44	Griffin, Ray	CB	5-10	186	4
36	Hargrove, Jim	RB	6-2	228	R
53	Harris, Bo	LB	6-3	226	7
83	Harris, M. L.	TE	6-5	238	2
27	Hicks, Bryan	S	6-0	192	2
71	Horn, Rod	NT	6-4	268	2
46	Johnson, Pete	RB	6-0	249	5
26	Kemp, Bobby	S	6-0	186	R
86	Kreider, Steve	WR	6-3	192	3
62	Lapham, Dave	G	6-4	262	8
55	LeClair, Jim	LB	6-3	234	10
87	McInally, Pat	P-WR	6-6	212	6
65	Montoya, Max	G	6-5	275	3
60	Moore, Blake	C-T	6-5	267	2
78	Munoz, Anthony	T	6-6	278	2
68	Obrovac, Mike	G	6-6	275	R
51	Razzano, Rick	LB	5-11	227	2
13	Riley, Ken	CB	6-0	183	13
89	Ross, Dan	TE	6-4	235	3
72	St. Clair, Mike	DE	6-5	254	6
15	Schonert, Turk	QB	6-1	185	2
25	Simmons, John	CB	5-11	192	R
12	Thompson, Jack	QB	6-3	217	3
81	Verser, David	WR	6-1	200	R
75	Whitley, Wilson	NT	6-3	265	5
57	Williams, Reggie	LB	6-0	228	6
77	Wilson, Mike	T	6-5	271	4

SUPER BOWL XVII

WASHINGTON 27, MIAMI 17

John Riggins pounded out 166 yards rushing, including the winning 43-yard touchdown run in the fourth quarter, and the Washington Redskins defeated the Miami Dolphins 27-17 to win their first championship since 1942.

The game had been billed as a duel between the offensive line of the Redskins, known as the Hogs, and the Killer Bees defense of the Dolphins. But the duel turned into a one-sided shooting, as the power running of Riggins and the short-passing game of Joe Theismann overcame several big plays by the Dolphins, who otherwise were shut down by a surprising—and unheralded—Washington defense.

Miami opened the scoring on its second possession. With a second and six at the Miami 24, quarterback David Woodley found wide receiver Jimmy Cefalo by himself 21 yards upfield. Cefalo outraced the Redskins' defense the remaining 55 yards, completing a 76-yard touchdown play.

The Dolphins started moving the next time they had the ball, but on first and 10 at the Redskins' 37, Woodley was sacked by Dexter Manley and fumbled. The ball was recovered by Dave Butz at Miami's 46. Nine plays later (five of them runs by Riggins), Mark Moseley kicked a 31-yard field goal to cut the Miami lead to 7-3.

Sparked by a 42-yard kickoff return by Fulton Walker, the Dolphins drove right back to score. A 13-play drive ended on the Redskins' 3, and Uwe von Schamann kicked a 20-yard field goal.

Then it was Washington's turn. Theismann hit four of four passes on the next drive, the last one a four-yarder for a touchdown to diminutive Alvin Garrett, which tied the score 10-10.

Walker took Jeff Hayes's subsequent kickoff and started upfield, angling to his right. Then he suddenly cut back to his left and was gone, 98 yards for a touchdown, the longest kickoff return in Super Bowl history and the first for a score.

Miami led 17-10 at halftime, despite having been outgained 191 yards to 142. But the Dolphins' day was over. They were to gain only 34 yards in the second half, including none passing on 11 attempts.

While Washington's defense was becoming impenetrable, its offense got into gear. On the second possession of the second half, Garrett gained 44 yards to the Miami 9 on a reverse. Four plays later, Moseley cut the deficit to 17-13 with a 20-yard field goal.

Late in the quarter, Theismann provided the play of the game—defensively. On a first and 10 at his own 18, Theismann's pass was batted into the air by Kim Bokamper. With Bokamper simultaneously trying to catch the ball and dash into the end zone, Theismann barely reached across the defender's body and jarred the ball loose, preventing what could have been the decisive score. The drive eventually ended with an interception by Lyle Blackwood at the Miami 1.

In the fourth quarter, Riggins began beating a tattoo on Miami's defense. Faced with a fourth and one at Miami's 43, the Redskins sent Riggins around left end. He shed a tackle attempt by Don McNeal and lumbered 43 yards for the go-ahead score.

On the next drive, Washington clinched the game. Riggins carried the ball eight times before Theismann capped the scoring for the day with a six-yard pass to Charlie Brown.

After the game, Riggins, the most valuable player, made the most of President Ronald Reagan's congratulatory phone call. "At least for tonight," Riggins said, "Ron may be President, but I'm the King."

Date—January 30, 1983
Site—Rose Bowl, Pasadena
Time—3:00 P.M. PST
Conditions—61 degrees, sunny
Playing Surface—Grass
Television—National Broadcasting Company (NBC)
Radio—Columbia Broadcasting System (CBS)
Regular Season Records—Miami, 7-2; Washington, 8-1
Conference Championships—Miami defeated the New York Jets 14-0 for the AFC title; Washington defeated the Dallas Cowboys 31-17 for the NFC title
Players' Shares—$36,000 to each member of the winning team; $18,000 to each member of the losing team
Attendance—103,667
Gross Receipts—$19,997,330.86
Officials—Referee, Jerry Markbreit; umpire, Art Demmas; line judge, Bill Reynolds; head linesman, Dale Hamer; back judge, Dick Hantak; side judge, Dave Parry; field judge, Don Orr
Coaches—Don Shula, Miami; Joe Gibbs, Washington

Miami	Starters, Offense	Washington
Duriel Harris	WR	Alvin Garrett
Jon Giesler	LT	Joe Jacoby
Bob Kuechenberg	LG	Russ Grimm
Dwight Stephenson	C	Jeff Bostic
Jeff Toews	RG	Fred Dean
Eric Laakso	RT	George Starke
Bruce Hardy	TE	Don Warren
Jimmy Cefalo	WR	Charlie Brown
David Woodley	QB	Joe Theismann
Andra Franklin	RB-TE	Rick Walker
Tony Nathan	RB	John Riggins
	Starters, Defense	
Doug Betters	LE	Mat Mendenhall
Bob Baumhower	NT-LT	Dave Butz
Kim Bokamper	RE-RT	Darryl Grant
Bob Brudzinski	LOLB-RE	Dexter Manley
A.J. Duhe	LILB-LLB	Mel Kaufman
Earnie Rhone	RILB-MLB	Neal Olkewicz
Larry Gordon	ROLB-RLB	Rich Milot
Gerald Small	LCB	Jeris White
Don McNeal	RCB	Vernon Dean
Glenn Blackwood	SS	Tony Peters
Lyle Blackwood	FS	Mark Murphy

Miami	7	10	0	0	—	17
Washington	0	10	3	14	—	27

Mia —Cefalo 76 pass from Woodley (von Schamann kick)
Wash—FG Moseley 31
Mia —FG von Schamann 20
Wash—Garrett 4 pass from Theismann (Moseley kick)
Mia —Walker 98 kickoff return (von Schamann kick)
Wash—FG Moseley 20
Wash—Riggins 43 run (Moseley kick)
Wash—Brown 6 pass from Theismann (Moseley kick)

TEAM STATISTICS	Mia	Wash
First downs	9	24
Rushing	7	14
Passing	2	9
By penalty	0	1
Total yardage	176	400
Net rushing yardage	96	276
Net passing yardage	80	124
Passes att.-comp.-had int.	17-4-1	23-15-2

RUSHING
Miami—Franklin, 16 for 49; Nathan, 7 for 26; Woodley, 4 for 16; Vigorito, 1 for 4; Harris, 1 for 1.
Washington—Riggins, 38 for 166, 1 TD; Garrett, 1 for 44; Harmon, 9 for 40; Theismann, 3 for 20; Walker, 1 for 6.
PASSING
Miami—Woodley, 4 of 14 for 97, 1 TD, 1 int.; Strock, 0 of 3.
Washington—Theismann, 15 of 23 for 143, 2 TDs, 2 int.
RECEIVING
Miami—Cefalo, 2 for 82, 1 TD; Harris, 2 for 15.
Washington—Brown, 6 for 60, 1 TD; Warren, 5 for 28; Garrett, 2 for 13, 1 TD; Walker, 1 for 27; Riggins, 1 for 15.
PUNTING
Miami—Orosz, 6 for 227, 37.8 average.
Washington—Hayes, 4 for 168, 42.0 average.
PUNT RETURNS
Miami—Vigorito, 2 for 22, 1 fair catch.
Washington—Nelms, 6 for 52.
KICKOFF RETURNS
Miami—Walker, 4 for 190, 1 TD; L. Blackwood, 2 for 32.
Washington—Nelms, 2 for 44; Wonsley, 1 for 13.
INTERCEPTIONS
Miami—Duhe, 1 for 0; L. Blackwood, 1 for 0.
Washington—Murphy, 1 for 0.

MIAMI DOLPHINS

No.	Name	Pos.	Ht.	Wt.	Year
73	Baumhower, Bob	NT	6-5	260	6
34	Bennett, Woody	RB	6-2	222	4
75	Betters, Doug	DE	6-7	260	5
72	Bishop, Richard	NT	6-1	265	7
47	Blackwood, Glenn	S	6-0	186	4
42	Blackwood, Lyle	S	6-1	188	10
58	Bokamper, Kim	DE	6-6	250	6
56	Bowser, Charles	LB	6-3	222	R
59	Brudzinski, Bob	LB	6-4	230	6
81	Cefalo, Jimmy	WR	5-11	188	5
76	Clark, Steve	DE	6-4	255	R
83	Den Herder, Vern	DE	6-6	252	12
63	Dennard, Mark	C	6-1	252	4
33	Diana, Rich	RB	5-9	220	R
77	Duhe, A.J.	LB	6-4	248	6
85	Duper, Mark	WR	5-9	185	R
61	Foster, Roy	G-T	6-4	275	R
37	Franklin, Andra	RB	5-10	225	2
79	Giesler, Jon	T	6-5	260	4
50	Gordon, Larry	LB	6-4	230	7
74	Green, Cleveland	T	6-3	262	4
84	Hardy, Bruce	TE	6-4	230	5
82	Harris, Duriel	WR	5-11	176	7
88	Heflin, Vince	WR	6-0	185	R
53	Hester, Ron	LB	6-1	218	R
31	Hill, Eddie	RB	6-2	210	4
11	Jensen, Jim	QB	6-4	212	2
49	Judson, William	CB	6-1	181	1
40	Kozlowski, Mike	S	6-0	198	3
67	Kuechenberg, Bob	G	6-2	255	13
68	Laakso, Eric	T	6-4	265	5
44	Lankford, Paul	CB	6-1	178	R
86	Lee, Ronnie	TE	6-3	236	4
28	McNeal, Don	CB	5-11	192	3
89	Moore, Nat	WR	5-9	188	9
22	Nathan, Tony	RB	6-0	206	4
3	Orosz, Tom	P	6-1	204	2
54	Potter, Steve	LB	6-3	235	2
55	Rhone, Earnie	LB	6-2	224	7
80	Rose, Joe	TE	6-3	230	3
52	Shull, Steve	LB	6-1	220	3
48	Small, Gerald	CB	5-11	192	5
57	Stephenson, Dwight	C	6-2	255	3
10	Strock, Don	QB	6-5	220	9
60	Toews, Jeff	G	6-3	255	4
32	Vigorito, Tom	RB-KR	5-10	197	2
5	von Schamann, Uwe	K	6-0	188	4
41	Walker, Fulton	CB-KR	5-10	193	2
16	Woodley, David	QB	6-2	204	3

WASHINGTON REDSKINS

No.	Name	Pos.	Ht.	Wt.	Year
53	Bostic, Jeff	C	6-2	245	3
69	Brooks, Perry	DT	6-3	265	5
87	Brown, Charlie	WR	5-10	179	1
65	Butz, Dave	DT	6-7	295	10
82	Caster, Rich	TE	6-5	230	13
51	Coleman, Monte	LB	6-2	235	4
54	Cronan, Pete	LB	6-2	238	5
63	Dean, Fred	G	6-3	255	5
32	Dean, Vernon	CB	5-11	178	R
86	Didier, Clint	TE	6-5	240	1
89	Garrett, Alvin	WR	5-7	178	3
30	Giaquinto, Nick	RB	5-11	204	3
77	Grant, Darryl	DT	6-2	265	2
68	Grimm, Russ	C-G	6-3	273	2
38	Harmon, Clarence	RB	5-11	209	6
5	Hayes, Jeff	P	5-11	175	R
8	Holly, Bob	QB	6-2	205	R
40	Jackson, Wilbur	RB	6-1	219	8
66	Jacoby, Joe	T	6-7	295	2
22	Jordan, Curtis	S	6-2	205	6
55	Kaufman, Mel	LB	6-2	218	2
50	Kubin, Larry	LB	6-2	234	1
62	Laster, Donald	T	6-5	285	R
20	Lavender, Joe	CB	6-4	188	10
79	Liebenstein, Todd	DE	6-6	245	R
56	Lowry, Quentin	LB	6-2	225	2
72	Manley, Dexter	DE	6-3	240	2
73	May, Mark	G	6-6	288	2
46	McDaniel, LeCharls	CB	5-9	169	2
78	McGee, Tony	DE	6-4	250	12
76	Mendenhall, Mat	DE	6-6	255	2
57	Milot, Rich	LB	6-4	237	4
3	Moseley, Mark	K	6-0	205	11
29	Murphy, Mark	S	6-4	210	6
21	Nelms, Mike	S-KR	6-1	185	3
52	Olkewicz, Neal	LB	6-0	230	4
17	Owen, Tom	QB	6-1	194	9
23	Peters, Tony	S	6-1	190	8
71	Puetz, Garry	T	6-4	265	10
44	Riggins, John	RB	6-2	235	11
80	Seay, Virgil	WR	5-8	175	2
74	Starke, George	T	6-5	260	10
7	Theismann, Joe	QB	6-0	198	9
88	Walker, Rick	TE	6-4	235	6
85	Warren, Don	TE	6-4	242	4
25	Washington, Joe	RB	5-10	179	6
45	White, Jeris	CB	5-10	188	9
47	Williams, Greg	S	5-11	185	R
39	Wonsley, Otis	RB	5-10	214	2

SUPER BOWL XVIII

LA RAIDERS 38, WASHINGTON 9

The Los Angeles Raiders' defense shut down the most prolific offense in NFL history, and Marcus Allen rushed for a Super Bowl-record 191 yards, as the Raiders defeated the Washington Redskins 38-9, then the biggest margin of victory in a Super Bowl.

In completing one of the most impressive runs through the playoffs ever, all three of the Raiders' platoons—offense, defense, and special teams—scored touchdowns.

Early in the first quarter, after Washington's first possession, the Raiders' Derrick Jensen broke through the Redskins' line, blocked Jeff Hayes's punt, and recovered it in the end zone to give Los Angeles a 7-0 advantage.

The Redskins' special teams had a chance to return the favor on the third play of the second quarter, but couldn't. A high snap sent punter Ray Guy leaping for the ball. Guy pulled it in with one hand, landed on his feet, and, unhurried by any rush, boomed a punt through Washington's end zone.

After holding the Redskins, the Raiders came out throwing. On first down, Jim Plunkett passed 50 yards down the middle to Cliff Branch. Two plays later, he found Branch again, for a 12-yard touchdown and a 14-0 lead.

The Redskins responded with a 13-play, 73-yard drive, but it netted only a 24-yard field goal by Mark Moseley. After holding the Raiders, Washington regained the ball on its own 12-yard line, with 12 seconds left in the half. Joe Theismann called a swing pass to halfback Joe Washington, a play that had gained 67 yards when the two clubs met earlier in the season. This time, linebacker Jack Squirek stepped in front of the intended receiver at the Washington 5 and dashed into the end zone for a touchdown and a 21-3 halftime lead.

After the intermission, the Redskins looked as if they were going to make a game of it. After receiving the second-half kickoff, Washington went 70 yards on three passes by Theismann and six runs by John Riggins, who scored on a one-yard plunge behind tackle George Starke. The momentum didn't remain long, however; reserve tight end Don Hasselbeck blocked Moseley's extra-point attempt.

Then the Raiders put the game away. Helped by a 38-yard pass interference penalty against Washington cornerback Darrell Green, Plunkett engineered an eight-play, 70-yard drive, which was capped by a five-yard touchdown run by Allen.

On the last play of the quarter, Allen struck again. On first and 10 at the Raiders' 26, he took a pitch, swept left, reversed his direction when he spotted safety Ken Coffey closing in, circled back to the middle, and cut upfield. Suddenly, he was in the open and on his way to a 74-yard touchdown run, the longest of his career and the longest in Super Bowl history. He was also on his way to the game's most-valuable-player honors.

The Raiders added a 21-yard field goal by Chris Bahr in the fourth quarter to break Green Bay's and Pittsburgh's Super Bowl record for points in a game. Meanwhile, the defense finished its day having held Riggins to a 2.5-yard rushing average while intercepting Theismann twice and sacking him six times. Nose tackle Reggie Kinlaw was the main force in stopping Riggins, while cornerbacks Mike Haynes and Lester Hayes held Washington wide receivers Charlie Brown and Art Monk to only four receptions, none in the decisive first half.

"I don't want to sound conceited, but . . . I knew we'd beat 'em today," Allen said after the game. "I think anybody who knew about football knew that."

Date—January 22, 1984
Site—Tampa Stadium, Tampa
Time—4:30 P.M. EST
Conditions—68 degrees, partly cloudy
Playing Surface—Grass
Television and Radio—Columbia Broadcasting Company (CBS)
Regular Season Records—Los Angeles, 12-4, Washington 14-2
Conference Championships—Los Angeles defeated the Seattle Seahawks 30-14 for the AFC title; Washington defeated the San Francisco 49ers 24-21 for the NFC title
Players' Shares—$36,000 to each member of the winning team; $18,000 to each member of the losing team
Attendance—72,920
Gross Receipts—$20,002,390.28
Officials—Referee, Gene Barth; umpire, Gordon Wells; line judge, Bob Beeks; head linesman, Jerry Bergman; back judge, Ben Tompkins; side judge, Gil Mace; field judge, Fritz Graf
Coaches—Joe Gibbs, Washington; Tom Flores, LA Raiders

Washington	Starters, Offense	LA Raiders
Charlie Brown	WR	Cliff Branch
Joe Jacoby	LT	Bruce Davis
Russ Grimm	LG	Charley Hannah
Jeff Bostic	C	Dave Dalby
Mark May	RG	Mickey Marvin
George Starke	RT	Henry Lawrence
Don Warren	TE	Todd Christensen
Art Monk	WR	Malcolm Barnwell
Joe Theismann	QB	Jim Plunkett
Rick Walker	TE-RB	Kenny King
John Riggins	RB	Marcus Allen
	Starters, Defense	
Todd Liebenstein	LE	Howie Long
Dave Butz	LT-NT	Reggie Kinlaw
Darryl Grant	RT-RE	Lyle Alzado
Dexter Manley	RE-LOLB	Ted Hendricks
Mel Kaufman	LLB-LILB	Matt Millen
Neal Olkewicz	MLB-RILB	Bob Nelson
Rich Milot	RLB-ROLB	Rod Martin
Darrell Green	LCB	Lester Hayes
Anthony Washington	RCB	Mike Haynes
Ken Coffey	SS	Mike Davis
Mark Murphy	FS	Vann McElroy

Washington	0	3	6	0	—	9
LA Raiders	7	14	14	3	—	38

Raiders—Jensen recovered blocked punt in end zone (Bahr kick)
Raiders—Branch 12 pass from Plunkett (Bahr kick)
Wash —FG Moseley 24
Raiders—Squirek 5 interception return (Bahr kick)
Wash —Riggins 1 run (kick blocked)
Raiders—Allen 5 run (Bahr kick)
Raiders—Allen 74 run (Bahr kick)
Raiders—FG Bahr 21

TEAM STATISTICS	Wash	Raiders
First downs	19	18
Rushing	7	8
Passing	10	9
By penalty	2	1
Total yardage	283	385
Net rushing yardage	90	231
Net passing yardage	193	154
Passes att.-comp.-had int.	35-16-2	25-16-0

RUSHING
Washington—Riggins, 26 for 64, 1 TD; Theismann, 3 for 18; J. Washington, 3 for 8.
LA Raiders—Allen, 20 for 191, 2 TDs; Pruitt, 5 for 17; King, 3 for 12; Willis, 1 for 7; Hawkins, 3 for 6; Plunkett, 1 for −2.
PASSING
Washington—Theismann, 16 of 35 for 243, 2 int.
LA Raiders—Plunkett, 16 of 25 for 172, 1 TD.
RECEIVING
Washington—Didier, 5 for 65; Brown, 3 for 93; J. Washington, 3 for 20; Giaquinto, 2 for 21; Monk, 1 for 26; Garrett, 1 for 17; Riggins, 1 for 1.
LA Raiders—Branch, 6 for 94, 1 TD; Christensen, 4 for 32; Hawkins, 2 for 20; Allen, 2 for 18; King, 2 for 8.
PUNTING
Washington—Hayes, 7 for 259, 37.0 average.
LA Raiders—Guy, 7 for 299, 42.7 average.
PUNT RETURNS
Washington—Green, 1 for 34; Giaquinto, 1 for 1, 2 fair catches.
LA Raiders—Pruitt, 1 for 8, 3 fair catches; Watts, 1 for 0.
KICKOFF RETURNS
Washington—Garrett, 5 for 100; Grant, 1 for 32; Kimball, 1 for 0.
LA Raiders—Pruitt, 1 for 17.
INTERCEPTIONS
Washington—None.
LA Raiders—Squirek, 1 for 5, 1 TD; Haynes, 1 for 0.

WASHINGTON REDSKINS

No.	Name	Pos.	Ht.	Wt.	Year
58	Anderson, Stuart	LB	6-1	224	2
53	Bostic, Jeff	C	6-2	250	4
69	Brooks, Perry	DT	6-3	270	6
87	Brown, Charlie	WR	5-10	179	2
65	Butz, Dave	DT	6-7	295	11
41	Carpenter, Brian	CB	5-10	167	2
48	Coffey, Ken	S	6-0	190	1
51	Coleman, Monte	LB	6-2	230	5
54	Cronan, Peter	LB	6-2	238	6
32	Dean, Vernon	CB	5-11	178	2
86	Didier, Clint	TE	6-5	240	2
26	Evans, Reggie	RB	5-11	201	1
89	Garrett, Alvin	WR	5-7	185	4
30	Giaquinto, Nick	RB	5-11	204	4
77	Grant, Darryl	DT	6-1	275	3
28	Green, Darrell	CB-KR	5-8	170	R
68	Grimm, Russ	G-C	6-3	275	3
5	Hayes, Jeff	P	5-11	175	2
8	Holly, Bob	QB	6-2	196	2
61	Huff, Ken	G	6-4	265	9
66	Jacoby, Joe	T	6-7	298	3
22	Jordan, Curtis	S	6-2	205	7
55	Kaufman, Mel	LB	6-2	218	3
67	Kimball, Bruce	G	6-2	260	2
50	Kubin, Larry	LB	6-2	238	2
12	Laufenberg, Babe	QB	6-2	195	R
79	Liebenstein, Todd	DE	6-6	255	2
72	Manley, Dexter	DE	6-3	250	3
71	Mann, Charles	DE	6-6	250	R
73	May, Mark	G	6-6	288	3
78	McGee, Tony	DE	6-3	249	13
83	McGrath, Mark	WR	5-11	175	2
57	Milot, Rich	LB	6-4	237	5
81	Monk, Art	WR	6-3	209	4
3	Moseley, Mark	K	6-0	204	12
29	Murphy, Mark	S	6-4	210	7
21	Nelms, Mike	WR-KR	6-1	184	4
52	Olkewicz, Neal	LB	6-0	233	5
44	Riggins, John	RB	6-2	235	12
80	Seay, Virgil	WR-KR	5-9	175	3
60	Simmons, Roy	G	6-3	264	4
74	Starke, George	T	6-5	260	11
7	Theismann, Joe	QB	6-0	198	10
88	Walker, Rick	TE	6-4	235	7
85	Warren, Don	TE	6-4	242	5
24	Washington, Anthony	CB	6-1	204	3
25	Washington, Joe	RB	5-10	179	7
47	Williams, Greg	S	5-11	185	2
84	Williams, Mike	TE	6-4	251	2
39	Wonsley, Otis	RB	5-10	214	3

LOS ANGELES RAIDERS

No.	Name	Pos.	Ht.	Wt.	Year
32	Allen, Marcus	RB	6-2	210	2
77	Alzado, Lyle	DE	6-3	260	13
10	Bahr, Chris	K	5-10	175	8
56	Barnes, Jeff	LB	6-2	230	7
80	Barnwell, Malcolm	WR	5-11	185	3
21	Branch, Cliff	WR	5-11	170	12
54	Byrd, Darryl	LB	6-1	220	R
57	Caldwell, Tony	LB	6-1	225	R
46	Christensen, Todd	TE	6-3	230	5
50	Dalby, Dave	C	6-3	250	12
79	Davis, Bruce	T	6-6	280	4
45	Davis, James	CB	6-0	190	2
36	Davis, Mike	S	6-3	205	6
8	Guy, Ray	P	6-3	190	11
73	Hannah, Charley	G	6-5	260	7
87	Hasselbeck, Don	TE	6-7	240	7
27	Hawkins, Frank	RB	5-9	210	3
37	Hayes, Lester	CB	6-0	200	7
22	Haynes, Mike	CB	6-2	190	8
83	Hendricks, Ted	LB	6-7	235	15
48	Hill, Kenny	S	6-0	195	3
11	Humm, David	QB	6-2	195	9
31	Jensen, Derrick	TE	6-1	220	5
64	Jordan, Shelby	T	6-7	285	7
33	King, Kenny	RB	5-11	205	5
62	Kinlaw, Reggie	NT	6-2	245	4
70	Lawrence, Henry	T	6-4	270	10
75	Long, Howie	DE	6-5	270	3
53	Martin, Rod	LB	6-2	225	7
65	Marvin, Mickey	G	6-4	265	7
26	McElroy, Vann	S	6-2	190	2
23	McKinney, Odis	S	6-2	190	6
55	Millen, Matt	LB	6-2	250	4
28	Montgomery, Cle	WR-KR	5-8	180	4
72	Mosebar, Don	G	6-6	265	R
82	Muhammad, Calvin	WR	5-11	190	2
51	Nelson, Bob	LB	6-4	235	6
71	Pickel, Bill	DE	6-5	260	R
16	Plunkett, Jim	QB	6-2	215	13
34	Pruitt, Greg	RB-KR	5-10	190	11
68	Robinson, Johnny	NT	6-2	260	3
58	Squirek, Jack	LB	6-4	225	2
61	Stalls, Dave	NT	6-4	250	7
66	Sylvester, Steve	C-G	6-4	260	9
93	Townsend, Greg	DE	6-3	240	R
20	Watts, Ted	CB	6-0	195	3
85	Williams, Dokie	WR	5-11	180	R
38	Willis, Chester	RB	5-11	195	3
6	Wilson, Marc	QB	6-6	205	4

SUPER BOWL XIX

SAN FRANCISCO 38, MIAMI 16

Joe Montana outdueled his more heralded counterpart, Dan Marino, and the San Francisco defense dominated a one-dimensional Miami offense, as the 49ers overran the Dolphins 38-16 to win their second Super Bowl in four years.

Going into the game, Miami's offense looked unstoppable behind the record-setting Marino, and the early stages of the contest gave no indication otherwise. After holding the 49ers on the game's initial possession, the Dolphins took over at the Miami 36. Marino completed four of five passes to set up a 37-yard field goal by Uwe von Schamann.

The 49ers counterpunched immediately. Montana nickeled-and-dimed his way to third and seven at the Miami 48. He then flashed the major difference between him and Marino when he ran 15 yards for a first down. On the next play, Montana hit Carl Monroe for a touchdown, giving the 49ers a 7-3 lead.

Miami quickly engineered its most effective drive of the day. Going without a huddle, Marino drove his team 70 yards in six plays, including five completions in a row, the last a two-yard touchdown to tight end Dan Johnson.

Yet, in a sense, Marino's lightning-quick strike helped undermine Miami's offense. It forced San Francisco head coach Bill Walsh to put in his elephant defense, a 4-2-5, in which Tom Holmoe became the Nickel back and rookie Jeff Fuller, in reality a defensive back, lined up at linebacker with Keena Turner to concentrate on short passes. It worked so well that Marino, who had completed 9 of 10 passes at the time, didn't complete another until after the two-minute warning, while the Dolphins' running game was totally shut down.

Early in the second quarter, the 49ers held Miami without a first down, and then, after a short punt by Reggie Roby, started a drive from Miami's 47. On first down, Montana ran 18 yards. He then passed 16 yards to Dwight Clark, and, two plays later, eight yards for a touchdown to Roger Craig.

The next four series were virtual replays. The Dolphins ran six plays netting only five yards. Meanwhile, the 49ers scored twice, on a six-yard run by Montana and a two-yard run by Craig, the latter giving them a 28-10 lead.

Facing a rout, the Dolphins scored two field goals in the last 12 seconds of the half, the second after San Francisco lineman Guy McIntyre fumbled a kickoff and Jim Jensen of Miami recovered.

But that was all for Miami. With Marino passing on almost every down in the second half, the 49ers turned loose their defensive line, which sacked him four times, pressured him constantly, and helped force two interceptions.

The 49ers, on the other hand, kept moving the ball relentlessly. Their first drive of the second half resulted in a 27-yard field goal by Ray Wersching. The second possession ended when Montana fired a 16-yard scoring pass to Craig, whose third touchdown of the day was a Super Bowl record. And in the fourth quarter, the 49ers mounted a 13-play, 78-yard drive that consumed almost eight minutes and wasn't stopped until Miami's defense held at its 2.

The result of San Francisco's offensive juggernaut was a game-record 537 yards. The key was Montana, the game's most valuable player, who completed 24 of 35 passes for a record 331 yards and also totaled 59 yards rushing, a record for quarterbacks.

"All week, all we heard was, 'Miami, Miami, Miami,'" Montana said. "That motivated us. We felt we had more tools than Miami—passing, running, a great defense—and we wanted to prove it."

Date—January 20, 1985
Site—Stanford Stadium, Stanford, California
Time—3:00 P.M. PST
Conditions—53 degrees, clearing fog
Playing Surface—Grass
Television—American Broadcasting Corporation (ABC)
Radio—Columbia Broadcasting System (CBS)
Regular Season Records—Miami, 14-2, San Francisco, 15-1
Conference Championships—Miami defeated the Pittsburgh Steelers 45-28 for the AFC title; San Francisco defeated the Chicago Bears 23-0 for the NFC title
Players' Shares—$36,000 to each member of the winning team; $18,000 to each member of the losing team
Attendance—84,059
Gross Receipts—$20,995,324.00
Officials—Referee, Pat Haggerty; umpire, Tom Hensley; line judge, Ray Dodez; head linesman, Leo Miles; back judge, Tom Kelleher; side judge, Bill Quinby; field judge, Bob Lewis
Coaches—Don Shula, Miami, Bill Walsh, San Francisco

Miami	Starters, Offense	San Francisco
Mark Duper	WR	Dwight Clark
Jon Giesler	LT	Bubba Paris
Roy Foster	LG	John Ayers
Dwight Stephenson	C	Fred Quillan
Ed Newman	RG	Randy Cross
Cleveland Green	RT	Keith Fahnhorst
Bruce Hardy	TE	Russ Francis
Mark Clayton	WR	Freddie Solomon
Dan Marino	QB	Joe Montana
Woody Bennett	RB	Roger Craig
Tony Nathan	RB	Wendell Tyler
	Starters, Defense	
Doug Betters	LE	Lawrence Pillers
Bob Baumhower	NT	Manu Tuiasosopo
Kim Bokamper	RE	Dwaine Board
Bob Brudzinski	LOLB	Dan Bunz
Jay Brophy	LILB	Riki Ellison
Mark Brown	RILB	Jack Reynolds
Charles Bowser	ROLB	Keena Turner
Don McNeal	LCB	Ronnie Lott
William Judson	RCB	Eric Wright
Glenn Blackwood	SS	Carlton Williamson
Lyle Blackwood	FS	Dwight Hicks

Miami	10	6	0	0	—	16
San Francisco	7	21	10	0	—	38

Mia—FG von Schamann 37
SF —Monroe 33 pass from Montana (Wersching kick)
Mia—D. Johnson 2 pass from Marino (von Schamann kick)
SF —Craig 8 pass from Montana (Wersching kick)
SF —Montana 6 run (Wersching kick)
SF —Craig 2 run (Wersching kick)
Mia—FG von Schamann 31
Mia—FG von Schamann 30
SF —FG Wersching 27
SF —Craig 16 pass from Montana (Wersching kick)

TEAM STATISTICS	Mia	SF
First downs	19	31
Rushing	2	16
Passing	17	15
By penalty	0	0
Total yardage	314	537
Net rushing yardage	25	211
Net passing yardage	289	326
Passes att.-comp.-had int.	50-29-2	35-24-0

RUSHING
Miami—Nathan, 5 for 18; Bennett, 3 for 7; Marino, 1 for 0.
San Francisco—Tyler, 13 for 65; Montana, 5 for 59, 1 TD; Craig, 15 for 58, 1 TD; Harmon, 5 for 20; Solomon, 1 for 5; Cooper, 1 for 4.

PASSING
Miami—Marino, 29 of 50 for 318, 1 TD, 2 int.
San Francisco—Montana, 24 of 35 for 331, 3 TDs.

RECEIVING
Miami—Nathan, 10 for 83; Clayton, 6 for 92; Rose, 6 for 73; D. Johnson, 3 for 28, 1 TD; Moore, 2 for 17; Cefalo, 1 for 14; Duper, 1 for 11.
San Francisco—Craig, 7 for 77, 2 TDs; D. Clark, 6 for 77; Francis, 5 for 60; Tyler, 4 for 70; Monroe, 1 for 33, 1 TD; Solomon, 1 for 14.

PUNTING
Miami—Roby, 6 for 236, 39.3 average.
San Francisco—Runager, 3 for 98, 32.7 average.

PUNT RETURNS
Miami—Walker, 2 for 15.
San Francisco—McLemore, 5 for 51.

KICKOFF RETURNS
Miami—Walker, 4 for 93; Hardy, 2 for 31; Hill, 1 for 16.
San Francisco—Harmon, 2 for 24; Monroe, 1 for 16; McIntyre, 1 for 0.

INTERCEPTIONS
Miami—None.
San Francisco—Williamson, 1 for 0; Wright, 1 for 0.

MIAMI DOLPHINS

No.	Name	Pos.	Ht.	Wt.	Year
70	Barnett, Bill	NT-DE	6-4	260	5
73	Baumhower, Bob	NT	6-5	265	8
34	Bennett, Woody	RB	6-2	225	7
78	Benson, Charles	DE	6-3	267	2
75	Betters, Doug	DE	6-7	265	7
47	Blackwood, Glenn	S	6-0	190	6
42	Blackwood, Lyle	S	6-1	190	12
58	Bokamper, Kim	DE	6-6	255	8
56	Bowser, Charles	LB	6-3	235	3
53	Brophy, Jay	LB	6-3	233	R
43	Brown, Bud	S	6-0	194	R
51	Brown, Mark	LB	6-2	225	2
59	Brudzinski, Bob	LB	6-4	223	8
23	Carter, Joe	RB	5-11	198	R
81	Cefalo, Jimmy	WR	5-11	188	6
71	Charles, Mike	DE	6-4	283	2
76	Clark, Steve	G	6-4	255	3
83	Clayton, Mark	WR	5-9	175	2
77	Duhe, A.J.	LB	6-4	235	8
85	Duper, Mark	WR	5-9	187	3
61	Foster, Roy	G	6-4	275	3
79	Giesler, Jon	T	6-5	260	6
74	Green, Cleveland	T	6-3	262	6
84	Hardy, Bruce	TE	6-5	232	7
88	Heflin, Vince	WR	6-0	185	3
31	Hill, Eddie	RB	6-2	210	6
11	Jensen, Jim	WR	6-4	215	4
87	Johnson, Dan	TE	6-3	240	3
46	Johnson, Pete	RB	6-0	250	8
49	Judson, William	CB	6-1	190	3
40	Kozlowski, Mike	S	6-1	198	5
44	Lankford, Paul	CB-S	6-2	184	3
72	Lee, Ronnie	T	6-4	265	6
13	Marino, Dan	QB	6-4	214	2
28	McNeal, Don	CB	5-11	192	4
89	Moore, Nat	WR	5-9	188	11
22	Nathan, Tony	RB	6-0	206	6
64	Newman, Ed	G	6-2	255	12
55	Rhone, Earnie	LB	6-2	224	9
4	Roby, Reggie	P	6-2	243	2
80	Rose, Joe	TE	6-3	230	5
50	Shipp, Jackie	LB	6-2	236	R
52	Shiver, Sanders	LB	6-2	235	9
45	Sowell, Robert	CB	5-11	175	2
57	Stephenson, Dwight	C	6-2	255	5
10	Strock, Don	QB	6-5	220	11
60	Toews, Jeff	G-C	6-3	255	6
5	von Schamann, Uwe	K	6-1	185	6
41	Walker, Fulton	CB	5-11	196	4

SAN FRANCISCO 49ERS

No.	Name	Pos.	Ht.	Wt.	Year
68	Ayers, John	G	6-5	265	8
76	Board, Dwaine	DE	6-5	248	5
57	Bunz, Dan	LB	6-4	225	6
95	Carter, Michael	NT	6-2	281	R
6	Cavanaugh, Matt	QB	6-2	212	7
87	Clark, Dwight	WR	6-4	215	6
29	Clark, Mario	CB	6-2	195	9
89	Cooper, Earl	TE	6-2	227	5
33	Craig, Roger	RB	6-0	222	2
51	Cross, Randy	G	6-3	265	9
74	Dean, Fred	DE	6-2	232	10
50	Ellison, Riki	LB	6-2	220	2
71	Fahnhorst, Keith	T	6-6	273	11
81	Francis, Russ	TE	6-6	242	9
86	Frank, John	TE	6-3	225	R
49	Fuller, Jeff	S	6-2	216	R
24	Harmon, Derrick	RB	5-10	202	R
22	Hicks, Dwight	S-CB	6-1	192	6
28	Holmoe, Tom	S	6-2	180	2
97	Johnson, Gary	DE	6-2	261	10
94	Kelcher, Louie	NT	6-5	310	10
66	Kennedy, Allan	T	6-7	275	3
42	Lott, Ronnie	CB-S	6-0	199	4
53	McColl, Milt	LB	6-6	230	4
62	McIntyre, Guy	G	6-3	271	R
43	McLemore, Dana	CB-KR	5-10	183	3
32	Monroe, Carl	RB-KR	5-8	166	2
16	Montana, Joe	QB	6-2	195	6
52	Montgomery, Blanchard	LB	6-2	236	2
83	Nehemiah, Renaldo	WR	6-1	183	3
77	Paris, Bubba	T	6-6	295	2
65	Pillers, Lawrence	DE	6-4	250	9
56	Quillan, Fred	C	6-5	266	7
64	Reynolds, Jack	LB	6-1	232	15
30	Ring, Bill	RB	5-10	205	4
4	Runager, Max	P	6-1	189	6
90	Shell, Todd	LB	6-4	225	R
67	Shields, Billy	T	6-8	279	10
88	Solomon, Freddie	WR	5-11	188	10
72	Stover, Jeff	DE	6-5	275	3
79	Stuckey, Jim	DE	6-4	253	5
78	Tuiasosopo, Manu	NT	6-3	252	6
58	Turner, Keena	LB	6-2	219	5
26	Tyler, Wendell	RB	5-10	200	7
99	Walters, Mike	LB	6-3	238	2
14	Wersching, Ray	K	5-11	210	12
27	Williamson, Carlton	S	6-0	204	4
85	Wilson, Mike	WR	6-3	210	4
21	Wright, Eric	CB	6-1	180	4

SUPER BOWL XX

CHI. BEARS 46, NEW ENGLAND 10

The Chicago defense forced six turnovers, returned one interception for a touchdown, scored a safety, and held the New England Patriots to 123 total yards and a record-low seven yards rushing, as the Bears recorded a 46-10 victory, the most lopsided score in Super Bowl history.

In a game that matched two outstanding defenses, the Bears proved superior; the Patriots couldn't stop Chicago's offense, which accounted for 408 yards and four long scoring drives.

The Patriots scored first, following Don Blackmon's recovery of Walter Payton's fumble on the second play of the game. The turnover gave New England the ball on the Chicago 19, but three incomplete passes led to a fourth and 10 and a 36-yard field goal by Tony Franklin.

The Bears came right back. On second and 10 at the 31, Jim McMahon completed a 43-yard pass to Willie Gault. Two runs by Matt Suhey picked up another first down, and, three plays later, Kevin Butler tied the score with a 28-yard field goal.

Two turnovers late in the first quarter helped put the Bears in charge of the game. First, Chicago defensive end Richard Dent, later named the game's most valuable player, sacked New England quarterback Tony Eason, who fumbled the ball away at his own 13. Butler kicked a 24-yard field goal for a 6-3 lead. On New England's first play after the kickoff, Craig James fumbled and Mike Singletary recovered at the Patriots' 13. On second down, Suhey blasted 11 yards for a touchdown.

In the second quarter, the Bears continued their domination on both sides of the line of scrimmage. McMahon scored from the 2 to cap a 10-play, 59-yard drive that built a 20-3 lead. Two series later, New England head coach Raymond Berry replaced an ineffective Eason with Steve Grogan. Eason had been zero-for-six passing, while being sacked three times. The Bears ended the half with an 11-play, 72-yard drive culminated by Butler's 24-yard field goal.

The halftime statistics provided ample proof of the Bears' effectiveness. They led in first downs 13 to 1, in rushing yards 92 to minus-5, in passing yards 144 to minus-14, and in total yards 236 to minus-19.

The Bears ended any lingering hopes the Patriots might have had the first time they touched the ball in the second half. With a first and 10 from his own 4-yard line following a punt, McMahon passed 60 yards to Gault. Eight plays later, McMahon sneaked over from the 1 for a 30-3 lead.

Three plays later, the Bears' defense got into the act again. Reserve cornerback Reggie Phillips intercepted Grogan's pass for tight end Derrick Ramsey and returned it 28 yards for a touchdown.

On New England's second play after the kickoff, Stanley Morgan fumbled after making a reception, and linebacker Wilber Marshall recovered, returning the ball to New England's 31. Three runs by Payton and a 27-yard pass from McMahon to Dennis Gentry gave the Bears a first-and-goal at the 1. Then came the moment America had been waiting for. Defensive tackle William (The Refrigerator) Perry was inserted at running back and banged into the end zone for a 44-3 lead.

The Patriots opened the fourth quarter with their only sustained drive of the day, 12 plays for 76 yards, capped by an eight-yard touchdown pass from Grogan to Irving Fryar. But the Bears had one final humiliation left for the Patriots. With four minutes left in the game, reserve defensive tackle Henry Waechter sacked Grogan in the end zone for a safety and the final 46-10 margin.

Date—January 26, 1986
Site—Louisiana Superdome, New Orleans
Time—4:20 P.M. CST
Conditions—70 degrees, indoors
Playing Surface—AstroTurf
Television and Radio—National Broadcasting Company (NBC)
Regular Season Records—New England, 11-5; Chi. Bears, 15-1
Conference Championships—New England defeated the Miami Dolphins 31-14 for the AFC title; Chi. Bears defeated the Los Angeles Rams 24-0 for the NFC title
Players' Shares—$36,000 to each member of the winning team; $18,000 to each member of the losing team
Attendance—73,818
Gross Receipts—$23,850,000.00
Officials—Referee, Red Cashion; umpire, Ron Botchan; line judge, Bama Glass; head linesman, Dale Williams; back judge, Al Jury; side judge, Bob Rice; field judge, Jack Vaughan
Coaches—Raymond Berry, New England; Mike Ditka, Chi. Bears

Chi. Bears	Starters, Offense	New England
Willie Gault	WR	Stanley Morgan
Jim Covert	LT	Brian Holloway
Mark Bortz	LG	John Hannah
Jay Hilgenberg	C	Pete Brock
Tom Thayer	RG	Ron Wooten
Keith Van Horne	RT	Steve Moore
Emery Moorehead	TE	Lin Dawson
Dennis McKinnon	WR	Stephen Starring
Jim McMahon	QB	Tony Eason
Matt Suhey	RB	Craig James
Walter Payton	RB	Tony Collins
	Starters, Defense	
Dan Hampton	LE	Garin Veris
Steve McMichael	LT-NT	Lester Williams
William Perry	RT-RE	Julius Adams
Richard Dent	RE-LOLB	Andre Tippett
Otis Wilson	LLB-LILB	Steve Nelson
Mike Singletary	MLB-RILB	Larry McGrew
Wilber Marshall	RLB-ROLB	Don Blackmon
Mike Richardson	LCB	Ronnie Lippett
Leslie Frazier	RCB	Raymond Clayborn
Dave Duerson	SS	Roland James
Gary Fencik	FS	Fred Marion

Chi. Bears	13	10	21	2	—	46
New England	3	0	0	7		10

NE —FG Franklin 36
ChiB—FG Butler 28
ChiB—FG Butler 24
ChiB—Suhey 11 run (Butler kick)
ChiB—McMahon 2 run (Butler kick)
ChiB—FG Butler 24
ChiB—McMahon 1 run (Butler kick)
ChiB—Phillips 28 interception return (Butler kick)
ChiB—Perry 1 run (Butler kick)
NE —Fryar 8 pass from Grogan (Franklin kick)
ChiB—Safety, Waechter tackled Grogan in end zone

TEAM STATISTICS	ChiB	NE
First downs	23	12
Rushing	13	1
Passing	9	10
By penalty	1	1
Total yardage	408	123
Net rushing yardage	167	7
Net passing yardage	241	116
Passes att.-comp.-had int.	24-12-0	36-17-2

RUSHING
Chi. Bears—Payton, 22 for 61; Suhey, 11 for 52, 1 TD; Gentry, 3 for 15; Sanders, 4 for 15; McMahon, 5 for 14, 2 TDs; Thomas, 2 for 8; Perry, 1 for 1, 1 TD; Fuller, 1 for 1.
New England—Collins, 3 for 4; Weathers, 1 for 3; Grogan, 1 for 3; C. James, 5 for 1; Hawthorne, 1 for -4.

PASSING
Chi. Bears—McMahon, 12 of 20 for 256; Fuller, 0 of 4.
New England—Grogan, 17 of 30 for 177, 1 TD, 2 int.; Eason, 0 of 6 for 0.

RECEIVING
Chi. Bears—Gault, 4 for 129; Gentry, 2 for 41; Margerum, 2 for 36; Moorehead, 2 for 22; Suhey, 1 for 24; Thomas, 1 for 4.
New England—Morgan, 7 for 70; Starring, 2 for 39; Fryar, 2 for 24, 1 TD; Collins, 2 for 19; Ramsey, 2 for 16; C. James, 1 for 6; Weathers, 1 for 3.

PUNTING
Chi. Bears—Buford, 4 for 173, 43.3 average.
New England—Camarillo, 6 for 263, 43.8 average.

PUNT RETURNS
Chi. Bears—Ortego, 2 for 20, 1 fair catch.
New England—Fryar, 2 for 22.

KICKOFF RETURNS
Chi. Bears—Gault, 4 for 49.
New England—Starring, 7 for 153.

INTERCEPTIONS
Chi. Bears—Morrissey, 1 for 47; Phillips, 1 for 28, 1 TD.
New England—None.

CHICAGO BEARS

No.	Name	Pos.	Ht.	Wt.	Year
60	Andrews, Tom	C	6-4	267	2
62	Bortz, Mark	G	6-6	269	3
8	Buford, Maury	P	6-1	191	4
6	Butler, Kevin	K	6-1	204	R
54	Cabral, Brian	LB	6-1	224	7
74	Covert, Jim	T	6-4	271	3
95	Dent, Richard	DE	6-5	263	3
22	Duerson, Dave	S	6-1	203	3
45	Fencik, Gary	S	6-1	196	10
21	Frazier, Leslie	CB	6-0	187	5
71	Frederick, Andy	T	6-6	265	9
4	Fuller, Steve	QB	6-4	195	7
83	Gault, Willie	WR	6-1	183	3
23	Gayle, Shaun	CB	5-11	193	2
29	Gentry, Dennis	RB	5-8	181	4
99	Hampton, Dan	DE-DT	6-5	267	7
73	Hartenstine, Mike	DE	6-3	254	11
63	Hilgenberg, Jay	C	6-3	258	5
75	Humphries, Stefan	G	6-3	263	2
98	Keys, Tyrone	DE	6-7	267	3
82	Margerum, Ken	WR	6-0	180	4
58	Marshall, Wilber	LB	6-1	225	2
85	McKinnon, Dennis	WR	6-1	185	3
9	McMahon, Jim	QB	6-1	190	4
76	McMichael, Steve	DT	6-2	260	6
87	Moorehead, Emery	TE	6-2	220	9
51	Morrissey, Jim	LB	6-3	215	R
89	Ortego, Keith	WR	6-0	180	R
34	Payton, Walter	RB	5-10	202	11
72	Perry, William	DT	6-2	308	R
48	Phillips, Reggie	CB	5-10	170	R
27	Richardson, Mike	CB	6-0	188	3
59	Rivera, Ron	LB	6-3	239	2
20	Sanders, Thomas	RB	5-11	203	R
50	Singletary, Mike	LB	6-0	228	5
26	Suhey, Matt	RB	5-11	216	6
31	Taylor, Ken	CB	6-1	185	R
57	Thayer, Tom	G-C	6-4	261	R
33	Thomas, Calvin	RB	5-11	245	4
52	Thrift, Cliff	LB	6-1	230	7
18	Tomczak, Mike	QB	6-1	195	R
78	Van Horne, Keith	T	6-6	280	5
70	Waechter, Henry	DT	6-5	275	4
55	Wilson, Otis	LB	6-2	232	6
80	Wrightman, Tim	TE	6-3	237	R

NEW ENGLAND PATRIOTS

No.	Name	Pos.	Ht.	Wt.	Year
85	Adams, Julius	DE	6-3	270	14
55	Blackmon, Don	LB	6-3	235	5
28	Bowman, Jim	S	6-2	210	R
58	Brock, Pete	C	6-5	275	10
3	Camarillo, Rich	P	5-11	185	5
26	Clayborn, Raymond	CB	6-0	186	9
33	Collins, Tony	RB	5-11	212	5
92	Creswell, Smiley	DE	6-4	251	1
87	Dawson, Lin	TE	6-3	240	5
11	Eason, Tony	QB	6-4	212	3
66	Fairchild, Paul	G	6-4	270	2
1	Franklin, Tony	K	5-8	182	7
80	Fryar, Irving	WR-KR	6-0	200	2
43	Gibson, Ernest	CB	5-10	185	2
14	Grogan, Steve	QB	6-4	210	11
73	Hannah, John	G	6-3	265	13
27	Hawthorne, Greg	WR-RB	6-2	225	7
76	Holloway, Brian	T	6-7	288	5
51	Ingram, Brian	LB	6-4	235	4
32	James, Craig	RB	6-0	215	2
38	James, Roland	S	6-2	191	6
83	Jones, Cedric	WR	6-1	184	4
42	Lippett, Ronnie	CB	5-11	180	3
31	Marion, Fred	S	6-2	191	4
50	McGrew, Larry	LB	6-5	233	5
23	McSwain, Rod	CB	6-1	198	2
67	Moore, Steve	T	6-4	285	3
86	Morgan, Stanley	WR	5-11	181	9
75	Morriss, Guy	C-G	6-4	255	13
57	Nelson, Steve	LB	6-2	230	12
98	Owens, Dennis	NT	6-1	258	4
70	Plunkett, Art	T	6-7	260	5
88	Ramsey, Derrick	TE	6-5	235	8
12	Ramsey, Tom	QB	6-1	189	1
52	Rembert, Johnny	LB	6-3	234	3
95	Reynolds, Ed	LB	6-5	230	3
81	Starring, Stephen	WR-KR	5-10	172	3
30	Tatupu, Mosi	RB	6-0	227	8
99	Thomas, Ben	DE	6-4	280	R
56	Tippett, Andre	LB	6-3	241	4
60	Veris, Garin	DE	6-4	255	R
24	Weathers, Robert	RB	6-2	222	4
54	Williams, Ed	LB	6-4	244	2
72	Williams, Lester	NT	6-3	272	4
61	Wooten, Ron	G	6-4	273	4

Championship Games

1932

CHI. BEARS 9, PORTSMOUTH 0

In each of the NFL's first 12 years, the league champion was the team that finished the schedule with the best winning percentage. In 1932, two teams tied for the first time. Although they had different overall records, the Chicago Bears (6-1-6) and the Portsmouth Spartans (6-1-4) both had winning percentages of .857. Immediately after the Bears' season-ending victory over the Green Bay Packers, the league office arranged a championship playoff to be held at Chicago's Wrigley Field one week later.

The Bears-Packers game had been played in the snow, so good weather wasn't expected for the championship. But the continuing heavy snow and the bitter cold, which got worse as the week progressed, convinced George Halas to move the game indoors to Chicago Stadium.

The trappings for the first championship game were unusual. A circus had just left the stadium, and the floors were covered with a layer of dirt. There was only room for an 80-yard field, which was surrounded by a fence three feet from each sideline.

The cramped quarters resulted in several rules alterations for the game. Each time a team crossed midfield, it was penalized 20 yards, in effect making the field 100 yards long. The goal posts were moved from the end line to the goal line, and the end zones were not of regulation size. Inbounds lines were created, and each time the ball was carried out of bounds, instead of being placed where it went out, it was returned to the inbounds lines for the next play.

The Bears entered the game at full strength, but the Spartans didn't. Portsmouth quarterback Earl (Dutch) Clark already had left the team for his off-season job as basketball coach at Colorado College and couldn't make it back in time for the game. He was replaced by Glenn Presnell.

For three quarters, neither team could score, and it looked as if the championship game, like the two times the teams had met in the regular season, might end in a tie.

Early in the fourth quarter, Chicago's Dick Nesbitt intercepted a pass by Leroy (Ace) Gutowsky at the Portsmouth 23-yard line and returned it to the 13. On first down, Bronko Nagurski carried the ball to the 7. On the next play, he took it to the 2. Several plays later, with the ball still on the 2, quarterback Carl Brumbaugh handed off to Nagurski, who faked a plunge into the line, backed up two steps, and fired a pass to Red Grange in the end zone.

The rules of pro football at the time stated that passes had to be thrown from at least five yards behind the line of scrimmage. Angry Portsmouth coach George (Potsy) Clark screamed that Nagurski's pass broke this rule. But his words fell on deaf ears.

Shortly before the end of the game, the Bears added a safety to win 9-0.

December 18, at Chicago

Chi. Bears	Starting Lineups	Portsmouth
Bill Hewitt	LE	Bill McKalip
Lloyd Burdick	LT	Ray Davis
Jules (Zuck) Carlson	LG	Maury Rodenger
Charles (Ookie) Miller	C	Clare Randolph
Joe Kopcha	RG	Grover (Ox) Emerson
Paul (Tiny) Engebretsen	RT	George Christensen
Luke Johnsos	RE	Harry Ebding
Keith Molesworth	QB	Roy Lumpkin
Red Grange	LH	Glenn Presnell
Dick Nesbitt	RH	Johnny Cavosie
Bronko Nagurski	FB	Leroy (Ace) Gutowsky

Chi. Bears	0	0	0	9	—	9
Portsmouth	0	0	0	0	—	0

ChiB—Grange 2 pass from Nagurski (Engebretsen kick)
ChiB—Safety, Wilson tackled in end zone
Attendance—11,198

1933

CHI. BEARS 23, NY GIANTS 21

In the first playoff game between the champions of the two new divisions, the Chicago Bears came from behind in the final three minutes to defeat the New York Giants 23-21. The Bears represented the Western Division and had compiled the best winning percentage (.833) in the NFL, while the Giants, the Eastern Division champs, had the most victories (11) in the NFL.

The Bears, trailing 7-6 at the half, 14-9 in the third quarter, and 21-16 in the fourth quarter, went ahead for the last time after the Giants' Ken Strong punted eight yards and Chicago took over on New York's 46-yard line. Keith Molesworth passed nine yards to Carl Brumbaugh. Bronko Nagurski, the Bears' leading rusher with 14 carries for 65 yards, gained four yards to the 33. On the next play, Nagurski threw a jump pass to Bill Hewitt. Hewitt gained 14 yards and lateraled to Bill Karr, who covered the remaining 19 yards for the winning score.

Fog hung over Wrigley Field and it misted in the first half, as both teams moved efficiently but scored very little. The Bears went ahead 6-0 on two field goals by Jack Manders. The Giants, who moved mainly through the air, took a 7-6 lead on Harry Newman's 29-yard touchdown pass to Morris (Red) Badgro and Strong's extra point.

In the third quarter, the Bears took the lead again on the third field goal of the day by Manders, who had kicked only five all season. The Giants came right back with a 61-yard drive for a score, and the Bears regained the lead after a six-play drive capped by Nagurski's first touchdown pass to Karr.

Newman, who completed 12 of 17 passes for 201 yards and two touchdowns, figured in the game's most exciting play on the first play of the fourth quarter. Newman began moving the Giants from their 26-yard line. Five successive pass completions put the ball on the Bears' 8. Strong took a handoff on the next play but became trapped near the sideline. He lateraled to the surprised Newman, who scrambled until he was trapped at the 15. Newman then threw a desperation pass to Strong, who had slipped free in the corner of the end zone and caught the ball for a touchdown.

December 17, at Chicago

NY Giants	Starting Lineups	Chi. Bears
Morris (Red) Badgro	LE	Bill Hewitt
Len Grant	LT	Roy (Link) Lyman
Denver (Butch) Gibson	LG	Jules Carlson
Mel Hein	C	Charles (Ookie) Miller
Tom (Pottsville) Jones	RG	Joe Kopcha
Steve Owen	RT	George Musso
Ray Flaherty	RE	Bill Karr
Harry Newman	QB	Carl Brumbaugh
Ken Strong	LH	Keith Molesworth
Dale Burnett	RH	Gene Ronzani
Bo Molenda	FB	Bronko Nagurski

NY. Giants	0	7	7	7	—	21
Chi. Bears	3	3	10	7	—	23

ChiB—FG Manders 16
ChiB—FG Manders 40
NYG—Badgro 29 pass from Newman (Strong kick)
ChiB—FG Manders 28
NYG—Krause 1 run (Strong kick)
ChiB—Karr 8 pass from Nagurski (Manders kick)
NYG—Strong 8 pass from Newman (Strong kick)
ChiB—Karr 19 lateral from Hewitt, who caught 14 pass from Nagurski (Brumbaugh kick)
Attendance—26,000

TEAM STATISTICS	NYG	ChiB
First downs	13	12
Rushing	4	9
Passing	8	3
By penalty	1	0
Total yardage	307	311
Net rushing yardage	99	161
Net passing yardage	208	150
Passes att.-comp.-had int.	20-14-1	16-7-1

1934

NY GIANTS 30, CHI. BEARS 13

In a rematch of the teams in the 1933 NFL Championship Game, the New York Giants rallied for 27 points in the fourth quarter to overcome a 13-3 Chicago lead and score a 30-13 victory in what has come to be known as the "Sneakers Game."

Although the Bears had recorded the best record in league history (13-0) and a late-season collapse had left the Giants with five losses and barely in control of the Eastern Division, the difference between the two teams wasn't as great as during the regular season, when the Bears twice defeated the Giants. Chicago entered the game without the services of Beattie Feathers, the NFL's first 1,000-yard rusher, and star guard Joe Kopcha. Moreover, an overnight freezing rain had turned the field into a sheet of ice, which would hurt the Bears' ground-oriented team more than the Giants' passing offense.

Giants' president John V. Mara inspected the playing field the morning of the game and reported the condition to head coach Steve Owen. The temperature was nine degrees. Owen and team captain Ray Flaherty discussed the idea of wearing basketball shoes. Some of the Giants' players were asked to bring their own sneakers to the game. Abe Cohen, a clubhouse equipment aide, made a trip to Manhattan College for additional pairs. There were no sporting goods stores open.

The Giants did not put on the rubber-soled shoes until the start of the third quarter. They trailed 10-3 at the half and fell behind 13-3 in the third quarter. The comeback did not begin until well into the final period. Rookie Ed Danowski, a midseason replacement for the injured Harry Newman at tailback in the Giants' Single-Wing formation, threw a 28-yard touchdown pass to Ike Frankian to make the score 13-10. The Bears did not advance on their next possession and, after a 20-yard punt, the Giants took over on Chicago's 42. Ken Strong, behind blocking from tackle Bill Morgan, fullback Bo Molenda, and Danowski, ran straight up the field for a touchdown to give New York a 17-13 lead. Shortly thereafter, Strong scored again, on an 11-yard run, and then Danowski kept around right end for a nine-yard touchdown and the final margin.

December 9, at New York

Chi. Bears	Starting Lineups	NY Giants
Bill Hewitt	LE	Ike Frankian
Roy (Link) Lyman	LT	Bill Morgan
Bert Pearson	LG	Denver (Butch) Gibson
Ed Kawal	C	Mel Hein
Jules Carlson	RG	Tom (Pottsville) Jones
George Musso	RT	Cecil (Tex) Irvin
Bill Karr	RE	Ray Flaherty
Carl Brumbaugh	QB	Ed Danowski
Gene Ronzani	LH	Dale Burnett
Keith Molesworth	RH	Ken Strong
Bronko Nagurski	FB	Bo Molenda

Chi. Bears	0	10	3	0	—	13
NY Giants	3	0	0	27	—	30

NYG—FG Strong 38
ChiB—Nagurski 1 run (Manders kick)
ChiB—FG Manders 17
ChiB—FG Manders 24
NYG—Frankian 28 pass from Danowski (Strong kick)
NYG—Strong 42 run (Strong kick)
NYG—Strong 11 run (kick failed)
NYG—Danowski 9 run (Molenda kick)
Attendance—35,059

TEAM STATISTICS	ChiB	NYG
First downs	10	12
Rushing	7	7
Passing	3	5
By penalty	0	0
Total yardage	169	282
Net rushing yardage	93	170
Net passing yardage	76	112
Passes att.-comp.-had int.	13-6-3	13-7-2

1935

DETROIT 26, NY GIANTS 7

The Detroit Lions took the opening kickoff, marched 61 yards to a touchdown, and never trailed the New York Giants on a day when wind, rain, sleet, and snow turned the University of Detroit field into a virtual swamp. The weather was especially merciless on the Giants, who relied on a passing game, while giving an advantage to run-oriented Detroit. The Lions' 26-7 victory marked their first NFL championship and it came two months after the baseball Tigers had won their first World Series.

The Lions scored on the opening series of the game. Helped by two long completed passes, Detroit's only two of the game, the Lions drove 61 yards to Leroy (Ace) Gutowsky's 2-yard touchdown run. New York responded with a drive of its own, but Ken Strong missed a 34-yard field goal and the Lions took over. Even more costly to the Giants was the loss of Tod Goodwin, the NFL's leading receiver, who suffered two broken ribs making a catch on the drive. Even a fumble recovery immediately after the missed field goal didn't help the Giants, who were held on downs.

Earl (Dutch) Clark increased the Lions' lead to 13-0 in the first period with a twisting run of 40 yards. The Giants did not score until midway through the second quarter, when Ed Danowski threw a pass to Strong. Gutowsky, who was defending on the play, deflected the ball with his fingertips, but Strong gained control and ran 31 yards to complete a 42-yard scoring play.

The Giants threatened to score several times early in the fourth quarter, but each time fell just short. With three minutes left in the game, Danowski tried a quick-kick, but the kick was low and hit the back of one of the Giants' blockers. Detroit's George Christiansen recovered on New York's 26-yard line. The Lions ran five plays into the line. On the sixth, from the 4-yard line, Clark faked into the middle and Ernie Caddel swept around the drawn-in defense for a touchdown.

Harry Newman returned the kickoff to the Giants' 32-yard line. Raymond (Buddy) Parker intercepted Danowski's pass in the flat on first down and ran 22 yards to the 10. Caddel ran four yards and Parker two before Parker scored on third down from the 4-yard line in the final seconds. Parker missed the extra point for a 26-7 final score.

December 15, at Detroit

NY Giants	Starting Lineups	Detroit
Ike Frankian	LE	Ed Klewicki
Bill Morgan	LT	John Johnson
Tom (Pottsville) Jones	LG	Regis Monahan
Mel Hein	C	Clare Randolph
Bill Owen	RG	Grover (Ox) Emerson
Len Grant	RT	George Christensen
Tod Goodwin	RE	John Schneller
Ed Danowski	QB	Glenn Presnell
Elvin (Kink) Richards	LH	Frank Christensen
Ken Strong	RH	Ernie Caddel
Les (Red) Corzine	FB	Leroy (Ace) Gutowsky

NY Giants	0	7	0	0	—	7
Detroit	13	0	0	13	—	26

Det —Gutowsky 2 run (Presnell kick)
Det —Clark 40 run (kick failed)
NYG—Strong 42 pass from Danowski (Strong kick)
Det —Caddel 4 run (Clark kick)
Det —Parker 4 run (kick failed)
Attendance—15,000

TEAM STATISTICS	NYG	Det
First downs	9	16
Rushing	4	14
Passing	3	2
By penalty	2	0
Total yardage	194	303
Net rushing yardage	106	235
Net passing yardage	88	68
Passes att.-comp.-had int.	13-4-2	5-2-0

1936

GREEN BAY 21, BOSTON 6

The Polo Grounds was the site of the championship game, although the participating teams were Green Bay and Boston. George Preston Marshall, the owner of the Redskins, moved the game from Boston to New York to show his contempt for what he considered Boston's poor support of his team. The Packers dominated the Redskins to win 21-6.

For the first time in the four-year history of the championship game, the weather was not severe. The temperature was 36 degrees and the sun was shining.

Boston's all-league halfback Cliff Battles, who gained 18 yards in his first two carries, was injured on the tenth play of the game. On that play, teammate Riley Smith fumbled Battles's lateral and Lou Gordon recovered for Green Bay on the Packers' 48-yard line. Three plays later Arnie Herber completed a 48-yard touchdown pass to Don Hutson on a sideline pattern.

Ernest (Pug) Rentner, the replacement for Battles, scored the Redskins' only touchdown on the first play of the second quarter. Rentner gained 18 yards on five carries and completed two passes for 41 yards in a 10-play, 78-yard drive that ended with him scoring from the 2. Riley Smith's conversion attempt was wide, however, and the Redskins still trailed 7-6.

Green Bay increased its lead to 14-6 in the third quarter on Herber's eight-yard pass to Milt Gantenbein. A 52-yard pass play—Herber to Johnny Blood (McNally)—set up the score.

The Packers' defense put the game away in the fourth quarter. Lon Evans blocked Riley Smith's punt on a play starting at Boston's 22-yard line. Clarke Hinkle recovered for the Packers on the 3-yard line. Bob Monnett, who was in the game for Herber, scored on the second play from the 2.

December 13, at New York

Green Bay	Starting Lineups	Boston
Milt Gantenbein	LE	Wayne Millner
Ernie Smith	LT	Glen (Turk) Edwards
Paul Engebretsen	LG	Les Olsson
George Svendsen	C	Frank Bausch
Lon Evans	RG	Jim Karcher
Lou Gordon	RT	Jim Barber
Don Hutson	RE	Charley Malone
Hank Bruder	QB	Riley Smith
George Sauer	LH	Cliff Battles
Arnie Herber	RH	Ed Justice
Clarke Hinkle	FB	Don Irwin

Green Bay	7	0	7	7	—	21
Boston	0	6	0	0	—	6

GB —Hutson 48 pass from Herber (E. Smith kick)
Bos—Rentner 2 run (kick failed)
GB —Gantenbein 8 pass from Herber (E. Smith kick)
GB —Monnett 2 run (Engebretsen kick)
Attendance—29,545

TEAM STATISTICS	GB	Bos
First downs	7	8
Rushing	2	4
Passing	4	3
By penalty	1	1
Total yardage	220	130
Net rushing yardage	67	39
Net passing yardage	153	91
Passes att.-comp.-had int.	23-9-2	26-7-1

RUSHING

Green Bay—Hinkle, 19 for 56; Sauer, 4 for 8; Blood (McNally), 2 for 8; Johnston, 2 for 4; Bruder, 1 for 0; Laws, 1 for 0; Herber, 2 for 0; Monnett, 12 for −2, 1 TD; Miller, 1 for −3.

Boston—Irwin, 13 for 37; Battles, 2 for 18; Rentner, 13 for 13, 1 TD; R. Smith, 5 for 0; Britt, 1 for −2.

PASSING

Green Bay—Herber, 6 of 15 for 140, 2 TDs, 1 int.; Monnett, 3 of 8 for 21, 1 int.

Boston—Rentner, 4 of 6 for 60; R. Smith, 2 of 13 for 21, 1 int.; Britt, 0 of 1; Pinckert, 0 of 1; E. Smith, 0 of 2.

RECEIVING

Green Bay—Hutson, 5 for 76, 1 TD; Blood (NcNally), 2 for 64; Gantenbein, 2 for 21, 1 TD.

Boston—Miller, 2 for 20; Justice, 1 for 32; Malone, 1 for 19; McChesney, 1 for 8; Irwin, 1 for 2.

1937

WASHINGTON 28, CHI. BEARS 21

Sammy Baugh completed 18 of 33 passes for 354 yards and three touchdowns, including scoring passes of 55, 78, and 35 yards in the third quarter as the Washington Redskins came from behind to defeat the Chicago Bears 28-21. Baugh's performance was achieved on an icy field in 15-degree weather.

Baugh, a rookie from TCU, established the Redskins' intentions on their first play from scrimmage. Passing from his own end zone, Baugh hit fullback Cliff Battles, who advanced the ball to Washington's 49, a gain of 42 yards. The Redskins were forced to punt, but the next time they had possession Baugh moved them 53 yards in 10 plays to a touchdown.

The Bears contained the Redskins for the remainder of the half and led 14-7 in the third quarter. Washington tied the score when Baugh passed to Wayne Millner, who ran a crossing pattern, caught the ball at Chicago's 35-yard line, and outran Bernie Masterson to complete a 55-yard play.

After Chicago went back in front 21-14 with a touchdown that concluded a 13-play, 73-yard advance, the Redskins struck quickly. They took the kickoff on their 22-yard line with 9:04 remaining in the quarter. On the first play, Baugh threw a 28-yard pass to Millner, who ran 50 yards, with Jack Manders and Bronko Nagurski in pursuit, to score. After the Bears punted following the next kickoff, Washington went 80 yards in 11 plays, Baugh combining with Ed Justice on a 35-yard scoring pass.

In the fourth quarter, the Bears drove to Washington's 23 and 14, but each time the Redskins held on downs.

December 12, at Chicago

Washington	Starting Lineups	Chi. Bears
Wayne Millner	LE	Edgar (Eggs) Manske
Glen (Turk) Edwards	LT	Joe Stydahar
Les Olsson	LG	Dan Fortmann
Ed Kawal	C	Frank Bausch
Jim Karcher	RG	George Musso
Jim Barber	RT	Del Bjork
Charley Malone	RE	George Wilson
Riley Smith	QB	Bernie Masterson
Sammy Baugh	LH	Ray Nolting
Erny Pinckert	RH	Jack Manders
Cliff Battles	FB	Bronko Nagurski

Washington	7	0	21	0	—	28
Chi. Bears	14	0	7	0	—	21

Wash—Battles 7 run (R. Smith kick)
ChiB —Manders 10 run (Manders kick)
ChiB —Manders 37 pass from Masterson (Manders kick)
Wash—Millner 55 pass from Baugh (R. Smith kick)
ChiB —Manske 4 pass from Masterson (Manders kick)
Wash—Millner 78 pass from Baugh (R. Smith kick)
Wash—Justice 35 pass from Baugh (R. Smith kick)
Attendance—15,870

TEAM STATISTICS	Wash	ChiB
First downs	18	11
Rushing	8	7
Passing	10	4
By penalty	0	0
Total yardage	481	332
Net rushing yardage	90	125
Net passing yardage	392	207
Passes att.-comp.-had int.	40-22-3	30-8-3

RUSHING

Chi. Bears—Manders, 10 for 64, 1 TD; Nagurski, 8 for 47; Nolting, 9 for 38; Rentner, 1 for 0; Ronzani, 1 for −3; Masterson, 2 for −9; Buivid, 3 for −12.

Washington—Battles, 19 for 43, 1 TD; Irwin, 10 for 33; Baugh, 4 for 6; Justice, 1 for 4; Krause, 1 for 4.

PASSING

Chi. Bears—Masterson, 4 of 17 for 131, 2 TDs, 2 int.; Buivid, 3 of 11 for 41, 1 int.; Molesworth, 1 of 1 for 35; Nagurski, 0 of 1.

Washington—Baugh, 18 of 33 for 354, 3 TDs, 1 int.; Battles, 3 of 5 for 21, 1 int.; R. Smith, 1 of 2 for 17, 1 int.

RECEIVING

Chi. Bears—Manske, 2 for 55, 1 TD; Plasman, 2 for 44; McDonald, 2 for 39; Manders, 1 for 37, 1 TD; Rentner, 1 for 32.

Washington—Millner, 9 for 179, 2 TDs; Battles, 3 for 80; Justice, 3 for 63, 1 TD; Malone, 3 for 25; R. Smith, 2 for 20; Pinckert, 1 for 18; Irwin, 1 for 7.

1938

NY GIANTS 23, GREEN BAY 17

The Green Bay Packers outgained the New York Giants 378-212 in total yardage, but the Giants' defense blocked two punts that led to nine points and a 23-17 victory. The crowd of 48,120 on a 31-degree afternoon in the Polo Grounds set a record.

The first blocked punt came on Green Bay's second possession of the day. On third and 11 at the Green Bay 11, Jim Lee Howell blocked Clarke Hinkle's punt and Leland Shaffer recovered for New York on the 7-yard line. After three plays netted only 1 yard, Ward Cuff kicked a 14-yard field goal.

Cecil Isbell's punt was blocked by Jim Poole with Howell recovering on Green Bay's 28 on the Packers' next possession. New York scored four plays later on a six-yard run by Alphonse (Tuffy) Leemans. Leemans caught one pass and carried the ball three times on the four plays. The Packers scored just before the half to cut New York's lead to two. An eight-play, 80-yard drive culminated in Hinkle's one-yard touchdown run.

Green Bay took a 17-16 lead in the third quarter when it marched 53 yards to Paul (Tiny) Engebretsen's 15-yard field goal. The Giants began the following series on their 39-yard line. Halfback Hank Soar carried the ball on five of the next six plays. He threw an incomplete pass on the seventh, then caught a pass for nine yards from quarterback Ed Danowski, and ran three yards to put the ball on Green Bay's 23-yard line. Danowski lofted a pass to the goal line. Soar and Poole leaped for the ball with two defenders. Soar made the catch and dragged Hinkle over the goal line for the winning touchdown.

December 11, at New York

Green Bay	Starting Lineups	NY Giants
Wayland Becker	LE	Jim Poole
Champ Seibold	LT	Ed Widseth
Russ Letlow	LG	John Dell Isola
Lee Mulleneaux	C	Mel Hein
Charles Goldenberg	RG	Orville Tuttle
Bill Lee	RT	Owen (Ox) Parry
Milt Gantenbein	RE	Jim Lee Howell
Herman Schneidman	QB	Ed Danowski
Cecil Isbell	LH	Hank Soar
Joe Laws	RH	Ward Cuff
Clarke Hinkle	FB	Leland Shaffer

Green Bay	0	14	3	0	—	17
NY Giants	9	7	7	0	—	23

NYG—FG Cuff 14
NYG—Leemans 6 run (kick failed)
GB —C. Mulleneaux 40 pass from Herber (Engebretsen kick)
NYG—Barnard 21 pass from Danowski (Cuff kick)
GB —Hinkle 1 run (Engebretsen kick)
GB —FG Engebretsen 15
NYG—Soar 23 pass from Danowski (Cuff kick)
Attendance—48,120

TEAM STATISTICS	GB	NYG
First downs	14	10
Rushing	9	6
Passing	4	2
By penalty	1	2
Total yardage	378	212
Net rushing yardage	164	115
Net passing yardage	214	97
Passes att.-comp.-had int.	19-8-1	15-8-1

RUSHING

NY Giants—Soar, 21 for 65; Leemans, 13 for 42, 1 TD; Barnum, 3 for 8; Danowski, 1 for 4; Karcis, 3 for 3; Cuff, 2 for −7.

Green Bay—Hinkle, 8 for 63, 1 TD; Monnett, 4 for 29; Herber, 3 for 22; Isbell, 11 for 20; Laws, 4 for 20; Jankowski, 3 for 14; Uram, 2 for −1; Miller, 1 for −3.

PASSING

NY Giants—Danowski, 7 of 11 for 77, 2 TDs; Leemans, 1 of 2 for 20, 1 int.; Barnum, 0 of 1; Soar, 0 of 1.

Green Bay—Herber, 5 of 14 for 123, 1 TD; Isbell, 3 of 5 for 91, 1 int.

RECEIVING

NY Giants—Soar, 3 for 41, 1 TD; Howell, 2 for 3; Barnard, 1 for 20, 1 TD; Barnum, 1 for 20; Leemans, 1 for 5; Perry, 0 for 8.

Green Bay—Becker, 2 for 79; C. Mulleneaux, 2 for 54, 1 TD; Uram, 1 for 24; Isbell, 1 for 22; Scherer, 1 for 19; Gantenbein, 1 for 6; Hutson, 0 for 10.

1939

GREEN BAY 27, NY GIANTS 0

Winds blowing across the Wisconsin flatlands through the open ends of Milwaukee's State Fair Park were measured in gusts up to 35 miles per hour. The Green Bay Packers' passers, Arnie Herber and Cecil Isbell, were intercepted three times, but they completed 7 of 10 attempts for 96 yards and two touchdowns. Giants passers completed 8 of 25 passes for 94 yards and had 6 intercepted as the Packers scored a 27-0 victory.

The Packers scored on a 54-yard drive in the first quarter when Herber passed seven yards to Milt Gantenbein, who was open between the goal posts in the end zone after the Giants assigned double coverage to Don Hutson. The score was 7-0 at the half. New York had three scoring opportunities, but Ward Cuff missed field-goal attempts of 42 and 41 yards, and Lem Barnum missed from 47. Cuff's first field-goal attempt was set up when Jim Poole blocked Clarke Hinkle's punt and Jim Lee Howell recovered in Green Bay territory.

Paul (Tiny) Engebretsen put the Packers in front 10-0 with a 29-yard field goal in the third quarter. Joe Laws returned a punt 30 yards to his 45 and the Packers moved 32 yards in seven plays to position Engebretsen. The score became 17-0 after Gantenbein intercepted a pass by Ed Danowski at the Giants' 33. Cecil Isbell threw a 26-yard pass on second down to Laws, who caught the ball over his shoulder on the 5-yard line and scored to complete a 31-yard play.

Ernie Smith's 42-yard field goal and Ed Jankowski's one-yard run finished the scoring in the fourth quarter. The Giants were on the 5-yard line when the game ended. Their deepest penetration had been the 16 in the third quarter, when the score was 17-0.

December 10, at Milwaukee

NY Giants	Starting Lineups	Green Bay
Jim Poole	LE	Don Hutson
Frank Cope	LT	Buford (Baby) Ray
John Dell Isola	LG	Russ Letlow
Mel Hein	C	Earl Svendsen
Orville Tuttle	RG	Charles Goldenberg
John Mellus	RT	Bill Lee
Jim Lee Howell	RE	Milt Gantenbein
Ed Danowski	QB	Larry Craig
Elvin (Kink) Richards	LH	Cecil Isbell
Ward Cuff	RH	Joe Laws
Nello Falaschi	FB	Clarke Hinkle

NY Giants	0	0	0	0	—	0
Green Bay	7	0	10	10	—	27

GB—Gantenbein 7 pass from Herber (Engebretsen kick)
GB—FG Engebretsen 29
GB—Laws 31 pass from Isbell (Engebretsen kick)
GB—FG E. Smith 42
GB—Jankowski 1 run (E. Smith kick)
Attendance—32,279

TEAM STATISTICS	NYG	GB
First downs	9	10
Rushing	5	6
Passing	3	2
By penalty	1	2
Total yardage	164	232
Net rushing yardage	70	136
Net passing yardage	94	96
Passes att.-comp.-had int.	25-8-6	10-7-3

RUSHING

Green Bay—Uram, 10 for 38; Isbell, 14 for 28; Hinkle, 13 for 25; Laws, 3 for 20; Jankowski, 7 for 14, 1 TD; Jacunski, 1 for 11; Herber, 3 for −3; Hutson, 1 for 3.

NY Giants—Leemans, 12 for 24; Miller, 3 for 10; Soar, 4 for 14; Richards, 7 for 12; Cuff, 2 for 7; Barnum, 4 for 4; Kline, 1 for 1; Owen, 1 for −2.

PASSING

Green Bay—Herber, 5 of 8 for 59, 1 TD, 3 int.; Isbell, 2 of 2 for 37, 1 TD.

NY Giants—Danowski, 4 of 12 for 48, 3 int.; Miller, 3 of 6 for 40, 1 int.; Leemans, 1 of 4 for 6, 1 int.; Barnum, 0 of 3, 1 int.

RECEIVING

Green Bay—Hutson, 2 for 21; Craig, 2 for 6; Jacunski, 1 for 31; Laws, 1 for 31, 1 TD; Gantenbein, 1 for 7, 1 TD.

NY Giants—Shaffer, 2 for 16; Falaschi, 2 for 6; Leemans, 1 for 37; Gelatka, 1 for 24; Barnum, 1 for 6; Cuff, 1 for 5.

1940

CHI. BEARS 73, WASHINGTON 0

Fullback Bill Osmanski of the Chicago Bears ran around left end for 68 yards and a touchdown on the second play of the game. The next time the Bears were on offense they held possession of the ball for 17 plays, marching 80 yards to score on quarterback Sid Luckman's one-foot plunge. The third time Chicago had the ball, fullback Joe Maniaci swept end for 42 yards and a touchdown on the first play. The Bears scored three touchdowns in the first 12:40 of the game; they rushed for 381 yards, amassed 519 total yards, intercepted eight passes, and won the NFL Championship Game 73-0 over the Washington Redskins, a team that had beaten them 7-3 three weeks before in the ninth game of the season. The game was a showcase for the Bears' T-formation at a time when the other NFL teams ran the Single Wing.

The Bears led 28-0 at the half after Luckman's 30-yard touchdown pass to Ken Kavanaugh. Luckman did not play the second half; quarterbacks Bernie Masterson, Bob Snyder, and Saul Sherman directed the team on four more scoring drives. The defense returned three passes for touchdowns. Redskins fans in Griffith Stadium began hooting in derision whenever the home team did something positive. The loudest demonstration came in the fourth quarter, when the score was 60-0 and the stadium public address made a "special announcement for 1941 Redskins season tickets."

December 8, at Washington

Chi. Bears	Starting Lineups	Washington
Bob Nowaskey	LE	Bob Masterson
Joe Stydahar	LT	Willie Wilkin
Dan Fortmann	LG	Dick Farman
Clyde (Bulldog) Turner	C	Bob Titchenal
George Musso	RG	Steve Slivinski
Lee Artoe	RT	Jim Barber
George Wilson	RE	Charley Malone
Sid Luckman	QB	Max Krause
Ray Nolting	LH	Sammy Baugh
George McAfee	RH	Ed Justice
Bill Osmanski	FB	Jim Johnston

Chi. Bears	21	7	26	19	—	73
Washington	0	0	0	0	—	0

ChiB—Osmanski 68 run (Manders kick)
ChiB—Luckman 1 run (Snyder kick)
ChiB—Maniaci 42 run (Martinovich kick)
ChiB—Kavanaugh 30 pass from Luckman (Snyder kick)
ChiB—Pool 15 interception return (Plasman kick)
ChiB—Nolting 23 run (kick failed)
ChiB—McAfee 34 interception return (Stydahar kick)
ChiB—Turner 24 interception return (kick failed)
ChiB—Clark 44 run (kick failed)
ChiB—Famiglietti 2 run (Maniaci pass from Sherman)
ChiB—Clark 1 run (pass failed)
Attendance—36,034

TEAM STATISTICS	ChiB	Wash
First downs	17	17
Rushing	13	4
Passing	3	10
By penalty	1	3
Total yardage	519	231
Net rushing yardage	381	5
Net passing yardage	138	226
Passes att.-comp.-had int.	10-7-0	51-20-8

RUSHING

Washington—Seymour, 4 for 17; Johnson, 4 for 14; Filchock, 3 for 3; Justice, 1 for 2; Zimmerman, 2 for −15; Baugh, 1 for −16.

Chi. Bears—Osmanski, 10 for 107, 1 TD; Clark, 7 for 75, 2 TD; Nolting, 11 for 67, 1 TD; Maniaci, 5 for 62, 1 TD; McAfee, 7 for 32: Famiglietti, 4 for 19, 1 TD; McLean, 3 for 18; Nowaskey, 1 for 7; Manders, 2 for 1; Luckman, 1 for 1, 1 TD; Snyder, 2 for −8.

PASSING

Washington—Filchock, 8 of 23 for 101, 4 int.; Baugh, 9 of 16 for 91, 2 int.; Zimmerman, 3 of 12 for 34, 2 int.

Chi. Bears—Luckman, 4 of 6 for 102, 1 TD; Snyder, 3 of 3 for 36; McAfee, 0 of 1.

RECEIVING

Washington—Millner, 6 for 94; Masterson, 3 for 34; Johnson, 3 for 9; Malone, 2 for 51; Hoffman, 2 for 8; Farkas, 1 for 19; Seymour, 1 for 7; Justice, 1 for 4; McChesney, 1 for 0.

Chi. Bears—Maniaci, 2 for 44; Kavanaugh, 2 for 32, 1 TD; Swisher, 1 for 38; Mihal, 1 for 14; Nolting, 1 for 12.

1941

CHI. BEARS 37, NY GIANTS 9

The Chicago Bears won their fourth championship game when they broke a 9-9 tie in the third quarter and defeated the New York Giants 37-9. The Wrigley Field crowd of 13,341 was the smallest in playoff history, coming one week after the Bears defeated Green Bay 33-14 for the Western Conference championship in a divisional playoff before 43,425.

The Bears trailed 6-3 at the end of the first quarter. They led 9-6 at the half after having possession of the ball 53 plays to the Giants' 10. Chicago controlled the ball for the first 10:34 of the first quarter, scoring on Bob Snyder's 14-yard field goal, which followed a series of penalties against Chicago and a blocked field goal that hit New York's Ken (Kayo) Lunday in the face but was recovered by the Bears. New York then scored its only touchdown. It marched 59 yards in four plays, scoring on a 31-yard pass from Alphonse (Tuffy) Leemans to George Franck.

The Bears, who had a total yardage edge of 389-157, began pulling away from the Giants after Ward Cuff's 16-yard field goal tied the score in the first three minutes of the third quarter. The Bears went 71, 66, and 54 yards for touchdowns. Their last score came in the final nine seconds of the game. The Giants' Hank Soar lateraled to Andy Marefos, who attempted to throw a pass on a halfback option. Marefos was hit by several Bears defenders and fumbled. Ken Kavanaugh picked up the ball and ran 42 yards. The final extra point was added on a dropkick, already a forgotten play in the NFL.

December 21, at Chicago

NY Giants	Starting Lineups	Chi. Bears
Jim Poole	LE	Dick Plasman
John Mellus	LT	Ed Kolman
Ken (Kayo) Lunday	LG	Dan Fortmann
Mel Hein	C	Clyde (Bulldog) Turner
Len Younce	RG	Ray Bray
Bill Edwards	RT	Lee Artoe
Jim Lee Howell	RE	John Siegal
Nello Falaschi	QB	Sid Luckman
George Franck	LH	Ray Nolting
Ward Cuff	RH	Hugh Gallarneau
Alphonse (Tuffy) Leemans	FB	Norm Standlee

NY Giants	6	0	3	0	—	9
Chi. Bears	3	6	14	14	—	37

ChiB—FG Snyder 14
NYG—Franck 31 pass from Leemans (kick failed)
ChiB—FG Snyder 39
ChiB—FG Snyder 37
NYG—FG Cuff 16
ChiB—Standlee 2 run (Snyder kick)
ChiB—Standlee 7 run (Maniaci kick)
ChiB—McAfee 5 run (Artoe kick)
ChiB—Kavanaugh 42 fumble return (McLean dropkick)
Attendance—13,341

TEAM STATISTICS	NYG	ChiB
First downs	8	20
Rushing	4	14
Passing	2	5
By penalty	2	1
Total yardage	157	389
Net rushing yardage	84	207
Net passing yardage	73	182
Passes att.-comp.-had int.	15-3-3	19-11-0

RUSHING
NY Giants—Leemans, 9 for 52; Franck, 2 for 30; Yeager, 2 for 7; Soar, 6 for 1; Eshmont, 1 for 0; Cuff, 3 for 0; Eakin, 1 for −1; Marefos, 1 for −5.
Chi. Bears—Standlee, 17 for 89, 2 TDs; McAfee, 14 for 81, 1 TD; McLean, 3 for 17; Osmanski, 5 for 15; Nolting, 4 for 13; Gallarneau, 7 for 6; Maniaci, 3 for 13; Bussey, 1 for −2; Snyder, 1 for −3; Luckman, 1 for −12.
PASSING
NY Giants—Leemans, 3 of 9 for 73, 1 TD, 3 int.; Eshmont, 0 of 1; Franck, 0 of 1; Soar, 0 of 4.
Chi. Bears—Luckman, 9 of 12 for 160; Bussey, 1 of 1 for 8; Snyder, 1 of 6 for 14.
RECEIVING
NY Giants—Cuff, 2 for 42; Franck, 1 for 31, 1 TD.
Chi. Bears—Plasman, 2 for 48; McAfee, 2 for 42; Standlee, 2 for 34; Siegal, 1 for 26; Kavanaugh, 1 for 14; Maniaci, 1 for 8; McLean, 1 for 5; Nowaskey, 1 for 5.

1942

WASHINGTON 14, CHI. BEARS 6

The Washington Redskins defeated the Chicago Bears 14-6 in a game in which the Bears were favored by 22 points. Chicago had won 24 games in a row, including postseason and preseason contests, and 39 of its previous 40 games. The Bears had not been beaten since a 16-14 loss to Green Bay on November 2, 1941.

Chicago took a 6-0 lead in the second quarter when Lee Artoe, a 230-pound tackle, ran 50 yards for a touchdown with a recovered fumble. The fumble resulted when Chicago's George Wilson tackled Dick Todd. However, Artoe's extra-point attempt was no good. The Redskins returned the following kickoff to the Bears' 42-yard line and scored in three plays, Sammy Baugh passing 38 yards to Wilbur Moore for the touchdown. Andy Farkas's one-yard run in the third quarter completed the scoring.

Baugh, who completed 5 of 13 passes for 66 yards, made one of the game's biggest defensive plays when he stopped a Bears' drive that had reached Washington's 12-yard line by intercepting a pass in the end zone. The Bears marched to the Redskins' 27- and 28-yard lines in the first period but came up empty when Artoe missed a 46-yard field goal the first time and they fumbled the second time. Chicago went 79 yards from its 20 to Washington's 1 in the fourth quarter. Halfback Hugh Gallarneau scored on the next play, but the Bears were penalized for backfield in motion. They surrendered the ball on downs and the Redskins controlled possession the last three minutes.

Washington and Chicago each finished the season with 11-1 records, including the championship playoff. The Redskins' loss was 14-7 to New York, which was beaten 26-7 by Chicago.

"I guess this kinda makes up for that thing in 1940, don't it," Baugh said after the game.

December 13, at Washington

Chi. Bears	Starting Lineups	Washington
Bob Nowaskey	LE	Bob Masterson
Ed Kolman	LT	Willie Wilkin
Dan Fortmann	LG	Dick Farman
Clyde (Bulldog) Turner	C	Ki Aldrich
Ray Bray	RG	Steve Slivinski
Lee Artoe	RT	Bill Young
George Wilson	RE	Ed Cifers
Sid Luckman	QB	Ray Hare
Ray Nolting	LH	Sammy Baugh
Hugh Gallarneau	RH	Ed Justice
Gary Famiglietti	FB	Andy Farkas

Chi. Bears	0	6	0	0	—	6
Washington	0	7	7	0	—	14

ChiB—Artoe 50 fumble return (kick failed)
Wash—Moore 38 pass from Baugh (Masterson kick)
Wash—Farkas 1 run (Masterson kick)
Attendance—36,006

TEAM STATISTICS	ChiB	Wash
First downs	10	9
Rushing	4	5
Passing	5	2
By penalty	1	2
Total yardage	188	170
Net rushing yardage	69	104
Net passing yardage	119	66
Passes att.-comp.-had int.	18-8-3	13-5-2

RUSHING
Washington—Farkas, 13 for 46, 1 TD; Seymour, 14 for 34; Todd, 2 for 12; Hare, 4 for 7; Baugh, 2 for 6; Masterson, 1 for −1.
Chi. Bears—Osmanski, 13 for 36; Nolting, 8 for 26; Famiglietti, 7 for 22; Maznicki, 5 for 14; McLean, 1 for 3; Gallarneau, 1 for 0; Patty, 3 for −1; Luckman, 3 for −33.
PASSING
Washington—Baugh, 5 of 13 for 66, 2 int., 1 TD.
Chi. Bears—Luckman, 5 of 11 for 9, 2 int.; O'Rourke, 4 of 6 for 110; Maznicki, 0 of 1, 1 int.
RECEIVING
Washington—Moore, 2 for 41, 1 TD; Todd, 1 for 9; Cifers, 1 for 8; Masterson, 1 for 8.
Chi. Bears—McLean, 3 for 26; Siegel, 2 for 11; Maznicki, 1 for 39; Nowaskey, 1 for 32; Nolting, 1 for 11.

1943

CHI. BEARS 41, WASHINGTON 21

Quarterback Sid Luckman completed 15 of 26 passes for 286 yards and five touchdowns and rushed for 64 yards in eight carries as the Chicago Bears defeated Washington 41-21.

The Bears, who were idle for 29 days after clinching the NFL West championship with a victory over the Chicago Cardinals, gained a total of 455 yards to the Redskins' 249 but trailed 7-0 after Andy Farkas concluded a 60-yard Redskins drive with a one-yard run in the second quarter. The Bears went 67 and 55 yards for touchdowns after the Washington score to take a 14-7 lead.

Redskins quarterback Sammy Baugh left the game after one play of the first quarter and sat on the bench weeping for the remainder of the half as physicians tried to determine the severity of a concussion he sustained when he was kicked in the head on the opening kickoff. Baugh returned in the second half and completed 8 of 12 passes for 123 yards and two touchdowns. His first-half replacement, George Cafego, completed 3 of 12 for 76 yards.

The championship game was the third in four years between the Bears and Washington. Typical of the rivalry between them was an incident in the first half when Redskins owner George Preston Marshall was ejected from the playing field after attempting to gain access to the Redskins' bench. Bears acting president Ralph Brizzolara ordered police to remove Marshall, who returned later and termed the Bears' action "a first-class, bush-league trick."

December 26, at Chicago

Washington	Starting Lineups	Chi. Bears
Bob Masterson	LE	Jim Benton
Lou Rymkus	LT	Dominic Sigillo
Clyde Shugart	LG	Dan Fortmann
George Smith	C	Clyde (Bulldog) Turner
Steve Slivinski	RG	George Musso
Joe Pasqua	RT	Al Hoptowit
Joe Aguirre	RE	George Wilson
Ray Hare	QB	Bob Snyder
Frank Seno	LH	Harry Clark
George Cafego	RH	Dante Magnani
Andy Farkas	FB	Bob Masters

Washington	0	7	7	7	—	21
Chi. Bears	0	14	13	14	—	41

Wash—Farkas 1 run (Masterson kick)
ChiB—Clark 31 pass from Luckman (Snyder kick)
ChiB—Nagurski 3 run (Snyder kick)
ChiB—Magnani 36 pass from Luckman (Snyder kick)
ChiB—Magnani 66 pass from Luckman (kick failed)
Wash—Farkas 17 pass from Baugh (Masterson kick)
ChiB—Benton 26 pass from Luckman (Snyder kick)
ChiB—Clark 16 pass from Luckman (Snyder kick)
Wash—Aguirre 25 pass from Baugh (Aguirre kick)
Attendance—34,320

TEAM STATISTICS	Wash	ChiB
First downs	11	14
Rushing	4	8
Passing	6	6
By penalty	1	0
Total yardage	249	455
Net rushing yardage	50	169
Net passing yardage	199	286
Passes att.-comp.-had int.	24-11-4	27-15-0

RUSHING
Washington—Farkas, 11 for 36, 1 TD; Seno, 4 for 17; Seymour, 3 for 4; Moore, 4 for 0; Cafego, 5 for −7.
Chi. Bears—Luckman, 8 for 64; Nagurski, 11 for 34, 1 TD; Nolting, 7 for 30; Clark, 9 for 21; Famiglietti, 3 for 9; Magnani, 2 for 6; Snyder, 2 for 4; Vodicka, 1 for 3; McLean, 1 for −2.
PASSING
Washington—Baugh, 8 for 12 for 123, 2 TDs, 1 int.; Cafego, 3 of 12 for 76, 3 int.
Chi. Bears—Luckman, 15 of 26 for 286, 5 TDs; Snyder, 0 of 1.
RECEIVING
Washington—Moore, 5 for 108; Aguirre, 1 for 25, 1 TD; Piasecky, 1 for 22; Farkas, 1 for 17, 1 TD; Masterson, 1 for 16; Lapka, 1 for 16; Seno, 1 for −5.
Chi. Bears—Magnani, 4 for 122, 2 TDs; Clark, 3 for 47, 2 TDs; Wilson, 3 for 29; Pool, 2 for 21; Benton, 1 for 29, 1 TD; McLean, 1 for 29; Nagurski, 1 for 9.

1944

GREEN BAY 14, NY GIANTS 7

The Green Bay Packers won their third NFL Championship Game and first in five years when they scored a 14-7 victory over the New York Giants, who were losers for the fifth time in seven championship games. The Giants had beaten the Packers 24-0 only four weeks earlier, assuring the New York team of the NFL's best record (8-1-1). This time, the Packers outgained the Giants 237-199 in total yards and scored both of their touchdowns in the second quarter on plays involving fullback Ted Fritsch.

Fritsch scored on a one-yard run early in the quarter, following a block by right guard Charles (Buckets) Goldenberg, the Packers' 33-year-old, 12-year veteran. The touchdown came on fourth down after the Giants had held the Packers without a gain for three downs.

Fritsch scored again on a 28-yard pass from Irv Comp. Don Hutson, the Packers' all-league end, figured prominently in the play. After Hutson gained 24 yards on a pass from Comp to put the ball on the 30, Hutson served as a decoy on the touchdown three plays later. He ran a crossing pattern from his left end position, drawing the Giants' secondary with him. Fritsch looped out of the backfield and caught Comp's pass on the 5. There wasn't a defender within 10 yards.

For most of the game, New York was without the services of Bill Paschal, the NFL's leading rusher, who had hurt his ankle in the season finale. The Giants, who did not advance beyond their own 35-yard line in the first half, scored on Ward Cuff's one-yard run in the fourth quarter. Cuff, who had played wingback in the Giants' Single-Wing formation for his entire eight-season career, scored from the tailback position. The touchdown was set up by a 41-yard pass from Arnie Herber to Frank Liebel. Herber, who had been out of pro football for three years before joining the Giants in 1944, played with the Packers from 1930 through 1940.

December 17, at New York

Green Bay	**Starting Lineups**	**NY Giants**
Don Hutson	LE	O'Neal Adams
Buford (Baby) Ray	LT	Frank Cope
Bill Kuusisto	LG	Len Younce
Charley Brock	C	Mel Hein
Charles Goldenberg	RG	Jim Sivell
Paul Berezney	RT	Vic Carroll
Harry Jacunski	RE	Frank Liebel
Larry Craig	QB	Len Calligaro
Irv Comp	LH	Arnie Herber
Joe Laws	RH	Ward Cuff
Ted Fritsch	FB	Howie Livingston

Green Bay	0	14	0	0	—	14
NY Giants	0	0	0	7	—	7

GB —Fritsch 1 run (Hutson kick)
GB —Fritsch 28 pass from Comp (Hutson kick)
NYG—Cuff 1 run (Strong kick)
Attendance—46,016

TEAM STATISTICS	**GB**	**NYG**
First downs	11	10
Rushing	9	5
Passing	2	4
By penalty	0	1
Total yardage	237	199
Net rushing yardage	163	85
Net passing yardage	74	114
Passes att.-comp.-had int.	11-3-3	22-8-4

RUSHING

NY Giants—Cuff, 12 for 76, 1 TD; Livingston, 12 for 22; Paschal, 2 for 4; Sulaitis, 1 for −1; Herber, 3 for −16.

Green Bay—Fritsch, 18 for 59, 1 TD; Laws, 13 for 72; Comp, 9 for 21; Duhart, 7 for 15; Perkins, 2 for −4.

PASSING

NY Giants—Herber, 8 of 22 for 114, 4 int.

Green Bay—Comp, 3 of 10 for 74, 1 TD, 3 int.; L. Brock, 0 of 1.

RECEIVING

NY Giants—Liebel, 3 for 70; Cuff, 2 for 23; Livingston, 2 for 21; Barker, 1 for 0.

Green Bay—Hutson, 2 for 46; Fritsch, 1 for 28, 1 TD.

1945

CLEVELAND 15, WASHINGTON 14

Two footballs that hit the crossbar of the goal posts were the difference in the NFL Championship Game, as the Cleveland Rams defeated the Washington Redskins 15-14. In the game, Bob Waterfield became the last rookie quarterback in NFL history to lead his team to the championship.

Early in the first quarter, the Redskins stopped a Rams drive at the Washington 5. Sammy Baugh dropped back into his end zone to unload a long pass, but it hit the crossbar and bounced back into the end zone, which was a safety under the current rules.

Baugh, who had been injured in the Redskins' victory over the New York Giants the week before, was taken out of the game in the first quarter and returned only to hold the ball on extra points. Frank Filchock, Baugh's replacement, helped put the Redskins ahead 7-2 with 9:29 left in the first half when he combined with halfback Steve Bagarus on a 38-yard pass play.

With three minutes remaining in the half, the Rams went back in front. Waterfield found Jim Benton alone and connected with him for a 37-yard touchdown pass. Waterfield's extra point was partially blocked and struck the goal-post crossbar, teetered for a moment, and dropped into the end zone, giving Cleveland a 9-7 lead.

The Rams increased their advantage to 15-7 in the third quarter, when Waterfield threw a 35-yard pass to Jim Gillette, who caught the ball over his shoulder and ran nine yards to complete a 44-yard touchdown. The Redskins later cut the lead to one. In the fourth quarter, Joe Aguirre missed two field goals, either of which could have won the game.

The game was played in six-degree weather. The Memorial Stadium sideline was piled with snow after workers arrived early to clear the playing area.

December 16, at Cleveland

Washington	**Starting Lineups**	**Cleveland**
Wayne Millner	LE	Floyd Konetsky
Fred Davis	LT	Eberle Schultz
Al Lolotai	LG	Riley Matheson
Ki Aldrich	C	Mike Scarry
Marvin Whited	RG	Milan Lazetich
Earl Audet	RT	Gil Bouley
Doug Turley	RE	Steve Pritko
Sammy Baugh	QB	Steve Nemeth
Dick Todd	LH	Fred Gehrke
Merlyn Condit	RH	Jim Gillette
Frank Akins	FB	Pat West

Washington	0	7	7	0	—	14
Cleveland	2	7	6	0	—	15

Cle —Safety, Baugh's pass hit goal post
Wash—Bagarus 38 pass from Filchock (Aguirre kick)
Cle —Benton 37 pass from Waterfield (Waterfield kick)
Cle —Gillette 44 pass from Waterfield (kick failed)
Wash—Seymour 8 pass from Filchock (Aguirre kick)
Attendance—32,178

TEAM STATISTICS	**Wash**	**Cle**
First downs	8	14
Rushing	3	9
Passing	4	4
By penalty	1	1
Total yardage	214	372
Net rushing yardage	35	180
Net passing yardage	179	192
Passes att.-comp.-had int.	20-9-2	27-14-2

RUSHING

Washington—Condit, 9 for 18; Rosato, 6 for 17; Akins, 6 for 16; DeFruiter, 1 for 15; Hare, 2 for 6; Todd, 1 for 1; deCorrevont, 1 for −2; Bagarus, 5 for −4; Filchock, 3 for −32.

Cleveland—Gillette, 17 for 101; Gehrke, 7 for 29; Greewood, 9 for 19; West, 3 for 17; Reisz, 3 for 14; Koch, 2 for 1; Waterfield, 3 for −1.

PASSING

Washington—Filchock, 8 of 14 for 172, 2 TDs, 2 int.; Baugh, 1 of 6 for 7.

Cleveland—Waterfield, 14 of 27 for 192, 2 TDs, 2 int.

RECEIVING

Washington—Bagarus, 3 for 95, 1 TD; Hare, 2 for 20; Dye, 1 for 44; Turley, 1 for 11; Seymour, 1 for 8, 1 TD; Condit, 1 for 1.

Cleveland—Benton, 9 for 125, 1 TD; Gillette, 2 for 45, 1 TD; Pritko, 2 for 17; West, 1 for 5.

1946

CHI. BEARS 24, NY GIANTS 14

The Chicago Bears won their sixth NFL Championship Game in 15 years when they scored a 24-14 victory over the New York Giants. A crowd of 58,346 in the Polo Grounds set a playoff record.

On the morning of the game, fullback Merle Hapes of the Giants was suspended by Commissioner Bert Bell. Hapes had declined a bribe to throw the game, but hadn't reported the attempt. Frank Filchock of the Giants was allowed to play, although he had been told by Hapes of the bribery attempt. With the crowd suspiciously watching his every move, Filchock played 50 minutes despite a broken nose, and threw two touchdown passes.

The Bears jumped to a 14-0 lead in the first nine minutes of the game, but Filchock cut it to 14-7 with a touchdown pass to end Frank Liebel late in the first quarter.

The Giants tied the score in the third quarter. Jim Lee Howell recovered Joe Osmanski's fumble on Chicago's 20. Three plays later, Filchock passed five yards for a touchdown to Steve Filipowicz.

With the score tied early in the fourth quarter, Bears quarterback Sid Luckman crossed up the Giants' defense and scored the winning touchdown. From the Giants' 19-yard line, Luckman looked over the defense and then called time out for a conference with coach George Halas. "Now?" Luckman inquired of the coach about a specially designed trap play. "Now," said Halas. Luckman faked a handoff to halfback George McAfee, hid the ball on his hip and ran to his right while the Giants' defense followed the Bears' line, which pulled to the left. Luckman scored his only touchdown of 1946 after shaking off a tackler at the 10-yard line and picking up blocks from center Clyde (Bulldog) Turner and guard Ray Bray.

December 15, at New York

Chi. Bears	**Starting Lineups**	**NY Giants**
Ken Kavanaugh	LE	Jim Poole
Fred Davis	LT	DeWitt (Tex) Coulter
Rudy Mucha	LG	Bob Dobelstein
Clyde (Bulldog) Turner	C	Chet Gladchuk
Ray Bray	RG	Len Younce
Mike Jarmoluk	RT	Jim White
George Wilson	RE	Jim Lee Howell
Joe Osmanski	QB	Steve Filipowicz
Dante Magnani	LH	Dave Brown
Hugh Gallarneau	RH	Howie Livingston
Bill Osmanski	FB	Ken Strong

Chi. Bears	14	0	0	10	—	24
NY Giants	7	0	7	0	—	14

ChiB—Kavanaugh 21 pass from Luckman (Maznicki kick)
ChiB—Magnani 19 pass interception (Maznicki kick)
NYG—Liebel 38 pass from Filchock (Strong kick)
NYG—Filipowicz 5 pass from Filchock (Strong kick)
ChiB—Luckman 19 run (Maznicki kick)
ChiB—FG Maznicki 26
Attendance—58,346

TEAM STATISTICS	**ChiB**	**NYG**
First downs	10	13
Rushing	5	6
Passing	4	4
By penalty	1	3
Total yardage	245	248
Net rushing yardage	101	120
Net passing yardage	144	128
Passes att.-comp.-had int.	22-9-2	26-9-6

RUSHING

Chi. Bears—Gallarneau, 6 for 24; B. Osmanski, 9 for 23; J. Osmanski, 8 for 20; Perkins, 4 for 18; Luckman, 4 for 8, 1 TD; McLean, 3 for 6; McAfee, 6 for 2.

NY Giants—Franck, 6 for 55; Filipowicz, 9 for 20; Filchock, 10 for 19; Livingston, 4 for 19; Doolan, 1 for 4; Reagan, 3 for 3.

PASSING

Chi. Bears—Luckman, 9 of 22 for 144, 1 TD, 2 int.

NY Giants—Filchock, 9 of 26 for 128, 2 TDs, 6 int.

RECEIVING

Chi. Bears—McAfee, 4 for 57; Kavanaugh, 2 for 53, 1 TD; Keane, 2 for 25; Sprinkle, 1 for 9.

NY Giants—Poole, 4 for 40; Filipowicz, 2 for 41, 1 TD; Liebel, 1 for 38, 1 TD; Doolan, 1 for 11; Gorgone, 1 for −2.

1947

CHI. CARDINALS 28, PHILADELPHIA 21

A frozen field in Comiskey Park did not prevent an offensive game as the Chicago Cardinals defeated the Philadelphia Eagles 28-21 in the first NFL championship playoff for either team. The Cardinals entered the game with an offensive plan designed to exploit the Eagles' tough 5-2-4 defense, which included a middle guard but no middle linebacker.

In a move reminiscent of the "Sneakers Game," the Cardinals started the game wearing basketball shoes. The Eagles followed suit a few minutes into the game.

Midway through the first quarter, the Cardinals double-teamed the Eagles' middle guard, and Charley Trippi raced 44 yards for a touchdown right up the middle. Early in the second quarter, the Cardinals ran a similar play, and Elmer Angsman went 70 yards for a touchdown, unhindered by any players past the line of scrimmage.

With the Cardinals holding NFL rushing leader Steve Van Buren to only 26 yards on 18 carries, the Eagles' offense could do very little until, with only a minute to go in the half, Tommy Thompson passed 36 yards to Pat McHugh, who ran in from the 17 to complete a 53-yard play.

The Eagles drove to two touchdowns in the second half, but still couldn't catch up because of the Cardinals' big plays. Midway through the third quarter, Trippi took a punt on his own 25, raced down the sideline before slipping on the Philadelphia 30, got to his feet, stumbled again on the 22, got up yet again, and went the rest of the way to complete a 75-yard touchdown return. Then, halfway through the fourth quarter, the Cardinals clinched the game when Angsman broke loose for another 70-yard touchdown run up the middle.

December 28, at Chicago

Philadelphia	Starting Lineups	Chi. Cardinals
Jack Ferrante	LE	Bill Blackburn
Vic Sears	LT	Dick Plasman
Cliff Patton	LG	Lloyd Arms
Alex Wojiechowicz	C	Vince Banonis
Frank (Bucko) Kilroy	RG	Hamilton Nichols
Al Wistert	RT	Stan Mauldin
Pete Pihos	RE	John Doolan
Pat McHugh	QB	Bill Campbell
Steve Van Buren	LH	John (Red) Cochran
Bosh Pritchard	RH	Marshall Goldberg
Joe Muha	FB	Walt Rankin

Philadelphia	0	7	7	7	—	21
Chi. Cardinals	7	7	7	7	—	28

ChiC—Trippi 44 run (Harder kick)
ChiC—Angsman 70 run (Harder kick)
Phil —McHugh 53 pass from Thompson (Patton kick)
ChiC—Trippi 75 punt return (Harder kick)
Phil —Van Buren 1 run (Patton kick)
ChiC—Angsman 70 run (Harder kick)
Phil —Craft 1 run (Patton kick)
Attendance—30,759

TEAM STATISTICS	Phil	ChiC
First downs	22	11
Rushing	10	8
Passing	11	2
By penalty	1	1
Total yardage	357	336
Net rushing yardage	60	282
Net passing yardage	297	54
Passes att.-comp.-had int.	44-27-3	14-3-2

RUSHING

Philadelphia—Muha, 8 for 31; Van Buren, 18 for 26, 1 TD; Craft, 6 for 8, 1 TD; Steele, 1 for 0; Thompson, 3 for 0; McHugh, 1 for −5.
Chi. Cardinals—Angsman, 10 for 159, 2 TDs; Trippi, 11 for 84, 1 TD; Harder, 10 for 37; Christman, 8 for 2.

PASSING

Philadelphia—Thompson, 27 of 44 for 297, 1 TD, 3 int.
Chi. Cardinals—Christman, 3 of 14 for 54, 2 int.

RECEIVING

Philadelphia—Ferrante, 8 for 73; Pritchard, 3 for 37; Pihos, 3 for 27; Craft, 3 for 27; McHugh, 2 for 55, 1 TD; Humbert, 2 for 30; Muha, 2 for 18; Armstrong, 2 for 16; Van Buren, 2 for 14.
Chi. Cardinals—Dewell, 1 for 38; Trippi, 1 for 20; Angsman, 1 for −4.

1948

PHILADELPHIA 7, CHI. CARDINALS 0

A protective tarpaulin was not removed from the playing field in Shibe Park until 30 minutes before the kickoff, but snow blanketed the entire field by game time. Of the 36,309 persons who bought tickets and assured a sellout, a total of 28,864 were on hand as the Philadelphia Eagles defeated the Chicago Cardinals 7-0 in a rematch of the teams that played for the NFL championship in 1947.

Conditions were so adverse that the stadium lights cast eerie shadows on the piles of snow along the sidelines and on the field. NFL Commissioner Bert Bell decreed that while the 10-yard first-down chain would be used there would be no measuring; the referee would be the final judge of all first downs. The sidelines were marked by ropes tied to stakes. Each time a field goal was tried, players from the kicking team would kneel and clear the snow with their hands to get a firmer footing.

The first time the Eagles had possession of the ball quarterback Tommy Thompson combined with end Jack Ferrante on a 65-yard pass play for a touchdown. An official's white penalty flag was thrown but it was invisible in the snow. When the Eagles realized the play would be called back because of an offside violation, Ferrante asked the official who had moved across the line of scrimmage before the snap of the ball. "You," said the official.

Turnovers gave both teams chances to score throughout the game. But missed field goals and tough defenses on fourth downs kept any points off the board until early in the fourth quarter. With less than a minute to go in the third quarter, Elmer Angsman fumbled at his 17-yard line, and Frank (Bucko) Kilroy of Philadelphia recovered. Bosh Pritchard took the ball to the 11 on the last play of the quarter. As the final quarter started, Joe Muha and Thompson gave the Eagles a first down with runs up the middle. Then Steve Van Buren plowed into the end zone from the five for the only score of the game.

The Cardinals played the entire game without injured quarterback Paul Christman.

December 19, at Philadelphia

Chi. Cardinals	Starters, Offense	Philadelphia
John (Red) Cochran	LE	John Green
Bob Zimny	LT	Jay MacDowell
Garrard (Buster) Ramsey	LG	Duke Maronic
Vince Banonis	C	Vic Lindskog
Plato Andros	RG	Frank (Bucko) Kilroy
Chet Bulger	RT	Al Wistert
Corwin Clatt	RE	Neill Armstrong
Jerry Davis	QB	Tommy Thompson
Charley Trippi	LH	Ernie Steele
Elmer Angsman	RH	Russ Craft
Pat Harder	FB	Joe Muha

Chi. Cardinals	0	0	0	0	—	0
Philadelphia	0	0	0	7	—	7

Phil—Van Buren 5 run (Patton kick)
Attendance—28,864

TEAM STATISTICS	ChiC	Phil
First downs	6	16
Rushing	3	15
Passing	3	0
By penalty	0	1
Total yardage	131	232
Net rushing yardage	96	225
Net passing yardage	35	7
Passes att.-comp.-had int.	11-3-1	12-2-2

RUSHING

Philadelphia—Van Buren, 26 for 98, 1 TD; Pritchard, 16 for 67; Thompson, 11 for 50; Myers, 2 for 7; Muha, 2 for 3.
Chi. Cardinals—Angsman, 10 for 33; Harder, 11 for 30; Trippi, 9 for 26; Mallouf, 2 for 5; Clatt, 1 for 2; Schwall, 1 for 0.

PASSING

Philadelphia—Thompson, 2 of 12 for 7, 2 int.
Chi. Cardinals—Mallouf, 3 of 7 for 35; Trippi, 0 of 2; Eikenburg, 0 of 2, 1 int.

RECEIVING

Philadelphia—Ferrante, 1 for 7; Pihos, 1 for 0.
Chi. Cardinals—Kutner, 2 for 19; Dewell, 1 for 16.

1949

PHILADELPHIA 14, LA RAMS 0

The NFL was finishing its thirtieth season, and the Philadelphia Eagles defeated the Los Angeles Rams 14-0 in the NFL Championship Game as fullback Steve Van Buren set records with 31 carries and 196 yards gained. Van Buren achieved the record after a storm that began 24 hours before kickoff dropped almost three inches of rain in Los Angeles. A crowd of more than 60,000, which would have set a playoff record, was expected before the storm. A total of 22,245 attended the game, which was played on a muddy field.

With Van Buren carrying the ball, the Eagles were able to maintain possession for 70 plays, compared to the Rams' 51. Philadelphia rushed for 274 yards, compared to 21 for Los Angeles. The Rams did not advance the ball further than the Eagles' 26-yard line. Philadelphia scored one of its touchdowns, the first of the game in the second quarter, on a 31-yard pass, quarterback Tommy Thompson to end Pete Pihos. It was Pihos's seventh touchdown in five games against Los Angeles. The score came after the only effective passing of the day. In a 63-yard drive, Thompson completed three key passes, one for 11 yards and a first down to Jack Ferrante, another for 16 yards and a first down to Ferrante, and then the touchdown pass.

The Eagles' other score came in the third quarter. Defensive end Len Skladany blocked Bob Waterfield's punt from the 5-yard line. The snap of the ball from center Don Paul was high and Waterfield had no chance to get the kick away. Skladany picked up the bouncing ball on the 2-yard line and scored.

The victory was Philadelphia's second in a row in the championship game, and it marked the Eagles' third straight appearance, climaxing the rise that began when Earle (Greasy) Neale was hired in 1941.

December 18, at Los Angeles

Philadelphia	Starting Lineups	LA Rams
Jack Ferrante	LE	Tom Fears
Vic Sears	LT	Dick Huffman
Cliff Patton	LG	Hal Dean
Vic Lindskog	C	John Martin
Frank (Bucko) Kilroy	RG	Ray Yagiello
Al Wistert	RT	Gil Bouley
Pete Pihos	RE	Bill Smyth
Tommy Thompson	QB	Bob Waterfield
Steve Van Buren	LH	Tom Kalmanir
Clyde (Smackover) Scott	RH	Verda (Vitamin T) Smith
John Myers	FB	Dick Hoerner

Philadelphia	0	7	7	0	—	14
LA Rams	0	0	0	0	—	0

Phil—Pihos 31 pass from Thompson (Patton kick)
Phil—Skladany 2 blocked punt return (Patton kick)
Attendance—22,245

TEAM STATISTICS	Phil	Rams
First downs	17	7
Rushing	12	0
Passing	4	6
By penalty	1	1
Total yardage	342	119
Net rushing yardage	274	21
Net passing yardage	68	98
Passes att.-comp.-had int.	9-5-2	27-10-1

RUSHING

Philadelphia—Van Buren, 31 for 196; Parmer, 15 for 41; Scott, 6 for 23; Thompson, 4 for 7; Ziegler, 3 for 4; Pritchard, 1 for 2; Myers, 1 for 1.
LA Rams—Gehrke, 3 for 13; Smith, 6 for 11; Hoerner, 7 for 10; Waterfield, 2 for 3; Hirsch, 2 for 0; Kalmanir, 2 for 0; Van Brocklin, 2 for −16.

PASSING

Philadelphia—Thompson, 5 of 9 for 68, 1 TD, 2 int.
LA Rams—Waterfield, 5 of 13 for 43, 1 int.; Van Brocklin, 5 of 15 for 55.

RECEIVING

Philadelphia—Ferrante, 2 for 27; Pihos, 1 for 31, 1 TD; Scott, 1 for 17; Thompson, 1 for −7.
LA Rams—Huffman, 2 for 26; Shaw, 2 for 21; Fears, 2 for 15; Smith, 2 for 11; Hoerner, 1 for 19; Younger, 1 for 6.

1950

CLEVELAND 30, LA RAMS 28

The Cleveland Browns, who joined the NFL in 1950 after winning four consecutive All-America Football Conference championships, defeated the Los Angeles Rams 30-28 on Lou Groza's 16-yard field goal with 28 seconds left in the game. Although the game was played on a frozen field amid snow flurries in 27-degree weather, the two teams unleashed potent passing attacks to set championship game records for passing yards and total yards.

On the first play from scrimmage, Bob Waterfield threw an 82-yard touchdown pass to Glenn Davis. But Cleveland came right back to score, with Otto Graham passing to Dub Jones for the tying touchdown. Eight plays after the kickoff, the Rams were back ahead again 14-7. Midway through the second period, Graham fired a strike to Dante Lavelli, who grabbed the pass between two Rams defenders on the 8-yard line and raced in for the score. Tommy James fumbled the snap on the extra point, and the Rams maintained a 14-13 halftime lead.

The Browns went ahead on another Graham-to-Lavelli touchdown pass in the third quarter, but then the Rams scored twice in 21 seconds. First, Dick Hoerner scored from the 1 on his seventh consecutive carry. Then, Marion Motley fumbled on the first play after the kickoff and Larry Brink picked up the ball and ran into the end zone for a touchdown.

Cleveland closed to a point with 4:35 left in the game, as Graham completed nine passes during a 65-yard drive, five in a row to Lavelli. Two minutes remained when the Browns took a Rams punt on their own 32. They moved to the 11 to position Groza's field goal.

December 24, at Cleveland

LA Rams	Starting Lineups	Cleveland
Tom Fears	LE	Mac Speedie
Dick Huffman	LT	Lou Groza
John Finlay	LG	Weldon Humble
Fred Naumetz	C	Frank Gatski
Harry Thompson	RG	Lin Houston
Bob Reinhard	RT	Lou Rymkus
Jack Zilly	RE	Dante Lavelli
Bob Waterfield	QB	Otto Graham
Glenn Davis	LH	Rex Bumgardner
Verda (Vitamin T) Smith	RH	Dub Jones
Dick Hoerner	FB	Marion Motley

LA Rams	14	0	14	0	—	28
Cleveland	7	6	7	10	—	30

Rams—Davis 82 pass from Waterfield (Waterfield kick)
Cle —Jones 27 pass from Graham (Groza kick)
Rams—Hoerner 3 run (Waterfield kick)
Cle —Lavelli 37 pass from Graham (kick failed)
Cle —Lavelli 39 pass from Graham (Groza kick)
Rams—Hoerner 1 run (Waterfield kick)
Rams—Brink 6 fumble return (Waterfield kick)
Cle —Bumgardner 14 pass from Graham (Groza kick)
Cle —FG Groza 16
Attendance—29,751

TEAM STATISTICS	Rams	Cle
First downs	22	22
Rushing	9	8
Passing	12	13
By penalty	1	1
Total yardage	418	414
Net rushing yardage	106	116
Net passing yardage	312	298
Passes att.-comp.-had int.	32-18-5	33-22-1

RUSHING
LA Rams—Hoerner, 24 for 86, 2 TDs; Smith, 4 for 11; Davis, 6 for 6; Waterfield, 1 for 2; Pasquariello, 1 for 1.
Cleveland—Graham, 12 for 99; Motley, 6 for 9; Jones, 2 for 4; Bumgardner, 5 for 2; Lavelli, 0 for 2.
PASSING
LA Rams—Waterfield, 18 of 31 for 312, 1 TD, 4 int.; Van Brocklin, 0 of 1, 1 int.
Cleveland—Graham, 22 of 32 for 298, 4 TDs, 1 int.
RECEIVING
LA Rams—Fears, 9 for 136; Hirsch, 4 for 42; Smith, 3 for 46; Davis, 2 for 88, 1 TD.
Cleveland—Lavelli, 11 for 128, 2 TDs; Jones, 4 for 80, 1 TD; Bumgardner, 4 for 46, 1 TD; Gillom, 1 for 29; Speedie, 1 for 17; Motley, 1 for −2.

1951

LA RAMS 24, CLEVELAND 17

The Los Angeles Rams won their first NFL championship since moving from Cleveland in 1946. The Rams defeated the Cleveland Browns 24-17 with the winning play a 73-yard pass and run involving quarterback Norm Van Brocklin and end Tom Fears. On third and three from the 27-yard line, Van Brocklin threw a 23-yard pass to Fears. Fears ran between defenders Cliff Lewis and Tom James, caught the ball at the 50-yard line, and ran to the end zone with 7:25 remaining in the game. The score came but 25 seconds after the Browns had tied the game on an eight-play, 70-yard drive culminated by Ken Carpenter's five-yard scoring run.

The Rams took a 7-0 lead in the second quarter on Dick Hoerner's one-yard run but they trailed 10-7 at the half after Lou Groza set a playoff record with a 52-yard field goal and Otto Graham threw a 17-yard touchdown pass to Dub Jones.

The Rams went back ahead in the third quarter. Graham fumbled on his own 24 when he was blind-sided by Larry Brink. Andy Robustelli advanced the fumble to the Browns' 2. On third down from the 1, Dan Towler blasted into the end zone. The Rams assumed a 17-10 lead early in the fourth quarter after a 17-yard field goal by Waterfield.

Fears described Van Brocklin's effort as "the best thrown pass I've ever caught. He laid it right in there full stride." Browns coach Paul Brown thought the play would not have worked if Lewis and James had not collided trying to cover Fears.

Despite suffering a championship-game loss for the first time ever, the Browns had a 372-334 edge in total offense.

December 23, at Los Angeles

Cleveland	Starting Lineups	LA Rams
Mac Speedie	LE	Tom Fears
Lou Groza	LT	Don Simensen
Abe Gibron	LG	Dick Daugherty
Frank Gatski	C	Leon McLaughlin
Bob Gaudio	RG	Bill Lange
Lou Rymkus	RT	Tom Dahms
Dante Lavelli	RE	Elroy (Crazylegs) Hirsch
Otto Graham	QB	Bob Waterfield
Ken Carpenter	LH	Dan Towler
Dub Jones	RH	Paul (Tank) Younger
Marion Motley	FB	Dick Hoerner

Cleveland	0	10	0	7	—	17
LA Rams	0	7	7	10	—	24

Rams—Hoerner 1 run (Waterfield kick)
Cle —FG Groza 52
Cle —Jones 17 pass from Graham (Groza kick)
Rams—Towler 1 run (Waterfield kick)
Rams—FG Waterfield 17
Cle —Carpenter 5 run (Groza kick)
Rams—Fears 73 pass from Van Brocklin (Waterfield kick)
Attendance—57,522

TEAM STATISTICS	Cle	Rams
First downs	22	20
Rushing	6	9
Passing	16	9
By penalty	0	2
Total yardage	372	334
Net rushing yardage	92	81
Net passing yardage	280	253
Passes att.-comp.-had int.	41-19-3	30-13-2

RUSHING
Cleveland—Graham, 5 for 43; Motley, 5 for 23; Carpenter, 4 for 14, 1 TD; Jones, 9 for 12.
LA Rams—Towler, 16 for 36, 1 TD; Younger, 4 for 20; Smith, 9 for 15; Waterfield, 2 for 8; Hoerner, 5 for 5, 1 TD; Van Brocklin, 1 for 3; Davis, 6 for −6.
PASSING
Cleveland—Graham, 19 of 40 for 280, 1 TD, 3 int.; Carpenter, 0 of 1.
LA Rams—Waterfield, 9 of 24 for 125, 1TD, 2 int.; Van Brocklin, 4 of 6 for 128.
RECEIVING
Cleveland—Speedie, 7 for 81; Lavelli, 4 for 66; Jones, 4 for 62, 1 TD; Carpenter, 3 for 48; Motley, 1 for 23.
LA Rams—Fears, 4 for 146, 1 TD; Hirsch, 4 for 66; Davis, 3 for 10; Smith, 1 for 18; Hoerner, 1 for 13.

1952

DETROIT 17, CLEVELAND 7

The Cleveland Browns outgained the Detroit Lions 384-258 and had 22 first downs to 10, but the Lions stopped Cleveland on their 21-, 21-, 24-, 5-, and 8-yard lines and scored a 17-7 victory for their first NFL championship since 1935. The Lions' most important defensive stand came in the fourth quarter when the score was 14-7. Cleveland fullback Marion Motley ran 43 yards to the Lions' 5. Motley was thrown for a five-yard loss on the next play. Then quarterback Otto Graham was thrown for a 12-yard loss attempting to pass. The Browns gained a yard on third down, and Graham threw an incomplete pass to Motley on fourth down.

Detroit went ahead early in the second quarter. Horace Gillom punted only 22 yards, and the Lions took over at midfield. On the eighth play of the drive, Bobby Layne scored on a quarterback sneak from the 2-yard line.

The score became 14-0 in the third quarter when halfback Doak Walker shook off a tackle by Bert Rechichar and ran 67 yards for a touchdown. Walker, who had been injured most of the season, had not scored a touchdown coming into the game. The Browns scored their touchdown on the following series, marching 67 yards in 11 plays. Fullback Harry (Chick) Jagade scored on a seven-yard run.

Pat Harder's 36-yard field goal in the fourth quarter clinched the victory for Detroit. The Lions had been forced to punt but Ken Carpenter fumbled the kick and Jim Martin recovered for Detroit on the 23. Following Harder's placement, the Browns moved from their 15-yard line to Detroit's 8. On fourth down, Graham passed to Ray Renfro in the end zone but Renfro deflected the ball to Darrell (Pete) Brewster. It was ruled an illegal catch—two offensive players made contact before a defensive player—and the ball, and the game, went over to Detroit.

December 28, at Cleveland

Detroit	Starters, Offense	Cleveland
Cloyce Box	LE	Darrell (Pete) Brewster
Bob Miller	LT	Lou Groza
Lou Creekmur	LG	Abe Gibron
Vince Banonis	C	Frank Gatski
Jim Martin	RG	Joe Skibinski
Gus Cifelli	RT	John Sandusky
Leon Hart	RE	Dante Lavelli
Bobby Layne	QB	Otto Graham
Doak Walker	LH	Ken Carpenter
Bob Hoernschemeyer	RH	Rex Bumgardner
Pat Harder	FB	Harry (Chick) Jagade

Detroit	0	7	7	3	—	17
Cleveland	0	0	7	0	—	7

Det—Layne 2 run (Harder kick)
Det—Walker 67 run (Harder kick)
Cle—Jagade 7 run (Groza kick)
Det—FG Harder 36
Attendance—50,934

TEAM STATISTICS	Det	Cle
First downs	10	22
Rushing	8	15
Passing	2	7
By penalty	0	0
Total yardage	258	384
Net rushing yardage	199	227
Net passing yardage	59	157
Passes att.-comp.-had int.	10-7-0	36-20-1

RUSHING
Detroit—Walker, 10 for 97, 1 TD; Layne, 9 for 47, 1 TD; Harder, 8 for 28; Hoernschemeyer, 7 for 27.
Cleveland—Jagade, 15 for 104, 1 TD; Motley, 6 for 74; Graham, 7 for 23; Carpenter, 3 for 13; Renfro, 3 for 13.
PASSING
Detroit—Layne, 7 of 9 for 68; Walker, 0 of 1.
Cleveland—Graham, 20 of 35 for 191, 1 int.; Motley, 0 of 1.
RECEIVING
Detroit—Harder, 2 for 18; Walker, 2 for 11; Hart, 1 for 15; Swiacki, 1 for 14; Box, 1 for 10.
Cleveland—Bumgardner, 4 for 43; Lavelli, 4 for 23; Renfro, 4 for 26; Motley, 3 for 21; Brewster, 2 for 53; Carpenter, 2 for 7; Gillom, 1 for 8.

1953

DETROIT 17, CLEVELAND 16

The Detroit Lions marched 80 yards to a touchdown late in the game to defeat the Cleveland Browns 17-16 in Briggs Stadium for their second straight NFL championship.

After Lou Groza kicked a 43-yard field goal to put the Browns ahead 16-10, the Lions took over on their 20-yard line with 4:10 remaining. Quarterback Bobby Layne passed 17 yards to Jim Doran on the first play. Two more passes were incomplete, but on third down Layne passed 18 yards to Doran for a first down on Cleveland's 45. Layne then passed nine yards to Cloyce Box, but Bob Hoernschemeyer was stopped for no gain. On third and one, Layne kept for three yards and a first down at Cleveland's 33. Layne then called a time out and discussed strategy with Lions coach Raymond (Buddy) Parker, who had been informed by coaches in the press box that the rush of Cleveland defensive end Len Ford created the possibility of the Lions succeeding on a screen pass to one of their running backs.

When Layne returned to the huddle he decided on another play. "Doran had been begging me to throw deep all day," Layne said. "Doran said he could get a step on Warren Lahr." The Lions' receiver was indeed open when he caught the ball on the 10-yard line. Doran, who was in the game because of an injury to starter Leon Hart, scored on the 33-yard pass with 2:08 remaining; Doak Walker's extra point provided the final margin.

In what was the worst day statistically of Otto Graham's career, the Lions scored after Graham fumbled and after he threw an interception, to lead 10-3 at the half. The Browns came back to go ahead on a touchdown by Harry (Chick) Jagade and two field goals by Groza.

December 27, at Detroit

Cleveland	Starting Lineups	Detroit
Darrell (Pete) Brewster	LE	Dorne Dibble
Lou Groza	LT	Lou Creekmur
Abe Gibron	LG	Harley Sewell
Frank Gatski	C	Vince Banonis
Chuck Noll	RG	Dick Stanfel
John Sandusky	RT	Ollie Spencer
Dante Lavelli	RE	Leon Hart
Otto Graham	QB	Bobby Layne
Ken Carpenter	LH	Doak Walker
Billy Reynolds	RH	Gene Gedman
Harry (Chick) Jagade	FB	Bob Hoernschemeyer

Cleveland	0	3	7	6	—	16
Detroit	7	3	0	7	—	17

Det—Walker 1 run (Walker kick)
Cle—FG Groza 13
Det—FG Walker 23
Cle—Jagade 9 run (Groza kick)
Cle—FG Groza 15
Cle—FG Groza 43
Det—Doran 33 pass from Layne (Walker kick)
Attendance—54,577

TEAM STATISTICS	Cle	Det
First downs	11	18
Rushing	9	10
Passing	1	7
By penalty	1	1
Total yardage	192	293
Net rushing yardage	182	129
Net passing yardage	10	164
Passes att.-comp.-had int.	16-3-2	26-12-2

RUSHING

Cleveland—Jagade, 15 for 104, 1 TD; Jones, 3 for 28; Reynolds, 6 for 16; Carpenter, 3 for 14; Renfro, 4 for 11; Graham, 5 for 9.
Detroit—Hoernschemeyer, 17 for 47; Layne, 11 for 46; Gedman, 8 for 29; Walker, 3 for 7, 1 TD.

PASSING

Cleveland—Graham, 2 of 15 for 20, 2 int.; Ratterman, 1 of 1 for 18.
Detroit—Layne, 12 of 25 for 179, 1 TD, 2 int.; Walker, 0 of 1.

RECEIVING

Cleveland—Jagade, 1 for 18; Lavelli, 1 for 13; Reynolds, 1 for 7.
Detroit—Doran, 4 for 95, 1 TD; Box, 4 for 54; Hoernschemeyer, 2 for −2; Dibble, 1 for 22; Walker, 1 for 10.

1954

CLEVELAND 56, DETROIT 10

In what he claimed was to be his last game, Otto Graham completed 9 of 12 passes for 163 yards and three touchdowns and ran for three touchdowns as the Cleveland Browns defeated the Detroit Lions 56-10.

The Browns had lost four games in a row to the Lions, including a 14-10 defeat in the final minute of the last regular-season game the week before. Cleveland had lost its league opener 28-10 to Philadelphia and had been beaten 55-27 by Pittsburgh in the third game. Although they had appeared in championship games every year since 1946, when they were members of the All-America Football Conference, the Browns had not won an NFL title since 1950, their first year in the league. They made up for those losses in a big way.

The Browns converted six Detroit turnovers (out of a total of nine) into touchdowns. A penalty on Gil Mains for roughing kicker Horace Gillom set up another. That came on a 35-yard pass, Graham to Ray Renfro, that gave Cleveland a 7-3 lead.

Renfro caught five passes and scored two touchdowns. The Browns had noticed that Bill Stits played close to the line when Cleveland was in a straight T-formation with no pass-receiving flanker in the loss to Detroit the previous week. The Browns decided to send Renfro out of the backfield on passes, and they engaged the Lions' safeties by sending their ends on crossing patterns. Stits did not have support and was unable to cover Renfro himself. Renfro's second touchdown, shortly before the half, increased the Browns' lead to 35-10.

December 26, at Cleveland

Detroit	Starters, Offense	Cleveland
Dorne Dibble	LE	Darrell (Pete) Brewster
Lou Creekmur	LT	Lou Groza
Harley Sewell	LG	Abe Gibron
Andy Miketa	C	Frank Gatski
Jim Martin	RG	Chuck Noll
Charlie Ane	RT	John Sandusky
Earl (Jug) Girard	RE	Dante Lavelli
Bobby Layne	QB	Otto Graham
Doak Walker	LH	Ray Renfro
Lew Carpenter	RH	Billy Reynolds
Bill Bowman	FB	Maurice Bassett

Detroit	3	7	0	0	—	10
Cleveland	14	21	14	7	—	56

Det—FG Walker 36
Cle—Renfro 35 pass from Graham (Groza kick)
Cle—Brewster 8 pass from Graham (Groza kick)
Cle—Graham 1 run (Groza kick)
Det—Bowman 5 run (Walker kick)
Cle—Graham 5 run (Groza kick)
Cle—Renfro 31 pass from Graham (Groza kick)
Cle—Graham 1 run (Groza kick)
Cle—Morrison 12 run (Groza kick)
Cle—Hanulak 10 run (Groza kick)
Attendance—43,827

TEAM STATISTICS	Det	Cle
First downs	16	17
Rushing	5	8
Passing	9	6
By penalty	2	2
Total yardage	331	303
Net rushing yardage	136	140
Net passing yardage	195	163
Passes att.-comp.-had int.	44-19-6	12-9-2

RUSHING

Detroit—Carpenter, 8 for 34; Bowman, 7 for 61, 1 TD; Walker, 3 for 13; Layne, 7 for 7; Hoernschemeyer, 2 for 2; Dublinski, 2 for −11.
Cleveland—Hanulak, 5 for 44, 1 TD; Graham, 9 for 27, 3 TDs; Bassett, 8 for 27; Morrison, 10 for 19, 1 TD; Reynolds, 6 for 16; Jones, 3 for 3; Renfro, 3 for 2; Ratterman, 1 for 2.

PASSING

Detroit—Layne, 18 of 42 for 177, 6 int.; Dublinski, 1 of 2 for 18.
Cleveland—Graham, 9 of 12 for 163, 3 TDs, 2 int.

RECEIVING

Detroit—Carpenter, 6 for 17; Girard, 5 for 57; Dibble, 4 for 63; Walker, 2 for 39; Hart, 1 for 19; Bowman, 1 for 0.
Cleveland—Renfro, 5 for 94, 2 TDs; Brewster, 2 for 53, 1 TD; Bassett, 1 for 10; Lavelli, 1 for 6.

1955

CLEVELAND 38, LA RAMS 14

Quarterback Otto Graham ended a 10-year professional football career by completing 14 of 25 passes for 209 yards and two touchdowns and scoring on runs of 1 and 15 yards as the Cleveland Browns defeated the Los Angeles Rams 38-14 before a record championship-playoff crowd of 85,693 persons. Graham announced his retirement after the game. In 10 seasons with the Browns, Graham was the quarterback in 10 championship games.

Graham had three passes intercepted, but the Rams were unable to convert. The Browns intercepted six of Los Angeles quarterback Norm Van Brocklin's passes. They converted four of the interceptions into a total of 24 points—the margin of difference.

The Rams moved from their 20 to Cleveland's 24 in the first quarter. Ken Konz intercepted Van Brocklin on first down and the Browns marched to Lou Groza's 26-yard field goal. In the second quarter, Van Brocklin was intercepted by Don Paul, who set a playoff record with a 65-yard return for a touchdown. After another interception by Tom James, Graham passed 50 yards to Dante Lavelli for a touchdown that made the score 17-7 at the half. After a drive that culminated in a 15-yard scoring run by Graham, an interception by Sam Palumbo set in motion a drive that ended with Graham's one-yard touchdown and a 31-7 lead with two minutes remaining in the third quarter. Graham accounted for another score 11 seconds into the final period, when he hit Ray Renfro with a 35-yard touchdown pass.

The Rams scored on a 67-yard pass play, Van Brocklin to Volney (Skeet) Quinlan, in the second quarter and on a four-yard run by Ron Waller in the fourth quarter.

December 26, at Los Angeles

Cleveland	Starting Lineups	LA Rams
Darrell (Pete) Brewster	LE	Tom Fears
Lou Groza	LT	Bob Cross
Abe Gibron	LG	Duane Putnam
Frank Gatski	C	Leon McLaughlin
Harold Bradley	RG	John Hock
Mike McCormack	RT	Charley Toogood
Dante Lavelli	RE	Elroy (Crazylegs) Hirsch
Otto Graham	QB	Norm Van Brocklin
Ray Renfro	LH	Ron Waller
Fred (Curly) Morrison	RH	Volney (Skeet) Quinlan
Ed Modzelewski	FB	Dan Towler

Cleveland	3	14	14	7	—	38
LA Rams	0	7	0	7	—	14

Cle —FG Groza 26
Cle —Paul 65 interception return (Groza kick)
Rams—Quinlan 67 pass from Van Brocklin (Richter kick)
Cle —Lavelli 50 pass from Graham (Groza kick)
Cle —Graham 15 run (Groza kick)
Cle —Graham 1 run (Groza kick)
Cle —Renfro 35 pass from Graham (Groza kick)
Rams—Waller 4 run (Richter kick)
Attendance—85,693

TEAM STATISTICS	Cle	Rams
First downs	17	17
Rushing	7	8
Passing	10	8
By penalty	0	1
Total yardage	371	259
Net rushing yardage	202	143
Net passing yardage	169	116
Passes att.-comp.-had int.	14-25-3	28-11-7

RUSHING

Cleveland—Modzelewski, 13 for 61; Bassett, 11 for 49; Morrison, 11 for 33; Graham, 9 for 21, 2 TDs; Jones, 1 for 3; Smith, 3 for 2.
LA Rams—Towler, 14 for 64; Waller, 11 for 48, 1 TD; Wade, 1 for 4.

PASSING

Cleveland—Graham, 14 of 25 for 209, 2 TDs, 3 int.
LA Rams—Van Brocklin, 11 of 25 for 166, 1 TD, 6 int.; Wade, 0 of 3, 1 int.

RECEIVING

Cleveland—Modzelewski, 5 for 34; Lavelli, 3 for 95, 1 TD; Renfro, 2 for 49, 1 TD; Jones, 1 for 11; Brewster, 1 for 9; Morrison, 1 for 7; Bassett, 1 for 4.
LA Rams—Quinlan, 5 for 116, 1 TD; Waller, 3 for 18; Fears, 1 for 16; Hirsch, 1 for 9; Towler, 1 for 7.

1956

NY GIANTS 47, CHI. BEARS 7

Gene Filipski returned George Blanda's opening kickoff 53 yards to the Chicago Bears' 39-yard line. The New York Giants scored four plays later on Mel Triplett's 17-yard run, signaling a 34-point first half en route to a 47-7 victory. The championship was the Giants' first since 1938 and was reminiscent of their victory over the Bears in the 1934 title game.

In 1934, the Giants beat the Bears 30-13 in the Polo Grounds in 9-degree weather on a frozen field after they switched from football cleats to basketball shoes in the second half. Before the 1956 game, which was played in 20-degree weather in Yankee Stadium, Giants' coach Jim Lee Howell sent Filipski and defensive back Ed Hughes to test the field. Hughes, who was wearing football shoes, slipped and fell after taking a few steps. Filipski maneuvered without trouble in basketball shoes. "Everyone wear sneakers," Howell announced to the team.

The Bears also wore rubber-soled shoes, but, hurt by two turnovers in the first quarter, they trailed 13-0 by the time Giants star quarterback Charlie Conerly made an appearance at the start of the second quarter, replacing Don Heinrich (who normally only probed the defenses so Conerly would know where to attack). Conerly directed three second-period touchdown drives and threw two touchdown passes in the second half. By the end of the game, third-string quarterback Bobby Clatterbuck was playing.

The Bears managed to score only after Emlen Tunnell fumbled away a punt on the Giants' 25-yard line.

December 30, at New York

Chi. Bears	Starting Lineups	NY Giants
Harlon Hill	LE	Kyle Rote
Bill Wightkin	LT	Roosevelt Brown
Herman Clark	LG	Bill Austin
Larry Strickland	C	Ray Wietecha
Stan Jones	RG	Jack Stroud
Kline Gilbert	RT	Dick Yelvington
Bill McColl	RE	Ken MacAfee
George Blanda	QB	Don Heinrich
Bob Watkins	LH	Frank Gifford
John Hoffman	RH	Alex Webster
Rick Casares	FB	Mel Triplett

Chi. Bears	0	7	0	0	—	7
NY Giants	13	21	6	7	—	47

NYG—Triplett 17 run (Agajanian kick)
NYG—FG Agajanian 17
NYG—FG Agajanian 43
NYG—Webster 3 run (Agajanian kick)
ChiB—Casares 9 run (Blanda kick)
NYG—Webster 1 run (Agajanian kick)
NYG—Moore blocked punt recovery in end zone (Agajanian kick)
NYG—Rote 9 pass from Conerly (kick failed)
NYG—Gifford 14 pass from Conerly (Agajanian kick)
Attendance—56,836

TEAM STATISTICS	ChiB	NYG
First downs	19	16
Rushing	8	8
Passing	10	8
By penalty	1	0
Total yardage	280	348
Net rushing yardage	67	126
Net passing yardage	213	222
Passes att.-comp.-had int.	47-20-2	20-11-0

RUSHING
Chi. Bears—Casares, 14 for 43, 1 TD; Caroline, 7 for 10; Watkins, 3 for 9; Blanda, 1 for 4; Hoffman, 1 for 3; Bingham, 1 for 1; Brown, 5 for −3.
NY Giants—Triplett, 13 for 71, 1 TD; Gifford, 5 for 30; Webster, 12 for 27, 2 TDs; Clatterbuck, 1 for 0; Filipski, 1 for 0; Moore, 1 for 0; Conerly, 1 for −2.

PASSING
Chi. Bears—Blanda, 12 of 27 for 140, 1 int.; Brown, 8 of 20 for 97, 1 int.
NY Giants—Conerly, 7 of 10 for 195, 2 TDs; Heinrich, 3 of 6 for 21; Clatterbuck, 1 of 3 for 12; Triplett, 0 of 1.

RECEIVING
Chi. Bears—Hill, 6 for 87; Dooley, 6 for 66; Casares, 4 for 41; McColl, 3 for 35; Caroline, 1 for 8.
NY Giants—Webster, 5 for 76; Gifford, 4 for 131, 1 TD; Chandler, 1 for 12; Rote, 1 for 9, 1 TD.

1957

DETROIT 59, CLEVELAND 14

The Detroit Lions defeated the Cleveland Browns 59-14 for their third NFL championship in six seasons, and four months and 19 days after coach Raymond (Buddy) Parker resigned at a "Meet the Lions" banquet at which he said, "I don't want to get involved in another losing season, so I'm leaving Detroit."

Quarterback Tobin Rote, acquired from Green Bay at the start of training camp and the Lions' regular since Bobby Layne was hurt late in the season's eleventh game against Cleveland, completed 12 of 19 passes for 280 yards and four touchdowns. One of Rote's most important passes came in the second quarter. Fullback Jim Brown had run 29 yards for a touchdown to end a drive of 78 yards that cut the score to 17-7 in favor of Detroit. The Lions moved to Cleveland's 26 on their next possession and apparently were going to attempt a field goal on fourth down. Rote kneeled to accept the snap from center and place the ball for kicker Jim Martin. But instead of acting as Martin's holder, Rote straightened up, moved to his right, and threw a 26-yard pass to Steve Junker that made the score 24-7.

The Browns never got closer than 17 points again, and when they cut the lead to 31-14 in the third quarter, Rote again snatched the momentum right back for Detroit. After the Lions returned the kickoff to the 22-yard line, Rote fired a 78-yard touchdown pass to Jim Doran to finish any Cleveland comeback hopes.

December 29, at Detroit

Cleveland	Starting Lineups	Detroit
Darrell (Pete) Brewster	LE	Jim Doran
Lou Groza	LT	Lou Creekmur
Herschel Forester	LG	Harley Sewell
Art Hunter	C	Frank Gatski
Fred Robinson	RG	Stan Campbell
Mike McCormack	RT	Ken Russell
Preston Carpenter	RE	Steve Junker
Tommy O'Connell	QB	Tobin Rote
Ray Renfro	LH	Gene Gedman
Lew Carpenter	RH	Howard Cassady
Jim Brown	FB	John Henry Johnson

Cleveland	0	7	7	0	—	14
Detroit	17	14	14	14	—	59

Det—FG Martin 31
Det—Rote 1 run (Martin kick)
Det—Gedman 1 run (Martin kick)
Cle—Brown 29 run (Groza kick)
Det—Junker 26 pass from Rote (Martin kick)
Det—Barr 19 interception return (Martin kick)
Cle—L. Carpenter 5 run (Groza kick)
Det—Doran 78 pass from Rote (Martin kick)
Det—Junker 23 pass from Rote (Martin kick)
Det—Middleton 32 pass from Rote (Martin kick)
Det—Cassady 16 pass from Reichow (Martin kick)
Attendance—55,263

TEAM STATISTICS	Cle	Det
First downs	17	22
Rushing	11	9
Passing	5	10
By penalty	1	3
Total yardage	313	438
Net rushing yardage	218	142
Net passing yardage	95	296
Passes att.-comp.-had int.	22-9-5	22-13-0

RUSHING
Detroit—Cassady, 8 for 48; Johnson, 8 for 40; Rote, 7 for 27, 1 TD; Gedman, 12 for 27, 1 TD; Reichow, 1 for 0.
Cleveland—L. Carpenter, 14 for 82, 1 TD; Brown, 20 for 69, 1 TD; Plum, 3 for 46; Renfro, 1 for 21.

PASSING
Detroit—Rote, 12 of 19 for 280, 4 TDs; Reichow, 1 of 3 for 16, 1 TD.
Cleveland—Plum, 5 of 13 for 51, 2 int.; O'Connell, 4 of 8 for 61, 2 int.; Hanulak, 0 for 1, 1 int.

RECEIVING
Detroit—Junker, 5 for 109, 2 TDs; Doran, 3 for 101, 1 TD; Cassady, 2 for 22, 1 TD; Middleton, 1 for 32, 1 TD; Johnson, 1 for 16; Tracy, 1 for 16.
Cleveland—P. Carpenter, 4 for 43; Brewster, 3 for 52; Renfro, 1 for 9; L. Carpenter, 1 for 8.

1958

BALTIMORE 23, NY GIANTS 17

The Baltimore Colts, who tied the game 17-17 on Steve Myhra's 20-yard field goal with seven seconds to play, defeated the New York Giants 23-17 in the first championship game to be decided in sudden-death overtime. The Colts marched 80 yards in 13 plays after taking a Giants punt in the extra period. Alan Ameche scored the winning touchdown on a one-yard run with 8:15 elapsed. Quarterback Johnny Unitas completed four passes during the drive, including two for 33 yards to end Raymond Berry. The key play in the march was a 23-yard run by Ameche that put the ball on the Giants' 20.

The Colts dominated the early action of the game despite trailing 3-0 after one quarter. By halftime, they led 14-3 after converting two fumbles by Frank Gifford into touchdowns.

The third quarter began with more of the same, as Baltimore, behind the precision passing of Unitas to Berry, drove to the Giants' 1-yard line. But on fourth down of a tremendous goal-line stand, linebacker Cliff Livingston dropped Ameche at the 5. The fired-up Giants then drove 95 yards for a touchdown, the big play being a 62-yard pass from Charlie Conerly to Kyle Rote. When Rote fumbled at Baltimore's 25, Alex Webster picked up the ball and ran it to the 1. The next play Mel Triplett scored, and, less than four minutes later, Conerly hooked up with Gifford on a 15-yard touchdown pass that put the Giants back ahead 17-14 with less than a minute elapsed in the fourth quarter.

With slightly more than two minutes left, Gifford was stopped inches short of a first down near midfield. The Giants chose to punt on fourth down, and, when the Colts took over, they had only two minutes to go 86 yards. That was enough time for Unitas.

December 28, at New York

Baltimore	Starting Lineups	NY Giants
Raymond Berry	LE	Kyle Rote
Jim Parker	LT	Roosevelt Brown
Art Spinney	LG	Al Barry
Madison (Buzz) Nutter	C	Ray Wietecha
Alex Sandusky	RG	Bob Mischak
George Preas	RT	Frank Youso
Jim Mutscheller	RE	Bob Schnelker
Johnny Unitas	QB	Don Heinrich
L.G. Dupre	LH	Frank Gifford
Lenny Moore	RH	Alex Webster
Alan Ameche	FB	Mel Triplett

Baltimore	0	14	0	3	6	—	23
NY Giants	3	0	7	7	0	—	17

NYG—FG Summerall 36
Balt —Ameche 2 run (Myhra kick)
Balt —Berry 15 pass from Unitas (Myhra kick)
NYG—Triplett 1 run (Summerall kick)
NYG—Gifford 15 pass from Conerly (Summerall kick)
Balt —FG Myhra 20
Balt —Ameche 1 run (no extra point attempted)
Attendance—64,185

TEAM STATISTICS	Balt	NYG
First downs	27	10
Rushing	9	3
Passing	17	7
By penalty	1	0
Total yardage	460	266
Net rushing yardage	138	88
Net passing yardage	322	178
Passes att.-comp.-had int.	40-26-1	18-12-0

RUSHING
NY Giants—Gifford, 12 for 60; Webster, 9 for 24; Triplett, 5 for 12, 1 TD; Conerly, 2 for 5; King, 3 for −13.
Baltimore—Ameche, 14 for 59, 2 TDs; Dupre, 11 for 30; Unitas, 4 for 26; Moore, 9 for 24.

PASSING
NY Giants—Conerly, 10 of 14 for 187, 1 TD; Heinrich, 2 of 4 for 13.
Baltimore—Unitas, 26 of 40 for 361, 1 TD, 1 int.

RECEIVING
NY Giants—Gifford, 3 for 14, 1 TD; Rote, 2 for 76; Schnelker, 2 for 63; Webster, 2 for 17; Triplett, 2 for 15; McAfee, 1 for 15.
Baltimore—Berry, 12 for 178, 1 TD; Moore, 5 for 99; Mutscheller, 4 for 63; Ameche, 3 for 14; Dupre, 2 for 7.

1959

BALTIMORE 31, NY GIANTS 16

A game that for three quarters was a nip-and-tuck repeat of the 1958 title game became a rout in the fourth quarter, as the Baltimore Colts scored 24 points to destroy the New York Giants 31-16.

Three field goals by Pat Summerall had overcome an early Baltimore lead of 7-0 built on a six-play, 80-yard drive culminating in Johnny Unitas's 60-yard touchdown pass to Lenny Moore. Leading 9-7 as the third period came to a close, the Giants faced a fourth and inches at the Baltimore 28. Spurning another field goal, quarterback Charlie Conerly sent Alex Webster into the line to gain the yardage. But he didn't.

When the Colts took possession, they suddenly had the flame they had missed all day, and Unitas marched them directly down to the go-ahead touchdown, which he scored himself on a four-yard sweep around right end.

Andy Nelson intercepted a pass by Conerly and returned the ball 17 yards to New York's 14 to set up Baltimore's next touchdown, a 12-yard pass from Unitas to Jerry Richardson. The Colts moved in front 28-9 when Johnny Sample intercepted a Conerly pass and ran 42 yards for a score. Sample intercepted another pass by Conerly, and his 24-yard return set up a 25-yard field goal by Steve Myhra.

Trailing 31-9, the Giants moved 70 yards, scoring with 32 seconds left in the game on Conerly's 32-yard pass to Bob Schnelker. The pass gave New York a final total-yardage advantage of 323-280 over the Colts, who were outrushed 118-73 and led only 207-205 in passing yardage.

December 27, at Baltimore

NY Giants	Starting Lineups	Baltimore
Kyle Rote	LE	Raymond Berry
Roosevelt Brown	LT	Jim Parker
Darrell Dess	LG	Art Spinney
Ray Wietecha	C	Madison (Buzz) Nutter
Jack Stroud	RG	Alex Sandusky
Frank Youso	RT	George Preas
Bob Schnelker	RE	Jim Mutscheller
Charlie Conerly	QB	Johnny Unitas
Frank Gifford	LH	Mike Sommer
Alex Webster	RH	Lenny Moore
Mel Triplett	FB	Alan Ameche

NY Giants	3	3	3	7	—	16
Baltimore	7	0	0	24	—	31

Balt —Moore 60 pass from Unitas (Myrha kick)
NYG—FG Summerall 23
NYG—FG Summerall 37
NYG—FG Summerall 23
Balt —Unitas 4 run (Myhra kick)
Balt —Richardson 12 pass from Unitas (Myhra kick)
Balt —Sample 42 interception return (Myrha kick)
Balt —FG Myrha 25
NYG—Schnelker 32 pass from Conerly (Summerall kick)
Attendance—57,545

TEAM STATISTICS	NYG	Balt
First downs	16	13
Rushing	4	3
Passing	11	10
By penalty	1	0
Total yardage	323	280
Net rushing yardage	118	73
Net passing yardage	205	207
Passes att.-comp.-had int.	38-17-3	29-18-0

RUSHING

Baltimore—Ameche, 9 for 30; Sommer, 6 for 15; Pricer, 4 for 14; Moore, 4 for 8; Unitas, 2 for 6, 1 TD.
NY Giants—Gifford, 9 for 50; Triplett, 6 for 39; Webster, 8 for 25; King, 2 for 4.

PASSING

Baltimore—Unitas, 18 of 29 for 265, 2 TDs.
NY Giants—Conerly, 16 of 35 for 234, 1 TD, 2 int.; Gifford, 1 of 2 for 19, 1 int.; King, 0 of 1.

RECEIVING

Baltimore—Berry, 5 for 68; Mutscheller, 5 for 40; Moore, 3 for 127, 1 TD; Price, 2 for 6; Ameche, 1 for 13; Richardson, 1 for 12, 1 TD; Sommer, 1 for −1.
NY Giants—Gifford, 9 for 50; Triplett, 6 for 39; Webster, 8 for 25; King, 2 for 4.

1960 AFL

HOUSTON 24, LA CHARGERS 16

The Houston Oilers defeated the Los Angeles Chargers 24-16 in the American Football League's first championship game, which was played in 50-degree weather at Jeppesen Stadium on the University of Houston campus. The rivalry between the teams, who divided two hotly contested regular-season games, was so intense that Los Angeles's Maury Schleicher and Houston's Julian Spence and Hogan Wharton were thrown out of the game for fighting.

The Chargers scored on their first two possessions. The Oilers came back to lead at halftime 10-9. George Blanda threw a touchdown pass to Dave Smith and then kicked a field goal after a 12-play, 40-yard drive on which he passed eight consecutive times.

Early in the fourth quarter, Houston still led by a point, but faced a third and nine at its own 12. Blanda threw a pass to Billy Cannon, who broke a tackle and outran the Chargers' secondary to complete an 88-yard touchdown play. Los Angeles moved to Houston's 22 in the final minute, but was stopped on fourth down. Had Los Angeles scored a touchdown, it would have tried for a two-point conversion that could have tied the game and created a sudden-death overtime.

January 1, 1961, at Houston

LA Chargers	Starters, Offense	Houston
Don Norton	SE	Bill Groman
Ernie Wright	LT	Al Jamison
Orlando Ferrante	LG	Bob Talamini
Don Rogers	C	George Belotti
Fred Cole	RG	Hogan Wharton
Ron Mix	RT	John Simerson
Dave Kocourek	TE	John Carson
Royce Womble	FL	Charley Hennigan
Jack Kemp	QB	George Blanda
Howie Ferguson	FB	Dave Smith
Paul Lowe	HB	Billy Cannon
	Starters, Defense	
Maury Schleicher	LE	Dalva Allen
Volney Peters	LT	Orville Trask
Gary Finneran	RT	George Shirkey
Ron Nery	RE	Dan Lanphear
Ron Botchan	LLB	Al Witcher
Emil Karas	MLB	Dennit Morris
Rommie Loudd	RLB	Mike Dukes
Charlie McNeil	LCB	Jim Norton
Dick Harris	RCB	Mark Johnston
Jim Sears	LS	Julian Spence
Bob Zeman	RS	Bobby Gordon

LA Chargers	6	3	7	0	—	16
Houston	0	10	7	7	—	24

LAC—FG Agajanian 38
LAC—FG Agajanian 22
Hou—Smith 17 pass from Blanda (Blanda kick)
Hou—FG Blanda 18
LAC—FG Agajanian 27
Hou—Groman 7 pass from Blanda (Blanda kick)
LAC—Lowe 2 run (Agajanian kick)
Hou—Cannon 88 pass from Blanda (Blanda kick)
Attendance—32,183

TEAM STATISTICS	LAC	Hou
First downs	21	17
Rushing	11	4
Passing	9	13
By penalty	1	0
Total yardage	333	401
Net rushing yardage	162	100
Net passing yardage	171	301
Passes att.-comp.-had int.	41-21-2	32-16-0

RUSHING

LA Chargers—Lowe, 21 for 165, 1 TD; Ferguson, 4 for 11; Ford, 2 for −5; Kemp, 6 for −9.
Houston—Cannon, 18 for 50; Smith, 19 for 45; Hall, 3 for 5.

PASSING

LA Chargers—Kemp, 21 of 41 for 171, 2 int.
Houston—Blanda, 16 of 31 for 301, 3 TDs; Cannon, 0 of 1.

RECEIVING

LA Chargers—Norton, 6 for 55; Womble, 6 for 29; Kocourek, 3 for 57; Lowe, 3 for 5; Ferguson, 2 for 19; Flowers, 1 for 6.
Houston—Smith, 5 for 52, 1 TD; Hennigan, 4 for 71; Cannon, 3 for 128, 1 TD; Groman, 3 for 37, 1 TD; Carson, 1 for 13.

1960 NFL

PHILADELPHIA 17, GREEN BAY 13

In his last game, Norm Van Brocklin had a little too much cunning and passing wizardry for the Green Bay Packers, as he led the Philadelphia Eagles to a 17-13 victory, marking the only championship loss ever for Vince Lombardi.

Billy Quinlan intercepted Van Brocklin's first pass on the second play of the game. The Packers gave up the ball on downs at the 5, but they regained possession when Ted Dean fumbled on the 22. Five plays later Paul Hornung kicked a 20-yard field goal. It was a key time for Philadelphia's defense—two turnovers deep in their territory, and the Eagles had given up only three points.

Although Hornung sent the Packers ahead 6-0 with a field goal in the second quarter, Van Brocklin brought the Eagles back. Taking over on his 43, Van Brocklin zipped a pass to Tommy McDonald for 22 yards and a first down. On the next play, Van Brocklin floated a pass up for McDonald, who caught it on the 5 and scored to send the Eagles ahead 7-6. Bobby Walston's 15-yard field goal and a 13-yard miss by Hornung left the Eagles ahead 10-6 at halftime.

Green Bay took a 13-10 lead in the fourth quarter on Bart Starr's seven-yard pass to Max McGee. Dean returned the ensuing kickoff 58 yards to the Packers' 39. A holding penalty moved the Eagles to the 32. Dean made six yards and Billy Barnes followed with six for a first down on the 20. Van Brocklin was thrown for a loss of seven, but he recovered with a 13-yard pass to Barnes. A run by Barnes and two by Dean put the ball in the end zone with 5:21 to play. But the Packers weren't dead. They drove to the Eagles' 22 with eight seconds left. Bart Starr passed to Jim Taylor, who reached the 8 before being dropped by Chuck Bednarik (who had played all 60 minutes) on the game's last play.

December 26, at Philadelphia

Green Bay	Starting Lineups	Philadelphia
Max McGee	SE	Bobby Walston
Bob Skoronski	LT	Jim McCusker
Fred (Fuzzy) Thurston	LG	Gerry Huth
Jim Ringo	C	Chuck Bednarik
Jerry Kramer	RG	Stan Campbell
Forrest Gregg	RT	J.D. Smith
Gary Knafelc	TE	Pete Retzlaff
Boyd Dowler	FL	Tommy McDonald
Bart Starr	QB	Norm Van Brocklin
Jim Taylor	FB	Ted Dean
Paul Hornung	HB	Billy Ray Barnes

Green Bay	3	3	0	7	—	13
Philadelphia	0	10	0	7	—	17

GB—FG Hornung 20
GB—FG Hornung 23
Phil—McDonald 35 pass from Van Brocklin (Walston kick)
Phil—FG Walston 15
GB—McGee 7 pass from Starr (Hornung kick)
Phil—Dean 5 run (Walston kick)
Attendance—67,325

TEAM STATISTICS	GB	Phil
First downs	22	13
Rushing	14	5
Passing	8	6
By penalty	0	2
Total yardage	401	296
Net rushing yardage	223	99
Net passing yardage	178	197
Passes att.-comp.-had int.	35-21-1	20-9-1

RUSHING

Philadelphia—Dean, 13 for 54, 1 TD; Barnes, 13 for 42; Van Brocklin, 2 for 3.
Green Bay—Taylor, 24 for 105; Hornung, 11 for 61; McGee, 1 for 35; Moore, 5 for 22; Starr, 1 for 0.

PASSING

Philadelphia—Van Brocklin, 9 of 20 for 204, 1 TD, 1 int.
Green Bay—Starr, 21 of 34 for 178, 1 TD, 1 int.; Hornung, 0 of 1.

RECEIVING

Philadelphia—McDonald, 3 for 90, 1 TD; Walston, 3 for 38; Retzlaff, 1 for 41; Dean, 1 for 22; Barnes, 1 for 13.
Green Bay—Knafelc, 6 for 76; Taylor, 6 for 46; Hornung, 4 for 14; McGee, 2 for 19, 1 TD; Moore, 2 for 9; Dowler, 1 for 14.

1961 AFL

HOUSTON 10, SAN DIEGO 3

The Houston Oilers defeated the San Diego Chargers 10-3 for the AFL championship in the season's fifth game between the teams. The Chargers defeated the Oilers twice in the 1961 preseason, and the teams divided two regular-season games, the Oilers winning the last meeting 33-13 to snap San Diego's 11-game winning streak.

Two of the AFL's top offenses were slowed all day by their own mistakes, as Houston turned the ball over seven times and San Diego six. The only score of the first half came on George Blanda's field goal after the Oilers gained good field position following a nine-yard San Diego punt.

The Oilers scored the game's only touchdown at the end of the only sustained march—going 80 yards in the third quarter. On third and five at San Diego's 35, Blanda was forced to leave the pocket when his receivers were covered. Running to his right, Blanda threw an 18-yard pass to Billy Cannon, who was running to his left and jumped to catch the ball. As Cannon came down, he shook off a tackler at the 17 and ran for a touchdown and 10-0 lead.

The Chargers' only score came with 12 seconds elapsed in the fourth quarter when George Blair kicked a 12-yard field goal. San Diego's last chance ended when Jack Kemp's pass was intercepted by Julian Spence in the final two minutes, the tenth interception of the game.

December 24, at San Diego

Houston	**Starters, Offense**	**San Diego**
Bill Groman	SE	Don Norton
Al Jamison	LT	Ernie Wright
Bob Talamini	LG	Ernie Barnes
Bob Schmidt	C	Don Rogers
Hogan Wharton	RG	Ron Mix
Rich Michael	RT	Sherman Plunkett
Willard Dewveall	TE	Dave Kocourek
Charley Hennigan	FL	Bob Scarpitto
George Blanda	QB	Jack Kemp
Charley Tolar	FB	Keith Lincoln
Billy Cannon	HB	Paul Lowe
	Starters, Defense	
Dalva Allen	LE	Earl Faison
George Shirkey	LT	Henry Schmidt
Ed Husmann	RT	Bill Hudson
Don Floyd	RE	Ron Nery
Doug Cline	LLB	Maury Schleicher
Dennit Morris	MLB	Emil Karas
Mike Dukes	RLB	Bob Laraba
Tony Banfield	LCB	Claude (Hoot) Gibson
Mark Johnston	RCB	Dick Harris
Jim Norton	LS	Charlie McNeil
Freddie Glick	RS	Bob Zeman

Houston	0	3	7	0	—	10
San Diego	0	0	0	3	—	3

Hou—FG Blanda 46
Hou—Cannon 35 pass from Blanda (Blanda kick)
SD —FG Blair 12
Attendance—29,556

TEAM STATISTICS	**Hou**	**SD**
First downs	18	15
Rushing	6	6
Passing	8	8
By penalty	4	1
Total yardage	256	256
Net rushing yardage	96	79
Net passing yardage	160	177
Passes att.-comp.-had int.	41-18-6	32-17-4

RUSHING
Houston—Tolar, 16 for 52; Cannon, 15 for 48; Blanda, 2 for −4.
San Diego—Roberson, 8 for 37; Lowe, 5 for 30; Lincoln, 3 for 7; Kemp, 4 for 5.
PASSING
Houston—Blanda, 18 of 40 for 160, 1 TD, 5 int.; Groman, 0 of 1, 1 int.
San Diego—Kemp, 17 of 32 for 226, 4 int.
RECEIVING
Houston—Cannon, 5 for 53, 1 TD; Hennigan, 5 for 43; Groman, 3 for 32; Dewveall, 2 for 10; Tolar, 2 for 2; McLeod, 1 for 20.
San Diego—Kocourek, 7 for 123; Norton, 3 for 48; Flowers, 2 for 17; Roberson, 1 for 11; Lowe, 1 for 10; Scarpitto, 1 for 9; Hayes, 1 for 5; Lincoln, 1 for 3.

1961 NFL

GREEN BAY 37, NY GIANTS 0

Paul Hornung, on leave from the U.S. Army, rushed for 89 yards in 20 carries and scored a record 19 points as the Green Bay Packers won their first championship in 17 years, defeating the New York Giants 37-0 in 21-degree weather at Lambeau Field. In their last appearance in a championship game, the Packers scored a 14-7 victory over the Giants.

Despite the cold, the field was in good condition. Fifty stadium workers had begun removing 14 inches of snow that covered 20 tons of hay at 6 A.M. the morning of the game. The bench areas of both teams were warmed by large infra-red heating units.

The Packers, who outgained New York 345-130 in total yardage, scored 24 points to break open the game in the second quarter following a scoreless first period. Hornung's six-yard run four seconds into the second quarter was followed by touchdown passes of 13 and 14 yards from Bart Starr to Boyd Dowler and Ron Kramer and a 17-yard field goal by Hornung just before halftime.

The Giants had threatened to score several times in the first quarter, but Kyle Rote dropped a sure touchdown pass deep in Green Bay territory, and halfback Bob Gaiters overthrew a wide-open Rote in the end zone.

December 31, at Green Bay

NY Giants	**Starters, Offense**	**Green Bay**
Del Shofner	SE	Max McGee
Roosevelt Brown	LT	Bob Skoronski
Darrell Dess	LG	Fred (Fuzzy) Thurston
Ray Wietecha	C	Jim Ringo
Jack Stroud	RG	Forrest Gregg
Greg Larson	RT	Norm Masters
Joe Walton	TE	Ron Kramer
Kyle Rote	FL	Boyd Dowler
Y.A. Tittle	QB	Bart Starr
Alex Webster	FB	Jim Taylor
Joel Wells	HB	Paul Hornung
	Starters, Defense	
Jim Katcavage	LE	Willie Davis
Dick Modzelewski	LT	Dave (Hawg) Hanner
Roosevelt Grier	RT	Henry Jordan
Andy Robustelli	RE	Bill Quinlan
Cliff Livingston	LLB	Dan Currie
Sam Huff	MLB	Ray Nitschke
Tom Scott	RLB	Bill Forester
Erich Barnes	LCB	Hank Gremminger
Dick Lynch	RCB	Jesse Whittenton
Joe Morrison	LS	John Symank
Jim Patton	RS	Willie Wood

NY Giants	0	0	0	0	—	0
Green Bay	0	24	10	3	—	37

GB—Hornung 6 run (Hornung kick)
GB—Dowler 13 pass from Starr (Hornung kick)
GB—R. Kramer 14 pass from Starr (Hornung kick)
GB—FG Hornung 17
GB—FG Hornung 22
GB—R. Kramer 13 pass from Starr (Hornung kick)
GB—FG Hornung 19
Attendance—39,029

TEAM STATISTICS	**NYG**	**GB**
First downs	6	19
Rushing	1	10
Passing	4	8
By penalty	1	1
Total yardage	130	345
Net rushing yardage	31	181
Net passing yardage	99	164
Passes att.-comp.-had int.	29-10-4	19-10-0

RUSHING
NY Giants—Webster, 7 for 19; Wells, 3 for 9; King, 2 for 5; Gaiters, 1 for 2; Tittle, 1 for −4.
Green Bay—Hornung, 20 for 89, 1 TD; Taylor, 14 for 69; Moore, 6 for 25; Pitts, 3 for 2; Roach, 1 for 0.
PASSING
NY Giants—Tittle, 6 of 20 for 65, 4 int.; Cornerly, 4 of 8 for 54; Gaiters, 0 of 1.
Green Bay—Starr, 10 of 17 for 164, 3 TDs; Hornung, 0 of 2.
RECEIVING
NY Giants—Rote, 3 for 54; Shofner, 3 for 41; Webster, 3 for 5; Walton, 1 for 19.
Green Bay—Kramer, 4 for 80, 2 TDs; Hornung, 3 for 47; Dowler, 3 for 37, 1 TD.

1962 AFL

DALLAS TEXANS 20, HOUSTON 17

The Dallas Texans won the longest game in the history of professional football (to that point) on Tommy Brooker's 25-yard field goal at 2:54 of the sixth quarter—after 17:54 of sudden-death overtime. Brooker's kick gave the Texans a 20-17 victory over the two-time defending champion Houston Oilers before a record AFL championship crowd of 37,981 in Jeppesen Stadium.

The kick also saved Abner Haynes, Dallas's all-league halfback and captain, from being an embarrassing footnote to history. When Haynes went to the center of the field to participate in the coin toss at the start of the fifth quarter, he put the Texans in jeopardy. Haynes won the toss and inadvertently said the Texans "would kick to the clock," not only giving the Oilers possession of the ball, but with the wind at their backs. Houston was not able to capitalize on the advantage, although at the end of the fifth quarter the Oilers got to Dallas's 35-yard line. On second down, a George Blanda pass was intercepted by Texans defensive end Bill Hull, who ran 23 yards to midfield. Dallas then started its winning drive. On third and eight at the Houston 48, Len Dawson threw complete to Jack Spikes for 10 yards. On the next play, Spikes burst through the left side for 19 yards and a first down at the Houston 19. On fourth and nine, Brooker kicked the winning field goal.

December 23, at Houston

Dallas Texans	**Starters, Offense**	**Houston**
Tommy Brooker	SE	Bob McLeod
Jim Tyrer	LT	Al Jamison
Marvin Terrell	LG	Bob Talamini
Jon Gilliam	C	Bob Schmidt
Al Reynolds	RG	Hogan Wharton
Jerry Cornelison	RT	Rich Michael
Fred Arbanas	TE	Willard Dewveall
Frank Jackson	FL	Charley Hennigan
Len Dawson	QB	George Blanda
Curtis McClinton	FB	Charley Tolar
Abner Haynes	HB	Billy Cannon
	Starters, Defense	
Curt Merz	LE	Gary Cutsinger
Paul Rochester	LT	Ed Culpepper
Jerry Mays	RT	Ed Husmann
Mel Branch	RE	Don Floyd
E.J. Holub	LLB	Doug Cline
Sherrill Headrick	MLB	Gene Babb
Walt Corey	RLB	Mike Dukes
Duane Wood	LCB	Tony Banfield
Dave Grayson	RCB	Bobby Jancik
Bobby Hunt	LS	Jim Norton
Bobby Ply	RS	Fred Glick

Dallas Texans	3	14	0	0	0	3	—	20
Houston	0	0	7	10	0	0	—	17

Dall—FG Brooker 16
Dall—Haynes 28 pass from Dawson (Brooker kick)
Dall—Haynes 2 run (Brooker kick)
Hou—Dewveall 15 pass from Blanda (Blanda kick)
Hou—FG Blanda 31
Hou—Tolar 1 run (Blanda kick)
Dall—FG Brooker 25
Attendance—37,981

TEAM STATISTICS	**Dall**	**Hou**
First downs	19	21
Rushing	10	6
Passing	5	15
By penalty	4	0
Total yardage	237	359
Net rushing yardage	199	98
Net passing yardage	38	261
Passes att.-comp.-had int.	14-9-0	46-23-5

RUSHING
Houston—Tolar, 17 for 58, 1 TD; Cannon, 11 for 37; Smith, 2 for 3.
Dallas Texans—Spikes, 11 for 77; McClinton, 24 for 70; Haynes, 14 for 26, 1 TD; Dawson, 5 for 26.
PASSING
Houston—Blanda, 23 of 46 for 261, 1 TD, 5 int.
Dallas Texans—Dawson, 9 of 14 for 88, 1 TD.
RECEIVING
Houston—Dewveall, 6 for 95, 1 TD; Cannon, 6 for 54; McLeod, 5 for 70, Hennigan, 3 for 37; Tolar, 1 for 8; 1 for 6; Jamison, 1 for −9.
Dallas Texans—Haynes, 3 for 45, 1 TD; Spikes, 2 for 24; Arbanas, 2 for 21; McClinton, 1 for 4; Bishop, 1 for −6.

1962 NFL

GREEN BAY 16, NY GIANTS 7

The Green Bay Packers fought off the New York Giants in 13-degree cold and winds that gusted up to 40 miles per hour in Yankee Stadium to score a 16-7 victory for their eighth NFL championship and second in a row. The Giants lost in the championship playoff for the fourth time in five years and the tenth time in thirteen appearances. Offensive backfield coach Kyle Rote, who retired as a Giants player after the 1961 season, remarked, "I never before saw a team that tried so hard and lost."

The Giants concentrated most of their efforts on fullback Jim Taylor, who tied a record with 31 carries. Taylor gained 85 yards, scored on a seven-yard touchdown run in the second quarter, and maintained a constant exchange with Giants defenders, challenging them to "hit me harder." The touchdown came late in the half, after Dan Currie tackled New York's Phil King, who fumbled on the Giants' 28, with the Packers recovering. On first down, Paul Hornung passed 21 yards to Boyd Dowler on a halfback option. On the next play, Taylor burst through the middle of the line to score.

Although they outgained Green Bay 291-244 in total yards, the Giants never led. Their only touchdown came when the score was 10-0 in the third quarter. Erich Barnes blocked Max McGee's punt and Jim Collier recovered in the end zone for a touchdown.

December 30, at New York

Green Bay	Starters, Offense	NY Giants
Max McGee	SE	Del Shofner
Norm Masters	LT	Roosevelt Brown
Fred (Fuzzy) Thurston	LG	Darrell Dess
Jim Ringo	C	Ray Wietecha
Jerry Kramer	RG	Greg Larson
Forrest Gregg	RT	Jack Stroud
Ron Kramer	TE	Joe Walton
Boyd Dowler	FL	Frank Gifford
Bart Starr	QB	Y.A. Tittle
Jim Taylor	FB	Alex Webster
Paul Hornung	HB	Phil King
	Starters, Defense	
Willie Davis	LE	Jim Katcavage
Dave (Hawg) Hanner	LT	Dick Modzelewski
Henry Jordan	RT	Roosevelt Grier
Bill Quinlan	RE	Andy Robustelli
Dan Currie	LLB	Bill Winter
Ray Nitschke	MLB	Sam Huff
Bill Forester	RLB	Tom Scott
Herb Adderley	LCB	Erich Barnes
Jesse Whittenton	RCB	Dick Lynch
Hank Gremminger	LS	Alan Webb
Willie Wood	RS	Jim Patton

Green Bay	3	7	3	3	—	16
NY Giants	0	0	7	0	—	7

GB —FG J. Kramer 26
GB —Taylor 7 run (J. Kramer kick)
NYG—Collier blocked punt recovery in end zone (Chandler kick)
GB —FG J. Kramer 29
GB —FG J. Kramer 30
Attendance—64,892

TEAM STATISTICS	GB	NYG
First downs	18	18
Rushing	11	5
Passing	6	11
By penalty	1	2
Total yardage	244	291
Net rushing yardage	148	94
Net passing yardage	96	197
Passes att.-comp.-had int.	22-10-0	41-18-1

RUSHING
Green Bay—Taylor, 31 for 85, 1 TD; Hornung, 8 for 35; Moore, 6 for 24; Starr, 1 for 4.
NY Giants—Webster, 15 for 56; King, 11 for 38.

PASSING
Green Bay—Starr, 9 of 21 for 85; Hornung, 1 of 1 for 21.
NY Giants—Tittle, 18 of 41 for 197, 1 int.

RECEIVING
Green Bay—Dowler, 4 for 48; Taylor, 3 for 20; R. Kramer, 2 for 25; McGee, 1 for 13.
NY Giants—Walton, 5 for 75; Shofner, 5 for 69; Gifford, 4 for 34; King, 2 for 14; Webster, 1 for 5; Morrison, 1 for 0.

1963 AFL

SAN DIEGO 51, BOSTON 10

Fullback Keith Lincoln of San Diego outgained the Boston Patriots 329-261 in total offense and led the Chargers to a 51-10 victory. Chargers coach Sid Gillman, pointing to the rival NFL, said after the game, "We're the champions of the world. If anyone wants to debate it, let them play us."

Lincoln gained 206 yards on 13 carries and caught seven passes for 123 yards. On the second play from scrimmage, he raced straight up the middle for a 56-yard gain. Seven plays later, Tobin Rote scored on a quarterback sneak. The next time the Chargers touched the ball, Lincoln was off again, running 67 yards for a touchdown. And then, after the Patriots scored to cut the lead to 14-7, the Chargers' Paul Lowe reeled off the third long run of the first quarter, going 58 yards for a touchdown. The Chargers increased their lead to 31-10 at halftime, and then kept the rout going, as reserve quarterback John Hadl passed for a touchdown and ran for a touchdown in the fourth quarter. San Diego finished with a record of 610 yards total offense.

January 5, 1964, at San Diego

Boston	Starters, Offense	San Diego
Gino Cappelletti	SE	Don Norton
Don Oakes	LT	Ernie Wright
Charlie Long	LG	Sam DeLuca
Walt Cudzik	C	Don Rogers
Billy Neighbors	RG	Pat Shea
Milt Graham	RT	Ron Mix
Tony Romeo	TE	Dave Kocourek
Jim Colclough	FL	Lance Alworth
Vito (Babe) Parilli	QB	Tobin Rote
Larry Garron	FB	Keith Lincoln
Ron Burton	HB	Paul Lowe
	Starters, Defense	
Larry Eisenhauer	LE	Earl Faison
Jesse Richardson	LT	Henry Schmidt
Houston Antwine	RT	George Gross
Bob Dee	RE	Bob Petrich
Tom Addison	LLB	Emil Karas
Nick Buoniconti	MLB	Chuck Allen
Jack Rudolph	RLB	Paul Maguire
Dick Felt	LCB	Bud Whitehead
Bob Suci	RCB	Dick Harris
Ron Hall	LS	George Blair
Ross O'Hanley	RS	Gary Glick

Boston	7	3	0	0	—	10
San Diego	21	10	7	13	—	51

SD —Rote 2 run (Blair kick)
SD —Lincoln 67 run (Blair kick)
Bos—Garron 7 run (Cappelletti kick)
SD —Lowe 58 run (Blair kick)
SD —FG Blair 11
Bos—FG Cappelletti 15
SD —Norton 14 pass from Rote (Blair kick)
SD —Alworth 48 pass from Rote (Blair kick)
SD —Lincoln 25 pass from Hadl (pass failed)
SD —Hadl 1 run (Blair kick)
Attendance—30,127

TEAM STATISTICS	Bos	SD
First downs	14	21
Rushing	6	11
Passing	8	9
By penalty	0	1
Total yardage	261	610
Net rushing yardage	75	318
Net passing yardage	186	292
Passes att.-comp.-had int.	37-17-2	26-17-0

RUSHING
San Diego—Lincoln, 13 for 206, 1 TD; Lowe, 12 for 94, 1 TD; Rote, 4 for 15, 1 TD; McDougall, 1 for 2; Hadl, 1 for 1, 1 TD; Jackson, 1 for 0.
Boston—Crump, 7 for 18; Garron, 3 for 15, 1 TD; Lott, 3 for 15; Yewcic, 1 for 14; Parilli, 1 for 10; Burton, 1 for 3.

PASSING
San Diego—Rote, 10 of 15 for 173, 2 TDs; Hadl, 6 of 10 for 112, 1 TD; Lincoln, 1 of 1 for 20.
Boston—Parilli, 14 of 29 for 189, 1 int.; Yewcic, 3 of 8 for 39, 1 int.

RECEIVING
San Diego—Lincoln, 7 for 123, 1 TD; Alworth, 4 for 77, 1 TD; Norton, 2 for 44, 1 TD; MacKinnon, 2 for 52; Kocourek, 1 for 5; McDougall, 1 for 4.
Boston—Burton, 4 for 12; Colclough, 3 for 26; Cappelletti, 2 for 72; Graham, 2 for 68; Crump, 2 for 28; Lott, 2 for 16; Garron, 2 for 6.

1963 NFL

CHI. BEARS 14, NY GIANTS 10

The sun was shining but the temperature was eight degrees at Wrigley Field, where the Chicago Bears intercepted five passes by New York Giants quarterback Y.A. Tittle, two of them setting up touchdowns in a 14-10 victory. Tittle played the second half with a severely strained knee, the result of a second-quarter tackle by Larry Morris.

The Giants scored first after Chicago quarterback Bill Wade fumbled on the New York 17. Tittle put together an 83-yard drive, culminating in his 14-yard touchdown pass to Frank Gifford. The Giants had a chance to further build their lead after recovering halfback Willie Galimore's fumble on the Bears' 31. But on the next play, Del Shofner dropped Tittle's perfect pass in the end zone, and New York never converted.

The Bears scored their first touchdown after linebacker Morris intercepted a screen pass intended for Phil King and returned the ball 61 yards to New York's 5-yard line. Wade scored on a two-yard run. The second touchdown followed an interception of another screen pass, by defensive end Ed O'Bradovich, who returned the ball 10 yards to the Giants' 14. Wade scored five plays later from the 1.

The Giants' defeat was their fifth in six years in the championship game. Their overall record was 3-11 since they lost to the Bears 23-21 in Wrigley Field in the NFL's first playoff game in 1933.

December 29, at Chicago

NY Giants	Starters, Offense	Chi. Bears
Del Shofner	SE	John Farrington
Roosevelt Brown	LT	Herman Lee
Darrell Dess	LG	Ted Karras
Greg Larson	C	Mike Pyle
Bookie Bolin	RG	Roger Davis
Jack Stroud	RT	Bob Wetoska
Joe Walton	TE	Mike Ditka
Frank Gifford	FL	Johnny Morris
Y.A. Tittle	QB	Bill Wade
Joe Morrison	FB	Joe Marconi
Phil King	HB	Willie Galimore
	Starters, Defense	
Jim Katcavage	LE	Ed O'Bradovich
Dick Modzelewski	LT	Stan Jones
John LoVetere	RT	Fred Williams
Andy Robustelli	RE	Doug Atkins
Jerry Hillebrand	LLB	Joe Fortunato
Sam Huff	MLB	Bill George
Tom Scott	RLB	Larry Morris
Erich Barnes	LCB	Bennie McRae
Dick Lynch	RCB	Dave Whitsell
Dick Pesonen	LS	Richie Petitbon
Jim Patton	RS	Roosevelt Taylor

NY Giants	7	3	0	0	—	10
Chi. Bears	7	0	7	0	—	14

NYG—Gifford 14 pass from Tittle (Chandler kick)
ChiB—Wade 2 run (Jencks kick)
NYG—FG Chandler 13
ChiB—Wade 1 run (Jencks kick)
Attendance—45,801

TEAM STATISTICS	NYG	ChiB
First downs	17	14
Rushing	8	6
Passing	9	7
By penalty	0	1
Total yardage	268	222
Net rushing yardage	128	93
Net passing yardage	140	129
Passes att.-comp.-had int.	30-11-5	28-10-0

RUSHING
NY Giants—Morrison, 18 for 61; King, 9 for 39; McElhenny, 7 for 19; Webster, 3 for 7; Tittle, 1 for 2.
Chi. Bears—Bull, 13 for 42; Wade, 8 for 34; 2 TDs; Galimore, 7 for 12; Marconi, 3 for 5.

PASSING
NY Giants—Tittle, 11 of 29 for 147, 1 TD, 5 int.; Griffing, 0 of 1.
Chi. Bears—Wade, 10 of 28 for 138.

RECEIVING
NY Giants—Gifford, 3 for 45, 1 TD; Morrison, 3 for 18; Thomas, 2 for 46; McElhenny, 2 for 20; Webster, 1 for 18.
Chi. Bears—Marconi, 3 for 64; Ditka, 3 for 38; J. Morris, 2 for 19; Coia, 1 for 22; Bull, 1 for −5.

1964 AFL

BUFFALO 20, SAN DIEGO 7

The San Diego Chargers scored on a 26-yard pass from quarterback Tobin Rote to end Dave Kocourek the first time they touched the ball, and were driving again on their second possession when Rote threw an 11-yard pass to fullback Keith Lincoln, who had swung out of the backfield. Buffalo linebacker Mike Stratton came up to make the tackle and hit Lincoln with such force that the San Diego star suffered a broken rib and had to be carried off the field. Lincoln, who also had rushed for 47 yards in three carries, including a 38-yard run that set up the touchdown, did not return. The Chargers struggled without him and dropped a 20-7 decision.

An AFL championship game record crowd of 40,242 persons in War Memorial Stadium saw the Bills take a 13-7 halftime lead on field goals of 12 and 17 yards by Pete Gogolak, sandwiched around a four-yard run by Wray Carlton.

The third quarter was scoreless, but the dominance of the Bills had been established. While the Chargers couldn't get any second-half offense mounted with either Rote or John Hadl at quarterback, in the fourth quarter, Jack Kemp passed 48 yards to end Glenn Bass to set up the Bills' final score. Kemp went over from the 1-yard line two plays later.

December 26, at Buffalo

San Diego	Starters, Offense	Buffalo
Don Norton	SE	Glenn Bass
Ernie Wright	LT	Stew Barber
Pat Shea	LG	Billy Shaw
Don Rogers	C	Walt Cudzik
Walt Sweeney	RG	Al Bemiller
Ron Mix	RT	Dick Hudson
Dave Kocurek	TE	Ernie Warlick
Jerry Robinson	FL	Elbert Dubenion
Tobin Rote	QB	Jack Kemp
Keith Lincoln	FB	Cookie Gilchrist
Paul Lowe	HB	Wray Carlton
	Starters, Defense	
Earl Faison	LE	Ron McDole
George Gross	LT	Jim Dunaway
Ernie Ladd	RT	Tom Sestak
Bob Petrich	RE	Tom Day
Ron Carpenter	LLB	John Tracey
Chuck Allen	MLB	Harry Jacobs
Frank Buncom	RLB	Mike Stratton
Jim Warren	LCB	Charley Warner
Dick Westmoreland	RCB	George (Butch) Byrd
Kenny Graham	SS	Gene Sykes
Bud Whitehead	FS	George Saimes

San Diego	7	0	0	0	—	7
Buffalo	3	10	0	7	—	20

SD —Kocourek 26 pass from Rote (Lincoln kick)
Buff—FG Gogolak 12
Buff—Carlton 4 run (Gogolak kick)
Buff—FG Gogolak 17
Buff—Kemp 1 run (Gogolak kick)
Attendance—40,242

TEAM STATISTICS	SD	Buff
First downs	15	21
Rushing	7	12
Passing	7	8
By penalty	1	1
Total yardage	259	387
Net rushing yardage	124	219
Net passing yardage	135	168
Passes att.-comp.-had int.	36-13-3	20-10-0

RUSHING

Buffalo—Gilchrist, 16 for 122; Carlton, 18 for 70, 1 TD; Kemp, 5 for 16, 1 TD; Dubenion, 1 for 9; Lamonica, 1 for 2.
San Diego—Lincoln, 3 for 47; Lowe, 7 for 34; MacKinnon, 1 for 17; Kinderman, 4 for 14; Hadl, 1 for 13; Rote, 1 for 6; Norton, 1 for −7.

PASSING

Buffalo—Kemp, 10 of 20 for 188.
San Diego—Rote, 10 of 26 for 118, 1 TD, 2 int.; Hadl, 3 of 10 for 31, 1 int.

RECEIVING

Buffalo—Dubenion, 3 for 36; Bass, 2 for 70; Warlick, 2 for 41; Gilchrist, 2 for 22; Ross, 1 for −1.
San Diego—Linderman, 4 for 52; MacKinnon, 3 for 12; Kocourek, 2 for 52, 1 TD; Lowe, 2 for 9; Norton, 1 for 13; Lincoln, 1 for 11.

1964 NFL

CLEVELAND 27, BALTIMORE 0

The Baltimore Colts entered the championship game with the most productive offense and the stingiest defense in the NFL. But the Cleveland defense shut down the Colts' high-powered attack while featuring a passing blitz on offense to register a 27-0 victory over one of the heaviest favorites in playoff history.

Both teams played conservatively in the first half, and no points were scored, despite the fact that each had averaged about 30 points per game during the regular season.

Early in the third quarter, however, the Browns got the first break of the game when Baltimore's Tom Gilburg shanked a punt and Cleveland took over in good field position. Lou Groza kicked a 43-yard field goal to snap the scoreless tie. Moments later, the Browns got the ball back, and Jim Brown blasted 46 yards deep into Baltimore territory. Cleveland went ahead 10-0 when Frank Ryan hit lanky flanker Gary Collins with an 18-yard touchdown pass. The Browns blew the game open just before the end of the quarter, when Ryan again connected with Collins for a touchdown, this time from 42 yards.

The Browns completed their rout with 10 fourth-quarter points. Lou Groza kicked a short field goal after a drive had stalled at the 2, and then Ryan threw his third touchdown pass of the day to Collins, from 51 yards away.

December 27, at Cleveland

Baltimore	Starters, Offense	Cleveland
Raymond Berry	SE	Paul Warfield
Bob Vogel	LT	Dick Schafrath
Jim Parker	LG	John Wooten
Dick Szymanski	C	John Morrow
Alex Sandusky	RG	Gene Hickerson
George Preas	RT	Monte Clark
John Mackey	TE	Johnny Brewer
Jimmy Orr	FL	Gary Collins
Johnny Unitas	QB	Frank Ryan
Jerry Hill	FB	Jim Brown
Lenny Moore	HB	Ernie Green
	Starters, Defense	
Gino Marchetti	LE	Paul Wiggin
Guy Reese	LT	Dick Modzelewski
Fred Miller	RT	Jim Kanicki
Ordell Braase	RE	Bill Glass
Steve Stonebreaker	LLB	Jim Houston
Bill Pellington	MLB	Vince Costello
Don Shinnick	RLB	Galen Fiss
Bobby Boyd	LCB	Bernie Parrish
Lenny Lyles	RCB	Walter Beach
Jerry Logan	SS	Larry Benz
Jim Welch	FS	Ross Fichtner

Baltimore	0	0	0	0	—	0
Cleveland	0	0	17	10	—	27

Cle—FG Groza 43
Cle—Collins 18 pass from Ryan (Groza kick)
Cle—Collins 42 pass from Ryan (Groza kick)
Cle—FG Groza 10
Cle—Collins 51 pass from Ryan (Groza kick)
Attendance—79,544

TEAM STATISTICS	Balt	Cle
First downs	11	20
Rushing	5	8
Passing	4	9
By penalty	2	3
Total yardage	181	339
Net rushing yardage	92	142
Net passing yardage	89	197
Passes att.-comp.-had int.	20-12-2	18-11-1

RUSHING

Baltimore—Moore, 9 for 40; Hill, 9 for 31; Unitas, 6 for 30; Boyd, 1 for −9.
Cleveland—Brown, 27 for 114; Green, 10 for 29; Ryan, 3 for 2; Warfield, 1 for −3.

PASSING

Baltimore—Unitas, 12 of 20 for 95, 2 int.
Cleveland—Ryan, 11 of 18 for 206, 3 TDs, 1 int.

RECEIVING

Baltimore—Berry, 3 for 38; Lorick, 3 for 18; Orr, 2 for 31; Moore, 2 for 4; Mackey, 1 for 2; Hill, 1 for 2.
Cleveland—Collins, 5 for 130, 3 TDs; Brown, 3 for 37; Brewer, 2 for 26; Warfield, 1 for 13.

1965 AFL

BUFFALO 23, SAN DIEGO 0

Mixing their defensive alignments, the Buffalo Bills used a three-man line with an end dropping off to cover passes and a safety blitz to confuse the San Diego Chargers' offense. They also assigned double coverage to pass receiver Lance Alworth, in addition to using two tight ends on offense. The result was a 23-0 victory over a team that had outgained them 816-381 in total offense in two regular-season games.

The Chargers never penetrated beyond Buffalo's 24-yard line. For the first 25 minutes of the game, San Diego's defense matched Buffalo's, but then the Bills scored on an 18-yard pass from Jack Kemp to Ernie Warlick. Shortly after that, the Chargers punted, and George (Butch) Byrd returned it 74 yards for a touchdown. That, combined with Buffalo's pressure defense, gave the Bills an almost insurmountable 14-0 halftime lead.

The second half meant more of the same for the San Diego offense. Paul Lowe, whose 1,121 yards rushing during the regular season had set an AFL record, was held to 57 yards, 47 of which came on one carry.

The Bills, meanwhile, added three field goals by Pete Gogolak, while first Kemp and then reserve Daryle Lamonica effectively moved the ball against the Chargers' defense.

December 26, at San Diego

Buffalo	Starters, Offense	San Diego
Charley Ferguson	SE	Don Norton
Stew Barber	LT	Ernie Wright
George Flint	LG	Ernest Park
Al Bemiller	C	Sam Gruneisen
Joe O'Donnell	RG	Walt Sweeney
Dick Hudson	RT	Ron Mix
Paul Costa	TE	Dave Kocourek
Bo Roberson	FL	Lance Alworth
Jack Kemp	QB	John Hadl
Wray Carlton	FB	Gene Foster
Billy Joe	HB	Paul Lowe
	Starters, Defense	
Ron McDole	LE	Earl Faison
Jim Dunaway	LT	George Gross
Tom Sestak	RT	Ernie Ladd
Tom Day	RE	Bob Petrich
John Tracey	LLB	Dick Degen
Harry Jacobs	MLB	Chuck Allen
Mike Stratton	RLB	Frank Buncom
Booker Edgerson	LCB	Jim Warren
George (Butch) Byrd	RCB	Leslie (Speedy) Duncan
Hagood Clarke	SS	Kenny Graham
George Saimes	FS	Bud Whitehead

Buffalo	0	14	6	3	—	23
San Diego	0	0	0	0	—	0

Buff—Warlick 18 pass from Kemp (Gogolak kick)
Buff—Byrd 74 interception return (Gogolak kick)
Buff—FG Gogolak 11
Buff—FG Gogolak 39
Buff—FG Gogolak 32
Attendance—30,361

TEAM STATISTICS	Buff	SD
First downs	23	12
Rushing	13	5
Passing	9	7
By penalty	1	0
Total yardage	260	229
Net rushing yardage	108	119
Net passing yardage	152	110
Passes att.-comp.-had int.	20-9-1	25-12-2

RUSHING

Buffalo—Carlton, 16 for 63; Joe, 16 for 35; Stone, 3 for 5; Smith, 1 for 5.
San Diego—Lowe, 12 for 57; Hadl, 8 for 24; Lincoln, 4 for 16; Foster, 2 for 9; Breaux, 1 for −2.

PASSING

Buffalo—Kemp, 8 of 19 for 155, 1 TD, 1 int.; Lamonica, 1 of 1 for 12.
San Diego—Hadl, 11 of 23 for 140, 2 int.; Breaux, 1 of 2 for 24.

RECEIVING

Buffalo—Roberson, 3 for 88; Warlick, 3 for 35, 1 TD; Costa, 2 for 32; Tracy, 1 for 12.
San Diego—Alworth, 4 for 82; Lowe, 3 for 3; Norton, 1 for 35; Farr, 1 for 24; MacKinnon, 1 for 10; Lincoln, 1 for 7; Kocourek, 1 for 3.

1965 NFL

GREEN BAY 23, CLEVELAND 12

Lambeau Field was cleared of four inches of snow, but a freezing rain turned the field into mud as the Green Bay Packers defeated the Cleveland Browns 23-12 and held fullback Jim Brown to 50 yards in 12 carries. Brown had led the NFL with 1,544 yards rushing during the season.

Packers runners Paul Hornung and Jim Taylor met with more success. Taylor never gained more than eight yards on a single attempt, but when the Packers controlled the ball for almost 14 minutes during two second-half drives to a touchdown and field goal, he was given the ball 12 times in 24 plays.

The Packers led 13-12 at halftime of a game that had been as close as the score would indicate. The Packers scored the first time they got the ball, Bart Starr passing 47 yards to Carroll Dale. The Browns came right back, scoring on a touchdown pass from Frank Ryan to Gary Collins. The extra point was missed, however. The teams traded field goals the rest of the half. But in the third quarter, an 11-play, 90-yard drive ending in Hornung's 13-yard touchdown run put the Browns too far behind to catch up.

"The snow and mud were our allies," said Packers coach Vince Lombardi. "When you have conditions like these, it's best to be basic, not fancy. And we're the most basic offensive team there is."

January 2, 1966, at Green Bay

Cleveland	Starters, Offense	Green Bay
Paul Warfield	SE	Boyd Dowler
John Brown	LT	Bob Skoronski
John Wooten	LG	Fred (Fuzzy) Thurston
John Morrow	C	Ken Bowman
Gene Hickerson	RG	Jerry Kramer
Monte Clark	RT	Forrest Gregg
Johnny Brewer	TE	Bill Anderson
Gary Collins	FL	Carroll Dale
Frank Ryan	QB	Bart Starr
Jim Brown	FB	Jim Taylor
Ernie Green	HB	Paul Hornung
	Starters, Defense	
Paul Wiggin	LE	Willie Davis
Dick Modzelewski	LT	Ron Kostelnik
Jim Kanicki	RT	Henry Jordan
Bill Glass	RE	Lionel Aldridge
Jim Houston	LLB	Dave Robinson
Vince Costello	MLB	Ray Nitschke
Galen Fiss	RLB	Lee Roy Caffey
Bernie Parrish	LCB	Herb Adderley
Walter Beach	RCB	Doug Hart
Ross Fichtner	SS	Tom Brown
Larry Benz	FS	Willie Wood

Cleveland	9	3	0	0	—	12
Green Bay	7	6	7	3	—	23

GB—Dale 47 pass from Starr (Chandler kick)
Cle—Collins 17 pass from Ryan (kick failed)
Cle—FG Groza 24
GB—FG Chandler 15
GB—FG Chandler 23
Cle—FG Groza 28
GB—Hornung 13 run (Chandler kick)
GB—FG Chandler 29
Attendance—50,777

TEAM STATISTICS	Cle	GB
First downs	8	21
Rushing	2	10
Passing	5	9
By penalty	1	2
Total yardage	161	332
Net rushing yardage	64	204
Net passing yardage	97	128
Passes att.-comp.-had int.	18-8-2	19-10-1

RUSHING
Cleveland—Brown, 12 for 50; Ryan, 3 for 9; Green, 3 for 5.
Green Bay—Hornung, 18 for 105, 1 TD; Taylor, 27 for 96; Moore, 2 for 3.
PASSING
Cleveland—Ryan, 8 of 18 for 115, 1 TD, 2 int.
Green Bay—Starr, 10 of 18 for 147, 1 TD, 1 int.; Hornung, 0 of 1.
RECEIVING
Cleveland—Brown, 3 for 44; Collins, 3 for 41, 1 TD; Warfield, 2 for 30.
Green Bay—Dowler, 5 for 59; Dale, 2 for 60, 1 TD; Taylor, 2 for 20; Hornung, 1 for 8.

1966 AFL

KANSAS CITY 31, BUFFALO 7

The Kansas City Chiefs qualified as the AFL's first representative to the Super Bowl when they defeated the Buffalo Bills 31-7. The Chiefs, who won the 1962 AFL title as the Dallas Texans, had a total yardage advantage of 277-255; their defense was responsible for the game's biggest play.

Trailing 14-7 near the end of the first half, Buffalo had the ball on the Chiefs' 10-yard line. Quarterback Jack Kemp passed to Bobby Crockett, but Chiefs safety Johnny Robinson intercepted the ball in the end zone and ran 72 yards. The Chiefs converted the interception into Mike Mercer's 32-yard field goal and led 17-7 at halftime. Instead of a possible tie with Kansas City, the Bills trailed by 10 points at the start of the second half.

The Chiefs had dominated the scoring in the first half with a strong passing game. Kansas City moved ahead early in the game on a 29-yard touchdown pass from Len Dawson to Fred Arbanas. The Bills struck right back with some passing of their own—69 yards and a touchdown from Jack Kemp to Elbert Dubenion. The Chiefs regained the lead on another touchdown pass by Dawson, this time to Otis Taylor.

In the second half, Kansas City turned to its time-consuming running game. It paid off with big dividends, as rookie Mike Garrett scored two touchdowns in the fourth quarter.

January 1, 1967, at Buffalo

Kansas City	Starters, Offense	Buffalo
Chris Burford	SE	Bobby Crockett
Jim Tyrer	LT	Stew Barber
Ed Budde	LG	Billy Shaw
Wayne Frazier	C	Al Bemiller
Curt Merz	RG	Joe O'Donnell
Dave Hill	RT	Dick Hudson
Fred Arbanas	TE	Paul Costa
Otis Taylor	FL	Elbert Dubenion
Len Dawson	QB	Jack Kemp
Curtis McClinton	FB	Wray Carlton
Mike Garrett	HB	Bobby Burnett
	Starters, Defense	
Jerry Mays	LE	Ron McDole
Ed Lothamer	LT	Jim Dunaway
Buck Buchanan	RT	Tom Sestak
Chuck Hurston	RE	Tom Day
Bobby Bell	LLB	John Tracey
Sherrill Headrick	MLB	Harry Jacobs
E.J. Holub	RLB	Mike Stratton
Fred Williamson	LCB	Tommy Janik
Willie Mitchell	RCB	George (Butch) Byrd
Bobby Hunt	SS	Hagood Clarke
Johnny Robinson	FS	George Saimes

Kansas City	7	10	0	14	—	31
Buffalo	7	0	0	0	—	7

KC—Arbanas 29 pass from Dawson (Mercer kick)
Buff—Dubenion 69 pass from Kemp (Lusteg kick)
KC—Taylor 29 pass from Dawson (Mercer kick)
KC—FG Mercer 32
KC—Garrett 1 run (Mercer kick)
KC—Garrett 18 run (Mercer kick)
Attendance—42,080

TEAM STATISTICS	KC	Buff
First downs	14	9
Rushing	6	2
Passing	8	7
By penalty	0	0
Total yardage	277	255
Net rushing yardage	113	40
Net passing yardage	164	215
Passes att.-comp.-had int.	24-16-0	27-12-2

RUSHING
Kansas City—Garrett, 13 for 39, 2 TDs; McClinton, 11 for 38; Dawson, 5 for 28; Coan, 2 for 6; E. Thomas, 2 for 2.
Buffalo—Carlton, 9 for 31; Burnett, 3 for 6; Kemp, 1 for 3.
PASSING
Kansas City—Dawson, 16 of 24 for 227, 2 TDs.
Buffalo—Kemp, 12 of 27 for 253, 1 TD, 2 int.
RECEIVING
Kansas City—Taylor, 5 for 78, 1 TD; Burford, 4 for 76; Garrett, 4 for 16; Arbanas, 2 for 44, 1 TD; McClinton, 1 for 13.
Buffalo—Burnett, 6 for 127; Dubenion, 2 for 79, 1 TD; Bass, 2 for 26; Crockett, 1 for 16; Carlton, 1 for 5.

1966 NFL

GREEN BAY 34, DALLAS 27

With less than two minutes remaining in the game, the Dallas Cowboys had a first down on the Green Bay Packers' 2-yard line, but they failed to score and the Packers won 34-27 in the Cotton Bowl.

The Packers jumped to a quick lead. Bart Starr threw a touchdown pass to Elijah Pitts. When Mel Renfro fumbled the ensuing kickoff, Green Bay's Jim Grabowski picked up the ball and ran it in for a touchdown. The Cowboys came back to tie the score at the end of the first quarter, and two field goals left them trailing only 21-20 in the third quarter. The Packers stormed back, scoring first on a pass from Bart Starr to Boyd Dowler and then, with 5:20 left in the game, on a pass from Starr to Max McGee.

It took the Cowboys a little more than a minute to score, on a 68-yard pass from Don Meredith to Frank Clarke. The Packers' next possession ended with a 16-yard punt by Chandler. Dallas took over on Green Bay's 47. On second down from the 22, Green Bay's Tom Brown was called for pass interference on Clarke in the end zone. That put the ball on the 2-yard line with 1:52 left. On fourth down, Meredith threw a pass that was intercepted by Brown in the end zone with 28 seconds remaining.

January 1, 1967, at Dallas

Green Bay	Starters, Offense	Dallas
Carroll Dale	SE	Bob Hayes
Bob Skoronski	LT	Jim Boeke
Fred (Fuzzy) Thurston	LG	Tony Liscio
Bill Curry	C	Dave Manders
Jerry Kramer	RG	Leon Donohue
Forrest Gregg	RT	Ralph Neely
Marv Fleming	TE	Pettis Norman
Boyd Dowler	FL	Pete Gent
Bart Starr	QB	Don Meredith
Jim Taylor	FB	Don Perkins
Elijah Pitts	HB	Dan Reeves
	Starters, Defense	
Willie Davis	LE	Willie Townes
Ron Kostelnik	LT	Jim Colvin
Henry Jordan	RT	Bob Lilly
Lionel Aldridge	RE	George Andrie
Dave Robinson	LLB	Chuck Howley
Ray Nitschke	MLB	Lee Roy Jordan
Lee Roy Caffey	RLB	Dave Edwards
Herb Adderley	LCB	Cornell Green
Bob Jeter	RCB	Warren Livingston
Tom Brown	SS	Mike Gaechter
Willie Wood	FS	Mel Renfro

Green Bay	14	7	7	6	—	34
Dallas	14	3	3	7	—	27

GB—Pitts 17 pass from Starr (Chandler kick)
GB—Grabowski 18 fumble return (Chandler kick)
Dall—Reeves 3 run (Villanueva kick)
Dall—Perkins 23 run (Villanueva kick)
GB—Dale 51 pass from Starr (Chandler kick)
Dall—FG Villanueva 11
Dall—FG Villanueva 32
GB—Dowler 16 pass from Starr (Chandler kick)
GB—McGee 28 pass from Starr (kick blocked)
Dall—Clarke 68 pass from Meredith (Villanueva kick)
Attendance—74,152

TEAM STATISTICS	GB	Dall
First downs	19	23
Rushing	3	12
Passing	14	10
By penalty	2	1
Total yardage	367	418
Net rushing yardage	102	187
Net passing yardage	265	231
Passes att.-comp.-had int.	28-19-0	31-15-1

RUSHING
Green Bay—Pitts, 12 for 66; Taylor, 10 for 37; Starr, 2 for −1.
Dallas—Perkins, 17 for 108, 1 TD; Reeves, 17 for 47, 1 TD; Meredith, 4 for 22; Norman, 2 for 10.
PASSING
Green Bay—Starr, 19 of 28 for 304, 4 TDs.
Dallas—Meredith, 15 of 31 for 238, 1 TD, int.
RECEIVING
Green Bay—Dale, 5 for 128, 1 TD; Taylor, 5 for 23; Fleming, 3 for 50; Dowler, 3 for 49, 1 TD; McGee, 1 for 28, 1 TD; Pitts, 1 for 17, 1 TD; Long, 1 for 9.
Dallas—Reeves, 4 for 77; Norman, 4 for 30; Clarke, 3 for 102, 1 TD; Gent, 3 for 28; Hayes, 1 for 1.

1967 AFL

OAKLAND 40, HOUSTON 7

The Oakland Raiders scored a touchdown on a fake field goal with 18 seconds remaining in the half and went on to defeat the Houston Oilers 40-7 for their first AFL championship. With the score 10-0, Oakland quarterback Daryle Lamonica took the snap from center for an apparent field-goal attempt by George Blanda from the Oilers' 17-yard line. Instead, Lamonica ran to his right and passed to end Dave Kocourek, who was open at the 10-yard line and scored to give Oakland a 17-0 lead at the half.

The Raiders had built a 10-0 lead on a 37-yard field goal by Blanda, who had been put on waivers by the Oilers before the season, and a 69-yard run by fullback Hewritt Dixon, who the Raiders had converted from tight end.

Needing a big play to get back into the game in the third quarter, the Oilers had a disaster instead. Zeke Moore fumbled the kickoff to open the second half, and Oakland recovered deep in Houston territory. Seven plays later, Lamonica scored on a 1-yard quarterback sneak. The Raiders steadily increased their lead to 30-0 in the fourth quarter before Houston finally scored on Pete Beathard's five-yard pass to Charlie Frazier.

December 31, at Oakland

Houston	Starters, Offense	Oakland
Lionel Taylor	SE	Bill Miller
Walt Suggs	LT	Bob Svihus
Bob Talamini	LG	Gene Upshaw
Bobby Maples	C	Jim Otto
Sonny Bishop	RG	Wayne Hawkins
Glen Ray Hines	RT	Harry Schuh
Alvin Reed	TE	Billy Cannon
Ode Burrell	FL	Fred Biletnikoff
Pete Beathard	QB	Daryle Lamonica
Hoyle Granger	RB	Hewritt Dixon
Woody Campbell	RB	Pete Banaszak
	Starters, Defense	
Pat Holmes	LE	Ike Lassiter
Willie Parker	LT	Dan Birdwell
George Rice	RT	Tom Keating
Richard Marshall	RE	Ben Davidson
George Webster	LLB	Bill Laskey
Garland Boyette	MLB	Dan Conners
Olen Underwood	RLB	Gus Otto
Miller Farr	LCB	Kent McCloughan
W.K. Hicks	RCB	Willie Brown
Ken Houston	SS	Warren Powers
Jim Norton	FS	Dave Grayson

Houston	0	0	0	7	—	7
Oakland	3	14	10	13	—	40

Oak —FG Blanda 37
Oak —Dixon 69 run (Blanda kick)
Oak —Kocourek 17 pass from Lamonica (Blanda kick)
Oak —Lamonica 1 run (Blanda kick)
Oak —FG Blanda 40
Oak —FG Blanda 42
Hous—Frazier 5 pass from Beathard (Wittenborn kick)
Oak —FG Blanda 36
Oak —Miller 12 pass from Lamonica (Blanda kick)
Attendance—53,330

TEAM STATISTICS	Hou	Oak
First downs	11	18
Rushing	4	11
Passing	6	6
By penalty	1	1
Total yardage	146	364
Net rushing yardage	38	263
Net passing yardage	108	101
Passes att.-comp.-had int.	35-15-1	26-10-0

RUSHING

Houston—Granger, 14 for 19; Campbell, 5 for 15; Blanks, 1 for 6; Beathard, 1 for −2.

Oakland—Dixon, 21 for 144, 1 TD; Banaszak, 15 for 116; Lamonica, 5 for 22, 1 TD; Hagberg, 2 for −1; Todd, 4 for −8; Biletnikoff, 1 for −10.

PASSING

Houston—Beathard, 15 of 35 for 142, 1 TD, 1 int.

Oakland—Lamonica, 10 of 24 for 111, 2 TDs; Blanda, 0 of 2.

RECEIVING

Houston—Frazier, 7 for 81, 1 TD; Reed, 4 for 60; Campbell, 2 for 5; Taylor, 1 for 6; Granger, 1 for −10.

Oakland—Miller, 3 for 32, 1 TD; Cannon, 2 for 31; Biletnikoff, 2 for 10; Kocourek, 1 for 17, 1 TD; Dixon, 1 for 8; Banaszak, 1 for 4.

1967 NFL

GREEN BAY 21, DALLAS 17

No professional football playoff ever took place in conditions to match the 13-below temperature and 15-miles-per-hour winds that enveloped Lambeau Field. Breathing steam and spitting ice, the Green Bay Packers and Dallas Cowboys came to the final 13 seconds, when Bart Starr scored a touchdown on a quarterback sneak to give Green Bay a 21-17 victory—its third consecutive NFL championship and fifth in seven years.

Starr slid across the goal line between blocks by center Ken Bowman and right guard Jerry Kramer on third down after Green Bay had taken its final time out. The score climaxed a 12-play, 68-yard drive that began with 4:50 left in the game. Dallas had gone ahead 17-14 on a 50-yard pass play, halfback Dan Reeves to flanker Lance Rentzel, eight seconds into the final quarter. The big play in the winning drive for the Packers was a short pass from Starr to fullback Chuck Mercein, who ran 19 yards to the Dallas 11. Mercein then gained eight yards to the 3. Starr scored three plays later.

The Packers jumped to a 14-0 lead in the second quarter. The Cowboys scored twice after Green Bay fumbles, the first time when Willie Townes hit Starr, who fumbled, with George Andrie scooping up the ball and running it in for a touchdown.

December 31, at Green Bay

Dallas	Starters, Offense	Green Bay
Bob Hayes	SE	Boyd Dowler
Tony Liscio	LT	Bob Skoronski
John Niland	LG	Gale Gillingham
Mike Connelly	C	Ken Bowman
Leon Donohue	RG	Jerry Kramer
Ralph Neely	RT	Forrest Gregg
Pettis Norman	TE	Marv Fleming
Lance Rentzel	FL	Carroll Dale
Don Meredith	QB	Bart Starr
Don Perkins	RB	Chuck Mercein
Dan Reeves	RB	Donny Anderson
	Starters, Defense	
Willie Townes	LE	Willie Davis
Jethro Pugh	LT	Ron Kostelnik
Bob Lilly	RT	Henry Jordan
George Andrie	RE	Lionel Aldridge
Chuck Howley	LLB	Dave Robinson
Lee Roy Jordan	MLB	Ray Nitschke
Dave Edwards	RLB	Lee Roy Caffey
Cornell Green	LCB	Herb Adderley
Mike Johnson	RCB	Bob Jeter
Mike Gaechter	SS	Tom Brown
Mel Renfro	FS	Willie Wood

Dallas	0	10	0	7	—	17
Green Bay	7	7	0	7	—	21

GB —Dowler 8 pass from Starr (Chandler kick)
GB —Dowler 46 pass from Starr (Chandler kick)
Dall—Andrie 7 fumble return (Villanueva kick)
Dall—FG Villanueva 21
Dall—Rentzel 50 pass from Reeves (Villanueva kick)
GB —Starr 1 run (Chandler kick)
Attendance—50,861

TEAM STATISTICS	Dall	GB
First downs	11	18
Rushing	4	5
Passing	6	10
By penalty	1	3
Total yardage	192	195
Net rushing yardage	92	80
Net passing yardage	100	115
Passes att.-comp.-had int.	26-11-1	24-14-1

RUSHING

Dallas—Perkins, 17 for 51; Reeves, 13 for 42; Meredith, 1 for 9; Baynham, 1 for −2; Clarke, 1 for −8.

Green Bay—Anderson, 18 for 35; Mercein, 6 for 20; Williams, 4 for 13; Wilson, 3 for 11; Starr, 1 for 1, 1 TD.

PASSING

Dallas—Meredith, 10 of 25 for 59, 1 int.; Reeves, 1 of 1 for 50, 1 TD.

Green Bay—Starr, 14 of 24 for 191, 2 TDs.

RECEIVING

Dallas—Hayes, 3 for 16; Reeves, 3 for 11; Rentzel, 2 for 61, 1 TD; Clarke, 2 for 24; Baynham, 1 for −3.

Green Bay—Dowler, 4 for 77, 2 TDs; Anderson, 4 for 44; Dale, 3 for 44; Mercein, 2 for 22; Williams, 1 for 4.

1968 AFL

NY JETS 27, OAKLAND 23

With two minutes left in the game, the Raiders had the ball on the Jets' 24-yard line. But when Daryle Lamonica threw a swing pass to halfback Charlie Smith, the rookie didn't catch it and then didn't cover it. Linebacker Ralph Baker recovered the ball, which was ruled a fumbled lateral rather than a forward pass, and the Jets were able to run the clock out to defeat the Raiders 27-23.

Despite icy winds, the Jets and Raiders raced up and down the field all day. The Jets scored after three minutes, on a 14-yard pass from Joe Namath to Don Maynard. They increased the lead to 10-0 before Lamonica hit Fred Biletnikoff with a 29-yard touchdown pass. At halftime, it was 13-10.

The Raiders tied the game early in the second half when George Blanda kicked a 9-yard field goal. Namath came right back with a 20-yard strike to tight end Pete Lammons for a 20-13 lead. Namath's passing backfired midway through the fourth quarter. George Atkinson returned an interception to the New York 5, and two plays later Pete Banaszak scored to put Oakland ahead. It took Namath less than a minute to finish the scoring for the day, throwing a six-yard touchdown pass to Maynard.

December 29, at New York

Oakland	Starters, Offense	NY Jets
Warren Wells	SE	George Sauer
Bob Svihus	LT	Winston Hill
Gene Upshaw	LG	Bob Talamini
Jim Otto	C	John Schmitt
Jim Harvey	RG	Randy Rasmussen
Harry Schuh	RT	Dave Herman
Billy Cannon	TE	Pete Lammons
Fred Biletnikoff	FL	Don Maynard
Daryle Lamonica	QB	Joe Namath
Hewritt Dixon	RB	Matt Snell
Charlie Smith	RB	Emerson Boozer
	Starters, Defense	
Isaac Lassiter	LE	Gerry Philbin
Dan Birdwell	LT	Paul Rochester
Carleton Oats	RT	John Elliott
Ben Davidson	RE	Verlon Biggs
Ralph (Chip) Oliver	LLB	Ralph Baker
Dan Conners	MLB	Al Atkinson
Gus Otto	RLB	Larry Grantham
George Atkinson	LCB	Johnny Sample
Willie Brown	RCB	Randy Beverly
Rodger Bird	SS	Jim Hudson
Dave Grayson	FS	Bill Baird

Oakland	0	10	3	10	—	23
NY Jets	10	3	7	7	—	27

NYJ—Maynard 14 pass from Namath (J. Turner kick)
NYJ—FG J. Turner 33
Oak—Biletnikoff 29 pass from Lamonica (Blanda kick)
NYJ—FG J. Turner 36
Oak—FG Blanda 26
Oak—FG Blanda 9
NYJ—Lammons 20 pass from Namath (J. Turner kick)
Oak—FG Blanda 20
Oak—Banaszak 5 run (Blanda kick)
NYJ—Maynard 6 pass from Namath (J. Turner kick)
Attendance—62,627

TEAM STATISTICS	Oak	NYJ
First downs	18	25
Rushing	3	9
Passing	14	15
By penalty	1	1
Total yardage	443	400
Net rushing yardage	50	144
Net passing yardage	393	256
Passes att.-comp.-had int.	47-20-0	49-19-1

RUSHING

Oakland—Dixon, 8 for 42; Banaszak, 3 for 6, 1 TD; Smith, 5 for 1; Lamonica, 3 for 1.

NY Jets—Snell, 19 for 71; Boozer, 11 for 51; Namath, 1 for 14; Mathis, 3 for 8.

PASSING

Oakland—Lamonica, 20 of 47 for 401, 1 TD.

NY Jets—Namath, 19 of 49 for 266, 3 TDs, 1 int.

RECEIVING

Oakland—Biletnikoff, 7 for 190, 1 TD; Dixon, 5 for 48; Cannon, 4 for 69; Wells, 3 for 83; Banaszak, 1 for 11.

NY Jets—Sauer, 7 for 70; Maynard, 6 for 118, 2 TDs; Lammons, 4 for 52, 1 TD; Snell, 1 for 15; Boozer, 1 for 11.

1968 NFL

BALTIMORE 34, CLEVELAND 0

The Baltimore Colts entered the NFL Championship Game as decided favorites, and with a motivation that accompanied their memories of having lost to Cleveland in a similar situation four years before. There would not be a repeat this time, however, as Baltimore's line dominated the Browns on both sides of the ball to post a 34-0 victory, only the second time the Browns ever had been shut out.

The Browns' only real scoring opportunity came in the first quarter, but the Colts' Bubba Smith blocked a 41-yard field-goal attempt by Don Cockroft.

Baltimore then broke the game open in the second quarter. After a field goal by Lou Michaels put them ahead 3-0, the Colts put together a 10-play, 60-yard drive that ended with Tom Matte's one-yard touchdown run. When Cleveland's Bill Nelsen tried to pass his team down the field, linebacker Mike Curtis intercepted and returned it to the Browns' 33. On first down, Matte ran 12 yards, and then Jerry Hill added 9 more. Matte scored his second touchdown on a run through the Browns' defense in which he showed cuts reminiscent of Lenny Moore.

The Browns seemed a beaten team at halftime, and the Colts took advantage of that to score 17 more points, including a third touchdown run by Matte from two yards out.

December 29, at Cleveland

Baltimore	Starters, Offense	Cleveland
Jimmy Orr	SE	Paul Warfield
Bob Vogel	LT	Dick Schafrath
Glenn Ressler	LG	John Demarie
Bill Curry	C	Fred Hoaglin
Dan Sullivan	RG	Gene Hickerson
Sam Ball	RT	Monte Clark
John Mackey	TE	Milt Morin
Willie Richardson	FL	Gary Collins
Earl Morrall	QB	Bill Nelsen
Jerry Hill	RB	Charley Harraway
Tom Matte	RB	Leroy Kelly
	Starters, Defense	
Bubba Smith	LE	Ron Snidow
Billy Ray Smith	LT	Jim Kanicki
Fred Miller	RT	Walter Johnson
Ordell Braase	RE	Jack Gregory
Mike Curtis	LLB	Jim Houston
Dennis Gaubatz	MLB	Bob Matheson
Don Shinnick	RLB	Dale Lindsey
Bobby Boyd	LCB	Erich Barnes
Lenny Lyles	RCB	Ben Davis
Jerry Logan	SS	Ernie Kellermann
Rick Volk	FS	Mike Howell

Baltimore	0	17	7	10	—	34
Cleveland	0	0	0	0	—	0

Balt—FG Michaels 28
Balt—Matte 1 run (Michaels kick)
Balt—Matte 12 run (Michaels kick)
Balt—Matte 2 run (Michaels kick)
Balt—FG Michaels 10
Balt—Brown 4 run (Michaels kick)
Attendance—78,410

TEAM STATISTICS	Balt	Cle
First downs	22	12
Rushing	13	2
Passing	8	8
By penalty	1	2
Total yardage	353	173
Net rushing yardage	184	56
Net passing yardage	169	117
Passes att.-comp.-had int.	25-11-1	32-13-2

RUSHING

Baltimore—Matte, 17 for 88, 3 TDs; Hill, 11 for 60; Brown, 5 for 18, 1 TD; Cole, 3 for 14; Mackey, 2 for 4; Morrall, 1 for 0.
Cleveland—Kelly, 13 for 28; Harraway, 6 for 26; E. Green, 1 for 2; Ryan, 2 for 0.

PASSING

Baltimore—Morrall, 11 of 25 for 169, 1 int.
Cleveland—Nelsen, 11 of 26 for 132, 2 int.; Ryan, 2 of 6 for 19.

RECEIVING

Baltimore—Richardson, 3 for 78; Mackey, 2 for 34; Orr, 2 for 33; Matte, 2 for 15; Mitchell, 1 for 7; Cole, 1 for 2.
Cleveland—Harraway, 4 for 40; Morin, 3 for 41; Kelly, 3 for 27; Warfield, 2 for 30; Collins, 1 for 13.

1969 AFL

KANSAS CITY 17, OAKLAND 7

The Kansas City Chiefs won the last championship of the AFL when they defeated the Oakland Raiders 17-7 after losing to that team twice in the regular season. The Chiefs turned the ball over three times inside their 30-yard line in the fourth quarter, but they intercepted three of Raiders quarterback Daryle Lamonica's passes during that time.

The Raiders opened the scoring in the first quarter when Charlie Smith scored from three yards out. But then Kansas City's Len Dawson, who had missed seven passes in a row in the early going, connected with Frank Pitts on a 41-yard pass that carried to the 1. Three plays later, Wendell Hayes smashed into the end zone.

The Chiefs broke the 7-7 tie in the third quarter. Faced with a third and 14 on his 2-yard line, Dawson scrambled out of trouble in his end zone and completed a 35-yard pass to Otis Taylor. That play ignited the 94-yard march to a five-yard run by Robert Holmes that made the score 14-7. The Raiders' first opportunity to tie came when Lamonica, who had returned to the game despite jamming his throwing hand against the helmet of Kansas City's Aaron Brown early in the quarter, moved Oakland from its 6-yard line to Kansas City's 39. Jim Kearney intercepted for Kansas City at the 24. Two series later Emmitt Thomas intercepted Lamonica, and the Chiefs went 62 yards to Jan Stenerud's 22-yard field goal.

January 4, 1970, at Oakland

Kansas City	Starters, Offense	Oakland
Frank Pitts	WR	Rod Sherman
Jim Tyrer	LT	Bob Svihus
Ed Budde	LG	Gene Upshaw
E.J. Holub	C	Jim Otto
Mo Moorman	RG	Jim Harvey
Dave Hill	RT	Harry Schuh
Fred Arbanas	TE	Billy Cannon
Otis Taylor	WR	Fred Biletnikoff
Len Dawson	QB	Daryle Lamonica
Robert Holmes	RB	Hewritt Dixon
Mike Garrett	RB	Charlie Smith
	Starters, Defense	
Jerry Mays	LE	Ike Lassiter
Curley Culp	LT	Carleton Oats
Buck Buchanan	RT	Tom Keating
Aaron Brown	RE	Ben Davidson
Bobby Bell	LLB	Ralph (Chip) Oliver
Willie Lanier	MLB	Dan Conners
Jim Lynch	RLB	Gus Otto
Jim Marsalis	LCB	Nemiah Wilson
Emmitt Thomas	RCB	Willie Brown
Jim Kearney	SS	George Atkinson
Johnny Robinson	FS	Dave Grayson

Kansas City	0	7	7	3	—	17
Oakland	7	0	0	0	—	7

Oak—Smith 3 run (Blanda kick)
KC —Hayes 1 run (Stenerud kick)
KC —Holmes 5 run (Stenerud kick)
KC —FG Stenerud 22
Attendance—53,564

TEAM STATISTICS	KC	Oak
First downs	13	18
Rushing	5	6
Passing	6	10
By penalty	2	2
Total yardage	207	233
Net rushing yardage	86	79
Net passing yardage	121	154
Passes att.-comp.-had int.	17-7-0	45-17-4

RUSHING

Kansas City—Hayes, 8 for 35, 1 TD; Garrett, 7 for 19; Holmes, 18 for 14, 1 TD; McVea, 3 for 13; Dawson, 3 for 5.
Oakland—Dixon, 12 for 36; Smith, 12 for 31, 1 TD; Banaszak, 2 for 8; Todd, 2 for 4.

PASSING

Kansas City—Dawson, 7 of 17 for 129.
Oakland—Lamonica, 15 of 39 for 167, 3 int.; Blanda, 2 of 6 for 24, 1 int.

RECEIVING

Kansas City—Taylor, 3 for 62; Holmes, 2 for 16; Pitts, 1 for 41; Arbanas, 1 for 10.
Oakland—Smith, 8 for 36; Sherman, 3 for 45; Cannon, 2 for 22; Banaszak, 2 for 13; Wells, 1 for 24; Dixon, 1 for 1.

1969 NFL

MINNESOTA 27, CLEVELAND 7

Snow was stacked along the sidelines and the temperature was eight degrees in Metropolitan Stadium as the Minnesota Vikings became the first expansion team to win the NFL championship when they defeated the Cleveland Browns 27-7.

It took the Vikings, who earlier in the season had whipped the Browns 51-3, less than four minutes to establish their dominance. On Minnesota's first possession, Gene Washington broke open when Cleveland cornerback Walt Sumner slipped on the slick field. Quarterback Joe Kapp hit Washington with a 33-yard pass to set up a touchdown. The score came on a seven-yard run by Kapp, who collided with Bill Brown in the backfield, then smashed through the middle of the Cleveland defense, shedding tacklers into the end zone.

On their next possession, the Vikings scored again. Washington got open again when cornerback Erich Barnes fell trying to cover him. Kapp hit Washington, who raced to the end zone, completing a 75-yard pass play.

The Vikings turned to their ground game, beating the Browns at the line of scrimmage and springing Dave Osborn for a 20-yard touchdown run late in the second quarter that opened the score up to 24-0.

The Browns couldn't score until the fourth quarter, when Bill Nelsen passed to wide receiver Gary Collins for a touchdown.

January 4, 1970, at Bloomington

Cleveland	Starters, Offense	Minnesota
Paul Warfield	WR	Gene Washington
Dick Schafrath	LT	Grady Alderman
John Demarie	LG	Jim Vellone
Fred Hoaglin	C	Mick Tingelhoff
Gene Hickerson	RG	Milt Sunde
Monte Clark	RT	Ron Yary
Milt Morin	TE	John Beasley
Gary Collins	WR	John Henderson
Bill Nelsen	QB	Joe Kapp
Bo Scott	RB	Bill Brown
Leroy Kelly	RB	Dave Osborn
	Starters, Defense	
Ron Snidow	LE	Carl Eller
Walter Johnson	LT	Gary Larsen
Jim Kanicki	RT	Alan Page
Jack Gregory	RE	Jim Marshall
Jim Houston	LLB	Roy Winston
Dale Lindsey	MLB	Lonnie Warwick
John Garlington	RLB	Wally Hilgenberg
Erich Barnes	LCB	Earsell Mackbee
Walt Sumner	RCB	Ed Sharockman
Ernie Kellermann	SS-LS	Karl Kassulke
Mike Howell	FS-RS	Paul Krause

Cleveland	0	0	0	7	—	7
Minnesota	14	10	3	0	—	27

Minn—Kapp 7 run (Cox kick)
Minn—Washington 75 pass from Kapp (Cox kick)
Minn—FG Cox 30
Minn—Osborn 20 run (Cox kick)
Minn—FG Cox 32
Cle —Collins 3 pass from Nelsen (Cockroft kick)
Attendance—46,503

TEAM STATISTICS	Cle	Minn
First downs	14	18
Rushing	4	13
Passing	10	5
By penalty	0	0
Total yardage	268	383
Net rushing yardage	97	222
Net passing yardage	171	161
Passes att.-comp.-had int.	33-17-2	13-7-0

RUSHING

Cleveland—Kelly, 15 for 80; Scott, 6 for 17.
Minnesota—Osborn, 18 for 108, 1 TD; Kapp, 8 for 57, 1 TD; Brown, 12 for 43; Jones, 2 for 7; Reed, 5 for 7.

PASSING

Cleveland—Nelsen, 17 of 33 for 181, 1 TD, 2 int.
Minnesota—Kapp, 7 of 13 for 169, 1 TD.

RECEIVING

Cleveland—Scott, 5 for 56; Collins, 5 for 43, 1 TD; Warfield, 4 for 47; Kelly, 2 for 17; Morin, 1 for 18.
Minnesota—Washington, 3 for 120, 1 TD; Henderson, 2 for 17; Brown, 1 for 20; Beasley, 1 for 12.

1970 AFC

BALTIMORE 27, OAKLAND 17

The Baltimore Colts became the first champion of the American Football Conference when they defeated the Oakland Raiders 27-17. The Raiders were an original AFL squad but the Colts joined the AFC with Pittsburgh and Cleveland from the NFL after the two leagues merged.

Baltimore built a 10-0 lead in the second quarter, with the passing of Johnny Unitas setting up a field goal and a touchdown run. The Raiders responded with the heroics of George Blanda, who entered the game after Daryle Lamonica pulled a thigh muscle when tackled by Bubba Smith early in the second period. Blanda's 48-yard field goal cut the halftime lead to 10-3.

In the third quarter, Blanda tied the score with a 38-yard touchdown pass to Fred Biletnikoff. But Unitas engineered two drives to put the Colts back on top 20-10.

Early in the fourth quarter, Blanda passed 15 yards to Warren Wells for a touchdown, cutting the deficit to three points. But the Raiders couldn't catch up. Two passes by Blanda were intercepted in the end zone. Then Unitas put the game away with a 68-yard touchdown pass to Ray Perkins, who was one of four Baltimore wide receivers on the play.

January 3, 1971, at Baltimore

Oakland	**Starters, Offense**	**Baltimore**
Warren Wells	WR	Eddie Hinton
Art Shell	LT	Bob Vogel
Gene Upshaw	LG	Glenn Ressler
Jim Otto	C	Dan Curry
Jim Harvey	RG	John Williams
Harry Schuh	RT	Dan Sullivan
Raymond Chester	TE	John Mackey
Fred Biletnikoff	WR	Roy Jefferson
Daryle Lamonica	QB	Johnny Unitas
Hewritt Dixon	RB	Tom Nowatzke
Charlie Smith	RB	Norm Bulaich
	Starters, Defense	
Tony Cline	LE	Bubba Smith
Carleton Oats	LT	Billy Ray Smith
Tom Keating	RT	Fred Miller
Ben Davidson	RE	Roy Hilton
Bill Laskey	LLB	Ray May
Dan Conners	MLB	Mike Curtis
Gus Otto	RLB	Ted Hendricks
Kent McCloughan	LCB	Charlie Stukes
Willie Brown	RCB	Jim Duncan
George Atkinson	SS	Jerry Logan
Dave Grayson	FS	Rick Volk

Oakland	0	3	7	7	—	17
Baltimore	3	7	10	7	—	27

Balt—FG O'Brien 16
Balt—Bulaich 2 run (O'Brien kick)
Oak—FG Blanda 48
Oak—Biletnikoff 38 pass from Blanda (Blanda kick)
Balt—FG O'Brien 23
Balt—Bulaich 11 run (O'Brien kick)
Oak—Wells 15 pass from Blanda (Blanda kick)
Balt—Perkins 68 pass from Unitas (O'Brien kick)
Attendance—54,799

TEAM STATISTICS	**Oak**	**Balt**
First downs	16	18
Rushing	5	7
Passing	10	11
By penalty	1	0
Total yardage	336	363
Net rushing yardage	107	126
Net passing yardage	229	237
Passes att.-comp.-had int.	36-18-3	30-11-0

RUSHING
Oakland—Dixon, 10 for 51; Smith, 9 for 44; Hubbard, 3 for 12.
Baltimore—Bulaich, 22 for 71, 2 TDs; Nowatzke, 8 for 32; Hill, 5 for 12; Unitas, 2 for 9; Havrilak, 1 for 2.
PASSING
Oakland—Blanda, 17 of 32 for 271, 2 TDs, 3 int.; Lamonica, 1 of 4 for 6.
Baltimore—Unitas, 11 of 30 for 245, 1 TD.
RECEIVING
Oakland—Wells, 5 for 108, 1 TD; Biletnikoff, 5 for 92, 1 TD; Dixon, 3 for 15; Chester, 2 for 36; Smith, 2 for 21; Hubbard, 1 for 5.
Baltimore—Hinton, 5 for 115; Jefferson, 3 for 36; Perkins, 2 for 80, 1 TD; Mackey, 1 for 14.

1970 NFC

DALLAS 17, SAN FRANCISCO 10

Rookie running back Duane Thomas rushed for 143 yards in 27 carries and scored on a 13-yard run as the Dallas Cowboys defeated the San Francisco 49ers 17-10 and won their first championship game after losses in the playoffs four consecutive years.

The game was a defensive deadlock through the first half, with each team scoring only a short field goal. However, in the third period, San Francisco quarterback John Brodie threw a short pass over the middle while under heavy pressure from defensive end Larry Cole. Linebacker Lee Roy Jordan intercepted at the 13. On the next play, Thomas scored. Brodie responded with a drive deep into Dallas territory, but Mel Renfro intercepted a pass on the 18. Dallas then pounded 82 yards, mostly on the ground, to a score that came on a five-yard pass from Craig Morton to running back Walt Garrison.

Trailing 17-3, the 49ers scored at the end of the third quarter on a 26-yard pass from Brodie to wide receiver Dick Witcher. But the Dallas defense, which had shut out Detroit the week before, stiffened, and the 49ers couldn't mount any threats the rest of the day. The game marked the 49ers' final appearance in Kezar Stadium, their home since they began play in the All-America Football Conference in 1946. They were scheduled to move into Candlestick Park in 1971.

January 3, 1971, at San Francisco

Dallas	**Starters, Offense**	**San Francisco**
Bob Hayes	WR	Dick Witcher
Ralph Neely	LT	Len Rohde
John Niland	LG	Randy Beisler
Dave Manders	C	Forrest Blue
Blaine Nye	RG	Woody Peoples
Rayfield Wright	RT	Cas Banaszek
Pettis Norman	TE	Bob Windsor
Reggie Rucker	WR	Gene Washington
Craig Morton	QB	John Brodie
Walt Garrison	RB	Doug Cunningham
Duane Thomas	RB	Ken Willard
	Starters, Defense	
Larry Cole	LE	Tommy Hart
Jethro Pugh	LT	Charlie Krueger
Bob Lilly	RT	Roland Lakes
George Andrie	RE	Bill Belk
Dave Edwards	LLB	Dave Wilcox
Lee Roy Jordan	MLB	Frank Nunley
Chuck Howley	RLB	Jim Sniadecki
Herb Adderley	LCB	Jimmy Johnson
Mel Renfro	RCB	Bruce Taylor
Cornell Green	SS	Mel Phillips
Charlie Waters	FS	Roosevelt Taylor

Dallas	0	3	14	0	—	17
San Francisco	3	0	7	0	—	10

SF —FG Gossett 16
Dall—FG Clark 21
Dall—Thomas 13 run (Clark kick)
Dall—Garrison 5 pass from Morton (Clark kick)
SF —Witcher 26 pass from Brodie (Gossett kick)
Attendance—59,364

TEAM STATISTICS	**Dall**	**SF**
First downs	22	15
Rushing	16	2
Passing	5	12
By penalty	1	1
Total yardage	319	307
Net rushing yardage	229	61
Net passing yardage	90	246
Passes att.-comp.-had int.	22-7-0	40-19-2

RUSHING
Dallas—Thomas, 27 for 143, 1 TD; Garrison, 17 for 71; Welch, 5 for 27; Reeves, 2 for − 12.
San Francisco—Willard, 13 for 42; Cunningham, 5 for 14; Thomas, 1 for 5.
PASSING
Dallas—Morton, 7 of 22 for 101, 1 TD.
San Francisco—Brodie, 19 of 40 for 262, 1 TD, 2 int.
RECEIVING
Dallas—Garrison, 3 for 51, 1 TD; Thomas, 2 for 24; Rucker, 1 for 21; Ditka, 1 for 5.
San Francisco—Washington, 6 for 88; Cunningham, 4 for 34; Windsor, 3 for 70; Witcher, 3 for 41, 1 TD; Willard, 2 for 22; Kwalick, 1 for 7.

1971 AFC

MIAMI 21, BALTIMORE 0

The changing of the AFC guard came in no uncertain fashion as the defending world champion Baltimore Colts, stocked with many aging players, were decisively beaten by the young and upcoming Miami Dolphins 21-0.

The Dolphins, a team that generally moved on the ground, wasted no time crossing up the Colts for a score. Midway through the first quarter, quarterback Bob Griese faked running back Larry Csonka into the line; the deception momentarily froze Baltimore safety Rick Volk. When Volk retreated to cover wide receiver Paul Warfield, he was too late to stop Griese's perfect pass —one that resulted in a 75-yard touchdown.

The Dolphins still led 7-0 in the third quarter when the Colts tried to go long themselves. Baltimore quarterback Johnny Unitas had Eddie Hinton open deep, but the ball was thrown short, and Hinton tipped it away from Miami's Curtis Johnson. Dick Anderson intercepted, setting off a chain reaction. One by one, six Baltimore players were knocked down in the open field by Miami blockers as Anderson weaved 62 yards to a touchdown. The last Colt in Anderson's way was Unitas, who was flattened by defensive tackle Bob Heinz.

Any comeback hopes the Colts had ended in the fourth quarter when Griese, who threw only eight times all day, hit Warfield again for 50 yards. That set up a five-yard touchdown run by Csonka.

January 2, 1972, at Miami

Baltimore	**Starters, Offense**	**Miami**
Eddie Hinton	WR	Paul Warfield
Bob Vogel	LT	Doug Crusan
Glenn Ressler	LG	Bob Kuechenberg
Bill Curry	C	Bob DeMarco
John Williams	RG	Larry Little
Dan Sullivan	RT	Norm Evans
Tom Mitchell	TE	Marv Fleming
Ray Perkins	WR	Howard Twilley
Johnny Unitas	QB	Bob Griese
Don Nottingham	RB	Larry Csonka
Don McCauley	RB	Jim Kiick
	Starters, Defense	
Bubba Smith	LE	Jim Riley
Billy Newsome	LT	Manny Fernandez
Fred Miller	RT	Bob Heinz
Roy Hilton	RE	Bill Stanfill
Ray May	LLB	Doug Swift
Mike Curtis	MLB	Nick Buoniconti
Ted Hendricks	RLB	Mike Kolen
Charlie Stukes	LCB	Tim Foley
Rex Kern	RCB	Curtis Johnson
Jerry Logan	SS	Jake Scott
Rick Volk	FS	Dick Anderson

Baltimore	0	0	0	0	—	0
Miami	7	0	7	7	—	21

Mia—Warfield 75 pass from Griese (Yepremian kick)
Mia—Anderson 62 interception return (Yepremian kick)
Mia—Csonka 5 run (Yepremian kick)
Attendance—76,622

TEAM STATISTICS	**Balt**	**Mia**
First downs	16	13
Rushing	6	8
Passing	10	4
By penalty	0	1
Total yardage	302	286
Net rushing yardage	93	144
Net passing yardage	209	142
Passes att.-comp.-had int.	36-20-3	8-4-1

RUSHING
Baltimore—McCauley, 15 for 50; Nottingham, 11 for 33; Unitas, 1 for 5; Nowatzke, 2 for 5.
Miami—Kiick, 18 for 66; Csonka, 15 for 63, 1 TD; Griese, 1 for 12; Morris, 1 for 3.
PASSING
Baltimore—Unitas, 20 of 36 for 224, 3 int.
Miami—Griese, 4 of 8 for 158, 1 TD, 1 int.
RECEIVING
Baltimore—Hinton, 6 for 98; Nottingham, 4 for 26; Perkins, 3 for 19; Havrilak, 2 for 31; McCauley, 2 for 24; Mitchell, 1 for 14; Matte, 1 for 6; Mackey, 1 for 6.
Miami—Warfield, 2 for 125, 1 TD; Twilley, 2 for 33.

1971 NFC

DALLAS 14, SAN FRANCISCO 3

The Dallas Cowboys broke a scoreless tie in the second quarter when defensive end George Andrie, hidden by San Francisco tackle Len Rohde, emerged to intercept John Brodie's screen pass to running back Ken Willard and ran the ball eight yards to the 49ers' 2-yard line. Calvin Hill scored from the 1 and Dallas went on to win its second straight NFC championship over San Francisco 14-3.

In a game dominated by defense, the Cowboys' defense proved to be a little better. The only time the 49ers managed to score was late in the third quarter, when Bruce Gossett kicked a 28-yard field goal to cut the margin to 7-3.

Dallas still held onto its slim lead when it put together an 80-yard drive in the fourth quarter. When the Cowboys reached the 49ers' 12, strong safety Mel Phillips went out with an ankle injury. Reacting immediately on third and two, Dallas coach Tom Landry sent in a pass play to tight end Mike Ditka. Ditka caught a five-yard pass from Roger Staubach to set up a two-yard touchdown run by Duane Thomas two plays later.

Dallas converted 8 of 14 third downs into first downs, including 4 on the 14-play drive that led to the final score. San Francisco converted only 1 of 11 third-down situations. The 49ers also were hurt by key interceptions by linebacker Lee Roy Jordan and safety Cliff Harris.

January 2, 1972, at Irving

San Francisco	**Starters, Offense**	**Dallas**
Dick Witcher	WR	Bob Hayes
Len Rohde	LT	Tony Liscio
Randy Beisler	LG	John Niland
Forrest Blue	C	Dave Manders
Woody Peoples	RG	Blaine Nye
Cas Banaszek	RT	Rayfield Wright
Ted Kwalick	TE	Mike Ditka
Gene Washington	WR	Lance Alworth
John Brodie	QB	Roger Staubach
Ken Willard	RB	Calvin Hill
Vic Washington	RB	Duane Thomas
	Starters, Defense	
Tommy Hart	LE	Larry Cole
Charlie Krueger	LT	Jethro Pugh
Earl Edwards	RT	Bob Lilly
Cedrick Hardman	RE	George Andrie
Dave Wilcox	LLB	Dave Edwards
Frank Nunley	MLB	Lee Roy Jordan
Skip Vanderbundt	RLB	Chuck Howley
Jimmy Johnson	LCB	Herb Adderley
Bruce Taylor	RCB	Mel Renfro
Mel Phillips	SS	Cornell Green
Roosevelt Taylor	FS	Cliff Harris

San Francisco	0	0	3	0	—	3
Dallas	0	7	0	7	—	14

Dall—Hill 1 run (Clark kick)
SF —FG Gossett 28
Dall—Thomas 2 run (Clark kick)
Attendance—63,409

TEAM STATISTICS	**SF**	**Dall**
First downs	9	16
Rushing	2	9
Passing	7	7
By penalty	0	0
Total yardage	239	244
Net rushing yardage	61	172
Net passing yardage	178	72
Passes att.-comp.-had int.	30-14-3	18-9-0

RUSHING
San Francisco—V. Washington, 10 for 58; Willard, 6 for 3.
Dallas—Staubach, 8 for 55; Garrison, 14 for 52; D. Thomas, 15 for 44, 1 TD; Hill, 9 for 21, 1 TD.

PASSING
San Francisco—Brodie, 14 of 30 for 184, 3 int.
Dallas—Staubach, 9 of 18 for 103.

RECEIVING
San Francisco—G. Washington, 4 for 88; Kwalick, 4 for 52; V. Washington, 3 for 28; Witcher, 1 for 6; Willard, 1 for 6; Cunningham, 1 for 4.
Dallas—Truax, 2 for 43; Hayes; 2 for 22; Alworth, 1 for 17; Reeves, 1 for 17; D. Thomas, 1 for 7; Ditka, 1 for 5; Garrison, 1 for −8.

1972 AFC

MIAMI 21, PITTSBURGH 17

Quarterback Bob Griese, sidelined since the fifth game of the season with a broken ankle, came off the bench at the start of the second half and directed touchdown marches of 80 and 49 yards that broke a 7-7 tie and led the Miami Dolphins to a 21-17 victory over the Pittsburgh Steelers.

Pittsburgh took a 7-0 lead in the first quarter after quarterback Terry Bradshaw fumbled into the Miami end zone and the ball was recovered by teammate Gerry Mullins. Bradshaw was knocked dizzy on the play, however, and had to be removed from the game. In the second quarter, Miami's Larry Seiple was in punt formation at Pittsburgh's 49 when he noticed that the defense had retreated to set up a punt return. Seiple ran instead of punting, gaining 37 yards to the 12 and setting up Miami's first touchdown. That came on a nine-yard pass from quarterback Earl Morrall to running back Larry Csonka.

After the Steelers took a 10-7 lead early in the third quarter, Griese helped put the Dolphins back on top. He hit Paul Warfield with a 52-yard pass; six plays later, the Dolphins scored on a two-yard run by Jim Kiick to go ahead 14-10. Another touchdown by Kiick put the Dolphins up 21-10 in the final period. Bradshaw returned with seven minutes left and threw a touchdown pass, but he also threw two interceptions to end Pittsburgh's hopes.

December 31, at Pittsburgh

Miami	**Starters, Offense**	**Pittsburgh**
Paul Warfield	WR	Al Young
Wayne Moore	LT	Jon Kolb
Bob Kuechenberg	LG	Sam Davis
Jim Langer	C	Ray Mansfield
Larry Little	RG	Bruce Van Dyke
Norm Evans	RT	Gerry Mullins
Marv Fleming	TE	John McMakin
Howard Twilley	WR	Ron Shanklin
Earl Morrall	QB	Terry Bradshaw
Larry Csonka	RB	John Fuqua
Eugene (Mercury) Morris	RB	Franco Harris
	Starters, Defense	
Vern Den Herder	LE	L.C. Greenwood
Manny Fernandez	LT	Joe Greene
Bob Heinz	RT	Ben McGee
Bill Stanfill	RE	Dwight White
Doug Swift	LLB	Jack Ham
Nick Buoniconti	MLB	Henry Davis
Mike Kolen	RLB	Andy Russell
Tim Foley	LCB	John Rowser
Curtis Johnson	RCB	Mel Blount
Jake Scott	SS	Glen Edwards
Dick Anderson	FS	Mike Wagner

Miami	0	7	7	7	—	21
Pittsburgh	7	0	3	7	—	17

Pitt —Mullins fumble recovery in end zone (Gerela kick)
Mia—Csonka 9 pass from Morrall (Yepremian kick)
Pitt —FG Gerela 14
Mia—Kiick 2 run (Yepremian kick)
Mia—Kiick 3 run (Yepremian kick)
Pitt —Young 12 pass from Bradshaw (Gerela kick)
Attendance—50,845

TEAM STATISTICS	**Mia**	**Pitt**
First downs	19	13
Rushing	11	6
Passing	6	6
By penalty	2	1
Total yardage	314	250
Net rushing yardage	193	128
Net passing yardage	121	122
Passes att.-comp.-had int.	16-10-1	20-10-2

RUSHING
Miami—Morris, 16 for 76; Csonka, 24 for 68; Seiple, 1 for 37; Kiick, 8 for 12, 2 TDs.
Pittsburgh—Harris, 16 for 76; Fuqua, 8 for 47; Bradshaw, 2 for 5.

PASSING
Miami—Morrall, 7 of 11 for 51, 1 TD, 1 int.; Griese, 3 of 5 for 70.
Pittsburgh—Bradshaw, 5 of 10 for 80, 1 TD, 2 int.; Hanratty, 5 of 10 for 57.

RECEIVING
Miami—Fleming, 5 for 50; Warfield, 2 for 63; Csonka, 1 for 9, 1 TD; Mandich, 1 for 5; Morris, 1 for −6.
Pittsburgh—Young, 4 for 54, 1 TD; Shankin, 2 for 49; Harris, 2 for 3; McMakin, 1 for 22; Brown, 1 for 9.

1972 NFC

WASHINGTON 26, DALLAS 3

Quarterback Billy Kilmer threw touchdown passes of 15 and 45 yards to wide receiver Charley Taylor and the Washington Redskins did not allow Dallas to move beyond its 30-yard line in the third quarter and not beyond midfield in the second half. The Redskins scored a 26-3 victory for their first championship since 1942.

The Redskins went into the game with two basic plans, and both worked to perfection. Defensively, Washington put a strong rush on Dallas quarterback Roger Staubach, who had missed most of the season before leading a comeback against San Francisco the week before. Although Staubach managed to scramble for 59 yards on five carries, he passed for only 98 yards, and the Dallas offense was ineffective all day.

Offensively, the Redskins wanted Taylor to attack the Cowboys' weak left cornerback position. In the first quarter, Taylor beat Charlie Waters on two important plays, the first a 51-yarder that set up Washington's first touchdown, and the second the touchdown itself. When Waters suffered a broken arm, Taylor gave some lessons to young Mark Washington, including his second touchdown reception. The rest of Washington's scoring was achieved on four field goals by Curt Knight, including three in the fourth quarter to break open a close game.

December 31, at Washington

Dallas	**Starters, Offense**	**Washington**
Ron Sellers	WR	Charley Taylor
Ralph Neely	LT	Terry Hermeling
John Niland	LG	Paul Laaveg
Dave Manders	C	Len Hauss
Blaine Nye	RG	John Wilbur
Rayfield Wright	RT	Walter Rock
Mike Ditka	TE	Jerry Smith
Lance Alworth	WR	Roy Jefferson
Roger Staubach	QB	Billy Kilmer
Walt Garrison	RB	Charley Harraway
Calvin Hill	RB	Larry Brown
	Starters, Defense	
Larry Cole	LE	Ron McDole
Jethro Pugh	LT	Manny Sistrunk
Bob Lilly	RT	Diron Talbert
Pat Toomay	RE	Verlon Biggs
Dave Edwards	LLB	Jack Pardee
Lee Roy Jordan	MLB	Myron Pottios
D.D. Lewis	RLB	Chris Hanburger
Charlie Waters	LCB	Pat Fischer
Mel Renfro	RCB	Mike Bass
Cornell Green	SS	Brig Owens
Cliff Harris	FS	Roosevelt Taylor

Dallas	0	3	0	0	—	3
Washington	0	10	0	16	—	26

Wash—FG Knight 18
Wash—Taylor 15 pass from Kilmer (Knight kick)
Dall —FG Fritsch 35
Wash—Taylor 45 pass from Kilmer (Knight kick)
Wash—FG Knight 39
Wash—FG Knight 46
Wash—FG Knight 45
Attendance—53,129

TEAM STATISTICS	**Dall**	**Wash**
First downs	8	16
Rushing	3	4
Passing	3	11
By penalty	2	1
Total yardage	169	316
Net rushing yardage	96	122
Net passing yardage	73	194
Passes att.-comp.-had int.	21-9-0	18-14-0

RUSHING
Dallas—Staubach, 5 for 59; Hill, 9 for 22; Garrison, 7 for 15.
Washington—Brown, 30 for 88; Harraway, 11 for 19; Kilmer, 3 for 15.

PASSING
Dallas—Staubach, 9 of 20 for 98; Hill, 0 of 1.
Washington—Kilmer, 14 of 18 for 194, 2 TDs.

RECEIVING
Dallas—Sellers, 2 for 29; Garrison, 2 for 18; Hill, 2 for 11; Parks, 1 for 21; Alworth, 1 for 15; Ditka, 1 for 4.
Washington—Taylor, 7 for 146, 2 TDs; Harraway, 3 for 13; Jefferson, 2 for 19; Brown, 2 for 16.

1973 AFC

MIAMI 27, OAKLAND 10

The Miami Dolphins scored a touchdown the first time they had the ball, marched 63 yards to another score in the closing seconds of the first half, and went on to a 27-10 victory over the Oakland Raiders for their third straight AFC championship. Dolphins quarterback Bob Griese, who scrambled 27 yards to the Raiders' 11 on the play before running back Larry Csonka scored Miami's first touchdown, only threw six passes as the Dolphins rushed for 266 yards and averaged better than five yards per carry. Csonka also scored Miami's second touchdown, blasting over from the 2-yard line. The Raiders' only threat of the first half ended when a holding penalty nullified a long pass into Miami territory.

The Raiders scored on George Blanda's 21-yard field goal to cut the score to 14-3 in the third quarter, but that was balanced on the next series by a 42-yard field goal by Garo Yepremian after Miami's Charlie Leigh returned the kickoff 52 yards. The Raiders made it 17-10 near the end of the quarter on a 25-yard pass from quarterback Ken Stabler to wide receiver Mike Siani. In the fourth quarter, the Dolphins put it away on Yepremian's second field goal and Csonka's third touchdown. The final score came after the Miami defense had stopped Oakland on fourth and inches late in the game.

December 30, at Miami

Oakland	Starters, Offense	Miami
Mike Siani	WR	Paul Warfield
Art Shell	LT	Wayne Moore
Gene Upshaw	LG	Bob Kuechenberg
Jim Otto	C	Jim Langer
George Buehler	RG	Larry Little
John Vella	RT	Norm Evans
Bob Moore	TE	Jim Mandich
Fred Biletnikoff	WR	Marlin Briscoe
Ken Stabler	QB	Bob Griese
Marv Hubbard	RB	Larry Csonka
Charlie Smith	RB	Eugene (Mercury) Morris
	Starters, Defense	
Tony Cline	LE	Vern Den Herder
Otis Sistrunk	LT	Manny Fernandez
Art Thoms	RT	Bob Heinz
Horace Jones	RE	Bill Stanfill
Phil Villapiano	LLB	Doug Swift
Dan Conners	MLB	Nick Buoniconti
Gerald Irons	RLB	Mike Kolen
Nemiah Wilson	LCB	Lloyd Mumphord
Willie Brown	RCB	Curtis Johnson
George Atkinson	SS	Jake Scott
Jack Tatum	FS	Dick Anderson

Oakland	0	0	10	0	—	10
Miami	7	7	3	10	—	27

Mia—Csonka 11 run (Yepremian kick)
Mia—Csonka 2 run (Yepremian kick)
Oak—FG Blanda 21
Mia—FG Yepremian 42
Oak—Siani 25 pass from Stabler (Blanda kick)
Mia—FG Yepremian 26
Mia—Csonka 2 run (Yepremian kick)
Attendance—74,384

TEAM STATISTICS	**Oak**	**Mia**
First downs	15	21
Rushing	4	18
Passing	9	2
By penalty	2	1
Total yardage	236	292
Net rushing yardage	107	266
Net passing yardage	129	26
Passes att.-comp.-had int.	23-15-1	6-3-1

RUSHING
Oakland—Hubbard, 10 for 54; Smith, 10 for 35; Davis, 4 for 15; Banaszak, 2 for 3.
Miami—Csonka, 29 for 117, 3 TDs; Morris, 14 for 86; Griese, 3 for 39; Kiick, 6 for 12; Nottingham, 1 for 12.
PASSING
Oakland—Stabler, 15 of 23 for 129, 1 TD, 1 int.
Miami—Griese, 3 of 6 for 34, 1 int.
RECEIVING
Oakland—Smith, 5 for 43; Siani, 3 for 45, 1 TD; Biletnikoff, 2 for 15; Hubbard, 2 for 11; Moore, 2 for 9; Davis, 1 for 6.
Miami—Warfield, 1 for 27; Driscoe, 1 for 0; Kiick, 1 for 1.

1973 NFC

MINNESOTA 27, DALLAS 10

The Minnesota Vikings took advantage of the bad back that kept Dallas defensive tackle Bob Lilly out of the lineup by running up the middle all day. The strategy worked, and the Vikings recorded a 27-10 victory.

Minnesota led 10-0 at the end of the first half after a 44-yard field goal by Fred Cox and a five-yard touchdown run by Chuck Foreman, the latter concluding an 86-yard drive. The Cowboys, without top running back Calvin Hill and with quarterback Roger Staubach throwing four interceptions, couldn't mount any offense all day.

In the third quarter, the Cowboys narrowed the margin when Golden Richards returned a punt 63 yards for a touchdown. Three plays later, Minnesota quarterback Fran Tarkenton combined with wide receiver John Gilliam, who had gotten a step behind cornerback Mel Renfro, on a 54-yard touchdown pass that restored the Vikings' 10-point lead.

In the fourth quarter, two interceptions killed the Cowboys' hopes. First, Bobby Bryant returned one 63 yards for a touchdown. Then, another set up the last score of the day, a 34-yard field goal by Cox. Late in the game, Dallas running back Walt Garrison fumbled the ball away on the Minnesota 2.

December 30, at Irving

Minnesota	Starters, Offense	Dallas
Carroll Dale	WR	Bob Hayes
Grady Alderman	LT	Ralph Neely
Ed White	LG	John Niland
Mick Tingelhoff	C	John Fitzgerald
Milt Sunde	RG	Blaine Nye
Ron Yary	RT	Rayfield Wright
Stu Voigt	TE	Billy Joe DuPree
John Gilliam	WR	Drew Pearson
Fran Tarkenton	QB	Roger Staubach
Oscar Reed	RB	Walt Garrison
Chuck Foreman	RB	Robert Newhouse
	Starters, Defense	
Carl Eller	LE	Larry Cole
Gary Larsen	LT	Jethro Pugh
Alan Page	RT	Bill Gregory
Jim Marshall	RE	Pat Toomay
Roy Winston	LLB	Dave Edwards
Jeff Siemon	MLB	Lee Roy Jordan
Wally Hilgenberg	RLB	D.D. Lewis
Nate Wright	LCB	Charlie Waters
Bobby Bryant	RCB	Mel Renfro
Jeff Wright	LS-SS	Cornell Green
Paul Krause	RS-FS	Cliff Harris

Minnesota	3	7	7	10	—	27
Dallas	0	0	10	0	—	10

Minn—FG Cox 44
Minn—Foreman 5 run (Cox kick)
Dall —Richards 63 punt return (Fritsch kick)
Minn—Gilliam 54 pass from Tarkenton (Cox kick)
Dall —FG Fritsch 17
Minn—Bryant 63 interception return (Cox kick)
Minn—FG Cox 34
Attendance—59,688

TEAM STATISTICS	**Minn**	**Dall**
First downs	20	9
Rushing	14	3
Passing	6	5
By penalty	0	1
Total yardage	306	153
Net rushing yardage	203	90
Net passing yardage	103	63
Passes att.-comp.-had int.	21-10-1	21-10-4

RUSHING
Minnesota—Foreman, 19 for 76, 1 TD; Reed, 18 for 75; Osborn, 4 for 27; Tarkenton, 4 for 16; B. Brown, 2 for 9.
Dallas—Newhouse, 14 for 50; Staubach, 5 for 30; Garrison, 5 for 9; Fugett, 1 for 1.
PASSING
Minnesota—Tarkenton, 10 of 21 for 133, 1 TD, 1 int.
Dallas—Staubach, 10 of 21 for 89, 4 int.
RECEIVING
Minnesota—Foreman, 4 for 28; Gilliam, 2 for 63, 1 TD; Voigt, 2 for 23; Lash, 1 for 11; Reed, 1 for 8.
Dallas—Hayes, 2 for 25; Pearson, 2 for 24; Montgomery, 2 for 15; DuPree, 1 for 20; Garrison, 1 for 10; Fugett, 1 for –1; Newhouse, 1 for –4.

1974 AFC

PITTSBURGH 24, OAKLAND 13

A defense that held the Oakland ground attack to 29 yards and an offense that scored three touchdowns in the fourth quarter combined to give the Pittsburgh Steelers a 24-13 victory and their first league or conference championship ever.

The Steelers trailed 10-3 at the end of the third quarter, but tied the score on Franco Harris's eight-yard run. Then the defense took over. Steelers linebacker Jack Ham intercepted a pass by Oakland quarterback Ken Stabler on the next series, and Pittsburgh converted it into a six-yard touchdown pass from quarterback Terry Bradshaw to wide receiver Lynn Swann.

Oakland had an opportunity to tie the score, but on a third-and-six situation at the Steelers' 12, Stabler had to throw the ball away under a heavy pass rush. The Raiders settled for a 24-yard field goal by George Blanda.

Late in the game, Pittsburgh was able to run out much of the clock by grinding out yardage on the ground. Even mistakes turned out positively. When Bradshaw fumbled at Oakland's 46, Raiders linebacker Gerald Irons could not get to the ball, and Rocky Bleier recovered for Pittsburgh, which gained a first down on the next play. The Steelers then drove to the clinching touchdown, a 21-yard run by Harris.

December 29, at Oakland

Pittsburgh	Starters, Offense	Oakland
Frank Lewis	WR	Cliff Branch
Jon Kolb	LT	Art Shell
Jim Clack	LG	Gene Upshaw
Ray Mansfield	C	Jim Otto
Gerry Mullins	RG	George Buehler
Gordon Gravelle	RT	John Vella
Larry Brown	TE	Bob Moore
Ron Shanklin	WR	Fred Biletnikoff
Terry Bradshaw	QB	Ken Stabler
Rocky Bleier	RB	Marv Hubbard
Franco Harris	RB	Clarence Davis
	Starters, Defense	
L.C. Greenwood	LE	Bubba Smith
Joe Greene	LT	Otis Sistrunk
Ernie Holmes	RT	Art Thoms
Dwight White	RE	Horace Jones
Jack Ham	LLB	Phil Villapiano
Jack Lambert	MLB	Dan Conners
Andy Russell	RLB	Gerald Irons
J.T. Thomas	LCB	Alonzo (Skip) Thomas
Mel Blount	RCB	Nemiah Wilson
Mike Wagner	SS	George Atkinson
Glen Edwards	FS	Jack Tatum

Pittsburgh	0	3	0	21	—	24
Oakland	3	0	7	3	—	13

Oak—FG Blanda 40
Pitt —FG Gerela 23
Oak—Branch 38 pass from Stabler (Blanda kick)
Pitt —Harris 8 run (Gerela kick)
Pitt —Swann 6 pass from Bradshaw (Gerela kick)
Oak—FG Blanda 24
Pitt —Harris 21 run (Gerela kick)
Attendance—53,023

TEAM STATISTICS	**Pitt**	**Oak**
First downs	20	15
Rushing	11	0
Passing	7	13
By penalty	2	2
Total yardage	305	278
Net rushing yardage	210	29
Net passing yardage	95	249
Passes att.-comp.-had int.	17-8-1	36-19-3

RUSHING
Pittsburgh—Harris, 29 for 111, 2 TDs; Bleier, 18 for 98; Bradshaw, 4 for 1.
Oakland—Davis, 10 for 16; Banaszak, 3 for 7; Hubbard, 7 for 16; Stabler, 1 for 0.
PASSING
Pittsburgh—Bradshaw, 8 of 17 for 95, 1 TD, 1 int.
Oakland—Stabler, 19 of 36 for 271, 1 TD, 3 int.
RECEIVING
Pittsburgh—Brown, 2 for 37; Bleier, 2 for 25; Swann, 2 for 17, 1 TD; Stallworth, 2 for 16.
Oakland—Branch, 9 for 186, 1 TD; Moore, 4 for 3; Biletnikoff, 3 for 45; Davis, 2 for 0; Banaszak, 1 for 0.

1974 NFC

MINNESOTA 14, LA RAMS 10

Minnesota was in the midst of a winter heat wave. It was 31 degrees and the sun was blinding as the Vikings defeated the Los Angeles Rams 14-10 in the Rams' first appearance in a championship game since 1955 and the Vikings' third appearance in six years.

The Vikings led 7-3 at halftime on the strength of a 29-yard touchdown pass from Fran Tarkenton to Jim Lash. The Rams scored on David Ray's 27-yard field goal.

The third quarter saw the key series of the game. Starting at their 1 after a perfect punt by Mike Eischeid, the Rams drove 98 yards. The big play was a 73-yard pass from quarterback James Harris to wide receiver Harold Jackson. Safety Jeff Wright knocked Jackson out of bounds on Minnesota's 2. On second down at the 1, Rams guard Tom Mack was called for illegal motion, moving the ball back to the 6. Harris ran for four yards to the 2, but his third-down pass to tight end Pat Curran was deflected by cornerback Jackie Wallace and caught in the end zone for a touchback by linebacker Wally Hilgenberg. Minnesota took over at its own 20-yard line. The Vikings then marched 80 yards in 15 plays to running back Dave Osborn's four-yard touchdown run. A 44-yard touchdown pass from Harris to Jackson was the Rams' final response. The Vikings ran out the final 5:37 of the game.

December 29, at Bloomington

LA Rams	Starters, Offense	Minnesota
Harold Jackson	WR	Jim Lash
Charlie Cowan	LT	Charles Goodrum
Tom Mack	LG	Andy Maurer
Ken Iman	C	Mick Tingelhoff
Joe Scibelli	RG	Ed White
John Williams	RT	Ron Yary
Bob Klein	TE	Stu Voigt
Jack Snow	WR	John Gilliam
James Harris	QB	Fran Tarkenton
Jim Bertelsen	RB	Dave Osborn
Lawrence McCutcheon	RB	Chuck Foreman
	Starters, Defense	
Jack Youngblood	LE	Carl Eller
Merlin Olsen	LT	Doug Sutherland
Larry Brooks	RT	Alan Page
Fred Dryer	RE	Jim Marshall
Ken Geddes	LLB	Roy Winston
Jack Reynolds	MLB	Jeff Siemon
Isiah Robertson	RLB	Wally Hilgenberg
Charlie Stukes	LCB	Nate Wright
Al Clark	RCB	Jackie Wallace
Dave Elmendorf	SS-LS	Jeff Wright
Bill Simpson	FS-RS	Paul Krause

LA Rams	0	3	0	7	—	10
Minnesota	0	7	0	7	—	14

Minn —Lash 29 pass from Tarkenton (Cox kick)
Rams—FG Ray 27
Minn —Osborn 4 run (Cox kick)
Rams —Jackson 44 pass from Harris (Ray kick)
Attendance—48,444

TEAM STATISTICS	**Rams**	**Minn**
First downs	15	18
Rushing	5	9
Passing	10	7
By penalty	0	2
Total yardage	340	269
Net rushing yardage	121	164
Net passing yardage	219	105
Passes att.-comp.-had int.	23-13-2	20-10-1

RUSHING

LA Rams—Bertelsen, 14 for 65; McCutcheon, 12 for 32; Harris, 3 for 17; Cappelletti, 3 for 8; Baker, 1 for −1.
Minnesota—Foreman, 22 for 80; Osborn, 20 for 76, 1 TD; Tarkenton, 4 for 5; Marinaro, 1 for 3.

PASSING

LA Rams—Harris, 13 of 23 for 248, 1 TD, 2 int.
Minnesota—Tarkenton, 10 of 20 for 123, 1 TD, 1 int.

RECEIVING

LA Rams—Bertelsen, 5 for 53; Jackson, 3 for 139, 1 TD; McCutcheon, 2 for 22; Snow, 1 for 19; Klein, 1 for 10; Cappelletti, 1 for 5.
Minnesota—Voigt, 4 for 43; Lash, 2 for 40; Gilliam, 2 for 33; Marinaro, 1 for 6; Osborn, 1 for 1.

1975 AFC

PITTSBURGH 16, OAKLAND 10

With snow in the 18-degree air and ice on the Three Rivers Stadium playing field, the Pittsburgh Steelers held off a late charge by the Oakland Raiders to win 16-10 for their second straight AFC championship.

With 17 seconds left in the game, Oakland trailed 16-7. On third and two at Pittsburgh's 24-yard line, Oakland's 48-year-old George Blanda kicked his longest field goal of the year, 41 yards. The Raiders attempted an onside kick on the ensuing kickoff. Marv Hubbard recovered the ball when Pittsburgh's Reggie Garrett fumbled. Seven seconds remained in the game. Quarterback Ken Stabler of Oakland threw a 37-yard pass to Cliff Branch, who caught the ball on the Steelers' 15. Time ran out before Branch could get out of bounds.

What ended up as an offensive display started as a grudging defensive struggle. Neither offense could move through the first 45 minutes of the game, with the only score in the first three periods being Roy Gerela's 36-yard field goal in the second quarter.

Then, in a span of six minutes, the two teams scored three times. Pittsburgh's Franco Harris blasted 25 yards for a touchdown. Oakland came right back with Stabler passing to Mike Siani for a 14-yard touchdown. And Terry Bradshaw hit John Stallworth with a 20-yard touchdown pass, setting up Oakland's last-minute flurry.

January 4, 1976, at Pittsburgh

Oakland	Starters, Offense	Pittsburgh
Cliff Branch	WR	Frank Lewis
Art Shell	LT	Jon Kolb
Gene Upshaw	LG	Jim Clack
Dave Dalby	C	Ray Mansfield
George Buehler	RG	Gerry Mullins
John Vella	RT	Gordon Gravelle
Bob Moore	TE	Larry Brown
Mike Siani	WR	Lynn Swann
Ken Stabler	QB	Terry Bradshaw
Marv Hubbard	RB	Rocky Bleier
Clarence Davis	RB	Franco Harris
	Starters, Defense	
Otis Sistrunk	LE	L.C. Greenwood
Art Thoms	NT-LT	Joe Greene
Horace Jones	RE-RT	Ernie Holmes
Phil Villapiano	LOLB-RE	Dwight White
Monte Johnson	LILB-LLB	Jack Ham
Gerald Irons	RILB-MLB	Jack Lambert
Ted Hendricks	ROLB-RLB	Andy Russell
Alonzo (Skip) Thomas	LCB	J.T. Thomas
Neal Colzie	RCB	Mel Blount
George Atkinson	SS	Mike Wagner
Jack Tatum	FS	Glen Edwards

Oakland	0	0	0	10	—	10
Pittsburgh	0	3	0	13	—	16

Pitt —FG Gerela 36
Pitt —Harris 25 run (Gerela kick)
Oak—Siani 14 pass from Stabler (Blanda kick)
Pitt —Stallworth 20 pass from Bradshaw (kick failed)
Oak—FG Blanda 41
Attendance—50,609

TEAM STATISTICS	**Oak**	**Pitt**
First downs	18	16
Rushing	3	5
Passing	13	10
By penalty	2	1
Total yardage	321	332
Net rushing yardage	93	117
Net passing yardage	228	215
Passes att.-comp.-had int.	42-18-2	25-15-3

RUSHING

Oakland—Banaszak, 8 for 33; Hubbard, 10 for 30; Davis, 13 for 29; J. Phillips, 1 for 1.
Pittsburgh—Harris, 27 for 79, 1 TD; Bradshaw, 2 for 22; Bleier, 10 for 16.

PASSING

Oakland—Stabler, 18 of 42 for 246, 1 TD, 2 int.
Pittsburgh—Bradshaw, 15 of 25 for 215, 1 TD, 3 int.

RECEIVING

Oakland—Siani, 5 for 80, 1 TD; Casper, 5 for 67; Branch, 2 for 56; Banaszak, 2 for 12; Moore, 2 for 12; Hart, 1 for 16; Davis, 1 for 3.
Pittsburgh—Harris, 5 for 58; Grossman, 4 for 36; Swann, 2 for 45; Stallworth, 2 for 30, 1 TD; Lewis, 1 for 33; L. Brown, 1 for 13.

1975 NFC

DALLAS 37, LA RAMS 7

Running back Preston Pearson, waived by Pittsburgh at the end of the preseason and signed as a free agent by Dallas, caught seven passes for 123 yards and three touchdowns as the wild card Cowboys upset the Los Angeles Rams 37-7.

Pearson took a short pass from Roger Staubach and scissored through the Rams' defense for 18 yards and Dallas's first touchdown one play after linebacker D.D. Lewis intercepted James Harris's first pass of the game. With 54 seconds left in the half, Pearson caught his second touchdown pass, from 15 yards, as the Cowboys went ahead 21-0. The Rams' only two scoring opportunities ended in a missed field goal and a blocked field-goal attempt.

The Cowboys put the game out of reach on their first possession of the second half, driving 69 yards to the touchdown that made it 28-0. On the drive, Staubach carried twice for 25 yards and twice connected with Pearson, the second time for a 19-yard touchdown on which Pearson caught the ball two yards deep in the backfield and weaved his way through the Rams for the score.

Early in the fourth quarter, the Rams scored to avoid their first home-field shutout in 30 years.

January 4, 1976, at Los Angeles

Dallas	Starters, Offense	LA Rams
Golden Richards	WR	Harold Jackson
Ralph Neely	LT	Charlie Cowan
Burton Lawless	LG	Tom Mack
John Fitzgerald	C	Rich Saul
Blaine Nye	RG	Joe Scibelli
Rayfield Wright	RT	John Williams
Jean Fugett	TE	Terry Nelson
Drew Pearson	WR	Ron Jessie
Roger Staubach	QB	James Harris
Robert Newhouse	RB	Cullen Bryant
Preston Pearson	RB	Lawrence McCutcheon
	Starters, Defense	
Ed (Too Tall) Jones	LE	Jack Youngblood
Jethro Pugh	LT	Merlin Olsen
Larry Cole	RT	Cody Jones
Harvey Martin	RE	Fred Dryer
Dave Edwards	LLB	Ken Geddes
Lee Roy Jordan	MLB	Jack Reynolds
D.D. Lewis	RLB	Isiah Robertson
Mark Washington	LCB	Eddie McMillan
Mel Renfro	RCB	Monte Jackson
Charlie Waters	SS	Dave Elmendorf
Cliff Harris	FS	Bill Simpson

Dallas	7	14	13	3	—	37
LA Rams	0	0	0	7	—	7

Dall—P. Pearson 18 pass from Staubach (Fritsch kick)
Dall—Richards 4 pass from Staubach (Fritsch kick)
Dall—P. Pearson 15 pass from Staubach (Fritsch kick)
Dall—P. Pearson 19 pass from Staubach (Fritsch kick)
Dall—FG Fritsch 40
Dall—FG Fritsch 26
Rams—Cappelletti 1 run (Dempsey kick)
Dall—FG Fritsch 26
Attendance—88,919

TEAM STATISTICS	**Dall**	**Rams**
First downs	24	9
Rushing	8	1
Passing	15	7
By penalty	1	1
Total yardage	441	118
Net rushing yardage	195	22
Net passing yardage	246	96
Passes att.-comp.-had int.	28-18-1	24-11-3

RUSHING

Dallas—Newhouse, 16 for 64; Staubach, 7 for 54; Dennison, 13 for 35; P. Pearson, 7 for 20; Young, 6 for 17; Fugett, 1 for 5.
LA Rams—Jaworski, 2 for 12; McCutcheon, 11 for 10; Cappelletti, 1 for 1, 1 TD. Scribner, 1 for 1; Bryant, 1 for −2.

PASSING

Dallas—Staubach, 16 of 26 for 220, 4 TDs, 1 int.; Longley, 2 of 2 for 26.
LA Rams—Jaworski, 11 of 22 for 147, 2 int.; Harris, 0 of 2, 1 int.

RECEIVING

Dallas—P. Pearson, 7 for 123, 3 TDs; D. Pearson, 5 for 46; Richards, 2 for 46, 1 TD; Fugett, 2 for 5; Young, 1 for 15; Dennison, 1 for 11.
LA Rams—Jessie, 4 for 52; McCutcheon, 3 for 39; T. Nelson, 3 for 28; Bryant, 1 for 28.

1976 AFC

OAKLAND 24, PITTSBURGH 7

After losses in the playoffs in seven of the eight previous years, the Oakland Raiders defeated the Pittsburgh Steelers 24-7 for their first conference championship since 1967.

Quarterback Ken Stabler completed 10 of 16 passes for 88 yards and two touchdowns as the Raiders broke to a 10-0 lead and put an important touchdown on the scoreboard in the last 19 seconds of the first half. With a first down on the Steelers' 4-yard line, the Raiders lined up with three tight ends as if to run. Pittsburgh braced with an eight-man line. Oakland quarterback Ken Stabler called for a fake run to the right side as tight end Warren Bankston slipped free to the left side and caught Stabler's pass for a 17-7 halftime lead.

Pittsburgh played without running backs Franco Harris and Rocky Bleier, and started the game with a three-tight-end offense with Reggie Harrison as the only back. The Raiders had no problems shutting down the Steelers' running game, while confusing quarterback Terry Bradshaw with a variety of looks.

The Raiders put the game away late in the third quarter when they moved 63 yards in 12 plays to a touchdown on a five-yard pass from Stabler to Pete Banaszak. Although Stabler was shaken up on the play and didn't return, his replacement, Mike Rae, helped the Raiders eat up time in the fourth quarter.

December 26, at Oakland

Pittsburgh	Starters, Offense	Oakland
Larry Brown	TE-WR	Fred Biletnikoff
Jon Kolb	LT	Art Shell
Sam Davis	LG	Gene Upshaw
Mike Webster	C	Dave Dalby
Jim Clack	RG	George Buehler
Gerry Mullins	RT	John Vella
Bennie Cunningham	TE	Dave Casper
Lynn Swann	WR	Cliff Branch
Terry Bradshaw	QB	Ken Stabler
Randy Grossman	TE-RB	Mark van Eeghen
Reggie Harrison	RB	Clarence Davis
	Starters, Defense	
L.C. Greenwood	LE	John Matuszak
Joe Greene	LT-NT	Dave Rowe
Ernie Holmes	RT-RE	Otis Sistrunk
Dwight White	RE-LOLB	Phil Villapiano
Jack Ham	LLB-LILB	Monte Johnson
Jack Lambert	MLB-RILB	Willie Hall
Andy Russell	RLB-ROLB	Ted Hendricks
J.T. Thomas	LCB	Alonzo (Skip) Thomas
Mel Blount	RCB	Willie Brown
Glen Edwards	SS	George Atkinson
Mike Wagner	FS	Jack Tatum

Pittsburgh	0	7	0	0	—	7
Oakland	3	14	7	0	—	24

Oak—FG Mann 39
Oak—Davis 1 run (Mann kick)
Pitt—Harrison 3 run (Mansfield kick)
Oak—Bankston 4 pass from Stabler (Mann kick)
Oak—Banaszak 5 pass from Stabler (Mann kick)
Attendance—53,739

TEAM STATISTICS	Pitt	Oak
First downs	13	15
Rushing	3	7
Passing	8	7
By penalty	2	1
Total yardage	237	228
Net rushing yardage	72	157
Net passing yardage	165	71
Passes att.-comp.-had int.	34-14-1	16-10-0

RUSHING

Pittsburgh—Harrison, 11 for 44, 1 TD; Fuqua, 8 for 24; Bradshaw, 1 for 4; Cunningham, 1 for 0.
Oakland—van Eeghen, 22 for 66; Davis, 11 for 54, 1 TD; Banaszak, 15 for 46; Garrett, 2 for 4; Casper, 1 for −13.

PASSING

Pittsburgh—Bradshaw, 14 of 35 for 176, 1 int.
Oakland—Stabler, 10 of 16 for 88, 2 TDs.

RECEIVING

Pittsburgh—Cunningham, 4 for 36; Swann, 3 for 58; Fuqua, 2 for 11; Harrison, 2 for 10; Brown, 1 for 32; Stallworth, 1 for 18; Lewis, 1 for 11.
Oakland—Branch, 3 for 46; Bankston, 2 for 11, 1 TD; Davis, 2 for 7; van Eeghen, 1 for 14; Banaszak, 1 for 5, 1 TD; Casper, 1 for 5.

1976 NFC

MINNESOTA 24, LA RAMS 13

The Minnesota Vikings became the first team to qualify for four Super Bowl appearances when they defeated the Los Angeles Rams 24-13 on a day when the temperature was 12 degrees under a bright sun and the wind-chill factor was 12 below.

The most important play of the game occurred in the first quarter. Behind the running of Lawrence McCutcheon, the Rams drove to a first down at the Minnesota 6. On fourth down, with the ball six inches short of the goal line, the Rams attempted a field goal. The kick was blocked by Nate Allen, and the ball was picked up at the 10 by Bobby Bryant, who scampered 90 yards for a touchdown.

Later in the quarter, the Rams had a first down at the Minnesota 21. Running back John Cappelletti fumbled, and Matt Blair recovered for Minnesota. Then in the second quarter, Blair blocked a punt by Rusty Jackson giving the ball to the Vikings on the Rams' 8. Four plays later, Fred Cox kicked a field goal to make the score 10-0 at halftime.

In the third quarter, Chuck Foreman slanted off right tackle and raced 62 yards to the Rams' 2. Two plays later he scored to put the Vikings up 17-0. The Rams responded with two touchdowns to cut the score to 17-13, but their last gasp ended with two minutes to play when Pat Haden's pass was intercepted at the Minnesota 8 by Bryant.

December 26, at Bloomington

LA Rams	Starters, Offense	Minnesota
Harold Jackson	WR	Ahmad Rashad
Doug France	LT	Steve Riley
Tom Mack	LG	Charles Goodrum
Rich Saul	C	Mick Tingelhoff
Dennis Harrah	RG	Ed White
John Williams	RT	Ron Yary
Bob Klein	TE	Stu Voigt
Ron Jessie	WR	Sammy White
Pat Haden	QB	Fran Tarkenton
John Cappelletti	RB	Brent McClanahan
Lawrence McCutcheon	RB	Chuck Foreman
	Starters, Defense	
Jack Youngblood	LE	Carl Eller
Merlin Olsen	LT	Doug Sutherland
Larry Brooks	RT	Alan Page
Fred Dryer	RE	Jim Marshall
Jim Youngblood	LLB	Matt Blair
Jack Reynolds	MLB	Amos Martin
Isiah Robertson	RLB	Wally Hilgenberg
Rod Perry	LCB	Nate Wright
Monte Jackson	RCB	Bobby Bryant
Dave Elmendorf	SS-LS	Jeff Wright
Bill Simpson	FS-RS	Paul Krause

LA Rams	0	0	13	0	—	13
Minnesota	7	3	7	7	—	24

Minn—Bryant 90 blocked field goal return (Cox kick)
Minn—FG Cox 25
Minn—Foreman 2 run (Cox kick)
Rams—McCutcheon 10 run (kick failed)
Rams—H. Jackson 5 pass from Haden (Dempsey kick)
Minn—Johnson 12 run (Cox kick)
Attendance—47,191

TEAM STATISTICS	Rams	Minn
First downs	21	13
Rushing	14	6
Passing	7	7
By penalty	0	0
Total yardage	336	267
Net rushing yardage	193	158
Net passing yardage	143	109
Passes att.-comp.-had int.	22-9-2	27-12-1

RUSHING

LA Rams—McCutcheon, 26 for 128, 1 TD; Cappelletti, 16 for 59; Jessie, 1 for 3; Haden, 3 for 3.
Minnesota—Foreman, 15 for 118, 1 TD; Miller, 10 for 28; Johnson, 2 for 12, 1 TD; McClanahan, 1 for 2; Tarkenton, 1 for −2.

PASSING

LA Rams—Haden, 9 of 22 for 161, 1 TD, 2 int.
Minnesota—Tarkenton, 12 of 27 for 143, 1 int.

RECEIVING

LA Rams—H. Jackson, 4 for 70, 1 TD; Jessie, 2 for 60; McCutcheon, 2 for 18; Cappelletti, 1 for 13.
Minnesota—Foreman, 5 for 81; Rashad, 3 for 28; Miller, 3 for 24; Grim, 1 for 10.

1977 AFC

DENVER 20, OAKLAND 17

Playing in a championship game for the first time in the history of the franchise, the Broncos used three big plays and one non-call to defeat the Raiders 20-17. The teams had met twice during the regular season, each winning once.

After the Raiders had gone ahead 3-0 on their initial drive, the Broncos needed only two plays to take a 7-3 lead. Craig Morton passed to Haven Moses 35 yards downfield and Moses outraced the Oakland defenders to the end zone, completing a 74-yard play.

The Broncos increased their advantage to 14-3 in the third period on a one-yard run by Jon Keyworth. Brison Manor's recovery of Clarence Davis's fumble at the Raiders' 17 set up the touchdown. On the play before the score, with a first and goal at the 2, Rob Lytle was hit by safety Jack Tatum as he dived over the line into the end zone. Lytle lost the ball, and Raiders nose tackle Mike McCoy picked it up and began to run the other way. The play was whistled dead, however. The officials ruled that it was Denver's ball.

After the Raiders scored early in the fourth quarter, Bob Swenson intercepted Ken Stabler's pass and brought it back to the Oakland 17, setting up the clinching touchdown pass from Morton to Moses three plays later.

January 1, 1978, at Denver

Oakland	Starters, Offense	Denver
Cliff Branch	WR	Jack Dolbin
Art Shell	LT	Andy Maurer
Gene Upshaw	LG	Tom Glassic
Dave Dalby	C	Mike Montler
George Buehler	RG	Paul Howard
Henry Lawrence	RT	Claudie Minor
Dave Casper	TE	Riley Odoms
Fred Biletnikoff	WR	Haven Moses
Ken Stabler	QB	Craig Morton
Mark van Eeghen	RB	Jon Keyworth
Clarence Davis	RB	Rob Lytle
	Starters, Defense	
Jonn Matuszak	LE	Barney Chavous
Dave Rowe	NT	Rubin Carter
Otis Sistrunk	RE	Lyle Alzado
Floyd Rice	LOLB	Bob Swenson
Monte Jackson	LILB	Joe Rizzo
Willie Hall	RILB	Randy Gradishar
Ted Hendricks	ROLB	Tom Jackson
Lester Hayes	LCB	Louis Wright
Willie Brown	RCB	Steve Foley
Alonzo (Skip) Thomas	SS	Billy Thompson
Jack Tatum	FS	Bernard Jackson

Oakland	3	0	0	14	—	17
Denver	7	0	7	6	—	20

Oak—FG Mann 20
Den—Moses 74 pass from Morton (Turner kick)
Den—Keyworth 1 run (Turner kick)
Oak—Casper 7 pass from Stabler (Mann kick)
Den—Moses 12 pass from Morton (pass failed)
Oak—Casper 17 pass from Stabler (Mann kick)
Attendance—74,982

TEAM STATISTICS	Oak	Den
First downs	20	16
Rushing	6	6
Passing	11	8
By penalty	3	2
Total yardage	298	308
Net rushing yardage	94	91
Net passing yardage	204	217
Passes att.-comp.-had int.	35-17-1	20-10-1

RUSHING

Oakland—van Eeghen, 20 for 71; Banaszak, 7 for 22; Davis, 9 for 1.
Denver—Perrin, 11 for 42; Lytle, 7 for 26; Keyworth, 8 for 19, 1 TD; Armstrong, 7 for 16; Jensen, 1 for 2; Morton, 2 for −4; Moses, 1 for −10.

PASSING

Oakland—Stabler, 17 of 35 for 215, 2 TDs, 1 int.
Denver—Morton, 10 of 20 for 224, 2 TDs, 1 int.

RECEIVING

Oakland—Casper, 5 for 71, 2 TDs; Biletnikoff, 4 for 38; Branch, 3 for 59; van Eeghen, 2 for 8; Bradshaw, 1 for 25; Siani, 1 for 12; Banaszak, 1 for 2.
Denver—Moses, 5 for 168, 2 TDs; Perrin, 2 for 20; Jensen, 1 for 20; Odoms, 1 for 13; Keyworth, 1 for 3.

1977 NFC

DALLAS 23, MINNESOTA 6

It was 30 degrees in Irving, but the Cowboys' defense was as hot as the day was cold. Led by defensive ends Harvey Martin and Ed (Too Tall) Jones, Dallas stopped the Vikings 23-6 and advanced to a record-tying fourth Super Bowl.

Dallas gained an early lead after Martin recovered Robert Miller's fumble on Minnesota's 39-yard line on the third play of the game. Two plays later, Roger Staubach threw a 32-yard touchdown pass to Golden Richards.

The Cowboys increased their lead to 13-0 with a five-yard touchdown run by Robert Newhouse in the second quarter. The score climaxed a 46-yard drive that had been kept alive by Danny White's 14-yard run out of punt formation. Dallas didn't complete a pass in the drive.

After a scoreless third quarter, the Cowboys put the game away midway through the final period. Faced with a fourth and 11 at the Dallas 12, White punted, but the ball was fumbled by Minnesota's Manfred Moore and recovered by tight end Jay Saldi of Dallas. Five plays later, Tony Dorsett scored from the 11.

The Cowboys' defense limited the Vikings to 22 yards rushing in the second half and 66 in the game. Jones made 12 tackles and recorded one sack, while Martin recovered two of the three fumbles the Vikings lost.

January 1, 1978, at Irving

Minnesota	Starters, Offense	Dallas
Ahmad Rashad	WR-TE	Jay Saldi
Steve Riley	LT	Ralph Neely
Charles Goodrum	LG	Herbert Scott
Mick Tingelhoff	C	John Fitzgerald
Ed White	RG	Tom Rafferty
Ron Yary	RT	Pat Donovan
Stu Voigt	TE	Billy Joe DuPree
Sammy White	WR	Drew Pearson
Bob Lee	QB	Roger Staubach
Robert Miller	RB	Robert Newhouse
Chuck Foreman	RB	Tony Dorsett
	Starters, Defense	
Carl Eller	LE	Ed Jones
Doug Sutherland	LT	Jethro Pugh
Alan Page	RT	Randy White
Jim Marshall	RE	Harvey Martin
Matt Blair	LLB	Thomas Henderson
Jeff Siemon	MLB	Bob Breunig
Fred McNeill	RLB	D. D. Lewis
Nate Wright	LCB	Benny Barnes
Bobby Bryant	RCB	Aaron Kyle
Jeff Wright	LS-SS	Charlie Waters
Paul Krause	RS-FS	Cliff Harris

Minnesota	0	6	0	0	—	6
Dallas	6	10	0	7	—	23

Dall —Richards 32 pass from Staubach (kick blocked)
Dall —Newhouse 5 run (Herrera kick)
Minn—FG Cox 33
Minn—FG Cox 37
Dall —FG Herrera 21
Dall —Dorsett 11 run (Herrera kick)
Attendance—61,968

TEAM STATISTICS	Min	Dall
First downs	12	16
Rushing	4	7
Passing	6	7
By penalty	2	2
Total yardage	214	328
Net rushing yardage	66	170
Net passing yardage	148	158
Passes att.-comp.-had int.	31-14-1	23-12-1

RUSHING
Minnesota—Foreman, 21 for 59; Miller, 8 for 5; Johnson, 1 for 2.
Dallas—Newhouse, 15 for 81, 1 TD; Dorsett, 19 for 71, 1 TD; D. White, 1 for 14; Staubach, 4 for 4.

PASSING
Minnesota—Lee, 14 of 31 for 158, 1 int.
Dallas—Staubach, 12 of 23 for 165, 1 TD, 1 int.

RECEIVING
Minnesota—Foreman, 5 for 36; S. White, 3 for 46; Rashad, 3 for 18; Miller, 2 for 39; Voigt, 1 for 19.
Dallas—D. Pearson, 5 for 62; P. Pearson, 3 for 48; Richards, 2 for 34, 1 TD; Newhouse, 2 for 5; DuPree, 1 for 16.

1978 AFC

PITTSBURGH 34, HOUSTON 5

A freezing rain, a smothering defense that came up with nine turnovers, and a 17-point outburst in a 48-second span were part of the Steelers' 34-5 rout of the Oilers, who were appearing in their first championship game since 1967.

The Steelers led the entire way, but broke the game open in the last minute of the first half. Touchdown runs by Franco Harris and Rocky Bleier had resulted in a 14-3 Steelers lead. The score by Harris was the only time in the game the Steelers had to drive far (57 yards) for their points. Bleier's touchdown was set up when Earl Campbell lost a fumble that was recovered by Jack Ham at the Houston 17. Then, with 1:23 left to go in the half, Houston's Ronnie Coleman fumbled. Moments later Terry Bradshaw passed 29 yards to Lynn Swann for a touchdown. Johnny Dirden fumbled the ensuing kickoff and the Steelers recovered at the Oilers' 17. Two plays later Bradshaw passed to John Stallworth for another touchdown. And after the Oilers took the next kickoff, Coleman fumbled on the first play from scrimmage, setting up Roy Gerela's field goal with four seconds left.

Defense dominated the second half, when the Steelers intercepted Dan Pastorini four times in the Oilers' six possessions.

January 7, 1979, at Pittsburgh

Houston	Starters, Offense	Pittsburgh
Ken Burrough	WR	John Stallworth
Greg Sampson	LT	Jon Kolb
George Reihner	LG	Sam Davis
Carl Mauck	C	Mike Webster
Ed Fisher	RG	Ray Pinney
Conway Hayman	RT	Larry Brown
Mike Barber	TE	Randy Grossman
Rich Caster	WR	Lynn Swann
Dan Pastorini	QB	Terry Bradshaw
Tim Wilson	RB	Rocky Bleier
Earl Campbell	RB	Franco Harris
	Starters, Defense	
James Young	LE	L.C. Greenwood
Curley Culp	NT-LT	Joe Greene
Elvin Bethea	RE-RT	Steve Furness
Robert Brazile	LOLB-RE	John Banaszak
Steve Kiner	LILB-LLB	Jack Ham
Gregg Bingham	RILB-MLB	Jack Lambert
Ted Washington	ROLB-RLB	Robin Cole
Willie Alexander	LCB	Ron Johnson
Greg Stemrick	RCB	Mel Blount
Bill Currier	SS	Donnie Shell
Mike Reinfeldt	FS	Mike Wagner

Houston	0	3	2	0	—	5
Pittsburgh	14	17	3	0	—	34

Pitt —Harris 7 run (Gerela kick)
Pitt —Bleier 15 run (Gerela kick)
Hou—FG Fritsch 19
Pitt —Swann 29 pass from Bradshaw (Gerela kick)
Pitt —Stallworth 17 pass from Bradshaw (Gerela kick)
Pitt —FG Gerela 37
Pitt —FG Gerela 22
Hou—Safety, Washington tackled Bleier in end zone
Attendance—49,417

TEAM STATISTICS	Hou	Pitt
First downs	10	21
Rushing	5	8
Passing	3	11
By penalty	2	2
Total yardage	142	379
Net rushing yardage	72	179
Net passing yardage	70	200
Passes att.-comp.-had int.	26-12-5	19-11-2

RUSHING
Houston—Campbell, 22 for 62; Woods, 1 for 9; T. Wilson, 2 for 6; Coleman, 1 for −5.
Pittsburgh—Harris, 20 for 51, 1 TD; Bleier, 10 for 45, 1 TD; Bradshaw, 7 for 29; Deloplaine, 3 for 28; Thornton, 3 for 22; Moser, 3 for 7; Kruczek, 1 for −3.

PASSING
Houston—Pastorini, 12 of 26 for 96, 5 int.
Pittsburgh—Bradshaw, 11 of 19 for 200, 2 TDs, 2 int.

RECEIVING
Houston—Caster, 5 for 44; T. Wilson, 5 for 33; Coleman, 1 for 15; Campbell, 1 for 4.
Pittsburgh—Swann, 4 for 98, 1 TD; Bleier, 4 for 42; Grossman, 2 for 43; Stallworth, 1 for 17, 1 TD.

1978 NFC

DALLAS 28, LA RAMS 0

An opportunistic Cowboys defense came up with five second-half turnovers, three of which set up touchdowns and the fourth of which was returned for a score, as the Cowboys defeated the Rams 28-0.

Both teams had scoring opportunities in the first half, but came up empty due to turnovers and missed field goals.

With 1:52 to go in the third quarter, Dallas strong safety Charlie Waters intercepted Pat Haden's pass and returned it to the Rams' 10-yard line. Five plays later Tony Dorsett scored from five yards out. Shortly before the end of the quarter, Waters intercepted another pass and returned it 29 yards to the Rams' 20 to set up a touchdown toss from Roger Staubach to Scott Laidlaw.

In the fourth quarter, the Rams put together their longest drive of the game, reaching the Dallas 10 chiefly on the strength of a 65-yard pass from Vince Ferragamo, who had replaced the injured Haden, to Willie Miller. On first down, Harvey Martin recovered a fumble, and the Cowboys then drove 89 yards in seven plays, scoring on an 11-yard pass from Staubach to tight end Billy Joe DuPree. The final Dallas score came with 1:19 remaining when linebacker Thomas (Hollywood) Henderson intercepted a pass from Ferragamo and returned it 68 yards down the left sideline.

January 7, 1979, at Los Angeles

Dallas	Starters, Offense	LA Rams
Tony Hill	WR	Willie Miller
Pat Donovan	LT	Doug France
Herbert Scott	LG	Tom Mack
John Fitzgerald	C	Rich Saul
Tom Rafferty	RG	Dennis Harrah
Rayfield Wright	RT	John Williams
Billy Joe DuPree	TE	Terry Nelson
Drew Pearson	WR	Ron Jessie
Roger Staubach	QB	Pat Haden
Scott Laidlaw	RB	John Cappelletti
Tony Dorsett	RB	Cullen Bryant
	Starters, Defense	
Ed Jones	LE	Jack Youngblood
Larry Cole	LT	Cody Jones
Randy White	RT	Mike Fanning
Harvey Martin	RE	Fred Dryer
Thomas Henderson	LLB	Jim Youngblood
Bob Breunig	MLB	Jack Reynolds
D.D. Lewis	RLB	Bob Brudzinski
Benny Barnes	LCB	Pat Thomas
Aaron Kyle	RCB	Rod Perry
Charlie Waters	SS	Dave Elmendorf
Cliff Harris	FS	Bill Simpson

Dallas	0	0	7	21	—	28
LA Rams	0	0	0	0	—	0

Dall—Dorsett 5 run (Septien kick)
Dall—Laidlaw 4 pass from Staubach (Septien kick)
Dall—DuPree 11 pass from Staubach (Septien kick)
Dall—Henderson 68 interception return (Septien kick)
Attendance—67,470

TEAM STATISTICS	Dall	Rams
First downs	16	15
Rushing	7	3
Passing	7	11
By penalty	2	1
Total yardage	235	277
Net rushing yardage	126	81
Net passing yardage	109	196
Passes att.-comp.-had int.	25-13-2	35-14-5

RUSHING
Dallas—Dorsett, 17 for 101, 1 TD; Laidlaw, 19 for 20; Staubach, 3 for 7; Newhouse, 1 for 4; DuPree, 1 for 3; Smith, 1 for −9.
LA Rams—Bryant, 20 for 52; Haden 2 for 20; Cappelletti, 3 for 19; Phillips, 3 for 2; Jodat, 2 for −5; Waddy, 1 for −7.

PASSING
Dallas—Staubach, 13 of 25 for 126, 2 TDs, 2 int.
LA Rams—Haden, 7 of 19 for 76, 3 int.; Ferragamo, 7 of 16 for 130, 2 int.

RECEIVING
Dallas—DuPree, 3 for 48, 1 TD; Johnson, 2 for 19; D. Pearson, 2 for 19; Dorsett, 2 for 15; P. Pearson, 2 for 12; Hill, 1 for 9; Laidlaw, 1 for 4, 1 TD.
LA Rams—Jessie, 4 for 42; Miller, 3 for 96; Waddy, 2 for 23; Bryant, 2 for 2; Scales, 1 for 18; Cappelletti, 1 for 15; Nelson, 1 for 10.

1979 AFC

PITTSBURGH 27, HOUSTON 13

The Steelers set an AFC Championship Game record by holding the Oilers to only 24 yards rushing, but had to withstand a brilliant passing attack by Houston's Dan Pastorini to win the game 27-13, and with it the right to go their fourth Super Bowl.

The Oilers jumped into an early lead when rookie strong safety Vernon Perry intercepted Terry Bradshaw and returned his pass 75 yards for a touchdown. Bradshaw bounced back to throw touchdown passes to Bennie Cunningham and John Stallworth to give the Steelers a 17-10 halftime lead.

The key play of the game came in the final minute of the third quarter. With a first and goal at the Pittsburgh 6, Pastorini threw a pass to Mike Renfro at the back of the end zone. The officials ruled the pass incomplete, saying Renfro didn't have possession until he crossed the end line. The Oilers protested, and television replays left the issue forever in doubt. Houston had to settle for a field goal on the first play of the fourth quarter, but Pittsburgh matched it immediately by driving 78 yards to score on Matt Bahr's kick. The Steelers clinched the game in the final minute on a four-yard touchdown run by Rocky Bleier after Donnie Shell recovered Guido Merkins's fumble on the Houston 45.

January 6, 1980, at Pittsburgh

Houston	Starters, Offense	Pittsburgh
Ken Burrough	WR	John Stallworth
Leon Gray	LT	Ted Peterson
David Carter	LG	Sam Davis
Carl Mauck	C	Mike Webster
Ed Fisher	RG	Steve Courson
Conway Hayman	RT	Larry Brown
Mike Barber	TE	Bennie Cunningham
Rich Caster	WR	Lynn Swann
Dan Pastorini	QB	Terry Bradshaw
Tim Wilson	RB	Rocky Bleier
Earl Campbell	RB	Franco Harris
	Starters, Defense	
Andy Dorris	LE	L.C. Greenwood
Curley Culp	NT-LT	Joe Greene
Elvin Bethea	RE-RT	Gary Dunn
Ted Washington	LOLB-RE	John Banaszak
Gregg Bingham	LILB-LLB	Dennis Winston
Art Stringer	RILB-MLB	Jack Lambert
Robert Brazile	ROLB-RLB	Robin Cole
J.C. Wilson	LCB	Ron Johnson
Greg Stemrick	RCB	Mel Blount
Vernon Perry	SS	Donnie Shell
Mike Reinfeldt	FS	J.T. Thomas

Houston	7	3	0	3	—	13
Pittsburgh	3	14	0	10	—	27

Hou—Perry 75 interception return (Fritsch kick)
Pitt —FG Bahr 21
Hou—FG Fritsch 27
Pitt —Cunningham 16 pass from Bradshaw (Bahr kick)
Pitt —Stallworth 20 pass from Bradshaw (Bahr kick)
Hou—FG Fritsch 23
Pitt —FG Bahr 39
Pitt —Bleier 4 run (Bahr kick)
Attendance—50,475

TEAM STATISTICS	Hou	Pitt
First downs	11	22
Rushing	2	9
Passing	7	13
By penalty	2	0
Total yardage	227	358
Net rushing yardage	24	161
Net passing yardage	203	197
Passes att.-comp.-had int.	29-20-1	30-18-1

RUSHING
Houston—Campbell, 17 for 15; Wilson, 4 for 9; Caster, 1 for 0.
Pittsburgh—Harris, 21 for 85; Bleier, 13 for 52, 1 TD; Bradshaw, 1 for 25; Thornton, 1 for −1.

PASSING
Houston—Pastorini, 19 of 28 for 203, 1 int.; Neilsen, 1 of 1 for 9.
Pittsburgh—Bradshaw, 18 of 30 for 219, 2 TDs, 1 int.

RECEIVING
Houston—Wilson, 7 for 60; Carpenter, 5 for 23; Renfro, 3 for 52; Coleman, 2 for 46; Merkins, 1 for 12; Campbell, 1 for 11; Barber, 1 for 8.
Pittsburgh—Harris, 6 for 50; Swann, 4 for 64; Stallworth, 3 for 52, 1 TD; Bleier, 3 for 39; Cunningham, 2 for 14, 1 TD.

1979 NFC

LA RAMS 9, TAMPA BAY 0

After four losses in the last five championship games, the Los Angeles Rams qualified for their first Super Bowl by defeating the Tampa Bay Buccaneers 9-0 in the first title game in which no touchdowns were scored.

Frank Corral accounted for all of the points in the game. The Rams were able to move the ball well, but couldn't get into the end zone. Corral kicked his first field goal on the first play of the second quarter, after the Rams drove 68 yards to the Tampa Bay 1, but couldn't get the ball in from there in two plays. At the end of the quarter, the Rams put together another drive, of 58 yards, that ended at the Tampa Bay 4 with Corral kicking a 21-yard field goal with 47 seconds left in the half.

The Rams clinched the game midway through the final period, when they drove 45 yards to a 23-yard field goal. The short drive was set up by a 16-yard punt return by Eddie Brown.

Meanwhile, the Rams' defense totally dominated the Buccaneers, holding them to just 13 yards in the first quarter and not allowing a first down until 7:55 remained in the second period. Ricky Bell gained 59 yards on 20 carries just one week after he set a playoff record with 38 carries for 142 yards. Tampa Bay's quarterbacks—Doug Williams and Mike Rae—completed only 4 of 26 passes and had absolutely no success in their plan to throw on cornerback Pat Thomas, who batted down five passes.

January 6, 1980, at Tampa

LA Rams	Starters, Offense	Tampa Bay
Billy Waddy	WR	Isaac Hagins
Doug France	LT	Dave Reavis
Kent Hill	LG	Greg Horton
Rich Saul	C	Steve Wilson
Dennis Harrah	RG	Greg Roberts
Jackie Slater	RT	Charley Hannah
Terry Nelson	TE	Jimmie Giles
Preston Dennard	WR	Larry Mucker
Vince Ferragamo	QB	Doug Williams
Cullen Bryant	RB	Ricky Bell
Wendell Tyler	RB-TE	Jim Obradovich
	Starters, Defense	
Jack Youngblood	LE	Wally Chambers
Mike Fanning	LT-NT	Randy Crowder
Larry Brooks	RT-RE	Lee Roy Selmon
Fred Dryer	RE-LOLB	David Lewis
Jim Youngblood	LLB-LILB	Dewey Selmon
Jack Reynolds	MLB-RILB	Richard Wood
Bob Brudzinski	RLB-ROLB	Cecil Johnson
Pat Thomas	LCB	Jeris White
Rod Perry	RCB	Mike Washington
Dave Elmendorf	SS	Mark Cotney
Nolan Cromwell	FS	Cedric Brown

LA Rams	0	6	0	3	—	9
Tampa Bay	0	0	0	0	—	0

Rams—FG Corral 19
Rams—FG Corral 21
Rams—FG Corral 23
Attendance—72,033

TEAM STATISTICS	Rams	TB
First downs	23	7
Rushing	13	3
Passing	8	4
By penalty	2	0
Total yardage	369	177
Net rushing yardage	216	92
Net passing yardage	153	85
Passes att.-comp.-had int.	23-12-0	27-5-1

RUSHING
LA Rams—Bryant, 18 for 106; Tyler, 28 for 86; McCutcheon, 6 for 26; Ferragamo, 1 for −2.
Tampa Bay—Bell, 20 for 59; Mucker, 1 for 24; Eckwood, 2 for 5; J. Davis, 2 for 4; Rae, 1 for 0.

PASSING
LA Rams—Ferragamo, 12 of 23 for 163.
Tampa Bay—Williams, 2 of 13 for 12, 1 int.; Rae, 2 of 13 for 42; Eckwood, 1 of 1 for 42.

RECEIVING
LA Rams—Bryant, 4 for 39; Dennard, 3 for 56; Young, 3 for 39; Nelson, 1 for 15; Tyler, 1 for 14.
Tampa Bay—Hagins, 2 for 42; Bell, 2 for 12; Mucker, 1 for 42.

1980 AFC

OAKLAND 34, SAN DIEGO 27

The Raiders jumped to a 28-7 lead and held on to defeat the Chargers 34-27 in a game matching two Western Division teams with identical records.

Jim Plunkett completed 14 of 18 passes for 261 yards and accounted for the three first-quarter scores for the Raiders. He threw a 65-yard touchdown pass to Raymond Chester, ran for a five-yard touchdown, and passed 21 yards to halfback Kenny King as Oakland built a 21-7 margin.

Chargers quarterback Dan Fouts and wide receiver Charlie Joiner connected for their second touchdown pass of the game 1:05 before the half to cut the Raiders' lead to 28-14.

The Chargers closed to 28-24 after their first two possessions of the third quarter, but could not get closer. On each of their next two possessions, the Raiders drove to field goals by Chris Bahr to up the lead to 34-24 early in the fourth quarter. The Chargers then put together a 12-play, 72-yard drive that took more than eight minutes off the clock and resulted only in another field goal. The Raiders ran off the last 6:43 of the game, without ever letting San Diego have the ball again.

January 11, 1981, at San Diego

Oakland	Starters, Offense	San Diego
Cliff Branch	WR	Charlie Joiner
Art Shell	LT	Billy Shields
Gene Upshaw	LG	Doug Wilkerson
Dave Dalby	C	Don Macek
Mickey Marvin	RG	Ed White
Henry Lawrence	RT	Dan Audick
Raymond Chester	TE	Kellen Winslow
Bob Chandler	WR	John Jefferson
Jim Plunkett	QB	Dan Fouts
Mark van Eeghen	RB	Chuck Muncie
Kenny King	RB-WR	Ron Smith
	Starters, Defense	
John Matuszak	LE	Leroy Jones
Reggie Kinlaw	NT-LT	Louie Kelcher
Dave Browning	RE-RT	Gary Johnson
Ted Hendricks	LOLB-RE	Fred Dean
Matt Millen	LILB-LLB	Ray Preston
Bob Nelson	RILB-MLB	Bob Horn
Rod Martin	ROLB-RLB	Woodrow Lowe
Lester Hayes	LCB	Willie Buchanon
Dwayne O'Steen	RCB	Mike Williams
Mike Davis	SS	Mike Fuller
Burgess Owens	FS	Glen Edwards

Oakland	21	7	3	3	—	34
San Diego	7	7	10	3	—	27

Oak—Chester 65 pass from Plunkett (Bahr kick)
SD —Joiner 48 pass from Fouts (Benirschke kick)
Oak—Plunkett 5 run (Bahr kick)
Oak—King 21 pass from Plunkett (Bahr kick)
Oak—van Eeghen 3 run (Bahr kick)
SD —Joiner 8 pass from Fouts (Benirschke kick)
SD —FG Benirschke 26
SD —Muncie 6 run (Benirschke kick)
Oak—FG Bahr 27
Oak—FG Bahr 33
SD —FG Benirschke 27
Attendance—52,428

TEAM STATISTICS	Oak	SD
First downs	21	26
Rushing	8	6
Passing	12	17
By penalty	1	3
Total yardage	362	434
Net rushing yardage	138	83
Net passing yardage	224	351
Passes att.-comp.-had int.	18-14-0	46-23-2

RUSHING
Oakland—van Eeghen, 20 for 85, 1 TD; King, 11 for 35; Jensen, 2 for 7; Plunkett, 4 for 6, 1 TD; Whittington, 5 for 5.
San Diego—Thomas, 12 for 48; Muncie, 9 for 34, 1 TD, Fouts, 1 for 2; Smith, 1 for −1.

PASSING
Oakland—Plunkett, 14 of 18 for 261, 2 TDs.
San Diego—Fouts, 22 of 45 for 336, 2 TDs, 2 int.; Winslow, 1 of 1 for 28.

RECEIVING
Oakland—Chester, 5 for 102, 1 TD; Branch, 3 for 78; King, 2 for 43, 1 TD; Chandler, 2 for 27; Whittington, 2 for 11.
San Diego—Joiner, 6 for 130, 2 TDs; Thomas, 5 for 40; Jefferson, 4 for 71; Smith, 3 for 76; Winslow, 3 for 42; Muncie, 2 for 5.

1980 NFC

PHILADELPHIA 20, DALLAS 7

With a 14-mile-per-hour wind and 16-degree temperature helping stall both teams' passing attacks, Wilbert Montgomery accounted for most of the offense as the Eagles advanced to their first Super Bowl with a 20-7 victory over the Cowboys.

Montgomery ran for 194 yards, only 2 short of the championship game record. He scored the Eagles' first touchdown on a 42-yard run through the Cowboys' defense after only 2:11 of play.

The Cowboys tied the score before the half on a three-yard touchdown run by Tony Dorsett, but didn't get past the Eagles' 39-yard line the rest of the game.

While the Eagles' defense controlled the Cowboys in the second half, the offense took advantage of two Dallas turnovers, which set up 10 third-quarter Philadelphia points. Tony Franklin kicked a 26 yard field goal four plays after Dennis Harrison sacked Danny White and recovered his fumble at the Cowboys' 11. After the next Dallas drive had reached the Philadelphia 40, Dorsett fumbled, and Jerry Robinson returned it 22 yards to the Dallas 38. Six plays later, Leroy Harris slashed off tackle, cut back to the middle, and pounded into the end zone from nine yards out for a 17-7 lead.

The only score of the fourth quarter came on a 20-yard field goal by Franklin after the Eagles had driven 62 yards to the Dallas 3.

January 11, 1981, at Philadelphia

Dallas	Starters, Offense	Philadelphia
Butch Johnson	WR	Harold Carmichael
Pat Donovan	LT	Stan Walters
Herbert Scott	LG	Petey Perot
Robert Shaw	C	Guy Morriss
Tom Rafferty	RG	Woody Peoples
Jim Cooper	RT	Jerry Sisemore
Billy Joe DuPree	TE	Keith Krepfle
Drew Pearson	WR	Rodney Parker
Danny White	QB	Ron Jaworski
Robert Newhouse	RB	Leroy Harris
Tony Dorsett	RB	Wilbert Montgomery
	Starters, Defense	
Ed Jones	LE	Dennis Harrison
Larry Cole	LT-NT	Charlie Johnson
Randy White	RT-RE	Carl Hairston
Harvey Martin	RE-LOLB	John Bunting
Guy Brown	LLB-LILB	Bill Bergey
Bob Breunig	MLB-RILB	Frank LeMaster
D.D. Lewis	RLB-ROLB	Jerry Robinson
Benny Barnes	LCB	Roynell Young
Aaron Mitchell	RCB	Herman Edwards
Charlie Waters	SS	Randy Logan
Dennis Thurman	FS	Brenard Wilson

Dallas	0	7	0	0	—	7
Philadelphia	7	0	10	3	—	20

Phil—Montgomery 42 run (Franklin kick)
Dall—Dorsett 3 run (Septien kick)
Phil—FG Franklin 26
Phil—Harris 9 run (Franklin kick)
Phil—FG Franklin 20
Attendance—70,696

TEAM STATISTICS	Dall	Phil
First downs	11	19
Rushing	5	13
Passing	6	5
By penalty	0	1
Total yardage	206	340
Net rushing yardage	90	263
Net passing yardage	116	77
Passes att.-comp.-had int.	32-12-1	29-9-2

RUSHING
Dallas—Newhouse, 7 for 44; Dorsett, 13 for 41, 1 TD; Johnson, 1 for 5; D. White, 1 for 0.
Philadelphia—Montgomery, 26 for 194, 1 TD; Harris, 10 for 60, 1 TD; Harrington, 1 for 4; Campfield, 1 for 3; Jaworski, 2 for 2.
PASSING
Dallas—D. White, 12 of 31 for 127, 1 int.; D. Pearson, 0 of 1.
Philadelphia—Jaworski, 9 of 29 for 91, 2 int.
RECEIVING
Dallas—Dorsett, 3 for 27; P. Pearson, 2 for 32; Johnson, 2 for 27; D. Pearson, 2 for 15; Springs, 2 for −2; Saldi, 1 for 28.
Philadelphia—Parker, 4 for 31; Krepfle, 2 for 22; Campfield, 1 for 17; Montgomery, 1 for 14; Carmichael, 1 for 7.

1981 AFC

CINCINNATI 27, SAN DIEGO 7

Amidst a temperature of nine degrees below zero and a 35-mile-per-hour wind that created a wind-chill factor of minus 59, the Bengals dominated the Chargers to win their first AFC Championship Game 27-7.

Dan Fouts had averaged more than 300 yards passing per game in the regular season, but the cruel weather helped limit the record-setting San Diego passing attack to only 173 net yards.

The Bengals scored on their second possession of the game, driving 51 yards to Jim Breech's 31-yard field goal. When James Brooks fumbled the ensuing kickoff, Don Bass recovered for the Bengals at the Chargers' 12. On second down, Ken Anderson passed eight yards for a touchdown to M. L. Harris.

The Chargers cut the lead to 10-7 in the second quarter. Fouts found tight end Kellen Winslow for a 33-yard touchdown pass. The Bengals struck right back after David Verser returned the kickoff to the 45. Anderson completed four out of five passes for 52 yards in a drive that culminated in Pete Johnson's one-yard touchdown run for a 17-7 halftime lead.

The Bengals' defense owned the second half. It shut out the Chargers and set up Breech's third-quarter field goal with a fumble recovery. In the fourth quarter, the Bengals drove 68 yards in 14 plays, almost entirely on the ground, for the clinching score.

January 10, 1982, at Cincinnati

San Diego	Starters, Offense	Cincinnati
Charlie Joiner	WR	Cris Collinsworth
Billy Shields	LT	Anthony Muñoz
Doug Wilkerson	LG	Dave Lapham
Don Macek	C	Blair Bush
Ed White	RG	Max Montoya
Russ Washington	RT	Mike Wilson
Kellen Winslow	TE	Dan Ross
Wes Chandler	WR	Isaac Curtis
Dan Fouts	QB	Ken Anderson
Chuck Muncie	RB	Pete Johnson
James Brooks	RB	Charles Alexander
	Starters, Defense	
Leroy Jones	LE	Eddie Edwards
Louie Kelcher	LT-NT	Wilson Whitley
Gary Johnson	RT-RE	Ross Browner
John Woodcock	RE-LOLB	Bo Harris
Linden King	LLB-LILB	Jim LeClair
Bob Horn	MLB-RILB	Glenn Cameron
Woodrow Lowe	RLB-ROLB	Reggie Williams
Willie Buchanon	LCB	Louis Breeden
Allan Ellis	RCB	Ken Riley
Pete Shaw	SS	Bobby Kemp
Glen Edwards	FS	Bryan Hicks

San Diego	0	7	0	0	—	7
Cincinnati	10	7	3	7	—	27

Cin—FG Breech 31
Cin—M. L. Harris 8 pass from Anderson (Breech kick)
SD—Winslow 33 pass from Fouts (Benirschke kick)
Cin—Johnson 1 run (Breech kick)
Cin—FG Breech 38
Cin—Bass 3 pass from Anderson (Breech kick)
Attendance—46,302

TEAM STATISTICS	SD	Cin
First downs	18	19
Rushing	11	8
Passing	7	11
By penalty	0	0
Total yardage	301	318
Net rushing yardage	128	143
Net passing yardage	173	175
Passes att.-comp.-had int.	28-15-2	23-15-0

RUSHING
San Diego—Muncie, 23 for 94; Brooks, 6 for 23; Fouts, 1 for 6; Cappelletti, 1 for 5.
Cincinnati—Johnson, 21 for 80, 1 TD; Anderson, 5 for 39; Alexander, 9 for 22; Collinsworth, 1 for 2.
PASSING
San Diego—Fouts, 15 of 28 for 185, 1 TD, 2 int.
Cincinnati—Anderson, 14 of 22 for 161, 2 TDs; Thompson, 1 of 1 for 14.
RECEIVING
San Diego—Chandler, 6 for 79; Winslow, 3 for 47, 1 TD; Joiner, 3 for 41; Brooks, 2 for 5; Sievers, 1 for 13.
Cincinnati—Ross, 5 for 69; Alexander, 3 for 25; Collinsworth, 2 for 28; Curtis, 2 for 28; Johnson, 1 for 14; M.L. Harris, 1 for 8, 1 TD; Bass, 1 for 3, 1 TD.

1981 NFC

SAN FRANCISCO 28, DALLAS 27

Joe Montana climaxed an 89-yard drive with a six-yard touchdown pass to Dwight Clark with 51 seconds left in the game, and the 49ers edged the Cowboys 28-27 in a see-saw battle.

The 49ers led early on a touchdown pass from Montana to Freddie Solomon, but the Cowboys drove right back to a field goal by Rafael Septien, and then seized the lead at the end of the first quarter with a two-play touchdown drive set up by Mike Hegman's recovery of a fumble by the 49ers' Bill Ring. Dallas scored on a touchdown pass from Danny White to Tony Hill.

Montana threw 20 yards to Clark for a 14-10 lead, but Dallas rebounded with a five-yard touchdown run by Tony Dorsett for a 17-14 halftime lead.

The 49ers scored next to go up 21-17, but a 21-yard pass from White to Doug Cosbie gave the Cowboys a 27-21 lead in the fourth quarter.

With 4:54 left in the game the 49ers gained possession on their own 11-yard line and drove 89 yards in 13 plays. On third down, Montana threw a high pass to the back of the end zone and Clark made a leaping catch for the winning score.

January 10, 1982, at San Francisco

Dallas	Starters, Offense	San Francisco
Tony Hill	WR	Mike Wilson
Pat Donovan	LT	Dan Audick
Herbert Scott	LG	John Ayers
Tom Rafferty	C	Fred Quillan
Kurt Peterson	RG	Randy Cross
Jim Cooper	RT	Keith Fahnhorst
Billy Joe DuPree	TE	Charle Young
Drew Pearson	WR	Mike Shumann
Danny White	QB	Joe Montana
Ron Springs	RB	Lenvil Elliott
Tony Dorsett	RB	Earl Cooper
	Starters, Defense	
Ed Jones	LE	Jim Stuckey
Larry Bethea	LT-NT	Archie Reese
Randy White	RT-RE	Dwaine Board
Harvey Martin	RE-LOLB	Willie Harper
Mike Hegman	LLB-LILB	Jack Reynolds
Bob Breunig	MLB-RILB	Craig Puki
D. D. Lewis	RLB-ROLB	Keena Turner
Everson Walls	LCB	Ronnie Lott
Dennis Thurman	RCB	Eric Wright
Charlie Waters	SS	Carlton Williamson
Michael Downs	FS	Dwight Hicks

Dallas	10	7	0	10	—	27
San Francisco	7	7	7	7	—	28

SF—Solomon 8 pass from Montana (Wersching kick)
Dall—FG Septien 44
Dall—Hill 26 pass from D. White (Septien kick)
SF—Clark 20 pass from Montana (Wersching kick)
Dall—Dorsett 5 run (Septien kick)
SF—Davis 2 run (Wersching kick)
Dall—FG Septien 22
Dall—Cosbie 21 pass from D. White (Septien kick)
SF—Clark 6 pass from Montana (Wersching kick)
Attendance—60,525

TEAM STATISTICS	Dall	SF
First downs	16	26
Rushing	5	6
Passing	9	17
By penalty	2	3
Total yardage	250	393
Net rushing yardage	115	127
Net passing yardage	135	266
Passes att.-comp.-had int.	24-16-1	35-22-3

RUSHING
Dallas—Dorsett, 22 for 91, 1 TD; J. Jones, 4 for 14; Springs, 5 for 10; D. White, 1 for 0.
San Francisco—Elliott, 10 for 48; Cooper, 8 for 35; Ring, 6 for 27; Solomon, 1 for 14; Easley, 2 for 6; Davis, 1 for 2, 1 TD; Montana, 3 for −5.
PASSING
Dallas—D. White, 16 of 24 for 173, 2 TDs, 1 int.
San Francisco—Montana, 22 of 35 for 286, 3 TDs, 3 int.
RECEIVING
Dallas—J. Jones, 3 for 17; DuPree, 3 for 15; Springs, 3 for 13; Hill, 2 for 43, 1 TD; Pearson, 1 for 31; Cosbie, 1 for 21, 1 TD; Johnson, 1 for 20; Saldi, 1 for 9; Donley, 1 for 4.
San Francisco—Clark, 8 for 120, 2 TDs; Solomon, 6 for 75, 1 TD; Young, 4 for 45; Cooper, 2 for 11; Elliott, 1 for 24; Shuman, 1 for 11.

1982 AFC

MIAMI 14, NY JETS 0

It was a day for the defenses at the rain-soaked Orange Bowl, and the most prominent defender was Miami linebacker A.J. Duhe. On a day when Miami's Killer Bees defense completely overwhelmed the Jets, Duhe scored one touchdown and set up another to lead Miami to a 14-0 victory.

With a muddy field and a slick ball helping them out, the Dolphins held NFL rushing leader Freeman McNeil to only 46 yards. They also intercepted Richard Todd five times and handcuffed his favorite receiver, old Miami nemesis Wesley Walker. The first half ended scoreless, with neither team really threatening, or even attempting a field goal.

On the first drive of the third quarter, a pass intended for Mike Augustyniak bounced off his hands and was intercepted by Duhe, who was downed at the Jets 48. Six plays later, with a third and three at the 28, Miami quarterback David Woodley threw complete to Duriel Harris for 14 yards, and on the same play an unsportsmanlike conduct penalty moved the ball to the New York 7. On first down, Woody Bennett blasted through the middle for a touchdown.

The Jets couldn't move the rest of the quarter. When they did get field position at their 41, Duhe intercepted his second pass of the day. Then, with two minutes gone in the fourth quarter, Todd threw a screen pass for Bruce Harper. Duhe picked it off in the left flat and raced down the sideline for a 35-yard touchdown return and the game's coup de grace.

January 23, 1983, at Miami

NY Jets	**Starters, Offense**	**Miami**
Wesley Walker	WR	Duriel Harris
Chris Ward	LT	Jon Giesler
Stan Waldemore	LG	Bob Kuechenberg
Joe Fields	C	Dwight Stephenson
Dan Alexander	RG	Jeff Toews
Marvin Powell	RT	Eric Laakso
Jerome Barkum	TE	Bruce Hardy
Johnny (Lam) Jones	WR	Jimmy Cefalo
Richard Todd	QB	David Woodley
Mike Augustyniak	RB	Andra Franklin
Freeman McNeil	RB-TE	Ronnie Lee
	Starters, Defense	
Mark Gastineau	LE	Kim Bokamper
Abdul Salaam	LT-NT	Bob Baumhower
Marty Lyons	RT-RE	Doug Betters
Kenny Neil	RE-LOLB	Bob Brudzinski
Greg Buttle	LLB-LILB	A. J. Duhe
Bob Crable	MLB-RILB	Earnie Rhone
Lance Mehl	RLB-ROLB	Larry Gordon
Bobby Jackson	LCB	Gerald Small
Jerry Holmes	RCB	Don McNeal
Ken Schroy	SS	Glenn Blackwood
Darrol Ray	FS	Lyle Blackwood

NY Jets	0	0	0	0	—	0
Miami	0	0	7	7	—	14

Mia—Bennett 7 run (von Schamann kick)
Mia—Duhe 35 interception return (von Schamann kick)
Attendance—67,396

TEAM STATISTICS	**NYJ**	**Mia**
First downs	10	13
Rushing	2	7
Passing	6	5
By penalty	2	1
Total yardage	139	198
Net rushing yardage	62	138
Net passing yardage	77	60
Passes att.-comp.-had int.	37-15-5	21-9-3

RUSHING
NY Jets—McNeil, 17 for 46; Todd, 4 for 10; Augustyniak, 2 for 5; Dierking, 1 for 1.
Miami—Woodley, 8 for 46; Franklin, 13 for 44; Nathan, 7 for 24; Bennett, 13 for 24, 1 TD.
PASSING
NY Jets—Todd, 15 of 37 for 103, 5 int.
Miami—Woodley, 9 of 21 for 87, 3 int.
RECEIVING
NY Jets—Harper, 4 for 14; J. Jones, 3 for 35; Barkum, 2 for 20; Augustyniak, 2 for 12; McNeil, 1 for 9; Gaffney, 1 for 7; Dierking, 1 for 6; Walker, 1 for 0.
Miami—Vigorito, 3 for 29; Harris, 2 for 28; Nathan, 2 for 4; Rose, 1 for 20; Lee, 1 for 6.

1982 NFC

WASHINGTON 31, DALLAS 17

Washington's relentless offense, moving at will behind the newly named Hogs offensive line, dominated the Dallas defense, and the Redskins won 31-17.

Although the Cowboys struck first by driving 75 yards to a field goal, the Redskins came back with an 84-yard march to a touchdown. In the second quarter, the Redskins got their first big break when Rod Hill bobbled a punt and Monte Coleman recovered at the Dallas 11. Four plays later, John Riggins dived over from the 1 to make it 14-3.

Shortly before the half, Dallas quarterback Danny White was run over by Dexter Manley and suffered a concussion. White never returned, but his understudy, Gary Hogeboom, led the Cowboys to a touchdown on their first possession of the second half.

Washington's Mike Nelms responded with a 76-yard kickoff return to the Dallas 20, and five plays later, Riggins scored from the 4. Again Hogeboom brought the Cowboys back, moving 84 yards for another touchdown. But there his magic ended.

In the fourth quarter, Mel Kaufman's interception led to a field goal. Then, Manley tipped Hogeboom's pass into the arms of Darryl Grant, who lumbered 10 yards for the final score of the game.

January 22, 1983, at Washington

Dallas	**Starters, Offense**	**Washington**
Tony Hill	WR	Charlie Brown
Pat Donovan	LT	Joe Jacoby
Howard Richards	LG	Russ Grimm
Tom Rafferty	C	Jeff Bostic
Kurt Peterson	RG	Mark May
Jim Cooper	RT	George Starke
Doug Cosbie	TE	Don Warren
Drew Pearson	WR	Alvin Garrett
Danny White	QB	Joe Theismann
Ron Springs	RB	John Riggins
Tony Dorsett	RB-TE	Rick Walker
	Starters, Defense	
Ed (Too Tall) Jones	LE	Mat Mendenhall
Don Smerek	LT	Dave Butz
Randy White	RT	Darryl Grant
Harvey Martin	RE	Dexter Manley
Mike Hegman	LLB	Mel Kaufman
Bob Breunig	MLB	Neal Olkewicz
Guy Brown	RLB	Rich Milot
Everson Walls	LCB	Jeris White
Dennis Thurman	RCB	Vernon Dean
Benny Barnes	SS	Tony Peters
Michael Downs	FS	Mark Murphy

Dallas	3	0	14	0	—	17
Washington	7	7	7	10	—	21

Dall —FG Septien 27
Wash —Brown 19 pass from Theismann (Moseley kick)
Wash —Riggins 1 run (Moseley kick)
Dall —Pearson 6 pass from Hogeboom (Septien kick)
Wash —Riggins 4 run (Moseley kick)
Dall —Johnson 23 pass from Hogeboom (Septien kick)
Wash —FG Moseley 29
Wash —Grant 10 interception return (Moseley kick)
Attendance—55,045

TEAM STATISTICS	**Dall**	**Wash**
First downs	21	18
Rushing	2	11
Passing	19	5
By penalty	0	2
Total yardage	340	260
Net rushing yardage	65	137
Net passing yardage	275	123
Passes att.-comp.-had int.	44-23-2	20-12-0

RUSHING
Dallas—Dorsett, 15 for 57; Springs, 4 for 15; Pearson, 1 for -1; T. Hill, 1 for -6.
Washington—Riggins, 36 for 140, 2 TDs; Washington, 2 for 2; Garrett, 1 for -2; Theismann, 1 for -3.
PASSING
Dallas—Hogeboom, 14 of 29 for 162, 2 TDs, 2 int.; D. White, 9 of 15 for 113.
Washington—Theismann, 12 of 20 for 150, 1 TD.
RECEIVING
Dallas—Johnson, 5 for 73, 1 TD; T. Hill, 5 for 59; Pearson, 5 for 55, 1 TD; Newsome, 3 for 24; Dorsett, 2 for 29; Cosbie, 2 for 26; DuPree, 1 for 9.
Washington—Garrett, 4 for 46; Brown, 3 for 54, 1 TD; Warren, 2 for 24; Washington, 1 for 13; Walker, 1 for 9; Harmon, 1 for 4.

1983 AFC

LA RAIDERS 30, SEATTLE 14

The Los Angeles Raiders shut down AFC rookie of the year Curt Warner and gained 401 total yards themselves to soundly defeat a Seattle team that had beaten them twice in the regular season. Warner was held to 26 yards in the Raiders' 30-14 victory.

Each of the Raiders' four first-half scores came after big plays, two by the offense and two by the defense. On Seattle's first possession of the game, Lester Hayes intercepted a pass by Dave Krieg to set up Chris Bahr's 20-yard field goal.

In the second quarter, Frank Hawkins scored twice, each following a long pass from Jim Plunkett to Malcolm Barnwell. The first pass was for 20 yards and set the Raiders up at Seattle's 14. Hawkins scored five plays later. The next big play went for 49 yards, setting the Raiders up at the 7. Hawkins scored to cap a four-play, 60-yard drive.

In the second half, Jim Zorn replaced Krieg for the Seahawks, but it was too little too late. Zorn threw two touchdown passes, but the Raiders had ended any doubts about a comeback when they went up 27-0 in the third quarter. The two-play drive consisted of Marcus Allen's 46-yard run and a three-yard scoring pass from Jim Plunkett to Allen.

January 8, 1984, at Los Angeles

Seattle	**Starters, Offense**	**LA Raiders**
Pete Metzelaars	TE	Don Hasselbeck
Ron Essink	LT	Bruce Davis
Edwin Bailey	LG	Charley Hannah
Blair Bush	C	Dave Dalby
Robert Pratt	RG	Mickey Marvin
Steve August	RT	Henry Lawrence
Charle Young	TE	Todd Christensen
Steve Largent	WR	Cliff Branch
Dave Krieg	QB	Jim Plunkett
Cullen Bryant	RB	Marcus Allen
Curt Warner	RB-WR	Malcolm Barnwell
	Starters, Defense	
Jacob Green	LE	Howie Long
Joe Nash	NT	Reggie Kinlaw
Jeff Bryant	RE	Lyle Alzado
Bruce Scholtz	LOLB	Ted Hendricks
Joe Norman	LILB	Matt Millen
Keith Butler	RILB	Bob Nelson
Greg Gaines	ROLB	Rod Martin
Kerry Justin	LCB	Lester Hayes
Dave Brown	RCB	Mike Haynes
Kenny Easley	SS	Mike Davis
John Harris	FS	Vann McElroy

Seattle	0	0	7	7	—	14
LA Raiders	3	17	7	3	—	30

Raiders —FG Bahr 20
Raiders —Hawkins 1 run (Bahr kick)
Raiders —Hawkins 5 run (Bahr kick)
Raiders —FG Bahr 45
Raiders —Allen 3 pass from Plunkett (Bahr kick)
Sea —Doornink 11 pass from Zorn (N. Johnson kick)
Raiders —FG Bahr 35
Sea —Young 9 pass from Zorn (N. Johnson kick)
Attendance—91,445

TEAM STATISTICS	**Sea**	**Raiders**
First downs	16	21
Rushing	4	10
Passing	10	11
By penalty	2	0
Total yardage	167	401
Net rushing yardage	65	205
Net passing yardage	102	196
Passes att.-comp.-had int.	37-17-5	24-17-2

RUSHING
Seattle—Warner, 11 for 26; Dixon, 3 for 24; Hughes, 3 for 14; C. Bryant, 1 for 1.
LA Raiders—Allen, 25 for 154; Plunkett, 7 for 26; Hawkins, 10 for 24, 2 TDs; Pruitt, 1 for 4; King, 2 for 0; Wilson, 1 for -3.
PASSING
Seattle—Zorn, 14 of 27 for 134, 2 TDs, 2 int.; Krieg, 3 of 9 for 12, 3 int.
LA Raiders—Plunkett, 17 of 24 for 214, 1 TD, 2 int.
RECEIVING
Seattle—Doornink, 6 for 48, 1 TD; Johns, 5 for 49; Largent, 2 for 25; Warner, 2 for 10; Young, 1 for 9, 1 TD; H. Jackson 1 for 5.
LA Raiders—Allen, 7 for 62, 1 TD; Barnwell, 5 for 116; Christensen, 3 for 14; Branch, 2 for 22.

1983 NFC

WASHINGTON 24, SAN FRANCISCO 21

Mark Moseley kicked a 25-yard field goal with 40 seconds to play in the game to give Washington a 24-21 victory despite one of the great comebacks in NFL playoff history.

For the first three quarters of the game, the Redskins looked like the team that had established the best record in the NFL during the regular season. Despite four missed field goals by the usually reliable Moseley and the negation of a touchdown by Darrell Green on a punt return that was called back due to an illegal lateral, the Redskins still led 21-0.

Early in the fourth quarter, however, Joe Montana, who set NFC Championship Game records with 27 completions in 48 attempts, got the 49ers rolling. In a little more than seven minutes, he threw three touchdown passes, the last a 12-yard strike to Mike Wilson, to tie the score.

But the Redskins were no strangers to last-minute heroics. Starting on their own 14, Joe Theismann put together a 13-play, 78-yard drive that took 6:12. The drive was aided greatly by two controversial penalties, one a pass-interference call against Eric Wright, the other holding against Ronnie Lott. On fourth down at the San Francisco 8, Moseley ended his day with his one successful field goal.

January 8, 1984, at Washington

San Francisco	Starters, Offense	Washington
Mike Wilson	WR	Charlie Brown
Bubba Paris	LT	Joe Jacoby
John Ayers	LG	Russ Grimm
Fred Quillan	C	Jeff Bostic
Randy Cross	RG	Mark May
Keith Fahnhorst	RT	George Starke
Russ Francis	TE	Don Warren
Freddie Solomon	WR	Art Monk
Joe Montana	QB	Joe Theismann
Roger Craig	RB	John Riggins
Wendell Tyler	RB-TE	Rick Walker
	Starters, Defense	
Lawrence Pillers	LE	Todd Liebenstein
Pete Kugler	NT-LT	Dave Butz
Dwaine Board	RE-RT	Darryl Grant
Willie Harper	LOLB-RE	Dexter Manley
Riki Ellison	LILB LLB	Mel Kaufman
Jack Reynolds	RILB-MLB	Neal Olkewicz
Keena Turner	ROLB-RLB	Rich Milot
Ronnie Lott	LCB	Darrell Green
Eric Wright	RCB	Anthony Washington
Carlton Williamson	SS	Ken Coffey
Dwight Hicks	FS	Mark Murphy

San Francisco	0	0	0	21	—	21
Washington	0	7	14	3	—	24

Wash —Riggins 4 run (Moseley kick)
Wash —Riggins 1 run (Moseley kick)
Wash —Brown 70 pass from Theismann (Moseley kick)
SF —Wilson 5 pass from Montana (Wersching kick)
SF —Solomon 76 pass from Montana (Wersching kick)
SF —Wilson 12 pass from Montana (Wersching kick)
Wash —FG Moseley 25
Attendance—55,363

TEAM STATISTICS	SF	Wash
First downs	19	24
Rushing	3	11
Passing	16	10
By penalty	0	3
Total yardage	434	410
Net rushing yardage	87	172
Net passing yardage	347	238
Passes att.-comp.-had int.	48-27-1	27-15-1

RUSHING
San Francisco—Tyler, 8 for 44; Montana, 5 for 40; Craig, 3 for 3.
Washington—Riggins, 36 for 123, 2 TDs; J. Washington, 6 for 23; Hayes, 1 for 14; Theismann, 2 for 12.

PASSING
San Francisco—Montana, 27 of 48 for 347, 3 TDs, 1 int.
Washington—Theismann, 14 of 26 for 229, 1 TD, 1 int.; Riggins, 1 for 1 for 36.

RECEIVING
San Francisco—Wilson, 8 for 57, 2 TDs; Solomon, 4 for 106, 1 TD; Francis, 4 for 48; Ramson, 3 for 47; Nehemiah, 3 for 46; Craig, 3 for 15; Tyler, 1 for 17; Cooper, 1 for 11.
Washington—Brown, 5 for 137, 1 TD; Didier, 3 for 61; Monk, 3 for 35; J. Washington, 3 for 21; Walker, 1 for 11.

1984 AFC

MIAMI 45, PITTSBURGH 28

Dan Marino had the kind of day most quarterbacks only dream about, in leading Miami to a 45-28 victory over Pittsburgh. Marino completed 21 of 32 passes for an AFC Championship Game-record 421 yards and another record four touchdowns.

Miami scored on its first possession, a 40-yard pass from Marino to Mark Clayton culminating a four-play, 67-yard drive. The Steelers' ground game kept them in the game, however, and, late in the second quarter Pittsburgh went ahead 14-10.

The Steelers' lead lasted only 82 seconds. Marino whisked the Dolphins 77 yards in five plays, ending with a 41-yard pass to Mark Duper. After an interception, the Dolphins scored again to lead 24-14 at the half.

The knockout punch came on the first possession of the second half. Marino took less than two minutes and only four plays to drive his team 78 yards, ending with a 36-yard pass to Duper. Mark Malone later threw two more touchdown passes for the Steelers, but they simply couldn't catch up.

January 6, 1985, at Miami

Pittsburgh	Starters, Offense	Miami
John Stallworth	WR	Mark Duper
Pete Rostosky	LT	Jon Giesler
Craig Wolfley	LG	Roy Foster
Mike Webster	C	Dwight Stephenson
Terry Long	RG	Ed Newman
Tunch Ilkin	RT	Cleveland Green
Bennie Cunningham	TE	Bruce Hardy
Louis Lipps	WR	Mark Clayton
Mark Malone	QB	Dan Marino
Frank Pollard	RB	Woody Bennett
Walter Abercrombie	RB	Tony Nathan
	Starters, Defense	
John Goodman	LE	Doug Betters
Gary Dunn	NT	Bob Baumhower
Edmund Nelson	RE	Kim Bokamper
Mike Merriweather	LOLB	Bob Brudzinski
David Little	LILB	Jay Brophy
Robin Cole	RILB	Mark Brown
Bryan Hinkle	ROLB	Charles Bowser
Dwayne Woodruff	LCB	Don McNeal
Sam Washington	RCB	William Judson
Donnie Shell	SS	Glenn Blackwood
Eric Williams	FS	Lyle Blackwood

Pittsburgh	7	7	7	7	—	28
Miami	7	17	14	7	—	45

Mia —Clayton 40 pass from Marino (von Schamann kick)
Pitt —Erenberg 7 run (Anderson kick)
Mia —FG von Schamann 26
Pitt —Stallworth 65 pass from Malone (Anderson kick)
Mia —Duper 41 pass from Marino (von Schamann kick)
Mia —Nathan 2 run (von Schamann kick)
Mia —Duper 36 pass from Marino (von Schamann kick)
Pitt —Stallworth 19 pass from Malone (Anderson kick)
Mia —Bennett 1 run (von Schamann kick)
Mia —Moore 6 pass from Marino (von Schamann kick)
Pitt —Capers 29 pass from Malone (Anderson kick)
Attendance—76,029

TEAM STATISTICS	Pitt	Mia
First downs	22	28
Rushing	8	10
Passing	14	18
By penalty	0	0
Total yardage	455	569
Net rushing yardage	143	134
Net passing yardage	312	435
Passes att.-comp.-had int.	36-20-3	33-22-1

RUSHING
Pittsburgh—Abercrombie, 15 for 68; Pollard, 11 for 48; Erenberg, 6 for 27, 1 TD.
Miami—Nathan, 19 for 64, 1 TD; P. Johnson, 10 for 39; Bennett, 8 for 33, 1 TD; Strock, 1 for -2.

PASSING
Pittsburgh—Malone, 20 of 36 for 312, 3 TDs, 3 int.
Miami—Marino, 21 of 32 for 421, 4 TDs, 1 int.; Nathan, 1 of 1 for 14.

RECEIVING
Pittsburgh—Erenberg, 5 for 59; Stallworth, 4 for 11, 2 TDs; Lipps, 3 for 45; Sweeney, 3 for 42; Pollard, 3 for 13; Capers, 1 for 29, 1 TD; Abercrombie, 1 for 13.
Miami—Nathan, 8 for 114; Duper, 5 for 148, 2 TDs; Clayton 4 for 95, 1 TD; Moore, 2 for 34, 1 TD; Hardy, 2 for 16; Rose, 1 for 28.

1984 NFC

SAN FRANCISCO 23, CHI. BEARS 0

The San Francisco defense slowed Chicago's running game and sacked quarterback Steve Fuller nine times to totally shut down the passing game, while the 49ers' offense eventually wore down the Bears en route to a 23-0 victory.

With the Bears' offense ineffective most of the day, the question was how long they could stop the 49ers. Safety Gary Fencik intercepted two of Joe Montana's passes—one in the end zone and the other on the 5—and the Bears only trailed 6-0 at halftime, after two field goals by Ray Wersching.

In the third quarter, the 49ers went to work. Following a 15-yard punt return by Dana McLemore, Montana drove his team 35 yards in five plays to a nine-yard touchdown run by Wendell Tyler. The Bears tried to get back into the game, driving 60 yards to the 49ers' 21. But sacks by Dwaine Board and Gary Johnson ended the Bears' threat.

When the 49ers took possession of the ball, they drove 88 yards for another touchdown. Montana completed four of four passes on the drive, but the key play was a 39-yard run off left tackle by Roger Craig. Another good punt return by McLemore late in the game again gave San Francisco good field position. Substitute quarterback Matt Cavanaugh led the 49ers to the game's final points.

January 6, 1985, at San Francisco

Chi. Bears	Starters, Offense	San Francisco
Willie Gault	WR	Dwight Clark
Jim Covert	LT	Bubba Paris
Mark Bortz	LG	John Ayers
Jay Hilgenberg	C	Fred Quillan
Kurt Becker	RG	Randy Cross
Keith Van Horne	RT	Keith Fahnhorst
Emery Moorehead	TE	Russ Francis
Dennis McKinnon	WR	Freddie Solomon
Steve Fuller	QB	Joe Montana
Matt Suhey	RB	Roger Craig
Walter Payton	RB	Wendell Tyler
	Starters, Defense	
Mike Hartenstine	LE	Lawrence Pillers
Steve McMichael	LT-NT	Manu Tuiasosopo
Dan Hampton	RT-RE	Dwaine Board
Richard Dent	RE LOLB	Dan Bunz
Otis Wilson	LLB-LILB	Riki Ellison
Mike Singletary	MLB-RILB	Jack Reynolds
Al Harris	RLB-ROLB	Keena Turner
Mike Richardson	LCB	Ronnie Lott
Leslie Frazier	RCB	Eric Wright
Todd Bell	SS	Carlton Williamson
Gary Fencik	FS	Dwight Hicks

Chi. Bears	0	0	0	0	—	0
San Francisco	3	3	7	10	—	23

SF—FG Wersching 21
SF—FG Wersching 22
SF—Tyler 9 run (Wersching kick)
SF—Solomon 10 pass from Montana (Wersching kick)
SF—FG Wersching 34
Attendance—61,336

TEAM STATISTICS	ChiB	SF
First downs	13	25
Rushing	9	9
Passing	3	14
By penalty	1	2
Total yardage	186	387
Net rushing yardage	149	159
Net passing yardage	37	228
Passes att.-comp.-had int.	22-13-1	35-19-2

RUSHING
Chi. Bears—Payton, 22 for 92; Fuller, 6 for 39; Suhey, 3 for 16; C. Thomas, 1 for 2.
San Francisco—Tyler, 10 for 68, 1 TD; Craig, 8 for 44; Montana, 5 for 22; Harmon, 3 for 18; Ring, 2 for 5; Cavanaugh, 1 for 2.

PASSING
Chi. Bears—Fuller, 13 of 22 for 87, 1 int.
San Francisco—Montana, 18 of 34 for 233, 1 TD, 2 int.; Cavanaugh, 1 of 1 for 3.

RECEIVING
Chi. Bears—Suhey, 4 for 11; McKinnon, 3 for 48; Payton, 3 for 11; Moorehead, 2 for 14; Dunsmore, 1 for 3.
San Francisco—Solomon, 7 for 73, 1 TD; D. Clark, 4 for 83; Wilson, 2 for 25; Tyler, 2 for 22; Francis, 2 for 20; Nehemiah, 1 for 10; Harmon, 1 for 3.

1985 AFC

NEW ENGLAND 31, MIAMI 14

New England snapped an 18-game losing streak in Miami (dating back to 1966), while handing the Dolphins their first-ever loss in the AFC Championship Game. The Patriots took advantage of six Miami turnovers, turning them into 24 points in a 31-14 victory.

The first break came on Miami's first offensive play. Tony Nathan fumbled and Garin Veris recovered for New England. Six plays later, Tony Franklin kicked a 23-yard field goal.

When Miami went ahead in the second quarter, New England came right back. Robert Weathers carried the ball four times for 57 yards in a 66-yard drive that ended with Tony Eason passing four yards to Tony Collins. When Dan Marino fumbled two plays after the kickoff, the Patriots recovered and powered right to the end zone, with Eason throwing to tight end Derrick Ramsey from the 1 for a 17-7 lead.

The Patriots blew it open at the beginning of the third quarter. Lorenzo Hampton fumbled the second-half kickoff, and Greg Hawthorne recovered for New England at the 25. On second and goal, Eason threw his third touchdown pass of the day, to Weathers.

Marino passed on 23 of 24 Miami plays in the fourth quarter, but the Dolphins could score only once and couldn't catch up.

January 12, 1986, at Miami

New England	Starters, Offense	Miami
Stanley Morgan	WR	Mark Duper
Brian Holloway	LT	Jon Giesler
John Hannah	LG	Roy Foster
Pete Brock	C	Dwight Stephenson
Ron Wooten	RG	Steve Clark
Steve Moore	RT	Ronnie Lee
Lin Dawson	TE	Bruce Hardy
Stephen Starring	WR	Mark Clayton
Tony Eason	QB	Dan Marino
Tony Collins	RB	Tony Nathan
Craig James	RB-WR	Nat Moore
	Starters, Defense	
Garin Veris	LE	Doug Betters
Lester Williams	NT	Mike Charles
Julius Adams	RE	Kim Bokamper
Andre Tippett	LOLB	Bob Brudzinski
Steve Nelson	LILB	Jay Brophy
Larry McGrew	RILB	Jackie Shipp
Don Blackmon	ROLB	Hugh Green
Ronnie Lippett	LCB	Paul Lankford
Raymond Clayborn	RCB	William Judson
Roland James	SS	Glenn Blackwood
Fred Marion	FS	Bud Brown

New England	3	14	7	7	—	31
Miami	0	7	0	7	—	14

NE —FG Franklin 23
Mia —Johnson 10 pass from Marino (Reveiz kick)
NE —Collins 4 pass from Eason (Franklin kick)
NE —D. Ramsey 1 pass from Eason (Franklin kick)
NE —Weathers 2 pass from Eason (Franklin kick)
Mia —Nathan 10 pass from Marino (Reveiz kick)
NE —Tatupu 1 run (Franklin kick)
Attendance—74,978

TEAM STATISTICS	NE	Mia
First downs	21	18
Rushing	15	3
Passing	6	15
By penalty	0	0
Total yardage	326	302
Net rushing yardage	255	68
Net passing yardage	71	234
Passes att.-comp.-had int.	12-10-0	48-20-2

RUSHING
New England—C. James, 22 for 105; Weathers, 16 for 87; Collins, 12 for 61; Tatupu, 6 for 9, 1 TD; Eason, 3 for -7.
Miami—Carter, 6 for 56; Davenport, 3 for 6; Nathan, 2 for 4; Bennett, 1 for 2; Marino, 1 for 0.

PASSING
New England—Eason, 10 of 12 for 71, 3 TDs.
Miami—Marino, 20 of 48 for 248, 2 TDs, 2 int.

RECEIVING
New England—D. Ramsey, 3 for 18, 1 TD; Collins, 3 for 15, 1 TD; Morgan, 2 for 30; Tatupu, 1 for 6; Weathers, 1 for 2, 1 TD.
Miami—Nathan, 5 for 57, 1 TD; Hardy, 3 for 52; Duper, 3 for 45; Clayton, 3 for 41; Davenport, 3 for 23; Johnson, 1 for 10, 1 TD; Moore, 1 for 10; Rose, 1 for 10.

1985 NFC

CHI. BEARS 24, LA RAMS 0

In a struggle between two outstanding defenses, the Bears proved stronger, holding the Rams off the scoreboard for a record second-consecutive playoff shutout, 24-0. The only previous time a playoff team had shut out its opponents in consecutive games, the contests had been a year apart. In 1948 and 1949, with only the championship game to play, Philadelphia shut out the Chicago Cardinals and the Rams.

The Bears scored on their first possession of the game. The five-play, 66-yard drive was capped by quarterback Jim McMahon's 16-yard scramble around left end for a touchdown. The next time they got the ball, the Bears raised their margin to 10-0 on a 34-yard field goal by Kevin Butler, following a 33-yard drive.

As the final seconds of the half ran down, the Rams lost their only scoring opportunity of the game. Although they had plenty of time, they didn't run a play, and the half ended with them inside the Chicago 3-yard line.

After increasing their lead to 17-0 on a 52-yard drive in the third quarter, the Bears finished the scoring late in the game when Richard Dent forced Rams quarterback Dieter Brock to fumble and linebacker Wilber Marshall recovered and ran 52 yards for a touchdown. The game, which had started in cool, gusty weather, ended in a snow flurry, appropriate for Chicago's first return to the championship in 22 years.

January 12, 1986, at Chicago

LA Rams	Starters, Offense	Chi. Bears
Henry Ellard	WR	Willie Gault
Irv Pankey	LT	Jim Covert
Kent Hill	LG	Mark Bortz
Tony Slaton	C	Jay Hilgenberg
Dennis Harrah	RG	Tom Thayer
Jackie Slater	RT	Keith Van Horne
David Hill	TE	Emery Moorehead
Ron Brown	WR	Dennis McKinnon
Dieter Brock	QB	Jim McMahon
Barry Redden	RB	Matt Suhey
Eric Dickerson	RB	Walter Payton
	Starters, Defense	
Doug Reed	LE	Dan Hampton
Charles DeJurnett	NT-LT	Steve McMichael
Reggie Doss	RE-RT	William Perry
Mel Owens	LOLB-RE	Richard Dent
Carl Ekern	LILB-LLB	Otis Wilson
Jim Collins	RILB-MLB	Mike Singletary
Mike Wilcher	ROLB-RLB	Wilber Marshall
Gary Green	LCB	Mike Richardson
LeRoy Irvin	RCB	Leslie Frazier
Nolan Cromwell	SS	Dave Duerson
Johnnie Johnson	FS	Gary Fencik

LA Rams	0	0	0	0	—	0
Chi. Bears	10	0	7	7	—	24

ChiB—McMahon 16 run (Butler kick)
ChiB—FG Butler 34
ChiB—Gault 22 pass from McMahon (Butler kick)
ChiB—Marshall 52 fumble return (Butler kick)
Attendance—63,522

TEAM STATISTICS	Rams	ChiB
First downs	9	13
Rushing	5	5
Passing	3	8
By penalty	1	0
Total yardage	130	232
Net rushing yardage	86	91
Net passing yardage	44	141
Passes att.-comp.-had int.	31-10-1	25-16-0

RUSHING
LA Rams—Dickerson, 17 for 46; Redden, 9 for 40.
Chi. Bears—Payton, 18 for 32; McMahon, 4 for 28, 1 TD; Suhey, 6 for 23; Gentry, 2 for 9; Thomas, 3 for -1.

PASSING
LA Rams—Brock, 10 of 31 for 66, 1 int.
Chi. Bears—McMahon, 16 of 25 for 164, 1 TD.

RECEIVING
LA Rams—Hunter, 3 for 29; Dickerson, 3 for 10; Brown, 2 for 14; Duckworth, 1 for 8; Ellard, 1 for 5.
Chi. Bears—Payton, 7 for 48; Gault, 4 for 56, 1 TD; Moorehead, 2 for 28; McKinnon, 1 for 17; Wrightman, 1 for 8; Suhey, 1 for 7.

Divisional Playoff Games

1941

CHI. BEARS 33, GREEN BAY 14

With the Chicago Bears trailing Green Bay 7-0 in the first quarter, rookie halfback Hugh Gallarneau returned a punt 81 yards for a touchdown, signaling the start of 30 consecutive points for the Bears, who led 30-7 at halftime on the way to a 33-14 victory over the Packers.

The game was the first non-championship playoff in NFL history; it was necessitated when both teams finished 10-1, with the Bears beating the Packers 25-17 and the Packers returning the favor 16-14. Coincidentally, during the preceding offseason, the NFL had taken care of the possibility of a divisional tie by establishing a new rule calling for a playoff game, with sudden-death overtime if necessary.

A crowd of 43,425 jammed Wrigley Field despite the fact that the temperature was only 16 degrees, recent snow was piled around the playing area, and the United States had entered World War II only one week before.

The action started immediately. Gallarneau fumbled the opening kickoff, and the Packers recovered, setting up a five-play, 18-yard drive that ended with Clarke Hinkle's one-yard touchdown run.

But then came Gallarneau's twisting-and-turning touchdown, preceding several long, slow scoring drives by the Bears, which took the heart out of the Packers. By halftime, reserve quarterback Bob Snyder had given the Bears their initial lead with a 24-yard field goal, fullback Norm Standlee had plowed over for two short touchdowns, and backup halfback Bob Swisher had bolted up the middle for a nine-yard scoring run.

The Bears used many reserves in an evenly played second half.

December 14, at Chicago

Green Bay	Starting Lineups	Chi. Bears
Don Hutson	LE	Dick Plasman
Buford (Baby) Ray	LT	Ed Kolman
Buckets Goldenberg	LG	Dan Fortmann
George Svendsen	C	Clyde (Bulldog) Turner
Lee McLaughlin	RG	Ray Bray
Charlie Schultz	RT	Lee Artoe
Ray Riddick	RE	John Siegal
Larry Craig	QB	Sid Luckman
Cecil Isbell	LH	Ray Nolting
Herman Rohrig	RH	Hugh Gallarneau
Clarke Hinkle	FB	Norm Standlee

Green Bay	7	0	7	0	—	14
Chi. Bears	6	24	0	3	—	33

GB —Hinkle 1 run (Hutson kick)
ChiB—Gallarneau 81 punt return (kick blocked)
ChiB—FG Snyder 24
ChiB—Standlee 3 run (Stydahar kick)
ChiB—Standlee 2 run (Stydahar kick)
ChiB—Swisher 9 run (Stydahar kick)
GB —Van Every 10 pass from Isbell (Hutson kick)
ChiB—FG Snyder 26
Attendance—43,425

TEAM STATISTICS	GB	ChiB
Total yardage	255	325
Net rushing yardage	33	277
Net passing yardage	222	48
Passes att.-comp.-had int.	27-11-2	12-5-0

RUSHING
Green Bay—Hinkle, 9 for 17, 1 TD; Canadeo, 5 for 7; Paskvan, 2 for 7; Van Every, 6 for 6; Jankowski, 3 for 4; Isbell, 11 for −8.
Chi. Bears—McAfee, 14 for 119; Standlee, 15 for 79, 2 TDs; Swisher, 5 for 38, 1 TD; Gallarneau, 3 for 11; Nolting, 3 for 9; Osmanski, 2 for 8; McLean, 2 for 7; Maniaci, 3 for 3; Luckman, 1 for 3.
PASSING
Green Bay—Isbell, 8 of 19 for 107, 1 TD; Van Every, 2 of 6 for 75, 1 int.; Canadeo, 1 of 2 for 40, 1 int.
Chi. Bears—Luckman, 4 of 9 for 41; Snyder, 1 of 3 for 7.
RECEIVING
Green Bay—Frutig, 3 for 75; Van Every, 2 for 24, 1 TD; Riddick, 1 for 45; Mulleneaux, 1 for 30; Hutson, 1 for 19; Jankowski, 1 for 19; Buhler, 1 for 8; Rohrig, 1 for 2.
Chi. Bears—McAfee, 2 for 27; Wilson, 1 for 15; Nowaskey, 1 for 7; Siegal, 1 for −1.

1943

WASHINGTON 28, NY GIANTS 0

Washington tailback Sammy Baugh, who had led the NFL in passing, punting, and interceptions during the regular season, put on a display of all those talents again to lead the Redskins to a 28-0 victory over the New York Giants.

Baugh completed 16 of 21 passes, intercepted two passes by New York's Alphonse (Tuffy) Leemans, and averaged more than 40 yards per punt as the Redskins avenged two season-closing losses (14-0 and 31-7) to the Giants that had dropped Washington into a tie with New York with a 6-3-1 record.

The playing surface at the Polo Grounds was frozen and the winter shadows and the winds blowing off the Harlem River compounded the chill, seemingly stopping everybody on the field except Baugh. But his play on both sides of the ball was all the Redskins needed.

After a slow first quarter, Baugh got his team cranked up in the second period. His passing to end Bob Masterson and halfback Wilbur Moore set up two touchdowns that made the score 14-0 at halftime. Fullback Andy Farkas, who totaled 60 yards on 22 carries, scored both times from two yards out.

In the third quarter, the Giants finally threatened when Leemans connected with halfback Ward Cuff on a 41-yard pass to the Washington 32. But the drive fizzled, and, the next time New York had the ball, Baugh intercepted Leemans and raced 28 yards to set up a third touchdown run by Farkas, this time from the 1.

Midway through the final period, Baugh started passing again, and the Redskins moved quickly downfield, scoring on Baugh's 11-yard touchdown pass to reserve end Ted Lapka, who caught two passes in a row after catching only two during the entire regular season.

The Giants didn't threaten again, and crossed midfield only one other time. Other than the long pass from Leemans to Cuff, they were held to 71 yards, only 16 through the air.

December 19, at New York

Washington	Starting Lineups	NY Giants
Bob Masterson	LE	Frank Liebel
Lou Rymkus	LT	Frank Cope
Clyde Shugart	LG	Len Younce
George Smith	C	Mel Hein
Steve Slivinski	RG	Vic Carroll
Joe Pasqua	RT	Al Blozis
Joe Aguirre	RE	Steve Pritko
Ray Hare	QB	Leland Shaffer
George Cafego	LH	Ward Cuff
Frank Seno	RH	Dave Brown
Andy Farkas	FB	Hank Soar

Washington	0	14	0	14	—	28
NY Giants	0	0	0	0	—	0

Wash—Farkas 2 run (Masterson kick)
Wash—Farkas 2 run (Masterson kick)
Wash—Farkas 1 run (Masterson kick)
Wash—Lapka 11 pass from Baugh (Masterson kick)
Attendance—42,800

TEAM STATISTICS	Wash	NYG
Total yardage	296	112
Net rushing yardage	83	55
Net passing yardage	213	57
Passes att.-comp.-had int.	22-17-2	20-4-3

RUSHING
Washington—Farkas, 22 for 60, 3 TDs; Hare, 3 for 9; Akins, 6 for 6; Seno, 1 for 6; Seymour, 4 for 4; Moore, 2 for 2; Cafego, 1 for −4.
NY Giants—Paschal, 16 for 56; Cuff, 9 for 23; Soar, 1 for 1; Leemans, 7 for −25.
PASSING
Washington—Baugh, 16 of 21 for 199, 1 TD, 2 int.; Farkas, 1 of 1 for 14.
NY Giants—Leemans, 2 of 10 for 44, 3 int.; Nix, 2 of 10 for 13.
RECEIVING
Washington—Masterson, 5 for 70; Moore, 4 for 57; Seno, 3 for 26; Lapka, 2 for 25, 1 TD; Aguirre, 2 for 21; Seymour, 1 for 14.
NY Giants—Cuff, 2 for 46; Blozis, 1 for 8; Walls, 1 for 3.

1947

PHILADELPHIA 21, PITTSBURGH 0

Philadelphia's special teams scored one touchdown and set up another as the Eagles won 21-0 over a Pittsburgh team torn by bitterness between the players and the coach.

Philadelphia and Pittsburgh had split two games during the regular season (with the Steelers winning 35-24 in Pittsburgh and the Eagles winning 21-0 in Philadelphia), but, while head coach Earle (Greasy) Neale's Eagles were developing into one of the great teams of all-time, the Steelers had internal problems. Several days before the franchise's first-ever playoff game, Pittsburgh's players publicly demanded they be paid overtime for the playoffs (their contracts didn't include any extra payment). Pittsburgh coach John (Jock) Sutherland, a strict disciplinarian, was outraged that his players would think of money when a championship was at stake and made his team practice in snow and sleet the day before the game. Although the players were paid, the bitterness carried into the game, and the Steelers didn't cross the Eagles' 45-yard line until late in the third quarter. By that time, the score was 21-0, and the game, for all purposes, was over.

Early in the game, the Eagles capitalized quickly on a Pittsburgh mistake. End Pete Pihos blocked a punt by Bob Cifers, and the Eagles recovered at the Pittsburgh 14. Two plays later, Tommy Thompson threw a 15-yard touchdown pass to halfback Steve Van Buren. In the second quarter, Thompson threw another touchdown pass, this one for 28 yards to end Jack Ferrante. The Steelers, meanwhile, couldn't pass at all, as tailback Johnny Clement, still nursing the effects of a dislocated elbow, completed only 4 of 16 attempts.

The Eagles closed out the scoring in the third period, when Cifers outkicked his coverage and Philadelphia halfback Bosh Pritchard snaked 79 yards through the Steelers for a touchdown.

Sutherland's team was the last Single-Wing offense to make the NFL playoffs. Sutherland died the next spring of a brain tumor.

December 21, at Pittsburgh

Philadelphia	Starting Lineups	Pittsburgh
Jack Ferrante	LE	Charles Mehelich
Jay MacDowell	LT	Jack Wiley
Cliff Patton	LG	Bill Moore
Alex Wojciechowicz	C	Chuck Cherundolo
Frank (Bucko) Kilroy	RG	John Mastrangelo
Al Wistert	RT	Frank Wydo
Pete Pihos	RE	Bob Davis
Tommy Thompson	QB	Charlie Seabright
Steve Van Buren	LH	Walter Slater
Bosh Pritchard	RH	Bob Cifers
Joe Muha	FB	Tony Compagno

Philadelphia	7	7	7	0	—	21
Pittsburgh	0	0	0	0	—	0

Phil— Van Buren 15 pass from Thompson (Patton kick)
Phil— Ferrante 28 pass from Thompson (Patton kick)
Phil— Pritchard 79 punt return (Patton kick)
Attendance—35,729

TEAM STATISTICS	Phil	Pitt
Total yardage	255	154
Net rushing yardage	124	102
Net passing yardage	131	52
Passes att.-comp.-had int.	18-11-0	18-4-0

RUSHING
Philadelphia—Van Buren, 18 for 45; Steele, 6 for 34; Muha, 7 for 15; Sherman, 2 for 12; Thompson, 4 for 7; Kish, 1 for 6; Craft, 10 for 3; Pritchard, 4 for 2.
Pittsburgh—Clement, 14 for 59; Cifers, 10 for 29; Compagno, 4 for 9; White, 1 for 5.
PASSING
Philadelphia—Thompson, 11 of 17 for 131, 2 TDs; Sherman, 0 of 1.
Pittsburgh—Clement, 4 of 16 for 52; Cifers, 0 of 2.
RECEIVING
Philadelphia—Ferrante, 5 for 73, 1 TD; Van Buren, 2 for 15, 1 TD; Craft, 2 for 14; Pihos, 1 for 10; Pritchard, 1 for 11.
Pittsburgh—Nickel, 2 for 32; Cifers, 1 for 18; Lach, 1 for 2.

1950

CLEVELAND 8, NY GIANTS 3

Lou Groza's 28-yard field goal with 58 seconds left broke a 3-3 tie as the Cleveland Browns beat the New York Giants 8-3 in a punishing defensive duel.

The Browns, who were in their first year in the NFL, and the Giants had tied for the Eastern Division title, although New York defeated Cleveland in both their regular-season games.

It was 10 degrees when the game began, and a numbing wind from Lake Erie left the wind-chill well below zero. The field was rock-hard and icy, and all of the players wore sneakers except for Groza, who wore one sneaker but had a cleated football shoe on his kicking foot.

The Browns scored in the first quarter on an 11-yard field goal by Groza, but that was all the points until the final period.

Early in the fourth quarter, swift Giants halfback Gene (Choo-Choo) Roberts broke into the clear on a reverse and raced toward what would have been the winning touchdown. Incredibly, Cleveland middle guard Bill Willis, well behind Roberts, chased him down at the 4-yard line. Then began a strange series of plays.

On third down from the 3, New York quarterback Charlie Conerly passed to end Bob McChesney in the end zone, but the Giants were penalized for being offside. On fourth down, Conerly's pass was intercepted by defensive back Tommy James, but Cleveland was penalized for holding. The Giants were penalized for being in motion before the snap of the ball on the next play, and the line of scrimmage was moved back to the 9. On the sixth play after Roberts's run, New York's Joe Scott collided with his blocker, Joe Sulaitis, and went down at the 13. Randy Clay then kicked a 20-yard field goal to tie the score 3-3.

With time running out, Otto Graham found a play the Giants couldn't stop — the quarterback draw. Running instead of passing, Graham set up Groza's winning field goal. Moments after the kick, Conerly dropped into his end zone while trying to pass, and Willis tackled him for a safety.

December 17, at Cleveland

NY Giants	Starting Lineups	Cleveland
Ellery Williams	LE	Mac Speedie
Arnie Weinmeister	LT	Lou Groza
Bill Milner	LG	Weldon Humble
John Rapacz	C	Frank Gatski
Bill Austin	RG	Lin Houston
Al DeRogatis	RT	Lou Rymkus
Bob McChesney	RE	Dante Lavelli
Travis Tidwell	QB	Otto Graham
Charlie Conerly	LH	Rex Bumgardner
Joe Scott	RH	Dub Jones
Eddie Price	FB	Marion Motley

NY Giants	0	0	0	3	—	3
Cleveland	3	0	0	5	—	8

Cle — FG Groza 11
NYG— FG Clay 20
Cle — FG Groza 28
Cle — Safety, Willis tackled Conerly in end zone
Attendance—33,754

TEAM STATISTICS	NYG	Cle
Total yardage	189	196
Net rushing yardage	141	153
Net passing yardage	48	43
Passes att.-comp.-had int.	15-3-2	9-3-1

RUSHING
NY Giants—Roberts, 12 for 76; Price, 21 for 65; Conerly, 1 for 2; Scott, 3 for −2.
Cleveland—Graham, 8 for 70; Bumgardner, 13 for 39; Jones, 12 for 32; Motley, 7 for 12.
PASSING
NY Giants—Conerly, 3 of 12 for 48, 2 int.; Tidwell, 0 of 3.
Cleveland—Graham, 3 of 9 for 43, 1 int.
RECEIVING
NY Giants—McChesney, 1 for 19; Roberts, 1 for 17; Sulaitis, 1 for 12.
Cleveland—Lavelli, 2 for 35; Bumgardner, 1 for 8.

1950

LA RAMS 24, CHI. BEARS 14

Los Angeles quarterback Bob Waterfield, unable to practice all week because of an attack of the flu, came off the bench in the second quarter and threw three touchdown passes to Tom Fears as the Rams defeated the Chicago Bears 24-14.

Waterfield almost hadn't dressed, and had to be assisted to the bench before the game after sitting out pregame drills on the 84-degree day in the Los Angeles Memorial Coliseum. But after taking over for starter Norm Van Brocklin, who had completed only 2 of 10 passes, Waterfield took control of the game.

"It was incredible," Fears said. "The more energy he expended, the stronger he seemed to get. It was so unbelievable that I feared a sudden and complete collapse. Until the end of the game, I was never convinced Bob would be able to keep the show on the road."

But he did. Waterfield entered the game with the Rams trailing 7-3, their only score having been his 43-yard field goal. Almost immediately, he led Los Angeles to a score, finding Fears alone for a 43-yard touchdown pass. The next time the Rams had the ball, he came back with a quick, 76-yard drive that culminated in a 68-yard touchdown pass to Fears for a 17-7 halftime lead.

In the third quarter, Waterfield continued his assault, driving the Rams to a 24-7 lead. The score came on a 27-yard pass to Fears, who caught seven passes for 198 yards, including six from Waterfield for 190 yards.

The Bears, who had moved the ball well all day only to be slowed by three interceptions and two fumbles, finally got on the scoreboard again in the fourth quarter, with Johnny Lujack moving them the length of the field to set up fullback Fred (Curly) Morrison's four-yard run.

December 17, at Los Angeles

Chi. Bears	Starting Lineups	LA Rams
Bill Wightkin	LE	Tom Fears
George Connor	LT	Dick Huffman
Dick Barwegan	LG	John Finlay
Clyde (Bulldog) Turner	C	Art Statuto
Ray Bray	RG	Dave Stephenson
Paul Stenn	RT	Bob Reinhard
Ed Sprinkle	RE	Elroy (Crazylegs) Hirsch
Johnny Lujack	QB	Norm Van Brocklin
George Gulyanics	LH	Glenn Davis
Julie Rykovich	RH	Verda (Vitamin T) Smith
Fred (Curly) Morrison	FB	Dick Hoerner

Chi. Bears	0	7	0	7	—	14
LA Rams	3	14	7	0	—	24

Rams— FG Waterfield 43
ChiB — Campana 23 run (Lujack kick)
Rams— Fears 43 pass from Waterfield (Waterfield kick)
Rams— Fears 68 pass from Waterfield (Waterfield kick)
Rams— Fears 27 pass from Waterfield (Waterfield kick)
ChiB — Morrison 4 run (Lujack kick)
Attendance—83,501

TEAM STATISTICS	ChiB	Rams
Total yardage	422	371
Net rushing yardage	229	74
Net passing yardage	193	297
Passes att.-comp.-had int.	29-15-3	31-16-1

RUSHING
Chi. Bears—Gulyanics, 15 for 94; Rykovich, 14 for 67; Campana, 4 for 29, 1 TD; Hoffman, 5 for 16; Morrison, 5 for 14, 1 TD; Huntsinger, 2 for 7; Lujack, 3 for 2.
LA Rams—Hoerner, 7 for 18; Barry, 8 for 16; Davis, 8 for 15; Smith, 3 for 12; Williams, 1 for 6; Pasquariello, 1 for 3; Waterfield, 2 for 2; Towler, 2 for 2.
PASSING
Chi. Bears—Lujack, 15 of 29 for 193, 3 int.
LA Rams—Waterfield, 14 of 21 for 280, 3 TDs, 1 int.; Van Brocklin, 2 of 10 for 17.
RECEIVING
Chi. Bears—Gulyanics, 6 for 67; Keane, 3 for 50; Morrison, 2 for 44; Boone, 1 for 13; Rykovich, 1 for 8; Kavanaugh, 1 for 6; Davis, 1 for 5.
LA Rams—Fears, 7 for 198, 3 TDs; Davis, 3 for 6; Hirsch, 2 for 46; Smith, 1 for 35; Hoerner, 1 for 9; Towler, 1 for 7; Boyd, 1 for −4.

1952

DETROIT 31, LA RAMS 21

Detroit fullback Pat Harder rushed for 72 yards and scored 19 points on two touchdowns, four extra points, and a field goal to lead the Lions to a 31-21 victory over the Los Angeles Rams in a cold, dense fog.

The Lions roared to a touchdown the first time they had the ball. With the Rams double-teaming Cloyce Box and Doak Walker on the outside, Bobby Layne passed to Leon Hart over the middle for gains of 22 and 13 yards, and Harder ended the drive with a 12-yard run around left end.

In the second quarter, Harder scored again on a four-yard run capping a long drive. Just before halftime, the Rams scored on Norm Van Brocklin's 15-yard touchdown pass to Tom Fears that made the score Harder 14, Rams 7.

In the third quarter, the Lions increased their margin to 24-7. Walker ended a drive with a 24-yard halfback pass to Hart in the end zone. Five minutes later, Harder kicked a 43-yard field goal.

The Rams came back in the fourth quarter behind veteran quarterback Bob Waterfield, who replaced Van Brocklin. Midway through the period, Waterfield pieced together a drive that culminated in (Deacon) Dan Towler's five-yard scoring run. Moments later, the Lions punted and Verda (Vitamin T) Smith zig-zagged his way 56 yards through the defenders for a touchdown that cut the margin to three points.

The Rams had one last chance to win. In the final minute, with the ball at the Los Angeles 11, Waterfield fired a pass to Elroy (Crazylegs) Hirsch. But linebacker LaVern Torgeson intercepted. With 30 seconds left, halfback Bob Hoernschemeyer hit left guard and ran nine yards for the clinching score. Harder converted for his nineteenth point of the day.

December 21, at Detroit

LA Rams	Starting Lineups	Detroit
Tom Fears	LE	Cloyce Box
Don Simensen	LT	Lou Creekmur
Dick Daugherty	LG	Jim Martin
Leon McLaughlin	C	Vince Banonis
Harry Thompson	RG	Dick Stanfel
Tom Dahms	RT	Gus Cifelli
Elroy (Crazylegs) Hirsch	RE	Leon Hart
Norm Van Brocklin	QB	Bobby Layne
(Deacon) Dan Towler	LH	Doak Walker
Verda (Vitamin T) Smith	RH	Byron Bailey
Paul (Tank) Younger	FB	Pat Harder

LA Rams	0	7	0	14	—	21
Detroit	7	7	10	7	—	31

Det — Harder 12 run (Harder kick)
Det — Harder 4 run (Harder kick)
Rams— Fears 14 pass from Van Brocklin (Waterfield kick)
Det — Hart 24 pass from Walker (Harder kick)
Det — FG Harder 43
Rams— Towler 5 run (Waterfield kick)
Rams— Smith 56 punt return (Waterfield kick)
Det — Hoernschemeyer 9 run (Harder kick)
Attendance—47,645

TEAM STATISTICS	Rams	Det
Total yardage	307	365
Net rushing yardage	128	173
Net passing yardage	179	192
Passes att.-comp.-had int.	28-18-1	23-11-4

RUSHING
LA Rams—Quinlan, 6 for 60; Towler, 13 for 54, 1 TD; Younger, 4 for 14; Myers, 2 for 8; Smith, 4 for −8.
Detroit—Harder, 8 for 72, 2 TDs; Hoernschemeyer, 11 for 49, 1 TD; Walker, 7 for 29; Layne, 6 for 20; Christiansen, 4 for 9; Cline, 3 for −6.
PASSING
LA Rams—Van Brocklin, 15 of 19 for 166, 1 TD; Waterfield, 3 of 9 for 13, 1 int.
Detroit—Layne, 9 of 21 for 144, 4 int.; Walker, 1 of 1 for 24, 1 TD; Hoernschemeyer, 1 of 1 for 24.
RECEIVING
LA Rams—Fears, 7 for 76, 1 TD; Hirsch, 5 for 46; Carey, 3 for 30; Myers, 2 for 6; Towler, 1 for 21.
Detroit—Hart, 5 for 86, 1 TD; Walker, 2 for 75; Box, 2 for 20; Harder, 1 for 6; Christiansen, 1 for 5.

1957

DETROIT 31, SAN FRANCISCO 27

The Detroit Lions, trailing 27-7 in the third quarter but fired up because they had overheard a premature celebration in the San Francisco locker room at halftime, scored three touchdowns in a period of 4:29 to shock the 49ers 31-27.

San Francisco started quickly. Midway through the first quarter, Y.A. Tittle threw a 34-yard Alley-Oop pass to R.C. Owens, who outjumped Jim David in the corner of the end zone for a touchdown and a 7-0 San Francisco lead. Three minutes later, Tittle fired a 47-yard scoring pass to Hugh McElhenny, who ran right between David and Yale Lary to score.

Although the Lions cut the lead to 14-7 with a 61-yard touchdown drive, Tittle came right back. He marched the 49ers 88 yards, capping the drive with a 12-yard touchdown pass to Billy Wilson. Gordy Soltau added a field goal before halftime.

San Francisco appeared to be on its way to another touchdown early in the third period when McElhenny broke loose for 71 yards to the Detroit 7. The Lions' defense held, however, and Soltau kicked another field goal.

Once again, San Francisco moved into Detroit territory, but Tittle fumbled at the 27, and Bob Long recovered for Detroit. In nine plays, the Lions drove 73 yards for a score, with Tom Tracy, in for John Henry Johnson, scoring from the 1. On the first play after a San Francisco punt, Tracy broke loose straight up the middle for a 58-yard scoring run.

The Lions' defense held once again, and the offense took over. Tobin Rote passed to Steve Junker for 36 yards to move the ball deep into San Francisco territory. Gene Gedman blasted into the end zone from two yards out only 44 seconds into the fourth quarter. The 49ers had four possessions in the final 14 minutes, but they turned the ball over each time.

December 22, at San Francisco

Detroit	Starting Lineups	San Francisco
Jim Doran	LE	Clyde Conner
Lou Creekmur	LT	Bob Cross
Harley Sewell	LG	Bruce Bosley
Frank Gatski	C	Frank Morze
Stan Campbell	RG	Lou Palatella
Charlie Ane	RT	Bob St. Clair
Steve Junker	RE	Billy Wilson
Tobin Rote	QB	Y.A. Tittle
Howard Cassady	LH	Hugh McElhenny
Dave Middleton	RH	R.C. Owens
John Henry Johnson	FB	Joe Perry

Detroit	0	7	14	10	—	31
San Francisco	14	10	3	10	—	27

SF — Owens 34 pass from Tittle (Soltau kick)
SF — McElhenny 47 pass from Tittle (Soltau kick)
Det— Junker 4 pass from Rote (Martin kick)
SF — Wilson 12 pass from Tittle (Soltau kick)
SF — FG Soltaut 25
SF — FG Soltau 10
Det— Tracy 1 run (Martin kick)
Det— Tracy 58 run (Martin kick)
Det— Gedman 2 run (Martin kick)
Det— FG Martin 13
Attendance—60,118

TEAM STATISTICS	Det	SF
Total yardage	343	375
Net rushing yardage	129	127
Net passing yardage	214	248
Passes att.-comp.-had int.	30-16-1	31-18-3

RUSHING
Detroit—Tracy, 11 for 86, 2 TDs; Johnson, 5 for 20; Gedman, 6 for 13, 1 TD; Rote, 4 for 5; Cassady, 3 for 5.
San Francisco—McElhenny, 14 for 82; Perry, 13 for 52; Babb, 2 for 3; Arenas, 1 for 2; Tittle, 3 for −12.

PASSING
Detroit—Rote, 16 of 30 for 214, 1 TD, 1 int.
San Francisco—Tittle, 18 of 31 for 248, 3 TDs; 3 int.

RECEIVING
Detroit—Junker, 8 for 92, 1 TD; Cassady, 3 for 37; Doran, 2 for 51; Middleton, 2 for 27; Tracy, 1 for 7.
San Francisco—Wilson, 9 for 107, 1 TD; McElhenny, 6 for 96, 1 TD; Owens, 1 for 34, 1 TD; Conner, 1 for 10; Babb, 1 for 1.

1958

NY GIANTS 10, CLEVELAND 0

The New York Giants' defense limited Cleveland to 86 total yards, holding Jim Brown (who had set the NFL record with 1,527 yards during the season) to eight yards on seven carries, as the Giants defeated the Browns 10-0. The previous week, with snow falling and less than a minute remaining, Pat Summerall had kicked a 49-yard field goal to give the Giants a 13-10 victory over the Browns and force the playoff.

The Browns had problems from the start, losing the ball on two of their first three plays from scrimmage. On the game's second play, Brown fumbled when he was hit by defensive end Jim Katcavage, and Rosey Grier recovered for the Giants. On second down, New York quarterback Don Heinrich's pass was intercepted at the Cleveland 42 by defensive back Junior Wren. The Browns gave it right back, however. On first down, Milt Plum went long for Preston Carpenter, and Lindon Crow intercepted at the New York 19.

Late in the first quarter, the Giants got the ball at their own 16 following a punt. Charlie Conerly replaced Heinrich, and the team started its first successful drive, helped by Conerly's conversion of a third and six with an 11-yard pass to Rote.

With a first and 10 at the 18, the Giants scored on a play they had practiced the week before the game. Alex Webster took a handoff from Conerly, then handed off to Frank Gifford on a reverse. Gifford ran eight yards to the Browns' 10 and lateraled to Conerly, who was trailing the play. Conerly ran for the touchdown. "The lateral was optional," Conerly said. "I was there if Gifford needed me."

Summerall added a field goal in the second period to build the lead to 10-0. The kick was set up by a 35-yard pass from Conerly to Bob Schnelker.

Cleveland moved to New York's 6-yard line early in the fourth quarter, but Sam Huff intercepted Plum's pass, and the Giants controlled the ball for 10 of the last 11 minutes.

December 21, at New York

Cleveland	Starting Lineups	NY Giants
Darrell (Pete) Brewster	LE	Kyle Rote
Lou Groza	LT	Roosevelt Brown
Jim Ray Smith	LG	Al Barry
Art Hunter	C	Ray Wietecha
Chuck Noll	RG	Jack Stroud
Willie McClung	RT	Frank Youso
Preston Carpenter	RE	Bob Schnelker
Mitt Plum	QB	Don Heinrich
Ray Renfro	LH	Frank Gifford
Bobby Mitchell	RH	Alex Webster
Jim Brown	FB	Mel Triplett

Cleveland	0	0	0	0	—	0
NY Giants	7	3	0	0	—	10

NYG— Conerly 10 lateral from Gifford, who had run 8 (Summerall kick)
NYG— FG Summerall 26
Attendance—61,274

TEAM STATISTICS	Cle	NYG
First downs	7	17
Rushing	2	12
Passing	5	5
By penalty	0	0
Total yardage	86	317
Net rushing yardage	24	211
Net passing yardage	62	106
Passes att.-comp.-had int.	27-10-3	18-8-2

RUSHING
Cleveland—Plum, 3 for 13; Brown, 7 for 8; L. Carpenter, 3 for 3.
NY Giants—Gifford, 23 for 95; Webster, 15 for 62; King, 10 for 26; Triplett, 5 for 18; Conerly, 0 for 10, 1 TD.

PASSING
Cleveland—Plum, 7 of 12 for 83, 2 int.; Ninowski, 3 of 15 for 31, 1 int.
NY Giants—Conerly, 7 of 11 for 75; Heinrich, 1 of 7 for 31, 2 int.

RECEIVING
Cleveland—Brewster, 3 for 56; P. Carpenter, 2 for 18; Brown, 2 for 18; L. Carpenter, 2 for 5; Renfro, 1 for 17.
NY Giants—Webster, 3 for 45; Schnelker, 2 for 46; Rote, 1 for 11; King, 1 for 6; Gifford, 1 for −1.

1963 AFL

BOSTON 26, BUFFALO 8

Boston fullback Larry Garron turned short pass receptions from Vito (Babe) Parilli into 59- and 17-yard touchdowns as the Patriots beat the Buffalo Bills 26-8 in 10-degree weather.

The Patriots and the Bills, the first teams to play one another in an AFL preseason game, recorded another first at War Memorial Stadium by playing in the first divisional playoff in league history.

All of the Patriots' points were accounted for by Garron and split end-kicker Gino Cappelletti. The Patriots scored the second time they had the ball on Cappelletti's 28-yard field goal. The next time Boston had the ball, Parilli flipped a pass to Garron in the flat. Garron broke two tackles and sprinted over the icy turf to score on a 59-yard play.

The Patriots increased their lead to 16-0 at halftime. In the third quarter, with the Bills pinned deep in their own territory, quarterback Daryle Lamonica, who had replaced ineffective starter Jack Kemp, threw long for flanker Elbert Dubenion, who outraced the Boston defenders to complete a 93-yard touchdown play. Lamonica then passed to linebacker John Tracey, an eligible receiver on the play, for a two-point conversion.

The Patriots ended any thoughts of a comeback by driving for another touchdown early in the fourth quarter. The score again came on a pass in the flat to Garron, who went 17 yards to the end zone.

December 28, at Buffalo

Boston	Starters, Offense	Buffalo
Gino Cappelletti	SE	Bill Miller
Don Oakes	LT	Stew Barber
Chuck Long	LG	Tom Day
Walt Cudzik	C	Al Bermiller
Billy Neighbors	RG	Billy Shaw
Milt Graham	RT	Ken Rice
Tony Romeo	TE	Ernie Warlick
Jim Colclough	FL	Glenn Bass
Vito (Babe) Parilli	QB	Jack Kemp
Larry Garron	FB	Cookie Gilchrist
Ron Burton	HB	Elbert Dubenion
	Starters, Defense	
Bob Dee	LE	Ron McDole
Houston Antwine	LT	Tom Sestak
Jesse Richardson	RT	Jim Dunaway
Jim Hunt	RE	Mack Yoho
Tom Addison	LLB	John Tracey
Nick Buoniconti	MLB	Harry Jacobs
Jack Rudolph	RLB	Mike Stratton
Dick Felt	LCB	Willie West
Bob Suci	RCB	Booker Edgerson
Ron Hall	LS	George Saimes
Ross O'Hanley	RS	Ray Abruzzese

Boston	10	6	0	10	—	26
Buffalo	0	0	8	0	—	8

Bos —FG Cappelletti 28
Bos —Garron 59 pass from Parilli (Cappelletti kick)
Bos —FG Cappelletti 12
Bos —FG Cappelletti 33
Buff—Dubenion 93 pass from Lamonica (Tracey pass from Lamonica)
Bos —Garron 17 pass from Parilli (Cappelletti kick)
Bos —FG Cappelletti 36
Attendance—33,044

TEAM STATISTICS	Bos	Buff
Total yardage	370	174
Net rushing yardage	83	7
Net passing yardage	287	167
Passes att.-comp.-had int.	35-14-1	45-19-4

RUSHING
Boston—Garron, 19 for 44; Neumann, 1 for 16; Burton, 8 for 12; Crump, 5 for 9; Lott, 2 for 2; Parilli, 1 for 0.
Buffalo—Gilchrist, 8 for 7; Bass, 2 for 4; Kemp, 2 for −4.

PASSING
Boston—Parilli, 14 of 35 for 300, 2 TDs, 1 int.
Buffalo—Kemp, 10 of 21 for 133, 1 int.; Lamonica, 9 of 24 for 168, 1 TD, 3 int.

RECEIVING
Boston—Garron, 4 for 120, 2 TDs; Cappelletti, 4 for 109; Burton, 3 for 22; Graham, 1 for 22; Lott, 1 for 18; Colclough, 1 for 9.
Buffalo—Ferguson, 4 for 47; Bass, 4 for 45; Dubenion, 3 for 115, 1 TD; Rutkowski, 3 for 45; Warlick, 3 for 33; Gilchrist, 1 for 11; Miller, 1 for 5.

1965 NFL

GREEN BAY 13, BALTIMORE 10

Green Bay's Don Chandler kicked two field goals, one to tie the game with 1:58 remaining in regulation, and one to win it after 13:39 of overtime, as the Packers defeated Baltimore 13-10.

The Colts entered the game with halfback Tom Matte playing quarterback because of injuries to Johnny Unitas and Gary Cuozzo. Matte, who had been a quarterback at Ohio State, ran the team from lists of plays taped to his wrist.

Baltimore took the lead after only 21 seconds. On the first play from scrimmage, Bart Starr passed to Bill Anderson, who fumbled. Linebacker Don Shinnick picked up the ball and returned it 25 yards for a touchdown. Starr suffered a rib injury on the play and missed the rest of the game. He was replaced by Zeke Bratkowski.

Trailing 10-0 late in the half, the Packers threatened to score, driving to a second and goal at the Baltimore 1. But, on fourth down, Jim Taylor fumbled, and the Colts took over.

Early in the third quarter, the Packers took over at the Baltimore 35 after a high snap from center prevented Tom Gilburg from getting off a punt. Bratkowski passed to Carroll Dale for 33 yards, and Paul Hornung scored from the 1. With nine minutes left, the Packers started a 15-play drive that ended with Chandler's field goal. The Colts disputed the call, saying the kick was just outside the upright.

December 26, at Green Bay

Baltimore	Starters, Offense	Green Bay
Raymond Berry	SE	Boyd Dowler
Bob Vogel	LT	Bob Skoronski
Jim Parker	LG	Fred (Fuzzy) Thurston
Dick Szymanski	C	Ken Bowman
Alex Sandusky	RG	Jerry Kramer
George Preas	RT	Forrest Gregg
John Mackey	TE	Bill Anderson
Jimmy Orr	FL	Carroll Dale
Tom Matte	QB	Bart Starr
Jerry Hill	FB	Jim Taylor
Lenny Moore	HB	Paul Hornung
	Starters, Defense	
Lou Michaels	LE	Willie Davis
Fred Miller	LT	Ron Kostelnik
Billy Ray Smith	RT	Henry Jordan
Ordell Braase	RE	Lionel Aldridge
Steve Stonebreaker	LLB	Dave Robinson
Dennis Gaubatz	MLB	Ray Nitschke
Don Shinnick	RLB	Lee Roy Caffey
Bobby Boyd	LCB	Herb Adderley
Lenny Lyles	RCB	Doug Hart
Jerry Logan	SS	Tom Brown
Wendell Harris	FS	Willie Wood

Baltimore	7	3	0	0	0	—	10
Green Bay	0	0	7	3	3	—	13

Balt— Shinnick 25 fumble return (Michaels kick)
Balt— FG Michaels 15
GB — Hornung 1 run (Chandler kick)
GB — FG Chandler 22
GB — FG Chandler 25
Attendance—50,484

TEAM STATISTICS	Balt	GB
First downs	9	23
Rushing	6	9
Passing	2	11
By penalty	1	3
Total yardage	175	362
Net rushing yardage	143	112
Net passing yardage	32	250
Passes att.-comp.-had int.	12-5-0	41-23-2

RUSHING
Baltimore—Hill, 16 for 57; Matte, 17 for 57; Moore, 12 for 33; Lorick, 1 for 1; Gilburg, 1 for −5.
Green Bay—Taylor, 23 for 60; Hornung, 10 for 33, 1 TD; Pitts, 3 for 14; Moore, 3 for 5.
PASSING
Baltimore—Matte, 5 of 12 for 40.
Green Bay—Bratkowski, 22 of 39 for 248, 2 int.; Starr, 1 of 1 for 10; Hornung, 0 of 1.
RECEIVING
Baltimore—Mackey, 3 for 25; Moore, 2 for 15.
Green Bay—Anderson, 8 for 78; Dowler, 5 for 50; Hornung, 4 for 42; Dale, 3 for 63; Taylor, 2 for 29; Moore, 1 for −4.

1967 NFL

DALLAS 52, CLEVELAND 14

Dallas split end Bob Hayes teamed with quarterback Don Meredith on an 86-yard touchdown pass and set up two other scores with punt returns of 68 and 64 yards, as the Cowboys crushed the Browns 52-14.

Even injuries couldn't slow down the Cowboys. When halfback Dan Reeves had to leave the game early in the first quarter, rookie Craig Baynham came in and scored three touchdowns. The first was on a three-yard pass from Meredith that opened the scoring. Before the first quarter was over, Dallas scored again when fullback Don Perkins blasted over from the 4. Then Hayes turned on the jets, catching the 86-yard touchdown pass from Meredith.

The Browns finally got on the scoreboard in the final minute of the first half against a relaxed Dallas defense. Frank Ryan threw a 13-yard touchdown pass to tight end Milt Morin.

The Cowboys came out supercharged again in the third quarter, pushing across two touchdowns on short runs before cornerback Cornell Green picked off one of Ryan's passes and raced 60 yards for a touchdown. At that stage, Meredith and most of the starting Cowboys came out of the game.

December 24, at Dallas

Cleveland	Starters, Offense	Dallas
Paul Warfield	SE	Bob Hayes
Dick Schafrath	LT	Tony Liscio
John Wooten	LG	John Niland
Fred Hoaglin	C	Mike Connelly
Gene Hickerson	RG	Leon Donohue
Monte Clark	RT	Ralph Neely
Ralph Smith	TE	Pettis Norman
Gary Collins	FL	Lance Rentzel
Frank Ryan	QB	Don Meredith
Ernie Green	RB	Don Perkins
Leroy Kelly	RB	Dan Reeves
	Starters, Defense	
Paul Wiggin	LE	Willie Townes
Walter Johnson	LT	Jethro Pugh
Jim Kanicki	RT	Bob Lilly
Bill Glass	RE	George Andrie
Jim Houston	LLB	Chuck Howley
Dale Lindsey	MLB	Lee Roy Jordan
John Brewer	RLB	Dave Edwards
Erich Barnes	LCB	Cornell Green
Mike Howell	RCB	Mike Johnson
Ernie Kellermann	SS	Mel Renfro
Ross Fichtner	FS	Phil Clark

Cleveland	0	7	0	7	—	14
Dallas	14	10	21	7	—	52

Dall— Baynham 3 pass from Meredith (Villanueva kick)
Dall— Perkins 4 run (Villanueva kick)
Dall— Hayes 86 pass from Meredith (Villanueva kick)
Dall— FG Villanueva 10
Cle — Morin 13 pass from Ryan (Groza kick)
Dall— Baynham 1 run (Villanueva kick)
Dall— Perkins 1 run (Villanueva kick)
Dall— Green 60 interception return (Villanueva kick)
Dall— Baynham 1 run (Villanueva kick)
Cle — Warfield 75 pass from Ryan (Groza kick)
Attendance—70,786

TEAM STATISTICS	Cle	Dall
First downs	15	22
Rushing	4	13
Passing	10	7
By penalty	1	2
Total yardage	322	401
Net rushing yardage	159	178
Net passing yardage	163	223
Passes att.-comp.-had int.	30-14-1	15-11-1

RUSHING
Cleveland—Kelly, 15 for 96; Green, 10 for 49; Ryan, 2 for 14.
Dallas—Perkins, 18 for 74, 2 TDs; Baynham, 13 for 50, 2 TDs; Garrison, 9 for 33; Clarke, 1 for 8; Reeves, 3 for 7; Meredith, 2 for 6.
PASSING
Cleveland—Ryan, 14 of 30 for 194, 2 TDs, 1 int.
Dallas—Meredith, 10 of 12 for 212, 2 TDs.; Morton, 1 of 3 for 13, 1 int.
RECEIVING
Cleveland—Kelly, 4 for 39; Warfield, 3 for 99, 1 TD; Morin, 3 for 35, 1 TD; Green, 3 for 18; Collins, 1 for 3.
Dallas—Hayes, 5 for 144, 1 TD; Rentzel, 3 for 65; Reeves, 1 for 9; Perkins, 1 for 4; Baynham, 1 for 3, 1 TD.

1967 NFL

GREEN BAY 28, LA RAMS 7

After losing in Los Angeles two weeks before, the Packers played a near-perfect game in defeating the Rams 28-7. Green Bay's defense shut down the top offense in the NFL, the Packers' offense ran and passed effectively, and the special teams set up two touchdowns.

The Rams scored first, with Roman Gabriel throwing a 29-yard touchdown pass to Bernie Casey in the first quarter. Shortly thereafter, the Rams drove into Green Bay territory and threatened again, but, when Bruce Gossett attempted a 24-yard field goal, Dave Robinson blocked it. The momentum of the game shifted in Green Bay's favor.

In the second quarter, Tom Brown returned a punt 39 yards to the Rams' 47. On second down, halfback Travis Williams shot through tackle and raced 46 yards for the tying touchdown. The Rams drove into Green Bay territory again, but Willie Wood returned a short field-goal attempt by Gossett 44 yards. Moments later, Starr connected with Carroll Dale on a 17-yard touchdown pass.

With the defense smothering the Rams, the Packers' punishing ground game put the game away in the third quarter, with Chuck Mercein scoring a six-yard touchdown on a draw play. In the final period, Starr found Dale with a 48-yard pass that carried to the Rams' 2 before Dale stumbled. Williams blasted two yards for the final score.

December 23, at Milwaukee

LA Rams	Starters, Offense	Green Bay
Jack Snow	SE	Boyd Dowler
Joe Carollo	LT	Bob Skoronski
Tom Mack	LG	Gale Gillingham
Ken Iman	C	Ken Bowman
Joe Scibelli	RG	Jerry Kramer
Charlie Cowan	RT	Forrest Gregg
Billy Truax	TE	Marv Fleming
Bernie Casey	FL	Carroll Dale
Roman Gabriel	QB	Bart Starr
Dick Bass	RB	Chuck Mercein
Les Josephson	RB	Donny Anderson
	Starters, Defense	
David (Deacon) Jones	LE	Willie Davis
Merlin Olsen	LT	Ron Kostelnik
Roger Brown	RT	Henry Jordan
Lamar Lundy	RE	Lionel Aldridge
Jack Pardee	LLB	Dave Robinson
Myron Pottios	MLB	Ray Nitschke
Maxie Baughan	RLB	Lee Roy Caffey
Clancy Williams	LCB	Herb Adderley
Irv Cross	RCB	Bob Jeter
Chuck Lamson	SS	Tom Brown
Eddie Meador	FS	Willie Wood

LA Rams	7	0	0	0	—	7
Green Bay	0	14	7	7	—	28

Rams— Casey 29 pass from Gabriel (Gossett kick)
GB — Williams 46 run (Chandler kick)
GB — Dale 17 pass from Starr (Chandler kick)
GB — Mercein 6 run (Chandler kick)
GB — Williams 2 run (Chandler kick)
Attendance—49,861

TEAM STATISTICS	Rams	GB
First downs	12	20
Rushing	2	11
Passing	9	8
By penalty	1	1
Total yardage	217	374
Net rushing yardage	75	163
Net passing yardage	142	211
Passes att.-comp.-had int.	31-11-1	23-17-1

RUSHING
LA Rams—Bass, 14 for 40; Josephson, 9 for 16; Mason, 2 for 13; Gabriel, 3 for 6.
Green Bay—Williams, 18 for 88, 2 TDs; Anderson, 12 for 52; Mercein, 12 for 13, 1 TD; Starr, 2 for 8; Wilson, 1 for 2.
PASSING
LA Rams—Gabriel, 11 of 31 for 186, 1 TD, 1 int.
Green Bay—Starr, 17 of 23 for 222, 1 TD, 1 int.
RECEIVING
LA Rams—Casey, 5 for 82, 1 TD; Truax, 2 for 45; Josephson, 2 for 30; Snow, 1 for 17; Pope, 1 for 12.
Green Bay—Dale, 6 for 109, 1 TD; Dowler, 3 for 35; Fleming, 3 for 30; Anderson, 2 for 30; Mercein, 2 for 10; Williams, 1 for 8.

1968 AFL

OAKLAND 41, KANSAS CITY 6

Quarterback Daryle Lamonica threw five touchdown passes and the Oakland defense held Kansas City without a touchdown for the first time since 1963 as the Raiders whipped the Chiefs 41-6.

Oakland blew the game open early, scoring on three of its first four possessions and leading 21-0 at the end of the first quarter. The first time the Raiders had the ball, Lamonica drove them 80 yards, hitting Fred Biletnikoff three times, including a 24-yard touchdown pass. The Raiders took over at the Kansas City 25 following a shanked punt, and three plays later Lamonica passed to Warren Wells for a touchdown. Lamonica completed a 70-yard drive with a 44-yard scoring pass to Biletnikoff.

The Chiefs threatened to get back into the game in the second quarter, driving to the Raiders' 3 and 2 on separate possessions. Each time they had to settle for short field goals. Then, taking the ball at the Oakland 20 with less than two minutes in the half, Lamonica provided the knockout punch. He drove the Raiders to the 46, from where, with 28 seconds left, he threw a 54-yard touchdown pass to Biletnikoff.

Lamonica finished his day's work on the second play of the fourth quarter, when he found Wells again for a 35-yard touchdown.

December 22, at Oakland

Kansas City	Starters, Offense	Oakland
Frank Pitts	SE	Warren Wells
Jim Tyrer	LT	Bob Svihus
Ed Budde	LG	Gene Upshaw
E. J. Holub	C	Jim Otto
Mo Moorman	RG	Jim Harvey
Dave Hill	RT	Harry Schuh
Fred Arbanas	TE	Billy Cannon
Otis Taylor	FL	Fred Biletnikoff
Len Dawson	QB	Daryle Lamonica
Robert Holmes	RB	Hewritt Dixon
Mike Garrett	RB	Charlie Smith
	Starters, Defense	
Jerry Mays	LE	Isaac Lassiter
Ed Lothamer	LT	Dan Birdwell
Buck Buchanan	RT	Carleton Oats
Aaron Brown	RE	Ben Davidson
Bobby Bell	LLB	Ralph (Chip) Oliver
Willie Lanier	MLB	Dan Conners
Jim Lynch	RLB	Gus Otto
Goldie Sellers	LCB	George Atkinson
Emmitt Thomas	RCB	Willie Brown
Jim Kearney	SS	Rodger Bird
Johnny Robinson	FS	Dave Grayson

Kansas City	0	6	0	0	—	6
Oakland	21	7	0	13	—	41

Oak—Biletnikoff 24 pass from Lamonica (Blanda kick)
Oak—Wells 23 pass from Lamonica (Blanda kick)
Oak—Biletnikoff 44 pass from Lamonica (Blanda kick)
KC —FG Stenerud 10
KC —FG Stenerud 8
Oak—Biletnikoff 54 pass from Lamonica (Blanda kick)
Oak—Wells 35 pass from Lamonica (Blanda kick)
Oak—FG Blanda 41
Oak—FG Blanda 40
Attendance—53,605

TEAM STATISTICS	KC	Oak
First downs	13	22
Rushing	3	7
Passing	9	14
By penalty	1	1
Total yardage	312	454
Net rushing yardage	70	118
Net passing yardage	242	336
Passes att.-comp.-had int.	36-17-4	39-19-0

RUSHING

Oakland—Smith, 13 for 74; Banaszak, 3 for 19; Dixon, 10 for 13; Hagberg, 4 for 12.

Kansas City—Holmes, 13 for 46; Hayes, 3 for 10; Dawson, 2 for 9; Garrett, 6 for 5.

PASSING

Oakland—Lamonica, 19 of 39 for 347, 5 TDs.

Kansas City—Dawson, 17 of 36 for 253, 4 int.

RECEIVING

Oakland—Biletnikoff, 7 for 180, 3 TDs; Smith, 5 for 52; Wells, 4 for 93, 2 TDs; Cannon, 2 for 15; Dixon, 1 for 7.

Kansas City—Pitts, 5 for 56; Taylor, 4 for 117; Garrett, 4 for 31; Richardson, 3 for 57; Holmes, 1 for −8.

1968 NFL

CLEVELAND 31, DALLAS 20

The Cleveland Browns turned five Dallas turnovers into 24 points, including two touchdowns in the first three minutes of the second half, and went on to defeat the Cowboys 31-20.

The Browns' defense didn't take long to get going. On the Cowboys' first possession, Mike Howell intercepted a pass by Don Meredith, setting up a 38-yard field goal by Don Cockroft.

The Dallas defense responded. Late in the first quarter, Chuck Howley picked up Bill Nelsen's fumble and ran 44 yards for a touchdown. Then, Mike Clark kicked a field goal following an interception by Dave Edwards.

The Browns tied the score 10-10 at halftime, driving 85 yards in six plays, and scoring on a 45-yard pass from Nelsen to Leroy Kelly.

Cleveland struck like lightning in the second half. On the first play from scrimmage, Dale Lindsey intercepted Meredith's pass and returned it 27 yards for a touchdown. On the third play following the kickoff, Ben Davis intercepted Meredith, and, two plays later, Kelly broke loose for a 35-yard touchdown run. Ernie Green added a touchdown following an interception by Erich Barnes.

December 21, at Cleveland

Dallas	Starters, Offense	Cleveland
Bob Hayes	SE	Paul Warfield
Tony Liscio	LT	Dick Schafrath
John Niland	LG	John Demarie
Malcolm Walker	C	Fred Hoaglin
John Wilbur	RG	Gene Hickerson
Ralph Neely	RT	Monte Clark
Pettis Norman	TE	Milt Morin
Lance Rentzel	FL	Gary Collins
Don Meredith	QB	Bill Nelsen
Don Perkins	RB	Charley Harraway
Craig Baynham	RB	Leroy Kelly
	Starters, Defense	
Larry Cole	LE	Ron Snidow
Jethro Pugh	LT	Walter Johnson
Bob Lilly	RT	Jim Kanicki
George Andrie	RE	Jack Gregory
Chuck Howley	LLB	Jim Houston
Lee Roy Jordan	MLB	Bob Matheson
Dave Edwards	RLB	Dale Lindsey
Cornell Green	LCB	Erich Barnes
Mel Renfro	RCB	Ben Davis
Mike Gaechter	SS	Ernie Kellermann
Dick Daniels	FS	Mike Howell

Dallas	7	3	3	7	—	20
Cleveland	3	7	14	7	—	31

Cle — FG Cockroft 38
Dall— Howley 44 fumble return (Clark kick)
Dall— FG Clark 16
Cle — Kelly 45 pass from Nelsen (Cockroft kick)
Cle — Lindsey 27 interception return (Cockroft kick)
Cle — Kelly 35 run (Cockroft kick)
Dall— FG Clark 47
Cle — Green 2 run (Cockroft kick)
Dall— Garrison 2 pass from Morton (Clark kick)
Attendance—81,497

TEAM STATISTICS	Dall	Cle
First downs	13	12
Rushing	5	4
Passing	8	8
By penalty	0	0
Total yardage	286	280
Net rushing yardage	86	102
Net passing yardage	200	178
Passes att.-comp.-had int.	32-12-4	25-13-1

RUSHING

Dallas—Perkins, 14 for 51; Morton, 2 for 14; Baynham, 10 for 7; Garrison, 1 for 6; Meredith, 1 for 5; Shy, 2 for 3.

Cleveland—Kelly, 20 for 87, 1 TD; Harraway, 5 for 12; Green, 3 for 5, 1 TD; Nelsen, 2 for −2.

PASSING

Dallas—Morton, 9 of 23 for 163, 1 TD, 1 int.; Meredith, 3 of 9 for 42, 3 int.

Cleveland—Nelsen, 13 of 25 for 203, 1 TD, 1 int.

RECEIVING

Dallas—Hayes, 5 for 83; Rentzel, 3 for 75; Garrison, 2 for 8, 1 TD; Baynham, 1 for 34; Norman, 1 for 5.

Cleveland—Warfield, 4 for 86; Morin, 4 for 47; Kelly, 2 for 46, 1 TD; Collins, 2 for 26; Harraway, 1 for −2.

1968 NFL

BALTIMORE 24, MINNESOTA 14

The Baltimore Colts scored two touchdowns in the space of two minutes and one second of the third quarter to break open a tough defensive struggle, and went on to beat Minnesota 24-14 in the Vikings' first playoff appearance.

The weather was miserable—30 degrees, 14-mile-per-hour winds, and sleet. Neither team scored for nearly 27 minutes, but then the Colts put together a 75-yard drive based primarily on two plays. On first down, Earl Morrall hit flanker Willie Richardson with a 39-yard pass to the Minnesota 36. On the next play, Morrall threw for the right corner of the field, and Richardson made a diving catch at the 3. Three plays later, Morrall dumped a three-yard scoring pass to tight end Tom Mitchell.

Morrall went to work again in the third quarter. A short punt put Baltimore at midfield. On second and nine, Morrall flipped a pass barely over the hands of linebacker Roy Winston to tight end John Mackey, who tore out of the grasp of Paul Krause and roared 49 yards to a touchdown. The Vikings moved to the Baltimore 30, but the Colts put on a nine-man rush. Bubba Smith hit Vikings quarterback Joe Kapp, the ball popped up in the air, and linebacker Mike Curtis grabbed it and raced 60 yards for the clinching touchdown.

December 22, at Baltimore

Minnesota	Starters, Offense	Baltimore
Gene Washington	SE	Jimmy Orr
Grady Alderman	LT	Bob Vogel
Jim Vellone	LG	Glenn Ressler
Mick Tingelhoff	C	Bill Curry
Milt Sunde	RG	Dan Sullivan
Doug Davis	RT	Sam Ball
John Beasley	TE	John Mackey
John Henderson	FL	Willie Richardson
Joe Kapp	QB	Earl Morrall
Bill Brown	RB	Preston Pearson
Dave Osborn	RB	Tom Matte
	Starters, Defense	
Carl Eller	LE	Bubba Smith
Alan Page	LT	Billy Ray Smith
Gary Larsen	RT	Fred Miller
Jim Marshall	RE	Ordell Braase
Roy Winston	LLB	Mike Curtis
Lonnie Warwick	MLB	Dennis Gaubatz
Wally Hilgenberg	RLB	Don Shinnick
Earsell Mackbee	LCB	Bobby Boyd
Ed Sharockman	RCB	Lenny Lyles
Karl Kassulke	LS-SS	Jerry Logan
Paul Krause	RS-FS	Rick Volk

Minnesota	0	0	0	14	—	14
Baltimore	0	7	14	3	—	24

Balt —Mitchell 3 pass from Morrall (Michaels kick)
Balt —Mackey 49 pass from Morrall (Michaels kick)
Balt —Curtis 60 fumble return (Michaels kick)
Minn—Martin 1 pass from Kapp (Cox kick)
Balt —FG Michaels 33
Minn—Brown 7 pass from Kapp (Cox kick)
Attendance—60,238

TEAM STATISTICS	Minn	Balt
First downs	22	15
Rushing	4	2
Passing	17	12
By penalty	1	1
Total yardage	351	295
Net rushing yardage	85	50
Net passing yardage	266	245
Passes att.-comp.-had int.	44-26-2	22-13-1

RUSHING

Minnesota—Kapp, 10 for 52; Brown, 10 for 30; Osborn, 5 for 4; Jones, 2 for 0; Lindsey, 1 for −1.

Baltimore—Matte, 14 for 31; Hill, 8 for 10; Mackey, 1 for 9; Pearson, 4 for 0.

PASSING

Minnesota—Kapp, 26 of 44 for 287, 2 TDs, 2 int.

Baltimore—Morrall, 13 of 22 for 280, 2 TDs, 1 int.

RECEIVING

Minnesota—Brown, 8 for 82, 1 TD; Washington, 5 for 95; Beasley, 5 for 69; Henderson, 5 for 33; Lindsey, 1 for 9; Martin, 1 for 1, 1 TD; Osborn, 1 for −2.

Baltimore—Richardson, 6 for 148; Mackey, 3 for 93, 1 TD; Orr, 2 for 36; Mitchell, 1 for 3, 1 TD; Pearson, 1 for 1.

1969 AFL

KANSAS CITY 13, NY JETS 6

Kansas City moved 80 yards in two plays early in the fourth quarter, scoring on Len Dawson's 19-yard pass to Gloster Richardson, and the Chiefs defeated the New York Jets 13-6.

Frigid weather and a blustery wind hampered both teams' passing attacks. The wind also held up Jan Stenerud's 40-yard field-goal attempt early in the game, dropping it just short of the goal posts. The Jets immediately mounted a threat of their own, with Joe Namath completing four of four passes on the way to Jim Turner's 27-yard field goal.

Two short field goals by Stenerud first tied the game 3-3 at halftime and then gave Kansas City a 6-3 lead in the third quarter, setting up the key defensive stand of the game. Following a pass-interference penalty on Emmitt Thomas in the end zone, the Jets' had a first and goal at the 1. But two runs and an incomplete pass didn't produce a score. On fourth down, Turner tied the game 6-6 with his second field goal.

Following the kickoff, the Chiefs took over at their 20. On first down, Dawson threw a long pass to Otis Taylor, who carried it to the Jets' 19 before being dragged down by Al Atkinson. On the next play, Dawson found Richardson alone in the end zone. Namath drove the Jets to the Kansas City 19 and 13 on the two following series, but both bids ended in failure.

December 20, at New York

Kansas City	Starters, Offense	NY Jets
Frank Pitts	WR	George Sauer
Jim Tyrer	LT	Winston Hill
Ed Budde	LG	Randy Rasmussen
E. J. Holub	C	John Schmitt
Mo Moorman	RG	Dave Herman
Dave Hill	RT	Roger Finnie
Fred Arbanas	TE	Pete Lammons
Otis Taylor	WR	Bake Turner
Len Dawson	QB	Joe Namath
Robert Holmes	RB	Matt Snell
Mike Garrett	RB	Emerson Boozer
	Starters, Defense	
Jerry Mays	LE	Gerry Philbin
Curley Culp	LT	Steve Thompson
Buck Buchanan	RT	John Elliott
Aaron Brown	RE	Verlon Biggs
Bobby Bell	LLB	Ralph Baker
Willie Lanier	MLB	Al Atkinson
Jim Lynch	RLB	Larry Grantham
Jim Marsalis	LCB	Cornell Gordon
Emmitt Thomas	RCB	Randy Beverly
Jim Kearney	SS	Jim Richards
Johnny Robinson	FS	Bill Baird

Kansas City	0	3	3	7	—	13
NY Jets	3	0	0	3	—	6

NYJ—FG J. Turner 27
KC —FG Stenerud 23
KC —FG Stenerud 25
NYJ—FG J. Turner 7
KC —Richardson 19 pass from Dawson (Stenerud kick)
Attendance—62,977

TEAM STATISTICS	KC	NYJ
First downs	14	19
Rushing	3	5
Passing	9	11
By penalty	2	3
Total yardage	276	235
Net rushing yardage	99	87
Net passing yardage	177	148
Passes att.-comp.-had int.	27-12-0	40-14-3

RUSHING

Kansas City—Garrett, 18 for 67; Hayes, 10 for 32; Holmes, 1 for 0; McVea, 1 for 0.

NY Jets—Snell, 12 for 61; Boozer, 3 for 14; Mathis, 6 for 11; Namath, 1 for 1.

PASSING

Kansas City—Dawson, 12 of 27 for 201, 1 TD.

NY Jets—Namath, 14 of 40 for 164, 3 int.

RECEIVING

Kansas City—Hayes, 5 for 46; Taylor, 2 for 74; Arbanas, 2 for 39; Holmes, 1 for 29; Richardson, 1 for 19, 1 TD; Pitts, 1 for −6.

NY Jets—Sauer, 5 for 61; Lammons, 3 for 37; B. Turner, 2 for 25; Maynard, 1 for 18; Boozer, 1 for 10; Snell, 1 for 9; Mathis, 1 for 4.

1969 AFL

OAKLAND 56, HOUSTON 7

Daryle Lamonica threw six touchdown passes, and Oakland scored four touchdowns in a span of 4:22, as the Raiders built a 28-0 lead after one quarter and coasted to a 56-7 victory over the Oilers.

The second time the Raiders had the ball, they took only five plays to drive 50 yards, scoring on Lamonica's 13-yard pass to Fred Biletnikoff. On the first play after the ensuing kickoff, George Atkinson intercepted Pete Beathard's pass and returned it 57 yards for a touchdown. The Oilers again lost the ball on the first play following the kickoff, with defensive tackle Carleton Oats recovering Hoyle Granger's fumble at the Houston 24. On first down, Lamonica passed to wide receiver Rod Sherman for the third Oakland touchdown in a span of 1:59. Following the kickoff, the Oilers held the ball slightly longer, but Beathard fumbled on the fourth play, and Tom Keating recovered for Oakland at the Houston 31. Again it took Oakland one play to score, Lamonica passing to Biletnikoff for a touchdown.

Lamonica threw three more touchdown passes in the game, driving the Raiders 71, 75, and 62 yards for scores before being replaced by George Blanda.

December 21, at Oakland

Houston	Starters, Offense	Oakland
Jim Beirne	WR	Rod Sherman
Walt Suggs	LT	Bob Svihus
Tom Regner	LG	Gene Upshaw
Bobby Maples	C	Jim Otto
Erwin (Sonny) Bishop	RG	Jim Harvey
Glen Ray Hines	RT	Harry Schuh
Alvin Reed	TE	Billy Cannon
Jerry LeVias	WR	Fred Biletnikoff
Pete Beathard	QB	Daryle Lamonica
Hoyle Granger	RB	Hewritt Dixon
Woody Campbell	RB	Charlie Smith
	Starters, Defense	
Pat Holmes	LE	Isaac Lassiter
Carel Stith	LT	Carleton Oats
Tom Domres	RT	Tom Keating
Elvin Bethea	RE	Ben Davidson
George Webster	LLB	Ralph (Chip) Oliver
Garland Boyette	MLB	Dan Conners
Olen Underwood	RLB	Gus Otto
Miller Farr	LCB	Nemiah Wilson
Zeke Moore	RCB	Willie Brown
Ken Houston	SS	George Atkinson
Johnny Peacock	FS	Dave Grayson

Houston	0	0	0	7	—	7
Oakland	28	7	14	7	—	56

Oak—Biletnikoff 13 pass from Lamonica (Blanda kick)
Oak—Atkinson 57 interception return (Blanda kick)
Oak—Sherman 24 pass from Lamonica (Blanda kick)
Oak—Biletnikoff 31 pass from Lamonica (Blanda kick)
Oak—Smith 60 pass from Lamonica (Blanda kick)
Oak—Sherman 23 pass from Lamonica (Blanda kick)
Oak—Cannon 3 pass from Lamonica (Blanda kick)
Hou—Reed 8 pass from Beathard (Gerela kick)
Oak—Hubbard 4 run (Blanda kick)
Attendance—53,539

TEAM STATISTICS	Hou	Oak
First downs	14	17
Rushing	1	5
Passing	10	11
By penalty	3	1
Total yardage	197	412
Net rushing yardage	28	110
Net passing yardage	169	302
Passes att.-comp.-had int.	46-18-3	22-14-3

RUSHING

Houston—Granger, 14 for 29; LeVias, 1 for 4; Campbell, 1 for 0; Beathard, 3 for −5.

Oakland—Dixon, 13 for 48; Todd, 8 for 31; Hubbard, 6 for 19, 1 TD; Hagberg, 2 for 9; C. Smith, 8 for 3.

PASSING

Houston—Beathard, 18 of 46 for 209, 1 TD, 3 int.

Oakland—Lamonica, 13 of 17 for 276, 6 TDs, 1 int.; Blanda, 1 of 5 for 33, 2 int.

RECEIVING

Houston—Reed, 7 for 81, 1 TD; Beirne, 5 for 48; Granger, 3 for 31; Haik, 2 for 42; LeVias, 1 for 7.

Oakland—C. Smith, 4 for 103, 1 TD; Sherman, 4 for 60, 2 TDs; Biletnikoff, 3 for 70, 2 TDs; Todd, 1 for 40; Hubbard, 1 for 33; Cannon, 1 for 3, 1 TD.

1969 NFL

CLEVELAND 38, DALLAS 14

Cleveland quarterback Bill Nelsen completed 15 of 22 passes for 184 yards in the first half, as the Browns took a 17-0 halftime lead over the favored Dallas Cowboys and went on to a 38-14 victory.

The Browns' offense was nearly flawless in the first half. One of the major keys was wide receiver Paul Warfield, who was double-teamed constantly, but still made eight receptions. Meanwhile, the Browns' defense totally shut down the Cowboys' wide receivers, Lance Rentzel and Bob Hayes.

The Browns took charge early, driving to Bo Scott's two-yard touchdown run. In the second quarter, Nelsen capped a drive by throwing a six-yard touchdown pass to tight end Milt Morin.

The Browns scored on their first possession of the third quarter to build their lead to 24-0. Then Craig Morton put together the Cowboys' first real drive of the day, finishing it off with a two-yard touchdown run. Morton started another drive, but the Cowboys' momentum was halted by linebacker Jim Houston's interception. After the Browns scored on a one-yard run by Leroy Kelly, Walt Sumner intercepted Morton again and raced 88 yards down the sideline for the Browns' final touchdown.

December 28, at Dallas

Cleveland	Starters, Offense	Dallas
Paul Warfield	WR	Bob Hayes
Dick Schafrath	LT	Tony Liscio
John Demarie	LG	John Niland
Fred Hoaglin	C	Malcolm Walker
Gene Hickerson	RG	John Wilbur
Monte Clark	RT	Ralph Neely
Milt Morin	TE	Pettis Norman
Gary Collins	WR	Lance Rentzel
Bill Nelsen	QB	Craig Morton
Bo Scott	RB	Walt Garrison
Leroy Kelly	RB	Calvin Hill
	Starters, Defense	
Ron Snidow	LE	Larry Cole
Walter Johnson	LT	Jethro Pugh
Jim Kanicki	RT	Bob Lilly
Jack Gregory	RE	George Andrie
Jim Houston	LLB	Dave Edwards
Dale Lindsey	MLB	Lee Roy Jordan
John Garlington	RLB	Chuck Howley
Erich Barnes	LCB	Cornell Green
Walt Sumner	RCB	Otto Brown
Ernie Kellermann	SS	Mike Gaechter
Mike Howell	FS	Mel Renfro

Cleveland	7	10	7	14	—	38
Dallas	0	0	7	7	—	14

Cle — Scott 2 run (Cockroft kick)
Cle — Morin 6 pass from Nelsen (Cockroft kick)
Cle — FG Cockroft 29
Cle — Scott 2 run (Cockroft kick)
Dall— Morton 2 run (Clark kick)
Cle — Kelly 1 run (Cockroft kick)
Cle — Sumner 88 interception return (Cockroft kick)
Dall— Rentzel 5 pass from Staubach (Clark kick)
Attendance—69,321

TEAM STATISTICS	Cle	Dall
First downs	22	17
Rushing	4	9
Passing	17	6
By penalty	1	2
Total yardage	344	217
Net rushing yardage	97	100
Net passing yardage	247	117
Passes att.-comp.-had int.	29-20-0	29-12-2

RUSHING

Cleveland—Kelly, 19 for 66, 1 TD; Scott, 11 for 33, 2 TDs; Morrison, 2 for 3; Cockroft, 1 for 0; Johnson, 2 for −5.

Dallas—Garrison, 9 for 49; Staubach, 3 for 22; Hill, 8 for 17; Morton, 4 for 12, 1 TD; Shy, 1 for 0.

PASSING

Cleveland—Nelsen, 18 of 27 for 219, 1 TD; Rhome, 2 of 2 for 35.

Dallas—Morton, 8 of 24 for 92, 2 int.; Staubach, 4 of 5 for 44, 1 TD.

RECEIVING

Cleveland—Warfield, 8 for 99; Morin, 4 for 52, 1 TD; Scott, 2 for 39; Collins, 2 for 19; Kelly, 2 for 10; Morrison, 1 for 18; Jones, 1 for 17.

Dallas—Hayes, 4 for 44; Rentzel, 3 for 41, 1 TD; Garrison, 2 for 15; Norman, 1 for 26; Hill, 1 for 7; Reeves, 1 for 3.

1969 NFL

MINNESOTA 23, LA RAMS 20

The Minnesota Vikings drove 65 yards to a fourth-quarter touchdown and added a safety 35 seconds later to upset the Los Angeles Rams 23-20.

On the second play of the game, Minnesota's Bill Brown fumbled, and Richie Petitbon recovered for the Rams at the Vikings' 45. The Rams quickly drove to Roman Gabriel's three-yard touchdown pass to Bob Klein, who was all alone in the end zone.

The Vikings came back, led by Joe Kapp's passes to Gene Washington, driving 75 yards in 10 plays to tie the game on Dave Osborn's one-yard run. Early in the second quarter, Bruce Gossett made a 20-yard field goal to put the Rams ahead 10-7. Then Gabriel took them 56 yards to his two-yard touchdown pass to Billy Truax with 48 seconds left in the half.

The Vikings drove 71 yards to a touchdown on their first possession of the second half. The big play was a 41-yard pass from Kapp to Washington on third and five.

A field goal gave the Rams a 20-14 lead early in the fourth quarter, but Kapp led the Vikings to the winning touchdown, passing for 40 yards and running for 14 on the drive. On the first play following the ensuing kickoff, Gabriel was dropped for a 12-yard loss and a safety by defensive end Carl Eller.

December 27, at Bloomington

LA Rams	Starters, Offense	Minnesota
Jack Snow	WR	Gene Washington
Charlie Cowan	LT	Grady Alderman
Tom Mack	LG	Jim Vellone
Ken Iman	C	Mick Tingelhoff
Mike LaHood	RG	Milt Sunde
Bob Brown	RT	Ron Yary
Billy Truax	TE	John Beasley
Wendell Tucker	WR	John Henderson
Roman Gabriel	QB	Joe Kapp
Les Josephson	RB	Bill Brown
Larry Smith	RB	Dave Osborn
	Starters, Defense	
David (Deacon) Jones	LE	Carl Eller
Merlin Olsen	LT	Gary Larsen
Coy Bacon	RT	Alan Page
Diron Talbert	RE	Jim Marshall
Jack Pardee	LLB	Roy Winston
Doug Woodlief	MLB	Lonnie Warwick
Maxie Baughan	RLB	Wally Hilgenberg
Clancy Williams	LCB	Earsell Mackbee
Jim Nettles	RCB	Ed Sharockman
Richie Petitbon	SS-LS	Karl Kassulke
Eddie Meador	FS-RS	Paul Krause

LA Rams	7	10	0	3	—	20
Minnesota	7	0	7	9	—	23

Rams— Klein 3 pass from Gabriel (Gossett kick)
Minn — Osborn 1 run (Cox kick)
Rams— FG Gossett 20
Rams— Truax 2 pass from Gabriel (Gossett kick)
Minn — Osborn 1 run (Cox kick)
Rams— FG Gossett 27
Minn — Kapp 2 run (Cox kick)
Minn — Safety, Eller tackled Gabriel in end zone
Attendance—47,900

TEAM STATISTICS	Rams	Minn
First downs	19	18
Rushing	10	7
Passing	9	10
By penalty	0	1
Total yardage	255	275
Net rushing yardage	126	97
Net passing yardage	129	178
Passes att.-comp.-had int.	32-22-1	19-12-2

RUSHING
LA Rams—L. Smith, 11 for 60; Gabriel, 4 for 26; Ellison, 4 for 22; Josephson, 10 for 16; Mason, 1 for 2.
Minnesota—Kapp, 7 for 42, 1 TD; Osborn, 13 for 30, 2 TDs; Brown, 8 for 22; Reed, 1 for 3.
PASSING
LA Rams—Gabriel, 22 of 32 for 150, 2 TDs, 1 int.
Minnesota—Kapp, 12 of 19 for 196, 2 int.
RECEIVING
LA Rams—Josephson, 7 for 41; L. Smith, 6 for 36; Truax, 5 for 47, 1 TD; Tucker, 3 for 23; Klein, 1 for 3, 1 TD.
Minnesota—Washington, 4 for 90; Henderson, 4 for 68; Brown, 2 for 20; Reed, 2 for 18.

1970 AFC

BALTIMORE 17, CINCINNATI 0

The Baltimore defense throttled the Cincinnati offense, holding it to 139 total yards and only 35 in the decisive first half and never allowing it past the Baltimore 42, as the Colts defeated the Bengals 17-0. The game was the first ever in the playoffs for the three-year-old Bengals, who proved to be no match for wily 15-year veteran Johnny Unitas.

The Colts scored the second time they had the ball, moving 74 yards on eight plays. Norm Bulaich powered Baltimore into Cincinnati territory, but when the Colts faced a third-and-nine situation, Unitas went long to Roy Jefferson. Jefferson caught the ball at the 12 after it grazed the hand of a Cincinnati defender and raced into the end zone, completing a 45-yard scoring play.

The next time the Colts gained possession, they drove 35 yards to set up a 44-yard field-goal attempt by rookie Jim O'Brien. The kick, which was made into a stiff 30-mile-per-hour wind, squeaked over the crossbar by inches to give Baltimore a 10-0 lead at halftime.

After a scoreless third quarter, the Colts added an insurance touchdown in the final period. Bulaich and Jerry Hill pounded out two first downs, and then, on third and 18, Unitas found Eddie Hinton with just enough room to spare for the first down. But Hinton eluded a tackler, and, behind a great block by Bulaich, sped 53 yards for a touchdown.

December 26, at Baltimore

Cincinnati	Starters, Offense	Baltimore
Chip Myers	WR	Eddie Hinton
Ernie Wright	LT	Bob Vogel
Rufus Mayes	LG	Glenn Ressler
Bob Johnson	C	Bill Curry
Pat Matson	RG	John Williams
Howard Fest	RT	Dan Sullivan
Bob Trumpy	TE	John Mackey
Speedy Thomas	WR	Roy Jefferson
Virgil Carter	QB	Johnny Unitas
Jess Phillips	RB	Tom Nowatzke
Paul Robinson	RB	Norm Bulaich
	Starters, Defense	
Royce Berry	LE	Bubba Smith
Mike Reid	LT	Billy Ray Smith
Steve Chomyszak	RT	Fred Miller
Ron Carpenter	RE	Roy Hilton
Al Beauchamp	LLB	Ray May
Bill Bergey	MLB	Mike Curtis
Ken Avery	RLB	Ted Hendricks
Lemar Parrish	LCB	Charlie Stukes
Ken Riley	RCB	Jim Duncan
Fletcher Smith	SS	Jerry Logan
Ken Dyer	FS	Rick Volk

Cincinnati	0	0	0	0	—	0
Baltimore	7	3	0	7	—	17

Balt— Jefferson 45 pass from Unitas (O'Brien kick)
Balt— FG O'Brien 44
Balt— Hinton 53 pass from Unitas (O'Brien kick)
Attendance—51,127

TEAM STATISTICS	Cin	Balt
First downs	7	15
Rushing	2	12
Passing	5	3
By penalty	0	0
Total yardage	139	299
Net rushing yardage	63	170
Net passing yardage	76	129
Passes att.-comp.-had int.	21-8-1	17-6-0

RUSHING
Cincinnati—Robinson, 5 for 25; Carter, 2 for 16; Phillips, 10 for 12; Lewis, 3 for 10; Johnson, 2 for 0.
Baltimore—Bulaich, 25 for 116; Nowatzke, 10 for 25; Unitas, 2 for 18; Hill, 3 for 11; Jefferson, 3 for 5; Havrilak, 3 for 0; Hinton, 1 for −5.
PASSING
Cincinnati—Carter, 7 of 20 for 64, 1 int.; Wyche, 1 of 1 for 29.
Baltimore—Unitas, 6 of 17 for 145, 2 TDs.
RECEIVING
Cincinnati—Myers, 4 for 66; Phillips, 2 for 12; Thomas, 1 for 9; Johnson, 1 for 6.
Baltimore—Hinton, 3 for 86, 1 TD; Jefferson, 2 for 51, 1 TD; Mackey, 1 for 8.

1970 AFC

OAKLAND 21, MIAMI 14

Two big plays, one by the defense and one by the offense, were the difference as Oakland defeated Miami 21-14 on a muddy field that slowed running attacks and destroyed kicking games. The game was the Dolphins' first-ever postseason appearance.

Both teams mounted good drives in the first quarter, but the Raiders' George Blanda and the Dolphins' Garo Yepremian both missed short field goals. In the second quarter, Charlie Smith fumbled at the Raiders' 20, and Bill Stanfill recovered for Miami. Two plays later, Bob Griese threw a 16-yard touchdown pass to Paul Warfield. Late in the quarter, Oakland quarterback Daryle Lamonica, who had been struggling, finally found his range. On successive third downs, he hit tight end Raymond Chester for 21 yards and Fred Biletnikoff for 11 yards. Then he passed 22 yards to Biletnikoff for a touchdown.

The Raiders opened the third quarter by driving 69 yards to a first down at the Miami 2. But then Smith fumbled again, and Jake Scott recovered for Miami at the 10. Shortly after that, cornerback Willie Brown intercepted Griese's pass and returned it 50 yards for a touchdown and a 14-7 Raiders lead.

Midway through the fourth quarter, on third and 12 at the 18, Lamonica guessed that flanker Rod Sherman would receive man-to-man coverage. He was right, and the result was an 82-yard touchdown pass that put the game away for the Raiders.

December 27, at Oakland

Miami	Starters, Offense	Oakland
Paul Warfield	WR	Warren Wells
Doug Crusan	LT	Art Shell
Bob Kuechenberg	LG	Gene Upshaw
Carl Mauck	C	Jim Otto
Larry Little	RG	Jim Harvey
Norm Evans	RT	Harry Schuh
Marv Fleming	TE	Raymond Chester
Howard Twilley	WR	Fred Biletnikoff
Bob Griese	QB	Daryle Lamonica
Larry Csonka	RB	Hewritt Dixon
Jim Kiick	RB	Charlie Smith
	Starters, Defense	
Jim Riley	LE	Tony Cline
Frank Cornish	LT	Carleton Oats
John Richardson	RT	Tom Keating
Bill Stanfill	RE	Ben Davidson
Doug Swift	LLB	Bill Laskey
Nick Buoniconti	MLB	Dan Conners
Mike Kolen	RLB	Gus Otto
Curtis Johnson	LCB	Kent McCloughan
Lloyd Mumphord	RCB	Willie Brown
Jake Scott	SS	George Atkinson
Dick Anderson	FS	Dave Grayson

Miami	0	7	0	7	—	14
Oakland	0	7	7	7	—	21

Mia —Warfield 16 pass from Griese (Yepremian kick)
Oak—Biletnikoff 22 pass from Lamonica (Blanda kick)
Oak—Brown 50 interception return (Blanda kick)
Oak—Sherman 82 pass from Lamonica (Blanda kick)
Mia —W. Richardson 7 pass from Griese (Yepremian kick)
Attendance—54,401

TEAM STATISTICS	Mia	Oak
First downs	16	12
Rushing	5	5
Passing	9	7
By penalty	2	0
Total yardage	242	307
Net rushing yardage	118	120
Net passing yardage	124	187
Passes att.-comp.-had int.	27-13-1	16-8-0

RUSHING
Miami—Kiick, 14 for 64; Morris, 8 for 29; Csonka, 10 for 23; Griese, 1 for 2.
Oakland—Hubbard, 18 for 58; Smith, 9 for 37; Dixon, 8 for 31; Banaszak, 1 for −6.
PASSING
Miami—Griese, 13 of 27 for 155, 2 TDs, 1 int.
Oakland—Lamonica, 8 of 16 for 187, 2 TDs.
RECEIVING
Miami—Warfield, 4 for 62, 1 TD; Kiick, 4 for 34; W. Richardson, 2 for 30, 1 TD; Morris, 2 for 15; Twilley, 1 for 14.
Oakland—Biletnikoff, 3 for 40, 1 TD, Chester, 2 for 47; Sherman, 1 for 82, 1 TD; Smith, 1 for 9; Dixon, 1 for 3.

1970 NFC

DALLAS 5, DETROIT 0

Dallas pounded out 209 yards on the ground against the NFL's best rushing defense, including 135 by rookie Duane Thomas, but it took a field goal and a safety to produce a 5-0 victory over Detroit.

Sensing that it would be tough to run against the Lions, Dallas head coach Tom Landry decided to pass frequently. But the strategy didn't work, as Craig Morton was able to complete only three passes in the first half. The only score came midway through the first quarter when Detroit quarterback Greg Landry fumbled near midfield, with Charlie Waters of the Cowboys returning it to the Detroit 46. When the Cowboys stalled at the 19, Mike Clark kicked a 26-yard field goal for a 3-0 lead.

The Lions, meanwhile, were unable to move except for one drive that carried to the Dallas 29. On third and one, Altie Taylor fumbled, with Waters again recovering for Dallas.

Because the Cowboys had gained 61 yards in the first half without much emphasis on the run, Landry switched to a power game in the second half. Early in the fourth quarter, Dallas started a drive of 76 yards in 15 plays and took almost eight minutes off the clock. But, on fourth and goal at the one-foot line, Thomas stumbled over his blocker, forcing Dallas to give up the ball. Three plays later, George Andrie sacked Landry for a safety and a 5-0 lead.

With two minutes left in the game, Bill Munson replaced Landry. Munson drove the Lions to the Dallas 29. On third and 10, his pass for tight end Charlie Sanders was high and cornerback Mel Renfro made a game-saving interception.

December 26, at Dallas

Detroit	Starters, Offense	Dallas
Earl McCullouch	WR	Bob Hayes
Roger Shoals	LT	Ralph Neely
Chuck Walton	LG	John Niland
Ed Flanagan	C	Dave Manders
Frank Gallagher	RG	Blaine Nye
Rockne (Rocky) Freitas	RT	Rayfield Wright
Charlie Sanders	TE	Pettis Norman
Larry Walton	WR	Reggie Rucker
Greg Landry	QB	Craig Morton
Altie Taylor	RB	Walt Garrison
Mel Farr	RB	Duane Thomas
	Starters, Defense	
Jim Mitchell	LE	Larry Cole
Alex Karras	LT	Jethro Pugh
Jerry Rush	RT	Bob Lilly
Larry Hand	RE	George Andrie
Paul Naumoff	LLB	Dave Edwards
Mike Lucci	MLB	Lee Roy Jordan
Wayne Walker	RLB	Chuck Howley
Lem Barney	LCB	Herb Adderley
Dick LeBeau	RCB	Mel Renfro
Mike Weger	SS	Cornell Green
Tom Vaughn	FS	Charlie Waters

Detroit	0	0	0	0	—	0
Dallas	3	0	0	2	—	5

Dall— FG Clark 26
Dall— Safety, Andrie tackled Landry in end zone
Attendance—73,167

TEAM STATISTICS	Det	Dall
First downs	7	14
Rushing	2	11
Passing	5	3
By penalty	0	0
Total yardage	156	231
Net rushing yardage	76	209
Net passing yardage	80	22
Passes att.-comp.-had int.	20-7-1	18-4-1

RUSHING
Detroit—Farr, 12 for 31; Taylor, 9 for 16; Landry, 3 for 15; Owens, 2 for 9; Walton, 1 for 5.
Dallas—Thomas, 30 for 135; Garrison, 17 for 72; Morton, 3 for 2.
PASSING
Detroit—Landry, 5 of 12 for 48; Munson, 2 of 8 for 44, 1 int.
Dallas—Morton, 4 of 18 for 38, 1 int.
RECEIVING
Detroit—Walton, 3 for 39; Taylor, 2 for 7; McCullouch, 1 for 39; Owens, 1 for 7.
Dallas—Garrison, 2 for 8; Hayes, 1 for 20; Norman, 1 for 10.

1970 NFC

SAN FRANCISCO 17, MINNESOTA 14

Nine-degree temperatures and winds of up to 15 miles per hour contributed to a classic battle for field position between two teams that knew one mistake could kill them. The difference was the play of San Francisco quarterback John Brodie, who ran for one touchdown and passed for another as the 49ers beat the Vikings 17-14.

Minnesota scored quickly to take a 7-0 lead. After driving deep into San Francisco territory, Gary Cuozzo's pass for Clint Jones was intercepted by linebacker Jim Sniadecki at the 6. On the 49ers' second play, Ken Willard fumbled, the ball popped into the hands of safety Paul Krause, and Krause raced 22 yards for a Minnesota touchdown.

The 49ers tied it late in the period. A 30-yard punt return by Bruce Taylor put San Francisco in good field position. Two plays later, Brodie threw a 24-yard touchdown pass to Dick Witcher. With less than four minutes left in the first half, Minnesota's Dave Osborn fumbled, and the 49ers converted it into Bruce Gossett's 40-yard field goal for a 10-7 lead.

Midway through the fourth quarter, the 49ers' Steve Spurrier punted to the Minnesota 1. When the Vikings couldn't move and punted, Taylor returned it 23 yards to the Minnesota 14. Five plays later, on third and goal, Brodie scored on a quarterback sneak with 1:20 left. The Vikings' final touchdown came with one second remaining.

December 27, at Bloomington

San Francisco	Starters, Offense	Minnesota
Gene Washington	WR	Gene Washington
Len Rohde	LT	Grady Alderman
Randy Beisler	LG	Jim Vellone
Forrest Blue	C	Mick Tingelhoff
Woody Peoples	RG	Milt Sunde
Cas Banaszek	RT	Ron Yary
Bob Windsor	TE	John Beasley
Dick Witcher	WR	John Henderson
John Brodie	QB	Gary Cuozzo
Ken Willard	RB	Clint Jones
Bill Tucker	RB	Dave Osborn
	Starters, Defense	
Tommy Hart	LE	Carl Eller
Charlie Krueger	LT	Gary Larsen
Roland Lakes	RT	Alan Page
Bill Belk	RE	Jim Marshall
Dave Wilcox	LLB	Roy Winston
Frank Nunley	MLB	Lonnie Warwick
Jim Sniadecki	RLB	Wally Hilgenberg
Jimmy Johnson	LCB	Bobby Bryant
Bruce Taylor	RCB	Ed Sharockman
Roosevelt Taylor	SS-LS	Karl Kassulke
Mel Phillips	FS-RS	Paul Krause

San Francisco	7	3	0	7	—	17
Minnesota	7	0	0	7	—	14

Minn—Krause 22 fumble return (Cox kick)
SF —Witcher 24 pass from Brodie (Gossett kick)
SF —FG Gossett 40
SF —Brodie 1 run (Gossett kick)
Minn—Washington 24 pass from Cuozzo (Cox kick)
Attendance—45,103

TEAM STATISTICS	SF	Minn
First downs	14	14
Rushing	5	7
Passing	8	6
By penalty	1	1
Total yardage	289	241
Net rushing yardage	96	117
Net passing yardage	193	124
Passes att.-comp.-had int.	32-16-0	27-9-2

RUSHING
San Francisco—Willard, 27 for 85; Tucker, 7 for 5; Brodie, 2 for 4, 1 TD; Kwalick, 1 for 2; Cunningham, 1 for 0.
Minnesota—Jones, 15 for 60; Osborn, 12 for 41; Cuozzo, 1 for 11; Brown, 2 for 5.
PASSING
San Francisco—Brodie, 16 of 32 for 201, 1 TD.
Minnesota—Cuozzo, 9 of 27 for 146, 1 TD, 2 int.
RECEIVING
San Francisco—Tucker, 6 for 48; Witcher, 4 for 45, 1 TD; Kwalick, 3 for 45; Washington, 2 for 45; Willard, 1 for 18.
Minnesota—Henderson, 5 for 80; Grim, 2 for 37; Washington, 1 for 24, 1 TD; Jones, 1 for 5.

1971 AFC

MIAMI 27, KANSAS CITY 24

Garo Yepremian kicked a 37-yard field goal after 7:40 of the sixth quarter to give Miami a 27-24 victory over Kansas City in the longest professional football game ever played. Until the kick, the game's hero had been Chiefs running back Ed Podolak, who gained 350 all-purpose yards, 85 rushing, 110 receiving, and 155 on kick returns.

The Chiefs scored the first two times they had the ball on a field goal by Jan Stenerud and Len Dawson's seven-yard pass to Podolak.

The Dolphins came right back, driving 80 yards to a one-yard run by Larry Csonka. Yepremian kicked a 14-yard field goal to knot the score at halftime.

The Chiefs drove 75 yards for a touchdown with the second-half kickoff, but the Dolphins matched that, going 71 yards to tie the score. The Chiefs then went 91 yards to Podolak's touchdown run. Then, the Dolphins drove 71 yards to a five-yard touchdown pass from Bob Griese to Marv Fleming.

Podolak returned the kickoff to the Miami 22 with 1:25 left, but Stenerud missed a field goal and the game went into overtime. In the fifth quarter, Stenerud had a field-goal attempt blocked, while Yepremian missed one. In the sixth period, Yepremian got another chance, and his aim was true.

December 25, at Kansas City

Miami	Starters, Offense	Kansas City
Paul Warfield	WR	Elmo Wright
Doug Crusan	LT	Jim Tyrer
Bob Kuechenberg	LG	Ed Budde
Bob DeMarco	C	Jack Rudnay
Larry Little	RG	Mo Moorman
Norm Evans	RT	Dave Hill
Marv Fleming	TE	Morris Stroud
Howard Twilley	WR	Otis Taylor
Bob Griese	QB	Len Dawson
Larry Csonka	RB	Wendell Hayes
Jim Kiick	RB	Ed Podolak
	Starters, Defense	
Jim Riley	LE	Marvin Upshaw
Manny Fernandez	LT	Curley Culp
Bob Heinz	RT	Buck Buchanan
Bill Stanfill	RE	Aaron Brown
Doug Swift	LLB	Bobby Bell
Nick Buoniconti	MLB	Willie Lanier
Bob Matheson	RLB	Jim Lynch
Tim Foley	LCB	Jim Marsalis
Curtis Johnson	RCB	Emmitt Thomas
Jake Scott	SS	Jim Kearney
Dick Anderson	FS	Johnny Robinson

Miami	0	10	7	7	0	3	—	27
Kansas City	10	0	7	7	0	0	—	24

KC — FG Stenerud 24
KC — Podolak 7 pass from Dawson (Stenerud kick)
Mia— Csonka 1 run (Yepremian kick)
Mia— FG Yepremian 14
KC — Otis 1 run (Stenerud kick)
Mia— Kiick 1 run (Yepremian kick)
KC — Podolak 3 run (Stenerud kick)
Mia— Fleming 5 pass from Griese (Yepremian kick)
Mia— FG Yepremian 37
Attendance—50,374

TEAM STATISTICS	Mia	KC
First downs	22	23
Rushing	6	13
Passing	14	10
By penalty	2	0
Total yardage	407	451
Net rushing yardage	144	213
Net passing yardage	263	238
Passes att.-comp.-had int.	35-20-2	26-18-2

RUSHING
Miami—Csonka, 24 for 86, 1 TD; Kiick, 15 for 56, 1 TD; Griese, 2 for 9; Warfield, 2 for −7.
Kansas City—Hayes, 22 for 100; Podolak, 17 for 85, 1 TD; Wright, 2 for 15; Otis, 3 for 13, 1 TD.
PASSING
Miami—Griese, 20 of 35 for 263, 1 TD, 2 int.
Kansas City—Dawson, 18 of 26 for 246, 1 TD, 2 int.
RECEIVING
Miami—Warfield, 7 for 140; Twilley, 5 for 58; Fleming, 4 for 37, 1 TD; Kiick, 3 for 24; Mandich, 1 for 4.
Kansas City—Podolak, 8 for 110, 1 TD; Wright, 3 for 104; Taylor, 3 for 12; Hayes, 3 for 6; Frazier, 1 for 14.

1971 AFC

BALTIMORE 20, CLEVELAND 3

Baltimore's number-one ranked defense held Cleveland's running game to 69 yards, and the Browns couldn't pass consistently against the Colts' zone defense. As a result, Baltimore jumped to a 14-0 halftime lead, then coasted to a 20-3 victory.

Cleveland had its chances early. Hoping to get a quick lead, the Browns went to the air on the fourth play of the game. Fair Hooker caught a pass from Bill Nelsen, which he carried 39 yards to the Colts' 12. There, however, cornerback Rex Kern stole the ball away. The next time the Browns had the ball, they drove to the Baltimore 4, but Bubba Smith blocked Don Cockroft's field-goal attempt.

The Colts took over at their 8, and moved 92 yards to a touchdown in 17 plays. Don Nottingham, who was starting in place of injured Norm Bulaich, scored from the 1. Midway through the second quarter, Baltimore scored again. Safety Rick Volk intercepted Nelsen's pass intended for Hooker and returned it 37 yards to the Cleveland 15. After a pass-interference penalty put the ball at the 7, Nottingham blasted seven yards behind right guard John Williams for the touchdown that made it 14-0.

The Browns' only threat of the second half ended with Cockroft's 14-yard field goal, but the Colts responded by driving down the field to a 42-yard field goal by Jim O'Brien. O'Brien kicked another field goal for the final points after Baltimore drove to the Cleveland 8 in the fourth quarter.

December 26, at Cleveland

Baltimore	Starters, Offense	Cleveland
Eddie Hinton	WR	Fair Hooker
Bob Vogel	LT	Doug Dieken
Glenn Ressler	LG	John Demarie
Bill Curry	C	Jim Copeland
John Williams	RG	Gene Hickerson
Dan Sullivan	RT	Bob McKay
Tom Mitchell	TE	Milt Morin
Ray Perkins	WR	Frank Pitts
Johnny Unitas	QB	Bill Nelsen
Don Nottingham	RB	Bo Scott
Tom Matte	RB	Leroy Kelly
	Starters, Defense	
Bubba Smith	LE	Ron Snidow
Billy Newsome	LT	Walter Johnson
Fred Miller	RT	Jerry Sherk
Roy Hilton	RE	Jack Gregory
Ray May	LLB	John Garlington
Mike Curtis	MLB	Jim Houston
Ted Hendricks	RLB	Bill Andrews
Charlie Stukes	LCB	Clarence Scott
Rex Kern	RCB	Ben Davis
Jerry Logan	SS	Walt Sumner
Rick Volk	FS	Mike Howell

Baltimore	0	14	3	3	—	20
Cleveland	0	0	3	0	—	3

Balt—Nottingham 1 run (O'Brien kick)
Balt—Nottingham 7 run (O'Brien kick)
Cle—FG Cockroft 14
Balt—FG O'Brien 42
Balt—FG O'Brien 15
Attendance—74,082

TEAM STATISTICS	Balt	Cle
First downs	16	11
Rushing	7	5
Passing	8	5
By penalty	1	1
Total yardage	271	165
Net rushing yardage	128	69
Net passing yardage	143	96
Passes att.-comp.-had int.	21-13-1	27-12-3

RUSHING

Baltimore—Nottingham, 23 for 92, 2 TDs; Matte, 16 for 26; McCauley, 3 for 9; Nowatzke, 1 for 1.
Cleveland—Kelly, 14 for 49; B. Scott, 8 for 25; Nelsen, 2 for −5.

PASSING

Baltimore—Unitas, 13 of 21 for 143, 1 int.
Cleveland—Nelsen, 9 of 21 for 104, 3 int.; Phipps, 3 of 6 for 27.

RECEIVING

Baltimore—Mitchell, 5 for 73; Matte, 3 for 22; Hinton, 2 for 30; Perkins, 1 for 10; Nottingham, 1 for 5; Havrilak, 1 for 3.
Cleveland—Scott, 5 for 41; Kelly, 4 for 24; Hooker, 1 for 39; Morin, 1 for 16; Glass, 1 for 11.

1971 NFC

DALLAS 20, MINNESOTA 12

Safety Cliff Harris intercepted a pass by Bob Lee to set up a 13-yard touchdown run by Duane Thomas that gave the Dallas Cowboys a 13-3 lead in the third quarter en route to a 20-12 victory over the Minnesota Vikings.

Both teams played conservative football in the first half, and the result was a 6-3 edge for the Cowboys, who scored one field goal after Dave Osborn fumbled at the Minnesota 36 and another after Chuck Howley returned an interception of a pass by Lee to the Minnesota 37.

On the second play of the third quarter, Lee threw a pass intended for Bob Grim, but Harris intercepted at the Minnesota 43 and returned it 30 yards. On first down, Thomas dashed right up the middle for a touchdown.

Dallas put the game away late in the third period. The Cowboys took over at their own 48 after a 24-yard punt return by Charlie Waters. On third and 15, Roger Staubach hit Lance Alworth for 30 yards and a critical first down. Five plays later, Staubach threw a nine-yard touchdown pass to Bob Hayes, who was alone in the corner of the end zone.

The Vikings scored nine points in the fourth quarter on a safety and a touchdown pass from Lee to tight end Stu Voigt.

December 25, at Bloomington

Dallas	Starters, Offense	Minnesota
Bob Hayes	WR	Gene Washington
Tony Liscio	LT	Grady Alderman
John Niland	LG	Ed White
Dave Manders	C	Mick Tingelhoff
Blaine Nye	RG	Milt Sunde
Rayfield Wright	RT	Ron Yary
Mike Ditka	TE	Bob Brown
Lance Alworth	WR	Bob Grim
Roger Staubach	QB	Bob Lee
Calvin Hill	RB	Clint Jones
Duane Thomas	RB	Dave Osborn
	Starters, Defense	
Larry Cole	LE	Carl Eller
Jethro Pugh	LT	Gary Larsen
Bob Lilly	RT	Alan Page
George Andrie	RE	Jim Marshall
Dave Edwards	LLB	Carl Winfrey
Lee Roy Jordan	MLB	Lonnie Warwick
Chuck Howley	RLB	Wally Hilgenberg
Herb Adderley	LCB	Bobby Bryant
Mel Renfro	RCB	Ed Sharockman
Cornell Green	SS-LS	Charlie West
Cliff Harris	FS-RS	Paul Krause

Dallas	3	3	14	0	—	20
Minnesota	0	3	0	9	—	12

Dall—FG Clark 26
Minn—FG Cox 27
Dall—FG Clark 44
Dall—D. Thomas 13 run (Clark kick)
Dall—Hayes 9 pass from Staubach (Clark kick)
Minn—Safety, Page tackled Staubach in end zone
Minn—Voigt 6 pass from Cuozzo (Cox kick)
Attendance—49,100

TEAM STATISTICS	Dall	Minn
First downs	10	17
Rushing	5	5
Passing	5	12
By penalty	0	0
Total yardage	183	311
Net rushing yardage	98	101
Net passing yardage	85	210
Passes att.-comp.-had int.	14-10-0	38-19-4

RUSHING

Dallas—D. Thomas, 21 for 66, 1 TD; Hill, 14 for 28; Garrison, 2 for 2; Staubach, 2 for 2.
Minnesota—Jones, 15 for 52; Lee, 3 for 28; Osborn, 6 for 13; Lindsey, 1 for 6; Grim, 1 for 2.

PASSING

Dallas—Staubach, 10 of 14 for 99, 1 TD.
Minnesota—Cuozzo, 12 of 22 for 124, 1 TD, 2 int.; Lee, 7 of 16 for 86, 2 int.

RECEIVING

Dallas—Hayes, 3 for 31, 1 TD; Alworth, 2 for 33; Ditka, 2 for 18; Hill, 2 for 14; D. Thomas, 1 for 3.
Minnesota—Washington, 5 for 70; Grim, 4 for 74; Voigt, 4 for 46, 1 TD; Reed, 4 for −3; Lindsey, 1 for 25; White, 1 for −2.

1971 NFC

SAN FRANCISCO 24, WASHINGTON 20

San Francisco came up with the big plays on offense and defense, and emerged with a 24-20 victory over Washington.

The Redskins scored first following Jon Jaqua's block and recovery of Steve Spurrier's punt at the San Francisco 28. Six plays later, Billy Kilmer passed to tight end Jerry Smith for a touchdown. With the score 10-3 in the final minute of the half, Ted Vactor returned Spurrier's punt 47 yards to the San Francisco 12. But the 49ers held, and Johnny Fuller blocked Curt Knight's field-goal attempt.

The Redskins opened the third quarter as if they were going to put the game away, driving to the 49ers' 11. But, on fourth and inches, linebacker Frank Nunley dropped Larry Brown for a two-yard loss. Three plays later, John Brodie threw a 78-yard touchdown pass to Gene Washington. On the fourth play after the kickoff, Roosevelt Taylor intercepted a pass by Kilmer, setting up Brodie's two-yard touchdown pass to tight end Bob Windsor.

With the score 17-13 late in the fourth quarter, Washington punter Mike Bragg had a poor snap from center roll through his legs. San Francisco defensive tackle Bob Hoskins recovered in the end zone for a touchdown that clinched the game.

December 26, at San Francisco

Washington	Starters, Offense	San Francisco
Clifton McNeil	WR	Dick Witcher
Jim Snowden	LT	Len Rohde
Ray Schoenke	LG	Randy Beisler
Len Hauss	C	Forrest Blue
John Wilbur	RG	Woody Peoples
Walt Rock	RT	Cas Banaszek
Jerry Smith	TE	Ted Kwalick
Roy Jefferson	WR	Gene Washington
Billy Kilmer	QB	John Brodie
Charley Harraway	RB	Vic Washington
Larry Brown	RB	Ken Willard
	Starters, Defense	
Ron McDole	LE	Tommy Hart
Manny Sistrunk	LT	Charlie Krueger
Diron Talbert	RT	Earl Edwards
Verlon Biggs	RE	Cedrick Hardman
Jack Pardee	LLB	Dave Wilcox
Myron Pottios	MLB	Frank Nunley
Chris Hamburger	RLB	Skip Vanderbundt
Pat Fischer	LCB	Jimmy Johnson
Mike Bass	RCB	Bruce Taylor
Richie Petitbon	SS	Mel Phillips
Brig Owens	FS	Roosevelt Taylor

Washington	7	3	3	7	—	20
San Francisco	0	3	14	7	—	24

Wash—Smith 5 pass from Kilmer (Knight kick)
SF—FG Gossett 23
SF—FG Knight 40
SF—G. Washington 78 pass from Brodie (Gossett kick)
SF—Windsor 2 pass from Brodie (Gossett kick)
Wash—FG Knight 36
SF—Hoskins, fumble recovery in end zone (Gossett kick)
Wash—Brown 16 pass from Kilmer (Knight kick)
Attendance—45,364

TEAM STATISTICS	Wash	SF
First downs	13	11
Rushing	6	2
Passing	5	9
By penalty	2	0
Total yardage	192	285
Net rushing yardage	99	112
Net passing yardage	93	173
Passes att.-comp.-had int.	27-11-1	19-10-0

RUSHING

Washington—Brown, 27 for 84; Harraway, 10 for 28; Kilmer, 1 for 0; Jefferson, 1 for −13.
San Francisco—V. Washington, 16 for 59; Willard, 19 for 46; Schreiber, 4 for 7.

PASSING

Washington—Kilmer, 11 of 27 for 106, 2 TDs, 1 int.
San Francisco—Brodie, 10 of 19 for 176, 2 TDs.

RECEIVING

Washington—Brown, 6 for 62, 1 TD; Smith, 3 for 32, 1 TD; Mason, 1 for 8; Harraway, 1 for 4.
San Francisco—Kwalick, 3 for 26; Witcher, 2 for 28; G. Washington, 1 for 78, 1 TD; Schreiber, 1 for 22; V. Washington, 1 for 10; Willard, 1 for 10; Windsor, 1 for 2, 1 TD.

1972 AFC

PITTSBURGH 13, OAKLAND 7

Pittsburgh came from behind to defeat Oakland 13-7 when Terry Bradshaw's scrambling fourth-down pass for John (Frenchy) Fuqua ricocheted off Oakland's Jack Tatum and was caught at the Raiders' 42-yard line by Franco Harris, who completed the 60-yard touchdown play with five seconds left. Harris's catch at his shoelaces became known at the Immaculate Reception.

For 56 minutes, the game was a brutal defensive struggle. The key play in the scoreless first half was Tatum's tackle of Fuqua for a gain of only one yard on a fourth-and-two situation at the Oakland 31.

The Steelers went ahead on the first possession of the third quarter. Bradshaw drove them 55 yards, setting up Roy Gerela's 18-yard field goal. In the fourth quarter, Gerela kicked a 29-yarder after Ken Stabler, who had replaced quarterback Daryle Lamonica, lost a fumble at the Raiders' 35.

With less than four minutes to go, the Raiders started their best drive of the day, and kept it alive with a conversion on a fourth-and-one play. With a first down at the Pittsburgh 30, Stabler read a Steelers blitz, circled left end, and ran untouched into the end zone for a 7-6 lead with 1:13 left.

After the kickoff, two passes by Bradshaw put the ball on the 40. Three consecutive incomplete passes left Bradshaw with a fourth and 10, and with history staring him in the face.

December 23, at Pittsburgh

Oakland	**Starters, Offense**	**Pittsburgh**
Mike Siani	WR	Al Young
Art Shell	LT	Jon Kolb
Gene Upshaw	LG	Sam Davis
Jim Otto	C	Ray Mansfield
George Buehler	RG	Bruce Van Dyke
Bob Brown	RT	Gerry Mullins
Raymond Chester	TE	John McMakin
Fred Biletnikoff	WR	Ron Shanklin
Daryle Lamonica	QB	Terry Bradshaw
Marv Hubbard	RB	John (Frenchy) Fuqua
Charlie Smith	RB	Franco Harris
	Starters, Defense	
Tony Cline	LE	L.C. Greenwood
Otis Sistrunk	LT	Joe Greene
Art Thoms	RT	Ben McGee
Horace Jones	RE	Dwight White
Phil Villapiano	LLB	Jack Ham
Dan Conners	MLB	Henry Davis
Gerald Irons	RLB	Andy Russell
Nemiah Wilson	LCB	John Rowser
Willie Brown	RCB	Mel Blount
George Atkinson	SS	Glen Edwards
Jack Tatum	FS	Mike Wagner

Oakland	0	0	0	7	—	7
Pittsburgh	0	0	3	10	—	13

Pitt —FG Gerela 18
Pitt —FG Gerela 29
Oak—Stabler 30 run (Blanda kick)
Pitt —Harris 60 pass from Bradshaw (Gerela kick)
Attendance—50,327

TEAM STATISTICS	**Oak**	**Pitt**
First downs	13	13
Rushing	9	7
Passing	4	6
By penalty	0	0
Total yardage	216	252
Net rushing yardage	138	108
Net passing yardage	78	144
Passes att.-comp.-had int.	30-12-2	25-11-1

RUSHING
Oakland—Smith, 14 for 57; Hubbard, 14 for 44; Stabler, 1 for 30, 1 TD; Davis, 2 for 7.
Pittsburgh—Harris, 18 for 64; Fuqua, 16 for 25; Bradshaw, 2 for 19.
PASSING
Oakland—Stabler, 6 of 12 for 57; Lamonica, 6 of 18 for 45, 2 int.
Pittsburgh—Bradshaw, 11 of 25 for 175, 1 TD, 1 int.
RECEIVING
Oakland—Chester, 3 for 40; Biletnikoff, 3 for 28; Smith, 2 for 8; Banaszak, 1 for 12; Siani, 1 for 7; J. Otto, 1 for 5; Hubbard, 1 for 2.
Pittsburgh—Harris, 5 for 96, 1 TD; Shanklin, 3 for 55; Fuqua, 1 for 11; McMakin, 1 for 9; Young, 1 for 4.

1972 AFC

MIAMI 20, CLEVELAND 14

Midway through the fourth quarter, Miami marched 80 yards to Jim Kiick's eight-yard touchdown run that gave the Dolphins a 20-14 victory over the Browns. The two big plays of the winning drive were passes of 15 and 35 yards from Earl Morrall to Paul Warfield. Two plays after the latter, linebacker Bill Andrews interfered with Warfield, giving the Dolphins a first down at the 8 and setting up Kiick's run.

The Dolphins jumped to a 10-0 lead in the first quarter. Charlie Babb blocked a punt by Don Cockroft at the 17, picked it up at the 5, and ran in for a touchdown. The next time the Dolphins had the ball, they drove 51 yards to set up Garo Yepremian's 40-yard field goal.

With the score still 10-0 in the third quarter, the Browns got back in the game. Thom Darden returned a punt 38 yards to the Miami 44, and Mike Phipps, who was intercepted five times, passed the Browns to the 5. Phipps scored from there on a run around right end.

The Dolphins increased their lead to 13-7 in the first two minutes of the final period, before the Browns drove 90 yards to take their only lead. The key play of the drive was Dick Anderson's interception of a pass by Phipps. But Anderson fumbled the ball, which was recovered by Cleveland's Fair Hooker for a first down. Two plays later, Phipps hit Hooker with a 27-yard touchdown pass.

December 24, at Miami

Cleveland	**Starters, Offense**	**Miami**
Fair Hooker	WR	Paul Warfield
Doug Dieken	LT	Wayne Moore
Gene Hickerson	LG	Bob Kuechenberg
Bob DeMarco	C	Jim Langer
John Demarie	RG	Larry Little
Bob McKay	RT	Norm Evans
Milt Morin	TE	Marv Fleming
Frank Pitts	WR	Howard Twilley
Mike Phipps	QB	Bob Griese
Bo Scott	RB	Larry Csonka
Leroy Kelly	RB	Jim Kiick
	Starters, Defense	
Nick Roman	LE	Vern Den Herder
Walter Johnson	LT	Manny Fernandez
Jerry Sherk	RT	Bob Heinz
Bob Briggs	RE	Bill Stanfill
Charlie Hall	LLB	Doug Swift
Dale Lindsey	MLB	Nick Buoniconti
Bill Andrews	RLB	Mike Kolen
Clarence Scott	LCB	Tom Foley
Ben Davis	RCB	Curtis Johnson
Thom Darden	SS	Jake Scott
Walt Sumner	FS	Dick Anderson

Cleveland	0	0	7	7	—	14
Miami	10	0	0	10	—	20

Mia—Babb 5 blocked punt return (Yepremian kick)
Mia—FG Yepremian 40
Cle—Phipps 5 run (Cockroft kick)
Mia—FG Yepremian 46
Cle—Hooker 27 pass from Phipps (Cockroft kick)
Mia—Kiick 8 run (Yepremian kick)
Attendance—80,010

TEAM STATISTICS	**Cle**	**Mia**
First downs	15	17
Rushing	9	11
Passing	6	4
By penalty	0	2
Total yardage	283	272
Net rushing yardage	165	198
Net passing yardage	118	74
Passes att.-comp.-had int.	23-9-5	13-6-0

RUSHING
Cleveland—B. Scott, 16 for 94; Phipps, 8 for 47, 1 TD; Brown, 4 for 13; Kelly, 4 for 11.
Miami—Morris, 15 for 72; Kiick, 14 for 50, 1 TD; Warfield, 2 for 41; Csonka, 12 for 32; Morrall, 4 for 3.
PASSING
Cleveland—Phipps, 9 of 23 for 131, 1 TD, 5 int.
Miami—Morrall, 6 of 13 for 88.
RECEIVING
Cleveland—B. Scott, 4 for 30; Hooker, 3 for 53, 1 TD; Kelly, 1 for 27; Morin, 1 for 21.
Miami—Twilley, 3 for 33; Warfield, 2 for 50; Kiick, 1 for 5.

1972 NFC

DALLAS 30, SAN FRANCISCO 28

Roger Staubach came off the bench late in the third quarter to lead the Cowboys to 17 points as Dallas overcame a 28-13 fourth-quarter deficit to defeat the 49ers 30-28.

San Francisco didn't waste time building a seemingly insurmountable lead. Vic Washington returned the game's opening kickoff 97 yards for a touchdown. With the score 7-3 at the end of the first quarter, Craig Morton fumbled at the Dallas 15, and the 49ers turned it into a one-yard touchdown run by Larry Schreiber. Schreiber scored again after a pass by Morton was intercepted by Skip Vanderbundt.

The Cowboys scored twice to make it 21-13 at halftime, but the 49ers increased their lead to 15 in the third quarter when Schreiber scored again.

Enter Staubach. First, he led the Cowboys 60 yards to a field goal. With less than two minutes left, he drove them 55 yards, passing 20 yards to Billy Parks for a touchdown. After Mel Renfro recovered an onside kick, Staubach ran for 21 yards, passed 19 yards to Parks, and passed to Ron Sellers for the winning score with 52 seconds left.

December 23, at San Francisco

Dallas	**Starters, Offense**	**San Francisco**
Ron Sellers	WR	Gene Washington
Ralph Neely	LT	Len Rohde
John Niland	LG	Randy Beisler
Dave Manders	C	Forrest Blue
Blaine Nye	RG	Woody Peoples
Rayfield Wright	RT	Cas Banaszek
Mike Ditka	TE	Ted Kwalick
Lance Alworth	WR	Preston Riley
Craig Morton	QB	John Brodie
Walt Garrison	RB	Larry Schreiber
Calvin Hill	RB	Vic Washington
	Starters, Defense	
Larry Cole	LE	Tommy Hart
Jethro Pugh	LT	Charlie Krueger
Bob Lilly	RT	Earl Edwards
Pat Toomay	RE	Cedrick Hardman
Dave Edwards	LLB	Dave Wilcox
Lee Roy Jordan	MLB	Ed Beard
D.D. Lewis	RLB	Skip Vanderbundt
Charlie Waters	LCB	Jimmy Johnson
Mel Renfro	RCB	Bruce Taylor
Cornell Green	SS	Windlan Hall
Cliff Harris	FS	Mike Simpson

Dallas	3	10	0	17	—	30
San Francisco	7	14	7	0	—	28

SF —V. Washington 97 kickoff return (Gossett kick)
Dall—FG Fritsch 37
SF —Schreiber 1 run (Gossett kick)
SF —Schreiber 1 run (Gossett kick)
Dall—FG Fritsch 45
Dall—Alworth 28 pass from Morton (Fritsch kick)
SF —Schreiber 1 run (Gossett kick)
Dall—FG Fritsch 27
Dall—Parks 20 pass from Staubach (Fritsch kick)
Dall—Sellers 10 pass from Staubach (Fritsch kick)
Attendance—61,214

TEAM STATISTICS	**Dall**	**SF**
First downs	22	13
Rushing	5	7
Passing	15	6
By penalty	2	0
Total yardage	402	255
Net rushing yardage	165	105
Net passing yardage	237	150
Passes att.-comp.-had int.	41-20-2	22-12-2

RUSHING
Dallas—Hill, 18 for 125; Staubach, 3 for 23; Garrison, 9 for 15; Morton, 1 for 2.
San Francisco—V. Washington, 10 for 56; Schreiber, 26 for 52, 3 TDs; Thomas, 1 for −3.
PASSING
Dallas—Staubach, 12 of 20 for 174, 2 TDs; Morton, 8 of 21 for 96, 1 TD.
San Francisco—Brodie, 12 of 22 for 150, 2 int.
RECEIVING
Dallas—Parks, 7 for 136, 1 TD; Garrison, 3 for 24; Alworth, 2 for 40, 1 TD; Sellers, 2 for 21, 1 TD; Montgomery, 2 for 19; Hayes, 1 for 13; Ditka, 1 for 9; Hill, 1 for 6; Truax, 1 for 2.
San Francisco—Riley, 4 for 41; G. Washington, 3 for 76; Schreiber, 3 for 20; V. Washington, 1 for 8; Kwalick, 1 for 5.

1972 NFC

WASHINGTON 16, GREEN BAY 3

A five-man defensive line helped Washington contain Green Bay's powerful running attack in the Redskins' 16-3 victory. Manny Sistrunk moved in over center on a line that limited Packers rookie running back John Brockington, who had gained 1,027 yards during the regular season, to 13 yards on nine carries.

After a scoreless first quarter, the Packers took a 3-0 lead when Chester Marcol capped a 60-yard drive with a 17-yard field goal with 5½ minutes left in the half. Then the Redskins struck suddenly. On second and five, Billy Kilmer sent Roy Jefferson deep down the middle for a 32-yard touchdown pass, despite the defensive efforts of Willie Buchanon. On Green Bay's next possession, Bill Brundige dropped Scott Hunter for an 11-yard loss at the Packers' 14. A short punt put the Redskins in position for a field goal with 33 seconds left in the half.

For most of the second half, Washington was content to play field-position football, with Mike Bragg keeping the Packers pinned deep in their own end of the field with a series of outstanding punts. At the beginning of the fourth quarter, the Redskins drove into Green Bay territory, where Curt Knight kicked a 35-yard field goal. The next time the Redskins had the ball, Knight added his third field goal of the day, from 46 yards. With time running out, Washington preserved its margin when Chris Hanburger intercepted Hunter's last pass of the day.

December 24, at Washington

Green Bay	**Starters, Offense**	**Washington**
Leland Glass	WR	Charley Taylor
Bill Hayhoe	LT	Terry Hermeling
Bill Lueck	LG	Paul Laaveg
Ken Bowman	C	Len Hauss
Malcolm Snider	RG	Ray Schoenke
Dick Himes	RT	Walt Rock
Len Garrett	TE	Mack Alston
Carroll Dale	WR	Roy Jefferson
Scott Hunter	QB	Billy Kilmer
John Brockington	RB	Charley Harraway
MacArthur Lane	RB	Larry Brown
	Starters, Defense	
Clarence Williams	LE	Ron McDole
Mike McCoy	LT	Bill Brundige
Bob Brown	RT	Diron Talbert
Alden Roche	RE	Verlon Biggs
Dave Robinson	LLB	Jack Pardee
Jim Carter	MLB	Myron Pottios
Fred Carr	RLB	Chris Hanburger
Willie Buchanon	LCB	Pat Fischer
Ken Ellis	RCB	Mike Bass
Al Matthews	SS	Brig Owens
Jim Hill	FS	Roosevelt Taylor

Green Bay	0	3	0	0	—	3
Washington	0	10	0	6	—	16

GB —FG Marcol 17
Wash—Jefferson 32 pass from Kilmer (Knight kick)
Wash—FG Knight 42
Wash—FG Knight 35
Wash—FG Knight 46
Attendance—53,140

TEAM STATISTICS	**GB**	**Wash**
First downs	10	13
Rushing	2	6
Passing	8	4
By penalty	0	3
Total yardage	211	232
Net rushing yardage	78	138
Net passing yardage	133	94
Passes att.-comp.-had int.	24-12-1	14-7-0

RUSHING
Green Bay—Lane, 14 for 56; Hunter, 2 for 13; Brockington, 13 for 9.
Washington—Brown, 25 for 101; Harraway, 10 for 34; Kilmer, 1 for 3.
PASSING
Green Bay—Hunter, 12 of 24 for 150, 1 int.
Washington—Kilmer, 7 of 14 for 100, 1 TD.
RECEIVING
Green Bay—Lane, 4 for 42; Dale, 2 for 28; Glass, 2 for 23; Brockington, 2 for 17; Staggers, 1 for 23; Garrett, 1 for 17.
Washington—Jefferson, 5 for 83, 1 TD; Taylor, 2 for 16.

1973 AFC

OAKLAND 33, PITTSBURGH 14

The Oakland Raiders were an irresistible force, controlling the ball and Pittsburgh in a 33-14 victory.

Although it's a hazard of conservative power football that uneven games on the field often stay close on the scoreboard, by early in the third quarter it was apparent that the game was a slow-motion rout, as the Raiders had driven 82, 60, 68, 57, 62, and 58 yards for scores.

The Raiders' first possession was their longest drive, 82 yards in 16 plays to a one-yard plunge off left tackle by Marv Hubbard. Early in the second quarter, they used more than six minutes on a drive to George Blanda's 25-yard field goal. A 20-yard punt return, followed by a 24-yard pass from Terry Bradshaw to Preston Pearson, put the Steelers in a position to make the game interesting at the half, which they did by scoring on Bradshaw's four-yard pass to Barry Pearson.

On their first two drives of the third quarter, the Raiders responded with two more field goals, building their lead to nine points. The knockout punch came in one swift motion. Willie Brown intercepted Bradshaw's pass and raced down the sideline 54 yards for a touchdown and a 23-7 lead.

December 22, at Oakland

Pittsburgh	**Starters, Offense**	**Oakland**
Frank Lewis	WR	Mike Siani
Jon Kolb	LT	Art Shell
Sam Davis	LG	Gene Upshaw
Ray Mansfield	C	Jim Otto
Bruce Van Dyke	RG	George Buehler
Glen Ray Hines	RT	John Vella
John McMakin	TE	Bob Moore
Barry Pearson	WR	Fred Biletnikoff
Terry Bradshaw	QB	Ken Stabler
Preston Pearson	RB	Marv Hubbard
Franco Harris	RB	Charlie Smith
	Starters, Defense	
L.C. Greenwood	LE	Tony Cline
Joe Greene	LT	Otis Sistrunk
Tom Keating	RT	Art Thoms
Dwight White	RE	Horace Jones
Jack Ham	LLB	Phil Villapiano
Henry Davis	MLB	Dan Conners
Andy Russell	RLB	Gerald Irons
John Rowser	LCB	Nemiah Wilson
Mel Blount	RCB	Willie Brown
Mike Wagner	SS	George Atkinson
Glen Edwards	FS	Jack Tatum

Pittsburgh	0	7	0	7	—	14
Oakland	7	3	13	10	—	33

Oak—Hubbard 1 run (Blanda kick)
Oak—FG Blanda 25
Pitt —B. Pearson 4 pass from Bradshaw (Gerela kick)
Oak—FG Blanda 31
Oak—FG Blanda 22
Oak—W. Brown 54 interception return (Blanda kick)
Oak—FG Blanda 10
Pitt —Lewis 26 pass from Bradshaw (Gerela kick)
Oak—Hubbard 1 run (Blanda kick)
Attendance—51,110

TEAM STATISTICS	**Pitt**	**Oak**
First downs	15	24
Rushing	2	14
Passing	10	8
By penalty	3	2
Total yardage	223	361
Net rushing yardage	65	232
Net passing yardage	167	129
Passes att.-comp.-had int.	25-12-3	17-14-0

RUSHING
Pittsburgh—Harris, 10 for 29; P. Pearson, 4 for 14; Fuqua, 3 for 13; Bradshaw, 3 for 9.
Oakland—Hubbard, 20 for 91, 2 TDs; C. Smith, 17 for 73; C. Davis, 12 for 48; Banaszak, 5 for 17; Moore, 1 for 3.
PASSING
Pittsburgh—Bradshaw, 12 of 25 for 167, 2 TDs, 3 int.
Oakland—Stabler, 14 of 17 for 142.
RECEIVING
Pittsburgh—Lewis, 4 for 70, 1 TD; Fuqua, 4 for 52; B. Pearson, 2 for 7, 1 TD; P. Pearson, 1 for 24; Williams, 1 for 14.
Oakland—Siani, 5 for 68; Moore, 3 for 26; C. Smith, 2 for 10; Hubbard, 1 for 17; Biletnikoff, 1 for 8; Branch, 1 for 8; Banaszak, 1 for 5.

1973 AFC

MIAMI 34, CINCINNATI 16

The Dolphins methodically took the Bengals apart in the first half, driving 80, 80, and 75 yards to touchdowns on three of their first four possessions en route to a 34-16 victory. When the Bengals got some easy points at the end of the half to draw near, Miami responded with two more scoring marches in the third quarter.

The Dolphins didn't wait to establish their dominance, putting together a 10-play drive the first time they had possession, ending with Bob Griese's 13-yard touchdown pass to Paul Warfield. Cincinnati came back with a 55-yard drive of its own to Horst Muhlmann's 24-yard field goal. But Miami retaliated, with Larry Csonka or Eugene (Mercury) Morris carrying on 9 of the team's 12 plays in a drive capped by Csonka's one-yard burst for a touchdown.

Early in the second quarter, Morris scored from four yards out. The next time the Dolphins had the ball, Neal Craig intercepted Griese's pass and returned it 45 yards for a touchdown. Two field goals before the end of the half gave Cincinnati hope and only a 21-16 deficit. But the Dolphins drove to scores the first two times they had the ball in the second half, to end any thoughts of an upset.

December 23, at Miami

Cincinnati	**Starters, Offense**	**Miami**
Charlie Joiner	WR	Paul Warfield
Rufus Mayes	LT	Wayne Moore
Howard Fest	LG	Bob Kuechenberg
Bob Johnson	C	Jim Langer
Pat Matson	RG	Larry Little
Vernon Holland	RT	Norm Evans
Bob Trumpy	TE	Jim Mandich
Isaac Curtis	WR	Marlin Briscoe
Ken Anderson	QB	Bob Griese
Boobie Clark	RB	Larry Csonka
Essex Johnson	RB	Eugene (Mercury) Morris
	Starters, Defense	
Royce Berry	LE	Vern Den Herder
Mike Reid	LT	Maulty Moore
Ron Carpenter	RT	Bob Heinz
Sherman White	RE	Bill Stanfill
Al Beauchamp	LLB	Doug Swift
Bill Bergey	MLB	Nick Buoniconti
Ken Avery	RLB	Mike Kolen
Lemar Parrish	LCB	Lloyd Mumphord
Ken Riley	RCB	Curtis Johnson
Neal Craig	SS	Jake Scott
Tommy Casanova	FS	Dick Anderson

Cincinnati	3	13	0	0	—	16
Miami	14	7	10	3	—	34

Mia— Warfield 13 pass from Griese (Yepremian kick)
Cin— FG Muhlmann 24
Mia— Csonka 1 run (Yepremian kick)
Mia— Morris 4 run (Yepremian kick)
Cin— Craig 45 interception return (Muhlmann kick)
Cin— FG Muhlmann 46
Cin— FG Muhlmann 10
Mia— Mandich 7 pass from Griese (Yepremian kick)
Mia— FG Yepremian 50
Mia— FG Yepremian 46
Attendance—74,770

TEAM STATISTICS	**Cin**	**Mia**
First downs	11	27
Rushing	5	18
Passing	6	9
By penalty	0	0
Total yardage	194	400
Net rushing yardage	97	241
Net passing yardage	97	159
Passes att.-comp.-had int.	27-14-1	19-11-2

RUSHING
Cincinnati—Clark, 7 for 40; Anderson, 3 for 26; E. Johnson, 2 for 17; Elliott, 7 for 15; Curtis, 1 for −1.
Miami—Morris, 20 for 106, 1 TD; Csonka, 20 for 71, 1 TD; Kiick, 10 for 51; Leigh, 1 for 8; Nottingham, 1 for 5.
PASSING
Cincinnati—Anderson, 14 of 27 for 114, 1 int.
Miami—Griese, 11 of 18 for 159, 2 TDs, 1 int.; Briscoe, 0 of 1, 1 int.
RECEIVING
Cincinnati—Elliott, 9 for 53; Joiner, 2 for 33; Clark, 2 for 18; Curtis, 1 for 9.
Miami—Warfield, 4 for 95, 1 TD; Mandich, 3 for 28, 1 TD; Kiick, 3 for 19; Briscoe, 1 for 17.

1973 NFC

MINNESOTA 27, WASHINGTON 20

Minnesota defensive end Carl Eller's raging halftime pep talk, punctuated when he smashed the team's blackboard to the floor, awoke the slumbering Vikings, who went on to defeat the Redskins 27-20. Washington entered the game as the wild card team.

Minnesota trailed 7-3 after a sloppily played first half. The Redskins' touchdown came on a three-yard run by Larry Brown after Bobby Bryant's fumble of a punt was recovered by special teams demon Bob Brunet at the Minnesota 21. Earlier, Curt Knight had missed a 17-yard field goal following a 76-yard drive by the Redskins. In the last minute of the half, an ill-advised pass by Fran Tarkenton was intercepted, depriving the Vikings of a score.

The Vikings got down to business in the second half, taking the kickoff and driving 79 yards. One play after Oscar Reed broke loose for 46 yards, Bill Brown drove in for a touchdown from the 2. The Redskins responded with field goals of 52 and 42 yards. Then Tarkenton capped a 71-yard drive with a 28-yard touchdown pass to John Gilliam. After a pass by Billy Kilmer was intercepted by Nate Wright on the first play following the ensuing kickoff, Tarkenton hit Gilliam with another touchdown, from eight yards out.

December 22, at Bloomington

Washington	**Starters, Offense**	**Minnesota**
Charley Taylor	WR	Carroll Dale
Terry Hermeling	LT	Grady Alderman
Paul Laaveg	LG	Ed White
Len Hauss	C	Mick Tingelhoff
John Wilbur	RG	Milt Sunde
George Starke	RT	Ron Yary
Jerry Smith	TE	Stu Voigt
Roy Jefferson	WR	John Gilliam
Billy Kilmer	QB	Fran Tarkenton
Charley Harraway	RB	Oscar Reed
Larry Brown	RB	Chuck Foreman
	Starters, Defense	
Ron McDole	LE	Carl Eller
Bill Brundige	LT	Gary Larsen
Diron Talbert	RT	Alan Page
Verlon Biggs	RE	Jim Marshall
Dave Robinson	LLB	Roy Winston
Myron Pottios	MLB	Jeff Siemon
Chris Hanburger	RLB	Wally Hilgenberg
Pat Fischer	LCB	Nate Wright
Mike Bass	RCB	Bobby Bryant
Ken Houston	SS-LS	Jeff Wright
Brig Owens	FS-RS	Paul Krause

Washington	0	7	3	10	—	20
Minnesota	0	3	7	17	—	27

Minn —FG Cox 19
Wash—L. Brown 3 run (Knight kick)
Minn —B. Brown 2 run (Cox kick)
Wash—FG Knight 52
Wash—FG Knight 42
Minn —Gilliam 28 pass from Tarkenton (Cox kick)
Minn —Gilliam 8 pass from Tarkenton (Cox kick)
Wash—Jefferson 28 pass from Kilmer (Knight kick)
Minn —FG Cox 30
Attendance—45,475

TEAM STATISTICS	**Wash**	**Minn**
First downs	18	17
Rushing	10	6
Passing	7	11
By penalty	1	0
Total yardage	314	359
Net rushing yardage	155	141
Net passing yardage	159	218
Passes att.-comp.-had int.	24-13-1	28-16-1

RUSHING
Washington—L. Brown, 29 for 115, 1 TD; Harraway, 13 for 40.
Minnesota—Reed, 17 for 95; Foreman, 11 for 40; Marinaro, 1 for 3; B. Brown, 1 for 2, 1 TD; Tarkenton, 4 for 1.

PASSING
Washington—Kilmer, 13 of 24 for 159, 1 TD, 1 int.
Minnesota—Tarkenton, 16 of 28 for 222, 2 TDs, 1 int.

RECEIVING
Washington—Jefferson, 6 for 84, 1 TD; Taylor, 4 for 56; L. Brown, 2 for 13; Harraway, 1 for 6.
Minnesota—Reed, 5 for 76; Voigt, 3 for 39; Foreman, 3 for 23; Gilliam, 2 for 36, 2 TDs; Dale, 2 for 31; Lash, 1 for 17.

1973 NFC

DALLAS 27, LA RAMS 16

The Cowboys took advantage of two turnovers on the Rams' first two plays of the game to gain a 14-0 advantage. When the Rams fought back to trail only 17-16, Roger Staubach hit Drew Pearson with an 83-yard touchdown pass to clinch a 27-17 victory.

On the game's first play from scrimmage, Lee Roy Jordan intercepted John Hadl's pass, setting the Cowboys up at the Los Angeles 26. Three runs by Calvin Hill produced a touchdown. On the first play after the kickoff, Lawrence McCutcheon fumbled at the 35 and Mel Renfro recovered, setting up Staubach's four-yard touchdown pass to Pearson.

By the end of the third quarter, Los Angeles had narrowed the Dallas lead to 17-6 on two field goals by David Ray, but Ray also had missed three medium-range attempts.

On the second play of the final period, Ray hit a 40-yard field goal. Shortly after that, Hill fumbled, with Fred Dryer recovering at the Dallas 17. Two plays later, Tony Baker smashed into the end zone and the Rams trailed by only one point.

Then came the play of the game. On third and 14, Pearson caught a 36-yard pass from Staubach between Steve Preece and Eddie McMillan and ran 47 yards for a touchdown.

December 23, at Irving

LA Rams	**Starters, Offense**	**Dallas**
Harold Jackson	WR	Bob Hayes
Charlie Cowan	LT	Ralph Neely
Tom Mack	LG	John Niland
Ken Iman	C	John Fitzgerald
Joe Scibelli	RG	Blaine Nye
John Williams	RT	Rayfield Wright
Bob Klein	TE	Billy Joe DuPree
Jack Snow	WR	Drew Pearson
John Hadl	QB	Roger Staubach
Jim Bertelsen	RB	Walt Garrison
Lawrence McCutcheon	RB	Calvin Hill
	Starters, Defense	
Jack Youngblood	LE	Larry Cole
Merlin Olsen	LT	Jethro Pugh
Larry Brooks	RT	Bob Lilly
Fred Dryer	RE	Pat Toomay
Ken Geddes	LLB	Dave Edwards
Jack Reynolds	MLB	Lee Roy Jordan
Isiah Robertson	RLB	D.D. Lewis
Charlie Stukes	LCB	Charlie Waters
Eddie McMillan	RCB	Mel Renfro
Dave Elmendorf	SS	Cornell Green
Steve Preece	FS	Cliff Harris

LA Rams	0	6	0	10	—	16
Dallas	14	3	0	10	—	27

Dall —Hill 3 run (Fritsch kick)
Dall —Pearson 4 pass from Staubach (Fritsch kick)
Dall —FG Fritsch 39
Rams—FG Ray 33
Rams—FG Ray 37
Rams—FG Ray 40
Rams—Baker 5 run (Ray kick)
Dall —Pearson 83 pass from Staubach (Fritsch kick)
Dall —FG Fritsch 12
Attendance—64,291

TEAM STATISTICS	**Rams**	**Dall**
First downs	11	15
Rushing	5	11
Passing	5	4
By penalty	1	0
Total yardage	192	298
Net rushing yardage	93	162
Net passing yardage	99	136
Passes att.-comp.-had int.	23-7-1	16-8-2

RUSHING
LA Rams—McCutcheon, 13 for 48; Bertelsen, 12 for 37; Hadl, 2 for 10; Baker, 1 for 5, 1 TD; L. Smith, 2 for −7.
Dallas—Hill, 25 for 97, 1 TD; Garrison, 10 for 30; Staubach, 4 for 30; Newhouse, 6 for 5.

PASSING
LA Rams—Hadl, 7 of 23 for 133, 1 int.; McCutcheon, 0 of 1.
Dallas—Staubach, 8 of 16 for 180, 2 TDs, 2 int.

RECEIVING
LA Rams—Snow, 3 for 77; L. Smith, 2 for 13; Jackson, 1 for 40; McCutcheon, 1 for 3.
Dallas—Pearson, 2 for 87, 2 TDs; Hill, 2 for 21; Fugett, 1 for 38; Hayes, 1 for 29; Garrison, 1 for 3; DuPree, 1 for 2.

1974 AFC

OAKLAND 28, MIAMI 26

As he was being sacked, Ken Stabler threw an eight-yard touchdown pass to triple-teamed Clarence Davis with 26 seconds left, and Oakland dethroned the two-time Super Bowl champion Dolphins 28-26.

In a game that was almost one continuous highlight film, Miami's Nat Moore returned the opening kickoff 89 yards for a touchdown. The Raiders tied it in the second quarter when Stabler passed to running back Charlie Smith for a 31-yard touchdown. Miami led 10-7 at the half and 16-14 after three quarters.

A field goal by Garo Yepremian early in the fourth quarter gave Miami a 20-14 advantage, but Stabler took only two plays to go 83 yards. With the ball at the Oakland 28, he went long for Cliff Branch, who made a diving catch at the Miami 27, got to his feet before defensive back Henry Stuckey could get to him, and sped the rest of the way for a touchdown and a 21-20 lead.

Miami came right back, going 68 yards in four plays, with Benny Malone sweeping right end for the last 23 yards and a touchdown with 2:08 to play.

But Stabler wasn't through. In a minute and a half he drove the Raiders to the Miami 8, converting two big third-down plays on the way.

December 21, at Oakland

Miami	**Starters, Offense**	**Oakland**
Paul Warfield	WR	Cliff Branch
Wayne Moore	LT	Art Shell
Bob Kuechenberg	LG	Gene Upshaw
Jim Langer	C	Jim Otto
Larry Little	RG	George Buehler
Norm Evans	RT	John Vella
Marv Fleming	TE	Bob Moore
Nat Moore	WR	Fred Biletnikoff
Bob Griese	QB	Ken Stabler
Larry Csonka	RB	Marv Hubbard
Benny Malone	RB	Clarence Davis
	Starters, Defense	
Vern Den Herder	LE	Bubba Smith
Manny Fernandez	LT	Otis Sistrunk
Bob Heinz	RT	Art Thoms
Bill Stanfill	RE	Horace Jones
Bob Matheson	LLB	Phil Villapiano
Nick Buoniconti	MLB	Dan Conners
Mike Kolen	RLB	Gerald Irons
Tim Foley	LCB	Alonzo (Skip) Thomas
Curtis Johnson	RCB	Nemiah Wilson
Jake Scott	FS	George Atkinson
Dick Anderson	SS	Jack Tatum

Miami	7	3	6	10	—	26
Oakland	0	7	7	14	—	28

Mia —N. Moore 89 kickoff return (Yepremian kick)
Oak—C. Smith 31 pass from Stabler (Blanda kick)
Mia —FG Yepremian 33
Oak—Biletnikoff 13 pass from Stabler (Blanda kick)
Mia —Warfield 16 pass from Griese (kick failed)
Mia —FG Yepremian 46
Oak—Branch 72 pass from Stabler (Blanda kick)
Mia —Malone 23 run (Yepremian kick)
Oak—Davis 8 pass from Stabler (Blanda kick)
Attendance—53,023

TEAM STATISTICS	**Mia**	**Oak**
First downs	18	19
Rushing	10	8
Passing	6	11
By penalty	2	0
Total yardage	294	411
Net rushing yardage	213	135
Net passing yardage	81	276
Passes att.-comp.-had int.	14-7-1	30-20-1

RUSHING
Miami—Csonka, 24 for 114; Malone, 14 for 83, 1 TD; Griese, 2 for 14; Kiick, 1 for 2.
Oakland—C. Davis, 12 for 59; Hubbard, 14 for 55; Banaszak, 3 for 14; Stabler, 3 for 7.

PASSING
Miami—Griese, 7 of 14 for 101, 1 TD, 1 int.
Oakland—Stabler, 20 of 30 for 293, 4 TDs, 1 int.

RECEIVING
Miami—Warfield, 3 for 47, 1 TD; N. Moore, 2 for 40; Nottingham, 1 for 9; Kiick, 1 for 5.
Oakland—Biletnikoff, 8 for 122, 1 TD; Branch, 3 for 84, 1 TD; B. Moore, 3 for 22; C. Smith, 2 for 35, 1 TD; C. Davis, 2 for 16, 1 TD; Hubbard, 1 for 9; Pitts, 1 for 5.

1974 AFC

PITTSBURGH 32, BUFFALO 14

Franco Harris scored three touchdowns within a span of four minutes and 52 seconds of the second quarter as Pittsburgh broke open a close game and coasted home with a 32-14 victory over Buffalo.

The Steelers marched 51 yards to Roy Gerela's field goal following the opening kickoff, but Buffalo grabbed its only lead late in the first quarter. Taking over at their own 44 following a short punt, the Bills quickly moved 56 yards, scoring on Joe Ferguson's 22-yard pass to tight end Paul Seymour.

The Steelers immediately drove 63 yards to retake the lead. Faced with a third and 10, Terry Bradshaw ran 12 yards for a first down. Two plays later, Bradshaw connected with Rocky Bleier on a 27-yard touchdown pass. The next time the Steelers had the ball, they drove 66 yards to Harris's one-yard touchdown run. On the first play after the kickoff, Buffalo's Jim Braxton broke loose for a 30-yard run, but Mike Wagner stripped him of the ball, which was recovered by Jack Ham. Two passes by Bradshaw set up another short touchdown run by Harris. After holding the Bills, the Steelers regained possession at their own 46, and quickly drove to Harris's third touchdown, a one-yard run with 16 seconds remaining in the half. O. J. Simpson of Buffalo scored the only touchdown of the second half.

December 22, at Pittsburgh

Buffalo	Starters, Offense	Pittsburgh
J.D. Hill	WR	Frank Lewis
Dave Foley	LT	Jon Kolb
Reggie McKenzie	LG	Jim Clack
Mike Montler	C	Ray Mansfield
Joe DeLamielleure	RG	Gerry Mullins
Donnie Green	RT	Gordon Gravelle
Paul Seymour	TE	Larry Brown
Ahmad Rashad	WR	Ron Shanklin
Joe Ferguson	QB	Terry Bradshaw
O.J. Simpson	RB	Franco Harris
Jim Braxton	RB	Rocky Bleier
	Starters, Defense	
Walt Patulski	LE	L.C. Greenwood
Mike Kadish	LT	Joe Greene
Earl Edwards	RT	Ernie Holmes
Dave Washington	RE	Dwight White
Jim Cheyunski	LLB	Jack Ham
Doug Allen	MLB	Jack Lambert
Bo Cornell	RLB	Andy Russell
Robert James	LCB	J.T. Thomas
Dwight Harrison	RCB	Mel Blount
Neal Craig	SS	Mike Wagner
Rex Kern	FS	Glen Edwards

Buffalo	7	0	7	0	—	14
Pittsburgh	3	26	0	3	—	32

Pitt —FG Gerela 21
Buff—Seymour 22 pass from Ferguson (Leypoldt kick)
Pitt —Bleier 27 pass from Bradshaw (kick blocked)
Pitt —Harris 1 run (Gerela kick)
Pitt —Harris 4 run (kick blocked)
Pitt —Harris 1 run (Gerela kick)
Buff—Simpson 3 pass from Ferguson (Leypoldt kick)
Pitt —FG Gerela 22
Attendance—48,321

TEAM STATISTICS	Buff	Pitt
First downs	15	29
Rushing	5	18
Passing	10	9
By penalty	0	2
Total yardage	264	438
Net rushing yardage	100	235
Net passing yardage	164	203
Passes att.-comp.-had int.	26-11-0	21-12-0

RUSHING
Buffalo—Simpson, 15 for 49; Braxton, 5 for 48; Ferguson, 1 for 3.
Pittsburgh—Harris, 24 for 74, 3 TDs; Bradshaw, 5 for 48; Bleier, 14 for 45; St. Davis, 5 for 32; Swann, 2 for 24; Gilliam, 1 for 12.
PASSING
Buffalo—Ferguson, 11 of 26 for 164, 2 TDs.
Pittsburgh—Bradshaw, 12 of 19 for 203, 1 TD; Gilliam, 0 of 2.
RECEIVING
Buffalo—Hill, 4 for 59; Simpson, 3 for 37, 1 TD; Seymour, 2 for 35, 1 TD; Rashad, 1 for 25; Braxton, 1 for 8.
Pittsburgh—Swann, 3 for 60; Bleier, 3 for 54, 1 TD; Lewis, 2 for 18; Brown, 1 for 29; McMakin, 1 for 22; Shanklin, 1 for 15; Harris, 1 for 5.

1974 NFC

MINNESOTA 30, ST. LOUIS 14

With the score 7-7 in the third quarter, Minnesota's Jeff Wright intercepted a pass by St. Louis quarterback Jim Hart to set up a field goal by Fred Cox. One minute later, Nate Wright picked up a fumble by Terry Metcalf and ran 20 yards to give the Vikings a 17-7 lead en route to a 30-14 victory.

The Cardinals controlled the first half, but came away only tied 7-7. In the first quarter, St. Louis had a third and one in Minnesota territory, but two running plays couldn't get a first down. Then, with three seconds in the half, Jim Bakken missed a 23-yard field goal.

The Vikings blew the game open in the third quarter, scoring three times in less than seven minutes. On the opening drive of the half, Jeff Wright intercepted Hart, and five plays later Cox converted. Two plays later, Metcalf's fumble was caused by devastating hits by Carl Eller and Alan Page. The Vikings held St. Louis on its next series, and Fran Tarkenton and Chuck Foreman drove Minnesota to another score, which came on Tarkenton's 38-yard pass to John Gilliam.

In the fourth quarter, the Vikings increased their lead to 30-7 with a 57-yard drive behind the power of Foreman and Dave Osborn, ending with Foreman's four-yard run behind guard Andy Maurer.

December 21, at Bloomington

St. Louis	Starters, Offense	Minnesota
Earl Thomas	WR	Jim Lash
Roger Finnie	LT	Charles Goodrum
Bob Young	LG	Andy Maurer
Tom Brahaney	C	Mick Tingelhoff
Conrad Dobler	RG	Ed White
Dan Dierdorf	RT	Ron Yary
Jackie Smith	TE	Stu Voigt
Mel Gray	WR	John Gilliam
Jim Hart	QB	Fran Tarkenton
Jim Otis	RB	Dave Osborn
Terry Metcalf	RB	Chuck Foreman
	Starters, Defense	
Council Rudolph	LE	Carl Eller
Leo Brooks	LT	Doug Sutherland
Bob Rowe	RT	Alan Page
Ron Yankowski	RE	Jim Marshall
Larry Stallings	LLB	Roy Winston
Mark Arneson	MLB	Jeff Siemon
Pete Barnes	RLB	Wally Hilgenberg
Norm Thompson	LCB	Nate Wright
Roger Wehrli	RCB	Jackie Wallace
Jim Tolbert	SS-LS	Jeff Wright
Clarence Duren	FS-RS	Paul Krause

St. Louis	0	7	0	7	—	14
Minnesota	0	7	16	7	—	30

StL —Thomas 13 pass from Hart (Bakken kick)
Minn—Gilliam 16 pass from Tarkenton (Cox kick)
Minn—FG Cox 37
Minn—N. Wright 20 fumble return (Cox kick)
Minn—Gilliam 38 pass from Tarkenton (kick failed)
Minn—Foreman 4 run (Cox kick)
StL —Metcalf 11 run (Bakken kick)
Attendance—44,626

TEAM STATISTICS	StL	Minn
First downs	17	19
Rushing	6	12
Passing	10	7
By penalty	1	0
Total yardage	284	363
Net rushing yardage	100	197
Net passing yardage	184	166
Passes att.-comp.-had int.	40-18-1	23-13-2

RUSHING
St. Louis—Metcalf, 15 for 55, 1 TD; Otis, 8 for 35; Hart, 1 for 10; Willard, 1 for 0.
Minnesota—Foreman, 23 for 114, 1 TD; Osborn, 16 for 67; Gilliam, 1 for 16; Tarkenton, 2 for 0.
PASSING
St. Louis—Hart, 18 of 40 for 200, 1 TD, 1 int.
Minnesota—Tarkenton, 13 of 23 for 169, 2 TDs, 2 int.
RECEIVING
St. Louis—Thomas, 6 for 64, 1 TD; Gray, 5 for 77; Metcalf, 4 for 43; Hammond, 1 for 10; Smith, 1 for 7; Otis, 1 for −1.
Minnesota—Foreman, 5 for 54; Osborn, 4 for 36; Gilliam, 2 for 54, 2 TDs; Voigt, 2 for 25.

1974 NFC

LA RAMS 19, WASHINGTON 10

Defensive tackle Merlin Olsen and linebacker Isiah Robertson came up with the big plays for Los Angeles as the Rams' defense held Washington to 99 yards in the second half and scored the clinching points in a 19-10 victory.

The Rams got on the scoreboard first, driving 67 yards in the opening period. James Harris completed four of four passes for 60 yards, including a 10-yard strike to Bob Klein for the touchdown. Buoyed by a 41-yard pass from Billy Kilmer to Charley Taylor, the Redskins came right back with a field goal.

In the second period, Pat Fischer intercepted a pass by Harris and returned it 40 yards to the Rams' 23. Helped by a pass-interference penalty in the end zone, the Redskins marched to a one-yard touchdown run by Moses Denson.

Late in the third period, the Rams tied the game on David Ray's field goal following a fumble by Larry Brown. Doug Cunningham fumbled the ensuing kickoff, setting up the Rams for another field goal, which put them ahead 13-10.

On the following series, Olsen put heavy pressure on Sonny Jurgensen (who had replaced Kilmer), who underthrew Brown. Robertson intercepted, and, with six Rams making clearing blocks, returned it for a touchdown.

December 22, at Los Angeles

Washington	Starters, Offense	LA Rams
Charley Taylor	WR	Harold Jackson
Ray Schoenke	LT	Charlie Cowan
Paul Laaveg	LG	Tom Mack
Len Hauss	C	Ken Iman
Walt Sweeney	RG	Joe Scibelli
George Starke	RT	John Williams
Jerry Smith	TE	Bob Klein
Roy Jefferson	WR	Jack Snow
Billy Kilmer	QB	James Harris
Moses Denson	RB	Jim Bertelsen
Larry Brown	RB	Lawrence McCutcheon
	Starters, Defense	
Ron McDole	LE	Jack Youngblood
Bill Brundige	LT	Merlin Olsen
Diron Talbert	RT	Larry Brooks
Verlon Biggs	RE	Fred Dryer
Dave Robinson	LLB	Ken Geddes
Rusty Tillman	MLB	Jack Reynolds
Chris Hanburger	RLB	Isiah Robertson
Pat Fischer	LCB	Charlie Stukes
Mike Bass	RCB	Al Clark
Ken Houston	SS	Dave Elmendorf
Brig Owens	FS	Bill Simpson

Washington	3	7	0	0	—	10
LA Rams	7	0	3	9	—	19

Rams— Klein 10 pass from Harris (Ray kick)
Wash— FG Bragg 35
Wash— Denson 1 run (Bragg kick)
Rams— FG Ray 37
Rams— FG Ray 26
Rams— Robertson 59 interception return (pass failed)
Attendance—80,118

TEAM STATISTICS	Wash	Rams
First downs	13	14
Rushing	4	8
Passing	7	6
By penalty	2	0
Total yardage	218	226
Net rushing yardage	49	131
Net passing yardage	169	95
Passes att.-comp.-had int.	30-13-3	24-8-2

RUSHING
Washington—Brown, 18 for 39; Denson, 7 for 5, 1 TD; Kilmer, 2 for 5.
LA Rams—McCutcheon, 26 for 71; Bertelsen, 6 for 34; Harris, 6 for 17; Cappelletti, 1 for 5; Scribner, 1 for 2; Baker, 2 for 2.
PASSING
Washington—Kilmer, 7 of 18 for 99; Jurgensen, 6 of 12 for 78, 3 int.
LA Rams—Harris, 8 of 24 for 95, 1 TD, 2 int.
RECEIVING
Washington—Taylor, 4 for 79; Evans, 4 for 31; J. Smith, 2 for 35; Denson, 2 for 17; Grant, 1 for 15.
LA Rams—Jackson, 2 for 35; Klein, 2 for 23, 1 TD; McCutcheon, 2 for 20; Curran, 1 for 12; Bertelsen, 1 for 5.

1975 AFC

PITTSBURGH 28, BALTIMORE 10

Pittsburgh's Steel Curtain defense scored once, set up two other touchdowns, sacked Baltimore's quarterbacks five times, and held the Colts to 154 yards (58 of which came on one pass late in the game) to lead the Steelers to a 28-10 victory.

The first score of the game came after Jack Ham intercepted a pass by Marty Domres to set the Steelers up at the Pittsburgh 39. Four plays later, Franco Harris scored from the 8. The Colts couldn't move until the second quarter, when Lloyd Mumphord's 58-yard interception return set up a 19-yard touchdown drive, which was capped by a five-yard pass from Domres to Glenn Doughty.

In the third quarter, the Colts took a 10-7 lead following a fumble by Harris on the Pittsburgh 19. Then the Steelers' defense took over. Late in the quarter, Mel Blount intercepted Domres and returned the ball to the Baltimore 7. On the next play, Rocky Bleier slanted over right tackle for a touchdown.

In the fourth quarter, a short punt set up the Steelers at the Baltimore 39. Behind the pounding of Harris, the Steelers drove to the 2, with Bradshaw scoring. Sparked by the long pass to Doughty, the Colts advanced to the Pittsburgh 3, but Bert Jones, who had returned from an early injury, fumbled when hit by Ham, and Andy Russell picked up the ball and ran 93 yards for a score.

December 27, at Pittsburgh

Baltimore	**Starters, Offense**	**Pittsburgh**
Roger Carr	WR	Frank Lewis
David Taylor	LT	Jon Kolb
Robert Pratt	LG	Jim Clack
Ken Mendenhall	C	Ray Mansfield
Elmer Collett	RG	Gerry Mullins
George Kunz	RT	Gordon Gravelle
Raymond Chester	TE	Larry Brown
Glenn Doughty	WR	Lynn Swann
Bert Jones	QB	Terry Bradshaw
Bill Olds	RB	Rocky Bleier
Lydell Mitchell	RB	Franco Harris
	Starters, Defense	
Fred Cook	LE	L.C. Greenwood
Mike Barnes	LT	Steve Furness
Joe Ehrmann	RT	Ernie Holmes
John Dutton	RE	Dwight White
Tom MacLeod	LLB	Jack Ham
Jim Cheyunski	MLB	Jack Lambert
Stan White	RLB	Andy Russell
Lloyd Mumphord	LCB	J.T. Thomas
Nelson Munsey	RCB	Mel Blount
Bruce Laird	SS	Mike Wagner
Jackie Wallace	FS	Glen Edwards

Baltimore	0	7	3	0	—	10
Pittsburgh	7	0	7	14	—	28

Pitt — Harris 8 run (Gerela kick)
Balt— Doughty 5 pass from Domres (Linhart kick)
Balt— FG Linhart 21
Pitt — Bleier 7 run (Gerela kick)
Pitt — Bradshaw 2 run (Gerela kick)
Pitt — Russell 93 fumble return (Gerela kick)
Attendance—49,053

TEAM STATISTICS	**Balt**	**Pitt**
First downs	10	16
Rushing	4	13
Passing	4	3
By penalty	2	0
Total yardage	154	287
Net rushing yardage	82	211
Net passing yardage	72	76
Passes att.-comp.-had int.	22-8-2	13-8-2

RUSHING

Baltimore—Mitchell, 26 for 63; Domres, 4 for 17; Olds, 5 for 6; Jones, 2 for 6; McCauley, 3 for 3; Carr, 1 for −13.

Pittsburgh—Harris, 27 for 153,1 TD; Bleier, 12 for 28, 1 TD; Bradshaw, 3 for 22, 1 TD; Collier, 1 for 8.

PASSING

Baltimore—Jones, 6 of 11 for 91; Domres, 2 of 11 for 9, 1 TD, 2 int.

Pittsburgh—Bradshaw, 8 of 13 for 103, 2 int.

RECEIVING

Baltimore—Mitchell, 4 for 20; Doughty, 2 for 63, 1 TD; McCauley, 1 for 9; Kennedy, 1 for 8.

Pittsburgh—Lewis, 3 for 65; Swann, 2 for 15; Bleier, 2 for 14; L. Brown, 1 for 9.

1975 AFC

OAKLAND 31, CINCINNATI 28

Ken Stabler led an offense that was nearly perfect as the Oakland Raiders built a 31-14 lead early in the fourth quarter, then held off Cincinnati 31-28.

Oakland's offense was unstoppable while building a 17-7 lead. Stabler threw two touchdown passes and George Blanda kicked a 27-yard field goal. On the Raiders' other possessions, Blanda missed one field goal and had another blocked.

The Raiders' offense continued its domination in the second half, scoring the first time it had the ball on a four-play, 35-yard drive. After a 91-yard touchdown drive by the Bengals cut the score to 24-14, Oakland drove 65 yards on 12 plays, scoring on a two-yard pass from Stabler to Dave Casper.

With 10 minutes remaining in the game, the Raiders faltered. Ken Riley intercepted a pass by Stabler, setting the Bengals up at the Oakland 9. Two plays later, Ken Anderson hit Charlie Joiner with a 25-yard touchdown pass. After Oakland punted, Anderson cut the lead to three points with a touchdown pass to Isaac Curtis. A fumble by Pete Banaszak at the Oakland 38 gave Cincinnati a chance to win it, but the Raiders' defense held on fourth down.

December 28, at Oakland

Cincinnati	**Starters, Offense**	**Oakland**
Isaac Curtis	WR	Cliff Branch
Rufus Mayes	LT	Art Shell
Howard Fest	LG	Gene Upshaw
Bob Johnson	C	Dave Dalby
John Shinners	RG	George Buehler
Vernon Holland	RT	John Vella
Bob Trumpy	TE	Bob Moore
Charlie Joiner	WR	Mike Siani
Ken Anderson	QB	Ken Stabler
Boobie Clark	RB	Marv Hubbard
Stan Fritts	RB	Clarence Davis
	Starters, Defense	
Ken Johnson	LE	Otis Sistrunk
Bob Brown	LT	Art Thoms
Ron Carpenter	RT	Horace Jones
Sherman White	RE	Ted Hendricks
Al Beauchamp	LLB	Phil Villapiano
Jim LeClair	MLB	Monte Jackson
Ron Pritchard	RLB	Gerald Irons
Lemar Parrish	LCB	Alonzo (Skip) Thomas
Ken Riley	RCB	Neal Colzie
Tommy Casanova	SS	George Atkinson
Bernard Jackson	FS	Jack Tatum

Cincinnati	0	7	7	14	—	28
Oakland	3	14	7	7	—	31

Oak—FG Blanda 27
Oak—Siani 9 pass from Stabler (Blanda kick)
Cin —Fritts 1 run (Green kick)
Oak—Moore 8 pass from Stabler (Blanda kick)
Oak—Banaszak 6 run (Blanda kick)
Cin —Elliott 6 run (Green kick)
Oak—Casper 2 pass from Stabler (Blanda kick)
Cin —Joiner 25 pass from Anderson (Green kick)
Cin —Curtis 14 pass from Anderson (Green kick)
Attendance—53,039

TEAM STATISTICS	**Cin**	**Oak**
First downs	17	27
Rushing	8	9
Passing	6	15
By penalty	3	3
Total yardage	258	358
Net rushing yardage	97	173
Net passing yardage	161	185
Passes att.-comp.-had int.	27-17-0	23-17-1

RUSHING

Cincinnati—B. Clark, 8 for 46; Elliott, 4 for 25, 1 TD; Fritts, 6 for 14, 1 TD; Anderson, 3 for 12; E. Johnson, 3 for 0; Williams, 1 for 0.

Oakland—C. Davis, 16 for 63; Banaszak, 17 for 62, 1 TD; Hubbard, 12 for 33; J. Phillips, 3 for 16; van Eeghen, 1 for 3; Stabler, 2 for −4.

PASSING

Cincinnati—Anderson, 17 of 27 for 201, 2 TDs.

Oakland—Stabler, 17 of 23 for 199, 3 TDs, 1 int.

RECEIVING

Cincinnati—B. Clark, 4 for 38; Myers, 3 for 67; Joiner, 3 for 60, 1 TD; Curtis, 3 for 20, 1 TD; Coslet, 2 for 14; Elliott, 1 for 9; Trumpy, 1 for −7.

Oakland—Moore, 6 for 57, 1 TD; Branch, 5 for 89; Siani, 3 for 35, 1 TD; C. Davis, 2 for 16; Casper, 1 for 2, 1 TD.

1975 NFC

LA RAMS 35, ST. LOUIS 23

Lawrence McCutcheon set NFC playoff records with 37 carries for 202 yards rushing, and the Los Angeles defense scored two touchdowns in the first 16 minutes, as the Rams raced by the Cardinals 35-23.

The Rams took charge immediately, driving 79 yards in 13 plays with the opening kickoff. Quarterback Ron Jaworski scored on a five-yard run. On the Cardinals' second play, Jim Hart's pass was intercepted by defensive end Jack Youngblood, who returned it 47 yards for a touchdown.

On the first play of the second quarter, the Rams increased their lead to 21-0 when safety Bill Simpson returned an interception for a touchdown. The Cardinals tried to get back in the game with a 59-yard drive to Jim Otis's three-yard touchdown run, but the Rams wrested control back when Jack Youngblood blocked Jim Bakken's extra-point attempt. On the first play after the kickoff, Jaworski passed to Harold Jackson for a 66-yard touchdown.

After the Cardinals cut the margin to 28-16, Simpson intercepted another pass. The Rams scored when McCutcheon fumbled at the 2, and Ron Jessie picked up the ball and ran it into the end zone.

December 27, at Los Angeles

St. Louis	**Starters, Offense**	**LA Rams**
J.V. Cain	TE-WR	Harold Jackson
Roger Finnie	LT	Doug France
Bob Young	LG	Tom Mack
Tom Banks	C	Rich Saul
Conrad Dobler	RG	Joe Scibelli
Dan Dierdorf	RT	John Williams
Jackie Smith	TE	Terry Nelson
Mel Gray	WR	Ron Jessie
Jim Hart	QB	Ron Jaworski
Jim Otis	RB	Cullen Bryant
Terry Metcalf	RB	Lawrence McCutcheon
	Starters, Defense	
Bob Bell	LE	Jack Youngblood
Charlie Davis	LT	Merlin Olsen
Bob Rowe	RT	Cody Jones
Ron Yankowski	RE	Fred Dryer
Larry Stallings	LLB	Ken Geddes
Greg Hartle	MLB	Jack Reynolds
Pete Barnes	RLB	Isiah Robertson
Norm Thompson	LCB	Eddie McMillan
Roger Wehrli	RCB	Monte Jackson
Ken Reaves	SS	Dave Elmendorf
Clarence Duren	FS	Bill Simpson

St. Louis	0	9	7	7	—	23
LA Rams	14	14	0	7	—	35

Rams— Jaworski 5 run (Dempsey kick)
Rams— Jack Youngblood 47 interception return (Dempsey kick)
Rams— Simpson 65 interception return (Dempsey kick)
StL — Otis 3 run (kick blocked)
Rams— H. Jackson 66 pass from Jaworski (Dempsey kick)
StL — FG Bakken 39
StL — Gray 11 pass from Hart (Bakken kick)
Rams— Jessie 2 fumble return (Dempsey kick)
StL — Jones 3 run (Bakken kick)
Attendance—72,650

TEAM STATISTICS	**StL**	**Rams**
First downs	22	26
Rushing	5	14
Passing	16	10
By penalty	1	2
Total yardage	363	440
Net rushing yardage	95	237
Net passing yardage	268	203
Passes att.-comp.-had int.	41-22-3	23-12-0

RUSHING

St. Louis—Otis, 12 for 38, 1 TD; Jones, 6 for 28, 1 TD; Metcalf, 8 for 27; Latin, 1 for 2.

LA Rams—McCutcheon, 37 for 202; Scribner, 4 for 16; Bryant, 3 for 12; Jaworski, 6 for 7, 1 TD.

PASSING

St. Louis—Hart, 22 of 41 for 291, 1 TD, 3 int.

LA Rams—Jaworski, 12 of 23 for 203, 1 TD.

RECEIVING

St. Louis—Metcalf, 6 for 94; Otis, 4 for 52; M. Gray, 3 for 52, 1 TD; Harris, 2 for 33; Latin, 2 for 23; Jones, 2 for 19; Cain, 2 for 17; Smith, 1 for 1.

LA Rams—Jessie, 4 for 52; McCutcheon, 3 for 8; J. Jackson, 2 for 84, 1 TD; Bryant, 2 for 26; T. Nelson, 1 for 33.

1975 NFC

DALLAS 17, MINNESOTA 14

Roger Staubach and Drew Pearson, two old hands at late-game theatrics, helped Dallas defeat Minnesota 17-14. Staubach's desperation pass to Pearson with 24 seconds remaining in the game covered 50 yards and turned a looming 14-10 loss into a victory. The miracle pass became known as the Hail Mary play.

The Cowboys more than doubled the Vikings in yards (158-78) in the first half, but trailed 7-0. Minnesota scored on Chuck Foreman's one-yard run three plays after a punt hit Cliff Harris and Fred McNeill recovered for Minnesota at the Dallas 4.

The Cowboys went ahead on their first two possessions of the second half. Doug Dennison finished a 72-yard drive by scoring from the 4, and Toni Fritsch kicked a 24-yard field goal.

With five minutes remaining, the Vikings took the lead. Brent McClanahan scored from the 1 to cap a 70-yard drive. With about two minutes left, the Vikings had a chance to run out the clock, but safety Charlie Waters blitzed Fran Tarkenton for a three-yard loss on third and two, and Minnesota punted.

Dallas took over at its 15 with 1:51 left. On third and one at the 24, Staubach passed to Pearson for seven yards and a first down. On fourth and 16 at the 25, Staubach completed a pass to Pearson at midfield for a first down with 44 seconds left. Then Staubach found him at the 5, and Pearson scored.

December 28, at Bloomington

Dallas	Starters, Offense	Minnesota
Golden Richards	WR	Jim Lash
Ralph Neely	LT	Steve Riley
Burton Lawless	LG	Andy Maurer
John Fitzgerald	C	Mick Tingelhoff
Blaine Nye	RG	Ed White
Rayfield Wright	RT	Ron Yary
Jean Fugett	TE	Stu Voigt
Drew Pearson	WR	John Gilliam
Roger Staubach	QB	Fran Tarkenton
Robert Newhouse	RB	Ed Marinaro
Preston Pearson	RB	Chuck Foreman
	Starters, Defense	
Ed (Too Tall) Jones	LE	Carl Eller
Jethro Pugh	LT	Doug Sutherland
Larry Cole	RT	Alan Page
Harvey Martin	RE	Jim Marshall
Dave Edwards	LLB	Fred McNeill
Lee Roy Jordan	MLB	Jeff Siemon
D. D. Lewis	RLB	Wally Hilgenberg
Mark Washington	LCB	Nate Wright
Mel Renfro	RCB	Bobby Bryant
Charlie Waters	SS-LS	Terry Brown
Cliff Harris	FS-RS	Paul Krause

Dallas	0	0	7	10	—	17
Minnesota	0	7	0	7	—	14

Minn—Foreman 1 run (Cox kick)
Dall —Dennison 4 run (Fritsch kick)
Dall —FG Fritsch 24
Minn—McClanahan 1 run (Cox kick)
Dalt —D. Pearson 50 pass from Staubach (Fritsch kick)
Attendance—46,425

TEAM STATISTICS	Dall	Minn
First downs	19	12
Rushing	7	6
Passing	11	6
By penalty	1	0
Total yardage	356	215
Net rushing yardage	131	115
Net passing yardage	225	100
Passes att.-comp.-had int.	29-17-0	26-12-1

RUSHING
Dallas—Dennison, 11 for 36, 1 TD; P. Pearson, 11 for 34; Newhouse, 12 for 33; Staubach, 7 for 24; Fugett, 1 for 4.
Minnesota—Foreman, 18 for 56, 1 TD; Tarkenton, 3 for 32; McClanahan, 4 for 22, 1 TD; Marinaro, 2 for 5.

PASSING
Dallas—Staubach, 17 of 29 for 246, 1 TD.
Minnesota—Tarkenton, 12 of 26 for 135; 1 int.

RECEIVING
Dallas—P. Pearson, 5 for 77; D. Pearson, 4 for 91, 1 TD; Newhouse, 2 for 25; Richards, 2 for 20; Fugett, 2 for 13; DuPree, 1 for 17; Dennison, 1 for 3.
Minnesota—Marinaro, 5 for 64; Foreman, 4 for 42; Gilliam, 1 for 15; Lash, 1 for 15; Voigt, 1 for −1.

1976 AFC

OAKLAND 24, NEW ENGLAND 21

In a game in which penalties played an uncommonly important part, Ken Stabler rolled left and dived untouched into the end zone with 10 seconds left to give Oakland a 24-21 victory over New England.

The Patriots took an early lead, driving 86 yards to Andy Johnson's one-yard touchdown run. With the score 7-3 and 2½ minutes left in the second quarter, Skip Thomas intercepted a pass by Steve Grogan. The Raiders drove 76 yards, the 31-yard touchdown coming on a leaping one-handed catch by Fred Biletnikoff in the end zone with 39 seconds left.

The Patriots regained the lead with two touchdown drives in the third quarter, each of which was aided by an Oakland penalty on fourth down.

With the score 21-17 late in the game, the Patriots were driving for the clinching score, but an illegal-motion penalty stalled them, and John Smith's 50-yard field-goal attempt was just short.

The Raiders drove 68 yards to Stabler's touchdown, with the big plays being two penalties. On third and 18, Stabler threw incomplete, but Ray Hamilton was penalized for roughing the passer. Then a personal foul penalty on third and one at the 4 gave the Raiders a first down at the 1.

December 18, at Oakland

New England	Starters, Offense	Oakland
Randy Vataha	WR	Cliff Branch
Leon Gray	LT	Art Shell
John Hannah	LG	Gene Upshaw
Bill Lenkaitis	C	Dave Dalby
Sam Adams	RG	George Buehler
Bob McKay	RT	John Vella
Russ Francis	TE	Dave Casper
Darryl Stingley	WR	Fred Biletnikoff
Steve Grogan	QB	Ken Stabler
Sam Cunningham	RB	Mark van Eeghen
Andy Johnson	RB	Clarence Davis
	Starters, Defense	
Mel Lunsford	LE	John Matuszak
Ray Hamilton	MG	Dave Rowe
Julius Adams	RE	Otis Sistrunk
Steve Zabel	OLB	Phil Villapiano
Sam Hunt	ILB	Monte Johnson
Steve Nelson	ILB	Willie Hall
Pete Barnes	OLB	Ted Hendricks
Bob Howard	LCB	Alonzo (Skip) Thomas
Mike Haynes	RCB	Willie Brown
Prentice McCray	SS	George Atkinson
Tim Fox	FS	Jack Tatum

New England	7	0	14	0	—	21
Oakland	3	7	0	14	—	24

NE —A. Johnson 1 run (Smith kick)
Oak—FG Mann 40
Oak—Biletnikoff 31 pass from Stabler (Mann kick)
NE —Francis 26 pass from Grogan (Smith kick)
NE —Phillips 3 run (Smith kick)
Oak—van Eeghen 1 run (Mann kick)
Oak—Stabler 1 run (Mann kick)
Attendance—53,045

TEAM STATISTICS	NE	Oak
First downs	23	20
Rushing	10	5
Passing	6	13
By penalty	7	2
Total yardage	331	282
Net rushing yardage	164	81
Net passing yardage	167	201
Passes att.-comp.-had int.	24-12-2	32-19-0

RUSHING
New England—Cunningham, 20 for 68; Grogan, 7 for 35; A. Johnson, 14 for 32, 1 TD; Calhoun, 5 for 17; J. Phillips, 3 for 12, 1 TD.
Oakland—van Eeghen, 11 for 39, 1 TD; C. Davis, 7 for 29; Banaszak, 4 for 8; Garrett, 1 for 4; Stabler, 1 for 1, 1 TD.

PASSING
New England—Grogan, 12 of 23 for 167, 1 TD, 1 int.; Francis, 0 of 1, 1 int.
Oakland—Stabler, 19 of 32 for 233, 1 TD.

RECEIVING
New England—Francis, 4 for 96, 1 TD; Stingley, 2 for 36; Cunningham, 2 for 14; A. Johnson, 2 for 13; Briscoe, 1 for 7; Chandler, 1 for 1.
Oakland—Biletnikoff, 9 for 137, 1 TD; Casper, 4 for 47; Branch, 3 for 32; van Eeghen, 1 for 8; C. Davis, 1 for 5; Garrett, 1 for 4.

1976 AFC

PITTSBURGH 40, BALTIMORE 14

Pittsburgh gained a divisional playoff record 526 yards while holding Baltimore to 170, as the Steelers rolled to a 40-14 victory. The game was so anticlimactic that the most exciting event of the day was when a small airplane crashed into the stands after the game. Because of the timing, few people remained in the area.

The Steelers wasted no time getting on the scoreboard. On third and eight at the Pittsburgh 24 on the first series of the game, the Colts rotated double coverage to Lynn Swann. Terry Bradshaw, who had missed six starts during the regular season with injuries, hit Frank Lewis with a bomb that produced a 76-yard touchdown.

Late in the first quarter, Bert Jones drove the Colts 69 yards to a touchdown (scored on a 17-yard pass to Roger Carr) that cut the Pittsburgh lead to 9-7. But that was Baltimore's first and last hurrah.

The Steelers scored on three of their next four possessions, driving 68 and 54 yards for touchdowns and getting a field goal with seven seconds left in the half following Glen Edwards's interception of a pass by Jones.

December 19, at Baltimore

Pittsburgh	Starters, Offense	Baltimore
Lynn Swann	WR	Roger Carr
Jon Kolb	LT	David Taylor
Sam Davis	LG	Robert Pratt
Mike Webster	C	Ken Mendenhall
Jim Clack	RG	Elmer Collett
Gerry Mullins	RT	George Kunz
Larry Brown	TE	Raymond Chester
Frank Lewis	WR	Glenn Doughty
Terry Bradshaw	QB	Bert Jones
Rocky Bleier	RB	Roosevelt Leaks
Franco Harris	RB	Lydell Mitchell
	Starters, Defense	
L. C. Greenwood	LE	Fred Cook
Joe Greene	LT	Mike Barnes
Ernie Holmes	RT	Joe Ehrmann
Dwight White	RE	John Dutton
Jack Ham	LLB	Derrel Luce
Jack Lambert	MLB	Jim Cheyunski
Andy Russell	RLB	Stan White
J. T. Thomas	LCB	Lloyd Mumphord
Mel Blount	RCB	Ray Oldham
Mike Wagner	SS	Bruce Laird
Glen Edwards	FS	Jackie Wallace

Pittsburgh	9	17	0	14	—	40
Baltimore	7	0	0	7	—	14

Pitt — Lewis 76 pass from Bradshaw (kick failed)
Pitt — FG Gerela 45
Balt— Carr 17 pass from Jones (Linhart kick)
Pitt — Harrison 1 run (Gerela kick)
Pitt — Swann 29 pass from Bradshaw (Gerela kick)
Pitt — FG Gerela 25
Pitt — Swann 11 pass from Bradshaw (Gerela kick)
Balt— Leaks 1 run (Linhart kick)
Pitt — Harrison 9 run (Mansfield kick)
Attendance—60,020

TEAM STATISTICS	Pitt	Balt
First downs	29	16
Rushing	12	4
Passing	15	8
By penalty	2	4
Total yardage	526	170
Net rushing yardage	225	71
Net passing yardage	301	99
Passes att.-comp.-had int.	24-19-0	25-11-2

RUSHING
Pittsburgh—Harris, 18 for 132; Fuqua, 11 for 54; Harrison, 10 for 40, 2 TDs; Bleier, 1 for −1.
Baltimore—Mitchell, 16 for 55; Leaks, 4 for 12, 1 TD; Jones, 2 for 3; McCauley, 1 for 1.

PASSING
Pittsburgh—Bradshaw, 14 of 18 for 264, 3 TDs; Kruczek, 5 of 6 for 44.
Baltimore—Jones, 11 of 25 for 144, 1 TD, 2 int.

RECEIVING
Pittsburgh—Swann, 5 for 77, 2 TDs; Harrison, 4 for 37; Harris, 3 for 24; Lewis, 2 for 103, 1 TD; Fuqua, 2 for 34; Bell, 2 for 25; Stallworth, 1 for 8.
Baltimore—Mitchell, 5 for 42; Chester, 3 for 42; Carr, 2 for 35, 1 TD; Doughty, 1 for 25.

1976 NFC

MINNESOTA 35, WASHINGTON 20

Minnesota dominated Washington with a ground game that produced two 100-yard rushers (Chuck Foreman and Brent McClanahan) and built a 35-6 third-quarter lead before coasting to a 35-20 victory.

The Vikings served notice on the first play from scrimmage that they had come prepared. Tight end Stu Voigt, left guard Charles Goodrum, and Foreman all blocked right, and McClanahan ran left for 41 yards. Three plays later, Fran Tarkenton threw to Voigt, who powered over two tacklers, ran 10 yards, and fell into the end zone to complete an 18-yard touchdown play.

With the score 7-3 late in the first quarter, and the Vikings facing a third and nine at the 27, Tarkenton threw to Sammy White on the 2. Ken Houston deflected the pass, but White grabbed it, juggled it as he fell, maintained possession, and rolled into the end zone for a touchdown.

The Vikings increased their halftime lead to 21-3 by driving 66 yards to Foreman's two-yard scoring run. The drive was sustained when Dan Nugent of Washington roughed Minnesota punter Neil Clabo. Drives of 51 and 76 yards gave the Vikings their biggest lead at the end of three quarters.

December 18, at Bloomington

Washington	Starters, Offense	Minnesota
Frank Grant	WR	Ahmad Rashad
Tim Stokes	LT	Steve Riley
Ron Saul	LG	Charles Goodrum
Len Hauss	C	Mick Tingelhoff
Terry Hermeling	RG	Ed White
George Starke	RT	Ron Yary
Jean Fugett	TE	Stu Voigt
Roy Jefferson	WR	Sammy White
Billy Kilmer	QB	Fran Tarkenton
John Riggins	RB	Brent McClanahan
Mike Thomas	RB	Chuck Foreman
	Starters, Defense	
Ron McDole	LE	Carl Eller
Dave Butz	LT	Doug Sutherland
Diron Talbert	RT	Alan Page
Dennis Johnson	RE	Jim Marshall
Brad Dusek	LLB	Matt Blair
Harold McLinton	MLB	Jeff Siemon
Chris Hanburger	RLB	Wally Hilgenberg
Pat Fischer	LCB	Nate Wright
Joe Lavender	RCB	Bobby Bryant
Ken Houston	SS-LS	Jeff Wright
Jake Scott	FS-RS	Paul Krause

Washington	3	0	3	14	—	20
Minnesota	14	7	14	0	—	35

Minn —Voigt 18 pass from Tarkenton (Cox kick)
Wash—FG Moseley 47
Minn —White 27 pass from Tarkenton (Cox kick)
Minn —Foreman 2 run (Cox kick)
Minn —Foreman 30 run (Cox kick)
Wash—FG Moseley 35
Minn —White 9 pass from Tarkenton (Cox kick)
Wash—Grant 12 pass from Kilmer (Moseley kick)
Wash—Jefferson 3 pass from Kilmer (Moseley kick)
Attendance—47,221

TEAM STATISTICS	Wash	Minn
First downs	19	21
Rushing	3	11
Passing	15	9
By penalty	1	1
Total yardage	365	384
Net rushing yardage	75	221
Net passing yardage	290	163
Passes att.-comp.-had int.	49-26-2	22-12-2

RUSHING
Washington—Thomas, 11 for 45; Riggins, 7 for 30.
Minnesota—Foreman, 20 for 105, 2 TDs; McClanahan, 20 for 101; Johnson, 2 for 11; Tarkenton, 1 for 3; Miller, 2 for 1; Lee, 1 for 0.

PASSING
Washington—Kilmer, 26 of 49 for 298, 2 TDs, 2 int.
Minnesota—Tarkenton, 12 of 21 for 170, 3 TDs, 2 int.; Lee, 0 of 1.

RECEIVING
Washington—Grant, 6 for 70, 1 TD; Fugett, 4 for 61; Jefferson, 4 for 59, 1 TD; Hill, 4 for 31; Riggins, 4 for 29; Thomas, 2 for 18; Smith, 1 for 30; L. Brown, 1 for 0.
Minnesota—S. White, 4 for 64, 2 TDs; Voigt, 4 for 42, 1 TD; McClanahan, 3 for 29; Rashad, 1 for 35.

1976 NFC

LA RAMS 14, DALLAS 12

A flurry of activity in the final quarter of a defensive struggle resulted in a score for the Rams, a score for the Cowboys, and a 14-12 Los Angeles victory.

The first big play of the day came late in the first half with the Rams leading 7-3. Charlie Waters blocked a punt by the Rams' Rusty Jackson, and the Cowboys turned it into Scott Laidlaw's one-yard touchdown run and a 10-7 halftime lead.

In the waning minutes of the third quarter, the Rams gained possession at the Dallas 39 when a hard hit by Larry Brooks forced Drew Pearson to fumble. Fred Dryer recovered for the Rams. On fourth and five at the Dallas 18, Tom Dempsey kicked a field goal to tie the score 10-10, but safety Cliff Harris was penalized for running into the kicker. The Rams took the first down at the 3. On third and goal at the 1, Lawrence McCutcheon was met by Thomas Henderson, lurched to his left, and forced his way into the end zone for a 14-10 lead.

With less than two minutes to go, Waters again blocked a punt by Jackson. On first down at the Los Angeles 17, Roger Staubach completed a pass to Butch Johnson, who could get only one foot in bounds as he came down in the end zone. The Rams held and took over on downs. On the Rams' fourth down, with four seconds left, Jackson took a snap in the end zone and ran to the right sideline as time ran out, giving the Cowboys a safety and two points.

December 19, at Irving

LA Rams	Starters, Offense	Dallas
Harold Jackson	WR	Golden Richards
Doug France	LT	Ralph Neely
Tom Mack	LG	Herbert Scott
Rich Saul	C	John Fitzgerald
Dennis Harrah	RG	Blaine Nye
John Williams	RT	Rayfield Wright
Bob Klein	TE	Billy Joe DuPree
Ron Jessie	WR	Drew Pearson
Pat Haden	QB	Roger Staubach
John Cappelletti	RB	Robert Newhouse
Lawrence McCutcheon	RB	Preston Pearson
	Starters, Defense	
Jack Youngblood	LE	Ed (Too Tall) Jones
Merlin Olsen	LT	Jethro Pugh
Larry Brooks	RT	Larry Cole
Fred Dryer	RE	Harvey Martin
Jim Youngblood	LLB	Bob Breunig
Jack Reynolds	MLB	Lee Roy Jordan
Isiah Robertson	RLB	D. D. Lewis
Rod Perry	LCB	Benny Barnes
Monte Jackson	RCB	Mark Washington
Dave Elmendorf	SS	Charlie Waters
Bill Simpson	FS	Cliff Harris

LA Rams	0	7	0	7	—	14
Dallas	3	7	0	2	—	12

Dall —FG Herrera 44
Rams—Haden 4 run (Dempsey kick)
Dall —Laidlaw 1 run (Herrera kick)
Rams—McCutcheon 1 run (Dempsey kick)
Dall —Safety, R. Jackson ran out of end zone
Attendance—62,436

TEAM STATISTICS	Rams	Dall
First downs	17	14
Rushing	6	4
Passing	8	9
By penalty	3	1
Total yardage	250	211
Net rushing yardage	120	85
Net passing yardage	130	126
Passes att.-comp.-had int.	21-10-3	37-15-3

RUSHING
LA Rams—McCutcheon, 21 for 58, 1 TD; Cappelletti, 19 for 54; Haden, 8 for 16, 1 TD; R. Jackson, 1 for −8.
Dallas—P. Pearson, 13 for 43; Newhouse, 9 for 25; Staubach, 2 for 8; D. Pearson, 1 for 4; Dennison, 1 for 3; Laidlaw, 2 for 2, 1 TD.

PASSING
LA Rams—Haden, 10 of 21 for 152, 3 int.
Dallas—Staubach, 15 of 37 for 150, 3 int.

RECEIVING
LA Rams—H. Jackson, 6 for 116; Cappelletti, 2 for 15; Klein, 1 for 12; McCutcheon, 1 for 9.
Dallas—P. Pearson, 6 for 41; D. Pearson, 3 for 38; DuPree, 3 for 34; Newhouse, 2 for 19; Johnson, 1 for 18.

1977 AFC

OAKLAND 37, BALTIMORE 31

Ken Stabler threw three touchdown passes to tight end Dave Casper, the last after 43 seconds of the sixth period, as Oakland defeated Baltimore 37-31 in the third-longest game in NFL history.

Both teams were cautious in the first half. A 30-yard run by Clarence Davis put the Raiders ahead, but Baltimore led 10-7 at the half.

On the Raiders' first possession of the second half, Stabler found Casper on an eight-yard touchdown pass. Baltimore's Marshall Johnson returned the ensuing kickoff 87 yards for a touchdown. Shortly after, Ted Hendricks blocked a Baltimore punt. Stabler and Casper then connected to make it 21-17.

The Colts drove 80 yards to Ron Lee's one-yard touchdown run to begin the fourth quarter, but the Raiders matched that with Pete Banaszak's score from the 1. Lee put Baltimore back on top with a 13-yard scoring run 78 seconds later. With time running out, Stabler connected with Casper again, this time on a 42-yard pass that gave the Raiders the ball at the Baltimore 14 and set up Errol Mann's tying field goal with 29 seconds left.

December 24, at Baltimore

Oakland	Starters, Offense	Baltimore
Cliff Branch	WR	Freddie Scott
Art Shell	LT	David Taylor
Gene Upshaw	LG	Robert Pratt
Dave Dalby	C	Ken Mendenhall
George Buehler	RG	Ken Huff
Henry Lawrence	RT	George Kunz
Dave Casper	TE	Raymond Chester
Fred Biletnikoff	WR	Glenn Doughty
Ken Stabler	QB	Bert Jones
Mark van Eeghen	RB	Roosevelt Leaks
Clarence Davis	RB	Lydell Mitchell
	Starters, Defense	
John Matuszak	LE	Fred Cook
Dave Rowe	NT-LT	Mike Barnes
Otis Sistrunk	RE-RT	Joe Ehrmann
Floyd Rice	LOLB-RE	John Dutton
Monte Johnson	LILB-LLB	Tom MacLeod
Willie Hall	RILB-MLB	Ed Simonini
Ted Hendricks	ROLB-RLB	Stan White
Lester Hayes	LCB	Norm Thompson
Willie Brown	RCB	Nelson Muncey
Alonzo (Skip) Thomas	SS	Bruce Laird
Jack Tatum	FS	Lyle Blackwood

Oakland	7	0	14	10	0	6	—	37
Baltimore	0	10	7	14	0	0	—	31

Oak—Davis 30 run (Mann kick)
Balt—Laird 61 interception return (Linhart kick)
Balt—FG Linhart 36
Oak—Casper 8 pass from Stabler (Mann kick)
Balt—Johnson 87 kickoff return (Linhart kick)
Oak—Casper 10 pass from Stabler (Mann kick)
Balt—R. Lee 1 run (Linhart kick)
Oak—Banaszak 1 run (Mann kick)
Balt—R. Lee 13 run (Linhart kick)
Oak—FG Mann 22
Oak—Casper 10 pass from Stabler (no kick) (0:43 of second extra period)
Attendance—59,925

TEAM STATISTICS	Oak	Balt
First downs	28	22
Rushing	8	10
Passing	17	8
By penalty	3	3
Total yardage	491	301
Net rushing yardage	167	187
Net passing yardage	324	114
Passes att.-comp.-had int.	40-21-2	26-12-0

RUSHING
Oakland—van Eeghen, 19 for 76; Davis, 16 for 48, 1 TD; Banaszak, 11 for 37, 1 TD; Garrett, 1 for 6.
Baltimore—Mitchell, 23 for 67; R. Lee, 11 for 46, 2 TDs; Leaks, 8 for 35; Jones, 6 for 30; McCauley, 2 for 9.

PASSING
Oakland—Stabler, 21 of 40 for 345, 3 TDs, 2 int.
Baltimore—Jones, 12 of 26 for 164.

RECEIVING
Oakland—Biletnikoff, 7 for 88; Branch, 6 for 113; Casper, 4 for 70, 3 TDs; van Eeghen, 2 for 39; Davis, 2 for 35.
Baltimore—Mitchell, 3 for 39; Scott, 2 for 45; R. Lee, 2 for 22; McCauley, 2 for 11; Chester, 1 for 30; Doughty, 1 for 20; Pratt, 1 for −3.

1977 AFC

DENVER 34, PITTSBURGH 21

Two fourth-quarter interceptions by linebacker Tom Jackson set up 10 points that broke open a close game and led the Broncos to a 34-21 victory over the Steelers in Denver's first playoff game ever.

The Steelers dominated the game in the first half, outgaining the Broncos 183-44 and holding onto the ball almost 21 minutes. But two Pittsburgh touchdown drives were offset by two big plays by Denver's defense and special teams, and the score was tied 14-14 at halftime. Denver scored first when John Schultz blocked a punt at the Pittsburgh 17. Rob Lytle carried four consecutive plays, scoring from the 4. After Pittsburgh had tied the score, Franco Harris fumbled at the Pittsburgh 45, and Jackson returned the ball to the 10. On first down, Otis Armstrong blasted off the right side for a touchdown.

With the game tied 21-21 in the fourth quarter, Jim Turner kicked a 44-yard field goal. Two plays later, Jackson intercepted Bradshaw's pass and returned it 32 yards to the Pittsburgh 9, setting up another field goal. With the Steelers driving, Jackson again intercepted, putting the ball on the Pittsburgh 33. Two plays later, Craig Morton connected with Jack Dolbin on a 34-yard touchdown pass.

December 24, at Denver

Pittsburgh	Starters, Offense	Denver
John Stallworth	WR	Haven Moses
Jon Kolb	LT	Andy Maurer
Sam Davis	LG	Tom Glassic
Mike Webster	C	Mike Montler
Jim Clack	RG	Paul Howard
Ray Pinney	RT	Claudie Minor
Larry Brown	TE	Riley Odoms
Lynn Swann	WR	Jack Dolbin
Terry Bradshaw	QB	Craig Morton
Rocky Bleier	RB	Jon Keyworth
Franco Harris	RB	Rob Lytle
	Starters, Defense	
Steve Furness	LE	Barney Chavous
Joe Greene	LT-NT	Rubin Carter
Ernie Holmes	RT-RE	Lyle Alzado
Dwight White	RE-LOLB	Bob Swenson
Jack Ham	LLB-LILB	Randy Gradishar
Jack Lambert	MLB-RILB	Tom Jackson
Loren Toews	RLB-ROLB	Joe Rizzo
J.T. Thomas	LCB	Louis Wright
Jimmy Allen	RCB	Steve Foley
Donnie Shell	SS	Billy Thompson
Glen Edwards	FS	Bernard Jackson

Pittsburgh	0	14	0	7	—	21
Denver	7	7	7	13	—	34

Den—Lytle 7 run (Turner kick)
Pitt —Bradshaw 1 run (Gerela kick)
Den—Armstrong 10 run (Turner kick)
Pitt —Harris 1 run (Gerela kick)
Den—Odoms 30 pass from Morton (Turner kick)
Pitt —Brown 1 pass from Bradshaw (Gerela kick)
Den—FG Turner 44
Den—FG Turner 25
Den—Dolbin 34 pass from Morton (Turner kick)
Attendance—75,059

TEAM STATISTICS	Pitt	Den
First downs	18	15
Rushing	10	5
Passing	8	9
By penalty	0	1
Total yardage	304	258
Net rushing yardage	127	103
Net passing yardage	177	155
Passes att.-comp.-had int.	37-19-3	23-11-0

RUSHING

Pittsburgh—Harris, 28 for 92, 1 TD; Bradshaw, 4 for 21, 1 TD; Bleier, 7 for 14.

Denver—Armstrong, 11 for 44, 1 TD; Lytle, 12 for 26, 1 TD; Keyworth, 5 for 20; Jensen, 4 for 13; Morton, 5 for 0.

PASSING

Pittsburgh—Bradshaw, 19 of 37 for 177, 1 TD, 3 int.

Denver—Morton, 11 of 23 for 164, 2 TDs.

RECEIVING

Pittsburgh—Stallworth, 4 for 80; Harris, 4 for 20; Cunningham, 3 for 42; Maxson, 3 for 11; Bleier, 2 for 10; Grossman, 1 for 7; Swann, 1 for 6; Brown, 1 for 1, 1 TD.

Denver—Odoms, 5 for 43, 1 TD; Moses, 2 for 45; Jensen, 2 for 33; Dolbin, 1 for 34, 1 TD; Armstrong, 1 for 0.

1977 NFC

DALLAS 37, CHI. BEARS 7

Dallas safety Charlie Waters set a divisional playoff record by intercepting three passes, and the Cowboys held the Bears scoreless until the fourth quarter to cruise to a 37-7 victory.

The Cowboys' defense took control at the very start of the game. On Chicago's first three possessions, the Bears netted only 13 yards and no first downs. Dallas, meanwhile, drove 79 and 74 yards for touchdowns. On the first drive, capped by Doug Dennison's two-yard touchdown run, Roger Staubach passed twice for 44 yards. On the second drive, Staubach completed two passes for 59 yards, 28 of them coming on a touchdown toss to tight end Billy Joe DuPree. The Cowboys added a field goal by Efren Herrera and an interception by Waters before halftime.

The second half was more of the same. D.D. Lewis intercepted Chicago quarterback Bob Avellini on the first play of the half. Two plays later, Tony Dorsett broke 23 yards for a touchdown. On the next Bears' possession, Avellini fumbled, Bill Gregory recovered for Dallas, and Herrera kicked a 31-yard field goal. A second interception by Waters didn't set up any points, but Avellini's fumble, which was recovered by Lewis, did. Dorsett's touchdown run started and concluded a one-play, seven-yard drive.

December 26, at Irving

Chi. Bears	Starters, Offense	Dallas
Bo Rather	WR	Golden Richards
Ted Albrecht	LT	Ralph Neely
Noah Jackson	LG	Herbert Scott
Dan Peiffer	C	John Fitzgerald
Revie Sorey	RG	Tom Rafferty
Dennis Lick	RT	Pat Donovan
Greg Latta	TE	Billy Joe DuPree
James Scott	WR	Drew Pearson
Bob Avellini	QB	Roger Staubach
Roland Harper	RB	Robert Newhouse
Walter Payton	RB	Tony Dorsett
	Starters, Defense	
Mike Hartenstine	LE	Ed Jones
Jim Osborne	LT	Jethro Pugh
Ron Rydalch	RT	Randy White
Billy Newsome	RE	Harvey Martin
Doug Buffone	LLB	Thomas Henderson
Tom Hicks	MLB	Bob Breunig
Waymond Bryant	RLB	D.D. Lewis
Allan Ellis	LCB	Benny Barnes
Virgil Livers	RCB	Aaron Kyle
Gary Fencik	SS	Charlie Waters
Doug Plank	FS	Cliff Harris

Chi. Bears	0	0	0	7	—	7
Dallas	7	10	17	3	—	37

Dall —Dennison 2 run (Herrera kick)
Dall —DuPree 28 pass from Staubach (Herrera kick)
Dall —FG Herrera 21
Dall —Dorsett 23 run (Herrera kick)
Dall —FG Herrera 31
Dall —Dorsett 7 run (Herrera kick)
Dall —FG Herrera 27
ChiB—Schubert 34 pass from Avellini (Thomas kick)
Attendance—63,260

TEAM STATISTICS	ChiB	Dall
First downs	15	20
Rushing	4	13
Passing	9	7
By penalty	2	0
Total yardage	224	365
Net rushing yardage	81	233
Net passing yardage	143	132
Passes att.-comp.-had int.	25-15-4	14-8-1

RUSHING

Chi. Bears—Payton, 19 for 60; Harper, 5 for 11; Earl, 2 for 6; Avellini, 1 for 4.

Dallas—Dorsett, 17 for 85, 2 TDs; Newhouse, 16 for 80; Dennison, 8 for 40, 1 TD; Staubach, 4 for 25; Brinson, 3 for 3.

PASSING

Chi. Bears—Avellini, 15 of 25 for 177, 1 TD, 4 int.

Dallas—Staubach, 8 of 13 for 134, 1 TD, 1 int.; D. White, 0 of 1.

RECEIVING

Chi. Bears—Schubert, 5 for 69, 1 TD; Payton, 3 for 33; Scott, 3 for 29; Latta, 2 for 25; Earl, 1 for 15; Harper, 1 for 6.

Dallas—D. Pearson, 2 for 30; Dorsett, 2 for 37; DuPree, 1 for 20, 1 TD; Newhouse, 1 for 13; Richards, 1 for 12; Brinson, 1 for 6.

1977 NFC

MINNESOTA 14, LA RAMS 7

Chuck Foreman ran for 101 yards in a torrential rainstorm to lead the Vikings to 14-7 victory over the interception-prone Rams. After three playoff games in Minnesota, the Rams thought they finally had the Vikings in good weather, but a major storm dropped 1½ inches of rain on Los Angeles.

Both teams wanted to score early—before the field turned into a quagmire. The Rams took the opening kickoff and drove to the Minnesota 30, where they were held on downs. With reserve quarterback Bob Lee, who was playing in place of injured Fran Tarkenton, hitting five of six passes, the Vikings drove 70 yards to Foreman's five-yard touchdown.

The Rams kept getting chances to score, but couldn't convert. In the second quarter, with a first and goal at the Minnesota 5, Pat Haden threw the ball directly to Minnesota cornerback Nate Allen in the end zone. On the Rams' next possession, Rafael Septien missed a short field goal.

Early in the fourth quarter, Manfred Moore's 21-yard punt return set up the Vikings' second score, a one-yard touchdown run by Sammy Johnson. The Rams quickly drove to the Minnesota 19, but on first down Haden again was intercepted.

With time running out, the Rams slipped and slid to their only score, a one-yard pass from Haden to Harold Jackson. With 53 seconds left, Jim Jodat recovered Septien's onside kick. The Rams reached the Vikings' 31 before Haden's pass was intercepted.

December 26, at Los Angeles

Minnesota	Starters, Offense	LA Rams
Ahmad Rashad	WR	Harold Jackson
Steve Riley	LT	Doug France
Charles Goodrum	LG	Tom Mack
Mick Tingelhoff	C	Rich Saul
Ed White	RG	Greg Horton
Ron Yary	RT	John Williams
Stu Voigt	TE	Terry Nelson
Sammy White	WR	Billy Waddy
Bob Lee	QB	Pat Haden
Robert Miller	RB	John Cappelletti
Chuck Foreman	RB	Lawrence McCutcheon
	Starters, Defense	
Carl Eller	LE	Jack Youngblood
Doug Sutherland	LT	Cody Jones
Alan Page	RT	Larry Brooks
Jim Marshall	RE	Fred Dryer
Matt Blair	LLB	Jim Youngblood
Jeff Siemon	MLB	Jack Reynolds
Fred McNeill	RLB	Isiah Robertson
Nate Wright	LCB	Pat Thomas
Bobby Bryant	RCB	Monte Jackson
Jeff Wright	LS-SS	Dave Elmendorf
Paul Krause	RS-FS	Nolan Cromwell

Minnesota	7	0	0	7	—	14
LA Rams	0	0	0	7	—	7

Minn — Foreman 5 run (Cox kick)
Minn — S. Johnson 1 run (Cox kick)
Rams— H. Jackson 1 pass from Haden (Septien kick)
Attendance—70,203

TEAM STATISTICS	Minn	Rams
First downs	14	14
Rushing	9	7
Passing	4	6
By penalty	1	1
Total yardage	189	267
Net rushing yardage	144	149
Net passing yardage	45	118
Passes att.-comp.-had int.	10-5-0	32-14-3

RUSHING

Minnesota—Foreman, 31 for 101, 1 TD; Miller, 12 for 52; Johnson, 3 for 1, 1 TD; Lee, 3 for − 10.

LA Rams—McCutcheon, 16 for 102; Haden, 3 for 27; Cappelletti, 7 for 11; Phillips, 1 for 9; Tyler, 1 for 0; Nelson, 1 for 0.

PASSING

Minnesota—Lee, 5 of 10 for 57.

LA Rams—Haden, 14 of 32 for 149, 1 TD; 3 int.

RECEIVING

Minnesota—Rashad, 2 for 37; Miller, 2 for 14; Foreman, 1 for 6.

LA Rams—Nelson, 5 for 85; H. Jackson, 3 for 21, 1 TD; McCutcheon, 2 for 15; Phillips, 2 for 0; Waddy, 1 for 5; Cappelletti, 1 for 4.

1978 AFC

PITTSBURGH 33, DENVER 10

The Pittsburgh Steelers broke open a close game with two long touchdown passes from Terry Bradshaw in a span of 34 seconds in the fourth quarter, and went on to defeat Denver 33-10.

The Broncos scored first on a 37-yard field goal by Jim Turner, but their lead didn't last long. The Steelers immediately drove 66 yards in eight plays, with Franco Harris blasting in behind left guard Sam Davis for a touchdown. The extra-point attempt was missed, but the next time Pittsburgh had the ball, Harris broke around right end for an 18-yard touchdown run and a 13-3 lead. Late in the half, trailing 16-3, the Broncos took advantage of a fumble by Bradshaw to move 49 yards to score.

The defensive play of the game and the Broncos' last gasp occurred simultaneously. Defensive tackle Joe Greene blocked Turner's short field-goal attempt in the third quarter. The Broncos couldn't mount another threat. In the fourth quarter, Bradshaw threw a 45-yard touchdown pass to John Stallworth, who set an AFC divisional playoff record with 10 catches. On the first play after the kickoff was fumbled, Bradshaw threw another touchdown pass.

December 30, at Pittsburgh

Denver	Starters, Offense	Pittsburgh
Jack Dolbin	WR	John Stallworth
Claudie Minor	LT	Jon Kolb
Tom Glassic	LG	Sam Davis
Billy Bryan	C	Mike Webster
Paul Howard	RG	Ray Pinney
Tom Novillo	RT	Larry Brown
Riley Odoms	TE	Randy Grossman
Haven Moses	WR	Lynn Swann
Craig Morton	QB	Terry Bradshaw
Jon Keyworth	RB	Rocky Bleier
Rob Lytle	RB	Franco Harris
	Starters, Defense	
Barney Chavous	LE	L.C. Greenwood
Rubin Carter	NT-LT	Joe Greene
Lyle Alzado	RE-RT	Steve Furness
Bob Swenson	LOLB-RE	John Banaszak
Joe Rizzo	LILB-LLB	Jack Ham
Randy Gradishar	RILB-MLB	Jack Lambert
Tom Jackson	ROLB-RLB	Robin Cole
Louis Wright	LCB	Ron Johnson
Steve Foley	RCB	Mel Blount
Billy Thompson	SS	Donnie Shell
Bernard Jackson	FS	Mike Wagner

Denver	3	7	0	0	—	10
Pittsburgh	6	13	0	14	—	33

Den—FG Turner 37
Pitt —Harris 1 run (kick failed)
Pitt —Harris 18 run (Gerela kick)
Pitt —FG Gerela 24
Den—Preston 3 run (Turner kick)
Pitt —FG Gerela 27
Pitt —Stallworth 45 pass from Bradshaw (Gerela kick)
Pitt —Swann 38 pass from Bradshaw (Gerela kick)
Attendance—50,230

TEAM STATISTICS	Den	Pitt
First downs	15	24
Rushing	5	9
Passing	8	11
By penalty	2	4
Total yardage	218	425
Net rushing yardage	87	153
Net passing yardage	131	272
Passes att.-comp.-had int.	22-12-0	29-16-1

RUSHING

Denver—Weese, 4 for 43; Preston, 4 for 14, 1 TD; Keyworth, 6 for 12; Perrin, 6 for 6; Lytle, 5 for 6; Canada, 1 for 3; Armstrong, 1 for 3.

Pittsburgh—Harris, 24 for 105, 2 TDs; Bleier, 8 for 26; Moser, 2 for 6; Bradshaw, 2 for 4; Thornton, 2 for 4; J. Smith, 1 for 4; Deloplaine, 1 for 4.

PASSING

Denver—Weese, 8 of 16 for 118; Morton, 3 for 5 for 34; Dilts, 1 of 1 for 16.

Pittsburgh—Bradshaw, 16 of 29 for 272, 2 TDs, 1 int.

RECEIVING

Denver—Dolbin, 4 for 77; Moses, 2 for 33; Preston, 2 for 19; Perrin, 2 for 16; Odoms, 1 for 24; Lytle, 1 for −1.

Pittsburgh—Stallworth, 10 for 156, 1 TD; Grossman, 4 for 64; Swann, 2 for 52, 1 TD.

1978 AFC

HOUSTON 31, NEW ENGLAND 14

Dan Pastorini threw three touchdown passes in the second quarter as Houston jumped to a 21-0 halftime lead and coasted to a 31-14 victory over the New England Patriots, whose coach, Chuck Fairbanks, was on the sidelines after having been suspended and then brought back for the playoffs.

After a scoreless first quarter, the Oilers opened up the game in the second period. On third and seven at the Houston 29, New England blitzed, leaving Ken Burrough and cornerback Mike Haynes one-on-one near the left sideline. Pastorini hit Burrough, who sidestepped Haynes and sprinted down the sideline for a 71-yard touchdown. On the next series, safety Mike Reinfeldt intercepted Steve Grogan's pass at the Houston 1. The Oilers then pounded out a 99-yard drive in 14 plays, scoring on Pastorini's 19-yard pass to tight end Mike Barber. Again New England threatened, but Reinfeldt intercepted Grogan once more, and the Oilers followed it with another touchdown pass, this one to Barber from 13 yards out with 36 seconds left in the half.

The Patriots scored in both the third and fourth quarters, but the Oilers used the running of Earl Campbell to set up two more scores and control the tempo of the game in the second half.

December 31, at Foxboro

Houston	Starters, Offense	New England
Ken Burrough	WR	Stanley Morgan
Greg Sampson	LT	Leon Gray
George Reihner	LG	John Hannah
Carl Mauck	C	Bill Lenkaitis
Ed Fisher	RG	Sam Adams
Conway Hayman	RT	Shelby Jordan
Mike Barber	TE	Russ Francis
Richard Caster	WR	Harold Jackson
Dan Pastorini	QB	Steve Grogan
Tim Wilson	RB	Sam Cunningham
Earl Campbell	RB	Andy Johnson
	Starters, Defense	
James Young	LE	Mel Lunsford
Curley Culp	NT	Ray Hamilton
Elvin Bethea	RE	Richard Bishop
Robert Brazile	LOLB	Steve Zabel
Gregg Bingham	LILB	Steve Nelson
Steve Kiner	RILB	Sam Hunt
Ted Washington	ROLB	Rod Shoate
Willie Alexander	LCB	Raymond Clayborn
Greg Stemrick	RCB	Mike Haynes
Bill Currier	SS	Doug Beaudoin
Mike Reinfeldt	FS	Tim Fox

Houston	0	21	3	7	—	31
New England	0	0	7	7	—	14

Hou—Burrough 71 pass from Pastorini (Fritsch kick)
Hou—Barber 19 pass from Pastorini (Fritsch kick)
Hou—Barber 13 pass from Pastorini (Fritsch kick)
Hou—FG Fritsch 30
NE —Jackson 24 pass from Johnson (Posey kick)
NE —Francis 24 pass from Owens (Posey kick)
Hou—Campbell 2 run (Fritsch kick)
Attendance—60,735

TEAM STATISTICS	Hou	NE
First downs	21	15
Rushing	11	6
Passing	8	8
By penalty	2	1
Total yardage	344	263
Net rushing yardage	174	83
Net passing yardage	170	180
Passes att.-comp.-had int.	15-12-1	35-16-3

RUSHING

Houston—Campbell, 27 for 118, 1 TD; T. Wilson, 14 for 26; Coleman, 7 for 19; Poole, 3 for 7; Duncan, 2 for 7; Nielsen, 1 for −3.

New England—Cunningham, 10 for 42; Grogan, 1 for 16; Johnson, 6 for 14; Ivory, 3 for 11.

PASSING

Houston—Pastorini, 12 of 15 for 200, 3 TDs, 1 int.

New England—Owen, 12 of 22 for 144, 1 TD, 1 int.; Grogan, 3 of 12 for 38, 2 int.; Johnson, 1 of 1 for 24, 1 TD.

RECEIVING

Houston—Barber, 5 for 83, 2 TDs; Burrough, 3 for 91, 1 TD; Caster, 2 for 12; Campbell, 1 for 10; Woods, 1 for 4.

New England—Francis, 8 for 101, 1 TD; Cunningham, 3 for 28; Morgan, 2 for 37; Johnson, 2 for 16; Jackson, 1 for 24, 1 TD.

1978 NFC

DALLAS 27, ATLANTA 20

Backup quarterback Danny White led the Cowboys to two touchdowns in the second half, when the Dallas defense shut down an explosive Atlanta team, and the Cowboys defeated the Falcons 27-20.

The Falcons were unstoppable in the first half, when they scored on each of their first four possessions. The Cowboys managed their only touchdown on a 13-yard run by Scott Laidlaw on a drive that was kept going when White ran for a first down from punt formation.

The game turned around on one play late in the first half. Linebacker Robert Pennywell knocked Dallas quarterback Roger Staubach out with a vicious hit after Staubach had already passed the ball. Inspired by the loss of their team leader, Dallas stopped the Falcons cold in the second half.

Meanwhile, the Dallas offense got going. In the third quarter, White drove the Cowboys 54 yards, passing two yards to Jackie Smith for a touchdown.

Early in the fourth quarter, the Cowboys took over at the Atlanta 30 after John James, hurried by Charlie Waters, managed only a 10-yard punt. Another personal foul by Pennywell and four carries by Laidlaw were enough to put Dallas ahead for good.

December 30, at Irving

Atlanta	Starters, Offense	Dallas
Wallace Francis	WR	Tony Hill
Mike Kenn	LT	Pat Donovan
Dave Scott	LG	Herbert Scott
Jeff Van Note	C	John Fitzgerald
R.C. Thielemann	RG	Tom Rafferty
Phil McKinnely	RT	Rayfield Wright
Jim Mitchell	TE	Billy Joe DuPree
Billy Ryckman	WR	Drew Pearson
Steve Bartkowski	QB	Roger Staubach
Bubba Bean	RB	Scott Laidlaw
Haskel Stanback	RB	Tony Dorsett
	Starters, Defense	
Jeff Yeates	LE	Ed Jones
Jim Bailey	LT	Larry Cole
Mike Lewis	RT	Randy White
Jeff Merrow	RE	Harvey Martin
Fulton Kuykendall	LLB	Thomas Henderson
Robert Pennywell	MLB	Bob Breunig
Greg Brezina	RLB	D.D. Lewis
Rolland Lawrence	LCB	Benny Barnes
Rick Byas	RCB	Aaron Kyle
Frank Reed	SS	Charlie Waters
Tom Pridemore	FS	Cliff Harris

Atlanta	7	13	0	0	—	20
Dallas	10	3	7	7	—	27

Dall—FG Septien 34
Atl —Bean 14 run (Mazzetti kick)
Dall—Laidlaw 13 run (Septien kick)
Atl —FG Mazzetti 42
Dall—FG Septien 48
Atl —Francis 17 pass from Bartkowski (Mazzetti kick)
Atl —FG Mazzetti 22
Dall—Smith 2 pass from D. White (Septien kick)
Dall—Laidlaw 1 run (Septien kick)
Attendance—63,406

TEAM STATISTICS	Atl	Dall
First downs	16	26
Rushing	10	9
Passing	5	15
By penalty	1	2
Total yardage	216	369
Net rushing yardage	164	148
Net passing yardage	52	221
Passes att.-comp.-had int.	23-8-3	37-17-1

RUSHING

Atlanta—Bean, 17 for 72, 1 TD; Stanback, 9 for 62; Franklin, 8 for 24; Esposito, 2 for 6.

Dallas—Laidlaw, 17 for 66, 2 TDs; Dorsett, 14 for 65; DuPree, 1 for 20; Staubach, 1 for 3; P. Pearson, 1 for −2; D. White, 3 for −4.

PASSING

Atlanta—Bartkowski, 8 of 23 for 95, 1 TD, 3 int.

Dallas—D. White, 10 of 20 for 127, 1 TD, 1 int.; Staubach, 7 of 17 for 105.

RECEIVING

Atlanta—Francis, 6 for 66, 1 TD; Ryckman, 1 for 22; Esposito, 1 for 7.

Dallas—DuPree, 5 for 59; D. Pearson, 4 for 75; Smith, 3 for 38, 1 TD; Hill, 3 for 36; Laidlaw, 1 for 15; Dorsett, 1 for 9.

1978 NFC

LA RAMS 34, MINNESOTA 10

After suffering four heartbreaking playoff losses to Minnesota in four meetings, the Los Angeles Rams broke a longtime jinx by shutting out the Vikings 24-0 in the second half for a 34-10 victory.

The Vikings led 3-0 at the end of the first quarter, but then the Rams began to take control. Early in the second period, Los Angeles drove 59 yards to a touchdown, which came when Pat Haden ended an extended scramble with a nine-yard pass to Willie Miller. After the Rams went ahead 10-3, cornerback Bobby Bryant intercepted a pass, setting the Vikings up at the Los Angeles 27 in the final two minutes of the half. A one-yard touchdown pass from Fran Tarkenton to Ahmad Rashad tied the game six seconds before halftime.

Early in the third quarter, a 21-yard punt return by Jackie Wallace set up the Rams' go-ahead touchdown, which was scored by Cullen Bryant on a three-yard run around right end. The next time the Rams touched the ball, they went 60 yards in five plays, scoring on a 27-yard pass from Haden to Ron Jessie, who dodged through the Vikings' defensive backs for the last 20 yards.

December 31, at Los Angeles

Minnesota	Starters, Offense	LA Rams
Ahmad Rashad	WR	Willie Miller
Frank Myers	LT	Doug France
Charles Goodrum	LG	Tom Mack
Mick Tingelhoff	C	Rich Saul
Wes Hamilton	RG	Dennis Harrah
Ron Yary	RT	John Williams
Bob Tucker	TE	Terry Nelson
Sammy White	WR	Ron Jessie
Fran Tarkenton	QB	Pat Haden
Rickey Young	RB	Cullen Bryant
Chuck Foreman	RB	John Cappelletti
	Starters, Defense	
Mark Mullaney	LE	Jack Youngblood
Doug Sutherland	LT	Cody Jones
James White	RT	Larry Brooks
Jim Marshall	RE	Fred Dryer
Matt Blair	LLB	Jim Youngblood
Jeff Siemon	MLB	Jack Reynolds
Fred McNeill	RLB	Bob Brudzinski
John Turner	LCB	Pat Thomas
Bobby Bryant	RCB	Rod Perry
Phil Wise	LS-SS	Dave Elmendorf
Tom Hannon	RS-FS	Bill Simpson

Minnesota	3	7	0	0	—	10
LA Rams	0	10	14	10	—	34

Minn — FG Danmeier 42
Rams— Miller 9 pass from Haden (Corral kick)
Rams— FG Corral 43
Minn — Rashad 1 pass from Tarkenton (Danmeier kick)
Rams— Bryant 3 run (Corral kick)
Rams— Jessie 27 pass from Haden (Corral kick)
Rams— FG Corral 28
Rams— Jodat 3 run (Corral kick)
Attendance—70,436

TEAM STATISTICS	Minn	Rams
First downs	12	25
Rushing	2	13
Passing	10	12
By penalty	0	0
Total yardage	244	409
Net rushing yardage	36	200
Net passing yardage	208	209
Passes att.-comp.-had int.	38-18-2	29-15-1

RUSHING

Minnesota—Foreman, 13 for 31; Kellar, 2 for 7; Tarkenton, 1 for −2.

LA Rams—Bryant, 27 for 100, 1 TD; Cappelletti, 10 for 44; Davis, 4 for 17; Haden, 2 for 15; Phillips, 2 for 10; Waddy, 1 for 9; Jodat, 1 for 3, 1 TD; Nelson, 1 for 2.

PASSING

Minnesota—Tarkenton, 18 of 37 for 219, 1 TD, 2 int.; Foreman, 0 of 1.

LA Rams—Haden, 15 of 29 for 209, 2 TDs, 1 int.

RECEIVING

Minnesota—Rashad, 7 for 84, 1 TD; Young, 4 for 49; Tucker, 4 for 48; Foreman, 3 for 38.

LA Rams—Jessie, 6 for 108, 1 TD; Young, 2 for 30; Miller, 2 for 29, 1 TD; Bryant, 2 for 13; Nelson, 1 for 13; Waddy, 1 for 10; Cappelletti, 1 for 6.

1979 AFC

HOUSTON 17, SAN DIEGO 14

Rookie strong safety Vernon Perry set a postseason-game record with four interceptions as Houston defeated San Diego 17-14 despite the absence of running back Earl Campbell, quarterback Dan Pastorini, and wide receiver Ken Burrough.

San Diego quarterback Dan Fouts passed the first seven plays the Chargers had the ball, as they drove 81 yards to a touchdown by Clarence Williams. On San Diego's next possession, however, Perry picked off a pass by Fouts at the Houston 18.

In the second quarter, Perry blocked a short field-goal attempt by Mike Wood, picked it up, and returned it 57 yards to the San Diego 28. Six plays later, Toni Fritsch kicked a field goal. On the third play after the kickoff, Perry intercepted Fouts again. Gifford Nielsen completed three passes to set up Fritsch's 18-yard field goal, but when the Chargers were called for illegal procedure, the Oilers took the ball on the 1 rather than the points. With 19 seconds in the half, Boobie Clark scored to make it 10-7.

At the beginning of the third quarter, Fouts guided the Chargers 65 yards to Lydell Mitchell's eight-yard touchdown run. Later, J.C. Wilson intercepted Fouts, giving the Oilers the ball at the San Diego 46. Three plays later, Nielsen passed to Mike Renfro for a 47-yard touchdown and a 17-14 lead. On each of the Chargers' last two possessions, Perry intercepted Fouts to check a Chargers comeback.

December 29, at San Diego

Houston	Starters, Offense	San Diego
Mike Renfro	WR	John Jefferson
Leon Gray	LT	Billy Shields
David Carter	LG	Doug Wilkerson
Carl Mauck	C	Bob Rush
Ed Fisher	RG	Ed White
Conway Hayman	RT	Russ Washington
Mike Barber	TE	Bob Klein
Richard Caster	WR	Charlie Joiner
Gifford Nielsen	QB	Dan Fouts
Tim Wilson	RB	Clarence Williams
Rob Carpenter	RB	Lydell Mitchell
	Starters, Defense	
Andy Dorris	LE	Leroy Jones
Curley Culp	NT-LT	Wilbur Young
Elvin Bethea	RE-RT	Gary Johnson
Ted Washington	LOLB-RE	Fred Dean
Gregg Bingham	LILB-LLB	Ray Preston
Art Stringer	RILB-MLB	Bob Horn
Robert Brazile	ROLB-RLB	Woodrow Lowe
J.C. Wilson	LCB	Willie Buchanon
Greg Stemrick	RCB	Mike Williams
Vernon Perry	SS	Mike Fuller
Mike Reinfeldt	FS	Pete Shaw

Houston	0	10	7	0	—	17
San Diego	7	0	7	0	—	14

SD —C. Williams 1 run (Wood kick)
Hou—FG Fritsch 26
Hou—Clark 1 run (Fritsch kick)
SD —Mitchell 8 run (Wood kick)
Hou—Renfro 47 pass from Nielsen (Fritsch kick)
Attendance—51,192

TEAM STATISTICS	Hou	SD
First downs	15	25
Rushing	9	6
Passing	5	17
By penalty	1	2
Total yardage	259	380
Net rushing yardage	148	63
Net passing yardage	111	317
Passes att.-comp.-had int.	19-10-1	47-25-5

RUSHING

Houston—Carpenter, 18 for 67; T. Wilson, 11 for 39; Clark, 9 for 30, 1 TD; Nielsen, 2 for 12.

San Diego—Mitchell, 8 for 33, 1 TD; C. Williams, 11 for 30, 1 TD.

PASSING

Houston—Nielsen, 10 of 19 for 111, 1 TD, 1 int.

San Diego—Fouts, 25 of 47 for 333, 5 int.

RECEIVING

Houston—Carpenter, 4 for 23; T. Wilson, 3 for 16; Renfro, 1 for 47, 1 TD; Coleman, 1 for 13; Barber, 1 for 12.

San Diego—Klein, 5 for 41; Joiner, 4 for 81; Jefferson, 4 for 70; C. Williams, 4 for 30; Mitchell, 4 for 26; Floyd, 3 for 51; McCrary, 1 for 34.

1979 AFC

PITTSBURGH 34, MIAMI 14

Pittsburgh's offense scored the first three times it had the ball and then turned the game over to the Steel Curtain defense, which limited Miami to 25 yards rushing in a 34-14 victory, the Steelers' fifteenth consecutive home triumph.

Pittsburgh was as close to perfection as possible in the first quarter. Taking the opening kickoff, the Steelers drove 62 yards in 13 plays to Sidney Thornton's one-yard scoring run. After holding Miami without a first down, they went 62 yards again, this time in nine plays, with Terry Bradshaw passing to John Stallworth for a 17-yard touchdown. Again the Dolphins couldn't pick up a first down and punted. On the sixth play of a 56-yard drive, Bradshaw escaped a heavy pass rush and threw 20 yards to Lynn Swann, who was alone in the right corner of the end zone.

After a scoreless second quarter, the Steelers' dominance was interrupted momentarily in the third quarter when the Dolphins recovered a punt touched by Dwayne Woodruff at the Pittsburgh 11. Two plays later, Bob Griese passed to Duriel Harris in the end zone to close the gap to 20-7.

The Steelers immediately asserted themselves, driving 69 yards on 12 plays to Rocky Bleier's one-yard touchdown run that put the game out of reach.

December 30, at Pittsburgh

Miami	Starters, Offense	Pittsburgh
Duriel Harris	WR	John Stallworth
Bob Kuechenberg	LT	Ted Peterson
Ed Newman	LG	Sam Davis
Mark Dennard	C	Mike Webster
Larry Little	RG	Steve Courson
Mike Current	RT	Larry Brown
Bruce Hardy	TE	Bennie Cunningham
Nat Moore	WR	Lynn Swann
Bob Griese	QB	Terry Bradshaw
Larry Csonka	RB	Sidney Thornton
Delvin Williams	RB	Franco Harris
	Starters, Defense	
Vern Den Herder	LE	L.C. Greenwood
Bob Baumhower	NT-LT	Joe Greene
A.J. Duhe	RE-RT	Gary Dunn
Kim Bokamper	LOLB-RE	John Banaszak
Steve Towle	LILB-LLB	Dennis Winston
Rusty Chambers	RILB-MLB	Jack Lambert
Larry Gordon	ROLB-RLB	Robin Cole
Norris Thomas	LCB	Ron Johnson
Gerald Small	RCB	Mel Blount
Tim Foley	SS	Donnie Shell
Neal Colzie	FS	J.T. Thomas

Miami	0	0	7	7	—	14
Pittsburgh	20	0	7	7	—	34

Pitt— Thornton 1 run (Bahr kick)
Pitt— Stallworth 17 pass from Bradshaw (kick blocked)
Pitt— Swann 20 pass from Bradshaw (Bahr kick)
Mia— D. Harris 7 pass from Griese (von Schamann kick)
Pitt— Bleier 1 run (Bahr kick)
Pitt— F. Harris 5 run (Bahr kick)
Mia— Csonka 1 run (von Schamann kick)
Attendance—50,214

TEAM STATISTICS	Mia	Pitt
First downs	16	27
Rushing	2	14
Passing	11	12
By penalty	3	1
Total yardage	249	379
Net rushing yardage	25	159
Net passing yardage	224	220
Passes att.-comp.-had int.	40-22-2	31-21-0

RUSHING

Miami—Csonka, 10 for 20, 1 TD; Davis, 2 for 12; Williams, 8 for 1; Griese, 1 for 1; Roberts, 1 for −9.

Pittsburgh—Harris, 21 for 83, 1 TD; Thornton, 12 for 52, 1 TD; Hawthorne, 2 for 15; Bleier, 4 for 13, 1 TD; A. Anderson, 1 for −4.

PASSING

Miami—Griese, 14 of 26 for 118, 1 TD, 1 int.; Strock, 8 of 14 for 125, 1 int.

Pittsburgh—Bradshaw, 21 of 31 for 230, 2 TD.

RECEIVING

Miami—Williams, 6 for 26; Moore, 5 for 93; Harris, 3 for 61, 1 TD; Nathan, 3 for 27; Davis 2 for 24; Hardy, 2 for 12; Torrey, 1 for 0.

Pittsburgh—Stallworth, 6 for 86, 1 TD; Harris, 5 for 32; Smith, 4 for 41; Swann, 3 for 37, 1 TD; Thornton, 3 for 34.

1979 NFC

TAMPA BAY 24, PHILADELPHIA 17

Ricky Bell ran for 142 yards and two touchdowns on a divisional-playoff-record 38 carries to power Tampa Bay to a 24-17 upset of Philadelphia.

The Buccaneers set the tone of the game on their opening drive, when they marched 80 yards on 18 plays and used up 9:34 before scoring on a four-yard run by Bell. Tampa Bay expanded its lead to 17-0 in the second quarter. A 10-play drive ended with Neil O'Donoghue's 40-yard field goal. On the second play after the ensuing kickoff, Wilbert Montgomery fumbled, and Randy Crowder recovered for Tampa Bay. A short drive culminated with Bell scoring from the 1 on fourth down.

Shortly before halftime, the Eagles got back into the game when Jerry Robinson intercepted a pass and returned it 37 yards to the Tampa Bay 11. Ron Jaworski passed to Charles Smith for a touchdown. The Eagles cut the margin to seven points in the third quarter, but then Doug Williams passed to Jimmie Giles for a touchdown and a 24-10 lead.

Late in the game, the Eagles had their last gasp. Jaworski took his team 80 yards, scoring on a 37-yard pass to Harold Carmichael. The Eagles got the ball back, but their hopes ended with 43 seconds left when they were unable to convert a fourth-down pass at midfield.

December 29, at Tampa

Philadelphia	**Starters, Offense**	**Tampa Bay**
Harold Carmichael	WR-TE	Jim Obradovich
Stan Walters	LT	Dave Reavis
Wade Key	LG	Greg Horton
Guy Morriss	C	Steve Wilson
Woody Peoples	RG	Greg Roberts
Jerry Sisemore	RT	Darryl Carlton
Keith Krepfle	TE	Jimmie Giles
Charles Smith	WR	Larry Mucker
Ron Jaworski	QB	Doug Williams
Leroy Harris	RB	Jerry Eckwood
Wilbert Montgomery	RB	Ricky Bell
	Starters, Defense	
Claude Humphrey	LE	Wally Chambers
Charlie Johnson	NT	Randy Crowder
Carl Hairston	RE	Lee Roy Selmon
John Bunting	LOLB	David Lewis
Jerry Robinson	LILB	Dewey Selmon
Frank LeMaster	RILB	Richard Wood
Reggie Wilkes	ROLB	Cecil Johnson
Bobby Howard	LCB	Jeris White
Herman Edwards	RCB	Mike Washington
Randy Logan	SS	Mark Cotney
John Sciarra	FS	Cedric Brown

Philadelphia	0	7	3	7	—	17
Tampa Bay	7	10	0	7	—	24

TB — Bell 4 run (O'Donoghue kick)
TB — FG O'Donoghue 40
TB — Bell 1 run (O'Donoghue kick)
Phil— Smith 11 pass from Jaworski (Franklin kick)
Phil— FG Franklin 42
TB — Giles 9 pass from Williams (O'Donoghue kick)
Phil— Carmichael 37 pass from Jaworski (Franklin kick)
Attendance—71,402

TEAM STATISTICS	**Phil**	**TB**
First downs	15	17
Rushing	4	10
Passing	10	6
By penalty	1	1
Total yardage	227	318
Net rushing yardage	48	186
Net passing yardage	179	132
Passes att.-comp.-had int.	39-15-0	15-7-1

RUSHING

Philadelphia—Montgomery, 13 for 35; Harris, 4 for 13; Jaworski, 1 for 0.

Tampa Bay—Bell, 38 for 142, 2 TDs; Eckwood, 8 for 19; Williams, 6 for 19; J. Davis, 3 for 6.

PASSING

Philadelphia—Jaworski, 15 of 39 for 199, 2 TDs.

Tampa Bay—Williams, 7 of 15 for 132, 1 TD, 1 int.

RECEIVING

Philadelphia—Montgomery, 4 for 35; Carmichael, 3 for 92, 1 TD; Smith, 3 for 49, 1 TD; Krepfle, 3 for 23; Harris, 1 for 2; Campfield, 1 for −2.

Tampa Bay—Giles, 3 for 43, 1 TD; Hagins, 2 for 34; Mucker, 1 for 34; Owens, 1 for 21.

1979 NFC

LA RAMS 21, DALLAS 19

Los Angeles quarterback Vince Ferragamo's third touchdown pass of the game, a 50-yarder to Billy Waddy with 2:06 left, lifted the Rams to a 21-19 victory over the Cowboys.

The Cowboys scored first, going ahead 2-0 in the first quarter when Ferragamo slipped in the end zone and was pinned there by Randy White. In the second quarter, Ferragamo hit running back Wendell Tyler with a 32-yard touchdown pass down the sidelines. Rafael Septien cut the lead to 7-5 with a 33-yard field goal with 52 seconds left, but the Rams moved 70 yards in four plays, with the score coming on a 43-yard pass from Ferragamo to Ron Smith, who made an acrobatic catch in the end zone with three seconds left in the half.

Ron Springs scored from one yard out to cap a 54-yard drive late in the third quarter that cut the Rams' lead to 14-12. In the fourth quarter, an interception by Cliff Harris set up Roger Staubach's two-yard touchdown pass to Jay Saldi and a 19-14 Dallas lead.

With time running out, the Rams' defense held the Cowboys and forced a punt, giving Los Angeles the ball at midfield. On first down, Ferragamo threw a pass over the middle that was tipped by linebacker Mike Hegman but still caught by Waddy, who outraced the Dallas defense to the end zone.

December 30, at Irving

LA Rams	**Starters, Offense**	**Dallas**
Billy Waddy	WR	Tony Hill
Doug France	LT	Pat Donovan
Kent Hill	LG	Herbert Scott
Rich Saul	C	John Fitzgerald
Dennis Harrah	RG	Tom Rafferty
Jackie Slater	RT	Rayfield Wright
Terry Nelson	TE	Billy Joe DuPree
Preston Dennard	WR	Drew Pearson
Vince Ferragamo	QB	Roger Staubach
Cullen Bryant	RB-TE	Doug Cosbie
Wendell Tyler	RB	Tony Dorsett
	Starters, Defense	
Jack Youngblood	LE	John Dutton
Mike Fanning	LT	Larry Cole
Larry Brooks	RT	Randy White
Fred Dryer	RE	Harvey Martin
Jim Youngblood	LLB	Mike Hegman
Jack Reynolds	MLB	Bob Breunig
Bob Brudzinski	RLB	D.D. Lewis
Dwayne O'Steen	LCB	Benny Barnes
Rod Perry	RCB	Aaron Kyle
Dave Elmendorf	SS	Randy Hughes
Nolan Cromwell	FS	Cliff Harris

LA Rams	0	14	0	7	—	21
Dallas	2	3	7	7	—	19

Dall — Safety, R. White tackled Ferragamo in end zone
Rams— Tyler 32 pass from Ferragamo (Corral kick)
Dall — FG Septien 33
Rams— R. Smith 43 pass from Ferragamo (Corral kick)
Dall — Springs 1 run (Septien kick)
Dall — Saldi 2 pass from Staubach (Septien kick)
Rams— Waddy 50 pass from Ferragamo (Corral kick)
Attendance—64,792

TEAM STATISTICS	**Rams**	**Dall**
First downs	16	16
Rushing	6	7
Passing	9	7
By penalty	1	2
Total yardage	361	280
Net rushing yardage	159	156
Net passing yardage	202	124
Passes att.-comp.-had int.	21-9-2	29-12-1

RUSHING

LA Rams—Tyler, 19 for 82; Bryant, 17 for 67; Cromwell, 1 for 7; Waddy, 1 for 3; Ferragamo, 1 for 0.

Dallas—Dorsett, 19 for 87; DuPree, 1 for 27; Newhouse, 7 for 21; Springs, 5 for 20, 1 TD; Staubach, 1 for 3; P. Pearson, 1 for −2.

PASSING

LA Rams—Ferragamo, 9 of 21 for 210, 3 TDs, 2 int.

Dallas—Staubach, 12 of 28 for 124, 1 TD, 1 int.; Springs, 0 of 1.

RECEIVING

LA Rams—Waddy, 3 for 97, 1 TD; Smith, 2 for 55, 1 TD; Tyler, 2 for 40, 1 TD; Dennard, 1 for 15; Bryant, 1 for 3.

Dallas—D. Pearson, 3 for 61; DuPree, 2 for 26; Saldi, 2 for 17, 1 TD; P. Pearson, 2 for 15; Johnson, 1 for 3; Springs, 1 for 2; Hill, 1 for 0.

1980 AFC

SAN DIEGO 20, BUFFALO 14

Dan Fouts threw a 50-yard touchdown pass to Ron Smith with only 2:08 left in the game as San Diego defeated Buffalo 20-14. On the play, San Diego's three 1,000-yard receivers—John Jefferson, Charlie Joiner, and Kellen Winslow—all lined up on the left, with Smith on the right. Smith cut over the middle and beat Bill Simpson for the touchdown.

The Chargers jumped to a 3-0 lead on their first possession, but the Bills dominated the rest of the half. Joe Ferguson's passing set up a one-yard touchdown run by Roosevelt Leaks on the second play of the second quarter, and then Ferguson threw a nine-yard touchdown pass to Frank Lewis with 22 seconds left in the half for a 14-3 lead.

Fouts brought the Chargers back on the opening drive of the third period, moving 70 yards in four plays to a nine-yard touchdown pass to Joiner. The big play was a 45-yard pass to Joiner.

Early in the fourth quarter, another field goal by Rolf Benirschke cut the San Diego deficit to one point, 14-13. With less than four minutes remaining, San Diego took over at its own 31. Two plays moved the ball to midfield. On second down, Buffalo cornerback Charles Romes stepped in front of Jefferson for an apparent interception, but the ball bounced off his chest. On the next play, Fouts passed to Smith for the game-winning score.

January 3, 1981, at San Diego

Buffalo	**Starters, Offense**	**San Diego**
Jerry Butler	WR	Charlie Joiner
Ken Jones	LT	Billy Shields
Reggie McKenzie	LG	Doug Wilkerson
Will Grant	C	Don Macek
Conrad Dobler	RG	Ed White
Joe Devlin	RT	Dan Audick
Mark Brammer	TE	Kellen Winslow
Frank Lewis	WR	John Jefferson
Joe Ferguson	QB	Dan Fouts
Curtis Brown	RB-TE	Gregg McCrary
Joe Cribbs	RB	Chuck Muncie
	Starters, Defense	
Ben Williams	LE	Leroy Jones
Fred Smerlas	NT-LT	Louie Kelcher
Sherman White	RE-RT	Gary Johnson
Lucius Sanford	LOLB-RE	Charles DeJurnett
Jim Haslett	LILB-LLB	Ray Preston
Shane Nelson	RILB-MLB	Bob Horn
Isiah Robertson	ROLB-RLB	Woodrow Lowe
Mario Clark	LCB	Willie Buchanon
Charles Romes	RCB	Mike Williams
Steve Freeman	SS	Mike Fuller
Bill Simpson	FS	Glen Edwards

Buffalo	0	14	0	0	—	14
San Diego	3	0	7	10	—	20

SD —FG Benirschke 22
Buff—Leaks 1 run (Mike-Mayer kick)
Buff—Lewis 9 pass from Ferguson (Mike-Mayer kick)
SD —Joiner 9 pass from Fouts (Benirschke kick)
SD —FG Benirschke 22
SD —Smith 50 pass from Fouts (Benirschke kick)
Attendance—52,253

TEAM STATISTICS	**Buff**	**SD**
First downs	17	21
Rushing	6	6
Passing	9	14
By penalty	2	1
Total yardage	244	397
Net rushing yardage	97	96
Net passing yardage	147	301
Passes att.-comp.-had int.	30-15-3	37-22-1

RUSHING

Buffalo—Cribbs, 18 for 53; Manucci, 2 for 21; Brown, 9 for 17; Leaks, 4 for 6, 1 TD.

San Diego—Muncie, 18 for 80; Thomas, 5 for 22; Fouts, 2 for −6.

PASSING

Buffalo—Ferguson, 15 of 29 for 180, 1 TD, 3 int.; Manucci, 0 of 1.

San Diego—Fouts, 22 of 37 for 314, 2 TDs, 1 int.

RECEIVING

Buffalo—Brammer, 4 for 62; Cribbs, 4 for 36; Lewis, 3 for 45, 1 TD; Butler, 2 for 19; Leaks, 1 for 17; Hooks, 1 for 1.

San Diego—Jefferson, 7 for 102; Muncie, 6 for 53; Joiner, 4 for 83, 1 TD; McCrary, 2 for 19; Smith, 1 for 50, 1 TD; Winslow, 1 for 5; Thomas, 1 for 2.

1980 AFC

OAKLAND 14, CLEVELAND 12

Oakland strong safety Mike Davis intercepted Brian Sipe's second-down pass intended for Ozzie Newsome in the end zone with 41 seconds remaining to preserve a 14-12 victory over Cleveland, which had marched from its own 14 to the Raiders' 13 in the last two minutes of the game.

Gusting winds and a temperature of one degree at game time pushed the chill factor to minus-37, resulting in slippery footing, stiff hands, and problems with both teams' passing and kicking games.

The first quarter was a punting duel. The Browns scored midway through the second period when cornerback Ron Bolton picked off Jim Plunkett's pass and returned it 42 yards for a touchdown. The extra point was blocked by Ted Hendricks. Taking the kickoff, the Raiders drove 64 yards to Mark van Eeghen's one-yard touchdown run with 22 seconds remaining in the half. The big play of the drive was a 28-yard pass from Plunkett to tight end Raymond Chester on third and 13. Chris Bahr's extra point put the Raiders ahead 7-6.

The Browns regained the lead on their first possession of the second half, scoring on a 30-yard field goal by Don Cockroft, who added a 30-yarder later in the period. With three seconds remaining in the third quarter, the Raiders started a 12-play, 80-yard drive that ended when van Eeghen scored again from the 1 with nine minutes left.

January 4, 1981, at Cleveland

Oakland	Starters, Offense	Cleveland
Cliff Branch	WR	Dave Logan
Art Shell	LT	Doug Dieken
Gene Upshaw	LG	Henry Sheppard
Dave Dalby	C	Tom DeLeone
Mickey Marvin	RG	Joe DeLamielleure
Henry Lawrence	RT	Cody Risien
Raymond Chester	TE	Ozzie Newsome
Bob Chandler	WR	Reggie Rucker
Jim Plunkett	QB	Brian Sipe
Mark van Eeghen	RB	Calvin Hill
Kenny King	RB	Mike Pruitt
	Starters, Defense	
John Matuszak	LE	Marshall Harris
Reggie Kinlaw	NT	Henry Bradley
Dave Browning	RE	Lyle Alzado
Ted Hendricks	LOLB	Charlie Hall
Matt Millen	LILB	R. L. Jackson
Bob Nelson	RILB	Dick Ambrose
Rod Martin	ROLB	Clay Matthews
Lester Hayes	LCB	Ron Bolton
Dwayne O'Steen	RCB	Clinton Burrell
Mike Davis	SS	Clarence Scott
Burgess Owens	FS	Thom Darden

Oakland	0	7	0	7	—	14
Cleveland	0	6	6	0	—	12

Cle —Bolton 42 interception return (kick blocked)
Oak—van Eeghen 1 run (Bahr kick)
Cle —FG Cockroft 30
Cle —FG Cockroft 30
Oak—van Eeghen 1 run (Bahr kick)
Attendance—78,245

TEAM STATISTICS	Oak	Cle
First downs	12	17
Rushing	4	6
Passing	8	8
By penalty	0	3
Total yardage	208	254
Net rushing yardage	76	85
Net passing yardage	132	169
Passes att.-comp.-had int.	30-14-2	40-13-3

RUSHING

Oakland—van Eeghen, 20 for 45, 2 TDs; King, 12 for 23; Plunkett, 4 for 8; Whittington, 1 for 1; Jensen, 1 for −1.
Cleveland—M. Pruitt, 13 for 48; Hill, 2 for 23; Sipe, 6 for 13; G. Pruitt, 4 for 11; Miller, 1 for 1; McDonald, 1 for −11.

PASSING

Oakland—Plunkett, 14 of 30 for 149, 2 int.
Cleveland—Sipe, 13 of 40 for 183, 3 int.

RECEIVING

Oakland—King, 4 for 14; Chester, 3 for 64; van Eeghen, 3 for 23; Branch, 2 for 23; Chandler, 1 for 15; Whittington, 1 for 10.
Cleveland—Newsome, 4 for 51; G. Pruitt, 3 for 54; Rucker, 2 for 38; Logan, 2 for 36; Hill, 2 for 4.

1980 NFC

PHILADELPHIA 31, MINNESOTA 16

The Eagles turned a game in which they were trailing midway through the third period into a 31-16 rout with the help of eight Minnesota turnovers in a span of 22 minutes.

The Vikings jumped to a lead the first time they had the ball, with Tommy Kramer passing to Sammy White for a 30-yard touchdown. Minnesota increased its lead to 14-0 in the second quarter on a one-yard touchdown run by Ted Brown. The Eagles came right back, with Jaworski capping an 85-yard drive with his tenth pass of the series, a nine-yard touchdown to Harold Carmichael.

On the opening drive of the third quarter, the Eagles tied the game on Wilbert Montgomery's eight-yard touchdown run. After the Vikings regained the lead with a safety, Montgomery scored again to put Philadelphia ahead for good.

Then the roof caved in. Eddie Payton fumbled away a punt near the end of the period, the first time the Vikings had dropped the ball in eight weeks. The next time the Vikings got possession, they fumbled again. And each of their final four possessions ended with an interception.

January 3, 1981, at Philadelphia

Minnesota	Starters, Offense	Philadelphia
Ahmad Rashad	WR	Harold Carmichael
Steve Riley	LT	Stan Walters
Brent Boyd	LG	Petey Perot
Dennis Swilley	C	Guy Morriss
Wes Hamilton	RG	Woody Peoples
Ron Yary	RT	Jerry Sisemore
Bob Tucker	TE	Keith Krepfle
Sammy White	WR	Scott Fitzkee
Tommy Kramer	QB	Ron Jaworski
Rickey Young	RB	Leroy Harris
Ted Brown	RB	Wilbert Montgomery
	Starters, Defense	
Mark Mullaney	LE	Dennis Harrison
James White	LT-NT	Charlie Johnson
Doug Sutherland	RT-RE	Carl Hairston
Doug Martin	RE-LOLB	John Bunting
Matt Blair	LLB-LILB	Bill Bergey
Scott Studwell	MLB-RILB	Frank LeMaster
Fred McNeill	RLB-ROLB	Jerry Robinson
John Turner	LCB	Roynell Young
Bobby Bryant	RCB	Herman Edwards
Tom Hannon	LS-SS	Randy Logan
Kurt Knoff	RS-FS	Brenard Wilson

Minnesota	7	7	2	0	—	16
Philadelphia	0	7	14	10	—	31

Minn—S. White 30 pass from Kramer (Danmeier kick)
Minn—Brown 1 run (Danmeier kick)
Phil —Carmichael 9 pass from Jaworski (Franklin kick)
Phil —Montgomery 8 run (Franklin kick)
Minn—Safety, Jaworski tackled in end zone by Martin and Blair
Phil —Montgomery 5 run (Franklin kick)
Phil —FG Franklin 33
Phil —Harrington 2 run (Franklin kick)
Attendance—70,178

TEAM STATISTICS	Minn	Phil
First downs	14	24
Rushing	3	12
Passing	10	12
By penalty	1	0
Total yardage	215	305
Net rushing yardage	36	126
Net passing yardage	179	179
Passes att.-comp.-had int.	39-19-5	38-17-2

RUSHING

Minnesota—Paschal, 4 for 26; Brown, 5 for 14, 1 TD; R. Miller, 1 for 2; Young, 2 for 0; S. White, 1 for −6.
Philadelphia—Montgomery, 26 for 74, 2 TDs; Harris, 7 for 27; Parker, 1 for 12; Giammona, 7 for 11; Harrington, 1 for 2, 1 TD.

PASSING

Minnesota—Kramer, 19 of 39 for 209, 1 TD, 5 int.
Philadelphia—Jaworski, 17 of 38 for 190, 1 TD, 2 int.

RECEIVING

Minnesota—Young, 6 for 57; Brown, 4 for 25; Senser, 4 for 25; S. White, 2 for 52, 1 TD; Rashad, 1 for 23; Paschal, 1 for 19; Bruer, 1 for 8.
Philadelphia—Carmichael, 7 for 84, 1 TD; Krepfle, 2 for 27; Montgomery, 2 for 26; Campfield, 2 for 21; Fitzkee, 2 for 19; Harris, 2 for 13.

1980 NFC

DALLAS 30, ATLANTA 27

Trailing 24-10 at the end of three quarters, Dallas exploded for three touchdowns in the final period, the last with 42 seconds left, to defeat Atlanta 30-27.

The Falcons scored the first two times they had the ball—on a 38-yard field goal by Tim Mazzetti and a 60-yard pass from Steve Bartkowski to Alfred Jenkins. The Cowboys tied it in the second quarter when Danny White passed to tight end Billy Joe DuPree for a five-yard touchdown. Atlanta came right back, Lynn Cain scoring on a one-yard run.

The Falcons extended their advantage to 24-10 in the third quarter. Bartkowski drove them 70 yards, with the score coming on a 12-yard pass to William Andrews.

Then White pulled the game out of the fire. First he took the Cowboys 85 yards to Robert Newhouse's one-yard touchdown. After the Falcons increased their lead to 27-17, White completed four of five passes as the Cowboys went 62 yards to a 14-yard touchdown pass to Drew Pearson. With less than two minutes remaining, White completed four of six passes for 70 yards, passing again to Pearson for 23 yards and the game winner.

January 4, 1981, at Atlanta

Dallas	Starters, Offense	Atlanta
Tony Hill	WR	Wallace Francis
Pat Donovan	LT	Mike Kenn
Herbert Scott	LG	Dave Scott
Robert Shaw	C	Jeff Van Note
Tom Rafferty	RG	R.C. Thielemann
Jim Cooper	RT	Warren Bryant
Billy Joe DuPree	TE	Junior Miller
Drew Pearson	WR	Alfred Jenkins
Danny White	QB	Steve Bartkowski
Robert Newhouse	RB	Lynn Cain
Tony Dorsett	RB	William Andrews
	Starters, Defense	
Ed Jones	LE	Jeff Yeates
Larry Cole	LT-NT	Don Smith
Randy White	RT-RE	Jeff Merrow
Harvey Martin	RE-LOLB	Al Richardson
Guy Brown	LLB-LILB	Fulton Kuykendall
Bob Breunig	MLB-RILB	Buddy Curry
D.D. Lewis	RLB-ROLB	Joel Williams
Benny Barnes	LCB	Rolland Lawrence
Aaron Mitchell	RCB	Kenny Johnson
Charlie Waters	SS	Bob Glazebrook
Dennis Thurman	FS	Tom Pridemore

Dallas	3	7	0	20	—	30
Atlanta	10	7	7	3	—	27

Atl —FG Mazzetti 38
Atl —Jenkins 60 pass from Bartkowski (Mazzetti kick)
Dall—FG Septien 38
Dall—DuPree 5 pass from White (Septien kick)
Atl —Cain 1 run (Mazzetti kick)
Atl —Andrews 12 pass from Bartkowski (Mazzetti kick)
Dall—Newhouse 1 run (Septien kick)
Atl —FG Mazzetti 34
Dall—D. Pearson 14 pass from White (Septien kick)
Dall—D. Pearson 23 pass from White (Septien kick)
Attendance—59,793

TEAM STATISTICS	Dall	Atl
First downs	22	18
Rushing	5	6
Passing	16	11
By penalty	1	1
Total yardage	422	371
Net rushing yardage	112	86
Net passing yardage	310	285
Passes att.-comp.-had int.	40-25-1	33-18-1

RUSHING

Dallas—Dorsett, 10 for 51; Newhouse, 6 for 31, 1 TD; P. Pearson, 1 for 11; D. Pearson, 1 for 9; DuPree, 1 for 5; Newsome, 1 for 4; D. White, 4 for 1.
Atlanta—Andrews, 14 for 43; Cain, 13 for 43, 1 TD.

PASSING

Dallas—D. White, 25 of 39 for 322, 3 TDs, 1 int.; Springs, 0 of 1.
Atlanta—Bartkowski, 18 of 33 for 320, 2 TDs, 1 int.

RECEIVING

Dallas—D. Pearson, 5 for 90, 2 TDs; Dorsett, 5 for 40; Hill, 4 for 53; P. Pearson, 4 for 51; Springs, 3 for 39; DuPree, 3 for 29, 1 TD; Johnson, 1 for 20.
Atlanta—Francis, 6 for 66; Jenkins, 4 for 155, 1 TD; Miller, 3 for 48; Cain, 2 for 20; Andrews, 2 for 19, 1 TD; Jackson, 1 for 12.

1981 AFC

SAN DIEGO 41, MIAMI 38

After 13:52 of overtime, Rolf Benirschke kicked a 29-yard field goal to give San Diego a 41-38 victory.

The game began as a rout. Miami's blunders and a blitzkrieg by San Diego left the Dolphins on the wrong end of a 24-0 score in the first quarter.

In the second period, Don Strock replaced David Woodley at quarterback for Miami. Behind Strock, the Dolphins drew even in the third quarter.

Miami took its first lead on Tony Nathan's 12-yard run. When Dan Fouts capped an 82-yard drive with a touchdown pass to James Brooks in the final minute, the game was tied at 38-38. Miami still had a chance, but San Diego tight end Kellen Winslow, who also caught 13 passes, blocked Uwe von Schamann's field-goal attempt on the last play of regulation.

After Benirschke missed and von Schamann had another field goal blocked in overtime, Fouts led the Chargers 74 yards to the game-winning kick.

January 2, 1982, at Miami

San Diego	Starters, Offense	Miami
Charlie Joiner	WR	Jimmy Cefalo
Billy Shields	LT	Jon Giesler
Doug Wilkerson	LG	Bob Kuechenberg
Don Macek	C	Mark Dennard
Ed White	RG	Ed Newman
Russ Washington	RT	Eric Laasko
Kellen Winslow	TE	Ronnie Lee
Wes Chandler	WR	Nat Moore
Dan Fouts	QB	David Woodley
John Cappelletti	RB-TE	Bruce Hardy
Chuck Muncie	RB	Andra Franklin
	Starters, Defense	
Leroy Jones	LE	Doug Betters
Louie Kelcher	LT-NT	Bob Baumhower
Gary Johnson	RT-RE	Vern Den Herder
John Woodcock	RE-LOLB	Bob Brudzinski
Linden King	LLB-LILB	Earnie Rhone
Bob Horn	MLB-RILB	A.J. Duhe
Woodrow Lowe	RLB-ROLB	Larry Gordon
Willie Buchanon	LCB	Fulton Walker
Mike Williams	RCB	Gerald Small
Pete Shaw	SS	Glenn Blackwood
Glen Edwards	FS	Lyle Blackwood

San Diego	24	0	7	7	3	—	41
Miami	0	17	14	7	0	—	38

SD — FG Benirschke 32
SD — Chandler 56 punt return (Benirschke kick)
SD — Muncie 1 run (Benirschke kick)
SD — Brooks 8 pass from Fouts (Benirschke kick)
Mia— FG von Schamann 34
Mia— Rose 1 pass from Strock (von Schamann kick)
Mia— Nathan 25 lateral from Harris after pass from Strock (von Schamann kick)
Mia— Rose 15 pass from Strock (von Schamann kick)
SD — Winslow 25 pass from Fouts (Benirschke kick)
Mia— Hardy 50 pass from Strock (von Schamann kick)
Mia— Nathan 12 run (von Schamann kick)
SD — Brooks 9 pass from Fouts (Benirschke kick)
SD — FG Benirschke 29
Attendance—73,735

TEAM STATISTICS	SD	Mia
First downs	34	25
Rushing	10	3
Passing	21	21
By penalty	3	1
Total yardage	564	472
Net rushing yardage	149	78
Net passing yardage	415	394
Passes att.-comp.-had int.	54-33-1	48-31-2

RUSHING
San Diego—Muncie, 24 for 120, 1 TD; Brooks, 3 for 19; Fouts, 2 for 10.
Miami—Nathan, 14 for 48, 1 TD; Woodley, 1 for 10; Hill, 3 for 8; Franklin, 9 for 6; Vigorito, 1 for 6.

PASSING
San Diego—Fouts, 33 of 53 for 433, 3 TDs, 1 int.; Muncie, 0 of 1.
Miami—Strock, 29 of 43 for 403, 4 TDs, 1 int.; Woodley, 2 for 5 for 20, 1 int.

RECEIVING
San Diego—Winslow, 13 for 166, 1 TD; Joiner, 7 for 108; Chandler, 6 for 106; Brooks, 4 for 31, 2 TDs; Muncie, 2 for 5; Scales, 1 for 17.
Miami—Nathan, 9 for 114, 1 TD; Harris, 6 for 106; Hardy, 5 for 89, 1 TD; Rose, 4 for 37, 2 TDs; Cefalo, 3 for 62; Vigorito, 2 for 12; Hill, 2 for 3.

1981 AFC

CINCINNATI 28, BUFFALO 21

With less than three minutes to play, Buffalo trailed 28-21 and faced a fourth-and-four situation at the Cincinnati 21. After a time-out, Joe Ferguson passed to Lou Piccone for a first down, but the Bills had used too much time and were assessed a delay-of-game penalty. On fourth and nine, Ferguson overthrew running back Roland Hooks in the end zone. The Bengals took over and ran out the clock for their first playoff victory ever.

The Bengals scored the first two times they had the ball, driving 58 and 52 yards to touchdown runs by Charles Alexander and Pete Johnson. They threatened to increase the lead in the second quarter, but Robb Riddick blocked Jim Breech's field-goal attempt. With less than two minutes in the half, Buffalo got back in the game. Ferguson passed to Jerry Butler for 54 yards to set up a one-yard touchdown run by Joe Cribbs to make the score 14-7.

Buffalo tied the game on its first possession of the third quarter, Cribbs scoring on a 44-yard run. But the Bengals came right back, driving 65 yards, with Alexander going 20 yards for the score.

Buffalo tied the game again in the fourth quarter, but the Bengals rebounded, going 78 yards for the winning points—a 16-yard pass from Ken Anderson to Cris Collinsworth.

January 3, 1982, at Cincinnati

Buffalo	Starters, Offense	Cincinnati
Jerry Butler	WR	Cris Collinsworth
Ken Jones	LT	Anthony Muñoz
Jon Borchardt	LG	Dave Lapham
Will Grant	C	Blair Bush
Tom Lynch	RG	Max Montoya
Joe Devlin	RT	Mike Wilson
Mark Brammer	TE	Dan Ross
Frank Lewis	WR	Isaac Curtis
Joe Ferguson	QB	Ken Anderson
Roosevelt Leaks	RB	Pete Johnson
Joe Cribbs	RB	Charles Alexander
	Starters, Defense	
Ben Williams	LE	Eddie Edwards
Fred Smerlas	NT	Wilson Whitley
Sherman White	RE	Ross Browner
Lucius Sanford	LOLB	Bo Harris
Jim Haslett	LILB	Jim LeClair
Phil Villapiano	RILB	Glenn Cameron
Isiah Robertson	ROLB	Reggie Williams
Mario Clark	LCB	Louis Breeden
Charles Romes	RCB	Ken Riley
Steve Freeman	SS	Bobby Kemp
Bill Simpson	FS	Bryan Hicks

Buffalo	0	7	7	7	—	21
Cincinnati	14	0	7	7	—	28

Cin —Alexander 4 run (Breech kick)
Cin —Johnson 1 run (Breech kick)
Buff—Cribbs 1 run (Mike-Mayer kick)
Buff—Cribbs 44 run (Mike-Mayer kick)
Cin —Alexander 20 run (Breech kick)
Buff—Butler 21 pass from Ferguson (Mike-Mayer kick)
Cin —Collinsworth 16 pass from Anderson (Breech kick)
Attendance—55,420

TEAM STATISTICS	Buff	Cin
First downs	21	22
Rushing	11	11
Passing	8	9
By penalty	2	2
Total yardage	336	305
Net rushing yardage	134	136
Net passing yardage	202	169
Passes att.-comp.-had int.	31-15-2	21-14-0

RUSHING
Buffalo—Cribbs, 15 for 90, 2 TDs; Hooks, 9 for 30; Leaks, 3 for 12; Brown, 1 for 2.
Cincinnati—Alexander, 13 for 72, 2 TDs; Johnson, 17 for 45, 1 TD; Anderson, 2 for 15; Griffin, 1 for 4.

PASSING
Buffalo—Ferguson, 15 of 31 for 202, 1 TD, 2 int.
Cincinnati—Anderson, 14 of 21 for 192, 1 TD.

RECEIVING
Buffalo—Butler, 4 for 98, 1 TD; Lewis, 3 for 38; Brammer, 3 for 23; Leaks, 2 for 16; Hooks, 2 for 15; Jessie, 1 for 12.
Cincinnati—Ross, 6 for 71; Johnson, 3 for 23; Collinsworth, 2 for 24, 1 TD; Kreider, 1 for 42; Curtis, 1 for 22; Alexander, 1 for 10.

1981 NFC

DALLAS 38, TAMPA BAY 0

The Dallas defensive line dominated the game, holding Tampa Bay to 74 yards rushing, sacking quarterback Doug Williams four times, and pressuring him into four interceptions and two throws that resulted in intentional grounding penalties as the Cowboys routed the Buccaneers 38-0.

"They mauled us on the line," said Tampa Bay head coach John McKay. "They did whatever they wanted and just kicked the hell out of us."

After a scoreless first quarter, the Cowboys got their offense moving in the second period. Danny White threw a nine-yard touchdown pass to Tony Hill for the only points Dallas would really need, and, in the last two minutes, a short drive set up Rafael Septien's 32-yard field goal.

The Dallas offensive line took control of the Buccaneers' defense in the third quarter. Dallas took the second-half kickoff and drove 80 yards for a touchdown that was scored on a one-yard run by Ron Springs. In the final minute and a half of the period, the Cowboys scored twice after interceptions. The Buccaneers, meanwhile, couldn't move at all on the ground, netting only two yards in the second half.

The Dallas reserves drove 90 yards in 12 plays to score the team's final touchdown midway through the fourth quarter.

January 2, 1982, at Irving

Tampa Bay	Starters, Offense	Dallas
Theo Bell	WR	Tony Hill
Gene Sanders	LT	Pat Donovan
Ray Snell	LG	Herbert Scott
Steve Wilson	C	Tom Rafferty
Greg Roberts	RG	Kurt Petersen
Charley Hannah	RT	Jim Cooper
Jimmie Giles	TE	Billy Joe DuPree
Kevin House	WR	Butch Johnson
Doug Williams	QB	Danny White
James Wilder	RB	Ron Springs
James Owens	RB	Tony Dorsett
	Starters, Defense	
Dave Stalls	LE	Ed Jones
David Logan	NT-LT	John Dutton
Lee Roy Selmon	RE-RT	Randy White
Andy Hawkins	LOLB-RE	Harvey Martin
Cecil Johnson	LILB-LLB	Mike Hegman
Richard Wood	RILB-MLB	Bob Breunig
Hugh Green	ROLB-RLB	D.D. Lewis
Norris Thomas	LCB	Everson Walls
Mike Washington	RCB	Dennis Thurman
Neal Colzie	SS	Charlie Waters
Cedric Brown	FS	Michael Downs

Tampa Bay	0	0	0	0	—	0
Miami	0	10	21	7	—	38

Dall— Hill 9 pass from White (Septien kick)
Dall— FG Septien 32
Dall— Springs 1 run (Septien kick)
Dall— Dorsett 5 run (Septien kick)
Dall— Jones 5 run (Septien kick)
Dall— Newsome 1 run (Septien kick)
Attendance—64,848

TEAM STATISTICS	TB	Dall
First downs	12	26
Rushing	3	15
Passing	7	10
By penalty	2	1
Total yardage	222	345
Net rushing yardage	74	212
Net passing yardage	148	133
Passes att.-comp.-had int.	29-10-4	26-15-0

RUSHING
Tampa Bay—Owens, 12 for 40; Wilder, 4 for 23; Williams, 2 for 9; Eckwood, 4 for 2.
Dallas—Dorsett, 16 for 86, 1 TD; Springs, 15 for 70, 1 TD; J. Jones, 9 for 32, 1 TD; Newhouse, 4 for 23; Newsome, 1 for 1, 1 TD; Cosbie, 1 for 0.

PASSING
Tampa Bay—Williams, 10 of 29 for 187, 4 int.
Dallas—D. White, 15 of 26 for 143, 1 TD.

RECEIVING
Tampa Bay—T. Bell, 3 for 36; Owens, 3 for 32; Giles, 2 for 98; Wilder, 1 for 11; House, 1 for 10.
Dallas—Dorsett, 4 for 48; DuPree, 3 for 22; Pearson, 2 for 21; Hill, 2 for 18, 1 TD; J. Jones, 2 for 15; Donley, 1 for 14; Cosbie, 1 for 5.

1981 NFC

SAN FRANCISCO 38, NY GIANTS 24

The New York Giants scored on several big plays, but that was all they could muster against San Francisco, while the 49ers showed the ability to score quickly, on long drives, or with their defense en route to a 38-24 victory.

The 49ers marched 85 yards in 13 plays with the opening kickoff for the game's first score, an eight-yard pass from Joe Montana to Charle Young. Later in the quarter, the Giants tied the score on a 72-yard pass from Scott Brunner to Earnest Gray.

With a 10-7 lead in the second quarter, the 49ers broke the game open. Ronnie Lott intercepted a pass, and, three plays later, Montana threw 58 yards to Freddie Solomon for a touchdown. Keena Turner recovered a fumble on the ensuing kickoff, and Ricky Patton scored on a 25-yard sweep.

The Giants fought back, cutting the margin to 24-17 in the third quarter. One play after Bill Currier intercepted Montana, Brunner passed 59 yards to Perkins for a touchdown.

San Francisco put the game away with a long drive resulting in Bill Ring's touchdown run, and Lott's 20-yard interception return for a score.

January 3, 1982, at San Francisco

NY Giants	Starters, Offense	San Francisco
Earnest Gray	WR	Mike Shumann
Jeff Weston	LT	Dan Audick
Billy Ard	LG	John Ayers
Jim Clack	C	Fred Quillan
J.T. Turner	RG	Randy Cross
Gordon King	RT	Keith Fahnhorst
Tom Mullady	TE	Charle Young
Johnny Perkins	WR	Mike Wilson
Scott Brunner	QB	Joe Montana
Leon Perry	RB	Ricky Patton
Rob Carpenter	RB	Earl Cooper
	Starters, Defense	
George Martin	LE	Jim Stuckey
Bill Neill	NT	Archie Reese
Gary Jeter	RE	Dwaine Board
Byron Hunt	LOLB	Willie Harper
Brian Kelley	LILB	Jack Reynolds
Harry Carson	RILB	Craig Puki
Lawrence Taylor	ROLB	Keena Turner
Mark Haynes	LCB	Ronnie Lott
Terry Jackson	RCB	Eric Wright
Bill Currier	SS	Carlton Williamson
Larry Flowers	FS	Dwight Hicks

NY Giants	7	3	7	7	—	24
San Francisco	7	17	0	14	—	38

SF — Young 8 pass from Montana (Wersching kick)
NYG— Gray 72 pass from Brunner (Danelo kick)
SF — FG Wersching 22
SF — Solomon 58 pass from Montana (Wersching kick)
SF — Patton 25 run (Wersching kick)
NYG— FG Danelo 48
NYG— Perkins 59 pass from Brunner (Danelo kick)
SF — Ring 3 run (Wersching kick)
SF — Lott 20 interception return (Wersching kick)
NYG— Perkins 17 pass from Brunner (Danelo kick)
Attendance—58,360

TEAM STATISTICS	NYG	SF
First downs	13	24
Rushing	3	8
Passing	9	13
By penalty	1	3
Total yardage	346	423
Net rushing yardage	65	135
Net passing yardage	281	288
Passes att.-comp.-had int.	37-16-2	31-20-1

RUSHING

NY Giants—Carpenter, 17 for 61; Bright, 1 for 5; Perry, 2 for 1; Brunner, 2 for −2.
San Francisco—Cooper, 7 for 52; Patton, 7 for 32, 1 TD; Ring, 10 for 29, 1 TD; Solomon, 1 for 12; Easley, 4 for 9; Clark, 1 fo 6; Davis, 1 for 4; Montana, 3 for −9.

PASSING

NY Giants—Brunner, 16 of 37 for 290, 3 TDs, 2 int.
San Francisco, Montana, 20 of 31 for 304, 2 TDs, 1 int.

RECEIVING

NY Giants—Perkins, 7 for 121, 2 TDs; Gray, 3 for 118, 1 TD; Carpenter, 3 for 18; Young, 2 for 15; Mistler, 1 for 18.
San Francisco—Solomon, 6 for 107, 1 TD; Clark, 5 for 104; Patton, 2 for 38; Young, 2 for 22, 1 TD; Wilson, 2 for 21; Ramson, 1 for 11; Elliott, 1 for 5; Ring, 1 for −4.

1982 AFC

NY JETS 17, LA RAIDERS 14

New York Jets linebacker Lance Mehl intercepted two of Jim Plunkett's passes in the final three minutes to preserve a slim 17-14 margin and lead the Jets to an upset of the Los Angeles Raiders.

The Jets led 10-0 at halftime, due in large part to the performance of Wesley Walker, who caught a first-quarter pass from Richard Todd for a 20-yard touchdown, then set up Pat Leahy's field goal with a 37-yard reception.

The Raiders grabbed the momentum and the lead in the third quarter. Plunkett led them 77 yards on 12 plays to a three-yard touchdown run by Marcus Allen. Then, Plunkett found Malcolm Barnwell with a 57-yard touchdown pass. When Lester Hayes intercepted Todd's pass in the final minute of the quarter to put the Raiders at the Jets' 41, it looked as if the Raiders were about to put the game away. But with a first down deep in Jets territory, Allen fumbled and Joe Klecko recovered for New York.

The Jets regained the lead with 3:45 to play on Scott Dierking's one-yard dive over the middle. Once again Walker had been the man of the moment, catching a 45-yard pass at the 1. Then it was time for Mehl. He intercepted Plunkett at the Jets' 35. Then, after Freeman McNeil fumbled the ball back to the Raiders, Mehl picked one off at the New York 26.

January 15, 1983, at Los Angeles

NY Jets	Starters, Offense	LA Raiders
Mickey Shuler	TE-WR	Cliff Branch
Chris Ward	LT	Bruce Davis
Stan Waldemore	LG	Curt Marsh
Joe Fields	C	Dave Dalby
Dan Alexander	RG	Mickey Marvin
Marvin Powell	RT	Henry Lawrence
Jerome Barkum	TE	Todd Christensen
Wesley Walker	WR	Malcolm Barnwell
Richard Todd	QB	Jim Plunkett
Mike Augustyniak	RB	Kenny King
Freeman McNeil	RB	Marcus Allen
	Starters, Defense	
Mark Gastineau	LE	Howie Long
Abdul Salaam	LT-NT	Reggie Kinlaw
Marty Lyons	RT-RE	Lyle Alzado
Kenny Neil	RE-LOLB	Ted Hendricks
Greg Buttle	LLB-LILB	Matt Millen
Stan Blinka	MLB-RILB	Bob Nelson
Lance Mehl	RLB-ROLB	Rod Martin
Bobby Jackson	LCB	Lester Hayes
Jerry Holmes	RCB	Ted Watts
Ken Schroy	SS	Mike Davis
Darrol Ray	FS	Burgess Owens

NY Jets	7	3	0	7	—	17
LA Raiders	0	0	14	0	—	14

NYJ — Walker 20 pass from Todd (Leahy kick)
NYJ — FG Leahy 30
Raiders— Allen 3 run (Bahr kick)
Raiders— Barnwell 57 pass from Plunkett (Bahr kick)
NYJ — Dierking 1 run (Leahy kick)
Attendance—90,038

TEAM STATISTICS	NYJ	Raiders
First downs	21	19
Rushing	8	7
Passing	11	11
By penalty	2	1
Total yardage	391	339
Net rushing yardage	139	93
Net passing yardage	252	246
Passes att.-comp.-had int.	24-15-2	33-21-3

RUSHING

NY Jets—McNeil, 23 for 105; Augustyniak, 4 for 22; Todd, 5 for 8; Dierking, 2 for 4, 1 TD.
LA Raiders—Allen, 15 for 36, 1 TD; Plunkett, 4 for 18; King, 5 for 16; Montgomery, 1 for 11; Hawkins, 3 for 4; Pruitt, 1 for 4; Barnwell, 1 for 4.

PASSING

NY Jets—Todd, 15 of 24 for 277, 1 TD, 2 int.
LA Raiders—21 of 33 for 266, 1 TD, 3 int.

RECEIVING

NY Jets—Walker, 7 for 169, 1 TD; J. Jones, 2 for 52; Augustyniak, 2 for 18; Barkum, 1 for 11; McNeil, 1 for 11; Shuler, 1 for 9; Dierking, 1 for 7.
LA Raiders—Allen, 6 for 37; Branch, 5 for 82; Christensen, 5 for 31; Barnwell, 2 for 83, 1 TD; Hawkins, 1 for 15; Ramsey, 1 for 14; King, 1 for 4.

1982 AFC

MIAMI 34, SAN DIEGO 13

The anticipated rematch between Miami and San Diego, the two teams that had battled to a 41-38 overtime thriller in 1981, turned out to be nothing but a good, old-fashioned drubbing as the Dolphins beat the Chargers on offense, defense, and special teams to record a 34-13 victory.

Miami capitalized on three early turnovers (including two fumbled kickoffs) to bolt to a 24-0 lead midway through the second quarter. Only one of the Dolphins' first four scores came following a drive of more than 30 yards.

The Chargers cut the halftime lead to 27-13 by scoring twice in the final four minutes of the second period, but then Miami's Killer Bees defense, the NFL's top-ranked unit, took over and grounded Air Coryell.

The Dolphins sacked Dan Fouts twice and intercepted him four times in the second half, including two by strong safety Glenn Blackwood.

Miami ended any doubt about the outcome by driving 62 yards to a touchdown that came on a seven-yard quarterback draw by David Woodley on the second play of the fourth quarter.

January 16, 1983, at Miami

San Diego	Starters, Offense	Miami
Charlie Joiner	WR	Duriel Harris
Billy Shields	LT	Jon Giesler
Doug Wilkerson	LG	Bob Kuechenberg
Don Macek	C	Dwight Stephenson
Ed White	RG	Jeff Toews
Russ Washington	RT	Eric Laakso
Kellen Winslow	TE	Bruce Hardy
Wes Chandler	WR	Jimmy Cefalo
Dan Fouts	QB	David Woodley
Larry Sievers	TE	Ronnie Lee
Chuck Muncie	RB	Tony Nathan
	Starters, Defense	
Leroy Jones	LE	Kim Bokamper
Louie Kelcher	LT-NT	Bob Baumhower
Gary Johnson	RT-RE	Doug Betters
Keith Ferguson	RE-LOLB	Bob Brudzinski
David Lewis	LLB-LILB	A.J. Duhe
Cliff Thrift	MLB-RILB	Earnie Rhone
Woodrow Lowe	RLB-ROLB	Larry Gordon
Jeff Allen	LCB	Gerald Small
Mike Williams	RCB	Don McNeal
Tim Fox	SS	Glenn Blackwood
Bruce Laird	FS	Lyle Blackwood

San Diego	0	13	0	0	—	13
Miami	7	20	0	7	—	34

Mia— Moore 3 pass from Woodley (von Schamann kick)
Mia— Franklin 3 run (von Schamann kick)
Mia— Lee 6 pass from Woodley (von Schamann kick)
Mia— FG von Schamann 24
SD — Joiner 28 pass from Fouts (kick failed)
Mia— FG von Schamann 23
SD — Muncie 1 run (Benirschke kick)
Mia— Woodley 7 run (von Schamann kick)
Attendance—71,383

TEAM STATISTICS	SD	Mia
First downs	17	29
Rushing	5	15
Passing	9	11
By penalty	3	3
Total yardage	247	413
Net rushing yardage	79	214
Net passing yardage	168	199
Passes att.-comp.-had int.	34-15-5	23-18-1

RUSHING

San Diego—Muncie, 11 for 62, 1 TD; Brooks, 3 for 9; Cappelletti, 1 for 5; Fouts, 1 for 3.
Miami—Franklin, 23 for 96, 1 TD; Nathan, 19 for 83; Bennett, 7 for 14; Woodley, 3 for 14, 1 TD; Orosz, 1 for 11; Vigorito, 1 for 2; Jensen, 2 for −6.

PASSING

San Diego—Fouts, 15 of 34 for 191, 1 TD, 5 int.
Miami—Woodley, 17 of 22 for 195, 2 TDs, 1 int.; Nathan, 1 of 1 for 20.

RECEIVING

San Diego—Muncie, 6 for 53; Chandler, 2 for 38; Brooks, 2 for 25; Sievers, 2 for 21; Joiner, 1 for 28, 1 TD; Winslow, 1 for 18; Holohan, 1 for 8.
Miami—Nathan, 8 for 55; Hardy, 3 for 45; Cefalo, 2 for 69; Vigorito, 2 for 22; Harris, 1 for 15; Lee, 1 for 6, 1 TD; Moore, 1 for 3, 1 TD

1982 NFC

WASHINGTON 21, MINNESOTA 7

John Riggins totaled a career-high 185 yards on 37 carries to lead the Washington Redskins to a 21-7 victory over the Minnesota Vikings.

"He was stupendous," said Washington coach Joe Gibbs. "The guy is remarkable, phenomenal. Two weeks ago he came to me and said he was excited about the playoffs. He said 'Give me the ball,' and he obviously meant he'd do something with it."

Washington got a quick 14-0 jump on Minnesota in the first quarter when the Redskins controlled the ball for nearly 12 minutes. The first touchdown came on the opening possession of the day, a 10-play, 66-yard drive capped by Joe Theismann's three-yard touchdown pass to tight end Don Warren. The Redskins scored again after moving 71 yards in only seven plays, the big one being a 46-yard pass from Theismann to Alvin Garrett. Riggins scored on fourth down from the 2.

"It's demoralizing the way they control the ball early and don't let you touch it," said Minnesota quarterback Tommy Kramer.

The Vikings reponded early in the second quarter with Ted Brown's 18-yard touchdown run. Theismann quickly matched those points, driving the Redskins to an 18-yard scoring pass to Garrett just more than three minutes later, for the final points in the game.

January 15, 1983, at Washington

Minnesota	Starters, Offense	Washington
Sammy White	WR	Charlie Brown
Steve Riley	LT	Joe Jacoby
Jim Hough	LG	Russ Grimm
Dennis Swilley	C	Jeff Bostic
Wes Hamilton	RG	Fred Dean
Tim Irwin	RT	George Starke
Joe Senser	TE	Don Warren
Sam McCullum	WR	Alvin Garrett
Tommy Kramer	QB	Joe Theismann
Tony Galbreath	RB-TE	Rick Walker
Ted Brown	RB	John Riggins
	Starters, Defense	
Doug Martin	LE	Mat Mendenhall
Charlie Johnson	NT-LT	Dave Butz
Mark Mullaney	RE-RT	Darryl Grant
Matt Blair	LOLB-RE	Dexter Manley
Scott Studwell	LILB-LLB	Mel Kaufman
Dennis Johnson	RILB-MLB	Neal Olkewicz
Fred McNeill	ROLB-RLB	Rich Milot
John Swain	LCB	Jeris White
Willie Teal	RCB	Vernon Dean
Tommy Hannon	LS-SS	Tony Peters
John Turner	RS-FS	Mark Murphy

Minnesota	0	7	0	0	—	7
Washington	14	7	0	0	—	21

Wash—Warren 3 pass from Theismann (Moseley kick)
Wash—Riggins 2 run (Moseley kick)
Minn —T. Brown 18 run (Danmeier kick)
Wash—Garrett 18 pass from Theismann (Moseley kick)
Attendance—54,593

TEAM STATISTICS	Minn	Wash
First downs	15	23
Rushing	3	12
Passing	11	11
By penalty	1	0
Total yardage	317	415
Net rushing yardage	79	204
Net passing yardage	238	211
Passes att.-comp.-had int.	39-18-0	23-17-1

RUSHING
Minnesota—T. Brown, 14 for 65, 1 TD; Young, 1 for 6; Nelson, 1 for 4; Galbreath, 1 for 4; Kramer, 1 for 0.
Washington—Riggins, 37 for 185, 1 TD; Washington, 1 for 11; Theismann, 3 for 4; Garrett, 1 for 4.

PASSING
Minnesota—Kramer, 8 of 39 for 252.
Washington—Theismann, 17 of 23 for 213, 2 TDs, 1 int.

RECEIVING
Minnesota—T. Brown, 7 for 62; McCullum, 3 for 63; LeCount, 3 for 57; Jordan, 2 for 11; Senser, 1 for 32; Jackson, 1 for 14; S. White, 1 for 13.
Washington—C. Brown, 5 for 59; Walker, 4 for 20, 1 TD; Garrett, 3 for 75, 1 TD; Giaquinto, 2 for 39; Walker, 2 for 15; Washington, 1 for 5.

1982 NFC

DALLAS 37, GREEN BAY 26

Dallas cornerback Dennis Thurman intercepted three passes, scoring on one in the second quarter and preserving a precarious lead with another in the fourth, to help the Cowboys to a 37-26 victory.

Dallas led 6-0 after the first quarter, but the Packers drove 79 yards to take the lead on a six-yard touchdown pass from Lynn Dickey to James Lofton. The Cowboys came back, driving 80 yards in 13 plays to go ahead 13-7. Then, on the first play after the kickoff, Thurman picked off Dickey's pass at the Packers' 39 and scored to make it 20-7 at halftime.

The Packers still trailed 23-13 at the end of three quarters, but, on the first play of the final period, Lofton took the ball on a reverse around right end and went 71 yards for a touchdown. The Cowboys responded with an 80-yard march to a touchdown, but Green Bay narrowed the gap again when Mark Lee scored on a 22-yard interception return.

Dallas finally pulled away when a 49-yard pass from Drew Pearson to Tony Hill set up a one-yard touchdown run by Robert Newhouse. Then Thurman made sure the Packers stayed at arm's length.

January 16, 1983, at Dallas

Green Bay	Starters, Offense	Dallas
James Lofton	WR	Tony Hill
Tim Stokes	LT	Pat Donovan
Tim Huffman	LG	Herbert Scott
Larry McCarren	C	Tom Rafferty
Leotis Harris	RG	Kurt Peterson
Greg Koch	RT	Jim Cooper
Paul Coffman	TE	Doug Cosbie
John Jefferson	WR	Drew Pearson
Lynn Dickey	QB	Danny White
Gerry Ellis	RB	Robert Newhouse
Eddie Lee Ivery	RB	Tony Dorsett
	Starters, Defense	
Mike Butler	LE	Ed Jones
Terry Jones	NT-LT	Don Smerek
Ezra Johnson	RE-RT	Randy White
John Anderson	LOLB-RE	Harvey Martin
Randy Scott	LILB-LLB	Mike Hegman
George Cumby	RILB-MLB	Bob Breunig
Mike Douglass	ROLB-RLB	Guy Brown
Mark Lee	LCB	Everson Walls
Mike McCoy	RCB	Dennis Thurman
Johnnie Gray	SS	Benny Barnes
Maurice Harvey	FS	Michael Downs

Green Bay	0	7	6	13	—	26
Dallas	6	14	3	14	—	37

Dall—FG Septien 50
Dall—FG Septien 34
GB —Lofton 6 pass from Dickey (Stenerud kick)
Dall—Newsome 2 run (Septien kick)
Dall—Thurman 39 interception return (Septien kick)
GB —FG Stenerud 30
GB —FG Stenerud 33
Dall—FG Septien 24
GB —Lofton 71 run (kick failed)
Dall—Cosbie 7 pass from D. White (Septien kick)
GB —Lee 22 interception return (Stenerud kick)
Dall—Newhouse 1 run (Septien kick)
Attendance—63,972

TEAM STATISTICS	GB	Dall
First downs	21	24
Rushing	5	10
Passing	16	13
By penalty	0	1
Total yardage	466	375
Net rushing yardage	158	109
Net passing yardage	308	266
Passes att.-comp.-had int.	36-19-3	37-24-1

RUSHING
Green Bay—Lofton, 1 for 71, 1 TD; Rodgers, 4 for 42; Ivery, 7 for 24; Ellis, 4 for 21; Dickey, 1 for 0.
Dallas—Dorsett, 27 for 99; Newhouse, 7 for 15, 1 TD; Newsome, 1 for 2, 1 TD; D. White, 4 for −7.

PASSING
Green Bay—Dickey, 19 of 36 for 332, 1 TD, 3 int.
Dallas—D. White, 23 of 36 for 225, 1 TD, 1 int.; Pearson, 1 of 1 for 49.

RECEIVING
Green Bay—Lofton, 5 for 109, 1 TD; Coffman, 5 for 72; Ellis, 5 for 30; Jefferson, 2 for 40; Ivery, 1 for 25; Epps, 1 for 16.
Dallas—T. Hill, 7 for 142; Newsome, 7 for 70; Cosbie, 4 for 36, 1 TD; Dorsett, 3 for 9; DuPree, 2 for 14; Pearson, 1 for 3.

1983 AFC

SEATTLE 27, MIAMI 20

It was cold and rainy in the Orange Bowl, but Miami's biggest chill came courtesy of Seattle, as the Seahawks stunned the Dolphins 27-20.

Miami was in control in the first half, when Dan Marino threw two touchdown passes. The first, a 19-yarder to tight end Dan Johnson, completed an 80-yard drive. The second touchdown was a spectacular 32-yard strike to Mark Duper, who made the catch on the left side of the end zone despite close coverage by Dave Brown and Kenny Easley. Miami's defense also was playing well, with the Seahawks' only score being set up by a 59-yard kickoff return.

In the second half, Miami's offense came apart at the seams. David Overstreet fumbled, and the Seahawks recovered at the 45. Eight plays later, Curt Warner scored from the 1, and Norm Johnson's extra point put Seattle ahead 14-13. After Marino was intercepted, Johnson padded the margin to 17-13 early in the fourth quarter.

The Dolphins regained the lead with less than four minutes to play, but Warner scored from the 2 following a 40-yard pass from Krieg to Steve Largent.

Miami never had a chance to come back. Fulton Walker fumbled on the kickoff, and, after Johnson kicked a 37-yard field goal with 1:37 left, Walker fumbled the next kickoff as well.

December 31, at Miami

Seattle	Starters, Offense	Miami
Pete Metzelaars	TE-WR	Mark Duper
Ron Essink	LT	Jon Giesler
Edwin Bailey	LG	Bob Kuechenberg
Blair Bush	C	Dwight Stephenson
Robert Pratt	RG	Ed Newman
Steve August	RT	Eric Laakso
Charle Young	TE	Dan Johnson
Steve Largent	WR	Nat Moore
Dave Krieg	QB	Dan Marino
Cullen Bryant	RB-TE	Bruce Hardy
Curt Warner	RB	Andra Franklin
	Starters, Defense	
Jacob Green	LE	Doug Betters
Joe Nash	NT	Bob Baumhower
Jeff Bryant	RE	Kim Bokamper
Bruce Scholtz	LOLB	Bob Brudzinski
Shelton Robinson	LILB	A.J. Duhe
Keith Butler	RILB	Earnie Rhone
Greg Gaines	ROLB	Charles Bowser
Kerry Justin	LCB	William Judson
Dave Brown	RCB	Gerald Small
Kenny Easley	SS	Glenn Blackwood
John Harris	FS	Lyle Blackwood

Seattle	0	7	7	13	—	27
Miami	0	13	0	7	—	20

Mia—Johnson 19 pass from Marino (kick failed)
Sea—C. Bryant 6 pass from Krieg (N. Johnson kick)
Mia—Duper 32 pass from Marino (von Schamann kick)
Sea—Warner 1 run (N. Johnson kick)
Sea—FG N. Johnson 27
Mia—Bennett 3 run (von Schamann kick)
Sea—Warner 2 run (N. Johnson kick)
Sea—FG N. Johnson 37
Attendance—74,136

TEAM STATISTICS	Sea	Mia
First downs	21	21
Rushing	12	9
Passing	9	11
By penalty	0	1
Total yardage	334	321
Net rushing yardage	151	128
Net passing yardage	183	193
Passes att.-comp.-had int.	29-15-1	26-15-2

RUSHING
Seattle—Warner, 29 for 113, 2 TDs; C. Bryant, 5 for 22; Hughes, 4 for 21; Krieg, 4 for −5.
Miami—Overstreet, 9 for 50; Bennett, 7 for 31, 1 TD; Franklin, 6 for 28; Nathan, 8 for 19.

PASSING
Seattle—Krieg, 15 of 28 for 192, 1 TD, 1 int.; Zorn, 0 of 1.
Miami—Marino, 15 of 25 for 193, 2 TDs, 2 int.; Clayton, 0 of 1.

RECEIVING
Seattle—Warner, 5 for 38; Johns, 4 for 60; Largent, 2 for 56; Doornink, 2 for 26; C. Bryant, 2 for 12, 1 TD.
Miami—Duper, 9 for 117, 1 TD; Johnson, 2 for 29, 1 TD; Moore, 2 for 26; Rose, 1 for 15; Nathan, 1 for 6.

1983 AFC

LA RAIDERS 38, PITTSBURGH 10

In front of an NFL playoff-record 90,380 onlookers at the Los Angeles Memorial Coliseum, the Los Angeles Raiders played virtually flawless football and dominated the Pittsburgh Steelers 38-10.

Though the Steelers scored first, on a 17-yard first-quarter field goal, it turned into an emotional advantage for the Raiders. Pittsburgh had driven 78 yards, but, on fourth and inches at goal line, head coach Chuck Noll went for a field goal by Gary Anderson.

"When they decided to take the three," said Raiders head coach Tom Flores, "it gave us a lift." So did an 18-yard interception return for a touchdown by cornerback Lester Hayes three minutes later. That made the score 7-3, and the rout was on.

The Raiders concluded an 80-yard drive in the second quarter with a four-yard touchdown run by Marcus Allen. Then they extended their lead to 17-3 with a field goal six seconds before halftime.

The Raiders scored all three times they had the ball in the third quarter, driving 72, 58, and 65 yards for touchdowns. The second drive lasted only two plays, the score coming on a 49-yard run by Allen, who went over right guard and broke up the middle.

January 1, 1984, at Los Angeles

Pittsburgh	**Starters, Offense**	**LA Raiders**
John Stallworth	WR	Cliff Branch
Tunch Ilkin	LT	Bruce Davis
Craig Wolfley	LG	Charley Hannah
Mike Webster	C	Dave Dalby
Steve Courson	RG	Mickey Marvin
Larry Brown	RT	Henry Lawrence
Bennie Cunningham	TE	Todd Christensen
Calvin Sweeney	WR	Malcolm Barnwell
Cliff Stoudt	QB	Jim Plunkett
Frank Pollard	RB	Kenny King
Franco Harris	RB	Marcus Allen
	Starters, Defense	
Edmund Nelson	LE	Howie Long
Gary Dunn	NT	Reggie Kinlaw
Keith Gary	RE	Lyle Alzado
Mike Merriweather	LOLB	Ted Hendricks
Jack Lambert	LILB	Matt Millen
David Little	RILB	Bob Nelson
Robin Cole	ROLB	Rod Martin
Dwayne Woodruff	LCB	Lester Hayes
Mel Blount	RCB	Mike Haynes
Donnie Shell	SS	Mike Davis
Rick Woods	FS	Vann McElroy

Pittsburgh	3	0	7	0	—	10
LA Raiders	7	10	21	0	—	38

Pitt — FG Anderson 17
Raiders— Hayes 18 interception return (Bahr kick)
Raiders— Allen 4 run (Bahr kick)
Raiders— FG Bahr 45
Raiders— King 9 run (Bahr kick)
Raiders— Allen 49 run (Bahr kick)
Pitt — Stallworth 58 pass from Stoudt (Anderson kick)
Raiders— Hawkins 2 run (Bahr kick)
Attendance—90,380

TEAM STATISTICS	**Pitt**	**Raiders**
First downs	17	24
Rushing	9	13
Passing	8	9
By penalty	0	2
Total yardage	331	413
Net rushing yardage	162	188
Net passing yardage	169	225
Passes att.-comp.-had int.	27-13-1	34-21-0

RUSHING
Pittsburgh—Stoudt, 9 for 50; Pollard, 9 for 37; Abercrombie, 6 for 36; F. Harris, 6 for 33; Odom, 1 for 4; T. Harris, 1 for 2.
LA Raiders—Allen, 13 for 121, 2 TDs; Hawkins, 10 for 25, 1 TD; Plunkett, 2 for 23; King, 6 for 20, 1 TD; Guy, 1 for 2; Wilson, 1 for −3.

PASSING
Pittsburgh—Stoudt, 10 of 20 for 187, 1 TD, 1 int.; Malone, 3 of 7 for 22.
LA Raiders—Plunkett, 21 of 34 for 232.

RECEIVING
Pittsburgh—F. Harris, 4 for 31; Capers, 2 for 54; Cunningham, 2 for 32; Sweeney, 2 for 24; Stallworth, 1 for 58, 1 TD; Odom, 1 for 6; Abercrombie, 1 for 4.
LA Raiders—Christensen, 7 for 88; Branch, 6 for 76; Allen, 5 for 38; Barnwell, 3 for 30.

1983 NFC

SAN FRANCISCO 24, DETROIT 23

With five seconds remaining in the game, Detroit's Ed Murray, who earlier had kicked a playoff-record 54-yard field goal, missed a 43-yard attempt, and the San Francisco 49ers beat the Lions 24-23.

That Murray, who already had kicked three field goals, was in a position to win the game was a bit remarkable in itself. The Lions had to overcome five interceptions thrown by Gary Danielson.

The Lions went ahead 3-0 on their opening drive. They threatened again before the end of the quarter, but Danielson was intercepted at the 15, and the 49ers drove 85 yards to score. On the first play after the kickoff, Danielson was intercepted, setting up Wendell Tyler's two-yard touchdown run.

Danielson was intercepted two more times in the first half, which ended with the score 14-9.

The 49ers led 17-9 at the end of the third quarter when Danielson finally started hitting his own receivers. The Lions drove to two touchdown runs by Billy Sims and a 23-17 lead with five minutes to play. But Joe Montana hit on six of six passes, the final one a 14-yard touchdown to Freddie Solomon.

There was time left for one quick drive. Four completions by Danielson set up Murray's attempt.

December 31, at San Francisco

Detroit	**Starters, Offense**	**San Francisco**
Mark Nichols	WR	Mike Wilson
Chris Dieterich	LT	Bubba Paris
Homer Elias	LG	John Ayers
Steve Mott	C	Fred Quillan
Don Greco	RG	Randy Cross
Keith Dorney	RT	Keith Fahnhorst
Ulysses Norris	TE	Russ Francis
Leonard Thompson	WR	Freddie Solomon
Gary Danielson	QB	Joe Montana
James Jones	RB	Roger Craig
Billy Sims	RB	Wendell Tyler
	Starters, Defense	
Curtis Green	LE	Jim Stuckey
William Gay	LT-NT	Pete Kugler
Doug English	RT-RE	Dwaine Board
Mike Cofer	RE-LOLB	Willie Harper
Garry Cobb	LLB-LILB	Riki Ellison
Ken Fantetti	MLB-RILB	Jack Reynolds
Jimmy Williams	RLB-ROLB	Keena Turner
Bobby Watkins	LCB	Ronnie Lott
Bruce McNorton	RCB	Eric Wright
William Graham	LS-SS	Carlton Williamson
Alvin Hall	RS-FS	Dwight Hicks

Detroit	3	6	0	14	—	23
San Francisco	7	7	3	7	—	24

Det— FG Murray 37
SF — Craig 1 run (Wersching kick)
SF — Tyler 2 run (Wersching kick)
Det— FG Murray 21
Det— FG Murray 54
SF — FG Wersching 19
Det— Sims 11 run (Murray kick)
Det— Sims 3 run (Murray kick)
SF — Solomon 14 pass from Montana (Wersching kick)
Attendance—59,979

TEAM STATISTICS	**Det**	**SF**
First downs	22	20
Rushing	9	9
Passing	11	10
By penalty	2	1
Total yardage	412	291
Net yards rushing	188	103
Net yards passing	224	188
Passes att.-comp.-had int.	38-24-5	31-18-1

RUSHING
Detroit—Sims, 20 for 114, 2 TDs; Jones, 10 for 33; L. Thompson, 1 for 24; Danielson, 4 for 17.
San Francisco—Tyler, 17 for 74, 1 TD; Montana, 3 for 16; Craig, 7 for 13, 1 TD.

PASSING
Detroit—Danielson, 24 of 38 for 236, 5 int.
San Francisco—Montana, 18 of 31 for 1 TD, 1 int.

RECEIVING
Detroit—L. Thompson, 6 for 74; Chadwick, 5 for 58; Jones, 5 for 44; Sims, 4 for 26; Scott, 3 for 29; Norris, 1 for 5.
San Francisco—Craig, 7 for 61; Francis, 4 for 75; Solomon, 2 for 16, 1 TD; Tyler, 2 for 15; Wilson, 1 for 26; Ramson, 1 for 4; Moore, 1 for 4.

1983 NFC

WASHINGTON 51, LA RAMS 7

The Washington offense scored on each of its first five possessions, while the defense intercepted Los Angeles quarterback Vince Ferragamo three times and held NFL rushing champion Eric Dickerson to 16 yards on 10 carries. The result of the combined effort was a devastating 51-7 victory for the Redskins, which was both the most lopsided victory ever for the Redskins and the worst defeat ever for the Rams.

Washington running back John Riggins, who rushed for 119 yards to go over the 100-yard mark for the fifth consecutive playoff game, opened the scoring midway through the first quarter. Riggins's three-yard run capped an eight-play, 65-yard drive on the Redskins' first possession of the day. After that, Washington kept scoring, building its lead to 17-0 after one quarter and 24-0 before the Rams finally scored on a 32-yard pass from Vince Ferragamo to wide receiver Preston Dennard. Riggins scored three touchdowns in the game.

The Redskins scored twice more before the half, setting an NFL playoff-game record with 38 first-half points.

January 1, 1984, at Washington

LA Rams	**Starters, Offense**	**Washington**
Preston Dennard	WR	Charlie Brown
Bill Bain	LT	Joe Jacoby
Kent Hill	LG	Russ Grimm
Doug Smith	C	Jeff Bostic
Dennis Harrah	RG	Mark May
Jackie Slater	RT	George Starke
Mike Barber	TE	Don Warren
George Farmer	WR	Art Monk
Vince Ferragamo	QB	Joe Theismann
Mike Guman	RB-TE	Rick Walker
Eric Dickerson	RB	John Riggins
	Starters, Defense	
Jack Youngblood	LE	Todd Liebenstein
Greg Meisner	NT-LT	Dave Butz
Reggie Doss	RE-RT	Darryl Grant
Mel Owens	LOLB-RE	Dexter Manley
Jim Collins	LILB-LLB	Mel Kaufman
Carl Ekern	RILB-MLB	Neal Olkewicz
George Andrews	ROLB-RLB	Rich Milot
Eric Harris	LCB	Darrell Green
LeRoy Irvin	RCB	Anthony Washington
Nolan Cromwell	SS	Ken Coffey
Johnnie Johnson	FS	Mark Murphy

LA Rams	0	7	0	0	—	7
Washington	17	21	6	7	—	51

Wash— Riggins 3 run (Moseley kick)
Wash— Monk 40 pass from Theismann (Moseley kick)
Wash— FG Moseley 42
Wash— Riggins 1 run (Moseley kick)
Rams— Dennard 32 pass from Ferragamo (Lansford kick)
Wash— Monk 21 pass from Theismann (Moseley kick)
Wash— Riggins 1 run (Moseley kick)
Wash— FG Moseley 36
Wash— FG Moseley 41
Wash— Green 72 interception return (Moseley kick)
Attendance—54,440

TEAM STATISTICS	**Rams**	**Wash**
First downs	12	23
Rushing	2	8
Passing	9	14
By penalty	1	1
Total yardage	204	445
Net rushing yardage	51	130
Net passing yardage	153	315
Passes att.-comp.-had int.	43-20-3	25-20-0

RUSHING
LA Rams—Jones, 4 for 28; Dickerson, 10 for 16; Redden, 2 for 7.
Washington—Riggins, 25 for 119, 3 TDs; Giaquinto, 4 for 9; Evans, 3 for 4; Wonsley, 2 for 3, Washington, 5 for −2; Holly, 1 for −3.

PASSING
LA Rams—Ferragamo, 20 of 43 for 175, 1 TD, 3 int.
Washington—Theismann, 18 of 23 for 202, 2 TDs; Holly, 2 of 2 for 13.

RECEIVING
LA Rams—Dickerson, 6 for 9; Guman, 5 for 29; Barber, 3 for 42; Ellard, 3 for 39; Dennard, 2 for 50, 1 TD; D. Hill, 1 for 6.
Washington—Brown, 6 for 171; Monk, 4 for 60, 2 TDs; Warren, 3 for 23; Giaquinto, 2 for 17; Garrett, 2 for 13; Walker, 1 for 14; Washington, 1 for 10; Didier, 1 for 7.

1984 AFC

MIAMI 31, SEATTLE 10

Looking to slow down Miami's scoring machine and grind out a victory the way it had the previous week against the Raiders, Seattle instead ground to a halt, as Miami's maligned defense controlled the game and helped the Dolphins to a 31-10 victory.

While the Dolphins held the Seahawks to 51 yards rushing, Miami's Tony Nathan gained 76 yards to open up the passing lanes for Dan Marino, who then picked Seattle apart. Nathan scored the first touchdown of the game on a 14-yard run. In the second period, two runs by Nathan and two passes by Marino were all the Dolphins needed to move 60 yards for a 14-3 lead. Late in the quarter, the Seahawks narrowed the margin to four when Dave Krieg connected with Steve Largent for a 56-yard touchdown.

The most important two series of the game opened the third quarter. The Seahawks put together an 11-play drive to the Miami 24, but missed a field goal. Then the Dolphins moved to the Seattle 3, where, on third down, Marino's pass was batted down in the end zone. An interference call on Keith Simpson gave Miami a first down, however, and two plays later the Dolphins scored on Marino's pass to tight end Bruce Hardy. The next time the Dolphins had the ball, Marino hit Mark Clayton with a 33-yard touchdown pass to clinch the win.

December 29, at Miami

Seattle	Starters, Offense	Miami
Mike Tice	TE-WR	Mark Duper
Ron Essink	LT	Jon Giesler
Edwin Bailey	LG	Roy Foster
Blair Bush	C	Dwight Stephenson
Robert Pratt	RG	Ed Newman
Bob Cryder	RT	Cleveland Green
Charle Young	TE	Bruce Hardy
Steve Largent	WR	Mark Clayton
Dave Krieg	QB	Dan Marino
David Hughes	RB	Woody Bennett
Dan Doornink	RB	Tony Nathan
	Starters, Defense	
Jacob Green	LE	Doug Betters
Joe Nash	NT	Bob Baumhower
Jeff Bryant	RE	Kim Bokamper
Bruce Scholtz	LOLB	Bob Brudzinski
Shelton Robinson	LILB	Jay Brophy
Keith Butler	RILB	Mark Brown
Greg Gaines	ROLB	Charles Bowser
Keith Simpson	LCB	Don McNeal
Dave Brown	RCB	William Judson
Kenny Easley	SS	Glenn Blackwood
John Harris	FS	Lyle Blackwood

Seattle	0	10	0	0	—	10
Miami	7	7	14	3	—	31

Mia— Nathan 14 run (von Schamann kick)
Sea— FG N. Johnson 27
Mia— Cefalo 34 pass from Marino (von Schamann kick)
Sea— Largent 56 pass from Krieg (N. Johnson kick)
Mia— Hardy 3 pass from Marino (von Schamann kick)
Mia— Clayton 33 pass from Marino (von Schamann kick)
Mia— FG von Schamann 37
Attendance—73,469

TEAM STATISTICS	Sea	Mia
First downs	8	22
Rushing	2	8
Passing	6	12
By penalty	0	2
Total yardage	267	405
Net rushing yardage	51	143
Net passing yardage	216	262
Passes att.-comp.-had int.	35-20-0	34-32-2

RUSHING

Seattle—Doornink, 10 for 35; Hughes, 7 for 14; Krieg, 1 for 2.
Miami—Nathan, 18 for 76, 1 TD; Bennett, 11 for 41; P. Johnson, 6 for 22; Carter, 1 for 4.

PASSING

Seattle—Krieg, 20 of 35 for 234, 1 TD.
Miami—Marino, 21 of 34 for 262, 3 TD, 2 int.

RECEIVING

Seattle—Largent, 6 for 128, 1 TD; Doornink, 6 for 23; Turner, 3 for 38; Skansi, 2 for 31; Hughes, 1 for 8; C. Young, 1 for 5; Krieg, 1 for 1.
Miami—Clayton, 5 for 72, 1 TD; Nathan, 4 for 20; Hardy, 3 for 48, 1 TD; Duper, 3 for 32; Cefalo, 2 for 43, 1 TD; Moore, 2 for 11; Bennett, 1 for 20; Rose, 1 for 13.

1984 AFC

PITTSBURGH 24, DENVER 17

The Steelers' lines dominated those of the Broncos, as Pittsburgh, the champion of what was considered by some the NFL's weakest division, upset the champion of the apparent strongest division 24-17.

The game was played on even terms in its opening stages, with the Broncos leading 7-0 at the end of the first quarter. John Elway passed nine yards for a touchdown to Jim Wright five plays after Tom Jackson recovered Mark Malone's fumble.

The Steelers came back to lead 10-7 at halftime. Gary Anderson kicked a 28-yard field goal, and Malone's passing and Frank Pollard's running set up Pollard's one-yard touchdown run with 1:14 left.

Denver tied it 10-10 early in the third quarter, blocking Craig Colquitt's punt to set up Rich Karlis's 21-yard field goal. The next time the Broncos had the ball, Elway, who was getting progressively less mobile due to a thigh injury, fired a 20-yard touchdown pass to Steve Watson. Pittsburgh came right back, driving 66 yards to a touchdown pass from Malone to Louis Lipps.

With a little more than three minutes left in the game, Eric Williams intercepted a pass by Elway and returned it to the Denver 2. Three plays later, Pollard plowed in for the winning touchdown.

December 30, at Denver

Pittsburgh	Starters, Offense	Denver
John Stallworth	WR	Don Summers
Pete Rostosky	LT	Dave Studdard
Craig Wolfley	LG	Keith Bishop
Mike Webster	C	Billy Bryan
Terry Long	RG	Paul Howard
Tunch Ilkin	RT	Ken Lanier
Darrell Nelson	TE	Clarence Kay
Louis Lipps	WR	Steve Watson
Mark Malone	QB	John Elway
Frank Pollard	RB-TE	Jim Wright
Walter Abercrombie	RB	Sammy Winder
	Starters, Defense	
John Goodman	LE	Barney Chavous
Gary Dunn	NT	Rubin Carter
Edmund Nelson	RE	Rulon Jones
Mike Merriweather	LOLB	Jim Ryan
David Little	LILB	Rick Dennison
Robin Cole	RILB	Steve Busick
Bryan Hinkle	ROLB	Tom Jackson
Dwayne Woodruff	LCB	Louis Wright
Sam Washington	RCB	Mike Harden
Donnie Shell	SS	Dennis Smith
Eric Williams	FS	Steve Foley

Pittsburgh	0	10	7	7	—	24
Denver	7	0	10	0	—	17

Den—J. Wright 9 pass from Elway (Karlis kick)
Pitt —FG Anderson 28
Pitt —Pollard 1 run (Anderson kick)
Den—FG Karlis 21
Den—Watson 20 pass from Elway (Karlis kick)
Pitt —Lipps 10 pass from Malone (Anderson kick)
Pitt —Pollard 2 run (Anderson kick)
Attendance—74,981

TEAM STATISTICS	Pitt	Den
First downs	25	15
Rushing	12	4
Passing	13	11
By penalty	0	0
Total yardage	381	250
Net rushing yardage	169	51
Net passing yardage	212	199
Passes att.-comp.-had int.	28-17-0	38-20-2

RUSHING

Pittsburgh—Pollard, 16 for 99, 2 TDs; Abercrombie, 17 for 75; Veals, 1 for 1; Lipps, 1 for 0; Malone, 5 for −6.
Denver—Winder, 15 for 37; Elway, 4 for 16; Willhite, 1 for 1; Parros, 1 for 0; Watson, 1 for −3.

PASSING

Pittsburgh—Malone, 17 of 28 for 224, 1 TD.
Denver—Elway, 19 of 37 for 184, 2 TDs, 2 int.; Willhite, 1 of 1 for 52.

RECEIVING

Pittsburgh—Lipps, 5 for 86, 1 TD; Pollard, 4 for 48; Stallworth, 3 for 38; Abercrombie, 3 for 18; Cunningham, 1 for 19; Thompson, 1 for 15.
Denver—Watson, 11 for 177, 1 TD; Winder, 4 for 22; J. Wright, 2 for 16, 1 TD; Willhite, 2 for 12; Alexander, 1 for 9.

1984 NFC

SAN FRANCISCO 21, NY GIANTS 10

Joe Montana threw three touchdown passes, and the 49ers' defense allowed the Giants only one field goal, as San Francisco defeated New York 21-10.

The 49ers had all the points they really needed in the first seven minutes of the game. On their first possession, Joe Montana completed three passes, the final one for 21 yards and a touchdown to Dwight Clark. Moments later the 49ers were in the end zone again. Phil Simms's pass for Lionel Manuel was tipped at the line by linebacker Dan Bunz, and the ball bounced off linebacker Riki Ellison and was intercepted by cornerback Ronnie Lott, who returned it 38 yards to New York's 12. Montana found Russ Francis in the end zone for a 14-0 lead.

At the end of the first quarter, the Giants started an 11-play drive that got them on the scoreboard with a field goal by Ali Haji-Sheikh. Midway through the second period, linebacker Harry Carson intercepted Montana's pass at the San Francisco 14 and bolted into the end zone for a touchdown that cut the lead to 14-10. Montana responded immediately, leading a five-play 72-yard drive that ended with his 29-yard touchdown pass to Freddie Solomon.

At that point the defenses took over, and, with an assist from three missed field goals, allowed no more points for the rest of the game.

December 29, at San Francisco

NY Giants	Starters, Offense	San Francisco
Earnest Gray	WR	Dwight Clark
William Roberts	LT	Bubba Paris
Brad Benson	LG	John Ayers
Kevin Belcher	C	Fred Quillan
Chris Godfrey	RG	Randy Cross
Karl Nelson	RT	Keith Fahnhorst
Zeke Mowatt	TE	Russ Francis
Bobby Johnson	WR	Freddie Solomon
Phil Simms	QB	Joe Montana
Rob Carpenter	RB	Roger Craig
Joe Morris	RB	Wendell Tyler
	Starters, Defense	
Curtis McGriff	LE	Lawrence Pillers
Jim Burt	NT	Manu Tuiasosopo
Leonard Marshall	RE	Dwaine Board
Carl Banks	LOLB	Dan Bunz
Gary Reasons	LILB	Riki Ellison
Harry Carson	RILB	Jack Reynolds
Lawrence Taylor	ROLB	Keena Turner
Kenny Daniel	LCB	Ronnie Lott
Perry Williams	RCB	Eric Wright
Bill Currier	SS	Carlton Williamson
Terry Kinard	FS	Dwight Hicks

NY Giants	0	10	0	0	—	10
San Francisco	14	7	0	0	—	21

SF — D. Clark 21 pass from Montana (Wersching kick)
SF — Francis 9 pass from Montana (Wersching kick)
NYG— FG Haji-Sheikh 46
NYG— Carson 14 interception return (Haji-Sheikh kick)
SF — Solomon 29 pass from Montana (Wersching kick)
Attendance—60,303

TEAM STATISTICS	NYG	SF
First downs	18	22
Rushing	7	5
Passing	10	16
By penalty	1	1
Total yardage	260	412
Net rushing yardage	87	131
Net passing yardage	173	281
Passes att.-comp.-had int.	44-25-2	39-25-3

RUSHING

NY Giants—Morris, 17 for 46; Galbreath, 4 for 34; Carpenter, 3 for 4; Simms, 1 for 3.
San Francisco—Montana, 3 for 63; Tyler, 14 for 35; Craig, 10 for 34; Harmon, 1 for −1.

PASSING

NY Giants—Simms, 25 of 44 for 218, 2 int.
San Francisco—Montana, 25 of 39 for 309, 3 TDs, 3 int.

RECEIVING

NY Giants—Mowatt, 5 for 49; Carpenter, 5 for 22; Morris, 4 for 45; Galbreath, 4 for 25; Johnson, 3 for 23; Manuel, 2 for 32; Mullady, 2 for 22.
San Francisco—D. Clark, 9 for 112, 1 TD; Solomon, 4 for 94, 1 TD; Craig, 4 for 31; Wilson, 3 for 37; Tyler, 2 for 26; Cooper, 2 for 0; Francis, 1 for 9, 1 TD.

1984 NFC

CHI. BEARS 23, WASHINGTON 19

The Chicago defense sacked Washington quarterback Joe Theismann seven times, intercepted him once, and recovered two fumbles to lead the Bears to a 23-19 upset, marking the first time the Redskins had lost a playoff game in Washington since 1940.

With the score tied 3-3 late in the second period, the Bears drove to the Washington 19. Walter Payton took a pitchout, faked a reverse to Dennis McKinnon, and threw a touchdown pass to tight end Pat Dunsmore, who was alone in the end zone.

Chicago quarterback Steve Fuller provided the knockout punch in the third quarter. On the second play of the half, Fuller read a Redskins blitz and threw a wobbly 10-yard pass to wide receiver Willie Gault at the sideline. Cornerback Darrell Green slipped as Gault made the catch and sped away untouched for a 75-yard score. The Redskins cut the lead to 16-10, but Fuller came through again. After Ken Coffey ran into Bears punter David Finzer, giving Chicago a first down, Fuller hit McKinnon with consecutive passes, the second a 16-yard touchdown. Again the Redskins drove to a score, but then the Bears' defense took over, and Washington scored only on an intentional safety by Finzer.

December 30, at Washington

Chi. Bears	Starters, Offense	Washington
Willie Gault	WR	Calvin Muhammad
Jim Covert	LT	Joe Jacoby
Mark Bortz	LG	Russ Grimm
Jay Hilgenberg	C	Rick Donnalley
Kurt Becker	RG	Ken Huff
Keith Van Horne	RT	Mark May
Emery Moorehead	TE	Don Warren
Dennis McKinnon	WR	Art Monk
Steve Fuller	QB	Joe Theismann
Matt Suhey	RB-TE	Clint Didier
Walter Payton	RB	John Riggins
	Starters, Defense	
Mike Hartenstine	LE	Charles Mann
Steve McMichael	LT	Dave Butz
Dan Hampton	RT	Darryl Grant
Richard Dent	RE	Dexter Manley
Otis Wilson	LLB	Mel Kaufman
Mike Singletary	MLB	Neal Olkewicz
Al Harris	RLB	Rich Milot
Mike Richardson	LCB	Darrell Green
Terry Schmidt	RCB	Vernon Dean
Todd Bell	SS	Ken Coffey
Gary Fencik	FS	Curtis Jordan

Chi. Bears	0	10	13	0	—	23
Washington	3	0	14	2	—	19

Wash—FG Moseley 25
ChiB—FG B. Thomas 34
ChiB—Dunsmore 19 pass from Payton (B. Thomas kick)
ChiB—Gault 75 pass from Fuller (kick failed)
Wash—Riggins 1 run (Moseley kick)
ChiB—McKinnon 16 pass from Fuller (B. Thomas kick)
Wash—Riggins 1 run (Moseley kick)
Wash—Safety, Finzer stepped out of end zone
Attendance—55,431

TEAM STATISTICS	ChiB	Wash
First downs	13	22
Rushing	5	6
Passing	7	14
By penalty	1	2
Total yardage	310	336
Net rushing yardage	114	93
Net passing yardage	196	243
Passes att.-comp.-had int.	17-10-0	42-22-1

RUSHING
Chi. Bears—Payton, 24 for 104; Suhey, 7 for 7; Fuller, 2 for 5; C. Thomas, 1 for 5; Finzer, 1 for −7.
Washington—Riggins, 21 for 50, 2 TDs; Theismann, 5 for 38; Washington, 1 for 5.
PASSING
Chi. Bears—Fuller, 9 of 15 for 211, 2 TDs; Payton, 1 of 2 for 19, 1 TD.
Washington—Theismann, 22 of 42 for 292, 1 int.
RECEIVING
Chi. Bears—McKinnon, 4 for 72, 1 TD; Gault, 1 for 75, 1 TD; Suhey, 1 for 33; Dunsmore, 1 for 19, 1 TD; C. Thomas, 1 for 13; Payton, 1 for 12; Moorehead, 1 for 6.
Washington—Monk, 10 for 122; Muhammad, 5 for 62; Didier, 4 for 85; Washington, 2 for 12; Warren, 1 for 11.

1985 AFC

MIAMI 24, CLEVELAND 21

Trailing 21-3 midway through the third quarter, Miami exploded for three touchdowns, the last with only 1:57 remaining, to defeat Cleveland 24-21.

The Dolphins scored the first time they had the ball on Fuad Reveiz's 51-yard field goal, but then Dan Marino and his passing offense disappeared until late in the third quarter.

With running backs Earnest Byner and Kevin Mack leading an attack that ran up 251 yards on the ground, the Browns scored in each of the first three periods. In the first quarter, they marched 82 yards in 10 plays to rookie quarterback Bernie Kosar's 16-yard touchdown pass to tight end Ozzie Newsome.

Late in the second period, Marino threw a pass to the Cleveland goal line, where safety Don Rogers intercepted and returned it to the 45. Eight plays later, Byner ran 21 yards for a touchdown. Byner tried to give the Dolphins a knockout punch in the third quarter, racing 66 yards for a touchdown.

The Dolphins responded, however. Marino drove them 74 yards, passing six yards to Nat Moore for a touchdown. The next time Miami had the ball, Ron Davenport ran 31 yards for a touchdown.

Late in the fourth quarter, the Dolphins took over at their 27. It took only eight plays to reach the Cleveland 1, from where Davenport scored again.

January 4, 1986, at Miami

Cleveland	Starters, Offense	Miami
Fred Banks	WR	Mark Duper
Rickey Bolden	LT	Jon Giesler
George Lilja	LG	Roy Foster
Mike Baab	C	Dwight Stephenson
Dan Fike	RG	Steve Clark
Cody Risien	RT	Ronnie Lee
Ozzie Newsome	TE	Bruce Hardy
Brian Brennan	WR	Mark Clayton
Bernie Kosar	QB	Dan Marino
Kevin Mack	RB	Woody Bennett
Earnest Byner	RB	Tony Nathan
	Starters, Defense	
Reggie Camp	LE	Doug Betters
Bob Golic	NT	Mike Charles
Carl Hairston	RE	Kim Bokamper
Chip Banks	LOLB	Bob Brudzinski
Eddie Johnson	LILB	Jay Brophy
Tom Cousineau	RILB	Mark Brown
Clay Matthews	ROLB	Hugh Green
Frank Minnifield	LCB	Paul Lankford
Hanford Dixon	RCB	William Judson
Al Gross	SS	Glenn Blackwood
Don Rogers	FS	Lyle Blackwood

Cleveland	7	7	7	0	—	21
Miami	3	0	14	7	—	24

Mia—FG Reveiz 51
Cle—Newsome 16 pass from Kosar (Bahr kick)
Cle—Byner 21 run (Bahr kick)
Cle—Byner 66 run (Bahr kick)
Mia—N. Moore, 6 pass from Marino (Reveiz kick)
Mia—Davenport 31 run (Reveiz kick)
Mia—Davenport 1 run (Reveiz kick)
Attendance—75,128

TEAM STATISTICS	Cle	Mia
First downs	17	20
Rushing	11	6
Passing	5	13
By penalty	1	1
Total yardage	313	330
Net rushing yardage	251	92
Net passing yardage	62	238
Passes att.-comp.-had int.	19-10-1	45-25-1

RUSHING
Cleveland—Byner, 16 for 161, 2 TDs; Mack, 13 for 56; Dickey, 6 for 28; Kosar, 2 for 6.
Miami—Davenport, 6 for 48, 2 TDs; Nathan, 7 for 21; Bennett, 4 for 17; Carter, 2 for 6.
PASSING
Cleveland—Kosar, 10 of 19 for 66, 1 TD, 1 int.
Miami—Marino, 25 of 45 for 238, 1 TD, 1 int.
RECEIVING
Cleveland—Byner, 4 for 25; Newsome, 2 for 22, 1 TD; Holt, 2 for 2; Cl. Weathers, 1 for 12; Fontenot, 1 for 5.
Miami—Nathan, 10 for 101; Hardy, 5 for 51; N. Moore, 4 for 29, 1 TD; D. Johnson, 2 for 17; Rose, 1 for 17; Clayton, 1 for 15, Bennett, 1 for 6; Carter, 1 for 2.

1985 AFC

NEW ENGLAND 27, LA RAIDERS 20

New England safety Jim Bowman recovered Sam Seale's fumble of a kickoff in the Los Angeles end zone for the go-ahead touchdown late in the third period, and the Patriots upset the Raiders 27-20.

The Patriots hoped to capitalize on turnovers. They did, collecting six that led to 17 points.

New England went ahead in the first quarter when Fulton Walker fumbled a punt at the Raiders' 21 and Bowman recovered. Tony Eason threw a 13-yard touchdown pass to tight end Lin Dawson.

Trailing 10-7, the Patriots dug a deep hole when Mosi Tatupu fumbled to the Raiders at the New England 17. On third down, Marcus Allen slashed to the 5 and leaped over Fred Marion into the end zone, completing an 11-yard scoring run.

The Patriots came right back, driving 80 yards to Craig James's 2-yard touchdown run. After Ronnie Lippett intercepted Marc Wilson's pass, Tony Franklin tied it 17-17. But the Raiders drove right back to a field goal by Matt Bahr six seconds before halftime.

Late in the third quarter, Eason engineered a 54-yard drive to Franklin's 32-yard field goal. That tied the game and set up the decisive kickoff play.

January 5, 1986, at Los Angeles

New England	Starters, Offense	LA Raiders
Stanley Morgan	WR	Jesse Hester
Brian Holloway	LT	Bruce Davis
John Hannah	LG	Charley Hannah
Pete Brock	C	Don Mosebar
Ron Wooten	RG	Mickey Marvin
Steve Moore	RT	Henry Lawrence
Lin Dawson	TE	Todd Christensen
Irving Fryar	WR	Dokie Williams
Tony Eason	QB	Marc Wilson
Craig James	RB	Frank Hawkins
Tony Collins	RB	Marcus Allen
	Starters, Defense	
Garin Veris	LE	Howie Long
Lester Williams	NT	Bill Pickel
Julius Adams	RE	Sean Jones
Andre Tippett	LOLB	Brad Van Pelt
Steve Nelson	LILB	Matt Millen
Larry McGrew	RILB	Reggie McKenzie
Don Blackmon	ROLB	Rod Martin
Ronnie Lippett	LCB	Lester Hayes
Raymond Clayborn	RCB	Mike Haynes
Roland James	SS	Mike Davis
Fred Marion	FS	Vann McElroy

New England	7	10	10	0	—	27
LA Raiders	3	17	0	0	—	20

NE—Dawson 13 pass from Eason (Franklin kick)
Raiders—FG Bahr 29
Raiders—Hester 16 pass from Wilson (Bahr kick)
Raiders—Allen 11 run (Bahr kick)
NE—C. James 2 run (Franklin kick)
NE—FG Franklin 45
Raiders—FG Bahr 32
NE—FG Franklin 32
NE—Bowman recovered fumble in end zone (Franklin kick)
Attendance—88,936

TEAM STATISTICS	NE	Raiders
First downs	15	17
Rushing	9	11
Passing	5	6
By penalty	1	0
Total yardage	254	287
Net rushing yardage	156	163
Net passing yardage	98	124
Passes att.-comp.-had int.	15-8-0	27-11-3

RUSHING
New England—C. James, 23 for 104, 1 TD; Collins, 9 for 18; Weathers, 9 for 18; Tatupu, 4 for 17; Fryar, 1 for 3; Eason, 3 for −4.
LA Raiders—Allen, 22 for 121, 1 TD; Hawkins, 4 for 33; Wilson, 1 for 9.
PASSING
New England—Eason, 7 of 14 for 117, 1 TD; C. James, 1 of 1 for 8.
LA Raiders—Wilson, 11 of 27 for 135, 1 TD, 3 int.
RECEIVING
New England—C. James, 3 for 48; D. Ramsey, 2 for 34; Morgan, 1 for 22; Dawson, 1 for 13, 1 TD; Collins, 1 for 8.
LA Raiders—Christensen, 4 for 70; Williams, 3 for 33; Allen, 3 for 8; Hootor, 1 for 16, 1 TD.

1985 NFC

LA RAMS 20, DALLAS 0

Eric Dickerson set an all-time NFL playoff record with 248 yards rushing and scored on two long runs to lead the Los Angeles Rams to a 20-0 victory over the Dallas Cowboys.

Except for Dickerson's two runs, the game was a tough defensive struggle. The only score of the first half came after Henry Ellard of the Rams returned Mike Saxon's punt 23 yards to the Dallas 38. On first down, Rams quarterback Dieter Brock connected with Ellard on a 21-yard completion. Four plays later, Mike Lansford kicked a 33-yard field goal.

The Rams broke the game open with two scores in the first minute and a half of the third quarter. First, a short kickoff was returned by Charles White to the Rams' 45. On first down, Dickerson broke straight up the middle and outraced the Dallas defenders 55 yards for a touchdown. On the ensuing kickoff, Kenny Duckett of the Cowboys fumbled when hit by Shawn Miller, and Vince Newsome recovered for the Rams at the Dallas 20. Four plays later, Lansford kicked his second field goal.

With 13 seconds left in the third quarter, Gordon Banks of the Cowboys fumbled on a punt return, and Tony Hunter recovered for the Rams at the Los Angeles 49. Moments later, Dickerson raced around right end and down the sidelines for a 40-yard touchdown. The Rams' defense, which allowed Dallas to the Los Angeles 30 only once all day, took over from there, stopping the Cowboys cold.

January 4, 1986, at Anaheim

Dallas	**Starters, Offense**	**LA Rams**
Tony Hill	WR	Henry Ellard
Chris Schultz	LT	Irv Pankey
Glen Titensor	LG	Kent Hill
Tom Rafferty	C	Tony Slaton
Kurt Peterson	RG	Dennis Harrah
Jim Cooper	RT	Jackie Slater
Doug Cosbie	TE	David Hill
Mike Renfro	WR	Ron Brown
Danny White	QB	Dieter Brock
Timmy Newsome	RB	Barry Redden
Tony Dorsett	RB	Eric Dickerson
	Starters, Defense	
Ed Jones	LE	Doug Reed
John Dutton	LT-NT	Charles DeJurnett
Randy White	RT-RE	Reggie Doss
Jim Jeffcoat	RE-LOLB	Mel Owens
Mike Hegman	LLB-LILB	Carl Ekern
Eugene Lockhart	MLB-RILB	Jim Collins
Jeff Rohrer	RLB-ROLB	Mike Wilcher
Everson Walls	LCB	Gary Green
Ron Fellows	RCB	LeRoy Irvin
Dextor Clinkscale	SS	Nolan Cromwell
Michael Downs	FS	Johnnie Johnson

Dallas	0	0	0	0	—	0
LA Rams	3	0	10	7	—	20

Rams—FG Lansford 33
Rams—Dickerson 55 run (Lansford kick)
Rams—FG Lansford 34
Rams—Dickerson 40 run (Lansford kick)
Attendance—66,581

TEAM STATISTICS	**Dall**	**Rams**
First downs	15	15
Rushing	3	11
Passing	12	3
By penalty	0	1
Total yardage	243	316
Net rushing yardage	61	269
Net passing yardage	182	47
Passes att.-comp.-had int.	43-24-3	22-6-1

RUSHING

Dallas—Dorsett, 17 for 58; Newsome, 1 for 3.

LA Rams—Dickerson, 34 for 248, 2 TDs; Redden, 6 for 21; Brock, 1 for 0.

PASSING

Dallas—D. White, 24 of 43 for 217, 3 int.

LA Rams—Brock, 6 of 22 for 50, 1 int.

RECEIVING

Dallas—Dorsett, 8 for 80; Cosbie, 6 for 61; Hill, 5 for 41; Newsome, 3 for 10; Powe, 1 for 19; J. Jones, 1 for 6.

LA Rams—Ellard, 2 for 33; Redden, 1 for 15; D. Hill, 1 for 3; Hunter, 1 for 3; Dickerson, 1 for −4.

1985 NFC

CHI. BEARS 21, NY GIANTS 0

The "Monsters of the Midway" were in fine form as the Chicago defense played its most inspired game to totally shut down the New York Giants 21-0.

Superlatives almost were inadequate to describe the Bears' defense. It held the Giants without a first down for 28 minutes in the first half. It recorded almost twice as much yardage in sacks (60) as it gave up rushing (32). In 11 third-quarter plays, it gave up minus-11 yards. With 12 minutes remaining in the game, it had given up only 67 net yards.

Despite such an effort, the Bears led only 7-0 at halftime, and it could have been closer. Midway through the first quarter, the Giants were forced to punt on fourth and 20 at the New York 12. However, the wind caught the ball before punter Sean Landeta kicked it, and it barely grazed the side of his foot. The ball was picked up by Shaun Gayle and returned five yards for a touchdown.

Late in the half, the Giants put together their first drive of the day. In the final 51 seconds, Phil Simms passed them to the Bears' 2, only to have a fourth-down field-goal attempt hit the left upright.

In the third quarter, the Bears scored twice to end the Giants' hopes. Jim McMahon passed 23 yards to Dennis McKinnon for one touchdown. Six minutes later, one play after McMahon hit tight end Tim Wrightman for a 46-yard gain, McMahon found McKinnon again, with a 20-yard touchdown pass.

January 6, 1986, at Chicago

NY Giants	**Starters, Offense**	**Chi. Bears**
Bobby Johnson	WR	Willie Gault
Brad Benson	LT	Jim Covert
Billy Ard	LG	Mark Bortz
Bart Oates	C	Jay Hilgenberg
Chris Godfrey	RG	Tom Thayer
Karl Nelson	RT	Keith Van Horne
Mark Bavaro	TE	Emery Moore
Lionel Manuel	WR	Dennis McKinnon
Phil Simms	QB	Jim McMahon
Rob Carpenter	RB	Matt Suhey
Joe Morris	RB	Walter Payton
	Starters, Defense	
Curtis McGriff	LE	Dan Hampton
Jim Burt	NT-LT	Steve McMichael
Leonard Marshall	RE-RT	William Perry
Byron Hunt	LOLB-RE	Richard Dent
Gary Reasons	LILB-LLB	Otis Wilson
Harry Carson	RILB-MLB	Mike Singletary
Lawrence Taylor	ROLB-RLB	Wilber Marshall
Elvis Patterson	LCB	Mike Richardson
Perry Williams	RCB	Leslie Frazier
Kenny Hill	SS	Dave Duerson
Terry Kinard	FS	Gary Fencik

NY Giants	0	0	0	0	—	0
Chi. Bears	7	0	14	0	—	21

ChiB—Gayle 5 punt return (Butler kick)
ChiB—McKinnon 23 pass from McMahon (Butler kick)
ChiB—McKinnon 20 pass from McMahon (Butler kick)
Attendance—62,076

TEAM STATISTICS	**NYG**	**ChiB**
First downs	10	17
Rushing	1	9
Passing	8	8
By penalty	1	0
Total yardage	181	363
Net rushing yardage	32	147
Net passing yardage	149	216
Passes att.-comp.-had int.	35-14-0	21-11-0

RUSHING

NY Giants—Morris, 12 for 32; Galbreath, 1 for 9; Williams, 1 for −9.

Chi. Bears—Payton, 27 for 93; Suhey, 6 for 33; McMahon, 5 for 18; Thomas, 4 for 11; Gentry, 1 for −1; McKinnon, 1 for −7.

PASSING

NY Giants—Simms, 14 of 35 for 209.

Chi. Bears—McMahon, 11 of 21 for 216, 2 TDs.

RECEIVING

NY Giants—Bavaro, 4 for 36; Adams, 3 for 65; Carpenter, 3 for 24; B. Williams, 1 for 33; McConkey, 1 for 23; Johnson, 1 for 17; Galbreath, 1 for 11.

Chi. Bears—Gault, 3 for 68; McKinnon, 3 for 52, 2 TDs; Suhey, 2 for 5; Wrightman, 1 for 46; Gentry, 1 for 41; Payton, 1 for 4.

Wild Card Games

1978 AFC

HOUSTON 17, MIAMI 9

Quarterback Dan Pastorini was the difference in a tough defensive struggle, leading Houston to a 17-9 upset of Miami.

The Dolphins got the first big break of the game. Miami was forced to punt from its 14. George Roberts boomed a 53-yard punt that Robert Woods fumbled and didn't chase down. Earnie Rhone recovered for the Dolphins at the Houston 21. Two plays later, Bob Griese passed over the middle to tight end Andre Tillman for a touchdown.

Houston responded with a 10-play, 71-yard touchdown drive. Pastorini completed six of seven passes for 66 yards, including a 13-yard strike to running back Tim Wilson to tie the score.

Neither team scored until the fourth quarter, although both had good opportunities. With a first and goal for the Dolphins, Leroy Harris fumbled the ball away. Later Griese threw an interception on the Houston 9. The Oilers, meanwhile, ended the half not scoring after being deep in Miami territory.

In the fourth quarter, Pastorini drove the Oilers to two scores. He completed four passes for 45 yards to set up the go-ahead field goal. Then, after Gregg Bingham intercepted Griese on the first play after the kickoff, Earl Campbell and Wilson carried on nine consecutive plays, with Campbell scoring from the 1.

December 24, at Miami

Houston	Starters, Offense	Miami
Ken Burrough	WR	Nat Moore
Greg Sampson	LT	Wayne Moore
Conway Hayman	LG	Bob Kuechenberg
Carl Mauck	C	Jim Langer
Ed Fisher	RG	Eric Laakso
Morris Towns	RT	Mike Current
Mike Barber	TE	Andre Tillman
Guido Merkins	WR	Duriel Harris
Dan Pastorini	QB	Bob Griese
Tim Wilson	RB	Leroy Harris
Earl Campbell	RB	Delvin Williams
	Starters, Defense	
Jim Young	LE	Vern Den Herder
Curley Culp	NT	Bob Baumhower
Elvin Bethea	RE	A.J. Duhe
Robert Brazile	LOLB	Kim Bokamper
Gregg Bingham	LILB	Steve Towle
Steve Kiner	RILB	Rusty Chambers
Ted Washington	ROLB	Larry Gordon
Willie Alexander	LCB	Norris Thomas
Greg Stemrick	RCB	Gerald Small
Bill Currier	SS	Tim Foley
Mike Reinfeldt	FS	Charlie Babb

Houston	7	0	0	10	—	17
Miami	7	0	0	2	—	9

Mia —Tillman 13 pass from Griese (Yepremian kick)
Hou—T. Wilson 13 pass from Pastorini (Fritsch kick)
Hou—FG Fritsch 35
Hou—Campbell 1 run (Fritsch kick)
Mia —Safety, Pastorini ran out of end zone
Attendance—72,445

TEAM STATISTICS	Hou	Mia
First downs	23	14
Rushing	9	6
Passing	14	7
By penalty	0	1
Total yardage	455	209
Net rushing yardage	165	91
Net passing yardage	290	118
Passes att.-comp.-had int.	30-20-0	30-12-3

RUSHING
Houston—Campbell, 26 for 84, 1 TD; Wilson, 14 for 76; Poole, 1 for 12; Coleman, 1 for 2; Pastorini, 3 for -9.
Miami—L. Harris, 9 for 43; Williams, 13 for 41; N. Moore, 1 for 7; Bulaich, 2 for 0.

PASSING
Houston—Pastorini, 20 of 29 for 306, 1 TD; Barber, 0 of 1.
Miami—Griese, 11 of 28 for 114, 1 TD, 2 int.; Strock, 1 of 2 for 23, 1 int.

RECEIVING
Houston—Burrough, 6 for 103; Wilson, 5 for 40, 1 TD; Barber, 4 for 112; Woods, 2 for 22; Campbell, 1 for 13; Caster, 1 for 11; Coleman, 1 for 5.
Miami—D. Harris, 4 for 42; N. Moore, 2 for 28; Tillman, 2 for 24, 1 TD; Bulaich, 2 for 14; L. Harris, 1 for 21; Williams, 1 for 8.

1978 NFC

ATLANTA 14, PHILADELPHIA 13

Quarterback Steve Bartkowski threw two touchdown passes in the final five minutes of the game to bring the Falcons back from a 13-0 deficit to a 14-13 victory, their first ever in a playoff game.

Neither team was effective in the first half, when Philadelphia built a 6-0 lead. Late in the first quarter, Atlanta wide receiver Billy Ryckman fumbled after returning Mike Michel's punt to the Atlanta 13. Cleveland Franklin recovered for the Eagles. On third down, Ron Jaworski hit Harold Carmichael for a touchdown. Michel missed the extra point.

With the help of a roughing the passer penalty, the Eagles drove 60 yards to a touchdown midway through the third quarter. Starting on first down at the 1, Philadelphia didn't find it easy to score, with Wilbert Montgomery finally blasting in on third down.

With 4:56 left to play, Bartkowski got the Falcons back in the game. He completed four of six passes for 88 yards and cut the score to 13-7 with a strike to tight end Jim Mitchell. The next time the Falcons touched the ball, Bartkowski hit three of four passes, including a 37-yard touchdown to Wallace Francis with 1:39 left to play.

Passing on eight consecutive plays, Jaworski led the Eagles to the Atlanta 16, but, with 13 seconds left, Michel missed a 34-yard field-goal attempt.

December 24, at Atlanta

Philadelphia	Starters, Offense	Atlanta
Harold Carmichael	WR	Wallace Francis
Stan Walters	LT	Mike Kenn
Wade Key	LG	Dave Scott
Guy Morriss	C	Jeff Van Note
Woody Peoples	RG	R.C. Thielemann
Jerry Sisemore	RT	Phil McKinnely
Richard Osborne	TE	Jim Mitchell
Bill Larson	TE-WR	Billy Ryckman
Ron Jaworski	QB	Steve Bartkowski
Mike Hogan	RB	Bubba Bean
Wilbert Montgomery	RB	Haskel Stanback
	Starters, Defense	
Dennis Harrison	LE	Jeff Yeates
Charlie Johnson	NT-LT	Jim Bailey
Carl Hairston	RE-RT	Mike Lewis
Reggie Wilkes	LOLB-RE	Jeff Merrow
Bill Bergey	LILB-LLB	Fulton Kuykendall
Frank LeMaster	RILB-MLB	Robert Pennywell
Ray Phillips	ROLB-RLB	Greg Brezina
Bobby Howard	LCB	Rolland Lawrence
Herman Edwards	RCB	Rick Byas
Randy Logan	SS	Frank Reed
John Sanders	FS	Tom Pridemore

Philadelphia	6	0	7	0	—	13
Atlanta	0	0	0	14	—	14

Phil—Carmichael 13 pass from Jaworski (kick failed)
Phil—Montgomery 1 run (Michel kick)
Atl —Mitchell 20 pass from Bartkowski (Mazzetti kick)
Atl —Francis 37 pass from Bartkowski (Mazzetti kick)
Attendance—59,403

TEAM STATISTICS	Phil	Atl
First downs	15	14
Rushing	4	4
Passing	10	9
By penalty	1	1
Total yardage	217	298
Net rushing yardage	53	75
Net passing yardage	164	223
Passes att.-comp.-had int.	35-19-0	32-18-2

RUSHING
Philadelphia—Hogan, 14 for 31; Montgomery, 16 for 19, 1 TD; Jaworski, 1 for 3; Campfield, 1 for 0.
Atlanta—Stanback, 16 for 58; Bean, 9 for 14; Bartkowski, 2 for 3.

PASSING
Philadelphia—Jaworski, 19 of 35 for 190, 1 TD.
Atlanta—Bartkowski, 18 of 32 for 243, 2 TD, 2 int.

RECEIVING
Philadelphia—Smith, 7 for 108; Carmichael, 5 for 45, 1 TD; Osborne, 3 for 15; Middlebrook, 1 for 11; Payne, 1 for 10; Hogan, 1 for 6; Montgomery, 1 for -5.
Atlanta—Francis, 6 for 135, 1 TD; Bean, 4 for 44; Mitchell, 3 for 35, 1 TD; Stanback, 2 for 7; Pearson, 1 for 13; Ryckman, 1 for 5; Jackson, 1 for 4.

1979 AFC

HOUSTON 13, DENVER 7

The Oilers' defense shut down the Broncos, and Houston won 13-7 despite the loss of Earl Campbell and Dan Pastorini for the second half due to injuries.

Houston scored on the opening series, following a 66-yard drive. The big play was a 41-yard pass from Pastorini to Ronnie Coleman. Toni Fritsch kicked a 31-yard field goal to put Houston up 3-0.

Denver marched right back for a touchdown, driving 80 yards in 13 plays and taking more than six minutes off the clock. The Broncos were helped by two penalties against the Oilers. Craig Morton passed seven yards to Dave Preston for the score.

With 2:33 to go in the half, the Oilers took over on their 26, and Pastorini whipped them 74 yards for the go-ahead touchdown in less than two minutes. Pastorini passed for 39 yards and Campbell ran for 20, including a three-yard touchdown. Campbell was hurt on the scoring run, however, and didn't return.

On the Oilers' first drive of the second half, Pastorini was sacked by Barney Chavous and left the game. He was replaced by Gifford Nielsen.

The Oilers' defense shut down every offensive thrust by the Broncos in the second half. Late in the game, Gregg Bingham intercepted a pass by Morton and returned it to the Denver 20. Rob Carpenter carried five consecutive times before Fritsch scored the game's last points on a 20-yard field goal.

December 23, at Houston

Denver	Starters, Offense	Houston
Rick Upchurch	WR	Ken Burrough
Dave Studdard	LT	Leon Gray
Tom Glassic	LG	David Carter
Bill Bryan	C	Carl Mauck
Paul Howard	RG	Ed Fisher
Claudie Minor	RT	Conway Hayman
Riley Odoms	TE	Mike Barber
Haven Moses	WR	Richard Caster
Craig Morton	QB	Dan Pastorini
Jon Keyworth	RB	Tim Wilson
Otis Armstrong	RB	Earl Campbell
	Starters, Defense	
Barney Chavous	LE	Andy Dorris
Rubin Carter	NT	Curley Culp
Brison Manor	RE	Elvin Bethea
Bob Swenson	LOLB	Ted Washington
Joe Rizzo	LILB	Gregg Bingham
Randy Gradishar	RILB	Art Stringer
Tom Jackson	ROLB	Robert Brazile
Louis Wright	LCB	J.C. Wilson
Steve Foley	RCB	Greg Stemrick
Billy Thompson	SS	Vernon Perry
Bernard Jackson	FS	Mike Reinfeldt

Denver	7	0	0	0	—	7
Houston	3	7	0	3	—	13

Hou—FG Fritsch 31
Den—Preston 7 pass from Morton (Turner kick)
Hou—Campbell 3 run (Fritsch kick)
Hou—FG Fritsch 20
Attendance—48,776

TEAM STATISTICS	Den	Hou
First downs	17	15
Rushing	7	8
Passing	9	6
By penalty	1	1
Total yardage	216	282
Net rushing yardage	112	135
Net passing yardage	104	147
Passes att.-comp.-had int.	27-14-1	22-10-2

RUSHING
Denver—Armstrong, 12 for 51; Canada, 4 for 29; Preston, 9 for 24; Jensen, 4 for 5; Upchurch, 1 for 3; Morton, 2 for 0.
Houston—Carpenter, 16 for 59; Campbell, 16 for 50, 1 TD; T. Wilson, 8 for 21; Coleman, 2 for 5.

PASSING
Denver—Morton, 14 of 27 for 144, 1 TD, 1 int.
Houston—Pastorini, 8 of 18 for 149, 1 int.; Nielsen, 2 of 4 for 9, 1 int.

RECEIVING
Denver—Preston, 4 for 40, 1 TD; Moses, 3 for 47; Armstrong, 2 for 22; Odom, 2 for 3; Egloff, 1 for 17; Jensen, 1 for 11; Canada, 1 for 4.
Houston—T. Wilson, 4 for 53; Carpenter, 3 for 26; Coleman, 1 for 41; Barber, 1 for 31; Campbell, 1 for 7.

1979 NFC

PHILADELPHIA 27, CHI. BEARS 17

Quarterback Ron Jaworski threw three touchdown passes, including two in a second-half comeback, as the Eagles overcame a 17-10 halftime deficit to win their first postseason game in 19 years.

Philadelphia scored after Wally Henry returned a punt 34 yards to Chicago's 26. Four running plays put the ball on the 17, from where Jaworski hit Harold Carmichael with a touchdown pass. Later in the quarter, the Bears tied the score on a two-yard run by Walter Payton. On the 82-yard drive, Mike Phipps completed five of six passes for 60 yards.

After the Eagles took a 10-7 lead, the Bears came back to score on another run by Payton. The big play in the drive was a 24-yard pass interference call against the Bears. Two plays after the kickoff, Jaworski fumbled and Alan Page recovered at the 17. With less than a minute in the half, a field goal by Bob Thomas put the Bears ahead 17-10.

Midway through the third quarter, Jaworski pulled the Eagles even. In a 67-yard drive, he completed three consecutive passes for 53 yards, including a 29-yard touchdown to Carmichael.

The next time the Eagles got the ball, Jaworski hit running back Billy Campfield for a 63-yard touchdown that provided the winning points.

December 23, at Philadelphia

Chi. Bears	Starters, Offense	Philadelphia
Rickey Watts	WR	Harold Carmichael
Tod Albrecht	LT	Stan Walters
Noah Jackson	LG	Wade Key
Dan Neal	C	Guy Morriss
Revie Sorey	RG	Woody Peoples
Dennis Lick	RT	Jerry Sisemore
Mike Cobb	TE	Keith Krepfle
Brian Baschnagel	WR	Charles Smith
Mike Phipps	QB	Ron Jaworski
Dave Williams	RB	Leroy Harris
Walter Payton	RB	Wilbert Montgomery
	Starters, Defense	
Dan Hampton	LE	Claude Humphrey
Jim Osborne	LT-NT	Charlie Johnson
Alan Page	RT-RE	Carl Hairston
Mike Hartenstine	RE-LOLB	John Bunting
Jerry Muckensturm	LLB-LILB	Jerry Robinson
Tom Hicks	MLB-RILB	Frank LeMaster
Gary Campbell	RLB-ROLB	Reggie Wilkes
Terry Schmidt	LCB	Bobby Howard
Allan Ellis	RCB	Herman Edwards
Gary Fencik	SS	Randy Logan
Doug Plank	FS	John Sciarra

Chi. Bears	7	10	0	0	—	17
Philadelphia	7	3	7	10	—	27

Phil —Carmichael 17 pass from Jaworski (Franklin kick)
ChiB—Payton 2 run (Thomas kick)
Phil —FG Franklin 29
ChiB—Payton 1 run (Thomas kick)
ChiB—FG Thomas 30
Phil —Carmichael 29 pass from Jaworski (Franklin kick)
Phil —Campfield 63 pass from Jaworski (Franklin kick)
Phil —FG Franklin 34
Attendance—69,397

TEAM STATISTICS	ChiB	Phil
First downs	15	18
Rushing	7	8
Passing	7	8
By penalty	1	2
Total yardage	241	315
Net rushing yardage	99	139
Net passing yardage	142	176
Passes att.-comp.-had int.	30-12-2	23-12-1

RUSHING
Chi. Bears—Payton, 16 for 67, 2 TDs; Williams, 10 for 23; McClendon, 2 for 6; Phipps, 1 for 3.
Philadelphia—Montgomery, 26 for 87; Harris, 8 for 33; Jaworski, 3 for 19.

PASSING
Chi. Bears—Phipps, 13 of 30 for 142, 2 int.
Philadelphia—Jaworski, 12 of 23 for 204, 3 TDs, 1 int.

RECEIVING
Chi. Bears—Payton, 3 for 52; Watts, 3 for 42; Baschnagel, 3 for 38; Latta, 2 for 6; Williams, 2 for 4.
Philadelphia—Carmichael, 6 for 111, 2 TDs; Campfield, 2 for 70, 1 TD; Montgomery, 2 for 0; Harris, 1 for 15; Smith, 1 for 8.

1980 AFC

OAKLAND 27, HOUSTON 7

The Oilers made more yards and more first downs and held onto the ball longer, but the Raiders' defense came up with the big plays to win the game 27-7.

On the first play from scrimmage, Earl Campbell fumbled and Mike Davis recovered at the Oilers' 24. Four plays later, Chris Bahr kicked a 47-yard field goal. Late in the first quarter, the Oilers went ahead, driving 55 yards on nine plays, seven of them runs by Campbell, who scored from the 1.

The Oilers had a chance to extend their lead in the second quarter, but Toni Fritsch missed a long field goal. A short while later, a good punt return set the Raiders up at the Houston 41. On second down, Jim Plunkett passed to Kenny King for 37 yards to the 2. Two plays later, Plunkett hit Todd Christensen with a one-yard scoring pass for a 10-7 lead.

In the third quarter, the Oilers drove to a first down at the Oakland 13, but Ken Stabler's pass for Mike Renfro was intercepted by Lester Hayes in the end zone. On the last play of the third quarter, Plunkett found Cliff Branch with a 33-yard completion. On the next play, Plunkett connected with running back Arthur Whittington down the right sideline for 44 yards and a touchdown. With six minutes left, Hayes intercepted another pass by Stabler and raced 20 yards for the final touchdown.

December 28, at Oakland

Houston	Starters, Offense	Oakland
Dave Casper	TE-WR	Cliff Branch
Angelo Fields	LT	Art Shell
Bob Young	LG	Gene Upshaw
Carl Mauck	C	Dave Dalby
Ed Fisher	RG	Mickey Marvin
Morris Towns	RT	Henry Lawrence
Mike Barber	TE	Raymond Chester
Mike Renfro	WR	Bob Chandler
Ken Stabler	QB	Jim Plunkett
Tim Wilson	RB	Mark van Eeghen
Earl Campbell	RB	Kenny King
	Starters, Defense	
Andy Dorris	LE	John Matuszak
Ken Kennard	NT	Reggie Kinlaw
Elvin Bethea	RE	Dave Browning
Ted Washington	LOLB	Ted Hendricks
Daryl Hunt	LILB	Matt Millen
Gregg Bingham	RILB	Bob Nelson
Robert Brazile	ROLB	Rod Martin
J.C. Wilson	LCB	Lester Hayes
Greg Stemrick	RCB	Dwayne O'Steen
Vernon Perry	SS	Mike Davis
Mike Reinfeldt	FS	Burgess Owens

Houston	7	0	0	0	—	7
Oakland	3	7	0	17	—	27

Oak—FG Bahr 47
Hou—Campbell 1 run (Fritsch kick)
Oak—Christensen 1 pass from Plunkett (Bahr kick)
Oak—Whittington 44 pass from Plunkett (Bahr kick)
Oak—FG Bahr 37
Oak—Hayes 20 interception return (Bahr kick)
Attendance—53,333

TEAM STATISTICS	Hou	Oak
First downs	18	12
Rushing	5	4
Passing	11	7
By penalty	2	1
Total yardage	275	250
Net rushing yardage	97	111
Net passing yardage	178	139
Passes att.-comp.-had int.	27-15-2	23-8-1

RUSHING
Houston—Campbell, 27 for 91, 1 TD; Carpenter, 5 for 9; T. Wilson, 1 for -3.
Oakland—King, 13 for 55; van Eeghen, 14 for 46; Whittington, 5 for 11; Jensen, 2 for 0; Plunkett, 1 for -1.

PASSING
Houston—Stabler, 15 of 26 for 243, 2 int.; Campbell, 0 of 1.
Oakland—Plunkett, 8 of 23 for 168, 2 TDs, 1 int.

RECEIVING
Houston—Barber, 4 for 83; Renfro, 3 for 69; Casper, 3 for 31; Carpenter, 3 for 26; Coleman, 1 for 23; B. Johnson, 1 for 11.
Oakland—Whittington, 2 for 64, 1 TD; Chester, 2 for 12; King, 1 for 37; Branch, 1 for 33; van Eeghen, 1 for 21; Christensen, 1 for 1, 1 TD.

1980 NFC

DALLAS 34, LA RAMS 13

Dallas quarterback Danny White threw touchdown passes in each of the Cowboys' first three possessions of the second half to break open a 13-13 tie and rout the Rams 34-13.

The Rams led 6-3 after the first quarter, when they drove 73 yards for a touchdown, the big plays being three passes from Vince Ferragamo to Preston Dennard for 43 yards. Frank Corral's extra-point attempt was blocked. In the second quarter, the Rams went ahead 13-6 on a touchdown pass from Ferragamo to Dennard, but the Cowboys tied it on Tony Dorsett's touchdown run.

With the Cowboys' offensive line controlling the line of scrimmage, and Dorsett and the other Dallas backs reeling off big chunks of yardage, the Rams fell further and further behind in the second half. White threw touchdown passes to end two quick third-quarter drives and then to finish a slow, sustained drive of 95 yards in the fourth quarter.

The Rams had defeated the Cowboys 38-14 with two weeks to go in the season, but it was a different Dallas team in the playoffs.

"I kept telling people all week that Dallas was going to be a lot tougher this time around," said Rams coach Ray Malavasi. "Well, you all saw what I was talking about."

December 28, at Irving

LA Rams	Starters, Offense	Dallas
Preston Dennard	WR	Tony Hill
Doug France	LT	Pat Donovan
Kent Hill	LG	Herbert Scott
Rich Saul	C	Robert Shaw
Dennis Harrah	RG	Tom Rafferty
Jackie Slater	RT	Jim Cooper
Victor Hicks	TE	Billy Joe DuPree
Billy Waddy	WR	Drew Pearson
Vince Ferragamo	QB	Danny White
Cullen Bryant	RB	Robert Newhouse
Jewerl Thomas	RB	Tony Dorsett
	Starters, Defense	
Jack Youngblood	LE	Ed Jones
Cody Jones	LT	Larry Cole
Larry Brooks	RT	Randy White
Fred Dryer	RE	Harvey Martin
Jim Youngblood	LLB	Mike Hegman
Jack Reynolds	MLB	Bob Breunig
George Andrews	RLB	D.D. Lewis
LeRoy Irvin	LCB	Benny Barnes
Rod Perry	RCB	Aaron Mitchell
Johnnie Johnson	SS	Charlie Waters
Nolan Cromwell	FS	Randy Hughes

LA Rams	6	7	0	0	—	13
Dallas	3	10	14	7	—	34

Dall —FG Septien 28
Rams—Thomas 1 run (kick blocked)
Dall —FG Septien 29
Rams—Dennard 21 pass from Ferragamo (Corral kick)
Dall —Dorsett 12 run (Septien kick)
Dall —Dorsett 10 pass from White (Septien kick)
Dall —Johnson 35 pass from White (Septien kick)
Dall —D. Pearson 11 pass from White (Septien kick)
Attendance—63,052

TEAM STATISTICS	Rams	Dall
First downs	15	29
Rushing	6	19
Passing	7	9
By penalty	2	1
Total yardage	260	528
Net rushing yardage	92	338
Net passing yardage	168	190
Passes att.-comp.-had int.	30-14-3	25-12-3

RUSHING
LA Rams—J. Thomas, 14 for 48, 1 TD; Bryant, 10 for 44.
Dallas—Dorsett, 22 for 160, 1 TD; Springs, 4 for 58; Newhouse, 11 for 46; J. Jones, 5 for 38; Newsome, 2 for 34; D. White, 2 for 2.

PASSING
LA Rams—Ferragamo, 14 of 30 for 175, 1 TD, 3 int.
Dallas—D. White, 12 of 25 for 190, 3 TDs, 3 int.

RECEIVING
LA Rams—Dennard, 6 for 117, 1 TD; J. Thomas, 3 for 26; Bryant, 2 for 7; Nelson, 1 for 12; Waddy, 1 for 9; Guman, 1 for 5.
Dallas—D. Pearson, 4 for 60, 1 TD; Dorsett, 3 for 28, 1 TD; Saldi, 2 for 52; Johnson, 1 for 35, 1 TD; Hill, 1 for 8; DuPree, 1 for 7.

1981 AFC

BUFFALO 31, NY JETS 27

Buffalo jumped to a 24-0 lead in the second quarter, then had to withstand a comeback by the New York Jets to win the first AFC Wild Card Game between teams from the same division, 31-27.

Bruce Harper of the Jets returned the game's opening kickoff to the 25, but fumbled when hit by Ervin Parker. Charles Romes picked up the ball and ran it in for a Buffalo touchdown. On Buffalo's second possession, Joe Ferguson hit wide receiver Frank Lewis with a 50-yard touchdown pass. Two interceptions off of Jets quarterback Richard Todd, who threw for 377 yards in the game, set up 10 more points, and gave the Bills a 24-0 lead.

By the end of the third quarter, the Jets had cut the margin to 24-13, but, with 10 minutes left, the Bills built what appeared to be an untouchable lead when Joe Cribbs ran 45 yards for a touchdown.

The Jets then started their comeback. First Todd passed to Bobby Jones for a touchdown. Then a one-yard run by Kevin Long made it 31-27. The Jets took over with 2:36 remaining, and, passing on every play, Todd drove them 69 yards to the Buffalo 11 with 10 seconds left. But safety Bill Simpson intercepted on the 1 with two seconds remaining.

December 27, at New York

Buffalo	**Starters, Offense**	**NY Jets**
Jerry Butler	WR	Wesley Walker
Ken Jones	LT	Chris Ward
Tom Lynch	LG	Randy Rasmussen
Will Grant	C	Joe Fields
Jon Borchardt	RG	Dan Alexander
Joe Devlin	RT	Marvin Powell
Mark Brammer	TE	Jerome Barkum
Frank Lewis	WR	Derrick Gaffney
Joe Ferguson	QB	Richard Todd
Roosevelt Leaks	RB	Tom Newton
Joe Cribbs	RB	Freeman McNeil
	Starters, Defense	
Ben Williams	LE	Mark Gastineau
Fred Smerlas	NT-LT	Abdul Salaam
Sherman White	RE-RT	Marty Lyons
Lucius Sanford	LOLB-RE	Joe Klecko
Jim Haslett	LILB-LLB	Greg Buttle
Phil Villapiano	RILB-MLB	Stan Blinka
Isiah Robertson	ROLB-RLB	Lance Mehl
Mario Clark	LCB	Donald Dykes
Charles Romes	RCB	Jerry Holmes
Steve Freeman	SS	Ken Schroy
Bill Simpson	FS	Darrol Ray

Buffalo	17	7	0	7	—	31
NY Jets	0	10	3	14	—	27

Buff—Romes 26 fumble recovery return (Mike-Mayer kick)
Buff—Lewis 50 pass from Ferguson (Mike-Mayer kick)
Buff—FG Mike-Mayer 29
Buff—Lewis 26 pass from Ferguson (Mike-Mayer kick)
NYJ—Shuler 30 pass from Todd (Leahy kick)
NYJ—FG Leahy 26
NYJ—FG Leahy 19
Buff—Cribbs 45 run (Mike-Mayer kick)
NYJ—B. Jones 30 pass from Todd (Leahy kick)
NYJ—Long 1 run (Leahy kick)
Attendance—57,050

TEAM STATISTICS	**Buff**	**NYJ**
First downs	15	23
Rushing	4	3
Passing	11	17
By penalty	0	3
Total yardage	321	419
Net rushing yardage	91	71
Net passing yardage	230	348
Passes att.-comp.-had int.	34-17-4	50-28-4

RUSHING
Buffalo—Cribbs, 14 for 83, 1 TD; Leaks, 6 for 12; Ferguson, 2 for -4.
NY Jets—McNeil, 12 for 32; Long, 8 for 28, 1 TD; Todd, 2 for 11.
PASSING
Buffalo—Ferguson, 17 of 34 for 268, 2 TDs, 4 int.
NY Jets—Todd, 28 of 50 for 377, 2 TDs, 4 int.
RECEIVING
Buffalo—Lewis, 7 for 158, 2 TDs; Cribbs, 4 for 64; Leaks, 3 for 23; Brammer, 2 for 17; Butler, 1 for 6.
NY Jets—Dierking, 7 for 52; Shuler, 6 for 116, 1 TD; B. Jones, 4 for 64, 1 TD; Gaffney, 4 for 64; Walker, 3 for 24; Barkum, 2 for 41; Newton, 1 for 12; Harper, 1 for 4.

1981 NFC

NY GIANTS 27, PHILADELPHIA 21

The New York Giants built a 20-0 first-quarter lead, then withstood a late Philadelphia rally to defeat the Eagles 27-21.

Philadelphia kick returner Wally Henry contributed to three of the Giants' scores. After the Eagles stopped the Giants on their first possession, Henry fumbled a punt at the 26, and Beasley Reece recovered for New York. Five carries by Rob Carpenter put the ball on the 4, and, after a penalty, Scott Brunner passed to Leon Bright for a touchdown.

The next time the Giants had the ball, they moved 62 yards to a touchdown. Henry took the ensuing kickoff at the 3 and fumbled. Mark Haynes recovered for the Giants in the end zone for a 20-0 lead.

Trailing 27-7 at halftime, the Eagles cut the margin to 13 on the first possession of the third quarter. They took 15 plays and almost eight minutes to drive 82 yards to Wilbert Montgomery's six-yard scoring run. But they couldn't move effectively again until six minutes remained in the game. Then Jaworski passed on 11 consecutive plays before Montgomery dove over the right side from the 1 with less than three minutes remaining.

The Eagles never had another chance, as the Giants used Rob Carpenter's runs to run out the clock.

December 27, at Philadelphia

NY Giants	**Starters, Offense**	**Philadelphia**
Earnest Gray	WR	Harold Carmichael
Jeff Weston	LT	Stan Walters
Billy Ard	LG	Steve Kenney
Jim Clack	C	Guy Morriss
J. T. Turner	RG	Ron Baker
Gordon King	RT	Jerry Sisemore
Gary Shirk	TE	Keith Krepfle
Johnny Perkins	WR-RB	Booker Russell
Scott Brunner	QB	Ron Jaworski
Leon Perry	RB	Hubert Oliver
Rob Carpenter	RB	Wilbert Montgomery
	Starters, Defense	
George Martin	LE	Dennis Harrison
Bill Neill	NT	Charlie Johnson
Gary Jeter	RE	Carl Hairston
Byron Hunt	LOLB	John Bunting
Brian Kelley	LILB	Al Chesley
Harry Carson	RILB	Frank LeMaster
Lawrence Taylor	ROLB	Jerry Robinson
Mark Haynes	LCB	Roynell Young
Terry Jackson	RCB	Herman Edwards
Bill Currier	SS	Randy Logan
Beasley Reece	FS	Brenard Wilson

NY Giants	20	7	0	0	—	27
Philadelphia	0	7	7	7	—	21

NYG—Bright 9 pass from Brunner (kick failed)
NYG—Mistler 10 pass from Brunner (Danelo kick)
NYG—Haynes recovered fumble in end zone (Danelo kick)
Phil —Carmichael 15 pass from Jaworski (Franklin kick)
NYG—Mullady 22 pass from Brunner (Danelo kick)
Phil —Montgomery 6 run (Franklin kick)
Phil —Montgomery 1 run (Franklin kick)
Attendance—71,611

TEAM STATISTICS	**NYG**	**Phil**
First downs	16	19
Rushing	10	8
Passing	6	8
By penalty	0	3
Total yardage	275	226
Net rushing yardage	183	93
Net passing yardage	92	133
Passes att.-comp.-had int.	14-9-1	24-13-0

RUSHING
NY Giants—Carpenter, 33 for 161; Brunner, 6 for 11; Perry, 3 for 11.
Philadelphia—Montgomery, 18 for 65, 2 TDs; Oliver, 5 for 12; Campfield, 1 for 10; Jaworski, 5 for 6.
PASSING
NY Giants—Brunner, 9 of 14 for 96, 3 TDs, 1 int.
Philadelphia—Jaworski, 13 of 24 for 154, 1 TD.
RECEIVING
NY Giants—Carpenter, 4 for 32; Mullady, 1 for 22, 1 TD; Gray, 1 for 12; Perkins, 1 for 11; Mistler, 1 for 10, 1 TD; Bright, 1 for 9, 1 TD.
Philadelphia—Montgomery, 3 for 32; R. Smith, 3 for 31; Carmichael, 2 for 40, 1 TD, C. Smith, 2 for 19, Krepfle, 1 for 18; Oliver, 1 for 7.

1982 AFC

MIAMI 28, NEW ENGLAND 13

Someone arranged for a tractor, along with some man-made snow, to be placed at one corner of the Orange Bowl, so the Patriots would feel at home, like when they beat the Dolphins 3-0 in the "snow-plow game" earlier in the year.

The Dolphins had the last laugh, however, as they beat the Patriots on the ground and in the air and stormed to a 28-13 victory.

New England scored first, in the second quarter, but the Dolphins drove right back down the field to take a 7-3 lead on a two-yard touchdown pass from David Woodley to Bruce Hardy, who did a juggling act in the back of the end zone. Miami had gone 79 yards on nine well-mixed plays, five runs and four passes. The next time the Dolphins had the ball, they scored again, driving 79 yards on nine plays to a one-yard touchdown run behind left tackle by Andra Franklin.

In the third quarter, New England cut the score to 14-6 on John Smith's second field goal, but the Dolphins again were up to the challenge, driving 74 yards in 11 plays for a touchdown. Miami made the result academic with its fourth long drive of the day in the final period. Woodley again hooked up with Hardy from two yards out to put the Dolphins up 28-6.

January 8, 1983, at Miami

New England	**Starters, Offense**	**Miami**
Stanley Morgan	WR-TE	Ronnie Lee
Brian Holloway	LT	Jon Giesler
John Hannah	LG	Bob Kuechenberg
Pete Brock	C	Dwight Stephenson
Ron Wooten	RG	Loren Toews
Shelby Jordan	RT	Eric Laakso
Don Hasselbeck	TE	Bruce Hardy
Preston Brown	WR	Jimmy Cefalo
Steve Grogan	QB	David Woodley
Lin Dawson	TE-RB	Andra Franklin
Mark van Eeghen	RB	Tommy Vigorito
	Starters, Defense	
Ken Sims	LE	Kim Bokamper
Lester Williams	NT	Bob Baumhower
Julius Adams	RE	Doug Betters
Larry McGrew	LOLB	Bob Brudzinski
Steve Nelson	LILB	A.J. Duhe
Clayton Weishuhn	RILB	Earnie Rhone
Don Blackmon	ROLB	Larry Gordon
Mike Haynes	LCB	Gerald Small
Raymond Clayborn	RCB	Don McNeal
Keith Lee	SS	Glenn Blackwood
Rick Sanford	FS	Lyle Blackwood

New England	0	3	3	7	—	13
Miami	0	14	7	7	—	28

NE —FG Smith 23
Mia —Hardy 2 pass from Woodley (von Schamann kick)
Mia —Franklin 1 run (von Schamann kick)
NE —FG Smith 42
Mia —Bennett 2 run (von Schamann kick)
Mia —Hardy 2 pass from Woodley (von Schamann kick)
NE —Hasselbeck 22 pass from Grogan (Smith kick)
Attendance—68,842

TEAM STATISTICS	**NE**	**Mia**
First downs	14	27
Rushing	6	12
Passing	8	14
By penalty	0	1
Total yardage	237	448
Net rushing yardage	77	214
Net passing yardage	160	234
Passes att.-comp.-had int.	30-16-2	19-16-0

RUSHING
New England—van Eeghen, 9 for 40; Collins, 7 for 35; Tatupu, 1 for 4; Morgan, 1 for -2.
Miami—Franklin, 26 for 112, 1 TD; Nathan, 12 for 71; Woodley, 1 for 16; Bennett, 5 for 10, 1 TD; Vigorito, 1 for 5.
PASSING
New England—Grogan, 16 of 30 for 189, 1 TD, 2 int.
Miami—Woodley, 16 of 19 for 246, 2 TD.
RECEIVING
New England—Hasselbeck, 7 for 87, 1 TD; Dawson, 4 for 49; Collins, 1 for 17; Toler, 1 for 16; Brown, 1 for 8; Johnson, 1 for 7; van Eeghen, 1 for 5.
Miami—Nathan, 5 for 68; Hardy, 3 for 23, 2 TDs; Rose, 2 for 47; Vigorito, 2 for 40; Cefalo, 2 for 27; Harris, 1 for 36; Diana, 1 for 5.

1982 AFC

LA RAIDERS 27, CLEVELAND 10

The Raiders dominated the game, rolling up 510 yards total offense, but couldn't put away the pesky Browns until the fourth quarter, finally emerging with a 27-10 victory.

On the first play of the game, Jim Plunkett threw long over the middle, hitting Cliff Branch with a 64-yard pass to the Browns' 15. Four plays later, Chris Bahr kicked a 27-yard field goal. Although the Raiders threatened twice more in the quarter, each time a pass by Plunkett was intercepted.

In the second quarter, the Browns tied the game on a field goal by Matt Bahr. The Raiders drove right back to score on a run by Marcus Allen, moving 88 yards, 75 of them coming on Plunkett's passing. With less than two minutes in the half, McDonald hooked up with Ricky Feacher on a 43-yard touchdown pass. But the Raiders raced to a field goal with six seconds left for a 13-10 halftime lead.

The Raiders established a commanding edge in the third quarter on a 12 play, 89 yard drive to Allen's second touchdown. The drive came after the Browns had reached the Raiders' 11, only to have Charles White fumble when tackled by Lyle Alzado.

The next time the Raiders had the ball, they put together a similar drive, moving 80 yards in 11 plays to a one-yard touchdown by Frank Hawkins.

January 8, 1983, at Los Angeles

Cleveland	Starters, Offense	LA Raiders
Dave Logan	WR	Cliff Branch
Doug Dieken	LT	Bruce Davis
Robert E. Jackson	LG	Curt Marsh
Mike Baab	C	Dave Dalby
Joe DeLamielleure	RG	Mickey Marvin
Cody Risien	RT	Henry Lawrence
Ozzie Newsome	TE	Todd Christensen
Ricky Feacher	WR	Malcolm Barnwell
Paul McDonald	QB	Jim Plunkett
Mike Pruitt	RB	Kenny King
Charles White	RB	Marcus Allen
	Starters, Defense	
Marshall Harris	LE	Howie Long
Bob Golic	NT	Reggie Kinlaw
Mike Robinson	RE	Lyle Alzado
Chip Banks	LOLB	Ted Hendricks
Tom Cousineau	LILB	Matt Millen
Tom Ambrose	RILB	Bob Nelson
Clay Matthews	ROLB	Rod Martin
Ron Bolton	LCB	Lester Hayes
Hanford Dixon	RCB	Ted Watts
Clarence Scott	SS	Mike Davis
Clinton Burrell	FS	Burgess Owens

Cleveland	0	10	0	0	—	10
LA Raiders	3	10	7	7	—	27

Raiders—FG C. Bahr 27
Cle —FG M. Bahr 52
Raiders—Allen 2 run (C. Bahr kick)
Cle —Feacher 43 pass from McDonald (M. Bahr kick)
Raiders—FG C. Bahr 37
Raiders—Allen 3 run (C. Bahr kick)
Raiders—Hawkins 1 run (C. Bahr kick)
Attendance—56,555

TEAM STATISTICS	Cle	Raiders
First downs	17	25
Rushing	1	11
Passing	11	14
By penalty	5	0
Total yardage	284	510
Net rushing yardage	56	140
Net passing yardage	228	370
Passes att.-comp.-had int.	37-18-0	37-24-2

RUSHING

Cleveland—White, 9 for 30; M. Pruitt, 8 for 19; McDonald, 1 for 7.
LA Raiders—Allen, 17 for 72, 2 TDs; King, 7 for 30; G. Pruitt, 3 for 15; Hawkins, 4 for 10; Plunkett, 2 for 10; Willis, 3 for 3.

PASSING

Cleveland—McDonald, 18 of 37 for 281, 1 TD.
LA Raiders—Plunkett, 24 of 37 for 386, 2 int.

RECEIVING

Cleveland—Feacher, 4 for 124, 1 TD; Newsome, 4 for 51; Walker, 4 for 47; M. Pruitt, 3 for 17; White, 2 for 15; Logan, 1 for 27.
LA Raiders—Christensen, 6 for 93; Allen, 6 for 75; Branch, 5 for 121; Barnwell, 2 for 38; G. Pruitt, 2 for 14; Ramsey, 1 for 25; King, 1 for 11; Hawkins, 1 for 9.

1982 AFC

NY JETS 44, CINCINNATI 17

New York running back Freeman McNeil rushed for 202 yards on 21 carries, scored once, and threw a touchdown pass to lead the Jets to a 44-17 victory over the favored Cincinnati Bengals.

The game wasn't all McNeil, however. For a while, it wasn't even all Jets. Cincinnati quarterback Ken Anderson threw first-quarter touchdown passes to Isaac Curtis and Dan Ross as the Bengals mounted a 14-3 lead. Then came the deluge.

After McNeil's touchdown pass to Derrick Gaffney opened the second quarter, an interception by Johnny Lynn set up an 85-yard drive that ended with a four-yard touchdown pass from Richard Todd to Wesley Walker for the Jets' first lead, 17-14.

The game remained close until the fourth quarter, which began with New York ahead 23-17. But McNeil scored on a 20-yard run and Darrol Ray returned an interception 98 yards for a touchdown to turn the game into a laugher.

January 9, 1983, at Cincinnati

NY Jets	Starters, Offense	Cincinnati
Wesley Walker	WR	Cris Collinsworth
Chris Ward	LT	Anthony Muñoz
Stan Waldemore	LG	Dave Lapham
Joe Fields	C	Blair Bush
Dan Alexander	RG	Glenn Bujnoch
Marvin Powell	RT	Mike Wilson
Jerome Barkum	TE	Dan Ross
Johnny (Lam) Jones	WR	Isaac Curtis
Richard Todd	QB	Ken Anderson
Mike Augustyniak	RB	Pete Johnson
Freeman McNeil	RB	Charles Alexander
	Starters, Defense	
Mark Gastineau	LE	Eddie Edwards
Abdul Salaam	LT-NT	Wilson Whitley
Marty Lyons	RT-RE	Ross Browner
Kenny Neil	RE-LOLB	Bo Harris
Greg Buttle	LLB-LILB	Jim LeClair
Stan Blinka	MLB-RILB	Glenn Cameron
Lance Mehl	RLB-ROLB	Reggie Williams
Bobby Jackson	LCB	Louis Breeden
Jerry Holmes	RCB	Ken Riley
Ken Schroy	SS	Bobby Kemp
Darrol Ray	FS	Mike Fuller

NY Jets	3	17	3	21	—	44
Cincinnati	14	0	3	0	—	17

Cin —Curtis 32 pass from Anderson (Breech kick)
NYJ—FG Leahy 32
Cin —Ross 2 pass from Anderson (Breech kick)
NYJ—Gaffney 14 pass from McNeil (Leahy kick)
NYJ—Walker 4 pass from Todd (Leahy kick)
NYJ—FG Leahy 24
NYJ—FG Leahy 47
Cin —FG Breech 20
NYJ—McNeil 20 run (Leahy kick)
NYJ—Ray 98 interception return (Leahy kick)
NYJ—Crutchfield 1 run (Leahy kick)
Attendance—57,560

TEAM STATISTICS	NYJ	Cin
First downs	27	23
Rushing	12	2
Passing	13	18
By penalty	2	3
Total yardage	508	395
Net rushing yardage	225	62
Net passing yardage	283	333
Passes att.-comp.-had int.	29-21-1	36-26-3

RUSHING

NY Jets—McNeil, 21 for 202, 1 TD; Dierking, 3 for 11; Newton, 2 for 6; Todd, 3 for 3; Augustyniak, 2 for 2; Crutchfield, 1 for 1, 1 TD; Harper, 1 for 0.
Cincinnati—Johnson, 9 for 26; A. Griffin, 3 for 17; Alexander, 7 for 14; Anderson, 2 for 5.

PASSING

NY Jets—Todd, 20 of 28 for 269, 1 TD, 1 int.; McNeil, 1 of 1 for 14, 1 TD.
Cincinnati—Anderson, 26 of 35 for 354, 2 TDs, 3 int.; Schonert, 0 of 1.

RECEIVING

NY Jets—Walker, 8 for 145, 1 TD; Gaffney, 4 for 50, 1 TD; Harper, 2 for 35; J. Jones, 2 for 22; Dierking, 2 for 9; McNeil, 1 for 9; Barkum, 1 for 9; Augustyniak, 1 for 4.
Cincinnati—Collinsworth, 7 for 120; Ross, 6 for 89, 1 TD; Curtis, 3 for 63, 1 TD; Kreider, 3 for 41; A. Griffin, 3 for 14; Johnson, 3 for 7; Harris, 1 for 20.

1982 AFC

SAN DIEGO 31, PITTSBURGH 28

Dan Fouts threw two fourth-quarter touchdown passes to Kellen Winslow, the second with only a minute left, to lead the Chargers to a scintillating, come-from-behind 31-28 victory over the Steelers.

San Diego had to survive the trauma of two fumbles by James Brooks in the first 30 seconds. His fumble of the opening kickoff cost seven points when Guy Ruff recovered in the end zone. Brooks almost created an instant replay when he fumbled the ensuing kickoff, but he recovered at his 1.

The Chargers kept their cool and clawed to a 17-14 halftime lead, including an 18-yard touchdown run by Brooks on the first play of the second quarter and a 10-yard touchdown pass from Fouts to backup tight end Eric Sievers with 32 seconds left in the half. The second score culminated a seven-play, 64-yard drive that took Fouts only 78 seconds.

Pittsburgh seemed to wrest control in the second half when Terry Bradshaw threw touchdown passes to Bennie Cunningham and John Stallworth, and the Steelers led 28-17 in the fourth quarter.

Then Fouts and Winslow showed why Air Coryell never could be counted out of a game.

January 9, 1983, at Pittsburgh

San Diego	Starters, Offense	Pittsburgh
Charlie Joiner	WR	John Stallworth
Billy Shields	LT	Ray Pinney
Doug Wilkerson	LG	Craig Wolfley
Don Macek	C	Mike Webster
Ed White	RG	Steve Courson
Russ Washington	RT	Larry Brown
Kellen Winslow	TE	Bennie Cunningham
Wes Chandler	WR	Lynn Swann
Dan Fouts	QB	Terry Bradshaw
John Cappelletti	RB	Frank Pollard
Chuck Muncie	RB	Franco Harris
	Starters, Defense	
Leroy Jones	LE	John Goodman
Louie Kelcher	LT-NT	Gary Dunn
Gary Johnson	RT-RE	Edmund Nelson
Keith Ferguson	RE-LOLB	Jack Ham
Linden King	LLB-LILB	Jack Lambert
Cliff Thrift	MLB-RILB	Loren Toews
Woodrow Lowe	RLB-ROLB	Robin Cole
Jeff Allen	LCB	Dwayne Woodruff
Mike Williams	RCB	Mel Blount
Tim Fox	SS	Donnie Shell
Bruce Laird	FS	Ron Johnson

San Diego	3	14	0	14	—	31
Pittsburgh	14	0	7	7	—	28

Pitt—Ruff fumble recovery in end zone (Anderson kick)
SD —FG Benirschke 25
Pitt—Bradshaw 1 run (Anderson kick)
SD —Brooks 18 run (Benirschke kick)
SD —Sievers 10 pass from Fouts (Benirschke kick)
Pitt—Cunningham 2 pass from Bradshaw (Anderson kick)
Pitt—Stallworth 9 pass from Bradshaw (Anderson kick)
SD —Winslow 8 pass from Fouts (Benirschke kick)
SD —Winslow 2 pass from Fouts (Benirschke kick)
Attendance—53,546

TEAM STATISTICS	SD	Pitt
First downs	29	26
Rushing	6	6
Passing	19	19
By penalty	4	1
Total yardage	479	422
Net rushing yardage	146	97
Net passing yardage	333	325
Passes att.-comp.-had int.	42-27-0	39-28-2

RUSHING

San Diego—Muncie, 25 for 126; Brooks, 3 for 20, 1 TD; Cappelletti, 1 for 0.
Pittsburgh—Pollard, 9 for 47; Harris, 10 for 35; Bradshaw, 2 for 12, 1 TD; Hawthorne, 2 for 3.

PASSING

San Diego—Fouts, 27 of 42 for 333, 3 TDs.
Pittsburgh—Bradshaw, 28 of 39 for 325, 2 TDs, 2 int.

RECEIVING

San Diego—Chandler, 9 for 124; Winslow, 7 for 102, 2 TDs; Joiner, 5 for 68; Sievers, 2 for 17, 1 TD; Muncie, 1 for 12; Fitzkee, 1 for 8; Brooks, 1 for 4; Cappelletti, 1 for -2.
Pittsburgh—Harris, 11 for 71; Stallworth, 8 for 116, 1 TD; Cunningham, 5 for 55, 1 TD; Pollard, 2 for 29; Smith, 1 for 40; Swann, 1 for 14.

1982 NFC

WASHINGTON 31, DETROIT 7

Washington's diminutive Alvin Garrett, normally a special-teams player, made the most of his chance to start in place of injured Art Monk by leading the Redskins to a 31-7 victory over the Detroit Lions. The five-foot, seven-inch Garrett caught six passes for 110 yards and three touchdowns.

The Redskins dominated the first half. On Detroit's second possession, safety Jeris White intercepted Eric Hipple's pass intended for Billy Sims and returned it 77 yards for a touchdown. Four plays after the kickoff, Hipple fumbled when sacked by blitzing Vernon Dean, and Darryl Grant recovered at the Detroit 19. Although a touchdown pass from Joe Theismann to tight end Don Warren was negated by a penalty, Mark Moseley kicked a 26-yard field goal.

The next three scores looked like replays of one another. In the second quarter, Theismann passed 21 yards to Garrett for a touchdown and then came back to do it again from the same distance. Then, on the first possession of the third quarter, Theismann hit Garrett from 27 yards out.

With the score 31-0, the Lions scored their only touchdown on a 15-yard pass from Hipple to David Hill. The score capped an 11-play, 83-yard drive. The fourth quarter saw Hipple try to pass on all 13 Detroit plays, while the Redskins were content to run the clock out behind John Riggins's carries.

January 8, 1983, at Washington

Detroit	Starters, Offense	Washington
Tracy Porter	WR	Charlie Brown
Chris Dieterich	LT	Joe Jacoby
Homer Elias	LG	Russ Grimm
Amos Fowler	C	Jeff Bostic
Don Greco	RG	Fred Dean
Keith Dorney	RT	George Starke
David Hill	TE	Don Warren
Leonard Thompson	WR	Alvin Garrett
Eric Hipple	QB	Joe Theismann
Dexter Bussey	RB-TE	Rick Walker
Billy Sims	RB	John Riggins
	Starters, Defense	
Dave Pureifory	LE	Mat Mendenhall
William Gay	LT	Dave Butz
Doug English	RT	Darryl Grant
Curtis Green	RE	Dexter Manley
Garry Cobb	LLB	Mel Kaufman
Ken Fantetti	MLB	Neal Olkewicz
Stan White	RLB	Rich Milot
Bobby Watkins	LCB	Jeris White
Al Latimer	RCB	Vernon Dean
William Graham	SS	Tony Peters
Alvin Hall	FS	Mark Murphy

Detroit	0	0	7	0	—	7
Washington	10	14	7	0	—	31

Wash—White 77 interception return (Moseley kick)
Wash—FG Moseley 26
Wash—Garrett 21 pass from Theismann (Moseley kick)
Wash—Garrett 21 pass from Theismann (Moseley kick)
Wash—Garrett 27 pass from Theismann (Moseley kick)
Det —Hill 15 pass from Hipple (Murray kick)
Attendance—55,045

TEAM STATISTICS	Det	Wash
First downs	20	18
Rushing	6	10
Passing	12	8
By penalty	2	0
Total yardage	364	366
Net rushing yardage	95	175
Net passing yardage	269	191
Passes att.-comp.-had int.	38-22-2	19-14-0

RUSHING
Detroit—Hipple, 6 for 47; Sims, 6 for 19; Bussey, 5 for 19; King, 4 for 10.
Washington—Riggins, 25 for 199; Jackson, 8 for 27; Walker, 2 for 14; Washington, 1 for 9; Theismann, 2 for 6.

PASSING
Detroit—Hipple, 22 of 38 for 298, 1 TD, 2 int.
Washington—Theismann, 14 of 19 for 210, 3 TDs.

RECEIVING
Detroit—Thompson, 7 for 150; Sims, 6 for 68; Hill, 3 for 29, 1 TD; Porter, 2 for 31; King, 2 for 8; Scott, 1 for 14; Bussey, 1 for -2.
Washington—Garrett, 6 for 110, 3 TDs; Walker, 4 for 16; Brown, 3 for 69; Washington, 1 for 15.

1982 NFC

GREEN BAY 41, ST. LOUIS 16

Green Bay did everything right offensively, while St. Louis piled up more yards (453 to 394) but offset them with four turnovers as the Packers whipped the Cardinals 41-16.

The Cardinals drove to Green Bay's 1-yard line on the opening possession of the game, but had to settle for a field goal. Before they scored again, however, they trailed 28-3. On four consecutive possessions, the Packers scored touchdowns, driving 73 yards on each of the first two, but only 39 and 12 after the next two, which were set up by Cardinals turnovers.

The Cardinals scored with nine seconds to go in the half, but, typical of the day they were having, missed the extra point.

The third quarter provided more of the same, with Green Bay adding 10 points while St. Louis missed a field goal and couldn't get any points out of a first down at the Green Bay 13. The Cardinals did score once in the fourth quarter, but, with time running out and quarterback Neil Lomax trying to make the score respectable, he was intercepted on the 1-yard line.

January 8, 1983, at Green Bay

St. Louis	Starters, Offense	Green Bay
Roy Green	WR	James Lofton
Luis Sharpe	LT	Tim Stokes
Terry Stieve	LG	Tim Huffman
Dan Dierdorf	C	Larry McCarren
Joe Bostic	RG	Leotis Harris
Tootie Robbins	RT	Greg Koch
Doug Marsh	TE	Paul Coffman
Pat Tilley	WR	John Jefferson
Neil Lomax	QB	Lynn Dickey
Wayne Morris	RB	Gerry Ellis
Ottis Anderson	RB	Eddie Lee Ivery
	Starters, Defense	
Elois Grooms	LE	Mike Butler
Mike Dawson	LT-NT	Terry Jones
David Galloway	RT-RE	Ezra Johnson
Curtis Greer	RE-LOLB	John Anderson
E.J. Junior	LLB-LILB	Randy Scott
Dave Ahrens	MLB-RILB	George Cumby
Charlie Baker	RLB-ROLB	Mike Douglass
Jeff Griffin	LCB	Mark Lee
Carl Allen	RCB	Mike McCoy
Lee Nelson	SS	Johnnie Gray
Benny Perrin	FS	Maurice Harvey

St. Louis	3	6	0	7	—	16
Green Bay	7	21	10	3	—	41

StL—FG O'Donoghue 18
GB—Jefferson 60 pass from Dickey (Stenerud kick)
GB—Lofton 20 pass from Dickey (Stenerud kick)
GB—Ivery 2 run (Stenerud kick)
GB—Ivery 4 pass from Dickey (Stenerud kick)
StL—Tilley 5 pass from Lomax (kick blocked)
GB—FG Stenerud 46
GB—Jefferson 7 pass from Dickey (Stenerud kick)
GB—FG Stenerud 34
StL—Shumann 18 pass from Lomax (O'Donoghue kick)
Attendance—54,282

TEAM STATISTICS	StL	GB
First downs	28	22
Rushing	8	7
Passing	19	13
By penalty	1	2
Total yardage	453	394
Net rushing yardage	106	108
Net passing yardage	347	286
Passes att.-comp.-had int.	51-32-2	26-19-0

RUSHING
St. Louis—Anderson, 8 for 58; Mitchell, 7 for 21; Morris, 3 for 14; Lomax, 4 for 9; Green, 1 for 4.
Green Bay—Ivery, 13 for 67, 1 TD; Ellis, 5 for 27; Rodgers, 6 for 18; Jensen, 3 for 10; Dickey, 1 for 0; Huckleby, 2 for -1; Lofton, 1 for -13.

PASSING
St. Louis—Lomax, 32 of 51 for 385, 2 TDs, 2 int.
Green Bay—Dickey, 17 of 23 for 260, 4 TDs; Ellis, 1 of 1 for 11; Campbell, 1 of 2 for 15.

RECEIVING
St. Louis—Green, 9 for 113; Tilley, 5 for 55, 1 TD; Shumann, 4 for 59, 1 TD; Mitchell, 4 for 57; Thompson, 3 for 41; Morris, 3 for 32; Marsh, 2 for 18; Harrell, 2 for 10.
Green Bay—Jefferson, 6 for 148, 2 TDs; Coffman, 4 for 39; Lofton, 3 for 52, 1 TD; Ellis, 3 for 29; Rodgers, 1 for 10; Ivery, 1 for 4, 1 TD; Jensen, 1 for 4.

1982 NFC

DALLAS 30, TAMPA BAY 17

The Dallas defense shut down Tampa Bay and made up for several of its offense's mistakes by scoring the winning points itself, as the Cowboys defeated the Buccaneers 30-17.

Dallas jumped to an early 6-0 lead on two field goals by Rafael Septien, the first of which was set up by Dextor Clinkscale's interception. Tampa Bay came back in the second quarter, when linebacker Hugh Green plucked Danny White's fumble from mid-air and raced 60 yards for a touchdown. The Buccaneers increased their lead to 10-6 when Bill Capece kicked a 32-yard field goal. Dallas regained the lead 35 seconds before halftime; White threw a touchdown pass to Ron Springs.

In the third quarter, a 17-play, 84-yard drive ended at the 1, and Septien kicked a field goal. The next time Dallas had the ball, White was intercepted, initiating a drive that culminated in Doug Williams passing 49 yards to Gordon Jones for a 17-16 lead.

The Cowboys, who more than doubled the Buccaneers' yardage in the game (456-218), still trailed as the fourth quarter began. But little-used rookie safety Monty Hunter picked off a pass by Williams and returned it 19 yards for a touchdown and a victory.

January 9, 1983, at Irving

Tampa Bay	Starters, Offense	Dallas
Gordon Jones	WR	Tony Hill
Dave Reavis	LT	Pat Donovan
Ray Snell	LG	Herbert Scott
Steve Wilson	C	Tom Rafferty
Sean Farrell	RG	Kurt Peterson
Charley Hannah	RT	Jim Cooper
Jimmie Giles	TE	Doug Cosbie
Kevin House	WR	Drew Pearson
Doug Williams	QB	Danny White
Melvin Carver	RB	Ron Springs
James Wilder	RB	Tony Dorsett
	Starters, Defense	
Dave Stalls	LE	Ed Jones
David Logan	NT-LT	John Dutton
Lee Roy Selmon	RE-RT	Randy White
Andy Hawkins	LOLB-RE	Harvey Martin
Cecil Johnson	LILB-LLB	Mike Hegman
Scot Brantley	RILB-MLB	Bob Breunig
Hugh Green	ROLB-RLB	Guy Brown
Norris Thomas	LCB	Everson Walls
John Holt	RCB	Dennis Thurman
Mark Cotney	SS	Benny Barnes
Neal Colzie	FS	Michael Downs

Tampa Bay	0	10	7	0	—	17
Dallas	6	7	3	14	—	30

Dall—FG Septien 33
Dall—FG Septien 33
TB —Green 60 fumble return (Capece kick)
TB —FG Capece 32
Dall—Springs 6 pass from D. White (Septien kick)
Dall—FG Septien 19
TB —Jones 49 pass from Williams (Capece kick)
Dall—Hunter 19 interception return (Septien kick)
Dall—Newsome 10 pass from D. White (Septien kick)
Attendance—65,042

TEAM STATISTICS	TB	Dall
First downs	8	29
Rushing	3	9
Passing	4	19
By penalty	1	1
Total yardage	218	456
Net rushing yardage	105	179
Net passing yardage	113	277
Passes att.-comp.-had int.	28-8-3	45-27-2

RUSHING
Tampa Bay—Wilder, 14 for 93; Carver, 7 for 12.
Dallas—Dorsett, 26 for 110; Donley, 1 for 25; Springs, 7 for 24; Newhouse, 5 for 15; Pearson, 1 for 4; DuPree, 1 for 1; D. White, 1 for 0.

PASSING
Tampa Bay—Williams, 8 of 28 for 113, 1 TD, 3 int.
Dallas—D. White, 27 of 45 for 312, 2 TDs, 2 int.

RECEIVING
Tampa Bay—House, 4 for 52; Wilder, 2 for 5; Jones, 1 for 49, 1 TD; Giles, 1 for 7.
Dallas—Pearson, 7 for 95; Johnson, 4 for 76; T. Hill, 4 for 45; Cosbie, 3 for 32; Springs, 3 for 16, 1 TD; Newsome, 2 for 14, 1 TD; Dorsett, 2 for 14; Newhouse, 1 for 11; DuPree, 1 for 9.

1982 NFC

MINNESOTA 30, ATLANTA 24

Quarterback Tommy Kramer orchestrated a 10-play, 72-yard drive, and running back Ted Brown scooted five yards around left end for a touchdown with 1:44 remaining in the game, to propel Minnesota to a 30-24 victory over the Atlanta Falcons.

The Vikings' defense stopped the Falcons all day long, intercepting Atlanta's Steve Bartkowski twice, sacking him three times, and pressuring him constantly. Despite not getting a touchdown from the offense, however, the Falcons were in a position to win the game 24-23 until the Vikings' winning drive.

Atlanta scored a little more than a minute into the game, when Paul Davis blocked a punt that Doug Rogers recovered in Minnesota's end zone. The Vikings came back to lead 13-7 at the half.

In the third quarter, Atlanta kicker Mick Luckhurst scrambled 17 yards for a touchdown with a lateral off a fake field goal. Less than two minutes later, safety Bob Glazebrook picked off a pass and returned it 35 yards for six points. After the Vikings went back ahead, Luckhurst kicked a 41-yard field goal to force Minnesota's final drive.

January 9, 1983, at Minneapolis

Atlanta	Starters, Offense	Minnesota
Alfred Jackson	WR	Sammy White
Mike Kenn	LT	Steve Riley
Pat Howell	LG	Jim Hough
Jeff Van Note	C	Dennis Swilley
R.C. Thielemann	RG	Wes Hamilton
Warren Bryant	RT	Tim Irwin
Russ Mikeska	TE	Joe Senser
Alfred Jenkins	WR	Sam McCullum
Steve Bartkowski	QB	Tommy Kramer
Keith Krepfle	TE-RB	Tony Galbreath
William Andrews	RB	Ted Brown
	Starters, Defense	
Jeff Yeates	LE	Doug Martin
Don Smith	NT	Charlie Johnson
Jeff Merrow	RE	Mark Mullaney
Al Richardson	LOLB	Matt Blair
Fulton Kuykendall	LILB	Jeff Siemon
Jim Laughlin	RILB	Dennis Johnson
Joel Williams	ROLB	Fred McNeill
Bobby Butler	LCB	John Swain
Kenny Johnson	RCB	Willie Teal
Bob Glazebrook	SS-LS	Tommy Hannon
Tom Pridemore	FS-RS	John Turner

Atlanta	7	0	14	3	—	24
Minnesota	3	10	3	14	—	30

Atl —Rogers recovered blocked punt in end zone (Luckhurst kick)
Minn—FG Danmeier 33
Minn—White 36 pass from Kramer (Danmeier kick)
Minn—FG Danmeier 30
Atl —Luckhurst 17 run (Luckhurst kick)
Atl —Glazebrook 35 interception return (Luckhurst kick)
Minn—FG Danmeier 39
Minn—McCullum 11 pass from Kramer (Danmeier kick)
Atl —FG Luckhurst 41
Minn—Brown 5 run (Luckhurst kick)
Attendance—60,560

TEAM STATISTICS	Atl	Minn
First downs	14	24
Rushing	5	8
Passing	5	12
By penalty	4	4
Total yardage	235	378
Net rushing yardage	120	125
Net passing yardage	115	253
Passes att.-comp.-had int.	23-9-2	34-20-1

RUSHING
Atlanta—Andrews, 11 for 48; Riggs, 9 for 38; Luckhurst, 1 for 17, 1 TD; Cain, 3 for 17.
Minnesota—Brown, 23 for 81, 1 TD; Nelson, 4 for 24; Kramer, 8 for 13; Galbreath, 6 for 10; S. White, 1 for -3.

PASSING
Atlanta—Bartkowski, 9 of 23 for 134, 2 int.
Minnesota—Kramer, 20 of 34 for 253, 2 TDs, 1 int.

RECEIVING
Atlanta—Jenkins, 2 for 52; Hodge, 2 for 29; Riggs, 2 for 16; Krepfle, 1 for 18; Cain, 1 for 14; A. Jackson, 1 for 5.
Minnesota—Senser, 6 for 81; McCullum, 4 for 51, 1 TD; Galbreath, 3 for 14; S. White, 2 for 61, 1 TD; LeCount, 2 for 24; Young, 2 for 13; Brown, 1 for 9.

1983 AFC

SEATTLE 31, DENVER 7

Normally conservative Seattle came out in the second half with a wide-open offense that disoriented the Denver Broncos and allowed the Seahawks to break open a close game. Coach Chuck Knox saw his team execute almost perfectly, as the Seahawks won their first-ever playoff game, 31-7.

The first half was played close to the vest. The Seahawks, who came out in their customary two-tight end offense, scored on their first possession. Using mainly the cut-back running of Curt Warner, Seattle drove to the Denver 17, where Dave Krieg hit Steve Largent with a touchdown pass.

Before the period ended, Denver tied the score, driving 76 yards on nine plays to Steve DeBerg's 13-yard strike to Wilbur Myles. In the second quarter, the Seahawks regained the lead when Kerry Justin intercepted a pass and returned it 45 yards to set up a 37-yard field goal by Norm Johnson.

With Dave Krieg taking to the air in the second half, the Seahawks scored on their first three possessions. Krieg drove the team 73 yards in five plays, ending with a touchdown pass to Pete Metzelaars. Then, he hit Paul Johns for 18 yards and a touchdown. Krieg set up a two-yard touchdown run by David Hughes with a 41-yard pass to Johns.

December 24, at Seattle

Denver	Starters, Offense	Seattle
Clint Sampson	WR-TE	Pete Metzelaars
Dave Studdard	LT	Ron Essink
Keith Bishop	LG	Edwin Bailey
Billy Bryan	C	Blair Bush
Paul Howard	RG	Robert Pratt
Ken Lanier	RT	Steve August
Ron Egloff	TE	Charle Young
Steve Watson	WR	Steve Largent
Steve DeBerg	QB	Dave Krieg
Nathan Poole	RB	Cullen Bryant
Sammy Winder	RB	Curt Warner
	Starters, Defense	
Barney Chavous	LE	Jacob Green
Rubin Carter	LT-NT	Joe Nash
Don Latimer	RT-RE	Jeff Bryant
Rulon Jones	RE-LOLB	Bruce Scholtz
Jim Ryan	LLB-LILB	Joe Norman
Randy Gradishar	MLB-RILB	Keith Butler
Tom Jackson	RLB-ROLB	Greg Gaines
Louis Wright	LCB	Kerry Justin
Mike Harden	RCB	Dave Brown
Dennis Smith	SS	Kenny Easley
Steve Foley	FS	John Harris

Denver	7	0	0	0	—	7
Seattle	7	3	7	14	—	31

Sea —Largent 17 pass from Krieg (N. Johnson kick)
Den—Myles 13 pass from DeBerg (Karlis kick)
Sea —FG N. Johnson 37
Sea —Metzelaars 5 pass from Krieg (N. Johnson kick)
Sea —Johns 18 pass from Krieg (N. Johnson kick)
Sea —Hughes 2 run (N. Johnson kick)
Attendance—64,275

TEAM STATISTICS	Den	Sea
First downs	21	17
Rushing	5	8
Passing	14	9
By penalty	2	0
Total yardage	360	324
Net rushing yardage	125	145
Net passing yardage	235	179
Passes att.-comp.-had int.	34-24-2	13-12-0

RUSHING
Denver—Winder, 16 for 59; Poole, 7 for 25; Elway, 3 for 16; Willhite, 5 for 16; Sampson, 1 for 8; Watson, 1 for 1.
Seattle—Warner, 23 for 99; Hughes, 3 for 16, 1 TD; C. Bryant, 5 for 15; Krieg, 3 for 9; Dixon, 3 for 4; Zorn, 1 for 2.

PASSING
Denver—DeBerg, 14 of 19 for 131, 1 TD, 1 int.; Elway, 10 of 15 for 123, 1 int.
Seattle—Krieg, 12 of 13 for 200, 3 TDs.

RECEIVING
Denver—Myles, 7 for 73, 1 TD; Watson, 4 for 51; Poole, 4 for 17; Sampson, 3 for 52; Winder, 2 for 13; Thomas, 1 for 19; Egloff, 1 for 16; Wilson, 1 for 12; Willhite, 1 for 1.
Seattle—Largent, 4 for 76, 1 TD; Warner, 3 for 22; Johns, 2 for 59, 1 TD; Young, 2 for 38; Metzelaars, 1 for 5, 1 TD.

1983 NFC

LA RAMS 24, DALLAS 17

The opportunistic Los Angeles Rams of rookie coach John Robinson turned three turnovers in the second half into 17 points and upset the Cowboys 24-17.

The halftime score was 7-7. With quarterback Vince Ferragamo hitting on four of four passes for 43 yards, the Rams drove 85 yards to score after only 3:35 of the game. The touchdown came on an 18-yard pass to David Hill. The rest of the half developed into a punt-swapping contest until Dallas took over on its 30 with 1:07 left. Danny White promptly hit five of six passes to take the Cowboys 70 yards to a 14-yard strike to Tony Hill.

The Cowboys took a quick 10-7 lead in the third period, but then began to self-destruct. First, Gary Allen muffed a punt that Mike Witcher recovered for the Rams at the Dallas 16. Presto—Ferragamo zipped a 16-yard touchdown pass to Preston Dennard. Next, 10 plays after linebacker Jim Collins had intercepted White, Ferragamo hit George Farmer with an eight-yard touchdown pass. Then, after White was intercepted by LeRoy Irvin, Mike Lansford kicked a 20-yard field goal to make it 24-10. The Cowboys scored with a minute left in the game, but then couldn't get the ball back.

December 26, at Irving

LA Rams	Starters, Offense	Dallas
Preston Dennard	WR	Tony Hill
Bill Bain	LT	Pat Donovan
Kent Hill	LG	Herbert Scott
Doug Smith	C	Tom Rafferty
Dennis Harrah	RG	Howard Richards
Jackie Slater	RT	Jim Cooper
Mike Barber	TE	Doug Cosbie
George Farmer	WR	Drew Pearson
Vince Ferragamo	QB	Danny White
Mike Guman	RB	Ron Springs
Eric Dickerson	RB	Tony Dorsett
	Starters, Defense	
Jack Youngblood	LE	Ed Jones
Greg Meisner	NT-LT	John Dutton
Reggie Doss	RE-RT	Randy White
Mel Owens	LOLB-RE	Harvey Martin
Jim Collins	LILB-LLB	Mike Hegman
Carl Ekern	RILB-MLB	Bob Breunig
George Andrews	ROLB-RLB	Anthony Dickerson
Eric Harris	LCB	Everson Walls
LeRoy Irvin	RCB	Dennis Thurman
Johnnie Johnson	SS	Bill Bates
Nolan Cromwell	FS	Michael Downs

LA Rams	7	0	7	10	—	24
Dallas	0	7	3	7	—	17

Rams—D. Hill 18 pass from Ferragamo (Lansford kick)
Dall —T. Hill 14 pass from D. White (Septien kick)
Dall —FG Septien 41
Rams—Dennard 16 pass from Ferragamo (Lansford kick)
Rams—Farmer 8 pass from Ferragamo (Lansford kick)
Rams—FG Lansford 20
Dall —Cosbie 2 pass from White (Septien kick)
Attendance—62,118

TEAM STATISTICS	Rams	Dall
First downs	19	24
Rushing	5	4
Passing	11	20
By penalty	3	0
Total yardage	243	363
Net rushing yardage	94	63
Net passing yardage	149	300
Passes att.-comp.-had int.	31-16-0	53-32-3

RUSHING
LA Rams—Dickerson, 23 for 99; Redden, 3 for 5; Ferragamo, 4 for -10.
Dallas—Dorsett, 17 for 59; Springs, 2 for 4; D. White, 1 for 0.

PASSING
LA Rams—Ferragamo, 15 of 30 for 162, 3 TDs; Dickerson, 1 of 1 for 1.
Dallas—D. White, 32 of 53 for 330, 2 TDs, 3 int.

RECEIVING
LA Rams—Farmer, 5 for 47, 1 TD; Dennard, 4 for 44, 1 TD; Barber, 2 for 20; D. Hill, 2 for 19, 1 TD; Dickerson, 2 for 11; Ellard, 1 for 22.
Dallas—T. Hill, 9 for 115, 1 TD; Springs, 6 for 38; Cosbie, 5 for 62, 1 TD; Dorsett, 4 for 12; Johnson, 3 for 20; Pearson, 2 for 49; Newsome, 2 for 25; DuPree, 1 for 9.

1984 AFC

SEATTLE 13, LA RAIDERS 7

The turning point of Seattle's 13-7 victory over Los Angeles came before the game started—when Seattle coach Chuck Knox decided to attack the Raiders' defense not with his record-setting passing attack, but with a ground game that had ranked twenty-fifth in the NFL.

The strategy caught the Raiders off balance. With Dave Krieg throwing only 10 passes, the Seahawks dominated the Raiders on the ground, rushing for 205 yards and keeping the ball for 35 minutes.

Seattle built a 13-0 lead in the fourth quarter behind a 26-yard touchdown pass from Krieg to Daryl Turner and two field goals by Norm Johnson. The catch by Turner was the only by a Seattle wide receiver all day, marking the first game since 1977 in which Steve Largent hadn't caught a pass.

The chief yardage-and-time eater for the Seahawks was Dan Doornink, who had the most productive game of his career, carrying 29 times for 126 yards. Doornink and teammate David Hughes continually ran off-tackle, cut back against the grain, and left the Raiders' linemen flat-footed.

Meanwhile, Seattle's defense was pressuring Jim Plunkett, who was sacked six times and intercepted twice. Plunkett did throw a 46-yard touchdown pass to Marcus Allen, but it came with five minutes left. That was far too late in the game given the way the Seahawks were controlling the ball.

December 22, at Seattle

LA Raiders	Starters, Offense	Seattle
Dave Casper	TE	Mike Tice
Bruce Davis	LT	Sid Abramowitz
Curt Marsh	LG	Edwin Bailey
Dave Dalby	C	Blair Bush
Mickey Marvin	RG	Robert Pratt
Henry Lawrence	RT	Bob Cryder
Todd Christensen	TE	Charle Young
Malcolm Barnwell	WR	Steve Largent
Jim Plunkett	QB	Dave Krieg
Kenny King	RB	David Hughes
Marcus Allen	RB	Dan Doornink
	Starters, Defense	
Howie Long	LE	Jacob Green
Reggie Kinlaw	NT	Joe Nash
Lyle Alzado	RE	Jeff Bryant
Brad Van Pelt	LOLB	Bruce Scholtz
Matt Millen	LILB	Shelton Robinson
Jack Squirek	RILB	Keith Butler
Rod Martin	ROLB	Greg Gaines
Lester Hayes	LCB	Keith Simpson
Mike Haynes	RCB	Dave Brown
Mike Davis	SS	Kenny Easley
Vann McElroy	FS	John Harris

LA Raiders	0	0	0	7	—	7
Seattle	0	7	3	3	—	13

Sea —Turner 26 pass from Krieg (N. Johnson kick)
Sea —FG N. Johnson 35
Sea —FG N. Johnson 44
Raiders—Allen 46 pass from Plunkett (Bahr kick)
Attendance—62,049

TEAM STATISTICS	Raiders	Sea
First downs	14	17
Rushing	5	12
Passing	8	4
By penalty	1	1
Total yardage	240	251
Net rushing yardage	105	205
Net passing yardage	135	46
Passes att.-comp.-had int.	27-14-2	10-4-0

RUSHING
LA Raiders—Allen, 17 for 61; Hawkins, 6 for 34; Pruitt, 1 for 6; King, 1 for 4.
Seattle—Doornink, 29 for 126; Hughes, 14 for 54; Lane, 4 for 17; Krieg, 3 for 10; Largent, 1 for -2.
PASSING
LA Raiders—Plunkett, 14 of 27 for 184, 1 TD, 2 int.
Seattle—Krieg, 4 of 10 for 70, 1 TD.
RECEIVING
LA Raiders—Allen, 5 for 90, 1 TD; Hawkins, 4 for 27; Barnwell, 3 for 34; Christensen, 1 for 21; King, 1 for 12.
Seattle—Turner, 1 for 26, 1 TD; Tice, 1 for 20; Doornink, 1 for 14; Hughes, 1 for 10.

1984 NFC

NY GIANTS 16, LA RAMS 13

The Los Angeles Rams' defense held the New York Giants to 40 yards rushing and 192 total yards, but the Giants made the key plays, both offensively and defensively, and won the game 16-13.

The Rams' defense had more to worry about than the Giants, however. The Rams' offense not only was plagued by penalties (10 for 75 yards) and inconsistency (just 214 net yards), it contributed to some of New York's points.

In the first quarter, with the Giants already leading 3-0, the Rams helped them build a 10-0 lead. Eric Dickerson fumbled and the ball was recovered by safety Bill Currier at the Rams' 23. Nine plays later, Rob Carpenter dove over for a touchdown.

After the teams swapped field goals, the Rams drove 78 yards in the third quarter. Dickerson scored on a 14-yard run, but the big play was a 45-yard pass-interference penalty against Terry Kinard.

Midway through the fourth quarter, trailing 16-10, the Rams drove for what they hoped would be the winning touchdown. With second and goal at the 4, the Rams tried to cross up the Giants' defense by giving the ball to Dwayne Crutchfield instead of Dickerson. Crutchfield was thrown for a three-yard loss, and the Rams had to settle for a field goal.

December 23, at Anaheim

NY Giants	Starters, Offense	LA Rams
Lionel Manuel	WR	Drew Hill
William Roberts	LT	Irv Pankey
Brad Benson	LG	Kent Hill
Kevin Belcher	C	Doug Smith
Chris Godfrey	RG	Dennis Harrah
Karl Nelson	RT	Bill Bain
Zeke Mowatt	TE	David Hill
Bobby Johnson	WR	Henry Ellard
Phil Simms	QB	Jeff Kemp
Rob Carpenter	RB-TE	James McDonald
Joe Morris	RB	Eric Dickerson
	Starters, Defense	
Curtis McGriff	LE	Jack Youngblood
Jim Burt	NT	Greg Meisner
Leonard Marshall	RE	Reggie Doss
Carl Banks	LOLB	Mel Owens
Gary Reasons	LILB	Carl Ekern
Harry Carson	RILB	Jim Collins
Lawrence Taylor	ROLB	Mike Wilcher
Kenny Daniel	LCB	Gary Green
Perry Williams	RCB	LeRoy Irvin
Bill Currier	SS	Vince Newsome
Terry Kinard	FS	Johnnie Johnson

NY Giants	10	0	6	0	—	16
LA Rams	0	3	7	3	—	13

NYG —FG Haji-Sheikh 37
NYG —Carpenter 1 run (Haji-Sheikh kick)
Rams —FG Lansford 38
NYG —FG Haji-Sheikh 39
Rams —Dickerson 14 run (Lansford kick)
NYG —FG Haji-Sheikh 36
Rams —FG Lansford 22
Attendance—67,037

TEAM STATISTICS	NYG	Rams
First downs	16	12
Rushing	5	5
Passing	8	5
By penalty	3	2
Total yardage	192	214
Net rushing yardage	40	107
Net passing yardage	152	107
Passes att.-comp.-had int.	31-22-0	15-11-0

RUSHING
NY Giants—Morris, 10 for 21; Carpenter, 13 for 20, 1 TD; Simms, 4 for -1.
LA Rams—Dickerson, 23 for 107, 1 TD; Kemp, 1 for 2; Crutchfield, 2 for -2.
PASSING
NY Giants—Simms, 22 of 31 for 179.
LA Rams—Kemp, 11 of 15 for 109.
RECEIVING
NY Giants—Mowatt, 7 for 73; Carpenter, 7 for 23; Manuel, 3 for 52; Gray, 2 for 20; Johnson, 1 for 6; Galbreath, 1 for 3; Morris, 1 for 2.
LA Rams—Brown, 3 for 32; Barber, 3 for 31; Ellard, 2 for 22; J. McDonald, 2 for 18; David Hill, 1 for 6.

1985 AFC

NEW ENGLAND 26, NY JETS 14

A fiery New England defense accounted for four turnovers, five sacks, and the clinching touchdown, as the Patriots defeated the Jets 26-14 to gain their first victory in the playoffs since 1963.

With the Jets leading 7-6 in the waning minutes of the first half, safety Fred Marion intercepted a pass by Ken O'Brien deep in Patriots territory and returned it to the 33. Six plays later, New England quarterback Tony Eason found a streaking Stanley Morgan down the left sideline for a 36-yard touchdown. When the Jets tried to use their two-minute offense, linebacker Andre Tippett hit O'Brien with such a jarring tackle that it put the NFL's leading passer out for the rest of the game.

The game slipped away from the Jets midway through the third quarter when Tony Franklin kicked the third of his four field goals. On the ensuing kickoff, Johnny Rembert stripped the ball away from Johnny Hector, picked it up, and ran 15 yards for a touchdown that made the score 23-7.

After the next kickoff, reserve quarterback Pat Ryan cut the margin to nine points by hitting tight end Mickey Shuler with a 12-yard touchdown pass. But the Jets could run only one play in Patriots territory the rest of the game.

December 28, at East Rutherford

New England	Starters, Offense	NY Jets
Stanley Morgan	WR	Al Toon
Brian Holloway	LT	Reggie McElroy
John Hannah	LG	Jim Sweeney
Pete Brock	C	Joe Fields
Ron Wooten	RG	Dan Alexander
Steve Moore	RT	Marvin Powell
Lin Dawson	TE	Mickey Shuler
Irving Fryar	WR	Wesley Walker
Tony Eason	QB	Ken O'Brien
Tony Collins	RB-TE	Rocky Klever
Craig James	RB	Freeman McNeil
	Starters, Defense	
Garin Veris	LE	Mark Gastineau
Lester Williams	NT-LT	Joe Klecko
Julius Adams	RE-RT	Barry Bennett
Andre Tippett	LOLB-RE	Marty Lyons
Steve Nelson	LILB-LLB	Kyle Clifton
Larry McGrew	RILB-MLB	Lance Mehl
Don Blackmon	ROLB-RLB	Bob Crable
Ronnie Lippett	LCB	Johnny Lynn
Raymond Clayborn	RCB	Russell Carter
Roland James	SS	Kirk Springs
Fred Marion	FS	Harry Hamilton

New England	3	10	10	3	—	26
NY Jets	0	7	7	0	—	14

NE —FG Franklin 33
NYJ—Hector 11 pass from O'Brien (Leahy kick)
NE —FG Franklin 41
NE —Morgan 36 pass from Eason (Franklin kick)
NE —FG Franklin 20
NE —Rembert 15 fumble return (Franklin kick)
NYJ—Shuler 12 pass from Ryan (Leahy kick)
NE —FG Franklin 26
Attendance—70,958

TEAM STATISTICS	NE	NYJ
First downs	12	15
Rushing	5	3
Passing	6	12
By penalty	1	0
Total yardage	258	240
Net rushing yardage	99	58
Net passing yardage	159	182
Passes att.-comp.-had int.	16-12-0	34-23-2

RUSHING
New England—James, 22 for 49; Collins, 11 for 36; Eason, 6 for 14.
NY Jets—McNeil, 16 for 41; Hector, 4 for 13; O'Brien, 1 for 4.
PASSING
New England—Eason, 12 of 16 for 179, 1 TD.
NY Jets—O'Brien, 13 of 17 for 149, 1 TD, 1 int.; Ryan, 10 of 17 for 84, 1 TD, 1 int.
RECEIVING
New England—Morgan, 4 for 62, 1 TD; Fryar, 2 for 47; C. James, 2 for 36; Dawson, 2 for 20; Collins, 2 for 14.
NY Jets—Toon, 9 for 93; Shuler, 5 for 53, 1 TD; Walker, 4 for 54; McNeil, 3 for 13; Hector, 1 for 11, 1 TD; Klever, 1 for 9.

1985 NFC

NY GIANTS 17, SAN FRANCISCO 3

Injuries, 10 dropped passes, and a fired-up New York defense combined to hold the NFC's number-two scoring team to a single field goal as the Giants defeated the 49ers 17-3.

San Francisco entered the game without guard Randy Cross and cornerback Eric Wright, and with quarterback Joe Montana and running back Roger Craig nursing injuries. New York, on the other hand, had a defense that played its most inspired game of the season and an unstoppable running back in little (5-7) Joe Morris, who gained 141 yards.

The Giants took the lead the first time they had the ball, with Eric Schubert kicking a 47-yard field goal less than three minutes into the game. Midway through the second period, they increased the score to 10-0 after Terry Kinard intercepted Montana and returned the ball to the San Francisco 38. Four plays later, Giants quarterback Phil Simms hit tight end Mark Bavaro, who made a sensational one-handed catch in the end zone. Helped by three penalties against the Giants' defense, the 49ers put together a 16-play, 85-yard drive for their only score of the game, cutting the halftime deficit to 10-3.

The Giants concluded the scoring on the opening drive of the third quarter, going 77 yards to a touchdown scored on Simms's pass to tight end Don Hasselbeck. The defense then took over the game.

December 29, at East Rutherford

San Francisco	Starters, Offense	NY Giants
Dwight Clark	WR	Bobby Johnson
Bubba Paris	LT	Brad Benson
John Ayers	LG	Billy Ard
Fred Quillan	C	Bart Oates
Guy McIntyre	RG	Chris Godfrey
Keith Fahnhorst	RT	Karl Nelson
Russ Francisc	TE	Mark Bavaro
Jerry Rice	WR	Lionel Manuel
Joe Montana	QB	Phil Simms
Roger Craig	RB	Rob Carpenter
Derrick Harmon	RB	Joe Morris
	Starters, Defense	
John Harty	LE	George Martin
Michael Carter	NT	Jim Burt
Dwaine Board	RE	Leonard Marshall
Todd Shell	LOLB	Byron Hunt
Riki Ellison	LILB	Gary Reasons
Mike Walter	RILB	Harry Carson
Keena Turner	ROLB	Lawrence Taylor
Dwight Hicks	LCB	Elvis Patterson
Tory Nixon	RCB	Perry Williams
Carlton Williamson	SS	Kenny Hill
Ronnie Lott	FS	Terry Kinard

San Francisco	0	3	0	0	—	3
NY Giants	3	7	7	0	—	17

NYG—FG Schubert 47
NYG—Bavaro 18 pass from Simms (Schubert kick)
SF —FG Wersching 21
NYG—Hasselbeck 3 pass from Simms (Schubert kick)
Attendance—75,842

TEAM STATISTICS	SF	NYG
First downs	19	21
Rushing	6	9
Passing	10	11
By penalty	3	1
Total yardage	362	355
Net rushing yardage	94	174
Net passing yardage	268	181
Passes att.-comp.-had int.	48-26-1	31-15-1

RUSHING

San Francisco—Tyler, 10 for 61; Craig, 9 for 23; Monroe, 1 for 10; Harmon, 1 for 0; Montana, 1 for 0.

NY Giants—Morris, 28 for 141; Carpenter, 4 for 25; Adams, 4 for 13; Simms, 5 for -5.

PASSING

San Francisco—Montana, 26 of 47 for 296, 1 int.; Rice, 0 of 1.

NY Giants—Simms, 15 of 31 for 181, 2 TDs, 1 int.

RECEIVING

San Francisco—Clark, 8 for 120; Rice, 4 for 45; Francis, 4 for 39; Frank, 3 for 25; Ring, 3 for 19; Craig, 2 for 18; Harmon, 1 for 16; Wilson, 1 for 14.

NY Giants—Bavaro, 5 for 67, 1 TD; Manuel, 3 for 56; Carpenter, 3 for 36; Galbreath, 1 for 9; Adams, 1 for 5; Morris, 1 for 5; Hasselbeck, 1 for 3, 1 TD.

The Playoff Bowl

1960

DETROIT 17, CLEVELAND 16

A blitzing Detroit defense harassed Cleveland's Milt Plum into five interceptions—three by safety Gary Lowe—and the Lions stopped the Browns 17-16. Detroit used a punishing ground attack, led by Nick Pietrosante, the game's most valuable player, to overcome a 7-0 halftime deficit and gain a 17-10 lead. Late in the game, Plum threw a short pass to Bobby Mitchell, who ran away from several Detroit defenders and raced 89 yards for a touchdown. On the extra point, the center snap was momentarily bobbled, and Dick (Night Train) Lane was able to block the kick to preserve the Detroit victory.

The game was nationally televised, and the NFL's share of the proceeds went to the Bert Bell NFL Player Benefit Plan for group medical, life insurance, and retirement benefits.

January 7, 1961, at Miami

Cleveland	**Starting Lineups**	**Detroit**
Gern Nagler	SE	Gail Cogdill
Dick Schafrath	LT	Willie McClung
Jim Ray Smith	LG	Harley Sewell
John Morrow	C	Bob Scholtz
Gene Hickerson	RG	John Gordy
Mike McCormack	RT	Ollie Spencer
Rich Kreitling	TE	Jim Gibbons
Ray Renfro	FL	Howard Cassady
Milt Plum	QB	Earl Morrall
Jim Brown	FB	Nick Pietrosante
Bobby Mitchell	HB	Dan Lewis

Cleveland	0	7	0	9	—	16
Detroit	0	0	10	7	—	17

Cle—Kreitling 9 pass from Plum (Baker kick)
Det—Pietrosante 5 run (Martin kick)
Det—FG Martin 12
Cle—FG Baker 27
Det—Webb 1 run (Martin kick)
Cle—Mitchell 89 pass from Plum (kick failed)
Attendance—34,981

1961

DETROIT 38, PHILADELPHIA 10

In 1961, Philadelphia's Sonny Jurgensen had passed for 700 yards more than any other NFL quarterback, but Detroit held him to 36 net yards. The Lions rolled up 331 total yards, mostly on power running.

January 6, 1962, at Miami

Detroit	**Starters, Offense**	**Philadelphia**
Gail Cogdill	SE	Bobby Walston
John Gonzaga	LT	Jim McCusker
Harley Sewell	LG	John Wittenborn
Bob Scholtz	C	Howard Keys
Ollie Spencer	RG	Stan Campbell
Danny LaRose	RT	J.D. Smith
Jim Gibbons	TE	Pete Retzlaff
Terry Barr	FL	Tommy McDonald
Jim Ninowski	QB	Sonny Jurgensen
Nick Pietrosante	FB	Clarence Peaks
Dan Lewis	HB	Billy Ray Barnes
	Starters, Defense	
Darris McCord	LE	Leo Sugar
Roger Brown	LT	Jess Richardson
Alex Karras	RT	Eddie Khayat
Bill Glass	RE	Marion Campbell
Carl Brettschneider	LLB	John Nocera
Joe Schmidt	MLB	Chuck Bednarik
Wayne Walker	RLB	Bob Pellegrini
Dick (Night Train) Lane	LCB	Jimmy Carr
Dick LeBeau	RCB	Irv Cross
Gary Lowe	LS	Don Burroughs
Yale Lary	RS	Bobby Freeman

Detroit	10	14	7	7	—	38
Philadelphia	0	0	10	0	—	10

Det—FG, Martin 38
Det—Barr 69 pass from Ninowski (Martin kick)
Det—Morrall 5 run (Martin kick)
Det—Studstill 18 pass from Morrall (Martin kick)
Phil—Retzlaff 9 pass from Hill (Walston kick)
Phil—FG Walston 22
Det—Barr 14 pass from Ninowski (Martin kick)
Det—Williams 19 pass from Morrall (Martin kick)
Attendance—25,612

1962

DETROIT 17, PITTSBURGH 10

Detroit won its third consecutive Playoff Bowl by shutting down the potent Steelers, holding Bobby Layne and his teammates to fewer than 100 yards in both passing and rushing. Milt Plum led the Lions with 274 yards passing, while fullback Ken Webb scored both Detroit touchdowns, one on the ground, the other on a pass from Plum.

January 6, 1963, at Miami

Pittsburgh	**Starters, Offense**	**Detroit**
Preston Carpenter	SE	Gail Cogdill
Dan James	LT	Bob Scholtz
Ray Lemek	LG	Harley Sewell
Madison (Buzz) Nutter	C	Bob Whitlow
Mike Sandusky	RG	John Gordy
Charlie Bradshaw	RT	Danny LaRose
John Burrell	TE	Jim Gibbons
Buddy Dial	FL	Pat Studstill
Bobby Layne	QB	Milt Plum
John Henry Johnson	FB	Ken Webb
Dick Hoak	HB	Dan Lewis
	Starters, Defense	
Ernie Stautner	LE	Darris McCord
Gene (Big Daddy) Lipscomb	LT	Roger Brown
Joe Krupa	RT	Alex Karras
Lou Michaels	RE	Sam Williams
Ken Kirks	LLB	Carl Brettschneider
Tom Bettis	MLB	Joe Schmidt
George Tarasovic	RLB	Wayne Walker
Brady Keys	LCB	Dick (Night Train) Lane
Clendon Thomas	RCB	Dick LeBeau
Willie Daniel	LS	Gary Lowe
Dick Haley	RS	Yale Lary

Pittsburgh	0	7	3	0	—	10
Detroit	0	10	7	0	—	17

Det—FG Walker 27
Pitt—Hoak 5 run (Michaels kick)
Det—Webb 20 pass from Plum (Walker kick)
Pitt—FG Michaels 40
Det—Webb 2 run (Walker kick)
Attendance—36,284

1963

GREEN BAY 40, CLEVELAND 23

Green Bay gained 490 yards, 259 on Bart Starr's passing, and controlled the game from the start.

January 5, 1964, at Miami

Green Bay	**Starters, Offense**	**Cleveland**
Max McGee	SE	Rich Kreitling
Bob Skoronski	LT	Dick Schafrath
Fred (Fuzzy) Thurston	LG	John Wooten
Jim Ringo	C	John Morrow
Jerry Kramer	RG	Gene Hickerson
Forrest Gregg	RT	John Brown
Ron Kramer	TE	Johnny Brewer
Boyd Dowler	FL	Gary Collins
Bart Starr	QB	Frank Ryan
Jim Taylor	FB	Jim Brown
Tom Moore	HB	Ernie Green
	Starters, Defense	
Willie Davis	LE	Paul Wiggin
Dave (Hawg) Hanner	LT	Dick Modzelewski
Henry Jordan	RT	Bob Gain
Urban Henry	RE	Bill Glass
Dan Currie	LLB	Jim Houston
Ray Nitschke	MLB	Vince Costello
Bill Forester	RLB	Galen Fiss
Herb Adderley	LCB	Bernie Parrish
Jesse Whittenton	RCB	Jim Shofner
Hank Gremminger	LS	Larry Benz
Willie Wood	RS	Ross Fichtner

Green Bay	14	14	7	5	—	40
Cleveland	0	10	0	13	—	23

GB—R. Kramer 18 pass from Starr (J. Kramer kick)
GB—Moore 99 pass from Starr (J. Kramer kick)
Cle—FG Groza 36
GB—McGee 15 pass from Starr (J. Kramer kick)
Cle—Green 5 run (Groza kick)
GB—Taylor 2 run (J. Kramer kick)
GB—Moore 2 run (J. Kramer kick)
GB—FG J. Kramer 8
Cle—Kreitling 20 pass from Ryan (Groza kick)
Cle—Crespino 25 pass from Ryan (kick failed)
GB—Safety, Aldridge tackled Ryan in end zone
Attendance—54,921

1964

ST. LOUIS 24, GREEN BAY 17

Little Billy Gambrell caught six passes for 184 yards and two touchdowns to earn most valuable player honors and help St. Louis upset Green Bay in the last postseason game a Vince Lombardi-coached team ever would lose.

January 3, 1965, at Miami

St. Louis	**Starters, Offense**	**Green Bay**
Billy Gambrell	SE	Boyd Dowler
Bob Reynolds	LT	Bob Skoronski
Ken Gray	LG	Fred (Fuzzy) Thurston
Bob DeMarco	C	Ken Bowman
Irv Goode	RG	Dan Grimm
Ernie McMillan	RT	Forrest Gregg
Jackie Smith	TE	Ron Kramer
Bobby Joe Conrad	FL	Bob Jeter
Charley Johnson	QB	Bart Starr
Bill (Thunder) Thornton	FB	Jim Taylor
Prentice Gautt	HB	Paul Hornung
	Starters, Defense	
Don Brumm	LE	Willie Davis
Sam Silas	LT	Ron Kostelnik
Luke Owens	RT	Henry Jordan
Joe Robb	RE	Lionel Aldridge
Larry Stallings	LLB	Dan Currie
Dale Meinert	MLB	Ray Nitschke
Bill Koman	RLB	Lee Roy Caffey
Pat Fischer	LCB	Herb Adderley
Jim Burson	RCB	Jesse Whittenton
Jerry Stovall	SS	Hank Gremminger
Larry Wilson	FS	Willie Wood

St. Louis	0	7	10	7	—	24
Green Bay	3	0	0	14	—	17

GB—FG Hornung 40
StL—Gambrell 80 pass from Johnson (Bakken kick)
StL—FG Bakken 7
StL—Gambrell 10 pass from Johnson (Bakken kick)
GB—Taylor 7 run (Hornung kick)
StL—Stovall 30 interception return (Bakken kick)
GB—Taylor 1 run (Hornung kick)
Attendance—56,218

1965

BALTIMORE 35, DALLAS 3

Halfback-turned-quarterback Tom Matte opened up his passing game, and the Colts bombed the Cowboys 35-3. Matte completed 7 of 17 passes for 165 yards and two touchdowns, while Baltimore outgained Dallas 347-176. The Cowboys suffered four turnovers and never mounted much of a threat.

January 9, 1966, at Miami

Baltimore	**Starters, Offense**	**Dallas**
Raymond Berry	SE	Bob Hayes
Bob Vogel	LT	Jim Boeke
Jim Parker	LG	Mike Connelly
Dick Szymanski	C	Dave Manders
Alex Sandusky	RG	Leon Donohue
George Preas	RT	Ralph Neely
John Mackey	TE	Frank Clarke
Jimmy Orr	FL	Buddy Dial
Tom Matte	QB	Don Meredith
Jerry Hill	FB	Don Perkins
Lenny Moore	HB	Dan Reeves
	Starters, Defense	
Lou Michaels	LE	Maury Youmans
Fred Miller	LT	Jim Colvin
Billy Ray Smith	RT	Bob Lilly
Ordell Braase	RE	George Andrie
Steve Stonebreaker	LLB	Chuck Howley
Dennis Gaubatz	MLB	Jerry Tubbs
Don Shinnick	RLB	Dave Edwards
Bobby Boyd	LCB	Cornell Green
Lenny Lyles	RCB	Warren Livingston
Jerry Logan	SS	Mel Renfro
Wendell Harris	FS	Obert Logan

Baltimore	0	14	14	7	—	35
Dallas	0	3	0	0	—	3

Balt—Moore 6 run (Michaels kick)
Dall—FG Villanueva 12
Balt—Hill 3 run (Michaels kick)
Balt—Hill 1 run (Michaels kick)
Balt—Orr 15 pass from Matte (Michaels kick)
Balt—Orr 20 pass from Matte (Michaels kick)
Attendance—65,569

1966

BALTIMORE 20, PHILADELPHIA 14

Tom Matte scored from one yard out with 14 seconds left to give the Colts a 20-14 victory. The score ended a 35-yard drive that followed an interception of a pass by Jack Concannon. Matte was the game's top rusher with 74 yards, but Izzy Lang of Philadelphia was selected most valuable player.

January 8, 1967, at Miami

Philadelphia	Starters, Offense	Baltimore
Fred Hill	SE	Raymond Berry
Dave Graham	LT	Bob Vogel
Ed Blaine	LG	Dan Sullivan
Jim Ringo	C	Dick Szymanski
Jim Skaggs	RG	Alex Sandusky
Bob Brown	RT	Jim Parker
Pete Retzlaff	TE	John Mackey
Ronnie Goodwin	FL	Jimmy Orr
Jack Concannon	QB	Johnny Unitas
Tom Woodeshick	FB	Jerry Hill
Tim Brown	HB	Tom Matte
	Starters, Defense	
Don Hultz	LE	Lou Michaels
Floyd Peters	LT	Fred Miller
John Meyers	RT	Billy Ray Smith
Gary Pettigrew	RE	Ordell Braase
Fred Whittingham	LLB	Mike Curtis
Dave Lloyd	MLB	Dennis Gaubatz
Harold Wells	RLB	Don Shinnick
Al Nelson	LCB	Bobby Boyd
Jim Nettles	RCB	Lenny Lyles
Nate Ramsey	SS	Jerry Logan
Joe Scarpati	FS	Alvin Haymond

Philadelphia	0	14	0	0	—	14
Baltimore	3	7	3	7	—	20

Balt—FG Michaels 23
Phil—K. Hill 1 run (Baker kick)
Balt—Berry 14 pass from Unitas (Michaels kick)
Phil—Lang 2 run (Baker kick)
Balt—FG Michaels 14
Balt—Matte 1 run (Michaels kick)
Attendance—58,088

1967

LA RAMS 30, CLEVELAND 6

Behind the passing of the game's most valuable player, Roman Gabriel, who threw for 223 yards and two touchdowns, Los Angeles moved seemingly at will to defeat Cleveland 30-6. The Rams almost doubled the Browns in total yardage, 385-205.

January 7, 1968, at Miami

LA Rams	Starters, Offense	Cleveland
Jack Snow	SE	Paul Warfield
Joe Carollo	LT	Dick Schafrath
Tom Mack	LG	John Wooten
Ken Iman	C	Fred Hoaglin
Joe Scibelli	RG	Gene Hickerson
Charlie Cowan	RT	Monte Clark
Billy Truax	TE	Ralph Smith
Bernie Casey	FL	Gary Collins
Roman Gabriel	QB	Frank Ryan
Dick Bass	RB	Ernie Green
Les Josephson	RB	Leroy Kelly
	Starters, Defense	
David (Deacon) Jones	LE	Paul Wiggin
Merlin Olsen	LT	Walter Johnson
Roger Brown	RT	Jim Kanicki
Lamar Lundy	RE	Bill Glass
Jack Pardee	LLB	Jim Houston
Myron Pottios	MLB	Dale Lindsey
Maxie Baughan	RLB	John Brewer
Clancy Williams	LCB	Erich Barnes
Irv Cross	RCB	Mike Howell
Chuck Lamson	SS	Ernie Kellermann
Eddie Meador	FS	Ross Fichtner

LA Rams	10	7	3	10	—	30
Cleveland	0	0	0	6	—	6

Rams—Casey 21 pass from Gabriel (Gossett kick)
Rams—FG Gossett 41
Rams—Truax 2 pass from Gabriel (Gossett kick)
Rams—FG Gossett 46
Cle—Kelly 2 run (kick failed)
Rams—Ellison 9 run (Gossett kick)
Rams—FG Gossett 19
Attendance—37,102

1968

DALLAS 17, MINNESOTA 13

Dallas quarterbacks Don Meredith and Craig Morton each threw a touchdown pass, as the Cowboys came back from a 13-0 first-quarter deficit to defeat Minnesota 17-13. Meredith, the game's most valuable player, completed 15 of 24 passes for 243 yards.

January 5, 1969, at Miami

Dallas	Starters, Offense	Minnesota
Bob Hayes	SE	Gene Washington
Tony Liscio	LT	Grady Alderman
John Niland	LG	Jim Vellone
Malcolm Walker	C	Mick Tingelhoff
John Wilbur	RG	Milt Sunde
Ralph Neely	RT	Doug Davis
Pettis Norman	TE	John Beasley
Lance Rentzel	FL	John Henderson
Craig Morton	QB	Joe Kapp
Don Perkins	RB	Bill Brown
Craig Baynham	RB	Dave Osborn
	Starters, Defense	
Larry Cole	LE	Carl Eller
Jethro Pugh	LT	Alan Page
Bob Lilly	RT	Gary Larsen
George Andrie	RE	Jim Marshall
Chuck Howley	LLB	Roy Winston
Lee Roy Jordan	MLB	Lonnie Warwick
Dave Edwards	RLB	Wally Hilgenberg
Cornell Green	LCB	Earsell Mackbee
Mel Renfro	RCB	Ed Sharockman
Mike Gaechter	SS	Karl Kassulke
Dick Daniels	FS	Paul Krause

Dallas	0	10	7	0	—	17
Minnesota	13	0	0	0	—	13

Minn—Bryant 81 punt return (Cox kick)
Minn—FG Cox 37
Minn—FG Cox 23
Dall—Hayes 51 pass from Meredith (Clark kick)
Dall—FG Clark 11
Dall—Baynham 20 pass from Morton (Clark kick)
Attendance—22,961

1969

LA RAMS 31, DALLAS 0

Roman Gabriel threw long touchdown passes the first two times Los Angeles had the ball, and the Rams coasted to an easy victory over the Cowboys in the final Playoff Bowl. Gabriel, who was named the game's most valuable player, hit 12 of 17 passes for 224 yards and four touchdowns. The shutout was the only one in the history of the game.

January 3, 1970, at Miami

Dallas	Starters, Offense	LA Rams
Bob Hayes	WR	Jack Snow
Tony Liscio	LT	Charlie Cowan
John Niland	LG	Tom Mack
Malcolm Walker	C	Ken Iman
John Wilbur	RG	Mike LaHood
Ralph Neely	RT	Bob Brown
Pettis Norman	TE	Billy Truax
Lance Rentzel	WR	Wendell Tucker
Craig Morton	QB	Roman Gabriel
Walt Garrison	RB	Larry Smith
Calvin Hill	RB	Les Josephson
	Starters, Defense	
Larry Cole	LE	David (Deacon) Jones
Jethro Pugh	LT	Merlin Olsen
Bob Lilly	RT	Coy Bacon
George Andrie	RE	Diron Talbert
Dave Edwards	LLB	Jack Pardee
Lee Roy Jordan	MLB	Doug Woodlief
Chuck Howley	RLB	Maxie Baughan
Cornell Green	LCB	Clancy Williams
Otto Brown	RCB	Jim Nettles
Mike Gaechter	SS	Richie Petitbon
Mel Renfro	FS	Eddie Meador

Dallas	0	0	0	0	—	0
LA Rams	14	0	7	10	—	31

Rams—Josephson 35 pass from Gabriel (Gossett kick)
Rams—Snow 67 pass from Gabriel (Gossett kick)
Rams—Klein 16 pass from Gabriel (Gossett kick)
Rams—Snow 49 pass from Gabriel (Gossett kick)
Rams—FG Gossett 42
Attendance—30,824

The Pro Bowl

1939

NY GIANTS 13, PRO ALL-STARS 10

Ward Cuff's 18-yard field goal with five minutes remaining in the game provided the New York Giants, 1938 NFL champions, with a 13-10 victory over the Pro All-Stars, comprised of players from other NFL teams and of the Los Angeles Bulldogs and the Hollywood Stars, two independent professional teams.

A crowd estimated at 20,000 watched at Wrigley Field, a baseball stadium in Los Angeles. Game officials predicted that 30,000 persons would attend and said the lower turnout was the result of a heavy fog that covered the Los Angeles basin.

The Giants trailed 10-3 entering the fourth quarter and tied the score on a 22-yard touchdown pass from Ed Danowski to Chuck Gelatka.

January 15, at Los Angeles

NY Giants	Starting Lineups	Pro All-Stars
Jim Lee Howell	LE	Gaynell Tinsley (Chi. Cards)
Ed Widseth	LT	Joe Stydahar (Chi. Bears)
Orville Tuttle	LG	Byron Gentry (Pittsburgh)
Mel Hein	C	John Wiatrak (Detroit)
Ken (Kayo) Lunday	RG	P. Mehringer (LA Bulldogs)
Owen (Ox) Parry	RT	Bruiser Kinard (Brooklyn)
Jim Poole	RE	Perry Schwartz (Brooklyn)
Nello Falaschi	QB	Erny Pinckert (Washington)
Hank Soar	LH	Sammy Baugh (Wash.)
Ward Cuff	RH	Lloyd Cardwell (Detroit)
Ed Danowski	FB	Clarke Hinkle (Green Bay)

Head coaches—Steve Owen, NY Giants; Ray Flaherty (Washington) and Elmer (Gus) Henderson (Detroit), Pro All-Stars

NY Giants	0	3	0	10	—	13
Pro All-Stars	0	3	7	0	—	10

NYG —FG Barnum 18
All-Stars—FG E. Smith 25
All-Stars—Cardwell 70 pass from Baugh (Stydahar kick)
NYG —Gelatka 22 pass from Danowski (Cuff kick)
NYG —FG Cuff 18
Attendance—20,000

JANUARY, 1940

GREEN BAY 16, NFL ALL-STARS 7

Cecil Isbell and Don Hutson combined to produce a 92-yard touchdown as the Green Bay Packers, winners of the 1939 NFL championship, defeated selected players from other NFL teams 16-7.

The Packers were leading 6-0 in the second quarter and had the ball on their 8-yard line. Isbell took the snap from center, faked a running play, and hurled a 61-yard pass to Hutson, sprinting free at the All-Stars' 31-yard line.

The game had been postponed a week because of threatening weather and rains that soaked the playing field in Gilmore Stadium, home field for the Hollywood Bears of the Pacific Coast League and a stadium built for football.

January 14, at Los Angeles

Green Bay	Starting Lineups	NFL All-Stars
Don Hutson	LE	Jim Poole (NY Giants)
Buford (Baby) Ray	LT	Joe Stydahar (Chi. Bears)
Paul Engebretsen	LG	Byron Gentry (Pittsburgh)
Tom Greenfield	C	Mel Hein (NY Giants)
Buckets Goldenberg	RG	Bruiser Kinard (Brooklyn)
Bill Lee	RT	Ray George (Detroit)
Milt Gantenbein	RE	Perry Schwartz (Brooklyn)
Larry Craig	QB	Fred Vanzo (Detroit)
Cecil Isbell	LH	Parker Hall (Cleveland)
Arnie Herber	RH	Erny Pinckert (Washington)
Clarke Hinkle	FB	Johnny Drake (Cleveland)

Head coaches—Earl (Curly) Lambeau, Green Bay; Steve Owen (NY Giants), NFL All-Stars

Green Bay	3	10	0	3	—	16
NFL All-Stars	0	0	7	0	—	7

GB —FG Hinkle 45
GB —FG Smith 15
GB —Hutson 92 pass from Isbell (Smith kick)
All-Stars—Carter 4 pass from O'Brien (Cuff kick)
GB —FG Smith 7
Attendance—18,000

DECEMBER, 1940

CHI. BEARS 28, NFL ALL-STARS 14

Dick Plasman intercepted a pass by Sammy Baugh and ran 26 yards to the 5-yard line, setting up the touchdown that broke a 14-14 tie and helped the Chicago Bears to a 28-14 victory over the NFL All-Stars before an overflow crowd of 21,624 at Gilmore Stadium in Los Angeles.

Bears quarterback Sid Luckman scored from the 1-yard line three plays after Plasman's interception to give Chicago a 21-14 lead. Plasman also figured in the Bears' first touchdown. He caught a 21-yard pass from Luckman, advanced two yards, then lateraled to Hampton Pool, the other end, who ran 48 yards to a touchdown.

December 29, at Los Angeles

Chi. Bears	Starting Lineups	NFL All-Stars
Dick Plasman	LE	Jim Poole (NY Giants)
Joe Stydahar	LT	Bruiser Kinard (Brooklyn)
Dan Fortmann	LG	Dick Bassi (Philadelphia)
Clyde (Bulldog) Turner	C	Mel Hein (NY Giants)
George Musso	RG	Doug Oldershaw (NY Giants)
Lee Artoe	RT	Jim Barber (Washington)
Hampton Pool	RE	Carl Mulleneaux (GB)
Sid Luckman	QB	Pug Manders (Brooklyn)
Ray Nolting	LH	Sammy Baugh (Wash.)
Gary Famiglietti	RH	Merlyn Condit (Pittsburgh)
Bill Osmanski	FB	Johnny Drake (Cleveland)

Head coaches—George Halas, Chi. Bears; Ray Flaherty (Washington), NFL All-Stars

Chi. Bears	7	7	7	7	—	28
NFL All-Stars	0	14	0	0	—	14

ChiB —Pool 48 lateral from Plasman, who caught 23 pass from Luckman (Martinovich kick)
All-Stars—Livingston 7 interception return (Hinkle kick)
ChiB —Clark 59 pass from Luckman (Snyder kick)
All-Stars—Looney 4 pass from Baugh (Hutson kick)
ChiB —Luckman 1 run (Snyder kick)
ChiB —Maniaci 2 run (Maniaci kick)
Attendance—21,624

JANUARY, 1942

CHI. BEARS 35, NFL ALL-STARS 24

The Chicago Bears scored three touchdowns in the second quarter and turned back an All-Stars threat in the third quarter to score a 35-24 victory. The game was moved to the Polo Grounds in New York because of the danger inherent in large gatherings in cities on the West Coast, which was protecting against the possibility of a Japanese attack not long after the bombing of Pearl Harbor in Hawaii.

The Bears drove 53 yards to their first score, George McAfee's three-yard touchdown run. McAfee gave them a 14-3 lead with a 68-yard punt return.

January 4, at New York

Chi. Bears	Starting Lineups	NFL All-Stars
Dick Plasman	LE	Perry Schwartz (Brooklyn)
Ed Kolman	LT	Willie Wilkin (Washington)
Dan Fortmann	LG	Jim Sivell (Brooklyn)
Clyde (Bulldog) Turner	C	Mel Hein (NY Giants)
Ray Bray	RG	Joe Kuharich (Chi. Cards)
Lee Artoe	RT	Bruiser Kinard (Brooklyn)
John Siegal	RE	Bill Dewell (Chi. Cards)
Sid Luckman	QB	Nello Falaschi (NY Giants)
Ray Nolting	LH	Frank Filchock (Wash.)
Hugh Gallarneau	RH	Ward Cuff (NY Giants)
Norm Standlee	FB	Pug Manders (Brooklyn)

Head coaches—George Halas, Chi. Bears; Steve Owen (NY Giants), NFL All-Stars

Chi. Bears	0	21	7	7	—	35
NFL All-Stars	3	0	14	7	—	24

All-Stars—FG Cuff 19
ChiB —McAfee 3 run (Snyder kick)
ChiB —McAfee 68 punt return (Artoe kick)
ChiB —Swisher 4 run (Stydahar kick)
All-Stars—Schwartz 15 pass from Baugh (Cuff kick)
All-Stars—Dewell 24 pass from Baugh (Cuff kick)
ChiB —McLean 20 pass from Luckman (Snyder kick)
ChiB —Kavanaugh 7 pass from Bussey (Stydahar kick)
All-Stars—Schwartz 20 pass from Baugh (Cuff kick)
Attendance—17,725

DECEMBER, 1942

NFL ALL-STARS 17, WASHINGTON 14

The Washington Redskins lost to the All-Stars in Philadelphia without star player Sammy Baugh.

Baugh explained that an automobile was supposed to have been provided by Redskins management to take him from Sweetwater, Texas (30 miles from his ranch in Rotan), to the airport in Dallas for an 11:50 P.M. flight the Friday before the Sunday game. Baugh said the car was not there, so he had the Sweetwater police call the airport in nearby Abilene. The police were told the last flight already had left Abilene at 6 P.M. Baugh said he then tried to get a taxi from Sweetwater to Dallas (230 miles away), "but the taxi driver was in a movie and when he got out it was too late. So I came home."

December 27, at Philadelphia

Washington	Starting Lineups	NFL All-Stars
Bob Masterson	LE	Perry Schwartz (Brooklyn)
Fred Davis	LT	John Woudenberg (Pitt.)
Dick Farman	LG	Augie Lio (Detroit)
Ki Aldrich	C	Chuck Cherundolo (Pitt.)
Steve Slivinski	RG	Enio Conti (Philadelphia)
Bill Young	RT	Chet Adams (Cleveland)
Ed Cifers	RE	Eddie Rucinski (Brooklyn)
Ray Hare	QB	Tommy Thompson (Phil.)
Roy Zimmerman	LH	Bill Dudley (Pittsburgh)
Ed Justice	RH	Merlyn Condit (Brooklyn)
Andy Farkas	FB	Harry Hopp (Detroit)

Head coaches—Ray Flaherty, Washington; Hunk Anderson (Chi. Bears), NFL All-Stars

Washington	7	0	7	0	—	14
NFL All-Stars	0	0	14	3	—	17

Wash —Aldrich 30 punt return (Masterson kick)
All-Stars—Dudley 97 interception return (Maznicki kick)
All-Stars—Petty 10 run (Maznicki kick)
Wash —Seymour 16 pass from Zimmerman (Masterson kick)
All-Stars—FG Artoe 43
Attendance—18,671

1951

AMERICAN 28, NATIONAL 27

Quarterback Otto Graham of the Cleveland Browns was named player of the game after scoring touchdowns on runs of 6 and 10 yards in the third quarter as the American Conference All-Stars overcame a 27-14 National Conference lead to win the first Pro Bowl in the game's revival in Memorial Coliseum. Graham also completed 19 of 27 passes.

Quarterbacks Bob Waterfield and Norm Van Brocklin of the Los Angeles Rams combined to complete 21 of 44 passes for 294 yards and three touchdowns for the National Conference.

January 14, at Los Angeles

American	Starting Lineups	National
Pete Pihos (Philadelphia)	LE	Tom Fears (LA Rams)
Lou Groza (Cleveland)	LT	Dick Huffman (LA Rams)
Weldon Humble (Cleveland)	LG	Dick Barwegan (Chi. Bears)
Bill Walsh (Pittsburgh)	C	Brad Ecklund (NY Yanks)
Bill Willis (Cleveland)	RG	Lou Creekmur (Detroit)
Al Wistert (Philadelphia)	RT	Thurman McGraw (Detroit)
Bob Shaw (Chi. Cardinals)	RE	Dan Edwards (NY Yanks)
Otto Graham (Cleveland)	QB	Bob Waterfield (LA Rams)
Gene Roberts (NY Giants)	LH	Glenn Davis (LA Rams)
E. Angsman (Chi. Cards)	RH	Billy Grimes (Green Bay)
Marion Motley (Cleveland)	FB	Dick Hoerner (LA Rams)

Head coaches—Paul Brown (Cleveland), American; Joe Stydahar (LA Rams), National

American	7	7	14	0	—	28
National	7	13	7	0	—	27

National —Fears 22 pass from Waterfield (Waterfield kick)
American—Dudley 47 punt return (Groza kick)
National —FG Waterfield 30
American—Shaw 49 pass from Graham (Groza kick)
National —FG Waterfield 27
National —Fears 5 pass from Van Brocklin (Waterfield kick)
National —Edwards 65 pass from Waterfield (Waterfield kick)
American—Graham 6 run (Harder kick)
American—Graham 10 run (Harder kick)
Attendance—53,678

1952

NATIONAL 30, AMERICAN 13

The National Conference All-Stars capitalized on two fourth-quarter fumbles by American Conference quarterback Sammy Baugh to score two touchdowns in a 20-point period in which they overcame a 13-10 American Conference lead to win 30-13. Baugh, playing in the fourth quarter, fumbled four times in a driving rain and had his only pass intercepted.

With the Nationals leading 16-13, Baugh fumbled on the Americans' 24. Defensive tackle Leo Nomellini picked up the ball on the 20 and ran for a touchdown that put the National team ahead 23-13.

January 12, at Los Angeles

National	Starting Lineups	American
Gordy Soltau (San Fran.)	LE	Fran Polsfoot (Chi. Cards)
George Connor (Chi. Bears)	LT	Lou Groza (Cleveland)
Lou Creekmur (Detroit)	LG	Bill Fischer (Chi. Cards)
Brad Ecklund (NY Yanks)	C	Bill Walsh (Pittsburgh)
Dick Barwegan (Chi. Bears)	RG	George Hughes (Pittsburgh)
M. McCormack (NY Yanks)	RT	Tex Coulter (NY Giants)
Elroy Hirsch (LA Rams)	RE	Dante Lavelli (Cleveland)
Bob Waterfield (LA Rams)	QB	Otto Graham (Cleveland)
Dan Towler (LA Rams)	LH	Ken Carpenter (Cleveland)
Tank Younger (LA Rams)	RH	Dub Jones (Cleveland)
John Dottley (Chi. Bears)	FB	Eddie Price (NY Giants)

Head coaches—Paul Brown (Cleveland), American; Raymond (Buddy) Parker (Detroit), National

National	3	7	0	20	—	30
American	7	6	0	0	—	13

American—Jones 44 pass from Graham (Graham kick)
National —FG Waterfield 30
American—FG Groza 45
American—FG Groza 11
National —Soltau 1 pass from Van Brocklin (Waterfield kick)
National Dottley 2 run (kick failed)
National —Nomellini 20 fumble return (Waterfield kick)
National —Hirsch 7 pass from Walker (Lujack kick)
Attendance—19,400

1953

NATIONAL 27, AMERICAN 7

Fullback Dan Towler took a handoff from quarterback Bobby Layne and threw a 13-yard pass to Hugh McElhenny for the game's first score in a 27-7 National Conference victory. The pass was the first Towler had thrown in three seasons as a professional.

Towler's Los Angeles Rams teammate, Norm Van Brocklin, replaced Layne at quarterback on the next offensive series. On Van Brocklin's first play, he threw a 39-yard pass to Green Bay's Billy Howton, who caught the ball on the American Conference's 35-yard line and ran for a touchdown that completed a 74-yard play. Later in the game, Van Brocklin threw a touchdown pass to McElhenny.

January 10, at Los Angeles

National	Starting Lineups	American
Cloyce Box (Detroit)	LE	Hugh Taylor (Wash.)
Lou Creekmur (Detroit)	LT	Lou Groza (Cleveland)
Dick Barwegan (Chi. Bears)	LG	Abe Gibron (Cleveland)
Bill Johnson (San Fran.)	C	Tex Coulter (NY Giants)
John Wozniak (Dallas)	RG	Bill Fischer (Chi. Cards)
Fred Williams (Chi. Bears)	RT	Bucko Kilroy (Phil.)
Elroy Hirsch (LA Rams)	RE	Elbie Nickel (Pittsburgh)
Bobby Layne (Detroit)	QB	Otto Graham (Cleveland)
B. Hoernschemeyer (Det.)	LH	Ray Mathews (Pittsburgh)
Billy Howton (Green Bay)	RH	Lynn Chandnois (Pitt.)
Dan Towler (LA Rams)	FB	Ollie Matson (Chi. Cards)

Head coaches—Paul Brown (Cleveland), American; Raymond (Buddy) Parker (Detroit), National

National	14	0	3	10	—	27
American	0	0	0	7	—	7

National —McElhenny 13 pass from Towler (Harder kick)
National —Howton 74 pass from Van Brocklin (Harder kick)
National —FG Harder 23
American—Graham 1 run (Groza kick)
National —FG Harder 13
National —McElhenny 7 pass from Van Brocklin (Harder kick)
Attendance—34,208

1954

EAST 20, WEST 9

Linebacker Chuck Bednarik of the Philadelphia Eagles returned an intercepted pass for a touchdown, recovered a fumble that led to a field goal, punted five times for a 43-yard average, and was named player of the game as the East scored a 20-9 victory.

The East took a 3-0 lead in the first quarter on an 11-yard field goal by Lou Groza that followed Joe Perry's fumble, which was recovered by Emlen Tunnell. Don Kindt tackled East quarterback Otto Graham in the end zone for a safety that made the score 3-2 at halftime.

West halfback Hugh McElhenny had 74 yards in 10 carries. Perry had 60 yards in 12 carries.

January 17, at Los Angeles

East	Starting Lineups	West
Pete Pihos (Philadelphia)	LE	Gordy Soltau (San Fran.)
Lou Groza (Cleveland)	LT	Lou Creekmur (Detroit)
Abe Gibron (Cleveland)	LG	Dick Barwegan (Baltimore)
Ken Farragut (Philadelphia)	C	Bill Johnson (San Fran.)
George Hughes (Pittsburgh)	RG	Dick Stanfel (Detroit)
Ken Snyder (Philadelphia)	RT	Leo Nomellini (San Fran.)
Dante Lavelli (Cleveland)	RE	Elroy Hirsch (LA Rams)
Otto Graham (Cleveland)	QB	Bobby Layne (Detroit)
Ray Renfro (Cleveland)	LH	Doak Walker (Detroit)
Lynn Chandnois (Pitt.)	RH	Tank Younger (LA Rams)
Chick Jagade (Cleve.)	FB	Joe Perry (San Francisco)

Head coaches—Paul Brown (Cleveland), East; Raymond (Buddy) Parker (Detroit), West

East	3	0	10	7	—	20
West	0	2	0	7	—	9

East —FG Groza 11
West—Safety, Kindt tackled Graham in end zone
East —FG Groza 25
East Bednarik 24 interception return (Groza kick)
West—Perry 16 run (Walker kick)
East —Renfro 25 run (Groza kick)
Attendance—44,214

1955

WEST 26, EAST 19

Player-of-the-game Billy Wilson caught 11 passes for 157 yards and one touchdown as the West overcame a 19-3 East lead in the second quarter to score a 26-19 victory.

Doak Walker's 30-yard field goal tied the game 19-19 with 11:31 remaining in the fourth quarter. On the East's next possession, quarterback Adrian Burk's pass was intercepted by LaVern Torgeson, who returned the ball 37 yards to the East's 4-yard line. Fullback Joe Perry gained three yards on the first play and scored from the 1 on the next play. Y.A. Tittle hit 16 of 26 passes for the West.

January 16, at Los Angeles

West	Starting Lineups	East
Harlon Hill (Chi. Bears)	LE	Pete Pihos (Philadelphia)
Lou Creekmur (Detroit)	LT	Lou Groza (Cleveland)
Bruno Banducci (S. Fran.)	LG	Bill Austin (NY Giants)
Leon McLaughlin (LA Rams)	C	Frank Gatski (Cleveland)
Duane Putnam (LA Rams)	RG	Abe Gibron (Cleveland)
Bill Bishop (Chi. Bears)	RT	Ken Snyder (Philadelphia)
Billy Wilson (San Fran.)	RE	Dante Lavelli (Cleveland)
Y.A. Tittle (San Fran.)	QB	Otto Graham (Cleveland)
J.H. Johnson (San Fran.)	LH	Ollie Matson (Chi. Cards)
Doak Walker (Detroit)	RH	Kyle Rote (NY Giants)
Joe Perry (San Francisco)	FB	Eddie Price (NY Giants)

Head coaches—Joe Kuharich (Washington), East; Lawrence (Buck) Shaw (San Francisco), West

West	3	6	7	10	—	26
East	13	6	0	0	—	19

East —Matson 6 pass from Graham (Groza kick)
East —Willey 5 fumble return (kick failed)
West—FG Walker 35
East —Taylor 33 pass from Burk (kick failed)
West—Wilson 14 pass from Tittle (kick failed)
West—Hill 42 pass from Tittle (Walker kick)
West—FG Walker 30
West—Perry 1 run (Walker kick)
Attendance—43,972

1956

EAST 31, WEST 30

The West's Jack Christiansen returned the opening kickoff 103 yards for a touchdown. The East's Ollie Matson returned the second half kickoff 91 yards.

After moving from its 24 to the West's 44 in nine plays, the East faced a fourth-and-three. On the first play of the fourth quarter, Lou Groza put the East ahead 24-23 with a 50-yard field goal.

Matson was named player of the game. He gained 83 yards in 11 carries and scored one touchdown, caught three passes for 9 yards, returned two punts 57 yards, and two kickoffs 137 yards.

January 15, at Los Angeles

West	Starting Lineups	East
Harlon Hill (Chi. Bears)	LE	Carlton Massey (Cleve.)
Lou Creekmur (Detroit)	LT	Lou Groza (Cleveland)
Duane Putnam (LA Rams)	LG	Abe Gibron (Cleveland)
Dick Szymanski (Balt.)	C	Harry Ulinski (Washington)
Stan Jones (Chi. Bears)	RG	Jack Stroud (NY Giants)
Bill Wightkin (Chi. Bears)	RT	Frank Varrichione (Pitt.)
Billy Wilson (San Fran.)	RE	Pete Pihos (Philadelphia)
Norm Van Brocklin (LA Rams)	QB	Adrian Burk (Philadelphia)
Ron Waller (LA Rams)	LH	Frank Gifford (NY Giants)
Doak Walker (Detroit)	RH	Ray Mathews (Pittsburgh)
Howie Ferguson (GB)	FB	Curly Morrison (Cleve.)

Head coaches—Joe Kuharich (Washington), East; Sid Gillman (LA Rams), West

West	7	7	9	7	—	30
East	7	0	14	10	—	31

West—Christiansen 103 kickoff return (Richter kick)
East —Pihos 12 pass from LeBaron (Groza kick)
West—Howton 73 pass from Brown (Richter kick)
East —Matson 91 kickoff return (Groza kick)
West—Ferguson 1 run (kick blocked)
East —Matson 15 run (Groza kick)
West—FG Rechichar 46
East —FG Groza 50
East —Mathews 20 pass from LeBaron (Groza kick)
West—Waller 3 run (Richter kick)
Attendance—37,867

1957

WEST 19, EAST 10

In a game in which the total offense of both teams was 229 yards, the West's Bert Rechichar provided the difference with field goals of 41, 44, 44, and 52 yards in a 19-10 victory by the West.

The West scored its touchdown after Joe Schmidt recovered Ollie Matson's fumble on the East's 12-yard line.

Pittsburgh's Ernie Stautner blocked Rechichar's first field goal attempt, from 47 yards in the first quarter. The East then marched 40 yards in 10 plays to score its only touchdown. Frank Gifford ran three yards to the 1-yard line and fumbled. Kyle Rote recovered in the end zone for the touchdown.

January 13, at Los Angeles

West	Starting Lineups	East
Harlon Hill (Chi. Bears)	LE	Darrell Brewster (Cleve.)
Lou Creekmur (Detroit)	LT	Roosevelt Brown (NYG)
Stan Jones (Chi. Bears)	LG	Buck Lansford (Phil.)
Charlie Ane (Detroit)	C	Jack Simmons (Chi. Cards)
Bill George (Chi. Bears)	RG	Dick Stanfel (Washington)
Bob St. Clair (San Fran.)	RT	Mike McCormack (Cleve.)
Billy Howton (Green Bay)	RE	Elbie Nickel (Pittsburgh)
Ed Brown (Chi. Bears)	QB	Charlie Conerly (NY Giants)
Hugh McElhenny (San Fran.)	LH	Frank Gifford (NY Giants)
Billy Wilson (San Fran.)	RH	Ollie Matson (Chi. Cards)
Rick Casares (Chi. Bears)	FB	Fran Rogel (Pittsburgh)

Head coaches—Jim Lee Howell (NY Giants), East; John (Paddy) Driscoll (Chi. Bears), West

West	7	3	3	6	—	19
East	0	7	3	0	—	10

West—Brown 1 run (Layne kick)
East —Rote fumble recovery in end zone (Baker kick)
West—FG Rechichar 41
East —FG Baker 52
West—FG Rechichar 44
West—FG Rechichar 44
West—FG Rechichar 52
Attendance—44,177

1958

WEST 26, EAST 7

The West trailed 7-6 after Earl Morrall's 39-yard touchdown pass to Ray Renfro in the second quarter. Bert Rechichar's nine-yard field goal with 38 seconds left in the half put the West back in front 9-7 and it never trailed again, scoring a 26-7 victory before a record crowd of 66,634.

West quarterbacks Y. A. Tittle and Johnny Unitas completed 15 of 25 passes for 159 yards and one touchdown. East quarterbacks Morrall and Eddie LeBaron completed 5 of 20 for 75 yards.

The West had a 17-7 advantage in first downs and outgained the East 340-149. Alan Ameche was the West's leading ground gainer with 85 yards in nine carries.

January 12, at Los Angeles

West	**Starting Lineups**	**East**
Billy Howton (Green Bay)	LE	Chuck Bednarik (Phil.)
Lou Creekmur (Detroit)	LT	Mike McCormack (Cleve.)
Duane Putnam (LA Rams)	LG	Bob Gain (Cleveland)
Jim Ringo (Green Bay)	C	Leo Sanford (Chi. Cards)
Harley Sewell (Detroit)	RG	Ernie Stautner (Pittsburgh)
Kline Gilbert (Chi. Bears)	RT	Roosevelt Brown (NYG)
Billy Wilson (San Fran.)	RE	Walt Michaels (Cleveland)
Y.A. Tittle (San Francisco)	QB	Eddie LeBaron (Wash.)
Jon Arnett (LA Rams)	LH	Emlen Tunnell (NY Giants)
Hugh McElhenny (San Fran.)	RH	Jerry Norton (Phil.)
Alan Ameche (Baltimore)	FB	Billy Ray Barnes (Phil.)

Head coaches—Raymond (Buddy) Parker (Pittsburgh), East; George Wilson (Detroit), West

West	6	3	10	7	—	26
East	0	7	0	0	—	7

West—Dillon 39 interception return (kick blocked)
East —Renfro 39 pass from Morrall (Groza kick)
West—FG Rechichar 9
West—FG Rechichar 23
West—Tom Wilson 10 run (Rechichar kick)
West—Ameche 8 pass from Unitas (Rechichar kick)
Attendance—66,634

1959

EAST 28, WEST 21

Frank Gifford, voted the game's most valuable player, gained 12 yards in six carries, caught three passes for 54 yards, and completed three of four passes for 75 yards and a touchdown.

Trailing 21-16 at the end of three quarters, the East scored a touchdown, a field goal, and a safety in the fourth quarter to win 28-21 before a record crowd of 72,250.

Each of the East's passers—Gifford, Eddie LeBaron, and Norm Van Brocklin—threw for a touchdown. They completed 16 of 34 passes for 214 yards.

January 11, at Los Angeles

East	**Starting Lineups**	**West**
Pete Retzlaff (Phil.)	LE	Raymond Berry (Baltimore)
Roosevelt Brown (NYG)	LT	Jim Parker (Baltimore)
Jim Ray Smith (Cleveland)	LG	Duane Putnam (LA Rams)
Jim Schrader (Washington)	C	Jim Ringo (Green Bay)
Dick Stanfel (Washington)	RG	Harley Sewell (Detroit)
Frank Varrichione (Pitt.)	RT	Bob St. Clair (San Fran.)
Bob Schnelker (NY Giants)	RE	Billy Wilson (San Fran.)
Norm Van Brocklin (Phil.)	QB	Johnny Unitas (Baltimore)
Frank Gifford (NY Giants)	LH	Jon Arnett (LA Rams)
Alex Webster (NY Giants)	RH	Lenny Moore (Baltimore)
Jim Brown (Cleveland)	FB	Alan Ameche (Baltimore)

Head coaches—Jim Lee Howell (NY Giants), East; Weeb Ewbank (Baltimore), West

East	9	7	0	12	—	28
West	7	7	7	0	—	21

West—Ameche 1 run (Richter kick)
East —FG Groza 25
East —Webster 40 pass from Gifford (kick blocked)
West—McElhenny 20 pass from Wade (Richter kick)
East —Nagler 7 pass from LeBaron (Groza kick)
West—Wade 10 run (Richter kick)
East —FG Groza 25
East —Retzlaff 15 pass from Van Brocklin (Groza kick)
East —Safety, Scott tackled McElhenny in end zone
Attendance—72,250

1960

WEST 38, EAST 21

Johnny Unitas and Y. A. Tittle combined to complete 27 of 40 passes for 365 yards and four touchdowns for the West, which led 31-14 at the half en route to a 38-21 victory. Unitas completed 14 of 22 passes for 187 yards and three touchdowns, ran for 43 yards, and was selected the most valuable player.

Unitas and Tittle threw to eight different receivers. Unitas's Baltimore Colts teammate Lenny Moore caught five for 103 yards and two touchdowns, and Del Shofner of the Los Angeles Rams caught six for 88. The West's Jon Arnett led rushers with 61 yards in 11 carries.

January 17, at Los Angeles

East	**Starting Lineups**	**West**
Bill Anderson (Washington)	LE	Del Shofner (LA Rams)
Roosevelt Brown (NYG)	LT	Jim Parker (Baltimore)
Ernie Stautner (Pittsburgh)	LG	Art Spinney (Baltimore)
Jim Schrader (Washington)	C	Jim Ringo (Green Bay)
John Nisby (Pittsburgh)	RG	Stan Jones (Chi. Bears)
Ken Panfil (Chi. Cardinals)	RT	Bob St. Clair (San Fran.)
Bob Schnelker (NY Giants)	RE	Raymond Berry (Baltimore)
Bobby Layne (Pittsburgh)	QB	Johnny Unitas (Baltimore)
Frank Gifford (NY Giants)	LH	Jon Arnett (LA Rams)
Tommy McDonald (Phil.)	RH	Lenny Moore (Baltimore)
Jim Brown (Cleveland)	FB	J.D. Smith (San Francisco)

Head coaches—Lawrence (Buck) Shaw (Philadelphia), East; Howard (Red) Hickey (San Francisco), West

East	7	7	0	7	—	21
West	10	21	0	7	—	38

East —Patton 22 interception return (Groza kick)
West—Berry 22 pass from Unitas (Hornung kick)
West—FG Hornung 16
East —McDonald 63 pass from Layne (Groza kick)
West—Moore 13 pass from Tittle (Hornung kick)
West—Moore 65 pass from Unitas (Hornung kick)
West—Smith 6 pass from Unitas (Hornung kick)
East —J. Brown 2 pass from Layne (Groza kick)
West—Hornung 2 run (Hornung kick)
Attendance—56,876

1961

WEST 35, EAST 31

The West and East divided eight touchdowns in the last three quarters, with the difference in the West's 35-31 victory coming in the first quarter, when it scored a touchdown on Jim Taylor's two-yard run and the East's Bobby Walston kicked a field goal.

Taylor scored three touchdowns and Sonny Randle scored two touchdowns for the East. West quarterback Johnny Unitas was voted the most valuable player after completing 10 of 18 passes for 218 yards and a touchdown and directing each of his team's five touchdown drives.

January 15, at Los Angeles

East	**Starting Lineups**	**West**
Bill Anderson (Washington)	LE	Gail Cogdill (Detroit)
Roosevelt Brown (NYG)	LT	Jim Parker (Baltimore)
Jim Ray Smith (Cleveland)	LG	Bruce Bosley (San Fran.)
Ray Wietecha (NY Giants)	C	Jim Ringo (Green Bay)
Jack Stroud (NY Giants)	RG	Stan Jones (Chi. Bears)
Mike McCormack (Cleve.)	RT	Bob St. Clair (San Fran.)
Sonny Randle (St. Louis)	RE	Red Phillips (LA Rams)
Norm Van Brocklin (Phil.)	QB	Johnny Unitas (Baltimore)
John David Crow (St. Louis)	LH	Paul Hornung (Green Bay)
Tommy McDonald (Phil.)	RH	Lenny Moore (Baltimore)
Jim Brown (Cleveland)	FB	Jim Taylor (Green Bay)

Head coaches—Lawrence (Buck) Shaw (Philadelphia), East; Vince Lombardi (Green Bay), West

East	3	14	7	7	—	31
West	7	14	7	7	—	35

West—Taylor 2 run (Hornung kick)
East —FG Walston 22
West—Taylor 1 run (Hornung kick)
East —Randle 51 pass from Plum (Walston kick)
East —McDonald 46 pass from Van Brocklin (Walston kick)
West—Moore 44 pass from Unitas (Hornung kick)
West—Taylor 1 run (Hornung kick)
East —Retzlaff 43 pass from Van Brocklin (Walston kick)
West—Arnett 20 run (Hornung kick)
East —Randle 36 pass from Van Brocklin (Walston kick)
Attendance—62,971

1962 AFL

WEST 47, EAST 27

January 7, at San Diego

East	**Starters, Offense**	**West**
Gino Cappelletti (Boston)	LE	Don Norton (San Diego)
Al Jamison (Houston)	LT	Ernie Wright (San Diego)
Chuck Leo (Boston)	LG	Ken Adamson (Denver)
Bob Schmidt (Houston)	C	Jim Otto (Oakland)
Bob Mischak (NY Titans)	RG	Bill Krisher (Dallas)
Ken Rice (Buffalo)	RT	Ron Mix (San Diego)
Bob McLeod (Houston)	RE	Dave Kocourek (San Diego)
George Blanda (Houston)	QB	Jack Kemp (San Diego)
Billy Cannon (Houston)	LH	Abner Haynes (Dallas)
Charley Hennigan (Hou.)	RH	Lionel Taylor (Denver)
Bill Mathis (NY Titans)	FB	Alan Miller (Oakland)
	Starters, Defense	
Laverne Torczon (Buffalo)	LE	Earl Faison (San Diego)
Chuck McMurtry (Buffalo)	LT	Bud McFadin (Denver)
Jim Hunt (Boston)	RT	Paul Rochester (Dallas)
Don Floyd (Houston)	RE	Mel Branch (Dallas)
Tom Addison (Boston)	LLB	Emil Karas (San Diego)
Archie Matsos (Buffalo)	MLB	Sherrill Headrick (Dallas)
Dennit Morris (Houston)	RLB	E.J. Holub (Dallas)
Tony Banfield (Houston)	LCB	Fred Williamson (Oakland)
Dick Felt (NY Titans)	RCB	Dave Webster (Dallas)
Bill Atkins (Buffalo)	LS	Austin Gonsoulin (Denver)
Fred Bruney (Boston)	RS	Charlie McNeil (San Diego)

Head coaches—Wally Lemm (Houston), East; Sid Gillman (San Diego), West

East	5	7	7	8	—	27
West	0	21	14	12	—	47

East —FG Blanda 32
East —Safety, Haynes tackled in end zone
West—Stone 45 pass from Davidson (Blair kick)
East —Cannon 34 pass from Blanda (Blanda kick)
West—Haynes 12 run (Blair kick)
West—Kocourek 24 pass from Davidson (Blair kick)
West—Haynes 66 punt return (Blair kick)
West—Norton 10 pass from Davidson (Blair kick)
East —Cappelletti 5 pass from Blanda (Blanda kick)
West—Williamson 53 interception return (kick failed)
East —Hennigan 3 pass from Dorow (Dorow run)
West—Stone 15 run (pass failed)
Attendance—20,973

1962 NFL

WEST 31, EAST 30

Jon Arnett scored a touchdown with 10 seconds left, and the West won a narrow 31-30 victory.

January 14, at Los Angeles

East	**Starters, Offense**	**West**
Del Shofner (NY Giants)	LE	Raymond Berry (Baltimore)
Ray Lemek (Washington)	LT	Jim Parker (Baltimore)
John Nisby (Pittsburgh)	LG	Stan Jones (Chi. Bears)
John Morrow (Cleveland)	C	Jim Ringo (Green Bay)
Jim Ray Smith (Cleveland)	RG	Ted Connolly (San Fran.)
Mike McCormack (Cleve.)	RT	Bob St. Clair (San Fran.)
Bobby Walston (Phil.)	RE	Red Phillips (LA Rams)
Y. A. Tittle (NY Giants)	QB	Bart Starr (Green Bay)
Don Perkins (Dallas)	LH	Jon Arnett (LA Rams)
Tommy McDonald (Phil.)	RH	Lenny Moore (Baltimore)
Jim Brown (Cleveland)	FB	Jim Taylor (Green Bay)
	Starters, Defense	
Jim Katcavage (NY Giants)	LE	Doug Atkins (Chi. Bears)
Bob Gain (Cleveland)	LT	Henry Jordan (Green Bay)
Bob Toneff (Washington)	RT	Alex Karras (Detroit)
Ernie Stautner (Pittsburgh)	RE	Gino Marchetti (Baltimore)
John Reger (Pittsburgh)	LLB	Bill Forester (Green Bay)
Sam Huff (NY Giants)	MLB	Joe Schmidt (Detroit)
Maxie Baughan (Phil.)	RLB	Bill George (Chi. Bears)
Erich Barnes (NY Giants)	LHB	Dick Lane (Detroit)
Jimmy Hill (St. Louis)	LHB	Jesse Whittenton (GB)
Jerry Norton (St. Louis)	LS	Abe Woodson (San Fran.)
Jim Patton (NY Giants)	RS	Eddie Dove (San Francisco)

Head coaches—Allie Sherman (NY Giants), East; Norm Van Brocklin (Minnesota), West

East	3	7	6	14	—	30
West	14	3	7	7	—	31

East —FG Walston 33
West—Berry 16 pass from Unitas (Martin kick)
West—Lane 42 pass interception (Martin kick)
East —Bielski 10 pass from Tittle (Walston kick)
West—FG Martin 27
West—McElhenny 10 pass from Starr (Martin kick)
East —Walston 12 pass from Plum (kick blocked)
East —Webster 2 pass from Tittle (Walston kick)
East —Brown 70 run (Walston kick)
West—Arnett 12 pass from Unitas (Martin kick)
Attendance—57,409

1963 AFL

WEST 21, EAST 14

Denver Broncos teammates Frank Tripucka and Lionel Taylor combined on a 20-yard pass with 8:56 remaining in the game for the touchdown that provided the West a 21-14 victory. Tripucka replaced Dallas's Len Dawson.

January 13, at San Diego

West	Starters, Offense	East
Reg Carolan (San Diego)	LE	Ernie Warlick (Buffalo)
Jim Tyrer (Dallas)	LT	Al Jamison (Houston)
Marvin Terrell (Dallas)	LG	Bob Talamini (Houston)
Jim Otto (Oakland)	C	Bob Schmidt (Houston)
Ron Mix (San Diego)	RG	Bob Mischak (NY Titans)
Jerry Cornelison (Dallas)	RT	Rich Michael (Houston)
Dave Kocourek (San Diego)	RE	Willard Dewveal (Houston)
Len Dawson (Dallas)	QB	George Blanda (Houston)
Abner Haynes (Dallas)	LH	Dick Christy (NY Titans)
Lionel Taylor (Denver)	RH	Charley Hennigan (Hou.)
Curtis McClinton (Dallas)	FB	Cookie Gilchrist (Buffalo)
	Starters, Defense	
Earl Faison (San Diego)	LE	Don Floyd (Houston)
Bud McFadin (Denver)	LT	Ed Husmann (Houston)
Ernie Ladd (San Diego)	RT	Tom Sestak (Buffalo)
Mel Branch (Dallas)	RE	Dick Klein (Boston)
Emil Karas (San Diego)	LLB	Tom Addison (Boston)
Sherrill Headrick (Dallas)	MLB	Arche Matsos (Buffalo)
Jim Fraser (Denver)	RLB	Marv Matuszak (Buffalo)
Fred Williamson (Oakland)	LCB	Tony Banfield (Houston)
Bob Zeman (Denver)	RCB	Fred Bruney (Boston)
Austin Gonsoulin (Denver)	LS	Jim Norton (Houston)
Dave Grayson (Dallas)	RS	Fred Glick (Houston)

Head coaches—Frank (Pop) Ivy (Houston), East; Hank Stram (Dallas), West

West	7	7	0	7	—	21
East	0	0	14	0	—	14

West—McClinton 64 run (Mingo kick)
West—Kocourek 11 pass from Dawson (Mingo kick)
East—Hennigan 8 pass from Blanda (Blanda kick)
East—Grantham 29 interception return (Blanda kick)
West—Taylor 20 pass from Tripucka (Mingo kick)
Attendance—27,641

1963 NFL

EAST 30, WEST 20

Jim Brown gained 144 yards and scored twice to give the East a 30-20 victory despite Johnny Unitas's 210 yards passing.

January 13, at Los Angeles

West	Starters, Offense	East
Gail Cogdill (Detroit)	LE	Del Shofner (NY Giants)
Jim Parker (Baltimore)	LT	Roosevelt Brown (NYG)
Harley Sewell (Detroit)	LG	Jim Ray Smith (Cleveland)
Jim Ringo (Green Bay)	C	Ray Wietecha (NY Giants)
Jerry Kramer (Green Bay)	RG	John Nisby (Washington)
Forrest Gregg (Green Bay)	RT	Mike McCormack (Cleve.)
Mike Ditka (Chi. Bears)	RE	Preston Carpenter (Pitt.)
Johnny Unitas (Baltimore)	QB	Y. A. Tittle (NY Giants)
Dick Bass (LA Rams)	LH	John David Crow (St. Louis)
Lenny Moore (Baltimore)	RH	Tommy McDonald (Phil.)
J.D. Smith (San Francisco)	FB	Jim Brown (Cleveland)
	Starters, Defense	
Doug Atkins (Chi. Bears)	LE	Lou Michaels (Pittsburgh)
Alex Karras (Detroit)	LT	Bob Gain (Cleveland)
Roger Brown (Detroit)	RT	Gene Lipscomb (Pitt.)
Gino Marchetti (Baltimore)	RE	Jim Katcavage (NY Giants)
Joe Fortunato (Chi. Bears)	LLB	Galen Fiss (Cleveland)
Joe Schmidt (Detroit)	MLB	Jerry Tubbs (Dallas)
Bill Forester (Green Bay)	RLB	Rod Breedlove (Wash.)
Dick Lane (Detroit)	LHB	Erich Barnes (NY Giants)
Abe Woodson (San Fran.)	RHB	Jimmy Hill (St. Louis)
Willie Wood (Green Bay)	LS	Jimmy Patton (NY Giants)
Yale Lary (Detroit)	RS	Larry Wilson (St. Louis)

Head coaches—Allie Sherman (NY Giants), East; Vince Lombardi (Green Bay), West

West	0	3	17	0	—	20
East	13	0	0	17	—	30

East—J. Brown 1 run (Michaels kick)
East—J. Brown 50 run (kick failed)
West—FG Davis 49
West—Bass 1 run (Davis kick)
West—FG Davis 32
West—Ditka 6 pass from Unitas (Davis kick)
East—Carpenter 19 pass from Tittle (Gain kick)
East—FG Michaels 27
East—Bishop 20 fumble return (Michaels kick)
Attendance—61,374

1964 AFL

WEST 27, EAST 24

Cotton Davidson threw a 25-yard pass to Oakland teammate Art Powell with 43 seconds left for a 27-24 West victory.

January 19, at San Diego

West	Starters, Offense	East
Art Powell (Oakland)	LE	Gino Cappelletti (Boston)
Jim Tyrer (Kansas City)	LT	Stew Barber (Buffalo)
Wayne Hawkins (Oakland)	LG	Billy Shaw (Buffalo)
Jim Otto (Oakland)	C	Bob Schmidt (Houston)
Ed Budde (Kansas City)	RG	Chuck Long (Boston)
Ron Mix (San Diego)	RT	Rich Michael (Houston)
Dave Kocourek (San Diego)	RE	Ernie Warlick (Buffalo)
Tobin Rote (San Diego)	QB	Babe Parilli (Boston)
Clem Daniels (Oakland)	LH	Larry Garron (Boston)
Lance Alworth (San Diego)	RH	Charley Hennigan (Hou.)
Keith Lincoln (San Diego)	FB	Cookie Gilchrist (Buffalo)
	Starters, Defense	
Earl Faison (San Diego)	LE	Bob Dee (Boston)
Dave Costa (Oakland)	LT	Ed Husmann (Houston)
Ernie Ladd (San Diego)	RT	Tom Sestak (Buffalo)
Mel Branch (Kansas City)	RE	Larry Eisenhauer (Boston)
Emil Karas (San Diego)	LLB	Nick Buoniconti (Boston)
Archie Matsos (Buffalo)	MLB	Tom Addison (Boston)
Jim Fraser (Denver)	RLB	Larry Grantham (NY Jets)
Fred Williamson (Oakland)	LCB	Galen Hall (NY Jets)
Austin Gonsoulin (Denver)	RCB	Tony Banfield (Houston)
Johnny Robinson (KC)	LS	Jim Norton (Houston)
Dave Grayson (Kansas City)	RS	Fred Glick (Houston)

Head coaches—Mike Holovak (Boston), East; Sid Gillman (San Diego), West

West	0	3	14	10	—	27
East	10	14	0	0	—	24

East—FG Cappelletti 35
East—Gilchrist 1 run (Cappelletti kick)
West—FG Fraser 19
East—Garron 12 pass from Parilli (Cappelletti kick)
East—Mathis 3 pass from Parilli (Cappelletti kick)
West—Lincoln 64 run (Fraser kick)
West—Lowe 5 run (Fraser kick)
West—FG Fraser 7
West—Powell 25 pass from Davidson (Fraser kick)
Attendance—20,016

1964 NFL

WEST 31, EAST 17

The West broke open the game with two quick touchdowns in the third quarter and won 31-17 over the East.

January 12, at Los Angeles

East	Starters, Offense	West
Del Shofner (NY Giants)	LE	Raymond Berry (Baltimore)
Dick Schafrath (Cleveland)	LT	Grady Alderman (Minn.)
Darrell Dess (NY Giants)	LG	John Gordy (Detroit)
Bob DeMarco (St. Louis)	C	Jim Ringo (Green Bay)
Ken Gray (St. Louis)	RG	Jerry Kramer (Green Bay)
Charlie Bradshaw (Pitt.)	RT	Forrest Gregg (Green Bay)
Pete Retzlaff (Philadelphia)	RE	Mike Ditka (Chi. Bears)
Charley Johnson (St. Louis)	QB	Johnny Unitas (Baltimore)
Bobby Mitchell (Wash.)	FL	Terry Barr (Detroit)
Timmy Brown (Philadelphia)	HB	Tommy Mason (Minnesota)
Jim Brown (Cleveland)	FB	Jim Taylor (Green Bay)
	Starters, Defense	
Bill Glass (Cleveland)	LE	Doug Atkins (Chi. Bears)
John LoVetere (NY Giants)	LT	Merlin Olsen (LA Rams)
Joe Krupa (Pittsburgh)	RT	Roger Brown (Detroit)
Jim Katcavage (NY Giants)	RE	Gino Marchetti (Baltimore)
Myron Pottios (Pittsburgh)	LLB	Wayne Walker (Detroit)
Galen Fiss (Cleveland)	MLB	Joe Fortunato (Chi. Bears)
Dale Meinert (St. Louis)	RLB	Rip Hawkins (Minnesota)
Erich Barnes (NY Giants)	LHB	Herb Adderley (Green Bay)
Dick Lynch (NY Giants)	RHB	Jesse Whittenton (GB)
Clendon Thomas (Pitt.)	LS	Richie Petitbon (Chi. Bears)
Larry Wilson (St. Louis)	RS	Roosevelt Taylor (Chi. Bears)

Head coaches—Allie Sherman (NY Giants), East; George Halas (Chi. Bears), West

East	3	0	0	14	—	17
West	7	7	14	3	—	31

East—FG Baker 30
West—Taylor 37 run (T. Davis kick)
West—Berry 4 pass from Unitas (T. Davis kick)
West—Whittenton 26 interception return (T. Davis kick)
West—Cogdill 5 pass from Unitas (T. Davis kick)
East—J. Brown 8 run (Baker kick)
West—FG T. Davis 38
East—J. Brown 3 run (Baker kick)
Attendance—67,242

1965 AFL

WEST 38, EAST 14

The game was scheduled for New Orleans but was moved the week of the game to Houston's Jeppesen Stadium. Keith Lincoln was named the outstanding offensive player for the second consecutive year.

January 16, at Houston

West	Starters, Offense	East
Art Powell (Oakland)	LE	Gino Cappelletti (Boston)
Jim Tyrer (Kansas City)	LT	Stew Barber (Buffalo)
Wayne Hawkins (Oakland)	LG	Billy Shaw (Buffalo)
Jim Otto (Oakland)	C	Jon Morris (Boston)
Walt Sweeney (San Diego)	RG	Bob Talamini (Houston)
Ron Mix (San Diego)	RT	Sherman Plunkett (NY Jets)
Dave Kocourek (San Diego)	RE	Ernie Warlick (Buffalo)
Len Dawson (Kansas City)	QB	Babe Parilli (Boston)
Clem Daniels (Oakland)	LH	Larry Garron (Boston)
Lance Alworth (San Diego)	RH	Charley Hennigan (Hou.)
Keith Lincoln (San Diego)	FB	Sid Blanks (Houston)
	Starters, Defense	
Bobby Bell (Kansas City)	LE	Bob Dee (Boston)
Jerry Mays (Kansas City)	LT	Tom Sestak (Buffalo)
Ernie Ladd (San Diego)	RT	Houston Antwine (Boston)
Earl Faison (San Diego)	RE	Larry Eisenhauer (Boston)
Jim Fraser (Denver)	LLB	Tom Addison (Boston)
Chuck Allen (San Diego)	MLB	Nick Buoniconti (Boston)
Frank Buncom (San Diego)	RLB	Larry Grantham (NY Jets)
Dave Grayson (Kansas City)	LCB	Pete Jaquess (Houston)
Willie Brown (Denver)	RCB	Butch Byrd (Buffalo)
Austin Gonsoulin (Denver)	LS	Fred Glick (Houston)
Bobby Hunt (Kansas City)	RS	George Saimes (Buffalo)

Head coaches—Lou Saban (Buffalo), East; Sid Gillman (San Diego), West

West	7	10	14	7	—	38
East	0	14	0	0	—	14

West—Lincoln 73 pass from Dawson (Brooker kick)
West—Daniels 5 pass from Hadl (Brooker kick)
East—Blanks 5 run (Cappelletti kick)
West—FG Brooker 46
East—Buoniconti 17 fumble return (Cappelletti kick)
West—Lincoln 80 run (Brooker kick)
West—Alworth 7 pass from Hadl (Brooker kick)
West—Powell 17 pass from Hadl (Brooker kick)
Attendance—15,446

1965 NFL

WEST 34, EAST 14

The West outgained the East 300-47 in the first half and led 17-7 on a 15-yard field goal by Wayne Walker and two touchdowns by Bill Brown.

January 10, at Los Angeles

West	Starters, Offense	East
Raymond Berry (Baltimore)	LE	Paul Warfield (Cleveland)
Bob Vogel (Baltimore)	LT	Dick Schafrath (Cleveland)
John Gordy (Detroit)	LG	Vince Promuto (Wash.)
Dick Szymanski (Baltimore)	C	Jim Ringo (Philadelphia)
Jim Parker (Baltimore)	RG	Ken Gray (St. Louis)
Forrest Gregg (Green Bay)	RT	Charlie Bradshaw (Pitt.)
Mike Ditka (Chi. Bears)	RE	Pete Retzlaff (Philadelphia)
Johnny Unitas (Baltimore)	QB	Frank Ryan (Cleveland)
Terry Barr (Detroit)	FL	Bobby Mitchell (Cleveland)
Lenny Moore (Baltimore)	HB	Charley Taylor (Wash.)
Jim Taylor (Green Bay)	FB	Jim Brown (Cleveland)
	Starters, Defense	
Willie Davis (Green Bay)	LE	Bill Glass (Cleveland)
Merlin Olsen (LA Rams)	LT	Bob Lilly (Dallas)
Roger Brown (Detroit)	RT	Floyd Peters (Philadelphia)
Gino Marchetti (Baltimore)	RE	John Paluck (Washington)
Wayne Walker (Detroit)	LLB	Maxie Baughan (Phil.)
Ray Nitschke (Green Bay)	MLB	Myron Pottios (Pittsburgh)
Joe Fortunato (Chi. Bears)	RLB	Jim Houston (Cleveland)
Bobby Boyd (Baltimore)	LHB	Pat Fischer (St. Louis)
Dick LeBeau (Detroit)	RHB	Irv Cross (Philadelphia)
Willie Wood (Green Bay)	LS	Mel Renfro (Dallas)
Eddie Meador (LA Rams)	RS	Paul Krause (Washington)

Head coaches—Blanton Collier (Cleveland), East; Don Shula (Baltimore), West

West	3	14	10	7	—	34
East	0	7	0	7	—	14

West—FG Walker 15
West—B. Brown 2 run (Walker kick)
East—Renfro 47 interception return (Baker kick)
West—B. Brown 2 pass from Tarkenton (Walker kick)
West—Nitschke 42 interception return (Walker kick)
West—FG Walker 28
West—Moore 2 run (Walker kick)
East—J. Brown 27 pass from Jurgensen (Baker kick)
Attendance—60,598

1966 AFL

AFL ALL-STARS 30, BUFFALO 19

A team of AFL All-Stars defeated the champion Bills behind the passing of rookie Joe Namath.

January 15, at Houston

Buffalo	**Starters, Offense**	**All-Stars**
Paul Costa	LE	Art Powell (Oakland)
Stew Barber	LT	Eldon Danenhauer (Denver)
Billy Shaw	LG	Bob Talamini (Houston)
Al Bemiller	C	Jim Otto (Oakland)
George Flint	RG	Wayne Hawkins (Oakland)
Dick Hudson	RT	Jim Tyrer (Kansas City)
Ernie Warlick	RE	Willie Frazier (Houston)
Jack Kemp	QB	John Hadl (San Diego)
Bob Smith	LH	Paul Lowe (San Diego)
Ed Rutowski	RH	Charley Hennigan (Hou.)
Billy Joe	FB	Cookie Gilchrist (Buffalo)
	Starters, Defense	
Tom Day	LE	Jerry Mays (Kansas City)
Dudley Meredith	LT	Ernie Ladd (San Diego)
Jim Dunaway	RT	Houston Antwine (Boston)
Ron McDole	RE	Earl Faison (San Diego)
Mike Stratton	LLB	Sherrill Headrick (KC)
Harry Jacobs	MLB	Nick Buoniconti (Boston)
John Tracey	RLB	Bobby Bell (Kansas City)
Booker Edgerson	LCB	Willie Brown (Denver)
Butch Byrd	RCB	Dave Grayson (Oakland)
Hagood Clark	LS	Kenny Graham (San Diego)
George Saimes	RS	Johnny Robinson (KC)

Head coaches—Sid Gillman (San Diego), AFL All-Stars; Lou Saban, Buffalo

Buffalo	10	3	0	6	—	19
AFL All-Stars	0	6	17	7	—	30

Buff —FG Gogolak 20
Buff —Saimes 61 fumble return (Gogolak kick)
All-Stars—FG Cappelletti 46
Buff —FG Gogolak 11
All-Stars—FG Cappelletti 14
All-Stars—FG Cappelletti 32
All-Stars—Lowe 1 run (Cappelletti kick)
All-Stars—Alworth 43 pass from Namath (Cappelletti kick)
All-Stars—Alworth 10 pass from Namath (Cappelletti kick)
Buff —Carlton 34 pass from Lamonica (run failed)
Attendance—35,572

1966 NFL

EAST 36, WEST 7

Fullback Jim Brown, the game's most valuable player, scored three touchdowns in his ninth Pro Bowl and final NFL game.

January 16, at Los Angeles

East	**Starters, Offense**	**West**
Sonny Randle (St. Louis)	LE	Dave Parks (San Francisco)
Roosevelt Brown (NYG)	LT	Bob Vogel (Baltimore)
John Wooten (Cleveland)	LG	Jim Parker (Baltimore)
Jim Ringo (Philadelphia)	C	Bruce Bosley (San Fran.)
Gene Hickerson (Cleve.)	RG	John Gordy (Detroit)
Bob Brown (Philadelphia)	RT	Walter Rock (San Fran.)
Pete Retzlaff (Philadelphia)	RE	John Mackey (Baltimore)
Frank Ryan (Cleveland)	QB	John Brodie (San Fran.)
Gary Collins (Cleveland)	FL	Tommy McDonald (LA Rams)
Timmy Brown (Philadelphia)	HB	Gale Sayers (Chi. Bears)
Jim Brown (Cleveland)	FB	Ken Willard (San Fran.)
	Starters, Defense	
Paul Wiggin (Cleveland)	LE	Willie Davis (Green Bay)
Sam Silas (St. Louis)	LT	Merlin Olsen (LA Rams)
Bob Lilly (Dallas)	RT	Roger Brown (Detroit)
George Andrie (Dallas)	RE	Doug Atkins (Chi. Bears)
Jim Houston (Cleveland)	LLB	Joe Fortunato (Chi. Bears)
Dale Meinert (St. Louis)	MLB	Dick Butkus (Chi. Bears)
Maxie Baughan (Phil.)	RLB	Lee Roy Caffey (GB)
Pat Fischer (St. Louis)	LHB	Herb Adderley (GB)
Irv Cross (Philadelphia)	RHB	Dick LeBeau (Detroit)
Mel Renfro (Dallas)	LS	Eddie Meador (LA Rams)
Paul Krause (Wash.)	RS	Willie Wood (GB)

Head coaches—Blanton Collier (Cleveland), East; Vince Lombardi (Green Bay), West

East	10	13	3	10	—	36
West	0	0	0	7	—	7

East —FG Bakken 41
East —J. Brown 2 run (Bakken kick)
East —J. Brown 2 run (Bakken kick)
East —J. Brown 1 run (kick failed)
East —FG Bakken 36
East —FG Bakken 42
East —Renfro 20 interception return (Bakken kick)
West —McDonald 31 pass from Brodie (Walker kick)
Attendance—60,124

1967 AFL

EAST 30, WEST 23

The East-West format was restored. Torrential rains flooded Oakland as the East rallied for a 30-23 win.

January 21, at Oakland

East	**Starters, Offense**	**West**
George Sauer (NY Jets)	SE	Art Powell (Oakland)
Stew Barber (Buffalo)	LT	Jim Tyrer (Kansas City)
Billy Shaw (Buffalo)	LG	Wayne Hawkins (Oakland)
Jon Morris (Boston)	C	Jim Otto (Oakland)
Bob Talamini (Houston)	RG	Ed Budde (Kansas City)
Sherman Plunkett (NY Jets)	RT	Ron Mix (San Diego)
Paul Costa (Buffalo)	TE	Jacque MacKinnon (SD)
Jack Kemp (Buffalo)	QB	Len Dawson (Kansas City)
Charley Frazier (Houston)	FL	Lance Alworth (San Diego)
Bobby Burnett (Buffalo)	HB	Clem Daniels (Oakland)
Matt Snell (NY Jets)	FB	Curtis McClinton (KC)
	Starters, Defense	
Larry Eisenhauer (Boston)	LE	Jerry Mays (Kansas City)
Jim Dunaway (Buffalo)	LT	Tom Keating (Oakland)
Houston Antwine (Boston)	RT	Buck Buchanan (KC)
Verlon Biggs (NY Jets)	RE	Ben Davidson (Oakland)
Mike Stratton (Buffalo)	LLB	Bobby Bell (Kansas City)
Nick Buoniconti (Boston)	MLB	Sherrill Headrick (KC)
Larry Grantham (NY Jets)	RLB	E. J. Holub (Kansas City)
W. K. Hicks (Houston)	LCB	Kent McCloughan (Oak.)
Butch Byrd (Buffalo)	RCB	Dave Grayson (Oakland)
Willie West (Miami)	LS	Austin Gonsoulin (Denver)
George Saimes (Buffalo)	RS	Johnny Robinson (KC)

Head coaches—Mike Holovak (Boston), East; John Rauch (Oakland), West

East	0	0	16	14	—	30
West	9	7	7	0	—	23

West—McClinton 31 pass from Dawson (Van Raaphorst kick)
West—Safety, center snap out of end zone
West—Dixon 17 pass from Flores (Van Raaphorst kick)
East —Safety, Dawson tackled in end zone
West—Buchanan 39 fumble return (Van Raaphorst kick)
East —Biggs 50 interception return (Cappelletti kick)
East —Carlton 3 pass from Parilli (Cappelletti kick)
East —Burnett 12 run (Cappelletti kick)
East —Frazier 17 pass from Parilli (Cappelletti kick)
Attendance—18,876

1967 NFL

EAST 20, WEST 10

The East scored a 20-10 victory, although Gale Sayers of the West was named outstanding back after gaining 110 yards in 11 carries, breaking runs of 52 and 42 yards on a muddy field slowed by heavy rains. Penalties spoiled 80- and 55-yard plays by Sayers.

January 22, at Los Angeles

West	**Starters, Offense**	**East**
Dave Parks (San Fran.)	LE	Bob Hayes (Dallas)
Grady Alderman (Minn.)	LT	Dick Schafrath (Cleveland)
Howard Mudd (San Fran.)	LG	John Wooten (Cleveland)
Mick Tingelhoff (Minn.)	C	Dave Manders (Dallas)
Milt Sunde (Minnesota)	RG	Gene Hickerson (Cleve.)
Forrest Gregg (Green Bay)	RT	Bob Brown (Philadelphia)
John Mackey (Baltimore)	RE	Jackie Smith (St. Louis)
Johnny Unitas (Baltimore)	QB	Don Meredith (Dallas)
Pat Studstill (Detroit)	FL	Gary Collins (Cleveland)
Gale Sayers (Chi. Bears)	HB	Leroy Kelly (Cleveland)
Dick Bass (LA Rams)	FB	Don Perkins (Dallas)
	Starters, Defense	
Deacon Jones (LA Rams)	LE	Joe Robb (St. Louis)
Merlin Olsen (LA Rams)	LT	Floyd Peters (Phil.)
Roger Brown (Detroit)	RT	Bob Lilly (Dallas)
Willie Davis (Green Bay)	RE	George Andrie (Dallas)
Dave Robinson (Green Bay)	LLB	Chuck Howley (Dallas)
Dick Butkus (Chi. Bears)	MLB	Tommy Nobis (Atlanta)
Maxie Baughan (LA Rams)	RLB	John Brewer (Cleveland)
Herb Adderley (Green Bay)	LH	Cornell Green (Dallas)
Dick LeBeau (Detroit)	RH	Brady Keys (Pittsburgh)
Willie Wood (Green Bay)	LS	Mel Renfro (Dallas)
Richie Petitbon (Chi. Bears)	RS	Larry Wilson (St. Louis)

Head coaches—Tom Landry (Dallas), East; George Allen (LA Rams), West

West	0	0	3	7	—	10
East	6	14	0	0	—	20

East —FG Clark 18
East —FG Clark 17
East —Roland 1 run (Clark kick)
East —Collins 18 pass from Ryan (Clark kick)
West —FG Gossett 27
West—Willard 51 pass from Starr (Gossett kick)
Attendance—15,062

1968 AFL

EAST 25, WEST 24

With 58 seconds left, guard Billy Shaw suggested Joe Namath try a quarterback sneak for the game-winning points. Namath did, and he scored.

January 21, at Jacksonville

East	**Starters, Offense**	**West**
George Sauer (NY Jets)	SE	Lance Alworth (San Diego)
Walt Suggs (Houston)	LT	Ron Mix (San Diego)
Bob Talamini (Houston)	LG	Walt Sweeney (San Diego)
Jon Morris (Boston)	C	Jim Otto (Oakland)
Billy Shaw (Buffalo)	RG	Wayne Hawkins (Oakland)
Don Oakes (Boston)	RT	Harry Schuh (Oakland)
Pete Lammons (NY Jets)	TE	Fred Arbanas (Kansas City)
Joe Namath (NY Jets)	QB	Daryle Lamonica (Oakland)
Don Maynard (NY Jets)	FL	Al Denson (Denver)
Keith Lincoln (Buffalo)	RB	Mike Garrett (Kansas City)
Jim Nance (Boston)	RB	Hewritt Dixon (Oakland)
	Starters, Defense	
Ron McDole (Buffalo)	LE	Jerry Mays (Kansas City)
Jim Hunt (Boston)	LT	Tom Keating (Oakland)
Jim Dunaway (Buffalo)	RT	Buck Buchanan (KC)
Verlon Biggs (NY Jets)	RE	Ben Davidson (Oakland)
Larry Grantham (NY Jets)	LLB	Bobby Bell (Kansas City)
Nick Buoniconti (Boston)	MLB	Dan Conners (Oakland)
Mike Stratton (Buffalo)	RLB	Frank Buncom (San Diego)
Miller Farr (Houston)	LCB	Willie Brown (Oakland)
Dick Westmoreland (Miami)	RCB	Speedy Duncan (SD)
George Saimes (Buffalo)	LS	Kenny Graham (San Diego)
Jim Norton (Houston)	RS	Johnny Robinson (KC)

Head coaches—Joe Collier (Buffalo), East; Lou Saban (Denver), West

East	3	10	0	12	—	25
West	7	14	0	3	—	24

East —FG Mercer 10
West—Duncan 90 kickoff return (Blanda kick)
West—Frazier 3 pass from Lamonica (Blanda kick)
East —Lammons 35 pass from Namath (Mercer kick)
West—Alworth 9 pass from Lamonica (Blanda kick)
East —FG Mercer 33
West—FG Blanda 28
East —Maynard 24 pass from Namath (pass failed)
East —Namath 1 run (run failed)
Attendance—40,103

1968 NFL

WEST 38, EAST 20

The West rallied for 21 fourth-quarter points and beat the East 38-20.

January 21, at Los Angeles

East	**Starters, Offense**	**West**
Bob Hayes (Dallas)	SE	Boyd Dowler (Green Bay)
Dick Schafrath (Clev.)	LT	Bob Vogel (Baltimore)
Ken Gray (St. Louis)	LG	Jerry Kramer (Green Bay)
Jim Ringo (Philadelphia)	C	Mick Tingelhoff (Minn.)
Gene Hickerson (Cleve.)	RG	Tom Mack (LA Rams)
Ralph Neely (Dallas)	RT	Forrest Gregg (Green Bay)
Jerry Smith (Washington)	TE	John Mackey (Baltimore)
Don Meredith (Dallas)	QB	Johnny Unitas (Baltimore)
Homer Jones (NY Giants)	FL	Willie Richardson (Balt.)
Leroy Kelly (Cleveland)	RB	Gale Sayers (Chi. Bears)
Don Perkins (Dallas)	RB	Bill Brown (Minnesota)
	Starters, Defense	
Paul Wiggin (Cleveland)	LE	Deacon Jones (LA Rams)
Floyd Peters (Phil.)	LT	Merlin Olsen (LA Rams)
Bob Lilly (Dallas)	RT	Roger Brown (LA Rams)
George Andrie (Dallas)	RE	Willie Davis, (Green Bay)
Chuck Howley (Dallas)	LLB	Dave Robinson (Green Bay)
Dale Meinert (St. Louis)	MLB	Dick Butkus (Chi. Bears)
Chris Hanburger (Wash.)	RLB	Maxie Baughan (LA Rams)
Cornell Green (Dallas)	LHB	Herb Adderley (Green Bay)
Dave Whitsell (N. Orleans)	RHB	Bob Jeter (Green Bay)
Jerry Stovall (St. Louis)	LS	Richie Petitbon (Chi. Bears)
Larry Wilson (St. Louis)	RS	Willie Wood (Green Bay)

Head coaches—Otto Graham (Washington), East; Don Shula (Baltimore), West

East	0	13	7	0	—	20
West	10	7	0	21	—	38

West—FG Chandler 26
West—Josephson 4 run (Chandler kick)
East —FG Bakken 45
East —FG Bakken 25
West—Farr 39 pass from Gabriel (Chandler kick)
East —Kelly 1 run (Bakken kick)
East —Taylor 9 pass from Meredith (Bakken kick)
West—Sayers 3 run (Chandler kick)
West—Petitbon 70 interception return (Chandler kick)
West—B. Brown 19 run (Chandler kick)
Attendance—53,289

1969 AFL

WEST 38, EAST 25

January 19, at Jacksonville

East	Starters, Offense	West
George Sauer (NY Jets)	SE	Warren Wells (Oakland)
Winston Hill (NY Jets)	LT	Jim Tyrer (Kansas City)
Billy Shaw (Buffalo)	LG	Ed Budde (Kansas City)
Jon Morris (Boston)	C	Jim Otto (Oakland)
Dave Herman (NY Jets)	RG	Walt Sweeney (San Diego)
Glen Ray Hines (Houston)	RT	Ron Mix (San Diego)
Alvin Reed (Houston)	TE	Jacque MacKinnon (SD)
Joe Namath (NY Jets)	QB	John Hadl (San Diego)
Don Maynard (NY Jets)	FL	Lance Alworth (San Diego)
Jim Kiick (Miami)	RB	Paul Robinson (Cin.)
Hoyle Granger (Houston)	RB	Hewritt Dixon (Oakland)
	Starters, Defense	
Gerry Philbin (NY Jets)	LE	Jerry Mays (Kansas City)
Jim Dunaway (Buffalo)	LT	Dan Birdwell (Oakland)
Houston Antwine (Boston)	LG	Buck Buchanan (KC)
Verlon Biggs (NY Jets)	C	Ben Davidson (Oakland)
George Webster (Houston)	LLB	Bobby Bell (Kansas City)
Garland Boyette (Houston)	MLB	Dan Conners (Oakland)
Mike Stratton (Buffalo)	RLB	Jim Lynch (Kansas City)
Miller Farr (Houston)	LCB	George Atkinson (Oakland)
Butch Byrd (Buffalo)	RCB	Willie Brown (Oakland)
Ken Houston (Houston)	LS	Kenny Graham (San Diego)
George Saimes (Buffalo)	RS	Johnny Robinson (KC)

Head coaches—George Wilson (Miami), East; Lou Saban (Denver), West

West	3	0	10	25	—	38
East	3	16	3	3	—	25

East —FG Turner 27
West—FG Stenerud 51
East —Kiick 2 run (Turner kick)
East —FG Turner 16
East —FG Turner 19
East —FG Turner 13
West—Trumpy 6 pass from Dawson (Stenerud kick)
East —FG Turner 18
West—FG Stenerud 30
East —FG Turner 21
West—Dixon 1 run (Stenerud kick)
West—Robinson 1 run (Robinson run)
West—Robinson 1 run (Stenerud kick)
West—FG Stenerud 32
Attendance—41,058

1969 NFL

WEST 10, EAST 7

The Los Angeles Rams' delegation played the major role in the West's 10-7 victory. George Allen was head coach, quarterback Roman Gabriel the outstanding back, and defensive tackle Merlin Olsen the outstanding lineman.

With 3:52 remaining in the game, Gabriel started the West on a march to the winning touchdown.

January 19, at Los Angeles

East	Starters, Offense	West
Homer Jones (NY Giants)	SE	Clifton McNeil (San Fran.)
Bob Reynolds (St. Louis)	LT	Charlie Cowan (LA Rams)
John Niland (Dallas)	LG	Tom Mack (LA Rams)
Len Hauss (Washington)	C	Mick Tingelhoff (Minn.)
Gene Hickerson (Cleveland)	RG	Howard Mudd (San Fran.)
Bob Brown (Philadelphia)	RT	Forrest Gregg (Green Bay)
Jackie Smith (St. Louis)	TE	John Mackey (Baltimore)
Don Meredith (Dallas)	QB	Earl Morrall (Baltimore)
Paul Warfield (Cleveland)	FL	Willie Richardson (Balt.)
Leroy Kelly (Cleveland)	RB	Tom Matte (Baltimore)
Don Perkins (Dallas)	RB	Ken Willard (San Francisco)
	Starters, Defense	
Don Brumm (St. Louis)	LE	Deacon Jones (LA Rams)
Walter Johnson (Cleve.)	LT	Merlin Olsen (LA Rams)
Bob Lilly (Dallas)	RT	Alan Page (Minnesota)
George Andrie (Dallas)	RE	Jim Marshall (Minnesota)
Chuck Howley (Dallas)	LLB	Mike Curtis (Baltimore)
Lee Roy Jordan (Dallas)	MLB	Dick Butkus (Chi. Bears)
Chris Hanburger (Wash.)	RLB	Maxie Baughan (LA Rams)
Erich Barnes (Cleveland)	LHB	Lem Barney (Detroit)
Mel Renfro (Dallas)	RHB	Kermit Alexander (SF)
Ernie Kellerman (Cleve.)	LS	Willie Wood (Green Bay)
Larry Wilson (St. Louis)	RS	Roosevelt Taylor (Chi. Bears)

Head coaches—Tom Landry (Dallas), East; George Allen (LA Rams), West

East	0	0	7	0	—	7
West	0	3	0	7	—	10

West—FG Gossett 20
East —Warfield 3 pass from Meredith (Baker kick)
West—Brown 1 run (Gossett kick)
Attendance—32,050

1970 AFL

WEST 26, EAST 3

The Houston Astrodome was the site of the final AFL All-Star game. John Hadl completed 18 of 26 passes for 224 yards and one touchdown in the West's 26-3 victory.

January 17, at Houston

East	Starters, Offense	West
George Sauer (NY Jets)	WR	Fred Biletnikoff (Oakland)
Winston Hill (NY Jets)	LT	Jim Tyrer (Kansas City)
Billy Shaw (Buffalo)	LG	Ed Budde (Kansas City)
Jon Morris (Boston)	C	Jim Otto (Oakland)
Dave Herman (NY Jets)	RG	Walt Sweeney (San Diego)
Glen Ray Hines (Houston)	RT	Harry Schuh (Oakland)
Alvin Reed (Houston)	TE	Billy Cannon (Oakland)
Ron Sellers (Boston)	WR	Lance Alworth (San Diego)
Mike Talliaferro (Boston)	QB	John Hadl (San Diego)
Carl Garrett (Boston)	RB	Dickie Post (San Diego)
Matt Snell (NY Jets)	RB	Robert Holmes (KC)
	Starters, Defense	
Gerry Philbin (NY Jets)	LE	Rich Jackson (Denver)
Jim Hunt (Boston)	LT	Curley Culp (Kansas City)
John Elliott (NY Jets)	RT	Buck Buchanan (KC)
Elvin Bethea (Houston)	RE	Steve DeLong (San Diego)
Garland Boyette (Houston)	LLB	Bobby Bell (Kansas City)
Nick Buoniconti (Miami)	MLB	Willie Lanier (Kansas City)
Larry Grantham (NY Jets)	RLB	Gus Otto (Oakland)
Miller Farr (Houston)	LCB	Jim Marsalis (Kansas City)
Butch Byrd (Buffalo)	RCB	Willie Brown (Oakland)
Ken Houston (Houston)	LS	Kenny Graham (San Diego)
Don Webb (Boston)	RS	Dave Grayson (Oakland)

Head coaches—George Wilson (Miami), East; Lou Saban (Denver), West

East	0	0	3	0	—	3
West	13	0	3	10	—	26

West—Post 1 run (pass failed)
West—Alworth 21 pass from Hadl (Stenerud kick)
West—FG Stenerud 38
East —FG Turner 44
West—FG Stenerud 30
West—Livingston 11 run (Stenerud kick)
Attendance—30,170

1970 NFL

WEST 16, EAST 13

Almost replaying the final minutes of the 1969 game, Los Angeles Rams quarterback Roman Gabriel marched the West 55 yards to the winning touchdown, overcoming a 13-9 East lead.

January 18, at Los Angeles

East	Starters, Offense	West
Paul Warfield (Cleveland)	WR	Gene Washington (Minn.)
Bob Reynolds (St. Louis)	LT	Grady Alderman (Minnesota)
John Niland (Dallas)	LG	Tom Mack (LA Rams)
Len Hauss (Washington)	C	Mick Tingelhoff (Minnesota)
Gene Hickerson (Cleve.)	RG	Gale Gillingham (Green Bay)
Ralph Neely (Dallas)	RT	Charlie Cowan (LA Rams)
Jerry Smith (Washington)	TE	Charlie Sanders (Detroit)
Roy Jefferson (Pitt.)	WR	Carroll Dale (Green Bay)
Bill Nelsen (Cleveland)	QB	Roman Gabriel (LA Rams)
Larry Brown (Washington)	RB	Gale Sayers (Chi. Bears)
Leroy Kelly (Cleveland)	RB	Tom Matte (Baltimore)
	Starters, Defense	
Tim Rossovich (Phil.)	LE	Carl Eller (Minnesota)
Walter Johnson (Cleve.)	LT	Merlin Olsen (LA Rams)
Bob Lilly (Dallas)	RT	Alan Page (Minnesota)
George Andrie (Dallas)	RE	Jim Marshall (Minnesota)
Chris Hanburger (Wash.)	LLB	Dave Robinson (Green Bay)
Dave Lloyd (Philadelphia)	MLB	Dick Butkus (Chi. Bears)
Chuck Howley (Dallas)	RLB	Dave Wilcox (San Fran.)
Pat Fischer (Wash.)	LCB	Lem Barney (Detroit)
Mel Renfro (Dallas)	RCB	Bob Jeter (Green Bay)
Jerry Stovall (St. Louis)	LS	Rick Volk (Baltimore)
Larry Wilson (St. Louis)	RS	Paul Krause (Minnesota)

Head coaches—Tom Fears (New Orleans), East; Norm Van Brocklin (Atlanta), West

East	7	6	0	0	—	13
West	0	7	0	9	—	16

East —Kelly 10 run (Dempsey kick)
East —FG Dempsey 46
West—Gabriel 1 run (Etter kick)
East —FG Dempsey 27
West—Safety, Brezina tackled Walden in end zone
West—Dale 28 pass from Gabriel (Etter kick)
Attendance—57,786

1971

NFC 27, AFC 6

Dallas's Mel Renfro broke open the first game between the all-stars of the American Football Conference and National Football Conference when he returned punts 82 and 56 yards for touchdowns.

January 24, at Los Angeles

AFC	Starters, Offense	NFC
Warren Wells (Oakland)	WR	Gene Washington (SF)
Jim Tyrer (Kansas City)	LT	Charlie Cowan (LA Rams)
Ed Budde (Kansas City)	LG	Tom Mack (LA Rams)
Jim Otto (Oakland)	C	Ed Flanagan (Detroit)
Walt Sweeney (San Diego)	RG	Gale Gillingham (GB)
Harry Schuh (Oakland)	RT	Ernie McMillan (St. Louis)
Raymond Chester (Oak.)	TE	Charlie Sanders (Detroit)
Marlin Briscoe (Buffalo)	WR	Gene Washington (Minn.)
Daryle Lamonica (Oakland)	QB	John Brodie (San Fran.)
Leroy Kelly (Cleveland)	RB	Larry Brown (Washington)
Hewritt Dixon (Oakland)	RB	MacArthur Lane (St. Louis)
	Starters, Defense	
Bubba Smith (Baltimore)	LE	Deacon Jones (LA Rams)
Joe Greene (Pittsburgh)	LT	Alan Page (Minnesota)
Buck Buchanan (KC)	RT	Bob Lilly (Dallas)
Rich Jackson (Denver)	RE	Carl Eller (Minnesota)
Bobby Bell (Kansas City)	LLB	Larry Stallings (St. Louis)
Willie Lanier (Kansas City)	MLB	Dick Butkus (Chi. Bears)
Andy Russell (Pittsburgh)	RLB	Fred Carr (Green Bay)
Jim Marsalis (Kansas City)	LCB	Jimmy Johnson (San Fran.)
Willie Brown (Oakland)	RCB	Mel Renfro (Dallas)
Ken Houston (Houston)	LS	Willie Wood (Green Bay)
Johnny Robinson (KC)	RS	Larry Wilson (St. Louis)

Head coaches—John Madden (Oakland), AFC; Dick Nolan (San Francisco), NFC

AFC	0	3	3	0	—	6
NFC	0	3	10	14	—	27

AFC—FG Stenerud 37
NFC—FG Cox 13
NFC—Osborn 23 pass from Brodie (Cox kick)
NFC—FG Cox 35
AFC—FG Stenerud 16
NFC—Renfro 82 punt return (Cox kick)
NFC—Renfro 56 punt return (Cox kick)
Attendance—48,222

1972

AFC 26, NFC 13

Len Dawson entered the game as quarterback in the third quarter and directed the AFC to two touchdowns and three field goals for a 26-13 victory.

January 23, at Los Angeles

NFC	Starters, Offense	AFC
Gene Washington (SF)	WR	Fred Biletnikoff (Oakland)
Ron Yary (Minnesota)	LT	Jim Tyrer (Kansas City)
John Niland (Dallas)	LG	Ed Budde (Kansas City)
Forrest Blue (San Fran.)	C	Bill Curry (Baltimore)
Gale Gillingham (GB)	RG	Walt Sweeney (San Diego)
George Kunz (Atlanta)	RT	Winston Hill (NY Jets)
Ted Kwalick (San Fran.)	TE	Raymond Chester (Oak.)
Dick Gordon (Chi. Bears)	WR	Paul Warfield (Miami)
Roger Staubach (Dallas)	QB	Bob Griese (Miami)
Larry Brown (Washington)	RB	Larry Csonka (Miami)
Steve Owens (Detroit)	RB	Floyd Little (Denver)
	Starters, Defense	
Claude Humphrey (Atlanta)	LE	Bubba Smith (Baltimore)
Alan Page (Minnesota)	LT	Joe Greene (Pittsburgh)
Bob Lilly (Dallas)	RT	Buck Buchanan (KC)
Cedric Hardman (SF)	RE	Elvin Bethea (Houston)
Dave Wilcox (San Fran.)	LLB	Ted Hendricks (Baltimore)
Dick Butkus (Chi. Bears)	MLB	Mike Curtis (Baltimore)
Chuck Howley (Dallas)	RLB	Bobby Bell (Kansas City)
Jimmy Johnson (San Fran.)	LCB	Emmitt Thomas (KC)
Roger Wehrli (St. Louis)	RCB	Willie Brown (Oakland)
Cornell Green (Dallas)	LS	Ken Houston (Houston)
Mel Renfro (Dallas)	RS	Rick Volk (Baltimore)

Head coaches—Don McCafferty (Baltimore), AFC; Dick Nolan (San Francisco), NFC

NFC	0	6	0	7	—	13
AFC	0	3	13	10	—	26

NFC—Grim 50 pass from Landry (kick failed)
AFC—FG Stenerud 25
AFC—FG Stenerud 23
AFC—FG Stenerud 48
AFC—Morin 5 pass from Dawson (Stenerud kick)
AFC—FG Stenerud 42
NFC—V. Washington 2 run (Knight kick)
AFC—F. Little 6 run (Stenerud kick)
Attendance—53,647

1973

AFC 33, NFC 28

The Pro Bowl left Los Angeles after 22 years.

January 21, at Irving

AFC	Starters, Offense	NFC
Otis Taylor (Kansas City)	WR	Gene Washington (SF)
Art Shell (Oakland)	LT	Ron Yary (Minnesota)
Gene Upshaw (Oakland)	LG	John Niland (Dallas)
Jim Otto (Oakland)	C	Forrest Blue (San Fran.)
Larry Little (Miami)	RG	Tom Mack (LA Rams)
Winston Hill (NY Jets)	RT	Rayfield Wright (Dallas)
Raymond Chester (Oakland)	TE	Ted Kwalick (San Fran.)
Gary Garrison (San Diego)	WR	John Gilliam (Minnesota)
Daryle Lamonica (Oakland)	QB	Billy Kilmer (Washington)
O. J. Simpson (Buffalo)	RB	Ron Johnson (NY Giants)
Franco Harris (Pittsburgh)	RB	John Brockington (GB)
	Starters, Defense	
Deacon Jones (San Diego)	LE	Claude Humphrey (Atlanta)
Joe Greene (Pittsburgh)	LT	Merlin Olsen (LA Rams)
Mike Reid (Cincinnati)	RT	Bob Brown (Green Bay)
Elvin Bethea (Houston)	RE	Coy Bacon (LA Rams)
Ted Hendricks (Baltimore)	LLB	Dave Wilcox (San Fran.)
Willie Lanier (Kansas City)	MLB	Tommy Nobis (Atlanta)
Andy Russell (Pittsburgh)	RLB	Chris Hanburger (Wash.)
Robert James (Buffalo)	LCB	Jimmy Johnson (SF)
Willie Brown (Oakland)	RCB	Lem Barney (Detroit)
Ken Houston (Houston)	LS	Cornell Green (Dallas)
Jake Scott (Miami)	RS	Bill Bradley (Philadelphia)

Head coaches—Chuck Noll (Pittsburgh), AFC; Tom Landry (Dallas), NFC

AFC	0	10	10	13	—	33
NFC	14	0	0	14	—	28

NFC—Brockington 1 run (Marcol kick)
NFC—Brockington 3 pass from Kilmer (Marcol kick)
AFC—Simpson 7 run (Gerela kick)
AFC—FG Gerela 18
AFC—FG Gerela 22
AFC—Hubbard 11 run (Gerela kick)
AFC—Taylor 5 pass from Lamonica (no kick; bad snap)
AFC—Bell 12 interception return (Gerela kick)
NFC—Brockington 1 run (Marcol kick)
NFC—Kwalick 12 pass from Snead (Marcol kick)
Attendance—47,879

1974

AFC 15, NFC 13

Garo Yepremian kicked five field goals in five attempts, the last with 21 seconds remaining, for all of the AFC's points in a 15-13 victory.

January 20, at Kansas City

NFC	Starters, Offense	AFC
Charley Taylor (Washington)	WR	Isaac Curtis (Cincinnati)
Ron Yary (Minnesota)	LT	Art Shell (Oakland)
Tom Mack (LA Rams)	LG	Gene Upshaw (Oakland)
Forrest Blue (San Fran.)	C	Jim Langer (Miami)
John Niland (Dallas)	RG	Larry Little (Miami)
Rayfield Wright (Dallas)	RT	Winston Hill (NY Jets)
Ted Kwalick (San Fran.)	TE	Riley Odoms (Denver)
Harold Jackson (LA Rams)	WR	Fred Biletnikoff (Oakland)
John Hadl (LA Rams)	QB	Ken Stabler (Oakland)
Chuck Foreman (Minn.)	RB	O. J. Simpson (Buffalo)
John Brockington (GB)	RB	Marv Hubbard (Oakland)
	Starters, Defense	
John Zook (Atlanta)	LE	L. C. Greenwood (Pitt.)
Merlin Olsen (LA Rams)	LT	Joe Greene (Pittsburgh)
Alan Page (Minnesota)	RT	Paul Smith (Denver)
Claude Humphrey (Atlanta)	RE	Elvin Bethea (Houston)
Dave Wilcox (San Fran.)	LLB	Ted Hendricks (Baltimore)
Jeff Siemon (Minnesota)	MLB	Willie Lanier (Kansas City)
Chris Hanburger (Wash.)	RLB	Andy Russell (Pittsburgh)
Lem Barney (Detroit)	LCB	Clarence Scott (Cleveland)
Mel Renfro (Dallas)	RCB	Willie Brown (Oakland)
Ken Houston (Washington)	LS	Dick Anderson (Miami)
Paul Krause (Minnesota)	RS	Jake Scott (Miami)

Head coach—John Madden (Oakland), AFC; Tom Landry (Dallas), NFC

NFC	0	10	0	3	—	13
AFC	3	3	3	6	—	15

AFC—FG Yepremian 16
NFC—FG Mike-Mayer 27
NFC—McCutcheon 14 pass from Gabriel (Mike-Mayer kick)
AFC—FG Yepremian 37
AFC—FG Yepremian 27
AFC—FG Yepremian 41
NFC—FG Mike-Mayer 21
AFC—FG Yepremian 42
Attendance—51,482

1975

NFC 17, AFC 10

James Harris, a pregame roster replacement for the injured Fran Tarkenton, and a second-quarter quarterback substitute for the injured Jim Hart, threw two eight-yard touchdown passes in the fourth quarter, and the NFC won the first night-time Pro Bowl game.

January 20, at Miami

NFC	Starters, Offense	AFC
Charley Taylor (Washington)	WR	Cliff Branch (Oakland)
Ron Yary (Minnesota)	LT	Art Shell (Oakland)
Tom Mack (LA Rams)	LG	Gene Upshaw (Oakland)
Jeff Van Note (Atlanta)	C	Jim Langer (Miami)
Gale Gillingham (GB)	RG	Larry Little (Miami)
Rayfield Wright (Dallas)	RT	Russ Washington (SD)
Charle Young (Philadelphia)	TE	Riley Odoms (Denver)
Drew Pearson (Dallas)	WR	Isaac Curtis (Cincinnati)
Jim Hart (St. Louis)	QB	Ken Stabler (Oakland)
Chuck Foreman (Minnesota)	RB	O. J. Simpson (Buffalo)
L. McCutcheon (LA Rams)	RB	Otis Armstrong (Denver)
	Starters, Defense	
Carl Eller (Minnesota)	LE	L. C. Greenwood (Pitt.)
Merlin Olsen (LA Rams)	LT	Joe Greene (Pittsburgh)
Alan Page (Minnesota)	RT	Jerry Sherk (Cleveland)
Claude Humphrey (Atlanta)	RE	Bill Stanfill (Miami)
Ted Hendricks (Green Bay)	LLB	Jack Ham (Pittsburgh)
Bill Bergey (Philadelphia)	MLB	Mike Curtis (Baltimore)
Chris Hanburger (Wash.)	RLB	Andy Russell (Pittsburgh)
Willie Buchanon (GB)	LCB	Robert James (Buffalo)
Roger Wehrli (St. Louis)	RCB	Emmitt Thomas (KC)
Ken Houston (Washington)	LS	Dick Anderson (Miami)
Paul Krause (Minnesota)	RS	Jack Tatum (Oakland)

Head coaches—John Madden (Oakland), AFC; Chuck Knox (LA Rams), NFC

NFC	0	3	0	14	—	17
AFC	0	0	10	0	—	10

NFC—FG Marcol 33
AFC—Warfield 32 pass from Griese (Gerela kick)
AFC—FG Gerela 33
NFC—Gray 8 pass from J. Harris (Marcol kick)
NFC—Taylor 8 pass from J. Harris (Marcol kick)
Attendance—26,484

1976

NFC 23, AFC 20

Quarterback replacement Mike Boryla threw two touchdown passes after entering the game with 5:39 remaining. Billy Johnson had 233 yards in returns.

January 26, at New Orleans

AFC	Starters, Offense	NFC
Isaac Curtis (Cincinnati)	WR	Mel Gray (St. Louis)
Art Shell (Oakland)	LT	Ron Yary (Minnesota)
Gene Upshaw (Oakland)	LG	Ed White (Minnesota)
Jim Langer (Miami)	C	Tom Banks (St. Louis)
Bob Kuechenberg (Miami)	RG	Conrad Dobler (St. Louis)
George Kunz (Baltimore)	RT	Dan Dierdorf (St. Louis)
Riley Odoms (Denver)	TE	Charle Young (Philadelphia)
Lynn Swann (Pittsburgh)	WR	John Gilliam (Minnesota)
Ken Anderson (Cincinnati)	QB	Jim Hart (St. Louis)
O. J. Simpson (Buffalo)	RB	Terry Metcalf (St. Louis)
Franco Harris (Pittsburgh)	RB	Chuck Foreman (Minnesota)
	Starters, Defense	
L. C. Greenwood (Pitt.)	LE	Jack Youngblood (LA Rams)
Joe Greene (Pittsburgh)	LT	Merlin Olsen (LA Rams)
Jerry Sherk (Cleveland)	RT	Alan Page (Minnesota)
John Dutton (Baltimore)	RE	Cedrick Hardman (SF)
Jack Ham (Pittsburgh)	LLB	Isiah Robertson (LA Rams)
Jack Lambert (Pittsburgh)	MLB	Jeff Siemon (Minnesota)
Andy Russell (Pittsburgh)	RLB	Chris Hanburger (Wash.)
Lemar Parrish (Cincinnati)	LCB	Lem Barney (Detroit)
Mel Blount (Pittsburgh)	RCB	Roger Wehrli (St. Louis)
Mike Wagner (Pittsburgh)	LS	Ken Houston (Washington)
Jake Scott (Miami)	RS	Cliff Harris (Dallas)

Head coaches—John Madden (Oakland), AFC; Chuck Knox (LA Rams), NFC

AFC	0	13	0	7	—	20
NFC	0	0	9	14	—	23

AFC—FG Stenerud 20
AFC—FG Stenerud 35
AFC—Burrough 64 pass from Pastorini (Stenerud kick)
NFC—FG Bakken 42
NFC—Foreman 4 pass from Hart (kick blocked)
AFC—Johnson 90 punt return (Stenerud kick)
NFC—Metcalf 14 pass from Boryla (Bakken kick)
NFC—Gray 8 pass from Boryla (Bakken kick)
Attendance—32,108

1977

AFC 24, NFC 14

The AFC intercepted six passes—five by members of the Pittsburgh Steelers, including two by cornerback Mel Blount—in a 24-14 victory. The crowd of 63,214 was the largest since 1964.

January 17, at Seattle

NFC	Starters, Offense	AFC
Mel Gray (St. Louis)	WR	Cliff Branch (Oakland)
Ron Yary (Minnesota)	LT	Art Shell (Oakland)
Ed White (Minnesota)	LG	John Hannah (New England)
Tom Banks (St. Louis)	C	Jim Langer (Miami)
Conrad Dobler (St. Louis)	RG	Joe DeLamielleure (Buffalo)
Dan Dierdorf (St. Louis)	RT	George Kunz (Baltimore)
Billy Joe DuPree (Dallas)	TE	Dave Casper (Oakland)
Drew Pearson (Dallas)	WR	Isaac Curtis (Cincinnati)
Roger Staubach (Dallas)	QB	Bert Jones (Baltimore)
Walter Payton (Chi. Bears)	RB	O. J. Simpson (Buffalo)
Delvin Williams (San Fran.)	RB	Lydell Mitchell (Baltimore)
	Starters, Defense	
Tommy Hart (San Francisco)	LE	Coy Bacon (Cincinnati)
Cleveland Elam (San Fran.)	LT	Curley Culp (Houston)
Wally Chambers (Chi. Bears)	RT	Jerry Sherk (Cleveland)
Jack Youngblood (LA Rams)	RE	John Dutton (Baltimore)
Isiah Robertson (LA Rams)	LLB	Jack Ham (Pittsburgh)
Bill Bergey (Philadelphia)	MLB	Jack Lambert (Pittsburgh)
Brad Van Pelt (NY Giants)	RLB	Robert Brazile (Houston)
Monte Jackson (LA Rams)	LCB	Lemar Parrish (Cincinnati)
Roger Wehrli (St. Louis)	RCB	Mel Blount (Pittsburgh)
Ken Houston (Washington)	LS	Tommy Casanova (Cin.)
Cliff Harris (Dallas)	RS	Glen Edwards (Pittsburgh)

Coaches—Chuck Noll (Pittsburgh), AFC; Chuck Knox (LA Rams), NFC.

NFC	0	14	0	0	—	14
AFC	10	7	0	7	—	24

AFC—Simpson 3 run (Linhart kick)
AFC—FG Linhart 31
NFC—Thomas 15 run (Bakken kick)
AFC—Joiner 12 pass from Anderson (Linhart kick)
NFC—McCutcheon 1 run (Bakken kick)
AFC—Branch 27 pass from Anderson (Linhart kick)
Attendance—63,214

1978

NFC 14, AFC 13

Quarterback Jim Hart replaced starter Pat Haden in the fourth quarter and completed five of six passes in a 63-yard drive that led to the winning touchdown. Player of the game Walter Payton gained 77 yards and scored the winning touchdown.

January 23, at Tampa

AFC	Starters, Offense	NFC
Lynn Swann (Pittsburgh)	WR	Drew Pearson (Dallas)
Art Shell (Oakland)	LT	Dan Dierdorf (St. Louis)
Gene Upshaw (Oakland)	LG	Ed White (Minnesota)
Jim Langer (Miami)	C	Tom Banks (St. Louis)
Joe DeLamielleure (Buffalo)	RG	Conrad Dobler (St. Louis)
George Kunz (Baltimore)	RT	Ron Yary (Minnesota)
Dave Casper (Oakland)	TE	Billy Joe DuPree (Dallas)
Nat Moore (Miami)	WR	Sammy White (Minnesota)
Bob Griese (Miami)	QB	Pat Haden (LA Rams)
Franco Harris (Pittsburgh)	RB	L. McCutcheon (LA Rams)
Lydell Mitchell (Baltimore)	RB	Walter Payton (Chi. Bears)
	Starters, Defense	
John Dutton (Baltimore)	LE	Jack Youngblood (LA Rams)
Mike Barnes (Baltimore)	LT	Cleveland Elam (San Fran.)
Curley Culp (Houston)	RT	Larry Brooks (LA Rams)
Lyle Alzado (Denver)	RE	Harvey Martin (Dallas)
Jack Ham (Pittsburgh)	LLB	Brad Van Pelt (NY Giants)
Randy Gradishar (Denver)	MLB	Bill Bergey (Philadelphia)
Robert Brazile (Houston)	RLB	Isiah Robertson (LA Rams)
Lemar Parrish (Cincinnati)	LCB	Rolland Lawrence (Atlanta)
Mike Haynes (New Eng.)	RCB	Roger Wehrli (St. Louis)
Billy Thompson (Denver)	LS	Charlie Waters (Dallas)
Tommy Casanova (Cin.)	RS	Cliff Harris (Dallas)

Coaches—Ted Marchibroda (Baltimore), AFC; Chuck Knox (LA Rams), NFC

AFC	3	10	0	0	—	13
NFC	0	0	7	7	—	14

AFC—FG Linhart 21
AFC—Branch 10 pass from Stabler (Linhart kick)
AFC—FG Linhart 39
NFC—Metcalf 4 pass from Haden (Herrera kick)
NFC—Payton 1 run (Herrera kick)
Attendance—51,337

1979

NFC 13, AFC 7

Quarterback Roger Staubach completed 9 of 15 passes for 125 yards, including one for the winning touchdown to Dallas Cowboys teammate Tony Hill in the third quarter. Ahmad Rashad caught five passes and was named player of the game. The victory gave the NFC a 5-4 advantage in AFC-NFC Pro Bowl games.

January 29, at Los Angeles

AFC	Starters, Offense	NFC
Lynn Swann (Pittsburgh)	WR	Harold Carmichael (Phil.)
Leon Gray (New England)	LT	Doug France (LA Rams)
John Hannah (New Eng.)	LG	Bob Young (St. Louis)
Mike Webster (Pittsburgh)	C	Tom Banks (St. Louis)
Joe DeLamielleure (Buffalo)	RG	Dennis Harrah (LA Rams)
Russ Washington (SD)	RT	Dan Dierdorf (St. Louis)
Dave Casper (Oakland)	TE	Billy Joe DuPree (Dallas)
Wesley Walker (NY Jets)	WR	Ahmad Rashad (Minnesota)
Terry Bradshaw (Pittsburgh)	QB	Roger Staubach (Dallas)
Earl Campbell (Houston)	RB	Tony Dorsett (Dallas)
Delvin Williams (Miami)	RB	Walter Payton (Chi. Bears)
	Starters, Defense	
Lyle Alzado (Denver)	LE	Jack Youngblood (LA Rams)
Joe Greene (Pittsburgh)	LT	Doug English (Detroit)
Louie Kelcher (San Diego)	RT	Dave Pear (Tampa Bay)
Elvin Bethea (Houston)	RE	Al Baker (Detroit)
Robert Brazile (Houston)	LLB	Matt Blair (Minnesota)
Randy Gradishar (Denver)	MLB	Bill Bergey (Philadelphia)
Jack Ham (Pittsburgh)	RLB	Brad Van Pelt (NY Giants)
Louis Wright (Denver)	LCB	Willie Buchanon (GB)
Mike Haynes (New Eng.)	RCB	Pat Thomas (LA Rams)
Billy Thompson (Denver)	LS	Charlie Waters (Dallas)
Thom Darden (Cleveland)	RS	Cliff Harris (Dallas)

Coaches—Chuck Fairbanks (New England), AFC; Bud Grant (Minnesota), NFC

AFC	0	7	0	0	—	7
NFC	0	6	7	0	—	13

NFC—Montgomery 2 run (kick failed)
AFC—Largent 8 pass from Griese (Yepremian kick)
NFC—T. Hill 19 pass from Staubach (Corral kick)
Attendance—46,281

1980

NFC 37, AFC 27

The game was the first played in a non-NFL city.

January 27, at Honolulu

NFC	Starters, Offense	AFC
Ahmad Rashad (Minnesota)	WR	John Stallworth (Pittsburgh)
Stan Walters (Philadelphia)	LT	Leon Gray (Houston)
Bob Young (St. Louis)	LG	John Hannah (New Eng.)
Rich Saul (LA Rams)	C	Mike Webster (Pittsburgh)
Dennis Harrah (LA Rams)	RG	Joe DeLamielleure (Buffalo)
Pat Donovan (Dallas)	RT	Russ Washington (SD)
Henry Childs (New Orleans)	TE	Dave Casper (Oakland)
Harold Carmichael (Phil.)	WR	John Jefferson (San Diego)
Roger Staubach (Dallas)	QB	Dan Fouts (San Diego)
Ottis Anderson (St. Louis)	RB	Earl Campbell (Houston)
Walter Payton (Chi. Bears)	RB	Franco Harris (Pittsburgh)
	Starters, Defense	
Jack Youngblood (LA Rams)	LE	L.C. Greenwood (Pitt.)
Charlie Johnson (Phil.)	LT	Joe Greene (Pittsburgh)
Randy White (Dallas)	RT	Bob Baumhower (Miami)
Harvey Martin (Dallas)	RE	Fred Dean (San Diego)
Brad Van Pelt (NY Giants)	LLB	Kim Bokamper (Miami)
Harry Carson (NY Giants)	MLB	Jack Lambert (Pittsburgh)
Jim Youngblood (LA Rams)	RLB	Robert Brazile (Houston)
Lemar Parrish (Wash.)	LCB	Louis Wright (Denver)
Roger Wehrli (St. Louis)	RCB	Mike Haynes (New Eng.)
Randy Logan (Philadelphia)	LS	Donnie Shell (Pittsburgh)
Tom Myers (New Orleans)	RS	Mike Reinfeldt (Houston)

Coaches—Don Coryell (San Diego), AFC; Tom Landry (Dallas), NFC

NFC	3	20	7	7	—	37
AFC	3	7	10	7	—	27

NFC—FG Moseley 37
AFC—FG Fritsch 19
NFC—Muncie 1 run (Moseley kick)
AFC—Pruitt 1 pass from Bradshaw (Fritsch kick)
NFC—D. Hill 13 pass from Manning (kick failed)
NFC—T. Hill 25 pass from Muncie (Moseley kick)
NFC—Henry 86 punt return (Moseley kick)
AFC—Campbell 2 run (Fritsch kick)
AFC—FG Fritsch 29
NFC—Muncie 11 run (Moseley kick)
AFC—Campbell 1 run (Fritsch kick)
Attendance—48,060

1981

NFC 21, AFC 7

Player of the game Ed Murray kicked four field goals, and Steve Bartkowski threw a 55-yard touchdown pass to Alfred Jenkins in the fourth quarter.

February 1, at Honolulu

AFC	Starters, Offense	NFC
Stanley Morgan (NE)	WR	Harold Carmichael (Phil.)
Doug Dieken (Cleveland)	LT	Mike Kenn (Atlanta)
John Hannah (New Eng.)	LG	Herbert Scott (Dallas)
Mike Webster (Pittsburgh)	C	Rich Saul (LA Rams)
Joe DeLamielleure (Cleve.)	RG	Kent Hill (LA Rams)
Marvin Powell (NY Jets)	RT	Dan Dierdorf (St. Louis)
Kellen Winslow (San Diego)	TE	Jimmie Giles (Tampa Bay)
John Jefferson (San Diego)	WR	James Lofton (Green Bay)
Brian Sipe (Cleveland)	QB	Steve Bartkowski (Atlanta)
Earl Campbell (Houston)	RB	Walter Payton (Chi. Bears)
Mike Pruitt (Cleveland)	RB	Ottis Anderson (St. Louis)
	Starters, Defense	
Art Still (Kansas City)	LE	Al Baker (Detroit)
Louie Kelcher (San Diego)	LT	Charlie Johnson (Phil.)
Gary Johnson (San Diego)	RT	Randy White (Dallas)
Fred Dean (San Diego)	RE	Lee Roy Selmon (TB)
Ted Hendricks (Oakland)	LLB	Brad Van Pelt (NY Giants)
Jack Lambert (Pittsburgh)	MLB	Bob Breunig (Dallas)
Robert Brazile (Houston)	RLB	Matt Blair (Minnesota)
Lester Hayes (Oakland)	LCB	Lemar Parrish (Washington)
Mike Haynes (New Eng.)	RCB	Rod Perry (LA Rams)
Donnie Shell (Pittsburgh)	LS	Randy Logan (Philadelphia)
Gary Barbaro (Kansas City)	RS	Nolan Cromwell (LA Rams)

Coaches—Sam Rutigliano (Cleveland), AFC; Leeman Bennett (Atlanta), NFC

AFC	0	7	0	0	—	7
NFC	3	6	0	12	—	21

NFC—FG Murray 31
AFC—Morgan 9 pass from Sipe (J. Smith kick)
NFC—FG Murray 31
NFC—FG Murray 34
NFC—Jenkins 55 pass from Bartkowski (Murray kick)
NFC—FG Murray 36
NFC—Safety, AFC holding in end zone
Attendance—47,879

1982

AFC 16, NFC 13

Nick Lowery kicked a 23-yard field goal with three seconds left in the game to give the AFC its first Pro Bowl victory in five years, 16-13. The NFC had tied the game just over two-and-a-half minutes earlier when Tony Dorsett scored on a four-yard run.

January 31, at Honolulu

NFC	Starters, Offense	AFC
James Lofton (Green Bay)	WR	Cris Collinsworth (Cin.)
Pat Donovan (Dallas)	LT	Anthony Muñoz (Cincinnati)
Herbert Scott (Dallas)	LG	Doug Wilkerson (San Diego)
Rich Saul (LA Rams)	C	Mike Webster (Pittsburgh)
Randy Cross (San Fran.)	RG	John Hannah (New Eng.)
Mike Kenn (Atlanta)	RT	Marvin Powell (NY Jets)
Jimmie Giles (Tampa Bay)	TE	Kellen Winslow (San Diego)
Alfred Jenkins (Atlanta)	WR	Frank Lewis (Buffalo)
Joe Montana (San Fran.)	QB	Ken Anderson (Cincinnati)
Tony Dorsett (Dallas)	RB	Pete Johnson (Cincinnati)
Billy Sims (Detroit)	RB	Joe Delaney (Kansas City)
	Starters, Defense	
Ed Jones (Dallas)	LE	Mark Gastineau (NY Jets)
Doug English (Detroit)	LT	Bob Baumhower (Miami)
Randy White (Dallas)	RT	Gary Johnson (San Diego)
Lee Roy Selmon (TB)	RE	Joe Klecko (NY Jets)
Lawrence Taylor (NYG)	LLB	Ted Hendricks (Oakland)
Harry Carson (NY Giants)	MLB	Jack Lambert (Pittsburgh)
Matt Blair (Minnesota)	RLB	Robert Brazile (Houston)
Roynell Young (Phil.)	LCB	Lester Hayes (Oakland)
Ronnie Lott (San Fran.)	RCB	Mel Blount (Pittsburgh)
Gary Fencik (Chi. Bears)	LS	Donnie Shell (Pittsburgh)
Nolan Cromwell (LA Rams)	RS	Gary Barbaro (Kansas City)

Coaches—Don Shula (Miami), AFC; John McKay (Tampa Bay), NFC

NFC	0	6	0	7	—	13
AFC	0	0	13	3	—	16

NFC—Giles 4 pass from Montana (kick blocked)
AFC—Muncie 2 run (kick failed)
AFC—Campbell 1 run (Lowery kick)
NFC—Dorsett 4 run (Septien kick)
AFC—FG Lowery 23
Attendance—50,402

1983

NFC 20, AFC 19

Danny White led the NFC on a 65-yard drive capped by an 11-yard touchdown pass to John Jefferson with 35 seconds left to give the NFC a 20-19 victory.

February 6, at Honolulu

AFC	Starters, Offense	NFC
Cris Collinsworth (Cin.)	WR	James Lofton (Green Bay)
Anthony Muñoz (Cincinnati)	LT	Pat Donovan (Dallas)
Doug Wilkerson (San Diego)	LG	R.C. Thielemann (Atlanta)
Mike Webster (Pittsburgh)	C	Jeff Van Note (Atlanta)
John Hannah (New Eng.)	RG	Randy Cross (San Fran.)
Marvin Powell (NY Jets)	RT	Mike Kenn (Atlanta)
Kellen Winslow (San Diego)	TE	Jimmie Giles (Tampa Bay)
Wes Chandler (San Diego)	WR	Dwight Clark (San Fran.)
Dan Fouts (San Diego)	QB	Joe Theismann (Wash.)
Chuck Muncie (San Diego)	RB	William Andrews (Atlanta)
Freeman McNeil (NY Jets)	RB	Tony Dorsett (Dallas)
	Starters, Defense	
Mark Gastineau (NY Jets)	LE	Ed Jones (Dallas)
Fred Smerlas (Buffalo)	LT	Doug English (Detroit)
Gary Johnson (San Diego)	RT	Randy White (Dallas)
Art Still (Kansas City)	RE	Lee Roy Selmon (TB)
Ted Hendricks (LA Raiders)	LLB	Lawrence Taylor (NYG)
Jack Lambert (Pittsburgh)	MLB	Harry Carson (NY Giants)
Robert Brazile (Houston)	RLB	Hugh Green (Tampa Bay)
Mike Haynes (New Eng.)	LCB	Mark Haynes (NY Giants)
Lester Hayes (LA Raiders)	RCB	Everson Walls (Dallas)
Donnie Shell (Pittsburgh)	SS	Tony Peters (Washington)
Gary Barbaro (Kansas City)	FS	Nolan Cromwell (LA Rams)

Coaches—Walt Michaels (NY Jets), AFC; Tom Landry (Dallas), NFC

AFC	9	3	7	0	—	19
NFC	0	10	0	10	—	20

AFC—Walker 34 pass from Fouts (Benirschke kick)
AFC—Safety, Still tackled Theismann in end zone
NFC—Andrews 3 run (Moseley kick)
NFC—FG Moseley 35
AFC—FG Benirschke 29
AFC—Allen 1 run (Benirschke kick)
NFC—FG Moseley 41
NFC—Jefferson 11 pass from D. White (Moseley kick)
Attendance—47,201

1984

NFC 45, AFC 3

Player of the game Joe Theismann set records with 21 completions and three touchdown passes, while throwing for 242 yards and rushing for 12 more.

January 29, at Honolulu

NFC	Starters, Offense	AFC
James Lofton (Green Bay)	WR	Carlos Carson (Kansas City)
Mike Kenn (Atlanta)	LT	Anthony Muñoz (Cincinnati)
Kent Hill (LA Rams)	LG	Chris Hinton (Baltimore)
Jeff Bostic (Washington)	C	Dwight Stephenson (Miami)
Russ Grimm (Washington)	RG	Ed Newman (Miami)
Joe Jacoby (Washington)	RT	Brian Holloway (New Eng.)
Paul Coffman (Green Bay)	TE	T. Christensen (LA Raiders)
Mike Quick (Philadelphia)	WR	Cris Collinsworth (Cin.)
Joe Theismann (Wash.)	QB	Dan Fouts (San Diego)
Eric Dickerson (LA Rams)	RB	Curt Warner (Seattle)
William Andrews (Atlanta)	RB	Earl Campbell (Houston)
	Starters, Defense	
Ed Jones (Dallas)	LE	Doug Betters (Miami)
Doug English (Detroit)	LT	Fred Smerlas (Buffalo)
Randy White (Dallas)	RT	Bob Baumhower (Miami)
Lee Roy Selmon (TB)	RE	Howie Long (LA Raiders)
Hugh Green (Tampa Bay)	LLB	Chip Banks (Cleveland)
Mike Singletary (Chi. Bears)	MLB	Jack Lambert (Pittsburgh)
Lawrence Taylor (NYG)	RLB	Rod Martin (LA Raiders)
Ronnie Lott (San Fran.)	LCB	Lester Hayes (LA Raiders)
Everson Walls (Dallas)	RCB	Gary Green (Kansas City)
Nolan Cromwell (LA Rams)	SS	Kenny Easley (Seattle)
Mark Murphy (Washington)	FS	Deron Cherry (Kansas City)

Coaches—Chuck Knox (Seattle), AFC; Bill Walsh (San Francisco), NFC

NFC	3	14	14	14	—	45
AFC	0	3	0	0	—	3

NFC—FG Haji-Sheikh 23
NFC—Andrews 16 pass from Theismann (Haji-Sheikh kick)
NFC—Andrews 2 pass from Montana (Haji-Sheikh kick)
AFC—FG Anderson 43
NFC—Cromwell 44 interception return (Haji-Sheikh kick)
NFC—Lofton 8 pass from Theismann (Haji-Sheikh kick)
NFC—Coffman 6 pass from Theismann (Haji-Sheikh kick)
NFC—Dickerson 14 run (Haji-Sheikh kick)
Attendance—50,445

1985

AFC 22, NFC 14

Art Still of Kansas City recovered a fumble and returned it 83 yards for a touchdown to clinch a 22–14 victory for the AFC. The teams combined for a record 17 sacks, 9 by the AFC and 8 by the NFC.

January 27, at Honolulu

AFC	Starters, Offense	NFC
Mark Duper (Miami)	WR	Roy Green (St. Louis)
Anthony Muñoz (Cincinnati)	LT	Joe Jacoby (Washington)
John Hannah (New Eng.)	LG	Russ Grimm (Washington)
Dwight Stephenson (Miami)	C	Fred Quillan (San Fran.)
Ed Newman (Miami)	RG	Randy Cross (San Fran.)
Brian Holloway (New Eng.)	RT	Mike Kenn (Atlanta)
Ozzie Newsome (Cleve.)	TE	Paul Coffman (Green Bay)
John Stallworth (Pitt.)	WR	James Lofton (Green Bay)
Dan Marino (Miami)	QB	Joe Montana (San Fran.)
Marcus Allen (LA Raiders)	RB	Eric Dickerson (LA Rams)
Sammy Winder (Denver)	RB	Walter Payton (Chi. Bears)
	Starters, Defense	
Mark Gastineau (NY Jets)	LE	Richard Dent (Chi. Bears)
Joe Nash (Seattle)	NT	Dan Hampton (Chi. Bears)
Howie Long (LA Raiders)	RE	Lee Roy Selmon (TB)
Mike Merriweather (Pitt.)	LOLB	Lawrence Taylor (NYG)
Steve Nelson (New Eng.)	LILB	Mike Singletary (Chi. Bears)
Robin Cole (Pittsburgh)	RILB	E.J. Junior (St. Louis)
Rod Martin (LA Raiders)	ROLB	Rickey Jackson (NO)
Lester Hayes (LA Raiders)	LCB	Ronnie Lott (San Fran.)
Dave Brown (Seattle)	RCB	Darrell Green (Washington)
Kenny Easley (Seattle)	SS	Todd Bell (Chi. Bears)
Vann McElroy (LA Raiders)	FS	Dwight Hicks (San Fran.)

Coaches—Chuck Noll (Pittsburgh), AFC; Mike Ditka (Chi. Bears), NFC

AFC	0	9	0	13	—	22
NFC	0	0	7	7	—	14

AFC—Safety, Gastineau tackled Dickerson in end zone
AFC—Allen 6 pass from Marino (Johnson kick)
NFC—Lofton 13 pass from Marino (Stenerud kick)
NFC—Payton 1 run (Stenerud kick)
AFC—Still 83 fumble return (Johnson kick)
AFC—FG Johnson 22
Attendance—50,385

1986

NFC 28, AFC 24

Player of the game Phil Simms threw three second-half touchdown passes, the last with 5:10 left, to lead the NFC from a 24-7 deficit to a 28-24 victory.

February 2, at Honolulu

NFC	Starters, Offense	AFC
Mike Quick (Philadelphia)	WR	Louis Lipps (Pittsburgh)
Jim Covert (Chi. Bears)	LT	Anthony Muñoz (Cincinnati)
Kent Hill (LA Rams)	LG	John Hannah (New Eng.)
Jay Hilgenberg (Chi. Bears)	C	Dwight Stephenson (Miami)
Russ Grimm (Washington)	RG	Mike Munchak (Houston)
Jackie Slater (LA Rams)	RT	Brian Holloway (New Eng.)
Doug Cosbie (Dallas)	TE	Ozzie Newsome (Cleve.)
Art Monk (Washington)	WR	Steve Largent (Seattle)
Phil Simms (NY Giants)	QB	Dan Fouts (San Diego)
Walter Payton (Chi. Bears)	RB	Marcus Allen (LA Raiders)
Roger Craig (San Fran.)	RB	Freeman McNeil (NY Jets)
	Starters, Defense	
Richard Dent (Chi. Bears)	LE	Mark Gastineau (NY Jets)
Randy White (Dallas)	NT	Joe Klecko (NY Jets)
Leonard Marshall (NYG)	RE	Howie Long (LA Raiders)
Lawrence Taylor (NYG)	LOLB	Andre Tippett (New Eng.)
Mike Singletary (Chi. Bears)	LILB	Karl Mecklenburg (Denver)
Harry Carson (NY Giants)	RILB	Steve Nelson (New Eng.)
Rickey Jackson (NO)	ROLB	Mike Merriweather (Pitt.)
Everson Walls (Dallas)	LCB	Mike Haynes (LA Raiders)
LeRoy Irvin (LA Rams)	RCB	Louis Wright (Denver)
Carlton Williamson (SF)	SS	Kenny Easley (Seattle)
Wes Hopkins (Philadelphia)	FS	Deron Cherry (Kansas City)

Coaches—Don Shula (Miami), AFC; John Robinson (LA Rams), NFC

NFC	0	7	7	14	—	28
AFC	7	17	0	0	—	24

AFC—Allen 2 run (Anderson kick)
NFC—Browner 48 interception return (Andersen kick)
AFC—Chandler 61 pass from Allen (Anderson kick)
AFC—FG Anderson 34
AFC—Lipps 11 pass from O'Brien (Anderson kick)
NFC—Monk 15 pass from Simms (Andersen kick)
NFC—Cosbie 2 pass from Simms (Andersen kick)
NFC—Giles 15 pass from Simms (Andersen kick)
Attendance—50,101

PRO BOWL SELECTIONS

The year shown refers to the year the game was played, not the season it followed. Twice, in 1940 and again in 1942, there were two games. The January games represented the 1939 and 1941 seasons, respectively. The December games represented the 1940 and 1942 seasons. An asterisk indicates that a player was selected but did not play.

A

Adamle, Tony, FB, Cleveland (2) 1951-52
Adams, Chet, T, Cleveland (2) Jan. 1942, Dec. 1942
Adams, Julius, DE, New England (1) 1981
Adamson, Ken, G, Denver (1) 1962
Adderley, Herb, CB, Green Bay (5) 1964-68
Addison, Tom, LB, Boston (4) 1962-65
Alban, Dick, HB, Washington (1) 1955
Albert, Frankie, QB, San Francisco (1) 1951
Alderman, Grady, T, Minnesota (6) 1964-68, 1970
Aldrich, Ki, C (2) Chi. Cardinals Jan. 1940; Washington Dec. 1942
Alexander, Kermit, S, San Francisco (1) 1969
Allen, Chuck, LB, San Diego (2) 1964-65
Allen, Marcus, RB, LA Raiders (3) 1983, 1985-86
Alworth, Lance, FL, San Diego (7) 1964-70
Alzado, Lyle, DE, Denver (2) 1978-79
Ameche, Alan, FB, Baltimore (4) 1956-59
Andersen, Morten, K, New Orleans (1) 1986
Anderson, Bill, E, Washington (2) 1960-61
Anderson, Dick, S, Miami (3) 1973-75
Anderson, Donny, HB, Green Bay (1) 1969
Anderson, Gary, K, Pittsburgh (2) 1985-86
Anderson, Ken, QB, Cincinnati (4) 1976-77, 1982-83
Anderson, Ottis, RB, St. Louis (2) 1980-81
Andrews, William, RB, Atlanta (4) 1981-84
Andrie, George, DE, Dallas (5) 1966-70
Ane, Charley, T, Detroit (2) 1957, 1959
Angsman, Elmer, HB, Chi. Cardinals (1) 1951
Antwine, Houston, DT, Boston (6) 1964*, 1965-69
Apolskis, Ray, C, Chi. Cardinals (1) Jan. 1942
Arbanas, Fred, TE (5) Dallas Texans 1963; Kansas City 1964*, 1965*, 1966, 1968
Armstrong, Otis, RB, Denver (2) 1975, 1977
Arnett, Jon, HB, LA Rams (5) 1958-62
Artoe, Lee, T, Chi. Bears (3) Dec. 1940, Jan. 1942, Dec. 1942
Atkins, Bill, S, Buffalo (1) 1962
Atkins, Doug, DE, Chi. Bears (8) 1958-64, 1966
Atkinson, Al, LB, NY Jets (1) 1969
Atkinson, George, CB, Oakland (2) 1969-70
Austin, Bill, G, NY Giants (1) 1955

B

Bacon, Coy, DE (3) LA Rams 1973; Cincinnati 1977-78
Baisi, Al, G, Chi. Bears (2) Dec. 1940, Jan. 1942
Baker, Al, DE, Detroit (3) 1979-81
Baker, Dave, S, San Francisco (1) 1960
Baker, Jon, G, NY Giants (2) 1952-53
Baker, Sam, HB-K (4) Washington 1957; Dallas 1964; Philadelphia 1965, 1969
Baker, Tony, RB, New Orleans (1) 1970
Bakken, Jim, K, St. Louis (4) 1966, 1968, 1976-77
Balaz, Frank, G, Green Bay (1) Jan. 1940
Ballman, Gary, HB-SE, Pittsburgh (2) 1965-66
Banducci, Bruno, G, San Francisco (1) 1955
Banfield, Tony, CB, Houston (3) 1962-64
Banks, Chip, LB, Cleveland (3) 1983-84, 1986*
Banks, Tom, C, St. Louis (4) 1976-79
Barbaro, Gary, S, Kansas City (3) 1981-83
Barber, Jim, T, Washington (1) Dec. 1940
Barber, Stew, T, Buffalo (5) 1964-68
Barkum, Jerome, WR, NY Jets (1) 1974
Barnard, Hap, E, NY Giants (1) 1939
Barnes, Billy Ray, FB-HB, Philadelphia (3) 1958-60
Barnes, Erich, DB (6) Chi. Bears 1960; NY Giants 1962-65; Cleveland 1969
Barnes, Mike, DT, Baltimore (1) 1978
Barnes, Walter (Piggy), G, Philadelphia (1) 1951
Barney, Lem, CB, Detroit (7) 1968-70, 1973-74, 1976-77
Barr, Terry, FL, Detroit (2) 1964-65
Bartkowski, Steve, QB, Atlanta (2) 1981-82
Barwegan, Dick, G (4) Chi. Bears 1951-53; Baltimore 1954
Bass, Dick, HB, LA Rams (3) 1963-64, 1967
Bassi, Dick, G, Philadelphia (1) Dec. 1940
Bates, Bill, ST, Dallas (1) 1985
Baugh, Sammy, HB-QB, Washington (5) 1939, Dec. 1940, Jan. 1942, Dec. 1942*, 1952
Baughan, Maxie, LB (9) Philadelphia 1961-62, 1964-66; LA Rams 1967-69, 1970*
Baumhower, Bob, DT-NT, Miami (5) 1980, 1982-84, 1985*
Bausch, Frank, C, Chi. Bears (1) Dec. 1940
Bednarik, Chuck, LB, Philadelphia (8) 1951-55, 1957-58, 1961
Behrman, Dave, LB, Buffalo (1) 1966*
Beinor, Ed, T, Washington (1) Dec. 1942*
Bierne, Jim, WR, Houston (1) 1970
Bell, Bobby, DE-LB, Kansas City (9) 1965-73
Bell, Todd, S, Chi. Bears (1) 1985
Bemiller, Al, C, Buffalo (1) 1966
Benirschke, Rolf, K, San Diego (1) 1893
Benton, Jim, E, Cleveland (1) Jan. 1940
Bergey, Bill, LB (5) Cincinnati 1970; Philadelphia 1975, 1977-79
Berry, Bob, QB, Atlanta (1) 1970
Berry, Raymond, SE, Baltimore (5) 1959-60, 1962, 1964-65
Bertelsen, Jim, RB, LA Rams (1) 1974
Bethea, Elvin, DE, Houston (8) 1970, 1972-76, 1979-80
Betters, Doug, DE, Miami (1) 1984
Bielski, Dick, E, Dallas Cowboys (1) 1962
Biggs, Verlon, DE, NY Jets (3) 1967-69
Biletnikoff, Fred, WR, Oakland (6) 1968, 1970-72, 1974-75
Bingaman, Les, G, Detroit (2) 1952, 1954
Birdsong, Carl, P, St. Louis (1) 1984
Birdwell, Dan, DE, Oakland (1) 1969
Bishop, Bill, T, Chi. Bears (1) 1955
Bishop, Don, CB, Dallas Cowboys (1) 1963
Bishop, Sonny, G, Houston (1) 1969
Bjork, Del, T, Chi. Bears (1) 1939
Blair, George, DB, San Diego (1) 1962
Blair, Matt, LB, Minnesota (6) 1978-83
Blanda, George, QB-K, (4) Houston 1962-64; Oakland 1968
Blanks, Sid, HB, Houston (1) 1965
Blazine, Tony, T, Chi. Cardinals (1) Jan. 1940
Blount, Mel, CB, Pittsburgh (5) 1976-77, 1979-80, 1982
Blozis, Al, T, NY Giants (1) Dec. 1942
Blue, Forrest, C, San Francisco (4) 1972-75
Bokamper, Kim, LB, Miami (1) 1980
Boozer, Emerson, HB, NY Jets (2) 1967, 1969
Boryla, Mike, QB, Philadelphia (1) 1976
Bosley, Bruce, G-C, San Francisco (4) 1961, 1966-68
Bosseler, Don, FB, Washington (1) 1960
Bostic, Jeff, C, Washington (1) 1984
Boyd, Bob, E, LA Rams (1) 1955
Boyd, Bobby, DB, Baltimore (2) 1965, 1969
Boyette, Garland, LB, Houston (2) 1969-70
Box, Cloyce, E, Detroit (2) 1951, 1953
Braase, Ordell, DE, Baltimore (2) 1967-68
Bradley, Bill, S, Philadelphia (3) 1972-74
Bradshaw, Charlie,T, Pittsburgh (2) 1964-65
Bradshaw, Terry, QB, Pittsburgh (3) 1976*, 1979-80
Bramlett, John, LB (2) Denver 1967; Miami 1968
Branch, Cliff, WR, Oakland (4) 1975-78
Branch, Mel, DE (3) Dallas Texans 1962-63; Kansas City 1964
Bray, Ray, G, Chi. Bears (4) Dec. 1940, Jan. 1942, 1951-52
Brazile, Robert, LB, Houston (7) 1977-83
Breedlove, Rod, LB, Washington (1) 1963
Breunig, Bob, LB, Dallas (3) 1980-81, 1983
Brewer, Johnny, LB, Cleveland (1) 1967
Brewster, Darrell (Pete), E, Cleveland (2) 1956-57
Brezina, Greg, LB, Atlanta (1) 1970
Brink, Larry, DE, LA Rams (2) 1951-52
Briscoe, Marlin, WR, Buffalo (1) 1971
Brito, Gene, DE, Washington (5) 1954, 1956-59
Brock, Charley, C, Green Bay (3) Jan. 1940, Dec. 1940, Dec. 1942
Brockington, John, RB, Green Bay (3) 1972-74
Brodie, John, QB, San Francisco (2) 1966, 1971
Brooker, Tommy, E, Kansas City (1) 1965
Brooks, Larry, DT, LA Rams (5) 1977-78, 1979*, 1980-81
Brooks, Leo, DT, St. Louis (1) 1977
Brookshier, Tom, CB, Philadelphia (2) 1960-61
Brown, Bill, FB, Minnesota (4) 1965-66, 1968-69
Brown, Bob, T, (6) Philadelphia 1966-67, 1969; LA Rams 1970*, 1971*; Oakland 1972*
Brown, Bob, DT, Green Bay (1) 1973
Brown, Charlie, WR, Washington (2) 1983-84
Brown, Dave, CB, Seattle (1) 1985
Brown, Ed, QB, Chi. Bears (2) 1956-57
Brown, Eddie, KR, Washington (2) 1977-78
Brown, Hardy, LB, San Francisco (1) 1953
Brown, Jim, FB, Cleveland (9) 1958-66
Brown, Larry, RB, Washington (4) 1970-72, 1973*
Brown, Larry, T, Pittsburgh (1) 1983
Brown, Roger, DT (6) Detroit 1963-67; LA Rams 1968
Brown, Ron, KR, LA Rams (1) 1986
Brown, Roosevelt, T, NY Giants (9) 1956-61, 1963, 1965-1966
Brown, Timmy, HB, Philadelphia (3) 1963-64, 1966
Brown, Willie, CB (9) Denver 1965-66; Oakland 1968-74
Browner, Joey, ST, Minnesota (1) 1986
Bruder, Hank, QB, Green Bay (1) Jan. 1940
Brumm, Don, DE, St. Louis (1) 1969
Bruney, Fred, S, Boston (2) 1962-63
Bryant, Bobby, CB, Minnesota (2) 1976, 1977*
Buchanan, Buck, DT, Kansas City (8) 1965-72
Buchanon, Willie, CB, Green Bay (3) 1974*, 1975, 1979
Budde, Ed, G, Kansas City (7) 1964, 1967-72
Buhler, Larry, FB, Green Bay (1) Jan. 1940
Bulaich, Norm, RB, Baltimore (1) 1972*
Buncom, Frank, LB, San Diego (3) 1965-66, 1968

Buoniconti, Nick, LB (8) Boston 1964-68; Miami 1970, 1973*, 1974
Burford, Chris, E, Dallas Texans (1) 1962
Burk, Adrian, QB, Philadelphia (2) 1955-56
Burnett, Bobby, HB, Buffalo (1) 1967
Burnett, Dale, HB, NY Giants (1) 1939
Burrell, Ode, HB, Houston (1) 1966
Burrough, Ken, WR, Houston (2) 1976, 1978
Bussey, Young, QB, Chi. Bears (2) Jan. 1942, Dec. 1942
Butkus, Dick, LB, Chi. Bears (8) 1966-73
Butler, Jack, DB, Pittsburgh (4) 1956-59
Butler, Jerry, WR, Buffalo (1) 1981
Butler, Jim, RB, Atlanta (1) 1970
Butz, Dave, DT, Washington (1) 1984
Byrd, Butch, CB, Buffalo (5) 1965-67, 1969-70

C

Caffey, Lee Roy, LB, Green Bay (1) 1966
Camarillo, Rich, P, New England (1) 1984
Campbell, Earl, RB, Houston (5) 1979-82, 1984
Campbell, Marion, DT, Philadelphia (2) 1960-61
Campbell, Woodie, HB, Houston (1) 1968*
Cannady, John, C, NY Giants (2) 1951, 1953
Cannon, Billy, HB-TE (2) Houston, 1962; Oakland, 1970
Cappelletti, Gino, E, Boston (5) 1962, 1964-67
Carapella, Al, T, San Francisco (1) 1955
Cardwell, Lloyd, HB, Detroit (1) 1939
Carlton, Wray, HB, Buffalo (2) 1966-67
Carmichael, Harold, WR, Philadelphia (4) 1974, 1979-81
Carolan, Reg, E, Dallas Texans (1) 1963
Caroline, J.C., HB, Chi. Bears (1) 1957
Carollo, Joe, T, LA Rams (1) 1969
Carpenter, Ken, HB, Cleveland (1) 1952
Carpenter, Preston, E, Pittsburgh (1) 1963
Carr, Fred, LB, Green Bay (3) 1971, 1973, 1976
Carr, Roger, WR, Baltimore (1) 1977
Carroll, Vic, G, Washington (1) Dec. 1942
Carson, Harry, LB, NY Giants (7) 1979*, 1980, 1982-86
Carson, Johnny, E, Washington (1) 1958
Carter, Jim, LB, Green Bay (1) 1974
Carter, Joe, E, Philadelphia (2) 1939, Jan. 1940
Carter, Michael, NT, San Francisco (1) 1986
Casanova, Tommy, S, Cincinnati (3) 1975, 1977-78
Casares, Rick, FB-HB, Chi. Bears (5) 1956-60
Casey, Bernie, FL, LA Rams (1) 1968
Cason, Jim, HB, San Francisco (2) 1952, 1955
Casper, Dave, TE (5) Oakland 1977-80; Houston 1981
Caster, Rich, TE, NY Jets (3) 1973, 1975-76
Chambers, Wally, DT, Chi. Bears (3) 1974, 1976-77
Chandler, Don, K, Green Bay (1) 1968
Chandler, Wes, WR (4) New Orleans 1980; San Diego 1983-84, 1986
Chandnois, Lynn, HB, Pittsburgh (2) 1953-54
Chapple, Dave, P, LA Rams (1) 1973
Cherry, Deron, S, Kansas City (3) 1984-86
Cherundolo, Chuck, C, Pittsburgh (2) Jan. 1942, Dec. 1942
Chesney, Chester, C, Chi. Bears (1) Dec. 1940
Chester, Raymond, TE, Oakland (4) 1971-73, 1980
Childs, Henry, TE, New Orleans (1) 1980
Christensen, Todd, TE, LA Raiders (3) 1984-86
Christiansen, Jack, S, Detroit (5) 1954-58
Christy, Dick, HB, NY Titans (1) 1963
Cifers, Ed, E, Washington (1) Dec. 1942
Clancy, Jack, SE, Miami (1) 1968
Clark, Bruce, DE, New Orleans (1) 1985
Clark, Dwight, WR, San Francisco (2) 1982-83
Clark, Harry, HB, Chi. Bears (2) Dec. 1940, Jan. 1942
Clark, Mike, K, Pittsburgh (1) 1967
Clarke, Hagood, DB, Buffalo (1) 1966
Clarke, Leon, E, LA Rams (2) 1956-57
Clayborn, Raymond, CB, New England (2) 1984, 1986
Clayton, Mark, WR, Miami (2) 1985-86
Coffman, Paul, TE, Green Bay (3) 1983-85
Cogdill, Gail, SE, Detroit (3) 1961, 1963-64
Colclough, Jim, E, Boston (1) 1963*
Cole, Pete, G, NY Giants (1) 1939
Cole, Robin, LB, Pittsburgh (1) 1985
Collett, Elmer, G, San Francisco (1) 1970
Collins, Gary, FL, Cleveland (2) 1966-67
Collins, Jim, LB, LA Rams (1) 1986
Collins, Ray, G, San Francisco (1) 1952
Collins, Tony, RB, New England (1) 1984
Collinsworth, Cris, WR, Cincinnati (3) 1982-84
Colo, Don, T, Cleveland (3) 1955-58, 1959
Condit, Merlyn, HB (2) Pittsburgh Dec. 1940; Brooklyn Dec. 1942
Conerly, Charlie, QB, NY Giants (2) 1951*, 1957
Conners, Dan, LB, Oakland (3) 1967-69
Connolly, Ted, G, San Francisco (1) 1962
Connor, George, T, Chi. Bears (4) 1951-54
Conrad, Bobby Joe, FL, St. Louis (1) 1965
Conti, Enio, G, Philadelphia (1) Dec. 1942
Cooke, Ed, DE, Miami (1) 1967
Coomer, Joe, T, Pittsburgh (1) Jan. 1942
Cope, Frank, T, NY Giants (2) 1939, Dec. 1940
Cordell, Ollie, HB, Cleveland (1) Dec. 1940
Corey, Walt, LB, Kansas City (1) 1964
Cornelison, Jerry, T, Dallas Texans (1) 1963
Corral, Frank, K, LA Rams (1) 1979
Cosbie, Doug, TE, Dallas (3) 1984-86
Costa, Dave, DT (4) Oakland 1964; Denver 1968-70
Costa, Paul, TE, Buffalo (2) 1966-67
Coulter, DeWitt (Tex), T, NY Giants (2) 1952-53
Covert, Jim, T, Chi. Bears (1) 1986
Cowan, Charlie, T, LA Rams (3) 1969-71
Cox, Fred, K, Minnesota (1) 1971
Craft, Russ, HB, Philadelphia (2) 1952-53
Craig, Larry, QB-E, Green Bay (3) Jan. 1940, Jan. 1942, Dec. 1942
Craig, Roger, RB, San Francisco (1) 1986
Creekmur, Lou, T, Detroit (8) 1951-58
Cribbs, Joe, RB, Buffalo (3) 1981, 1982*, 1984
Cromwell, Nolan, S, LA Rams (4) 1981-84
Cross, Irv, CB, Philadelphia (2) 1965-66
Cross, Randy, G, San Francisco (3) 1982-83, 1985
Crow, John David, HB (4) Chi. Cardinals 1960; St. Louis 1961, 1963; San Francisco 1966
Crow, Lindon, DB (3) Chi. Cardinals 1957-58; NY Giants 1960
Csonka, Larry, RB, Miami (5) 1971-72, 1973*, 1974*, 1975
Cuff, Ward, HB, NY Giants (3) 1939, Jan. 1940, Jan. 1942
Culp, Curley, DT (6) Kansas City 1970, 1972; Houston 1976-79
Cunningham, Sam, RB, New England (1) 1979
Current, Mike, T, Denver (1) 1970
Currie, Dan, LB, Green Bay (1) 1961
Curry, Bill, C, Baltimore (2) 1972-73
Curtis, Isaac, WR, Cincinnati (4) 1974-77
Curtis, Mike, LB, Baltimore (4) 1959, 1971-72, 1975

D

Dalby, Dave, C, Oakland (1) 1978
Dale, Carroll, WR, Green Bay (3) 1969-71
Danenhauer, Eldon, T, Denver (2) 1963, 1966
Daniels, Clem, HB, Oakland (4) 1964-67
Danowski, Ed, FB, NY Giants (1) 1939
Darden, Thom, S, Cleveland (1) 1979
Daughtery, Dick, LB, LA Rams (1) 1958
David, Jim, DB, Detroit (6) 1955-60
Davidson, Ben, DE, Oakland (3) 1967-69
Davidson, Cotton, QB (2) Dallas Texans 1962; Oakland 1964
Davis, Ben, CB, Cleveland (1) 1973
Davis, Fred, T (2) Washington Dec. 1942; Chi. Bears 1951
Davis, Glenn, HB, LA Rams (1) 1951
Davis, Tommy, K, San Francisco (2) 1963-64
Davis, Willie, DE, Green Bay (5) 1964-68
Dawson, Len, QB (7) Dallas Texans 1963; Kansas City 1965, 1967-69, 1970*, 1972
Day, Tom, DE, Buffalo (1) 1966
Deal, Rufus, FB, Washington (1) Dec. 1942
Dean, Fred, DE (4) San Diego 1980-81; San Francisco 1982, 1984
Dean, Ted, HB, Philadelphia (1) 1962
Dee, Bob, DE, Boston (4) 1962, 1964-66
DeLamielleure, Joe, G (6) Buffalo 1976-80; Cleveland 1981
Delaney, Joe, RB, Kansas City (1) 1982
DeLeone, Tom, C, Cleveland (2) 1980-81
DeLong, Steve, DE, San Diego (1) 1970
DeMarco, Bob, C, St. Louis (3) 1964, 1966, 1968*
Dempsey, Tom, K, New Orleans (1) 1970
Denson, Al, FL, Denver (2) 1968, 1970
Dent, Richard, DE, Chi. Bears (2) 1985-86
Derby, Dean, DB, Pittsburgh (1) 1960
DeRogatis, Al, T, NY Giants (2) 1951-52
Dess, Darrell, G, NY Giants (2) 1963-64
Dewell, Bill, E, Chi. Cardinals (1) Jan. 1942
Dewveall, Willard, E, Houston (1) 1963
Dial, Buddy, FL, Pittsburgh (2) 1962, 1964*
Dickerson, Eric, RB, LA Rams (2) 1984-85
Dieken, Doug, T, Cleveland (1) 1981
Dierdorf, Dan, T, St. Louis (6) 1975-79, 1981
Dillon, Bobby, HB, Green Bay (4) 1956-59
Ditka, Mike, TE, Chi. Bears (5) 1962-66
Dixon, Hewritt, FB, Oakland (4) 1967-69, 1971
Dobler, Conrad, G, St. Louis (3) 1976-78
Dodrill, Dale, G, Pittsburgh (4) 1954-56, 1958
Doll, Don, HB (4) Detroit 1951-53; Washington 1954
Donovan, Art, DT, Baltimore (5) 1954-58
Donovan, Pat, T, Dallas (4) 1980-83
Doran, Jim, E, Dallas Cowboys (1) 1961
Dorney, Keith, T, Detroit (1) 1983
Dorow, Al, QB (2) Washington 1957; NY Titans 1962
Dorsett, Tony, RB, Dallas (4) 1979, 1982-84
Dottley, John, FB, Chi. Bears (1) 1952
Dougherty, Phil, C, Chi. Cardinals (1) 1939
Dove, Bob, E, Chi. Cardinals (1) 1951
Dove, Eddie, S, San Francisco (1) 1962
Dowler, Boyd, FL, Green Bay (2) 1966, 1968
Drake, Johnny, FB, Cleveland (3) 1939, Jan. 1940, Dec. 1940
Drazenovich, Chuck, LB, Washington (4) 1956-59
Drulis, Chuck, G, Chi. Bears (1) Dec. 1942
Dryer, Fred, DE, LA Rams (1) 1976
Dubenion, Elbert, FL, Buffalo (1) 1965
Dudley, Bill, HB (3) Pittsburgh Dec. 1942; Washington 1951-52
Duerson, Dave, S, Chi. Bears (1) 1986
Duhe, A.J., LB, Miami (1) 1985
Dunaway, Jim, DT, Buffalo (4) 1966-69
Duncan, Leslie (Speedy), DB-KR (4) San Diego 1966-68; Washington 1972
Duper, Mark, WR, Miami (2) 1984-85
DuPree, Billy Joe, TE, Dallas (3) 1977-79
Dutton, John, DE, Baltimore (3) 1976-78

E

Easley, Kenny, S, Seattle (4) 1983-86
Ecklund, Brad, C, NY Yanks (2) 1951-52
Edgerson, Booker, DB, Buffalo (1) 1966
Edwards, Dan, E, NY Giants (1) 1951
Edwards, Glen (Turk), T, Washington (1) Jan. 1940
Edwards, Glen, S, Pittsburgh (2) 1976-77
Eisenhauer, Larry, DE, Boston (4) 1963-65, 1967
Elam, Cleveland, DT, San Francisco (2) 1977-78
Ellard, Henry, KR, LA Rams (1) 1985
Eller, Carl, DE, Minnesota (6) 1969-72, 1974*, 1975
Elliott, John, DT, NY Jets (3) 1969-71
Ellis, Allan, CB, Chi. Bears (1) 1978
Ellis, Ken, CB, Green Bay (2) 1974-75
Ellison, Willie, RB, LA Rams (1) 1972*
Elter, Leo, HB, Washington (1) 1957
Engebretsen, Paul, G, Green Bay (1) Jan. 1940
English, Doug, DT, Detroit (4) 1979, 1982-84
Erlandson, Tom, LB, Miami (1) 1967
Etter, Bob, K, Atlanta (1) 1970
Evans, Norm, T, Miami (2) 1973, 1975

F

Fahnhorst, Keith, T, San Francisco (1) 1985
Faison, Earl, DE, San Diego (5) 1962-66
Falaschi, Nello, QB, NY Giants (2) 1939, Jan. 1942
Famiglietti, Gary, HB, Chi. Bears (3) Dec. 1940, Jan. 1942, Dec. 1942
Farkas, Andy, FB, Washington (2) Jan. 1940, Dec. 1942
Farman, Dick, G, Washington (1) Dec. 1942
Farr, Mel, RB, Detroit (2) 1968, 1971
Farr, Miller, CB, Houston (3) 1968-70
Farragut, Ken, C, Philadelphia (1) 1954
Fears, Tom, E, LA Rams (1) 1951
Federovich, John, T, Chi. Bears (1) Jan. 1942
Felt, Dick, CB (2) NY Titans 1962; Boston 1963
Fencik, Gary, S, Chi. Bears (2) 1981-82
Ferguson, Charley, E, Buffalo (1) 1966*
Ferguson, Howie, FB, Green Bay (1) 1956
Fields, Joe, C, NY Jets (2) 1982-83
Filchock, Frank, HB, Washington (2) Jan. 1940, Jan. 1942
Finks, Jim, QB, Pittsburgh (1) 1953
Fischer, Bill, G, Chi. Cardinals (3) 1951-53
Fischer, Pat, CB (3) St. Louis 1965-66; Washington 1970
Fiss, Galen, LB, Cleveland (2) 1963-64
Flanagan, Ed, C, Detroit (4) 1970-72, 1974
Flatley, Paul, SE, Minnesota (1) 1967
Flint, George, G, Buffalo (1) 1966
Flores, Tom, QB, Oakland (1) 1967
Floyd, Don, DE, Houston (2) 1962-63
Foley, Dave, T, Buffalo (1) 1974
Foley, Tim, S, Miami (1) 1980
Folkins, Lee, TE, Dallas (1) 1964
Ford, Len, DE, Cleveland (4) 1952-55
Foreman, Chuck, RB, Minnesota (5) 1974-76, 1977*, 1978
Forester, Bill, LB, Green Bay (4) 1960-63
Forte, Aldo, G, Chi. Bears (2) Dec. 1940, Jan. 1942
Fortmann, Dan, G, Chi. Bears (3) Dec. 1940, Jan. 1942, Dec. 1942
Fortunato, Joe, LB, Chi. Bears (5) 1959, 1963-66
Foster, Roy, G, Miami (1) 1986
Fouts, Dan, QB, San Diego (6) 1980-84, 1986
Fox, Tim, S, New England (1) 1981
France, Doug, T, LA Rams (2) 1978-79
Francis, Russ, TE, New England (3) 1977, 1978*, 1979
Franklin, Andra, RB, Miami (1) 1983
Fraser, Jim, LB, Denver (3) 1963-65
Frazier, Charlie, TE, Houston (1) 1967
Frazier, Willie, TE, San Diego (3) 1966, 1968, 1970
Frederickson, Tucker, FB, NY Giants (1) 1966
Freitas, Rockne (Rocky), T, Detroit (1) 1973*
Fritsch, Toni, K, Houston (1) 1980
Fryar, Irving, KR, New England (1) 1986
Fugett, Jean, TE, Washington (1) 1978
Fuller, Frank, T, Chi. Cardinals (1) 1960

G

Gabriel, Roman, QB (4) LA Rams 1968-70; Philadelphia 1974
Gain, Bob, DT-DE, Cleveland (5) 1958-60, 1962-63
Galazin, Stan, C, NY Giants (1) 1939
Galimore, Willie, HB, Chi. Bears (1) 1959
Gallarneau, Hugh, HB, Chi. Bears (1) Jan. 1942
Gantenbein, Milt, E, Green Bay (1) Jan. 1940
Garrett, Carl, RB, Boston (1) 1970
Garrett, Mike, HB, Kansas City (2) 1967-68
Garrison, Gary, WR, San Diego (4) 1969, 1971*, 1972-73
Garrison, Walt, RB, Dallas (1) 1973
Garron, Larry, HB, Boston (4) 1962, 1964-65, 1968
Gastineau, Mark, DE, NY Jets (5) 1982-86
Gatski, Frank, C, Cleveland (1) 1956
Gelatka, Chuck, E, NY Giants (1) 1939

Gentry, Byron, G, Pittsburgh (2) 1939, Jan. 1940
George, Bill, MG-LB, Chi. Bears (8) 1955-1962
George, Ray, T, Detroit (1) Jan. 1940
Gerela, Roy, K, Pittsburgh (2) 1973, 1975
Geri, Joe, HB, Pittsburgh (2) 1951-52
Gibbons, Jim, TE, Detroit (3) 1961-62, 1965
Gibron, Abe, G, Cleveland (4) 1953-56
Gifford, Frank, HB, NY Giants (7) 1954-57, 1959-60, 1964
Gilbert, Kline, T, Chi. Bears (1) 1958
Gilchrist, Cookie, FB (4) Buffalo 1963-65; Denver 1966
Gildea, Johnny, QB, NY Giants (1) 1939
Giles, Jimmie, TE, Tampa Bay (4) 1981-83, 1986
Gilliam, John, WR, Minnesota (4) 1973-76
Gilliam, Jon, C-LB, Dallas Texans (1) 1962
Gillingham, Gale, G, Green Bay (5) 1970-72, 1974*, 1975
Gillom, Horace, E, Cleveland (1) 1953
Gilmer, Harry, QB, Washington (2) 1951, 1953
Glass, Bill, DE, Cleveland (4) 1963-65, 1968
Glick, Fred, DB, Houston (3) 1963-65
Goddard, Ed, QB, Cleveland (1) 1939
Goeddeke, George, G, Denver (1) 1970
Gogolak, Pete, K, Buffalo (1) 1966
Goldenberg, Charles (Buckets), G, Green Bay (1) Jan. 1940
Golic, Bob, NT, Cleveland (1) 1986
Gonsoulin, Austin (Goose), S, Denver (5) 1962-65, 1967
Goode, Rob, FB, Washington (2) 1952, 1955
Goode, Irv, G, St. Louis (2) 1965, 1968
Goode, Tom, C, Miami (1) 1970
Gordon, Dick, WR, Chi. Bears (2) 1971*, 1972
Gordy, John, G, Detroit (3) 1964-1966
Gore, Gordon, HB, LA Bulldogs (1) 1939
Gossett, Bruce, K, LA Rams (2) 1967, 1969
Gradishar, Randy, LB, Denver (7) 1976, 1978-80, 1982-84
Graham, Kenny, S, San Diego (4) 1966, 1968-70
Graham, Otto, QB, Cleveland (5) 1951-55
Granger, Hoyle, FB, Houston (2) 1968-69
Grantham, Larry, LB (5) NY Titans 1963; NY Jets 1964-65, 1967, 1970
Gray, Ken, G, St. Louis (6) 1962, 1964-65, 1967-69
Gray, Leon, T (4) New England 1977, 1979; Houston 1980, 1982
Gray, Mel, WR, St. Louis (4) 1975-78
Grayson, Dave, CB-S (6) Dallas Texans 1963; Kansas City 1964-65; Oakland 1966-67, 1970
Green, Bobby Joe, P, Chi. Bears (1) 1971
Green, Cornell, CB, Dallas (5) 1966-68, 1972-73
Green, Darrell, CB, Washington (1) 1985
Green, Ernie, FB, Cleveland (2) 1967-68
Green, Gary, CB (4) Kansas City 1982-84; LA Rams 1986
Green, Hugh, LB, Tampa Bay (2) 1983-84
Green, John, E, Philadelphia (1) 1951
Green, Roy, WR, St. Louis (2) 1984-85
Green, Tony, KR, Washington (1) 1979
Greene, Joe, DT, Pittsburgh (10) 1970-77, 1979-80
Greene, Tony, S, Buffalo (1) 1978
Greenfield, Tom, C, Green Bay (1) Jan. 1940
Greenwood, L.C., DE, Pittsburgh (6) 1974-77, 1979-80
Gregg, Forrest, T, Green Bay (9) 1960-65, 1967-69
Gregory, Jack, DE (2) Cleveland 1970; NY Giants 1973
Grgich, Visco, G, San Francisco (1) 1951
Grier, Roosevelt, DT, NY Giants (3) 1954*, 1957, 1961
Griese, Bob, QB, Miami (8) 1968-69, 1971-72, 1974-75, 1978-79
Grim, Bob, WR, Minnesota (1) 1972
Grimes, Billy, HB, Green Bay (2) 1951-52
Grimm, Russ, G, Washington (3) 1984-86
Groom, Jerry, T, Chi. Cardinals (1) 1955
Groza, Lou, T, Cleveland (9) 1951-56, 1958-60
Grupp, Bob, P, Kansas City (1) 1980
Guy, Ray, P, Oakland (7) 1974-79, 1981

H

Haden, Jack, T, NY Giants (1) 1939
Haden, Pat, QB, LA Rams (1) 1978
Hadl, John, QB (6) San Diego 1965-66, 1969-70, 1973; LA Rams 1974
Haji-Sheikh, Ali, K, NY Giants (1) 1984
Hall, Parker, HB, Cleveland (1) Jan. 1940
Hall, Ron, DB, Boston (1) 1964
Ham, Jack, LB, Pittsburgh (8) 1974*, 1975-79, 1980*, 1981
Hampton, Dan, DE-DT-NT, Chi. Bears (4) 1981, 1983, 1985-86
Hanburger, Chris, LB, Washington (9) 1967-70, 1973-76, 1977*
Hanken, Ray, E, NY Giants (1) 1939
Hannah, John, G, New England (9) 1977, 1979-83, 1984*, 1985-86
Hanner, Dave, DT, Green Bay (2) 1954-55
Hansen, Brian, P, New Orleans (1) 1985
Hansen, Owen, HB, Hollywood (1) 1939
Harder, Pat, FB (2) Chi. Cardinals 1951; Detroit 1953
Hardman, Cedrick, DE, San Francisco (2) 1972, 1976
Hardy, Jim, QB, Chi. Cardinals (1) 1951
Hare, Cecil, HB, Washington (2) Jan. 1942, Dec. 1942
Hare, Ray, QB, Washington (1) Dec. 1942
Harrah, Dennis, G, LA Rams (4) 1979-81, 1986
Harris, Cliff, S, Dallas (5) 1975-76, 1978-80
Harris, Dick, CB, San Diego (1) 1962
Harris, Franco, RB, Pittsburgh (9) 1973-76, 1977*, 1978-81
Harris, James, QB, LA Rams (1) 1975
Harrison, Dennis, DE, Philadelphia (1) 1983
Hart, Jim, QB, St. Louis (4) 1975-78
Hart, Leon, E, Detroit (1) 1952*
Hart, Tommy, DE, San Francisco (1) 1977
Hatcher, Dale, P, LA Rams (1) 1986
Hauss, Len, C, Washington (5) 1967, 1969-71, 1973
Hawkins, Rip, LB, Minnesota (1) 1964
Hawkins, Wayne, G, Oakland (5) 1964-68
Hayes, Bob, SE, Dallas (3) 1966-68
Hayes, Lester, CB (5) Oakland 1981-82; LA Raiders 1983-85
Haynes, Abner, HB (3) Dallas Texans 1962-63; Kansas City 1965
Haynes, Mark, CB, NY Giants (3) 1983-84, 1985*
Haynes, Mike, CB (8) New England 1977*, 1978-81, 1983; LA Raiders 1985-86
Hazeltine, Matt, LB, San Francisco (2) 1963, 1965
Headrick, Sherrill, LB (4) Dallas Texans 1962-63; Kansas City 1966-67
Hein, Mel, C, NY Giants (4) 1939, Jan. 1940, Dec. 1940, Jan. 1942
Henderson, Thomas, LB, Dallas (1) 1979
Hendricks, Ted, LB (8) Baltimore 1972-74; Green Bay 1975; Oakland 1981-82; LA Raiders 1983-84
Henke, Ed, E, San Francisco (1) 1953
Hennigan, Charley, E, Houston (5) 1962-66
Henry, Wally, KR, Philadelphia (1) 1980
Herber, Arnie, QB, Green Bay (1) Jan. 1940
Herman, Dave, G, NY Jets (2) 1969-70
Herrera, Efren, K, Dallas (1) 1978
Hickerson, Gene, G, Cleveland (6) 1966-71
Hicks, Dwight, S, San Francisco (4) 1982-85
Hicks, W.K., CB, Houston (1) 1967
Hilgenberg, Jay, C, Chi. Bears (1) 1986
Hill, Calvin, RB, Dallas (4) 1970*, 1973, 1974*, 1975
Hill, David, TE, Detroit (2) 1979-80
Hill, Harlon, E, Chi. Bears (3) 1955-57
Hill, J.D., WR, Buffalo (1) 1973
Hill, Jimmy, DB, St. Louis (3) 1961-63
Hill, Kent, G, LA Rams (5) 1981, 1983-86
Hill, Mack Lee, FB, Kansas City (1) 1965
Hill, Tony, WR, Dallas (3) 1979-80, 1986
Hill, Winston, G-T, NY Jets (8) 1965, 1968-74
Hines, Glen Ray, T, Houston (2) 1969-70
Hinkle, Clarke, FB, Green Bay (3) 1939, Jan. 1940, Dec. 1940
Hinton, Chris, G-T (2) Baltimore 1984; Indianapolis 1986
Hirsch, Elroy (Crazylegs), E, LA Rams (3) 1952-54
Hoaglin, Fred, C, Cleveland (1) 1970
Hoak, Dick, HB, Pittsburgh (1) 1959
Hock, John, G, LA Rams (1) 1957
Hoerner, Dick, FB, LA Rams (1) 1951
Hoernschemeyer, Bob (Hunchy), HB, Detroit (2) 1952-53
Hoffman, John, E-HB, Chi. Bears (2) 1954, 1956
Holloway, Brian, T, New England (3) 1984-86
Holmes, Pat, DE, Houston (2) 1968-69
Holmes, Robert, RB, Kansas City (1) 1970
Holub, E.J., LB (5) Dallas Texans 1962, 1963*; Kansas City 1965*, 1966-67
Hopkins, Wes, S, Philadelphia (1) 1986
Hopp, Harry, FB, Detroit (1) Dec. 1942
Hornung, Paul, HB, Green Bay (2) 1960-61
Houston, Jim, LB, Cleveland (4) 1965-66, 1970-71
Houston, Ken, S (12) Houston 1969-73; Washington 1974-79, 1980*
Howell, Jim Lee, E, NY Giants (1) 1939
Howley, Chuck, LB, Dallas (6) 1966-70, 1972
Howton, Billy, E, Green Bay (4) 1953, 1956-58
Hubbard, Marv, RB, Oakland (3) 1972-74
Hubbert, Brad, FB, San Diego (1) 1968
Hudson, Bill, DT, San Diego (1) 1962
Hudson, Dick, T, Buffalo (1) 1966
Huff, Sam, LB (5) NY Giants 1959-62; Washington 1965
Huffman, Dick, T, LA Rams (1) 1951
Hughes, Bill, C, Chi. Bears (1) Jan. 1942
Hughes, George, G, Pittsburgh (2) 1952, 1954
Humbert, Dick, E, Philadelphia (1) Jan. 1942
Humble, Weldon, G, Cleveland (1) 1951
Humphrey, Claude, DE, Atlanta (6) 1971-75, 1978
Hunt, Bobby, DB, Kansas City (1) 1965
Hunt, Jim, DT, Boston (4) 1962*, 1967-68, 1970
Hunter, Art, C, Cleveland (1) 1960
Husmann, Ed, DT, Houston (3) 1962-64
Hutson, Don, E, Green Bay (4) Jan. 1940, Dec. 1940, Jan. 1942, Dec. 1942*

I

Irvin, LeRoy, CB, LA Rams (1) 1986
Isbell, Cecil, QB, Green Bay (4) 1939, Jan. 1940, Jan. 1942, Dec. 1942*
Ivy, Frank (Pop), E, Chi. Cardinals (1) Dec. 1942

J

Jackson, Earnest, RB, San Diego (1) 1985
Jackson, Frank, SE, Kansas City (1) 1966
Jackson, Harold, WR (5) Philadelphia 1970, 1973; LA Rams 1974, 1976, 1978
Jackson, Monte, CB, LA Rams (2) 1977, 1978*
Jackson, Rich, DE, Denver (3) 1969-71
Jackson, Rickey, LB, New Orleans (3) 1984-86
Jackson, Tom, LB, Denver (3) 1978-80
Jacobs, Harry, LB, Buffalo (2) 1966, 1970
Jacoby, Joe, T, Washington (3) 1984-86
Jacunski, Harry, E, Green Bay (1) Jan. 1940
Jagade, Harry (Chick), FB, Cleveland (1) 1954
James, Craig, RB, New England (1) 1986
James, Dick, HB, Washington (1) 1962
James, John, P, Atlanta (3) 1976-78
James, Robert, CB, Buffalo (3) 1973-75
James, Tommy, HB, Cleveland (1) 1954
Jamison, Al, T, Houston (2) 1962-63
Janik, Tom, DB, Buffalo (2) 1966, 1968
Jankowski, Eddie, HB, Green Bay (1) Jan. 1940
Jaquess, Pete, DB, Houston (1) 1965
Jarmoluk, Mike, T, Philadelphia (1) 1952
Jauron, Dick, KR, Detroit (1) 1975
Jaworski, Ron, QB, Philadelphia (1) 1981
Jefferson, John, WR (4) San Diego 1979-81; Green Bay 1983
Jefferson, Roy, WR (3) Pittsburgh 1969-70; Washington 1972
Jenkins, Alfred, WR, Atlanta (2) 1981-82
Jennings, Dave, P, NY Giants (4) 1979-81, 1983
Jessie, Ron, WR, LA Rams (1) 1977
Jeter, Bob, DB, Green Bay (2) 1968, 1970
Joe, Billy, HB, Buffalo (1) 1966
Johnson, Bill, C, San Francisco (2) 1953-54
Johnson, Billy (White Shoes), KR (3) Houston 1976, 1978; Atlanta 1984
Johnson, Bob, C, Cincinnati (1) 1969
Johnson, Charley, QB, St. Louis (1) 1964
Johnson, Charlie, DT, Philadelphia (3) 1980-82
Johnson, Curley, P, NY Jets (1) 1966
Johnson, Ezra, DE, Green Bay (1) 1979
Johnson, Gary, DT, San Diego (4) 1980-83
Johnson, Jimmy, CB, San Francisco (5) 1970*, 1971-73, 1975*
Johnson, John, T, Detroit (1) Jan. 1940
Johnson, John Henry, FB-HB (4) San Francisco 1955; Pittsburgh 1963-65
Johnson, Larry, C, NY Giants (1) 1939
Johnson, Norm, K, Seattle (1) 1985
Johnson, Pete, RB, Cincinnati (1) 1982
Johnson, Ron, RB, NY Giants (2) 1971, 1973
Johnson, Walter, DT, Cleveland (3) 1968-70
Johnston, Mark, DB, Houston (1) 1962
Joiner, Charlie, WR, San Diego (3) 1977, 1980-81
Jones, Art, HB, Pittsburgh (1) Jan. 1942
Jones, Bert, QB, Baltimore (1) 1977
Jones, Cody, DT, LA Rams (1) 1979
Jones, David (Deacon), DE (8) LA Rams 1965-71; San Diego 1973
Jones, Dub, HB, Cleveland (1) 1952
Jones, Ed (Too Tall), DE, Dallas (3) 1982-84
Jones, Homer, SE, NY Giants (2) 1968-69
Jones, Rulon, DE, Denver (1) 1986
Jones, Stan, G, Chi. Bears (7) 1956-62
Jordan, Henry, DT, Green Bay (4) 1961-62, 1964, 1967
Jordan, Lee Roy, LB, Dallas (5) 1968-69, 1970*, 1974*, 1975
Josephson, Les, HB, LA Rams (1) 1968
Joyce, Don, DE, Baltimore (1) 1959
Junior, E.J., LB, St. Louis (2) 1985-86
Jurgensen, Sonny, QB (5) Philadelphia 1962*; Washington 1965, 1967*, 1968*, 1970*
Justice, Ed, HB, Washington (1) Dec. 1942

K

Kaminski, Larry, C, Denver (1) 1968
Kapp, Joe, QB, Minnesota (1) 1970*
Karas, Emil, LB, San Diego (3) 1962-64
Karcis, John, FB, NY Giants (1) 1939
Karras, Alex, DT, Detroit (4) 1961-63, 1966
Kassulke, Karl, S, Minnesota (1) 1971
Katcavage, Jim, DE, NY Giants (3) 1962-64
Kavanaugh, Ken, E, Chi. Bears (2) Dec. 1940, Jan. 1942
Keane, Tom, HB, Baltimore (1) 1954
Keating, Tom, DT, Oakland (2) 1967-68
Kelcher, Louie, DT, San Diego (3) 1978-79, 1981
Kell, Paul, T, Green Bay (1) Jan. 1940
Kellerman, Ernie, DB, Cleveland (1) 1969
Kelly, Leroy, HB, Cleveland (6) 1967-72
Kemp, Jack, QB (7) San Diego 1962; Buffalo 1963, 1964*, 1965-67, 1970
Kenn, Mike, T, Atlanta (5) 1981-85
Kenney, Bill, QB, Kansas City (1) 1984
Keys, Brady, DB, Pittsburgh (1) 1967
Khayat, Bob, G-K, Washington (1) 1961
Kiick, Jim, RB, Miami (2) 1969-70
Kilmer, Billy, QB, Washington (1) 1973
Kilroy, Frank (Bucko), G, Philadelphia (3) 1953-55
Kinard, Frank (Bruiser), T, Brooklyn (5) 1939, Jan. 1940, Dec. 1940, Jan. 1942, Dec. 1942
Kindt, Don, HB, Chi. Bears (1) 1954
King, Kenny, RB, Oakland (1) 1981*
Klecko, Joe, DE-DT-NT, NY Jets (4) 1982, 1984-86
Klein, Dick, E, Boston (1) 1963
Knight, Curt, K, Washington (1) 1972
Kocourek, Dave, TE, San Diego (4) 1962-65
Kolman, Ed, T, Chi. Bears (3) Dec. 1940, Jan. 1942, Dec. 1942
Koman, Bill, DE, St. Louis (2) 1963, 1965

Konz, Kenny, HB, Cleveland (1) 1956
Koy, Ernie, HB, NY Giants (1) 1968
Kramer, Jerry, G, Green Bay (3) 1963-64, 1968
Kramer, Ron, TE, Green Bay (1) 1963
Krause, Paul, S (8) Washington 1965-66; Minnesota 1970, 1972-76
Krieg, Dave, QB, Seattle (1) 1985
Krisher, Bill, G, Dallas Texans (1) 1962
Krouse, Ray, T, NY Giants (1) 1955
Krueger, Al, E, Washington (1) Dec. 1942*
Krueger, Charlie, DT, San Francisco (2) 1961, 1965
Krupa, Joe, DT, Pittsburgh (1) 1964
Kuechenberg, Bob, G, Miami (6) 1975-76, 1978-79, 1983-84
Kuharich, Joe, G, Chi. Cardinals (1) Jan. 1942
Kunz, George, T (8) Atlanta 1970, 1972-74; Baltimore 1975-78
Kupp, Jake, G, New Orleans (1) 1970
Kwalick, Ted, TE, San Francisco (3) 1972-74

L

Ladd, Ernie, DT, San Diego (4) 1963-66
Lahar, Harold, G, Chi. Bears (1) Jan. 1942
Laird, Bruce, CB, Baltimore (1) 1973
Lambert, Jack, LB, Pittsburgh (9) 1976-84
Lammons, Pete, TE, NY Jets (1) 1968
Lamonica, Daryle, QB (5) Buffalo 1966; Oakland 1968, 1970*, 1971, 1973
Landry, Greg, QB, Detroit (1) 1972
Landry, Tom, DB, NY Giants (1) 1955
Lane, Dick (Night Train), DB (7) Chi. Cardinals 1955-57, 1959; Detroit 1961-63
Lane, MacArthur, RB, St. Louis (1) 1971
Langer, Jim, C, Miami (6) 1974-79
Lanier, Willie, LB, Kansas City (8) 1969-75, 1976*
Lansford, Buck, G, Philadelphia (1) 1957
Largent, Steve, WR, Seattle (5) 1979, 1980*, 1982, 1985-86
Larsen, Gary, DT, Minnesota (2) 1970-71
Larson, Greg, C, NY Giants (1) 1969
Lary, Yale, S, Detroit (9) 1954, 1957-63, 1965
Laskey, Bill, LB, Buffalo (1) 1966
Lassiter, Isaac, DE, Oakland (1) 1967
Lattner, Johnny, HB, Pittsburgh (1) 1955
Lavelli, Dante, E, Cleveland (3) 1952, 1954-55
Lavender, Joe, CB, Washington (2) 1980-81
Lawrence, Henry, T, LA Raiders (2) 1984-85
Lawrence, Jimmy, HB, Chi. Cardinals-Green Bay (1) Jan. 1940
Lawrence, Rolland, CB, Atlanta (1) 1978
Laws, Joe, HB, Green Bay (1) Jan. 1940
Layne, Bobby, QB (5) Detroit 1952-54, 1957; Pittsburgh 1960
LeBaron, Eddie, QB (4) Washington 1956, 1958-59; Dallas Cowboys 1963
LeBeau, Dick, DB, Detroit (3) 1965-67
LeClair, Jim, LB, Cincinnati (1) 1977
Lee, Bill, T, Green Bay (1) Jan. 1940
Leemans, Alphonse (Tuffy), HB, NY Giants (2) 1939, Jan. 1942
LeMaster, Frank, LB, Philadelphia (1) 1982
Lemek, Ray, T, Washington (1) 1962
Leo, Charlie, G, Boston (1) 1962
Letlow, Russ, G, Green Bay (2) 1939, Jan. 1940
LeVias, Jerry, WR, Houston (1) 1970*
Lewis, David, LB, Tampa Bay (1) 1981
Lewis, Frank, WR, Buffalo (1) 1982
Lewis, Woodley, HB, LA Rams (1) 1951
Lilly, Bob, DT, Dallas (11) 1963, 1965-72, 1973*, 1974*
Lincoln, Keith, HB-FB (5) San Diego 1963-66; Buffalo 1968
Linhart, Toni, K, Baltimore (2) 1977-78
Lio, Augie, G, Detroit (2) Jan. 1942, Dec. 1942
Lipps, Louis, KR-WR, Pittsburgh (2) 1985-86
Lipscomb, Gene (Big Daddy), DT (3) Baltimore 1959-60; Pittsburgh 1963
Lipscomb, Paul, T, Washington (4) 1951-54
Little, Floyd, RB, Denver (5) 1969-72, 1974
Little, Larry, G, Miami (5) 1970, 1972-75
Livingston, Andy, RB, New Orleans (1) 1970
Livingston, Mike, QB, Kansas City (1) 1970
Livingston, Ted, G, Cleveland (1) Dec. 1940
Lloyd, Dave, LB, Philadelphia (1) 1970
Lockhart, Carl (Spider), DB, NY Giants (2) 1967, 1969
Lofton, James, WR, Green Bay (7) 1979, 1981-86
Logan, Jerry, S, Baltimore (3) 1966, 1971-72
Lomax, Neil, QB, St. Louis (1) 1985
Long, Charley, T-G, Boston (2) 1963-64
Long, Howie, DE, LA Raiders (3) 1984-86
Looney, Don, E, Philadelphia (1) Dec. 1940
Lott, Ronnie, CB, San Francisco (4) 1982-85
LoVetere, John, DT, NY Giants (1) 1964
Lowe, Paul, HB, San Diego (2) 1964, 1966
Lowery, Nick, K, Kansas City (1) 1982
Lucci, Mike, LB, Detroit (1) 1982
Luckman, Sid, QB, Chi. Bears (3) Dec. 1940, Jan. 1942, Dec. 1942
Lujack, Johnny, QB, Chi. Bears (2) 1951-52
Lunday, Kenneth (Kayo), G, NY Giants (1) 1939
Lundy, Lamar, DE, LA Rams (1) 1960
Lyles, Lenny, DB, Baltimore (1) 1967
Lynch, Dick, CB, NY Giants (1) 1964
Lynch, Jim, LB, Kansas City (1) 1969

M

Mack, Kevin, RB, Cleveland (1) 1986
Mack, Tom, G, LA Rams (11) 1968-76, 1978-79
Mackey, John, TE, Baltimore (5) 1964, 1966-69
MacKinnon, Jacque, TE, San Diego (2) 1967, 1969
Magnani, Dante, HB, Cleveland (1) Dec. 1942
Maguire, Paul, LB (2) San Diego 1963; Buffalo 1966
Malone, Charley, E, Washington (1) Dec. 1942*
Manders, Clarence (Pug), QB, Brooklyn (3) Jan. 1940, Dec. 1940, Jan. 1942
Manders, Dave, C, Dallas (1) 1967
Maniaci, Joe, FB, Chi. Bears (2) Dec. 1940, Jan. 1942
Manning, Archie, QB, New Orleans (2) 1979-80
Manske, Edgar (Eggs), E, Chi. Bears (1) Dec. 1940
Maples, Bobby, C, Houston (1) 1969
Marchetti, Gino, DE, Baltimore (10) 1955-58, 1960-65
Marcol, Chester, K, Green Bay (2) 1973, 1975
Marconi, Joe, FB, Chi. Bears (1) 1964
Marinkovic, John, E, Green Bay (2) 1954, 1956
Marino, Dan, QB, Miami (3) 1984*, 1985, 1986*
Marion, Fred, S, New England (1) 1986
Marsalis, Jim, CB, Kansas City (2) 1970-71
Marshall, Jim, DE, Minnesota (2) 1969-70
Marshall, Leonard, DE, NY Giants (1) 1986
Martin, Harvey, DE, Dallas (4) 1977-78, 1979*, 1980
Martin, Jim, K, Detroit (1) 1962
Martin, Rod, LB, LA Raiders (2) 1984-85
Martinovich, Phil, G, Chi. Bears (1) Dec. 1940
Mason, Tommy, HB, Minnesota (3) 1963-65
Massey, Carlton, E, Cleveland (1) 1956
Masterson, Bernie, QB, Chi. Bears (1) Dec. 1940
Masterson, Bob, E, Washington (1) Dec. 1942
Mathews, Ray, HB, Pittsburgh (2) 1953, 1956
Mathis, Bill, FB-HB (2) NY Titans 1962; NY Jets 1964
Matson, Ollie, HB, Chi. Cardinals (5) 1953, 1955-58
Matsos, Archie, LB (3) Buffalo 1962-63; Oakland 1964
Matte, Tom, HB, Baltimore (2) 1969-70
Matthews, Clay, LB, Cleveland (1) 1986
Matuszak, Marv, G-LB (3) Pittsburgh 1954; San Francisco 1958; Buffalo 1963
Matuza, Al, C, Chi. Bears (1) Jan. 1942
Maynard, Don, FL, NY Jets (4) 1966, 1968-69, 1970*
Mays, Jerry, DE-DT (7) Dallas Texans 1963; Kansas City 1965-69, 1971
Maznicki, Frank, HB, Chi. Bears (1) Dec. 1942
McAfee, George, HB, Chi. Bears (1) Jan. 1942
McCarren, Larry, C, Green Bay (2) 1983-84
McChesney, Bob, E, Washington (2) 1939, Dec. 1942
McClairen, Jack, E, Pittsburgh (1) 1958
McClinton, Curtis, FB (3) Dallas Texans 1963; Kansas City 1967-68
McCloughan, Kent, CB, Oakland (2) 1967, 1968*
McCord, Darris, T-E, Detroit (1) 1958
McCormack, Mike, T (6) NY Yanks 1952; Cleveland 1957-58, 1961-63
McCutcheon, Lawrence, RB, LA Rams (5) 1974-78
McDole, Ron, DE, Buffalo (2) 1966, 1968
McDonald, Tommy, HB-E (6) Philadelphia 1959-63; LA Rams 1966
McElhenny, Hugh, HB (6) San Francisco 1953-54, 1957-59; Minnesota 1962
McElroy, Vann, S, LA Raiders (2) 1984-85
McFadin, Bud, T-DT (5) LA Rams 1956-57; Denver 1962-64
McGee, Ben, DE, Pittsburgh (2) 1967, 1969
McGee, Max, E, Green Bay (1) 1962
McGraw, Thurman, T, Detroit (1) 1951
McInally, Pat, P, Cincinnati (1) 1982
McKeever, Marlin, TE, LA Rams (1) 1967
McLaughlin, Leon, C, LA Rams (1) 1955
McLean, Ray (Scooter), HB, Chi. Bears (2) Dec. 1940, Jan. 1942
McLeod, Bob, E, Houston (1) 1962
McMahon, Jim, QB, Chi. Bears (1) 1986
McMillan, Ernie, T, St. Louis (4) 1966, 1968, 1970-71
McMurty, Chuck, DT, Buffalo (1) 1962
McNeil, Charlie, S, San Diego (1) 1962
McNeil, Clifton, FL, San Francisco (1) 1969
McNeil, Freeman, RB, NY Jets (3) 1983, 1985-86
McPeak, Bill, E, Pittsburgh (3) 1953-54, 1957
Meador, Eddie, DB, LA Rams (5) 1961, 1965-67, 1969
Mecklenburg, Karl, LB, Denver (1) 1986
Mehl, Lance, LB, NY Jets (1) 1986
Mehringer, Pete, G, LA Bulldogs (1) 1939
Meinert, Dale, LB, St. Louis (3) 1964, 1966, 1968
Mellus, John, T, NY Giants (2) 1939, Jan. 1942
Mercer, Mike, K, Buffalo (1) 1968
Meredith, Don, QB, Dallas (3) 1967-69
Meredith, Dudley, DT, Buffalo (1) 1966
Merriweather, Mike, LB, Pittsburgh (2) 1985-86
Mertens, Jerry, HB, San Francisco (1) 1959
Metcalf, Terry, RB, St. Louis (3) 1975-76, 1978
Michael, Rich, T, Houston (2) 1963-64
Michaels, Lou, DE-K, Pittsburgh (2) 1963-64
Michaels, Walt, MG-LB, Cleveland (5) 1956-60
Michalik, Art, G, San Francisco (1) 1954
Middleton, Terdell, RB, Green Bay (1) 1979
Mihal, Joe, T, Chi. Bears (2) Dec. 1940, Jan. 1942
Mike-Mayer, Nick, K, Atlanta (1) 1974
Miller, Alan, FB, Oakland (1) 1962
Miller, Fred, DT, Baltimore (3) 1968-69, 1970*
Miller, Junior, TE, Atlanta (2) 1981-82
Miller, Paul, DE, LA Rams (2) 1956-57
Mills, Pete, DE, Buffalo (1) 1966
Mingo, Gene, HB, Denver (1) 1963
Mischak, Bob, G, NY Titans (2) 1962-63
Mitchell, Bobby, HB-FL (4) Cleveland 1961; Washington 1963-65
Mitchell, Jim, TE, Atlanta (2) 1970, 1973
Mitchell, Leroy, DB, Boston (1) 1969
Mitchell, Lydell, RB, Baltimore (3) 1976-78
Mix, Ron, T-G, San Diego (8) 1962-69
Modzelewski, Dick, DT, Cleveland (1) 1965
Moegle, Dickie, HB, San Francisco (1) 1956
Monk, Art, WR, Washington (2) 1985-86
Montana, Joe, QB, San Francisco (4) 1982, 1984-85, 1986*
Montgomery, Wilbert, RB, Philadelphia (2) 1979-80
Moore, Al, E, Green Bay (1) Jan. 1940
Moore, Bill, E, LA Bulldogs (1) 1939
Moore, Lenny, HB, Baltimore (7) 1957, 1959-63, 1965
Moore, Nat, WR, Miami (1) 1978
Moore, Tom, HB, Green Bay (1) 1963
Moore, Wayne, T, Miami (1) 1974*
Moore, Wilbur, HB, Washington (1) Dec. 1942
Moore, Zeke, CB, Houston (2) 1970-71
Morgan, Stanley, WR, New England (2) 1980-81
Morin, Milt, TE, Cleveland (2) 1969, 1972
Morrall, Earl, QB (2) Pittsburgh 1958; Baltimore 1969
Morris, Dennit, LB, Houston (1) 1962
Morris, Eugene (Mercury), RB-KR, Miami (3) 1972-73, 1974*
Morris, Joe, RB, NY Giants (1) 1986
Morris, Johnny, FL, Chi. Bears (1) 1961
Morris, Jon, C, Boston (7) 1965-71
Morrison, Fred (Curly), FB, Cleveland (1) 1956
Morrow, John, C, Cleveland (2) 1962, 1964
Moseley, Mark, K, Washington (2) 1980, 1983
Moses, Haven, WR (2) Buffalo 1970; Denver 1974
Motley, Marion, FB, Cleveland (1) 1951
Mudd, Howard, G, San Francisco (3) 1967-69
Mul-Key, Herb, KR, Washington (1) 1974
Mulleneaux, Carl, E, Green Bay (2) Jan. 1940, Dec. 1940
Munchak, Mike, G, Houston (2) 1985-86
Muncie, Chuck, RB (3) New Orleans 1980; San Diego 1982-83
Muñoz, Anthony, T, Cincinnati (5) 1982-86
Murphy, Mark, S, Washington (1) 1984
Murray, Ed, K, Detroit (1) 1981
Musso, George, G, Chi. Bears (3) Jan. 1940, Dec. 1940, Jan. 1942
Mutscheller, Jim, E, Baltimore (1) 1958
Myers, Chip, WR, Cincinnati (1) 1973
Myers, Tommy, S, New Orleans (1) 1980

N

Nagler, Gern, E, Chi. Cardinals (1) 1959
Namath, Joe, QB, NY Jets (5) 1966, 1968-69, 1970*, 1973*
Nance, Jim, FB, Boston (2) 1967*, 1968
Nash, Joe, NT, Seattle (1) 1985
Naumoff, Paul, LB, Detroit (1) 1971
Neal, Ed, C, Green Bay (1) 1951
Neely, Ralph, T, Dallas (2) 1968, 1970
Neighbors, Billy, G, Boston (1) 1964
Nelms, Mike, KR, Washington (3) 1981-83
Nelsen, Bill, QB, Cleveland (1) 1970
Nelson, Andy, S, Baltimore (1) 1961
Nelson, Steve, LB, New England (3) 1981, 1985-86
Neville, Tom, T-C, Boston (1) 1967
Newman, Ed, G, Miami (4) 1982, 1983*, 1984-85
Newsome, Ozzie, TE, Cleveland (3) 1982, 1985-86
Nickel, Elbie, E, Pittsburgh (3) 1953-54, 1957
Niemi, Laurie, T, Washington (2) 1952-53
Niland, John, G, Dallas (6) 1969-74
Nisby, John, G (3) Pittsburgh 1960, 1962; Washington 1963
Nitschke, Ray, LB, Green Bay (1) 1965
Nobis, Tommy, LB, Atlanta (5) 1967-69, 1971, 1973
Nolting, Ray, HB, Chi. Bears (2) Dec. 1940, Jan. 1942
Nomellini, Leo, DT, San Francisco (10) 1951-54, 1957-1962
Noonan, Karl, FL, Miami (1) 1969
Norton, Don, E, San Diego (2) 1962, 1963*
Norton, Jerry, S (5) Philadelphia 1958-59; Chi. Cardinals 1960; St. Louis 1961-62
Norton, Jim, S, Houston (3) 1963-64, 1968
Nowaskey, Bob, E, Chi. Bears (2) Dec. 1940, Jan. 1942
Nutter, Madison (Buzz), C, Pittsburgh (1) 1963
Nye, Blaine, G, Dallas (2) 1975, 1977

O

Oakes, Don, T, Boston (1) 1968
O'Brien, Davey, QB, Philadelphia (1) Jan. 1940
O'Brien, Ken, QB, NY Jets (1) 1986
Odom, Steve, KR, Green Bay (1) 1976
Odoms, Riley, TE, Denver (4) 1974-76, 1979
O'Donnell, Joe, T, Buffalo (1) 1966
Oldershaw, Doug, G, NY Giants (1) Dec. 1940
Olsen, Merlin, DT, LA Rams (14) 1963-70, 1971*, 1972-76
Olson, Harold, T, Buffalo (1) 1962
Olszewski, Johnny, FB, Chi. Cardinals (2) 1954, 1956

Orr, Jimmy, FL (2) Pittsburgh 1960; Baltimore 1966
Osborn, Dave, RB, Minnesota (1) 1971
Osmanski, Bill, FB, Chi. Bears (2) Dec. 1940, Jan. 1942
Otis, Jim, RB, St. Louis (1) 1976
Otto, Gus, LB, Oakland (1) 1970
Otto, Jim, C, Oakland (12) 1962-73
Owens, Steve, RB, Detroit (1) 1972

P

Page, Alan, DT, Minnesota (9) 1969-76, 1977*
Paluck, John, DE, Washington (1) 1965
Panfil, Ken, T, Chi. Cardinals (1) 1960
Pardee, Jack, LB, LA Rams (1) 1964
Parilli, Vito (Babe), QB, Boston (3) 1964-65, 1967
Parker, Jim, T-G, Baltimore (8) 1959-66
Parks, Dave, E, San Francisco (3) 1965-67
Parrish, Bernie, DB, Cleveland (2) 1961, 1964
Parrish, Lemar, CB-KR (8) Cincinnati 1971-72, 1975-78; Washington 1980-81
Parry, Owen (Ox), T, NY Giants (1) 1939
Pastorini, Dan, QB, Houston (1) 1976
Patton, Jim, S, NY Giants (5) 1959-63
Paul, Don, C, LA Rams (3) 1952-54
Paul, Don, HB-S (4) Chi. Cardinals 1954; Cleveland 1957-59
Paulson, Dainard, DB, NY Jets (2) 1965-66
Payton, Walter, RB, Chi. Bears (8) 1977-81, 1984-86
Pear, Dave, DT, Tampa Bay (1) 1979
Pearson, Drew, WR, Dallas (3) 1975, 1977-78
Peoples, Woody, G, San Francisco (2) 1973-74
Perkins, Don, HB-FB, Dallas (6) 1962-64, 1967-69
Perry, Joe, FB, San Francisco (3) 1953-55
Perry, Rod, CB, LA Rams (2) 1979, 1981*
Peters, Floyd, DT, Philadelphia (3) 1965, 1967-68
Peters, Tony, S, Washington (1) 1983
Peters, Volney, T, Washington (1) 1956
Petitbon, Richie, S, Chi. Bears (4) 1963-64, 1967-68
Petty, John, FB, Chi. Bears (1) Dec. 1942
Philbin, Gerry, DE, NY Jets (2) 1969-70
Phillips, Jim, E, LA Rams (3) 1961-63
Pietrosante, Nick, FB, Detroit (2) 1961-62
Pihos, Pete, E, Philadelphia (6) 1951-56
Pinckert, Erny, QB, Washington (2) 1939, Jan. 1940
Plasman, Dick, E, Chi. Bears (2) Dec. 1940, Jan. 1942
Plum, Milt, QB, Cleveland (2) 1961-62
Plunkett, Sherman, T, NY Jets (2) 1965, 1967
Podoley, Jim, HB, Washington (1) 1958
Poillon, Dick, HB, Washington (1) Dec. 1942
Polsfoot, Fran, E, Chi. Cardinals (1) 1952
Pool, Hampton, E, Chi. Bears (2) Dec. 1940, Jan. 1942
Poole, Jim, E, NY Giants (3) 1939, Jan. 1940, Dec. 1940
Post, Dickie, HB, San Diego (2) 1968*, 1970
Pottios, Myron, LB, Pittsburgh (3) 1962, 1964-65
Powell, Art, SE, Oakland (4) 1964-67
Powell, Marvin, T, NY Jets (5) 1980-83, 1984*
Prestridge, Luke, P, Denver (1) 1983
Price, Charles (Cotton), QB, Detroit (1) Dec. 1940
Price, Eddie, FB, NY Giants (3) 1952-53,1955
Pritchard, Bosh, HB, Philadelphia (1) Dec. 1942
Promuto, Vince, G, Washington (2) 1964-65
Pruitt, Greg, KR-RB (5) Cleveland 1974-75, 1977-78; LA Raiders 1984
Pruitt, Mike, RB, Cleveland (2) 1980-81
Putnam, Duane, G, LA Rams (4) 1955-56, 1958-59
Pyle, Mike, C, Chi. Bears (1) 1964

Q

Quick, Mike, WR, Philadelphia (3) 1984-86
Quillan, Fred, C, San Francisco (2) 1985-86
Quinlan, Volney (Skeet), HB, LA Rams (1) 1955

R

Radovich, Bill, G, Detroit (1) 1939
Randle, Sonny, SE, St. Louis (4) 1961-63, 1966
Rashad, Ahmad, WR, Minnesota (4) 1979-82
Ray, Buford (Baby), T, Green Bay (1) Jan. 1940
Reaves, Ken, CB, Atlanta (1) 1970
Rechichar, Bert, HB, Baltimore (3) 1956-58
Redman, Rick, LB, San Diego (1) 1968
Reed, Alvin, TE, Houston (2) 1969-70
Reger, John, LB, Pittsburgh (3) 1960-62
Reichow, Jerry, E, Minnesota (1) 1962
Reid, Mike, DT, Cincinnati (2) 1973, 1974*
Reinfeldt, Mike, S, Houston (1) 1980
Renfro, Mel, CB-S, Dallas (10) 1965-72, 1973*, 1974
Renfro, Ray, HB, Cleveland (3) 1954, 1958, 1961
Retzlaff, Pete, E, Philadelphia (5) 1959, 1961, 1964-66
Reynolds, Bob, T, St. Louis (3) 1967, 1969-70
Reynolds, Jack, LB, LA Rams (2) 1976, 1981
Rice, Ken, T, Buffalo (1) 1962
Richards, Elvin (Kink), FB-HB, NY Giants (2) 1939, Dec. 1940
Richardson, Jess, T, Philadelphia (1) 1960
Richardson, Willie, FL, Baltimore (2) 1968-69
Richter, Les, LB, LA Rams (8) 1955-62
Riffle, Dick, HB, Pittsburgh (1) Jan. 1942
Riggins, John, RB, NY Jets (1) 1976
Riggs, Gerald, RB, Atlanta (1) 1986
Ringo, Jim, C (10) Green Bay 1958-64; Philadelphia 1965-66, 1968
Roaches, Carl, KR, Houston (1) 1982
Robb, Joe, DE, St. Louis (1) 1967
Roberson, Bo, SE, Buffalo (1) 1966
Roberts, Gene, HB, NY Giants (1) 1951
Robertson, Isiah, LB, LA Rams (6) 1972, 1974-78
Robinson, Dave, LB, Green Bay (3) 1967-68, 1970
Robinson, Jerry, LB, Philadelphia (1) 1982
Robinson, Johnny, S, Kansas City (7) 1964, 1965*, 1966-69, 1971
Robinson, Paul, RB, Cincinnati (2) 1969-70
Robinson, Wayne, LB, Philadelphia (2) 1955-56
Robustelli, Andy, DE (7) LA Rams 1954, 1956; NY Giants 1957-58, 1960-62
Roby, Reggie, P, Miami (1) 1985
Rochester, Paul, DT, Dallas Texans (1) 1962
Rock, Walter, T, San Francisco (1) 1966
Rogel, Fran, FB, Pittsburgh (1) 1957
Rogers, George, RB, New Orleans (2) 1982-83
Rohde, Len, T, San Francisco (1) 1971
Roland, Johnny, HB, St. Louis (2) 1967, 1968*
Ross, Dan, TE, Cincinnati (1) 1983
Rossovich, Tim, LB, Philadelphia (1) 1970
Rote, Kyle, HB-E, NY Giants (4) 1954*, 1955-57
Rote, Tobin, QB (2) Green Bay, 1957; San Diego, 1964
Rowe, Bob, DT, St. Louis (1) 1969
Rucinski, Eddie, E, Brooklyn (1) Dec. 1942
Rudnay, Jack, C, Kansas City (4) 1974-77
Russell, Andy, LB, Pittsburgh (7) 1969, 1971-76
Rutgens, Joe, DT, Washington (2) 1964, 1966
Rutkowski, Ed, FL, Buffalo (1) 1966
Ryan, Frank, QB, Cleveland (3) 1965-67

S

Saimes, George, S, Buffalo (5) 1965-69
St. Clair, Bob, T, San Francisco (5) 1957, 1959-62
St. Jean, Len, G, Boston (1) 1967
Sanders, Charlie, TE, Detroit (7) 1969-72, 1975-77
Sanders, Orban (Spec), DB, NY Yanks (1) 1951
Sandusky, Mike, G, Pittsburgh (1) 1961
Sanford, Leo, LB-C, Chi. Cardinals (2) 1957-58
Sauer, George, SE, NY Jets (4) 1967-70
Saul, Rich, C, LA Rams (6) 1977-82
Sayers, Gale, HB, Chi. Bears (4) 1966-68, 1970
Scarpitto, Bob, E, Denver (1) 1967
Schafrath, Dick, T, Cleveland (6) 1964-69
Schmidt, Bob, C, Houston (3) 1962-64
Schmidt, Henry, DT, Buffalo (1) 1966
Schmidt, Joe, LB, Detroit (9) 1955-63
Schnelker, Bob, E, NY Giants (2) 1959-60
Schnellbacher, Otto, HB, NY Giants (2) 1951-52
Schottenheimer, Marty, LB, Buffalo (1) 1966
Schrader, Jim, C, Washington (3) 1959-60, 1962
Schroeder, Gene, E, Chi. Bears (1) 1953
Schuh, Harry, T, Oakland (3) 1968, 1970-71
Schultz, Charles, T, Green Bay (1) Jan. 1940
Schwartz, Perry, E, Brooklyn (4) 1939, Jan. 1940, Jan. 1942, Dec. 1942
Scibelli, Joe, G, LA Rams (1) 1969
Scott, Clarence, CB, Cleveland (1) 1974
Scott, Herbert, G, Dallas (3) 1980-82
Scott, Jake, S, Miami (5) 1972*, 1973-74, 1975*, 1976
Scott, Tom, E, Philadelphia (2) 1958-59
Scudero, Joe (Scooter), HB, Washington (1) 1965
Sellers, Ron, WR, Boston (1) 1970
Selmon, Lee Roy, DE, Tampa Bay (6) 1980*, 1981-85
Senser, Joe, TE, Minnesota (1) 1982*
Septien, Rafael, K, Dallas (1) 1982
Sestak, Tom, DT, Buffalo (4) 1963-65, 1966*
Sewell, Harley, G, Detroit (4) 1958-60, 1963
Seymour, Bob, HB, Washington (1) Dec. 1942
Shaffer, Leland, QB, NY Giants (1) 1939
Shanklin, Ron, WR, Pittsburgh (1) 1974*
Shaw, Billy, G, Buffalo (8) 1963-70
Shaw, Bob, E, Chi. Cardinals (1) 1951
Shell, Art, T, Oakland (8) 1973-79, 1981
Shell, Donnie, S, Pittsburgh (5) 1979-83
Sherk, Jerry, DT, Cleveland (4) 1974-77
Sherman, Saul, QB, Chi. Bears (1) Dec. 1940*
Sherman, Will, S, LA Rams (2) 1956, 1959
Shipkey, Jerry, FB, Pittsburgh (3) 1951-53
Shirk, John, E, Chi. Cardinals (1) Dec. 1940
Shofner, Del, SE, (5) LA Rams 1959-60; NY Giants 1962-64
Shonta, Chuck, DB, Boston (1) 1967
Shugart, Clyde, G, Washington (2) Jan. 1942, Dec. 1942*
Siegal, John, E, Chi. Bears (3) Dec. 1940, Jan. 1942, Dec. 1942
Siemon, Jeff, LB, Minnesota (4) 1974, 1976-78
Silas, Sam, DT, St. Louis (1) 1966
Simington, Milt, G, Pittsburgh (1) Dec. 1942*
Simmons, Jack, C, Chi. Cardinals (1) 1957
Simms, Phil, QB, NY Giants (1) 1986
Simpson, O.J., RB, Buffalo (6) 1970, 1973-77
Sims, Billy, RB, Detroit (3) 1981-83
Singletary, Mike, LB, Chi. Bears (3) 1984-86
Sipe, Brian, QB, Cleveland (1) 1981
Sisemore, Jerry, T, Philadelphia (2) 1980, 1982
Sistrunk, Otis, DT, Oakland (1) 1975
Sivell, Jim, G, Brooklyn (1) Jan. 1942
Skladany, Tom, P, Detroit (1) 1982
Skoronski, Bob, T, Green Bay (1) 1967
Slater, Jackie, T, LA Rams (2) 1984, 1986
Slivinski, Steve, G, Washington (1) Dec. 1942
Smerlas, Fred, DT, Buffalo (4) 1981-84
Smith, Bill, E, Chi. Cardinals (1) Jan. 1940
Smith, Bob, HB, Detroit (1) 1953
Smith, Bob, HB, Buffalo (1) 1966
Smith, Bubba, DE, Baltimore (2) 1971-72
Smith, Dennis, S, Denver (1) 1986
Smith, Doug, C, LA Rams (2) 1985, 1986*
Smith, Ernie, T (2) Hollywood 1939; Green Bay Jan. 1940
Smith, George, C, Washington (1) Dec. 1942
Smith, Harry, G, Detroit (1) Dec. 1940
Smith, J.D., FB, San Francisco (2) 1960, 1963
Smith, J.D., T, Philadelphia (1) 1962*
Smith, J.T., KR, Kansas City (1) 1981
Smith, Jackie, TE, St. Louis (5) 1967-71
Smith, Jerry, TE, Washington (2) 1968, 1970
Smith, Jim Ray, G, Cleveland (5) 1959, 1960*, 1961-63
Smith, John, K, New England (1) 1981
Smith, Paul, DT, Denver (2) 1973-74
Smith, Ron, KR, Chi. Bears (1) 1973
Smith, Stu, QB, Pittsburgh (1) 1939
Snead, Norm, QB (3) Washington 1964; Philadelphia 1966; NY Giants 1973
Snell, Matt, FB, NY Jets (3) 1965*, 1967, 1970
Snow, Jack, SE, LA Rams (1) 1968*
Snyder, Bob, QB, Chi. Bears (2) Dec. 1940, Jan. 1942
Snyder, Ken, T, Philadelphia (2) 1954-55
Soar, Hank, HB, NY Giants (1) 1939
Soltau, Gordy, E, San Francisco (3) 1952-54
Spadaccini, Vic, QB, Cleveland (1) 1940
Speedie, Mac, E, Cleveland (1) 1951
Spinney, Art, G, Baltimore (2) 1960-61
Sprinkle, Ed, E, Chi. Bears (4) 1951-53, 1955
Stabler, Ken, QB, Oakland (4) 1974-75, 1977*, 1978
Stacy, Billy, DB, St. Louis (1) 1962
Stallings, Larry, LB, St. Louis (1) 1971
Stallworth, John, WR, Pittsburgh (4) 1980, 1983-85
Standlee, Norm, FB (2) Chi. Bears Jan. 1942; San Francisco 1951
Stanfel, Dick, G (5) Detroit 1954; Washington 1956-59
Stanfill, Bill, DE, Miami (5) 1970, 1972, 1973*, 1974*, 1975
Stark, Rohn, P, Indianapolis (1) 1986
Starr, Bart, QB, Green Bay (4) 1961-63, 1967
Staubach, Roger, QB, Dallas (6) 1972, 1976*, 1977, 1978*, 1979-80
Stautner, Ernie, T-DE, Pittsburgh (9) 1953-54, 1956-62
Stemrick, Greg, CB, Houston (1) 1981
Stenerud, Jan, K (6) Kansas City 1969-72, 1976; Minnesota 1985
Stephenson, Dwight, C, Miami 1984-86
Still, Art, DE, Kansas City (4) 1981-83, 1985
Stits, Bill, HB, Detroit (1) 1955
Stone, Donnie, HB, Denver (1) 1962
Stovall, Jerry, DB, St. Louis (3) 1967-68, 1970
Stralka, Clem, G, Washington (1) Dec. 1942
Stratton, Mike, LB, Buffalo (6) 1964-69
Strickland, Larry, C, Chi. Bears (1) 1957
Stroud, Jack, G, NY Giants (3) 1956, 1958, 1961
Stryzkalski, Johnny (Strike), HB, San Francisco (1) 1951
Studstill, Pat, FL-P, Detroit (2) 1966-67
Sturm, Jerry, G-C, Denver (2) 1965, 1967
Stydahar, Joe, T, Chi. Bears (4) 1939, Jan. 1940, Dec. 1940, Jan. 1942
Sugar, Leo, DE (2) Chi. Cardinals 1959; St. Louis 1961
Suggs, Walt, T, Houston (2) 1968-69
Sunde, Milt, G, Minnesota (1) 1967
Svendsen, Bud, C, Green Bay (1) Jan. 1940
Svoboda, Bill, HB, Chi. Cardinals (1) 1954
Swann, Lynn, WR, Pittsburgh (3) 1976, 1978-79
Sweeney, Walt, G, San Diego (9) 1965-73
Swenson, Bob, LB, Denver (1) 1982
Swisher, Bob, HB, Chi. Bears (2) Dec. 1940, Jan. 1942
Szymanski, Dick, C, Baltimore (3) 1956, 1963, 1965

T

Talamini, Bob, G, Houston (6) 1963-68
Talbert, Diron, DT, Washington (1) 1975
Taliaferro, George, HB (3) NY Yanks 1952; Dallas Texans 1953; Baltimore 1954
Taliaferro, Mike, QB, Boston (1) 1970
Tarkenton, Fran, QB, (9) Minnesota 1965-66, 1975*, 1976*, 1977*; NY Giants 1968-71
Tatum, Jack, S, Oakland (3) 1974-75, 1976*
Taylor, Bruce, CB, San Francisco (1) 1972*
Taylor, Charley, HB-WR, Washington (8) 1965-68, 1973-76
Taylor, Hugh (Bones), E, Washington (2) 1953, 1955
Taylor, Jim, FB, Green Bay (5) 1961-62, 1963*, 1964-65
Taylor, Lawrence, LB, NY Giants (5) 1982-86
Taylor, Lionel, E, Denver (3) 1962-63, 1966*
Taylor, Otis, WR, Kansas City (3) 1967, 1972-73
Taylor, Roosevelt, S, Chi. Bears (2) 1964, 1969
Terrell, Marvin, G, Dallas Texans (1) 1963
Teteak, Deral, G, Green Bay (1) 1953
Theismann, Joe, QB, Washington (2) 1983-84
Thielemann, R.C., G, Atlanta (3) 1982-84

Thomas, Aaron, E, NY Giants (1) 1965
Thomas, Clendon, S, Pittsburgh (1) 1964
Thomas, Emmitt, CB, Kansas City (5) 1969, 1972-73, 1975-76
Thomas, J.T., CB, Pittsburgh (1) 1977
Thomas, John, G, San Francisco (1) 1967
Thomas, Mike, RB, Washington (1) 1977
Thomas, Pat, CB, LA Rams (2) 1979, 1981
Thomason, Bobby, QB, Philadelphia (3) 1954, 1956-57
Thompson, Billy, S, Denver (3) 1978-79, 1982
Thompson, Tommy, QB, Philadelphia (1) Dec. 1942
Tilley, Pat, WR, St. Louis (1) 1981*
Tingelhoff, Mick, C, Minnesota (6) 1965-70
Tinsley, Gaynell, E, Chi. Cardinals (1) 1939
Tinsley, Pete, G, Green Bay (1) Jan. 1940
Tippett, Andre, LB, New England (2) 1985-86
Titchenal, Bob, C, Washington (1) Dec. 1942*
Tittle, Y.A., QB (6) San Francisco 1954-55, 1958, 1960; NY Giants 1962-63
Todd, Dick, HB, Washington (2) Dec. 1940, Dec. 1942*
Tolar, Charlie, FB, Houston (2) 1962-63
Toneff, Bob, DT (4) San Francisco 1956; Washington 1960-62
Tonnemaker, Clayton, LB, Green Bay (1) 1954
Torczon, Laverne, DE, Buffalo (1) 1962
Torgeson, LaVern, C-LB (3) Detroit 1955; Washington 1956-57
Torrance, Jack, T, Chi. Bears (1) Dec. 1940
Toth, Zollie, FB, NY Yanks (1) 1951
Towler, Dan, FB-HB, LA Rams (4) 1952-55
Tracey, John, LB, Buffalo (2) 1966-67
Tracy, Tom (The Bomb), FB, Pittsburgh (2) 1959, 1961
Trippi, Charley, QB-HB, Chi. Cardinals (2) 1953-54
Tripson, John, E, Detroit (1) Jan. 1942
Tripucka, Frank, QB, Denver (1) 1963
Trumpy, Bob, TE, Cincinnati (4) 1969, 1970*, 1971, 1974
Tubbs, Jerry, LB, Dallas (1) 1963
Tunnell, Emlen, S (9) NY Giants 1951-58; Green Bay 1960
Turner, Bake, SE, NY Jets (1) 1964
Turner, Cecil, KR, Chi. Bears (1) 1971
Turner, Clyde (Bulldog), C, Chi. Bears (4) Dec. 1940, Jan. 1942, 1951-52
Turner, Jim, K, NY Jets (2) 1969-70
Turner, Keena, LB, San Francisco (1) 1985
Tuttle, Orville, G, NY Giants (2) 1939, Jan. 1940
Tyler, Wendell, RB, San Francisco (1) 1985
Tyrer, Jim, T (9) Dallas Texans 1963; Kansas City 1964-67, 1969-72

U

Ulinski, Harry, C, Washington (1) 1956
Unitas, Johnny, QB, Baltimore (10) 1958-65, 1967-68
Upchurch, Rick, KR, Denver (4) 1977, 1979-80, 1983
Upshaw, Gene, G, Oakland (7) 1969, 1973-78
Uram, Andy, HB, Green Bay (1) Jan. 1940

V

Van Brocklin, Norm, QB (9) LA Rams 1951-56; Philadelphia 1959, 1960*, 1961
Van Dyke, Bruce, G, Pittsburgh (1) 1974
van Eeghen, Mark, RB, Oakland (1) 1978
Van Note, Jeff, C, Atlanta (5) 1975-76, 1981-83
Van Pelt, Brad, LB, NY Giants (5) 1977-81
Van Raaphorst, Dick, K, San Diego (1) 1967
Vanzo, Fred, QB, Detroit (1) Jan. 1940
Varrichione, Frank, T (5) Pittsburgh 1956, 1958-59, 1961; LA Rams 1963
Villapiano, Phil, LB, Oakland (4) 1974-77
Vogel, Bob, T, Baltimore (5) 1965-66, 1968, 1969*, 1972
Volk, Rick, DB, Baltimore (3) 1968, 1970, 1972

W

Wade, Bill, QB (2) LA Rams 1959; Chi. Bears 1964
Wagner, Mike, S, Pittsburgh (2) 1976-77
Walden, Bobby, P, Pittsburgh (1) 1970
Walker, Chuck, DT, St. Louis (1) 1967
Walker, Doak, HB, Detroit (5) 1951-52, 1954-56
Walker, Wayne, LB-K, Detroit (3) 1964-66
Walker, Wesley, WR, NY Jets (2) 1979, 1983
Waller, Ron, HB, LA Rams (1) 1956
Wallner, Fred, G, Chi. Cardinals (1) 1956
Walls, Everson, CB, Dallas (4) 1982-84, 1986
Walsh, Bill, C, Pittsburgh (2) 1951-52
Walston, Bobby, E-K, Philadelphia (2) 1961-62
Walters, Stan, T, Philadelphia (2) 1979-80
Warfield, Paul, WR (8) Cleveland 1965, 1969-70; Miami 1971-72, 1973*, 1974*, 1975
Warlick, Ernie, E, Buffalo (4) 1963-66
Warner, Charley, DB, Buffalo (1) 1966
Warner, Curt, RB, Seattle (1) 1984
Warren, Jim, DB, Miami (1) 1967
Washington, Dave, LB, San Francisco (1) 1977
Washington, Gene, WR, Minnesota (2) 1970-71
Washington, Gene, WR, San Francisco (4) 1970-73
Washington, Joe, RB, Baltimore (1) 1980
Washington, Russ, T, San Diego (5) 1975-76, 1978-80
Washington, Vic, RB, San Francisco (1) 1972
Waterfield, Bob, QB, LA Rams (2) 1951-52
Waters, Charlie, S, Dallas (3) 1977-79
Watson, Steve, WR, Denver (1) 1982
Watts, George, T, Washington (1) Dec. 1942*
Weatherall, Jim, T, Philadelphia (2) 1956-57
Webb, Don, S, Boston (1) 1970
Webster, Alex, FB, NY Giants (2) 1959, 1962
Webster, David, S, Dallas Texans (1) 1962
Webster, George, LB, Houston (3) 1968*, 1969, 1970*
Webster, Mike, C, Pittsburgh (8) 1979-86
Wehrli, Roger, CB, St. Louis (7) 1971-72, 1975-78, 1980
Weinmeister, Arnie, T, NY Giants (4) 1951-54
Weisgerber, Dick, QB, Green Bay (1) Jan. 1940
Wells, Billy, HB, Washington (1) 1955
Wells, Warren, WR, Oakland (2) 1969, 1971
West, Stan, G, LA Rams (2) 1952-53
West, Willie, S (2) Buffalo 1964; Miami 1967
Westmoreland, Dick, CB, Miami (1) 1968
Wham, Tom, E, Chi. Cardinals (1) 1952
White, Arthur (Tarzan), G, NY Giants (1) 1939
White, Danny, QB, Dallas (1) 1983
White, Dwight, DE, Pittsburgh (2) 1973-74
White, Ed, G (4) Minnesota 1976-78; San Diego 1980
White, Randy, DT-NT, Dallas (9) 1978-86
White, Sammy, WR, Minnesota (2) 1977-78
Whited, Marv, QB, Washington (1) Dec. 1942*
Whitsell, Dave, DB, New Orleans (1) 1968
Whittenton, Jesse, DB, Green Bay (2) 1962, 1964
Wiatrak, John, C, Cleveland (1) 1939
Widby, Ron, P, Dallas (1) 1972
Widseth, Ed, T, NY Giants (1) 1939
Wietecha, Ray, C, NY Giants (4) 1958-59, 1961, 1963
Wiggin, Paul, DE, Cleveland (2) 1966, 1968
Wightkin, Bill, T, Chi. Bears (1) 1956
Wilcox, Dave, LB, San Francisco (7) 1967, 1969-70, 1971*, 1972-74
Wilder, James, RB, Tampa Bay (1) 1985
Wildung, Dick, T, Green Bay (1) 1952
Wilkerson, Doug, G, San Diego (3) 1981-83
Wilkin, Willie, T, Washington (3) Dec. 1940, Jan. 1942, Dec. 1942
Willard, Ken, FB, San Francisco (4) 1966-67, 1969-70
Willey, Norm, E, Philadelphia (2) 1955-56
Williams, Ben, DE, Buffalo (1) 1983
Williams, Delvin, RB (2) San Francisco 1977; Miami 1979
Williams, Fred, T, Chi. Bears (4) 1953-54; 1959-60
Williams, Johnny, HB, Washington (1) 1953
Williams, Willie, DB, NY Giants (1) 1970
Williamson, Carlton, S, San Francisco (2) 1985-86
Williamson, Fred, DB, Oakland (3) 1962-64
Willis, Bill, G, Cleveland (3) 1951-53
Wilson, Billy, E, San Francisco (6) 1955-60
Wilson, George, E, Chi. Bears (3) Dec. 1940, Jan. 1942, Dec. 1942
Wilson, Jerrel, P, Kansas City (3) 1971-73
Wilson, Larry, S, St. Louis (8) 1963-64, 1966-71
Wilson, Nemiah, CB, Oakland (1) 1968
Wilson, Otis, LB, Chi. Bears (1) 1986
Wilson, Tom, HB, LA Rams (1) 1958
Wimberly, Abner, E, Green Bay (1) 1953
Winder, Sammy, RB, Denver (1) 1985
Winkler, Jim, T, LA Rams (1) 1953
Winslow, Kellen, TE, San Diego (4) 1981-84
Wistert, Al, T, Philadelphia (1) 1951
Wittum, Tom, P, San Francisco (2) 1974-75
Wolfe, Hugh, FB, NY Giants (1) 1939
Wood, Duane, DB, Kansas City (1) 1964
Wood, Willie, S, Green Bay (8) 1963, 1965-71
Woodeshick, Tom, FB, Philadelphia (1) 1969
Woodson, Abe, DB, San Francisco (5) 1960-64
Woodson, Marv, DB, Pittsburgh (1) 1968
Wooten, John, G, Cleveland (2) 1966-67
Woudenberg, John, T, Pittsburgh (1) Dec. 1942
Wozniak, John, G, Dallas Texans (1) 1953
Wright, Eric, CB, San Francisco (2) 1985, 1986*
Wright, Ernie, T, San Diego (3) 1962, 1964, 1966
Wright, Louis, CB, Denver (5) 1978-80, 1984, 1986
Wright, Rayfield, T, Dallas (6) 1972-77

Y

Yary, Ron, T, Minnesota (7) 1972-78
Yepremian, Garo, K, Miami (2) 1974, 1979
Young, Bill, T, Washington (1) Dec. 1942
Young, Bob, G, St. Louis (2) 1979-80
Young, Buddy, HB, Baltimore (1) 1955
Young, Charle, TE, Philadelphia (3) 1974-76
Young, Fredd, ST, Seattle (2) 1985-86
Young, Roynell, CB, Philadelphia (1) 1982
Youngblood, Jack, DE, LA Rams (7) 1974-80
Youngblood, Jim, LB, LA Rams (1) 1980
Younger, Paul (Tank), FB-HB, LA Rams (4) 1952-54, 1956*

Z

Zarnas, Gust, G, Green Bay (1) Jan. 1940
Zatkoff, Roger, LB, Green Bay (3) 1955-57
Zeman, Bob, DB, Denver (1) 1963
Zeno, Joe, G, Washington (1) Dec. 1942*
Zimmerman, Roy, QB, Washington (1) Dec. 1942
Zook, John, DE, Atlanta (1) 1974

Chicago College All-Star Games

1934

CHI. BEARS 0, ALL-STARS 0

The first Chicago College All-Star Game ended in a scoreless tie, punctuated by 12 punts by the Chicago Bears and 11 by the College All-Stars. The All-Stars outgained the Bears 143-123 and had six first downs to the Bears' three.

Chicago moved to the collegians' 9-yard line in the second quarter, but end Bill Hewitt fumbled on a reverse and Ed (Moose) Krause of Notre Dame recovered on the 19-yard line. The All-Stars' Bill Smith attempted a 41-yard field goal on the last play of the game, but it was blocked and recovered by Chicago's Carl Brumbaugh. Smith also missed a 32-yard attempt.

The game matched the 1933 champions of the National Football League and graduated college seniors who were selected in a poll conducted by the sponsoring *Chicago Tribune* and 105 associated newspapers throughout the United States. A crowd of 79,432 was in attendance.

August 31, at Soldier Field

Chi. Bears	**Starting Lineups**	**College All-Stars**
Bill Hewitt	LE	Edgar Manske (N'western)
Roy (Link) Lyman	LT	Ed Krause (Notre Dame)
Jules Carlson	LG	Frank Walton (Pittsburgh)
Charles (Ookie) Miller	C	Chuck Bernard (Michigan)
Joe Zeller	RG	Fritz Febel (Purdue)
George Musso	RT	Ade Schwammel (Ore. St.)
Luke Johnsos	RE	Joe Skladany (Pittsburgh)
Carl Brumbaugh	QB	Homer Griffith (USC)
Gene Ronzani	LH	Beattie Feathers (Tenn.)
George Corbett	RH	Joe Laws (Iowa)
Bronko Nagurski	FB	Mike Mikulak (Oregon)

Head coaches—George Halas, Chi. Bears; Nobel Kizer (Purdue), College All-Stars

Chi. Bears	0	0	0	0	—	0
College All-Stars	0	0	0	0	—	0

Attendance—79,432

1935

CHI. BEARS 5, ALL-STARS 0

The Chicago Bears, runners-up to the New York Giants for the 1934 NFL championship, combined a field goal and a safety to defeat the College All-Stars in a game that was finished in a driving rainstorm.

The Bears' Jack Manders kicked a 27-yard field goal in the first quarter. All-Stars punter Bill Shepherd of Western Maryland fumbled a snap from center in the fourth quarter and recovered in the end zone, where he was downed for a safety.

The All-Stars had a first down on the Bears' 8-yard line in the fourth quarter, but gave up possession on downs without gaining a yard.

Chicago led 168-62 in total yardage and had nine first downs to five. The punting game dominated the contest. Each team punted 14 times, the Bears averaging 43.2 yards a kick, the All-Stars 37.1.

August 29, at Soldier Field

Chi. Bears	**Starting Lineups**	**College All-Stars**
Bill Hewitt	LE	Don Hutson (Alabama)
Art Buss	LT	Tony Blazine (Illinois Wes.)
Ray Richards	LG	Regis Monahan (Ohio State)
Ed Kawal	C	George Shotwell (Pitt.)
Joe Kopcha	RG	Billy Bevan (Minnesota)
George Musso	RT	Jim Barber (San Francisco)
Bill Karr	RE	Ray Fuqua (SMU)
Bernie Masterson	QB	Miller Munjas (Pittsburgh)
Beattie Feathers	LH	Bill Shepherd (W. Maryland)
John Sisk	RH	Al Nichelini (St. Mary's)
Jack Manders	FB	Stan Kostka (Minnesota)

Head coaches—George Halas, Chi. Bears; Frank Thomas (Alabama), College All-Stars

Chi. Bears	3	0	0	2	—	5
College All-Stars	0	0	0	0	—	0

Chi—FG Manders 27
Chi—Safety, Shepherd downed in end zone after fumbled center snap
Attendance—77,450

1936

DETROIT 7, ALL-STARS 7

Fullback Sheldon Beise and tailback Vernal (Babe) LeVoir, teammates on the University of Minnesota's 1934-35 national collegiate champion teams, combined their efforts to score the first touchdown of the three-year-old series as the All-Stars battled the Detroit Lions, 1935 NFL champions, to a 7-7 tie.

On fourth-and-eight at the Lions' 17-yard line in the second quarter, Beise faked a plunge into the line, then pitched the ball back to LeVoir, who cut over tackle behind good blocking and scored, ending a five-play, 61-yard drive.

Detroit's touchdown came with slightly more than two minutes remaining in the game. Ernie Caddel ran eight yards on fourth and one.

The game was delayed 24 hours because of rain. The All-Stars led in total yardage 184-128 and had nine first downs to the Lions' six.

September 3, at Soldier Field

Detroit	**Starting Lineups**	**All-Stars**
Ed Klewicki	LE	Wayne Millner (Notre Dame)
John Johnson	LT	Dick Smith (Minnesota)
Frank Knox	LG	Paul Tangora (N'western)
Clare Randolph	C	Gomer Jones (Ohio State)
Grover (Ox) Emerson	RG	Vernon Oech (Minnesota)
George Christensen	RT	Truman Spain (SMU)
John Schneller	RE	Keith Topping (Stanford)
Earl (Dutch) Clark	QB	Riley Smith (Alabama)
Frank Christensen	LH	Jay Berwanger (Chicago)
Ernie Caddel	RH	Bill Shakespeare (N. Dame)
Raymond (Buddy) Parker	FB	Sheldon Beise (Minnesota)

Head coaches—George (Potsy) Clark, Detroit; Bernie Bierman (Minnesota), College All-Stars

Detroit	0	0	0	7	—	7
College All-Stars	0	7	0	0	—	7

All-Stars—LeVoir 17 run (Fromhart kick)
Det —Caddel 8 run (Clark dropkick)
Attendance—76,361

1937

ALL-STARS 6, GREEN BAY 0

Tailback Sammy Baugh of TCU completed 7 of 13 passes for 115 yards and one touchdown and intercepted two passes as the College All-Stars defeated the Green Bay Packers 6-0.

After replacing Pittsburgh's Bobby LaRue on the second play of the game, Baugh teamed with Gaynell Tinsley on a first-quarter touchdown pass play that covered 47 yards. The All-Stars threatened three other times but two field goal attempts by Nebraska's Sam Francis and one by Minnesota's Bud Wilkinson failed.

Green Bay, which outgained the collegians 298-180 in total offense and led 17-8 in first downs, moved from its 24-yard line to the All-Stars' 3 in the fourth quarter. On fourth down, Arnie Herber passed in the flat to Don Hutson, who was tackled for no gain by Johnny Drake of Purdue. Herber completed 14 of 38 passes for 202 yards.

September 1, at Soldier Field

Green Bay	**Starting Lineups**	**College All-Stars**
Don Hutson	LE	Gaynell Tinsley (LSU)
Ernie Smith	LT	Ed Widseth (Minnesota)
Paul Engebretsen	LG	Max Starcevich (Wash.)
George Svendsen	C	Earl Svendsen (Minnesota)
Lon Evans	RG	Steve Reid (Northwestern)
Lou Gordon	RT	Averell Daniell (Pitt.)
Milt Gantenbein	RE	Merle Wendt (Ohio State)
Hank Bruder	QB	Vern Huffman (Indiana)
George Sauer	LH	Bobby LaRue (Pittsburgh)
Arnie Herber	RH	Johnny Drake (Purdue)
Clarke Hinkle	FB	Sam Francis (Nebraska)

Head coaches—Earl (Curly) Lambeau, Green Bay; Charles (Gus) Dorais (Detroit), College All-Stars

Green Bay	0	0	0	0	—	0
College All-Stars	6	0	0	0	—	6

All-Stars—Tinsley 47 pass from Baugh (kick failed)
Attendance—84,560

1938

ALL-STARS 28, WASHINGTON 16

Cecil Isbell of Purdue threw a 40-yard touchdown pass to Northwestern's John Kovatch, Bill Dougherty of Santa Clara intercepted a pass and ran 40 yards for a touchdown, and Andy Uram of Minnesota returned another interception for a score as the College All-Stars scored four touchdowns in the second half to defeat the Washington Redskins 28-16.

Isbell was named the most valuable player after completing 7 of 14 passes for 160 yards and a touchdown. The All-Stars trailed 10-3 at halftime after a four-yard touchdown run by Washington's Max Krause and a 30-yard field goal by Riley Smith.

August 31, at Soldier Field

Washington	**Starting Lineups**	**College All-Stars**
Wayne Millner	LE	Perry Schwartz (California)
Glen (Turk) Edwards	LT	Fred Shirey (Nebraska)
Les Olsson	LG	Joe Routt (Texas A&M)
Vic Carroll	C	Ralph Wolf (Ohio State)
Jim Karcher	RG	Leroy Monsky (Alabama)
Jim Barber	RT	Vic Markov (Washington)
Charley Malone	RE	Chuck Sweeney (N. Dame)
Riley Smith	QB	Andy Puplis (Notre Dame)
Sammy Baugh	LH	Cecil Isbell (Purdue)
Erny Pinckert	RH	Andy Uram (Minnesota)
Max Krause	FB	Frank Patrick (Pittsburgh)

Head coaches—Ray Flaherty, Washington; Alvin (Bo) McMillin (Indiana), College All-Stars

Washington	7	3	0	6	—	16
College All-Stars	3	0	12	13	—	28

All-Stars—FG McDonald 15
Wash —Krause 4 run (Smith kick)
Wash —FG Smith 30
All-Stars—Kovatch 40 pass from Isbell (kick failed)
All-Stars—Dougherty 40 interception return (kick failed)
All-Stars—Davis 4 run (kick blocked)
Wash —Karamatic 2 run (kick blocked)
All-Stars—Uram 47 interception return (Patrick kick)
Attendance—74,250

1939

NY GIANTS 9, ALL-STARS 0

Field goals of 34 yards by Ward Cuff and 22 and 41 yards by Ken Strong elevated the New York Giants to a 9-0 victory over the College All-Stars.

The game marked Strong's first appearance in a Giants' uniform since the 1935 season. He played for the New York Yankees of the American Football League in 1936-37 and for the Jersey City Giants of the American Professional Football Association in 1938. The APFL was a minor professional football league.

The All-Stars advanced to the Giants' 34-yard line in the second quarter and gave up the ball on downs. Len Barnum's intercepted pass stopped a collegiate drive at New York's 31 in the fourth quarter, and John Mellus's interception at the 22 stopped the All-Stars as the game ended.

August 30, at Soldier Field

NY Giants	**Starting Lineups**	**College All-Stars**
Jim Poole	LE	Bowden Wyatt (Tennessee)
Frank Cope	LT	Joe Mihal (Purdue)
John Dell Isola	LG	Francis Twedell (Minn.)
Mel Hein	C	Charley Brock (Nebraska)
Orville Tuttle	RG	Ralph Heikkinen (Michigan)
John Mellus	RT	Bob Haak (Indiana)
Jim Lee Howell	RE	Earl Brown (Notre Dame)
Ed Danowski	QB	Davey O'Brien (TCU)
Ward Cuff	LH	Marshall Goldberg (Pitt.)
Leland Shaffer	RH	Bob MacLeod (Dartmouth)
John Karcis	FB	Howard Weiss (Wisconsin)

Head coaches—Steve Owen, NY Giants; Elmer Layden (Notre Dame), College All-Stars

NY Giants	3	3	0	3	—	9
College All-Stars	0	0	0	0	—	0

NYG—FG Cuff 34
NYG—FG Strong 22
NYG—FG Strong 41
Attendance—81,456

1940

GREEN BAY 45, ALL-STARS 28

Cecil Isbell and Arnie Herber combined to complete 11 of 20 passes for 306 yards and five touchdowns as the Green Bay Packers outscored the All-Stars.

Ambrose Schindler of USC, who was selected the game's most valuable All-Star, put the All-Stars ahead with a one-yard run in the first quarter. The score was tied 14-14 in the second quarter, and the All-Stars still were within reach of the Packers at 35-28 in the fourth. Isbell threw for three touchdowns, and Don Hutson caught three.

August 29, at Soldier Field

Green Bay	Starting Lineups	College All-Stars
Don Hutson	LE	Bill Fisk (USC)
Buford (Baby) Ray	LT	Nick Cutlich (Northwestern)
Russ Letlow	LG	Jim Logan (Indiana)
George Svendsen	C	Clyde Turner (Hard.-Sim.)
Buckets Goldenberg	RG	Harry Smith (USC)
Bill Lee	RT	Tad Harvey (Notre Dame)
Milt Gantenbein	RE	Esco Sarkkinen (Ohio State)
Larry Craig	QB	Ambrose Schindler (USC)
Cecil Isbell	LH	Nile Kinnick (Iowa)
Joe Laws	RH	Lou Brock (Purdue)
Clarke Hinkle	FB	Joe Thesing (Notre Dame)

Head coaches—Earl (Curly) Lambeau, Green Bay; Eddie Anderson (Iowa), College All-Stars

Green Bay	14	14	7	10	—	45
College All-Stars	7	14	0	7	—	28

All-Stars—Schindler 1 run (Kinnick dropkick)
GB —Hutson 81 pass from Isbell (Smith kick)
GB —Mulleneaux 26 pass from Isbell (Smith kick)
All-Stars—Washington 1 run (Kellogg kick)
GB —Uram 60 pass from Herber (Engebretsen kick)
GB —Hutson 35 pass from Isbell (Smith kick)
All-Stars—McFadden 56 pass from Kinnick (Kinnick dropkick)
GB —Hutson 29 pass from Herber (Smith kick)
All-Stars—Schindler 1 run (Kinnick dropkick)
GB —FG Smith 34
GB —Isbell 4 run (Hutson kick)
Attendance—84,567

1941

CHI. BEARS 37, ALL-STARS 13

The Chicago Bears marched 45, 71, and 82 yards for touchdowns in the final 12 minutes of play to defeat the College All-Stars 37-13.

The All-Stars trailed 16-6 at the end of the third quarter and closed the score to 16-13 early in the fourth quarter when Charlie O'Rourke of Boston College passed to Jackie Robinson of UCLA.

Harry Clark scored from the one on the Bears' next possession to give Chicago a 23-13 lead. Sid Luckman passed to George McAfee to increase Chicago's advantage to 30-13. George Franck of Minnesota was the game's most valuable All-Star.

August 28, at Soldier Field

Chi. Bears	Starting Lineups	College All-Stars
Dick Plasman	LE	Dave Rankin (Purdue)
Joe Stydahar	LT	Ernie Pannell (Texas A&M)
Danny Fortmann	LG	Augie Lio (Georgetown)
Clyde (Bulldog) Turner	C	Rudy Mucha (Washington)
George Musso	RG	Tommy O'Boyle (Tulane)
Lee Artoe	RT	Nick Drahos (Cornell)
George Wilson	RE	Ed Rucinski (Indiana)
Sid Luckman	QB	Forest Evashevski (Mich.)
Ray Nolting	LH	Tom Harmon (Michigan)
George McAfee	RH	George Franck (Minn.)
Bill Osmanski	FB	George Paskvan (Wis.)

Head coaches—George Halas, Chi. Bears; Carl Snavely (Cornell), College All-Stars

Chi. Bears	6	7	3	21	—	37
College All-Stars	6	0	0	7	—	13

Chi —Kavanaugh 34 pass from Luckman (kick blocked)
All-Stars—Franck 22 pass from Harmon (kick blocked)
Chi —Clark 1 run (Manders kick)
Chi —FG Artoe 46
All-Stars—Robinson 46 pass from O'Rourke (Lio kick)
Chi —Clark 1 run (Manders kick)
Chi —McAfee 25 pass from Luckman (Manders kick)
Chi —Nowaskey 9 pass from Bussey (Manders kick)
Attendance—98,203

1942

CHI. BEARS 21, ALL-STARS 0

The Chicago Bears' dominance of the College All-Stars was more apparent than the final score of 21-0. The Bears outrushed the collegians 268-36 and outpassed them 203-77 for a total yardage advantage of 471-113.

The Bears' first touchdown was scored by Hugh Gallarneau on a four-yard run on fourth down after 8:40 of the first quarter. Steve Juzwik of Notre Dame returned the kickoff 91 yards from the All-Stars' 3-yard line to the Bears' 6. But the All-Stars did not score, giving up the ball on downs.

Juzwik's fumble at the collegians' 23 in the second period set up Chicago's second touchdown, a 24-yard pass, Young Bussey to Hampton Pool. Gallarneau scored Chicago's final touchdown in the third quarter on an eight-yard run.

August 28, at Soldier Field

Chi. Bears	Starting Lineups	College All-Stars
John Siegal	LE	Mal Kutner (Texas)
Ed Kolman	LT	Jim Daniell (Ohio State)
Danny Fortmann	LG	Rob Jeffries (Missouri)
Clyde (Bulldog) Turner	C	Vince Banonis (Detroit)
Ray Bray	RG	Bernie Crimmins (N. Dame)
Lee Artoe	RT	Al Blozis (Georgetown)
Hampton Pool	RE	Judd Ringer (Minnesota)
Sid Luckman	QB	Dick Erdlitz (Northwestern)
Ray Nolting	LH	Bruce Smith (Minnesota)
Hugh Gallarneau	RH	Steve Juzwik (Notre Dame)
Bill Osmanski	FB	Jack Graf (Ohio State)

Head coaches—George Halas, Chi. Bears; Bob Zuppke (Illinois), College All-Stars

Chi. Bears	7	7	7	0	—	21
College All-Stars	0	0	0	0	—	0

Chi —Gallarneau 4 run (Stydahar kick)
Chi—Pool 24 pass from Bussey (Stydahar kick)
Chi—Gallarneau 8 run (Stydahar kick)
Attendance—101,103

1943

ALL-STARS 27, WASHINGTON 7

The College All-Stars defeated the Washington Redskins 27-7 for their first victory in five years over an NFL champion. The All-Stars' roster was selected by team coaches instead of by a nationwide newspaper poll. The site of the game was switched to Dyche Stadium on the Northwestern University campus.

The All-Stars scored first when Missouri's Bob Steuber returned a punt 50 yards down the sideline for a touchdown.

The All-Stars began pulling away on a 37-yard touchdown pass play, Glenn Dobbs to Pat Harder, who ran the final 20 yards. Washington moved from its 43 to the All-Stars' 18 in the third quarter; Otto Graham intercepted a pass on the 3 and returned the ball 97 yards for a touchdown.

August 25, at Evanston, Illinois

Washington	Starting Lineups	College All-Stars
Bob Masterson	LE	Pete Pihos (Indiana)
Willie Wilkin	LT	Al Wistert (Michigan)
Dick Farman	LG	Felix Bucek (Texas A&M)
George Smith	C	Vic Lindskog (Stanford)
Steve Slivinski	RG	Buster Ramsey (Wm. & M.)
Clyde Shugart	RT	Dick Wildung (Minnesota)
Bob McChesney	RE	Bill Huber (Notre Dame)
Ray Hare	QB	Dick Renfro (Wash. St.)
Sammy Baugh	LH	Otto Graham (Northwestern)
Wilbur Moore	RH	Bob Steuber (Missouri)
Bob Seymour	FB	Pat Harder (Wisconsin)

Head coaches—Arthur (Dutch) Bergman, Washington; Harry Stuhldreher (Wisconsin), College All-Stars

Washington	0	7	0	0	—	7
College All-Stars	7	7	6	7	—	27

All-Stars—Steuber 50 punt return (Harder kick)
Wash —Aguirre 6 pass from Baugh (Masterson kick)
All-Stars—Harder 37 pass from Dobbs (Harder kick)
All-Stars—Graham 97 interception return (kick blocked)
All-Stars—Harder 33 run (Graham kick)
Attendance—48,471

1944

CHI. BEARS 24, ALL-STARS 21

Pete Gudauskas's 13-yard field goal with 10:42 left in the game gave the Chicago Bears a 24-21 victory.

Tulsa halfback Glenn Dobbs, making his second appearance in the game as a collegian under wartime eligibility rules, threw a four-yard pass to Notre Dame's Creighton Miller for the All-Stars' first touchdown. That concluded a 33-yard drive after a short Bears punt. The All-Stars went ahead 14-0 later in the first quarter when Dobbs fumbled and teammate John Tavener of Indiana picked up the ball and ran 12 yards for a touchdown. Dobbs was selected the game's most valuable All-Star.

August 30, at Evanston, Illinois

Chi. Bears	Starting Lineups	College All-Stars
Jim Benton	LE	John Dugger (Ohio State)
Dominic Sigillo	LT	Bill Willis (Ohio State)
Pete Gudauskas	LG	Dick Barwegan (Purdue)
Clyde (Bulldog) Turner	C	John Tavener (Indiana)
George Zorich	RG	Lin Houston (Ohio State)
Al Hoptowit	RT	Bob Zimny (Indiana)
George Wilson	RE	John Yonakor (Notre Dame)
John Long	QB	Lou Saban (Indiana)
Ray Nolting	LH	Glenn Dobbs (Tulsa)
Doug McEnulty	RH	Charley Trippi (Georgia)
Gary Famiglietti	FB	Creighton Miller (N. Dame)

Head coaches—Heartley (Hunk) Anderson and Luke Johnsos, Chi. Bears; Lynn (Pappy) Waldorf (Northwestern), College All-Stars

Chi. Bears	0	14	7	3	—	24
College All-Stars	14	0	7	0	—	21

All-Stars—Miller 4 pass from Dobbs (Saban kick)
All-Stars—Tavener 12 fumble return (Saban kick)
Chi —Famiglietti 3 run (Gudauskas kick)
Chi —Benton 12 pass from Luckman (Gudauskas kick)
All-Stars—Saban 1 run (Saban kick)
Chi —McLean 19 run (Gudauskas kick)
Chi —FG Gudauskas 13
Attendance—48,769

1945

GREEN BAY 19, ALL-STARS 7

Don Hutson intercepted a pass by Perry Moss of Tulsa in the first minute of the fourth quarter and ran 85 yards for the final touchdown in the Green Bay Packers' 19-7 victory over the College All-Stars. The game was returned to Soldier Field.

The All-Stars scored on a 63-yard pass play, Bob Kennedy of Washington State to Nick Scollard of St. Joseph's. Earlier, Kennedy had intercepted Irv Comp's pass in the end zone, returned it to the 2, then stepped back into the end zone for a safety.

The collegians advanced to the Packers' 24-yard line in the second quarter, but Michigan's Tom Harmon fumbled after a 46-yard run. Georgia's Charley Trippi ran to Green Bay's 2-yard line in the fourth quarter, but again the All-Stars fumbled.

August 30, at Soldier Field

Green Bay	Starting Lineups	College All-Stars
Don Hutson	LE	Ted Cook (Alabama)
Buford (Baby) Ray	LT	Bob Zimny (Indiana)
Bill Kuusisto	LG	Damon Tassos (Texas A&M)
Charley Brock	C	Tex Warrington (Auburn)
Buckets Goldenberg	RG	Glen Burgeis (Tulsa)
Paul Berezney	RT	Ralph Foster (Okla. St.)
Joel Mason	RE	Bill Huber (Notre Dame)
Larry Craig	QB	Charles Mitchell (Tulsa)
Irv Comp	LH	Charley Trippi (Georgia)
Lou Brock	RH	Don Greenwood (Illinois)
Ted Fritsch	FB	Bob Kennedy (Wash. St.)

Head coaches—Earl (Curly) Lambeau, Green Bay; Bernie Bierman (Minnesota), College All-Stars

Green Bay	3	9	0	7	—	19
College All-Stars	0	7	0	0	—	7

GB —FG Hutson 12
GB —Safety, Kennedy stepped into end zone
GB —McKay 20 pass from Rohrig (Hutson kick)
All-Stars—Scollard 63 pass from Kennedy (Harmon kick)
GB —Hutson 85 interception return (Hutson kick)
Attendance—92,753

1946

ALL-STARS 16, LA RAMS 0

Elroy (Crazylegs) Hirsch of the University of Wisconsin ran 68 yards for a first-quarter touchdown and turned a 32-yard pass from Northwestern's Otto Graham into a 62-yard touchdown in the third quarter of the College All-Stars' 16-0 victory over the Los Angeles Rams.

The Rams, representing Los Angeles for the first time since moving from Cleveland after the 1945 season, had the ball on the collegians' 19, 29, 18, 10, and 36 in the first half, but could not score. The All-Stars fumbled seven times in the game and the Rams recovered four.

Because they had played as underclassmen during World War II eligibility rules, some of the players on the college roster were making their second and third appearances in the game.

August 23, at Soldier Field

LA Rams	Starting Lineups	College All-Stars
Howard (Red) Hickey	LE	Jack Russell (Baylor)
Eberle Schultz	LT	Martin Ruby (Texas A&M)
Riley Matheson	LG	Visco Grgich (Santa Clara)
Bob DeLauer	C	Bill Godwin (Georgia)
Milan Lazetich	RG	Buster Ramsey (Wm. & M.)
Gil Bouley	RT	Derrell Palmer (TCU)
Steve Pritko	RE	Ralph Heywood (USC)
Bob Waterfield	QB	Otto Graham (Northwestern)
Fred Gehrke	LH	Billy Hillenbrand (Indiana)
Jim Gillette	RH	Dub Jones (Tulane)
Pat West	FB	Pat Harder (Wisconsin)

Head coaches—Adam Walsh, LA Rams; Alvin (Bo) McMillin (Indiana), College All-Stars

LA Rams	0	0	0	0	—	0
College All-Stars	7	0	7	2	—	16

All-Stars—Hirsch 68 run (Harder kick)
All-Stars—Hirsch 62 pass from Graham (Harder kick)
All-Stars—Safety, Walker tackled Washington in end zone
Attendance—97,380

1947

ALL-STARS 16, CHI. BEARS 0

A record crowd of 105,840 persons, attracted partly by the presence of the hometown Bears and an All-Stars team coached by Notre Dame University's Frank Leahy, saw the collegians score a 16-0 victory, their second shutout in a row by that margin.

The All-Stars used a T-formation offense for the first time in the series. It was an offense made famous by the Bears earlier in the decade. The collegians outgained the professionals 340-116 in total yards and outrushed them 189-35.

The All-Stars went 82 yards in 11 plays the first time they had the ball and 87 in two plays on their second series. Illinois's Buddy Young set up both touchdowns by running 31 yards on one play in the first drive and moving 41 yards with a pass in the second drive; he was named most valuable player.

August 22, at Soldier Field

Chi. Bears	Starting Lineups	College All-Stars
Ken Kavanaugh	LE	Bob Skoglund (Notre Dame)
Fred Davis	LT	Dick Barwegan (Purdue)
Chuck Drulis	LG	Alex Agase (Illinois)
Clyde (Bulldog) Turner	C	John Cannady (Indiana)
Ray Bray	RG	Weldon Humble (Rice)
Walt Stickel	RT	John Mastrangelo (N. Dame)
Ed Sprinkle	RE	Joe Tereschinski (Georgia)
Sid Luckman	QB	George Ratterman (N. Dame)
Ray (Scooter) McLean	LH	Buddy Young (Illinois)
Hugh Gallarneau	RH	Doc Blanchard (Army)
Joe Osmanski	FB	Tony Adamle (Ohio State)

Head coaches—George Halas, Chi. Bears; Frank Leahy (Notre Dame), College All-Stars

Chi. Bears	0	0	0	0	—	0
College All-Stars	13	0	3	0	—	16

All-Stars—Mello 6 run (kick blocked)
All-Stars—Zilly 46 pass from Ratterman (Case kick)
All-Stars—FG Case 21
Attendance—105,840

1948

CHI. CARDINALS 28, ALL-STARS 0

The Chicago Cardinals moved 80 yards to a touchdown the second time they had possession of the ball and went on to a 28-0 victory over the College All-Stars. Charley Trippi, who scored the Cardinals' final touchdown on a 13-yard pass from Ray Mallouf, was appearing in his fifth All-Star game, but his first as a professional.

The Cardinals outgained the All-Stars 333-235. The All-Stars marched 84 yards and two feet to the Cardinals' 1-foot line in the third quarter, when the score was 14-0, but Floyd Simmons of Notre Dame was stopped by Marshall Goldberg on fourth down.

Vince Banonis intercepted a pass by Perry Moss of Illinois and ran 31 yards for a touchdown to give Chicago a 21-0 lead in the fourth quarter.

August 20, at Soldier Field

Chi. Cardinals	Starting Lineups	College All-Stars
Bill Dewell	LE	Paul Cleary (USC)
Chet Bulger	LT	George Connor (N. Dame)
Lloyd Arms	LG	Arnie Weinmeister (Wash.)
Vince Banonis	C	Dick Scott (Navy)
Garrard (Buster) Ramsey	RG	Howard Brown (Indiana)
Stan Mauldin	RT	Ziggy Czarobski (N. Dame)
Mal Kutner	RE	Len Ford (Michigan)
Paul Christman	QB	Johnny Lujack (N. Dame)
Charley Trippi	LH	Bob Chappuis (Michigan)
Marshall Goldberg	RH	Charlie Conerly (Miss.)
Pat Harder	FB	Bump Elliott (Michigan)

Head coaches—Jimmy Conzelman, Chi. Cardinals; Frank Leahy (Notre Dame), College All-Stars

Chi. Cardinals	7	7	0	14	—	28
College All-Stars	0	0	0	0	—	0

Chi—Angsman 2 run (Harder kick)
Chi—Schwall 14 run (Harder kick)
Chi—Banonis 31 interception return (Harder kick)
Chi—Trippi 13 pass from Mallouf (Harder kick)
Attendance—101,220

1949

PHILADELPHIA 38, ALL-STARS 0

The day before the game with the Philadelphia Eagles, Bud Wilkinson, coach of the College All-Stars, said, "We haven't got a chance . . . and I'm not kidding." The Eagles shut down the All-Stars' passing game for three yards in losses, outrushed the collegians 228-116 for a 358-113 total yardage advantage, and won 38-0.

The Eagles defensed the collegians' split T formation with an eight-man line. Their three-man secondary also was close to the line. The professionals penetrated so quickly the All-Stars were unable to set up a passing attack.

Philadelphia broke a scoreless tie in the second quarter by marching 71 yards to a touchdown.

August 12, at Soldier Field

Philadelphia	Starting Lineups	College All-Stars
Jack Ferrante	LE	Barney Poole (Mississippi)
Vic Sears	LT	George Petrovich (Texas)
Cliff Patton	LG	Marty Wendell (Notre Dame)
Vic Lindskog	C	Chuck Bednarik (Penn.)
Frank (Bucko) Kilroy	RG	Bill Fischer (Notre Dame)
Al Wistert	RT	Al DeRogatis (Duke)
Pete Pihos	RE	Mel Sheehan (Missouri)
Tommy Thompson	QB	Jack Mitchell (Oklahoma)
Steve Van Buren	LH	George Taliaferro (Indiana)
Bosh Pritchard	RH	Jerry Williams (Wash. St.)
Joe Muha	FB	Joe Geri (Georgia)

Head coaches—Earle (Greasy) Neale, Philadelphia; Bud Wilkinson (Oklahoma), College All-Stars

Philadelphia	0	17	7	14	—	38
College All-Stars	0	0	0	0	—	0

Phil—Van Buren 1 run (Patton kick)
Phil—FG Patton 14
Phil—Craft 4 run (Patton kick)
Phil—Pihos 7 pass from Thompson (Patton kick)
Phil—Doss 4 run (Patton kick)
Phil—Armstrong 13 pass from Mackrides (Patton kick)
Attendance—93,780

1950

ALL-STARS 17, PHILADELPHIA 7

Halfback Charlie (Choo-Choo) Justice of North Carolina gained 133 yards in nine carries, scored on a 35-yard pass from quarterback Eddie LeBaron of Pacific, and was voted his team's most valuable player as the College All-Stars defeated the Philadelphia Eagles 17-7. The game was televised nationally for the first time on a 29-station network.

Justice gained 31 and 12 yards as the All-Stars marched 54 yards in six plays to a touchdown on their second series. They led 14-0 at the half after Santa Clara's Hall Haynes recovered a fumble by Clyde (Smackover) Scott at the Eagles' 35; LeBaron scrambled away from a strong rush and dumped the ball to Justice, who caught the pass at the line of scrimmage and weaved his way to a touchdown.

August 11, at Soldier Field

Philadelphia	Starting Lineups	College All-Stars
Jack Ferrante	LE	Art Weiner (North Carolina)
Vic Sears	LT	Don Campora (Pacific)
Cliff Patton	LG	Porter Payne (Georgia)
Vic Lindskog	C	Clayton Tonnemaker (Minn.)
Frank (Bucko) Kilroy	RG	George Hughes (Wm. & M.)
Al Wistert	RT	Leon Manley (Oklahoma)
Pete Pihos	RE	Jim Martin (Notre Dame)
Tommy Thompson	QB	Travis Tidwell (Auburn)
Steve Van Buren	LH	Doak Walker (SMU)
Clyde (Smackover) Scott	RH	Hall Haynes (Santa Clara)
Joe Muha	FB	Curly Morrison (Ohio St.)

Head coaches—Earle (Greasy) Neale, Philadelphia; Eddie Anderson (Holy Cross), College All-Stars

Philadelphia	0	0	0	7	—	7
College All-Stars	7	7	0	3	—	17

All-Stars—Pasquariello 1 run (Soltau kick)
All-Stars—Justice 35 pass from LeBaron (Soltau kick)
Phil —Van Buren 1 run (Patton kick)
All-Stars—FG Soltau 23
Attendance—88,885

1951

CLEVELAND 33, ALL-STARS 0

Halfback Dub Jones rushed for 105 yards and two touchdowns and quarterback Otto Graham completed 16 of 30 passes for 263 yards and two touchdowns as the Cleveland Browns outgained the College All-Stars 425-126 and posted a 33-0 victory.

The All-Stars made only five first downs; their longest gain was a 23-yard run by SMU's Kyle Rote, who had 45 yards in eight carries.

The Browns took a 2-0 lead in the first quarter when Rote fumbled a handoff from Notre Dame quarterback Bob Williams, who recovered the ball in the end zone but was downed by Len Ford for a safety. Bud McFadin of Texas was the All-Stars' most valuable player.

August 17, at Soldier Field

Cleveland	Starting Lineups	College All-Stars
Mac Speedie	LE	Don Stonesifer (N'western)
Lou Groza	LT	Bob Gain (Kentucky)
Abe Gibron	LG	Bud McFadin (Texas)
Frank Gatski	C	Jerry Groom (Notre Dame)
Lin Houston	RG	Lynn Lynch (Illinois)
Lou Rymkus	RT	Mike McCormack (Kansas)
Dante Lavelli	RE	Bob Wilkinson (UCLA)
Otto Graham	QB	Bob Williams (Notre Dame)
Rex Bumgardner	LH	Wilford White (Arizona St.)
Dub Jones	RH	Kyle Rote (SMU)
Emerson Cole	FB	Dan Dufek (Michigan)

Head coaches—Paul Brown, Cleveland; Herman Hickman (Yale), College All-Stars

Cleveland	2	10	7	14	—	33
College All-Stars	0	0	0	0	—	0

Cle—Safety, Ford downed Williams in end zone
Cle—Jones 2 run (Groza kick)
Cle—FG Groza 17
Cle—Jones 3 run (Groza kick)
Cle—Lavelli 14 pass from Graham (Groza kick)
Cle—Cole 8 pass from Graham (Groza kick)
Attendance—92,180

1952

LA RAMS 10, ALL-STARS 7

The Los Angeles Rams drove 51 yards midway in the fourth quarter to position Bob Waterfield for a 24-yard field goal that gave the Rams a 10-7 victory.

The All-Stars led 7-0 going into the final quarter after a 69-yard touchdown drive that ended with Ohio State's Vic Janowicz running three yards in the second quarter. Quarterback Babe Parilli, who gained 68 yards in seven carries, contributed a 41-yard run to the march.

The professionals tied the score in the early minutes of the fourth period on a three-yard pass, Norm Van Brocklin to Paul (Tank) Younger. The score was set up by a penalty against San Francisco's Ollie Matson, who drew pass interference defending a Van Brocklin to Volney (Skeet) Quinlan pass that put the ball on the 7-yard line.

August 15, at Soldier Field

LA Rams	Starting Lineups	College All-Stars
Tom Fears	LE	Leo Sugar (Purdue)
Don Simensen	LT	Harold Mitchell (UCLA)
Dick Daugherty	LG	Don Coleman (Michigan St.)
Leon McLaughlin	C	Doug Mosley (Kentucky)
Bill Lange	RG	Bob Ward (Maryland)
Tom Dahms	RT	Bill Pearman (Tennessee)
Elroy (Crazylegs) Hirsch	RE	Billy Howton (Rice)
Bob Waterfield	QB	Babe Parilli (Kentucky)
Dan Towler	LH	Vic Janowicz (Ohio State)
Verda (Vitamin T) Smith	RH	Hugh McElhenny (Wash.)
John Myers	FB	Ed Modzelewski (Maryland)

Head coaches—Joe Stydahar, LA Rams; Bobby Dodd (Georgia Tech), College All-Stars

LA Rams	0	0	0	10	—	10
College All-Stars	0	7	0	0	—	7

All-Stars—Janowicz 3 run (Janowicz kick)
LA —Younger 3 pass from Van Brocklin (Waterfield kick)
LA —FG Waterfield 24
Attendance—88,316

1953

DETROIT 24, ALL-STARS 10

Detroit's Bobby Layne set a passing yardage record by completing 21 of 31 passes for 323 yards as the Lions rolled up a record 21 first downs and outgained the College All-Stars 473-187 in a 24-10 victory.

Layne's primary receivers were ends Leon Hart, who caught seven passes for 106 yards, and Cloyce Box, five for 108, and halfback Doak Walker, eight for 97. Three All-Star quarterbacks completed only 9 of 27 passes for 81 yards.

The Lions' first touchdown was typical of their free-wheeling attack. They drove 80 yards, with the big play a Layne-to-Hart pass with a lateral from Hart to Walker that covered 47 yards, setting up Bob Hoernschemeyer's five-yard scoring run.

August 14, at Soldier Field

Detroit	Starting Lineups	College All-Stars
Cloyce Box	LE	Bernie Flowers (Purdue)
Lou Creekmur	LT	Kline Gilbert (Mississippi)
Jim Martin	LG	Donn Moomaw (UCLA)
Vince Banonis	C	George Morris (Ga. Tech)
Dick Stanfel	RG	Harley Sewell (Texas)
Gus Cifelli	RT	J.D. Kimmel (Houston)
Leon Hart	RE	Tom Scott (Virginia)
Bobby Layne	QB	Jack Scarbath (Maryland)
Doak Walker	LH	Fred Bruney (Ohio State)
Bob Hoernschemeyer	RH	Jim Sears (USC)
Pat Harder	FB	Buck McPhail (Oklahoma)

Head coaches—Raymond (Buddy) Parker, Detroit; Bobby Dodd (Georgia Tech), College All-Stars

Detroit	7	3	7	7	—	24
College All-Stars	0	3	0	7	—	10

Det —Hoernschemeyer 5 run (Harder kick)
Det —FG Walker 10
All-Stars—FG Dawson 23
Det —Box 8 pass from Layne (Harder kick)
Det —Hoernschemeyer 2 run (Harder kick)
All-Stars—Dawson 17 run (Samuels kick)
Attendance—93,818

1954

DETROIT 31, ALL-STARS 6

The Detroit Lions played without starting quarterback Bobby Layne, but reserve quarterback Tom Dublinski completed 10 of 15 passes for 103 yards as the Lions outgained the College All-Stars 361-144 in total yardage and won 31-6.

Layne did not play because the Lions feared he would be injured by also participating on defense. The game was conducted under collegiate rules as stipulated in the contract between the sponsoring *Chicago Tribune* and NFL. Colleges played one-platoon football in 1953. The Lions and other professional teams played with two platoons. It was the first time in 10 years the All-Star Game was played with limited substitution.

August 13, at Soldier Field

Detroit	Starting Lineups	College All-Stars
Dorne Dibble	LE	Carlton Massey (Texas)
Lou Creekmur	LT	Bob Morgan (Maryland)
Jim Martin	LG	Jerry Hilgenberg (Iowa)
LaVern Torgeson	C	Ed Beatty (Mississippi)
Harley Sewell	RG	Menil Mavraides (N. Dame)
Charlie Ane	RT	Stan Jones (Maryland)
Leon Hart	RE	Dick Deitrick (Pittsburgh)
Tom Dublinski	QB	Zeke Bratkowski (Georgia)
Doak Walker	LH	Chet Hanulak (Maryland)
Jack Christiansen	RH	Johnny Lattner (Notre Dame)
Lew Carpenter	FB	Neil Worden (Notre Dame)

Head coaches—Raymond (Buddy) Parker, Detroit; Jim Tatum (Maryland), College All-Stars

Detroit	17	0	7	7	—	31
College All-Stars	0	0	6	0	—	6

Det —FG Martin 46
Det —Walker 5 run (Walker kick)
Det —Carpenter 4 run (Girard kick)
All-Stars—Lattner 4 run (kick blocked)
Det —Carpenter 1 run (Martin kick)
Det —Doran 34 fumble return (Walker kick)
Attendance—93,470

1955

ALL-STARS 30, CLEVELAND 27

The College All-Stars broke a string of four straight victories by the NFL champion and improved their record in the series to 7 victories against 13 losses and 2 ties with a 30-27 win over the Cleveland Browns.

Tad Weed, a 5-foot 6-inch, 146-pound kicker from Ohio State, made field goals of 21, 19, and 41 yards, the last giving the Collegians a 30-20 lead with six minutes remaining.

The Browns went ahead for the final time 20-17 with 19 seconds remaining in the half on a 25-yard pass from George Ratterman to Ray Renfro.

August 12, at Soldier Field

Cleveland	Starting Lineups	College All-Stars
Darrell (Pete) Brewster	LE	Max Boydston (Oklahoma)
Lou Groza	LT	Jim Ray Smith (Baylor)
Abe Gibron	LG	Hank Bullough (Mich. St.)
Frank Gatski	C	Dick Szymanski (N. Dame)
Harold Bradley	RG	Bud Brooks (Arkansas)
Mike McCormack	RT	Frank Varrichione (N. Dame)
Dante Lavelli	RE	Henry Hair (Georgia Tech)
George Ratterman	QB	Ralph Guglielmi (N. Dame)
Ray Renfro	LH	Dickie Moegle (Rice)
Dub Jones	RH	Dave Middleton (Auburn)
Maurice Bassett	FB	Alan Ameche (Wisconsin)

Head coaches—Paul Brown, Cleveland; Earl (Curly) Lambeau, College All-Stars

Cleveland	7	13	0	7	—	27
College All-Stars	3	14	3	10	—	30

All-Stars—FG Weed 21
Cle —Ratterman 1 run (Groza kick)
All-Stars—Eidom 2 run (Weed kick)
Cle —Renfro 18 run (Groza kick)
All-Stars—Hair 5 pass from Guglielmi (Weed kick)
Cle —Renfro 25 pass from Ratterman (kick blocked)
All-Stars—FG Weed 19
All-Stars—Triplett 1 run (Leggett run)
All-Stars—FG Weed 41
Cle —Morrison 5 run (Groza kick)
Attendance—75,000

1956

CLEVELAND 26, ALL-STARS 0

The Cleveland Browns drove 80 yards the first time they had the ball and went on to win 26-0.

On the first series of plays, Michigan State quarterback Earl Morrall passed 11 yards to Navy's Ron Beagle, ran 10 yards himself, and handed off to Ohio State's Howard (Hopalong) Cassady for a nine-yard gain, moving the All-Stars to Cleveland's 34. Morrall was shaken up, however, on the play involving Cassady, and Jerry Reichow of Iowa replaced him. Reichow threw a pass on his first play and the Browns' Warren Lahr intercepted in the end zone. Cleveland took over on its 20 and moved to the first touchdown. Groza kicked field goals of 38, 30, 24, and 27 yards.

August 10, at Soldier Field

Cleveland	Starting Lineups	College All-Stars
Darrel (Pete) Brewster	LE	Ron Beagle (Navy)
Lou Groza	LT	Frank D'Agostino (Auburn)
Abe Gibron	LG	Hugh Pitts (TCU)
Frank Gatski	C	Bob Pellegrini (Maryland)
Herschel Forester	RG	Sam Huff (West Virginia)
Mike McCormack	RT	Bob Skoronski (Indiana)
Dante Lavelli	RE	Don Holleder (Army)
George Ratterman	QB	Earl Morrall (Michigan St.)
Fred (Curly) Morrison	LH	Howard Cassady (Ohio St.)
Ray Renfro	RH	Don McIlhenny (SMU)
Ed Modzelewski	FB	Don Schaefer (Notre Dame)

Head coaches—Paul Brown, Cleveland; Earl (Curly) Lambeau, College All-Stars

Cleveland	7	6	6	7	—	26
College All-Stars	0	0	0	0	—	0

Cle—Morrison 13 pass from Ratterman (Groza kick)
Cle—FG 38 Groza
Cle—FG 30 Groza
Cle—FG 24 Groza
Cle—FG 27 Groza
Cle—Filipski 3 run (Groza kick)
Attendance—75,000

1957

NY GIANTS 22, ALL-STARS 12

Quarterback Charlie Conerly and end Ken McAfee combined on touchdown pass plays of 38 and 10 yards as the New York Giants overcame an early deficit to score a 22-12 victory.

Wake Forest's Billy Barnes ran two yards for a touchdown to end a 55-yard drive that began when Wayne Bock of Illinois recovered a fumble by Alex Webster on the collegians' 45-yard line.

A fumble by Barnes later in the first quarter was recovered by Charlie Toogood and the Giants converted the turnover into a 33-yard field goal by Ben Agajanian.

August 9, at Soldier Field

NY Giants	Starting Lineups	College All-Stars
Kyle Rote	LE	Ron Kramer (Michigan)
Roosevelt Brown	LT	Carl Vereen (Georgia Tech)
Gerald Huth	LG	Dalton Truax (Tulane)
Ray Wietecha	C	Joe Amstutz (Indiana)
Jack Stroud	RG	Mike Sandusky (Maryland)
Dick Yelvington	RT	Earl Leggett (LSU)
Ken McAfee	RE	Tom Maentz (Michigan)
Don Heinrich	QB	John Brodie (Stanford)
Frank Gifford	LH	Jon Arnett (USC)
Alex Webster	RH	Abe Woodson (Illinois)
Mel Triplett	FB	Don Bosseler (Miami)

Head coaches—Jim Lee Howell, NY Giants; Earl (Curly) Lambeau, College All-Stars

NY Giants	3	7	7	5	—	22
College All-Stars	6	3	0	3	—	12

All-Stars—Barnes 2 run (kick failed)
NYG —FG Agajanian 33
NYG —McAfee 38 pass from Conerly (Agajanian kick)
All-Stars—FG Cothren 12
NYG —McAfee 10 pass from Conerly (Agajanian kick)
NYG —FG Agajanian 45
All-Stars—FG Cothren 33
NYG —Safety, Nolan tackled Woodson in end zone
Attendance—75,000

1958

ALL-STARS 35, DETROIT 19

The Detroit Lions outrushed the College All-Stars 179-3 and had 22 first downs to 11, but the collegians struck for 20 points in the second quarter and went on to win 35-19.

The Lions led 7-0 at the end of the first quarter, but the All-Stars intercepted Bobby Layne three times and scored on two passes from Jim Ninowski of Michigan State to Bobby Mitchell of Illinois to take a 20-7 halftime lead. The collegians intercepted five passes, while outpassing Detroit 291-193.

August 15, at Soldier Field

Detroit	**Starting Lineups**	**College All-Stars**
Jim Doran	LE	C. Krueger (Texas A&M)
Lou Creekmur	LT	Lou Michaels (Kentucky)
Harley Sewell	LG	Jerry Kramer (Idaho)
Charlie Ane	C	Dan Currie (Michigan State)
Stan Campbell	RG	Bill Krisher (Oklahoma)
Ken Russell	RT	Gene Hickerson (Miss.)
Steve Junker	RE	Jim Gibbons (Iowa)
Tobin Rote	QB	King Hill (Rice)
Gene Gedman	LH	Jim Pace (Michigan)
Howard Cassady	RH	B. Joe Conrad (Texas A&M)
John Henry Johnson	FB	Walt Kowalczyk (Mich. St.)

Head coaches—George Wilson, Detroit; Otto Graham, College All-Stars

Detroit	7	0	6	6	—	19
College All-Stars	0	20	2	13	—	35

Det —Doran 24 pass from Rote (Layne kick)
All-Stars—FG Conrad 19
All-Stars—Mitchell 84 pass from Ninowski (Conrad kick)
All-Stars—Mitchell 18 pass from Ninowski (Conrad kick)
All-Stars—FG Conrad 33
All-Stars—Safety, Jobko tackled Rote in end zone
Det —Gedman 9 run (kick blocked)
All-Stars—FG Conrad 24
All-Stars—FG Conrad 24
All-Stars—Howley 29 interception return (Conrad kick)
Det —Pfeifer 1 run (kick blocked)
Attendance—70,000

1959

BALTIMORE 29, ALL-STARS 0

The College All-Stars had a 19-18 edge in first downs, but the Baltimore Colts converted three turnovers into touchdowns and scored all of their points in the first half en route to a 29-0 victory.

Center Dan James of Ohio State snapped the ball over the head of Southern Methodist punter Dave Sherer and the ball went out of the end zone for a safety. The Colts' Carl Taseff returned the ensuing free kick 42 yards. Johnny Unitas passed 33 yards to Jim Mutscheller and three yards to Raymond Berry for a touchdown and an 8-0 lead.

Billy Stacy of Mississippi State fumbled a punt in the second quarter and Baltimore's Tom Addison recovered, setting up a 29-yard touchdown pass, Unitas to Mutscheller.

August 14, at Soldier Field

Baltimore	**Starting Lineups**	**College All-Stars**
Raymond Berry	LE	Buddy Dial (Rice)
Jim Parker	LT	Gene Selawski (Purdue)
Art Spinney	LG	Mike Rabold (Indiana)
Madison (Buzz) Nutter	C	Dan James (Ohio State)
Alex Sandusky	RG	Andy Cvercko (N'western)
George Preas	RT	Fran O'Brien (Michigan St.)
Jim Mutscheller	RE	Dave Sherer (SMU)
Johnny Unitas	QB	Lee Grosscup (Utah)
L.G. Dupre	LH	Don Brown (Houston)
Lenny Moore	RH	Dick Haley (Pittsburgh)
Alan Ameche	FB	Nick Pietrosante (N. Dame)

Head coaches—Weeb Ewbank, Baltimore; Otto Graham (Coast Guard), College All-Stars

Baltimore	8	21	0	0	—	29
College All-Stars	0	0	0	0	—	0

Balt—Safety, James centered ball out of end zone
Balt—Berry 3 pass from Unitas (kick failed)
Balt—Mutscheller 29 pass from Unitas (Rechichar kick)
Balt—Dupre 13 pass from Unitas (Rechichar kick)
Balt—Davis 36 interception return (Rechichar kick)
Attendance—70,000

1960

BALTIMORE 32, ALL-STARS 7

Quarterback Johnny Unitas completed 22 of 42 passes for 281 yards and three touchdowns, and the Baltimore Colts outgained the College All-Stars 416-128 in total offense and posted a 32-7 victory.

Baltimore moved 69 yards in seven plays the second time it had the ball to take a 7-0 lead. The All-Stars moved to the Colts' 5-yard line in the second quarter, but quarterback Don Meredith of Southern Methodist fumbled. The Colts' Gino Marchetti recovered, and Baltimore marched 95 yards to a touchdown.

August 12, at Soldier Field

Baltimore	**Starting Lineups**	**College All-Stars**
Raymond Berry	LE	Carroll Dale (Virginia Tech)
George Preas	LT	Bob Denton (Pacific)
Art Spinney	LG	Chuck Janerette (Penn St.)
Madison (Buzz) Nutter	C	Bill Lapham (Iowa)
Alex Sandusky	RG	Mike McGee (Duke)
Jim Parker	RT	Gene Gossage (N'western)
Jim Mutscheller	RE	Hugh McInnis (So. Miss.)
Johnny Unitas	QB	George Izo (Notre Dame)
Lenny Moore	LH	Prentice Gautt (Oklahoma)
Alan Ameche	RH	Tom Moore (Vanderbilt)
L.G. Dupre	FB	Frank Mestnik (Marquette)

Head coaches—Weeb Ewbank, Baltimore; Otto Graham (Coast Guard), College All-Stars

Baltimore	7	17	5	3	—	32
College All-Stars	0	0	0	7	—	7

Balt —Moore 4 pass from Unitas (Myhra kick)
Balt —Moore 3 pass from Unitas (Myhra kick)
Balt —FG Myhra 38
Balt —Moore 14 pass from Unitas (Myhra kick)
Balt —Safety, Lipscomb and Joyce tackled Izo in end zone
Balt —FG Myhra 27
All-Stars—Gautt 60 pass from Meredith (Khayat kick)
Balt —FG Myhra 26
Attendance—70,000

1961

PHILADELPHIA 28, ALL-STARS 14

Trapped behind the line of scrimmage, quarterback Sonny Jurgensen improvised with a behind-the-back pass to Pete Retzlaff for a first down that sustained the first of four touchdown drives in the Philadelphia Eagles' 28-14 victory over the College All-Stars.

August 5, at Soldier Field

Philadelphia	**Starters, Offense**	**College All-Stars**
Pete Retzlaff	LE	Aaron Thomas (Oregon St.)
Jim McCusker	LT	Roland Lakes (Wichita St.)
John Wittenborn	LG	Billy Shaw (Georgia Tech)
Chuck Bednarik	C	Greg Larson (Minnesota)
Stan Campbell	RG	Houston Antwine (S. Illinois)
J. D. Smith	RT	Jim Tyrer (Ohio State)
Bobby Walston	RE	Mike Ditka (Pittsburgh)
Sonny Jurgensen	QB	Norm Snead (Wake Forest)
Billy Barnes	LH	Pervis Atkins (N.M. St.)
Tommy McDonald	RH	Bernie Casey (Bowl. Green)
Clarence Peaks	FB	Bill Brown (Illinois)
	Starters, Defense	
Leo Sugar	LE	Earl Faison (Indiana)
Jess Richardson	LT	Joe Rutgens (Illinois)
Ed Khayat	RT	Ernie Ladd (Grambling)
Marion Campbell	RE	Bob Lilly (TCU)
John Nocera	LLB	Frank Visted (Navy)
Chuck Weber	MLB	E. J. Holub (Texas Tech)
Maxie Baughan	RLB	Fred Hageman (Kansas)
Jim Carr	LHB	Ed Sharockman (Pitt.)
Tom Brookshier	RHB	Claude Gibson (N.C. St.)
Bob Freeman	LS	Tom Matte (Ohio State)
Don Burroughs	RS	Joe Krakoski (Illinois)

Head coaches—Nick Skorich, Philadelphia; Otto Graham (Coast Guard), College All-Stars

Philadelphia	14	7	0	7	—	28
College All-Stars	0	0	0	14	—	14

Phil —McDonald 27 pass from Jurgensen (Walston kick)
Phil —Retzlaff 25 pass from Jurgensen (Walston kick)
Phil —McDonald 24 pass from Hill (Walston kick)
Phil —McDonald 24 pass from Jurgensen (Walston kick)
All-Stars—Gregory 18 pass from Kilmer (Fleming kick)
All-Stars—Grecni 57 interception return (Fleming kick)
Attendance—66,000

1962

GREEN BAY 42, ALL-STARS 20

Quarterback Bart Starr completed 13 of 22 passes for 255 yards and a record five touchdowns.

August 3, at Soldier Field

Green Bay	**Starters, Offense**	**College All-Stars**
Max McGee	LE	Reg Carolan (Idaho)
Bob Skoronski	LT	Fate Echols (Northwestern)
Fred (Fuzzy) Thurston	LG	Bill Hudson (Memphis St.)
Jim Ringo	C	Wayne Frazier (Auburn)
Jerry Kramer	RE	Roy Winston (LSU)
Forrest Gregg	RT	Joe Carollo (Notre Dame)
Ron Kramer	RE	Chuck Bryant (Ohio State)
Bart Starr	QB	John Hadl (Kansas)
Paul Hornung	LH	Curtis McClinton (Kansas)
Boyd Dowler	RH	Lance Alworth (Arkansas)
Jim Taylor	FB	Earl Gros (LSU)
	Starters, Defense	
Willie Davis	LE	Frank Parker (Okla. State)
Dave Hanner	LT	Merlin Olsen (Utah State)
Henry Jordan	RT	John Meyers (Washington)
Bill Quinlan	RE	Clark Miller (Utah State)
Dan Currie	LLB	Bill Saul (Penn State)
Ray Nitschke	MLB	Larry Onesti (Northwestern)
Bill Forester	RLB	Frank Buncom (USC)
Hank Gremminger	LHB	James Saxton (Texas)
Jesse Whittenton	RHB	Wendell Harris (LSU)
John Symank	LS	Tom Dellinger (N.C. St.)
Willie Wood	RS	Angelo Dabiero (N. Dame)

Head coaches—Vince Lombardi, Green Bay; Otto Graham (Coast Guard), College All-Stars

Green Bay	7	7	7	21	—	42
College All-Stars	7	3	10	0	—	20

All-Stars—Gros 1 run (Mather kick)
GB —Dowler 22 pass from Starr (Hornung kick)
All-Stars—FG Mather 26
GB —R. Kramer 4 pass from Starr (Hornung kick)
All-Stars—Bryant 21 pass from Hadl (Mather kick)
GB —Dowler 22 pass from Starr (Hornung kick)
All-Stars—FG Mather 15
GB —McGee 20 pass from Starr (Hornung kick)
GB —McGee 36 pass from Starr (Hornung kick)
GB —Pitts 3 run (Hornung kick)
Attendance—65,000

1963

ALL-STARS 20, GREEN BAY 17

A third-down pass from quarterback Ron VanderKelen to Pat Richter, VanderKelen's University of Wisconsin teammate, resulted in the All-Stars' first victory in the series since 1958.

August 2, at Soldier Field

Green Bay	**Starters, Offense**	**College All-Stars**
Max McGee	LE	Pat Richter (Wisconsin)
Bob Skoronski	LT	Bob Vogel (Ohio State)
Fred (Fuzzy) Thurston	LG	Ed Budde (Michigan St.)
Jim Ringo	C	Dave Behrman (Mich. St.)
Jerry Kramer	RG	Don Chuy (Clemson)
Forrest Gregg	RT	Daryl Sanders (Ohio State)
Ron Kramer	RE	Bob Jencks (Miami, Ohio)
Bart Starr	QB	Ron VanderKelen (Wis.)
Boyd Dowler	FL	Paul Flatley (Northwestern)
Tom Moore	HB	Larry Ferguson (Iowa)
Jim Taylor	FB	Bill Thornton (Nebraska)
	Starters, Defense	
Willie Davis	LE	Fred Miller (LSU)
Dave Hanner	LT	Charles Sieminski (Penn St.)
Henry Jordan	RT	Jim Dunaway (Mississippi)
Urban Henry	RE	Don Brumm (Purdue)
Dan Currie	LLB	Dave Robinson (Penn St.)
Ken Iman	MLB	Lee Roy Jordan (Alabama)
Bill Forester	RLB	Bobby Bell (Minnesota)
Herb Adderley	LHB	Tom Janik (Texas A&I)
Jesse Whittenton	RHB	Larry Glueck (Villanova)
Hank Gremminger	LS	Lonnie Sanders (Mich. St.)
Willie Wood	RS	Kermit Alexander (UCLA)

Head coaches—Vince Lombardi, Green Bay; Otto Graham (Coast Guard), College All Stars

Green Bay	7	3	0	7	—	17
College All-Stars	3	7	0	10	—	20

GB —Taylor 2 run (J. Kramer kick)
All-Stars—FG Jencks 20
All-Stars—Ferguson 6 run (Jencks kick)
GB —FG J. Kramer 21
All-Stars—FG Jencks 33
All-Stars—Richter 73 pass from VanderKelen (Jencks kick)
GB —Taylor 1 run (J. Kramer kick)
Attendance—65,000

1964

CHI. BEARS 28, ALL-STARS 17

The Chicago Bears overcame the College All-Stars' 10-7 halftime lead with three consecutive touchdowns in the third and fourth quarters on their way to a 28-17 victory.

August 7, at Soldier Field

Chi. Bears	**Starters, Offense**	**College All-Stars**
Gary Barnes	LE	Chuck Logan (N'western)
Herman Lee	LT	Lloyd Voss (Nebraska)
Ted Karras	LG	Harrison Rosdahl (Penn St.)
Mike Pyle	C	Ray Kubala (Texas A&M)
Jim Cadile	RG	Dick Evey (Tennessee)
Bob Wetoska	RT	Ernie Borghetti (Pittsburgh)
Mike Ditka	RE	Ted Davis (Georgia Tech)
Bill Wade	QB	Pete Beathard (USC)
Johnny Morris	FL	Paul Warfield (Ohio State)
Ron Bull	HB	Tony Lorick (Arizona State)
Joe Marconi	FB	Willis Crenshaw (Kan. St.)
	Starters, Defense	
Ed O'Bradovich	LE	George Seals (Missouri)
Stan Jones	LT	Tom Keating (Michigan)
Earl Leggett	RT	George Bednar (N. Dame)
Doug Atkins	RE	Ed Lothamer (Michigan)
Joe Fortunato	LLB	Wally Hilgenberg (Iowa)
Bill George	MLB	Mike Reilly (Iowa)
Larry Morris	RLB	Dave Wilcox (Oregon)
Bennie McRae	LHB	George Rose (Auburn)
Dave Whitsell	RHB	J. Richardson (W. Texas St.)
Richie Petitbon	LS	Perry Lee Dunn (Miss.)
Roosevelt Taylor	RS	Mel Renfro (Oregon)

Head coaches—George Halas, Chi. Bears; Otto Graham (Coast Guard), College All-Stars

Chi. Bears	0	7	14	7	—	28
College All-Stars	0	10	0	7	—	17

All-Stars—FG Van Raaphorst 14
Chi —Ditka 13 pass from Wade (Jencks kick)
All-Stars—Davis 14 pass from Taylor (Van Raaphorst kick)
Chi —Wade 1 run (Jencks kick)
Chi —Barnes 20 pass from Wade (Jencks kick)
Chi —Bivins 30 pass from Bukich (Jencks kick)
All-Stars—Taylor 5 pass from Mira (Van Raaphorst kick)
Attendance—65,000

1965

CLEVELAND 24, ALL-STARS 16

Cleveland's Jamie Caleb blocked a punt by Mississippi's Frank Lambert when the College All-Stars had 10 men on the field, and Stan Sczurek recovered in the end zone for the go-ahead score.

August 6, at Soldier Field

Cleveland	**Starters, Offense**	**College All-Stars**
Paul Warfield	LE	Bob Hayes (Florida A&M)
Dick Schafrath	LT	Ralph Neely (Oklahoma)
John Wooten	LG	Bob Breitenstein (Tulsa)
John Morrow	C	Bill Curry (Georgia Tech)
Gene Hickerson	RG	Jim Wilson (Georgia)
Monte Clark	RT	Harry Schuh (Memphis St.)
Johnny Brewer	RE	Fred Brown (Miami)
Frank Ryan	QB	Roger Staubach (Navy)
Gary Collins	FL	Fred Biletnikoff (Florida St.)
Ernie Green	HB	Pat Donnelly (Navy)
Jim Brown	FB	Ken Willard (North Carolina)
	Starters, Defense	
Paul Wiggin	LE	Jim Garcia (Purdue)
Dick Modzelewski	LT	Joe Szczecko (N'western)
Jim Kanicki	RT	Jim Norton (Washington)
Bill Glass	RE	Verlon Biggs (Jackson St.)
Jim Houston	LLB	Don Croftcheck (Indiana)
Vince Costello	MLB	Dick Butkus (Illinois)
Galen Fiss	RLB	Marty Schottenheimer (Pitt.)
Bernie Parrish	LHB	Clancy Williams (Wash. St.)
Walter Beach	RHB	Roy Jefferson (Utah)
Ross Fichtner	LS	Al Nelson (Cincinnati)
Larry Benz	RS	George Donnelly (Illinois)

Head coaches— Blanton Collier, Cleveland; Otto Graham (Coast Guard), College All-Stars

Cleveland	7	10	7	0	—	24
College All-Stars	0	3	6	7	—	16

Cle —Brown 7 run (Groza kick)
All-Stars—FG Mercein 36
Cle —Sczurek, blocked punt recovery in end zone
Cle —FG Groza 30
Cle —Collins 10 pass from Ryan (Groza kick)
All-Stars—Mercein 5 pass from Huarte (kick failed)
All-Stars—Rentzel 5 pass from Huarte (Mercein kick)
Attendance—68,000

1966

GREEN BAY 38, ALL-STARS 0

Quarterback Steve Sloan of Alabama fumbled on the game's first play from scrimmage, and Green Bay's Lionel Aldridge recovered on the College All-Stars' 33-yard line. Five plays later the Packers scored.

August 5, at Soldier Field

Green Bay	**Starters, Offense**	**College All-Stars**
Carroll Dale	LE	G. Garrison (San Diego St.)
Bob Skoronski	LT	Dave McCormick (LSU)
Fred (Fuzzy) Thurston	LG	John Niland (Iowa)
Ken Bowman	C	Pat Killorin (Syracuse)
Jerry Kramer	RG	Tom Mack (Michigan)
Forrest Gregg	RT	Francis Peay (Missouri)
Bill Anderson	RE	Milt Morin (Massachusetts)
Bart Starr	QB	Steve Sloan (Alabama)
Boyd Dowler	FL	D. Anderson (Texas Tech)
Paul Hornung	HB	Roy Shivers (Utah State)
Jim Taylor	FB	Johnny Roland (Missouri)
	Starters, Defense	
Willie Davis	LE	Stan Hindman (Mississippi)
Ron Kostelnik	LT	Jerry Shay (Purdue)
Henry Jordan	RT	George Rice (LSU)
Lionel Aldridge	RE	Aaron Brown (Minnesota)
Dave Robinson	LLB	Doug Buffone (Louisville)
Ray Nitschke	MLB	Tommy Nobis (Texas)
Lee Roy Caffey	RLB	Don Hansen (Illinois)
Herb Adderley	LHB	Stan Quintana (N.Mex.)
Bob Jeter	RHB	Charlie King (Purdue)
Willie Wood	LS	Doug McFalls (Georgia)
Tom Brown	RS	Nick Rassas (Notre Dame)

Head coaches—Vince Lombardi, Green Bay; John Sauer, College All-Stars

Green Bay	7	21	10	0	—	38
College All-Stars	0	0	0	0	—	0

GB—Dowler 10 pass from Starr (Chandler kick)
GB—B. Anderson 13 pass from Starr (Chandler kick)
GB—Taylor 1 run (Chandler kick)
GB—Adderley 36 interception return (Chandler kick)
GB—FG Chandler 17
GB—Taylor 13 run (Chandler kick)
Attendance—72,000

1967

GREEN BAY 27, ALL-STARS 0

Quarterback Bart Starr completed 15 of 21 passes for 212 yards and two touchdowns and turned nine third-down situations into six first downs before leaving the game at the end of the half with the Green Bay Packers leading the College All-Stars 20-0.

August 4, at Soldier Field

Green Bay	**Starters, Offense**	**College All-Stars**
Boyd Dowler	LE	Gene Washington (Mich. St.)
Bob Skoronski	LT	Gene Upshaw (Texas A&I)
Gale Gillingham	LG	Tom Regner (Notre Dame)
Ken Bowman	C	Bob Hyland (Boston Coll.)
Jerry Kramer	RG	Norman Davis (Grambling)
Forrest Gregg	RT	Mike Current (Ohio State)
Allen Brown	TE	Tom Beer (Houston)
Bart Starr	QB	Steve Spurrier (Florida)
Carroll Dale	FL	Dave Williams (Wash.)
Elijah Pitts	RB	Floyd Little (Syracuse)
Ben Wilson	RB	Mel Farr (UCLA)
	Starters, Defense	
Willie Davis	LE	Leo Carroll (San Diego St.)
Ron Kostelnik	LT	Bubba Smith (Michigan St.)
Henry Jordan	RT	Dave Rowe (Penn State)
Lionel Aldridge	RE	Alan Page (Notre Dame)
Dave Robinson	LLB	George Webster (Mich. St.)
Ray Nitschke	MLB	Jim Lynch (Notre Dame)
Lee Roy Caffey	RLB	Paul Naumoff (Tennessee)
Herb Adderley	LHB	Bob Grim (Oregon State)
Bob Jeter	RHB	Phil Clark (Northwestern)
Tom Brown	LS	Rick Volk (Michigan)
Willie Wood	RS	Henry King (Utah State)

Head coaches—Vince Lombardi, Green Bay; John Sauer, College All-Stars

Green Bay	6	14	0	7	—	27
College All-Stars	0	0	0	0	—	0

GB—FG Chandler 13
GB—FG Chandler 14
GB—Dowler 11 pass from Starr (Chandler kick)
GB—Long 22 pass from Starr (Chandler kick)
GB—Grabowski 22 run (Chandler kick)
Attendance—70,934

1968

GREEN BAY 34, ALL-STARS 17

Quarterback Bart Starr completed 17 of 23 passes for 288 yards and three touchdowns.

August 2, at Soldier Field

Green Bay	**Starters, Offense**	**College All-Stars**
Boyd Dowler	SE	Bob Wallace (Texas-El Paso)
Bob Skoronski	LT	Mo Moorman (Texas A&M)
Gale Gillingham	LG	Bill Leuck (Arizona)
Ken Bowman	C	Bob Johnson (Tennessee)
Jerry Kramer	RG	John Williams (Minnesota)
Forrest Gregg	RT	Ron Yary (USC)
Marv Fleming	TE	Charlie Sanders (Minn.)
Bart Starr	QB	Gary Beban (UCLA)
Carroll Dale	FL	Dennis Homan (Alabama)
Elijah Pitts	RB	MacArthur Lane (Utah St.)
Jim Grabowski	RB	Larry Csonka (Syracuse)
	Starters, Defense	
Willie Davis	LE	Claude Humphrey (Tenn. St.)
Ron Kostelnik	LT	Curley Culp (Arizona State)
Henry Jordan	RT	Bill Staley (Utah State)
Lionel Aldridge	RE	Marvin Upshaw (Trinity)
Dave Robinson	LLB	Fred Carr (Texas-El Paso)
Ray Nitschke	MLB	Mike McGill (Notre Dame)
Lee Roy Caffey	RLB	Adrian Young (USC)
Herb Adderley	LHB	Jon Henderson (Colo. St.)
Bob Jeter	RHB	Jim Smith (Oregon)
Tom Brown	LS	Major Hazelton (Fla. A&M)
Willie Wood	RS	Bob Atkins (Grambling)

Head coaches—Phil Bengtson, Green Bay; Norm Van Brocklin, College All-Stars

Green Bay	7	17	0	10	—	34
College All-Stars	0	3	7	7	—	17

GB —Anderson 1 run (Kramer kick)
GB —Dale 20 pass from Starr (Kramer kick)
GB —Dale 36 pass from Starr (Kramer kick)
All-Stars—FG DePoyster 22
GB —FG Traynham 30
All-Stars—McCullouch 7 pass from Beban (DePoyster kick)
GB —Dale 23 pass from Starr (Kramer kick)
GB —FG Kramer 47
All-Stars—McCullouch 24 pass from Landry (DePoyster kick)
Attendance—69,917

1969

NY JETS 26, ALL-STARS 24

The New York Jets scored a 26-24 victory.

August 1, at Soldier Field

NY Jets	**Starters, Offense**	**College All-Stars**
George Sauer	WR	Jim Seymour (Notre Dame)
Winston Hill	LT	Dave Foley (Ohio State)
Randy Rasmussen	LG	Mike Montler (Colorado)
John Schmitt	C	Jon Kolb (Oklahoma State)
Dave Herman	RG	John Shinners (Xavier)
Sam Walton	RT	George Kunz (Notre Dame)
Pete Lammons	TE	Bob Klein (USC)
Don Maynard	WR	Jerry LeVias (SMU)
Joe Namath	QB	Terry Hanratty (Notre Dame)
Emerson Boozer	RB	Altie Taylor (Utah State)
Matt Snell	RB	Paul Gipson (Houston)
	Starters, Defense	
Gerry Philbin	LE	Bill Stanfill (Georgia)
Paul Rochester	LT	Rich Moore (Villanova)
John Elliott	RT	Rolf Krueger (Texas A&M)
Verlon Biggs	RE	Fred Dryer (San Diego St.)
John Neidert	LLB	Ron Pritchard (Arizona St.)
Al Atkinson	MLB	Bill Bergey (Arkansas State)
Ralph Baker	RLB	Bob Babich (Miami, Ohio)
Johnny Sample	LCB	Jim Marsalis (Tenn. St.)
Randy Beverly	RCB	Billy Thompson (Md.-E.S.)
Bill Baird	LS	Gene Epps (Texas-El Paso)
Jim Hudson	RS	Roger Wehrli (Missouri)

Head coaches—Weeb Ewbank, NY Jets; Otto Graham, College All-Stars

NY Jets	6	7	10	3	—	26
College All-Stars	0	0	17	7	—	24

NYJ —FG J. Turner 43
NYJ —FG J. Turner 16
NYJ —Snell 3 run (J. Turner kick)
NYJ —FG J.Turner 42
All-Stars—Washington 17 pass from Cook (Gerela kick)
All-Stars—FG Gerela 28
NYJ —Snell 35 run (J. Turner kick)
All-Stars—Klein 12 pass from Cook (Gerela kick)
NYJ —FG J. Turner 18
All-Stars—LeVias 19 pass from Cook (Gerela kick)
Attendance—74,208

1970

KANSAS CITY 24, ALL-STARS 3

Len Dawson was successful on 17 of 21 passes, including 12 of 14 for 117 yards and one touchdown in the first half, as the Kansas City Chiefs defeated the College All-Stars 24-3.

Dawson's 25-yard pass to Frank Pitts put Kansas City ahead 7-0 the first time it had the ball.

July 31, at Soldier Field

Kansas City	Starters, Offense	College All-Stars
Frank Pitts	WR	Jerry Hendren (Idaho)
Jim Tyrer	LT	Bob McKay (Texas)
Ed Budde	LG	Doug Wilkerson (N.C. Cent.)
E. J. Holub	C	Sid Smith (USC)
Mo Moorman	RG	Chuck Hutchison (Ohio St.)
Dave Hill	RT	Bob Asher (Vanderbilt)
Fred Arbanas	TE	Rich Caster (Jackson St.)
Otis Taylor	WR	Ron Shanklin (N. Texas St.)
Len Dawson	QB	Dennis Shaw (San Diego St.)
Mike Garrett	RB	Bob Anderson (Colorado)
Robert Holmes	RB	Art Malone (Arizona State)
	Starters, Defense	
Jerry Mays	LE	Al Cowlings (USC)
Curley Culp	LT	Mike McCoy (Notre Dame)
Buck Buchanan	RT	Mike Reid (Penn State)
Aaron Brown	RE	C. Hardman (N. Texas St.)
Bobby Bell	LLB	John Small (Citadel)
Willie Lanier	MLB	Steve Zabel (Oklahoma)
Jim Lynch	RLB	Jim Files (Oklahoma)
Jim Marsalis	LCB	Bruce Taylor (Boston U.)
Emmitt Thomas	RCB	Al Mathews (Texas A&I)
Jim Kearney	LS	Steve Tannen (Florida)
Johnny Robinson	RS	Charlie Waters (Clemson)

Head coaches—Hank Stram, Kansas City; Otto Graham, College All-Stars

Kansas City	10	14	0	0	—	24
College All-Stars	0	0	3	0	—	3

KC —Pitts 25 pass from Dawson (Stenerud kick)
KC —FG Stenerud 43
KC —McVea 3 run (Stenerud kick)
KC —Kearney 65 interception return (Stenerud kick)
All-Stars—FG Delaney 26
Attendance—69,940

1971

BALTIMORE 24, ALL-STARS 17

The Baltimore Colts' 24-17 victory over the College All-Stars was the professionals' eighth in a row and gave them a record of 27 victories, 9 losses, and 2 ties in the series.

July 30, at Soldier Field

Baltimore	Starters, Offense	College All-Stars
Eddie Hinton	WR	J. D. Hill (Arizona State)
Bob Vogel	LT	Marv Montgomery (USC)
Glenn Ressler	LG	Steve Lawson (Kansas)
Bill Curry	C	Warren Koegel (Penn State)
John Williams	RG	H. Allison (San Diego St.)
Dan Sullivan	RT	Vern Holland (Tenn. State)
John Mackey	TE	Bob Moore (Stanford)
Ray Perkins	WR	Ernie Jennings (Air Force)
Earl Morrall	QB	Jim Plunkett (Stanford)
Tom Matte	RB	John Brockington (Ohio St.)
Norm Bulaich	RB	Mike Adamle (N'western)
	Starters, Defense	
Bubba Smith	LE	Jack Youngblood (Florida)
Jim Bailey	LT	Julius Adams (Texas So.)
Billy Newsome	RT	Tony McGee (Bishop)
Roy Hilton	RE	Richard Harris (Grambling)
Ray May	LLB	Ron Hornsby (SE Louisiana)
Mike Curtis	MLB	Isiah Robertson (Southern)
Ted Hendricks	RLB	Jack Ham (Penn State)
Charlie Stukes	LCB	Clarence Scott (Kansas St.)
Jim Duncan	RCB	Ike Thomas (Bishop)
Jerry Logan	LS	Charlie Hall (Pittsburgh)
Rick Volk	RS	Jack Tatum (Ohio State)

Head coaches—Don McCafferty, Baltimore; Blanton Collier, College All-Stars

Baltimore	7	7	3	7	—	24
College All-Stars	0	10	0	7	—	17

Balt —Perkins 24 pass from Morrall (O'Brien kick)
All-Stars—Brockington 1 run (Pastorini kick)
Balt —Matte 15 pass from Morrall (O'Brien kick)
All-Stars—FG Jacobs 40
Balt —FG O'Brien 22
Balt —Mitchell 44 pass from Morrall (O'Brien kick)
All-Stars—Ham 47 fumble return (Jacobs kick)
Attendance—52,289

1972

DALLAS 20, ALL-STARS 7

The Dallas Cowboys converted a pass interception and recovered fumble into 10 points.

Mel Renfro intercepted a pass by Jerry Tagge at the All-Stars' 30 in the first quarter; the Cowboys turned the mistake into Mike Clark's 31-yard field goal.

July 28, at Soldier Field

Dallas	Starters, Offense	College All-Stars
Bob Hayes	WR	Mike Siani (Villanova)
Ralph Neely	LT	Lionel Antoine (So. Illinois)
John Niland	LG	Reggie McKenzie (Mich.)
Dave Manders	C	Bob Kuziel (Pittsburgh)
Blaine Nye	RG	Steve Okoniewski (Mont.)
Rayfield Wright	RT	Dan Yockum (Syracuse)
Mike Ditka	TE	Riley Odoms (Houston)
Lance Alworth	WR	Glenn Doughty (Michigan)
Roger Staubach	QB	Jerry Tagge (Nebraska)
Duane Thomas	RB	Jeff Kinney (Nebraska)
Walt Garrison	RB	Franco Harris (Penn State)
	Starters, Defense	
Larry Cole	LE	Walt Patulski (Notre Dame)
Jethro Pugh	LT	J. Mendenhall (Grambling)
Bob Lilly	RT	Pete Lazetich (Stanford)
George Andrie	RE	Sherman White (California)
Dave Edwards	LLB	Willie Hall (USC)
Lee Roy Jordan	MLB	Jeff Siemon (Stanford)
Chuck Howley	RLB	Mike Taylor (Michigan)
Herb Adderley	LCB	W. Buchanon (San Diego St.)
Mel Renfro	RCB	Tommy Casanova (LSU)
Cornell Green	LS	Thom Darden (Michigan)
Cliff Harris	RS	Craig Clemons (Iowa)

Head coaches—Tom Landry, Dallas; Bob Devaney (Nebraska), College All-Stars

Dallas	3	7	7	3	—	20
College All-Stars	0	0	0	7	—	7

Dall —FG Clark 31
Dall —Sellers 18 pass from Morton (Clark kick)
Dall —Hayes 24 pass from Morton (Fritsch kick)
Dall —FG Fritsch 33
All-Stars—Newhouse 1 run (Marcol kick)
Attendance—54,162

1973

MIAMI 14, ALL-STARS 3

The Miami Dolphins marched 66 yards to Larry Csonka's three-yard touchdown run the first time they had the ball and went on to defeat the College All-Stars 14-3.

Csonka gained 76 yards in 17 carries as the professionals outgained the collegians 251-133 in total offense.

July 27, at Soldier Field

Miami	Starters, Offense	College All-Stars
Paul Warfield	WR	Barry Smith (Florida State)
Wayne Moore	LT	Paul Seymour (Michigan)
Bob Kuechenberg	LG	Pete Adams (USC)
Jim Langer	C	Dave Brown (USC)
Larry Little	RG	John Hannah (Alabama)
Norm Evans	RT	Jerry Sisemore (Texas)
Marv Fleming	TE	Charle Young (USC)
Howard Twilley	WR	Steve Holden (Arizona St.)
Bob Griese	QB	Bert Jones (LSU)
Jim Kiick	RB	T. Metcalf (Long Beach St.)
Larry Csonka	RB	Chuck Foreman (Miami)
	Starters, Defense	
Vern Den Herder	LE	W. Chambers (E. Kentucky)
Manny Fernandez	LT	John Grant (USC)
Bob Heinz	RT	Rich Glover (Nebraska)
Bill Stanfill	RE	John Matuszak (Tampa)
Doug Swift	LLB	Jim Merlo (Stanford)
Nick Buoniconti	MLB	J. Youngblood (Tenn. Tech)
Bob Matheson	RLB	Gary Weaver (Fresno State)
Tim Foley	LCB	Burgess Owens (Miami)
Curtis Johnson	RCB	Mike Holmes (Texas So.)
Charlie Babb	LS	J. T. Thomas (Florida State)
Dick Anderson	RS	Jackie Wallace (Arizona)

Head coaches—Don Shula, Miami; John McKay (USC), College All-Stars

Miami	7	0	0	7	—	14
College All-Stars	0	3	0	0	—	3

Mia —Csonka 3 run (Yepremian kick)
All-Stars—FG Guy 10
Mia —Csonka 7 run (Yepremian kick)
Attendance—54,103

1974

NO GAME

The forty-first Chicago All-Star game was canceled by the sponsoring *Chicago Tribune* after the NFL Players' Association said it would not give full sanction to the game between the College All-Stars and Miami Dolphins.

The Players' Association and NFL owners were involved in a collective bargaining dispute that had resulted in some of the Association's members striking their summer training camps. The All-Stars voted not to continue preparation for the contest unless the players and owners settled their dispute.

1975

PITTSBURGH 21, ALL-STARS 14

Trailing 14-7 at the half, the Pittsburgh Steelers rallied for a 21-14 victory over the College All-Stars behind quarterback Joe Gilliam, who passed for two touchdowns in the fourth quarter.

Gilliam replaced starter Terry Bradshaw.

August 1, at Soldier Field

Pittsburgh	Starters, Offense	College All-Stars
Frank Lewis	WR	Pat McInally (Harvard)
Jon Kolb	LT	Dennis Harrah (Miami)
Jim Clack	LG	Ken Huff (North Carolina)
Ray Mansfield	C	Kyle Davis (Oklahoma)
Gerry Mullins	RG	Lynn Boden (So. Dakota St.)
Gordon Gravelle	RT	Kurt Schumacher (Ohio St.)
Larry Brown	TE	Russ Francis (Oregon)
Ron Shanklin	WR	Emmett Edwards (Kansas)
Terry Bradshaw	QB	Steve Bartkowski (Cal.)
Rocky Bleier	RB	Walter Payton (Jackson St.)
Franco Harris	RB	Stan Winfrey (Arkansas St.)
	Starters, Defense	
L. C. Greenwood	LE	Mike Fanning (Notre Dame)
Joe Greene	LT	Mike Hartenstine (Penn St.)
Ernie Holmes	RT	Randy White (Maryland)
Dwight White	RE	Robert Brazile (Jackson St.)
Jack Ham	LLB	Glenn Cameron (Florida)
Jack Lambert	MLB	Ralph Ortega (Florida)
Andy Russell	RLB	Richard Wood (USC)
J. T. Thomas	LCB	Neal Colzie (Ohio State)
Mel Blount	RCB	Louis Wright (San Jose St.)
Mike Wagner	LS	Charles Phillips (USC)
Glen Edwards	RS	Marvin Cobb (USC)

Head coaches—Chuck Noll, Pittsburgh; John McKay (USC), College All-Stars

Pittsburgh	0	7	0	14	—	21
College All-Stars	7	7	0	0	—	14

All-Stars—McInally 28 pass from Bartkowski (Mike-Mayer kick)
Pitt —Grossman 2 pass from Bradshaw (Gerela kick)
All-Stars—Livers 88 punt return (Mike-Mayer kick)
Pitt —Bleier 6 pass from Gilliam (Gerela kick)
Pitt —Lewis 21 pass from Gilliam (Gerela kick)
Attendance-54,562

1976

PITTSBURGH 24, ALL-STARS 0

The Pittsburgh Steelers won 24-0 in the last Chicago College All-Star Game. It was called with 1:22 left in the third quarter. A thunderstorm flooded the field and 12 minutes later game officials agreed with NFL Commissioner Pete Rozelle to suspend play.

July 23, at Soldier Field

Pittsburgh	**Starters, Offense**	**College All-Stars**
Frank Lewis	WR	Duriel Harris (N. Mexico St.)
Jon Kolb	LT	Mark Koncar (Colorado)
Jim Clack	LG	Tom Glassic (Virginia)
Mike Webster	C	Pete Brock (Colorado)
Gerry Mullins	RG	Jackie Slater (Jackson St.)
Gordon Gravelle	RT	Dennis Lick (Wisconsin)
Larry Brown	TE	B. Cunningham (Clemson)
Lynn Swann	WR	Brian Baschnagel (Ohio St.)
Terry Bradshaw	QB	M. Kruczek (Boston Coll.)
Rocky Bleier	RB	Joe Washington (Oklahoma)
Franco Harris	RB	Tony Galbreath (Missouri)
	Starters, Defense	
L. C. Greenwood	LE	Troy Archer (Colorado)
Joe Greene	LT	Lee Roy Selmon (Oklahoma)
Ernie Holmes	RT	Dewey Selmon (Oklahoma)
Dwight White	RE	James White (Oklahoma St.)
Jack Ham	LLB	Kevin McLain (Colorado St.)
Jack Lambert	MLB	Ed Simonini (Texas A&M)
Andy Russell	RLB	Larry Gordon (Arizona St.)
J. T. Thomas	LCB	Aaron Kyle (Wyoming)
Mel Blount	RCB	Mario Clark (Oregon)
Mike Wagner	LS	Shafer Suggs (Ball State)
Glen Edwards	RS	Ed Lewis (Kansas)

Head coaches—Chuck Noll, Pittsburgh; Ara Parseghian (Notre Dame), College All-Stars

Pittsburgh	3	6	15	—	24
College All-Stars .	0	0	0	—	0

Pitt—FG Gerela 29
Pitt—FG Gerela 32
Pitt—FG Gerela 23
Pitt—Safety, Pinney centered ball out of end zone
Pitt—Harris 21 run (Gerela kick)
Pitt—Reamon 2 run (kick failed)
Attendance—52,895

ALL-STAR SELECTIONS

The position listed after a player's name is the position he played in the Chicago College All-Star Game, even if it isn't the position he played in college or in professional football. Although the All-Star roster normally was limited to players who had completed their senior years, several players participated more than once. Due to the large number of players going into the service after or during college in World War II, successful undergraduates often were chosen to participate in the game. They still were eligible to play following their senior seasons, even if the war had ended. Dick Barwegan of Purdue and Charley Trippi of Georgia played in the most games as collegians, each appearing four times, in 1943, 1944, 1945, and 1947.

A

Abel, George, C, Nebraska 1942
Adamle, Mike, RB, Northwestern 1971
Adamle, Tony, B, Ohio State 1947
Adams, John, FB, Cal State-Los Angeles 1959
Adams, Julius, DT, Texas Southern 1971
Adams, Pete, G, USC 1973
Adderley, Herb, HB, Michigan State 1961
Agase, Alex, G, Illinois 1947
Agase, Lou, T, Illinois 1948
Agett, Al, B, Michigan State 1937
Alderton, John, E, Maryland 1953
Aldrich, Ki, C, TCU 1939
Aldworth, Bill, T, Minnesota 1944
Alexander, Kermit, S, UCLA 1963
Alfonse, Jules, B, Minnesota 1937
Alfson, Warren, G, Nebraska 1941
Allen, Doug, LB, Penn State 1974
Allen, Ed, B, Pennsylvania 1945
Allerdice, Dave, B, Princeton 1941
Allis, Harry, E, Michigan State 1951
Allison, Henry, G, San Diego State 1971
Allman, Tom, FB, West Virginia 1954
Alvarez, Don, G, Dartmouth 1947
Alward, Tom, G, Nebraska 1976
Alworth, Lance, HB, Arkansas 1962
Alzado, Lyle, DE, Yankton 1971
Ameche, Alan, FB, Wisconsin 1955
Amstutz, Joe, C, Indiana 1957
Amundson, George, RB, Iowa State 1973
Anahu, Bill, E, Santa Clara 1940
Anderson, Billy Guy, QB, Tulsa 1966
Anderson, Bob, RB, Colorado 1970
Anderson, Dave, B, California 1939
Anderson, Donny, HB, Texas Tech 1966
Anderson, Max, RB, Arizona State 1968
Anderson, Stan, T, Stanford 1940
Andretich, John, B, Purdue 1943, 1944
Andrews, John, TE, Indiana 1971
Angsman, Elmer, B, Notre Dame 1946
Antil, Ray, E, Minnesota 1937
Antoine, Lionel, T, Southern Illinois 1972
Antonini, Ettore, E, Indiana 1936
Antwine, Houston, G, Southern Illinois 1961
Apolskis, Ray, C, Marquette 1941
Appleby, Gordon, C, Ohio State 1944, 1945
Appleton, Scott, DT, Texas 1964
Arbanas, Fred, E, Michigan State 1961
Archer, Troy, DE, Colorado 1976
Armstrong, Otis, RB, Purdue 1973
Arneson, Mark, LB, Arizona 1972
Arnett, Jon, HB, USC 1957
Artoe, Lee, T, California 1940
Asa, Marion, G, Bradley 1941
Aschenbrenner, Frank, B, Northwestern 1949
Ashbaugh, Pete, QB, Notre Dame 1948
Ashcom, Rich, T, Oregon 1943
Asher, Bob, T, Vanderbilt 1970
Astroth, Liz, QB, Illinois 1942, 1943
Athey, Bill, G, Baylor 1953
Atkins, Billy, HB, Auburn 1958
Atkins, Bob, S, Grambling 1968
Atkins, Pervis, HB, New Mexico State 1961
Aucreman, Ted, E, Indiana 1960
Austin, Bill, B, Rutgers 1959

B

Babartsky, Al, T, Fordham 1938
Babcock, Harry, E, Georgia 1953
Babich, Bob, LB, Miami (Ohio) 1969
Babinecz, John, LB, Villanova 1972
Bagdon, Ed, G, Michigan State 1950
Bagnell, Reds, B, Pennsylvania 1951
Bahr, Chris, K, Penn State 1976
Bain, Bill, G, USC 1975
Baker, Art, B, Syracuse 1961
Baker, David, B, Oklahoma 1959
Baker, John, T, North Carolina Central 1958
Baker, Johnny, LB, Mississippi State 1963
Baker, Ralph, LB, Penn State 1964
Baker, Terry, QB, Oregon State 1964
Balazs, Frank, B, Iowa 1939
Baldwin, Burr, E, UCLA 1947
Ball, Sam, T, Kentucky 1966
Banaszek, Cas, TE, Northwestern 1967
Banducci, Bruno, G, Stanford 1944
Bannon, Bruce, LB, Penn State 1973
Banonis, Vince, C, Detroit 1942
Banta, Jack, B, USC 1941
Barber, Jim, T, San Francisco 1935
Barber, Mike, TE, Louisiana Tech 1976
Barber, Stew, T, Penn State 1961
Barclay, George, G, North Carolina 1935
Barnes, Billy Ray, HB, Wake Forest 1957
Barnes, Walt, C, Nebraska 1966
Barnes, Walter (Piggy), T, LSU 1944
Barr, Terry, HB, Michigan 1957
Barrett, Jean, T, Tulsa 1972
Bartkowski, Steve, QB, California 1975
Barton, Tom, G, Clemson 1953
Barwegen, Dick, T, Purdue 1943, 1944, 1945, 1947
Barzilauskas, Carl, DT, Indiana 1974
Baschnagel, Brian, WR, Ohio State 1976
Basrak, Mike, C, Duquesne 1937
Bass, Dick, HB, Pacific 1960
Bassi, Dick, G, Santa Clara 1937
Bauer, Ed, T, Notre Dame 1976
Baugh, Sammy, B, TCU 1937
Baughan, Maxie, C, Georgia Tech 1960
Bauman, Alf, T, Northwestern 1942
Baumgardner, Max, E, Texas 1948
Beach, Walter, B, Central Michigan 1960
Beagle, Ron, E, Navy 1956
Beasley, Terry, WR, Auburn 1972
Beathard, Pete, QB, USC 1964
Beatty, Ed, C, Mississippi 1954
Beaty, Harold, E, Oklahoma State 1961
Beban, Gary, QB, UCLA 1968
Beck, Ken, T, Texas A&M 1959
Beck, Ray, G, Georgia Tech 1952
Beck, Ted, G-T, Western Illinois 1959
Bednar, George, DT, Notre Dame 1964
Bednarik, Chuck, C, Pennsylvania 1949
Bedsole, Hal, E, USC 1964
Beer, Tom, TE, Houston 1967
Behrman, Dave, C, Michigan State 1963
Beinor, Ed, T, Notre Dame 1939
Beise, Sheldon, B, Minnesota 1936
Beisler, Randy, DE, Indiana 1966
Belcher, Curg, S, BYU 1967
Bell, Bob, DT, Cincinnati 1971
Bell, Bobby, LB, Minnesota 1963
Bell, Ed, G, Indiana 1945, 1946
Bell, Eddie, E, Pennsylvania 1953
Bell, George, C, Purdue 1937
Bell, Harace, G, Minnesota 1939
Bellino, Joe, HB, Navy 1961
Bendrick, Ben, E, Wisconsin 1949
Bengston, Phil, T, Minnesota 1935
Benton, Jim, E, Arkansas 1938
Bentz, Roman, T, Tulane 1944, 1945
Bergey, Bill, LB, Arkansas State 1969
Bernard, Chuck, C, Michigan 1934
Bernardi, Frank, HB, Colorado 1955
Bernet, Ed, E, SMU 1955
Bertelli, Angelo, QB, Notre Dame 1943
Bertelsen, Jim, RB, Texas 1972
Berwanger, Jay, B, Chicago 1936
Berzinski, Willis, HB, Wisconsin-LaCrosse 1956
Beson, Warren, E, Minnesota 1949
Bettis, Tom, G, Purdue 1955
Bevan, Billy, G, Minnesota 1935
Beynon, Jack, QB, Illinois 1935
Bielski, Dick, FB, Maryland 1955
Biggs, Verlon, DE, Jackson State 1965
Biles, Shelton, T, Army 1947
Biletnikoff, Fred, FL, Florida State 1965
Bill, Bob, T, Notre Dame 1962
Billingsley, Ron, DE, Wyoming 1967
Bird, Rodger, CB, Kentucky 1966
Birdwell, Dan, C, Houston 1962
Birr, Jim, E, Indiana 1938
Bjork, Del, T, Oregon 1937
Black, Blondy, B, Mississippi State 1946
Blackaby, Inman, B, Butler 1938
Blackburn, Bill, C, Rice 1946
Blahak, Joe, S, Nebraska 1973
Blaine, Ed, T, Missouri 1962
Blair, George, HB, Mississippi 1961
Blair, Matt, LB, Iowa State 1974
Blanchard, Felix (Doc), B, Army 1947

Blandin, Ernie, T, Tulane 1946
Blazer, Phil, T, North Carolina 1959
Blazine, Tony, T, Illinois Wesleyan 1935
Bleick, Tom, S, Georgia Tech 1974
Blount, Mel, CB, Southern 1970
Blozis, Al, T, Georgetown (Washington D.C.) 1942
Blue, Forrest, C, Auburn 1968
Bock, Ed, G, Iowa State 1939
Bock, Wayne, T, Illinois 1957
Boden, Lynn, G, South Dakota State 1975
Bodney, Al, E, Tulane 1941
Boerio, Chuck, C, Illinois 1952
Bogdanski, Joe, E, Colgate 1935
Boggan, Rex, T, Mississippi 1955
Bokamper, Kim, LB, San Jose State 1976
Bomba, Brad, E, Indiana 1957
Bonelli, Ernie, B, Pittsburgh 1945
Boor, Don, B, Michigan 1943
Booth, Barrett, QB, LSU 1939
Borden, Les, E, Fordham 1935
Borghetti, Ernie, T, Pittsburgh 1964
Borries, Fred, B, Navy 1935
Bosley, Bruce, T, West Virginia 1956
Bosseler, Don, FB, Miami 1957
Bottari, Vic, B, California 1939
Bowman, Ken, C, Wisconsin 1964
Boydston, Max, E, Oklahoma 1955
Boydstun, Frank, B, Baylor 1951
Boyle, Joe, E, Creighton 1942
Bozich, Craig, LB, BYU 1969
Brabham, Danny, LB, Arkansas 1963
Brackett, M.L., T, Auburn 1956
Bradley, Bill, S, Texas 1969
Bradley, Dave, T, Penn State 1969
Brahaney, Tom, C, Oklahoma 1973
Branch, Phil, G, Texas 1954
Bratkowski, Zeke, QB, Georgia 1954
Brazile, Robert, DE, Jackson State 1975
Breitenstein, Bob, G, Tulsa 1965
Brennan, Terry, B, Notre Dame 1949
Breslin, Jack, B, Michigan State 1946
Brewer, Homer, B, Mississippi 1960
Brewer, Johnny, E, Mississippi 1961
Brewer, Mel, G, Illinois 1940
Brewster, Darrell (Pete), E, Purdue 1952
Brieske, Jim, C, Michigan 1948
Brinkley, Lorenzo, CB, Missouri 1972
Britt, Charley, B, Georgia 1960
Brock, Charley, C, Nebraska 1939
Brock, Clyde, T, Utah State 1962
Brock, Lou, B, Purdue 1940
Brock, Pete, C, Colorado 1976
Brockington, John, RB, Ohio State 1971
Brodie, John, QB, Stanford 1957
Brodnax, George, E, Georgia Tech 1949
Brooks, Billy, WR, Oklahoma 1976
Brooks, Bud, G, Arkansas 1955
Brooks, Jon, G, Kent State 1967
Brown, Aaron, DE, Minnesota 1966
Brown, Allen, E, Mississippi 1965
Brown, Barry, TE, Florida 1966
Brown, Bill, B, Illinois 1961
Brown, Dave, C, USC 1973
Brown, Dave, CB, Michigan 1975
Brown, Don, T, Oklahoma 1954
Brown, Don, HB, Houston 1959
Brown, Earl, E, Notre Dame 1939
Brown, Earle, G, Tennessee 1945
Brown, Eddie, S, Tennessee 1974
Brown, Fred, E, Miami 1965
Brown, Howard, G, Indiana 1948
Brown, Jim, FB, Syracuse 1957
Brown, Larry, TE, Kansas 1971
Brown, Ray, QB, Mississippi 1958
Brown, Roger, T, Maryland-Eastern Shore 1960
Brown, Sam, C, Georgia Tech 1953
Brown, Stan, WR, Purdue 1971
Brown, Terry, S, Oklahoma State 1969
Brown, Willie, FL, USC 1964
Browne, Gordie, T, Boston College 1974
Brownson, Van, QB, Nebraska 1972
Brumm, Don, DE, Purdue 1963
Brundige, Bill, DE, Colorado 1970
Bruney, Fred, HB, Ohio State 1953
Brunner, Warren, B, Tulane 1939
Bruno, Spuds, G, West Chester 1945
Bryant, Chuck, E, Ohio State 1962
Bryant, Cullen, S, Colorado 1973
Bryant, Goble, T, Texas A&M 1944, Army 1949
Bryant, Waymond, LB, Tennessee State 1974
Bryant, William, S, Grambling 1974
Buccianeri, Mike, G, Indiana 1941
Bucek, Felix, G, Texas A&M 1943
Buchanan, Buck, DT, Grambling 1963
Buchanon, Willie, CB, San Diego State 1972
Buda, Carl, G, Tulsa 1945
Budde, Ed, G, Michigan State 1963
Buffone, Doug, LB, Louisville 1966
Buhler, Larry, B, Minnesota 1939
Buivid, Ray, B, Marquette 1937
Bujan, George, C, Illinois 1946
Bull, Ronnie, FB, Baylor 1962
Bullough, Hank, G, Michigan State 1955
Buncom, Frank, LB, USC 1962
Burgeis, Glen, T, Tulsa 1945
Burgoon, Charley, LB, North Park 1971
Burk, Adrian, QB, Baylor 1950
Burke, Nick, G, Northwestern 1946
Burkett, Jackie, C, Auburn 1960
Burl, Alex, HB, Colorado State 1954
Burnine, Hank, E, Missouri 1956
Burns, Leon, RB, Long Beach State 1971
Burrell, Ode, HB, Mississippi State 1964
Burris, Bo, S, Houston 1967
Burris, Bob, HB, Oklahoma 1956
Burris, Buddy, G, Oklahoma 1949
Burrough, Ken, WR, Texas Southern 1970
Burton, Larry, WR, Purdue 1975
Butkus, Dick, LB, Illinois 1965
Butler, Earl, T, North Carolina 1960
Butler, Gary, TE, Rice 1973
Buttle, Greg, LB, Penn State 1976
Byers, Ken, T, Cincinnati 1962
Bykowski, Frank, G, Purdue 1940
Byrd, Dennis, DT, North Carolina State 1968

C

Cafego, George, B, Tennessee 1940
Caffey, Lee Roy, LB, Texas A&M 1963
Cahill, Bill, S, Washington 1973
Cain, Jim, B, Washington 1937
Cain, Jim, E, Alabama 1949
Cain, J.V., TE, Colorado 1974
Calcagni, Ralph, T, Pennsylvania 1945
Calhoun, Clay, B, Loyola (Chicago) 1938
Callanan, Jim, E, USC 1947
Calligaro, Len, QB, Wisconsin 1943
Calloway, Ernie, LB, Texas Southern 1969
Calvano, Mike, G, Northwestern 1938
Calvelli, Tony, C, Stanford 1939
Cameron, Glenn, LB, Florida 1975
Cameron, Paul, HB, UCLA 1954
Campbell, Dick, B, Wyoming 1951
Campbell, Hugh, E, Washington State 1963
Campbell, Marion, T, Georgia 1952
Campora, Don, T, Pacific 1950
Canada, Bud, E, Arkansas 1949
Cannady, John, C, Indiana 1944, 1947
Canrinus, Fred, E, St. Mary's (California) 1934
Cappelletti, John, RB, Penn State 1974
Carapella, Al, T, Miami 1951
Cardwell, Lloyd, B, Nebraska 1937
Carey, Bob, E, Michigan State 1952
Carey, Tom, QB, Notre Dame 1955
Carlisle, Duke, QB, Texas 1964
Carlson, Harold, T, DePaul 1937
Carlson, Ray, E, Marquette 1943
Carlton, Darryl, T, Tampa 1975
Carney, Don, B, Rockhurst 1940
Carolan, Reg, E, Idaho 1962
Carollo, Joe, T, Notre Dame 1962
Carpenter, Ken, B, Oregon State 1950
Carpenter, Preston, HB, Arkansas 1956
Carpenter, Ron, DE, North Carolina State 1970
Carr, Fred, LB, Texas-El Paso 1968
Carr, Roger, WR, Louisiana Tech 1974
Carroll, Leo, DE, San Diego State 1967
Carroll, Maurice, B, Catholic 1938
Carson, John, E, Georgia 1954
Carter, Jim, B, Purdue 1935
Carter, Louis, RB, Maryland 1975
Caruthers, Robert, C, Lake Forest 1940
Casanova, Tommy, CB, LSU 1972
Casares, Rick, FB, Florida 1954
Case, Ernie, QB, UCLA 1947
Casey, Bernie, FL, Bowling Green 1961
Casper, Dave, TE, Notre Dame 1974
Cassady, Howard (Hopalong), HB, Ohio State 1956
Cassiano, Dick, B, Pittsburgh 1940
Castelo, Bob, E, Illinois 1939
Caster, Rich, TE, Jackson State 1970
Catlin, Tom, C, Oklahoma 1953
Cavazos, Bobby, HB, Texas Tech 1954
Caveness, Ronnie, LB, Arkansas 1965
Cavigga, Al, G, LSU 1945
Ceithaml, George, B, Michigan 1946
Cerne, Joe, C, Northwestern 1965
Chadwick, Bill, C, Beloit 1942
Chambers, Dean, T, Washington 1954
Chambers, Wally, DE, Eastern Kentucky 1973
Chandler, Don, HB, Florida 1956
Chandnois, Lynn, B, Michigan State 1950
Chappuis, Bob, B, Michigan 1948
Charles, John, CB, Purdue 1967
Cheatham, Lloyd, QB, Auburn 1942
Cheshire, Chuck, B, UCLA 1936
Chester, Raymond, TE, Morgan State 1970
Childress, Joe, FB, Auburn 1956
Chollet, Hillary, B, Cornell 1950
Christensen, Erik, E, Richmond 1956
Christiansen, Bob, TE, UCLA 1972
Christiansen, Marty, B, Minnesota 1940
Christman, Paul, QB, Missouri 1941
Christy, Dick, HB, North Carolina State 1958
Churchwell, Don, G, Mississippi 1959
Chuy, Don, G, Clemson 1963
Clabo, Neil, P, Tennessee 1975
Clancy, Jack, SE, Michigan 1967
Claridge, Dennis, QB, Nebraska 1964
Clark, Gail, LB, Michigan State 1973
Clark, Jim, G, Oregon State 1952
Clark, Mario, CB, Oregon 1976
Clark, Phil, CB, Northwestern 1967
Clatt, Corwin, B, Notre Dame 1943, 1944, 1945
Clawson, Don, B, Northwestern 1946
Cleary, Paul, E, USC 1948
Clem, Jerry, G, SMU 1954
Clemons, Craig, S, Iowa 1972
Clemons, Ray, G, St. Mary's (California) 1947
Cline, Ollie, B, Ohio State 1948
Cobb, Marvin, S, USC 1975
Cockroft, Don, K, Adams State 1967
Cody, Ed, B, Purdue 1947
Coffee, J.C., G, Indiana 1944, 1945
Coffey, Junior, HB, Washington 1965
Coffis, Jim, B, Stanford 1938
Cogdill, Gail, E, Washington State 1960
Coleman, Don, G, Michigan State 1952
Coleman, Herb, C, Notre Dame 1946
Colhauer, Jake, G-T, Oklahoma State 1945, 1946
Collins, Gary, E, Maryland 1962
Collins, Spot, G, Texas 1947
Colzie, Neal, CB, Ohio State 1975
Concannon, Jack, QB, Boston College 1964
Conerly, Charlie, QB, Mississippi 1948
Conlee, Gerry, C, St. Mary's (California) 1937
Conners, Dan, LB, Miami 1964
Connor, George, T, Notre Dame 1948
Conrad, Bobby Joe, HB, Texas A&M 1958
Cook, Dave, B, Illinois 1934
Cook, Greg, QB, Cincinnati 1969
Cook, Ted, E, Alabama 1945
Cook, Walter, B, Purdue 1943
Cooke, Ed, E, Maryland 1958
Cooper, Bill, B, Muskingum 1961
Cooper, Harden, T, Tulsa 1947
Corbett, Steve, C, Boston College 1974
Cordileone, Lou, T, Clemson 1960
Cordill, Ollie, B, Rice 1940
Coronado, Bob, HB, Pacific 1959
Cosgrove, Tom, C, Maryland 1953
Cothren, Paige, FB, Mississippi 1957
Coughlan, Jim, E, Santa Clara 1939
Coutre, Larry, B, Notre Dame 1950
Cowhig, Gerry, B, Notre Dame 1947
Cowlings, Al, DE, USC 1970
Cox, Jim, TE, Miami 1968
Craft, Russ, B, Alabama 1945
Cramer, Carl, QB, Ohio State 1934
Crawford, Bill, G, TCU 1942
Crawford, Darrell, QB, Georgia Tech 1952
Crawford, Denver, T, Tennessee 1945
Crawford, Fred, T, Duke 1934
Crawford, Jim, G, Mississippi 1950
Crayne, Dick, B, Iowa 1936
Creaney, Mike, TE, Notre Dame 1973
Creekmur, Lou, T, William & Mary 1950
Crenshaw, Willis, FB, Kansas State 1964
Crespino, Bobby, B, Mississippi 1961
Crimmins, Bernie, G, Notre Dame 1942
Crockett, Bobby, SE, Arkansas 1966
Croft, Abe, E, SMU 1944
Croftcheck, Don, LB, Indiana 1965
Crow, John David, HB, Texas A&M 1958
Crow, Lindon, HB, USC 1955
Cruice, Wally, B, Northwestern 1936
Crutcher, Tommy, LB, TCU 1964
Csonka, Larry, RB, Syracuse 1968
Culp, Curley, DT, Arizona State 1968
Cunningham, Bennie, TE, Clemson 1976
Cunningham, Sam, RB, USC 1973
Current, Mike, T, Ohio State 1967
Currie, Dan, C, Michigan State 1958
Currivan, Don, E, Boston College 1943
Curry, Bill, C, Georgia Tech 1965
Curtis, Bucky, E, Vanderbilt 1951
Curtis, Isaac, WR, San Diego State 1973
Cushing, Bud, C, Cornell 1944
Cutlich, Nick, T, Northwestern 1940
Cverko, Andy, T, Northwestern 1959
Czarobski, Ziggy, T, Notre Dame 1948

D

Dabiero, Angelo, HB, Notre Dame 1962

Daddio, Bill, E, Pittsburgh 1939
D'Agostino, Frank, T, Auburn 1956
Dahlgren, Gordon, G, Michigan State 1937
Dalby, Dave, C, UCLA 1972
Dale, Carroll, E, Virginia Tech 1960
Daley, Bill, B, Minnesota 1946
Daly, Bob, E, Northwestern 1940
Danbom, Larry, B, Notre Dame 1937
Dancewicz, Frank, QB, Notre Dame 1946
Daney, George, G, Texas-El Paso 1968
Daniell, Ave, T, Pittsburgh 1937
Daniell, Jim, T, Ohio State 1942
Darden, Thom, S, Michigan 1972
Darnell, Grant, G, Texas A&M 1946
Darnell, Len, E, Duke 1941
Darre, Bernie, T, Tulane 1961
Davidson, Ben, T, Washington 1961
Davidson, Cotton, QB, Baylor 1954
Davidson, Jim, T, Ohio State 1965
Davis, Art, HB, Mississippi State 1956
Davis, Bob, T, Georgia Tech 1948
Davis, Corby, B, Indiana 1938
Davis, Dave, QB, USC 1937
Davis, Don, DT, Cal State-Los Angeles 1966
Davis, Ernie, HB, Syracuse 1962
Davis, Glenn, B, Army 1947
Davis, Harper, B, Mississippi State 1949
Davis, Jasper, B, Duke 1941
Davis, Kyle, C, Oklahoma 1975
Davis, Lamar, E, Georgia 1944
Davis, Norman, G, Grambling 1967
Davis, Roger, G, Syracuse 1960
Davis, Ted, E, Georgia Tech 1964
Dawson, Gib, HB, Texas 1953
Dawson, Len, QB, Purdue 1957
Dawson, Mike, DT, Arizona 1976
Deal, Russ, T, Indiana 1947
Dean, Floyd, B, Iowa 1941
Dean, Floyd, LB, Florida 1963
Dean, Ted, B, Wichita State 1960
DeCarlo, Art, HB, Georgia 1953
DeCorrevont, Bill, B, Northwestern 1942
Deitrich, Dick, E, Pittsburgh 1954
Dekdebrun, Allan, QB, Cornell 1946
Dekker, Paul, E, Michigan State 1953
Delaney, Mike, K, American International 1970
DeLeone, Tom, C, Ohio State 1972
Dellastatious, Bill, B, Missouri 1944
Dellinger, Floyd, B, Texas Tech 1959
Dellinger, Tom, B, North Carolina State 1962
DeLong, Steve, DE, Tennessee 1965
DeLuca, Sam, T, South Carolina 1957
DeMaria, Pete, G, Purdue 1943
Demmerle, Pete, WR, Notre Dame 1975
Dennerlein, Jerry, T, St. Mary's (California) 1937
Denton, Bob, T, Pacific 1960
DePoyster, Jerry, K, Wyoming 1968
DeRogatis, Al, T, Duke 1949
Dethman, Bob, QB, Oregon State 1942
Deutsch, Leo, E, Benedictine 1937
Devlin, Joe, T, Iowa 1976
Dewar, Jim, B, Indiana 1943, 1944, 1945
Dial, Buddy, E, Rice 1959
Dick, George, E, Kansas 1944
Dickerson, Ronald, CB, Kansas State 1971
Dickey, Len, T, Texas A&M 1947
Diehl, Bill, C, Iowa 1942
Diercks, Bobby, QB, Wisconsin 1943
Dierdorf, Dan, T, Michigan 1971
DiFrancesca, Vince, G, Northwestern 1948
Dillon, Bobby, HB, Texas 1952
DiMarco, Alfonzo, QB, Iowa 1949
Dimitro, Mike, G, UCLA 1949
Ditka, Mike, E, Pittsburgh 1961
Dittrich, John, G, Wisconsin 1956
Dixon, Felix, T, Boston U. 1938
Dobbs, Glenn, B, Tulsa 1943, 1944
Dodrill, Dale, G, Colorado State 1951
Doelling, Fred, B, Pennsylvania 1960
Doll, Don, B, USC 1949
Donnelly, George, S, Illinois 1965
Donnelly, Pat, HB, Navy 1965
Dooley, Jim, HB, Miami 1952
Dooley, Vince, QB, Auburn 1954
Dorow, Al, HB, Michigan State 1952
Doss, Noble, B, Texas 1946
Dotson, Al, DT, Grambling 1965
Dottley, John, B, Mississippi 1951
Doud, Chuck, T, UCLA 1954
Dougherty, Bill, C, Santa Clara 1938
Douglass, Bobby, QB, Kansas 1969
Douglass, Paul, B, Illinois 1951
Doughty, Glenn, RB, Michigan 1972
Dove, Eddie, HB, Colorado 1959
Dowd, Jerry, C, St. Mary's (California) 1939
Dowler, Boyd, B, Colorado 1959
Doyle, Dennis, G, Tulane 1951
Dragash, Nick, G, South Dakota State 1938
Drahos, Nick, T, Cornell 1941
Drake, Johnny, B, Purdue 1937
Drone, Ed, B, St. Louis 1937
Dryer, Fred, DE, San Diego State 1969
Drzewiecki, Ron, HB, Marquette 1955
Dubenion, Elbert, HB, Bluffton 1959
Dudley, Bill, B, Virginia 1942
Dufek, Dan, B, Michigan 1951
Dugan, Fred, E, Dayton 1958
Dugger, Dean, E, Ohio State 1955
Dugger, Jack, E, Ohio State 1944, 1945
Duke, Paul, C, Georgia Tech 1947
Dunaway, Jim, DT, Mississippi 1963
Duncan, Jimmy, S, Maryland-Eastern Shore 1968
Dunlap, Leonard, CB, North Texas State 1971
Dunn, Perry Lee, S, Mississippi 1964
Dupre, L.G., HB, Baylor 1955
Duranko, Pete, DT, Notre Dame 1967
Duvall, Hugh, B, Northwestern 1936
Dye, Bill, QB, Ohio State 1937
Dykstra, Gene, T, Illinois 1937

E

Eason, Roger, T, Oklahoma 1942
Ebli, Ray, T, Notre Dame 1942, 1943
Echols, Fate, T, Northwestern 1962
Eddins, Jo Jo, T, Auburn 1945
Eddy, Nick, RB, Notre Dame 1967
Edwards, Dan, E, Georgia 1948
Edwards, Emmett, WR, Kansas 1975
Edwards, Weldon, T, TCU 1948
Egler, Alan, B, Colgate 1951
Eidom, Frank, HB, SMU 1955
Eidson, Jim, T, Mississippi State 1976
Eigelberger, Bob, C, Missouri 1944
Eller, Carl, DE, Minnesota 1964
Ellersick, Don, E, Washington State 1960
Elliott, Bump, B, Michigan 1948
Elliott, Pete, QB, Michigan 1949
Ellis, Clarence, S, Notre Dame 1972
Ellzey, Charley, C, Southern Mississippi 1960
Elrod, Buddy, E, Mississippi State 1941
Elser, Don, B, Notre Dame 1936
Emanuel, Frank, LB, Tennessee 1966
Emmons, Frank, B, Oregon 1940
Engles, Rick, P, Tulsa 1976
Enich, Steve, G, Marquette 1945
Enos, Jim, C, Army 1947
Enyart, Bill, RB, Oregon State 1969
Epping, Ed, DT, Air Force 1970
Epps, Gene, S, Texas-El Paso 1969
Erdelatz, Eddie, E, St. Mary's (California) 1936
Erdlitz, Dick, QB, Northwestern 1942
Erickson, Bud, C, Washington 1938
Eshmont, Len, B, Fordham 1941
Esser, Clarence, T, Wisconsin 1947
Estes, Don, T, LSU 1963
Evans, Dick, E, Iowa 1940
Evashevski, Forest, QB, Michigan 1941
Everhardus, Herman, B, Michigan 1934
Evey, Dick, G, Tennessee 1964

F

Fairband, Bill, LB, Colorado 1967
Faison, Earl, E, Indiana 1961
Famiglietti, Gary, B, Boston U. 1938
Fanning, Mike, DE, Notre Dame 1975
Farkas, Andy, B, Detroit 1938
Farr, Mel, RB, UCLA 1967
Farragut, Ken, C, Mississippi 1951
Farris, Tom, QB, Wisconsin 1942, 1943
Faunce, Ev, B, Minnesota 1949
Faust, George, QB, Minnesota 1939
Faverty, Hal, E, Wisconsin 1952
Fay, Pete, B, Stanford 1939
Fears, Tom, E, UCLA 1948
Feathers, Beattie, B, Tennessee 1934
Febel, Fritz, G, Purdue 1934
Fekete, Gene, B, Ohio State 1944
Felker, Art, E, Marquette 1951
Felton, Ralph, FB, Maryland 1954
Fenimore, Bob, B, Oklahoma State 1947
Fenton, Bill, E, Iowa 1954
Fenton, Jack, B, Michigan State 1943
Ferguson, Bob, FB, Ohio State 1962
Ferguson, Joe, QB, Arkansas 1973
Ferguson, Larry, HB, Iowa 1963
Fichtner, Ross, QB, Purdue 1960
Filchock, Frank, QB, Indiana 1938
Files, Jim, LB, Oklahoma 1970
Filipowicz, Steve, B, Fordham 1943
Fischer, Bill, G, Notre Dame 1949
Fisher, Dick, B, Ohio State 1942
Fisk, Bill, E, USC 1940
Fitch, Bob, E, Minnesota 1942, 1946
Flanagan, Phil, G, Holy Cross 1936
Flanigan, Jim, LB, Pittsburgh 1967
Flatley, Paul, FL, Northwestern 1963
Fleming, George, B, Washington 1961
Flood, Dave, HB, Notre Dame 1953
Flowers, Bernie, E, Purdue 1953
Flowers, Clyde, T, TCU 1945
Flowers, Keith, HB, TCU 1952
Foldberg, Hank, E, Army 1948
Foley, Dave, T, Ohio State 1969
Ford, Gerald, C, Michigan 1935
Ford, Jimmy, B, Tulsa 1944
Ford, Len, E, Ohio State 1948
Foreman, Chuck, RB, Miami 1973
Forester, Bill, LB, SMU 1953
Forester, Herschel, G, SMU 1952
Forrestal, Tom, QB, Navy 1958
Fortmann, Dan, G, Colgate 1936
Foster, Ralph, T, Oklahoma State 1945
Fournet, Sid, T, LSU 1955
Fowler, Willmer, HB, Northwestern 1959
Francis, Russ, TE, Oregon 1975
Francis, Sam, B, Nebraska 1937
Franck, George, B, Minnesota 1941
Franklin, Bobby, B, Mississippi 1960
Frankowski, Ray, G, Washington 1942
Franks, Julius, G, Michigan 1943
Frazier, Cliff, DT, UCLA 1976
Frazier, Wayne, C, Auburn 1962
Frederickson, Tucker, FB, Auburn 1965
Freeman, Mike, CB, Fresno State 1968
Freitas, Jesse, QB, San Diego State 1974
Freitas, Rockne, C, Oregon State 1967
Fromhart, Wally, QB, Notre Dame 1936
Frutig, Ed, E, Michigan 1941
Fuchs, Bob, C, Missouri 1950
Fuell, Don, QB, Southern Mississippi 1962
Fugate, Bill, G, Marquette 1942
Fullerton, Ed, HB, Maryland 1953
Funchess, Tom, T, Jackson State 1968
Fuqua, Ray, E, SMU 1935

G

Gabriel, Roman, QB, North Carolina State 1962
Gafford, Monk, B, Auburn 1946
Gagne, Vern, E, Minnesota 1949
Gagner, Larry, G, Florida 1966
Gailus, Joe, G, Ohio State 1934
Gain, Bob, T, Kentucky 1951
Gaiters, Bob, B, New Mexico State 1961
Galbreath, Tony, RB, Missouri 1976
Gallagher, Dave, DE, Michigan 1974
Gallagher, Frank, C, Yale 1938
Gallarneau, Hugh, B, Stanford 1941
Galovich, Sam, G, Knox 1937
Gandee, Sonny, E, Ohio State 1952
Garcia, Jim, DE, Purdue 1965
Garcia, Rod, K, Stanford 1974
Garlington, John, LB, LSU 1968
Garnaas, Bill, QB, Minnesota 1946
Garrett, Bobby, QB, Stanford 1954
Garrett, Carl, RB, New Mexico Highlands 1969
Garrett, Dub, T, Mississippi State 1948
Garrett, Mike, HB, USC 1966
Garrison, Gary, SE, San Diego State 1966
Garrison, Walt, FB, Oklahoma State 1966
Gaskin, Dreher, E, Clemson 1954
Gaul, Frank, T, Notre Dame 1949
Gautt, Prentice, B, Oklahoma 1960
Gay, Billy, B, Notre Dame 1951
Gaziano, Frank, G, Holy Cross 1944
Gelatka, Chuck, E, Mississippi State 1937
George, Charlie, T, Wake Forest 1952
Gerela, Roy, K, New Mexico State 1969
Geremia, Frank, T, Notre Dame 1959
Geri, Joe, B, Georgia 1949
Getty, Charlie, T, Penn State 1974
Geyer, Paul, B, Northwestern 1937
Giannelli, Mario, G, Boston College 1948
Gibbons, Jim, E, Iowa 1958
Gibbons, Tom, B, St. Viator 1937
Gibbs, Sonny, QB, TCU 1963
Gibson, Claude, B, North Carolina State 1961
Gibson, Merle, E, TCU 1945
Gifford, Frank, HB, USC 1952
Gilbert, Kline, T, Mississippi 1953
Gillette, Walker, WR, Richmond 1970
Gillingham, Gale, T, Minnesota 1966
Gillman, Sid, E, Ohio State 1934
Gillom, Horace, E, Nevada-Reno 1947
Gipson, Paul, RB, Houston 1969
Girard, Jug, B, Wisconsin 1948
Gladchuck, Chester, C, Boston College 1941
Glassford, Bill, G, Pittsburgh 1937
Glassic, Tom, G, Virginia 1976
Glick, Gary, B, Colorado State 1956
Glover, Rich, DT, Nebraska 1973
Glueck, Larry, CB, Villanova 1963
Gmitro, Rudy, B, Minnesota 1939
Goddard, Ed, B, Washington State 1937
Godwin, Bill, C, Georgia 1946

Goeddeke, George, C, Notre Dame 1967
Gogolak, Charlie, K, Princeton 1966
Goldberg, Marshall, B, Pittsburgh 1939
Goldsberry, John, T, Indiana 1949
Golemgeske, John, T, Wisconsin 1937
Gompers, Bill, B, Notre Dame 1948
Good, Dick, B, Illinois 1943
Goode, Irv, C, Kentucky 1962
Goode, Rob, B, Texas A&M 1949
Gordon, Bobby, HB, Tennessee 1958
Gordon, Larry, LB, Arizona State 1976
Gordy, John, T, Tennessee 1957
Gorman, Tom, C, Notre Dame 1934
Gorski, Stan, E, Northwestern 1948
Goss, Don, G, SMU 1957
Gossage, Gene, T, Northwestern 1960
Governali, Paul, B, Columbia 1943
Grabowski, Jim, FB, Illinois 1966
Gradishar, Randy, LB, Ohio State 1974
Graf, Jack, B, Ohio State 1942
Graff, Stan, E, Stanford 1941
Graham, Otto, B, Northwestern 1943, 1946
Graiziger, Bob, G, Minnesota 1944
Grandelius, Sonny, B, Michigan State 1951
Grant, John, DT, USC 1973
Gravelle, Gordon, G, BYU 1972
Graves, Johnny, B, California 1948
Gray, Bill, C, Oregon State 1947
Gray, Gordon, B, USC 1948
Gray, Joe, B, Oregon State 1938
Gray, Sam, E, Tulsa 1945
Gray, Tim, S, Texas A&M 1975
Greathouse, Merle, B, Oklahoma 1949
Grecni, Dick, C, Ohio U. 1961
Green, Sammy, LB, Florida 1976
Green, Woody, RB, Arizona State 1974
Greene, John, T, Michigan 1944
Greenwood, Don, B, Illinois 1944, 1945
Grefe, Ted, E, Northwestern 1944
Gregg, Forrest, G, SMU 1956
Gregory, Bill, DT, Wisconsin 1971
Gregory, Glynn, HB, SMU 1961
Gressette, Nate, T, Clemson 1954
Grgich, Visco, Santa Clara 1946
Grier, Rosey, T, Penn State 1955
Griese, Bob, QB, Purdue 1967
Griffin, Archie, RB, Ohio State 1976
Griffin, Bob, C, Arkansas 1952
Griffin, Don, B, Illinois 1946
Griffin, John, CB, Memphis State 1963
Griffing, Glynn, QB, Mississippi 1963
Griffith, Homer, QB, USC 1934
Grim, Bob, CB, Oregon State 1967
Groom, Jerry, C, Notre Dame 1951
Gros, Earl, B, LSU 1962
Gross, Charley, G, Bradley 1939
Grosscup, Lee, QB, Utah 1959
Grottkau, Bob, G, Oregon 1959
Gryboski, Ed, G, Illinois 1936
Gude, Bob, C, Vanderbilt 1942
Guepe, Art, QB, Marquette 1937
Guerre, George, B, Michigan State 1949
Guglielmi, Ralph, QB, Notre Dame 1955
Gundlach, Herman, G, Harvard 1935
Gunner, Harry, DE, Oregon State 1968
Gustafson, Ed, C, George Washington 1947
Gustafson, Harlan, E, Pennsylvania 1940
Gustitus, Joe, T, St. Ambrose 1938
Guy, Louis, HB, Mississippi 1963
Guy, Ray, P, Southern Mississippi 1973
Guzik, John, G, Pittsburgh 1959

H

Haak, Bob, T, Indiana 1939
Haas, Ken, T, Missouri 1940
Habig, Neil, C, Purdue 1958
Hackney, Elmore, B, Duke 1938
Hadl, John, QB, Kansas 1962
Hafeli, Dwight, E, St. Louis 1937
Hafen, Banard, E, Utah 1949
Hageman, Fred, C, Kansas 1961
Hager, Allen, G, Purdue 1953
Hahnenstein, Ollie, B, Northwestern 1941
Haines, By, B, Washington 1937
Hair, Henry, E, Georgia Tech 1955
Hale, I.B., T, TCU 1939
Haley, Dick, HB, Pittsburgh 1959
Hall, Charlie, S, Pittsburgh 1971
Hall, Ken, E, North Texas State 1954
Hall, Parker, B, Mississippi 1939
Hall, Pete, QB, Marquette 1960
Hall, Willie, LB, USC 1972
Halliday, Sid, E, SMU 1948
Haluska, Jim, QB, Wisconsin 1956
Ham, Jack, LB, Penn State 1971
Haman, Johnny, C, Northwestern 1940
Hamilton, Andy, WR, LSU 1972
Hammack, Malcolm, FB, Florida 1955
Hamrick, Charlie, T, Ohio State 1937
Hand, Tom, C, Iowa 1943
Hanifan, Jim, E, California 1955
Hankins, Cecil, B, Oklahoma State 1945, 1946
Hanley, Dan, B, Notre Dame 1935
Hannah, John, G, Alabama 1973
Hanratty, Terry, QB, Notre Dame 1969
Hansen, Don, LB, Illinois 1966
Hanson, Rod, E, Illinois 1958
Hantla, Bob, G, Kansas 1954
Hanulak, Chet, HB, Maryland 1954
Hapes, Merle, B, Mississippi 1942
Hardeman, Don, RB, Texas A&I 1975
Harder, Pat, B, Wisconsin 1943, 1946
Hardman, Cedrick, DE, North Texas State 1970
Hargrave, Bob, QB, Notre Dame 1942
Harmon, Tom, B, Michigan 1941, 1945
Harper, Charlie, G, Oklahoma State 1966
Harrah, Dennis, T, Miami 1975
Harrell, Willard, RB, Pacific 1975
Harris, Dick, C, Texas 1949
Harris, Duriel, WR, New Mexico State 1976
Harris, Franco, RB, Penn State 1972
Harris, Jimmy, QB, Oklahoma 1957
Harris, Mike, G, Mississippi State 1947
Harris, Richard, DE, Grambling 1971
Harris, W.F., C, Auburn 1946
Harris, Wendell, HB, LSU 1962
Hart, Jeff, T, Oregon State 1975
Hart, Leon, E, Notre Dame 1950
Hartenstine, Mike, DT, Penn State 1975
Hartman, Fred, T, Rice 1941
Harvey, Tad, T, Notre Dame 1940
Hasse, Adrian, E, Amherst 1946
Hawkins, Ben, FL, Arizona State 1966
Hawkins, Rip, C, North Carolina 1961
Hayes, Bob, E, Florida A&M 1965
Hayes, Tom, E, Army 1947
Haynes, Hall, B, Santa Clara 1950
Haynes, Mike, CB, Arizona State 1976
Hazeltine, Matt, C, California 1955
Hazelton, Major, S, Florida A&M 1968
Healy, Jack, G, Maryland 1958
Heap, Don, B, Northwestern 1938
Heap, Joe, HB, Notre Dame 1955
Heath, Leon, B, Oklahoma 1951
Heath, Stan, QB, Nevada-Reno 1949
Hecht, George, G, Alabama 1944
Hecker, Fred, B, Purdue 1934
Heekin, Dick, B, Ohio State 1936
Hegarty, Bill, T, Villanova 1953
Heidel, Jimmy, S, Mississippi 1966
Heikkinen, Ralph, G, Michigan 1939
Heineman, Ken, QB, Texas-El Paso 1940
Heinz, Bob, DT, Pacific 1969
Hekkers, Frank, T, Wisconsin 1946
Hellinghausen, Bob, C, Tulsa 1947
Henderson, Jon, CB, Colorado State 1968
Hendren, Jerry, WR, Idaho 1970
Hendricks, Ted, LB, Miami 1969
Hennis, Ted, QB, Purdue 1940
Henrion, Nestor, G, Carnegie-Mellon 1937
Henson, Champ, RB, Ohio State 1976
Herbert, Eddie, QB, Indiana 1942
Herchman, Bill, T, Texas Tech 1956
Herkommer, Karl, HB, Purdue 1954
Herndon, Clarence, T, Nebraska 1942
Heywood, Ralph, E, USC 1946
Hickerson, Gene, T, Mississippi 1958
Hickman, Larry, FB, Baylor 1959
Hicks, John, G, Ohio State 1974
Hiemenz, Paul, C, Northwestern 1941
Hilgenberg, Jerry, G, Iowa 1954
Hilgenberg, Wally, LB, Iowa 1964
Hill, Dan, C, Duke 1939
Hill, David, TE, Texas A&I 1976
Hill, Fred, E, USC 1965
Hill, J.D., WR, Arizona State 1971
Hill, Jim, S, Texas A&I 1968
Hill, Jimmy, B, Tennessee 1951
Hill, King, QB, Rice 1958
Hillenbrand, Billy, B, Indiana 1944, 1946
Hilliard, Bohn, B, Texas 1935
Hindman, Stan, DE, Mississippi 1966
Hines, Glen Ray, T, Arkansas 1966
Hinton, Charles, CB, USC 1973
Hinton, Chuck, G-T, North Carolina 1962
Hinton, Eddie, WR, Oklahoma 1969
Hirsch, Ed, B-G, Northwestern 1943, 1947
Hirsch, Elroy (Crazylegs), B, Wisconsin 1946
Hixson, Chuck, QB, SMU 1971
Hoernschemeyer, Bob, B, Indiana 1946
Hofer, Bill, QB, Notre Dame 1939
Hoffman, Bob, B, USC 1940
Holdash, Irv, C, North Carolina 1951
Holden, Sam, G, Grambling 1971
Holden, Steve, WR, Arizona State 1973
Holland, Vernon, T, Tennessee A&I 1971
Holleder, Don, E, Army 1956
Holmes, Mike, CB, Texas Southern 1973
Holub, E.J., C, Texas Tech 1961
Homan, Dennis, FL, Alabama 1968
Hoptowit, Alphonse, G, Washington State 1938
Hornsby, Ronnie, LB, Southeastern Louisiana 1971
Hornung, Paul, QB, Notre Dame 1957
Horton, Charley, HB, Vanderbilt 1956
Horvath, Les, B, Ohio State 1945
Houston, Jim, E, Ohio State 1960
Houston, Lin, G, Ohio State 1944
Hovland, Lynn, G, Wisconsin 1939
Howard, Paul, G, BYU 1973
Howlett, Pat, B, DePaul 1938
Howley, Chuck, G, West Virginia 1958
Howton, Billy, E, Rice 1952
Hrivnak, Gary, DT, Purdue 1973
Huarte, John, QB, Notre Dame 1965
Huber, Bill, E, Notre Dame 1943, 1944, 1945
Hudock, Mike, C, Miami 1957
Hudson, Bill, T, Memphis State 1962
Huey, Warren, E, Michigan State 1949
Huff, Ken, G, North Carolina 1975
Huff, Sam, G, West Virginia 1956
Huffman, Vern, QB, Indiana 1937
Hughes, Bill, C, Michigan State 1952
Hughes, George, G, William & Mary 1950
Hughes, Tom, T, Purdue 1944
Hull, Bill, E, Wake Forest 1962
Hull, Mike, RB, USC 1968
Humble, Weldon, G, Rice 1947
Humphrey, Buddy, QB, Baylor 1959
Humphrey, Claude, DE, Texas A&I 1968
Humphrey, Paul, C, Purdue 1939
Hunsinger, Chuck, B, Florida 1950
Hunt, John, B, Marshall 1942
Hunter, Art, T, Notre Dame 1954
Hunter, James, CB, Grambling 1976
Hupke, Tom, G, Alabama 1934
Hutchinson, Bill, B, Dartmouth 1940
Hutchinson, Tom, E, Kentucky 1963
Hutchison, Chuck, G, Ohio State 1970
Hutson, Don, E, Alabama 1935
Hyatt, Freddie, SE, Auburn 1968
Hyland, Bob, C-G, Boston College 1967

I

Ice, Harry, B, Missouri 1942
Ingalls, Don, C, Michigan 1942
Ippolito, Tony, B, Purdue 1939
Irish, John, T, Arizona 1934
Irwin, Don, B, Colgate 1936
Isbell, Cecil, B, Purdue 1938
Isenbarger, John, RB, Indiana 1970
Ison, J.D., E, Baylor 1950
Ivory, Bob, G, Detroit 1945
Ivy, Frank (Pop), E, Oklahoma 1940
Izo, George, QB, Notre Dame 1960

J

Jabbusch, Bob, G, Ohio State 1944
Jackson, Bobby, B, Alabama 1959
Jackson, Ken, T, Texas 1951
Jackson, Leroy, HB, Western Illinois 1962
Jacobs, Bob, K, Wyoming 1971
Jacobs, Harry, T, Bradley 1959
Jacobs, Jack, B, Oklahoma 1942
Jacobs, Proverb, G, California 1958
Jacobs, Ray, G-T, Howard Payne 1962
Jacobson, Larry, DT, Nebraska 1972
Jacoby, Chuck, B, Indiana 1944, 1946
Jacoby, George, G, Ohio State 1954
Jacunski, Harry, E, Fordham 1939
Jagade, Harry (Chick), B, Indiana 1949
Jagielski, Harry, T, Indiana 1954
James, Dan, C, Ohio State 1959
James, Tommy, B, Ohio State 1943, 1947
Janerette, Charley, G, Penn State 1960
Janet, Ernie, G, Washington 1971
Janik, Tom, CB, Texas A&I 1963
Janke, Fred, T, Michigan 1939
Jankowski, Ed, B, Wisconsin 1937
Janowicz, Vic, HB, Ohio State 1952
Jaynes, David, QB, Kansas 1974
Jefferson, Bernie, B, Northwestern 1939
Jefferson, Roy, CB, Utah 1965
Jeffries, Rob, G, Missouri 1942
Jencks, Bob, E, Miami (Ohio) 1963
Jenkins, Al, G, Tulsa 1969
Jenkins, Tom, G, Ohio State 1964
Jennings, Ernie, WR, Air Force 1971
Jensen, Alva, B, Rockhurst 1941
Jensen, Jim, RB, Iowa 1976
Jewett, Bob, E, Michigan State 1958
Joachim, Steve, QB, Temple 1975
Jobko, Bill, G, Ohio State 1958
Johnson, Al, QB, Hardin-Simmons 1948
Johnson, Bob, C, Tennessee 1968

Johnson, Clyde, T, Kentucky 1944, 1945
Johnson, Don, E, Miami 1957
Johnson, Gary, DT, Grambling 1975
Johnson, Harvey, B, William & Mary 1946
Johnson, Jimmy, B, UCLA 1961
Johnson, Tom, T, Michigan 1952
Johnson, Walter, DT, Cal State-Los Angeles 1965
Johnston, Jimmy, B, Washington 1939
Jones, Art, B, Richmond 1941
Jones, Bert, QB, LSU 1973
Jones, Bob, G, Indiana 1934
Jones, Bob, SE, San Diego State 1967
Jones, Clint, RB, Michigan State 1967
Jones, Dub, B, Tulane 1946
Jones, Ed (Too Tall), DE, Tennessee State 1974
Jones, Ellis, G, Tulsa 1944, 1945
Jones, Gomer, C, Ohio State 1936
Jones, Harry, FL, Arkansas 1967
Jones, Jim, HB, Washington 1958
Jones, Joe, DE, Tennessee State 1970
Jones, Ken, G, Arkansas State 1976
Jones, Ray, CB, Southern 1970
Jones, Spike, K, Georgia 1970
Jones, Stan, T, Maryland 1954
Jones, Tom, T, Miami (Ohio) 1955
Jordan, Henry, T, Virginia 1957
Jordan, Jeff, E, Tulsa 1965
Jordan, Lee Roy, LB, Alabama 1963
Jorgensen, Wagner, C, St. Mary's (California) 1936
Joyce, Don, T, Tulane 1951
Jungmichel, Buddy, G, Texas 1946
Junker, Steve, E, Xavier 1957
Justice, Charlie (Choo-Choo), B, North Carolina 1950
Juzwik, Steve, B, Notre Dame 1942

K

Kabealo, Mike, QB, Ohio State 1939
Kadish, Mike, DT, Notre Dame 1972
Kalbaugh, Elwood, C, Princeton 1935
Kammerer, Carl, G, Pacific 1961
Kanicki, Jim, DT, Michigan State 1963
Kapter, Alex, G, Northwestern 1943, 1946
Karas, Emil, T, Dayton 1959
Karcher, Jim, G, Ohio State 1936
Karmazin, Andy, E, Wake Forest 1945
Karras, Alex, T, Iowa 1958
Karras, Johnny, HB, Illinois 1952
Karras, Lou, T, Purdue 1950
Karwales, Jack, E, Michigan 1943
Katcavage, Jim, E, Dayton 1956
Kavanaugh, Ken, E, LSU 1940
Kawal, Al, G, Northwestern 1935
Kay, Bill, T, Iowa 1949
Keating, Howard, E, Detroit 1942
Keating, Tom, DT, Michigan 1964
Kekeris, Jim, T, Missouri 1944
Keller, Mike, LB, Michigan 1972
Kellogg, Bob, B, Tulane 1940
Kelly, Ellison, LB, Michigan State 1959
Kelly, Tim, LB, Notre Dame 1971
Kempthorn, Dick, B, Michigan 1950
Kenfield, Ted, B, Nebraska 1944
Kennedy, Bob, B, Washington State 1943, 1945
Kensler, Ed, HB, Maryland 1952
Kerasiotis, Nick, G, St. Ambrose 1941
Kerr, Bud, E, Notre Dame 1940
Kersulis, Walt, E, Illinois 1950
Keuper, Ken, QB, Georgia 1944
Kevorkian, Alex, T, Harvard 1938
Khayat, Bob, G, Mississippi 1960
Kiick, Jim, RB, Wyoming 1968
Kiilsgaard, Carl, T, Idaho 1950
Kilgrow, Joe, B, Alabama 1938
Killorin, Pat, C, Syracuse 1966
Kilmer, Billy, QB, UCLA 1961
Kimbrough, Al, E, Northwestern 1961
Kimmel, J.D., T, Houston 1953
Kinard, Frank (Bruiser), T, Mississippi 1938
Kindle, Greg, T, Tennessee State 1974
Kinek, Mike, E, Michigan State 1940
King, Charlie, CB, Purdue 1966
King, Henry, S, Utah State 1967
King, Phil, HB, Vanderbilt 1958
Kinney, Jeff, RB, Nebraska 1972
Kinnick, Nile, B, Iowa 1940
Kinson, Roger, C, Missouri 1952
Kirk, Ken, C, Mississippi 1960
Kischer, Everett, QB, Iowa State 1939
Kish, Ben, QB, Pittsburgh 1940
Klawitter, Dick, T, South Dakota State 1956
Klein, Bob, TE, USC 1969
Kmetovic, Pete, B, Stanford 1942
Knafelc, Gary, E. Colorado 1954
Knezovich, John, C, Bradley 1944
Knotts, Ernie, G, Duke 1947
Knutson, Steve, T, USC 1975
Kochman, Roger, HB, Penn State 1963
Kockel, Mike, G, Fordham 1939
Kodba, Joe, C, Purdue 1947
Kodros, Archie, C, Michigan 1940
Koegel, Warren, C, Penn State 1971
Kohl, Ralph, T, Michigan 1949
Kolb, Jon, C, Oklahoma State 1969
Kolesar, Bob, G, Michigan 1944
Kollar, Bill, DT, Montana State 1974
Kolman, Ed, T, Temple 1940
Koncar, Mark, T, Colorado 1976
Konz, Ken, B, LSU 1951
Kopcha, Mike, C, Tennessee-Chattanooga 1940
Kopczak, Frank, T, Notre Dame 1937
Kortas, Ken, DT, Louisville 1964
Koslowski, Stan, B, Holy Cross 1946
Kostka, Stan, B, Minnesota 1935
Kovac, Ed, B, Cincinnati 1960
Kovatch, John, E, Northwestern 1938
Kovatch, John, E, Notre Dame 1942
Kowalczyk, Walt, HB, Michigan State 1958
Koy, Ted, RB, Texas 1970
Kozar, Andy, FB, Tennessee 1953
Kracum, George, B, Pittsburgh 1941
Kraemer, Eldred, G, Pittsburgh 1955
Krakoski, Joe, B, Illinois 1961
Kramer, Jerry, G, Idaho 1958
Kramer, Ron, E, Michigan 1957
Krause, Ed (Moose), T, Notre Dame 1934
Krause, Paul, S, Iowa 1964
Kreitling, Rich, E, Illinois 1959
Krisher, Bill, G, Oklahoma 1958
Krouse, Ray, T, Maryland 1951
Kruczek, Mike, QB, Boston College 1976
Krueger, Art, C, Marquette 1934
Krueger, Charlie, T, Texas A&M 1958
Krueger, Rolf, DT, Texas A&M 1969
Krupa, Joe, T, Purdue 1956
Krutko, Larry, FB, West Virginia 1958
Kubala, Ray, C, Texas A&M 1964
Kuharich, Joe, G, Notre Dame 1938
Kuhn, Cliff, G, Illinois 1937
Kuhn, Gil, C, USC 1937
Kunz, George, T, Notre Dame 1969
Kupcinet, Irv, QB, North Dakota 1935
Kutner, Mal, E, Texas 1942
Kuziel, Bob, C, Pittsburgh 1972
Kyle, Aaron, CB, Wyoming 1976

L

Lach, Steve, B, Duke 1942
Ladd, Ernie, T, Grambling 1961
Lakes, Roland, C, Wichita State 1961
Lakos, Mick, HB, Vanderbilt 1953
Lamb, Walter (Dub), E, Oklahoma 1945
Lambert, Frank, E, Mississippi 1965
Lamone, Gene, G, West Virginia 1955
Lamson, Chuck, B, Wyoming 1962
Landry, Greg, QB, Massachusetts 1968
Lane, Gary, QB, Missouri 1966
Lane, MacArthur, RB, Utah State 1968
Lansdell, Grenny, B, USC 1940
Lansford, Buck, T, Texas 1955
Lapham, Bill, C, Iowa 1960
Lapham, Dave, G, Syracuse 1974
LaPrade, Loren, C, Stanford 1944
LaRose, Dan, E, Missouri 1961
Larson, Frank, E, Minnesota 1935
Larson, Greg, C, Minnesota 1961
Larson, Leon, E, Wisconsin-River Falls 1939
Larson, Lynn, G, Kansas State 1970
Larson, Paul, QB, California 1955
LaRue, Bobby, B, Pittsburgh 1937
Lattner, Johnny, HB, Notre Dame 1954
Lauricella, Hank, HB, Tennessee 1952
Lautar, John, G, Notre Dame 1937
Lawless, Burton, G, Florida 1975
Lawrence, Henry, T, Florida A&M 1974
Lawrence, Jim, B, TCU 1936
Laws, Joe, B, Iowa 1934
Lawson, Steve, G, Kansas 1971
Layden, Mike, B, Notre Dame 1936
Layden, Pete, B, Texas 1944
Layne, Bobby, QB, Texas 1948
Lazetich, Pete, DT, Stanford 1972
LeBaron, Eddie, QB, Pacific 1950
LeClerc, Roger, C, Trinity (Connecticut) 1960
Lee, Bill, T, Alabama 1935
Leemans, Alfonse (Tuffy), B, George Washington 1936
Leeper, Harry, E, Northwestern 1935
Leggett, Dave, QB, Ohio State 1955
Leggett, Earl, T, LSU 1957
Lemmon, Dick, E, California 1952
Lemonick, Bernie, G, Pennsylvania 1951
Lenc, George, E, Augustana (Illinois) 1939
Lenkaitis, Bill, C, Penn State 1968
Leo, Jim, E, Cincinnati 1960
Lesnick, Ed, C, Illinois State 1938
Lester, Darrell, C, TCU 1936
Leuthauser, Dennis, K, Air Force 1970
LeVias, Jerry, WR, SMU 1969
LeVoir, Vernal (Babe), QB, Minnesota 1936
Levy, Leonard, G, Minnesota 1942
Lewis, D.D., LB, Mississippi State 1968
Lewis, Eddie, S, Kansas 1976
Lewis, Frank, WR, Grambling 1971
Lewis, Mac, T, Iowa 1959
Lick, Dennis, T, Wisconsin 1976
Lillis, Paul, T, Notre Dame 1942
Lilly, Bob, T, TCU 1961
Lincoln, Keith, HB, Washington State 1961
Lind, Al, C, Northwestern 1936
Lindberg, Les, B, Illinois 1936
Lindsey, Jim, FL, Arkansas 1966
Lindskog, Vic, C, Stanford 1942, 1943, 1944
Lio, Augie, G, Georgetown (Washington D.C.) 1941
Liscio, Tony, T, Tulsa 1963
Lister, Jack, E, Missouri 1943
Little, Floyd, RB, Syracuse 1967
Little, Jack, T, Texas A&M 1953
Livers, Virgil, CB, Western Kentucky 1975
Livingstone, Bob, B, Notre Dame 1948
Loebs, Frank, E, Purdue 1936
Logan, Chuck, E, Northwestern 1964
Logan, Dave, WR, Colorado 1976
Logan, Jim, G, Indiana 1940
Lokanc, Joe, G, Northwestern 1941
Long, R.A., B, Tennessee 1945
Longhi, Ed, C, Notre Dame 1939
Looney, Joe Don, HB, Oklahoma 1964
Lopp, Frank, T, Wisconsin 1945
Lorick, Tony, FB, Arizona State 1964
Losch, Jack, HB, Miami 1956
Lothamer, Ed, DE, Michigan State 1964
Louderback, Tommy, G, San Jose State 1955
Lucci, Mike, C, Tennessee 1962
Luciano, Ron, T, Syracuse 1959
Luckman, Sid, QB, Columbia 1939
Lueck, Bill, G, Arizona 1968
Lujack, Johnny, QB, Notre Dame 1948
Lukats, Nick, B, Notre Dame 1934
Lund, Francis (Pug), B, Minnesota 1935
Lundy, Lamar, E, Purdue 1957
Lutz, Larry, T, California 1936
Lyles, Lenny, HB, Louisville 1958
Lynch, Dick, HB, Notre Dame 1958
Lynch, Jim, LB, Notre Dame 1967
Lynch, Lynn, G, Illinois 1951

M

Macek, Don, G, Boston College 1976
Mack, Tom, G, Michigan 1966
Mackenzie, Jim, G, Kentucky 1952
Mackey, John, E, Syracuse 1963
Mackiewicz, Felix, E, Purdue 1940
MacLeod, Bob, B, Dartmouth 1939
Macrae, Don, G, Northwestern 1952
Maczuzak, John, DT, Pittsburgh 1964
Maddock, Bob, G, Notre Dame 1942
Maddock, George, T, Northwestern 1949
Maddox, George, T, Kansas State 1935
Maentz, Tom, E, Michigan 1957
Magac, Mike, T, Missouri 1960
Mahalic, Drew, LB, Notre Dame 1975
Maher, Bruce, B, Detroit 1960
Mallouf, Ray, B, SMU 1941
Malone, Art, RB, Arizona State 1970
Malone, Benny, RB, Arizona State 1974
Maloney, Norm, E, Purdue 1948
Manders, Clarence (Pug), B, Drake 1939
Maneikis, Walter, T, Chicago 1934
Maniaci, Joe, B, Fordham 1936
Manley, Leon, T, Oklahoma 1950
Mann, Bob, E, Michigan 1948
Mansfield, Ray, C. Washington 1963
Manske, Edgar (Eggs), E, Northwestern 1934
Manton, Taldon (Tillie), B, TCU 1936
Marchetti, Gino, T, San Francisco 1952
Marcol, Chester, K, Hillsdale 1972
Marconi, Joe, HB, West Virginia 1956
Marino, Vic, G, Ohio State 1940
Marker, Curt, G, Northern Michigan 1967
Markov, Vic, T, Washington 1938
Markovich, Mark, G, Penn State 1974
Marsalis, Jim, CB, Tennessee State 1969
Martha, Paul, S, Pittsburgh 1964
Martin, Jim, E, Notre Dame 1950
Marx, Greg, DE, Notre Dame 1973
Mason, Tommy, HB, Tulane 1961
Massey, Carlton, E, Texas 1954
Masterson, Bernie, QB, Nebraska 1934
Mastrangeli, Al, C, Illinois 1949
Mastrangelo, John, G, Notre Dame 1947
Mather, Greg, E, Navy 1962
Matheson, Bob, LB, Duke 1967
Mathews, George, B, Georgia Tech 1948
Matsko, John, C, Michigan State 1957
Matson, Ollie, HB, San Francisco 1952

Matte, Tom, B, Ohio State 1961
Matthews, Al, CB, Texas A&I 1970
Matthews, Bo, RB, Colorado 1974
Matuszak, John, DE, Tampa 1973
Matuszak, Marv, T, Tulsa 1953
Matuszczak, Walt, QB, Cornell 1941
Maves, Earl, B, Wisconsin 1948
Mavraides, Menil, G, Notre Dame 1954
Maxwell, Tom, CB, Texas A&M 1969
Mayes, Clair, G, Oklahoma 1951
Mayes, Rufus, T, Ohio State 1969
Mayther, Bill, C, Oregon 1944, 1945
McAdams, Carl, LB, Oklahoma 1966
McAdams, Dean, B, Washington 1941
McAuliffe, Don, HB, Michigan State 1953
McBride, Bob, G, Notre Dame 1947
McCafferty, Don, T, Ohio State 1944, 1945
McCaffrey, Mike, LB, California 1969
McCartney, Ron, LB, Tennessee 1976
McCarty, Pat, C, Notre Dame 1938
McChesney, Howard, E, Hardin-Simmons 1950
McClarence, Bill, B, Bradley 1938
McClinton, Curtis, HB, Kansas 1962
McClowry, Terry, LB, Michigan State 1975
McColl, Bill, E, Stanford 1952
McCord, Darris, T, Tennessee 1955
McCormack, Mike, T, Kansas 1951
McCormick, Dave, T, LSU 1966
McCormick, Nevin, B, Notre Dame 1938
McCoy, Mike, DT, Notre Dame 1970
McCoy, Mike, CB, Colorado 1976
McCullouch, Earl, SE, USC 1968
McCurry, Bob, C, Michigan State 1949
McCusker, Jim, T, Pittsburgh 1958
McDermott, John, B, Detroit 1940
McDonald, Jim, QB, Ohio State 1938
McDonald, Jim, C, Illinois 1939
McDonald, Ray, RB, Idaho 1967
McDonald, Tommy, HB, Oklahoma 1957
McElhenny, Hugh, HB, Washington 1952
McElroy, Bucky, HB, Southern Mississippi 1954
McFadden, Banks, B, Clemson 1940
McFadin, Bud, G, Texas 1951
McFalls, Doug, S, Georgia 1966
McFalls, Jim, T, Virginia Military 1959
McGannon, Bill, B, Notre Dame 1941
McGee, John, E, Regis 1941
McGee, Mike, G, Duke 1960
McGee, Tony, DT, Bishop 1971
McGill, Mike, LB, Notre Dame 1968
McGoldrick, Jim, G, Notre Dame 1939
McGurn, George, B, Northwestern 1940
McHan, Lamar, QB, Arkansas 1954
McHenry, Bill, C, Washington & Lee 1954
McIlhenny, Don, HB, SMU 1956
McInally, Pat, WR, Harvard 1975
McInnis, Hugh, E, Southern Mississippi 1960
McKay, Bob, T, Texas 1970
McKay, Roy Dale, B, Texas 1943, 1944
McKeever, Donald, B, Benedictine 1941
McKeever, Marlin, E, USC 1961
McKenzie, Reggie, G, Michigan 1972
McLain, Kevin, LB, Colorado State 1976
McMahon, Bill, G, Rockhurst 1941
McNeill, Rod, RB, USC 1974
McPartland, Jim, T, St. Mary's (California) 1947
McPhail, Buck, FB, Oklahoma 1953
McWilliams, Tom (Shorty), B, Mississippi State 1949
Mead, Jack, E, Wisconsin 1946
Meadows, Ed, T, Duke 1954
Meek, Billy, B, Tennessee 1945
Meek, John, QB, California 1938
Mehringer, Pete, T, Kansas 1934
Meilinger, Steve, E, Kentucky 1954
Melinkovich, George, B, Notre Dame 1935
Mello, Jim, B, Notre Dame 1947
Melton, Tom, G, Purdue 1942
Mendenhall, John, DT, Grambling 1972
Mendenhall, Ken, C, Oklahoma 1970
Mense, Jim, C, Notre Dame 1956
Mercein, Chuck, FB, Yale 1965
Meredith, Don, QB, SMU 1960
Merlo, Jim, LB, Stanford 1973
Merrick, Ed, C, Richmond 1940
Merrill, Walter, T, Alabama 1940
Messner, Max, G, Cincinnati 1960
Mestnik, Frank, B, Marquette 1960
Metcalf, Terry, RB, Long Beach State 1973
Method, Harold, G, Northwestern 1940
Meyer, Charles (Monk), B, Army 1937
Meyer, Fred, E, Stanford 1942
Meyers, John, T, Washington 1962
Meylan, Wayne, LB, Nebraska 1968
Michael, Bill, E, Ohio State 1957
Michaels, Ed, G, Villanova 1958
Michaels, Lou, T, Kentucky 1958
Michels, John, G, Tennessee 1953
Middleton, Dave, HB, Auburn 1955
Middleton, Rick, LB, Ohio State 1974
Midler, Lou, G, Minnesota 1938
Mieszkowski, Ed, T, Notre Dame 1946
Mihal, Joe, T, Purdue 1939
Mike-Mayer, Steve, K, Maryland 1975
Mikulak, Mike, B, Oregon 1934
Miller, Bill, E, Miami 1962
Miller, Bob, TE, USC 1969
Miller, Clark, T, Utah State 1962
Miller, Creighton, B, Notre Dame 1943, 1944
Miller, Fred, DE, LSU 1963
Miller, Hal, T, Georgia Tech 1953
Millner, Wayne, E, Notre Dame 1936
Mims, Crawford, G, Mississippi 1954
Minarik, Hank, E, Michigan State 1951
Mincevich, Frank, G, South Carolina 1955
Mira, George, QB, Miami 1964
Mischak, Bob, E, Army 1954
Mitchell, Bobby, HB, Illinois 1958
Mitchell, Charley, HB, Washington 1963
Mitchell, Charlie, B, Tulsa 1945
Mitchell, Charlie, G, Florida 1958
Mitchell, Emery, B, Stanford 1950
Mitchell, Harold, T, UCLA 1952
Mitchell, Jack, QB, Oklahoma 1949
Mitchell, Lydell, RB, Penn State 1972
Mitchell, Mack, DE, Houston 1975
Mitchell, Paul, T, Minnesota 1943, 1946
Mitinger, Bob, E, Penn State 1962
Modzelewski, Dick, T, Maryland 1953
Modzelewski, Ed, FB, Maryland 1952
Moegle, Dickie, HB, Rice 1955
Mohrbacher, Stan, T, Iowa 1945
Molnar, Jim, B, Bradley 1940
Momsen, Bob, G, Ohio State 1951
Monachino, Jim, B, California 1951
Monahan, Regis, G, Ohio State 1935
Moncrief, Monte, T, Texas A&M 1944, 1945, 1947
Mondala, Stan, B, Missouri 1938
Monsky, Leroy, G, Alabama 1938
Mont, Tommy, QB, Maryland 1947
Montgomery, Cliff, QB, Columbia 1934
Montgomery, Marv, T, USC 1971
Montgomery, Randy, CB, Weber State 1970
Montler, Mike, G, Colorado 1969
Moomaw, Donn, LB, UCLA 1953
Moore, Bill (Red), T, Penn State 1947
Moore, Bob, TE, Stanford 1971
Moore, Bobby, RB, Oregon 1972
Moore, Derland, DT, Oklahoma 1973
Moore, Henry, HB, Arkansas 1956
Moore, Joe, RB, Missouri 1971
Moore, Lenny, HB, Penn State 1956
Moore, Lynn, RB, Army 1970
Moore, Manfred, RB, USC 1974
Moore, Rich, DT, Villanova 1969
Moore, Tom, B, Vanderbilt 1960
Moorhead, Bobby, HB, Georgia Tech 1953
Mooring, John, T, Tampa 1971
Moorman, Mo, T, Texas A&M 1968
Mooty, Jim, B, Arkansas 1960
Moran, Jim, DT, Idaho 1964
Morgan, Bob, T, Maryland 1954
Morin, Milt, TE, Massachusetts 1966
Morrall, Earl, QB, Michigan State 1956
Morris, Cecil, G, Oklahoma 1956
Morris, Chuck, CB, Mississippi 1963
Morris, George, LB, Georgia Tech 1953
Morris, Jon, C, Holy Cross 1964
Morris, Larry, C, Georgia Tech 1955
Morris, Max, E, Northwestern 1946
Morrison, Curly, B, Ohio State 1950
Morrison, Joe, HB, Cincinnati 1959
Morriss, Guy, C, TCU 1973
Morrow, Bob, B, Illinois Wesleyan 1941
Morse, Ray, E, Oregon 1935
Morton, Craig, QB, California 1965
Morton, John, E, Missouri 1944
Morze, Frank, C, Boston College 1955
Moser, Bob, C, Pacific 1951
Moser, Derace, B, Texas A&M 1942
Moses, Haven, FL, San Diego State 1968
Mosley, Doug, C, Kentucky 1952
Moss, Bobby, HB, West Virginia 1956
Moss, Joe, T, Maryland 1952
Moss, Perry, QB, Tulsa 1945, Illinois 1948
Mucha, Chuck, G, Washington 1935
Mucha, Rudy, C, Washington 1941
Mullaney, Mark, DE, Colorado State 1975
Mullen, Tom, G, Southwest Missouri State 1974
Mumley, Nick, T, Purdue 1959
Muncie, Chuck, RB, California 1976
Munger, Willis, G, Illinois College 1936
Munjas, Miller, QB, Pittsburgh 1935
Murakowski, Art, B, Northwestern 1950
Murley, Dick, T, Purdue 1956
Myers, Tommy, S, Syracuse 1972

N

Nabors, Tuffy, C, Texas Tech 1948
Nagle, Fran, QB, Nebraska 1951
Nakken, Herb, HB, Utah 1956
Naumoff, Paul, LB, Tennessee 1967
Nebel, Fred, C, Xavier 1938
Neely, Ralph, T, Oklahoma 1965
Negus, Fred, C, Wisconsin 1947
Neils, Steve, LB, Minnesota 1974
Nelson, Al, S, Cincinnati 1965
Nelson, Bob, C, Baylor 1941
Nelson, Herb, E, Pennsylvania 1943
Nelson, Ken, E, Illinois 1937
Newhouse, Robert, RB, Houston 1972
Newman, Bobby, QB, Washington State 1959
Newton, Bob, T, Nebraska 1971
Nicely, Joe, G, West Virginia 1958
Nichelni, Al, B, St. Mary's (California) 1935
Niedziela, Bruno, T, Iowa 1947
Niehaus, Steve, DT, Notre Dame 1976
Niemi, Laurie, T, Washington State 1949
Niland, John, G, Iowa 1966
Ninowski, Jim, QB, Michigan State 1958
Nisby, John, G, Pacific 1957
Nitschke, Ray, FB, Illinois 1958
Nix, Jack, B, Mississippi State 1940
Nobis, Tommy, LB, Texas 1966
Nolan, Dick, HB, Maryland 1954
Nolan, Jack, T, Penn State 1948
Nomellini, Leo, C, Minnesota 1950
Nomina, Tom, G, Miami (Ohio) 1963
North, John, E, Vanderbilt 1948
Norton, Jerry, HB, SMU 1954
Norton, Jim, DT, Washington 1965
Novak, Jack, G, Miami 1961
Novak, Ken, DT, Purdue 1976
Novak, Tom, C, Nebraska 1950
Nugent, Phil, QB, Tulane 1961
Nunamaker, Julian, DE, Tennessee 1969
Nussbaumer, Bob, B, Michigan 1946

O

O'Boyle, Tommy, G, Tulane 1941
Obradovich, Jim, TE, USC 1975
O'Brien, Davey, QB, TCU 1939
O'Brien, Emile, E, Tulane 1949
O'Brien, Fran, T, Michigan State 1959
O'Connell, Tommy, QB, Illinois 1953
O'Connor, Bill F. (Zeke), E, Notre Dame 1948
O'Connor, Bill J. (Bucky), G, Notre Dame 1948
Odom, Steve, WR, Utah State 1974
Odoms, Riley, TE, Houston 1972
O'Donahue, Pat, E, Wisconsin 1952
Odson, Urban, T, Minnesota 1942
Oech, Vernon, G, Minnesota 1936
Ognovich, Nick, B, Wake Forest 1948
Okland, Jack, T, Utah 1944
Okoniewski, Steve, T, Montana 1972
Olds, Bill, RB, Nebraska 1973
Olenski, Mitchell, T, Alabama 1946
Oliver, Vince, QB, Indiana 1939
Olsen, Merlin, T, Utah State 1962
Olsen, Phil, DT, Utah State 1970
Olsonoski, Larry, G, Minnesota 1948
Olszewski, Johnny, HB, California 1953
O'Neil, Ed, LB, Penn State 1974
O'Neill, Joe, E, Notre Dame 1937
Onesti, Larry, C, Northwestern 1962
Onkotz, Dennis, LB, Penn State 1970
Oravec, John, B, Willamette 1936
O'Reilly, Phil, T, Purdue 1949
Oriard, Mike, C, Notre Dame 1970
O'Rourke, Charlie, B, Boston College 1941
Ortega, Ralph, LB, Florida 1975
Ortmann, Chuck, B, Michigan 1951
Orvis, Herb, DE, Colorado 1972
O'Shea, Mike, WR, Utah State 1969
Osmanski, Bill, B, Holy Cross 1939
Osmond, John, C, Tulsa 1966
Osterman, Bob, C, Notre Dame 1941
Ottmar, Dave, P, Stanford 1974
Owens, Burgess, CB, Miami 1973
Owens, Don, T, Southern Mississippi 1957
Owens, Ike, E, Illinois 1948
Owens, Jim, E, Oklahoma 1950
Owens, Steve, RB, Oklahoma 1970

P

Pace, Jim, HB, Michigan 1958
Padley, Jack, B, Dayton 1940
Paffrath, Bob, QB, Minnesota 1941
Page, Alan, DE, Notre Dame 1967
Pajaczkowski, Frank, HB, Richmond 1956
Palmer, Derrell, T, TCU 1946
Paluck, John, E, Pittsburgh 1956
Palumbo, Sam, G, Notre Dame 1955
Panelli, Johnny, B, Notre Dame 1949
Panish, Ted, B, Bradley 1939

Pannell, Ernie, T, Texas A&M 1941
Papit, Johnny, B, Virginia 1951
Pardee, Jack, FB, Texas A&M 1957
Pardonner, Paul, QB, Purdue 1934
Paremore, Bob, HB, Florida A&M 1963
Parilli, Vito (Babe), QB, Kentucky 1952
Park, Ralph, B, Texas 1944, 1945
Parker, Artimus, S, USC 1974
Parker, Frank, E, Oklahoma State 1962
Parker, Jim, G, Ohio State 1957
Parks, Dave, E, Texas Tech 1964
Parson, Ray, T, Minnesota 1970
Paskvan, George, B, Wisconsin 1941
Pasquariello, Ralph, B, Villanova 1950
Pastorini, Dan, QB, Santa Clara 1971
Patanelli, Matt, E, Michigan 1937
Patera, Jack, G, Oregon 1955
Patrick, Frank, B, Pittsburgh 1938
Patterson, Billy, QB, Baylor 1939
Patulski, Walt, DE, Notre Dame 1972
Paulman, Bill, B, Stanford 1939
Pavelec, Ted, T, Detroit 1941
Pawlowski, Joe, G, Illinois 1945
Payne, Porter, G, Georgia 1950
Payton, Walter, RB, Jackson State 1975
Peaks, Clarence, HB, Michigan State 1957
Pearman, Bill (Pug), T, Tennessee 1952
Peay, Francis, T, Missouri 1966
Pedersen, Win, T, Minnesota 1940
Pellegrini, Bob, C, Maryland 1956
Penaluna, Bob, G, Iowa 1943
Penrose, Craig, QB, San Diego State 1976
Perkins, Don, B, New Mexico 1960
Pertel, Joe, G, Navy 1953
Perucca, John, T, North Central College 1947
Petchel, Elwood, B, Penn State 1949
Peters, Marty, E, Notre Dame 1936
Peters, Tony, S, Oklahoma 1975
Petitbon, John, HB, Notre Dame 1952
Petitbon, Richie, B, Tulane 1959
Petrick, Frank, E, Indiana 1939
Petrovich, George, T, Texas 1949
Pettit, Ken, E, Iowa 1941
Petty, George, G, Lake Forest 1943
Pfefferle, Dick, T, Notre Dame 1936
Pfeifer, Al, E, Fordham 1951
Phillips, Bill, B, DePaul 1937
Phillips, Charles, S, USC 1975
Phillips, Jim, E, Auburn 1958
Philyaw, Charles, DE, Texas Southern 1976
Phipps, Mike, QB, Purdue 1970
Piccone, Cammille, B, Notre Dame 1943
Piepul, Milt, B, Notre Dame 1941
Pietrosante, Nick, FB, Notre Dame 1959
Pihos, Pete, E, Indiana 1943
Pillath, Roger, T, Wisconsin 1964
Pincura, Stan, B, Ohio State 1936
Pingel, Johnny, B, Michigan State 1939
Pinion, Ray, G, TCU 1962
Pinney, Ray, C, Washington 1976
Pitts, Hugh, G, TCU 1956
Plummer, Bobby, T, TCU 1962
Plunkett, Jim, QB, Stanford 1971
Ply, Bobby, QB, Baylor 1962
Podolak, Ed, RB, Iowa 1969
Podoley, Jim, HB Central Michigan 1957
Poltl, Randy, S, Stanford 1974
Poole, Barney, E, Mississippi 1949
Poole, Ray, E, Mississippi 1947
Popovich, Milt, B, Montana 1938
Potsklan, Johnny, E, Penn State 1948
Pottios, Myron, LB, Notre Dame 1961
Prashaw, Milt, G, Michigan 1946
Prchlik, Johnny, G, Yale 1948
Pregulman, Marv, C, Michigan 1946
Prestel, Jim, T, Idaho 1960
Preston, Ben, E, Auburn 1958
Preston, Fred, E, Nebraska 1942
Prewitt, Felto, C, Tulsa 1946
Price, Ernie, DT, Texas A&I 1973
Price, Jerrell, G, Texas Tech 1952
Price, Jim, LB, Auburn 1963
Principe, Dom, B, Fordham 1940
Pritchard, Ron, LB, Arizona State 1969
Pritula, Bill, T, Michigan 1948
Prochaska, Ray, E, Nebraska 1941
Profit, Joe, RB, Northeast Louisiana 1971
Profit, Mel, E, UCLA 1964
Provost, Ted, CB, Ohio State 1970
Pruitt, Greg, RB, Oklahoma 1973
Pruitt, Mike, RB, Purdue 1976
Prymuski, Bob, T, Illinois 1949
Przybycki, Joe, G, Michigan State 1968
Psaltis, Jim, HB, USC 1953
Ptacek, Bob, QB, Michigan 1959
Pugh, Marion, QB, Texas A&M 1941
Pukema, Helge, G, Minnesota 1942
Puplis, Andy, QB, Notre Dame 1938
Purvis, Duane, B, Purdue 1935
Pyle, Mike, C, Yale 1961

Q

Quintana, Stan, CB, New Mexico 1966

R

Rabold, Mike, G, Indiana 1959
Raid, Gary, T, Willamette 1959
Raimondi, Ben, QB, Indiana 1947
Ramsey, Buster, G, William & Mary 1943, 1946
Ramsey, Knox, G, William & Mary 1948
Ramsey, Ray, B, Bradley 1947
Randolph, Alvin, CB, Iowa 1966
Rankin, Dave, E, Purdue 1941
Rapacz, John, C, Oklahoma 1948
Rassas, Nick, S, Notre Dame 1966
Rast, Holt, E, Alabama 1942
Ratterman, George, QB, Notre Dame 1947
Rauch, John, QB, Georgia 1949
Ravensberg, Bob, E, Indiana 1944
Rechichar, Bert, HB, Tennessee 1952
Redmond, Rudy, CB, Pacific 1969
Reece, Geoff, C, Washington State 1975
Reed, Jim, G, Texas Tech 1947
Reed, Oscar, RB, Colorado State 1968
Reeder, Jim, T, Illinois 1940
Rees, Trevor, E, Ohio State 1936
Reese, Don, DT, Jackson State 1974
Regeczi, John, B, Michigan 1935
Regner, Tom, G, Notre Dame 1967
Reichardt, Bill, FB, Iowa 1952
Reichow, Jerry, QB, Iowa 1956
Reid, Mike, DT, Penn State 1970
Reid, Steve, G, Northwestern 1937
Reifsnyder, Bob, T, Navy 1959
Reilly, Jim, G, Notre Dame 1970
Reilly, Mike, LB, Iowa 1964
Reinhard, Bob, B, California 1944
Relyea, Ken, T, Colgate 1937
Remington, Bill, C, Washington State 1943
Renfro, Dick, QB, Washington State 1943
Renfro, Mel, S, Oregon 1964
Renfroe, Joe, B, Tulane 1945
Rennebohm, Dale, C, Minnesota 1936
Renner, Bill, B, Michigan 1936
Rentzel, Lance, FL, Oklahoma 1965
Renzel, Doug, B, Marquette 1942
Repko, Joe, T, Boston College 1946
Ressler, Glenn, G, Penn State 1965
Routz, Joe, G, Notre Dame 1938
Reynolds, Billy, HB, Pittsburgh 1953
Reynolds, Bob, T, Bowling Green 1963
Reynolds, Bobby, T, Stanford 1936
Reynolds, Jack, LB, Tennessee 1970
Reynolds, Jim, B, Oklahoma State 1946
Rhea, Floyd, G, Oregon 1943
Rhodemyre, Jay, C, Kentucky 1948
Rhoden, Don, LB, Rice 1953
Rice, George, DT, LSU 1966
Rice, Ken, T, Auburn 1961
Richardson, Jerry, CB, West Texas State 1964
Richardson, Willie, FL, Jackson State 1963
Richter, Les, G, California 1952
Richter, Pat, E, Wisconsin 1963
Ridlon, Jimmy, HB, Syracuse 1957
Rifenburg, Dick, E, Michigan 1949
Riffle, Chuck, G, Notre Dame 1940
Riggins, John, RB, Kansas 1971
Riley, Jim, DT, Oklahoma 1967
Riley, Joe, B, Alabama 1937
Riley, Steve, T, USC 1974
Rimkus, Vic, T, Holy Cross 1953
Ringer, Judd, E, Minnesota 1942
Rissmiller, Ray, T, Georgia 1965
Rivera, Hank, HB, Oregon State 1962
Robbins, Jack, QB, Arkansas 1938
Roberts, Gene (Choo-Choo), B, Tennessee-Chattanooga 1947
Robertson, Bill, E, Memphis State 1951
Robertson, Bobby, B, USC 1942
Robertson, Isiah, LB, Southern 1971
Robesky, Ken, G, Stanford 1942
Robinson, Dave, LB, Penn State 1963
Robinson, Jackie, B, UCLA 1941
Rochester, Paul, T, Michigan State 1960
Rock, Walt, G, Maryland 1963
Rogers, Cullen, B, Texas A&M 1945
Rohm, Charles (Pinky), B, LSU 1938
Rohrig, Herman, B, Nebraska 1941
Rokisky, John, E, Duquesne 1942
Roland, Johnny, FB, Missouri 1966
Roscoe, George, B, Minnesota 1936
Rosdahl, Harrison, G, Penn State 1964
Rose, George, CB, Auburn 1964
Rosenberg, Aaron, G, USC 1934
Rosequist, Ted, T, Ohio State 1934
Ross, Larry, E, Denver 1956
Rossovich, Tim, LB, USC 1968
Rote, Kyle, B, SMU 1951
Rotela, Jamie, LB, Tennessee 1973
Roussel, Tom, LB, Southern Mississippi 1968
Routt, Bill, T, Texas A&M 1941
Routt, Joe, T, Texas A&M 1938
Rowan, Rip, B, Army 1949
Rowden, Jake, C, Maryland 1951
Rowe, Bob, DE, Western Michigan 1967
Rowe, Dave, DT, Penn State 1967
Rowe, Red, E, Dartmouth 1950
Ruby, Martin, T, Texas A&M 1946
Rucinski, Eddie, E, Indiana 1941
Rudnay, Jack, C, Northwestern 1969
Ruffa, Tony, T, Duke 1941
Ruman, Bob, B, Arizona 1944
Rupert, Dick, G, Nebraska 1972
Rush, Jerry, DT, Michigan State 1965
Russell, Jack, E, Baylor 1946
Rutgens, Joe, T, Illinois 1961
Ryba, Jim, T, Alabama 1938
Rykovich, Julie, B, Illinois 1947

S

Saban, Lou, QB, Indiana 1944, 1946
Sabol, Joe, HB, UCLA 1953
Sacco, Tony, QB, St. Ambrose 1940
Saggau, Bob, B, Notre Dame 1941
Saia, Joe, G, St. Viator 1937
Salatino, Joe, QB, Santa Clara 1935
Salsbury, Jim, G, UCLA 1955
Sample, Johnny, HB, Maryland-Eastern Shore 1958
Sampson, Greg, DT, Stanford 1972
Samuels, Dale, QB, Purdue 1953
Sanders, Charlie, TE, Minnesota 1968
Sanders, Daryle, T, Ohio State 1963
Sanders, Lonnie, S, Michigan State 1963
Sandifer, Dan, B, LSU 1948
Sandusky, John, T, Villanova 1950
Sandusky, Mike, T, Maryland 1957
Sardisco, Tony, G, Tulane 1956
Sarkisian, Alex, C, Northwestern 1949
Sarkkinen, Esco, E, Ohio State 1940
Sarno, Amerino, T, Fordham 1936
Sarringhaus, Paul, B, Ohio State 1944
Sartori, Larry, G, Fordham 1942
Sauer, George, B, Nebraska 1934
Saul, Bill, C, Penn State 1962
Savitsky, George, T, Pennsylvania 1948
Saxton, James, HB, Texas 1962
Sayers, Gale, HB, Kansas 1965
Sayers, Ron, RB, Nebraska Omaha 1969
Scarbath, Jack, QB, Maryland 1953
Schabarum, Pete, B, California 1951
Schaefer, Don, FB, Notre Dame 1956
Schafrath, Dick, G, Ohio State 1959
Schiechl, John, C, Santa Clara 1940
Schindler, Ambrose, QB, USC 1940
Schlralll, Rocco, G, Notre Dame 1935
Schleicher, Maurice, E, Penn State 1959
Schlinkman, Walt, B, Texas Tech 1945
Schoenbaum, Alex, T, Ohio State 1939
Schottenheimer, Marty, LB, Pittsburgh 1965
Schrader, Dick, C, Notre Dame 1954
Schreyer, Marty, T, Purdue 1938
Schroeder, Gene, E, Virginia 1951
Schuh, Harry, T, Memphis State 1965
Schulte, George, QB, Rockhurst 1941
Schulte, Tom, E, East Kentucky State 1958
Schumacher, Kurt, T, Ohio State 1975
Schwall, Vic, B, Northwestern 1947
Schwammel, Ade, T, Oregon State 1934
Schwartz, Perry, E, California 1938
Schweder, John (Bull), G, Pennsylvania 1950
Scollard, Nick, E, St. Joseph's (Indiana) 1945, 1946
Scorsone, Vince, G, Pittsburgh 1957
Scott, Clarence, CB, Kansas State 1971
Scott, Clyde (Smackover), B, Arkansas 1949
Scott, Dick, C, Navy 1948
Scott, Tom, E, Virginia 1953
Scruggs, Ted, E, Rice 1947
Seals, George, DE, Missouri 1964
Sears, Jim, HB, USC 1953
Sebastian, Mike, B, Pittsburgh 1934
Seeman, Bob, E, Nebraska 1940
Seidel, Gerhard, B, Columbia 1939
Seidel, Glenn, QB, Minnesota 1936
Seiler, Paul, T, Notre Dame 1967
Selawski, Gene, T, Purdue 1959
Selmon, Dewey, DT, Oklahoma 1976
Selmon, Lee Roy, DT, Oklahoma 1976
Severin, Paul, E, North Carolina 1941
Sewell, Harley, G, Texas 1953
Seymour, Jim, WR, Notre Dame 1969
Seymour, Paul, T, Michigan 1973
Shakespeare, Bill, E, Notre Dame 1936
Shalosky, Bill, G, Cincinnati 1953
Shanklin, Ron, WR, North Texas State 1970
Sharockman, Ed, B, Pittsburgh 1961

Shaw, Billy, G, Georgia Tech 1961
Shaw, Dennis, QB, San Diego State 1970
Shaw, George, QB, Oregon 1955
Shay, Jerry, DT, Purdue 1966
Shedlosky, Ed, B, Tulsa 1945
Sheehan, Mel, E, Missouri 1949
Sheetz, Paul, G, Xavier 1940
Shepherd, Bill, B, Western Maryland 1935
Sherer, Dave, E, SMU 1959
Sheridan, Benny, B, Notre Dame 1940
Sherman, Rod, FL, USC 1967
Sherman, Saul, B, Chicago 1939
Sherrill, J.W., B, Tennessee 1951
Sherrod, Bobby, G, TCU 1946
Sherrod, Bud, E, Tennessee 1951
Shinners, John, G, Xavier 1969
Shinnick, Don, FB, UCLA 1957
Shires, Marshall, T, Tennessee 1941
Shirey, Fred, T, Nebraska 1938
Shivers, Roy, HB, Utah State 1966
Shofner, Del, HB, Baylor 1957
Shofner, Jim, HB, TCU 1958
Shotwell, George, C, Pittsburgh 1935
Siani, Mike, WR, Villanova 1972
Siegel, Don, T, Michigan 1939
Siemering, Larry, C, San Francisco 1935
Sieminski, Chuck, DT, Penn State 1963
Siemon, Jeff, LB, Stanford 1972
Signaigo, Joe, G, Notre Dame 1948
Silovich, Joe, B, Minnesota 1943
Silovich, Martin, C, Marquette 1945, 1946
Simmons, Dave, LB, Georgia Tech 1965
Simmons, Floyd, B, Notre Dame 1948
Simonini, Ed, LB, Texas A&M 1976
Simpson, Bill, S, Michigan State 1974
Sims, George, B, Baylor 1949
Sims, Hosea, E, Marquette 1954
Singer, Bernie, B, Arizona 1945
Sisemore, Jerry, T, Texas 1973
Sitko, Emil, B, Notre Dame 1950
Sitko, Steve, QB, Notre Dame 1940
Sizemore, Paul, E, Furman 1943, 1944, 1945
Skaggs, Jim, G, Washington 1962
Skladany, Joe (Mugsy), E, Pittsburgh 1934
Skoglund, Bob, E, Notre Dame 1947
Skoronski, Bob, T, Indiana 1956
Skorupan, John, LB, Penn State 1973
Slater, Jackie, G, Jackson State 1976
Sloan, Steve, QB, Alabama 1966
Small, Eldridge, CB, Texas A&I 1972
Small, John, LB, Citadel 1970
Smeja, Rudy, E, Michigan 1943
Smilanich, Bronko, B, Arizona 1939
Smith, Barry, WR, Florida State 1973
Smith, Bill, E, Washington 1934
Smith, Bill, T, North Carolina 1948
Smith, Bobby, HB, North Texas State 1964
Smith, Bruce, B, Minnesota 1942
Smith, Bubba, DT, Michigan State 1967
Smith, Charles (Rabbit), B, Georgia 1947
Smith, Dick, T, Minnesota 1936
Smith, Harry, G, USC 1940
Smith, Iwood, G, Ohio State 1937
Smith, Jim (Yazoo), CB, Oregon 1968
Smith, Jim Ray, T, Baylor 1955
Smith, Pete, E, Oklahoma 1938
Smith, Riley, QB, Alabama 1936
Smith, Royce, G, Georgia 1972
Smith, Sid, C, USC 1970
Smith, Zeke, G, Auburn 1960
Snead, Norm, QB, Wake Forest 1961
Snell, Matt, FB, Ohio State 1964
Snorton, Matt, E, Michigan State 1964
Snow, Jack, E, Notre Dame 1965
Snyder, Lum, T, Georgia Tech 1952
Soboleski, Joe, G, Michigan 1949
Sobrero, Frank, B, Santa Clara 1935
Sohn, Ben, G, USC 1941
Solomon, Freddie, QB-WR, Tampa 1975
Soltau, Gordy, E, Minnesota 1950
Sommer, Mike, HB, George Washington 1958
Souders, Cy, E, Ohio State 1947
Spadaccini, Vic, QB, Minnesota 1938
Spain, Truman, T, SMU 1936
Speegle, Cliff, C, Oklahoma 1945
Spencer, Maurice, CB, North Carolina Central 1974
Spilis, John, WR, Northern Illinois 1969
Spurrier, Steve, QB, Florida 1967
Stacy, Billy, B, Mississippi State 1959
Stalcup, Jerry, G, Wisconsin 1960
Staley, Bill, DT, Utah State 1968
Stallings, Don, T, North Carolina 1960
Standlee, Norm, B, Stanford 1941
Stanfel, Dick, G, San Francisco 1951
Stanfill, Bill, DE, Georgia 1969
Stanley, C.B., T, Tulsa 1946
Stanton, Hank, E, Arizona 1942
Starcevich, Max, G, Washington 1937
Staton, Jim, T, Wake Forest 1951
Statuto, Art, C, Notre Dame 1948
Staubach, Roger, QB, Navy 1965
Stautzenberger, Odell, G, Texas A&M 1949
Steen, Jim, T, Syracuse 1935
Steere, Dick, T, Drake 1951
Steffy, Joe, G, Army 1949
Stegent, Larry, RB, Texas A&M 1970
Steinkemper, Bill, T, Notre Dame 1937
Stephenson, Jack, T, Ohio State 1942
Steuber, Bob, B, Missouri 1943
Stickles, Monty, E, Notre Dame 1960
Stingley, Darryl, WR, Purdue 1973
Stith, Carel, DT, Nebraska 1967
Stockert, Ernie, E, UCLA 1953
Stonesifer, Don, E, Northwestern 1951
Storti, Tony, B, Illinois 1944
Stremic, Tony, G, Navy 1958
Striegel, Bill, G, Pacific 1958
Strohmeyer, George, C, Notre Dame 1948
Stromberg, Woody, E, Army 1937
Stroud, Jack, T, Tennessee 1951
Strugar, George, T, Washington 1957
Strzykalski, Johnny, B, Marquette 1945
Stuart, Bob, B, Army 1949
Stydahar, Joe, T, West Virginia 1936
Stynchula, Andy, T, Penn State 1960
Sucic, Steve, B, Illinois 1945
Suffridge, Bob, G, Tennessee 1941
Sugar, Leo, E, Purdue 1952
Suggs, Shafer, S, Ball State 1976
Suhey, Steve, G, Penn State 1948
Sullivan, Dan, T, Boston College 1962
Sullivan, George, T, Notre Dame 1948
Sullivan, Joe, B, Dartmouth 1949
Sullivan, Pat, QB, Auburn 1972
Susoeff, Nick, E, Washington State 1943
Sutton, Archie, T, Illinois 1965
Sutton, Ed, HB, North Carolina 1957
Sutton, Mitch, DT, Kansas 1974
Svendsen, Earl, C, Minnesota 1937
Svoboda, Bill, B, Tulane 1950
Swann, Lynn, WR, USC 1974
Sweeney, Chuck, E, Notre Dame 1938
Sweeney, Walt, G, Syracuse 1963
Sweiger, Bob, B, Minnesota 1942
Swiacki, Bill, E, Columbia 1948
Swisher, Bob, B, Northwestern 1938
Swistowicz, Mike, B, Notre Dame 1950
Switzer, Veryl, HB, Kansas State 1954
Szafaryn, Len, T, North Carolina 1949
Szczecko, Joe, DT, Northwestern 1965
Szymakowski, Dave, SE, West Texas State 1968
Szymanski, Dick, C, Notre Dame 1955
Szymanski, Frank, C, Notre Dame 1943

T

Tagge, Jerry, QB, Nebraska 1972
Taliaferro, George, B, Indiana 1949
Tamburo, Dick, LB, Michigan State 1953
Tangora, Paul, G, Northwestern 1936
Tannen, Steve, S, Florida 1970
Tanner, Ted, C, Stanford 1954
Tarasovic, George, C, LSU 1952
Tarbox, Bruce, G, Syracuse 1961
Tarver, John, RB, Colorado 1972
Tassos, Damon, G, Texas A&M 1945
Tatarek, Bob, DT, Miami 1968
Tate, Al, T, Illinois 1951
Tate, John, LB, Jackson State 1975
Tatum, Jack, S, Ohio State 1971
Tavener, John, C, Indiana 1944, 1945, 1946
Tavzel, Harold, T, Army 1947
Taylor, Altie, RB, Utah State 1969
Taylor, Bruce, CB, Boston U. 1970
Taylor, Charley, HB, Arizona State 1964
Taylor, Jim, C, Baylor 1956
Taylor, Jim, FB, LSU 1958
Taylor, Mike, LB, Michigan 1972
Temp, Jim, E, Wisconsin 1955
Templeton, Dave, G, Ohio State 1949
Tereshinski, Joe, E, Georgia 1947
Terrio, Bob, RB, Nebraska 1972
Thesing, Joe, B, Notre Dame 1940
Thomas, Aaron, E, Oregon State 1961
Thomas, Clendon, HB, Oklahoma 1958
Thomas, Duane, RB, West Texas State 1970
Thomas, George, B, Oklahoma 1950
Thomas, Ike, CB, Bishop 1971
Thomas, J.T., S, Florida State 1973
Thomas, John, E, Oregon State 1952
Thomason, Jim, B, Texas A&M 1941
Thompson, Billy, CB, Maryland-Eastern Shore 1969
Thompson, Dave, C, Clemson 1971
Thompson, Norm, S, Utah 1971
Thompson, Rocky, WR, West Texas State 1971
Thompson, Tommy, C, William & Mary 1949
Thornton, Bill, FB, Nebraska 1963
Tidwell, Billy, QB, Texas A&M 1952
Tidwell, Travis, QB, Auburn 1950
Tigart, Thurman, G, Oklahoma 1946
Timberlake, Bob, QB, Michigan 1965
Timberlake, George, G, USC 1954
Tinker, Gerald, WR, Kent State 1974
Tinsley, Gaynell, E, LSU 1937
Tisdale, Stu, QB, Yale 1951
Todd, Larry, HB, Arizona State 1965
Todd, Richard, QB, Alabama 1976
Tokarczyk, Dolph, G, Pennsylvania 1949
Toler, Burl, T, San Francisco 1952
Tomasi, Dom, G, Michigan 1949
Tomasic, Andy, B, Temple 1942
Toneff, Bob, T, Notre Dame 1952
Tonelli, Mario, B, Notre Dame 1939
Tonnemaker, Clayton, C, Minnesota 1950
Topping, Keith, E, Stanford 1936
Toth, Steve, B, Northwestern 1937
Triplett, Mel, FB, Toledo 1955
Trippi, Charley, B, Georgia 1943, 1944, 1945, 1947
Tripucka, Frank, QB, Notre Dame 1949
Trosch, Gene, DE, Miami 1967
Truax, Dalton, G, Tulane 1957
Tubbs, Jerry, C, Oklahoma 1957
Tucker, Arnold, QB, Army 1947
Turner, Clyde (Bulldog), C, Hardin-Simmons 1940
Twedell, Fred, G, Minnesota 1939
Tyrer, Jim, T, Ohio State 1961
Tyrrell, Bob, G, St. Ambrose 1939

U

Ulinski, Harry, C, Kentucky 1950
Underwood, Ronnie, HB, Arkansas 1957
Upshaw, Gene, T, Texas A&I 1967
Upshaw, Marvin, DE, Trinity (Texas) 1968
Uram, Andy, B, Minnesota 1938
Urban, Gaspar, T, Notre Dame 1948
Uremovich, Emil, T, Indiana 1941
Urlaub, Bill, C, Northwestern 1943

V

Van Brocklin, Norm, QB, Oregon 1949
Van Buren, Steve, B, LSU 1944
VanderKelen, Ron, QB, Wisconsin 1963
Van Every, Hal, B, Minnesota 1940
Van Raaphorst, Dick, K, Ohio State 1964
Van Ranst, Al, C, Cornell 1939
Vanzo, Fred, QB, Northwestern 1938
Varrichione, Frank, T, Notre Dame 1955
Vereen, Carl, T, Georgia Tech 1957
Verry, Norm, G, USC 1946
Villapiano, Phil, LB, Bowling Green 1971
Vincent, Eddie, HB, Iowa 1956
Visted, Frank, LB, Navy 1961
Vogds, Evan, G, Wisconsin 1946
Vogel, Bob, T, Ohio State 1963
Vohaska, Bill, C, Illinois 1951
Voigts, Bob, T, Northwestern 1939
Volk, Rick, S, Michigan 1967
Volm, Frank, QB, Marquette 1951
Vosberg, Don, E, Marquette 1941
Voss, Lloyd, T, Nebraska 1964
Vuchnich, Mike, B, Ohio State 1934

W

Wade, Bill, QB, Vanderbilt 1952
Wagner, Steve, S, Wisconsin 1976
Wahl, Al, T, Michigan 1951
Waldorf, Bob, G, Missouri 1940
Walker, Blake, QB, Yale 1946
Walker, Cornelius, DT, Rice 1975
Walker, Doak, B, SMU 1950
Walker, Jim, T, Iowa 1942
Walker, Malcolm, C, Rice 1965
Walker, Paul, E, Yale 1946
Walker, Val Joe, HB, SMU 1953
Walker, Wayne, C, Idaho 1958
Wallace, Bob, SE, Texas-El Paso 1968
Wallace, Jackie, S, Arizona 1973
Wallace, Stan, HB, Illinois 1954
Waller, Ron, HB, Maryland 1955
Walsh, Bill, C, Notre Dame 1949
Walters, Rod, G, Iowa 1970
Walton, Frank (Tiger), G, Pittsburgh 1934
Walton, Joe, E, Pittsburgh 1957
Warburton, Cotton, QB, USC 1935
Ward, Bob, G, Maryland 1952
Ward, John, G, Oklahoma State 1970
Warfield, Paul, FL, Ohio State 1964
Warrington, Tex, C, Auburn 1945
Washington, Gene, SE, Michigan State 1967
Washington, Gene, WR, Stanford 1969
Washington, Joe, RB, Oklahoma 1976
Washington, Kenny, B, UCLA 1940
Washington, Mike, CB, Alabama 1975
Washington, Russ, T, Missouri 1968
Wasicek, Charles, T, Colgate 1936

Wasick, Dave, DE, San Jose State 1975
Waters, Charlie, S, Clemson 1970
Watkins, Bobby, HB, Ohio State 1955
Watson, Joe, C, Rice 1950
Wayt, Russell, LB, Rice 1965
Weatherall, Jim, T, Oklahoma 1952
Weaver, Charlie, LB, USC 1971
Weaver, Gary, LB, Fresno State 1973
Weaver, John, HB, Navy 1955
Webb, Jimmy, DT, Mississippi State 1975
Webster, George, LB, Michigan State 1967
Webster, Mike, C, Wisconsin 1974
Wedemeyer, Herman, B, St. Mary's (California) 1948
Weed, Tad, HB, Ohio State 1955
Wegner, Erwin, C, Northwestern 1938
Wehrli, Roger, S, Missouri 1969
Weiner, Art, E, North Carolina 1950
Weinmeister, Arnie, G, Washington 1948
Weiss, Howard, B, Wisconsin 1939
Wellman, Vere, T, Wichita State 1956
Welsh, George, QB, Navy 1956
Wendell, Marty, G, Notre Dame 1949
Wendt, Fred, B, Texas-El Paso 1949
Wendt, Merle, E, Ohio State 1937
Wenskunas, Mac, C, Illinois 1947
Werder, Bus, C, Georgetown (Washington D.C.) 1948
Werkheiser, Eldon, G, Dubuque 1943
Werner, Clyde, LB, Washington 1970
West, Stan, G, Oklahoma 1950
Westfall, Bob, B, Michigan 1942
Wetoska, Bob, E, Notre Dame 1959
Wetzel, Damon, B, Ohio State 1935
Wharton, Al, T, Maryland 1957
Wheeler, Wayne, WR, Alabama 1974
White, Byron (Whizzer), B, Colorado 1938
White, Ed, DE, California 1969
White, Gene, G, Indiana 1946
White, Jack, B, Princeton 1938
White, Jack, C, Michigan 1948
White, James, DE, Oklahoma State 1976
White, Jeris, CB, Hawaii 1974
White, Lee, RB, Weber State 1968
White, Randy, DT, Maryland 1975
White, Sammy, WR, Grambling 1970
White, Sherman, DE, California 1972
White, Walter, TE, Maryland 1975
White, Wilford (Whizzer), B, Arizona State 1951
Whiteaker, Dave, T, Purdue 1954
Whitlow, Ken, C, Rice 1941
Whitmire, Wilson, C, Navy 1957
Wiatrak, John, C, Washington 1937
Widseth, Ed, T, Minnesota 1937
Wiggin, Paul, T, Stanford 1957
Wightkin, Bill, E, Notre Dame 1950
Wilcox, Dave, LB, Oregon 1964
Wildung, Dick, T, Minnesota 1943
Wilke, Bob, B, Notre Dame 1937
Wilkerson, Doug, G, North Carolina Central 1970
Wilkinson, Bob, E, UCLA 1951
Wilkinson, Bud, B, Minnesota 1937
Willard, Ken, FB, North Carolina 1965
Williams, Bob, QB, Notre Dame 1951
Williams, Broughton, E, Florida 1947
Williams, Charlie, WR, Prairie View A&M 1970
Williams, Clancy, CB, Washington State 1965
Williams, Dave, FL, Washington 1967
Williams, Fred, T, Arkansas 1952
Williams, Jerry, B, Washington State 1949
Williams, John, G, Minnesota 1968
Williams, Morgan, G, TCU 1954
Williams, Roy, DT, Pacific 1963
Williams, Sammy, E, Michigan State 1959
Williams, Wayne, B, Minnesota 1944
Willingham, Larry, CB, Auburn 1971
Willis, Bill, T, Ohio State 1944, 1945
Wilson, Ben, FB, USC 1963
Wilson, Billy, T, Auburn 1962
Wilson, Bob, B, SMU 1936
Wilson, Bobby, HB, Alabama 1953
Wilson, Jim, G, Georgia 1965
Wilson, Tommy, B, Illinois 1937
Wimberly, Abner, E, LSU 1949
Winans, Jeff, DT, USC 1973
Winfrey, Stan, RB, Arkansas State 1975
Wingate, Elmer, E, Maryland 1951
Winkler, Joe, C, Purdue 1943
Winslow, Bob, E, USC 1940
Winslow, Don, G, Iowa 1950
Winston, Roy, G, LSU 1962
Wistert, Al, T, Michigan 1943
Wodziak, Frank, E, Illinois 1953
Wolf, Jim, T, Louisville 1956
Wolf, Joe, T, North Carolina 1943
Wolf, Ralph, C, Ohio State 1938
Wolfe, Hugh, B, Texas 1938
Wolff, Alvord, T, Santa Clara 1939
Woltman, Clem, T, Purdue 1938
Wood, Richard, LB, USC 1975
Woodcock, John, LB, Hawaii 1976
Woods, Robert, T, Tennessee State 1973
Woodson, Abe, HB, Illinois 1957
Wooten, John, G, Colorado 1959
Wooten, W.G. (Dub), E, Oklahoma 1944
Worden, Neil, FB, Notre Dame 1954
Wotkyns, Haskell (Inky), B, USC 1935
Wozniak, John, G, Alabama 1948
Wright, Elmo, WR, Houston 1971
Wright, Louis, CB, San Jose State 1975
Wyatt, Bowden, E, Tennessee 1939
Wylie, Joe, RB, Oklahoma 1973
Wysocki, John, E, Villanova 1939

Y

Yagiello, Ray, T, Catawba 1948
Yary, Ron, T, USC 1968
Yates, Paul, B, Texas A&M 1945
Yearby, Bill, DE, Michigan 1966
Yerges, Howard, QB, Michigan 1948
Yockum, Dan, G, Syracuse 1972
Yonakor, John, E, Notre Dame 1944, 1946
Youell, Jim, QB, Iowa 1943
Youman, Maury, T, Syracuse 1960
Young, Adrian, LB, USC 1968
Young, Buddy, B, Illinois 1947
Young, Charle, TE, USC 1973
Young, Roland, E, Oklahoma 1939
Young, Wilbur, DT, William Penn 1971
Youngblood, Jack, DE, Florida 1971
Youngblood, Jim, LB, Tennessee Tech 1973
Youso, Frank, T, Minnesota 1958
Yowarsky, Walt, T, Kentucky 1951

Z

Zabel, Steve, LB, Oklahoma 1970
Zachary, Jim, E, Purdue 1938
Zapalac, Willie, B, Texas A&M 1943
Zarnas, Gust, G, Ohio State 1938
Zarza, Lou, E, Michigan State 1936
Zatkoff, Roger, LB, Michigan 1953
Zeno, Mike, G, Virginia Tech 1961
Ziemba, Wally, C, Notre Dame 1943
Zilly, Jack, E, Notre Dame 1947
Zimny, Bob, T, Indiana 1943, 1944, 1945
Zitko, John, E, Northwestern 1937
Zontini, Lou, B, Notre Dame 1940
Zwernemann, Ron, G, East Texas State 1967

All-Pros

In 1920, the American Professional Football Association (which became the NFL two years later) was formed. That same year, the first all-pro team was named. The selections were made by Bruce Copeland, the sports editor of the Rock Island *Argus,* and a close follower of the early pro game. No one named an all-pro team in 1921.

In 1922, two NFL player-coaches, George Halas of the Chicago Bears and Guy Chamberlin of the Canton Bulldogs, named all-pro teams. Their respective selections are indicated by an H or a C.

An all-pro poll that appeared annually in the Green Bay *Press-Gazette* began in 1923 and received recognition in league cities, where, unlike in many larger metropolitan areas, pro football was covered thoroughly. The poll ran from 1923-1931; the voters consisted of, at varying times, sportswriters from league cities, game officials, team coaches, and team owners.

In 1931, the results of the *Press-Gazette* poll gave the league its first official all-pro team. From 1932 through 1942, the NFL's official team was selected by coaches throughout the league. The practice continued until 1943, the first year of the news service teams. *Associated Press* (AP) and *United Press* (UP; *United Press International* [UPI] since 1958) picked the all-pro teams until 1960. From 1961-69, AP, UPI, and *Newspaper Enterprise Association* (NEA) picked the all-pro teams for the NFL.

The AFL all-pro teams were picked by the players in 1960 and from 1962-66; the coaches picked the team in 1961. In 1964, AP and UPI started picking AFL all-pro teams, joining the players from 1964-66. In 1967, the players stopped their picks and the wire services were the only AFL all-pro teams in 1967 and 1968.

In 1969, the first combined NFL-AFL all-pro team was picked by the Pro Football Hall of Fame. AP, UPI, and NEA each picked both an AFL all-pro team and an NFL all-pro team. In 1970-71, the wire services picked all-conference teams; the official all-pro team was chosen by the Professional Football Writers Association (PFWA). From 1972-75, both the PFWA and the NEA picked all-pro teams. Since 1976, the PFWA, NEA, and AP have picked teams.

1920	
Guy Chamberlin, Decatur	E
Oke Smith, Rock Island	E
Wilbur (Pete) Henry, Canton	T
Hugh Blacklock, Decatur	T
Fred Denfield, Rock Island	G
Dewey Lyle, Rock Island	G
George Trafton, Decatur	C
John (Paddy) Driscoll, Chi. Cardinals	QB
Eddie Novak, Rock Island	HB
Fritz Pollard, Akron	HB
Rip King, Akron	FB

1922	
Eddie Anderson, Chi. Cardinals (C)	E
Elmer (Bird) Carroll, Canton (C)	E
Guy Chamberlin, Canton (H)	E
Luke Urban, Buffalo (H)	E
Wilbur (Pete) Henry, Canton (C,H)	T
Hugh Blacklock, Chi. Bears (H)	T
Clarence (Steamer) Horning, Toledo (C)	T
Herb Stein, Toledo (C, H)	G
Ed Healey, Rock Island-Chi. Bears (H)	G
Duke Osborn, Canton (C)	G
Joe Alexander, Rochester (C, H)	C
Tommy Hughitt, Buffalo (H)	QB
Harry Robb, Canton (C)	QB
John (Paddy) Driscoll, Chi. Cardinals (C, H)	HB
Pete Stinchcomb, Chi. Bears (C, H)	HB
Doc Elliott, Canton (C)	FB
Rip King, Akron (H)	FB

1923	
Jay (Inky) Williams, Hammond	E
Gus Tebell, Columbus	E
Ed Healey, Chi. Bears	T
Wilbur (Pete) Henry, Canton	T
Adolph (Swede) Youngstrom, Buffalo	G
Raymond (Bub) Weller, St. Louis	G
Harry Mehre, Minneapolis	C
John (Paddy) Driscoll, Chi. Cardinals	QB
Jim Thorpe, Oorang	HB
Al Michaels, Akron	HB
Doc Elliott, Canton	FB

1924	
Joe Little Twig, Rock Island	E
Walter (Tillie) Voss, Green Bay	E
Ed Healey, Chi. Bears	T
Boni Petcoff, Columbus	T
Adolph (Swede) Youngstrom, Buffalo	G
Stan Muirhead, Dayton	G
George Trafton, Chi. Bears	C
Joe Sternaman, Chi. Bears	QB
Charlie Way, Frankford	HB
Benny Boynton, Buffalo	HB
Doc Elliott, Cleveland	FB

1925	
Charlie Berry, Pottsville	E
Ed Lynch, Rochester	E
Ed Healey, Chi. Bears	T
Gus Sonnenberg, Detroit	T
Art Carney, NY Giants	G
Jim McMillen, Chi. Bears	G
Ralph Claypool, Chi. Cardinals	C
Joe Sternaman, Chi. Bears	QB
John (Paddy) Driscoll, Chi. Cardinals	HB
Dave Noble, Cleveland	HB
Jack McBride, NY Giants	FB

1926	
Harold (Brick) Muller, LA Buccaneers	E
Charlie Berry, Pottsville	E
Ed Healey, Chi. Bears	T
Walt Ellis, Chi. Cardinals	T
Johnny Budd, Frankford	G
Gus Sonnenberg, Detroit	G
Clyde Smith, Kansas City	C
Tut Imlay, LA Buccaneers	QB
John (Paddy) Driscoll, Chi. Bears	HB
Verne Lewellen, Green Bay	HB
Ernie Nevers, Duluth	FB

1927	
Lavern Dilweg, Green Bay	E
Cal Hubbard, NY Giants	E
Gus Sonnenberg, Providence	T
Ed Wier, Frankford	T
Mike Michalske, NY Yankees	G
Steve Owen, NY Giants	G
Clyde Smith, Cleveland	C
Benny Friedman, Cleveland	QB
Verne Lewellen, Green Bay	HB
John (Paddy) Driscoll, Chi. Bears	HB
Ernie Nevers, Duluth	FB

1928	
Lavern Dilweg, Green Bay	E
Ray Flaherty, NY Yankees-NY Giants	E
Bill Owen, Detroit	T
Russell (Bull) Behman, Frankford	T
Mike Michalske, NY Yankees	G
Jim McMillen, Chi. Bears	G
Clyde Smith, Providence	C
Benny Friedman, Detroit	QB
George (Wildcat) Wilson, Providence	HB
Verne Lewellen, Green Bay	HB
Wally Diehl, Frankford	FB

1929	
Lavern Dilweg, Green Bay	E
Ray Flaherty, NY Giants	E
Russell (Bull) Behman, Frankford	T
Bob Beattie, Orange	T
Mike Michalske, Green Bay	G
Milt Rehnquist, Providence	G
Joe Westoupal, NY Giants	C
Benny Friedman, NY Giants	QB
Verne Lewellen, Green Bay	HB
Tony Plansky, NY Giants	HB
Ernie Nevers, Chi. Cardinals	FB

1930	
Lavern Dilweg, Green Bay	E
Luke Johnsos, Chi. Bears	E
Forrest (Jap) Douds, Providence-Portsmouth	T
Roy (Link) Lyman, Chi. Bears	T
Mike Michalske, Green Bay	G
Walt Kiesling, Chi. Cardinals	G
Rudolph (Swede) Hagberg, Brooklyn	C
Benny Friedman, NY Giants	QB
Harold (Red) Grange, Chi. Bears	HB
Ken Strong, Staten Island	HB
Ernie Nevers, Chi. Cardinals	FB

1931	
Lavern Dilweg, Green Bay	E
Morris (Red) Badgro, NY Giants	E
Cal Hubbard, Green Bay	T
George Christensen, Portsmouth	T
Mike Michalske, Green Bay	G
Denver (Butch) Gibson, NY Giants	G
Frank McNally, Chi. Cardinals	C
Earl (Dutch) Clark, Portsmouth	QB
Harold (Red) Grange, Chi. Bears	HB
Johnny Blood (McNally), Green Bay	HB
Ernie Nevers, Chi. Cardinals	FB

1932	
Ray Flaherty, NY Giants	E
Luke Johnsos, Chi. Bears	E
Cal Hubbard, Green Bay	T
Glen (Turk) Edwards, Boston	T
Jules (Zuck) Carlson, Chi. Bears	G
Walt Kiesling, Chi. Cardinals	G
Nate Barrager, Green Bay	C
Earl (Dutch) Clark, Portsmouth	QB
Arnie Herber, Green Bay	HB
Roy (Father) Lumpkin, Portsmouth	HB
Bronko Nagurski, Chi. Bears	FB

1933	
Bill Hewitt, Chi. Bears	E
Morris (Red) Badgro, NY Giants	E
Cal Hubbard, Green Bay	T
Glen (Turk) Edwards, Boston	T
Herman Hickman, Brooklyn	G
Joe Kopcha, Chi. Bears	G
Mel Hein, NY Giants	C
Harry Newman, NY Giants	QB
Glenn Presnell, Portsmouth	HB
Cliff Battles, Boston	HB
Bronko Nagurski, Chi. Bears	FB

1934	
Bill Hewitt, Chi. Bears	E
Morris (Red) Badgro, NY Giants	E
George Christensen, Detroit	T
Bill Morgan, NY Giants	T
Denver (Butch) Gibson, NY Giants	G
Joe Kopcha, Chi. Bears	G
Mel Hein, NY Giants	C
Earl (Dutch) Clark, Detroit	QB
Beattie Feathers, Chi. Bears	HB
Ken Strong, NY Giants	HB
Bronko Nagurski, Chi. Bears	FB

1935	
Bill Smith, Chi. Cardinals	E
Bill Karr, Chi. Bears	E
Bill Morgan, NY Giants	T
George Musso, Chi. Bears	T
Joe Kopcha, Chi. Bears	G
Mike Michalske, Green Bay	G
Mel Hein, NY Giants	C
Earl (Dutch) Clark, Detroit	QB
Ed Danowski, NY Giants	HB
Ernie Caddel, Detroit	HB
Mike Mikulak, Chi. Cardinals	FB

1936	
Bill Hewitt, Chi. Bears-Philadelphia	E
Don Hutson, Green Bay	E
Glen (Turk) Edwards, Boston	T
Ernie Smith, Green Bay	T
Lon Evans, Green Bay	G
Grover (Ox) Emerson, Detroit	G
Mel Hein, NY Giants	C
Earl (Dutch) Clark, Detroit	QB
Cliff Battles, Boston	HB
Alphonse (Tuffy) Leemans, NY Giants	HB
Clarke Hinkle, Green Bay	FB

1937	
Bill Hewitt, Philadelphia	E
Gaynell Tinsley, Chi. Cardinals	E
Joe Stydahar, Chi. Bears	T
Glen (Turk) Edwards, Washington	T
Lon Evans, Green Bay	G
George Musso, Chi. Bears	G
Mel Hein, NY Giants	C
Earl (Dutch) Clark, Detroit	QB
Cliff Battles, Washington	HB
Sammy Baugh, Washington	HB
Clarke Hinkle, Green Bay	FB

1938	
Don Hutson, Green Bay	E
Gaynell Tinsley, Chi. Cardinals	E
Ed Widseth, NY Giants	T
Joe Stydahar, Chi. Bears	T
Dan Fortmann, Chi. Bears	G
Russ Letlow, Green Bay	G
Mel Hein, NY Giants	C
Clarence (Ace) Parker, Brooklyn	QB
Ed Danowski, NY Giants	HB
Lloyd Cardwell, Detroit	HB
Clarke Hinkle, Green Bay	FB

1939	
Don Hutson, Green Bay	E
Jim Poole, NY Giants	E
Joe Stydahar, Chi. Bears	T
Jim Barber, Washington	T
Dan Fortmann, Chi. Bears	G
John Dell Isola, NY Giants	G
Mel Hein, NY Giants	C
Davey O'Brien, Philadelphia	QB
Alphonse (Tuffy) Leemans, NY Giants	HB

Andy Farkas, Washington ..... HB
Bill Osmanski, Chi. Bears ..... FB

1940

Don Hutson, Green Bay ..... E
Perry Schwartz, Brooklyn ..... E
Joe Stydahar, Chi. Bears ..... T
Frank (Bruiser) Kinard, Brooklyn ..... T
Dan Fortmann, Chi. Bears ..... G
John Wiethe, Detroit ..... G
Mel Hein, NY Giants C
Clarence (Ace) Parker, Brooklyn ..... QB
Sammy Baugh, Washington ..... HB
Byron (Whizzer) White, Detroit ..... HB
Johnny Drake, Cleveland ..... FB

1941

Don Hutson, Green Bay ..... E
Perry Schwartz, Brooklyn ..... E
Frank (Bruiser) Kinard, Brooklyn ..... T
Willie Wilkin, Washington ..... T
Dan Fortmann, Chi. Bears ..... G
Joe Kuharich, Chi. Cardinals ..... G
Clyde (Bulldog) Turner, Chi. Bears C
Sid Luckman, Chi. Bears ..... QB
Cecil Isbell, Green Bay ..... HB
George McAfee, Chi. Bears ..... HB
Clarke Hinkle, Green Bay ..... FB

1942

Don Hutson, Green Bay ..... E
Bob Masterson, Washington ..... E
Willie Wilkin, Washington ..... T
Lee Artoe, Chi. Bears ..... T
Dan Fortmann, Chi. Bears ..... G
Bill (Monk) Edwards, NY Giants ..... G
Clyde (Bulldog) Turner, Chi. Bears C
Sid Luckman, Chi. Bears ..... QB
Cecil Isbell, Green Bay ..... HB
Bill Dudley, Pittsburgh ..... HB
Gary Famiglietti, Chi. Bears ..... FB

1943

Don Hutson, Green Bay (AP, UP) ..... E
Ed Rucinzki, Chi. Cardinals (AP, UP) ..... E
Al Blozis, NY Giants (AP, UP) ..... T
Frank (Bruiser) Kinard, Brooklyn (AP) ..... T
Vic Sears, Phil-Pitt (UP) ..... T
Dan Fortmann, Chi. Bears (AP, UP) ..... G
Dick Farman, Washington (AP, UP) ..... G
Clyde (Bulldog) Turner, Chi. Bears (AP, UP) C
Sid Luckman, Chi. Bears (AP, UP) ..... QB
Sammy Baugh, Washington (AP, UP) ..... HB
Harry Clark, Chi. Bears (AP, UP) ..... HB
Tony Canadeo, Green Bay (AP) ..... FB
Ward Cuff, NY Giants (UP) ..... FB

1944

Don Hutson, Green Bay (AP, UP) ..... E
Joe Aguirre, Washington (AP, UP) ..... E
Al Wistert, Philadelphia (AP, UP) ..... T
Frank (Bruiser) Kinard, Brooklyn (AP) ..... T
Frank Cope, NY Giants (UP) ..... T
Len Younce, NY Giants (AP, UP) ..... G
Riley Matheson, Cleveland (AP, UP) ..... G
Clyde (Bulldog) Turner, Chi. Bears (AP, UP) C
Sid Luckman, Chi. Bears (AP) ..... QB
Leroy Zimmerman, Philadelphia (UP) ..... QB
Frank Sinkwich, Detroit (AP, UP) ..... HB
Steve Van Buren, Philadelphia (AP) ..... HB
Ward Cuff, NY Giants (UP) ..... HB
Bill Paschal, NY Giants (AP, UP) ..... FB

1945

Don Hutson, Green Bay (AP, UP) ..... E
Jim Benton, Cleveland (AP) ..... E
Steve Pritko, Cleveland (UP) ..... E
Al Wistert, Philadelphia (AP, UP) ..... T
Frank Cope, NY Giants (AP) ..... T
Emil Uremovich, Detroit (UP) ..... T
Riley Matheson, Cleveland (AP, UP) ..... G
Bill Radovich, Detroit (AP, UP) ..... G
Charley Brock, Green Bay (AP, UP) C
Bob Waterfield, Cleveland (AP) ..... QB
Sammy Baugh, Washington (UP) ..... QB
Steve Van Buren, Philadelphia (AP, UP) ..... HB
Steve Bagarus, Washington (AP) ..... HB
Bob Waterfield, Cleveland (UP) ..... HB
Bob Westfall, Detroit (AP) ..... FB
Ted Fritsch, Green Bay (UP) ..... FB

1946

Jim Benton, LA Rams (AP, UP) ..... E
Jim Poole, NY Giants (AP) ..... E
Ken Kavanaugh, Chi. Bears (UP) ..... E
Al Wistert, Philadelphia (AP, UP) ..... T
Jim White, NY Giants (AP, UP) ..... T
Riley Matheson, LA Rams (AP, UP) ..... G
Len Younce, NY Giants (AP) ..... G
Augie Lio, Philadelphia (UP) ..... G
Clyde (Bulldog) Turner, Chi. Bears (AP, UP) C
Bob Waterfield, LA Rams (AP, UP) ..... QB
Bill Dudley, Pittsburgh (AP, UP) ..... HB
Sid Luckman, Chi. Bears (AP) ..... HB
Frank Filchock, NY Giants (UP) ..... HB
Ted Fritsch, Green Bay (AP, UP) ..... FB

1947

Ken Kavanaugh, Chi. Bears (AP, UP) ..... E
Mal Kutner, Chi. Cardinals (AP, UP) ..... E
Al Wistert, Philadelphia (AP, UP) ..... T
Dick Huffman, LA Rams (AP) ..... T
Fred Davis, Chi. Bears (UP) ..... T
Riley Matheson, LA Rams (AP) ..... G
Garrard (Buster) Ramsey, Chi. Cardinals (AP) ..... G
Len Younce, NY Giants (UP) ..... G
Bill Moore, Pittsburgh (UP) ..... G
Clyde (Bulldog) Turner, Chi. Bears (AP) C
Vince Banonis, Chi. Cardinals (UP) C
Sid Luckman, Chi. Bears (AP, UP) ..... QB
Steve Van Buren, Philadelphia (AP, UP) ..... HB
Sammy Baugh, Washington (AP, UP) ..... HB
John Clement, Pittsburgh (AP) ..... FB
Pat Harder, Chi. Cardinals (UP) ..... FB

1948

Pete Pihos, Philadelphia (AP, UP) ..... E
Mal Kutner, Chi. Cardinals (AP, UP) ..... E
Dick Huffman, LA Rams (AP, UP) ..... T
Fred Davis, Chi. Bears (AP) ..... T
Al Wistert, Philadelphia (UP) ..... T
Garrard (Buster) Ramsey, Chi. Cardinals (AP, UP) ..... G
Chuck Drulis, Chi. Bears (AP) ..... G
Ray Bray, Chi. Bears (UP) ..... G
Clyde (Bulldog) Turner, Chi. Bears (AP) C
Fred Naumetz, LA Rams (UP) C
Sammy Baugh, Washington (AP, UP) ..... QB
Steve Van Buren, Philadelphia (AP, UP) ..... HB
Charley Trippi, Chi. Cardinals (AP, UP) ..... HB
Tommy Thompson, Philadelphia (AP) ..... FB
Pat Harder, Chi. Cardinals (UP) ..... FB

1949

Pete Pihos, Philadelphia (AP, UP) ..... E
Tom Fears, LA Rams (AP, UP) ..... E
Dick Huffman, LA Rams (AP, UP) ..... T
George Connor, Chi. Bears (AP) ..... T
Vic Sears, Philadelphia (UP) ..... T
Ray Bray, Chi. Bears (AP, UP) ..... G
Garrard (Buster) Ramsey, Chi. Cardinals (AP, UP) ..... G
Fred Naumetz, LA Rams (AP, UP) C
Bob Waterfield, LA Rams (AP, UP) ..... QB
Steve Van Buren, Philadelphia (AP, UP) ..... HB
Tony Canadeo, Green Bay (AP, UP) ..... HB
Elmer Angsman, Chi. Cardinals (AP) ..... FB
Pat Harder, Chi. Cardinals (UP) ..... FB

1950

Tom Fears, LA Rams (AP, UP) ..... E
Dan Edwards, NY Yanks (AP) ..... E
Mac Speedie, Cleveland (UP) ..... E
George Connor, Chi. Bears (AP, UP) ..... T
Arnie Weinmeister, NY Giants (AP, UP) ..... T
Dick Barwegan, Chi. Bears (AP, UP) ..... G
Joe Signaigo, NY Yanks (AP) ..... G
Bill Willis, Cleveland (UP) ..... G
Chuck Bednarik, Philadelphia (AP) C
Clayton Tonnemaker, Green Bay (UP) C
Johnny Lujack, Chi. Bears (AP, UP) ..... QB
Doak Walker, Detroit (AP, UP) ..... HB
Joe Geri, Pittsburgh (AP, UP) ..... HB
Marion Motley, Cleveland (AP, UP) ..... FB

1951

Offense

Elroy (Crazylegs) Hirsch, LA Rams (AP, UP) ..... E
Leon Hart, Detroit (AP) ..... E
Dante Lavelli, Cleveland (UP) ..... E
George Connor, Chi. Bears (AP) ..... T
Lou Groza, Cleveland (UP) ..... T
Leo Nomellini, San Francisco (AP) ..... T
DeWitt (Tex) Coulter, NY Giants (UP) ..... T
Lou Creekmur, Detroit (AP, UP) ..... G
Dick Barwegan, Chi. Bears (AP, UP) ..... G
Vic Lindskog, Philadelphia (AP) C
Frank Gatski, Cleveland (UP) C
Otto Graham, Cleveland (AP, UP) ..... QB
Doak Walker, Detroit (AP, UP) ..... HB
Dub Jones, Cleveland (AP, UP) ..... HB
Eddie Price, NY Giants (AP) ..... FB
(Deacon) Dan Towler, LA Rams (UP) ..... FB

Defense

Len Ford, Cleveland (AP, UP) ..... DE
Larry Brink, LA Rams (AP) ..... DE
Leon Hart, Detroit (UP) ..... DE
Arnie Weinmeister, NY Giants (AP, UP) ..... DT
Al DeRogatis, NY Giants (AP) ..... DT
George Connor, Chi. Bears (UP) ..... DT
Bill Willis, Cleveland (AP, UP) ..... MG
Les Bingaman, Detroit (AP) ..... MG
Jon Baker, NY Giants (UP) ..... MG
Chuck Bednarik, Philadelphia (AP, UP) ..... LB
Paul (Tank) Younger, LA Rams (AP) ..... LB
Tony Adamle, Cleveland (UP) ..... LB
Otto Schnellbacher, NY Giants (AP, UP) ..... DB
Jerry Shipkey, Pittsburgh (AP) ..... DB
Warren Lahr, Cleveland (UP) ..... DB
Emlen Tunnell, NY Giants (AP, UP) ..... DB

1952

Offense

Gordy Soltau, San Francisco (AP, UP) ..... E
Cloyce Box, Detroit (AP) ..... E
Mac Speedie, Cleveland (UP) ..... E
Leo Nomellini, San Francisco (AP, UP) ..... T
George Connor, Chi. Bears (AP) ..... T
Lou Groza, Cleveland (UP) ..... T
Lou Creekmur, Detroit (AP, UP) ..... G
Lou Groza, Cleveland (AP) ..... G
Bill Fischer, Chi. Cardinals (UP) ..... G
Frank Gatski, Cleveland (AP) C
Bill Walsh, Pittsburgh (UP) C
Bobby Layne, Detroit (AP) ..... QB
Otto Graham, Cleveland (UP) ..... QB
Hugh McElhenny, San Francisco (AP, UP) ..... HB
(Deacon) Dan Towler, LA Rams (AP, UP) ..... HB
Eddie Price, NY Giants (AP, UP) ..... FB

Defense

Len Ford, Cleveland (AP, UP) ..... DE
Larry Brink, LA Rams (UP) ..... DE
Pete Pihos, Philadelphia (AP) ..... DE
Arnie Weinmeister, NY Giants (AP, UP) ..... DT
Thurman (Fum) McGraw, Detroit (AP, UP) ..... DT
Stan West, LA Rams (AP, UP) ..... MG
Bill Willis, Cleveland (AP) ..... MG
Les Bingaman, Detroit (UP) ..... MG
Chuck Bednarik, Philadelphia (AP, UP) ..... LB
Jerry Shipkey, Pittsburgh (AP) ..... LB
George Connor, Chi. Bears (UP) ..... LB
Jack Christiansen, Detroit (AP) ..... DB
Ollie Matson, Chi. Cardinals (AP) ..... DB
Bob Smith, Detroit (UP) ..... DB
Herb Rich, LA Rams (UP) ..... DB
Emlen Tunnell, NY Giants (AP, UP) ..... DB

1953

Offense

Pete Pihos, Philadelphia (AP, UP) ..... E
Dante Lavelli, Cleveland (UP) ..... E
Elroy (Crazylegs) Hirsch, LA Rams (AP) ..... E
George Connor, Chi. Bears (AP) ..... T
Lou Groza, Cleveland (AP, UP) ..... T
Lou Creekmur, Detroit (UP) ..... T
Dick Stanfel, Detroit (AP, UP) ..... G
Lou Creekmur, Detroit (AP) ..... G
Bruno Banducci, San Francisco (UP) ..... G
Frank Gatski, Cleveland (AP, UP) C
Otto Graham, Cleveland (AP, UP) ..... QB
Hugh McElhenny, San Francisco (AP, UP) ..... HB
Doak Walker, Detroit (AP) ..... HB
(Deacon) Dan Towler, LA Rams (UP) ..... HB
Joe Perry, San Francisco (AP, UP) ..... FB

Defense

Len Ford, Cleveland (AP, UP) ..... DE
Andy Robustelli, LA Rams (AP) ..... DE
Norm Willey, Philadelphia (UP) ..... DE
Arnie Weinmeister, NY Giants (AP, UP) ..... DT
Leo Nomellini, San Francisco (AP, UP) ..... DT
Les Bingaman, Detroit (AP, UP) ..... MG
Bill Willis, Cleveland (AP) ..... MG
Dale Dodrill, Pittsburgh (UP) ..... MG
Chuck Bednarik, Philadelphia (AP) ..... LB
Don Paul, LA Rams (AP) ..... LB
Tommy Thompson, Cleveland (UP) ..... LB
George Connor, Chi. Bears (UP) ..... LB
Tom Keane, Baltimore (AP, UP) ..... DB
Tommy Thompson, Cleveland (AP) ..... DB
Jack Christiansen, Detroit (AP, UP) ..... DB
Ken Gorgal, Cleveland (UP) ..... DB

1954

Offense

Pete Pihos, Philadelphia (AP, UP) ..... E
Bob Boyd, LA Rams (AP) ..... E
Harlon Hill, Chi. Bears (UP) ..... E
Lou Creekmur, Detroit (AP, UP) ..... T
Lou Groza, Cleveland (AP, UP) ..... T
Dick Stanfel, Detroit (AP, UP) ..... G
Bruno Banducci, San Francisco (AP, UP) ..... G
Bill Walsh, Pittsburgh (AP, UP) C
Otto Graham, Cleveland (AP, UP) ..... QB
Doak Walker, Detroit (AP, UP) ..... HB
Ollie Matson, Chi. Cardinals (AP, UP) ..... HB
Joe Perry, San Francisco (AP, UP) ..... FB

Defense

Len Ford, Cleveland (AP, UP) ..... DE
Norm Willey, Philadelphia (AP, UP) ..... DE
Leo Nomellini, San Francisco (AP, UP) ..... DT
Art Donovan, Baltimore (AP, UP) ..... DT
Les Bingaman, Detroit (AP, UP) ..... MG
Dale Dodrill, Pittsburgh (AP) ..... MG
Frank (Bucko) Kilroy, Philadelphia (UP) ..... MG
Chuck Bednarik, Philadelphia (AP, UP) ..... LB
Joe Schmidt, Detroit (AP) ..... LB
Roger Zatkoff, Green Bay (UP) ..... LB
Tom Landry, NY Giants (AP, UP) ..... DB
Bobby Dillon, Green Bay (AP) ..... DB
Jim David, Detroit (UP) ..... DB
Jack Christiansen, Detroit (AP, UP) ..... DB

1955

Offense

Harlon Hill, Chi. Bears (AP, UP) . . . E
Billy Wilson, San Francisco (UP) . . . E
Pete Pihos, Philadelphia (AP) . . . E
Lou Groza, Cleveland (AP, UP) . . . T
Bill Wightkin, Chi. Bears (AP) . . . T
Bob St. Clair, San Francisco (UP) . . . T
Stan Jones, Chi. Bears (AP) . . . G
Duane Putnam, LA Rams (AP) . . . G
Abe Gibron, Cleveland (UP) . . . G
Bill Austin, NY Giants (UP) . . . G
Frank Gatski, Cleveland (AP, UP) . . . C
Otto Graham, Cleveland (AP, UP) . . . QB
Ollie Matson, Chi. Cardinals (AP, UP) . . . HB
Frank Gifford, NY Giants (AP) . . . HB
Ron Waller, LA Rams (UP) . . . HB
Alan Ameche, Baltimore (AP, UP) . . . FB

Defense

Gene Brito, Washington (AP, UP) . . . DE
Andy Robustelli, LA Rams (AP) . . . DE
Len Ford, Cleveland (UP) . . . DE
Art Donovan, Baltimore (AP, UP) . . . DT
Bob Toneff, San Francisco (AP) . . . DT
Don Colo, Cleveland (UP) . . . DT
Bill George, Chi. Bears (AP) . . . MG
Dale Dodrill, Pittsburgh (UP) . . . MG
Chuck Bednarik, Philadelphia (UP) . . . LB
George Connor, Chi. Bears (UP) . . . LB
Roger Zatkoff, Green Bay (AP) . . . LB
Joe Schmidt, Detroit (AP) . . . LB
Bobby Dillon, Green Bay (AP, UP) . . . DB
Will Sherman, LA Rams (AP, UP) . . . DB
Jack Christiansen, Detroit (AP, UP) . . . DB
Emlen Tunnell, NY Giants (AP) . . . DB
Don Paul, Cleveland (UP) . . . DB

1956

Offense

Harlon Hill, Chi. Bears (AP, UP) . . . E
Billy Howton, Green Bay (AP, UP) . . . E
Lou Creekmur, Detroit (AP, UP) . . . T
Roosevelt Brown, NY Giants (AP, UP) . . . T
Stan Jones, Chi. Bears (AP, UP) . . . G
Dick Stanfel, Washington (AP, UP) . . . G
Larry Strickland, Chi. Bears (AP) . . . C
Charlie Ane, Detroit (UP) . . . C
Bobby Layne, Detroit (AP, UP) . . . QB
Frank Gifford, NY Giants (AP, UP) . . . HB
Ollie Matson, Chi. Cardinals (AP, UP) . . . HB
Rick Casares, Chi. Bears (AP, UP) . . . FB

Defense

Andy Robustelli, NY Giants (AP, UP) . . . DE
Gene Brito, Washington (AP, UP) . . . DE
Rosey Grier, NY Giants (AP, UP) . . . DT
Art Donovan, Baltimore (AP) . . . DT
Ernie Stautner, Pittsburgh (UP) . . . DT
Bill George, Chi. Bears (AP, UP) . . . MG
Joe Schmidt, Detroit (AP, UP) . . . LB
Les Richter, LA Rams (AP) . . . LB
Chuck Bednarik, Philadelphia (UP) . . . LB
Dick (Night Train) Lane, Chi. Cardinals (AP, UP) . . . DB
Emlen Tunnell, NY Giants (AP, UP) . . . DB
Jack Christiansen, Detroit (AP, UP) . . . DB
Yale Lary, Detroit (AP) . . . DB
Bobby Dillon, Green Bay (UP) . . . DB

1957

Offense

Billy Wilson, San Francisco (AP, UP) . . . E
Billy Howton, Green Bay (AP, UP) . . . E
Roosevelt Brown, NY Giants (AP, UP) . . . T
Lou Creekmur, Detroit (AP) . . . T
Lou Groza, Cleveland (UP) . . . T
Duane Putnam, LA Rams (AP, UP) . . . G
Dick Stanfel, Washington (AP, UP) . . . G
Jim Ringo, Green Bay (AP) . . . C
Larry Strickland, Chi. Bears (UP) . . . C
Y. A. Tittle, San Francisco (AP, UP) . . . QB
Frank Gifford, NY Giants (AP, UP) . . . HB
Ollie Matson, Chi. Cardinals (AP, UP) . . . HB
Jim Brown, Cleveland (AP, UP) . . . FB

Defense

Gino Marchetti, Baltimore (AP, UP) . . . DE
Andy Robustelli, NY Giants (UP) . . . DE
Gene Brito, Washington (AP) . . . DE
Leo Nomellini, San Francisco (AP, UP) . . . DT
Art Donovan, Baltimore (AP, UP) . . . DT
Joe Schmidt, Detroit (AP, UP) . . . LB
Marv Matuszak, San Francisco (AP, UP) . . . LB
Bill George, Chi. Bears (AP, UP) . . . LB
Jack Christiansen, Detroit (AP, UP) . . . DB
Bobby Dillon, Green Bay (AP, UP) . . . DB
Jack Butler, Pittsburgh (AP, UP) . . . DB
Yale Lary, Detroit (UP) . . . DB
Milt Davis, Baltimore (AP) . . . DB

1958

Offense

Raymond Berry, Baltimore (AP, UPI) . . . E
Del Shofner, LA Rams (AP, UPI) . . . E
Roosevelt Brown, NY Giants (AP, UPI) . . . T
Jim Parker, Baltimore (AP, UPI) . . . T
Dick Stanfel, Washington (AP, UPI) . . . G
Duane Putnam, LA Rams (AP, UPI) . . . G
Ray Wietecha, NY Giants (AP, UPI) . . . C
Johnny Unitas, Baltimore (AP, UPI) . . . QB
Lenny Moore, Baltimore (AP, UPI) . . . HB
Jon Arnett, LA Rams (AP, UPI) . . . HB
Jim Brown, Cleveland (AP, UPI) . . . FB

Defense

Gino Marchetti, Baltimore (AP, UPI) . . . DE
Andy Robustelli, NY Giants (AP) . . . DE
Gene Brito, Washington (UPI) . . . DE
Gene (Big Daddy) Lipscomb, Baltimore (AP, UPI) . . . DT
Ernie Stautner, Pittsburgh (AP, UPI) . . . DT
Joe Schmidt, Detroit (AP, UPI) . . . LB
Sam Huff, NY Giants (AP, UPI) . . . LB
Bill George, Chi. Bears (AP, UPI) . . . LB
Jack Butler, Pittsburgh (AP, UPI) . . . DB
Yale Lary, Detroit (AP, UPI) . . . DB
Jim Patton, NY Giants (AP, UPI) . . . DB
Bobby Dillon, Green Bay (AP, UPI) . . . DB

1959

Offense

Raymond Berry, Baltimore (AP, UPI) . . . E
Del Shofner, LA Rams (AP, UPI) . . . E
Roosevelt Brown, NY Giants (AP, UPI) . . . T
Jim Parker, Baltimore (AP, UPI) . . . T
Jim Ray Smith, Cleveland (AP, UPI) . . . G
Stan Jones, Chi. Bears (AP) . . . G
Art Spinney, Baltimore (UPI) . . . G
Jim Ringo, Green Bay (AP, UPI) . . . C
Johnny Unitas, Baltimore (AP, UPI) . . . QB
Frank Gifford, NY Giants (AP, UPI) . . . HB
Lenny Moore, Baltimore (AP) . . . HB
J.D. Smith, San Francisco (UPI) . . . HB
Jim Brown, Cleveland (AP, UPI) . . . FB

Defense

Gino Marchetti, Baltimore (AP, UPI) . . . DE
Andy Robustelli, NY Giants (AP, UPI) . . . DE
Gene (Big Daddy) Lipscomb, Baltimore (AP, UPI) . . . DT
Leo Nomellini, San Francisco (AP, UPI) . . . DT
Joe Schmidt, Detroit (AP, UPI) . . . LB
Sam Huff, NY Giants (AP, UPI) . . . LB
Bill George, Chi. Bears (AP, UPI) . . . LB
Abe Woodson, San Francisco (AP, UPI) . . . DB
Jack Butler, Pittsburgh (AP, UPI) . . . DB
Jim Patton, NY Giants (AP, UPI) . . . DB
Dean Derby, Pittsburgh (UPI) . . . DB
Andy Nelson, Baltimore (AP) . . . DB

1960 NFL

Offense

Raymond Berry, Baltimore (AP, UPI) . . . E
Sonny Randle, St. Louis (AP, UPI) . . . E
Jim Parker, Baltimore (AP, UPI) . . . T
Forrest Gregg, Green Bay (AP) . . . T
Roosevelt Brown, NY Giants (UPI) . . . T
Jim Ray Smith, Cleveland (AP, UPI) . . . G
Stan Jones, Chi. Bears (UPI) . . . G
Jerry Kramer, Green Bay (AP) . . . G
Jim Ringo, Green Bay (AP, UPI) . . . C
Norm Van Brocklin, Philadelphia (AP, UPI) . . . QB
Paul Hornung, Green Bay (AP, UPI) . . . HB
Lenny Moore, Baltimore (AP, UPI) . . . HB
Jim Brown, Cleveland (AP, UPI) . . . FB

Defense

Gino Marchetti, Baltimore (AP, UPI) . . . DE
Andy Robustelli, NY Giants (AP) . . . DE
Doug Atkins, Chi. Bears (UPI) . . . DE
Henry Jordan, Green Bay (AP, UPI) . . . DT
Alex Karras, Detroit (AP, UPI) . . . DT
Chuck Bednarik, Philadelphia (AP, UPI) . . . LB
Bill Forester, Green Bay (AP, UPI) . . . LB
Bill George, Chi. Bears (AP, UPI) . . . LB
Tom Brookshier, Philadelphia (AP, UPI) . . . DB
Abe Woodson, San Francisco (AP) . . . DB
Dick (Night Train) Lane, Detroit (UPI) . . . DB
Jerry Norton, St. Louis (AP, UPI) . . . DB
Jim Patton, NY Giants (AP, UPI) . . . DB

1960 AFL

Offense

Bill Groman, Houston . . . E
Lionel Taylor, Denver . . . E
Rich Michael, Houston . . . T
Ron Mix, LA Chargers . . . T
Bill Krisher, Dallas Texans . . . G
Bob Mischak, NY Titans . . . G
Jim Otto, Oakland . . . C
Jack Kemp, LA Chargers . . . QB
Abner Haynes, Dallas Texans . . . HB
Paul Lowe, LA Chargers . . . HB
Dave Smith, Houston . . . FB

Defense

Laverne Torczon, Buffalo . . . DE
Mel Branch, Dallas Texans . . . DE
Bud McFadin, Denver . . . DT
Volney Peters, LA Chargers . . . DT
Archie Matsos, Buffalo . . . LB
Sherrill Headrick, Dallas Texans . . . LB
Tom Addison, Boston . . . LB
Richie McCabe, Buffalo . . . DB
Dick Harris, LA Chargers . . . DB
Ross O'Hanley, Boston . . . DB
Austin (Goose) Gonsoulin, Denver . . . DB

1961 NFL

Offense

Del Shofner, NY Giants (AP, UPI, NEA) . . . E
Jim (Red) Phillips, LA Rams (AP, UPI) . . . E
Mike Ditka, Chi. Bears (NEA) . . . E
Roosevelt Brown, NY Giants (AP, UPI, NEA) . . . T
Jim Parker, Baltimore (AP, NEA) . . . T
Forrest Gregg, Green Bay (UPI) . . . T
Jim Ray Smith, Cleveland (AP, UPI, NEA) . . . G
Fred (Fuzzy) Thurston, Green Bay (AP, UPI, NEA) . . . G
Jim Ringo, Green Bay (AP, UPI, NEA) . . . C
Sonny Jurgensen, Philadelphia (AP, UPI) . . . QB
Y.A. Tittle, NY Giants (NEA) . . . QB
Lenny Moore, Baltimore (AP, UPI, NEA) . . . HB
Paul Hornung, Green Bay (AP, UPI) . . . HB
Jim Taylor, Green Bay (NEA) . . . HB
Jim Brown, Cleveland (AP, UPI, NEA) . . . FB

Defense

Gino Marchetti, Baltimore (AP, UPI, NEA) . . . DE
Jim Katcavage, NY Giants (AP, UPI) . . . DE
Doug Atkins, Chi. Bears (NEA) . . . DE
Henry Jordan, Green Bay (AP, UPI, NEA) . . . DT
Alex Karras, Detroit (AP, UPI) . . . DT
Gene (Big Daddy) Lipscomb, Pittsburgh (NEA) . . . DT
Joe Schmidt, Detroit (AP, UPI, NEA) . . . LB
Dan Currie, Green Bay (UPI, NEA) . . . LB
Bill George, Chi. Bears (AP, NEA) . . . LB
Bill Forester, Green Bay (AP, UPI) . . . LB
Dick (Night Train) Lane, Detroit (AP, NEA) . . . DB
Jesse Whittenton, Green Bay (AP, UPI) . . . DB
Erich Barnes, NY Giants (AP, UPI) . . . DB
Jimmy Hill, St. Louis (NEA) . . . DB
Jim Patton, NY Giants (AP, UPI, NEA) . . . DB
Johnny Sample, Pittsburgh (UPI) . . . DB
Jerry Norton, St. Louis (NEA) . . . DB

1961 AFL

Offense

Lionel Taylor, Denver . . . E
Charley Hennigan, Houston . . . E
Ron Mix, San Diego . . . T
Al Jamison, Houston . . . T
Bob Mischak, NY Titans . . . G
Chuck Leo, Boston . . . G
Jim Otto, Oakland . . . C
George Blanda, Houston . . . QB
Abner Haynes, Dallas Texans . . . HB
Billy Cannon, Houston . . . HB
Billy Mathis, NY Titans . . . FB

Defense

Earl Faison, San Diego . . . DE
Don Floyd, Houston . . . DE
Bud McFadin, Denver . . . DT
Chuck McMurtry, Buffalo . . . DT
Sherrill Headrick, Dallas Texans . . . LB
Archie Matsos, Buffalo . . . LB
Chuck Allen, San Diego . . . LB
Tony Banfield, Houston . . . DB
Dick Harris, San Diego . . . DB
Dave Webster, Dallas Texans . . . DB
Charlie McNeil, San Diego . . . DB

1962 NFL

Offense

Del Shofner, NY Giants (AP, UPI, NEA) . . . SE
Mike Ditka, Chi. Bears (UPI, NEA) . . . TE
Ron Kramer, Green Bay (AP) . . . TE
Bobby Mitchell, Washington (AP, UPI, NEA) . . . FL
Forrest Gregg, Green Bay (AP, UPI, NEA) . . . T
Roosevelt Brown, NY Giants (AP, UPI) . . . T
Jim Parker, Baltimore (NEA) . . . T
Jerry Kramer, Green Bay (AP, UPI, NEA) . . . G
Jim Parker, Baltimore (AP) . . . G
Jim Ray Smith, Cleveland (NEA) . . . G
Fred (Fuzzy) Thurston, Green Bay (UPI) . . . G
Jim Ringo, Green Bay (AP, UPI, NEA) . . . C
Y.A. Tittle, NY Giants (AP, UPI, NEA) . . . QB
Jim Taylor, Green Bay (AP, UPI, NEA) . . . RB
Don Perkins, Dallas Cowboys (AP, NEA) . . . RB
Dick Bass, LA Rams (UPI) . . . RB

Defense

Gino Marchetti, Baltimore (AP, UPI, NEA) . . . DE
Jim Katcavage, NY Giants (UPI, NEA) . . . DE
Willie Davis, Green Bay (AP) . . . DE
Roger Brown, Detroit (AP, UPI, NEA) . . . DT
Alex Karras, Detroit (UPI, NEA) . . . DT
Henry Jordan, Green Bay (AP) . . . DT
Joe Schmidt, Detroit (AP, UPI, NEA) . . . MLB
Dan Currie, Green Bay (AP, UPI, NEA) . . . LB
Bill Forester, Green Bay (AP, UPI, NEA) . . . LB
Dick (Night Train) Lane, Detroit (AP, UPI, NEA) . . . CB
Herb Adderley, Green Bay (AP, UPI) . . . CB
Abe Woodson, San Francisco (NEA) . . . CB
Yale Lary, Detroit (AP, UPI, NEA) . . . S

Jim Patton, NY Giants (AP, UPI, NEA) ... S

1962 AFL

Offense

Charley Hennigan, Houston ... SE
Dave Kocourek, San Diego ... TE
Chris Burford, Dallas Texans ... FL
Eldon Danenhauer, Denver ... T
Jim Tyrer, Dallas Texans ... T
Bob Talamini, Houston ... G
Ron Mix, San Diego ... G
Jim Otto, Oakland ... C
Len Dawson, Dallas Texans ... QB
Abner Haynes, Dallas Texans ... HB
Cookie Gilchrist, Buffalo ... FB

Defense

Don Floyd, Houston ... DE
Mel Branch, Dallas Texans ... DE
Bud McFadin, Denver ... DT
Jerry Mays, Dallas Texans ... DT
Sherrill Headrick, Dallas Texans ... MLB
Larry Grantham, NY Titans ... LB
E.J. Holub, Dallas Texans ... LB
Tony Banfield, Houston ... CB
Fred Williamson, Oakland ... CB
Austin (Goose) Gonsoulin, Denver ... S
Bob Zeman, Denver ... S

1963 NFL

Offense

Del Shofner, NY Giants (AP, UPI, NEA) ... SE
Mike Ditka, Chi. Bears (AP, UPI, NEA) ... TE
Bobby Joe Conrad, St. Louis (AP, UPI) ... FL
Bobby Mitchell, Washington (NEA) ... FL
Forrest Gregg, Green Bay (AP, UPI, NEA) ... T
Roosevelt Brown, NY Giants (UPI, NEA) ... T
Dick Schafrath, Cleveland (AP) ... T
Jerry Kramer, Green Bay (AP, UPI, NEA) ... G
Jim Parker, Baltimore (AP, NEA) ... G
Ken Gray, St. Louis (UPI) ... G
Jim Ringo, Green Bay (AP, UPI, NEA) ... C
Y.A. Tittle, NY Giants (AP, UPI, NEA) ... QB
Tommy Mason, Minnesota (AP, UPI, NEA) ... RB
Jim Brown, Cleveland (AP, UPI, NEA) ... RB

Defense

Doug Atkins, Chi. Bears (AP, UPI, NEA) ... DE
Jim Katcavage, NY Giants (AP, UPI) ... DE
Gino Marchetti, Baltimore (NEA) ... DE
Henry Jordan, Green Bay (AP, UPI, NEA) ... DT
Roger Brown, Detroit (AP, UPI, NEA) ... DT
Bill George, Chi. Bears (AP, UPI) ... MLB
Joe Schmidt, Detroit (NEA) ... MLB
Joe Fortunato, Chi. Bears (AP, UPI, NEA) ... LB
Jack Pardee, LA Rams (AP) ... LB
Myron Pottios, Pittsburgh (NEA) ... LB
Bill Forester, Green Bay (UPI) ... LB
Dick Lynch, NY Giants (AP, UPI, NEA) ... CB
Herb Adderley, Green Bay (AP) ... CB
Abe Woodson, San Francisco (NEA) ... CB
Dick (Night Train) Lane, Detroit (UPI) ... CB
Roosevelt Taylor, Chi. Bears (AP, NEA) ... S
Richie Petitbon, Chi. Bears (AP, UPI) ... S
Willie Wood, Green Bay (NEA) ... S
Larry Wilson, St. Louis (UPI) ... S

1963 AFL

Offense

Art Powell, Oakland ... SE
Fred Arbanas, Kansas City ... TE
Lance Alworth, San Diego ... FL
Ron Mix, San Diego ... T
Jim Tyrer, Kansas City ... T
Billy Shaw, Buffalo ... G
Bob Talamini, Houston ... G
Jim Otto, Oakland ... C
Tobin Rote, San Diego ... QB
Clem Daniels, Oakland ... HB
Keith Lincoln, San Diego ... FB

Defense

Larry Eisenhauer, Boston ... DE
Earl Faison, San Diego ... DE
Tom Sestak, Buffalo ... DT
Houston Antwine, Boston ... DT
Archie Matsos, Oakland ... MLB
E.J. Holub, Kansas City ... LB
Tom Addison, Boston ... LB
Dave Grayson, Kansas City ... CB
Fred Williamson, Oakland ... CB
Fred Glick, Houston ... S
Austin (Goose) Gonsoulin, Denver ... S

1964 NFL

Offense

Frank Clarke, Dallas (AP) ... SE
Paul Warfield, Cleveland (NEA) ... SE
Bobby Mitchell, Washington (UPI) ... SE
Mike Ditka, Chi. Bears (AP, UPI, NEA) ... TE
Johnny Morris, Chi. Bears (AP, UPI, NEA) ... FL
Forrest Gregg, Green Bay (AP, UPI, NEA) ... T
Dick Schafrath, Cleveland (AP, UPI) ... T
Bob Vogel, Baltimore (NEA) ... T
Jim Parker, Baltimore (AP, UPI, NEA) ... G
Ken Gray, St. Louis (AP, UPI) ... G
John Gordy, Detroit (NEA) ... G
Mick Tingelhoff, Minnesota (AP, UPI) ... C
Bob DeMarco, St. Louis (NEA) ... C
Johnny Unitas, Baltimore (AP, UPI, NEA) ... QB
Lenny Moore, Baltimore (AP, UPI, NEA) ... RB
Jim Brown, Cleveland (AP, UPI, NEA) ... RB

Defense

Willie Davis, Green Bay (AP, UPI, NEA) ... DE
Gino Marchetti, Baltimore (AP, UPI, NEA) ... DE
Bob Lilly, Dallas (AP, UPI, NEA) ... DT
Henry Jordan, Green Bay (AP, UPI) ... DT
Merlin Olsen, LA Rams (NEA) ... DT
Ray Nitschke, Green Bay (AP, UPI) ... MLB
Dale Meinert, St. Louis (NEA) ... MLB
Joe Fortunato, Chi. Bears (AP, UPI, NEA) ... LB
Maxie Baughan, Philadelphia (AP) ... LB
Jim Houston, Cleveland (NEA) ... LB
Wayne Walker, Detroit (UPI) ... LB
Pat Fischer, St. Louis (AP, UPI, NEA) ... CB
Bobby Boyd, Baltimore (AP, UPI) ... CB
Erich Barnes, NY Giants (NEA) ... CB
Paul Krause, Washington (AP, UPI, NEA) ... S
Willie Wood, Green Bay (AP, UPI, NEA) ... S

1964 AFL

Offense

Charley Hennigan, Houston (AP, UPI, PL) ... SE
Art Powell, Oakland (PL) ... SE
Fred Arbanas, Kansas City (AP, UPI, PL) ... TE
Lance Alworth, San Diego (AP, UPI, PL) ... FL
Ron Mix, San Diego (AP, UPI, PL) ... T
Stew Barber, Buffalo (AP, UPI) ... T
Jim Tyrer, Kansas City (PL) ... T
Billy Shaw, Buffalo (AP,UPI, PL) ... G
Billy Neighbors, Boston (AP, UPI) ... G
Bob Talamini, Houston (PL) ... G
Jim Otto, Oakland (AP, UPI, PL) ... C
Babe Parilli, Boston (AP, UPI, PL) ... QB
Keith Lincoln, San Diego (AP, UPI, PL) ... HB
Cookie Gilchrist, Buffalo (AP, UPI, PL) ... FB

Defense

Earl Faison, San Diego (AP, UPI, PL) ... DE
Larry Eisenhauer, Boston (AP, PL) ... DE
Bobby Bell, Kansas City (UPI) ... DE
Tom Sestak, Buffalo (AP, UPI, PL) ... DT
Ernie Ladd, San Diego (AP, UPI) ... DT
Jerry Mays, Kansas City (PL) ... DT
Nick Buoniconti, Boston (AP, UPI, PL) ... MLB
Larry Grantham, NY Jets (AP, UPI, PL) ... LB
Mike Stratton, Buffalo (AP, UPI) ... LB
Tom Addison, Boston (PL) ... LB
Willie Brown, Denver (AP, UPI, PL) ... CB
Dave Grayson, Kansas City (AP, PL) ... CB
Fred Williamson, Kansas City (UPI) ... CB
Ron Hall, Boston (AP, UPI) ... S
Dainard Paulson, NY Jets (UPI, PL) ... S
Fred Glick, Houston (PL) ... S
George Saimes, Buffalo (AP) ... S

1965 NFL

Offense

Dave Parks, San Francisco (AP, UPI, NEA) ... SE
Pete Retzlaff, Philadelphia (AP, UPI, NEA) ... TE
Jimmy Orr, Baltimore (AP, NEA) ... FL
Gary Collins, Cleveland (UPI) ... FL
Bob Brown, Philadelphia (AP, NEA) ... T
Dick Schafrath, Cleveland (AP, UPI) ... T
Forrest Gregg, Green Bay (UPI) ... T
Bob Vogel, Baltimore (NEA) ... T
Jim Parker, Baltimore (AP, UPI, NEA) ... G
John Gordy, Detroit (NEA) ... G
Ken Gray, St. Louis (UPI) ... G
Forrest Gregg, Green Bay (AP) ... G
Mick Tingelhoff, Minnesota (AP, UPI, NEA) ... C
Johnny Unitas, Baltimore (AP, UPI, NEA) ... QB
Gale Sayers, Chi. Bears (AP, UPI, NEA) ... RB
Jim Brown, Cleveland (AP, UPI, NEA) ... RB

Defense

Willie Davis, Green Bay (AP, UPI, NEA) ... DE
David (Deacon) Jones, LA Rams (AP, UPI, NEA) ... DE
Alex Karras, Detroit (AP, UPI, NEA) ... DT
Bob Lilly, Dallas (AP, UPI, NEA) ... DT
Dick Butkus, Chi. Bears (AP, NEA) ... MLB
Ray Nitschke, Green Bay (UPI) ... MLB
Wayne Walker, Detroit (AP, UPI, NEA) ... LB
Joe Fortunato, Chi. Bears (AP, NEA) ... LB
Jim Houston, Cleveland (UPI) ... LB
Bobby Boyd, Baltimore (AP, UPI, NEA) ... CB
Herb Adderley, Green Bay (AP, UPI, NEA) ... CB
Willie Wood, Green Bay (AP, UPI, NEA) ... S
Paul Krause, Washington (AP, UPI) ... S
Mel Renfro, Dallas (NEA) ... S

1965 AFL

Offense

Lionel Taylor, Denver (AP, UPI, PL) ... SE
Art Powell, Oakland (PL) ... SE
Willie Frazier, Houston (AP, UPI, PL) ... TE
Lance Alworth, San Diego (AP, UPI, PL) ... FL
Jim Tyrer, Kansas City (AP, UPI, PL) ... T
Ron Mix, San Diego (AP, UPI) ... T
Eldon Danenhauer, Denver (PL) ... T
Billy Shaw, Buffalo (AP, UPI, PL) ... G
Bob Talamini, Houston (AP, UPI, PL) ... G
Jim Otto, Oakland (AP, UPI, PL) ... C
Jack Kemp, Buffalo (AP, UPI, PL) ... QB
Paul Lowe, San Diego (AP, UPI, PL) ... HB
Cookie Gilchrist, Denver (AP, UPI, PL) ... FB
Pete Gogolak, Buffalo (PL) ... K

Defense

Earl Faison, San Diego (AP, UPI, PL) ... DE
Jerry Mays, Kansas City (AP, PL) ... DE
Ron McDole, Buffalo (UPI) ... DE
Tom Sestak, Buffalo (AP, UPI, PL) ... DT
Ernie Ladd, San Diego (AP, UPI, PL) ... DT
Nick Buoniconti, Boston (AP, UPI, PL) ... MLB
Mike Stratton, Buffalo (AP, UPI, PL) ... LB
Bobby Bell, Kansas City (AP, UPI, PL) ... LB
Dave Grayson, Oakland (AP, UPI, PL) ... CB
George (Butch) Byrd, Buffalo (AP, PL) ... CB
Fred Williamson, Kansas City (UPI) ... CB
George Saimes, Buffalo (AP, UPI, PL) ... S
Johnny Robinson, Kansas City (AP, PL) ... S
Dainard Paulson, NY Jets (UPI) ... S
Curley Johnson, NY Jets (PL) ... P

1966 NFL

Offense

Bob Hayes, Dallas (AP, UPI) ... SE
Dave Parks, San Francisco (NEA) ... SE
John Mackey, Baltimore (AP, UPI, NEA) ... TE
Pat Studstill, Detroit (AP, UPI) ... FL
Bob Hayes, Dallas (NEA) ... FL
Bob Brown, Philadelphia (AP, UPI, NEA) ... T
Forrest Gregg, Green Bay (AP, UPI, NEA) ... T
Jerry Kramer, Green Bay (AP, UPI) ... G
John Thomas, San Francisco (AP, NEA) ... G
John Gordy, Detroit (UPI) ... G
Gene Hickerson, Cleveland (NEA) ... G
Mick Tingelhoff, Minnesota (AP, UPI, NEA) ... C
Bart Starr, Green Bay (AP, UPI, NEA) ... QB
Leroy Kelly, Cleveland (AP, UPI, NEA) ... RB
Gale Sayers, Chi. Bears (AP, UPI, NEA) ... RB

Defense

Willie Davis, Green Bay (AP, UPI, NEA) ... DE
David (Deacon) Jones, LA Rams (AP, UPI, NEA) ... DE
Bob Lilly, Dallas (AP, UPI, NEA) ... DT
Merlin Olsen, LA Rams (AP, UPI, NEA) ... DT
Ray Nitschke, Green Bay (AP, UPI, NEA) ... MLB
Chuck Howley, Dallas (AP, UPI, NEA) ... LB
Lee Roy Caffey, Green Bay (AP, UPI) ... LB
Maxie Baughan, LA Rams (NEA) ... LB
Herb Adderley, Green Bay (AP, UPI, NEA) ... CB
Cornell Green, Dallas (AP, NEA) ... CB
Bobby Boyd, Baltimore (UPI) ... CB
Larry Wilson, St. Louis (AP, UPI, NEA) ... S
Willie Wood, Green Bay (AP, UPI, NEA) ... S

1966 AFL

Offense

Otis Taylor, Kansas City (AP, UPI) ... SE
Art Powell, Oakland (PL) ... SE
Fred Arbanas, Kansas City (AP, UPI, PL) ... TE
Lance Alworth, San Diego (AP, UPI, PL) ... FL
Jim Tyrer, Kansas City (AP, UPI, PL) ... T
Ron Mix, San Diego (AP, UPI) ... T
Sherman Plunkett, NY Jets (PL) ... T
Billy Shaw, Buffalo (AP, UPI, PL) ... G
Bob Talamini, Houston (PL) ... G
Ed Budde, Kansas City (AP) ... G
Wayne Hawkins, Oakland (UPI) ... G
Jon Morris, Boston (AP) ... C
Jim Otto, Oakland (UPI, PL) ... C
Len Dawson, Kansas City (AP, UPI, PL) ... QB
Clem Daniels, Oakland (AP, UPI, PL) ... HB
Jim Nance, Boston (AP, UPI, PL) ... FB
Gino Cappelletti, Boston (PL) ... K

Defense

Jerry Mays, Kansas City (AP, UPI, PL) ... DE
Larry Eisenhauer, Boston (PL) ... DE
Ron McDole, Buffalo (AP) ... DE
Verlon Biggs, N.Y. Jets (UPI) ... DE
Buck Buchanan, Kansas City (AP, UPI, PL) ... DT
Jim Dunaway, Buffalo (AP) ... DT
Houston Antwine, Boston (UPI, PL) ... DT
Nick Buoniconti, Boston (AP, UPI, PL) ... MLB
Mike Stratton, Buffalo (AP, UPI, PL) ... LB
Bobby Bell, Kansas City (AP, UPI, PL) ... LB
George (Butch) Byrd, Buffalo (AP, UPI, PL) ... CB
Dave Grayson, Oakland (PL) ... CB
Kent McCloughan, Oakland (AP, UPI) ... CB
Johnny Robinson, Kansas City (AP, UPI, PL) ... S
Kenny Graham, San Diego (AP, UPI) ... S
George Saimes, Buffalo (PL) ... S
Bob Scarpitto, Denver (PL) ... P

1967 NFL

Offense

Charley Taylor, Washington (AP, UPI, NEA) ... WR
Homer Jones, NY Giants (UPI, NEA) ... WR
Willie Richardson, Baltimore (AP) ... WR

John Mackey, Baltimore (AP, NEA) ... TE
Jackie Smith, St. Louis (UPI) ... TE
Ralph Neely, Dallas (AP, UPI) ... T
Forrest Gregg, Green Bay (AP, UPI) ... T
Ernie McMillan, St. Louis (NEA) ... T
Bob Vogel, Baltimore (NEA) ... T
Gene Hickerson, Cleveland (AP, UPI, NEA) ... G
Jerry Kramer, Green Bay (AP, UPI) ... G
Howard Mudd, San Francisco (NEA) ... G
Mick Tingelhoff, Minnesota (UPI, NEA) ... C
Bob DeMarco, St. Louis (AP) ... C
Johnny Unitas, Baltimore (AP, UPI, NEA) ... QB
Leroy Kelly, Cleveland (AP, UPI, NEA) ... RB
Gale Sayers, Chi. Bears (AP, UPI, NEA) ... RB

Defense

Willie Davis, Green Bay (AP, UPI, NEA) ... DE
David (Deacon) Jones, LA Rams (AP, UPI, NEA) ... DE
Bob Lilly, Dallas (AP, UPI, NEA) ... DT
Merlin Olsen, LA Rams (AP, UPI, NEA) ... DT
Dick Butkus, Chi. Bears (UPI, NEA) ... MLB
Tommy Nobis, Atlanta (AP) ... MLB
Dave Robinson, Green Bay (AP, UPI, NEA) ... LB
Chuck Howley, Dallas (AP) ... LB
Maxie Baughan, LA Rams (UPI) ... LB
Dave Wilcox, San Francisco (NEA) ... LB
Bob Jeter, Green Bay (AP, UPI, NEA) ... CB
Cornell Green, Dallas (AP, UPI, NEA) ... CB
Willie Wood, Green Bay (AP, UPI) ... S
Eddie Meador, LA Rams (UPI, NEA) ... S
Larry Wilson, St. Louis (AP, NEA) ... S

1967 AFL

Offense

George Sauer, NY Jets (AP, UPI) ... SE
Billy Cannon, Oakland (AP, UPI) ... TE
Lance Alworth, San Diego (AP, UPI) ... FL
Ron Mix, San Diego (AP, UPI) ... T
Jim Tyrer, Kansas City (AP) ... T
Harry Schuh, Oakland (UPI) ... T
Bob Talamini, Houston (AP, UPI) ... G
Walt Sweeney, San Diego (AP, UPI) ... G
Jim Otto, Oakland (AP, UPI) ... C
Daryle Lamonica, Oakland (AP, UPI) ... QB
Mike Garrett, Kansas City (AP, UPI) ... RB
Jim Nance, Boston (AP, UPI) ... RB

Defense

Ben Davidson, Oakland (AP, UPI) ... DE
Pat Holmes, Houston (AP, UPI) ... DE
Buck Buchanan, Kansas City (AP, UPI) ... DT
Tom Keating, Oakland (AP, UPI) ... DT
Nick Buoniconti, Boston (AP, UPI) ... MLB
George Webster, Houston (AP, UPI) ... LB
Bobby Bell, Kansas City (AP, UPI) ... LB
Miller Farr, Houston (AP, UPI) ... CB
Kent McCloughan, Oakland (AP, UPI) ... CB
George Saimes, Buffalo (AP, UPI) ... S
Johnny Robinson, Kansas City (AP, UPI) ... S

1968 NFL

Offense

Clifton McNeil, San Francisco (AP, UPI, NEA) ... WR
Paul Warfield, Cleveland (UPI, NEA) ... WR
Bob Hayes, Dallas (AP) ... WR
John Mackey, Baltimore (AP, UPI, NEA) ... TE
Ralph Neely, Dallas (AP, UPI, NEA) ... T
Bob Brown, Philadelphia (AP, NEA) ... T
Bob Vogel, Baltimore (UPI) ... T
Gene Hickerson, Cleveland (AP, UPI, NEA) ... G
Howard Mudd, San Francisco (AP, UPI, NEA) ... G
Mick Tingelhoff, Minnesota (AP, UPI, NEA) ... C
Earl Morrall, Baltimore (AP, UPI, NEA) ... QB
Leroy Kelly, Cleveland (AP, UPI, NEA) ... RB
Gale Sayers, Chi. Bears (AP, UPI, NEA) ... RB

Defense

David (Deacon) Jones, LA Rams (AP, UPI, NEA) ... DE
Carl Eller, Minnesota (AP, UPI, NEA) ... DE
Merlin Olsen, LA Rams (AP, UPI, NEA) ... DT
Bob Lilly, Dallas (AP, UPI, NEA) ... DT
Dick Butkus, Chi. Bears (AP, UPI, NEA) ... MLB
Mike Curtis, Baltimore (AP, UPI) ... LB
Chuck Howley, Dallas (AP, NEA) ... LB
Dave Robinson, Green Bay (UPI, NEA) ... LB
Lem Barney, Detroit (AP, UPI, NEA) ... CB
Bobby Boyd, Baltimore (AP, UPI) ... CB
Cornell Green, Dallas (NEA) ... CB
Larry Wilson, St. Louis (AP, UPI, NEA) ... S
Eddie Meador, LA Rams (AP) ... S
Willie Wood, Green Bay (UPI) ... S
Rick Volk, Baltimore (NEA) ... S

1968 AFL

Offense

Lance Alworth, San Diego (AP, UPI) ... WR
George Sauer, NY Jets (AP, UPI) ... WR
Jim Whalen, Boston (AP, UPI) ... TE
Ron Mix, San Diego (AP, UPI) ... T
Jim Tyrer, Kansas City (AP, UPI) ... T
Walt Sweeney, San Diego (AP, UPI) ... G
Gene Upshaw, Oakland (AP, UPI) ... G
Jim Otto, Oakland (AP, UPI) ... C
Joe Namath, NY Jets (AP, UPI) ... QB
Paul Robinson, Cincinnati (AP, UPI) ... RB
Hewritt Dixon, Oakland (AP, UPI) ... RB

Defense

Gerry Philbin, NY Jets (AP, UPI) ... DE
Rich Jackson, Denver (AP, UPI) ... DE
Buck Buchanan, Kansas City (AP, UPI) ... DT
Dan Birdwell, Oakland (AP, UPI) ... DT
Willie Lanier, Kansas City (AP) ... MLB
Dan Conners, Oakland (UPI) ... MLB
George Webster, Houston (AP, UPI) ... LB
Bobby Bell, Kansas City (AP, UPI) ... LB
Miller Farr, Houston (AP, UPI) ... CB
Willie Brown, Oakland (AP, UPI) ... CB
Dave Grayson, Oakland (AP, UPI) ... S
Johnny Robinson, Kansas City (AP, UPI) ... S

1969 NFL

Offense

Roy Jefferson, Pittsburgh (AP, UPI, NEA) ... WR
Gary Collins, Cleveland (AP, UPI) ... WR
Dan Abramowicz, New Orleans (AP) ... WR
Paul Warfield, Cleveland (NEA) ... WR
Jerry Smith, Washington (AP, UPI, NEA) ... TE
Bob Brown, LA Rams (AP, UPI, NEA) ... T
Ralph Neely, Dallas (AP, UPI, NEA) ... T
Gene Hickerson, Cleveland (AP, UPI) ... G
Tom Mack, LA Rams (UPI, NEA) ... G
Gale Gillingham, Green Bay (NEA) ... G
John Niland, Dallas (AP) ... G
Mick Tingelhoff, Minnesota (AP, UPI, NEA) ... C
Roman Gabriel, LA Rams (AP, UPI) ... QB
Sonny Jurgensen, Washington (NEA) ... QB
Gale Sayers, Chicago (AP, UPI, NEA) ... RB
Calvin Hill, Dallas (AP, UPI) ... RB
Leroy Kelly, Cleveland (NEA) ... RB

Defense

Carl Eller, Minnesota (AP, UPI, NEA) ... DE
David (Deacon) Jones, LA Rams (AP, UPI, NEA) ... DE
Merlin Olsen, LA Rams (AP, UPI, NEA) ... DT
Bob Lilly, Dallas (AP, NEA) ... DT
Alan Page, Minnesota (UPI) ... DT
Dick Butkus, Chi. Bears (AP, UPI, NEA) ... MLB
Chuck Howley, Dallas (AP, UPI, NEA) ... LB
Dave Robinson, Green Bay (AP, UPI, NEA) ... LB
Lem Barney, Detroit (AP, UPI, NEA) ... CB
Herb Adderley, Green Bay (AP) ... CB
Cornell Green, Dallas (UPI) ... CB
Jimmy Johnson, San Francisco (NEA) ... CB
Larry Wilson, St. Louis (AP, UPI, NEA) ... S
Eddie Meador, LA Rams (AP, UPI) ... S
Mel Renfro, Dallas (NEA) ... S

1969 AFL

Offense

Lance Alworth, San Diego (UPI, NEA) ... WR
Fred Biletnikoff, Oakland (AP, NEA) ... WR
Don Maynard, NY Jets (AP) ... WR
Warren Wells, Oakland (UPI) ... WR
Bob Trumpy, Cincinnati (AP, UPI, NEA) ... TE
Jim Tyrer, Kansas City (AP, UPI, NEA) ... T
Harry Schuh, Oakland (AP, UPI) ... T
Winston Hill, NY Jets (NEA) ... T
Ed Budde, Kansas City (AP, NEA) ... G
Walt Sweeney, San Diego (UPI, NEA) ... G
Gene Upshaw, Oakland (AP, UPI) ... G
Jim Otto, Oakland (AP, UPI, NEA) ... C
Daryle Lamonica (AP, UPI) ... QB
Joe Namath, NY Jets (NEA) ... QB
Floyd Little, Denver (AP, UPI, NEA) ... RB
Matt Snell, NY Jets (AP, UPI, NEA) ... RB

Defense

Rich Jackson, Denver (AP, UPI, NEA) ... DE
Gerry Philbin, NY Jets (AP, UPI) ... DE
Ron McDole, Buffalo (NEA) ... DE
John Elliott, NY Jets (AP, UPI, NEA) ... DT
Buck Buchanan, Kansas City (AP, UPI) ... DT
Tom Keating, Oakland (NEA) ... DT
Nick Buoniconti, Miami (AP, UPI, NEA) ... MLB
Bobby Bell, Kansas City (AP, UPI, NEA) ... LB
George Webster, Houston (AP, UPI, NEA) ... LB
Willie Brown, Oakland (AP, UPI, NEA) ... CB
George (Butch) Byrd, Buffalo (AP, UPI, NEA) ... CB
Dave Grayson, Oakland (AP, UPI, NEA) ... S
Johnny Robinson, Kansas City (AP, UPI, NEA) ... S

1969 Combined

Offense

Lance Alworth, San Diego ... WR
Paul Warfield, Cleveland ... WR
Bob Trumpy, Cincinnati ... TE
Bob Brown, LA Rams ... T
Jim Tyrer, Kansas City ... T
Tom Mack, LA Rams ... G
Gene Hickerson, Cleveland ... G
Mick Tingelhoff, Minnesota ... C
Roman Gabriel, LA Rams ... QB
Gale Sayers, Chi. Bears ... RB
Calvin Hill, Dallas ... RB
Jan Stenerud, Kansas City ... K

Defense

David (Deacon) Jones, LA Rams ... DE
Carl Eller, Minnesota ... DE
Merlin Olsen, LA Rams ... DT
Bob Lilly, Dallas ... DT
Dick Butkus, Chi. Bears ... MLB
Bobby Bell, Kansas City ... LB
Chuck Howley, Dallas ... LB
Lem Barney, Detroit ... CB
Willie Brown, Oakland ... CB
Larry Wilson, St. Louis ... S
Johnny Robinson, Kansas City ... S
David Lee, Baltimore ... P

1970

Offense

Gene Washington, San Francisco ... WR
Dick Gordon, Chi. Bears ... WR
Charlie Sanders, Detroit ... TE
Jim Tyrer, Kansas City ... T
Bob Brown, LA Rams ... T
Gene Upshaw, Oakland ... G
Gene Hickerson, Cleveland ... G
Mick Tingelhoff, Minnesota ... C
John Brodie, San Francisco ... QB
Larry Brown, Washington ... RB
Ron Johnson, NY Giants ... RB
Jan Stenerud, Kansas City ... K

Defense

Carl Eller, Minnesota ... DE
Rich Jackson, Denver ... DE
Alan Page, Minnesota ... DT
Merlin Olsen, LA Rams ... DT
Dick Butkus, Chi. Bears ... MLB
Bobby Bell, Kansas City ... LB
Chuck Howley, Dallas ... LB
Willie Brown, Oakland ... CB
Jimmy Johnson, San Francisco ... CB
Johnny Robinson, Kansas City ... S
Larry Wilson, St. Louis ... S
Dave Lewis, Cincinnati ... P

1971

Offense

Otis Taylor, Kansas City ... WR
Paul Warfield, Miami ... WR
Charlie Sanders, Detroit ... TE
Ron Yary, Minnesota ... T
Rayfield Wright, Dallas ... T
Larry Little, Miami ... G
John Niland, Dallas ... G
Forrest Blue, San Francisco ... C
Bob Griese, Miami ... QB
John Brockington, Green Bay ... RB
Larry Csonka, Miami ... RB
Garo Yepremian, Miami ... K
Jan Stenerud, Kansas City ... K

Defense

Carl Eller, Minnesota ... DE
Bubba Smith, Baltimore ... DE
Bob Lilly, Dallas ... DT
Alan Page, Minnesota ... DT
Willie Lanier, Kansas City ... MLB
Ted Hendricks, Baltimore ... LB
Dave Wilcox, San Francisco ... LB
Jimmy Johnson, San Francisco ... CB
Willie Brown, Oakland ... CB
Rick Volk, Baltimore ... S
Bill Bradley, Philadelphia ... S
Jerrel Wilson, Kansas City ... P

1972

Offense

Gene Washington, San Francisco (PFWA) ... WR
Otis Taylor, Kansas City (PFWA) ... WR
Fred Biletnikoff, Oakland (NEA) ... WR
Paul Warfield, Miami (NEA) ... WR
Bob Tucker, NY Giants (PFWA) ... TE
Ted Kwalick, San Francisco (NEA) ... TE
Rayfield Wright, Dallas (PFWA, NEA) ... T
Bob Brown, Oakland (PFWA) ... T
George Kunz, Atlanta (NEA) ... T
Larry Little, Miami (PFWA, NEA) ... G
Gene Upshaw, Oakland (PFWA) ... G
Blaine Nye, Dallas (NEA) ... G
Forrest Blue, San Francisco (PFWA) ... C
Len Hauss, Washington (NEA) ... C
Joe Namath, NY Jets (PFWA, NEA) ... QB
Larry Brown, Washington (PFWA, NEA) ... RB
O.J. Simpson, Buffalo (PFWA, NEA) ... RB
Chester Marcol, Green Bay (PFWA, NEA) ... K

Defense

Claude Humphrey, Atlanta (PFWA, NEA) ... DE
Jack Gregory, NY Giants (PFWA, NEA) ... DE
Joe Greene, Pittsburgh (PFWA, NEA) ... DT
Mike Reid, Cincinnati (PFWA, NEA) ... DT
Dick Butkus, Chi. Bears (PFWA, NEA) ... MLB
Dave Wilcox, San Francisco (PFWA, NEA) ... LB
Chris Hanburger, Washington (PFWA, NEA) ... LB
Willie Brown, Oakland (PFWA, NEA) ... CB
Jimmy Johnson, San Francisco (PFWA, NEA) ... CB
Dick Anderson, Miami (PFWA, NEA) ... S
Bill Bradley, Philadelphia (PFWA, NEA) ... S

Jerrel Wilson, Kansas City (PFWA) ... P
Don Cockroft, Cleveland (NEA) ... P

1973

Offense

Harold Jackson, LA Rams (PFWA, NEA) ... WR
Harold Carmichael, Philadelphia (PFWA) ... WR
John Gilliam, Minnesota (NEA) ... WR
Charle Young, Philadelphia (PFWA) ... TE
Riley Odoms, Denver (NEA) ... TE
Ron Yary, Minnesota (PFWA) ... T
Rayfield Wright, Dallas (PFWA) ... T
Art Shell, Oakland (NEA) ... T
George Kunz, Atlanta (NEA) ... T
Larry Little, Miami (PFWA, NEA) ... G
Reggie McKenzie, Buffalo (PFWA) ... G
Joe Scibelli, LA Rams (NEA) ... G
Forrest Blue, San Francisco (PFWA) ... C
Bob Johnson, Cincinnati (NEA) ... C
John Hadl, LA Rams (PFWA) ... QB
Fran Tarkenton, Minnesota (NEA) ... QB
O.J. Simpson, Buffalo (PFWA, NEA) ... RB
Calvin Hill, Dallas (PFWA) ... RB
John Brockington, Green Bay (NEA) ... RB
Garo Yepremian, Miami (PFWA, NEA) ... K

Defense

Bill Stanfill, Miami (PFWA, NEA) ... DE
Claude Humphrey, Atlanta (PFWA) ... DE
Alan Page, Minnesota (NEA) ... DE
Joe Greene, Pittsburgh (PFWA, NEA) ... DT
Alan Page, Minnesota (PFWA) ... DT
Mike Reid, Cincinnati (NEA) ... DT
Lee Roy Jordan, Dallas (PFWA, NEA) ... MLB
Dave Wilcox, San Francisco (PFWA, NEA) ... LB
Isiah Robertson, LA Rams (PFWA) ... LB
Chris Hanburger, Washington (NEA) ... LB
Willie Brown, Oakland (PFWA, NEA) ... CB
Mel Renfro, Dallas (PFWA, NEA) ... CB
Dick Anderson, Miami (PFWA, NEA) ... S
Jake Scott, Miami (PFWA) ... S
Bill Bradley, Philadelphia (NEA) ... S
Ray Guy, Oakland (PFWA, NEA) ... P

1974

Offense

Cliff Branch, Oakland (PFWA, NEA) ... WR
Drew Pearson, Dallas (PFWA) ... WR
Mel Gray, St. Louis (NEA) ... WR
Riley Odoms, Denver (PFWA, NEA) ... TE
Ron Yary, Minnesota (PFWA, NEA) ... T
Art Shell, Oakland (PFWA, NEA) ... T
Tom Mack, LA Rams (PFWA) ... G
Larry Little, Miami (PFWA) ... G
Ed White, Minnesota (NEA) ... G
Gale Gillingham, Green Bay (NEA) ... G
Jim Langer, Miami (PFWA, NEA) ... C
Ken Stabler, Oakland (PFWA, NEA) ... QB
O.J. Simpson, Buffalo (PFWA, NEA) ... RB
Otis Armstrong, Denver (PFWA) ... RB
Lawrence McCutcheon, LA Rams (NEA) ... RB
Chester Marcol, Green Bay (PFWA) ... K
Jan Stenerud, Kansas City (NEA) ... K

Defense

Jack Youngblood, LA Rams (PFWA) ... DE
L.C. Greenwood, Pittsburgh (PFWA) ... DE
Claude Humphrey, Atlanta (NEA) ... DE
Fred Dryer, LA Rams (NEA) ... DE
Joe Greene, Pittsburgh (PFWA, NEA) ... DT
Alan Page, Minnesota (PFWA, NEA) ... DT
Bill Bergey, Philadelphia (PFWA) ... MLB
Willie Lanier, Kansas City (NEA) ... MLB
Jack Ham, Pittsburgh (PFWA, NEA) ... LB
Ted Hendricks, Green Bay (PFWA, NEA) ... LB
Robert James, Buffalo (PFWA, NEA) ... CB
Emmitt Thomas, Kansas City (PFWA) ... CB
Roger Wehrli, St. Louis (NEA) ... CB
Tony Greene, Buffalo (PFWA, NEA) ... S
Ken Houston, Washington (PFWA) ... S
Dick Anderson, Miami (NEA) ... S
Ray Guy, Oakland (PFWA, NEA) ... P

1975

Offense

Lynn Swann, Pittsburgh (PFWA) ... WR
Mel Gray, St. Louis (PFWA) ... WR
Cliff Branch, Oakland (NEA) ... WR
Isaac Curtis, Cincinnati (NEA) ... WR
Charle Young, Philadelphia (PFWA, NEA) ... TE
Ron Yary, Minnesota (PFWA, NEA) ... T
Dan Dierdorf, St. Louis (PFWA) ... T
Rayfield Wright, Dallas (NEA) ... T
Larry Little, Miami (PFWA) ... G
Joe DeLamielleure, Buffalo (PFWA) ... G
Bob Kuechenberg, Miami (NEA) ... G
Ed White, Minnesota (NEA) ... G
Jim Langer, Miami (PFWA, NEA) ... C
Fran Tarkenton, Minnesota (PFWA, NEA) ... QB
O.J. Simpson, Buffalo (PFWA, NEA) ... RB
Chuck Foreman, Minnesota (PFWA, NEA) ... RB
Jim Bakken, St. Louis (PFWA, NEA) ... K

Defense

Jack Youngblood, LA Rams (PFWA, NEA) ... DE
L.C. Greenwood, Pittsburgh (PFWA, NEA) ... DE
Curley Culp, Houston (PFWA, NEA) ... DT
Alan Page, Minnesota (PFWA) ... DT
Wally Chambers, Chi. Bears (NEA) ... DT
Jack Lambert, Pittsburgh (PFWA) ... MLB
Willie Lanier, Kansas City (NEA) ... MLB
Jack Ham, Pittsburgh (PFWA, NEA) ... LB
Andy Russell, Pittsburgh (PFWA) ... LB
Isiah Robertson, LA Rams (NEA) ... LB
Mel Blount, Pittsburgh (PFWA, NEA) ... CB
Roger Wehrli, St. Louis (PFWA) ... CB
Emmitt Thomas, Kansas City (NEA) ... CB
Ken Houston, Washington (PFWA, NEA) ... S
Paul Krause, Minnesota (PFWA) ... S
Cliff Harris, Dallas (NEA) ... S
Ray Guy, Oakland (PFWA, NEA) ... P

1976

Offense

Cliff Branch, Oakland (PFWA, NEA, AP) ... WR
Drew Pearson, Dallas (PFWA, AP) ... WR
Isaac Curtis, Cincinnati (NEA) ... WR
Dave Casper, Oakland (PFWA, NEA, AP) ... TE
Dan Dierdorf, St. Louis (PFWA, NEA, AP) ... T
Ron Yary, Minnesota (PFWA, NEA, AP) ... T
Joe DeLamielleure, Buffalo (PFWA, NEA, AP) ... G
John Hannah, New England (PFWA, AP) ... G
Conrad Dobler, St. Louis (NEA) ... G
Jim Langer, Miami (PFWA, NEA) ... C
Tom Banks, St. Louis (AP) ... C
Bert Jones, Baltimore (PFWA, NEA, AP) ... QB
O.J. Simpson, Buffalo (PFWA, NEA, AP) ... RB
Walter Payton, Chi. Bears (PFWA, AP) ... RB
Chuck Foreman, Minnesota (NEA) ... RB
Jim Bakken, St. Louis (PFWA, NEA, AP) ... K
Rick Upchurch, Denver (AP) ... KR

Defense

Jack Youngblood, LA Rams (PFWA, NEA, AP) ... DE
Tommy Hart, San Francisco (PFWA, NEA) ... DE
John Dutton, Baltimore (AP) ... DE
Wally Chambers, Chi. Bears (PFWA, NEA, AP) ... DT
Jerry Sherk, Cleveland (PFWA, NEA, AP) ... DT
Jack Lambert, Pittsburgh (PFWA, NEA, AP) ... MLB
Jack Ham, Pittsburgh (PFWA, NEA, AP) ... LB
Robert Brazile, Houston (PFWA) ... LB
Chris Hanburger, Washington (NEA) ... LB
Isiah Robertson, LA Rams (AP) ... LB
Monte Jackson, LA Rams (PFWA, NEA, AP) ... CB
Roger Wehrli, St. Louis (PFWA, AP) ... CB
Lemar Parrish, Cincinnati (NEA) ... CB
Cliff Harris, Dallas (PFWA, NEA, AP) ... S
Ken Houston, Washington (PFWA, NEA) ... S
Tommy Casanova, Cincinnati (AP) ... S
Ray Guy, Oakland (PFWA, NEA, AP) ... P

1977

Offense

Drew Pearson, Dallas (AP, NEA, PFWA) ... WR
Nat Moore, Miami (AP, PFWA) ... WR
Cliff Branch, Oakland (NEA) ... WR
Dave Casper, Oakland (AP, NEA, PFWA) ... TE
Dan Dierdorf, St. Louis (AP, NEA, PFWA) ... T
Art Shell, Oakland (AP, NEA, PFWA) ... T
Joe DeLamielleure, Buffalo (AP, NEA, PFWA) ... G
Gene Upshaw, Oakland (AP, PFWA) ... G
Larry Little, Miami (PFWA) ... G
John Hannah, New England (NEA) ... G
Jim Langer, Miami (AP, NEA, PFWA) ... C
Bob Griese, Miami (AP, NEA, PFWA) ... QB
Franco Harris, Pittsburgh (AP, NEA, PFWA) ... RB
Walter Payton, Chi. Bears (AP, NEA, PFWA) ... RB
Efren Herrera, Dallas (AP, NEA, PFWA) ... K
Billy Johnson, Houston (AP, PFWA) ... KR

Defense

Harvey Martin, Dallas (AP, NEA, PFWA) ... DE
Lyle Alzado, Denver (AP, PFWA) ... DE
Claude Humphrey, Atlanta (NEA) ... DE
Cleveland Elam, San Francisco (AP, NEA, PFWA) ... DT
Louie Kelcher, San Diego (NEA) ... DT
Larry Brooks, LA Rams (PFWA) ... DT
Joe Greene, Pittsburgh (AP) ... DT
Bill Bergey, Philadelphia (NEA, PFWA) ... MLB
Randy Gradishar, Denver (AP) ... MLB
Jack Ham, Pittsburgh (AP, NEA, PFWA) ... LB
Tom Jackson, Denver (AP, PFWA) ... LB
Robert Brazile, Houston (NEA) ... LB
Rolland Lawrence, Atlanta (AP, PFWA) ... CB
Roger Wehrli, St. Louis (AP, NEA) ... CB
Monte Jackson, LA Rams (PFWA) ... CB
Mel Blount, Pittsburgh (NEA) ... CB
Cliff Harris, Dallas (AP, NEA, PFWA) ... S
Ken Houston, Washington (NEA) ... S
Bill Thompson, Denver (AP) ... S
Charlie Waters, Dallas (PFWA) ... S
Ray Guy, Oakland (AP, NEA, PFWA) ... P

1978

Offense

Lynn Swann, Pittsburgh (AP, NEA, PFWA) ... WR
Wesley Walker, NY Jets (AP, NEA, PFWA) ... WR
Dave Casper, Oakland (AP, NEA, PFWA) ... TE
Dan Dierdorf, St. Louis (AP, NEA, PFWA) ... T
Leon Gray, New England (AP, PFWA) ... T
Russ Washington, San Diego (NEA) ... T
John Hannah, New England (AP, NEA, PFWA) ... G
Joe DeLamielleure, Buffalo (NEA, PFWA) ... G
Bob Kuechenberg, Miami (AP) ... G
Mike Webster, Pittsburgh (AP, NEA, PFWA) ... C
Terry Bradshaw, Pittsburgh (AP, PFWA) ... QB
Jim Zorn, Seattle (NEA) ... QB
Earl Campbell, Houston (AP, NEA, PFWA) ... RB
Walter Payton, Chi. Bears (NEA, PFWA) ... RB
Delvin Williams, Miami (AP) ... RB
Frank Corral, LA Rams (NEA, PFWA) ... K
Pat Leahy, NY Jets (AP) ... K
Rick Upchurch, Denver (AP, PFWA) ... KR

Defense

Al (Bubba) Baker, Detroit (AP, NEA, PFWA) ... DE
Jack Youngblood, LA Rams (AP, NEA, PFWA) ... DE
Randy White, Dallas (AP, NEA, PFWA) ... DT
Louie Kelcher, San Diego (AP, NEA, PFWA) ... DT
Randy Gradishar, Denver (AP, NEA, PFWA) ... MLB
Jack Ham, Pittsburgh (AP, NEA, PFWA) ... LB
Robert Brazile, Houston (AP, NEA, PFWA) ... LB
Louis Wright, Denver (AP, NEA, PFWA) ... CB
Willie Buchanon, Green Bay (AP, PFWA) ... CB
Mike Haynes, New England (NEA, PFWA) ... CB
Charlie Waters, Dallas (NEA, PFWA) ... S
Thom Darden, Cleveland (NEA, PFWA) ... S
Cliff Harris, Dallas (AP, PFWA) ... S
Ken Houston, Washington (AP) ... S
Ray Guy, Oakland (AP, NEA, PFWA) ... P

1979

Offense

John Jefferson, San Diego (AP, NEA, PFWA) ... WR
John Stallworth, Pittsburgh (AP, NEA, PFWA) ... WR
Dave Casper, Oakland (AP) ... TE
Raymond Chester, Oakland (NEA) ... TE
Ozzie Newsome, Cleveland (PFWA) ... TE
Leon Gray, Houston (AP, NEA, PFWA) ... T
Marvin Powell, NY Jets (AP, PFWA) ... T
Jon Kolb, Pittsburgh (NEA) ... T
John Hannah, New England (AP, NEA, PFWA) ... G
Joe DeLamielleure, Buffalo (NEA, PFWA) ... G
Bob Young, St. Louis (AP) ... G
Mike Webster, Pittsburgh (AP, NEA, PFWA) ... C
Dan Fouts, San Diego (AP, NEA, PFWA) ... QB
Earl Campbell, Houston (AP, NEA, PFWA) ... RB
Ottis Anderson, St. Louis (AP, PFWA) ... RB
Walter Payton, Chi. Bears (NEA) ... RB
Toni Fritsch, Houston (AP, NEA, PFWA) ... K
Tony Nathan, Miami (AP) ... KR
Rick Upchurch, Denver (PFWA) ... KR
J.T. Smith, Kansas City (PFWA) ... PR

Defense

Lee Roy Selmon, Tampa Bay (AP, NEA, PFWA) ... DE
Jack Youngblood, LA Rams (AP, NEA, PFWA) ... DE
Randy White, Dallas (AP, NEA, PFWA) ... DT
Larry Brooks, LA Rams (AP) ... DT
Joe Greene, Pittsburgh (PFWA) ... DT
Charlie Johnson, Philadelphia (NEA) ... DT
Jack Lambert, Pittsburgh (AP, NEA) ... MLB
Randy Gradishar, Denver (PFWA) ... MLB
Robert Brazile, Houston (AP, NEA, PFWA) ... LB
Jack Ham, Pittsburgh (AP, NEA, PFWA) ... LB
Lemar Parrish, Washington (AP, NEA, PFWA) ... CB
Louis Wright, Denver (AP, NEA, PFWA) ... CB
Mike Reinfeldt, Houston (AP, NEA, PFWA) ... S
Donnie Shell, Pittsburgh (AP, NEA) ... S
Gary Fencik, Chi. Bears (PFWA) ... S
Bob Grupp, Kansas City (NEA, PFWA) ... P
Dave Jennings, NY Giants (AP) ... P

1980

Offense

John Jefferson, San Diego (AP, NEA, PFWA) ... WR
James Lofton, Green Bay (NEA, PFWA) ... WR
Charlie Joiner, San Diego (AP) ... WR
Kellen Winslow, San Diego (AP, NEA, PFWA) ... TE
Mike Kenn, Atlanta (AP, NEA, PFWA) ... T
Leon Gray, Houston (AP, PFWA) ... T
Dan Dierdorf, St. Louis (NEA) ... T
John Hannah, New England (AP, NEA, PFWA) ... G
Herbert Scott, Dallas (AP, NEA) ... G
Joe DeLamielleure, Cleveland (PFWA) ... G
Mike Webster, Pittsburgh (AP, NEA, PFWA) ... C
Brian Sipe, Cleveland (AP, NEA, PFWA) ... QB
Earl Campbell, Houston (AP, NEA, PFWA) ... RB
Walter Payton, Chi. Bears (AP, NEA, PFWA) ... RB
Ed Murray, Detroit (AP, NEA, PFWA) ... K
Horace Ivory, New England (PFWA) ... KR
J.T. Smith, Kansas City (AP) ... KR
J.T. Smith, Kansas City (PFWA) ... PR

Defense

Lee Roy Selmon, Tampa Bay (NEA, PFWA) ... DE
Art Still, Kansas City (NEA, PFWA) ... DE
Lyle Alzado, Cleveland (AP) ... DE
Fred Dean, San Diego (AP) ... DE
Gary Johnson, San Diego (AP, NEA, PFWA) ... DT

Randy White, Dallas (NEA, PFWA) .... DT
Charlie Johnson, Philadelphia (AP) .... DT
Jack Lambert, Pittsburgh (AP, NEA, PFWA) .... MLB
Ted Hendricks, Oakland (AP, NEA, PFWA) .... LB
Robert Brazile, Houston (NEA, PFWA) .... LB
Matt Blair, Minnesota (AP) .... LB
Lester Hayes, Oakland (AP, NEA, PFWA) .... CB
Lemar Parrish, Washington (NEA, PFWA) .... CB
Pat Thomas, LA Rams (AP) .... CB
Nolan Cromwell, LA Rams (AP, NEA, PFWA) .... S
Donnie Shell, Pittsburgh (AP, NEA, PFWA) .... S
Dave Jennings, NY Giants (AP, NEA, PFWA) .... P

1981

Offense

James Lofton, Green Bay (AP, NEA, PFWA) .... WR
Alfred Jenkins, Atlanta (AP, NEA, PFWA) .... WR
Kellen Winslow, San Diego (AP, NEA, PFWA) .... TE
Anthony Muñoz, Cincinnati (AP, NEA, PFWA) .... T
Marvin Powell, NY Jets (AP, NEA, PFWA) .... T
John Hannah, New England (AP, NEA, PFWA) .... G
Randy Cross, San Francisco (NEA, PFWA) .... G
Herbert Scott, Dallas (AP) .... G
Mike Webster, Pittsburgh (AP, NEA, PFWA) C
Ken Anderson, Cincinnati (AP, NEA, PFWA) .... QB
Tony Dorsett, Dallas (AP, NEA, PFWA) .... RB
Billy Sims, Detroit (NEA, PFWA) .... RB
George Rogers, New Orleans (AP) .... RB
Rafael Septien, Dallas (AP, PFWA) .... K
Nick Lowery, Kansas City (NEA) .... K
LeRoy Irvin, LA Rams (AP, PFWA) .... KR
Mike Nelms, Washington (PFWA) .... PR

Defense

Joe Klecko, NY Jets (AP, NEA, PFWA) .... DE
Fred Dean, San Francisco (AP, PFWA) .... DE
Ed Jones, Dallas (NEA) .... DE
Randy White, Dallas (AP, NEA, PFWA) .... DT
Gary Johnson, San Diego (AP, PFWA) .... DT
Doug English, Detroit (NEA) .... DT
Charlie Johnson, Philadelphia (AP) .... NT
Jack Lambert, Pittsburgh (AP, NEA, PFWA) .... MLB
Lawrence Taylor, NY Giants (AP, NEA, PFWA) .... LB
Bob Swenson, Denver (AP, NEA) .... LB
Jerry Robinson, Philadelphia (PFWA) .... LB
Ronnie Lott, San Francisco (AP, NEA, PFWA) .... CB
Mel Blount, Pittsburgh (AP, PFWA) .... CB
Mark Haynes, NY Giants (NEA) .... CB
Nolan Cromwell, LA Rams (AP, NEA, PFWA) .... S
Gary Barbaro, Kansas City (NEA, PFWA) .... S
Gary Fencik, Chi. Bears (AP) .... S
Pat McInally, Cincinnati (AP, PFWA) .... P
Tom Skladany, Detroit (NEA) .... P

1982

Offense

Wes Chandler, San Diego (AP, NEA, PFWA) .... WR
Dwight Clark, San Francisco (AP, NEA, PFWA) .... WR
Kellen Winslow, San Diego (AP, NEA, PFWA) .... TE
Anthony Muñoz, Cincinnati (AP, NEA, PFWA) .... T
Marvin Powell, NY Jets (AP, NEA, PFWA) .... T
Doug Wilkerson, San Diego (AP, NEA, PFWA) .... G
John Hannah, New England (PFWA) .... G
Ed Newman, Miami (NEA) .... G
R.C. Thielemann, Atlanta (AP) .... G
Joe Fields, NY Jets (AP, NEA) C
Mike Webster, Pittsburgh (PFWA) C
Dan Fouts, San Diego (AP, NEA, PFWA) .... QB
Marcus Allen, LA Raiders (AP, NEA, PFWA) .... RB
Freeman McNeil, NY Jets (AP, NEA, PFWA) .... RB
Mark Moseley, Washington (AP, NEA, PFWA) .... K
Mike Nelms, Washington (PFWA) .... KR
Rich Upchurch, Denver (AP) .... KR
LeRoy Irvin, LA Rams (PFWA) .... PR

Defense

Mark Gastineau, NY Jets (AP, NEA, PFWA) .... DE
Lee Roy Selmon, Tampa Bay (NEA, PFWA) .... DE
Ed Jones, Dallas (AP) .... DE
Randy White, Dallas (AP, NEA, PFWA) .... DT
Dan Hampton, Chi. Bears (NEA, PFWA) .... DT
Doug English, Detroit (AP) .... DT
Fred Smerlas, Buffalo (AP) .... NT
Jack Lambert, Pittsburgh (AP, NEA, PFWA) .... MLB
Lawrence Taylor, NY Giants (AP, NEA, PFWA) .... LB
Hugh Green, Tampa Bay (PFWA) .... LB
Ted Hendricks, LA Raiders (AP) .... LB
Rod Martin, LA Raiders (NEA) .... LB
Louis Breeden, Cincinnati (AP, NEA) .... CB
Mark Haynes, NY Giants (AP, PFWA) .... CB
Mike Haynes, New England (NEA) .... CB
Everson Walls, Dallas (PFWA) .... CB
Nolan Cromwell, LA Rams (AP, PFWA) .... S
Donnie Shell, Pittsburgh (AP, PFWA) .... S
Gary Barbaro, Kansas City (NEA) .... S
Kenny Easley, Seattle (NEA) .... S
Dave Jennings, NY Giants (NEA, PFWA) .... P
Luke Prestridge, Denver (AP) .... P

1983

Offense

Roy Green, St. Louis (AP, NEA, PFWA) .... WR
Mike Quick, Philadelphia (AP, NEA) .... WR
James Lofton, Green Bay (PFWA) .... WR
Todd Christensen, LA Raiders (AP, NEA, PFWA) .... TE
Joe Jacoby, Washington (AP, NEA, PFWA) .... T
Anthony Muñoz, Cincinnati (AP, PFWA) .... T
Keith Fahnhorst, San Francisco (NEA) .... T
Russ Grimm, Washington (AP, NEA, PFWA) .... G
John Hannah, New England (AP, NEA, PFWA) .... G
Dwight Stephenson, Miami (NEA, PFWA) C
Mike Webster, Pittsburgh (AP) C
Joe Theismann, Washington (AP, NEA, PFWA) .... QB
Eric Dickerson, LA Rams (AP, NEA, PFWA) .... RB
John Riggins, Washington (AP, PFWA) .... RB
William Andrews, Atlanta (NEA) .... RB
Ali Haji-Sheikh, NY Giants (AP, NEA, PFWA) .... K
Mike Nelms, Washington (AP) .... KR
Fulton Walker, Miami (PFWA) .... KR
Billy Johnson, Atlanta (PFWA) .... PR

Defense

Doug Betters, Miami (AP, NEA, PFWA) .... DE
Howie Long, LA Raiders (NEA, PFWA) .... DE
Mark Gastineau, NY Jets (AP) .... DE
Dave Butz, Washington (AP, NEA) .... DT
Randy White, Dallas (AP, PFWA) .... DT
Doug English, Detroit (PFWA) .... DT
Bob Baumhower, Miami (AP) .... NT
Fred Smerlas, Buffalo (NEA) .... NT
Jack Lambert, Pittsburgh (AP, NEA, PFWA) .... ILB
Mike Singletary, Chi. Bears (NEA) .... ILB
Lawrence Taylor, NY Giants (AP, NEA, PFWA) .... OLB
Chip Banks, Cleveland (AP, PFWA) .... OLB
Rod Martin, LA Raiders (NEA) .... OLB
Gary Green, Kansas City (NEA, PFWA) .... CB
Ronnie Lott, San Francisco (PFWA) .... CB
Ken Riley, Cincinnati (AP) .... CB
Everson Walls, Dallas (AP) .... CB
Louis Wright, Denver (NEA) .... CB
Kenny Easley, Seattle (AP, NEA, PFWA) .... S
Mark Murphy, Washington (AP, PFWA) .... S
Johnnie Johnson, LA Rams (NEA) .... S
Rich Camarillo, New England (NEA, PFWA) .... P
Rohn Stark, Baltimore (AP) .... P

1984

Offense

Roy Green, St. Louis (AP, NEA, PFWA) .... WR
Art Monk, Washington (AP, PFWA) .... WR
James Lofton, Green Bay (NEA) .... WR
Ozzie Newsome, Cleveland (AP, NEA, PFWA) .... TE
Keith Fahnhorst, San Francisco (AP, NEA, PFWA) .... T
Joe Jacoby, Washington (AP, PFWA) .... T
Anthony Muñoz, Cincinnati (NEA) .... T
Russ Grimm, Washington (AP, NEA, PFWA) .... G
John Hannah, New England (NEA, PFWA) .... G
Ed Newman, Miami (AP) .... G
Dwight Stephenson, Miami (AP, NEA, PFWA) C
Dan Marino, Miami (AP, NEA, PFWA) .... QB
Eric Dickerson, LA Rams (AP, NEA, PFWA) .... RB
Walter Payton, Chi. Bears (AP, NEA, PFWA) .... RB
Norm Johnson, Seattle (AP, PFWA) .... K
Jan Stenerud, Minnesota (NEA) .... K
Henry Ellard, LA Rams (AP) .... KR
Bobby Humphery, NY Jets (PFWA) .... KR
Louis Lipps, Pittsburgh (PFWA) .... PR

Defense

Mark Gastineau, NY Jets (AP, NEA, PFWA) .... DE
Howie Long, LA Raiders (AP, NEA, PFWA) .... DE
Randy White, Dallas (AP, NEA, PFWA) .... DT
Dan Hampton, Chi. Bears (AP, NEA) .... DT
Joe Nash, Seattle (AP) .... NT
E.J. Junior, St. Louis (AP, NEA, PFWA) .... ILB
Mike Singletary, Chi. Bears (AP, NEA, PFWA) .... ILB
Lawrence Taylor, NY Giants (AP, NEA, PFWA) .... OLB
Rod Martin, LA Raiders (AP, PFWA) .... OLB
Clay Matthews, Cleveland (NEA) .... OLB
Mike Haynes, LA Raiders (AP, NEA, PFWA) .... CB
Mark Haynes, NY Giants (AP, NEA) .... CB
Lester Hayes, LA Raiders (PFWA) .... CB
Kenny Easley, Seattle (AP, NEA, PFWA) .... S
Deron Cherry, Kansas City (AP) .... S
Michael Downs, Dallas (PFWA) .... S
Wes Hopkins, Philadelphia (NEA) .... S
Reggie Roby, Miami (AP, NEA, PFWA) .... P

1985

Offense

Steve Largent, Seattle (AP, PFWA) .... WR
Louis Lipps, Pittsburgh (NEA, PFWA) .... WR
Mike Quick, Philadelphia (AP, NEA) .... WR
Todd Christensen, LA Raiders (AP, NEA, PFWA) .... TE
Jim Covert, Chi. Bears (AP, NEA, PFWA) .... T
Anthony Muñoz, Cincinnati (AP, NEA, PFWA) .... T
Russ Grimm, Washington (AP, NEA, PFWA) .... G
John Hannah, New England (AP, PFWA) .... G
Randy Cross, San Francisco (NEA) .... G
Dwight Stephenson, Miami (AP, NEA, PFWA) C
Dan Marino, Miami (AP, PFWA) .... QB
Dan Fouts, San Diego (NEA) .... QB
Marcus Allen, LA Raiders (AP, NEA, PFWA) .... RB
Walter Payton, Chi. Bears (AP, NEA, PFWA) .... RB
Nick Lowery, Kansas City (AP, NEA) .... K
Ron Brown, LA Rams (AP) .... KR

Defense

Howie Long, LA Raiders (AP, NEA, PFWA) .... DE
Richard Dent, Chi. Bears (AP, PFWA) .... DE
Mark Gastineau, NY Jets (NEA) .... DE
Randy White, Dallas (AP, NEA) .... DT
Steve McMichael, Chi. Bears (AP) .... DT
Joe Klecko, NY Jets (AP, NEA, PFWA) .... NT
Karl Mecklenburg, Denver (AP, NEA, PFWA) .... ILB
Mike Singletary, Chi. Bears (AP, NEA, PFWA) .... ILB
Lawrence Taylor, NY Giants (AP, NEA, PFWA) .... OLB
Andre Tippett, New England (AP, NEA, PFWA) .... OLB
Mike Haynes, LA Raiders (AP, NEA, PFWA) .... CB
Eric Wright, San Francisco (AP, NEA) .... CB
Everson Walls, Dallas (PFWA) .... CB
Kenny Easley, Seattle (AP, NEA, PFWA) .... S
Wes Hopkins, Philadelphia (AP, NEA, PFWA) .... S
Dale Hatcher, LA Rams (AP) .... P
Rohn Stark, Indianapolis (NEA) .... P

ALL-PRO SQUAD OF THE 1920s

The team chosen by the Hall of Fame Selection Committee

Name	Pos.	Ht.	Wt.	Teams
Guy Chamberlin	End	6-2	210	Decatur 1920; Chi. Staleys 1921; Canton 1922-23; Cleveland 1924; Frankford 1925-26; Chi. Cardinals 1927
Lavern Dilweg	End	6-3	203	Milwaukee 1926; Green Bay 1927-34
George Halas	End	6-1	180	Decatur 1920; Chi. Staleys 1921; Chi. Bears 1922-29
Ed Healey	Tackle	6-3	220	Rock Island 1920-22; Chi. Bears 1922-27
Wilbur (Pete) Henry	Tackle	6-0	250	Canton 1920-23, 1925-26; NY Giants 1927; Pottsville 1927-28
Cal Hubbard	Tackle	6-5	250	NY Giants 1927-28, 1936; Green Bay 1929-33, 1935; Pittsburgh 1936
Steve Owen	Tackle	6-2	235	Kansas City 1924-25; NY Giants 1926-31, 1933
Hunk Anderson	Guard	5-11	195	Chi. Bears 1922-25
Walt Kiesling	Guard	6-2	245	Duluth 1926-27; Pottsville 1928; Chi. Cardinals 1929-33; Chi. Bears 1934; Green Bay 1935-36; Pittsburgh 1937-38
Mike Michalske	Guard	6-0	209	NY Yankees 1926-28; Green Bay 1929-35, 1937
George Trafton	Center	6-2	235	Decatur 1920; Chi. Staleys 1921; Chi. Bears 1922-32
Jimmy Conzelman	Quarterback	6-0	180	Decatur 1920; Rock Island 1921-22; Milwaukee 1923-24; Detroit 1925-26; Providence 1927-29
John (Paddy) Driscoll	Quarterback	5-11	160	Chi. Cardinals 1920-25; Decatur 1920; Chi. Bears 1926-29
Harold (Red) Grange	Halfback	6-0	185	Chi. Bears 1925, 1929-34; NY Yankees 1926-27
Joe Guyon	Halfback	6-1	180	Canton 1920; Cleveland 1921; Washington 1921; Oorang 1922-23; Rock Island 1924; Kansas City 1924-26; NY Giants 1927
Earl (Curly) Lambeau	Halfback	6-0	195	Green Bay 1921-29
Jim Thorpe	Halfback	6-1	190	Canton 1920, 1926; Cleveland 1921; Oorang 1922-23; Toledo 1923; Rock Island 1924; NY Giants 1925; Chi. Cardinals 1928
Ernie Nevers	Fullback	6-1	205	Duluth 1926-27; Chi. Cardinals 1929-31

ALL-PRO SQUAD OF THE 1930s

The team chosen by the Hall of Fame Selection Committee

Name	Pos.	Ht.	Wt.	Teams
Bill Hewitt	End	5-11	191	Chi. Bears 1932-36; Philadelphia 1937-39; Phil-Pitt 1943
Don Hutson	End	6-1	180	Green Bay 1935-45
Wayne Millner	End	6-0	191	Boston 1936; Washington 1937-41, 1945
Gaynell Tinsley	End	6-1	200	Chi. Cardinals 1937-38, 1940
George Christensen	Tackle	6-2	238	Portsmouth 1931-33; Detroit 1934-38
Frank Cope	Tackle	6-3	234	NY Giants 1938-47
Glen (Turk) Edwards	Tackle	6-2	260	Boston 1932-36; Washington 1937-40
Bill Lee	Tackle	6-2	235	Brooklyn 1935-37; Green Bay 1937-42, 1946
Joe Stydahar	Tackle	6-4	230	Chi. Bears 1936-42; 1945-46
Grover (Ox) Emerson	Guard	6-0	190	Portsmouth 1931-33; Detroit 1934-37; Brooklyn 1938
Dan Fortmann	Guard	6-0	207	Chi. Bears 1936-43
Charles (Buckets) Goldenberg	Guard	5-10	222	Green Bay 1933-45
Russ Letlow	Guard	6-0	212	Green Bay 1936-42, 1946
Mel Hein	Center	6-2	225	NY Giants 1931-45
George Svendsen	Center	6-4	240	Green Bay 1935-37, 1940-41
Earl (Dutch) Clark	Quarterback	6-0	185	Portsmouth 1931-32; Detroit 1934-38
Arnie Herber	Quarterback	6-1	200	Green Bay 1930-40; NY Giants 1944-45
Cecil Isbell	Quarterback	6-0	190	Green Bay 1938-42
Cliff Battles	Halfback	6-1	201	Boston 1932-36; Washington 1937
Johnny Blood (McNally)	Halfback	6-0	185	Milwaukee 1925-26; Duluth 1926-27; Pottsville 1928; Green Bay 1929-33, 1935-36; Pittsburgh 1934, 1937-39
Beattie Feathers	Halfback	5-11	177	Chi. Bears 1934-37; Brooklyn 1938-39; Green Bay 1940
Alphonse (Tuffy) Leemans	Halfback	6-0	200	NY Giants 1936-43
Ken Strong	Halfback	5-11	210	Staten Island 1929-32; NY Giants 1933-35, 1939, 1944-45; NY Yanks (AFL) 1936-37
Clarke Hinkle	Fullback	5-11	191	Green Bay 1932-41
Bronko Nagurski	Fullback	6-2	225	Chi. Bears 1930-37, 1943

ALL-PRO SQUAD OF THE 1940s

The team chosen by the Hall of Fame Selection Committee

Name	Pos.	Ht.	Wt.	Teams
Jim Benton	End	6-3	210	Cleveland 1938-40, 1942, 1944-45; Chi. Bears 1943; LA Rams 1946-47
Jack Ferrante	End	6-1	205	Philadelphia 1941, 1944-50
Ken Kavanaugh	End	6-3	205	Chi. Bears 1940-41, 1945-50
Dante Lavelli	End	6-0	192	Cleveland 1946-56
Pete Pihos	End	6-1	210	Philadelphia 1947-55
Mac Speedie	End	6-3	205	Cleveland 1946-52
Ed Sprinkle	End	6-1	207	Chi. Bears 1944-55
Al Blozis	Tackle	6-7	250	NY Giants 1942-44
George Connor	Tackle	6-3	240	Chi. Bears 1948-55
Frank (Bucko) Kilroy	Tackle	6-2	244	Phil-Pitt 1943; Philadelphia 1944-55
Buford (Baby) Ray	Tackle	6-6	250	Green Bay 1938-48
Vic Sears	Tackle	6-3	236	Philadelphia 1941-42, 1945-53; Phil-Pitt 1943
Al Wistert	Tackle	6-1	214	Phil-Pitt 1943; Philadelphia 1944-51
Bruno Banducci	Guard	5-11	220	Philadelphia 1944-45; San Francisco 1946-54
Bill Edwards	Guard	6-3	218	NY Giants 1940-42, 1946
Garrard (Buster) Ramsey	Guard	6-1	220	Chi. Cardinals 1946-51
Bill Willis	Guard	6-2	215	Cleveland 1946-53
Len Younce	Guard	6-1	210	NY Giants 1941, 1943-44, 1946-48
Charley Brock	Center	6-2	210	Green Bay 1939-47
Clyde (Bulldog) Turner	Center	6-2	235	Chi. Bears 1940-52
Alex Wojciechowicz	Center	6-0	235	Detroit 1938-46; Philadelphia 1946-50
Sammy Baugh	Quarterback	6-2	180	Washington 1937-52
Sid Luckman	Quarterback	6-0	195	Chi. Bears 1939-50
Bob Waterfield	Quarterback	6-2	200	Cleveland 1945; LA Rams 1946-52
Tony Canadeo	Halfback	5-11	195	Green Bay 1941-44, 1946-52
Bill Dudley	Halfback	5-10	176	Pittsburgh 1942, 1945-46; Detroit 1947-49; Washington 1950-51, 1953
George McAfee	Halfback	6-0	177	Chi. Bears 1940-41, 1945-50
Charley Trippi	Halfback	6-0	185	Chi. Cardinals 1947-55
Steve Van Buren	Halfback	6-1	200	Philadelphia 1944-51
Byron (Whizzer) White	Halfback	6-1	188	Pittsburgh 1938; Detroit 1940-41
Pat Harder	Fullback	5-11	205	Chi. Cardinals 1946-50; Detroit 1951-53
Marion Motley	Fullback	6-1	238	Cleveland 1946-53; Pittsburgh 1955
Bill Osmanski	Fullback	5-11	200	Chi. Bears 1939-43, 1946-47

ALL-PRO SQUAD OF THE 1950s

The team chosen by the Hall of Fame Selection Committee

OFFENSE

Name	Pos.	Ht.	Wt.	Teams
Raymond Berry	End	6-2	187	Baltimore 1955-67
Tom Fears	End	6-2	215	LA Rams 1948-56
Bobby Walston	End	6-0	195	Philadelphia 1951-62
Elroy (Crazylegs) Hirsch	Halfback-End	6-2	190	Chi. Rockets (AAFC) 1946-48; LA Rams 1949-57
Roosevelt Brown	Tackle	6-3	255	NY Giants 1953-65
Bob St. Clair	Tackle	6-9	265	San Francisco 1953-63
Dick Barwegan	Guard	6-1	228	NY Yankees (AAFC) 1947; Baltimore (AAFC) 1948-49; Chi. Bears 1950-52; Baltimore 1953-54
Jim Parker	Guard	6-3	273	Baltimore 1957-67
Dick Stanfel	Guard	6-3	240	Detroit 1952-55; Washington 1956-58
Chuck Bednarik	Center	6-3	230	Philadelphia 1949-62
Otto Graham	Quarterback	6-1	195	Cleveland 1946-55
Bobby Layne	Quarterback	6-2	190	Chi. Bears 1948; NY Bulldogs 1949; Detroit 1950-58; Pittsburgh 1958-62
Norm Van Brocklin	Quarterback	6-1	190	LA Rams 1949-57; Philadelphia 1958-60
Frank Gifford	Halfback	6-1	200	NY Giants 1952-60; 1962-64
Ollie Matson	Halfback	6-2	220	Chi. Cardinals 1952, 1954-58; LA Rams 1959-62; Detroit 1963; Philadelphia 1964-66
Hugh McElhenny	Halfback	6-1	198	San Francisco 1952-60; Minnesota 1961-62; NY Giants 1963; Detroit 1964
Lenny Moore	Halfback	6-1	190	Baltimore 1956-67
Alan Ameche	Fullback	6-1	220	Baltimore 1955-60
Joe Perry	Fullback	6-0	200	San Francisco 1948-60, 1963; Baltimore 1961-62
Lou Groza	Kicker	6-3	250	Cleveland 1946-59, 1961-67

DEFENSE

Name	Pos.	Ht.	Wt.	Teams
Len Ford	End	6-5	248	LA Dons (AAFC) 1948-49; Cleveland 1950-57; Green Bay 1958
Gino Marchetti	End	6-4	245	Dallas 1952; Baltimore 1953-64, 1966
Art Donovan	Tackle	6-3	265	Baltimore 1950, 1953-61; NY Yanks 1951; Dallas 1952
Leo Nomellini	Tackle	6-3	264	San Francisco 1950-63
Ernie Stautner	Tackle	6-2	235	Pittsburgh 1950-63
Joe Fortunato	Linebacker	6-1	225	Chi. Bears 1955-66
Bill George	Linebacker	6-2	230	Chi. Bears 1952-65; LA Rams 1966
Sam Huff	Linebacker	6-1	230	NY Giants 1956-63; Washington 1964-67, 1969
Joe Schmidt	Linebacker	6-0	222	Detroit 1953-65
Jack Butler	Halfback	6-1	193	Pittsburgh 1951-59
Dick (Night Train) Lane	Halfback	6-2	210	LA Rams 1952-53; Chi. Cardinals 1954-59; Detroit 1960-65
Jack Christiansen	Safety	6-1	185	Detroit 1951-58
Yale Lary	Safety	5-11	190	Detroit 1952-53, 1956-64
Emlen Tunnell	Safety	6-1	200	NY Giants 1948-58; Green Bay 1959-61

ALL-PRO SQUAD OF THE 1960s

The team chosen by the Hall of Fame Selection Committee

OFFENSE

Name	Pos.	Ht.	Wt.	Teams
Del Shofner	Split End	6-3	190	LA Rams 1957-60; NY Giants 1961-67
Charley Taylor	Split End	6-3	210	Washington 1964-75, 1977
Gary Collins	Flanker	6-4	215	Cleveland 1962-71
Boyd Dowler	Flanker	6-5	225	Green Bay 1959-69; Washington 1971
John Mackey	Tight End	6-2	224	Baltimore 1963-71; San Diego 1972
Bob Brown	Tackle	6-4	295	Philadelphia 1964-68; LA Rams 1969-70; Oakland 1971-73
Forrest Gregg	Tackle	6-4	250	Green Bay 1956, 1958-70; Dallas 1971
Ralph Neely	Tackle	6-6	265	Dallas 1965-77
Gene Hickerson	Guard	6-3	260	Cleveland 1958-60, 1962-73
Jerry Kramer	Guard	6-3	254	Green Bay 1958-68
Howard Mudd	Guard	6-2	254	San Francisco 1964-69; Chi. Bears 1969-70
Jim Ringo	Center	6-2	230	Green Bay 1953-63; Philadelphia 1964-67
Sonny Jurgensen	Quarterback	6-0	203	Philadelphia 1957-63; Washington 1964-74
Bart Starr	Quarterback	6-1	190	Green Bay 1956-71
Johnny Unitas	Quarterback	6-2	196	Baltimore 1956-72; San Diego 1973
John David Crow	Halfback	6-2	224	Chi. Cardinals 1958-59; St. Louis 1960-64; San Francisco 1965-68
Paul Hornung	Halfback	6-2	215	Green Bay 1957-62, 1964-66
Leroy Kelly	Halfback	6-0	200	Cleveland 1964-73
Gale Sayers	Halfback	6-0	198	Chi. Bears 1965-71
Jim Brown	Fullback	6-2	232	Cleveland 1957-65
Jim Taylor	Fullback	6-0	215	Green Bay 1958-66; New Orleans 1967
Jim Bakken	Kicker	6-0	200	St. Louis 1962-78

DEFENSE

Name	Pos.	Ht.	Wt.	Teams
Doug Atkins	End	6-8	270	Cleveland 1953-54; Chi. Bears 1955-66; New Orleans 1967-69
Willie Davis	End	6-3	245	Cleveland 1958-59; Green Bay 1960-69
David (Deacon) Jones	End	6-5	260	LA Rams 1961-71; San Diego 1972-73; Washington 1974
Alex Karras	Tackle	6-2	245	Detroit 1958-62, 1964-70
Bob Lilly	Tackle	6-5	260	Dallas 1961-74
Merlin Olsen	Tackle	6-5	270	LA Rams 1962-76
Dick Butkus	Linebacker	6-3	245	Chi. Bears 1965-73
Larry Morris	Linebacker	6-2	220	LA Rams 1955-57; Chi. Bears 1959-65; Atlanta 1966
Ray Nitschke	Linebacker	6-3	240	Green Bay 1958-72
Tommy Nobis	Linebacker	6-2	235	Atlanta 1966-76
Dave Robinson	Linebacker	6-3	240	Green Bay 1963-72; Washington 1973-74
Herb Adderley	Cornerback	6-0	200	Green Bay 1961-69; Dallas 1970-72
Lem Barney	Cornerback	6-0	202	Detroit 1967-77
Bobby Boyd	Cornerback	5-10	192	Baltimore 1960-68
Eddie Meador	Safety	5-11	199	LA Rams 1959-70
Larry Wilson	Safety	6-0	190	St. Louis 1960-72
Willie Wood	Safety	5-10	190	Green Bay 1960-71
Don Chandler	Punter	6-2	210	NY Giants 1956-64; Green Bay 1965-67

ALL-TIME AFL TEAM

Chosen by AFL members of the Hall of Fame Selection Committee

OFFENSE

Name	Pos.	Ht.	Wt.	Teams
Lance Alworth	Flanker	6-0	180	San Diego 1962-70; Dallas 1971-72
Don Maynard	Split End	6-1	179	NY Giants 1958; NY Titans 1960-62; NY Jets 1963-72; St. Louis 1973
Fred Arbanas	Tight End	6-3	240	Dallas Texans 1962; Kansas City 1963-70
Ron Mix	Tackle	6-4	250	LA Chargers 1960; San Diego 1961-69; Oakland 1971
Jim Tyrer	Tackle	6-6	274	Dallas Texans 1961-62; Kansas City 1963-73; Washington 1974
Ed Budde	Guard	6-5	265	Kansas City 1963-76
Billy Shaw	Guard	6-2	258	Buffalo 1961-69
Jim Otto	Center	6-2	248	Oakland 1960-74
Joe Namath	Quarterback	6-2	195	NY Jets 1965-76; LA Rams 1977
Clem Daniels	Running Back	6-1	220	Dallas Texans 1960; Oakland 1961-67; San Francisco 1968
Paul Lowe	Running Back	6-0	205	LA Chargers 1960; San Diego 1961, 1963-68; Kansas City 1968-69
George Blanda	Kicker	6-2	215	Chi. Bears 1949-58; Baltimore 1950; Houston 1960-66; Oakland 1967-75

DEFENSE

Name	Pos.	Ht.	Wt.	Teams
Jerry Mays	End	6-4	252	Dallas Texans 1961-62; Kansas City 1963-70
Gerry Philbin	End	6-2	245	NY Jets 1964-72; Philadelphia 1973
Houston Antwine	Tackle	6-1	270	Boston 1961-70; New England 1971
Tom Sestak	Tackle	6-4	260	Buffalo 1962-68
Bobby Bell	Linebacker	6-4	228	Kansas City 1963-74
Nick Buoniconti	Linebacker	5-11	220	Boston 1962-68; Miami 1969-74, 1976
George Webster	Linebacker	6-4	223	Houston 1967-72; Pittsburgh 1972-73; New England 1974-76
Willie Brown	Cornerback	6-1	190	Denver 1963-66; Oakland 1967-78
Dave Grayson	Cornerback	5-10	187	Dallas Texans 1961-62; Kansas City 1963-64; Oakland 1965-70
Johnny Robinson	Safety	6-1	205	Dallas Texans 1960-62; Kansas City 1963-71
George Saimes	Safety	5-11	186	Buffalo 1963-69; Denver 1970-72
Jerrel Wilson	Punter	6-2	222	Kansas City 1963-77; New England 1978

ALL-TIME ALL-PROS

The team chosen by the Hall of Fame Selection Committee in 1969

OFFENSE

Name	Pos.	Ht.	Wt.	Teams
Don Hutson	Split End	6-1	180	Green Bay 1935-45
John Mackey	Tight End	6-2	224	Baltimore 1963-71; San Diego 1972
Cal Hubbard	Tackle	6-5	250	NY Giants 1927-28, 1936; Green Bay 1929-33; Pittsburgh 1936
Jerry Kramer	Guard	6-3	254	Green Bay 1958-68
Chuck Bednarik	Center	6-3	230	Philadelphia 1949-62
Elroy Hirsch	Flanker	6-2	190	Chi. Rockets (AAFC) 1946-48; LA Rams 1949-57
Johnny Unitas	Quarterback	6-1	196	Baltimore 1956-72; San Diego 1973
Jim Thorpe	Halfback	6-1	190	Canton 1920, 1926; Cleveland 1921; Oorang 1922-23; Toledo 1923; Rock Island 1924; NY Giants 1925; Chi. Cardinals 1928
Gale Sayers	Halfback	6-0	198	Chi. Bears 1965-71
Jim Brown	Fullback	6-2	232	Cleveland 1957-65
Lou Groza	Kicker	6-3	250	Cleveland 1946-59, 1961-67

DEFENSE

Name	Pos.	Ht.	Wt.	Teams
Gino Marchetti	End	6-4	245	Dallas 1952; Baltimore 1953-64, 1966
Leo Nomellini	Tackle	6-3	264	San Francisco 1950-63
Ray Nitschke	Linebacker	6-3	240	Green Bay 1958-72
Dick (Night Train) Lane	Cornerback	6-2	210	LA Rams 1952-53; Chi. Cardinals 1954-59; Detroit 1960-65
Emlen Tunnell	Safety	6-1	200	NY Giants 1949-58; Green Bay 1959-61

RUNNERS-UP

OFFENSE

Name	Pos.	Ht.	Wt.	Teams
Raymond Berry	Split End	6-2	187	Baltimore 1955-67
Dante Lavelli	Split End	6-0	192	Cleveland 1946-56
Mike Ditka	Tight End	6-3	230	Chi. Bears 1961-66; Philadelphia 1967-68; Dallas 1969-72
Ron Kramer	Tight End	6-3	230	Green Bay 1957, 1959-65; Detroit 1965-67
Forrest Gregg	Tackle	6-4	250	Green Bay 1956, 1958-70; Dallas 1971
Joe Stydahar	Tackle	6-4	230	Chi. Bears 1936-42, 1945-46
Dan Fortmann	Guard	6-0	207	Chi. Bears 1936-43
Jim Parker	Guard	6-3	273	Baltimore 1957-67
Mel Hein	Center	6-2	225	NY Giants 1931-45
Alex Wojciechowicz	Center	6-0	235	Detroit 1938-46; Philadelphia 1946-50
Boyd Dowler	Flanker	6-5	225	Green Bay 1959-69; Washington 1971
Lenny Moore	Flanker	6-1	190	Baltimore 1956-67
Sammy Baugh	Quarterback	6-2	180	Washington 1937-52
Norm Van Brocklin	Quarterback	6-1	190	LA Rams 1949-57; Philadelphia 1958-60
Harold (Red) Grange	Halfback	6-0	185	Chi. Bears 1925, 1929-34; NY Yankees 1926-27
Hugh McElhenny	Halfback	6-1	198	San Francisco 1952-60; Minnesota 1961-62; NY Giants 1963; Detroit 1964
Bronko Nagurski	Fullback	6-2	225	Chi. Bears 1930-37, 1943
Joe Perry	Fullback	6-0	200	San Francisco 1948-60, 1963; Baltimore 1961-62
Ernie Nevers	Kicker	6-1	205	Duluth 1926-27; Chi. Cardinals 1929-31
Ken Strong	Kicker	6-1	210	Stapleton 1929-32; NY Giants 1933-35, 1939, 1944-47; NY Yanks (AFL) 1936-37

DEFENSE

Name	Pos.	Ht.	Wt.	Teams
Len Ford	End	6-5	248	LA Dons (AAFC) 1948-49; Cleveland 1950-57; Green Bay 1958
David (Deacon) Jones	End	6-5	260	LA Rams 1961-71; San Diego 1972-73; Washington 1974
Art Donovan	Tackle	6-3	265	Baltimore 1950; NY Yankees 1951; Dallas 1952; Baltimore 1953-61
Ernie Stautner	Tackle	6-2	235	Pittsburgh 1950-63
Joe Schmidt	Linebacker	6-0	222	Detroit 1953-65
Clyde (Bulldog) Turner	Linebacker	6-2	235	Chi. Bears 1940-52
Herb Adderley	Cornerback	6-0	200	Green Bay 1961-69; Dallas 1970-72
Jack Butler	Cornerback	6-1	193	Pittsburgh 1951-59
Jack Christiansen	Safety	6-1	185	Detroit 1951-58
Larry Wilson	Safety	6-0	190	St. Louis 1960-72

ALL-PRO SQUAD OF THE 1970s

The team chosen by the Hall of Fame Selection Committee

OFFENSE

Name	Pos.	Ht.	Wt.	Teams
Harold Carmichael	Wide Receiver	6-8	225	Philadelphia 1971-83; Dallas 1984
Drew Pearson	Wide Receiver	6-0	183	Dallas 1973-83
Lynn Swann	Wide Receiver	6-0	180	Pittsburgh 1974-82
Paul Warfield	Wide Receiver	6-0	188	Cleveland 1964-69, 1976-77; Miami 1970-74
Dave Casper	Tight End	6-4	230	Oakland 1974-80; Houston 1980-83; Minnesota 1983; LA Raiders 1984
Charlie Sanders	Tight End	6-4	230	Detroit 1966-77
Dan Dierdorf	Tackle	6-3	288	St. Louis 1971-83
Art Shell	Tackle	6-5	286	Oakland 1968-81; LA Raiders 1982
Rayfield Wright	Tackle	6-6	260	Dallas 1967-79
Ron Yary	Tackle	6-6	255	Minnesota 1968-81; LA Rams 1982
Joe DeLamielleure	Guard	6-3	245	Buffalo 1973-79, 1985; Cleveland 1980-84
John Hannah	Guard	6-2	265	New England 1973-85
Larry Little	Guard	6-1	265	San Diego 1967-68; Miami 1969-80
Gene Upshaw	Guard	6-5	255	Oakland 1967-81; LA Raiders 1982
Jim Langer	Center	6-2	257	Miami 1970-80; Minnesota 1980-81
Mike Webster	Center	6-2	255	Pittsburgh 1974-85
Terry Bradshaw	Quarterback	6-3	215	Pittsburgh 1970-83
Ken Stabler	Quarterback	6-3	215	Oakland 1970-79; Houston 1980-81; New Orleans 1982-84
Roger Staubach	Quarterback	6-3	197	Dallas 1969-79
Earl Campbell	Running Back	5-11	224	Houston 1978-84; New Orleans 1984-85
Franco Harris	Running Back	6-3	230	Pittsburgh 1972-83; Seattle 1984
Walter Payton	Running Back	5-10	202	Chi. Bears 1975-85
O.J. Simpson	Running Back	6-1	216	Buffalo 1969-77; San Francisco 1978-79
Garo Yepremian	Kicker	5-8	175	Detroit 1966-67; Miami 1970-78; New Orleans 1979; Tampa Bay 1980-81

DEFENSE

Name	Pos.	Ht.	Wt.	Teams
Carl Eller	End	6-6	247	Minnesota 1964-78; Seattle 1979
L.C. Greenwood	End	6-6	245	Pittsburgh 1969-81
Harvey Martin	End	6-5	250	Dallas 1973-83
Jack Youngblood	End	6-4	244	LA Rams 1971-84
Joe Greene	Tackle	6-4	275	Pittsburgh 1969-81
Bob Lilly	Tackle	6-5	260	Dallas 1961-74
Merlin Olsen	Tackle	6-5	270	LA Rams 1962-78
Alan Page	Tackle	6-4	245	Minnesota 1967-78; Chi. Bears 1978-81
Bobby Bell	Linebacker	6-4	228	Kansas City 1963-74
Robert Brazile	Linebacker	6-4	238	Houston 1975-84
Dick Butkus	Linebacker	6-3	245	Chi. Bears 1965-73
Jack Ham	Linebacker	6-1	225	Pittsburgh 1971-82
Ted Hendricks	Linebacker	6-7	225	Baltimore 1969-73; Green Bay 1974; Oakland 1975-81; LA Raiders 1982-83
Jack Lambert	Linebacker	6-4	220	Pittsburgh 1974-84
Willie Brown	Cornerback	6-1	190	Denver 1963-66; Oakland 1967-78
Jimmy Johnson	Cornerback	6-2	185	San Francisco 1961-76
Roger Wehrli	Cornerback	6-0	190	St. Louis 1969-82
Louis Wright	Cornerback	6-2	200	Denver 1975-85
Dick Anderson	Safety	6-2	196	Miami 1968-77
Cliff Harris	Safety	6-1	192	Dallas 1970-79
Ken Houston	Safety	6-3	198	Houston 1967-72; Washington 1973-80
Larry Wilson	Safety	6-0	190	St. Louis 1960-73
Ray Guy	Punter	6-3	195	Oakland 1973-81; LA Raiders 1982-85

AFL-NFL 1960-84 ALL-STAR TEAM

The 25-year team chosen by the Hall of Fame Selection Committee

OFFENSE

Name	Pos.	Ht.	Wt.	Teams
Lance Alworth	Flanker	6-0	180	San Diego 1962-70; Dallas 1971-72
Raymond Berry	Split End	6-2	187	Baltimore 1955-67
Kellen Winslow	Tight End	6-5	242	San Diego 1979-85
Forrest Gregg	Tackle	6-4	240	Green Bay 1956, 1958-70; Dallas 1971
Ron Mix	Tackle	6-4	250	LA Chargers 1960; San Diego 1961-69; Oakland 1971
John Hannah	Guard	6-2	265	New England 1973-85
Jim Parker	Guard	6-3	273	Baltimore 1957-67
Jim Otto	Center	6-2	248	Oakland 1960-74
Johnny Unitas	Quarterback	6-1	196	Baltimore 1956-72; San Diego 1973
Jim Brown	Running Back	6-2	232	Cleveland 1957-65
O.J. Simpson	Running Back	6-1	216	Buffalo 1969-77; San Francisco 1978-79
Jan Stenerud	Kicker	6-2	190	Kansas City 1967-79; Green Bay 1980-83; Minnesota 1984-85
Gale Sayers	Kick Returner	6-0	198	Chi. Bears 1965-71
Rick Upchurch	Kick Returner	5-10	180	Denver 1975-83

DEFENSE

Name	Pos.	Ht.	Wt.	Teams
Willie Davis	End	6-3	245	Cleveland 1958-59; Green Bay 1960-69
Gino Marchetti	End	6-4	245	Dallas Texans 1952; Baltimore 1953-64, 1966
Bob Lilly	Tackle	6-5	260	Dallas 1961-74
Merlin Olsen	Tackle	6-5	270	LA Rams 1962-76
Dick Butkus	Linebacker	6-3	245	Chi. Bears 1965-73
Jack Lambert	Linebacker	6-4	220	Pittsburgh 1974-84
Ray Nitschke	Linebacker	6-3	240	Green Bay 1958-72
Willie Brown	Cornerback	6-1	190	Denver 1963-66; Oakland 1967-78
Dick (Night Train) Lane	Cornerback	6-2	210	LA Rams 1952-53; Chi. Cardinals 1954-59; Detroit 1960-65
Yale Lary	Safety	5-11	190	Detroit 1952-53, 1956-64
Larry Wilson	Safety	6-0	190	St. Louis 1960-72
Ray Guy	Punter	6-3	195	Oakland 1973-81; LA Raiders 1982-85

NFL Honors

SUPER BOWL MOST VALUABLE PLAYER

Super Bowl I Bart Starr, QB, Green Bay
Super Bowl II Bart Starr, QB, Green Bay
Super Bowl III Joe Namath, QB, NY Jets
Super Bowl IV Len Dawson, QB, Kansas City
Super Bowl V Chuck Howley, LB, Dallas
Super Bowl VI Roger Staubach, QB, Dallas
Super Bowl VII Jake Scott, S, Miami
Super Bowl VIII Larry Csonka, RB, Miami
Super Bowl IX Franco Harris, RB, Pittsburgh
Super Bowl X Lynn Swann, WR, Pittsburgh
Super Bowl XI Fred Biletnikoff, WR, Oakland
Super Bowl XII Harvey Martin, DE, Dallas
Randy White, DT, Dallas
Super Bowl XIII Terry Bradshaw, QB, Pittsburgh
Super Bowl XIV Terry Bradshaw, QB, Pittsburgh
Super Bowl XV Jim Plunkett, QB, Oakland
Super Bowl XVI Joe Montana, QB, San Francisco
Super Bowl XVII John Riggins, RB, Washington
Super Bowl XVIII Marcus Allen, RB, LA Raiders
Super Bowl XIX Joe Montana, QB, San Francisco
Super Bowl XX Richard Dent, DE, Chi. Bears

PRO BOWL PLAYER OF THE GAME
(Dan McGuire Award)

1951 Otto Graham, QB, Cleveland
1952 Dan Towler, FB, LA Rams
1953 Don Doll, DB, Detroit
1954 Chuck Bednarik, LB, Philadelphia
1955 Billy Wilson, E, San Francisco
1956 Ollie Matson, HB, Chi. Cardinals
1957 Bert Rechichar, HB, Baltimore (Back)
Ernie Stautner, T, Pittsburgh (Lineman)
1958 Hugh McElhenny, HB, San Francisco (Back)
Gene Brito, DE, Washington (Lineman)
1959 Frank Gifford, HB, NY Giants (Back)
Doug Atkins, DE, Chi. Bears (Lineman)
1960 Johnny Unitas, QB, Baltimore (Back)
Gene (Big Daddy) Lipscomb, DT, Pittsburgh (Lineman)
1961 Johnny Unitas, QB, Baltimore (Back)
Sam Huff, LB, NY Giants (Lineman)
1962A Cotton Davidson, QB, Dallas Texans
1962N Jim Brown, FB, Cleveland (Back)
Henry Jordan, DT, Green Bay (Lineman)
1963A Curtis McClinton, FB, Dallas Texans (Offense)
Earl Faison, DE, San Diego (Defense)
1963N Jim Brown, FB, Cleveland (Back)
Gene (Big Daddy) Lipscomb, DT, Pittsburgh (Lineman)
1964A Keith Lincoln, FB, San Diego (Offense)
Archie Matsos, LB, Oakland (Defense)
1964N Johnny Unitas, QB, Baltimore (Back)
Gino Marchetti, DE, Baltimore (Lineman)
1965A Keith Lincoln, FB, San Diego (Offense)
Willie Brown, CB, Denver (Defense)
1965N Fran Tarkenton, QB, Minnesota (Back)
Terry Barr, FL, Detroit (Lineman)
1966A Joe Namath, QB, NY Jets (Offense)
Frank Buncom, LB, San Diego (Defense)
1966N Jim Brown, FB, Cleveland (Back)
Dale Meinert, LB, St. Louis (Lineman)
1967A Vito (Babe) Parilli, QB, Boston (Offense)
Verlon Biggs, DE, NY Jets (Defense)
1967N Gale Sayers, HB, Chi. Bears (Back)
Floyd Peters, DT, Philadelphia (Lineman)
1968A Joe Namath, QB, NY Jets (Offense)
Don Maynard, FL, NY Jets (Offense)
Leslie (Speedy) Duncan, DB, San Diego (Defense)
1968N Gale Sayers, RB, Chi. Bears (Back)
Dave Robinson, LB, Green Bay (Lineman)
1969A Len Dawson, QB, Kansas City (Offense)
George Webster, LB, Houston (Defense)
1969N Roman Gabriel, QB, LA Rams (Back)
Merlin Olsen, DT, LA Rams (Lineman)
1970A John Hadl, QB, San Diego
1970N Gale Sayers, RB, Chi. Bears (Back)
George Andrie, DE, Dallas (Lineman)
1971 Mel Renfro, S, Dallas (Back)
Fred Carr, LB, Green Bay (Lineman)
1972 Jan Stenerud, K, Kansas City (Offense)
Willie Lanier, LB, Kansas City (Defense)
1973 O.J. Simpson, RB, Buffalo
1974 Garo Yepremian, K, Miami
1975 James Harris, QB, LA Rams
1976 Billy Johnson, KR, Houston
1977 Mel Blount, CB, Pittsburgh
1978 Walter Payton, RB, Chi. Bears
1979 Ahmad Rashad, WR, Minnesota
1980 Chuck Muncie, RB, New Orleans
1981 Ed Murray, K, Detroit
1982 Kellen Winslow, TE, San Diego
Lee Roy Selmon, DE, Tampa Bay
1983 Dan Fouts, QB, San Diego
John Jefferson, WR, Green Bay
1984 Joe Theismann, QB, Washington
1985 Mark Gastineau, DE, NY Jets
1986 Phil Simms, QB, NY Giants

CHICAGO COLLEGE ALL-STAR GAME
MOST VALUABLE ALL-STAR

1940 Ambrose Schindler, QB, USC
1941 George Franck, HB, Minnesota
1942 Bruce Smith, HB, Minnesota
1943 Pat Harder, FB, Wisconsin
1944 Glen Dobbs, HB, Tulsa
1945 Charley Trippi, HB, Georgia
1946 Elroy Hirsch, HB, Wisconsin
1947 Buddy Young, HB, Illinois
1948 Jay Rhodemyre, C, Kentucky
1949 Bill Fischer, G, Notre Dame
1950 Charlie (Choo-Choo) Justice, HB, North Carolina
1951 Bud McFadin, G, Texas
1952 Vito (Babe) Parilli, QB, Kentucky
1953 Gib Dawson, HB, Texas
1954 Johnny Lattner, HB, Notre Dame
1955 Tad Weed, K, Ohio State
1956 Sam Huff, G, West Virginia
1957 Jon Arnett, HB, USC
1958 Jim Ninowski, QB, Michigan State
Bobby Mitchell, HB, Illinois
1959 Buddy Dial, E, Rice
1960 Prentice Gautt, HB, Oklahoma
1961 Billy Kilmer, QB, UCLA
1962 John Hadl, QB, Kansas
1963 Ron VanderKelen, QB, Wisconsin
1964 Charley Taylor, HB, Arizona State
1965 John Huarte, QB, Notre Dame
1966 Tommy Nobis, LB, Texas
1967 Jack Clancy, SE, Michigan
1968 Earl McCullouch, SE, USC
1969 Greg Cook, QB, Cincinnati

MOST VALUABLE PLAYER AWARDS
Joe F. Carr Trophy—Official NFL MVP

1938 Mel Hein, C, NY Giants
1939 Parker Hall, HB, Cleveland
1940 Clarence (Ace) Parker, HB, Brooklyn
1941 Don Hutson, E, Green Bay
1942 Don Hutson, E, Green Bay
1943 Sid Luckman, QB, Chi. Bears
1944 Frank Sinkwich, QB, Detroit
1945 Bob Waterfield, QB, Cleveland
1946 Bill Dudley, HB, Pittsburgh

Professional Football Writers Association

1976 Bert Jones, QB, Baltimore
1977 Walter Payton, RB, Chi. Bears
1978 Earl Campbell, RB, Houston
1979 Earl Campbell, RB, Houston
1980 Brian Sipe, QB, Cleveland
1981 Ken Anderson, QB, Cincinnati
1982 Dan Fouts, QB, San Diego
1983 Joe Theismann, QB, Washington
1984 Dan Marino, QB, Miami
1985 Marcus Allen, RB, LA Raiders

Maxwell Club
(Bert Bell Trophy)

1959 Johnny Unitas, QB, Baltimore
1960 Norm Van Brocklin, QB, Philadelphia
1961 Paul Hornung, HB, Green Bay
1962 Andy Robustelli, DE, NY Giants
1963 Jim Brown, FB, Cleveland
1964 Johnny Unitas, QB, Baltimore
1965 Pete Retzlaff, TE, Philadelphia
1966 Don Meredith, QB, Dallas
1967 Johnny Unitas, QB, Baltimore
1968 Leroy Kelly, RB, Cleveland
1969 Roman Gabriel, QB, LA Rams
1970 George Blanda, QB-K, Oakland
1971 Roger Staubach, QB, Dallas
1972 Larry Brown, RB, Washington
1973 O.J. Simpson, RB, Buffalo
1974 Merlin Olsen, DT, LA Rams
1975 Fran Tarkenton, QB, Minnesota
1976 Ken Stabler, QB, Oakland
1977 Bob Griese, QB, Miami
1978 Terry Bradshaw, QB, Pittsburgh
1979 Earl Campbell, RB, Houston
1980 Ron Jaworski, QB, Philadelphia
1981 Ken Anderson, QB, Cincinnati
1982 Joe Theismann, QB, Washington
1983 John Riggins, RB, Washington
1984 Dan Marino, QB, Miami
1985 Walter Payton, RB, Chi. Bears

Associated Press

1974 Ken Stabler, QB, Oakland
1975 Fran Tarkenton, QB, Minnesota
1976 Bert Jones, QB, Baltimore
1977 Walter Payton, RB, Chi. Bears
1978 Terry Bradshaw, QB, Pittsburgh
1979 Earl Campbell, RB, Houston
1980 Brian Sipe, QB, Cleveland
1981 Ken Anderson, QB, Cincinnati
1982 Mark Moseley, K, Washington
1983 Joe Theismann, QB, Washington
1984 Dan Marino, QB, Miami
1985 Marcus Allen, RB, LA Raiders

United Press International
(NFL Player of the Year 1953-1969; NFC 1970-85)

1953 Otto Graham, QB, Cleveland
1954 Joe Perry, FB, San Francisco
1955 Otto Graham, QB, Cleveland
1956 Frank Gifford, HB, NY Giants
1957 Y.A. Tittle, QB, San Francisco
1958 Jim Brown, FB, Cleveland
1959 Johnny Unitas, QB, Baltimore
1960 Norm Van Brocklin, QB, Philadelphia
1961 Paul Hornung, HB, Green Bay
1962 Y.A. Tittle, QB, NY Giants
1963 Jim Brown, FB, Cleveland
1964 Johnny Unitas, QB, Baltimore
1965 Jim Brown, FB, Cleveland
1966 Bart Starr, QB, Green Bay
1967 Johnny Unitas, QB, Baltimore
1968 Earl Morrall, QB, Baltimore
1969 Roman Gabriel, QB, LA Rams
1970 John Brodie, QB, San Francisco
1971 Alan Page, DT, Minnesota
1972 Larry Brown, RB, Washington
1973 John Hadl, QB, LA Rams
1974 Jim Hart, QB, St. Louis
1975 Fran Tarkenton, QB, Minnesota
1976 Chuck Foreman, RB, Minnesota
1977 Walter Payton, RB, Chi. Bears
1978 Archie Manning, QB, New Orleans
1979 Ottis Anderson, RB, St. Louis
1980 Ron Jaworski, QB, Philadelphia
1981 Tony Dorsett, RB, Dallas
1982 Mark Moseley, K, Washington
1983 Eric Dickerson, RB, LA Rams
1984 Eric Dickerson, RB, LA Rams
1985 Walter Payton, RB, Chi. Bears

United Press International
(AFL Player of the Year 1960-69; AFC 1970-85)

1960 Abner Haynes, HB, Dallas Texans
1961 George Blanda, QB, Houston
1962 Cookie Gilchrist, FB, Buffalo
1963 Lance Alworth, FL, San Diego
1964 Gino Cappelletti, FL-K, Boston
1965 Paul Lowe, HB, San Diego
1966 Jim Nance, FB, Boston
1967 Daryle Lamonica, QB, Oakland
1968 Joe Namath, QB, NY Jets
1969 Daryle Lamonica, QB, Oakland
1970 George Blanda, QB-K, Oakland
1971 Otis Taylor, WR, Kansas City
1972 O.J. Simpson, RB, Buffalo
1973 O.J. Simpson, RB, Buffalo
1974 Ken Stabler, QB, Oakland
1975 O.J. Simpson, RB, Buffalo
1976 Bert Jones, QB, Baltimore
1977 Craig Morton, QB, Denver
1978 Earl Campbell, RB, Houston
1979 Dan Fouts, QB, San Diego
1980 Brian Sipe, QB, Cleveland
1981 Ken Anderson, QB, Cincinnati
1982 Dan Fouts, QB, San Diego
1983 Curt Warner, RB, Seattle
1984 Dan Marino, QB, Miami
1985 Marcus Allen, RB, LA Raiders

The Sporting News
(NFC Player of the Year 1970-79; NFL 1980-85)

1970 John Brodie, QB, San Francisco
1971 Roger Staubach, QB, Dallas
1972 Larry Brown, RB, Washington
1973 John Hadl, QB, LA Rams
1974 Chuck Foreman, RB, Minnesota
1975 Fran Tarkenton, QB, Minnesota
1976 Walter Payton, RB, Chi. Bears
1977 Walter Payton, RB, Chi. Bears
1978 Archie Manning, QB, New Orleans
1979 Ottis Anderson, RB, St. Louis
1980 Brian Sipe, QB, Cleveland
1981 Ken Anderson, QB, Cincinnati
1982 Mark Moseley, K, Washington
1983 Eric Dickerson, RB, LA Rams
1984 Dan Marino, QB, Miami
1985 Marcus Allen, RB, LA Raiders

The Sporting News
(AFL Player of the Year 1960-69; AFC 1970-79)

1960 Abner Haynes, HB, Dallas Texans
1961 George Blanda, QB, Houston
1962 Len Dawson, QB, Kansas City
1963 Clem Daniels, HB, Oakland
1964 Gino Cappelletti, FL-K, Boston
1965 Paul Lowe, HB, San Diego
1966 Jim Nance, FB, Boston
1967 Daryle Lamonica, QB, Oakland

1968 Joe Namath, QB, NY Jets
1969 Daryle Lamonica, QB, Oakland
1970 George Blanda, QB-K, Oakland
1971 Bob Griese, QB, Miami
1972 Earl Morrall, QB, Miami
1973 O.J. Simpson, RB, Buffalo
1974 Ken Stabler, QB, Oakland
1975 O.J. Simpson, RB, Buffalo
1976 Ken Stabler, QB, Oakland
1977 Craig Morton, QB, Denver
1978 Earl Campbell, RB, Houston
1979 Dan Fouts, QB, San Diego

OFFENSIVE PLAYER-OF-THE-YEAR AWARDS
Associated Press
1974 Ken Stabler, QB, Oakland
1975 Fran Tarkenton, QB, Minnesota
1976 Bert Jones, QB, Baltimore
1977 Walter Payton, RB, Chi. Bears
1978 Earl Campbell, RB, Houston
1979 Earl Campbell, RB, Houston
1980 Earl Campbell, RB, Houston
1981 Ken Anderson, QB, Cincinnati
1982 Dan Fouts, QB, San Diego
1983 Joe Theismann, QB, Washington
1984 Dan Marino, QB, Miami
1985 Marcus Allen, RB, LA Raiders

DEFENSIVE PLAYER-OF-THE-YEAR AWARDS
Associated Press
1974 Joe Greene, DT, Pittsburgh
1975 Mel Blount, CB, Pittsburgh
1976 Jack Lambert, LB, Pittsburgh
1977 Harvey Martin, DE, Dallas
1978 Randy Gradishar, LB, Denver
1979 Lee Roy Selmon, DE, Tampa Bay
1980 Lester Hayes, CB, Oakland
1981 Lawrence Taylor, LB, NY Giants
1982 Lawrence Taylor, LB, NY Giants
1983 Doug Betters, DE, Miami
1984 Kenny Easley, S, Seattle
1985 Mike Singletary, LB, Chi. Bears

ROOKIE OF THE YEAR AWARDS
Associated Press (Offense)
1974 Don Woods, RB, San Diego
1975 Mike Thomas, RB, Washington
1976 Sammy White, WR, Minnesota
1977 Tony Dorsett, RB, Dallas
1978 Earl Campbell, RB, Houston
1979 Ottis Anderson, RB, St. Louis
1980 Billy Sims, RB, Detroit
1981 George Rogers, RB, New Orleans
1982 Marcus Allen, RB, LA Raiders
1983 Eric Dickerson, RB, LA Rams
1984 Louis Lipps, WR, Pittsburgh
1985 Eddie Brown, WR, Cincinnati

Associated Press (Defense)
1974 Jack Lambert, LB, Pittsburgh
1975 Robert Brazile, LB, Houston
1976 Mike Haynes, CB, New England
1977 A.J. Duhe, DE, Miami
1978 Al Baker, DE, Detroit
1979 Jim Haslett, LB, Buffalo
1980 Al Richardson, LB, Atlanta
Buddy Curry, LB, Atlanta
1981 Lawrence Taylor, LB, NY Giants
1982 Chip Banks, LB, Cleveland
1983 Vernon Maxwell, LB, Baltimore
1984 Bill Maas, NT, Kansas City
1985 Duane Bickett, LB, Indianapolis

United Press International
(NFL 1955-69; NFC 1970-85)
1955 Alan Ameche, FB, Baltimore
1956 Lenny Moore, HB, Baltimore
1957 Jim Brown, FB, Cleveland
1958 Jimmy Orr, FL, Baltimore
1959 Boyd Dowler, FL, Green Bay
1960 Gail Cogdill, SE, Detroit
1961 Mike Ditka, TE, Chi. Bears
1962 Ronnie Bull, FB, Chi. Bears
1963 Paul Flatley, FL, Minnesota
1964 Charley Taylor, HB, Washington
1965 Gale Sayers, HB, Chi. Bears
1966 Johnny Roland, HB, St. Louis
1967 Mel Farr, RB, Detroit
1968 Earl McCullouch, FL, Detroit
1969 Calvin Hill, RB, Dallas
1970 Bruce Taylor, CB, San Francisco
1971 John Brockington, RB, Green Bay
1972 Chester Marcol, K, Green Bay
1973 Charle Young, TE, Philadelphia
1974 John Hicks, G, NY Giants
1975 Mike Thomas, RB, Washington
1976 Sammy White, WR, Minnesota
1977 Tony Dorsett, RB, Dallas
1978 Al (Bubba) Baker, DE, Detroit
1979 Ottis Anderson, RB, St. Louis
1980 Billy Sims, RB, Detroit
1981 George Rogers, RB, New Orleans
1982 Jim McMahon, QB, Chi. Bears
1983 Eric Dickerson, RB, LA Rams
1984 Paul McFadden, K, Philadelphia
1985 Jerry Rice, WR, San Francisco

United Press International
(AFL 1960-69; AFC 1970-85)
1960 Abner Haynes, HB, Dallas Texans
1961 Earl Faison, DE, San Diego
1962 Curtis McClinton, FB, Dallas Texans
1963 Billy Joe, FB, Denver
1964 Matt Snell, FB, NY Jets
1965 Joe Namath, QB, NY Jets
1966 Bobby Burnett, HB, Buffalo
1967 George Webster, LB, Houston
1968 Paul Robinson, RB, Cincinnati
1969 Greg Cook, QB, Cincinnati
1970 Dennis Shaw, QB, Buffalo
1971 Jim Plunkett, QB, New England
1972 Franco Harris, RB, Pittsburgh
1973 Boobie Clark, RB, Cincinnati
1974 Don Woods, RB, San Diego
1975 Robert Brazile, LB, Houston
1976 Mike Haynes, CB, New England
1977 A.J. Duhe, DE, Miami
1978 Earl Campbell, RB, Houston
1979 Jerry Butler, WR, Buffalo
1980 Joe Cribbs, RB, Buffalo
1981 Joe Delaney, RB, Kansas City
1982 Marcus Allen, RB, LA Raiders
1983 Curt Warner, RB, Seattle
1984 Louis Lipps, WR, Pittsburgh
1985 Kevin Mack, RB, Cleveland

The Sporting News
(NFC 1970-79; NFL 1980-85)
1970 Bruce Taylor, CB, San Francisco
1971 John Brockington, RB, Green Bay
1972 Chester Marcol, K, Green Bay
1973 Chuck Foreman, RB, Minnesota
1974 Wilbur Jackson, RB, San Francisco
1975 Steve Bartkowski, QB, Atlanta
1976 Sammy White, WR, Minnesota
1977 Tony Dorsett, RB, Dallas
1978 Al (Bubba) Baker, DE, Detroit
1979 Ottis Anderson, RB, St. Louis
1980 Billy Sims, RB, Detroit
1981 George Rogers, RB, New Orleans
1982 Marcus Allen, RB, LA Raiders
1983 Dan Marino, QB, Miami
1984 Louis Lipps, WR, Pittsburgh
1985 Eddie Brown, WR, Cincinnati

The Sporting News
(AFL 1960-69; AFC 1970-79)
1960 Abner Haynes, HB, Dallas Texans
1961 Earl Faison, DE, San Diego
1962 Curtis McClinton, FB, Dallas Texans
1963 Billy Joe, FB, Denver
1964 Matt Snell, FB, NY Jets
1965 Joe Namath, QB, NY Jets
1966 Bobby Burnett, HB, Buffalo
1967 Dickie Post, RB, San Diego
1968 Paul Robinson, RB, Cincinnati
1969 Carl Garrett, RB, Boston
1970 Dennis Shaw, QB, Buffalo
1971 Jim Plunkett, QB, New England
1972 Franco Harris, RB, Pittsburgh
1973 Boobie Clark, RB, Cincinnati
1974 Don Woods, RB, San Diego
1975 Robert Brazile, LB, Houston
1976 Mike Haynes, CB, New England
1977 A.J. Duhe, DE, Miami
1978 Earl Campbell, RB, Houston
1979 Jerry Butler, WR, Buffalo

COACH OF THE YEAR AWARDS
Associated Press
1974 Don Coryell, St. Louis
1975 Ted Marchibroda, Baltimore
1976 Forrest Gregg, Cleveland
1977 Robert (Red) Miller, Denver
1978 Jack Patera, Seattle
1979 Jack Pardee, Washington
1980 Chuck Knox, Buffalo
1981 Bill Walsh, San Francisco
1982 Joe Gibbs, Washington
1983 Joe Gibbs, Washington
1984 Chuck Knox, Seattle
1985 Mike Ditka, Chi. Bears

United Press International
(NFL 1955-69; NFC 1970-85)
1955 Joe Kuharich, Washington
1956 Raymond (Buddy) Parker, Detroit
1957 Paul Brown, Cleveland
1958 Weeb Ewbank, Baltimore
1959 Vince Lombardi, Green Bay
1960 Lawrence (Buck) Shaw, Philadelphia
1961 Allie Sherman, NY Giants
1962 Allie Sherman, NY Giants
1963 George Halas, Chi. Bears
1964 Don Shula, Baltimore
1965 George Halas, Chi. Bears
1966 Tom Landry, Dallas
1967 George Allen, LA Rams
1968 Don Shula, Baltimore
1969 Harry (Bud) Grant, Minnesota
1970 Alex Webster, NY Giants
1971 George Allen, Washington
1972 Dan Devine, Green Bay
1973 Chuck Knox, LA Rams
1974 Don Coryell, St. Louis
1975 Tom Landry, Dallas
1976 Jack Pardee, Chi. Bears
1977 Leeman Bennett, Atlanta
1978 Dick Vermeil, Philadelphia
1979 Jack Pardee, Washington
1980 Leeman Bennett, Atlanta
1981 Bill Walsh, San Francisco
1982 Joe Gibbs, Washington
1983 John Robinson, LA Rams
1984 Bill Walsh, San Francisco
1985 Mike Ditka, Chi. Bears

United Press International
(AFL 1960-69; AFC 1970-85)
1960 Lou Rymkus, Houston
1961 Wally Lemm, Houston
1962 Jack Faulkner, Denver
1963 Al Davis, Oakland
1964 Lou Saban, Buffalo
1965 Lou Saban, Buffalo
1966 Mike Holovak, Boston
1967 Johnny Rauch, Oakland
1968 Hank Stram, Kansas City
1969 Paul Brown, Cincinnati
1970 Don Shula, Miami
1971 Don Shula, Miami
1972 Chuck Noll, Pittsburgh
1973 John Ralston, Denver
1974 Sid Gillman, Houston
1975 Ted Marchibroda, Baltimore
1976 Chuck Fairbanks, New England
1977 Robert (Red) Miller, Denver
1978 Walt Michaels, NY Jets
1979 Sam Rutigliano, Cleveland
1980 Sam Rutigliano, Cleveland
1981 Forrest Gregg, Cincinnati
1982 Tom Flores, LA Raiders
1983 Chuck Knox, Seattle
1984 Chuck Knox, Seattle
1985 Raymond Berry, New England

The Sporting News
1970 Don Shula, Miami
1971 George Allen, Washington
1972 Don Shula, Miami
1973 Chuck Knox, LA Rams
1974 Don Coryell, St. Louis
1975 Ted Marchibroda, Baltimore
1976 Chuck Fairbanks, New England
1977 Robert (Red) Miller, Denver
1978 Jack Patera, Seattle
1979 Dick Vermeil, Philadelphia
1980 Chuck Knox, Buffalo
1981 Bill Walsh, San Francisco
1982 Joe Gibbs, Washington
1983 Joe Gibbs, Washington
1984 Chuck Knox, Seattle
1985 Mike Ditka, Chi. Bears

The Hall of Fame

HALL OF FAME CLASSES

INDUCTEES

New members of the Pro Football Hall of Fame are elected annually by a 29-member national board of selectors, made up of media representatives from every league city and the president of the Pro Football Writers Association. Currently, between four and seven new enshrinees are elected each year. An affirmative vote of approximately 80 percent is needed for election.

Any fan may nominate any eligible player, coach, or contributor simply by writing the Pro Football Hall of Fame. Players must be retired five years to be eligible, while a coach need only be retired, with no time limit specified. Contributors (owners, administrators, etc.) may be elected while they still are active.

The charter class of 17 enshrinees was elected in 1963, and the honor roll now stands at 133.

PRESENTERS

Presenters make the speeches of presentation for inductees at the annual ceremonies at the Pro Football Hall of Fame during "Football's Greatest Weekend" in Canton, Ohio. At first presenters were appointed by the Hall of Fame, but later the policy was changed allowing each nominee to choose the person who would present him for induction.

Inductee	**Presenter**
1963	
Charter members	
September 7, 1963	
Sammy Baugh	Harry Stuhldreher
Bert Bell	David McDonald
Art Rooney accepted for the late Bell	
Johnny Blood (McNally)	Supreme Court Justice Byron (Whizzer) White
Joe Carr	Earl Schreiber
Dan Tehan accepted for the late Carr	
Earl (Dutch) Clark	Senator Philip A. Hart
Harold (Red) Grange	Jimmy Conzelman
George Halas	David L. Lawrence
Mel Hein	Frank T. Bow
Wilbur (Pete) Henry	E.E. (Rip) Miller
Harry Robb accepted for the late Henry	
Cal Hubbard	Paul Kerr
Don Hutson	Dante Lavelli
Earl (Curly) Lambeau	Jim Crowley
Tim Mara	Art Daley
Jack Mara accepted for his late father	
George Preston Marshall	General Harry W. Abendroth
Bronko Nagurski	Don Miller
Ernie Nevers	Elmer Layden
Jim Thorpe	Henry A. Roemer
Pete Calac accepted for the late Thorpe	
1964	
September 6, 1964	
Jimmy Conzelman	Supreme Court Justice William O. Douglas
Ed Healey	Harry Stuhldreher
Clarke Hinkle	Bronko Nagurski
Roy (Link) Lyman	William E. Umstattd
Mike Michalske	L.C. Timm
Art Rooney, Sr.	David L. Lawrence
George Trafton	Ernie Nevers
1965	
September 12, 1965	
Guy Chamberlin	Wallace (Doc) Elliott
John (Paddy) Driscoll	Jimmy Conzelman
Dan Fortmann	Andy Kerr
Otto Graham	Paul Brown
Sid Luckman	Lou Little
Steve Van Buren	Clarke Hinkle
Bob Waterfield	Pat O'Brien
1966	
September 17, 1966	
Bill Dudley	Bob Waterfield
Joe Guyon	Jimmy Conzelman
Arnie Herber	Clarke Hinkle
Walt Kiesling	Supreme Court Justice Byron (Whizzer) White
George McAfee	Dick Gallagher
Steve Owen	Mel Hein
Jim Lee Howell accepted for the late Owen	
Hugh (Shorty) Ray	Dan Tehan
Hugh L. Ray, Jr. accepted for his late father	
Clyde (Bulldog) Turner	Ed Healey
1967	
August 5, 1967	
Chuck Bednarik	Earle (Greasy) Neale
Charles W. Bidwill, Sr.	Art Rooney, Sr.
Charles W. (Stormy) Bidwill, Jr. accepted for his late father	
Paul Brown	Otto Graham
Bobby Layne	Raymond (Buddy) Parker
Daniel F. Reeves	Bob Waterfield
Ken Strong	Chick Meehan
Joe Stydahar	Dr. Dan Fortmann
Emlen Tunnell	Father Benedict Dudley
1968	
August 3, 1968	
Cliff Battles	Edward Bennett Williams
Art Donovan	Jim Mutscheller
Elroy (Crazylegs) Hirsch	Hampton Pool
Wayne Millner	Ray Flaherty
Marion Motley	Bill Willis
Charley Trippi	Paul Shebby
Alex Wojciechowicz	Earle (Greasy) Neale
1969	
September 13, 1969	
Glen (Turk) Edwards	Mel Hein
Earle (Greasy) Neale	Chuck Bednarik
Leo Nomellini	Mrs. Vic Morabito
Joe Perry	Mrs. Tony Morabito
Ernie Stautner	Art Rooney, Sr.
1970	
August 8, 1970	
Jack Christiansen	Raymond (Buddy) Parker
Tom Fears	Hal Dean
Hugh McElhenny	Lou Spadia
Pete Pihos	Howard Brown
1971	
July 31, 1971	
Jim Brown	Ken Malloy
Bill Hewitt	Upton Bell
Mrs. Mary Ellen Concozza accepted for her late father	
Frank (Bruiser) Kinard	Jack White
Vince Lombardi	Wellington Mara
Vince Lombardi, Jr. accepted for his late father	
Andy Robustelli	J. Walter Kennedy
Y.A. Tittle	Wellington Mara
Norm Van Brocklin	Rankin Smith
1972	
July 29, 1972	
Lamar Hunt	William H. Sullivan, Jr.
Gino Marchetti	Carroll Rosenbloom
Ollie Matson	Joe Kuharich
Clarence (Ace) Parker	Jack White
1973	
July 28, 1973	
Raymond Berry	Weeb Ewbank
Jim Parker	Woody Hayes
Joe Schmidt	William Clay Ford
1974	
July 27, 1974	
Tony Canadeo	Dick Bourguignon
Bill George	Ed McCaskey
Lou Groza	Paul Brown
Dick (Night Train) Lane	W.E. Pigford
1975	
August 2, 1975	
Roosevelt Brown	Talmadge Hill
George Connor	George Halas
Dante Lavelli	Paul Brown
Lenny Moore	Andy Stopper
1976	
July 24, 1976	
Ray Flaherty	Jim Barber
Len Ford	Ted McIntyre
Debbie Ford accepted for her late father	
Jim Taylor	Marie Lombardi
1977	
July 30, 1977	
Frank Gifford	Wellington Mara
Forrest Gregg	Marie Lombardi
Gale Sayers	George Halas
Bart Starr	Bill Moseley
Bill Willis	Paul Brown
1978	
July 29, 1978	
Lance Alworth	Al Davis
Weeb Ewbank	Paul Brown
Alphonse (Tuffy) Leemans	Peter Guzy
Ray Nitschke	Phil Bengtson
Larry Wilson	Jack Curtice
1979	
July 28, 1979	
Dick Butkus	Pete Elliott
Yale Lary	Garrard (Buster) Ramsey
Ron Mix	Joe Madro
Johnny Unitas	Frank Gitschier
1980	
August 2, 1980	
Herb Adderley	Willie Davis
David (Deacon) Jones	George Allen
Bob Lilly	Tom Landry
Jim Otto	Al Davis
1981	
August 1, 1981	
Morris (Red) Badgro	Mel Hein
George Blanda	Al Davis
Willie Davis	Eddie Robinson
Jim Ringo	Willard (Whiz) Rinehart
1982	
August 7, 1982	
Doug Atkins	Ed McCaskey
Sam Huff	Tom Landry
George Musso	George Halas
Merlin Olsen	Tony Knap
1983	
July 30, 1983	
Bobby Bell	Hank Stram
Sid Gillman	Joe Madro
Sonny Jurgensen	Edward Bennett Williams
Bobby Mitchell	Edward Bennett Williams
Paul Warfield	Gene Slaughter
1984	
July 28, 1984	
Willie Brown	Al Davis
Mike McCormack	Paul Brown
Charley Taylor	Tom Skinner
Arnie Weinmeister	John A. Cherberg
1985	
August 3, 1985	
Frank Gatski	Abe Gibron
Joe Namath	Larry Bruno
Pete Rozelle	Tex Schramm
O.J. Simpson	Lou Saban
Roger Staubach	Tom Landry
1986	
August 2, 1986	
Paul Hornung	Max McGee
Ken Houston	Wally Lemm
Willie Lanier	Lamar Hunt
Fran Tarkenton	Max Winter
Doak Walker	Bobby Layne

Herb Adderley

Cornerback. 6-1, 200. Born in Philadelphia, Pennsylvania, June 8, 1939. Michigan State. Inducted in 1980. 1961-69 Green Bay Packers, 1970-72 Dallas Cowboys.

Herb Adderley came out of Michigan State in 1961 as a first-round draft choice with a reputation as an offensive performer. Though he was switched to defense in the NFL, Adderley did compile some impressive offensive figures for a cornerback. Of his six interceptions in 1965, he returned three for touchdowns, which stood as an NFL single-season record until 1971. Counting kickoff returns and interceptions, Adderley scored nine touchdowns. He played in five consecutive Pro Bowls (1963-67) and was named all-pro four times. While with the Packers he played in Super Bowls I and II. He announced his retirement following the 1969 season, a year in which he led the NFL in interception-return yardage, but decided to continue playing after he was traded to the Dallas Cowboys. He played three years with Dallas and appeared in Super Bowls V and VI.

INTERCEPTIONS

Year	Team	No.	Yards	Avg.	Long	TD
1961	Green Bay	1	9	9.0	9	0
1962	Green Bay	7	132	18.9	50t	1
1963	Green Bay	5	86	17.2	39	0
1964	Green Bay	4	56	14.0	35	0
1965	Green Bay	6	175	29.2	44	3
1966	Green Bay	4	125	31.3	68t	1
1967	Green Bay	4	16	4.0	12t	1
1968	Green Bay	3	27	9.0	17	0
1969	Green Bay	5	169	33.8	80t	1
1970	Dallas	3	69	23.0	30	0
1971	Dallas	6	182	30.3	46	0
1972	Dallas	0	0	0.0	0	0
Totals		48	1,046	21.8	80t	7

KICKOFF RETURNS

120, 3,080 Yards, 25.7 Avg., 103 Long, 2 TD

Lance Alworth

Flanker. 6-0, 184. Born in Houston, Texas, August 3, 1940. Arkansas. Inducted in 1978. 1962-70 San Diego Chargers, 1971-72 Dallas Cowboys.

Lance Alworth was the first American Football League player to be inducted into the Hall of Fame. An All-America halfback at Arkansas, he was drafted by the Oakland Raiders in 1962 and immediately traded to the Chargers for three players. Alworth was nicknamed "Bambi" because of his boyish looks, speed, grace, and leaping ability. He was the AFL's leading receiver three times (1966, 1968-69) and was named all-AFL seven consecutive years. With San Diego (from 1962-69) he caught passes in 96 consecutive games, surpassing Hall of Fame member Don Hutson's NFL record of 95 games (the record has since been broken). He also set a record by gaining more than 1,000 yards receiving in seven consecutive seasons. In nine years with the Chargers he played on one AFL championship team (1963) and two Western Division champions (1964-65). With Dallas, he scored the first touchdown in Super Bowl VI, which Dallas won 24-3 against Miami.

RECEIVING

Year	Team	No.	Yards	Avg.	Long	TD
1962	San Diego	10	226	22.6	67	3
1963	San Diego	61	1,205	19.8	85	11
1964	San Diego	61	1,235	20.2	82	13
1965	San Diego	69	1,602	23.2	85	14
1966	San Diego	73	1,383	18.9	78	13
1967	San Diego	52	1,010	19.4	71t	9
1968	San Diego	68	1,312	19.3	80t	10
1969	San Diego	64	1,003	15.7	76t	4
1970	San Diego	35	608	17.4	80t	4
1971	Dallas	34	487	14.3	26	2
1972	Dallas	15	195	13.0	30	2
Totals		542	10,266	18.9	85	85

RUSHING

24 Att., 129 Yards, 5.4 Avg., 35 Long, 2 TD

PUNT RETURNS

29, 309 Yards, 10.7 Avg., 61 Long, 0 TD

KICKOFF RETURNS

10, 216 Yards, 21.6 Avg., 34 Long, 0 TD

Doug Atkins

Defensive end. 6-8, 275. Born in Humboldt, Tennessee, May 8, 1930. Tennessee. Inducted in 1982. 1953-54 Cleveland Browns, 1955-66 Chicago Bears, 1967-69 New Orleans Saints.

Only one lineman (Jim Marshall, 1960-79) in the history of the NFL played more than the 17 seasons completed by Doug Atkins. Few played as well. One of only a handful of stars of the 1950s and 1960s who wouldn't be undersize by today's standards, he combined strength, size, skill, agility, and aggressiveness. Atkins was a relentless pass rusher, often hurdling blockers to get to the quarterback. He was equally as strong against the running game. Atkins, who originally attended college on a basketball scholarship, was an all-pro in 1960, 1961, and 1963. He was named to the Pro Bowl eight times in a nine-year span (1958-66) and was selected as the outstanding lineman of the 1959 game. Thought to be near the end of his career when traded to the expansion New Orleans Saints in 1967, Atkins turned in three strong seasons before retiring. At that time, his 205 games were second only to kicker-tackle Lou Groza's 216 in the NFL length-of-service record column.

Morris (Red) Badgro

End. 6-0, 190. Born in Orilla, Washington, December 1, 1902. USC. Inducted in 1981. 1927 New York Yankees, 1930-35 New York Giants, 1936 Brooklyn Dodgers.

NFL players in Red Badgro's era were sixty-minute men. They played on offense, defense, and special teams. Their statistics wouldn't elicit a second look in most cases today, but there were those who were a cut above in the league's pioneer days. Badgro was one of them. Badgro was a versatile athlete, who went to USC on a basketball scholarship. His pro football career began in 1927 with the New York Yankees and was renewed with the Giants in 1930 after two years in professional baseball. Badgro was a rugged blocker and tough defender, who played his way into the record books as a receiver. He scored the first touchdown in the 1933 NFL Championship Game and tied for the league lead in receptions in 1934 with 16. He was on the all-pro teams in 1931, 1933, and 1934.

Cliff Battles

Halfback. 6-1, 201. Born in Akron, Ohio, May 1, 1910. Died April 27, 1981. West Virginia Wesleyan. Inducted in 1968. 1932 Boston Braves, 1933-36 Boston Redskins, 1937 Washington Redskins.

Cliff Battles played only six seasons in the NFL, but he gained 3,622 yards for the Braves and Redskins, finishing his career as the NFL's all-time rushing leader. Big and fast, he was the first NFL runner to rush for more than 200 yards in a game, gaining 215 in 16 carries against the Giants in 1933. A Phi Beta Kappa scholar, he was one of the first professional stars to come from a small college, West Virginia Wesleyan. His final season, 1937, was a memorable one in which he gained 874 yards, won his second rushing title, and earned all-pro honors for the third time in six years.

RUSHING

Year	Team	Att.	Yards	Avg.	TD
1932	Boston	148	576	3.9	3
1933	Boston	146	737	5.0	3
1934	Boston	103	511	5.0	6
1935	Boston	84	310	3.7	1
1936	Boston	176	614	3.5	5
1937	Washington	216	874	4.0	5
Totals		873	3,622	4.1	23

SCORING

31 TD, 1 FG, 1 PAT, 190 Points

PASSING

107 Att., 36 Comp., 476 Yards, 1 TD

RECEIVING

37, 546 Yards, 14.8 Avg., 54 Long, 3 TD

Sammy Baugh

Halfback-Quarterback. 6-2, 180. Born in Temple, Texas, March 17, 1914. TCU. Inducted in 1963. 1937-52 Washington Redskins.

In his 16-year career in the pros, Sammy Baugh led the league in passing six times. When he retired he held NFL career records for pass attempts, completions, passing yards, touchdown passes, and completion percentage. He also held season marks for completions and yards. All of that is even more remarkable when you consider that he came to pro football from TCU as a Single-Wing tailback and had to make a transition to T-formation quarterback halfway through his career. Baugh set the NFL record for career and season punting average, made 28 interceptions while playing safety in the one-platoon era (even though the category wasn't officially recorded the first three years of his career), and in 1943 led the league in passing, punting, and interceptions. Baugh later served as the first-ever head coach of the New York Titans and as head coach of the Houston Oilers.

PASSING

Year	Team	Att.	Comp.	Yards	TD	Int.
1937	Washington	171	81	1,127	8	14
1938	Washington	128	63	853	5	11
1939	Washington	96	53	518	6	9
1940	Washington	177	111	1,367	12	10
1941	Washington	193	106	1,236	10	19
1942	Washington	225	132	1,524	16	11
1943	Washington	239	133	1,754	23	19
1944	Washington	146	82	849	4	8
1945	Washington	182	128	1,669	11	4
1946	Washington	161	87	1,163	8	17
1947	Washington	354	210	2,938	25	15
1948	Washington	315	185	2,599	22	23
1949	Washington	255	145	1,903	18	14
1950	Washington	166	90	1,130	10	11
1951	Washington	154	67	1,104	7	17
1952	Washington	33	20	152	2	1
Totals		2,995	1,693	21,886	187	203

PUNTING

Year	Team	No.	Yards	Avg.	Long	Blk.
1937	Washington					
1938	Washington					
1939	Washington	26		38.0	69	
1940	Washington	35		51.3	85	
1941	Washington	30		48.7	75	0
1942	Washington	37		46.6	74	0
1943	Washington	50		45.9	81	3
1944	Washington	44		40.6	76	1
1945	Washington	33		43.3	57	0
1946	Washington	33		45.1	60	0
1947	Washington	35		43.7	67	2
1948	Washington	0	0	0.0	0	0
1949	Washington	1	53	53.0	53	0
1950	Washington	9		39.1	58	1
1951	Washington	4		55.3	58	0
1952	Washington	1	48	48.0	48	0
Totals		338	15,245	45.1	85	7

INTERCEPTIONS

Year	Team	No.	Yards	Avg.	Long	TD
1937	Washington					
1938	Washington					
1939	Washington					
1940	Washington					
1941	Washington	4	83	20.8	35	0
1942	Washington	5	77	15.4	29	0
1943	Washington	11	112	10.2	23	0
1944	Washington	4	21	5.3	18	0
1945	Washington	4	114	28.5	74	0
1946	Washington					
1947	Washington					
1948	Washington					
1949	Washington					
1950	Washington					
1951	Washington					
1952	Washington					
Totals		28	407	14.5	74	0

RUSHING

324 Att., 325 Yards, 1.0 Avg., 41 Long, 9 TD

SCORING

9 TD, 1 PAT, 55 Points

Chuck Bednarik

Center-Linebacker. 6-3, 230. Born in Bethlehem, Pennsylvania, May 1, 1925. Pennsylvania. Inducted in 1967. 1949-62 Philadelphia Eagles.

Pro football was a highly specialized game by 1960, but Chuck Bednarik, at 35, played both offensively and defensively in a string of key games that helped the Eagles into the NFL title game, where he played more than 50 minutes. His tackle of Jim Taylor, nine yards short of the goal line, preserved Philadelphia's win over Green Bay on the game's final play. In 14 seasons, the durable Bednarik missed only three games. He won all-pro honors both as a center and a linebacker. A two-time All-America at Pennsylvania, Bednarik was the NFL's bonus draft choice in 1949. He played in eight Pro Bowls and was honored as player of the game in the 1954 game.

Bert Bell

Commissioner-Team owner. Born in Philadelphia, Pennsylvania, February 25, 1895. Died October 11, 1959. Pennsylvania. Inducted in 1963. 1933-40 Philadelphia Eagles, 1941-46 Pittsburgh Steelers.

Bert Bell, who was elected Commissioner in 1946, saw the NFL through a bitter and costly power struggle with the rival All-America Football Conference. Bell provided strong leadership until his death in the grandstands at an Eagles-Steelers game in 1959. He was a football man most of his life, having played at Pennsylvania and later coaching there and at other schools. Bell, who took charge of the newly formed Philadelphia Eagles in 1933, sought to increase competitive balance in the NFL by proposing the college player draft in 1935. After serving the Eagles as general manager, ticket manager, publicity director, and head coach, he joined the Steelers as co-owner and head coach in 1941. In later work as Commissioner he laid down strong anti-gambling policies and instituted the home television blackout of NFL games.

Bobby Bell

Linebacker. 6-4, 225. Born in Shelby, North Carolina, June 17, 1940. Minnesota. Inducted in 1983. 1963-74 Kansas City Chiefs.

The only problem Kansas City head coach Hank Stram ever had with Bobby Bell was deciding where to play him. Bell had the strength of a lineman, the quickness of a back, and the ability to play almost any position. After winning the Outland Trophy as a tackle at Minnesota, Bell shocked the football world by signing with the Chiefs instead of the Minnesota Vikings, who also had drafted him. After two years of alternating between defensive end (where he was selected all-AFL) and linebacker, Bell finally settled at linebacker. For six consecutive years, he was all-AFL and played in the AFL All-Star Game. He was selected as the AFL's defensive player of the year in 1969 and was chosen on the AFL's all-time team. After the merger, he made all-pro three times and played in three AFC-NFC Pro Bowls. Bell not only finished his career with 26 career interceptions and eight touchdowns scored, until he retired he continued to play center on field goals and punts.

Raymond Berry

End. 6-2, 187. Born in Corpus Christi, Texas, February 27, 1933. SMU. Inducted in 1973. 1955-67 Baltimore Colts.

Raymond Berry proved that dedication, concentration, and long hours of practice can compensate for limited physical skills. He had average size and speed, but when he retired he was the leading receiver in the history of the NFL, with 631 receptions. Berry was chosen as a future out of SMU; in the NFL, he worked with Johnny Unitas to form a remarkable passing combination, perfecting the sideline pass. Berry's 12 receptions in the memorable 1958 NFL Championship Game are still a record. Berry was far ahead of his time in his training methods—he used gadgets such as tinted goggles to gain an advantage over his opponents, practiced long after regular sessions were over, and did constant hand and wrist exercises to prevent fumbling. In 13 years, he fumbled only once. Berry led the NFL in receiving three times, was on all-pro teams three times, and played in five Pro Bowls. In 1984, he was named the head coach of New England, and the next year he took the Patriots to their first-ever Super Bowl.

RECEIVING

Year	Team	No.	Yards	Avg.	Long	TD
1955	Baltimore	13	205	15.8	45	0
1956	Baltimore	37	601	16.2	54	2
1957	Baltimore	47	800	17.0	67t	6
1958	Baltimore	56	794	14.2	54	9
1959	Baltimore	66	959	14.5	55t	14
1960	Baltimore	74	1,298	17.5	70t	10
1961	Baltimore	75	873	11.6	44	0
1962	Baltimore	51	687	13.5	37	3
1963	Baltimore	44	703	16.0	64t	3
1964	Baltimore	43	663	15.4	46	6
1965	Baltimore	58	739	12.7	40	7
1966	Baltimore	56	786	14.0	40t	7
1967	Baltimore	11	167	15.2	40	1
Totals		631	9,275	14.7	70t	68

SCORING

68 TD, 408 Points

Charles W. Bidwill, Sr.

Team owner. Born in Chicago, Illinois, September 16, 1895. Died April 19, 1947. Loyola (Chicago). Inducted in 1967. 1933-47 Chicago Cardinals.

Charles Bidwill's interest in pro football preceded his ownership of the Chicago Cardinals by some years. His financial support enabled George Halas to retain ownership of the Chicago Bears during the early days of the Depression. Bidwill took over the Cardinals in 1933. The team lost games but he kept his faith in the sport. After World War II, Bidwill signed Charley Trippi to a $100,000 contract to complete a "dream backfield" that also included Paul Christman, Marshall Goldberg, and Pat Harder. But Bidwill wasn't around to see his team win the NFL championship in 1947. He died in April of that year. The ownership of the team passed to his wife, Violet, and eventually to his sons, Charles, Jr., and Bill. A non-conformist, Bidwill was often called "Blue Shirt" Bidwill because he spurned traditional white shirts and businessmen's shoes in favor of blue shirts and high boots.

George Blanda

Quarterback-Kicker. 6-2, 215. Born in Youngwood, Pennsylvania, September 17, 1927. Kentucky. Inducted in 1981. 1949-58 Chicago Bears, 1950 Baltimore Colts, 1960-66 Houston Oilers, 1967-75 Oakland Raiders.

George Blanda became a folk hero at age 43, when he passed or kicked the Oakland Raiders to a final-second tie and four last-minute victories in a five-week period. He played five more seasons, becoming the oldest player in NFL history. Blanda's career lasted 26 seasons, an NFL record. He played 10 years with the Bears, becoming the team's all-time scoring leader. Blanda signed with Houston for the AFL's first season and led the Oilers to the 1960 and 1961 championships. In 1961, he set a record with 36 touchdown passes. He retired as pro football's career scoring leader.

SCORING

Year	Team	TD	FG	PAT	Points
1949	Chi. Bears	1	7-15	0-0	27
1950	Baltimore	0	0-0	0-0	0
	Chi. Bears	0	6-15	0-0	18
1951	Chi. Bears	0	6-17	26-26	44
1952	Chi. Bears	1	6-25	30-30	54
1953	Chi. Bears	0	7-20	27-27	48
1954	Chi. Bears	0	8-16	23-23	47
1955	Chi. Bears	2	11-16	37-37	82
1956	Chi. Bears	0	12-28	45-47	81
1957	Chi. Bears	1	14-26	23-23	71
1958	Chi. Bears	0	11-23	36-37	69
1959	Did not play pro football				
1960	Houston	4	15-34	46-47	115
1961	Houston	0	16-26	64-65	112
1962	Houston	0	11-26	48-49	81
1963	Houston	0	9-22	39-39	66
1964	Houston	0	13-29	37-38	76
1965	Houston	0	11-21	28-28	61
1966	Houston	0	16-30	39-40	87
1967	Oakland	0	20-30	56-57	116
1968	Oakland	0	21-34	54-54	117
1969	Oakland	0	20-37	45-45	105
1970	Oakland	0	16-29	36-36	84
1971	Oakland	0	15-22	41-42	86
1972	Oakland	0	17-26	44-44	95
1973	Oakland	0	23-33	31-31	100
1974	Oakland	0	11-17	44-46	77
1975	Oakland	0	13-21	44-48	83
Totals		9	335-638	943-959	2,002

PASSING

Year	Team	Att.	Comp.	Yards	TD	Int.
1949	Chi. Bears	21	9	197	0	5
1950	Baltimore	0	0	0	0	0
	Chi. Bears	0	0	0	0	0
1951	Chi. Bears	0	0	0	0	0
1952	Chi. Bears	131	47	664	8	11
1953	Chi. Bears	362	169	2,164	14	23
1954	Chi. Bears	281	131	1,929	15	17
1955	Chi. Bears	97	42	459	4	7
1956	Chi. Bears	69	37	439	7	4
1957	Chi. Bears	19	8	65	0	3
1958	Chi. Bears	7	2	19	0	0
1959	Did not play pro football					
1960	Houston	363	169	2,413	24	22
1961	Houston	362	187	3,330	36	22
1962	Houston	418	197	2,810	27	42
1963	Houston	423	224	3,003	24	25
1964	Houston	505	262	3,287	17	27
1965	Houston	442	186	2,542	20	30
1966	Houston	271	122	1,764	17	21
1967	Oakland	38	15	285	3	3
1968	Oakland	49	30	522	6	2
1969	Oakland	13	6	73	2	1
1970	Oakland	55	29	461	6	5
1971	Oakland	58	32	378	4	6
1972	Oakland	15	5	77	1	0
1973	Oakland	0	0	0	0	0
1974	Oakland	4	1	28	1	0
1975	Oakland	3	1	11	0	1
Totals		4,007	1,911	26,920	236	277

RUSHING

135 Att., 344 Yards, 2.5 Avg., 19 Long, 9 TD

PUNTING

20, 39.3 Avg., Long 57, 0 Blk.

Johnny Blood (McNally)

Halfback. 6-0, 185. Born in New Richmond, Wisconsin, November 27, 1903. Died November 28, 1985. St. John's (Minnesota). Inducted in 1963. 1925-26 Milwaukee Badgers, 1926-27 Duluth Eskimos, 1928 Pottsville Maroons, 1929-33, 1935-36 Green Bay Packers, 1934 Pittsburgh Pirates; player-coach 1937-39 Pittsburgh Pirates.

Johnny Blood took his name from a movie marquee for the Rudolph Valentino film, *Blood and Sand*. A free spirit, Blood was also a superbly gifted athlete. He made a reputation as a pass receiver and a breakaway runner when straight-ahead power football was still the accepted method of attack. Despite his eccentric behavior, he was a vital part of four Green Bay Packers championship teams. He scored 37 touchdowns and 224 points and played 15 seasons, a record for the most years in the league at the time he retired. His last three years were spent as player-coach with Pittsburgh.

Jim Brown

Fullback. 6-2, 232. Born in St. Simons, Georgia, February 17, 1936. Syracuse. Inducted in 1971. 1957-65 Cleveland Browns.

The amazingly durable Jim Brown never missed a game in nine years of NFL play, during which he gained a then-record 12,312 rushing yards. A player who had the perfect combination of size, speed, and power, Brown is considered by many the finest runner ever in football. He led the NFL in rushing in eight of his nine seasons, made an all-pro team eight times, and played in nine straight Pro Bowls. He scored 756 points, the highest NFL total by a non-kicker. Only twice did he fail to go over the 1,000-yard rushing mark, his first season and 1962, when he played with a severely sprained wrist. The former Syracuse fullback rushed for more than 100 yards a game 58 times, almost half his pro starts. Brown still holds the NFL career record of 5.22 yards per carry. He retired at the top of his game, prior to the 1966 season, to pursue an acting career.

RUSHING

Year	Team	Att.	Yards	Avg.	Long	TD
1957	Cleveland	202	942	4.7	69t	9
1958	Cleveland	257	1,527	5.9	65t	17
1959	Cleveland	290	1,329	4.6	70t	14
1960	Cleveland	215	1,257	5.8	71t	9
1961	Cleveland	305	1,408	4.6	38	8
1962	Cleveland	230	996	4.3	31	13
1963	Cleveland	291	1,863	6.4	80t	12
1964	Cleveland	280	1,446	5.2	71	7
1965	Cleveland	289	1,544	5.3	67	17
Totals		2,359	12,312	5.2	80t	106

RECEIVING

Year	Team	No.	Yards	Avg.	Long	TD
1957	Cleveland	16	55	3.4	12	1
1958	Cleveland	16	138	8.6	46	1
1959	Cleveland	24	190	7.9	25	0
1960	Cleveland	19	204	10.7	37t	2
1961	Cleveland	46	459	10.0	77t	2
1962	Cleveland	47	517	11.0	53t	5
1963	Cleveland	24	268	11.2	83t	3
1964	Cleveland	36	340	9.4	40t	2
1965	Cleveland	34	328	9.6	32t	4
Totals		262	2,499	9.5	83t	20

SCORING

126 TD, 756 Points

KICKOFF RETURNS

29, 648 Yards, 22.3 Avg., 35 Long, 0 TD

Paul Brown

Coach. Born in Norwalk, Ohio, September 7, 1908. Miami (Ohio). Inducted in 1967. 1946-62 Cleveland Browns, 1968-75 Cincinnati Bengals.

Many of the things that are part of pro football today—full-time coaching staffs, calling plays via messengers, precise pass routes, classroom study, and extensive college scouting—were either Paul Brown innovations or were raised to a higher level of efficiency by him. Brown was hired by the Cleveland Browns of the newly organized All-America Football Conference in 1945, when he was still coaching at Great Lakes Naval Training Station. He had earned a national reputation when he guided Ohio State to the 1942 national championship. He took over in Cleveland in 1946, and the Browns won league championships all four seasons of the AAFC's existence. In 1950, after the AAFC merged with the NFL, Brown and the Browns again won the championship, and they were in the title game the next five seasons. Brown's Cleveland teams won three NFL titles and seven divisional championships in 13 seasons. Only once—the year after Otto Graham retired—did a Paul Brown Cleveland team finish below .500. Brown began a second successful coaching career with the Cincinnati Bengals in 1968, a year after his induction into the Hall of Fame. It took Brown only three years to win the AFC Central title in 1970, the quickest ever for an expansion team in the NFL. He retired as a coach after the 1975 season.

Roosevelt Brown

Offensive tackle. 6-3, 255. Born in Charlottesville, Virginia, October 20, 1932. Morgan State. Inducted in 1975. 1953-65 New York Giants.

Almost any biography of Roosevelt (Rosey) Brown mentions him as one of the NFL's most notable "sleeper" draft choices. He was picked on the twenty-seventh round in 1953. He became a starter his first season and remained so for 13 years. From 1956 through 1963, Brown made all-pro each year; he also played in nine Pro Bowl games. The Giants made excellent use of Brown's outstanding speed by designing special plays that used him as a pulling blocker from his tackle position. Prior to this, pulling was done mainly by offensive guards. Brown was also used defensively on goal-line stands. Phlebitis forced his retirement in 1966.

Willie Brown

Cornerback. 6-2, 190. Born in Yazoo City, Mississippi, December 2, 1940. Grambling. Inducted in 1984. 1963-66 Denver Broncos, 1967-78 Oakland Raiders.

Willie Brown went from almost not making it in professional football to being one of the premier defensive backs of all time. He reported to Houston in 1963 as a free agent but was cut before the season began. He was picked up at the last minute by Denver, and the next year was named all-AFL after intercepting nine passes, including four in one game against the Jets. Brown was traded to Oakland in 1967 and started a string of seven consecutive years in which he played in either the AFL All-Star Game or the AFC-NFC Pro Bowl. Brown saved his biggest moment for his biggest game. In Super Bowl XI, he returned an interception 75 yards for the Raiders' last score in a 32-14 Oakland victory. He finished his career with 54 interceptions.

INTERCEPTIONS

Year	Team	No.	Yards	Avg.	Long	TD
1963	Denver	1	0	1.0	0	0
1964	Denver	9	140	15.6	45	0
1965	Denver	2	18	9.0	18	0
1966	Denver	3	37	12.3	31	0
1967	Oakland	7	33	4.7	25t	1
1968	Oakland	2	27	13.5	27t	1
1969	Oakland	5	111	22.2	30	0
1970	Oakland	3	0	0.0	0	0
1971	Oakland	2	2	1.0	2	0
1972	Oakland	4	26	6.5	13	0
1973	Oakland	3	−1	−0.3	0	0
1974	Oakland	1	31	31.0	31	0
1975	Oakland	4	−1	−0.3	0	0
1976	Oakland	3	25	8.3	22	0
1977	Oakland	4	24	6.0	18	0
1978	Oakland	1	0	0.0	0	0
Totals		54	472	8.7	45	2

Dick Butkus

Linebacker. 6-3, 245. Born in Chicago, Illinois, December 9, 1942. Illinois. Inducted in 1979. 1965-73 Chicago Bears.

When he was 10 years old, Dick Butkus decided on his future occupation—pro football player. He pursued his goal through an all-state scholastic career and an All-America collegiate career at Illinois. Butkus joined the Bears as a first-round draft choice in 1965—the same season that Gale Sayers, also a member of the Hall of Fame, was another Bears first-round selection. Butkus played in eight Pro Bowl games in his nine-year career, which was shortened considerably by injuries. He also was named to the all-pro team six times. Butkus is considered by many to have been the game's premier middle linebacker and most intimidating player. The 25 opponents' fumbles Butkus recovered during his career is the second-highest total in league history.

Tony Canadeo

Halfback. 5-11, 195. Born in Chicago, Illinois, May 5, 1919. Gonzaga. Inducted in 1974. 1941-44, 1946-52 Green Bay Packers.

Tony Canadeo was a versatile, two-way performer. He ran, passed, punted, returned punts and kickoffs, caught passes, and played defense. He was adept at all of them. Taking all categories into account, Canadeo averaged 75 yards a game over his 11 seasons. Before entering the service, he was the Packers' leading passer. Upon his return, he was their heavy-duty runner. In 1949, he became only the third man in NFL history to rush for more than 1,000 yards in a season; he rushed for 4,197 yards in his career. A fiery competitor, Canadeo refused to let tacklers help him to his feet.

RUSHING

Year	Team	Att.	Yards	Avg.	Long	TD
1941	Green Bay	43	137	3.2	16	3
1942	Green Bay	89	272	3.1	50	3
1943	Green Bay	94	489	5.2	35	3
1944	Green Bay	31	149	4.8	34	0
1945	Military service					
1946	Green Bay	122	476	3.9	27	0
1947	Green Bay	103	464	4.5	35	2
1948	Green Bay	123	589	4.8	49	4
1949	Green Bay	208	1,052	5.1	54	4
1950	Green Bay	93	247	2.6	15	4
1951	Green Bay	54	131	2.4	15	1
1952	Green Bay	65	191	2.9	35	2
Totals		1,025	4,197	4.1	54	26

PASSING
268 Att., 105 Comp., 1,642 Yards, 16 TD, 20 Int.

RECEIVING
69, 579 Yards, 8.4 Avg., 46 Long, 5 TD

INTERCEPTIONS
9, 129 Yards, 14.3 Avg., 35 Long, 0 TD

PUNTING
45, 1,669 Yards, 37.1 Avg., 62 Long, 0 Blk.

PUNT RETURNS
46, 513 Yards, 11.2 Avg., 26 Long, 0 TD

KICKOFF RETURNS
71, 1,626 Yards, 22.9 Avg., 55 Long, 0 TD

SCORING
31 TD, 186 Points

Joe Carr

NFL President. Born in Columbus, Ohio, October 22, 1880. Died May 20, 1939. Did not attend college. Inducted in 1963. President, 1921-39 National Football League.

A sports promoter and sportswriter, Joe Carr was involved in pro football long before there was an NFL. He founded the Columbus Panhandles in 1904. Carr was also a pro basketball and minor league baseball executive. In 1921 he became President of the American Professional Football Association, which changed its name to the National Football League in 1922. During his tenure, the league moved from sandlots and rickety ballparks to the nation's largest stadiums. In 1927, Carr was responsible for the re-organization of the NFL and its reduction to a manageable 12 teams. Carr was a pioneer in other areas, too. He introduced the standard player contract and barred any collegiate player from signing with an NFL team until his class graduated. As President, he set down guidelines followed in later years by other NFL leaders. His administration, regarded as strict but fair, ended with his death in 1939.

Guy Chamberlin

End-Coach. 6-2, 210. Born in Blue Springs, Nebraska, January 16, 1894. Died April 4, 1967. Nebraska. Inducted in 1965. 1920 Decatur Staleys, 1921 Chicago Staleys, 1922-23 Canton Bulldogs, 1924 Cleveland Bulldogs, 1925-26 Frankford Yellow Jackets, 1927 Chicago Cardinals.

Wherever Guy Chamberlin went, victories seemed to follow. He established a reputation as a fine pass-catcher at a time when passing wasn't commonplace. And he also turned end-around plays into long gainers. It was said he was never hurt, as a collegian or pro. In 1920 and 1921 Chamberlin was paired with another of football's biggest names—George Halas—at end for the Decatur and Chicago Staleys. The ex-Nebraska All-America served as a part-time player as well as a coach from 1922-26, when he helped win four NFL championships with three different teams—Canton, Cleveland, and Frankford. At Cleveland in 1924, Chamberlin was one of the first coaches to institute planned, daily practices. His coaching record was 60-16-6. Chamberlin was named as an end on the all-decade team of the 1920s.

Jack Christiansen

Defensive Back. 6-1, 185. Born in Sublette, Kansas, December 20, 1928. Died June 29, 1986. Colorado State. Inducted in 1970. 1951-58 Detroit Lions.

As a rookie in 1951, Jack Christiansen set an NFL record by returning four punts for touchdowns. The record wasn't matched until Denver's Rick Upchurch tied it in 1976. Christiansen's two touchdowns in a single game on punt returns in 1951 set another record. In eight years, Christiansen scored a record eight times on punt returns. He led the NFL in interceptions in 1953 and 1957 on the way to a career total of 46. The Lions' secondary was called Chris's Crew after him. He was one of the first defensive specialists to become a dangerous weapon. Opponents passed and punted the ball away from him.

INTERCEPTIONS

Year	Team	No.	Yards	Avg.	Long	TD
1951	Detroit	2	53	26.5	53	0
1952	Detroit	2	47	23.5	32	0
1953	Detroit	12	238	19.8	92t	1
1954	Detroit	8	84	10.5	30t	1
1955	Detroit	3	49	16.3	29	0
1956	Detroit	8	109	13.6	33	0
1957	Detroit	10	137	13.7	52	1
1958	Detroit	1	0	0.0	0	0
Totals		46	717	15.6	92t	3

PUNT RETURNS

Year	Team	No.	Yards	Avg.	Long	TD
1951	Detroit	18	343	19.1	89t	4
1952	Detroit	15	322	21.5	79t	2
1953	Detroit	8	22	2.8	10	0
1954	Detroit	23	225	9.8	61t	1
1955	Detroit	12	87	7.3	42	0
1956	Detroit	6	73	12.2	66t	1
1957	Detroit	3	12	4.0	8	0
1958	Detroit	0	0	0.0	0	0
Totals		85	1,084	12.8	89t	8

KICKOFF RETURNS

59, 1,329 Yards, 22.5 Avg., 46 Long, 0 TD

Earl (Dutch) Clark

Quarterback-Halfback. 6-0, 185. Born in Fowler, Colorado, October 11, 1906. Died August 5, 1978. Colorado College. Inducted in 1963. 1931-32 Portsmouth Spartans, 1934-38 Detroit Lions.

Earl (Dutch) Clark was a scoring threat from anywhere, in any manner. As a tailback in the Single Wing, he was a legitimate triple-threat. He scored by running, passing, and kicking. He was the last of the NFL's dropkickers. He was the Lions' player-coach in 1937 and 1938. Clark, the only All-America football player ever produced at Colorado College, made an all-pro team in six of his seven seasons. He led NFL scorers three times—in 1932, 1935, and 1936. Clark also served as head coach of the Cleveland Rams from 1939-42.

RUSHING

Year	Team	Att.	Yards	Avg.	TD
1931	Portsmouth				
1932	Portsmouth	111	461	4.2	2
1933	Did not play football				
1934	Detroit	123	763	6.2	6
1935	Detroit	120	412	3.4	4
1936	Detroit	123	628	5.1	6
1937	Detroit	96	468	4.9	5
1938	Detroit	7	25	3.6	0
Totals		580	2,757	4.8	23

PASSING

249 Att., 114 Comp., 1,507 Yards, 10 TD, 14 Int.

RECEIVING

29, 341 Yards, 11.8 Avg., 3 TD

SCORING

42 TD, 15 FG, 72 PAT, 369 Points

George Connor

Tackle-Linebacker. 6-3, 240. Born in Chicago, Illinois, January 1, 1925. Holy Cross, Notre Dame. Inducted in 1975. 1948-55 Chicago Bears.

George Connor was an All-America at both Holy Cross and Notre Dame. He was all-pro at three positions: offensive tackle, defensive tackle, and linebacker. Connor played for Holy Cross in 1942-43 and for Notre Dame in 1946-47. He was drafted by the New York Giants in 1946, when his original Holy Cross class graduated. The rights to him were traded by the Giants in 1948 to the Boston Yanks for quarterback Paul Governali, and the Yanks in turn traded his rights to the Bears for end-tackle Mike Yarmaluk. Connor joined the Bears as a two-way tackle. But in 1949 the Bears moved him to linebacker, where he became one of the prototypes for the big, fast, agile, and aggressive men who play that position in today's NFL. He was strong enough to meet and stop the power plays smaller linebackers couldn't handle, and he also was an intelligent player who was good at reading plays. In three years, he made all-pro teams on both offense and defense, and he played in four Pro Bowls. A leg injury ended his career at age 30.

Jimmy Conzelman

Quarterback-Coach-Team owner. 6-0, 180. Born in St. Louis, Missouri, March 6, 1898. Died July 31, 1970. Washington (St. Louis). Inducted in 1964. 1920 Decatur Staleys, 1921-22 Rock Island Independents, 1923-24 Milwaukee Badgers; player coach 1925-26 Detroit Panthers, 1927-29 Providence Steam Roller; coach 1930 Providence Steam Roller, 1940-42, 1946-48 Chicago Cardinals.

As a collegian Jimmy Conzelman played in the 1919 Rose Bowl. He then was a teammate of George Halas at Great Lakes Naval Training Station. As a two-way professional player, he starred with five teams, including Halas's 1920 Decatur Staleys, before a knee injury ended his playing career in 1929. As player-coach in 1928, he led Providence to an NFL championship. He owned and coached the Detroit Panthers in the mid-1920s. As a non-playing coach, he took a floundering Chicago Cardinals team and won two divisional titles and, in 1947, an NFL championship. He also was an actor, author, executive, songwriter, and orator.

Willie Davis

Defensive end. 6-3, 245. Born in Lisbon, Louisiana, July 24, 1934. Grambling. Inducted in 1981. 1958-59 Cleveland Browns, 1960-69 Green Bay Packers.

The early part of Willie Davis's career showed no indication of eventual enshrinement in the Hall of Fame. He was drafted on the fifteenth round by Cleveland in 1956 as a guard out of Grambling. After three weeks in training camp he was drafted again, this time by the U.S. Army. After two years in the service, Davis returned to the Browns and played two seasons as a defensive end; he also played offensive tackle. In 1960, he was traded to the Packers and started his march to the Hall of Fame. He played 10 years at one position—defensive end—as the Packers became the NFL's dominant team. Davis earned all-pro honors five times (1962, 1964-67) in a six-year span and was selected to play in five consecutive Pro Bowls (1964-68).

Art Donovan

Defensive tackle. 6-3, 265. Born in Bronx, New York, June 5, 1925. Boston College. Inducted in 1968. 1950 Baltimore Colts, 1951 New York Yanks, 1952 Dallas Texans, 1953-61 Baltimore Colts.

Art Donovan didn't come into the NFL until he was 25, because of Marine Corps service. After playing on mediocre teams the first part of his career he became a star on the Colts' championship teams. He was a complete defensive lineman, outstanding against both the run and the pass. Donovan was on all-pro teams four times and appeared in five Pro Bowls. His father was a boxing referee and his grandfather was a middleweight boxing champion.

John (Paddy) Driscoll

Halfback-Quarterback. 5-11, 160. Born in Evanston, Illinois, January 11, 1896. Died June 29, 1968. Northwestern. Inducted in 1965. 1920-25 Chicago Cardinals, 1920 Decatur Staleys, 1926-29 Chicago Bears.

Had there been a most valuable player elected in the American Pro Football Association in 1920, it most likely would have been Paddy Driscoll. A former teammate of George Halas's at Great Lakes Naval Training Station during World War I, Driscoll was the tailback for the Chicago Cardinals in 1920, when he earned a reputation as a fine all-around ball player, especially adept at kicking. He also was a slick broken-field runner and an accurate passer throwing the large football of his day. Late in the year, Halas even hired Driscoll away from the Cardinals for one game between the Decatur Staleys and the Akron Pros. Driscoll served as player-coach for the Cardinals from 1920-22, and remained with the team as a player through 1925, when he was booed for punting away from Red Grange in Grange's first appearance as a pro. Driscoll's contract was sold to the Bears in 1926, and he played the rest of his career with them. He was selected all-pro six times. Driscoll took over as coach of the Bears in 1956 and 1957, winning a divisional championship his first year. He stayed with the team in various jobs until his death in 1968.

Bill Dudley

Halfback. 5-10, 176. Born in Bluefield, Virginia, December 24, 1921. Virginia. Inducted in 1966. 1942, 1945-46 Pittsburgh Steelers, 1947-49 Detroit Lions, 1950-51, 1953 Washington Redskins.

(Bullet) Bill Dudley threw sidearm passes. He got most of his rushing yardage through effective use of blockers rather than his own speed. He didn't use any approach steps as a placekicker. He simply stood where the ball was to be placed down, swung his right leg back, and then forward as he kicked. Dudley led the NFL in rushing, interceptions, and punt returns in 1946. Dudley was the NFL's first draft choice in 1942 after an All-America career at Virginia, and he rushed for a league-leading 696 yards his first season. Dudley divided his nine-year pro career into three segments with Pittsburgh, Detroit, and Washington, and he remains among the most popular players ever to perform in those cities. He gained 8,157 combined yards on rushing, receiving, and returns.

RUSHING

Year	Team	Att.	Yards	Avg.	Long	TD
1942	Pittsburgh	162	696	4.3	66	5
1943	Military service					
1944	Military service					
1945	Pittsburgh	57	204	3.5	32	3
1946	Pittsburgh	146	604	4.1	41	3
1947	Detroit	80	302	3.8	28	2
1948	Detroit	33	97	2.9	11	0
1949	Detroit	125	402	3.2	26	3
1950	Washington	66	339	5.1	27	1
1951	Washington	91	398	4.4	40	2
1952	Did not play football					
1953	Washington	5	15	3.0	7	0
Totals		765	3,057	4.0	66	19

PUNT RETURNS

Year	Team	No.	Yards	Avg.	Long	TD
1942	Pittsburgh	20	271	13.6	47	0
1943	Military service					
1944	Military service					
1945	Pittsburgh	5	20	4.0	6	0
1946	Pittsburgh	27	385	14.3	52	0
1947	Detroit	11	182	16.5	84t	1
1948	Detroit	8	67	8.4	18	0
1949	Detroit	11	199	18.1	67t	1
1950	Washington	12	185	15.4	96t	1
1951	Washington	22	172	7.8	27	0
1952	Did not play football					
1953	Washington	8	34	4.3	16	0
Totals		124	1,515	12.2	96t	3

PASSING

222 Att., 81 Comp., 985 Yards, 6 TD, 17 Int.

RECEIVING

123, 1,383 Yards, 11.2 Avg., 18 TD

INTERCEPTIONS

23, 459 Yards, 20.0 Avg., 80 Long, 2 TD

PUNTING

191, 38.2 Avg., 4 Blk.

KICKOFF RETURNS

78, 1,743 Yards, 22.3 Avg., 1 TD

SCORING

44 TD, 33 FG, 121 PAT, 484 Points

Glen (Turk) Edwards

Tackle. 6-2, 260. Born in Mold, Washington, September 28, 1907. Died January 10, 1973. Washington State. Inducted in 1969. 1932 Boston Braves, 1933-36 Boston Redskins, 1937-40 Washington Redskins.

At 260 pounds Glen (Turk) Edwards was bigger than most linemen of his time. He made all-pro teams in 1932, 1933, 1936, and 1937. Edwards was outstanding both as an offensive blocker and as a defender, largely because of his unusual quickness and agility. An All-America and Rose Bowl star at Washington State, Edwards played for $150 a game when he joined the Boston Braves in 1932. His career ended in a strange way. After meeting Mel Hein—his former Washington State teammate and the New York Giants' center and captain—at the center of the field for a pregame coin toss, Edwards turned to go back to the bench. But his knee collapsed, and he never played again. Edwards was the Redskins' head coach from 1946-48.

Weeb Ewbank

Coach. Born in Richmond, Indiana, May 6, 1907. Miami (Ohio). Inducted in 1978. 1954-62 Baltimore Colts, 1963-73 New York Jets.

Weeb Ewbank is the only head coach to win world championships in both the National Football League and the American Football League. His title teams were the 1958 and 1959 Baltimore Colts and the 1968 New York Jets, who defeated the Colts in Super Bowl III. Ewbank, one of many NFL coaches from Miami's "Cradle of Coaches," began his career with the Cleveland Browns in 1949 as an assistant under Paul Brown. He took part in the development of two of the game's most renowned quarterbacks, Johnny Unitas and Joe Namath. Although his overall record was only one game above .500 (130-129-7), Ewbank undertook and completed successful rebuilding projects with both franchises.

Tom Fears

End. 6-2, 215. Born in Los Angeles, California, December 3, 1923. UCLA. Inducted in 1970. 1948-56 Los Angeles Rams.

Tom Fears came into pro football projected as a defensive specialist, but in each of his first three seasons, he led the NFL in pass receiving. In 1950, Fears caught 84 passes, a record that stood for a decade. His 18 catches in one game against the Packers that season is still a record. In his career, Fears, who was not only big and fast but ran precise patterns, caught 400 passes for 5,397 yards and 38 touchdowns. He made three touchdown catches as the Rams won a divisional playoff game in 1950, and in 1951 he scored on a 73-yard pass-and-run play as the Rams beat the Cleveland Browns and won their only NFL title in Los Angeles.

RECEIVING

Year	Team	No.	Yards	Avg.	Long	TD
1948	LA Rams	51	698	13.7	80t	4
1949	LA Rams	77	1,013	13.2	51t	9
1950	LA Rams	84	1,116	13.3	53t	7
1951	LA Rams	32	528	16.5	54	3
1952	LA Rams	48	600	12.5	36	6
1953	LA Rams	23	278	12.1	31	4
1954	LA Rams	36	546	15.2	43	3
1955	LA Rams	44	569	12.9	31	2
1956	LA Rams	5	49	9.8	18	0
Totals		400	5,397	13.5	80t	38

SCORING

39 TD, 1 FG, 12 PAT, 249 Points

Ray Flaherty

End-Coach. 6-0, 190. Born in Spokane, Washington, September 1, 1904. Gonzaga. Inducted in 1976. 1926 Los Angeles Wildcats (AFL), 1927 New York Yankees, 1928-29, 1931-35 New York Giants; coach 1936 Boston Redskins, 1937-42 Washington Redskins, 1946-48 New York Yankees (AAFC), 1949 Chicago Hornets (AAFC).

Ray Flaherty was an all-pro end with the New York Giants in 1928, 1929, and 1932, leading the NFL in pass receptions in 1932, the first season official statistics were kept. He was captain and assistant coach of the Giants before taking over the Redskins as head coach in 1936. Flaherty won four Eastern Division titles and two world championships with the Redskins and his record overall was 80-37-5. His All-America Football Conference New York Yankees won divisional titles in 1946 and 1947 but lost the title game to the Cleveland Browns in both years. It was Flaherty who suggested the use of sneakers in the 1934 NFL Championship Game won by the Giants over the Bears. In college at Gonzaga a heel bruise forced him to wear tennis shoes in practice one day and he found they gave him excellent traction on frozen fields.

Len Ford

End. 6-5, 260. Born in Washington, D.C., February 18, 1926. Died March 14, 1972. Michigan. Inducted in 1976. 1948-49 Los Angeles Dons (AAFC), 1950-57 Cleveland Browns, 1958 Green Bay Packers.

Len Ford entered professional football as a two-way end and caught 67 passes for the Los Angeles Dons of the All-America Football Conference in 1948 and 1949. But when the AAFC folded, Ford was acquired by Cleveland and used exclusively as a defensive end. He made all-pro teams five consecutive years, 1951-55, and played in the Pro Bowl four times. Ford was one of the first defensive ends to be known for his all-out pass rush—he often leaped over blockers to get to the quarterback. Ford recovered 20 fumbles during his career. After missing much of the 1950 season because of severe facial injuries, he wore a special mask and played an outstanding game in the Browns' 1950 championship victory over the Rams.

Dan Fortmann

Guard. 6-0, 207. Born in Pearl River, New York, April 11, 1916. Colgate. Inducted in 1965. 1936-43 Chicago Bears.

George Halas of the Chicago Bears reportedly chose Dan Fortmann of Colgate as he was making the last selection of the 1936 college player draft because he liked the sound of Fortmann's name. Fortmann was small for a lineman even for that day, and his football career also appeared unpromising because he wanted to become a doctor. But he played eight years. He became one of the best linemen of all time, making all-pro six consecutive years, 1938-43, playing offensively and defensively. A Phi Beta Kappa student in college, Fortmann was one of a group whose members attended medical or dental school while playing for Chicago. Fortmann was a practicing physician before he retired as a Bears player in 1943. He later served the Los Angeles Rams as team doctor.

Frank Gatski

Center. 6-3, 240. Born in Farmington, West Virginia, March 13, 1922. Auburn. Inducted in 1985. 1946-56 Cleveland Browns, 1957 Detroit Lions.

Frank Gatski was the greatest winner—if championship games are a measure—of any non-kicker in pro football history. In his 12-year career, he appeared in 11 championship games, including eight victories. Gatski, a center and linebacker, joined the Cleveland Browns when they were formed. Although he wasn't as well known as some of his former Browns teammates, he was the dominant center in the NFL in the 1950s, being named all-pro in 1951, 1952, 1953, and 1955. He was an exceptional pass blocker and had almost unbelievable durability. He never missed a game or practice in his entire career—high school, college, and pro. Gatski was traded to Detroit for his final season, and the Lions won the NFL championship.

Bill George

Linebacker. 6-2, 230. Born in Waynesburg, Pennsylvania, October 27, 1930. Wake Forest. Inducted in 1974. 1952-65 Chicago Bears, 1966 Los Angeles Rams.

The Chicago Bears thought so highly of Bill George they selected him on the second round of the 1951 draft, when he still had a year of eligibility left. He reported in 1952 and went on to play 15 years. He played middle linebacker and called defensive signals. He recovered 16 fumbles and made 18 interceptions. George played in eight Pro Bowl games and made all-pro as many times. Early in his career he placekicked, scoring 26 points on four field goals and 14 extra points.

Frank Gifford

Halfback. 6-1, 195. Born in Santa Monica, California, August 16, 1930. USC. Inducted in 1977. 1952-60, 1962-64 New York Giants.

The New York Giants made the NFL title game five times with Frank Gifford on the team. In 1956, the season they won the NFL championship 47-7 over the Bears, he finished fifth in the league in rushing, with 819 yards, and third in receiving, with 51 catches for 603 yards. He also caught a touchdown pass in the championship game. Gifford, who had been a college star at USC, played halfback, flanker, and—early in his career—defensive back. He was all-pro in 1955, 1956, 1957, and 1959, and played in seven Pro Bowls. After missing 1961 with an injury, he returned to average 20.4 yards per catch in 1962.

RUSHING

Year	Team	Att.	Yards	Avg.	Long	TD
1952	NY Giants	38	116	3.1	15	0
1953	NY Giants	50	157	3.1	15	2
1954	NY Giants	66	368	5.6	30	2
1955	NY Giants	86	351	4.1	49	3
1956	NY Giants	159	819	5.2	69	5
1957	NY Giants	136	528	3.9	41	5
1958	NY Giants	115	468	4.1	33	8
1959	NY Giants	106	540	5.1	79	3
1960	NY Giants	77	232	3.0	13	4
1961	Did not play football					
1962	NY Giants	2	18	9.0	12	1
1963	NY Giants	4	10	2.5	12	0
1964	NY Giants	1	2	2.0	2t	1
Totals		840	3,609	4.3	79	34

RECEIVING

Year	Team	No.	Yards	Avg.	Long	TD
1952	NY Giants	5	36	7.2	11	0
1953	NY Giants	18	292	16.2	49t	4
1954	NY Giants	14	154	11.0	35t	1
1955	NY Giants	33	437	13.2	54	4
1956	NY Giants	51	603	11.8	48	4
1957	NY Giants	41	588	14.3	63	4
1958	NY Giants	29	330	11.4	41	2
1959	NY Giants	42	768	18.3	77t	4
1960	NY Giants	24	344	14.3	44t	3
1961	Did not play football					
1962	NY Giants	39	796	20.4	63t	7
1963	NY Giants	42	657	15.6	64	7
1964	NY Giants	29	429	14.8	40t	3
Totals		367	5,434	14.8	77t	43

PASSING

63 Att., 29 Comp., 823 Yards, 14 TD, 6 Int.

INTERCEPTIONS

2, 112 Yards, 56.0 Avg., 1 TD

PUNT RETURNS

25, 121 Yards, 4.8 Avg., 0 TD

KICKOFF RETURNS

23, 594 Yards, 25.8 Avg., 0 TD

SCORING

78 TD, 2 FG, 10 PAT, 484 Points

Sid Gillman

Coach. Born in Minneapolis, Minnesota, October 26, 1911. Ohio State. Inducted in 1983. 1955-59 Los Angeles Rams, 1960 Los Angeles Chargers, 1961-69, 1971 San Diego Chargers, 1973-74 Houston Oilers.

Sid Gillman had one of the most imaginative and versatile minds in professional football history. His special legacy was his leadership role in the development of the modern passing game. Gillman entered the NFL with the Rams after coaching Miami (Ohio) and Cincinnati to a combined record of 81-19-2. In his first year in Los Angeles, Gillman coached the Rams to the Western Conference title. In 1960, he moved to the Los Angeles Chargers of the new AFL, bringing the new league a measure of respect and credibility it desperately needed. Gillman's Chargers won five AFC Western Division titles and one league championship in the league's first six years. Following his retirement as a head coach in 1974, Gillman continued to serve as an offensive consultant to the Bears and the Eagles. Gillman helped develop the talents of a number of quarterbacks, including Norm Van Brocklin, Bill Wade, Zeke Bratkowski, Frank Ryan, Jack Kemp, John Hadl, and Ron Jaworski.

Otto Graham

Quarterback. 6-1, 195. Born in Waukegan, Illinois, December 6, 1921. Northwestern. Inducted in 1965. 1946-55 Cleveland Browns.

Otto Graham not only was one of the best passers in NFL history, he was perhaps the greatest winner ever. He also was versatile; he was converted from a college Single-Wing tailback to a T-formation quarterback in pro football. In 10 seasons with the Browns, he led them into 10 championship games. Graham personified everything Paul Brown wanted in a football player, both on and off the field. He led the All-America Football Conference in passing each of his four years in that league, and the NFL twice. In the 1950 NFL Championship Game, Graham passed for four touchdowns. In the 1954 title game, he threw for three and ran for three. In addition to becoming a star football player at Northwestern, Graham was a basketball All-America. He served as head coach of the Washington Redskins from 1966-68.

PASSING

Year	Team	Att.	Comp.	Yards	TD	Int.
1946	Cleveland (AAFC)	174	95	1,834	17	5
1947	Cleveland (AAFC)	269	163	2,753	25	11
1948	Cleveland (AAFC)	333	173	2,713	25	15
1949	Cleveland (AAFC)	285	161	2,785	19	10
1950	Cleveland	253	137	1,943	14	20
1951	Cleveland	265	147	2,205	17	16
1952	Cleveland	364	181	2,816	20	24
1953	Cleveland	258	167	2,722	11	9
1954	Cleveland	240	142	2,092	11	17
1955	Cleveland	185	98	1,721	15	8
NFL Totals		1,565	872	13,499	88	94
Pro Totals		2,626	1,464	23,584	174	135

RUSHING

NFL—306 Att., 682 Yards, 2.2 Avg., 36 Long, 33 TD

Pro—405 Att., 882 Yards, 2.2 Avg., 36 Long, 44 TD

Harold (Red) Grange

Halfback. 6-0, 185. Born in Forksville, Pennsylvania, June 13, 1903. Illinois. Inducted in 1963. 1925 Chicago Bears, 1926 New York Yankees (AFL), 1927 New York Yankees, 1929-34 Chicago Bears.

Red Grange's reputation as a runner was already established when he joined the Chicago Bears on Thanksgiving Day in 1925. The man nicknamed the Galloping Ghost had been one of the most famous college players ever, and his name brought the first huge crowds to pro football, helping a number of financially troubled franchises and perhaps assuring a successful future of the sport. Grange and the Bears went on an 18-game coast-to-coast tour after the 1925 season, giving the game an audience it had never had. Grange and his personal manager, C. C. (Cash and Carry) Pyle, established the first American Football League in 1926. It folded after one season, and Grange and other players joined the NFL. A knee injury caused Grange to miss all of the 1928 season and robbed him of much elusiveness, but he remained a fine defensive player and a big box-office attraction.

Forrest Gregg

Tackle. 6-4, 250. Born in Sulphur Springs, Texas, October 18, 1933. SMU. Inducted in 1977. 1956, 1958-70 Green Bay Packers, 1971 Dallas Cowboys.

Forrest Gregg joined Green Bay in 1956, and his career was interrupted by 21 months of military service. Gregg came back in 1958, Vince Lombardi became Packers' coach in 1959, and the team made one of the most dramatic turnarounds in NFL history. Gregg was a key player at tackle and guard (he was named all-pro at both in 1965 after taking over for injured Jerry Kramer), and was named to the Pro Bowl nine times in the 1960s. He played on three Super Bowl-winning teams, two in Green Bay and one in Dallas, his last season as an active player. Gregg, who was called by Lombardi, "the finest player I have ever coached," has since served as head coach of Cleveland, Cincinnati, and Green Bay.

Lou Groza

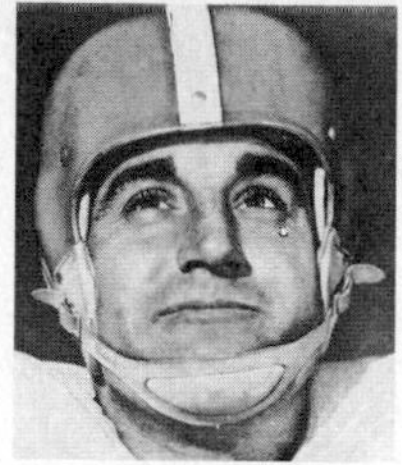

Tackle-Kicker. 6-3, 250. Born in Martin's Ferry, Ohio, January 25, 1924. Ohio State. Inducted in 1974. 1946-59, 1961-67 Cleveland Browns.

Lou (The Toe) Groza was one of the greatest kickers in NFL history. He scored 1,349 points in the NFL. His field goal with 20 seconds left won the 1950 NFL Championship Game 30-28 for the Browns over the Rams. Altogether, he played in 13 championship games, four in the All-America Football Conference, nine in the NFL. He played in nine Pro Bowls. And he was more than just a kicker. He was also an excellent tackle, six times all-pro, pass blocking for Otto Graham and opening holes for Marion Motley, Dub Jones, Bobby Mitchell, and Jim Brown. A back injury forced him to retire in 1960 but he came back in 1961 and played strictly as a kicker for seven more years.

SCORING

Year	Team	FG	PAT	Points
1946	Cleveland (AAFC)	13-29	45-47	84
1947	Cleveland (AAFC)	7-21	39-42	60
1948	Cleveland (AAFC)	8-19	51-52	75
1949	Cleveland (AAFC)	2- 7	34-35	40
1950	Cleveland	13-19	29-29	*74
1951	Cleveland	10-23	43-43	73
1952	Cleveland	19-33	32-32	89
1953	Cleveland	23-26	39-40	108
1954	Cleveland	16-24	37-38	85
1955	Cleveland	11-22	44-45	77
1956	Cleveland	11-20	18-18	51
1957	Cleveland	15-22	32-32	77
1958	Cleveland	8-19	36-38	60
1959	Cleveland	5-16	33-37	48
1960	Retired from football			
1961	Cleveland	16-23	37-38	85
1962	Cleveland	14-31	33-35	75
1963	Cleveland	15-23	40-43	85
1964	Cleveland	22-33	49-49	115
1965	Cleveland	16-25	45-45	93
1966	Cleveland	9-23	51-52	*78
1967	Cleveland	11-23	43-43	76
NFL Totals		234-405	641-657	*1,349
Pro Totals		264-481	810-834	1,608

*Includes a touchdown.

Joe Guyon

Halfback. 6-1, 180. Born in Mahnomen, Minnesota, November 26, 1892. Died November 27, 1971. Carlisle, Georgia Tech. Inducted in 1966. 1920 Canton Bulldogs, 1921 Cleveland Indians, 1921 Washington Senators, 1922-23 Oorang Indians, 1924 Rock Island Independents, 1924-25 Kansas City Cowboys, 1927 New York Giants.

The career of Joe Guyon, a Chippewa Indian from Minnesota, roughly paralleled that of Jim Thorpe. Guyon played with Thorpe at Carlisle Indian School. Then Guyon was an All-America tackle at Georgia Tech. He was a triple-threat halfback in the pros. He played on four different teams with Thorpe. In 1927, a touchdown pass by Guyon gave the New York Giants a victory over the Chicago Bears and won the NFL championship for the Giants. Guyon didn't confine his athletic activity to football. He played minor league baseball in the summers—when football started later and the baseball season was shorter. A baseball injury in 1928 ended Guyon's pro football career.

George Halas

End-Coach-Team owner. 6-0, 175. Born in Chicago, Illinois, February 2, 1895. Died October 31, 1983. Illinois. Inducted in 1963. 1920 Decatur Staleys, 1921 Chicago Staleys, 1922-29 Chicago Bears; coach 1933-42, 1946-55, 1958-67 Chicago Bears.

George Halas's career paralleled the history of the NFL. He attended college at Illinois. Playing for Great Lakes in the 1919 Rose Bowl, Halas was named the game's most valuable player. Halas was in Canton on September 17, 1920 when the NFL's second organizational meeting was held. He remained active in the administration of the Chicago Bears for the next 63 years. Halas, known as "Papa Bear," coached the Chicago team for 40 seasons and his 325 NFL victories were the most by any coach. Before settling into coaching and administration, Halas was a top two-way end for 11 seasons. In 1923, he picked up a Jim Thorpe fumble and ran it back 98 yards for a touchdown, an NFL record for a fumble return until it was broken in 1972. He coached the Bears to seven NFL championships.

Ed Healey

Tackle. 6-3, 220. Born in Indian Orchard, Massachusetts, December 28, 1894. Died December 9, 1978. Dartmouth. Inducted in 1964. 1920-22 Rock Island Independents, 1922-27 Chicago Bears.

After playing at Dartmouth, Ed Healey went into coaching—until he decided to try out in the new professional league at Rock Island, Illinois, in 1920 and made the team. While playing for the Rock Island Independents in 1922, Healey impressed George Halas and the Chicago coach made one of the first player deals to get him. Healey's contract was transferred to the Bears for $100. Halas later called Healey "the most versatile tackle ever." Healey's teammate, Red Grange, said, "He loved to come downfield under a punt. He was an absolutely vicious player." Healey made all-pro the year he played for both Rock Island and Chicago and then four more times with the Bears. He also was outstanding in the Bears' long barnstorming tour after the 1925 season.

Mel Hein

Center. 6-2, 225. Born in Redding, California, August 22, 1909. Washington State. Inducted in 1963. 1931-45 New York Giants.

Mel Hein was outstanding as a center, guard, and tackle at Washington State, but he had to write to three NFL teams offering his services before he was signed by the New York Giants for $150 a game. He became the Giants' regular center and started for 15 seasons. He never missed a game and he rarely played less than 60 minutes. He was a strong blocker despite having to deliver accurate long snaps before blocking opposing linemen. On defense, he covered passes and tackled as well as any linebacker in the league. He was all-pro for eight consecutive seasons, 1933-40. Hein was the NFL's first official most valuable player.

Wilbur (Pete) Henry

Tackle. 6-0, 250. Born in Mansfield, Ohio, October 31, 1897. Died February 7, 1952. Washington & Jefferson. Inducted in 1963. 1920-23, 1925-26 Canton Bulldogs, 1927 New York Giants, 1927-28 Pottsville Maroons.

Wilbur Henry was a hefty player nicknamed "Fats." But he was a quick and powerful man who did many things well. He played tackle, but sometimes he was used as a power ball carrier, or as the receiver on a tackle-eligible pass play. He was called the best kick-blocker of his time, and he was named all-pro three times. He also kicked, sharing the record for the longest dropkick field goal (50 yards) with fellow Hall of Famer Paddy Driscoll. A three-time college All-America at Washington & Jefferson, Henry signed with the Canton Bulldogs the day the NFL was organized in that Ohio town, and he was an offensive and defensive standout as the team won consecutive NFL titles in 1922 and 1923. He played for the Pottsville Maroons in 1924, before they were in the NFL.

Arnie Herber

Quarterback. 6-1, 200. Born in Green Bay, Wisconsin, April 2, 1910. Died October 14, 1969. Wisconsin, Regis. Inducted in 1966. 1930-40 Green Bay Packers, 1944-45 New York Giants.

Pro football's first heralded passing combination was quarterback Arnie Herber of the Green Bay Packers to receiver Don Hutson in the 1930s. Herber predated Hutson by five seasons, and had built a reputation as a star by the time Hutson arrived. In the days when the forward pass was mostly a desperation play, Herber and the Packers used it anytime and anywhere with great success. He was especially effective throwing long. Herber played on four NFL champions with Green Bay and was the league's top passer three seasons—1932, 1934, and 1936. He retired in 1940, but came back in 1944 with the New York Giants and led them to the Eastern Division title. His lifetime statistics show 8,033 yards passing and 79 touchdown passes, despite the fact he had small fingers and had to pass a melon-shaped ball the first three seasons of his career.

PASSING

Year	Team	Att.	Comp.	Yards	TD	Int.
1930	Green Bay					
1931	Green Bay					
1932	Green Bay	101	37	639	9	9
1933	Green Bay	126	56	656	4	12
1934	Green Bay	115	42	799	8	12
1935	Green Bay	106	40	729	8	6
1936	Green Bay	173	77	1,239	11	13
1937	Green Bay	104	47	676	7	10
1938	Green Bay	55	22	336	4	4
1939	Green Bay	139	57	1,107	8	9
1940	Green Bay	89	38	560	5	7
1941	Retired from football					
1942	Retired from football					
1943	Retired from football					
1944	N.Y. Giants	86	36	651	6	8
1945	N.Y. Giants	80	35	641	9	8
Totals		1,174	487	8,033	79	98

Bill Hewitt

End. 5-11, 191. Born in Bay City, Michigan, October 8, 1909. Died January 14, 1947. Michigan. Inducted in 1971. 1932-36 Chicago Bears, 1937-39 Philadelphia Eagles, 1943 Phil-Pitt.

Bill Hewitt was not especially big, but he was an intense player. His initial charge was so quick that opponents often claimed he was offside. Hewitt played without a helmet from 1932-39 and his return to the league from retirement in 1943 may have prompted the rules change making the wearing of helmets mandatory. He was one of the first linemen to pursue all over the field. He made an all-pro team with two different clubs, the Chicago Bears in 1933 and 1934 and the Philadelphia Eagles in 1937. In 1936, Hewitt made all-pro even though he was traded from the Bears to the Eagles midway through the season. He had perhaps his finest game in the NFL when he led the Bears to victory in the 1933 Championship Game against the New York Giants. He was killed in an automobile accident in Pennsylvania in January, 1947.

RECEIVING

Year	Team	No.	Yards	Avg.	TD
1932	Chi. Bears	4	44	11.0	0
1933	Chi. Bears	16	274	17.1	2
1934	Chi. Bears	10	151	15.1	5
1935	Chi. Bears	5	80	16.0	0
1936	Chi. Bears-Philadelphia	15	358	23.9	6
1937	Philadelphia	16	197	12.3	5
1938	Philadelphia	18	237	13.2	4
1939	Philadelphia	15	243	16.2	1
1940	Retired from football				
1941	Retired from football				
1942	Retired from football				
1943	Phil-Pitt	2	22	11.0	0
Totals		101	1,606	15.9	23

Clarke Hinkle

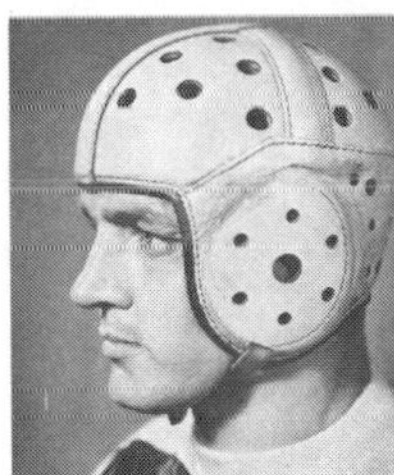

Fullback. 5-11, 201. Born in Toronto, Ohio, April 10, 1912. Bucknell. Inducted in 1964. 1932-41 Green Bay Packers.

Hinkle has been called the fiercest competitor ever in football. He had stirring personal duels with Bronko Nagurski of the Bears. Hinkle was a battering-ram runner and a hard-tackling linebacker but he also passed, punted, placekicked, caught passes and defended against them. An all-pro choice four times, he was the NFL's all-time leading ground gainer when he retired, with 3,860 yards. He had a 43.4-yard punting average. Hinkle also led the NFL in scoring in 1938 and in field goals in 1940 and 1941.

RUSHING

Year	Team	Att.	Yards	Avg.	Long	TD
1932	Green Bay	95	331	3.5	27	3
1933	Green Bay	139	413	3.0	33	4
1934	Green Bay	144	359	2.5	32	1
1935	Green Bay	77	273	3.5	17	2
1936	Green Bay	100	476	4.8	57	5
1937	Green Bay	129	552	4.3	41	5
1938	Green Bay	114	299	2.6	46	3
1939	Green Bay	135	381	2.8	29	5
1940	Green Bay	109	383	3.5	31	2
1941	Green Bay	129	393	3.0	20	5
Totals		1,171	3,860	3.3	57	35

RECEIVING

48, 552 Yards, 11.5 Avg., 9 TD

SCORING

44 TD, 26 FG, 28 PAT, 370 Points

Elroy (Crazylegs) Hirsch

Halfback-End. 6-2, 190. Born in Wausau, Wisconsin, June 17, 1923. Wisconsin, Michigan. Inducted in 1968. 1946-48 Chicago Rockets (AAFC), 1949-57 Los Angeles Rams.

Elroy Hirsch is remembered mostly as one of the most spectacular pass receivers ever to play in the NFL, but he got his nickname—Crazylegs—because of his unusual running style. He was one of the first backs to be moved out wide and made a flanker, with the Los Angeles Rams in 1950. A star with the Chicago Rockets of the All-America Football Conference before coming to the NFL, Hirsch teamed with fellow Hall of Famers Tom Fears, Bob Waterfield, and Norm Van Brocklin to set numerous passing and scoring records. In 1951, Hirsch caught 66 passes for 1,495 yards and a record 17 touchdowns. He was honored as the flanker on the all-time NFL team in 1969. He ended his career in 1957 with 343 catches for 6,299 yards and 53 touchdowns. He played the title role in his film biography and starred in two other movies.

RECEIVING

Year	Team	No.	Yards	Avg.	Long	TD
1946	Chi. Rockets (AAFC)	27	347	12.9		3
1947	Chi. Rockets (AAFC)	10	282	28.2		3
1948	Chi. Rockets (AAFC)	7	101	14.4		1
1949	LA Rams	22	326	14.8	48t	4
1950	LA Rams	42	687	16.4	58t	7
1951	LA Rams	66	1,495	22.7	91t	17
1952	LA Rams	25	590	23.6	84t	4
1953	LA Rams	61	941	15.4	70	4
1954	LA Rams	35	720	20.6	66	3
1955	LA Rams	25	460	18.4	72t	2
1956	LA Rams	35	603	17.2	76t	6
1957	LA Rams	32	477	14.9	45	6
NFL Totals		343	6,299	18.4	91t	53
Pro Totals		387	7,029	18.2	91t	60

RUSHING

NFL—74 Att., 317 Yards, 4.3 Avg., 51 Long, 2 TD
Pro—207 Att., 687 Yards, 3.3 Avg., 51 Long, 4 TD

Paul Hornung

Halfback. 6-2, 220. Born in Louisville, Kentucky, December 23, 1935. Notre Dame. Inducted in 1986. 1957-62, 1964-66 Green Bay Packers.

Paul Hornung had all the skills of a great offensive player. He could pass, run, catch, block, and kick, and do all of them at a level that few others in the NFL could match. Hornung won the Heisman Trophy at Notre Dame, then was the bonus pick in the 1957 NFL draft. After playing quarterback, fullback, and halfback as a rookie, he settled in at halfback under new head coach Vince Lombardi, and led the NFL in scoring three consecutive years, 1959-61. In 1960, he set the all-time record with 176 points on 15 touchdowns, 15 field goals, and 41 extra points. The next year, in the NFL Championship Game, he set a record by scoring 19 points in the Packers' 37-0 victory over the Giants. Hornung missed the 1963 season after being suspended by Commissioner Pete Rozelle, but he came back to play three more years for the Packers.

RUSHING

Year	Team	Att.	Yards	Avg.	Long	TD
1957	Green Bay	60	319	5.3	72	3
1958	Green Bay	69	310	4.5	55	2
1959	Green Bay	152	681	4.5	63	7
1960	Green Bay	160	671	4.2	37	13
1961	Green Bay	127	597	4.7	55	8
1962	Green Bay	57	219	3.8	37	5
1963	Suspended					
1964	Green Bay	103	415	4.0	40	5
1965	Green Bay	89	299	3.4	17	5
1966	Green Bay	76	200	2.6	9	2
Totals		893	3,711	4.2	72	50

SCORING

Year	Team	TD	FG	PAT	Points
1957	Green Bay	3	0-4	0-0	18
1958	Green Bay	2	11-21	22-23	67
1959	Green Bay	7	7-17	31-32	94
1960	Green Bay	15	15-28	41-41	176
1961	Green Bay	10	15-22	41-41	146
1962	Green Bay	7	6-10	14-14	74
1963	Suspended				
1964	Green Bay	5	12-38	41-43	107
1965	Green Bay	8	0-0	0-0	48
1966	Green Bay	5	0-0	0-0	30
Totals		62	66-140	190-194	760

RECEIVING

130, 1,480 Yards, 11.4 Avg., 12 TD

PASSING

55 Att., 24 Comp., 383 Yards, 5 TD, 4 Int.

Ken Houston

Safety. 6-3, 198. Born in Lufkin, Texas, November 12, 1944. Prairie View A&M. Inducted in 1986. 1967-72 Houston Oilers, 1973-80 Washington Redskins.

When Ken Houston was selected on the ninth round of the first AFL-NFL combined draft in 1967, not much was expected of him. However, he became a starter midway through his rookie season, and, when he retired 14 years later, he not only held the NFL record with nine interceptions returned for touchdowns, he had been named all-pro or all-conference eight times and had been chosen for two AFL All-Star Games and a record 10 consecutive AFC-NFC Pro Bowls. Houston possessed all the tools to become the perfect strong safety—he was quick, agile, and a punishing tackler. The Redskins wanted Houston so much that they traded five players to the Oilers for him in 1973. He scored 12 touchdowns in his career, 9 on interceptions and 1 each on a blocked field goal, a fumble return, and a punt return.

INTERCEPTIONS

Year	Team	No.	Yards	Avg.	Long	TD
1967	Houston	4	151	37.8	78	2
1968	Houston	5	160	32.0	66t	2
1969	Houston	4	87	21.8	51t	1
1970	Houston	3	32	10.7	11	0
1971	Houston	9	220	24.4	48t	4
1972	Houston	0	0	0.0	0	0
1973	Washington	6	32	5.3	22	0
1974	Washington	2	40	20.0	37	0
1975	Washington	4	33	8.3	19	0
1976	Washington	4	25	6.3	12	0
1977	Washington	5	69	13.8	31	0
1978	Washington	2	29	14.5	29	0
1979	Washington	1	20	20.0	20	0
1980	Washington	0	0	0.0	0	0
Totals		49	898	18.3	78	9

Cal Hubbard

Tackle-End. 6-5, 250. Born in Keytesville, Missouri, October 11, 1900. Died October 17, 1977. Centenary, Geneva. Inducted in 1963. 1927-28, 1936 New York Giants, 1929-33, 1935 Green Bay Packers, 1936 Pittsburgh Pirates.

Cal Hubbard is the only man to be enshrined in both the Pro Football Hall of Fame and the Baseball Hall of Fame. He was the most feared lineman of his era and one of the few early pros who was as large as today's players. As a rookie in 1927, he was a keystone in the New York Giants' championship defense, which limited opponents to 20 points for the season. A powerful blocker, he stood out on offense, too. Hubbard played end his first two years, and he was named all-pro as a rookie. The Packers moved him to tackle, where he made all-pro three more times. He was selected as a tackle on the NFL's all-time team, chosen in 1969. After retiring from football, Hubbard was a respected American League baseball umpire and became umpire-in-chief.

Sam Huff

Linebacker. 6-1, 230. Born in Morgantown, West Virginia, October 4, 1934. West Virginia. Inducted in 1982. 1956-63 New York Giants, 1964-67, 1969 Washington Redskins.

In the 1950s, Sam Huff was the first defensive player to attain the type of notoriety previously reserved for offensive players. As an integral part of a strong Giants defense, Huff helped defenders, and more particularly linebackers, gain public recognition; a half-hour television special in 1961, "The Violent World of Sam Huff," also helped. So did the fact that the Giants won a world championship (1956) and six division titles while Huff played for them. Huff came to the Giants as a third-round choice in the 1956 draft. He played in five Pro Bowls (1959-62, 1965) and was named outstanding lineman of the 1961 game. Huff was traded to the Redskins in 1964, where he played through 1967. After a one-year retirement, Huff came back in 1969 as a player-coach under Vince Lombardi. During Huff's early career, Lombardi was a Giants assistant.

Lamar Hunt

Team owner-Founder. Born in El Dorado, Arkansas, August 2, 1932. SMU. Inducted in 1972. 1960-62 Dallas Texans, 1963-86 Kansas City Chiefs.

Lamar Hunt failed several times in a bid to gain an NFL franchise for his home state of Texas in the 1950s. He formed the American Football League in 1959, and it began play in 1960. Hunt was owner and founder of the Dallas Texans. After a difficult struggle the league merged with the NFL in 1966. Hunt moved the Dallas franchise to Kansas City in 1963, and it became one of football's strongest organizations, winning Super Bowl IV in 1970. Hunt once played end behind Raymond Berry at SMU. When he was elected to the Hall of Fame, he said it was a triumph symbolic of all the officials, coaches, and players of the AFL.

Don Hutson

End. 6-1, 180. Born in Pine Bluff, Arkansas, January 31, 1913. Alabama. Inducted in 1963. 1935-45 Green Bay Packers.

Don Hutson entered the NFL in the mid-1930s, but he was similar to today's receivers in his style of play. He had everything—good hands, outstanding moves, and 9.8 speed in the 100-yard dash (an incredibly fast time in the 1930s). He dominated the NFL. He was an all-pro nine times, and he led the NFL in receptions eight times. Five times he topped the league's scorers. He caught at least one pass in 95 consecutive games from 1937 through 1945, a record that lasted almost a quarter century. During his 11-year career, Hutson caught 488 passes, 99 of them for touchdowns (a mark that still is a record). Early in his career he was a two-way end, and he was named to the NFL's all-time team at that position in 1969. He later played defensive safety and led the NFL in interceptions in 1940. Hutson also kicked extra points and field goals, scoring 823 lifetime points.

RECEIVING

Year	Team	No.	Yards	Avg.	Long	TD
1935	Green Bay	18	420	23.3	83	6
1936	Green Bay	34	536	15.8	87	8
1937	Green Bay	41	552	13.5	78	7
1938	Green Bay	32	548	17.1	54	9
1939	Green Bay	34	846	24.9	92	6
1940	Green Bay	45	664	14.8	36	7
1941	Green Bay	58	738	12.7	45	10
1942	Green Bay	74	1,211	16.4	73	17
1943	Green Bay	47	776	16.5	79	11
1944	Green Bay	58	866	14.9	55t	9
1945	Green Bay	47	834	17.7	75t	9
Totals		488	7,991	16.4	92	99

SCORING

Year	Team	TD	FG	PAT	Points
1935	Green Bay	7	0-	1-	43
1936	Green Bay	9	0-	0-	54
1937	Green Bay	7	0-	0-	42
1938	Green Bay	9	0-	3-	57
1939	Green Bay	6	0-0	2-	38
1940	Green Bay	7	0-0	15-	57
1941	Green Bay	12	1-2	20-24	95
1942	Green Bay	17	1-4	33-34	138
1943	Green Bay	12	3-5	36-36	117
1944	Green Bay	9	0-3	31-33	85
1945	Green Bay	10	2-4	31-35	97
Totals		105	7-18	172-	823

RUSHING

62 Att., 284 Yards, 4.6 Avg., 27 Long, 3 TD

INTERCEPTIONS

30, 389 Yards, 13.0 Avg., 84 Long, 1 TD

David (Deacon) Jones

Defensive end. 6-5, 250. Born in Eatonville, Florida, December 9, 1938. Mississippi Valley State. Inducted in 1980. 1961-71 Los Angeles Rams, 1972-73 San Diego Chargers, 1974 Washington Redskins.

When David Jones arrived in Los Angeles as a fourteenth-round draft choice he found 10 pages of Joneses in the telephone book, and about 20 David Joneses. To establish an identity he nicknamed himself Deacon. Later he was called the Secretary of Defense. Credited with coining the term sack, Jones elevated pass-rushing technique to the point where the fan could see and appreciate defensive linemen. Anchored by Jones and fellow Hall of Fame member Merlin Olsen, the Rams' defensive line became known as the Fearsome Foursome. Jones was traded to the San Diego Chargers in 1972, and finished his career with the Washington Redskins. Jones was named all-pro five times (in 11 seasons with Los Angeles) and played in eight Pro Bowls.

Sonny Jurgensen

Quarterback. 6-0, 203. Born in Wilmington, North Carolina, August 23, 1934. Duke. Inducted in 1983. 1957-63 Philadelphia Eagles, 1964-74 Washington Redskins.

Nearly everyone who came in contact with Sonny Jurgensen—coaches, scouts, receivers, teammates, and opponents—agreed he was the best pure passer they ever had seen. Jurgensen is the third-rated passer in NFL history, with the number-one ranking among players with more than 3,000 attempts. What makes Jurgensen's ranking even more noteworthy is that he spent much of his career with non-contenders and continually was faced with playing catch-up. During the early part of his career, Jurgensen backed up Norm Van Brocklin. In 1961, his first year as a starter, he set NFL records for completions, yards, and touchdown passes and was named all-pro. Jurgensen was traded to Washington for Norm Snead. With the Redskins, Jurgensen led the NFL in passing twice and the NFC once, tied the league mark with a 99-yard touchdown pass to Gerry Allen, and, in 1967, set new league records for attempts, completions, and yards. Jurgensen was selected to play in three Pro Bowls.

PASSING

Year	Team	Att.	Comp.	Yards	TD	Int.
1957	Philadelphia	70	33	470	5	8
1958	Philadelphia	22	12	259	0	1
1959	Philadelphia	5	3	27	1	0
1960	Philadelphia	44	24	486	5	1
1961	Philadelphia	416	235	3,723	32	24
1962	Philadelphia	366	196	3,261	22	26
1963	Philadelphia	184	99	1,413	11	13
1964	Washington	385	207	2,934	24	13
1965	Washington	356	190	2,367	15	16
1966	Washington	436	254	3,209	28	19
1967	Washington	508	288	3,747	31	16
1968	Washington	292	167	1,980	17	11
1969	Washington	442	274	3,102	22	15
1970	Washington	337	202	2,354	23	10
1971	Washington	28	16	170	0	2
1972	Washington	59	39	633	2	4
1973	Washington	145	87	904	6	5
1974	Washington	167	107	1,185	11	5
Totals		4,262	2,433	32,224	255	189

RUSHING

181 Att., 493 Yards, 2.7 Avg., 15 TD

Walt Kiesling

Guard-Coach. 6-2, 245. Born in St. Paul, Minnesota, March 27, 1903. Died March 2, 1962. St. Thomas (Minnesota). Inducted in 1966. 1926-27 Duluth Eskimos, 1928 Pottsville Maroons, 1929-33 Chicago Cardinals, 1934 Chicago Bears, 1935-36, Green Bay Packers, 1937-38 Pittsburgh Pirates; Coach 1939-40 Pittsburgh Pirates, 1941-42 Pittsburgh Steelers; Co-coach 1943 Phil-Pitt, 1944 Card-Pitt; Coach 1954-56 Pittsburgh Steelers.

As a player and coach, Walt Kiesling was in the NFL 34 years. He spent 13 of those years as a guard for six different teams. As a coach, he spent most of his time as a Steelers assistant, but also was head coach of the team twice, a dozen years apart. And during World War II, he was co-head coach of the 1943 Phil-Pitt and 1944 Card-Pitt merged teams. Kiesling helped give perennial loser Pittsburgh its first winning season in 1942. As a player he had a tackle's size but was used at guard offensively because of his quickness in pulling to lead plays. Defensively, he was one of the league's best. His best playing years were with the Cardinals in 1929-33 when he made all-pro teams almost every season, and 1934, when he starred for the unbeaten Chicago Bears.

Frank (Bruiser) Kinard

Tackle. 6-1, 210. Born in Pelahatchie, Mississippi, October 23, 1914. Mississippi. Inducted in 1971. 1938-44 Brooklyn Dodgers-Tigers, 1946-47 New York Yankees (AAFC).

A two-time All-America at Mississippi, Frank (Bruiser) Kinard was a second-round draft choice of the Brooklyn Dodgers in 1938. At 6 feet 1 inch and 210 pounds, he was small for the tackle position, but he also was tough, aggressive, fast, and durable. A 60-minute performer, he was outstanding as a blocker and smothering as a tackler, and was out of a game with injuries only once in his nine-year career. He was the first man to be an all-pro in both the NFL (1940, 1941, 1943, and 1944) and the All-America Football Conference (1946). In 1945, he was named all-Armed Services. Kinard came from a football family. His brother, George, was a teammate on the Dodgers and a younger brother, Billy, also played pro football.

Earl (Curly) Lambeau

Coach. Born in Green Bay, Wisconsin, April 9, 1898. Died June 1, 1965. Notre Dame. Inducted in 1963. 1919-49 Green Bay Packers, 1950-51 Chicago Cardinals, 1952-53 Washington Redskins.

Earl (Curly) Lambeau and the Green Bay Packers joined the NFL in 1921. Lambeau, who had played at Notre Dame under Knute Rockne, was an outstanding passer, and is credited with having been the first pro coach to exploit the forward pass as an important part of a team's offense. Later, he had players such as Arnie Herber and Cecil Isbell throwing to receivers such as Don Hutson and Johnny Blood (McNally). The Packers won six NFL championships under Lambeau, and his 230 career victories in league play are fourth-most in NFL history, ranking him behind only George Halas, Don Shula, and Tom Landry. In addition to having been a successful coach, Lambeau was a star player for nearly a dozen years. The support of the citizens and Lambeau's commitment to the team helped it survive as the NFL's only "town team." In 1922, Lambeau purchased the Green Bay franchise back from the NFL, after the original owners had withdrawn from the league.

Dick (Night Train) Lane

Defensive Back. 6-2, 210. Born in Austin, Texas, April 16, 1928. Scottsbluff Junior College. Inducted in 1974. 1952-53 Los Angeles Rams, 1954-59 Chicago Cardinals, 1960-65 Detroit Lions.

Dick (Night Train) Lane tried out for the Los Angeles Rams' team in 1952. He had only one season of junior college football and some service ball as experience. But the Rams took a chance, signing him to a free-agent contract. As a rookie, Lane set an NFL record of 14 interceptions in one season. In 1954, the Rams traded him to the Chicago Cardinals, where he continued to play defensive back and saw occasional activity as a receiver. One of those appearances got him into the NFL record book again. He was on the receiving end in a 98-yard pass play. Later in his career, Lane was traded to Detroit. Lane was all-pro five times and played in six Pro Bowls. He retired in 1965 with a total of 68 interceptions, the second-most at the time. He was voted to the all-time NFL team in 1969.

INTERCEPTIONS

Year	Team	No.	Yards	Avg.	Long	TD
1952	LA Rams	14	298	21.3	80	2
1953	LA Rams	3	9	3.0	8	0
1954	Chi. Cardinals	10	181	18.1	64	0
1955	Chi. Cardinals	6	69	11.5	26	0
1956	Chi. Cardinals	7	206	29.4	66t	1
1957	Chi. Cardinals	2	47	23.5	33	0
1958	Chi. Cardinals	2	0	0.0	0	0
1959	Chi. Cardinals	3	125	41.7	69	1
1960	Detroit	5	102	20.4	80t	1
1961	Detroit	6	73	12.2	32	0
1962	Detroit	4	16	4.0	13	0
1963	Detroit	5	70	14.0	33	0
1964	Detroit	1	11	11.0	11	0
1965	Detroit	0	0	0.0	0	0
Totals		68	1,207	17.8	80t	5

Willie Lanier

Linebacker. 6-1, 245. Born in Clover, Virginia, August 21, 1945. Morgan State. Inducted in 1986. 1967-77 Kansas City Chiefs.

Ermal Allen of the Dallas Cowboys once said, "You hear a lot about Dick Butkus and Tommy Nobis, but this Willie Lanier is really the best middle linebacker in pro football." There are those who would argue he was the best ever. Lanier was nicknamed "Contact" for his powerful hits. He also was an important part of the Chiefs' pass defense, intercepting at least two passes every season except his first and last and finishing with a career total of 27 (along with 15 fumble recoveries). Lanier became a starter as a rookie. The next year was the first of eight consecutive years he was selected to either the AFL All-Star Game or the AFC-NFC Pro Bowl; he was the defensive most valuable player of the 1971 game. Lanier was named all-pro, all-league, or all-conference eight times.

INTERCEPTIONS

27, 440 Yards, 16.3 Avg., 75 Long, 2 TD

Yale Lary

Safety-Punter. 5-11, 189. Born in Fort Worth, Texas, November 24, 1930. Texas A&M. Inducted in 1979. 1952-53, 1956-64 Detroit Lions.

Yale Lary truly was multi-talented. The Texas A&M product was the right safety in Detroit's famed Chris's Crew, the secondary led by Hall of Fame member Jack Christiansen. Three times (1959, 1961, 1963) Lary led the NFL in punting; he narrowly missed a fourth. He was second in career punting average at the time of his retirement. In addition, Lary was a dangerous kick returner. He was an all-pro four times and participated in nine Pro Bowls. Lary was at his best under pressure. Teammate (and Hall of Fame member) Joe Schmidt said, "Yale invariably put the ball across midfield when punting from the end zone. He made us [the defense] look good by giving us room to work." Lary served in the Texas legislature while a player.

INTERCEPTIONS

Year	Team	No.	Yards	Avg.	Long	TD
1952	Detroit	4	61	15.3	53	0
1953	Detroit	5	98	19.6	32	0
1954	Military service					
1955	Military service					
1956	Detroit	8	182	22.8	73t	1
1957	Detroit	2	64	32.0	63	0
1958	Detroit	3	70	23.3	31	0
1959	Detroit	3	0	0.0	0	0
1960	Detroit	3	44	14.7	22	0
1961	Detroit	6	95	15.8	42	0
1962	Detroit	8	51	6.4	32	0
1963	Detroit	2	21	10.5	21t	1
1964	Detroit	6	101	16.8	30	0
Totals		50	787	15.7	73t	2

PUNTING

Year	Team	No.	Yards	Avg.	Long	Blk.
1952	Detroit	5		36.2	43	0
1953	Detroit	28		39.7	61	0
1954	Military service					
1955	Military service					
1956	Detroit	42		40.4	61	0
1957	Detroit	54		39.9	66	0
1958	Detroit	59		42.8	62	1
1959	Detroit	45	2,118	47.1	67	0
1960	Detroit	64	2,802	43.8	63	2
1961	Detroit	52		48.4	71	0
1962	Detroit	52	2,402	45.3	68	1
1963	Detroit	35	1,713	48.9	73	0
1964	Detroit	67	3,099	46.3	74	0
Totals		503		44.3	74	4

PUNT RETURNS
126, 752 Yards, 6.0 Avg., 74 Long, 3 TD

KICKOFF RETURNS
22, 495 Yards, 22.5 Avg., 41 Long, 0 TD

Dante Lavelli

End. 6-0, 199. Born in Hudson, Ohio, February 23, 1923. Ohio State. Inducted in 1975. 1946-56 Cleveland Browns.

Dante Lavelli was another player who didn't figure to star in the National Football League. When he reported to the Cleveland Browns' camp in 1946 (when the team was in the All-America Football Conference) he had played in only three varsity games at Ohio State, then served in the infantry for several years. But he became a starter his first season, and tied for the AAFC lead in receptions. Early in his career he teamed with Mac Speedie to give the Browns a set of great pass-catching ends. Lavelli had unusually large hands, and rarely dropped a ball. In the Browns' first NFL Championship Game, in 1950, he caught all 11 passes Otto Graham threw him. He has a record 24 receptions in championship play. His last year, 1956, was the only one in which Lavelli didn't play in a championship game. He made all-pro teams four times, twice each in the AAFC and NFL.

RECEPTIONS

Year	Team	No.	Yards	Avg.	Long	TD
1946	Cleveland (AAFC)	40	843	21.8		8
1947	Cleveland (AAFC)	49	799	16.3		9
1948	Cleveland (AAFC)	25	463	18.5		5
1949	Cleveland (AAFC)	28	475	17.0		7
1950	Cleveland	37	565	15.3	43	5
1951	Cleveland	43	586	13.6	47	6
1952	Cleveland	21	336	16.0	41	4
1953	Cleveland	45	783	17.4	55t	6
1954	Cleveland	47	802	17.1	64	7
1955	Cleveland	31	492	15.9	49	4
1956	Cleveland	20	344	17.2	68t	1
NFL Totals		244	3,908	16.0	68t	33
Pro Totals		386	6,488	16.8	68t	62

Bobby Layne

Quarterback. 6-2, 190. Born in Santa Anna, Texas, December 19, 1926. Texas. Inducted in 1967. 1948 Chicago Bears, 1949 New York Bulldogs, 1950-58 Detroit Lions, 1958-62 Pittsburgh Steelers.

Bobby Layne was as good a clutch player as any who ever played the game. He was a master of the two-minute offense at the end of a half or a game. After spending a year each with the Chicago Bears and the New York Bulldogs, the fun-loving Texan came into his own in Detroit, where he led the Lions to four divisional and three NFL championships in the 1950s. After being traded to Pittsburgh, Layne gave that long-struggling franchise the most potent offense it ever had known. He completed 1,814 passes in 3,700 attempts for 26,768 yards and 196 touchdowns, all NFL career records when he retired, but Layne's greatest skills were in more intangible areas—play-calling and leadership.

PASSING

Year	Team	Att.	Comp.	Yards	TD	Int.
1948	Chi. Bears	52	16	232	3	2
1949	NY Bulldogs	299	155	1,796	9	18
1950	Detroit	336	152	2,323	16	18
1951	Detroit	332	152	2,403	26	23
1952	Detroit	287	139	1,999	19	20
1953	Detroit	273	125	2,088	16	21
1954	Detroit	246	135	1,818	14	12
1955	Detroit	270	143	1,830	11	17
1956	Detroit	244	129	1,909	9	17
1957	Detroit	179	87	1,169	6	12
1958	Detroit	26	12	171	0	2
	Pittsburgh	268	133	2,339	14	10
1959	Pittsburgh	297	142	1,986	20	21
1960	Pittsburgh	209	103	1,814	13	17
1961	Pittsburgh	149	75	1,205	11	16
1962	Pittsburgh	233	116	1,686	9	17
Totals		3,700	1,814	26,768	196	243

RUSHING

Year	Team	Att.	Yards	Avg.	Long	TD
1948	Chi. Bears	13	80	6.2	18	1
1949	NY Bulldogs	54	196	3.6	27	3
1950	Detroit	56	250	4.5	30	4
1951	Detroit	61	290	4.8	36	1
1952	Detroit	94	411	4.4	29	1
1953	Detroit	87	343	3.9	23	0
1954	Detroit	30	119	4.0	34	2
1955	Detroit	31	111	3.6	19	0
1956	Detroit	46	169	3.7	20	5
1957	Detroit	24	99	4.1	21	0
1958	Detroit	5	12	2.4	7	0
	Pittsburgh	35	142	4.1	21	3
1959	Pittsburgh	33	181	5.5	21	2
1960	Pittsburgh	19	12	0.6	13	2
1961	Pittsburgh	8	11	1.4	10	0
1962	Pittsburgh	15	25	1.7	17	1
Totals		611	2,451	4.0	36	25

SCORING
25 TD, 34 FG, 120 PAT, 372 Points

Alphonse (Tuffy) Leemans

Fullback. 6-0, 200. Born in Superior, Wisconsin, November 12, 1912. Died January 19, 1979. George Washington. Inducted in 1978. 1937-43 New York Giants.

For someone from a relatively small-time football program, Tuffy (after the age of 10 few people called him Alphonse) Leemans made a major impact on the NFL in his rookie season. He led the league in rushing in 1936 on the way to becoming a vital and versatile part of strong Giants teams through 1943. In eight seasons, he was the team's top rusher five times. He also led the Giants in passing three times and receiving once and was the Giants' play-caller. Like others from the era, Leemans's statistics aren't overpowering by today's standards, but he was one of the brightest stars in the game during his career.

RUSHING

Year	Team	Att.	Yards	Avg.	Long	TD
1936	NY Giants	206	830	4.0		2
1937	NY Giants	144	429	3.0		0
1938	NY Giants	121	463	3.8		4
1939	NY Giants	128	429	3.4		3
1940	NY Giants	132	474	3.6		1
1941	NY Giants	100	332	3.3	26	4
1942	NY Giants	51	116	2.3	16	3
1943	NY Giants	37	69	1.9	13	0
Totals		919	3,142	3.4		17

PASSING

Year	Team	Att.	Comp.	Yards	TD	Int.
1936	NY Giants	42	13	258	3	6
1937	NY Giants	20	5	64	1	1
1938	NY Giants	42	19	249	3	6
1939	NY Giants	26	12	198	0	2
1940	NY Giants	31	15	159	2	3
1941	NY Giants	66	31	475	4	5
1942	NY Giants	69	35	555	7	4
1943	NY Giants	87	37	366	5	5
Totals		383	167	2,324	25	32

RECEIVING

28, 422 Yards, 15.1 Avg., 3 TD

Bob Lilly

Defensive tackle. 6-4, 260. Born in Olney, Texas, July 24, 1939. TCU. Inducted in 1980. 1961-74 Dallas Cowboys.

The first player the Dallas Cowboys ever drafted was Bob Lilly. Tom Landry, the Cowboys' coach, said, "A player like Bob Lilly comes along once in a coach's lifetime." Lilly was amazingly quick and agile for someone his size (6-4, 260). His pursuit was so intense that teams found it best to run plays directly at him. Although this often required double- and triple-team blocking, Lilly was seldom completely neutralized. For 14 seasons, 11 of which saw him named to the Pro Bowl squad, he was the keystone of Dallas's Doomsday Defense. Lilly was named all-pro seven times, including six in a row (1964-69).

Vince Lombardi

Coach. Born in Brooklyn, New York, June 11, 1913. Died September 3, 1970. Fordham. Inducted in 1971. 1959-67 Green Bay Packers, 1969 Washington Redskins.

Vince Lombardi didn't get his first head coaching job above the high school level until he was 45. But he turned the Green Bay Packers into league champions within three years and built one of the dynasties of sports. In nine seasons he compiled a 99-31-4 record, as his Packers won five NFL titles. In addition, his club won the first two Super Bowls. Lombardi was a strict coach who thought execution, rather than razzle-dazzle, was the way to win. He retired as Green Bay coach after Super Bowl II. After serving as general manager of the Packers in 1968, Lombardi returned to coach the Washington Redskins in 1969 and gave them their first winning season, 7-5-2, since 1953. Lombardi died of cancer in 1970.

Sid Luckman

Quarterback. 6-0, 195. Born in Brooklyn, New York, November 21, 1916. Columbia. Inducted in 1965. 1939-50 Chicago Bears.

After an All-America career as a tailback at Columbia, Sid Luckman became the first of pro football's great T-formation quarterbacks. He had a rare combination of mental and athletic brilliance. He mastered the Bears' highly complex offense and executed it flawlessly. The near-perfect performance of Luckman and the Bears in a 73-0 win over Washington in the 1940 title game caused a sudden switch to the T-formation with man-in-motion at all levels of football. Luckman was all-pro six times. He was a superb ball-handler and play-caller and also excelled on defense and as a punter.

PASSING

Year	Team	Att.	Comp.	Yards	TD	Int.
1939	Chi. Bears	51	23	636	5	4
1940	Chi. Bears	105	48	941	4	9
1941	Chi. Bears	119	68	1,181	9	6
1942	Chi. Bears	105	57	1,023	10	13
1943	Chi. Bears	202	110	2,194	28	12
1944	Chi. Bears	143	71	1,018	11	11
1945	Chi. Bears	217	117	1,725	14	10
1946	Chi. Bears	229	110	1,826	17	16
1947	Chi. Bears	323	176	2,712	24	31
1948	Chi. Bears	163	89	1,047	13	14
1949	Chi. Bears	50	22	200	1	3
1950	Chi. Bears	37	13	180	1	2
Totals		1,744	904	14,683	137	131

INTERCEPTIONS

17, 310 Yards, 18.2 Avg., 54 Long, 2 TD

PUNTING

230, 8,842 Yards, 38.4 Avg., 78 Long, 1 Blk.

Roy (Link) Lyman

Tackle. 6-2, 252. Born in Table Rock, Nebraska, November 30, 1898. Died December 28, 1972. Nebraska. Inducted in 1964. 1922-23 Canton Bulldogs, 1924 Cleveland Bulldogs, 1925 Canton Bulldogs, 1925 Frankford Yellow Jackets, 1926-28, 1930-31, 1933-34 Chicago Bears.

Roy (Link) Lyman is credited with pioneering the "stunting and gambling" style of tackle play. At times, he would change positions as the ball was about to be snapped, a maneuver unheard of at the time. Lyman was a standout on four NFL championship teams, the 1922 and 1923 Canton Bulldogs, 1924 Cleveland Bulldogs, and 1933 Chicago Bears. He joined the Bears for Red Grange's barnstorming tour after the 1925 season and remained with them the rest of his career. In 16 seasons of college and pro football, he was on only one losing team. He retired at 36, when he still was an effective player.

Tim Mara

Team owner. Born in New York, New York, July 29, 1887. Died February 17, 1959. Did not attend college. Inducted in 1963. 1925-59 New York Giants.

Reasoning that "a New York franchise for anything ought to be worth $500," Tim Mara paid that price to buy a team in the NFL in 1925. The move helped give the league the major status it sought and needed; it had been centered in the small cities of the Midwest. Hampered by bad weather, the Giants suffered heavy financial losses in 1925, but when Red Grange and the Bears appeared at the Polo Grounds that December, the team's fortunes improved. Mara still faced a struggle, however. He had to fight the first American Football League in 1926 and the All-America Football Conference in 1946. Mara's Giants survived the confrontations as one of the NFL's most stable franchises. Under Mara, the team won three NFL and eight divisional titles.

Gino Marchetti

Defensive end. 6-4, 245. Born in Antioch, California, January 2, 1927. San Francisco. Inducted in 1972. 1952 Dallas Texans, 1953-64, 1966 Baltimore Colts.

Gino Marchetti was selected the best defensive end in the NFL's first 50 years in 1969. He played his position as few have and was especially adept at rushing the passer. Marchetti played in 10 Pro Bowls. He made all-pro teams for seven years, 1956-1962. Marchetti was first tried as an offensive tackle but he quickly found a place at defensive end. More than anyone, he proved that speed could be coupled with size at that position. As a collegian, Marchetti played on the great University of San Francisco teams that sent nearly a dozen players to the pros, including fellow Hall of Famer Ollie Matson.

George Preston Marshall

Team owner. Born in Grafton, West Virginia, October 11, 1897. Died August 9, 1969. Randolph-Macon. Inducted in 1963. 1932 Boston Braves, 1933-36 Boston Redskins, 1937-69 Washington Redskins.

George Preston Marshall brought showmanship to the NFL. He popularized the marching band and the spectacular halftime show. He was an early exponent of publicity and public relations. He conceived a far-flung radio network that carried Redskins' games throughout the South, and later covered the same area with televised games. But Marshall was more than just a showman. It was at his suggestion—despite the fact he'd been in the league just one season—that most of the sweeping rules changes of 1933 took place. The changes, which opened up the game, included a set schedule, two divisions with a championship playoff, moving the goal posts to the goal line, and a slimmed-down football for more passing.

Ollie Matson

Halfback. 6-2, 220. Born in Trinity, Texas, May 1, 1930. San Francisco. Inducted in 1972. 1952, 1954-58 Chicago Cardinals, 1959-62 Los Angeles Rams, 1963 Detroit Lions, 1964-66 Philadelphia Eagles.

While others were preparing for their rookie seasons in the NFL, Ollie Matson was competing in the 1952 Olympics, where he won a bronze medal in the 400-meter run. Playing for the Chicago Cardinals that fall, he made more than 1,000 all-purpose yards—rushing, receiving, and returning punts and kickoffs. He went on to become one of the most versatile and productive backs in NFL history. The Los Angeles Rams so coveted him that in 1959 they traded nine players to get him. During his career he was constantly shifted from position to position and platoon to platoon. He retired with 12,844 combined net yards—3,746 of them on kickoff returns, on which he was very dangerous. He was an all-pro four consecutive years, 1954-57.

RUSHING

Year	Team	Att.	Yards	Avg.	Long	TD
1952	Chi. Cardinals	96	344	3.6	25	3
1953	Military service					
1954	Chi. Cardinals	101	506	5.0	79t	4
1955	Chi. Cardinals	109	475	4.4	54	1
1956	Chi. Cardinals	192	924	4.8	79t	5
1957	Chi. Cardinals	134	577	4.3	56t	6
1958	Chi. Cardinals	129	505	3.9	55t	5
1959	LA Rams	161	863	5.4	50	6
1960	LA Rams	61	170	2.9	27	1
1961	LA Rams	24	181	7.5	69t	2
1962	LA Rams	3	0	0.0	2	0
1963	Detroit	13	20	1.5	9	0
1964	Philadelphia	96	404	4.2	63	4
1965	Philadelphia	22	103	4.7	22	2
1966	Philadelphia	29	101	3.5	28	1
Totals		1,170	5,173	4.4	79t	40

RECEIVING

Year	Team	No.	Yards	Avg.	Long	TD
1952	Chi. Cardinals	11	187	17.0	47t	3
1953	Military service					
1954	Chi. Cardinals	34	611	18.0	70	3
1955	Chi. Cardinals	17	237	13.9	70t	2
1956	Chi. Cardinals	15	199	13.3	45t	2
1957	Chi. Cardinals	20	451	22.6	75t	3
1958	Chi. Cardinals	33	465	14.1	59	3
1959	LA Rams	18	130	7.2	49	0
1960	LA Rams	15	98	6.5	24	0
1961	LA Rams	29	537	18.5	96t	3
1962	LA Rams	3	49	16.3	20t	1
1963	Detroit	2	20	10.0	17	0
1964	Philadelphia	17	242	14.2	32	1
1965	Philadelphia	2	29	14.5	20	1
1966	Philadelphia	6	30	5.0	11	1
Totals		222	3,285	14.8	96t	23

KICKOFF RETURNS

Year	Team	No.	Yards	Avg.	Long	TD
1952	Chi. Cardinals	20	624	31.2	100t	2
1953	Military service					
1954	Chi. Cardinals	17	449	26.4	91t	1
1955	Chi. Cardinals	15	368	24.5	37	0
1956	Chi. Cardinals	13	362	27.8	105t	1
1957	Chi. Cardinals	7	154	22.0	32	0
1958	Chi. Cardinals	14	497	35.5	101t	2
1959	LA Rams	16	367	22.9	48	0
1960	LA Rams	9	216	24.0	42	0
1961	LA Rams	0	0	0.0	0	0
1962	LA Rams	0	0	0.0	0	0
1963	Detroit	3	61	20.3	30	0
1964	Philadelphia	3	104	34.7	43	0
1965	Philadelphia	0	0	0.0	0	0
1966	Philadelphia	26	544	20.9	31	0
Totals		143	3,746	26.2	105t	6

PUNT RETURNS

65, 595 Yards, 9.2 Avg., 78 Long, 3 TD

SCORING

73 TD, 438 Points

George McAfee

Halfback. 6-0, 177. Born in Ironton, Ohio, March 13, 1918. Duke. Inducted in 1966. 1940-41, 1945-50 Chicago Bears.

Military service caused him to miss three seasons at his peak, but George McAfee was still a great NFL breakaway runner. He was sometimes called "One-Play McAfee." Most of his 39 touchdowns in the NFL were on long, spectacular plays. Lean and lightning fast, McAfee was at his best running the ball, but he also was an accomplished left-footed punter and left-handed passer. He was used as a defensive back after his return from World War II, and intercepted 21 passes.

RUSHING

Year	Team	Att.	Yards	Avg.	Long	TD
1940	Chi. Bears	47	253	5.4		2
1941	Chi. Bears	65	474	7.3	70	6
1942	Military service					
1943	Military service					
1944	Military service					
1945	Chi. Bears	16	139	8.6	38	3
1946	Chi. Bears	14	53	3.8	14	0
1947	Chi. Bears	63	209	3.3	39	3
1948	Chi. Bears	92	392	4.3	23	5
1949	Chi. Bears	42	161	3.8	23	3
1950	Chi. Bears	2	4	2.0	4	0
Totals		341	1,685	4.9	70	22

PUNT RETURNS

Year	Team	No.	Yards	Avg.	Long	TD
1940	Chi. Bears					
1941	Chi. Bears	5	158	31.6	74t	1
1942	Military service					
1943	Military service					
1944	Military service					
1945	Chi. Bears	1	8	8.0	8	0
1946	Chi. Bears	1	24	24.0	24	0
1947	Chi. Bears	18	261	14.5	35	0
1948	Chi. Bears	30	417	13.9	60t	1
1949	Chi. Bears	24	279	11.6	33	0
1950	Chi. Bears	33	284	8.6	25	0
Totals		112	1,431	12.8	74t	2

RECEIVING

85, 1,357 Yards, 16.0 Avg., 65 Long, 11 TD

INTERCEPTIONS

21, 294 Yards, 14.0 Avg., 1 TD

Mike McCormack

Tackle. 6-4, 250. Born in Chicago, Illinois, June 21, 1930. Kansas. Inducted in 1984. 1951 New York Yanks, 1954-62 Cleveland Browns.

Cleveland was so eager to obtain the services of tackle Mike McCormack that it acquired his playing rights while he still had a year to serve in the U.S. Army. McCormack had played his rookie year with the New York Yanks, but in 1953, while he was in the service, the new Baltimore Colts received his rights. The Colts, in turn, swapped him to the Browns as part of a 15-player deal, in which he was the key player. When he joined the Browns, McCormack played at middle guard for a while, but he made his lasting mark at offensive tackle. He made six appearances in the Pro Bowl and played in three NFL Championship Games. McCormack later served as head coach of Philadelphia from 1973-75, Baltimore from 1980-81, and Seattle in 1982. He was named president of the Seahawks in 1983.

Hugh McElhenny

Halfback. 6-1, 198. Born in Los Angeles, California, December 31, 1928. Washington. Inducted in 1970. 1952-60 San Francisco 49ers, 1961-62 Minnesota Vikings, 1963 New York Giants, 1964 Detroit Lions.

Few NFL players ever have enjoyed a finer season than Hugh McElhenny did as a rookie in 1952. He led the league in rushing average with seven yards a carry, scored 60 points, and was named rookie of the year. Nicknamed "The King," he made instinctive moves no one duplicated, sometimes going 40 yards criss-crossing the field to make a five-yard gain. He was an all-pro in 1952 and 1953, and played in six Pro Bowls. Thought to be over the hill by the 49ers because his knees had worn down after so much twisting and turning, McElhenny was drafted by the expansion Vikings in 1961 and contributed more than 1,000 total yards that season. He had 11,369 total yards.

RUSHING

Year	Team	Att.	Yards	Avg.	Long	TD
1952	San Francisco	98	684	7.0	89t	6
1953	San Francisco	112	503	4.5	33	3
1954	San Francisco	64	515	8.0	60t	6
1955	San Francisco	90	327	3.6	44	4
1956	San Francisco	185	916	5.0	86t	8
1957	San Francisco	102	478	4.7	61	1
1958	San Francisco	113	451	4.0	34	6
1959	San Francisco	18	67	3.7	19	1
1960	San Francisco	95	347	3.7	38	0
1961	Minnesota	120	570	4.8	41	3
1962	Minnesota	50	200	4.0	27	0
1963	NY Giants	55	175	3.2	23	0
1964	Detroit	22	48	2.2	14	0
Totals		1,124	5,281	4.7	89t	38

RECEIVING

Year	Team	No.	Yards	Avg.	Long	TD
1952	San Francisco	26	367	14.1	77	3
1953	San Francisco	30	474	15.8	71	2
1954	San Francisco	8	162	20.3	53	0
1955	San Francisco	11	203	18.5	55t	2
1956	San Francisco	16	193	12.1	22	0
1957	San Francisco	37	458	12.4	43	2
1958	San Francisco	31	366	11.8	59t	2
1959	San Francisco	22	329	15.0	62t	3
1960	San Francisco	14	114	8.1	45	1
1961	Minnesota	37	283	7.6	26	3
1962	Minnesota	16	191	11.9	41	0
1963	NY Giants	11	91	8.3	24	2
1964	Detroit	5	16	3.2	27	0
Totals		264	3,247	12.3	77	20

PUNT RETURNS
126, 920 Yards, 7.3 Avg., 94 Long, 2 TD

KICKOFF RETURNS
83, 1,921 Yards, 23.1 Avg., 55 Long, 0 TD

SCORING
60 TD, 360 Points

Mike Michalske

Guard. 6-0, 209. Born in Cleveland, Ohio, April 24, 1903. Penn State. Inducted in 1964. 1926 New York Yankees (AFL), 1927-28 New York Yankees, 1929-35, 1937 Green Bay Packers.

After making All-America at Penn State, Mike Michalske joined the New York Yankees of the American Football League in 1926. He and the Yankees moved to the NFL in 1927, and he was traded to Green Bay in 1929. The Packers were NFL champions in 1929-31 when Michalske had his greatest years. Offensively, Michalske led interference on most plays, regardless of which direction they went. Defensively, he had a style like today's blitzing linebackers and was adept at stopping power thrusts. Michalske was named all-pro six times. He later was the first guard inducted into the Hall of Fame.

Wayne Millner

End. 6-0, 191. Born in Roxbury, Massachusetts, January 31, 1913. Died November 19, 1976. Notre Dame. Inducted in 1968. 1936 Boston Redskins, 1937-41, 1945 Washington Redskins.

Wayne Millner was one of the main reasons the Washington Redskins won NFL championships under Ray Flaherty. He had excellent statistics as a pass receiver but his value to the team was enhanced by his aggressive line and downfield blocking and his defensive play. "I always knew if I got open," Hall of Fame running back Cliff Battles said, "Millner would be there to throw a block for me." In the 1937 NFL Championship Game, Millner caught two touchdown passes—for 78 and 55 yards—as the Redskins won 28-21. An All-America at Notre Dame, Millner caught 124 passes as a pro. He missed three years of football because of military service.

RECEIVING

Year	Team	No.	Yards	Avg.	Long	TD
1936	Boston	18	211	11.7		0
1937	Washington	14	216	15.4		2
1938	Washington	18	232	12.9		1
1939	Washington	19	294	15.5		4
1940	Washington	22	233	10.6		3
1941	Washington	20	262	13.1	55	0
1942	Military service					
1943	Military service					
1944	Military service					
1945	Washington	13	130	10.0	11	2
Totals		124	1,578	12.7		12

Bobby Mitchell

Halfback-Wide receiver. 6-0, 195. Born in Hot Springs, Arkansas, June 6, 1935. Illinois. Inducted in 1983. 1958-61 Cleveland Browns, 1962-68 Washington Redskins.

Bobby Mitchell started his career as one of the top halfbacks in the NFL; he finished it as one of the top wide receivers. Mitchell served notice of his ability early—he caught two touchdown passes in the All-Stars' upset of the Detroit Lions in the 1958 Chicago College All-Star Game. As a rookie with the Cleveland Browns, Mitchell earned the starting halfback position next to Jim Brown. In four years, he ran for 2,297 yards and caught passes for 1,462 more. In 1962, Mitchell was traded to Washington, where he was moved to flanker. In his first year at the position, he led the NFL in receiving; the next year he led it in receiving yards. In 1963, he also caught a 99-yard touchdown pass from George Izo. During his first six years with the Redskins, Mitchell never caught fewer than 58 passes. When he retired, he was the number-two career receiver in NFL history. Today, he's the assistant general manager of the Redskins.

RUSHING

Year	Team	Att.	Yards	Avg.	Long	TD
1958	Cleveland	80	500	6.3	63t	1
1959	Cleveland	131	743	5.7	90t	5
1960	Cleveland	111	506	4.6	50	5
1961	Cleveland	101	548	5.4	65t	5
1962	Washington	1	5	5.0	5	0
1963	Washington	3	24	8.0	21	0
1964	Washington	2	33	16.5	19	0
1965	Washington	0	0	0.0	0	0
1966	Washington	13	141	10.8	48	1
1967	Washington	61	189	3.1	16	1
1968	Washington	10	46	4.6	13	0
Totals		513	2,735	5.3	90t	18

RECEIVING

Year	Team	No.	Yards	Avg.	Long	TD
1958	Cleveland	16	131	8.2	25	3
1959	Cleveland	35	351	10.0	76t	4
1960	Cleveland	45	612	13.6	69t	6
1961	Cleveland	32	368	11.5	55	3
1962	Washington	72	1,384	19.2	81t	11
1963	Washington	69	1,436	20.8	99t	7
1964	Washington	60	904	15.1	60	10
1965	Washington	60	867	14.5	80t	6
1966	Washington	58	905	15.6	70t	9
1967	Washington	60	866	14.4	65t	6
1968	Washington	14	130	9.3	18	0
Totals		521	7,954	15.3	99t	65

PUNT RETURNS
69, 699 Yards, 10.1 Avg., 78 Long, 3 TD

KICKOFF RETURNS
102, 2,690 Yards, 26.4 Avg., 98 Long, 5 TD

SCORING
91 TD, 546 Points

Ron Mix

Tackle. 6-4, 250. Born in Los Angeles, California, March 10, 1938. USC. Inducted in 1979. 1960 Los Angeles Chargers, 1961-69 San Diego Chargers, 1971 Oakland Raiders.

To have played on the offensive line and to be only the second AFL player enshrined in the Hall of Fame indicates the stature Ron Mix earned as a player. He was an All-America at USC in 1959 and the first draft choice of the AFL's Boston Patriots and the NFL's Baltimore Colts in 1960. The Patriots traded Mix to San Diego. According to records kept by the Chargers, Mix had only two holding calls made against him in his 10 seasons with the team. After sitting out the 1970 season, he came back to play one year with the Oakland Raiders. Mix, who earned a law degree while still an active player, was named all-AFL nine times and was selected to the all-time all-AFL team.

Lenny Moore

Halfback-Flanker. 6-1, 198. Born in Reading, Pennsylvania, November 25, 1933. Penn State. Inducted in 1975. 1956-67 Baltimore Colts.

Opponents often knew if Lenny Moore was flanked wide, he was going to catch a pass; if he was in the backfield, he was going to run the ball. Knowing this, they still had trouble stopping him. In 12 NFL seasons, he made more than 12,000 all-purpose yards. He made all-pro teams for five years, and played in seven Pro Bowls. Only Jim Brown, with 126 touchdowns, scored more than Moore's 113. Moore put together a string of 18 consecutive games in which he scored at least one touchdown. After missing most of the 1963 season he earned comeback player of the year honors in 1964, gaining more than 1,000 yards rushing and receiving, and scoring 20 touchdowns.

RUSHING

Year	Team	Att.	Yards	Avg.	Long	TD
1956	Baltimore	86	649	7.5	79t	8
1957	Baltimore	98	488	5.0	55t	3
1958	Baltimore	82	598	7.3	73t	7
1959	Baltimore	92	422	4.6	31t	2
1960	Baltimore	91	374	4.1	57t	4
1961	Baltimore	92	648	7.0	54t	7
1962	Baltimore	106	470	4.4	25	2
1963	Baltimore	27	136	5.0	25t	2
1964	Baltimore	157	584	3.7	32t	16
1965	Baltimore	133	464	3.5	28t	5
1966	Baltimore	63	209	3.3	18	3
1967	Baltimore	42	132	3.1	21	4
Totals		1,069	5,174	4.8	79t	63

RECEIVING

Year	Team	No.	Yards	Avg.	Long	TD
1956	Baltimore	11	102	9.3	27	1
1957	Baltimore	40	687	17.2	82t	7
1958	Baltimore	50	938	18.5	77t	7
1959	Baltimore	47	846	18.0	71	6
1960	Baltimore	45	936	20.8	80t	9
1961	Baltimore	49	728	14.9	72t	8
1962	Baltimore	18	215	11.9	80t	2
1963	Baltimore	21	288	13.7	34	2
1964	Baltimore	21	472	22.5	74t	3
1965	Baltimore	27	414	15.3	52t	3
1966	Baltimore	21	260	12.4	36	0
1967	Baltimore	13	153	11.8	37	0
Totals		363	6,039	16.6	82t	48

KICKOFF RETURNS

49, 1,180 Yards, 24.1 Avg., 92 Long, 1 TD

SCORING

113 TD, 678 Points

Marion Motley

Fullback. 6-1, 238. Born in Leesburg, Georgia, June 5, 1920. Nevada-Reno. Inducted in 1968. 1946-53 Cleveland Browns, 1955 Pittsburgh Steelers.

Marion Motley grew up in Canton, site of the Hall of Fame, and starred for McKinley High. A devastating power runner of the post-World War II years, Motley contributed to the Browns in many ways. He protected for Otto Graham on pass plays, and he was perhaps the most effective back in pro football on draw plays. When Graham did get in trouble, Motley almost always could turn a short dump-off pass into a good gain. He was a top linebacker early in his career, too, and was used often on Cleveland's goal-line defense. Motley was the career rushing leader in the All-America Football Conference, and led the NFL in his first season in the league in 1950.

RUSHING

Year	Team	Att.	Yards	Avg.	Long	TD
1946	Cleveland (AAFC)	73	601	8.2		5
1947	Cleveland (AAFC)	146	889	6.1		8
1948	Cleveland (AAFC)	157	964	6.1		5
1949	Cleveland (AAFC)	113	570	5.0		8
1950	Cleveland	140	810	5.8	69t	3
1951	Cleveland	61	273	4.5	26	1
1952	Cleveland	104	444	4.3	59	1
1953	Cleveland	32	161	5.0	34	0
1954	Did not play football					
1955	Pittsburgh	2	8	4.0	8	0
NFL Totals		339	1,696	5.0	69t	5
Pro Totals		828	4,720	5.7	69t	31

RECEIVING

NFL—40, 463 Yards, 11.6 Avg., 68 Long, 3 TD
Pro—85, 1,107 Yards, 13.0 Avg., 7 TD

George Musso

Guard-Tackle. 6-2, 270. Born in Collinsville, Illinois, April 8, 1910. Millikin. Inducted in 1982. 1933-44 Chicago Bears.

George Musso was one of the first Bears to join the team from a little-known college, a Chicago tradition even before today's sophisticated scouting. A versatile player, Musso played both guard and tackle, making all-pro at both positions. Musso was a 60-minute man playing offense and defense. He was as responsible as anyone for the Bears of his era being known as the Monsters of the Midway. During Musso's 12-year career, the Bears were division champions seven times and NFL champions four times (1933, 1940, 1941, and 1943). That Musso had to wait 38 years after retiring to be selected to the Hall of Fame can be explained in part by the others associated with his Bears teams. Dan Fortmann, Red Grange, George Halas, Sid Luckman, George McAfee, Bronko Nagurski, Joe Stydahar, and Clyde (Bulldog) Turner all preceded him into the Hall of Fame. In 1929, Musso played against Ronald Reagan, a guard for Eureka College. In 1935, he went against Gerald Ford, a center from Michigan playing in the Chicago College All-Star Game.

Bronko Nagurski

Fullback. 6-2, 225. Born in Rainy River, Ontario, Canada, November 3, 1908. Minnesota. Inducted in 1963. 1930-37, 1943 Chicago Bears.

Bronko Nagurski is still the standard by which power runners are measured. He came out of Minnesota after having made All-America teams as both a tackle and a fullback. He teamed with Red Grange in his early pro years to give Chicago the league's best running game, and Nagurski's blocking enabled Beattie Feathers to rush for 1,004 yards in 1934, the first NFL runner to top 1,000. He retired in 1937 to become a professional wrestler, but he came back for the 1943 season. He was used mostly at tackle but he played fullback in the final game win over the Chicago Cardinals that clinched the divisional championship. The Bears won the NFL title the following week. He also was a remarkable linebacker.

RUSHING

Year	Team	Att.	Yards	Avg.	Long	TD
1930	Chi. Bears					
1931	Chi. Bears					
1932	Chi. Bears	111	496	4.5		4
1933	Chi. Bears	128	533	4.2		1
1934	Chi. Bears	123	586	4.8		7
1935	Chi. Bears	37	137	3.7		1
1936	Chi. Bears	122	529	4.3		3
1937	Chi. Bears	73	343	4.7		1
1938	Retired from football					
1939	Retired from football					
1940	Retired from football					
1941	Retired from football					
1942	Retired from football					
1943	Chi. Bears	16	84	5.3	11	1

Joe Namath

Quarterback. 6-2, 200. Born in Beaver Falls, Pennsylvania, May 31, 1943. Alabama. Inducted in 1985. 1965-76 New York Jets, 1977 Los Angeles Rams.

When Joe Namath guaranteed a New York Jets victory over the Baltimore Colts in Super Bowl III, then helped produce a 16-7 upset three days later, he became an American folk hero. The Super Bowl victory was the zenith for Namath's career, which had begun on a high point. Once called "the greatest athlete I have ever coached," by Paul (Bear) Bryant, Namath signed with the Jets in 1965 for $400,000, the largest pro football contract ever at the time. He was the AFL's most expensive victory in the costly interleague war. Namath was worth the price, however. In 1965, he was named rookie of the year and most valuable player of the AFL All-Star Game. Two years later, he became the first player to pass for more than 4,000 yards in a season.

PASSING

Year	Team	Att.	Comp.	Yards	TD	Int.
1965	NY Jets	340	164	2,220	18	15
1966	NY Jets	471	232	3,379	19	27
1967	NY Jets	491	258	4,007	26	28
1968	NY Jets	380	187	3,145	15	17
1969	NY Jets	361	185	2,734	19	17
1970	NY Jets	179	90	1,259	5	12
1971	NY Jets	59	28	537	5	6
1972	NY Jets	324	162	2,816	19	21
1973	NY Jets	133	68	966	5	6
1974	NY Jets	361	191	2,616	20	22
1975	NY Jets	326	157	2,286	15	28
1976	NY Jets	230	114	1,090	4	16
1977	LA Rams	107	50	606	3	5
Totals		3,762	1,886	27,663	173	220

RUSHING

71 Att., 140 Yards, 2.0 Avg., 7 TD

Earle (Greasy) Neale

Coach. Born in Parkersburg, West Virginia, November 5, 1891. Died November 2, 1973. West Virginia Wesleyan. Inducted in 1969. 1941-50 Philadelphia Eagles.

Earle (Greasy) Neale played major league baseball (he was the Cincinnati Reds' leading hitter in the 1919 World Series) at about the same time he was starting his pro football career with the pre-NFL Canton Bulldogs of 1917, under an assumed name. Later he was to have an extensive college coaching career before he finally entered the NFL as coach of the Philadelphia Eagles in 1941. The Eagles had been a perennial second-division club since they were founded in 1933 but Neale built them into a power. They were runners-up in 1944, 1945, and 1946, then won the Eastern Division championship in 1947 and were NFL champions in 1948 and 1949. His 1948 and 1949 clubs won the titles with back-to-back shutouts in the championship games. He devised the Eagle defense, one of the forerunners of the four-three.

Ernie Nevers

Fullback. 6-1, 205. Born in Willow River, Minnesota, June 11, 1903. Died May 3, 1976. Stanford. Inducted in 1963. 1926-27 Duluth Eskimos, 1929-31 Chicago Cardinals.

Of all the men in the Hall of Fame, Ernie Nevers's career was the briefest—just five NFL seasons. But he was a brilliant player. He was an iron man who missed only 26 minutes of play in 1926. The 40 points he scored—six touchdowns and four extra points—for the Cardinals against the Chicago Bears in 1929 is still an NFL record. Glenn (Pop) Warner, who had coached Jim Thorpe earlier, said Nevers was "the greatest player I ever coached." Warner coached Nevers at Stanford, where Nevers was an All-America. Nevers's signing with Duluth in 1926 had almost as much of an impact as Red Grange's had the year before. Nevers was player-coach with the Chicago Cardinals. In addition to football, he also was a pitcher for the St. Louis Browns and played professional basketball.

Ray Nitschke

Linebacker. 6-3, 235. Born in Elmwood Park, Illinois, December 29, 1936. Illinois. Inducted in 1978. 1958-72 Green Bay Packers.

During the 1960s, defense was an important factor in the Green Bay Packers' unparalleled success. Ray Nitschke, the middle linebacker, was the linchpin of the unit. For 15 seasons he provided leadership and direction on the field, calling defensive signals for much of his career. Nitschke, one of the hardest tacklers ever to play the game, was named the most valuable player in the 1962 NFL Championship Game. He was one of several Packers who blossomed after Vince Lombardi arrived as head coach in 1959. During his career, Nitschke played on two Super Bowl championship teams and five NFL title teams. He was named to the all-time NFL team chosen in 1969.

Leo Nomellini

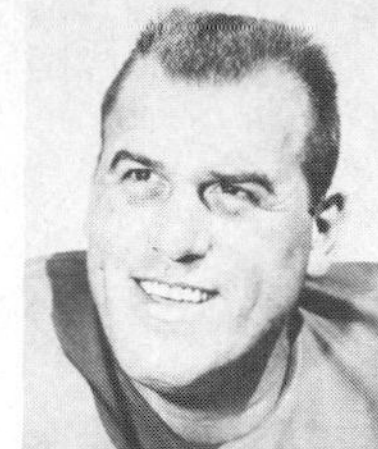

Defensive tackle. 6-3, 264. Born in Lucca, Italy, June 19, 1924. Minnesota. Inducted in 1969. 1950-63 San Francisco 49ers.

Military service delayed Leo Nomellini's debut until he was 26, but he made up for the late start, playing until he was 39. Nomellini, who was nicknamed "The Lion," didn't miss a game during his entire 14-year career. His 174 consecutive games were an NFL record when he retired. Counting preseason, regular season, playoff, and Pro Bowl games, Nomellini's string was 266 games. He cleared the way for Hugh McElhenny, Joe Perry, J.D. Smith, and John Henry Johnson on offense, but it was on defense where he earned his greatest reputation. He was named the defensive tackle on the NFL's all-time team in 1969.

Merlin Olsen

Defensive tackle. 6-5, 270. Born in Logan, Utah, September 15, 1940. Utah State. Inducted in 1982. 1962-76 Los Angeles Rams.

Merlin Olsen seemed destined for greatness. He was a consensus All-America and Phi Beta Kappa his senior year at Utah State and Los Angeles's first-round pick in the 1962 NFL draft. In his first NFL season, Olsen was named rookie of the year and elected to the Pro Bowl squad. He repeated as a Pro Bowl selection 13 more times, missing only in his fifteenth and final professional season. No one ever has played in more (14) postseason all-star games. Olsen teamed with David (Deacon) Jones—another member of the Hall of Fame—Rosey Grier or Roger Brown, and Lamar Lundy to form the Rams' Fearsome Foursome in the 1960s. The Fearsome Foursome eventually broke up, but Olsen continued his high caliber of play with the Rams. He was named NFL player of the year by the Maxwell Club in 1974, and was an all-pro six times (1966-70, 1973). For six consecutive seasons Olsen was voted by Rams teammates as either the team's most valuable player or outstanding defensive lineman. After retiring, Olsen became a successful television football analyst and actor.

Jim Otto

Center. 6-2, 255. Born in Wausau, Wisconsin, January 5, 1938. Miami. Inducted in 1980. 1960-74 Oakland Raiders.

Because he weighed 205 pounds in college, Jim Otto was considered too light to play in the NFL. The birth of the American Football League gave Otto the opportunity to prove the reports inaccurate. He virtually grew up with the league. Otto, who wore number 00 after his rookie year, became an immediate starter at center for the Raiders and held the job for 15 seasons. He appeared in 210 consecutive regular-season games, in addition to numerous preseason, postseason, and all-star games. Otto was the only all-league center the AFL had in its 10-year existence, and he was voted to the all-time AFL team. He played in the AFL All-Star Game or the Pro Bowl 13 times. He is a graduate of Wausau High School, the same school attended by Elroy (Crazylegs) Hirsch.

Steve Owen

Tackle-Coach. 6-0, 235. Born in Cleo Springs, Oklahoma, April 21, 1898. Died May 17, 1964. Phillips. Inducted in 1966. 1924 Kansas City Blues, 1925 Kansas City Cowboys, 1926-30 New York Giants. Coach, 1931-53 New York Giants.

Steve Owen was a defensive coaching genius; he devised the Umbrella defense. He also played what he called the A-formation. He was one of the first coaches to exploit the field goal as a scoring weapon. Owen learned football through his line play in the early NFL. He was big and rough, the equal of any tackle in the game. Starting in 1931, he coached the New York Giants for 23 years "on a handshake" each season with owner Tim Mara; Owen never signed a formal contract. His record was 153-108-17 and his teams won eight divisional and two NFL championships.

Clarence (Ace) Parker

Halfback-Quarterback. 5-11, 168. Born in Portsmouth, Virginia, May 17, 1912. Duke. Inducted in 1972. 1937-41 Brooklyn Dodgers, 1945 Boston Yanks, 1946 New York Yankees (AAFC).

Clarence (Ace) Parker was a celebrated All-America tailback at Duke who joined the Brooklyn football Dodgers in 1937. He signed with them but expected to play pro football only briefly because he'd also signed a major league baseball contract with the Philadelphia Athletics. He stayed with the Dodgers, however, and won all-pro honors in 1938 and 1940. Parker, a triple-threat, two-way back despite the fact that he wasn't very big or very fast, led the Dodgers to their best seasons in 1940 and 1941. After his return from World War II service, he helped lead the New York Yankees to the All-America Football Conference Eastern Division title in 1946.

RUSHING

Year	Team	Att.	Yards	Avg.	Long	TD
1937	Brooklyn	34	26	0.8		1
1938	Brooklyn	93	253	2.7		2
1939	Brooklyn	104	271	2.6		5
1940	Brooklyn	89	306	3.4		3
1941	Brooklyn	85	301	3.5	60	0
1942	Military serrvice					
1943	Military service					
1944	Military service					
1945	Boston	18	-49	-2.7	7	0
1946	NY Yankees (AAFC)	75	184	2.5		3
NFL Totals		423	1,108	2.6		11
Pro Totals		498	1,292	2.6		14

PASSING

Year	Team	Att.	Comp.	Yards	TD	Int.
1937	Brooklyn	61	28	514	1	7
1938	Brooklyn	148	63	865	5	7
1939	Brooklyn	157	72	977	4	13
1940	Brooklyn	111	49	817	10	7
1941	Brooklyn	102	51	642	2	8
1942	Military service					
1943	Military service					
1944	Military service					
1945	Boston	24	10	123	0	5
1946	NY Yankees (AAFC)	115	62	763	8	3
NFL Totals		603	273	3,938	22	47
Pro Totals		718	335	4,701	30	50

Jim Parker

Guard-Tackle. 6-3, 273. Born in Macon, Georgia, April 3, 1934. Ohio State. Inducted in 1973. 1957-67 Baltimore Colts.

Jim Parker, a two-time All-America at Ohio State and winner of the 1956 Outland Trophy as the nation's top college lineman, was the first lineman elected to the Hall of Fame exclusively as an offensive performer. Noted for his defensive skills at Ohio State, Parker was thought by many to be destined for pro duty on defense, too, but from his first day of pro practice he was at left tackle on offense. That's where he stayed until midway through his sixth season, when he was moved to left guard, despite the great difference in requirements at the positions. He was outstanding as a blocker both on passing and running plays. His special assignment was to protect quarterback Johnny Unitas, which he did superbly. Parker played in eight Pro Bowls. He was named all-pro eight consecutive years, four at tackle, three at guard, and one (in 1962) at both.

Joe Perry

Fullback. 6-0, 200. Born in Stevens, Arkansas, January 27, 1927. Compton Junior College. Inducted in 1969. 1948-60, 1963 San Francisco 49ers, 1961-62 Baltimore Colts.

Joe Perry, nicknamed "The Jet" by 49ers quarterback Frankie Albert because of his quick starts, came into the pros without having played college football, only junior college and Navy football. In 16 seasons, the longest career ever for a running back, Perry became one of the leading ground gainers in pro football history. He was the first NFL runner to put together back-to-back 1,000-yard seasons, in 1953 and 1954. In the early 1950s, Perry was a member of the 49ers' "Million Dollar Backfield," which also included Y.A. Tittle, Hugh McElhenny, and John Henry Johnson. Perry was all-AAFC in 1949 and all-NFL in 1953 and 1954. He played in three Pro Bowls.

RUSHING

Year	Team	Att.	Yards	Avg.	Long	TD
1948	San Francisco (AAFC)	77	562	7.3		10
1949	San Francisco (AAFC)	115	783	6.8		8
1950	San Francisco	124	647	5.2	78t	5
1951	San Francisco	136	677	5.0	58t	3
1952	San Francisco	158	725	4.6	78t	8
1953	San Francisco	192	1,018	5.3	51t	10
1954	San Francisco	173	1,049	6.1	58	8
1955	San Francisco	156	701	4.5	42	2
1956	San Francisco	115	520	4.5	39	3
1957	San Francisco	97	454	4.7	34	3
1958	San Francisco	125	758	6.1	73t	4
1959	San Francisco	139	602	4.4	40	3
1960	San Francisco	36	95	2.6	21	1
1961	Baltimore	168	675	4.0	27	3
1962	Baltimore	94	359	3.8	21	0
1963	San Francisco	24	98	4.1	16	0
NFL Totals		1,737	8,378	4.8	78t	53
Pro Totals		1,929	9,723	5.0	78t	71

RECEIVING

Year	Team	No.	Yards	Avg.	Long	TD
1948	San Francisco (AAFC)	8	79	9.9		1
1949	San Francisco (AAFC)	11	146	13.3		3
1950	San Francisco	13	69	5.3	16	1
1951	San Francisco	18	167	9.3	35	1
1952	San Francisco	15	81	5.4	17	0
1953	San Francisco	19	191	10.1	60t	3
1954	San Francisco	26	203	7.8	70	0
1955	San Francisco	19	55	2.9	19	1
1956	San Francisco	18	104	5.8	20	0
1957	San Francisco	15	130	8.7	17	0
1958	San Francisco	23	218	9.5	64t	1
1959	San Francisco	12	53	4.4	15	0
1960	San Francisco	3	-3	-1.0	3	0
1961	Baltimore	34	322	9.5	27	1
1962	Baltimore	22	194	8.8	32	0
1963	San Francisco	4	12	3.0	8	0
NFL Totals		241	1,796	7.4	70	8
Pro Totals		260	2,021	7.8	70	12

SCORING

NFL—61 TD, 1 FG, 6 PAT, 375 Points
Pro—84 TD, 1 FG, 6 PAT, 513 Points

KICKOFF RETURNS

NFL—15, 276 Yards, 18.4 Avg., 0 TD
Pro—33, 758 Yards, 23.0 Avg., 1 TD

Pete Pihos

End. 6-1, 210. Born in Orlando, Florida, October 22, 1923. Indiana. Inducted in 1970. 1947-55 Philadelphia Eagles.

Throughout his nine-year career with the Philadelphia Eagles, Pete Pihos was moved from platoon to platoon, and even played the full 60 minutes at times. Playing primarily on offense, he was an all-pro in 1948 and 1949. In 1952, he made it on defense. Back on offense, he was all-pro in 1953, 1954, and 1955; he was also the NFL's leading pass catcher in each of those years. Pihos was chosen to play in five Pro Bowl games in a row. He had been drafted by the Eagles in 1945 but military service delayed the completion of his education at Indiana and he didn't report to the pros until 1947. Despite his service on defense, Pihos had 373 receptions, good for 5,619 yards and 61 touchdowns.

RECEIVING

Year	Team	No.	Yards	Avg.	Long	TD
1947	Philadelphia	23	382	16.6	66t	7
1948	Philadelphia	46	766	16.7	48	11
1949	Philadelphia	34	484	14.2	49	4
1950	Philadelphia	38	447	11.8	43	6
1951	Philadelphia	35	536	15.3	38t	5
1952	Philadelphia	12	219	18.3	47	1
1953	Philadelphia	63	1,049	16.7	59	10
1954	Philadelphia	60	872	14.5	34	10
1955	Philadelphia	62	864	13.9	40t	7
Totals		373	5,619	15.1	66t	61

SCORING

63 TD, 378 Points

Hugh (Shorty) Ray

Supervisor of officials. Born in Highland Park, Illinois, September 21, 1884. Died September 16, 1956. Illinois. Inducted in 1966.

Hugh (Shorty) Ray is not an instantly recognizable pro football name, but his contributions to the game were great. As technical advisor and supervisor of officials for the NFL from 1938 to 1956, Ray was responsible for much of the streamlining that made pro football the fast-moving, exciting game it has become. Armed with a stopwatch, pencils, charts, and field glasses, Ray observed hundreds of games and thousands of plays, making countless notations. All of them were designed to make the game faster and safer. Ray toured the league's training camps annually to clarify and explain the game's rules to players and coaches. He also worked tirelessly to improve the techniques and quality of officiating.

Daniel F. Reeves

Team owner. Born in New York, New York, June 30, 1912. Died April 15, 1971. Georgetown. Inducted in 1967. 1941-45 Cleveland Rams, 1946-71 Los Angeles Rams.

Dan Reeves's interest in professional football stemmed from his friendship with schoolmate Jack Mara, son of Giants' owner Tim Mara. Reeves purchased the Cleveland Rams in 1941, and, when he moved the title-winning club of 1945 to Los Angeles for the 1946 season, he was responsible for making the NFL a coast-to-coast league. Many NFL owners were reluctant to approve the move but Reeves persuaded them to go along with him. He was also the first NFL owner after World War II to sign black players, the first of whom were Kenny Washington and Woody Strode. The Rams also signed the first player from a predominantly black college, Paul (Tank) Younger of Grambling in 1949. Reeves loved the draft and developed many of the scouting techniques that later became common. He became known for trading outstanding young players for draft choices, so he could select more young players in the draft.

Jim Ringo

Center. 6-1, 235. Born in Orange, New Jersey, November 21, 1932. Syracuse. Inducted in 1981. 1953-63 Green Bay Packers, 1964-67 Philadelphia Eagles.

Jim Ringo was an all-pro and Pro Bowl choice when Green Bay was the Siberia of the NFL. He continued to perform at an all-star level after Vince Lombardi turned the league's smallest city into Titletown. Ringo was the pivotal man in an offensive line that made the Packers' power sweep the most feared play of the era. He was not especially big, but he was very quick, smart, and durable. He played in 182 consecutive games, an NFL career record at the time. Ringo was selected to the all-pro team six times, and played in 10 Pro Bowls—7 with Green Bay and 3 with Philadelphia (he was traded to the Eagles on May 6, 1964). He was a seventh-round draft choice in 1953. Ringo served as head coach of Buffalo in 1976 and 1977.

Andy Robustelli

Defensive end. 6-0, 230. Born in Stamford, Connecticut, December 6, 1925. Arnold College. Inducted in 1971. 1951-55 Los Angeles Rams, 1956-64 New York Giants.

Arnold College (onetime enrollment 350) doesn't even exist anymore, but it sent Andy Robustelli to pro football and the Hall of Fame. He was chosen by the Rams on the nineteenth round of the 1951 draft. Used as both an offensive and defensive end early in his career, he eventually settled into the defensive end position when two-platoon football became dominant. He was a two-time all-pro with the Rams, and, after being traded to the Giants, he was all-pro five more times. He was an important part of the Giants' heralded defensive unit during the mid and late 1950s and the early 1960s. Robustelli was intelligent, quick, strong, and durable. He missed only one game in 14 years. He played in eight NFL Championship Games and in seven Pro Bowls.

Art Rooney, Sr.

Team owner. Born in Coulterville, Pennsylvania, January 27, 1901. Georgetown, Duquesne. Inducted in 1964. 1933-40 Pittsburgh Pirates, 1941-42 Pittsburgh Steelers, 1943 Phil-Pitt, 1944 Card-Pitt, 1945-86 Pittsburgh Steelers.

In 1933, Art Rooney purchased an NFL franchise for Pittsburgh for $2,500. His teams always seemed to be luckless, ill-fated, and, in some cases, just plain bad. He survived the Depression and the talent-thin times of World War II, when he twice was forced to merge his struggling franchise with another. When the man who had supported pro, semipro, and amateur sports of all types in western Pennsylvania even before he bought the Steelers, finally realized his first championships—victories in Super Bowls IX and X—the sports world gave him the acclaim he never had enjoyed before. Rooney's Steelers teams also won Super Bowls XIII and XIV, giving him more Super Bowl championships than any other owner.

Pete Rozelle

Commissioner. Born in South Gate, California, March 1, 1926. San Francisco. Inducted in 1985. 1960-86 NFL Commissioner.

When 33-year-old Pete Rozelle became a compromise choice as Commissioner of the NFL in 1960, following the death of Bert Bell, pro football still was a second banana to college football in popularity. That scenario changed under Rozelle, whose career had begun in public relations. He had gone from sports information director at the University of San Francisco to public relations director of the Los Angeles Rams to publicist for the 1956 Melbourne Olympic Games to general manager of the Rams to the Commissioner of the NFL. In a tenure longer than any of his predecessors, Rozelle helped elevate pro football to an important place not only in the entertainment industry, but in the sociological structure of the United States. In 1962, he negotiated the NFL's first single-network television agreement. The next year, he preserved the integrity of the game with the gambling-related suspensions of Alex Karras and Paul Hornung, for which Rozelle was named Sportsman of the Year by *Sports Illustrated*. Rozelle helped maintain the NFL's stability throughout the conflict with the AFL and was a key figure in the merger and the subsequent restructuring of the league, completed in 1970. Rozelle also was one of the primary forces in making the Super Bowl the most popular single-day sports attraction in the world.

Gale Sayers

Running back. 6-0, 200. Born in Wichita, Kansas, May 30, 1943. Kansas. Inducted in 1977. 1965-71 Chicago Bears.

A pair of injured knees stopped Gale Sayers after just seven pro seasons, and only five of them had been even partially healthy ones for him. But they were among the most brilliant any running back has had. Sayers gained 4,956 total yards on 991 carries, and twice went over 1,000 yards, in 1966 and 1969. When Sayers did it the second time, he had just recovered from knee surgery. In his last two seasons, Sayers played in only four games. In the five seasons preceding 1970, however, he set half a dozen NFL records and 16 Bears team records. As a rookie, the "Kansas Comet" was second in the NFL in rushing, punt returns, and kickoff returns, and set an NFL record (since broken) with 22 touchdowns. He also tied another record by scoring six touchdowns against San Francisco. Sayers led the NFL in kickoff returns in 1966 and remains the career kickoff-return leader. He had almost incredible quickness and balance when he was healthy, and earned a reputation as one of the all-time "mudder" backs of the game, able to play as well on a bad field as a good one. He was named all-pro each of his first five years.

RUSHING

Year	Team	Att.	Yards	Avg.	Long	TD
1965	Chi. Bears	166	867	5.2	61t	14
1966	Chi. Bears	229	1,231	5.4	58t	8
1967	Chi. Bears	186	880	4.7	70	7
1968	Chi. Bears	138	856	6.2	63	2
1969	Chi. Bears	236	1,032	4.4	28	8
1970	Chi. Bears	23	52	2.3	15	0
1971	Chi. Bears	13	38	2.9	9	0
Totals		991	4,956	5.0	70	39

RECEIVING

Year	Team	No.	Yards	Avg.	Long	TD
1965	Chi. Bears	29	507	17.5	80t	6
1966	Chi. Bears	34	447	13.1	80t	2
1967	Chi. Bears	16	126	7.9	32	1
1968	Chi. Bears	15	117	7.8	21	0
1969	Chi. Bears	17	116	6.8	25	0
1970	Chi. Bears	1	-6	-6.0	-6	0
1971	Chi. Bears	0	0	0.0	0	0
Totals		112	1,307	11.6	80t	9

PUNT RETURNS

Year	Team	No.	Yards	Avg.	Long	TD
1965	Chi. Bears	16	238	14.9	85t	1
1966	Chi. Bears	6	44	7.3	27	0
1967	Chi. Bears	3	80	26.7	58	1
1968	Chi. Bears	2	29	14.5	18	0
1969	Chi. Bears	0	0	0.0	0	0
1970	Chi. Bears	0	0	0.0	0	0
1971	Chi. Bears	0	0	0.0	0	0
Totals		27	391	14.5	85t	2

KICKOFF RETURNS

Year	Team	No.	Yards	Avg.	Long	TD
1965	Chi. Bears	21	660	31.4	96t	1
1966	Chi. Bears	23	718	31.2	93t	2
1967	Chi. Bears	16	603	37.7	103t	3
1968	Chi. Bears	17	461	27.1	46	0
1969	Chi. Bears	14	339	24.2	52	0
1970	Chi. Bears	0	0	0.0	0	0
1971	Chi. Bears	0	0	0.0	0	0
Totals		91	2,781	30.6	103t	6

SCORING

56 TD, 336 Points

Joe Schmidt

Linebacker. 6-0, 222. Born in Pittsburgh, Pennsylvania, January 19, 1932. Pittsburgh. Inducted in 1973. 1953-65 Detroit Lions.

Injuries in college kept Joe Schmidt from being a high pro draft choice. He wasn't selected until the seventh round in 1953. But he moved into the then-evolving middle linebacker position almost immediately and became an NFL institution. He was chosen all-pro nine times and played in nine consecutive Pro Bowls. He was the Lions' team leader, and was named the team's most valuable player four times. Schmidt led by example. Not especially big or fast, he had an exceptional knack for diagnosing a play, moving to the point of attack, and making the tackle. He also made 24 career interceptions. Schmidt served as head coach of the Lions from 1967-72.

O.J. Simpson

Running back. 6-1, 212. Born in San Francisco, California, July 9, 1947. USC. Inducted in 1985. 1969-77 Buffalo Bills, 1978-79 San Francisco 49ers.

If injuries hadn't slowed down O.J. Simpson after five consecutive 1,000-yard seasons, he might be the leading rusher in the history of pro football. Simpson remains the ultimate combination of speed and power. He was the first player selected in the draft after winning the Heisman Trophy and running on USC's world-record-setting 440-yard relay team. After three unspectacular years in the pros, Simpson took off when Lou Saban became Buffalo's head coach. In a five-year period (1972-76), he led the NFL in rushing four times, including 1973, when he set an all-time record with 2,003 yards. That year he also set a game record with 250 yards; in 1976, he broke his own mark with 273 yards against Detroit. Simpson also led the league in scoring in 1975, when he set a record with 23 touchdowns. He was named all-pro five consecutive years and played in one AFL All-Star Game and five AFC-NFC Pro Bowls.

RUSHING

Year	Team	Att.	Yards	Avg.	Long	TD
1969	Buffalo	181	697	3.9	32t	2
1970	Buffalo	120	488	4.1	56t	5
1971	Buffalo	183	742	4.1	46t	5
1972	Buffalo	292	1,251	4.3	94t	6
1973	Buffalo	332	2,003	6.0	80t	12
1974	Buffalo	270	1,125	4.2	41t	3
1975	Buffalo	329	1,817	5.5	88t	16
1976	Buffalo	290	1,503	5.2	75t	8
1977	Buffalo	126	557	4.4	39	0
1978	San Francisco	161	593	3.7	34	1
1979	San Francisco	120	460	3.8	22	3
Totals		2,404	11,236	4.7	94t	61

RECEIVING

203, 2,142 Yards, 10.6 Avg., 64 Long, 14 TD

KICKOFF RETURNS

33, 990 Yards, 30.0 Avg., 95 Long, 1 TD

SCORING

76 TD, 456 Points

Bart Starr

Quarterback. 6-1, 200. Born in Montgomery, Alabama, January 9, 1934. Alabama. Inducted in 1977. 1956-71 Green Bay Packers.

Bart Starr had an injury-plagued career at the University of Alabama, and he wasn't drafted by Green Bay until the seventeenth round in 1956. For four seasons, he had to share quarterbacking duties with several other Packers quarterbacks. But he gained regular status late in 1959 under Vince Lombardi and helped Green Bay to its first winning season in 12 years. Together, Lombardi and Starr—along with many talented compatriots—made history. Starr led the NFL's passers three times—in 1963, 1964, and 1966. It was his brilliance in postseason play that set Starr apart. In six NFL title games, he completed 84 of 145 passes for 1,090 yards and 11 touchdowns, and he was intercepted only once. He was even more deadly in Green Bay's two Super Bowl wins. Starr later became head coach of the Packers, compiling a 53-77-3 record.

PASSING

Year	Team	Att.	Comp.	Yards	TD	Int.
1956	Green Bay	44	24	325	2	3
1957	Green Bay	215	117	1,489	8	10
1958	Green Bay	157	78	875	3	12
1959	Green Bay	134	70	972	6	7
1960	Green Bay	172	98	1,358	4	8
1961	Green Bay	295	172	2,418	16	16
1962	Green Bay	285	178	2,438	12	9
1963	Green Bay	244	132	1,855	15	10
1964	Green Bay	272	163	2,144	15	4
1965	Green Bay	251	140	2,055	16	9
1966	Green Bay	251	156	2,257	14	3
1967	Green Bay	210	115	1,823	9	17
1968	Green Bay	171	109	1,617	15	8
1969	Green Bay	148	92	1,161	9	6
1970	Green Bay	255	140	1,645	8	13
1971	Green Bay	45	24	286	0	3
Totals		3,149	1,808	24,718	152	138

RUSHING

247 Att., 1,308 Yards, 5.3 Avg., 39 Long, 15 TD

Roger Staubach

Quarterback. 6-3, 202. Born in Cincinnati, Ohio, February 5, 1942. Navy. Inducted in 1985. 1969-79 Dallas Cowboys.

Roger Staubach had an abundance of all the abilities that make a quarterback great. He was an outstanding passer, leading the NFL in that category in 1971, 1973, 1978, and 1979, and the NFC in 1977. He finished his career as the all-time passing leader, and still ranks number two. He was an effective runner, averaging 5.5 yards per carry during his career. He also was a leader and, because of his knack of coming up with the big play, a crowd-pleaser. But the thing that set Staubach apart from other quarterbacks was his ability to bring his team back from the edge of defeat. In his career, Staubach led the Cowboys to an almost unbelievable 23 come-from-behind victories. Staubach's exploits started at the U.S. Naval Academy, where he won the Heisman Trophy as a junior. After spending four years in the Navy, Staubach joined the Cowboys in 1969 as a 27-year-old rookie. Midway through his third year, he became a starter and led the Cowboys to Super Bowl VI, where he was the most valuable player. He helped lead the Cowboys to five NFC titles and two Super Bowl victories, and was selected to the AFC-NFC Pro Bowl six times.

PASSING

Year	Team	Att.	Comp.	Yards	TD	Int.
1969	Dallas	47	23	421	1	2
1970	Dallas	82	44	542	2	8
1971	Dallas	211	126	1,882	15	4
1972	Dallas	20	9	98	0	2
1973	Dallas	286	179	2,428	23	15
1974	Dallas	360	190	2,552	11	15
1975	Dallas	348	198	2,666	17	16
1976	Dallas	369	208	2,715	14	11
1977	Dallas	361	210	2,620	18	9
1978	Dallas	413	231	3,190	25	16
1979	Dallas	461	267	3,586	27	11
Totals		2,958	1,685	22,700	153	109

RUSHING

410 Att., 2,264 Yards, 5.5 Avg., 20 TD

Ernie Stautner

Defensive tackle. 6-2, 235. Born in Cham, Bavaria, Germany, April 20, 1925. Boston College. Inducted in 1969. 1950-63 Pittsburgh Steelers.

Ernie Stautner was small by later standards for NFL defensive tackles but the Pittsburgh Steelers chose him on the second round of the 1950 draft and he responded with 14 starring seasons. As much as anyone, it was Stautner who gave the Steelers of the 1950s a reputation as a team that could not be beaten physically, even though it was losing on the scoreboard. Stautner played in nine Pro Bowls. He recovered 21 opponents' fumbles, a total among the best in NFL history, and he recorded three safeties. When he retired, the Steelers retired his jersey. Since 1966, he has been the defensive line coach for the Dallas Cowboys.

Ken Strong

Halfback. 5-11, 210. Born in New Haven, Connecticut, August 6, 1906. Died October 5, 1979. NYU. Inducted in 1967. 1929-32 Staten Island Stapletons, 1933-35, 1939, 1944-47 New York Giants, 1936-37 New York Yanks (AFL).

Ken Strong, ex-NYU All-America, was an efficient kicker for a long time. He also was one of the most versatile backs ever to play in the NFL. He ran, passed, punted, placekicked, and played defense. He was the man Steve Owen chose to kick when he decided to turn the field goal into a more frequently used weapon. In the 1934 title game against the Chicago Bears, Strong scored 17 points on two touchdowns, two extra points, and a field goal as New York came from behind to win with a 27-point rally in the fourth quarter.

SCORING

Year	Team	TD	FG	PAT	Points
1929	Staten Island	4	0-	9-13	33
1930	Staten Island	7	1-	8-11	53
1931	Staten Island	7	2-	5- 8	53
1932	Staten Island	4	1-	6- 8	33
1933	NY Giants	6	5-	13-14	64
1934	NY Giants	6	4-11	8- 9	56
1935	NY Giants	1	4-	11-12	29
1936	NY Yanks (AFL)				
1937	NY Yanks (AFL)				
1938	Did not play football				
1939	NY Giants	0	4- 8	7- 7	19
1940	Military service				
1941	Military service				
1942	Military service				
1943	Military service				
1944	NY Giants	0	6-12	23-24	41
1945	NY Giants	0	6-13	23-23	41
1946	NY Giants	0	4- 9	32-32	44
1947	NY Giants	0	2- 5	24-25	30
NFL Totals		35	39- 1	169-186	496

RUSHING

NFL—363 Att., 1,321 Yards, 3.6 Avg., 24 TD

PASS RECEIVING

NFL—19, 254 Yards, 13.4 Avg., 6 TD

Joe Stydahar

Tackle. 6-4, 230. Born in Kaylor, Pennsylvania, March 3, 1912. Died March 23, 1977. West Virginia. Inducted in 1967. 1936-42, 1945-46 Chicago Bears.

The college draft was held for the first time in 1936, and, on his first pick, George Halas of the Chicago Bears chose Joe Stydahar, tackle from West Virginia. Starting as a rookie, the man nicknamed "Jumbo Joe" went on to become all-pro four consecutive seasons, and was an integral part of a Bears team that appeared in five NFL title games and won three of them. A two-way tackle, Stydahar was especially effective on defense, where he was both extremely powerful and very agile. Like other pros of his era, Stydahar spurned helmets until rules required them. Stydahar was away from the Bears two seasons because of military service, then came back to the team for two more years. He was head coach of the Los Angeles Rams in 1950-51, guiding them to two conference titles and one NFL championship. He also was head coach of the Chicago Cardinals in 1953-54.

Fran Tarkenton

Quarterback. 6-0, 185. Born in Richmond, Virginia, February 3, 1940. Georgia. Inducted in 1986. 1961-66, 1972-78 Minnesota Vikings, 1967-71 New York Giants.

If statistics are the measure of a player, then Fran Tarkenton is in a class by himself. In his 18-year career, Tarkenton passed more times, for more completions, more yards, and more touchdowns than any other quarterback in pro football history. He also did it about as well as anyone else—he currently ranks tenth in career passing efficiency. Tarkenton started as a rookie for the expansion Minnesota Vikings, throwing four touchdown passes in his first NFL game against the Bears. Early in his career, he gained much notoriety for his seemingly endless scrambles away from defensive linemen. In 1967, he was traded to the New York Giants, for whom he played five years before coming back to Minnesota in 1972. In his last seven years with the Vikings, he led Minnesota to six NFC Central Division titles and three Super Bowl appearances. He was selected to play in nine Pro Bowls.

PASSING

Year	Team	Att.	Comp.	Yards	TD	Int.
1961	Minnesota	280	157	1,997	18	17
1962	Minnesota	329	163	2,595	22	25
1963	Minnesota	297	170	2,311	15	15
1964	Minnesota	306	171	2,506	22	11
1965	Minnesota	329	171	2,609	19	11
1966	Minnesota	358	192	2,561	17	16
1967	NY Giants	377	204	3,088	29	19
1968	NY Giants	337	182	2,555	21	12
1969	NY Giants	409	220	2,918	23	8
1970	NY Giants	389	219	2,777	19	12
1971	NY Giants	386	226	2,567	11	21
1972	Minnesota	378	215	2,651	18	13
1973	Minnesota	274	169	2,113	15	7
1974	Minnesota	351	199	2,598	17	12
1975	Minnesota	425	273	2,994	25	13
1976	Minnesota	412	255	2,961	17	8
1977	Minnesota	258	155	1,734	9	14
1978	Minnesota	572	345	3,468	25	32
Totals		6,467	3,686	47,003	342	266

RUSHING

675 Att., 3,674 Yards, 5.4 Avg., 32 TD

Charley Taylor

Halfback-Wide receiver. 6-3, 210. Born in Grand Prairie, Texas, September 28, 1941. Arizona State. Inducted in 1984. 1964-75, 1977 Washington Redskins.

Charley Taylor could have been one of the best running backs of his time in the NFL; instead, he was one of the best wide receivers of all time. Taylor was a first-round draft choice by Washington in 1964, and he earned rookie-of-the-year honors after rushing for 755 yards and catching 53 passes. Two years later, however, he was moved to split end midway through the season, which he finished as the leading pass catcher in the NFL, with 72 receptions. Taylor led the NFL in receiving again in 1967, and he finished second in 1969 and 1973. Through the first 12 years of his career, he caught fewer than 40 passes in a season only once, set an NFL record by making 50 or more receptions seven times, and finished among the top five receivers in the NFL seven times. Taylor ended his career as pro football's all-time receiving leader, breaking Don Maynard's NFL record with 649 receptions. He appeared in eight Pro Bowls.

RECEIVING

Year	Team	No.	Yards	Avg.	Long	TD
1964	Washington	53	814	15.4	80t	5
1965	Washington	40	577	14.4	69	3
1966	Washington	72	1,119	15.5	86t	12
1967	Washington	70	990	14.1	86t	9
1968	Washington	48	650	13.5	47	5
1969	Washington	71	883	12.4	88t	8
1970	Washington	42	593	14.1	41	8
1971	Washington	24	370	15.4	71t	4
1972	Washington	49	673	13.7	70t	7
1973	Washington	59	801	13.6	53	7
1974	Washington	54	738	13.7	51	5
1975	Washington	53	774	14.6	64	6
1976	Did not play football					
1977	Washington	14	158	11.3	19	0
Totals		649	9,140	14.1	88t	79

RUSHING

442 Att., 1,488 Yards, 3.4 Avg., 11 TD

SCORING

90 TD, 540 Points

Jim Taylor

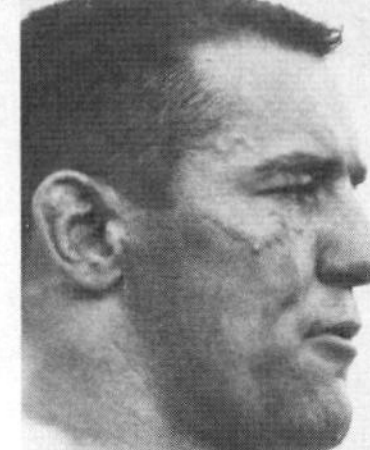

Fullback. 6-0, 216. Born in Baton Rouge, Louisiana, September 20, 1935. Louisiana State. Inducted in 1976. 1958-66 Green Bay Packers, 1967 New Orleans Saints.

Jim Taylor was overshadowed by Jim Brown during their playing careers, but Taylor accomplished something Brown never did—he gained more than 1,000 yards in five consecutive seasons. Taylor was called "the most determined runner I've ever seen" by his coach, Vince Lombardi. Taylor typified the rugged power of the Packers' championship teams. His personal duels in those games with the Giants' linebacker Sam Huff were sensational. In 1962, Taylor led the NFL in rushing, the only time anyone beat out Brown for the title. His 19 rushing touchdowns that season also were a record, and he led the NFL in scoring. Taylor gained 8,207 yards in nine seasons with the Packers, and another 390 in a final season in his native Louisiana with the expansion New Orleans Saints. He retired as the career rushing leader for both teams.

RUSHING

Year	Team	Att.	Yards	Avg.	Long	TD
1958	Green Bay	52	247	4.8	25	1
1959	Green Bay	120	452	3.8	21	6
1960	Green Bay	230	1,101	4.8	32	11
1961	Green Bay	243	1,307	5.4	53	15
1962	Green Bay	272	1,474	5.4	51	19
1963	Green Bay	248	1,018	5.1	40t	9
1964	Green Bay	235	1,169	5.0	84t	12
1965	Green Bay	207	734	3.5	35	4
1966	Green Bay	204	705	3.5	19	4
1967	New Orleans	130	390	3.0	16	2
Totals		1,941	8,597	4.4	84t	83

RECEIVING

Year	Team	No.	Yards	Avg.	Long	TD
1958	Green Bay	4	72	18.0	31t	1
1959	Green Bay	9	71	7.9	20t	2
1960	Green Bay	15	121	8.1	27	0
1961	Green Bay	25	175	7.0	18	1
1962	Green Bay	22	106	4.8	25	0
1963	Green Bay	13	68	5.2	27t	1
1964	Green Bay	38	354	9.3	35t	3
1965	Green Bay	20	207	10.4	41	0
1966	Green Bay	41	331	8.1	21	2
1967	New Orleans	38	251	6.6	27	0
Totals		225	1,756	7.8	41	10

SCORING

93 TD, 558 Points

Jim Thorpe

Halfback. 6-1, 190. Born in Prague, Oklahoma, May 28, 1888. Died March 28, 1953. Carlisle. Inducted in 1963. 1920, 1926 Canton Bulldogs, 1921 Cleveland Indians, 1922-23 Oorang Indians, 1923 Toledo Maroons, 1924 Rock Island Independents, 1925 New York Giants, 1928 Chicago Cardinals.

Jim Thorpe's success in the 1912 Olympics made him the nation's number-one sports figure. Myth and legend surround the Sac and Fox Indian's career, but he is regarded by many as America's greatest all-around athlete. Before there was a National Football League, Thorpe did much to give pro football acceptance by signing with the Canton Bulldogs in 1915. He also played major league baseball. By the time the NFL was organized, Thorpe was past his peak as a player, but the newly formed league unanimously named him its charter president. After leaving Canton in 1921, Thorpe played with numerous NFL teams until he was almost 40 years old. His salary was $250 a game, in a time when the average player was paid almost nothing. In 1950 Thorpe was voted America's male athlete of the first half century.

Y.A. Tittle

Quarterback. 6-0, 200. Born in Marshall, Texas, October 24, 1926. LSU. Inducted in 1971. 1948-50 Baltimore Colts, 1951-60 San Francisco 49ers, 1961-64 New York Giants.

Success followed Y.A. Tittle everywhere he went. A record-setting quarterback at LSU, Tittle signed with the Baltimore Colts of the All-America Football Conference despite being the top draft choice of the Detroit Lions. In his pro debut, Tittle threw four touchdown passes in an upset of the New York Yankees. When the Colts folded after the 1950 season and their players were made eligible to be drafted, Tittle was the first choice of San Francisco. The balding, ungainly-looking Tittle spent 10 years with the 49ers, beating out Frankie Albert for the starting position his first year, and holding onto it until his final season with the club, when he was replaced by John Brodie. Tittle then spent four seasons with the New York Giants, leading them to three NFL Championship Games. In 1962, he set the NFL record with 33 touchdown passes, and the next year he broke it with 36. When he retired, he had passed for 28,339 yards, the most in NFL history, and had been selected to six Pro Bowls.

PASSING

Year	Team	Att.	Comp.	Yards	TD	Int.
1948	Baltimore (AAFC)	289	161	2,522	16	9
1949	Baltimore (AAFC)	289	148	2,209	14	18
1950	Baltimore	315	161	1,884	8	19
1951	San Francisco	114	63	808	8	9
1952	San Francisco	208	106	1,407	11	12
1953	San Francisco	259	149	2,121	20	16
1954	San Francisco	295	170	2,205	9	9
1955	San Francisco	287	147	2,185	17	28
1956	San Francisco	218	124	1,641	7	12
1957	San Francisco	279	176	2,157	13	15
1958	San Francisco	208	120	1,467	9	15
1959	San Francisco	199	102	1,331	10	15
1960	San Francisco	127	69	694	4	3
1961	NY Giants	285	163	2,272	17	12
1962	NY Giants	375	200	3,224	33	20
1963	NY Giants	367	221	3,145	36	14
1964	NY Giants	281	147	1,798	10	22
NFL Totals		3,817	2,118	28,339	212	221
Pro Totals		4,395	2,427	33,070	242	248

RUSHING

NFL—291 Att., 999 Yards, 3.4 Avg., 45 Long, 33 TD
Pro—372 Att., 1,245 Yards, 3.3 Avg., 45 Long, 39 TD

George Trafton

Center. 6-2, 235. Born in Chicago, Illinois, December 6, 1896. Died September 5, 1971. Notre Dame. Inducted in 1964. 1920 Decatur Staleys, 1921 Chicago Staleys, 1922-32 Chicago Bears.

George Trafton became a charter player in the NFL with the Decatur Staleys in 1920, after only one season of football at Notre Dame, and he stayed on to become a fixture in each of the league's first 13 seasons. He was a man fans loved to hate, especially in Green Bay, because of his flamboyant, even roughhouse, play. Trafton was the first center to make a one-handed snap, in the days when the center had to snap the ball long to a tailback. He also excelled on defense, where he was an innovator in the "roving" style of play from sideline to sideline. Trafton was the first all-pro center, in 1920.

Charley Trippi

Halfback. 6-0, 185. Born in Pittston, Pennsylvania, December 14, 1922. Georgia. Inducted in 1968. 1947-55 Chicago Cardinals.

Charley Trippi of Georgia was a Single-Wing tailback when he came to the Chicago Cardinals, but he played many positions in nine pro seasons. He was primarily a halfback for five, a quarterback for two, and a defensive back for two. He excelled at each position. Drafted as a future on the first round in 1945, Trippi found himself in the middle of a bidding war between the NFL and the All-America Football Conference. He signed a multi-year contract in 1947 for $100,000 despite rumors he was offered more by the AAFC. Trippi became the final piece in the Cardinals' Dream Backfield, and in the NFL Championship Game in 1947 he scored two touchdowns—one on a 44-yard run, the other on a 75-yard punt return. In 1948, his average of 5.4 yards a carry topped the NFL. Because of unique wartime rules, Trippi played in four Chicago College All-Star games as a collegian.

RUSHING

Year	Team	Att.	Yards	Avg.	Long	TD
1947	Chi. Cardinals	83	401	4.8	41	2
1948	Chi. Cardinals	128	690	5.4	50t	6
1949	Chi. Cardinals	112	553	4.9	55	3
1950	Chi. Cardinals	99	426	4.3	22	3
1951	Chi. Cardinals	78	501	6.4	32	4
1952	Chi. Cardinals	72	350	4.9	59t	4
1953	Chi. Cardinals	97	433	4.5	21	0
1954	Chi. Cardinals	18	152	8.4	57t	1
1955	Chi. Cardinals	0	0	0.0	0	0
Totals		687	3,506	5.1	59t	23

PASSING

434 Att., 205 Comp., 2,547 Yards, 16 TD, 31 Int.

RECEIVING

130, 1,321 Yards, 10.2 Avg., 11 TD

PUNT RETURNS

63, 864 Yards, 13.7 Avg., 67 Long, 2 TD

KICKOFF RETURNS

66, 1,457 Yards, 22.1 Avg., 50 Long, 0 TD

SCORING

37 TD, 222 Points

Emlen Tunnell

Safety. 6-1, 200. Born in Bryn Mawr, Pennsylvania, March 29, 1925. Died July 23, 1975. Iowa. Inducted in 1967. 1948-58 New York Giants, 1959-61 Green Bay Packers.

Like Dick (Night Train) Lane, Emlen Tunnell walked into a team office and asked for a pro tryout. He soon became a key in the New York Giants' Umbrella defense. He was called the team's "offense on defense" because of his yardage totals on punt returns and interceptions. His lifetime interceptions (79), interception yardage (1,282), and punt return yards (2,209) set NFL records. The interception-yardage record still stands. Tunnell played in nine Pro Bowls and was all-pro four times. During much of Tunnell's time with the Giants, Vince Lombardi was one of the Giants' assistant coaches. Lombardi took Tunnell with him to Green Bay, where he finished his career.

INTERCEPTIONS

Year	Team	No.	Yards	Avg.	Long	TD
1948	NY Giants	7	116	16.6	43t	1
1949	NY Giants	10	251	25.1	55t	2
1950	NY Giants	7	167	23.9	35	0
1951	NY Giants	9	74	8.2	30	0
1952	NY Giants	7	149	21.3	40	0
1953	NY Giants	6	117	19.5	44	0
1954	NY Giants	8	108	13.5	43	0
1955	NY Giants	7	76	10.9	26	0
1956	NY Giants	6	87	14.5	23	0
1957	NY Giants	6	87	14.5	52t	1
1958	NY Giants	1	8	8.0	8	0
1959	Green Bay	2	20	10.0	18	0
1960	Green Bay	3	22	7.3	22	0
1961	Green Bay	0	0	0.0	0	0
Totals		79	1,282	16.2	55t	4

PUNT RETURNS

Year	Team	No.	Yards	Avg.	Long	TD
1948	NY Giants	12	115	9.6	25	0
1949	NY Giants	26	315	12.1	67t	1
1950	NY Giants	31	305	9.8	43	0
1951	NY Giants	34	489	14.4	81t	3
1952	NY Giants	30	411	13.7	60	0
1953	NY Giants	38	223	5.9	37	0
1954	NY Giants	21	70	3.3	12	0
1955	NY Giants	25	98	3.9	66t	1
1956	NY Giants	22	120	5.5	14	0
1957	NY Giants	12	60	5.0	23	0
1958	NY Giants	6	0	0.0	0	0
1959	Green Bay	1	3	3.0	3	0
1960	Green Bay	0	0	0.0	0	0
1961	Green Bay	0	0	0.0	0	0
Totals		258	2,209	8.6	81t	5

KICKOFF RETURNS

46, 1,215 Yards, 26.4 Avg., 100 Long, 1 TD

Clyde (Bulldog) Turner

Center. 6-2, 235. Born in Sweetwater, Texas, November 10, 1919. Hardin-Simmons. Inducted in 1966. 1940-52 Chicago Bears.

Long before other teams in the NFL began doing it, the Chicago Bears used the draft to select players from obscure colleges. Clyde (Bulldog) Turner was one of the best examples. His college was Hardin-Simmons, but Turner was a first-round choice by the Bears. He became an all-pro seven times. Turner was a student of football; his grasp of the Bears' T-formation was on a par with that of quarterback Sid Luckman. He was effective both as an offensive blocker and as a linebacker. In 1942, he led the league in interceptions. Turner played on four NFL championship teams, and in the five title games in which he participated, he made four interceptions. He was the head coach of the New York Titans in 1962.

Johnny Unitas

Quarterback. 6-1, 195. Born in Pittsburgh, Pennsylvania, May 7, 1933. Louisville. Inducted in 1979. 1956-72 Baltimore Colts, 1973 San Diego Chargers.

The Cinderella story of Johnny Unitas is well-documented: A small college career at Louisville; drafted and waived by the Pittsburgh Steelers; earned $6.00 a game with the Bloomfield (a section of Pittsburgh) Rams; offered a $7,000 contract with the Baltimore Colts on a 65¢ telephone call. Unitas, considered by many to be the premier quarterback in NFL history, retired after the 1973 season holding nearly every meaningful career passing record: most attempts, most completions, most yardage, most 300-yard games, and most touchdown passes. From 1956 to 1960 he set a record by throwing at least one touchdown pass in 47 consecutive games. What do not show in Unitas's statistics are the coolness and poise he exhibited under pressure. His tying and winning drives in the 1958 NFL title game remain textbook examples of the two-minute drill.

PASSING

Year	Team	Att.	Comp.	Yards	TD	Int.
1956	Baltimore	198	110	1,498	9	10
1957	Baltimore	301	172	2,550	24	17
1958	Baltimore	263	136	2,007	19	7
1959	Baltimore	367	193	2,899	32	14
1960	Baltimore	378	190	3,099	25	24
1961	Baltimore	420	229	2,990	16	24
1962	Baltimore	389	222	2,967	23	23
1963	Baltimore	410	237	3,481	20	12
1964	Baltimore	305	158	2,824	19	6
1965	Baltimore	282	164	2,530	23	12
1966	Baltimore	348	195	2,748	22	24
1967	Baltimore	436	255	3,428	20	16
1968	Baltimore	32	11	139	2	4
1969	Baltimore	327	178	2,342	12	20
1970	Baltimore	321	166	2,213	14	18
1971	Baltimore	176	92	942	3	9
1972	Baltimore	157	88	1,111	4	6
1973	San Diego	76	34	471	3	7
Totals		5,186	2,830	40,239	290	253

RUSHING

450 Att., 1,777 Yards, 3.9 Avg., 34 Long, 13 TD

Norm Van Brocklin

Quarterback. 6-1, 190. Born in Eagle Butte, South Dakota, March 15, 1926. Died May 1, 1983. Oregon. Inducted in 1971. 1949-57 Los Angeles Rams, 1958-60 Philadelphia Eagles.

Norm Van Brocklin always had an ace up his sleeve for the rest of the NFL. In 1948, he wrote a letter to Rams owner Dan Reeves telling him he had enough units to graduate early if the Rams wanted to draft him. Once with the Rams, "The Dutchman" proved to be one of the best passers and field leaders the game ever has had. His first four years he shared the quarterback position with Hall of Famer Bob Waterfield. But he still starred. In the 1951 NFL Championship Game, his 73-yard touchdown pass to Tom Fears in the fourth quarter earned the Rams their only world championship in Los Angeles. In 1958, Van Brocklin was traded to Philadelphia, and in 1960 his passing was the key as the Eagles beat the Green Bay Packers in Vince Lombardi's only defeat in a championship game. Van Brocklin led the NFL in passing three times and in punting twice. In 1951, he set a record with 554 yards passing against the New York Yanks. He played in eight Pro Bowls. Van Brocklin was the first head coach of the Minnesota Vikings (1961-66) and the second coach of the Atlanta Falcons (1968-74).

PASSING

Year	Team	Att.	Comp.	Yards	TD	Int.
1949	LA Rams	58	32	601	6	2
1950	LA Rams	233	127	2,061	18	14
1951	LA Rams	194	100	1,725	13	11
1952	LA Rams	205	113	1,736	14	17
1953	LA Rams	286	156	2,393	19	14
1954	LA Rams	260	139	2,637	13	21
1955	LA Rams	272	144	1,890	8	15
1956	LA Rams	124	68	966	7	12
1957	LA Rams	265	132	1,105	20	21
1958	Philadelphia	374	198	2,409	15	20
1959	Philadelphia	340	191	2,617	16	14
1960	Philadelphia	284	153	2,471	24	17
Totals		2,895	1,553	23,611	173	178

PUNTING

Year	Team	No.	Avg.	Long	Blk.
1949	LA Rams	2	45.5	46	0
1950	LA Rams	11	42.4	51	0
1951	LA Rams	48	41.5	62	1
1952	LA Rams	29	43.1	66	0
1953	LA Rams	60	42.2	57	0
1954	LA Rams	44	42.6	61	0
1955	LA Rams	60	44.6	61	0
1956	LA Rams	48	43.1	72	0
1957	LA Rams	54	44.3	71	0
1958	Philadelphia	54	41.2	58	1
1959	Philadelphia	53	42.7	59	1
1960	Philadelphia	60	43.1	70	0
Totals		523	42.9	72	3

RUSHING

102 Att., 40 Yards, 0.4 Avg., 16 Long, 11 TD

Steve Van Buren

Halfback. 6-1, 200. Born in La Ceiba, Honduras, December 28, 1920. LSU. Inducted in 1965. 1944-51 Philadelphia Eagles.

Steve Van Buren was a runner who combined speed, power, and elusiveness. He had halfback speed and fullback size. In 1947, he became only the second man in NFL history to gain more than 1,000 yards. He led the NFL's rushers four times in his eight-year pro career. Three were consecutive (1947-49), and he went over 1,000 yards twice. He finished his career with a record 5,860 yards (since broken). As a rookie in 1944, Van Buren led the league in punt returns; he set the pace in kickoff returns, rushing, and scoring the following year. He was a blocking back early in his college career for baseball star Alvin Dark, but finished second in the nation in rushing and scoring as a senior. As a professional, he doubled as a defensive back much of his career.

RUSHING

Year	Team	Att.	Yards	Avg.	Long	TD
1944	Philadelphia	80	444	5.6	70t	5
1945	Philadelphia	143	832	5.8	69t	15
1946	Philadelphia	116	529	4.6	58	5
1947	Philadelphia	217	1,008	4.6	45	13
1948	Philadelphia	201	945	4.7	29	10
1949	Philadelphia	263	1,146	4.4	41	11
1950	Philadelphia	188	629	3.3	41	4
1951	Philadelphia	112	327	2.9	17	6
Totals		1,320	5,860	4.4	70t	60

RECEIVING

45, 503 Yards, 11.2 Avg., 50 Long, 3 TD

PUNT RETURNS

34, 473 Yards, 13.9 Avg., 55 Long, 2 TD

KICKOFF RETURNS

76, 2,030 Yards, 26.7 Avg., 98 Long, 3 TD

SCORING

77 TD, 2 PAT, 464 Points

Doak Walker

Halfback. 5-11, 173. Born in Dallas, Texas, January 1, 1927. SMU. Inducted in 1986. 1950-55 Detroit Lions.

Doak Walker might have been the best all-around back in the history of college football. Although he played only six years, he was just as effective as a pro, joining former Highland Park High School (Dallas) teammate Bobby Layne to lead the Lions to three divisional titles and two league championships. Walker, a three-time consensus All-America at SMU and the Heisman Trophy winner as a junior, could do everything—run, pass, catch, kick, return kicks, and play defense. He led the NFL in scoring as a rookie, with 128 points, the second-most in NFL history at the time. In 1952, after missing much of the season with injuries, he scored the decisive touchdown in the Lions' 17-7 victory over Cleveland in the NFL Championship Game. The next year, he scored 11 points, including the winning extra point, in a 17-16 title-game victory over the Browns. Walker led the NFL in scoring again in 1955, his final season. Except in 1952, he never finished lower than third in the NFL in scoring. Although his career was short, he was named all-pro four times and was selected to five Pro Bowls.

RUSHING

Year	Team	Att.	Yards	Avg.	Long	TD
1950	Detroit	83	386	4.7	30t	5
1951	Detroit	79	356	4.5	34	2
1952	Detroit	26	106	4.1	20	0
1953	Detroit	66	337	5.1	50t	2
1954	Detroit	32	240	7.5	38	1
1955	Detroit	23	95	4.1	51	2
Totals		309	1,520	4.9	51	12

RECEIVING

Year	Team	No.	Yards	Avg.	Long	TD
1950	Detroit	35	534	15.3	43	6
1951	Detroit	22	421	19.1	63	4
1952	Detroit	11	90	8.2	18	0
1953	Deroit	30	502	16.7	83t	3
1954	Detroit	32	564	17.6	66t	3
1955	Detroit	22	428	19.5	70t	5
Totals		152	2,539	16.7	83t	21

SCORING

Year	Team	TD	FG	PAT	Points
1950	Detroit	11	8-18	38-41	128
1951	Detroit	6	6-12	43-44	97
1952	Detroit	0	3- 5	5- 5	14
1953	Detroit	5	12-29	27-29	93
1954	Detroit	5	11-17	43-43	106
1955	Detroit	7	9-16	27-29	96
Totals		34	49-87	183-191	534

KICKOFF RETURNS

38, 968 Yards, 25.5 Avg., 0 TD

Paul Warfield

Wide receiver. 6-0, 188. Born in Warren, Ohio, November 28, 1942. Ohio State. Inducted in 1983. 1964-69, 1976-77 Cleveland Browns, 1970-74 Miami Dolphins, 1975 Memphis Southmen (WFL).

Few receivers have had the overall talents of Paul Warfield, and fewer still ever have used them as well. Warfield had 9.6 speed in the 100-yard dash and was an NCAA runner-up in the long jump. Warfield had been an outstanding halfback at Ohio State, but the Cleveland Browns moved him to wide receiver, and he became one of the most feared deep threats of all time. Warfield, who had incredibly fluid, graceful moves, averaged more than 20 yards per reception seven consecutive years (1966-72), and his 20.1-yard career average is one of the best in NFL history. Warfield was traded to Miami in 1970 and promptly set several records. He helped the Dolphins win Super Bowls VII and VIII. When he retired, he had caught 85 touchdown passes, the third-most ever at the time. He was named all-pro four times and was selected to play in eight Pro Bowls.

RECEIVING

Year	Team	No.	Yards	Avg.	Long	TD
1964	Cleveland	52	920	17.7	62t	9
1965	Cleveland	3	30	10.0	13	0
1966	Cleveland	36	741	20.6	51	5
1967	Cleveland	32	702	21.3	49t	8
1968	Cleveland	50	1,067	21.3	65t	12
1969	Cleveland	42	886	21.1	82t	10
1970	Miami	28	703	25.1	54	6
1971	Miami	43	996	23.2	86t	11
1972	Miami	29	606	20.9	47	3
1973	Miami	29	514	17.7	45t	11
1974	Miami	27	536	19.9	54	2
1975	Memphis (WFL)	25	422	16.9	47t	3
1976	Cleveland	38	613	16.1	37t	6
1977	Cleveland	18	251	13.9	52t	2
NFL Totals		427	8,565	20.1	86t	85
Pro Totals		452	8,987	19.9	86t	88

Bob Waterfield

Quarterback. 6-2, 200. Born in Elmira, New York, July 26, 1920. Died April 25, 1983. UCLA. Inducted in 1965. 1945 Cleveland Rams, 1946-52 Los Angeles Rams.

Bob Waterfield led his team to an NFL championship in his first pro season; no rookie quarterback has done that since. His two touchdown passes provided the victory in the 1945 title game. A cool, gifted performer in all phases of athletics, Waterfield led the league in passing in 1946 and 1951 and in field goals in 1947, 1949, and 1951. In his career he made 315 extra points and 60 field goals. His punting average was 42.4 yards. On defense, he made 20 interceptions, and he still is thought of as the best defensive back the Rams ever had. He was one of the first quarterbacks to throw the long pass consistently on third down. He retired in 1952, at the height of his career. Waterfield served as head coach of the Rams from 1960-62.

PASSING

Year	Team	Att.	Comp.	Yards	TD	Int.
1945	Cleveland	171	89	1,609	14	17
1946	LA Rams	251	127	1,747	17	17
1947	LA Rams	221	96	1,210	8	18
1948	LA Rams	180	87	1,354	14	18
1949	LA Rams	296	154	2,168	17	24
1950	LA Rams	213	122	1,540	11	13
1951	LA Rams	176	88	1,566	13	10
1952	LA Rams	109	51	655	3	11
Totals		1,617	814	11,849	97	128

PUNTING

Year	Team	No.	Yards	Avg.	Long	Blk.
1945	Cleveland	39	1,588	40.7	68	1
1946	LA Rams	39	1,745	44.6	65	0
1947	LA Rams	59	2,500	42.4	86	1
1948	LA Rams	43	1,843	42.6	88	0
1949	LA Rams	49	2,177	44.4	61	1
1950	LA Rams	52	2,087	40.1	61	2
1951	LA Rams	4	166	41.5	52	0
1952	LA Rams	30	1,276	42.5	88	0
Totals		315	13,382	42.4	88	5

INTERCEPTIONS

20, 228 Yards, 11.4 Avg., 35 Long, 0 TD

SCORING

13 TD, 60 FG, 315 PAT, 573 Points

Arnie Weinmeister

Defensive tackle. 6-4, 235. Born in Rhein, Saskatchewan, Canada, March 23, 1923. Washington. Inducted in 1984. 1948-49 New York Yankees (AAFC), 1950-53 New York Giants.

Few players ever have dominated a position like Arnie Weinmeister did in his six years in the All-America Football Conference and the NFL. One of the first defensive players to captivate fans the way an offensive back does, Weinmeister had good size and was widely considered to be the fastest lineman in pro football. He had an extremely keen football instinct, and was a master at diagnosing offensive plays and then stopping them before they could get under way. Weinmeister had been a fullback at Washington, but New York Yankees coach Ray Flaherty made him a two-way tackle. In his second year, he was named all-AAFC. Weinmeister moved to the Giants in 1950 when the AAFC merged into the NFL. He was named all-pro and selected to the Pro Bowl each of the next four years. Weinmeister was in his prime when he ended his NFL career to play football in his native Canada.

Bill Willis

Guard. 6-2, 215. Born in Columbus, Ohio, October 5, 1921. Ohio State. Inducted in 1977. 1946-53 Cleveland Browns.

Bill Willis was one of the two black players signed by Paul Brown of the Cleveland Browns in 1946 (Marion Motley was the other) when the Browns became the first All-America Football Conference team to sign black players. The Los Angeles Rams recently had broken the 12-year-old color line in the NFL with the signing of Kenny Washington and Woody Strode. Willis, a smallish lineman out of Ohio State, excelled for four seasons as the Browns won four straight AAFC titles, and was with them four more years when they moved to the NFL. A three-time all-league player in the AAFC, Willis was all-pro all four years in the NFL. Although he was a solid blocker, he dominated at middle guard on defense, where his quickness allowed him to easily penetrate the backfield.

Larry Wilson

Safety. 6-0, 190. Born in Rigby, Idaho, March 24, 1938. Utah. Inducted in 1978. 1960-72 St. Louis Cardinals.

One way or another, Larry Wilson left a lasting impression on nearly all the quarterbacks he faced in his 13-year NFL career. If he wasn't smothering them in their own backfields with a safety blitz, he was intercepting their passes downfield. He compiled impressive offensive statistics during a career at Utah as a two-way halfback, but defense was his forte. He got his chance to play safety in the final preseason game of 1960, his rookie year, and became a fixture at the position. Of Wilson's 52 career interceptions, perhaps the most dramatic was one he made against the Pittsburgh Steelers in 1965; he had casts on both hands, which were broken. Bobby Layne once called Wilson "pound-for-pound, the toughest player in the NFL."

INTERCEPTIONS

Year	Team	No.	Yards	Avg.	Long	TD
1960	St. Louis	2	4	2.0	4	0
1961	St. Louis	3	36	12.0	25	0
1962	St. Louis	2	59	29.5	57t	1
1963	St. Louis	4	67	16.8	36	0
1964	St. Louis	3	44	14.7	42t	1
1965	St. Louis	6	153	25.5	96t	1
1966	St. Louis	10	180	18.0	91t	2
1967	St. Louis	4	75	18.8	44	0
1968	St. Louis	4	14	3.5	8	0
1969	St. Louis	2	15	7.5	15	0
1970	St. Louis	5	72	14.4	22	0
1971	St. Louis	4	46	11.5	23	0
1972	St. Louis	3	35	11.7	24	0
Totals		52	800	15.4	96t	5

Alex Wojciechowicz

Center. 6-0, 235. Born in South River, New Jersey, August 12, 1915. Fordham. Inducted in 1968. 1938-46 Detroit Lions, 1946-50 Philadelphia Eagles.

Alex Wojciechowicz's name was hard to pronounce and equally hard to spell, but he was a great player. He came into pro football with much expected of him. He was a two-time All-America at Fordham and, with Vince Lombardi, one of the "Seven Blocks of Granite" in that school's line. The Detroit Lions made him their number-one draft pick. Even though the team was not a contender in his era, he was a top-flight, two-way center. Midway through his eighth season in the league, he was acquired by the Eagles and Earle (Greasy) Neale made him a full-time linebacker. Wojciechowicz excelled at the role. He was solid against running plays, but he also was noted for his play against the pass. He was the NFL's best at chucking receivers. As a center, he was known for his unusually wide stance over the ball.

NFL Coaches

The roster includes head coaches in the National Football League (1920-85), the fourth American Football League (1960-69), and the All-America Football Conference (1946-49). To qualify, one must have been at least the nominal head coach of a team for one game during the regular season or playoffs.

In the early days of the NFL, most head coaches were player-coaches because the rules prohibited coaching from the sidelines. Not infrequently, early teams had two player-coaches, who are listed as co-coaches for the appropriate years. In modern times there also have been several instances when teams have had co-coaches, usually after a head coach was released late in the season and was replaced temporarily by two or three assistants working jointly.

The records for the coaches include regular season and playoff games. The records occasionally differ from other sources in that they include both the results of AAFC games and the results of the Playoff Bowls, which were held from 1960-69.

To qualify for the list of the top 10 coaches according to winning percentage, one must have been a head coach for a minimum 75 games. In figuring winning percentages, ties count half a win and half a loss, as they do in today's standings. Until relatively recent years, ties had not counted at all in the standings, as if they hadn't been played.

A

Abbott, Fay, Dayton 1928-29: 0-13-0
Albert, Frankie, San Francisco 1956-58: 19-17-1
Alexander, Joe, NY Giants 1926: 8-4-1
Allen, George, LA Rams 1966-70; Washington 1971-77: 120-54-5
Anderson, Hunk, Chi. Bears 1942-45 (Co-coach): 23-12-2
Andrews, LeRoy, Kansas City 1924-26; Cleveland 1927; Detroit 1928; NY Giants 1929-30; Chi. Cardinals 1931: 53-28-3
Armstrong, Johnny, Rock Island 1924: 6-2-2
Armstrong, Neill, Chi. Bears 1978-81: 30-35-0
Arnsparger, Bill, NY Giants 1974-76: 7-28-0
Austin, Bill, Pittsburgh 1966-68; Washington 1970: 17-36-3

B

Bach, Joe, Pittsburgh 1935-36, 1952-53: 21-27-0
Ball, Herman, Washington 1949-51: 4-16-0
Barr, Wallace (Shorty), Racine 1926 (Co-coach): 1-4-0
Barry, Norman, Chi. Cardinals 1925-26: 16-8-2
Batterson, Dim, Buffalo 1927: 0-5-0
Battles, Cliff, Brooklyn (AAFC) 1946-47: 4-16-1
Baugh, Sammy, NY Titans 1960-61; Houston 1964: 18-24-0
Behman, Russell (Bull), Frankford 1929-31: 14-23-7
Bell, Bert, Philadelphia 1936-40; Pittsburgh 1941: 10-46-2
Bengtson, Phil, Green Bay 1968-70: 20-21-1
Bennett, Leeman, Atlanta 1977-82; Tampa Bay 1985: 49-58-0
Bergman, Arthur (Dutch), Washington 1943: 7-4-1
Berry, George, Akron 1925: 4-0-2
Berry, Raymond, New England 1984-85: 18-10-0
Berryman, Robert (Punk), Frankford 1924; Brooklyn 1926: 14-10-1
Bettis, Tom, Kansas City 1977: 1-6-0
Bezdek, Hugo, Cleveland 1937-38: 1-13-0
Biles, Ed, Houston 1981-83: 8-23-0
Blackbourn, Lisle, Green Bay 1954-57: 17-31-0
Blood (McNally), Johnny, Pittsburgh 1937-39: 6-19-0
Boland, Pat, Chi. Rockets (AAFC) 1946: 2-3-1
Brandy, Joe, Minneapolis 1924: 0-6-0
Brewer, Brooke, Akron 1922 (Co-coach): 3-5-2
Brickley, Charley, NY Giants 1921: 0-2-0
Brown, Paul, Cleveland 1946-62; Cincinnati 1968-75: NFL 170-109-6, Pro 222-113-9
Bruney, Fred, Philadelphia 1985: 1-0-0
Bryan, John, Milwaukee 1925-26: 2-13-0
Bullough, Hank, New England 1978 (Co-coach); Buffalo 1985: 2-11-0

C

Campbell, Hugh, Houston 1984-85: 8-22-0
Campbell, Marion, Atlanta 1974-76; Philadelphia 1983-85: 23-48-1
Casey, Eddie, Boston 1935: 2-8-1
Cawthorn, Pete, Brooklyn 1943-44: 2-18-0
Chamberlin, Guy, Canton 1922-23; Cleveland 1924; Frankford 1925-26; Chi. Cardinals 1927: 58-16-6
Checkaye, Severin (Cooney), Muncie 1921: 0-2-0
Chevigny, Jack, Chi. Cardinals 1932: 2-6-2
Christiansen, Jack, San Francisco 1963-67: 26-38-3
Clark, Algy, Cincinnati 1934: 0-8-0
Clark, Earl (Dutch), Detroit 1937-38, Cleveland 1939-42: 30-34-2
Clark, George (Potsy), Portsmouth 1930-33; Detroit 1934-36, 1940; Brooklyn 1937-39: 70-48-15
Clark, Monte, San Francisco 1976; Detroit 1978-84: 51-69-1
Cofall, Stanley, Cleveland 1920: 0-2-1
Collier, Blanton, Cleveland 1963-70: 79-40-2
Collier, Joe, Buffalo 1966-68: 13-17-1
Conkright, William (Red), Oakland 1962: 1-8-0
Conzelman, Jimmy, Rock Island 1921-22; Milwaukee 1923-24; Detroit 1925-26; Providence 1927-30; Chi. Cardinals 1940-42, 1946-48: 92-69-17
Cornsweet, Al, Cleveland 1932 (Co-coach): 2-8-0
Coryell, Don, St. Louis 1973-77; San Diego 1978-85: 113-82-1
Coughlin, Frank, Rock Island 1921: 1-1-1
Cramer, Carl, Akron 1923: 1-6-0
Creighton, Milan, Chi. Cardinals 1935-38: 16-26-4
Crowe, Clem, Buffalo (AAFC) 1949; Baltimore 1950: NFL 1-11-0, Pro 5-13-1
Crowley, Jim, Chi. Rockets (AAFC) 1947: 1-12-0

D

Davis, Al, Oakland 1963-65: 23-16-3
Dawson, Lowell (Red), Buffalo (AAFC) 1946-49: 20-26-4
DeGroot, Dudley, Washington 1944-45; LA Dons (AAFC) 1946-47: NFL 14-6-1, Pro 26-16-3
Depler, John, Orange 1929; Newark 1930; Brooklyn 1931: 6-26-5
Devine, Dan, Green Bay 1971-74: 25-28-4
Devore, Hugh, Green Bay 1953 (Co-coach); Philadelphia 1956-57: 7-18-1
Dietz, William (Lone Star), Boston 1933-34: 11-11-2
DiMelio, Luby, Pittsburgh 1934: 2-10-0
Ditka, Mike, Chi. Bears 1982-85: 40-22-0
Doherty, Bill, Cincinnati 1921: 1-3-0
Donelli, Aldo (Buff), Pittsburgh 1941; Cleveland 1944: 4-11-0
Dooley, Jim, Chi. Bears 1968-71: 20-36-0
Dorais, Gus, Detroit 1943-47: 20-31-2
Douds, Forrest (Jap), Pittsburgh 1933: 3-6-2
Dove, Bob, Chi. Rockets (AAFC) 1946 (Co-coach): 2-2-1
Dowhower, Rod, Indianapolis 1985: 5-11-0
Driscoll, John (Paddy), Chi. Cardinals 1920-22; Chi. Bears 1956-57: 31-18-5
Driskill, Walt, Baltimore (AAFC) 1949: 1-7-0
Drulis, Chuck, St. Louis 1961 (Co-coach): 2-0-0

E

Edwards, Bill, Detroit 1941-42: 4-9-1
Edwards, Gene, Canton 1921; Cleveland 1923, 1925: 14-11-7
Edwards, Glen (Turk), Washington 1946-48: 16-18-1
Erdelatz, Eddie, Oakland 1960-61: 6-10-0
Erhardt, Ron, New England 1978 (Co-coach), 1979-81: 21-28-0
Ewart, Charley, NY Bulldogs 1949: 1-10-1
Ewbank, Weeb, Baltimore 1954-62; NY Jets 1963-73: 134-130-7

F

Fairbanks, Chuck, New England 1973-78: 46-41-0
Falcon, Gil, Chi. Tigers 1920; Toledo 1922: 7-7-3
Faulkner, Jack, Denver 1962-64: 9-22-1
Fausch, Frank, Evansville 1921-22: 3-5-0
Fears, Tom, New Orleans 1967-70: 13-34-2
Feldman, Marty, Oakland 1961-62: 2-15-0
Filchock, Frank, Denver 1960-61: 7-20-1
Flaherty, Ray, Boston 1936; Washington 1937-42; NY Yankees (AAFC) 1946-48; Chi. Hornets (AAFC) 1949: NFL 56-23-2, Pro 82-41-4
Flores, Tom, Oakland 1979-81; LA Raiders 1982-85: 78-38-0
Flower, Jim, Akron 1924: 2-6-0
Folwell, Bob, NY Giants 1925: 8-4-0
Forsyth, Jack, Rochester 1920: 6-3-2
Forzano, Rick, Detroit 1974-76: 15-17-0
Friedman, Benny, Brooklyn 1932: 3-9-0

G

Getto, Mike, Brooklyn 1942: 3-8-0
Gibbs, Joe, Washington 1981-85: 57-24-0
Gibron, Abe, Chi. Bears 1972-74: 11-30-1
Gibson, George, Minneapolis 1930: 1-7-1
Gillies, Fred, Chi. Cardinals 1928: 1-5-0
Gillman, Sid, LA Rams 1955-59; LA Chargers 1960; San Diego 1961-69, 1971; Houston 1973-74: 123-104-7
Gillo, Hank, Hammond 1920-21; Racine 1926 (Co-coach): 4-12-1
Gilmer, Harry, Detroit 1965-66: 10-26-2
Glanville, Jerry, Houston 1985: 0-2-0
Golembeski, Archie, Providence 1925: 6-5-1
Graham, Otto, Washington 1966-68: 17-22-3
Grant, Harry (Bud), Minnesota 1967-83, 1985: 168-109-5
Gregg, Forrest, Cleveland 1975-77; Cincinnati 1980-83; Green Bay 1984-85: 68-66-0
Griggs, Cecil (Tex), Rochester 1925: 0-6-1

H

Haines, Hinky, Staten Island 1931: 4-6-1
Halas, George, Decatur 1920; Chi. Staleys 1921; Chi. Bears 1922-29, 1933-42, 1946-55, 1958-67: 325-151-31
Handler, Phil, Chi. Cardinals 1943, 1945; Card-Pitt 1944 (Co-coach); Chi. Cardinals 1949, 1951 (Co-coach): 4-34-0
Hanifan, Jim, St. Louis 1980-85: 39-50-1
Hanley, Dick, Chi. Rockets (AAFC) 1946: 1-1-1
Hanson, Hal, Staten Island 1932: 2-7-3
Hecker, Norb, Atlanta 1966-68: 4-26-1
Hefferle, Ernie, New Orleans 1975: 1-7-0
Hegarty, Jack, Washington 1921: 1-2-0
Hein, Mel, LA Dons (AAFC) 1947 (Co-coach): 2-2-0
Heldt, John, Columbus 1926: 1-6-0
Henderson, Elmer (Gus), Detroit 1939: 6-5-0
Henning, Dan, Atlanta 1983-85: 15-33-0
Henry, Wilbur (Pete), Canton 1926 (Co-coach); Pottsville 1928: 3-17-3
Hickey, Howard (Red), San Francisco 1959-63: 27-27-1
Higgins, Austin, Louisville 1921: 0-2-0
Hollway, Bob, St. Louis 1971-72: 8-18-2
Holovak, Mike, Boston 1961-68; NY Jets 1976: 53-48-9
Holtz, Lou, NY Jets 1976: 3-10-0
Horning, Clarence (Steamer), Toledo 1923: 2-3-2
Horween (McMahon), Arnold, Chi. Cardinals 1923-24: 13-8-1
Howell, Jim Lee, NY Giants 1954-60: 54-29-4
Hudspeth, Tommy, Detroit 1976-77: 11-13-0
Huffine, Ken, Muncie 1920: 0-1-0
Hughes, Ed, Houston 1971: 4-9-1
Hughitt, Tommy, Buffalo 1920-24: 33-15-7
Hunter, Hal, Indianapolis 1984: 0-1-0

I

Imlay, Tut, LA Buccaneers 1926 (Co-coach): 6-3-1
Isbell, Cecil, Baltimore (AAFC) 1947-49; Chi. Cardinals 1951 (Co-coach): NFL 1-1-0, Pro 10-24-1
Ivy, Frank (Pop), Chi. Cardinals 1958-59; St. Louis 1960-61; Houston 1962-63: 34-41-2

J

Joesting, Herb, Minneapolis 1929: 1-9-0
Johnson, Bill, Cincinnati 1976-78: 18-15-0
Johnson, Harvey, Buffalo 1968, 1971: 2-23-1
Johnsos, Luke, Chi. Bears 1942-45 (Co-coach): 23-12-1
Jolley, Al, Buffalo 1929; Brooklyn 1930; Cincinnati 1933: 8-14-2
Jones, Ralph, Chi. Bears 1930-32: 24-10-7

K

Karcis, John, Detroit 1942: 0-8-0
Kendrick, Jim, Louisville 1923; Buffalo 1926: 4-7-2
Keough, Jack, Hartford 1926: 3-7-0
Khayat, Eddie, Philadelphia 1971-72: 8-15-2
Kiesling, Walt, Pittsburgh 1939-42, 1954-56; Phil-Pitt 1943 (Co-coach); Card-Pitt 1944 (Co-coach): 30-55-5
Knox, Chuck, LA Rams 1973-77; Buffalo 1978-82; Seattle 1983-85: 127-79-1
Kopf, Herb, Boston 1944-46: 7-22-2
Koppisch, Walt, Buffalo 1925: 1-6-2
Kraehe, Ollie, St. Louis 1923: 1-4-2
Kuharich, Joe, Chi. Cardinals 1952; Washington 1954-58; Philadelphia 1964-68: 58-82-3
Kush, Frank, Baltimore 1982-83; Indianapolis 1984: 11-28-1

L

Laird, Jim, Providence 1926: 5-7-1
Lambeau, Earl (Curly), Green Bay 1921-49; Chi. Cardinals 1950-51; Washington 1952-53: 229-134-22
Landry, Tom, Dallas 1960-85: 254-150-6
Lemm, Wally, Houston 1961, 1966-70; St. Louis 1962-65: 66-66-7
Leonard, Jim, Pittsburgh 1945: 2-8-0
Levy, Marv, Kansas City 1978-82: 31-42-0
Lewis, Art, Cleveland 1938: 4-4-0
Lombardi, Vince, Green Bay 1959-67; Washington 1969: 106-36-6
Lyons, Leo, Rochester 1921-23: 2-9-1

M

Mackovic, John, Kansas City 1983-85: 20-28-0
Madden, John, Oakland 1969-78: 112-39-7
Mahrt, Lou, Dayton 1927: 1-6-1
Malavasi, Ray, Denver 1966; LA Rams 1978-82: 47-44-0
Marchibroda, Ted, Baltimore 1975-79: 41-36-0
Marshall, Billy, Detroit 1920-21: 3-8-4
Mathews, Ned, Chi. Rockets (AAFC) 1946 (Co-coach): 2-2-1
Mazur, John, Boston 1970; New England 1971-72: 9-21-0
McCafferty, Don, Baltimore 1970-72; Detroit 1973: 32-18-2
McCormack, Mike, Philadelphia 1973-75; Baltimore 1980-81; Seattle 1982: 29-51-1
McCulley, Pete, San Francisco 1978: 1-8-0
McEwen, John (Cap), Brooklyn 1933-34: 9-11-1
McKay, John, Tampa Bay 1976-84: 45-91-1
McKeever, Ed, Chi. Rockets (AAFC) 1948: 1-13-0
McLean, Ray (Scooter), Green Bay 1953 (Co-coach), 1958: 1-12-1
McMillin, Alvin (Bo), Detroit 1948-50; Philadelphia 1951: 14-24-0
McPeak, Bill, Washington 1961-65: 21-46-3
McVay, John, NY Giants 1976-78: 14-23-0
Meagher, Jack, Miami (AAFC) 1946: 1-5-0
Mehre, Harry, Minneapolis 1923: 2-5-2
Meyer, Ken, San Francisco 1977: 5-9-0
Meyer, Ron, New England 1982-84: 18-16-0
Michaels, Walt, NY Jets 1977-82: 41-49-1
Michelosen, John, Pittsburgh 1948-51: 20-26-2
Miller, Robert (Red), Denver 1977-80: 42-25-0
Millner, Wayne, Philadelphia 1951: 2-8-0

Modzelewski, Dick, Cleveland 1977: 0-1-0
Molesworth, Keith, Baltimore 1953: 3-9-0
Moran, Charley, Frankford 1927: 2-4-1
Muller, Brick, LA Buccaneers 1926 (Co-coach): 6-3-1

N

Neale, Earle (Greasy), Philadelphia 1941-42, 1944-50; Phil-Pitt 1943 (Co-coach): 66-44-5
Nesser, Frank, Columbus 1922: 0-7-0
Nesser, Ted, Columbus 1920-21: 3-14-2
Nevers, Ernie, Duluth 1927; Chi. Cardinals 1930-31, 1939: 12-26-2
Nixon, Mike, Washington 1959-60; Pittsburgh 1965: 6-30-2
Nolan, Dick, San Francisco 1968-75; New Orleans 1978-80: 71-85-5
Noll, Chuck, Pittsburgh 1969-85: 164-104-1
Noonan, Jerry, Rochester 1924: 0-7-0
North, John, New Orleans 1973-75: 11-23-0

O

O'Connor, Fred, San Francisco 1978: 1-6-0
Owen, Steve, NY Giants 1931-53: 153-108-17

P

Palm, Mike, Cincinnati 1933; St. Louis 1934: 4-5-1
Parcells, Bill, NY Giants 1983-85: 24-27-1
Pardee, Jack, Chi. Bears 1975-77; Washington 1978-80: 44-47-0
Parker, Raymond (Buddy), Chi. Cardinals 1949 (Co-coach for first six games); Detroit 1951-56; Pittsburgh 1957-64: 107-77-9
Patera, Jack, Seattle 1976-82: 35-59-0
Peppler, Pat, Atlanta 1976: 3-6-0
Perkins, Ray, NY Giants 1979-82: 24-35-0
Peterson, Bill, Houston 1972-73: 1-18-0
Phelan, Jimmy, LA Dons (AAFC) 1948-49; Dallas 1952: NFL 1-11-0, Pro 12-26-0
Phillips, O.A. (Bum), Houston 1975-80; New Orleans 1981-85: 86-80-0
Phillips, Wade, New Orleans 1985: 1-3-0
Pierotti, Al, Cleveland 1920: 2-2-1
Pollard, Fritz, Akron 1920-21 (Co-coach); Milwaukee 1922; Hammond 1923-25; Akron 1925, 1926 (Co-coach): 23-23-12
Pool, Hampton, Miami (AAFC) 1946; Chi. Rockets (AAFC) 1947; LA Rams 1952-54: NFL 23-11-2, Pro 25-18-2
Potteiger, Earl, Kenosha 1924; NY Giants 1927-28: 15-13-4
Prochaska, Ray, St. Louis 1961 (Co-coach): 2-0-0
Prothro, Tommy, LA Rams 1971-72, San Diego 1974-78: 35-51-2

R

Ralston, John, Denver 1972-76: 34-33-3
Ramsey, Garrard (Buster), Buffalo 1960-61: 11-16-1
Rauch, Dick, Pottsville 1925-27; NY Yankees 1928; Boston 1929: 33-24-2
Rauch, Johnny, Oakland 1966-68; Buffalo 1969-70: 42-30-2
Reeves, Dan, Denver 1981-85: 45-30-0
Rice, Homer, Cincinnati 1978-79: 8-19-0
Richards, Ray, Chi. Cardinals 1955-57: 14-21-1
Ringo, Jim, Buffalo 1976-77: 3-20-0
Robb, Harry, Canton 1925, 1926 (Co-coach): 5-13-3
Roberts, J.D., New Orleans 1970-72: 7-25-3
Robinson, Ed, Providence 1931: 4-4-3
Robinson, John, LA Rams 1983-85: 32-21-0
Rogers, Darryl, Detroit 1985: 7-9-0
Ronzani, Gene, Green Bay 1950-53: 14-31-1
Rose, Tam, Tonawanda 1921: 0-1-0
Ruetz, Babe, Racine 1922: 6-4-1
Rush, Clive, Boston 1969-70: 5-16-0
Rutigliano, Sam, Cleveland 1978-84: 47-52-0
Rymkus, Lou, Houston 1960-61: 12-7-1

S

Saban, Lou, Boston 1960-61; Buffalo 1962-65, 1972-76; Denver 1967-71: 97-101-7
Sachs, Len, Louisville 1926: 0-4-0
Sandusky, John, Baltimore 1972: 4-5-0
Scanlon, Dewey, Duluth 1924-26; Chi. Cardinals 1929: 19-15-4
Schissler, Paul, Chi. Cardinals 1933-34; Brooklyn 1935-36: 14-29-3
Schmidt, Joe, Detroit 1967-72: 43-35-7
Schnellenberger, Howard, Baltimore 1973-74: 4-13-0
Schottenheimer, Marty, Cleveland 1984-85: 12-12-0
Scott, Ralph, NY Yankees 1927: 7-8-1
Scott, Tom, Brooklyn (AAFC) 1946: 1-0-0
Shaughnessy, Clark, LA Rams 1948-49: 14-8-3
Shaw, Lawrence (Buck), San Francisco 1946-54; Philadelphia 1958-60: NFL 53-41-3, Pro 92-56-5
Sheeks, Paul, Akron 1922 (Co-coach): 3-5-2
Sherman, Allie, NY Giants 1961-68: 57-54-4
Shipkey, Ted, LA Dons (AAFC) 1947 (Co-coach): 2-2-0
Shipp, Ken, NY Jets 1975: 1-4-0
Shula, Don, Baltimore 1963-69; Miami 1970-85: 257-99-6
Sies, Dale, Rock Island 1923: 2-3-3
Skorich, Nick, Philadelphia 1961-63; Cleveland 1971-74: 45-51-5
Smith, Jerry, Denver 1971: 2-3-0
Smith, Maurice (Clipper), Boston 1947-48: 7-16-1
Snyder, Bob, LA Rams 1947: 6-6-0
Speedie, Mac, Denver 1964-66: 6-19-1
Stanfel, Dick, New Orleans 1980: 1-3-0
Starr, Bart, Green Bay 1975-83: 53-77-3
Steckel, Les, Minnesota 1984: 3-13-0
Stephenson, Kay, Buffalo 1983-85: 10-26-0
Sternaman, Joey, Duluth 1923: 4-3-0
Stevens, Mal, Brooklyn (AAFC) 1946: 1-4-1
Stinchcomb, Pete, Columbus 1923: 1-2-1
Storck, Carl, Dayton 1922-26: 12-26-4
Strader, Norman (Red), NY Yankees (AAFC) 1948-49; NY Yanks 1950-51; San Francisco 1955: NFL 12-22-2, Pro 25-32-2
Stram, Hank, Dallas Texans 1960-62; Kansas City 1963-74; New Orleans 1976-77: 136-100-10
Studley, Chuck, Houston 1983: 2-8-0
Stydahar, Joe, LA Rams 1950-52; Chi. Cardinals 1953-54: 22-29-1
Sutherland, John (Jock), Brooklyn 1940-41; Pittsburgh 1946-47: 30-17-1
Svare, Harland, LA Rams 1962-65; San Diego 1971-73: 21-48-5

T

Talbott, Nelson, Dayton 1920-21: 9-6-3
Taylor, Hugh (Bones), Houston 1965: 4-10-0
Tebell, Gus, Columbus 1923: 4-2-0
Thomas, Joe, Baltimore 1974: 2-9-0
Thorpe, Jim, Canton 1920: Cleveland 1921; Oorang 1922-23: 13-25-2
Tobin, Elgie, Akron 1920-21 (Co-coach): 16-3-4
Todd, Dick, Washington 1951: 5-4-0
Trimble, Jim, Philadelphia 1952-55: 25-20-3
Turner, Clyde (Bulldog), NY Titans 1962: 5-9-0

U

Ursella, Rube, Rock Island 1920, 1925; Minneapolis 1921; Akron 1926 (Co-coach): 13-12-9

V

Van Brocklin, Norm, Minnesota 1961-66; Atlanta 1968-74: 66-100-7
Vermeil, Dick, Philadelphia 1976-82: 57-51-0
Voyles, Carl, Brooklyn (AAFC) 1948: 2-12-0

W

Waller, Charlie, San Diego 1969-70: 9-7-3
Waller, Ron, San Diego 1973: 1-5-0
Walsh, Adam, Cleveland 1945; LA Rams 1946: 16-5-1
Walsh, Bill, San Francisco 1979-85: 66-48-0
Walton, Joe, NY Jets 1983-85: 25-24-0
Waterfield, Bob, LA Rams 1960-62: 9-24-1
Weaver, Jim (Red), Columbus 1924-25: 4-13-0
Webster, Alex, NY Giants 1969-73: 29-40-1
Weir, Ed, Frankford 1928: 11-3-2
Whelchel, John, Washington 1949: 3-3-1
Wiggin, Paul, Kansas City 1975-77: 11-24-0
Wiggs, Hubert, Louisville 1922: 1-3-0
Wilkin, Willie, Chi. Rockets (AAFC) 1946 (Co-coach): 2-2-1
Wilkinson, Bud, St. Louis 1978-79: 9-20-0
Williams, Jerry, Philadelphia 1969-71: 7-22-2
Willsey, Ray, St. Louis 1961 (Co-coach): 2-0-0
Wilson, George, Detroit 1957-64; Miami 1966-69: 73-84-8
Wilson, Larry, St. Louis 1979: 2-1-0
Winner, Charley, St. Louis 1966-70; NY Jets 1974-75: 44-44-5
Workman, Harry (Hoge), Cleveland 1931 (Co-coach): 2-8-0
Wray, Lud, Boston 1932; Philadelphia 1933-35: 13-25-3
Wyche, Sam, Cincinnati 1984-85: 15-17-0
Wycoff, Doug, Staten Island 1929-30: 8-9-5

Y

Young, Doc, Hammond 1925-26: 0-5-0
Youngstrom, Adolph (Swede), Frankford 1927: 4-5-2

Top 10 Coaches—Victories

Coach	Team(s)	Yrs.	Won	Lost	Tied	Pct.
George Halas	Chi. Bears	40	325	151	31	.672
Don Shula	Baltimore, Miami	23	257	99	6	.718
Tom Landry	Dallas	26	254	150	6	.627
Earl (Curly) Lambeau	Green Bay, Chi. Cardinals, Washington	33	229	134	22	.623
Paul Brown	Cleveland, Cincinnati	25	222	113	9	.658
Harry (Bud) Grant	Minnesota	18	168	109	5	.605
Chuck Noll	Pittsburgh	17	164	104	1	.612
Steve Owen	NY Giants	23	153	108	17	.581
Hank Stram	Dallas Texans, Kansas City, New Orleans	17	136	100	10	.573
Weeb Ewbank	Baltimore, NY Jets	20	134	130	7	.507

Top 10 Coaches—Winning Percentage

Coach	Team(s)	Yrs.	Won	Lost	Tied	Pct.
Guy Chamberlin	Canton, Cleveland, Frankford, Chi. Cardinals	6	58	16	6	.763
Vince Lombardi	Green Bay, Washington	10	106	36	6	.736
John Madden	Oakland	10	112	39	7	.731
Don Shula	Baltimore, Miami	23	257	99	6	.718
Joe Gibbs	Washington	5	57	24	0	.704
George Allen	LA Rams, Washington	12	120	54	5	.684
Tom Flores	Oakland, LA Raiders	7	78	38	0	.672
George Halas	Chi. Bears	40	325	151	31	.672
Ray Flaherty	Boston, Washington, NY Yankees (AAFC), Chi. Hornets (AAFC)	11	82	41	4	.661
Blanton Collier	Cleveland	8	79	40	2	.661

NFL Superlatives

TOP 10 SCORERS

Player	Years	TD	FG	PAT	TP
George Blanda	26	9	335	943	2,002
Jan Stenerud	19	0	373	580	1,699
Jim Turner	16	1	304	521	1,439
Jim Bakken	17	0	282	534	1,380
Fred Cox	15	0	282	519	1,365
Lou Groza	17	1	234	641	1,349
Mark Moseley	15	0	288	457	1,321
Gino Cappelletti	11	42	176	350	1,130
Don Cockroft	13	0	216	432	1,080
Garo Yepremian	14	0	210	444	1,074

Cappelletti's total includes four two-point conversions.

TOP 10 TOUCHDOWN SCORERS

Player	Years	Rush	Pass Rec.	Returns	Total TD
Jim Brown	9	106	20	0	126
John Riggins	14	104	12	0	116
Lenny Moore	12	63	48	2	113
Walter Payton	11	98	11	0	109
Don Hutson	11	3	99	3	105
Franco Harris	13	91	9	0	100
Jim Taylor	10	83	10	0	93
Bobby Mitchell	11	18	65	8	91
Leroy Kelly	10	74	13	3	90
Charley Taylor	13	11	79	0	90

TOP 10 RUSHERS

Player	Years	Att.	Yards	Avg.	Long	TD
Walter Payton	11	3,371	14,860	4.4	76	98
Jim Brown	9	2,359	12,312	5.2	80	106
Franco Harris	13	2,949	12,120	4.1	75	91
John Riggins	14	2,916	11,352	3.9	66	104
O.J. Simpson	11	2,404	11,236	4.7	94	61
Tony Dorsett	9	2,441	10,832	4.4	99	66
Earl Campbell	8	2,187	9,407	4.3	81	74
Jim Taylor	10	1,941	8,597	4.4	84	83
Joe Perry	14	1,737	8,378	4.8	78	53
Larry Csonka	11	1,891	8,081	4.3	54	64

TOP 10 PASSERS

Player	Years	Att.	Comp.	Pct. Comp.	Yards	TD	Pct. TD	Int.	Pct. Int.	Avg. Gain	Rating
Joe Montana	7	2,571	1,627	63.3	19,262	133	5.2	67	2.6	7.49	92.4
Roger Staubach	11	2,958	1,685	57.0	22,700	153	5.2	109	3.7	7.67	83.4
Sonny Jurgensen	18	4,262	2,433	57.1	32,224	255	6.0	189	4.4	7.56	82.6
Len Dawson	19	3,741	2,136	57.1	28,711	239	6.4	183	4.9	7.67	82.6
Neil Lomax	5	1,826	1,047	57.3	13,406	79	4.3	55	3.0	7.34	82.3
Danny White	10	2,393	1,422	59.4	17,911	130	5.4	107	4.5	7.48	82.3
Ken Anderson	15	4,452	2,643	59.4	32,667	196	4.4	158	3.5	7.34	82.0
Dan Fouts	13	4,810	2,839	59.0	37,492	228	4.7	205	4.3	7.79	81.8
Bart Starr	16	3,149	1,808	57.4	24,718	152	4.8	138	4.4	7.85	80.5
Fran Tarkenton	18	6,467	3,686	57.0	47,003	342	5.3	266	4.1	7.27	80.4

1,500 or more attempts. The passing ratings are based on performance standards established for completion percentage, interception percentage, touchdown percentage, and average gain. Passers are allocated points according to how their marks compare with those standards.

TOP 10 PASS RECEIVERS

Player	Years	No.	Yards	Avg.	Long	TD
Charlie Joiner	17	716	11,706	16.3	87	63
Charley Taylor	13	649	9,110	14.0	88	79
Don Maynard	15	633	11,834	18.7	87	88
Raymond Berry	13	631	9,275	14.7	70	68
Steve Largent	10	624	10,059	16.1	74	78
Harold Carmichael	14	590	8,985	15.2	85	79
Fred Biletnikoff	14	589	8,974	15.2	82	76
Harold Jackson	16	579	10,372	17.9	79	76
Lionel Taylor	10	567	7,195	12.7	80	45
Lance Alworth	11	542	10,266	18.9	85	85

TOP 10 INTERCEPTORS

Player	Years	No.	Yards	Avg.	Long	TD
Paul Krause	16	81	1,185	14.6	81	3
Emlen Tunnell	14	79	1,282	16.2	55	4
Dick (Night Train) Lane	14	68	1,207	17.8	80	5
Ken Riley	15	65	596	9.2	66	5
Dick LeBeau	13	62	762	12.3	70	3
Emmitt Thomas	13	58	937	16.2	73	5
Bobby Boyd	9	57	994	17.4	74	4
Johnny Robinson	12	57	741	13.0	57	1
Mel Blount	14	57	736	12.9	52	2
Lem Barney	11	56	1,077	19.2	71	7
Pat Fischer	17	56	941	16.8	69	4

TOP 10 PUNTERS

Player	Years	No.	Yards	Avg.	Long	Blk.
Rohn Stark	4	313	14,135	45.2	72	2
Sammy Baugh	16	338	15,245	45.1	85	9
Tommy Davis	11	511	22,833	44.7	82	2
Yale Lary	11	503	22,279	44.3	74	4
Horace Gillom	7	385	16,872	43.8	80	5
Jerry Norton	11	358	15,671	43.8	78	2
Don Chandler	12	660	28,678	43.5	90	4
Rich Camarillo	5	317	13,687	43.2	76	0
Jerrel Wilson	16	1,072	46,139	43.0	72	12
Norm Van Brocklin	12	523	22,413	42.9	72	3

300 or more punts.

TOP 10 PUNT RETURNERS

Player	Years	No.	Yards	Avg.	Long	TD
Henry Ellard	3	83	1,121	13.5	83	4
George McAfee	8	112	1,431	12.8	74	2
Jack Christiansen	8	85	1,084	12.8	89	8
Claude Gibson	5	110	1,381	12.6	85	3
Louis Lipps	2	89	1,093	12.3	76	3
Bill Dudley	9	124	1,515	12.2	96	3
Billy Johnson	11	250	3,036	12.1	87	6
Rick Upchurch	9	248	3,008	12.1	92	8
Mack Herron	3	84	982	11.7	66	0
Billy Thompson	13	157	1,814	11.6	60	0

75 or more returns.

TOP 10 KICKOFF RETURNERS

Player	Years	No.	Yards	Avg.	Long	TD
Gale Sayers	7	91	2,781	30.6	103	6
Lynn Chandnois	7	92	2,720	29.6	93	3
Abe Woodson	9	193	5,538	28.7	105	5
Buddy Young	6	90	2,514	27.9	104	2
Travis Williams	5	102	2,801	27.5	105	6
Joe Arenas	7	139	3,798	27.3	96	1
Clarence Davis	8	79	2,140	27.1	76	0
Steve Van Buren	8	76	2,030	26.7	98	3
Lenny Lyles	12	81	2,161	26.7	103	3
Eugene (Mercury) Morris	8	111	2,947	26.5	105	3

75 or more returns.

1,000 YARDS RUSHING IN A SEASON

Year	Player, Team	Att.	Yards	Avg.	Long	TD
1934	**Beattie Feathers, Chi. Bears**	101	1,004	9.9	82	8
1947	Steve Van Buren, Philadelphia	217	1,008	4.6	45	13
1949	Steve Van Buren, Philadelphia[2]	263	1,146	4.4	41	11
	Tony Canadeo, Green Bay	208	1,052	5.1	54	4
1953	Joe Perry, San Francisco	192	1,018	5.3	51	10
1954	Joe Perry, San Francisco[2]	173	1,049	6.1	58	8
1956	Rick Casares, Chi. Bears	234	1,126	4.8	68	12
1958	Jim Brown, Cleveland	257	1,527	5.9	65	17
1959	Jim Brown, Cleveland[2]	290	1,329	4.6	70	14
	J. D. Smith, San Francisco	207	1,036	5.0	73	10
1960	Jim Brown, Cleveland[3]	215	1,257	5.8	71	9
	Jim Taylor, Green Bay	230	1,101	4.8	32	11
	John David Crow, St. Louis	183	1,071	5.9	57	6
1961	Jim Brown, Cleveland[4]	305	1,408	4.6	38	8
	Jim Taylor, Green Bay[2]	243	1,307	5.4	53	15
1962	Jim Taylor, Green Bay[3]	272	1,474	5.4	51	19
	John Henry Johnson, Pittsburgh	251	1,141	4.5	40	7
	Cookie Gilchrist, Buffalo	214	1,096	5.1	44	13
	Abner Haynes, Dallas Texans	221	1,049	4.7	71	13
	Dick Bass, LA Rams	196	1,033	5.3	57	6
	Charlie Tolar, Houston	244	1,012	4.1	25	7
1963	Jim Brown, Cleveland[5]	291	1,863	6.4	80	12
	Clem Daniels, Oakland	215	1,099	5.1	74	3
	Jim Taylor, Green Bay[4]	248	1,018	4.1	40	9
	Paul Lowe, San Diego	177	1,010	5.7	66	8
1964	Jim Brown, Cleveland[6]	280	1,446	5.2	71	7
	Jim Taylor, Green Bay[5]	235	1,169	5.0	84	12
	John Henry Johnson, Pittsburgh[2]	235	1,048	4.5	45	7
1965	Jim Brown, Cleveland[7]	289	1,544	5.3	67	17
	Paul Lowe, San Diego[2]	222	1,121	5.0	59	7
1966	Jim Nance, Boston	299	1,458	4.9	65	11
	Gale Sayers, Chi. Bears	229	1,231	5.4	58	8
	Leroy Kelly, Cleveland	209	1,141	5.5	70	15
	Dick Bass, LA Rams[2]	248	1,090	4.4	50	8
1967	Jim Nance, Boston[2]	269	1,216	4.5	53	7
	Leroy Kelly, Cleveland[2]	235	1,205	5.1	42	11
	Hoyle Granger, Houston	236	1,194	5.1	67	6
	Mike Garrett, Kansas City	236	1,087	4.6	58	9
1968	Leroy Kelly, Cleveland[3]	248	1,239	5.0	65	16
	Paul Robinson, Cincinnati	238	1,023	4.3	87	8
1969	Gale Sayers, Chi. Bears[2]	236	1,032	4.4	28	8
1970	Larry Brown, Washington	237	1,125	4.7	75	5
	Ron Johnson, NY Giants	263	1,027	3.9	68	8
1971	Floyd Little, Denver	284	1,133	4.0	40	6
	John Brockington, Green Bay	216	1,105	5.1	52	4
	Larry Csonka, Miami	195	1,051	5.4	28	7
	Steve Owens, Detroit	246	1,035	4.2	23	8
	Willie Ellison, LA Rams	211	1,000	4.7	80	4
1972	O.J. Simpson, Buffalo	292	1,251	4.3	94	6
	Larry Brown, Washington[2]	285	1,216	4.3	38	8
	Ron Johnson, NY Giants[2]	298	1,182	4.0	35	9

	Larry Csonka, Miami[2]	213	1,117	5.2	45	6
	Marv Hubbard, Oakland	219	1,100	5.0	39	4
	Franco Harris, Pittsburgh	188	1,055	5.6	75	10
	Calvin Hill, Dallas	245	1,036	4.2	26	6
	Mike Garrett, San Diego[2]	272	1,031	3.8	41	6
	John Brockington, Green Bay[2]	274	1,027	3.7	30	8
	Eugene (Mercury) Morris, Miami	190	1,000	5.3	33	12
1973	O.J. Simpson, Buffalo[2]	332	2,003	6.0	80	12
	John Brockington, Green Bay[3]	265	1,144	4.3	53	3
	Calvin Hill, Dallas[2]	273	1,142	4.2	21	6
	Lawrence McCutcheon, LA Rams	210	1,097	5.2	37	2
	Larry Csonka, Miami[3]	219	1,003	4.6	25	5
1974	Otis Armstrong, Denver	263	1,407	5.3	43	9
	Don Woods, San Diego	227	1,162	5.1	56	7
	O.J. Simpson, Buffalo[3]	270	1,125	4.2	41	3
	Lawrence McCutcheon, LA Rams[2]	236	1,109	4.7	23	3
	Franco Harris, Pittsburgh[2]	208	1,006	4.8	54	5
1975	O.J. Simpson, Buffalo[4]	329	1,817	5.5	88	16
	Franco Harris, Pittsburgh[3]	262	1,246	4.8	36	10
	Lydell Mitchell, Baltimore	289	1,193	4.1	70	11
	Jim Otis, St. Louis	269	1,076	4.0	30	5
	Chuck Foreman, Minnesota	280	1,070	3.8	31	13
	Greg Pruitt, Cleveland	217	1,067	4.9	50	8
	John Riggins, NY Jets	238	1,005	4.2	42	8
	Dave Hampton, Atlanta	250	1,002	4.0	22	5
1976	O.J. Simpson, Buffalo[5]	290	1,503	5.2	75	8
	Walter Payton, Chi. Bears	311	1,390	4.5	60	13
	Delvin Williams, San Francisco	248	1,203	4.9	80	7
	Lydell Mitchell, Baltimore[2]	289	1,200	4.2	43	5
	Lawrence McCutcheon, LA Rams[3]	291	1,168	4.0	40	9
	Chuck Foreman, Minnesota[2]	278	1,155	4.2	46	13
	Franco Harris, Pittsburgh[4]	289	1,128	3.9	30	14
	Mike Thomas, Washington	254	1,101	4.3	28	5
	Rocky Bleier, Pittsburgh	220	1,036	4.7	28	5
	Mark van Eeghen, Oakland	233	1,012	4.3	21	3
	Otis Armstrong, Denver[2]	247	1,008	4.1	31	5
	Greg Pruitt, Cleveland[2]	209	1,000	4.8	64	4
1977	Walter Payton, Chi. Bears[2]	339	1,852	5.5	73	14
	Mark van Eeghen, Oakland[2]	324	1,273	3.9	27	7
	Lawrence McCutcheon, LA Rams[4]	294	1,238	4.2	48	7
	Franco Harris, Pittsburgh[5]	300	1,162	3.9	61	11
	Lydell Mitchell, Baltimore[3]	301	1,159	3.9	64	3
	Chuck Foreman, Minnesota[3]	270	1,112	4.1	51	6
	Greg Pruitt, Cleveland[3]	236	1,086	4.6	78	3
	Sam Cunningham, New England	270	1,015	3.8	31	4
	Tony Dorsett, Dallas	208	1,007	4.8	84	12
1978	**Earl Campbell, Houston**	302	1,450	4.8	81	13
	Walter Payton, Chi. Bears[3]	333	1,395	4.2	76	11
	Tony Dorsett, Dallas[2]	290	1,325	4.6	63	7
	Delvin Williams, Miami[2]	272	1,258	4.6	58	8
	Wilbert Montgomery, Philadelphia	259	1,220	4.7	47	9
	Terdell Middleton, Green Bay	284	1,116	3.9	76	11
	Franco Harris, Pittsburgh[6]	310	1,082	3.5	37	8
	Mark van Eeghen, Oakland[3]	270	1,080	4.0	34	9
	Terry Miller, Buffalo	238	1,060	4.5	60	7
	Tony Reed, Kansas City	206	1,053	5.1	62	5
	John Riggins, Washington[2]	248	1,014	4.1	31	5
1979	Earl Campbell, Houston[2]	368	1,697	4.6	61	19
	Walter Payton, Chi. Bears[4]	369	1,610	4.4	43	14
	Ottis Anderson, St. Louis	331	1,605	4.8	76	8
	Wilbert Montgomery, Philadelphia[2]	338	1,512	4.5	62	9
	Mike Pruitt, Cleveland	264	1,294	4.9	77	9
	Ricky Bell, Tampa Bay	283	1,263	4.5	49	7
	Chuck Muncie, New Orleans	238	1,198	5.0	69	11
	Franco Harris, Pittsburgh[7]	267	1,186	4.4	71	11
	John Riggins, Washington[3]	260	1,153	4.4	66	9
	Wendell Tyler, LA Rams	218	1,109	5.1	63	9
	Tony Dorsett, Dallas[3]	250	1,107	4.4	41	6
	William Andrews, Atlanta	239	1,023	4.3	23	3
1980	Earl Campbell, Houston[3]	373	1,934	5.2	55	13
	Walter Payton, Chi. Bears[5]	317	1,460	4.6	69	6
	Ottis Anderson, St. Louis[2]	301	1,352	4.5	52	9
	William Andrews, Atlanta[2]	265	1,308	4.9	33	4
	Billy Sims, Detroit	313	1,303	4.2	52	13
	Tony Dorsett, Dallas[4]	278	1,185	4.3	56	11
	Joe Cribbs, Buffalo	306	1,185	3.9	48	11
	Mike Pruitt, Cleveland[2]	249	1,034	4.2	56	6
1981	**George Rogers, New Orleans**	378	1,674	4.4	79	13
	Tony Dorsett, Dallas[5]	342	1,646	4.8	75	4
	Billy Sims, Detroit[2]	296	1,437	4.9	51	13
	Wilbert Montgomery, Philadelphia[3]	286	1,402	4.9	41	8
	Ottis Anderson, St. Louis[3]	328	1,376	4.2	28	9
	Earl Campbell, Houston[4]	361	1,376	3.8	43	10
	William Andrews, Atlanta[3]	289	1,301	4.5	29	10
	Walter Payton, Chi. Bears[6]	339	1,222	3.6	39	6
	Chuck Muncie, San Diego[2]	251	1,144	4.6	73	19
	Joe Delaney, Kansas City	234	1,121	4.8	82	3
	Mike Pruitt, Cleveland[3]	247	1,103	4.5	21	7
	Joe Cribbs, Buffalo[2]	257	1,097	4.3	35	3
	Pete Johnson, Cincinnati	274	1,077	3.9	39	12
	Wendell Tyler, LA Rams[2]	260	1,074	4.1	69	12
	Ted Brown, Minnesota	274	1,063	3.9	34	6
1983	**Eric Dickerson, LA Rams**	390	1,808	4.6	85	18
	William Andrews, Atlanta[4]	331	1,567	4.7	27	7
	Curt Warner, Seattle	335	1,449	4.3	60	13
	Walter Payton, Chi. Bears	314	1,421	4.5	49	6
	John Riggins, Washington[4]	375	1,347	3.6	44	24
	Tony Dorsett, Dallas[6]	289	1,321	4.6	77	8
	Earl Campbell, Houston[5]	322	1,301	4.0	42	12
	Ottis Anderson, St. Louis[4]	296	1,270	4.3	43	5
	Mike Pruitt, Cleveland[4]	293	1,184	4.0	27	10
	George Rogers, New Orleans[2]	256	1,144	4.5	76	5
	Joe Cribbs, Buffalo[3]	263	1,131	4.3	45	3
	Curtis Dickey, Baltimore	254	1,122	4.4	56	4
	Tony Collins, New England	219	1,049	4.8	50	10
	Billy Simms, Detroit[3]	220	1,040	4.7	41	7
	Marcus Allen, LA Raiders	266	1,014	3.8	19	9
	Franco Harris, Pittsburgh[8]	279	1,007	3.6	19	5
1984	Eric Dickerson, LA Rams[2]	379	2,105	5.6	66	14
	Walter Payton, Chi. Bear[8]	381	1,684	4.4	72	11
	James Wilder, Tampa Bay	407	1,544	3.8	37	13
	Gerald Riggs, Atlanta	353	1,486	4.2	57	13
	Wendell Tyler, San Francisco[3]	246	1,262	5.1	40	7
	John Riggins, Washington[5]	327	1,239	3.8	24	14
	Tony Dorsett, Dallas[7]	302	1,189	3.9	31	6
	Earnest Jackson, San Diego	296	1,179	4.0	32	8
	Ottis Anderson, St. Louis[5]	289	1,174	4.1	24	6
	Marcus Allen, LA Raiders[2]	275	1,168	4.2	52	13
	Sammy Winder, Denver	296	1,153	3.9	24	4
	Greg Bell, Buffalo	262	1,100	4.2	85	7
	Freeman McNeil, NY Jets	229	1,070	4.7	53	5
1985	Marcus Allen, LA Raiders[3]	390	1,759	4.6	61	11
	Gerald Riggs, Atlanta[2]	397	1,719	4.3	50	10
	Walter Payton, Chi. Bears[9]	324	1,551	4.8	40	9
	Joe Morris, NY Giants	294	1,336	4.5	65	21
	Freeman McNeil, NY Jets[2]	294	1,331	4.5	69	3
	Tony Dorsett, Dallas[8]	305	1,307	4.3	60	7
	James Wilder, Tampa Bay[2]	365	1,300	3.6	28	10
	Eric Dickerson, LA Rams[3]	292	1,234	4.2	43	12
	Craig James, New England	263	1,227	4.7	65	5
	Kevin Mack, Cleveland	222	1,104	5.0	61	7
	Curt Warner, Seattle[2]	291	1,094	3.8	38	8
	George Rogers, Washington[3]	231	1,093	4.7	35	7
	Roger Craig, San Francisco	214	1,050	4.9	62	9
	Earnest Jackson, Philadelphia[2]	282	1,028	3.6	59	5
	Stump Mitchell, St. Louis	183	1,006	5.5	64	7
	Earnest Byner, Cleveland	244	1,002	4.1	36	8

1,000 YARDS PASS RECEIVING IN A SEASON

Year	Player, Team	No.	Yards	Avg.	Long	TD
1942	Don Hutson, Green Bay	74	1,211	16.4	73	17
1945	Jim Benton, Cleveland	45	1,067	23.7	84	8
1949	Bob Mann, Detroit	66	1,014	15.4	64	4
	Tom Fears, LA Rams	77	1,013	13.2	51	9
1950	Tom Fears, LA Rams[2]	84	1,116	13.3	53	7
	Cloyce Box, Detroit	50	1,009	20.2	82	11
1951	Elroy (Crazylegs) Hirsch, LA Rams	66	1,495	22.7	91	17
1952	**Billy Howton, Green Bay**	53	1,231	23.2	90	13
1953	Pete Pihos, Philadelphia	63	1,049	16.7	59	10
1954	Bob Boyd, LA Rams	53	1,212	22.9	80	6
	Harlan Hill, Chi. Bears	45	1,124	25.0	76	12
1956	Billy Howton, Green Bay[2]	55	1,188	21.6	66	12
	Harlon Hill, Chi. Bears[2]	47	1,128	24.0	79	11
1958	Del Shofner, LA Rams	51	1,097	21.5	92	8
1960	**Bill Groman, Houston**	72	1,473	20.5	92	12
	Raymond Berry, Baltimore	74	1,298	17.5	70	10
	Don Maynard, NY Titans	72	1,265	17.6	65	6
	Lionel Taylor, Denver	92	1,235	13.4	80	12
	Art Powell, NY Titans	69	1,167	16.9	76	14
1961	Charley Hennigan, Houston	82	1,746	21.3	80	12
	Lionel Taylor, Denver[2]	100	1,176	11.8	52	4
	Bill Groman, Houston[2]	50	1,175	23.5	80	17
	Tommy McDonald, Philadelphia	64	1,144	17.9	66	13
	Del Shofner, NY Giants[2]	68	1,125	16.5	46	11
	Jim (Red) Phillips, LA Rams	78	1,092	14.0	69	5
	Mike Ditka, Chi. Bears	56	1,076	19.2	76	12
	Dave Kocourek, San Diego	55	1,055	19.2	76	4
	Buddy Dial, Pittsburgh	53	1,047	19.8	88	12
	R.C. Owens, San Francisco	55	1,032	18.8	54	5
1962	Bobby Mitchell, Washington	72	1,384	19.2	81	11
	Sonny Randle, St. Louis	63	1,158	18.4	86	7
	Tommy McDonald, Philadelphia[2]	58	1,146	19.8	60	10
	Del Shofner, NY Giants[3]	53	1,133	21.4	69	12
	Art Powell, NY Titans[2]	64	1,130	17.7	80	8
	Frank Clarke, Dallas Cowboys	47	1,043	22.2	66	14
	Don Maynard, NY Titans[2]	56	1,041	18.6	86	8
1963	Bobby Mitchell, Washington[2]	69	1,436	20.8	99	7
	Art Powell, Oakland[3]	73	1,304	17.9	85	16
	Buddy Dial, Pittsburgh[2]	60	1,295	21.6	83	9
	Lance Alworth, San Diego	61	1,205	19.8	85	11
	Del Shofner, NY Giants[4]	64	1,181	18.5	70	9
	Lionel Taylor, Denver[3]	78	1,101	14.1	72	10
	Terry Barr, Detroit	66	1,086	16.5	75	13
	Charley Hennigan, Houston[2]	61	1,051	17.2	83	10
	Sonny Randle, St. Louis[2]	51	1,014	19.9	68	12
	Bake Turner, NY Jets	71	1,009	14.2	53	6
1964	Charley Hennigan, Houston[3]	101	1,546	15.3	53	8
	Art Powell, Oakland[4]	76	1,361	17.9	77	11
	Lance Alworth, San Diego[2]	61	1,235	20.2	82	13
	Johnny Morris, Chi. Bears	93	1,200	12.9	63	10
	Elbert Dubenion, Buffalo	42	1,139	27.1	72	10
	Terry Barr, Detroit[2]	57	1,030	18.1	58	9
1965	Lance Alworth, San Diego[3]	69	1,602	23.2	85	14
	Dave Parks, San Francisco	80	1,344	16.8	53	12
	Don Maynard, NY Jets[3]	68	1,218	17.9	56	14

	Pete Retzlaff, Philadelphia	66	1,190	18.0	78	10
	Lionel Taylor, Denver[4]	85	1,131	13.3	63	6
	Tommy McDonald, LA Rams[3]	67	1,036	15.5	51	9
	Bob Hayes, Dallas	46	1,003	21.8	82	12
1966	Lance Alworth, San Diego[4]	73	1,383	18.9	78	13
	Otis Taylor, Kansas City	58	1,297	22.4	89	8
	Pat Studstill, Detroit	67	1,266	18.9	99	5
	Bob Hayes, Dallas[2]	64	1,232	19.3	95	13
	Charlie Frazier, Houston	57	1,129	19.8	79	12
	Charley Taylor, Washington	72	1,119	15.5	86	12
	George Sauer, NY Jets	63	1,081	17.2	77	5
	Homer Jones, NY Giants	48	1,044	21.8	98	8
	Art Powell, Oakland[5]	53	1,026	19.4	46	11
1967	Don Maynard, NY Jets[4]	71	1,434	20.2	75	10
	Ben Hawkins, Philadelphia	59	1,265	21.4	87	10
	Homer Jones, NY Giants[2]	49	1,209	24.7	70	13
	Jackie Smith, St. Louis	56	1,205	21.5	76	9
	George Sauer, NY Jets[2]	75	1,189	15.9	61	6
	Lance Alworth, San Diego[5]	52	1,010	19.4	71	9
1968	Lance Alworth, San Diego[6]	68	1,312	19.3	80	10
	Don Maynard, NY Jets[5]	57	1,297	22.8	87	10
	George Sauer, NY Jets[3]	66	1,141	17.3	43	3
	Warren Wells, Oakland	53	1,137	21.5	94	11
	Gary Garrison, San Diego	52	1,103	21.2	84	10
	Roy Jefferson, Pittsburgh	58	1,074	18.5	62	11
	Paul Warfield, Cleveland	50	1,067	21.3	65	12
	Homer Jones, NY Giants[3]	45	1,057	23.5	84	7
	Fred Biletnikoff, Oakland	61	1,037	17.0	82	6
	Lance Rentzel, Dallas	54	1,009	18.7	65	6
1969	Warren Wells, Oakland[2]	47	1,260	26.8	80	14
	Harold Jackson, Philadelphia	65	1,116	17.2	65	9
	Roy Jefferson, Pittsburgh[2]	67	1,079	16.1	63	9
	Dan Abramowicz, New Orleans	73	1,015	13.9	49	7
	Lance Alworth, San Diego[7]	64	1,003	15.7	76	4
1970	Gene Washington, San Francisco	53	1,100	20.8	79	12
	Marlin Briscoe, Buffalo	57	1,036	18.2	48	8
	Dick Gordon, Chi. Bears	71	1,026	14.5	69	13
	Gary Garrison, San Diego[2]	44	1,006	22.9	67	12
1971	Otis Taylor, Kansas City	57	1,110	19.5	82	7
1972	Harold Jackson, Philadelphia[2]	62	1,048	16.9	77	4
	John Gilliam, Minnesota	47	1,035	22.0	66	7
1973	Harold Carmichael, Philadelphia	67	1,116	16.7	73	9
1974	Cliff Branch, Oakland	60	1,092	18.2	67	13
	Drew Pearson, Dallas	62	1,087	17.5	50	2
1975	Ken Burrough, Houston	53	1,063	20.1	77	8
1976	Roger Carr, Baltimore	43	1,112	25.9	79	11
	Cliff Branch, Oakland[2]	46	1,111	24.2	88	12
	Charlie Joiner, San Diego	50	1,056	21.1	81	7
1978	Wesley Walker, NY Jets	48	1,169	24.4	77	8
	Steve Largent, Seattle	71	1,168	16.5	57	8
	Harold Carmichael, Philadelphia[2]	55	1,072	19.5	56	8
	John Jefferson, San Diego	56	1,001	17.9	46	13
1979	Steve Largent, Seattle[2]	66	1,237	18.7	55	9
	John Stallworth, Pittsburgh	70	1,183	16.9	65	8
	Ahmad Rashad, Minnesota	80	1,156	14.5	52	9
	John Jefferson, San Diego[2]	61	1,090	17.9	65	10
	Frank Lewis, Buffalo	54	1,082	20.0	55	2
	Wes Chandler, New Orleans	65	1,069	16.4	85	6
	Tony Hill, Dallas	60	1,062	17.7	75	10
	Drew Pearson, Dallas[2]	55	1,026	18.7	56	8
	Wallace Francis, Atlanta	74	1,013	13.7	42	8
	Harold Jackson, New England[3]	45	1,013	22.5	59	7
	Charlie Joiner, San Diego[2]	72	1,008	14.0	39	4
	Stanley Morgan, New England	44	1,002	22.8	63	12
1980	John Jefferson, San Diego[2]	82	1,340	16.3	58	13
	Kellen Winslow, San Diego	89	1,290	14.5	65	9
	James Lofton, Green Bay	71	1,226	17.3	47	4
	Charlie Joiner, San Diego[3]	71	1,132	15.9	51	4
	Ahmad Rashad, Minnesota[2]	69	1,095	15.9	76	5
	Steve Largent, Seattle[3]	66	1,064	16.1	67	6
	Tony Hill, Dallas[2]	60	1,055	17.6	58	8
	Alfred Jenkins, Atlanta	57	1,026	18.0	57	6
1981	Alfred Jenkins, Altanta[2]	70	1,358	19.4	67	13
	James Lofton, Green Bay[2]	71	1,294	18.2	75	8
	Frank Lewis, Buffalo[2]	70	1,244	17.8	33	4
	Steve Watson, Denver	60	1,244	20.7	95	13
	Steve Largent, Seattle[4]	75	1,224	16.3	57	9
	Charlie Joiner, San Diego[4]	70	1,188	17.0	57	7
	Kevin House, Tampa Bay	56	1,176	21.0	84	9
	Wes Chandler, N.O.-San Diego[2]	69	1,142	16.6	51	6
	Dwight Clark, San Francisco	85	1,105	13.0	78	4
	John Stallworth, Pittsburgh[2]	63	1,098	17.4	55	5
	Kellen Winslow, San Diego[2]	88	1,075	12.2	67	10
	Pat Tilley, St. Louis	66	1,040	15.8	75	3
	Stanley Morgan, New England[2]	44	1,029	23.4	76	6
	Harold Carmichael, Philadelphia[3]	61	1,028	16.9	85	6
	Freddie Scott, Detroit	53	1,022	19.3	48	5
	Cris Collinsworth, Cincinnati	67	1,009	15.1	74	8
	Joe Senser, Minnesota	79	1,004	12.7	53	8
	Ozzie Newsome, Cleveland	69	1,002	14.5	62	6
	Sammy White, Minnesota	66	1,001	15.2	53	3
1982	Wes Chandler, San Diego[3]	49	1,032	21.1	66	9
1983	Mike Quick, Philadelphia	69	1,409	20.4	83	13
	Carlos Carson, Kansas City	80	1,351	16.9	50	7
	James Lofton, Green Bay[3]	58	1,300	22.4	74	8
	Todd Christensen, LA Raiders	92	1,247	13.6	45	12
	Roy Green, St. Louis	78	1,227	15.7	71	14
	Charlie Brown, Washington	78	1,225	15.7	75	8
	Tim Smith, Houston	83	1,176	14.2	47	6
	Kellen Winslow, San Diego[3]	88	1,172	13.3	46	8
	Earnest Gray, NY Giants	78	1,139	14.6	62	5
	Steve Watson, Denver[2]	59	1,133	19.2	78	5
	Cris Collinsworth, Cincinnati[2]	66	1,130	17.1	63	5
	Steve Largent, Seattle[5]	72	1,074	14.9	46	11
	Mark Duper, Miami	51	1,003	19.7	85	10
1984	Roy Green, St. Louis[2]	78	1,555	19.9	83	12
	John Stallworth, Pittsburgh[3]	80	1,395	17.4	51	11
	Mark Clayton, Miami	73	1,389	19.0	65	18
	Art Monk, Washington	106	1,372	12.9	72	7
	James Lofton, Green Bay[4]	62	1,361	22.0	79	7
	Mark Duper, Miami[2]	71	1,306	18.4	80	8
	Steve Watson, Denver[3]	69	1,170	17.0	73	7
	Steve Largent, Seattle[6]	74	1,164	15.7	65	12
	Tim Smith, Houston[2]	69	1,141	16.5	75	4
	Stacey Bailey, Atlanta	67	1,138	17.0	61	6
	Carlos Carson, Kansas City[2]	57	1,078	18.9	57	4
	Mike Quick, Philadelphia[2]	61	1,052	17.2	90	9
	Todd Christensen, LA Raiders[2]	80	1,007	12.6	38	7
	Kevin House, Tampa Bay[2]	76	1,005	13.2	55	5
	Ozzie Newsome, Cleveland[2]	89	1,001	11.2	52	5
1985	Steve Largent, Seattle[7]	79	1,287	16.3	43	6
	Mike Quick, Philadelphia[3]	73	1,247	17.1	99	11
	Art Monk, Washington[2]	91	1,226	13.5	53	2
	Wes Chandler, San Diego[4]	67	1,199	17.9	75	10
	Drew Hill, Houston	64	1,169	18.3	57	9
	James Lofton, Green Bay[5]	69	1,153	16.7	56	4
	Louis Lipps, Pittsburgh	59	1,134	19.2	51	12
	Cris Collinsworth, Cincinnati[3]	65	1,125	17.3	71	5
	Tony Hill, Dallas[3]	74	1,113	15.0	53	7
	Lionel James, San Diego	86	1,027	11.9	67	6
	Roger Craig, San Francisco	92	1,016	11.0	73	6

200 YARDS RUSHING IN A GAME

Date	Player, Team, Opponent	Att.	Yards	TD
Oct. 8, 1933	Cliff Battles, Boston vs. NY Giants	16	215	1
Nov. 27, 1949	Steve Van Buren, Philadelphia vs. Pittsburgh	27	205	0
Nov. 12, 1950	Gene Roberts, NY Giants vs. Chi. Cardinals	26	218	2
Nov. 22, 1953	Dan Towler, LA Rams vs. Baltimore	14	205	1
Dec. 16, 1956	Tom Wilson, LA Rams vs. Green Bay	23	223	0
Nov. 24, 1957	Jim Brown, Cleveland vs. LA Rams	31	237	4
Nov. 15, 1959	Bobby Mitchell, Cleveland vs. Washington	14	232	3
Dec. 18, 1960	John David Crow, St. Louis vs. Pittsburgh	24	203	0
Nov. 19, 1961	Jim Brown, Cleveland vs. Philadelphia	34	237	4
Dec. 10, 1961	Billy Cannon, Houston vs. NY Titans	25	216	3
Sept. 22, 1963	Jim Brown, Cleveland vs. Dallas	20	232	2
Oct. 20, 1963	Clem Daniels, Oakland vs. NY Jets	27	200	2
Nov. 3, 1963	Jim Brown, Cleveland vs. Philadelphia	28	223	1
Dec. 8, 1963	Cookie Gilchrist, Buffalo vs. NY Jets	36	243	5
Oct. 10, 1964	John Henry Johnson, Pittsburgh vs. Cleveland	30	200	3
Oct. 30, 1966	Jim Nance, Boston vs. Oakland	38	208	2
Nov. 3, 1968	Gale Sayers, Chi. Bears vs. Green Bay	24	205	0
Dec. 20, 1970	John (Frenchy) Fuqua, Pitt. vs. Philadelphia	20	218	2
Dec. 5, 1971	Willie Ellison, LA Rams vs. New Orleans	26	247	1
Sept. 16, 1973	O.J. Simpson, Buffalo vs. New England	29	250	2
Dec. 9, 1973	O.J. Simpson, Buffalo vs. New England	22	219	1
Dec. 16, 1973	O.J. Simpson, Buffalo vs. NY Jets	34	200	1
Sept. 28, 1975	O.J. Simpson, Buffalo vs. Pittsburgh	28	227	1
Dec. 14, 1975	Greg Pruitt, Cleveland vs. Kansas City	26	214	3
Oct. 24, 1976	Chuck Foreman, Minnesota vs. Philadelphia	28	200	2
Nov. 25, 1976	O.J. Simpson, Buffalo vs. Detroit	29	273	2
Dec. 5, 1976	O.J. Simpson, Buffalo vs. Miami	24	203	1
Oct. 30, 1977	Walter Payton, Chi. Bears vs. Green Bay	23	205	2
Nov. 20, 1977	Walter Payton, Chi. Bears vs. Minnesota	40	275	1
Dec. 4, 1977	Tony Dorsett, Dallas vs. Philadelphia	23	206	2
Nov. 26, 1978	Terry Miller, Buffalo vs. NY Giants	21	208	2
Oct. 19, 1980	Earl Campbell, Houston vs. Tampa Bay	33	203	0
Oct. 26, 1980	Earl Campbell, Houston vs. Cincinnati	27	202	2
Nov. 16, 1980	Earl Campbell, Houston vs. Chi. Bears	31	206	0
Dec. 21, 1980	Earl Campbell, Houston vs. Minnesota	29	203	1
Sept. 4, 1983	George Rogers, New Orleans vs. St. Louis	24	206	2
Sept. 18, 1983	Tony Collins, New England vs. NY Jets	23	212	3
Nov. 6, 1983	James Wilder, Tampa Bay vs. Minnesota	31	219	1
Nov. 27, 1983	Curt Warner, Seattle vs. Kansas City (OT)	32	207	3
Sept. 2, 1984	Gerald Riggs, Atlanta vs. New Orleans	35	202	2
Nov. 4, 1984	Eric Dickerson, LA Rams vs. St. Louis	21	208	2
Nov. 18, 1984	Greg Bell, Buffalo vs. Dallas	27	206	1
Dec. 9, 1984	Eric Dickerson, LA Rams vs. Houston	27	215	2
Dec. 21, 1985	George Rogers, Washington vs. St. Louis	34	206	1
Dec. 21, 1985	Joe Morris, NY Giants vs. Pittsburgh	36	202	3

400 YARDS PASSING IN A GAME

Date	Player, Team, Opponent	Att.	Comp.	Yards	TD
Nov. 14, 1943	Sid Luckman, Chi. Bears vs. NY Giants	32	21	433	7
Oct. 31, 1948	Sammy Baugh, Washington vs. Boston	24	17	446	4
Oct. 31, 1948	Jim Hardy, LA Rams vs. Chi. Cardinals	53	28	406	3
Dec. 11, 1949	Johnny Lujack, Chi. Bears vs. Chi. Cardinals	39	24	468	6
Sept. 28, 1951	Norm Van Brocklin, LA Rams vs. NY Yanks	41	27	554	5
Oct. 4, 1952	Otto Graham, Cleveland vs. Pittsburgh	49	21	401	3
Nov. 8, 1953	Bobby Thomason, Philadelphia vs. NY Giants	44	22	437	4
Dec. 13, 1958	Bobby Layne, Pittsburgh vs. Chi. Cardinals	49	23	409	2
Oct. 13, 1961	Jacky Lee, Houston vs. Boston	41	27	457	2
Oct. 29, 1961	George Blanda, Houston vs. Buffalo	32	18	464	4
Oct. 29, 1961	Sonny Jurgensen, Philadelphia vs. Wash.	41	27	436	3
Nov. 19, 1961	George Blanda, Houston vs. NY Titans	32	20	410	7
Dec. 17, 1961	Sonny Jurgensen, Philadelphia vs. Detroit	42	27	403	3

Sept. 15, 1962	Frank Tripucka, Denver vs. Buffalo	56	29	447	2
Oct. 28, 1962	Y.A. Tittle, NY Giants vs. Washington	39	27	505	7
Nov. 18, 1962	Bill Wade, Chi. Bears vs. Dallas Cowboys	46	28	466	2
Dec. 16, 1962	Sonny Jurgensen, Philadelphia vs. St. Louis	34	15	419	5
Oct. 13, 1963	Charley Johnson, St. Louis vs. Pittsburgh	41	20	428	2
Nov. 10, 1963	Don Meredith, Dallas vs. San Francisco	48	30	460	3
Nov. 17, 1963	Norm Snead, Washington vs. Pittsburgh	40	23	424	2
Dec. 22, 1963	Tom Flores, Oakland vs. Houston	29	17	407	6
Oct. 16, 1964	Babe Parilli, Boston vs. Oakland	47	25	422	4
Oct. 25, 1964	Cotton Davidson, Oakland vs. Denver	36	23	427	5
Nov. 1, 1964	Len Dawson, Kansas City vs. Denver	38	23	435	6
Oct. 24, 1965	Fran Tarkenton, Minnesota vs. San Francisco	35	21	407	3
Nov. 28, 1965	Sonny Jurgensen, Washington vs. Dallas	43	26	411	3
Nov. 13, 1966	Don Meredith, Dallas vs. Washington	29	21	406	2
Sept. 17, 1967	Johnny Unitas, Baltimore vs. Atlanta	32	22	401	2
Oct. 1, 1967	Joe Namath, NY Jets vs. Miami	39	23	415	3
Nov. 26, 1967	Sonny Jurgensen, Washington vs. Cleveland	50	32	418	3
Sept. 9, 1968	Pete Beathard, Houston vs. Kansas City	48	23	413	2
Sept. 28, 1969	Joe Kapp, Minnesota vs. Baltimore	43	28	449	7
Dec. 21, 1969	Don Horn, Green Bay vs. St. Louis	31	22	410	5
Sept. 24, 1972	Joe Namath, NY Jets vs. Baltimore	28	15	496	6
Dec. 11, 1972	Joe Namath, NY Jets vs. Oakland	46	25	403	1
Nov. 18, 1974	Charley Johnson, Denver vs. Kansas City	42	28	445	2
Nov. 17, 1975	Ken Anderson, Cincinnati vs. Buffalo	46	30	447	2
Oct. 3, 1976	James Harris, LA Rams vs. Miami	29	17	436	2
Sept. 21, 1980	Richard Todd, NY Jets vs. San Francisco	60	42	447	3
Oct. 12, 1980	Lynn Dickey, Green Bay vs. Tampa Bay	51	35	418	1
Oct. 19, 1980	Dan Fouts, San Diego vs. NY Giants	41	26	444	3
Nov. 16, 1980	Doug Williams, Tampa Bay vs. Minnesota	55	30	486	4
Dec. 14, 1980	Tommy Kramer, Minnesota vs. Cleveland	49	38	456	4
Oct. 11, 1981	Tommy Kramer, Minnesota vs. San Diego	43	27	444	4
Oct. 25, 1981	Brian Sipe, Cleveland vs. Baltimore	41	30	444	4
Oct. 25, 1981	David Woodley, Miami vs. Dallas	37	21	408	3
Nov. 15, 1981	Steve Bartkowski, Atlanta vs. Pittsburgh	50	33	416	2
Nov. 21, 1982	Joe Montana, San Francisco vs. St. Louis	39	26	408	3
Dec. 11, 1982	Dan Fouts, San Diego vs. San Francisco	48	33	444	5
Dec. 20, 1982	Dan Fouts, San Diego vs. Cincinnati	40	25	435	1
Dec. 20, 1982	Ken Anderson, Cincinnati vs. San Diego	56	40	416	2
Dec. 26, 1982	Vince Ferragamo, LA Rams vs. Chi. Bears	46	30	509	3
Sept. 25, 1983	Richard Todd, NY Jets vs. LA Rams (OT)	50	37	446	2
Oct. 2, 1983	Joe Theismann, Washington vs. LA Raiders	39	23	417	3
Oct. 9, 1983	Joe Ferguson, Buffalo vs. Miami (OT)	55	38	419	5
Nov. 20, 1983	Dave Krieg, Seattle vs. Denver	42	31	418	3
Dec. 11, 1983	Bill Kenney, Kansas City vs. San Diego	41	31	411	4
Sept. 2, 1984	Phil Simms, NY Giants vs. Philadelphia	30	23	409	4
Sept. 30, 1984	Dan Marino, Miami vs. St. Louis	36	24	429	3
Oct. 21, 1984	Dan Fouts, San Diego vs. LA Raiders	45	24	410	3
Nov. 4, 1984	Dan Marino, Miami vs. NY Jets	42	23	422	2
Nov. 25, 1984	Dave Krieg, Seattle vs. Denver	44	30	406	3
Dec. 2, 1984	Dan Marino, Miami vs. LA Raiders	57	35	470	4
Dec. 9, 1984	Dan Marino, Miami vs. Indianapolis	41	29	404	4
Dec. 16, 1984	Neil Lomax, St. Louis vs. Washington	46	37	468	2
Sept. 15, 1985	Dan Fouts, San Diego vs. Seattle	43	29	440	4
Sept. 19, 1985	Tommy Kramer, Minnesota vs. Chi. Bears	55	28	436	3
Oct. 6, 1985	Phil Simms, NY Giants vs. Dallas	36	18	432	3
Oct. 6, 1985	Joe Montana, San Francisco vs. Atlanta	57	37	429	5
Oct. 13, 1985	Phil Simms, NY Giants vs. Cincinnati	62	40	513	1
Oct. 13, 1985	Dave Krieg, Seattle vs. Atlanta	51	33	405	4
Nov. 10, 1985	Dan Fouts, San Diego vs. LA Raiders (OT)	41	26	436	4
Dec. 20, 1985	John Elway, Denver vs. Seattle	42	24	432	1

4,000 YARDS PASSING IN A SEASON

Year	Player, Team	Att.	Comp.	Yards	TD	Int.
1967	Joe Namath, NY Jets	491	258	4,007	26	28
1979	Dan Fouts, San Diego[1]	530	332	4,082	24	24
1980	Dan Fouts, San Diego[2]	589	348	4,715	30	24
	Brian Sipe, Cleveland	554	337	4,132	30	14
1981	Dan Fouts, San Diego[3]	609	360	4,802	33	17
1983	Lynn Dickey, Green Bay	484	289	4,458	32	29
	Bill Kenney, San Diego	603	346	4,348	24	18
1984	Dan Marino, Miami[1]	564	362	5,084	48	17
	Neil Lomax, St. Louis	560	345	4,614	28	16
	Phil Simms, NY Giants	533	286	4,044	22	18
1985	Dan Marino, Miami[2]	567	336	4,137	30	21

250 YARDS RECEIVING IN A GAME

Date	Player, Team, Opponent	No.	Yards	TD
Nov. 22, 1945	Jim Benton, Cleveland vs. Detroit	10	303	1
Dec. 3, 1950	Cloyce Box, Detroit vs. Baltimore	12	302	4
Oct. 21, 1956	Billy Howton, Green Bay vs. LA Rams	7	257	2
Oct. 13, 1961	Charley Hennigan, Houston vs. Boston	13	272	1
Oct. 28, 1962	Del Shofner, NY Giants vs. Washington	11	269	1
Nov. 4, 1962	Sonny Randle, St. Louis vs. NY Giants	16	256	1
Sept. 23, 1979	Jerry Butler, Buffalo vs. NY Jets	10	255	4
Dec. 20, 1982	Wes Chandler, San Diego vs. Cincinnati	10	260	2
Dec. 22, 1985	Stephone Paige, Kansas City vs. San Diego	8	309	2

300 COMBINED NET YARDS GAINED IN A GAME

Date	Player, Team, Opponent	No.	Yards	TD
Nov. 22, 1945	Jim Benton, Cleveland vs. Detroit	10	303	1
Oct. 29, 1950	Wally Triplett, Detroit vs. LA Rams	11	331	1
Dec. 3, 1950	Cloyce Box, Detroit vs. Baltimore	13	302	4
Nov 19, 1961	Jim Brown, Cleveland vs. Philadelphia	38	313	4
Dec. 10, 1961	Billy Cannon, Houston vs. NY Titans	32	373	5
Dec. 16, 1962	Timmy Brown, Philadelphia vs. St. Louis	19	341	2
Nov. 17, 1963	Gary Ballman, Pittsburgh vs. Washington	12	320	2
Dec. 12, 1965	Gale Sayers, Chi. Bears vs. San Francisco	17	336	6
Dec. 18, 1966	Gale Sayers, Chi. Bears vs. Minnesota	20	339	2
Nov. 2, 1969	Travis Williams, Green Bay vs. Pittsburgh	11	314	3
Dec. 6, 1969	Jerry LeVias, Houston vs. NY Jets	18	329	1
Oct. 4, 1970	O.J. Simpson, Buffalo vs. NY Jets	26	303	2
Nov. 1, 1970	Eugene (Mercury) Morris, Miami vs. Baltimore	17	302	0
Nov. 23, 1975	Greg Pruitt, Cleveland vs. Cincinnati	28	304	2
Dec. 21, 1975	Walter Payton, Chi. Bears vs. New Orleans	32	300	1
Sept. 22, 1985	Lionel James, San Diego vs. Cincinnati	20	316	2
Nov. 10, 1985	Lionel James, San Diego vs. LA Raiders (OT)	23	345	0
Dec. 22, 1985	Stephone Paige, Kansas City vs. San Diego	8	309	2

2,000 COMBINED NET YARDS IN A SEASON

Year	Player, Team	Rushing Att.-Yards	Receptions	Punt Returns	Kickoff Returns	Fumble Runs	Total Yards
1960	**Abner Haynes, Dallas Texans**	156 875	55-576	14-215	19-434	4-0	248-2,100
1961	Billy Cannon, Houston	200-948	43-586	9-70	18-439	2-0	272-2,043
1962	Tim Brown, Philadelphia	137-545	52-849	6-81	30-831	4-0	229-2,306
	Dick Christy, NY Titans	114-535	62-538	15-250	38-824	2-0	231-2,147
1963	Timmy Brown, Philadelphia	192-841	36-487	16-152	33-945	2-3	279-2,428
	Jim Brown, Cleveland	291-1,863	24-268	0-0	0-0	0-0	315-2,131
1965	**Gale Sayers, Chi. Bears**	166-867	29-507	16-238	21-660	4-0	236-2,272
1966	Gale Sayers, Chi. Bears	229-1,231	34-447	6-44	23-718	3-0	295-2,440
	Leroy Kelly, Cleveland	209-1,141	32-366	13-104	19-403	0-0	273-2,014
1973	O.J. Simpson, Buffalo	332-2,003	6-70	0-0	0-0	0-0	338-2,073
1974	Mack Herron, New England	231-824	38-474	35-517	28-629	3-0	335-2,444
	Otis Armstrong, Denver	263-1,407	38-405	0-0	16-386	1-0	318-2,198
	Terry Metcalf, St. Louis	152-718	50-377	26-340	20-623	7-0	255-2,058
1975	Terry Metcalf, St. Louis	165-816	43-378	23-285	35-960	2-23	268-2,462
	O.J. Simpson, Buffalo	329-1,817	28-426	0-0	0-0	1-0	358-2,243
1977	Walter Payton, Chi. Bears	339-1,852	27-269	0-0	2-95	5-0	373-2,216
	Terry Metcalf, St. Louis	149-739	34-403	14-108	32-772	1-0	230-2,022
1978	Bruce Harper, NY Jets	58-303	13-196	30-378	55-1,280	1-0	157-2,157
1979	Wilbert Montgomery, Philadelphia	338-1,512	41-494	0-0	1-6	2-0	382-2,012
1980	Bruce Harper, NY Jets	45-126	50-634	28-242	49-1,070	3-0	175-2,072
1981	**James Brooks, San Diego**	109-525	46-329	22-290	40-949	1-0	218-2,093
	William Andrews, Atlanta	289-1,301	81-735	0-0	0-0	1-0	371-2,036
1983	**Eric Dickerson, LA Rams**	390-1,808	51-404	0-0	0-0	1-0	442-2,212
	William Andrews, Atlanta	331-1,567	59-609	0-0	0-0	2-0	392-2,176
	Walter Payton, Chi. Bears	314-1,421	53-607	0-0	0-0	2-0	369-2,028
1984	Eric Dickerson, LA Rams	379-2,105	21-139	0-0	0-0	4-15	404-2,259
	James Wilder, Tampa Bay	407-1,544	86-685	0-0	0-0	4-0	497-2,229
	Walter Payton, Chi. Bears	381-1,684	45-368	0-0	0-0	1-0	427-2,052
1985	Lionel James, San Diego	105-516	86-1,027	25-213	36-779	1-0	253-2,535
	Marcus Allen, LA Raiders	380-1,759	67-555	0-0	0-0	2-(−6)	449-2,308
	Roger Craig, San Francisco	214-1,050	92-1,016	0-0	0-0	0-0	306-2,066
	Walter Payton, Chi. Bears	324-1,551	49-483	0-0	0-0	1-0	374-2,034

Bold face—first year in the league.

ANNUAL RUSHING LEADERS

Year	Player, Team	Att.	Yards	Avg.	TD
1932	**Cliff Battles, Boston**	148	576	3.9	3
1933	Jim Musick, Boston	173	809	4.7	5
1934	**Beattie Feathers, Chi. Bears**	101	1,004	9.9	8
1935	Doug Russell, Chi. Cardinals	140	499	3.6	0
1936	**Alphonse (Tuffy) Leemans, NY Giants**	206	830	4.0	2
1937	Cliff Battles, Washington	216	874	4.0	5
1938	**Byron (Whizzer) White, Pittsburgh**	152	567	3.7	4
1939	**Bill Osmanski, Chi. Bears**	121	699	5.8	7
1940	Byron (Whizzer) White, Detroit	146	514	3.5	5
1941	Clarence (Pug) Manders, Brooklyn	111	486	4.4	5
1942	**Bill Dudley, Pittsburgh**	162	696	4.3	5
1943	**Bill Paschal, NY Giants**	147	572	3.9	10
1944	Bill Paschal, NY Giants	196	737	3.8	9
1945	Steve Van Buren, Philadelphia	143	832	5.8	15
1946	Bill Dudley, Pittsburgh	146	604	4.1	3
1947	Steve Van Buren, Philadelphia	217	1,008	4.6	13
1948	Steve Van Buren, Philadelphia	201	945	4.7	10
1949	Steve Van Buren, Philadelphia	263	1,146	4.4	11
1950	**Marion Motley, Cleveland**	140	810	5.8	3
1951	Eddie Price, NY Giants	271	971	3.6	7
1952	Dan Towler, LA Rams	156	894	5.7	10
1953	Joe Perry, San Francisco	192	1,018	5.3	10
1954	Joe Perry, San Francisco	173	1,049	6.1	8
1955	**Alan Ameche, Baltimore**	213	961	4.5	9
1956	Rick Casares, Chi. Bears	234	1,126	4.8	12
1957	**Jim Brown, Cleveland**	202	942	4.7	9
1958	Jim Brown, Cleveland	257	1,527	5.9	17
1959	Jim Brown, Cleveland	290	1,329	4.6	14
1960	Jim Brown, Cleveland, NFL	215	1,257	5.8	9
	Abner Haynes, Dallas Texans, AFL	157	875	5.6	9
1961	Jim Brown, Cleveland, NFL	305	1,408	4.6	8
	Billy Cannon, Houston, AFL	200	948	4.7	6
1962	Jim Taylor, Green Bay, NFL	272	1,474	5.4	19
	Cookie Gilchrist, Buffalo, AFL	214	1,096	5.1	13
1963	Jim Brown, Cleveland, NFL	291	1,863	6.4	12
	Clem Daniels, Oakland, AFL	215	1,099	5.1	3
1964	Jim Brown, Cleveland, NFL	280	1,446	5.1	7
	Cookie Gilchrist, Buffalo, AFL	230	981	4.3	6
1965	Jim Brown, Cleveland, NFL	289	1,544	5.3	17
	Paul Lowe, San Diego, AFL	222	1,121	5.0	7
1966	Jim Nance, Boston, AFL	299	1,458	4.9	11
	Gale Sayers, Chi. Bears, NFL	229	1,231	5.4	8
1967	Jim Nance, Boston, AFL	269	1,216	4.5	7
	Leroy Kelly, Cleveland, NFL	235	1,205	5.1	11
1968	Leroy Kelly, Cleveland, NFL	248	1,239	5.0	16
	Paul Robinson, Cincinnati, AFL	238	1,023	4.3	8
1969	Gale Sayers, Chi. Bears, NFL	236	1,032	4.4	8
	Dickie Post, San Diego, AFL	182	873	4.8	6
1970	Larry Brown, Washington, NFC	237	1,125	4.7	5
	Floyd Little, Denver, AFC	209	901	4.3	3
1971	Floyd Little, Denver, AFC	284	1,133	4.0	6
	John Brockington, Green Bay, NFC	216	1,105	5.1	4
1972	O.J. Simpson, Buffalo, AFC	292	1,251	4.3	6
	Larry Brown, Washington, NFC	285	1,216	4.3	8
1973	O.J. Simpson, Buffalo, AFC	332	2,003	6.0	12
	John Brockington, Green Bay, NFC	265	1,144	4.3	3
1974	Otis Armstrong, Denver, AFC	263	1,407	5.3	9
	Lawrence McCutcheon, LA Rams, NFC	236	1,109	4.7	3
1975	O.J. Simpson, Buffalo, AFC	329	1,817	5.5	16
	Jim Otis, St. Louis, NFC	269	1,076	4.0	5
1976	O.J. Simpson, Buffalo, AFC	290	1,503	5.2	8
	Walter Payton, Chi. Bears, NFC	311	1,390	4.5	13
1977	Walter Payton, Chi. Bears, NFC	339	1,852	5.5	14
	Mark van Eeghen, Oakland, AFC	324	1,273	3.9	7
1978	**Earl Campbell, Houston, AFC**	302	1,450	4.8	13
	Walter Payton, Chi. Bears, NFC	333	1,395	4.2	11
1979	Earl Campbell, Houston, AFC	368	1,697	4.6	19
	Walter Payton, Chi. Bears, NFC	369	1,610	4.4	14
1980	Earl Campbell, Houston, AFC	373	1,934	5.2	13
	Walter Payton, Chi. Bears, NFC	317	1,460	4.6	6
1981	**George Rogers, New Orleans, NFC**	378	1,674	4.4	13
	Earl Campbell, Houston, AFC	361	1,376	3.9	10
1982	Freeman McNeil, NY Jets, AFC	151	786	5.2	6
	Tony Dorsett, Dallas, NFC	177	745	4.2	5
1983	**Eric Dickerson, LA Rams, NFC**	390	1,808	4.6	18
	Curt Warner, Seattle, AFC	335	1,449	4.3	13
1984	Eric Dickerson, LA Rams, NFC	379	2,105	5.6	14
	Earnest Jackson, San Diego, AFC	296	1,179	4.0	8
1985	Marcus Allen, LA Raiders, AFC	380	1,759	4.6	11
	Gerald Riggs, Atlanta, NFC	397	1,719	4.3	10

Bold face—first year in the league.

PASSING

Year	Player, Team	Att.	Comp.	Yards	TD	Int.
1932	Arnie Herber, Green Bay	101	37	639	9	9
1933	**Harry Newman, NY Giants**	136	53	973	11	17
1934	Arnie Herber, Green Bay	115	42	799	8	12
1935	Ed Danowski, NY Giants	113	57	794	10	9
1936	Arnie Herber, Green Bay	173	77	1,239	11	13
1937	**Sammy Baugh, Washington**	171	81	1,127	8	14
1938	Ed Danowski, NY Giants	129	70	848	7	8
1939	**Parker Hall, Cleveland**	208	106	1,227	9	13
1940	Sammy Baugh, Washington	177	111	1,367	12	10
1941	Cecil Isbell, Green Bay	206	117	1,479	15	11
1942	Cecil Isbell, Green Bay	268	146	2,021	24	14
1943	Sammy Baugh, Washington	239	133	1,754	23	19
1944	Frank Filchock, Washington	147	84	1,139	13	9
1945	Sammy Baugh, Washington	182	128	1,669	11	4
	Sid Luckman, Chi. Bears	217	117	1,725	14	10
1946	Bob Waterfield, LA Rams	251	127	1,747	18	17
1947	Sammy Baugh, Washington	354	210	2,938	25	15
1948	Tommy Thompson, Philadelphia	246	141	1,965	25	11
1949	Sammy Baugh, Washington	255	145	1,903	18	14
1950	Norm Van Brocklin, LA Rams	233	127	2,061	18	14
1951	Bob Waterfield, LA Rams	176	88	1,566	13	10
1952	Norm Van Brocklin, LA Rams	205	113	1,736	14	17
1953	Otto Graham, Cleveland	258	167	2,722	11	9
1954	Norm Van Brocklin, LA Rams	260	139	2,637	13	21
1955	Otto Graham, Cleveland	185	98	1,721	15	8
1956	Ed Brown, Chi. Bears	168	96	1,667	11	12
1957	Tommy O'Connell, Cleveland	110	63	1,229	9	8
1958	Eddie LeBaron, Washington	145	79	1,365	11	10
1959	Charlie Conerly, NY Giants	194	113	1,706	14	4
1960	Milt Plum, Cleveland, NFL	250	151	2,297	21	5
	Jack Kemp, LA Chargers, AFL	406	211	3,018	20	25
1961	George Blanda, Houston, AFL	362	187	3,330	36	22
	Milt Plum, Cleveland, NFL	302	177	2,416	18	10
1962	Len Dawson, Dallas Texans, AFL	310	189	2,759	29	17
	Bart Starr, Green Bay, NFL	285	178	2,438	12	9
1963	Y.A. Tittle, NY Giants, NFL	367	221	3,145	36	14
	Tobin Rote, San Diego, AFL	286	170	2,510	20	17
1964	Len Dawson, Kansas City, AFL	354	199	2,879	30	18
	Bart Starr, Green Bay, NFL	272	163	2,144	15	4
1965	Rudy Bukich, Chi. Bears, NFL	312	176	2,641	20	9
	John Hadl, San Diego, AFL	348	174	2,798	20	21
1966	Bart Starr, Green Bay, NFL	251	156	2,257	14	3
	Len Dawson, Kansas City, AFL	284	159	2,527	26	10
1967	Sonny Jurgensen, Washington, NFL	508	288	3,747	31	16
	Daryle Lamonica, Oakland, AFL	425	220	3,228	30	20
1968	Len Dawson, Kansas City, AFL	224	131	2,109	17	9
	Earl Morrall, Baltimore, NFL	317	182	2,909	26	17
1969	Sonny Jurgensen, Washington, NFL	442	274	3,102	22	15
	Greg Cook, Cincinnati, AFL	197	106	1,854	15	11
1970	John Brodie, San Francisco, NFC	378	223	2,941	24	10
	Daryle Lamonica, Oakland, AFC	356	179	2,516	22	15
1971	Roger Staubach, Dallas, NFC	211	126	1,882	15	4
	Bob Griese, Miami, AFC	263	145	2,089	19	9
1972	Norm Snead, NY Giants, NFC	325	196	2,307	17	12
	Earl Morrall, Miami, AFC	150	83	1,360	11	7
1973	Roger Staubach, Dallas, NFC	286	179	2,428	23	15
	Ken Stabler, Oakland, AFC	260	163	1,997	14	10
1974	Ken Anderson, Cincinnati, AFC	328	213	2,667	18	10
	Sonny Jurgensen, Washington, NFC	167	107	1,185	11	5
1975	Ken Anderson, Cincinnati, AFC	377	228	3,169	21	11
	Fran Tarkenton, Minnesota, NFC	425	273	2,994	25	13
1976	Ken Stabler, Oakland, AFC	291	194	2,737	27	17
	James Harris, LA Rams, NFC	158	91	1,460	8	6
1977	Bob Griese, Miami, AFC	307	180	2,252	22	13
	Roger Staubach, Dallas, NFC	361	210	2,620	18	9
1978	Roger Staubach, Dallas, NFC	413	231	3,190	25	16
	Terry Bradshaw, Pittsburgh, AFC	368	207	2,915	28	20
1979	Roger Staubach, Dallas, NFC	461	267	3,586	27	11
	Dan Fouts, San Diego, AFC	530	332	4,082	24	24
1980	Brian Sipe, Cleveland, AFC	554	337	4,132	30	14
	Ron Jaworski, Philadelphia, NFC	451	257	3,529	27	12
1981	Ken Anderson, Cincinnati, AFC	479	300	3,753	29	10
	Joe Montana, San Francisco, NFC	488	311	3,565	19	12
1982	Ken Anderson, Cincinnati, AFC	309	218	2,495	12	9
	Joe Theismann, Washington, NFC	252	161	2,033	13	9
1983	Steve Bartkowski, Atlanta, NFC	432	274	3,167	22	5
	Dan Marino, Miami, AFC	296	173	2,210	20	6
1984	Dan Marino, Miami, AFC	564	362	5,084	48	17
	Joe Montana, San Francisco, NFC	432	279	3,630	28	10
1985	Ken O'Brien, NY Jets, AFC	488	297	3,888	25	8
	Joe Montana, San Francisco, NFC	494	303	3,653	27	13

PASS RECEIVING

Year	Player, Team	No.	Yards	Avg.	TD
1932	Ray Flaherty, NY Giants	21	350	16.7	3
1933	John (Shipwreck) Kelly, Brooklyn	22	246	11.2	3
1934	Joe Carter, Philadelphia	16	238	14.9	4
	Morris (Red) Badgro, NY Giants	16	206	12.9	1
1935	**Tod Goodwin, NY Giants**	26	432	16.6	4
1936	Don Hutson, Green Bay	34	536	15.8	8
1937	Don Hutson, Green Bay	41	552	13.5	7
1938	Gaynell Tinsley, Chi. Cardinals	41	516	12.6	1
1939	Don Hutson, Green Bay	34	846	24.9	6
1940	**Don Looney, Philadelphia**	58	707	12.2	4
1941	Don Hutson, Green Bay	58	738	12.7	10
1942	Don Hutson, Green Bay	74	1,211	16.4	17
1943	Don Hutson, Green Bay	47	776	16.5	11
1944	Don Hutson, Green Bay	58	866	14.9	9
1945	Don Hutson, Green Bay	47	834	17.7	9
1946	Jim Benton, LA Rams	63	981	15.6	6
1947	Jim Keane, Chi. Bears	64	910	14.2	10
1948	**Tom Fears, LA Rams**	51	698	13.7	4
1949	Tom Fears, LA Rams	77	1,013	13.2	9
1950	Tom Fears, LA Rams	84	1,116	13.3	7
1951	Elroy (Crazylegs) Hirsch, LA Rams	66	1,495	22.7	17
1952	Mac Speedie, Cleveland	62	911	14.7	5
1953	Pete Pihos, Philadelphia	63	1,049	16.7	10
1954	Pete Pihos, Philadelphia	60	872	14.5	10
	Billy Wilson, San Francisco	60	830	13.8	5
1955	Pete Pihos, Philadelphia	62	864	13.9	7
1956	Billy Wilson, San Francisco	60	889	14.8	5
1957	Billy Wilson, San Francisco	52	757	14.6	6
1958	Raymond Berry, Baltimore	56	794	14.2	9
	Pete Retzlaff, Philadelphia	56	766	13.7	2
1959	Raymond Berry, Baltimore	66	959	14.5	14
1960	Lionel Taylor, Denver, AFL	92	1,235	13.4	12
	Raymond Berry, Baltimore, NFL	74	1,298	17.5	10
1961	Lionel Taylor, Denver, AFL	100	1,176	11.8	4
	Jim (Red) Phillips, LA Rams, NFL	78	1,092	14.0	5
1962	Lionel Taylor, Denver, AFL	77	908	11.8	4
	Bobby Mitchell, Washington, NFL	72	1,384	19.2	11
1963	Lionel Taylor, Denver, AFL	78	1,101	14.1	10
	Bobby Joe Conrad, St. Louis, NFL	73	967	13.2	10
1964	Charley Hennigan, Houston, AFL	101	1,546	15.3	8
	Johnny Morris, Chi. Bears, NFL	93	1,200	12.9	10
1965	Lionel Taylor, Denver, AFL	85	1,131	13.3	6
	Dave Parks, San Francisco, NFL	80	1,344	16.8	12
1966	Lance Alworth, San Diego, AFL	73	1,383	18.9	13
	Charley Taylor, Washington, NFL	72	1,119	15.5	12
1967	George Sauer, NY Jets, AFL	75	1,189	15.9	6
	Charley Taylor, Washington, NFL	70	990	14.1	9
1968	Clifton McNeil, San Francisco, NFL	71	994	14.0	7
	Lance Alworth, San Diego, AFL	68	1,312	19.3	10
1969	Dan Abramowicz, New Orleans, NFL	73	1,015	13.9	7
	Lance Alworth, San Diego, AFL	64	1,003	15.7	4
1970	Dick Gordon, Chi. Bears, NFC	71	1,026	14.5	13
	Marlin Briscoe, Buffalo, AFC	57	1,036	18.2	8
1971	Fred Biletnikoff, Oakland, AFC	61	929	15.2	9
	Bob Tucker, NY Giants, NFC	59	791	13.4	4
1972	Harold Jackson, Philadelphia, NFC	62	1,048	16.9	4
	Fred Biletnikoff, Oakland, AFC	58	802	13.8	7
1973	Harold Carmichael, Philadelphia, NFC	67	1,116	16.7	9
	Fred Willis, Houston, AFC	57	371	6.5	1
1974	Lydell Mitchell, Baltimore, AFC	72	544	7.6	2
	Charle Young, Philadelphia, NFC	63	696	11.0	3
1975	Chuck Foreman, Minnesota, NFC	73	691	9.5	9
	Reggie Rucker, Cleveland, AFC	60	770	12.8	3
1976	MacArthur Lane, Kansas City, AFC	66	686	10.4	1
	Drew Pearson, Dallas, NFC	58	806	13.9	6
1977	Lydell Mitchell, Baltimore, AFC	71	620	8.7	4
	Ahmad Rashad, Minnesota, NFC	51	681	13.4	2
1978	Rickey Young, Minnesota, NFC	88	704	8.0	5
	Steve Largent, Seattle, AFC	71	1,168	16.5	8
1979	Joe Washington, Baltimore, AFC	82	750	9.1	3
	Ahmad Rashad, Minnesota, NFC	80	1,156	14.5	9
1980	Kellen Winslow, San Diego, AFC	89	1,290	14.5	9
	Earl Cooper, San Francisco, NFC	83	567	6.8	4
1981	Kellen Winslow, San Diego, AFC	88	1,075	12.2	10
	Dwight Clark, San Francisco, NFC	85	1,105	13.0	4
1982	Dwight Clark, San Francisco, NFC	60	913	12.2	5
	Kellen Winslow, San Diego, AFC	54	721	13.4	6
1983	Todd Christensen, LA Raiders, AFC	92	1,247	13.6	12
	Roy Green, St. Louis, NFC	78	1,227	15.7	14
	Charlie Brown, Washington, NFC	78	1,225	15.7	8
	Earnest Gray, NY Giants, NFC	78	1,139	14.6	5
1984	Art Monk, Washington, NFC	106	1,372	12.9	7
	Ozzie Newsome, Cleveland, AFC	89	1,001	11.2	5
1985	Roger Craig, San Francisco, NFC	92	1,016	11.0	6
	Lionel James, San Diego, AFC	86	1,027	11.9	6

SCORING

Year	Player, Team	TD	FG	PAT	TP
1932	Earl (Dutch) Clark, Portsmouth	6	3	10	55
1933	Ken Strong, NY Giants	6	5	13	64
	Glenn Presnell, Portsmouth	6	6	10	64
1934	Jack Manders, Chi. Bears	3	10	31	79
1935	Earl (Dutch) Clark, Detroit	6	1	16	55
1936	Earl (Dutch) Clark, Detroit	7	4	19	73
1937	Jack Manders, Chi. Bears	5	8	15	69
1938	Clarke Hinkle, Green Bay	7	3	7	58
1939	Andy Farkas, Washington	11	0	2	68
1940	Don Hutson, Green Bay	7	0	15	57
1941	Don Hutson, Green Bay	12	1	20	95
1942	Don Hutson, Green Bay	17	1	33	138
1943	Don Hutson, Green Bay	12	3	36	117
1944	Don Hutson, Green Bay	9	0	31	85
1945	Steve Van Buren, Philadelphia	18	0	2	110
1946	Ted Fritsch, Green Bay	10	9	13	100
1947	Pat Harder, Chi. Cardinals	7	7	39	102
1948	Pat Harder, Chi. Cardinals	6	7	53	110
1949	Pat Harder, Chi. Cardinals	8	3	45	102
	Gene Roberts, NY Giants	17	0	0	102
1950	**Doak Walker, Detroit**	11	8	38	128
1951	Elroy (Crazylegs) Hirsch, LA Rams	17	0	0	102
1952	Gordy Soltau, San Francisco	7	6	34	94
1953	Gordy Soltau, San Francisco	6	10	48	114
1954	Bobby Walston, Philadelphia	11	4	36	114
1955	Doak Walker, Detroit	7	9	27	96
1956	Bobby Layne, Detroit	5	12	33	99
1957	Sam Baker, Washington	1	14	29	77
	Lou Groza, Cleveland	0	15	32	77
1958	Jim Brown, Cleveland	18	0	0	108
1959	Paul Hornung, Green Bay	7	7	31	94
1960	Paul Hornung, Green Bay, NFL	15	15	41	176
	Gene Mingo, Denver, AFL	6	18	33	123
1961	Gino Cappelletti, Boston, AFL	8	17	48	147
	Paul Hornung, Green Bay, NFL	10	15	41	146
1962	Gene Mingo, Denver, AFL	4	27	32	137
	Jim Taylor, Green Bay, NFL	19	0	0	114
1963	Gino Cappelletti, Boston, AFL	2	22	35	113
	Don Chandler, NY Giants, NFL	0	18	52	106
1964	Gino Cappelletti, Boston, AFL	7	25	36	155
	Lenny Moore, Baltimore, NFL	20	0	0	120
1965	**Gale Sayers, Chi. Bears, NFL**	22	0	0	132
	Gino Cappelletti, Boston, AFL	0	17	27	132
1966	Gino Cappelletti, Boston, AFL	6	16	35	119
	Bruce Gossett, LA Rams, NFL	0	28	29	113
1967	Jim Bakken St. Louis, NFL	0	27	36	117
	George Blanda, Oakland, AFL	0	20	56	116
1968	Jim Turner, NY Jets, AFL	0	34	43	145
	Leroy Kelly, Cleveland, NFL	20	0	0	120
1969	Jim Turner, NY Jets, AFL	0	32	33	129
	Fred Cox, Minnesota, NFL	0	26	43	121
1970	Fred Cox, Minnesota, NFC	0	30	35	125
	Jan Stenerud, Kansas City, AFC	0	30	26	116
1971	Garo Yepremian, Miami, AFC	0	28	33	117
	Curt Knight, Washington, NFC	0	29	27	114
1972	**Chester Marcol, Green Bay, NFC**	0	33	29	128
	Bobby Howfield, NY Jets, AFC	0	27	40	121
1973	David Ray, LA Rams, NFC	0	30	40	130
	Roy Gerela, Pittsburgh, AFC	0	29	36	123
1974	Chester Marcol, Green Bay, NFC	0	25	19	94
	Roy Gerela, Pittsburgh, AFC	0	20	33	93
1975	O.J. Simpson, Buffalo, AFC	23	0	0	138
	Franco Harris, Pittsburgh, AFC	14	0	0	84
1976	Chuck Foreman, Minnesota, NFC	14	0	0	84
	Chuck Foreman, Minnesota, NFC	22	0	0	132
1977	Errol Mann, Oakland, AFC	0	20	39	99
	Walter Payton, Chi. Bears, NFC	16	0	0	96
1978	**Frank Corral, LA Rams, NFC**	0	29	31	118
	Pat Leahy, NY Jets, AFC	0	22	41	107
1979	John Smith, New England, AFC	0	23	46	115
	Mark Moseley, Washington, NFC	0	25	39	114
1980	John Smith, New England, AFC	0	26	51	129
	Ed Murray, Detroit, NFC	0	27	35	116
1981	Ed Murray, Detroit, NFC	0	25	46	121
	Rafael Septien, Dallas, NFC	0	27	40	121
	Jim Breech, Cincinnati, AFC	0	22	49	115
	Nick Lowery, Kansas City, AFC	0	26	37	115
1982	**Marcus Allen, LA Raiders, AFC**	14	0	0	84
	Wendell Tyler, LA Rams, NFC	13	0	0	78
1983	Mark Moseley, Washington, NFC	0	33	62	161
	Gary Anderson, Pittsburgh, AFC	0	27	38	119
1984	Ray Wersching, San Francisco, NFC	0	25	56	131
	Gary Anderson, Pittsburgh, AFC	0	24	45	117
1985	**Kevin Butler, Chi. Bears, NFC**	0	31	51	144
	Gary Anderson, Pittsburgh, AFC	0	33	40	139

FIELD GOALS

Year	Player, Team	Attempts	Made	Pct.
1932	Earl (Dutch) Clark, Portsmouth		3	
1933	**Jack Manders, Chi. Bears**		6	
	Glenn Presnell, Portsmouth		6	
1934	Jack Manders, Chi. Bears		10	
1935	Armand Niccolai, Pittsburgh		6	
	Bill Smith, Chi. Cardinals		6	
1936	Jack Manders, Chi. Bears		7	
	Armand Niccolai, Pittsburgh		7	
1937	Jack Manders, Chi. Bears		8	
1938	Ward Cuff, NY Giants	9	5	55.6
	Ralph Kercheval, Brooklyn	13	5	38.5
1939	Ward Cuff, NY Giants	16	7	43.8
1940	Clarke Hinkle, Green Bay	14	9	64.3
1941	Clarke Hinkle, Green Bay	14	6	42.9
1942	Bill Daddio, Chi. Cardinals	10	5	50.0
1943	Ward Cuff, NY Giants	9	3	33.3
	Don Hutson, Green Bay	5	3	60.0
1944	Ken Strong, NY Giants	12	6	50.0
1945	Joe Aguirre, Washington	13	7	53.8
1946	Ted Fritsch, Green Bay	17	9	52.9
1947	Ward Cuff, Green Bay	16	7	43.8
	Pat Harder, Chi. Cardinals	10	7	70.0
	Bob Waterfield, LA Rams	16	7	43.8
1948	Cliff Patton, Philadelphia	12	8	66.7
1949	Cliff Patton, Philadelphia	18	9	50.0
	Bob Waterfield, LA Rams	16	9	56.3
1950	**Lou Groza, Cleveland**	19	13	68.4
1951	Bob Waterfield, LA Rams	23	13	56.5
1952	Lou Groza, Cleveland	33	19	57.6
1953	Lou Groza, Cleveland	26	23	88.5
1954	Lou Groza, Cleveland	24	16	66.7
1955	Fred Cone, Green Bay	24	16	66.7
1956	Sam Baker, Washington	25	17	68.0
1957	Lou Groza, Cleveland	22	15	68.2
1958	Paige Cothren, LA Rams	25	14	56.0
	Tom Miner, Pittsburgh	28	14	50.0
1959	Pat Summerall, NY Giants	29	20	69.0
1960	Tommy Davis, San Francisco, NFL	32	19	59.4
	Gene Mingo, Denver, AFL	28	18	64.3
1961	Steve Myhra, Baltimore, NFL	39	21	53.8
	Gino Cappelletti, Boston, AFL	32	17	53.1
1962	Gene Mingo, Denver, AFL	39	27	69.2
	Lou Michaels, Pittsburgh, NFL	42	26	61.9
1963	Jim Martin, Baltimore, NFL	39	24	61.5
	Gino Cappelletti, Boston, AFL	39	22	57.9
1964	Jim Bakken, St. Louis, NFL	38	25	65.8
	Gino Cappelletti, Boston, AFL	39	25	64.1
1965	Pete Gogolak, Buffalo, AFL	46	28	60.9
	Fred Cox, Minnesota, NFL	35	23	65.7
1966	Bruce Gossett, LA Rams, NFL	49	28	57.1
	Mike Mercer, Oakland-Kansas City, AFL	30	21	70.0
1967	Jim Bakken, St. Louis, NFL	39	27	69.2
	Jan Stenerud, Kansas City, AFL	36	21	58.3
1968	Jim Turner, NY Jets, AFL	46	34	73.9
	Mac Percival, Chi. Bears, NFL	36	25	69.4
1969	Jim Turner, NY Jets, AFL	47	32	68.1
	Fred Cox, Minnesota, NFL	37	26	70.3
1970	Fred Cox, Minnesota, NFC	46	30	65.2
	Jan Stenerud, Kansas City, AFC	42	30	71.4
1971	Curt Knight, Washington, NFC	49	29	59.2
	Garo Yepremian, Miami, AFC	40	28	70.0
1972	**Chester Marcol, Green Bay, NFC**	48	33	68.8
	Roy Gerela, Pittsburgh, AFC	41	28	68.3
1973	David Ray, LA Rams, NFC	47	30	63.8
	Roy Gerela, Pittsburgh, AFC	43	29	67.4
1974	Chester Marcol, Green Bay, NFC	39	25	64.1
	Roy Gerela, Pittsburgh, AFC	29	20	69.0
1975	Jan Stenerud, Kansas City, AFC	32	22	68.8
	Toni Fritsch, Dallas, NFC	35	22	62.9
1976	Mark Moseley, Washington, NFC	34	22	64.7
	Jan Stenerud, Kansas City, AFC	38	21	55.3
1977	Mark Moseley, Washington, NFC	37	21	56.8
	Errol Mann, Oakland, AFC	28	20	71.4
1978	**Frank Corral, LA Rams, NFC**	43	29	67.4
	Pat Leahy, NY Jets, AFC	30	22	73.3
1979	Mark Moseley, Washington, NFC	33	25	75.8
	John Smith, New England, AFC	33	23	69.7
1980	**Ed Murray, Detroit, NFC**	42	27	64.3
	John Smith, New England, AFC	34	26	76.5
	Fred Steinfort, Denver, AFC	34	26	76.5
1981	Rafael Septien, Dallas, NFC	35	27	77.1
	Nick Lowery, Kansas City, AFC	36	26	72.2
1982	Mark Moseley, Washington, NFC	21	20	95.2
	Nick Lowery, Kansas City, AFC	24	19	79.2
1983	**Ali Haji-Sheikh, NY Giants, NFC**	42	35	83.3
	Raul Allegre, Baltimore, AFC	35	30	85.7
1984	**Paul McFadden, Philadelphia, NFC**	37	30	81.1
	Gary Anderson, Pittsburgh, AFC	32	24	75.0
	Matt Bahr, Cleveland, AFC	32	24	75.0
1985	Gary Anderson, Pittsburgh, AFC	42	33	78.6
	Morten Andersen, New Orleans, NFC	35	31	88.6
	Kevin Butler, Chi. Bears, NFC	37	31	83.8

Bold face—first year in the league.

INTERCEPTIONS

Year	Player, Team	No.	Yards	TD
1940	Clarence (Ace) Parker, Brooklyn	6	146	1
	Kent Ryan, Detroit	6	65	0
	Don Hutson, Green Bay	6	24	0
1941	Marshall Goldberg, Chi. Cardinals	7	54	0
	Art Jones, Pittsburgh	7	35	0
1942	**Clyde (Bulldog) Turner, Chi. Bears**	8	96	1
1943	Sammy Baugh, Washington	11	112	0
1944	**Howard Livingston, NY Giants**	9	172	1
1945	Roy Zimmerman, Philadelphia	7	90	0
1946	Bill Dudley, Pittsburgh	10	242	1
1947	Frank Reagan, NY Giants	10	203	0
	Frank Seno, Boston	10	100	0
1948	**Dan Sandifer, Washington**	13	258	2
1949	Bob Nussbaumer, Chi. Cardinals	12	157	0
1950	**Orban (Spec) Sanders, NY Yanks**	13	199	0
1951	Otto Schnellbacher, NY Giants	11	194	2
1952	**Dick (Night Train) Lane, LA Rams**	14	298	2
1953	Jack Christiansen, Detroit	12	238	1
1954	Dick (Night Train) Lane, Chi. Cardinals	10	181	0
1955	Will Sherman, LA Rams	11	101	0
1956	Lindon Crow, Chi. Cardinals	11	170	0
1957	**Milt Davis, Baltimore**	10	219	2
	Jack Christiansen, Detroit	10	137	1
	Jack Butler, Pittsburgh	10	85	0
1958	Jim Patton, NY Giants	11	183	0
1959	Dean Derby, Pittsburgh	7	127	0
	Milt Davis, Baltimore	7	119	1
	Don Shinnick, Baltimore	7	70	0
1960	**Austin (Goose) Gonsoulin, Denver, AFL**	11	98	0
	Dave Baker, San Francisco, NFL	10	96	0
	Jerry Norton, St. Louis, NFL	10	96	0
1961	Billy Atkins, Buffalo, AFL	10	158	0
	Dick Lynch, NY Giants, NFL	9	60	0
1962	Lee Riley, NY Titans, AFL	11	122	0
	Willie Wood, Green Bay, NFL	9	132	0
1963	Fred Glick, Houston, AFL	12	180	1
	Dick Lynch, NY Giants, NFL	9	251	3
	Roosevelt Taylor, Chi. Bears, NFL	9	172	1
1964	Dainard Paulson, NY Jets, AFL	12	157	1
	Paul Krause, Washington, NFL	12	140	1
1965	W.K. Hicks, Houston, AFL	9	156	0
	Bob Boyd, Baltimore, NFL	9	78	1
1966	Larry Wilson, St. Louis, NFL	10	180	2
	Johnny Robinson, Kansas City, AFL	10	136	1
	Bobby Hunt, Kansas City, AFL	10	113	0
1967	Miller Farr, Houston, AFL	10	264	3
	Lem Barney, Detroit, NFL	10	232	3
	Tom Janik, Buffalo AFL	10	222	2
	Dave Whitsell, New Orleans, NFL	10	178	2
	Dick Westmoreland, Miami, AFL	10	127	1
1968	Dave Grayson, Oakland, AFL	10	195	1
	Willie Williams, NY Giants, NFL	10	103	0
1969	Mel Renfro, Dallas, NFL	10	118	0
	Emmitt Thomas, Kansas City, AFL	9	146	1
1970	Johnny Robinson, Kansas City, AFC	10	155	0
	Dick LeBeau, Detroit, NFC	9	96	0
1971	Bill Bradley, Philadelphia, NFC	11	248	0
	Ken Houston, Houston, AFC	9	220	4
1972	Bill Bradley, Philadelphia, NFC	9	73	0
	Mike Sensibaugh, Kansas City, AFC	8	65	0
1973	Dick Anderson, Miami, AFC	8	163	2
	Mike Wagner, Pittsburgh, AFC	8	134	0
	Bobby Bryant, Minnesota, NFC	7	105	1
1974	Emmitt Thomas, Kansas City, AFC	12	214	2
	Ray Brown, Atlanta, NFC	8	164	1
1975	Mel Blount, Pittsburgh, AFC	11	121	0
	Paul Krause, Minnesota, NFC	10	201	0
1976	Monte Jackson, LA Rams, NFC	10	173	3
	Ken Riley, Cincinnati, AFC	9	141	1
1977	Lyle Blackwood, Baltimore, AFC	10	163	0
	Roland Lawrence, Atlanta, NFC	7	138	0
1978	Thom Darden, Cleveland, AFC	10	200	0
	Ken Stone, St. Louis, NFC	9	139	0
	Willie Buchanon, Green Bay, NFC	9	93	1
1979	Mike Reinfeldt, Houston, AFC	12	205	0
	Lemar Parrish, Washington, NFC	9	65	0
1980	Lester Hayes, Oakland, AFC	13	273	1
	Nolan Cromwell, LA Rams, NFC	8	140	1
1981	**Everson Walls, Dallas, NFC**	11	133	0
	John Harris, Seattle, AFC	10	155	2
1982	Everson Walls, Dallas, NFC	7	61	0
	Ken Riley, Cincinnati, AFC	5	88	1
	Bobby Jackson, NY Jets, AFC	5	84	1
	Dwayne Woodruff, Pittsburgh, AFC	5	53	0
	Donnie Shell, Pittsburgh, AFC	5	27	0
1983	Mark Murphy, Washington, NFC	9	127	0
	Ken Riley, Cincinnati, AFC	8	89	2
	Vann McElroy, LA Raiders, AFC	8	68	0
1984	Kenny Easley, Seattle, AFC	10	126	2
	Tom Flynn, Green Bay, NFC	9	106	0
1985	Everson Walls, Dallas, NFC	9	31	0
	Albert Lewis, Kansas City, AFC	8	59	0
	Eugene Daniel, Indianapolis, AFC	8	53	0

PUNTING

Year	Player, Team	No.	Avg.	Long
1939	**Parker Hall, Cleveland**	58	40.8	80
1940	Sammy Baugh, Washington	35	51.4	85
1941	Sammy Baugh, Washington	30	48.7	75
1942	Sammy Baugh, Washington	37	48.2	74
1943	Sammy Baugh, Washington	50	45.9	81
1944	Frank Sinkwich, Detroit	45	41.0	73
1945	Roy McKay, Green Bay	44	41.2	73
1946	Roy McKay, Green Bay	64	42.7	64
1947	Jack Jacobs, Green Bay	57	43.5	74
1948	Joe Muha, Philadelphia	57	47.3	82
1949	**Mike Boyda, NY Bulldogs**	56	44.2	61
1950	**Fred (Curly) Morrison, Chi. Bears**	57	43.3	65
1951	Horace Gillom, Cleveland	73	45.5	66
1952	Horace Gillom, Cleveland	61	45.7	73
1953	Pat Brady, Pittsburgh	80	46.9	64
1954	Pat Brady, Pittsburgh	66	43.2	72
1955	Norm Van Brocklin, LA Rams	60	44.6	61
1956	Norm Van Brocklin, LA Rams	48	43.1	72
1957	Don Chandler, NY Giants	60	44.6	61
1958	Sam Baker, Washington	48	45.4	64
1959	Yale Lary, Detroit	45	47.1	67
1960	Jerry Norton, St. Louis, NFL	39	45.6	62
	Paul Maguire, LA Chargers, AFL	43	40.5	61
1961	Yale Lary, Detroit, NFL	52	48.4	71
	Billy Atkins, Buffalo, AFL	85	44.5	70
1962	Tommy Davis, San Francisco, NFL	48	45.6	82
	Jim Fraser, Denver, AFL	55	43.6	75
1963	Yale Lary, Detroit, NFL	35	48.9	73
	Jim Fraser, Denver, AFL	81	44.4	66
1964	**Bobby Walden, Minnesota, NFL**	72	46.4	73
	Jim Fraser, Denver, AFL	73	44.2	67
1965	Gary Collins, Cleveland, NFL	65	46.7	71
	Jerrel Wilson, Kansas City, AFL	68	46.1	64
1966	Bob Scarpitto, Denver, AFL	76	45.8	70
	David Lee, Baltimore, NFL	49	45.6	64
1967	Bob Scarpitto, Denver, AFL	105	44.9	73
	Billy Lothridge, Atlanta, NFL	87	43.7	62
1968	Jerrel Wilson, Kansas City, AFL	63	45.1	70
	Billy Lothridge, Atlanta, NFL	75	44.3	70
1969	David Lee, Baltimore, NFL	57	45.3	66
	Dennis Partee, San Diego, AFL	71	44.6	62
1970	**Dave Lewis, Cincinnati, AFC**	79	46.2	63
	Julian Fagan, New Orleans, NFC	77	42.5	64
1971	Dave Lewis, Cincinnati, AFC	72	44.8	56
	Tom McNeill, Philadelphia, NFC	73	42.0	64
1972	Jerrel Wilson, Kansas City, AFC	66	44.8	69
	Dave Chapple, LA Rams, NFC	53	44.2	70
1973	Jerrel Wilson, Kansas City, AFC	80	45.5	68
	Tom Wittum, San Francisco, NFC	79	43.7	62
1974	Ray Guy, Oakland, AFC	74	42.2	66
	Tom Blanchard, New Orleans, NFC	88	42.1	71
1975	Ray Guy, Oakland, AFC	68	43.8	64
	Herman Weaver, Detroit, NFC	80	42.0	61
1976	Marv Bateman, Buffalo, AFC	86	42.8	78
	John James, Atlanta, NFC	101	42.1	67
1977	Ray Guy, Oakland, AFC	59	43.3	74
	Tom Blanchard, New Orleans, NFC	82	42.4	66
1978	Pat McInally, Cincinnati, AFC	91	43.1	65
	Tom Skladany, Detroit, NFC	86	42.5	63
1979	**Bob Grupp, Kansas City, AFC**	89	43.6	74
	Dave Jennings, NY Giants, NFC	104	42.7	72
1980	Dave Jennings, NY Giants, NFC	94	44.8	63
	Luke Prestridge, Denver, AFC	70	43.9	57
1981	Pat McInally, Cincinnati, AFC	72	45.4	62
	Tom Skladany, Detroit, NFC	64	43.5	74
1982	Luke Prestridge, Denver, AFC	45	45.0	65
	Carl Birdsong, St. Louis, NFC	54	43.8	65
1983	Rohn Stark, Baltimore, AFC	91	45.3	68
	Frank Garcia, Tampa Bay, NFC	95	42.2	64
1984	Jim Arnold, Kansas City, AFC	98	44.9	63
	Brian Hansen, New Orleans, NFC	69	43.8	66
1985	Rohn Stark, Indianapolis, AFC	78	45.9	68
	Rick Donnelly, Atlanta, NFC	59	43.6	68

PUNT RETURNS

Year	Player, Team	No.	Yards	Avg.	Long	TD
1941	Byron (Whizzer) White, Detroit	19	262	13.8	64	0
1942	Merlyn Condit, Brooklyn	21	210	10.0	23	0
1943	Andy Farkas, Washington	15	168	11.2	33	0
1944	**Steve Van Buren, Philadelphia**	15	230	15.3	55	1
1945	**Dave Ryan, Detroit**	15	220	14.7	56	0
1946	Bill Dudley, Pittsburgh	27	385	14.2	52	0
1947	**Walt Slater, Pittsburgh**	28	435	15.5	33	0
1948	George McAfee, Chi. Bears	30	417	13.9	60	1
1949	Verda (Vitamin T) Smith, LA Rams	27	427	15.8	85	1
1950	**Herb Rich, Baltimore**	12	276	23.0	86	1
1951	Claude (Buddy) Young, NY Yanks	12	231	19.3	79	1
1952	Jack Christiansen, Detroit	15	322	21.5	79	2
1953	Charley Trippi, Chi. Cardinals	21	239	11.4	38	0
1954	**Veryl Switzer, Green Bay**	24	306	12.8	93	1
1955	Ollie Matson, Chi. Cardinals	13	245	18.8	78	2
1956	Kenny Konz, Cleveland	13	187	14.4	65	1
1957	Bert Zagers, Washington	14	217	15.5	76	2
1958	Jon Arnett, LA Rams	18	223	12.4	58	0
1959	Johnny Morris, Chi. Bears	14	171	12.2	78	1
1960	**Abner Haynes, Dallas Texans, AFL**	14	215	15.4	46	0
	Abe Woodson, San Francisco, NFL	13	174	13.4	48	0
1961	Dick Christy, NY Titans, AFL	18	383	21.3	70	2
	Willie Wood, Green Bay, NFL	14	225	16.1	72	2
1962	Dick Christy, NY Titans, AFL	15	250	16.7	73	2
	Pat Studstill, Detroit, NFL	29	457	15.8	44	0
1963	Dick James, Washington, NFL	16	214	13.4	39	0
	Claude (Hoot) Gibson, Oakland, AFL	26	307	11.8	85	2
1964	Bobby Jancik, Houston, AFL	12	220	18.3	82	1
	Tom Watkins, Detroit, NFL	16	238	14.9	68	2
1965	Leroy Kelly, Cleveland, NFL	17	265	15.6	67	2
	Les (Speedy) Duncan, San Diego, AFL	30	464	15.5	66	2
1966	Les (Speedy) Duncan, San Diego, AFL	18	238	13.2	81	1
	Johnny Roland, St. Louis, NFL	20	221	11.1	86	1
1967	Floyd Little, Denver, AFL	16	270	16.9	72	1
	Ben Davis, Cleveland, NFL	18	229	12.7	52	1
1968	Bob Hayes, Dallas, NFL	15	312	20.8	90	2
	Noland Smith, Kansas City, AFL	18	270	15.0	80	1
1969	Alvin Haymond, LA Rams, NFL	33	435	13.2	52	0
	Billy Thompson, Denver, AFL	25	288	11.5	40	0
1970	Ed Podolak, Kansas City, AFC	23	311	13.5	60	0
	Bruce Taylor, San Francisco, NFC	43	516	12.0	76	0
1971	Les (Speedy) Duncan, Washington, NFC	22	233	10.6	33	0
	Leroy Kelly, Cleveland, AFC	30	292	9.7	74	0
1972	**Ken Ellis, Green Bay, NFC**	14	215	15.4	80	1
	Chris Farasopoulos, NY Jets, AFC	17	179	10.5	65	1
1973	Bruce Taylor, San Francisco, NFC	15	207	13.8	61	0
	Ron Smith, San Diego, AFC	27	352	13.0	84	2
1974	Lemar Parrish, Cincinnati, AFC	18	338	18.8	90	2
	Dick Jauron, Detroit, NFC	17	286	16.8	58	0
1975	Billy Johnson, Houston, AFC	40	612	15.3	83	3
	Terry Metcalf, St. Louis, NFC	23	285	12.4	69	1
1976	Rick Upchurch, Denver, AFC	39	536	13.7	92	4
	Eddie Brown, Washington, NFC	48	646	13.5	71	1
1977	Billy Johnson, Houston, AFC	35	539	15.4	87	2
	Larry Marshall, Philadelphia, NFC	46	489	10.6	48	0
1978	Rick Upchurch, Denver, AFC	36	493	13.7	75	1
	Jackie Wallace, LA Rams, NFC	52	618	11.9	58	0
1979	John Sciarra, Philadelphia, NFC	16	182	11.4	38	0
	Tony Nathan, Miami, AFC	28	306	10.9	86	1
1980	J. T. Smith, Kansas City, AFC	40	581	14.5	75	2
	Kenny Johnson, Atlanta, NFC	23	281	12.2	56	0
1981	LeRoy Irvin, LA Rams, NFC	46	615	13.4	84	3
	James Brooks, San Diego, AFC	22	290	13.2	42	0
1982	Rick Upchurch, Denver, AFC	15	242	16.1	78	2
	Billy Johnson, Atlanta, NFC	24	273	11.4	71	0
1983	**Henry Ellard, LA Rams, NFC**	16	217	13.6	72	1
	Kirk Springs, NY Jets, AFC	23	287	12.5	76	1
1984	Mike Martin, Cincinnati, AFC	24	376	15.7	55	0
	Henry Ellard, LA Rams, NFC	30	403	13.4	83	2
1985	Irving Fryar, New England, AFC	37	520	14.1	85	2
	Henry Ellard, LA Rams, NFC	37	501	13.5	80	1

KICKOFF RETURNS

Year	Player, Team	No.	Yards	Avg.	Long	TD
1941	Marshall Goldberg, Chi. Cardinals	12	290	24.2	41	0
1942	Marshall Goldberg, Chi. Cardinals	15	393	26.2	95	1
1943	Ken Heineman, Brooklyn	16	444	27.8	69	0
1944	Bob Thurbon, Card-Pitt	12	291	24.3	55	0
1945	Steve Van Buren, Philadelphia	13	373	28.7	98	1
1946	Abe Karnofsky, Boston	21	599	28.5	97	1
1947	Ed Saenz, Washington	29	797	27.4	94	2
1948	**Joe Scott, NY Giants**	20	569	28.5	99	1
1949	**Don Doll, Detroit**	21	536	25.5	56	0
1950	Verda (Vitamin T) Smith, LA Rams	22	724	33.7	97	3
1951	Lynn Chandois, Pittsburgh	12	390	32.5	55	0
1952	Lynn Chandois, Pittsburgh	17	599	35.2	93	2
1953	Joe Arenas, San Francisco	16	551	34.4	82	0
1954	Billy Reynolds, Cleveland	14	413	29.5	51	0
1955	Al Carmichael, Green Bay	14	418	29.9	100	1
1956	**Tom Wilson, LA Rams**	15	477	31.8	103	1
1957	**Jon Arnett, LA Rams**	18	504	28.0	98	1
1958	Ollie Matson, Chi. Cardinals	14	497	35.5	101	2
1959	Abe Woodson, San Francisco	13	382	29.4	105	1
1960	**Tom Moore, Green Bay, NFL**	12	397	33.1	84	0
	Ken Hall, Houston, AFL	19	594	31.3	104	1
1961	Dick Bass, LA Rams, NFL	23	698	30.3	64	0
	Dave Grayson, Dallas Texans, AFL	16	453	28.3	73	0
1962	Abe Woodson, San Francisco, NFL	37	1,157	31.3	79	0
	Bobby Jancik, Houston, AFL	24	726	30.3	61	0
1963	Abe Woodson, San Francisco, NFL	29	935	32.2	103	3
	Bobby Jancik, Houston, AFL	45	1,317	29.3	53	0
1964	**Clarence Childs, NY Giants, NFL**	34	987	29.0	100	1
	Bo Roberson, Oakland, AFL	36	975	27.1	59	0
1965	Tommy Watkins, Detroit NFL	17	584	34.4	94	0
	Abner Haynes, Denver, AFL	34	901	26.5	60	0
1966	Gale Sayers, Chi. Bears, NFL	23	718	31.2	93	2
	Goldie Sellers, Denver, AFL	19	541	28.5	100	2
1967	**Travis Williams, Green Bay, NFL**	18	739	41.1	104	4
	Zeke Moore, Houston, AFL	14	405	28.9	92	1
1968	Preston Pearson, Baltimore, NFL	15	527	35.1	102	2
	George Atkinson, Oakland, AFL	32	802	25.1	60	0
1969	Bobby Williams, Detroit, NFL	17	563	33.1	96	1
	Billy Thompson, Denver, AFL	18	513	28.5	63	0
1970	Jim Duncan, Baltimore, AFC	20	707	35.4	99	1
	Cecil Turner, Chi. Bears, NFC	23	752	32.7	96	4
1971	Travis Williams, LA Rams, NFC	25	743	29.7	105	1
	Eugene (Mercury) Morris, Miami, AFC	15	423	28.2	94	1
1972	Ron Smith, Chi. Bears, NFC	30	924	30.8	94	1
	Bruce Laird, Baltimore, AFC	29	843	29.1	73	0
1973	Carl Garrett, Chi. Bears, NFC	16	486	30.4	67	0
	Wallace Francis, Buffalo, AFC	23	687	29.9	101	2
1974	Terry Metcalf, St. Louis, NFC	20	623	31.2	94	1
	Greg Pruitt, Cleveland, AFC	22	606	27.5	88	1
1975	**Walter Payton, Chi. Bears, NFC**	14	444	31.7	70	0
	Harold Hart, Oakland, AFC	17	518	30.5	102	1
1976	**Duriel Harris, Miami, AFC**	17	559	32.9	69	0
	Cullen Bryant, LA Rams, NFC	16	459	28.7	90	1
1977	**Raymond Clayborn, New England, AFC**	28	869	31.0	101	3
	Wilbert Montgomery, Philadelphia, NFC	23	619	26.9	99	1
1978	Steve Odom, Green Bay, NFC	25	677	27.1	95	1
	Keith Wright, Cleveland, AFC	30	789	26.3	86	0
1979	Larry Brunson, Oakland, AFC	17	441	25.9	89	0
	Jimmy Edwards, Minnesota, NFC	44	1,103	25.1	83	0
1980	Horace Ivory, New England, AFC	36	992	27.6	98	1
	Rich Mauti, New Orleans, NFC	31	798	25.7	52	0
1981	Mike Nelms, Washington, NFC	37	1,099	29.7	84	0
	Carl Roaches, Houston, AFC	28	769	27.5	96	1
1982	**Mike Mosley, Buffalo, AFC**	18	487	27.1	66	0
	Alvin Hall, Detroit, NFC	16	426	26.6	96	1
1983	Fulton Walker, Miami, AFC	36	962	26.7	78	0
	Darrin Nelson, Minnesota, NFC	18	445	24.7	50	0
1984	**Bobby Humphery, NY Jets, AFC**	22	675	30.7	97	1
	Barry Redden, LA Rams, NFC	23	530	23.0	40	0
1985	Ron Brown, LA Rams, NFC	28	918	32.8	98	3
	Glen Young, Cleveland, AFC	35	898	25.7	63	0

Bold face—first year in the league.

POINTS SCORED

Year	Team	Points
1932	Green Bay	152
1933	NY Giants	244
1934	Chi. Bears	286
1935	Chi. Bears	192
1936	Green Bay	248
1937	Green Bay	220
1938	Green Bay	223
1939	Chi. Bears	298
1940	Washington	245
1941	Chi. Bears	396
1942	Chi. Bears	376
1943	Chi. Bears	303
1944	Philadelphia	267
1945	Philadelphia	272
1946	Chi. Bears	289
1947	Chi. Bears	363
1948	Chi. Cardinals	395
1949	Philadelphia	364
1950	LA Rams	466
1951	LA Rams	392
1952	LA Rams	349
1953	San Francisco	372
1954	Detroit	337
1955	Cleveland	349
1956	Chi. Bears	363
1957	LA Rams	307
1958	Baltimore	381
1959	Baltimore	374
1960	NY Titans, AFL	382
	Cleveland, NFL	362
1961	Houston, AFL	513
	Green Bay, NFL	391
1962	Green Bay, NFL	415
	Dallas Texans, AFL	389
1963	NY Giants, NFL	448
	San Diego, AFL	399
1964	Baltimore, NFL	428
	Buffalo, AFL	400
1965	San Francisco, NFL	421
	San Diego, AFL	340
1966	Kansas City, AFL	448
	Dallas, NFL	445
1967	Oakland, AFL	468
	LA Rams, NFL	398
1968	Oakland, AFL	453
	Dallas, NFL	431
1969	Minnesota, NFL	379
	Oakland, AFL	377
1970	San Francisco, NFC	352
	Baltimore, AFC	321
1971	Dallas, NFC	400
	Oakland, AFC	344
1972	Miami, AFC	385
	San Francisco, NFC	353
1973	LA Rams, NFC	388
	Denver, AFC	354
1974	Oakland, AFC	355
	Washington, NFC	320
1975	Buffalo, AFC	420
	Minnesota, NFC	377
1976	Baltimore, AFC	417
	LA Rams, NFC	351
1977	Oakland, AFC	351
	Dallas, NFC	345
1978	Dallas, NFC	384
	Miami, AFC	372
1979	Pittsburgh, AFC	416
	Dallas, NFC	371
1980	Dallas, NFC	454
	New England, AFC	441
1981	San Diego, AFC	478
	Atlanta, NFC	426
1982	San Diego, AFC	288
	Dallas, NFC	226
	Green Bay, NFC	226
1983	Washington, NFC	541
	LA Raiders, AFC	442
1984	Miami, AFC	513
	San Francisco, NFC	475
1985	San Diego, AFC	467
	Chi. Bears, NFC	456

TOTAL YARDS GAINED

Year	Team	Yards
1932	Chi. Bears	2,755
1933	NY Giants	2,973
1934	Chi. Bears	3,900
1935	Chi. Bears	3,454
1936	Detroit	3,703
1937	Green Bay	3,201
1938	Green Bay	3,037
1939	Chi. Bears	3,988
1940	Green Bay	3,400
1941	Chi. Bears	4,265
1942	Chi. Bears	3,900
1943	Chi. Bears	4,045
1944	Chi. Bears	3,239
1945	Washington	3,549
1946	LA Rams	3,793
1947	Chi. Bears	5,053
1948	Chi. Cardinals	4,705
1949	Chi. Bears	4,873
1950	LA Rams	5,420
1951	LA Rams	5,506
1952	Cleveland	4,352
1953	Philadelphia	4,811
1954	LA Rams	5,187
1955	Chi. Bears	4,316
1956	Chi. Bears	4,537
1957	LA Rams	4,143
1958	Baltimore	4,539
1959	Baltimore	4,458
1960	Houston, AFL	4,936
	Baltimore, NFL	4,245
1961	Houston, AFL	6,288
	Philadelphia, NFL	5,112
1962	NY Giants, NFL	5,005
	Houston, AFL	4,971
1963	San Diego, AFL	5,153
	NY Giants, NFL	5,024
1964	Buffalo, AFL	5,206
	Baltimore, NFL	4,779
1965	San Francisco, NFL	5,270
	San Diego, AFL	5,188
1966	Dallas, NFL	5,145
	Kansas City, AFL	5,114
1967	NY Jets, AFL	5,152
	Baltimore, NFL	5,008
1968	Oakland, AFL	5,696
	Dallas, NFL	5,117
1969	Dallas, NFL	5,112
	Oakland, AFL	5,036
1970	Oakland, AFC	4,829
	San Francisco, NFC	4,503
1971	Dallas, NFC	5,035
	San Diego, AFC	4,738
1972	Miami, AFC	5,036
	NY Giants, NFC	4,483
1973	LA Rams, NFC	4,906
	Oakland, AFC	4,773
1974	Dallas, NFC	4,983
	Oakland, AFC	4,718
1975	Buffalo, AFC	5,467
	Dallas, NFC	5,025
1976	Baltimore, AFC	5,236
	St. Louis, NFC	5,136
1977	Dallas, NFC	4,812
	Oakland, AFC	4,736
1978	New England, AFC	5,965
	Dallas, NFC	5,959
1979	Pittsburgh, AFC	6,258
	Dallas, NFC	5,968
1980	San Diego, AFC	6,410
	LA Rams, NFC	6,006
1981	San Diego, AFC	6,744
	Detroit, NFC	5,933
1982	San Diego, AFC	4,048
	San Francisco, NFC	3,242
1983	San Diego, AFC	6,197
	Green Bay, NFC	6,172
1984	Miami, AFC	6,936
	San Francisco, NFC	6,366
1985	San Diego, AFC	6,535
	San Francisco, NFC	5,920

YARDS RUSHING

Year	Team	Yards
1932	Chi. Bears	1,770
1933	Boston	2,260
1934	Chi. Bears	2,847
1935	Chi. Bears	2,096
1936	Detroit	2,885
1937	Detroit	2,074
1938	Detroit	1,893
1939	Chi. Bears	2,043
1940	Chi. Bears	1,818
1941	Chi. Bears	2,263
1942	Chi. Bears	1,881
1943	Phil-Pitt	1,730
1944	Philadelphia	1,661
1945	Cleveland	1,714
1946	Green Bay	1,765
1947	LA Rams	2,171
1948	Chi. Cardinals	2,560
1949	Philadelphia	2,607
1950	NY Giants	2,336
1951	Chi. Bears	2,408
1952	San Francisco	1,905
1953	San Francisco	2,230
1954	San Francisco	2,498
1955	Chi. Bears	2,388
1956	Chi. Bears	2,468
1957	LA Rams	2,142
1958	Cleveland	2,526
1959	Cleveland	2,149
1960	St. Louis, NFL	2,356
	Oakland, AFL	2,056
1961	Green Bay, NFL	2,350
	Dallas Texans, AFL	2,189
1962	Buffalo, AFL	2,480
	Green Bay, NFL	2,460
1963	Cleveland, NFL	2,639
	San Diego, AFL	2,203
1964	Green Bay, NFL	2,276
	Buffalo, AFL	2,040
1965	Cleveland, NFL	2,331
	San Diego, AFL	2,085
1966	Kansas City, AFL	2,274
	Cleveland, NFL	2,166
1967	Cleveland, NFL	2,139
	Houston, AFL	2,122
1968	Chi. Bears, NFL	2,377
	Kansas City, AFL	2,227
1969	Dallas, NFL	2,276
	Kansas City, AFL	2,220
1970	Dallas, NFC	2,300
	Miami, AFC	2,082
1971	Miami, AFC	2,429
	Detroit, NFC	2,376
1972	Miami, AFC	2,960
	Chi. Bears, NFC	2,360
1973	Buffalo, AFC	3,088
	LA Rams, NFC	2,925
1974	Dallas, NFC	2,454
	Pittsburgh, AFC	2,417
1975	Buffalo, AFC	2,974
	Dallas, NFC	2,432
1976	Pittsburgh, AFC	2,971
	LA Rams, NFC	2,528
1977	Chi. Bears, NFC	2,811
	Oakland, AFC	2,627
1978	New England, AFC	3,165
	Dallas, NFC	2,783
1979	NY Jets, AFC	2,646
	St. Louis, NFC	2,582
1980	LA Rams, NFC	2,799
	Houston, AFC	2,635
1981	Detroit, NFC	2,795
	Kansas City, AFC	2,633
1982	Buffalo, AFC	1,371
	Dallas, NFC	1,313
1983	Chi. Bears, NFC	2,727
	Baltimore, AFC	2,695
1984	Chi. Bears, NFC	2,974
	NY Jets, AFC	2,189
1985	Chi. Bears, NFC	2,761
	Indianapolis, AFC	2,439

YARDS PASSING

Leadership in this category has been based on net yards since 1952.

Year	Team	Yards
1932	Chi. Bears	1,013
1933	NY Giants	1,348
1934	Green Bay	1,165
1935	Green Bay	1,449
1936	Green Bay	1,629
1937	Green Bay	1,398
1938	Washington	1,536
1939	Chi. Bears	1,965
1940	Washington	1,887
1941	Chi. Bears	2,002
1942	Green Bay	2,407
1943	Chi. Bears	2,310
1944	Washington	2,021
1945	Chi. Bears	1,857
1946	LA Rams	2,080
1947	Washington	3,336
1948	Washington	2,861
1949	Chi. Bears	3,055
1950	LA Rams	3,709
1951	LA Rams	3,296
1952	Cleveland	2,566
1953	Philadelphia	3,089
1954	Chi. Bears	3,104
1955	Philadelphia	2,472
1956	LA Rams	2,419
1957	Baltimore	2,388
1958	Pittsburgh	2,752
1959	Baltimore	2,753
1960	Houston, AFL	3,203
	Baltimore, NFL	2,956
1961	Houston, AFL	4,392
	Philadelphia, NFL	3,605
1962	Denver, AFL	3,404
	Philadelphia, NFL	3,385
1963	Baltimore, NFL	3,296
	Houston, AFL	3,222
1964	Houston, AFL	3,527
	Chi. Bears, NFL	2,841
1965	San Francisco, NFL	3,487
	San Diego, AFL	3,103
1966	NY Jets, AFL	3,464
	Dallas, NFL	3,023
1967	NY Jets, AFL	3,845
	Washington, NFL	3,730
1968	San Diego, AFL	3,623
	Dallas, NFL	3,026
1969	Oakland, AFL	3,271
	San Francisco, NFL	3,158
1970	San Francisco, NFC	2,923
	Oakland, AFC	2,865
1971	San Diego, AFC	3,134
	Dallas, NFC	2,786
1972	NY Jets, AFC	2,777
	San Francisco, NFC	2,735
1973	Philadelphia, NFC	2,998
	Denver, AFC	2,519
1974	Washington, NFC	2,978
	Cincinnati, AFC	2,804
1975	Cincinnati, AFC	3,241
	Washington, NFC	2,917
1976	Baltimore, AFC	2,933
	Minnesota, NFC	2,855
1977	Buffalo, AFC	2,530
	St. Louis, NFC	2,499
1978	San Diego, AFC	3,375
	Minnesota, NFC	3,243
1979	San Diego, AFC	3,915
	San Francisco, NFC	3,641
1980	San Diego, AFC	4,531
	Minnesota, NFC	3,688
1981	San Diego, AFC	4,739
	Minnesota, NFC	4,333
1982	San Diego, AFC	2,927
	San Francisco, NFC	2,502
1983	San Diego, AFC	4,661
	Green Bay, NFC	4,365
1984	Miami, AFC	5,018
	St. Louis, NFC	4,257
1985	San Diego, AFC	4,870
	Dallas, NFC	3,861

FEWEST POINTS ALLOWED

Year	Team	Points
1932	Chi. Bears	44
1933	Brooklyn	54
1934	Detroit	59
1935	Green Bay	96
	NY Giants	96
1936	Chi. Bears	94
1937	Chi. Bears	100
1938	NY Giants	79
1939	NY Giants	85
1940	Brooklyn	120
1941	NY Giants	114
1942	Chi. Bears	84
1943	Washington	137
1944	NY Giants	75
1945	Washington	121
1946	Pittsburgh	117
1947	Green Bay	210
1948	Chi. Bears	151
1949	Philadelphia	134
1950	Philadelphia	141
1951	Cleveland	152
1952	Detroit	192
1953	Cleveland	162
1954	Cleveland	162
1955	Cleveland	218
1956	Cleveland	177
1957	Cleveland	172
1958	NY Giants	183
1959	NY Giants	170
1960	San Francisco, NFL	205
	Dallas Texans, AFL	253
1961	San Diego, AFL	219
	NY Giants, NFL	220
1962	Green Bay, NFL	148
	Dallas Texans, AFL	233
1963	Chi. Bears, NFL	144
	San Diego, AFL	255
1964	Baltimore, NFL	225
	Buffalo, AFL	242
1965	Green Bay, NFL	224
	Buffalo, AFL	226
1966	Green Bay, NFL	163
	Buffalo, AFL	255
1967	LA Rams, NFL	196
	Houston, AFL	199
1968	Baltimore, NFL	144
	Kansas City, AFL	170
1969	Minnesota, NFL	133
	Kansas City, AFL	177
1970	Minnesota, NFC	143
	Miami, AFC	228
1971	Minnesota, NFC	139
	Baltimore, AFC	140
1972	Miami, AFC	171
	Washington, NFC	218
1973	Miami, AFC	150
	Minnesota, NFC	168
1974	LA Rams, NFC	181
	Pittsburgh, AFC	189
1975	LA Rams, NFC	135
	Pittsburgh, AFC	162
1976	Pittsburgh, AFC	138
	Minnesota, NFC	176
1977	Atlanta, NFC	129
	Denver, AFC	148
1978	Pittsburgh, AFC	195
	Dallas, NFC	208
1979	Tampa Bay, NFC	237
	San Diego, AFC	246
1980	Philadelphia, NFC	222
	Houston, AFC	251
1981	Philadelphia, NFC	221
	Miami, AFC	275
1982	Washington, NFC	128
	Miami, AFC	131
1983	Miami, AFC	250
	Detroit, NFC	286
1984	San Francisco, NFC	227
	Denver, AFC	241
1985	Chi. Bears, NFC	198
	NY Jets, AFC	264

FEWEST TOTAL YARDS ALLOWED

Year	Team	Yards
1933	Brooklyn	1,789
1934	Chi. Cardinals	1,539
1935	Boston	1,996
1936	Boston	2,181
1937	Washington	2,123
1938	NY Giants	2,029
1939	Washington	2,116
1940	NY Giants	2,219
1941	NY Giants	2,368
1942	Chi. Bears	1,703
1943	Chi. Bears	2,262
1944	Philadelphia	1,943
1945	Philadelphia	2,073
1946	Washington	2,451
1947	Green Bay	3,396
1948	Chi. Bears	2,931
1949	Philadelphia	2,831
1950	Cleveland	3,154
1951	NY Giants	3,250
1952	Cleveland	3,075
1953	Philadelphia	2,998
1954	Cleveland	2,658
1955	Cleveland	2,841
1956	NY Giants	3,081
1957	Pittsburgh	2,791
1958	Chi. Bears	3,066
1959	NY Giants	2,843
1960	St. Louis, NFL	3,029
	Buffalo, AFL	3,866
1961	San Diego, AFL	3,726
	Baltimore, NFL	3,782
1962	Detroit, NFL	3,217
	Dallas Texans, AFL	3,951
1963	Chicago, NFL	3,176
	Boston, AFL	3,834
1964	Green Bay, NFL	3,179
	Buffalo, AFL	3,878
1965	San Diego, AFL	3,262
	Detroit, NFL	3,557
1966	St. Louis, NFL	3,492
	Oakland, AFL	3,910
1967	Oakland, AFL	3,294
	Green Bay, NFL	3,300
1968	LA Rams, NFL	3,118
	NY Jets, AFL	3,363
1969	Minnesota, NFL	2,720
	Kansas City, AFL	3,163
1970	Minnesota, NFC	2,803
	NY Jets, AFC	3,655
1971	Baltimore, AFC	2,852
	Minnesota, NFC	3,406
1972	Miami, AFC	3,297
	Green Bay, NFC	3,474
1973	LA Rams, NFC	2,951
	Oakland, AFC	3,160
1974	Pittsburgh, AFC	3,074
	Washington, NFC	3,285
1975	Minnesota, NFC	3,153
	Oakland, AFC	3,629
1976	Pittsburgh, AFC	3,323
	San Francisco, NFC	3,562
1977	Dallas, NFC	3,213
	New England, AFC	3,638
1978	LA Rams, NFC	3,893
	Pittsburgh, AFC	4,168
1979	Tampa Bay, NFC	3,949
	Pittsburgh, AFC	4,270
1980	Buffalo, AFC	4,101
	Philadelphia, NFC	4,443
1981	Philadelphia, NFC	4,447
	NY Jets, AFC	4,871
1982	Miami, AFC	2,312
	Tampa Bay, NFC	2,442
1983	Cincinnati, AFC	4,327
	New Orleans, NFC	4,691
1984	Chi. Bears, NFC	3,863
	Cleveland, AFC	4,641
1985	Chi. Bears, NFC	4,135
	LA Raiders, AFC	4,603

FEWEST YARDS RUSHING ALLOWED

Year	Team	Yards
1933	Brooklyn	964
1934	Chi. Cardinals	954
1935	Boston	988
1936	Boston	1,148
1937	Chi. Bears	933
1938	Detroit	1,081
1939	Chi. Bears	812
1940	NY Giants	977
1941	Washington	1,042
1942	Chi. Bears	519
1943	Phil-Pitt	793
1944	Philadelphia	558
1945	Philadelphia	817
1946	Chi. Bears	1,060
1947	Philadelphia	1,329
1948	Philadelphia	1,209
1949	Chi. Bears	1,196
1950	Detroit	1,367
1951	NY Giants	913
1952	Detroit	1,145
1953	Philadelphia	1,117
1954	Cleveland	1,050
1955	Cleveland	1,189
1956	NY Giants	1,443
1957	Baltimore	1,174
1958	Baltimore	1,291
1959	NY Giants	1,261
1960	St. Louis, NFL	1,212
	Dallas Texans, AFL	1,338
1961	Boston, AFL	1,041
	Pittsburgh, NFL	1,463
1962	Detroit, NFL	1,231
	Dallas Texans, AFL	1,250
1963	Boston, AFL	1,107
	Chi. Bears, NFL	1,442
1964	Buffalo, AFL	913
	LA Rams, NFL	1,501
1965	San Diego, AFL	1,094
	LA Rams, NFL	1,409
1966	Buffalo, AFL	1,051
	Dallas, NFL	1,176
1967	Dallas, NFL	1,081
	Oakland, AFL	1,129
1968	Dallas, NFL	1,195
	NY Jets, AFL	1,195
1969	Dallas, NFL	1,050
	Kansas City, AFL	1,091
1970	Detroit, NFC	1,152
	NY Jets, AFC	1,283
1971	Baltimore, AFC	1,113
	Dallas, NFC	1,144
1972	Dallas, NFC	1,515
	Miami, AFC	1,548
1973	LA Rams, NFC	1,270
	Oakland, AFC	1,470
1974	LA Rams, NFC	1,302
	New England, AFC	1,587
1975	Minnesota, NFC	1,532
	Houston, AFC	1,680
1976	Pittsburgh, AFC	1,457
	LA Rams, NFC	1,564
1977	Denver, AFC	1,531
	Dallas, NFC	1,651
1978	Dallas, NFC	1,721
	Pittsburgh, AFC	1,774
1979	Denver, AFC	1,693
	Tampa Bay, NFC	1,873
1980	Detroit, NFC	1,599
	Cincinnati, AFC	1,680
1981	Detroit, NFC	1,623
	Kansas City, AFC	1,747
1982	Pittsburgh, AFC	762
	Detroit, NFC	854
1983	Washington, NFC	1,289
	Cincinnati, AFC	1,499
1984	Chi. Bears, NFC	1,377
	Pittsburgh, AFC	1,617
1985	Chi. Bears, NFC	1,319
	NY Jets, AFC	1,516

FEWEST YARDS PASSING ALLOWED

Leadership in this category has been based on net yards since 1952.

Year	Team	Yards
1933	Portsmouth	558
1934	Philadelphia	545
1935	Chi. Cardinals	793
1936	Philadelphia	853
1937	Detroit	804
1938	Chi. Bears	897
1939	Washington	1,116
1940	Philadelphia	1,012
1941	Pittsburgh	1,168
1942	Washington	1,093
1943	Chi. Bears	980
1944	Chi. Bears	1,052
1945	Washington	1,121
1946	Pittsburgh	939
1947	Green Bay	1,790
1948	Green Bay	1,626
1949	Philadelphia	1,607
1950	Cleveland	1,581
1951	Pittsburgh	1,687
1952	Washington	1,580
1953	Washington	1,751
1954	Cleveland	1,608
1955	Pittsburgh	1,295
1956	Cleveland	1,103
1957	Cleveland	1,300
1958	Chi. Bears	1,769
1959	NY Giants	1,582
1960	Chi. Bears, NFL	1,388
	Buffalo, AFL	2,124
1961	Baltimore, NFL	1,913
	San Diego, AFL	2,363
1962	Green Bay, NFL	1,746
	Oakland, AFL	2,306
1963	Chi. Bears, NFL	1,734
	Oakland, AFL	2,589
1964	Green Bay, NFL	1,647
	San Diego, AFL	2,518
1965	Green Bay, NFL	1,981
	San Diego, AFL	2,168
1966	Green Bay, NFL	1,959
	Oakland, AFL	2,118
1967	Green Bay, NFL	1,377
	Buffalo, AFL	1,825
1968	Houston, AFL	1,671
	Green Bay, NFL	1,796
1969	Minnesota, NFL	1,631
	Kansas City, AFL	2,072
1970	Minnesota, NFC	1,438
	Kansas City, AFC	2,010
1971	Atlanta, NFC	1,638
	Baltimore, AFC	1,739
1972	Minnesota, NFC	1,699
	Cleveland, AFC	1,736
1973	Miami, AFC	1,290
	Atlanta, NFC	1,430
1974	Pittsburgh, AFC	1,466
	Atlanta, NFC	1,572
1975	Minnesota, NFC	1,621
	Cincinnati, AFC	1,729
1976	Minnesota, NFC	1,575
	Cincinnati, AFC	1,758
1977	Atlanta, NFC	1,384
	San Diego, AFC	1,725
1978	Buffalo, AFC	1,960
	LA Rams, NFC	2,048
1979	Tampa Bay, NFC	2,076
	Buffalo, AFC	2,530
1980	Washington, NFC	2,171
	Buffalo, AFC	2,282
1981	Philadelphia, NFC	2,696
	Buffalo, AFC	2,870
1982	Miami, AFC	1,027
	Tampa Bay, NFC	1,384
1983	New Orleans, NFC	2,691
	Cincinnati, AFC	2,828
1984	New Orleans, NFC	2,453
	Cleveland, AFC	2,696
1985	Washington, NFC	2,746
	Pittsburgh, AFC	2,783

PROGRESSION OF RECORDS

RUSHING YARDS

Year	Player, Team	Yards
1932	Cliff Battles, Boston	576
1933	Jim Musick, Boston	809
1934	Beattie Feathers, Chi. Bears	1,004
1947	Steve Van Buren, Philadelphia	1,008
1949	Steve Van Buren, Philadelphia	1,146
1958	Jim Brown, Cleveland	1,527
1963	Jim Brown, Cleveland	1,863
1973	O.J. Simpson, Buffalo	2,003
1984	Eric Dickerson, LA Rams	2,105

RUSHING ATTEMPTS

Year	Player, Team	Att.
1932	Cliff Battles, Boston	148
1933	Jim Musick, Boston	173
1936	Alphonse (Tuffy) Leemans, NY Giants	206
1937	Cliff Battles, Washington	216
1947	Steve Van Buren, Philadelphia	217
1949	Steve Van Buren, Philadelphia	263
1951	Eddie Price, NY Giants	271
1959	Jim Brown, Cleveland	290
1961	Jim Brown, Cleveland	305
1973	O.J. Simpson, Buffalo	332
1977	Walter Payton, Chi. Bears	339
1979	Walter Payton, Chi. Bears	369
1980	Earl Campbell, Houston	373
1981	George Rogers, New Orleans	378
1983	Eric Dickerson, LA Rams	390
1984	James Wilder, Tampa Bay	407

TOUCHDOWNS RUSHING

Year	Player, Team	TD
1932	Earl (Dutch) Clark, Portsmouth	6
1933	Glenn Presnell, Portsmouth	6
1934	Earl (Dutch) Clark, Detroit	8
	Beattie Feathers, Chi. Bears	8
1939	Johnny Drake, Cleveland	9
1940	Johnny Drake, Cleveland	9
1943	Bill Paschal, NY Giants	10
1945	Steve Van Buren, Philadelphia	15
1958	Jim Brown, Cleveland	17
1962	Jim Taylor, Green Bay	19
1979	Earl Campbell, Houston	19
1981	Chuck Muncie, San Diego	19
1983	John Riggins, Washington	24

PASSING YARDS

Year	Player, Team	Att.
1932	Arnie Herber, Green Bay	639
1933	Harry Newman, NY Giants	973
1936	Arnie Herber, Green Bay	1,239
1939	Davey O'Brien, Philadelphia	1,324
1940	Sammy Baugh, Washington	1,367
1941	Cecil Isbell, Green Bay	1,479
1942	Cecil Isbell, Green Bay	2,021
1943	Sid Luckman, Chi. Bears	2,194
1947	Sammy Baugh, Washington	2,938
1960	Johnny Unitas, Baltimore	3,099
1961	Sonny Jurgensen, Philadelphia	3,723
1967	Joe Namath, NY Jets	4,007
1979	Dan Fouts, San Diego	4,082
1980	Dan Fouts, San Diego	4,715
1981	Dan Fouts, San Diego	4,802
1984	Dan Marino, Miami	5,084

PASSING ATTEMPTS

Year	Player, Team	Att.
1932	Arnie Herber, Green Bay	101
1933	Harry Newman, NY Giants	136
1936	Arnie Herber, Green Bay	173
1939	Parker Hall, Cleveland	208
1940	Davey O'Brien, Philadelphia	277
1942	Bud Schwenk, Chi. Cardinals	295
1943	Sammy Baugh, Washington	329
1947	Sammy Baugh, Washington	354
1952	Otto Graham, Cleveland	364
1954	Tobin Rote, Green Bay	382
1960	Frank Tripucka, Denver	478
1964	George Blanda, Houston	505
1967	Sonny Jurgensen, Washington	508
1978	Fran Tarkenton, Minnesota	572
1979	Steve DeBerg, San Francisco	578
1980	Dan Fouts, San Diego	589
1981	Dan Fouts, San Diego	609

PASSING COMPLETIONS

Year	Player, Team	Comp.
1932	Arnie Herber, Green Bay	37
1933	Harry Newman, NY Giants	53
1935	Ed Danowski, NY Giants	57
1936	Arnie Herber, Green Bay	77
1937	Sammy Baugh, Washington	81
1939	Parker Hall, Cleveland	106
1940	Davey O'Brien, Philadelphia	124
1942	Cecil Isbell, Green Bay	146
1947	Sammy Baugh, Washington	210
1960	Frank Tripucka, Denver	248
1964	George Blanda, Houston	262
1967	Sonny Jurgensen, Washington	288
1978	Fran Tarkenton, Minnesota	345
1979	Steve DeBerg, San Francisco	347
1980	Dan Fouts, San Diego	348
1981	Dan Fouts, San Diego	360
1984	Dan Marino, Miami	362

COMPLETION PERCENTAGE

Year	Player, Team	Pct.
1933	Benny Friedman, Brooklyn	52.5
1936	Earl (Dutch) Clark, Detroit	53.5
1938	Bob Monnett, Green Bay	54.4
1939	Frank Filchock, Washington	61.8
1940	Sammy Baugh, Washington	62.7
1945	Sammy Baugh, Washington	70.3
1982	Ken Anderson, Cincinnati	70.6

TOUCHDOWN PASSES

Year	Player, Team	TD
1932	Arnie Herber, Green Bay	9
1933	Harry Newman, NY Giants	11
1935	Ed Danowski, NY Giants	11
1936	Arnie Herber, Green Bay	11
1939	Frank Filchock, Washington	11
1940	Sammy Baugh, Washington	12
1941	Cecil Isbell, Green Bay	15
1942	Cecil Isbell, Green Bay	24
1943	Sid Luckman, Chi. Bears	28
1959	Johnny Unitas, Baltimore	32
1961	George Blanda, Houston	36
1963	Y.A. Tittle, NY Giants	36
1984	Dan Marino, Miami	48

RECEPTIONS

Year	Player, Team	No.
1932	Ray Flaherty, NY Giants	21
1933	John (Shipwreck) Kelly	22
1935	Tod Goodwin, NY Giants	26
1936	Don Hutson, Green Bay	34
1937	Don Hutson, Green Bay	41
1938	Gaynell Tinsley, Chi. Cardinals	41
1940	Don Looney, Philadelphia	58
1941	Don Hutson, Green Bay	58
1942	Don Hutson, Green Bay	74
1949	Tom Fears, LA Rams	77
1950	Tom Fears, LA Rams	84
1960	Lionel Taylor, Denver	92
1961	Lionel Taylor, Denver	100
1964	Charley Hennigan, Houston	101
1984	Art Monk, Washington	106

RECEIVING YARDS

Year	Player, Team	Yards
1932	Ray Flaherty, NY Giants	350
1933	Paul Moss, Pittsburgh	383
1935	Charley Malone, Boston	433
1936	Don Hutson, Green Bay	526
1937	Gaynell Tinsley, Chi. Cardinals	675
1939	Don Hutson, Green Bay	846
1942	Don Hutson, Green Bay	1,211
1951	Elroy (Crazylegs) Hirsch, LA Rams	1,495
1961	Charley Hennigan, Houston	1,746

TOUCHDOWN RECEPTIONS

Year	Player, Team	TD
1932	Three Players	3
1933	Five players	3
1934	Bill Hewitt, Chi. Bears	5
1935	Don Hutson, Green Bay	7
1936	Don Hutson, Green Bay	8
1938	Don Hutson, Green Bay	9
1941	Don Hutson, Green Bay	10
1942	Don Hutson, Green Bay	17
1951	Elroy (Crazylegs) Hirsch, LA Rams	17
1961	Bill Groman, Houston	17
1984	Mark Clayton, Miami	18

INTERCEPTIONS

Year	Player, Team	Int.
1940	Don Hutson, Green Bay	6
	Clarence (Ace) Parker, Brooklyn	6
	Kent Ryan, Detroit	6
1941	Marshall Goldberg, Chi. Cardinals	7
	Art Jones, Pittsburgh	7
1942	Clyde (Bulldog) Turner, Chi. Bears	8
1943	Sammy Baugh, Washington	11
1948	Dan Sandifer, Washington	13
1952	Dick (Night Train) Lane, LA Rams	14

PUNTING AVERAGE

Year	Player, Team	Avg.
1939	Parker Hall, Cleveland	40.8
1940	Sammy Baugh, Washington	51.4

POINTS

Year	Player, Team	Points
1932	Earl (Dutch) Clark, Portsmouth	55
1933	Ken Strong, NY Giants	64
	Glenn Presnell, Portsmouth	64
1934	Jack Manders, Chi. Bears	79
1941	Don Hutson, Green Bay	95
1942	Don Hutson, Green Bay	138
1960	Paul Hornung, Green Bay	176

TOUCHDOWNS

Year	Player, Team	TD
1939	Andy Farkas, Washington	11
1941	Don Hutson, Green Bay	12
	George McAfee, Chi. Bears	12
1942	Don Hutson, Green Bay	17
1945	Steve Van Buren, Philadelphia	18
1958	Jim Brown, Cleveland	18
1961	Bill Groman, Houston	18
1962	Jim Taylor, Green Bay	19
	Abner Haynes, Dallas Texans	19
1965	Gale Sayers, Chi. Bears	22
1975	O.J. Simpson, Buffalo	23
1983	John Riggins, Washington	24

FIELD GOALS

Year	Player, Team	FG
1932	Earl (Dutch) Clark, Portsmouth	3
1933	Jack Manders, Chi. Bears	6
	Glenn Presnell, Portsmouth	6
1934	Jack Manders, Chi. Bears	10
1950	Lou Groza, Cleveland	13
1951	Bob Waterfield, LA Rams	13
1952	Lou Groza, Cleveland	19
1953	Lou Groza, Cleveland	23
1962	Gene Mingo, Denver	27
1965	Pete Gogolak, Buffalo	28
1966	Bruce Gossett, LA Rams	28
1968	Jim Turner, NY Jets	34
1983	Ali Haji-Sheikh, NY Giants	35

POINTS AFTER TOUCHDOWN

Year	Player, Team	PAT
1932	Earl (Dutch) Clark, Portsmouth	10
1933	Jack Manders, Chi. Bears	14
1934	Jack Manders, Chi. Bears	31
1942	Don Hutson, Green Bay	33
1943	Bob Snyder, Chi. Bears	39
1947	Ray McLean, Chi. Bears	44
1948	Pat Harder, Chi. Cardinals	53
1950	Bob Waterfield, LA Rams	54
1961	George Blanda, Houston	64
1984	Uwe von Schamann, Miami	66

The Draft

The format of the NFL draft has changed many times since the brainchild of former NFL Commissioner and club owner Bert Bell was accepted by the league owners on May 19, 1935.

Bell's idea was to help the weaker teams by allowing them first choice of the top college players. Teams would draft in an inverse order of their finish, with the league champion selecting last, regardless of its record. Prior to that time, players had been able to sign with any club. Open signing tended to make the strong get stronger.

The initial draft was held February 8, 1936, at the Ritz-Carlton Hotel in Philadelphia. The first player chosen was Heisman Trophy winner Jay Berwanger, a halfback from the University of Chicago. But Berwanger never signed with either the Eagles, who selected him, or the Bears, after they traded for his rights. The first drafted player who did play was the number-two pick, halfback Riley Smith of Alabama, who was selected by the Boston Redskins.

It took only one year for the format of the draft to change. The December 1936 draft had 10 rounds, one more than the first year. In 1939, the draft increased to 20 rounds; at the start of World War II, it was expanded to 30 rounds, the assumption being that many of those drafted also would be drafted by the Armed Forces. During the war, the NFL voted to stop using the term "draft" and referred to players as being on the "preferred negotiations list."

Following World War II, the All-America Football Conference operated for four years, and held drafts prior to three of them, 1947-49. Those drafts are included after the NFL drafts of the same years.

From 1947 to 1958, the bonus pick rule was in effect. Each year one team received the first pick in the draft, usually in exchange for its thirtieth-round choice. In 1949 and 1950, the bonus pick was a true bonus. In each of those years, the team selecting didn't lose its final-round choice; Philadelphia had a twenty-fifth-round selection in 1949 (when, for one year, the draft dropped to 25 rounds), and Detroit had a thirtieth-round choice in 1950. Each team was eligible for the bonus pick only once, and it was selected by lottery.

When the AFL was founded prior to the 1960 season, the two leagues began drafting many of the same players. That same season the NFL draft was shortened to 20 rounds. After its initial draft, the AFL varied the length of its drafts from 34 to 20 rounds.

Part of the merger agreement between the AFL and NFL was to hold a combined draft, which started in 1967 and was shortened to 17 rounds. The draft was further reduced to 12 rounds in 1977; the same year it was moved to late April or May.

The format of the following all-time draft list changes several times. In the early years of the draft, the league kept only scant records, listing each team's order of selection, from first pick to thirtieth. But those picks didn't necessarily correspond to rounds 1 through 30. In the several years in which more complete records were kept, the teams that finished in the bottom half of the league standings received either more selections, or more selections higher in the draft, than teams in the top half of the standings. Records from other early years make it impossible to determine the round in which a player was chosen. Thus, from 1936-1947 (except in 1938), the numbers before each player generally indicate nothing more than a team's order of selection. Beginning in 1948, the numbers indicate the rounds in which players were selected and include more than one player per round when choices were traded.

In the 1930s, it was common for a team to trade an established player for the rights to sign a draftee, who had been selected with that team in mind. Teams also traded actual draft positions for players, as is done today. But in 1940, rules were passed prohibiting the sale or trading of a team's first two draft positions or of a team's first two selections until one playing season after that selection. Shortly thereafter, the rule involving draft positions was expanded to include all rounds, and in that form remained in effect until 1947, when the Chicago Bears received two draft choices in trades, the Chicago Cardinals' third-round and Philadelphia's fourth-round. Again because of inadequate records, the trading of draft positions isn't indicated prior to 1947, except in 1939.

Throughout the first four decades of the draft, players occasionally (or in some years frequently) were selected who hadn't completed their college eligibility. These players were divided into two groups—"future picks" and players ineligible for the draft.

The future pick was based on the old NFL rule that a player could be chosen if his class had graduated even if he hadn't completed his eligibility. Thus, if a player had been redshirted in college, had sat out a year while transferring from one school to another, or otherwise would have completed his four years of eligibility in five years, he could be drafted after his fourth year, and his rights would remain with the team that selected him, even if he didn't sign for a year.

Most early future picks were not recorded as such, but they were made as long ago as 1949. In the 1960s, with the AFL and NFL each trying to get a draft advantage, future picks became more and more frequent; in 1965 and 1966, the AFL actually held separate drafts for futures. At the time of the merger, in 1967, the leagues agreed to eliminate future picks.

Today a player is required to have graduated or to have completed his eligibility before he can be drafted, unless he is a fifth-year student who announces his intention to forgo his final year of eligibility.

In the unusual circumstance that a player loses his eligibility after the draft, a supplemental draft can be held. In the same order as the previous draft, each team has the opportunity to offer its first-round pick of the next year for the athlete. The process continues through the rounds until he is chosen.

In the draft list, a future pick is indicated by an "F" after the player's school. No future picks are shown prior to 1949. Those obtainable for the NFL, such as all that were made by San Francisco, are indicated through 1961. All AFL future picks and those of the NFL from 1962-66 are indicated.

Through the years, many players were selected who still had college eligibility remaining but weren't eligible to be drafted as futures. These selections basically were mistakes that were made before scouting became as exact as it is today. Generally, these players were drafted again the next year, sometimes even by the same team. A selection that was voided by the league because the player who was drafted was ineligible is indicated by an asterisk at the end of the information about the player.

Notes included with each year refer only to that year, unless otherwise indicated.

1936

Held February 8, 1936

BOSTON

1. Smith, Riley, B, Alabama
2. Topping, Keith, E, Stanford
3. Smith, Ed, B, NYU
4. Tangora, Paul, G, Northwestern
5. Groseclose, Wilson, T, TCU
6. Lutz, Larry, T, California
7. Irwin, Don, B, Colgate
8. Millner, Wayne, E, Notre Dame
9. Saunders, Marcel, G, Loyola (Los Angeles)

BROOKLYN

1. Crayne, Dick, B, Iowa
2. LeVoir, Vernal (Babe), B, Minnesota
3. Jorgenson, Wagner, C, St. Mary's (California)
4. Bryant, Paul (Bear), E, Alabama
5. Wilson, Bob, B, SMU
6. Maniaci, Joe, B, Fordham
7. Schreiber, Herb, B, St. Mary's (California)
8. Hamilton, Bob (Bones), B, Stanford
9. Moscrip, Jim (Monk), E, Stanford

CHI. BEARS

1. Stydahar, Joe, T, West Virginia
2. Michaels, Eddie, G, Villanova
3. Roscoe, George, B, Minnesota
4. Allman, Bob, E, Michigan State
5. Oech, Vern, T, Minnesota
6. Christofferson, Ted, B, Washington State
7. Smith, Dick, T, Minnesota
8. Sylvester, John, E, Rice
9. Fortmann, Dan, G, Colgate

CHI. CARDINALS

1. Lawrence, Jim, B, TCU
2. Jones, Gomer, C, Ohio State
3. Erdelatz, Eddie, E, St. Mary's (California)
4. Brett, Ed, E, Washington State
5. Riordan, Stan, E, Oregon
6. Antonini, Ettore, E, Indiana
7. Dennis, Tack, B, Tulsa
8. Carter, Ross, G, Oregon
9. Larsen, Niels, T, Stanford

DETROIT

1. Wagner, Sid, G, Michigan State
2. Cheshire, Chuck, B, UCLA
3. Pilney, Andy, B, Notre Dame
4. Biese, Sheldon, B, Minnesota
5. Francis, Kavanaugh, C, Alabama
6. Mickal, Abe, B, LSU
7. Wasicek, Charlie, T, Colgate
8. Rennebohn, Dale, C, Minnesota
9. Train, Bob (Choo-Choo), E, Yale

GREEN BAY

1. Letlow, Russ, G, San Francisco
2. Wheeler, J.W., T, Oklahoma
3. Scherer, Bernie, E, Nebraska
4. Ward, Theron, B, Idaho
5. Lester, Darrell, C, TCU
6. Reynolds, Bob, T, Stanford
7. Fromhart, Wally, B, Notre Dame
8. Cruice, Wally, B, Northwestern
9. Wetsel, J.C., G, SMU

NY GIANTS

1. Lewis, Art (Pappy), T, Ohio U.
2. Leemans, Alphonse (Tuffy), B, George Washington
3. Loebs, Frank (Butch), E, Purdue
4. Rose, Roy, E, Tennessee
5. Jontos, Ed, G, Syracuse
6. Durner, Gus, T, Duke
7. Peeples, Bob, T, Marquette
8. Heekin, Dick, B, Ohio State
9. Flanagan, Phil, G, Holy Cross

PHILADELPHIA

1. Berwanger, Jay, B, Chicago
2. McCauley, John, B, Rice
3. Muller, Wes, C, Stanford
4. Wallace, Bill, B, Rice
5. Shuford, Harry, B, SMU
6. Barabas, Al, B, Columbia
7. Weller, Jack, G, Princeton
8. Constable, Pepper, B, Princeton
9. Pauk, Paul, B, Princeton

PITTSBURGH

1. Shakespeare, Bill, B, Notre Dame
2. Barnum, Len, B, West Virginia Wesleyan
3. Grayson, Bobby, B, Stanford
4. Spain, Truman, T, SMU
5. Sandefur, Wayne, B, Purdue
6. Orr, Maurice, T, SMU
7. Peters, Marty, E, Notre Dame
8. Karpowich, Ed, T, Catholic
9. Meglen, Joe, B, Georgetown (Washington D.C.)

1937

Held December 12, 1936

President Joe Carr stated at the draft meeting that because there was a possibility of adding a tenth franchise to the league prior to the opening of the season, 10 players should be drafted for the new team. It was decided that the league would draft for the new franchise, selecting in last place in each round. It was agreed that if no additional team was admitted, the players selected by the league were to revert to the remaining clubs, with preference for selection being given in the same order as in the regular draft. Before the 1937 season, the Cleveland Rams were admitted as the tenth team in the league.

BOSTON

1. Baugh, Sammy, B, TCU
2. Falaschi, Nello, B, Santa Clara
3. Eldar, Maurice, B, Kansas State
4. Bassi, Dick, G, Santa Clara
5. Bond, Chuck, T, Washington
6. Cain, Jimmie, B, Washington
7. Holland, Rolla, G, Kansas State
8. Eaves, Joel, E, Auburn
9. Docherty, Bill, T, Temple
10. Cara, Dom (Mac), E, North Carolina State

BROOKLYN

1. Goddard, Ed, B, Washington State

2. Parker, Clarence (Ace), B, Duke
3. Starcevich, Max, G, Washington
4. Kurlish, Bill, B, Pennsylvania
5. Johnson, Al, B, Kentucky
6. Golemgeske, John, T, Wisconsin
7. Funk, Fred, B, UCLA
8. Reid, Steve, G, Northwestern
9. Nowogrowski, Ed, B, Washington
10. Kuhn, Gil, T, USC

CHI. BEARS
1. McDonald, Les, E, Nebraska
2. Stewart, Marv, C, LSU
3. Plasman, Dick, E, Vanderbilt
4. Hammond, Henry, E, Southwestern (Kansas)
5. Conkright, Bill (Red), C, Oklahoma
6. Bjork, Del, T, Oregon
7. Friedman, J.W. (Buck), B, Rice
8. Toth, Steve, B, Northwestern
9. Guepe, Al, B, Marquette
10. Wade, Ed (Red), T, Utah State

CHI. CARDINALS
1. Buivid, Ray (Buzz), B, Marquette
2. Tinsley, Gaynell, E, LSU
3. Guepe, Art, B, Marquette
4. Bryan, H.K. (Bucky), B, Tulane
5. Harmon, Ham, C, Tulsa
6. Dickens, Phil, B, Tennessee
7. Dickerson, Herm, B, Virginia Tech
8. Reynolds, John, C, Baylor
9. Hafeli, Dwight, E, Washington (St. Louis)
10. Fitzsimmons, Middleton, G, Georgia Tech

DETROIT
1. Cardwell, Lloyd, B, Nebraska
2. Hamrick, Charley, T, Ohio State
3. Huffman, Vern, B, Indiana
4. Glassford, Bill, G, Pittsburgh
5. Patt, Maury, E, Carnegie-Mellon
6. Bell, George, G, Purdue
7. Sprague, John, E, SMU
8. Sayre, Elvin, C, Illinois
9. Kelley, Larry, E, Yale
10. Bell, Kay, T, Washington State

GREEN BAY
1. Jankowski, Eddie, B, Wisconsin
2. Daniell, Ave, T, Pittsburgh
3. Wilkinson, Charles (Bud), T, Minnesota
4. Gibson, Dewitt, T, Northwestern
5. Wendt, Merle, E, Ohio State
6. Baldwin, Marv, T, TCU
7. Chapman, Les, T, Tulsa
8. Dahlgren, Gordon, G, Michigan State
9. Gavin, Dave, T, Holy Cross
10. Did not choose

NY GIANTS
1. Widseth, Ed, T, Minnesota
2. White, Arthur (Tarzan), G, Alabama
3. Dennerlein, Gerry, T, St. Mary's (California)
4. Cuff, Ward, B, Marquette
5. Kobrosky, Mickey, B, Trinity (Connecticut)
6. Farley, Jim, G, Virginia Military
7. Poole, Jim, E, Mississippi
8. Meyers, Gene, G, Kentucky
9. Scheyer, Dwight, T, Washington State
10. Gelatka, Chuck, E, Mississippi State

PHILADELPHIA
1. Francis, Sam, B, Nebraska
2. Murray, Franny, B, Pennsylvania
3. Ellis, Drew, T, TCU
4. Gilbert, Walt, B, Auburn
5. Drobnitch, Alex, G, Denver
6. Guckeyson, Bill, B, Maryland
7. Barna, Herb, E, West Virginia
8. Henrion, Nestor, E, Carnegie-Mellon
9. Fanning, Paul, T, Kansas State
10. Antil, Ray, E, Minnesota

PITTSBURGH
1. Basrak, Mike, C, Duquesne
2. Finley, Bob, B, SMU
3. Breeden, Bill, E, Oklahoma
4. Hewes, Elmo (Bo), B, Oklahoma
5. Frye, Jack, B, Missouri
6. Roach, Walt, E, TCU
7. Haines, Byron, E, Washington
8. Kordick, Marty, G, St. Mary's (California)
9. Patanelli, Matt, E, Michigan
10. Nevers, Stan, T, Kentucky

LEAGUE
1. Drake, Johnny, B, Purdue
2. Alphonse, Jules, B, Michigan
3. LaRue, Bobby, B, Pittsburgh
4. Wiatrak, John, C, Washington
5. Smith, Inwood, G, Ohio State
6. Del Sasso, Chris, T, Indiana
7. Schoen, Norm, B, Baldwin-Wallace
8. Schmarr, Herm, E, Catholic
9. Johnson, Ray, B, Denver
10. Holt, Solon, G, TCU

1938
Held December 12, 1937

After each team made its first-round selection, the five teams that finished lowest in the 1937 standings made an extra selection. This process was repeated after the second round.

BROOKLYN
1. Brumbaugh, Boyd, B, Duquesne
   Kilgrow, Joe, B, Alabama
2. Kinard, Frank (Bruiser), T, Mississippi
   Moore, Gene, C, Colorado
3. Merlin, Ed, G, Vanderbilt
4. Schwartz, Perry, E, California
5. Monsky, Leroy, G, Alabama
6. Noyes, Lon, T, Montana
7. Stringham, John, B, BYU
8. Sivell, Jim, G, Auburn
9. Druze, Johnny, E, Fordham
10. Mark, Lou, C, North Carolina State

CHI. BEARS
1. Gray, Joe, B, Oregon State
2. Famiglietti, Gary, B, Boston U.
3. Zarnas, Gust, G, Ohio State
4. Masterson, Bob, E, Miami
5. Ramsey, Frank, G, Oregon State
6. Sims, Fletcher, B, Georgia Tech
7. Schwarz, Alex, T, San Francisco
8. Weger, John, T, Butler
9. Mickovsky, Ray, B, Case Western Reserve
10. Dreher, Fred, E, Denver

CHI. CARDINALS
1. Robbins, Jack, B, Arkansas
   Popovich, Milt, B, Montana
2. Patrick, Frank, B, Pittsburgh
   Herwig, Bob, C, California
3. Babartsky, Al, T, Fordham
4. Brunansky, Joe, T, Duke
5. Cherry, Ed, B, Hardin-Simmons
6. Lavington, Leon, E, Colorado
7. Dougherty, Phil, C, Santa Clara
8. Sloan, Dwight, B, Arkansas
9. Kenderdine, Bob, E, Indiana
10. Maulner, Bob, C, Holy Cross

CLEVELAND
1. Davis, Corbett, B, Indiana
   Benton, Jim, E, Arkansas
2. Routt, Joe, G, Texas A&M
   Markov, Vic, T, Washington
3. Franco, Ed, G, Fordham
4. Hamilton, Ray, G, Arkansas
5. Chesbro, Marcel (Red), Colgate
6. Mayberry, Walt (Tiger), B, Florida
7. Ream, Chuck, E, Ohio State
8. Maras, Joe, T, Duquesne
9. Hoptowit, Al, T, Washington State
10. Spadaccini, Vic, B, Minnesota

DETROIT
1. Wojciechowicz, Alex, C, Fordham
2. Smith, Pete, E, Oklahoma
3. Bershak, Andy, E, North Carolina
4. Schleckman, Karl, T, Utah
5. Szakash, Paul, B, Montana
6. Nardi, Dick, B, Ohio State
7. Sirtosky, Jim, G, Indiana
8. Wolf, Ralph, C, Ohio State
9. Douglass, Clarence, B, Kansas
10. Frank, Clint, B, Yale

GREEN BAY
1. Isbell, Cecil, B, Purdue
2. Schreyer, Marty, T, Purdue
3. Sweeney, Chuck, E, Notre Dame
4. Uram, Andy, B, Minnesota
5. Kovatch, Johnny, E, Northwestern
6. Ragazzo, Phil, T, Case Western Reserve
7. Howell, Johnny, B, Nebraska
8. Barnhart, Frank, G, Northern Colorado
9. Tinsley, Pete, G, Georgia
10. Falkenstein, Tony, B, St. Mary's (California)

NY GIANTS
1. Karamatic, George, B, Gonzaga
2. Vanzo, Fred, B, Northwestern
3. Konemann, Marion (Dutch), B, Georgia Tech
4. Souchak, Frank, E, Pittsburgh
5. Moan, Kelly, B, West Virginia
6. Doyle, Ted, T, Nebraska
7. Mellus, John, T, Villanova
8. Grimstead, Bob, T, Washington State
9. Oldershaw, Doug, G, Cal-Santa Barbara
10. Hackney, Elmore, B, Duke

PHILADELPHIA
1. McDonald, Jim, B, Ohio State
   Riffle, Dick, B, Albright
2. Bukant, Joe, B, Washington (St. Louis)
   Meek, John, B, California
3. Shirley, Fred, T, Nebraska
4. Ramsey, Herschel, E, Texas Tech
5. Lannon, Bob, E, Iowa
6. Woltman, Clem, T, Purdue
7. Kolberg, Elmer, B, Oregon State
8. Kriel, Emmett, T, Baylor
9. Hinkle, Carl, C, Vanderbilt
10. Michelosen, Johnny, B, Pittsburgh

PITTSBURGH
1. White, Byron (Whizzer), B, Colorado
   Filchock, Frank, B, Indiana
2. Wolfe, Hugh, B, Texas
   Matisi, Tony, T, Pittsburgh
3. Midler, Lou, T, Minnesota
4. Platukis, George, E, Duquesne
5. King, Ray, E, Minnesota
6. Burnette, Tom, B, North Carolina
7. McDonough, Paul, E, Utah
8. McCarty, Pat, C, Notre Dame
9. Krause, Bill, T, Baldwin-Wallace
10. Kuharich, Joe, G, Notre Dame

WASHINGTON
1. Farkas, Andy, B, Detroit
2. Chapman, Sam, B, California
3. Price, Dave, C, Mississippi State
4. Dohrmann, Elmer, E, Nebraska
5. Young, Roy, T, Texas A&M
6. Hartman, Bill, B, Georgia
7. Parks, Ed, C, Oklahoma
8. Abbitt, Jack, B, Elon
9. Johnston, Jimmy, B, Washington
10. Bartos, Henry, G, North Carolina

1939
Held December 8, 1938

BROOKLYN
1. Mac Leod, Bob, B, Dartmouth
2. Manders, Clarence (Pug), B, Drake, from Pittsburgh
   Haak, Bob, T, Indiana
3. Young, Walt, E, Oklahoma
4. Bottari, Vic, B, California
   Beiner, Ed, T, Notre Dame, from Chi. Bears
5. Kinnison, Jack, C, Missouri
6. Janiak, Len, B, Ohio U.
7. Schoenbaum, Alex, T, Ohio State
8. Hill, Dan (Tiger), C, Duke
9. Kline, Forrest, G, TCU
10. Bradley, Kimble, B, Mississippi
    Kaplanoff, Carl, T, Ohio State, from Green Bay
11. Lenc, George, E, Augustana (Illinois)
12. Heikkenen, Ralph, G, Michigan
13. Gembis, George, B, Wayne State
14. Carnelly, Ray, B, Carnegie-Mellon
15. Trunzo, Lou, G, Wake Forest
16. Gross, Charley, G, Bradley
17. Siegal, Johnny, E, Columbia
18. Morin, Paul, T, Iowa State
19. Anderson, Ferrel, G, Kansas
20. Popp, Tony, E, Toledo

CHI. BEARS
1. Luckman, Sid, QB, Columbia, from Pittsburgh
   Osmanski, Bill, B, Holy Cross
2. Wysocki, John, E, Villanova
3. Delaney, Joe, T, Holy Cross
4. Choice to Brooklyn
5. Heileman, Charlie, E, Iowa State
6. Dannies, Bob, C, Pittsburgh
7. Bray, Ray, G, Western Michigan
8. Wood, Walt, B, Tennessee
9. Braga, Al, B, San Francisco
10. Roise, Hal, B, Idaho
11. Bock, Ed, G, Iowa State
12. Stolfa, Anton, B, Luther
13. Voigts, Bob, T, Northwestern
14. Armstrong, Ken, T, Tarkio
15. Masters, Raphael, E, Newberry
16. Sherman, Solly, B, Chicago
17. Simonich, Ed, B, Notre Dame
18. Vogeler, George, C, Oklahoma State
19. Forte, Aldo, T, Montana
20. Kircher, Everett, B, Iowa State

CHI. CARDINALS
1. Aldrich, Ki, C, TCU
2. Goldberg, Marshall (Biggie), B, Pittsburgh
3. Wolff, Alvord, T, Santa Clara
4. Stebbins, Hal (Curly), B, Pittsburgh
5. Daddio, Bill, E, Pittsburgh
6. Faust, George, B, Minnesota
7. Dwyer, Bill, B, New Mexico
8. Hinkebein, Sherm, C, Kentucky
9. Brown, Earl, E, Notre Dame
10. Crowder, Earl, QB, Oklahoma
11. Sabodos, Andy, G, Citadel
12. Miatovich, Blase, T, San Francisco
13. Clarke, Russ, G, Santa Clara
14. Goins, Gus, E, Clemson
15. Elkins, Everett, B, Marshall
16. Huffman, Frank, E, Marshall
17. Kochel, Mike, G, Fordham
18. Rice, Tom, T, San Francisco
19. Did not choose
20. Did not choose

CLEVELAND
1. Hall, Parker, B, Mississippi
2. Smith, Gaylon, B, Southwestern
3. Tarbox, Elmer, B, Texas Tech
4. Garard, Wally, T, St. Mary's (California)
5. Gatto, Eddie, T, LSU
6. McGarry, Bernie, T, Utah
7. Dowd, Gerry, C, St. Mary's (California)
8. Brunner, Warren (Bronco), B, Tulane
9. Bostick, Lew, G, Alabama
10. Petrick, Frank, E, Indiana
11. Roth, Sid, G, Cornell
12. Adams, Chet, T, Ohio U.
13. Hitt, Joel, E, Mississippi College
14. Ryland, John, C, UCLA
15. Friend, Ben, T, LSU
16. Reupke, Gordon, B, Iowa State
17. Perrie, Mike, B, St. Mary's (California)
18. Atty, Alex, G, West Virginia
19. Lane, Bill, B, Bucknell
20. Graham, Paul, B, Indiana

DETROIT
1. Pingel, John, B, Michigan State
2. Weiss, Howie, B, Wisconsin
3. Maronic, Steve, T, North Carolina
4. Wendlick, Joe, E, Oregon State
5. Tutty, Darrell, B, East Texas State
6. Trzuskowski, Dick, T, Idaho
7. Callihan, Bill, B, Nebraska
8. George, Ray, T, USC
9. Calvelli, Tony, C, Stanford
10. Coughlan, Jim, E, Santa Clara
11. Hutchins, Prescott, G, Oregon State
12. Means, Art, G, Washington
13. Hodge, Gene, E, East Texas State
14. Lazetich, Bill, B, Montana
15. Neihaus, Ralph, T, Dayton
16. Niemant, Dutch, B, New Mexico
17. Tonelli, Amerigo (Tony), G, USC
18. McDonald, Jim, C, Illinois
19. Waters, Merrill, E, BYU
20. Howe, Al, T, Xavier

GREEN BAY
1. Buhler, Larry, B, Minnesota
2. Brock, Charley, C, Nebraska
3. Hovland, Lynn, G, Wisconsin
4. Craig, Larry, E, South Carolina
5. Twedell, Francis, T, Minnesota
6. Kell, Paul, T, Notre Dame
7. Hall, John, B, TCU
8. Gavre, Vince, B, Wisconsin
9. Sprague, Charley, E, SMU
10. Choice to Brooklyn
11. Elmer, Dan, C, Minnesota
12. Badgett, Bill, T, Georgia
13. Greenfield, Tom, C, Arizona
14. Bellin, Roy, B, Wisconsin

15. Yerby, John, E, Oregon
16. Balaz, Frank, B, Iowa
17. Brennan, Jack, G, Michigan
18. Schultz, Charley, T, Minnesota
19. Hofer, Willard, B, Notre Dame
20. Gunther, Bill, B, Santa Clara

NY GIANTS
1. Nielson, Walt, B, Arizona
2. Chickerneo, John, B, Pittsburgh
3. Willis, Don, B, Clemson
4. Ginney, Jerry, G, Santa Clara
5. Woodell, Lloyd, C, Arkansas
6. Zagar, Pete, T, Stanford
7. Mills, Bob, T, Nebraska
8. Roberts, Tom, T, DePaul
9. Miller, Merl, B, Washington
10. Schroeder, Bruno, E, Texas A&M
11. Allis, Sam, B, Centenary
12. Watson, George, B, North Carolina
13. Duggan, Gil, T, Oklahoma
14. Panish, Ted, B, Bradley
15. Sanders, Jack, T, SMU
16. Dolman, Will, E, California
17. Paulman, Bill, B, Stanford
18. Smith, Lyle, G, Tulane
19. Tonelli, Mario, B, Notre Dame
20. Rhodes, Jack, G, Texas

PHILADELPHIA
1. O'Brien, Davey, B, TCU
2. Newton, Charlie, B, Washington
3. Mihal, Joe, T, Purdue
4. Dewell, Bill, E, SMU
5. Coston, Fred, G, Texas A&M
6. Schuehle, Carl, B, Rice
7. Ippolito, Tony, B, Purdue
8. Somers, George, T, La Salle
9. Britt, Rankin, E, Texas A&M
10. McKeever, Bill, T, Cornell
11. Humphrey, Paul, C, Purdue
12. Kraynick, Jack, B, North Carolina
13. White, Allie, T, TCU
14. Aleskus, Joe, T, Ohio State
15. Watkins, Forrest, B, West Texas State
16. Hall, Irv, B, Brown
17. Riddell, Bob, E, South Dakota State
18. Gainor, Charley, E, North Dakota
19. White, Morris, B, Tulsa
20. Gormley, Dick, C, LSU

PITTSBURGH
1. Choice to Chi. Bears
2. Choice to Brooklyn
3. Patterson, Bill, B, Baylor
4. McCullough, Hugh, B, Oklahoma
5. Wheeler, Ernie, B, North Dakota State
6. Boyd, Sam, E, Baylor
7. Palumbo, Eddie, B, Detroit
8. Nelson, Ole, E, Michigan State
9. Petro, Steve, G, Pittsburgh
10. Lee, Jack, B, Carnegie-Mellon
11. Tomasetti, Lou, B, Bucknell
12. Cochran, Denny, B, St. Louis
13. Hoffman, Fabian, E, Pittsburgh
14. Clary, Ed, B, South Carolina
15. Tosi, John, C, Niagara
16. Lezouski, Al, G, Pittsburgh
17. Longhi, Ed, C, Notre Dame
18. Shirk, Dave, E, Kansas
19. Peters, Frank, E, Washington
20. Sheldrake, Tom, E, Washington

WASHINGTON
1. Hale, I.B., T, TCU
2. Holm, Charley, B, Alabama
3. Todd, Dick, B, Texas A&M
4. Anderson, Dave, B, California
5. Lumpkin, Quinton, C, Georgia
6. Russell, Torrance (Bo), T, Auburn
7. Moore, Wilbur, B, Minnesota
8. Johnston, Jimmy, B, Washington
9. German, Jim, B, Centre
10. O'Mara, Bob, B, Duke
11. Slivinski, Steve, G, Washington
12. Hoffman, Bob, B, USC*
13. Tipton, Eric, B, Duke
14. Farman, Dick, T, Washington State
15. Shugart, Clyde, T, Iowa State
16. Morgan, Boyd, B, USC
17. Smith, Paul, T, Benedictine
18. Coop, Paul, T, Centre
19. Kuber, Matt, G, Villanova
20. Cruver, Al, B, Washington State

1940
Held December 9, 1939

BROOKLYN
1. McFadden, Banks, B, Clemson
2. Kinnick, Nile, B, Iowa
3. Shetley, Rhoten, B, Furman
4. Bailey, Bill, E, Duke
5. Merrill, Walt, T, Alabama
6. Murray, Jack, C, Wisconsin
7. Coon, Ed, T, North Carolina State
8. Zadworney, Frank, B, Ohio State
9. Jocher, Art, T, Manhattan
10. Turner, Jim, G, Holy Cross
11. Cutlich, Nick, T, Northwestern
12. Dougherty, George, B, Howard
13. Gussie, Mike, G, West Virginia
14. Coffman, Len, B, Tennessee
15. Conlin, Jim, C, NYU
16. Donovan, Dennis, B, Oregon
17. Funair, Frank, B, Bucknell
18. Strosser, Walt, B, St. Vincent
19. Hydock, Steve, E, Albright
20. Howell, Milt, G, Auburn

CHI. BEARS
1. Turner, Clyde (Bulldog), C, Hardin-Simmons
2. Kavanaugh, Ken, E, LSU
3. Kolman, Ed, T, Temple
4. Woudenberg, John, T, Denver
5. Akin, Leonard, G, Baylor
6. Fordham, Jim, B, Georgia
7. Pool, Hampton, G, Stanford
8. Pace, Tom, B, Utah
9. Artoe, Lee, T, California
10. McCubbin, Bill, E, Kentucky
11. Clark, Harry, B, West Virginia
12. Crisci, Frank, T, Case Western Reserve
13. Barnes, Sherm, E, Baylor
14. Christianson, Al, B, Knox
15. White, Wilbur, T, Bradley
16. Schlosser, Ralph, C, Gonzaga
17. Popov, John, B, Cincinnati
18. Bussey, Young, B, LSU
19. McLaran, Ray, B, St. Anselm
20. Kichefski, Walt, E, Miami

CHI. CARDINALS
1. Cafego, George, B, Tennessee
2. Stirnweiss, George (Snuffy), B, North Carolina
3. Madden, Lloyd, B, Colorado Mines
4. Shirk, Jack, E, Oklahoma
5. Christiansen, Marty, B, Minnesota
6. Reginato, Vic, E, Oregon
7. Chisick, Andy, C, Villanova
8. Kish, Ben, B, Pittsburgh
9. Pappas, Luke, T, Utah
10. Roche, Jack, B, Santa Clara
11. Davis, Bill, T, Texas Tech
12. Andersen, Stan, T, Stanford
13. Coppage, Alton, E, Oklahoma
14. Hudson, Judson, B, Davis & Elkins
15. Ziembra, Joe, E, Benedictine
16. Clark, Beryl, B, Oklahoma
17. Foster, Ralph, T, Oklahoma State
18. Bryant, Lowell, B, Clemson
19. Buckley, Russ, B, Gustavus Aldophus
20. Pate, Rupert, T, Wake Forest

CLEVELAND
1. Cordill, Ollie, B, Rice
2. Condit, Merlyn, B, Carnegie-Mellon
3. Haman, Jack, C, Northwestern
4. Wood, Bob, T, Alabama
5. Myers, Park, T, Texas
6. Heineman, Ken, B, Texas-El Paso
7. Nowasky, Bob, E, George Washington
8. Anahu, Bob, E, Santa Clara
9. Thorpe, Wilfrid, G, Arkansas
10. Smith, Herb, B, St. Mary's (California)
11. Clay, Boyd, T, Tennessee
12. Goolsby, Jim, C, Mississippi State
13. Gregory, Jack, T, Tennessee-Chattanooga
14. Bogden, Pete, E, Utah
15. Goodnight, Owen, B, Hardin-Simmons
16. Kohler, Morris, B, Oregon State
17. Nix, Jack, B, Mississippi State
18. Stevenson, Ralph, G, Oklahoma
19. Magnani, Dante, B, St. Mary's (California)
20. Linden, Luke, T, Kentucky

DETROIT
1. Nave, Doyle, B, USC
2. Fisk, Bill, E, USC
3. Smith, Harry, G, USC
4. Rike, Jim, C, Tennessee
5. Winslow, Bob, E, USC
6. Tranavitch, Bill, B, Rutgers
7. Haas, Bob, T, Missouri
8. DeWitte, Leon, B, Purdue
9. Prasse, Erwin, E, Iowa
10. Binder, Ken, B, Carroll (Wisconsin)
11. Bowers, Justin, T, Oklahoma
12. Morlock, Jack, B, Marshall
13. Rouse, Stillman, E, Missouri
14. Padley, Jack, B, Dayton
15. Hackenbruck, John, T, Oregon State
16. Ribar, Frank, G, Duke
17. McCarthy, Herb, B, Denver
18. Parten, Dub, T, Centenary
19. Morgan, Malvern, C, Auburn
20. Orf, Bob, E, Missouri

GREEN BAY
1. Van Every, Hal, B, Minnesota
2. Brock, Lou, B, Purdue
3. Sarkkinen, Esco, E, Ohio State
4. Cassiano, Dick, B, Pittsburgh
5. White, Millard, T, Tulane
6. Seeman, George, E, Nebraska
7. Manley, J.R., G, Oklahoma
8. Brown, Jack, B, Purdue
9. Guritz, Don, G, Northwestern
10. Gaspar, Phil, T, USC
11. Schindler, Ambrose, B, USC
12. Kerr, Bill, E, Notre Dame
13. Brewer, Mel, G, Illinois
14. Andrus, Ray, B, Vanderbilt
15. Kodros, Archie, C, Michigan
16. Gillette, Jim, B, Virginia
17. Matuza, Al, C, Georgetown (Washington D.C.)
18. Reeder, Jim, T, Illinois
19. Eichler, Vince, B, Cornell
20. Luebcke, Henry, T, Iowa

NY GIANTS
1. Lansdell, Grenny, B, USC
2. McLaughry, John, B, Brown
3. Tomaselli, Carl, E, Scranton
4. Smith, Lou, B, California
5. Williams, Rex, C, Texas Tech
6. Pederson, Win, T, Minnesota
7. Principe, Dom, B, Fordham
8. Clark, Earl, B, TCU
9. McKibben, John, E, Tulsa
10. McGee, Ed, G, Temple
11. Payne, Joe, G, Clemson
12. Smith, Bob, B, Oregon
13. Turner, Othel, T, Tulsa
14. Swan, Ned, C, Drake
15. Rogalia, John, B, Scranton
16. Edwards, Bennett, T, Baylor
17. Walden, Cecil, G, Oregon
18. Sullivan, John, E, San Francisco
19. Barnum, Weenie, B, Centenary
20. Claxton, Myron, T, Whittier

PHILADELPHIA
1. McAfee, George, B, Duke
2. Schiechl, Johnny, C, Santa Clara
3. Favor, Dick, B, Oklahoma
4. Schultz, Eberle, G, Oregon State
5. Emmons, Frank, B, Oregon
6. Singer, Saul, T, Arkansas
7. Pegg, Hal, C, Bucknell
8. Looney, Don, E, TCU
9. Jones, Don, B, Washington
10. Maher, Frank, B, Toledo
11. Hackney, Elmer, B, Kansas State
12. Hoerner, Durward, E, TCU
13. Hennis, Ted, B, Purdue
14. Bunsen, Bill, B, Kansas
15. Crumbaker, Don, E, Kansas State
16. Green, J.R., T, Rice
17. Molnar, Jim, B, Bradley
18. Schwartzer, Ernie, G, Boston College
19. Schneider, Bill, B, Mississippi State
20. DeBord, Bill, T, Kansas State

PITTSBURGH
1. Eakin, Kay, QB, Arkansas
2. Wenzel, Ralph, E, Tulane
3. Kiick, George, B, Bucknell
4. Ivy, Frank (Pop), E, Oklahoma
5. Goff, Clark, T, Florida
6. Bykowski, Frank, G, Purdue
7. Cignetti, Pete, B, Boston College
8. Nery, Carl, G, Duquesne
9. Boisseau, Dick, T, Washington & Lee
10. Shu, Paul, B, Virginia Military
11. Cox, Cary, C, Alabama
12. Pirro, Rocco, B, Catholic
13. Noppenberg, John, B, Miami
14. Stublar, Nick, T, Santa Clara
15. McCarthy, Ray, B, Santa Clara
16. Gajecki, Leon, C, Penn State
17. Sullivan, Mike, E, North Carolina State
18. Daly, Seaton, T, Gonzaga
19. Harvey, Thad, T, Notre Dame
20. Katzenstein, Marvin, T, Colorado Mines

WASHINGTON
1. Boell, Ed, B, NYU
2. Banker, Burton (Buddy), B, Tulane
3. Kirchem, Bill, T, Tulane
4. Boyd, Joe, T, Texas A&M
5. Zimmerman, Leroy, B, San Jose State
6. Orr, Roland (Bud), E, Missouri
7. Hoffman, Bob, B, USC
8. Seymour, Bob, B, Oklahoma
9. Stoecker, Howard, T, USC
10. Johnson, Allen, G, Duke
11. Bartholomew, Sam, B, Tennessee
12. Lain, Ernie, B, Rice
13. Sanford, Hayward, E, Alabama
14. Perdue, Willard (Bolo), E, Duke
15. Andrako, Steve, C, Ohio State
16. Graybeal, Jay, B, Oregon
17. Slagle, Charley, B, North Carolina
18. Murphy, Buck, B, Georgia Tech
19. Wetzel, Mel, T, Missouri
20. Sitko, Steve, B, Notre Dame

1941
Held December 10, 1940

BROOKLYN
1. McAdams, Dean, B, Washington
2. Stasica, Leo, B, Colorado
3. Frick, Ray, C, Pennsylvania
4. Rucinski, Eddie, E, Indiana
5. Newman, Hal, E, Alabama
6. Jackson, Glenn, C, Texas
7. Toczylowski, Henry, B, Boston College
8. Langhurst, Jim, B, Ohio State
9. Weiner, Bernie, T, Kansas State
10. Johnson, Harvey, B, Mississippi State*
11. Kinard, George, G, Mississippi
12. Cheatham, Lloyd, B, Auburn
13. Jurich, Mike, T, Denver
14. Alfson, Warren, G, Nebraska
15. McGowen, Dick, B, Auburn
16. McCurry, Lonnie, G, Texas Tech
17. Parker, Dave, E, Hardin-Simmons
18. Ungerer, Joe, T, Fordham
19. Koshlap, Jules, B, Georgetown (Washington D.C.)
20. Whitlow, Ken, C, Rice

CHI. BEARS
1. Harmon, Tom, B, Michigan
2. Standlee, Norm, B, Stanford
3. Scott, Don, B, Ohio State
4. Gallarneau, Hugh, B, Stanford
5. O'Rourke, Charley, B, Boston College
6. O'Boyle, Tommy, G, Tulane
7. Federovich, John (Ace), T, Davis & Elkins
8. Hartman, Fred, T, Rice
9. Rankin, Dave, E, Purdue
10. Matuza, Al, C, Georgetown (Washington D.C.)
11. Laher, Hal, G, Oklahoma
12. LaLanne, Jim, B, North Carolina
13. Hardin, Jim, E, Kentucky
14. Morrow, Bob, B, Illinois Wesleyan
15. Johnson, Jim, B, Santa Clara
16. Martin, Johnny, B, Oklahoma
17. Mulkey, Jack, E, Fresno State
18. Osterman, Bob, C, Notre Dame
19. Glenn, Bill, B, Eastern Illinois
20. Hahnenstein, Ollie, B, Northwestern

CHI. CARDINALS
1. Kimbrough, John (Jarrin' John), B, Texas A&M
2. Christman, Paul, QB, Missouri
3. Foxx, Bob, B, Tennessee
4. Clement, Johnny (Zero), B, SMU
5. Apolskis, Ray, C, Marquette
6. Robnett, Marshall, G, Texas A&M
7. Kuzman, George, T, Fordham
8. Kracum, George, B, Pittsburgh
9. Vargo, Tom, E, Penn State
10. Mallouf, Ray, B, SMU
11. Sommers, Jack, C, UCLA
12. Armstrong, Charley, B, Mississippi College
13. Pitts, Wayne, B, Arizona State
14. Lokanc, Joe, G, Northwestern
15. White, Claude, C, Ohio State

16. Kimball, Gates, T, North Carolina
17. Schultz, Ray, G, Missouri
18. Harris, Fred, T, SMU
19. Aussieker, Mel, B, St. Louis
20. Platt, Frank, T, Penn State

CLEVELAND

1. Mucha, Rudy, C, Washington
2. Shires, Marshall, T, Tennessee
3. MacDowell, Jay, E, Washington
4. Luther, Walt, B, Nebraska
5. Haliski, Chet, B, Oregon
6. Kisselburgh, Jim, B, Oregon State
7. Prochaska, Ray, E, Nebraska
8. Gallovich, Tony, B, Wake Forest
9. Simington, Milt, G, Arkansas
10. Pendergast, John, C, Wake Forest
11. Drahos, Nick, T, Cornell
12. Punches, Harold, G, Colorado
13. McMurray, Bill, E, Murray State
14. Elmore, Bill, B, California
15. Desmore, Warren, C, Toledo
16. Wilson, Gordon, G, Texas-El Paso
17. Hershey, Kirk, E, Cornell
18. Lee, Cobbie, B, Murray State
19. Hursh, Harold, B, Indiana
20. Barnes, Leo, T, LSU

DETROIT

1. Thomason, Jim, B, Texas A&M
2. Goodreault, Gene, E, Boston College
3. Hopp, Harry, B, Nebraska
4. Lio, Augie, G, Georgetown (Washington D.C.)
5. Nelson, Bob, C, Baylor
6. Tripson, John, T, Mississippi State
7. Jett, John, E, Wake Forest
8. Manzo, Joe, T, Boston College
9. Davis, Jasper, B, Duke
10. Pavelec, Ted, T, Detroit
11. Piepul, Milt, B, Notre Dame
12. Jefferson, Billy, B, Mississippi State
13. Britt, Maurice, E, Arkansas
14. Schibanoff, Alex, T, Franklin & Marshall
15. Scott, Perry, E, Muhlenberg
16. Sarres, George, C, Providence
17. Gage, Fred, B, Wisconsin
18. Ishmael, Charlie, B, Kentucky
19. Isberg, Len, B, Oregon
20. Friedlander, Paul, B, Carnegie-Mellon

GREEN BAY

1. Paskvan, George, B, Wisconsin
2. Paffrath, Bob, B, Minnesota
3. Frutig, Ed, E, Michigan
4. Rohrig, Herman, B, Nebraska
5. Telesmanic, Bill, E, San Francisco
6. Kuusisto, Bill, G, Minnesota
7. Canadeo, Tony, B, Gonzaga
8. Byelene, Mike, B, Purdue
9. Heimenz, Paul, C, Northwestern
10. Enich, Mike, T, Iowa
11. Heffernan, Ed, B, St. Mary's (California)
12. Lyman, Del, T, UCLA
13. Frieberger, Johnny, E, Arkansas
14. Pannell, Ernie, T, Texas A&M
15. Saggau, Bob, B, Notre Dame
16. Pukema, Heige, G, Minnesota
17. Hayes, Bob, E, Toledo
18. Strasbaugh, Jim, B, Ohio State
19. Bailey, Joe, C, Kentucky
20. Malinowski, Bruno, B, Holy Cross

NY GIANTS

1. Franck, George, B, Minnesota
2. Reagan, Frankie, B, Pennsylvania
3. Eshmont, Len, B, Fordham
4. DeFilippo, Lou, C, Fordham
5. Vosberg, Don, E, Marquette
6. Younce, Len, G, Oregon State
7. Sohn, Ben, G, USC
8. Matuszczak, Walt, B, Cornell
9. Peoples, Bobby, B, USC
10. Marefos, Andy, B, St. Mary's (California)
11. Brovarney, Cass, G, Detroit
12. Moore, Arnie, E, Mississippi State
13. Black, Johnny, B, Arizona
14. Lucas, Wilson, E, Baylor
15. Anderson, Jack, T, Baylor
16. Allerdice, Dave, B, Princeton
17. Peters, Chuck, B, Penn State
18. Stone, Earl, C, Washington State
19. Dungan, Jack, T, Arizona
20. Fisher, Ted, E, Carnegie-Mellon

PHILADELPHIA

1. Jones, Art, B, Richmond
2. Pugh, Marion, B, Texas A&M
3. Ghesquiere, Al, B, Detroit
4. Kahler, Royal, T, Nebraska
5. Hickey, Howard (Red), E, Arkansas
6. Battista, Julius (Mush), G, Florida
7. Rogers, P.K., B, East Texas State
8. Williams, Don, T, Texas
9. Stenstrom, Marshall, B, Oregon
10. Patrick, John, B, Penn State
11. Hoague, Joe, B, Colgate
12. Dodson, Les, B, Mississippi
13. Lukachick, Alex, E, Boston College
14. Conatser, Bill, B, Texas A&M
15. Yauckoes, John, T, Boston College
16. McFadden, Joe, B, Georgetown (Washington D.C.)
17. Shonk, John, E, West Virginia
18. Russell, L.B., B, Hardin-Simmons
19. Henke, Charley, G, Texas A&M
20. Fernella, Mike, T, Akron

PITTSBURGH

1. Gladchuk, Chet, C, Boston College
2. Knolla, Johnny, B, Creighton
3. Ringgold, Jim, B, Wake Forest
4. Sears, Vic, T, Oregon State
5. Suffridge, Bob, G, Tennessee
6. Roberts, Jim, C, Marshall
7. Elrod, Buddy, E, Mississippi State
8. Fritz, Ralph, G, Michigan
9. Uremovich, Emil, T, Indiana
10. Severin, Paul, E, North Carolina
11. Cotton, Russ, B, Texas-El Paso
12. Goree, J.W., G, LSU
13. Eibner, John, T, Kentucky
14. McAfee, Wes, B, Duke
15. Fox, Terry, B, Miami
16. Cornwall, Bill, T, Furman
17. Kerr, George, G, Boston College
18. Bjorcklund, Bob, E, Minnesota
19. Castiglia, Jim, B, Georgetown (Washington D.C.)
20. Landsberg, Mort, B, Cornell

WASHINGTON

1. Evashevski, Forest, B, Michigan
2. Davis, Fred, T, Alabama
3. Stuart, Jim, T, Oregon
4. Cifers, Ed, E, Tennessee
5. Krueger, Al, E, USC
6. Wilder, Henry, B, Iowa State
7. Grimmett, Bill, E, Tulsa
8. Hickerson, Ed, G, Alabama
9. Aguirre, Joe, E, St. Mary's (California)
10. Banta, Jack, B, USC
11. Conn, Roy, T, Arizona
12. Tornell, Deward, B, San Jose State
13. Buckingham, Morris, C, San Jose State
14. Dow, Ken, B, Oregon State
15. McRae, Stan, E, Michigan State
16. Osmanski, Joe, B, Holy Cross
17. Fullilove, Earl, T, Georgetown (Washington D.C.)
18. Hiestand, Ed, E, Vanderbilt
19. Riggs, Tom, T, Illinois
20. Gentry, Lee, B, Tulsa

1942

Held December 22, 1941

BROOKLYN

1. Robertson, Bobby, B, USC
2. Mechan, Curt, B, Oregon
3. Francis, Vike, B, Nebraska
4. Stanton, Henry, E, Arizona
5. Goldsmith, Wayne, B, Emporia State
6. Flanagan, Preston, E, Texas
7. Gifford, Bob, B, Denver
8. Petro, Joe, G, Muhlenberg
9. Donlan, Fraser (Pat), T, Manhattan
10. Thibaut, Jim, B, Tulane
11. Deremer, Art, C, Niagara
12. Gervelis, Stan, E, Pittsburgh
13. Davis, Gene, B, Pennsylvania
14. Masloski, Ed, B, Scranton
15. Pitts, R.C., E, Arkansas
16. Miller, Ralph, B, Kansas
17. Elliot, Wilson, T, Tennessee-Chattanooga
18. Polantonio, Bill, G, Elon
19. Hayes, Bert, B, Wichita State
20. Fedora, Walt, B, George Washington

CHI. BEARS

1. Albert, Frankie, B, Stanford
2. Boratyn, Joe, B, Holy Cross
3. Ruby, Martin, T, Texas A&M
4. Burrus, H.C., E, Hardin-Simmons
5. Jeffries, Bob, G, Missouri
6. Maznicki, Frank, B, Boston College
7. Petty, John, B, Purdue
8. Mullins, Noah (Moon), B, Kentucky
9. Geyer, Bill, B, Colgate
10. Daniell, Jim, T, Ohio State
11. Hunt, Jack, B, Marshall
12. Gude, Henry, C, Vanderbilt
13. Krutulis, Joe, E, Miami
14. Abel, George, G, Nebraska
15. Edmiston, Don, T, Tennessee
16. Rast, Holt, E, Alabama
17. Jones, Edgar (Special Delivery), B, Pittsburgh
18. Tessendorf, Bill, T, Gonzaga
19. Kissell, Adolph, B, Boston College
20. Clarkson, Stu, C, Texas A&I

CHI. CARDINALS

1. Lach, Steve, B, Duke
2. Cheatham, Lloyd, B, Auburn
3. Schwenk, Wilson (Bud), B, Washington (St. Louis)
4. Banonis, Vince, C, Detroit
5. Reinhard, Bob, T, California
6. Daniel, Chal, G, Texas
7. Thornton, Rupe, G, Santa Clara
8. Renzel, Doug, B, Marquette
9. Wetterlund, Chet, B, Illinois Wesleyan
10. Ringer, Jud, E, Minnesota
11. Fitzharris, Jim, E, St. Thomas (Minnesota)
12. Brye, Dick, T, Marquette
13. Givler, Charley, G, Wake Forest
14. Swink, Hugh, T, Oklahoma State
15. Harshman, Marv, B, Pacific Lutheran
16. Arabian, George, B, St. Mary's (California)
17. Crain, Jackie, B, Texas
18. Suntheimer, Carl, C, North Carolina
19. Nelson, Jimmy, B, Alabama
20. Wallach, Norvell, T, Missouri

CLEVELAND

1. Wilson, Jack, B, Baylor
2. Jacobs, (Indian) Jack, B, Oklahoma
3. Eason, Roger, T, Oklahoma
4. Levy, Len, G, Minnesota
5. Matthews, Orville, B, Oklahoma
6. Sweeney, Mike, E, Texas
7. Rossi, Italo, T, Purdue
8. Brumley, Bob, B, Rice
9. Ulrich, Hubert, E, Kansas
10. deLauer, Bob, T, USC
11. Hightower, Ben, E, Sam Houston State
12. Zirinsky, Walt, B, Lafayette
13. Bradfield, Ray, E, Santa Clara
14. Greene, Tom, T, Georgia
15. Peel, Ike, B, Tennessee
16. Henicle, Glenn, G, Tulsa
17. Clawson, Don, B, Northwestern
18. Graf, Jack, B, Ohio State
19. Regner, Bill, E, Oregon
20. Conley, Gene, T, Washington

DETROIT

1. Westfall, Bob, B, Michigan
2. Bauman, Alf, T, Northwestern
3. Dethman, Bob, B, Oregon State
4. Sanzotta, Dom, B, Case Western Reserve
5. Blalock, Joe, E, Clemson
6. Evans, Murray, B, Hardin-Simmons
7. Colella, Tommy, B, Canisius
8. Franceski, Joe, T, Scranton
9. Banjavic, Emil, B, Arizona
10. Diehl, Bill, C, Iowa
11. Polanski, John, B, Wake Forest
12. Stringfellow, Joe, E, Southern Mississippi
13. Arena, Tony, C, Michigan State
14. Heinberg, Wolf, T, Cal-Santa Barbara
15. Speedie, Mac, E, Utah
16. Bynum, Firman, T, Arkansas
17. Fisher, Dick, B, Ohio State
18. Speth, George, T, Murray State
19. Heaton, Blair, E, Susquehanna
20. Collins, Ben, B, West Texas State

GREEN BAY

1. Odson, Urban, T, Minnesota
2. Frankowski, Ray, G, Washington
3. Green, Bill, B, Iowa
4. Krivonak, Joe, G, South Carolina
5. Johnston, Preston, B, SMU
6. Rogers, Joe, E, Michigan
7. Langdale, Noah, T, Alabama
8. Flick, Gene, C, Minnesota
9. Farris, Tom, B, Wisconsin
10. Richardson, Jimmy, B, Marquette
11. Smith, Bruce, B, Minnesota
12. Applegate, Bill, G, South Carolina
13. Trimble, Jim, T, Indiana
14. Kinkade, Tom, B, Ohio State
15. Preston, Fred, E, Nebraska
16. Ingalls, Bob, C, Michigan
17. Benson, George, B, Northwestern
18. Young, Horace (Deacon), B, SMU
19. Woronicz, Henry, E, Boston College
20. Adams, Woody, T, TCU

NY GIANTS

1. Hapes, Merle, B, Mississippi
2. Sweiger, Bob, B, Minnesota
3. Blozis, Al, T, Georgetown (Washington D.C.)
4. Glass, Bob, B, Tulane
5. Prothro, Tommy, B, Duke
6. Kearns, Tom, T, Miami
7. Merker, Bob, E, Millikin
8. Kopcik, Mike, E, Georgetown (Washington D.C.)
9. Solic, John, C, St. Francis (New York)
10. Krouse, Len, B, Penn State
11. Barnett, Bob, C, Duke
12. Layden, Pete, B, Texas
13. Jungmichel, Buddy, G, Texas
14. Doggett, Keith, T, Wichita State
15. Miller, Verne, T, Harvard
16. Hovious, Junie, B, Mississippi
17. Price, Owen, B, Texas-El Paso
18. Kretowicz, Adam, E, Holy Cross
19. Blumenstock, Jim, B, Fordham
20. Hull, Milt, T, Florida

PHILADELPHIA

1. Kmetovic, Pete, B, Stanford
2. Lindskog, Vic, C, Stanford
3. Williams, Ted, B, Boston College
4. Paschka, Gordon, G, Minnesota
5. Blandin, Ernie, T, Tulane
6. Younglove, Earl, E, Washington
7. Sewell, Billy, B, Washington State
8. Halverson, Bill, G, Oregon State
9. Graves, Ray, C, Tennessee
10. Stackpool, Jack, B, Washington
11. Doss, Noble, B, Texas
12. Meyer, Fred, E, Stanford
13. Brenton, Bob, T, Missouri
14. Wyhonic, John, G, Alabama
15. Griffin, O'Dell, G, Baylor
16. Smaltz, Bill, B, Penn State
17. Moinoro, Arnio, E, Stanford
18. Braun, Bill, T, Santa Clara
19. Dvoracek, Charley, B, Texas Tech
20. Tommervik, Marv, B, Pacific Lutheran

PITTSBURGH

1. Dudley, (Bullet) Bill, B, Virginia
2. Martin, Vern, B, Texas
3. Casanega, Ken, B, Santa Clara
4. Kutner, Mal, E, Texas
5. Sandig, Curt, B, St. Mary's (Texas)
6. Greene, Charley, T, Tulsa
7. Butler, Johnny, B, Tennessee
8. Spendlove, Floyd, T, Utah
9. Chase, Rayburn, B, Missouri
10. Steele, Ernie, B, Washington
11. Wood, Thornley, B, Columbia
12. Roach, Bill, E, TCU
13. Holt, Wayne, G, Tulsa
14. Mosher, Clure, C, Louisville
15. Law, Hubbard, B, Sam Houston State
16. Tomasic, Andy, B, Temple
17. Chamberlain, Garth, T, BYU
18. Rokisky, John, E, Duquesne
19. Jenkins, Ray (Earthquake), B, Colorado
20. Kapriva, Frank, G, Wake Forest

WASHINGTON

1. Sanders, Orban (Spec), B, Texas
2. Deal, Rufus, B, Auburn
3. Zeno, Joe, G, Holy Cross
4. McCollum, Harley, T, Tulane
5. Fitch, Bob, E, Minnesota
6. Peters, George, B, Oregon State
7. Swiger, Frank, B, Duke
8. Goodyear, Johnny, B, Marquette
9. Demao, Al, C, Duquesne
10. Ahwesh, Phil, B, Duquesne
11. Kovatch, John, E, Notre Dame
12. deCorrevant, Bill, B, Northwestern
13. Whited, Marvin, B, Oklahoma
14. Chipman, Dean, B, BYU
15. Watts, George, T, Appalachian State
16. Stewart, Gene, B, Willamette
17. Timmons, Charlie, B, Clemson
18. Croft, Milburn (Tiny), T, Ripon

19. Juzwik, Steve, B, Notre Dame
20. Couppee, Al, B, Iowa

1943

Held April 8, 1943

Although the Philadelphia and Pittsburgh franchises merged for the 1943 season, at the time of the draft they still were independent franchises, and each selected separately. Neither gave up its rights to any players while the merger was in effect. The Cleveland franchise participated in the draft, but then was granted permission to suspend operations for one year. It retained the rights to the players it had selected.

BROOKLYN
1. Governali, Paul, B, Columbia
2. Black, Blondy, B, Mississippi State
3. Ceithaml, George, B, Michigan
4. Domnanovich, Joe, C, Alabama
5. Comer, Marty, E, Tulane
6. Johnson, Harvey, B, William & Mary
7. Matisi, John, T, Duquesne
8. Ferguson, John, E, California
9. Rason, Ray, G, SMU
10. Schleich, Vic, T, Nebraska
11. Sabasteanski, Joe, C, Fordham
12. Thomas, Lou, B, Tulane
13. Stiff, Bert, B, Pennsylvania
14. Fekete, John, B, Ohio U.
15. Rhea, Floyd, G, Oregon
16. Burkett, Bill, E, Iowa
17. Onofrio, Al, B, Arizona State
18. Schoonover, Ken, T, Penn State
19. Barnette, Quentin, B, West Virginia
20. Bledsoe, Bill, E, USC
21. Coutchie, Bob, E, Arizona
22. Reece, Don, B, Missouri
23. Gibson, W.J., E, North Carolina State
24. Dent, Lou, B, Colorado State
25. Lee, Gene, C, Florida
26. Hardy, Harvey, G, Georgia Tech
27. Green, Bob, T, Arkansas
28. Poleshuk, Steve, G, Colgate
29. Sabo, Al, B, Alabama
30. Allshouse, George, C, Pittsburgh

CHI. BEARS
1. Steuber, Bob, B, Missouri
2. Evans, Fred (Dippy), B, Notre Dame
3. Stamm, Ed, T, Stanford
4. Palmer, Derrell, T, TCU
5. Vucinich, Milt, C, Stanford
6. Beals, Alyn, E, Santa Clara
7. Jurkovich, Jim, B, California
8. Lamb, W.G. (Dub), E, Oklahoma
9. Hammett, Ray (Duke), B, Stanford
10. Zikmund, Al, B, Nebraska
11. Wood, Clark, T, Kentucky
12. Arms, Loyd, T, Oklahoma State
13. Sturdy, Lyle, B, Wichita State
14. Tomlinson, Buddy, T, Hardin-Simmons
15. Preston, Pat, T, Wake Forest
16. Norberg, Hank, E, Stanford
17. Lyons, Pat, E, Wisconsin
18. Butler, Marion, B, Clemson
19. Santucci, Al, C, Santa Clara
20. Johnson, Orville, G, SMU
21. Boudreau, Wally, B, Boston College
22. Baumann, Bob, T, Wisconsin
23. Holtscher, Elwood, C, Shurtleff
24. Keller, Ben, G, Duquesne
25. Block, Charley, E, Shurtleff
26. Brannon, Ted, T, Rice
27. Wayne, Lou, E, Texas
28. Creevy, Dick, B, Notre Dame
29. Buffington, Bill, B, Purdue
30. Peterson, Woody, B, Utah

CHI. CARDINALS
1. Dobbs, Glenn, B, Tulsa
2. Grigas, Johnny, B, Holy Cross
3. Currivan, Don, E, Boston College
4. Hust, Al, E, Tennessee
5. Hecht, George, G, Alabama
6. Klug, Al, T, Marquette
7. Mauldin, Stan, T, Texas
8. Godwin, Bill, C, Georgia
9. Storer, Moffatt, B, Duke
10. Mitchell, Fondren, B, Florida
11. Lussow, Emil, E, Dubuque
12. Hirsbrunner, Paul, T, Wisconsin
13. Baumgartner, Bill, E, Minnesota
14. Ramsey, Garrard (Buster), G, William & Mary
15. Doloway, Earl, B, Indiana
16. Burke, Nick, G, Northwestern
17. Campbell, Bill, B, Oklahoma
18. Booth, Clarence, T, SMU
19. Simmons, Elvis (Boots), E, Texas A&M
20. Ericson, Roy, G, Villanova
21. Smith, George (Locomotive), B, Villanova
22. Sutch, George, B, Temple
23. Kimsey, Cliff, B, Georgia
24. Humble, Weldon, G, Rice
25. Purdin, Cal, B, Tulsa
26. McGovern, Eddie, B, Illinois
27. Drulis, Al, G, Temple
28. MacDonald, Ken, C, Rutgers
29. Edwards, Bill, G, LSU
30. Hecomovich, Pete, B, Idaho

CLEVELAND
1. Holovak, Mike, B, Boston College
2. Farmer, Tom, B, Iowa
3. Naumetz, Fred, C, Boston College
4. Taylor, Chuck, G, Stanford
5. Johnson, Clyde, T, Kentucky
6. Horvath, Les, B, Ohio State
7. Henderson, Bill, E, Texas A&M
8. Parker, Bill, E, Iowa
9. Solari, Al, B, UCLA
10. Simmons, Homer, T, Oklahoma
11. Roblin, Tom, B, Oregon
12. Vickroy, Bill, C, Ohio State
13. Alerghini, Tom, G, Holy Cross
14. Sharp, Sam, E, Alabama
15. Kieppe, Dick, B, Michigan State
16. Rogers, Cullen, B, Texas A&M
17. Ruark, Walt, C, Georgia
18. Davis, Bert, C, Utah
19. Fidler, Jay, T, Brown
20. Falk, Carl, T, Washington
21. Coll, Tom, E, St. Mary's (California)
22. McCorkle, Mark, B, Washington
23. Moshofsky, Ed, T, Oregon
24. Adams, Hal, B, Missouri
25. Shephard, Jim, E, Oregon
26. Stetler, Jack, B, Pittsburgh
27. Davis, Jeff, C, Missouri
28. Pritko, Steve, E, Villanova
29. Konetsky, Floyd, G, Florida
30. Miller, Willie, G, LSU

DETROIT
1. Sinkwich, Frank, B, Georgia
2. Schreiner, Dave, E, Wisconsin
3. Ashcom, Dick, T, Oregon
4. Hamer, Ralph, B, Furman
5. Wickett, Lloyd, T, Oregon State
6. Jones, Casey, B, Union (Tennessee)
7. Sizemore, Paul, E, Furman
8. Poschner, George, E, Georgia
9. Irish, Jack, T, Arizona
10. Fenton, Jack, B, Michigan State
11. Renfro, Dick, B, Washington State
12. Kolesar, Bob, G, Michigan
13. Huntsinger, Del, B, Portland
14. Dernoncourt, Ellard, E, St. Louis
15. Woodward, Dick, E, Colorado
16. Bass, Marv, T, William & Mary
17. Peelish, Vic, G, West Virginia
18. Maeda, Chet, B, Colorado State
19. Kuszynski, Bernie, E, Pennsylvania
20. Scanland, Al, B, Oklahoma State
21. Lohry, Royal (Ace), B, Iowa State
22. Holland, Percy, G, LSU
23. Fitzgerald, Mike, G, Missouri
24. Remington, Will, C, Washington State
25. Hamm, Huel, B, Oklahoma
26. Konopka, Irv, T, Idaho
27. Fears, Chuck, T, UCLA
28. Ekern, Bert, E, Missouri
29. Wagner, Virgil, B, Millikin
30. Kaplan, Manny, B, Western Maryland

GREEN BAY
1. Wildung, Dick, T, Minnesota
2. Comp, Irv, B, Benedictine
3. McKay, Roy Dale, B, Texas
4. Susoeff, Nick, E, Washington State
5. Snelling, Ken, E, UCLA
6. Gatewood, Les, C, Baylor
7. Verry, Norm, T, USC
8. Barnett, Solon, G, Baylor
9. Forte, Bob, B, Arkansas
10. Davis, Van, E, Georgia
11. Brock, Tom, C, Notre Dame
12. Tate, Ralph, B, Oklahoma State
13. Carlson, Don, T, Denver
14. Welch, Mike, B, Minnesota
15. Thomas, Ron, G, USC
16. Powers, Jim, T, St. Mary's (California)
17. Prescott, Harold (Ace), E, Hardin-Simmons
18. Forrest, Eddie, C, Santa Clara
19. Wasserbach, Lloyd, T, Wisconsin
20. Hoskins, Mark, B, Wisconsin
21. Bennett, Earl, G, Hardin-Simmons
22. Zellick, George, E, Oregon State
23. Bierhaus, Gene, E, Minnesota
24. Makris, George, G, Wisconsin
25. Susick, Pete, B, Washington
26. Hasse, Bud, E, Northwestern
27. Thornally, Dick, T, Wisconsin
28. Ray, Bob, B, Wisconsin
29. Christensen, Brunel, T, California
30. Roskie, Ken, B, USC

NY GIANTS
1. Filipowicz, Steve, B, Fordham
2. Proctor, Dewey, B, Furman
3. Culwell, Val, G, Oregon
4. Reynolds, Jim, B, Auburn
5. Palazzi, Lou, C, Penn State
6. Visnic, Larry, G, Benedictine
7. Caraway, Doyle, G, Texas Tech
8. Piccolo, Bill, C, Canisius
9. Knox, Glenn, E, William & Mary
10. Domina, Walt, B, Norwich
11. McCafferty, Don, T, Ohio State
12. Stoves, Jay, B, Washington State
13. Currie, Howard, T, Geneva
14. Keithley, N.A., B, Tulsa
15. Lister, Jack, E, Missouri
16. Holshouser, Dwight, B, Catawba
17. Lushine, Jim, T, Minnesota
18. Berllus, Veto, E, Idaho
19. Marshall, Fred, G, North Carolina
20. Korczowski, John, B, William & Mary
21. Hoeman, Gene, E, Oklahoma State
22. Beebe, Keith, B, Occidental
23. Brown, Dave, B, Alabama
24. Hail, Maurice, G, Tulsa
25. McNamara, Ed, T, Holy Cross
26. Drake, Dick, T, Ohio Wesleyan
27. Ritinski, Stan, E, Fordham
28. Mollenhoff, Clark, T, Drake
29. Adams, Verlin, G, Morris Harvey
30. Brundage, Bob, B, Pennsylvania

PHILADELPHIA
1. Muha, Joe, B, Virginia Military
2. Davis, Lamar (Racehorse), B, Georgia
3. Gafford, Monk, B, Auburn
4. Kennedy, Bob, B, Washington State
5. Wistert, Al (Whitey), T, Michigan
6. Banducci, Bruno, T, Stanford
7. Harrison, Walt, C, Washington
8. Alford, Bruce, E, TCU
9. Canale, Rocco, G, Boston College
10. Conoly, Zuehl, T, Texas
11. Billman, John, G, Minnesota
12. Donaldson, Jack, T, Pennsylvania
13. Erickson, Bill, C, Georgetown (Washington D.C.)
14. Weeks, George, E, Alabama
15. Craft, Russ, B, Alabama
16. Darling, Paul, B, Iowa State
17. Gorinski, Walt, B, LSU
18. Friedman, Bob, T, Washington
19. Bezemes, Johnny, B, Holy Cross
20. Mutryn, Chet, B, Xavier
21. Manzini, Baptiste, C, St. Vincent
22. Gillespie, Bernie, E, Scranton
23. Lawhon, Jay, T, Arkansas
24. Zachem, Vince, C, Morehead State
25. Schwarting, Joe, E, Texas
26. Neff, Bob, T, Notre Dame
27. Macioszczyk, Art, B, Western Michigan
28. Arata, Jim, T, Xavier
29. Scott, Wally, E, Texas
30. Jaworowski, Stan, T, Georgetown (Washington D.C.)

PITTSBURGH
1. Daley, Bill, B, Minnesota
2. Russell, Jack, E, Baylor
3. Connolly, Harry, B, Boston College
4. Sossamon, Lou, C, South Carolina
5. Ratto, Al, C, St. Mary's (California)
6. Curry, Ray, E, St. Mary's (California)
7. Murphy, Ed, E, Holy Cross
8. Dwelle, Dick, B, Rice
9. Wukits, Al, C, Duquesne
10. Repko, Joe, T, Boston College
11. Boltrek, Pete, T, North Carolina State
12. Shiekman, Mort, G, Pennsylvania
13. Crain, Milt, B, Baylor
14. Kielbasa, Max, B, Duquesne
15. Skorich, Nick, G, Cincinnati
16. Field, Jackie, B, Texas
17. Bucek, Felix, G, Texas A&M
18. Welsh, Johnny, B, Pennsylvania
19. Compagno, Tony, B, St. Mary's (California)
20. Zapalac, Willie, B, Texas A&M
21. Bain, George, T, Oregon State
22. Wynne, Clay, T, Arkansas
23. Cibulas, Joe, T, Duquesne
24. Yambrick, Bill, C, Western Michigan
25. Freeman, Jack, G, Texas
26. Goode, Joe, B, Duquesne
27. Durishan, Jack, T, Pittsburgh
28. Lobpries, Fritz, G, Texas
29. Jones, Art, B, Haverford
30. Ruman, Bob, B, Arizona

WASHINGTON
1. Jenkins, Jack, B, Missouri
2. Dutton, Bill, B, Pittsburgh
3. Dove, Bob, E, Notre Dame
4. Ziemba, Wally, C, Notre Dame
5. Rymkus, Lou, T, Notre Dame
6. Leon, Tony, G, Alabama
7. Motl, Bob, E, Northwestern
8. McDonald, Walt, B, Tulane
9. Perpich, George, T, Georgetown (Washington D.C.)
10. Wood, Dan, C, Mississippi
11. Wright, Harry, G, Notre Dame
12. Britt, Oscar, G, Mississippi
13. Weber, Dick, G, Syracuse
14. Day, Joe, B, Oregon State
15. Dornfeld, Frank, B, Georgetown (Washington D.C.)
16. Baklarz, John, T, Arizona State
17. Mogus, Leo, E, Youngstown State
18. Secrest, Dick B, Rochester
19. Nolander, Don, C, Minnesota
20. Barrett, Johnny, B, Georgetown (Washington D.C.)
21. Vohs, Tom, T, Colgate
22. Yancey, Charlie, B, Mississippi State
23. Bentz, Roman, T, Tulane
24. Berthold, Paul (Swifty), E, Syracuse
25. Pacewic, Vince, B, Loyola (Los Angeles)
26. Riccardi, Joe, T, Ohio U.
27. Jaffurs, Johnny, G, Penn State
28. Akins, Frank, B, Washington State
29. Corry, Bill, B, Florida
30. Bogovich, Bo, G, Delaware

1944

Held April 19, 1944

Although the Pittsburgh and Chicago Cardinals franchises merged for the 1944 season, at the time of the draft they still were independent franchises, and each selected separately. Neither gave up its rights to any players while the merger was in effect. Philadelphia and Pittsburgh, which had been merged in 1943, alternately selected fourth (for their fifth-place finish) and ninth (last of the teams playing the previous season). Cleveland, which was given permission to resume operations for 1944, selected tenth. The expansion Boston Yanks had the first overall selection in the draft, and then selected last in each following round.

BOSTON
1. Bertelli, Angelo, QB, Notre Dame
2. Dimancheff, Boris (Babe), B, Purdue
3. Rice, Larry, C, Tulane
4. Parker, John (Butch), T, Loyola (Los Angeles)
5. Andrews, Mike, E, North Carolina State
6. Musick, Bob, B, USC
7. Warrington, Caleb (Tex), C, Auburn
8. Sisti, Angelo, T, Boston College
9. Long, Gene, G, Kansas
10. Fiorentino, Ed, E, Boston College
11. Zeleznak, Mike, B, Kansas State
12. Maskas, John, T, Virginia Tech
13. Bond, John, B, TCU
14. Antaya, Roger, G, Dartmouth
15. Shurnas, Marshall, E, Missouri
16. Bennett, Reldon, T, LSU
17. Faircloth, Art, B, North Carolina State
18. Bilotti, Tony, G, St. Mary's (California)
19. Furman, Bill, T, Washington & Lee
20. Morford, Clare, G, Oklahoma
21. Richmond, Dilton, E, LSU
22. Lawlor, Courtney, B, Richmond
23. Debus, Howard, B, Nebraska

24. Portwood, Bill, E, Kentucky
25. Collins, Harold, G, Southwestern (Texas)
26. Gill, Aubrey, C, Texas
27. Wasilewski, Chet, B, Holy Cross
28. Letchas, Gus, B, Georgia
29. Calcagni, Ralph, T, Pennsylvania
30. Roberts, Walton, B, Texas

BROOKLYN

1. Miller, Creighton, B, Notre Dame
2. Callahan, J.R., B, Texas
3. Park, Ralph, B, Texas
4. Sikich, Rudy, T, Minnesota
5. Ullom, Verne, E, Cincinnati
6. McDonald, Bruce, E, Illinois State
7. Graiziger, Bob, G, Minnesota
8. Sachse, Jack, C, Texas
9. Olenski, Mitch, T, Alabama
10. Cenci, Aldo, B, Penn State
11. Bicaninch, John, G, Minnesota
12. Tyree, Jim, E, Oklahoma
13. Wright, Jim, C, SMU
14. Genis, John, T, Illinois
15. Murphy, Billie (Spook), B, Mississippi State
16. Essick, Doug, E, USC
17. Maley, Howard (Red), B, SMU
18. Willer, Don, T, USC
19. Callanan, Howard, B, USC
20. Doherty, George, T, Louisiana Tech
21. Mihalic, Mike, G, Mississippi State
22. Cook, Ted, E, Alabama
23. Gillenwater, Bucky, T, Texas Tech
24. Baldwin, Jack, C, Centenary
25. Manning, Dick, B, USC
26. Grierson, Ray, E, Illinois
27. Golding, Joe, B, Oklahoma
28. Zimny, Bob, T, Indiana
29. Frohm, Marty, T, Mississippi State
30. Blose, Howard, B, Cornell

CHI. BEARS

1. Evans, Ray, B, Kansas
2. Smeja, Rudy, E, Michigan
3. Croft, Abe, E, SMU
4. Stanley, C.B., T, Tulsa
5. Seeley, Darwin, C, Stanford
6. Fawcett, Randall (Buck), B, Stanford
7. Morton, Jack, E, Missouri
8. Starford, Bill, C, Wake Forest
9. Houston, Lin, G, Ohio State
10. Moore, J.P., B, Vanderbilt
11. Duffey, Bill, E, Georgetown (Washington D.C.)
12. Hartley, Joe, T, LSU
13. Milner, Bill, G, Duke
14. Hirsch, Ed (Buckets), B, Northwestern
15. Ryckeley, Ed, E, Georgia Tech
16. Plasman, Howdy, B, Miami
17. French, Barry (Bear), T, Purdue
18. Taylor, Paul, B, USC
19. Margarita, Hank, B, Brown
20. Davis, Ed, B, Oklahoma
21. Jamison, Dick, T, USC
22. Bortka, Jack, B, Kansas State
23. Ruskusky, Roy, E, St. Mary's (California)
24. Franck, Harry, B, Northwestern
25. McKewan, Jack, T, Alabama
26. Mitchell, Charley, B, Tulsa
27. Boyle, Pat, G, Wisconsin
28. Pepper, Bernie, T, Missouri
29. Vogt, Karl, T, Villanova
30. Endres, Bob, T, Colgate

CHI. CARDINALS

1. Harder, Pat, B, Wisconsin
2. Mitchell, Paul, T, Minnesota
3. Judd, Saxon, E, Tulsa
4. Tavener, Jack, C, Indiana
5. Blackburn, Bill, C, Rice
6. Garnaas, Bill, B, Minnesota
7. Smith, Rodger, B, Texas Tech
8. Cochran, John (Red), B, Wake Forest
9. Scanlan, Frank, B, Loyola (Los Angeles)
10. Saban, Lou, B, Indiana
11. Griffin, Fran, T, Holy Cross
12. Daniels, Leo, B, Texas A&M
13. Dobbs, Bobby, B, Tulsa
14. Hall, Van, B, TCU
15. Carpenter, Jack, T, Missouri
16. Csuri, Charley, T, Ohio State
17. Magliolo, Joe, B, Texas
18. Szot, Walt, T, Bucknell
19. Adams, Jack, E, Presbyterian
20. Kuffel, Ray, E, Marquette
21. West, Jack, E, Texas
22. Escorcia, Jack, B, Illinois State
23. Buffmire, Don, B, Northwestern
24. Nanni, Bob, T, Duke
25. McGinnis, John, E, Notre Dame
26. Hodges, Warren, T, Kansas
27. Earley, Bill, B, Notre Dame
28. Davis, Bob, G, Oregon
29. DiFrancesca, Vince, T, Northwestern*
30. Ott, Lloyd, C, North Carolina State

CLEVELAND

1. Butkovich, Tony, B, Illinois
2. Bouley, Gil, T, Boston College
3. Waterfield, Bob, B, UCLA
4. Akins, Al, B, Washington State
5. Cheverko, George, B, Fordham
6. Stasica, Stan, B, South Carolina
7. Boensch, Fred, T, Stanford
8. Shaw, Bob, E, Ohio State
9. Andrejco, Joe, B, Fordham
10. Filley, Pat, G, Notre Dame
11. Erickson, Bob, B, Washington
12. Maceau, Mel, C, Marquette
13. Hubbell, Frank, E, Tennessee
14. Aguirre, John, T, USC
15. Clayton, Aubrey, B, Auburn
16. Zamlynski, Ziggy, B, Villanova
17. McBride, Bob, G, Notre Dame
18. Yackanich, Joe, T, Fordham
19. Creevey, John, B, Notre Dame
20. Jones, David Paul, B, Arkansas
21. Pharr, Jim, C, Auburn
22. Warlick, Joe, B, Mississippi State
23. Gianelli, Bert, G, Santa Clara
24. Kuhn, Charley, B, Kentucky
25. Smith, Jim, T, Colorado
26. Donelli, Ray, B, Duquesne
27. Hughes, John, E, Mississippi State
28. McPhee, Dick, B, Georgia
29. McLeod, Jim, E, LSU
30. Kudlacz, Stan, C, Notre Dame

DETROIT

1. Graham, Otto, B, Northwestern
2. Cifers, Bob, B, Tennessee
3. Heywood, Ralph, E, USC
4. Betteridge, George, B, Utah
5. Greene, John, T, Michigan
6. Alliquie, Ed, T, Santa Clara
7. Briggs, Paul, T, Colorado
8. Giske, Rod, G, Washington State
9. Bolger, Matthew, E, Notre Dame
10. Hein, Herb, E, Minnesota
11. White, Paul, B, Michigan
12. Lescoulie, Jack, G, UCLA
13. Rehor, Doug, B, Dickinson
14. Pritula, Bill, C, Michigan
15. Molich, Jim, E, Fresno State
16. Yakapovich, Jules, B, Colgate
17. Helms, J.A., T, Georgia Tech
18. Madarik, Elmer, B, Detroit
19. Eubank, Bill, E, Mississippi State
20. Ahlstrom, Ray, B, St. Mary's (California)
21. Kapter, Alex, G, Northwestern
22. Clark, Vic, B, Texas-El Paso
23. Fischer, Max, C, Oklahoma
24. Jacoby, Chuck, B, Indiana
25. McCarthy, Bob, E, St. Mary's (California)
26. Hendrickson, Stan, E, Colorado
27. Bouldin, Fred, B, Missouri
28. McElwee, Dick, B, West Virginia
29. Derleth, Bob, T, Michigan
30. Dick, George, E, Kansas

GREEN BAY

1. Pregulman, Merv, G, Michigan
2. Kuzma, Tom, B, Michigan
3. McPartland, Bill, T, St. Mary's (California)
4. McCardle, Mickey, B, USC
5. Tracy, Jack, E, Washington
6. Agase, Alex, G, Illinois
7. Whitmire, Don, T, Alabama, Navy
8. Koch, Bob, B, Oregon
9. Johnson, Virgil, E, Arkansas
10. Giusti, Roy, B, St. Mary's (California)
11. Baughman, Bill, C, Alabama
12. Griffin, Don, B, Illinois
13. Gissler, Bert, E, Nebraska
14. Shelton, Lou, B, Oregon State
15. Cusick, Charley, G, Colgate
16. Cox, Hugh, B, North Carolina
17. Davis, Kermit, E, Mississippi State
18. Johnson, Bob, C, Purdue
19. Cox, Jim, T, Stanford
20. Anderson, Cliff, E, Minnesota
21. Perry, John Wesley, B, Duke
22. DeMaria, Pete, G, Purdue
23. Liss, Len, T, Marquette
24. Jordon, Ray, B, North Carolina
25. Grubaugh, Al, T, Nebraska
26. Howard, A.B., E, Mississippi State
27. Paladino, Paul, G, Arkansas
28. Butchofsky, Bob, B, Texas A&M
29. Deal, Russ, G, Indiana
30. Gonzales, Abel (Frito), B, SMU

NY GIANTS

1. Hillenbrand, Billy, B, Indiana
2. Blount, Lamar, B, Mississippi State
3. Flowers, Clyde, T, TCU
4. Kane, Herb, T, East Central (Oklahoma)
5. Maitland, Vic, T, Hobart
6. Okland, Jack, T, Utah State
7. Frickey, Herm, B, Minnesota
8. Clay, Roy, B, Colorado State
9. Sanchez, Johnny, T, San Francisco
10. Beamer, Ernie, E, Duke
11. Grate, Carl, G, Georgia
12. Mont, Tommy, B, Maryland
13. Poole, Ray, E, Mississippi
14. Corley, Elbert, C, Mississippi State
15. Poole, Ollie, E, Mississippi
16. Ellsworth, Ralph, B, Texas
17. Schneider, Ed, T, Washburn
18. Gres, Marcel, T, Texas
19. Brooks, Neil, B, Washington
20. Kane, Pete, B, Geneva
21. Kittrell, M.L. (Kit), B, Baylor
22. Renfro, Roy, G, Fresno State
23. Dubzinski, John, G, Boston College
24. Beyer, Howard, C, Michigan State
25. Babula, Ben, B, Fordham
26. Fitanides, Ted, B, New Hampshire
27. Bires, Andy, E, Alabama
28. Rock, Tom, E, Columbia
29. Cyhel, Walt, T, Creighton
30. Nelson, Francis, B, Baylor

PHILADELPHIA

1. Van Buren, Steve, B, LSU
2. La Prade, Loren, G, Stanford
3. Parker, Joe, E, Texas
4. Horne, Hillary, T, Mississippi State
5. Kulbitski, Vic, B, Minnesota
6. Phillips, George, B, UCLA
7. Sarringhaus, Paul, B, Ohio State
8. Perko, John, G, Minnesota
9. Ormsbee, Elliot, B, Bradley
10. Parsons, Earl, B, USC
11. Hanzlik, Bob, E, Wisconsin
12. Talley, Jim, C, LSU
13. Fusci, Dom, T, South Carolina
14. Green, Johnny, E, Tulsa
15. Freeman, Jackie, B, William & Mary
16. Kane, Joe, B, Pennsylvania
17. Schiro, Tony, G, Santa Clara
18. Michael, Norm, B, Syracuse
19. Kulakowski, Eddie, T, West Virginia
20. Postus, Al, B, Villanova
21. Smith, Milt, E, UCLA
22. Klapstein, Earl, T, Pacific
23. Frisbee, Bob, B, Stanford
24. Eiden, Ed, B, Scranton
25. Burdick, Barney, E, Creighton
26. Daukas, Nick, T, Dartmouth
27. Darone, Pasquale, G, Boston College
28. Clark, Bill, T, Colorado College
29. Pasko, Pete, E, East Stroudsburg
30. Majewski, Myron, T, American International

PITTSBURGH

1. Podesto, Johnny, B, St. Mary's (California)
2. Odell, Bob, E, Pennsylvania
3. Gantt, Bob, E, Duke
4. McCaffray, Art, T, Pacific
5. Owen, George, G, Wake Forest
6. Savage, Dan, B, Brown
7. Freitas, Jesse, B, Santa Clara
8. Titus, George, C, Holy Cross
9. Stofko, Ed, B, St. Francis
10. Jansante, Val, E, Duquesne
11. Buda, Carl, G, Tulsa
12. Gray, Sam, E, Tulsa
13. Longacre, Bob, B, William & Mary
14. Zetty, Les, E, Muhlenberg
15. Myers, Jim, G, Tennessee
16. Gottlieb, Joe, B, Duquesne
17. Davis, Hugh, B, Michigan State
18. Sullivan, Bill, E, Villanova
19. Woodside, Jimmy, C, Temple
20. Miller, Bill, B, Pennsylvania
21. Lawson, Bob, E, Holy Cross
22. Caver, Hank, B, Presbyterian
23. Carter, Paul, T, Michigan State
24. Holben, Dick, T, Muhlenberg
25. Tippee, Howard, B, Iowa State
26. Malmberg, Charley, T, Rice
27. Ashbaugh, Russ, B, Notre Dame
28. Petroski, Pat, G, Miami
29. Tosti, Joe, E, Scranton
30. Seelinger, Len, B, Wisconsin

WASHINGTON

1. Micka, Mike, B, Colgate
2. Audet, Earl, T, USC
3. Doherty, Ed, B, Boston College
4. Fellows, Jackie, B, Fresno State
5. Fischer, Hal, G, Texas
6. White, Cliff, T, Murray State
7. Ogdahl, Ted, B, Willamette
8. Sneddon, Bob, B, St. Mary's (California)
9. Aldworth, Bill, T, Minnesota
10. Joslyn, Bill, B, Stanford
11. Walker, Charley, C, Kentucky
12. Clement, Boyd, C, Oregon State
13. Gaffney, Jim, B, Tennessee
14. Ossowski, Ted, T, Oregon State
15. Davis, Tom, B, Duke
16. Batorski, John, E, Colgate
17. Ehrhardt, Clyde, C, Georgia
18. Brown, Dave, E, UCLA
19. Ivy, Bill, T, Northwestern
20. Babcock, Bruce, B, Rochester
21. Reinhard, Bill, B, California
22. Bauer, Ed, G, South Carolina
23. Martin, (Smokey) Joe, B, Cornell
24. Gustafson, Lee, B, Oregon State
25. Pappas, Nick, T, Utah
26. Bowen, Lindsey, E, Rice
27. Gustafson, Bill, T, Washington State
28. Yablonski, Bill, C, Holy Cross
29. Hollingbery, Buster, C, Washington State
30. Sheller, Willard, B, Stanford

1945

Held April 6, 1945

Although the Boston and Brooklyn franchises merged for the 1945 season, at the time of the draft they still were independent franchises, and each selected separately. Neither gave up its rights to any players while the merger was in effect. Pittsburgh and the Chicago Cardinals, which had been merged in 1944, alternately selected first, second, and third (with Brooklyn) for their last-place finish the previous season.

In 1944, the league had passed a special one-year rule allowing a handful of players who still had college eligibility to play one year in the NFL and then to be returned to the preferred negotiations list in 1945. This rule primarily was aimed at those players who were unable to play collegiately because their programs had dropped football, but also included some who had left school but then had been ineligible to serve in the Armed Forces. In 1945, three such players were selected after a year in the NFL: Paul Duhart (Pittsburgh, second round), Russ Lowther (Detroit, sixth round), and John Morelli (Boston, twenty-eighth round). One other player—John Itzel (Pittsburgh, seventeenth round)—was granted special permission to be selected and to play in 1945, returning to the preferred negotiations list in 1946.

BOSTON

1. Prokop, Eddie, B, Georgia Tech
2. Dean, Tom, T, SMU
3. Tassos, Damon, G, Texas A&M
4. Deeks, Don, T, Washington
5. Strzykalski, Johnny (Strike), B, Marquette*
6. Mello, Jim, B, Notre Dame
7. Silovich, Marty, C, Marquette
8. Jones, Ellis, G, Tulsa
9. Lambert, Earl, B, Manhattan
10. Kasprzak, Don, B, Dartmouth
11. Jones, Ben, E, Arkansas
12. Coleman, Herb, C, Notre Dame
13. Pezelski, Joe, B, Villanova
14. DiGangi, John, T, Holy Cross
15. Highsmith, Chan, C, North Carolina
16. Costello, Mike, E, Georgetown (Washington D.C.)
17. Dromgoole, Paul, E, Manhattan
18. Czekala, Dolph, T, Syracuse
19. Drumm, Joe, T, Georgetown (Washington D.C.)
20. Gianelli, Mario, T, Boston College

21. Jamison, Eric, T, San Francisco
22. Kretz, Walt, B, Cornell
23. Grbovaz, Marty, E, San Francisco*
24. Gory, Ziggy, C, Villanova
25. Iancelli, Bill, E, William & Mary*
26. Kull, Al, T, Fordham
27. Mangene, Bob, B, Boston College
28. Morelli, John, G, Georgetown (Washington D.C.)
29. Fisher, John, C, Harvard
30. Oberto, Elmer, G, Georgetown (Washington D.C.)

BROOKLYN
1. Renfroe, Joe, B, Tulane
2. Williams, Wayne, B, Minnesota
3. Gray, Cecil, C, Oregon
4. Enich, Steve, G, Marquette
5. Kowalski, Al, QB, Tulsa
6. Barwegen, Dick, G, Purdue
7. Futrell, Louie, B, Fresno State
8. Dodds, John, G, California
9. Johnson, Elting, B, Bucknell
10. Cross, Roy, E, Tennessee
11. Haury, Earl, T, Kansas State
12. Martin, John, B, East Tennessee State
13. McDonald, George, T, South Carolina
14. Self, Hal, B, Alabama
15. Reilly, Tom, G, Fordham
16. Harrison, Skimp, E, South Carolina
17. Weinmeister, Arnie, E, Washington
18. Eikenberg, Virgil, B, Rice
19. Kasulin, Al, B, Villanova
20. Lively, Charley, T, Arkansas
21. Curran, Ted, B, Iowa
22. Fabling, Don, B, Colorado*
23. Crittenden, Wally, B, USC
24. Taddie, Jules, C, Rochester
25. Whitney, Jerry, B, USC
26. Trapani, Felix, G, LSU*
27. Finney, Hal, B, USC
28. Fauble, Don, B, Oklahoma
29. Studen, Nick, B, Denver
30. Dykstra, LaMar, B, Colorado*

CHI. BEARS
1. Lund, Don, B, Michigan
2. Allen, Charley, B, SMU
3. Masterson, Forest, C, Iowa
4. Shaw, Wayne, B, SMU
5. Burgeis, Glen, T, Tulsa
6. O'Brien, Pat, T, Purdue
7. Mayther, Bill, C, Oregon
8. Poe, Bill, B, Clemson
9. Avery, Chuck, B, Minnesota
10. Boyd, Jack, B, UCLA
11. Ellsworth, Ralph, B, Texas
12. Mattioli, Frank, G, Pittsburgh
13. Gibson, Merle, E, TCU
14. Creevey, John, B, Notre Dame
15. Sacrinty, Nick, B, Wake Forest
16. Keane, Jim, C, Iowa
17. Niedziela, Bruno, T, Iowa
18. Williams, Broughton, E, Florida
19. Stickel, Walt, T, Pennsylvania
20. Livingston, Bob, B, Notre Dame
21. Vargon, Mike, E, Kansas State
22. Wright, Charley, G, Iowa State
23. Green, Jack, G, Alabama
24. Gambino, Lu, B, Maryland
25. Jones, Ray, B, Texas
26. Hary, Bob, B, Minnesota
27. Forkovich, Nick, B, William & Mary
28. Robinson, Don, B, Michigan
29. Johnston, Wayne (Rusty), B, Marquette
30. Groves, George, C, Marquette

CHI. CARDINALS
1. Trippi, Charley, B, Georgia
2. Collins, Paul, B, Missouri
3. Watt, Walt, B, Miami
4. Dobelstein, Bob, G, Tennessee
5. Chronister, Zeke, E, TCU
6. Clatt, Corwin, B, Notre Dame
7. Czarobski, Ziggy, T, Notre Dame
8. Harrington, John, E, Marquette
9. Meeks, Gene, B, Kentucky
10. Huber, Bill, E, Notre Dame
11. Heard, Halley, T, LSU
12. Cowan, Bob, B, Indiana
13. Luper, Elmore (Buddy), B, Duke
14. Barnett, Solon, G, Baylor
15. Carver, Gordon, B, Duke
16. Cannady, John, B, Indiana*
17. Cittadino, Ben, E, Duke
18. Strayhorn, Ralph, G, North Carolina
19. Andretich, John, B, Purdue
20. Kramer, John, T, Marquette

21. Cheek, J.D., G, Baylor*
22. Grant, Fred, B, Wake Forest
23. Cook, Johnny, B, Georgia*
24. McClure, Ardie, T, Georgia
25. Norige, Hugo, B, Wooster
26. Knight, Gene (Red), B, LSU*
27. Fambrough, Don, B, Texas
28. Williams, Garland (Bulldog), T, Duke
29. Dusek, Ed, B, Texas A&M
30. Payne, Otto, B, Texas A&M

CLEVELAND
1. Hirsch, Elroy (Crazylegs), B, Michigan, Wisconsin
2. Lazetich, Milan, T, Michigan
3. Wooten, W.G. (Dub), E, Oklahoma
4. Zilly, Jack, E, Notre Dame
5. Harding, Roger, C, California
6. Cowhig, Jerry, B, Notre Dame
7. Negus, Fred, C, Wisconsin
8. August, Johnny, B, Alabama
9. Huffman, Dick, T, Tennessee
10. Walters, Vern, B, Alma
11. Fears, Tom, E, UCLA
12. Winkler, Joe, C, Purdue
13. Aland, Jack, T, Alabama
14. Uknes, Chuck, B, Iowa
15. Lund, Bill, B, Case Western Reserve*
16. Barton, Bob, E, Holy Cross
17. Hoerner, Dick, B, Iowa
18. Kennon, Lee, T, Oklahoma
19. Matulich, Eagle, B, Mississippi State
20. Griffin, Bill, T, Kentucky
21. Erickson, Leroy, B, Oregon
22. Evans, Ray, T, Texas-El Paso*
23. Higgins, Luke, T, Notre Dame
24. Nowak, Stan, E, South Carolina
25. Konopka, Gene, G, Villanova
26. Florek, Ray, B, Illinois
27. Perry, Russ, B, Wake Forest
28. West, Pat, B, USC
29. Davis, Bill, B, Oregon
30. Compton, Charley, T, Alabama

DETROIT
1. Szymanski, Frank, C, Notre Dame
2. Mohrbacher, Stan, G, Iowa
3. Wiese, Bob, B, Michigan
4. Fekete, Gene, B, Ohio State
5. Jarmoluk, Mike, T, Temple
6. Lowther, Russ, B, Detroit
7. Joop, Les, T, Illinois
8. Walker, Paul, E, Yale
9. Hansen, Howie, T, Utah State
10. Kasap, Mike, T, Illinois
11. Hopp, Wally, B, Nebraska
12. Trickey, Ben, B, Iowa
13. Williams, Windell, E, Rice
14. Flanigan, Wayne, E, Denver
15. Key, O.J., B, Tulane
16. McWhorter, Jim, B, Alabama
17. LeForce, Clyde, B, Tulsa
18. Castronis, Mike, G, Georgia
19. Currier, Ken, G, Wisconsin
20. Verutti, Jack, B, St. Mary's (California)
21. Olsen, Ray, B, Tulane
22. Morrow, Russ, C, Tennessee
23. Green, Stan, T, Oklahoma
24. Ivory, Bob, G, Detroit
25. Taylor, Dell, B, Tulsa
26. Ciesla, Len, B, Creighton
27. Lopp, Frank, T, Wisconsin
28. Limont, Paul, E, Notre Dame
29. Schadler, Ben, B, Northwestern*
30. Dorais, Tom, B, Detroit

GREEN BAY
1. Schlinkman, Walt, B, Texas Tech
2. Goodnight, Clyde, E, Tulsa
3. Graham, Joe, E, Florida
4. Wells, Don, T, Georgia
5. Stephenson, Casey, B, Tennessee
6. Collins, Toby, T, Tulsa
7. Dingler, Lamar, E, Arkansas
8. Helscher, Hal, B, LSU
9. Hammond, Ralph, C, Pittsburgh
10. Podgorski, Ed, T, Lafayette
11. Hackett, Bill, G, Ohio State
12. Lindsey, Marv, B, Arkansas
13. McClure, Robert (Buster), T, Nevada-Reno*
14. Pieper, Harry, C, California
15. Kula, Bob, B, Minnesota
16. Hazard, Frank, G, Nebraska
17. Jeffers, Ed, T, Oklahoma State
18. Prentice, Bill, B, Santa Clara
19. Fuller, Warren, E, Fordham
20. Neilsen, Fred, T, St. Mary's (California)

21. Gilmore, Bob, B, Washington
22. Baxter, Lloyd, C, SMU
23. Luhn, Nolan, E, Tulsa
24. Blanco, Nestor, G, Colorado Mines
25. Chestnut, Bill, B, Kansas
26. Thompson, Jim, B, Washington State
27. Evans, Jim, E, Idaho
28. Nichols, Ham, G, Rice*
29. Priday, John, B, Ohio State
30. Aldridge, Billy Joe, B, Oklahoma State

NY GIANTS
1. Barbour, Elmer, B, Wake Forest
2. Appleby, Gordon, C, Ohio State
3. Castleberry, Ed, B, West Texas State
4. Poole, Barney, E, Mississippi, Army
5. Mead, Jack, E, Wisconsin
6. Vodick, Nick, B, Northwestern
7. Rudan, John, B, Marquette
8. Smith, Vic, B, UCLA
9. Young, Jim, T, Arkansas
10. Bevis, Billy, B, Tennessee
11. Boozer, Bob, T, Arkansas
12. Rhoades, Stan, B, Mississippi State
13. Wink, Jack, B, Wisconsin
14. Little, Jim, T, Kentucky
15. Jabbusch, Bob, G, Ohio State
16. Byrd, Bill, C, Maryland
17. Morries, Glenn, T, Texas
18. Davis, Pete, B, Santa Clara
19. Vacanti, Sam, B, Iowa
20. Oliver, Vern, C, Washington State
21. Chadwell, Jim, T, Tennessee
22. Mroz, Vince, E, Michigan State
23. Kita, George, B, Drake
24. Graham, Doug, T, Stanford
25. Dillon, Jack, E, Texas Tech
26. J'Anthony, Charley, B, Brown
27. Pipkin, Ray, B, Arkansas
28. Wolf, Joe, C, USC
29. Broderick, T, Utah
30. Staples, John, G, Alabama

PHILADELPHIA
1. Yonaker, John, E, Notre Dame
2. Dark, Alvin, B, LSU
3. Pihos, Pete, E, Indiana
4. Dellago, Chuck, G, Minnesota
5. Gonzales, Morales, B, St. Mary's (California)
6. Robinson, Sam, B, Washington
7. Hall, Forrest, B, San Francisco
8. Sadonis, Joe, T, Fordham
9. Mobley, Rudy, B, Hardin-Simmons
10. Newmeyer, Jim, T, St. Vincent
11. Chambers, Bill, T, UCLA
12. Duda, John, B, Virginia*
13. Montgomery, Bill, B, LSU
14. Werner, Howard, E, Syracuse
15. Austin, Jim, B, Missouri
16. Klenk, Quentin, T, USC
17. Spencer, Joe, T, Oklahoma State
18. Pratt, Leo, T, Oklahoma State
19. Teschner, Phil, T, Brown
20. Magee, Johnny, G, Rice
21. Mosley, Norm, B, Alabama
22. Brown, Blair, G, Oklahoma State
23. Hall, Bob, E, Stanford
24. Talcott, Don, T, Nevada-Reno
25. Thompson, Bill, T, New Mexico
26. Fleming, Al, C, Wichita State
27. Benjamin, Leo, C, West Virginia
28. Dougherty, Jim, B, Miami (Ohio)
29. Reese, Ken, B, Alabama
30. Braner, Loren, C, Pittsburgh

PITTSBURGH
1. Duhart, Paul, B, Florida
2. Dugger, Jack, E, Ohio State
3. Dellastatious, Bill, B, Missouri*
4. Adams, Roger, C, Florida*
5. Mehelich, Chuck, E, Duquesne
6. Browning, Greg, E, Denver
7. Wolak, Mike, B, Duquesne
8. Hughes, Tom, T, Missouri
9. Pense, Leon, B, Arkansas
10. Brandau, Art, C, Tennessee
11. Ball, Ray, B, Holy Cross
12. Basilone, Frank, B, Duquesne*
13. Monahan, John, E, Dartmouth
14. Odelli, Mel, B, Duquesne
15. Connor, George, T, Notre Dame*
16. Ungles, Jim, B, Kansas State
17. Itzel, John, B, Pittsburgh
18. Wizbicki, Alex, B, Holy Cross
19. Landrigan, Jim, T, Dartmouth
20. Lilienthal, Bill, T, Villanova
21. Price, Art, B, Rutgers

22. Malmberg, Don, B, UCLA
23. Hartwell, Everett, E, Auburn
24. Cain, Ed, B, Rice
25. Carlaccini, Angelo, B, Pittsburgh
26. Burns, Ed, B, Boston College
27. Stough, Glen, T, Duke
28. Marsh, Jim, T, Oklahoma State
29. Grant, Ralph, B, Bucknell*
30. Kondrla, John, T, St. Vincent

WASHINGTON
1. Hardy, Jim, QB, USC
2. Adams, John (Tree), T, Notre Dame
3. Bujan, George, C, Oregon
4. North, Johnny, E, Vanderbilt
5. Steber, John, G, Georgia Tech
6. Porter, Art, E, Tulane
7. Kuykendall, Curt, B, Auburn
8. Brogger, Frank, E, Michigan State
9. Creger, Mack, B, Northwestern
10. McKee, Paul, E, Syracuse
11. Conerly, Charlie, QB, Mississippi
12. Putnik, John, E, Utah State
13. Saenz, Eddie, B, USC
14. Fusci, Dom, T, South Carolina
15. Jenkins, Bobby Tom, B, Alabama
16. Stacco, Ed, T, Colgate*
17. Bradshaw, Jim, C, Auburn
18. Shipkey, Bill, B, Stanford
19. Halliday, Sid, T, SMU
20. Davidson, Chick, T, Cornell*
21. Martin, Gabby, E, SMU
22. McCurdy, Jim, C, Stanford
23. Souders, Cecil (Cy), E, Ohio State
24. Wall, Ben, B, Western Michigan*
25. Hillery, George, E, Texas-El Paso
26. Dreblow, Milford, B, USC
27. Irwin, Frank, T, Duke*
28. Diner, Leon, E, Denver
29. Cummings, Bob, C, Vanderbilt
30. Nolander, Don, T, Minnesota

1946
Held January 14, 1946

BOSTON
1. Dancewicz, Frank (Boley), QB, Notre Dame
2. Scollard, Nick, E, St. Joseph's (Indiana)
3. McClure, Robert (Buster), T, Nevada-Reno
4. Breslin, Jack, B, Michigan State
5. Bourgeois, Gaston, B, Tulane
6. Tigart, Thurman, G, Oklahoma
7. Mieszkowski, Ed, T, Notre Dame
8. Lipka, Chet, E, Boston College
9. Dekdebrun, Al, B, Cornell
10. John, Rex, T, Wisconsin
11. West, Bob, B, Colorado
12. Dodge, Max, E, Nevada-Reno
13. Kirkland, Joe, T, Virginia
14. Ventresco, Ralph, B, Penn State
15. Furey, John, T, Boston College
16. Swiacki, Bill, E, Columbia
17. Tiedeman, Charley, B, Brown
18. Alverez, Don, G, Dartmouth
19. Burns, Jack, B, Temple
20. Ruggerio, Frank, B, Notre Dame
21. Price, Jack, B, Baylor
22. Igleheart, Elliot (Ike), G, Tulane
23. Levitt, Bill, C, Miami
24. Karmazin, Mike, E, Duke
25. Latcham, Chet, G, Denver
26. Botsford, Gordon, E, Boston U.
27. Kauffman, John, G, Oregon
28. Glaesner, Don, E, Maryland
29. McKinnon, Carl, G, Dartmouth
30. Klutka, Nick, E, Florida

CHI. BEARS
1. Lujack, Johnny, QB, Notre Dame
2. Rykovich, Julie, B, Illinois
3. Broyles, Frank, QB, Georgia Tech
4. Knotts, Ernie, G, Duke
5. Schneider, Don, B, Pennsylvania
6. Scruggs, Ted, E, Rice
7. Beard, Wendell, T, California
8. Ziegler, John, B, Colorado
9. Dropo, Walt, E, Connecticut
10. Harris, Bill, C, Auburn
11. Allen, Eddie, B, Pennsylvania
12. Bauman, Frank, E, Illinois
13. Nostrum, Reed, T, Utah
14. Chatterton, Dick, B, BYU
15. Timko, Johnny, C, Temple
16. Hazelwood, Ted, T, North Carolina
17. Johnson, Dick, C, Baylor

18. Boettcher, Art, B, Shurtleff
19. Gallagher, Tom, B, Illinois
20. Adams, Johnny, B, Denver
21. Widseth, Dean, T, Bemidji State
22. Kochins, George, T, Bucknell
23. Hoisch, Al, B, Stanford
24. Grgich, Visco, E, Santa Clara
25. Richards, Allen, B, Cincinnati
26. Tunstill, Jess, B, Kentucky
27. Smock, Ken, B, Purdue
28. Weldon, Howard, G, North Carolina
29. Cook, Johnny, B, Georgia
30. Franck, Harry, B, Northwestern

CHI. CARDINALS
1. Jones, Dub, B, Tulane
2. Wenskunas, Mac, C, Illinois
3. Angsman, Elmer, B, Notre Dame
4. Nichols, Ham, G, Rice
5. Golding, Joe, B, Oklahoma
6. Dickey, Len, T, Texas A&M
7. Lenshan, Pat, E, Tennessee
8. Tinsley, Phil, E, Alabama
9. Colhouer, J.C., G, Oklahoma State
10. Barber, Tom, T, Tennessee-Chattanooga
11. Loepfe, Dick, T, Wisconsin
12. Yablonski, Venton, B, Columbia
13. Lewis, Lee, B, Washington
14. Russell, Bob, B, Miami (Ohio)
15. Rovai, Fred, G, Notre Dame
16. Evans, Ray, T, Texas-El Paso
17. Loubie, Bob, B, Miami (Ohio)
18. Irwin, Frank, T, Duke
19. Ratteree, Pride, G, Wake Forest
20. Heywood, Bill, B, Notre Dame
21. Traught, Al, B, Miami (Ohio)
22. Andrulewicz, Clem, T, Villanova
23. Rakowski, Adam, E, Pennsylvania
24. McKenzie, Jack, B, Northwestern
25. Worthington, Tom,T, Tulsa
26. Vugrin, Jim, G, Tennessee
27. Herschbarger, Jesse, E, SMU
28. Ledbetter, Newman, T, Texas Tech
29. Baldwin, Alton, E, Arkansas
30. LaRue, Jim, B, Duke

DETROIT
1. Dellastatious, Bill, B, Missouri
2. Thomas, Russ, T, Ohio State*
3. Harris, Dave, E, Wake Forest
4. Eddins, Joe, G, Auburn
5. Berezney, Pete, T, Notre Dame
6. DeCourcey, Keith, B, Washington
7. Hedges, Bill, T, West Texas State
8. Dixon, Thornton, T, Ohio State
9. Stevens, Bob, B, Oregon State
10. Farris, Pat, T, Texas Tech
11. Copoulos, Paul, B, Marquette
12. Irby, Ty, B, Auburn
13. Thrash, Pat, E, South Carolina
14. Mote, Kelly, E, Duke
15. Scrugg, Bill, B, Rice
16. Wall, Ben, B, Central Michigan
17. Kispert, Merlin, B, Minnesota
18. Malmberg, Don, T, UCLA
19. Maloney, Norm, E, Purdue
20. Simmons, Jack, B, Detroit
21. Pulte, Joe, E, Detroit
22. Funderberg, Bob, B, Northwestern
23. Stacco, Ed, T, Colgate
24. Anderson, Roger, G, Oregon State
25. Murdock, Chuck, E, Georgia Tech
26. Van Duesen, Dick, C, Minnesota
27. Agnew, Bill, B, California
28. Panos, Tom, G, Utah
29. Palesse, Orlando, E, Marquette
30. Schellstede, Otis, G, Oklahoma State

GREEN BAY
1. Strzykalski, Johnny (Strike), B, Marquette
2. Nussbaumer, Bob, B, Michigan
3. Cody, Ed, B, Purdue
4. Ferraro, John, T, USC
5. Renner, Art, E, Michigan
6. Cole, Bert, T, Oklahoma State
7. Darnell, Grant, G, Texas A&M
8. McAfee, Joe, B, Holy Cross
9. Conroy, Steve, B, Holy Cross
10. Hildebrand, Billy, E, Mississippi State
11. Hand, Tom, C, Iowa
12. Hills, George, G, Georgia Tech
13. Hough, Jim, B, Clemson
14. Gaines, Dean, T, Georgia Tech
15. Miller, J.P., G, Georgia
16. Morse, Boyd, E, Arizona
17. Bradford, Joe, C, USC
18. DeRosa, Bill, B, Boston College
19. Grant, Ralph, B, Bucknell
20. Brown, Howard, G, Indiana
21. Kosmac, Andy, C, LSU
22. Stacy, Maurice, B, Washington
23. Davidson, Chick, T, Cornell
24. Norton, John, B, Washington
25. Holtsinger, Ed, B, Georgia Tech
26. Campbell, Joe, E, Holy Cross
27. Saunders, Francis, T, Clemson
28. Sparlis, Al, G, UCLA
29. Clymer, Ralph, G, Purdue
30. Henderson, Joervin, C, Missouri

LA RAMS
1. Sitko, Emil (Red), B, Notre Dame
2. Samuel, Don, B, Oregon State
3. Paul, Don, C, UCLA*
4. Oestreich, Newell (Ace), B, California
5. King, Lafayette (Dolly), E, Georgia
6. Whisler, Joe, B, Ohio State
7. Schumchyk, Mike, E, Arkansas
8. Signaigo, Joe, G, Notre Dame
9. Phillips, Tom, B, Ohio State
10. Strojny, Ted, T, Holy Cross
11. Strohmeyer, George, C, Notre Dame
12. Palladino, Bob, B, Notre Dame
13. Lorenz, Dick, E, Oregon State
14. Bouley, Larry, B, Georgia
15. Urban, Gasper, G, Notre Dame
16. Wise, Bob, G, Colorado
17. Ford, Jerry, E, Notre Dame
18. Albrecht, Bob, B, Marquette
19. Lewis, Cliff, B, Duke
20. Richardson, Bob, T, Marquette
21. Lebow, Derald, B, Oklahoma
22. Lippincott, Bill, B, Washington State
23. Jamison, Kay, E, Florida
24. Gambrell, D.J., C, Alabama
25. Dickey, Joe Ben, B, Colorado
26. Grbovaz, Marty, E, San Francisco
27. Perrin, Jay, T, USC
28. Plant, Frank, C, Georgia
29. Cowan, Dale, T, Kansas State
30. West, John, B, Oklahoma

NY GIANTS
1. Connor, George, T, Notre Dame
2. Jones, Elmer, G, Wake Forest
3. Rodgers, Hosea, B, North Carolina
4. Duke, Paul, C, Georgia Tech
5. Stout, Pete, B, TCU
6. Lalikos, Jim, T, Brown
7. Plyler, Jim, T, Texas
8. Roberts, Gene (Choo-Choo), B, Tennessee-Chattanooga
9. Harris, Mike, G, Mississippi State
10. Clay, Walt, B, Colorado
11. Amling, Warren, G, Ohio State
12. Bush, Al, T, Duke
13. Reiman, Bob, B, Oregon State
14. Hazelhurst, Bob, B, Denver
15. Stapley, Stan, T, Utah
16. Terlizzi, Nick, T, Alabama
17. Justak, Ray, G, Northwestern
18. Morris, Bob, B, USC
19. Loflin, Tom, E, LSU
20. Kelly, Dick, B, Minnesota
21. Patton, Mel, B, Santa Clara
22. Stiers, Bill, B, UCLA
23. Hare, Vernon, B, Santa Clara
24. Scully, Neil, B, Dayton
25. Miller, George, T, Denver
26. White, Barney, E, Tulsa
27. Kalens, Butch, G, Illinois
28. Ellis, Charlie, B, Virginia
29. Lucas, Steve, E, Duke
30. Voris, Bill, B, North Carolina

PHILADELPHIA
1. Riggs, Leo, B, USC
2. Gray, Gordon, E, USC
3. Slater, Walt, B, Tennessee
4. Prewitt, Felto, C, Tulsa
5. Robotham, George, E, UCLA
6. Lecture, Jim, G, Northwestern
7. Lewis, Ernie, B, Colorado
8. Vandeweghe, Al, E, William & Mary
9. Iancelli, Bill, E, Franklin & Marshall
10. McHugh, Pat, P, Georgia Tech
11. Wingender, John, B, Washington
12. Paine, Homer, T, Tulsa
13. Kerns, John, T, Ohio U.
14. Hubbard, Buddy, B, William & Mary
15. Smith, Allen, B, Tulsa
16. Millham, Bernie, E, Fordham
17. Mauss, Lawrence, C, Utah
18. Butcher, Dave, B, William & Mary
19. Fabling, Don, B, Colorado
20. Feldman, George, B, Tufts
21. Cameron, Ed, G, Miami (Ohio)
22. Steed, Charley, B, Arkansas-Monticello
23. Grygiel, Ed, B, Dartmouth
24. Raimondi, Ben, B, Indiana*
25. Bailey, Sam, E, Georgia
26. Long, Bob, B, Tennessee
27. Fisher, Bill, T, Harvard
28. Slusser, George, B, Ohio State
29. Itzel, John, B, Pittsburgh
30. Kirkman, Larry, B, Boston U.

PITTSBURGH
1. Blanchard, Felix (Doc), B, Army
2. Clark, George, B, Duke
3. Rowe, Harmon, B, San Francisco
4. Tepsic, Joe, B, Penn State
5. Seiferling, Jack, B, Utah State
6. Woods, Marion, G, Clemson
7. Reinhardt, Tom, T, Minnesota
8. Ponsetto, Joe, B, Michigan
9. Evans, Bob, B, Pennsylvania
10. Bonwell, Mel, B, Central (Iowa)
11. Holloway, Doc, G, William & Mary
12. Owen, Carroll, B, Catawba
13. Poppin, George, T, New Mexico
14. McCain, Bob, E, Mississippi
15. Tallchief, Tom, T, Oklahoma
16. Perl, Al, B, Youngstown State
17. Lopez, Russ, C, West Virginia
18. Garrison, Charles (Buck), G, Wake Forest
19. Cloud, Bill, T, Temple
20. Garbinski, Mike, B, Penn State
21. Loiacano, Charley, C, Lafayette
22. Johnson, George, T, Pittsburgh
23. Leitheiser, Bill, G, Duke
24. Adams, Roger, C, Florida
25. Verkins, Bob, B, Tulsa
26. Castle, Clarence, B, Mississippi
27. Marino, Marchi, T, Penn State
28. Hansen, Bob, E, UCLA
29. Graves, Larry, T, Newberry
30. Bruce, Gail, E, Washington

WASHINGTON
1. Rossi, Cal, B, UCLA*
2. Koslowski, Stan, B, Holy Cross
3. Adelt, Gay, B, Utah
4. Trojanowski, Walt, B, Connecticut
5. Hendren, Bob, T, Culver-Stockton
6. Callanan, George, B, USC
7. Skoglund, Bob, E, Notre Dame
8. Leicht, Jake, B, Oregon
9. Maggioli, Achille (Chick), B, Illinois
10. Moncrief, Monte, T, Texas A&M*
11. Tereshinski, Joe, E, Georgia
12. Sprague, Stan, E, Illinois
13. Adelman, Harry, E, USC
14. Butchofsky, Bob, B, Texas A&M
15. Prashaw, Mike, T, Michigan
16. Robnett, Ed, B, Texas Tech
17. Dykstra, LaMar, B, Colorado
18. Ward, Bob, B, San Jose State
19. Pehar, John, T, USC
20. Robinson, Roger, B, Syracuse
21. Cadenhead, Charley, C, Mississippi State
22. Rodas, Bob, G, Santa Clara
23. Webb, Charlie, E, LSU
24. Flanagan, Marion, B, Texas A&M
25. Phillips, Roland, T, Georgia Tech
26. Hallmark, Jim, B, Texas A&M
27. Mills, Fay, T, Alabama
28. Ritter, William (Tex), B, Georgia Tech
29. Takesian, Sarkis, B, California
30. Campbell, Mike, E, Mississippi

1947 NFL
Held December 16, 1946

BOSTON
1. Barzilauskas, Fritz, G, Yale
2. Heap, Walt, B, Texas
3. Rapacz, John, C, Oklahoma
4. Baldwin, Alton, E, Arkansas
5. Vogelaar, Carroll, T, San Francisco
6. Sullivan, George, T, Notre Dame
7. Watt, Joe, B, Syracuse
8. Chipley, Bill, E, Washington & Lee
9. Malinowski, Gene, C, Detroit
10. Hazelhurst, Bob, B, Denver
11. Sidorik, Al, T, Mississippi State
12. Roberts, Wally, E, Holy Cross
13. Sullivan, Bob, B, Iowa
14. Long, Leo, B, Duke
15. Parker, Frank, T, Holy Cross
16. Marcolini, Hugo, B, St. Bonaventure
17. Shirley, Marion, T, Oklahoma City
18. Nabors, Roland, C, Texas Tech
19. Kennelly, Pat, E, Southeastern Louisiana
20. Waller, Darrell, B, Washington State
21. Hart, Paul, B, Delaware
22. Lamoure, Gene, G, Fresno State
23. Kolaskinski, Hank, B, Wyoming
24. Heap, Ed, T, Texas
25. Polzin, John, G, TCU
26. Bloxom, Dave, B, TCU
27. Stautzenberger, Odell, G, Texas A&M
28. Chatterton, Dick, B, BYU
29. Rodgers, Tom, T, Bucknell
30. Prchlik, John, G, Yale

CHI. BEARS
BONUS CHOICE: Fenimore, Bob, B, Oklahoma State
1. Kindt, Don, B, Wisconsin
2. Minini, Frank, B, San Jose State
3. Canady, Jim, B, Texas
   Merriman, Lloyd, B, Stanford, from Chi. Cardinals
4. Wetz, Harlan, T, Texas
   Stephens, Roger, B, Cincinnati, from Philadelphia
5. Moseley, Reid, E, Georgia
6. Smith, H.A., E, Mississippi
7. Eddleman, Dwight (Dike), B, Illinois
8. Tucker, Arnold, B, Army
9. Hatch, Larry, B, Washington
10. Adamle, Tony, C, Ohio State
11. Fritz, Emil, G, Maryland
12. Turner, Jim, T, California
13. Goodall, Wayne, E, Oklahoma City
14. Gagne, Verne, E, Minnesota
15. Dreyer, Wally, B, Wisconsin
16. Pupa, Walt, B, North Carolina
17. McLellan, John, T, Montana State
18. Cromer, Bill, B, Texas
19. Reader, Russ, B, Michigan State
20. Batchelor, Jim, B, East Texas State
21. Lawler, Allen, B, Texas
22. Berlin, Gordon, C, Washington
23. Cunningham, John, E, California
24. Morris, Max, B, Northwestern
25. Morris, Bill, E, Oklahoma
26. Baumgardner, Joe Bill, B, Texas
27. McCarthy, Jerry, E, Pennsylvania
28. Pierce, Jack, B, Illinois
29. Ehlers, Ed, B, Purdue

CHI. CARDINALS
1. Coulter, DeWitt (Tex), T, Army
2. Allen, Ermal, B, Kentucky
3. Choice to Chi. Bears
4. Raimondi, Ben, B, Indiana
5. Turner, Howard, B, North Carolina State
6. Maddock, George, T, Northwestern
7. Dufelmeier, Art, B, Illinois
8. Ramsey, Ray, B, Bradley
9. Wallace, Dave, B, Oklahoma
10. Sarratt, Charley, B, Oklahoma
11. Cooper, Hardin, T, Tulsa
12. Russ, Carl, B, Rice*
13. Mulligan, Buddy, B, Duke
14. Smith, Charlie, B, Georgia
15. Ravensburg, Bob, E, Indiana
16. Barnett, Barney, E, Northeastern Oklahoma
17. Deeds, Scotty, B, BYU
18. Esser, Clarence, T, Wisconsin
19. Ballard, Shelton, C, LSU
20. Walker, Wade, T, Oklahoma
21. Carroll, Tom, T, Minnesota
22. Dorsey, Tom, B, Brown
23. Schnellbacher, Otto, E, Kansas
24. Joe, Larry, B, Penn State
25. Abrams, Dick, B, Washington State
26. Smith, Joe, E, Texas Tech
27. Rotunno, Tony, B, St. Ambrose
28. Lindsey, Clyde, E, LSU
29. Callahan, Bob, C, Michigan
30. Karamigios, Johnny, B, Denver

DETROIT
1. Davis, Glenn, B, Army
2. Thomas, Russ, T, Ohio State
3. Kekeris, Jim, T, Missouri
4. Hoover, Charley, C, Vanderbilt
5. Chappuis, Bob, B, Michigan
6. Gallagher, Bernie, T, Pennsylvania
7. Grain, Ed, G, Pennsylvania
8. James, Harvey, C, Miami
9. Alexander, Kale, T, South Carolina
10. Elliott, Chalmers (Bump), B, Michigan
11. Sullivan, Pete, T, Detroit
12. Camaratta, LaVerne, B, Iowa State

13. Vezmar, Walt, G, Michigan State
14. Hagen, Dick, E, Washington
15. Meeks, J.W., B, East Texas State
16. Nilsen, Reed, C, BYU
17. James, Tommy, B, Ohio State
18. Maugham, Ralph, E, Utah State
19. Baty, Buryl, B, Texas A&M
20. Madar, Elmer, E, Michigan
21. White, J.T., E, Michigan
22. Schuette, Carl, B, Marquette
23. Cipot, Steve, T, St. Bonaventure
24. Cadenhead, Bill, B, Alabama
25. Cody, Jim, T, East Texas State
26. Maves, Earl, B, Wisconsin
27. Hillman, Bill, B, Tennessee
28. Kelly, Arch, E, Detroit
29. Tulis, Bob, T, Texas A&M
30. McAfee, Howard, T, Tulane

GREEN BAY
1. Case, Ernie, B, UCLA
2. Baldwin, Burr, E, UCLA
3. Burris, Paul (Buddy), G, Oklahoma
4. Wilson, Gene, E, SMU
5. Connors, Dick, B, Northwestern
6. Moncrief, Monte, T, Texas A&M
7. McDougal, Bob, B, Miami
8. Kelly, Bob, B, Notre Dame
9. Moulton, Tom, C, Oklahoma State
10. Hills, George, G, Georgia Tech
11. Skoglund, Bob, E, Notre Dame
12. Mitchell, Jack, B, Oklahoma
13. Crawford, Denver, T, Tennessee
14. Callanan, Jim, E, USC
15. Scalissi, Ted, B, Ripon
16. Goodman, Jim, T, Indiana
17. Miller, Dick, G, Lawrence
18. Ecklund, Brad (Whitey), C, Oregon
19. West, Bob, B, Colorado
20. Reilly, Tex, B, Colorado
21. Sockolov, Ron, T, California
22. St. John, Herb, G, Georgia
23. Redeker, Fred, B, Cincinnati
24. Lubker, Herm, E, Arkansas
25. Palladino, Bob, B, Notre Dame
26. Baxter, Jerrell, T, North Carolina
27. Sellers, Ray, E, Georgia
28. Carle, Jerry, B, Northwestern
29. Hogan, Bill, B, Kansas
30. Olsen, Ralph, E, Utah

LA RAMS
1. Wedemeyer, Herman, B, St. Mary's (California)
2. Paul, Don, C, UCLA
3. Gray, Gordon, B, USC
4. Evenson, Paul, T, Oregon State
5. Smyth, Bill, T, Cincinnati
6. McGovern, Bill, C, Washington
7. Partin, Max, B, Tennessee
8. Samuelson, Carl, T, Nebraska
9. Steger, Russ, B, Illinois*
10. Lavelli, Dante, E, Ohio State
11. Dimitro, Mike, G, UCLA
12. Kissell, John, T, Boston College
13. Fuchs, George, B, Wisconsin
14. Chubb, Ralph, B, Michigan
15. Hardy, Don, E, USC
16. Champagne, Ed, T, LSU
17. Dewar, Jimmy, B, Indiana
18. Reiges, Bernie, B, UCLA
19. McLaughlin, Leon, C, UCLA
20. Elliott, Charley, T, Oregon
21. Levanti, Lou, C, Illinois
22. Cheek, J.D., T, Oklahoma State*
23. Dal Porto, Bob, B, California
24. Standefer, Gene, B, Texas Tech
25. David, Bob, B, Villanova

NY GIANTS
1. Schwall, Vic, B, Northwestern
2. Cannady, John, C, Indiana
3. Greene, Nelson, T, Tulsa
4. Davis, Bob, T, Georgia Tech
5. Iversen, Chris (Duke), B, Oregon
6. Muelheuser, Frank, B, Colgate
7. Novitsky, John, T, Oklahoma City
8. Mullis, Fred, B, Tennessee-Chattanooga
9. Hoernschemeyer, Bob (Hunchy), B, Indiana
10. Brown, Hardy (Thumper), B, Tulsa*
11. Hachten, Bill, G, Stanford
12. Fuson, Herschel (Ug), B, Army
13. Fallon, John, T, Notre Dame
14. Orlando, Bob, G, Colgate
15. Pullatie, Frank, B, SMU
16. Brinkley, Dick, B, Wake Forest
17. Guess, Frank, B, Texas
18. Landry, Tom, B, Texas, F
19. Ponsetto, Joe, B, Michigan
20. Donovan, Art, T, Boston College
21. Schoener, Hal, E, Iowa
22. Moll, Bill, B, Connecticut
23. Thomas, Dick, G, Southern Mississippi
24. Stewart, Ralph, C, Notre Dame
25. Bibighaus, George, E, Muhlenberg

PHILADELPHIA
1. Armstrong, Neill, E, Oklahoma State
2. Mackrides, Bill, B, Nevada-Reno
3. Savitsky, George, T, Pennsylvania
4. Choice to Chi. Bears
5. Yovicsin, Tony, E, Miami
6. Satterfield, Alf, T, Vanderbilt
7. Leonetti, Bob, G, Wake Forest
8. Cornogg, Ulysses, T, Wake Forest
9. Sarkisian, Alex, C, Northwestern
10. D'Arcy, Jerry, C, Tulsa
11. Hamberger, John, T, SMU
12. Johnson, Alvin, B, Hardin-Simmons
13. Cook, Joe, B, Hardin-Simmons
14. Durkota, Jeff, B, Penn State, F
15. Shurtz, Hubert, T, LSU
16. Bell, Hal, B, Muhlenberg
17. Campion, Tom, T, Southeastern Louisiana
18. Hall, Fred, G, LSU
19. Clayton, Jim, T, Wyoming
20. Blomquist, George, E, North Carolina State
21. Haynes, Joe, G, Tulsa
22. Hense, Stanton, E, Xavier
23. Kelly, Johnny, B, Rice
24. Roberts, H.J., G, Rice
25. Cutchin, Phil, B, Kentucky
26. Wakefield, Charley, T, Stanford
27. Lagenbeck, Dick, T, Cincinnati
28. Winkler, Bernie, T, Texas Tech
29. Stephens, Bill, T, Baylor
30. Kalash, Mike, E, Wisconsin-La Crosse

PITTSBURGH
1. Bechtol, Hub, E, Texas
2. Mastrangelo, John, G, Notre Dame
3. Wydo, Frank, T, Cornell
4. Aschenbrenner, Frank, B, Northwestern
5. Meeks, Bryant (Meatball), C, South Carolina
6. Shipkey, Jerry, B, UCLA
7. Vander Clute, Bert, G, Wesleyan
8. Gibson, Paul, E, North Carolina State
9. Medd, Jack, C, Wesleyan
10. Fitch, Jack, B, North Carolina
11. Parseghian, Ara, B, Miami (Ohio), F
12. Moore, Bill (Red), T, Penn State
13. Bruno, Larry, B, Geneva
14. Jenkins, Ralph, C, Clemson
15. Nickel, Elbie, E, Cincinnati
16. Cregar, Bill, C, Holy Cross
17. Mulready, Jerry, B, North Dakota State
18. Smith, Warren, T, Kansas Wesleyan
19. Hamilton, Fred, T, Vanderbilt
20. Taylor, Fred, E, TCU
21. Bushmaier, Binks, B, Vanderbilt
22. Davis, Paul, B, Otterbein
23. Kalmanir, Tommy (Cricket), B, Nevada-Reno, F
24. Mohr, Don, E, Baldwin-Wallace
25. Young, Art, G, Dartmouth
26. Sazio, Ralph, T, William & Mary
27. Pitzer, Dick, E, Army
28. Stalloni, Tom, T, Delaware
29. DiFrancesca, Vince, G, Northwestern
30. Lahr, Warren, B, Case Western Reserve

WASHINGTON
1. Rossi, Cal, B, UCLA
2. Knight, Gene (Red), B, LSU
3. Foldberg, Hank, E, Army
4. Garzoni, Mike, G, USC
5. Gray, Bill, C, Oregon State
6. Harris, Hank, T, Texas
7. Karrasch, Roy, E, UCLA
8. Williamson, Ernie, T, North Carolina
9. Carmody, L.G., B, Central Washington
10. Savage, U.S., E, Richmond
11. Steckroth, Bob, E, William & Mary
12. Edwards, Weldon, T, TCU
13. Wheeler, Earl, C, Arkansas
14. Gold, Billy, B, Tennessee
15. Hart, Jack, T, Detroit
16. Nichols, Tom, B, Richmond
17. Dowda, Harry, B, Wake Forest
18. Webb, Charlie, E, LSU
19. Bond, Elmo, T, Washington State
20. Hefti, Jim, B, St. Lawrence
21. Dudley, Tom, E, Virginia
22. Smith, Jim, B, Iowa
23. Mullins, Hal, T, Duke
24. Bocoka, Francis, E, Washington State
25. Sacrinty, Otis, B, Wake Forest
26. Dropo, Milt, C, Connecticut
27. Brownson, Lynn, B, Stanford
28. Colone, Joe, B, Penn State
29. Schoener, Herb, E, Iowa
30. Plevo, Bob, T, Purdue

1947 AAFC
Held December 20-21, 1946

The AAFC's first draft was held in the same manner as the NFL draft—teams drafting in inverse order of finish. Buffalo, which had finished the 1946 season with the same record as Brooklyn, drafted second in each round, however, with Brooklyn drafting third. Although Miami was no longer in the league by the time the 1947 season was played, it was at the time of the draft. Miami's selections later were granted to the new Baltimore Colts. Prior to the regular draft, "special selections" were made. It is not known why these selections weren't part of the regular draft or in what order they were made. All teams had two, except Buffalo, which had five, and the Los Angeles Dons and San Francisco, which had one each. Most likely, Los Angeles and San Francisco each traded one of its choices to Buffalo. The regular draft was 15 rounds, followed by a "supplemental draft," in which various teams didn't get choices. From rounds 16 through 20, Cleveland and the New York Yankees didn't make selections. From rounds 21 through 25, Cleveland, New York, San Francisco, and Los Angeles didn't receive selections. Like current NFL drafts, the AAFC drafts indicated an overall order of selection, which is shown by a number after each player's school.

BROOKLYN
Blanchard, Felix (Doc), FB, Army
Roberts, Gene (Choo-Choo), B, Tennessee-Chattanooga
1. Armstrong, Neill, E, Oklahoma State, 3
2. Conerly, Charlie, QB, Mississippi, 11
3. Barzilauskas, Fritz, G, Yale, 19
4. Wright, Jim, G, SMU, 27
5. Wetz, Harlan, T, Texas, 35
6. Bushmaier, Binks, B, Vanderbilt, 43
7. Williams, Garland, T, Georgia, 51
8. Hefti, Jim, B, St. Lawrence, 59
9. Burris, Paul (Buddy), G, Oklahoma, 67
10. Milner, Bill, G, Duke, 75
11. Smith, Jim, T, Colorado, 83
12. Goodman, Marv, E, Willamette, 91
13. Scruggs, Ted, E, Rice, 99
14. Nelsen, Reed, C, BYU, 107
15. Shannon, Gus, G, Colorado, 115
16. Cook, Joe, B, Hardin-Simmons, 123
17. Laurinaitas, Frank, G, Richmond, 129
18. Gustafson, Edsel, C, George Washington, 135
19. Hagen, Dick, E, Washington, 141
20. Foldberg, Hank, E, Army, 147
21. Furman, Harry, T, Cornell, 153
22. Kretz, Walt, B, Cornell, 157
23. Monahan, John, E, Dartmouth, 161
24. Bailey, Bruce, B, Virginia, 165
25. Evans, Ray, B,Texas-El Paso, 169

BUFFALO
Fenimore, Bob, B, Oklahoma State
Aschenbrenner, Frank, B, Northwestern
Richardson, Cal, E, Tulsa
Cochran, John (Red), B, Wake Forest
1. Baldwin, Alton, E, Arkansas, 2
2. Davis, Bob, T, Georgia Tech, 10
3. Kuffel, Ray, E, Marquette, 18
4. Andrejko, Joe, B, Fordham, 26
5. Mastrangelo, John, G, Notre Dame, 34
6. Corley, Elbert, C, Mississippi State, 42
7. Knotts, Ernie, G, Duke, 50
8. Watt, Joe, B, Syracuse, 58
9. Gibson, Paul, E, North Carolina State, 66
10. Maskas, John, T, Virginia Tech, 74
11. Jarrell, Baxter, T, North Carolina, 82
12. Liptka, Chet, T, Boston College, 90
13. Sowinski, Joe, G, Indiana, 98
14. Chipley, Bill, E, Washington & Lee, 106
15. Kosanovich, Bronco, C, Penn State, 114
16. Kosikowski, Frank, E, Notre Dame, 122
17. Serini, Wash, T, Kentucky, 128
18. Yablonski, Ventan, B, Columbia, 134
19. Compton, Chuck, T, Alabama, 140
20. Swiacki, Bill, E, Columbia, 146
21. Nichols, Hamilton, G, Rice, 152
22. Furey, John, T, Boston College, 156
23. Schneider, Don, B, Pennsylvania, 160
24. Highsmith, Chan, C, North Carolina, 164
25. Wydo, Frank, T, Cornell, 168

CHI. ROCKETS
Lujack, Johnny, QB, Notre Dame
Gallagher, Bernie, T, Pennsylvania
1. Sullivan, George, T, Notre Dame, 4
2. Manieri, Ray, B, Wake Forest, 12
3. Derleth, Bob, T, Michigan, 20
4. Reagan, Johnny, B, Montana State, 28
5. Pharr, Jim, C, Auburn, 36
6. Sandberg, Bob, B, Minnesota, 44
7. Allen, Ed, B, Pennsylvania, 52
8. Bolger, Matt, E, Notre Dame, 60
9. Eikenberg, Virgil, B, Rice, 68
10. Allen, Ermal, QB, Kentucky, 76
11. Chaves, Marty, G, Oregon State, 84
12. Jernigan, George, G, Georgia, 92
13. Jordan, R.J., E, Georgia Tech, 100
14. Livingstone, Bob, B, Notre Dame, 108
15. Ivy, Bill, T, Northwestern, 116
16. Niedziela, Bruno, T, Iowa, 124
17. Mackrides, Bill, QB, Nevada-Reno, 130
18. Wenskunas, Mac, C, Illinois, 136
19. Graham, Tony, C, St. Mary's (Minnesota), 142
20. Benda, Russ, G, Iowa, 148
21. Watkins, George, T, Texas, 154
22. Vacanti, Sam, B, Nebraska, 158
23. Zenkevitch, Len, T, Idaho, 162
24. Day, Dave, G, Iowa, 166
25. Franks, Bill, T, Illinois, 170

CLEVELAND
Hoerner, Dick, B, Iowa
Rice, Robert Lawrence, C, Tulane
1. Chappuis, Bob, B, Michigan, 8
2. Cowhig, Gerry, B, Notre Dame, 16
3. Carpenter, Jack, T, Missouri, Michigan, 24
4. Cowan, Bob, B, Indiana, 32
5. Griffen, Bill, T, Kentucky, 40
6. Bush, Jack, T, Georgia, 48
7. Rapacz, John, C, Oklahoma, 56
8. Hazelhurst, Al, B, Denver, 64
9. Ellsworth, Ralph, B, Texas, 72
10. Dewar, Jim, H. Indiana, 80
11. Huber, Bill, E, Illinois, 88
12. Giannella, Mario, G, Boston College, 96
13. Shurnas, Marshall, E, Missouri, 104
14. Signaigo, Joe, B, Notre Dame, 112
15. Widseth, Dean, T, Minnesota, 120

LA DONS
Wedemeyer, Herman, B, St. Mary's (California)
1. Baldwin, Burr, E, UCLA, 5
2. Skipkey, Jerry, B, UCLA, 13
3. Merriman, Lloyd, B, Stanford, 21
4. Rossi, Cal, B, UCLA, 29
5. Clement, Boyd, T, Oregon State, 37
6. Zapalac, Willie, B, Texas A&M, 45
7. Savitsky, George, T, Pennsylvania, 53
8. Paul, Don, C, UCLA, 61
9. Hart, Paul, B, Delaware, 69
10. Heap, Walt, QB, Texas, 77
11. Dimitro, Mike, G, UCLA, 85
12. Moore, Bill, T, Penn State, 93
13. Martin, Joe, B, Cornell, 101
14. Wilson, Eugene, E, SMU, 109
15. Muelheuser, Frank, B, Colgate, 117
16. Cody, Ed, B, Purdue, 125
17. Sullivan, Bob, B, Iowa, 131
18. Cullen, Louis, B, New Mexico, 137
19. Killelea, John, B, Boston College, 143
20. Andros, Dee, G, Oklahoma, 149

MIAMI
Tucker, Arnold, QB, Army
Case, Ernie, B, UCLA
1. Madar, Elmer, E, Michigan, 1
2. Bechtol, Hub, E, Texas, 9
3. Mont, Tommy, B, Maryland, 17
4. Humble, Weldon, G, Rice, 25
5. Deal, Russ, T, Indiana, 33
6. Malmberg, Don, T, UCLA, 41
7. Schwall, Vic, B, Northwestern, 49
8. Turner, Howard, B, North Carolina State, 57
9. Hubbell, Franklin, E, Tennessee, 65
10. Burgeois, Gaston, G, Tulane, 73
11. Brieske, Jim, C, Michigan, 81

12. Mobley, Rudy, B, Hardin-Simmons, 89
13. Doherty, Gerry, B, Delaware, 97
14. Baumgartner, Bill, E, Minnesota, 105
15. Kekeris, Jim, T, Missouri, 113
16. North, John, E, Vanderbilt, 121
17. Canady, Jim, B, Texas, 127
18. Brown, Harold, G, Indiana, 133
19. Sims, John, B, Tulane, 139
20. Vanderclutte, Bert, G, Wesleyan, 145
21. Stalloni, Tony, T, Delaware, 151
22. Lamoure, Gene, G, Fresno State, 155
23. Daniels, Leo, B, Texas A&M, 159
24. Reilly, Tex, B, Colorado, 163
25. Landrigan, Jim, T, Holy Cross, 167

NY YANKEES

Young, Buddy, B, Illinois
Trippi, Charley, B, Georgia
1. Raimondi, Ben, B, Indiana, 7
2. Moncreif, Monte, T, Texas A&M, 15
3. Collins, Bill (Spot), G, Texas, 23
4. Tereshinski, Joe, E, Georgia Tech, 31
5. Durishan, Jack, T, Pittsburgh, 39
6. Dropo, Walter, E, Connecticut, 47
7. Nabors, Roland, C, Texas Tech, 55
8. Strohmeyer, George, C, Notre Dame, 63
9. Ossowski, Ted, T, Oregon State, 71
10. Werder, Dick, G, Georgetown (Washington D.C.), 79
11. Healey, Bill, G, Georgia Tech, 87
12. Sikorski, Ed, B, Muhlenberg, 95
13. Miklich, Bill, B, Idaho, 103
14. Elliott, Chuck, T, Oregon, 111
15. Grain, Ed, G, Pennsylvania, 119

SAN FRANCISCO

Davis, Glenn, B, Army
1. LeForce, Clyde, B, Tulsa, 6
2. Wiese, Bob, B, Michigan, 14
3. Duke, Paul, C, Georgia Tech, 22
4. Samuel, Don, B, Oregon State, 30
5. Satterfield, Alf, T, Vanderbilt, 38
6. Zilly, John, E, Notre Dame, 46
7. Knight, Gene (Red), B, LSU, 54
8. Malmberg, Charlie, T, Rice, 62
9. Leonetti, Bob, G, Wake Forest, 70
10. Broyles, Frank, QB, Georgia Tech, 78
11. Tyree, Jim, E, Oklahoma, 86
12. Robnett, Ed, B, Texas Tech, 94
13. Slater, Walter, B, Tennessee, 102
14. Wheeler, Earl, C, Arkansas, 110
15. Proctor, Les, G, Texas, 118
16. DeRogatis, Al, T, Duke, 126
17. Tullos, Earl, T, LSU, 132
18. Meeks, Bryant, C, South Carolina, 138
19. Royston, Ed, G, Wake Forest, 144
20. Bumgardner, Max, E, Texas, 150

1948 NFL

Held December 19, 1947

BOSTON

1. Mancha, Vaughn, C, Alabama
2. Cook, Earl, G, SMU
3. Nolan, John, T, Penn State, from NY Giants
Healey, Bill, G, Georgia Tech
4. Slosburg, Phil, B, Temple
5. Choice to LA Rams
6. Furse, Robert (Tex), B, Yale
7. Burton, Jim, E, Wesleyan
8. Forbes, Bob, B, Florida
9. Roman, George, T, Case Western Reserve
10. Wimberly, Abner, E, LSU
11. Jensen, Bob, E, Iowa State
12. Entsminger, Hal (Bus), B, Missouri
13. Ragonese, Carmen, B, New Hampshire
14. Ratterman, George, QB, Notre Dame
15. Trotter, Nute, T, Oklahoma
16. Mendel, Jack, E, Canisius
17. Jowell, Mel, G, McMurry
18. Nelson, Frank, B, Utah
19. Lukens, Jim, E, Washington & Lee
20. O'Brien, Fran, B, Dartmouth
21. Zito, Jim, T, Michigan State
22. Roderick, Jack, E, Yale
23. Sikorski, Eddie, B, Muhlenberg
24. Mather, Bruce, B, New Hampshire
25. Shoaf, Jim, T, Iowa*
26. McCary, Joe, B, Virginia
27. Sica, Al, B, Pennsylvania
28. Bonk, Harry, B, Maryland
29. Langsjoen, Bernor, B, Gustavus Adolphus
30. Neff, George, B, Virginia

CHI. BEARS

1. Layne, Bobby, QB, Texas, from Detroit through Pittsburgh
Bumgardner, Max, E, Texas
2. Garrett, Dub, T, Mississippi State
3. Ramsey, Knox, G, William & Mary
4. Brugge, Bob, B, Ohio State
5. Choice to Detroit
6. McWilliams, Tom (Shorty), B, Army, Mississippi State
7. Mills, Malachi, T, Virginia Military
8. Flanagan, Dick, E, Ohio State
9. McDowell, Jim, G, William & Mary
10. Sheehan, Mel, E, Missouri
11. Scott, Dick, C, Navy
12. Cline, Ollie, B, Ohio State
13. Goode, Rob, B, Texas A&M*
14. Grimenstein, Clyde, E, Purdue
15. Fallon, John, G, Notre Dame
16. Brown, Ray, B, Virginia
17. Hileman, Bob, C, California
18. Gay, Thurman, T, Oklahoma State
19. Blount, Ralph (Peppy), E, Texas
20. Boone, J.R., B, Tulsa
21. Duncan, Jim, E, Wake Forest
22. Gatewood, Jimmy, B, Georgia
23. Brumm, George, C, Pacific
24. Dietzel, Paul, C, Miami (Ohio)
25. Clasby, Ed, B, Boston College
26. Hardison, Fred, E, Duke
27. Van Deren, Frank, E, California
28. Pietkiewicz, Al, E, San Francisco
29. Cox, Norm, B, TCU
30. Smith, Truett, B, Mississippi St.*

CHI. CARDINALS

1. Spavital, Jim, B, Oklahoma State
2. Smith, Bill, T, North Carolina
3. Smith, Jay, E, Southern Mississippi
4. Choice to Pittsburgh
5. Cason, Jim, B, LSU
6. Camp, Jim, B, North Carolina
7. Choice to NY Giants
8. Weisner, Carl, E, St. Louis
9. Corum, Gene, G, West Virginia
10. Self, Clarence, B, Wisconsin
11. Hollar, John, B, Appalachian State
12. Hanlon, Bob, B, Loras
13. Petrovich, George, T, Texas
14. Still, Jim, B, Georgia Tech
15. Davis, Clay, C, Oklahoma State
16. Caughron, Harry, T, William & Mary
17. Davis, Jerry, B, Southeastern Louisiana
18. Dwyer, Gene, E, St. Ambrose
19. Waters, Harry, B, Colorado College
20. Monroe, Dick, C, Kansas
21. Reynolds, H.M. (Hindu), E, Southern Mississippi
22. Wedel, Dick, G, Wake Forest
23. Shoults, Paul, B, Miami (Ohio)
24. Wendt, Fred, B, Texas-El Paso
25. Belden, Doug, B, Florida
26. Stackhouse, Ray, T, Xavier
27. Reid, Bernie, G, Georgia
28. Powell, Jim, E, Tennessee
29. Polidor, Bob, B, Villanova
30. Fischer, Bill, G, Notre Dame*

DETROIT

1. Choice to Chi. Bears through Pittsburgh
Tittle, Y.A., QB, LSU, from LA Rams
2. Quist, George, B, Stanford
3. Bingaman, Les, T, Illinois
4. Minor, Jim, T, Arkansas
5. Choice to Green Bay
Schwab, Moroni, T, Utah State, from Chi. Bears
6. Williamson, Bob, T, Hobart
7. Enke, Fred, B, Arizona
8. Choice to NY Giants
9. Doll, Don, B, USC
10. Cleary, Paul, E, USC
11. Land, Fred, T, LSU
12. Choice to NY Giants
13. Steger, Russ, B, Illinois*
14. Enstice, Hal, B, Union (New York)
15. Elliott, Pete, B, Michigan, F
16. Templeton, Dave, G, Ohio State
17. Sickels, Quentin, G, Michigan
18. Spruill, Jim, T, Rice
19. Hafen, Bernie, E, Utah
20. Dellosobelle, Aldo, T, Loyola (Los Angeles)
21. Dill, Dean, B, USC
22. McEwen, Jack, B, Colorado
23. Steiner, Roy (Rebel), E, Alabama*
24. Saurez, Joe, G, St. Mary's (California)
25. McGee, Coy, B, Notre Dame
26. Alexander, Phil, T, South Carolina
27. Pizza, Frank, T, Toledo
28. Schutte, George, T, USC
29. Pabalis, Tony, B, Central Michigan
30. McCurry, Bob, C, Michigan State

GREEN BAY

1. Girard, Earl (Jug), B, Wisconsin
2. Smith, Oscar, B, Texas-El Paso
3. Sellers, Weyman, E, Georgia
4. Olsonoski, Larry, G, Minnesota
5. Richards, Don, T, Arkansas, from Detroit
Rhodemyre, Jay, C, Kentucky
6. Cunz, Bob, T, Illinois
7. Choice to NY Giants
8. Walmsley, George, B, Rice
9. Hodges, Bob, T, Bradley
10. Rennebohm, Bob, E, Wisconsin
11. Moss, Perry, B, Illinois
12. Provo, Fred, B, Washington
13. Agase, Lou, T, Illinois
14. Raven, Travis, B, Texas
15. Choice to Washington
16. Balge, Ken, E, Michigan State
17. Tatom, Charley, T, Texas
18. Thomas, Floyd, C, Arkansas
19. St. John, Herb, G, Georgia
20. Anderson, Don, B, Rice
21. Kling, Fred, B, Missouri
22. Biggers, Clyde, T, Catawba
23. Heath, Stan, QB, Nevada-Reno*
24. Allen, Aubrey, T, Colorado
25. Gorski, Stan, E, St. Mary's (Minnesota)
26. Sharp, Don, C, Tulsa
27. Panelli, John (Pep), B, Notre Dame*
28. McGeary, Clarence (Clink), T, North Dakota State
29. Mills, Mike, E, BYU
30. Earhart, Ralph, E, Texas Tech

LA RAMS

1. Choice to Detroit
2. Keane, Tom, B, West Virginia
3. Bailey, Bruce, B, Virginia
4. Grimes, George, B, Virginia
5. Ruszkowski, Gene, T, Ohio U., from Boston
Cudd, Noel, T, West Texas State
6. Walker, Bob, B, Colorado Mines
7. Graham, Mike, B, Cincinnati
8. Johnson, Glenn, T, Arizona State
9. Zisch, Johnny, E, Colorado
10. Phleger, Atherton (Pinky), T, Stanford
11. Heck, Bob, E, Purdue
12. Schroll, Bill, B, LSU
13. Dement, Bob, T, Southern Mississippi
14. Schoenherr, Charley, B, Wheaton
15. Brink, Larry, E, Northern Illinois
16. O'Connor, Bill (Zeke), G, Notre Dame
17. Nelson, Bill, B, Montana State
18. Rees, Jim, T, North Carolina State
19. Borneman, Ray, B, Texas
20. Yagiello, Ray, T, Catawba
21. Pesek, John, E, Nebraska
22. DeAutremont, Charlie, B, Southern Oregon
23. Levenhagen, Bob, G, Washington
24. Cooper, Leon, T, Hardin-Simmons, Albright
25. Wade, Jim, B, Oklahoma City
26. Sinofsky, Ken, G, Nevada-Reno
27. Stuart, Bobby Jack, B, Tulsa, Army
28. Crum, Hilliard (Junior), E, Arizona
29. Kunkiewicz, Tony, B, Trinity (Connecticut)
30. Taylor, Bill, E, Rice

NY GIANTS

1. Minisi, Tony (Skippy), B, Pennsylvania, Navy
2. Scott, Joe, B, San Francisco
3. Choice to Boston
4. Gehrke, Bruce, E, Columbia
5. Wolosky, Johnny, C, Penn State
6. Erickson, Bill, T, Mississippi
7. Pfohl, Bob, B, Purdue
Wiltgen, Ken, E, Northwestern, from Green Bay
Royston, Ed, G, Wake Forest, from Chi. Cardinals
8. Hutchinson, Ralph, T, Tennessee-Chattanooga
Coates, Ray, B, LSU, from Detroit
9. Ottele, Dick, B, Washington
10. Magdziak, Stan, B, William & Mary
11. Lanzi, Pete, E, Youngstown State
12. Modzeleski, Len, T, Scranton
Brieske, Jim, C, Michigan, from Detroit
13. Hatch, Bob, B, Boston U.
14. Hansel, John, G, Guilford
15. Garza, Dan, E, Oregon
16. Yovetich, Dan, E, Montana State
17. Grothus, Joe, G, Iowa
18. Mathews, George, B, Georgia Tech
19. Ettinger, Don (Red Dog), G, Kansas
20. Williams, Frank, B, Utah State
21. Woodward, Dick, C, Iowa
22. Kisiday, George, T, Columbia
23. Roberts, Theron, G, Arkansas
24. McCormick, Walt, C, USC
25. Wilkins, Dick, E, Oregon
26. Marotta, Vince, B, Mount Union
27. Salisbury, Tom, T, Clemson
28. Lilja, Roy, C, Colorado College
29. Greenhalgh, Bobby, B, San Francisco
30. Kelley, Ed, T, Texas

PHILADELPHIA

1. Scott, Clyde (Smackover), B, Arkansas, Navy
2. Campbell, Paul, QB, Texas
3. Myers, Jack (Moose), B, UCLA
4. Duncan, Howard, C, Ohio State
5. Tinsley, Buddy, T, Baylor
6. Wendell, Marty, G, Notre Dame
7. Beasley, Scott, E, Nevada-Reno
8. Richeson, Ray, G, Alabama
9. Johnson, Gil, QB, SMU
10. Wyman, Bill, T, Rice*
11. Walthall, Jim, B, West Virginia
12. Kempthorn, Dick, B, Michigan
13. Rifenburg, Dick, E, Michigan
14. Stanton, Don, T, Oregon
15. Kohl, Ralph, T, Michigan
16. Fowler, Aubrey, B, Arkansas
17. Krall, Rudy, B, New Mexico
18. Claunch, Ed, C, LSU
19. Norton, Negley, T, Penn State
20. Frizzell, Lockwood, C, Virginia
21. Swaner, Jack, B, California
22. Littleton, Art, E, Pennsylvania
23. Parmer, Jim, B, Oklahoma State
24. Creekmur, Lou, T, William & Mary
25. Stanton, Bill, E, North Carolina State
26. Ellender, Benny, B, Tulane
27. Grossman, Rex, B, Indiana
28. Kitchens, A.B., T, Tulsa
29. Statuto, Art, C, Notre Dame
30. Novak, Tom, C, Nebraska

PITTSBURGH

1. Edwards, Dan, E, Georgia
2. Nuzum, Jerry, B, New Mexico State
3. Wozniak, John, G, Alabama
4. Gasparella, Joe, B, Notre Dame
O'Reilly, Phil, T, Purdue, from Chi. Cardinals
5. Luongo, Bill, B, Pennsylvania
6. Cooper, Jim, C, North Texas State
7. Ryan, Ed, E, St. Mary's (California)
8. Deranek, Dick, B, Indiana
9. Redfield, Paul, T, Colgate
10. Papach, George, B, Purdue
11. Finical, Tom, E, Princeton
12. Lane, Clayton, T, New Hampshire
13. Mazuca, Dick, G, Canisius
14. McPeak, Bill, E, Pittsburgh
15. Messoline, Frank, B, Scranton
16. Lane, Tom, T, Muhlenburg
17. Barbolak, Pete, T, Purdue
18. Folger, Fred, B, Duke
19. Snyder, Charley, T, Marshall
20. Stevens, Tally, E, Utah
21. Norman, Dike, C, Washington & Lee
22. Simmons, Floyd, B, Notre Dame
23. Hausser, Paul, T, Wichita State
24. Ramsey, Bob, B, SMU
25. Whitlow, Felton, T, North Texas State
26. Bowen, Dinky, B, Georgia Tech
27. Gibron, Abe, G, Purdue
28. Hilkene, Bruce, T, Michigan
29. Zuchowski, Ted, T, Toledo
30. DeMatteo, Tony, B, Pittsburgh

WASHINGTON

BONUS CHOICE: Gilmer, Harry, B, Alabama
1. Tew, Lowell, B, Alabama
2. Thompson, Tommy, C, William & Mary
3. Sandifer, Dan, B, LSU
4. Weisenburger, Jack, B, Michigan
5. Kurkowski, Jack, B, Detroit
6. Cady, Jerry, T, Gustavus Adolphus
7. Anderson, Bob, B, Stanford
8. Katrishen, Mike, T, Southern Mississippi
9. Marshall, Ed, T, Pennsylvania
10. Andrus, Ted, G, Southwestern Louisiana

11. Russ, Carl, B, Rice
12. Jagade, Harry (Chick), B, Indiana
13. Quirk, Eddie, B, Missouri
14. Pollard, Art, B, Arizona
15. Newman, Chuck, E, Louisiana Tech
    Schwartzkopf, Dale, E, Texas, from Green Bay
16. Pearcy, Ray, C, Oklahoma
17. Vellela, Gene, T, Scranton
18. Box, Cloyce, B, West Texas State
19. Bell, Bryan, B, Washington & Lee
20. Williams, Joel, C, Texas
21. Hoitsma, Lou, E, William & Mary
22. Lawhorn, Floyd, G, Texas Tech
23. West, Dick, B, Princeton
24. Oakes, Roland, E, Missouri
25. Watkins, Ed, T, Idaho
26. Corbitt, Don, C, Arizona
27. Bowen, Buddy, B, Mississippi
28. Paulson, Vic, E, Cal-Santa Barbara
29. Welch, Barney, B, Texas A&M

1948 AAFC

Held December 16, 1947

The draft increased to 30 rounds, and the best teams from the preceding season again received fewer choices, but this year those lost selections were earlier in the draft than in 1947. Each team selected in the first round. The next nine rounds varied greatly. In the second round, only the Chicago Rockets and Baltimore received a choice. In the third, seventh, and ninth rounds, each team made a selection. In the fourth and sixth rounds, Cleveland and the New York Yankees didn't receive selections. In the fifth round, only the Rockets, Baltimore, and Brooklyn received picks. And in the eighth and tenth rounds, only the Rockets, Baltimore, Brooklyn, and the Los Angeles Dons received picks. After the tenth round, each team made selections throughout the next 20 rounds.

BALTIMORE

1. Layne, Bobby, QB, Texas, 2
2. Garrett, Dub, T, Mississippi State, 10
3. Cooke, Earl, G, SMU, 12
4. Sandifer, Don, B, LSU, 20
5. Smith, Joe, E, Texas Tech, 26
6. Raczkowski, Gene, T, Ohio U., 29
7. Batchelor, Jim, B, East Texas State, 35
8. Olson, Rex, B, BYU, 43
9. Fowler, Aubrey, B, Arkansas, 47
10. Fitch, Jack, B, North Carolina, 55
11. Ettinger, Don, T, Kansas, 59
12. Redfield, Paul, T, Colgate, 67
13. Madgziak, Stan, B, William & Mary, 75
14. Deranek, Dick, B, Indiana, 83
15. Norman, Dike, B, Washington & Lee, 91
16. Working, Dick, B, Washington & Lee, 99
17. Sparter, George, C, North Carolina, 107
18. Prather, Rollin, E, Kansas State, 115
19. Mosely, Monk, B, Alabama, 123
20. Ragonese, Carmen, B, New Hampshire, 131
21. Walker, Bob, B, Colorado Mines, 139
22. Borneman, Ray, B, Texas, 147
23. Tillman, Pete, C, Oklahoma, 155
24. Phofl, Bob, B, Purdue, 163
25. Levanti, Lou, C, Illinois, 171
26. Zatkoff, Sam, E, Illinois, 179*
27. Jagade, Harry (Chick), B, Indiana, 187
28. Bendrick, Ben, B, Wisconsin, 195*
29. Grossman, Rex, B, Indiana, 203
30. Reinking, Dick, E, SMU, 211

BROOKLYN

1. Gilmer, Harry, QB, Alabama, 3
3. Edwards, Dan, E, Georgia, 13
4. Spencer, Joe, T, Oklahoma State, 21
5. Binganan, Les, T, Illinois, 27
6. Smith, Jim, E, Southern Mississippi, 30
7. Paine, Homer, T, Oklahoma, 36
8. Gehrke, Bruce, E, Columbia, 44
9. Minor, Jim, T, Arkansas, 48
10. St. John, Herb, G, Georgia, 56
11. Newman, Chuck, E, Louisiana Tech, 60
12. Camp, Jim, B, North Carolina, 68
13. Koch, Bob, B, Oregon, 76
14. White, John, C, Michigan, 84
15. Terry, Bob, T, Texas A & M, 92*
16. Woznick, John, G, Alabama, 100
17. Jensen, Bob, E, Iowa State, 108
18. Jurich, Joe, E, West Chester, 116
19. Cromer, Bill, B, North Texas State, 124
20. Scott, Dick, C, Navy, 132
21. Marusa, Walt, G, Delaware, 140
22. Dobkins, Knute, E, Butler, 148
23. Westphal, Fred, E, Cornell, 156
24. Dinkins, Merle, E, Oklahoma, 164
25. Pupa, Walt, B, North Carolina, 172
26. Richeson, Ray, G, Alabama, 180
27. Hurrle, Ott, C, Butler, 188
28. Lowans, Warren, T, West Chester, 196
29. Littleton, Art, E, Pennsylvania, 204
30. McGeary, Clarence (Clink), T, North Dakota State, 212

BUFFALO

1. Scott, Clyde (Smackover), B, Arkansas, Navy, 6
3. Gompers, Bill, B, Notre Dame, 16
4. O'Connor, Bill, E, Notre Dame, 24
6. Wendell, Marty, G, Notre Dame, 33
7. Brugge, Bob, B, Ohio State, 39
9. King, Louis, B, Iowa, 51
11. Finney, John, B, Compton J.C., 63
12. Johnson, Dick, G, Baylor, 71
13. Grimes, George, B, Virginia, 79
14. Joe, Larry, B, Penn State, 87
15. Ballard, Frank, G, Virginia Tech, 95
16. Walthall, Jim, B, West Virginia, 103
17. Coates, Ray, B, LSU, 111
18. Waybright, Dud, E, Notre Dame, 119
19. Walker, Wade, T, Oklahoma, 127
20. Stephens, Roger, B, Cincinnati, 135
21. Duncan, Howard, C, Ohio State, 143
22. Sazio, Ralph, T, William & Mary, 151
23. Bloomquist, George, E, North Carolina State, 159
24. Cheek, J.D., T, Oklahoma State, 167
25. Rennebohm, Bob, E, Wisconsin, 175
26. Andrus, Ted, G, Southwestern Louisiana, 183
27. Brown, Ray, B, Virginia, 191
28. Corriere, Lou, B, Buffalo, 199
29. Wosloski, John, C, Penn State, 207
30. Stevens, Talley, E, Utah State, 215*

CHI. ROCKETS

1. Minisi, Tony (Skippy), B, Pennsylvania, 1
2. Samuelson, Carl, T, Nebraska, 9
3. Nolan, John, T, Penn State, 11
4. Cleary, Paul, E, USC, 19
5. Walsh, John, C, Notre Dame, 25*
6. DiFrancisca, Vince, G, Northwestern, 28
7. Rhodemyer, John, C, Kentucky, 34
8. Turner, Jim, T, California, 42
9. Miller, Myron, C, Oklahoma State, 46
10. Schlosburg, Phil, B, Temple, 54
11. Swaner, Jack, B, California, 58
12. Gay, Thurman, T, Oklahoma State, 66
13. Parker, Frank, T, Holy Cross, 74*
14. Agase, Lou, T, Illinois, 82
15. McCarthy, J.F., E, Pennsylvania, 90
16. Krall, Rudy, B, New Mexico, 98
17. Flanagan, Dick, B, Ohio State, 106
18. Ryan, Ed, E, St. Mary's (California), 114
19. Gillory, Byron, B, Texas, 122*
20. Doll, Don, B, USC, 130
21. Provo, Fred, B, Washington, 138
22. Tinsley, Phil, E, UCLA, 146
23. Treichler, Glen, B, Colgate, 154
24. Owen, Ike, E, Illinois, 162
25. Sockalov, Ron, T, California, 170
26. Corum, Gene, G, West Virginia, 178
27. Daniels, John, C, Cal-Santa Barbara, 186
28. Hoisch, Al, B, UCLA, 194
29. Wedel, Dick, G, Wake Forest, 202
30. Finical, Tom, E, Princeton, 210

CLEVELAND

1. Durkota, Jeff, B, Penn State, 8
3. Cline, Ollie, B, Ohio State, 18
7. Thompson, Tommy, C, William & Mary, 41
9. Smith, Bill, T, North Carolina, 53
11. Maughan, Ralph, C, Utah State, 65
12. Sensenbaugher, Dean, B, Ohio State, 73
13. Rubish, Mike, E, North Carolina, 81*
14. Sarkesian, Alex, C, Northwestern, 89
15. Dworsky, Dan, B, Michigan, 97*
16. Beasley, Scott, E, Nevada-Reno, 105
17. Steger, Russ, B, Illinois, 113
18. Hoistma, Lou, E, William & Mary, 121
19. Ashbaugh, Pete, B, Notre Dame, 129
20. Templeton, Dave, G, Ohio State, 137
21. Eddleman, Dwight, B, Illinois, 145
22. Gambino, Lou, B, Maryland, 153
23. McDowell, Jim, G, William & Mary, 161
24. Fowle, Heywood, T, North Carolina, 169
25. Parseghian, Ara, B, Miami (Ohio), 177
26. Saylor, Todd, E, Lafayette, 185
27. Caughron, Harry, T, William & Mary, 193
28. Lanzi, Pete, E, Youngstown State, 201
29. Roman, George, T, Case Western Reserve, 209
30. Sheehan, Mel, E, Missouri, 217

LA DONS

1. Mancha, Vaughn, C, Alabama, 4
3. Ford, Len, E, Michigan, 14
4. Novitsky, John, T, Oklahoma City, 22
5. Sexton, Linwood, B, Wichita State, 31
7. Edwards, Weldon, T, TCU, 37
8. Spavital, Jim, B, Oklahoma State, 45
9. Ramsey, Knox, G, William & Mary, 49
10. Mills, Malachi, G, Virginia Military, 57
11. Mihajlovich, Lou, E, Indiana, 61
12. Davis, Harper, B, Mississippi State, 69
13. Graham, Mike, B, Cincinnati, 77
14. Winkler, Bernie, T, Texas Tech, 85
15. Erickson, Bill, T, Mississippi, 93
16. McWilliams, Tom (Shorty), B, Army, Mississippi State, 101
17. Levenhagen, Bob, G, Washington, 109
18. Sellers, Wayman, E, Georgia, 117
19. Wimberly, Abner, E, LSU, 125
20. Ziegler, Frank, B, Georgia Tech, 133
21. Smith, Ed, B, Texas-El Paso, 141
22. Mortelello, Paul, G, Florida, 149
23. Kenfield, Ted, B, California, 157
24. Mulligan, Buddy, B, Duke, 165
25. Lambert, George, T, Mississippi, 173
26. Still, Jim, QB, Georgia Tech, 181
27. Tatom, Charley, G, Texas, 189
28. Creekmur, Lou, T, William & Mary, 197
29. McLoughlin, Leon, C, UCLA, 205
30. Kitchens, A.B., T, Tulsa, 213

NY YANKEES

1. Tew, Lowell, B, Alabama, 7
3. Schnellenbacher, Otto, E, Kansas, 17
7. Stout, Pete, B, TCU, 40
9. Poole, Barney, E, Army, Mississippi, 52, F
11. Weisenberger, Jack, B, Michigan, 64
12. Hendren, Bob, T, USC, 72
13. Ottelle, Dick, B, Washington, 80
14. McKissack, Dick, B, SMU, 88*
15. Magliolo, Joe, B, Texas, 96
16. Ramsey, Bob, B, SMU, 104
17. Wright, Charles, E, Texas A & M, 112
18. Shirley, Marion, T, Oklahoma City, 120
19. Landry, Tom, B, Texas, 128
20. Forbes, Bobby, B, Florida, 136
21. Russ, Carl, B, Rice, 144
22. Enke, Fred, B, Arizona, 152*
23. Cunningham, John, E, California, 160
24. Ognovich, Nick, B, Wake Forest, 168
25. Zelezanak, Mike, B, Kansas State, 176
26. Panelli, John (Pep), B, Notre Dame, 184*
27. Girard, Earl (Jug), B, Wisconsin, 192
28. Collins, Albin (Rip), B, LSU, 200*
29. Nelson, Frank, B, Utah, 208
30. Clements, Bill, E, UCLA, 216

SAN FRANCISCO

1. Scott, Joe, B, San Francisco, 5
3. Cason, Jim, B, LSU, 15
4. McCormick, Walt, C, USC, 23
6. Land, Fred, T, LSU, 32
7. O'Reilly, Phil, T, Purdue, 38
9. Luongo, Bill, B, Pennsylvania, 50
11. Steckroth, Bob, E, William & Mary, 62
12. Malinowski, Gene, C, Detroit, 70
13. Modzelski, Len, T, Scranton, 78
14. Rideout, Les, T, Bowling Green, 86
15. Olsonoski, Larry, T, Purdue, 94
16. Matulich, Wally, B, Mississippi State, 102
17. Ravensberg, Bob, E, Indiana, 110
18. Pritula, Bill, T, Michigan, 118
19. Fitzgerald, Art, B, Yale, 126
20. Barbolak, Pete, T, Purdue, 134
21. Loepfe, Dick, T, Wisconsin, 142
22. Heck, Bob, E, Purdue, 150
23. Lanhorne, Floyd, G, Texas Tech, 158
24. Bryant, Goble, T, Army, 166
25. Talarico, Bill, B, Pennsylvania, 174
26. Marshall, Everett, T, Pennsylvania, 182
27. Moss, Perry, B, Illinois, 190
28. Bell, Bill, QB, Muhlenberg, 198
29. Siegert, Herb, G, Illinois, 206
30. Williams, Frank, B, Utah State, 214

1949 NFL

Held December 21, 1948

Although before the start of the 1949 season Ted Collins moved his franchise to New York, where it was named the Bulldogs, at the time of the draft, it still was located in Boston.

BOSTON

1. Walker, Doak, B, SMU, F
2. DeMoss, Bob, B, Purdue
3. Colella, Phil, B, St. Bonaventure
    Chewning, Lynn, B, Hampden-Sydney, from Chi. Cardinals
4. Keeney, Huey, B, Rice
5. Boyda, Mike, B, Washington & Lee
6. Collins, Albin (Rip), B, LSU
    Tamburo, Sam, E, Penn State, from Philadelphia
7. Wismann, Pete, C, St. Louis
8. Rubish, Mike, E, North Carolina
9. Craig, Bernie, T, Denver
10. Geary, John, T, Wesleyan
11. Mencotti, Edo, B, Detroit
12. Maenhout, Mornane, E, St. John's (Minnesota)
13. Dieckelman, Jim, E, Holy Cross
14. Toscani, Ed, B, Dayton
15. Ramacorti, George, G, Boston U.
16. Bruce, Jack, B, William & Mary
17. Beson, Warren, C, Minnesota
18. Gould, Albie, E, Boston College
19. Reich, Bob, T, Colgate
20. Gaul, Frank, T, Notre Dame
21. Pierce, Sammy, B, Baylor
22. Lail, Jim, B, Wake Forest
23. Lanza, Nick, B, Rice
24. Ponsalle, Joe, T, Trinity (Connecticut)
25. Girolamo, Paul, B, Cornell

CHI. BEARS

1. Harris, Dick, C, Texas
2. Grimes, Billy, B, Oklahoma State
3. O'Quinn, Johnny (Red), E, Wake Forest, F
4. Bendrick, Ben, B, Wisconsin
5. Hoffman, John, B, Arkansas
6. Krall, Jerry, B, Ohio State, F
7. Jones, Wally (Wah-Wah), E, Kentucky
8. Weatherly, Gerry (Bones), C, Rice, from Detroit
    Wightkin, Bill, E, Notre Dame, F
9. Tokarczyk, Dolph, G, Pennsylvania
10. Malley, Lee, B, Carson-Newman
11. Tiblier, Jerry, B, Mississippi
12. Blanda, George, QB, Kentucky
13. Taliaferro, George, B, Indiana
14. Keily, Ernie, G, Texas-El Paso*
15. Faverty, Hal, G, Wisconsin
16. Wahl, Al, T, Michigan*
17. Corbisiero, John, B, Middlebury
18. Moran, Jim, B, John Carroll
19. Mitten, Bob, G, North Carolina
20. Heck, Bob, B, Pacific
21. Duncan, Jim, E, Duke
22. Bertuzzi, Dick, B, Kansas
23. Kane, Harry, C, Pacific*
24. Smith, Bernie, T, Texas-El Paso
25. Marczyk, Stan, T, North Carolina

CHI. CARDINALS

1. Fischer, Bill, G, Notre Dame
2. McKissack, Dick, B, SMU*
3. Choice to Boston
4. Goldsberry, John, T, Indiana
5. Wham, Tom, E, Furman
6. Hanula, Bernie, T, Wake Forest
7. Greathouse, Myrl, B, Oklahoma, from Detroit
    Cain, Jim, E, Alabama
8. Brown, Joe E., B, Georgia Tech
9. Herring, Hal, C, Auburn
10. Hecker, Bob, B, Baldwin-Wallace
11. Flowers, Stan, E, Redlands
12. Stone, Billy, B, Bradley
13. Todd, Bob, T, Louisville
14. Klimek, Tony, E, Illinois, F
15. McQuade, Bob, B, Xavier
16. Murdock, Tom, B, Appalachian State
17. Rupp, Eddie, B, Denison
18. Halbert, Webb, B, Iowa
19. Laun, Dean, E, Iowa State
20. Rowan, Earl, T, Hardin-Simmons*
21. Joslin, Leon, B, TCU
22. Sprang, Bill, C, Purdue
23. Cox, Bob, E, North Carolina
24. Szymakowski, Stan, B, Lehigh
25. Choice to NY Giants

DETROIT
1. Rauch, Johnny, QB, Georgia
2. Panelli, John (Pep), B, Notre Dame
3. Kusserow, Lou, B, Columbia
4. Sullivan, Joe, B, Dartmouth
5. Brodnax, George, E, Georgia Tech
6. Meinert, Bob, B, Oklahoma State
7. Choice to Chi. Cardinals
8. Choice to Chi. Bears
9. Drazenovich, Chuck, B, Penn State, F
10. Davis, Bill, G, Duke
11. Settembre, Ernie, T, Miami
12. Boteler, Virgil, C, New Mexico
13. Russas, Al, E, Tennessee
14. Panter, Dale, T, Utah State
15. Pifferini, Bob, C, San Jose State
16. Merrill, Kimball, T, BYU
17. Thigpen, Zealand, B, Vanderbilt
18. Wehr, Bill, C, Denison
19. Triplett, Wally, B, Penn State
20. Romano, Joe, T, North Carolina
21. Lininger, Jack, C, Ohio State, F
22. Tobler, Gil, B, Utah
23. Patterson, R.B., G, Mississippi State
24. Clark, Oswald, E, Michigan
25. Cowan, Les, E, McMurry

GREEN BAY
1. Heath, Stan, QB, Nevada-Reno
2. Dworsky, Dan, C, Michigan
3. Ferry, Lou, T, Villanova
4. Summerhays, Bob, B, Utah
5. Lewis, Glenn, B, Texas Tech
6. Ethridge, Joe, T, SMU
7. Choice to LA Rams
8. Orlich, Dan, E, Nevada-Reno
9. Faunce, Everett, B, Minnesota
10. Choice to LA Rams through Detroit
11. Larche, Harry, T, Arkansas State
12. Steiner, Roy (Rebel), E, Alabama, F
13. Mastrangeli, Al, C, Illinois
14. Williams, Bobby, C, Texas Tech
15. Cooper, Ken, G, Vanderbilt
16. Hemenar, Gene, T, West Virginia
17. Devine, Paul, B, Heidelberg
18. Lewis, Floyd, G, SMU
19. Folsom, Bobby, E, SMU
20. Cooney, Larry, B, Penn State
21. Kranz, Ken, B, Wisconsin-Milwaukee
22. Kordick, John, B, USC
23. Kelly, Bill, E, Texas Tech
24. Ford, Jimmy, B, Tulsa
25. Lambright, Frank, G, Arkansas

LA RAMS
1. Thomason, Bobby, B, Virginia Military
2. Sims, George, B, Baylor
3. Winkler, Jim, T, Texas A&M
4. Van Brocklin, Norm, QB, Oregon
5. Howell, Earl, B, Mississippi
6. Reynolds, Charles, B, Texas Tech
7. Williams, Jerry, B, Washington State, from Green Bay
   Baker, Jon, G, California
8. Waldrum, John, G, Sul Ross
9. Smith, Johnny, E, Arizona*
10. Buksar, George, B, Purdue, from Green Bay
   Minnich, Max, B, Bowling Green
11. Cozad, Jim, T, Iowa
12. Renna, Bill, C, Santa Clara
13. Barry, Paul, B, Tulsa
14. Carmichael, Ed, T, Oregon State
15. Dodd, J.C., B, Sul Ross
16. Morgan, Joe, G, Southern Mississippi
17. Sheffield, Dick, E, Tulane
18. Chollet, Hillary, B, Cornell
19. Leonard, Joe, T, Virginia
20. Eisenberg, Lloyd, T, Duke
21. Teufel, George, B, Lock Haven
22. Hamilton, Ed, E, Arkansas
23. Kersulis, Walt, E, Illinois*
24. Klemenok, Fred, B, San Francisco
25. Matthews, Clay, T, Georgia Tech

NY GIANTS
1. Page, Paul, B, SMU
2. DeRogatis, Al, T, Duke
3. Olson, Bill, B, Columbia
4. Kay, Bill, T, Iowa
5. Cheek, J.D., G, Oklahoma State
6. Gibron, Abe, G, Purdue
7. Lovuolo, Frank, E, St. Bonaventure
8. Salscheider, John, B, St. Thomas (Minnesota)
9. Soboleski, Joe, G, Michigan
10. Rossides, Gene, B, Columbia
11. Hensley, Dick, E, Kentucky
12. Sundheim, George, B, Northwestern
13. Austin, Bill, T, Oregon State
14. Adams, Norb, B, Purdue
15. Pickelsimer, Ralph, C, Otterbein
16. Morrical, Jerry, T, Indiana
17. Teninga, Wally, B, Michigan
18. Nutt, Dick, B, North Texas State
19. McCall, Ken, B, Georgia
20. O'Sullivan, Pat, C, Alabama
21. Cate, A.D., G, North Texas State
22. Fetzer, Tom, B, Wake Forest
23. Fischer, Cletus, B, Nebraska
24. McAuliffe, Don, B, Notre Dame
25. Degyanski, Gene, E, Baldwin-Wallace
   Doran, Ralph, B, Iowa, from Chi. Cardinals

PHILADELPHIA
BONUS CHOICE: Bednarik, Chuck, C, Pennsylvania
1. Tripucka, Frank, QB, Notre Dame
2. Burns, Frank, B, Rutgers
3. Ziegler, Frank, B, Georgia Tech
4. Panciera, Don, B, San Francisco
5. Brennan, Terry, B, Notre Dame
6. Huey, Warren, E, Michigan State, from Washington
   Choice to Boston
7. Gillespie, Frank, G, Clemson
8. Dean, Bob, B, Cornell
9. Jenkins, Jonathan, T, Dartmouth
10. Lester, Roy, E, West Virginia
11. Wilson, Bobby, B, Mississippi
12. Armstrong, Dale, E, Dartmouth
13. Button, Lyle, T, Illinois*
14. Lund, Bobby, B, Tennessee
15. Copp, Carl, T, Vanderbilt
16. Reno, Frank, E, West Virginia
17. Skladany, Leo, E, Pittsburgh
18. Strait, Russ, B, Muhlenberg
19. Odom, Paul, G, Rollins
20. Brinkman, Lloyd, B, Missouri
21. Futrell, Lou, B, USC
22. Kingry, Harvey, B, Colorado Mines
23. Kalver, Hank, T, Oklahoma City
24. Leon, Fred, T, Nevada-Reno
25. Schweder, John (Bull), G, Pennsylvania

PITTSBURGH
1. Gage, Bobby, B, Clemson
2. Davis, Harper, B, Mississippi State
3. Walsh, Bill, C, Notre Dame
4. Geri, Joe, B, Georgia
5. Long, Bill, E, Oklahoma State
6. Brightwell, Doug, C, TCU
7. Talarico, Bill, B, Pennsylvania
8. Brown, George, G, TCU
9. Brennan, Tom, T, Boston College
10. Hood, Bob, E, Alabama
11. Sanders, Al, C, Southern Mississippi
12. Finks, Jim, B, Tulsa
13. Walston, R.R., G, North Texas State
14. Moon, Dave, B, SMU
15. Sobczak, Ed, E, Michigan
16. Snell, Denvard, T, Auburn
17. Kissell, Veto, B, Holy Cross
18. Shipman, Clint, T, East Texas State
19. McBride, Jack, E, Rice
20. Mann, Ben, G, Mississippi
21. Jackura, Joe, C, Georgia
22. Johnson, Lloyd, B, West Texas State
23. Owens, Jim, E, Oklahoma
24. Snowden, Ivan, T, Texas A&I
25. Goff, Bobby, B, Texas A&M

WASHINGTON
1. Goode, Rob, B, Texas A&M
2. Niemi, Laurie, T, Washington State
3. Szafaryn, Len, T, North Carolina
4. DeNoia, Mike, B, Scranton
5. Berrang, Eddie, E, Villanova
6. Choice to Philadelphia
7. Fritz, Chet, G, Missouri
8. Kennedy, Bob, B, North Carolina
9. McNeil, Ed, E, Michigan
10. Vasicek, Vic, G, Texas
11. Hobbs, Homer, G, Georgia
12. Varner, Harry, T, Arizona
13. Henke, Ed, T, USC
14. Haggerty, Pat, E, William & Mary
15. Frassetto, Gene, T, California
16. Flowers, Dick, T, Alabama
17. Pritchard, Ross, B, Arkansas
18. Siegert, Herb, G, Illinois
19. Hainlen, Bob, B, Colorado State
20. Fletcher, Ollie, E, USC
21. Hughes, Tommy, B, Duke
22. Clements, Bill, E, UCLA
23. Pattee, Frank, B, Kansas
24. Cullom, Jim, G, California*
25. Sebek, Nick, B, Indiana

1949 AAFC SECRET
Held July 8, 1948

A secret, two-round draft was held for players who were to be seniors in the 1948 season. The purpose was for the struggling AAFC to be able to get a jump on wooing the top college players before the NFL teams could talk to them. Two of the selections were voided by AAFC Commissioner O.O. Kessing because the players were not seniors and had college eligibility remaining for the 1949 season. Dick Harris, the first selection of Baltimore, later was assigned to Cleveland by the Commissioner.

BALTIMORE
1. Harris, Dick, C, Texas
2. Jackson, Levi, B, Yale*

BROOKLYN
1. Bednarik, Chuck, C, Pennsylvania
2. Choice to NY Yankees

BUFFALO
1. Gibron, Abe, G, Purdue
2. Tripucka, Frank, QB, Notre Dame

CHI. ROCKETS
1. Brennan, Terry, B, Notre Dame
   Elliott, Pete, B, Michigan, from NY Yankees
2. Fisher, Bill, G, Notre Dame

CLEVELAND
1. Derricotte, Gene, B, Michigan
2. Kempthorn, Dick, B, Michigan

LA DONS
1. Dworsky, Dan, C, Michigan
2. Price, Jack, B, Baylor

NY YANKEES
1. Choice to Chi. Rockets
2. Kusserow, Lou, B, Columbia, from Brooklyn
   Rauch, Johnny, QB, Georgia

SAN FRANCISCO
1. Stautner, Ernie, T, Boston College*
2. Winkler, Jim, T, Texas A&M

1949 AAFC
Held December 21, 1948

In determining the draft order, the divisional playoff game between Buffalo and Baltimore was added to the regular season finish. This made the order of selection for the three teams that had tied during the regular season Baltimore (7-8), the Los Angeles Dons (7-7), and Buffalo (8-7). For the first time in the AAFC, there were several trades for selections. There were 29 rounds, and again the teams with a lower finish in 1948 received more selections. Each team received a first-round choice. The Chicago Rockets, the New York Yankees, and Baltimore received a second-round selection, and Brooklyn received a third-round pick. Every team then selected in each round through the sixteenth. Everyone but Cleveland and San Francisco made choices from rounds 17 through 21, and then just Chicago, Brooklyn, and New York from rounds 22 through 24. Each selected again in round 25, and each team except Chicago, Brooklyn, and New York from rounds 26 through 30.

BALTIMORE
1. Sims, George, B, Baylor, 4
2. Gage, Bob, B, Clemson, 14
4. Kohl, Ralph, T, Michigan, 25
5. Jones, Wally (Wah-Wah), E, Kentucky, 33
6. Pattee, Frank, B, Kansas, 41
7. Folger, Frank, B, Duke, 49
8. Prymunski, Bob, T, Illinois, 57
9. Faunce, Everett, B, Minnesota, 65
10. Alexander, Kale, T, South Carolina, 73
11. Page, Paul, B, SMU, 81
12. Owens, Jim, E, Oklahoma, 89
13. Beson, Warren, C, Minnesota, 97
14. Moon, David, B, SMU, 105
15. Jenkins, John, T, Dartmouth, 113
16. O'Quinn, John, E, Wake Forest, 121
17. Geary, Clyde, T, Connecticut Wesleyan, 129
18. Sanders, Al, T, Southern Mississippi, 135
19. Sundheim, Guy, C, Northwestern, 141*
20. Lazier, Mernie, B, Illinois, 147
21. Larche, Harry, T, Arkansas State, 153
25. Grothus, Joe, G, Iowa, 168
26. Gillory, Byron, B, Texas, 173
27. Cox, Bob, E, North Carolina, 178
28. DeMoss, Bob, B, Purdue, 183
29. Pryor, George, F, Wake Forest, 188

BROOKLYN
1. Sullivan, Joe, B, Dartmouth, 2
2. Szafaryn, Len, T, North Carolina, 10
   Walsh, Bill, C, Notre Dame, 11
   Ferry, Lou, T, Villanova, 12
3. Triplett, Wally, B, Penn State, 16
4. Tokarczyk, Dolph, G, Pennsylvania, 23
5. Quinn, Joe, G, Cornell, 31*
6. Skladany, Leo, E, Pittsburgh, 39
7. Chewning, Lynn, B, Hampden-Sydney, 47
8. McCurry, Bob, C, Michigan State, 55
9. Klemovitch, Chuck, G, Columbia, 63
10. Duncan, Bob, E, Duke, 71*
11. Chollet, Hilary, B, Cornell, 79*
12. Davis, Bill, G, Duke, 87
13. Dale, Roland, T, Mississippi, 95
14. Alexander, Murry, E, Mississippi State, 103
15. Derrick, Howard, B, Tennessee-Chattanooga, 111
16. Armstrong, Dale, E, Dartmouth, 119
17. Younger, Paul (Tank), B, Grambling, 127
18. Holgren, Mitchell, T, Hartford, 133
19. Weaver, Frank, B, Moravian, 139
20. Price, Eddie, B, Tulane, 145
21. Geosits, John, T, Bucknell, 151
22. Brennan, Tom, G, Boston College, 157
23. Mc Bride, Jack, E, Rice, 160
24. Folson, Bobby, E, SMU, 163
25. Long, Bill, E, Oklahoma State, 166

BUFFALO
1. Kay, Bill, T, Iowa, 6
3. Keeney, Hugh, B, Rice, from Chi. Hornets, 15
   Kissell, Vito, B, Holy Cross, 19
4. Volz, Wilbur, B, Missouri, 27
5. Gaul, Frank, G, Notre Dame, 35
6. Guess, Frank, B, Texas, 43
7. Ensminger, Harold, QB, Missouri, 51
8. Vasicek, Vic, G, Texas, 59
9. Verdova, Alex, B, Ohio State, 67
10. Russas, Al, E, Tennessee, 75
11. Settembre, Ernie, T, Miami, 83
12. Kormarnicki, Milt, C, Villanova, 91*
13. Songin, Butch, QB, Boston College, 99*
14. Cooper, Leon, T, Hardin-Simmons, 107
15. Tonnemaker, Clayton, C, Minnesota, 115*
16. Goode, Rob, B, Texas A & M, 123
17. Donovan, Art, G, Boston College, 131
18. Goodman, Jim, T, Maryland, 137
19. London, Merlin, E, Oklahoma State, 143
20. Breen, Marty, C, Canisius, 149
21. Simon, John, G, Penn State, 155
25. Hanula, Bernie, T, Wake Forest, 170
26. Deuber, Bob, B, Pennsylvania, 175
27. Lewis, Floyd, G, SMU, 180
28. Cochran, Leon, B, Auburn, 185
29. Leonard, Joe, T, Virginia, 190*

CHI. HORNETS
1. Heath, Stan, QB, Nevada-Reno, 1
2. Blanda, George, QB, Kentucky, 9
3. Choice to Buffalo
4. Finks, Jim, QB, Tulsa, 22
5. Falcone, Carmen, B, Pennsylvania, 30
6. Tamburo, Sam, B, Penn State, 38
7. Hutchinson, Ralph, T, Tennessee-Chattanooga, 46
8. Cain, Jim, E, Alabama, 54
9. Sabulo, Tino, C, San Francisco, 62*
10. Huey, Warren, E, Michigan State, 70
11. Van Brocklin, Norm, QB, Oregon, 78
12. Van Noy, Jay, B, Utah State, 86*
13. Wham, Tom, E, Furman, 94
14. Snowden, Ivan, T, Texas A & I, 102
15. Reynolds, Abbie, B, Texas Tech, 110*
16. Monroe, Dick, C, Kansas, 118
17. Guerre, George, B, Michigan State, 126
18. Phillips, John, B, Southern Mississippi, 132*
19. Smith, Verda (Vitamin T), B, Abilene Christian, 138
20. Davis, Clayton, C, Oklahoma State, 144

21. Benigni, George, E, Georgetown (Washington D.C.), 150
22. Patterson, R.M., T, McMurry, 156
23. Kemplin, Bill, E, North Texas State, 159*
24. Cadenhead, Bill, B, Alabama, 162*
25. Poole, Phil, G, Mississippi, 165

CLEVELAND
1. Mitchell, Jack, QB, Oklahoma, 8
3. Collins, Albin (Rip), B, LSU, 21
4. McLellan, Bill, T, Brown, 29
5. McNeill, Ed, E, Michigan, 37
6. O'Malley, Tom, B, Cincinnati, 45
7. Alexander, Phil, T, South Carolina, 53
8. Cannevino, Mike, B, Ohio State, 61
9. Walker, Doak, B, SMU, 69, F
10. Adams, Norb, B, Purdue, 77
11. Norton, Negley, T, Penn State, 85
12. Burns, Frank, B, Rutgers, 93
13. Self, Clarence, B, Wisconsin, 101
14. Kersulis, Walt, E, Illinois, 109
15. Stuart, Bobby Jack, B, Army, 117
16. Bowen, Dinkey, B, Georgia Tech, 125
25. Cooney, Larry, B, Penn State, 172
26. Lininger, Ray, C, Ohio State, 177
27. Gagne, Verne, E, Minnesota, 182
28. Moran, Jim, B, John Carroll, 187
29. Soboleski, Joe, T, Michigan, 192

LA DONS
1. Taliaferro, George, B, Indiana, 5
3. Rodgers, Hosea, B, North Carolina, 18
4. Meinert, Bob, B, Oklahoma State, 26
5. Grimes, Bill, B, Oklahoma State, 34
6. Geri, Joe, B, Georgia, 42
7. Renna, Bill, C, Santa Clara, 50
8. Austin, Bill, T, Oregon State, 58
9. Rubish, Mike, E, North Carolina, 66
10. Krall, Jerry, B, Ohio State, 74
11. Drazenovich, Chuck, B, Penn State, 82
12. Klosterman, Larry, G, North Carolina, 90
13. Blake, Tom, G, Cincinnati, 98
14. Lorenz, Dick, E, Oregon State, 106
15. Bastian, Bob, G, USC, 114
16. Steffen, Art, B, UCLA, 122
17. Gannon, Tom (Chip), B, Harvard, 130
18. Hatch, Larry, B, Washington, 136
19. Tiblier, Jerry, B, Mississippi, 142
20. Frasseto, Gene, T, California, 148
21. Clark, Jim, G, Mississippi, 154
25. Ralston, Ed, B, Richmond, 169
26. Donaldson, John, B, Georgia, 174
27. Eisenberg, Lloyd, T, Duke, 179
28. Pastre, George, T, UCLA, 184
29. Ethridge, Joe, G, SMU, 189

NY YANKEES
1. Thomason, Bobby, QB, Virginia Military, 3
2. Panelli, John (Pep), B, Notre Dame, 13
3. Howard, Sherman, B, Nevada-Reno, 17
4. Rifenburg, Dick, E, Michigan, 24
5. Maddock, George, T, Northwestern, 32
6. Panciera, Don, QB, San Francisco, 40
7. Garza, Dan, E, Oregon, 48
8. Bell, Brian, B, Washington & Lee, 56
9. Mastrangeli, Al, C, Illinois, 64
10. Goldsberry, John, T, Indiana, 72
11. Bendrick, Ben, B, Wisconsin, 80
12. Van Deren, Frank, E, California, 88*
13. Berrang, Ed, E, Villanova, 96
14. Doornink, Bob, T, Washington State, 104
15. Glenn, Jack, T, Georgia Tech, 112
16. Bruce, Jack, B, William & Mary, 120
17. Johnson, Gil, B, SMU, 128
18. Hafen, Banard, E, Utah, 134
19. Jensen, Hal, B, San Francisco, 140
20. Kalmanir, Tommy (Cricket), B, Nevada, 146
21. Beasley, Al, G, St. Mary's (California), 152
22. Tolman, Ernie, E, USC, 158
23. Morrical, Gerry, T, Indiana, 161
24. Hood, Bob, E, Alabama, 164
25. Nagel, Ross, T, St. Louis, 167

SAN FRANCISCO
1. Fritz, Chester, T, Missouri, 7
3. Lovuolo, Frank, E, St. Bonaventure, 20
4. De Noia, Mike, B, Scranton, 28
5. Brodnax, George, E, Georgia Tech, 36
6. Hamberger, John, T, SMU, 44
7. Steigman, Dan, C, North Carolina, 52
8. Reid, Bernie, G, Georgia, 60
9. Wendt, Fred, B, Texas-El Paso, 68
10. Flowers, Dick, T, Alabama, 76
11. Lund, Bob, B, Tennessee, 84
12. Baker, Jon, G, California, 92
13. Reichert, Jim, G, Arkansas, 100
14. Garlin, Don, B, California, 108
15. Wismann, Pete, C, St. Louis, 116
16. Hobbs, Homer, G, Georgia, 124
25. Schoultz, Paul, B, Miami (Ohio), 171
26. Kelly, Jack, T, Louisiana Tech, 176
27. Flanakin, Jasper, E, Baylor, 181
28. Smith, Rudy, T, Louisiana Tech, 186
29. Long, Gordon, B, Arkansas, 191

1950

Held January 21-22, 1950

When the NFL and the AAFC merged on December 9, 1949, the NFL draft, like the league, increased by three teams—the Baltimore Colts, the Cleveland Browns, and the San Francisco 49ers. At the draft, members of the 1949 New York Bulldogs' active roster and reserve list were eligible to be selected along with the college seniors. Such players have NY Bulldogs in parentheses after their school.

Shortly after the draft, the New York Yankees of the AAFC were divided between the New York Giants and the Bulldogs. The rest of the AAFC players went into a special allocation pool from which they were selected by the NFL teams. Each team received 10 choices in the allocation draft, except for Baltimore, which received 15. Before the start of the 1950 season, the Bulldogs-Yankees team was renamed the New York Yanks.

BALTIMORE
1. Burk, Adrian, QB, Baylor
2. Campbell, Leon (Muscles), B, Arkansas
3. Colo, Don, T, Brown
4. Murray, Earl, G, Purdue
5. Halliday, Jack, G, SMU
6. Rich, Herb, B, Vanderbilt
7. Bok, Art, B, Dayton
8. Harris, Dick, C, Texas
9. Bass, Bill, B, Arkansas
10. Fry, Errol, G, Texas
11. Romanosky, Joe, T, St. Bonaventure
12. Dey, Bill, B, Dartmouth
13. Stone, Ray, E, Texas
14. Smiarowski, Mitch, C, St. Bonaventure
15. Spinney, Art, E, Boston College
16. Fisher, Dave, B, Southwestern Louisiana
17. Murphy, Ralph, G, Rice
18. Schoolmaster, Charley, C, Western Michigan
19. Waddail, Bill, B, Auburn
20. Dunlap, Sheldon, G, Cincinnati
21. Phillips, Tom, B, Baldwin-Wallace
22. Armstrong, Chip, C, Occidental
23. Wettlaufer, Harry, E, Pennsylvania
24. Petroski, Bill, T, Holy Cross
25. Pepper, Jim, G, Syracuse
26. Mazzanti, Gino, B, Arkansas
27. Johnson, Mitford, B, Baylor
28. Adcock, John, T, Auburn
29. Graham, Bob (Snakey), B, Pennsylvania
30. Blake, Tom, G, Cincinnati (NY Bulldogs)

CHI. BEARS
1. Hunsinger, Chuck, B, Florida, from NY Bulldogs
   Morrison, Fred (Curly), B, Ohio State
2. Dottley, John (Kayo), B, Mississippi
3. Romanik, Steve, B, Villanova
4. Novak, Tom, C, Nebraska, from Pittsburgh
   Papaleo, Dom, G, Boston College
5. Zalejski, Ernie, B, Notre Dame
6. Perricone, Gaspar, B, Northwestern, from NY Giants
   Hansen, Wayne, C, Texas-El Paso
7. Prather, Rollin, E, Kansas State
8. Nevills, Sam, T, Oregon
9. Reid, Floyd, B, Georgia, from NY Bulldogs
   Braznell, Dick, B, Missouri
10. Wahl, Al, T, Michigan
11. Helwig, John, G, Notre Dame
12. Roof, Kenny, B, Oklahoma State
13. Dempsey, Frank, T, Florida
14. Hover, Al, G, LSU
15. Glisson, Jimmy, B, Tulane
16. Bradley, Ed, E, Wake Forest
17. Janaszek, Ray, B, Dayton
18. Andrews, Rupert, B, Stanford
19. Bye, Billy, B, Minnesota
20. Crawford, Jim (Tank), G, Mississippi
21. Angle, Bob, B, Iowa State
22. Byler, Jim, G, North Carolina State
23. Bigham, Bill, T, Harding
24. Polenske, Walt, B, Pacific
25. Samuels, Perry, B, Texas
26. Sella, George, B, Princeton
27. Davis, Wilton, B, Hardin-Simmons
28. Kenary, Jim, B, Harvard
29. Nadherny, Ferd, B, Yale
30. Markert, Allen, T, Minnesota

CHI. CARDINALS
1. Choice to LA Rams
2. Jennings, Jack, T, Ohio State
3. Svoboda, Bill, B, Tulane, from NY Bulldogs
   Polsfoot, Fran, E, Washington State
4. Paul, Don, B, Washington State
5. Kiilsgaard, Carl, T, Idaho
6. Wood, Warren, G, Puget Sound
7. Gay, Billy, B, Notre Dame, from NY Giants, F
   Bagdon, Eddie, G, Michigan State
8. Hock, John, T, Santa Clara
9. Ragazzo, Vito, E, William & Mary
10. Grothaus, Walt, C, Notre Dame
   Lavigne, Milt, B, Southeastern Louisiana, from Pittsburgh
11. Ison, J.D., E, Baylor
12. Wallheiser, Frank, E, Western Kentucky
   Sharpe, Bob, G, Davidson, from Pittsburgh
13. Hennessey, Jerry, E, Santa Clara
14. Andros, Dee, G, Oklahoma
15. Langford, Al, B, Howard Payne
16. Bierman, Harry, E, Furman
17. Palmer, Tom, T, Wake Forest
18. Espenan, Ray, E, Notre Dame
19. Day, Loran, B, Northwestern
20. Halbert, Webb, B, Iowa State
21. Blumhardt, Howard, B, South Dakota
22. Lipinski, Jim, T, Fairmont State
23. Montgomery, Bill, B, Fresno State
24. Gambold, Bob, B, Washington State, F
25. Truman, Lee, B, Kentucky
26. Pittman, Jim, B, Mississippi State
27. Bienemann, Tom, E, Drake*
28. Jones, Sonny, B, Wyoming
29. Montagne, Bill, B, California
30. Banonis, Vic, C, Georgetown (Washington D.C.)

CLEVELAND
1. Carpenter, Ken, B, Oregon State
2. Sandusky, John, T, Villanova, from Detroit
   Martin, Jim, E, Notre Dame
3. Robinson, Jimmy Joe, B, Pittsburgh
4. Wilson, Bob (Red), C, Wisconsin
5. Phelps, Don (Dopey), B, Kentucky
6. Gorgal, Ken, B, Purdue
7. Carter, Win, B, Missouri
8. Frizzell, Russ, T, Tulsa
9. Duncan, Jim, E, Wake Forest
10. O'Pella, Frank, B, William & Mary
11. Plotz, Bob, G, Pittsburgh
12. Cole, Emerson, B, Toledo
13. Wright, Rupe, G, Baylor
14. Harrington, Packard, C, St. Mary's California)
15. Meland, Ted, G, Oregon
16. King, Art, G, Ball State
17. McKinney, Hal, G, Missouri Valley
18. Travue, Joe, B, Louisville
19. Songin, Eddie (Butch), B, Boston College
20. Hackney, John, G, Murray State
21. Vogts, Leroy, G, Washington (St. Louis)
22. Dowling, Jim, G, Santa Clara
23. Moselle, Don, B, Wisconsin-Superior
24. Woodland, Jack, B, Bowling Green
25. Brasher, Jim, C, Maryland
26. Toogood, Charley, T, Nebraska*
27. Gray, Dick, B, Oregon State
28. Pyle, Billy, B, Texas
29. Schnelker, Bob, E, Bowling Green
30. Massey, Jim, B, Detroit

DETROIT
BONUS CHOICE: Hart, Leon, E, Notre Dame
1. Watson, Joe, C, Rice
2. Choice to Cleveland
   McGraw, Thurman (Fum), T, Colorado State, from Philadelphia
3. Murakowski, Art, B, Northwestern
4. Kiely, Ernie, G, Texas-El Paso
5. Fitkin, Hal, B, Dartmouth
6. Jaszewski, Floyd, T, Minnesota
7. Leverman, Bill, B, St. Edward's
8. McAllister, Ralph, B, Minnesota
9. Wood, Ed, G, Detroit
10. Malcolm, Roland, B, Gustavus Adolphus
11. Wilson, Jack, T, Ohio State
12. Walters, Bucky, T, Brown
13. Ryan, Jim, B, San Francisco
14. Squires, Cliff, C, Nebraska Wesleyan
15. Worthington, Tom, B, Northwestern
16. Greiner, Jerry, C, Detroit
17. Callahan, Connie, B, Morningside
18. Stansauk, Don, T, Denver
19. Cifelli, Gus, T, Notre Dame
20. Davis, Fred, E, Maryland
21. Brewer, George, B, Oklahoma
22. Tate, Jim, T, Purdue
23. Heller, Irv, T, Boston U.
24. McDowell, Jim, G, William & Mary
25. Glick, Gene, B, Michigan State
26. Lee, Bobby Coy, B, Texas
27. Johnson, Elbert, E, Texas Tech
28. Karras, Johnny, B, Illinois*
29. Steger, Russ, B, Illinois
30. DeRoin, Rube, C, Oklahoma State

GREEN BAY
1. Tonnemaker, Clayton, C, Minnesota
2. Rote, Tobin, QB, Rice
3. Soltau, Gordy, E, Minnesota
4. Coutre, Larry, B, Notre Dame
5. Choice to Pittsburgh
6. Cloud, Jack, B, William & Mary
7. Manley, Leon, G, Oklahoma
8. Szulborski, Harry, B, Purdue
9. Wilson, Roger, E, South Carolina
10. Mealey, Bob, T, Minnesota
11. Lorendo, Gene, E, Georgia
12. Pavich, Andy, E, Denver
13. Elliott, Carlton, E, Virginia
14. Leon, Fred, T, Nevada-Reno
15. Huebner, Gene, C, Baylor
16. Kuzma, Frank, B, Minnesota
17. Otterback, Hal, G, Wisconsin
18. Galiffa, Arnold, QB, Army
19. Rowan, Earl, T, Hardin-Simmons
20. Howe, Jim, B, Kentucky
21. Evans, Gene, B, Wisconsin
22. Beatty, Chuck, C, Penn State
23. Mattey, George, G, Ohio State
24. Delph, Don, B, Dayton
25. Waters, Frank, B, Michigan State
26. Radtke, Claude, E, Lawrence
27. Osborne, Bill, B, Nevada-Reno
28. Hering, Herm, B, Rutgers
29. Zaranka, Ben, E, Kentucky
30. Mallouf, Ray, B, SMU (NY Bulldogs)

LA RAMS
1. Pasquariello, Ralph, B, Villanova, from Chi. Cardinals
   West, Stan, G, Oklahoma
2. Fuchs, Bob, C, Missouri
3. Murray, Don, T, Penn State
4. Proctor, Ben, E, Texas
5. McKissack, Dick, B, SMU
6. Langrell, Orville, T, Oklahoma City
7. Coggin, Cliff, E, Southern Mississippi
8. Lewis, Woodley, B, Oregon
9. Cowan, Les, E, McMurry, F
10. Van Noy, Jay, B, Utah State
11. Roundy, Jay, B, USC, from NY Giants
   Stuvek, Fred, G, West Virginia
12. Lunney, John, G, Arkansas
13. Winbigler, Tom, B, College of Idaho
14. Trautwein, Bill, T, Ohio State
15. Stephenson, Dave (Trapper), C, West Virginia
16. Maloney, Jim, E, Fordham
17. Neugold, Harry, T, Rensselaer
18. Collier, Bobby, T, SMU, F
19. Smith, Johnny, E, Arizona
20. Young, Bill, B, Hillsdale
21. Klein, Bill, E, Hanover
22. Barber, Doug, B, Dakota Wesleyan
23. Bird, Jim, T, USC
24. Joiner, Joe, E, Austin
25. Towler, (Deacon) Dan, B, Washington & Jefferson
26. Haldy, Otto, T, Mankato State
27. Kilman, Hal, T, TCU
28. Morgan, Junior, E, San Jose State
29. Heck, Bob, B, Pacific
30. Lange, Bill, G, Dayton

NY BULLDOGS
1. Choice to Chi. Bears
2. Weiner, Art, E, North Carolina
3. Choice to Chi. Cardinals
4. Toth, Zollie, B, LSU

5. Swistowicz, Mike, B, Notre Dame
6. Aldridge, Ben, B, Oklahoma State
7. Narrell, Don, T, TCU
8. Archer, Jack, B, TCU
9. Choice to Chi. Bears
10. Lyle, Melvin, E, LSU
11. McAuley, Roger, G, TCU
12. Hillhouse, Andy, Texas A&M
13. Morton, Jack, B, West Virginia
14. Carmichael, Ed, G, Oregon State
15. Messeroll, Norm, T, Tennessee
16. Stetter, Bill, C, Holy Cross
17. Tidwell, Joe Dean, B, Harding (Tennessee)
18. Champion, Jim, T, Mississippi State
19. Griffin, Bob, B, Baylor
20. Royal, Darrell, B, Oklahoma
21. French, Bud, B, Kansas
22. Johnson, R.V., T, St. Mary's (California)
23. Sheffield, Dick, E, Tulane
24. DeYoung, Bill, B, Stanford
25. Dotur, Steve, G, Oregon
26. Noonan, Red, B, Alabama
27. Olson, Chuck, E, Washington
28. Petty, Ed, C, Hardin-Simmons
29. Jasonek, Ed, B, Furman
30. Poulos, John, B, Pacific

NY GIANTS
1. Tidwell, Travis, B, Auburn
2. Price, Eddie, B, Tulane
3. Clay, Randy, B, Texas
4. Payne, Porter, G, Georgia
5. Griffith, Forrest, B, Kansas
6. Choice to Chi. Bears
7. Choice to Chi. Cardinals
8. Van Buren, Ebert, B, LSU*
9. Cisterna, Vince, E, Northern Arizona
10. Wilkinson, Bob, E, UCLA, F
11. Choice to LA Rams
12. Wietecha, Ray, C, Northwestern
13. Kelly, Joe, C, Wisconsin
14. Fritz, Gene, T, Minnesota
15. Roberson, Bill, T, Stephen F. Austin
16. Jackson, Bob (Stonewall), B, North Carolina A&T
17. Hatfield, Steve, B, Shippensburg
18. Roman, George, T, Case Western Reserve (NY Bulldogs)
19. Barzilauskas, Fritz, G, Yale (NY Bulldogs)
20. Tangaro, Joe, T, Utah
21. Stribling, Bill, E, Mississippi, F
22. DeMoss, Bob, B, Purdue (NY Bulldogs)
23. Davis, Warren, C, Colgate
24. Finnin, Tom, T, Detroit
25. Beiersdorf, Ken, B, Minnesota
26. Copp, Carl, T, Vanderbilt
27. Sweet, Art, B, Baylor
28. McAuliffe, Don, B, Michigan State, F
29. Boyda, Mike, B, Washington & Lee (NY Bulldogs)
30. Tanner, Hampton, T, Georgia

PHILADELPHIA
1. Grant, Harry (Bud), E, Minnesota
2. Choice to Detroit
3. Sandoro, Bob, B, Oregon
4. McChesney, Bob, E, Hardin-Simmons
5. Kaysserian, Mike, B, Detroit
6. McDermott, Lloyd, T, Kentucky
7. Olix, Mel, B, Miami (Ohio)
8. O'Hanlon, Dick, T, Ohio State
9. Wilson, Bobby, B, Mississippi
10. Johnson, Ernie, B, UCLA
11. Lantrip, Bobby, B, Rice
12. Mahoney, Frank, E, Brown
13. Willey, Norm (Wildman), B, Marshall
14. Hix, Billy, E, Arkansas
15. Carey, Herb, B, Dartmouth
16. Marck, Jim, T, Xavier
17. Taylor, Jerry, C, Mississippi State
18. Tunnicliff, Ed, B, Northwestern
19. Robinson, Darrell, E, Oregon
20. Pregulman, Merv, G, Michigan (NY Bulldogs)
21. Cross, Marv, B, Washington State
22. Hague, Jim, E, Ohio State
23. Lesko, Al, T, St. Bonaventure
24. DeSylvia, Tom, G, Oregon State
25. Eagles, Jim, C, North Texas State
26. Franz, Rod, G, California
27. Martin, Bill, B, USC
28. Burson, Don, B, Northwestern
29. Curtier, Wes, T, Richmond
30. Parker, Dud, B, Baylor

PITTSBURGH
1. Chandnois, Lynn, B, Michigan State
2. Stautner, Ernie, T, Boston College
3. Hughes, George, G, William & Mary
4. Choice to Chi. Bears
5. Rowe, Tom, E, Dartmouth, from Green Bay
   Allen, Lou, T, Duke
6. Mattson, Ed, B, Trinity (Texas)
7. Smith, Truett, B, Mississippi State
8. Rogel, Fran, B, Penn State
9. Druen, Max, T, Tulane
10. Choice to Chi. Cardinals
11. Williams, Charley, E, Sam Houston State
12. Choice to Chi. Cardinals
13. Norton, Negley, T, Penn State
14. Kynes, Jim, C, Florida
15. Russell, Harry, B, San Jose State
16. Barkouskie, Bernie, G, Pittsburgh
17. Bodine, Al, B, Georgia
18. Powell, Kenneth, E, North Carolina
19. Gaul, Frank, T, Notre Dame
20. DeNoia, Mike, B, Scranton
21. Tomlinson, Dick, G, Kansas
22. Burak, Stan, B, George Washington
23. Kersulis, Walt, E, Illinois
24. Weaver, John, G, Miami (Ohio)
25. Numbers, Bob, C, Lehigh
26. Vaccaro, Nick, B, Florida
27. Kreiser, Elmer, E, Bloomsburg
28. Diehl, Jerry, B, Idaho
29. DePasqua, Carl, B, Pittsburgh
30. Hudak, Ed, T, Notre Dame

SAN FRANCISCO
1. Nomellini, Leo, T, Minnesota
2. Campora, Don, T, Pacific
3. Collins, Ray, T, LSU
4. Bailey, Morris, E, TCU
5. Kane, Harry, C, Pacific
6. Van Pool, Don, E, Oklahoma State
7. Berry, Lindy, B, TCU
8. Williams, Ellery, E, Santa Clara
9. Zinach, Pete, B, West Virginia
10. Celeri, Bob, B, California
11. Dow, Harley, T, San Jose State
12. Burke, Don, B, USC
13. Cecconi, Lou (Bimbo), B, Pittsburgh
14. Payne, Tom, E, Santa Clara
15. Crampsey, Leo, E, St. Bonaventure
16. Shaw, Charley, G, Oklahoma State
17. Van Meter, Cliff, B, Tulane
18. Genito, Ralph, B, Kentucky
19. Klein, Forest, G, California
20. Nix, Jack, E, USC
21. Alker, Guerin, C, Loyola (Los Angeles)
22. Wilson, Billy, E, San Jose State, F
23. Williams, Jim (Froggy), E, Rice
24. Wyman, Bill, T, Rice
25. Dunn, Bob, G, Dayton
26. Powers, Jim, B, USC
27. Johnson, Ken, G, Pacific
28. Hall, Charley, B, Arizona
29. Whelan, Bob, B, Boston U.
30. Stillwell, Bob, E, USC

WASHINGTON
1. Thomas, George, B, Oklahoma
2. Haynes, Hall, B, Santa Clara
3. Karras, Lou, T, Purdue
4. Ulinski, Harry, C, Kentucky
5. Spaniel, Frank, B, Notre Dame
6. Pepper, Gene, G, Missouri
7. Houghton, Jerry, T, Washington State
8. Rohde, John, E, Pacific
9. Winslow, Don, T, Iowa
10. LeBaron, Eddie, QB, Pacific
11. Brown, Dan, E, Villanova
12. Chauncey, Bill, B, Iowa State
13. Davis, Clay, C, Oklahoma State
14. Button, Lyle, T, Illinois
15. Loyd, Alex, E, Oklahoma State
16. Justice, Charlie (Choo-Choo), B, North Carolina
17. Cullom, Jim, G, California
18. Duke, Alvin, B, Arkansas
19. White, Ed, E, Alabama
20. Bayer, George, T, Washington
21. Witucki, Cas (Slug), G, Indiana
22. deLaurentis, John, T, Waynesburg
23. Zuravleff, Joe, E, Northwestern
24. Tilton, Dick, T, Nevada-Reno
25. Stewart, Art, B, Southeastern Oklahoma
26. Roth, Earl, B, Maryland
27. Lee, Ed, T, Kansas
28. Shoaf, Ralph, B, Virginia
29. Lundin, Johnny, G, Minnesota
30. Noppinger, Bob, E, Georgetown (Washington D.C.)

1951

Held January 18-19, 1951

After the Baltimore franchise disbanded following the 1950 season, players from its active roster and reserve list were made eligible for the draft along with college seniors. Such players have Baltimore in parentheses after their school.

CHI. BEARS
1. Williams, Bob, QB, Notre Dame, from Baltimore
   Stone, Billy, B, Bradley, from NY Yanks (Baltimore)
   Schroeder, Gene, E, Virginia
2. George, Bill, T, Wake Forest
3. White, Wilford (Whizzer), B, Arizona State
4. Moser, Bob, C, Pacific
   Jelley, Tom, E, Miami, from NY Giants
5. Rowland, Brad, B, McMurry
6. Falkenberg, Herb, B, Trinity (Texas)
7. Lea, Paul, T, Tulane
8. Mayes, Clair, G, Oklahoma
9. Gregus, Bill, Wake Forest
10. Sherrill, J.W., B, Tennessee
11. Hardiman, Tom, B, Georgetown (Washington D.C.)
12. Hairston, Lawrence (Punjab), T, Nevada-Reno
13. Wright, Charley, B, West Texas State
14. Woods, Bailey, B, Abilene Christian
15. Hall, Sid, C, Pacific
16. Volm, Frank, E, Marquette
17. Dufek, Don, B, Michigan
18. Brown, Chuck, G, Illinois
19. Lisak, Ed, B, Oklahoma
20. Smith, Larry, C, South Carolina
21. Higgins, Larry, B, Fordham
22. Hanson, Bob, G, Montana
23. Hlavac, Rene, T, Nebraska-Omaha
24. Dokas, Pete, E, Mansfield
25. Miller, Johnny, B, Northwestern
26. Rogers, Buddy, B, Arkansas
27. Taylor, Jerry, C, Wyoming
28. Campbell, Leon (Muscles), B, Arkansas (Baltimore)
29. Justice, John, G, Santa Clara
30. Butler, Charley, E, George Washington

CHI. CARDINALS
1. Groom, Jerry, C, Notre Dame
2. Joyce, Don, T, Tulane
3. Stonesifer, Don, E, Northwestern
4. Doyne, Dick, B, Lehigh
5. Lynch, Lynn, G, Illinois, from Washington
   Choice to San Francisco
6. Jasonek, Ed, B, Furman
7. Punches, Dick, T, Colorado
8. Sanford, Leo, C, Louisiana Tech
9. Schmidt, Neil, B, Purdue
10. Cooper, Ken, G, Vanderbilt (Baltimore)
11. Bienemann, Tom, E, Drake
12. Landry, Jack, B, Notre Dame
13. Peters, Volney, T, USC
14. Leskovar, Bill, B, Kentucky
15. Simcic, John, G, Wisconsin
16. Miller, Gene, B, Northwestern
17. May, Henry, C, Southwest Missouri State
18. Pomeroy, Russ, T, Stanford
19. Ackerman, Gene, E, Missouri
20. Wallner, Fred, G, Notre Dame
21. Bunting, Dick, E, Drake
22. Whitman, S.J., B, Tulsa
23. Owens, Jim, E, Oklahoma (Baltimore)
24. Cross, Billy, B, West Texas State
25. Quick, Vernon, G, Wofford
26. Fleischmann, Jeff, B, Cornell
27. Huxhold, Ken, T, Wisconsin
28. Martin, Dick, B, Kentucky
29. Livingston, Bob, B, Notre Dame (Baltimore)
30. Root, Leon, B, Rutgers

CLEVELAND
1. Konz, Kenny, B, LSU
2. Curtis, Bucky, E, Vanderbilt
3. Helluin, Jerry, T, Tulane, F
4. Oristaglio, Bob, E, Pennsylvania, from San Francisco (Baltimore)
   Smith, Bob, B, Texas A&M, from Green Bay
   Donovan, Art, T, Boston College (Baltimore)
5. Loomis, Ace, B, Wisconsin-La Crosse
6. Rogas, Dan, G, Tulane
7. Holdash, Irv, C, North Carolina, from NY Yanks
   Michaels, Walt, B, Washington & Lee
8. Spinney, Art, E, Boston College, from Green Bay (Baltimore)
   Clark, Max, B, Houston
9. Toler, Burl, G, San Francisco, from Detroit
   Shula, Don, B, John Carroll
10. Gierula, Chet, G, Maryland
11. Custis, Bernie, B, Syracuse
12. Seillers, Milan, B, Florida State, from Detroit
    Kirtley, Stew, E, Morehead State
13. Voskuhl, Bob, C, Georgetown (Kentucky)
14. Cernoch, Rudy, T, Northwestern
15. Skibinski, Joe, G, Purdue, F
16. Pasky, Ed, B, South Carolina
17. Ka-Ne, Leroy, B, Dayton
18. DeRoin, Rube, C, Oklahoma State
19. Solari, Ray, G, California
20. Crocher, Jack, B, Tulsa
21. Stone, Ray, E, Texas
22. Taseff, Carl, B, John Carroll
23. Champion, Johnny, B, SMU
24. Benner, Wayne, B, Florida State
25. Knispel, John, T, Wisconsin-La Crosse
26. Williams, Fred, T, Arkansas, F
27. Jones, Jack, B, Livingston
28. Thrift, Roger, B, East Carolina
29. Driver, Bill, B, Florida State
30. Averno, Sisto, G, Muhlenberg (Baltimore)

DETROIT
1. Choice to Philadelphia
2. Stanfel, Dick, G, San Francisco
3. Dibble, Dorne, E, Michigan State
4. D'Alonzo, Pete, B, Villanova
5. Doran, Jim, E, Iowa State
   Torgeson, LaVern, C, Washington State, from NY Yanks
6. Christiansen, Jack, B, Colorado State
7. Monsen, Bob, T, Ohio State
8. Raklovits, Dick, B, Illinois
9. Choice to Cleveland
10. Shoaf, Jim, G, LSU
11. Anderson, Frankie, E, Oklahoma
12. Choice to Cleveland
13. Siegert, Wayne, T, Illinois
14. Wittmer, Lee, T, Detroit
15. Hill, Jimmie, B, Tennessee
16. Geremsky, Ted, E, Pittsburgh
17. Meisenheimer, Darrell, B, Oklahoma State
18. Wolgast, Eddie, B, Arizona
19. Hanson, Gordy, T, Washington State
20. Gibbons, Harry, B, South Dakota State
21. Block, King, B, Idaho
22. Foldberg, Dan, E, Army
23. Gabriel, Dick, B, Lehigh
24. Buksar, George, B, Purdue (Baltimore)
25. Harris, Dick, C, Texas (Baltimore)
26. Kazmierski, Frank, C, West Virginia
27. Allis, Harry, E, Michigan
28. Peot, Dick, T, South Dakota State
29. Womack, Bruce, T, West Texas State
30. Horwath, Ron, B, Detroit

GREEN BAY
1. Gain, Bob, T, Kentucky
2. Collins, Albin (Rip), B, LSU (Baltimore)
3. Cone, Fred, B, Clemson
4. Choice to Cleveland
5. Stinson, Wade, B, Kansas
6. Holowenko, Sig, T, John Carroll
7. Sutherland, Bill, E, St. Vincent
8. Choice to Cleveland
9. McWilliams, Dick, T, Michigan
10. Noppinger, Bob, T, Georgetown (Washington D.C.)
11. Rooks, George, B, Morgan State
12. Kreager, Carl, C, Michigan
13. Stephens, Ed, B, Missouri
14. Bauer, Ray, E, Montana
15. Ernst, Joe, B, Tulane
16. Afflis, Dick (The Bruiser), T, Nevada-Reno
17. Pelfrey, Ray, B, Eastern Kentucky
18. Petela, Ed, B, Boston College
19. Liber, Jim, B, Xavier
20. Johnson, Dick, T, Virginia
21. Edling, Art, E, Minnesota
22. Felker, Art, E, Marquette
23. Chamberlain, Tubba, G, Wisconsin-Eau Claire
24. Christie, Dick, B, Nebraska-Omaha
25. Monte, Charlie, B, Hillsdale
26. Miller, Bill, T, Ohio State
27. Bossons, Bob, C, Georgia Tech
28. Ayre, Bill, B, Abilene Christian

29. Fieler, Ralph, E, Miami
30. Withers, Ed, B, Wisconsin

LA RAMS
1. McFadin, Bud, G, Texas
2. Rich, Herb, B, Vanderbilt (Baltimore)
3. Toogood, Charley, T, Nebraska
4. Kinek, George, B, Tulane
5. Momsen, Tony, C, Michigan
6. Hecker, Norb, E, Baldwin-Wallace
7. Egler, Alan, B, Colgate
8. Primiani, Hugo, T, Boston U.
9. Lang, Nolan, B, Oklahoma
10. Kirkby, Roland, B, Washington
11. Natyshak, John, B, Tampa
12. Hardey, Don, B, Pacific
13. Reid, Joe, C, LSU
14. McCoy, Rob, B, Georgia Tech
15. Posey, Obie, B, Southern
16. Robertson, Bill, E, Memphis State
17. Riley, Hal, E, Baylor
18. Daugherty, Dick, G, Oregon
19. Robustelli, Andy, E, Arnold
20. Nutter, Jim, B, Wichita State
21. Stelle, Earl, B, Oregon
22. Baggett, Billy, B, LSU
23. Thomas, Dean, T, Michigan State
24. Abeltin, Harry, T, Colgate
25. Calvert, Jackie, T, Clemson
26. Ruetz, Howie, T, Loras
27. Brosky, Al, B, Illinois, F
28. Wingo, Sterling, B, Virginia Tech
29. Jackson, Earl, B, Texas Tech
30. Hanley, Alvin, B, Kentucky State

NY GIANTS
BONUS CHOICE: Rote, Kyle, B, SMU
1. Spavital, Jim, B, Oklahoma State (Baltimore)
2. Krouse, Ray, T, Maryland
3. Grandelius, Sonny, B, Michigan State
4. Choice to Chi. Bears
5. Stroud, Jack, T, Tennessee
6. Hannah, Herb, T, Alabama
7. Williams, Joel, C, Texas (Baltimore)
8. Benners, Fred, B, SMU, F
9. Donan, Holland, T, Princeton
10. Murray, Earl, G, Purdue (Baltimore)
11. Bagnell, Reds, B, Pennsylvania
12. Hudson, Bob, E, Clemson
13. Douglass, Paul, B, Illinois
14. Flanagan, Pat, T, Marquette
15. Vykukal, Gene, T, Texas
16. Pfeifer, Alan, E, Fordham
17. Sherrod, Bud, E, Tennessee
18. Smith, Frank, B, Miami
19. Conn, Billy, B, Auburn
20. Albright, Bill, T, Wisconsin
21. Lemonick, Bernie, G, Pennsylvania
22. Binkley, Waldo, T, Austin Peay
23. Yelvington, Dick, T, Georgia
24. Kuh, Dick, G, Michigan State
25. Lagod, Chet, T, Tennessee-Chattanooga
26. Armstrong, Quincy, C, North Texas State
27. Hubbard, Charley, E, Morris Harvey
28. Quinn, Hal, G, SMU
29. Considine, John, T, Purdue

NY YANKS
1. Choice to Chi. Bears
2. Jackson, Ken, T, Texas
3. McCormack, Mike, T, Kansas
4. Wingate, Elmer, E, Maryland
5. Choice to Detroit
6. Musacco, George, B, Loyola (Los Angeles)
7. Choice to Cleveland
8. Lauer, Larry, C, Alabama
9. Colo, Don, T, Brown (Baltimore)
10. Thomas, Jesse, B, Michigan State
11. Wyndham, Steve, B, Clemson
12. Lary, Al, E, Alabama
13. Thomas, John, E, Oregon State*
14. Rapp, Charley, B, Duquesne
15. Wanamaker, Bill, G, Kentucky
16. Fray, Bill, T, Idaho
17. Rowan, Dick, C, Texas
18. Watson, Bob, E, UCLA
19. Longmore, Ralph, B, Duquesne
20. Price, Jerrell, T, Texas Tech
21. Pollard, Al, B, Army
22. King, Ed, C, Boston College (Baltimore)
23. Cunningham, Dave, B, Utah
24. Stroschein, Breck, E, UCLA
25. Boudreaux, Roy, T, Southwestern Louisiana
26. Sherman, Will, B, St. Mary's (California)
27. Price, Ed, B, Texas Tech
28. Chadband, Jim, B, Idaho
29. Kissell, Veto, B, Holy Cross (Baltimore)
30. Shinn, Joe, E, Tulane

PHILADELPHIA
1. Van Buren, Ebert, B, LSU
Mutryn, Chet, B, Xavier, from Detroit (Baltimore)
2. Choice to Washington
3. Bruno, Al, E, Kentucky
4. Nagle, Fran, B, Nebraska
5. Dwyer, Jack, B, Loyola (Los Angeles)
6. Farragut, Ken, C, Mississippi
7. Boydston, Frank, B, Baylor
8. Richards, Jack, E, Arkansas
9. Doyle, Denny, G, Tulane
10. Schaufele, Louis, B, Arkansas
11. Pope, Bob, T, Kentucky
12. Rich, Henry, B, Arizona State
13. Mastellone, Pete, C, Miami
14. Walston, Bobby, E, Georgia
15. North, Bobby, B, Georgia Tech
16. Hatfield, Hal, E, USC
17. Waggoner, Hal, B, Tulane
18. Weeks, Bill, B, Iowa State
19. Bove, Jack, T, West Virginia
20. Glorioso, John, B, Missouri
21. Franklin, Neal, T, SMU
22. Rucker, Jack, B, Mississippi State
23. Bighead, Jack, E, Pepperdine*
24. Kotowski, Tony, E, Mississippi State
25. Drahn, Glenn, B, Iowa
26. Stewart, Billy, B, Mississippi State
27. Winship, Bob, T, Rice
28. Stendel, Marv, E, Arkansas
29. Hansen, Roscoe, T, North Carolina
30. Ford, John (Model-T), QB, Hardin-Simmons

PITTSBURGH
1. Avinger, Clarence (Butch), B, Alabama
2. Ortmann, Chuck, B, Michigan
3. Sulima, George, E, Boston U.
4. French, Barry (Bear), T, Purdue (Baltimore)
5. Sampson, Floyd, B, McMurry
6. Dodrill, Dale, G, Colorado State
7. Mathews, Ray, B, Clemson
8. Minarik, Hank, E, Michigan State
9. Schweder, John (Bull), G, Pennsylvania (Baltimore)
10. Salata, Paul, E, USC (Baltimore)
11. McCutcheon, Joe, C, Washington & Lee
12. Brandt, Jim, B, St. Thomas (Minnesota)
13. Szabo, Bill, T, Bucknell
14. Mizerany, Mike, G, Alabama
15. Webb, Clay, B, Kentucky
16. Oberg, Lambert, C, Trinity (Connecticut)
17. Gehlmann, Ted, T, William & Mary
18. Field, Pat, B, Georgia
19. Pavlikowski, Bill, B, Boston U.
20. Donnelly, Tom, T, Holy Cross
21. Cheatam, Ernie, T, Loyola (Los Angeles)
22. Hendley, Dick, B, Clemson
23. Minor, Joe, E, John Carroll
24. Alois, Art, C, San Francisco
25. Calvin, Tommy, B, Alabama
26. Pearman, Bill (Pug), G, Tennessee
27. Radcliffe, Bob, B, Wisconsin
28. Hansen, Howie, B, UCLA
29. Smith, Fred, E, Tulsa
30. Gruble, John, E, Tennessee

SAN FRANCISCO
1. Tittle, Y.A., QB, LSU (Baltimore)
2. Schabarum, Pete, B, California
3. Mixon, Bill, B, Georgia
4. Choice to Cleveland
5. Steere, Dick, T, Drake
Carapella, Al, T, Miami, from Chi. Cardinals
6. Strickland, Bishop, B, South Carolina
7. Forbes, Dick, E, St. Ambrose
8. Arenas, Joe, B, Nebraska-Omaha
9. Van Alstyne, Bruce, E, Stanford
10. Feher, Nick, G, Georgia
11. Jessup, Bill, E, USC
12. Monachino, Jim, B, California
13. Harvin, Dick, E, Georgia Tech
14. Berry, Rex, B, BYU
15. Sparks, Dave, G, South Carolina
16. White, Bob, B, Stanford
17. Michalik, Art, G, St. Ambrose
18. Murphy, Jim, T, Xavier
19. Phillips, John, B, Southern Mississippi
20. Tate, Al, T, Illinois
21. Brown, Hardy (Thumper), B, Tulsa
22. Winslow, Dwight, B, Boise J.C.
23. Brunswald, Wally, B, Gustavus Adolphus
24. Kingsford, Tom, B, Montana
25. Peterson, Mike, E, Denver
26. Carpenter, Keith, T, San Jose State
27. Lung, Ray, G, Oregon
28. Rohan, Jack, B, Loras
29. Garnett, S.P., T, Kansas
30. Faske, Jerry, B, Iowa

WASHINGTON
1. Heath, Leon, B, Oklahoma
2. Salem, Eddie, B, Alabama
Staton, Jim, T, Wake Forest, from Philadelphia
3. Yowarsky, Walt, T, Kentucky
4. Giroski, Paul, T, Rice
5. Choice to Chi. Cardinals
6. Martinkovic, John, E, Xavier
7. Papit, Johnny, B, Virginia
8. Cox, Billy, B, Duke
9. Rowden, Jake, C, Maryland
10. Jensen, Bob, E, Iowa State (Baltimore)
11. DeChard, Bill, B, Holy Cross
12. Applegate, Al, G, Scranton
13. Campbell, Dick, B, Wyoming
14. Burk, Adrian, QB, Baylor (Baltimore)
15. Thomas, Vic, T, Colorado
16. Bates, Bob, C, Texas A&M
17. Brito, Gene, E, Loyola (Los Angeles)
18. Fucci, Dom, B, Kentucky
19. Brown, Buddy, G, Arkansas
20. Kerestes, John, B, Purdue
21. Marable, Clarence, T, TCU
22. Speed, Elliot, C, Alabama
23. Martin, Cecil, B, North Texas State
24. Powers, Tom, B, Duke
25. Chubb, Bob, E, Shippensburg
26. Williams, Johnny, B, USC
27. Johnson, Bill, B, Stetson
28. Kadlec, John, G, Missouri
29. Stewart, Art, B, Southeastern Oklahoma
30. Bolkovac, Nick, T, Pittsburgh

1952

Held January 17, 1952

Prior to the draft, the New York Yanks franchise was returned to the league. The franchise and assets were granted to a Dallas, Texas, group. The team originally was known —and drafted—as the Texas Football Rangers. By the time a team was fielded, however, it was known as the Dallas Texans.

CHI. BEARS
1. Dooley, Jim, B, Miami
2. Macon, Eddie, B, Pacific
3. McColl, Bill, E, Stanford
4. Clark, Herman, T, Oregon State
5. Hoffman, Jack, E, Xavier, from Pittsburgh
Williams, Fred, T, Arkansas
6. Brown, Ed, B, San Francisco
7. Fortunato, Joe, B, Mississippi State
8. Bishop, Bill, T, North Texas State, from Pittsburgh
Jurney, Billy, E, Arkansas
9. Cross, Bobby, T, Stephen F. Austin
10. Choice to Green Bay
11. Miller, Bill, B, Wake Forest
12. Kozar, Andy, B, Tennessee
13. Athan, Rich, B, Northwestern
14. Galloway, Gale, C, Baylor
15. Kazmaier, Dick, B, Princeton
16. Spears, Bob, B, Yale
17. Carroll, John, T, Houston
18. O'Connell, Tommy, B, Illinois, F
19. Reidenbach, Ken, T, Drake
20. Lesane, Jimmy, B, Virginia
21. Daffer, Ted, G, Tennessee
22. Gregory, Dick, B, Minnesota
23. Nestor, Paul, T, Maryland
24. Mundinger, Dick, T, Minnesota
25. Stoddard, Bob, T, Utah State
26. McElroy, Bucky, B, Southern Mississippi*
27. Reid, Bob, B, Baylor
28. Scioscia, Karney, B, Maryland
29. Riggs, Teddy, B, Rice
30. Shemonski, Bob, B, Maryland

CHI. CARDINALS
1. Matson, Ollie, B, San Francisco
2. Karras, Johnny, B, Illinois
Brewster, Darrell (Pete), E, Purdue, from Detroit
3. Choice to San Francisco
4. Choice to LA Rams
5. Fugler, Dick, T, Tulane
6. Hancock, John, G, Baylor
7. Jabbusch, Harry, C, South Carolina
8. Coleman, Don, G, Michigan State
9. Cook, Malcolm, B, Georgia
10. Feltch, John, T, Holy Cross
11. Sugar, Leo, E, Purdue
12. Masnaghetti, Joe, T, Marquette
13. Massucco, Mel, B, Holy Cross
14. Tofaute, Tom, C, North Carolina State
15. Davis, John, B, Indiana
16. Mergen, Mike, G, San Francisco
17. Crawford, Darrell, B, Georgia Tech
18. Pyron, Bill, T, Mississippi State
19. Listopad, Ed, T, Wake Forest
20. Fischel, Frank, E, Arkansas
21. Musgrove, Wade, G, Hardin-Simmons
22. Lippman, Glenn, B, Texas A&M
23. Stephens, Louis (Red), G, San Francisco
24. Moore, E.J., G, Abilene Christian
25. Anderson, Cliff, E, Indiana
26. Fry, Charley, T, Maryland
27. Moses, Sam, T, Texas A&M
28. Lutz, Harold, E, Alabama
29. Kasperan, Don, B, Purdue
30. Stolk, Will, B, Miami

CLEVELAND
1. Rechichar, Bert, B, Tennessee, from Detroit
Agganis, Harry, QB, Boston U., F
2. Hughes, Bill, C, Michigan State
3. Klosterman, Don, QB, Loyola (Los Angeles), from Texas
Campanella, Joe, T, Ohio State
4. Renfro, Ray, B, North Texas State
Costa, Elmer, G, North Carolina State, from Green Bay
5. Jankovich, Keever, E, Pacific
6. Shields, Burrell, B, John Carroll
7. Pace, John, T, Mississippi State
8. Williams, Stan, E, Baylor, from Texas
Forester, Herschel, G, SMU
9. Finnell, Bob, B, Xavier
10. Ribiero, Pat, T, Pacific
11. Logan, Dick, T, Ohio State
12. Thompson, Roy, B, Florida State
13. Cosgrove, Tom, C, Maryland, F
14. Ruzich, Steve, G, Ohio State
15. Alpin, Holly, E, Tampa
16. Neathery, Herb, B, Illinois, from Detroit
Rowland, Ed, T, Oklahoma
17. Sheets, Stew, T, Penn State
18. Mirchi, Ken, G, Santa Clara
19. Talarico, Sam, T, Indiana, from San Francisco
Maccioli, Mike, B, Purdue
20. Brandenberry, Bob, B, Kansas
21. Calhoun, Dick, G, Baylor
22. Johnson, Howard (Corky), T, Cal-Santa Barbara
23. Greene, Don, T, Miami (Ohio), from LA Rams
Robertson, Bobby, B, Indiana
24. Wren, Junior, B, Missouri
25. Reddell, Billy, B, Florida
26. Vernasco, Joe, E, Illinois
27. Maletzky, Bill, G, Maryland, F
28. Pietro, John, G, Brown
29. Klevay, Walt, B, Ohio State
30. Saban, John, B, Xavier

DETROIT
1. Choice to Cleveland
2. Choice to Chi. Cardinals
3. Lary, Yale, B, Texas A&M
4. Summerall, Pat, E, Arkansas
5. Miller, Bob, T, Virginia
6. Cooper, Gordon, E, Denver
7. Gardner, Wes, C, Utah
8. Dublinski, Tom, B, Utah
9. Gandee, Sherwin (Sonny), E, Ohio State
10. Dowden, Steve, T, Baylor
11. Flowers, Keith, C, TCU
12. Roshto, Jim, B, LSU
13. McDonald, Carroll, C, Florida
14. Oliverson, Ray, B, BYU
15. Burgamy, John, G, Georgia
16. Choice to Cleveland
17. Lauricella, Hank, B, Tennessee
18. Campbell, Stan, G, Iowa State
19. Earon, Blaine, E, Duke
20. Mains, Gil, T, Murray State
21. Boykin, Arnold (Showboat), B, Mississippi

22. David, Jim, E, Colorado State
23. Maxwell, Hal, E, Mississippi
24. Werckle, Bob, T, Vanderbilt
25. Bailey, By, B, Washington State
26. Terry, Buddy, E, Stephen F. Austin
27. Trout, Bob, E, Baylor
28. Turner, Hal, E, Tennessee State
29. Hudson, Art, B, Western Illinois
30. Dillon, Ray Don, B, Prairie View A&M

GREEN BAY

1. Parilli, Vito (Babe), QB, Kentucky
2. Howton, Billy, E, Rice
3. Dillon, Bobby, B, Texas
4. Choice to Cleveland
5. Hanner, Dave (Hawg), T, Arkansas
6. Johnson, Tom, T, Michigan
7. Reichardt, Bill, B, Iowa
8. Becket, Mel, C, Indiana
9. Teteak, Deral, G, Wisconsin
10. Kleinschmidt, Art, G, Tulane
Roffler, Bud, B, Washington State, from Chicago
11. Burkhalter, Billy, B, Rice
12. Wilson, Bill, T, Texas
13. Hair, Billy, B, Clemson
14. Morgan, Jack, T, Michigan State
15. Floyd, Bobby Jack, B, TCU
16. Coatta, Johnny, B, Wisconsin
17. Peterson, Don, B, Michigan
18. Tisdale, Howard, T, Stephen F. Austin
19. Pont, Johnny, B, Miami (Ohio)
20. Boerio, Chuck, C, Illinois
21. Zimmerman, Herb, G, TCU
22. Kluckhorn, Karl, E, Colgate
23. Kapral, Frank, G, Michigan State
24. Schuetzner, John, E, South Carolina
25. LaPradd, Charlie, T, Florida
26. Stokes, Charlie, T, Tennessee
27. Russell, I.D., B, SMU
28. Barrett, Billy, B, Notre Dame
29. Stratton, Bill, B, Lewis
30. Fulkerson, Jack, T, Southern Mississippi

LA RAMS

BONUS CHOICE: Wade, Bill, QB, Vanderbilt
1. Carey, Bob, E, Michigan State
2. Griffin, Bob, T, Arkansas
3. McConnell, Dewey, E, Wyoming
4. Casner, Ken, T, Baylor, from Chi. Cardinals
Quinlan, Volney (Skeet), B, San Diego State
5. Polofsky, Gordon, B, Tennessee
6. Putnam, Duane, G, Pacific, from Pittsburgh
Price, Jerrell, T, Texas Tech
7. Delevan, Burt, T, Pacific, F
8. McCormick, Tom, B, Pacific, F
9. Townsend, Byron, B, Texas
10. Welch, Luke, T, Baylor
11. Baker, Sam, B, Oregon State, F
12. Roberts, Jake, B, Tulsa
13. Phillips, Aubrey (Red), C, Texas Tech
14. Moss, Joe, T, Maryland
15. Hegarty, Bill, T, Villanova, F
16. Hooks, Bob, E, USC
17. Griggs, John, C, Kentucky
18. Dees, Bob, T, Southwest Missouri State
19. Geldien, Harry, B, Wyoming
20. Weber, Ed, B, William & Mary
21. Preston, Art, B, San Diego State
22. Pahr, Joe, B, Valparaiso
23. Choice to Cleveland
24. Kelnhofer, Rich, G, St. Ambrose
25. Teeuws, Len, T, Tulane
26. Fuller, Frank, T, Kentucky, F
27. Meyer, Hugh, C, Texas A&M
28. Hart, Granville, B, Southern Mississippi
29. Perry, Gerry, T, California, F

NY GIANTS

1. Gifford, Frank, B, USC
2. Beck, Ray, G, Georgia Tech
3. Heinrich, Don, QB, Washington, F
4. Hodel, Merwin, B, Colorado, from Texas
Menasco, Don, E, Texas
5. Patton, Bob, T, Clemson
6. MacKenzie, Jim, T, Kentucky
7. Walker, Val Joe, B, SMU, F
8. Shipp, Billy, T, Alabama, F
9. Kastan, John, B, Boston U.
10. Knight, Pat, E, SMU
11. Harris, Charlie, C, California
12. Ochoa, Dick, B, Texas
13. Brady, Pat, B, Nevada-Reno
14. Mitchell, Hal, T, UCLA
15. Bischoff, Paul, E, West Virginia
16. Burns, Paul, G, Notre Dame
17. Karpe, Bob, T, California
18. Little, Gene, G, Rice
19. Cahill, Frank, E, Northern Illinois
20. Boggan, Rex, T, Mississippi, F
21. Creamer, Jim, C, Michigan State
22. Raley, Bob, B, Texas
23. Bickel, Bob, B, Duke
24. Mitchell, Wes, E, Pacific
25. Kelley, Bill, C, Pacific
26. Lavery, Tom, E, Boston U.
27. Morrison, Duane, B, Arizona State
28. Patterson, Alton, T, McMurry
29. Dillon, Jim, B, California
30. Arnold, Joe, G, Texas

PHILADELPHIA

1. Bright, Johnny, B, Drake
2. Weatherall, Jim, T, Oklahoma
3. Snyder, Lum, T, Georgia Tech
4. Ulrich, Chuck, T, Illinois
5. Choice to Texas
6. Lemmon, Dick, B, California
7. Thomas, John, E, Oregon State
8. Robinson, Wayne, C, Minnesota
9. Nipp, Maury, G, Loyola (Los Angeles)
10. McGinley, Gerry, G, Pennsylvania
11. Goldston, Ralph, B, Youngstown State
12. Blount, Jack, T, Mississippi State
13. Hamilton, Ed, B, Kentucky
14. Stringer, Bob, B, Tulsa
15. Schmidt, Malcolm, E, Iowa State
16. Brewer, Jim, G, North Texas State
17. Weigle, John, E, Oklahoma State
18. Romanowski, Ed, B, Scranton
19. Trammell, Talbott, E, Washington & Lee
20. Blaik, Bobby, B, Army, Colorado College
21. Wheeler, Les, G, Abilene Christian
22. Turco, Johnny, B, Holy Cross
23. Schnell, Maury, B, Iowa State
24. Tyrrell, Joe, G, Temple
25. Kelley, Bob, C, West Texas State
26. Albert, Bob, B, Bucknell
27. Hill, Chuck, B, New Mexico
28. Brewer, Johnny, B, Louisville
29. Morocco, Tony (Zippy), B, Georgia
30. Stevens, Don, B, Illinois

PITTSBURGH

1. Modzelewski, Ed, B, Maryland
2. Tarasovic, George, C, LSU
3. Wadiak, Steve, B, South Carolina
4. Gearding, Jack, T, Xavier
5. Choice to Chi. Bears
6. Choice to LA Rams
7. Hipps, Claude, B, Georgia
8. Choice to Chi. Bears
9. Payne, Hal (Herky), B, Tennessee
10. Gilmartin, George, B, Xavier
11. Spinks, Jack, B, Alcorn State
12. McFadden, Marv, T, Michigan State
13. Flood, Dave, B, Notre Dame
14. Davis, June, G, Texas
15. Pivirotto, Dick, B, Princeton
16. Ladygo, Pete, G, Maryland
17. Smithwick, Pat, E, St. Norbert
18. MacDonald, Andy, B, Central Michigan
19. Kerkorian, Gary, QB, Stanford
20. Simeone, Dan, T, Villanova
21. Babcock, Harry, E, Georgia*
22. Byrne, Bob, B, Montana State
23. Pollock, Vic, B, Army
24. Bestwick, Bob, B, Pittsburgh
25. Robinson, Bill, B, Lincoln (Missouri)
26. Wilson, Bobby, B, Alabama
27. Doyle, Dick (Skippy), B, Ohio State, F
28. Hanifan, Jerry, B, St. Bonaventure
29. Warriner, Chris, E, Pittsburgh
30. Kissell, Ed, B, Wake Forest

SAN FRANCISCO

1. McElhenny, Hugh (The King), B, Washington
2. Toneff, Bob, T, Notre Dame
3. Shannon, Gene, B, Houston, from Chi. Cardinals
Tidwell, Billy, B, Texas A&M
4. Campbell, Marion, T, Wisconsin
5. O'Donahue, Pat, E, Wisconsin
6. Beasley, Jim, C, Tulsa
7. Robison, Don, B, California
8. Smith, Jerry, T, Wisconsin
9. Christian, Glen, B, Idaho
10. West, Carl, B, Mississippi
11. Kimmel, J.D., T, Army, Houston
12. Snyder, Fred, E, Loyola (Los Angeles)
13. Yeager, Rudy, T, LSU
14. Simons, Frank, E, Nebraska
15. Norman, Haldo, E, Gustavus Adolphus
16. Meyers, Bob, B, Stanford
17. Baldock, Al, E, USC
18. Carey, Bill, E, Michigan State
19. Choice to Cleveland
20. Yates, Jess, E, LSU
21. Offield, Gene, C, Hardin-Simmons
22. Cozad, Jim, T, Santa Clara
23. Glazier, Bill, E, Arizona
24. Kreuger, Ralph, T, California
25. Laughlin, Bud, B, Kansas, F
26. Kane, Dick, G, Cincinnati
27. Schaaf, Waldo, T, Oklahoma State
28. Palumbo, Joe, G, Virginia
29. Mosher, Chuck, E, Colorado
30. Patrick, Dick, C, Oregon

TEXAS

1. Richter, Les, G, California
2. Marchetti, Gino, T, San Francisco
3. Choice to Cleveland
4. Choice to NY Giants
5. Jorgenson, Jack, T, Colorado
Sinquefield, Mel, C, Mississippi, from Philadelphia
6. Cianelli, Dave, C, Maryland
7. Petitbon, John, B, Notre Dame
8. Choice to Cleveland
9. Lansford, Jim, T, Texas
10. Hammond, Jim, B, Wisconsin
11. Cannamela, Pat, G, USC
12. Mutscheller, Jim, E, Notre Dame
13. Ward, Bill, G, Arkansas
14. Williams, Paul, E, Texas
15. Bighead, Jack, E, Pepperdine
16. Kaseta, Vince, E, Tennessee
17. Horn, Dick, B, Stanford
18. Molnar, Les, T, Buffalo
19. Felker, Gene, E, Wisconsin
20. Adams, John, E, Texas
21. Hugasian, Harry, B, Stanford
22. Freeman, Chet, B, LSU
23. Ward, Bob, G, Maryland
24. Monihan, Jim, B, Rutgers
25. Young, George, T, Bucknell
26. Bartosh, Gil, B, TCU
27. Moseley, Doug, C, Kentucky
28. Hudeck, Russ, T, Texas A&M
29. Suchy, Ray, G, Nevada-Reno

WASHINGTON

1. Isbell, Larry, B, Baylor
2. Davis, Andy, B, George Washington
3. Dorow, Al, B, Michigan State
4. Hightower, Dick, C, SMU
5. Clark, Jim, G, Oregon State
6. Kensler, Ed, G, Maryland
7. Janowicz, Vic, B, Ohio State
8. Johnston, Hubert, T, Iowa
9. Alban, Dick, B, Northwestern
10. Ostrowski, Chet, E, Notre Dame
11. Mazza, Orlando, E, Michigan State
12. Middendorf, Frank, C, Cincinnati
13. Potter, Ray, T, LSU
14. Conway, Doug, T, TCU
15. Wittman, Julius, T, Ohio State
16. Berschet, Marv, T, Illinois
17. Bocetti, Gil, B, Washington & Lee
18. Bartlett, Ed, E, California
19. Marvin, Joe, B, UCLA
20. Kinson, Roger, C, Missouri
21. Jenkins, Dick, T, Illinois
22. O'Rourke, Jim, B, North Carolina State
23. Barfield, Ken, T, Mississippi
24. Kirkland, Ted, E, Vanderbilt
25. Gero, Sal, T, Elon
26. Goode, Dunny, B, Hardin-Simmons
27. White, Ben, E, SMU
28. Engel, Ron, B, Minnesota
29. Pappa, John, B, California
30. Linn, Bob, B, Case Western Reserve

1953

Held January 22, 1953

The Baltimore Colts didn't officially enter the NFL until January 23, 1953, the day after the draft. The Colts' selections were made by their coaching and scouting staff, however.

BALTIMORE

1. Vessels, Billy, B, Oklahoma
2. Flowers, Bernie, E, Purdue
3. McPhail, Buck, B, Oklahoma
4. Catlin, Tom, C, Oklahoma
5. Little, Jack, T, Texas A&M
6. Sears, Jim, B, USC
7. Athey, Bill, G, Baylor
8. Prewett, Jim, T, Tulsa
9. Blair, Bob, E, TCU
10. Cole, John, B, Arkansas
11. Rossi, Gene, B, Cincinnati
12. Vaughn, Kaye, G, Tulsa
13. Morehead, Bobby, B, Georgia Tech
14. Continetti, Frank, G, George Washington
15. Sutton, Buddy, B, Arkansas
16. Currin, Jim, E, Dayton
17. Rambour, George, T, Dartmouth
18. Labat, LeRoy, B, LSU
19. Powell, Bill, B, California
20. Russo, Pete, T, Indiana
21. Kirby, Frank, T, Bucknell
22. Gish, Merlin, C, Kansas
23. Housepian, Mike, G, Tulane
24. Brethauer, Monte, E, Oregon
25. Szombathy, Joe, E, Syracuse
26. Prescott, Scott, C, Minnesota
27. Graves, Ray, B, Texas A&M
28. Sabol, Joe, B, UCLA
29. Alessandrini, Jack, G, Notre Dame
30. Roche, Tom, T, Northwestern

CHI. BEARS

1. Anderson, Billy, B, Compton J.C.
2. Bratkowski, Zeke, QB, Georgia, F
3. Rowekamp, Bill, B, Army, Missouri
4. Koch, Joe, B, Wake Forest
5. Jones, Stan, T, Maryland, F
6. DeCarlo, Art, B, Georgia
Gilbert, Kline, T, Mississippi, from San Francisco
7. McElroy, Bucky, B, Southern Mississippi, from Washington
Bingham, Don, B, Sul Ross
8. Kreamcheck, John, T, William & Mary
9. Ashley, Bruno, T, East Texas State
10. Moore, Jimmy, B, Florida A&M
11. Slowey, Jim, C, Georgetown (Washington D.C.)
Charney, Ralph, B, Kentucky, from Pittsburgh
12. Lawrence, Jim, T, Duke
13. Strickland, Larry, C, North Texas State
14. Carl, Harland, B, Wisconsin
15. Jecha, Ralph, G, Northwestern
16. Hatley, John, T, Sul Ross
17. Beal, Bob, E, California
18. Shirley, Jim, B, Clemson
19. Byrus, Bill, T, Iowa State
20. Mahin, Tom, T, Purdue
21. Martin, Wayne, E, TCU
22. Wood, Wayne, T, Memphis State
23. Mask, Jim, E, Mississippi
24. Hatcher, Paul, C, Arkansas City J.C.
25. Pickard, Clyde, G, Wake Forest
26. Evans, Bob, T, Pennsylvania
27. Wahlin, Marvin, B, Arizona State
28. Caldwell, Jim, T, Tennessee State
29. Lewis, Jack, E, Wake Forest
30. Brehany, Bill, QB, Virginia Military

CHI. CARDINALS

1. Olszewski, Johnny, B, California
2. Psaltis, Jim, B, USC
3. Samuels, Dale, QB, Purdue
4. Martin, Buck, E, Georgia Tech
5. Shalosky, Bill, G, Cincinnati
6. Curcillo, Tony, B, Ohio State
Higgins, Tom, T, North Carolina, from Philadelphia
7. Choice to Philadelphia
8. Watford, Jerry, G, Alabama
9. Husmann, Ed, G, Nebraska, from Washington
Stone, Avatus, B, Syracuse
10. Berndt, Charley, T, Wisconsin
11. Woodsum, Ed, E, Yale
12. Spaulding, Chuck, B, Wyoming
13. McPhee, Frank, E, Princeton, from Washington
Morris, Ronnie, B, Tulsa
14. Sprague, Dick, B, Washington
15. Chickillo, Nick, G, Miami
16. Lear, Jimmy, B, Mississippi
17. Heninger, Earl, B, Purdue
18. Yukica, Joe, E, Penn State
19. Donahue, Tom, C, Wake Forest
20. D'Errico, Len, G, Boston U.
21. Curtis, Joe, E, Alabama
22. Lokovsek, Hal, T, Washington State
23. Root, Jim, B, Miami (Ohio)
24. Glass, Brad, G, Princeton
25. Sullivan, Haywood, B, Florida
26. Ringe, Don, T, Idaho

27. Brocato, C.O., C, Baylor
28. Prokopiak, Mike, B, New Mexico
29. Wrightenberry, Earl, T, Clemson
30. Gaudreau, Bill, B, Notre Dame

CLEVELAND
1. Atkins, Doug, T, Tennessee
2. Reynolds, Billy, B, Pittsburgh
3. Bruney, Fred, B, Ohio State
Donaldson, Gene, G, Kentucky, from Detroit
4. Tamburo, Dick, C, Michigan State
5. Van Doren, Bob, E, USC
6. Steinbrunner, Don, E, Washington State
7. Filipski, Gene, B, Army, Villanova, F
8. Massey, Carlton, E, Texas, F
9. McNamara, Bob, B, Minnesota
10. Natali, Elmo, B, California (Pennsylvania)
11. Hilinski, Dick, T, Ohio State, F
12. Willhoite, Elmer, G, USC
13. Fiss, Galen, B, Kansas
14. Nagler, Gern, E, Santa Clara
15. Carson, Johnny, E, Georgia, F
16. Kuykendall, Eric, B, Illinois
17. Bean, George, B, Utah
18. Batten, Dick, T, Pacific
19. Cain, Tom, G, Colorado
20. Noll, Chuck, T, Dayton
21. Crockett, Bill, G, Rice
22. Looper, Byrd, B, Duke
23. Kent, Ronnie, B, Tulane
24. Labenda, John, T, Wittenberg
25. Ellis, Jim, B, Michigan State
26. Hoag, Charley, B, Kansas
27. Sisco, Jack, C, Baylor
28. Verkirk, Ray, T, North Texas State
29. Hobson, Clell, B, Alabama
30. Myers, Andy, G, Tennessee

DETROIT
1. Sewell, Harley, G, Texas
2. Gedman, Gene, B, Indiana
3. Choice to Cleveland
4. Ane, Charlie, T, USC
5. Choice to Philadelphia
6. Spencer, Ollie, T, Kansas
7. Schmidt, Joe, C, Pittsburgh
8. Carpenter, Lew, B, Arkansas
9. McCormick, Carlton, C, TCU
10. Gaskin, Dreher, E, Clemson
11. Messenger, Elmer, G, Washington State
12. Spencer, Larry, B, Wake Forest
13. Thomas, Bob, E, Washington & Lee
14. Barger, Jack, T, New Mexico
15. Topor, Ted, B, Michigan
16. Volonnino, Bob, G, Army, Villanova
17. Green, Ray, T, Duke
18. Mioduszewski, Ed, B, William & Mary
19. Held, Paul, B, San Diego State, F
20. Hart, Gerry, T, Army, Mississippi State
21. Tata, Bob, B, Virginia
22. Retzlaff, Pete, B, South Dakota State
23. Karilivacz, Carl, B, Syracuse
24. Grant, Truett, T, Duke
25. Brown, Marv, B, East Texas State
26. Dooley, Jim, C, Penn State
27. Parker, Jackie, B, Mississippi State*
28. Pepper, Laurin, B, Southern Mississippi*
29. Rector, Harley, T, Wayne State (Nebraska)
30. Maus, Hal, E, Montana

GREEN BAY
1. Carmichael, Al, B, USC
2. Reich, Gil, B, Army, Kansas
3. Forester, Bill, T, SMU
4. Dawson, Gib, B, Texas
5. Zatkoff, Roger, T, Michigan
6. Kennedy, Bob, G, Wisconsin
7. Ringo, Jim, C, Syracuse
8. Hargrove, Lauren, B, Georgia
9. Harrawood, Floyd, T, Tulsa
10. Rimkus, Vic, G, Holy Cross
11. Johnson, Joe, B, Boston College, F
12. Curran, Dick, B, Arizona State
13. Orders, Bob, C, Army, West Virginia
14. Wrenn, Charley, T, TCU
15. Helwig, Gene, B, Tulsa
16. Hlay, John, B, Ohio State
17. Georges, Bill, E, Texas
18. Philbee, Jim, B, Bradley
19. Lucky, Bill, T, Baylor*
20. Harville, John, B, TCU
21. Conway, Bob, B, Alabama
22. Turnbeaugh, Bill, T, Auburn
23. Murray, Bill, E, American International
24. Haslam, Jim, T, Tennessee
25. Jones, Ike, E, UCLA
26. Bozanic, George, B, USC
27. McConaughey, Jim, E, Houston
28. Jordan, Zack, B, Colorado
29. O'Brien, Henry, G, Boston College
30. Barry, Al, G, USC

LA RAMS
1. Moomaw, Donn, C, UCLA, from Philadelphia
Barker, Ed, E, Washington State
2. Bukich, Rudy, B, USC
3. Fry, Bob, T, Kentucky
4. Roberts, Willie, E, Tulsa
5. Scott, Tom, E, Virginia
6. Miller, Paul, T, LSU, from Washington, F
Waugh, Howie, B, Tulsa
7. Reynolds, Bobby, B, Nebraska
8. Morgan, Bob, T, Maryland, F
9. Myers, Brad, B, Bucknell
10. Lakos, Mick, B, Vanderbilt
11. Bailey, Jim, B, Miami (Ohio)
12. Doud, Chuck, G, UCLA
13. Matto, Andy, T, Cincinnati
14. James, Frank, G, Houston
15. Carroll, Tom, B, Oklahoma
16. DeLoe, Ben, T, Mississippi State
17. Svare, Harland, E, Washington State
18. Jones, Lew, T, Wabash
19. Ellena, Jack, T, UCLA, F
20. Morford, Bob, B, College of Idaho
21. Gordon, Dick, T, Toledo
22. Porter, George, T, Southwest Texas State
23. Willoughby, Larry, B, Fresno State
24. Gudmundson, Marlow, B, North Dakota State
25. Clemens, Ed, C, Dayton
26. Yourkowski, Louie, T, Washington
27. Welsh, Lou, C, USC
28. Murray, Jim, T, Montana
29. Lewis, Ray, E, Boise J.C.
30. Phren, Fritz, B, College of the Ozarks

NY GIANTS
1. Marlow, Bobby, B, Alabama
2. Crowder, Eddie, QB, Oklahoma
3. Roberts, Cal, T, Gustavus Adolphus
4. Douglas, Everett, T, Florida
5. Long, Buford, B, Florida
6. Peviani, Bob, G, USC
7. Branby, Don, E, Colorado
8. Beck, Don, B, Army, Notre Dame
9. Gray, Jim, B, Panola J.C.
10. Cooper, Darrow, E, Texas A&M, from Washington
Maloy, Charlie, QB, Holy Cross
11. Ruehl, Jim, C, Ohio State
12. Matesic, Joe, T, Arizona State
13. McShulski, Jack, E, Army, Kansas State
14. Hall, J.L., B, Florida
15. Bowman, Dick, G, Oklahoma
16. Skyinskus, Bill, G, Syracuse
17. Rhoden, Don, C, Rice
18. Suwall, Phil, B, Western Maryland
19. Lehman, Hal, T, Southern Mississippi
20. Christiansen, Dick, E, Arizona
21. Bullard, Gene, T, Louisiana College
22. Kelley, Mike, E, Florida
23. Kukowski, Ted, C, Navy, Syracuse
24. Kubes, Charley, G, Minnesota
25. Drake, Dan, B, Rice
26. Wetzel, Bill, B, Syracuse
27. Brown, Roosevelt (Rosey), T, Morgan State
28. Ramona, Joe, G, Santa Clara
29. Griffis, Bob, G, Furman
30. Canakes, Stavros, G, Minnesota

PHILADELPHIA
1. Choice to LA Rams
2. Conway, Al, B, Army, William Jewell
3. Johnson, Don, B, California
4. Mrkonic, George, G, Kansas
5. Bell, Eddie, E, Pennsylvania
Smith, Rex, E, Illinois, from Detroit
6. Choice to Chi. Cardinals
7. Erickson, Jack, T, Army, Beloit, from Chi. Cardinals
Malavasi, Ray, G, Army, Mississippi State
8. Richardson, Jess, T, Alabama
9. French, Roger, E, Minnesota
10. Brookshier, Tom, B, Colorado
11. Pollard, Bob, B, Penn State
12. Porter, George, T, San Jose State
13. Westort, Ray, G, Utah
14. Bailey, Roy, B, Tulane
15. Irvin, Willie, E, Florida A&M
16. Wallace, Bud, B, North Carolina
17. Rados, Tony, B, Penn State
18. Trauth, Marv, T, Mississippi
19. Bachouros, Pete, B, Illinois
20. Arns, Rollie, C, Iowa State
21. Brooks, Hal, T, Washington & Lee
22. LeClaire, Laurie, B, Michigan
23. Knox, Jeff, E, Georgia Tech
24. Romero, Eli, B, Wichita State
25. Michels, Johnny, G, Tennessee
26. Achziger, Harvey, T, Colorado State
27. Hersh, Earl, B, West Chester
28. Gratson, Joe, B, Penn State
29. Paolone, Ralph, B, Kentucky
30. Hren, Chuck, B, Northwestern

PITTSBURGH
1. Marchibroda, Ted, QB, Detroit
2. Johnson, John Henry, B, Arizona State
3. Matuszak, Marv, T, Tulsa
4. Colteryahn, Lloyd, E, Maryland
5. Gaona, Bob, T, Wake Forest
6. Barton, Tom, G, Clemson
7. Alderton, John, E, Maryland
8. Perry, Lowell, E, Michigan
9. Sarnese, Pat, T, Temple
10. Holohan, Frank, T, Tennessee
11. Choice to Chi. Bears
12. Robertson, Jerry, B, Kansas
13. Davis, Leo, E, Bradley
14. Montgomery, Charley, T, Mississippi
15. O'Neil, Bob, E, Notre Dame
16. Zachary, John, B, Miami (Ohio)
17. Quinn, Reed, B, Florida
18. Holben, Carl, T, Duke
19. Williams, Jim, B, Louisville
20. Hayley, Will Lee, E, Auburn
21. Earley, Don, G, South Carolina
22. O'Connor, Ed, T, Maryland
23. Correll, Ray, G, Kentucky
24. Schneidenbach, Bob, B, Miami
25. Hampel, Vic, E, Houston
26. McClairen, Jack (Goose), E, Bethune-Cookman
27. Delaney, Jack, B, Cincinnati
28. Cimini, Joe, T, Mississippi State
29. Massaro, Art, B, Washington & Jefferson
30. Tepe, Lou, C, Duke

SAN FRANCISCO
BONUS CHOICE: Babcock, Harry, E, Georgia
1. Stolhanske, Tom, E, Texas
2. Morris, George, C, Georgia Tech
3. St. Clair, Bob, T, San Francisco
4. Fullerton, Ed, B, Maryland
5. Miller, Hal, T, Georgia Tech
6. Choice to Chi. Bears
7. Carr, Paul, B, Houston*
8. Hogland, Doug, T, Oregon State
9. Ledyard, Hal, B, Tennessee-Chattanooga
10. Brown, Pete, G, Georgia Tech
11. Charlton, Al, B, Washington State
12. Leach, Carson (Red), G, Duke
13. Earley, Bill, B, Washington
14. Fletcher, Tom, B, Arizona State
15. Genthner, Charley, T, Texas
16. Durig, Fred, E, Bowling Green
17. Latham, Hugh, T, San Diego State
18. Wacholz, Stan, E, San Jose State
19. DuClos, King, T, Texas-El Paso
20. Huizinga, Ray, T, Northwestern
21. Bahnsen, Ken, E, North Texas State
22. Robbins, Laverne, G, Midwestern State (Texas)
23. Hunt, Travis, T, Alabama
24. Morgan, Ed, B, Tennessee
25. Stockert, Ernie, E, UCLA
26. Cooper, Harley, B, Arizona State
27. McCleod, Ralph, E, LSU
28. Novikoff, Tom, B, Oregon
29. Stillwell, Don, E, USC

WASHINGTON
1. Scarbath, Jack, B, Maryland
2. Modzelewski, Dick, T, Maryland
3. Dekker, Paul, E, Michigan State
4. Boll, Don, G, Nebraska
5. Carras, Nick, B, Missouri
6. Choice to LA Rams
7. Choice to Chi. Bears
8. Weidensaul, Lew, E, Maryland
9. Choice to Chi. Cardinals
10. Choice to NY Giants
11. Webster, Alex, B, North Carolina State
12. Nutter, Madison (Buzz), C, Virginia Tech
13. Choice to Chi. Cardinals
14. Timmerman, Ed, B, Michigan State
15. Suminski, Dave, T, Wisconsin
16. Slay, Jim, E, Mississippi
17. Haner, Bob, B, Villanova
18. Turner, Jim, B, Texas Tech
19. Flyzik, Tom, T, George Washington
20. Link, Bill, G, Wake Forest
21. Dublinski, Jim, C, Utah
22. Pucci, Ed, G, USC
23. Bierne, Ed, E, Detroit
24. Butterworth, Stan, B, Bucknell
25. Hurd, Art, G, Maryland
26. Ashcraft, Walt, T, USC
27. Zanetti, John, T, John Carroll
28. Buckley, Bob, B, USC
29. Shires, Pat, B, Tennessee
30. Mathias, Bob, B, Stanford

1954
Held January 28, 1954

BALTIMORE
1. Davidson, Cotton, QB, Baylor
2. Grigg, Larry, B, Oklahoma
3. Choice to LA Rams
4. Choice to Green Bay
5. Ellis, Don, B, Texas A&M
6. Choice to Cleveland
7. Turner, Glenn, B, Georgia Tech
8. McCotter, Dennis, G, Detroit
9. Adams, Bob, G, Shippensburg
10. Schoonmaker, Bob, B, Missouri
11. Leberman, Bob, B, Syracuse
12. Chelf, Don, T, Iowa
13. McMillan, Dave, B, John Carroll
14. Braase, Ordell, T, South Dakota
15. D'Agostino, Joe, G, Florida
16. Sandusky, Alex, E, Clarion
17. Adkins, Tommy, C, Kentucky
18. Shinaut, Dick, B, Texas-El Paso
19. Wenzlau, Charley, E, Miami (Ohio)
20. Berry, Raymond, E, SMU, F
21. Lade, Bob, G, Wayne State
22. Meyer, Bob, T, Ohio State
23. Hardeman, Leon, B, Georgia Tech
24. Kerlin, Don, B, Concordia (Minnesota)
25. Rodgers, Pepper, B, Georgia Tech
26. Esparza, Jesus, T, New Mexico State
27. Sennett, Bill, E, Georgia Tech
28. Ecstrom, Ray, C, Westminster (Pennsylvania)
29. Taliaferro, Claude, B, Illinois
30. Abbruzzi, Pat, B, Rhode Island*

CHI. BEARS
1. Wallace, Stan, B, Illinois
2. Casares, Rick, B, Florida
3. Meadows, Ed, T, Duke
4. Paterra, Fran, B, Notre Dame
5. Griffis, Bob, G, Furman
6. Hudson, John, G, Rice
7. Cecere, Ralph, B, Villanova
8. Garlington, Tom, T, Arkansas
9. Giel, Paul, B, Minnesota
10. Andrews, D.C., E, Hardin-Simmons
11. Wallin, Ron, B, Minnesota
12. Faragalli, Joe, G, Villanova
13. Seaholm, Julius, G, Texas
14. Miller, Ken, B, Illinois
15. Hill, Harlon, E, North Alabama
16. Lindley, Earl, B, Utah State
17. Woodard, Lou, C, Sam Houston State
18. Moore, McNeil, B, Sam Houston State
19. Lum, Jim, T, Louisiana Tech
20. Ladd, Jim, E, Bowling Green
21. Cleere, Sonny, T, Abilene Christian
22. Sumner, Charlie, B, William & Mary
23. Lee, Herman, T, Florida A&M
24. Jarrett, Bill, B, West Virginia
25. Feamster, Tom, E, Florida State*
26. Petroka, Lou, B, Boston U.
27. Oniskey, Dick, C, Tennessee-Chattanooga
28. Underwood, P.W., G, Mississippi State
29. Beale, Alvin, B, Trinity (Texas)
30. Haluska, Jim, B, Wisconsin

CHI. CARDINALS
1. McHan, Lamar, QB, Arkansas
2. Knafelc, Gary, E, Colorado
3. Cavazos, Bobby, B, Texas Tech
4. Bredde, Bill, B, Oklahoma State
5. Dohoney, Don, E, Michigan State
6. McHugh, Tom, B, Notre Dame
7. Mann, Dave, B, Oregon State
8. Larson, Paul, B, California, F

9. Chambers, Dean, T, Washington
10. Lewis, Tommy, B, Alabama
11. Smith, Homer, B, Princeton
12. Pitt, Howard, E, Duke
13. Goble, Les, B, Alfred
14. Dumas, Sammy, G, Arkansas
15. Harp, Cecil, E, Pacific
16. Kilgore, Al, T, Kent State
17. Troxell, Jack, B, Arkansas
18. Young, Dick, B, Tennessee-Chattanooga
19. Sazio, Jerry, T, William & Mary
20. Huntsman, Stan, B, Wabash
21. Stander, Jim, T, Colorado
22. Fanucchi, Ledio, T, Fresno State
23. Oakley, Charley, B, LSU
24. Sawchik, Lou, E, Ohio U.
25. Marchand, Jerry, B, LSU
26. Carrigan, Ralph, C, Alabama
27. Culver, John, B, Harvard
28. Koller, Tom, B, William & Mary
29. Albrecht, Bill, B, Washington
30. Burl, Alex, B, Colorado State

CLEVELAND

BONUS CHOICE: Garrett, Bobby, QB, Stanford
1. Bauer, John, G, Illinois
2. Hanulak, Chet (The Jet), B, Maryland
3. Bassett, Maurice, B, Langston
4. Hilgenberg, Jerry, C, Iowa
5. Lucky, Bill, T, Baylor
6. Smith, Jim Ray, G, Baylor, from Baltimore
   Jenkins, Asa, B, Toledo
7. Miller, Don, B, SMU
8. Barbish, Bill, B, Tennessee, from San Francisco
   Harris, Charlie, B, Georgia
9. Jones, Tom, T, Miami (Ohio), F
10. Goss, Don, G, SMU, from San Francisco
   Pagna, Tom, B, Miami (Ohio)
11. Schuebel, Max, T, Rice
12. Bruenich, Tom, T, Maryland
13. Cummins, George, T, Tulane
14. Head, Jim, B, Iowa
15. Lyssy, Chet, B, Hardin Simmons
16. Raidel, Rich, G, Kent State
17. Chapman, Howard, T, Florida
18. Wohrman, Bill, B, South Carolina
19. Taylor, John, C, Austin
20. Pierce, Hugh, C, North Carolina State
21. Baughman, Jim, G, Illinois
22. Caudle, Lloyd, B, Duke
23. Mischak, Bob, E, Army
24. Grambling, Johnny, B, South Carolina
25. Hughes, Tom, T, Virginia Tech
26. Lundy, Joe, G, Kansas
27. Mapp, Johnny, B, Virginia Military
28. Vergara, Vince, B, Syracuse & Army
29. Carter, Troy, B, Virginia Military

DETROIT

1. Chapman, Dick, T, Rice
2. Neal, Jim, C, Michigan State
3. Bowman, Bill, B, William & Mary
4. Stits, Bill, B, UCLA, from Washington
   McCants, Howard, E, Washington State
5. Parozzo, George, T, William & Mary
6. Dacus, Pence, B, Southwest Texas State, from Green Bay
   Kercher, Dick, B, Tulsa
7. Cross, Jack, B, Utah
8. Davis, Milt, B, UCLA
9. Lawson, Bob, B, Cal Poly-SLO
10. Carroll, Jack, E, Holy Cross
11. Schwenk, Milt, T, Washington State
12. Hartman, Bob, T, Oregon State
13. Swierczek, Jim, B, Marshall
14. Novak, Ray, B, Nebraska
15. Hinderlider, Kirk, E, Colorado State
16. Chuoke, Bob, T, Houston
17. Kaser, Rick, B, Toledo
18. Hayes, Norm, T, Idaho
19. Graves, Buster, T, Arkansas
20. Durrant, Jim, G, Utah
21. Kistler, Jack, B, Duke
22. Brundage, Dewey, E, BYU
23. Shanafelt, Jack, T, Pennsylvania
24. Burrows, Bobby, G, Duke
25. Woit, Dick, B, Arkansas State
26. George, Jim, T, Syracuse
27. Rzeszut, Dick, C, Benedictine
28. Rutschman, Dolph, B, Linfield
29. Bertrand, Mel, C, Idaho
30. Horton, Ellis, B, Eureka (Illinois)

GREEN BAY

1. Hunter, Art, T, Notre Dame
   Switzer, Veryl, B, Kansas State, from NY Giants
2. Fleck, Bob, T, Syracuse
3. Timberlake, George, G, USC
4. Choice to Washington
   Allman, Tommy, B, West Virginia, from Baltimore
5. McGee, Max, B, Tulane
6. Choice to Detroit
7. Marshall, Sam, T, Florida A&M
8. Williams, Jimmie, T, Texas Tech
9. Davis, Dave, E, Georgia Tech
10. Knutson, Gene, E, Michigan
11. Hall, Ken, E, North Texas State
12. Oliver, Bill, B, Alabama
13. Takacs, Mike, G, Ohio State
14. Johnson, Dave (Kosse), B, Rice
15. Choice to San Francisco
16. Koch, Des, B, USC
17. Roberts, J.D., G, Oklahoma
18. Barnes, Emery, E, Oregon
19. Hall, Ken, C, Springfield
20. Herbert, Lowell, G, Pacific
21. Liebscher, Art, B, Pacific
22. Buford, Willie, T, Morgan State
23. Sathrum, Clint, B, St. Olaf
24. Tennefoss, Marv, E, Stanford
25. Smalley, John, T, Alabama
26. Baierl, Ralph, T, Maryland
27. Sims, Hosea, E, Marquette
28. Slonac, Evan, B, Michigan State
29. Dufek, Jerry, T, St. Norbert
30. Campbell, Terry, B, Washington State

LA RAMS

1. Beatty, Ed, C, Mississippi
2. Gillioz, Buddy, T, Houston
3. Kincaid, Jim, B, South Carolina, from Baltimore
   Nickoloff, Tom, E, USC, from Washington
   Hair, Henry, E, Georgia Tech
4. McClelland, Lester, T, Syracuse, from Pittsburgh
   Nygaard, Norm, B, San Diego State
5. Allen, Charlie, T, San Jose State, from Philadelphia
   Hauser, Art, T, Xavier
6. Panfil, Ken, T, Purdue, F
7. Weeks, Charley, T, USC
8. Black, George, E, Washington
9. Bravo, Alex, B, Cal Poly-SLO
10. Hughes, Ed, B, Tulsa, from Philadelphia
   Katchik, Joe, E, Notre Dame
11. Wardlow, Duane, T, Washington
12. Maultsby, Jack, T, North Carolina
13. Hensley, Sam, E, Georgia Tech
14. Johnson, Mitchell, B, Bishop
15. Elliot, Ed, B, Richmond
16. Frey, Roger, T, Georgia Tech
17. Wilhelm, Ed, C, Houston
18. Sheriff, Stan, C, Cal Poly-SLO
19. Givens, Frank, T, Georgia Tech
20. Dougherty, Bob, B, Cincinnati
21. Cooper, Jerry, T, West Virginia
22. Pacer, Ray, T, Purdue
23. Marks, Don, B, California
24. Brookman, Ed, T, West Virginia
25. Miller, Dick, B, Baldwin-Wallace
26. Holtzman, Glen, T, North Texas State
27. Shine, Entee, E, Notre Dame
28. Mann, Dick, B, Case Western Reserve
29. Dietrick, Dick, E, Pittsburgh
30. Metzke, Frank, T, Marquette

NY GIANTS

1. Choice to Green Bay
2. Buck, Ken, E, Pacific
3. Bennett, Clyde, E, South Carolina
4. Nolan, Dick, B, Maryland
5. Putman, Earl, T, Arizona State
6. Jacoby, George, T, Ohio State
7. Berry, Wayne, B, Washington State
8. Starkey, Ralph, T, West Virginia
9. O'Garra, Pete, E, UCLA
10. Steinberg, John, E, Stanford
11. Fitzpatrick, Tom, G, Villanova
12. Gulseth, Wendell, T, Wisconsin
13. Topp, Bob, E, Michigan
14. Epps, Bobby, B, Pittsburgh
15. Swan, Jim, G, Denver
16. Rice, George, B, Iowa
17. Parker, Jackie, B, Mississippi State
18. Mims, Crawford, G, Mississippi
19. King, Bob, G, South Carolina
20. Snipes, Gene, E, Austin
21. Corless, Rex, B, Michigan State
22. Collier, Joe, E, Northwestern
23. Mangum, Pete, B, Mississippi
24. Harris, Bill, T, LSU
25. Baker, Bill, B, Washburn
26. Van Zandt, George, B, Long Beach C.C.
27. Clatterbuck, Bobby, B, Houston
28. Partridge, Jim, B, Tulane
29. Mote, Bill, T, Florida State
30. Gibson, Jim, T, USC

PHILADELPHIA

1. Worden, Neil, B, Notre Dame
2. Ryan, Rocky, E, Illinois
3. Connor, Ted, T, Nebraska
4. Mavraides, Menil (Minnie), G, Notre Dame
5. Choice to LA Rams
6. Lambert, Hal, T, TCU
7. Norton, Jerry, B, SMU
8. Hunter, Dan, T, Florida
9. Branch, Phil, G, Texas
10. Choice to LA Rams
11. McLaughlin, Dave, E, Dartmouth
12. Clasby, Dick, B, Harvard
13. Mehalick, Joe, T, Virginia
14. Patterson, Hal, B, Kansas
15. McKown, Ray, B, TCU
16. Grant, Charlie, C, Utah
17. Knowles, Bob, T, Baylor
18. Mrvos, Sam, G, Georgia
19. Clem, Jerry, G, SMU
20. Bailes, Tommy, B, Houston
21. Crouch, Johnny, E, TCU*
22. Wojciehowski, Jim, E, Purdue
23. Lofton, Harold, B, Mississippi
24. Gressette, Nate, T, Clemson
25. Zambiasi, Ray, B, Detroit
26. Smith, Charley, B, Baylor
27. Addiego, Ben, B, Villanova
28. Gerdes, John, T, Cornell
29. Stone, Jack, B, West Virginia
30. Woodlee, Tommy, B, South Carolina

PITTSBURGH

1. Lattner, Johnny, B, Notre Dame
2. Stark, Pat, B, Syracuse
3. Miner, Tom, E, Tulsa
4. Choice to LA Rams
5. Choice to San Francisco
6. Pepper, Laurin, B, Southern Mississippi
7. O'Brien, Jack, E, Florida
8. Cameron, Paul, B, UCLA
9. Zombek, Joe, E, Pittsburgh
10. Fisher, Bob, T, Tennessee
11. Cimarolli, Lou, B, Pittsburgh
12. Fritz, Don, E, Cincinnati
13. Lattimer, Charley, C, Maryland
14. Bradford, Roger, E, Waynesburg
15. Drake, Tom, G, Tennessee-Chattanooga
16. Krol, Cas, T, Detroit
17. Fulwyler, Joe, C, Oregon State
18. Penza, Don, E, Notre Dame
19. Rydalch, Don, B, Utah
20. Prender, Fred, B, West Chester
21. Tassotti, Dan, T, Miami
22. Lapsley, John, G, Northeastern
23. Pascarella, Joe, T, Penn State
24. Flanagan, Jack, E, Detroit
25. Barron, Jim, T, Mississippi State
26. Varaitis, Joe, B, Pennsylvania
27. Yewcic, Tom, QB, Michigan State
28. Bush, Joe, G, Notre Dame
29. Fagan, Joe, T, John Carroll
30. Sweatte, Juel, B, Oklahoma

SAN FRANCISCO

1. Faloney, Bernie, B, Maryland
2. Rucka, Leo, C, Rice
3. Korcheck, Steve, C, George Washington
4. Boxhold, Charlie, B, Maryland
5. Hantla, Bob, G, Kansas, from Pittsburgh
   Mincevich, Frank, G, South Carolina
6. Sagely, Floyd, E, Arkansas
7. Youngelman, Sid, T, Alabama
8. Choice to Cleveland
9. Connolly, Ted, G, Tulsa
10. Choice to Cleveland
11. Skocko, John, E, USC
12. Easterwood, Hal, C, Mississippi State
13. Williams, Morgan, G, TCU
14. Williams, Sammy, B, California
15. Gossage, Ed, T, Georgia Tech, from Green Bay
   Palumbo, Sam, G, Notre Dame*
16. Fiveash, Bobby, B, Florida State
17. Kautz, Carl, T, Texas Tech
18. Kay, Morris, E, Kansas
19. Edmiston, Bob, T, Temple
20. DePietro, Frank, B, Georgia
21. Alsup, Howard, T, Middle Tennessee State
22. Reynolds, Ralph, B, North Texas State
23. Fenstemaker, LeRoy, B, Rice
24. Daniels, Jerry, T, Tennessee Tech
25. Platt, John, B, Elon
26. Bello, Pete, C, Pasadena C.C.
27. Baker, Gayford, G, Nebraska-Omaha
28. Garbrecht, Bob, B, Rice
29. Dunn, Ted, B, Murray State
30. Folks, Don, E, Houston

WASHINGTON

1. Meilinger, Steve, E, Kentucky
2. Schrader, Jim, C, Notre Dame
3. Choice to LA Rams
4. Felton, Ralph, B, Maryland, from Green Bay
   Choice to Detroit
5. Wells, Billy, B, Michigan State
6. McHenry, Bill, C, Washington & Lee
7. Jagielski, Harry, T, Indiana
8. Marker, Bill, E, West Virginia
9. Minnick, Jerry, T, Nebraska
10. Green, Merrill, B, Oklahoma
11. Wilson, Gene, B, South Carolina
12. Dunkerly, Ben, T, West Virginia
13. Dornburg, Roger, B, Wisconsin
14. Nelson, Roger, T, Oklahoma
15. Merck, Hugh, T, South Carolina
16. Spring, Gilmer, E, Texas
17. Coody, Jerry, B, Baylor
18. Cudzik, Walt, C, Purdue
19. Witt, Jerry, B, Wisconsin
20. Morley, Sam, E, Stanford
21. Cavaglieri, John, T, North Texas State
22. Schmaling, Max, B, Purdue
23. Carrieri, Pete, G, Villanova
24. Hentro, Will, E, Memphis State
25. Rosso, George, B, Ohio State
26. Gibson, Dorsey, B, Oklahoma State
27. Yarborough, Ken, E, North Carolina
28. Hansen, Ron, T, Minnesota
29. Kress, Ted, B, Michigan
30. Rondou, Don, B, Northwestern

1955

Held January 27-28, 1955

BALTIMORE

BONUS CHOICE: Shaw, George, B, Oregon
1. Ameche, Alan (The Horse), B, Wisconsin
2. Szymanski, Dick, C, Notre Dame
3. Dupre, L.G. (Long Gone), B, Baylor
4. Choice to LA Rams
   Patera, Jack, G, Oregon, from NY Giants
5. Preas, George, G, Virginia Tech
6. Lewis, Leo, B, Lincoln (Missouri)
7. McDonald, Frank, E, Miami
8. Meinert, Dale, G, Oklahoma State
9. Walter, Bryan, B, Texas Tech
   Evans, Bill, G, Miami (Ohio), from NY Giants
10. Choice to LA Rams
11. Radik, Emil, B, Nebraska-Omaha
12. Chorovich, Dick, T, Miami (Ohio)
13. Abbruzzi, Pat, B, Rhode Island
14. Lee, John, B, Georgia Tech
15. Peterson, Gerry, T, Texas, F
16. Laswell, Dick, T, TCU
17. Clark, Wes, T, Southern Mississippi
18. Shephard, Charley, B, North Texas State
19. Cobb, Jim, T, Abilene Christian
20. Cianciola, Charley, E, Lawrence
21. Manych, Nick, E, Eastern Michigan
22. Welch, Jerry, B, South Dakota State
23. McNamara, Dick, B, Minnesota
24. Esquivel, Alex, B, Mexico City College
25. Grann, Dick, T, Rhode Island
26. Minker, Marion, T, Bucknell
27. Locke, Jim, T, Virginia Tech
28. Meyer, Bob, T, Ohio State
29. Waters, Bill, T, Austin

CHI. BEARS

1. Drzewiecki, Ron, B, Marquette
2. Watkins, Bobby, B, Ohio State
3. Choice to Cleveland
4. O'Malley, Joe, E, Georgia
5. Kendall, Leland, T, Oklahoma State

6. Shannon, Dan, E, Notre Dame, from Washington
Mosely, Henry, B, Morris Brown
7. Sturgess, Bruce, B, William & Mary
8. Verkerk, Gene, T, North Texas State
9. Lavery, Jim, B, Scranton
10. Allen, John, E, Arizona State
11. Redfield, Tom, E, Delaware
12. Bratt, Clarence, B, Wisconsin
13. Cash, Norm, B, Sul Ross
14. Nickla, Ed, G, Tennessee
15. Smith, J.D., B, North Carolina A&T
16. Choice to Chi. Cardinals
17. Harrison, Mel, C, Sam Houston State
18. Roach, Claude, G, TCU
19. Jones, Allen, B, Baylor
20. James, Joe, T, Howard Payne
21. Hall, Choyce, C, Midwestern State (Texas)
22. Allison, Carl, B, Oklahoma
23. Barger, Jerry, B, Duke
24. Young, Joe, E, Marquette
25. Dees, Charley, T, Tyler J.C.
26. Jeter, Perry, B, Cal Poly-SLO
27. Kinley, Joel, G, Tennessee
28. Wright, Charley, E, Prairie View A&M
29. Klein, Dick, T, Iowa
30. Fouts, Jerry, B, Midwestern State (Texas)

CHI. CARDINALS
1. Boydston, Max, E, Oklahoma
2. Crow, Lindon, B, USC
3. Hammack, Mal, B, Florida
Pasquesi, Tony, T, Notre Dame, from NY Giants
4. Bernardi, Frank, B, Colorado
5. DaRe, Mario, T, USC
6. Bowersox, Jack, G, Maryland
7. Leggett, Dave, B, Ohio State
8. Irvine, Sam, C, Maryland
9. McGinty, Charlie, E, North Texas State
10. Scaffidi, Frank, T, Marquette
11. Pepsin, Tom, E, Miami
12. Sandstrom, Dale, B, Concordia (Minnesota)
13. McLuckie, Tom, G, Maryland
14. Brown, Gordy, E, Louisiana Tech
15. Brubaker, Dick, E, Ohio State
16. Herndon, Bob, B, Oklahoma
Dennis, Al, E, Middlebury, from Chi. Bears
17. White, Larry, C, New Mexico
18. Campbell, Fred, T, Duke
19. Coy, Dick, T, St. John's (Minnesota)
20. Burst, Jim, B, Washington (St. Louis)
21. Wright, Howie, B, Virginia Tech
22. Berra, Vic, E, Montana State
23. Bays, Karl, T, Eastern Kentucky
24. Pierce, Max, B, Utah
25. Scott, Bob, E, Evansville
26. Hooper, Billy, B, Baylor
27. Schwager, Bruce, T, Merchant Marine
28. Ems, Bob, B, Southern Illinois
29. Renzi, Gene, T, Northeastern
30. Sweet, Bob, B, Trinity (Texas)

CLEVELAND
1. Burris, Kurt, C, Oklahoma
2. Renfro, Dean, B, North Texas State
3. Hall, John, T, Iowa, from Chi. Bears
Freeman, Bobby, B, Auburn
4. Reynolds, Paul, B, Notre Dame, from Green Bay
Palumbo, Sam, C, Notre Dame
5. Dandoy, Aramis, B, USC
6. Bolden, Leroy, B, Michigan State
7. Locklear, Jack, C, Auburn
8. Choice to Detroit
9. Ford, Henry, B, Pittsburgh
10. Dillon, Glen, E, Pittsburgh
11. Knebel, Eric, T, SMU
12. Eaton, Jack, T, New Mexico
13. Borton, Johnny, QB, Ohio State
14. Robinson, Fred, G, Washington, F
15. Smith, Bob, B, Nebraska
16. Suchy, Don, C, Iowa
17. Leonard, Bob, B, Purdue
18. Champlin, Steve, T, Oklahoma
19. Ebert, Tom, E, Kansas State
20. Proctor, Bill, T, Florida State
21. Spinks, Rick, B, Texas Tech
22. Stone, Jerry, T, Southeastern Louisiana
23. Greer, Jim, E, Elizabeth City State
24. Matsock, John, B, Michigan State
25. Lindo, Ernie, B, Pacific
26. Fife, Don, C, Purdue
27. Baldwin, Bobby, B, Sam Houston State
28. Tokus, Ed, E, Georgia
29. Robinson, Tex, B, Temple
30. Leachman, Lamar, C, Tennessee

DETROIT
1. Middleton, Dave, B, Auburn
2. Salsbury, Jim, G, UCLA
3. McCord, Darris, T, Tennessee
4. Malloy, Gordon, B, Miami, from Washington
Riley, Lee, B, Detroit
5. Brooks, Bud, G, Arkansas
6. Childers, Elijah, T, Prairie View A&M
7. Zagers, Bert, B, Michigan State
8. Cunningham, Leon, C, South Carolina, from Pittsburgh
Holland, Lamoine, E, Rice, from Cleveland
Walker, Bill, E, Maryland
9. Jenkins, Walt, T, Wayne State
10. Gastall, Tom, B, Boston U.
11. McDermott, Herb, T, Iowa State
12. Goist, Dick, B, Cincinnati
13. Henderson, Don, T, Utah
14. Gajda, Jerry, B, Benedictine
15. Atkins, George, G, Auburn
16. Marr, Al, E, Bradley
17. Daly, Don, B, Eastern Kentucky
18. Oleksiak, Pat, B, Tennessee
19. Muller, Bob, C, Eastern Kentucky
20. Mahaffey, Fred, B, Denver
21. Walters, Jim, T, Mississippi
22. Albrecht, George, B, Maryland
23. Galuska, George, B, Wyoming
24. Flacke, Bob, G, Holy Cross
25. Miller, Dick, T, Illinois
26. McDonald, Duncan, B, Michigan
27. Troka, Mike, B, Trinity (Connecticut)
28. Lovell, Harry, G, South Carolina
29. Dearing, Bill, B, Florida
30. Hatch, Charley, E, Utah State

GREEN BAY
1. Bettis, Tom, G, Purdue
2. Temp, Jim, E, Wisconsin
3. Leake, Buddy, B, Oklahoma
4. Choice to Cleveland
5. Bullough, Hank, G, Michigan State
6. Amundsen, Norm, G, Wisconsin
7. Clemens, Bob, B, Georgia
8. Crouch, Johnny, E, TCU
9. Culpepper, Ed, T, Alabama
10. Rogers, George, T, Auburn
11. Clark, Ron, B, Nebraska
12. Walker, Art, T, Michigan
13. Adams, Ed, B, South Carolina
14. Baer, Fred, B, Michigan
15. Machoukas, George, C, Toledo
16. Brackins, Charley, QB, Prairie View A&M
17. Beightol, Lynn, B, Maryland
18. Nix, Doyle, B, SMU
19. Carter, Bob, T, Grambling
20. Bolt, Carl, B, Southern Mississippi
Antkowiak, Bob, E, Bucknell, from NY Giants
21. Isbell, Lavell, T, Houston
22. Brunner, Bill, B, Arkansas Tech
23. Shaw, Elton, T, LSU
24. Bryant, Charley, G, Nebraska
25. Borden, Nate, E, Indiana
26. Jennings, Jim, E, Missouri
27. Peringer, Bob, E, Washington State
28. Spears, Jack, T, Tennessee-Chattanooga
29. Pino, Sam, B, Boston U.
30. Saia, Bob, B, Tulane

LA RAMS
1. Morris, Larry, C, Georgia Tech
2. Waller, Ron, B, Maryland, from Washington
Long, Bob, B, UCLA, from Pittsburgh
Taylor, Corky, B, Kansas State
Fournet, Sid, T, LSU, from NY Giants
3. Choice to NY Giants
4. Feamster, Tom, E, Florida State, from Baltimore
Fouch, Ed, T, USC
5. Kelley, Ed, B, Texas
6. Tharp, Corky, B, Alabama
7. Clayton, Frank, B, USC
8. Teas, Billy, B, Georgia Tech
9. Witte, John, T, Oregon State
10. Arnelle, Jesse, E, Penn State, from Baltimore
Harland, Claude, E, Texas Tech
11. Ray, Joe, T, UCLA
12. Hanifan, Jim, E, California
13. Parkinson, Dave, B, Texas
14. Elliot, George, B, Northeastern Oklahoma
15. Hoerning, Bob, B, St. Norbert
16. Coates, Charley, T, Tulane
17. Mitcham, Gene, E, Arizona State
18. Sweeney, Clyde, T, West Virginia
19. Davis, John, E, Miles
20. Muldowney, Jack, T, Dayton
21. Cvengros, Jerry, T, Wisconsin
22. Elmore, Ken, T, Texas Tech
23. Medved, George, T, Florida
24. Andrews, Bill, B, Trinity (Texas)
25. Cook, Ralph, T, Ball State
26. Hallow, Lou, C, Wake Forest
27. Nevitt, Bruce, C, Washington State
28. Hoffman, Jim, B, Cincinnati
29. Howe, Bob, B, Cincinnati
30. Jones, K.C., E, San Francisco

NY GIANTS
1. Heap, Joe, B, Notre Dame
2. Choice to LA Rams
3. Grier, Roosevelt (Rosey), T, Penn State, from LA Rams
Choice to Chi. Cardinals
4. Choice to Baltimore
5. Triplett, Mel, B, Toledo
6. Locklin, Ron, E, Wisconsin
7. Choice to Washington
8. Patton, Jimmy, B, Mississippi
9. Choice to Baltimore
10. Paslay, Lea, B, Mississippi
11. Hillen, Bill, E, West Virginia
12. Burnine, Hank, E, Missouri, F
13. Damore, John, C, Northwestern
14. Kettler, Elwood, B, Texas A&M
15. Stowers, Ed, E, Wake Forest
16. Kragthorpe, Dave, G, Utah State
17. Bills, Bob, B, BYU
18. Stout, Joe, B, Temple
19. Jacobs, John, E, Colby
20. Choice to Green Bay
21. Dilby, Gary, C, LSU
22. Doggett, Al, B, LSU
23. Callahan, Jerry, B, Colorado State
24. Vujevich, Matt, B, San Jose State
25. Dement, Ken, T, Southeast Missouri State
26. Cohen, Abe, G, Tennessee-Chattanooga
27. Blanda, Paul, B, Pittsburgh
28. Crow, Al, T, William & Mary
29. Jackson, Harold, B, Southern
30. Toole, Bill, B, Oregon

PHILADELPHIA
1. Bielski, Dick, B, Maryland
2. Lansford, Buck, T, Texas
3. Eidom, Frank, B, SMU
4. Dugger, Dean, E, Ohio State
5. Lamone, Gene, G, West Virginia
6. Quinn, Billy, B, Texas
7. McKenna, Bill, E, Brandeis
8. Watson, Herman, T, Vanderbilt
9. Morgan, Von, E, Abilene Christian
10. Washington, Talmadge (Duke), B, Washington State
11. Hardy, Bob, B, Kentucky
12. Nacrelli, Andy, E, Fordham
13. Krisher, Jerry, C, Ohio State
14. Bell, Tommy, B, Army
15. Brougher, Don, C, Maryland
16. White, Clyde, G, Clemson
17. Maravic, Nick, B, Wake Forest
18. Nutt, Duane, B, SMU
19. Fails, Terry, E, Vanderbilt
20. Wade, Jimmy, B, Tennessee
21. Anderson, John, E, Kansas
22. Lewis, Ernie, G, Arizona
23. Ingram, Cecil, B, Alabama
24. Postula, Vic, B, Michigan State
25. Pavich, Frank, G, USC
26. Palahunik, George, G, Maryland
27. Gringrass, Bob, B, Wisconsin
28. Avery, Wingo, C, Clemson
29. Lloyd, Ron, T, Bucknell
30. Finney, Dave, B, TCU

PITTSBURGH
1. Varrichione, Frank, T, Notre Dame
2. Choice to LA Rams
3. Bernet, Ed, E, SMU
4. Broussard, Fred, C, Northwestern State (Louisiana)
5. Mason, George, T, Alabama
6. Harkey, Lem, B, Emporia State
7. Reeve, Hal, T, Oregon
8. Choice to Detroit
9. Unitas, Johnny, QB, Louisville
10. Boyle, Terry, T, Cincinnati
11. Eaton, Vic, B, Missouri
12. Cooke, Jim, E, Lincoln (Pennsylvania)
13. Whitmer, Jim, B, Purdue
14. Byrne, John (Buck), G, John Carroll
15. Duckett, Ellis, B, Michigan State
16. Vincent, Frank, C, Glenville State
17. Merchant, Ed, B, Miami (Ohio)
18. Maier, Albie, G, Marshall
19. Smith, Ed, B, Texas Southern
20. Matykiewicz, Lou, E, Iowa
21. Phenix, Rees, T, Georgia Tech
22. McCabe, Richie, B, Pittsburgh
23. Holz, Gordy, T, Minnesota
24. Mayock, Mike, E, Villanova
25. Bull, Charlie, G, Missouri
26. Soltau, Jim, E, Minnesota
27. Sanford, Bill, B, Hofstra
28. Williams, Dave, G, Ohio State
29. Sinclair, Bernie, E, Texas A&M
30. Caruzzi, Jim, B, Marquette

SAN FRANCISCO
1. Moegle, Dickie, B, Rice
2. Morze, Frank, C, Boston College
3. Hardy, Carroll, B, Colorado
4. Hazeltine, Matt, C, California
5. Kraemer, Eldred, T, Pittsburgh
6. Luna, Bobby, B, Alabama
7. Dean, Johnny, B, Virginia Tech
8. Meyers, Freddie, B, Oklahoma State, F
9. Preziosio, Fred, T, Purdue, F
10. Aschbacker, Ron, E, Oregon State
11. Rotella, Rudy, E, Nebraska-Omaha
12. Palatella, Lou, T, Pittsburgh, F
13. Gaskell, Richie, E, George Washington
14. McKeithan, Nick, B, Duke
15. Hess, Burdette, G, Idaho
16. Hall, Jim, E, Auburn
17. Newton, Bob, G, San Diego State
18. Pheister, Ron, C, Oregon
19. Garzoli, John, T, California
20. Dyer, Glen, B, Texas
21. Maderos, George, E, Cal State-Chico
22. Vann, Pete, QB, Army
23. Gunnari, Tom, E, Washington State, F
24. Heaston, Bob, G, Cal Poly-SLO
25. Wade, Dewey, E, Kansas State
26. Kerr, Johnny, E, Purdue
27. Shockey, Dick, B, Marquette, F
28. Sanders, Don, B, Stanford
29. Kniedinger, Otto, T, Penn State, F
30. Gongola, Bob, B, Illinois, F

WASHINGTON
1. Guglielmi, Ralph, QB, Notre Dame
2. Choice to LA Rams
3. Perkins, Ray, B, Syracuse
4. Choice to Detroit
5. Glantz, Don, T, Nebraska
6. Choice to Chi. Bears
7. Christensen, Erik, E, Richmond
Marciniak, Ron, G, Kansas State, from NY Giants
8. Allen, John, C, Purdue
9. Miller, John, T, Boston College, F
10. Louderback, Tom, G, San Jose State
11. Parker, Larry, B, North Carolina
12. Barish, John, T, Waynesburg
13. Oniskey, Len, T, Cornell
14. Braatz, Tom, E, Marquette
15. Horton, Charley, B, Vanderbilt
16. Norris, Hal, B, California
17. Shea, Don, G, Georgia
18. Bailey, Don, B, Penn State
19. Dee, Bob, E, Holy Cross
20. Geyer, Ron, T, Michigan
21. George, Buck, B, Clemson
22. Boland, Joe, B, George Washington
23. Donaldson, Chick, C, West Virginia
24. Ready, Bob, T, Notre Dame
25. Radella, Frank, C, Wyoming
26. Houston, Wally, G, Purdue
27. Baker, A.J., B, Arkansas
28. Cassidy, Arch, T, Florida
29. Bordier, Bing, E, USC
30. Petty, Tom, E, Virginia Tech

1956

Held November 29, 1955 (Rounds 1-3) and January 12, 1956 (Rounds 4-30)

The first three rounds were held two months earlier than recent drafts in order to give NFL teams an even start with the Canadian Football League in signing top players. The CFL had been attempting to build its popularity by

signing big-name players from the United States. Rounds 4-30 were held in January. The NFL also had early drafts the next two years, when the first four rounds were picked in November or December.

BALTIMORE
1. Moore, Lenny, B, Penn State
2. Donlin, Dick, E, Hamline
3. Pascal, Bob, B, Duke
4. Inabinet, Ben, T, Clemson
5. Gray, Herb, E, Texas
6. Schmidt, Don, B, Texas Tech
7. Waters, Bill, T, Austin
8. Koman, Bill, G, North Carolina
9. Lewis, John, E, Michigan State
10. Scott, Gene, B, Centre
11. Shaw, Dennis, E, North Texas State
12. Myrha, Steve, G, North Dakota
13. Hill, Jack, B, Utah State
14. Schwanger, Ted, B, Tennessee Tech
15. Polzer, John, LB, Virginia
16. Hendrik, Gene (Moose), B, Drake
17. Danenhauer, Bill, E, Emporia State
18. Looman, Earl, G, Stetson
19. Fyvie, Bob, T, Lafayette
20. Hill, Rob, B, Jackson State
21. Harness, Jim, B, Mississippi State
22. Del Vicaro, Pat, G, Southern Mississippi
23. Stephenson, Al (Bear), T, Idaho State
24. Fox, Bobby, QB, East Texas State
25. Mills, Brad, B, Kentucky
26. Lohr, Jim, T, Southwest Missouri State
27. Hartwell, Herb, B, Virginia
28. Shearer, John, QB, Shepherd
29. Rusher, Jim, E, Kansas State
30. Sweeney, Terry, B, Middle Tennessee State

CHI. BEARS
1. Schriewer, Menan (Tex), E, Texas
2. Brackett, M.L., T, Auburn
3. Choice to Cleveland
4. Mellekas, John, T, Arizona
5. Galimore, Willie, B, Florida A&M
6. Choice to Cleveland
7. Caroline, J.C., B, Illinois
8. Klawitter, Dick, C, South Dakota State
9. Vargo, Ken, C, Ohio State
10. Lucas, Dick, E, Boston College
11. Jankans, John, E, Arizona State
12. Cruze, Buddy, E, Tennessee
13. Grogg, Dick, G, Minnesota
14. Graham, Milt, E, Colgate
15. Fitzgerald, Dick, B, Notre Dame
16. Brown, Ray, B, Florida
17. Adams, Tom, E, UCLA
18. Payton, Earl, B, Prairie View A&M
19. Smith, John, B, UCLA
20. Maxime, Charley, G, Auburn
21. Waddell, Jimmy, B, Compton J.C.
22. Billings, Joe, T, Memphis State
23. Holt, Lou, E, Howard Payne
24. Castete, Jess, B, McNeese State
25. Hentschel, Jerry, T, Sam Houston State
26. Orr, Don, B, Vanderbilt
27. Buchanan, Waylon, E, East Texas State
28. Alexander, Bob, B, Trinity (Connecticut)
29. Krietemeyer, Billy, B, Vanderbilt
30. Buckler, Jim, G, Alabama

CHI. CARDINALS
1. Childress, Joe, B, Auburn
2. Masters, Norm, T, Michigan State
3. Roach, John, QB, SMU
4. Salerno, Sam, T, Colorado
5. Choice to LA Rams
6. Dupre, Charlie, B, Baylor
7. Konovsky, Bob, T, Wisconsin
8. Lunceford, Dave, T, Baylor, F
9. Lovely, Bob, T, Tampa
10. Towne, Willis, E, Wichita State
11. James, Fob, B, Auburn
12. Walker, Jerry, T, Texas Tech
13. Bolinger, Bo, G, Oklahoma
14. Neuman, Carnell, B, Illinois
15. Anderson, Charley, E, Louisiana Tech
    Spiers, Tom, QB, Arkansas State, from Washington
16. Welsh, George, QB, Navy
17. Beagle, Ron, E, Navy
18. Brown, Jim, G, UCLA
19. Zagar, Ray, B, Marquette
20. Mattison, Dickie, B, Georgia Tech
21. Herr, Ronnie, B, Texas Tech
22. Murphy, Jim, T, Stephen F. Austin
23. Branoff, Tony, B, Michigan
24. Trask, Orville, T, Rice
25. Wheeler, Bill, T, Kentucky
26. Zickefoose, Chuck, E, Kansas State
27. Hutchinson, Jack, T, Oklahoma State
28. Miller, Jim, QB, Wisconsin
29. Troglio, Jim, B, Northwestern
30. Kucera, Bill, T, Colorado

CLEVELAND
1. Carpenter, Preston, B, Arkansas
2. Kinard, Billy, B, Mississippi
3. Ross, Larry, E, Denver, from Chi. Bears
   Quinlan, Billy, E, Michigan State
4. Moss, Bobby, B, West Virginia
5. Clarke, Frank, E, Colorado, F
6. Plunkett, Sherman, E, Maryland-Eastern Shore, from Chi. Bears
   Wiggin, Paul, E, Stanford, F
7. Griffith, Chuck, E, USC
8. Hellyer, Len, B, Marshall
9. Hecker, Jack, E, Bowling Green
10. Rayburn, Eddie, T, Rice
11. Underdonk, Bill, T, West Virginia
12. Javernick, Harry, T, Colorado
13. Furey, Jim, C, Kansas State
14. Sidwell, Charlie, B, William & Mary
15. Davis, Willie, E, Grambling
16. Cooper, Thurlow, E, Maine
17. West, Eddie, QB, North Carolina State
18. Carroll, Hal (Candy), B, Case Western Reserve
19. Sebest, John, E, Eastern Kentucky
20. Mobra, Jim, E, Oklahoma
21. Kapish, Gene, E, Notre Dame
22. Brown, Sam (First Down), B, UCLA
23. Althouse, Don, E, Syracuse
24. Hughes, Jim, G, San Jose State
25. Davenport, Bob, B, UCLA
26. Kammerman, Jack, E, Utah
27. Dwyer, Ed, E, Purdue
28. Sparks, Ollie, G, Iowa State
29. Battos, John, E, Vanderbilt
30. Bartholomew, Bob, T, Wake Forest

DETROIT
1. Cassady, Howard (Hopalong), B, Ohio State
2. Choice to LA Rams
3. McIlhenny, Don, B, SMU
4. Reichow, Jerry, QB, Iowa
5. Tracy, Tom (The Bomb), B, Tennessee
6. Lusk, Bob, C, William & Mary
7. Cronin, Gene, G, Pacific
8. Powell, Jack, T, Texas A&M
9. Jones, Calvin, G, Iowa
10. Silas, Joe, DE, South Carolina
11. Wacker, Lew, B, Richmond
    Selep, Tom, B, Maryland, from Pittsburgh
12. Nunnery, Bob, T, LSU
13. Ferguson, O.K., B, LSU
14. Falls, Ronnie, LB, Duke
15. Allert, Horace (Buzzy), DE, Southwest Texas State
16. Zyzda, Len, DE, Purdue
17. Wind, Ken, E, Houston
18. Petrarca, Emidio, B, Boston College
19. Vaughn, Dale, B, Virginia Military
20. Stephenson, Joe, E, Vanderbilt
21. Blechen, Bob, C, Whittier
22. Marazza, Dick, T, Clemson
23. Garrard, Bob, B, Georgia
24. Walz, Jarv, E, Central Michigan
25. Hall, Jerry, B, Rice
26. Walden, Joe, B, West Texas State
27. Burnthorne, Bryan, G, Tulane
28. Smith, John, G, Northwestern
29. Peters, Doug, B, UCLA
30. Gibbens, John, T, Southwest Texas State

GREEN BAY
1. Losch, Jack, B, Miami
2. Gregg, Forrest, T, SMU
3. Choice to LA Rams
4. Morris, Cecil, G, Oklahoma
5. Skoronski, Bob, T, Indiana
6. Burris, Bob, B, Oklahoma
7. Gremminger, Hank, E, Baylor
8. Dennis, Russ, E, Maryland
9. Duvall, Gordy, B, USC
10. Laugherty, Bob, B, Maryland
11. Hudock, Mike, C, Miami
12. Burnett, Max, B, Arizona
13. Mense, Jim, C, Notre Dame
14. Thomas, Charlie, B, Wisconsin
15. Alliston, Buddy, G, Mississippi
16. Lynch, Curtis, T, Alabama
17. Starr, Bart, QB, Alabama
18. Intihar, Stan, E, Cornell
19. Vakey, Ken, E, Texas Tech
20. Letbetter, Clyde, T, Baylor
21. O'Brien, Hal, B, SMU
22. Popson, Johnny, B, Furman
23. Birchfield, Jesse, G, Duke
24. Wilson, Don, C, Rice
25. Koeneke, Franz, E, Minnesota
26. Goehe, Dick, T, Mississippi
27. Kolian, Dick, E, Wisconsin
28. Lance, Bobby, QB, Florida
29. Newcomb, Vester, C, Southwest J.C. (Mississippi)
30. Hermes, Rod, QB, Beloit

LA RAMS
1. Marconi, Joe, B, West Virginia, from NY Giants
   Horton, Charlie, B, Vanderbilt
2. Clarke, Leon, E, USC, from Detroit
   Pitts, Hugh, C, TCU
3. Williams, A.D., DE, Pacific, from Green Bay
   Marshall, John, B, SMU
4. Berzinski, Willis, B, Wisconsin-La Crosse, from Washington
   Carmichael, Jim, E, California
5. Freeman, Jim, E, Iowa, from San Francisco
   Nakken, Herb, B, Utah, from Chi. Cardinals
   Whittenton, Jesse, DB, Texas-El Paso
6. Vincent, Eddie, B, Iowa
7. Morris, Jack, B, Oregon, F
8. Boyer, George, LB, Florida State
9. Woolford, Maury, T, Louisville
10. Sticka, Charlie, B, Trinity (Connecticut)
11. Decker, Jim, B, UCLA
12. Lindbeck, Em, QB, Illinois
13. Norcia, Mike, B, Kent State
14. Runnels, Tom, B, North Texas State
15. Shatto, Dick, B, Kentucky
16. Pelluer, Arnie, E, Washington State
17. Butler, Jack, T, Kentucky
18. Klotz, Jack, T, Widener
19. Dees, Charlie, T, McNeese State
20. Coyne, John, T, West Chester
21. Robichaux, Milt, E, Trinity (Texas)
22. Fouts, Dick, E, Missouri
23. Paulson, Al, B, Washington State
24. Williams, Sam, DE, Michigan State, F
25. Tunning, Glen, G, Pittsburgh
26. Cureton, Hardiman, T, UCLA
27. Siesel, Roger, T, Miami (Ohio)
28. Morrow, John, T, Michigan
29. Bates, Mickey, B, Illinois
30. Kackmeister, Dick, C, Central Michigan

NY GIANTS
1. Choice to LA Rams
2. Moore, Henry, B, Arkansas
3. Huff, Sam, T, West Virginia
4. Katcavage, Jim, E, Dayton
5. Chandler, Don, B, Florida
6. Cason, Fred, B, Florida
7. Nery, Ron, T, Kansas State
8. Holleder, Don, E, Army
9. Braden, Ken, C, East Texas State
10. Hermann, Johnny, B, UCLA
11. Moloney, Dick, B, Kentucky
12. Choice to Washington
13. Crawford, Eddie, B, Mississippi, F
14. McMullan, John, G, Notre Dame
15. Melnik, Ron, T, Army
16. Portney, Al, T, Missouri
17. Mooney, Tom, T, Miami (Ohio)
18. Boone, Matt, B, North Carolina Central
19. Detring, Ray, B, Missouri
20. Falls, Mike, G, Minnesota
21. McComb, Don, E, Villanova
22. Harkrader, Jerry, B, Ohio State
23. McCool, Bob (Slick), B, Mississippi
24. Huth, Gerry, G, Wake Forest
25. Speers, Harry, B, Florida
26. Buller, Bev, B, Kansas
27. Nesbitt, Gerry, B, Arkansas
28. Fuller, Bill, T, Arkansas
29. Nelson, Jim, G, Duke
30. Williams, Wayne, E, Southern Illinois

PHILADELPHIA
1. Pellegrini, Bob, C, Maryland
2. D'Agostino, Frank, T, Auburn
3. Schaffer, Don, B, Notre Dame
4. Choice to Washington
5. Thurston, Fred (Fuzzy), G, Valparaiso
6. Burton, Tirrel, B, Miami (Ohio)
7. Waedekin, John, T, Hardin-Simmons
8. Payne, Elroy, B, McMurry
9. Bredice, Johnny, E, Boston U.
10. Dimmick, Tom, C, Houston
11. Keller, Kenny, B, North Carolina
12. Harkins, Tommy, E, Vanderbilt
13. Sides, James, B, Texas Tech
14. Reich, Frank, C, Penn State
15. Brant, Don, B, Montana
16. Hix, Billy, T, Middle Tennessee State
17. Mastrogiovanni, Joe, B, Wyoming
18. Consoles, Nick, QB, Wake Forest
19. Womack, Delano, B, Texas
20. Glover, Darrell, T, Maryland-Eastern Shore
21. Adams, Jack, T, San Jose State
22. Miller, Joe, B, Cincinnati
23. Spencer, Chet, E, Oklahoma State
24. Parham, John, B, Wake Forest
25. Grogan, Johnny, T, Dayton
26. Lunsford, Earl, B, Oklahoma State
27. Ellett, Al, T, Alabama
28. Strawn, Bill, LB, Western Kentucky
29. Hughes, Bob, B, Southern Mississippi
30. Ulm, Joe, B, San Jose State

PITTSBURGH
BONUS CHOICE: Glick, Gary, QB, Colorado State
1. Davis, Art, B, Mississippi State
2. Krupa, Joe, T, Purdue
3. Taylor, Jim, C, Baylor
4. Murley, Dick, G, Purdue
5. Murakowski, Bill, B, Purdue
6. Taylor, Ray, B, TCU
7. Gaspari, Dick, C, George Washington
8. Wellman, Vere, G, Wichita State
9. Edmonds, Wayne, G, Notre Dame
10. Baldacci, Lou, B, Michigan
    Nolan, Bob, E, Miami, from Washington
11. Choice to Detroit
12. Tarasovic, Phil, E, Yale
13. Holley, Weldon, B, Baylor
14. Emmons, Jim, T, Alabama
15. Choice to San Francisco
16. Reed, Lionel, B, Central State (Oklahoma)
17. Schmidt, Bill, G, Pittsburgh
18. Stephens, John, QB, Holy Cross
19. Jacobs, Jerry, G, Florida State
20. Glatz, Fred, E, Pittsburgh
21. Martell, Gene, T, Notre Dame
22. DiPasquale, Ray, B, Pittsburgh
23. Neft, Pete, QB, Pittsburgh
24. Engram, Bryan, E, TCU
25. O'Dell, Bill, B, Clemson
26. Sweeney, Frank, G, Xavier
27. Benson, Buddy, B, Arkansas
28. DeGraaf, Bill, B, Cornell
29. Thompson, Wes, T, Alabama

SAN FRANCISCO
1. Morrall, Earl, QB, Michigan State
2. Bosley, Bruce, T, West Virginia
3. Herschman, Bill, T, Texas Tech
4. Pajaczkowski, Frank, B, Richmond
5. Choice to LA Rams
6. Sardisco, Tony, LB, Tulane
7. Barnes, Larry, B, Colorado State, F
8. Smith, Charley, E, Abilene Christian
9. Cox, Jim, E, Cal Poly-SLO
10. Zaleski, Jerry, B, Colorado State
11. Pell, Stew, T, North Carolina
12. Swedberg, Roger, T, Iowa
13. Moody, Ralph, B, Kansas
14. Owens, R.C., E, College of Idaho, F
15. Henderson, Reed, T, Utah State
    Boyd, Gene, B, Abilene Christian, from Pittsburgh
16. Herring, George, QB, Southern Mississippi
17. Weiss, Dick, T, Mississippi
18. Yelverton, Billy, T, Mississippi, F
19. Arrigoni, Pete, B, Arizona
20. Scarbrough, Bob, C, Auburn
21. Joyner, L.C., E, Contra Costa J.C.
22. Wessman, Clarence, E, San Jose State
23. Monroe, Mike, B, Washington
24. Wallace, Ed, T, San Diego J.C.
25. Goad, Paul, B, Abilene Christian
26. Loudd, Rommie, E, UCLA
27. Gustafson, Jerry, QB, Stanford
28. Drew, Jerry, B, California, F
29. Benson, Dean, B, Willamette
30. Mitchell, Bob, T, Puget Sound, F

WASHINGTON
1. Vereb, Ed, B, Maryland
2. Paluck, John, E, Pittsburgh
3. Wyant, Fred, B, West Virginia
4. Choice to LA Rams
   Machinsky, Fran, T, Ohio State, from Philadelphia

5. Lowe, Gary, B, Michigan State
6. Choice to Chi. Cardinals
7. Caraway, Donnie, B, Houston*
8. James, Dick, B, Oregon
9. Rouviere, Francis (Whitey), B, Miami
10. Choice to Pittsburgh
11. Powell, Tom, G, Colgate
12. Planutis, Gerry, B, Michigan State, from NY Giants
Moreno, Gil, T, UCLA
13. Ward, Jerry, G, Dayton
14. Uebel, Pat, B, Army
15. Choice to Chi. Cardinals
16. Gray, Wells, G, Wisconsin
17. Day, Eagle, QB, Mississippi
18. Pyburn, Jim, E, Auburn
19. Lemek, Ray, G, Notre Dame
20. Gonzales, Vince, B, LSU
21. Schnellenberger, Howard, E, Kentucky
22. Nicula, George, T, Notre Dame
23. St. John, Don, B, Xavier
24. Tatum, Johnny, C, Texas
25. Brooks, Franklin, G, Georgia Tech
26. Burnham, Dave, B, Wheaton
27. Flippin, Royce, B, Princeton
28. Hicks, Billy, B, North Alabama
29. Bisceglia, Pat, G, Notre Dame
30. Nystrom, Buck, G, Michigan State

1957

Held November 27, 1956 (Rounds 1-4) and January 31, 1957 (Rounds 5-30)

BALTIMORE
1. Parker, Jim, G, Ohio State
2. Shinnick, Don, LB, UCLA
3. Owens, Luke, T, Kent State
4. Simpson, Jackie, B, Florida
5. Underwood, Ronnie, B, Arkansas
6. Pricer, Billy, B, Oklahoma
7. Saage, Reuben, B, Baylor
8. Harmon, Jack, E, Eastern Oregon
9. White, Bob, T, Otterbein
10. Grisham, Joe, E, Austin Peay
11. Nelson, Andy, QB, Memphis State
12. Simonic, Don, T, Tennessee Tech
13. Call, Jack, B, Colgate
14. Guido, Joe, B, Youngstown State
15. Whitley, Hall, C, Texas A&I
16. Prelock, Ed, T, Kansas
Canavino, Joe, HB, Ohio State, from Pittsburgh
17. Wisniewski, Dan, G, Pittsburgh
18. Villa, Jim, B, Allegheny
19. Froehle, Charlie, G, St. John's (Minnesota)
20. Livingston, Walt, B, Heidelberg
21. Mulholland, Owen, B, Houston
22. Van Atta, Chet, T, Kansas
23. Baird, Connie, E, Hardin-Simmons
24. Hoeft, Harwood, E, South Dakota State
25. Geach, Harlan, T, College of Idaho
26. Unitas, Joe, T, Louisville
27. DeMalon, Len, G, St. Vincent
28. Schnieter, Walt, T, Colorado
29. Rasmussen, Bob, G, Minnesota
30. Bailey, Bob, E, Thiel

CHI. BEARS
1. Leggett, Earl, T, LSU
2. Swink, Jim, B, TCU
3. Knox, Ronnie, QB, UCLA
4. Johnson, Jack, B, Miami
5. Zucco, Vic, B, Michigan State
6. Dickinson, Bo, B, Southern Mississippi
7. DeLuca, Gerry, T, Middle Tennessee State
8. Ward, Al, B, Yale, from Pittsburgh
Kilcullen, Bob, T, Texas Tech
9. Brown, Bill, G, Syracuse
10. Murphy, Bill, E, Fresno State
11. Hampton, Roger, B, McNeese State
12. Sorenson, Larry, T, Utah State
13. Williams, Don, B, Texas Tech
14. Schmidt, Bob, B, Memphis State
15. Hosek, Tony, E, West Virginia
16. Heuring, Ed, E, Maryland
17. Heine, Don, E, Murray State
18. Wharton, Al, G, Maryland
19. Hermsen, Lee, B, Marquette
20. Frazier, Al, B, Florida A&M
21. Janes, Jerry, E, LSU
22. Dalzell, Tom, T, Virginia Tech
23. Peroyea, Don, T, Southeastern Louisiana
24. Lutterbock, Ken, B, Evansville
25. Ryan, Joe, C, Villanova
26. Harris, Gehrig, B, Grambling
27. Brown, Nick, G, Fresno State
28. Emerson, Tom, G, Oklahoma
29. Caraway, Donnie, B, Houston*
30. Wesley, Sam, B, Oregon State

CHI. CARDINALS
1. Tubbs, Jerry, C, Oklahoma
2. Maentz, Tom, E, Michigan
3. Hudson, Bill, T, Clemson
4. Choice to San Francisco
5. Bock, Wayne, T, Illinois
6. Choice to Green Bay
7. Choice to Cleveland through NY Giants
8. Choice to LA Rams
9. McCumby, Don, T, Washington
10. Carouthers, Don, E, Bradley
11. Kraus, Bob, G, Kansas
12. Derrick, Bob, B, Oklahoma
13. Ritt, Ed, T, Montana State
14. Fee, Bob, B, Indiana
15. Livingston, Bill, C, SMU
16. Hurley, Terry, E, Montana
17. Terry, Buddy, T, Houston
18. Smith, Hal, B, UCLA
19. Barrington, Paul, G, Minnesota
20. Horner, Tom, T, Kansas
21. Kopnisky, Joe, E, West Virginia
22. Sizemore, Don, B, Hardin-Simmons
23. Konicek, Milt, T, Duke
24. Klim, Ron, C, West Virginia
25. Volz, Ray, B, Denison
26. Rohde, Ted, B, Kansas
27. Butorovich, Bob, T, Montana State
28. Husser, Hugh, E, Southeastern Louisiana
29. Corso, Lee, B, Florida State
30. Gibson, Frank, T, Kansas

CLEVELAND
1. Brown, Jim, B, Syracuse
2. Plum, Milt, QB, Penn State
3. Walker, George, B, Arkansas
4. Camera, Paul, E, Stanford
5. Jordan, Henry, T, Virginia, from Green Bay
Campbell, Milt, B, Indiana
6. Amstutz, Joe, G, Indiana, from Green Bay
Martin, Harley, T, California
7. Hickerson, Gene, T, Mississippi, F
Rotunno, Mike, C, Michigan, from Chi. Cardinals through NY Giants
8. Gillis, Don, C, Rice
9. Comstock, Don, B, Alabama
10. Reinhart, Bob, B, San Jose State
11. Cummings, Bill, T, Ohio State
12. Spitzenberger, Rudy, G, Houston
13. Sansom, Jerry, E, Auburn
14. Feller, Don, B, Kansas
15. Kaiser, Dave, E, Michigan State
16. Bayuk, John (The Beast), B, Colorado
17. Tamburello, Frank, B, Maryland
18. Torczon, Laverne, G, Nebraska
19. Ploen, Kenny, QB, Iowa
20. Stillwell, Jack, E, North Carolina
21. Juneau, Curry, E, Southern Mississippi
22. Winters, Bob, QB, Utah State
23. Frazer, Jim, T, Hampden-Sydney
24. Napolean, Allen, B, Stanford
25. Dimitroff, Tom, B, Miami (Ohio)
26. Bliss, Allen, E, Miami (Ohio)
27. Okulovich, Andy, B, Ohio State
28. Cockrell, Gene, T, Hardin-Simmons
29. Trozzo, Bill, T, West Virginia
30. McKiever, Bob, B, Northwestern

DETROIT
1. Glass, Bill, G, Baylor
2. Gordy, John, T, Tennessee
3. Barr, Terry, B, Michigan
4. Junker, Steve, E, Xavier
5. Barrow, John, G, Florida
6. Russell, Ken, T, Bowling Green
7. Leahy, Gerry, E, Colorado
8. Liddick, Dave, T, George Washington
9. Nikkel, John, E, TCU
10. Rychlec, Tom, E, American International
11. Osterich, Carl, C, Missouri
12. O'Brien, Charlie, E, Valparaiso
13. West, Bill, B, Eastern Oregon
14. Smith, Phil, B, Jacksonville State
15. Alderton, Gene, C, Maryland
16. Olson, Hillmer, C, Virginia Tech
17. Kemp, Jack, QB, Occidental
18. Weenig, Jay, G, BYU
19. Gunderman, Bob, E, Virginia
20. Lazzerino, Alex, T, South Carolina
21. Meredith, Dudley, T, Lamar
22. Schulte, Tom, E, Eastern Kentucky
23. Gillar, George, B, Texas A&M
24. Scales, Joe, B, Vanderbilt
25. Johnson, Carl, B, South Dakota
26. Muelhaupt, Ed, G, Iowa State
27. Trafas, Dick, E, St. Thomas (Minnesota)
28. Smith, Joe, B, Houston
29. Martin, Hugh, G, Pomona
30. Shill, Mike, T, Furman

GREEN BAY
BONUS CHOICE: Hornung, Paul, QB, Notre Dame
1. Kramer, Ron, E, Michigan
2. Wells, Joel, D, Clemson
3. Truax, Dalton, T, Tulane
4. Vereen, Carl, T, Georgia Tech
5. Choice to Cleveland
6. Choice to Cleveland
Nisby, Jack, G, Pacific, from Chi. Cardinals
7. Gilliam, Frank, E, Iowa
8. Belotti, George, C, USC
9. Wineberg, Ken, B, TCU
10. Gustafson, Gary, G, Gustavus Adolphus
11. Roseboro, Jim, D, Ohio State
12. Sullivan, Ed, C, Notre Dame
Bestor, Glenn, B, Wisconsin, from NY Giants
13. Morse, Jim, B, Notre Dame
14. Schoendorf, Rudy, T, Miami (Ohio)
15. Hinton, Pat, G, Louisiana Tech
16. Buckingham, Ed, T, Minnesota
17. Boudreaux, Don, T, Houston
18. Green, Credell, B, Washington
19. Danjean, Ernie, G, Auburn
20. Oliver, Percy, G, Illinois
21. Mehrer, Chuck, T, Missouri
22. Quillian, Ronnie, QB, Tulane
23. Symank, John, B, Florida
24. Leyendecker, Charlie, T, SMU
25. Johnson, Jerry, T, St. Norbert
26. Bass, Buddy, E, Duke
27. Booher, Marty, T, Wisconsin
28. Herbold, Dave, G, Minnesota
29. Dare, Howie, B, Maryland

LA RAMS
1. Arnett, Jon, B, USC
Shofner, Del, B, Baylor, from NY Giants
2. Pardee, Jack, B, Texas A&M
3. Smith, Billy Ray, T, Arkansas
Strugar, George, T, Washington, from San Francisco
4. Cox, Bobby, QB, Minnesota
Lundy, Lamar, E, Purdue, from NY Giants
5. Derby, Dean, B, Washington
Enright, Dick, G, USC, from Washington
6. Wilkins, Roy, E, Georgia
7. Gray, Ed, T, Oklahoma
8. Hord, Roy, T, Duke
Bradshaw, Charlie, T, Baylor, from Chi. Cardinals, F
9. Mitchell, John, C, TCU
10. Spragg, Warren, T, Hillsdale
11. Smith, Don, T, Miami (Ohio)
12. Klochak, Don, B, North Carolina
13. Wolfenden, Bob, B, Virginia Tech
14. Lazzarino, Joe, T, Maryland
15. Hinman, Ed, B, Wichita State
16. Luck, John, T, Georgia
17. Trippett, Dave, T, Hillsdale
18. Cook, Clarence, E, Nebraska
19. Zuhowski, Bill, T, Arizona State
20. Beams, Byron, T, Notre Dame
21. Pinkston, Pat, E, UCLA
22. Cothren, Paige, B, Mississippi
23. Allen, Dalva, T, Houston
24. Rogers, Darryl, B, Fresno State
25. Orr, Jimmy, B, Georgia
26. Blakely, Dick, B, Minnesota
27. Osborne, Clancy, E, Arizona State
28. Gudath, Bob, E, Compton J.C.
29. Maas, Dean, C, Minnesota
30. Williams, Lee, B, Ohio State

NY GIANTS
1. Choice to LA Rams
2. DeLuca, Sam, T, South Carolina
3. Mendyk, Dennis, B, Michigan State
4. Choice to LA Rams
5. Wesley, Larry, T, Florida
6. Hobert, Bob, T, Minnesota
7. Curtis, Chuck, QB, TCU
8. Bookman, John, B, Florida
9. Maynard, Don, B, Texas-El Paso
10. Massa, Gordon, C, Holy Cross
11. Burke, Pat, G, John Carroll
12. Choice to Green Bay
13. Bennett, Ron, E, Mississippi State
14. Hesse, Dean, T, East Texas State
15. Derrick, Julius, E, South Carolina
16. Deutschmann, Lou, B, LSU
17. Stone, Jerry, C, Mississippi
18. Eaton, Jim, E, Florida
19. Morris, Ronnie, B, Tulsa
20. Roberts, Laneair, E, Georgia
21. Smaltz, Joe, B, John Carroll
22. Niemann, Jim, B, Cincinnati
23. Healy, Jack, B, Maryland
24. Hicks, Don, T, Florida
25. Goebel, Jerry, C, Michigan
26. Zalenka, Emmett, G, Tulane
27. Brawley, Carl, T, Sul Ross
28. Gaines, Corky, G, South Carolina
29. Bowman, Mike, G, Princeton
30. Gest, Don, E, Washington State

PHILADELPHIA
1. Peaks, Clarence, B, Michigan State
2. Barnes, Billy Ray, B, Wake Forest
3. McDonald, Tommy, B, Oklahoma
4. Jurgensen, Sonny, QB, Duke
5. Harris, Jimmy, QB, Oklahoma
6. Choice to San Francisco
7. Saidock, Tom, T, Michigan State
8. McElhaney, Hal, B, Duke
9. Davis, Hal, B, Westminster (Pennsylvania)
10. Bruhns, Don, C, Drake
11. Shoaf, Gil, T, Wabash
12. Dike, Buddy, B, TCU
13. Bobo, Hubert, B, Ohio State
14. Cashman, Jerry, T, Syracuse
15. Moriarity, Mort, E, Texas
16. Nocera, John, B, Iowa
17. Radakovich, Dan, C, Penn State
18. Kelley, Billy, T, Baylor
19. Harasimowicz, Paul, T, Vermont
20. Thompson, Leroy, B, Butler
21. Brooks, Charley, E, Michigan
22. Simerson, John, T, Purdue
23. Lovely, Lou, G, Boston U.
24. McGill, Dennis, B, Yale
25. Ratliff, Bob, B, West Texas State
26. Richardson, Alvin, T, Grambling
27. Hall, Frank, B, USC
28. Corona, Clem, G, Michigan
29. Niznik, John, E, Wake Forest
30. Hubbard, Larry, E, Marquette

PITTSBURGH
1. Dawson, Len, QB, Purdue
2. Michael, Bill, T, Ohio State
3. Owens, Don, T, Southern Mississippi
4. Choice to Washington
5. Richards, Perry, E, Detroit
6. Volkert, George, B, Georgia Tech
7. Johnson, Curley, B, Houston
8. Choice to Chi. Bears
9. Hutchings, Charley, T, Miami
10. Jelic, Ralph, B, Pittsburgh
11. Hughes, Dick, B, Tulsa
12. Ellison, Vern, G, Oregon State
13. Underwood, Dwaine, T, Oklahoma State
14. Crawford, Jim, B, Wyoming
15. Canil, Herman, T, Pittsburgh
16. Choice to Baltimore
17. Salvaterra, Corny, QB, Pittsburgh
18. Bigbee, Len, E, East Texas State
19. Bennett, Phil, E, Miami
20. Szuehan, John, T, North Carolina State
21. Chichowski, Gene, QB, Indiana
22. Thomas, Aurelius, G, Ohio State
23. Pollock, Bob, T, Pittsburgh
24. Francis, Gary, E, Illinois
25. Hinesley, Jim, E, Michigan State
26. Swann, Bob, T, Vanderbilt
27. Konkoly, Bob, B, Xavier
28. Kolinsky, Frank, T, Tennessee
29. Ramage, Tom, G, Utah State
30. Serier, Don, E, Arkansas State

SAN FRANCISCO
1. Brodie, John, QB, Stanford
2. Woodson, Abe, B, Illinois
3. Choice to LA Rams
4. Ridlon, Jim, B, Syracuse
Sandusky, Mike, T, Maryland, from Chi. Cardinals
5. Rubke, Karl, C, USC
6. Rhodes, Bill, B, Western State (Colorado), from Philadelphia
Hunter, Jim, B, Missouri

7. Dugan, Fred, E, Dayton, F
8. Pitts, Ernie, E, Denver
9. Brueckman, Charlie, C, Pittsburgh, F
10. Hurst, Jerry, E, Middle Tennessee State, F
11. Davis, Tommy, B, LSU, F
12. Sington, Fred, T, Alabama, F
13. Mackey, Charley, E, Arizona State
14. Warzeka, Ron, T, Montana State
15. Kaiser, Earl, B, Houston, F
16. Kristopaitis, Vic, B, Dayton
17. Kuhn, Dave, C, Kentucky
18. Guy, Dick, G, Ohio State
19. Babb, Gene, B, Austin
20. DeLoatch, Sid, G, Duke
21. Wilcox, Fred, B, Tulane
22. Tripp, Paul, T, Idaho State
23. Thomas, John, E, Pacific
24. Ladner, John, E, Wake Forest
25. Meyer, Ray, B, Lamar
26. Topping, Tom, T, Duke, F
27. Vicic, Don, B, Ohio State
28. Curtis, Bill, B, TCU
29. Hallbeck, Vern, B, TCU
30. Parks, George, B, Lamar

WASHINGTON
1. Bosseler, Don, B, Miami
2. Walton, Joe, E, Pittsburgh
3. Sutton, Eddie, B, North Carolina
4. Podoley, Jim, B, Central Michigan, from Pittsburgh
   Scorsone, Vince, G, Pittsburgh
5. Choice to LA Rams
6. Frankenberger, J.T., T, Kentucky
7. Merz, Wally, T, Colorado
8. Lopata, Paul, E, Yale
9. Laack, Galen, G, Pacific
10. Dobrino, Don, B, Iowa
11. Foster, Dick, T, Idaho
12. Mitchell, Wade, QB, Georgia Tech
13. Austin, Claude, B, George Washington
14. Rice, George, T, Wofford
15. Bomba, Brad, E, Indiana
16. Brodolky, Joe, B, Florida
17. Brock, Fred, B, Wheaton
18. Sakach, Ed, G, George Washington
19. Bauer, John, B, Villanova
20. Frick, Buddy, E, South Carolina
21. Owen, Sam, B, Georgia Tech
22. Voytek, Ed, G, Purdue
23. Viola, Al, G, Northwestern
24. Jennings, Bob, C, Furman
25. Sassels, Dick, T, Catawba
26. Rotenberry, Paul, B, Georgia Tech
27. Anderson, Ormand, T, Georgia Tech
28. Martin, Guy, B, Colgate
29. Benedict, George, E, Springfield
30. Luppino, Art, B, Arizona

1958

Held December 2, 1957 (Rounds 1-4) and January 28, 1958 (Rounds 5-30)

BALTIMORE
1. Lyles, Lenny, B, Louisville
2. Stransky, Bob, B, Colorado
3. Nicely, Joe, G, West Virginia
4. Walters, Les, E, Penn State
5. Brown, Ray, B, Mississippi, from Chi. Cardinals
   Choice to NY Giants
6. Taylor, Bob, E, Vanderbilt
7. Sample, Johnny, B, Maryland-Eastern Shore, from Pittsburgh
   Diehl, John, T, Virginia
8. Peters, Floyd, G, Cal State-San Francisco
9. Bullard, Hal, B, Lenoir-Rhyne
10. Schamber, Ray, E, South Dakota
11. Jordan, Bobby, B, Virginia Military
12. Addison, Tommy, G, South Carolina
13. Richardson, Jerry, E, Wofford
14. Hall, Ken, B, Texas A&M
15. Carney, Les, B, Ohio U.
16. Matsos, Archie, G, Michigan State, F
17. Reese, Jim, B, Minnesota
18. Lloyd, Dave, C, Georgia*
19. Murnen, John, G, Bowling Green
20. Forrestal, Tom, QB, Navy
21. Faulk, Jim, B, TCU
22. McKee, Bob, E, Monmouth
23. Parslow, Phil, B, UCLA
24. Sandlin, Bobby, B, Tennessee
25. Rountree, Jim, B, Florida
26. Grimes, Bob, T, Central Michigan
27. Dintiman, George, B, Lock Haven
28. Murphy, Jim, T, East Tennessee State
29. Padgett, Doug, E, Duke
30. Lund, Gary, G, Utah State

CHI. BEARS
1. Howley, Chuck, G, West Virginia
2. Dewveall, Willard, E, SMU
3. Cooke, Ed, E, Maryland
   Healy, Don, T, Maryland, from Cleveland
4. Barnes, Erich, B, Purdue
5. Jewett, Bob, E, Michigan State
6. Douglas, Merrill, B, Utah
7. Bentley, Gene, B, Texas Tech
8. Rutsch, Ed, T, George Washington
9. Anderson, Ralph, E, Cal State-Los Angeles
10. Lewis, Aubrey, B, Notre Dame
11. Cinelli, Rocco, T, Wisconsin
12. Morris, Johnny, B, Cal-Santa Barbara
13. Choice to NY Giants
14. Melnik, Bill, T, Army
15. Harryman, Jim, B, Compton J.C.
16. Pleger, Ken, T, Capital
17. Eaton, Dick, C, Richmond
18. Dupler, Phil, B, Duke
19. Roehnelt, Bill, G, Bradley, from Green Bay
   Chancey, Bill, E, West Virginia
20. Rutledge, Les, T, Michigan State
21. Miller, Bill, T, New Mexico Highlands
22. Carter, Al, B, Tennessee
23. Daw, Ken, B, Sam Houston State
24. Moon, Russ, T, Virginia Tech
25. Barron, Bob, C, St. Norbert
26. Lyles, Bob, B, Memphis State
27. Napolski, Ben, E, Northwestern
28. Main, Wilbur, B, Maryland
29. Hakes, Glen, G, New Mexico
30. Halum, Bobby, B, Middle Tennessee State

CHI. CARDINALS
BONUS CHOICE: Hill, King, QB, Rice
1. Crow, John David, B, Texas A&M
2. McCusker, Jim, T, Pittsburgh
   Oliver, Bobby Jack, T, Rice, from Detroit
3. Cowart, Larry, C, Baylor
4. Choice to LA Rams
5. Choice to Baltimore
6. Gordon, Bobby, B, Tennessee
7. Jelacic, Jon, E, Minnesota
8. Choice to San Francisco
9. Keelan, John, T, Kansas State
10. Robertshaw, Gil, T, Brown
11. Philpot, Dean, B, Fresno State
12. Hinton, Bill, G, Louisiana Tech
13. Jackson, Charlie, B, SMU
14. Schmidt, Bob, T, Minnesota
15. Dunlap, Ray, B, Marshall
16. Patterson, Wade, E, Idaho
17. Starnes, Mac, C, Abilene Christian
18. Cheppo, Mario, E, Louisville
19. Randle, Sonny, B, Virginia, F
20. Matheny, Jim, C, UCLA
21. Toole, Ray, B, North Texas State
22. Aloisio, Tony, E, Indiana
23. Harbour, John, T, Southeast Missouri State
24. Soesbe, Eric, T, Vanderbilt
25. Riekenberg, J.C., B, Northwestern State (Louisiana)
26. Masters, Ray, B, SMU
27. Lewis, Will, B, Tennessee-Chattanooga
28. McGinty, Gale, B, West Texas State
29. Irby, Ken, T, Mississippi State

CLEVELAND
1. Shofner, Jim, B, TCU
2. Mitchell, Charley, G, Florida
3. Choice to Chi. Bears
   Guy, Buzz, T, Duke, from Detroit
4. Ninowski, Jim, QB, Michigan State
5. Funston, Farrell, E, Pacific
   Gibbons, Jim, E, Iowa, from Detroit
6. Wulff, Jim, B, Michigan State, F
7. Mitchell, Bobby, B, Illinois
8. Lattimore, Bert, E, Duke
9. Parrish, Bernie, B, Florida
10. Russavage, Leo, T, North Carolina
11. Bowermaster, Russ, E, Ohio State
12. Brodhead, Bob, B, Duke
13. Williams, Hal, B, Miami (Ohio)
14. Miller, Ken, T, TCU
15. Hoelscher, Howard, B, Rice
16. Cornelison, Jerry, T, SMU
17. Osborne, Roddy, B, Texas A&M
18. Johnson, Alvin, T, Idaho
19. Brown, Ed, G, Arizona
20. Serieka, Ed, B, Xavier
21. Martin, Bill, E, Iowa State
22. Renn, Bob, B, Florida State
23. Verhey, Dan, T, Washington State
24. O'Connor, Jim, T, Marshall
25. Peters, Bobby, B, Baylor
26. Thompson, Frank, T, Wake Forest
27. Thelen, Dave, B, Miami (Ohio)
28. Boykin, Bill, T, Michigan State
29. Czapla, Frank, T, Missouri
30. Svendsen, Bern, C, Minnesota

DETROIT
1. Karras, Alex, T, Iowa
2. Choice to Chi. Cardinals
3. Choice to Cleveland
4. Walker, Wayne, C, Idaho
5. Choice to Cleveland
6. Lewis, Danny, B, Wisconsin
7. Pfeifer, Ralph, B, Kansas State, from San Francisco
   Outten, Hal, T, Virginia
8. Koepfer, Karl, G, Bowling Green, from Pittsburgh
   Blazer, Phil, T, North Carolina
9. Loftin, Jim, B, Alabama, from Pittsburgh
   Paolucci, Ben, T, Wayne State
10. Schaubach, Elliot, T, William & Mary
11. Chaney, Claude, B, Dayton
12. Boutte, Hal, E, San Jose State
13. Maroney, Barry, B, Cincinnati
14. Webb, Ken, B, Presbyterian
15. Scheldrup, John, E, Iowa State, from San Francisco
   Mohlman, Jerry, B, Benedictine
16. Ringquist, Gordon, T, Central Michigan
17. Gurasich, Walt, G, USC
18. Austin, Bill, C, Auburn, from Pittsburgh
   Carrier, Larry, B, Kansas
19. Bottos, Dave, B, Murray State
20. Curry, Bill, T, Western Kentucky
21. Wagstaff, Jim, B, Idaho State
22. Nidiffer, Buddy, E, South Carolina
23. Destino, Frank, B, South Carolina
24. Whitsell, Dave, B, Indiana
25. Cook, Jim, B, Auburn
26. Bruce, Joe, T, Middle Tennessee State
27. Agers, Don, T, Missouri-Rolla
28. Pitt, Jack, E, South Carolina
29. Herzog, Henry, B, Kentucky
30. Bronson, Tommy, B, Tennessee

GREEN BAY
1. Currie, Dan, C, Michigan State
2. Taylor, Jim, B, LSU
3. Christy, Dick, B, North Carolina State
   Nitschke, Ray, B, Illinois, from NY Giants
4. Kramer, Jerry, G, Idaho
5. Francis, Joe, B, Oregon State
6. Gray, Ken, T, Howard Payne
7. Mainson, Doug, B, Hillsdale
8. Bill, Mike, C, Syracuse
9. Jarock, Norm, B, St. Norbert
10. Johnson, Carl, T, Illinois
11. Horton, Harry, E, Wichita State
12. Miller, Wayne, E, Baylor
13. Cook, Gene, E, Toledo
14. Hauffe, Harry T, South Dakota
15. Newell, Tom, B, Drake
16. Finley, Arley, T, Georgia Tech
17. Reese, Joe, E, Arkansas Tech
18. Strid, Chuck, G, Syracuse
19. Choice to Chi. Bears
20. DuBose, John, B, Trinity (Texas)
21. Kershner, Jerry, T, Oregon
22. Maggard, Dick, B, College of Idaho
23. Ashton, Jack, G, South Carolina
24. Jereck, John, T, Detroit
25. Plenty, Larry, B, Boston College
26. Harris, Esker, G, UCLA
27. Habig, Neil, C, Purdue
28. Crowell, Dave, G, Washington State
29. Haynes, Bob, T, Sam Houston State
30. Peters, John, T, Houston

LA RAMS
1. Michaels, Lou, T, Kentucky, from Washington
   Phillips, Jim (Red), E, Auburn
2. Thomas, Clendon, B, Oklahoma
3. Jones, Jim, B, Washington
4. Henry, Urban, T, Georgia Tech, from Chi. Cardinals
   Woidzik, Frank, T, Buffalo, from Pittsburgh
   Guzik, John, G, Pittsburgh, F
5. Baker, John, T, North Carolina Central
   Ryan, Frank, QB, Rice, from Pittsburgh
6. Iglehart, Floyd, B, Wiley
7. Jobko, Bill, G, Ohio State
8. Marks, Bobby, B, Texas A&M
9. Selawski, Gene, T, Purdue, F
10. Jacks, Al, QB, Penn State
11. Schweitzer, Gerry, E, Pacific
12. Clairborne, Ron, T, Kansas
13. Kolodziej, Tony, E, Michigan State
14. Mason, Bill, B, UCLA
15. Johnston, Dick, C, Southern Mississippi
16. Westemeyer, Clint, E, St. Ambrose
17. Thomas, Bill, C, Clemson
18. Scott, Coy, T, McNeese State
19. Dorsey, Dick, E, USC
20. Colbert, George, B, Denver
21. Parrish, Ron, B, Linfield
22. Steiger, Bill, E, Washington State
23. Berry, Gary, B, East Texas State
24. Harding, Larry, E, Michigan State
25. Atkins, Bill, T, San Jose State
26. Bridges, Corky, B, Central Washington
27. Vereen, Alonzo, B, Florida A&M
28. Morrow, Gordy, E, Michigan
29. Bourgeois, O'Jay, B, Arizona State
30. Fondren, Walt, B, Texas

NY GIANTS
1. King, Phil, B, Vanderbilt
2. Youso, Frank, T, Minnesota
3. Choice to Green Bay
4. Caraway, Donnie, B, Houston
5. Day, Dick, T, Washington
   Conrad, Bobby Joe, B, Texas A&M, from Baltimore
6. Lott, Billy, B, Mississippi
7. Vaughn, Vernon, E, Maryland-Eastern Shore
8. Sutherin, Don, B, Ohio State
9. Kissell, Ron, T, Pittsburgh
10. Drummond, Herb, B, Central State (Ohio)
11. Williams, Sid, B, Wisconsin
12. Hershey, Gerry, T, Syracuse
13. Kurker, George, T, Tufts, from Chi. Bears
   Herndon, Don, B, Tampa
14. Roberts, C.R., B, USC
15. Sixta, Norm, T, Minnesota
16. West, John, T, Mississippi
17. Harrison, Jack, C, Duke
18. Fusco, Dick, T, Middlebury
19. Jackson, Ernie, B, Syracuse
20. Clements, Joe, B, Texas
21. Hansen, Charlie, C, Tulane
22. Wester, Cleve, T, Auburn
23. Hurst, Billy, B, Mississippi
24. Brod, Max, B, Texas Tech
25. Haensel, Wayne, T, South Dakota
26. Burkholder, Dave, G, Minnesota
27. Bronson, Dick, T, USC
28. Watters, Bob, E, Lincoln (Missouri)
29. Pitney, Lou, C, New Haven
30. Lumpkin, Billy, E, North Alabama

PHILADELPHIA
1. Kowalczyk, Walt, B, Michigan State
2. Jacobs, Proverb, T, California
3. Choice to Washington
4. Rigney, Frank, T, Iowa
5. Mulgado, Bobby, B, Arizona State
6. Kersey, John, T, Duke
7. Mansfield, Len, T, Pittsburg State
8. Striegel, Bill, LB, Pacific
9. Choice to Pittsburgh
10. Sapp, Theron, B, Georgia, F
11. Dillard, Mel, B, Purdue
12. Crabtree, Jack, B, Oregon
13. Trimarki, Mickey, QB, West Virginia
14. Lapham, Bill, C, Iowa
15. Hinos, Stan, T, Mississippi Valley State
16. Meatheringham, Mike, T, Georgia
17. Van Buren, Bill, C, Iowa
18. Burroughs, John, T, Iowa
19. Sabal, Ron, G, Purdue
20. Lovelace, Kent, B, Mississippi
21. Madden, John, T, Cal Poly-SLO
22. Sherwood, George, E, St. Joseph's (Indiana)
23. Templeton, Billy, E, Mississippi
24. Padgett, Jim, C, Clemson
25. Divine, Hal, T, Memphis State
26. MacLean, Neil, B, Wake Forest
27. Wall, Hindman, E, Auburn
28. Gossage, Gene, T, Northwestern
29. McDonald, Don, B, Houston
30. Thompson, Jim, E, Temple

PITTSBURGH
1. Choice to San Francisco
2. Krutko, Larry, B, West Virginia

3. Krisher, Bill, G, Oklahoma
4. Choice to LA Rams
5. Choice to LA Rams
6. Lasse, Dick, E, Syracuse
7. Choice to Baltimore
8. Choice to Detroit
9. Henry, Mike, T, USC, from Philadelphia
   Choice to Detroit
10. Campbell, Dick, C, Marquette
11. Aldrich, Larry, E, Idaho
12. Reed, Leroy, B, Mississippi
13. Choice to San Francisco
14. Jennings, Doyle, T, Oklahoma
15. Sears, Ed, B, Florida
16. Perkins, John, T, Southern Mississippi
17. Lewis, Joe, T, Compton J.C.
18. Choice to Detroit
19. Keady, Gene, B, Kansas State
20. Johnson, George, T, Wake Forest
21. Jones, Everett, G, Utah
22. Thompson, Bill, E, Duke
23. Trowbridge, Ken, B, North Carolina State
24. Roberts, Norm, E, East Texas State
25. Groce, Bill, B, North Texas State
26. Evans, Jon, E, Oklahoma State
27. Dellinger, Floyd, B, Texas Tech
28. Akin, Dean, E, Jacksonville State
29. Fuquay, Mert, E, Baylor
30. Scherer, Dick, E, Pittsburgh

SAN FRANCISCO
1. Pace, Jim, B, Michigan, from Pittsburgh
   Krueger, Charlie, T, Texas A&M
2. Newman, Bob, B, Washington State, F
3. Hoppe, Bob, B, Auburn
4. Varone, John, B, Miami
5. Atkins, Billy, B, Auburn
6. Schmidt, Henry, T, USC
7. Choice to Detroit
8. Burton, Leon, B, Arizona State, from Chi. Cardinals, F
   Mills, Ron, B, West Texas State
9. Troutman, George, T, Capital
10. Heckman, Vel, T, Florida, F
11. Wharton, Bob, T, Houston, F
12. Williams, Pete, T, Lehigh
13. Yore, Jim, B, Indiana, from Pittsburgh
   Dukes, Hal, E, Michigan State
14. Fields, Max, B, Whittier
15. Choice to Detroit
16. Shirkey, George, T, Stephen F. Austin
17. Wittenborn, John, T, Southeast Missouri State
18. Morris, Dennit, B, Oklahoma
19. Mushatt, Ronnie, C, Grambling
20. Mertens, Jerry, E, Drake
21. Christian, Don, B, Arkansas
22. Hartman, Bruce, T, Luther
23. Fields, Larry, B, Utah
24. Mackey, Dee, E, East Texas State, F
25. Kaczmarek, Bill, C, Southwest Missouri State
26. Hill, Hillard, E, USC, F
27. Witucki, Bob, E, Texas Tech
28. Warren, Garland, C, North Texas State
29. Hodges, Herman, B, Sam Houston State
30. Stahura, Ted, T, Kansas State, F

WASHINGTON
1. Choice to LA Rams
2. Sommer, Mike, B, George Washington
3. Anderson, Bill, B, Tennessee, from Philadelphia
   Flowers, Stan, B, Georgia Tech
4. Nolan, Dan, QB, Lehigh
5. Van Pelt, Jim, QB, Michigan
6. Lynch, Dick, B, Notre Dame
7. Bennett, Leon, T, Boston College
8. Payne, Buddy, E, North Carolina
9. Kuchta, Frank, C, Notre Dame
10. Preston, Ben, T, Auburn
11. Dess, Darrell, T, North Carolina State
12. Michaels, Eddie, G, Villanova
13. Ford, Ken (Model-T), QB, Hardin-Simmons
14. Farls, Jack, E, Penn State
15. Davis, Jack, T, Arizona
16. Polzer, Fred, E, Virginia
17. Wilt, Fred, T, Richmond
18. King, Lennie, B, Connecticut
19. Stephenson, Don, C, Georgia Tech
20. Pelham, Lou, E, Florida
21. Simpson, Jackie, G, Mississippi
22. Sanders, Charley, B, West Texas State
23. Schomburger, Ron, E, Florida State
24. Hanson, Rod, E, Illinois
25. Groom, John, G, TCU
26. Bloomquist, Frank, G, Iowa
27. Gehring, Perry, E, Minnesota
28. Biggs, Joe, G, Hardin-Simmons
29. Coffin, Ed, B, Syracuse
30. Smith, Ted, E, Georgia Tech

1959
Held December 2, 1958

BALTIMORE
1. Burkett, Jackie, C, Auburn
2. Sherer, Dave, E, SMU
3. Choice to Detroit
4. Smith, Zeke, G, Auburn
5. Churchwell, Don, G, Mississippi
6. Pyle, Palmer, T, Michigan State
7. Lewis, Hal, B, Houston
8. Coffey, Tommy Joe, B, West Texas State
9. Brown, Tom, G, Minnesota
10. Stewart, Don, E, SMU
11. Stephens, Tom, B, Syracuse
12. Wood, Dick, QB, Auburn
13. Smith, Rudi, T, Mississippi
14. Burket, Ferdie, B, Southeastern Oklahoma
15. Foret, Ted, T, Auburn
16. Keller, Morris, T, Clemson
17. Bergan, Leroy, T, South Dakota State
18. Bandy, Opie, T, Tulsa
19. Crain, Milt, C, Mississippi
20. Balonick, Paul, C, North Carolina State
21. Hernstein, John, B, Michigan
22. Leatherman, Lonny, E, TCU
23. Davis, Bob, B, Houston
24. Novagratz, Bob, G, Army
25. Kieffer, Ed, B, Syracuse
26. Lorio, Rene, B, Southern Mississippi
27. Thurman, Terry, B, Rice
28. Long, Fred, B, Iowa
29. McGriff, Perry, E, Florida
30. Weese, Blair, B, West Virginia Tech

CHI. BEARS
1. Clark, Don, B, Ohio State
2. Petitbon, Richie, QB, Tulane
3. Johnson, Pete, B, Virginia Military
4. Choice to LA Rams
5. Adams, John, B, Cal State-Los Angeles
6. Cole, Fred, G, Maryland
7. Tucker, Jim, E, Tennessee-Chattanooga, from Philadelphia
8. Clark, Dick, B, Baylor
   Smith, Willie, T, Michigan, from NY Giants
9. Youmans, Maury, T, Syracuse
10. Coronado, Bobby, E, Pacific
11. Gray, Ed, T, North Texas State
12. Rowland, Justin, E, TCU
13. Jones, Gene, B, Rice
14. Robb, Joe, T, TCU
15. LeClerc, Roger, C, Trinity (Connecticut), F
16. Redding, Don, T, North Carolina
17. Neal, Willie, B, Jackson State
18. Asbury, Ken, B, Missouri Valley
19. Plain, Chris, T, Stanford
20. Carcaterra, Tony, E, Elon
21. Stone, Donnie, B, Arkansas
22. Rubal, Lennie, B, William & Mary
23. Haller, Bob, T, Northwest Missouri State
24. Spain, Bob, T, Baylor
25. Huhn, Tom, C, St. Joseph's (Indiana)
26. Kunde, Bob, T, Capital
27. Aveni, John, E, Indiana
28. Williams, Bob, B, Notre Dame
29. Southern, Eddie, E, Texas
30. Jackson, Cliff, B, North Carolina Central

CHI. CARDINALS
1. Stacy, Billy, B, Mississippi State
2. Wilson, Jerry, E, Auburn
3. Butler, Jimmy, B, Vanderbilt
4. Beck, Ken, T, Texas A&M
5. Schleicher, Maury, E, Penn State
   Bates, Ted, T, Oregon State, from Washington
6. Redmond, Tom, T, Vanderbilt
   Lewis, Mac, T, Iowa, from Detroit
7. Choice to San Francisco
8. Choice to Cleveland
9. Ferguson, Gary, T, SMU
10. DeCantis, Emil, B, North Carolina
11. Faucette, Floyd, B, Georgia Tech
12. Edmondson, Ted, E, Hardin-Simmons
13. Lamberti, Pat, E, Richmond
14. Bobo, Bob, T, Texas-El Paso
15. Schroeder, John, E, North Carolina
16. Dingens, John, T, Detroit
17. Hart, Pete, B, Hardin-Simmons
18. DeDecker, Darrell, T, Illinois
19. Dunn, Billy, B, SMU
20. Murphy, Jerry Lee, T, Ohio State
21. Memmelaar, Dale, G, Wyoming
22. Shamblin, Glenn, B, West Virginia
23. Glick, Freddie, B, Colorado State
24. Reed, Jim, G, East Texas State
25. Jeffery, Jim, T, Auburn
26. Chuha, Joe, C, USC
27. Corrigan, Bob, G, Indiana
28. Fleming, Don, B, Florida
29. O'Connor, Jim, C, Marshall
30. Walton, Rabe, B, North Carolina

CLEVELAND
1. Kreitling, Rich, E, Illinois
2. Schafrath, Dick, G, Ohio State
3. O'Brien, Fran, T, Michigan State
4. Prahst, Gary, E, Michigan, from Green Bay
   Lloyd, Dave, C, Georgia
5. Wooten, John, G, Colorado, from Detroit
   LeBeau, Dick, B, Ohio State
6. Denton, Bob, E, Pacific
   Prestel, Jim, T, Idaho, from NY Giants
7. Miller, Gene, T, Rice
8. Ptacek, Bob, QB, Michigan, from Chi. Cardinals
   Choice to Green Bay
9. Wilson, Kirk, B, UCLA
10. Zeman, Bob, B, Wisconsin
11. King, Jerry, G, Kent State
12. Palandrani, Frank, T, North Carolina State
13. Reese, Ray, B, Bowling Green
14. Dubenion, Elbert (Golden Wheels), B, Bluffton
15. Salwocki, Tom, C, Pittsburgh
16. Caleb, Jamie, B, Grambling
17. Schmittan, Homer, E, Tennessee Tech
18. Hill, Ed, G, Miami (Ohio)
19. Schroeder, Joe, T, Xavier
20. McClain, Al, T, Shaw
21. Fraser, Jim, G, Wisconsin
22. Wenzel, Joe, E, Lehigh
23. Gardner, Jim, T, Duke
24. Goings, Russ, G, Xavier
25. Spycholski, Ernie, T, Ohio State
26. Floyd, Homer, B, Kansas
27. Baker, Larry, T, Bowling Green
28. Abadie, Pete, E, Tulane
29. Nietupski, Ron, T, Illinois
30. Ketchie, Carl, B, Washington State

DETROIT
1. Pietrosante, Nick, B, Notre Dame
2. Horton, Charley, G, Baylor
   Rabold, Mike, T, Indiana, from Pittsburgh
3. Koes, Ron, C, North Carolina
   Luciano, Ron, T, Syracuse, from Baltimore
4. Brandriff, Art, B, Virginia Military
   Grottkau, Bob, G, Oregon State, from NY Giants
5. Choice to Cleveland
6. Choice to Chi. Cardinals
   Guesman, Dick, T, West Virginia, from Pittsburgh
7. Donnell, Ben, C, Vanderbilt
8. Lenden, Jim, T, Oregon
9. Smith, Carl, B, Tennessee
10. Laraway, Jack, B, Purdue
11. Jacobs, Harry, G, Bradley
12. Stehouwer, Ron, T, Colorado State
13. Steffen, Jim, B, UCLA
14. Baldwin, Jim, C, McMurry
15. Maher, Bruce, B, Detroit
16. McGee, George, T, Southern
17. Rudolph, Jack, E, Georgia Tech
18. Holden, Dave, T, Cal State-Los Angeles
19. Granderson, Rufus, T, Prairie View A&M
20. McGrew, Dan, C, Purdue
21. Davis, Buddy, B, Richmond
22. Shields, Lebron, T, Tennessee, F
23. Cesario, Sal, T, Denver
24. Riddle, Fred, B, Pittsburgh
25. Chamberlain, Dan, E, Cal State-Sacramento
26. Bradley, Jim, B, Lincoln (Missouri)
27. Jerry, Bill, T, South Carolina
28. Matthews, Vince, B, Texas
29. Sime, Dave, E, Duke
30. Stover, Ron, E, Oregon

GREEN BAY
1. Duncan, Randy, QB, Iowa
2. Hawkins, Alex, B, South Carolina
3. Dowler, Boyd, B, Colorado
4. Choice to Cleveland
5. Choice to Washington
   Cverko, Andy, C, Northwestern, from Pittsburgh
6. Taylor, Willie, C, Florida A&M
7. Jackson, Bobby, B, Alabama
   Raid, Gary, T, Willamette, from NY Giants
8. Mayfield, Buddy, E, South Carolina
   Laraba, Bob, B, Texas-El Paso, from Cleveland
9. Dixon, George, B, Bridgeport
10. Tuccio, Sam, T, Southern Mississippi
11. Webb, Bob, B, St. Ambrose
12. Hall, Larry, G, Missouri Valley
13. Hurd, Jim, B, Albion
14. Kerr, Ken, G, Arizona State
15. Teteak, Dick, G, Wisconsin
16. Edgington, Dan, E, Florida
17. Secules, Tom, B, William & Mary
18. Nearents, Dick, T, Eastern Washington
19. Butler, Bill, B, Tennessee-Chattanooga
20. Sample, Charley, B, Arkansas
21. Smith, Dave, B, Ripon
22. Anderson, Charlie, E, Drake
23. Lawver, Ben, T, Lewis & Clark
24. Hergert, Joe, C, Florida
25. Hardee, Leroy, B, Florida A&M
26. Higginbotham, Ken, E, Trinity (Texas)
27. Brown, Tim, B, Ball State
28. Epps, Jerry, G, West Texas State
29. Flara, Jack, B, Pittsburgh
30. Emerich, Dick, T, West Chester

LA RAMS
1. Bass, Dick, B, Pacific, from Philadelphia
   Dickson, Paul, T, Baylor
2. Humphrey, Buddy, QB, Baylor, from Washington
   Brown, Don, B, Houston
3. Franckhauser, Tom, E, Purdue, from Pittsburgh
   Hickman, Larry, B, Baylor
4. Tracey, John, E, Texas A&M, from Chi. Bears
   Martin, Blanche, B, Michigan State
   Reifsnyder, Bob, T, Navy, from Pittsburgh
5. Lands, John, E, Montana State
6. Painter, Dave, C, Tulane
7. Meador, Eddie, B, Arkansas Tech
8. Conner, Bill, E, Jackson State
9. Cundiff, Larry, T, Michigan State
10. Goldstein, Alan, E, North Carolina
11. Kelly, Joe, B, New Mexico State
12. Connelly, Mike, C, Utah State
13. Witcher, Al, E, Baylor
14. Davidson, Pete, T, Citadel
15. Kelly, Walt, B, Houston
16. Royal, Ted, C, Duke
17. Wilemon, Dave, T, SMU
18. Van Metre, Dave, E, Colorado College
19. Shannon, Carver, B, Southern Illinois
20. Coyle, Ross, E, Oklahoma
21. Bergmann, Marv, T, Washington
22. Meglen, Bill, G, Utah State
23. Deiderich, George, G, Vanderbilt
24. Campbell, Tom, B, Indiana
25. Borah, Bob, E, Houston
26. Strumke, Bill, B, Georgia
27. Kroll, Alex, C, Rutgers, F
28. Johnson, Rafer, B, UCLA
29. Moore, Ernie, E, Alabama State
30. Millich, Don, B, Washington

NY GIANTS
1. Grosscup, Lee, QB, Utah
2. Dial, Buddy, E, Rice
3. Morrison, Joe, B, Cincinnati
4. Choice to Detroit
5. Kelly, Ellison, G, Michigan State
6. Choice to Cleveland
7. Choice to Green Bay
8. Choice to Chi. Bears
9. Delveaux, Jack, B, Illinois
10. Pepe, Bob, E, North Carolina State
11. Sawyer, Bob, B, Wyoming
12. Flowers, Charlie, B, Mississippi
13. Kompara, John, T, South Carolina
14. Ellis, Roger, C, Maine
15. Bercich, Bob, B, Michigan State
16. Soltis, Bob, B, Minnesota
17. Gonsoulin, Austin (Goose), E, Baylor*
18. Ecuyer, Al, G, Notre Dame
19. Scott, George, B, Miami (Ohio)
20. Shetler, Jerry, G, Minnesota
21. Swearingen, Fred, G, North Carolina
22. Gibson, Gale, E, Iowa State

23. Kremblas, Frank, QB, Ohio State
24. James, Charley, B, Missouri
25. Reale, Lou, C, Buffalo
26. Doretti, Frank, C, California
27. Biscaha, Joe, E, Richmond
28. Williams, Dolphus, T, Morgan State
29. Christopher, Henry, E, SMU
30. Sington, Dave, T, Alabama

PHILADELPHIA
1. Choice to LA Rams
2. Smith, J.D., T, Rice
3. Carlton, Wray, B, Duke
4. Grazione, Jim, QB, Villanova
5. Mumley, Nick, T, Purdue
6. Benecick, Al, G, Syracuse
7. Choice to Chi. Bears
8. Fowler, Wilmer, B, Northwestern
9. Johnson, Gene, B, Cincinnati
10. West, Rollie, B, Villanova
11. Powell, Art, E, San Jose State
12. Keys, Howard, T, Oklahoma State
13. Stillwagon, Dick, B, Purdue
14. Smith, Jack, T, Clemson
15. Poteete, Jim, C, Mississippi State
16. Paduch, Ken, T, Auburn
17. Craig, Bill, T, Villanova
18. Benson, Jim, B, Georgia Tech
19. Miller, Alan, B, Boston College
20. Payne, Jim, G, Clemson
21. Salerno, Bob, G, Colorado
22. Bowie, Jim, T, Kentucky
23. Williams, Dick, E, Southern
24. Benn, Gerry, T, Oklahoma State
25. Jamieson, Dick, QB, Bradley
26. Burks, Jim, T, Virginia Tech
27. Jenkins, Lowell, T, Wisconsin
28. Sexton, Leo, E, Auburn
29. Stolte, John, T, Kansas State
30. Mosca, Angelo, T, Notre Dame

PITTSBURGH
1. Choice to San Francisco
2. Choice to Detroit
3. Choice to LA Rams
4. Choice to LA Rams
5. Choice to Green Bay
6. Choice to Detroit
7. Choice to Washington
8. Barnett, Tom, B, Purdue
9. Davis, Hal, G, Houston
10. Gunnels, Riley, T, Georgia
11. Curtis, Overton, B, Utah State
12. Pavliska, Bill, B, Baylor
13. Bohling, Dewey, B, Hardin-Simmons
14. Peppercorn, John, E, Kansas
15. Brodnax, J.W. (Red), B, LSU
16. Carrico, Bill, G, North Texas State
17. Leeka, Bill, T, UCLA
18. Seinturier, John, T, USC
19. Kocourek, Dave, E, Wisconsin
20. Hayes, Rudy, B, Clemson
21. Green, Johnny, QB, Tennessee-Chattanooga
22. Polk, Burley, T, Hardin-Simmons
23. Davis, Ernye, B, McMurry
24. Farmer, Wayne, T, Purdue
25. Miller, Ron, E, Vanderbilt
26. Scott, John, T, Ohio State
27. Tolar, Charley, B, Northwestern State (Louisiana)
28. Hall, Ronnie, B, Missouri Valley
29. Loncar, Dick, T, Notre Dame
30. Fjerstad, Willus, B, Minnesota

SAN FRANCISCO
1. Baker, Dave, QB, Oklahoma
   James, Dan, C, Ohio State, from Pittsburgh
2. Harrison, Bob, C, Oklahoma
3. Dove, Eddie, B, Colorado
4. Clark, Monte, T, USC
5. Geremia, Frank, T, Notre Dame
6. Bavaro, Tony, T, Holy Cross
7. Rogers, Don, T, South Carolina, from Chi. Cardinals
   Colchico, Dan, E, San Jose State, F
8. Aiken, Lew, E, Vanderbilt
9. Green, Bobby Joe, B, Florida
10. Nagurski, Bronko, T, Notre Dame
11. Hayes, Jack, B, Trinity (Texas)
12. Korutz, Bill, C, Dayton
13. Lopasky, Bill, G, West Virginia
14. Dukes, Mike, B, Clemson
15. Belland, Joe, B, Arizona State
16. Cook, Bob, B, Idaho State
17. Jurczak, Jerome, C, Benedictine
18. Cowley, Jack, T, Trinity (Texas)
19. Osborne, Tom, B, Hastings, F
20. Deese, Toby, T, Georgia Tech, F
21. Carr, Luther, B, Washington
22. McQueen, Burnio, E, North Carolina A&T
23. Dollahan, Bruce, T, Illinois
24. Chudy, Craig, E, UCLA
25. Gee, Roy, G, Trinity (Texas), F
26. Young, Ed, E, Louisville
27. Semenko, Mel, T, Colorado
28. McCluskey, Mike, B, Washington
29. Bolton, Jack, T, Puget Sound
30. Carter, Bob, T, Denver

WASHINGTON
1. Allard, Don, QB, Boston College
2. Choice to LA Rams
3. Karas, Emil, T, Dayton
4. Wood, Jim, E, Oklahoma State
5. Wetoska, Bob, T, Notre Dame, from Green Bay
   Choice to Chi. Cardinals
6. McFalls, Jim, T, Virginia Military
7. Lawrence, Don, T, Notre Dame
   Ogiego, Mitch, QB, Iowa, from Pittsburgh
   Kenney, Jim, E, Boston U., from Chi. Bears
8. O'Pella, Gene, E, Villanova
9. Haley, Dick, B, Pittsburgh
10. Toth, Ron, B, Notre Dame
11. Marciniak, Gerry, G, Michigan
12. Wypyszynski, Roger, T, St. Norbert
13. Shoemake, Billy, E, LSU
14. Schwarz, Kurt, G, Maryland
15. Hood, Fred, E, Northeastern Oklahoma
16. Splain, Dick, T, New Haven
17. Healy, Jim, G, Holy Cross
18. Kapp, Joe, QB, California
19. Lauder, Bobby, B, Auburn
20. Brewer, Billy, B, Mississippi
21. Reight, Mel, B, West Virginia
22. Gob, Art, E, Pittsburgh
23. Alexander, Clarence, B, Southeastern Louisiana
24. Darrah, George, B, Franklin & Marshall
25. Sargent, Bob, T, Colby
26. Grabosky, Gene, T, Syracuse
27. Odyniec, Norm, B, Notre Dame
28. Austin, Billy, B, Rutgers
29. Lockwood, Don, G, Tulane
30. Colclough, Jim, B, Boston College

1960 NFL

Date unknown

The NFL held an early secret draft so that its teams could get a jump on the new AFL teams in signing players, and so that the AFL teams couldn't use the NFL draft list to help them sign quality players. Although the Cardinals played the 1960 season in St. Louis, at the time of the draft the franchise still was located in Chicago.

The expansion Dallas Rangers were admitted to the league too late to participate in the 1960 draft. Owner Clint Murchison did sign two players—Don Meredith of SMU and Don Perkins of New Mexico—to personal services contracts before the draft, however. At the draft, the Chicago Bears drafted Meredith in the third round so that, according to George Halas, no other teams would draft him and cause trouble over the contract. The Colts, apparently unaware of Perkins's status, drafted him in the ninth round. The Rangers retained both players, but had to give up their third-round and ninth-round choices in 1962 to the Bears and Colts, respectively.

On March 13, 1960, the Rangers selected 36 players in an expansion draft. Each of the other 12 NFL teams froze 25 players from its 36-man roster. The Rangers then were given 24 hours to pick three veterans from those unfrozen by each other team. Murchison changed the name of his team from the Rangers to the Cowboys before the start of the 1960 season.

BALTIMORE
1. Mix, Ron, T, USC
2. Terrell, Marvin (Bo), G, Mississippi, from NY Giants
   Floyd, Don, T, TCU
3. Welch, Jim, HB, SMU
4. Schwedes, Gerhard, HB, Syracuse
5. Lasater, Marv, B, TCU
6. Bansavage, Al, G, USC
7. Beabout, Jerry, T, Purdue
8. Colvin, Jim, T-E, Houston
9. Hall, Bob, T, Army, from Philadelphia
   Perkins, Don, B, New Mexico
10. Barnes, Ernie, T, North Carolina Central, from Washington
   Boyd, Bobby, B, Oklahoma
11. Wehking, Bob, C, Florida
12. Bucek, Bill, HB, Rice
13. Nemeth, Jim, C, South Carolina
14. Johannsen, Dale, T, Augustana (South Dakota)
15. Grantham, Larry, E, Mississippi
16. Boynton, George, B, North Texas State
17. Beaver, Jim, T, Florida
18. Sheehan, Dan, T, Tennessee-Chattanooga
19. Carpenter, Bill, E, Army
20. Hogue, Bob, T, Shepherd

CHI. BEARS
1. Davis, Roger, G, Syracuse
2. Choice to Washington
3. Meredith, Don, QB, SMU
4. Martin, Billy, B, Minnesota
5. Norman, Dick, QB, Stanford
6. Kovac, Ed, B, Cincinnati
7. Bivins, Charley, B, Morris Brown
8. Manning, Pete, E, Wake Forest
9. Kirk, Ken, C, Mississippi
10. Choice to Pittsburgh
11. Fanning, Stan, T, Idaho, from Philadelphia
   Shaw, Glenn, HB, Kentucky
12. Budrewicz, Tom, T, Brown
13. Spada, Bob, E, Duke
14. Sorey, Jim, T, Texas Southern
15. Lashua, Warren, B, Whitworth
16. Farrington, John (Bo), E, Prairie View A&M
17. Hanna, Jim, E, USC
18. King, Claude, B, Houston
19. Roberts, Lloyd, T, Georgia
20. Coia, Angelo, B, USC

CHI. CARDINALS
1. Izo, George, B, Notre Dame
2. Olson, Harold, T, Clemson
   McGee, Mike, G, Duke, from LA Rams
3. McInnis, Hugh, E, Southern Mississippi
   Ellzey, Charley, C, Southern Mississippi, from Green Bay
4. West, Willie, HB, Oregon
   Woods, Silas, E, Marquette, from LA Rams
5. Burrell, Bill, LB, Illinois
   Phelps, George, B, Cornell College (Iowa), from Pittsburgh
   Mazurek, Ed, T, Xavier, from NY Giants
6. Lee, Jacky, QB, Cincinnati
7. Wilson, Larry, HB, Utah
8. Crow, Wayne, HB, California
9. Hoopes, Dewitt, T, Northwestern
10. Johnson, Charley, QB, New Mexico State, F
   Oglesby, Paul, T, UCLA, from Green Bay
11. Towns, Bobby, HB, Georgia
12. Chapman, Tom, E, Detroit
13. Jones, Vic, HB, Indiana
14. DeMarco, Bob, T, Dayton, F
15. Mestnik, Frank, FB, Marquette
16. Hunt, Jim (Earthquake), T, Prairie View A&M
17. Davis, Joe, T, Citadel
18. Haas, Bob, HB, Missouri
19. Alexander, Herman, T, Findlay
20. Day, Tom, G, North Carolina A&T

CLEVELAND
1. Houston, Jim, E, Ohio State
2. Stephens, Larry, T, Texas, from Pittsburgh
   Gautt, Prentice, FB, Oklahoma
3. Fichtner, Ross, B, Purdue
4. Brewer, Johnny, E, Mississippi, from Green Bay
   Marshall, Jim, T, Ohio State
5. Jarus, Bob, FB, Purdue, from Green Bay
   Choice to Pittsburgh
6. Khayat, Bob, G, Mississippi
7. Anderson, Taz, FB, Georgia Tech
8. White, Bob, B, Ohio State
9. Burford, Chris, E, Stanford
10. Washington, Clyde, HB, Purdue
11. Franklin, Bobby, B, Mississippi
12. Mostardo, Rich, B, Kent State
13. Grecni, Rich, C, Ohio U.
14. Dumbauld, Bill, T, West Virginia
15. Watkins, Tom, HB, Iowa State
16. Waldon, Jim, QB, Wyoming
17. Coleman, Lovell, B, Western Michigan
18. Hanlon, Jack, B, Pennsylvania
19. Campbell, Jack, E, Toledo
20. Nelson, Bob, C, Wisconsin

DALLAS RANGERS (Expansion)
Ane, Charlie, C, USC, from Detroit
Barry, Al, G, USC, from NY Giants
Bielski, Dick, TE, Maryland, from Philadelphia
Bolden, Leroy, HB, Michigan State, from Cleveland
Borden, Nate, DE, Indiana, from Green Bay
Braatz, Tom, LB, Marquette, from Washington
Butler, Bill, S, Tennessee-Chattanooga, from Green Bay
Clarke, Frank, TE-FL, Colorado, from Cleveland
Cronin, Gene, LB, Pacific, from Detroit
Cross, Bobby, T, Stephen F. Austin, from Chi. Cardinals
DeLucca, Jerry, T, Tennessee, from Philadelphia
Doran, Jim, SE, Iowa State, from Detroit
Dugan, Fred, SE, Dayton, from San Francisco
Dupre, L.G., HB, Baylor, from Baltimore
Fisher, Ray, DT, Eastern Illinois, from Pittsburgh
Franckhauser, Tom, DB, Purdue, from LA Rams
Fry, Bob, T, Kentucky, from LA Rams
Gonzaga, John, DE, from San Francisco
Guy, Buzz, G, Duke, from NY Giants
Healy, Don, DT, Maryland, from Chi. Bears
Heinrich, Don, QB, Washington, from NY Giants
Husmann, Ed, DT, Nebraska, from Chi. Cardinals
Johnson, Jack, DB, Miami, from Chi. Bears
Johnson, Pete, DB, Virginia Military, from Chi. Bears
Krouse, Ray, DT, Maryland, from Baltimore
Luna, Bobby, DB, Alabama, from Pittsburgh
Mathews, Ray, FL, Clemson, from Pittsburgh
McIlhenny, Don, HB, SMU, from Green Bay
Modzelewski, Ed, FB, Maryland, from Cleveland
Nicely, Joe, G, West Virginia, from Washington
Nix, Doyle, DB, SMU, from Washington
Patera, Jack, LB, Oregon, from Chi. Cardinals
Putnam, Duane, G, Pacific, from LA Rams
Sherer, Dave, P, SMU, from Baltimore
Striegel, Bill, G, Pacific, from Philadelphia
Tubbs, Jerry, LB, Oklahoma, from San Francisco

DETROIT
1. Robinson, Johnny, HB, LSU
2. Rabb, Warren, QB, LSU
3. Scholtz, Bob, C, Notre Dame
4. Andreotti, Jim, C, Northwestern
   Brown, Roger, T, Maryland-Eastern Shore, from Pittsburgh
5. Choice to Green Bay
6. Cogdill, Gail, E, Washington State
7. Norton, Jim, E, Idaho
8. Choice to Washington
9. Messner, Max, T, Cincinnati
10. Alderman, Grady, T, Detroit
   O'Brien, Jim, T, Boston College, from Philadelphia
11. Aucerman, Ted, E, Indiana
12. Ross, Dave, E, Cal State-Los Angeles
13. Tunney, Pete, HB, Occidental
14. Glasgow, Jim, T, Jacksonville State
15. Harper, Darrell, HB, Michigan
16. Rasso, Steve, B, Cincinnati
17. Hudson, Bob, E, Louisiana Tech
18. Walton, Frank, HB, John Carroll
19. Prebola, Gene, E, Boston U.
20. Look, Dean, QB, Michigan State

GREEN BAY
1. Moore, Tom, B, Vanderbilt
2. Jeter, Bob, HB, Iowa
3. Choice to Chi. Cardinals
4. Choice to Cleveland
5. Hackbart, Dale, B, Wisconsin, from Detroit
   Choice to Cleveland
6. Wright, Mike, T, Minnesota

7. Phares, Kirk, G, South Carolina
8. Hitt, Don, C, Oklahoma State
9. Brixius, Frank, T, Minnesota
10. Choice to Chi. Cardinals
11. Ray, Ron, T, Howard Payne
12. Ball, Harry, T, Boston College
13. Winslow, Paul, B, North Carolina Central
14. Gilliam, Jon, C, East Texas State
15. Henley, Garney, B, Huron
16. Littlejohn, John, B, Kansas State
17. Gomes, Joe, B, South Carolina
18. Whittington, Royce, T, Southwestern Louisiana
19. Brooks, Rich, E, Purdue
20. Lewis, Gilmer, T, Oklahoma

LA RAMS

1. Cannon, Billy, B, LSU
2. Choice to Chi. Cardinals
3. Britt, Charley, QB, Georgia
   Atkins, Pervis, HB, New Mexico State, from Pittsburgh
4. Choice to Chi. Cardinals
5. Janerette, Charley, T, Penn State
6. Stalcup, Jerry, G, Wisconsin
   Ellersick, Don, E, Washington State, from Pittsburgh
7. Morrison, Ron, T, New Mexico
8. Dale, Carroll, E, Virginia Tech
9. Luster, Marv, E, UCLA
10. McClinton, Curtis, HB, Kansas
11. Young, Ken, HB, Valparaiso
12. Brown, Doug Pat, G, Fresno State, F
13. Jones, James, E, SMU
14. Stanger, Harold, C, North Texas State
15. Rakowski, Harry, C, Citadel
16. Kaczmarek, Don, T, North Dakota
17. Congedo, Emanuel, E, Villanova
18. Gates, Tom, B, San Bernardino Valley College
19. Boeke, Jim, T, Heidelberg
20. Shelton, Royce, HB, Stephen F. Austin

NY GIANTS

1. Cordileone, Lou, T, Clemson
2. Choice to Baltimore
3. Leo, Jim, E, Cincinnati
4. Choice to Washington
5. Choice to Chi. Cardinals
6. Blair, George, B, Mississippi
7. Yates, Bob, T, Syracuse
8. Hageman, Fred, C, Kansas
9. Anderson, Bob, HB, Army
10. Simms, Bob, E, Rutgers
11. Rems, Dale, T, Purdue
12. Hall, Pete, QB, Marquette
13. Varnado, Jim, FB, Southern
14. Cline, Doug, FB, Clemson
15. Beach, Walter, HB, Central Michigan
16. Beck, Bill, T, Gustavus Adolphus
17. Baker, Dave, E, Syracuse
18. Polychronis, Tony, T, Utah
19. Webster, Jim, HB, Marquette
20. Gorman, Bill, T, McMurry

PHILADELPHIA

1. Burton, Ron, HB, Northwestern
2. Baughan, Maxie, C, Georgia Tech
3. Merz, Curt, E, Iowa
4. Dean, Ted, B, Wichita State, from Washington
   Cummings, Jack, QB, North Carolina
5. Norton, Don, E, Iowa
6. Wilson, Emmett, T, Georgia Tech
7. Wilkins, John, T, USC
8. Lee, Monte, E, Texas
9. Choice to Baltimore
10. Choice to Detroit
11. Choice to Chi. Bears
12. Grosz, Dave, QB, Oregon
13. Graham, Dave, E, Virginia
14. Petersen, Ray, B, West Virginia
15. Wilcox, John, T, Oregon
16. Lancaster, Larry, T, Georgia
17. Graney, Mike, E, Notre Dame
18. Turner, Emory, G, Purdue
19. Hain, Bob, T, Iowa
20. Armstrong, Ramon, G, TCU

PITTSBURGH

1. Spikes, Jack, FB, TCU
2. Choice to Cleveland
3. Choice to LA Rams
4. Choice to Detroit
5. Choice to Chi. Cardinals
   Haynes, Abner, B, North Texas State, from Cleveland
6. Choice to LA Rams
7. Wilson, Leonard, B, Purdue, from Washington
   Dennis, Lonnie, G, BYU
8. Lanphear, Dan, T, Wisconsin
9. Harris, Marshall, HB, TCU
10. Kapele, John, T, BYU
    Martin, Arvie, C, TCU, from Chi. Bears
11. Choice to San Francisco
12. Butler, Earl, T, North Carolina
13. Womack, Larry, HB, Cal State-Los Angeles
14. Keyes, Brady, HB, Colorado State
15. Essenmacker, Larry, T, Alma
16. Ames, Dave, B, Richmond
17. Chamberlain, Dale, FB, Miami (Ohio)
18. Lee, Charley, T, Iowa
19. Turley, Howard, E, Louisville
20. Hershberger, George, T, Wichita State

SAN FRANCISCO

1. Stickles, Monty, E, Notre Dame
2. Kammerer, Carl, G, Pacific, F
   Magac, Mike, G, Missouri, from Washington
3. Breedlove, Rod, G, Maryland
4. Norton, Ray, HB, San Jose State
5. Rohde, Len, T, Utah State
6. Murchison, Ola Lee, E, Pacific
7. Waters, Bobby, QB, Presbyterian
8. Mathis, Bill, HB, Clemson, from Washington
   Fugler, Max, C, LSU
9. Wasden, Bobby, E, Auburn
10. Branch, Mel, E, LSU
11. Pitts, Ed, T, South Carolina, from Pittsburgh
    Hansen, Ernie, C, Northern Arizona, F
12. Williams, Jim, G, North Carolina
13. Hinshaw, Dean, T, Stanford, F
14. Campbell, Gary, B, Whittier
15. Dowdle, Mike, B, Texas
16. Heinke, Jim, T, Wisconsin
17. Gonsoulin, Austin (Goose), B, Baylor
18. Robinson, Carl, T, South Carolina State
19. Pate, Bobby, B, Presbyterian
20. Woodward, Jim, T, Lamar

WASHINGTON

1. Lucas, Richie, QB, Penn State
2. Choice to San Francisco
   Horner, Sam, HB, Virginia Military, from Chi. Bears
3. Stynchula, Andy, T, Penn State
4. Choice to Philadelphia
   Promuto, Vince, G, Holy Cross, from NY Giants
5. Stallings, Don, T, North Carolina
6. Hudson, Dave, E, Florida
7. Choice to Pittsburgh
8. Kohlhaas, Earl, G, Penn State, from Detroit
   Choice to San Francisco
9. Bumgarner, Dwight, E, Duke
10. Choice to Baltimore
11. Eifrid, Jim, C, Colorado State
12. Crotty, Jim, HB, Notre Dame
13. Herron, Bill, E, Georgia
14. Milstead, Charley, B, Texas A&M
15. Darre, Bernard, G, Tulane
16. Kulbacki, Joe, B, Purdue
17. Roland, Billy, G, Georgia
18. Lawrence, John, G, North Carolina State
19. Maltony, Ron, G, Purdue
20. Wolf, Jimmy, HB, Panhandle State

1960 AFL

Held November 22, 1959 (First selections) and December 2, 1959 (Second selections)

When the first AFL draft was held, no front offices or coaching staffs were yet complete. No more than half of the eight teams even had any scouts or personnel staff. In order to be equitable to all eight teams, all information on college players was pooled. The four people responsible for the information used in the draft were Don Rossi, the general manager of the Dallas Texans; Dean Griffing, the general manager of the Denver Broncos; John Breen, the director of player personnel for the Houston Oilers; and Frank Leahy, the general manager of the Los Angeles Chargers.

To begin the draft, each team received one territorial, or bonus, pick. The purpose of the selection was to gain the rights to a player who not only would be one of the main building blocks of the team, but who, being a star of regional or national scope, would help sell tickets and assure the financial success of the franchise. The territorial picks were not made in any order. They were agreed upon unanimously by the clubs. The territorial picks were as follows: Boston, Gerhard Schwedes, HB, Syracuse; Buffalo, Richie Lucas, QB, Penn State; Dallas Texans, Don Meredith, QB, SMU; Denver, Roger LeClerc, C, Trinity (Connecticut); Houston, Billy Cannon, HB, LSU; Los Angeles Chargers, Monty Stickles, E, Notre Dame; Minneapolis, Dale Hackbart, QB, Wisconsin; and New York Titans, George Izo, QB, Notre Dame.

After the territorial picks, a consensus was reached by Rossi, Griffing, Breen, and Leahy as to who were the best eight players in the country at each offensive position. (Due to limited substitution rules at the time, college football players generally were listed only by their offensive positions.) The names of each position were put into a box and drawn for by each club. If a club already had a player at a certain position due to its territorial pick, it was left out of the first selection for that position. For example, the first time ends were selected, only seven names instead of eight were placed in the box and drawn, and Los Angeles didn't receive a choice. When each team had completed a full offensive team, the process was repeated, with the players deemed the ninth through sixteenth best in the country. This selection process continued through 33 selections per team, or three full offensive platoons.

Shortly after the draft was completed, the teams decided there was a need for a wider base from which to attempt to sign players. Two weeks after the first selections, a second draft was held. The second draft consisted of 20 rounds and was conducted under the same guidelines. Occasionally the lists of players at each position didn't work out to be evenly divisible by eight. Therefore, although each team received 20 picks, some received a player more at one position than did others.

Since there was no real order of priority for the players selected, they were listed in alphabetical order under the headings "First selections" and "Second selections." Since the players selected simply were rated as the top collegians in the country, some of them were juniors, and were selected as future picks. One, Doug Pat Brown of Fresno State, was a sophomore, but his selection by the Dallas Texans was upheld despite not following traditional guidelines of future picks.

Shortly after the draft, Minneapolis was offered a franchise in the NFL, and, on January 27, 1960, withdrew from the AFL. Three days later, Oakland was admitted as the eighth AFL team, and the new club inherited Minneapolis' draft list. In the interim period, however, AFL clubs had signed a number of players drafted by Minneapolis. In order to stock the Oakland franchise with players, the AFL held an allocation draft. The other seven teams froze 11 players, after which Oakland chose a varying number of players from each unfrozen list, totaling 24 players.

BOSTON
(First Selections)

Allen, Buddy, HB, Utah State
Burton, Ron, HB, Northwestern
Chamberlain, Dale, FB, Miami (Ohio)
Christopher, Henry, E, SMU
Colchicco, Dan, E, San Jose State
Cummings, Jack, QB, North Carolina State
Davis, James, C, Oklahoma
Fazio, Serafino (Foge), C, Pittsburgh
Fugler, Max, C, LSU
Gardner, Tim, T, Duke
Goodyear, James, T-G, Wake Forest
Harris, Dave, HB, Kansas
Henderson, Al, T, Colorado State
Hickman, Jim, T-G, Penn State
Kranz, Bob, FB, Penn State
Kulbacki, Joe, HB, Purdue
Mackey, Dee, E, East Texas State
Manley, Leon, G, West Texas State
Manning, Cliff, T-G, Hardin-Simmons
Manning, Pete, E, Wake Forest
Mazurek, Ed, T, Xavier
Meglen, Bill, G, Utah State
Mestnik, Frank, FB, Marquette
Mix, Ron, T, USC
Nikolai, Irv, E, Stanford
Prestel, Jim, T, Idaho
Salerno, Bob, G, Colorado
Schwedes, Gerhard, HB, Syracuse
Soergel, Dick, QB, Oklahoma State
Wagner, Larry, T, Vanderbilt
White, Harvey, QB, Clemson
Wilemon, Tirey, HB, SMU
Wisener, Gary, E, Baylor

(Second Selections)

Ames, Dave, HB, Richmond
Boeke, Jim, T-G, Heidelberg
Brewer, Billy, QB, Mississippi
Congedo, Emanuel, T-G, Villanova
Dye, Pat, T-G, Georgia
Farrington, John (Bo), E, Prairie View A&M
Grecni, Rich, C, Ohio U., F
Jones, Bud, E, SMU
Kacmarek, Don, T-G, North Dakota
Lawrence, John, T-G, North Carolina State
Maltony, Ron, T-G, Purdue, F
Pate, Bobby, HB, Presbyterian
Rudolph, Jack, LB, Georgia Tech
Sally, Frank, T-G, California
Spada, Bob, E, Duke, F
Tunney, Pete, HB, Occidental
Webster, Jim, HB, Marquette
Wilcox, John, T-G, Oregon

BUFFALO
(First Selections)

Arnold, Birtho, T-G, Ohio State
Bivins, Charlie, HB, Morris Brown
Black, Don, E, New Mexico
Burrell, Bill, G, Illinois
Choquette, Paul, FB, Brown
Connelly, Mike, C, Utah State
Conroy, Jim, FB, USC
Coogan, Bob, T-G, Utah
Cordileone, Lou, T, Clemson
Dean, Ted, FB, Wichita State
Evans, Willie, HB, Buffalo
Fichtner, Ross, QB, Purdue
Gilliam, Jon, C, East Texas State
Goldstein, Al, E, North Carolina
Houston, Jim, E, Ohio State
Jauch, Ray, HB, Iowa
Khayat, Bob, T, Mississippi
Kirk, Ken, C, Mississippi
Leo, Jim, E, Cincinnati
Lucas, Richie, QB, Penn State
McMurtry, Chuck, T-G, Whittier
Meyer, Bubba, E, TCU
Miller, Ron, E, Vanderbilt
Oliver, Gale, T, Texas A&M
Olson, Harold, T, Clemson
Peterson, Ray, HB, West Virginia
Promuto, Vince, G, Holy Cross
Ramirez, Rene, HB, Texas
Rohde, Len, T, Utah State
Schaffer, Joe, T, Tennessee
Schneider, Wayne, HB, Colorado State
Toncic, Ivan, QB, Pittsburgh
Wilson, Larry, HB, Utah

(Second Selections)

Bumgarner, Dwight, E, Duke, F
Day, Tom, T-G, North Carolina A&T
Dreymala, Babe, T-G, Texas
Gomes, Joe, HB, South Carolina
Graney, Mike, E, Notre Dame
Hall, Pete, QB, Marquette
Hanna, Jim, E, USC
Hanson, Ernie, C, Northern Arizona, F
Harper, Darrell, HB, Michigan, F
Littlejohn, John, HB, Kansas State
Luster, Marv, E, UCLA, F
Nichols, Dwight, HB, Iowa State
Priddy, Merlin, HB, TCU
Rakowski, Harry, HB, Citadel, F
Rems, Dale, T-G, Purdue, F
Robison, Carl, T-G, South Carolina State
Sliva, Bob, T-G, Stephen F. Austin
Sorey, James, T-G, Texas Southern
Thompson, Jerry, T-G, Oklahoma
Whittington, Royce, T-G, Southeastern Louisiana, F

DALLAS TEXANS
(First Selections)

Atcheson, Jack, E, Western Illinois
Boone, George, T, Kentucky
Burford, Chris, E, Stanford
Butler, Earl Ray, T, North Carolina
Cogdill, Gail, E, Washington State
Crotty, Jim, HB, Notre Dame
Ferguson, Gary, T, SMU
Glynn, Tom, C, Boston College, F
Gossage, Gene, T, Northwestern

Heineke, Jim, T, Wisconsin
Jerry, William, T-G, South Carolina
Kapele, John, T, BYU
Kelley, Louis, FB, New Mexico State
Lewis, Gilmer, T-G, Oklahoma
Malmberg, John, T-G, Knox
Martin, Arvie, C, TCU, F
Meredith, Don, QB, SMU
Moore, Tom, HB, Vanderbilt
Murchison, Ola Lee, E, Pacific
Nelson, Bob, C, Wisconsin
Norton, Jim, E, Idaho
Rabb, Warren, QB, LSU
Ringwood, Howard, HB, BYU
Robinson, Johnny, HB, LSU
Saunders, John, FB, South Carolina
Shaw, Glenn, FB, Kentucky
Speer, Gordon, HB, Rice
Stone, Jack, G, Oregon
Terrell, Marvin (Bo), G, Mississippi
Turner, Emery, G, Purdue
Vader, Joe, E, Kansas State
Zaruba, Carroll, HB, Nebraska
(Second Selections)
Alderman, Grady, T-G, Detroit
Alexander, Herman, T-G, Findlay
Anderson, Taz, HB, Georgia Tech, F
Beaver, Jim, T-G, Florida
Beck, Bill, T-G, Gustavus Adolphus, F
Brown, Doug Pat, T-G, Fresno State, F
Campbell, Gary, HB, Whittier
Cole, Vernon, QB, North Texas State
Deese, Toby, T-G, Georgia Tech
Dumbald, Carl, T-G, West Virginia
Elizey, Charley, C, Southern Mississippi
Gates, Tom, HB, San Bernardino Valley College
Gonsoulin, Austin (Goose), HB, Baylor
Holden, Clark, HB, USC
Hoopes, Dewitt, T-G, Northwestern
Leebern, Don, T-G, Georgia
Thompson, Bill, C, Georgia
Tranum, Billy, E, Arkansas
Vickers, Jim, E, Georgia
Ward, Larry, E, Lamar
Winslow, Paul, HB, North Carolina Central

DENVER
(First Selections)
Ball, Harry, T, Boston College
Britt, Charley, QB, Georgia
Canary, Dave, E, Cincinnati
Candro, Paul, HB, Boston U.
Carrico, Bill, G, North Texas State
Cundiff, Larry, C, Michigan State
Darre, Bernard, T, Tulane, F
Davis, Roger, T, Syracuse
Dennis, Lonnie, G, BYU
Dingens, John, T-G, Detroit
Doke, Maurice, G, Texas
Dowdle, Mike, FB, Texas
Hawkins, Wayne, T, Pacific
Huber, Gary, C, Miami (Ohio)
Hudson, Dave, E, Florida
King, Claude, HB, Houston
Klochak, Don, FB, North Carolina
LeClerc, Roger, C, Trinity (Connecticut)
Look, Dean, QB, Michigan State
Mathis, Bill, HB, Clemson
McNeece, Ken, T-G, San Jose State
Monroe, James, QB, Arkansas
Norton, Ray, HB, San Jose State
Rosbaugh, Bob, HB, Miami
Semenko, Mel, E, Colorado, F
Shields, Lebron, T, Tennessee
Spikes, Jack, FB, TCU
Turley, Howard, E, Louisville
Walden, Jim, QB, Wyoming
West, Willie, HB, Oregon
Willener, John, G, Oregon
Yates, Bob, T, Syracuse
Young, Ken, E, Valparaiso
Zimpfer, Bob, T-G, Bowling Green
(Second Selections)
Branch, Mel, T-G, LSU
Cain, Ronnie, E, Kentucky
Campbell, Jack, E, Toledo, F
Chapman, Tom, E, Detroit
Coleman, LeVelle, HB, Western Michigan
Colvin, Jim, T-G, Houston
Foret, Teddy, T-G, Auburn
Green, Bobby Joe, HB, Florida
Hanlon, Jack, HB, Penn State
Hershberger, George, T-G, Wichita State
Horner, Sam, HB, Virginia Military
Hudson, Bob, E, Lamar
Jones, Vic, HB, Indiana
Luplow, Billy, T-G, Arkansas

Phelps, George, HB, Cornell College (Iowa)
Roberts, Tom, T-G, Georgia Tech
Stenger, Sam, C, Denver
Treadway, Olin, QB, Iowa
Wilkins, John, T-G, USC, F
Wilson, Emmet, T-G, Georgia Tech

HOUSTON
(First Selections)
Arena, Pete, G, Northwestern
Bass, Dick, HB, Pacific
Bohler, Bill, E-T, St. Ambrose
Cadwell, Larry, G-T, Louisville
Cannon, Billy, HB, LSU
Cline, Doug, FB, Clemson
Coleman, DeJustice, HB, Illinois
Crandall, Bob, HB, New Mexico
Drinnon, Cleatus, C, Hardin-Simmons
Gremer, John, G, Illinois
Herring, George, G-T, North Texas State
Hitt, Don, C, Oklahoma State
Johnson, Steve, QB, Pepperdine
Lands, John, E, Montana
Lee, Jacky, QB, Cincinnati
Maher, Bruce, HB, Detroit
Mattson, Don, T, USC
McGee, Mike, G, Duke
McInnis, Hugh, E, Southern Mississippi
Messner, Max, T, Cincinnati
Mulholland, George, E, New Mexico State
O'Steen, Gary, HB, Alabama
Prebola, Gene, E, Boston U.
Pyle, Palmer, T, Michigan State
Roach, William, T, TCU
Simms, Bob, E, Rutgers
Snowden, Philip, QB, Missouri
Underwood, Don, G-T, McNeese State
Whetstone, Duane, FB, George Washington
White, Bob, FB, Ohio State
Youmans, Maury, T, Syracuse
(Second Selections)
Branch, Clair, HB, Texas
Chamberlain, Dave, HB, Miami (Ohio)
Cochran, Don, T-G, Alabama
Fanning, Stan, T-G, Idaho
Glasgow, Jim, T-G, Jackson State
Graham, Dave, E, Virginia
Haas, Bob, HB, Missouri
Hughes, Lowell, QB, Kent State
Johannson, Dale, T-G, Augustana (South Dakota), F
Marshall, Jim, T-G, Ohio State
Morrison, Ron, T-G, New Mexico
Muennink, Jerry, C, Texas
Oglesby, Paul, T-G, UCLA
Peppercorn, John, E, Kansas
Peterson, Bob, C, Oregon
Talamini, Bob, T-G, Kentucky
Towns, Bob, E, Georgia
Wasden, Bob, E, Auburn
Welch, Jim, HB, SMU
Wolff, Jim, HB, Panhandle State

LA CHARGERS
(First Selections)
Aucreman, Ted, E, Indiana
Bercich, Bob, HB, Michigan State
Berlinger, Barney, E, Penn
Boone, Charley, C, Richmond
Boyd, Bobby, QB, Oklahoma
Bradfute, Byron, T-G, Southern Mississippi
Breedlove, Rod, G, Maryland
Budrewicz, Tom, T, Brown
Cameron, Jim, C, East Texas State
Crouthamel, Jake, HB, Dartmouth
Davidson, Pete, T-G, Citadel
Faucette, Floyd, HB, Georgia Tech
Franklin, Bobby, QB, Mississippi
Flowers, Charley, FB, Mississippi
Horn, Don, FB, Iowa
Jeter, Bob, HB, Iowa
Lindner, Bill, T, Pittsburgh
Locklin, Billy Ray, T, New Mexico State
Lopasky, Bill, G, West Virginia
Maguire, Paul, E, Citadel
McDaniel, Edward (Wahoo), E, Oklahoma
Milstead, Charley, QB, Texas A&M
Pitts, Ed, T, South Carolina
Serieka, Ed, FB, Xavier
Schlotz, Bob, C, Notre Dame
Sloan, Russ, E, Missouri
Stehouwer, Ron, T, Colorado
Stewart, Wayne, G, Citadel
Stickles, Monty, E, Notre Dame
Stolte, John, T, Kansas City
Wilson, Leonard, HB, Purdue
Zeman, Bob, HB, Wisconsin

(Second Selections)
Beabout, Jerry, T-G, Purdue, F
Blair, George, HB, Mississippi, F
Brixius, Frank, T-G, Minnesota, F
Davis, Joe, T-G, Citadel
Demarco, Bob, T-G, Dayton, F
Hain, Bob, T-G, Iowa
Janssen, Chuck, T-G, Tulsa
Kelley, Gordon, E, Georgia
Lancaster, Larry, G-T, Georgia
Lasater, Marv, HB, TCU
Lashua, Warren, E, Whitworth
McGriff, Perry, E, Florida
Phares, Kirk, T-G, South Carolina
Rawson, Lamar, HB, Auburn
Ray, Ronald, T-G, Howard Payne
Talkington, Ken, QB, Texas Tech
Talley, John, QB, Northwestern
Waters, Bobby, HB, Presbyterian
Wehking, Bob, C, Florida
Womack, Larry, HB, Colorado State

MINNEAPOLIS
(First Selections)
Andreotti, Jim, C, Northwestern
Baughan, Maxie, C, Georgia Tech
Blanch, George, HB, Texas
Boyette, Cloyd, T-G, Texas Southern
Boykin, Willie, T, Michigan State
Cavelli, Carmen, E, Richmond
Chastain, Jim, T-G, Michigan State
Curci, Fran, QB, Miami
Carroll, Dale, E, Virginia Tech
Daniels, Purcell, FB, Pepperdine
Deskin, Don, T, Michigan
Dumbroski, Leon, T-G, Delaware
Fitch, Ken, T, Kansas
Hackbart, Dale, QB, Wisconsin
Haynes, Abner, HB, North Texas State
Hogan, Vin, HB, Boston College
Jarus, Bob, HB, Purdue
Kohlhaas, Earl, G, Penn State
Lackey, Bobby, QB, Texas
MacLean, Neil, FB, Wake Forest
Muff, Larry, E, Benedictine
Norton, Don, E, Iowa
O'Brien, Jim, T, Boston College
Otto, Jim, C, Miami
Pollard, Chuck, E, Rice
Roland, Billy, G, Georgia
Smith, Ray, FB, UCLA
Smith, Wade, HB, North Carolina
Stalcup, Jerry, G, Wisconsin
Wilcox, John, T, Oregon
Witcher, Al, E, Baylor
Woods, Silas, HB, Marquette
Wright, Mike, T, Minnesota
(Second Selections)
Alexander, C.J., HB, Southeastern
Atkins, Pervis, HB, New Mexico State, F
Bansavage, Al, T-G, USC
Beach, Walter, HB, Central Michigan
Brewer, Johnny, E, Mississippi, F
Edington, Don, E, Florida
Evans, Howard, C, Houston
Hageman, Fred, C, Kansas, F
Herron, Bill, E, Georgia
Hogue, Bob, T-G, Shepherd, F
Lambert, Gerald, T-G, Texas A&I
McCord, Sam, QB, East Texas State
Mostardo, Rich, HB, Kent State
Parker, Bob, T-G, East Texas State
Polychronis, Tony, T-G, Utah, F
Sheehan, Dan, T-G, Tennessee-Chattanooga, F
Turley, Howard, E, Louisville
Williams, Jim, T-G, North Carolina
Woodward, Jim, T-G, Lamar

NY TITANS
(First Selections)
Akin, Lewis, E, Vanderbilt
Allen, Chuck, T, Alabama
Bucek, Bill, HB, Rice
Burkett, Jackie, C, Auburn
Coia, Angelo, HB, USC
Eifrid, Jim, C, Colorado State
Ellersick, Don, E, Washington State
Floyd, Don, T, TCU
Gautt, Prentice, FB, Oklahoma
Genyk, George, G, Michigan
Grantham, Larry, E, Mississippi
Graybeal, Joe, C, Eastern Kentucky
Groner, Jack, QB, Washington & Lee
Izo, George, QB, Notre Dame
Kaohelaulii, Ed, T, Oregon State
Kovac, Ed, HB, Cincinnati
Magac, Mike, T, Missouri

Martin, Blanche, FB, Michigan State
Merz, Curt, E, Iowa
Meyer, Eddie, T-G, West Texas State
Miller, Gene, T-G, Rice
Mooty, Jim, HB, Arkansas
Morin, Mike, HB, Knox
Patella, Nick, G, Wake Forest
Perkins, Don, HB, New Mexico
Ross, David, E, Cal State-Los Angeles
Smith, Roger, G, Auburn
Stallings, Don, T, North Carolina State
Stephens, Larry, T-G, Texas
St. Clair, Jim, QB, Cal-Santa Barbara
Stinnette, Jim, FB, Oregon State
Wilemon, David, T, SMU
(Second Selections)
Abadie, Pete, E, Tulane
Armstrong, Ramon, T-G, TCU
Baker, Dave, E, Syracuse, F
Brooks, Richard, E, Purdue
Brown, Roger, T-G, Maryland-Eastern Shore
Budrewicz, Tom, T-G, Brown
Colburn, Bob, QB, Bowling Green
Essenmacker, Larry, T-G, Alma
Gorman, Jim, T-G, McMurry
Hall, Bob, T-G, Kent State, F
Harris, Marshall, HB, TCU
Henley, Garney, HB, Huron
Hunt, Jim, T-G, Purdue
Leboeuf, Gordon, HB, Texas A&M
Nemeth, Jim, C, South Carolina, F
Rasso, Steve, HB, Cincinnati
Shelton, Royce, HB, Stephen F. Austin, F
Sknoeckni, Gary, E, Syracuse
Stynchula, Andy, T-G, Penn State
Walton, Frank, HB, John Carroll

OAKLAND (Allocation)
Armstrong, Ramon, T, TCU, from NY Titans
Blanch, George, HB, Texas, from Houston
Cannivino, Joe, DB, Ohio State, from Buffalo
Carr, Luther, T, Washington, from LA Chargers
Cavalli, Carmen, DE, Richmond, from Buffalo
Churchwell, Don, G, Mississippi, from Houston
Curci, Fran, QB, Miami, from Houston
Daniels, Purcell, DB, Pepperdine, from Houston
Deskins, Don, G, Michigan, from LA Chargers
Edington, Don, E, Florida, from Boston
Epps, Jerry, G, West Texas State, from NY Titans
Goldstein, Alan, E, North Carolina, from Buffalo
Harrison, Bob, LB, Arizona State, from LA Chargers
Hawkins, Wayne, G, Pacific, from Denver
Holden, Clark, HB, USC, from Dallas Texans
Jones, Stan, G, Maryland-Eastern Shore, from Dallas Texans
Lancaster, Larry, G-T, Georgia, from LA Chargers
Lott, Billy, HB, Mississippi, from Houston
Nelson, Bob, C, Wisconsin, from Boston
Newhouse, Ron, LB, Michigan, from NY Titans
Peterson, Ray, HB, West Virginia, from Buffalo
Prebola, Gene, E, Boston U., from Houston
Starnes, Mack, DB, USC, from Houston
Woodward, Jim, G, North Carolina Central, from Houston

1961 NFL
Held December 27-28, 1960

The expansion Minnesota Vikings received the first choice in each round. The draft consisted of 280 selections.

In February, the Vikings selected 36 players in an expansion draft. Each of the other 13 NFL teams, except Dallas, froze 30 players from its 38-man roster. The Vikings chose three players per team from those remaining.

BALTIMORE
1. Matte, Tom, HB, Ohio State
2. Gilburg, Tom, T, Syracuse
3. Hill, Jerry, HB, Wyoming
4. Gregory, Ken, E, Whittier
5. Dyas, Ed, B, Auburn, from Pittsburgh
   Osborne, Ron, T, Clemson
6. Kern, Don, HB, Virginia Military

7. Grimsley, Ike, HB, Michigan State
8. Terhes, Paul, B, Bucknell
9. Nicklas, Pete, T, Baylor
10. Clemens, Bob, B, Pittsburgh
11. White, Ralph, T, Bowling Green
12. Reynolds, Dick, T, North Carolina State
13. Garber, Dallas, B, Marietta
14. Hunt, Bob, T, SMU
15. Sims, E.A., E, New Mexico State
16. Weisner, Tom, B, Wisconsin
17. Jastrzembski, Steve, B, Pittsburgh
18. Allison, Wilson, T, Baylor
19. Novsek, Joe, T, Tulsa
20. Kimbrough, Albert, B, Northwestern

CHI. BEARS
1. Ditka, Mike, E, Pittsburgh
2. Brown, Bill, B, Illinois
3. Gibson, Claude (Hoot), B, North Carolina State
4. Ladd, Ernie, T, Grambling
5. Lincoln, Keith, B, Washington State
6. Fleming, George, B, Washington
7. Pyle, Mike, C, Yale
8. Ryan, Ed, B, Michigan State
9. Bethune, Bob, B, Mississippi State
10. Harness, Jason, E, Michigan State
11. Fewell, Sam, T, South Carolina
12. Dyer, Howard, QB, Virginia Military
13. McLeod, Bob, E, Abilene Christian
14. Tyrer, Jim, T, Ohio State
15. Linning, Chuck, T, Miami
16. Frazier, Wayne, C, Auburn
17. Barfield, Rossie, E, North Carolina Central
18. Finn, John, T, Louisville
19. Charles, Ben, QB, South Carolina
20. Mason, Gordon, B, Tennessee Tech

CLEVELAND
1. Crespino, Bobby, E, Mississippi, from Detroit
   Choice to Dallas Cowboys
2. Nutting, Ed, T, Georgia Tech
3. Choice to LA Rams
4. Brown, John, T, Syracuse, F
5. Lucci, Mike, C, Tennessee, F
6. Parker, Frank, T, Oklahoma State, from Detroit
   Choice to St. Louis
7. Powell, Preston, B, Grambling
8. Frongillo, John, T, Baylor, F
   Cox, Fred, HB, Pittsburgh, from Green Bay, F
9. Gibbs, Jake, QB, Mississippi
10. Wolff, Wayne, G, Wake Forest, from Washington
    Ericson, Ken, E, Syracuse
11. Gault, Billy, B, TCU
12. Lage, Dick, E, Lenoir-Rhyne
13. Wilson, Jack, B, Duke
14. Lohman, Phil, C, Oklahoma
15. Taylor, Charley, B, Mississippi
16. Shoals, Roger, T, Maryland
17. Bird, Calvin, B, Kentucky
18. Morris, Ed, T, Indiana
19. Minihane, Bob, G, Boston U.
20. Baker, Charlie, T, Tennessee, F

DALLAS COWBOYS
1. Choice to Washington
   Lilly, Bob, T, TCU, from Cleveland
2. Holub, E.J., C, Texas Tech
3. Barber, Stew, G, Penn State
4. Davis, Arnold, E, Baylor
5. Choice to San Francisco
6. Choice to Washington
7. Gilmore, Art, B, Oregon State
8. Talbert, Don, T, Texas, F
9. Gregory, Glynn, B, SMU
10. Choice to Green Bay
11. Stevenson, Norris, B, Missouri
12. Shingler, Lowndes, QB, Clemson
13. Goodman, Don, B, Florida
14. Shaw, Billy, T, Georgia Tech
15. Varnado, Julius, T, Cal State-San Francisco
16. Steffen, Jerry, B, Colorado
17. Cloud, Everett, B, Maryland
18. Williams, Randy, B, Indiana
19. Hoyem, Lynn, C, Long Beach State
20. Morgan, Jerry, B, Iowa State

DETROIT
1. Choice to Cleveland
2. LaRose, Danny, E, Missouri
3. Mills, Dick, T, Pittsburgh, from Pittsburgh
   Antwine, Houston, G, Southern Illinois
4. Hartline, Ron, FB, Oklahoma
5. Faison, Earl, E, Indiana
   Puckett, Ron, T, Cal State-Los Angeles, from Philadelphia
6. Choice to Cleveland
7. Choice to St. Louis
8. Muff, Larry, E, Benedictine
9. Brooks, Bob, FB, Ohio U.
10. Linden, Errol, E, Houston
11. Vargo, Larry, E, Detroit, F
12. Rodgers, Tom, B, Kentucky
13. Hodge, Paul, LB, Pittsburgh
14. Bowers, Charley, HB, Arizona State
15. Lauber, Mike, E, Wisconsin-River Falls
16. Krantz, Gus, T, Northern Michigan
17. Goode, Tom, LB, Mississippi State
18. Gregor, John, T, Montana
19. Valesano, Gene, B, Northern Michigan
20. Lewis, Tom, B, Lake Forest

GREEN BAY
1. Adderley, Herb, B, Michigan State
2. Kostelnik, Ron, T, Cincinnati
3. Nugent, Phil, B, Tulane
4. Dudley, Paul, B, Arkansas
   LeSage, Joe, G, Tulane, from Philadelphia
5. Novak, Jack, G, Miami
6. Folkins, Lloyd, E, Washington
7. Johnson, Lewis, B, Florida A&M
8. Choice to Cleveland
9. Flanagan, Vester, T, Cal State-Humboldt
10. Hagberg, Roger, B, Minnesota, from Dallas Cowboys
    McLeod, Buck, T, Baylor
11. Keckin, Val, B, Southern Mississippi
12. Denvir, John, T, Colorado
13. Pitts, Elijah, B, Philander Smith
14. Toburen, Nelson, E, Wichita State
15. Lardani, Ray, T, Miami
16. Mason, Clarence, E, Bowling Green
17. Brewington, Jim, T, North Carolina Central
18. Sims, Arthur, B, Texas A&M
19. Bondhus, Leland, T, South Dakota State
20. Ratkowski, Ray, B, Notre Dame

LA RAMS
1. McKeever, Marlin, LB, USC
2. Kimbrough, Elbert, E, Northwestern
3. Beaty, Harold, G, Oklahoma State
   Miller, Ron, QB, Wisconsin, from Cleveland, F
4. Cowan, Charlie, T, New Mexico Highlands, from Washington
   Choice to NY Giants
5. Hector, Willie, G, Pacific
6. Olderman, Bruce, T, Allegheny
   Wood, Larry, B, Northwestern, from Pittsburgh
7. Smith, Bobby, B, UCLA, F
8. Carolan, Reg, E, Idaho, F
9. Allen, Duane, E, Santa Ana J.C.
10. Scibelli, Joe, T, Notre Dame
11. Lane, Bob, E, Baylor, F
12. Mince, Walt, B, Arizona
13. McKeever, Mike, G, USC
14. Jones, David (Deacon), T, Mississippi Valley State
15. Wright, Ernie, T, Ohio State
16. Zeno, Mike, G, Virginia Tech
17. Allen, Chuck, G, Washington
18. Williamson, Bill, T, Bakersfield J.C.
19. Zivkovich, Lou, T, New Mexico State
20. Lederle, Al, E, Georgia Tech

MINNESOTA
1. Mason, Tommy, HB, Tulane
2. Hawkins, Rip, LB, North Carolina
3. Tarkenton, Fran, QB, Georgia
4. Lamson, Chuck, HB, Wyoming, F
5. Sharockman, Ed, HB, Pittsburgh
6. Burch, Jerry, E, Georgia
7. Ferrie, Allan, E, Wagner
8. Lindquist, Paul, T, New Hampshire
9. Sheehan, Dan, T, Tennessee-Chattanooga
10. Mayberry, Doug, FB, Utah State
11. Mays, Jerry, T, SMU
12. Stonebreaker, Steve, E, Detroit, F
13. Hayes, Ray, FB, Central State (Oklahoma)
14. Peterson, Ken, T, Utah
15. Mercer, Mike, E, Arizona State
16. Karpowicz, Ted, HB, Detroit
17. Jones, Willie, B, Purdue
18. Voight, Bob, T, Cal State-Los Angeles, F
19. Hill, Bill, FB, Presbyterian
20. McFarland, Mike, QB, Western Illinois

MINNESOTA (Expansion)
Alderman, Grady, G, Detroit, from Detroit
Barnett, Tom, HB, Purdue, from Pittsburgh
Beams, Byron, T, Notre Dame, from Pittsburgh
Beck, Ken, DT, Texas A&M, from Green Bay
Bishop, Bill, DT, North Texas State, from Chi. Bears
Boll, Don, T, Nebraska, from NY Giants
Culpepper, Ed, DT, Alabama, from St. Louis
Ellersick, Don, FL, Washington State, from LA Rams
Haley, Dick, DB, Pittsburgh, from Washington
Huth, Gerry, G, Wake Forest, from Philadelphia
Janerette, Charlie, G, Penn State, from LA Rams
Johnson, Gene, DB, Cincinnati, from Philadelphia
Joyce, Don, DE, Tulane, from Baltimore
Kimber, Bill, E, Florida State, from NY Giants
Lapham, Bill, C, Iowa, from Philadelphia
McElhenny, Hugh, HB, Washington, from San Francisco
Middleton, Dave, E, Auburn, from Detroit
Morris, Jack, DB, Oregon, from Pittsburgh
Mostardi, Rich, DB, Kent State, from Cleveland
Murphy, Fred, E, Georgia Tech, from Cleveland
Osborne, Clancy, LB, Arizona State, from San Francisco
Pesonen, Dick,DB, Minnesota-Duluth, from Green Bay
Rabold, Mike, G, Indiana, from St. Louis
Richards, Perry, SE, Detroit, from St. Louis
Roehnelt, Bill, LB, Bradley, from Washington
Rubke, Karl, LB, USC, from San Francisco
Selawski, Gene, T, Purdue, from Cleveland
Shaw, Glenn, FB, Kentucky, from Chi. Bears
Shields, Lebron, DT, Tennessee, from Baltimore
Smith, Zeke, LB, Auburn, from Baltimore
Stalcup, Jerry, LB, Wisconsin, from LA Rams
Stephens, Louis (Red), G, San Francisco, from Washington
Sumner, Charlie, DB, William & Mary, from Chi. Bears
Whitsell, Dave, DB, Indiana, from Detroit
Winslow, Paul, HB, North Carolina Central, from Green Bay
Youso, Frank, T, Minnesota, from NY Giants

NY GIANTS
1. Choice to San Francisco through Baltimore
2. Gaiters, Bob, B, New Mexico State, from Washington
   Tarbox, Bruce, G, Syracuse
3. Choice to Washington
4. Davidson, Ben, T, Washington, from LA Rams
   Choice to Philadelphia
5. Daniels, Jerry, E, Mississippi
6. Larson, Greg, C, Minnesota
7. Collier, Jimmy, E, Arkansas
8. Green, Allen, C, Mississippi
9. Gray, Moses, T, Indiana
10. Knight, Glen, E, Shaw
11. Benton, Bob, T, Mississippi
12. Moynihan, Jack, QB, Holy Cross
13. Fields, Jerry, B, Ohio State
14. White, Eugene, B, Florida A&M
15. Binkley, Cody, C, Vanderbilt
16. Vishneski, Bernie, T, Virginia Tech
17. Cooper, Sylvester, T, Bakersfield J.C.
18. DesMarais, Ken, C, Holy Cross
19. Reublin, Bob, B, Bowling Green
20. McKeta, Don, B, Washington

PHILADELPHIA
1. Baker, Art, FB, Syracuse
2. Strange, Bo, C, LSU
3. Wright, James Earl, QB, Memphis State, from St. Louis, F
   Oakes, Don, T, Virginia Tech
4. Ficca, Dan, G, USC, from NY Giants
   Choice to Green Bay
5. Choice to Detroit
6. Balme, Ben, G, Yale
7. Cross, Irv, B, Northwestern
8. Beaver, Jim, G, Florida
9. Fontes, Wayne, HB, Michigan State, F
10. Hayes, Luther, E, USC
11. Hicks, L.E., T, Florida
12. Majors, Billy, B, Tennessee
13. Jonas, Don, B, Penn State
14. Fleming, Willie, HB, Iowa
15. Richards, Bobby, T, LSU
16. Clapp, G.W., G, Auburn
17. Lavery, Larry, T, Illinois
18. Maravich, Nick, T, North Carolina State
19. Wilson, Dick, C, Penn State
20. MacKinnon, Jacque, B, Colgate

PITTSBURGH
1. Choice to San Francisco
2. Pottios, Myron, LB, Notre Dame
3. Choice to Detroit
4. Choice to San Francisco
5. Mautino, Fred, E, Syracuse, from Washington
   Choice to Baltimore
6. Choice to LA Rams
7. Hoak, Dick, B, Penn State
8. Balthazar, George, T, Tennessee State
9. Choice to San Francisco
10. Mack, Bill (Red), B, Notre Dame
11. Clement, Harry, B, North Carolina
12. Jackunas, Frank, T, Detroit, F
13. Choice to San Francisco
14. Schmitz, Bob, G, Montana State
15. McCown, Ray, B, West Texas State
16. Scott, Wilbert, B, Indiana
17. Nofsinger, Terry, QB, Utah
18. Simko, John, E, Augustana (North Dakota)
19. Wyatt, Bernard, B, Iowa
20. Jones, Mike, QB, San Jose State

ST. LOUIS
1. Rice, Ken, T, Auburn
2. Arbanas, Fred, E, Michigan State
3. Wilson, Billy, T, Auburn, from Washington, F
   Choice to Philadelphia
4. McDole, Ron, T, Nebraska
5. Bass, Glen, E, East Carolina
6. Evans, Dale, B, Kansas State
   Thornton, Dick, QB, Northwestern, from Cleveland, F
7. Hultz, George, T, Southern Mississippi, F
   Bemiller, Al, C, Syracuse, from Detroit
8. Starks, Marshall, HB, Illinois
9. Graning, Chick, HB, Georgia Tech, F
10. King, Jimmy, T, Clemson, F
11. Kinnune, Bill, G, Washington
12. Stock, Mike, B, Northwestern
13. McMillan, Ernie, E, Illinois
14. Elliot, Bob, FB, North Carolina
15. West, Mel, B, Missouri
16. Bradley, Jake, T, Florida A&M
17. Fischer, Pat, B, Nebraska
18. Browning, Art, G, Duke
19. Schnell, Dick, T, Wyoming
20. Reed, Leo, E, Colorado State

SAN FRANCISCO
1. Johnson, Jimmy, B, UCLA, from Pittsburgh
   Casey, Bernie, B, Bowling Green
   Kilmer, Billy, B, UCLA, from Baltimore
2. Lakes, Roland, C, Wichita State
3. Cooper, Bill, B, Muskingum
4. Thomas, Aaron, E, Oregon State, from Pittsburgh
   Messer, Dale, B, Fresno State
5. McCreary, Bob, T, Wake Forest
   Miller, Clark, T, Utah State, from Dallas Cowboys, F
6. McClellan, Mike, B, Oklahoma, F
7. Purdin, Ray, B, Northwestern
8. Plumley, Neill, T, Oregon
9. Donahue, Leon, T, San Jose State, from Pittsburgh, F
   Nino, Everisto, T, East Texas State
10. Hynes, Paul, FB, Louisiana Tech
11. Parrilli, Tony, G, Illinois
12. Coffey, Don, E, Memphis State, F
13. Hackler, Tommy, E, Tennessee Tech, from Pittsburgh
    Fincke, Julius, T, McNeese State, F
14. Worrell, Bill, T, Georgia
15. Sams, Bob, T, Central State (Oklahoma)
16. Fuller, Charlie, HB, Cal State-San Francisco
17. Jewell, Tom, T, Idaho State
18. McFarland, Kay, HB, Colorado State, F
19. Simpson, Tom, T, Davidson
20. Perry, Jerry, G, Central State (Oklahoma)

WASHINGTON
1. Snead, Norm, QB, Wake Forest, from Dallas Cowboys
   Rutgens, Joe, T, Illinois

2. Choice to NY Giants
3. Choice to St. Louis
Cunningham, Jim, B, Pittsburgh, from NY Giants
4. Choice to LA Rams
5. Choice to Pittsburgh
6. Krakoski, Joe, B, Illinois, from Dallas Cowboys
O'Day, John, T, Miami
7. Kerr, Jim, B, Penn State
8. Barnes, Charley, E, Northeast Louisiana
9. Arrington, Joel, B, Duke
10. Choice to Cleveland
11. Mattson, Riley, T, Oregon
12. Coolbaugh, Bob, E, Richmond
13. Elmore, Doug, B, Mississippi, F
14. Schick, Doyle, B, Kansas
15. Johnson, Bob, E, Michigan
16. Petty, Ron, T, Louisville
17. Bellino, Joe, B, Navy
18. Tolford, George, T, Ohio State
19. Romeo, Tony, E, Florida State
20. Ingram, Mike, G, Ohio State

1961 AFL

Held November 23, 1960 (Rounds 1-6) and December 5, 1960 (Rounds 7-30)

The AFL established the same draft format as the NFL used—teams drafting in an inverse order of finish. One difference from the NFL was that no future picks could be made until the fourteenth round. Each team could protect two players within its geographical territory through the first two rounds, in order to assure itself the right to players whose signing might help the financial success of the franchise. The territorial draft rule was used again in the 1962 draft, before being eliminated on January 8, 1962. Although the Chargers played the 1961 season in San Diego, at the time of the draft, the franchise still was located in Los Angeles.

BOSTON
1. Mason, Tommy, HB, Tulane
2. Hawkins, Rip, C, North Carolina
3. LaRose, Danny, E, Missouri
4. Zeno, Mike, G, Virginia Tech
5. Tarkenton, Fran, QB, Georgia
6. Eisenhauer, Larry, T, Boston College
7. Terhes, Paul, QB, Bucknell
8. Long, Charley, G, Tennessee-Chattanooga
9. Lakes, Roland, C, Wichita State
10. Mueller, Dick, E, Kentucky
11. West, Mel, HB , Missouri
12. Harris, Wayne, C, Arkansas
13. Underwood, Dan, T, McNeese State
14. Wright, James Earl, QB, Memphis State, F
15. Choice to Dallas Texans
16. Balthazar, George, T, Tennessee State
17. Ratkowski, Ray, HB, Notre Dame
18. Rodgers, Tom, HB, Kentucky
19. Bellino, Joe, HB, Navy
20. Childs, Clarence, HB, Florida A&M
21. Oakes, Dan, G, Virginia Tech
22. Johnson, Bob, E, Michigan
23. DeDecker, Darrel, C, Illinois
24. Webb, Don, HB, Iowa State
25. Minihane, Bob, T, Boston U.
26. Granger, Charles, T, Southern
27. Huxhold, Terry, T, Wisconsin
28. Harvard, Bryant, QB, Auburn
29. McMillan, Ernie, T, Illinois
30. Hultz, George, T, Southern Mississippi, F

BUFFALO
1. Rice, Ken, T, Auburn
2. Shaw, Billy, T, Georgia Tech
3. Baker, Art, FB, Syracuse
Gilburg, Tom, T, Syracuse, from NY Titans
4. Barber, Stew, T, Penn State
5. Snead, Norm, QB, Wake Forest
6. Brown, Fred, HB, Georgia
7. Bemiller, Al, C, Syracuse
8. Linning, Chuck, T, Miami
9. Majors, Billy, HB, Tennessee
10. Kern, Don, HB, Virginia Military
11. Wall, Roy (Milam), HB, North Carolina
12. Powers, Floyd, G, Mississippi State
13. Causey, Tom, E, Louisiana Tech
14. Kostelnik, Ron, T, Cincinnati
15. Frye, Jerry, E, South Carolina
16. Scott, Vince, E, Maryland
17. Wolff, Wayne, T, Wake Forest
18. Bodkin, John, G, South Carolina
19. Barnes, Charley, E, Northeast Louisiana
20. Cloud, Everett, HB, Maryland
21. Vargo, Larry, E, Detroit, F
22. Baker, Charlie, T, Tennessee, F
23. Mack, Bill (Red), HB, Notre Dame
24. Jackunas, Frank, C, Detroit, F
25. Harbaugh, Jack, HB, Bowling Green
26. Stanford, Lorenzo, T, North Carolina A&I
27. Allen, Bob, E, Wake Forest
28. Harness, Jason, E, Michigan State
29. Stock, Mike, HB, Northwestern
30. Martin, Billy, HB, Minnesota

DALLAS TEXANS
1. Holub, E.J., C, Texas Tech
2. Lilly, Bob, T, TCU
3. Tyrer, Jim, T, Ohio State
4. Moorman, Claude, E, Duke
5. Mays, Jerry, T, SMU
6. Choice to LA Chargers
7. Arbanas, Fred, E, Michigan State
8. O'Day, John, T, Miami
9. Mills, Dick, T, Pittsburgh
10. Daniels, Jerry, E, Mississippi
11. Tibbets, Marvin, HB, Georgia Tech
12. Hynes, Paul, HB, Louisiana Tech
13. Gregory, Glynn, HB, SMU
14. McClinton, Curtis, HB, Kansas, F
15. Nutting, Ed, T, Georgia Tech, from Boston
Rambo, Roy Lee, G, TCU
16. Thomas, Aaron, E, Oregon State
17. Williams, Jarrell, HB, Arkansas
18. Hartline, Ron, FB, Oklahoma
19. Jackson, Frank, HB, SMU
20. Lane, Bob, E, Baylor, F
21. Thornton, Dick, QB, Northwestern, F
22. Sharockman, Ed, HB, Pittsburgh
23. Zivkovich, Lou, T, New Mexico State, F
24. Dye, Pat, G, Georgia
25. Ramsey, Ray, QB, Adams State
26. House, Danny, HB, Davidson
27. Schloredt, Bob, QB, Washington
28. Stine, Bill, G, Michigan
29. Caddell, Lonnie, FB, Rice, F
30. Price, Cedric, E, Kansas State

DENVER
1. Gaiters, Bob, HB, New Mexico State
2. Hill, Jerry, HB, Wyoming
3. Strange, Bo, C, LSU
4. McDole, Ron, T, Nebraska
Davis, Sonny, E, Baylor, from NY Titans
5. Cowan, Charlie, E, New Mexico Highlands
6. Evans, Dale, HB, Kansas State
7. Patchen, Pat, E, Florida
8. Choice to Oakland
9. Nugent, Phil, QB, Tulane
10. Sturgeon, Charley, HB, Kentucky
11. Simko, John, E, Augustana (South Dakota)
12. Miller, Jerry, E, Howard Payne
13. Greene, Ron, G, Washington State
14. Cooper, Bill, FB, Muskingum
15. Crafts, Willlie, G, Texas A&I
16. Larkin, Jim, T, Hillsdale
17. Weiss, Chuck, FB, Colorado
18. Graning, Chick, HB, Georgia Tech, F
19. Hobbs, John, G, Maryland-Eastern Shore
20. McLeod, Buck, T, Baylor
21. Morgan, Jim, HB, Iowa State
22. Hackler, Tom, E, Tennessee Tech
23. Jewel, Tom, T, Idaho State
24. Simms, E.A., E, New Mexico State
25. Samms, Pete, T, Central State (Oklahoma)
26. Smith, Sam, HB, North Alabama
27. Olson, Don, HB, Nebraska
28. Lee, Wayne, G, Colorado State
29. Cobb, Archie, T, Nebraska, F
30. Mills, Dave, HB, Northeast Missouri State

HOUSTON
1. Ditka, Mike, E, Pittsburgh
2. Goode, Tom, C, Mississippi State
3. Suggs, Walt, T, Mississippi State
4. Walden, Bobby, HB, Georgia
5. Lee, Monte, G, Texas
6. Gibbs, Jake, QB, Mississippi
7. Reynolds, Dick, T, North Carolina State
8. Antwine, Houston, G, Southern Illinois
9. White, Ralph, T, Bowling Green
10. Lee, Charley, C, Iowa
11. Bird, Bob, G, Bowling Green
12. McLeod, Bob, E, Abilene Christian
13. Hinton, Gerald, G, Louisiana Tech
14. King, Jimmy, T, Clemson, F
15. Ferriter, Dennis, C, Marquette
16. Wood, Larry, HB, Northwestern
17. Fewell, Sam, T, South Carolina
18. Grimsley, Ike, HB, Michigan State
19. Pearson, Myron, HB, Colorado State
20. Johnson, Lewis, HB, Florida A&M
21. Miller, Ron, QB, Wisconsin, F
22. Kelly, Bob, E, New Mexico State
23. Anderson, Jim, FB, Mississippi
24. Gregory, Ken, E, Whittier
25. Kreider, Jack, HB, Tulsa, F
26. Fuell, Don, QB, Southern Mississippi, F
27. King, Boyd, C, Rice
28. Frongillo, John, T, Baylor, F
29. Lewis, Tom, E, Lake Forest, from NY Titans
Linden, Errol, E, Houston
30. Stroud, Jim, T, Rice

LA CHARGERS
1. Faison, Earl, E, Indiana
2. Lincoln, Keith, HB, Washington State
3. McKeever, Marlin, E, USC
4. Johnson, Jimmy, HB, UCLA
5. Kilmer, Billy, HB-QB, UCLA
6. Bird, Calvin, HB, Kentucky, from Dallas Texans
Roberts, Cliff, T, Illinois
7. Gibson, Claude (Hoot), HB, North Carolina State
8. Johnson, Charley, QB, New Mexico State
9. Scarpitto, Bob, HB, Notre Dame
10. Hector, Willie, G, Pacific
11. Larson, Greg, C, Minnesota
12. Braxton, Hezekiah, FB, Virginia Union
13. Messer, Dale, FB, Fresno State
14. Wilson, Billy, T, Auburn, F
15. Ladd, Ernie, T, Grambling
16. Whitehead, Bud, HB, Florida State
17. Carolan, Reg, E, Idaho, F
18. Dyas, Ed, FB, Auburn
19. Espenship, Jack, HB, Florida
20. Lucci, Mike, C, Tennessee, F
21. Gaines, Gene, HB, UCLA
22. Brown, John, T, Syracuse, F
23. Bass, Glenn, HB, East Carolina
24. Balme, Ben, G, Yale
25. Coffey, Don, E, Memphis State, F
26. Kinnune, Bill, G, Washington
27. Hayes, Luther, E, USC
28. Allen, Chuck, G, Washington
29. Ficca, Dan, T, USC
30. McKeever, Mike, G, USC

NY TITANS
1. Brown, Tom, G, Minnesota
2. Adderley, Herb, HB, Michigan State
3. Choice to Buffalo
4. Choice to Denver
5. Matte, Tom, QB, Ohio State
6. Brown, Bill, FB, Illinois
7. Mautino, Fred, E, Syracuse
8. Beaty, Harold, T, Oklahoma State
9. Casey, Bernie, FB, Bowling Green
10. Scibelli, Joe, T, Notre Dame
11. Gilmore, Art, HB, Oregon State
12. Stevenson, Norris, HB, Missouri
13. Wendryhoski, Joe, T, Illinois
14. Cunningham, Jim, FB, Pittsburgh
15. Cross, Irv, E, Northwestern
16. Steffen, Jerry, HB, Colorado
17. Pyle, Mike, T, Yale
18. Bentley, Alfred, E, Arkansas State
19. Kerr, Jim, HB, Penn State
20. Plumley, Neil, T, Oregon State
21. Brooks, Bob, FB, Ohio U.
22. Fontes, Wayne, HB, Michigan State, F
23. Walker, Mickey, LB, Michigan State
24. Dyer, Howard, QB, Virginia Military
25. Griffith, Andy, HB, American International
26. Smith, Bobby, HB, UCLA, F
27. Gray, Moses, T, Indiana
28. Cox, Fred, HB, Pittsburgh, F
29. Choice to Houston
30. Minnerly, Bill, HB, Connecticut

OAKLAND
1. Rutgens, Joe, T, Illinois
2. Fleming, George, HB, Washington
3. Pottios, Myron, G, Notre Dame
4. Kimbrough, Elbert, E, Northwestern
5. Norman, Dick, QB, Stanford
6. Crespino, Bobby, HB, Mississippi
7. Purdin, Ray, HB, Northwestern
8. Watkins, Tom, HB, Iowa State, from Denver
Price, Dick, G, Mississippi
9. Shingler, Lowndes, QB, Clemson
10. Peterson, Ken, T, Utah
11. Mayberry, Doug, FB, Utah State
12. Schmitz, Bob, G, Montana State
13. Burch, Gerald, E, Georgia Tech
14. Miller, Clark, T, Utah State, F
15. Coolbaugh, Bob, E, Richmond
16. Lamson, Chuck, HB, Wyoming, F
17. Novsek, Joe, T, Tulsa
18. Krakoski, Joe, HB, Illinois
19. Fuller, Charles, HB, Cal State-San Francisco
20. Powell, Preston, FB, Grambling
21. Jones, Mike, QB, San Jose State
22. Jones, Blayne, G, Idaho State
23. Fisher, Roger, C, Utah State
24. Novak, Jack, G, Miami
25. Yanke, Paul, E, Northwestern
26. Hinshaw, Dean, T, Stanford
27. Appledoorn, Clair, E, San Jose State
28. Grosz, Dave, QB, Oregon
29. Morris, Ed, T, Indiana
30. Face, Bill, HB, Stanford

1962 NFL

Held December 4, 1961

BALTIMORE
1. Harris, Wendell, B, LSU
2. Saul, Bill, LB, Penn State
3. Sullivan, Dan, T, Boston College
4. Dillard, Jim, B, Oklahoma State
5. Croft, Jerry, G, Bowling Green, from Pittsburgh
6. Choice to Green Bay
7. Miller, Fred, T, LSU, F
8. Brokaw, Pete, B, Syracuse
9. Walker, Roy, FB, Purdue, from Dallas Cowboys, F
Rappold, Walt, QB, Duke, F
10. Moore, Fred, T, Memphis State, F
11. Tyler, Scott, B, Miami (Ohio), F
12. Turner, Bake, HB, Texas Tech
13. Holmes, Charles, FB, Maryland-Eastern Shore
14. Jones, Stinson, B, Virginia Military
15. Monte, Joe, G, Furman, F
16. Abruzzeze, Ray, HB, Alabama
17. Knocke, Bill, HB, Fresno State, F
18. Rideout, Mel, QB, Richmond, F
19. Gillett, Fred, B, Cal State-Los Angeles
20. McKee, Herm, B, Washington State, F

CHI. BEARS
1. Bull, Ronnie, B, Baylor
2. Brock, Clyde, T, Utah State, from Pittsburgh
McRae, Bennie, B, Michigan
3. Bates, Jim, E, USC, from Dallas Cowboys
Hull, Bill, E, Wake Forest
4. Cadile, Jim, T, San Jose State
5. Burton, Mac, E, San Jose State, from Washington
Tunnicliff, Bill, FB, Michigan
6. Choice to Philadelphia
7. O'Bradovich, Ed, E, Illinois
8. Reynolds, Ed, T, Tulane, F
Onesti, Larry, C, Northwestern, from NY Giants
9. Winston, Kelton, HB, Wiley
10. Weaver, LeRoy, B, Adams State
11. Robinson, Jerry, HB, Grambling
12. Watts, Bill, T, Miami
13. Perkowski, Joe, B, Notre Dame
14. Von Sonn, Andy, C, UCLA, F
15. Martin, Kent, T, Wake Forest, F
16. Nelson, John, C, Xavier
17. Glass, Glenn, HB, Tennessee
18. Neck, Tommy, B, LSU
19. Kellum, Bill, T, Tulane, F
20. Roberts, Jack, T, Ohio State

CLEVELAND
1. Collins, Gary, E, Maryland, from Dallas Cowboys
Jackson, Leroy, B, Western Illinois
2. Hinton, Chuck, T, North Carolina Central, from Minnesota
Stephens, Sandy, B, Minnesota
3. Choice to Dallas Cowboys
Furman, John, QB, Texas-El Paso, from Green Bay
4. Sczurek, Stan, G, Purdue
5. Rivera, Henry, HB, Oregon State

6. Tidmore, Sam, E, Ohio State
7. Havlicek, John, E, Ohio State
8. Choice to Detroit
9. Dickerson, Charles, T, Illinois, F
10. Goerlitz, Jerry, C, Northern Michigan, from Minnesota
White, Albert, B, Capital
11. Meyers, Ronnie, E, Villanova, from Minnesota
McNeil, Clifton, E, Grambling
12. Stute, Ted, E, Ohio U.
13. Gardner, Frank, T, North Carolina Central
14. Shorter, Jim, B, Detroit
15. Goosby, Tom, G, Baldwin-Wallace, F
16. Biodrowski, Dennis, E, Memphis State, F
17. Harlan, Herbert, E, Baylor, F
18. Bishop, Sonny, G, Fresno State
19. Anabo, John, QB, Fresno State
20. Flatley, Paul, B, Northwestern*

DALLAS COWBOYS
1. Choice to Cleveland
2. Gibbs, Sonny, QB, TCU, F
3. Choice to Chi. Bears
Plummer, Bobby, T, TCU, from Cleveland
4. Choice to San Francisco
5. Choice to LA Rams
6. Davis, Donnie, E, Southern
Andrie, George, E, Marquette, from NY Giants
7. Choice to LA Rams
8. Tureaud, Ken, B, Michigan
9. Choice to Baltimore
10. Longmeyer, John, G, Southern Illinois
11. Hudas, Larry, E, Michigan State
12. Choice to Green Bay
13. Moses, Bob, E, Texas
14. Hays, Harold, G, Southern Mississippi, F
15. Reese, Guy, T, SMU
16. Johnston, Bob, T, Rice
17. Jacobs, Ray, T, Howard Payne
18. Cloutier, Dave, B, Maine
19. Holmes, Paul, T, Georgia, F
20. Bullocks, Amos, B, Southern Illinois

DETROIT
1. Hadl, John, B, Kansas
2. Wilson, Eddie, QB, Arizona
3. Thompson, Bobby, HB, Arizona
4. Lomakoski, John, T, Western Michigan, from Pittsburgh
Ferguson, Larry, B, Iowa, F
5. Birdwell, Dan, C, Houston
6. Bundra, Mike, T, USC
7. Hall, Tom, E, Minnesota
8. Hooper, Murdock, T, Houston
Imperiale, Frank, G, Southern Illinois, from Cleveland
9. Grant, Todd, C, Michigan
10. Archer, Jerry, C, Pittsburg State, F
11. Anderson, Karl, T, Bowling Green
12. Sprute, Gale, C, Winona State
13. Knight, Sherlock, T, Central State (Ohio)
14. Davidson, Jim, B, Maryland
15. Broadbent, Dick, E, Delaware
16. Sesták, Tom, E, McNeese State
17. Wickline, Rucker, C, Marshall
18. Zuger, Joe, QB, Arizona State
19. Bernhardt, Jim, T, Linfield
20. Brown, Bob, E, Michigan, F

GREEN BAY
1. Gros, Earl, B, LSU
2. Blaine, Ed, G, Missouri
3. Barnes, Gary, E, Clemson, from New York Giants
Choice to Cleveland
4. Gassert, Ron, T, Virginia
5. Morris, Chuck, B, Mississippi, from Baltimore, F
Schopf, Jon, G, Michigan
6. Sutro, John, T, San Jose State, from Baltimore
Donahue, Oscar, E, San Jose State
7. Cutsinger, Gary, T, Oklahoma State
8. Tullis, Jim, B, Florida A&M, F
9. Schenck, Peter, B, Washington State
10. Weidner, Gale, QB, Colorado
11. Thrush, Jim, T, Xavier, F
12. Thorne, Joe, B, South Dakota State, from Dallas Cowboys
Pennington, Tom, B, Georgia
13. Kepner, Tom, T, Villanova
14. Green, Ernie, B, Louisville
15. Holdinsky, Roger, B, West Virginia
16. Field, Jimmy, B, LSU, F
17. Buchannan, Buck, T, Grambling*
18. Joiner, Bob, QB, Presbyterian
19. Scattini, Jerry, B, California
20. Snodgrass, Mike, C, Western Michigan

LA RAMS
1. Gabriel, Roman, QB, North Carolina State, from Minnesota
Olsen, Merlin, T, Utah State
2. Carollo, Joe, T, Notre Dame
3. Meyers, John, T, Washington
Cornett, John, T, Rice, from Pittsburgh
4. Perkins, Art, FB, North Texas State
5. Choice to NY Giants
Smith, Jim, T, Penn State, from Dallas Cowboys
Wilson, Ben, FB, USC, from Philadelphia, F
6. Choice to NY Giants
7. Thorson, Sherwyn, G, Iowa
Bakken, Jim, QB, Wisconsin, from Dallas Cowboys
8. Farris, Dick, G, North Texas State, F
9. Lassiter, Ike, T, St. Augustine
10. Norris, Jim, T, Houston
11. Wilder, Bert, T, North Carolina State, F
12. Marinovich, Marv, T, USC, F
13. Fearnside, Bob, HB, Bowling Green
14. Henson, Gary, E, Colorado
15. Nikirk, Walter, T, Houston, F
16. Skufca, Ron, T, Purdue, F
17. Steadman, Dave, T, Georgia Tech, F
18. Furlow, Charlie, QB, Mississippi State, F
19. Barto, Gerard, T, Drake, F
20. Andersen, Foster, T, UCLA

MINNESOTA
1. Choice to LA Rams
2. Choice to Cleveland
3. Miller, Bill, E, Miami
4. Winston, Roy, G, LSU
5. Choice to NY Giants
6. Bowie, Larry, T, Purdue
7. Choice to Philadelphia
8. White, Paul, HB, Florida
9. Shirk, Marshall, T, UCLA
10. Choice to Cleveland
11. Choice to Cleveland
12. Fallon, Gary, HB, Syracuse
13. Van Cleef, Roger, T, Southwestern Oklahoma
14. Russ, Patrick, T, Purdue
15. Guilford, Larry, E, Pacific
16. Contoulis, John, T, Connecticut, F
17. Staley, Ron, E, Wisconsin
18. Hawthorne, Junior, T, Kentucky, F
19. Minter, Tommy, B, Baylor
20. Cagaanan, Terry, B, Utah State, F

NY GIANTS
1. Hillebrand, Jerry, E, Colorado
2. Bill, Bob, T, Notre Dame
3. Choice to Green Bay
4. Griffing, Glynn, QB, Mississippi, F
5. Bolin, Bookie, G, Mississippi, from Minnesota
Miranda, Curtis, C, Florida A&M, from LA Rams
Choice to St. Louis
6. Triplett, Bill, B, Miami (Ohio), from LA Rams
Choice to Dallas Cowboys
7. Byers, Ken, T, Cincinnati
8. Choice to Chi. Bears
9. Bohovich, Reed, T, Lehigh
10. Williams, J.R., C, Fresno State, F
11. Bishop, Dave, B, Connecticut
12. Gursky, Al, HB, Penn State, F
13. Booth, Billy Joe, T, LSU
14. Mather, Greg, E, Navy
15. Taylor, Joe, HB, North Carolina A&T
16. Johnson, Roger, HB, Oregon State
17. Schaffer, Ken, T, Marquette
18. Winter, Bill, FB, St. Olaf
19. Stem, Bob, C, Syracuse
20. Moss, Jim, T, South Carolina

PHILADELPHIA
1. Choice to St. Louis
2. Case, Pete, T, Georgia
3. Holmes, Pat, T, Texas Tech
4. Byrne, Bill, G, Boston College
5. Choice to LA Rams
6. Gonzales, Gus, G, Tulane, from Chi. Bears
McGeever, John, HB, Auburn
7. Perkins, Jim, T, Colorado, from Minnesota
Budd, Frank, B, Villanova
8. Smith, Ralph (Catfish), E, Mississippi
9. Butler, Bob, T, Kentucky
10. Skaggs, Jim, G, Washington
11. Horne, George, T, BYU
12. Thompson, Larry, C, Tulane
13. McKinney, George, B, Arkansas
14. Schwab, Jim, E, Penn State
15. Woulfe, Mike, G, Colorado, F
16. Mazzanti, Jerry, T, Arkansas, F
17. Martin, Mike, T, Washington State
18. Larscheid, Tom, B, Utah State
19. Ericksen, Harold, G, Georgia Tech
20. Turner, Ron, E, Wichita State

PITTSBURGH
1. Ferguson, Bob, B, Ohio State
2. Choice to Chi. Bears
3. Choice to LA Rams
4. Choice to Detroit
5. Choice to Baltimore
6. Choice to San Francisco
7. Collins, Jack, HB, Texas
8. Ballman, Gary, B, Michigan State
9. Powers, John, E, Notre Dame
10. Vignali, Larry, G, Pittsburgh
11. Wills, Bob, E, California
12. Mudie, Sam, B, Rutgers
13. Woodward, Dave, T, Auburn
14. Whitaker, Jim, E, Nevada-Reno
15. Hatch, Vern, E, North Carolina Central
16. Ply, Bobby, B, Baylor
17. Tucker, Nat, B, Florida A&M
18. Yarbrough, Ferrell, T, Northwestern State (Louisiana)
19. Kuprok, John, E, Pittsburgh
20. Knight, John, B, Valparaiso

ST. LOUIS
1. Echols, Fate, T, Northwestern
Goode, Irv, C, Kentucky, from Philadelphia
2. Jackson, Bob, FB, New Mexico State
3. Bryant, Chuck, E, Ohio State
4. Kochman, Roger, HB, Penn State, F
5. Choice to San Francisco
Rice, Bill, E, Alabama, from NY Giants
6. Elwell, John, E, Purdue
7. Kirchiro, Bill, G, Maryland
8. Gross, George, T, Auburn, F
9. Hollis, Wilburn, QB, Iowa
10. Francovitch, George, G, Syracuse
11. Saxton, James, B, Texas
12. O'Billovich, Bob, B, Montana State
13. Diamond, Bill, G, Miami
14. Mans, George, E, Michigan
15. Barlund, Dick, E, Maryland
16. Wegener, Bill, G, Missouri
17. Kasso, Don, HB, Oregon State
18. Donatelli, Don, C, Florida State
19. Smith, Don, B, Langston
20. Dickson, Judge, B, Minnesota

SAN FRANCISCO
1. Alworth, Lance, B, Arkansas
2. Pine, Ed, C, Utah
3. Adams, Billy Ray, FB, Mississippi
4. Dean, Floyd, T, Florida, F
Sieminski, Chuck, T, Penn State, from Dallas Cowboys, F
5. Woods, Ted, HB, Colorado, from St. Louis
Lind, Mike, HB, Notre Dame, F
6. Luhnow, Keith, B, Santa Ana, from Washington
Brown, Jerry, G, Mississippi, from Pittsburgh
Winter, Bill, T, West Virginia
7. Burrell, John, E, Rice
8. Vollenweider, Jim, B, Miami
9. Roberts, Jim, T, Mississippi, F
10. Coustillac, Regis, G, Pittsburgh
11. Jepson, Larry, C, Furman
12. McPike, Milt, E, Kirksville
13. Pierovich, George, B, California
14. Easterly, Dick, B, Syracuse
15. Osborne, Ray, T, Mississippi State
16. Frank, Ron, T, South Dakota State
17. Foltz, Wally, E, De Pauw
18. Brown, Gary, T, Illinois
19. Burton, Bob, T, Murray State
20. McFarland, Roger, B, Kansas, F

WASHINGTON
1. Davis, Ernie, B, Syracuse
2. Hernandez, Joe, B, Arizona
3. Mitinger, Bob, E, Penn State
4. Neighbors, Billy, T, Alabama
5. Choice to Chi. Bears
6. Choice to San Francisco
7. Coan, Bert, HB, Kansas, F
8. Hatcher, Ron, FB, Michigan State
9. Viti, Dave, E, Boston U.
10. Childress, John, G, Arkansas
11. Palazzo, Carl, T, Adams State
12. Terrebonne, Terry, HB, Tulane, F
13. Whisler, Bill, E, Iowa
14. Costen, Jim, HB, South Carolina
15. Velia, Len, T, Georgia
16. Brooker, Tommy, E, Alabama
17. Miller, Alan, G, Ohio U.
18. Charon, Carl, B, Michigan State
19. Crabb, Claude, B, Colorado
20. Trancygier, Ed, QB, Florida State, F

1962 AFL

Held December 2, 1961 (Rounds 1-25) and December 16, 1961 (Rounds 26-34)

The AFL initially held its 25-round draft as planned. Two days later, however, the NFL draft included many future picks that the AFL teams had not made. In order to be competitive with the NFL teams for those players chosen by the NFL as future picks, the AFL teams selected nine more rounds of future picks in a continuation of their earlier draft.

BOSTON
1. Collins, Gary, E, Maryland
2. Jackson, Leroy, HB, Western Illinois
3. Thorson, Sherwyn, G, Iowa
4. Choice to Houston
5. Choice to Dallas Texans
6. Neighbors, Billy, T, Alabama
7. Schopf, John, T, Michigan
8. McRae, Benny, HB, Michigan
9. Triplett, Bill, FB, Miami (Ohio)
10. Knight, John, HB, Valparaiso
11. Choice to Buffalo
12. Choice to Oakland
13. Buoniconti, Nick, G, Notre Dame
14. Sieminski, Chuck, T, Penn State, F
15. Goerlitz, Gerry, C, Northern Michigan
16. Byers, Ken, G, Cincinnati
17. Maentz, Scott, E, Michigan
18. Chandler, Tom, T, Florida A&M
19. Meyers, Ron, E, Villanova
20. Neck, Tommy, HB, LSU
21. Traynham, John, HB, Virginia Military
22. Asack, Bob, T, Columbia
23. Crate, Walt, HB, Widener
24. Christman, Don, C, Richmond
25. Stem, Bob, C, Syracuse
26. Field, Jimmy, QB, LSU, F
27. Gursky, Al, HB, Penn State, F
28. Dickerson, Charlie, T, Illinois, F
29. Fincke, Julius, T, McNeese State, F
30. Finn, John, T, Louisville, F
31. Ingram, Mike, G, Ohio State, F
32. Taylor, Charley, HB, Mississippi, F
33. Jastrzembski, Steve, E, Pittsburgh, F
34. Lardani, Ray, T, Miami, F

BUFFALO
1. Davis, Ernie, HB, Syracuse
2. Glass, Glenn, HB, Tennessee
3. Elwell, John, E, Purdue
4. Choice to Dallas Texans
5. Dellinger, Tom, HB, North Carolina State
6. Viti, Dave, E, Boston U.
7. LeCompte, Jim, G, North Carolina
8. White, Paul, HB, Florida
9. Saul, Bill, C, Penn State
10. Bullocks, Amos, HB, Southern Illinois
11. Croft, Jerry, G, Bowling Green
Pennington, Tom, E, Georgia, from Boston
12. Choice to Oakland
13. Gassert, Ron, T, Virginia, from Dallas Texans
Stratton, Mike, E, Tennessee
14. Scufca, Ron, T, Purdue, F
15. Kochman, Roger, HB, Penn State, F
16. Imperiale, Frank, T, Southern Illinois
17. Sestak, Tom, E, McNeese State
18. Kehoe, Joe, E, Virginia*
19. Johnson, Bill, LB, Southeastern Louisiana
20. Tidmore, Sam, E, Ohio State
21. Henley, Carey, HB, Tennessee-Chattanooga

22. Hall, Tom, E, Minnesota
23. Abruzzese, Ray, HB, Alabama
24. Sczurek, Stan, G, Purdue
25. Gash, Dave, E, Kentucky, F
26. Reynolds, Ed, T, Tulane, F
27. Crabb, Claude, HB, Colorado, F
28. Walker, Roy, FB, Purdue, F
29. Beaver, Jim, G, Florida, F
30. Binkley, Cody, C, Vanderbilt, F
31. Collier, Jim, E, Arkansas, F
32. Erickson, Ken, E, Syracuse, F
33. Parilli, Tony, G, Illinois, F
34. Charles, Ben, QB, USC, F

DALLAS TEXANS
1. Bull, Ronnie, HB, Baylor
2. Miller, Bill, E, Miami
3. Wilson, Eddie, QB, Arizona
4. Hinton, Chuck, T, North Carolina Central
   Goode, Irv, C, Kentucky, from Buffalo
5. Plummer, Bobby, T, TCU
   Ply, Bobby, QB, Baylor, from NY Titans
   Hull, Bill, E, Wake Forest, from Boston
6. Hinton, Al, E, Iowa
7. Choice to San Diego
8. Bowie, Larry, T, Purdue
9. Shirk, Marshall, T, UCLA
10. Saxton, James, HB, Texas
11. Hunt, Bobby, QB, Auburn, from Oakland
    Reese, Guy, T, SMU
12. Thompson, Bobby, HB, Arizona
13. Choice to Buffalo
14. Bolin, Bookie, G, Mississippi, F
15. Graham, Dave, T, Virginia, F
16. Norman, Pettis, E, Johnson C. Smith
17. Brooker, Tommy, E, Alabama
18. Carollo, Joe, T, Notre Dame
19. Welch, Lee, HB, Mississippi State
20. Semcheski, Mike, G, Lehigh
21. Martin, Kent, T, Wake Forest, F
22. Bernhardt, Jim, T, Linfield
23. Foret, Russ, T, Georgia Tech
24. Trammell, Pat, QB, Alabama
25. Burrell, John, E, Rice
26. Rappold, Walt, QB, Duke, F
27. Tyler, Scott, HB, Miami (Ohio), F
28. Thrush, Jim, T, Xavier, F
29. Ryan, Ed, HB, Michigan State, F
30. Goodman, Don, HB, Florida, F
31. Nino, Everisto, T, East Texas State, F
32. Arrington, Joel, HB, Duke, F
33. Wilson, Jack, HB, Duke, F
34. Shoals, Rodger, C, Maryland, F

DENVER
1. Olsen, Merlin, T, Utah State
2. Hillebrand, Jerry, E, Colorado
3. Holmes, Charles, FB, Maryland-Eastern Shore
4. Furman, John, QB, Texas-El Paso
5. Choice to San Diego
6. Choice to San Diego
7. McGeever, John, HB, Auburn
8. Harris, Elbert, HB, Southeastern Louisiana
9. Jepson, Larry, C, Furman
10. Weidner, Gale, QB, Colorado
11. Kline, Mike, G, Oregon State
12. Choice to NY Titans
13. Cegelski, Bob, C, Montana State
14. Gibbs, Sonny, QB, TCU, F
15. Louden, Bill, G, Benedictine
16. Ballman, Gary, HB, Michigan State
17. Tarr, Jerry, E, Oregon
18. Schenk, Pete, E, Washington State
19. Choice to Oakland
20. Martin, Mike, E, Washington State
21. Perkins, Jim, T, Colorado
22. Kasso, Don, HB, Oregon State
23. Tureaud, Ken, HB, Michigan
24. Thomas, Neil, G, Hillsdale
25. Edwards, Dave, E, Auburn
26. Roberts, Jim, T, Mississippi, F
27. Von Sonn, Andy, C, UCLA, F
28. Holmes, Paul, T, Georgia, F
29. Hoyem, Lynn, C, Long Beach State, F
30. Mince, Walt, HB, Arizona, F
31. Williamson, Bill, T, Bakersfield J.C., F
32. Flanagan, Vester, T, Cal State-Humboldt, F
33. Allen, Duane, E, Santa Ana J.C., F
34. Stonebreaker, Steve, E, Detroit, F

HOUSTON
1. Jacobs, Ray, T, Howard Payne
2. Gros, Earl, FB, LSU
3. Case, Pete, T, Georgia
4. Cutsinger, Gary, T, Oklahoma State, from Boston
   Choice to San Diego
5. Rice, Bill, E, Alabama
6. Pinion, Ray, G, TCU
7. Gonzales, Gus, G, Tulane
8. Brock, Clyde, T, Utah State
9. Onesti, Larry, C, Northwestern
10. Moses, Bob, E, Texas
11. Thomas, John, G, McMurry
12. Collins, Jack, HB, Texas
13. Cassell, Royce, E, New Mexico State
14. Griffing, Glynn, QB, Mississippi, F
15. Shaffer, Ken, T, Marquette
16. Adams, Billy Ray, FB, Mississippi
17. Miller, Bill, T, New Mexico Highlands
18. Perkins, Art, FB, North Texas State
19. Jancik, Bobby, HB, Lamar
20. Isbell, Joe Bob, G, Houston
21. Jackson, Roland, FB, Rice
22. Bolin, Kenny, HB, Houston
23. Van Buren, Bill, C, Iowa
24. Melvin, Boyd, T, Northwestern
25. Johnson, Bob, T, Rice
26. Hays, Harold, G, Southern Mississippi, F
27. McFarland, Roger, HB, Kansas, F
28. Henson, Gary, E, Colorado, F
29. Osborne, Ron, T, Clemson, F
30. Clemens, Bob, HB, Pittsburgh, F
31. Kimbrough, Al, HB, Northwestern, F
32. Wyatt, Bernard, HB, Iowa, F
33. Lerderle, Al, E, Georgia Tech, F
34. Talbert, Don, T, Texas, F

NY TITANS
1. Stephens, Sandy, QB, Minnesota
2. Kroll, Alex, C, Rutgers
3. Echols, Fate, T, Northwestern
4. Blaine, Ed, G, Missouri
5. Choice to Dallas Texans
6. Melin, Mel, QB, Washington State
7. Mans, George, E, Michigan
8. Lomakoski, John, T, Western Michigan
9. Barnes, Gary, E, Clemons
10. Stute, Ted, T, Ohio U.
11. Miranda, Curtis, C, Florida A&M
12. Winter, Bill, T, West Virginia, from Denver
    Choice to San Diego
13. Hollis, Wilburn, QB, Iowa
14. Wilder, Bert, T, North Carolina State, F
15. Mudie, Sam, HB, Rutgers
16. Smith, Jim, T, Penn State
17. Miller, Allen, G, Ohio U.
18. Iles, Buddy, E, TCU
19. Bohovich, Reed, T, Lehigh
20. Dickson, Judge, FB, Minnesota
21. Hatcher, Ron, FB, Michigan State
22. Nolan, Tom, T, Widener
23. Kuprok, John, E, Pittsburgh
24. Counts, Johnny, HB, Illinois
25. Warren, Russ, HB, Columbia
26. Morris, Chuck, HB, Mississippi, F
27. Archer, Jerry, C, Pittsburg State, F
28. Nikirk, Walter, T, Houston, F
29. Parker, Frank, T, Oklahoma State, F
30. McClellan, Mike, HB, Oklahoma, F
31. Hicks, L.E., T, Florida, F
32. Jonas, Don, HB, Penn State, F
33. Maravich, Nick, T, North Carolina State, F
34. Wilson, Dick, C, Penn State, F

OAKLAND
1. Gabriel, Roman, QB, North Carolina State
2. Choice to San Diego
3. Pine, Ed, C, Utah
4. Meyers, John, T, Washington
5. Hernandez, Joe, HB, Arizona
6. Birdwell, Dan, C, Houston
7. Norris, Jim, T, Houston
8. Yarborough, Ferrell, E, Northwestern State (Louisiana)
9. Dillard, Jim, HB, Oklahoma State
10. Rivera, Henry, HB, Oregon State
11. Choice to Dallas Texans
12. Skaggs, Jim, G, Washington
    Schwertfeger, Gary, LB, Montana, from Buffalo
    Donahue, Oscar, E, San Jose State, from Boston
13. Pierovich, George, FB, California
14. Choice to San Diego
15. Dean, Floyd, E, Florida, F
16. Russ, Pat, T, Purdue
17. Ferguson, Larry, HB, Iowa, F
18. Vollenweider, Jim, FB, Miami
19. Spurlock, Dennis, QB, Whitworth
    Horne, Kent, T, BYU, from Denver
20. Sutro, John, G, San Jose State
21. Tunnicliff, Bill, FB, Michigan
22. Cadile, Jim, E, San Jose State
23. Basham, Elvin, G, Kansas
24. Bruce, Mickey, HB, Oregon
25. Cagaanan, Tom, HB, Utah State, F
26. Miller, Fred, T, LSU, F
27. Luhnow, Keith, FB, Santa Ana J.C., F
28. Marinovich, Marv, T, USC, F
29. Donahue, Leon, E, San Jose State, F
30. Nicklas, Pete, T, Baylor, F
31. Elliott, Bob, FB, North Carolina, F
32. Richards, Bob, T, LSU, F
33. White, Eugene, HB, Florida A&M, F
34. Worrell, Bill, T, Georgia, F

SAN DIEGO
1. Ferguson, Bob, FB, Ohio State
2. Alworth, Lance, HB, Arkansas, from Oakland
   Hudson, Dick, T, Memphis State
3. Hadl, John, QB, Kansas
4. Bill, Bob, T, Notre Dame, from Houston
   Burton, Mack, HB, San Jose State
5. Mitinger, Bob, E, Penn State, from Denver
   Cornett, John, T, Rice
6. Winston, Roy, G, LSU, from Denver
   Buncom, Frank, LB, USC
7. Harris, Wendell, HB, LSU, from Dallas Texans
   Jackson, Bob, FB, New Mexico State
8. Robinson, Jerry, HB, Grambling
9. Minter, Tom, HB, Baylor
10. Sullivan, Dan, T, Boston College
11. Bishop, Irv, G, Fresno State
12. Smith, Ralph, E, Mississippi, from NY Titans
    Andrio, George, E, Marquette
13. Bryant, Charles, E, Ohio State
14. Coan, Bert, HB, Kansas, from Oakland, F
    Bates, Jim, HB, USC, F
15. Moore, Fred, T, Memphis State, F
16. Gross, George, T, Auburn, F
17. Gardner, Frank, T, North Carolina Central
18. Biodrowski, Dennis, E, Memphis State, F
19. Lind, Mike, FB, Notre Dame, F
20. Herman, Ron, QB, Bradley
21. Williams, Jesse, C, Fresno State, F
22. Thibert, Jim, E, Toledo, F
23. Farris, Dick, G, North Texas State, F
24. Jones, Homer, HB, Texas Southern, F*
25. Gruneisen, Sam, E, Villanova
26. Woulfe, Mike, G, Colorado, F
27. Rideout, Mel, QB, Richmond, F
28. Wilson, Ben, FB, USC, F
29. Dudley, Paul, HB, Arkansas, F
30. Denvir, John, T, Colorado, F
31. Elmore, Doug, HB, Mississippi, F
32. Frazier, Wayne, C, Auburn, F
33. MacKinnon, Jacque, HB, Colgate, F
34. Lohman, Phil, C, Oklahoma, F

1963 NFL
Held December 3, 1962

BALTIMORE
1. Vogel, Bob, T, Ohio State
2. Mackey, John, E, Syracuse
   Wilson, Butch, B, Alabama, from Pittsburgh
3. Choice to St. Louis
4. Logan, Jerry, B, West Texas State
   Fullwood, Harlow, G-T, Virginia, from Chi. Bears
5. Ventura, Bill, T-E, Richmond
6. Cook, Jerry, B, Texas
7. Richardson, Willie, E, Jackson State
8. Hayes, Dave, B, Penn State
9. Trull, Don, QB, Baylor, F
10. Sierkerski, Bill, G-T, Missouri
11. Hill, Winston, T, Texas Southern
12. Maples, Jimmy, C-LB, Baylor
13. Watters, Paul, T, Miami (Ohio), F
14. Petties, Neil, E-B, San Diego State, F
15. Mavity, Leon, DB, Colorado, F
16. Quast, Dick, G, Memphis State, F
17. Carson, Kern, B, San Diego State, F
18. Woodruff, Luther, T, North Carolina State, F
19. Berzansky, Steve, B, West Virginia, F
20. Hurd, D.L., E, Cal State-San Francisco

CHI. BEARS
1. Choice to LA Rams
   Behrman, Dave, C, Michigan State, from Pittsburgh
2. Barnett, Steve, T, Oregon, from Dallas Cowboys
   Jencks, Bob, E, Miami (Ohio)
3. Glueck, Larry, DB, Villanova
4. Sanders, Stan, E, Whittier, from San Francisco
   Mitchell, Charley, HB, Washington, from Pittsburgh
   Choice to Baltimore
5. Choice to San Francisco
6. Johnson, John, T, Indiana, from Pittsburgh
   Mathieson, Dave, QB, Washington State, F
7. Underhill, Paul, B, Missouri, F
8. Harmon, Dennis, DB, Southern Illinois
9. Day, Monte, T, Fresno State, from Dallas Cowboys, F
   Watson, Dave, LB, Georgia Tech
10. Hoerster, Ed, LB, Notre Dame
11. Tullis, James, DB, Florida A&M, F
12. Drummond, Dick, B, George Washington, F
13. Szumczyk, John, B, Trinity (Connecticut)
14. Banks, Gordon, B, Fisk
15. Dentel, Bob, C-LB, Miami
16. Caylor, Lowell, DB, Miami (Ohio)
17. Sisk, John, B, Miami, F
18. Slabaugh, Jeff, E, Indiana
19. Yaksick, Bob, DB, Rutgers
20. Gregory, John, E, Baldwin-Wallace

CLEVELAND
1. Hutchinson, Tom, E, Kentucky
2. Kanicki, Jim, T, Michigan State
3. Choice to LA Rams
4. Munsey, Bill, B, Minnesota
5. Choice to Pittsburgh
   Baker, Frank, B, Toledo, from Detroit
6. Borghetti, Ernie, T, Pittsburgh, from Minnesota, F
   Bloom, Tom, B, Purdue, from Philadelphia
   Choice to LA Rams
7. Choice to Green Bay
8. Sweeney, Walt, E, Syracuse
9. Raimey, Dave, B, Michigan
10. Bobbitt, Jim, G, Michigan State
11. Graham, Art, E, Boston College
12. Infante, Lindy, B, Florida
13. Katterhenrich, Dave, B, Ohio State
14. Faulkner, Staley, T, Texas, F
15. Reade, Lynn, T, USC, F
16. Kelly, Dick, G, Georgia, F
17. Anderson, Dick, E, Penn State, F
18. Garvin, Bobby, T, Mississippi State
19. Sherman, Gary, LB, Bowling Green
20. Shaw, Steve, B, Vanderbilt, F

DALLAS COWBOYS
1. Jordan, Lee Roy, LB, Alabama
2. Choice to Chi. Bears
3. Price, Jim, LB, Auburn
4. Hall, Whaley, T, Mississippi, F
5. Choice to NY Giants
6. Choice to Green Bay
7. Clothier, Marv, G, Kansas
8. Choice to Green Bay
9. Choice to Chi. Bears
10. Scheyer, Rod, T, Washington
11. Schoenke, Ray, C, SMU
12. Perkins, Bill, FB, Iowa
13. Wicker, Paul, T, Fresno State, F
14. Cioci, Lou, LB, Boston College
15. Overton, Jerry, DHB, Utah
16. Golden, Dennis, T, Holy Cross
17. Parks, Ernie, G, McMurry, F
18. Frank, Bill, T, Colorado
19. Stiger, Jim, B, Washington
20. Lucas, Tommy, E, Texas

DETROIT
1. Sanders, Daryl, T, Ohio State
2. Williams, Roy, T, Pacific
3. Choice to Philadelphia
4. Walton, Dick, G, Iowa State
5. Choice to Cleveland
6. King, Don, HB, Syracuse
7. Gamble, John, G, Pacific
8. Gaubatz, Dennis, LB, LSU
9. Dill, Ken, LB, Mississippi, F
10. Ryder, Nick, B, Miami
11. Kassulke, Karl, B, Drake
12. Janik, Tom, B, Texas A&I
13. Clark, Ernie, LB, Michigan State
14. O'Brien, Bill, T, Xavier
15. Simon, Jim, E-LB, Miami
16. Johnson, Charlie, T, Villanova
17. Frantz, Gene, B, BYU

18. Greer, Al, E, Jackson State
19. Reeberg, Lucian, T, Hampton
20. Scarborough, Gordon, B, East Texas State, F

GREEN BAY
1. Robinson, Dave, E, Penn State
2. Brown, Tom, B, Maryland
3. Claridge, Dennis, B, Nebraska, from Pittsburgh, F
   Liscio, Tony, T, Tulsa
4. Aldridge, Lionel, G, Utah State, from NY Giants
   Simons, Carlton, C, Stanford
5. Cverko, Jack, G, Northwestern, from Washington, F
   Grimm, Dan, T, Colorado
6. Simmons, John, E, Tulsa, from Dallas Cowboys, F
   Barrett, Jan, E, Fresno State
7. Kroner, Gary, B, Wisconsin, from Cleveland
   Hill, Olin, T, Furman, from Pittsburgh
   Todd, Turnley, LB, Virginia, F
8. Kinderman, Keith, B, Florida State, from Dallas Cowboys
   Rettino, Louis, B, Villanova
9. Freeman, Bill, T, Southern Mississippi, F
10. McQuiston, Earl, G, Iowa
11. Fleming, Marv, E, Utah
12. Lamonica, Daryle, QB, Notre Dame
13. Kellum, Bill, T, Tulane, F
14. Holler, James (Punkey), LB, South Carolina
15. Breen, Gene, T, Virginia Tech, F
16. Hunt, Coolidge, B, Texas Tech
17. Walker, Thurman, E, Illinois
18. Hernandez, Luis, G, Texas-El Paso
19. Hamp, Herman, B, Fresno State, F
20. Brezina, Bobby, B, Houston

LA RAMS
1. Baker, Terry, B, Oregon State
   Guthrie, Rufus, G, Georgia Tech, from Chi. Bears
2. Nomina, Tom, T, Miami (Ohio)
3. Costa, Dave, G, Utah
   Baker, John, LB, Mississippi State, from Cleveland
4. Griffin, John, B, Memphis State
5. Auer, Joe, B, Georgia Tech, F
   Benson, Roland, T, Miami, from Philadelphia, F
   Chuy, Don, T, Clemson, from Pittsburgh
6. Saimes, George, B, Michigan State
   Monaghan, Terry, T, Penn State, from Cleveland, F
7. Zorn, Bill, T, Michigan State
8. Peters, Anton, T, Florida
9. Profit, Mel, E, UCLA, F
10. Farrier, Curt, T, Montana State
11. Theisen, Dave, B, Nebraska, F
12. Moody, Billy, B, Arkansas
13. Hildebrand, Al, T, Stanford, F
14. Arbuse, Alan, T, Rhode Island
15. Campbell, Larry, E, Toledo, F
16. Burden, Walter, LB, McNeese State
17. Wilson, Jerrel, LB-K, Southern Mississippi
18. Soefker, Buddy, B, LSU, F
19. Nelson, Dornel, B, Arizona State
20. Redell, Bill, DHB, Occidental, F

MINNESOTA
1. Dunaway, Jim, T, Mississippi
2. Bell, Bobby, T, Minnesota
3. Poage, Ray, B, Texas
4. Flatley, Paul, E, Northwestern
5. Kaltenbach, Gary, T, Pittsburgh
6. Choice to Cleveland
7. Choice to NY Giants
8. O'Mahoney, Jim, LB, Miami
9. Hoover, Bob, B, Florida
10. Kosens, Terry, B, Hofstra
11. Campbell, John, LB, Minnesota
12. Sklopan, John, B, Southern Mississippi
13. O'Brien, Dave, T, Boston College
14. Ferrisi, Ralph, B, Southern Connecticut State
15. Murio, John, E, Whitworth
16. Mirich, Rex, T, Arizona State, F
17. Munsey, Tom, B, Concord
18. McIntyre, Tom, T, St. John's (Minnesota)
19. Horvath, Frank, B, Youngstown State
20. Kent, Mailon, B, Auburn, F

NY GIANTS
1. Choice to St. Louis
2. Lasky, Frank, T, Florida, F
3. Skelly, Dick, B, Florida
4. Choice to Green Bay
5. Hill, Dave, T, Auburn, from Dallas Cowboys
   Slaby, Lou, B, Pittsburgh
6. Petrich, Bob, T, West Texas State
7. Hoppmann, Dave, B, Iowa State, from Minnesota
   Petkus, Burt, G, Northwestern
8. Herman, Dave, G, Michigan State, F
9. Taylor, Bob, T, Maryland-Eastern Shore
10. Taliaferro, Mike, B, Illinois, F
11. McKinnon, Don, C, Dartmouth
12. Adamchik, Ed, G, Pittsburgh, F
13. Moss, Jim, B, West Virginia
14. Williams, Joe, B, Iowa
15. Howell, Lane, C, Grambling
16. Killett, Charlie, B, Memphis State, F
17. McAdams, Bob, T, North Carolina Central
18. Pashe, Bill, B, George Washington
19. Buchanan, Buck, T, Grambling
20. Jones, Homer, B, Texas Southern, F

PHILADELPHIA
1. Budde, Ed, T, Michigan State
2. Mansfield, Ray, T, Washington
3. Crossan, Dave, G-C, Maryland
   Guy, Louis, B, Mississippi, from Detroit
4. Choice to San Francisco
5. Choice to LA Rams
6. Choice to Cleveland
7. Caffey, Lee Roy, B-LB, Texas A&M
8. Woodeshick, Tom, B, West Virginia
   Sykes, Gene, B, LSU, from Washington
9. Ward, Dennis, T, Oklahoma
10. Liske, Pete, B, Penn State, F
11. Heck, Ralph, LB, Colorado
12. Gill, Roger, B, Texas Tech, F
13. Iacone, Joe, B, West Chester
14. Ramsey, Nate, B, Indiana
15. Heard, George, E, New Mexico
16. Goodwin, Ronnie, B, Baylor
17. Rush, Gordon, B, Tulane
18. Mathews, Rudy, T, TCU
19. Wasdovich, Mike, G, Indiana
20. Rizzo, Ben, B, Miami

PITTSBURGH
1. Choice to Chi. Bears
2. Choice to Baltimore
3. Choice to Green Bay
4. Choice to Chi. Bears
5. Choice to LA Rams
6. Choice to Chi. Bears
7. Choice to Green Bay
8. Atkinson, Frank, T, Stanford
9. Carrington, Gene, T, Boston College
10. Nelsen, Bill, B, USC
11. Dixon, Hewritt, B, Florida A&M
12. Curry, Roy, B, Jackson State, F
13. Gray, Harold, LB, Cal State-Los Angeles
14. Dickerson, Robert, E, Bethune-Cookman
15. Szykowny, Matt, B, Iowa
16. Russell, Andy, B, Missouri
17. Stein, Tim, C, Miami (Ohio), F
18. Bradshaw, Jim, B, Tennessee-Chattanooga
19. Berg, Roger, T, St. Thomas (Minnesota)
20. Traficant, Jim, B, Pittsburgh

ST. LOUIS
1. Stovall, Jerry, B, LSU
   Brumm, Don, DE, Purdue, from NY Giants
2. Reynolds, Bob, T, Bowling Green
3. Brabham, Danny, DE, Arkansas
   Fracchia, Mike, B, Alabama, from Baltimore, F
4. Estes, Don, T, LSU
5. Thornton, Bill (Thunder), B, Nebraska
6. Paremore, Bob, B, Florida A&M
7. Moss, Jim, T, South Carolina
8. Cook, Jim, G, Oklahoma
9. Crenshaw, Willis, B, Kansas State, F
10. Smith, Jackie, E, Northwestern State (Louisiana)
11. Burson, Jim, B, Auburn
12. Walker, Chuck, G, Duke, F
13. Zyskowski, Alex, B, Wichita State
14. Lea, Paul, B, Oklahoma
15. Scrutchins, Ed, E, Toledo
16. Slafkosky, John, T, Notre Dame
17. Meggyesy, Dave, LB, Syracuse
18. Stallings, Larry, T, Georgia Tech
19. Haney, Darnell, T, Utah State
20. Clay, Bill, E, Arkansas, F

SAN FRANCISCO
1. Alexander, Kermit, B, UCLA
2. Rock, Walter, G, Maryland
3. Lisbon, Don, B, Bowling Green
4. Rosdahl, Harrison, G, Penn State, from Philadelphia, F
   Choice to Chi. Bears
   Campbell, Hugh, E, Washington State, from Washington
5. Burke, Vern, E, Oregon State, F
   Pilot, Jim (Preacher), B, New Mexico State, from Pittsburgh, F
   Moeller, Gary, G-LB, Ohio State, from Chi. Bears
6. Emerick, Pat, G, Western Michigan
7. DeCourley, Ernest, T, Moorhead State
8. Locke, Roger, E, Arizona State, F
9. Maczuzak, John, T, Pittsburgh, F
10. Lopour, Dick, B, Huron
11. Shafer, Steve, B, Utah State
12. Benton, Bob, T, Mississippi State
13. Schultz, Dick, T, Ohio
14. Tobin, Bill, B, Missouri
15. Ross, Oliver, B, West Texas State, F
16. Bogdalek, Jim, T, Toledo
17. Reed, Ken, G, Tulsa
18. Sellers, John, T, Bakersfield J.C., F
19. Price, Bob, G, North Texas State
20. Davis, Don, B, McMurry

WASHINGTON
1. Richter, Pat, E, Wisconsin
2. Sanders, Lonnie, B, Michigan State
3. Snidow, Ron, T, Oregon
4. Choice to San Francisco
5. Choice to Green Bay
6. Nickoson, Charley, T, Ohio U.
7. Francis, Dave, B, Ohio State
8. Choice to Philadelphia
9. Joe, Billy, B, Villanova
10. Foster, Rod, G, Ohio State
11. Schau, Allen, E, Western Michigan
12. Caldwell, Bob, C, Georgia Tech
13. Greiner, John, E, Purdue
14. Winingder, Tom, B, Georgia Tech
15. Butsko, Harry, LB, Maryland
16. Adams, Dave, G, Arkansas, F
17. Whaley, Ron, DHB, Tennessee-Chattanooga, F
18. Roberts, Drew, E, Cal State-Humboldt
19. Turner, Jim, QB, Utah State
20. Baughan, Joe, T, Auburn

1963 AFL

Held December 1, 1962

Although the two franchises played the 1963 season as the Kansas City Chiefs and the New York Jets, at the time of the draft they still were known as the Dallas Texans and the New York Titans, respectively.

Boston became the only franchise ever to select the same player twice in the same draft. In the thirteenth round, the Patriots chose Dave Adams of Arkansas as a future, but the selection was voided because future picks couldn't be made until the fourteenth round. The Patriots again chose Adams in the twenty-seventh round, when he was eligible as a future pick.

BOSTON
1. Graham, Art, E, Boston College
2. Jordan, Lee Roy, C, Alabama
3. Vogel, Bob, T, Ohio State
4. Reynolds, Bob, T, Bowling Green
5. Cioci, Lou, G, Boston College
6. Silas, Sam, T, Southern Illinois
7. Williamson, Dick, E, Alabama
8. Foster, Rod, G, Ohio State
9. Simon, Jim, E, Miami
10. McKinnon, Don, C, Dartmouth
11. Hayes, Dave, FB, Penn State, from Houston
    Watson, Dave, G, Georgia Tech
12. Gambrell, Billy, HB, South Carolina, from Buffalo
    Gauntner, Tim, HB, John Carroll
13. Adams, Dave, T, Arkansas, F*
    Ferrissi, Ralph, FB, Southern Connecticut State
14. Hall, Whaley, T, Mississippi, F
15. Dentel, Bob, C, Miami
16. Bryant, Wes, T, Arkansas*
17. Neumann, Tom, HB, Michigan
18. O'Brien, Dave, T, Boston College
19. McCarthy, Pat, QB, Holy Cross
20. Bradshaw, Jim, HB, Tennessee-Chattanooga
21. Sherman, Gary, B, Bowling Green
22. Craddock, Nate, FB, Parsons
23. Snyder, Al, HB, Holy Cross
24. Schultz, Dick, T, Ohio U.
25. Gaubatz, Dennis, G, LSU
26. Tullis, Jim, HB, Florida A&M, F
27. Adams, Dave, T, Arkansas, F
28. Whaley, Ron, HB, Tennessee-Chattanooga, F
29. Kelly, Dick, G, Georgia, F

BUFFALO
1. Behrman, Dave, C, Michigan State
2. Dunaway, Jim, T, Mississippi, from Oakland
   Hutchinson, Tom, E, Kentucky
3. Brown, Tom, HB, Maryland
4. Woodeshick, Tom, HB, West Virginia
5. Jencks, Bob, E, Miami (Ohio)
6. Saimes, George, FB, Michigan State, from Dallas Texans
   Moss, Jim, LB, South Carolina
7. Kanicki, Jim, T, Michigan State
8. Choice to Denver
9. Stallings, Larry, LB, Georgia Tech
10. Snidow, Ron, T, Oregon
11. Infante, Lindy, HB, Florida, from NY Jets
    Choice to Houston
12. Choice to Boston
13. Choice to Boston
14. Simmons, J.B., E, Tulsa, F
15. Underhill, Paul, FB, Missouri, F
16. Hoerster, Ed, LB, Notre Dame
17. Slabaugh, Jeff, T, Indiana
18. Paterra, Herb, LB, Michigan State
19. Sykes, Gene, E, LSU
20. Fullwood, Harlow, T, Virginia
21. Adamchak, Ed, T, Pittsburgh, F
22. Walker, Chuck, T, Duke, F
23. Middleton, Bob, E, Ohio State
24. Lamonica, Daryle, QB, Notre Dame
25. Carlson, Ron, E, Wisconsin
26. Crenshaw, Willis, FB, Nebraska, F
27. Quast, Dick, G, Memphis State, F
28. Mavity, Leon, HB, Colorado, F
29. Killett, Charlie, HB, Memphis State, F

DALLAS TEXANS
1. Buchanan, Buck, T, Grambling, from Oakland
   Budde, Ed, T, Michigan State
2. Rock, Walter, T, Maryland
3. Brumm, Don, T, Purdue
4. Sanders, Daryl, G, Ohio State
5. Campbell, John, E, Minnesota
6. Choice to Buffalo
7. Bell, Bobby, T, Minnesota
8. Sklopan, John, HB, Southern Mississippi
9. Barrett, Jan, E, Fresno State
10. Farrier, Curt, T, Montana State
11. Goodwin, Ronnie, HB, Baylor, from Oakland
    Wilson, Jerrel, FB, Southern Mississippi
12. Choice to NY Titans
13. Choice to Houston
14. Johnson, Stone, HB, Grambling, from Oakland
    Pilot, Jim (Preacher), HB, New Mexico State, F
15. Auer, Joe, HB, Georgia Tech, F
16. Profit, Mel, E, UCLA, F
17. Moore, Billy, QB, Arkansas
18. Freeman, Bill, T, Southern Mississippi, F
19. Choice to Denver
20. Vaught, Lowell, T, Southwestern Louisiana, F
21. Borghetti, Ernie, T, Pittsburgh, F
22. Maczuzak, John, T, Pittsburgh, F
23. Yaksick, Bob, HB, Rutgers
24. Hill, Dave, T, Auburn
25. Hughes, John, G, SMU, F
26. Todd, Turnley, C, Virginia, F
27. Clay, Billy, E, Arkansas, F
28. Scarborough, Gordon, E, East Texas State, F
29. Sisk, John, HB, Miami, F

DENVER
1. Alexander, Kermit, HB, UCLA
2. Poage, Ray, FB, Texas, from NY Jets
   Nomina, Tom, T, Miami (Ohio)
3. Janik, Tom, HB, Texas A&I
4. Slaby, Lou, LB, Pittsburgh
5. Mansfield, Ray, C, Washington
6. Peters, Anton, T, Florida

7. Slaughter, Mickey, QB, Louisiana Tech, from San Diego
Flatley, Paul, E, Northwestern
8. Dixon, Hewritt, FB, Florida A&M, from Buffalo
Griffin, John, HB, Memphis State
9. Fleming, Marv, E, Utah
10. Sanders, Lonnie, HB, Michigan State
Richter, Pat, E, Wisconsin, from Houston
11. Joe, Billy, FB, Villanova
12. Gamble, John, E, Pacific
13. Maples, Jimmy, C, Baylor
14. Choice to San Diego
15. Freeman, Winston, E, North Texas State
16. Crossan, Dave, G, Maryland
17. Paremore, Bob, HB, Florida A&M
18. Mitchell, Charley, HB, Washington
19. Baker, Frank, FB, Toledo
Starling, Bruce, HB, Florida, from Dallas Texans
20. Grimm, Dan, G, Colorado
21. Nolan, Ross, E, Northeast Louisiana
22. Mathiesen, Dave, QB, Washington State, F
23. Mooty, Billy, HB, Arkansas
24. Simons, C.B., LB, Stanford
25. Farmer, Forest, LB, Purdue
26. Day, Monte, T, Fresno State, F
27. Sellers, John, T, Bakersfield J.C., F
28. Reddell, Bill, HB, Occidental, F
29. Carson, Kern, HB, San Diego State, F

HOUSTON
1. Brabham, Danny, FB, Arkansas
2. Estes, Don, T, LSU
3. Cook, Jerry, HB, Texas
4. Caffey, Lee Roy, FB, Texas A&M, from Oakland
Hopkins, Jerry, C, Texas A&M
5. Jones, Homer, HB, Texas Southern, from Oakland
Chuy, Don, T, Clemson
6. Aldridge, Lionel, T, Utah State
7. Baker, John, E, Mississippi State
8. Burson, Jim, HB, Auburn
9. Burke, Ed, T, Notre Dame
10. Choice to Denver
11. Brown, Tom, G, Pittsburgh, from Buffalo
Choice to Boston
12. Choice to Oakland
13. Choice to Oakland
Ward, Dennis, G, Oklahoma, from Dallas Texans
14. Trull, Don, QB, Baylor, F
15. Looney, Joe Don, HB, Oklahoma*
16. Benson, Rex, T, Miami, F
17. Griffin, Jerry, E, Louisiana Tech
18. Lea, Paul, HB, Oklahoma
19. Hoover, Bob, HB, Florida
20. Lee, Wayne, C, Oklahoma
21. Faulkner, Staley, T, Texas, F
22. Byer, Sam, FB, Texas A&M
23. Raesz, Gene, E, Rice
24. Burton, Bob, T, Grambling
25. Kaltenbach, Gary, T, Pittsburgh
26. Thiesen, Dave, HB, Nebraska, F
27. Hildebrand, Al, T, Stanford, F
28. Stein, Tim, C, Miami (Ohio), F
29. Ross, Oliver, T, West Texas State, F

NY TITANS
1. Stovall, Jerry, HB, LSU
2. Choice to Denver
3. Richardson, Willie, E, Jackson State
4. Contoulis, John, T, Connecticut
5. Mackey, John, E, Syracuse
6. Price, Jim, LB, Auburn
7. Guy, Lou, HB, Mississippi
8. King, Bill, QB, Dartmouth
9. Sanders, Stan, E, Whittier
10. Liscio, Tony, T, Tulsa
11. Choice to Buffalo
12. Craver, Joe, LB, North Carolina
Lucas, Tommy, E, Texas, from Dallas Texans
13. Hill, Olin, T, Furman
14. Choice to San Diego
15. Liske, Pete, QB, Penn State, F
16. Ryder, Nick, HB, Miami
17. Johnson, Charley, G, Villanova
18. Munsey, Bill, HB, Minnesota
19. Kroner, Gary, HB, Wisconsin
20. Johnson, John, T, Indiana
21. VanderKelen, Ron, QB, Wisconsin
22. Thornton, Bill (Thunder), FB, Nebraska
23. Rettino, Lou, FB, Villanova
24. Caylor, Lowell, HB, Miami (Ohio)
25. Baughan, Joe, T, Auburn
26. Monaghan, Terry, T, Penn State, F
27. Herman, Dave, G, Michigan State, F
28. Taliaferro, Mike, QB, Illinois, F
29. Wicker, Paul, T, Fresno State, F

OAKLAND
1. Choice to Dallas Texans
2. Choice to Buffalo
3. Choice to San Diego
4. Choice to Houston
5. Choice to Houston
6. Wilson, Butch, HB, Alabama
7. Costa, Dave, T, Utah
8. Locke, Roger, E, Arizona State
9. Logan, Jerry, HB, West Texas State
10. Schoenke, Ray, G, SMU
11. Choice to Dallas Texans
12. Burdin, Walt, LB, McNeese State
Branson, Doyle, HB, Southern Oregon, from Houston
13. Haney, Darnel, E, Utah State
Roberts, Drew, E, Cal State-Humboldt, from Houston
14. Choice to Dallas Texans
15. Burke, Vern, E, Oregon, F
16. Moss, Jim, HB, West Virginia
17. Murio, John, HB, Whitworth
18. Dillon, Terry, HB, Montana
Hogan, George, G, Texas A&M, from San Diego
19. Fiorentino, Tony, G, UCLA
20. Mirich, Rex, T, Arizona State, F
21. Petties, Neal, HB, San Diego State, F
22. Campbell, Hugh, E, Washington State
23. Anabo, Jon, QB, Fresno State
24. Peters, Dick, T, Whittier
25. McFarland, Bill, FB, Oklahoma State
26. Claridge, Dennis, QB, Nebraska, F
27. Skelly, Dick, HB, Florida, F
28. Campbell, Larry, FB, Utah State, F
29. Anderson, Dick, E, Penn State, F

SAN DIEGO
1. Sweeney, Walt, E, Syracuse
2. Guthrie, Rufus, G, Georgia Tech
3. Kinderman, Keith, HB, Florida State
Robinson, Dave, E, Penn State, from Oakland
4. Williams, Roy, T, Pacific
5. Glueck, Larry, HB, Villanova
6. Emerick, Pat, LB, Western Michigan
7. Choice to Denver
8. Heeter, Gene, E, West Virginia
9. Barnett, Steve, T, Oregon
10. Scott, Don, T, Tampa
11. Petrich, Bob, T, West Texas State
12. Baker, Terry, QB, Oregon State
13. Walton, Dick, G, Iowa State
14. Lasky, Frank, T, Florida, F
Rosdahl, Harrison, G, Penn State, from NY Jets, F
Cverko, Jack, G, Northwestern, from Denver, F
15. Fracchia, Mike, HB, Alabama, F
16. Breen, Gene, LB, Virginia Tech, F
17. Drummond, Dick, HB, George Washington, F
18. Choice to Oakland
19. Park, Ernie, T, McMurry
20. Soefker, Buddy, LB, LSU, F
21. Points, Dan, T, Cincinnati, F
22. Gill, Roger, HB, Texas Tech, F
23. Watters, Paul, T, Miami (Ohio), F
24. Frank, Bill, T, Colorado
25. Mazzanti, Jerry, T, Arkansas
26. Dill, Ken, C, Mississippi, F
27. Butsko, Harry, G, Maryland, F
28. Berzansky, Steve, FB, West Virginia, F
29. Hamp, Herman, HB, Fresno State, F

1964 NFL
Held December 2, 1963

BALTIMORE
1. Woodson, Marv, HB, Indiana
2. Lorick, Tony, HB, Arizona State
3. Choice to Green Bay
4. Davis, Ted, E-LB, Georgia Tech
5. Lothamer, Ed, T, Michigan State
6. Mazurek, Jim, T, Syracuse
7. Sugarman, Ken, T, Whitworth
8. Williamson, John, LB, Louisiana Tech
9. Turner, Vince, B, Missouri
10. Choice to Detroit
11. Paglio, John, T, Syracuse
12. Graham, Kenny, HB, Washington State
13. Parker, Charlie, T, Southern Mississippi
14. Case, John, E, Clemson
15. Kramer, Larry, T, Nebraska, F
16. Lopes, Roger, FB, Michigan State
17. Green, Don, HB, Susquehanna
18. Haymond, Alvin, HB, Southern
19. Dejanovich, Owen, T, Northern Arizona
20. Butler, John, FB, San Diego State, F

CHI. BEARS
1. Evey, Dick, T, Tennessee
2. Choice to Pittsburgh
Martin, Billy, E, Georgia Tech, from LA Rams
Crain, Pat, HB, Clemson, from Pittsburgh, F
3. Blanks, Sid, HB, Texas A&I
4. Budka, Frank, HB, Notre Dame
Reilly, Mike, LB, Iowa, from Minnesota
5. Conners, Dan, T, Miami
6. Jones, Jimmy, E, Wisconsin, F
7. Logan, Chuck, E, Northwestern
8. Rakestraw, Larry, QB, Georgia
9. Wilkinson, Jay, HB, Duke
10. Brown, Mike, B, Delaware
11. Leeuwenberg, Dick, T, Stanford, F
12. Horton, Bob, FB, Boston U.
13. Webb, Cloyd, E, Iowa
14. Francisco, Kent, T, UCLA, F
15. Burman, George, T, Northwestern
16. Butler, Roderick, HB, Eastern Illinois
17. Kasapis, Constantinos, T, Iowa
18. Batts, Bob, HB, Texas Southern
19. Whitehead, Jim, T, Georgia, F
20. Niglio, Dick, FB, Yale, F

CLEVELAND
1. Warfield, Paul, HB, Ohio State
2. Truax, Billy, DE, LSU
3. Choice to LA Rams
4. Shackelford, Don, T, Pacific
5. Klein, Dick, T, Wichita State, F
6. Choice to Dallas
7. Odom, Sammy, LB, Northwestern State (Louisiana)
8. Kelly, Leroy, HB, Morgan State
9. Briscoe, John, LB, Arizona, F
10. Van Raaphorst, Dick, K, Ohio State
Robinson, Bobby, G, Mississippi, from Pittsburgh, F
11. Versprille, Eddie, FB, Alabama
12. Mitchell, Ed, T, Southern, F
13. Meehan, Bob, G, Syracuse
14. Sieg, Terry, HB, Virginia, F
15. Houtman, John, T, Michigan
16. Williams, Sid, E, Southern
17. Bartolameolli, Larry, T, Western Michigan, F
18. Lewis, Sherman, HB, Michigan State
19. Higgins, Jim, G, Xavier
20. Archer, Dave, T, Syracuse, F

DALLAS
1. Appleton, Scott, T, Texas
2. Renfro, Mel, B, Oregon
3. Choice to LA Rams
4. Dunn, Perry Lee, QB, Mississippi
5. Choice to Green Bay
6. Lothridge, Billy, QB, Georgia Tech
Curry, Jim, E, Cincinnati, from Cleveland
Evans, Jim, E, Texas-El Paso, from Green Bay
7. Hayes, Bob, HB, Florida A&M, F
8. Geverink, Al, HB, UCLA
9. Kupp, Jake, E, Washington
10. Staubach, Roger, QB, Navy, F
11. Crenshaw, Bob, G, Baylor
12. Norman, Johnny, E, Northwestern State (Louisiana)
13. Rhome, Jerry, QB, Tulsa, F
14. Worden, Jim, LB, Wittenberg
15. Van Burkleo, Bill, B, Tulsa, F
16. Cercel, Paul, C, Pittsburgh, F
17. Abell, Bud, E, Missouri, F
18. Viltz, Theo, DB, USC, F*
19. Murphy, H.D., B, Oregon
20. Hughes, John, LB, SMU

DETROIT
1. Beathard, Pete, QB, USC
2. Snorton, Matt, E, Michigan State
3. Philbin, Gerry, T, Buffalo
Batten, Pat, HB, Hardin-Simmons, from Philadelphia
4. Hilgenberg, Wally, G, Iowa
5. Nelson, Benny, HB, Alabama
6. Hilton, John, E, Richmond, F
7. Parcells, Bill, T, Wichita State
8. Choice to St. Louis
9. Rasmussen, Wayne, HB, South Dakota State
10. Hand, Larry, T, Appalachian State, F
Holton, Glenn, HB, West Virginia, from Baltimore
11. Hyne, Don, T, Baldwin-Wallace
12. Wells, Warren, E, Texas Southern
13. Miller, John, T, Idaho State
14. Bickle, Doug, E, Hillsdale, F
15. LaLonde, Roger, T, Muskingum
16. Robinson, Allan, HB, BYU, F
17. Provenzano, Joe, T, Kansas State
18. Langley, Willis, T, LSU
19. Zellmer, Bruce, HB, Winona State
20. Barilla, Steve, T, Wichita State

GREEN BAY
1. Voss, Lloyd, T, Nebraska
2. Morris, Jon, C, Holy Cross
3. Crutcher, Tommy, B, TCU
Burrell, Ode, B, Mississippi State, from Baltimore
O'Donnell, Joe, G, Michigan, from NY Giants
4. Costa, Paul, B, Notre Dame, F
Long, Bob, E, Wichita State, from Philadelphia
5. Wright, Steve, T, Alabama
Carlisle, Duke, B, Texas, from Dallas
6. Choice to Dallas
7. Herzing, Dick, T, Drake, F
8. Bowman, Ken, C, Wisconsin
9. McDowell, John, T, St. John's (Minnesota)
10. Jacobs, Allen, B, Utah, F
11. Petersen, Jack, T, Nebraska-Omaha
12. Bean, Dwain, B, North Texas State
13. Mauro, Jack, T, Northern Michigan
14. O'Grady, Tom, E, Northwestern
15. Zenko, Alex, T, Kent State, F
16. Ireland, Andrew, B, Utah, F
17. St. Jean, Len, E, Northern Michigan
18. Hicks, Mike, G, Marshall
19. Baker, John, E, Virginia Union
20. Curry, Bill, C, Georgia Tech, F

LA RAMS
1. Munson, Bill, QB, Utah State
2. Choice to Chi. Bears
3. Richardson, Jerry, B, West Texas State
Mims, John, T, Rice, from Washington
Brown, Willie, B, USC, from Dallas
Pillath, Roger, T, Wisconsin, from Cleveland
4. Choice to NY Giants
5. Henson, Ken, C, TCU, F
6. Johnson, Herman, HB, Michigan State, F
7. Varnell, John, T, West Texas State
8. Pope, Bucky, E, Catawba
9. Burton, Jerry, B, Northwestern State (Louisiana)
10. Larsen, Gary, T, Concordia (Minnesota)
Smith, Ron, QB, Richmond, from Minnesota, F
11. Farris, John, T, San Diego State, F
12. Dawson, Bill, E, Florida State, F
13. Harris, Marvin, C, Stanford
14. Garrett, John, LB, Oklahoma, F
15. Mayne, Mike, E, Idaho, F
16. Zera, Phil, B, St. Joseph's (Indiana), F
17. Galmin, Jim, E, Tampa
18. Smith, Tom, G, Villanova, F
19. Cherry, Bob, E, Wittenberg
20. Hohn, Bob, HB, Nebraska, F

MINNESOTA
1. Eller, Carl, T, Minnesota
2. Bedsole, Hal, E, USC
3. Rose, George, HB, Auburn
4. Choice to Chi. Bears
Keating, Tom, T, Michigan, from NY Giants
5. Kirby, John, LB, Nebraska
6. Lacey, Bob, E, North Carolina
7. Bryant, Wes, T, Arkansas
8. McWatters, Bill, FB, North Texas State
9. Lester, Darrell, FB, McNeese State
10. Choice to LA Rams
11. Estes, H.O., G, East Central (Oklahoma)
12. Sands, Sandy, E, Texas, F
13. Vollmer, Russ, HB, Memphis State
14. Michel, Tom, HB, East Carolina
15. Kiffin, Monte, T, Nebraska
16. Oats, Carlton, E, Florida A&M, F
17. McClurg, Jerry, E, Colorado, F
18. Robinson, Carl, T, Prairie View A&M

19. Schott, Dick, E, Louisville, F
20. Sunde, Milt, T, Minnesota

NY GIANTS
1. Looney, Joe Don, B, Oklahoma
2. Thurlow, Steve, HB, Stanford
3. Choice to Green Bay
4. Choice to Minnesota
   Snell, Matt, FB, Ohio State, from LA Rams
   Seals, George, E, Missouri, from St. Louis
5. DiMidio, Tony, T, West Chester
6. Schichtle, Henry, QB, Wichita State
7. Anderson, Roger, T, Virginia Union
8. Wood, Gary, B, Cornell
   Popp, Ray, G, Pittsburgh, from Philadelphia, F
9. Bitsko, Mickey, LB, Dayton, F
10. Moran, Jim, T, Idaho
11. Condren, Glen, T, Oklahoma, F
12. McNaughton, Jim, E, Utah State
13. Deibert, John, T, Penn State, F
14. Harris, Bill, HB, Colorado
15. Hinton, Chuck, G, Mississippi, F
16. Lembright, Wynn, T, Toledo
17. Humenik, Dave, T, Notre Dame, F
18. Garrett, Jim, HB, Grambling
19. Kinard, Frank, HB, Mississippi, F
20. Gibbons, Tony, T, John Carroll

PHILADELPHIA
1. Brown, Bob, G, Nebraska
2. Concannon, Jack, QB, Boston College
3. Choice to Detroit
4. Choice to Green Bay
   Kubala, Ray, C, Texas A&M, from Washington
5. Babb, Mickey, E-LB, Georgia
6. Denson, Al, E, Florida A&M
7. Goimarac, Pete, C, West Virginia
8. Choice to NY Giants
9. Smith, Larry, B, Mississippi
10. Boris, Tom, B, Purdue
11. Berry, Bob, B, Oregon, F
12. Sapinsky, John, T, William & Mary
13. Kindig, Howard, C, Cal State-Los Angeles, F
14. Arizzi, Ernie, B, Maryland
15. Burrows, Bob, T, East Texas State, F
16. Radosevich, Will, T, Wyoming, F
17. Morgan, Mike, E, LSU
18. Lang, Izzy, B, Tennessee State, F
19. Bowe, Dick, T, Rice, F
20. Lucas, Tommy, G, Mississippi, F

PITTSBURGH
1. Martha, Paul, HB, Pittsburgh
2. Choice to Chi. Bears
   Kelly, Jim, E, Notre Dame, from Chi. Bears
3. Baker, Ralph, LB, Penn State
4. McGee, Ben, T, Jackson State
5. Alley, T.W., T, William & Mary
6. Gibson, Tom, G, South Carolina
7. Smith, Bobby, HB, North Texas State
8. Currington, Bobby, HB, North Carolina Central
9. Nichols, Bob, T, Stanford, F
10. Choice to Cleveland
11. Soleau, Bob, G, William & Mary
12. Sherman, Bob, HB, Iowa
13. Baker, Glenn, T, Washington State
14. Jenkins, Tom, G, Ohio State
15. Brown, Barry, E, Florida, F
16. Kesler, Ed, FB, North Carolina, F
17. Shaw, Dennis, C, Detroit
18. Dobbins, Oliver, HB, Morgan State
19. Marshall, Don, T, Lehigh
20. Generalovich, Bryan, E, Pittsburgh, F

ST. LOUIS
1. Kortas, Ken, T, Louisville
2. Turner, Herschel, G, Kentucky
3. Prudhomme, Remi, T, LSU, F
4. Choice to NY Giants
5. Brooks, Charley, E, Memphis State, F
6. Bowman, Dick, E, Syracuse
7. Lamb, Jerry, E, Arkansas, F
8. Johnson, Bob, E, Wisconsin
   Bednar, George, G, Notre Dame, from Detroit
9. Ross, Willie, B, Nebraska
10. Lawrence, Tony, T, Bowling Green, F
11. Hard, Richard, T, Wenatchee Valley J.C.
12. Sortun, Rick, G, Washington
13. Adams, Jake, E, Virginia Tech
14. Slaby, Len, C, Syracuse
15. Stallings, Cliff, B, New Mexico
16. Ankerson, Jack, QB, Ripon
17. Evans, John, T, Memphis State, F
18. Hoover, Dave, B, Iowa State
19. Young, Dick, T, Howard Payne, F
20. Kubinski, Ralph, G, Missouri

SAN FRANCISCO
1. Parks, Dave, E, Texas Tech
2. Mira, George, QB, Miami
3. Wilcox, Dave, DE, Oregon
4. Wilson, Jim, G, Georgia, F
5. Johnson, Rudy, B, Nebraska
6. Lewis, Gary, B, Arizona State
7. Clarke, Hagood, B, Florida
8. Daugherty, Bob, B, Tulsa, F
   Poole, Bob, E, Clemson, from Washington
9. Mudd, Howard, G, Hillsdale
10. Polser, Fred, T, East Texas State, F
11. Almquist, Dennis, G, Idaho
12. Long, Jim, B, Fresno State, F
13. Brown, Bob, T, Arkansas A&M
14. Beard, Ed, T, Tennessee
15. Griffin, Jim, E, Grambling
16. Gordon, Cornell, B, North Carolina A&T, F
17. Brusven, Ken, T, Oregon State, F
18. Cole, Jerry, E, Southwest Texas State, F
19. Rawson, Larry, B, Auburn
20. Baker, Gene, G, Whitworth

WASHINGTON
1. Taylor, Charley, HB, Arizona State
2. Krause, Paul, B, Iowa
3. Choice to LA Rams
4. Choice to Philadelphia
5. Snowden, Jim, FB, Notre Dame, F
6. Brown, Russ, E, Florida
7. Shiner, Dick, QB, Maryland
8. Choice to San Francisco
9. Hauss, Len, C, Georgia
10. Leeson, Rick, B, Pittsburgh
11. Donaldson, Gene, LB, Purdue
12. Zvolerin, Bob, T, Tennessee
13. MacDonald, Tom, B, Notre Dame
14. Urbanik, Tom, B, Penn State, F
15. Evers, Dick, T, Colorado State, F
16. Walters, Tommy, B, Southern Mississippi
17. Clay, Ozzie, B, Iowa State
18. Jones, Bob, G, Nebraska
19. Seedborg, John, G, Arizona State
20. Guest, Gordon, B, Arkansas, F

1964 AFL

Held November 30, 1963

BOSTON
1. Concannon, Jack, QB, Boston College
2. Kelly, Jim, E, Notre Dame
3. Choice to Denver
4. Morris, Jon, E, Holy Cross
5. Choice to San Diego
6. Mazurek, Jim, G, Syracuse
7. Alley, T.W., T, William & Mary
8. Garrett, J.D., HB, Grambling, from Buffalo
   LaLonde, Roger, T, Muskingum
9. St. Jean, Len, E, Northern Michigan
10. Choice to Buffalo
11. Barrett, John, HB, Boston College
12. Choice to Boston through Kansas City
13. Scarpati, Joe, DB, North Carolina State
14. Wilson, Jim, T, Georgia, F
15. Gibbons, Tony, T, John Carroll
16. Pedro, Pete, HB, West Texas State
17. Wood, Gary, QB-HB, Cornell
18. Tiller, Joe, T, Montana State
19. Dawson, Bill, E, Florida State, F
20. Farmer, Lonnie, LB, Tennessee-Chattanooga
21. Lawrence, Tony, T, Bowling Green, F
22. Archer, Dave, T, Syracuse, F
23. Humenik, Dave, T, Notre Dame, F
24. Bartolameoli, Larry, T, Western Michigan, F
25. Generalovich, Bryan, E, Pittsburgh, F
26. Niglio, Dick, HB, Yale, F

BUFFALO
1. Eller, Carl, T, Minnesota
2. Evey, Dick, DE, Tennessee
3. Rose, George, DB, Auburn
4. Byrd, George (Butch), HB, Boston U., from Denver
   Warfield, Paul, HB, Ohio State
5. Keating, Tom, T, Michigan, from Kansas City
   Reilly, Mike, LB, Iowa
6. Choice to Kansas City
7. Pillath, Roger, T, Wisconsin
8. Choice to Boston
9. Martha, Paul, HB, Pittsburgh
10. Simpson, Howard, E, Auburn
    Lattimer, Earl, FB-LB, Michigan State, from Boston
11. Smith, Bobby, HB, North Texas State, from Denver
    Webb, Cloyd, E, Iowa
12. Ross, Willie, HB, Nebraska
    Gogolak, Pete, K, Cornell, from Boston through Kansas City
13. O'Donnell, Joe, G-LB, Michigan
14. Prudhomme, Remi, T, LSU, F
15. Simpson, Bill, T, Baylor, F
16. Hilton, John, E, Richmond, F
17. Kramer, Larry, T, Nebraska, F
18. Clarke, Hagood, HB, Florida
19. Montgomery, Don, E, North Carolina State
20. Dugan, Bob, T, Mississippi State
21. Deibert, John, T, Penn State, F
22. Briscoe, John, LB, Arizona, F
23. Evans, John, T, Memphis State, F
24. Schott, Dick, T, Louisville, F
25. Urbanik, Tom, DB, Penn State, F
26. Jacobs, Allen, FB, Utah, F

DENVER
1. Brown, Bob, T, Nebraska
2. Choice to Houston
3. Woodson, Marv, DB, Indiana
   Snorton, Matt, E, Michigan State, from Boston
4. Choice to Buffalo
5. Choice to Houston
6. Shackleford, Don, T, Pacific
   Denson, Al, FL, Florida A&M, from Oakland
7. Kubala, Ray, C-T, Texas A&M
   Richardson, Jerry, LB, West Texas State, from Houston
8. Hilgenberg, Wally, G-LB, Iowa
9. Mims, John, T, Rice
10. Choice to San Diego through Kansas City
11. Choice to Buffalo
12. Krause, Paul, DB, Iowa
13. Parker, Charlie, G, Southern Mississippi
14. Hayes, Bob, HB, Florida A&M, F
15. Logan, Chuck, E, Northwestern
16. Cherry, Bob, E, Wittenburg
17. McNaughton, Jim, E, Utah State
18. Mira, George, QB, Miami
19. Barry, Odell, FL, Findlay
20. Choice to Kansas City
21. Herzing, Dick, T, Drake, F
22. Lewis, Gary, HB, Arizona State, F
23. Brusvan, Ken, T, Oregon State, F
24. Bitsko, Mickey, LB, Dayton, F
25. Jones, Jim, E, Wisconsin, F
26. Berry, Bob, QB, Oregon, F

HOUSTON
1. Appleton, Scott, T, Texas
2. Taylor, Charley, HB, Arizona State, from Denver
   Truax, Billy, DE, LSU
3. Crenshaw, Bobby, T, Baylor
4. Burrell, Ode, HB, Mississippi State
5. Varnell, John, T, West Texas State, from Denver
   Blanks, Sid, HB, Texas A&I
6. Wilcox, Dave, G, Oregon
7. Choice to Denver
8. Seals, Ezell, HB, Prairie View A&M
9. Burton, Jerry, HB, Northwestern State (Louisiana)
10. Odom, Sammy, LB, Northwestern State (Louisiana)
11. Dejanovich, Owen, G, Northern Arizona
12. Nelson, Benny, DB, Alabama
13. Choice to Kansas City
14. Henson, Ken, C, TCU, F
15. Crain, Pat, FB, Clemson, F
16. Munson, Bill, QB, Utah State
17. Leeuwenburg, Dick, T, Stanford, F
18. Nichols, Bob, T, Stanford, F
19. Robinson, Carl, T, Prairie View A&M
20. Jaquess, Pete, HB, Eastern New Mexico
21. Cole, Jerry, HB, Southwest Texas State, F
22. Kessler, Ed, FB, North Carolina, F
23. Whitehead, Jim, T, Georgia, F
24. Garrett, John, LB, Oklahoma, F
25. Bowe, Dick, T, Rice, F
26. Zenko, Alex, T, Kent State, F

KANSAS CITY
1. Beathard, Pete, QB, USC
2. Martin, Billy, E, Georgia Tech
3. Kortas, Ken, T, Louisville
4. Lothamer, Ed, T, Michigan State
5. Choice to Buffalo
6. Carlisle, Duke, DB, Texas
   Looney, Joe Don, HB, Oklahoma, from Buffalo
7. Simon, John, E, Notre Dame
8. Bedsole, Hal, E, USC
9. DiMidio, Tony, T, West Chester
10. Stephens, Clay, E, Notre Dame
11. Crutcher, Tommy, LB, TCU
12. Adams, Jack, E, Virginia Tech
13. Hudson, Orville, E, East Texas State
    Wilkinson, Jay, HB, Duke, from Houston
14. Costa, Paul, HB, Notre Dame, F
15. Snowden, Jim, FB, Notre Dame, F
16. Staubach, Roger, QB, Navy, F
17. Peterson, Jack, T, Nebraska-Omaha
18. Knoll, Jerry, T, Washington, F
19. Lamb, Jerry, E, Arkansas, F
20. Sands, Sandy, E, Texas, from Denver, F
    Hohn, Bob, HB, Nebraska, F
21. Burrows, Bob, T, East Texas State, F
22. Evers, Dick, T, Colorado State, F
23. Abell, Bud, E, Missouri, F
24. Young, Bob, T, Austin, F
25. McClurg, Jerry, T, Colorado, F
26. Zera, Phil, HB, St. Joseph's (Indiana), F

NY JETS
1. Snell, Matt, FB, Ohio State
2. Voss, Lloyd, T, Nebraska
3. Philbin, Gerry, LB, Buffalo
4. Evans, Jim, FL, Texas-El Paso
5. McGee, Ben, DT, Jackson State
6. Baker, Ralph, LB, Penn State
7. Choice to San Diego
8. Wright, Steve, T, Alabama
9. Lewis, Sherman, HB, Michigan State
10. Bowman, Ken, C, Wisconsin
11. Lacey, Bob, E, North Carolina
12. Johnson, Rudy, FB, Nebraska
13. Ware, Jeff, LB, Pittsburgh
14. Brooks, Charley, E, Memphis State, F
15. Johnson, Herman, DB, Michigan State, F
16. Popp, Ray, LB, Pittsburgh, F
17. Lehman, Bob, G-LB, Notre Dame
18. Scott, Bill, G, Memphis State
19. Condren, Glenn, T, Oklahoma, F
20. Shiner, Dick, QB, Maryland
21. Hand, Larry, T, Appalachian State, F
22. Radosevich, Will, T, Wyoming, F
23. Gordon, Cornell, HB, North Carolina A&T, F
24. Mayne, Mike, E, Idaho, F
25. Rhome, Jerry, QB, Tulsa, F
26. Butler, John, FB, San Diego State, F

OAKLAND
1. Lorick, Tony, HB, Arizona State
2. Conners, Dan, T, Miami
3. Bednar, George, T, Notre Dame
4. Budness, Bill, LB, Boston U.
5. Green, Don, DB, Susquehanna
6. Choice to Denver
7. Sapinsky, John, T, William & Mary
8. Petno, Vince, DB, Citadel
9. Williamson, John, G, Louisiana Tech
   Turner, Herschel, T, Kentucky, from San Diego
10. Renfro, Mel, HB, Oregon
11. Rakestraw, Larry, QB, Georgia
12. Lothridge, Billy, QB, Georgia Tech
13. Babb, Mickey, E, Georgia
14. Polser, Fred, G, East Texas State, F
15. Geirs, Mike, T, USC, F
16. Wilkening, Ron, HB, North Dakota, F
17. Lewis, Fred, HB, Massachusetts, F
18. Calcagno, Ron, QB, Santa Clara
19. Michel, Tom, FB, East Carolina
20. Beard, Ed, T, Tennessee
21. Oates, Carlton, E, Florida A&M, F
22. Long, Jim, FB, Fresno State, F
23. Curry, Bill, C, Georgia Tech, F
24. Francisco, Kent, T, UCLA, F
25. Sieg, Terry, HB, Virginia, F
26. Guest, Gordon, QB, Arkansas, F

SAN DIEGO
1. Davis, Ted, E, Georgia Tech
2. Kirby, John, LB, Nebraska

3. Dunn, Perry Lee, DB, Mississippi
4. Parks, Dave, E, Texas Tech
5. Kirner, Gary, T, USC, from Boston
   Goimarac, Pete, C, West Virginia
6. Brown, Willie, HB, USC
7. Batten, Pat, FB, Hardin-Simmons, from NY Jets
   Anderson, Roger, T, Virginia Union
8. Seals, George, DE, Missouri
9. Choice to Oakland
10. Bowman, Dick, E, Syracuse, from Denver through Kansas City
    Long, Bob, E, Wichita State
11. Horton, Bob, FB, Boston U.
12. Carpenter, Ron, E, Texas A&M
13. Graham, Kenny, HB, Washington State
14. Kindig, Howard, C, Cal State-Los Angeles, F
15. Mitchell, Ed, T, Southern, F
16. Daugherty, Bob, HB, Tulsa, F
17. Farris, John, T, San Diego State, F
18. Robinson, Bob, G-LB, Mississippi, F
19. Cercel, Paul, C-LB, Pittsburgh, F
20. Klein, Dick, T, Wichita State, F
21. Robinson, Allen, HB, BYU, F
22. Hinton, Charles, C, Mississippi, F
23. Smith, Ron, QB, Richmond, F
24. Van Burkleo, Bill, HB, Tulsa, F
25. Lucas, Tommy, G, Mississippi, F
26. Kinard, Frank, FB, Mississippi, F

1965 NFL
Held November 28, 1964

BALTIMORE
1. Curtis, Mike, LB, Duke
2. Neely, Ralph, T, Oklahoma
3. Choice to San Francisco
   Ressler, Glenn, C, Penn State, from Minnesota
4. Johnson, Dave, E, San Jose State
   Schottenheimer, Marty, LB, Pittsburgh, from Washington
5. McGuire, John, E, Syracuse, F
6. Atkinson, Al, T, Villanova
   Felts, Bobby, HB, Florida A&M, from NY Giants
7. Kolocek, John, T, Corpus Christi State
8. Davis, Roosevelt, T, Tennessee State
9. Bleick, Tom, B, Georgia Tech, F
10. Harold, George, B, Allen
11. Richardson, Lamar, E, Fisk
12. Rodosovich, Ted, G, Cincinnati
13. Airheart, Bruce, HB, North Dakota State
14. Fishman, Jerry, LB, Maryland
15. Hilton, Roy, FB, Jackson State
16. Tensi, Steve, QB, Florida State
17. Reichardt, Fred, HB, Wisconsin
18. King, Charley, HB, Purdue, F
19. Brown, Barry, E-LB, Florida, F
20. Haffner, George, QB, McNeese State, F
    Johnson, Ray, C, Prairie View A&M, from Washington, F

CHI. BEARS
1. Sayers, Gale, HB, Kansas
   Butkus, Dick, LB, Illinois, from Pittsburgh
   DeLong, Steve, T, Tennessee, from Washington
2. Choice to Cleveland
3. Choice to Cleveland
4. Nance, Jim, FB, Syracuse
5. Choice to LA Rams
6. Carey, Tony, HB, Notre Dame, F
7. Gordon, Dick, HB, Michigan State
   Sutton, Mickey, B, Auburn, from Washington
8. Schweda, Brian, T, Kansas
9. Ambrusko, Ken, B, Maryland, F
10. Murphy, Dennis, T, Florida
11. Cornish, Frank, T, Grambling, F
12. Cox, Steve, T, South Carolina, F
13. Daniels, Dave, T, Florida A&M, F
14. Pivec, Dave, E, Notre Dame
15. Robinson, Art, B, Cal State-Los Angeles
16. Pitts, Frank, E, Southern
17. LaFramboise, Tom, QB, Louisville
18. Schwager, Mike, T, Northwestern
19. Bobich, Lou, K, Michigan State
20. Kurek, Ralph, FB, Wisconsin

CLEVELAND
1. Choice to San Francisco
2. Garcia, Jim, T, Purdue, from Chi. Bears
   Bussell, Gerry, HB, Georgia Tech, from LA Rams
   Johnson, Walter, DT, Cal State-Los Angeles
3. Scott, Bo, HB, Ohio State, from Chi. Bears
   Maples, Bobby, LB, Baylor
4. Choice to Minnesota
5. Irwin, Bill, T, Mississippi
6. Simkus, Arnie, T, Michigan, from San Francisco
   Aldredge, Corwyn, E, Northwestern State (Louisiana)
7. Lindsey, Dale, LB, Western Kentucky
8. Howell, Mike, B, Grambling
9. Lane, Gary, QB, Missouri, F
10. Screen, Pat, QB, LSU, F
11. Cordill, Ollie, B, Memphis State, F
12. Canale, Justin, G, Mississippi State
13. Pickett, Henry, HB, Baylor, F
14. Simrell, Dan, QB, Toledo
15. Gagner, Larry, T, Florida, F
16. Anthony, Mel, FB, Michigan
17. Boyette, John, T, Clemson, F
18. Arrington, Dick, G, Notre Dame, F
19. Orazen, Ed, G, Ohio State
20. Goldberg, Frank, LB, Central Michigan

DALLAS
1. Morton, Craig, QB, California
2. Walker, Malcolm, LB, Rice
3. Choice to NY Giants through Green Bay
4. Sidle, Jimmy, HB, Auburn
   Svihus, Bob, T, USC, from Detroit
5. Pettee, Roger, LB, Florida
6. Utz, Sonny, FB, Virginia Tech
7. Owens, Brig, QB, Cincinnati
8. Wayt, Russell, LB, Rice
9. Zanios, Jim, FB, Texas Tech
10. McCullough, Gaylon, C, Alabama
11. Pugh, Jethro, T, Elizabeth City State
12. Kellerman, Ernie, QB, Miami (Ohio)
13. Schraub, Jack, E, California
14. Porterfield, Gary, E, Tulsa
15. Foster, Gene, B, Arizona State
16. McDougal, Doug, E, Oregon State
17. Johnson, Mitch, T, UCLA
18. Amsler, Marty, T, Evansville
19. Rettenmund, Marv, HB, Ball State
20. Barlow, Don, T, Kansas State

DETROIT
1. Nowatzke, Tom, FB, Indiana
2. Rush, Jerry, T, Michigan State
3. Biletnikoff, Fred, FL, Florida State
4. Choice to Dallas
   Myers, Tommy, QB, Northwestern, from Pittsburgh
5. Flynn, John, E, Oklahoma
   Vaughn, Tommy, B, Iowa State, from NY Giants
   Flanagan, Ed, C, Purdue, from Minnesota
6. Hawkins, Earl, B, Emory & Henry
7. Kowalkowski, Bob, G, Virginia, F
   Kent, Gregg, T, Utah, from Minnesota, F
8. Harbin, Larry, B, Appalachian State
9. McLenna, Bruce, B, Hillsdale, F
10. Pennie, Frank, T, Florida, F
11. Kearney, Jim, B, Prairie View A&M
12. Moore, Jim, LB, North Texas State
13. Jacobson, Jack, B, Oklahoma State
14. Brown, Larry, B, Oklahoma, F
15. Dickey, Wallace, E, Southwest Texas State
16. Smith, John, T, Maryland-Eastern Shore
17. Odom, Sonny, HB, Duke, F
18. Sweetan, Karl, QB, Wake Forest
19. Love, Preston, B, Nebraska
20. Wilson, George, QB, Xavier, F

GREEN BAY
1. Anderson, Donny, HB, Texas Tech, from Philadelphia, F
   Elkins, Lawrence, E, Baylor
2. Dotson, Alphonse, T, Grambling
3. Brown, Allen, E, Mississippi
4. Mahle, Wally, B, Syracuse
5. Goodwin, Doug, FB, Maryland-Eastern Shore
   Harvey, Jim, T, Mississippi, from Pittsburgh, F
6. Symons, Bill, HB, Colorado
   Koeper, Rich, T, Oregon State, from Pittsburgh
7. Coffey, Junior, FB, Washington
   Roberts, Jerry, B, Baldwin-Wallace, from NY Giants
   Jacobazzi, Roger, T, Wisconsin, from San Francisco
8. Shinn, Mike, E, Kansas, F
9. Bulaich, Larry, B, TCU
10. Marshall, Bud, T, Stephen F. Austin
11. Weatherwax, Jim, T, Cal State-Los Angeles, F
12. Jeter, Gene, HB, Arkansas-Pine Bluff
13. Schmidt, Roy, G, Long Beach State, F
14. Putnam, John, FB, Drake
15. Hurston, Chuck, T, Auburn
16. Vandersea, Phil, FB, Massachusetts, F
17. Clark, Steve, K, Oregon State
18. White, Jeff, E, Texas Tech, F
19. Sears, Len, T, South Carolina, F
20. Chandler, Jim, FB, Benedictine

LA RAMS
1. Williams, Clancy, HB, Washington State
2. Choice to Cleveland
3. Brown, Fred, E-LB, Miami
4. Strofolino, Mike, LB, Villanova
5. Woodlief, Doug, E, Memphis State
   Marchlewski, Frank, C, Minnesota, from Chi. Bears
6. Harrison, Bill, E, Elon
7. Guillory, Tony, G, Lamar
8. Dzura, Stan, T, California, F
9. Caveness, Ronnie, LB, Arkansas
10. Burt, Jim, HB, Western Kentucky
11. Walet, Merlin, FB, McNeese State, F
12. Werl, Bob, E, Miami, F
13. Berry, Brent, T, San Jose State, F
14. Robertson, Bill, E, Austin
15. Davis, Marvin, E, Wichita State, F
16. Brown, Charlie, T, Tulsa, F
17. Blecksmith, Ed, B, USC, F
18. Lowery, Leo, FB, Texas Tech, F
19. Anderson, Billy Guy, QB, Tulsa, F
20. Scott, Billy, E, Northeastern Oklahoma, F

MINNESOTA
1. Snow, Jack, E, Notre Dame
2. Rentzel, Lance, HB, Oklahoma
   Sutton, Archie, T, Illinois, from NY Giants
3. Choice to Baltimore
4. Whalen, Jim, E, Boston College
   Harris, Jim, T, Utah State, from Cleveland
5. Choice to Detroit
6. Grisham, Jim, B, Oklahoma
7. Choice to Detroit
8. Jordon, Jeff, B, Tulsa
   Hankinson, John, QB, Minnesota, from San Francisco, F
9. McClendon, Frank, T, Alabama
10. Schweiger, Jerald, T, Wisconsin-Superior
11. Thomas, John, E, USC, F
12. Tilleman, Mike, T, Montana
13. Osborn, Dave, B, North Dakota
14. Leetzow, Max, E, Idaho
15. Morgan, Phillip, B, East Tennessee State
16. Labinski, Paul, T, St. John's (Minnesota)
17. Smith, Veran, B, Utah State
18. Kotite, Rich, E, Wagner, F
19. Johnson, Ellis, HB, Southeastern Louisiana
20. Iacavazzi, Cosmo, B, Princeton

NY GIANTS
1. Frederickson, Tucker, B, Auburn
2. Choice to Minnesota
3. Choice to San Francisco
   Mercein, Chuck, FB, Yale, from Pittsburgh
   Timberlake, Bob, QB, Michigan, from Dallas through Green Bay
4. Carr, Henry, HB, Arizona State
5. Choice to Detroit
   Lambert, Frank, E, Mississippi, from Washington
6. Choice to Baltimore
7. Choice to Green Bay
8. Williams, Willie, B, Grambling
9. Frick, John, E, Ohio U.
10. Crenshaw, Ben, B, Jackson State
11. Koy, Ernie, B, Texas
12. Carroll, Jim, LB, Notre Dame
13. Lockhart, Carl, B, North Texas State
14. Underwood, Olin, E, Texas
15. Giers, Mike, G, USC
16. Good, Tom, B, Marshall, F
17. Powless, Dave, G, Illinois
18. Ciccolello, Mike, LB, Dayton, F
19. Reed, Smith, B, Alcorn State
20. Torok, John, QB, Arizona State

PHILADELPHIA
1. Choice to Green Bay
2. Rissmiller, Ray, T, Georgia
3. Nelson, Al, HB, Cincinnati
4. Hill, Fred, E, USC
5. Henderson, John, E, Michigan
6. Huarte, John, QB, Notre Dame
   Garrison, Gary, E, San Diego State, from Washington, F
7. Will, Erwin, T, Dayton
8. Piraino, Al, T, Wisconsin
9. Hudlow, Floyd, B, Arizona
10. Redman, Rick, G, Washington
11. James, Louis, HB, Texas-El Paso
12. Kuznieski, John, HB, Purdue, F
13. Fouse, John, E, Arizona
14. Longo, Tom, B, Notre Dame, F
15. Taylor, Otis, B, Prairie View A&M
16. Gray, Jim, B, Toledo
17. Austin, Dave, E, Georgia Tech, F
18. Marcordes, Bill, E, Bradley
19. Englehart, Charley, T, John Carroll
20. Shann, Bobby, E, Boston College

PITTSBURGH
1. Choice to Chi. Bears
2. Jefferson, Roy, HB, Utah
3. Choice to NY Giants
4. Choice to Detroit
5. Choice to Green Bay
6. Choice to Green Bay
7. Browning, Charley, B, Washington
8. Howley, Bill, E, Pittsburgh
9. Neville, Tom, T, Mississippi State
10. Tobey, Dave, C, Oregon, F
11. Molden, Frank, T, Jackson State
12. Lofquist, Craig, B, Minnesota
13. Wilburn, J.R., B, South Carolina, F
14. Butler, Jim (Cannonball), B, Edward Waters
15. Carrell, John, T, Texas Tech, F
16. Dusenbury, Doug, K, Kansas State
17. Canale, Whit, FB, Tennessee
18. Howard, Bob, B, Stanford
19. Price, Lonnie, B, Southwestern Louisiana, F
20. Fertig, Craig, QB, USC

ST. LOUIS
1. Namath, Joe, QB, Alabama
2. Simmons, Dave, LB, Georgia Tech
3. Ogden, Ray, E, Alabama
4. Roland, Johnny, HB, Missouri, F
5. Bonds, Bob, HB, San Jose State
6. Hines, Glen Ray, T, Arkansas, F
7. Roy, Frank, E, Utah
8. Meyer, John, LB, Notre Dame
9. Heidel, Jimmy, B, Mississippi, F
10. Drulis, Chuck, E, Duke, F
11. French, Bud, B, Alabama
12. Sasser, Glen, E, North Carolina State
13. Murphy, Steve, HB, Northwestern
14. Alford, Mike, C, Auburn
15. Lane, Harlan, B, Baylor, F
16. Silvestri, Carl, B, Wisconsin
17. Melinkovich, Mike, T, Gray's Harbor J.C.
18. McQuarters, Ed, G, Oklahoma
19. Shivers, Roy, HB, Ohio State, F
20. Giacobazzi, Tony, E, Iowa

SAN FRANCISCO
1. Willard, Ken, FB, North Carolina
   Donnelly, George, B, Illinois, from Cleveland
2. Cerne, Joe, C, Northwestern
3. Norton, Jim, T, Washington
   Schweickert, Bob, B, Virginia Tech, from NY Giants
   Chapple, Jack, LB, Stanford, from Baltimore
4. Todd, Larry, FL, Arizona State
5. McCormick, Dave, T, LSU, F
6. Choice to Cleveland
7. Choice to Green Bay
8. Choice to Minnesota
9. Swinford, Wayne, HB, Georgia
10. Cappadona, Bob, FB, Northeastern, F
11. Mass, Steve, T, Detroit, F
12. Plump, Dave, HB, Fresno State, F
13. Schumacher, Gregg, E, Illinois
14. Andruski, Frank, HB, Utah
15. Pabian, Joe, T, West Virginia
16. Hettema, Dave, T, New Mexico, F
17. Frketich, Len, E, Oregon State
18. Standridge, Leon, E, San Diego State, F
19. Ford, Dale, HB, Washington State
20. Duncan, Dennis, B, Louisiana College

WASHINGTON
1. Choice to Chi. Bears
2. Breitenstein, Bob, T, Tulsa

3. McCloughan, Kent, B, Nebraska
4. Choice to Baltimore
5. Choice to NY Giants
6. Choice to Philadelphia
7. Choice to Chi. Bears
8. Croftcheck, Don, G-LB, Indiana
9. Smith, Jerry, E, Arizona State
10. Briggs, Bob, FB, Central State (Oklahoma)
11. Adams, Willie, G, New Mexico State
12. Strohmeyer, John, T, Nebraska, F
13. Bracy, Biff, HB, Duke, F
14. Estrada, Dave, HB, Arizona State
15. Baldwin, Ben, B, Vanderbilt
16. Reed, Robert, G, Tennessee A&I
17. Hart, Gary, E, Vanderbilt
18. Hanburger, Chris, C-LB, North Carolina
19. Ellerbe, Roosevelt, B, Iowa State, F
20. Choice to Baltimore

1965 AFL

Held November 28, 1964

BOSTON

1. Rush, Jerry, T, Michigan State
2. Choice to Houston
3. Whalen, Jim, E, Boston College
4. Johnson, Ellis, HB, Southeastern Louisiana
5. Aldredge, Corwyn, E, Northwestern State (Louisiana)
6. Canale, Justin, G, Mississippi State
7. Neville, Tom, T, Mississippi State
8. Brown, Fred, E, Miami
9. Malone, Bob, T, Louisiana Tech
10. Choice to Buffalo
11. Frechette, John, T, Boston College
12. Weatherly, Jim, DB, Mississippi
13. Green, Charlie, QB, Wittenberg
14. Cunningham, Jay, HB, Bowling Green
15. Rodosevitch, Ted, G, Cincinnati
16. Pyne, George, T, Olivet
17. Graves, White, DB, LSU
Lee, David, E, Louisiana Tech, from NY Jets
18. Meixler, Ed, LB, Boston U.
19. Nance, Jim, FB, Syracuse
20. Fugazzi, Fred, FB, Missouri Valley

BUFFALO

1. Davidson, Jim, T, Ohio State
2. Choice to Kansas City
3. Atkinson, Alan, T, Villanova
4. Choice to Kansas City
5. Simmons, Dave, LB, Georgia Tech
6. Rentzel, Lance, HB, Oklahoma
7. Schottenheimer, Marty, LB, Pittsburgh
8. Rissmiller, Ray, T, Georgia
9. Nelson, Al, DB, Cincinnati
10. Mercein, Chuck, FB, Yale
Hudlow, Floyd, DB, Arizona, from Boston
11. Goodwin, Doug, FB, Maryland-Eastern Shore
12. Hurston, Chuck, T, Auburn
Mills, Pete, HB, Wichita State, from Oakland
13. Timberlake, Bob, QB, Michigan
14. Hart, Lyn, DB, Virginia State
15. Meyer, John, LB, Notre Dame
16. Airheart, Bruce, HB, North Dakota State
17. Henderson, John, E, Michigan
18. Hinze, Ray, T, Texas A&M
Fouse, John, E, Arizona, from Denver
19. Marchlewski, Frank, LB, Minnesota
20. Henry, John, DT, Boston U.

DENVER

1. Choice to NY Jets
2. Butkus, Dick, LB, Illinois
3. Ressler, Glenn, C, Penn State
4. Donnelly, George, DB, Illinois
5. Breitenstein, Bob, T, Tulsa
Leetzow, Max, DT, Idaho, from Oakland
6. Wilhelm, Tom, T, Syracuse
7. Garcia, Jim, DE, Purdue
8. Hohman, John, G, Wisconsin
9. Bussell, Garry, DB, Georgia Tech
10. Jeter, Gene, LB, Arkansas-Pine Bluff
11. Vaughn, Tommy, HB, Iowa State
12. Myers, Tommy, QB, Northwestern
13. Strofalino, Mike, LB, Villanova
14. Frick, John, G, Ohio U.
15. Jordan, Jeff, DB, Tulsa
16. Schweda, Brian, T, Kansas
17. Choice to Boston
18. Dupree, Larry, HB, Florida, from NY Jets
Choice to Buffalo
19. Oelschlager, Ron, HB, Kansas
20. Metchner, Terry, G, Albion

HOUSTON

1. Elkins, Lawrence, E, Baylor
2. Walker, Malcolm, LB, Rice
Neely, Ralph, T, Oklahoma, from Boston
3. Koy, Ernie, FB, Texas
4. Maples, Bobby, LB, Baylor
5. Molden, Frank, T, Jackson State
6. Murphy, Dennis, T, Florida
Wayt, Russ, LB, Rice, from Oakland
7. Choice to Kansas City
8. Ogden, Ray, FB, Alabama
Hilton, Roy, LB, Jackson State, from Oakland
9. Kinney, George, DE, Wiley
10. Williams, Maxie, T, Southeastern Louisiana
11. McCloughan, Kent, HB, Nebraska
12. Reed, Bob, G, Tennessee State
13. Felts, Bob, DB, Florida A&M
14. Evans, Norm, T, TCU
15. Guillory, Tony, T, Lamar
16. Coffey, Junior, HB, Washington
17. Grisham, Jim, FB, Oklahoma
18. Mundy, Russ, HB, West Texas State
19. Fox, Frank, T, Sam Houston State
20. Brezina, Gus, G, Houston

KANSAS CITY

1. Sayers, Gale, HB, Kansas
2. Chapple, Jack, G, Stanford
Caveness, Ronnie, LB, Arkansas, from Buffalo
3. Curtis, Mike, FB, Duke
4. Taylor, Otis, E, Prairie View A&M
Pitts, Frank, HB, Southern, from Buffalo
5. Reed, Smith, HB, Alcorn State
6. Sutton, Mickey, DB, Auburn
7. Richardson, Gloster, E, Jackson State, from Houston
Bobich, Lou, DB-K, Michigan State
8. Thomas, Danny, QB-K, SMU
9. Cerne, Joe, C, Northwestern
10. Howard, Bob, DB, Stanford
11. Piraino, Al, T, Wisconsin
12. Cox, Mike, LB, Iowa State
13. Bonds, Bob, DB-E, San Jose State
14. Dotson, Fred, DB, Wiley
15. Powless, Dave, G, Illinois
16. Irvine, Stan, T, Colorado
17. Croftcheck, Don, LB, Indiana
18. Smith, Jerry, E, Arizona State
19. Alford, Mike, C, Auburn
20. Symons, Bill, HB, Colorado

NY JETS

1. Namath, Joe, QB, Alabama, from Denver
Nowatzke, Tom, FB, Indiana
2. Huarte, John, QB, Notre Dame
3. Biggs, Verlon, T, Jackson State
4. Schweickert, Bob, HB, Virginia Tech
5. Sasser, Glenn, DE, North Carolina State
6. Hoovler, Don, LB, Ohio U.
7. Harris, Jim, DT, Utah State
Roberts, Archie, QB, Columbia, from Oakland
8. McCurdy, Rick, DE, Oklahoma
9. Sidle, Jimmy, HB, Auburn
10. Lambert, Frank, K-E, Mississippi
11. Gray, Jim, DB, Toledo
12. Berrington, John, LB-C, Iowa State
13. Utz, Sonny, FB, Virginia Tech
14. Plumlee, Gary, DT-DE, New Mexico
15. Burt, Jim, DB, Western Kentucky
16. Cartwright, Seth, DT, Prairie View A&M
17. Browning, Charles, DB, Washington
18. Choice to Denver
19. Dudek, Frank, G, Xavier
20. Allen, Troy, DB, Western Michigan

OAKLAND

1. Schuh, Harry, T, Memphis State
2. Biletnikoff, Fred, E, Florida State
3. Svihus, Bob, T, USC
4. Otto, Gus, FB, Missouri
5. Choice to Denver
6. Choice to Houston
7. Choice to NY Jets
8. Choice to Houston
9. Zecher, Rich, T, Utah State
10. Morton, Craig, QB, California
11. Minor, Bill, LB, Illinois
12. Choice to Buffalo
13. Mahle, Wally, DB, Syracuse
14. Hawley, Loren, DB, California
15. Cronin, Bill, DE, Boston College
16. Hill, Fred, E, USC
17. Porterfield, Gary, E, Tulsa
18. Dugan, John, T, Holy Cross
19. McClendon, Frank, T, Alabama
20. Scott, Bo, HB, Ohio State

SAN DIEGO

1. DeLong, Steve, G, Tennessee
2. Jefferson, Roy, E, Utah
3. Brown, Allen, E, Mississippi
4. Tensi, Steve, QB, Florida State
5. Redman, Rick, LB, Washington
6. Beasley, Will, FB, North Carolina A&T
7. Snow, Jack, E, Notre Dame
8. Williams, Clancy, HB, Washington
9. Whelchel, Jerry, QB, Massachusetts
10. Foster, Gene, HB, Arizona State
11. Smith, Veran, G, Utah State
12. Allison, Jim, FB, San Diego State
13. Quigley, Bill, LB, Villanova
14. Floyd, Don, E, Florida State
15. Howell, Mike, DB, Grambling
16. Godden, John, LB, San Diego State
17. Hardy, Leon, T, Texas Southern
18. Evans, Bobby, T, Texas A&M
19. Beck, Braden, K, Stanford
20. Edwards, Jack, C, Florida State

1965 AFL REDSHIRT

Held November 28, 1964

A separate, 12-round redshirt draft was held, and no future picks were made in the regular draft. The AFL repeated the redshirt draft in 1966.

BOSTON

1. McCormick, Dave, T, LSU
2. Kowlowski, Bob, T, Virginia
3. Cappadonna, Bob, FB, Northeastern
4. Arrington, Dick, G, Notre Dame
5. Smith, Dennis, DE, Cincinnati
6. Ezell, Billy, DB, LSU
7. Hankinson, John, QB, Minnesota
8. Colle, Beau, DB, LSU
9. Brown, Charley, T, Tulsa
10. Hettema, Dave, T, New Mexico
11. Schmidt, Roy, G, Long Beach State
12. Standridge, Leon, E, San Diego State

BUFFALO

1. Ambrusko, Ken, HB, Maryland
2. Lane, Gary, QB, Missouri
3. Kuzniewski, John, FB, Purdue
4. Davis, Roger, HB, Virginia
5. Boyette, John, T, Clemson
6. Strohmeyer, John, DE, Nebraska
7. Wilburn, J.R., E, South Carolina
8. King, Charley, DB, Purdue
9. Hawkins, Earl, HB, Emory & Henry
10. Odom, Sonny, HB, Duke
11. Johnson, Ray, G, Prairie View A&M
12. Wilson, George, QB, Xavier

DENVER

1. Farr, Miller, HB, Wichita State
2. Johnson, Walter, G, Cal State-Los Angeles
3. Davis, Marvin, DE, Wichita State
4. Brown, Barry, E, Florida
5. Tilleman, Mike, T, Montana State
6. Inman, Jerry, T, Oregon
7. Tobey, Dave, LB, Oregon
8. Maddox, John, E, Mississippi
9. Vandersea, Phil, FB, Massachusetts
10. Walet, Merlin, FB, McNeese State
11. Fishman, Jerry, LB, Maryland
12. Bracy, Biff, HB, Duke

HOUSTON

1. Anderson, Donny, HB, Texas Tech
2. Hines, Glen Ray, T, Arkansas
3. Shinn, Mike, DE, Kansas
4. Cordill, Ollie, QB, Memphis State
5. Crumpler, Jerry, T, Mississippi
6. Daniels, Dave, T, Florida A&M
7. Lowery, Leo, HB, Texas Tech
8. Sears, Len, T, South Carolina
9. Bleick, Tom, HB, Georgia Tech
10. Hafner, George, QB, McNeese State
11. Anderson, Billy Guy, QB, Tulsa
12. Lane, Harlan, FL, Baylor

KANSAS CITY

1. Dotson, Alphonse, T, Grambling
2. Cornish, Frank, DT, Grambling
3. Carr, Henry, HB, Arizona State
4. Cox, Steve, T, South Carolina
5. Thomas, John, E, USC
6. Wilburn, John, G, Stanford
7. Moore, Bill, HB, Mississippi State
8. Ellerbe, Roosevelt, DB, Iowa State
9. McLenna, Bruce, HB, Hillsdale
10. Drulis, Chuck, E, Duke
11. Scott, Bill, E, Northeastern Oklahoma
12. Price, Lonnie, HB, Southwestern Louisiana

NY JETS

1. Roland, Johnny, HB, Missouri
2. McGuire, John, TE-DE, Syracuse
3. Heidel, Jimmy, DB, Mississippi
4. Werl, Bob, DE, Miami
5. Sauer, George, FL, Texas
6. Lindsey, Dale, LB, Western Kentucky
7. Barlow, Ron, FB, Kansas State
8. Mallendick, Bob, T, Hillsdale
9. Kotite, Rich, E, Wagner
10. Austin, Dave, E, Georgia Tech
11. Marshall, Richard, T, Stephen F. Austin
12. Screen, Pat, QB, LSU

OAKLAND

1. Todd, Larry, HB, Arizona State
2. Harvey, Jim, T, Mississippi
3. Mass, Steve, T, Detroit
4. Cox, Mickey, T, LSU
5. Taylor, Bob, G, Cincinnati
6. Kent, Gregg, T, Utah
7. Carroll, John, T, Texas Tech
8. Pickett, Henry, HB, Baylor
9. Pennie, Frank, T, Florida State
10. Berry, Brent, T, San Jose State
11. Longo, Tom, DB, Notre Dame
12. Duncan, Dennis, HB, Louisiana College

SAN DIEGO

1. Garrison, Gary, E, San Diego State
2. Martin, Larry, T, San Diego State
3. Dzura, Stan, T-DE, California
4. Woodlief, Doug, LB, Memphis State
5. Weatherwax, Jim, T, Cal State-Los Angeles
6. Good, Tom, LB, Marshall
7. Waff, Wayne, E, East Tennessee State
8. Shivers, Roy, HB, Utah
9. Carey, Tony, HB, Notre Dame
10. Plump, Dave, HB, Fresno State
11. White, Jeff, E, Texas Tech
12. Cicollella, Mike, LB, Dayton

1966 NFL

Held November 27, 1965

The expansion Atlanta Falcons received the first and last choices in each of the first five rounds, and the first choice in rounds 6-20. The draft consisted of 305 selections.

On February 15, the Falcons selected 42 players in an expansion draft. Each of the other 14 NFL teams froze 29 players from its 40-man roster. The Falcons chose one player from those remaining on each team. Then the other teams froze two additional players, leaving eight on each list, from which the Falcons chose two more each.

ATLANTA

1. Nobis, Tommy, LB, Texas
Johnson, Randy, QB, Texas A&I
2. Rassas, Nick, DB, Notre Dame
Jones, Jerry, T, Bowling Green
3. Dennis, Mike, HB, Mississippi
Sheridan, Phil, E, Notre Dame
4. Reaves, Ken, DB, Virginia State
Asbury, Willie, HB, Kent State
5. Wolski, Bill, HB, Notre Dame
Kahn, Martin, T, North Texas State
6. Casey, Charley, FL, Florida
7. Johnson, William, FB, University of the South
8. Goss, Bill, LB, Tulane
9. Sanders, Bob, C, North Texas State
10. Bender, Mike, G, Arkansas
11. Sloan, Steve, QB, Alabama
12. Hollister, Ken, T, Indiana
13. Collins, Bob, T, South Carolina
14. Ecker, Steve, K, Shippensburg
15. Tolleson, Tom, FL, Alabama
16. Vining, Jim, G, Rice
17. Archambeau, Lurley, C, Toledo
18. Korver, Doug, C, Northern Iowa
19. Mainer, Walt, DB, Xavier
20. Riggle, Bob, DB, Penn State

ATLANTA (Expansion)
Anderson, Roger, DT, from NY Giants
Benz, Larry, S, Northwestern, from Cleveland
Calland, Lee, DB, Louisville, from Minnesota
Claridge, Dennis, QB, Nebraska, from Green Bay
Coffey, Junior, FB, Washington, from Green Bay
Cook, Ed, G, Notre Dame, from St. Louis
Crossan, Dave, C, Maryland, from Washington
Dunn, Perry Lee, HB, Mississippi, from Dallas
Franklin, Bobby, S, Mississippi, from Cleveland
Grimm, Dan, G, Colorado, from Green Bay
Hawkins, Alex, FL, South Carolina, from Baltimore
Heck, Ralph, LB, Colorado, from Philadelphia
Jencks, Bob, TE-K, Miami (Ohio), from Washington
Jobko, Bill, LB, Ohio State, from Minnesota
Johnson, Rudy, HB, Nebraska, from San Francisco
Lasky, Frank, T, Florida, from NY Giants
Lewis, Danny, FB, Wisconsin, from Washington
Linden, Errol, T, Houston, from Minnesota
Mack, Bill (Red), FL, Notre Dame, from Pittsburgh
Marchlewski, Frank, C, Minnesota, from LA Rams
Martin, Billy, TE, Georgia Tech, from Chi. Bears
Memmelaar, Dale, G, Wyoming, from Cleveland
Messer, Dale, FL, Fresno State, from San Francisco
Messner, Max, LB, Cincinnati, from Pittsburgh
Murphy, Dennis, DT, Florida, from Chi. Bears
Petties, Neal, SE, San Diego State, from Baltimore
Powell, Tim, DE, Northwestern, from LA Rams
Recher, Dave, C, Iowa, from Philadelphia
Reese, Guy, T, SMU, from Baltimore
Richards, Bob, DE, LSU, from Philadelphia
Richardson, Jerry, DB, West Texas State, from LA Rams
Rushing, Marion, LB, Southern Illinois, from St. Louis
Sherman, Bob, DB, Iowa, from Pittsburgh
Sieminski, Chuck, DT, Penn State, from San Francisco
Silvestri, Carl, DB, Wisconsin, from St. Louis
Simon, Jim, G-T, Miami, from Detroit
Smith, Ron, DB, Wisconsin, from Chi. Bears
Talbert, Don, T, Texas, from Dallas
Wheelwright, Ernie, FB, Southern Illinois, from NY Giants
Whitlow, Bob, C, Arizona, from Detroit
Williams, Sam, DE, Michigan State, from Detroit
Youmans, Maury, DE, Syracuse, from Dallas

BALTIMORE
1. Ball, Sam, T, Kentucky
2. Allison, Butch, T, Missouri
3. Kestner, Rick, FL, Kentucky
4. Sherman, Rod, FL, USC, from Dallas, F
   Granger, Hoyle, FB, Mississippi State
5. Choice to Dallas
6. Maliszewski, Stas, LB, Princeton
7. Ellis, Dave, DE-T, North Carolina State, from San Francisco
   Perkins, Ray, E, Alabama, F
8. Allen, Gerry, HB, Nebraska-Omaha, from Minnesota
   White, Jack, QB, Penn State, F
9. Gross, Jerry, HB, Auburn
10. Brownlee, Claude, DE, Benedictine
11. Crabtree, Eric, HB, Pittsburgh
12. Carter, Jim, G, Tennessee State
13. Hadrick, Bob, E, Purdue
14. Ward, Jim, QB, Gettysburg
15. Garner, Lee, LB, Mississippi, F
16. Stewart, Rod, E, Duke
17. Matson, Randy, T, Texas A&M, F
18. Toner, Ed, T, Massachusetts, F
19. Duke, Ken, HB, Morgan State
20. Carr, Tom, T, Morgan State

CHI. BEARS
1. Rice, George, T, LSU
2. Brown, Charlie, DB, Syracuse
3. Pickens, Bob, T, Nebraska, F
4. Jackson, Randy, T, Florida, from Pittsburgh
   Buffone, Doug, LB, Louisville
5. Choice to Minnesota
6. Brewster, Dennis, T, BYU, from Washington
   McRae, Franklin, DT, Tennessee State
7. Myer, Ron, QB, South Dakota State
8. McFalls, Doug, DB, Georgia
9. Greenlee, Fritz, E, Arizona, F
10. Burnett, Bobby, HB, Arkansas
11. Owens, Terry, E, Jacksonville State
12. Page, Wayne, DE, Clemson
13. Becker, Wayne, T, Montana, F
14. Buckner, Mike, DB, Northwestern
15. Kollman, Jim, G, Oregon, F
16. Senkbeil, Lynn, LB, Nebraska, F
17. Gentry, Curtis, DB, Maryland-Eastern Shore
18. Kines, Charley, T, Michigan
19. Haberer, Roger, HB, Eastern Illinois
20. Sellers, Goldie, HB, Grambling

CLEVELAND
1. Morin, Milt, E, Massachusetts
2. Norton, Rick, QB, Kentucky
3. Choice to Green Bay
4. Duranko, Pete, DE-LB, Notre Dame, F
5. Schultz, Randy, FB, Northern Iowa, from Detroit
   Fulford, Dan, E, Auburn, F
6. Battle, Jim, DE, Southern, from NY Giants
   Hoaglin, Fred, C, Pittsburgh
7. Carter, Leroy, FL, Grambling, F
8. Talaga, Tom, E, Notre Dame
9. Gregory, Jack, DE, Tennessee-Chattanooga, F
10. Ledbetter, Monty, E, Northwestern State (Louisiana)
11. Fire, Tony, T, Bowling Green
12. Czap, Rich, T, Nebraska, F
13. Boudreaux, Jim, T, Louisiana Tech
14. Lammons, Pete, E, Texas
15. Ellis, Bob, DE, Massachusetts
16. Ray, David, E, Alabama
17. Modzelewski, Gene, T, New Mexico State
18. Harraway, Charley, FB, San Jose State
19. Singer, Karl, T, Purdue
20. Petro, Joe, DB, Temple

DALLAS
1. Niland, John, G, Iowa
2. Townes, Willie, T, Tulsa
3. Choice to San Francisco
4. Choice to Baltimore
5. Choice to San Francisco
   Garrison, Walt, HB, Oklahoma State, from Baltimore
6. Dunlevy, Bob, E, West Virginia
7. Robinson, Arthur, E, Florida A&M
8. Kunit, Don, HB, Penn State
9. Elam, Darrell, E, West Virginia Tech
10. Mitchell, Mason, HB, Washington
11. Denny, Austin, E, Tennessee, F
12. Shy, Les, DB, Long Beach State, from Pittsburgh
    Baynham, Craig, HB, Georgia Tech, F
13. Lamb, Ron, HB, South Carolina
14. Turner, Lewis, HB, Norfolk State
15. Gartung, Mark, T, Oregon State, F
16. Piggee, Tom, HB, Cal State-San Francisco
17. Allen, George, T, West Texas State
18. Orr, Steve, T, Washington
19. Johnson, Byron, T, Central Washington
20. Hudson, Lou, FL, Minnesota

DETROIT
1. Choice to Green Bay
2. Eddy, Nick, HB, Notre Dame, F
3. Malinchak, Bill, E, Indiana
4. Van Horn, Doug, G, Ohio State, from NY Giants
   Walker, Willie, FL, Tennessee State
5. Cody, Bill, LB, Auburn, from Pittsburgh
   Choice to Cleveland
6. De Sutter, Wayne, T, Western Illinois, from Minnesota
   Choice to Philadelphia
7. Robinson, Johnnie, E, Tennessee State
8. Pincavage, John, HB, Virginia
9. Cunningham, Dick, G, Arkansas, F
10. Yates, Bruce, T, Auburn, from Minnesota
    Brigham, Tom, DE, Wisconsin
11. O'Billovich, Jack, LB, Oregon State
12. Winkler, Randy, T, Tarleton State, F
13. Maselter, Bill, T, Wisconsin
14. Moore, Denis, T, USC, F
15. Sullivan, Bill, DE, West Virginia
16. Gendron, Jerry, E, Wisconsin-Eau Claire
17. Dunlap, Ralph, DE, Baylor
18. Johnson, Bill, E, Livingston
19. Baier, Bob, T, Simpson
20. Smith, Allen, HB, Findlay, F

GREEN BAY
1. Grabowski, Jim, FB, Illinois, from Detroit
   Gillingham, Gale, T, Minnesota
2. Cichowski, Tom, T, Maryland, F
3. Heron, Fred, T, San Jose State
   Jeter, Tony, E, Nebraska, from Cleveland
4. Roderick, John, FL, SMU
5. Choice to LA Rams
6. Choice to Washington
7. Miller, Ray, DE, Idaho, F
8. McLean, Ken, FL, Texas A&M
9. Rector, Ron, HB, Northwestern
10. Montgomery, Sam, DE, Southern
11. Wenzel, Ralph, G, San Diego State
12. Mankins, Jim, FB, Florida State, F
13. King, Ed, LB, USC, F
14. Hanson, Ron, FL, North Dakota State
15. Bolton, Grady, T, Mississippi State
16. Schultz, Bob, DE, Wisconsin-Stevens Point
17. Hatcock, David, DB, Memphis State
18. Jones, Jim, DE, Nebraska-Omaha
19. Moton, Dave, E, USC
20. Maras, Ed, E, South Dakota State

LA RAMS
1. Mack, Tom, T, Michigan
2. Garrett, Mike, HB, USC
3. Tyson, Dick, G, Tulsa
4. Dyer, Henry, FB, Grambling
5. Talbert, Diron, T, Texas, F
   Arndt, Dick, T, Idaho, from Green Bay, F
6. Anderson, Bruce, T, Willamette
7. Youngblood, George, DB, Cal State-Los Angeles
8. Ezerins, Vilnis, HB, Wisconsin-Whitewater
9. Matthies, Burton, HB, Wayne State
10. Capshaw, Mike, T, Abilene Christian
11. Hoover, Darrell, HB, Arizona
12. Clayton, George, DB, Fairmont State
13. David, Jake, HB, Lamar, F
14. Parks, Terry, T, Cal State-Los Angeles, F
15. Sullivan, Mike, E, Oregon State, F
16. O'Brien, Joe, E, Texas-Arlington, F
17. Gilbert, Dan, T, Arkansas Tech
18. Johnson, Ray, LB, Whitworth
19. Williams, Homer, FL, USC, F
20. Harrington, Bud, FB, Tulsa, F

MINNESOTA
1. Shay, Jerry, T, Purdue
2. Lindsey, Jim, HB, Arkansas
3. Hansen, Don, LB, Illinois
4. Acks, Ron, DE, Illinois
5. Davis, Doug, T, Kentucky
   Hall, Bob, DB, Brown, from Chi. Bears
6. Aylor, Wilbur, T, Southwest Texas State, from Pittsburgh
   Choice to Detroit
7. Meers, Bob, E, Massachusetts
8. Choice to Baltimore
9. Green, Ron, FL, North Dakota
10. Choice to Detroit
11. Quintana, Stan, DB, New Mexico
12. Petrella, Bob, DB, Tennessee
13. Martin, Larry, T, San Diego State
14. Twilley, Howard, E, Tulsa
15. Wright, Hugh, HB, Adams State, F
16. Williams, Jim, DE, Arkansas
17. Beard, Monroe, HB, Virginia Union
18. Greco, Dale, DT, Illinois
19. Stokes, Jessie, HB, Corpus Christi State
20. Choice to Philadelphia

NY GIANTS
1. Peay, Francis, T, Missouri
2. Davis, Don, T, Cal State-Los Angeles
3. Fisher, Tom, LB, Tennessee, F
4. Choice to Detroit
5. Briggs, Bill, DE, Iowa
6. Choice to Cleveland
7. Harris, Phil, HB, Texas
8. Harper, Charlie, T, Oklahoma State, from Pittsburgh
   Matan, Bill, E, Kansas State
9. White, Freeman, E, Nebraska
10. Smith, Jeff, LB, USC
11. Wilder, Cliff, E, Iowa
12. Avery, Ken, LB, Southern Mississippi, F
13. Fulgham, Jim, T, Minnesota
14. McCard, Howard, G, Syracuse
15. Bowman, Steve, HB, Alabama
16. Price, Sam, HB, Illinois
17. Eickman, Gary, T, Illinois
18. Anderson, Kai, C, Illinois, F
19. Crockett, Bobby, E, Arkansas
20. Minniear, Randy, HB, Purdue

PHILADELPHIA
1. Beisler, Randy, DE, Indiana
2. Pettigrew, Gary, DE, Stanford
3. Hawkins, Ben, FL, Arizona State
4. Emanuel, Frank, LB, Tennessee
5. Berry, Dan, HB, California, F
6. Sherlag, Bob, DB, Memphis State
   Tom, Mel, LB, San Jose State, from Detroit, F
7. Lince, David, T, North Dakota
8. Mason, John, E, Stanford, F
9. Todd, Jim, HB, Ball State
10. Osmond, John, C, Tulsa
11. Walton, Welford, DE, Nevada-Reno
12. Van Dyke, Bruce, G, Missouri
13. Bohl, Jim, HB, New Mexico State, F
14. Medved, Ron, HB, Washington
15. Day, Harry, T, Memphis State
16. Vasys, Arunas, LB, Notre Dame
17. Kelley, Ike, LB, Ohio State
18. Moorer, Bill, C, Georgia Tech, F
19. Reed, Taft, DB, Jackson State
20. Risio, Bill, T, Boston College, F
    Circo, Gerald, K, Cal State-Chico, from Minnesota

PITTSBURGH
1. Leftridge, Dick, FB, West Virginia
2. Gagner, Larry, G, Florida
3. Killorin, Pat, C, Syracuse
4. Choice to Chi. Bears
5. Choice to Detroit
6. Choice to Minnesota
7. Boozer, Emerson, HB, Maryland Eastern Shore
8. Choice to NY Giants
9. Stewart, Dale, DE, Pittsburgh
10. Marion, Jay, DB, Wyoming, F
11. Washington, Charley, HB, Grambling
12. Choice to Dallas
13. Dial, Benjy, QB, Eastern New Mexico
14. Novogratz, Joe, LB, Pittsburgh
15. Dobson, Joe, T, Idaho
16. Long, Jim, E, Purdue
17. Brundage, Mike, QB, Oregon, F
18. Lucas, Ken, QB, Pittsburgh
19. Neilson, Dave, QB, Albion
20. Springer, Ron, T, Albion

ST. LOUIS
1. McAdams, Carl, LB, Oklahoma
2. Lucas, Harold, T, Michigan State
3. Long, Dave, DE, Iowa
4. Snook, Gary, QB, Iowa
5. Clancy, Jack, FL, Michigan, F
6. Van Galder, Tim, QB, Iowa State, F
7. Arkwright, Charley, T, Georgia, F
8. Goich, Dan, E, California, F
9. Bryant, Charlie, FL, Allen
10. Ringer, Mike, HB, Oklahoma
11. Williams, Bobby, HB, Central State (Oklahoma)
12. Johnson, Rickey, T, Clemson
13. Brown, Jim, G, Nebraska
14. Pratt, LaVerle, LB, Idaho, F
15. Alleman, Darryl, E, Wyoming
16. Kasperek, Dick, C, Iowa State
17. Russell, Benny, QB, Louisville, F
18. Jones, Willie, DE, Kansas State
19. Golmont, Tony, DB, North Carolina State
20. Gallagher, Tom, DE, Indiana

SAN FRANCISCO
1. Hindman, Stan, T, Mississippi
2. Windsor, Bob, E, Kentucky, F
3. Randolph, Al, HB, Iowa, from Dallas
   Bland, Dan, DB, Mississippi State
4. Parker, Don, G, Virginia, F
5. Phillips, Mel, DB, North Carolina A&T, from Dallas
   Smith Steve, E, Michigan
6. Johnson, Charlie, DT, Louisville
7. Choice to Baltimore
8. Witcher, Dick, E, UCLA

9. Kramer, Kent, E, Minnesota
10. Sbranti, Ron, DE, Utah State
11. Ridlehuber, Preston, HB, Georgia
12. Loebach, Lyle, T, Simpson
13. Jackson, Jim, HB, Western Illinois, F
14. Collett, Elmer, C, Cal State-San Francisco, F
15. Saffold, Saint (St.), E, San Jose State, F
16. LeClair, Jim, QB, C.W. Post
17. Breeland, Jim, C, Georgia Tech, F
18. Parson, Ron, E, Austin Peay, F
19. Fitzgerald, Dick, T, Nebraska, F
20. Walker, Willie, E, Baylor, F

WASHINGTON
1. Gogolak, Charlie, K, Princeton
2. Barnes, Walter, T, Nebraska
3. Barrington, Tom, FB, Ohio State
4. Clay, Bill, DB, Mississippi
5. Lemay, Dick, T, Vanderbilt
6. Choice to Chi. Bears
Yates, Earl, T, Duke, from Green Bay
7. Patton, George, T, Georgia, F
8. Mitchell, Stan, FB, Tennessee
9. Shinholser, Jack, LB, Florida State
10. Belser, Caesar, DB, Arkansas-Monticello
11. Reding, Dick, FL, Northwestern State (Louisiana), F
12. Stipech, John, LB, Utah, F
13. Wingate, Heath, C, Bowling Green, F
14. Lovelace, Jerry, HB, Texas Tech, F
15. Seymour, Hal, HB-K, Florida
16. Wantland, Hal, HB, Tennessee
17. Zalnasky, Mitch, E, Pittsburgh
18. Burson, Joe, HB, Georgia
19. White, Andre, E, Florida A&M, F
20. Kelly, John, C, Florida A&M

1966 AFL
Held November 28, 1965

The expansion Miami Dolphins received the first two choices in the first round and the first choice in each subsequent round. The draft consisted of 181 selections.

On January 15, 1966, the Dolphins selected 32 players in an expansion draft, four from each of the other eight AFL teams.

BOSTON
1. Singer, Karl, T, Purdue
2. Boudreaux, Jim, T, Louisiana Tech
3. Lucas, Harold, T, Michigan State
4. Choice to NY Jets
5. Mangum, John, T, Southern Mississippi
6. Irby, Dan, T, Louisiana Tech
7. Battle, Jim, T, Southern
8. Montgomery, Sam, DB, Southern
9. Satcher, Doug, LB, Southern Mississippi
10. Brewster, Dennis, T, BYU
11. Choice to NY Jets
12. Fugere, Dick, LB, Cincinnati
13. Carr, Tom, FB, Bates
14. Hall, Bob, DB, Brown
15. Laird, Billy, QB, Louisiana Tech
16. Owens, Buddy, G, Michigan State
17. Capp, Dick, DE, Boston College
18. Pincavage, John, E-DB, Virginia
19. Novogratz, Joe, G, Pittsburgh
20. Soule, Paul, HB, Bowdoin

BUFFALO
1. Dennis, Mike, HB, Mississippi
2. Lindsey, Jim, HB, Arkansas
3. Jackson, Randy, T, Florida
4. Burnett, Bobby, HB, Arkansas
5. Sherlag, Bob, DB, Memphis State
6. Johnson, Bill, HB, University of the South
7. Choice to Denver
8. Guidry, Paul, E, McNeese State
9. Carter, Jim, DE, Tennessee State
10. Crockett, Bobby, E, Arkansas
11. Stewart, Dale, HB, Pittsburgh
12. DeSutter, Wayne, T, Western Illinois
13. McFarlane, Al, HB-K, Louisville
14. Golmont, Tony, DB, North Carolina State
15. Smith, Allen, HB, Fort Valley State
16. Russell, Ed, T, Illinois
17. Earhart, Bill, DT, Bowling Green
18. Lashutka, Greg, E, Ohio State
19. Phillips, Mel, HB, North Carolina A&T
20. McLean, Ken, E, Texas A&M

DENVER
1. Shay, Jerry, T, Purdue
2. White, Freeman, E, Nebraska
3. Hadrick, Bob, E, Purdue
4. Johnson, Randy, QB, Texas A&I
5. Clay, Billy, DB, Mississippi
6. Fulgham, James, T, Minnesota
7. Jones, Jerry, G, Bowling Green
Glacken, Scotty, QB, Duke, from Buffalo
8. Sellers, Goldie, DB, Grambling
9. Sbranti, Ron, LB, Utah State
10. Cox, Larry, T, Abilene Christian
11. Burns, James, G, Northwestern
12. Choice to NY Jets
13. Crabtree, Eric, DB, Pittsburgh
14. Forseberg, Fred, DT, Washington
15. Ringer, Mike, DB, Oklahoma
16. Rogers, Frank, K, Colorado
17. Eickman, Gary, DE, Illinois
18. Talaga, Tom, T, Notre Dame
19. Coughlin, Tom, DE, Miami
20. Hysell, Cliff, T, Montana State

HOUSTON
1. Nobis, Tommy, LB, Texas
2. Hindman, Stan, G, Mississippi
3. Rice, George, T, LSU
4. Allen, George, T, West Texas State
5. Granger, Hoyle, FB, Mississippi State
6. Long, Dave, DE-LB, Iowa
7. Menefee, Hartwell, DB, New Mexico State
8. Bland, Dan, HB, Mississippi State
9. Suffel, Dick, DB, Southwest Texas State
10. Aylor, Wilbur, DT, Southwest Texas State
11. Ledbetter, Monty, E, Northwestern State (Louisiana)
12. Day, Harry, DE, Memphis State
13. Zimmerman, Fred, LB, Toledo
14. Lince, Butch, DT, North Dakota
15. Dillard, Tom, T, Austin Peay
16. Smith, Steve, DE, Michigan
17. Loebach, Lyle, T, Simpson
18. Buzzell, Ed, QB, Ottawa
19. Fuller, Frank, DT, Drake
20. Odegaard, Dave, C, Bemidji State

KANSAS CITY
1. Brown, Aaron, E, Minnesota
2. Peay, Francis, T, Missouri
3. Barnes, Walter, G, Nebraska
4. Gibson, Elijah, HB, Bethune-Cookman
5. Van Horn, Doug, G, Ohio State
6. Osmond, John, C, Tulsa
7. Gogolak, Charlie, K, Princeton
8. Smith, Fletcher, DB, Tennessee State
9. Smith, Dick, E-DB, Northwestern
10. Dawston, Fred, DB, South Carolina State
11. Smith, Willie Ray, DB, Kansas
12. Bonds, Bill, DB, McMurry
13. Walker, Wayne, E-K, Northwestern State (Louisiana)
14. Harraway, Charley, FB, San Jose State
15. Van Dyke, Bruce, G, Missouri
16. Barrington, Tom, FB, Ohio State
17. Garrison, Walt, FB, Oklahoma State
18. Seymour, Hal, DB, Florida
19. Dunlevy, Bob, E, West Virginia
20. Garrett, Mike, HB, USC

MIAMI
1. Grabowski, Jim, FB, Illinois
Norton, Rick, QB, Kentucky
2. Emanuel, Frank, LB, Tennessee
3. Gagner, Larry, G, Florida
4. Leftridge, Dick, FB, West Virginia
5. Bolton, Grady, T, Mississippi State
6. Weisacosky, Ed, LB, Miami
7. Hansen, Don, LB, Illinois
8. Petrella, Bob, HB, Tennessee
9. Matan, Bill, DE, Kansas State
10. Killorin, Pat, C, Syracuse
11. Price, Sam, HB, Illinois
12. Twilley, Howard, E, Tulsa
13. Kramer, Kent, E, Minnesota
14. Scoggin, Phil, K, Texas A&M
15. Oliver, Jerry, T, Southwest Texas State
16. Lorenz, Don, DE, Stephen F. Austin
17. Bender, Mike, G, Arkansas
18. Kestner, Rich, E, Kentucky
19. Moreau, Doug, E-K, LSU
20. Tooker, John, DB, Adams State

MIAMI (Expansion)
Branch, Mel, DE, LSU, from Kansas City
Caveness, Ronnie, LB, Arkansas, from Kansas City
Cooke, Ed, DE, Maryland, from Denver
Davidson, Jim, T, Ohio State, from Buffalo
Dotson, Al, DT, Grambling, from Kansas City
Erlandson, Tom, LB, Washington State, from Denver
Evans, Norm, T, TCU, from Houston
Goode, Tom, C, Mississippi State, from Houston
Huddock, Mike, C, Miami, from NY Jets
Jackson, Frank, WR, SMU, from Kansas City
Joe, Billy, FB, Villanova, from Buffalo
Kocourek, Dave, TE, Wisconsin, from San Diego
McDaniel, Edward (Wahoo), LB, Oklahoma, from NY Jets
McGeever, John, S, Auburn, from Denver
Mingo, Gene, K, from Oakland
Neighbors, Billy, G, Alabama, from Boston
Nomina, Tom, DT, Miami (Ohio), from Denver
O'Hanley, Ross, S, Boston College, from Boston
Park, Ernie, G, McMurry, from San Diego
Rice, Ken, G, Auburn, from Oakland
Roberson, Bo, WR, Cornell, from Buffalo
Rudolph, Jack, LB, Georgia Tech, from Boston
Simpson, Howard, DT, Auburn, from Buffalo
Spikes, Jack, FB, TCU, from Houston
Torczon, Laverne, DE, Nebraska, from NY Jets
Warren, Jimmy, CB, Illinois, from San Diego
West, Willie, S, Oregon, from NY Jets
Westmoreland, Dick, CB, North Carolina A&T, from San Diego
Williams, Maxie, T, Southeastern Louisiana, Wilson, Eddie, QB, Arizona, from Boston
Wood, Dick, QB, Auburn, from Oakland
Zecher, Rich, DT, Utah State, from Oakland

NY JETS
1. Yearby, Bill, T, Michigan
2. Ball, Sam, T, Kentucky
3. McAdams, Carl, LB, Oklahoma
4. Waskiewicz, Jim, C-LB, Wichita State, from Boston
Sheridan, Phil, E, Notre Dame
5. Hawkins, Ben, E, Arizona State
6. Boozer, Emerson, FB, Maryland-Eastern Shore
Lemay, Dick, G, Vanderbilt, from Oakland
7. Dobson, Joe, T, Idaho
8. Lammons, Pete, E, Texas
9. Jones, James, E, Nebraska-Omaha
10. Wolski, Bill, HB, Notre Dame
11. Allen, Gerry, HB, Nebraska-Omaha, from Boston
Walton, Bob, T, Auburn
12. Chomyszak, Steve, DT, Syracuse, from Denver
Hollister, Ken, DE, Indiana
13. Maliszewski, Stas, LB, Princeton
14. Quintana, Stan, DB, New Mexico
15. Cody, Steve, LB, Auburn
16. Acks, Ron, DB, Illinois
17. Tolleson, Tom, DB, Alabama
18. Mosher, Gerry, E, California
19. Ridlehuber, Preston, HB, Georgia
20. Schultz, Randy, HB, Cedar Fort State

OAKLAND
1. Bird, Rodger, HB, Kentucky
2. Allison, Butch, T, Missouri
3. Mitchell, Tom, E, Bucknell
4. Tyson, Richard, G, Tulsa
5. Banaszak, Pete, HB, Miami
6. Choice to NY Jets
7. McRae, Franklin, T, Tennessee State
8. Choice to Denver
9. Kinney, Clifton, LB, San Diego State
10. Jeter, Tony, E, Nebraska
11. Labruzzo, Joe, HB, LSU
12. Foster, Wayne, T, Washington State
13. Niland, John, G, Iowa
14. Johnson, Mike, HB, Kansas
15. Renko, Steve, FB, Kansas
16. Ritchey, Craig, DB, Stanford
17. Holman, Ted, DB, Syracuse
18. Robinson, Art, E, Florida A&M
19. Shinholser, Jack, LB, Florida State
20. Bowman, Steve, FB, Alabama

SAN DIEGO
1. Davis, Don, T, Cal State-Los Angeles
2. Rassas, Nick, HB, Notre Dame
3. Morin, Milt, E, Massachusetts
4. Brown, Charlie, HB, Syracuse
5. Smith, Russ, HB, Miami
6. Pettigrew, Gary, DE, Stanford
7. Tolbert, Jim, E, Lincoln (Missouri)
8. Buffone, Doug, LB, Louisville
9. Reed, Taft, E-DB, Jackson State
10. Pride, Danny, LB, Tennessee State
11. Owens, Terry, E, Jacksonville State
12. Jones, Ray, HB, Cal State-Los Angeles
13. Ridge, Houston, DE, San Diego State
14. London, Mike, E, Wisconsin
15. Novack, Shelly, E, Long Beach State
16. Scott, Bill, DB, Idaho
17. Ogle, Ron, DT, Long Beach State
18. Travis, John, HB, San Jose State
19. Bell, Jerome, E-K, Central State (Oklahoma)
20. McDowell, Bill, LB, Florida State

1966 AFL REDSHIRT
Held November 28, 1965

BOSTON
1. Townes, Willie, T, Tulsa
2. Avery, Ken, LB, Southern Mississippi
3. Toner, Ed, G, Massachusetts
4. Wingate, Heath, T, Bowling Green
5. Perkins, Ray, E, Alabama
6. Avezzano, Joe, G, Florida State
7. Caston, Brent, DB, Mississippi
8. Schaefer, Tom, FB, Tennessee-Chattanooga
9. White, Jack, QB, Penn State
10. Ellis, Bob, HB, Massachusetts
11. Marion, Jay, HB, Wyoming

BUFFALO
1. Gregory, Jack, E, Tennessee-Chattanooga
2. Robinson, John, E, Tennessee State
3. King, Tony, E, Findlay
4. Cunningham, Dick, LB, Arkansas
5. Czap, Dick, T, Nebraska
6. Carter, Leroy, HB, Grambling
7. Weeks, Dick, B, Texas-El Paso
8. Phelps, Monroe, HB, Missouri
9. King, Ed, LB, USC
10. Moorer, Bill, C, Georgia Tech
11. Russell, Benny, QB, Louisville

DENVER
1. Eddy, Nick, HB, Notre Dame
2. Duranko, Pete, E, Notre Dame
3. Arndt, Dick, T, Idaho
4. Gartung, Mark, T, Oregon State
5. Hatfield, Art, E, Cal State-Los Angeles
6. Durling, Jerald, T, Wyoming
7. Mason, John, E, Stanford
8. Sorrell, Henry, LB, Tennessee-Chattanooga
9. Harrington, Bud, FB, Tulsa
10. White, Andre, E, Florida A&M
11. Sullivan, Mike, E, Oregon State

HOUSTON
1. Fisher, Tom, LB, Tennessee
2. Van Galder, Tim, QB, Iowa State
3. Dunlap, Ralph, DT, Baylor
4. Davis, Bill, QB, Lamar
5. Glover, Richard, T, Virginia State
6. Gary, John, DT, Grambling
7. Pettaway, Clyde, T, North Carolina A&T
8. Marshall, Roger, QB, Baylor
9. Garner, Lee, LB, Mississippi
10. Goich, Dan, T, California
11. Arkwright, Charley, T, Georgia

KANSAS CITY
1. Youngblood, George, E-DB, Cal State-Los Angeles
2. Pickens, Bob, T, Nebraska
3. Stenerud, Jan, K, Montana State
4. Berry, Dan, HB, California
5. Senkbeil, Lynn, LB, Nebraska
6. Reding, Dick, DB, Northwestern State (Louisiana)
7. Ogle, Bill, T, Stanford
8. Myricks, Melvin, DB, Washburn
9. Parks, Perry, DT, Cal State-Los Angeles
10. Collett, Elmer, C, Cal State-San Francisco
11. Moore, Denis, T, USC

MIAMI
1. Roderick, John, E, SMU
2. Fulford, Harold, E, Auburn
3. Clancy, Jack, E, Michigan
4. Mankins, Jim, FB, Florida
5. Greenlee, Fritz, E, Arizona
6. Darnell, Bill, DB, North Carolina
7. Williams, Don, DT, Wofford
8. Brittenum, Jon, QB, Arkansas
9. Baynham, Craig, E, Georgia Tech

10. Winkler, Randy, T, Tarleton State
11. Anderson, Kai, C, Illinois

NY JETS
1. Parker, Don, E, Virginia
2. Denney, Austin, E, Tennessee
3. Lovelace, Jerry, HB, Texas Tech
4. Burnett, Tom, E, Arkansas
5. Miller, Ray, T, Idaho
6. Smith, Allen, HB, Findlay
7. Smith, Randy, LB, Clemson
8. Campbell, Joe, DB, Auburn
9. Stipech, John, T, Utah
10. Fitzgerald, Dick, T, Nebraska
11. Kollman, Jim, G, Oregon

OAKLAND
1. Sherman, Rod, HB, USC
2. Cichowski, Tom, T, Maryland
3. Parson, Ron, E, Austin Peay
4. Crumbacher, John, T, Tennessee
5. Patton, George, T, Georgia
6. Archer, Dan, T, Oregon
7. Thomas, Bill, HB, Oklahoma
8. Schmautz, Ray, LB, San Diego State
9. Tom, Mel, LB, San Jose State
10. O'Brien, Joe, FB, Texas-Arlington
11. Brundage, Mike, QB, Oregon

SAN DIEGO
1. Windsor, Bob, E, Kentucky
2. Talbert, Diron, T, Texas
3. Staggs, Jeff, LB, San Diego State
4. Pratt, LaVerle, LB, Idaho
5. Nixon, Rhome, E, Southern
6. Beauchamp, Joe, E-DB, Iowa
7. Saffold, S.T., E, San Jose State
8. Hubbert, Brad, HB, Arizona
9. Page, Wayne, DB, Clemson
10. Becker, Wayne, T, Montana
11. Wright, Hugh, FB, Adams State

1967

Held March 14, 1967

The first combined AFL-NFL draft was held. A player's order of selection among the 445 players drafted was designated by a number after his college. The expansion New Orleans Saints received first and last choices in each round and one additional choice at the end of the second, third, and fourth rounds.

On February 10, the Saints selected 42 players in an expansion draft, using the same procedures as in the formation of the Atlanta Falcons in 1966. The Falcons were exempted from the expansion draft in 1967, thus leaving 14 teams from whom the Saints selected players.

ATLANTA
1. Choice to San Francisco
2. Carroll, Leo, DE, San Diego State, 31
3. Jordan, Jim, HB, Florida, 57
4. Choice to Cleveland
5. Delaney, Bill, TE, American International, 112
   Matson, Randy, DT, Texas A&M, from San Francisco, 120
6. Choice to Baltimore
   Snipes, Eugene, HB, Elizabeth City State, from LA Rams, 148
   Bircher, Martine, DB, Arkansas, from Baltimore, 151
7. Colehour, Corey, QB, North Dakota, 162
8. Choice to Washington
9. Moton, Bob, FL, Bishop, 215
10. Schafroth, Dick, T, Iowa State, 240
11. Walker, John, LB, Jackson State, 268
12. Gentry, Bill, LB, North Carolina State, 293
13. Szabo, Sandor, K, Ithaca, 317
14. Bryan, Tom, FB, Auburn, 346
15. Nicholas, Al, FB, Cal State-Sacramento, 371
16. Chester, Larry, DB, Allen, 396
17. Buckner, Bill, QB, Delta State, 424

BALTIMORE
1. Smith, Bubba, DT, Michigan State, from New Orleans, 1
   Detwiler, Jim, HB, Michigan, 20
2. Volk, Rick, DB, Michigan, 45
3. Davis, Norman, T, Grambling, from New Orleans, 54
   Ward, Leon, LB, Oklahoma State, 71
4. Stukes, Charlie, HB, Maryland-Eastern Shore, 100
5. Porter, Ron, LB, Idaho, 126
6. Southall, Terry, QB, Baylor, from Atlanta, 137
   Choice to Atlanta
7. Rein, Bo, FL, Ohio State, 179
8. Anderson, Lee, T, Bishop, from St. Louis, 202
   Johnson, Cornelius, LB, Virginia Union, 204
9. Kirkland, Ron, HB, Nebraska, 229
10. Gilbert, Leigh, TE, Northern Illinois, 258
11. Reed, Herman, T, St. Augustine, 290
12. Pearson, Preston, DB, Illinois, from Pittsburgh, 298
    Christian, J.B., G, Oklahoma State, 307
13. Allen, Marc, DE, West Texas State, 335
14. Conley, Pat, LB, Purdue, 359
15. Wade, Bob, DB, Morgan State, 385
16. Alley, Don, FL, Adams State, 413
17. Choice to New Orleans

BOSTON
1. Charles, John, DB, Purdue, 21
2. Choice to Kansas City
3. Choice to NY Jets
4. Philpott, Ed, DE, Miami (Ohio), 101
5. Witt, Melvin, DE, Texas-Arlington, 128
6. Medlen, Ron, DE, SMU, 154
7. Leo, Bobby, HB, Harvard, 180
8. Fussell, Tom, DT, LSU, 206
9. Thornhill, Charlie, DB, Michigan State, 232
10. Runnels, John, LB, Penn State, 257
11. Mitchell, Leroy, FL, Texas Southern, 283
12. Davis, Dave, T, Harvard, 310
13. Ilg, Ray, LB, Colgate, 336
14. Beaird, Bobby, DB, Auburn, 361
15. Folliard, Tom, LB, Mississippi State, 388
16. Nocera, Dick, HB, Southern Connecticut, 414
17. Nichols, Bobby, TE, Boston U., 440

BUFFALO
1. Pitts, John, FL-DB, Arizona State, 22
2. LeMoine, Jim, TE, Utah State, from Oakland, 42
   Choice to San Diego
3. Rhoads, Tom, DE, Notre Dame, from Oakland through Denver, 70
   Choice to Oakland
4. Bugenhagen, Gary, T, Syracuse, 102
5. Choice to Miami
6. Wilkerson, Bill, DE, Texas El Paso, from Oakland, 149
   Choice to Oakland
7. Gaiser, George, T, SMU, 181
8. Luke, Tommy, DB, Mississippi, 207
9. Seither, Gerald, E, Kent State, 233
10. Croft, Tom, DB, Louisiana Tech, 259
11. Tomich, Paul, T, Drake, 284
12. Ames, Ernie, DT, Kent State, from Houston, 292
    Bonner, Bob, DT, Southern, 311
13. Finley, Howard, DB, Tennessee State, from Miami, 318
    Carter, George, HB, St. Bonaventure, from Houston, 319
    Wheeler, Randy, HB, Georgia, 337
14. Moore, Vern, HB, Central State (Oklahoma), 362
15. Martinsen, Grant, DB, Utah State, 389
16. Irwin, Mike, HB, Penn State, 415
17. Smith, Grover, HB, Fort Valley State, 441

CHI. BEARS
1. Phillips, Loyd, DE, Arkansas, 10
2. Jones, Bob, DB, San Diego State, 36
3. Lyle, Gary, HB, George Washington, 63
4. Dodd, Al, DB, Northwestern State (Louisiana), 90
   Greenlee, Tom, DB, Washington, from LA Rams, 95
5. Alford, Bruce, K, TCU, 119
6. Carter, Virgil, QB, BYU, 142
   Kriewald, Doug, G, West Texas State, 143
7. Truitt, John, E, Indiana State, 169
8. Murphy, Roger, E, Northwestern, 195
   Griffin, Jerry, LB, SMU, 200
9. Cass, Greg, C, Washington, 221
10. Choice to Washington
11. Mayo, Earl, HB, Morgan State, 273
12. Green, Bruce, E, Midland Lutheran, 299
13. Carstens, Kaye, DB, Nebraska, 326
14. Nesbitt, Lynn, G, Wake Forest, 351
15. Oakes, Terry, DE, Cal State-San Francisco, 377
16. Rogers, Bill, DB, Weber State, 403*
17. Myers, Jack, LB, Western State (Colorado), 429

CLEVELAND
1. Matheson, Bob, LB, Duke, 18
2. Conjar, Larry, FB, Notre Dame, 46
3. Cockroft, Don, K, Adams State, from NY Giants, 55
   Barney, Eppie, E, Iowa State, 72
4. Ward, Carl, HB, Michigan, from Atlanta, 83
   Taffoni, Joe, T, Tennessee-Martin, 98
5. Choice to Houston through Dallas
6. DeMarie, John, DE, LSU, 152
7. House, Bill, T, Youngstown State, 177
8. Devrow, Bill, DB, Southern Mississippi, 205
9. Dowdy, Cecil, LB, Alabama, 230
10. Copeland, Jim, G, Virginia, 255
11. Sabatino, Bill, DE, Colorado, 282
12. Fowler, Charlie, T, Houston, 308
13. Andrews, Billy, LB, Southeastern Louisiana, 333
14. Rogers, Floyd, T, Clemson, 360
15. Williamson, Dennis, DB, Wisconsin-Whitewater, 386
16. Williams, Don, E, Akron, 411
17. Davis, Ben, HB, Defiance, 439

DALLAS
1. Choice to Houston
2. Choice to Houston
3. Clark, Phil, DB, Northwestern, 76
4. Marker, Curtis, G, Northern Michigan, 103
5. Choice to Green Bay
6. Stokes, Sims, FL, Northern Arizona, 157
7. Wright, Rayfield, DT, Fort Valley State, 182
8. Laub, Steve, QB, Illinois Wesleyan, 208
9. Morgan, Byron, DB, Findlay, 234
10. Bowens, Eugene, HB, Tennessee State, 260
11. Riley, Pat, FL, Kentucky, 285
12. Deters, Harold, K, North Carolina State, 312
13. Kerkian, Al, DE, Akron, 338
14. Boyd, Tommy, G, Tarleton State, 364
15. David, Leavie, DB, Edward Waters, 390
16. Brothers, Paul, QB, Oregon State, 416
17. Adams, George, LB, Morehead State, 442

DENVER
1. Little, Floyd, HB, Syracuse, 6
2. Beer, Tom, TE, Houston, 32
3. Current, Mike, T, Ohio State, from Miami, 58
   Goeddeke, George, C, Notre Dame, 59
4. Cunningham, Carl, DE, Houston, 85
5. Lynch, Fran, FB, Hofstra, from Miami, 110
   Huard, John, LB, Maine, 113
6. Sweeney, Neal, E, Tulsa, 139
7. Richter, Frank, G, Georgia, 165
8. Cassese, Tom, E, C.W. Post, 191
9. Summers, Jim, DB, Michigan State, 217
10. Krause, Paul, QB, Dubuque, 243
11. Andrus, Lou, DE, BYU, 269
12. Choice to Miami
13. Furjanic, Dennis, DE, Houston, 321
14. Francisco, Tom, HB, Virginia Tech, 347
15. Smith, Don, G, Florida A&M, 373
16. Lentz, Jack, QB, Holy Cross, 399
17. Valley, Wayne, T, Oregon State, 425

DETROIT
1. Farr, Mel, HB, UCLA, 7
2. Barney, Lem, DB, Jackson State, 34
3. Naumoff, Paul, LB, Tennessee, 60
4. Kamanu, Lew, DE, Weber State, 88
5. Choice to Philadelphia
6. Jones, Tim, QB, Weber State, 141
   McCambridge, John, DE, Northwestern, from Washington, 144
7. Tuinstra, Ted, T, Iowa State, 166
8. Choice to St. Louis
9. Weger, Mike, DB, Bowling Green, 218
10. Hayhoe, Jerry, G, USC, 245
11. Shirley, Ray, T, Arizona State, 270
12. Watts, Eric, DB, San Jose State, 297
13. Wright, Lamar, G, Georgia Tech, 322
14. Robinson, Cleveland, DE, South Carolina State, 349
15. Burke, Sam, DB, Georgia Tech, 374
16. Zawadzkas, Jerry, TE, Columbia, 401
17. Ramsey, Ken, DT, Northwestern, 426

GREEN BAY
1. Hyland, Bob, G, Boston College, 9
   Horn, Don, QB, San Diego State, 25
2. Dunaway, Dave, FL, Duke, from LA Rams, 41
   Flanigan, Jim, LB, Pittsburgh, 51
3. Rowser, John, DB, Michigan, 78
4. Williams, Travis, HB, Arizona State, from Washington, 93
   Choice to St. Louis
5. Hood, Dwight, DT, Baylor, from Pittsburgh, 116
   Tate, Richard, DB, Utah, from Dallas, 130
   Bachman, Jay, C, Cincinnati, 132
6. Williams, Stew, FB, Bowling Green, 158
7. Ziolkowski, Bob, T, Iowa, from NY Giants, 161
   Powell, Bill, LB, Missouri, 184
8. Miles, Clarence, DT, Trinity (Texas), 210
9. Reed, Harlan, TE, Mississippi State, 236
10. Shear, Bill, K, Cortland State, 262
11. Bennett, Dave, QB, Springfield, 287
12. Bass, Mike, DB, Michigan, 314
13. Brown, Keith, FL, Central Missouri State, 340
14. James, Claudis, HB, Jackson State, 366
15. Schneider, Jim, DT, Colgate, 392
16. Cassidy, Fred, HB, Miami, 418
17. Elias, Jeff, TE, Kansas, 444

HOUSTON
1. Webster, George, LB, Michigan State, 5
   Regner, Tom, G, Notre Dame, from Dallas, 23
2. Davis, Bob, QB, Virginia, 30
   Hopkins, Roy, HB, Texas Southern, from Dallas, 49
3. Carwell, Larry, DB, Iowa State, 56
4. Stith, Carel, T, Nebraska, 85
5. Johns, Peter, DB, Tulane, 111
   Parker, Willie, DT, Arkansas-Pine Bluff, from Washington through Dallas, 118
   Moore, Zeke, DB, Lincoln (Missouri), from Cleveland through Dallas, 127
6. Barnes, Pete, LB, Southern, 136
7. Carrington, Ed, FL, Virginia, 164
8. Brunson, John, HB, Benedictine, 189
   Washington, Sharon, FL, Northeast Missouri State, from Oakland, 201
9. Houston, Ken, DB, Prairie View A&M, 214
10. Campbell, Woody, HB, Northwestern, 242
    Sheehan, Tim, C, Stanford, from Kansas City, 261
11. Decker, Harold, DE, Kalamazoo, 267
12. Choice to Buffalo
13. Choice to Buffalo
14. Hailstock, Henry, G, Lincoln (Missouri), 345
15. McQueen, Marvin, LB, Mississippi, 370
16. Keeling, Rex, FL, Samford, 398
17. Lee, Larry, FL, Texas A&M, 423

KANSAS CITY
1. Trosch, Gene, DT, Miami, 24
2. Lynch, Jim, LB, Notre Dame, from Boston, 47
   Lanier, Willie, LB, Morgan State, 50
3. Masters, Billy, TE, LSU, 77
4. Zwernemann, Ron, G, East Texas State, 104
5. Choice to Oakland through Buffalo
6. Smith, Noland, HB, Tennessee State, 156
7. Erickson, Dick, C, Wisconsin-Stout, 183
8. Altemeier, Tom, T, Luther, 209
9. Pope, Ed, DT, Jackson State, 235
10. Choice to Houston
11. Braswell, Bill, G, Auburn, 286
12. Kolonski, Dick, C, Lake Forest, from San Diego, 303
    Lashley, Kent, FL, Northeastern Oklahoma, 313
13. Simmons, Linwood, FB, Edward Waters, 339
14. Bishop, John, DT, Delta State, 365
15. Caponi, Dennis, FB, Xavier, 391
16. Noggle, Charlie, HB, North Carolina State, 417
17. Lattin, Dave, FL, Texas-El Paso, 443

LA RAMS
1. Choice to Minnesota
2. Ellison, Willie, HB, Texas Southern, from Minnesota, 33
   Choice to Green Bay
3. Choice to Philadelphia
4. Choice to Chi. Bears
5. Shaw, Nate, DB, USC, 122
6. Choice to Atlanta

7. Choice to Philadelphia
8. Choice to Chi. Bears
9. Smith, Tommie, HB, San Jose State, 226
10. Moore, Leon, DB, Tennessee State, 252
11. Horak, Frank, DB, TCU, 278
12. Badjek, Pat, LB, Franklin, 304
13. Erisman, John, E, Miami (Ohio), 330
14. Richardson, Walt, DT, Fresno State, 356
15. Bunker, Steve, TE, Oregon, 382
16. Sack, Allen, LB, Notre Dame, 408
17. Barnes, Bill, C, Washington, 434

MIAMI
1. Griese, Bob, QB, Purdue, 4
2. Riley, Jim, T, Oklahoma, 29
3. Choice to Denver
4. Greenlee, Bob, T, Yale, 84
5. Choice to Denver
   Tucker, Gary, HB, Tennessee-Chattanooga, from Buffalo, 129
6. Norris, Bud, TE, Washington State, 138
7. Seiple, Larry, HB, Kentucky, 163
8. Choice to Oakland
9. Richardson, John, DT, UCLA, 216
10. Beier, Tom, DB, Miami, 241
11. Pyburn, Jack, T, Texas A&M, 266
12. Juk, Stan, LB, South Carolina, 294
   Whitaker, Jim, DB, Missouri, from Denver, 295
13. Choice to Buffalo
14. Stikes, Charles, DB, Kent State, 344
15. Ferro, Jake, LB, Youngstown State, 372
16. Calhoun, Maurice, FB, Central State (Ohio), 397
17. Kissam, Larry, T, Florida State, 422

MINNESOTA
1. Jones, Clint, HB, Michigan State, from NY Giants, 2
   Washington, Gene, FL, Michigan State, 8
   Page, Alan, DE, Notre Dame, from LA Rams, 15
2. Grim, Bob, HB, Oregon State, from NY Giants, 28
   Choice to LA Rams
3. Denny, Earl, FL, Missouri, 61
4. Coleman, Alvin, DB, Tennessee A&I, 87
5. Last, Ken, E, Minnesota, 115
6. Choice to Pittsburgh
7. Bryant, Bobby, DB, South Carolina, 167
8. Choice to Pittsburgh
   Beasley, John, TE, California, from Washington, 197
9. Morris, Bill, G, Holy Cross, 219
10. Tatman, Pete, FB, Nebraska, 244
11. Trygstad, Bob, DT, Washington State, 271
12. Cremer, Fred, G, St. John's (Minnesota), 296
13. Hardt, Charley, DB, Tulsa, 323
14. Hargrove, Jimmy, LB, Howard Payne, 348
15. Shea, Jimmy, DB, Eastern New Mexico, 375
16. Beard, Gene, DB, Virginia Union, 400
17. Wagoner, Dick, DB, Bowling Green, 427

NEW ORLEANS
1. Choice to Baltimore
   Kelley, Les, HB, Alabama, 26
2. Burris, Bo, QB-DB, Houston, 27
   Gilliam, John, FL, South Carolina State, 52
   Rowe, Dave, T, Penn State, 53
3. Choice to Baltimore
   Williams, Del, C, Florida State, 79
   Hart, Ben, HB, Oklahoma, 80
4. Widby, Ron, K, Tennessee, 81
   Carr, Bill, C, Florida, 106
   Stangle, Tom, T, Dayton, 107
5. McCall, Don, HB, USC, 108
   Douglas, John, DB, Texas Southern, 133
6. Harvey, George, G, Kansas, 134
   Wood, Bo, LB, North Carolina, 159
7. Hertzog, Gary, G, Willamette, 160
   McKelvey, Bob, HB, Northwestern, 185
8. Harris, Sam, TE, Colorado, 186
   Siler, Barry, LB, Albion, 211
9. Lavens, Tim, TE, Idaho, 212
   Ross, Eugene, DB, Oklahoma, 237
10. Brown, Charlie, FL, Missouri, 238
   Robertson, Roosevelt, FL, North Carolina Central, 263
11. Benson, Jim, G, Florida, 264
   Corbin, Bernard, DB, Alabama A&M, 288
12. Pack, Ronnie, G, Texas Tech, 289
   Robinson, John, FL, Tennessee State, 315
13. Stetz, Bill, LB, Boston College, 316
   Grossnickle, Gary, DB, Missouri, 341
14. Hester, Jim, TE, North Dakota, 342
   Stetter, George, DB, Virginia, 367
15. Snow, John, T, Wake Forest, 368
   Johnson, Darrell, HB, Lamar, 393
16. Rhoden, Marcus, FL, Mississippi State, 394
   Cortez, Bruce, DB, Parsons, 419
17. Abramowicz, Dan, HB, Xavier, 420
   Stewart, Billy Bob, LB, SMU, from Baltimore, 438
   Walker, Jimmy, E, Providence, 445

NEW ORLEANS (Expansion)
Barrington, Tom, FB, Ohio State, from Washington
Battle, Jim, T, Southern, from Cleveland
Bradshaw, Charlie, T, Baylor, from Pittsburgh
Burkett, Jackie, LB, Auburn, from Baltimore
Cahill, Dave, DT, Arizona State, from Philadelphia
Cody, Bill, LB, Auburn, from Detroit
Croftcheck, Don, G, Indiana, from Washington
Curry, Bill, C, Georgia Tech, from Green Bay
Davis, Ted, LB, Georgia Tech, from Baltimore
Garcia, Jim, DE, Cal State-Chico, from NY Giants
Hall, Tom, FL, Minnesota, from Minnesota
Heckard, Steve, FL, Davidson, from LA Rams
Heidel, Jimmy, DB, Mississippi, from St. Louis
Hornung, Paul, HB, Notre Dame, from Green Bay
Kilmer, Billy, QB, UCLA, from San Francisco
Kimbrough, Elbert, DB, Northwestern, from San Francisco
Kramer, Kent, TE, Minnesota, from San Francisco
Kupp, Jake, G, Washington, from Washington
Leggett, Earl, DT, LSU, from LA Rams
Logan, Obert, DB, Trinity (Texas), from Dallas
Mattson, Riley, T, Oregon, from Chi. Bears
Morrow, John, C, Michigan, from Cleveland
Ogden, Ray, TE, Alabama, from St. Louis
Rissmiller, Ray, T, Georgia, from Philadelphia
Roberts, Walter (The Flea), FL, San Jose State, from Cleveland
Rose, George, DB, Auburn, from Minnesota
Sandeman, Bill, T, Pacific, from Dallas
Scholtz, Bob, T, Notre Dame, from NY Giants
Schweda, Brian, DE, Kansas, from Chi. Bears
Simmons, Dave, LB, Georgia Tech, from St. Louis
Simmons, Jerry, SE, Bethune-Cookman, from Pittsburgh
Smith, Bob, HB, North Texas State, from Pittsburgh
Smith, Bobby Lee, DB, UCLA, from Detroit
Stephens, Larry, DT, Texas, from Dallas
Stonebreaker, Steve, LB, Detroit, from Baltimore
Tilleman, Mike, DT, Montana, from Minnesota
Vandersea, Phil, LB, Masschusetts, from Green Bay
Walker, Willie, SE, Tennessee State, from Detroit
Wendryhoski, Joe, G, Illinois, from LA Rams
Whitsell, Dave, DB, Indiana, from Chi. Bears
Whittingham, Fred, LB, Cal Poly-SLO, from Philadelphia
Wood, Gary, QB, Cornell, from NY Giants

NY GIANTS
1. Choice to Minnesota
2. Choice to Minnesota
3. Choice to Cleveland
4. Thompson, Louis, DT, Alabama, 82
5. Lewis, Dave, QB, Stanford, 109
6. Choice to Washington through Minnesota
7. Choice to Green Bay
8. Eaton, Scott, DB, Oregon State, 187
9. Freeman, Fred, T, Mississippi Valley State, 213
10. Stebbins, Dick, E, Grambling, 239
11. Pifer, Pete, FB, Oregon State, 265
12. Shortal, Bob, LB, Dayton, 291
13. Stidham, Tom, K, Oklahoma, 320
14. Bates, Bill, K, Missouri, 343
15. Reale, Tom, T, Southern Connecticut State, 369
16. Seman, Bill, G, Northeast Missouri State, 395
17. Rowe, Gary, HB, North Carolina State, 421

NY JETS
1. Seiler, Paul, G, Notre Dame, 12
2. Sheron, Rich, TE, Washington State, 37
3. Randall, Dennis, DE, Oklahoma State, 66
   King, Henry, DB, Utah State, from Boston, 74
4. Gray, Julian, DB, Grambling, 92
5. Jackson, Louis, DB, Grambling, 117
6. Richardson, Jeff, DE, Michigan State, 146
7. Elliott, John, G, Texas, 171
8. Bledsoe, Gene, G, Texas, 196
9. Scott, Ray, DE, Prairie View A&M, 224
10. Brown, Raymond, DB, Alcorn State, 249
11. Slattery, Herb, G, Delaware, 274
12. Rasmussen, Randy, G, Kearney State, 302
13. Emmer, Jack, FL, Rutgers, 327
14. Stromberg, Mike, LB, Temple, 352
15. Schweberger, Jack, FL, Vermont, 380
16. Archibald, Doug, DB, Tennessee, 405
17. Biletnikoff, Bob, QB, Miami, 430

OAKLAND
1. Upshaw, Gene, G-T, Texas A&I, 17
2. Choice to Buffalo
3. Choice to Buffalo through Denver
   Fairband, Bill, LB, Colorado, from Buffalo, 75
4. Jackson, James Roy, E, Oklahoma, 96
5. Warfield, Gerald, HB, Mississippi, 124
   Hibler, Mike, LB, Stanford, from Buffalo through Kansas City, 131
6. Choice to Buffalo
   Egloff, Rick, QB, Wyoming, from Buffalo, 155
7. Lewellen, Ron, DT, Tennessee-Martin, 176
8. Banks, Estes, HB, Colorado, from Miami, 188
   Choice to Houston
9. DeVilling, Mark, LB, Muskingum, 228
10. Sligh, Richard, T, North Carolina Central, 253
11. Benson, Dwayne, LB, Hamline, 280
12. Kruse, Bob, T, Wayne State, 306
13. Kleinpeter, Len, E, Southwestern Louisiana, 332
14. Boyett, Casey, E, BYU, 363*
15. Woodson, Ben, HB, Utah, 384
16. Bruce, Don, G, Virginia Tech, 409
17. Cullin, Mike, DE, Slippery Rock, 436

PHILADELPHIA
1. Jones, Harry, HB, Arkansas, 19
2. Brooks, John, G, Kent State, 44
3. Wilson, Harry, HB, Nebraska, from LA Rams, 68
   Choice to Pittsburgh
4. Hughes, Chuck, FL, Texas-El Paso, 99
5. Van Pelt, Bob, C, Indiana, from Detroit, 114
   Absher, Dick, TE, Maryland, 125
6. Hughes, Bob, DE, Jackson State, 153
7. Williams, John, DB, San Diego State, from LA Rams, 174
   Crenshaw, Bob, G, New Mexico State, 178
8. Klacking, Don, FB, Wyoming, 203
9. Stancell, Harold, DB, Tennessee, 231
10. Bates, Maurice, DE, Northern State (South Dakota), 256
11. Parker, Omar, G, Washington, 281
12. Monroe, Ben, QB, New Mexico, 309
13. Downs, Bill, DT, Louisville, 334
14. Kenney, Dick, K, Michigan State, 358
15. Poche, David, T, McNeese State, 387
16. Baker, Lynn, DB, Colorado, 412
17. Catavolos, George, DB, Purdue, 437

PITTSBURGH
1. Choice to Green Bay
2. Shy, Don, HB, San Diego State, 35
3. Choice to San Francisco
   Freitas, Rockne, C, Oregon State, from Philadelphia, 73
4. May, Ray, LB, USC, 89
5. Choice to Green Bay
6. Haggerty, Mike, T, Miami, from Minnesota, 140
   Choice to Chi. Bears through Atlanta
7. Choice to Washington
8. Foruria, John, QB, Idaho, from Minnesota, 192
   Barnes, Mike, T, Purdue, 194
9. Otis, Paul, DT, Houston, 221
10. Wilsey, Bill, LB, Fresno State, 246
11. Whitcomb, Jim, FL, Emporia State, 272
12. Choice to Baltimore
13. Homan, Jim, G, USC, 324
14. Anderson, Chet, TE, Minnesota, 350
15. Love, Mike, FB, Abilene Christian, 376
16. Smith, Bill, C, Oregon, 402
17. Davenport, Mike, FB, Wyoming, 428

ST. LOUIS
1. Williams, Dave, FL, Washington, 16
2. Rowe, Bob, DE, Western Michigan, 43
3. Carlin, Vidal, QB, North Texas State, 69
4. Barnes, Mike, DB, Texas-Arlington, 97
   Bowling, Andy, LB, Virginia Tech, from Green Bay, 105
5. Rivers, Jamie, TE, Bowling Green, 123
6. Campbell, Mike, HB, Lenoir-Rhyne, 150
7. Randall, Joe, K, Brown, 175
8. Gold, Mike, T, Utah State, from Detroit, 193
   Choice to Baltimore
9. Wheeler, Ted, TE, West Texas State, 227
10. Barrs, Lavern, DB, Furman, 255
11. Marcontell, Ed, G, Lamar, 279
12. Dundas, Steve, FL, Pomona, 305
13. Duncum, Bob, T, West Texas State, 331
14. Hickey, Bo, FB, Maryland, 357
15. Wosilius, Bill, LB, Syracuse, 383
16. Spiller, Phil, DB, Cal State-Los Angeles, 410
17. Bacigalupo, Terry, DE, Oklahoma State, 435

SAN DIEGO
1. Billingsley, Ron, DT, Wyoming, 14
2. McCall, Ron, LB, Weber State, 40
   Howard, Bob, DB, San Diego State, from Buffalo, 48
3. Akin, Harold, T, Oklahoma State, 67
4. Post, Dickie, HB, Houston, 94
5. Erickson, Bernard, LB, Abilene Christian, 121
6. Johns, Nate, FL, San Diego State, 147
7. Conway, David, K, Texas, 173
8. Mills, John, E, Tennessee, 199
9. Newell, Steve, E, Long Beach State, 225
10. Ossmo, Torre, T, Western Michigan, 251
11. Jarvis, Carroll, HB, Virginia, 277
12. Choice to Kansas City
13. Carr, Leon, DB, Prairie View A&M, 329
14. Baccaglio, Martin, DT, San Jose State, 355
15. Scoggins, Craig, E, San Diego State, 381
16. Phillips, Paul, T, South Carolina, 407
17. Gibbs, John, HB, South Carolina State, 433

SAN FRANCISCO
1. Spurrier, Steve, QB, Florida, from Atlanta, 3
   Banaszek, Cas, TE-LB, Northwestern, 11
2. Holzer, Tom, T, Louisville, 39
3. Nunley, Frank, LB, Michigan, from Pittsburgh, 62
   Tucker, Bill, HB, Tennessee State, 65
4. Trimble, Wayne, DB, Alabama, 91
5. Choice to Atlanta
6. Cunningham, Doug, HB, Mississippi, 145
7. Jackson, Milt, DB, Tulsa, 170
8. Johnson, Walter, LB, Tuskegee, 198
9. Briggs, Bob, T, Heidelberg, 223
10. Myers, Phil, FL, Northwestern Oklahoma, 248
11. Carmann, Ken, DT, Kearney State, 276
12. Hall, James, LB, Tuskegee, 301
13. Gibbs, Rich, DB, Iowa, 325
14. Leblanc, Dalton, FL, Northeast Louisiana, 354
15. Spencer, Clarence, FL, Louisville, 379*
16. Templeman, Bart, C, Eastern Montana, 404
17. Talbott, Danny, QB, North Carolina, 432

WASHINGTON
1. McDonald, Ray, HB, Idaho, 13

2. Musgrove, Spain, DT, Utah State, 38
3. Belcher, Curg, DB, BYU, 64
4. Choice to Green Bay
5. Choice to Houston through Dallas
6. Bandy, Don, T, Tulsa, from NY Giants through Minnesota, 135
Choice to Detroit
7. Matte, Bruce, QB-HB, Miami (Ohio), from Pittsburgh, 168
Love, John, FL, North Texas State, 172
8. Hendershot, Larry, G-LB, Arizona State, from Atlanta, 190
Choice to Minnesota
9. Larsen, Pete, HB, Cornell, 222
10. Houlton, Tim, DT, St. Norbert, from Chi. Bears, 247
Sullivan, Bruce, DB, Illinois, 250
11. Brown, Bill, C, Texas-El Paso, 275
12. Sepic, Ron, E, Ohio State, 300
13. Rodwell, Bob, LB, Eastern Michigan, 328
14. Socha, Andy, HB, Marshall, 353
15. Breding, Ed, G, Texas A&M, 378
16. Avila, Alfredo, DB, Sul Ross, 406
17. Baucom, Lyle, T, Cal State-San Francisco, 431

1968

Held January 30-31, 1968

Minnesota had the first selection in the draft due to a trade with the New York Giants. Despite a 7-7 record in 1967, under the merger agreement the Giants had received the first choice overall as compensation for accepting the Jets as a New York entry into the merged league. The expansion Cincinnati Bengals received the first and last choices in each round (the second choice in the first round); one additional choice at the end of the second, third, and fourth rounds; and all AFL sixth-round selections except Miami's. Atlanta, with the worst record in pro football in 1967, received the third pick in the first round and the second in each subsequent round.

On January 21, the Bengals selected 40 players in an expansion draft, taking five from each AFL team except the Miami Dolphins.

ATLANTA

1. Humphrey, Claude, DE, Tennessee State, 3
2. Dabney, Carlton, DE, Morgan State, 29
Wright, John, FL, Illinois, from Green Bay through LA Rams, 53
3. Choice to Chi. Bears
4. Choice to St. Louis
5. Choice to Washington
6. Hagle, Jim, RB, SMU, 140
Wynns, Joe, DB, South Carolina State, from Pittsburgh, 147
Eber, Rick, FL, Tulsa, from Baltimore, 162
7. Choice to Minnesota
8. Jeffords, Ray, TE, Georgia, 194
9. Holland, Henry, C, North Texas State, 221
10. Tomasini, Mike, DT, Colorado State, 248
11. Brezina, Greg, LB, Houston, 275
12. Vaughn, A.J., RB, Wayne State, 302
13. Harris, Bill, RB, Colorado, 329
14. Polk, Joe, RB, Livingstone, 356
15. Bean, Don, FL, Houston, 383
16. Hall, Roy, T, San Jose State, 410
17. Schmidt, Jim, DB, Cal State-San Francisco, 437

BALTIMORE

1. Williams, John, T, Minnesota, 23
2. Grant, Bob, LB, Wake Forest, 50
3. O'Hara, Rich, FL, Northern Arizona, 78
4. Duncan, Jim, RB, Maryland-Eastern Shore, 107
5. Elzey, Paul, LB, Toledo, from NY Giants, 126
Choice to Cleveland
6. Choice to Atlanta
7. Andrews, Anthony, RB, Hampton, 188
8. Davis, Tommy, G, Tennessee State, 216
9. Cole, Terry, RB, Indiana, 242
10. Austin, Ocie, DB, Utah State, from Washington, 257
Tomlin, Ed, RB, Hampton, 270
11. Pickens, Bill, G, Houston, 296
12. Jackson, James, T, Jackson State, 324
13. Tennebar, Howard, T, Kent State, 350
14. Mitchell, Charles, TE, Alabama State, 378
15. Beaver, Jeff, QB, North Carolina, 404
16. Blackledge, Walt, FL, San Jose State, 432
17. Pederson, Roy, LB, Northern Iowa, 458

BOSTON

1. Byrd, Dennis, DT, North Carolina State, 6
2. Funchess, Tom, T, Jackson State, 32
3. Marsh, Aaron, FL, Eastern Kentucky, 60
4. Gamble, R.C., RB, South Carolina State, 88
5. Smithberger, Jim, DB, Notre Dame, 116
6. Choice to Cincinnati
7. Schneider, John, QB, Toledo, 170
8. Johnson, Daryl, DB, Morgan State, 197
9. Choice to Houston
10. Outlaw, Johnny, DB, Jackson State, 249
11. Feldhausen, Paul, T, Northland, 278
12. Cheyunski, Jim, LB, Syracuse, 305
13. Huber, Max, T, BYU, 332
14. McKay, Henry, E, Guilford, 358
15. McMahon, Art, DB, North Carolina State, 385
16. Fulton, Charley, RB, Tennessee, 413
17. Koontz, Ed, LB, Catawba, 440

BUFFALO

1. Moses, Haven, E, San Diego State, 9
2. Tatareck, Bob, DT, Miami, 34
3. Trapp, Richard, E, Florida, 63
4. Chandler, Edgar, T-K, Georgia, from Denver, 86
Choice to Kansas City
5. Gregory, Ben, RB, Nebraska, from Denver through Cincinnati, 114
McBath, Mike, DE, Penn State, through Kansas City, 119
Anderson, (Mini) Max, RB, Arizona State, from Kansas City, 132
6. Choice to Cincinnati
7. Richardson, Pete, DB, Dayton, 173
8. Kalsu, Bob, T, Oklahoma, 199
9. McDermott, Gary, RB, Tulsa, 227
10. Lawson, Jerome, DB, Utah, 251
11. Plagge, Dick, RB, Auburn, 281
12. Pipes, Greg, LB, Baylor, 306
13. Darragh, Dan, QB, William & Mary, 336
14. DeVliegher, Chuck, DT, Memphis State, 361
15. Gilmore, John, DT, Peru State, 389
16. Frantz, John, C, California, 415
17. Hines, Dick, DT, Kentucky State, 443

CHI. BEARS

1. Hull, Mike, RB, USC, 16
2. Wallace, Bob, E, Texas-El Paso, 46
3. Hazelton, Major, DB, Florida A&M, from Atlanta, 57
Choice to Dallas
4. Mass, Wayne, T, Clemson, 99
Bush, Alan, G, Mississippi, from LA Rams, 106
5. Turner, Cecil, FL, Cal Poly-SLO, 127
6. Schmedding, Jim, C, Weber State, 154
7. Holmon, Willie, DE, South Carolina State, 181
8. Bell, Wayne, RB, Lenoir-Rhyne, 208
9. Moore, Sam, T, Mississippi Valley State, 235
10. Davis, Fred, G, Doane, 262
11. Coady, Rich, TE, Memphis State, 289
12. Vallez, Emilio, LB, New Mexico, 316
13. Dearion, Willie, FL, Prairie View A&M, 343
14. Gargus, Harold, DT, New Mexico State, 370
15. Jaeger, Rich, C, Gustavus Adolphus, 397
16. Murphy, Jim, K, Utah State, 424
17. Layton, Gene, DT, Colorado State, 451

CINCINNATI

1. Johnson, Bob, C, Tennessee, 2
Choice to Miami
2. Staley, Bill, DE, Utah State, 28
Choice to Miami
Smiley, Tom, RB, Lamar, 55
3. Davis, Gary, QB, Vanderbilt, 56
Robinson, Paul, RB, Arizona, 82
Livingston, Dale, K, Western Michigan, 83
4. Phillips, Jess, DB, Michigan State, 84
McVea, Warren, RB, Houston, 109
Choice to Denver
5. Middendorf, Dave, G, Washington State, 112
Beauchamp, Al, LB, Southern, 138
6. Fest, Howard, T, Texas, 139
Kendricks, Billy, T, Alabama A&M, from Boston, 143
Neidert, John, LB, Louisville, from Buffalo, 145
Warren, Dewey, QB, Tennessee, from San Diego, 155
Johnson, Essex, DB, Grambling, from NY Jets, 156
Maple, Elmo, FL, Southern, from Kansas City, 158
Ellis, Sidney, DB, Jackson State, from Houston, 160
Williams, Charles, RB, Arkansas-Pine Bluff, from Oakland, 163
Johnson, James, DB, South Carolina State, 165
7. Smith, Steve, TE, Miami, 166
Bean, Wes, LB, Grambling, 192
8. Gunner, Harry, LB, Oregon State, 193
Brantley, Ed, T, North Texas State, 219
9. Johnson, Phil, DB, Long Beach State, 220
Hanrahan, Steve, DT, Weber State, 246
10. Patrick, Wayne, RB, Louisville, 247
Russell, James, E, North Texas State, 273
11. Scott, Wally, DB, Arizona, 274
Banks, Jeff, LB, Pacific, 300
12. Trumpy, Bob, TE, Utah, 301
Jones, Harold, T, Grambling, 327
13. Bivins, James, LB, Texas Southern, 328
Washington, Teddy, RB, San Diego State, 354
14. Webster, Les, RB, Iowa State, 355
Lewicke, Steve, E, Texas-El Paso, 381
15. Palmore, Harvey, G, Morgan State, 382
Mira, Joe, FL, Miami, 408
16. Williams, Monk, DB, Alcorn State, 409
Marks, Brown, LB, Indiana, 435
17. Manning, Don, LB, UCLA, 436
Smith, Jimmy, TE, Jackson State, 462

CINCINNATI (Expansion)

Archer, Dan, T, Oregon, from Oakland
Banks, Estes, RB, Colorado, from Oakland
Bellino, Joe, RB, Navy, from Boston
Boudreaux, Jim, DT, Louisiana Tech, from Boston
Brabham, Danny, LB, Arkansas, from Houston
Brannan, Solomon, DB, Morris Brown, from NY Jets
Brown, Bill, T, Texas-El Paso, from NY Jets
Bugenhagen, Gary, T, Syracuse, from Buffalo
Buncom, Frank, LB, USC, from San Diego
Burford, Chris, SE, Stanford, from Kansas City
Burnett, Bobby, RB, Arkansas, from Buffalo
Garrett, J.D., RB, Grambling, from Boston
Gilchrist, Cookie, RB, from Denver
Graves, White, DB, LSU, from Boston
Griffin, Jim, DE, Grambling, from San Diego
Hall, Ron, DB, Missouri Valley, from Boston
Headrick, Sherrill, LB, TCU, from Kansas City
Hunt, Bobby, DB, Auburn, from Kansas City
Isbell, Joe Bob, G, Houston, from Houston
Johns, Nate, RB, San Diego State, from Oakland
Jones, Willie, DE, Kansas, from Houston
Kellogg, Mike, RB, Santa Clara, from Denver
King, Charley, DB, Purdue, from Buffalo
Marsh, Frank, RB, Oregon State, from San Diego
Matlock, John, C, Miami, from NY Jets
Matson, Pat, G, Oregon, from Denver
Perreault, Pete, G, Boston U., from NY Jets
Poole, Bob, TE, Clemson, from Houston
Reynolds, Al, G, Tarkio, from Kansas City
Rice, Andy, DT, Texas Southern, from Houston
Schmidt, Bob, T, Minnesota, from Buffalo
Sherman, Rod, FL, USC, from Oakland
Sligh, Richard, DT, North Carolina Central, from Oakland
Smith, Fletcher, DB, Tennessee, from Kansas City
Sorrell, Henry, LB, Tennessee-Chattanooga, from Denver
Van Raaphorst, Dick, K, Ohio State, from San Diego
Waskiewicz, Jim, C-LB, Wichita State, from NY Jets
Wright, Ernie, T, Ohio State, from San Diego
Wright, Lonnie, DB, Colorado State, from Denver
Zecher, Rich, DT, Utah State, from Buffalo

CLEVELAND

1. Upshaw, Marvin, DE, Trinity (Texas), 21
2. Garlington, John, LB, LSU, 47
3. Olszewski, Harry, G, Clemson, from Pittsburgh, 64
Morrison, Reece, RB, Southwest Texas State, from Washington, 66
Choice to Detroit through LA Rams
4. Meylan, Wayne, LB, Nebraska, 104
5. Wempe, Mike, T, Missouri, 131
Jackson, Jackie, RB, Clemson, from Baltimore, 134
6. James, Nathaniel, DB, Florida A&M, from NY Giants, 152
7. Brady, Dale, RB, Memphis State, 186
8. Schoen, Tom, DB, Notre Dame, 212
9. Porter, David, DT, Michigan, 238
10. Greer, James, DE, Stephen F. Austin, from Pittsburgh, 255
Mitchell, Alvin, FL, Morgan State, 267
11. Alcorn, Jim, QB, Clarion, 293
12. Beutler, Tom, LB, Toledo, 319
13. Sellers, Terry, DB, Georgia, 348
14. Whipps, Edgar, RB, Jackson State, 374
15. Baxter, Bob, FL, Memphis State, 400
16. Sievert, Dick, DE, Wisconsin-River Falls, 429
17. McDuffie, Wayne, C, Florida State, 455

DALLAS

1. Homan, Dennis, E, Alabama, 20
2. McDaniels, Dave, E, Mississippi Valley State, 45
3. Harmon, Ed, LB, Louisville, from Chi. Bears, 71
Choice to Minnesota
4. Douglas, John, LB, Missouri, from NY Giants, 97
Choice to New Orleans
5. Nye, Blaine, T, Stanford, 130
6. Lewis, D.D., LB, Mississippi State, 159
7. Taucher, Bob, T, Nebraska, 185
8. Brown, Frank, DT, Albany State, 211
9. Kmiec, Ken, DB, Illinois, 241
10. Olison, Ben, FL, Kansas, 266
11. Shotts, Ron, RB, Oklahoma, 292
12. Whitty, Wilson, LB, Boston U., 321
13. Lord, Carter, FL, Harvard, 347
14. Williams, Ron, DB, West Virginia, 373
15. Lunceford, Tony, K, Auburn, 402
16. Cole, Larry, T, Hawaii, 428
17. Nordgren, George, RB, Houston, 454

DENVER

1. Choice to San Diego
2. Culp, Curley, DE, Arizona State, 31
3. Ford, Garrett, RB, West Virginia, 58
Vaughn, Bob, T, Mississippi, from Kansas City, 75
4. Choice to Buffalo
Lambert, Gordon, LB, Tennessee-Martin, from Miami, 91
Garrett, Drake, DB, Michigan State, from Kansas City, 102
Holloman, Gus, DB, Houston, from Cincinnati, 111
5. Choice to Buffalo through Cincinnati
6. Choice to Miami
7. Choice to Oakland
8. Holloway, Steve, DB, Weber State, 196
9. Smith, Paul, LB, New Mexico, 222
10. Langford, Bob, T, Middle Tennessee State, 252
11. Choice to Oakland
12. Hendrix, Bobby, T, Mississippi, 304
13. Greer, Charlie, DB, Colorado, 330
14. Briscoe, Marlin, RB, Nebraska-Omaha, 357
15. Kuhman, Jeff, LB, Vermont, 386
16. Brown, Adin, LB, William & Mary, 412
17. Grady, Steve, RB, USC, 438

DETROIT

1. Landry, Greg, QB, Massachusetts, 11
McCullouch, Earl, E, USC, from LA Rams, 24
2. DePoyster, Jerry, K, Wyoming, 37
3. Choice to San Francisco
Sanders, Charlie, TE, Minnesota, from Cleveland through LA Rams, 74
4. Mooney, Ed, LB, Texas Tech, 93
5. Odle, Phil, E, BYU, 120
6. Spitzer, Mike, DE, San Jose State, 148
7. Choice to New Orleans
8. Miller, Terry, LB, Illinois, 202
9. Barton, Greg, QB, Tulsa, 229
10. Liggins, Granville, LB, Oklahoma, 256
11. Little, Dwight, G, Kentucky, 283

12. Caruthers, Ed, DB, Arizona, 310
13. Bailey, Chuck, T, Cal State-Humboldt, 337
14. Davis, Richie, E, Upsala, 364
15. Oliver, Jim, RB, Colorado State, 391
16. Rokita, Bob, DE, Arizona State, 418
17. Choice to Minnesota

GREEN BAY
1. Carr, Fred, LB, Texas-El Paso, from New Orleans, 5
   Lueck, Bill, G, Arizona, 26
2. Choice to Atlanta through LA Rams
3. Stevens, Billy, QB, Texas-El Paso, from St. Louis, 67
   Himes, Dick, T, Ohio State, 81
4. McCarthy, Brendan, RB, Boston College, from Pittsburgh, 92
   Robinson, John, FL, Tennessee State, 108
5. Duich, Steve, T, San Diego State, from Pittsburgh, 121
   Winkler, Francis, DE, Memphis State, 137
6. Chadwick, Walter, RB, Tennessee, 164
7. Beath, Andy, DB, Duke, 191
8. Owens, Tom, G, Missouri-Rolla, 218
9. Apisa, Bob, RB, Michigan State, 245
10. Cash, Rick, T, Northeast Missouri State, from NY Giants, 260
   Worthen, Ron, C, Arkansas State, 272
11. Rule, Gordon, DB, Dartmouth, 299
12. Porter, Dennis, T, Northern Michigan, 325
13. Geiselman, Frank, FL, Rhode Island, 353
14. Farler, John, E, Colorado, 380
15. Gibson, Ridley, DB, Baylor, 407
16. Groves, Al, T, St. Norbert, 434
17. Rota, Ken, RB, North Dakota State, 461

HOUSTON
1. Choice to Kansas City
2. Haik, Mac, E, Mississippi, 49
3. Bethea, Elvin, T, North Carolina A&T, 77
4. Beirne, Jim, E, Purdue, 105
5. Longo, Bob, E, Pittsburgh, 137
6. Choice to Cincinnati
7. Toscano, Paul, DB, Wyoming, 187
8. Choice to NY Jets
9. Robertson, Bob, C, Illinois, from Boston, 224
   Choice to Miami
10. Peace, Joe, LB, Louisiana Tech, from San Diego, 263
   Domres, Tom, DE, Wisconsin, 268
11. Halley, Bill, E, La Verne, 295
12. Lischner, Barry, RB, Missouri, 322
13. Dousay, Jimmy, RB, LSU, 349
14. Stotter, George, G, Houston, 376
15. Choice to San Diego
16. Smith, Bob, DB, Miami (Ohio), 430
17. Alsbrooks, Billy, DB, North Carolina Central, 457

KANSAS CITY
1. Moorman, Mo, G, Texas A&M, 19
   Daney, George, G, Texas-El Paso, from Houston, 22
2. Livingston, Mike, QB, SMU, 48
3. Choice to Denver
4. McCarty, Mickey, TE, TCU, from Buffalo, 90
   Choice to Denver
5. Choice to Buffalo
6. Choice to Cincinnati
7. Grezaffi, Sammy, DB, LSU, 184
8. Endsley, Lindon, C, North Texas State, 213
9. McClure, Mac, LB, Mississippi, 239
10. Gehrke, Jack, FL, Utah, 265
11. Nosewicz, Tom, DE, Tulane, 294
12. Johns, Bobby, DB, Alabama, 320
13. Kavanagh, Jim, FL, Boston College, 346
14. Holmes, Robert, RB, Southern, 375
15. Chambless, Bill, G, Miami, 401
16. Talbert, Pat, T, Southwest Missouri State, 427
17. Williams, Wesley, LB, Texas Southern, 456

LA RAMS
1. Choice to Detroit
2. Beban, Gary, QB, UCLA, from New Orleans, 30
   La Hood, Mike, G, Wyoming, 51
3. Choice to Pittsburgh
4. Choice to Chicago
5. Martin, Don, K, Washington, 135
6. Webb, Bobby, C, Southern Mississippi, 161
7. Choice to Pittsburgh
8. Williams, Joe, FL, Florida A&M, 215
9. Richardson, Bob, T, Washington, 243
10. Marcelin, Allen, FL, Parsons, 269
11. Pergine, John, LB, Notre Dame, 297
12. Jackson, Harold, FL, Jackson State, 323
13. Halverson, Dean, LB, Washington, 351
14. Jackson, Cephus, DB, Jackson State, 377
15. Yell, Dennis, T, Moorhead State, 405
16. Raye, Jimmy, QB-DB, Michigan State, 431
17. Choice to Philadelphia

MIAMI
1. Csonka, Larry, RB, Syracuse, 8
   Crusan, Doug, T, Indiana, from Cincinnati, 27
2. Keyes, Jimmy, LB-K, Mississippi, 35
   Cox, Jim, E, Miami, from Cincinnati, 54
3. Urbanek, Jim, T, Mississippi, 62
   Anderson, Dick, DB, Colorado, from San Diego, 73
4. Choice to Denver
5. Kiick, Jim, RB, Wyoming, 118
6. Hammond, Kim, QB, Florida State, from Denver, 142
   Hines, Jimmy, FL, Texas Southern, 146
7. Boynton, John, T, Tennessee, 172
8. Choice to NY Jets
   Edmonds, Randall, LB, Georgia Tech, from Oakland, 217
9. McDowell, Sam, T, Southwest Missouri State, 226
   Paciorek, Tom, DB, Houston, from Houston, 240
10. Mirto, Joe, T, Miami, 253
11. Cooper, Cornelius, T, Prairie View A&M, 280
12. Paxton, Paul, T, Akron, 307
13. Joswick, Bob, DT, Tulsa, 334
14. Blunk, Ray, TE, Xavier, 362
15. Corbin, Ken, LB, Miami, 388
16. Still, Henry, DT, Bethune-Cookman, 416
17. Nemeth, Bill, C, Arizona, 442

MINNESOTA
1. Yary, Ron, T, USC, from NY Giants, 1
   Choice to New Orleans
2. West, Charlie, DB, Texas-El Paso, 33
3. Choice to Pittsburgh
   McGill, Mike, LB, Notre Dame, from Dallas, 76
4. Freeman, Mike, DB, Fresno State, 89
5. Choice to Washington
6. Goodridge, Bob, FL, Vanderbilt, 144
7. Reed, Oscar, Colorado State, from Atlanta, 167
   Snow, Lenny, RB, Georgia Tech, 171
8. Urbanowicz, Hank, DT, Miami, 198
9. Donohoe, Mike, TE, San Francisco, 225
10. Sakal, Tom, DB, Minnesota, 250
11. Haas, Bill, E, Nebraska-Omaha, 279
12. Small, Howie, C, Rhode Island, 308
13. Wherry, Rich, E, Northern State (South Dakota), 333
14. Evans, Don, T, Arkansas Pine Bluff, 360
15. Haynie, Jim, QB, West Chester, 387
16. Kuharich, Larry, DB, Boston College, 414
17. Lee, Bob, QB, Pacific, 441
   Hull, Bill, G, Tennessee Tech, from Detroit, 445

NEW ORLEANS
1. Choice to Green Bay
   Hardy, Kevin, DE, Notre Dame, from Minnesota, 7
2. Choice to LA Rams
3. Szymakowski, Dave, E, West Texas State, 59
4. Crittendon, Willie, DT, Tulsa, 85
   Sartin, Dan, T, Mississippi, from Dallas, 103
5. South, Ronnie, QB, Arkansas, 115
6. Choice to San Francisco
7. Phillips, Ray, G, Michigan, 169
   Howard, Eugene, FL, Langston, from Detroit, 175
8. Southland, Dick, G-T, Notre Dame, 195
9. Blake, Joe, T, Tulsa, 223
10. Robinson, Doug, DB, Iowa State, 254
11. Blocker, Bennie, RB, South Carolina State, 276
12. Beck, John, DB, San Diego State, 303
13. Trepanier, K.O., DE, Montana State, 331
14. Covington, Herb, RB, Memphis State, 359
15. Cooks, Wilmer, RB, Colorado, 384
16. Ghattas, Elie, G, Ball State, 411
17. Ferguson, Jim, LB, USC, 439

NY GIANTS
1. Choice to Minnesota
2. Buzin, Rich, T, Penn State, 41
3. Duhon, Bobby, RB, Tulane, 70
4. Choice to Dallas
5. Choice to Baltimore
6. Choice to Cleveland
7. Chatman, Doug, DE, Jackson State, 180
8. Choice to San Francisco
9. Koontz, Joe, E, Cal State-San Francisco, 234
10. Choice to Green Bay
11. Davis, Henry, DE, Grambling, 288
12. Holifield, Jimmy, DB, Jackson State, 314
13. Gallagher, John, DE, Boston U., 342
14. Moreman, Bill, RB, Florida State, 368
15. Boston, McKinley, G, Minnesota, 396
16. Parker, Ken, DB, Fordham, 422
17. Kohn, Larry, TE, Georgia, 450

NY JETS
1. White, Lee, RB, Weber State, 17
2. Thompson, Steve, DE, Washington, 44
3. Walton, Sam, T, East Texas State, 72
4. Magner, Gary, DT, USC, 101
5. Jacobsen, Lee, LB, Kearney State, 128
6. Choice to Cincinnati
7. Lubke, Oscar, T, Ball State, 182
8. Taylor, Bob, RB, Maryland-Eastern Shore, from Miami, 200
   Richards, Jim, DB, Virginia Tech, 210
   Henke, Karl, DT, Tulsa, from Houston, 214
9. Houser, Gary, TE-K, Oregon State, 236
10. D'Amato, Mike, DB, Hofstra, 264
11. Owens, Henry, FL, Weber State, 290
12. Hayes, Ray, DT, Toledo, 318
13. Myslinski, Tom, G, Maryland, 344
14. Nairn, Harvey, RB, Southern, 372
15. Ehrig, Ronnie, DB, Texas, 398*
16. Bilotta, Tom, G, Adams State, 426
17. Strasser, Myles, RB, Wisconsin-Oshkosh, 452

OAKLAND
1. Dickey, Eldridge, QB, Tennessee State, 25
2. Stabler, Ken, QB, Alabama, 52
3. Shell, Art, T, Maryland-Eastern Shore, 80
4. Smith, Charlie, RB, Utah, 110
5. Naponic, John, T, Virginia, 136
6. Choice to Cincinnati
7. Harper, John, C, Adams State, from Denver, 168
   Atkinson, George, DB, Morris Brown, 190
8. Choice to Miami
9. Eason, John, TE, Florida A&M, 244
10. Owens, Rick, DB, Pennsylvania, 271
11. Hubbard, Marv, TE, Colgate, from Denver, 277
   Oliver, Ralph (Chip), LB, USC, 298
12. Plantz, Larry, FL, Colorado, 326
13. Blackstone, Larry, RB, Fairmont State, 352
14. Carlson, Ray, LB, Hamline, 379
15. Leinert, Mike, RB, Texas Tech, 406
16. Morrison, David, DB, Southwest Texas State, 433
17. Berry, Steve, E, Catawba, 460

PHILADELPHIA
1. Rossovich, Tim, DE, USC, 14
2. Pinder, Cyril, RB, Illinois, 39
3. Young, Adrian, LB, USC, 68
4. McNeil, Len, G, Fresno State, 95
5. Dirks, Mike, T, Wyoming, from Washington, 122
   Nordquist, Mark, T, Pacific, 124
6. Randle, Thurman, T, Texas-El Paso, 150
   Martin, Dave, DB, Notre Dame, from Cleveland, 157
7. Przybycki, Joe, G, Michigan State, 178
8. Lavan, Al, DB, Colorado State, 204
9. Evans, Mike, C, Boston College, 232
10. Mallory, John, DB, West Virginia, 258
11. Persin, Len, DE, Boston College, 286
12. Taylor, Thurston, TE, Florida State, 312
13. Barron, George, T, Mississippi State, 340
14. Williamson, Dan, LB, West Virginia, 366
15. Graham, Joe, G, Tennessee, 394
16. Creel, Phil, Northwestern State (Louisiana), 420
17. Forzani, Joe, LB, Utah State, 448
   Antonini, Frank, RB, Parsons, from LA Rams, 459

PITTSBURGH
1. Taylor, Mike, T, USC, 10
2. Ruple, Ernie, T, Arkansas, 36
3. Henderson, Jon, DB, Colorado State, from Minnesota, 61
   Choice to Cleveland
   Hebert, Ken, FL-K, Houston, from LA Rams, 79
4. Choice to Green Bay
5. Choice to Green Bay
6. Choice to Atlanta
7. Dalton, Doug, RB, New Mexico State, 174
   Glennon, Bill, DT, Washington, from LA Rams, 189
8. Holman, Danny, QB, San Jose State, 201
9. Knight, John, DE, Weber State, 228
10. Choice to Cleveland
11. King, Kim, QB, Georgia Tech, 282
12. Wheeler, Sam, LB, Wisconsin, 309
13. Roundy, Joe, G, Puget Sound, 335
14. Harris, Lou, DB, Kent State, 363
15. Lanning, Bob, DE, Northern Montana, 390
16. Bleier, Rocky, RB, Notre Dame, 417
17. Cole, Bob, LB, South Carolina, 444

ST. LOUIS
1. Lane, MacArthur, RB, Utah State, 13
2. Hyatt, Freddie, FL, Auburn, 40
   Atkins, Bob, DB, Grambling, from San Francisco, 42
3. Choice to Green Bay
4. Fitzgerald, Don, RB, Kent State, from Atlanta, 87
   Schniesing, Joe, LB, New Mexico State, 96
5. Rosema, Rocky, LB, Michigan, 123
6. Lane, Frank, LB, Stephen F. Austin, 151
7. Henry, Ken, FL, Wake Forest, 177
8. Daanen, Jerry, FL, Miami, 205
9. Sinkule, Billy, DE, Central Michigan, 231
10. Busch, Tom, FL-K, Iowa State, 259
11. Slagle, Larry, G, UCLA, 285
12. Emerson, Vernon, T, Minnesota-Duluth, 313
13. Sauls, Mack, DB, Southwest Texas State, 339
14. Bender, Vic, C, Northeast Louisiana, 367
15. Lovich, Dave, DE, Northwestern State (Louisiana), 393
16. Lankas, Dan, LB, Kansas State, 421
17. Lee, Bob, FL, Minnesota, 447

SAN DIEGO
1. Washington, Russ, T, Missouri, from Denver, 4
   Hill, Jim, DB, Texas A&I, 18
2. Lenkaitis, Bill, C, Penn State, 43
3. Choice to Miami
4. Dyer, Ken, FL, Arizona State, 100
5. Perry, Bill, TE, Kent State, 129
6. Choice to Cincinnati
7. Fenner, Lane, FL, Florida State, 183
8. Gammage, Elliott, TE, Tennessee, 209
9. Harris, Grundy, RB, Southern, 237
10. Choice to Houston
11. Partee, Dennis, K, SMU, 291
12. Queen, Jeff, LB, Morgan State, 317
13. Combs, Fred, DB, North Carolina State, 345
14. Campbell, Jim, LB, West Texas State, 371
15. Kramarczyk, Dan, T, Dayton, 399
   Wells, Robert, T, Johnson C. Smith, from Houston, 403
16. Farley, Dick, DB, Boston U., 425
17. Andrews, Dan, TE, West Texas State, 453

SAN FRANCISCO
1. Blue, Forrest, C, Auburn, 15
2. Choice to St. Louis
3. Olssen, Lance, T, Purdue, from Detroit, 65
   Vanderbundt, Skip, LB, Oregon State, 69
4. Fuller, Johnny, E, Lamar, 98
5. Lee, Dwight, RB, Michigan State, 125
6. Johnson, Leo, FL, Tennessee State, from New Orleans, 141
   Belk, Bill, DE, Maryland-Eastern Shore, 153
7. Richardson, Jerry, LB, Mississippi, 179
8. Brown, Charley, T, Augustana (South Dakota), from NY Giants, 206

Gray, Tom, FL, Morehead State, 207
9. Boyett, Casey, E, BYU, 233*
10. Hart, Tommy, LB, Morris Brown, 261
11. Fitzgibbons, Dennis, G, Syracuse, 287
12. Johnson, Henry, QB, Fisk, 315
13. Mitrakos, Tom, C, Pittsburgh, 341
14. Moore, Alex, RB, Norfolk State, 369
15. Spencer, Clarence, FL, Louisville, 395
16. Rosenow, Tom, DT, Northern Illinois, 423
17. Patera, Dennis, K, BYU, 449

WASHINGTON
1. Smith, Jim (Yazoo), DB, Oregon, 12
2. Roussel, Tom, LB, Southern Mississippi, 38
3. Choice to Cleveland
4. Crane, Dennis, DT, USC, 94
5. Barefoot, Ken, TE, Virginia Tech, from Atlanta, 113
Bragg, Mike, K, Richmond, from Minnesota, 117
Choice to Philadelphia
6. Banks, Willie, G, Alcorn State, 149
7. Brunet, Bob, RB, Louisiana Tech, 176
8. Magnuson, Brian, RB, Montana, 203
9. Liberatore, Frank, DB, Clemson, 230
10. Choice to Baltimore
11. Garretson, Tom, DB, Northwestern, 284
12. Weedman, Dave, DT, Western Washington, 311
13. St. Louis, Mike, T, Central Missouri State, 338
14. Zivich, Dave, T, Cal-Santa Barbara, 365
15. Coverson, Coger, G, Texas Southern, 392
16. Turner, Willie, RB, Jackson State, 419
17. Bosch, Frank, DT, Colorado, 446

1969
Held January 28-29, 1969

ATLANTA
1. Kunz, George, T, Notre Dame, 2
2. Gipson, Paul, RB, Houston, 29
3. Snider, Malcolm, T, Stanford, 54
Sandstrom, Jon, G, Oregon State, from NY Giants through LA Rams, 67
4. Mitchell, Jim, TE, Prairie View A&M, 81
Lyons, Dickie, DB, Kentucky, from Baltimore, 103
5. Choice to Minnesota
Pleviak, Tony, DE, Illinois, from Dallas through Baltimore, 127
6. Choice to LA Rams
Oyler, Wally, DB, Louisville, from Detroit, 137
7. Enderle, Dick, G, Minnesota, 158
Cottrell, Ted, LB, Delaware Valley, from Detroit, 164
8. Callahan, Jim, FL, Temple, 185
9. Choice to Baltimore
10. Stanciel, Jeff, RB, Mississippi Valley State, 237
11. Van Note, Jeff, LB, Kentucky, 262
12. Samples, Denver, DT, Texas-El Paso, 289
13. Carpenter, Harry, T, Tennessee State, 313
14. Hunt, Billy, DB, Kansas, 341
15. Weatherford, Jim, DB, Tennessee, 366
16. Hughes, Ed, RB, Texas Southern, 393
17. Williams, Paul, RB, California, 418

BALTIMORE
1. Hinton, Eddie, FL, Oklahoma, 25
2. Hendricks, Ted, LB, Miami, from New Orleans, 33
Maxwell, Tom, DB, Texas A&M, 51
3. Nelson, Dennis, T, Illinois State, 77
4. Stewart, Jacky, RB, Texas Tech, from Washington, 87
Choice to Atlanta
5. Dunlap, King, DT, Tennessee State, 129
6. Fortier, Bill, T, LSU, 154
7. Fleming, Gary, DE, Samford, from New Orleans, 163
Moss, Roland, RB, Toledo, 181
8. Havrilak, Sam, QB, Bucknell, 207
9. Wright, George, DT, Sam Houston State, from Atlanta, 210
Good, Larry, QB, Georgia Tech, 232
10. Griffin, Marion, TE, Purdue, 259
11. Delaney, Ken, T, Akron, 285
12. Riley, Butch, LB, Texas A&I, 310
13. Mauck, Carl, LB, Southern Illinois, 337
14. Bartelt, Dave, LB, Colorado, 363
15. Thompson, George, DB, Marquette, 389
16. McMillan, Jim, RB-FL, Citadel, 415
17. Cowan, Joe, FL, Johns Hopkins, 441

BOSTON
1. Sellers, Ron, SE, Florida State, 6
2. Montler, Mike, G, Colorado, 32
3. Garrett, Carl, RB, New Mexico Highlands, 58
4. Choice to Denver through Kansas City
5. Jackson, Onree, QB, Alabama A&M, 110
6. Choice to Oakland
7. Hackley, Rick, T, New Mexico State, 162
8. Gladieux, Bob, RB, Notre Dame, 188
9. Alexakos, Steve, G-LB, San Jose State, from Buffalo, 209
Walker, Joe, DE, Albany State, 214
10. Devlin, Dennis, DB, Wyoming, 240
11. Gallup, Barry, SE, Boston College, 266
12. Lee, Richard, DT, Grambling, 292
13. Leasy, Joe, LB, Alcorn State, 318
14. Cagle, John, LB, Clemson, 344
15. Conley, Brant, RB-P, Tulsa, 370
16. Vuono, Jim, LB, Adams State, 396
17. Muse, George, LB-DB, Grambling, 422

BUFFALO
1. Simpson, O.J., RB, USC, 1
2. Enyart, Bill, RB, Oregon State, 27
3. Nunamaker, Julian, DE, Tennessee-Martin, 53
4. Richey, Mike, T, North Carolina, 79
5. Mayes, Ben, DT, Drake, 105
6. Choice to Denver
7. Helton, John, DE, Arizona State, 157
8. Harvey, Jim, T, Virginia Tech, 183
Harris, James, QB, Grambling, from Denver, 192
9. Choice to Boston
10. Baines, Ron, FL, Montana, 235
11. Hall, Bobby, DB, North Carolina State, 261
12. Pate, Lloyd, RB, Cincinnati, 287
13. Lovelace, Leon, T, Texas Tech, 312
14. Thornton, Bubba, FL, TCU, 339
15. Wilson, Karl, RB, Olivet, 365
16. Kirk, Robert, G, Indiana, 391
17. Lineberry, Wayne, LB, East Carolina, 417

CHI. BEARS
1. Mayes, Rufus, T, Ohio State, 14
2. Douglass, Bobby, QB, Kansas, 41
3. Montgomery, Ross, RB, TCU, 66
4. Redmond, Rudy, DB, Pacific, 91
5. Winegardner, Jim, TE, Notre Dame, 119
6. Nicholson, Bill, DE, Stanford, 144
7. Copeland, Ron, FL, UCLA, 169
8. Hubbell, Webb, G, Arkansas, 197
9. Aluise, Joe, RB, Arizona, 222
10. Pearson, Ron, TE-LB, Maryland, 247
11. Campbell, Sam, DT, Iowa State, 275
12. Hale, Dave, DE, Ottawa, 300
13. Quinn, Tom, DB, Notre Dame, 325
14. Ehrig, Ronnie, DB, Texas, 353
15. Coble, Bob, P, Kansas State, 378
16. Stydahar, Dave, G, Purdue, 403
17. Long, Bob, SE, Texas A&M, 431

CINCINNATI
1. Cook, Greg, QB, Cincinnati, 5
2. Bergey, Bill, LB, Arkansas State, 31
3. Thomas, Louis, SE, Utah, 57
4. Turner, Clem, RB, Cincinnati, 83
5. Dennis, Guy, G, Florida, 109
6. Riley, Ken, DB, Florida A&M, 135
7. Berry, Royce, DE, Houston, 161
8. Buchanan, Tim, LB, Hawaii, 187
9. Stripling, Mike, RB, Tulsa, 213
10. Howell, Steve, TE, Ohio State, 239
11. Stewart, Mark, DB, Georgia, 265
12. Paige, Lonnie, DT, North Carolina Central, 291
13. Benson, Chuck, SE, Southern Illinois, 316
14. Wilson, Mike, RB, Dayton, 343
15. Shoemaker, Bill, K, Stanford, 369
16. Schmidt, Bill, LB, Missouri, 395
17. Story, Terry, T, Georgia Tech, 421

CLEVELAND
1. Johnson, Ron, RB, Michigan, 20
2. Choice to Washington
3. Jenkins, Al, G, Tulsa, from Philadelphia, 55
Glass, Chip, TE, Florida State, 72
4. Summers, Freddie, DB, Wake Forest, 98
5. Hooker, Fair, FL, Arizona State, 124
6. Adams, Larry, DT, TCU, from NY Giants, 145
Righetti, Joe, DT, Waynesburg, 150
7. Sumner, Walt, DB, Florida State, 176
8. Reynolds, Chuck, C, Tulsa, 202
9. Kamzelski, Ron, DT, Minnesota, 228
10. Shelly, Greg, G, Virginia, 254
11. Jones, Dave, FL, Kansas State, 280
12. Davis, Dick, RB, Nebraska, 306
13. Boutwell, Tommy, QB, Southern Mississippi, 332
14. Smaha, Jiggy, DT, Georgia, 358
15. Stevenson, Joe, TE, Georgia Tech, 384
16. Lowe, James, FL, Tuskegee, 410
17. Oliver, Bob, DE, Abilene Christian, 436

DALLAS
1. Hill, Calvin, RB, Yale, 24
2. Flowers, Richmond, FL, Tennessee, 49
3. Stinic, Tom, LB, Michigan, from San Francisco, 68
Hagen, Halvor, DT, Weber State, 74
4. Choice to New Orleans
5. Kyle, Chuck, LB, Purdue, from LA Rams, 125
Choice to Atlanta through Baltimore
6. Shaw, Rick, FL, Arizona State, 152
7. Bales, Larry, FL, Emory & Henry, 180
8. Benhardt, Elmer, LB, Missouri, 205
9. Welch, Claxton, RB, Oregon, 230
10. Gottlieb, Stuart, T, Weber State, 258
11. Williams, Clarence, DT, Prairie View A&M, 283
12. Belden, Bob, QB, Notre Dame, 308
13. Matison, Rene, FL, New Mexico, 336
14. Lutri, Gerald, T, Northern Michigan, 361
15. Justus, Bill, DB, Tennessee, 386
16. Kerr, Floyd, DB, Colorado State, 414
17. Bailey, Bill, DT, Lewis & Clark, 439

DENVER
1. Choice to San Diego
2. Cavness, Grady, DB, Texas-El Paso, 36
3. Thompson, Billy, DB, Maryland-Eastern Shore, 61
4. Schnitker, Mike, LB, Colorado, from Boston through Kansas City, 84
Hayes, Ed, DB, Morgan State, 88
5. Quayle, Frank, RB, Virginia, 113
6. Williams, Wandy, RB, Hofstra, from Buffalo, 131
Coleman, Mike, RB, Tampa, 140
7. Giffin, Al, TE, Auburn, 165
8. Choice to Buffalo
9. Jones, Henry, RB, Grambling, 217
10. Smith, Jim, DB, Utah State, 244
11. Pastrana, Alan, QB, Maryland, 270
12. Plummer, Wes, DB, Arizona State, 196
13. Sias, Johnny, SE, Georgia Tech, 321
14. Crane, Gary, LB, Arkansas State, 348
15. Kahoun, Errol, G, Miami (Ohio), 373
16. Woods, Billy, DB, North Texas State, 400
17. O'Brien, Buster, QB, Richmond, 425

DETROIT
1. Choice to LA Rams
2. Taylor, Altie, RB, Utah State, 34
Yarbrough, Jim, TE, Florida, from LA Rams, 47
3. Walton, Larry, FL, Arizona State, from New Orleans, 59
Choice to NY Giants
4. Choice to San Francisco
5. Choice to Minnesota through Pittsburgh
6. Choice to Atlanta
7. Choice to Atlanta
8. Carr, Jim, T, Jackson State, 190
9. Rasley, Rocky, G, Oregon State, 216
10. Bergum, Bob, DE, Wisconsin-Platteville, 242
11. Walker, Ron, DE, Morris Brown, 268
12. Hadlock, Bob, DT, George Fox, 294
13. Bowie, Wilson, RB, USC, 320
14. Hoey, George, FL, Michigan, 346
15. Gough, Fred, LB, Texas-Arlington, 372
16. Spain, Ken, DE, Houston, 398
Stahl, John, G, Fresno State, from Minnesota, 407
17. Steele, Gary, TE, Army, 424

GREEN BAY
1. Moore, Rich, DT, Villanova, 12
2. Bradley, Dave, T, Penn State, 38
3. Spilis, John, FL, Northern Illinois, 64
4. Williams, Perry, RB, Purdue, 90
5. Hayhoe, Bill, DT, USC, 116
6. Jones, Ron, TE, Texas-El Paso, from Pittsburgh, 134
Vinyard, Kenny, K, Texas Tech, 142
7. Agajanian, Larry, DT, UCLA, 168
8. Gosnell, Doug, DT, Utah State, 194
9. Hampton, Dave, RB, Wyoming, 220
10. Nelson, Bruce, T, North Dakota State, 246
11. Harden, Leon, DB, Texas-El Paso, 272
12. Buckman, Tom, TE, Texas A&M, 298
13. Koinzan, Craig, LB, Doane, 324
14. Voltzke, Rich, RB, Minnesota, 350
15. Eckstein, Dan, DB, Presbyterian, 376
16. Hewins, Dick, FL, Drake, 402
17. Mack, John, RB, Central Missouri State, 428

HOUSTON
1. Pritchard, Ron, LB, Arizona State, 15
2. LeVias, Jerry, FL, SMU, 40
3. Drungo, Elbert, T, Tennessee State, 65
Johnson, Rich, RB, Illinois, from NY Jets, 78
4. Joiner, Charlie, DB, Grambling, 93
Gerela, Roy, P, New Mexico State, from San Diego, 96
5. Peacock, John, DB, Houston, 118
6. Grate, Willie, FL, South Carolina State, 143
7. Richardson, Mike, RB, SMU, 171
8. Woods, Glenn, DE, Prairie View A&M, 196
9. Watson, Ed, LB, Grambling, 221
10. Pryor, Joe, DE, Boston College, 249
Naponic, Bob, QB, Illinois, from Oakland, 256
11. May, Terry, C, SMU, 274
12. Resley, George, DT, Texas A&M, 299
13. Pickens, Richard, RB, Tennessee, 327
14. Reeves, Roy, DB, South Carolina, 352
15. Tyszkiewicz, John, G, Tennessee-Chattanooga, 377
16. Wainscott, Loyd, DT, Texas, 405
17. Autry, Hank, C, Southern Mississippi, 430

KANSAS CITY
1. Marsalis, Jim, DB, Tennessee State, 23
2. Podolak, Ed, RB, Iowa, 48
3. Stroud, Morris, TE, Clark, 76
4. Rudnay, Jack, C, Northwestern, 101
5. Stein, Bob, LB, Minnesota, 126
6. Pleasant, John, RB, Alabama State, 155
7. Nettles, Tom, FL, San Diego State, 179
8. King, Clanton, T, Purdue, 204
LeBlanc, Maurice, DB, LSU, from Oakland, 206
9. Klepper, Dan, G, Nebraska-Omaha, 231
10. Sponheimer, John, DT, Cornell, 257
11. Wupper, Skip, DE, C.W. Post, 282
12. Lavin, John, LB, Notre Dame, 309
13. Piland, Rick, G, Virginia Tech, 335
14. Bream, Al, DB, Iowa, 360
15. Winston, Leland, T, Rice, 388
16. Johnson, Eural, DB, Prairie View A&M, 413
17. Jenkins, Ralph, DB, Tuskegee, 438

LA RAMS
1. Smith, Larry, RB, Florida, from Detroit, 8
Seymour, Jim, SE, Notre Dame, from Washington, 10
Klein, Bob, TE, USC, 21
2. Choice to Detroit
3. Choice to St. Louis through Detroit
4. Zook, John, DE, Kansas, 99
5. Choice to Dallas
6. Drones, A.Z., T, West Texas State, from Atlanta, 133
Curran, Pat, LB, Lakeland, 151
7. Hawkins, James, DB, Nebraska, 177
8. Harvey, Richard, DB, Jackson State, 203
9. Foote, Mike, LB, Oregon State, 229
10. Gordon, Jerry, T, Auburn, 255
11. Svendsen, Dave, FL, Eastern Washington, 281
12. Carr, Tim, QB, C.W. Post, 307
13. Williams, Roger, DB, Grambling, 333
14. Stephens, Ray, RB, Minnesota, 359
15. Jugum, George, LB, Washington, 385
16. Hipps, Henry, LB, North Carolina State, 411
17. Thorpe, Jim, DB, Hofstra, 437

MIAMI
1. Stanfill, Bill, DE, Georgia, 11
2. Heinz, Bob, T, Pacific, 37
3. Morris, Eugene (Mercury), RB, West Texas State, 63
4. McBride, Norm, LB, Utah, 89
5. Pearson, Willie, DB, North Carolina A&T, 115
Kremser, Karl, K, Tennessee, from Oakland, 128
6. Tuck, Ed, G, Notre Dame, 141
7. Eagan, John, C, Boston College, 167
Kulka, John, G, Penn State, from San Diego, 174
8. Weinstein, Bruce, TE, Yale, 193
9. Powell, Jesse, LB, West Texas State, 219
10. Mertens, Jim, TE, Fairmont State, 245
11. Berdis, Mike, T, North Dakota State, 271
12. McCullers, Dale, LB, Florida State, 297
13. Ayres, Amos, DB, Arkansas-Pine Bluff, 323
14. Thompson, Glenn, T, Troy State, 349
15. McGeehan, Chick, FL, Tennessee, 375
16. Mumford, Lloyd, DB, Texas Southern, 401
17. Krallman, Tom, DE, Xavier, 427

MINNESOTA
1. Choice to New Orleans
2. White, Ed, G, California, from NY Giants, 39
Murphy, Volly, FL, Texas-El-Paso, 43
3. Choice to Philadelphia
4. McCaffrey, Mike, LB, California, 95
5. Barnes, Jim, G, Arkansas, from Atlanta, 106
O'Shea, Mike, SE, Utah State, from Detroit through Pittsburgh, 112
Davis, Cornelius, RB, Kansas State, 121
6. Bates, Marion, DB, Texas Southern, 148
7. Choice to Washington
8. Wood, Harris, FL, Washington, 199
9. Fink, Tom, G, Minnesota, 225
10. McCauley, Tom, SE, Wisconsin, 253
11. Dowling, Brian, QB, Yale, 277
12. Jenke, Noel, LB, Minnesota, 303
13. Moylan, Jim, DT, Texas Tech, 329
14. Head, Tommy, C, Southwest Texas State, 355
15. Mosley, Eugene, TE, Jackson State, 381
16. Choice to Detroit
17. Housely, Wendell, RB, Texas A&M, 433

NY GIANTS
1. Dryer, Fred, DE, San Diego State, 13
2. Choice to Minnesota
3. Vanoy, Vernon, DE, Kansas, from Detroit, 60
Choice to Atlanta through LA Rams
4. Houston, Rich, FL, East Texas State, 92
5. Choice to New Orleans
6. Choice to Cleveland
7. Brenner, Al, DB, Michigan State, 170
8. Irby, George, RB, Tuskegee, 195
9. Hickl, Ray, LB, Texas A&I, 223
10. Galiardi, Lou, DT, Dayton, 248
11. Fuqua, John (Frenchy), RB, Morgan State, 273
12. Blackney, Harry, RB, Maryland, 301
13. Perrin, Richard, DB, Bowling Green, 326
14. Smith, Steve, K, Weber State, 351
15. Herrmann, Don, FL, Waynesburg, 379
16. Jones, Byron, LB, West Texas State, 404
17. Riley, Ken, LB, Texas-Arlington, 429

NY JETS
1. Foley, Dave, T, Ohio State, 26
2. Woodall, Al, QB, Duke, 52
3. Choice to Houston
4. Jones, Ezell, T, Minnesota, 104
5. Gilbert, Chris, RB, Texas, 130
6. Jones, Jimmy, LB, Wichita State, 156
7. Larson, Cliff, DE, Houston, 182
8. Leonard, Cecil, DB, Tuskegee, 208
9. Peters, Frank, T-C, Ohio U., 233
10. Hall, Mike, LB, Alabama, 260
11. Roberts, Gary, G, Purdue, 286
12. Battle, Mike, DB, USC, 311
13. O'Neal, Steve, P, Texas A&M, 338
14. Finnie, Roger, DE, Florida A&M, 364
15. Stewart, Wayne, TE, California, 390
16. Nock, George, RB, Morgan State, 416
17. Zirkle, Fred, DT, Duke, 442

NEW ORLEANS
1. Choice to San Francisco
Shinners, John, G, Xavier, from Minnesota, 17
2. Choice to Baltimore
Neal, Richard, DE, Southern, from St. Louis, 45
3. Choice to Detroit
4. Hale, Dennis, DB, Minnesota, 85
Hudspeth, Bob, T, Southern Illinois, from Dallas, 102
5. Kyasky, Tony, DB, Syracuse, 111
Christensen, Keith, T, Kansas, from NY Giants, 117
6. Miller, Bob, TE, USC, 138
7. Choice to Baltimore
8. Lawrence, Jim, FL, USC, 189
9. Owens, Joe, LB, Alcorn State, 215
10. Reynolds, McKinley, RB, Hawaii, 241
11. Morel, Tommy, FL, LSU, 267
12. Broadhead, Tom, RB, Cal-Santa Barbara, 293
13. Robillard, Joe, DB, Linfield, 319
14. Loyd, Gary, K, California Lutheran, 345
15. Waller, Bill, FL, Xavier, 371
16. Hargett, Ed, QB, Texas A&M, 397
17. Kurzawski, Chico, DB, Northwestern, 423

OAKLAND
1. Thoms, Art, DT, Syracuse, 22
2. Buehler, George, G, Stanford, 50
3. Edwards, Lloyd, TE, San Diego State, 75
4. Jackson, Ruby, T, New Mexico State, 100
5. Choice to Miami
6. Newfield, Ken, RB, LSU, from Boston, 136
Allen, Jackie, DB, Baylor, 153
7. Taylor, Finnis, DB, Prairie View A&M, 178
8. Choice to Kansas City
9. Buie, Drew, E, Catawba, 234
10. Choice to Houston
11. Rice, Harold, LB, Tennessee State, 284
12. Goddard, Al, DB, Johnson C. Smith, 317
13. Husted, Dave, LB, Wabash, 334
14. Busby, Harold, E, UCLA, 362
15. Presnell, Alvin, RB, Alabama A&M, 387
16. Davis, Bill, LB, Alabama, 412
17. Austin, Billy, TE, Arkansas-Pine Bluff, 440

PHILADELPHIA
1. Keyes, Leroy, RB, Purdue, 3
2. Calloway, Ernie, LB, Texas Southern, 28
3. Choice to Cleveland
Bradley, Bill, DB, Texas, from Minnesota, 69
4. Kuechenberg, Bob, G, Notre Dame, 80
5. Anderson, Jim, G, Missouri, 107
6. Barnhorst, Dick, TE, Xavier, 132
7. Schmeising, Mike, RB, St. Olaf, 159
8. Hobbs, Bill, LB, Texas A&M, 184
9. Lawrence, Kent, FL, Georgia, 211
Buss, Lynn, LB, Wisconsin, from Washington, 218
10. Wade, Sonny, QB, Emory & Henry, 236
Shanklin, Donnie, RB, Kansas, from Washington, 243
11. Marcum, Jim, DB, Texas-Arlington, 263
12. Adams, Gary, DB, Arkansas, 288
13. Key, Wade, TE, Southwest Texas State, 314
14. Ross, Jim, T, Bishop, 340
15. Angevine, Leon, SE, Penn State, 367
16. McClinton, Tom, DB, Southern, 392
17. Haack, Bob, T, Linfield, 419

PITTSBURGH
1. Greene, Joe, DT, North Texas State, 4
2. Hanratty, Terry, QB, Notre Dame, 30
Bankston, Warren, RB, Tulane, from San Francisco through Cleveland, 42
3. Kolb, Jon, C, Oklahoma State, 56
4. Campbell, Bob, RB, Penn State, 82
5. Choice to St. Louis
6. Choice to Green Bay
7. Beatty, Charles, DB, North Texas State, 160
Brown, Chadwick, T, East Texas State, from St. Louis through Minnesota, 175
8. Cooper, Joe, FL, Tennessee State, 186
9. Sodaski, John, DB, Villanova, 212
10. Greenwood, L.C., DE, Arkansas-Pine Bluff, 238
11. Washington, Clarence, DT, Arkansas-Pine Bluff, 264
12. Fisher, Doug, LB, San Diego State, 290
13. Lynch, John, LB, Drake, 315
14. Houmard, Bob, RB, Ohio U., 342
15. Liberto, Ken, SE, Louisiana Tech, 368
16. Mosley, Dock, FL, Alcorn State, 394
17. Eppright, Bill, K, Kent State, 420

ST. LOUIS
1. Wehrli, Roger, DB, Missouri, 19
2. Krueger, Rolf, DT, Texas A&M, from Washington, 35
Choice to New Orleans
3. Healy, Chip, LB, Vanderbilt, 71
Brown, Terry, DB, Oklahoma State, from LA Rams through Detroit, 73
4. Rhodes, Bill, G, Florida State, 97
5. Shockley, Walt, RB, San Jose State, from Pittsburgh, 108
Huey, Gene, FL, Wyoming, 123
6. Van Pelt, Amos, RB, Ball State, 149
7. Choice to Pittsburgh through Minnesota
8. Mulligan, Wayne, C, Clemson, 201
9. Snowden, Cal, DE, Indiana, 227
10. Warren, Gerald, K, North Carolina State, 252
11. Kerl, Gary, LB, Utah, 279
12. Taylor, Howard, RB, New Mexico State, 305
13. Heinz, Dick, DT, Cal-Santa Barbara, 331
14. Roseborough, Ed, QB, Arizona State, 356
15. Latham, Fritz, T, Tuskegee, 383
16. Riggins, Junior, RB, Kansas, 409
17. Hummer, George, C, Arizona State, 435

SAN DIEGO
1. Domres, Marty, QB, Columbia, from Denver, 9
Babich, Bob, LB, Miami (Ohio), 18
2. Sayers, Ron, RB, Nebraska-Omaha, 44
3. Ferguson, Gene, T, Norfolk State, 70
4. Choice to Houston
5. Orszulak, Harry, FL, Pittsburgh, 122
6. Swarn, Terry, FL, Colorado State, 147
7. Choice to Miami
8. Cotton, Craig, FL, Youngstown State, 200
9. Williams, Joe, DB, Southern, 226
10. Arnold, David, G, Northwestern State (Louisiana), 251
11. Norwood, Willie, TE, Alcorn State, 278
12. White, Jim, RB, Arkansas-Pine Bluff, 304
13. Simpson, M.H., DB, Houston, 330
14. Ackman, Bill, DT, New Mexico State, 356
15. Jarvis, Charlie, RB, Army, 382
16. Davenport, Willie, FL, Southern, 408
17. Rentz, Larry, DB, Florida, 434

SAN FRANCISCO
1. Kwalick, Ted, TE, Penn State, from New Orleans, 7
Washington, Gene, FL, Stanford, 16
2. Choice to Pittsburgh through Cleveland
3. Choice to Dallas
4. Sniadecki, Jim, LB, Indiana, from Detroit, 86
Moore, Gene, RB, Occidental, 94
5. Edwards, Earl, DT, Wichita State, 120
6. Thomas, Jimmy, RB, Texas-Arlington, 146
7. Van Sinderen, Steve, T, Washington State, 172
8. Loper, Mike, T, BYU, 198
9. Crawford, Hilton, DB, Grambling, 224
10. Chapple, Dave, K, Cal-Santa Barbara, 250
11. Peake, Willie, T, Alcorn State, 276
12. O'Malley, Jack, T, USC, 302
13. Champlin, Paul, DB, Eastern Montana, 328
14. Black, Tom, FL, East Texas State, 354
15. Golden, Gary, DB, Texas Tech, 380
16. Hoskins, Bob, LB, Wichita State, 406
17. Rushing, Joe, LB, Memphis State, 432

WASHINGTON
1. Choice to LA Rams
2. Choice to St. Louis
Epps, Eugene, DB, Texas-El Paso, from Cleveland, 46
3. Cross, Ed, RB, Arkansas-Pine Bluff, 62
4. Choice to Baltimore
5. Kishman, Bill, DB, Colorado State, 114
6. McLinton, Harold, LB, Southern, 139
7. Anderson, Jeff, RB, Virginia, 166
Didion, John, C, Oregon State, from Minnesota, 173
8. Brown, Larry, RB, Kansas State, 191
9. Choice to Philadelphia
10. Choice to Philadelphia
11. Norri, Eric, DT, Notre Dame, 269
12. Shannon, Bob, DB, Tennessee State, 295
13. Shook, Mike, DB, North Texas State, 322
14. Brand, Rick, DT, Virginia, 347
15. Rogers, Paul, T, Virginia, 374
16. Washington, Mike, LB, Southern, 399
17. Dobbert, Rich, DE, Springfield, 426

1970

Held January 27-28, 1970

ATLANTA
1. Small, John, LB, Citadel, 12
2. Malone, Art, RB, Arizona State, 39
3. Maurer, Andy, G, Oregon, 64
Snyder, Todd, WR, Ohio U., from NY Giants, 65
4. Reed, Paul, T, Johnson C. Smith, from Philadelphia, 84
Choice to St. Louis
5. Van Ness, Bruce, RB, Rutgers, from Philadelphia through NY Giants, 112
Mendenhall, Ken, C, Oklahoma, 116
6. Herron, Mack, RB, Kansas State, 143
Butcher, Jade, WR, Indiana, from Washington, 147
Marshall, Randy, DE, Linfield, from LA Rams, 152
7. Choice to LA Rams
Orcutt, Gary, WR, USC, from NY Giants, 169
8. Brewer, Larry, TE, Louisiana Tech, from NY Giants, 194
Miller, Seth, DB, Arizona State, 195
9. Robinson, Roy, DB, Montana, 220
10. Hatcher, Jim, DB, Kansas, 246
11. Brunson, Mike, RB, Arizona State, 272
12. Holton, Lonnie, RB, Northern Michigan, 298
13. Stepanek, Rich, DT, Iowa, 324
14. Wald, Chuck, WR, North Dakota State, 351
15. Mauney, Keith, DB, Princeton, 376
16. Parnell, Steve, WR, Massachusetts, 403
17. Bell, Bill, K, Kansas, 428

BALTIMORE
1. Bulaich, Norm, RB, TCU, 18
2. Bailey, Jim, DT, Kansas, 44
3. O'Brien, Jim, WR, Cincinnati, 70
Person, Ara, TE, Morgan State, from LA Rams through Philadelphia, 74
4. Smear, Steve, LB, Penn State, from Washington, 95
Choice to Green Bay
5. Newsome, Billy, DE, Grambling, 122
6. Gardin, Ron, DB, Arizona, 148
7. Slade, Gordon, QB, Davidson, 174
8. Bouley, Bob, T, Boston College, 199
9. Harris, Barney, DB, Texas A&M, 226
10. Palmer, Dick, LB, Kentucky, 252
11. Edwards, George, RB, Fairmont State, 278
12. Burrell, Don, WR, Angelo State, 304
13. Polak, Dave, LB, Bowling Green, 330
14. Curtis, Tom, DB, Michigan, 356
15. Gary, Phillip, DE, Kentucky State, 382
16. Maitland, Jack, RB, Williams, 408
17. Pearman, Alvin, WR, Colgate, 434

BOSTON
1. Olsen, Phil, DT, Utah State, 4
2. Choice to Houston
3. Ballou, Mike, LB, UCLA, 56
4. Ray, Eddie, DB, LSU, 83
5. Olson, Bob, LB, Notre Dame, from Miami, 107
Choice to NY Jets
6. Choice to Buffalo
7. Lawson, Odell, RB, Langston, 160
8. Choice to NY Jets
9. Wirgowski, Dennis, DE, Purdue, 212
10. Brown, Henry, K-WR, Missouri, 239
11. Bramlett, Dennis, T, Texas-El Paso, 264
12. Roero, Greg, DT, New Mexico Highlands, 291
13. Shelley, Ronnie, DB, Troy State, 316
14. Craw, Garvie, RB-TE, Michigan, 343
15. Schoolfield, Kent, WR, Florida A&M, 368

16. McDaniel, Otis, DE, Tuskegee, 395
17. Killingsworth, Joe, WR, Oklahoma, 420

BUFFALO
1. Cowlings, Al, DE, USC, 5
2. Shaw, Dennis, QB, San Diego State, 30
3. Reilly, Jim, G, Notre Dame, 57
   Alexander, Glenn, DB, Grambling, from San Diego, 67
4. Gantt, Jerry, DE, North Carolina Central, 82
5. Starnes, Steve, LB, Tampa, 109
6. Edwards, Ken, RB, Virginia Tech, 134
   Guthrie, Grant, K, Florida State, from Boston, 135
7. Fowler, Wayne, T, Richmond, 161
8. Cheek, Richard, T, Auburn, 186
9. Bridges, Bill, G, Houston, 213
10. Dixon, Willie, DB, Albany State, 238
11. Williams, Terry, RB, Grambling, 265
12. Simpson, Dave, T, Drake, 290
13. Schroeder, Stefan, K, Pacific, 317
14. Costen, Bill, T, Morris Brown, 342
15. Farris, Dave, TE, Central Michigan, 369
16. Davis, Larry, WR, Rice, 394
17. Bevan, George, DB, LSU, 421

CHI. BEARS
1. Choice to Green Bay
2. Choice to Dallas
3. Farmer, George, WR, UCLA, 54
4. Larson, Lynn, T, Kansas State, 79
   Brupbacher, Ross, LB, Texas A&M, from LA Rams, 100
5. Choice to New Orleans
6. Cutburth, Bobby, QB, Oklahoma State, 133
   Curchin, Jeff, T, Florida State, from St. Louis, 139
7. Choice to Philadelphia
8. Stephenson, Dana, DB, Nebraska, 183
9. Cole, Linzy, TCU, 210
10. Holloway, Glen, G, North Texas State, 235
11. Rose, Ted, TE, Northern Michigan, 262*
12. Davis, Butch, DB, Missouri, 287
13. Gunn, Jimmy, DB, USC, 314
14. Morgan, Jim, WR, Henderson State, 339
15. Abraira, Phil, DB, Florida State, 366
16. Helterbran, Bob, G, North Texas State, 390
17. Brunson, Joe, DT, Furman, 416

CINCINNATI
1. Reid, Mike, DT, Penn State, 7
2. Carpenter, Ron, DT, North Carolina State, 32
3. Bennett, Chip, LB, Abilene Christian, 60
4. Stephen, Joe, G, Jackson State, 85
   Hayes, Billie, DB, San Diego State, from Kansas City, 104
5. Choice to Houston through NY Jets
6. Durko, Sandy, DB, USC, 137
7. Parrish, Lamar, DB, Lincoln (Missouri), 163
8. Trout, Bill, DT, Miami, 188
9. Bolden, Bill, RB, UCLA, 216
10. Roman, Nick, DE, Ohio State, 241
11. Wallace, Sam, LB, Grambling, 266
12. Truesdell, Tom, DT, Ohio Wesleyan, 294
13. Dunn, Paul, WR, U.S. International, 319
14. Johnson, Joe, WR, Johnson C. Smith, 344*
15. Weeks, Marvin, DB, Alcorn State, 372
16. Ely, Larry, LB, Iowa, 397
17. Smith, Dick, RB, Washington State, 422

CLEVELAND
1. Phipps, Mike, QB, Purdue, from Miami, 3
   McKay, Bob, T, Texas, 21
2. Jones, Joe, DE, Tennessee State, from New Orleans, 36
   Sherk, Jerry, DT, Oklahoma State, 47
3. Choice to Dallas
4. Stevenson, Ricky, DB, Arizona, 99
5. Engel, Steve, DB, Colorado, 125
6. Cilek, Mike, QB, Iowa, 151
7. Wycinsky, Craig, G, Michigan State, 177
8. Davidson, Honester, DB, Bowling Green, 203
9. Brown, Geoff, LB, Pittsburgh, 229
10. Yanchar, Bill, DT, Purdue, 255
11. Benner, Gene, WR, Maine, 281
12. Sanders, Jerry, K, Texas Tech, 307
13. Roberts, Larry, RB, Central Missouri State, 333
14. Tharpe, Jim, LB, Lincoln (Missouri), 359
15. Homoly, Guy, DB, Illinois State, 385
16. Redebough, John, TE, Bemidji State, 410
17. Tabb, Charles, RB, McMurry, 436

DALLAS
1. Thomas, Duane, RB, West Texas State, 23
2. Asher, Bob, T, Vanderbilt, from Chi. Bears, 27
   Adkins, Margene, WR, Henderson J.C., 49
3. Waters, Charlie, DB, Clemson, from Houston through Cleveland, 66
   Kiner, Steve, LB, Tennessee, from Cleveland, 73
   Fox, Denton, DB, Texas Tech, 75
4. Fitzgerald, John, T, Boston College, 101
5. Choice to St. Louis
6. Toomay, Pat, DE, Vanderbilt, 153
7. Abbey, Don, LB, Penn State, 179
8. Dossey, Jerry, G, Arkansas, 205
9. Andrusyshyn, Zenon, K, UCLA, 231
10. Athas, Pete, DB, Tennessee, 257
11. Southerland, Ivan, T, Clemson, 283
12. Williams, Joe, RB, Wyoming, 309
13. Washington, Mark, DB, Morgan State, 335
14. Martin, Julian, WR, North Carolina Central, 361
15. DeLong, Ken, TE, Tennessee, 387
16. Hill, Seabern, DB, Arizona State, 411
17. Patterson, Glenn, C, Nebraska, 438

DENVER
1. Anderson, Bobby, RB, Colorado, 11
2. Roche, Alden, DE, Southern, 37
3. Kohler, John, T, South Dakota, 63
4. Hendren, Jerry, WR, Idaho, 89
5. McKoy, Bill, LB, Purdue, 115
6. Mosier, John, TE, Kansas, 141
7. Montgomery, Randy, DB, Weber State, 167
8. Choice to Kansas City
   Porter, Lewis, RB, Southern, from Kansas City, 208
9. Washington, Dave, LB, Alcorn State, 219
10. Fullerton, Maurice, DT, Tuskegee, 247
11. Bryant, Cleve, DB, Ohio U., 271
12. Jones, Greg, RB, Wisconsin Whitewater, 301
13. McKoy, Jim, DB, Parsons, 323
14. Slipp, Jeff, DE, BYU, 349
15. Barakat, Maher, K, South Dakota Tech, 375
16. Stewart, Bobby, QB, Northern Arizona, 401
17. Kalfoss, Frank, K, Montana State, 427

DETROIT
1. Owens, Steve, RB, Oklahoma, 19
2. Parsons, Ray, DE, Minnesota, 45
3. Mitchell, Jim, DE, Virginia State, 71
4. Choice to NY Giants
5. Parker, Bob, G, Memphis State, 123
6. Terry, Tony, DT, USC, 149
7. Geddes, Ken, LB, Nebraska, 175
8. Choice to St. Louis
9. Weaver, Herman, P, Tennessee, 227
10. Maxwell, Bruce, RB, Arkansas, 253
11. Laird, Roger, DB, Kentucky State, 279
12. Murrell, Emanuel, DB, Cal Poly-SLO, 305
13. Haverdick, Dave, DT, Morehead State, 331
14. Brown, Charlie, WR, Northern Arizona, 357
15. Haney, Bob, T, Idaho, 383
16. Todd, Jerry, DB, Memphis State, 409
17. Marshall, Jesse, DT, Centenary, 435

GREEN BAY
1. McCoy, Mike, DT, Notre Dame, from Chi. Bears, 2
   McGeorge, Rich, TE, Elon, 16
2. Matthews, Al, DB, Texas A&M, 41
3. Carter, Jim, LB, Minnesota, 68
4. Ellis, Ken, WR, Southern, 93
   Butler, Skip, K, Texas-Arlington, from Baltimore, 96
5. Pryor, Cecil, DE, Michigan, 120
6. Hunt, Ervin, DB, Fresno State, 145
7. Walker, Cleo, C, Louisville, 172
8. Mjos, Tim, RB, North Dakota State, 197
9. Reinhard, Bob, G, Stanford, 224
10. Melby, Russ, DT, Weber State, 248
    Patrick, Frank, TE, Nebraska, from Washington, 251
11. Hook, Dan, LB, Cal State-Humboldt, 276
12. Foreman, Frank, WR, Michigan State, 300
13. Smith, Dave, RB, Utah, 328
14. Lints, Bob, G, Eastern Michigan, 353
15. Carter, Mike, WR, Cal State-Sacramento, 380
16. Heacock, Jim, DB, Muskingum, 405
17. Krause, Larry, RB, St. Norbert, 432

HOUSTON
1. Wilkerson, Doug, G, North Carolina Central, 14
2. Brooks, Leo, DT, Texas, from Boston, 31
   Dusenbery, Bill, RB, Johnson C. Smith, 40
3. Choice to Dallas through Cleveland
4. Jones, John, P, Georgia, 92
5. Saul, Ron, G, Michigan State, from Cincinnati through NY Jets, 110
   Duley, Ed, DT, Northern Arizona, 118
6. Johnson, Benny, DB, Johnson C. Smith, 144
7. Olson, Charley, DB, Concordia (Minnesota), 170
8. McClish, Mike, T, Wisconsin, 196
9. Blossoms, Charley, DE, Texas Southern, 222
10. Dawkins, Joe, RB, Wisconsin, 249
11. Morris, Bob, C, Duke, 274
12. Dawkins, Richard, TE, Johnson C. Smith, 299*
13. Lewis, Jess, LB, Oregon State, 326
14. Rasmussen, Clair, G, Wisconsin-Oshkosh, 352
15. Sharp, Dave, T, Stanford, 378
16. Myers, Chris, WR, Kenyon, 404*
17. Fagan, Julian, P, Mississippi, 430

KANSAS CITY
1. Smith, Sid, T, USC, 26
2. Werner, Clyde, LB, Washington, 52
3. Barnett, Billy Bob, DE, Texas A&M, from San Francisco, 61
   Hadley, David, DB, Alcorn State, 78
4. Choice to Cincinnati
5. Oriard, Mike, C, Notre Dame, 130
6. Hews, Bob, T, Princeton, 156
7. Glosson, Clyde, WR, Texas-El Paso, 182
8. Barry, Fred, DB, Boston U., from Denver, 193
   Choice to Denver
9. Evans, Charley, T, Texas Tech, 234
10. Stankovich, Bob, G, Arkansas, 259
11. O'Neal, Bill, RB, Grambling, 285
12. Fedorchak, Rod, G, Pittsburgh, 312
13. Patridge, Troy, DE, Texas-Arlington, 338
14. Dumont, Glen, RB, American International, 364
15. Liggett, Bob, DT, Nebraska, 389
16. Ross, Randy, LB, Kansas State, 413
17. Jenkins, Rayford, DB, Alcorn State, 442

LA RAMS
1. Reynolds, Jack, LB, Tennessee, 22
2. Williams, Charlie, WR, Prairie View A&M, 35
   Choice to San Francisco through Philadelphia
3. Choice to Baltimore through Philadelphia
4. Choice to Chi. Bears
5. Choice to New Orleans
6. Choice to Atlanta
7. Provost, Ted, DB, Ohio State, from Philadelphia, 162
   Nelson, Bill, DT, Oregon State, from Atlanta, 168
   Choice to Washington
8. Saul, Rich, LB, Michigan State, 204
9. Graham, Dave, T, New Mexico Highlands, 230
10. Opalsky, Vince, RB, Miami, 256
11. Bookert, David, RB, New Mexico, 282
12. Arnold, Larry, QB, Hawaii, 308
13. Jones, Melvin, WR, Florida A&M, 334
14. Geddes, Bob, LB, UCLA, 360
15. Azam, Dag, G, West Texas State, 386
16. Reichardt, Roland, K, West Texas State, 412
17. Crenshaw, Don, DB, USC, 437

MIAMI
1. Choice to Cleveland
2. Mandich, Jim, TE, Michigan, 29
3. Foley, Tim, DB, Purdue, 55
4. Johnson, Curtis, DB, Toledo, 81
5. Choice to Boston
6. Campbell, Dave, DE, Auburn, 132
7. Scott, Jake, DB, Georgia, 159
8. Chavers, Narvel, RB, Jackson State, 185
9. Ginn, Hubert, RB, Florida A&M, 211
10. Nittenger, Dick, G, Tampa, 237
11. Wheless, Brownie, T, Rice, 263*
12. Kolen, Mike, LB, Auburn, 289
13. Buddington, Dave, RB, Springfield, 315
14. Brackett, Gary, G, Holy Cross, 341
15. Hauser, Pat, WR, East Tennessee State, 367
16. Williams, Charlie, G, Tennessee State, 393
17. Myles, George, DT, Morris Brown, 419

MINNESOTA
1. Ward, John, T, Oklahoma State, 25
2. Cappleman, Bill, QB, Florida State, 51
3. Burgoon, Chuck, LB, North Park, 77
4. Choice to Washington through LA Rams and New Orleans
5. Jones, Greg, RB, UCLA, 129
6. Choice to Pittsburgh
7. Farber, Hap, LB, Mississippi, 181
8. Carroll, Mike, G, Missouri, 206
9. Morrow, George, DE, Mississippi, 233
10. Voight, Stu, TE, Wisconsin, 260
11. Zaunbrecher, Godfrey, C, LSU, 286
12. Holland, James, DB, Jackson State, 311
13. Pearce, Bob, DB, Stephen F. Austin, 337
14. Spinks, Tommy, WR, Louisiana Tech, 363
15. Francis, Bennie, DE, Chadron State, 388
16. Cerone, Bruce, WR, Emporia State, 417
17. Healy, Brian, DB, Michigan, 441

NEW ORLEANS
1. Burrough, Ken, WR, Texas Southern, 10
2. Choice to Cleveland
3. Swinney, Clovis, DE, Arkansas State, 62
4. Howell, Delles, DB, Grambling, 88
5. Cannon, Glenn, DB, Mississippi, from Chi. Bears, 106
   Choice to Washington
   Ramsey, Steve, QB, North Texas State, from LA Rams, 126
6. Easley, Mel, DB, Oregon State, 140
7. Woodard, Lon, DE, San Diego State, 166
8. Estes, Lawrence, DE, Alcorn State, 192
9. Otis, Jim, RB, Ohio State, 218
10. Brumfield, Jim, RB, Indiana State, 244
11. Klahr, Gary, LB, Arizona, 270
12. Davenport, Willie, DB, Southern, 296
13. Miller, Ralph, TE, Alabama State, 322*
14. Sutherland, Doug, DE, Wisconsin-Superior, 348
15. Vest, Jim, DE, Washington State, 374
16. Gaspar, Cliff, DT, Grambling, 400
17. Wyatt, Doug, DB, Tulsa, 426

NY GIANTS
1. Files, Jim, LB, Oklahoma, 13
2. Choice to St. Louis
3. Choice to Atlanta
4. Choice to Pittsburgh
   Grant, Wes, DE, UCLA, from Detroit, 97
5. Brumfield, Claude, G, Tennessee State, 117
6. Miller, Duane, WR, Drake, 142
7. Choice to Atlanta
8. Choice to Atlanta
9. Hughes, Pat, C, Boston U., 221
10. Fortier, Matt, DE, Fairmont State, 245
11. Pitcaithley, Alan, RB, Oregon, 273
12. Nels, Larry, LB, Wyoming, 297
13. Inskeep, Gary, T, Wisconsin-Stout, 325
14. Brand, Rodney, C, Arkansas, 350
15. Muir, Warren, RB, South Carolina, 377
16. Nolting, Vic, DB, Xavier, 402
17. Breaux, Walter, DT, Grambling, 429

NY JETS
1. Tannen, Steve, DB, Florida, 20
2. Caster, Richard, WR, Jackson State, 46
3. Onkotz, Dennis, LB, Penn State, 72
4. Ebersole, John, DE, Penn State, 98
5. McClain, Cliff, RB, South Carolina State, from Boston, 108
   Arthur, Gary, TE, Miami (Ohio), 124

6. Stewart, Terry, DB, Arkansas, 150
7. Williams, Jim, DB, Virginia State, 176
8. Porter, Jack, G, Oklahoma, from Boston, 187
Lomas, Mark, DE, Northern Arizona, 202
9. Bell, Eddie, WR, Idaho State, 228
10. Dickerson, Cleve, RB, Miami (Ohio), 254
11. Thomas, Earlie, DB, Colorado State, 280
12. Pierson, Bill, C-G, San Diego State, 306
13. Groth, Walter, DT, Baylor, 332
14. Little, John, LB, Oklahoma State, 358
15. Bayless, Tom, DT, Purdue, 384
16. Herard, Claude, DT, Mississippi, 418
17. Beard, Dick, RB, Kentucky, 440

OAKLAND
1. Chester, Raymond, TE, Morgan State, 24
2. Koy, Ted, RB, Texas, 50
3. Irons, Gerald, DE-DT, Maryland-Eastern Shore, 76
4. Cline, Tony, LB, Miami, 102
5. Laster, Art, T, Maryland-Eastern Shore, 128
6. Wyatt, Alvin, DB, Bethune-Cookman, 154
7. Svitak, Steve, LB, Boise State, 180
8. Wynn, Mike, DE-DT, Nebraska, 207
9. Hill, Ike, DB, Catawba, 232
10. Bosserman, Gordon, T, UCLA, 258
11. Hicks, Emery, LB, Kansas, 284
12. De Loach, Gerry, G, Cal-Davis, 310
13. Highsmith, Don, RB, Michigan State, 336
14. Riley, John, K-P, Auburn, 362
15. Moore, Fred, WR, Washington State, 392
16. Roth, Tim, DB, South Dakota State, 414
17. Stolberg, Eric, WR, Indiana, 439

PHILADELPHIA
1. Zabel, Steve, TE, Oklahoma, 6
2. Jones, Ray, DB, Southern, 34
3. Bouggess, Lee, RB, Louisville, 59
4. Choice to Atlanta
5. Choice to Atlanta through NY Giants
6. Choice to St. Louis
7. Brennan, Terry, T, Notre Dame, from Chi. Bears, 158
Choice to LA Rams
8. Gordon, Ira, T, Kansas State, 190
9. King, David, LB, Stephen F. Austin, 215
10. Jaggard, Steve, DB, Memphis State, 240
11. Walik, Billy, DB, Villanova, 268
12. Jones, Robert, DT, Grambling, 293
13. Stevens, Richard, T, Baylor, 318
14. Moseley, Mark, K, Stephen F. Austin, 346
15. Carlos, John, WR, San Jose State, 371
16. Uperesa, Tuufuli, T, Montana, 396
17. Sizelove, Mike, TE, Idaho, 424

PITTSBURGH
1. Bradshaw, Terry, QB, Louisiana Tech, 1
2. Shanklin, Ronnie, WR, North Texas State, 28
3. Blount, Mel, DB, Southern, 53
4. George, Ed, T, Wake Forest, 80
Evenson, Jim, RB, Oregon, from NY Giants, 90
5. Staggers, Jon, DB, Missouri, 105
6. Barrera, Manuel, LB, Kansas State, 131
Kegler, Clarence, T, South Carolina State, from Minnesota, 155
7. Griffin, Danny, RB, Texas-Arlington, 157
8. Smith, Dave, WR, Indiana (Pennsylvania), 184
9. Crennel, Carl, LB, West Virginia, 209
10. Brown, Isaiah, DB, Stanford, 236
11. Hunt, Calvin, C, Baylor, 261
12. Sharp, Rick, DT, Washington, 288
13. Main, Billy, RB, Oregon State, 313
14. Askson, Bert, LB, Texas Southern, 340
15. Keppy, Glen, DT, Wisconsin-Platteville, 365
16. Yanossy, Frank, DT, Tennessee, 391
17. Key, Harry, TE, Mississippi Valley State, 415

ST. LOUIS
1. Stegent, Larry, RB, Texas A&M, 8
2. Corrigall, Jim, LB, Kent State, 33
Hutchison, Chuck, G, Ohio State, from NY Giants, 38
3. Pittman, Charlie, RB, Penn State, 58
Harris, Eric, DB, Colorado, from Washington, 69
4. Lens, Greg, DT, Trinity (Texas), 86
Parish, Don, LB, Stanford, from Atlanta, 91
5. Lloyd, Tom, T, Bowling Green, 111
Pierson, Barry, DB, Michigan, from Dallas, 127
6. Manuel, James, T, Toledo, from Philadelphia, 136
Choice to Chi. Bears
7. McFarland, Jim, TE, Nebraska, 164
8. Banks, Tom, C, Auburn, 189
Holmgren, Mike, QB, USC, from Detroit, 201
9. White, Paul, RB, Texas-El Paso, 214
10. Plummer, Tony, DB, Pacific, 242
11. Siwek, Mike, DT, Western Michigan, 267
12. Collins, Charles, WR, Kansas State, 292
13. Thomas, Jack, G, Mississippi State, 320
14. Groth, Ray, WR, Utah, 345
15. Wilson, Ron, WR, West Illinois, 370
16. Fowler, Gary, RB, California, 398
17. Powell, Cliff, LB, Arkansas, 423

SAN DIEGO
1. Gillette, Walker, WR, Richmond, 15
2. Williams, Tom, DT, Cal-Davis, 42
3. Choice to Buffalo
4. Maddox, Bill, TE, Syracuse, 94
5. Farrar, Pettus, RB, Norfolk State, 119
6. Parks, Billy, WR, Long Beach State, 146
7. Fabish, Jim, DB, Texas-El Paso, 171
8. Clark, Wayne, QB, U.S. International, 198
9. Fletcher, Chris, DB, Temple, 213
10. Steen, Mac, G, Florida, 250
11. Protz, John, LB, Syracuse, 275
12. Gravelle, Howard, TE, Cal-Davis, 302
13. Bradley, Bernard, DB, Utah State, 327
14. Caldwell, Tyrone, DT, South Carolina State, 354
15. Childs, Eugene, RB, Texas-El Paso, 379
16. Green, Mike, RB, Nebraska, 406
17. Sanks, Dave, G, Louisville, 431

SAN FRANCISCO
1. Hardman, Cedrick, DE, North Texas State, 9
Taylor, Bruce, DB, Boston U., from Washington, 17
2. Choice to LA Rams
Isenbarger, John, RB, Indiana, from LA Rams through Philadelphia, 48
3. Choice to Kansas City
4. Washington, Vic, WR, Wyoming, 87
5. McArthur, Gary, T, USC, 113
6. Clark, Rusty, QB, Houston, 138
7. Strong, Jim, RB, Houston, 165
8. Campbell, Carter, LB, Weber State, 191
9. Riley, Preston, DB-WR, Memphis State, 217
10. Schreiber, Larry, RB, Tennessee Tech, 243
11. Crockett, Dan, WR, Toledo, 269
12. Tant, Bill, T, Dayton, 295
13. Vanderslice, Jim, LB, TCU, 321
14. King, Jack, G, Clemson, 347
15. Delsignore, Dave, WR, Youngstown State, 373
16. Perkins, Produs, DB, Livingstone, 399
17. Culton, Mike, P, La Verne, 425

WASHINGTON
1. Choice to St. Louis
2. Brundige, Bill, DE, Colorado, 43
3. Choice to St. Louis
4. Choice to Baltimore
Laaveg, Paul, T, Iowa, from Minnesota through LA Rams and New Orleans, 103
5. Sistrunk, Manny, DT, Arkansas-Pine Bluff, from New Orleans, 114
Pierce, Danny, RB, Memphis State, 121
6. Choice to Atlanta
7. Merritt, Roland, WR, Maryland, 173
Harris, Jimmy, DB, Howard Payne, from LA Rams, 178
8. Johnson, Paul, DB, Penn State, 200
9. Sonntag, Ralph, T, Maryland, 225
10. Choice to Green Bay
11. Alston, Mack, TE, Maryland-Eastern Shore, 277
12. Kates, Jim, LB, Penn State, 303
13. Patterson, Joe, T, Lawrence, 329
14. Moro, Tony, RB, Dayton, 355
15. Lewandowski, Vic, C, Holy Cross, 381
16. Bushore, Steve, WR, Emporia State, 407
17. Maxfield, Earl, DT, Baylor, 433

1971

Held January 28-29, 1971

Although the Patriots' franchise played the 1971 season as New England, at the time of the draft it still was located in Boston.

ATLANTA
1. Profit, Joe, RB, Northeast Louisiana, 7
2. Burrow, Ken, WR, San Diego State, 33
3. Hart, Leo, QB, Duke, 59
4. Potchad, Mike, T, Pittsburg State, 85
5. Jarvis, Ray, WR, Norfolk State, 111
6. Hayes, Tom, DB, San Diego State, 137
Brown, Ray, DB, West Texas State, from NY Giants, 148
7. Chesson, Wes, WR, Duke, 163
8. Havig, Dennis, G, Colorado, 189
9. Griffin, Alvin, WR, Tuskegee, 215
10. Tillman, Faddie, DE, Boise State, 241
11. Shears, Larry, DB, Lincoln (Missouri), 267
12. Lowe, Ronnie, WR, Ft. Valley State, 293
13. Crooks, Dan, DB, Wisconsin, 319
14. Comer, Deryl, TE, Texas, 345
15. Clark, Wallace, RB, Auburn, 371
16. James, Lindsey, RB, San Diego State, 397
17. Martin, Willie, RB, Johnson C. Smith, 423

BALTIMORE
1. McCauley, Don, RB, North Carolina, from Miami, 22
Dunlap, Leonard, DB, North Texas State, 26
2. Atessis, Bill, DE, Texas, 52
3. Douglas, Karl, QB, Texas A&I, 78
4. Choice to Pittsburgh
5. Andrews, John, TE, Indiana, 130
6. Frith, Ken, DT, Northeast Louisiana, 156
7. Bowdell, Gordon, WR, Michigan State, 182
8. Bogan, Willie, DB, Dartmouth, 207
9. Burnett, Bill, RB, Arkansas, 234
10. Kern, Rex, QB, Ohio State, 260
11. Jones, Dave, LB, Baylor, 286
12. Wuensch, Bobby, T, Texas, from Pittsburgh, 294
Triplett, Bill, WR, Michigan State, 312
13. Neville, Tom, LB, Yale, 338
14. Mikolayunas, Mike, RB, Davidson, 364
15. Hogan, Mike, LB, Michigan State, 390
16. Harrington, Rich, DB, Houston, 416
17. Nottingham, Don, RB, Kent State, 441

BOSTON
1. Plunkett, Jim, QB, Stanford, 1
2. Adams, Julius, DT, Texas Southern, 27
3. Choice to Buffalo through Oakland
4. Choice to Denver
5. Kelly, Tim, LB, Notre Dame, 105
6. Hardt, David, TE, Kentucky, 131
7. Choice to Oakland
8. Choice to Buffalo
9. Ashton, Josh, RB, Tulsa, 209
10. McDowell, Layne, T, Iowa, 235
11. Schneiss, Dan, TE, Nebraska, 261
12. Rodman, John, T, Northwestern, 287
13. Swain, Lewis, DB, Alabama A&M, 313
14. Sykes, Alfred, WR, Florida A&M, 339
15. McGarry, Nick, TE, Massachusetts, 365
16. Zikmund, Jim, DB, Kearney State, 391
17. Leigh, Ronald, DE, Elizabeth City State, 417

BUFFALO
1. Hill, J.D, WR, Arizona State, 4
2. White, Jan, TE, Ohio State, 29
3. Jarvis, Bruce, C, Washington, from Boston through Oakland, 53
Braxton, Jim, RB, West Virginia, 57
4. Choice to New Orleans
5. Green, Donnie, T, Purdue, 107
Beamer, Tim, DB, Johnson C. Smith, from Denver, 113
6. Choice to Chi. Bears
McKinley, Bill, DE, Arizona, from Cincinnati, 145
7. Chandler, Bob, WR, USC, 160
8. Ross, Louis, DE, South Carolina State, from Boston, 183
Walls, Tyrone, RB, Missouri, 185
9. Strickland, Bob, LB, Auburn, 213
10. Choice to Oakland
11. Browder, Andy, T, Texas A&I, 263
12. Sheffield, Jim, K, Texas A&M, 291
13. Underwood, Busty, QB, TCU, 316
14. Hoots, Jim, DE, Missouri Southern, 341
15. Cole, Charley, RB, Toledo, 369
16. Hunter, Billy, DB, Utah, 394
17. Morrison, Pat, TE, Arkansas, 419

CHI. BEARS
1. Moore, Joe, RB, Missouri, 11
2. Harrison, Jim, RB, Missouri, from New Orleans, 28
Ford, Charles, DB, Houston, 36
3. McGee, Tony, DE, Bishop, 64
Newton, Bob, T, Nebraska, from LA Rams, 71
4. Moore, Jerry, DB, Arkansas, 89
5. Choice to San Francisco
6. Thomas, Earl, TE, Houston, from Buffalo, 135
7. Lee, Buddy, QB, LSU, 167
Ferris, Dennis, RB, Pittsburgh, from LA Rams, 176
8. Weiss, Karl, T, Vanderbilt, 192
9. McClain, Lester, WR, Tennessee, 220
10. Rowden, Larry, LB, Houston, 245
11. Hardy, Cliff, DB, Michigan State, 270
12. Booras, Steve, DE, Mesa J.C., 298*
13. Nicholas, Ed, T, North Carolina State, 323
14. Lewis, Willie, RB, Arizona, 347
15. Maciejowski, Ron, QB, Ohio State, 376
16. Bailey, Sid, DE, Texas-Arlington, 401
17. Garganes, Ray, LB, Millersville, 426

CINCINNATI
1. Holland, Vernon, T, Tennessee State, 15
2. Lawson, Steve, G, Kansas, 41
3. Anderson, Ken, QB, Augustana (Illinois), 67
4. Willis, Fred, RB, Boston College, 93
5. May, Arthur, DE, Tuskegee, from NY Jets, 110
Choice to San Diego
6. Choice to Buffalo
7. Craig, Neal, DB, Fisk, 171
8. Herring, Fred, DB, Tennessee State, 197
9. Gustafson, Gary, LB, Montana State, 223
10. Stambaugh, Jack, G, Oregon, 249
11. Marshall, Ed, WR, Cameron, 275
12. Hayden, James, DE, Memphis State, 301
13. Knapman, David, TE, Central Washington, 327
14. Mallory, Irvin, DB, Virginia Union, 353
15. Thomas, Bob, RB, Arizona State, 379
16. Debevc, Mark, LB, Ohio State, 405
17. Pearson, Sam, DB, Western Kentucky, 432

CLEVELAND
1. Scott, Clarence, DB, Kansas State, 14
2. Cornell, Bo, RB, Washington, 40
3. Staroba, Paul, WR, Michigan, 66
Hall, Charlie, LB, Houston, from Kansas City, 68
4. Pena, Bubba, G, Massachusetts, 92
5. Brown, Stan, WR, Purdue, 118
6. Dieken, Doug, T, Illinois, from Chi. Bears, 142
Dixon, Jay, DE, Boston U., 144
7. Jacobs, Bob, K, Wyoming, 170
8. Zelina, Larry, RB, Ohio State, 196
9. Levels, Wilmur, DB, North Texas State, 222
10. Casteel, Steve, LB, Oklahoma, 248
11. Sikich, Mike, G, Northwestern, 274
12. Blanchard, Tony, TE, North Carolina, 300
13. Jamula, Thad, T, Lehigh, 326
14. Kingrea, Rick, LB, Tulane, 352
15. Green, Bill, DB, Western Kentucky, 378
16. Smith, Dave, WR, Mississippi State, 404
17. Dillon, Leo, C, Dayton, 430

DALLAS
1. Smith, Tody, DE, USC, 25
2. Thomas, Ike, DB, Bishop, 51
3. Scarber, Sam, RB, New Mexico, from St. Louis, 69
Gregory, Bill, DT, Wisconsin, 77
4. Carter, Joe, TE, Grambling, from New Orleans, 80
Mitchell, Adam, T, Mississippi, 103
5. Kadziel, Ron, LB, Stanford, 129
6. Maier, Steve, WR, Northern Arizona, 155
7. Griffin, Bill, T, Catawba, 181

8. Jessie, Ron, WR, Kansas, 206
9. Jackson, Honor, WR, Pacific, 233
10. Wallace, Rodney, DT, New Mexico, 259
11. Bonwell, Ernest, DT, Lane, 285
12. Goepel, Steve, QB, Colgate, 311
13. Ford, Jim, RB, Texas Southern, 337
14. Covey, Tyrone, DB, Utah State, 363
15. Young, Bob, TE, Delaware, 389
16. Brennan, John, T, Boston College, 415
17. Bomer, John, C, Memphis State, 440

DENVER
1. Choice to Green Bay
   Montgomery, Marv, T, USC, from Green Bay, 12
2. Harrison, Dwight, WR, Texas A&I, 35
3. Choice to St. Louis
4. Alzado, Lyle, DE, Yankton, from Boston, 79
   Johnson, Cleo, DB, Alcorn State, 87
5. Choice to Buffalo
6. Phillips, Harold, DB, Michigan State, 139
7. Adams, Doug, LB, Ohio State, 165
8. Beard, Tom, C, Michigan State, from Houston, 187
   Choice to Kansas City
9. Handy, John, LB, Purdue, 217
10. Harris, Carlis, WR, Idaho State, 243
11. Roitsch, Roger, DT, Rice, 269
12. Franks, Floyd, WR, Mississippi, 295
13. Blackford, Craig, QB, Evansville, 321
14. Lyons, Tommy, C, Georgia, 350
15. James, Larry, RB, Norfolk State, 373
16. Thompson, Steve, DT, Minnesota, 399
17. Simcsak, Jack, K, Virginia Tech, 425

DETROIT
1. Bell, Bob, DT, Cincinnati, 21
2. Thompson, Dave, C-G, Clemson, from Philadelphia, 30
   Weaver, Charlie, LB, USC, 48
3. Clark, Al, DB, Eastern Michigan, 72
4. Woods, Larry, DT, Tennessee State, 100
5. Newell, Pete, G, Michigan, 125
6. Harris, Frank, QB, Boston College, from LA Rams through Philadelphia, 150
   Franklin, Herman, WR, USC, 152
7. Wheless, Brownie, T, Rice, 177
8. Lee, Ken, LB, Washington, 204
9. Zofko, Mickey, RB, Auburn, 229
10. Choice to Philadelphia
11. Webb, Phil, DB, Colorado State, 281
12. Pilconis, Bill, WR, Pittsburgh, 308
13. Abercrombie, David, RB, Tulane, 332
14. Lorenz, Tom, TE, Iowa State, 360
15. Coates, Ed, WR, Central Missouri State, 385
16. Kutchinski, Tom, DB, Michigan State, 411
17. Jolley, Gordon, T, Utah, 436

GREEN BAY
1. Brockington, John, RB, Ohio State, from Denver, 9
   Choice to Denver
2. Choice to San Francisco
   Robinson, Virgil, RB, Grambling, from LA Rams, 46
3. Hall, Charlie, DB, Pittsburgh, 62
4. Choice to LA Rams
5. Choice to San Diego
   Smith, Donnell, DE, Southern, from Washington, 116
   Stillwagon, Jim, LB, Ohio State, from LA Rams through Washington, 124
6. Hunter, Scott, QB, Alabama, 140
7. Davis, Dave, WR, Tennessee State, 168
   Johnson, James, WR, Bishop, from Oakland, 175
8. Headley, Win, C, Wake Forest, 193
9. Mayer, Barry, RB, Minnesota , 218
10. Hunt, Kevin, T, Doane, 246
11. Lanier, John, RB, Parsons, 271
12. Hendren, Greg, G, California, 296
13. Martin, Jack, RB, Angelo State, 324
14. Spears, LeRoy, DE, Moorhead State, 348
15. Garrett, Len, TE, New Mexico Highlands, 374
16. O'Donnell, Jack, G, Central State (Oklahoma), 402
17. Johnson, Monty, DB, Oklahoma, 427

HOUSTON
1. Pastorini, Dan, QB, Santa Clara, 3
2. Choice to New Orleans
3. Dickey, Lynn, QB, Kansas City, 56
4. Jackson, Larron, T, Missouri, 81
5. Armstrong, Willie, RB, Grambling, 109
6. Alexander, Willie, DB, Alcorn State, 134
7. Croyle, Phil, LB, California, 159
   Watson, Larry, T, Morgan State, from NY Giants, 174
8. Choice to Denver
9. Rice, Floyd, TE-LB, Alcorn State, 212*
10. Price, Russell, DE, North Carolina Central, 237
11. Hughes, Macon, WR, Rice, 265
12. Thompson, John, G, Minnesota, 290
13. Hoing, Joe, G, Arkansas Tech, 315
14. Adams, Dick, DB, Miami (Ohio), 343
15. Hopkins, Andy, RB, Stephen F. Austin, 368
16. Denson, Moses, RB, Maryland-Eastern Shore, 393*
17. Fox, Calvin, LB, Michigan State, 421

KANSAS CITY
1. Wright, Elmo, WR, Houston, 16
2. Young, Wilber, DT, William Penn, from San Diego, 39
   Lewis, Scott, DE, Grambling, 42
3. Choice to Cleveland
4. Robinson, David, TE, Jacksonville State, 94
5. Adamle, Mike, RB, Northwestern, 120
6. Reardon, Kerry, DB, Iowa, 146
7. Choice to New Orleans
8. Sensibaugh, Mike, DB, Ohio State, from Denver, 191
   Telander, Rick, DB, Northwestern, 198
9. Hawes, Alvin, T, Minnesota, 224
10. Jankowski, Bruce, WR, Ohio State, 250
11. Allen, Nate, DB, Texas Southern, 276
12. Esposito, Tony, RB, Pittsburgh, 302
13. Hixson, Chuck, QB, SMU, 328
14. Bergey, Bruce, DE, UCLA, 354
15. Montgomery, Mike, DB, Southwest Texas State, 380
16. Jansonius, Darrell, G, Iowa State, 406
17. Hill, Travis, DB, Prairie View A&M, 431*

LA RAMS
1. Robertson, Isiah, LB, Southern, from Washington, 10
   Youngblood, Jack, DE, Florida, 20
2. Choice to Green Bay
3. Elmendorf, Dave, DB, Texas A&M, from Washington, 63
   Choice to Chicago
4. Worster, Steve, RB, Texas, from Green Bay, 90
   Choice to New Orleans
5. Choice to Green Bay through Washington
6. Choice to Detroit through Philadelphia
7. Choice to Chi. Bears
8. Garay, Tony, DE, Hofstra, 202
9. Schmidt, Joe, WR, Miami, 228
10. Popplewell, Don, C, Colorado, 254
11. Richards, Charlie, QB, Richmond, 280
12. Behrendt, Kirk, T, Wisconsin-Whitewater, 306
13. Harrison, Russell, RB, Kansas State, 331
14. Coleman, Lionel, DB, Oregon, 358
15. Kos, Gary, G, Notre Dame, 384
16. Boice, Ross, LB, Pacific Lutheran, 409
17. Vataha, Randy, WR, Stanford, from New Orleans, 418
   Sweet, Joe, WR, Tennessee State, 435

MIAMI
1. Choice to Baltimore
2. Stowe, Otto, WR, Iowa State, 47
3. Farley, Dale, LB, West Virginia, 74
4. Theismann, Joe, QB, Notre Dame, 99
5. Choice to Pittsburgh
6. Coleman, Dennis, LB, Mississippi, 151
7. Dickerson, Ron, DB, Kansas State, 178
8. Choice to Pittsburgh
9. Den Herder, Vern, DE, Central Iowa, 230
10. Maree, Ron, DT, Purdue, 255
11. Surma, Vic, T, Penn State, 282
12. Byars, Leroy, RB, Alcorn State, 307
13. Hepburn, Lionel, DB, Texas Southern, 333
14. Vaughn, David, TE, Memphis State, 359
15. Richards, Bob, G, California, 386
16. Myers, Chris, WR, Kenyon, 410
17. Mark, Curt, LB, Mayville, 437

MINNESOTA
1. Hayden, Leo, RB, Ohio State, 24
2. Choice to Philadelphia
3. Hackett, Eddie, WR, Alcorn State, 76
4. Clements, Vince, RB, Connecticut, 102
5. Choice to Pittsburgh
6. Choice to Philadelphia
7. Mack, Gene, LB, Texas-El Paso, 180
8. Farley, John, DE, Johnson C. Smith, 208
9. Sullivan, Tim, RB, Iowa, 232
10. Morris, Chris, G, Indiana, 258
11. Walker, Mike, LB, Tulane, 284
12. Holmes, Reggie, DB, Wisconsin-Stout, 310
13. Fry, Benny, C, Houston, 336
14. Gallagher, Jim, LB, Yale, 362
15. Wright, Jeff, DB, Minnesota, 388
16. Edmonds, Greg, WR, Penn State, 413
17. Duncan, Ken, P, Tulsa, 439

NEW ORLEANS
1. Manning, Archie, QB, Mississippi, 2
2. Choice to Chi. Bears
   Holden, Sam, G, Grambling, from Houston, 31
3. Lee, Bivian, DB, Prairie View A&M, 54
4. Choice to Dallas
   Bell, Carlos, RB, Houston, from Buffalo, 82
   Winther, Wimpy, C, Mississippi, from Washington, 88
   Martin, D'Artagnan, DB, Kentucky State, from San Diego, 91
   Morrison, Don, T, Texas-Arlington, from LA Rams, 98
5. Choice to Pittsburgh
6. Moorhead, Don, RB, Michigan, 132
7. DiNardo, Larry, G, Notre Dame, 158
   Newland, Bob, WR, Oregon, from Kansas City, 172
8. Choice to Pittsburgh
   Elder, Jimmy, DB, Southern, from Washington, 194
   Gresham, Bob, RB, West Virginia, from Oakland, 201
9. Williams, Tom, DB, Willamette, 210
10. Choice to San Francisco
   Pamplin, Rocky, RB, Hawaii, from Philadelphia, 239
11. Pollard, Bob, DE, Weber State, 262
12. Gathright, Ron, DB, Morehead State, 288
13. Burchfield, Don, TE, Ball State, 314
14. Scott, Bobby, QB, Tennessee, 340
15. Graves, Bart, T-DE, Tulane, 366
16. Robinson, Craig, T, Houston, 392
17. Choice to LA Rams
   Eben, Hermann, WR, Oklahoma State, from Washington, 428

NY GIANTS
1. Thompson, Rocky, WR, West Texas State, 18
2. Walton, Wayne, T, Abilene Christian, 44
3. Hornsby, Ronnie, LB, Southeastern Louisiana, 70
4. Tipton, Dave, DT, Stanford, 96
5. Choice to San Francisco
6. Choice to Atlanta
7. Choice to Houston
8. Gregory, Ted, DE-LB, Delaware, 200
9. Thomas, Ed, LB, Lebanon Valley, 226
10. Reed, Henry, LB, Weber State, 252
11. Ellison, Marshall, G, Dayton, 278
12. Blanchard, Tom, QB-K, Oregon, 304
13. Roller, Dave, DT, Kentucky, 330
14. Evans, Charlie, RB, USC, 356
15. Wright, Jim, LB, Notre Dame, 382
16. Gibbs, Dick, TE, Texas-El Paso, 408
17. Zeno, Coleman, WR, Grambling, 434

NY JETS
1. Riggins, John, RB, Kansas, 6
2. Mooring, John, T, Tampa, 32
3. Farasopoulos, Chris, DB, BYU, 58
4. Zapalac, Bill, LB, Texas, 84
5. Choice to Cincinnati
6. Wise, Phil, TE, Nebraska-Omaha, 136
7. Palmer, Scott, DT, Texas, 162
8. Kirksey, Roy, G, Maryland-Eastern Shore, 188
9. Curtis, John, TE, Springfield, 214
10. Bettis, Jim, DB, Michigan, 240
11. Studdard, Vern, WR, Mississippi, 266
12. Sowells, Rich, DB, Alcorn State, 292
13. Eggold, John, DE, Arizona, 318
14. Harpring, John, G, Michigan 344
15. Dyches, Dan, C, South Carolina, 370
16. Harkey, Steve, RB, Georgia Tech, 396
17. Flaska, Greg, DE, Western Michigan, 422

OAKLAND
1. Tatum, Jack, DB, Ohio State, 19
2. Villapiano, Phil, LB, Bowling Green, 45
3. Koegel, Warren, C, Penn State, 73
4. Davis, Clarence, RB, USC, 97
5. Moore, Bob, TE, Stanford, 123
6. Slough, Greg, LB, USC, 149
7. Martin, Don, DB, Yale, from Boston, 157
   Choice to Green Bay
8. Choice to New Orleans
9. Garnett, Dave, RB, Pittsburgh, 227
10. West, Bill, DB, Tennessee State, from Buffalo, 238
   Oesterling, Tim, DT, UCLA, 253
11. Poston, Jim, DT, South Carolina, 279
12. Jones, Horace, DT, Louisville, 305
13. Natzel, Mick, DB, Central Michigan, 334
14. Gipson, Tom, DT, North Texas State, 357
15. Giles, Andy, DE, William & Mary, 383
16. Stawarz, Tony, DB, Miami, 412
17. Hill, Charles, WR, Sam Houston State, 442

PHILADELPHIA
1. Harris, Richard, DE, Grambling, 5
2. Choice to Detroit
   Allison, Henry, G, San Diego State, from Minnesota, 50
3. Choice to San Francisco
4. Feller, Happy, K, Texas, 83
5. Shellabarger, Tom, T, San Diego State, 108
6. Smith, Jack, DB, Troy State, 133
   Neely, Wyck, DB, Mississippi, from Minnesota, 154
7. Carmichael, Harold, WR, Southern, 161
8. Gotschalk, Len, C, Cal State-Humboldt, 186
9. Pettigrew, Len, LB, Ashland, 211
10. Choice to New Orleans
   Bailey, Tom, Florida State, from Detroit, 256
11. Davis, Albert, RB, Tennessee State, 264
12. Saathoff, Rich, DE, Northern Arizona, 289
13. Lester, Danny, DB, Texas, 317
14. Creech, Robert, LB, TCU, 342
15. Fisher, Ed, G, Prairie View, 367
16. James, Bruce, LB, Arkansas, 395
17. Sage, John, LB, LSU, 420

PITTSBURGH
1. Lewis, Frank, WR, Grambling, 8
2. Ham, Jack, LB, Penn State, 34
3. Davis, Steve, RB, Delaware State, 60
4. Mullins, Gerry, TE, USC, 86
   White, Dwight, DE, East Texas State, from Baltimore, 104
5. Brown, Larry, TE, Kansas, from New Orleans, 106
   Holmes, Mel, T, North Carolina A&T, 112
   Anderson, Ralph, DB, West Texas State, from Miami, 126
   Brister, Fred, LB, Mississippi, from Minnesota, 128
6. Hanneman, Craig, T, Oregon State, 138
7. McClure, Worthy, T-G, Mississippi, 164
8. Crowe, Larry, RB, Texas Southern, from New Orleans, 184
   Rogers, Paul, K, Nebraska, 190
   Holmes, Ernie, DT, Texas Southern, from Miami, 203
9. Anderson, Mike, LB, LSU, 216
10. O'Shea, Jim, TE, Boston College, 242
11. Wagner, Mike, DB, Western Illinois, 268
12. Choice to Baltimore
13. Young, Al, WR, South Carolina State, 320
14. Evans, McKinney, DB, New Mexico Highlands, 346
15. Makin, Ray, G, Kentucky, 372
16. Huntley, Walter, DB, Trinity (Texas), 398
17. Ehle, Danny, RB, Howard Payne, 424

ST. LOUIS
1. Thompson, Norm, DB, Utah, 17
2. Dierdorf, Dan, T, Michigan, 43
3. Livesay, Jim, WR, Richmond, from Denver, 61
   Choice to Dallas
4. Willingham, Larry, DB, Auburn, 95
5. Wallace, Rocky, LB, Missouri, 121
6. Gray, Mel, WR, Missouri, 147
7. Cooch, James, DB, Colorado, 173
8. Yankowski, Ron, DE, Kansas State, 199
9. Savoy, Mike, WR, Black Hills State, 225
10. Miller, Ron, T, McNeese State, 251
11. Ogle, Rick, LB, Colorado, 277
12. Von Dulm, Tim, QB, Portland State, 303

13. Allen, Jeff, DB, Iowa State, 329
14. Klausen, Doug, T, Arizona, 355
15. Heiskell, Ted, RB, Houston, 381
16. Brame, Lawrence, LB, Western Kentucky, 407
17. Watkins, Preston, WR, Bluefield, 433

SAN DIEGO
1. Burns, Leon, RB, Long Beach State, 13
2. Choice to Kansas City
3. Montgomery, Mike, RB, Kansas State, 65
4. Choice to New Orleans
5. Salter, Bryant, DB, Pittsburgh, from Green Bay, 115
   White, Ray, LB, Syracuse, 117
   Asack, Phil, DE, Duke, from Cincinnati, 119
6. Mayes, Jacob, RB, Tennessee State, 143
7. Dicus, Chuck, WR, Arkansas, 169
8. Van Gorkum, Leon, DE, San Diego State, 195
9. Tanner, John, TE, Tennessee Tech, 221
10. Nowak, Gary, TE, Michigan State, 247
11. Pinson, Don, DB, Tennessee State, 273
12. Garnett, Wes, WR, Utah State, 299
13. Milner, Sammy, WR, Mississippi State, 325
14. O'Daniel, Edward, DE, Texas Southern, 351
15. Humston, Eric, LB, Muskingum, 377
16. Foote, Ed, C, Hawaii, 403
17. Kell, Chip, C, Tennessee, 429

SAN FRANCISCO
1. Anderson, Tim, DB, Ohio State, 23
2. Janet, Ernie, G, Washington, from Green Bay, 37
   Orduna, Joe, RB, Nebraska, 49
3. Dickerson, Sam, WR, USC, from Philadelphia, 55
   Parker, Willie, C, North Texas State, 75
4. Harris, Tony, RB, Toledo, 101
5. Shaternick, Dean, T, Kansas State, from Chi. Bears, 114
   Wells, George, LB, New Mexico State, from NY Giants, 122
   Huff, Marty, LB, Michigan, 127
6. Bresler, Al, WR, Auburn, 153
7. Watson, John, T, Oklahoma, 179
8. McCann, Jim, K, Arizona State, 205
9. Couch, Therman, LB, Iowa State, 231
10. Cardo, Ron, RB, Wisconsin-Oshkosh, from New Orleans, 236
   Jennings, Ernie, WR, Air Force, 257
11. Reed, Joe, QB, Mississippi State, 283
12. Bunch, Jim, DT, Wisconsin-Platteville, 309
13. Bullock, John, RB, Purdue, 335
14. Dunstan, Bill, DE, Utah State, 361
15. Lennon, John, T, Colgate, 387
16. Purcell, Dave, DT, Kentucky, 414
17. Charlton, Leroy, DB, Florida A&M, 438*

WASHINGTON
1. Choice to LA Rams
2. Speyrer, Cotton, WR, Texas, 38
3. Choice to LA Rams
4. Choice to New Orleans
5. Choice to Green Bay
6. Hayman, Conway, G, Delaware, 141
7. Germany, Willie, DB, Morgan State, 166
8. Choice to New Orleans
9. Fanucci, Mike, DE, Arizona State, 219
10. Taylor, Jesse, RB, Cincinnati, 244
11. Starke, George, T, Columbia, 272
12. Severson, Jeff, DB, Long Beach State, 297
13. Ryczek, Dan, C, Virginia, 322
14. Bynum, Bill, QB, Western New Mexico, 349
15. Christnovich, Anthony, G, Wisconsin-LaCrosse, 375
16. Tucker, Glenn, LB, North Texas State, 400
17. Choice to New Orleans

1972
Held February 1-2, 1972

ATLANTA
1. Ellis, Clarence, DB, Notre Dame, 15
2. Sullivan, Pat, QB, Auburn, from Philadelphia through Detroit, 40
   Okoniewski, Steve, T, Montana, from Detroit, 41
   Manning, Roosevelt, DT, Northeastern Oklahoma, 42
3. Goodman, Les, RB, Yankton, 67
4. Howard, Andrew, DT, Grambling, 94
5. Taylor, Billy, RB, Michigan, from Houston through Denver and Buffalo, 109
   Cindrich, Ralph, LB, Pittsburgh, 119
6. Perfetti, Mike, DB, Minnesota, from New England through NY Giants, 140
   Riley, Fred, WR, Idaho, 146
7. Moon, Lance, RB, Wisconsin, 171
8. Brandon, Henry, RB, Southern, 198
9. Easterling, Ray, DB, Richmond, 223
10. Choice to St. Louis
11. Phillips, Jack, WR, Grambling, 275
12. Mialik, Larry, TE, Wisconsin, 302
13. Sovio, Henry, TE, Hawaii, 327
14. Chandler, Tom, LB, Minnesota, 354
15. Jenkins, Oscar, DB, Virginia Union, 379
16. Butler, Larry, LB, Stanford, 406
17. Holland, Bill, RB, USC, 431

BALTIMORE
1. Drougas, Tom, T, Oregon, 22
2. Mildren, Jack, DB, Oklahoma, from Oakland, 46
   Doughty, Glenn, WR, Michigan, from Washington, 47
   Mitchell, Lydell, RB, Penn State, 48
3. Choice to New Orleans through Oakland
4. Choice to Oakland
   Allen, Eric, WR, Michigan State, from Dallas through New Orleans and San Diego, 104
5. Croft, Don, DT, Texas-El Paso, from New England, 115
   Choice to New Orleans
6. Laird, Bruce, DB, American International, 152
7. Sykes, John, RB, Morgan State, from NY Jets through Washington, 169
   Choice to Oakland
8. Qualls, Al, LB, Oklahoma, from San Diego, 191
   Brownson, Van, QB, Nebraska, 204
9. Hambell, Gary, DT, Dayton, from Green Bay, 215
   Choice to Cleveland
10. Schilling, Dave, RB, Oregon State, from New England, 256
11. DeBernardi, Fred, DE, Texas-El Paso, 282
12. Theiler, Gary, TE, Tennessee, 308
13. Washington, Herb, WR, Michigan, 334
14. Morris, John, C, Missouri Valley, 359
15. Parkhouse, Robin, LB, Alabama, 386
16. Wichard, Gary, QB, C.W. Post, 412
17. White, Stan, LB, Ohio State, 438

BUFFALO
1. Patulski, Walt, DE, Notre Dame, 1
2. McKenzie, Reggie, G, Michigan, 27
3. Swendsen, Fred, DE, Notre Dame, 53
4. Jackson, Randy, RB, Wichita State, 79
5. Garror, Leon, DB, Alcorn State, 105
   Penchion, Robert, G, Alcorn State, from Denver, 108
6. Choice to Oakland
7. Stepaniak, Ralph, DB, Notre Dame, 157
8. Gibson, Paul, WR, Texas-El Paso, 183
9. Vogel, Steve, LB, Boise State, 209
10. Tyler, Maurice, DB, Morgan State, 235
11. Light, Bill, LB, Minnesota, 271
12. Baker, Jeff, WR, U.S. International, 287
13. Moss, Ed, RB, Southeast Missouri State, 313
14. Salb, Karl, DT,Kansas, 340
15. Choice to Oakland
16. Linstrom, Brian, QB, Arizona, 391
17. Shelley, John, DB, Oklahoma, 417

CHI. BEARS
1. Antoine, Lionel, T, Southern Illinois, from NY Giants, 3
   Clemons, Craig, DB, Iowa, 12
2. Choice to Philadelphia
3. Musso, Johnny, RB, Alabama, 62
4. Choice to LA Rams
5. Parsons, Bob, TE, Penn State, 117
6. Pifferini, Bob, LB, UCLA, from Cincinnati, 133
   Choice to Green Bay
7. Fassel, Jim, QB, Long Beach State, 167
   Osborne, Jim, DT, Southern, from Dallas, 182
8. Wirtz, Ralph, WR, North Dakota State, 192
9. Horton, Larry, DE, Iowa, 219
10. Turnbull, Jack, C, Oregon State, 247
11. Wimberly, Ed, DB, Jackson State, 272
12. Neill, Doug, RB, Texas A&M, 297
13. Rood, Jay, T, South Dakota-Springfield, 322
14. Brown, Bob, WR, Rice, 347
15. Lawson, Roger, RB, Western Michigan, 377
16. McKinney, Bill, LB, West Texas State, 402
17. Dickinson, LaVerne, DB, Southern, 427

CINCINNATI
1. White, Sherman, DE, California, 2
2. Casanova, Tommy, DB, LSU, 29
3. LeClair, Jim, LB, North Dakota, 54
4. Jackson, Bernard, DB, Washington State, 81
5. De Leone, Tom, C, Ohio State, 106
6. Choice to Chi. Bears
7. Conley, Steve, RB, Kansas, 158
8. Kratzer, Dan, WR, Missouri Valley, 185
9. Walters, Stan, T, Syracuse, 210
10. Foster, Brian, DB, Colorado, 237
11. Pederson, Kent, TE, Cal-Santa Barbara, 261
12. Wegis, Fredrick, DB, Cal Poly-SLO, 289
13. Hamilton, James, QB, Arkansas State, 314
14. Porter, Steve, WR, Indiana, 341
15. Minnieweather, Hosea, DT, Jackson State, 366
16. Wiegmann, John, WR, Cal Poly-Pomona, 393
17. Green, David, K, Ohio U., 418

CLEVELAND
1. Darden, Thom, DB, Michigan, 18
2. Brooks, Clifford, DB, Tennessee State, 45
   Sims, Lester, DE, Alabama, from Miami, 51
3. Choice to LA Rams
4. Choice to Kansas City
5. Hunt, George, K, Tennessee, 122
   Kucera, Greg, RB, Northern Colorado, from Minnesota through LA Rams, 128
6. Forey, Leonard, G, Texas A&M, 149
7. Wesley, Don, T, Maryland-Eastern Shore, 174
8. McKinnis, Hugh, RB, Arizona State, 201
9. McKee, Larry, G, Arizona, 226
   LeFear, Billy, WR-RB, Henderson State, from Baltimore, 230
10. Mosier, Herschell, DT, Northwestern Oklahoma, 253
11. Long, Mel, LB, Toledo, 278
12. Chapman, Bernie, DB, Texas-El Paso, 305
13. Sipe, Brian, QB, San Diego State, 330
14. Stewart, Ed, G, East Central (Oklahoma), 357
15. McCullar, Jewel, LB, Cal State-Chico, 382
16. Wakefield, Dick, WR, Ohio State, 409
17. Portz, Bill, DB, Sterling, 434

DALLAS
1. Thomas, Bill, RB, Boston College, 26
2. Newhouse, Robert, RB, Houston, from New England, 35
   Babinecz, John, LB, Villanova, from NY Jets through Oakland and New Orleans, 39
   McKee, Charlie, WR, Arizona, 52
3. Keller, Mike, LB, Michigan, from New England, 64
   Bateman, Marv, K, Utah, 78
4. Kearney, Tim, LB, North Michigan, from Denver through New Orleans, 83
   West, Robert, WR, San Diego State, from New England, 90
   Zapiec, Charlie, LB, Penn State, from Detroit, 93
   Choice to Baltimore through New Orleans and San Diego
5. Choice to San Diego
6. Bolden, Charles, DB, Iowa, 156
7. Choice to Chi. Bears
8. Coleman, Ralph, LB, North Carolina A&T, 208
9. Bell, Roy, RB, Oklahoma, 234
10. Amman, Richard, DE, Florida State, 260
11. Leonard, Lonnie, DE, North Carolina A&T, 286
12. Harris, Jimmy, WR, Ohio State, 312
13. Fugett, Jean, TE, Amherst, 338
14. Thompson, Alan, RB, Wisconsin, 363
15. Alvarez, Carlos, WR, Florida, 390
16. Longmire, Gordon, QB, Utah, 416
17. Cain, Alfonso, DT, Bethune-Cookman, 442

DENVER
1. Odoms, Riley, TE, Houston, 5
2. Choice to LA Rams through San Diego
3. Phillips, Bill, LB, Arkansas State, 58
4. Choice to Dallas through New Orleans
   Graham, Tom, LB, Oregon, from Minnesota, 102
5. Choice to Buffalo
   Krieg, Jim, WR, Washington, from Philadelphia, 118
6. Choice to Houston
7. Choice to Miami
8. Estay, Ronnie, DT-LB, LSU, 186
9. Priester, Floyd, DB, Boston U., 214
10. Wilkins, Richard, DE, Maryland-Eastern Shore, 239
11. Brunson, Larry, WR, Colorado, 263
12. McDougall, Randy, WR-DB, Weber State, 292
13. Warner, Bob, RB, Bloomsburg, 317
14. Kundich, Jerome, G, Texas-El Paso, 342
15. Parmenter, Harold, DT, Massachusetts, 370
16. Bougus, Tom, RB, Boston College, 395
17. Harris, Lou, RB, USC, 420

DETROIT
1. Orvis, Herb, DE, Colorado, 16
2. Choice to Atlanta
3. Sanders, Ken, DE, Howard Payne, from Philadelphia, 65
   Choice to Philadelphia
4. Choice to Dallas
5. Choice to LA Rams
6. Potts, Charlie, DB, Purdue, 145
7. Stoudamire, Charles, WR, Portland State, 172
8. Stuckey, Henry, DB, Missouri, 197
9. McClintock, Bill, DB, Drake, 224
10. Teal, Jim, LB, Purdue, 249
11. Waldron, Bob, DT, Tulane, 276
12. Bradley, Paul, WR, SMU, 301
13. Kirschner, John, TE, Memphis State, 328
14. Kelly, Eric, T, Whitworth, 353
15. Roach, Steve, LB, Kansas, 380
16. Jenkins, Leon, DB, West Virginia, 405
17. Tyler, Mike, DB, Rice, 432

GREEN BAY
1. Buchanon, Willie, DB, San Diego State, 7
   Tagge, Jerry, QB, Nebraska, from San Diego, 11
2. Marcol, Chester, K, Hillsdale, 34
3. Choice to Minnesota
4. Patton, Eric, LB, Notre Dame, 86
5. Choice to New Orleans
6. Ross, Nathaniel, DB, Bethune-Cookman, 138
   Pureifory, Dave, LB, Eastern Michigan, from Chi. Bears, 142
   Hudson, Robert, RB, Northeastern Oklahoma, from LA Rams, 147
7. Bushong, Bill, DT, Kentucky, 163
8. Glass, Leland, WR, Oregon, 190
9. Choice to Baltimore
10. Wortman, Keith, G, Nebraska, 242
11. Bailey, David, WR, Alabama, 266
12. Rich, Mike, RB, Florida, 294
13. Lakes, Jesse, RB, Central Michigan, 319
14. Hefner, Larry, LB, Clemson, 346
15. Thone, Rich, WR, Arkansas Tech, 371
16. Burrell, Charles, DT, Arkansas-Pine Bluff, 398
17. Choice to San Diego

HOUSTON
1. Sampson, Greg, DE, Stanford, 6
2. Choice to New Orleans
3. Jolley, Lewis, RB, North Carolina, 56
   Freelon, Solomon, G, Grambling, from Kansas City, 75
4. Choice to St. Louis
5. Choice to Atlanta through Denver and Buffalo
6. Bullard, Joe, DB, Tulane, 134
   Allen, Elmer, LB, Mississippi, from Denver, 136
7. Hutchinson, Eric, DB, Northwestern, 162
8. Roberts, Guy, LB, Maryland, 187
9. Postler, Willie, T, Montana, 212
10. Dawson, Rhett, WR, Florida State, 240
   Butler, Jim, TE, Tulsa, from Miami, 259
11. Evans, Ron, T, Baylor, 264
12. Rodgers, Willie, RB, Kentucky State, 290

13. Roberts, Willie, DB, Houston, 318
14. Crockett, Gary, C, Lamar, 343
15. Choice to Pittsburgh
16. Murdock, Guy, C, Michigan, 396
17. Cochrane, Kelly, QB, Miami, 421

KANSAS CITY
1. Kinney, Jeff, RB, Nebraska, 23
2. Choice to New England
3. Choice to Houston
4. Hamilton, Andy, WR, LSU, from Cleveland, 97
   Choice to New Orleans
5. Davis, Milt, DE, Texas-Arlington, 127
6. Kahler, John, DE, Long Beach State, 153
7. Carlson, Dean, QB, Iowa State, 179
8. Mahoney, Scott, G, Colorado, 205
9. Taylor, Dave, DT, Weber State, 231
10. Ruppert, Rich, T, Hawaii, 257
11. Walker, Elbert, T, Wisconsin, 283
12. Williams, Mike, DT, Oregon, 309
13. Hellams, Tyler, DB, South Carolina, 335
14. Chaney, Dave, LB, San Jose State, 360
15. Marshall, Larry, DB, Maryland, 387
16. Johnson, Bob, DE, Hanover, 413
17. Washington, Ted, LB, Mississippi Valley State, 439

LA RAMS
1. Choice to NY Giants through New England
2. Bertelsen, Jim, RB, Texas, from Denver through San Diego, 30
   Choice to Oakland
3. Choice to NY Giants
   McCutcheon, Lawrence, RB, Colorado State, from Cleveland, 70
4. Saunders, John, DB, Toledo, from Chi. Bears, 87
   Phillips, Eddie, DB, Texas, 95
5. Childs, Bob, G, Kansas, from Detroit, 120
   Choice to NY Giants through Washington
   Christiansen, Bob, TE, UCLA, from Washington, 125
6. Choice to Green Bay
   Herbert, Eddie, DT, Texas Southern, from Washington, 151
7. Choice to Oakland
8. Graham, Tom, WR, Baldwin-Wallace, 199
9. Howard, Harry, DB, Ohio State, 225
10. Massey, Jim, DB, Linfield, 251
11. Choice to Oakland
    Schmidt, Albert, RB, Pittsburg State, from Oakland, 280
12. Hoot, Dave, DB, Texas A&M, 303
13. Nunez, Jaime, K, Weber State, 329
14. Brooks, Larry, T, Virginia State, 355
15. Page, Kenny, LB, Kansas, 381
16. Kirby, Jim, WR, Long Beach State, 407
17. Palmer, Luther, TE, Virginia Union, 433
    McKean, John, C, Oregon, from Oakland, 436

MIAMI
1. Kadish, Mike, DT, Notre Dame, 25
2. Choice to Cleveland
3. Kosins, Gary, RB, Dayton, 77
4. Ball, Larry, DE, Louisville, from San Diego, 91
   Benton, Al, T, Ohio U., 103
5. Babb, Charlie, DB, Memphis State, 129
6. Nettles, Ray, LB, Tennessee, 155
7. Adams, Bill, G, Holy Cross, from Denver, 161
   Harrell, Calvin, RB, Arkansas State, 180
8. Curry, Craig, QB, Minnesota, 207
9. Johnson, Greg, DB, Wisconsin, 233
10. Choice to Houston
11. Jenkins, Ed, WR, Holy Cross, 285
12. Bell, Ashley, TE, Purdue, 311
13. Robinson, Archie, DB, Hillsdale, 337
14. Jones, Willie, LB, Tampa, 362
15. Davis, Bill, DT, William & Mary, 389
16. Hannah, Al, WR, Wisconsin, 415
17. Brown, Vern, DB, Western Michigan, 441

MINNESOTA
1. Siemon, Jeff, LB, Stanford, from New England, 10
   Choice to NY Giants
2. Marinaro, Ed, RB, Cornell, 50
3. Beutow, Bart, T, Minnesota, from Green Bay, 59
   Choice to Philadelphia
4. Choice to Denver
5. Choice to Cleveland through LA Rams
6. Martin, Anthony, LB, Louisville, 154
7. Slater, Bill, DE, Western Michigan, 181
8. Demery, Calvin, WR, Arizona State, 206
9. Goodrum, Charles, G, Florida A&M, 232
10. Aldridge, Willie, RB-DB, South Carolina State, 258
11. McKelton, Willie, DB, Southern, 284
12. Banaugh, Bob, DB, Montana State, 310
13. Roberts, Franklin, RB, Alcorn State, 336
14. Owens, Marv, WR-RB, San Diego State, 361
15. Sivert, Mike, G, East Tennessee State, 388
16. Graff, Neil, QB, Wisconsin, 414
17. Schmalz, Dick, WR, Auburn, 440

NEW ENGLAND
1. Choice to Minnesota
2. Choice to Dallas
   Reynolds, Tom, WR, San Diego State, from Kansas City, 49
3. Choice to Dallas
   White, Jim, DE, Colorado State, from Washington through LA Rams, 73
4. Choice to Dallas
5. Choice to Baltimore
   Bolton, Ron, DB, Norfolk State, from Oakland, 124
6. Choice to Atlanta through NY Giants
7. Hoss, Clark, TE, Oregon State, 165
   Tarver, John, RB, Colorado, from San Diego, 166
8. Beyrle, Steve, G, Kansas State, 195
9. Kelson, Mike, T, Arkansas, 220
10. Caraway, Mel, DB, Northwestern Oklahoma, 245
11. Cason, Rodney, T, Angelo State, 269
12. Booras, Steve, DE, Mesa J.C., 296
13. Elmore, Sam, DB, Eastern Michigan, 325
14. Rideout, Eddie, WR, Boston College, 350
15. Klimek, Joel, TE, Pittsburgh, 375
16. Dahl, Eric, DB, San Jose State, 400
17. Ah You, Junior, LB, Arizona State, 425

NEW ORLEANS
1. Smith, Royce, G, Georgia, 8
2. Hall, Willie, LB, USC, from Houston, 31
   Choice to Oakland
3. Kuziel, Bob, C, Pittsburgh, 60
   Myers, Tommy, DB, Syracuse, from Baltimore through Oakland, 74
4. Crangle, Mike, DE, Tennessee-Martin, 85
   Federspiel, Joe, LB, Kentucky, from Washington through LA Rams and Philadelphia, 99
   Coleman, Mike, DE, Knoxville, from Kansas City, 101
5. Butler, Bill, RB, Kansas State, from Green Bay, 111
   Johnson, Carl, T, Nebraska, 112
   Davies, Bob, DB, South Carolina, from Baltimore, 126
6. Dorton, Wayne, G, Arkansas State, 137
   Watson, Curt, RB, Tennessee, from Oakland, 150
7. Jackson, Ernie, DB, Duke, 164
8. Vinson, Ron, WR, Abilene Christian, 189
9. Branstetter, Kent, DT, Houston, 216
10. Kupp, Andy, G, Idaho, 241
11. Dongieux, Paul, LB, Mississippi, 267
12. Lockhart, Steve, TE, Arkansas State, 293
13. Weatherspoon, Cephus, WR, Ft. Lewis, 320
14. Barrios, Steve, WR, Tulane, 345
15. Lachaussee, Rusty, QB, Tulane, 372
16. Balthrop, Joe, G, Tennessee, 397
17. Graham, Dick, R, Oklahoma State, 424

NY GIANTS
1. Choice to Chi. Bears
   Small, Eldridge, DB, Texas A&I, from LA Rams through New England, 17
   Jacobson, Larry, DE, Nebraska, from Minnesota, 24
2. Choice to San Francisco
3. Mendenhall, John, T, Grambling, 55
   Mozisek, Tommy, RB, Houston, from LA Rams, 69
4. Choice to Pittsburgh
5. Gatewood, Tom, WR, Notre Dame, 107
   Edwards, Larry, LB, Texas A&I, from LA Rams through Washington, 121
6. Hill, John, C, Lehigh, 132
7. Choice to Pittsburgh
   Zikas, Mike, DT, Notre Dame, from Washington, 177
8. Mabry, Tom, T, Arkansas, 184
9. Richardson, Ed, RB, Southern, 211
10. Odom, John, DB, Texas Tech, 236
11. Robertson, John, DB, Kansas State, 262
12. Anderson, Jay, DT, Mayville, 288
13. Heard, Chuck, DE, Georgia, 315
14. Evans, James, LB, South Carolina State, 339
15. Kavanaugh, Ken, TE, LSU, 367
16. Greyer, Neovia, DB, Wisconsin, 392
17. Seyferth, Fritz, RB, Michigan, 419

NY JETS
1. Barkum, Jerome, WR, Jackson State, 9
   Taylor, Mike, LB, Michigan, from Washington, 20
2. Choice to Dallas through New Orleans and Oakland
3. Hammond, Gary, WR, SMU, 66
4. Galigher, Ed, DE, UCLA, 89
5. Harris, Dick, DB, South Carolina, 114
6. Jackson, Joe, DE, New Mexico State, 139
7. Choice to Baltimore through Washington
8. Latimore, Marion, G, Kansas State, 194
9. Ford, Jeff, DB, Georgia Tech, 218
10. Turner, Harley, DB, Tennessee-Chattanooga, 244
11. Stevenson, Robert, LB, Tennessee State, 268
12. Bjorklund, Hank, RB, Princeton, 299
13. Sullivan, Steve, T, North Texas State, 324
14. Age, Louis, G, Southwestern Louisiana, 349
15. Sullivan, Phil, DB, Georgia, 374
16. Kipfmiller, Gary, C, Nebraska-Omaha, 399
17. Gamble, Ken, P, Fayetteville, 429

OAKLAND
1. Siani, Mike, WR, Villanova, 21
2. Korver, Kelvin, T, Northwestern (Iowa), from New Orleans, 33
   Choice to Baltimore
   Vella, John, T, USC, from LA Rams, 43
3. Lunsford, Mel, DT, Central State (Ohio), 72
4. Branch, Cliff, WR, Colorado, 98
   Dalby, Dave, C, UCLA, from Baltimore, 100
5. Choice to New England
6. Medlin, Dan, DT, North Carolina State, from Buffalo, 131
   Choice to New Orleans
7. Jamieson, Ray, RB, Memphis State, from LA Rams, 173
   Thomas, Alonzo (Skip), DB, USC, 176
   Pete, Dennis, DB, Cal State-San Francisco, from Baltimore, 178
8. Brown, Jackie, RB, Stanford, 202
9. Bigler, Dave, RB, Morningside, 228
10. Price, Phillip, DB, Idaho State, 254
11. Carroll, Joe, LB, Pittsburgh, from LA Rams, 277
    Choice to LA Rams
12. Gaydos, Kent, TE, Florida State, 306
13. Covington, Ted, WR, Cal State-Northridge, 333
14. Cambal, Dennis, RB, William & Mary, 358
15. Hester, Charles, RB, Central State (Ohio), from Buffalo, 364
    Snesrud, Dave, LB, Hamline, 384
16. Wright, Willie, TE, North Carolina A&T, 410
17. Choice to LA Rams

PHILADELPHIA
1. Reaves, John, QB, Florida, 14
2. Yochum, Dan, T, Syracuse, from Chi. Bears, 37
   Choice to Atlanta through Detroit
3. Choice to Detroit
   Luken, Tom, G, Purdue, from Detroit, 68
   Majors, Bobby, DB, Tennessee, from Minnesota, 76
4. James, Ron (Po), RB, New Mexico State, 92
5. Choice to Denver
6. Winfield, Vern, G, Minnesota, 144
7. Foster, Will, LB, Eastern Michigan, 170
8. Ratcliff, Larry, RB, Eastern Michigan, 196
9. Gibbs, Pat, DB, Lamar, 222
10. Bunting, John, LB, North Carolina, 248
11. Sweeney, Dennis, DE, Western Michigan, 274
12. Zimmerman, Don, WR, Northeast Louisiana, 300
13. Carpenter, Preston, DE, Mississippi, 326
14. Overmyer, Bill, LB, Ashland, 352
15. Sullivan, Tom, RB, Miami, 378
16. Bielenberg, Steve, LB, Oregon State, 404
17. Nash, Tom, T, Georgia, 430

PITTSBURGH
1. Harris, Franco, RB, Penn State, 13
2. Gravelle, Gordon, T, BYU, 38
3. McMakin, John, TE, Clemson, 63
4. Brinkley, Lorenzo, DB, Missouri, from NY Giants, 80
   Bradley, Ed, LB, Wake Forest, 88
5. Furness, Steve, DE, Rhode Island, 113
6. Meyer, Dennis, DB, Akansas State, 143
7. Colquitt, Joe, DE, Kansas State, from NY Giants, 159
   Kelly, Robert, DB, Jackson State, 168
8. Vincent, Stahle, RB, Rice, 193
9. Kelley, Don, DB, Clemson, 217
10. Brown, Bob, DT, Tampa, 243
11. Gilliam, Joe, QB, Tennessee State, 273
12. Curl, Ron, T, Michigan State, 298
13. Messmer, Ernie, T, Villanova, 323
14. Durrance, Tommy, RB, Florida, 348
15. Hulecki, John, G, Massachusetts, from Houston, 368
    Harrington, Charles, G, Wichita State, 373
16. Hawkins, Nate, WR, Nevada-Las Vegas, 403
17. Linehan, Ron, LB, Idaho, 428

ST. LOUIS
1. Moore, Bobby, (Ahmad Rashad), RB-WR, Oregon, 4
2. Arneson, Mark, LB, Arizona, 32
3. Beckman, Tom, DE, Michigan, 57
4. Lyman, Jeff, LB, BYU, 82
   Imhof, Martin, DT, San Diego State, from Houston, 84
5. Dobler, Conrad, G, Wyoming, 110
6. Heater, Don, RB, Montana Tech, 135
7. Rudolph, Council, DE, Kentucky State, 160
8. Wicks, Bob, WR, Utah State, 188
9. Macken, Gene, C, South Dakota, 213
10. Washington, Eric, DB, Texas-El Paso, 238
    Franks, Mike, QB, Eastern New Mexico, from Atlanta, 250
11. Jones, Ron, LB, Arkansas, 265
12. Gay, Tommy, DT, Arkansas-Pine Bluff, 291
13. Campana, Tom, DB, Ohio State, 316
14. McTeer, Pat, K, New Mexico State, 344
15. Herman, Mark, TE, Yankton, 369
16. Alford, Henry, DE, Pittsburgh, 394
17. Carter, Kent, LB, USC, 422

SAN DIEGO
1. Choice to Green Bay
2. Lazetich, Pete, DE, Stanford, 36
3. McClard, Bill, K, Arkansas, 61
4. Choice to Miami
5. Bishop, Jim, TE, Tennessee Tech, 116
5. Gooden, Harry, DE, Alcorn State, 130
6. Ward, Bruce, G, San Diego State, 141
7. Choice to New England
8. Choice to Baltimore
9. Schmitz, Fran, DT, St. Norbert, 221
10. Kolstad, Lon, LB, Wisconsin Whitewater, 246
11. Turner, John, TE, Long Beach State, 270
12. Key, Sam, LB, Elon, 295
13. Selfridge, Andy, LB, Virginia, 321
14. Van Reenen, John, DE, Washington State, 351
15. Neugent, Charles, DB, Tuskegee, 376
16. Shaw, James, DB, Tulsa, 401
17. Dragon, Oscar, RB, Arizona State, from Green Bay, 423
    Tackett, Bob, T, Texas-El Paso, 426

SAN FRANCISCO
1. Beasley, Terry, WR, Auburn, 19
2. McGill, Ralph, RB, Tulsa, from NY Giants, 28
   Barrett, Jean, T, Tulsa, 44
3. Dunbar, Jubilee, WR, Southern, 71
4. Hall, Windlan, DB, Arizona State, 96
5. Greene, Mike, LB, Georgia, 123
6. Walker, Jackie, DB, Tennessee, 148
7. Hardy, Edgar, G, Jackson State, 175
8. Wittum, Tom, K, Northern Illinois, 200
9. Brown, Jerry, DB, Northwestern, 227
10. Williams, Steve, DT, Western Carolina, 252
11. Laputka, Tom, DE, Southern Illinois, 279
12. Setzler, Steve, DE, St. John's (Minnesota), 304
13. Pettigrew, Leon, T, Cal State-Northridge, 331
14. Guthrie, Eric, QB, Boise State, 356
15. Maddox, Bob, DE, Frostburg State, 383

16. Davis, Ron, G, Virginia State, 408
17. Alexander, Ted, RB, Langston, 435

WASHINGTON
1. Choice to NY Jets
2. Choice to Baltimore
3. Choice to New England through LA Rams
4. Choice to New Orleans through LA Rams and Philadelphia
5. Choice to LA Rams
6. Choice to LA Rams
7. Choice to NY Giants
8. Denson, Moses, RB, Maryland-Eastern Shore, 203
9. Boekholder, Steve, DE, Drake, 229
10. Oldham, Mike, WR, Michigan, 255
11. Welch, Jeff, DB, Arkansas Tech, 281
12. Bunce, Don, QB, Stanford, 307
13. Grant, Frank, WR, Southern Colorado, 332
14. O'Quinn, Mike, G, McNeese State, 365
15. Taibi, Carl, DE, Colorado, 385
16. Higginbotham, Steve, DB, Alabama, 411
17. Clemente, Kevin, LB, Boston College, 437

1973
Held January 30-31, 1973

ATLANTA
1. Choice to Houston
2. Marx, Greg, DT, Notre Dame, 39
3. Choice to San Diego through Oakland
4. Choice to Detroit
   Geredine, Tom, WR, Northeast Missouri State, from NY Giants, 94
5. Choice to Washington
6. Bebout, Nick, T, Wyoming, 142
7. Campbell, George, DB, Iowa State, 170
8. Reed, Tom, G, Arkansas, 195
9. Ingram, Russell, C, Texas Tech, 220
10. Mike-Mayer, Nick, K, Temple, 248
11. Buelow, Byron, DB, Wisconsin-LaCrosse, 273
12. Samples, Mike, LB, Drake, 298
13. Stecher, Chris, T, Claremont-Mudd-Scripps, 326
14. Madeya, John, QB, Louisville, 351
15. Gage, Thomas, DB, Lamar, 376
16. Ferguson, Rufus, RB, Wisconsin, 404
17. Hodge, Jim, WR, Arkansas, 428

BALTIMORE
1. Jones, Bert, QB, LSU, from New Orleans, 2
   Ehrmann, Joe, DT, Syracuse, 10
2. Barnes, Mike, DE, Miami, 35
3. Olds, Bill, RB, Nebraska, from Denver through Houston, 61
   Rotella, Jamie, LB, Tennessee, 62
4. Palmer, Gery, T, Kansas, from Chi. Bears through Philadelphia, 83
   Smith, Ollie, WR, Tennessee State, from San Diego, 85
   Choice to New Orleans
5. Taylor, David, G, Catawba, 114
6. Choice to Minnesota through New Orleans
7. Choice to Denver
8. Oldham, Ray, DB, Middle Tennessee State, from San Diego, 189
   Windauer, Bill, G, Iowa, 191
9. Choice to Washington
10. Choice to NY Jets
11. Neal, Dan, C, Kentucky, 270
12. Thomas, Bernard, DE, Western Michigan, 295
13. Pierantozzi, Tom, QB, West Chester, 322
14. Williams, Ed, RB, West Virginia, 347
15. Brown, Jackie, DB, South Carolina, 374
16. Januszkiewicz, Marty, RB, Syracuse, 399
17. Falkenhagen, Guy, T, Northern Michigan, 426

BUFFALO
1. Seymour, Paul, T, Michigan, 7
   DeLamielleure, Joe, G, Michigan State, from Miami, 26
2. Winans, Jeff, DT, USC, 32
3. Ferguson, Joe, QB, Arkansas, 57
   Kampa, Bob, DT, California, from Washington, 77
4. Walker, Don, DB, Central State (Ohio), 87
   Yeates, Jeff, DT, Boston College, from Washington, 103
5. Francis, Wallace, WR, Arkansas-Pine Bluff, from San Diego, 110
   Choice to Miami
6. Skorupan, John, LB, Penn State, 136
7. McConnell, Brian, LB, Michigan State, 162
   Ford, John, TE, Henderson State, from Washington, 181
8. Fobbs, Lee, RB, Grambling, 190
9. Reppond, Mike, WR, Arkansas, 215
10. Reed, Matthew, QB, Grambling, 240
    LeHeup, John, LB, South Carolina, from Washington, 259
11. Earl, Richard, T, Tennessee, 265
12. Carroll, Ron, DT, Sam Houston State, 294
13. Choice to Denver
14. Krakau, Merv, LB, Iowa State, 344
15. Rizzo, Joe, LB, Merchant Marine, 369
    O'Neil, Vince, RB, Kansas, from Kansas City, 379
16. Choice to Denver
17. Stearns, John (Bad Dude), DB, Colorado, 423

CHI. BEARS
1. Chambers, Wally, DE, Eastern Kentucky, 8
2. Huff, Gary, QB, Florida State, 32
   Hrivnak, Gary, DT, Purdue, from Dallas, 48
3. Choice to Detroit
4. Choice to Baltimore through Philadelphia
5. Ellis, Allan, DB, UCLA, from Philadelphia, 107
   Choice to San Francisco
6. Creaney, Mike, C, Notre Dame, 138
7. Choice to LA Rams
8. Graham, Conrad, DB, Tennessee, 187
9. Deutsch, Mike, RB, North Dakota, 216
10. Barry, Bill, WR, Mississippi, 241
11. Seigler, Ed, K, Clemson, 266
12. Griffin, Mike, G, Arkansas, 291
13. Cieszkowski, John, RB, Notre Dame, 320
14. Juenger, Dave, WR, Ohio U., 345
15. Rives, Don, LB, Texas Tech, 370
16. Hart, Bill, C, Michigan, 395
17. Roach, Larry, DB, Oklahoma, 424

CINCINNATI
1. Curtis, Isaac, WR, San Diego State, 15
2. Chandler, Al, TE, Oklahoma, 43
3. George, Tim, WR, Carson-Newman, 68
4. Choice to Cleveland through Baltimore
5. McCall, Bob, RB, Arizona, 121
6. Jones, Bob, DB, Virginia Union, 146
7. Maddox, Robert, DE, Frostburg, 171
8. Wilson, Joe, RB, Holy Cross, 199
9. Dampeer, John, G, Notre Dame, 224
10. Elliott, Lenvil, RB, Northeast Missouri State, 249
11. Montgomery, William, DB, Morehouse, 277
12. Clark, Boobie, RB, Bethune-Cookman, 302
13. West, Brooks, DT, Texas-El Paso, 327
14. Scales, Hurles, DB, North Texas State, 355
15. McNulty, Ted, QB, Indiana, 380
16. Unger, Harry, RB, Auburn, 405
17. Estabrook, Wayne, QB, Whittier, 433

CLEVELAND
1. Holden, Steve, WR, Arizona State, from NY Giants, 16
   Adams, Pete, T, USC, 22
2. Pruitt, Greg, RB, Oklahoma, from New England through NY Giants, 30
   Stienke, Jim, DB, Southwest Texas State, 47
3. Crum, Bob, DE, Arizona, from Kansas City through Baltimore, 67
4. Dorris, Andy, LB, New Mexico State, from Cincinnati through Baltimore, 93
   Mattingly, Randy, QB, Evansville, 100
5. Choice to San Diego
6. Green, Van, DB, Shaw, 150
7. Choice to Miami
8. Choice to Detroit
9. Wester, Curtis, G, East Texas State, 228
10. Humphrey, Tom, T, Abilene Christian, 256
11. Barisich, Carl, DT, Princeton, 281
12. Simmons, Stan, TE, Lewis & Clark, 306
13. Romaniszyn, Jim, RB, Edinboro, 334
14. Popelka, Robert, DB, SMU, 359
15. Sullivan, Dave, WR, Virginia, 384
16. Greenfield, George, RB, Murray State, 412
17. McClowry, Robert, C, Michigan State, 437

DALLAS
1. DuPree, Billy Joe, TE, Michigan State, 20
2. Richards, Golden, WR, Hawaii, from Green Bay, 46
   Choice to Chi. Bears
3. Martin, Harvey Banks, DE, East Texas State, from Houston through New Orleans, 53
   Choice to New England
4. Scrivener, Drane, DB, Tulsa, 98
5. Walton, Bruce, T, UCLA, 126
6. Leyen, Bob, G, Yale, 151
7. Barnes, Rodrigo, LB, Rice, 176
8. Werner, Dan, QB, Michigan State, 204
9. White, Mike, DB, Minnesota, 229
10. Johnson, Carl, LB, Tennessee, 254
11. Caswell, Gerald, G, Colorado State, 282
12. Arneson, Jim, G, Arizona, 307
13. Smith, John, WR, UCLA, 332
14. Thornton, Bob, G, North Carolina, 360
15. Baisy, Walt, LB, Grambling, 385
16. Conley, John, TE, Hawaii, 410
17. Strayhorn, Les, RB, East Carolina, 438

DENVER
1. Armstrong, Otis, RB, Purdue, 9
2. Chavous, Barney, DE, South Carolina State, 36
3. Howard, Paul, G, BYU, from New Orleans through Washington and Cleveland, 54
   Choice to Baltimore through Houston
   Wood, John, DT, LSU, from San Francisco through Washington and San Diego, 70
4. Jackson, Tom, LB, Louisville, 88
5. McTorry, Charles, DB, Tennessee State, 113
6. Choice to Pittsburgh
7. Askea, Mike, T, Stanford, 165
   Grant, John, DE, USC, from Baltimore, 166
8. Choice to Pittsburgh
9. Blackwood, Lyle, DB, TCU, 217
10. Marshall, Al, WR, Boise State, 244
11. Brown, Elton, DE, Utah State, 269
12. O'Malley, Jim, LB, Notre Dame, 296
13. Smith, Ed, DE, Colorado College, from Buffalo, 319
    White, Ed, RB, Tulsa, 321
14. Hufnagel, John, QB, Penn State, 348
15. Jones, Calvin, DB, Washington, 373
16. Ross, Oliver, RB, Alabama A&M, from Buffalo, 398
    Muhlbeier, Ken, C, Idaho, 200
17. Morgan, Kenneth, TE, Elon, 425

DETROIT
1. Price, Ernie, DE, Texas A&I, 17
2. Crosswhite, Leon, RB, Oklahoma, 44
3. Brady, John, TE, Washington, from Chi. Bears, 58
   Laslavic, Jim, LB, Penn State, 71
   Johnson, Levi, DB, Texas A&I, from Oakland through LA Rams, 75
4. Hennigan, Mike, LB, Tennessee Tech, from New Orleans, 81
   Jauron, Dick, RB, Yale, from Atlanta, 91
   Hooks, Jim, RB, Central State (Oklahoma), 96
5. Choice to San Diego through Washington
6. Choice to St. Louis
7. Andrews, John, DT, Morgan State, 175
8. McCray, Prentice, DB, Arizona State, 200
   Bledsoe, John, RB, Ohio State, from Cleveland, 203
9. Dean, Ira, DB, Baylor, 227
10. Bonner, Ray, DB, Middle Tennessee State, 252
11. Freeman, Scott, WR, Wyoming, 279
12. Scott, Tom, WR, Washington, 304
13. Moss, John, LB, Pittsburgh, 331
14. Corey, Jay, T, Santa Clara, 356
15. Hansen, Dan, DB, BYU, 383
16. Nickels, Larry, WR, Dayton, 408
17. Belgrave, Earl, T, Ohio State, 435

GREEN BAY
1. Smith, Barry, WR, Florida State, 21
2. Choice to Dallas
3. MacLeod, Tom, LB, Minnesota, 74
4. Choice to LA Rams
5. Choice to Oakland
6. Toner, Tom, LB, Idaho State, 152
7. Muller, John, T, Iowa, 177
8. Austin, Hise, DB, Prairie View A&M, 202
9. Brown, Rick, LB, South Carolina, 230
10. Allen, Larry, LB, Illinois, 255
11. Engle, Phil, DT, South Dakota State, 280
12. McCarren, Larry, C, Illinois, 308
13. Alderson, Tim, DB, Minnesota, 333
14. Anderson, James, DT, Northwestern, 358
15. Echols, Reggie, WR, UCLA, 386
16. Pretty, Keith, TE, Western Michigan, 411
17. Sampson, Harold, DT, Southern, 436

HOUSTON
1. Matuszak, John, DE, Tampa, 1
   Amundson, George, RB, Iowa State, from Atlanta, 14
2. Choice to Kansas City
3. Choice to Dallas through New Orleans
4. Bingham, Gregg, LB, Purdue, 79
5. Garrison, Edesel, WR, USC, 105
6. Mayo, Ron, TE, Morgan State, 131
7. Jordan, Shelby, T, Washington (St. Louis), 157
8. Blahak, Joe, DB, Nebraska, 183
9. Williams, Mark, K-P, Rice, 209
10. Vaughn, Darrell, DT, Northern Colorado, 235
11. Eaglin, Lawrence, DB, Stephen F. Austin, 261
12. Lyman, Brad, WR, UCLA, 287
13. Martin, Willie, G, Northeastern Oklahoma, 313
14. Lou, Ron, C, Arizona State, 339
15. Goree, Roger, LB, Baylor, 365
16. Dameron, Tim, WR, East Carolina, 390
17. Braband, Randy, LB, Texas, 417

KANSAS CITY
1. Choice to Detroit through Chi. Bears
2. Butler, Gary, TE, Rice, from Houston, 27
   Choice to LA Rams
3. Choice to Cleveland through Baltimore
   Krause, Paul, T, Central Michigan, from Cleveland, 72
4. Lohmeyer, John, DE, Emporia State, from Minnesota, 89
   Choice to LA Rams
5. Grambau, Fred, DE, Michigan, 120
6. Jones, Doug, DB, Cal State-Northridge, 145
7. Smith, Donn, T, Purdue, 173
8. Palewicz, Al, LB, Miami, 197
9. Story, Bill, DT, Southern Illinois, 223
10. Osley, Willie, DB, Illinois, 251
11. Eley, Monroe, RB, Arizona State, 276*
12. Ramsey, Tom, DT, Northern Arizona, 301
13. Metallo, Paul, DB, Massachusetts, 329
14. White, Albert, WR, Fort Valley State, 354
15. Choice to Buffalo
16. Grooms, Wilbur, LB, Tampa, 407
17. Korver, Clayton, TE, SMU, 431

LA RAMS
1. Choice to New England
2. Bryant, Cullen, DB, Colorado, from San Diego, 31
   Jaworski, Ron, QB, Youngstown State, 37
   Youngblood, Jim, LB, Tennessee Tech, from Kansas City, 42
3. Stokes, Tim, T, Oregon, from San Diego, 60
   Choice to St. Louis
4. Choice to Oakland
   McMillan, Eddie, DB, Florida State, from Kansas City, 95
   Nelson, Terry, TE, Arkansas-Pine Bluff, from Green Bay, 99
5. Jones, Steve, RB, Duke, 115
   Jones, Cody, DE, San Jose State, from Washington, 129
6. Peterson, Jim, DE, San Diego State, from New Orleans through Washington, 133
   Caldwell, Jason, WR, North Carolina Central, 141
7. Brown, Steve, LB, Oregon State, from Chi. Bears, 161
   Dulac, Bill, G, Eastern Michigan, 167
8. Choice to Washington
9. Nicholson, Jim, T, Michigan State, 219
10. Choice to Washington
11. Inmon, Jeff, RB, North Carolina Central, 271
    Jackson, Willie, WR, Florida, from Washington, 285
12. Storck, Robert, DT, Wisconsin, 297
13. Milburn, Rod, WR, Southern, 323
    Spearman, Clint, LB, Michigan, from Oakland, 335
14. Rhone, Walter, DB, Central State (Missouri), 349

15. Bond, Jerry, DB, Weber State, 375
Matter, Kurt, DE, Washington, from Washington, 393
16. Cherry, Fuller, DB, Arkansas-Monticello, 401
17. Henry, Fred, RB, New Mexico, 427

MIAMI
1. Choice to Buffalo
2. Bradley, Chuck, C, Oregon, 52
3. Gray, Leon, T, Jackson State, 78
4. Rather, Bo, WR, Michigan, 104
5. Strock, Don, QB, Virginia Tech, from Buffalo, 111
McCurry, Dave, DB, Iowa State, 130
6. Newman, Ed, G, Duke, 156
7. Reilly, Kevin, LB, Villanova, from New England, 160
Shepherd, Benny, RB, Arkansas Tech, from San Diego, 163
Hatter, Willie, WR, Northern Illinois, from Cleveland, 178
Smith, Tom, RB, Miami, 182
8. Pearmon, Archie, DE, Northeastern Oklahoma, 208
9. Lorch, Karl, DE, USC, 234
10. Fernandes, Ron, DE, Eastern Michigan, 260
11. Kete, Chris, C, Boston College, 286
12. Mullen, Mike, LB, Tulane, 312
13. Booker, Joe, HB, Miami (Ohio), 338
14. Boyd, Greg, RB, Arizona, 364
15. Palmer, Bill, TE, St. Thomas (Minnesota), 389
16. Jackson, James, DE, Norfolk State, 416
17. Wade, Charlie, WR, Tennessee State, 442

MINNESOTA
1. Foreman, Chuck, RB, Miami, 12
2. Wallace, Jackie, DB, Arizona, from St. Louis, 34
Choice to NY Giants
3. Lash, Jim, WR, Northwestern, 65
4. Wells, Mike, QB, Illinois, from Philadelphia, 80
Choice to Kansas City
5. McClanahan, Brent, RB, Arizona State, 118
6. Kingsriter, Doug, TE, Minnesota, from Baltimore through New Orleans, 139
Abbott, Fred, LB, Florida, 143
7. Brown, Josh, RB, Southwest Texas State, 168
8. Darling, Craig, T, Iowa, 196
9. Dibbles, Larry, DE, New Mexico, 221
10. Lee, Randy, DB-P, Tulane, from Philadelphia, 236
Mason, Dave, DB, Nebraska, 246
11. Murdock, Geary, G, Iowa State, 274
12. Spencer, Alan, WR, Pittsburg State, 299
13. Just, Ron, G, Minot State, 324
14. Bishop, Eddie, DB, Southern, 352*
15. Chandler, Tony, RB, Missouri Valley, 377
16. Smiley, Larry, DE, Texas Southern, 402
17. Winfield, Dave, TE, Minnesota, 429

NEW ENGLAND
1. Hannah, John, G, Alabama, 4
Cunningham, Sam, RB, USC, from LA Rams, 11
Stingley, Darryl, WR, Purdue, from Chi. Bears, 19
2. Choice to Cleveland through NY Giants
3. Dusek, Brad, DB, Texas A&M, 56
Davis, Charles, RB, Alcorn State, from Dallas, 73
4. Gallaher, Allen, T, USC, 82
5. Dumler, Doug, C, Nebraska, 108
6. Choice to New Orleans
7. Choice to Miami
8. Brown, Isaac, RB, Western Kentucky, 186
9. Callaway, David, T, Texas A&M, 212
10. Ruster, Dan, DB, Oklahoma, 238
11. May, Homer, TE, Texas A&M, 264
12. Barnes, Bruce, P, UCLA, 290
13. Lowry, Alan, DB, Texas, 316
14. Hamilton, Ray (Sugar Bear), LB, Oklahoma, 342
15. Pugh, Condie, RB, Norfolk State, 368
16. Kutter, Mike, DE, Concordia, 394
17. McAshan, Eddie, QB-DB, Georgia Tech, 420

NEW ORLEANS
1. Choice to Baltimore
2. Moore, Derland, DE, Oklahoma, 29
Baumgartner, Steve, DE, Purdue, from Washington through NY Jets, 51
3. Choice to Denver through Washington and Cleveland
Van Valkenburg, Pete, RB, BYU, from NY Jets, 66
4. Choice to Detroit
Merlo, Jim, LB, Stanford, from Baltimore, 86
5. Choice to Pittsburgh through Denver
6. Choice to LA Rams through Washington
Shuford, Marty, RB, Arizona, from New England, 134
7. Cahill, Bill, DB, Washington, 158
8. Peterson, Bob, G, Utah, 185
Winslow, Doug, WR, Drake, from Washington, 207
9. Fink, Mike, DB, Missouri, 210
10. Horsley, Jeff, RB, North Carolina Central, 237
11. Owens, James, RB, Auburn, 262
12. Orndorff, Paul, RB, Tampa, 289
13. Watkins, Richard, DT, Weber State, 314
14. Fersen, Paul, T, Georgia, 341
15. Evenson, Mike, C, North Dakota State, 366
16. Stevens, Howard, RB, Louisville, 392
17. Garner, Bobby, TE, Winston-Salem, 418

NY GIANTS
1. Choice to Cleveland
2. Van Pelt, Brad, LB, Michigan State, from Minnesota, 40
Choice to San Francisco
3. Glover, Rich, DT, Nebraska, 69
4. Choice to Atlanta
5. McQuay, Leon, RB, Tampa, 119
6. Brantley, Wade, DT, Troy State, 147
7. Freeman, Rod, TE, Vanderbilt, 172
8. Hasenohrl, George, DT, Ohio State, 198
9. Paine, Ty, QB, Washington State, 225
10. Love, Walter, DB, Westminster (Utah), 250
11. Wideman, William, DT, North Carolina A&T, 275
12. Lumpkin, Ron, DB, Arizona State, 303
13. Davis, Clifton, RB, Alcorn State, 328
14. Kelley, Brian, LB, California Lutheran, 353
15. Schaukowitch, Carl, G, Penn State, 381
16. Nitka, Ben, K, Colorado College, 406
17. Billizon, John, DE, Grambling, 430

NY JETS
1. Owens, Burgess, DB, Miami, 13
2. Woods, Robert, T, Tennessee State, 38
3. Choice to New Orleans
4. Ferguson, Bill, LB, San Diego State, 90
5. Bannon, Bruce, LB, Penn State, 116
6. Roach, Travis, G, Texas, 144
Harrell, Rick, C, Clemson, from Washington, 155
7. Haggard, Mike, WR, South Carolina, 169
8. Seifert, Rick, DB, Ohio State, 194
9. Spicer, Robin, LB, Indiana, 222
10. Carbone, Joe, LB, Delaware, from Baltimore, 243
Krempin, James, T, Texas A&I, 247
11. Knight, David, WR, William & Mary, 272
12. Puetz, Gary, T, Valparaiso, 300
13. Parrish, Robert, DT, Duke, 325
14. Schwartz, Joe, RB, Toledo, 350
15. Williams, Mahlon, TE, North Carolina Central, 378
16. Cerwinski, John, T, Bowling Green, 403
17. Foote, Jim, P, Delaware Valley, 432

OAKLAND
1. Guy, Ray, K-P, Southern Mississippi, 23
2. Johnson, Monte, DT, Nebraska, 49
3. Choice to Detroit through LA Rams
4. Smith, Perry, DB, Colorado State, from LA Rams, 92
Wylie, Joe, WR, Oklahoma, 101
5. Neal, Louis, WR, Prairie View A&M, from Green Bay, 124
Mikolajczyk, Ron, T, Tampa, 127
6. Myers, Brent, T, Purdue, 153
7. Weaver, Gary, LB, Fresno State, 179
8. Rae, Mike, QB, USC, 205
9. Sweeney, Steve, TE, California, 231
10. Allen, Leo, RB, Tuskegee, 257
11. List, Jerry, RB, Nebraska, 283
12. Krapf, Jim, G-LB, Alabama, 309
13. Choice to LA Rams
14. Polen, Bruce, DB, William Penn, 361
15. Leffers, Dave, C, Vanderbilt, 387
16. Gadlin, Jerry, WR, Wyoming, 413
17. Ryan, Mike, G, USC, 439

PHILADELPHIA
1. Sisemore, Jerry, T, Texas, 3
Young, Charle, TE, USC, from San Diego, 6
2. Morriss, Guy, G, TCU, 28
3. Logan, Randy, DB, Michigan, 55
4. Choice to Minnesota
5. Choice to Chi. Bears
6. Picard, Bob, WR, Eastern Washington, 132
7. Wynn, Will, DE, Tennessee State, 159
8. Lintner, Dan, DB, Indiana, 184
9. Nokes, John, LB, Northern Illinois, 211
10. Choice to Minnesota
11. Van Elst, Gary, DT, Michigan State, 263
12. Lavender, Joe, DB, San Diego State, 288
13. Davis, Stan, WR, Memphis State, 315
14. Sacra, Ralph, T, Texas A&M, 340
15. Schlezes, Ken, DB, Notre Dame, 367
16. Dowsing, Frank, DB, Mississippi State, 391
17. Oliver, Greg, RB, Trinity (Texas), 419

PITTSBURGH
1. Thomas, J.T., DB, Florida State, 24
2. Phares, Ken, DB, Mississippi State, 50
3. Bernhardt, Roger, G, Kansas, 76
4. Clark, Gail, LB, Michigan State, 102
5. Reavis, Dave, DE, Arkansas, from New Orleans through Washington, 106
Clark, Larry, LB, Northern Illinois, 128
6. Bell, Ron, RB, Illinois State, from Denver, 140
Scolnik, Glen, WR, Indiana, 154
7. Dorsey, Nate, DE, Mississippi Valley State, 180
8. Toews, Loren, LB, California, from Denver, 192
Janssen, Bill, T, Nebraska, 206
9. Bonham, Braccy, G, North Carolina Central, 232
10. Wunderly, Don, DT, Arkansas, 258
11. White, Bob, DB, Arizona, 284
12. Lee, Willie, RB, Indiana State, 310
13. Fergerson, Rick, WR, Kansas State, 336
14. Cowan, Roger, DE, Stanford, 362
15. Cross, Charles, DB, Iowa, 388
16. Nardi, Glen, DT, Navy, 414
17. Shannon, Mike, DT, Oregon State, 440

ST. LOUIS
1. Butz, Dave, DT, Purdue, 5
2. Choice to Minnesota
Keithley, Gary, QB, Texas El Paso, from San Francisco, 45
3. Sturt, Fred, G, Bowling Green, 59
Metcalf, Terry, RB, Long Beach State, from LA Rams, 63
4. Choice to San Diego through Chi. Bears
5. Brahaney, Tom, C, Oklahoma, 109
6. Crump, Dwayne, DB, Fresno State, 137
Andre, Phil, DB, Washington, from Detroit, 148
7. Jones, Ken, T, Oklahoma, 164
8. Garrett, Ken, RB, Wake Forest, 188
9. King, Ken, LB, Kentucky, 213
10. Sloan, Bonnie, DT, Austin Peay, 242
11. Sanspree, Dan, DE, Auburn, 267
12. Unruh, Dean, T, Oklahoma, 292
13. Robinson, Ed, DB, Lamar, 317
14. Peiffer, Dan, G, Southeast Missouri State, 346
15. Parker, Mel, LB, Duke, 371
16. Hann, Jim, LB, Montana, 396
17. Crone, Eric, QB, Harvard, 421

SAN DIEGO
1. Choice to Philadelphia
Rodgers, Johnny, WR, Nebraska, from Washington through Baltimore, 25
2. Choice to LA Rams
3. Choice to LA Rams
Fouts, Dan, QB, Oregon, from Atlanta through Oakland, 64
4. Thaxton, James, TE, Tennessee State, from St. Louis through Chi. Bears, 84
Choice to Baltimore
Singletary, Bill, LB, Temple, from San Francisco through Washington, 97
5. Choice to Buffalo
McGee, Willie, WR, Alcorn State, from Detroit through Washington, 123
Knoble, Jon, LB, Weber State, from Cleveland, 125
6. Roberts, Marvin, C, Michigan State, 135
7. Choice to Miami through New England
8. Choice to Baltimore
9. Bennett, Tab, LB, Illinois, 214
10. Burnett, Cliff, DE, Montana, 239
11. Douglas, Jay, C, Memphis State, 268
12. Ahrens, Lynn, T, Eastern Montana, 293
13. Reese, Alfred, RB, Tennessee State, 318
14. Adams, Tony, QB, Utah State, 343
15. Parris, Gary, TE, Florida State, 372
16. Petty, Joe, DB, Arizona State, 397
17. Darrow, Barry, T, Montana, 422

SAN FRANCISCO
1. Holmes, Mike, DB, Texas Southern, 18
2. Harper, Willie, LB, Nebraska, from NY Giants, 41
Choice to St. Louis
3. Choice to Denver through Washington and San Diego
4. Choice to San Diego through Washington
5. Fulk, Mike, LB, Indiana, from Chi. Bears, 112
Beverly, Ed, WR, Arizona State, 122
6. Moore, Arthur, DT, Tulsa, 149
7. Mitchell, John, LB, Alabama, 174
8. Atkins, Dave, RB, Texas-El Paso, 201
9. Praetorius, Roger, RB, Syracuse, 226
10. Hunt, Charlie, LB, Florida State, 253
11. Dahlberg, Tom, RB, Gustavus Adolphus, 278
12. Pettus, Larry, T, Tennessee State, 305
13. Kelso, Alan, C, Washington, 330
14. Morrison, Dennis, QB, Kansas State, 357
15. Bettiga, Mike, WR, Cal State-Humboldt, 382
16. Oven, Mike, TE, Georgia Tech, 409
17. Erickson, Bob, G, North Dakota State, 434

WASHINGTON
1. Choice to San Diego through Baltimore
2. Choice to New Orleans through NY Jets
3. Choice to Buffalo
4. Choice to Buffalo
5. Cantrell, Charley, G, Lamar, from Atlanta, 117
Choice to LA Rams
6. Choice to NY Jets
7. Choice to Buffalo
8. Choice to New Orleans
Hancock, Mike, TE, Idaho State, from LA Rams, 193
9. Galbos, Rich, RB, Ohio State, from Baltimore, 218
Sheats, Eddie, LB, Kansas, 233
10. Stone, Ken, DB, Vanderbilt, from LA Rams, 245
11. Choice to LA Rams
12. Webster, Ernie, G, Pittsburgh, 311
13. Johnson, Dennis, DT, Delaware, 337
14. Marshall, Herb, DB, Cameron, 363
15. Choice to LA Rams
16. Wedman, Mike, K, Colorado, 415
17. Davis, Jeff, RB, Mars Hills, 441

1974
Held January 29-30, 1974

ATLANTA
1. Choice to Minnesota
2. Tinker, Gerald, WR, Kent State, 44
3. McQuilken, Kim, QB, Lehigh, 69
Spencer, Maurice, DB, North Carolina Central, from Oakland through New Orleans, 71
4. Kendrick, Vince, RB, Florida, 96
5. Childs, Henry, TE, Kansas State, from Baltimore through Detroit, 109
Choice to New Orleans
Eley, Monroe, RB, Arizona State, from LA Rams through Minnesota and Philadelphia, 128
6. Orange, Doyle, RB, Southern Mississippi, 147
7. Coode, James, T-G, Michigan, 173
8. Choice to Green Bay through New Orleans
9. Bailey, Larry, DT, Pacific, 225
10. Ryczek, Paul, C, Virginia, 252
11. Wilson, Eddie, WR, Albany State, 277
12. Koegel, Vic, LB, Ohio State, 304
13. Powell, Ralph, RB, Nebraska, 329
14. Givens, John, G, Villanova, 356
15. Jones, Willie, WR, Iowa State, 381

16. McGee, Sylvester, RB, Rhode Island, 408
17. Davis, Al, G-T, Boise State, 433

BALTIMORE
1. Dutton, John, DE, Nebraska, 5
   Carr, Roger, WR, Louisiana Tech, from LA Rams, 24
2. Cook, Fred, DE, Southern Mississippi, 32
   Shuttlesworth, Ed, RB, Michigan, from Philadelphia, 37
3. Robinson, Glenn, LB-DE, Oklahoma State, 57
   Pratt, Robert, G, North Carolina, from Denver, 67
4. Bell, Tony, DB, Bowling Green, 84
5. Choice to Atlanta through Detroit
   Nettles, Doug, DB, Vanderbilt, from Minnesota, 129
6. Choice to Miami
   Rhodes, Danny, LB, Arkansas, from New England, 140
7. Jackson, Noah, G, Tampa, 161
   Dickel, Dan, LB, Iowa, from Denver, 170
   Scott, Freddie, WR, Amherst, from Buffalo, 174
8. Latta, Greg, TE, Morgan State, 188
   Miles, Paul, Bowling Green, from Denver, 198
9. Choice to LA Rams through Washington
10. Van Duyne, Bob, G, Idaho, 240
   Ellis, Glenn, DT, Elon, from LA Rams, 257
11. Rudnick, Tim, DB, Notre Dame, 265
12. Simonson, Dave, T, Minnesota, 292
   Bobrowski, Bo, QB, Purdue, from Washington, 307
13. Hall, Randy, DB, Idaho, 317
14. Collins, Ed, WR, Rice, 344
15. Kelly, Pat, LB, Richmond, 369
16. Margavage, Dave, T, Kentucky, 396
17. Berra, Tim, WR, Massachusetts, 421
   Lewis, Buzzy, DB, Florida State, from Washington, 436

BUFFALO
1. Gant, Reuben, TE, Oklahoma State, 18
2. Allen, Doug, LB, Penn State, from Houston, 27
   Choice to San Diego
3. Marangi, Gary, QB, Boston College, 70
4. Crumpler, Carlester, RB, East Carolina, 95
5. Hayman, Gary, WR, Penn State, from San Diego, 106
   Guy, Tim, T, Oregon, 122
6. Choice to Cleveland
7. Choice to Baltimore
8. Choice to Cleveland
   Hare, Gregg, QB, Ohio State, from Washington, 203
9. Doherty, Brian, P, Notre Dame, 226
10. Cameron, Art, TE, Albany State (Georgia), from St. Louis, 241
   Calhoun, Don, RB, Kansas State, from Cleveland, 249
   Choice to St. Louis through Denver
11. Kirby, Rod, LB, Pittsburgh, 278
12. Means, Dave, DE, Southeast Missouri State, 303
13. Gatewood, Ed, LB, Tennessee State, 331
14. Lamm, Paul, DB, North Carolina, from Houston, 339
   Gurbada, Phil, DB, Mayville State, 355
15. Williams, Ken, LB, Southwestern Louisiana, 382
16. Qvale, Sanford, T, North Dakota State, 406
17. Casola, Sal, K, Cincinnati, 434

CHI. BEARS
1. Bryant, Waymond, LB, Tennessee State, 4
   Gallagher, Dave, DE-DT, Michigan, from Washington through LA Rams, 20
2. Choice to New England
3. Wheeler, Wayne, WR, Alabama, from San Diego, 54
   Horton, Greg, G-T, Colorado, 56
   Taylor, Cliff, RB, Memphis State, from New England through Washington, 62
4. Choice to Pittsburgh through New England
5. Choice to Philadelphia
6. Choice to Green Bay
7. Ettinger, Jack, WR, Arkansas, 160
8. Chadwick, Alan, QB, East Tennessee State, 186
   Grandberry, Ken, RB, Washington from New England, 190
9. Choice to Miami
10. Choice to Cleveland
11. Hodgins, Norm, DB, LSU, 264
12. Sevy, Jeff, DT, California, 290
13. Barnes, Joe, QB, Texas Tech, 316
14. Vellano, Paul, DT, Maryland, 342
15. Alexander, Oliver, TE, Grambling, 368
16. Geist, Randy, DB, Colorado, 394
17. Holland, Craig, QB, Texas-Arlington, 420

CINCINNATI
1. Kollar, Bill, DT, Montana State, 23
2. Davis, Charlie, RB, Colorado, 48
3. Lapham, Dave, G, Syracuse, from New Orleans, 61
   Jolitz, Evan, LB, Cincinnati, 73
4. Boryla, Mike, QB, Stanford, from New England, 87
   White, Daryl, G, Nebraska, 98
   Williams, Richard, WR, Abilene Christian, from Minnesota, 103
5. Stanback, Haskel, RB, Tennessee, from New Orleans, 114
   Bishop, Richard, DT, Louisville, 127
6. Sinclair, Robin, DB, Washington State, 152
   Byrant, William, DB, Grambling, from Washington through New Orleans, 153
7. Sawyer, Ken, DB, Syracuse, 177
8. McDaniel, John, WR, Lincoln (Missouri), 202
9. Johnson, Ed, DE, SMU, 231
10. Herd, Charles, WR, Penn State, 256
11. Kezirian, Ed, T, UCLA, 281
12. McClinon, Rudy, DB, Xavier, 306
13. Jornov, Ted, LB, Iowa State, 335
14. Phillips, Mike, T, Cornell, 360
15. Jackson, Isaac, RB, Kansas State, 385
16. Bishop, Darryl, DB, Kentucky, 410
17. Smith, Jim, RB, North Carolina Central, 439*

CLEVELAND
1. Choice to San Diego
2. Corbett, Billy, T, Johnson C. Smith, 40
3. Choice to Denver
4. Choice to Oakland
5. Ilgenfritz, Mark, DE, Vanderbilt, 118
6. Pritchett, Billy, RB, West Texas State, from Buffalo, 146
   Choice to Pittsburgh through Denver
7. Herrick, Bob, WR, Purdue, from St. Louis, 163
   Sullivan, Gerry, C-T, Illinois, 171
8. Choice to Washington
   Brown, Eddie, DB, Tennessee, from Buffalo, 199
9. Scott, Dan, G, Ohio State, 224
10. Puestow, Mike, WR, North Dakota State, from Chi. Bears, 238
   Choice to Buffalo
11. Gooden, Tom, K, Harding, 274
12. McNeil, Ron, DE, North Carolina Central, 302
13. Seifert, Mike, DE, Wisconsin, 327
14. Hunt, Bob, RB, Heidelberg, 352
15. Terrell, Ransom, LB, Arizona, 380
16. Anderson, Preston, DB, Rice, 407
17. Buchanan, Carlton, DT, Southwestern Oklahoma, 430

DALLAS
1. Jones, Ed (Too Tall), DE, Tennessee State, from Houston, 1
   Young, Charley, RB, North Carolina State, 22
2. Choice to Miami
3. White, Danny, QB, Arizona State, from Houston, 53
   Peterson, Cal, LB, UCLA, 72
4. Hutcherson, Ken, LB, Livingston, from Oakland, 97
   Andrade, Andy, RB, Northern Michigan, 101
5. Kelsey, Jon, T, Missouri, 126
6. Bright, Jimmy, DB, UCLA, 151
7. Nester, Raymond, LB, Michigan State, 176
8. Holt, Mike, DB, Michigan State, 205
9. Dulin, Bill, T, Johnson C. Smith, 230
10. Morgan, Dennis, RB, Western Illinois, 255
11. McGee, Harvey, WR, Southern Mississippi, 280
12. Bobo, Keith, QB, SMU, 209
13. Lima, Fred, K, Colorado, 334
14. Richards, Doug, DB, BYU, 359
15. Craft, Bruce, T, Geneva, 384
16. Killian, Gene, G-T, Tennessee, 413
17. Skolrood, Lawrie, T, North Dakota, 438

DENVER
1. Gradishar, Randy, LB, Ohio State, 14
2. Wafer, Carl, DT, Tennessee State, 42
3. Choice to Baltimore
   Minor, Claudie, T, San Diego State, from Cleveland, 68
4. Collier, Ozell, DB, Colorado, 92
5. Choice to Minnesota
6. Winesberry, John, WR, Stanford, 145
7. Choice to Baltimore
8. Choice to Baltimore
9. Choice to Pittsburgh
10. Johnson, Charlie, DB, Southern, 248
11. Buchanan, Steve, RB, Holy Cross, 276
12. Cameron, Larry, LB, Alcorn State, 301
13. Clerkley, John, DT, Fort Valley State, 326
14. Marks, Rich, DB, Northern Illinois, 354
15. Pennington, Piel, QB, Massachusetts, 379
16. Austin, Darrell, T, South Carolina, 404
17. Brown, Boyd, TE, Alcorn State, 432

DETROIT
1. O'Neil, Ed, LB, Penn State, from New Orleans, 8
   Choice to New Orleans
2. Howard, Billy, DT, Alcorn State, 39
3. Bussey, Dexter, RB, Texas-Arlington, 65
4. Choice to St. Louis
5. Capria, Carl, DB, Purdue, 117
6. Burden, Willie, RB, North Carolina State, from New Orleans, 139
   Davis, Jim, G, Alcorn State, 143
7. Herrera, Efren, K, UCLA, 169
8. Denimarck, Mike, LB, Emporia State, 195
9. Choice to LA Rams
10. Wooley, David, RB, Central State (Oklahoma), 247
11. Blair, T.C., TE, Tulsa, 273
12. Wakefield, Mark, WR, Tampa, 299
13. Rothwell, Fred, C, Kansas State, 325
14. Jones, David, DB, Howard Payne, 351
15. Wells, John, G, Kansas State, 377
16. Wilson, Myron, DB, Bowling Green, 403
17. Temple, Collis, DE, LSU, 429

GREEN BAY
1. Smith, Barty, RB, Richmond, 12
2. Choice to Miami
3. Choice to Minnesota through San Diego
4. Choice to San Francisco
5. Odom, Steve, WR, Utah, 116
6. Woods, Don, RB, New Mexico, from Chi. Bears, 134
   Payne, Ken, WR, Langston, 142
7. Purvis, Bart, T, Maryland, 168
8. Doris, Monte, LB, USC, 194
   Guillet, Ned, DB, Boston College, from Atlanta through New Orleans, 200
9. Holton, Harold, G, Texas-El Paso, 220
10. Troszak, Doug, DT, Michigan, 246
11. Torkelson, Eric, RB, Connecticut, 272
12. Walker, Randy, K, Northwestern State (Louisiana), 298
13. Armstrong, Emanuel, LB, San Jose State, 324
14. Neloms, Andrew, DT, Kentucky State, 350
15. Wannstedt, Dave, T, Pittsburgh, 376
16. Cooney, Mark, LB, Colorado, 402
17. Woodfield, Randy, WR, Portland State, 428

HOUSTON
1. Choice to Dallas
2. Choice to Buffalo
3. Choice to Dallas
4. Manstedt, Steve, LB, Nebraska, 79
5. Choice to San Diego through Washington
6. Choice to Kansas City through New Orleans
   Brown, Booker, G, USC, from LA Rams, 154
7. Fairley, Leonard, DB, Alcorn State, 157
8. McCoy, Mike, DB, Western Kentucky, 183
9. Choice to New England
10. Choice to New Orleans
11. Taylor, Steve, C, Auburn, 261
12. Browne, Ricky, LB, Florida, 287
13. Dixon, Dan, G, Boise State, 313
14. Choice to Buffalo
15. Johnson, Billy (White Shoes), WR, Widener, 365
16. Williams, Mathew, RB, Northeast Louisiana, 391
17. Hedge, Bill, T, Northeast Missouri State, 417

KANSAS CITY
1. Green, Woody, RB, Arizona State, 16
2. Getty, Charlie, T, Penn State, 41
3. Jaynes, David, QB, Kansas, 66
4. Herkenhoff, Matt, T, Minnesota, 94
5. Choice to NY Giants
6. Washington, Jim, RB, Clemson, from Houston through New Orleans, 131
   Choice to Washington
7. Hegge, Leroy, DE, South Dakota—Springfield, 172
8. Choice to NY Jets
9. Jennings, Jim, RB, Rutgers, 222
10. Condon, Tom, G, Boston College, 250
11. Thornbladh, Bob, RB, Michigan, 275
12. Brown, Carl, WR, West Texas State, 300
13. Romagnoli, Norm, LB, Kentucky State, 328
14. Pomarico, Frank, G, Notre Dame, 353
15. Burnham, Lem, LB, U. S. International, 378
16. Beers, Barry, G, William & Mary, 405
17. Langner, David, DB, Auburn, 431

LA RAMS
1. Cappelletti, John, RB, Penn State, from Philadelphia, 11
   Choice to Baltimore
2. Simpson, Bill, DB, Michigan State, 50
3. Oliver, Al, T, UCLA, 76
4. Weese, Norris, DB, Mississippi, from Washington, 99
   Johnson, Frank, T, Cal-Riverside, 102
5. Choice to Atlanta through Minnesota and Philadelphia
6. Choice to Houston
7. Harvey, John, RB, Texas-Arlington, from San Diego, 158
   Choice to Washington
8. Choice to San Diego
9. Hutt, Don, WR, Boise State, from Baltimore through Washington, 213
   Williams, Derek, DB, Cal-Riverside, from Detroit, 221
   Choice to Washington
10. Choice to Baltimore
11. Hayes, Rick, T, Washington, 284
12. Freberg, Roger, G, UCLA, 310
13. Solverson, Pete, T, Drake, 336
14. Carson, Ananias, WR, Langston, 362
15. Thomas, Bob, K, Notre Dame, 388
16. Ottmar, Dave, P, Stanford, 414
17. Townsend, Willie, WR, Notre Dame, 440

MIAMI
1. Reese, Don, DE, Jackson State, 26
2. Tillman, Andre, TE, Texas Tech, from Green Bay, 38
   Malone, Benny, RB, Arizona State, from Dallas, 47
   White, Jeris, DB, Hawaii, 52
3. Moore, Nat, WR, Florida, 78
4. Stevenson, Bill, DT, Drake, 104
5. Vann, Cleveland, LB, Oklahoma State, 130
6. Crowder, Randy, DE, Penn State, from Baltimore, 136
   Wolfe, Bob, T, Nebraska, 156
7. Swierc, Carl, WR, Rice, from New Orleans, 164
   Sullivan, Joe, G, Boston College, 182
8. Baker, Melvin, WR, Texas Southern, 208
9. Wickert, Tom, G, Washington State, from Chi. Bears, 212
   Lally, Bob, LB, Cornell, 234
10. Valbuena, Gary, QB, Tennessee, 260
11. Roberts, Gerry, DE, UCLA, 286
12. Revels, Jim, DB, Florida, 312
13. Heath, Clayton, RB, Wake Forest, 338
14. Johnson, Sam, LB, Arizona State, 364
15. Cates, Larry, DB, Western Michigan, 390
16. Wolf, Jessie, DT, Prairie View A&M, 416
17. Dickerson, Ken, DB, Tuskegee, 442

MINNESOTA
1. McNeill, Fred, LB, UCLA, from Atlanta, 17
   Riley, Steve, T, USC, 25
2. Holland, John, WR, Tennessee State, from San Diego, 29
   Blair, Matt, LB, Iowa State, 51
3. Craig, Steve, TE, Northwestern, from Green Bay through San Diego, 64
   Anderson, Scott, C, Missouri, 77
4. Townsend, Mike, DB, Notre Dame, from New Orleans, 86
   Choice to Cincinnati
5. Ferguson, Jim, DB, Stanford, from Denver, 120

Choice to Baltimore
6. Kellar, Mark, RB, Northern Illinois, 155
7. Tabron, Fred, RB, Southwest Missouri State, 181
8. Simmons, Berl, K, TCU, 207
9. McCullum, Sam, WR, Montana State, 232
10. Reed, Barry, RB, Peru State, 259
11. Boone, Dave, DE, Eastern Michigan, 285
12. Poltl, Randy, DB, Stanford, 311
13. Keller, Gary, DT, Utah, 337
14. Dixon, Alan, RB, Harding, 363
15. Wachtler, Kurt, DT, St. John's (Minnesota), 289
16. Goebel, John, RB, St. Thomas (Minnesota), 415
17. Garrett, Earl, DB, Massachusetts-Boston, 441

NEW ENGLAND
1. Choice to San Francisco
2. Corbett, Steve, G, Boston College, from Chi. Bears, 30
Nelson, Steve, LB, North Dakota State, 34
3. Choice to Chi. Bears through Washington
4. Choice to Cincinnati
5. Johnson, Andy, RB, Georgia, 113
Battle, Charlie, LB-DE, Grambling, from Washington through New Orleans, 124
6. Choice to Baltimore
Ramsey, Chuck, P, Wake Forest, from Philadelphia, 141
7. Choice to Pittsburgh
Damkroger, Maury, LB, Nebraska, from Washington, 178
8. Choice to Chi. Bears
9. McCartney, Ed, LB, Northwestern Oklahoma, from Houston, 209
Choice to Washington
10. Choice to Pittsburgh
11. Gibson, Archie, RB, Utah State, 268
12. Foster, Eddie, T, Oklahoma, 296
13. Bennett, Phil, RB, Boston College, 321
14. Bowens, Cecil, RB, Kentucky, 346
15. Hunt, Sam, LB, Stephen F. Austin, 374
16. Selmon, Lucious, DT, Oklahoma, 399
17. Hudson, Gary, DB, Boston College, 424

NEW ORLEANS
1. Choice to Detroit
Middleton, Rick, LB, Ohio State, from Detroit, 13
2. Seal, Paul, TE, Michigan, 36
3. Choice to Cincinnati
4. Choice to Minnesota
McNeill, Rod, RB, USC, from San Francisco, 88
5. Parker, Joel, WR, Florida, from San Francisco, 113
Choice to Cincinnati
Schmidt, Terry, DB, Ball State, from Atlanta, 121
6. Choice to Detroit
7. Choice to Miami
8. Choice to NY Jets
Maxson, Alvin, RB, SMU, from Oakland, 201
9. La Porta, Phil, T, Penn State, 217
10. Anderson, Frosty, WR, Nebraska, from Houston, 235
Thibodeaux, Tommy, G, Tulane, 242
11. Merritt, Kent, WR, Virginia, 270
12. Buckmon, James, DE, Pittsburgh, 295
13. Truax, Mike, LB, Tulane, 320
14. Marshall, Kent, DB, TCU, 348
15. Cipa, Larry, QB, Michigan, 373
16. Coleman, Don, LB, Michigan, 398
17. Williams, Marvin, WR, Western Illinois, 426

NY GIANTS
1. Hicks, John, G, Ohio State, 3
2. Mullen, Tom, G, Southwest Missouri State, 28
3. Dvorak, Rick, DE-LB, Wichita State, 55
4. Summerell, Carl, QB, East Carolina, 80
5. Clune, Don, WR, Penn State, 107
Powers, Clyde, DB, Oklahoma, from Kansas City, 119
6. Pietrzak, Jim, T, Eastern Michigan, 132
7. Woolbright, Marty, TE, South Carolina, 159
8. Bibbs, Ezil, DE, Grambling, 184
9. Rathje, Jim, RB, Northern Michigan, 211
10. Rhodes, Ray, WR, Tulsa, 236
11. Brooks, Bobby, DB, Bishop, 263
12. Sims, James, DB, USC, 288
13. Colvin, Dennis, T, Southwest Texas State, 315
14. Hayes, Mike, T, Virginia State, 340
15. Jones, Larry, WR, Northeast Missouri State, 367
16. Brown, Buddy, G, Alabama, 392
17. Crosby, Steve, RB, Ft. Hays State, 419

NY JETS
1. Barzilauskas, Carl, DT, Indiana, 6
2. Browne, Gordon, T, Boston College, 31
3. Turk, Godwin, LB, Southern, 58
Word, Roscoe, DB, Jackson State, from Washington, 74
4. Choice to San Francisco through New Orleans
5. Baccus, Gary, LB, Oklahoma, 110
6. Wyman, Bill, C, Texas, 135
Jones, Wayne, RB, Mississippi State, from St. Louis, 137
7. Veazey, Burney, TE, Mississippi, 162
8. Gantt, Greg, K, Alabama, 187
Lightfoot, Larry, RB, Livingston, from New Orleans, 192
Rydalch, Ron, DT, Utah, from Kansas City, 197
9. Burns, Robert, RB, Georgia, 214
10. Baker, Sam, G, Georgia, 239
11. Bird, Eugene, DB, Southern Mississippi, 266
Buckley, Bill, WR, Mississippi State, from St. Louis, 267
12. Ricca, John, DE, Duke, 291
13. Tate, John, LB, Jackson State, 318*
14. Fountain, Greg, G, Mississippi State, 343
15. Brister, Willie, TE, Southern, 370
16. Jackson, Clarence, RB, Western Kentucky, 395
17. Lowrey, Doug, G-C, Arkansas State, 422

OAKLAND
1. Lawrence, Henry, T, Florida A&M, 19
2. Casper, Dave, TE, Notre Dame, 45
3. Choice to Atlanta through New Orleans
van Eeghen, Mark, RB, Colgate, from Pittsburgh, 75
4. Bradshaw, Morris, RB, Ohio State, from Cleveland, 93
Choice to Dallas
5. Wessel, Pete, DB, Northwestern, 128
6. McAlister, James, RB, UCLA, 148
7. Garcia, Rod, K, Stanford, 175
8. Choice to New Orleans
9. Pope, Kenith, DB, Oklahoma, 227
10. Arnold, Chris, DB, Virginia State, 253
11. Hart, Harold, RB, Texas Southern, 279
12. Gonzalez, Noe, RB, Southwest Texas State, 305
13. Dennery, Mike. LB, Southern Mississippi, 330
14. Willingham, Don, RB, Wisconsin-Milwaukee, 357
15. Mathis, Greg, DB, Idaho State, 383
16. Robinson, Delario, WR, Kansas, 409
17. Morris, James, DT, Missouri Valley, 435

PHILADELPHIA
1. Choice to LA Rams
2. Choice to Baltimore
3. Sutton, Mitch, DT, Kansas, 63
4. LeMaster, Frank, LB, Kentucky, 89
5. Cagle, Jim, DT, Georgia, from Chi. Bears, 108
Krepfle, Keith, TE, Iowa State, 115
6. Choice to New England
7. Cullars, Willie, DE, Kansas State, 167
8. Woods, Robert, LB, Howard Payne, 193
9. Sheridan, Mark, WR, Holy Cross, 219
10. Polak, Phil, RB, Bowling Green, 245
11. Brittain, Bill, C, Kansas State, 271
12. Parker, Artimus, DB, USC, 297
13. Ditley, Lars, DE, South Dakota Tech, 323
14. Smith, Dave, LB, Oklahoma, 349
15. Bond, Sid, T, TCU, 375
16. Smith, Jim, LB, Monmouth, 401
17. Brown, Cliff, RB, Notre Dame, 427

PITTSBURGH
1. Swann, Lynn, WR, USC, 21
2. Lambert, Jack, LB, Kent State, 46
3. Choice to Oakland
4. Stallworth, John, WR, Alabama A&M, from Chi. Bears through New England, 82
Allen, Jimmy, DB, UCLA, 100
5. Webster, Mike, C, Wisconsin, 125
6. Wolfe, James, DE, Prairie View A&M, from Cleveland through Denver, 149
Druschel, Rick, G, North Carolina State, 150
7. Sitterle, Allen, T, North Carolina State, from New England, 165
Garske, Scott, TE, Eastern Michigan, 179
8. Gefert, Mark, LB, Purdue, 204
9. Reamon, Tommy, RB, Missouri, from Denver, 223
Davis, Charlie, T, TCU, 229
10. Kregel, Jim, G, Ohio State, from New England, 243
Atkinson, Dave, DB, BYU, 254
11. Morton, Dickie, RB, Arkansas, 283
12. Lickiss, Hugh, LB, Simpson, 308
13. Kolch, Frank, QB, Eastern Michigan, 333
14. Henley, Bruce, DB, Rice, 358
15. Hunt, Larry, DT, Iowa State, 387
16. Morgan, Octavus, LB, Illinois, 412
17. Moore, Larry, DE, Angelo State, 437

ST. LOUIS
1. Cain, J.V., TE, Colorado, 7
2. Kindle, Greg, T, Tennessee State, 33
3. Choice to San Diego
George, Steve, DT, Houston, from San Francisco, 60
4. Keeton, Durwood, DB, Oklahoma, 85
Harris, Ike, WR, Iowa State, from Detroit, 91
5. Neils, Steve, LB, Minnesota, 111
6. Choice to NY Jets
7. Choice to Cleveland
8. Albert, Sergio, K, U.S. International, 189
9. Harrison, Reggie, RB, Cincinnati, 215
10. Choice to Buffalo
Hartle, Greg, LB, Newberry, from Buffalo through Denver, 251
11. Choice to NY Jets
12. Wallace, Roger, WR, Bowling Green, 293
13. Poulos, Jimmy, RB, Georgia, 319
14. Smith, Charles, RB, Yankton, 345
15. Ancell, Vincent, DB, Arkansas State, 371
16. Emery, Alonzo, RB, Arizona State, 397
17. Moseley, John, DB, Missouri, 423

SAN DIEGO
1. Matthews, Bo, RB, Colorado, 2
Goode, Don, LB, Kansas, from Cleveland, 15
2. Choice to Minnesota
Markovich, Mark, C, Penn State, from Buffalo, 43
3. Choice to Chi. Bears
Rudder, Bill, RB, Tennessee, from St. Louis, 59
4. Davis, Harrison, WR, Virginia, 81
5. Teerlinck, John, DT, Western Illinois, from Houston through Washington, 105
Choice to Buffalo
6. Freitas, Jesse, QB, San Diego State, 133
7. Choice to LA Rams
8. Forrest, Tom, G, Cincinnati, 185
Boatwright, Bon, T, Oklahoma State, from LA Rams, 206
9. Colbert, Danny, DB, Tulsa, 210
10. Ketchoyian, John, LB, Santa Clara, 237
11. Grannell, Dave, TE, Arizona State, 262
12. Williams, Sam, DB, California, 289
13. Vertefeuille, Brian, T, Idaho State, 314
14. Bailey, Greg, DB, Long Beach State, 341
15. Anthony, Charles, LB, USC, 366
Meczka, Greg, TE, Bowling Green, from Washington, 386
16. Skarin, Neal, DE, Arizona State, 393
17. DeJurnett, Charles, DT, San Jose State, 418

SAN FRANCISCO
1. Jackson, Wilbur, RB, Alabama, from New England, 9
Sandifer, Bill, DT, UCLA, 10
2. Fahnhorst, Keith, TE, Minnesota, 35
Williams, Delvin, RB, Kansas, from Washington, 49
3. Choice to St. Louis
4. Haslerig, Clint, WR, Michigan, from NY Jets through New Orleans, 83
Choice to New Orleans
Johnson, Sammy, RB, North Carolina, from Green Bay, 90
5. Choice to New Orleans
6. Raines, Mike, DT, Alabama, 138
7. Johnson, Kermit, RB, UCLA, 166
8. Schneitz, Jim, G, Missouri, 191
9. Moore, Manfred, RB, USC, 216
10. Gaspard, Glen, LB, Texas, 244
11. Battle, Greg, DB, Colorado State, 269
12. Hull, Tom, LB, Penn State, 294
13. Owen, Tom, QB, Wichita State, 322
14. Williamson, Walt, DE, Michigan, 347
15. Gray, Leonard, TE, Long Beach State, 372
16. Conners, Jack, DB, Oregon, 400
17. Stanley, Levi, G, Hawaii, 425

WASHINGTON
1. Choice to Chi. Bears through LA Rams
2. Choice to San Francisco
3. Choice to NY Jets
4. Choice to LA Rams
5. Choice to New England through New Orleans
6. Keyworth, Jon, TE, Colorado, from Kansas City, 144
Choice to Cincinnati through New Orleans
7. Choice to New England
Varty, Mike, LB, Northwestern, from LA Rams, 180
8. Robinson, Darwin, RB, Dakota State (South Dakota), from Cleveland, 196
Choice to Buffalo
9. Sens, Mark, DE, Colorado, from New England, 218
Flater, Mike, K, Colorado Mines, 228
Kennedy, Jim, TE, Colorado State, from LA Rams, 233
10. Vann, Johnny, DB, South Dakota, 258
11. Miller, Joe, T, Villanova, 282
12. Choice to Baltimore
13. O'Dell, Stu, LB, Indiana, 332
14. Van Galder, Don, QB, Utah, 361
15. Choice to San Diego
16. Anderson, Nate, RB, Eastern Illinois, 411
17. Choice to Baltimore

1975
Held January 28-29, 1975

ATLANTA
1. Bartkowski, Steve, QB, California, from Baltimore, 1
Choice to Baltimore
2. Ortega, Ralph, LB, Florida, 29
3. Choice to Cincinnati
Thompson, Woody, RB, Miami, from Houston, 65
4. Nessel, John, G, Penn State, 81
5. Choice to Denver
McCrary, Greg, TE, Clark, from Buffalo, 123
6. Kuykendall, Fulton, LB, UCLA, from Baltimore, 132
Payton, Doug, G, Colorado, 133
7. Esposito, Mike, RB, Boston College, 159
8. Adams, Brent, T, Tennessee-Chattanooga, 185
9. Davis, Brad, RB, LSU, 211
10. Mills, Marshall, WR, West Virginia, 237
11. Merrow, Jeff, DT, West Virginia, 263
12. Pickett, Alonzo, T-G, Texas Southern, 289
13. Russ, Carl, LB, Michigan, 315
14. Robinson, Steve, DT, Tuskegee, 340
15. Robinson, Jim, WR, Georgia Tech, 367
16. Knutson, Steve, T, USC, 393
17. Anderson, Mitch, QB, Northwestern, 418

BALTIMORE
1. Choice to Atlanta
Huff, Ken, G, North Carolina, from Atlanta, 3
2. Choice to LA Rams through Green Bay
3. Washington, Mike, DB, Alabama, 53
Pear, Dave, DT, Washington, from Chi. Bears, 56
4. Johnson, Marshall, RB, Houston, 80
Linford, Paul, DT, BYU, from NY Jets, 93
5. Leaks, Roosevelt, RB, Texas, 105
6. Choice to Atlanta
Westbrook, Don, WR, Nebraska, from NY Giants, 131
7. Jones, Kim, RB, Colorado State, 157
Joachim, Steve, QB, Temple, from Chi. Bears, 160
Luce, Derrel, LB, Baylor, from NY Jets through Chi. Bears, 168
8. Bushong, John, DE, Western Kentucky, 184
Denboer, Greg, TE, Michigan, from Chi. Bears through Denver, 187
Cage, Mario, RB, Northwestern State (Louisiana), from Green Bay, 192

9. McKinney, Royce, DB, Kentucky State, 209
10. Waganheim, Phil, P, Maryland, 236
11. Hazel, Dave, WR, Ohio State, 261
12. Storm, Brad, LB, Iowa State, 288
13. Roman, John, G, Idaho State, 313
14. Smith, Mike, C, SMU, 339
15. Goodie, John, RB, Langston, 365
16. Malouf, Bill, QB, Mississippi, 392
Evavold, Mike, DT, Macalester, from San Francisco, 399
Smith, Robert, DB, Maryland, from Oakland, 419
17. McKnight, David, LB, Georgia, 416
Bengard, Mike, DE, Northwestern (Iowa), from San Francisco, 426
Russel, Frank, WR, Maryland, from Oakland, 440

BUFFALO
1. Ruud, Tom, LB, Nebraska, 19
2. Choice to Oakland
Nelson, Bob, LB, Nebraska, from Philadelphia, 42
Lott, Glenn, DB, Drake, from Oakland, 50
3. Choice to San Francisco
4. Choice to Cincinnati
Donchez, Tom, RB, Penn State, from Washington, 102
5. Choice to Atlanta
McCrumbly, John, LB, Texas A&M, from Houston through Oakland, 115
6. Choice to New Orleans
7. Chapman, Gil, RB, Michigan, from San Francisco, 166
Cherry, Reggie, RB, Houston, from Denver, 174
Banks, Harry, DB, Michigan, 175
8. Hill, John, DT, Duke, 201
9. Choice to Cincinnati
10. Hooks, Roland, RB, North Carolina State, 253
11. Drake, Tom, DB, Michigan, 279
12. Johnson, Mark, DE, Missouri, 305
13. Dienhart, Mark, T, St. Thomas (Minnesota), 331
14. Evans, Robert, WR, Morris Brown, 350
15. Kupec, Chris, QB, North Carolina, 383
16. Fine, Tom, TE, Notre Dame, 408
17. Turcotte, Jeff, DE, Colorado, 435

CHI. BEARS
1. Payton, Walter, RB, Jackson State, 4
2. Hartenstine, Mike, DE, Penn State, 31
3. Choice to Baltimore
4. Livers, Virgil, DB, Western Kentucky, 83
5. Choice to Washington
Sorey, Revie, G, Illinois, from New Orleans, 110
6. Avellini, Bob, QB, Maryland, 135
Hicks, Tom, LB, Illinois, from LA Rams through San Diego, 151
7. Choice to Baltimore
Douthitt, Earl, DB, Iowa, from Washington through St. Louis, 178
8. Choice to Baltimore through Denver
Harris, Joe, LB, Georgia Tech, from New England, 197
9. Stillwell, Roger, DT, Stanford, 212
10. Choice to Miami
Julius, Mike, G, St. Thomas (Minnesota), from LA Rams, 254
11. Dean, Mike, K, Texas, 264
12. Plank, Doug, DB, Ohio State, 291
13. McDaniel, Charles, RB, Louisiana Tech, 316
14. Hartfield, Walter, RB, Southwest Texas State, 342
15. Marcantonio, Steve, WR, Miami, 368
16. Beckman, Witt, WR, Miami, 395
17. Harper, Roland, RB, Louisiana Tech, 420

CINCINNATI
1. Cameron, Glenn, LB, Florida, 14
2. Krevis, Al, T, Boston College, 39
3. Burley, Gary, DE, Pittsburgh, from Atlanta, 55
Sheide, Gary, QB, BYU, 64
Harris, Bo, LB, LSU, from Minnesota, 77
4. Choice to Minnesota
Fritts, Stan, RB, North Carolina State, from Buffalo, 97
5. McInally, Pat, WR, Harvard, 120
West, Jeff, TE-P, Cincinnati, from Dallas, 122
6. Shuman, Tom, QB, Penn State, from Philadelphia, 142
Smith, Rollen, DB, Arkansas, 145
7. Devlin, Chris, LB, Penn State, 170
8. Davis, Ricky, DB, Alabama, 195
9. Dubinetz, Greg, G-C, Yale, 220
Williams, Lofell, WR, Virginia Union, from Buffalo, 227
10. Felker, Rocky, DB, Mississippi State, 245
11. Cobb, Marvin, DB, USC, 276
12. Novak, Jack, TE, Wisconsin, 301
13. Rosenberg, Ron, LB, Montana, 326
14. Haywood, Frank, DT, North Carolina State, 351
15. Enright, Greg, K, Southern Oregon, 376
16. Tuttle, John, WR, Kansas State, 401
17. Charity, Elvin, DB, Yale, 432

CLEVELAND
1. Mitchell, Mack, DE, Houston, 5
2. Choice to San Diego
3. Roan, Oscar, WR, SMU, 57
4. Peters, Tony, DB, Oklahoma, 82
5. Zimba, John, DE, Villanova, 109
Cope, Jim, LB, Ohio State, from Detroit, 119
6. Choice to San Diego
Miller, Charles, DB, West Virginia, from Washington, 150
Hynoski, Henry, RB, Temple, from Oakland, 154
7. Wang, Merle, T, TCU, 161
8. Santini, Barry, TE, Purdue, 186
9. Poole, Larry, RB, Kent State, 213
Hogan, Floyd, DB, Arkansas, from Kansas City, 215
10. Lewis, Stan, DE, Wayne, 238
11. Marinelli, Tom, G, Boston College, 265
12. Ambrose, Dick, LB, Virginia, 290
13. Armstead, Willie, WR, Utah, 317
14. Barrett, Tim, RB, John Carroll, 341
15. Moore, Willie, DT, Johnson C. Smith, 369
16. McKay, John (J.K.), WR, USC, 394
17. Graf, Dave, LB, Penn State, 421

DALLAS
1. White, Randy, LB, Maryland, from NY Giants, 2
Henderson, Thomas, LB, Langston, 18
2. Lawless, Burton, G, Florida, 44
3. Breunig, Bob, LB, Arizona State, 70
4. Donovan, Pat, DE, Stanford, from Houston, 90
Hughes, Randy, DB, Oklahoma, 96
5. Davis, Kyle, C, Oklahoma, from Green Bay, 113
Choice to Cincinnati
6. Woolsey, Rolly, DB, Boise State, 148
7. Hegman, Mike, LB, Tennessee State, 173
8. Hoopes, Mitch, P, Arizona, 200
9. Jones, Ed, DB, Rutgers, 226
10. Booker, Dennis, RB, Millersville, 252
11. Krpalek, Greg, C, Oregon State, 278
12. Bland, Chuck, DB, Cincinnati, 304
13. Scott, Herbert, G, Virginia Union, 330
14. Laidlaw, Scott, RB, Stanford, 356
15. Hamilton, Willie, RB, Arizona, 382
16. Clark, Pete, TE, Colorado State, 407
17. Testerman, Jim, TE, Dayton, 434

DENVER
1. Wright, Louis, DB, San Jose State, 17
2. Smith, Charles, DE, North Carolina Central, 43
3. Franckowiak, Mike, QB, Central Michigan, from NY Giants, 54
Mahalic, Drew, LB, Notre Dame, 69
4. Taylor, Steve, DB, Georgia, from Kansas City, 84
Upchurch, Rich, WR, Minnesota, 95
5. Rogers, Stan, T, Maryland, from Atlanta, 107
Carter, Rubin, DT, Miami, 121
6. Choice to Washington
7. Choice to Buffalo
8. Foley, Steve, QB, Tulane, 199
9. Williams, Roussell, DB, Arizona, 225
10. Engelhardt, Hank, C, Pacific, from Kansas City, 240
Haggerty, Steve, WR, Nevada-Las Vegas, 251
11. Choice to Washington
12. Walters, Harry, LB, Maryland, 303
13. Penick, Eric, RB, Notre Dame, 329
14. Arnold, Jerry, G, Oklahoma, 355
15. Shelton, Ken, TE, Virginia, 381
16. Bridges, Bubba, DT, Colorado, 409
17. Sherman, Lester, RB, Albany State, 433

DETROIT
1. Boden, Lynn, G, South Dakota State, 13
2. English, Doug, DT, Texas, 38
3. Choice to New Orleans through Minnesota
4. Hertwig, Craig, T, Georgia, 94
5. Choice to Cleveland
6. Cooper, Fred, DB, Purdue, from New Orleans, 138
King, Horace, RB, Georgia, from New England, 141
Franklin, Dennis, QB-WR, Michigan, 144
7. Murphy, Mike, WR, Drake, 169
8. Thompson, Leonard, RB, Oklahoma State, 194
9. Strinko, Steve, LB, Michigan, 219
10. Boyd, Brad, TE, LSU, 250
11. Myers, Steve, G, Ohio State, 275
12. Roundtree, Andre, LB, Iowa State, 300
13. Smith, Jim, RB, North Carolina Central, 325
14. McMillan, Jim, QB, Boise State, 350
15. Green, Rudy, RB, Yale, 375
16. Chaves, Les, DB, Kansas State, 406
17. Lancaster, Mark, G, Tulsa, 431

GREEN BAY
1. Choice to LA Rams
2. Choice to Miami
Bain, Bill, G, USC, from Washington, 47
3. Choice to LA Rams
Harrell, Willard, RB, Pacific, from San Diego, 58
4. Luke, Steve, DB, Ohio State, 88
5. Choice to Dallas
6. Choice to LA Rams
7. Giaquinto, Tony, WR, Central Connecticut State, 165
8. Choice to Baltimore
9. Hodgin, Jay Lynn, RB, South Carolina, 217
10. Cooke, William, DE, Massachusetts, 244
11. Martin, Bob, DE, Washington, 269
12. Brown, Carlos, QB, Pacific, 296
13. Fuhriman, Bob, DB, Utah State, 321
14. Blackmon, Stan, TE, North Texas State, 348
15. Allen, Randy, WR, Southern, 373
16. McCaffrey, Bob, C, USC, 400
17. Ray, Tom, DB, Central Michigan, 425

HOUSTON
1. Brazile, Robert, LB, Jackson State, from Kansas City, 6
Hardeman, Don, RB, Texas A&I, 15
2. Edwards, Emmett, WR, Kansas, 40
3. Choice to Atlanta
4. Choice to Dallas
5. Choice to Buffalo through Oakland
6. O'Neal, Jesse, DE, Grambling, 146
7. Biehle, Mike, T, Miami (Ohio), from Kansas City, 162
Cotney, Mark, DB, Cameron, 171
8. Lawrence, Jerry, DT, South Dakota State, 196
9. Bruer, Bob, TE, Mankato State, 221
10. Pringle, Alan, K, Rice, 246
11. Sawyer, John, TE, Southern Mississippi, 271
12. Miller, Willie, WR, Colorado State, 302
13. Scales, Ricky, WR, Virginia Tech, 327
14. Medford, Jody, G, Rice, 352
15. Holmes, Jack, RB, Texas Southern, 377
16. Lambert, Ken, DB, Virginia Tech, 402
17. Seeker, Ricky, C, Texas A&M, 427

KANSAS CITY
1. Choice to Houston
2. Stephens, Elmore, TE, Kentucky, 34
3. Walker, Cornelius, DT, Rice, 59
4. Choice to Denver
5. Choice to LA Rams
6. LaGrand, Morris, RB, Tampa, 137
Wasick, Dave, LB, San Jose State, from San Francisco, 139
7. Choice to Houston
8. Choice to Pittsburgh
Hoffman, Wayne, TE, Oklahoma, from San Diego through Washington, 189
9. Choice to Cleveland
10. Choice to Denver
11. Hegland, Dale, G, Minnesota, 268
12. Rackley, James, RB, Florida A&M, 293
13. Snider, John, LB, Stanford, 318
14. Moshier, Gene, G, Vanderbilt, 346
15. Choice to Pittsburgh
16. Peterson, Mark, DE, Illinois, 396
17. Bulino, Mike, DB, Pittsburgh, 424

LA RAMS
1. Fanning, Mike, DT, Notre Dame, from Green Bay, 9
Harrah, Dennis, T, Miami, from Philadelphia, 11
France, Doug, T, Ohio State, 20
2. Jackson, Monte, DB, San Diego State, from Baltimore through Green Bay, 28
Jones, Leroy, DE, Norfolk State, 48
3. Choice to San Diego through Chi. Bears
Reece, Geoff, C, Washington State, from Green Bay, 61
Nugent, Dan, TE, Auburn, from Philadelphia, 67
4. Perry, Rod, DB, Colorado, 98
5. Hammond, Wayne, DT, Montana State, from Kansas City, 112
Nuzum, Rick, C, Kentucky, 126
6. Choice to Chi. Bears through San Diego
McCarthy, Darius, WR, South Carolina State, from Green Bay, 140
7. Haden, Pat, QB, USC, 176
8. Washington, John, DB, Tulane, 204
9. Riegel, Gordy, LB, Stanford, 229
10. Choice to Chi. Bears
11. Strickland, Howard, RB, California, 281
12. Williams, Chandler, WR, Lincoln (Missouri), 307
13. Jacobs, A.J., DB, Louisville, 332
14. Allen, Arthur, WR, Clark, 360
15. White, Alvin, QB, Oregon State, 385
16. Reynolds, Francis, RB, Alcorn State, 410
17. Boyd, Skip, P, Washington, 438

MIAMI
1. Carlton, Darryl, T, Tampa, 23
2. Solomon, Freddie, QB, Tampa, from Green Bay, 36
Winfrey, Stan, RB, Arkansas State, 49
3. Hill, Gerald, LB, Houston, 75
4. Elia, Bruce, LB, Ohio State, 100
5. Owens, Morris, WR, Arizona State, from NY Giants, 106
Hill, Barry, DB, Iowa State, 127
6. Choice to NY Jets
Towle, Steve, LB, Kansas, from NY Jets, 143
7. Kent, Phillip, RB, Baylor, 179
8. Crawford, Barney, DT, Harding, 205
9. Wilson, James, G, Clark, 231
10. Russell, Clyde, RB, Oklahoma, from Chi. Bears, 239
Jackson, Joe, TE, Penn State, from Washington, 256
Danelo, Joe, K, Washington State, 257
11. Dilworth, John, DB, Northwestern State (Louisiana), 283
12. Yancey, Joe, T, Henderson State, 309
13. Isabell, Leonard, WR, Tulsa, 334
14. Lewis, James, DB, Tennessee State, from NY Giants, 338
Graham, John, QB, Colorado State, 361
15. Johns, Skip, RB, Carson-Newman, 387
16. Smith, Vernon, C, Georgia, 413
17. Copeland, Dwaine, RB, Middle Tennessee State, 439

MINNESOTA
1. Mullaney, Mark, DE, Colorado State, 25
2. Riley, Art, DT, USC, 52
3. Choice to Cincinnati
4. Henson, Harold (Champ), RB, Ohio State, from Cincinnati, 89
Adams, Bruce, WR, Kansas, 103
5. Miller, Robert, RB, Kansas, 129
6. Broussard, Bubba, LB, Houston, 155
7. Greene, Henry, RB, Southern, 181
8. Hollimon, Joe, DB, Arkansas State, 207
9. Passananti, John, G, Western Illinois, 233
10. Clabo, Neil, P, Tennessee, 258
11. Spencer, Ike, RB, Utah, 285
12. Beamon, Autry, DB, East Texas State, 311
13. Hurd, Mike, WR, Michigan State, 336
14. Strickland, Mike, RB, Eastern Michigan, 363
15. Bakken, Ollie, LB, Minnesota, 388
16. Goedjen, Tom, K, Iowa State, 414
17. Bellizeare, Adolph, RB, Pennsylvania, 441

NEW ENGLAND
1. Francis, Russ, TE, Oregon, 16
2. Shoate, Rod, LB, Oklahoma, 41
3. Cusick, Pete, DT, Ohio State, 66
4. Carter, Allen, RB, USC, from San Diego through Cleveland, 86
Burks, Steve, WR, Arkansas State, 91
5. Grogan, Steve, QB, Kansas State, 116

Freeman, Steve, DB, Mississippi State, from Philadelphia, 117
6. Choice to Detroit
7. Williams, Lawrence, WR, Texas Tech, 172
8. Choice to Chi. Bears
9. Choice to Pittsburgh
10. Choice to Pittsburgh
11. Garnett, Rene, DB, Idaho State, 272
12. Kendon, Matt, DT, Idaho State, 297
Holloway, Condredge, QB-DB, Tennessee, from Washington, 306
13. Harvey, Joe, DE, Northern Michigan, 328
14. Gossom, Tom, WR, Auburn, 353
15. Clayton, Don, RB, Murray State, 378
16. Marbury, Kerry, RB, West Virginia, 403
17. Horton, Myke, T, UCLA, 428

NEW ORLEANS
1. Burton, Larry, WR, Purdue, 7
Schumacher, Kurt, T, Ohio State, from NY Jets, 12
2. Gross, Lee, C, Auburn, 32
3. Jones, Andrew, RB, Washington State, 60
Grooms, Elois, DE, Tennessee Tech, from Detroit through Minnesota, 63
4. Choice to San Francisco
Starkebaum, John, DB, Nebraska, from Philadelphia, 92
Hall, Charlie, DE, Tulane, from St. Louis, 99
5. Choice to Chi. Bears
6. Choice to Detroit
Lemon, Mike, LB, Kansas, from Buffalo, 149
7. Rogers, Steve, RB, LSU, 163
8. Choice to St. Louis
9. Strachan, Mike, RB, Iowa State, 216
10. Heater, Chuck, RB, Michigan, 241
11. Lee, Danny, P, Northeast Louisiana, 266
12. Gustafson, Ron, WR, North Dakota, 294
13. Upchurch, Jim, RB, Arizona, 319
14. Rhino, Randy, DB, Georgia Tech, 343
15. Burget, Grant, RB, Oklahoma, 372
16. McDonald, Mike, LB, Catawba, 397
17. Westbrooks, Greg, LB, Colorado, 422

NY GIANTS
1. Choice to Dallas
2. Simpson, Al, T, Colorado State, 27
3. Choice to Denver
Buggs, Danny, WR, West Virginia, from San Francisco, 62
4. Giblin, Robert, DB, Houston, 79
5. Choice to Miami
6. Choice to Baltimore
7. Obradovich, Jim, TE, USC, 158
8. Tate, John, LB, Jackson State, 183
9. Mahoney, Mike, WR, Richmond, 210
10. McClowry, Terry, LB, Michigan State, 235
11. Martin, George, DE, Oregon, 262
12. White, Marsh, RB, Arkansas, 287
13. Townsend, Ricky, K, Tennessee, 314
14. Choice to Miami
15. O'Connor, Jim, RB, Drake, 366
16. Micklos, Jim, TE, Ball State, 391
17. Colbert, Rondy, DB, Lamar, 417

NY JETS
1. Choice to New Orleans
2. Davis, Anthony, RB, USC, 37
3. Wood, Richard, LB, USC, 68
4. Choice to Baltimore
5. Wysocki, Joe, G, Miami, 118
6. Choice to Miami
Alward, Tom, G, Nebraska, from Miami, 153
7. Choice to Baltimore through Chi. Bears
8. Scott, James, WR, Henderson J.C., 193
9. Taylor, Everett, DB, Memphis State, 224
10. James, Charles, DB, Jackson State, 249
11. Bradford, Jon, RB, Central State (Ohio), 274
12. Cooper, Bert, LB, Florida State, 299
13. Spivey, Dan, DT, Georgia, 324
14. Fields, Joe, C, Widener, 349
15. Manor, Brison, DT, Arkansas, 380
16. Wells, Greg, G, Albany State, 405
17. Bartoszek, Mike, TE, Ohio State, 430

OAKLAND
1. Colzie, Neal, DB, Ohio State, 24
2. Phillips, Charles, DB, USC, from Buffalo, 45
Choice to Buffalo
3. Carter, Louis, RB, Maryland, 76
4. Choice to San Diego
5. Humm, David, QB, Nebraska, 128
6. Choice to Cleveland
7. Daniels, James, DB, Texas A&M, 180
8. Choice to San Diego
9. Knight, Harry, QB, Richmond, 232
10. Sylvester, Steve, T, Notre Dame, 259
11. Choice to San Diego
12. Magee, Jack, C, Boston College, 310
13. Choice to San Diego
14. Doyle, Tom, QB, Yale, 362
15. Careathers, Paul, RB, Tennessee, 389
16. Choice to Baltimore
17. Choice to Baltimore

PHILADELPHIA
1. Choice to LA Rams
2. Choice to Buffalo
3. Choice to LA Rams
4. Choice to New Orleans
5. Choice to New England
6. Choice to Cincinnati
7. Capraun, Bill, T, Miami, 167
8. Bleamer, Jeff, T, Penn State, 198
9. Choice to San Francisco
10. Schroy, Ken, DB, Maryland, 248
11. Rowen, Keith, G, Stanford, 273
12. Pawlewicz, Dick, RB, William & Mary, 298
13. Ehlers, Tom, LB, Kentucky, 324
14. O'Rourke, Larry, DT, Ohio State, 355
15. Korver, Clayton, DE, Northwestern (Iowa), 379*
16. Jones, Calvin, WR, Texas Tech, 404
17. Webb, Gary, DE, Temple, 429

PITTSBURGH
1. Brown, Dave, DB, Michigan, 26
2. Barber, Bob, DE, Grambling, 51
3. White, Walter, TE, Maryland, 78
4. Evans, Harold, LB, Houston, 104
5. Sexton, Brent, DB, Elon, 130
6. Crenshaw, Marvin, T, Nebraska, 156
7. Mattingly, Wayne, T, Colorado, 185
8. Kropp, Tom, LB, Kearney State, from Kansas City, 190
Humphrey, Al, DE, Tulsa, 208
9. Clark, Eugene, G, UCLA, from New England, 222
Reimer, Bruce, RB, North Dakota State, 234
10. Heyer, Kirt, DT, Kearney State, from New England, 247
Gray, Archie, WR, Wyoming, 260
11. Little, Randy, TE, West Liberty, 286
12. Murphy, Greg, DE, Penn State, 312
13. Gaddis, Bob, WR, Mississippi Valley State, 337
14. Collier, Mike, RB, Morgan State, 364
15. Thatcher, James, WR, Langston, from Kansas City, 371
Smith, Marty, DT, Louisville, 390
16. Bassler, Miller, TE, Houston, 415
17. Hegener, Stan, G, Nebraska, 442

ST. LOUIS
1. Gray, Tim, DB, Texas A&M, 21
2. Germany, Jim, RB, New Mexico State, 46
3. Choice to San Francisco
4. Choice to New Orleans
5. Goodman, Harvey, T, Colorado, 124
6. Jameson, Larry, DT, Indiana, 152
7. Beaird, Steve, RB, Baylor, 177
8. Adams, John, DT, West Virginia, from New Orleans, 188
Lauriano, Louis, DB, Long Beach State, 202
9. Choice to San Francisco
10. McGraw, Mike, LB, Wyoming, 255
11. Latin, Jerry, RB, Northern Illinois, 280
12. Jones, Ben, WR, LSU, 308
13. Lindgren, Steve, DE, Hamline, 333
14. Bahe, Ritch, WR, Nebraska, 358
15. Franklin, Ron, DT, Boise State, 386
16. Miller, Mark, WR, Missouri, 411
17. Monroe, Ken, RB, Indiana State, 436

SAN DIEGO
1. Johnson, Gary, DT, Grambling, 8
Williams, Mike, DB, LSU, from Washington, 22
2. Kelcher, Louie, DT, SMU, from Cleveland, 30
Dean, Fred, LB, Louisiana Tech, 33
3. Choice to Green Bay
Fuller, Mike, DB, Auburn, from LA Rams through Chi. Bears, 73
4. Choice to New England through Cleveland
Bernich, Ken, LB, Auburn, from Oakland, 101
5. Nosbusch, Kevin, DT, Notre Dame, 111
Waddell, Charles, TE, North Carolina, from Washington through LA Rams and Buffalo, 125
6. Carroll, John, WR, Oklahoma, from Cleveland, 134
Shields, Billy, T, Georgia Tech, 136
7. Young, Rickey, RB, Jackson State, 164
8. Choice to Kansas City through Washington
Collier, Barry, T, Georgia, from Washington, 203
Peretta, Ralph, G, Purdue, from Oakland, 206
9. Keller, Larry, LB, Houston, 214
10. Bradley, Otha, DT, USC, 242
11. Phason, Vince, DB, Arizona, 267
McBee, Ike, WR, San Jose State, from Oakland, 284
12. Dahl, Jerry, LB, North Dakota State, 292
13. Demmerle, Pete, WR, Notre Dame, 320
Printers, Glen, RB, South Colorado State, from Oakland, 335
14. Barnett, Reggie, DB, Notre Dame, 345
15. Roush, John, G, Oklahoma, 370
16. Salvestrini, Chip, G, Yankton, 398
17. Jeffrey, Neal, QB, Baylor, 423

SAN FRANCISCO
1. Webb, Jimmy, DT, Mississippi State, 10
2. Collins, Greg, LB, Notre Dame, 35
3. Choice to NY Giants
Hart, Jeff, T, Oregon State, from Buffalo, 71
Mike-Mayer, Steve, K, Maryland, from Washington, 72
Baker, Wayne, DT, BYU, from New Orleans, 74
4. Elam, Cleveland, DE, Tennessee State, from New Orleans, 85
Oliver, Frank, DB, Kentucky State, 87
5. Bullock, Wayne, RB, Notre Dame, 114
6. Choice to Kansas City
7. Choice to Buffalo
8. Kendrick, Preston, LB, Florida, 191
9. Johnson, James, DB, Tennessee State, 218
Natale, Dan, TE, Penn State, from Philadelphia, 223
Douglas, Caesar, T, Illinois Weslyan, from St. Louis, 230
10. Layton, Donnie, RB, South Carolina State, 243
11. Hernandez, Gene, DB, TCU, 270
12. Worley, Rick, QB, Howard Payne, 295
13. Mitchell, Dale, LB, USC, 322
14. Henson, David, WR, Abilene Christian, 347
15. Lavin, Rich, TE, Western Illinois, 374
16. Choice to Baltimore
17. Choice to Baltimore

WASHINGTON
1. Choice to San Diego
2. Choice to Green Bay
3. Choice to San Francisco
4. Choice to Buffalo
5. Choice to San Diego through LA Rams and Buffalo
Thomas, Mike, RB, Nevada-Las Vegas, from Chi. Bears, 108
6. Choice to Cleveland
Doak, Mark, T, Nebraska, from Denver, 147
7. Choice to Chi. Bears through St. Louis
8. Choice to San Diego
9. Hickman, Dallas, DE, California, 228
10. Choice to Miami
11. Johnson, Ardell, DB, Nebraska, from Denver, 277
Hackenbruck, Jerry, DE, Oregon State, 282
12. Choice to New England
13. McKie, Morris, DB, North Carolina A&T, 344
14. Benson, Dave, LB, Weber State, 359
15. Kuehn, Art, C, UCLA, 384
16. Pavelka, Dennis, G, Nebraska, 412
17. Taylor, Carl, DE, Memphis State, 437

1976

Held April 8-9, 1976

There were 487 selections instead of 492. Five teams forfeited choices: the Chicago Bears and New York Giants each a sixth-round pick, Washington a seventh-round pick, and Atlanta and the New York Jets each a tenth-round pick.

The expansion Tampa Bay Buccaneers and Seattle Seahawks alternated making the first and second selections of each round. Each new team also received two choices at the end of the second, third, fourth, and fifth rounds.

On March 30-31, Tampa Bay and Seattle each selected 39 players in an expansion draft. Each of the other 26 teams froze 29 players from its roster. Tampa Bay and Seattle alternated making selections from the remaining pool of players. When the first player was chosen from each team, that team then froze two additional players. Tampa Bay and Seattle continued making their selections until three players had been chosen from each existing team.

ATLANTA
1. Bean, Bubba, RB, Texas A&M, 9
2. Collins, Sonny, RB, Kentucky, 36
3. Scott, Dave, T, Kansas, 71
4. Brett, Walt, G-T, Montana, 102
5. Choice to Minnesota
Choice to Buffalo
6. Varner, Stan, DT-DE, BYU, from Denver, 169
7. Farmer, Karl, WR, Pittsburgh, 193
8. Reed, Frank, DB, Washington, 219
9. McKinnely, Phil, T, UCLA, 246
10. Choice forfeited
11. Brislin, Chuck, T, Mississippi State, 302
12. Bolton, Pat, K, Montana State, 329
13. Williams, Mike, T, Florida, 356
14. Husfloen, Mark, DE, Washington State, 383
15. Olson, Ron, DB, Washington, 414
16. Curto, Pat, LB, Ohio State, 441
17. Green, Tony, DB, Texas Tech, 468

BALTIMORE
1. Novak, Ken, DT, Purdue, 20
2. Choice to Pittsburgh
3. Simonini, Ed, LB, Texas A&M, 81
Lee, Ron, RB, West Virginia, from Tampa Bay, 90
4. Choice to Pittsburgh
5. Shiver, Sanders, LB, Carson-Newman, from Chi. Bears through Miami and Chi. Bears, 134
Kirkland, Mike, QB, Arkansas, 143
6. Choice to Buffalo
7. Choice to New Orleans through Chi. Bears and Oakland
8. Thompson, Rick, WR, Baylor, 228
9. Levenick, Stu, T, Illinois, 258
10. Baylor, Tim, DB, Morgan State, 283
11. Gibney, Rick, DT, Georgia Tech, 310
12. Stavroff, Frank, K, Indiana, 339
13. Choice to Oakland
14. Cummings, Jeremiah, DE, Albany State, 394
15. Alexander, Gary, T, Clemson, 424
16. Fuhrman, Mike, TE, Memphis State, from Washington through Baltimore and San Francisco, 449
Ludwig, Steve, C, Miami, 451
17. Choice to Oakland

BUFFALO
1. Clark, Mario, DB, Oregon, 18
2. Jones, Ken, G, Arkansas State, 45
Devlin, Joe, T, Iowa, from St. Louis, 52
3. Williams, Ben, DT, Mississippi, 78
4. Jilek, Dan, LB, Michigan, 78
5. Coleman, Fred, TE, Northeast Louisiana, 142
6. Benson, Leslie, DE, Baylor, from Atlanta, 164
Piper, Scott, WR, Arizona, 171
Powell, Darnell, RB, Tennessee-Chattanooga, from Baltimore, 175
7. Williams, Jackie, DB, Texas A&M, from NY Giants, 195
Choice to NY Jets
8. Gardner, Scott, QB, Virginia, from Cleveland, 215
Easter, Bobby Joe, RB, Middle Tennessee State, 226
Meadowcroft, Art, G, Minnesota, from Washington through Atlanta, 227
9. Turner, Jeff, LB, Kansas, from San Diego, 241
Kotzur, Bob, DT, Southwest Texas State, 255

10. Moody, Keith, DB, Syracuse, 280
11. Smith, Forry, WR, Iowa State, 309
12. Lowery, Joe, RB, Jackson State, 336
13. Wilcox, Will, G, Texas, 365
14. Williams, Tony, WR, Middle Tennessee State, 392
15. Robinson, Arnold, LB, Bethune-Cookman, 421
16. Gorrell, Gary, LB, Boise State, 448
17. Berg, Bob, K, New Mexico, 477

CHI. BEARS
1. Lick, Dennis, T, Wisconsin, from Green Bay through LA Rams and Detroit, 8
Choice to Detroit
2. Choice to Pittsburgh
3. Baschnagel, Brian, RB-WR, Ohio State, from New England, 66
Choice to Detroit
4. Sciarra, John, DB, UCLA, 103
Rhodes, Wayne, DB, Alabama, from Detroit through Miami, 108
5. Choice to Baltimore through Miami and Chi. Bears
6. Jiggetts, Dan, T, Harvard, from Cleveland, 161
Choice forfeited
7. Muckensturm, Jerry, LB, Arkansas State, 190
8. Choice to Oakland through San Diego
9. Choice to Philadelphia
10. Choice to Washington
11. Andersen, Norm, WR, UCLA, 299
12. O'Leary, John, RB, Nebraska, 330
13. Kasowski, Dale, RB, North Dakota, 357
14. Cuie, Ron, RB, Oregon State, 384
15. Meyers, Jerry, DT, Northern Illinois, 411
16. Parker, Ronald, TE, TCU, 442
17. Malham, Mike, LB, Arkansas State, 469

CINCINNATI
1. Brooks, Billy, WR, Oklahoma, from Philadelphia, 11
Griffin, Archie, RB, Ohio State, 24
2. Bujnoch, Glenn, Texas A&M, from Philadelphia, 38
Bahr, Chris, K, Penn State, 51
3. Reece, Danny, DB, USC, from Philadelphia, 69
Williams, Reggie, LB, Dartmouth, 82
4. Davis, Tony, RB, Nebraska, from Kansas City, 106
Fairchild, Greg, G, Tulsa, 116
5. Shelby, Willie, DB, Alabama, from San Francisco, 138
Perry, Scott, DB, Williams, 147
6. Nelson, Orlando, TE, Utah State, 176
7. Bateman, Bob, QB, Brown, from New England, 187
Rome, Pete, DB, Miami (Ohio), from Green Bay, 192
Kuhn, Ken, LB, Ohio State, 205
8. Hunt, Ron, T, Oregon, 232
9. Allgood, Lonnie, WR, Syracuse, 259
10. Klaban, Tom, K, Ohio State, 287
11. Morgan, Melvin, Mississippi Valley State, 314
12. Harris, Joe Dale, WR, Alabama, 340
13. Walker, Randy, RB, Miami (Ohio), 371
14. Coleman, Greg, P, Florida A&M, 398
15. Hieber, Lynn, QB, Indiana (Pennsylvania), 425
16. Demopoulos, George, C, Miami, 455
17. Dannelley, Scott, G, Ohio State, 482

CLEVELAND
1. Pruitt, Mike, RB, Purdue, 7
2. Choice to Oakland
3. Logan, Dave, WR-TE, Colorado, 65
4. Swick, Gene, QB, Toledo, from New England through Philadelphia, 97
St. Clair, Mike, DE, Grambling, 99
5. Sheppard, Henry, T, SMU, 130
6. Choice to Chi. Bears
7. Cassidy, Steve, DT, LSU, 189
8. Choice to Buffalo
9. Reed, James, RB, Mississippi, 242
Nagel, Craig, QB, Purdue, from Oakland, 261
10. Kleber, Doug, T, Illinois, 271
11. Celek, Doug, DE, Kent State, 297
12. Choice to Houston
13. Murray, Brian, T, Arizona, 354
14. Smalzer, Joe, TE, Illinois, 381
15. Philyaw, Luther, DB, Loyola (Los Angeles), 408
16. Lorenzen, Chris, DT, Arizona State, 438
17. Fleming, Tom, WR, Dartmouth, 464

DALLAS
1. Kyle, Aaron, DB, Wyoming, 27
2. Jensen, Jim, RB, Iowa, from NY Giants, 40
Eidson, Jim, G, Mississippi State, 55
3. Fergerson, Duke, WR, San Diego State, from San Francisco, 73
Smith, John, RB, Boise State, from Denver, 75
Johnson, Butch, WR, Cal-Riverside, 87
4. Rafferty, Tom, G, Penn State, 119
5. Pesuit, Wally, T, Kentucky, 151
6. McGuire, Greg, T, Indiana, 181
7. Schaum, Greg, DT, Michigan State, from San Diego, 186
Williams, Dave, RB, Colorado, 208
8. Laws, Henry, DB, South Carolina, 236
9. Reece, Beasley, DB, North Texas State, 264
10. Cook, Leroy, DE, Alabama, 290
11. Greene, Cornelius, QB, Ohio State, 317
12. McShane, Charles, LB, California Lutheran, 346
13. Driscoll, Mark, QB, Colorado State, 374
14. Mushinskie, Larry, TE, Nebraska, 402
15. Curry, Dale, LB, UCLA, 430
16. Costanzo, Rick, T, Nebraska, 458
17. Woodfill, Stan, K, Oregon, 486

DENVER
1. Glassic, Tom, G, Virginia, 15
2. Knoff, Kurt, DB, Kansas, 43
3. Choice to Dallas
4. Penrose, Craig, QB, San Diego State, 107
5. Perrin, Lonnie, RB, Illinois, 139
6. Choice to Atlanta
7. Choice to Houston
8. Betterson, James, RB, North Carolina, 224
9. Czirr, Jim, C, Michigan, 252
Lisko, Jim, LB, Arkansas State, from St. Louis, 260
10. Gilliam, Art, DE, Grambling, 278
11. Pittman, Greg, LB, Iowa State, 306
12. Moore, Randy, DT, Arizona State, 334
13. McGraw, Donnie, RB, Houston, 362
14. Evans, Larry, LB, Mississippi College, 390
15. Summers, Wilbur, P, Louisville, 418
16. Huddleston, John, LB, Utah, 446
17. Cozens, Randy, DE, Pittsburgh, 474

DETROIT
1. Hunter, James, DB, Grambling, from Chi. Bears, 10
Gaines, Lawrence, RB, Wyoming, 16
2. Long, Ken, G, Purdue, 44
Hill, David, TE, Texas A&I, from Washington through San Diego, 46
3. Bolinger, Russ, T, Long Beach State, from Chi. Bears, 68
Woodcock, John, DT, Hawaii, 76
4. Choice to Chi. Bears through Miami
5. Choice to San Francisco
Scavella, Steadman, LB, Miami, from Miami, 145
Choice to New England
7. Ten Napel, Garth, LB, Texas A&M, 198
8. Sorenson, Rich, K, Cal State-Chico, from Philadelphia through New England, 217
Braswell, Charles, DB, West Virginia, 225
9. Jones, Leanell, TE, Long Beach State, 253
10. Bowerman, Bill, QB, New Mexico State, 279
11. Shugrue, Gary, DE-LB, Villanova, 307
12. McCabe, Mike, C, South Carolina, 335
13. Jacobs, Mel, WR-KR, San Diego State, 363
14. Elston, Leonard, WR, Kentucky State, 391
15. Smock, Trent, WR, Indiana, 419
16. McCurdy, Craig, LB, William & Mary, 447
17. Meeks, Jim, DB, Boise State, 475

GREEN BAY
1. Choice to Chi. Bears through LA Rams and Detroit
Koncar, Mark, T, Colorado, from Oakland, 23
2. Choice to LA Rams
3. Choice to Pittsburgh
McCoy, Mike, DB, Colorado, from Kansas City, 72
4. Perko, Tom, LB, Pittsburgh, 101
5. Thompson, Aundra, RB, East Texas State, 132
6. Choice to Kansas City through Houston
7. Choice to Cincinnati
8. Burrow, Jim, DB, Nebraska, 218
9. Gueno, Jim, LB, Tulane, 245
10. Green, Jessie, WR, Tulsa, 274
11. Leak, Curtis, WR, Johnson C. Smith, 301
12. Jackson, Mel, G, USC, 328
13. Bowman, Bradley, DB, Southern Mississippi, 355
14. Henson, John, RB, Cal Poly-SLO, 386
15. Dandridge, Jerry, LB, Memphis State, 413
16. Timmermans, Mike, G, Northern Iowa, 440
17. Hall, Ray, TE, Cal Poly-SLO, 467

HOUSTON
1. Choice to New England through San Francisco
2. Barber, Mike, TE, Louisiana Tech, 48
3. Choice to Kansas City
4. Choice to San Diego through Oakland
Largent, Steve, WR, Tulsa, from LA Rams through Philadelphia and Green Bay, 117
5. Choice to Kansas City
6. Simonsen, Todd, T, South Dakota State, 173
7. Harris, Larry, DT, Oklahoma State, from Denver, 197
Choice to New England
8. Simon, Bobby, T, Grambling, 229
9. Stringer, Art, LB, Ball State, 256
10. Kincannon, Steve, QB, Cal State-Humboldt, 284
11. Walker, Skip, RB, Texas A&M, 311
12. Bell, Larry, DT, East Texas State, from Cleveland, 324
Choice to San Diego
13. O'Rourke, Dan, WR, Colorado, 368
14. Reimer, John, T, Wisconsin, 395
15. Byars, Bobby, DB, Cheyney, 422
16. Johnson, Claude, LB, Florida A&M, 452
17. Misher, Allen, WR, LSU, 479

KANSAS CITY
1. Walters, Rod, G, Iowa, 14
2. Frazier, Cliff, DT, UCLA, 41
3. Simons, Keith, DT, Minnesota, from New Orleans through San Francisco, 63
Choice to Green Bay
Barbaro, Gary, DB, Nicholls State, from NY Giants through Green Bay, 74
Marshall, Henry, WR, Missouri, from Houston, 79
4. Choice to Cincinnati
5. Lee, Willie, DT, Bethune-Cookman, 137
Elrod, Jimbo, LB, Oklahoma, from Houston, 144
6. Taylor, Steve, DB, Kansas, from Green Bay through Houston, 166
Gregolunas, Bob, LB, Northern Illinois, 167
Harper, Calvin, T, Illinois State, from Washington, 172
7. Wellington, Rod, RB, Iowa, 196
8. Olsen, Orrin, C, BYU, 222
9. Collier, Tim, East Texas State, 249
10. Paul, Whitney, DE, Colorado, 277
11. Squires, Bob, TE, Hastings, 304
12. Porter, Harold, WR, Southwestern Louisiana, 331
13. Bruner, Joe, QB, Northeast Louisiana, 361
14. Thurman, Rick, T, Texas, 388
15. Rozumek, Dave, LB, New Hampshire, 415
16. Anderson, Dennis, P-DB, Arizona, 445
17. McNeil, Pat, RB, Baylor, 472

LA RAMS
1. McLain, Kevin, LB, Colorado State, 26
2. Thomas, Pat, DB, Texas A&M, from Green Bay, 39
McCartney, Ron, LB, Tennessee, 53
3. Slater, Jackie, G, Jackson State, 86
4. Taylor, Gerald, WR, Texas A&I, from Tampa Bay, 96
Choice to Houston through Philadelphia and Green Bay
5. Ekern, Carl, LB, San Jose State, from San Diego, 128
Bordelon, Ken, DE, LSU, 149
Scales, Dwight, WR, Grambling, from Tampa Bay, 155
6. Choice to Washington
7. Buie, Larry, DB, Mississippi State, 207
8. Choice to Washington
9. Church, Jeb, DB, Stanford, 263
10. Johns, Freeman, WR, SMU, 288
11. Nemeth, Brian, TE, South Carolina, 316
12. Jodat, Jim, RB, Carthage, 344
13. Hamilton, Steve, QB, Emporia State, 373
14. Burleson, Al, DB, Washington, 400
15. Campbell, Malcolm, WR, Cal State-Los Angeles, 429
16. Gage, Rick, WR, Arkansas Tech, 456
17. Shaw, Gary, DB, BYU, 485

MIAMI
1. Gordon, Larry, LB, Arizona State, from Washington, 17
Bokamper, Kim, LB, San Jose State, 18
2. McCreary, Loaird, TE, Tennessee State, 49
3. Harris, Duriel, WR, New Mexico State, 80
4. Mitchell, Melvin, G, Tennessee State, from NY Jets through Chi. Bears, 98
Choice to Philadelphia
5. Choice to Detroit
6. Davis, Gary, RB, Cal Poly-SLO, 174
7. Ingersoll, Joe, G, Nevada-Las Vegas, from New Orleans, 185
Owens, John, DE, Tennessee State, 200
8. Simpson, Bob, T, Colorado, 230
9. Thomas, Norris, DB, Southern Mississippi, 257
10. Fencik, Gary, DB, Yale, from Washington, 281
Testerman, Don, RB, Clemson, 282
11. Pride, Dexter, RB, Minnesota, 312
12. Young, Randy, T, Iowa State, 338
Brandford, Darryl, DT, Northwestern, from St. Louis, 341
13. Head, Bernie, C, Tulsa, 366
14. Gissler, Bob, LB, South Dakota State, 396
15. Holmes, Ron, Utah State, 423
16. Green, Mike, K, Ohio U., 450
17. Grantz, Jeff, QB, South Carolina, 480

MINNESOTA
1. White, James (Duck), DT, Oklahoma State, 25
2. White, Sammy, WR, Grambling, 54
3. Hamilton, Wes, G, Tulsa, 85
4. Willis, Leonard, WR, Ohio State, 118
5. Wagner, Steve, DB, Wisconsin, from Atlanta, 133
Barnette, Keith, RB, Boston College, 150
6. Egerdahl, Terry, DB, Minnesota-Duluth, 180
7. Brune, Larry, DB, Rice, 206
8. Choice to New England
9. Hagins, Isaac, WR, Southern, 262
10. Salmon, Bill, QB, Northern Iowa, 289
11. Kracher, Steve, RB, Montana State, 318
12. Sparks, Robert, DB, Cal State-San Francisco, 345
13. Pauson, Gary, DE, Colorado State, 372
14. Stapleton, Jeff, T, Purdue, 401
15. Groce, Ron, RB, Macalester, 428
16. Hickel, Randy, DB, Montana State, 457
17. Lukowski, Rich, West Virginia, 484

NEW ENGLAND
1. Haynes, Mike, DB, Arizona State, 5
Brock, Pete, C, Colorado, from San Francisco, 12
Fox, Tim, DB, Ohio State, from Houston through San Francisco, 21
2. Forte, Ike, RB, Arkansas, 35
3. Choice to Chi. Bears
4. Choice to Cleveland through Philadelphia
5. Choice to San Diego
6. Choice to NY Giants
Boyd, Greg, DE, San Diego State, 170
7. Choice to Cincinnati
Brooks, Perry, DT, Southern, from Houston, 202
8. Choice to Philadelphia
Betts, Stu, RB, Northern Michigan, from Minnesota, 235
9. Beaudoin, Doug, DB, Minnesota, 243
10. Feacher, Ricky, WR, Mississippi Valley State, 270
11. Thomas, Donnie, LB, Indiana, 298
12. Bell, Nathaniel, DT, Tulane, 325
13. Jones, James, DB, Central Michigan, 352
14. Quehl, Dave, WR, Holy Cross, 382
15. Coleman, Bernard, WR, Bethune-Cookman, 409
16. Brown, Clifford, DT, Tuskegee, 436
17. Anderson, Todd, C, Stanford, 465

NEW ORLEANS
1. Muncie, Chuck, RB, California, 3

2. Galbreath, Tony, RB, Missouri, 32
3. Choice to Kansas City from San Francisco
Simmons, Bob, T, Texas, from Washington through San Diego, 77
4. Owens, Tinker, WR, Oklahoma, 95
5. Parrish, Scott, T, Utah State, 127
6. Stieve, Terry, G, Wisconsin, 160
7. Choice to Miami
Bauer, Ed, G, Notre Dame, from Baltimore through Chi. Bears and Oakland, 201
8. Cassady, Craig, DB, Ohio State, 213
9. Peiffer, Warren, DT, Iowa, 240
10. Hardin, Junior, LB, Eastern Kentucky, 269
11. Kokal, Greg, QB, Kent State, 294
12. Butts, Milton, T, North Carolina, 323
13. Downing, Kenny, DB, Missouri, 350
14. Hucke, Rich, DE, Western Montana, 379
15. Seminoff, Steve, DT, Wichita State, 406
16. Jones, Gene, T, Bowling Green, 435
17. MacDonald, Scott, TE, West Virginia, 462

NY GIANTS
1. Archer, Troy, DE, Colorado, 13
2. Choice to Dallas
3. Choice to Kansas City through Green Bay
4. Bell, Gordon, RB, Michigan, from San Francisco, 104
Carson, Harry, LB, South Carolina State, 105
5. Wilson, Melvin, DB, Cal State-Northridge, 136
6. Lloyd, Dan, LB, Washington, from New England, 162
Choice forfeited
7. Choice to Buffalo
8. Jordan, John, DT, Indiana, 221
9. Choice to San Diego
10. Thomas, John, RB, Valley City, 276
11. Brantley, Craig, WR, Clemson, 303
12. Golsteyn, Jerry, QB, Northern Illinois, 333
13. Caswell, Rick, KR, Western Kentucky, 360
14. Mullane, Jerry, LB, Lehigh, 387
15. Morgan, Eddie, DT, Arkansas State, 417
16. Lawson, Dave, K, Air Force, 444
17. Curnutte, Steve, DB, Vanderbilt, 471

NY JETS
1. Todd, Richard, QB, Alabama, 6
2. Suggs, Shafer, DB, Ball State, 33
3. Buttle, Greg, LB, Penn State,67
4. Choice to Miami through Chi. Bears
5. King, Steve, T, Michigan, 129
6. Martin, Bob, LB, Nebraska, 163
7. Faulk, Larry, (Abdul Salaam), DE, Kent State, 188
Richards, James, RB, Florida, from Buffalo,199
8. Davis, Joe, G, USC, from Tampa Bay, 211
Giammona, Louie, RB, Utah State, 214
9. Moore, Ronnie, WR, Virginia Military, 244
10. Choice forfeited
11. Pillers, Lawrence, LB, Alcorn State, 296
12. Buckey, Don, WR, North Carolina State, 326
Buckey, Dave, QB, North Carolina State, from Philadelphia, 327
13. Choice to Philadelphia
14. Gluchoski, Al, C, West Virginia, 380
15. Faulk, Rick, P, Cal State-San Francisco, 410
16. Godwin, James, RB, Fayetteville State, 437
17. Willie, Darwin, TE, Tulane, 466

OAKLAND
1. Choice to Green Bay
2. Philyaw, Charles, DT, Texas Southern, from Cleveland, 34
Blount, Jeb, QB, Tulsa, 50
3. Bonness, Rik, LB, Nebraska, 84
4. McMath, Herb, LB, Morningside, from Washington through San Diego, 110
Choice to San Diego
5. Steinfort, Fred, K, Boston College, 146
6. Choice to San Diego
7. Chapman, Clarence, WR, Eastern Michigan, 204
8. Dove, Jerome, DB, Colorado State, from Chi. Bears through San Diego, 220
Kunz, Terry, RB, Colorado, 231
9. Choice to Cleveland
10. Lewis, Dwight, DB, Purdue, 286
11. Jennings, Rick, RB, Maryland, 313
12. Brown, Cedric, DB, Kent State, 343
13. Crnick, Craig, DE, Idaho, from Baltimore, 367
Young, Mark, T, Washington State, 370
14. Young, Calvin, RB, Fresno State, 397
15. Hargrave, Carl, DB, Upper Iowa, 427
16. Hogan, Doug, DB, USC, 454
17. Tate, Buddy, DB, Tulsa, from Baltimore, 478
Beasley, Nate, RB, Delaware, 481

PHILADELPHIA
1. Choice to Cincinnati
2. Choice to Cincinnati
3. Choice to Cincinnati
4. Choice to San Francisco
Smith, Mike, DE, Florida, from Miami, 111
5. Johnson, Greg, DT, Florida State, 135
6. Johnson, Kirk, T, Howard Payne, 165
7. Hairston, Carl, DE, Maryland-Eastern Shore, 191
8. La Fargue, Richard, C, Arkansas, from New England, 216
Choice to Detroit through New England
9. Hogan, Mike, RB, Tennessee-Chattanooga, from Chi. Bears, 247
Osborne, Richard, TE, Texas A&M, 248
10. Lusk, Herb, RB, Long Beach State, 273
11. Gilbert, Mike, DT-DE, San Diego State, 300
12. Choice to NY Jets
13. Tautolo, Terry, LB, UCLA, from NY Jets, 353
Ebbecke, Steve, DB, Villanova, 358
14. Shy, Melvin, DB, Tennessee State, 385
15. White, Brett, P, UCLA, 412
16. Campassi, Steve, RB, Kentucky, 439
17. Terry, Anthony, DB, Cal-Davis, 470

PITTSBURGH
1. Cunningham, Bennie, TE, Clemson, 28
2. Pinney, Ray, C, Washington, from Chi. Bears, 37
Kruczek, Mike, QB, Boston College, from Baltimore, 47
Files, James, C, McNeese State, 56
3. Coder, Ron, DT, Penn State, from Green Bay, 70
Pough, Ernest, WR, Texas Southern, 88
4. Monds, Wonder, DB, Nebraska, from Baltimore, 112
Bell, Theo, WR, Arizona, 120
5. Norton, Rodney, LB, Rice, 152
6. Dunn, Gary, DT, Miami, from San Diego through St. Louis, 159
Deloplaine, Jack, RB, Salem, 182
7. Burton, Barry, TE, Vanderbilt, 209
8. McAleney, Ed, DT, Massachusetts, 237
9. Gaines, Wentford, DB, Cincinnati, 265
10. Campbell, Gary, LB, Colorado, 291
11. Fuchs, Rolland, RB, Arkansas, 319
12. Carroll, Bill, WR, East Texas State, 347
13. Kain, Larry, TE, Ohio State, 375
14. Fields, Wayne, DB, Florida, 403
15. Davis, Mel, DE, North Texas State, 431
16. Butts, Randy, RB, Kearney State, 459
17. Kirk, Kelvin, WR, Dayton, 487

ST. LOUIS
1. Dawson, Mike, DT, Arizona, 22
2. Choice to Buffalo
3. Oates, Brad, T, BYU, 82
4. Tilley, Pat, WR, Louisiana Tech, 114
5. Morris, Wayne, RB, SMU, from Washington, 141
Choice to Washington
6. Choice to San Francisco
7. Rogers, Phil, RB, Virginia Tech, 203
8. Burks, Randy, WR, Southeastern Oklahoma, 233
9. Choice to Denver
10. Walker, Randy, RB, Bethune-Cookman, 285
11. Akins, Marty, DB, Texas, 315
12. Choice to Miami
13. Brewton, Greg, DT, Michigan State, 369
14. Crosier, Raymond, DE, Abilene Christian, 399
15. Choice to Washington
Nelson, Lee, DB, Florida State, from Washington, 420
16. Beaird, Cecil, WR, Fisk, 453
17. Myers, Dan, DB, Georgia Tech, 483

SAN DIEGO
1. Washington, Joe, RB, Oklahoma, 4
2. Macek, Don, G, Boston College, 31
3. Dorsey, Larry, WR, Tennessee State, 64
4. Horn, Bob, LB, Oregon State, 94
Singleton, Ron, TE, Grambling, from Houston through Oakland, 113
Owens, Artie, WR, West Virginia, from Oakland, 115
5. Choice to LA Rams
Lowe, Woodrow, LB, Alabama, from New England, 131
6. Choice to Pittsburgh through St. Louis
Lane, Calvin, DB, Fresno State, from Oakland, 178
7. Choice to Dallas
8. DiRienzo, Tony, K, Oklahoma, 212
9. Choice to Buffalo
Harrison, Glynn, RB, Georgia, from NY Giants, 251
10. Perlinger, Jeff, DE, Michigan, 268
11. Preston, Ray, LB, Syracuse, 295
12. Lee, Ron, DB, Oregon, 322
Harris, Herman, DB, Mississippi Valley State, from Houston, 337
13. Lee, John, DT, Nebraska, 351
14. Jones, Ed, G, Cincinnati, 378
15. Hoffman, Jack, DT-DE, Indiana, 407
16. Harrison, Jack, G, California, 434
17. Sanders, Clarence, LB, Cincinnati, 463

SAN FRANCISCO
1. Choice to New England
2. Cross, Randy, C, UCLA, 42
Lewis, Eddie, DB, Kansas, from Tampa Bay, 57
3. Choice to Dallas
4. Rivera, Steve, WR, California, from Philadelphia, 100
Choice to NY Giants
5. Choice to Cincinnati
Leonard, Anthony, DB, Virginia Union, from Detroit, 140
6. Penneywell, Robert, LB, Grambling, 168
Bull, Scott, QB, Arkansas, from St. Louis, 177
7. Chesley, Jay, DB, Vanderbilt, 194
8. Ayers, John, T, West Texas State, 223
9. Harrison, Kenny, WR, SMU, 250
10. Ross, Robin, T, Washington State, 275
11. Hofer, Paul, RB, Mississippi, 305
12. Loper, Gerald, G, Florida, 332
13. Brumfield, Larry, DB, Indiana State, 359
14. Miller, Johnny, LB, Livingstone, 389
15. Stidham, Howard, LB, Tennessee Tech, 416
16. Lewis, Reggie, DE, San Diego State, 443
17. Jenkins, Darryl, RB, San Jose State, 473

SEATTLE
1. Niehaus, Steve, DT, Notre Dame, 2
2. Green, Sammy, LB, Florida, 29
Smith, Sherman, RB, Miami (Ohio), 58
Raible, Steve, WR, Georgia Tech, 59
3. Lloyd, Jeff, DE, West Texas State, 62
Engles, Rick, P, Tulsa, 89
Bitterlich, Don, K, Temple, 92
4. Myer, Steve, QB, New Mexico, 93
Johnson, Randy, G, Georgia, 122
Bolton, Andy, RB, Fisk, 123
5. Dufek, Don, DB, Michigan, 126
Jones, Ernie, DB, Miami, 153
Bates, Larry, RB, Miami, 156
6. Darby, Alvis, TE, Florida, 157
7. Dixon, Lodie, DT, Arkansas State, 184
8. Shipp, Larry, WR, LSU, 210
9. Bos, Bob, T, Iowa State, 239
10. Coffield, Randy, LB, Florida State, 266
11. Muehr, Keith, P, Southwestern Louisiana, 293
12. Barnett, Ronnie, WR, Texas-Arlington, 320
13. Reid, Andy, RB, Georgia, 349
14. Blinks, Jarvis, DB, Northwestern State (Louisiana), 376
15. Smith, Dan, T, Washington State, 405
16. Urczyk, Jeff, G, Georgia Tech, 432
17. Rowland, Chris, QB, Washington, 461

SEATTLE (Expansion)
Baker, Wayne, DT, BYU, from San Francisco
Barisch, Carl, DT, Princeton, from Cleveland
Bebout, Nick, T, Wyoming, from Atlanta
Blackwood, Lyle, DB, TCU, from Cincinnati
Bradley, Ed, LB, Wake Forest, from Pittsburgh
Brown, Dave, DB, Michigan, from Pittsburgh
Clune, Don, WR, Pennsylvania, from NY Giants
Colbert, Rondy, DB, Lamar, from NY Giants
Crump, Dwayne, DB, Fresno State, from St. Louis
Curtis, Mike, LB, Duke, from Baltimore
Davis, Jerry, DB, Morris Brown, from NY Jets
Demarie, John, G, LSU, from Cleveland
Evans, Norm, T, TCU, from Miami
Geddes, Ken, LB, Nebraska, from LA Rams
Graff, Neil, QB, Wisconsin, from New England
Hansen, Don, LB, Illinois, from Atlanta
Hayman, Gary, RB, Penn State, from Buffalo
Hoaglin, Fred, C, Pittsburgh, from Houston
Howard, Ron, TE, Seattle, from Dallas
Hutcherson, Ken, LB, Livingston State, from Green Bay
Jolley, Gordon, T, Utah, from Detroit
Keithley, Gary, QB, Texas-El Paso, from St. Louis
Kuehn, Art, C, UCLA, from Washington
Marbury, Kerry, RB, West Virginia, from New England
Matthews, Al, DB, Texas A&I, from Green Bay
McCullum, Sam, WR, Montana State, from Minnesota
McMakin, John, TE, Clemson, from Detroit
McMillan, Eddie, DB, Florida State, from LA Rams
Olds, Bill, RB, Nebraska, from Baltimore
O'Neal, Jesse, DE, Grambling, from Houston
Owens, Joe, DE, Alcorn State, from New Orleans
Penchion, Bob, G, Alcorn State, from San Francisco
Picard, Bob, WR, Eastern Washington State, from Philadelphia
Rasley, Rocky, G, Oregon State, from Kansas City
Taylor, Steve, DB, Kansas, from Denver
Tipton, Dave, DE, Stanford, from San Diego
Waddell, Charles, TE, North Carolina, from San Diego
Woods, Larry, DT, Tennessee State, from NY Jets
Woolsey, Rolly, DB, Boise State, from Dallas

TAMPA BAY
1. Selmon, Lee Roy, DE, Oklahoma, 1
2. DuBose, Jimmy, RB, Florida, 30
Choice to San Francisco
Selmon, Dewey, DT, Oklahoma, 60
3. Young, Steve, T, Colorado, 61
Choice to Baltimore
Maughan, Steve, LB, Utah State, 91
4. Choice to LA Rams
Appleby, Richard, WR, Georgia, 121
Little, Charles, G, Houston, 124
5. Kelson, Mishael, DB, West Texas State, 125
Wilson, Steve, T, Georgia, 154
Choice to LA Rams
6. Jordan, Curtis, DB, Texas Tech, 158
7. Dickinson, Parnell, QB, Mississippi Valley State, 183
8. Choice to NY Jets
9. Welch, Bruce, G, Texas A&M, 238
10. Smith, Sid, LB, BYU, 267
11. Washington, Melvin, DB, Colorado State, 297
12. Ragsdale, George, RB, North Carolina A&T, 321
13. Jenkins, Brad, TE, Nebraska, 348
14. Roaches, Carl, KR, Texas A&M, 377
15. Dzierzak, Bob, DT, Utah State, 404
16. West, Tommy, LB, Tennessee, 433
17. Berry, Jack, QB, Washington & Lee, 460

TAMPA BAY (Expansion)
Ball, Larry, LB, Louisville, from Detroit
Blahak, Joe, DB, Nebraska, from Minnesota
Bridges, Bubba, DT, Colorado, from Denver
Broussard, Bubba, LB, Houston, from Chi. Bears
Carter, Louis, RB, Maryland, from Oakland

Colavito, Steve, LB, Wake Forest, from Philadelphia
Cotney, Mark, DB, Cameron State, from Houston
Current, Mike, T, Ohio State, from Denver
Davis, Anthony, RB, USC, from NY Jets
Davis, Ricky, Alabama, DB, from Cincinnati
Douthitt, Earl, DB, Iowa, from Chi. Bears
Elia, Bruce, LB, Ohio State, from Miami
Ely, Larry, LB, Iowa, from Chi. Bears
Fest, Howard, G, Texas, from Cincinnati
Gordon, Ira, G, Kansas State, from San Diego
Gunn, Jimmy, LB, USC, from NY Giants
Hart, Harold, RB, Texas Southern, from Oakland
Keeton, Durwood, DB, Oklahoma, from New England
Kendrick, Vince, RB, Florida, from Atlanta
LaGrand, Morris, RB, Tampa, from New Orleans
McGee, Willie, WR, Alcorn State, from LA Raiders
McKay, John (J.K.), WR, USC, from Cleveland
Moore, Bob, TE, Stanford, from Oakland
Moore, Manfred, RB, USC, from San Francisco
Oliver, Frank, DB, Kentucky State, from Buffalo
Pear, Dave, DT, Washington, from Baltimore
Peterson, Cal, LB, UCLA, from Dallas
Reavis, Dave, T, Arkansas, from Pittsburgh
Rudolph, Council, DE, Kentucky State, from St. Louis
Ryczek, Dan, C, Virginia, from Washington
Smith, Barry, WR, Florida State, from Green Bay
Stone, Ken, DB, Vanderbilt, from Washington
Swift, Doug, LB, Amherst, from Miami
Thompson, Dave, T-C, Clemson, from New Orleans
Toomay, Pat, DE, Vanderbilt, from Buffalo
Ward, John, C-G, Oklahoma State, from Minnesota
Williams, Lawrence, WR, Texas Tech, from Kansas City
Yochum, Dan, T, Syracuse, from Philadelphia

WASHINGTON
1. Choice to Miami
2. Choice to Detroit through San Diego
3. Choice to New Orleans through San Diego
4. Choice to Oakland through San Diego
5. Choice to St. Louis
   Hughes, Mike, G, Baylor, from St. Louis, 148
6. Choice to Kansas City
   Marvaso, Tom, DB, Cincinnati, from LA Rams, 179
7. Choice forfeited
8. Choice to Buffalo through Atlanta
   Fryer, Bryan, WR, Alberta, from LA Rams, 234*
9. Akins, Curtis, G-C, Hawaii, 254
10. Strohmeier, Paul, LB, Washington, from Chi. Bears, 272
    Choice to Miami
11. Gissler, Dean, DE, Nebraska, 308
12. Tullis, Walter, DB, Delaware State, 342
13. Britt, Waymon, DB-WR, Michigan, 364
14. Buckner, Quinn, DB, Indiana, 393*
15. Choice to St. Louis
    Monroe, John, RB, Bluefield, from St. Louis, 426
16. Choice to Baltimore through Baltimore and San Francisco
17. Wills, Chuck, DB, Oregon, 476

1977
Held May 3-4, 1977

There were 335 selections instead of 336. Houston forfeited its fifth-round choice.

ATLANTA
1. Bryant, Warren, T, Kentucky, 6
   Faumuina, Wilson, DT, San Jose State, from St. Louis, 20
2. Thielemann, R.C., C, Arkansas, 36
3. Fields, Edgar, DT, Texas A&M, 63
4. Leavitt, Allan, K, Georgia, 89
5. Diggs, Shelton, RB, USC, 120
6. Choice to San Diego
   Jenkins, Keith, DB, Cincinnati, from Washington, 161
7. Choice to Cleveland
8. Packer, Walter, WR, Mississippi State, 203
9. Maxwell, John, T, Boston College, 230
   Speer, Robert, DE, Arkansas State, from Washington, 242
10. Ryckman, Billy, WR, Louisiana Tech, 257
11. Farmer, Dave, RB, USC, 287
12. Parrish, Don, DE, Pittsburgh, 314

BALTIMORE
1. Burke, Randy, WR, Kentucky, 26
2. Ozdowski, Mike, DE, Virginia, 53
3. Choice to St. Louis
4. Choice to Cleveland through Washington, Miami, and Chi. Bears
5. Choice to New Orleans
6. O'Neal, Calvin, LB, Michigan, 163
7. Carter, Blanchard, T, Nevada-Las Vegas, 193
8. Helvis, Ken, T-C, Georgia, 220
9. Capriola, Glen, RB, Boston College, 247
10. Baker, Ron, G, Oklahoma State, 277
11. Ruff, Brian, LB, Citadel, 304
12. Deutsch, Bill, RB, North Dakota, 331

BUFFALO
1. Choice to Cincinnati
2. Dokes, Phil, DT, Oklahoma State, from Detroit, 12
   Choice to Seattle through Dallas
3. Brown, Curtis, RB, Missouri, 59
   Kimbrough, John, WR, St. Cloud State, from Cleveland, 73
4. Dean, Jimmy, DT, Texas A&M, 86
5. Besana, Fred, QB, California, 115
   O'Donoghue, Neil, K, Auburn, from San Francisco, 127
6. Choice to San Francisco
   Pruitt, Ron, DE, Nebraska, from Cleveland, 157
7. Nelms, Mike, DB, Baylor, 170
8. Morton, Greg, DT, Michigan, 197
9. Choice to Kansas City
10. Choice to Pittsburgh
11. Jackson, Nate, RB, Tennessee State, 282
12. Romes, Charles, DB, North Carolina Central, 309

CHI. BEARS
1. Albrecht, Ted, T, California, 15
2. Spivey, Mike, DB, Colorado, 43
3. Earl, Robin, RB, Washington, from NY Giants, 61
   Choice to Miami
4. Choice to Pittsburgh
5. Choice to Oakland
6. Evans, Vince, QB, USC, from Tampa Bay, 140
   Choice to Philadelphia
7. Butler, Gerald, WR, Nicholls State, 182
8. Choice to NY Jets
9. Buonamici, Nick, DT, Ohio State, 238
10. Breckner, Dennis, DE, Miami, 266
11. Zelencik, Connie, C, Purdue, 294
12. Irvin, Terry, DB, Jackson State, 322

CINCINNATI
1. Edwards, Eddie, DT, Miami, from Buffalo, 3
   Whitley, Wilson, DT, Houston, from Philadelphia, 8
   Cobb, Mike, TE, Michigan State, 22
2. Johnson, Pete, RB, Ohio State, 49
3. Voight, Mike, RB, North Carolina, 76
4. Walker, Rick, TE, UCLA, from Tampa Bay, 85
   Wilson, Mike, T, Georgia, 103
   Anderson, Jerry, DB, Oklahoma, from St. Louis, 105
5. Phillips, Ray, LB, Nebraska, 133
6. Duniven, Tommy, QB, Texas Tech, 160
7. Breeden, Louis, DB, North Carolina Central, 187
   Corbett, Jim, TE, Pittsburgh, from Minnesota, 194
8. St. Victor, Jose, G, Syracuse, 214
9. Zachary, Willie, WR, Central State (Ohio), 245
10. Bialik, Bob, P, Hillsdale, 272
11. Parrish, Joel, G, Georgia, from San Diego, 292
    Allen, Carl, DB, Southern Mississippi, 299
12. Percival, Alex, WR, Morehouse, 326

CLEVELAND
1. Jackson, Robert, LB, Texas A&M, 17
2. Skladany, Tom, P-K, Ohio State, 46
3. Choice to Buffalo
4. Davis, Oliver, DB, Tennessee State, 102
   Sims, Robert, DT, South Carolina State, from Baltimore through Washington, Miami, and Chi. Bears, 110
5. Choice to San Diego
6. Choice to Buffalo
7. Randle, Kenny, WR, SMU, from Atlanta, 173
   Smith, Blane, TE, Purdue, 184
   Lingenfelter, Bob, T, Nebraska, from St. Louis, 188
8. Armstrong, Bill, DB, Wake Forest, 213
9. Brown, Daryl, DB, Tufts, 240
10. Burkett, Tom, T, North Carolina, 269
11. Nash, Charles, WR, Arizona, 296
12. Tierney, Leo, C, Georgia Tech, 325

DALLAS
1. Dorsett, Tony, RB, Pittsburgh, from Seattle, 2
   Choice to San Diego
2. Carano, Glenn, QB, Nevada-Las Vegas, 54
3. Hill, Tony, WR, Stanford, from Philadelphia, 62
   Belcher, Val, G, Houston, 81
4. Brown, Guy, LB, Houston, 108
5. Frederick, Andy, DT, New Mexico, 137
6. Cooper, Jim, T, Temple, 164
7. Stalls, Dave, DE, Northern Colorado, 191
8. Cleveland, Al, DE, Pacific, from San Diego, 208
   Williams, Fred, RB, Arizona State, 221
9. Cantrell, Mark, C, North Carolina, 248
10. DeBerg, Steve, QB, San Jose State, 275
11. Wardlow, Don, TE, Washington, 305
12. Peters, Greg, G, California, 332

DENVER
1. Schindler, Steve, G, Boston College, 18
2. Lytle, Rob, RB, Michigan, 45
3. Choice to Green Bay
4. Bryan, Billy, C, Duke, 101
5. Choice to NY Jets
6. Choice to LA Rams
7. Swider, Larry, P, Pittsburgh, 185
8. Culliver, Calvin, RB, Alabama, 212
9. Jackson, Charles, DT, Washington, 241
10. Middlebrook, Orna, WR, Arkansas State, 268
11. Heck, Phil, LB, California, 297
12. Levenhagen, Scott, TE, Western Illinois, 324

DETROIT
1. Choice to Buffalo
2. Williams, Walt, DB, New Mexico State, 42
3. Kane, Rick, RB, San Jose State, 69
4. Blue, Luther, WR, Iowa State, 96
5. Crosby, Ron, LB, Penn State, from Seattle, 114
   Choice to Pittsburgh
6. Choice to San Diego
   Pinkney, Reggie, DB, East Carolina, from Minnesota through New England, 166
7. Black, Tim, LB, Baylor, 179
8. Griffin, Mark, T, North Carolina, 209
9. Mathieson, Steve, QB, Florida State, 236
10. Anderson, Gary, G, Stanford, 263
11. Daykin, Tony, LB, Georgia Tech, 293
12. Greenwood, Dave, G-C, Iowa State, 320

GREEN BAY
1. Butler, Mike, DE, Kansas, 9
   Johnson, Ezra, DE, Morris Brown, from Oakland, 28
2. Koch, Greg, DT, Arkansas, 39
3. Choice to Houston
   Scribner, Rick, G, Idaho State, from Denver, 74
4. Choice to Pittsburgh
5. Simpson, Nate, RB, Tennessee State, 122
6. Moresco, Tim, DB, Syracuse, 149
7. Gofourth, Derrel, C, Oklahoma State, from NY Giants, 172
   Tipton, Rell, G, Baylor, 176
8. Whitehurst, David, QB, Furman, 206
9. Mullins, Joel, T, Arkansas State, 233
10. Culbreath, Jim, RB, Oklahoma, 260
11. Randolph, Terry, DB, American International, 290
12. Choice to Oakland

HOUSTON
1. Towns, Morris, T, Missouri, 11
2. Reihner, George, G, Penn State, 38
3. Choice to San Francisco
   Wilson, Tim, RB, Maryland, from Green Bay, 66
   Giles, Jimmie, TE, Alcorn State, from Miami, 70
   Carpenter, Rob, RB, Miami (Ohio), from Oakland through Buffalo, 84
4. Choice to Kansas City
   Anderson, Warren, WR, West Virginia State, from San Diego through Miami, 98
5. Choice forfeited
6. Woolford, Gary, DB, Florida State, 148
   Carter, David, C, Western Kentucky, from New England, 165
7. Choice to NY Giants
8. Davis, Steve, WR, Georgia, from Seattle, 198
   Foster, Eddie, WR, Houston, 205
9. Currier, Bill, DB, South Carolina, 232
10. Hull, Harvey, LB, Mississippi State, 262
11. Romano, Al, LB, Pittsburgh, 289
12. Johansson, Ove, K, Abilene Christian, 316

KANSAS CITY
1. Green, Gary, DB, Baylor, 10
2. Reed, Tony, RB, Colorado, 37
3. Howard, Thomas, LB, Texas Tech, 67
4. Bailey, Mark, RB, Long Beach State, from Philadelphia, 92
   Samuels, Andre, TE, Bethune-Cookman, 94
   Helton, Darius, G, North Carolina Central, from Houston, 95
   Harris, Eric, DB, Memphis State, from Washington, 104
5. Choice to Pittsburgh
6. Burleson, Rick, DE, Texas, 150
   Herrera, Andre, RB, Southern Illinois, from Oakland through Tampa Bay and Chi. Bears, 167
7. Golub, Chris, DB, Kansas, 177
8. Olsonoski, Ron, LB, St. Thomas (Minnesota), 204
   Smith, Waddell, WR, Kansas, from Washington, 215
9. Glanton, Derrick, DE, Bishop, from Buffalo, 226
   Green, Dave, T, New Mexico, 235
10. Vitali, Mark, QB, Purdue, 261
11. Mitchell, Maurice, WR, Northern Michigan, 288
12. Burks, Raymond, LB, UCLA, 318

LA RAMS
1. Brudzinski, Bob, LB, Ohio State, 23
2. Cromwell, Nolan, DB, Kansas, from Seattle, 31
   Waddy, Billy, RB-WR, Colorado, from Washington through San Diego, 50
   Choice to Seattle
3. Fulton, Ed, G, Maryland, from San Diego, 68
   Tyler, Wendell, RB, UCLA, 79
4. Ferragamo, Vince, QB, Nebraska, from New Orleans, 91
   Jones, Eary, DE, Memphis State, 107
5. Hickman, Donnie, G, USC, from Washington, 130
   Williams, Jeff, G, Rhode Island, 134
6. Best, Art, RB, Kent State, from Denver, 156
   Choice to New Orleans
7. Choice to Washington
8. Bockwoldt, Rod, DB, Weber State, 218
9. Choice to Washington
10. Petersen, Don, TE, Boston College, 274
11. Long, Carson, K, Pittsburgh, 302
12. Caudill, Barry, C, Southern Mississippi, 330

MIAMI
1. Duhe, A.J., DT, LSU, 13
2. Baumhower, Bob, DT, Alabama, 40
3. Choice to Houston
   Watson, Mike, T, Miami (Ohio), from Chi. Bears, 71
4. Choice to Washington
5. Michel, Mike, K, Stanford, from Tampa Bay, 113

Harris, Leroy, RB, Arkansas State, 123
6. Choice to NY Giants
7. Herron, Bruce, LB, New Mexico, 180
8. Perkins, Horace, DB, Colorado, 207
9. Turner, Robert, RB, Oklahoma State, 237
10. Carter, Mark, T, Eastern Michigan, 264
11. Alexander, John, DE, Rutgers, 291
12. Anderson, Terry, WR, Bethune-Cookman, 321

MINNESOTA
1. Kramer, Tommy, QB, Rice, 27
2. Swilley, Dennis, G, Texas A&M, 55
3. Hannon, Tom, DB, Michigan State, 83
4. Choice to Seattle
5. Moore, Ken, TE, Northern Illinois, 138
6. Choice to Detroit through New England
7. Choice to Cincinnati
8. Strozier, Clint, DB, USC, 222
9. Studwell, Scott, LB, Illinois, 250
10. Beaver, Dan, K, Illinois, 278
11. Hartwig, Keith, WR, Arizona, 306
12. Kelleher, Jim, RB, Colorado, 335

NEW ENGLAND
1. Clayborn, Raymond, DB, Texas, from San Francisco, 16
Morgan, Stanley, WR, Tennessee, 25
2. Ivory, Horace, RB, Oklahoma, from San Francisco, 44
Hasselbeck, Don, TE, Colorado, 52
3. Brown, Sidney, DB, Oklahoma, 82
4. Skinner, Gerald, T, Arkansas, 109
5. Choice to St. Louis
6. Choice to Houston
7. Smith, Ken, WR, Arkansas-Pine Bluff, 192
8. Benson, Brad, G, Penn State, 219
9. Vogele, Jerry, LB, Michigan, 249
10. Rasmussen, John, T, Wisconsin, 276
Alexander, Giles, DE, Tulsa, from Oakland, 279
11. Costict, Ray, LB, Mississippi State, 303
12. Preston, Dave, RB, Bowling Green, 333

NEW ORLEANS
1. Campbell, Joe, DE, Maryland, 7
2. Fultz, Mike, DT, Nebraska, 34
3. Watts, Bob, LB, Boston College, 64
4. Choice to LA Rams
5. Lafary, Dave, T, Purdue, 118
Hubbard, Dave, T, BYU, from Baltimore, 136
6. Parsley, Cliff, P, Oklahoma State, 147
Shick, Tom, G, Maryland, from LA Rams, 162
7. Boykin, Greg, RB, Northwestern, 174
8. Stewart, Jim, DB, Tulsa, 201
9. Knowles, Dave, T, Indiana, 231
10. Septien, Rafael, K, Southwestern Louisiana, 258
11. Blain, John, T, San Jose State, 285
12. Dalton, Oakley, DE, Jackson State, 315

NY GIANTS
1. Jeter, Gary, DT, USC, 5
2. Perkins, Johnny, WR, Abilene Christian, 32
3. Choice to Chi. Bears
4. Vaughan, Mike, T, Oklahoma, 88
5. Dean, Randy, QB, Northwestern, 117
6. Jordan, Bob, T, Memphis State, 143
Moorehead, Emery, WR-RB, Colorado, from Miami, 153
7. Choice to Green Bay
Dixon, Al, TE, Iowa State, from Houston, 178
8. Rice, Bill, DT, BYU, 199
Rodgers, Otis, LB, Iowa State, from San Francisco, 211
9. Mullins, Ken, DE, Florida A&M, 228
10. Jones, Mike, WR, Minnesota, 255
11. Helms, Bill, TE, San Diego State, 284
12. Simmons, Elmo, RB, Texas-Arlington, 311

NY JETS
1. Powell, Marvin, T, USC, 4
2. Walker, Wesley, WR, California, 33
3. Choice to Pittsburgh
Marshall, Charles (Tank), DE, Texas A&M, from San Francisco, 72
4. Dierking, Scott, RB, Purdue, 90
5. Griggs, Perry, WR, Troy State, 116
Gregory, Gary, T, Baylor, from Denver, 129
6. Klecko, Joe, DT, Temple, 144
7. White, Charles, RB, Bethune-Cookman, from Tampa Bay, 168
Grupp, Bob, DB, Duke, 171
Long, Kevin, RB, South Carolina, from Oakland, 195
8. Alexander, Dan, DT, LSU, 200
Thompson, Ed, LB, Ohio State, from Chi. Bears, 210
9. Robinson, Matt, QB, Georgia, 227
10. Hennessy, John, DE, Michigan, 256
11. Choice to Philadelphia
Butterfield, Dave, DB, Nebraska, from Oakland, 307
12. Gargis, Phil, RB-DB, Auburn, 312
Conrad, Dave, T, Maryland, from Philadelphia, 313

OAKLAND
1. Choice to Green Bay
2. Davis, Mike, DB, Colorado, from Philadelphia, 35
McKnight, Ted, RB, Minnesota-Duluth, 57
3. Choice to Houston through Buffalo
4. Marvin, Mickey, G, Tennessee, 112
5. Hayes, Lester, DB, Texas A&M, from Chi. Bears, 126
Barnes, Jeff, LB, California, 139
6. Choice to Kansas City through Tampa Bay and Chi. Bears
7. Martini, Rich, WR, Cal-Davis, from Washington through Houston and NY Giants, 190
Choice to NY Jets
8. Robiskie, Terry, RB, LSU, 223
9. Choice to Tampa Bay
10. Choice to New England
11. Choice to NY Jets
12. Martin, Rod, LB, USC, from Green Bay, 317
Benirschke, Rolf, K, Cal-Davis, 334

PHILADELPHIA
1. Choice to Cincinnati
2. Choice to Oakland
3. Choice to Dallas
4. Choice to Kansas City
5. Sharp, Skip, DB, Kansas, 119
6. Russell, Kevin, DB, Tennessee State, 145
Montgomery, Wilbert, RB, Abilene Christian, from Chi. Bears, 154
Mitchell, Martin, DB, Tulane, from St. Louis through Washington, 158
7. Johnson, Charlie, DT, Colorado, 175
8. Franklin, Cleveland, RB, Baylor, 202
9. Humphreys, T.J., G, Arkansas State, 229
10. Mastronardo, John, WR, Villanova, 259
11. Moore, Rocco, T, Western Michigan, from NY Jets, 283
Cordova, Mike, QB, Stanford, 286
12. Choice to NY Jets

PITTSBURGH
1. Cole, Robin, LB, New Mexico, 21
2. Thornton, Sidney, RB, Northwestern State (Louisiana), 48
3. Beasley, Tom, DT, Virginia Tech, from NY Jets, 60
Smith, Jim, WR, Michigan, 75
4. Petersen, Ted, C, Eastern Illinois, from Green Bay, 93
Smith, Laverne, RB, Kansas, from Chi. Bears, 99
Audick, Dan, G, Hawaii, 106
5. Stoudt, Cliff, QB, Youngstown State, from Kansas City, 121
Courson, Steve, G, South Carolina, from Detroit, 125
Winston, Dennis, LB, Arkansas, 132
6. Harris, Paul, LB, Alabama, 159
7. Frisch, Randy, DT, Missouri, 186
8. August, Phil, WR, Miami, 217
9. Kelly, Roosevelt, TE, Eastern Kentucky, 244
10. Cowans, Alvin, DB, Florida, from Buffalo, 253
LaCrosse, Dave, LB, Wake Forest, 271
11. West, Lou, DB, Cincinnati, 298
12. Stephens, Jimmy, TE, Florida, from Seattle, 310
Choice to Seattle

ST. LOUIS
1. Pisarkiewicz, Steve, QB, Missouri, from Washington, 19
Choice to Atlanta
2. Franklin, George, RB, Texas A&I, 47
3. Allerman, Kurt, LB, Penn State, 78
Middleton, Terdell, RB, Memphis State, from Baltimore, 80
4. Choice to Cincinnati
5. Lee, Ernest, DT, Texas, 131
Spiva, Andy, LB, Tennessee, from New England, 135
6. Choice to Philadelphia through Washington
7. Choice to Cleveland
8. Williams, Eric, LB, USC, 216
9. Jackson, Johnny, DT, Southern, 243
10. LeJay, Jim, WR, San Jose State, 270
11. Lee, Greg, DB, Western Illinois, 301
12. Fenlaw, Rick, LB, Texas, 328

SAN DIEGO
1. Choice to Seattle through Dallas
Rush, Bob, C, Memphis State, from Dallas, 24
2. Choice to Seattle through Dallas
3. Choice to LA Rams
King, Linden, DB, Colorado State, from Washington, 77
4. Choice to Houston through Miami
5. Williams, Clarence, RB, South Carolina, 124
Olander, Cliff, QB, New Mexico State, from Cleveland, 128
6. Lindstrom, Dave, DE, Boston U., from Atlanta, 146
Barnes, Larry, RB, Tennessee State, 151
Shaw, Pete, DB, Northwestern, from Detroit, 152
7. Bush, Ron, DB, USC, 181
8. Choice to Dallas
9. Washington, Gene, WR, Georgia, 234
10. Townsend, Curtis, LB, Arkansas, 265
11. Choice to Cincinnati
12. Stansik, Jim, TE, Eastern Michigan, 319

SAN FRANCISCO
1. Choice to New England
2. Choice to New England
3. Boyd, Elmo, WR, Eastern Kentucky, from Houston, 65
Choice to NY Jets
4. Black, Stan, DB, Mississippi State, 100
5. Choice to Buffalo
6. Burns, Mike, DB, USC, from Buffalo, 141
Harlan, Jim, C, Howard Payne, 155
7. Van Wagner, Jim, RB, Michigan Tech, 183
8. Choice to NY Giants
9. Posey, David, K, Florida, 239
10. Choice to Tampa Bay
11. Billick, Brian, TE, BYU, 295
12. Martin, Scott, G, North Dakota, 323

SEATTLE
1. Choice to Dallas
August, Steve, G, Tulsa, from San Diego through Dallas, 14
2. Lynch, Tom, T, Boston College, from Buffalo through Dallas, 30
Choice to LA Rams
Beeson, Terry, LB, Kansas, from San Diego through Dallas, 41
Cronan, Pete, LB, Boston College, from LA Rams, 51
3. Boyd, Dennis, DE, Oregon State, 58
4. Yarno, John, C, Idaho, 87
Seivers, Larry, WR, Tennessee, from Minnesota, 111
5. Choice to Detroit
6. Benjamin, Tony, RB, Duke, 142
7. Sims, David, RB, Georgia Tech, 169
8. Choice to Houston
9. Adzick, George, DB, Minnesota, 225
10. Adkins, Sam, QB, Wichita State, 254
11. Westbeld, Bill, T, Dayton, 281
12. Choice to Pittsburgh
Wilson, I.V., DT, Tulsa, from Pittsburgh, 329

TAMPA BAY
1. Bell, Ricky, RB, USC, 1
2. Lewis, David, LB, USC, 29
3. Hannah, Charley, DE, Alabama, 56
4. Choice to Cincinnati
5. Choice to Miami
6. Choice to Chi. Bears
7. Choice to NY Jets
8. Hedberg, Randy, QB, Minot State, 196
9. Hemingway, Byron, LB, Boston College, 224
Mucker, Larry, WR, Arizona State, from Oakland, 251
10. Morgan, Robert, RB, Florida, 252
Ball, Aaron, LB, Cal State-Fullerton, from San Francisco, 267
11. Rodgers, Chuck, DB, North Dakota State, 280
12. Sheffield, Chip, WR, Lenoir-Rhyne, 308

WASHINGTON
1. Choice to St. Louis
2. Choice to LA Rams through San Diego
3. Choice to San Diego
4. McColl, Duncan, DE, Stanford, from Miami, 97
Choice to Kansas City
5. Choice to LA Rams
6. Choice to Atlanta
7. Choice to Oakland through Houston and NY Giants
Haynes, Reggie, TE, Nevada-Las Vegas, from LA Rams, 189
8. Choice to Kansas City
9. Choice to Atlanta
Northington, Mike, RB, Purdue, from LA Rams, 246
10. Sykes, James, RB, Rice, 273
11. Harris, Don, DB, Rutgers, 300
12. Kirkland, Curtis, DE, Missouri, 327

1978
Held May 2-3, 1978

There were 334 selections instead of 336. Seattle gave up its fourth-round choice in a 1977 supplemental draft. Green Bay forfeited its fourth-round pick.

ATLANTA
1. Kenn, Mike, T, Michigan, 13
2. Stewart, Steve, LB, Minnesota, 43
3. Waldemore, Stan, G, Nebraska, 70
4. Cabral, Brian, LB, Colorado, 95
5. Pearson, Dennis, WR, San Diego State, 125
6. Parker, Rodney, WR, Tennessee State, 152
7. Jackson, Alfred, WR, Texas, from Tampa Bay, 167
Wright, James, TE, TCU, 179
8. Adkins, David, LB, Ohio State, 209
Williams, David, DB, Tennessee-Martin, from Washington, 216
9. Pridemore, Tom, DB, West Virginia, 236
10. Patton, Ricky, RB, Jackson State, from Philadelphia, 257
Strong, Ray, RB, Nevada-Las Vegas, 263
11. Reed, Milton, DB, Baylor, 293
12. Butler, Daria, LB, Oklahoma State, 320

BALTIMORE
1. McCall, Reese, TE, Auburn, 25
2. Woods, Mike, LB, Cincinnati, 52
3. Choice to San Francisco
4. Choice to Detroit
5. Myers, Frank, T, Texas A&M, from San Francisco, 117
Choice to Kansas City
6. Garry, Ben, RB, Southern Mississippi, 161
7. Logan, Jeff, RB, Ohio State, 191
8. Anthony, Monte, RB, Nebraska, 218
9. Studdard, Dave, T, Texas, 245
10. Owens, Dallas, DB, Kentucky, 275
11. Mason, Henry, WR, Central Missouri, 302
12. Allen, Bruce, P, Richmond, 329

BUFFALO
1. Miller, Terry, RB, Oklahoma State, 5
2. Hardison, Dee, DE, North Carolina, 32
Hutchinson, Scott, DE, Florida, from San Francisco, 38
3. Johnson, Dennis, RB, Mississippi State, 59
Fulton, Danny, WR, Nebraska-Omaha, from San Francisco, 65
4. Sanford, Lucius, LB, Georgia Tech, 89
5. Spaeth, Ken, TE, Nebraska, 114
6. Choice to NY Jets
Smith, Eric, T, Southern Mississippi, from Philadelphia, 145
7. Celotto, Mario, LB, USC, 171
Powell, Steve, RB, Northeast Missouri State, from Houston, 183
8. Choice to New England through Philadelphia
9. Choice to NY Jets
10. Grant, Will, C, Kentucky, 255
11. Blanton, Jerry, LB, Kentucky, 282
12. Crump, Richard, RB, Northeastern Oklahoma, 308

CHI. BEARS
1. Choice to LA Rams through Cleveland
2. Choice to San Francisco
3. Shearer, Brad, DT, Texas, 74
4. Choice to Kansas City
5. Choice to Cincinnati
6. Skibinski, John, RB, Purdue, from Kansas City, 139
Ieremia, Mekeli, DE, BYU, 158
7. Jones, Herman, WR, Ohio State, 185
8. Freitas, George, TE, California, 212
9. Martin, Mike, LB, Kentucky, 244
10. Zambiasi, Ben, LB, Georgia, 271
11. Underwood, Walt, DE, USC, 298
12. Sibley, Lew, LB, LSU, 325

CINCINNATI
1. Browner, Ross, DT, Notre Dame, from Philadelphia, 8
Bush, Blair, C, Washington, 16
2. Griffin, Ray, DB, Ohio State, from Philadelphia, 35
Turner, Dave, RB, San Diego State, 45
3. Vincent, Ted, DT, Wichita State, 72
Bass, Dan, WR, Houston, from Denver, 83
4. Law, Dennis, WR, East Tennessee State, 99
5. Dinkel, Tom, LB, Kansas, 126
Hertel, Rob, QB, USC, from Chi. Bears, 131
6. Geise, Steve, RB, Penn State, 155
7. Branson, Joe, DB, Livingstone, 182
Bass, Dan, G, Elon, from Denver, 193
8. Miller, Bill, T, Western Illinois, 211
9. Shumon, Ron, LB, Wichita State, 238
10. DePaso, Tom, LB, Penn State, 267
11. Prince, Calvin, RB, Louisville, from St. Louis, 293
Donahue, Mark, G, Michigan, 294
12. Featsent, Kim, WR, Kent State, 323

CLEVELAND
1. Matthews, Clay, LB, USC, 12
Newsome, Ozzie, WR, Alabama, from LA Rams, 23
2. Evans, Johnny, P-QB, North Carolina State, 39
3. Collins, Larry, RB, Texas A&I, from Detroit, 67
Miller, Mark, QB, Bowling Green, 68
4. Choice to Miami
Pullara, Pete, G, Tennessee-Chattanooga, from Washington through LA Rams, 103
5. Wright, Keith, WR, Memphis State, 122
6. Pitts, Al, C, Michigan State, 149
7. Choice to Miami
8. Turnbow, Jesse, DT, Tennessee, 205
9. Kramer, Jon, G, Baylor, 234
10. Watson, Brent, T, Tennessee, 261
11. Gillard, Larry, DT, Mississippi State, 290
12. Biedermann, Leo, T, California, 317

DALLAS
1. Bethea, Larry, DE, Michigan State, 28
2. Christensen, Todd, RB, BYU, 56
3. Hudgens, Dave, DT, Oklahoma, 84
4. Blackwell, Alois, RB, Houston, 110
5. Rosen, Rich, G, Syracuse, 138
6. Randolph, Harold, LB, East Carolina, 166
7. Randall, Tom, DT-DE, Iowa State, 194
8. Butler, Homer, WR, UCLA, 222
9. Williams, Russ, DB, Tennessee, 250
10. Tomasetti, Barry, G, Iowa, 278
11. Thurman, Dennis, DB, USC, 306
12. Washburn, Lee, G, Montana State, 334

DENVER
1. Latimer, Don, DT, Miami, 27
2. Gay, William, TE, USC, 55
3. Choice to Cincinnati
4. Choice to Detroit
5. Choice to NY Giants
6. Choice to Detroit
7. Choice to Cincinnati
8. Smith, Frank, T, Alabama A&M, 221
9. Choice to San Francisco
10. Kenney, Vince, WR, Maryland, 277
11. Brumley, Lacy, T, Clemson, 305
12. Choice to Miami

DETROIT
1. Bradley, Luther, DB, Notre Dame, 11
2. Baker, Al, DE, Colorado State, 40
3. Choice to Cleveland
4. Fifer, William, T, West Texas State, 94
Elias, Homer, G, Tennessee State, from Baltimore, 107
5. Tearry, Larry, C, Wake Forest, from Denver, 109
Fowler, Amos, G, Southern Mississippi, 121
Gray, Dan, DE, Rutgers, from San Diego, 123
6. Hicks, Dwight, DB, Michigan, 150
Ardizzone, Tony, G, Northwestern, from San Diego, 153
Thompson, Jesse, WR, California, from Denver, 165
7. Gibson, Bruce, RB, Pacific, 177
8. Breech, Jim, K, California, 206
9. Choice to San Francisco
10. Arrington, Fred, LB, Purdue, 262
11. Murray, Richard, DT, Oklahoma, 289
12. Patterson, Mark, DB, Washington State, 318

GREEN BAY
1. Lofton, James, WR, Stanford, 6
Anderson, John, LB, Michigan, from Oakland, 26
2. Hunt, Mike, LB, Minnesota, 34
3. Hood, Estus, DB, Illinois State, 62
4. Choice forfeited
5. Douglass, Mike, LB, San Diego State, 116
Wilder, Willie, RB, Florida, from Pittsburgh, 128
6. Harris, Leotis, G, Arkansas, 144
7. Plasketes, George, LB, Mississippi, 172
8. Sproul, Dennis, QB, Arizona State, 200
9. Myers, Keith, QB, Utah State, 228
10. Key, Larry, RB, Florida State, 256
Totten, Mark, C, Florida, from NY Giants, 259
11. Jones, Terry, DT, Alabama, 284
12. Ramson, Eason, TE, Washington State, 312

HOUSTON
1. Campbell, Earl, RB, Texas, from Tampa Bay, 1
Choice to Tampa Bay
2. Choice to Tampa Bay
3. Nielsen, Gifford, QB, BYU, 73
4. Renfro, Mike, WR, TCU, 98
5. Choice to San Francisco through Kansas City and Chi. Bears
6. Rucker, Conrad, TE, Southern, 154
7. Choice to Buffalo
8. Wilson, J.C., DB, Pittsburgh, 210
9. Mol, Jim, DE, Morningside, 239
10. Young, Steve, TE, Wake Forest, 266
11. Thicklen, Willie, WR, Alabama State, 295
12. Schuhmacher, John, G, USC, 322

KANSAS CITY
1. Still, Art, DE, Kentucky, 2
2. Hicks, Sylvester, DE, Tennessee State, 29
3. Spani, Gary, LB, Kansas State, 58
4. Johnson, Danny, LB, Tennessee State, 85
Woods, Pete, QB, Missouri, from Chi. Bears, 104
5. McRae, Jerrold, WR, Tennessee State, 112
Carey, Dwight, DT, Texas-Arlington, from Philadelphia, 118
Woods, Robert, WR-KR, Grambling, from Baltimore, 134
6. Choice to Chi. Bears
7. Odom, Ricky, DB, USC, 168
Kellar, Bill, WR, Stanford, from Washington, 184
8. White, John Henry, RB, Louisiana Tech, 195
9. Brown, Larry, T, Miami, 224
10. Bryant, Earl, DE, Jackson State, 251
11. Milo, Ray, DB, New Mexico State, 280
12. Brock, Willie, C, Colorado, 310

LA RAMS
1. Peacock, Elvis, RB, Oklahoma, from Chi. Bears through Cleveland, 20
Choice to Cleveland
2. Johnson, Stan, DT, Tennessee State, from Washington, 46
Smith, Ronnie, WR, San Diego State, 53
3. Corral, Frank, P, UCLA, from Washington, 78
White, Leon, C, Colorado, 80
4. Manges, Mark, QB, Maryland, 105
5. Choice to San Diego
6. Choice to Tampa Bay
7. Doss, Reggie, DE, Hampton, 189
8. Choice to Washington
9. Anderson, Andre, DE, New Mexico State, 246
10. Peal, Charles, T, Indiana, 273
11. Hostetler, Ron, LB, Penn State, 303
12. Coppens, Gus, T, UCLA, 330

MIAMI
1. Choice to San Francisco
2. Benjamin, Guy, QB, Stanford, 51
3. Smith, Lyman, DT, Duke, from NY Giants, 64
Cefalo, Jimmy, WR, Penn State, 81
4. Small, Gerald, DB, San Jose State, from Cleveland, 93
Laakso, Eric, T, Tulane, 106
5. Burgmeier, Ted, DB, Notre Dame, from Tampa Bay, 111
Choice to San Francisco
6. Betters, Doug, DE, Nevada-Reno, 163
7. Baldischwiler, Karl, T, Oklahoma, from Cleveland, 178
Henry, Lloyd, WR, Northeast Missouri State, 190
8. Clancy, Sean, LB, Amherst, 217
9. Hardy, Bruce, TE, Arizona State, 247
10. Dennard, Mark, C, Texas A&M, 274
11. Choice to Seattle
12. Moore, Mike, RB, Middle Tennessee, 331
Kenney, Bill, QB, Northern Colorado, from Denver, 333

MINNESOTA
1. Holloway, Randy, DE, Pittsburgh, 21
2. Turner, John, DB, Miami, 48
3. Walton, Whip, LB, San Diego State, 75
4. Hough, Jim, C, Utah State, 100
5. Choice to NY Giants
6. Choice to Washington through San Francisco
7. Choice to Philadelphia
8. Wood, Mike, K, Southeast Missouri State, from Seattle, 204
Choice to NY Jets
9. Deutsch, Mike, P, Colorado State, 240
10. Shaw, Hughie, RB, Texas A&I, 272
11. Harris, Ron, RB, Colorado State, 299
12. Morrow, Jeff, T, Minnesota, 326

NEW ENGLAND
1. Cryder, Bob, G, Alabama, 18
2. Cavanaugh, Matt, QB, Pittsburgh, 50
3. Pennywell, Carlos, WR, Grambling, 77
4. Wheeler, Dwight, T, Tennessee State, 102
5. Matthews, Bill, LB, South Dakota State, 129
6. Coleman, Kem, LB, Mississippi, 156
7. Hawkins, Mike, LB, Texas A&I, 188
8. Falcon, Terry, G, Montana, from Buffalo through Philadelphia, 198
Tatupu, Mosi, RB, USC, 215
9. Petersen, Tim, LB, Arizona State, 242
10. Ferguson, Bryan, DB, Miami, 269
11. Williams, Charlie, LB, Florida, 296
12. Gibney, John, C, Colgate, 328

NEW ORLEANS
1. Chandler, Wes, WR, Florida, 3
2. Taylor, James, T, Missouri, 33
3. Bennett, Barry, DT, Concordia (Minnesota), 60
4. Schwartz, Don, DB, Washington State, 87
5. Felton, Eric, DB, Texas Tech, 115
6. Rieker, Mike, QB, Lehigh, 141
Chesley, Francis, LB, Wyoming, from Washington through Houston, 157
7. Choice to NY Jets
8. Williams, Brooks, TE, North Carolina, 199
9. Carter, Richard, DB, North Carolina State, 226
10. Choice to NY Giants
11. Besaint, Nathan, DT, Southern, 283
Riley, Dave, RB, West Virginia, from Seattle, 285
12. Hardy, Larry, TE, Jackson State, 309

NY GIANTS
1. King, Gordon, T, Stanford, 10
2. McKinney, Odis, DB, Colorado, 37
3. Choice to Miami
4. Taylor, Billy, RB, Texas Tech, 90
5. Jackson, Terry, DB, San Diego State, 120
Krahl, Jim, DT, Texas Tech, from Minnesota, 132
DeRoo, Brian, WR, Redlands, from Denver, 137
6. Pass, Randy, G-C, Georgia Tech, 147
7. Doornink, Dan, RB, Washington State, 174
8. Grady, Jeff, LB, Florida A&M, 201
9. Swiacki, Bill, TE, Amherst, 232
10. Jorgensen, Greg, G, Nebraska, from New Orleans, 253
Choice to Green Bay
11. Heim, Dennis, DT, Southwest Missouri State, 286
12. Lawson, Greg, RB, Western Illinois, 313

NY JETS
1. Ward, Chris, T, Ohio State, 4
2. Merrill, Mark, LB, Minnesota, 31
3. Shuler, Mickey, TE, Penn State, 61
4. Donnell, Dodie, RB, Nebraska, 88
5. Sidler, Randy, LB, Penn State, 113
6. Jackson, Bobby, DB, Florida State, from Buffalo, 140
Robinson, Gregg, DT, Dartmouth, 142
7. Armstrong, Levi, DB, UCLA, from New Orleans, 169
Earley, James, RB, Michigan State, 170
8. Gaffney, Derrick, WR, Florida, 197
Mock, Mike, P-LB, Texas Tech, from Philadelphia, 203
Eppes, Roy, DB, Clemson, from Minnesota, 213
9. Grant, Reggie, DB, Oregon, from Buffalo, 225
Hutton, Neil, DB, Penn State, 227
10. Richardson, Louis, DE, Florida State, 254
11. Ryan, Pat, QB, Tennessee, 281
12. Williams, Alan, P, Florida, 311

OAKLAND
1. Choice to Green Bay
2. Browning, Dave, DE, Washington, 54
3. Jensen, Derrick, RB, Texas-Arlington, from Tampa Bay, 57
Mason, Lindsey, T, Kansas, 82
4. Harvey, Maurice, DB, Ball State, from Tampa Bay, 86
Stewart, Joe, WR, Missouri, 108
5. Ramsey, Derrick, TE, Kentucky, 136
6. Davis, Tom, C, Nebraska, from Tampa Bay, 143
Levenseller, Mike, WR, Washington State, 164
7. Whittington, Arthur, RB, SMU, from Philadelphia, 176
Inman, Earl, LB, Bethune-Cookman, 192
8. Nichols, Mark, DE, Colorado State, from San Diego, 207
Choice to San Diego
9. Choice to San Diego
10. Choice to Pittsburgh through Tampa Bay
11. Jones, Dean, DB, Fresno State, from San Diego, 291
Glazebrook, Bob, DB, Fresno State, 304
12. Conron, Joe, WR, Pacific, 332

PHILADELPHIA
1. Choice to Cincinnati
2. Choice to Cincinnati
3. Wilkes, Reggie, LB, Georgia Tech, 66
4. Harrison, Dennis, DT, Vanderbilt, 92
5. Choice to Kansas City
Banks, Norris, RB, Kansas, from Washington, 130
6. Choice to Buffalo
7. Choice to Oakland
Marshall, Greg, DT, Oregon State, from Minnesota, 186
8. Choice to NY Jets
9. Williams, Charles, DB, Jackson State, 230
10. Choice to Atlanta
11. Campfield, Bill, RB, Kansas, 288
12. Slater, Mark, C, Minnesota, 315

PITTSBURGH
1. Johnson, Ron, DB, Eastern Michigan, 22
2. Fry, Willie, DE, Notre Dame, 49
3. Colquitt, Craig, P, Tennessee, 76
4. Anderson, Larry, DB, Louisiana Tech, 101
5. Choice to Green Bay
6. Reutershan, Randy, WR, Pittsburgh, 160
7. Dufresne, Mark, TE, Nebraska, 187
8. Moser, Rich, RB, Rhode Island, from St. Louis, 208
Keys, Andre, WR, Cal Poly-SLO, 214
9. Reynolds, Lance, T, BYU, 241
10. Becker, Doug, LB, Notre Dame, 268
Jurich, Tom, K, Northern Arizona, from Oakland through Tampa Bay, 276
11. Terry, Nat, DB, Florida State, from Tampa Bay, 279
Brzoza, Tom, C, Pittsburgh, 300
12. Carr, Brad, LB, Maryland, 327

ST. LOUIS
1. Little, Steve, K, Arkansas, 15
Greene, Ken, DB, Washington State, from Washington, 19
2. Barefield, John, LB, Texas A&I, 42
3. Greene, Doug, DB, Texas A&I, 69
4. Collins, George, G, Georgia, from San Diego, 96
Childs, Jim, WR, Cal Poly-SLO, 97
5. Carr, Earl, RB, Florida, 124
6. Williams, Jack, DE, Bowling Green, 151
7. Stief, Dave, WR, Portland State, 181
8. Choice to Pittsburgh
9. Mosley, Joe, TE, Central State (Ohio), 235
10. Gill, Randy, LB, San Jose State, 265
11. Choice to Cincinnati
12. Clay, Anthony, LB, South Carolina State, 319

SAN DIEGO
1. Jefferson, John, WR, Arizona State, 14
2. Hardaway, Milton, T, Oklahoma State, 41
3. Anderson, Rickey, RB, South Carolina State, 71
4. Choice to St. Louis
5. Choice to Detroit
Choma, John, G, Virginia, from LA Rams, 135
6. Choice to Detroit
7. Featherstone, Cliff, DB, Colorado State, 180
8. Choice to Oakland
Hedrick, Gavin, P, Washington State, from Oakland, 220
9. Bradley, Henry, DT, Alcorn State, 237
Whitlatch, Blake, LB, LSU, from Oakland, 248
10. Price, Charles, TE, Cincinnati, 264
11. Choice to Oakland
12. Bell, Kevin, WR, Lamar, 321

SAN FRANCISCO
1. MacAfee, Ken, TE, Notre Dame, 7
Bunz, Dan, LB, Long Beach State, from Miami, 24
2. Choice to Buffalo
Downing, Walt, G, Michigan, from Chi. Bears, 47
3. Choice to Buffalo
Hughes, Ernie, G, Notre Dame, from Baltimore, 79
4. LeCount, Terry, WR, Florida, 91
5. Choice to Baltimore
Reese, Archie, DT, Clemson, from Houston through Kansas City and Chi. Bears, 127
Threadgill, Bruce, DB, Mississippi State, from Miami, 133
6. Walker, Elliott, RB, Pittsburgh, 148
7. Quillan, Fred, C, Oregon, 175
8. Choice to Washington
9. Redden, Herman, DB, Howard, 229
Moore, Dean, LB, Iowa, from Detroit, 233
McDaniels, Steve, T, Notre Dame, from Denver, 249
10. Connell, Mike, P, Cincinnati, 260
11. McCray, Willie, DE, Troy State, 287
12. Irons, Dan, T, Texas Tech, 314

SEATTLE
1. Simpson, Keith, DB, Memphis State, 9
2. Butler, Keith, LB, Memphis State, 36
3. Jury, Bob, DB, Pittsburgh, 63
4. Choice exercised in 1977 supplemental draft (Hunter, Al, RB, Notre Dame)
5. Bullard, Louis, T, Jackson State, 119
6. Starks, Glenn, WR, Texas A&I, 146
7. Harris, John, DB, Arizona State, 173
8. Choice to Minnesota
9. Grimmett, Rich, T, Illinois, 231
10. Stewart, Rob, WR, Lafayette, 258
11. Choice to New Orleans
Halas, George, LB, Miami, from Miami, 301
12. Bergeron, Jeff, RB, Lamar, 316

TAMPA BAY
1. Choice to Houston
Williams, Doug, QB, Grambling, from Houston, 17
2. Davis, Johnny, RB, Alabama, 30
Moritz, Brett, G, Nebraska, from Houston, 44
3. Choice to Oakland
4. Choice to Oakland
5. Choice to Miami
6. Choice to Oakland
Marshall, Elijah, WR, North Carolina State, from LA Rams, 162
7. Choice to Atlanta
8. McGriff, John, LB, Miami, 196
9. Taylor, Willie, WR, Pittsburgh, 223
10. Brown, Aaron, LB, Ohio State, 252
11. Choice to Pittsburgh
12. McLee, Kevin, RB, Georgia, 307

WASHINGTON
1. Choice to St. Louis
2. Choice to LA Rams
3. Choice to LA Rams
4. Choice to Cleveland through LA Rams
5. Choice to Philadelphia
6. Choice to New Orleans through Houston
Green, Tony, RB, Florida, from Minnesota through San Francisco, 159
7. Choice to Kansas City
8. Lee, Walker, WR, North Carolina, from San Francisco, 202
Choice to Atlanta
Hover, Don, LB, Washington State, from LA Rams, 219
9. Hurley, John, QB, Santa Clara, 243
10. Hertenstein, Scott, DE, Azusa Pacific, 270
11. Williams, Mike, DB, Texas A&M, 297
12. McCabe, Steve, G, Bowdoin, 324

1979

Held May 3-4, 1979

There were 330 selections instead of 336. Houston gave up its tenth-round choice and San Francisco its twelfth-round pick in 1978 supplemental drafts. Four teams forfeited choices: Minnesota and Pittsburgh each a third-round pick, the Los Angeles Rams a fifth-round pick, and New England a seventh-round pick.

ATLANTA
1. Smith, Don, DE, Miami, 17
2. Howell, Pat, G, USC, 49
3. Mayberry, James, RB, Colorado, 75
Andrews, William, RB, Auburn, from Miami, 79
4. Cain, Lynn, RB, USC, from Philadelphia, 100
Johnson, Charles, DB, Grambling, 101
5. Zele, Mike, DT, Kent State, 127
6. Moroski, Mike, QB, Cal-Davis, 154
7. Westlund, Roger, T, Washington, 186
8. Miller, Keith, LB, Northeastern Oklahoma, 212
9. Parkins, Dave, DB, Utah State, 239
10. Beekley, Bruce, LB, Oregon, 266
11. Leer, Bill, C, Colorado State, 292
12. Walker, Stuart, LB, Colorado, 323

BALTIMORE
1. Krauss, Barry, LB, Alabama, 6
2. Choice to Tampa Bay
3. Choice to Tampa Bay
Anderson, Kim, DB, Arizona State, from Washington through Houston, 69
4. Choice to Detroit
5. Braziel, Larry, DB, USC, 115
6. Choice to Buffalo
Moore, Jimmy, T, Ohio State, from Washington, 150
7. Choice to Houston
8. Heimkreiter, Steve, LB, Notre Dame, 197
Glasgow, Nesby, DB, Washington, from Minnesota, 207
9. Henderson, Russ, P, Virginia, 224
10. Stephens, Steve, TE, Oklahoma State, 254
11. Priestner, John, LB, Western Ontario, 280
12. Green, Charlie, WR, Kansas State, 306

BUFFALO
1. Cousineau, Tom, LB, Ohio State, from San Francisco, 1
Butler, Jerry, WR, Clemson, 5
2. Smerlas, Fred, DT, Boston College, 32
Haslett, Jim, LB, Indiana (Pennsylvania), from Denver, 51
3. Borchardt, Jon, T, Montana State, 62
4. Johnson, Ken, DE, Knoxville, from San Francisco, 83
Nixon, Jeff, DB, Richmond, 87
5. Kush, Rod, DB, Nebraska-Omaha, 114
Manucci, Dan, QB, Kansas State, from Tampa Bay through Seattle, 116
6. Choice to Houston
Burrow, Mike, G, Auburn, from Baltimore, 141
7. Mullady, Tom, TE, Southwestern (Memphis), 170
8. Choice to Philadelphia
9. Baker, Kevin, DE, William Penn, 226
10. Marler, David, QB, Mississippi State, 253
11. Lawler, Paul, DB, Colgate, 279
12. Harris, Mike, RB, Arizona State, 308

CHI. BEARS
1. Hampton, Dan, DT, Arkansas, from Tampa Bay, 4
Harris, Al, DE, Arizona State, 9
2. Watts, Rickey, WR, Tulsa, 39
3. McClendon, Willie, RB, Georgia, 66
4. Choice to Cincinnati
5. Choice to Dallas
6. Sullivan, John, LB, Illinois, 147
7. Kunz, Lee, LB, Nebraska, 174
8. Moss, Rick, DB, Purdue, 203
9. Heavens, Jerome, RB, Notre Dame, 230
10. Restic, Joe, DB, Notre Dame, 257
11. Wright, Bob, T, Cincinnati, 286
12. Becker, Dave, DB, Iowa, 312

CINCINNATI
1. Thompson, Jack, QB, Washington State, 3
Alexander, Charles, RB, LSU, from Washington, 12
2. Ross, Dan, TE, Northeastern, 30
3. Cotton, Barney, G, Nebraska, 59
4. White, James, DT, Albany State, 84
Lusby, Vaughn, DB, Arkansas, from Chi. Bears, 91
5. Merrill, Casey, DE, Cal-Davis, 113
6. Kreider, Steve, WR, Lehigh, 139
7. Montoya, Max, T, UCLA, 168
8. Kurnick, Howie, LB, Cincinnati, 194
9. Burk, Scott, DB, Oklahoma State, 223
10. Poole, Nathan, RB, Louisville, 250
11. Bungarda, Ken, DT, Missouri, 278
12. Browner, Jim, DB, Notre Dame, 304

CLEVELAND
1. Choice to San Diego
Adams, Willis, WR, Houston, from San Diego, 20
2. Johnson, Lawrence, DB, Wisconsin, 40
Claphan, Sam, T, Oklahoma, from San Diego, 47
3. Ramey, Jim, DE, Kentucky, 70
4. Miller, Matt, T, Colorado, 95
5. Choice to LA Rams
Dimler, Rich, DT, USC, from Washington through LA Rams, 124
6. Burrell, Clinton, DB, LSU, 151
Ronan, Jim, DT, Minnesota, from LA Rams, 163
7. Choice to Philadelphia
Risien, Cody, T, Texas A&M, from Oakland, 183
8. Perkov, Kent, DE, San Diego State, 204
9. McGee, Carl, LB, Duke, 234
Weathers, Curtis, TE, Mississippi, from Oakland, 241
10. Smith, John, WR, Tennessee State, 261
11. Poeschl, Randy, DE, Nebraska, 287
12. Choice to Oakland
Methvin, Dewitt, C, Tulane, from Washington, 315

DALLAS
1. Shaw, Robert, C, Tennessee, 27
2. Mitchell, Aaron, DB, Nevada-Las Vegas, 55
3. Cosbie, Doug, TE, Santa Clara, from Seattle, 76
Choice to San Francisco through Seattle
4. DeLoach, Ralph, DE, California, 109
5. Hukill, Bob, G, North Carolina, from Chi. Bears, 121
Andersen, Curtis, DE, Central State (Ohio), from Seattle, 128
Springs, Ron, RB, Ohio State, 136
6. Lavender, Tim, DB, USC, from Seattle, 155
Salzano, Mike, G, North Carolina, from Denver, 160
De France, Chris, WR, Arizona State, 164
7. Fitzpatrick, Greg, LB, Youngstown State, 191
8. Thornton, Bruce, DT, Illinois, 219
9. Cobb, Garry, LB, USC, 247
10. Calhoun, Mike, DT, Notre Dame, 274
11. Choice to Detroit
12. Lowry, Quentin, LB, Youngstown State, 329

DENVER
1. Clark, Kelvin, T, Nebraska, 22
2. Choice to Buffalo
3. Radford, Bruce, DE, Grambling, 77
4. Jefferson, Charles, DB, McNeese State, 105
5. Leach, Rick, QB, Michigan, 132
6. McIntyre, Jeff, LB, Arizona State, from Detroit, 148
Choice to Dallas
7. Prestridge, Luke, P, Baylor, 188
8. Choice to Miami
9. Taylor, Charlie, WR, Rice, 242
10. Choice to New England
11. Dixon, Zachary, RB, Temple, 297
12. Jacobs, Dave, K, Syracuse, 325

DETROIT
1. Dorney, Keith, T, Penn State, 10
2. Fantetti, Ken, LB, Wyoming, 37
3. Robinson, Bo, RB, West Texas State, 67
4. Norris, Ulysses, TE, Georgia, from Baltimore, 88
Brooks, Jon, LB, Clemson, 92
5. Choice to San Francisco
Brown, Walt, C, Pittsburgh, from San Diego through Baltimore, 131
6. Choice to Denver
7. Choice to Oakland through Cleveland
8. Choice to NY Giants
Mohring, John, LB, C.W. Post, from Seattle, 213
9. Komlo, Jeff, QB, Delaware, 231
10. Choice to Miami
11. Choice to NY Giants
Cole, Eddie, LB, Mississippi, from Dallas, 302
12. Forster, Bob, C-G, Brown, 313
Sweeney, Bryan, WR, Texas A&I, from New England, 326

GREEN BAY
1. Ivery, Eddie Lee, RB, Georgia Tech, 15
2. Atkins, Steve, RB, Maryland, 44
3. Johnson, Charles, DT, Maryland, 71
4. Choice to NY Jets
5. Choice to NY Jets
6. Simmons, Dave, LB, North Carolina, 153
7. Monroe, Henry, DB, Mississippi State, 180
Wingo, Rich, LB, Alabama, from San Diego, 184
8. Cassidy, Ron, WR, Utah State, from San Francisco, 193
Partridge, Rick, P, Utah, 208
9. Thompson, John, TE, Utah State, 235
10. Lockett, Frank, WR, Nebraska, 264
11. Thorson, Mark, DB, Ottawa, 290
12. Moats, Bill, P, South Dakota, 318

HOUSTON
1. Choice to Kansas City
2. Stensrud, Mike, DE, Iowa State, from Kansas City, 31
Baker, Jesse, DE, Jacksonville State, 50
3. King, Kenny, RB, Oklahoma, from Oakland through Baltimore
Choice to Tampa Bay
4. Choice to San Diego
5. Choice to Tampa Bay
6. Hunt, Daryl, LB, Oklahoma, from Buffalo, 143
Murphy, Mike, LB, Southwest Missouri State, 159
7. Ries, Tim, DB, Southwest Missouri State, from Baltimore, 171
Choice to NY Jets
8. Hartwig, Carter, DB, USC, 214
9. Ellender, Richard, WR, McNeese State, 243
10. Choice exercised in 1978 supplemental draft (Dirden, Johnnie, WR, Sam Houston State)
11. Taylor, Mike, T, Georgia Tech, 298
12. Wilson, Wayne, RB, Shepherd, 324

KANSAS CITY
1. Bell, Mike, DE, Colorado State, 2
Fuller, Steve, QB, Clemson, from Houston, 23
2. Choice to Houston
3. Choice to LA Rams
4. Manumaleuna, Frank, LB, San Jose State, 85
5. Gant, Earl, RB, Missouri, 112
6. Gaines, Robert, WR, Washington, 140

7. Kremer, Ken, DE, Ball State, 167
8. Williams, Mike, RB, New Mexico, 195
Brewer, Robert, G, Temple, from LA Rams through St. Louis, 218
9. Folston, James, TE, Cameron, 222
Robinson, Joe, T, Ohio State, from New Orleans, 229
10. DuPree, Mike, LB, Florida, 251
Jackson, Gerald, DB, Mississippi State, from Washington, 260
11. Rome, Stan, WR, Clemson, 277
12. Forrest, Michael, RB, Arkansas, 305

LA RAMS
1. Andrews, George, LB, Nebraska, from Oakland, 19
Hill, Kent, T, Georgia Tech, 26
2. Hill, Eddie, RB, Memphis State, 54
3. Moore, Jeff, WR, Tennessee, from Kansas City, 58
Wellman, Mike, C, Kansas, from New England, 81
Choice to Tampa Bay through Washington, Miami, and Oakland
4. Tucker, Derwin, DB, Illinois, from San Diego, 99
Wilkinson, Jerry, DT, Oregon State, 108
5. Choice forfeited
Hicks, Victor, TE, Oklahoma, from Cleveland, 122
6. Choice to Cleveland
7. Delaney, Jeff, DB, Pittsburgh, 190
8. Choice to Kansas City
9. Rutledge, Jeff, QB, Alabama, 246
10. Willis, Larry, WR, Alcorn State, from Kansas City, 268
Ebensberger, Grady, DT, Houston, 273
11. Deramus, Jesse, DT, Tennessee State, 301
12. Hill, Drew, WR, Georgia Tech, 328

MIAMI
1. Giesler, Jon, T, Michigan, 24
2. Toews, Jeff, T, Washington, 53
3. Nathan, Tony, RB, Alabama, from Tampa Bay, 61
Land, Mel, LB, Michigan State, from NY Giants, 63
Lee, Ron, TE, Baylor, from New Orleans, 65
Choice to Atlanta
4. Howell, Steve, RB, Baylor, 107
5. Bessillieu, Don, DB, Georgia Tech, 134
6. Lindquist, Steve, G, Nebraska, 162
7. von Schamann, Uwe, K, Oklahoma, 189
8. Groth, Jeff, WR, Bowling Green, from Washington, 206
Choice to Tampa Bay
Blackwood, Glenn, DB, Texas, from Denver, 215
9. Weston, Jeff, DT, Notre Dame, 244
10. Stanton, Jerome, DB, Michigan State, from Detroit, 258
Kozlowski, Mike, RB, Colorado, 272
11. Blanton, Mike, DE, Georgia Tech, 299
12. Fortner, Larry, QB, Miami (Ohio), 327

MINNESOTA
1. Brown, Ted, RB, North Carolina State, 16
2. Huffman, Dave, C, Notre Dame, 43
3. Choice forfeited
4. Dils, Steve, QB, Stanford, 97
5. Meter, Jerry, LB, Michigan, 129
6. Senser, Joe, TE, West Chester, 152
7. Winkel, Bob, DT, Kentucky, 181
8. Choice to Baltimore
9. Diggs, Billy, WR, Winston-Salem State, 236
10. Choice to NY Jets
11. Nelson, Brian, WR, Texas Tech, 291
12. Stephens, David, LB, Kentucky, 317

NEW ENGLAND
1. Sanford, Rick, DB, South Carolina, 25
2. Golic, Bob, LB, Notre Dame, 52
3. Choice to LA Rams
4. Hare, Eddie, P, Tulsa, 106
5. Zamberlin, John, LB, Pacific Lutheran, 135
6. Choice to Pittsburgh
7. Flint, Judson, DB, Memphis State, from Washington, 177
Choice forfeited
8. Love, Randy, RB, Houston, 216
9. Spagnola, John, TE, Yale, 245
10. Cox, Martin, WR, Vanderbilt, from Denver, 270
Clark, Allan, RB, Northern Arizona, 271
11. Choice to Washington
12. Choice to Detroit

NEW ORLEANS
1. Erxleben, Russell, K-P, Texas, 11
2. Mathis, Reggie, LB, Oklahoma, 38
3. Choice to Miami
4. Kovach, Jim, LB, Kentucky, 93
5. Huckleby, Harlan, RB, Michigan, 120
6. Ray, Ricky, DB, Norfolk State, 146
7. Sytsma, Stan, LB, Minnesota, 176
8. Panfil, Doug, G, Tulsa, 202
9. Choice to Kansas City
10. Choice to Oakland
11. Hall, David, WR, Missouri-Rolla, 285
12. Finch, Kelsey, RB, Tennessee, 311

NY GIANTS
1. Simms, Phil, QB, Morehead State, 7
2. Gray, Earnest, WR, Memphis State, 36
3. Choice to Miami
4. Tabor, Phil, DE, Oklahoma, 90
5. Jackson, Cleveland, TE, Nevada-Las Vegas, 117
6. Torrey, Bob, RB, Penn State, 145
Hicks, Eddie, RB, East Carolina, from Philadelphia, 158
7. Alvers, Steve, TE, Miami, 172
8. Perry, D.K., DB, SMU, 200
Simmons, Roy, G, Georgia Tech, from Detroit, 201
9. Rusk, Tom, LB, Iowa, 227
10. Fowler, Dan, G, Kentucky, 256
11. Mince, Mike, DB, Fresno State, 282
Johnson, Ken, RB, Miami, from Detroit, 284
12. Gillespie, Tim, G, North Carolina State, 310

NY JETS
1. Lyons, Marty, DE, Alabama, 14
2. Gastineau, Mark, DE, East Central (Oklahoma), 41
3. Dykes, Donald, DB, Southeastern Louisiana, 68
4. Cunningham, Eric, G, Penn State, 96
Lynn, Johnny, DB, UCLA, from Green Bay, 98
5. Kirchbaum, Kelly, LB, Kentucky, 123
Blinka, Stan, LB, Sam Houston State, from Green Bay, 125
6. Dufek, Bill, G, Michigan, 149
7. King, Emmett, RB, Houston, 179
Brown, Keith, Minnesota, from Houston, 187
8. Harris, Marshall, DT, TCU, from Tampa Bay, 198
Beamon, Willie, LB, Boise State, 205
9. Spratler, Gordy, RB, North Dakota State, 232
10. Sybeldon, Steve, T, North Dakota, 262
McGlasson, Ed, C, Youngstown State, from Minnesota, 263
11. Sanders, Dan, QB, Carson-Newman, 288
12. Darby, Paul, WR, Southwest Texas State, 314

OAKLAND
1. Choice to LA Rams
2. Jones, Willie, DE, Florida State, from Washington through St. Louis, 42
Choice to St. Louis
3. Choice to Houston through Baltimore
4. Choice to Washington
5. Choice to St. Louis
6. Matthews, Ira, KR, Wisconsin, from Tampa Bay, 142
Williams, Henry, DB, San Diego State, 156
7. Matia, Jack, T, Drake, from Detroit through Cleveland, 175
Choice to Cleveland
8. Hawkins, Robert, RB, Kentucky, 209
9. Choice to Cleveland
Rourke, Jim, T, Boston College, from Philadelphia, 238
10. Choice to Kansas City
Smith, Ricky, DB, Tulane, from New Orleans, 259
11. Davis, Bruce, T, UCLA, 294
12. Abernathy, Dirk, DB, Bowling Green, from Cleveland, 316
Kinlaw, Reggie, DT, Oklahoma, 320

PHILADELPHIA
1. Robinson, Jerry, LB, UCLA, 21
2. Perot, Petey, G, Northwestern State (Louisiana), 48
3. Franklin, Tony, K, Texas A&M, 74
4. Cowins, Ben, RB, Arkansas, from Washington, 94
Choice to Atlanta
5. Fitzkee, Scott, WR, Penn State, 126
6. Choice to NY Giants
7. Swafford, Don, T, Florida, from Cleveland, 178
Bunche, Curtis, DE, Albany State, 185
8. Correal, Chuck, C, Penn State, from Buffalo, 196
Runager, Max, P, South Carolina, 211
9. Choice to Oakland
10. Choice to San Diego
11. Chesley, Al, LB, Pittsburgh, 296
12. Choice to Pittsburgh

PITTSBURGH
1. Hawthorne, Greg, RB, Baylor, 28
2. Valentine, Zack, LB, East Carolina, 56
3. Choice forfeited
4. Davis, Russell, RB, Michigan, from Tampa Bay through Detroit, 86
Sweeney, Calvin, WR, USC, 110
5. Board, Dwaine, DE, North Carolina A&T, 137
6. Murrell, Bill, TE, Winston-Salem State, from San Diego, 157
Woodruff, Dwayne, DB, Louisville, from New England, 161
Bahr, Matt, K, Penn State, 165
7. Kimball, Bruce, G, Massachusetts, 192
8. Graves, Tom, LB, Michigan State, 220
9. Kirk, Richard, DE, Denison, 248
10. Thompson, Tod, TE, BYU, 275
11. Moore, Charlie, C, Wichita State, 303
12. Smith, Ed, LB, Vanderbilt, from Philadelphia, 322
Almond, Mike, WR, Northwestern State (Louisiana), 330

ST. LOUIS
1. Anderson, Otis, RB, Miami, 8
2. Brown, Theotis, RB, UCLA, 35
Favron, Calvin, LB, Southeastern Louisiana, from Oakland, 46
3. Bostic, Joe, T, Clemson, 64
4. Green, Roy, DB, Henderson State, 89
5. Henry, Steve, DB, Emporia State, 118
Bell, Mark R., WR, Colorado State, from Oakland, 130
6. Lott, Thomas, RB, Oklahoma, 144
7. Gibson, Kirk, WR, Michigan State, 173
8. Miller, Larry, LB, BYU, 199
9. Rozier, Bob, DE, California, 228
10. Holloway, Jerry, TE, Western Illinois, 255
11. Henderson, Nate, T, Florida State, 283
12. McBride, Ricky, LB, Georgia, 309

SAN DIEGO
1. Winslow, Kellen, TE, Missouri, from Cleveland, 13
Choice to Cleveland
2. Choice to Cleveland
3. Thrift, Cliff, LB, East Central (Oklahoma), 73
4. Choice to LA Rams
Floyd, John, WR, Northeast Louisiana, from Houston, 104
5. Choice to Detroit
6. Choice to Pittsburgh
7. Choice to Green Bay
8. Haslip, Wilbert, RB, Hawaii, 210
9. Garrett, Alvin, WR, Angelo State, 237
10. Petruccio, Tony, DT, Penn State, from Philadelphia, 265
Green, Al, DB, LSU, 269
11. Rader, Dave, QB, Tulsa, 295
12. Duncan, Frank, DB, Cal State-San Francisco, 321

SAN FRANCISCO
1. Choice to Buffalo
2. Owens, James, WR, UCLA, 29
3. Choice to Seattle
Montana, Joe, QB, Notre Dame, from Dallas through Seattle, 82
4. Choice to Buffalo
5. Seabron, Tom, LB, Michigan, 111
Aldridge, Jerry, RB, Angelo State, from Detroit, 119
6. Vaughan, Ruben, DT, Colorado, 138
7. Francis, Phil, RB, Stanford, 166
8. Choice to Green Bay
9. Hamilton, Steve, DT, Missouri, 221
10. Clark, Dwight, WR, Clemson, 249
Ballage, Howard, DB, Colorado, from Tampa Bay, 252
11. McBride, Billy, DB, Tennessee State, 276
12. Choice exercised in 1978 supplemental draft (Connors, Rod, RB, USC)

SEATTLE
1. Tuiasosopo, Manu, DT, UCLA, 18
2. Norman, Joe, LB, Indiana, 45
3. Jackson, Michael, LB, Washington, from San Francisco, 57
Choice to Dallas
4. Bell, Mark E., TE, Colorado State, 102
5. Choice to Dallas
6. Choice to Dallas
7. Polowski, Larry, LB, Boise State, from Tampa Bay through Washington, 169
Choice to Washington
8. Choice to Detroit
9. Tate, Ezra, RB, Mississippi College, 240
10. Hardy, Robert, DT, Jackson State, 267
11. Hinesly, Jim, G, Michigan State, 293
12. Moore, Jeff, RB, Jackson State, 319

TAMPA BAY
1. Choice to Chicago
2. Roberts, Greg, G, Oklahoma, from Baltimore, 33
Jones, Gordon, WR, Pittsburgh, 34
3. Eckwood, Jerry, RB, Arkansas, from Baltimore, 60
Choice to Miami
Lewis, Reggie, DE, North Texas State, from Houston, 78
Berns, Rick, RB, Nebraska, from LA Rams through Washington, Miami, and Oakland, 80
4. Choice to Pittsburgh through Detroit
5. Choice to Buffalo
Fusina, Chuck, QB, Penn State, from Houston, 133
6. Choice to Oakland
7. Choice to Seattle through Washington
8. Sanders, Eugene, DT, Texas A&M, from Miami, 217
Choice to NY Jets
9. Vereen, Henry, WR, Nevada-Las Vegas, 225
10. Choice to San Francisco
11. Rippentrop, Bob, TE, Fresno State, 281
12. Logan, David, DT, Pittsburgh, 307

WASHINGTON
1. Choice to Cincinnati
2. Choice to Oakland through St. Louis
3. Choice to Baltimore through Houston
4. Choice to Philadelphia
Warren, Don, TE, San Diego State, from Oakland through Green Bay, 103
5. Choice to Cleveland
6. Choice to Baltimore
7. Choice to New England
Milot, Rich, LB, Penn State, from Seattle, 182
8. Choice to Miami
9. Haines, Kris, WR, Notre Dame, 233
10. Coleman, Monte, LB, Central Arkansas, 289
Hall, Tony, WR, Knoxville, from New England, 300
12. Choice to Cleveland

1980
Held April 29-30, 1980

There were 333 selections instead of 336. Buffalo gave up its sixth-round choice in a 1979 supplemental draft. Philadelphia and Oakland forfeited their third-round and fourth-round choices, respectively.

ATLANTA
1. Miller, Junior, TE, Nebraska, 7
2. Curry, Buddy, LB, North Carolina, 36
3. Jones, Earl, DB, Norfolk State, 63
4. Laughlin, Jim, LB, Ohio State, 91
Hipp, I.M., RB, Nebraska, from Philadelphia, 104
5. Vassar, Brad, LB, Pacific, 117
Johnson, Kenny, DB, Mississippi State, from LA Rams through Washington, 137
6. Davis, Mike, DB, Colorado, 146
7. Smith, Mike, WR, Grambling, 172
8. Richardson, Al, LB, Georgia Tech, 201
9. Keller, Glen, C, West Texas State, 228

10. Bellamy, Walt, DB, Virginia Military, 257
11. Babb, Mike, DB, Oklahoma, 284
12. Jones, Quinn, RB, Tulsa, 313

BALTIMORE
1. Dickey, Curtis, RB, Texas A&M, 5
   Hatchett, Derrick, DB, Texas, from Dallas, 24
2. Donaldson, Ray, C, Georgia, 32
   Foley, Tim, T, Notre Dame, from Dallas, 51
3. Choice to Detroit
4. Butler, Raymond, WR, USC, 88
5. Choice to Kansas City
6. Foote, Chris, C, USC, 144
7. Roberts, Wesley, DE, TCU, 170
8. Walter, Ken, T, Texas Tech, from Detroit, 195
   Choice to Denver
9. Bright, Mark, RB, Temple, 227
10. Stewart, Larry, T, Maryland, 254
11. Whitley, Eddy, TE, Kansas State, 280
12. Bielski, Randy, K, Towson State, 311
   Sims, Marvin, RB, Clemson, from Denver, 324

BUFFALO
1. Choice to Seattle
   Ritcher, Jim, C, North Carolina State, from Seattle, 16
2. Cribbs, Joe, RB, Auburn, from San Francisco, 29
   Bradley, Gene, QB, Arkansas State, 37
3. Brammer, Mark, TE, Michigan State, 67
   Schmeding, John, G, Boston College, from Seattle, 71
4. Parker, Ervin, LB, South Carolina State, 93
5. Pyburn, Jeff, DB, Georgia, 119
   Lee, Keith, DB, Colorado State, from Washington, 129
6. Choice exercised in 1979 supplemental draft (Stewart, Rod, RB, Kentucky)
7. Choice to San Diego
8. Krueger, Todd, QB, Northern Michigan, 202
9. Davis, Kent, DB, Southeast Missouri State, 231
10. Cater, Greg, P, Tennessee-Chattanooga, 259
11. Gordon, Joe, DT, Grambling, 286
12. Lapham, Roger, TE, Maine, 316

CHI. BEARS
1. Wilson, Otis, LB, Louisville, 19
2. Suhey, Matt, RB, Penn State, 46
3. Choice to Dallas
4. Thompson, Arland, G, Baylor, 103
5. Tabor, Paul, C, Oklahoma, 130
6. Guess, Mike, DB, Ohio State, 156
7. Tolbert, Emanuel, WR, SMU, 183
8. Clark, Randy, G, Northern Illinois, 215
9. Schonert, Turk, QB, Stanford, 242
10. Stephens, Willie, DB, Texas Tech, 269
11. Judge, Chris, DB, TCU, 296
12. Fisher, Robert, TE, SMU, 323

CINCINNATI
1. Muñoz, Anthony, T, USC, 3
2. Criswell, Kirby, LB, Kansas, 31
3. Horn, Rod, DT, Nebraska, 59
4. Glass, Bill, G, Baylor, 86
5. Hicks, Bryan, DB, McNeese State, 113
6. Heath, Jo Jo, DB, Pittsburgh, 141
   Melontree, Andrew, LB, Baylor, from Tampa Bay, 159
7. Simpkins, Ron, LB, Michigan, from San Francisco, 167
   Johnson, Gary Don, DT, Baylor, 168
8. Lyles, Mark, RB, Florida State, 196
9. Bright, Greg, DB, Morehead State, 224
10. Vitiello, Sandro, K, Massachusetts, 252
11. Alexis, Alton, WR, Tulane, 281
12. Wright, Mike, QB, Vanderbilt, 308

CLEVELAND
1. Choice to LA Rams
   White, Charles, RB, USC, from LA Rams, 27
2. Choice to Denver
   Crosby, Cleveland, DE, Arizona, from San Diego through LA Rams, 54
3. Odom, Cliff, LB, Texas-Arlington, 72
4. Crews, Ron, DE, Nevada-Las Vegas, 99
   McDonald, Paul, QB, USC, from LA Rams, 109
5. Franks, Elvis, DE, Morgan State, from Green Bay through LA Rams, 116
   Choice to Oakland
6. Choice to San Diego
7. Choice to NY Giants
8. Copeland, Jeff, LB, Texas Tech, 209
9. Dewalt, Roy, RB, Texas-Arlington, 236
10. Fidel, Kevin, C, San Diego State, 263
11. Sales, Roland, RB, Arkansas, 294
12. Jackson, Marcus, DT, Purdue, 321

DALLAS
1. Choice to Baltimore
2. Choice to Baltimore
3. Roe, Bill, LB, Colorado, from Chi. Bears, 78
   Jones, James, RB, Mississippi State, 80
4. Petersen, Kurt, DE, Missouri, 105
5. Hogeboom, Gary, QB, Central Michigan, 133
6. Newsome, Timmy, RB, Winston-Salem State, 162
7. Brown, Lester, RB, Clemson, 189
8. Savage, Larry, LB, Michigan State, 216
9. Flowers, Jackie, WR, Florida State, 246
10. Teague, Matthew, DE, Prairie View A&M, 273
11. Padjen, Gary, LB, Arizona State, 300
12. Wells, Norm, DE, Northwestern, 330

DENVER
1. Choice to San Francisco through NY Jets
2. Jones, Rulon, DE, Utah State, from Cleveland, 42
   Choice to NY Jets
3. Carter, Larry, DB, Kentucky, 74
4. Parros, Rick, RB, Utah State, 107
5. Harden, Mike, DB, Michigan, 131
   Short, Laval, DT, Colorado, from San Diego through Washington and Cleveland, 136
6. Bishop, Keith, G, Baylor, 157
7. Havekost, John, G, Nebraska, 184
8. Coleman, Don, WR, Oregon, from Baltimore, 197
   Choice to St. Louis
9. Bracelin, Greg, LB, California, 243
10. Seay, Virgil, WR, Troy State, 270
11. Farris, Phil, WR, North Carolina, 297
12. Choice to Baltimore

DETROIT
1. Sims, Billy, RB, Oklahoma, 1
2. Choice to Minnesota through San Francisco
3. Turnure, Tom, C, Washington, 57
   Friede, Mike, WR, Indiana, from Baltimore, 62
4. Hipple, Eric, QB, Utah State, 85
5. Streeter, Mark, DB, Arizona, 111
   Ginn, Tommie, G, Arkansas, from Kansas City, 120
6. Dieterich, Chris, T, North Carolina State, 140
7. Murray, Ed, K, Tulane, 166
8. Choice to Baltimore
9. Jett, DeWayne, WR, Hawaii, 222
   Tuinei, Tom, DT, Hawaii, from San Francisco through Kansas City, 223
10. Henderson, Henry (Donnie), DB, Utah State, 251
11. Smith, Wayne, DB, Purdue, 278
12. Williams, Ray, KR, Washington State, 307

GREEN BAY
1. Clark, Bruce, DE, Penn State, 4
   Cumby, George, LB, Oklahoma, from San Diego, 26
2. Lee, Mark, DB, Washington, 34
3. Kitson, Syd, G, Wake Forest, 61
4. Nixon, Fred, WR, Oklahoma, 87
5. Choice to Cleveland through LA Rams
6. Swanke, Karl, G, Boston College, 143
7. Aydelette, Buddy, T, Alabama, 169
8. Smith, Tim, DB, Oregon State, 199
9. Saalfeld, Kelly, C, Nebraska, 226
10. White, Jafus, DB, Texas A&I, 253
11. Skiles, Ricky, LB, Louisville, 283
12. Stewart, James, DB, Memphis State, 310

HOUSTON
1. Choice to New England
2. Fields, Angelo, T, Michigan State, from Kansas City, 38
   Skaugstad, Daryle, DT, California, 52
3. Smith, Tim, WR-P, Nebraska, 79
4. Combs, Chris, TE, New Mexico, 106
5. Corker, John, LB, Oklahoma State, 134
6. Choice to New England
7. Bradshaw, Craig, QB, Utah State, from Oakland, 182
   Choice to NY Jets
8. Bailey, Harold, RB, Oklahoma State, 217
9. Harris, Ed, RB, Bishop, 244
10. Choice to Seattle
11. Preston, Eddie, WR, Western Kentucky, 301
12. Pitts, Wiley, WR, Temple, 328

KANSAS CITY
1. Budde, Brad, G, USC, 11
2. Choice to Houston
3. Hadnot, James, RB, Texas Tech, 66
4. Klug, Dave, LB, Concordia, 94
5. Carson, Carlos, WR, LSU, from Baltimore, 114
   Pensick, Dan, DT, Nebraska, from St. Louis, 115
   Choice to Detroit
6. Garcia, Bubba, WR, Texas-El Paso, 147
   Heater, Larry, RB, Arizona, from LA Rams, 164
7. Choice to LA Rams
8. Stepney, Sam, LB, Boston U., 203
9. Donovan, Tom, WR, Penn State, 230
10. Martinovich, Rob, T, Notre Dame, 261
11. Markham, Dale, DT, North Dakota, 287
12. Brewington, Mike, LB, East Carolina, 314

LA RAMS
1. Johnson, Johnnie, DB, Texas, from Cleveland, 17
   Choice to Cleveland
2. Pankey, Irv, T, Penn State, from Washington, 50
   Choice to Washington
3. Thomas, Jewerl, RB, San Jose State, from San Francisco, 58
   Irvin, LeRoy, DB, Kansas, from Oakland, 70
   Murphy, Phil, DT, South Carolina State, 82
4. Choice to Cleveland
5. Choice to Atlanta through Washington
6. Guman, Mike, RB, Penn State, from New England through Cleveland, 154
   Choice to Kansas City
7. Collins, Kirk, DB, Baylor, from Kansas City, 176
   Ellis, Gerry, RB, Missouri, 192
8. Pettigrew, Tom, T, Eastern Illinois, 220
9. Farmer, George, WR, Southern, 248
10. Gruber, Bob, T, Pittsburgh, 276
11. Greer, Terry, WR, Alabama State, 304
12. Scanlon, Kevin, QB, Arkansas, 332

MIAMI
1. McNeal, Don, DB, Alabama, 21
2. Stephenson, Dwight, C, Alabama, 48
3. Barnett, Bill, DE, Nebraska, 75
4. Bailey, Elmer, WR, Minnesota, 100
5. Choice to Seattle through Washington
6. Byrd, Eugene, WR, Michigan State, 158
7. Rose, Joe, TE, California, 185
8. Allen, Jeff, DB, Cal-Davis, 212
   Woodley, David, QB, LSU, from Washington, 214
9. Goodspeed, Mark, T, Nebraska, 239
10. Lantz, Doug, C, Miami (Ohio), 271
   Long, Ben, LB, South Dakota, from Philadelphia, 272
11. Driscoll, Phil, DE, Mankato State, from San Francisco, 279
   Choice to Philadelphia
12. Stone, Chuck, G, North Carolina State, 325

MINNESOTA
1. Martin, Doug, DT, Washington, 9
2. Teal, Willie, DB, LSU, from Detroit through San Francisco, 30
   Choice to San Francisco
3. Choice to San Francisco
   Boyd, Brent, C, UCLA, from New Orleans, 68
4. Johnson, Dennis, LB, USC, 92
5. Paschal, Doug, RB, North Carolina, 121
   Jones, Paul, RB, California, from New Orleans, 122
6. Yakavonis, Ray, DE, East Stroudsburg, 148
7. Johnson, Henry, LB, Georgia Tech, 174
8. Choice to Seattle
9. Mosley, Dennis, RB, Iowa, 232
10. Brown, Kenny, WR, Nebraska, 258
11. Harrell, Sam, RB, East Carolina, 288
12. Lane, Thomas, DB, Florida A&M, 315

NEW ENGLAND
1. James, Roland, DB, Tennessee, 14
   Ferguson, Vagas, RB, Notre Dame, from Houston, 25
2. McGrew, Larry, LB, USC, 45
3. McMichael, Steve, DT, Texas, 73
4. Choice to San Francisco through LA Rams
5. McDougald, Doug, DE-DT, Virginia Tech, 124
6. Choice to LA Rams through Cleveland
   Brown, Preston, WR, Vanderbilt, from Houston, 160
7. Kearns, Tom, G, Kentucky, 180
8. House, Mike, TE, Pacific, 208
9. Burget, Barry, LB, Oklahoma, 235
10. Daniel, Tom, C, Georgia Tech, 266
11. Hubach, Mike, P, Kansas, 293
12. Jordan, Jimmy, QB, Florida State, 320

NEW ORLEANS
1. Brock, Stan, T, Colorado, 12
2. Waymer, Dave, DB, Notre Dame, 41
3. Choice to Minnesota
4. Jolly, Mike, DB, Michigan, 96
5. Choice to Minnesota
6. Boyd, Lester, LB, Kentucky, 150
7. Morucci, Mike, RB, Bloomsburg, 177
8. Evans, Chuck, LB, Stanford, 206
9. Mordica, Frank, RB, Vanderbilt, 233
10. Webb, Tanya, DE, Michigan State, 262
11. Woodard, George, RB, Texas A&M, 289
12. Lewis, Kiser, LB, Florida A&M, 318

NY GIANTS
1. Haynes, Mark, DB, Colorado, 8
2. Choice to Pittsburgh
3. Lapka, Myron, DT, USC, 64
4. Pittman, Danny, WR, Wyoming, 90
5. Blount, Tony, DB, Virginia, 118
6. Brunner, Scott, QB, Delaware, 145
7. Choice to Oakland
   Hebert, Darryl, DB, Oklahoma, from Seattle, 179
   Linnin, Chris, DE, Washington, from Cleveland, 181
8. Harris, Ken, RB, Alabama, 200
9. Wonsley, Otis, RB, Alcorn State, 229
10. Sanford, Joe, T, Washington, 256
11. Bernish, Steve, DE, South Carolina, 285
12. Lansford, Mike, K, Washington, 312

NY JETS
1. Jones, Johnny (Lam), WR, Texas, from San Francisco, 2
   Choice to San Francisco
2. Ray, Darrol, DB, Oklahoma, 40
   Clayton, Ralph, WR-RB, Michigan, from Denver, 47
3. Mehl, Lance, LB, Penn State, 69
4. Johnson, Jesse, DB, Colorado, 95
5. Zidd, Jim, LB, Kansas, 123
6. Visger, George, DE-DT, Colorado, 149
   Schremp, Tom, DE-DT, Wisconsin, from Oakland, 152
7. Batton, Bob, RB, Nevada-Las Vegas, 178
   Leverett, Bennie, RB, Bethune-Cookman, from Houston, 190
8. Dziama, Jeff, LB, Boston College, 205
9. Peters, Joe, DT, Arizona State, 234
10. Bingham, Guy, C, Montana, 260
11. Zachery, James, LB, Texas A&M, 290
12. Dumars, David, DB, Northeast Louisiana, 317

OAKLAND
1. Wilson, Marc, QB, BYU, 15
2. Millen, Matt, LB, Penn State, 43
3. Choice to LA Rams
4. Choice forfeited
5. Lewis, Kenny, LB, Virginia Tech, from Cleveland, 125
   Adams, John, LB, LSU, 126
   Bowens, William, LB, North Alabama, from Tampa Bay, 128
6. Choice to NY Jets
7. Barnwell, Malcolm, WR, Virginia Union, from NY Giants, 173
   Choice to Houston
8. Hill, Kenny, DB, Yale, from San Francisco, 194
   Choice to San Francisco
9. Choice to San Francisco
10. Carter, Walter, DT, Florida State, 264
11. Massey, Mike, LB, Arkansas, 291
12. Muhammad, Calvin, WR, Texas Southern, 322

PHILADELPHIA
1. Young, Roynell, DB, Alcorn State, 23
2. Harrington, Perry, RB, Jackson State, 53
3. Choice forfeited
4. Choice to Atlanta
5. Rivers, Nate, WR, South Carolina State, 135
6. Murtha, Greg, T, Minnesota, 161
7. Ward, Terrell, DB, San Diego State, 188
8. Curcio, Mike, LB, Temple, 218
9. Harris, Bob, T, Bowling Green, 245
10. Choice to Miami
11. Jukes, Lee, WR, North Carolina State, from Miami, 298
Brown, Thomas, DE, Baylor, 302
12. Fields, Howard, DB, Baylor, 329

PITTSBURGH
1. Malone, Mark, QB, Arizona State, 28
2. Kohrs, Bob, LB, Arizona State, from NY Giants, 35
Goodman, John, DE, Oklahoma, 56
3. Sydnor, Ray, TE, Wisconsin, 83
4. Hurley, Bill, QB, Syracuse, 110
5. Wolfley, Craig, G, Syracuse, 138
6. Ilkin, Tunch, C, Indiana State, 165
7. Johnson, Nate, WR, Hillsdale, 193
8. Walton, Ted, DB, Connecticut, 221
9. McCall, Ron, WR, Arkansas-Pine Bluff, 249
10. Wilson, Woodrow, DB, North Carolina State, from San Francisco, 250
Fritz, Ken, G, Ohio State, 277
11. Pollard, Frank, RB, Baylor, 305
12. Vaclavik, Charles, DB, Texas, from San Francisco, 306
McGriff, Tyrone, G, Florida A&M, 333

ST. LOUIS
1. Greer, Curtis, DE, Michigan, 6
2. Marsh, Doug, TE, Michigan, 33
3. Sinnott, John, T, Brown, 60
Baker, Charlie, LB, New Mexico, from San Diego, 81
4. Lisch, Rusty, QB, Notre Dame, 89
5. Choice to Kansas City
6. Acker, Bill, DT, Texas, 142
7. Apuna, Ben, LB, Arizona State, 171
8. Branch, Dupree, DB, Colorado State, 198
Hudson, Grant, DT, Virginia, from Denver, 211
9. Mays, Stafford, DE, Washington, 225
10. Brown, Rush, DT, Ball State, 255
11. Brown, Delrick, DB, Houston, 282
12. Gray, Tyrone, WR, Washington State, 309

SAN DIEGO
1. Choice to Green Bay
2. Choice to Cleveland through LA Rams
3. Choice to St. Louis
4. Luther, Ed, QB, San Jose State, from Tampa Bay, 101
Gregor, Bob, DB, Washington State, 108
5. Choice to Denver through Washington and Cleveland
6. Harrington, LaRue, RB, Norfolk State, from Cleveland, 151
Hamilton, Wayne, LB, Alabama, 163
7. Loewen, Chuck, G, South Dakota State, from Buffalo, 175
Dodds, Stuart, P, Montana State, 191
8. Sirmones, Curtis, RB, North Alabama, 219
9. Whitman, Steve, RB, Alabama, 247
10. Choice to Tampa Bay
11. Singleton, John, DE, Texas-El Paso, 303
12. Price, Harry, WR, McNeese State, 331

SAN FRANCISCO
1. Choice to NY Jets
Cooper, Earl, RB, Rice, from NY Jets, 13
Stuckey, Jim, DT, Clemson, from Denver through NY Jets, 20
2. Choice to Buffalo
Turner, Keena, LB, Purdue, from Minnesota, 39
3. Choice to LA Rams
Miller, Jim, P, Mississippi, from Minnesota, 65
Puki, Craig, LB, Tennessee, from Washington through LA Rams, 77
4. Churchman, Ricky, DB, Texas, 84
Hodge, David, LB, Houston, from New England through LA Rams, 98
5. Times, Kenneth, DT, Southern, 112
6. Williams, Herb, DB, Southern, 139
7. Choice to Cincinnati
8. Choice to Oakland
Leopold, Bobby, LB, Notre Dame, from Oakland, 210
9. Choice to Detroit through Kansas City
Hartwig, Dan, QB, California Lutheran, from Oakland, 237
10. Choice to Pittsburgh
11. Choice to Miami
12. Choice to Pittsburgh

SEATTLE
1. Green, Jacob, DE, Texas A&M, from Buffalo, 10
Choice to Buffalo
2. Hines, Andre, T, Stanford, 44
3. Choice to Buffalo
4. Dion, Terry, DE, Oregon, 97
5. Steele, Joe, RB, Washington, 127
Jacobs, Daniel, DE, Winston-Salem State, from Miami through Washington, 132
6. McNeal, Mark, DE, Idaho, 153
7. Choice to NY Giants
8. Minor, Vic, DB, Northeast Louisiana, from Minnesota, 204
Cosgrove, Jack, C, Pacific, 207
9. Swift, Jim, T, Iowa, 238
10. Essink, Ron, T, Grand Valley State, 265
Reaves, Billy, WR, Morris Brown, from Houston, 274
11. Ena, Tali, RB, Washington State, 292
12. Gilbert, Presnell, DB, U.S. International, 319

TAMPA BAY
1. Snell, Ray, G, Wisconsin, 22
2. House, Kevin, WR, Southern Illinois, 49
3. Brantley, Scot, LB, Florida, 76
4. Choice to San Diego
Flowers, Larry, DB, Texas Tech, from Washington, 102
5. Choice to Oakland
6. Choice to Cincinnati
7. Leonard, Jim, C, Santa Clara, 186
8. Goodard, Derrick, DB, Drake, 213
9. Carter, Gerald, WR, Texas A&M, 240
10. Hawkins, Andy, LB, Texas A&I, 267
Davis, Brett, RB, Nevada-Las Vegas, from San Diego, 275
11. Jones, Terry, DE, Central State (Oklahoma), 299
12. Coleman, Gene, DB, Miami, 326

WASHINGTON
1. Monk, Art, WR, Syracuse, 18
2. Choice to LA Rams
Mendenhall, Mat, DE, BYU, from LA Rams, 55
3. Choice to San Francisco through LA Rams
4. Choice to Tampa Bay
5. Choice to Buffalo
6. Bell, Farley, LB, Cincinnati, 155
7. Jones, Melvin, G, Houston, 187
8. Choice to Miami
9. McCullough, Lawrence, WR, Illinois, 241
10. Walker, Lewis, RB, Utah, 268
11. Matocha, Mike, DE, Texas-Arlington, 295
12. Emmett, Marcene, DB, North Alabama, 327

1981
Held April 28-29, 1981

There were 332 selections instead of 336. Atlanta gave up its seventh-round pick and San Diego its ninth-round choice in 1980 supplemental drafts. Denver and Oakland forfeited their third-round and fifth-round choices, respectively.

ATLANTA
1. Butler, Bobby, DB, Florida State, 25
2. White, Lyman, LB, LSU, 54
3. Woerner, Scott, DB, Georgia, 80
4. Scully, John, C, Notre Dame, 109
5. Sanders, Eric, T, Nevada-Reno, 136
6. Stanback, Harry, DT, North Carolina, 164
7. Choice exercised in 1980 supplemental draft (Teague, Matthew, DE, Prairie View A&M)
8. Toney, Clifford, DB, Auburn, 219
9. Fance, Calvin, RB, Rice, 245
10. Murphy, Robert, DB, Ohio State, 274
11. Chappelle, Keith, WR, Iowa, 301
12. McCants, Mark, DB, Temple, 330

BALTIMORE
1. McMillan, Randy, RB, Pittsburgh, 12
Thompson, Donnell, DT, North Carolina, from Minnesota, 18
2. Choice to Minnesota
3. Van Divier, Randy, T, Washington, 68
4. Sherwin, Tim, TE, Boston College, 94
5. Choice to Minnesota
6. Green, Bubba, DT, North Carolina State, 149
7. Ariri, Obed, K, Clemson, 178
8. Sitton, Ken, DB, Oklahoma, 204
Taylor, Hosea, DT, Houston, from Philadelphia, 220
9. Gooch, Tim, DT, Kentucky, 233
10. Gerken, Gregg, LB, Northern Arizona, from San Francisco, 256
Bryant, Trent, DB, Arkansas, 259
11. Smith, Holden, WR, California, 288
12. Scoggins, Eric, LB, USC, 315

BUFFALO
1. Choice to Oakland
Moore, Booker, RB, Penn State, from Oakland, 28
2. Williams, Chris, DB, LSU, from Cleveland, 49
Franklin, Byron, WR, Auburn, 50
3. Mosley, Mike, WR, Texas A&M, 76
Geathers, Robert, DT, South Carolina State, from Oakland
4. Choice to LA Rams
5. Clark, Calvin, DE, Purdue, 135
6. Holt, Robert, WR, Baylor, 161
7. Doolittle, Steve, LB, Colorado, 188
8. Choice to New Orleans
9. Riddick, Robb, RB, Millersville, 241
10. Cross, Justin, T, Western Colorado, 272
11. Barnett, Buster, TE, Jackson State, 299
12. Clark, Keith, LB, Memphis State, 326

CHI. BEARS
1. Van Horne, Keith, T, USC, 11
2. Singletary, Mike, LB, Baylor, from San Francisco, 38
Choice to San Francisco
3. Margerum, Ken, WR, Stanford, 67
4. Bell, Todd, DB, Ohio State, 95
5. Choice to San Francisco
6. Henderson, Reuben, DB, San Diego State, 150
7. Fisher, Jeff, DB, USC, 177
8. Zettek, Scott, DT, Notre Dame, 205
9. Ditta, Frank, G, Baylor, 232
10. Clifford, Tim, QB, Indiana, 260
11. Johnson, Lonnie, RB, Indiana, 287
12. Shupryt, Bob, LB, New Mexico, 316

CINCINNATI
1. Verser, David, WR, Kansas, 10
2. Collinsworth, Chris, WR, Florida, 37
3. Simmons, John, DB, SMU, 64
4. Frazier, Guy, LB, Wyoming, 93
5. Pryor, Benjie, TE, Pittsburgh, 120
6. Robinson, Rex, K, Georgia, 146
7. Schuh, Jeff, LB, Minnesota, 176
8. Kemp, Bobby, DB, Cal State-Fullerton, 202
9. Hannula, Jim, T, Northern Illinois, 229
Samoa, Samoa, RB, Washington State, from San Francisco, 230
10. Simpson, Hubert, RB, Tennessee, 258
11. Jackson, Robert, DB, Central Michigan, 285
12. O'Connell, Mark, QB, Ball State, 312

CLEVELAND
1. Dixon, Hanford, DB, Southern Mississippi, 22
2. Choice to Buffalo
3. Choice to Kansas City through Denver
4. Choice to San Diego
Robinson, Mike, DE, Arizona, from Washington, 92
5. Cox, Steve, K, Arkansas, 134
6. Simmons, Ron, DT, Florida State, 160
7. Johnson, Eddie, LB, Louisville, 187
8. Choice to NY Jets
9. Schleusener, Randy, G, Nebraska, 244
10. Prater, Dean, DE, Oklahoma State, 271
11. Friday, Larry, DB, Mississippi State, 298
12. McGill, Kevin, T, Oregon, 325

DALLAS
1. Richards, Howard, T, Missouri, 26
2. Donley, Doug, WR, Ohio State, 53
3. Titensor, Glen, DE, BYU, 81
4. Pelluer, Scott, LB, Washington State, from San Francisco, 91
Nelson, Derrie, LB, Nebraska, 108
5. Spradlin, Danny, LB, Tennessee, 137
6. Skillings, Vince, DB, Ohio State, 163
7. Fellows, Ron, DB, Missouri, from Tampa Bay, 173
Miller, Ken, DB, Eastern Michigan, 191
8. Piurowski, Paul, LB, Florida State, 218
9. Wilson, Mike, WR, Washington State, 246
10. Graham, Pat, DT, California, 273
11. Morrison, Tim, G, Georgia, 302
12. Lundy, Nate, WR, Indiana, 329

DENVER
1. Smith, Dennis, DB, USC, 15
2. Brown, Clay, TE, BYU, 42
3. Choice forfeited
4. Herrmann, Mark, QB, Purdue, 98
5. Lanier, Ken, T, Florida State, 125
6. Lewis, Alvin, RB, Colorado State, 151
7. Busick, Steve, LB, USC, 181
8. Choice to NY Giants
9. Olsen, Rusty, DE, Washington, 234
10. Choice to St. Louis
11. Walker, Pat, WR, Miami, 290
12. Hankerd, John, LB, Notre Dame, 317
Robinson, Mandel, RB, Wyoming, from Detroit, 321

DETROIT
1. Nichols, Mark, WR, San Jose State, 16
2. Green, Curtis, DE, Alabama State, 46
3. Greco, Don, G, Western Illinois, 72
4. Porter, Tracy, WR, LSU, 99
5. Lee, Larry, G, UCLA, 129
6. Johnson, Sam, DB, Maryland, 155
7. Spivey, Lee, T, SMU, 182
8. Niziolek, Bob, TE, Colorado, 211
9. Jernigan, Hugh, DB, Arkansas, 238
Martin, Dave, DB, Villanova, from New England, 240
10. Cannavino, Andy, LB, Michigan, 264
11. Jackson, Willie, DB, Mississippi State, 294
12. Choice to Denver

GREEN BAY
1. Campbell, Rich, QB, California, 6
2. Lewis, Gary, TE, Texas-Arlington, 35
3. Stachowicz, Ray, P, Michigan State, 62
Choice to Washington
4. Turner, Richard, DT, Oklahoma from LA Rams through Washington, 105
5. Braggs, Byron, DT, Alabama, 117
6. Choice to NY Giants
7. Whitaker, Bill, DB, Missouri, 172
8. Werts, Larry, LB, Jackson State, 200
9. Huffman, Tim, T, Notre Dame, 227
10. Hall, Nickie, QB, Tulane, 255
11. Valora, Forrest, LB, Oklahoma, 282
12. Lewis, Cliff, LB, Southern Mississippi, 311

HOUSTON
1. Choice to Oakland
2. Choice to Oakland
3. Holston, Michael, WR, Morgan State, 79
4. Eyre, Nick, T, BYU, 106
5. Fowler, Delbert, LB, West Virginia, 133
6. Kay, Bill, DB, Purdue, 159
7. Choice to Seattle
Washington, Don, DB, Texas A&I, from Oakland, 193
8. Tullis, Willie, WR, Troy State, 217
9. Riley, Avon, LB, UCLA, 243
10. Jones, Larry, RB, Colorado State, 270
11. Mathews, Claude, G, Auburn, 297
12. Capece, Bill, K, Florida State, 324

KANSAS CITY
1. Scott, Willie, TE, South Carolina, 14
2. Delaney, Joe, RB, Northwestern State (Louisiana), 41
3. Harvey, Marvin, TE, Southern Mississippi, 70
Taylor, Roger, T, Oklahoma State, from Cleveland through Denver, 75
Burruss, Lloyd, DB, Maryland, from LA Rams, 78
4. Washington, Ron, WR, Arizona State, 97
5. Thomas, Todd, T, North Dakota, 124
6. Luckie, Dock, DT, Florida, 153
7. Jackson, Billy, RB, Alabama, 180
8. Dorri, David, WR, Rutgers, 206
9. Vereen, Anthony, DB, Southeastern Louisiana, 237
10. Studdard, Les, G, Texas, 262

11. Case, Frank, DE, Penn State, 289
12. Gagliano, Bob, QB, Utah State, 319

LA RAMS
1. Owens, Mel, LB, Michigan, from Washington, 9
   Choice to Washington
2. Choice to Minnesota through Washington and Baltimore
   Collins, Jim, LB, Syracuse, from Miami, 43
3. Choice to Kansas City
   Meisner, Greg, DT, Pittsburgh, from Tampa Bay, 63
   Cobb, Robert, DE, Arizona, from Washington, 66
4. Lilja, George, C, Michigan, from Buffalo, 104
   Choice to Green Bay through Washington
5. Choice to Washington
6. Daniels, William, DT, Alabama State, 158
7. Battle, Ron, TE, North Texas State, from Washington, 175
   Clark, Mike, DE, Florida, 190
8. Plunkett, Art, T, Nevada-Las Vegas, 216
9. Seawell, Ron, LB, Portland State, 242
10. Alexander, Robert, RB, West Virginia, 269
11. Greene, Marcellus, DB, Arizona, 296
12. Penaranda, Jairo, RB, UCLA, 328

MIAMI
1. Overstreet, David, RB, Oklahoma, 13
2. Choice to LA Rams
   Franklin, Andra, RB, Nebraska, from Oakland through LA Rams, 56
3. Choice to LA Rams
4. Greene, Sam, WR, Nevada-Las Vegas, from New Orleans, 84
   Wright, Brad, QB, New Mexico, 96
5. Poole, Ken, DE, Northeast Louisiana, 126
   Vigorito, Tommy, RB, Virginia, from Philadelphia, 138
6. Moore, Mack, DE, Texas A&M, 152
   Walker, Fulton, DB, West Virginia, from Minnesota, 154
7. Daum, Mike, T, Cal Poly-SLO, 179
8. Judson, William, DB, South Carolina State, 208
9. Noonan, John, WR, Nebraska, 235
10. Folsom, Steve, TE, Utah, 261
11. Jensen, Jim, QB, Boston U., 291
12. Alford, John, DT, South Carolina State, 318

MINNESOTA
1. Choice to Baltimore
2. McDole, Mardye, WR, Mississippi State, from Baltimore, 39
   Sendlein, Robin, LB, Texas, 45
   Redwine, Jarvis, RB, Nebraska, from LA Rams through Washington and Baltimore, 52
3. Choice to New Orleans
   Irwin, Tim, T, Tennessee, from New England, 74
4. Swain, John, DB, Miami, 101
5. Choice to New Orleans
   Ray, Wendell, DE, Missouri, from Baltimore, 123
6. Choice to Miami
7. Shaver, Don, RB, Kutztown, 184
8. Wilson, Wade, QB-P, East Texas State, 210
9. Choice to Seattle
10. Murphy, James, WR, Utah State, 266
11. Stephanos, Bill, T, Boston College, 293
12. Williams, Brian, TE, Southern, 320

NEW ENGLAND
1. Holloway, Brian, T, Stanford, 19
2. Collins, Tony, RB, East Carolina, 47
3. Choice to Minnesota
4. Blackmon, Don, LB, Tulsa, 102
5. Clark, Steve, DT, Kansas State, 130
6. Wooten, Ron, G, North Carolina, 157
7. Toler, Ken, WR, Mississippi, 185
8. Naber, Ken, K-P, Stanford, from New Orleans, 194
   Dawson, Lin, TE, North Carolina State, 212
9. Choice to Detroit
10. Choice to Cleveland
11. Buckley, Brian, QB, Harvard, 295
12. Crissy, Cris, DB, Princeton, 323

NEW ORLEANS
1. Rogers, George, RB, South Carolina, 1
2. Gary, Russell, DB, Nebraska, 29
   Jackson, Rickey, LB, Pittsburgh, from San Diego, 51
3. Warren, Frank, DE, Auburn, 57
   Brenner, Hoby, TE, USC, from Minnesota, 71
4. Choice to Miami
5. Oubre, Louis, T, Oklahoma, 112
   Boyarsky, Jerry, DT, Pittsburgh, from Minnesota, 128
6. Hudson, Nat, G, Georgia, 139
   Poe, Johnnie, DB, Missouri, from Tampa Bay, 144
   Redd, Glen, LB, BYU, from Oakland, 166
7. Williams, Kevin, WR, USC, 167
8. Choice to New England
   Gladys, Gene, LB, Penn State, from Buffalo, 214
   Evans, Kevin, DB, Arkansas, from San Diego, 215
9. Tyler, Toussaint, RB, Washington, 222
10. Gajan, Hokie, RB, LSU, 249
11. Mickens, Lester, WR, Kansas, 277
12. Wilks, Jim, DT, San Diego State, 305

NY GIANTS
1. Taylor, Lawrence, LB, North Carolina, 2
2. Young, Dave, TE, Purdue, 32
3. Mistler, John, WR, Arizona State, 59
4. Chatman, Clifford, RB, Central State (Oklahoma), 85
5. Neill, Bill, DT, Pittsburgh, 115
6. Choice to San Diego
   Hoover, Mel, WR, Arizona State, from Green Bay, 145
   O'Neal, Edward, RB, Tuskegee, 165
7. Jackson, Louis, RB, Cal Poly-SLO, 168
8. Powers, John, G, Michigan, 197
   Reed, Mark, QB, Moorhead State, from Denver, 207
   Ard, Billy, G, Wake Forest, from Oakland, 221
9. Hunt, Byron, LB, SMU, 224
10. Barker, Mike, DT, Grambling, 250
11. Choice to San Diego
12. Maher, Mike, TE, Western Illinois, 307

NY JETS
1. McNeil, Freeman, RB, UCLA, 3
2. Barber, Marion, RB, Minnesota, 30
3. Rudolph, Ben, DT, Long Beach State, 60
4. Washington, Al, LB, Ohio State, 86
5. Keys, Tyrone, DE, Mississippi State, 113
6. Woodring, John, LB, Brown, 142
7. Neil, Kenny, DE, Iowa State, 169
8. Jones, Lloyd, WR, BYU, 195
   Watts, J.C., DB, Oklahoma, from Cleveland, 213
9. Larry, Admiral Dewey, DB, Nevada-Las Vegas, 225
10. Wetzel, Marty, LB, Tulane, 251
11. Gall, Ed, DT, Maryland, 278
12. Moeller, Mike, T, Drake, 308

OAKLAND
1. Watts, Ted, DB, Texas Tech, from Houston, 21
   Marsh, Curt, T, Washington, from Buffalo, 23
   Choice to Buffalo
2. Long, Howie, DT, Villanova, from Houston, 48
   Choice to Miami through LA Rams
3. Choice to Buffalo
4. Robinson, Johnny, DT, Louisiana Tech, 111
5. Davis, James, DB, Southern, from Tampa Bay, 118
   Choice forfeited
6. Choice to New Orleans
7. Choice to Houston
8. Choice to NY Giants
9. Mohl, Curt, T, UCLA, 248
10. Hawkins, Frank, RB, Nevada-Reno, 276
11. Willis, Chester, RB, Auburn, 304
12. Nelson, Phil, TE, Delaware, 332

PHILADELPHIA
1. Mitchell, Leonard, DE, Houston, 27
2. Miraldi, Dean, G, Utah, 55
3. LaFleur, Greg, TE, LSU, 82
4. Murray, Calvin, RB, Ohio State, 110
5. Choice to Miami
6. Choice to NY Giants
7. Duncan, Alan, K, Tennessee, from San Francisco, 174
   Field, Doak, LB, Baylor, 192
8. Choice to Baltimore
9. Commiskey, Chuck, C, Mississippi, 247
10. Oliver, Hubie, RB, Arizona, 275
11. Davis, Gail, DT, Virginia Union, 303
12. Ellis, Ray, DB, Ohio State, 331

PITTSBURGH
1. Gary, Keith, DE, Oklahoma, 17
2. Washington, Anthony, DB, Fresno State, 44
3. Donnalley, Rick, C-G, North Carolina, 73
4. Martin, Robbie, WR, Cal Poly-SLO, 100
5. Martin, Ricky, WR, New Mexico, 127
6. Hinkle, Bryan, LB, Oregon, 156
7. Little, David, LB, Florida, 183
8. Wilson, Frank, RB, Rice, 209
9. Hunter, James, T, USC, 239
10. Mayock, Mike, DB, Boston College, 265
11. Trocano, Rick, QB, Pittsburgh, 292
12. Choice to San Francisco

ST. LOUIS
1. Junior, E.J., LB, Alabama, 5
2. Lomax, Neil, QB, Portland State, 33
3. Griffin, Jeff, DB, Utah, 61
4. Rhodes, Steve, WR, Oklahoma, 88
5. Gillen, John, LB, Illinois, 116
6. Ahrens, Dave, LB, Wisconsin, 143
7. Donnalley, Kevin, DB, North Dakota State, 171
8. Fisher, Mike, WR, Baylor, 198
9. Mitchell, Stump, RB, Citadel, 226
10. Mallard, James, WR, Alabama, 253
    Joiner, Jim, WR, Miami, from Denver, 263
11. Sherrod, Mike, TE, Illinois, 281
12. Adams, Joe, G, Nebraska, 309

SAN DIEGO
1. Brooks, James, RB, Auburn, 24
2. Choice to New Orleans
3. Phillips, Irvin, DB, Arkansas Tech, 77
4. Lawrence, Amos, RB, North Carolina, 103
   Sievers, Eric, TE, Maryland, from Cleveland, 107
5. Ferguson, Keith, LB, Ohio State, 131
6. Gissinger, Andrew, T, Syracuse, from NY Giants, 141
   Duckworth, Bobby, WR, Arkansas, 162
7. Holohan, Pete, TE, Notre Dame, 189
8. Choice to New Orleans
9. Choice exercised in 1980 supplemental draft (Mullins, Billy, WR, USC)
10. Parham, Robert, RB, Grambling, 268
11. Petrzelka, Matt, T, Iowa, from NY Giants, 280
    Bradley, Carlos, LB, Wake Forest, 300
12. Charles, Stacy, WR, Bethune-Cookman, 327

SAN FRANCISCO
1. Lott, Ronnie, DB, USC, 8
2. Harty, John, DT, Iowa, from Washington, 36
   Choice to Chi. Bears
   Wright, Eric, DB, Missouri, from Chi. Bears, 40
3. Williamson, Carlton, DB, Pittsburgh, 65
4. Choice to Dallas
5. Thomas, Lynn, DB, Pittsburgh, 121
   Jones, Arrington, RB, Winston-Salem State, from Chi. Bears, 122
6. Kugler, Pete, DT, Penn State, 147
7. Choice to Philadelphia
8. White, Garry, RB, Minnesota, 203
9. Choice to Cincinnati
10. Choice to Baltimore
11. DeBose, Ronnie, TE, UCLA, 286
12. Ogilvie, Major, RB, Alabama, 313
    Adams, Joe, QB, Tennessee State, from Pittsburgh, 322

SEATTLE
1. Easley, Kenny, DB, UCLA, 4
2. Hughes, David, RB, Boise State, 31
3. Dugan, Bill, G, Penn State, 58
4. Phillips, Scott, WR, BYU, 87
5. Bailey, Edwin, G, South Carolina State, 114
6. Durham, Steve, DE, Clemson, 140
7. Johnson, Ron, WR, Long Beach State, 170
   Scovill, Brad, TE, Penn State, from Houston, 186
8. Lane, Eric, RB, BYU, 196
9. Stone, Jim, RB, Notre Dame, 223
   Whatley, Jim, WR, Washington State, from Minnesota, 236
10. Dawson, Ken, RB, Savannah State, 252
11. Olander, Lance, RB, Colorado, 279
12. Bednarek, Jeff, DT, Pacific, 306

TAMPA BAY
1. Green, Hugh, LB, Pittsburgh, 7
2. Wilder, James, RB, Missouri, 34
3. Choice to LA Rams
4. Holt, John, DB, West Texas State, 89
5. Choice to Oakland
6. Choice to New Orleans
7. Choice to Dallas
8. Johnson, Denver, T, Tulsa, 199
9. Ford, Mike, QB, SMU, 228
10. McCune, Ken, DE, Texas, 254
11. Smith, Johnny Ray, DB, Lamar, 283
12. White, Brad, DT, Tennessee, 310

WASHINGTON
1. Choice to LA Rams
   May, Mark, T, Pittsburgh, from LA Rams, 20
2. Choice to San Francisco
3. Choice to LA Rams
   Grimm, Russ, C, Pittsburgh, from Miami through LA Rams, 69
4. Flick, Tom, QB, Washington, from Green Bay, 90
   Choice to Cleveland
5. Manley, Dexter, DE, Oklahoma State, 119
   Sayre, Gary, G, Cameron, from LA Rams, 132
6. Kubin, Larry, LB, Penn State, 148
7. Choice to LA Rams
8. Brown, Charlie, WR, South Carolina State, 201
9. Grant, Darryl, G, Rice, 231
10. Kessel, Phil, QB, Northern Michigan, 257
    Kennedy, Allan, T, Washington State, from New England through Cleveland, 267
11. Hill, Jerry, WR, North Alabama, 284
12. Didier, Clint, WR, Portland State, 314

1982

Held April 27-28, 1982

There were 334 selections instead of 336. New Orleans gave up its first-round pick and New England its eleventh round pick in 1981 supplemental drafts. Although the Raiders played the 1982 season in Los Angeles, at the time of the draft, the franchise still was located in Oakland.

ATLANTA
1. Riggs, Gerald, RB, Arizona State, 9
2. Rogers, Doug, DE, Stanford, 36
3. Bailey, Stacey, WR, San Jose State, 63
4. Brown, Reggie, RB, Oregon, 95
5. Mansfield, Von, DB, Wisconsin, 122
6. Kelley, Mike, QB, Georgia Tech, 149
7. Toloumu, David, RB, Hawaii, 176
8. Eberhardt, Ricky, DB, Morris Brown, 203
9. Horan, Mike, P, Long Beach State, 235
10. Stowers, Curtis, LB, Mississippi State, 262
11. Keller, Jeff, WR, Washington State, 288
12. Levenick, Dave, LB, Wisconsin, 315

BALTIMORE
1. Cooks, Johnie, LB, Mississippi State, 2
   Schlichter, Art, QB, Ohio State, from LA Rams, 4
2. Wisniewski, Leo, DT, Penn State, 28
   Stark, Rohn, P, Florida State, from LA Rams, 34
3. Burroughs, James, DB, Michigan State, 57
4. Pagel, Mike, QB, Arizona State, 84
5. Crouch, Terry, G, Oklahoma, 113
6. Beach, Pat, TE, Washington State, 140
7. Jenkins, Fletcher, DT, Washington, 169
8. Loia, Tony, G, Arizona State, 196
9. Berryhill, Tony, C, Clemson, 225
10. Deery, Tom, DB, Widener, 252
11. Meacham, Lamont, DB, Western Kentucky, 280
12. Wright, Johnnie, RB, South Carolina, 307

BUFFALO
1. Tuttle, Perry, WR, Clemson, from Denver, 19
   Choice to Denver
2. Kofler, Matt, QB, San Diego State, 48
3. Marve, Eugene, LB, Saginaw Valley State, from Cleveland, 59

Choice to Seattle
4. Williams, Van, RB, Carson-Newman, from St. Louis, 93
Choice to Denver
5. Choice to Washington
6. Chivers, DeWayne, TE, South Carolina, 160
7. Anderson, Gary, K, Syracuse, from Cleveland, 171
Choice to Detroit through LA Rams
8. Tousignant, Luc, QB, Fairmont State, 218
9. Edwards, Dennis, DT, USC, 245
10. James, Vic, DB, Colorado, 272
11. Kalil, Frank, G, Arizona, 298
12. Suber, Tony, DT, Gardner-Webb, 329

CHI. BEARS
1. McMahon, Jim, QB, BYU, 5
2. Choice to Tampa Bay
3. Wrightman, Tim, TE, UCLA, 62
4. Gentry, Dennis, RB, Baylor, 89
5. Hartnett, Perry, G, SMU, 116
Tabron, Dennis, DB, Duke, from San Diego, 134
6. Becker, Kurt, G, Michigan, 146
7. Waechter, Henry, DT, Nebraska, 173
8. Doerger, Jerry, T, Wisconsin, 200
9. Hatchett, Mike, DB, Texas, 230
10. Turner, Joe, DB, USC, 257
11. Boliaux, Guy, LB, Wisconsin, 283
12. Young, Ricky, LB, Oklahoma State, 313

CINCINNATI
1. Collins, Glen, DE, Mississippi State, 26
2. Weaver, Emanuel, DT, South Carolina, 54
3. Holman, Rodney, TE, Tulane, 82
4. Tate, Rodney, RB, Texas, 110
5. Sorensen, Paul, DB, Washington State, 138
6. King, Arthur, DT, Grambling, 166
7. Needham, Ben, LB, Michigan, 194
8. Yli-Renko, Kari, T, Cincinnati, 222
9. Bennett, James, WR, Northwestern State (Louisiana), 250
10. Hogue, Larry, DB, Utah State, 278
11. Davis, Russell, RB, Idaho, 350
12. Feraday, Dan, QB, Toronto, 333

CLEVELAND
1. Banks, Chip, LB, USC, 3
2. Baldwin, Keith, DE, Texas A&M, 31
3. Choice to Buffalo
4. Walker, Dwight, WR, Nicholls State, 87
5. Babb, Mike, C, Texas, 115
6. Choice to Dallas
Whitwell, Mike, WR, Texas A&M, from Denver, 162
7. Choice to Buffalo
8. Kafentzis, Mark, DB, Hawaii, 199
Heflin, Van, TE, Vanderbilt, from Oakland, 204
Jackson, Bill, DB, North Carolina, from Washington, 211
9. Baker, Milton, TE, West Texas State, 227
10. Floyd, Ricky, RB, Southern Mississippi, 255
11. Michuta, Steve, QB, Grand Valley State, 282
12. Nicolas, Scott, LB, Miami, 310

DALLAS
1. Hill, Rod, DB, Kentucky State, 25
2. Rohrer, Jeff, LB, Yale, 53
3. Eliopulos, Jim, LB, Wyoming, 81
4. Carpenter, Brian, DB, Michigan, from Tampa Bay, 101
5. Hunter, Monty, DB, Salem (West Virginia), 109
Pozderac, Phil, T, Notre Dame, 137
6. Hammond, Ken, G, Vanderbilt, from Cleveland, 143
Daum, Charles, DT, Cal Poly-SLO, 165
7. Purifoy, Bill, DE, Tulsa, 193
8. Peoples, George, RB, Auburn, from Denver through Buffalo, 216
Sullivan, Dwight, RB, North Carolina State, 221
9. Gary, Joe, DT, UCLA, 249
10. Eckerson, Todd, T, North Carolina State, 277
11. Thompson, George, WR, Albany State (Georgia), from Tampa Bay, 295
Whiting, Mike, RB, Florida State, 304
12. Burtness, Rich, G, Montana, 332

DENVER
1. Choice to Buffalo
Willhite, Gerald, RB, San Jose State, from Buffalo, 21
2. McDaniel, Orlando, WR, LSU, 50
3. Choice to Houston through LA Rams
4. Choice to Kansas City
Plater, Dan, WR, BYU, from Buffalo, 106
5. Winder, Sammy, RB, Southern Mississippi, 131
6. Choice to Cleveland
7. Ruben, Alvin, DE, Houston, 189
8. Choice to Dallas through Buffalo
9. Uecker, Keith, T, Auburn, 243
10. Woodward, Ken, LB, Tuskegee, 274
11. Yatsko, Stuart, G, Oregon, 300
12. Clark, Brian, G, Clemson, 327

DETROIT
1. Williams, Jimmy, LB, Nebraska, 15
2. Watkins, Bobby, DB, Southwest Texas State, 42
3. Doig, Steve, LB, New Hampshire, 69
4. McNorton, Bruce, DB, Georgetown (Kentucky), 96
5. Graham, William, DB, Texas, 127
6. Machurek, Mike, QB, Idaho State, 154
7. Bates, Phil, RB, Nebraska, from Houston, 175
Choice to LA Rams
Simmons, Victor, WR, Oregon State, from Buffalo through LA Rams, 187
8. Moss, Martin, DE, UCLA, 208
9. Wagoner, Danny, DB, Kansas, from Oakland through LA Rams, 231
Choice to Miami
10. Barnes, Roosevelt, LB, Purdue, 266
11. Lee, Edward, WR, South Carolina State, 292
12. Porter, Ricky, RB, Slippery Rock, 319
Rubick, Rob, TE, Grand Valley State, from San Diego, 326

GREEN BAY
1. Choice to New Orleans through San Diego
Hallstrom, Ron, G, Iowa, from San Diego, 22
2. Choice to New England through San Diego
3. Rodgers, Del, RB, Utah, 71
4. Brown, Robert, LB, Virginia Tech, 98
5. Meade, Mike, RB, Penn State, 126
6. Parlavecchio, Chet, LB, Penn State, 152
7. Whitley, Joey, DB, Texas-El Paso, 183
8. Boyd, Thomas, LB, Alabama, 210
9. Riggins, Charles, DE, Bethune-Cookman, 237
10. Garcia, Eddie, K, SMU, 264
11. Macaulay, John, C, Stanford, 294
12. Epps, Phillip, WR, TCU, 321

HOUSTON
1. Munchak, Mike, G, Penn State, 8
2. Choice to Oakland
Luck, Oliver, QB, West Virginia, from Tampa Bay through Miami and LA Rams, 44
3. Choice to LA Rams
Edwards, Stan, RB, Michigan, from NY Giants, 72
Abraham, Robert, LB, North Carolina State, from Denver through LA Rams, 77
4. Bryant, Steve, WR, Purdue, 94
5. Taylor, Malcolm, DE, Tennessee State, 121
6. Allen, Gary, RB, Hawaii, 148
7. Choice to Detroit
8. Choice to LA Rams
9. Bradley, Matt, DB, Penn State, 234
10. Reeves, Ron, QB, Texas Tech, 261
11. Campbell, Jim, TE, Kentucky, 287
12. Craft, Donnie, RB, Louisville, 314

KANSAS CITY
1. Hancock, Anthony, WR, Tennessee, from St. Louis, 11
Choice to St. Louis
2. Daniels, Calvin, LB, North Carolina, 46
3. Choice to St. Louis
4. Haynes, Louis, LB, North Texas State, 100
Anderson, Stuart, LB, Virginia, from Denver, 104
5. Thompson, Delbert, RB, Texas-El Paso, 130
6. Roquemore, Durwood, DB, Texas A&I, 157
7. Smith, Greg, DT, Kansas, 184
8. DeBruijn, Case, P-K, Idaho State, 214
9. Byford, Lyndle, T, Oklahoma, 241
10. Brodsky, Larry, WR, Miami, 268
11. Carter, Bob, WR, Arizona, 297
12. Miller, Mike, DB, Southwest Texas State, 324

LA RAMS
1. Choice to Baltimore
Redden, Barry, RB, Richmond, from Washington, 14
2. Choice to Baltimore
3. Choice to Washington
Bechtold, Bill, C, Oklahoma, from Houston, 67
4. Gaylord, Jeff, LB, Missouri, 88
5. Kersten, Wally, T, Minnesota, from Seattle, 117
Barnett, Doug, DE, Azusa Pacific, 118
6. Locklin, Kerry, TE, New Mexico State, 145
7. Choice to Pittsburgh through Washington
Shearin, Joe, G, Texas, from Detroit, 181
8. Jones, A.J. (Jam), RB, Texas, 202
Reilly, Mike, DE, Oklahoma, from Houston, 207
9. Speight, Bob, T, Boston U., 229
10. McPherson, Miles, DB, New Haven, 256
11. Coffman, Ricky, WR, UCLA, 285
12. Coley, Raymond, DT, Alabama A&M, 312

MIAMI
1. Foster, Roy, G, USC, 24
2. Duper, Mark, WR, Northwestern State (Louisiana), 52
3. Lankford, Paul, DB, Penn State, 80
4. Bowser, Charles, LB, Duke, 108
5. Nelson, Bob, DT, Miami, from Minnesota, 120
Diana, Rich, RB, Yale, 136
6. Tutson, Tom, DB, South Carolina State, from San Diego, 161
Hester, Ron, LB, Florida State, 164
7. Johnson, Dan, TE, Iowa State, from New Orleans, 170
Cowan, Larry, RB, Jackson State, 192
8. Randle, Tate, DB, Texas Tech, 220
9. Clark, Steve, DE, Utah, from Detroit, 239
Boatner, Mack, RB , Southeastern Louisiana, 248
10. Fisher, Robin, LB, Florida, from Philadelphia, 271
Jones, Wayne, T, Utah, 276
11. Crum, Gary, T, Wyoming, 303
12. Rodrique, Mike, WR, Miami, 331

MINNESOTA
1. Nelson, Darrin, RB, Stanford, 7
2. Tausch, Terry, T, Texas, 39
3. Choice to New Orleans
4. Fahnhorst, Jim, LB, Minnesota, 92
5. Choice to Miami
6. Storr, Greg, LB, Boston College, 147
7. Jordan, Steve, TE, Brown, 179
8. Harmon, Kirk, LB, Pacific, 206
9. Howard, Bryan, DB, Tennessee State, 233
10. Lucear, Gerald, WR, Temple, 260
11. Rouse, Curtis, G, Tennessee-Chattanooga, 286
12. Milner, Hobson, RB, Cincinnati, 318

NEW ENGLAND
1. Sims, Ken, DE, Texas, 1
Williams, Lester, DT, Miami, from San Francisco, 27
2. Choice to San Francisco
Weathers, Robert, RB, Arizona State, from Green Bay through San Diego, 40
Tippett, Andre, LB, Iowa, from Washington through San Francisco, 41
Haley, Darryl, T, Utah, from San Francisco, 55
3. Jones, Cedric, WR, Duke, 56
Weishuhn, Clayton, LB, Angelo State, from Seattle, 60
4. Crump, George, DE, East Carolina, 85
Ingram, Brian, LB, Tennessee, from San Francisco, 111
5. Marion, Fred, DB, Miami, 112
6. Smith, Ricky, DB, Alabama State, 141
7. Roberts, Jeff, LB, Tulane, 168
8. Collins, Ken, LB, Washington State, 197
9. Murdock, Kelvin, WR, Troy State, 224
10. Clark, Brian, K, Florida, 253
11. Choice exercised in 1981 supplemental draft (Davidson, Chy, WR, Rhode Island)
12. Sandon, Steve, QB, Northern Iowa, from NY Giants, 296
Taylor, Greg, KR, Virginia, 308

NEW ORLEANS
1. Choice exercised in 1981 supplemental draft (Wilson, Dave, QB, Illinois)
Scott, Lindsay, WR, Georgia, from Green Bay through San Diego, 13
2. Edelman, Brad, C, Missouri, 30
3. Lewis, Rodney, DB, Nebraska, 58
Goodlow, Eugene, WR, Kansas State, from Minnesota, 66
Duckett, Kenny, WR, Wake Forest, from Washington, 68
Krimm, John, DB, Notre Dame, from San Diego, 76
4. Andersen, Morten, K, Michigan State, 86
5. Elliott, Tony, DE, North Texas State, 114
6. Lewis, Marvin, RB, Tulane, 142
7. Choice to Miami
8. Slaughter, Chuck, T, South Carolina, 198
9. Choice to Washington
10. Choice to Washington
11. Choice to Washington
12. Choice to Washington

NY GIANTS
1. Woolfolk, Butch, RB, Michigan, 18
2. Morris, Joe, RB, Syracuse, 45
3. Choice to Houston
4. Raymond, Gerry, G, Boston College, 102
5. Umphrey, Rich, C, Colorado, 129
6. Nicholson, Darrell, LB, North Carolina, 156
7. Wiska, Jeff, G, Michigan State, 186
8. Hubble, Robert, TE, Rice, 213
9. Higgins, John, DB, Nevada-Las Vegas, 240
10. Baldinger, Rich, T, Wake Forest, 270
11. Choice to New England
12. Seale, Mark, DT, Richmond, 323

NY JETS
1. Crable, Bob, LB, Notre Dame, 23
2. McElroy, Reggie, T, West Texas State, 51
3. Crutchfield, Dwayne, RB, Iowa State, 79
4. Floyd, George, DB, Eastern Kentucky, 107
5. Jerue, Mark, LB, Washington, 135
6. Phea, Lonell, WR, Houston, 163
7. Coombs, Tom, TE, Idaho, 191
8. Texada, Lawrence, RB, Henderson State, 219
9. Klever, Rocky, RB, Montana, 247
10. Hemphill, Darryl, DB, West Texas State, 275
11. Parmelee, Perry, WR, Santa Clara, 302
12. Carlstrom, Tom, G, Nebraska, 330

OAKLAND
1. Allen, Marcus, RB, USC, 10
2. Squirek, Jack, LB, Illinois, from Houston, 35
Romano, Jim, C, Penn State, 37
3. McElroy, Vann, DB, Baylor, 64
4. Muransky, Ed, T, Michigan, 91
5. Jackson, Ed, LB, Louisiana Tech, 123
6. Choice to San Francisco
7. Jackson, Jeff, DE, Toledo, 177
8. Choice to Cleveland
9. Choice to Detroit through LA Rams
10. D'Amico, Rich, LB, Penn State, 263
11. Turner, Willie, WR, LSU, 289
12. Smith, Randy, WR, East Texas State, 316

PHILADELPHIA
1. Quick, Mike, WR, North Carolina State, 20
2. Sampleton, Lawrence, TE, Texas, 47
3. Kab, Vyto, TE, Penn State, 78
4. Griggs, Anthony, LB, Ohio State, 105
5. DeVaughn, Dennis, DB, Bishop, 132
6. Grieve, Curt, WR, Yale, 159
7. Armstrong, Harvey, DT, SMU, 190
8. Fritzsche, Jim, T, Purdue, 217
9. Woodruff, Tony, WR, Fresno State, 244
10. Choice to Miami
11. Ingram, Ron, WR, Oklahoma State, 301
12. Taylor, Rob, T, Northwestern, 328

PITTSBURGH
1. Abercrombie, Walter, RB, Baylor, 12
2. Meyer, John, T, Arizona State, 43
3. Merriweather, Mike, LB, Pacific, 70
4. Woods, Rick, DB, Boise State, 97
5. Dallafior, Ken, T, Minnesota, 124
6. Perko, Mike, DT, Utah State, 155
Bingham, Craig, LB, Syracuse, from San Francisco through New Orleans, 167

7. Nelson, Edmund, DT, Auburn, from LA Rams, 172
Boures, Emil, C, Pittsburgh, 182
8. Goodson, John, P, Texas, 209
9. Hirn, Mike, TE, Central Michigan, 236
10. Sunseri, Sal, LB, Pittsburgh, 267
11. Sorboor, Mikal Abdul, G, Morgan State, 293
12. Hughes, Al, DE, Western Michigan, 320

ST. LOUIS
1. Choice to Kansas City
Sharpe, Luis, T, UCLA, from Kansas City, 16
2. Galloway, David, DT, Florida, 38
3. Perrin, Benny, DB, Alabama, 65
Guilbeau, Rusty, DE, McNeese State, from Kansas City, 73
4. Robbins, Tootie, T, East Carolina, from Seattle, 90
5. Bedford, Vance, DB, Texas, 119
Ferrell, Earl, RB, East Tennessee State, from Washington, 125
6. Shaffer, Craig, LB, Indiana State, 150
7. Sebro, Bob, C, Colorado, 178
8. Lindstrom, Chris, DT, Boston U., 205
9. Dalley, Darnell, LB, Maryland, 232
10. McGill, Eddie, TE, Western Carolina, 259
11. Williams, James, DE, North Carolina A&T, 290
12. Atha, Bob, K, Ohio State, 317

SAN DIEGO
1. Choice to Green Bay
2. Choice to Washington through LA Rams
3. Choice to New Orleans
4. Choice to Tampa Bay
5. Choice to Chi. Bears
6. Choice to Miami
7. Hall, Hollis, DB, Clemson, 188
8. Buford, Maury, P, Texas Tech, 215
9. Lyles, Warren, DT, Alabama, 246
10. Young, Andre, DB, Louisiana Tech, 273
11. Watson, Anthony, DB, New Mexico State, 299
12. Choice to Detroit

SAN FRANCISCO
1. Choice to New England
2. Paris, Bubba, T, Michigan, from New England, 29
Choice to New England
3. Choice to Tampa Bay through San Diego
4. Choice to New England
5. Williams, Newton, RB, Arizona State, 139
6. Choice to Pittsburgh through New Orleans
Williams, Vince, RB, Oregon, from Oakland, 151
7. Ferrari, Ron, LB, Illinois, 195
8. Choice to Washington through New Orleans
9. Clark, Bryan, QB, Michigan State, 251
10. McLemore, Dana, KR, Hawaii, from Tampa Bay, 269
Barbian, Tim, DT, Western Illinois, 279
11. Gibson, Gary, LB, Arizona, 306
12. Washington, Tim, DB, Fresno State, 334

SEATTLE
1. Bryant, Jeff, DE, Clemson, 6
2. Scholtz, Bruce, LB, Texas, 33
3. Choice to New England
Metzelaars, Pete, TE, Wabash, from Buffalo, 75
4. Choice to St. Louis
5. Choice to LA Rams
6. Campbell, Jack, T, Utah, 144
7. Williams, Eugene, LB, Tulsa, 174
8. Cooper, Chester, WR, Minnesota, 201
9. Jefferson, David, LB, Miami, 228
10. Austin, Craig, LB, South Dakota, 258
11. Clancy, Sam, DE-DT, Pittsburgh, 284
12. Naylor, Frank, C, Rutgers, 311

TAMPA BAY
1. Farrell, Sean, G, Penn State, 17
2. Choice to Houston through Miami and LA Rams
Reese, Booker, DE, Bethune-Cookman, from Chi. Bears, 32
3. Bell, Jerry, TE, Arizona State, 74
Cannon, John, DE, William & Mary, from San Francisco through San Diego, 83
4. Choice to Dallas
Barrett, Dave, RB, Houston, from San Diego, 103
5. Davis, Jeff, LB, Clemson, 128
6. Tyler, Andre, WR, Stanford, 158
7. Morris, Tom, DB, Michigan State, 185
8. Atkins, Kelvin, LB, Illinois, 212
9. Lane, Bob, QB, Northeast Louisiana, 242
10. Choice to San Francisco
11. Choice to Dallas
12. Morton, Michael, KR, Nevada-Las Vegas, 325

WASHINGTON
1. Choice to Baltimore through LA Rams
2. Choice to New England through San Francisco
Dean, Vernon, DB, San Diego State, from San Diego through LA Rams, 49
3. Powell, Carl, WR, Jackson State, from LA Rams, 61
Choice to New Orleans
4. Liebenstein, Todd, DE, Nevada-Las Vegas, 99
5. Choice to St. Louis
Williams, Michael, TE, Alabama A&M, from Buffalo, 133
6. Jeffers, Lamont, LB, Tennessee, 153
7. Schachtner, John, LB, Northern Arizona, 180
8. Choice to Cleveland
Warthen, Ralph, DT, Gardner-Webb, from San Francisco through New Orleans, 223
9. Coffey, Ken, DB, Southwest Texas State, from New Orleans, 226
Trautman, Randy, DT, Boise State, 238
10. Smith, Harold, DE, Kentucky State, from New Orleans, 254
Daniels, Terry, DB, Tennessee, 265
11. Miller, Dan, K, Miami, from New Orleans, 281
Holly, Bob, QB, Princeton, 291
12. Laster, Don, T, Tennessee State, from New Orleans, 309
Goff, Jeff, LB, Arkansas, 322

1983
Held April 26-27, 1983

There were 335 selections instead of 336. Detroit gave up its ninth-round pick in a 1982 supplemental draft.

ATLANTA
1. Pitts, Mike, DE, Alabama, 16
2. Britt, James, DB, LSU, 43
3. Provence, Andrew, DE, South Carolina, 75
4. Harper, John, LB, Southern Illinois, 102
5. Miller, Brett, T, Iowa, 129
6. Allen, Anthony, WR, Washington, 156
7. Turk, Jeff, DB, Boise State, 183
8. Rade, John, LB, Boise State, 215
9. Choice to Baltimore
10. Giacomarro, Ralph, P, Penn State, 268
11. Salley, John, DB, Wyoming, 295
12. Matthews, Allama, TE, Vanderbilt, 322

BALTIMORE
1. Elway, John, QB, Stanford, 1
2. Maxwell, Vernon, LB, Arizona State, 29
3. Achica, George, DT, USC, 57
4. Smith, Phil, WR, San Diego State, 85
5. Abramowitz, Sid, T, Tulsa, 113
6. Choice to San Diego
Feasel, Grant, C, Abilene Christian, from San Diego, 161
7. Moore, Alvin, RB, Arizona State, 169
8. Choice to Denver
9. Mills, Jim, T, Hawaii, 225
Rose, Chris, T, Stanford, from Atlanta, 241
10. Hopkins, Ronald, DB, Murray State, 252
11. Taylor, Jim Bob, QB, Georgia Tech, 280
12. Williams, Carl, WR, Texas Southern, 308

BUFFALO
1. Hunter, Tony, TE, Notre Dame, 12
Kelly, Jim, QB, Miami, from Cleveland, 14
2. Talley, Darryl, LB, West Virginia, 39
3. Choice to New Orleans through St. Louis
4. Junkin, Trey, LB, Louisiana Tech, 93
Payne, Jimmy, DE, Georgia, from Washington through New Orleans, 112
5. Vandenboom, Matt, DB, Wisconsin, 126
6. Choice to NY Giants through LA Rams
7. Brown, Gurnest, DT, Maryland, 180
8. Durham, James, DB, Houston, 207
9. Parker, George, RB, Norfolk State, 234
10. Tharpe, Richard, DT, Louisville, 260
11. White, Larry, DE, Jackson State, 293
12. Dawkins, Julius, WR, Pittsburgh, 320

CHI. BEARS
1. Covert, Jim, T, Pittsburgh, 6
Gault, Willie, WR, Tennessee, from Tampa Bay, 18
2. Richardson, Mike, DB, Arizona State, 33
3. Duerson, Dave, DB, Notre Dame, 64
4. Thayer, Tom, C, Notre Dame, 91
Dunsmore, Pat, TE, Drake, from San Diego, 107
5. Choice to New England
6. Choice to Cleveland
7. Choice to Cleveland
8. Dent, Richard, DE, Tennessee State, 203
Bortz, Mark, DT, Iowa, from San Diego, 219
9. Fada, Rob, G, Pittsburgh, 230
Zavagnin, Mark, LB, Notre Dame, from Cleveland through San Francisco, 235
10. Hutchison, Anthony, RB, Texas Tech, 256
11. Worthy, Gary, RB, Wilmington, 286
12. Williams, Oliver, WR, Illinois, from San Francisco, 313
Choice to San Diego

CINCINNATI
1. Rimington, Dave, C, Nebraska, 25
2. Horton, Ray, DB, Washington, 53
3. Turner, Jim, DB, UCLA, 81
4. Maidlow, Steve, LB, Michigan State, 109
5. Christensen, Jeff, QB, Eastern Illinois, 137
6. DeAyala, Kiki, LB, Texas, from New Orleans, 152
Kinnebrew, Larry, RB, Tennessee State, 165
7. Griffin, James, DB, Middle Tennessee State, 193
8. Martin, Mike, WR, Illinois, 221
9. Wilson, Stanley, RB, Oklahoma, 248
10. Krumrie, Tim, DT, Wisconsin, 276
11. Williams, Gary, WR, Ohio State, 304
12. Young, Andre, LB, Bowling Green, 332

CLEVELAND
1. Choice to Buffalo
2. Brown, Ron, WR, Arizona State, 41
3. Camp, Reggie, DE, California, 68
4. Choice to San Diego
5. Contz, Bill, T, Penn State, 122
6. Stracka, Tim, TE, Wisconsin, from Chi. Bears, 145
Puzzuoli, Dave, DT, Pittsburgh, 149
7. Belk, Rocky, WR, Miami, from Chi. Bears, 176
Choice to Philadelphia
8. McClearn, Mike, G, Temple, 209
9. Choice to Chi. Bears through San Francisco
10. Hopkins, Thomas, T, Alabama A&M, 262
11. Green, Boyce, RB, Carson-Newman, 288
McAdoo, Howard, LB, Michigan State, from LA Raiders, 305
12. Farren, Paul, T, Boston U., 316

DALLAS
1. Jeffcoat, Jim, DE, Arizona State, 23
2. Walter, Mike, DE, Oregon, 50
3. Caldwell, Bryan, DE, Arizona State, 77
4. Faulkner, Chris, TE, Florida, 108
5. McSwain, Chuck, RB, Clemson, 135
6. Collier, Reggie, QB, Southern Mississippi, 162
7. Schultz, Chris, T, Arizona, 189
8. Ricks, Lawrence, RB, Michigan, 220
9. Gross, Al, DB, Arizona, 246
10. Moran, Eric, T, Washington, 273
11. Taylor, Dan, T, Idaho State, 300
12. Bouier, Lorenzo, RB, Maine, 331

DENVER
1. Hinton, Chris, G, Northwestern, 4
2. Cooper, Mark, T, Miami, 31
3. Sampson, Clint, WR, San Diego State, 60
4. Choice to LA Rams through San Francisco
5. Harris, George, LB, Houston, 116
Baldwin, Bruce, DB, Harding, from New Orleans, 125
6. Heflin, Victor, DB, Delaware State, 143
7. Dupree, Myron, DB, North Carolina Central, 172
8. Kubiak, Gary, QB, Texas A&M, from Baltimore, 197
Choice to Pittsburgh
9. Hawkins, Brian, DB, San Jose State, 228
10. Bowyer, Walt, DE, Arizona State, 254
11. Bailey, Don, C, Miami, 283
12. Mecklenburg, Karl, DT, Minnesota, 310

DETROIT
1. Jones, James, RB, Florida, 13
2. Strenger, Rich, T, Michigan, 40
3. Cofer, Mike, DE, Tennessee, 67
4. Curley, August, LB, USC, 94
5. Johnson, Demetrious, DB, Missouri, from LA Rams, 115
Mott, Steve, C, Alabama, 121
6. Brown, Todd, WR, Nebraska, 154
7. Black, Mike, P, Arizona State, 181
8. Stapleton, Bill, DB, Washington, 208
9. Choice used in 1982 supplemental draft (Robinson, Kevin, DB, North Carolina A&T)
10. Laube, Dave, G, Penn State, 261
11. Tate, Ben, RB, North Carolina Central, 287
12. Lane, Jim, C, Idaho State, 321

GREEN BAY
1. Lewis, Tim, DB, Pittsburgh, from New Orleans, 11
Choice to San Diego
2. Drechsler, Dave, G, North Carolina, 48
3. Choice to Miami through Houston
4. Miller, Mike, WR, Tennessee, 104
5. Thomas, Bryan, RB, Pittsburgh, 132
6. Sams, Ron, G, Pittsburgh, 160
7. Clark, Jessie, RB, Arkansas, 188
8. Briscoe, Carlton, DB, McNeese State, 216
9. Ham, Robin, C, West Texas State, 243
10. Williams, Byron, WR, Texas-Arlington, from Houston, 253
Thomas, Jimmy, DB, Indiana, 271
11. Scribner, Bucky, P, Kansas, 299
12. Harvey, John, DT, USC, 327

HOUSTON
1. Choice to LA Rams
Matthews, Bruce, T, USC, from Seattle, 9
2. Salem, Harvey, T, California, 30
Bostic, Keith, DB, Michigan, from Seattle, 42
3. Joiner, Tim, LB, LSU, 58
Dressel, Chris, TE, Stanford, from Seattle, 69
Brown, Steve, DB, Oregon, from Miami, 83
4. Hill, Greg, DB, Oklahoma State, 86
McCloskey, Mike, TE, Penn State, from LA Rams, 88
5. Moriarty, Larry, RB, Notre Dame, 114
Foster, Jerome, DT, Ohio State, from Miami, 139
6. Haworth, Steve, DB, Oklahoma, 142
7. Walls, Herkie, WR, Texas, 170
8. Thompson, Robert, LB, Michigan, 198
9. Potter, Kevin, DB, Missouri, 226
10. Choice to Green Bay
11. Choice to NY Giants
12. Choice to NY Giants

KANSAS CITY
1. Blackledge, Todd, QB, Penn State, 7
2. Lutz, Dave, T, Georgia Tech, 34
3. Lewis, Albert, DB, Grambling, 61
4. Wetzel, Ron, TE, Arizona State, 92
5. Arnold, Jim, P, Vanderbilt, 119
6. Gardner, Ellis, T, Georgia Tech, 146
7. Thomas, Ken, RB, San Jose State, 173
Posey, Daryl, RB, Mississippi College, from New Orleans, 179
8. Eatman, Irv, T, UCLA, 204
9. Lingner, Adam, C, Illinois, 231
10. Shumate, Mark, DT, Wisconsin, 257
11. Jackson, DeWayne, DE, South Carolina State, 284
12. Jones, Ken, T, Tennessee, 315

LA RAIDERS
1. Mosebar, Don, T, USC, 26
2. Pickel, Bill, DT, Rutgers, 54
3. Caldwell, Tony, LB, Washington, 82
4. Townsend, Greg, DE, TCU, 110
5. Williams, Dokie, WR, UCLA, 138
6. Choice to Washington
7. McCall, Jeff, RB, Clemson, 194
8. Dotterer, Mike, RB, Stanford, 222
9. Jordan, Kent, TE, St. Mary's (California), 249

10. Fernandez, Mervyn, WR, San Jose State, 277
11. Choice to Cleveland
12. Lindquist, Scott, QB, Northern Arizona, 333

LA RAMS
1. Dickerson, Eric, RB, SMU, from Houston, 2
Choice to Seattle through Houston
2. Ellard, Henry, WR, Fresno State, 32
Wilcher, Mike, LB, North Carolina, from San Francisco, 36
3. Choice to San Francisco
4. Nelson, Chuck, K, Washington, from Denver through San Francisco, 87
Choice to Houston
Newsome, Vince, DB, Washington, from NY Giants, 97
Reed, Doug, DT, San Diego State, from Miami, 111
5. Choice to Detroit
Grant, Otis, WR, Michigan State, from San Diego, 134
6. Kowalski, Gary, T, Boston College, 144
7. Simmons, Jeff, WR, USC, 171
8. West, Troy, DB, USC, 200
9. Belcher, Jack, C, Boston College, 227
10 Choice to Minnesota
11. Triplett, Danny, LB, Clemson, 282
12. Casper, Clete, QB, Washington State, 311

MIAMI
1. Marino, Dan, QB, Pittsburgh, 27
2. Charles, Mike, DT, Syracuse, 55
3. Benson, Charles, DE, Baylor, from Green Bay through Houston, 76
Choice to Houston
4. Choice to LA Rams
5. Choice to Houston
6. Roby, Reggie, P, Iowa, 167
7. Woetzel, Keith, LB, Rutgers, 195
8. Clayton, Mark, WR, Louisville, 223
9. Brown, Mark, LB, Purdue, 250
10. Reed, Anthony, RB, South Carolina State, 278
11. Lukens, Joe, G, Ohio State, 306
12. Carter, Anthony, WR, Michigan, 334

MINNESOTA
1. Browner, Joey, DB, USC, 19
2. Choice to Philadelphia
3. Ashley, Walker Lee, LB, Penn State, 73
4. Rush, Mark, RB, Miami, 100
5. Stewart, Mark, LB, Washington, 127
6. Jones, Mike, WR, Tennessee State, 159
7. Lee, Carl, DB, Marshall, 186
8. Brown, Norris, TE, Georgia, 213
9. Achter, Rod, WR, Toledo, 239
10. Brown, Melvin, DB, Mississippi, from LA Rams, 255
Tate, Walter, C, Tennessee State, 266
11. Butcher, Brian, G, Clemson, 298
12. Turner, Maurice, RB, Utah State, 325

NEW ENGLAND
1. Eason, Tony, QB, Illinois, 15
2. Wilson, Darryal, WR, Tennessee, 47
3. Starring, Stephen, WR, McNeese State, 74
Moore, Steve, G, Tennessee State, from San Diego, 80
4. Rembert, Johnny, LB, Clemson, 101
5. Creswell, Smiley, DE, Michigan State, from Chi. Bears, 118
Lewis, Darryl, TE, Texas-Arlington, 128
6. Bass, Mike, K, Illinois, 155
7. James, Craig, RB, SMU, 187
8. Lippett, Ronnie, DB, Miami, 214
9. Williams, Ricky, RB, Langston, from New Orleans, 233
Keel, Mark, TE, Arizona, 240
10. Williams, James, TE, Wyoming, from NY Giants, 264
Williams, Toby, DE, Nebraska, from New Orleans, 265
Ramsey, Tom, QB, UCLA, 267
11. Parker, Steve, WR, Abilene Christian, from New Orleans, 292
Eason, Calvin, DB, Houston, 294
12. Kelly, Waddell, RB, Arkansas State, from New Orleans, 319
Ekern, Andy, T, Missouri, 326

NEW ORLEANS
1. Choice to Green Bay
2. Korte, Steve, G, Arkansas, 38
3. Tice, John, TE, Maryland, 65
Austin, Cliff, RB, Clemson, from Buffalo through St. Louis, 66
4. Lewis, Gary, NT, Oklahoma State, 98
5. Choice to Denver
6. Choice to Cincinnati
7. Choice to Kansas City
8. Greenwood, David, DB, Wisconsin, 206
9. Choice to New England
10. Choice to New England
11. Choice to New England
12. Choice to New England

NY GIANTS
1. Kinard, Terry, DB, Clemson, 10
2. Marshall, Leonard, DT, LSU, 37
3. Williams, Jamie, TE, Nebraska, from San Francisco through LA Rams, 63
Nelson, Karl, T, Iowa State, 70
4. Choice to LA Rams
5. Scott, Malcolm, TE, LSU, 124
6. Patterson, Darrell, LB, TCU, 151
Belcher, Kevin, G, Texas-El Paso, from Buffalo through LA Rams, 153
7. Williams, Perry, DB, North Carolina State, 178
8. Headen, Andy, LB, Clemson, 205
9. Haji-Sheikh, Ali, K, Michigan, 237
10. Choice to New England
11. Jenkins, Lee, DB, Tennessee, from Houston, 281
Pierson, Clenzie, DT, Rice, 291
12. Jones, Robbie, LB, Alabama, from Houston, 309
Magwood, Frank, WR, Clemson, 318
Tuggle, John, RB, California, from Washington, 335

NY JETS
1. O'Brien, Ken, QB, Cal-Davis, 24
2. Hector, Johnny, RB, Texas A&M, 51
3. Townsell, JoJo, WR, UCLA, 78
4. Howell, Wes, TE, California, 105
5. Walker, John, DT, Nebraska-Omaha, 136
6. White, Vincent, RB, Stanford, 163
7. Newbold, Darrin, LB, Southwest Missouri State, 190
8. Mullen, Davlin, DB, Western Kentucky, 217
9. Humphrey, Bobby, WR, New Mexico State, 247
10. Fike, Dan, T, Florida, 274
11. Harmon, Mike, WR, Mississippi, 301
12. Crum, Stu, K, Tulsa, 328

PHILADELPHIA
1. Haddix, Michael, RB, Mississippi State, 8
2. Hopkins, Wes, DB, SMU, 35
Schulz, Jody, LB, East Carolina, from Minnesota, 46
3. Young, Glen, WR, Mississippi State, 62
4. Williams, Michael, RB, Mississippi College, 89
5. Darby, Byron, DT, USC, 120
6. Oatis, Victor, WR, Northwestern State (Louisiana), 147
7. Edgar, Anthony, RB, Hawaii, 174
Schultheis, Jon, G, Princeton, from Cleveland, 182
8. Kraynak, Rich, LB, Pittsburgh, 201
9. Pelzer, Rich, T, Rhode Island, 232
10. Strauthers, Thomas, DE, Jackson State, 258
11. Sebahar, Steve, C, Washington State, 285
12. Mangrum, David, QB, Baylor, 312

PITTSBURGH
1. Rivera, Gabriel, DT, Texas Tech, 21
2. Capers, Wayne, WR, Kansas, 52
3. Seabaugh, Todd, LB, San Diego State, 79
4. Metcalf, Bo Scott, DB, Baylor, 106
5. Skansi, Paul, WR, Washington, 133
Garrity, Gregg, WR, Penn State, from Washington, 140
6. Williams, Eric, DB, North Carolina State, 164
7. Kirchner, Mark, G, Baylor, 191
8. Odom, Henry, RB, South Carolina State, from Denver, 199
Dunaway, Craig, TE, Michigan, 218
9. Wingle, Blake, G, UCLA, 244
10. Straughter, Roosevelt, DB, Northeast Louisiana, 275
11. Raugh, Mark, TE, West Virginia, 302
12. Wiley, Roger, RB, Sam Houston State, 330

ST. LOUIS
1. Smith, Leonard, DB, McNeese State, 17
2. Mack, Cedric, DB, Baylor, 44
3. Dardar, Ramsey, DT, LSU, 71
4. Duda, Mark, DT, Maryland, from Seattle, 96
Washington, Lionel, DB, Tulane, 103
5. Bird, Steve, WR, Eastern Kentucky, 130
6. Schmitt, George, DB, Delaware, 157
7. Scott, Carlos, C, Texas-El Paso, 184
8. Harris, Bob, DB, Auburn, 211
9. Brown, Otis, RB, Jackson State, 242
10. Lucas, Tim, LB, California, 269
11. Williams, Aaron, WR, Washington, 296
12. Lane, James, LB, Alabama State, 323

SAN DIEGO
1. Smith, Billy Ray, LB, Arkansas, from San Francisco, 5
Anderson, Gary, WR-RB, Arkansas, from Green Bay, 20
Byrd, Gill, DB, San Jose State, 22
2. Choice to San Francisco
3. Choice to New England
4. Walters, Danny, DB, Arkansas, from Cleveland, 95
Choice to Chi. Bears
5. Choice to LA Rams
6. Johnson, Trumaine, WR, Grambling, from Baltimore, 141
Choice to Baltimore
7. Elko, Bill, DT, LSU, 192
8. Jackson, Earnest, RB, Texas A&M, from San Francisco, 202
Choice to Chi. Bears
9. Green, Mike, LB, Oklahoma State, 245
10. Mathison, Bruce, QB, Nebraska, 272
11. Kearse, Tim, WR, San Jose State, 303
Spencer, Tim, RB, Ohio State, from Washington, 307
12. Blaylock, Billy, DB, Tennessee Tech, from Chi. Bears, 314
Ehin, Chuck, DT, BYU, 329

SAN FRANCISCO
1. Choice to San Diego
2. Choice to LA Rams
Craig, Roger, RB, Nebraska, from San Diego, 49
3. Montgomery, Blanchard, LB, UCLA, from LA Rams, 59
Choice to NY Giants through LA Rams
4. Holmoe, Tom, DB, BYU, 90
5. Gray, Riki, LB, USC, 117
6. Choice to Tampa Bay
7. Moten, Gary, LB, SMU, 175
8. Choice to San Diego
9. Mularkey, Mike, TE, Florida, 229
10. Merrell, Jeff, DT, Nebraska, 259
11. Sapolu, Jesse, G, Hawaii, 289
12. Choice to Chi. Bears

SEATTLE
1. Warner, Curt, RB, Penn State, from LA Rams through Houston, 3
Choice to Houston
2. Choice to Houston
3. Choice to Houston
4. Choice to St. Louis
5. Castor, Chris, WR, Duke, 123
6. Gipson, Reginald, RB, Alabama A&M, 150
7. Merriman, Sam, LB, Idaho, 177
8. Hernandez, Matt, T, Purdue, 210
9. Clasby, Bob, T, Notre Dame, 236
10. Speros, Pete, G, Penn State, 263
11. Mayberry, Bob, G, Clemson, 290
12. Dow, Don, T, Washington, 317

TAMPA BAY
1. Choice to Chi. Bears
2. Grimes, Randy, C, Baylor, 45
3. Castille, Jeremiah, DB, Alabama, 72
4. Thomas, Kelly, T, USC, 99
5. Chickillo, Tony, DT, Miami, 131
6. Branton, Rheugene, WR, Texas Southern, from San Francisco, 148
Kaplan, Ken, T, New Hampshire, 158
7. Ledbetter, Weldon, RB, Oklahoma, 185
8. Samuelson, John, LB, Azusa Pacific, 212
9. Arbubakrr, Hasson, DT, Texas Tech, 238
10. Durham, Darius, WR, San Diego State, 270
11. Witte, Mark, TE, North Texas State, 297
12. Higgenbotham, John, DT, Northeastern Oklahoma, 324

WASHINGTON
1. Green, Darrell, DB, Texas A&I, 28
2. Williams, Richard, RB, Memphis State, 56
3. Mann, Charles, DE, Nevada-Reno, 84
4. Choice to Buffalo through New Orleans
5. Choice to Pittsburgh
6. Winckler, Bob, T, Wisconsin, from LA Raiders, 166
Laufenberg, Babe, QB, Indiana, 168
7. Bryant, Kelvin, RB, North Carolina, 196
8. Hallstrom, Todd, T, Minnesota, 224
9. Gilbert, Marcus, RB, TCU, 251
10. Gandy, Geff, LB, Baylor, 279
11. Choice to San Diego
12. Choice to NY Giants

1984
Held May 1-2, 1984

ATLANTA
1. Bryan, Rick, DT, Oklahoma, 9
2. Case, Scott, DB, Oklahoma, from Philadelphia, 32
Benson, Thomas, LB, Oklahoma, 36
3. McSwain, Rod, DB, Clemson, 63
4. Malancon, Rydell, LB, LSU, 94
5. Choice to San Francisco
Benson, Cliff, TE, Purdue, from Denver through San Francisco, 132
6. Bennett, Ben, QB, Duke, 148
Ralph, Dan, DT, Oregon, from San Francisco, 163
7. Dodge, Kirk, LB, Nevada-Las Vegas, 175
8. Jackson, Jeff, LB, Auburn, 206
9. Howe, Glen, T, Southern Mississippi, 233
10. Franklin, Derrick, DB, Fresno State, 260
11. Norman, Tommy, WR, Jackson State, 287
12. Holmes, Don, WR, Mesa, 318

BUFFALO
1. Choice to Miami
Bell, Greg, RB, Notre Dame, from Miami, 26
2. Richardson, Eric, WR, San Jose State, 41
3. Choice to New Orleans
Bellinger, Rodney, DB, Miami, from Cleveland, 77
McNanie, Sean, DE, San Diego State, from Pittsburgh through Miami, 79
Neal, Speedy, RB, Miami, from Miami, 82
4. Brookins, Mitchell, WR, Illinois, 95
5. Kidd, John, P, Northwestern, 128
6. Slaton, Tony, C, USC, 155
7. David, Stan, DB, Texas Tech, 182
8. Rayfield, Stacy, DB, Texas-Arlington, 209
9. Howell, Leroy, DE, Appalachian State, 236
10. Azelby, Joe, LB, Harvard, 263
11. White, Craig, WR, Missouri, 299
12. Davis, Russell, WR, Maryland, 322

CHI. BEARS
1. Marshall, Wilber, LB, Florida, 11
2. Rivera, Ron, LB, California, 44
3. Humphries, Stefan, G, Michigan, 71
4. Andrews, Tom, G, Louisville, 98
5. Choice to Washington through San Diego, Seattle, and NY Giants
6. Choice to Dallas
7. Robertson, Dakita, RB, Central Arkansas, 179
8. Anderson, Brad, WR, Arizona, 212
9. Choice to San Francisco
Casale, Mark, QB, Montclair State, from Cleveland, 244
10. Vestman, Kurt, TE, Idaho, 266
Gayle, Shaun, DB, Ohio State, from Cleveland, 271
11. Choice to LA Rams
Butkus, Mark, DT, Illinois, from Cleveland, 297
12. Choice to Miami through San Francisco
Jordan, Donald, RB, Houston, from Cleveland, 330

CINCINNATI
1. Hunley, Ricky, LB, Arizona, 7
Koch, Pete, Maryland, from New England, 16
Blados, Brian, T, North Carolina, from LA Raiders through New England, 28
2. Esiason, Boomer, QB, Maryland, 38
3. Jennings, Stanford, RB, Furman, 65
4. Farley, John, RB, Cal State-Sacramento, 92

5. Bussey, Barney, DB, South Carolina State, 119
6. Kern, Don, TE, Arizona State, 150
7. Barker, Leo, LB, New Mexico State, 177
8. Reimers, Bruce, T, Iowa State, 204
9. Kozerski, Bruce, C, Holy Cross, 231
10. Jackson, Aaron, LB, North Carolina, 262
Ziegler, Brent, RB, Syracuse, from New England, 265
11. McKeaver, Steve, RB, Central State (Oklahoma), 289
12. Raquet, Steve, LB, Holy Cross, 316

CLEVELAND
1. Rogers, Don, DB, UCLA, 18
2. Rockins, Chris, DB, Oklahoma State, from LA Rams, 48
Davis, Bruce, WR, Baylor, 50
3. Choice to Buffalo
4. Bolden, Rickey, TE, SMU, from New Orleans through Denver, 96
Brennan, Brian, WR, Boston College, 104
5. Piepkorn, Dave, T, North Dakota State, 131
6. Nugent, Terry, QB, Colorado State, 158
7. Dumont, Jim, LB, Rutgers, 190
8. Choice to NY Jets
9. Jones, Don, WR, Texas A&M, from Philadelphia, 227
Choice to Chi. Bears
10. Choice to Chi. Bears
Byner, Earnest, RB, East Carolina, from LA Raiders, 280
11. Choice to Chi. Bears
12. Choice to Chi. Bears

DALLAS
1. Cannon, Billy, LB, Texas A&M, 25
2. Scott, Victor, DB, Colorado, from Minnesota through Houston, 40
Choice to Houston
3. Cornwell, Fred, TE, USC, 81
4. DeOssie, Steve, LB, Boston College, 110
5. Pelluer, Steve, QB, Washington, from Tampa Bay, 113
Granger, Norm, RB, Iowa, 137
6. Lockhart, Eugene, LB, Houston, from Chi. Bears, 152
Levelis, Joe, G, Iowa, 166
7. Martin, Ed, LB, Indiana State, 193
8. Revell, Mike, RB, Bethune-Cookman, 222
9. Hunt, John, G, Florida, from Indianapolis, 232
Maune, Neil, G, Notre Dame, 249
10. Salonen, Brian, TE, Montana, 278
11. Aughtman, Dowe, DT, Auburn, 304
12. Lewis, Carl, WR, Houston, 334

DENVER
1. Choice to Indianapolis
2. Townsend, Andre, DE, Mississippi, 46
3. Lilly, Tony, DB, Florida, 78
4. Robbins, Randy, DB, Arizona, from San Diego through Tampa Bay, 89
Choice to NY Giants
5. Choice to Atlanta through San Francisco
6. Smith, Aaron, LB, Utah State, 159
7. Kay, Clarence, TE, Georgia, 186
8. Hood, Winford, T, Georgia, from Green Bay, 207
Garnett, Scott, DT, Washington, 218
9. Brewer, Chris, RB, Arizona, 245
10. Micho, Bobby, TE, Texas, 272
11. Lang, Gene, RB, LSU, 298
12. Jarmin, Murray, WR, Clemson, 326

DETROIT
1. Lewis, David, TE, California, 20
2. Mandley, Pete, WR, Northern Arizona, 47
3. Williams, Eric, DT, Washington State, from San Diego through St. Louis, 62
Anderson, Ernest, RB, Oklahoma State, 74
Baack, Steve, DE, Oregon, from LA Rams, 75
4. D'Addio, Dave, RB, Maryland, 106
5. Choice to LA Rams
6. Witkowski, John, QB, Columbia, 160
7. Carter, Jimmie, LB, New Mexico, from Indianapolis, 178
Atkins, Renwick, T, Kansas, 187
8. Jones, David, C, Texas, 214
9. Hollins, Rich, WR, West Virginia, 246
10. Frizzell, William, DB, North Carolina Central, from Indianapolis, 259
Thaxton, James, DB, Louisiana Tech, 273
11. Saxon, Mike, P, San Diego State, 300
12. Streno, Glenn, C, Tennessee, 327

GREEN BAY
1. Carreker, Alphonso, DE, Florida State, 12
2. Choice to NY Jets through San Diego
3. Humphrey, Donnie, DT, Auburn, 72
4. Dorsey, John, LB, Connecticut, 99
5. Flynn, Tom, DB, Pittsburgh, 126
6. Wright, Randy, QB, Wisconsin, 153
7. Jones, Daryll, DB, Georgia, 181
8. Choice to Denver
9. Choice to Kansas City
10. Hoffman, Gary, T, Santa Clara, 267
11. Cannon, Mark, C, Texas-Arlington, 294
12. Taylor, Lenny, WR, Tennessee, from San Diego, 313
Emans, Mark, LB, Bowling Green, 323

HOUSTON
1. Steinkuhler, Dean, T, Nebraska, 2
2. Smith, Doug, DE, Auburn, 29
Eason, Bo, DB, Cal-Davis, from Dallas, 54
3. Meads, Johnny, LB, Nicholls State, 58
4. Studaway, Mark, DE, Tennessee, 85
Allen, Patrick, DB, Utah State, from Minnesota, 100
5. Lyles, Robert, LB, TCU, 114
6. Grimsley, John, LB, Kentucky, 141
Mullins, Eric, WR, Stanford, from LA Rams, 161
7. Joyner, Willie, RB, Maryland, 170
8. Baugh, Kevin, WR, Penn State, 197
9. Donaldson, Jeff, DB, Colorado, 226
Johnson, Mike, DE, Illinois, from NY Giants, 228
Russell, Mike, LB, Toledo, from LA Raiders, 252
10. Choice to LA Rams
11. Choice to LA Raiders
12. Choice to LA Rams

INDIANAPOLIS
1. Coleman, Leonard, DB, Vanderbilt, 8
Solt, Ron, G, Maryland, from Denver, 19
2. Winter, Blaise, DT, Syracuse, 35
3. Scott, Chris, DT, Purdue, 66
4. Curry, Craig, DB, Texas, 93
Wonsley, George, RB, Mississippi State, from Seattle, 103
5. Tate, Golden, WR, Tennessee State, 120
Call, Kevin, T, Colorado State, from Seattle, 130
6. Beverly, Dwight, RB, Illinois, 147
7. Choice to Detroit
8. Daniel, Eugene, DB, LSU, 205
9. Choice to Dallas
10. Choice to Detroit
11. Stowe, Bob, T, Illinois, 290
12. Hathaway, Steve, LB, West Virginia, 317

KANSAS CITY
1. Maas, Bill, DT, Pittsburgh, 5
Alt, John, T, Iowa, from LA Rams, 21
2. Radecic, Scott, LB, Penn State, 34
3. Heard, Herman, RB, Southern Colorado, 61
4. Robinson, Mark, DB, Penn State, 90
5. Holle, Eric, DE, Texas, 117
Paine, Jeff, LB, Texas A&M, from LA Rams, 134
6. Stevens, Rufus, WR, Grambling, 146
7. Ross, Kevin, DB, Temple, 173
8. Clark, Randy, DB, Florida, 202
9. Auer, Scott, T, Michigan State, 229
Hestera, Dave, TE, Colorado, from Green Bay, 240
10. Wenglikowski, Al, LB, Pittsburgh, 258
11. Johnson, Bobby, RB, San Jose State, 285
12. Lang, Mark, LB, Texas, 314

LA RAIDERS
1. Choice to Cincinnati through New England
2. Jones, Sean, DE, Northeastern, from San Francisco, 51
Choice to San Francisco
3. McCall, Joe, RB, Pittsburgh, 84
4. Choice to Tampa Bay
5. Parker, Andy, TE, Utah, from Minnesota, 127
Choice to Minnesota
6. Toran, Stacey, DB, Notre Dame, 168
7. Willis, Mitch, DE, SMU, from New Orleans, 183
Choice to Minnesota
8. Seale, Sam, WR, Western State (Colorado), 224
9. Choice to Houston
10. Choice to Cleveland
11. Williams, Gardner, DB, St. Mary's (California), from Houston, 282
Choice to Minnesota
12. Essington, Randy, QB, Colorado, 336

LA RAMS
1. Choice to Kansas City
2. Choice to Cleveland
3. Choice to Detroit
4. Choice to Washington through Houston
5. Stephens, Hal, DE, East Carolina, from Detroit, 133
Choice to Kansas City
6. Choice to Houston
7. Radachowsky, George, DB, Boston College, 188
8. Brady, Ed, LB, Illinois, 215
9. Reynolds, George, P, Penn State, 242
10. Vann, Norwood, TE, East Carolina, from Houston, 253
Dooley, Joe, C, Ohio State, 274
11. Harper, Michael, RB, USC, from Chi. Bears, 293
Love, Dwayne, RB, Houston, 301
12. Fisher, Rod, DB, Oklahoma State, from Houston, 309
Bias, Moe, LB, Illinois, 328

MIAMI
1. Shipp, Jackie, LB, Oklahoma, from Buffalo, 14
Choice to Buffalo
2. Brophy, Jay, LB, Miami, 53
3. Choice to Buffalo
4. Carter, Joe, RB, Alabama, 109
5. May, Dean, QB, Louisville, 138
6. Tatum, Rowland, LB, Ohio State, 165
7. Carvalho, Bernard, G, Hawaii, 194
8. Landry, Ronnie, RB, McNeese State, 221
9. Boyle, Jim, T, Tulane, 250
10. Chesley, John, TE, Oklahoma State, 277
11. Brown, Bud, DB, Southern Mississippi, 305
12. Devane, William, DT, Clemson, from Chi. Bears through San Francisco, 320
Weingrad, Mike, LB, Illinois, 333

MINNESOTA
1. Millard, Keith, DE, Washington State, 13
2. Choice to Dallas through Houston
3. Anderson, Alfred, RB, Baylor, 67
4. Choice to Houston
5. Choice to LA Raiders
Rice, Allen, RB, Baylor, from LA Raiders, 140
6. Collins, Dwight, WR, Pittsburgh, 154
7. Haines, John, DT, Texas, 180
Lewis, Loyd, G, Texas A&I, from LA Raiders, 196
8. Sverchek, Paul, DT, Cal Poly-SLO, 208
9. Kidd, Keith, WR, Arkansas, 235
10. Spencer, James, LB, Oklahoma State, 268
11. Pickett, Edgar, LB, Clemson, 295
Thompson, Lawrence, WR, Miami, from LA Raiders, 308
12. Jones, Mike, RB, North Carolina A&T, 321

NEW ENGLAND
1. Fryar, Irving, WR, Nebraska, from Tampa Bay through Cincinnati, 1
Choice to Cincinnati
2. Williams, Ed, LB, Texas, 43
3. Williams, Jon, RB, Penn State, 70
4. Choice to New Orleans
5. Fairchild, Paul, G, Kansas, 124
6. Gibson, Ernest, DB, Furman, 151
7. Kallmeyer, Bruce, K, Kansas, 184
Williams, Derwin, WR, New Mexico, from San Francisco, 192
8. Keyton, James, T, Arizona State, 211
9. Bolzan, Scott, T, Northern Illinois, 238
Windham, David, LB, Jackson State, from Washington, 251
10. Choice to Cincinnati
11. Flager, Charlie, G, Washington State, 292
12. Howell, Harper, TE, UCLA, 319

NEW ORLEANS
1. Choice to NY Jets
2. Geathers, James, DE, Wichita State, 42
3. Hoage, Terry, DB, Georgia, from Buffalo, 68
Anthony, Tyrone, RB, North Carolina, 69
4. Choice to Cleveland through Denver
Hilgenberg, Joel, C, Iowa, from New England, 97
5. Fields, Jitter, DB, Texas, 123
6. Thorp, Don, DT, Illinois, 156
7. Choice to LA Raiders
8. Terrell, Clemon, RB, Southern Mississippi, 210
9. Hansen, Brian, P, Sioux Falls, 237
10. Gray, Paul, LB, Western Kentucky, 264
11. Bourgeau, Michel, DE, Boise State, 291
12. Nelson, Byron, T, Arizona, 324

NY GIANTS
1. Banks, Carl, LB, Michigan State, 3
Roberts, William, T, Ohio State, from Washington, 27
2. Choice to Washington
3. Hostetler, Jeff, QB, West Virginia, 59
4. Goode, Conrad, T, Missouri, 87
Reasons, Gary, LB, Northwestern State (Louisiana) from Denver, 105
5. Harris, Clint, DB, East Carolina, 115
6. Scott, Jim, DE, Clemson, 143
7. Manuel, Lionel, WR, Pacific, 171
8. Choice to San Diego
9. Choice to Houston
10. Jordan, David, G, Auburn, 255
Golden, Heyward, DB, South Carolina State, from San Diego, 257
11. Cephous, Frank, RB, UCLA, 283
12. Green, Lawrence, LB, Tennessee-Chattanooga, 311

NY JETS
1. Carter, Russell, DB, SMU, 10
Faurot, Ron, DE, Arkansas, from New Orleans, 15
2. Sweeney, Jim, C, Pittsburgh, 37
Dennison, Glenn, TE, Miami, from Green Bay through San Diego, 39
3. Clifton, Kyle, LB, TCU, 64
4. Bell, Bobby, LB, Missouri, 91
5. Armstrong, Tron, WR, Eastern Kentucky, 122
6. Paige, Tony, RB, Virginia Tech, 149
7. Hamilton, Harry, DB, Penn State, 176
8. Griggs, Billy, TE, Virginia, 203
Wright, Brett, P, Southeastern Louisiana, from Cleveland, 217
9. Baldwin, Tom, DT, Tulsa, 234
10. Cone, Ronny, RB, Georgia Tech, 261
11. Martin, Dan, T, Iowa State, 288
12. Roberson, David, WR, Houston, 315

PHILADELPHIA
1. Jackson, Kenny, WR, Penn State, 4
2. Choice to Atlanta
3. Russell, Rusty, T, South Carolina, 60
4. Cooper, Evan, DB, Michigan, 88
5. Hardy, Andre, RB, St. Mary's (California), 116
6. Raridon, Scott, T, Nebraska, 145
7. Hayes, Joe, RB, Central State (Oklahoma), 172
8. Matsakis, Manny, K, Capital, 200
9. Choice to Cleveland
10. Thomas, John, DB, TCU, 256
11. Robertson, John, T, East Carolina, 284
12. McFadden, Paul, K, Youngstown State, 312

PITTSBURGH
1. Lipps, Louis, WR, Southern Mississippi, 23
2. Kolodziejski, Chris, TE, Wyoming, 52
3. Choice to Buffalo through Miami
4. Thompson, Weegie, WR, Florida State, 108
Long, Terry, G, East Carolina, from Washington, 111
5. Hughes, Van, DT, Southwest Texas State, 135
6. Brown, Chris, DB, Notre Dame, 164
7. Campbell, Scott, QB, Purdue, 191
8. Rasmussen, Randy, C, Minnesota, 220
9. Erenberg, Rich, RB, Colgate, 247
10. McJunkin, Kirk, T, Texas, 276
11. Veals, Elton, RB, Tulane, 303
12. Gillespie, Fernandars, RB, William Jewell, 332

ST. LOUIS
1. Duncan, Clyde, WR, Tennessee, 17
2. Dawson, Doug, G, Texas, 45
3. Choice to San Francisco
McIvor, Rick, QB, Texas, from San Francisco, 80
4. Bayless, Martin, DB, Bowling Green, 101

5. Leiding, Jeff, LB, Texas, 129
Goode, John, TE, Youngstown State, from San Francisco, 136
6. Clark, Rod, LB, Southwest Texas State, 157
7. Walker, Quentin, RB, Virginia, 185
8. Noga, Niko, LB, Hawaii, from San Diego, 201
Paulling, Bob, K, Clemson, 213
9. Walker, John, RB, Texas, 241
10. Smythe, Mark, DT, Indiana, 269
11. Mackey, Kyle, QB, East Texas State, 296
12. Parker, Paul, G, Oklahoma, 325

SAN DIEGO
1. Cade, Mossy, DB, Texas, 6
2. Guendling, Mike, LB, Northwestern, 33
3. Choice to Detroit through St. Louis
4. Choice to Denver through Tampa Bay
5. James, Lionel, KR, Auburn, 118
6. Guthrie, Keith, DT, Texas A&M, 144
7. Bendross, Jesse, WR, Alabama, 174
8. Woodard, Ray, DT, Texas, from NY Giants, 199
Choice to St. Louis
Craighead, Bob, RB, Northeast Louisiana, from San Francisco, 219
9. Barnes, Zack, DT, Alabama State, 230
10. Choice to NY Giants
11. McGee, Buford, RB, Mississippi, 286
12. Choice to Green Bay
Harper, Maurice, WR, LaVerne, from San Francisco, 331

SAN FRANCISCO
1. Shell, Todd, LB, BYU, 24
2. Choice to LA Raiders
Frank, John, TE, Ohio State, from LA Raiders, 56
3. McIntyre, Guy, G, Georgia, from St. Louis, 73
Choice to St. Louis
4. Choice to Tampa Bay through San Diego
5. Carter, Michael, DT, SMU, from Atlanta, 121
Choice to St. Louis
Fuller, Jeff, LB, Texas A&M, from Washington through LA Raiders, 139
6. Choice to Atlanta
7. Choice to New England
8. Choice to San Diego
9. Miller, Lee, DB, Cal State-Fullerton, from Chi. Bears 239
Harmon, Derrick, RB, Cornell, 248
10. Moritz, Dave, WR, Iowa, 275
11. Pendleton, Kirk, WR, BYU, 307
12. Choice to San Diego

SEATTLE
1. Taylor, Terry, DB, Southern Illinois, 22
2. Turner, Daryl, WR, Michigan State, 49
3. Young, Fred, LB, New Mexico State, 76
Hagood, Rickey, DT, South Carolina, from Tampa Bay through San Francisco, 86
4. Choice to Indianapolis
5. Choice to Indianapolis
6. Kaiser, John, LB, Arizona, 162
7. Slater, Sam, T, Weber State, 189
8. Puzar, John, C, Long Beach State, 216
9. Schreiber, Adam, G, Texas, 243
10. Morris, Randall, RB, Tennessee, 270
11. Gemza, Steve, T, UCLA, 302
12. Windham, Theodis, DB, Utah State, 329

TAMPA BAY
1. Choice to New England through Cincinnati
2. Browner, Keith, LB, USC, 30
3. Acorn, Fred, DB, Texas, 57
4. Choice to Seattle through San Francisco
Gunter, Michael, RB, Tulsa, from San Francisco through San Diego, 107
Heller, Ron, T, Penn State, from LA Raiders, 112
5. Choice to Dallas
6. Washington, Chris, LB, Iowa State, 142
7. Carroll, Jay, TE, Minnesota, 169
8. Robinson, Fred, DE, Miami, 198
9. Mallory, Rick, G, Washington, 225
10. Gallery, Jim, K, Minnesota, 254
11. Kiel, Blair, QB, Notre Dame, 281
12. Jemison, Thad, WR, Ohio State, 310

WASHINGTON
1. Choice to NY Giants
2. Slater, Bob, DT, Oklahoma, from NY Giants, 31
Hamilton, Steve, DE, East Carolina, 55
3. Schroeder, Jay, QB, UCLA, 83
4. Smith, Jimmy, RB, Elon, from LA Rams through Houston, 102
Choice to Pittsburgh
5. Pegues, Jeff, LB, East Carolina, from Chi. Bears through San Diego, Seattle, and NY Giants, 125
Choice to San Francisco through LA Raiders
6. Singer, Curt, T, Tennessee, 167
7. Smith, Mark, WR, North Carolina, 195
8. Smith, Jeff, DB, Missouri, 223
9. Choice to New England
10. Griffin, Keith, RB, Miami, 279
11. Jones, Anthony, TE, Wichita State, 306
12. Thomas, Curtland, WR, Missouri, 335

1984 SUPPLEMENTAL
Held June 5, 1984

A supplemental draft was held for those players who had been eligible to be drafted by NFL teams, but who hadn't been due to contracts with other professional leagues. The draft gave NFL teams the league rights to the players should they ever become free agents.

ATLANTA
1. Jones, Joey, WR, Alabama, 9 (Birmingham)
2. McInnis, Mike, DT, Arkansas-Pine Bluff, 36 (Philadelphia)
3. Woodberry, Dennis, DB, Southern Arkansas, 63 (Birmingham)

BUFFALO
1. Drane, Dwight, DB, Oklahoma, 14 (LA Express)
2. Hart, Darryl, DB, Lane, 41 (Oakland)
3. Corbin, Don, T, Kentucky, 68 (Pittsburgh)

CHICAGO
1. Choice to Cleveland
2. Choice to Cleveland
3. Choice to Cleveland

CINCINNATI
1. Peace, Wayne, QB, Florida, 7 (Tampa Bay)
2. Johnson, Bill, RB, Arkansas State, 38 (Denver)
3. Kilkenny, Tom, LB, Temple, 65 (Chi. Blitz)

CLEVELAND
1. Mack, Kevin, RB, Clemson, from Chi. Bears, 11 (LA Express)
Johnson, Mike, LB, Virginia Tech, 18 (Philadelphia)
2. McNeil, Gerald, WR, Baylor, from Chi. Bears, 44 (Houston)
Robison, Tommy, T, Texas A&M, 50 (Houston)
3. West, Doug, LB, UCLA, from Chi. Bears, 71 (Jacksonville)
Bond, John, QB, Mississippi State, 77 (Saskatchewan)

DALLAS
1. Fowler, Todd, TE, Stephen F. Austin, 25 (Houston)
2. Moore, Malcolm, WR, USC, 54 (LA Express)
3. Spek, Jeff, TE, San Diego State, 81 (New Jersey)

DENVER
1. Gilbert, Freddie, DE, Georgia, 19 (New Jersey)
2. Massie, Rick, WR, Kentucky, 46 (Calgary)
3. Smith, Reggie, T, Kansas, 78 (Tampa Bay)

DETROIT
1. Williams, Alphonso, WR, Nevada-Reno, 20 (Oklahoma)
2. Jamison, George, LB, Cincinnati, 47 (Philadelphia)
3. Hollie, Doug, DE, SMU, 74 (Pittsburgh)

GREEN BAY
1. Jordan, Buford, RB, McNeese State, 12 (New Orleans)
2. Clanton, Chuck, DB, Auburn, 39 (Birmingham)
3. Sullivan, John, DB, California, 72 (Oakland)

HOUSTON
1. Rozier, Mike, RB, Nebraska, 2 (Pittsburgh)
2. Maggs, Don, T, Tulane, 29, (Pittsburgh)
3. Madsen, Lynn, DT, Washington, 58, (New Jersey)

INDIANAPOLIS
1. Bergmann, Paul, TE, UCLA, 8 (Jacksonville)
2. Bentley, Albert, RB, Miami, 35 (Michigan)
3. Smith, Byron, DT, California, 66 (Saskatchewan)

KANSAS CITY
1. Adickes, Mark, T, Baylor, 5 (LA Express)
2. Sanchez, Lupe, DB, UCLA, 34 (Arizona)
3. Lane, Garcia, DB, Ohio State, 61 (Philadelphia)

LA RAIDERS
1. Woods, Chris, WR, Auburn, 28 (Edmonton)
2. Hill, Stewart, LB, Washington, 56 (Edmonton)
3. Farr, James, G, Clemson, 84 (Washington)

LA RAMS
1. Fuller, William, DE, North Carolina, 21 (Philadelphia)
2. Johnson, Rick, QB, Southern Illinois, 48 (Oklahoma)
3. Byrne, Jim, DT, Wisconsin-LaCrosse, 75 (New Jersey)

MIAMI
1. Knight, Danny, WR, Mississippi State, 26 (New Jersey)
2. Forte, Dewey, DE, Bethune-Cookman, 53 (LA Express)
3. Hanks, Duan, WR, Stephen F. Austin, 82 (Philadelphia)

MINNESOTA
1. Smith, Allanda, DB, TCU, 13 (LA Express)
2. Smith, Robert, DE, Grambling, 40 (Arizona)
3. Howard, Davie, LB, Long Beach State, 67 (LA Express)

NEW ENGLAND
1. Sanders, Ricky, WR-PR, Southwest Texas State, 16 (Houston)
2. Jordan, Eric, RB, Purdue, 43 (Oakland)
3. Lewis, Walter, QB, Alabama, 70 (Memphis)

NEW ORLEANS
1. Johnson, Vaughan, LB, North Carolina State, 15 (Jacksonville)
2. Gray, Mel, RB, Purdue, 42 (LA Express)
3. Bearden, Steve, LB, Vanderbilt, 69 (Memphis)

NY GIANTS
1. Zimmerman, Gary, G, Oregon, 3 (LA Express)
2. Robinson, James, DT, Clemson, 31 (LA Express)
3. Warren, Kirby, RB, Pacific, 59 (LA Express)

NY JETS
1. Hobart, Ken, QB, Idaho, 10 (Denver)
2. Sandusky, Jim, WR, San Diego State, 37 (British Columbia)
3. Gill, Turner, QB, Nebraska, 64 (Montreal)

PHILADELPHIA
1. White, Reggie, DE, Tennessee, 4 (Memphis)
2. Goodlow, Darryl, LB, Oklahoma, 32 (Oklahoma)
3. Carter, Thomas, LB, San Diego State, 60 (Oakland)

PITTSBURGH
1. Gunn, Duane, WR, Indiana, 23 (LA Express)
2. Dixon, Tom, C, Michigan, 52 (Michigan)
3. Boren, Phillip, T, Arkansas, 79 (Birmingham)

SEATTLE
1. Hudson, Gordon, TE, BYU, 22 (LA Express)
2. Powell, Alvin, G, Winston-Salem State, 49 (Oklahoma)
3. Seurer, Frank, QB, Kansas, 76 (LA Express)

ST. LOUIS
1. Ruether, Mike, C, Texas, 17 (LA Express)
2. Kennard, Derek, G, Nevada-Reno, 45 (LA Express)
3. Riordan, Tim, QB, Temple, 73 (Philadelphia)

SAN DIEGO
1. Williams, Lee, DE, Bethune-Cookman, 6 (LA Express)
2. Smith, Steve, QB, Michigan, 33 (Montreal)
3. Collins, Clarence, WR, Illinois State, 62 (New Jersey)

SAN FRANCISCO
1. Crawford, Derrick, WR, Memphis State, 24 (Memphis)
2. Conwell, Joe, T, North Carolina, 51 (Philadelphia)
3. Schellen, Mark, RB, Nebraska, 80 (New Orleans)

TAMPA BAY
1. Young, Steve, QB, BYU, 1 (LA Express)
2. Nelson, Kevin, RB, UCLA, 30 (LA Express)
3. Clark, Alex, DB, LSU, 57 (New Orleans)

WASHINGTON
1. Zendejas, Tony, K, Nevada-Reno, 27 (LA Express)
2. Clark, Gary, WR, James Madison, 55 (Jacksonville)
3. Verdin, Clarence, WR, Southwestern Louisiana, 83 (Houston)

1985
Held April 30-May 1, 1985

ATLANTA
1. Fralic, Bill, T, Pittsburgh, from Houston through Minnesota, 2
Choice to Minnesota
2. Choice to Washington
Gann, Mike, DE, Notre Dame, from St. Louis, 45
3. Choice to Minnesota
4. Harry, Emile, WR, Stanford, 89
5. Choice to St. Louis
6. Choice to Miami
Pleasant, Reggie, DB, Clemson, from New Orleans, 152
7. Choice to Cincinnati
8. Lee, Ashley, DB, Virginia Tech, 201
Washington, Ronnie, LB, Northeast Louisiana, from New England, 215
9. Moon, Micah, LB, North Carolina, 228
10. Martin, Brent, C, Stanford, 257
11. Ayres, John, DB, Illinois, 284
12. Whisenhunt, Ken, TE, Georgia Tech, 313

BUFFALO
1. Smith, Bruce, DE, Virginia Tech, 1
Burroughs, Derrick, DB, Memphis State, from Green Bay, 14
2. Traynowicz, Mark, T, Nebraska, 29
Burkett, Chris, WR, Jackson State, from Green Bay, 42
3. Reich, Frank, QB, Maryland, 57
Garner, Hal, LB, Utah State, from Cleveland, 63
4. Reed, Andre, WR, Kutztown, 86
Hellestrae, Dale, T, SMU, from San Francisco, 112
5. Choice to LA Rams
Teal, Jimmy, WR, Texas A&M, from Dallas, 130
6. Hamby, Mike, DT, Utah State, 141
7. Pitts, Ron, DB, UCLA, 169
8. Robinson, Jacque, RB, Washington, 197
9. Jones, Glenn, DB, Norfolk State, 225
10. Babyar, Chris, G, Illinois, 253
11. Seawright, James, LB, South Carolina, 282
12. Choice to Washington
Woodside, Paul, K, West Virginia, from Seattle, 333

CHI. BEARS
1. Perry, William, DT, Clemson, 22
2. Phillips, Reggie, DB, SMU, 49
3. Maness, James, WR, TCU, 78
4. Butler, Kevin, K, Georgia, 105
5. Choice to NY Jets
6. Choice to LA Rams
7. Bennett, Charles, DE, Southwestern Louisiana, 190
8. Buxton, Steve, T, Indiana State, 217
9. Sanders, Thomas, RB, Texas A&M, 250
10. Coryatt, Pat, DT, Baylor, 273
11. Morrissey, Jim, LB, Michigan State, 302
12. Choice to San Diego

CINCINNATI
1. Brown, Eddie, WR, Miami, 13
   King, Emanuel, LB, Alabama, from Seattle, 25
2. Zander, Carl, LB, Tennessee, 43
3. Thomas, Sean, DB, TCU, 70
4. Tuggle, Anthony, DB, Nicholls State, 97
5. Degrate, Tony, DT, Texas, 127
   Davis, Lee, DB, Mississippi, from New England, 129
6. Stokes, Eric, T, Northeastern, from Tampa Bay, 148
   Lester, Keith, TE, Murray State, 154
7. Locklin, Kim, RB, New Mexico State, from Atlanta, 172
   Walter, Joe, T, Texas Tech, 181
8. Strobel, Dave, LB, Iowa, 211
9. Cruise, Keith, DE, Northwestern, 238
10. King, Bernard, LB, Syracuse, 265
11. Stanfield, Harold, TE, Mississippi College, 296
12. Garza, Louis, T, New Mexico State, 322

CLEVELAND
1. Choice to Green Bay through Buffalo
2. Allen, Greg, RB, Florida State, 35
3. Choice to Buffalo
4. Choice to Miami
5. Choice to Dallas through Buffalo
6. Krerowicz, Mark, G, Ohio State, 147
7. Langhorne, Reggie, WR, Elizabeth City State, 175
8. Banks, Fred, WR, Liberty Baptist, 203
9. Choice to Philadelphia
10. Williams, Larry, G, Notre Dame, 259
11. Tucker, Travis, TE, Southern Connecticut, 287
12. Swanson, Shane, WR, Nebraska, 315

DALLAS
1. Brooks, Kevin, DE, Michigan, 17
2. Penn, Jesse, LB, Virginia Tech, 44
3. Ker, Crawford, G, Florida, 76
4. Lavette, Robert, RB, Georgia Tech, 103
5. Walker, Herschel, RB, Georgia, from Houston, 114
   Darwin, Matt, C, Texas A&M, from Cleveland through Buffalo, 119
   Choice to Buffalo
6. Ploeger, Kurt, DE, Gustavus Adolphus, from Indianapolis, 144
   Moran, Matt, G, Stanford, 157
7. Powe, Karl, WR, Alabama State, from NY Jets through Kansas City, 178
   Herrmann, Jim, DE, BYU, 184
8. Gonzales, Leon, WR, Bethune-Cookman, 216
9. Strasburger, Scott, LB, Nebraska, 243
10. Jones, Joe, TE, Virginia Tech, 270
11. Dellocono, Neal, LB, UCLA, 297
12. Jordan, Karl, LB, Vanderbilt, 324

DENVER
1. Sewell, Steve, RB, Oklahoma, 26
2. Johnson, Vance, WR, Arizona, from Houston, 31
   Fletcher, Simon, DE, Houston, 54
3. Choice to Houston
4. McGregor, Keli, TE, Colorado State, 110
5. Choice to Houston
   Hinson, Billy, G, Florida, from Miami, 139
6. Choice to NY Jets
7. Cameron, Dallas, NT, Miami, 194
8. Riley, Eric, DB, Florida State, 222
9. Smith, Daryl, DB, North Alabama, 249
10. Funck, Buddy, QB, New Mexico, from New England, 269
   Anderson, Ron, LB, SMU, 278
11. Rolle, Gary, WR, Florida, 306
12. Lynch, Dan, G, Washington State, 334

DETROIT
1. Brown, Lomas, T, Florida, 6
2. Glover, Kevin, C, Maryland, 34
3. Johnson, James, LB, San Diego State, 62
4. Hancock, Kevin, LB, Baylor, 90
5. McIntosh, Joe, RB, North Carolina State, 118
6. Short, Stan, G, Penn State, 146
7. Staten, Tony, DB, Angelo State, 174
8. Caldwell, Scotty, RB, Texas-Arlington, 202
9. James, June, LB, Texas, 230
10. Beauford, Clayton, WR, Auburn, 258
11. Harris, Kevin, DB, Georgia, 286
12. Weaver, Mike, G, Georgia, 314

GREEN BAY
1. Ruettgers, Ken, T, USC, from Cleveland through Buffalo, 7
   Choice to Buffalo
2. Choice to Buffalo
3. Moran, Rich, G, San Diego State, 71
4. Stanley, Walter, WR, Mesa, 98
5. Noble, Brian, LB, Arizona State, 125
6. Lewis, Mark, TE, Texas A&M, 155
7. Wilson, Eric, LB, Maryland, from Minnesota, 171
   Ellerson, Gary, RB, Wisconsin 182
8. Stills, Ken, DB, Wisconsin, 209
9. Johnson, Morris, G, Alabama A&M, 239
10. Burgess, Ronnie, DB, Wake Forest, 266
11. Shield, Joe, QB, Trinity (Connecticut), 294
12. Meyer, Jim, P, Arizona State, 323

HOUSTON
1. Choice to Atlanta through Minnesota
   Childress, Ray, DE, Texas A&M, from Minnesota, 3
   Johnson, Richard, DB, Wisconsin, from New Orleans, 11
2. Choice to Denver
   Byrd, Richard, DE, Southern Mississippi, from Tampa Bay through Denver, 36
3. Choice to NY Giants
   Kelley, Mike, C, Notre Dame, from Denver, 82
4. Briehl, Tom, LB, Stanford, 87
5. Choice to Dallas
   Bush, Frank, LB, North Carolina State, from LA Rams through Kansas City, 133
   Johnson, Lee, K, BYU, from Denver, 138
6. Choice to LA Raiders
   Krakoski, Joe, LB, Washington, from Kansas City, 153
7. Akiu, Mike, WR, Hawaii, 170
8. Thomas, Chuck, C, Oklahoma, 199
9. Tasker, Steve, KR, Northwestern, 226
10. Golic, Mike, DE, Notre Dame, 255
11. Drewrey, Willie, KR, West Virginia, 281
12. Vonder Haar, Mark, DT, Minnesota, 311

INDIANAPOLIS
1. Bickett, Duane, LB, USC, 5
2. Anderson, Don, DB, Purdue, 32
3. Young, Anthony, DB, Temple, 61
4. Broughton, Willie, DE, Miami, 88
5. Caron, Roger, T, Harvard, 117
6. Choice to Dallas
7. Harbour, James, WR, Mississippi, 173
8. Nichols, Ricky, WR, East Carolina, 200
9. Boyer, Mark, TE, USC, 229
10. Pinesett, Andre, DT, Cal State-Fullerton, 256
11. Choice to LA Rams
12. Burnette, Dave, T, Central Arkansas, 312

KANSAS CITY
1. Horton, Ethan, RB, North Carolina, 15
2. Hayes, Jonathan, TE, Iowa, 41
3. Choice to San Diego
4. Olderman, Bob, G, Virginia, 99
5. King, Bruce, RB, Purdue, 126
6. Bostic, Jonathan, DB, Bethune-Cookman, from Philadelphia, 149
   Choice to Houston
7. Thomson, Vince, DE, Missouri Western, from San Diego, 180
   Heffernan, Dave, G, Miami, 183
8. Hillary, Ira, WR, South Carolina, 210
9. Armentrout, Mike, DB, Southwest Missouri State, 237
10. Smith, Jeff, RB, Nebraska, 267
11. Jackson, Chris, C, SMU, 293
12. LeBel, Harper, C, Colorado State, 321

LA RAIDERS
1. Hester, Jessie, WR, Florida State, 23
2. Choice to New England
3. Moffett, Tim, WR, Mississippi, 79
   Adams, Stefon, DB, East Carolina, from Washington through Houston, 80
4. Kimmel, Jamie, LB, Syracuse, from Washington, 107
   Choice to New England
5. Reeder, Dan, RB, Delaware, 135
6. Hilger, Rusty, QB, Oklahoma State, from Houston, 143
   Choice to Minnesota
7. Belcher, Kevin, T, Wisconsin, from NY Giants, 186
   Pattison, Mark, WR, Washington, from New England, 188
   Clark, Bret, DB, Nebraska, 191
   Haden, Nick, C, Penn State, from Washington through New England, 192
8. Wingate, Leonard, DT, South Carolina State, 220
9. Sydnor, Chris, DB, Penn State, 246
10. McKenzie, Reggie, LB, Tennessee, from Washington, 275
   Myres, Albert, DB, Tulsa, 276
11. Strachan, Steve, RB, Boston College, 303
12. Polk, Raymond, DB, Oklahoma State, 332

LA RAMS
1. Gray, Jerry, DB, Texas, 21
2. Scott, Chuck, WR, Vanderbilt, 50
3. Hatcher, Dale, P, Clemson, 77
4. Choice to Minnesota
5. Greene, Kevin, LB, Auburn, from Buffalo, 113
   Choice to Houston through Kansas City
6. Young, Mike, WR, UCLA, from Chi. Bears, 161
   Johnson, Damone, TE, Cal Poly-SLO, 162
7. Bradley, Danny, RB, Oklahoma, 189
8. McIntyre, Marlon, RB, Pittsburgh, 218
9. Swanson, Gary, LB, Cal Poly-SLO, 245
10. Love, Duval, G, UCLA, 274
11. Flutie, Doug, QB, Boston College, from Indianapolis, 285
   Brown, Kevin, DB, Northwestern, 301
12. Choice to Tampa Bay

MIAMI
1. Hampton, Lorenzo, RB, Florida, 27
2. Choice to San Diego
3. Little, George, DT, Iowa, from Philadelphia, 65
   Moyer, Alex, LB, Northwestern, 83
4. Smith, Mike, DB, Texas-El Paso, from Cleveland, 91
   Dellenbach, Jeff, T, Wisconsin, 111
5. Choice to Denver
6. Shorthose, George, WR, Missouri, from Atlanta, 145
   Davenport, Ron, RB, Louisville, 167
7. Reveiz, Fuad, K, Tennessee, 195
8. Sharp, Dan, TE, TCU, 223
9. Hinds, Adam, DB, Oklahoma State, 251
10. Pendleton, Mike, DB, Indiana, 279
11. Jones, Mike, RB, Tulane, 307
12. Noble, Ray, DB, California, 335

MINNESOTA
1. Choice to Houston
   Doleman, Chris, LB, Pittsburgh, from Atlanta, 4
2. Holt, Issiac, DB, Alcorn State, 30
3. Lowdermilk, Kirk, C, Ohio State, 59
   Meamber, Tim, LB, Washington, from Atlanta, 60
   Long, Tim, T, Memphis State, from San Diego, 66
4. Rhymes, Buster, WR, Oklahoma, 85
   Morrell, Kyle, DB, BYU, from LA Rams, 106
5. MacDonald, Mark, G, Boston College, 115
6. Bono, Steve, QB, UCLA, 142
   Newton, Tim, NT, Florida, from LA Raiders, 164
7. Choice to Green Bay
8. Blair, Nikita, LB, Texas-El Paso, 198
9. Covington, Jaime, RB, Syracuse, 227
10. Johnson, Juan, WR, Langston, 254
11. Williams, Tim, DB, North Carolina A&T, 283
12. Jones, Byron, NT, Tulsa, 310

NEW ENGLAND
1. Choice to San Francisco
   Matich, Trevor, C, BYU, from San Francisco, 28
2. Veris, Garin, DE, Stanford, 48
   Bowman, Jim, DB, Central Michigan, from LA Raiders, 52
   Thomas, Ben, DE, Auburn, from San Francisco, 56
3. Choice to San Francisco
   McMillian, Audrey, DB, Houston, from San Francisco, 84
4. Toth, Tom, T, Western Michigan, 102
   Phelan, Gerard, WR, Boston College, from LA Raiders, 108
5. Choice to Cincinnati
6. Choice to Philadelphia
7. Choice to LA Raiders
8. Choice to Atlanta
   Hodge, Milford, DT, Washington State, from San Francisco, 224
9. Choice to Pittsburgh
10. Choice to Denver
11. Lewis, Paul, RB, Boston U., 295
12. Mumford, Tony, RB, Penn State, 328

NEW ORLEANS
1. Choice to Houston
   Toles, Alvin, LB, Tennessee, from Washington, 24
2. Gilbert, Daren, T, Cal State-Fullerton, 38
3. Del Rio, Jack, LB, USC, 68
4. Allen, Billy, DB, Florida State, 95
5. Choice to Washington
6. Choice to Atlanta
7. Martin, Eric, WR, LSU, 179
8. Kohlbrand, Joe, DE, Miami, 206
9. Johnson, Earl, DB, South Carolina, 236
10. Choice to Washington
11. Choice to Washington
12. Songy, Treg, DB, Tulane, 320

NY GIANTS
1. Adams, George, RB, Kentucky, 19
2. Robinson, Stacy, WR, North Dakota State, 46
3. Davis, Tyrone, DB, Clemson, from Houston, 58
   Johnston, Brian, C, North Carolina, 73
4. Bavaro, Mark, TE, Notre Dame, 100
5. Henderson, Tracy, WR, Iowa State, 132
6. Oliver, Jack, G, Memphis State, 159
   Pembrook, Mark, DB, Cal State-Fullerton, from Seattle, 165
7. Choice to LA Raiders
8. Rouson, Lee, RB, Colorado, 213
9. Wright, Frank, NT, South Carolina, 240
10. Dubroc, Gregg, LB, LSU, 272
11. Young, Allen, DB, Virginia Tech, 299
12. Welch, Herb, DB, UCLA, 326

NY JETS
1. Toon, Al, WR, Wisconsin, 10
2. Lyles, Lester, DB, Virginia, 40
3. Elder, Donnie, DB, Memphis State, 67
4. Allen, Doug, WR, Arizona State, 94
5. Benson, Troy, LB, Pittsburgh, from Tampa Bay, 120
   Luft, Brian, DT, USC, 124
   Smith, Tony, WR, San Jose State, from Chi. Bears, 134
6. Deaton, Jeff, G, Stanford, 151
   Miano, Rich, DB, Hawaii, from Denver, 166
7. Choice to Dallas through Kansas City
8. Monger, Matt, LB, Oklahoma State, 208
9. Waters, Mike, RB, San Diego State, 235
10. Glenn, Kerry, DB, Minnesota, 262
11. White, Brad, DE, Texas Tech, 292
12. Wallace, Bill, WR, Pittsburgh, 319

PHILADELPHIA
1. Allen, Kevin, T, Indiana, 9
2. Cunningham, Randall, QB-P, Nevada-Las Vegas, 37
3. Choice to Miami
4. Naron, Greg, G, North Carolina, 93
5. Jiles, Dwayne, LB, Texas Tech, 121
6. Choice to Kansas City
   Reeves, Ken, T, Texas A&M, from New England, 156
7. Choice to Washington
8. Polley, Tom, LB, Nevada-Las Vegas, 205
9. Toub, Dave, C, Texas-El Paso, from Cleveland, 231
   Drake, Joe, DT, Arizona, 233
10. Kelso, Mark, DB, William & Mary, 261
11. Hunter, Herman, RB, Tennessee State 289
12. Russell, Todd, DB, Boston College, 317

PITTSBURGH
1. Sims, Darryl, DE, Wisconsin, 20

2. Behning, Mark, T, Nebraska, 47
3. Hobley, Liffort, DB, LSU, 74
4. Turk, Dan, C, Wisconsin, 101
5. Choice to Seattle
Jacobs, Cam, LB, Kentucky, from Washington, 136
6. Carr, Gregg, LB, Auburn, 160
7. Andrews, Alan, TE, Rutgers, 187
8. Newsome, Harry, P, Wake Forest, 214
9. Small, Fred, LB, Washington, 241
Harris, Andre, DB, Minnesota, from New England, 242
10. White, Oliver, TE, Kentucky, 268
11. Matichak, Terry, DB, Missouri, 300
12. Sanchez, Jeff, DB, Georgia, 327

ST. LOUIS
1. Nunn, Freddie Joe, LB, Mississippi, 18
2. Choice to Atlanta
Bergold, Scott, T, Wisconsin, from Washington through Atlanta, 51
3. Smith, Lance, T, LSU, 72
4. Wolfley, Ron, RB, West Virginia, 104
5. Dunn, K.D., TE, Clemson, from Atlanta, 116
Wong, Louis, G, BYU, 131
6. Novacek, Jay, WR, Wyoming, 158
7. Choice to Washington through Kansas City
8. Monaco, Rob, G, Vanderbilt, 212
9. Williams, Scott, TE, Georgia, 244
10. Williams, Dennis, RB, Furman, 271
11. Anderson, Ricky, K, Vanderbilt, 298
12. Young, Lonnie, DB, Michigan State, 325

SAN DIEGO
1. Lachey, Jim, G, Ohio State, 12
2. Davis, Wayne, DB, Indiana State, 39
Dale, Jeffery, DB, LSU, from Miami, 55
3. Choice to Minnesota
Hendy, John, DB, Long Beach State, from Kansas City, 69
4. Mojsiejenko, Ralf, K, Michigan State, 96
5. Choice to Seattle
6. Lewis, Terry, DB, Michigan State, 150
7. Choice to Kansas City
Fellows, Mark, LB, Montana State, from San Francisco, 196
8. Adams, Curtis, RB, Central Michigan, 207
9. Berner, Paul, QB, Pacific, 234
Remsberg, Dan, T, Abilene Christian, from San Francisco, 252
10. King, David, DB, Auburn, 264
11. Smith, Jeff, NT, Kentucky, 291
12. Simmons, Tony, DE, Tennessee, 318
Pearson, Bret, TE, Wisconsin, from Chi. Bears, 329

SAN FRANCISCO
1. Rice, Jerry, WR, Mississippi Valley State, from New England, 16
Choice to New England
2. Choice to New England
3. Moore, Ricky, RB, Alabama, from New England,75
Choice to New England
4. Choice to Buffalo
5. Collie, Bruce, T, Texas-Arlington, 140
6. Barry, Scott, QB, Cal-Davis, 168
7. Choice to San Diego
8. Choice to New England
9. Choice to San Diego
10. Choice to Seattle
11. Wood, David, DE, Arizona, 308
12. Chumley, Donald, DT, Georgia, 336

SEATTLE
1. Choice to Cincinnati
2. Gill, Owen, RB, Iowa, 53
3. Greene, Danny, WR, Washington, 81
4. Davis, Tony, TE, Missouri, 109
5. Napolitan, Mark, C, Michigan State, from San Diego, 123
Brown, Arnold, DB, North Carolina Central, from Pittsburgh, 128
Jones, Johnnie, RB, Tennessee, 137
6. Choice to NY Giants
7. Mattes, Ron, T, Virginia, 193
8. Lewis, Judious, WR, Arkansas State, 221
9. Otto, Bob, DE, Idaho State, 248
10. Conner, John, QB, Arizona, 277
Bowers, James, DB, Memphis State, from San Francisco, 280
11. Cooper, Louis, LB, Western Carolina, 305
12. Choice to Buffalo

TAMPA BAY
1. Holmes, Ron, DE, Washington, 8
2. Choice to Houston through Denver
3. Randle, Ervin, LB, Baylor, 64
4. Heaven, Mike, DB, Illinois, 92
5. Choice to NY Jets
6. Choice to Cincinnati
7. Prior, Mike, DB, Illinois State, 176
8. Freeman, Phil, WR, Arizona, 204
9. Calabria, Steve, QB, Colgate, 232
10. Igwebuike, Donald, K, Clemson, 260
11. Williams, James, RB, Memphis State, 288
12. Rockford, Jim, DB, Oklahoma, 316
Melka, Jim, LB, Wisconsin, from LA Rams, 330

WASHINGTON
1. Choice to New Orleans
2. Nixon, Tory, DB, San Diego State, from Atlanta, 33
Choice to St. Louis through Atlanta
3. Choice to LA Raiders through Houston
4. Choice to LA Raiders
5. Cherry, Raphel, RB, Hawaii, from New Orleans, 122
Choice to Pittsburgh
6. Lee, Danzell, TE, Lamar, 163
7. Harris, Jamie, KR, Oklahoma State, from Philadelphia, 177
Vital, Lionel, RB, Nicholls State, from St. Louis through Kansas City, 185
Choice to LA Raiders through New England
8. Wilburn, Barry, DB, Mississippi, 219
9. Geier, Mitch, G, Troy State, 247
10. Orr, Terry, RB, Texas, from New Orleans, 263
Choice to LA Raiders
11. McKenzie, Raleigh, G, Tennessee, from New Orleans, 290
Kimble, Garry, DB, Sam Houston State, 304
12. Hamel, Dean, DT, Tulsa, from Buffalo, 309
Winn, Bryant, LB, Houston, 331

1986
Held April 29-30, 1986

There were 333 choices instead of 336. Cleveland gave up a first-round choice and San Francisco a ninth-round choice in 1985 supplemental drafts. New England forfeited its fourth-round selection.

ATLANTA
1. Casillas, Tony, NT, Oklahoma, 2
Green, Tim, LB, Syracuse, from Washington, 17
2. Choice to Washington
3. Choice to Cincinnati
4. Choice to LA Raiders
5. Choice to Washington
6. Choice to Kansas City through Washington
Dixon, Floyd, WR, Stephen F. Austin, from Cleveland through Buffalo, 154
Williams, Keith, RB, Southwest Missouri State, from Washington, 159
7. Choice to Philadelphia
8. Hudgens, Kevin, DE, Idaho State, 197
9. Starks, Kevin, TE, Minnesota, 224
10. Baker, Tony, RB, East Carolina, 252
11. Hegg, Chris, QB, Northeast Missouri State, 280
12. Griffin, Steve, WR, Purdue, 308

BUFFALO
1. Choice to Cleveland
Harmon, Ronnie, RB, Iowa, from Cleveland, 16
Wolford, Will, T, Vanderbilt, from Dallas through San Francisco, 20
2. Choice to Detroit through San Francisco
3. Choice to San Francisco
Burton, Leonard, C, South Carolina State, from LA Rams, 77
4. Choice to Green Bay
5. Byrum, Carl, RB, Mississippi Valley State, 111
6. Choice to Dallas
7. Choice to Cleveland
Williams, Bob, TE, Penn State, from Tampa Bay, 168
Pike, Mark, DT, Georgia Tech, from Detroit, 178
Rolle, Butch, TE, Michigan State, from Seattle, 180
8. Choice to Kansas City
Furjanic, Tony, LB, Notre Dame, from Kansas City, 202
9. Bynum, Reggie, WR, Oregon State, 222
10. Teafatiller, Guy, NT, Illinois, 251
11. Garbarczyk, Tony, NT, Wake Forest, 278
Witt, Billy, DE, North Alabama, from Indianapolis, 282
12. Choice to Dallas
McClure, Brian, QB, Bowling Green, from Kansas City, 313
Christian, Derek, LB, West Virginia, from Green Bay, 331

CHI. BEARS
1. Anderson, Neal, RB, Florida, 27
2. Jackson, Vestee, DB, Washington, 55
3. Williams, David, WR, Illinois, 82
4. Blair, Paul, T, Oklahoma State, 110
5. Barnes, Lew, WR, Oregon, 138
6. Powell, Jeff, RB, Tennessee, 166
7. Jones, Bruce, DB, North Alabama, 194
8. Douglass, Maurice, DB, Kentucky, 221
9. Teltschik, John, P, Texas, 249
10. Hundley, Barton, DB, Kansas State, 277
11. Kozlowski, Glen, WR, BYU, 305
12. Choice to San Diego

CINCINNATI
1. Kelly, Joe, LB, Washington, 11
McGee, Tim, WR, Tennessee, from Denver, 21
2. Billups, Lewis, DB, North Alabama, 38
3. Skow, Jim, DE, Nebraska, from Atlanta, 58
Hammerstein, Mike, DT, Michigan, 65
Fulcher, David, DB, Arizona State, from Denver, 78
4. Kattus, Eric, TE, Michigan, 91
Gaynor, Doug, QB, Long Beach State, from Seattle, 99
5. White, Leon, LB, BYU, 123
6. Hunt, Gary, DB, Memphis State, 152
7. Franklin, Pat, RB, Southwest Texas State, 177
8. Douglas, David, G, Tennessee, 204
9. Whittingham, Cary, LB, BYU, 230
10. Shaw, Jeff, NT, Salem (West Virginia), 262
11. Stone, Tim, T, Kansas State, 289
Flaherty, Tom, LB, Northwestern, from Green Bay, 294
12. Bradley, Steve, QB, Indiana, 316

CLEVELAND
1. Choice exercised in 1985 supplemental draft (Kosar, Bernie, QB, Miami), from Buffalo
Choice to Buffalo
2. Slaughter, Webster, WR, San Diego State, 43
3. Choice to Detroit
4. Choice to San Francisco through LA Rams
5. Miller, Nick, LB, Arkansas, 127
6. Choice to Atlanta through Buffalo
7. Meyer, Jim, T, Illinois State, from Buffalo, 167
Norseth, Mike, QB, Kansas, from Kansas City, 174
Choice to Seattle
8. Choice to Philadelphia
9. Taylor, Danny, DB, Texas-El Paso, 238
10. Smith, Willie, TE, Miami, 265
11. Dausin, Randy, G, Texas A&M, 292
12. Simmons, King, DB, Texas Tech, 319

DALLAS
1. Sherrard, Mike, WR, UCLA, from San Francisco, 18
Choice to Buffalo through San Francisco
2. Clack, Darryl, RB, Arizona State, from Indianapolis, 33
Choice to Indianapolis
3. Walen, Mark, DT, UCLA, 74
4. Zendejas, Max, K, Arizona, 100
5. Choice to San Francisco
6. Chandler, Thornton, TE, Alabama, from Buffalo, 140
Gelbaugh, Stan, QB, Maryland, from Detroit, 150
Yancey, Lloyd, G, Temple, 158
7. Holloway, Johnny, WR, Kansas, 185
8. Clemons, Topper, RB, Wake Forest, 212
9. Ionata, John, G, Florida State, 242
10. Chester, Bryan, G, Texas, 269
11. Jax, Garth, LB, Florida State, 296
12. Duliban, Chris, LB, Texas, from Buffalo, 307
Flack, Tony, DB, Georgia, 322

DENVER
1. Choice to Cincinnati
2. Choice to NY Giants
3. Choice to Cincinnati
4. Juriga, Jim, T, Illinois, 104
5. Colorito, Tony, NT, USC, 134
6. Mobley, Orson, TE, Salem (West Virginia), from Green Bay, 151
Jackson, Mark, WR, Purdue, 161
7. Phillips, Raymond, LB, North Carolina State, 188
8. Klostermann, Bruce, LB, South Dakota State, 217
9. Thomas, Joe, WR, Mississippi Valley State, 244
10. Hall, Victor, TE, Jackson State, 271
11. Dendy, Thomas, RB, South Carolina, 301
12. Choice to LA Rams

DETROIT
1. Long, Chuck, QB, Iowa, 12
2. James, Garry, RB, LSU, from Buffalo through San Francisco, 29
3. Choice to San Francisco
3. Milinichik, Joe, T, North Carolina State, from Cleveland, 69
Choice to LA Rams through San Francisco
4. Mitchell, Devon, DB, Iowa, 92
5. Smith, Oscar, RB, Nicholls State, 119
6. Choice to Dallas
7. Choice to Buffalo
8. Griffin, Allyn, WR, Wyoming, 205
9. Pickens, Lyle, DB, Colorado, 231
10. Johnson, Tracy, LB, Morningside, 258
11. Melvin, Leland, WR, Richmond, 290
12. Durden, Allan, DB, Arizona, 317

GREEN BAY
1. Choice to Minnesota through San Diego
2. Davis, Kenneth, RB, TCU, 41
3. Bosco, Robbie, QB, BYU, 72
4. Harris, Tim, LB, Memphis State, from Buffalo, 84
Knight, Dan, T, San Diego State, 98
5. Koart, Matt, DT, USC, 125
6. Dent, Burnell, LB, Tulane, from St. Louis, 143
Choice to Denver
7. Berry, Ed, DB, Utah State, 183
8. Cline, Michael, NT, Arkansas State, 210
9. Moore, Brent, DT, USC, 236
10. Spann, Gary, LB, TCU, 263
11. Choice to Cincinnati
12. Choice to Buffalo

HOUSTON
1. Everett, Jim, QB, Purdue, 3
2. Givins, Ernest, WR, Louisville, 34
3. Pinkett, Allen, RB, Notre Dame, 61
4. Choice to Kansas City
5. Parks, Jeff, TE, Auburn, 114
6. Wallace, Ray, RB, Purdue, 145
7. Choice to Indianapolis through LA Rams
8. Griffin, Larry, DB, North Carolina, 199
9. Sebring, Bob, LB, Illinois, 225
10. Sommer, Don, G, Texas-El Paso, 256
11. Cochran, Mark, T, Baylor, 283
12. Banks, Chuck, RB, West Virginia Tech, 310

INDIANAPOLIS
1. Hand, Jon, DE, Alabama, from New Orleans, 4
Choice to New Orleans
2. Choice to Dallas
Trudeau, Jack, QB, Illinois, from Dallas, 47
3. Choice to New Orleans
4. Brooks, Bill, WR, Boston U., 86
5. Kellar, Scott, DE, Northern Illinois, 117
Walker, Gary, C, Boston U., from San Diego, 124
6. Choice to LA Rams
7. O'Malley, Steve, NT, Northern Illinois, 171
White, Chris, K, Illinois, from Houston through LA Rams, 172
Sims, Tommy, DB, Tennessee, from LA Rams, 190
8. Hooper, Trell, DB, Memphis State, 198
9. Brotzki, Bob, T, Syracuse, 228
10. Choice to St. Louis
Anderson, Pete, G, Georgia, from San Diego, 266
11. Choice to Buffalo
12. Wade, Steve, DT, Vanderbilt, 309
Williams, Isaac, DT, Florida State, from LA Rams, 326

KANSAS CITY
1. Jozwiak, Brian, T, West Virginia, 7
2. Hackett, Dino, LB, Appalachian State, 35
3. Griffin, Leonard, DE, Grambling, 63
4. Baugh, Tom, C, Southern Illinois, from Houston, 87
   Fox, Chas, WR, Furman, 90
5. Choice to San Diego
6. Hagood, Kent, RB, South Carolina, from Atlanta through Washington, 141
   Choice to Washington
7. Choice to Cleveland
8. Colbert, Lewis, P, Auburn, from Buffalo, 196
   Choice to Buffalo
9. Baldinger, Gary, DE, Wake Forest, 229
10. Readon, Ike, NT, Hampton, 257
11. Pearson, Aaron, LB, Mississippi State, 285
12. Choice to Buffalo

LA RAIDERS
1. Buczkowski, Bob, DE, Pittsburgh, 24
2. Choice to NY Giants through Minnesota
3. Cochran, Brad, DB, Michigan, 80
4. Wise, Mike, DE, Cal-Davis, from Atlanta, 85
   Mueller, Vance, RB, Occidental, from NY Giants, 103
   McCallum, Napoleon, RB, Navy, 108
5. Choice to Pittsburgh
6. Marrone, Doug, T, Syracuse, 164
7. Lewis, Bill, C, Nebraska, 191
8. Mauntel, Joe, LB, Eastern Kentucky, 219
9. Lee, Zeph, RB, USC, 246
10. Reinke, Jeff, DE, Mankato State, 275
11. Webster, Randell, LB, Southwestern Oklahoma, 302
12. Shepherd, Larry, WR, Houston, 330

LA RAMS
1. Schad, Mike, T, Queen's (Ontario), 23
2. Newberry, Tom, G, Wisconsin-La Crosse, 50
3. Millen, Hugh, QB, Washington, from Detroit through San Francisco, 71
   Choice to Buffalo
4. Choice to Philadelphia
5. Choice to San Diego
6. Cox, Robert, T, UCLA, from Indianapolis, 144
   Williams, Lynn, RB, Kansas, 160
7. Choice to Indianapolis
8. Jarecki, Steve, LB, UCLA, from Tampa Bay, 195
   Goebel, Hank, T, Cal State-Fullerton, 216
9. Watts, Elbert, DB, USC, 243
10. Breeland, Garrett, LB, USC, 273
11. Schwanke, Chul, RB, South Dakota, 300
12. Choice to Indianapolis
   Dupree, Marcus, RB, Oklahoma, from Denver, 327

MIAMI
1. Choice to Tampa Bay
2. Offerdahl, John, LB, Western Michigan, 52
3. Turner, T.J., DT, Houston, 81
4. Pruitt, James, WR, Cal State-Fullerton, 107
5. Wyatt, Kevin, DB, Arkansas, 136
6. Sowell, Brent, DT, Alabama, 163
7. Kolic, Larry, LB, Ohio State, 193
8. Stuart, John, T, Texas, 218
9. Thompson, Reyna, DB, Baylor, 247
10. Wickersham, Jeff, QB, LSU, 274
11. Franklin, Arnold, TE, North Carolina, 303
12. Isom, Rickey, RB, North Carolina State, 329

MINNESOTA
1. Choice to San Diego
   Robinson, Gerald, DE, Auburn, from Green Bay through San Diego, 14
2. Choice to Tampa Bay through Miami
3. Choice to San Diego
4. Phillips, Joe, DT, SMU, 93
5. Jones, Hassan, WR, Florida State, 120
6. Rooks, Thomas, RB, Illinois, 147
7. Hilton, Carl, TE, Houston, 179
8. Schippang, Gary, T, West Chester, 206
9. Slaton, Mike, DB, South Dakota, 232
10. Cormier, Joe, WR, USC, 259
11. Armstrong, John, DB, Richmond, 286
12. Solomon, Jesse, LB, Florida State, 318

NEW ENGLAND
1. Dupard, Reggie, RB, SMU, 26
2. Ruth, Mike, NT, Boston College, from Seattle, 42
   Glenn, Vencie, DB, Indiana State, 54
3. Forfeited
4. Gieselman, Scott, TE, Boston College, 109
5. Robinson, Greg, G, Cal State-Sacramento, 137
6. Choice to Tampa Bay
7. McDonald, Ray, WR, Florida, from San Francisco, 187
   Williams, Brent, DE, Toledo, 192
8. Baty, Greg, TE, Stanford, 220
9. Colton, George, G, Maryland, 248
10. Jones, Cletis, RB, Florida State, 276
11. Thomas, Gene, WR, Pacific, 304
12. McAulay, Don, K, Syracuse, 332

NEW ORLEANS
1. Choice to Indianapolis
   Dombrowski, Jim, T, Virginia, from Indianapolis, 6
2. Hilliard, Dalton, RB, LSU, 31
3. Mayes, Rueben, RB, Washington State, from Tampa Bay, 57
   Swilling, Pat, LB, Georgia Tech, from Indianapolis, 60
   Word, Barry, RB, Virginia, 62
4. Edwards, Kolvin, WR, Liberty Baptist, 88
5. Sutton, Reggie, DB, Miami, 115
6. Thompson, Robert, WR, Youngstown State, 142
7. Fenerty, Gill, RB, Holy Cross, 173
8. Mokofisi, Filipo, LB, Utah, 200
9. Jones, Merlon, LB, Florida A&M, 226
10. Dumbauld, Jon, DE, Kentucky, 253
11. Swoopes, Pat, NT, Mississippi State, 284
12. Brown, Sebastian, WR, Bethune-Cookman, 311

NY GIANTS
1. Dorsey, Eric, DE, Notre Dame, 19
2. Collins, Mark, DB, Cal State-Fullerton, from San Diego through Minnesota, 44
   Howard, Erik, NT, Washington State, 46
   Johnson, Pepper, LB, Ohio State, from Denver, 51
   Lasker, Greg, DB, Arkansas, from LA Raiders through Minnesota, 53
3. Washington, John, DE, Oklahoma State, 73
4. Choice to LA Raiders
5. Warren, Vince, WR, San Diego State, 130
6. Brown, Ron, WR, Colorado, from Tampa Bay through Denver, 139
   Miller, Solomon, WR, Utah State, 157
7. Francis, Jon, RB, Boise State, 184
8. Cisowski, Steve, T, Santa Clara, 214
9. Luebbers, Jim, DE, Iowa State, 241
10. Kimmel, Jerry, LB, Syracuse, 268
11. Lynch, Len, G, Maryland, 295
12. Choice to Philadelphia

NY JETS
1. Haight, Mike, T, Iowa, 22
2. Williams, Doug, T, Texas A&M, 49
3. Crawford, Tim, LB, Texas Tech, 79
4. Alexander, Rogers, LB, Penn State, 105
5. Hadley, Ron, LB, Washington, 132
6. Choice to San Francisco
7. White, Bob, T, Rhode Island, 189
8. Ducksworth, Robert, DB, Southern Mississippi, 215
9. Faaola, Nuu, RB, Hawaii, 245
10. Carr, Carl, LB, North Carolina, 272
11. Amoia, Vince, RB, Arizona State, 299
12. Cesario, Sal, T, Cal Poly-SLO, 328

PHILADELPHIA
1. Byars, Keith, RB, Ohio State, 10
2. Toney, Anthony, RB, Texas A&M, 37
   Johnson, Alonzo, LB, Florida, from Washington through LA Raiders, 48
3. Choice to San Francisco
4. Choice to San Diego
   Darwin, Matt, C, Texas A&M, from LA Rams, 106
5. Criswell, Ray, P, Florida, 121
   McMillen, Dan, DE, Colorado, from Washington through Atlanta, 128
6. Landsee, Bob, C, Wisconsin, 149
7. Redick, Corn, WR, Cal State-Fullerton, from Atlanta, 169
   Lee, Byron, LB, Ohio State, 176
8. Choice to San Francisco
   Joyner, Seth, LB, Texas-El Paso, from Cleveland, 208
9. Simmons, Clyde, DE, Western Carolina, 233
10. Tautalatasi, Junior, RB, Washington State, 261
11. Bogdalek, Steve, G, Michigan State, 288
12. Singletary, Reggie, DE, North Carolina State, 315
   Howard, Bobby, RB, Indiana, from NY Giants, 325

PITTSBURGH
1. Rienstra, John, G, Temple, 9
2. Williams, Gerald, DE, Auburn, 36
3. Brister, Walter, QB, Northeast Louisiana, 67
4. Callahan, Bill, DB, Pittsburgh, 94
5. Tucker, Erroll, DB, Utah, 122
   Jones, Brent, TE, Santa Clara, from LA Raiders, 135
6. Bryant, Domingo, DB, Texas A&M, 148
7. Carter, Rodney, RB, Purdue, 175
8. Boso, Cap, TE, Illinois, 207
9. Henton, Anthony, LB, Troy State, 234
10. Seitz, Warren, WR, Missouri, 260
11. Station, Larry, LB, Iowa, 287
12. Williams, Mike, LB, Tulsa, 314

ST. LOUIS
1. Bell, Anthony, LB, Michigan State, 5
2. Lee, John, K, UCLA, 32
3. Chilton, Gene, C, Texas, 59
4. Carter, Carl, DB, Texas Tech, 89
5. Tupper, Jeff, DE, Oklahoma, 116
6. Choice to Green Bay
7. Swanson, Eric, WR, Tennessee, 170
8. Brown, Ray, G, Arkansas State, 201
9. Kafentzis, Kent, DB, Hawaii, 227
10. Sikahema, Vai, RB, BYU, 254
   Smith, Wes, WR, East Texas State, from Indianapolis, 255
11. Dillard, Wayne, LB, Alcorn State, 281
12. Austin, Kent, QB, Mississippi, 312

SAN DIEGO
1. O'Neal, Leslie, DE, Oklahoma State, from Minnesota, 8
   FitzPatrick, James, T, USC, 13
2. Choice to NY Giants through Minnesota
3. Unrein, Terry, DE, Colorado State, from Minnesota, 66
4. Walker, Jeff, T, Memphis State, 70
   Allert, Ty, LB, Texas, from Philadelphia, 95
   Taylor, Tommy, LB, UCLA, 97
5. Landry, Doug, LB, Louisiana Tech, from Kansas City, 118
   Choice to Indianapolis
   Brown, Donald, DB, Maryland, from San Francisco, 129
   Johnson, Matt, DB, USC, from LA Rams, 133
6. Pardridge, Curt, WR, Northern Illinois, 155
7. Smalls, Fred, LB, West Virginia, 182
8. Perrino, Mike, T, Notre Dame, 209
9. Zordich, Mike, DB, Penn State, 235
10. Choice to Indianapolis
11. Sanders, Chuck, RB, Slippery Rock, 293
   Smetana, Drew, T, Oregon, from San Francisco, 298
12. Sprowls, Jeff, DB, BYU, 320
   Travis, Mike, DB, Georgia Tech, from Chi. Bears, 333

SAN FRANCISCO
1. Choice to Dallas
2. Roberts, Larry, DE, Alabama, from Detroit, 39
   Choice to Washington
3. Rathman, Tom, RB, Nebraska, from Buffalo, 56
   McKyer, Tim, DB, Texas-Arlington, from Philadelphia, 64
   Taylor, John, WR, Delaware State, 76
4. Haley, Charles, LB, James Madison, from Cleveland through LA Rams, 96
   Wallace, Steve, T, Auburn, from Washington through LA Rams, 101
   Fagan, Kevin, DT, Miami, 102
5. Choice to San Diego
   Miller, Patrick, LB, Florida, from Dallas, 131
6. Choice to Washington
   Griffin, Don, DB, Middle Tennessee State, from NY Jets, 162
7. Choice to New England
8. Popp, Jim, TE, Vanderbilt, from Philadelphia, 203
   Choice exercised in 1985 supplemental draft (Snipes, Roosevelt, RB, Florida State)
9. Cherry, Tony, RB, Oregon, 240
10. Stinson, Elliston, WR, Rice, 267
   Hallman, Harold, LB, Auburn, from Washington, 270
11. Choice to San Diego
12. Choice to Tampa Bay

SEATTLE
1. Williams, John L., RB, Florida, 15
2. Choice to New England
3. Hunter, Patrick, DB, Nevada-Reno, 68
4. Choice to Cincinnati
5. Edmonds, Bobby Joe, WR, Arkansas, 126
6. Anderson, Eddie, DB, Fort Valley State, 153
7. Choice to Buffalo
   Miles, Paul, RB, Nebraska, from Cleveland, 181
8. Mitz, Alonzo, DE, Florida, 211
9. Black, Mike, T, Cal State-Sacramento, 237
10. Fairbanks, Don, DE, Colorado, 264
11. Norrie, David, QB, UCLA, 291
12. McVeigh, John, LB, Miami, 321

TAMPA BAY
1. Jackson, Bo, RB, Auburn, 1
   Jones, Roderick, DB, SMU, from Miami, 25
2. Walker, Jackie, LB, Jackson State, 28
   Murphy, Kevin, LB, Oklahoma, from Minnesota through Miami, 40
3. Choice to New Orleans
4. Swoope, Craig, DB, Illinois, 83
5. Maarleveld, J.D., T, Maryland, 112
6. Choice to NY Giants through Denver
   Walker, Kevin, DB, East Carolina, from New England, 165
7. Choice to Buffalo
8. Choice to LA Rams
9. Barnhardt, Tommy, P, North Carolina, 223
10. Reed, Benton, DE, Mississippi, 250
11. Drenth, Mark, T, Purdue, 279
12. Miller, Clay, G, Michigan, 306
   Crawford, Mike, RB, Arizona State, from San Francisco, 324

WASHINGTON
1. Choice to Atlanta
2. Koch, Markus, DE, Boise State, from Atlanta
   Murray, Walter, WR, Hawaii, from San Francisco, 45
   Choice to Philadelphia through LA Raiders
3. Walton, Alvin, DB, Kansas, 75
4. Choice to San Francisco through LA Rams
5. Caldwell, Ravin, LB, Arkansas, from Atlanta, 113
   Choice to Philadelphia through Atlanta
6. Rypien, Mark, QB, Washington State, from Kansas City, 146
   Huddleston, Jim, G, Virginia, from San Francisco, 156
   Choice to Atlanta
7. Badanjek, Rick, RB, Maryland, 186
8. Gouveia, Kurt, LB, BYU, 213
9. Asberry, Wayne, DB, Texas A&M, 239
10. Choice to San Francisco
11. Fells, Kenny, RB, Henderson State, 297
12. Yarber, Eric, WR, Idaho, 323

Rules of the NFL

DIGEST OF NFL RULES

RULE 1 THE FIELD

It is 360 feet long and 160 feet wide. The end zones are 30 feet, or 10 yards, deep. The hashmarks or inbounds lines are 70 feet 9 inches from each side line. The lines used for tries-for-point are two yards from each goal line.

Sidelines and end lines are out of bounds. The goal line is in the end zone. A player with the ball in his possession scores when the ball is on, above, or over the goal line.

Goal posts must be the single standard type, offset from the end line and painted bright gold. The actual goal is the plane extending indefinitely above the crossbar between the outer edges of the posts. Goal posts must be 18 feet 6 inches wide and the top face of the crossbar 10 feet above the ground. The post must extend at least 30 feet above the crossbar.

Decorations in the end zone and at the 50-yard line must be approved by the commissioner to avoid confusing where the goal lines, sidelines, and end lines are.

RULE 2 THE BALL

The ball must be a Wilson ball bearing the signature of Commissioner Pete Rozelle.

It shall be made of an inflated rubber bladder enclosed in a pebble-grained leather case of natural tan color without corrugations of any kind. It shall have the form of a prolate spheroid. It shall be inflated to 12½ to 13½ pounds.

The home team must have 24 balls available for testing by the referee one hour before each game.

RULE 3 DEFINITIONS

Chucking is warding off an opponent who is in front of a defender by contacting him with a quick extension of the arm or arms, followed by the return of the arm or arms to a flexed position, thereby breaking the original contact.

Clipping is throwing the body across the back of an opponent's leg or hitting him from the back while moving up from behind unless the opponent is a runner or the action is in close line play.

Close line play is the area between the positions normally occupied by the offensive tackles, extending three yards on each side of the line of scrimmage.

A dead ball is a ball not in play.

A double foul is a foul by each team during the same down.

A down is the period of action that starts when the ball is put in play and ends when it is dead.

Encroachment occurs when a player enters the neutral zone and makes contact with an opponent before the ball is snapped.

A fair catch is an unhindered catch of a kick by a member of the receiving team, who must raise one arm at full length above his head and wave it from side to side while the kick is in flight.

A foul is any violation of a playing rule.

A free kick is a kickoff, a kick after a safety, or a kick after a fair catch. It may be a placekick, a dropkick, or punt, except a punt may not be used on a kickoff.

A fumble is the loss of possession of the ball.

Impetus is the action of a player that gives momentum to the ball.

A live ball is a ball legally free kicked or snapped and it continues in play until the down ends.

A loose ball is a live ball not in the possession of any player.

A muff is the touching of a loose ball by a player in an unsuccessful attempt to obtain possession.

The neutral zone is the space the length of the ball between the two scrimmage lines.

Offside means a player has any part of his body beyond his scrimmage or free kick line when the ball is snapped.

Possession of a pass is when a player controls the ball throughout the act of clearly touching both feet, or any other part of his body other than the hand(s), to the ground inbounds.

A punt is a kick made when a player drops the ball and kicks it while it is in flight.

A safety is when the ball is dead on or behind a team's own goal if the impetus comes from a player of that team. Two points are scored for the opposing team.

A shift is the movement of two or more offensive players at the same time before the snap.

Sudden death is the continuation of a tied game into sudden death overtime in which the team scoring first by safety, field goal, or touchdown wins.

A touchback is when a ball is dead on or behind a team's own goal line and the impetus came from an opponent and the play was not a touchdown or missed field goal.

A touchdown is when any part of the ball, legally in possession of a player inbounds, is on, above, or over the opponent's goal line, provided it is not a touchback.

Unsportsmanlike conduct is any act contrary to the generally understood principles of sportsmanship.

RULE 4 HOW THE GAME IS STARTED, CONDUCTED, AND TIMED

A game is 60 minutes long, divided into four periods of 15 minutes each. Halftime is 15 minutes long, unless otherwise specified.

The stadium clock is official. The line judge supervises the timing. The clock operator starts and stops the clock upon the signal of any official.

The toss of the coin takes place within three minutes of the kickoff. The visiting captain calls the toss. The winner of the toss makes one of two choices, whether his team will receive or kick or secondly, the goal his team will defend. The loser of the toss gets the other choice. For the second half, the loser of the toss has the first choice of the two privileges.

The teams change goals at the end of the first and third periods.

The clock operator starts the clock when the ball is kicked off to start the game, and thereafter, following any time out, the clock starts when the ball is snapped or free kicked.

Three charged team time outs are allowed each team during each half.

Time outs last one minute 30 seconds. Time outs during the last two minutes of a half are one minute.

The referee may allow two minutes for an injured player and three minutes for repair of equipment.

The offense has 30 seconds to put the ball in play.

The clock starts when the ball is snapped following a change of possession.

In the last two minutes of each half the clock does not start on a kickoff until the ball has been legally touched by a player of either team in the field of play.

A team cannot "buy" an extra time out and take a penalty in the last two minutes of each half. But a fourth time out is allowed without a penalty for an injured player who must be removed immediately. A fifth time out or more is allowed for an injury and a five-yard penalty is assessed if the clock was running. In addition, if the clock is running and the score is tied or the team in possession is losing, the ball cannot be put in play for at least 10 seconds on the fourth or more time out. The half or game can end while those 10 seconds are being run off the clock.

The down is replayed on a foul by the defense on the last play of the half or game if the penalty is accepted by the offense.

The down is not replayed on a foul by the offense on the last play of the half or game, and the play in which the foul was committed is nullified. Exceptions are fair catch interference, a foul following a change of possession, and illegal touching. No score by the offense counts.

The down is replayed when a double foul occurs on the last play of the half or game.

RULE 5 THE PLAYERS, SUBSTITUTES, AND THEIR EQUIPMENT

Each team is permitted 11 men on the field at the snap.

All players must be numbered according to their positions as follows: quarterbacks and kickers, 1-19; all backs, running and defensive, 20-49; centers and linebackers, 50-59; defensive linemen and interior offensive linemen, including centers, 60-79; further, defensive linemen and linebackers also may be numbered 90-99; wide receivers and tight ends, 80-89. All players who had been in the NFL in 1972 may use their old numbers. Otherwise, any and all players entering the league must be numbered in accordance with the preceding rules. An offensive player who comes into a game wearing an illegal number for the position he takes must report to the referee, who in turn will report same to the defensive captain.

Substitutes may not enter the field while the ball is in play. They may enter at any time while the ball is dead, provided the players they replace have cleared the field on their own side between the end lines prior to the snap or free kick. Players who have been substituted for may not linger on the field. If they do it is unsportsmanlike conduct.

A substitute is not to report to any official. He becomes a player when he informs a teammate he is replacing him; a teammate voluntarily withdraws upon his entering; he participates in at least one play after communicating with a teammate; or, in the absence of any of these, he is on the field at the time of the snap or free kick.

No player can wear equipment that, in the opinion of the officials, endangers other players.

RULE 6 THE FREE KICK

A free kick called a kickoff puts the ball in play at the start of each half, after a try for point, and after a successful field goal. The free kick line is the 35.

The kicker may use a tee up to three inches high on a kickoff.

A kickoff is illegal unless it travels 10 yards or is touched by the receiving team. It is a free ball once it is touched by the receiving team. The receiving team may recover and advance it. The kicking team may recover but not advance it unless it was first possessed and lost by the receiving team. If it recovers it in the end zone it is a touchdown.

When a kickoff goes out of bounds between the goal lines without being touched by the receiving team it must be kicked again and there is a five-yard penalty against the kicking team. If the kicking team either illegally kicks off out of bounds or is guilty of a short free kick on two or more consecutive kickoffs, receiver shall have an option of either a rekick with a five-yard penalty, or they may take possession of the ball at the dead ball spot, out of bounds spot, or spot of illegal touch.

A kick after a safety and a kick after a fair catch are also free kicks. In each case a dropkick, placekick, or punt may be used.

On a kick after a fair catch the receiving team has the option to put the ball in play by a punt, dropkick, or placekick without a tee, or by a snap. If the team dropkicks or placekicks and the ball goes between the uprights of the opponent's goal it is a field goal.

RULE 7 THE SCRIMMAGE

The offensive team must have at least seven players on the line of scrimmage at the snap.

Offensive players not on the line of scrimmage, except for the player who takes the snap, must be at least one yard back except for the player who takes the snap.

No player of either team may enter the neutral zone before the snap.

All offensive players must be stationary at the snap, except that one back may be in motion parallel to the line of scrimmage or backward from it. No interior linemen may move after taking or simulating a three-point stance.

A quarterback can be called for a false start penalty if his action is judged to be an obvious attempt to draw an opponent offside.

After a shift all offensive players must come to an absolute stop for at least one second before the snap.

RULE 8 FORWARD AND BACKWARD PASS AND FUMBLE

The offense may make only one forward pass each play.

The passer must be behind his line of scrimmage.

A forward pass may be touched or caught only by an eligible player—offensive players on either end of the line or at least one yard behind the line at the snap, except for the T-formation quarterback, or any defensive player.

Any eligible offensive player may catch a forward pass. If a pass is touched by one offensive player and touched or caught by a second eligible offensive player, pass completion is legal. Further, all offensive players become eligible once a pass is touched by an eligible receiver or any defensive player.

If a forward pass is caught simultaneously by eligible players of both teams it goes to the passing team.

A pass is incomplete and the ball is dead if the pass hits the ground or goes out of bounds, hits the goal post or the crossbar of either team, is caught by an offensive player after touching an ineligible receiver, or is caught by the passer.

A forward pass is complete when a receiver clearly touches the ground with both feet inbounds while in possession of the ball. If he is carried out of bounds by an opponent while in possession in the air, the pass is complete where he went out of bounds.

If a pass is incomplete on fourth down on a play that starts inside the opponent's 20-yard line, the defense gets the ball at the line of scrimmage.

It is intentional grounding when the ball strikes the ground after the passer throws, tosses, or lobs it to prevent loss of yards by his team.

No defensive player may run into a passer of a legal forward pass after the ball has left the passer's hand. The referee must determine whether the opponent had a reasonable chance to stop his momentum during an attempt to block the pass or tackle the passer while he still had the ball.

A pass begins when the passer starts to bring his hand forward. If the ball then hits the ground it is an incomplete pass. If the passer loses control of it before he brings his hand forward it is a fumble.

The restriction against pass interference begins for the passing team at the snap. The restriction begins for the defensive team when the ball leaves the passer's hand. The restrictions end for both when the ball is touched by anyone.

If there is defensive pass interference in the end zone, it is first down for the offense on the defense's 1-yard line.

It is pass interference by either team when any player movement beyond the offensive line significantly hinders the progress of an eligible player or such player's opportunity to catch the ball during a legal forward pass. When a player establishes a position to catch the ball in which an opponent cannot reach the ball without first contacting the player in a manner that prevents the player from catching the ball, such action by the opponent shall be considered interference. Provided an eligible player is not interfered with in such a manner, the following exceptions to pass interference will prevail: If neither player is looking for the ball and there is incidental contact in the act of moving to the ball that does not materially affect the route of an eligible player, there is no interference. If there is any question whether the incidental contact materially affects the route, the ruling shall be no interference. Inadvertent tripping is not a foul in this situation. Any eligible player looking for and intent on playing the ball who initiates contact, however severe, while attempting to move to the spot of completion or interception will not be called for interference. Any eligible player who makes contact, however severe, with one or more eligible players while looking for and making a genuine attempt to catch or bat a reachable ball, will not be called for interference. It must be remembered that defensive players have as much right to the ball as offensive eligible receivers. Pass interference by the defense is not to be called when the forward pass is clearly uncatchable. There is no defensive pass interference behind the line.

Any pass that is not a foward pass is a backward pass, or lateral.

A runner may pass backward at any time.

Any player on either team may catch the backward pass or recover the ball after it touches the ground. The offense can recover and advance it but the defense can only recover it, unless it is in the air, and in that case the defense can both recover and advance it.

A fumble may be advanced by any player on either team regardless of whether it is recovered before or after the ball hits the ground.

If an offensive player fumbles anywhere on the field during a fourth-down play, or if a player fumbles on any down after the two-minute warning, only the fumbling player is permitted to recover and/or advance the ball. If the ball is recovered by any other offensive player, the ball is dead at the spot of the fumble unless it is recovered behind the spot of the fumble. Any defensive player may recover and/or advance any fumble. The fourth-down fumble rule does not apply if any player touches, but does not possess a direct snap from center. A fumble in the last two minutes that goes forward and out of bounds is dead at the spot of the fumble.

RULE 9 THE SCRIMMAGE KICK

Scrimmage kicks are punts, dropkicks, and placekicks.

During a scrimmage kick only the end men on the line of scrimmage at the snap may go beyond the line before the ball is kicked. If there is an eligible receiver aligned or in motion behind the line and more than one yard outside the end man on his side, clearly making him the outside receiver, he may replace the end man as the player eligible to go downfield before the snap.

Any punt that is blocked and does not cross the line of scrimmage may be recovered and advanced by either team. If the offensive team recovers after the ball has been touched by the defensive team, the offensive team must make the yardage necessary for its first down, if it is fourth down, to retain possession of the ball.

The kicking team may never advance its own kick beyond the line of scrimmage.

No player on the receiving team may run into or rough the kicker.

The penalty for running into the kicker is 5 yards and for roughing the kicker it is 15. If the roughing the kicker penalty is flagrant it is disqualification.

It is legal for a player on the receiving team to run into or rough the kicker if the contact is incidental to and after the receiving team player has touched the ball in flight; the contact is caused by the kicker's own motions; or, the contact occurs during a quick kick or a kick made after a run or when the kicker recovers a loose ball. It is a loose ball when the kicker muffs the snap or the snap hits the ground.

If a member of the kicking team who is attempting to down the ball on or inside the opponent's 5-yard line carries it into the end zone, it is a touchback.

Any member of the punting team may down the ball anywhere in the field of play.

If the receiving team commits a foul before gaining possession and the ball is still in the air or rolling on the ground after a punt or field goal attempt, the receiving team will retain possession of the ball and be penalized for its foul.

The defensive team may advance all kicks from scrimmage, including missed field goals, whether the ball crosses the defensive team's goal line or not.

It is illegal for a defensive player to stand on, jump on, or be picked up by a teammate or use a hand or hands on a teammate to gain additional height in an attempt to block a kick.

When a field goal is missed and the line of scrimmage is beyond the 20, the defensive team gets the ball at the line of scrimmage. When a field goal is missed inside the 20, the ball reverts to the 20.

RULE 10 THE FAIR CATCH

It is a legal fair catch signal when one arm is raised at full length above the head and waved from side to side while the ball is in flight.

No opponent may interfere with the fair catcher, the ball, or his path to the ball.

The fair catcher is not required to catch the ball.

After signaling, he cannot block or initiate contact with any opponent until the ball touches someone.

The fair catch signal is off if the ball is touched by a member of the kicking team while it is in flight, or it hits the ground.

It is delay of game and a five-yard penalty if the fair catcher unduly advances the ball. The ball is dead at the spot of the catch.

If time expires while the ball is in play and a fair catch is awarded, the receiving team may choose to extend the period with one free-kick down.

RULE 11 SCORING

A touchdown counts six points, a field goal three, a safety two, and a successful try for point one.

The ball is automatically dead at the instant of legal player possession on, above, or behind the opponent's goal line.

The referee may award a touchdown when the offended team is deprived of one by a palpably unfair act, such as the act of a player coming off the bench and tackling a runner apparently en route to a touchdown.

The ball may be spotted for a try for point anywhere between the inbounds lines, two or more yards from the goal line.

A successful conversion counts one point whether it is by run, pass, or kick.

RULE 12 CONDUCT OF PLAYERS

A runner may ward off opponents with his hands and arms but no other player on offense may use his hands or arms to obstruct an opponent by grasping with the hands or pushing or encircling any part of his body during a block.

No offensive player may assist the runner except by blocking for him. There can be no interlocking interference.

Any offensive player who pretends to possess the ball or to whom a teammate pretends to give the ball may be tackled, provided he is crossing his scrimmage line between the ends of a normal tight offensive line.

An offensive player who lines up more than two yards outside his own tackle or a player who, at the snap, is in a backfield position and subsequently takes a position more than two yards outside a tackle, may not clip an opponent anywhere nor may he contact an opponent below the waist if the blocker is moving toward the ball and if contact is made within an area five yards on either side of the line.

Pass blocking is the obstruction of an opponent by the use of that part of the body above the knees. During a legal block, hands (open or closed) must be inside the blocker's elbows and can be thrust forward to contact an opponent as long as the contact is inside the frame. Hands cannot be thrust forward above the frame to contact an opponent on the neck, face, or head. The blocker cannot use his hands or arms to push from behind, hang onto, or encircle an opponent in a manner that restricts his movements as the play develops. The blocker may ward off an opponent's attempt to grasp his jersey or arms and prevent legal contact to the head.

Run blocking is an aggressive action by a blocker to obstruct an opponent from the ball carrier. During a legal block, contact can be made with the head, shoulders, hands, and/or outer surface of the forearm, or any other part of the body. Hands with extended arms can be thrust forward to contact an opponent as long as the contact is inside the frame and outside the pocket area. As the play develops, a blocker is permitted to work for and maintain position on an opponent as long as he does not push from behind or clip (outside legal clip zone). A blocker who makes contact with extended arms within the pocket area may maintain such contact outside of the pocket area as long as the action is continuous. A blocker cannot make initial contact with extended arms outside the pocket area. A blocker lined up more than two yards outside the tackle is subject to the crackback rule.

A defensive player may not tackle or hold an opponent other than the runner.

A defensive player may use his hands and arms only to ward off an obstructing opponent, to push or pull an opponent out of the way on the line of scrimmage, in an actual attempt to get at or tackle the runner, to push or pull an opponent out of the way in a legal attempt to recover a loose ball, during a legal block on an opponent who is not an eligible pass receiver; and when legally blocking an eligible pass receiver above the waist.

A defensive player must not contact an opponent above the shoulders with the palm of his hand—head slap—except during his initial charge or to ward him off the line. It cannot be a repeated act against the same opponent during any one contact.

A defensive player may use his hands or arms to contact an eligible receiver only to a point five yards beyond the line of scrimmage. Beyond this limitation, a defender may use his hands or arms only to defend or protect himself against impending contact caused by a receiver.

A defensive player may block an eligible receiver below the waist—roll block him—provided the receiver is within three yards of the line of scrimmage and lined up within two yards of the tackle.

A player may bat or punch a loose ball in the field of play but not toward the opponent's goal line. In either end zone, he may not bat or punch a loose ball in any direction.

A player may not bat or punch a ball while it is in player possession.

A player may not kick at a ball except as a punt, dropkick, or placekick.

A player may not strike with the fists, kick, knee, or strike on the head, neck, or face with the heel, back, or side of the hand, wrist, forearm, elbow, or clasped hands.

A player may not grasp the facemask of an opponent.

There shall be no piling on, unnecessary roughness, clipping, crawling, or any form of unsportsmanlike conduct.

Clipping is legal in close line play, in an area extending laterally to the positions originally occupied by the offensive tackles and longitudinally three yards on either side of the line of scrimmage.

RULE 13 CONDUCT OF NON-PLAYERS

There shall be no unsportsmanlike conduct by a substitute, coach, attendants, or any other non-player.

Coaches may move in an area extending 18 yards in both directions from the middle of the team's bench.

Each team may have no more than 15 non-players in its bench area.

RULE 14 ENFORCEMENT PENALTIES

Penalties are enforced from four spots: (1) the previous spot is where the ball was put in play; (2) the spot of the foul is where it occurred; (3) the spot of the snap, pass, fumble, return kick, or free kick is where one of those things occurred; (4) the succeeding spot is where the ball would be put in play if no distance penalty were to be enforced.

Fouls by the offense behind the line of scrimmage and on the field of play are penalized from the previous spot.

If there is a double foul during a down in which there is a change of possession, the team last gaining possession may keep the ball unless its foul was committed prior to the change of possession.

If there is a double foul after a change of possession the defensive team retains the ball at the spot of its foul or dead ball spot.

If one of the fouls of a double foul involves disqualification the player must be removed but no penalty yardage is assessed.

The penalty is assessed on the following kickoff when a team scores and either team commits a personal foul, unsportsmanlike conduct, or any obviously unfair act.

RULE 15 OFFICIALS DUTIES

They are the referee, umpire, head linesman, line judge, back judge, side judge, and field judge.

If one of them is absent, the crew is to be arranged on the most feasible basis.

All officials have concurrent jurisdiction over any foul.

The referee has general oversight and control of the game. He is the final authority for the score and number of the down. He sees that the ball is properly put in play. He notifies the coach and captain when a team has used its three time outs and he notifies both coaches when two minutes remain in a half.

The umpire has primary jurisdiction over the equipment of the players and the conduct and action of the players on the line of scrimmage.

The head linesman is primarily responsible for offside, encroaching, any actions pertaining to the scrimmage line prior to the snap, and the work of the chain crew.

The line judge times the game and, in case the stadium clock becomes inoperative, takes over the timing on the field. He works on the side of the field opposite the head linesman and is primarily responsible for watching illegal motion behind the line at the snap and illegal shifts. He fires a pistol signaling that time has expired at the end of a period.

The back judge works on the same side of the field as the line judge, 17 yards deep. He is responsible for watching all eligible receivers on his side of the field. After receivers have cleared the line of scrimmage, he concentrates on action in the area between the umpire and the field judge.

The field judge is in the defensive secondary 25 yards deep and watches forward passes, kicks from scrimmage, loose balls out of the range of the umpire, back judge, or head linesman, times the 30 seconds the offensive team has to put the ball in play, and checks for illegal substitutions.

The side judge works on the same side of the field as the head linesman, 17 yards deep. He is responsible for all eligible receivers on his side of the field. After the receivers have cleared the line of scrimmage, the side judge concentrates on action in the area between the umpire and field judge. The side judge also is responsible for counting the number of players on the field at the time of the snap.

RULE 16 SUDDEN DEATH

Sudden death prevails for all games, but preseason and regular season games have a maximum of one 15-minute period of overtime.

The team scoring first during overtime play is the winner of the game.

RULE 17 HANDLING AN EMERGENCY

If any non-player enters the field or end zones and in the judgment of an official interferes with play, the referee, after consulting with the crew, shall enforce any such penalty or score as the interference warrants.

MAJOR RULES CHANGES

The rules of football had already gone through a half-century of development before the league that became the NFL arrived in 1920.

College football was by then a major part of American life. And just as millions followed the sport in the huge arenas where it was played or through newspaper accounts of the game's heroes, the way it was played and governed was also of great interest. The decisions reached at the annual meeting of the rules committee were reported and studied and argued over.

By the time of the NFL, this annual process had been going on for a long time. The colleges had already established the major rules that laid the foundation for the game: the field 100 by 53 yards (1876); 11 players on a side (1880); three downs to make five yards (1881), later settling at four downs to make 10 yards (1912); seven men required on the offensive line at the snap (1895); the ball a prolate spheroid (1897); a neutral zone between the lines (1906); three points for a field goal (1909) and six for a touchdown (1912); and a four-man officials' crew of referee, umpire, field judge, and head linesman (1907).

The rule books used today in professional, college, and high school football resemble very much the single rule book used in the nineteenth century in its headings and the way it was organized. A chapter in a rule book is a "rule." The headings in today's books resemble those in the book of 1900—"Rule 1, The Field; Rule 2, The Ball; Rule 3, Players and Substitutes, etc."

The subdivisions of today's rule books are the same as those in the book used at the turn of the century by men of property such as Walter Camp and Walter Okeson who also dabbled in football and set up the rules in the language of a legal covenant —rule, section, article. Just as any legal document has a chapter on the definitions of the agreement, so does a football rule book, only in this case what it defines are fair catches, field goals, huddles, and the line of scrimmage.

No one in pro football "wrote the rule book." Building on the original book of Camp and others, the governing bodies of professional, college, and high school football made committees that wrote changes to meet their needs. The NFL made no major changes in the rules for 13 years—until the league meetings of 1933 and 1934, when it invented hashmarks or inbounds lines, moved the goal posts to the goal line (a rules change it would find necessary to undo in the seventies), and allowed forward passes from anywhere behind the line of scrimmage.

One of the persons who had the greatest influence on the NFL rules and how they are enforced was Hugh (Shorty) Ray, the league's "technical advisor" from 1938 until 1956. So great were Ray's contributions that he was elected to the Hall of Fame in 1966.

Ray advised the NFL owners on rules changes to be considered each year. Ray selected, tested, graded, and supervised the work of NFL officials. He improved the way officials work, made the game safer, and made it move faster.

A small (5 feet 6 inches), squeaky-voiced mechanical drawing instructor at Harrison High School in Chicago, Ray was one of the best game officials in the Big Ten Conference when George Halas of the Chicago Bears recommended that the NFL hire him. Ray became technical advisor and rule book associate editor for the National Federation of State High School Associations at the same time he was also employed by the NFL. For that reason, the rules of high school and professional football were similar in Ray's years and immediately thereafter.

Ray constantly pushed NFL officials to be the best in the sport. He held clinics for them, made them take tests, mailed them open-book examinations to take and return to him for grading, and mailed them a steady stream of announcements, approved rules, and the annual "play situation book," forerunner of the present-day "case books."

"He pounded the rules into his officials so they could average ninety-five percent on a test on even the most difficult problems," George Halas recalled.

During games, Ray and his part-time assistants watched officials from the press box or grandstands with watches, clipboards, and pencils at the ready, timing every move. If Ray did not get an eyewitness report on a game, he studied movies of the game with his time and motion movie projector. When the season ended, he presented his conclusions to league meetings in voluminous ring binders packed with data on every NFL game played, every down, every play situation.

As a result, NFL officials learned to work efficiently and at high speed because they knew they were being watched and graded every play. The pros began to run off more plays and their games ended sooner.

A summary of the important year-by-year changes in the NFL rules follows.

1929 A fourth official, the line judge, is added.

1933 The ball will be moved in 10 yards to the hashmarks or inbounds lines whenever it is in play within five yards of the sidelines.

The clipping penalty is increased to 25 yards. The goal posts are moved to the goal lines.

1934 A player entering the game may communicate with his teammates immediately instead of waiting until one play is completed.

Officials must notify the coach when a team has exhausted its three legal time outs in each half.

A forward pass made hand-to-hand behind the line of scrimmage that becomes incomplete is a fumble and may be advanced by either team.

Within 10 yards of the goal, a defensive team can be penalized only half the distance for offside violations.

The second incomplete pass over the goal line in the same series or a fourth down incompletion in the end zone results in a touchback.

Forward passing is legalized from any spot behind the line of scrimmage.

A runner who falls to the ground, or who is tackled, may advance unless a defender continues to hold him on the ground.

Flying blocks and flying tackles are permitted.

Players of the receiving team may be stationed at any place on the field, so long as they do not advance within 10 yards of the ball before it is kicked.

The ball may be kicked off from a dirt tee.

A fumbled ball, except fumbles resulting from lateral passes, may be advanced by either team, no matter whether the ball strikes the ground or not. If the defense recovers a fumbled lateral, the ball is dead; if the offense recovers a fumbled lateral, it may advance.

When a team completes a legal forward pass, which is in turn followed by a second forward pass, the penalty will be loss of five yards from the point of the second and illegal forward pass.

1935 All penalties will be enforced from the point where the ball was put in play and not from the point where the foul occurred.

A pass thrown beyond the line of scrimmage intended as a lateral but going forward will be declared downed at the point of throwing.

The ball, when fumbled, is free except when kicked or thrown.

A fourth down incomplete pass, or a second incomplete pass in the same series that goes into the end zone, is returned to the point where the ball was put in play, except when the previous play originated inside the 20-yard line.

The hashmarks or inbounds lines are moved for the second time: a ball out of bounds will be brought in 15 yards.

1936 When the goal posts interfere with the play of the team that is in possession of the ball, it will have the privilege of moving the ball five yards to either side of the goal posts without penalty.

1937 No changes.

1938 After a kickoff goes out of bounds, the ball will be put in play on the receiving team's 45-yard line.

Any two players withdrawn from a game during the fourth quarter may re-enter once.

All penalties against the defense within the 10-yard line will be half the distance to the goal line.

The referee may penalize 15 yards for deliberate roughing of a passer after the ball has left his hand.

The penalty for a second forward pass behind the line of scrimmage is loss of down instead of loss of down and five yards.

If a kickoff goes out of bounds between the goal lines, the opponents will have the option of putting it in play by a scrimmage anywhere on their 45-yard line or at a point 15 yards in from where the ball crossed the side line. If the ball is last touched by the receivers, the ball will be put in play at the inbounds spot.

1939 During the last two minutes of the second half, additional time outs by the offense after its third legal one are not allowed unless it is for a designated injured player who is to be removed. A fourth time out under these conditions is not penalized, but additional time outs are treated as excess time outs.

During a kickoff, the kicking team may use only a natural tee made of the soil in the immediate vicinity of the kick and it must not be more than three inches in height.

The penalty for a forward pass touching an ineligible player on or behind his line of scrimmage is loss of down and 15 yards from the previous spot, and this penalty may not be declined.

The penalty for a forward pass striking an ineligible player beyond the line of scrimmage will be loss of the ball at the previous spot.

Before a forward pass is thrown from behind the line of scrimmage, ineligible players may not legally cross that line except in an initial line charge while blocking an opponent. The penalty is loss of down and 15 yards.

1940 The clipping penalty is reduced to 15 yards.

The defense has the choice of loss of down and 15 yards from the previous spot or a touchback for pass interference by the offense behind the defense's goal line.

The penalty for a forward pass not from scrimmage is five yards.

A penalty enforced in the field of play cannot carry the ball more than one half the distance to the offenders' goal line.

The penalty for a foul prior to a kick or pass from behind the line is enforced from the previous spot or behind that spot if the offensive team commits a foul behind the previous spot.

1941 The penalty for an illegal shift is five yards.

A kick from scrimmage or a return kick crossing the receivers' goal line from the impetus of the kick is a touchback.

The penalty for a personal foul by the opponents of the scoring team is enforced on the kickoff.

Illegal touching of a kicked ball is not an offset foul and the ball is dead when illegally recovered.

The penalty for a disqualifying foul is 15 yards.

The penalty for an illegal bat or kick is 15 yards.

The umpire is to time the game and the head linesman and field judge are to supervise substitutions.

1942 The snapper is not offside unless some portion of his body is ahead of the defense's line.

A free kick cannot be made in a side zone.

A detachable kicking toe is illegal.

Pass interference by the offense in the defense's end zone is a touchback during any down.

A forward pass that has touched a second eligible or an ineligible player may be intercepted.

The coach's area is to extend 10 yards in both directions from the center of his team's bench.

1943 Free substitution is permitted.

The time out rule applies at the end of both halves.

Players must wear helmets.

The offense may intercept and advance the defense's illegal pass from end zone.

1944 A substitute is not required to report to an official and he becomes a player when he informs a teammate that he is replacing him or when he communicates with any teammate.

All enforcements for fouls during a free kick, except fair catch interference, are from the previous spot.

Communication between players and their coach is legal provided the coach is in his prescribed area and it does not cause delay.

Offensive pass interference in the end zone is not a touchback.

A designated center, guard, or tackle or one shifted to an end or back position may return to any position if he is withdrawn for one play.

1945 The hashmarks or inbounds lines are moved a third time, to a point 20 yards from the sideline.

It is mandatory to enforce a penalty for encroachment if the defensive signal caller is beyond his line after the neutral zone is established.

A player under the center who extends his hands must receive the snap.

When the snap in flight is muffed by the receiver and then touches the ground, the defense may recover and advance.

The ball is dead when any receiver catches after a fair catch signal unless the kick is touched in flight by the members of the kicking team.

It is first and 10 for the offense when it recovers a kick from scrimmage anywhere in the field of play after it has first been touched by the defense beyond the line.

A player, in blocking, may not strike an opponent below the shoulders with elbows by pivoting or turning his trunk at the waist.

Players must wear long stockings in league games.

During a try, the snap may be made two or more yards from the goal line.

The referee is to designate an offending player when known.

A rule regarding attempts to consume or conserve time at the end of the second and fourth periods is extended to also include the first and third periods.

On a personal foul prior to a completion or an interception of a legal pass by the offended team, it will have the choice of the usual penalty or 15 yards from the spot of the dead ball.

1946 An offensive player is on his line provided one hand is touching the ground and it is on or within one foot of his line.

When a forward pass from behind the line touches either team's goal post or crossbar it is incomplete.

The toss of the coin must be held before the teams leave the field at the conclusion of pregame warm-ups.

The captains are to meet at the center of the field at the usual three minutes before game time, but only the receivers and their goal are to be indicated.

The penalty for an invalid fair catch signal is five yards from the spot of the signal.

The penalty for illegal equipment is five yards for delay and suspension for at least one down.

Substitution is limited to no more than three men at one time.

The receiving team is permitted to run punts and unsuccessful field goal attempts out from behind the goal line.

1947 The officials automatically will re-spot the ball on the nearest inbounds line when the spot of the snap is between the inbounds lines and inside the offense's 10-yard line.

When a team has less than 11 players on the field prior to the snap or free kick, officials are not to inform them.

During a try, if the kick is not successful, the ball becomes dead as soon as the failure is evident.

When a scrimmage or return kick crosses the receivers' goal line from the impetus of the kick, it is a touchback.

The kicker loses his usual protection if he kicks after recovering a loose ball on the ground.

A fifth official, the back judge, is added.

During a forward pass if the spot of a pass violation is behind the offense's goal line, the penalty is enforced from previous spot.

The field judge may use his whistle to assist the referee or other officials in declaring the ball dead.

Sudden death is adopted for divisional playoffs and championship games.

1948 Officials notifying each team that there are five minutes before the start of the second half must notify the head coach personally.

If an intended pass is downed behind the line, it is a referee's time out until any players who have gone downfield for a pass have had a reasonable time to return.

Plastic helmets are prohibited and coaches are to assume primary responsibility for the use of equipment that endangers their own or opponents' players.

A flexible artificial tee may be used at the kickoff.

If a foul occurs beyond the line during a backward pass or a fumble from scrimmage, the basic spot of enforcement is the spot of the pass or fumble.

It is illegal to bat or punch a ball in any direction while it is in player's possession.

When a player is disqualified, the referee must notify his coach.

1949 Any number of substitutes may enter while the ball is dead during time in.

Eligible pass receivers of a given team may wear different color helmets than their teammates. All the receivers must wear the same color.

Both the players' benches may be located on the same side of the field.

Plastic helmets are permitted.

1950 Free substitution is readopted.

A backward pass going out of bounds between the goal lines belongs to the team last in possession.

1951 Aluminum shoe cleats are illegal.

A center, guard, or tackle is not eligible to touch a forward pass from scrimmage even when he is on the end of the line.

An illegal-touching violation by a member of the kicking team does not offset a foul by the receivers.

1952 All players must be numbered according to their position "except as provided for nationally known players."

A player is not considered to be illegally in motion provided he is not going forward at the snap.

The penalty for offensive pass interference is 15 yards from the previous spot and not loss of down.

1953 Withdrawn players and substitutes do not have to participate for at least one play or down.

A foul between downs must occur after the play has definitely ended.

Rules regarding hurdling cover only the act of a runner.

Players must be moving forward to be considered illegally in motion.

1954 The referee is the sole judge of and must pressure gauge all game balls on the field prior to the start of a game.

In case of rain or a wet or slippery field, playable balls can be requested at any time by the offensive team, and are to be furnished by the home team attendant from the sidelines.

There will be a referee's time out for at least 10 seconds during change of possession, longer when required.

The use of a tee for a free kick after a fair catch is prohibited.

Illegal "kicking" of ball must be with the foot to be considered a foul.

1955 The ball is put in play at the spot of the interception when intercepting momentum causes the ball to be declared dead in the end zone possession.

Ten seconds may be run off the clock for the team in possession during the last two minutes of a half if it is behind in the score or the game is tied.

If a player touches the ground with any part of his body, except his hands or feet, while in the grasp of an opponent and irrespective of the grasp being broken, the ball is declared dead immediately.

A player on the kicking team who has been out of bounds may not touch, recover, or advance a scrimmage kick beyond the line.

1956 When a runner is contacted by a defensive player and he touches the ground with any part of his body except his hands or feet, the ball shall be declared dead immediately.

A brown ball with white stripes will be used for night games.

No artificial material shall be permitted to assist in the execution of a field goal or try-for-point.

Halftime will be 20 minutes long.

It is illegal to grab or grasp face guards, except the ball carrier's.

Loudspeaker coaching from the sidelines is not permitted.

When an interior lineman takes a three-point stance and moves after taking that stance, he must be ruled offside or illegally in motion.

1957 On all requested time outs the referee will not sound his whistle for play to start until 60 seconds have elapsed.

Head linesmen will use a clamp on the chains when measuring for a first down.

1958 The back judge will be the official timer of the game.

On all requested time outs, the referee will not signify that the ball will be put in play prior to one minute and 30 seconds of elapsed time.

1959 No changes.

1960 American Football League permits one- or two-point conversion.

The official time is kept on the scoreboard clock in the AFL.

1961 No changes.

1962 No player shall grasp the facemask of an opponent. A flagrant offender will be disqualified.

The sudden death rule applies to the Pro Bowl game.

1963 When the spot of the snap is inside the offense's 15-yard line and between the inbounds lines, the ball is spotted at the nearest inbound line.

1964 No changes.

1965 The color of the officials' flags will be bright gold.

A sixth official, the line judge, is added.

A shift will begin after players assume a set position instead of when they come out of the huddle.

1966 Goal posts will be offset from the goal line and the uprights will extend a minimum of 20 feet above the crossbar and will be painted bright gold in color.

1967 A player who signals for a fair catch may not block or initiate contact with one of the kickers until the ball touches a player.

Goal posts will be single standard.

Fields will be rimmed by a white border, six feet wide.

1968 No changes.

1969 Kicking shoes will be of standard production and not subsequently modified in any manner.

The referee can charge a team time out when it is apparent an injured player cannot leave the field under his own power. The referee does not have to wait until the captain requests the team time out.

The kicker as well as the holder may be beyond the line when a placekick is made.

1970 The official time will be kept on the scoreboard clock.

1971 A team will not be charged a time out for an injured player unless the injury occurs in the last two minutes of either half.

The defense may advance on unsuccessful field goal attempt after it crosses the defense's goal line.

Holding, illegal use of hands, and clipping fouls committed by the offensive team behind the line of scrimmage during forward passes will be penalized from the previous spot.

If there is a double foul during a down in which there is a change of possession, the team last gaining possession may keep the ball after enforcement for its foul, provided its foul was not prior to the final change of possession—the "clean hands" rule.

A new pass blocking definition is added. Pass blocking is the obstruction of an opponent by the use of that part of the blocker's body above his knees. During a legal block, the hands must be cupped or closed and remain inside the blocker's elbows and must remain inside the frame of the opponent as well as the blocker's body. The arms must be in a flexed position, but cannot be fully extended to create a push. By use of up and down action of flexed arms, the blocker is permitted to ward off the opponent's attempt to grasp his jersey or arms and prevent legal contact to his head. The blocker is not permitted to push, clamp down on, hang on to, or encircle the opponent.

A passer can be penalized when he throws, tosses, or lobs the ball away with a deliberate attempt to prevent a loss of yardage by his team.

1972 The inbounds lines or hashmarks are moved to 70 feet, 9 inches from the sidelines.

When it is fourth down for the offense at or inside

its 15-yard line, the ball will be spotted 20 yards from the sideline.

The penalty for an illegal receiver accidentally going out of bounds and returning to touch a pass is reduced from 15 yards and loss of down to loss of down.

The penalty for grasping a facemask, unless flagrantly, is reduced to five yards.

The commissioner will notify teams when a brown ball with white stripes will be used for a late-starting game.

A kick from scrimmage that crosses the goal line may be advanced by the defensive team into the field of play.

All fouls by the offense behind the line of scrimmage in the field of play will be penalized from the previous spot.

Disqualified players may not re-enter during overtime periods.

1973 The clock will start on the snap following all changes of team possession.

Periods can be extended if there is a change of team possession after there is a foul by the offense.

All players are to be numbered according to their positions.

Close line play is defined as the area ordinarily occupied by offensive tackles and longitudinally three yards on either side of the line of scrimmage.

A defensive player who jumps or stands on a teammate or who is picked up by a teammate cannot attempt to block a kick.

If the receiving team commits a foul during a kick from scrimmage after the ball is kicked, it will not lose the ball as part of its penalty.

1974 The goal posts are moved from the goal line to the end line.

Kickoffs will be made from the 35- not the 40-yard line.

During a kick from scrimmage, only the end men are permitted to go beyond the line of scrimmage before the ball is kicked.

Field goals attempted and missed from the scrimmage line beyond the 20-yard line will result in the defensive team taking possession of the ball at the line of scrimmage. Field goals attempted and missed from the line of scrimmage inside the 20-yard line will result in the defensive team taking possession at the 20-yard line.

When the spot of enforcement for holding, illegal use of hands, arms, or body on offense as well as tripping fouls is not in the field of play at or behind the line of scrimmage or no deeper than three yards beyond the line of scrimmage, the penalty will be 10 yards.

Eligible pass receivers can only be chucked once by any defender after the receiver has gone three yards beyond the line of scrimmage.

Eligible receivers who line up in a position within two yards of a tackle may be legally blocked below the waist at the line of scrimmage.

Eligible receivers who line up more than two yards from a tackle may not be blocked below the waist at or behind the line of scrimmage.

It is illegal for an offensive player to block an opponent below the waist within an area three yards on either side of the line of scrimmage if the blocker is aligned in a position more than two yards outside his tackle and is moving in toward the position of the ball, either at the snap or after it is made—an illegal crackback.

A broken limit line is to encompass the entire field two feet outside the white border except in the coaching areas.

The sudden death system of determining the winner when the score is tied at end of regulation playing time is in effect for preseason and regular season games except that the playing time will be limited to a maximum of one 15-minute period.

1975 End zone markings and club identification at the 50-yard line must be approved by the commissioner.

Pylons not flags will be used for goal line and end line markings.

There will be standard sideline markers and chain crews will be uniformly attired.

Ball boys will be clearly identifiable.

Unsportsmanlike conduct includes lingering on the field when being substituted for.

A team may use a double shift on or inside the opponent's 20-yard line after showing it at least three times previously in the game.

A fourth down pass that is incomplete in or through the end zone when the line of scrimmage is inside the 20 will result in the opponent taking possession at the previous line of scrimmage.

If there are penalties on each team on the same play and one results in disqualification, the penalties will be offsetting, but the disqualification will stand.

The penalty for an ineligible player downfield on a forward pass is reduced from 15 to 10 yards.

The penalty for offensive pass interference is reduced from 15 to 10 yards.

Penalties for defensive holding or illegal use of hands will be assessed from the previous line of scrimmage rather than from the spot where the ball is blown dead if that spot is behind the line of scrimmage.

1976 There will be 24 not 12 footballs available each game.

Footballs with stripes will no longer be used.

The toss of the coin will be held three minutes before the kickoff, not 30 minutes before.

A delay of game penalty will no longer be enforced when a runner carries the ball in a manner clearly designed to consume playing time.

Any foul committed by the defense which prevents the try-for-point from being attempted will result in the down being replayed and the kicking team having the option as to when the yardage penalty will be assessed—on the next try or on the ensuing kickoff. Any foul committed by the defense on a successful try will result in a distance penalty being assessed on the following kickoff.

It is illegal for a defender to use a hand or hands on a teammate to gain additional height in an attempt to block a kick.

Each team may not have more than 15 persons in addition to its uniformed players on each sideline.

When spectators enter the playing field before the game is over, the field must be cleared in order to allow completion of the game.

Two 30-second clocks visible to players, officials, and fans will be displayed, noting the official time between the ready-for-play signal and the snap of the ball.

A ribbon 2 inches by 36 inches long will be attached to the top of each goal post to assist in determining wind direction.

A player who reports a change in his eligibility, prior to a touchdown, can legally return to his original position for a try-for-point attempt without having to leave the field for one play.

A defender is not permitted to rough a ball carrier who falls to the ground untouched by running or diving into him.

Whenever a disqualified player is banished from a game, he must leave the entire playing field area.

1977 It is illegal for a defensive lineman to strike an opponent above the shoulders or to make a head slap.

The coin toss may be held at any time within three minutes of kickoff.

It is illegal for a back who lines up inside a tight end to move to the outside and then back inside again to crack back on a defender below the waist.

An offensive lineman who takes a two point stance must have some part of his body within one foot of his end of the ball to be legally on the line of scrimmage.

Any shoe worn by a player with an artificial limb must have its kicking surface conform to that of a normal kicking toe.

If the kicking team fouls during a punt before possession changes and the receiving team fouls after possession changes, the penalties will offset and the down will be replayed.

A defender will be permitted to make contact with an eligible receiver either in the three-yard zone beyond the line of scrimmage or once beyond that zone, but not both.

A team will lose its coin toss option and sustain a 15-yard penalty if it does not arrive on the field for warmup at least 15 minutes before the scheduled kickoff.

It is illegal for a wide receiver to clip an opponent anywhere, including in the legal clipping zone.

Kicking a loose ball is a foul only if the act is deliberate.

1978 Extended arms and open hands are permissible in pass blocking.

During the last two minutes of a half, it is the responsibility of the defensive team to line up properly when the referee signals ready for play.

The officials have the right to not stop the clock or to run 10 seconds off a stopped clock when a team deliberately attempts to conserve time in the last two minutes of a half.

When the ball is carried across the line of scrimmage, no legal forward pass can be thrown.

A double touch of a forward pass is legal, but batting a pass in flight toward an opponent's goal line is illegal.

The penalty for intentional grounding in the field of play is reduced from a loss of down and 15 yards to a loss of down and 10 yards. It is a safety when a passer illegally grounds a ball in the end zone.

Defenders are permitted to maintain contact with receivers in a five-yard zone beyond the line of scrimmage, but contact is restricted beyond that point.

Hurdling is no longer a foul.

Taunting or baiting opponents is an unsportsmanlike conduct penalty.

A 15-yard penalty will be assessed during a down involving a double foul without change of possession when one foul carries a 15-yard penalty and the other only five yards.

There will be seven game officials instead of six. A side judge was added.

All 15-yard penalties are reduced to 10 yards except those involving unnecessary roughness, unsportsmanlike conduct, personal fouls, disqualification, or palpably unfair acts.

If there is a defensive foul behind the line of scrimmage during a play in which a runner is downed behind the line, the offensive team will be awarded sufficient penalty yardage to advance the ball to at least the former line of scrimmage and a first down.

1979 The captain who lost the pregame coin toss can delay his second-half choice until immediately before the start of the second half.

A team whose player is injured by a personal foul committed during the last two minutes of a half will not be charged with a time out if the player is disabled after the penalty has been assessed.

There will be a consistent length of time for the clock to be stopped before it is restarted again whenever a quarterback is sacked behind the line of scrimmage.

Defensive linemen can wear numbers in the nineties.

Any time a player leaves the field on the wrong side of the field or over the end line of the end zone, his team will be penalized five yards from the previous spot of the ball, whether the violation is discovered during the down or at the end of the down.

If an offensive player fumbles anywhere on the field during a fourth-down play, or if a player fumbles on any down after the two-minute warning in a half, only the fumbling player can recover and/or advance the ball.

If a member of the receiving team touches a scrimmage kick in the field of play or in the end zone, and a member of the kicking team legally recovers the ball in the end zone, the kicking team will retain possession either at the spot the ball was first touched by the receiving team or at the 1-yard line.

No player on the receiving team can block opponents below the waist during a kickoff, punt, or field goal attempt.

The prohibited crackback zone on either side of the line of scrimmage is extended from three yards to five.

Officials are to blow the play dead as soon as the quarterback is clearly in the grasp and control of any tackler.

A player will be penalized for unsportsmanlike conduct when he commits a non-contact act such as throwing a punch or a forearm or kicking at an opponent.

It is illegal for a player to use his helmet to butt or ram an opponent, or to use the crown of the helmet unnecessarily (spearing).

A period can be extended to permit a team whose opportunity to catch a scrimmage kick has been interfered with on the last play. The offended team can run one play from scrimmage, attempt a field goal, or attempt a free kick.

1980 Members of both teams may talk to their respective coaches during any injury time out.

A time out for injury will not be charged to a team if any foul committed by an opponent in the last two minutes of a half caused the injury.

It is illegal for a player to strike, swing, or club an opponent in the head, neck, or face even if the initial contact is below the head.

It is mandatory for the official to run the clock for 10 seconds before permitting the ball to be put in play when officials rule that a team has used illegal efforts to conserve time during the last two minutes of a half.

A team that has signaled and made a fair catch, or was interfered with, may elect to put the ball in play with a free kick, but a team that does not signal fair catch cannot attempt a free kick even if the receiver is interfered with.

1981 It is illegal for players to use any form of adhesive substance while participating in a game.

A player will be credited with a catch if he controls the ball when his second foot clearly lands on the ground inbounds.

Players who change their eligibility by virtue of a change of position must report such change to the referee before the start of each play.

An intentional grounding penalty will result in a loss of down and the ball will be put in play at the spot of the foul if that spot was more than 10 yards behind the line of scrimmage.

When an ineligible receiver touches a forward pass on or behind the line of scrimmage, the penalty will be loss of down. When an ineligible receiver is touched beyond the line of scrimmage, the penalty will be a loss of 10 yards.

The penalty for offensive blocking from behind above the waist is 10 yards.

The penalty for defensive fouls committed behind the line when the runner or intended passer is tackled behind the line will be enforced from the spot of the foul, or the spot where the ball becomes dead.

The spot where possession was lost is eliminated as a potential spot of enforcement for a personal foul committed prior to a completion or interception of a pass. The penalty will be assessed from the previous spot and the offended team will retain possession of the ball.

The fourth-down fumble rule will no longer apply when a player touches, but does not possess, a snap from center, unless there is a hand-to-hand exchange.

1982 There will be no automatic first down if the defense is penalized for incidental grasping of the facemask.

The player possession rule was altered to read: A player other than an eligible receiver is in possession when he has held the ball firmly in his grasp long enough to have established control. In order for an eligible receiver of a forward pass to be in possession, he must control the ball throughout the act of clearly touching both feet, or any other part of his body other than his hand(s), to the ground inbounds. If the player is hit, causing the ball to come loose simultaneously while clearly touching both feet or any other part of his body except the hand(s) inbounds, there is no possession.

Illegal uniform items now include hard or soft hip pads that are not covered by the outer uniform.

Rules covering the showing of a double shift inside the opponent's 20-yard line and the shortening of the length of the game were eliminated.

The penalties for illegal batting or punching the ball, and illegal kicking of the ball with the foot or leg are 10 yards (instead of 15). Neither is a personal foul.

1983 Any player on the field is permitted to call a team time out.

All mandatory player equipment must be designed and made by a professional manufacturer and such equipment may not be altered, except by direction of the team physician.

In case of question on the part of an official there is no pass interference if there is incidental contact that does not materially affect the route of a receiver or a defender.

There will be automatic disqualification of a player who uses a helmet he is not wearing as a weapon.

There will be consistent spot of enforcement for a foul committed by a player signaling for a fair catch whether the loose ball is in the field of play or in the end zone at the time of the foul.

If, during the final 30 seconds of either half, the defensive team is behind in the score and commits a foul when it has no time outs left, the offensive team is permitted to decline the penalty for the foul and have the time on the clock expire.

A team no longer will be allowed to build a natural tee made of soil in order to elevate the ball for a kicker.

1984 Linebackers are permitted to wear jersey numerals in the 90s.

The procedure in which the referee starts the clock five seconds after a quarterback sack will be limited to the last two minutes of a half rather than throughout the entire game.

It is illegal for a defender to take a running start from beyond the line of scrimmage in an attempt to block a field goal or point after touchdown.

A punter, placekicker, or holder will be penalized for unsportsmanlike conduct if he simulates being roughed by a defensive player.

The encroachment rule will be in effect when contact is made by an opponent prior to the snap rather than by having a player line up in the neutral zone.

Players will wear a one-piece exterior stocking that combines solid white and individual team colors.

Offensive players will be permitted to block opponents with extended arms in the pocket area on running plays. This pocket area includes contact made three yards beyond the line of scrimmage.

Spiking by the scoring player will be allowed. However, any prolonged, excessive, or premeditated celebration by individual players or groups of players will incur a five-yard penalty for unsportsmanlike conduct.

If the kicking team either illegally kicks off out of bounds or is guilty of a short free kick on two or more consecutive kickoffs, the receivers have the options of either a re-kick with a five-yard penalty, or they will be permitted to take possession of the ball at the dead ball spot, out-of-bounds spot, or spot of illegal touch.

1985 The length of a team time out during the final two minutes of either half will be reduced from 90 seconds to 60 seconds.

A fair catch signal is valid only when a receiver waves his extended arm from side to side above his head.

Offensive linemen are permitted to interlock legs.

A play ends automatically whenever a quarterback kneels or simulates kneeling on the ground during the last two minutes of a half.

A play ends when any runner slides to the ground feet first, thereby declaring himself down.

It will be illegal for a team to change the color of hand and arm coverings on a week-to-week basis.

With the exception of the last two minutes, if the scoreboard clock is stopped to assess and mark off a penalty, it will be restarted when the ball is declared ready for play unless the clock has been stopped otherwise by rule. Under these circumstances and during the last two minutes of a half, the clock will be started on the snap.

There will be an experimental use of instant replay as an electronic aid to officiating during nine nationally televised preseason games.

A player who legally changes his eligibility in a series of downs will be permitted to return to his original position at the end of a quarter.

Clarifications: the general rule involving pass interference (the exceptions concerning incidental contact are more specific); the rule when a defender is blocked into a kicker to make it clear that a penalty for running into the kicker won't be assessed; and the rule prohibiting attempts to block field goals and points after touchdowns.

1986 By rule, it will be illegal for a player to wear equipment that tends to advertise or has markings other than the team logo.

An instant replay system as an aid to officiating is established.

The provision for a specific five-yard area in determining when the player's intercepting momentum carries him into the end zone is deleted.

A fumble that is not recovered will return to the fumbling team at the spot of the fumble if it goes forward unless the ball goes out of bounds in the opponent's end zone. In this case, the defensive team will take possession at the spot of the fumble.

The rule regarding equipment requirements for kicking shoes was clarified.

Only the player who gives a fair catch signal and muffs the ball will be given the opportunity to make the catch free from interference.

If the clock is stopped to mark off a penalty and the offensive team then commits a foul between downs before the two-minute warning in a half, the clock will start on the snap.

The rule concerning no blocking below the waist on punts is extended through the entire down (from the snap until the play ends).

League policy on chop blocks is extended to include a player lined up outside of a tackle and who deliberately blocks (chops) an opponent in the area of the thigh or lower even though the tackle shows pass set and does not engage the opponents being blocked.

A History of Football Equipment

Equipment may or may not be able to turn losers into winners, but it definitely performs a large function: It protects players and prevents injuries. It is an obvious fact, however, that football players still get injured. That is why manufacturers keep devising better equipment, and teams and leagues keep insisting that they do so.

The game Princeton and Rutgers played in 1869, called the first college football game in America, involved no equipment at all other than the ball. The players merely "laid aside their hats, coats, and vests," according to Allison Danzig. "Neither team was in uniform, although some Rutgers players wore scarlet stocking-caps."

When Harvard played McGill University of Montreal in 1874, the Harvard players wore sweaters and handkerchiefs around their heads, and the McGill players wore white trousers, striped jerseys, and turbans, according to Rawlings Sporting Goods. Princeton or Yale in 1876 may have been the first to wear a complete uniform in its games.

A. G. Spalding & Company Sporting Goods was the first manufacturer of athletic equipment. Others sprang up rapidly and played an important role in the growth of the game of football.

There was a time when it appeared that manufacturers of football equipment would become extinct, and equipment would become unnecessary. "The roughness of the game has been practically eliminated by the new rules," the 1909 *Spalding Guide* said. "Still, shin guards and shoulder pads are sometimes needed."

That report proved optimistic. Football players did not begin to wear fewer pads but in fact became covered with them. And the rules organizations for high school, college, and—after 1920—professional football went right on changing the game and writing strict rules about equipment.

The first major rules change the NFL made having to do with equipment was the seemingly long-overdue requirement in 1943 that players wear helmets.

Elmer Layden, Commissioner of the NFL from 1941-46, believed that many of the players in the league had rather bad-looking legs, and he considered it one of the momentous acts of his administration that he pushed through a rule in 1945 requiring them to wear long stockings. Equipment changes since then have been for both safety and style.

Beginning in 1970, the members of the league required themselves—not in their rules, but in their by-laws—to give the commissioner a year's notice before changing their uniform.

I. THE BALL

The unusual shape of a football—which is defined as a prolate spheroid—contributes immeasurably to the variety of the sport played with it and the fascination others have for it. Not being round, it bounces oddly. Being elliptical, it is aerodynamically superior to a round ball, so it passes better. It can be handed off and carried more easily than a round ball of the same size.

The word prolate is from the Latin *prolatus,* meaning stretched out. The polar axis is longer than its equatorial diameter. Most of the sports balls in the world are round. Of all the sports shown in a 1974 book, *Rules of the Game,* only four used prolate balls. They were rugby and American, Australian, and Canadian football.

The game between Princeton and Rutgers in 1869 was played with a round English soccer ball. Rugby gained the upper hand, however, when McGill University of Montreal put it on display in games against Harvard in 1874. Rugby football went on to become, simply, football.

As its name implies, football was originally played only with the feet. Rugby brought the hands into play in 1823. The ball could be picked up and passed. Nearly another century went by, however, before it could be passed *forward.*

Traditions die hard. The rule permitting the forward pass in 1906 was virtually ignored until well-known teams—for example, the 1913 Notre Dame team with Gus Dorais at tailback and Knute Rockne at end—began using the forward pass. Changes in the ball's specifications were ordered. It became slimmer, lighter, and easier to pass.

Five rules were made—all by college and not professional football—affecting the football's shape. Its weight was set at 14 to 15 ounces in 1912. Its long axis became 28" to 28½" the same year. Its short axis—around the middle—went from 22½" to 23" in 1912, to 22" to 22½" in 1929, to 21¼" to 21½" in 1934. Its length became 11 to 11¼" in 1931. And the amount of air that can be pumped into it was set at 12½ to 13½ pounds in 1934.

Manufacturers met those specifications in varying degrees. The Pro Football Hall of Fame has on display a half-moon templet used before games in the early days of football. The ball was lowered into it to determine whether it had the proper shape and amount of inflation. A similar operation is performed before games today; the referee personally checks every football, 24 in all, to make sure each has 12½ to 13½ pounds of air pressure in it.

The rules changes affecting the shape of the football ended in 1934. That roughly coincided with the NFL's rules changes of 1933, the first significant ones it ever made, creating inbounds lines or hashmarks to which the ball had to be returned for the start of a new play whenever it was carried near or over the sideline, and allowing forward passes from anywhere behind the line of scrimmage. The colleges had been responsible for slimming the football. The pros were responsible for removing puritanical strictures limiting the amount of passing in a game, and moving the ball nearer the center of the field, opening the way for rollout, bootleg, and sprintout passing.

For decades, footballs have been referred to as pigskins. Yet the preferred material for quality footballs always has been steerhide. Cowhide has been second best, and bullhide was never used because bull's have been left to father new offspring. Rubber gained a foothold in the football world in 1951, but its stay was brief.

The bladder in a football, on the other hand, is made of rubber. Inflating it and keeping it inflated was a problem that plagued the sport for 50 years. The ball in the second game in 1869 between Rutgers and Princeton, according to Allison Danzig, kept losing its shape and "several times during the game play had to be stopped, and a little key was brought out from the sideline to unlock the small nozzle tucked into the ball. The players took turns blowing the ball up."

In 1886, the Peck & Snyder Sporting Goods catalog advertised a device resembling a syringe called "The New Patent Foot Ball Inflator." It was "far superior, in every respect, to the old style large brass pumps. With it the largest ball can be inflated to its fullest capacity in five minutes time while the old way took half an hour.

"It is not advisable to inflate Foot Balls with the breath, as the moisture that collects in them soon rots the bladder."

Stem valves that protruded from the ball and had to be tucked in during play gave way to metal valves such as those on automobile tires. They were considered unsafe and so rubber valves were developed for footballs. The final step in making an efficient ball was prelacing; it developed about 1920 and after that the ball no longer had to unlaced to be inflated.

White footballs were used for a time, too. In 1956, the NFL okayed the use of white footballs in night games. For the next 20 years, there were "night footballs" with white stripes around each end. They were prohibited in 1976 because the paint made the balls slick. The rules continued to call for a ball that is ". . . a pebble grained, leather case of natural tan color."

The Spalding J5-V was the official NFL ball from 1920 until 1940, and it was used in the AFL between 1960 and 1969. Spalding named the ball "The Duke" during the 1930s. "The Duke" was the boyhood nickname of Wellington Mara of the New York Giants. Thorp Sporting Goods began making a ball called "The Duke," and sold the registered name to Spalding. Wilson Sporting Goods took it over when it became the manufacturer of official NFL footballs in 1941. "The Duke" was retired in 1969 and Wilson's ball renamed, simply, "NFL."

The leather Wilson uses comes primarily from the Horween Leather Company, originally owned and operated by Arnold Horween, Sr., who was the coach at Harvard from 1926-30. The hides are tanned and sold to Wilson, which uses only full grain steerhide, the full thickness of the hide, in NFL footballs. The four panels for the ball are cut in such a way that any blemishes on the hide are avoided. The panels are skived to a specified thickness and then weighed to make sure they meet specifications and checked to make sure their appearance is uniform.

Linings for each panel and reinforcements for the bladder opening and the valve ring are added. The panels are sewn together inside out. The ball is then turned through the lace opening using an iron post, in an operation that requires strength and dexterity. The bladder is inserted and the ball is laced. It is inflated to 80 pounds, 65 above the required amount of pressure, so it can be examined for appearance, stitching, and shape. If it meets every requirement, it is stamped "NFL," deflated, and delivered. It is then used in an NFL game, the only truly essential piece of equipment.

II. PANTS AND JERSEYS

The first football pants and jerseys, in the 1870s, were made of canvas. They were knee-length togs or breeches and long- or short-sleeved jackets that laced in the front. Canvas is sturdy and durable; it is good for making tents. After a long, hot game in which the players had perspired freely, football uniforms made of canvas must not have needed folding; they probably would have stood up by themselves.

Moleskin, "a heavy-napped cotton twill fabric," replaced canvas in football pants. The tolerance for canvas jerseys waned, too; in the 1890s, according to a Rawlings Sporting Goods publication, "No player was seen without his turtle neck sweater."

The most significant thing that happened to pants and jerseys, however, was that they were sewn together to make one unit, an all-purpose football-playing suit of canvas, moleskin, or leather into which a player gradually inserted himself, laced it up all around, and went out to scrimmage. The Smock football suit, the varsity union suit, and "Whitley's Football Armor" were examples. They became museum pieces about the turn of the century, and pants and jerseys went back to being worn separately.

Football was a furious sport at the turn of the century, and manufacturers took steps to make equipment safer. New types of pads appeared to protect the knees, thighs, hips, kidneys, and ribs. The best way to hold them in place, it seemed, was to lace them to or hang them from the player's pants. Experiments began to find the right way to connect pads and pants, and went on for the next 25 years.

Strips of cane sewn into the lining for thigh pads appeared in 1906; these hard strips must have been a bellringer for a head-on tackler. The next step was laces around each leg, permitting the thigh pads to be raised and lowered. There was a period of time in which manufacturers came to see the pants as merely a "shell" on which all manner of pads were to be hung. In 1915, Spalding offered a "complete padded harness with heavy felt hip pad connected with wide elastic belt at back, fiber thigh guards laced in special canvas and webbing reinforced pockets all securely mounted on simple but strong skeleton pants form."

At last, a simpler pair of pants emerged. They had pockets on the inside for the player to insert his thigh and knee pads; all other pads were strapped on independent of the pants.

Beginning with canvas, moleskin, and leather, a great variety of fabrics have been used in football pants. Khaki cloth or drill, fustian cloth, and duckcloth were first used about 1910. According to Rawling Sporting Goods, "Duck became the primary pants material for over 30 years."

Spalding's "Intercollegiate" pants in 1931 were made of Army duck. But in 1933 its "College Speed Pants," the top of the Spalding line, were made of "Skookum Cloth, the strongest, lightest fabric suitable for football pants."

There was, however, a family of new synthetic fibers that would make Skookum Cloth obsolete for football pants. Knits first appeared in 1934, according to Rawling Sporting Goods. "The first all-knit shell was introduced in 1936 and the first half-fabric, half-knit model made its bow in 1937. Many different combinations of knit materials have been developed through the years, with the latest knit incorporating the highly-popular Spandex, a stretch polyurethane material."

Spandex was the principal fiber in the most expensive model pants displayed in the catalogs of Rawlings and two other major manufacturers. It actually is the general term for all fibers that resemble rubber in that they have a high extensibility and highly retractive forces that derive from their chemical nature. Its special properties make it very good for football pants and a far cry from the materials of the early 1900s.

Jerseys have a somewhat more limited history. Canvas was the first fabric used in them; before the turn of the century, players sometimes were called "canvasbacks" because of the sleeveless canvas vests they wore over their turtlenecks.

The first real football jerseys were made of cotton and wool and those fabrics prevailed for 40 years, until the arrival of synthetics in jerseys in about 1950. They were, according to Rawlings Sporting Goods, rayon-durene, nylon-durene, rayon-cotton, and nylon-cotton. Nylon-mesh jerseys were even lighter and more comfortable that the rest; even the NFL teams in the coolest climates favored them, wearing them on cold days over thermal underwear.

Among the innovations in jerseys that did not succeed were Rawlings's 1928-29 model, which featured "grip-sure cloth, sewn to the jersey front to aid in holding onto the ball," and tear-away jerseys, which allowed a runner to rip free from the grasp of a tackler holding onto his shirt, but which threatened to bankrupt the teams that used them as they struggled to keep their running backs in jerseys game after game.

Decorations on jerseys go back at least as far as 1876, when each Princeton player wore a "P" on his sweater in a game against Pennsylvania. Either Amos Alonzo Stagg or Glenn (Pop) Warner invented jersey numbers about 1905. Manufacturers arrayed the numbers and stripes on jerseys in a great variety that knew little restraint. The Canton Bulldogs of 1921 wore horizontal stripes around their middles, which only accentuated the considerable girth of their star tackle, Wilbur (Pete) Henry. The St. Louis Gunners of 1934 wore jerseys with a cannon superimposed on a patriotic shield. They left history a photograph of one of their players wearing this creation; the player was Homer Reynolds, "The Human Cannon."

III. THE HELMET

Jerseys and pants identify players. Helmets and pads protect them. The one event that more than any other was responsible for making these articles of protection necessary took place in 1888. The annual rules convention for the emerging sport of college football passed a rule permitting tackling below the waist. Football changed dramatically. Teams no longer arrayed themselves across the entire breadth of the field. Teams bunched themselves around the runner to block for him. The wedge and mass play arrived. Football became, for a time, a savage sport full of fights, brawling, even fatalities.

Grudgingly, football players accepted the wearing of protective equipment. Step-by-step, players braved being called sissies to wear pads of various types that in just a few years would be considered essential.

The article they accepted last of all was the helmet. The banal head harnesses and then the leather helmets that emerged were always disdained by a macho few. Even Glenn (Pop) Warner counseled his Carlisle players against them in 1912. "Playing without helmets gives players more confidence, saves their heads from many hard jolts, and keeps their ears from becoming torn or sore," he said. "I do not encourage their use. I have never seen an accident to the head which was serious, but I have many times seen cases when hard bumps on the head so dazed the player receiving them that he lost his memory for a time and had to be removed from the game."

Gerald Ford, who later became President of the United States, played center for Michigan in 1932-34 without a helmet. It was not a required article of equipment in college football until 1939.

The National Football League did not require the wearing of helmets until 1943, although the great majority of professional players had long since taken to wearing them. The last NFL player to play in a game without a helmet probably was end Dick Plasman of the Chicago Bears in 1940. There is a photo of him without one, taken during the 1940 championship game in which Chicago crushed the Washington Redskins 73-0.

End Bill Hewitt of the Bears and Philadelphia Eagles was another player who took the field without anything covering his head, and he eventually was elected to the Hall of Fame, making him far better known than Plasman. Hewitt, however, retired in 1939. He came back for one season during World War II, 1943, but by then the rules required him to put on a helmet.

Ivy League teams played in the first games, wrote the first rules, and formed the first college football association. In 1889, Princeton players adopted the practice of growing their hair long to protect themselves against head injuries. According to researcher Paul Quam, "this fad swept the country, and football players with their unsightly mops of hair became the delight of cartoonists."

Wearing long hair while playing football went out of fashion, according to Quam, "when a championship Yale team appeared with close-cropped heads in 1895." (The crew-cut became *de rigueur* and remained in fashion for nearly 70 years.) The next phase in the development of the helmet began with the appearance of the head harness. Its name had a little of the livery stable in it, and that is not surprising since the age of the automobile in America was just beginning.

George Barclay of Lafayette College probably developed the head harness in 1896. He designed a headgear which had three thick leather straps forming a tight fit around his head, and had it made by a harness maker. It was only logical that it became known as a head harness.

Contraptions made of an assortment of straps and pads turned into leather caps. They acquired ear flaps and then the flaps acquired ear holes, which must have improved communication greatly. There is no way these things could have provided anything more than rudimentary protection to the portion of the football-playing population that wore them.

Nose protectors were an interesting by-product of the head harness era. Edgar Allen Poe was an All-America back at Princeton as well as a grand-nephew of the famous author of the same name. He used a nose guard against Yale in 1890. Other players started using it. A hard leather proboscis hung from a strap around the forehead, fit over the nose, and had an extension at the bottom that the wearer clenched in his teeth to hold the device in place. They interfered with good vision and that even more important requisite of a person going through strenuous activity—the ability to breathe easily. "No player should wear a nose protector unless he has a sore nose," said Pop Warner in 1912. One of the oddest creations in the history of football equipment soon went out of style.

The head harness began to take the shape and appearance we would recognize today as a football helmet. That soon became its name, instead of head harness. But it still had a serious deficiency. As long as it sat right down on the skull, it was only pretending to protect the wearer. Then suspension appeared, probably in 1917, to cradle the skull away from the leather shell. Straps of fabric formed a pattern inside the helmet. They absorbed and distributed the impact better, and they allowed for ventilation. It was a tremendous breakthrough in helmet-making. Rawlings introduced the Zuppke helmet, designed by the Illinois coach, and Spalding introduced the first of what would become a well-known line, its "ZH" helmets, in 1925.

An innovation 14 years later, however, dwarfed all that had gone before. Gerry E. Morgan and other employees of the John T. Riddell Company in Chicago, manufacturers of sporting goods, invented and patented a plastic football helmet in 1939. It was a single molded shell. It was stronger, more durable, and lighter than leather helmets, and it wouldn't rot or mildew the way they did when damp. It had a revolutionary web suspension inside it.

In 1940, Riddell devised the first chinstrap worn on the chin and not the Adam's apple, and the first plastic face mask.

Most plastics are synthetic. They are derived from petroleum, coal, salt, air, and water. They are light in weight, but for their weight they are prodigiously strong. Thermoplastics are one type; the name means they are remeltable. Among the 15 or more types of thermoplastics are acrylonitrile-butadiene-styrene (ABS) and polycarbonate. Their features are excellent toughness and high impact strength. They are the plastics used in football helmets.

Riddell made its plastic helmets and they were worn for the first time in a game by some of the players in the Chicago College All-Star Game of 1939. The company also had another first. Founder John T. Riddell and owner-coach George Halas of the Bears devised low-cut football shoes, and the 1940 Bears became the first team ever to wear such shoes.

Riddell's plastic helmet was a little flat on top at first but it gradually changed to its characteristic teardrop shape, which allowed the impact of a blow to slide to one side or the other rather than be met head-on. Its web suspension could be raised or lowered to fit the head of whatever person pulled it on.

The eve of a world war, however, was not the best time to come up with a new sports invention. Football was not an essential industry, and Riddell could not get plastic. The full-fledged assault on the leather helmet had to wait until the war ended.

The fact that the United States Military Academy football team of 1944 became the first to ever wear plastic helmets may have resulted from the Army being privy to Riddell's research, or it may have been because Army was coached by a bright, innovative, and far-thinking man, Earl (Red) Blaik. He won national championships in 1944 and 1945 with a pair of backs, Felix (Doc) Blanchard and Glenn Davis, who wore the new Riddell plastic helmets.

There were problems, however. The plastic in the helmets of Riddell and those of competitors who entered the market was sometimes brittle; a drill boring a hole to attach a face mask would pop right through. The plastic's resistance to blows was in doubt after linebacker Fred Naumetz of the Los Angeles Rams split nine plastic helmets in one season. They were banned from use in the NFL in 1948. Riddell's future was in doubt. It was apparently saved by the intercession in its behalf of Halas of the Bears. The plastic helmet was restored for 1949, and the leather helmet became extinct.

Paint on football helmets goes back almost as far as helmets themselves. Rawlings introduced a white helmet in 1920 that it said "may be kept white with gasoline or painted in college colors if desired." The Brooklyn Dodgers had silver helmets in 1937. Halfback Fred Gehrke of the Los Angeles Rams, who had studied art at the University of Utah, painted a horn design on the Rams' helmets in 1948, the first helmet emblem. Distinctive designs became the trademarks of pro football teams.

Gehrke's paint kept chipping off every game, however, and he and his teammates had to paint the emblems back on the helmets constantly. The legalization of plastic helmets in 1949 made it possible to bake color into helmets and greatly expand its use on them. As a result, football became far more colorful. Helmets became coordinated with jerseys and pants.

The nose protector was the forerunner of the face mask. Nose protector helmets were found during the transition to face masks. The manufacturers began making them as early as 1927; that was the first year one appeared in the *Spalding Guide*. A molded piece of leather with holes for the eyes and mouth covered the entire face. It looked like a ski mask or the visor of a knight errant. Without a doubt, it was the most bizarre-looking piece of football apparel ever made. The dearth of photographs of anyone wearing one of them bears out their confirmed lack of acceptance, probably because they were unbearably hot.

The first person to devise a bar face mask on a football helmet was Vern McMillan, the owner of a sporting goods store in Terre Haute, Indiana. It was a rubber-covered wire mask on a leather helmet. Such masks were used in the mid-1930s. There is a face mask on the helmet of a New York Giants player in a photo in a 1937 issue of *SPORT*.

The superior rigidity of the plastic helmet made the universality of the face mask possible. The hole drilled for the bolt holding the mask would not expand the way it would if it was drilled through leather. And the sides of the plastic helmet would not collapse, driving the nut into the wearer's face.

As use of the plastic helmet spread, so did makeshift face masks. Linemen needed them more than backs, and began crafting odd cages of leather- and tape-covered wire. When Joe Perry of the San Francisco 49ers suffered a broken jaw in 1954, he wore a face mask manufactured of clear lucite plastic. Lucite, however, frequently shattered and it was banned. The breakthrough in face masks came in 1955. G. E. Morgan, a consultant to Riddell, and Paul Brown, coach of the Cleveland Browns, invented the BT-5 face mask for quarterback Otto Graham, who was dominating pro football and against whom pass rushers sometimes led with the elbow. The "BT" in the invention's name was for bar tubular; it was a single tubular bar that was a combination of rubber and plastic. Graham wore it one year and retired from pro football.

From the BT-5 came a variety of single bars, double bars, triple bars, masks, cages, and "birdcages." Plastic and rubber tubing or welded steel or aluminum with a vinyl plastisol coating were used in their construction. Cages once reserved only for linemen came to be adopted by backs as well. Bobby Layne of the Pittsburgh Steelers, who retired in 1962, was one of the last players to play without a face mask. Years later, Billy Kilmer of the Washington Redskins was one of the few men still playing with only a single bar.

Morgan and Brown came up with another invention the year after their BT-5 face mask. They put a citizen's band radio in quarterback George Ratterman's helmet. Brown, who was on the sideline, had a transmitter and Ratterman had a receiver. The quarterback couldn't talk back to the coach. The experiment with this device in a game was brief. There was interference on the frequency. Expecting to hear Brown call the next play, Ratterman instead heard two women talking incoherently. The experiment ended, and the next year the NFL banned radio-equipped football helmets.

Chinstraps were improved by the addition of ribbed vinyl-coated chincups. College football, intent on preventing injuries by keeping the helmet securely on the head, began requiring four-point chinstraps in 1976; they snapped onto the helmet at four places instead of two.

Mouthpieces also became a requisite in college football and some players continued to wear them as they entered pro football. Others complained that the rubber mouthpieces made it difficult to speak or even breathe at times and could even induce gagging and nausea.

Energy-absorbing helmets of the space age entered pro football in 1971. Morgan, by then chairman of the board of Riddell, was granted a patent for "Energy Absorbing and Sizing Means for Helmets." The result was the company's new HA-91 and HA-92 energy-absorbing, "microfit" helmets. They had valves on their crown to allow air to be pumped into vinyl cushions that were crammed into every available space inside the helmet. The player put it on and then had it pumped up by the equipment manager to fit firmly around the player's head. Fluid could be pumped in, too. These were the so-called "water helmets." Actually, an anti-freeze solvent was used, to prevent a helmet from freezing atop a player's head in the middle of a cold day at Green Bay or Bloomington.

Riddell's older TK-2 web suspension helmet, however, refused to give way to the microfits. Veterans everywhere in the NFL who had worn Riddell's and other suspension helmets stayed with them. Among other things, they said, suspension provided better ventilation. Players at the speed positions such as running back, wide receiver, and cornerback preferred suspension helmets because they were lighter.

Riddell's PAC-3, a "padded aero cell," made its debut in 1974. This time the vinyl cushions did not have to be pumped up; maintenance was reduced and players did not have to stand in line at the equipment manager's desk to have their helmets blown up. The PAC-3 had 32 individual vinyl air cushions with layers of energy-absorbing foam. Small holes in the crown allowed the cushions inside to dissipate the force of the impact and carry it away through the orifices in the surface.

Linemen have the most collisions and so they need the best padding and the largest cages or face masks. With all this hardware on and in the helmet, it can get rather heavy. Norm Evans, a tackle for the Seattle Seahawks and the Miami Dolphins, said in *On the Line*, "Until I learned to do exercises to strengthen my neck, the hardest part of every training camp for me was starting to wear a helmet again. The first time I'd put the helmet on, my head would go *clunk*! over to one side. You know those things weigh about two-and-a-half pounds. After a few days I'd get to where I could draw my head down into my neck. Then there's a way I could tilt the face mask at a certain angle. Between the two positions, I could keep my helmet upright."

The Stanford Research Institute noted in its 1974 study that helmets "have gradually become thicker and more rigid." The NFL, NCAA, and National Federation of State High School Associations make it mandatory that all players wear helmets that meet test standards of the National Operating Committee on Standards for Athletic Equipment.

IV. PADS

"Football isn't a contact sport," the saying goes. "Dancing is a contact sport; football is a *collision* sport." People who play it are therefore required to wear pads. Of all the ones they wear, the most obvious are the shoulder pads. They make massive NFL linemen appear even more massive. Shoulder pads are an elaborate apparatus of straps, foam, and plastic. Their mission is to protect the clavicle.

At one time, shoulder pads were flimsy contraptions that slumped weakly over the crown of each shoulder. The principle of cantilevering appeared in them about 1935. Straps held the epaulets of the pads away from the shoulder, high above it, to absorb shock. Cantilever shoulder pads transformed many skinny high school youngsters into fearsome-looking football players.

Elastic underarm straps, deeper chest plates, "snubbers" to hold the flap in place under the epaulet, and nylon covering and stitching were further breakthroughs in shoulder pads. Varying sizes were developed—massive sets for big linemen, smaller models for linebackers and running backs, and an even smaller size for quarterbacks, wide receivers, defensive backs, and kickers.

Thigh and knee pads are molded foam rubber parts that are inserted in pockets inside football players' pants. Shin, elbow, and forearm pads, and padded, fingerless gloves, are articles of padding that players may tape onto themselves. Shin guards protect against leg-whipping. Elbow pads prevent artificial turf burns. Forearm pads and gloves traditionally aided defensive and offensive linemen, but in the 1980s wide receivers adopted gloves. In 1985, for the first time, quarterbacks also started wearing gloves.

No player wants to play without protection. All are concerned about their safety and having a long, profitable career. The cutaway photos of players covered from head to toe in padding, which appear in sporting goods catalogs and in sports magazines, are a sales manager's fondest dream and not a reality. Few players, if any, wear every possible pad. Gerald (Dad) Braiser, former equipment manager of the Green Bay Packers, says rib pads are worn by players only when they're hurt, and Don Hewitt of the Los Angeles Rams says, "There is hardly a player in the NFL wearing hip pads."

In the last few seasons some players have started using a new kind of equipment that is lighter and less bulky than the traditional pads. Designed by Byron Donzis, these new pads use air-filled channels to absorb impact. Donzis's protective equipment was first used in the NFL in the 1978 playoffs, when Houston Oilers quarterback Dan Pastorini wore a flak jacket to protect injured ribs.

Since then Donzis has designed pads for specific players and positions.

V. SHOES

Football had been played for a number of years. Players had tried a variety of footwear. Then a breakthrough occurred—white football shoes! A sporting goods company advertised them as its number-one model. You can plainly see it right there in the Peck & Snyder catalog. The year? 1886.

The idea, however, did not catch on and another 80 years went by before quarterback Joe Namath of the New York Jets popularized white football shoes once more.

Shoes show off players' individualism. They are compelled to wear jerseys, pants, helmets, and stockings the same as everyone else. In their shoes, however, they express themselves. Because of this, and because of the advent of artificial turf and the many models made especially for it, an almost endless variety of football shoes is available.

Baseball shoes were the first football shoes. They looked like the shoes of Whistler's mother. Kangaroo leather instead of cowhide arrived not in some postwar "modern" era but as early as 1906; in fact, Spalding said then that it had been making kangaroo leather shoes for Yale, Princetown, Penn, and other college teams for years. The farmer's brogan style gave way to low-cut oxfords in 1940. A roof was built over a stadium, the Houston Astrodome, in 1965, and a carpet floor called "artificial turf" was laid in it. Other fields, indoors and out, took on artificial turf. The manufacturers raced to make the best shoe for it.

Inverted truncated pyramid football cleats appeared in the 1890s. They were made of pieces of leather glued together and nailed to the shoe. One-piece fiber cleats, once again nailed to the shoe, appeared in 1915. Interchangeable cleats arrived in 1921; they screwed on and off a metal post jutting from the sole of the shoe.

It is not hard to imagine what a threat to safety these metal posts posed if a cleat came off during the course of a game. In 1939, the college football rules committee ordered a change. "Female" football cleats were outlawed; that is, the cleat had to become the "male" part with the metal post, the shoe the "female" part into which the post was inserted.

Fiber gave way to rubber, and rubber gave way to aluminum and nylon, steel-tipped cleats. Aluminum, however, was banned from use in cleats by the NFL in 1951.

Cleats lock in the ground and that can be a major cause of knee injuries. Of all the countless inventions that have been offered to prevent cleat-lock in football shoes, perhaps none was more interesting and compelling than Dr. Bruce Cameron's swivel shoe, which he called the "Wolverine Swivler." An orthopedic surgeon in Houston, he offered the product for the first time in about 1970. It had a swivel cleat on the front of the sole that turned 360 degrees, but, he said, "It is not free-swinging; the wedge joint sets with the body weight. It takes about a week for a player to get used to it."

The Stanford Research Institute study of 1974 offered more orthodox solutions for the problems cleats cause. It recommended more and shorter cleats, and the manufacturers of soccer-style football shoes for artificial surfaces have begun to make them. The SRI study called for an end to the use of the traditional long conical cleat on natural turf and said the more cleats, the better, to keep them from locking into the turf. Today's cleats, like all of the equipment, are the safest and best modern technology can develop.

PHOTOGRAPHY CREDITS

Bill Amatucci 65c
Charles Aqua Viva 49a, 50e
Baltimore Colts 427b
Vernon Biever 33ae, 62d, 63b, 411a, 414d, 415f, 418d, 424c, 428c
David Boss 62a, 65b, 76a, 411c, 414c, 417f, 424g, 426a, 428e, 431d, 432b, 433b
Clifton Boutelle 421e
George Brace 418c, 427e, 434b
Chance Brockway 51ac, 62g
Brown University 18a
Greg Cava 77c
Chicago Bears 20a, 415d, 417d, 425c, 431a, 435a
Chicago Cardinals 434c
Cleveland Browns 418e, 423b, 425d, 427c
Cleveland Plain Dealer 433c
Christine Cotter 74c
Thomas J. Croke 75c, 76b
Dave Cross 75a, 77b
Dallas Cowboys 424b, 432a
Detroit Lions 422d
Malcolm Emmons 50f, 64b, 75d, 433a
Nate Fine 31b, 76c, 424d
Paul Fine 60b
George Gellatly 415b, 423ac, 436a
George Gojkovich 64a
Green Bay Packers 414e, 420b, 421c
Green Bay Press Gazette 419g
Rod Hanna 60de, 61c, 412d
H. Lee Hansen 31d
Ken Hardin 50d
Kansas City Chiefs 421b
Don Lansu 63d
Laughead Photographers 47c, 48b
Hank LeFebvre 419e, 422c
Ross Lewis 420c, 422e, 430e
Los Angeles Rams 417a, 420a, 425b, 435c
Fred Matthes 34a
Minnesota Vikings 432e
Bill Mount 64c
New York Giants 411d, 419c, 434d
New York Jets 74b, 416d
Darryl Norenberg 48g, 50c, 62c, 412e, 415g, 421d, 427a, 429b, 431b
Ohio State University 437a
Philadelphia Eagles 21b, 412b, 429d, 430b, 435d
Pittsburgh Press 430d
Pro Football Hall of Fame 18bc, 19ac, 21a, 30ab, 31c, 411e, 412c, 413ac, 414f, 415ace, 416ab, 417bce, 418bf, 419bdf, 420d, 422ab, 424aef, 425a, 426b, 427d, 428abg, 429ae, 432cd, 436d, 437c
Russ Reed 33f, 61b
Frank Rippon 32a, 33d, 35a, 60a, 74a
Fred Roe 34bc, 51d
Art Rogers 436c
Ron Ross 63c, 65e
Dan Rubin 46c, 47bd, 414b, 417g, 421a, 430c, 434a
Manny Rubio 65d, 414a
Russ Russell 65a, 75b
St. Louis Cardinals 48c
San Diego Chargers 411b, 418a
San Francisco 49ers 428d, 429c
Bill Smith 419a
Robert L. Smith 48e, 62b, 431c
Sports Illustrated 32c, 35c
Vic Stein 32b, 33bc, 35b, 46abd, 63a, 430a
George F. Taubeneck 20b
George Tiedemann 60c
Tony Tomsic 48f, 49b, 50b, 51b, 413d, 435b, 436b
Corky Trewin 76d
United Press International 19b, 20c, 21c, 31a
Bob Verlin 49c
Fred Vuich 77a
Washington Redskins 412a, 416c, 426cd
Herb Weitman 61a, 62ef, 427f, 437b
Lou Witt 47a, 48ad, 50a, 413b
Michael Zagaris 428f